A CONCORDANCE TO

The Poetry of Robert Frost

This concordance was prepared at
Dartmouth College

programmed under the supervision of
JOHN G. KEMENY
at the Kiewit Computation Center
by RICHARD A. JENSON

A CONCORDANCE TO

The Poetry of Robert Frost

Edited by

EDWARD CONNERY LATHEM

New York · Chicago · San Francisco

Holt Information Systems

a division of Holt, Rinehart and Winston

THIS CONCORDANCE

is based upon the text of
the standard edition of Mr. Frost's verse,
The Poetry of Robert Frost, edited by Edward Connery Lathem
and published in 1969 by Holt, Rinehart and Winston,
a volume that incorporates the contents
of the following eleven books by the poet,
which were originally issued in the years specified:

A Boy's Will (1913)
North of Boston (1914)
Mountain Interval (1916)
New Hampshire (1923)
West-Running Brook (1928)
A Further Range (1936)
A Witness Tree (1942)
A Masque of Reason (1945)
Steeple Bush (1947)
A Masque of Mercy (1947)
In the Clearing (1962)

Editor's Preface

THE ORIGIN of this concordance may be traced back in time to a luncheon in the summer of 1968. My table companion was John G. Kemeny, then Professor of Mathematics at Dartmouth, subsequently her Albert Bradley Third Century Professor, and now President of the College. We had met to talk about another matter entirely, but in the course of our conversation I mentioned my interest in a series of computer-produced literary concordances which had been issued in recent years by one of the country's leading university presses. I indicated that I was myself currently preparing for publication a new volume of Robert Frost's poetry, one intended by Mr. Frost's estate to constitute a standard edition—involving, thus, the establishment of what would be a stable body of text for some years to come—and it had occurred to me to wonder whether it might be possible to produce locally, at Dartmouth's computer facility, a Frost concordance.

Professor Kemeny, a pioneer in electronic-computing developments within the academic world, had little doubt that this could be done. Indeed, if I were disposed to assume editorial responsibility for such an enterprise, he would, he declared, gladly assign one of his own assistants to the project and would, moreover, himself personally supervise the programming.

By the following summer my editing of the collection entitled *The Poetry of Robert Frost* had been completed, and the book was at its page-proofs stage. During July, therefore, in keeping with his generous offer, John Kemeny directed the attention of Richard A. Jenson, a mathematics

v

major who had just been graduated from Dartmouth with the Class of 1969, to the task of beginning the programming work, responsive to my specifications of desired features for the concordance.

After a succession of preliminary approaches, accompanied by brief, sample computer-output trials, a full run of the Kemeny-Jenson program, incorporating all five-hundred-odd pages of input from the new *Poetry* volume, was achieved in September. Thereafter, in order to provide for certain adjustments and further refinements, additional program revisions were made by Richard Jenson, under Professor Kemeny's guidance, during the winter of 1969–70. These were introduced with the aid of Randolph M. Brodersen (Dartmouth 1970), an experienced undergraduate programmer, and that of John S. McGeachie, Assistant Director for System Development in the College's Kiewit Computation Center. The final, production run of the program was accomplished in May of 1970, using Dartmouth's GE-635 computer, and the output was then transferred to tape for printing at Information Services Incorporated, Babson Park, Wellesley, Massachusetts, under the direction of Leonard L. Ily, Operations Supervisor of that organization. Grateful acknowledgment is made to Messrs. Brodersen, McGeachie, and Ily for their valuable help and for their kind offices generally.

John G. Kemeny and Richard A. Jenson, as collaborators with the editor in bringing this volume into being, are cited on the page facing the title page, where their responsibility for the programming is recorded. The concordance itself constitutes a tribute to their efforts, and the extent and character of their attainments will be readily evident to the book's users. I should like, however, to add here a personal expression of admiration and warm gratitude for the care, skill, sensitive understanding, and limitless patience exhibited by both men throughout the period of our working together on this project.

BASED ON the text of *The Poetry of Robert Frost* (New York: Holt, Rinehart and Winston, 1969), this concordance has been prepared with the consent and generous cooperation of Alfred C. Edwards, sole executor and trustee of the Estate of Robert Frost and former chief executive of the firm that for over half a century has been Mr. Frost's principal publisher—Henry Holt and Company, which in 1959 changed its corporate designation to Holt, Rinehart and Winston.

As is usual with compilations of this sort, certain high-frequency, non-significant words have been omitted from the indexing, as have

vi

been, for consistency's sake, most compounds (either in full or in contracted form) made up of such words. All of these are, however, noted in their proper places within the alphabetic sequence of the concordance, bearing the subjunction ---NOT INDEXED. They are:

A	HASN'T	ME	THAT'D	WE'LL
ALTHOUGH	HAVE	MIGHTN'T	THAT'S	WERE
AM	HAVEN'T	MUST	THE	WE'RE
AN	HE	MUSTN'T	THEIR	WEREN'T
AND	HE'D	MY	THEIRS	WE'VE
ANOTHER	HE'LL	NO	THEM	WHAT
ANOTHER'S	HER	NOR	THEN	WHAT'LL
ARE	HERE	NOT	THEN'S	WHAT'S
AREN'T	HERE'S	NOW	THERE	WHEN
AT	HERS	NOW'S	THERE'D	WHEN'S
BE	HE'S	OF	THERE'S	WHERE
BECAUSE	HIM	ON	THESE	WHERE'S
BEEN	HIS	OR	THEY	WHICH
BUT	HOW	OTHER	THEY'D	WHO
BY	I	OTHERS	THEY'LL	WHO'D
CANNOT	I'D	OTHERS'	THEY'RE	WHOM
CAN'T	IF	OTHER'S	THEY'VE	WHO'S
COULD	I'LL	OUR	THIS	WHOSE
COULDN'T	I'M	OURS	THOSE	WHY
DID	IN	SHALL	THOUGH	WITH
DIDN'T	INTO	SHAN'T	THROUGH	WON'T
DO	IS	SHE	TO	WOULD
DOES	ISN'T	SHE'D	TOO	WOULDN'T
DOESN'T	IT	SHE'LL	UPON	YOU
DON'T	IT'D	SHE'S	US	YOU'D
FOR	ITS	SHOULD	WAS	YOU'LL
FROM	IT'S	SHOULDN'T	WASN'T	YOUR
HAD	I'VE	SO	WE	YOU'RE
HADN'T	MAYN'T	SO'S	WE'D	YOURS
HAS		THAT		YOU'VE

In addition, five other words have been omitted from the indexing in all instances except when used as nouns: CAN MAY MIGHT MINE WILL

and these words have been identified as - - -NOT INDEXED- - -EXCEPT FOR: following which citation are entered those lines that contain the specified word as a noun.

Although of relatively high incidence, and therefore sometimes not indexed in concordances, both AS and LIKE have been fully indexed herein, because of the importance of these words with respect to similes in the poetry. Archaisms, rare in Robert Frost's writings, have been retained, despite the fact that comparable modern or presently-common forms are omitted; accordingly, for example, DIDST, THEE, and THINE are indexed, while DID, YOU, and YOUR are not. All unusual contractions have been included in the indexing, as have contractions beginning with an apostrophe, even though some are in fact contracted from single or compound words that would themselves be omitted. Also, hyphenated words have been cross-referenced from the element or elements which follow hyphens therein.

Entries within the concordance give, under the word being indexed, each line in which that word is present, the appropriate page reference to *The Poetry of Robert Frost*, identification of the title that is involved, and a notation of the line number or other symbol establishing specific location. Titles of poems and books, as well as subtitles and dedications, have all been indexed, and the abbreviations used in the concordance's LINE column to designate these elements are T, S, and D, respectively. Entries are also given for titles of the individual parts of poems, successive part-titles being indicated as 1P, 2P, and so forth. Where poem titles are more than twenty-three units in length (each alphabetic or numerical character, space, and punctuation mark counting as a unit), it has been necessary to abbreviate them for inclusion in the TITLE column of the concordance. This is also true of the title for the section of text called "'An Afterword' from Complete Poems," which becomes AFTERWORD FROM COMPLETE as it appears in the TITLE column. The poem titles that have been abbreviated are listed below, given in the order of the poems' appearance in *The Poetry of Robert Frost* and with their deleted parts set off by pointed brackets:

from *North of Boston*—
⟨THE⟩ DEATH OF THE HIRED MAN

from *Mountain Interval*—
⟨AN⟩ OLD MAN'S WINTER NIGHT
⟨THE⟩ LAST WORD OF A BLUEBIRD

viii

from *New Hampshire*—

⟨THE⟩ PAUPER WITCH OF GRAFTON

A FOUNTAIN, A BOTTLE⟨, A DONKEY'S EARS, AND SOME BOOKS⟩

STOPPING BY WOODS ⟨ON A SNOWY EVENING⟩

FOR ONCE⟨, THEN,⟩ SOMETHING

LOOKING FOR ⟨A⟩ SUNSET BIRD ⟨IN WINTER⟩

EVENING ⟨IN⟩ A SUGAR ORCHARD

⟨THE⟩ VALLEY'S SINGING DAY

ON A TREE FALLEN ACROSS ⟨THE ROAD⟩

⟨THE⟩ NEED OF BEING VERSED ⟨IN COUNTRY THINGS⟩

from *West-Running Brook*—

ACQUAINTED WITH ⟨THE⟩ NIGHT

THE LOVELY ⟨SHALL⟩ BE CHOOSERS

SITTING BY A BUSH ⟨IN BROAD SUNLIGHT⟩

ON LOOKING UP BY CHANCE ⟨AT THE CONSTELLATIONS⟩

from *A Further Range*—

⟨A⟩ BLUE RIBBON AT AMESBURY

⟨THE⟩ OLD BARN AT THE BOTTOM ⟨OF THE FOGS⟩

ON ⟨THE⟩ HEART'S BEGINNING TO ⟨CLOUD THE MIND⟩

⟨THE⟩ FIGURE IN THE DOORWAY

LEAVES COMPARED WITH ⟨FLOWERS⟩

ON TAKING FROM THE TOP ⟨TO BROADEN THE BASE⟩

⟨THEY WERE⟩ WELCOME TO THEIR BELIEF

⟨THE⟩ STRONG ⟨ARE⟩ SAYING NOTHING

NEITHER OUT FAR NOR IN ⟨DEEP⟩

⟨ON⟩ A BIRD SINGING IN ⟨ITS⟩ SLEEP

⟨THE⟩ HARDSHIP OF ACCOUNTING

⟨THE⟩ BEARER OF EVIL TIDINGS

from *A Witness Tree*—

HAPPINESS MAKES UP ⟨IN HEIGHT FOR WHAT IT LACKS IN LENGTH⟩

I COULD GIVE ALL ⟨TO TIME⟩

NEVER ⟨AGAIN⟩ WOULD BIRDS' SONG ⟨BE THE SAME⟩

⟨THE⟩ QUEST OF ⟨THE⟩ PURPLE-FRINGED

⟨THE⟩ DISCOVERY OF ⟨THE⟩ MADEIRAS

⟨TO⟩ A MOTH SEEN IN WINTER

⟨IT IS⟩ ALMOST ⟨THE YEAR⟩ TWO THOUSAND

⟨ON OUR⟩ SYMPATHY WITH ⟨THE⟩ UNDER DOG

OF ⟨THE⟩ STONES OF THE PLACE
A SERIOUS STEP LIGHTLY ⟨TAKEN⟩
THE LITERATE FARMER AND ⟨THE PLANET VENUS⟩

from *Steeple Bush*—
AN UNSTAMPED LETTER IN ⟨OUR RURAL LETTER BOX⟩
⟨ON⟩ MAKING CERTAIN ANYTHING ⟨HAS HAPPENED⟩
⟨THE⟩ MIDDLENESS OF THE ROAD
LUCRETIUS VERSUS ⟨THE LAKE⟩ POETS

from *"An Afterword" from Complete Poems*—
⟨TAKE⟩ SOMETHING LIKE A STAR

from *In the Clearing*—
FOR JOHN F. KENNEDY ⟨HIS INAUGURATION⟩
⟨A⟩ CONCEPT SELF-CONCEIVED
DOES NO ONE AT ALL EVER ⟨FEEL THIS WAY IN THE LEAST?⟩
⟨THE⟩ OBJECTION TO BE⟨ING⟩ STEPPED ⟨ON⟩
HOW HARD ⟨IT IS⟩ TO KEEP FROM ⟨BEING KING WHEN IT'S IN YOU
    AND IN THE SITUATION⟩
LINES ⟨WRITTEN⟩ IN DEJECTION ⟨ON THE EVE OF GREAT SUCCESS⟩
⟨THE⟩ MILKY WAY IS A COWPATH
⟨ON BEING⟩ CHOSEN POET OF VERMONT
IN WINTER IN THE WOODS⟨. . .⟩

Because *The Poetry of Robert Frost* is not intended to be a definitive edition (it makes no attempt, for instance, to collate manuscript texts), variant readings are not included in this concordance, nor are word-frequency counts tabulated. These and other features will, of course, be appropriate for inclusion in a subsequent concordance based on the exhaustive, variorum edition of Robert Frost's poems which will one day be produced.

E.C.L.

Dartmouth College
June 1970

The Concordance

A---NOT INDEXED   PAGE TITLE   LINE

ABANDON
    FOR, DEAR ME, WHY ABANDON A BELIEF . . . . 58 THE BLACK COTTAGE . . 105
    TO CLOSE A ROAD, ABANDON A FARM, ... 263 THE TIMES TABLE . . . 18
A-B-C
    THAT IS, A B C, ... 436 KITTY HAWK 273
ABDICATION
    SO THE TWO MAKING GOOD THEIR ABDICATION . . . . . . 454 HOW HARD TO KEEP FROM 10
ABEDNEGO
    LIKE SHADRACH, MESHACH, AND ABEDNEGO. . . . . 516 A MASQUE OF MERCY . . 604
ABHORRENCE
    IT'S HARD TO TELL WHICH IS THE WORSE ABHORRENCE, . . . 321 BUILD SOIL 155
ABIDE
    AND TELL YOU THAT I SAW DOES STILL ABIDE. . . . . . 16 A DREAM PANG . . 12
    BUT JUST THE KIND THAT KINSFOLK CAN'T ABIDE. . . . . 39 DEATH OF THE HIRED MAN 141
ABIDED
    SO CLOSE YET SURE TO BE ABIDED BY, ... 423 FOR JOHN F. KENNEDY . 56
ABIDING
    AT HOME IN HER ABIDING PEN, ... 280 BLUE RIBBON AT AMESBURY 14
ABISHAG
    WAS ONCE THE BEAUTY ABISHAG, ... 307 PROVIDE, PROVIDE . . 3
ABJECT
    I AM ABJECT BEFORE YOU," SAID DARIUS. . . . . . . 458 HOW HARD TO KEEP FROM 145
ABLE
    YOU MAY TAUNT ME WITH NOT BEING ABLE TO FLEE THE EARTH. . 306 NOT QUITE SOCIAL . . 9
ABLEST
    THE ABLEST ACTORS I CAN LAY MY HANDS ON. . . . . . 481 A MASQUE OF REASON . 226
ABNEGATION
    GREED HAS BEEN TAUGHT A LITTLE ABNEGATION . . . . . 319 BUILD SOIL 117
ABODE
    IN THAT VANISHED ABODE THERE FAR APART . . . . . . 6 GHOST HOUSE . . . 12
    (TWO MILES IT WAS) TO HIS ABODE. . . . . 139 BROWN'S DESCENT . . . 48
A-BOUNCING
    AS WE CAN FALL AND KEEP A-BOUNCING ON OUR FEET. . . . 215 A FOUNTAIN, A BOTTLE . 62
ABOUT
    AND HUSH AND CLUCK AND FLUTTER ABOUT: . . . . . . 6 GHOST HOUSE . . . 17
    PERHAPS IT WAS SOMETHING ABOUT THE HEAT OF THE SUN, . . 17 MOWING 4
    SOMETHING, PERHAPS, ABOUT THE LACK OF SOUND-- . . . 17 MOWING 5
    I TRIED TO MAKE HIM TALK ABOUT HIS TRAVELS. . . . . 36 DEATH OF THE HIRED MAN 42
    HE'D KEEP SO STILL ABOUT HIM ALL THIS TIME?" . . . . 39 DEATH OF THE HIRED MAN 138
    BUT WHAT WOULD INTEREST YOU ABOUT THE BROOK, ... 42 THE MOUNTAIN . . . 48
    ABOUT ITS BEING THERE. I NEVER SAW IT. . . . . . 42 THE MOUNTAIN . . . 67
    "BUT A LAKE'S DIFFERENT. WHAT ABOUT THE SPRING?" . . . 43 THE MOUNTAIN . . . 77
    TO WHIPS AND POLES. THERE'S NOBODY ABOUT. . . . . 49 A HUNDRED COLLARS . 136
    TELL ME ABOUT IT IF IT'S SOMETHING HUMAN. . . . . 53 HOME BURIAL . . . 58
    AND TALK ABOUT YOUR EVERYDAY CONCERNS. . . . . . 54 HOME BURIAL . . . 86
    SHE ALWAYS, WHEN SHE TALKED ABOUT THE WAR, ... 56 THE BLACK COTTAGE . 26
    "I WONDER YOU DIDN'T SEE LOREN ABOUT." . . . . . 60 BLUEBERRIES 33
    ABOUT MY FACE AND BODY AND THROUGH MY WRAPPER, . . . 63 A SERVANT TO SERVANTS 29
    IN A BOOK ABOUT FERNS? LISTEN TO THAT! . . . . . 63 A SERVANT TO SERVANTS 35
    SPRAWLING ABOUT THE KITCHEN WITH THEIR TALK . . . . 65 A SERVANT TO SERVANTS 77
    ANYWAY ALL HE TALKED ABOUT WAS LOVE. . . . . . 66 A SERVANT TO SERVANTS 110
    WHAT FORM MY DREAMING WAS ABOUT TO TAKE. . . . . 68 AFTER APPLE-PICKING . 17
    "WHAT DID I SAY?" / "ABOUT OUR TAKING PAINS." . . . 70 THE CODE 11
    I'D SEEN ABOUT ENOUGH OF HIS BULLING TRICKS . . . . 71 THE CODE 47
    AND SORT OF WAITING TO BE ASKED ABOUT IT, ... 72 THE CODE 82
    I WENT ABOUT TO KILL HIM FAIR ENOUGH." . . . . . 73 THE CODE 112
    AND PERHAPS HEAR SOME WORD ABOUT THE WEATHER. . . . 74 THE GENERATIONS OF MEN 33
    DRAWN INTO TOWN ABOUT THIS CELLAR HOLE . . . . . 76 THE GENERATIONS OF MEN 89
    "TELL ME ABOUT HER. DOES SHE LOOK LIKE ME?" . . . . 77 THE GENERATIONS OF MEN 110
    AND THOSE WILL BEAR SOME KEEPING STILL ABOUT." . . . 80 THE GENERATIONS OF MEN 198
    MY FINGERS ARE ABOUT ALL I'VE THE USE OF . . . . 81 THE HOUSEKEEPER . . 6
    "YES, WHAT'S IT ALL ABOUT? WHEN DID SHE GO?" . . . 82 THE HOUSEKEEPER . . 21
    AND NO ONE HERE BUT HENS BLOWING ABOUT. . . . . 83 THE HOUSEKEEPER . . 47
    THERE WAS NO QUARREL ABOUT PROPERTY." . . . . . 84 THE HOUSEKEEPER . . 94
    ONE THING YOU CAN'T HELP LIKING ABOUT JOHN, ... 85 THE HOUSEKEEPER . . 115
    "BUT WHAT ABOUT YOUR FLORA OF THE VALLEY?" . . . . 95 THE SELF-SEEKER . . 80
    ABOUT MY CYPRIPEDIUM REGINAE; . . . . 95 THE SELF-SEEKER . . 86
    YOU DON'T KNOW WHAT I MEAN ABOUT THE FLOWERS. . . . 100 THE SELF-SEEKER . . 226
    THESE LATTER ABOUT TO FALL. I THOUGHT THAT ONLY . . 102 THE WOOD-PILE . . . 34
    HAD WORN THEM REALLY ABOUT THE SAME, ... 105 THE ROAD NOT TAKEN . 10
    WITH HILLS AND CIRCLING ARMS ABOUT-- . . . . . 120 BOND AND FREE . . . 2
    WITH ALL HER MATTER OF FACT ABOUT THE ICE STORM, . . 121 BIRCHES 22
    TO LEARN ABOUT NOT LAUNCHING OUT TOO SOON . . . . 122 BIRCHES 33
    TO SEE FOR MYSELF ABOUT THE BIRCH . . . . . . 123 PEA BRUSH 3
    THEY LOOKED ABOUT FOR SOMEONE TO HAVE DONE IT. . . . 132 THE BONFIRE . . . 89
    ABOUT THE SHIPS WHERE WAR HAS FOUND THEM OUT . . . 132 THE BONFIRE . . . 104
    AT SEA, ABOUT THE TOWNS WHERE WAR HAS COME . . . . 132 THE BONFIRE . . . 105
    IN CASTING ABOUT FOR A CORNER . . . . 133 A GIRL'S GARDEN . . 9
    HE TOLD ME A LITTLE ABOUT HIMSELF. . . . . . . 140 THE GUM-GATHERER . . 12
    THE RED MAN GAVE IN POKING ABOUT THE MILL, ... 142 THE VANISHING RED . 15
    WHAT? WE'VE FOUND OUT IN ONE HOUR MORE ABOUT HIM . . 152 SNOW 252
    WE'RE GLAD. OH, SAY NO MORE ABOUT IT, MAN. . . . . 155 SNOW 332
    I WONDER ABOUT THE TREES. . . . . 156 THE SOUND OF TREES . 1
    "ABOUT THE BRITISH ARCTIC. THAT'S WHAT COMES . . . 159 NEW HAMPSHIRE . . 23
    ABOUT DISPOSING OF IT. DO YOU KNOW, ... 164 NEW HAMPSHIRE . . 169
    ANYTHING I CAN SAY ABOUT NEW HAMPSHIRE . . . . . 165 NEW HAMPSHIRE . . 210
    WILL SERVE ALMOST AS WELL ABOUT VERMONT, ... 165 NEW HAMPSHIRE . . 211
    ABOUT THE PEOPLE BEING BETTER THERE . . . . . 167 NEW HAMPSHIRE . . 255
    I DON'T KNOW WHAT TO SAY ABOUT THE PEOPLE. . . . . 167 NEW HAMPSHIRE . . 265
    ABOUT OUR PLACE AMONG THE INFINITIES. . . . . . 168 NEW HAMPSHIRE . . 305
    ABOUT IMPROVING PEOPLE IN THE WORLD, ... 169 NEW HAMPSHIRE . . 336
    ABOUT THE NEW SCHOOL OF THE PSEUDO-PHALLIC, . . . 170 NEW HAMPSHIRE . . 359
    HOW ABOUT BEING A GOOD GREEK, FOR INSTANCE? . . . 171 NEW HAMPSHIRE . . 404
    AND RESTFUL JUST TO THINK ABOUT NEW HAMPSHIRE. . . . 172 NEW HAMPSHIRE . . 412
    ABOUT THE HOUSE--ABOUT THE PEOPLE NOT THERE. . . . 175 THE CENSUS-TAKER . 49
    ABOUT OUR PLACE AMONG THE INFINITIES. . . . . . 177 THE STAR-SPLITTER . 19
    MEAN LAUGHTER WENT ABOUT THE TOWN THAT DAY . . . . 177 THE STAR-SPLITTER . 40
    ABOUT HIS TELESCOPE. BEYOND THE AGE . . . . . 178 THE STAR-SPLITTER . 54

- 1 -

ABOUT (CONTINUED)
AS FATHERS ABOUT CHILDREN, YOU TELL TEACHER. . . . . . . 180 MAPLE 6
ABOUT THE DIFFERENT TREES, AND SOMETHING, TOO, ... 180 MAPLE 27
ABOUT YOUR MOTHER THAT PERHAPS MAY HELP." . . . . 180 MAPLE 28
WHAT WAS IT ABOUT HER NAME? ITS STRANGENESS LAY . . . . 181 MAPLE 44
SOMETHING ABOUT WAVE OFFERING, IT SAID." . . . . 183 MAPLE 107
ABOUT THE WAY HE SAW IT WAS WITH YOU . . . . 183 MAPLE 128
LAID SCARLET AND PALE PINK ABOUT HER FEET. . . . . . . 184 MAPLE 147
WHAT IT WAS ALL ABOUT. THERE MIGHT BE SOMETHING . . . . 185 THE AX-HELVE . . . 15
WHERE I MUST JUDGE IF WHAT HE KNEW ABOUT AN AX . . . . . 186 THE AX-HELVE . . . 41
DO YOU KNOW, WHAT WE TALKED ABOUT WAS KNOWLEDGE? . . . . 188 THE AX-HELVE . . . 82
BAPTISTE ON HIS DEFENSE ABOUT THE CHILDREN . . . . . . 188 THE AX-HELVE . . . 83
THE ONE ABOUT HIS JUMPING SO'S TO LAND . . . . 192 PAUL'S WIFE . . . 50
AND TELL PAUL WHAT HE OUGHT TO DO ABOUT IT. . . . . . . 193 PAUL'S WIFE . . . 79
ABOUT HIS WIFE TO KEEP HER TO HIMSELF. . . . . 195 PAUL'S WIFE . . . 149
WOULDN'T BE SPOKEN TO ABOUT A WIFE . . . . 196 PAUL'S WIFE . . . 156
"WHY, IF SHE ISN'T SERIOUS ABOUT IT! . . . . 198 WILD GRAPES . . . 81
I DON'T KNOW MUCH ABOUT THE LETTING DOWN; . . . . 198 WILD GRAPES . . . 84
LABAN HAD KNOWN ABOUT WHAT IT WOULD BE . . . . 201 PLACE FOR A THIRD . . 73
WE WERE ABOUT IT ONE NIGHT IN THE CELLAR. . . . . 206 THE WITCH OF COOS . . 142
ABOUT WHERE HENRY HUDSON'S GONE, ... 211 AN EMPTY THREAT . . 16
LET'S TALK ABOUT IT." / "LET'S GO SEE THE PLACE." . . . 213 A FOUNTAIN, A BOTTLE . 16
AND HAD IT PUBLISHED. IT WAS ALL ABOUT . . . . 215 A FOUNTAIN, A BOTTLE . 79
BOOKS WERE NOT THROWN IRREVERENTLY ABOUT. . . . . 216 A FOUNTAIN, A BOTTLE . 117
BUT ONE THING ABOUT IT, IT MUSTN'T GET WARM. . . . . . 228 GOOD-BY AND KEEP COLD . 16
A NUMBER IN. BUT WHAT ABOUT THE BROOK . . . . 231 A BROOK IN THE CITY . 3
DUST ALWAYS BLOWING ABOUT THE TOWN, ... 249 A PECK OF GOLD . . . 1
FATE HAD HER IMAGINATION ABOUT HER, ... 252 TREE AT MY WINDOW . . 14
THE LIGHT WAS WHAT IT WAS ALL ABOUT: . . . . 253 THE THATCH 5
THEY COULD NOT GO FLYING ABOUT IN SEARCH . . . . 253 THE THATCH 23
OF WHIRLING HANDS AND ARMS ABOUT THE HEAD . . . . 277 THE WHITE-TAILED HORNET . 9
YET HOW ABOUT THE INSECT CERTAINTY . . . . 277 THE WHITE-TAILED HORNET . 12
HAWKING FOR FLIES ABOUT THE KITCHEN DOOR, ... 278 THE WHITE-TAILED HORNET . 24
ABOUT MY CREVICE AND BURROW. . . . . 282 A DRUMLIN WOODCHUCK . 32
ABOUT WHO IS TOO OLD TO GO WALKING, ... 294 A RECORD STRIDE . . 11
ABOUT BEING PAST-ACTIVE SHOES. . . . . 295 A RECORD STRIDE . . 32
TILL ABOUT THE RIGHT CONSISTENCE. . . . . 304 CLEAR AND COLDER . . 6
ABOUT THE WORLD'S DESPAIR; . . . . 309 NOT ALL THERE . . . 2
YOU LIKE TO HEAR ABOUT GOLD. . . . . 310 THE VINDICTIVES . . 1
IF EARTH WERE THOUGHT ABOUT TO CHANGE ITS AXIS, ... 317 BUILD SOIL 58
JUST WHAT AM I SUPPOSED TO DO ABOUT IT? . . . . 322 BUILD SOIL 205
WITH A LENGTH OF CORDAGE ABOUT THE WAIST. . . . . 346 DISCOVERY OF MADEIRAS . 77
THEY ADDED CLASPS ABOUT THE NECK . . . . 346 DISCOVERY OF MADEIRAS . 83
ONE MORE MILLENNIUM'S ABOUT TO END. . . . . 352 THE LESSON FOR TODAY . 46
TAKE COMFORT IN ABOUT THE SAME COMPLAINT. . . . . 353 THE LESSON FOR TODAY . 82
(MAKE NO MISTAKE ABOUT ITS BEING BONES); . . . . 354 THE LESSON FOR TODAY . 132
ABOUT HOW LONG A MAN MAY THINK TO LIVE, ... 354 THE LESSON FOR TODAY . 135
WHEN SOMETHING STRANGE ABOUT IT MADE ME THINK. . . . . 357 A CONSIDERABLE SPECK . 6
AS GRAVE AS HE ABOUT THE WORLD'S DEFEAT. . . . . 359 THE LOST FOLLOWER . . 24
SOMETHING ABOUT A KINGDOM IN THE SKY . . . . 359 THE LOST FOLLOWER . . 35
ABOUT WHEN BEST TO HAVE US IN OUR ORBIT, ... 361 A LOOSE MOUNTAIN . . 20
"TRAVELER, I'M GLAD YOU ASKED ABOUT THAT LIGHT. . . . . 368 THE LITERATE FARMER AND 23
SAY ABOUT HALFWAY UP THE WESTERN SKY, ... 370 THE LITERATE FARMER AND 66
ABOUT IT, THOUGH. WE HAVEN'T GOT THE MIND. . . . . . . 372 THE LITERATE FARMER AND 133
AND THERE'S A STORY IN A BOOK ABOUT IT: . . . . 377 DIRECTIVE 13
'TWAS SOMETHING WE KNEW ALL ABOUT TO BEGIN WITH . . . . 380 TOO ANXIOUS FOR RIVERS . 24
THAT MEN HAVE THOUGHT ABOUT IN VAIN. . . . . 381 AN UNSTAMPED LETTER IN . 37
THEN FROM THE WORK YOU WENT ABOUT . . . . 381 AN UNSTAMPED LETTER IN . 48
THE ONLY THING I WORRY ABOUT IS THE SUN. . . . . 392 IT BIDS PRETTY FAIR . 3
I GRANT YOU--IF YOU'RE SURE ABOUT THE WORD. . . . . . . 394 LUCRETIUS VERSUS POETS . 11
AND ALL THE GREAT CONVENTION WAS ABOUT. . . . . 400 THE BROKEN DROUGHT . . 5
SO IF THEY FOUGHT ABOUT EQUALITY . . . . 404 FROM PLANE TO PLANE . 5
OR YOU'D FEEL DIFFERENTLY ABOUT THE CLASSES. . . . . . 406 FROM PLANE TO PLANE . 78
TODAY I WANT TO TALK ABOUT THE SUN. . . . . 406 FROM PLANE TO PLANE . 87
"ALL RIGHT, LET'S HARMONIZE ABOUT THE DOCTOR. . . . . . 407 FROM PLANE TO PLANE . 102
THAT SHOULD IF NOT BE TALKED THEN SUNG ABOUT. . . . . . 411 POD OF THE MILKWEED . 9
BUT HOW ABOUT THE WHEREWITHAL? . . . . 416 AMERICA IS HARD TO SEE . 4
IS ABOUT TIRED OF BEING LOOTED . . . . 419 AMERICA IS HARD TO SEE . 81
NEXT MORNING THE MINUTE I WAS ABOUT . . . . 420 ONE MORE BREVITY . . 44
AND YET DONE NOTHING ABOUT IT IN SONG. . . . . 421 ONE MORE BREVITY . . 65
THEY WOULD BRING EMPIRES DOWN ABOUT OUR EARS . . . . . 423 FOR JOHN F. KENNEDY . 29
LOVE IS ALL ABOUT. . . . . 429 KITTY HAWK 31
HOW ABOUT THE LIE . . . . 430 KITTY HAWK 64
ASKED ABOUT MY SOUL . . . . 432 KITTY HAWK 143
DARE TO SPEAK OUT AND TELL ME ABOUT MYSELF. . . . . . . 456 HOW HARD TO KEEP FROM . 100
WHERE HOMER BEGGED. HE'LL TELL YOU ABOUT FREEDOM. . . . 459 HOW HARD TO KEEP FROM . 183
WITH ALL THIS TALK ABOUT THE HOPE OF YOUTH . . . . . . 462 HOW HARD TO KEEP FROM . 257
WORKED UP ABOUT IT. BUT SHE REALLY HASN'T-- . . . . . 476 A MASQUE OF REASON . 94
THAN THE DAY SHE WAS BORN / THAT'S ABOUT RIGHT, ... 479 A MASQUE OF REASON . 158
I NEED SOME HELP ABOUT THIS REASON PROBLEM . . . . . . 479 A MASQUE OF REASON . 165
BUT WHAT IS ALL THIS SECRECY ABOUT? . . . . 483 A MASQUE OF REASON . 272
IT COMES DOWN TO A DOUBT ABOUT THE WISDOM . . . . 483 A MASQUE OF REASON . 291
SO THERE IS NOTHING WE CAN DO ABOUT IT. . . . . 483 A MASQUE OF REASON . 293
I STICK TO THAT. BUT TALK ABOUT CONFUSION!-- . . . . . 485 A MASQUE OF REASON . 336
I'D HAD ABOUT ENOUGH OF HIS DERISION . . . . 485 A MASQUE OF REASON . 349
SOMETHING ABOUT--(THE THREE MEN LAUGH.) . . . . 487 A MASQUE OF REASON . 400
ABOUT HIS BLINDNESS. / OH, HE SPEAKS! HE CAN SPEAK! . . 488 A MASQUE OF REASON . 417
HE HAS HIS BUSINESS HE MUST BE ABOUT. . . . . 489 A MASQUE OF REASON . 431
DON'T YOU BE BITTER ABOUT IT. I'M NOT BITTER. . . . . . 494 A MASQUE OF MERCY . . 26
ABOUT A WHALE. / OH, YOU MEAN MOBY DICK . . . . 495 A MASQUE OF MERCY . . 48
HOW ABOUT LOVING GOD? / YOU MAKE ME SHRUG.-- . . . . . 499 A MASQUE OF MERCY . . 164
ABOUT OUR OWN OR ANYBODY'S END. . . . . 507 A MASQUE OF MERCY . . 354
WE'VE HAD ABOUT ENOUGH OF THESE SENSATIONS. . . . . . . 508 A MASQUE OF MERCY . . 396
YOU SAY IT, PAUL. / YOU MEAN ABOUT SUCCESS, ... 509 A MASQUE OF MERCY . . 409
TO EMBROIL THE VERY GODS ABOUT THEIR SPHERES . . . . . 511 A MASQUE OF MERCY . . 471
BUT LET'S BE SERIOUS ABOUT PAUL'S OFFER. . . . . 513 A MASQUE OF MERCY . . 519
I WON'T DECEIVE MYSELF ABOUT SUCCESS. . . . . 513 A MASQUE OF MERCY . . 525
SOMETHING TO BE FANATICAL ABOUT, ... 515 A MASQUE OF MERCY . . 570

ABOUT (CONTINUED)
   NAIVENESS ABOUT JUSTICE OUT OF HIM, ... 517 A MASQUE OF MERCY . . 640
   WAS ABOUT ALL THERE EVER WAS TO ME. . . . . 518 A MASQUE OF MERCY . . 658
ABOVE
   THAT SUDDENLY ABOVE THE BEES IS HEARD, ... 12 A PRAYER IN SPRING . . 10
   THE WHICH IT IS RESERVED FOR GOD ABOVE . . . . . . 12 A PRAYER IN SPRING . . 14
   THEY FALL FROM GIVING SHADE ABOVE, ... 25 IN HARDWOOD GROVES . . 2
   THE CROWS ABOVE THE FOREST CALL; . . . . 27 OCTOBER 5
   TOSSED, TANGLED, WHIRLED AND WHIRLED ABOVE, ... 28 MY BUTTERFLY 16
   TO HAVE SOME HEAD OF WATER FROM ABOVE, ... 43 THE MOUNTAIN 70
   A MAN? A BRUTE. NAKED ABOVE THE WAIST, ... 46 A HUNDRED COLLARS . . 50
   KEEPING HIS HEAD ABOVE. 'DAMN YE,' I SAYS, ... 72 THE CODE 77
   UP TO THE BRIM, AND EVEN ABOVE THE BRIM. . . . . . 122 BIRCHES 38
   WE TALKED LIKE BARKING ABOVE THE DIN . . . . 140 THE GUM-GATHERER . . 7
   THAT JANGLED EVEN ABOVE THE GENERAL NOISE, ... 142 THE VANISHING RED . . 25
   PILING IT WELL ABOVE THE WINDOWSILLS. . . . . . . 149 SNOW 179
   THAN THE MAN FIGHTING IT TO KEEP ABOVE IT, ... 151 SNOW 225
   AND A VAGUE ALL-DISTURBING ROAR ABOVE THE RIVER . . 182 MAPLE 83
   OR STAINED BY VEGETATION FROM ABOVE, ... 214 A FOUNTAIN, A BOTTLE . 39
   AND BLUE SO FAR ABOVE US COMES SO HIGH, ... 220 FRAGMENTARY BLUE . . 7
   DREAD FIFTY ABOVE MORE THAN FIFTY BELOW." . . . . . 228 GOOD-BY AND KEEP COLD . 19
   WHERE THE CHIMNEY STARTED ABOVE THE STOVE. . . . . 232 THE KITCHEN CHIMNEY . 12
   ABOVE A HAZY TREE-AND-FARMHOUSE CLUSTER . . . . . 245 THE FREEDOM OF THE MOON 2
   HURRYING LOW ABOVE THE GROVE, SOME WAIF . . . . . 249 ACCEPTANCE 9
   THE BEAR PUTS BOTH ARMS AROUND THE TREE ABOVE HER . 268 THE BEAR 1
   ONE WHO WOULD NEVER HANG ABOVE A BOOKCASE . . . . 278 THE WHITE-TAILED HORNET 17
   GODS ABOVE ARE NOT ABOVE IT. . . . . 304 CLEAR AND COLDER . . 23
   MADE PUBLICLY IN SCHOOL, ABOVE SUSPICION . . . . . 324 BUILD SOIL 274
   ABOVE SOME MORE RELIGION IN A MANGER. . . . . . . 369 THE LITERATE FARMER AND 35
   LIKE TROUBLE IN THE BROW ABOVE THE EYES: . . . . . 399 THE INGENUITIES OF DEBT 3
   TWO THOUSAND FEET ABOVE THE OCEAN LEVEL. . . . . . 400 TO THE RIGHT PERSON . 6
   THAT HANGS PERCEPTIBLY ABOVE THE SCENE. . . . . . 412 POD OF THE MILKWEED . 29
ABREAST
   AND MAKES GAPS EVEN TWO CAN PASS ABREAST. . . . . 33 MENDING WALL 4
ABROAD
   SINCE EVER THEY FLUNG ABROAD IN SPRING . . . . . . 236 MISGIVING 5
   SOMEHOW MUST HAVE GOTTEN ABROAD, ... 251 BEREFT 14
ABRUPTION
   AND THE MOST SACRED THING OF ALL'S ABRUPTION. . . . 510 A MASQUE OF MERCY . . 435
ABRUPTLY
   AND SLOW ME DOWN--AND I ABRUPTLY SLOWED, ... 189 THE GRINDSTONE . . . 32
ABSENCE
   TO THE DARK HOUSE AFTER SO LONG AN ABSENCE, ... 89 THE FEAR 18
ABSENT
   BUT ON THE MEMORY OF ONE ABSENT, MOST, ... 15 WAITING 26
ABSENTIA
   PERICLES SENT ASPASIA IN ABSENTIA: . . . . 461 HOW HARD TO KEEP FROM 250
ABSENT-SPIRITED
   I AM TOO ABSENT-SPIRITED TO COUNT; . . . . 296 DESERT PLACES . . . 7
ABSOLUTE
   WITH THE ABSOLUTE FLIGHT AND REST . . . . 388 MIDDLENESS OF THE ROAD 14
   THROUGH TEMPERATURE OF ABSOLUTE ZERO? . . . . . . 395 WHY WAIT FOR SCIENCE . 8
ABSOLUTELY
   ARE ABSOLUTELY SURE TO COME TO GRIEF. . . . . . . 394 HAEC FABULA DOCET . . 20
   AND HELD THEM ABSOLUTELY PARALLEL . . . . 396 ANY SIZE WE PLEASE . . 6
ABSORB
   SO WE WON'T SIMPLY TAKE IT AND ABSORB IT. . . . . . 361 A LOOSE MOUNTAIN . . 21
ABSTRACT
   TO KEEP OUR ABSTRACT VERSE FROM BEING DRY. . . . . 395 ETHEREALIZING . . . 14
   OF COURSE, IN THE ABSTRACT HIGH SINGULAR . . . . . 478 A MASQUE OF REASON . 137
ABSTRACTION
   EXCEPT AS AN ABSTRACTION OF THE MIND. . . . . . . 318 BUILD SOIL 71
ABSURD
   WHICH MAKES OPPOSING IT TO ART ABSURD . . . . . . 394 LUCRETIUS VERSUS POETS 10
   INDULGING AN ABSURD DRAMATIC SPELL, ... 396 ANY SIZE WE PLEASE . . 3
ABSURDLY (SEE SOLEMN-ABSURDLY)
   BOTH ARE DELIGHTFUL STATES FOR THEIR ABSURDLY . . . 165 NEW HAMPSHIRE . . . 186
ABUSED
   THAT THEY MAY BE ABUSED AND TAKEN ADVANTAGE OF . . . 322 BUILD SOIL 189
A-BUTTONING
   A-BUTTONING COATS, TO ASK HIM WHO HE WAS. . . . . 106 CHRISTMAS TREES . . . 8
ABYSMAL
   LONG SINCE IN SOME ABYSMAL CITY STREET, ... 359 THE LOST FOLLOWER . . 22
ABYSS
   IN THE ABYSS OF ODOR AND RUSTLE AT MY BACK, ... 14 WAITING 19
   ACROSS THE SOUL-FROM-SOUL ABYSS, ... 328 A MISSIVE MISSILE . . 49
ABYSS'S
   TO FILL THE ABYSS'S VOID WITH EMPTINESS. . . . . . 259 WEST-RUNNING BROOK . . 49
ACCELERATING
   IT SEEMS TO START RIGHT OFF ACCELERATING. . . . . 489 A MASQUE OF REASON . 450
ACCENT
   HIS ACCENT WAS NOT GOOD. . . . . 366 NOT OF SCHOOL AGE . . 17
ACCEPT
   AND BOW AND ACCEPT THE END . . . . 30 RELUCTANCE 23
   "I WON'T ACCEPT THE SUBSTITUTE. IT'S EMPTY." . . . 214 A FOUNTAIN, A BOTTLE . 43
   BUT IF YOU WILL ACCEPT THE TIP, ... 326 TO A THINKER . . . 18
   HELP ME ACCEPT ITS FATE WITH CHRISTMAS FEELING. . . 350 TO A YOUNG WRETCH . . 24
   COWER DOWN IN DESPERATION TO ACCEPT . . . . 357 A CONSIDERABLE SPECK . 22
   SHE'S HAD SOME LOSS SHE CAN'T ACCEPT FROM GOD-- . . 501 A MASQUE OF MERCY . . 204
   THAT IS THE MYSTERY YOU MUST ACCEPT.-- . . . . . . 512 A MASQUE OF MERCY . . 511
   DO YOU ACCEPT IT, MASTER JONAS DOVE? . . . . . . 512 A MASQUE OF MERCY . . 512
ACCEPTABLE
   BE FOUND ACCEPTABLE IN HEAVEN'S SIGHT. . . . . . . 520 A MASQUE OF MERCY . . 722
   BE FOUND ACCEPTABLE IN HEAVEN'S SIGHT. . . . . . . 520 A MASQUE OF MERCY . . 725
ACCEPTANCE
   ACCEPTANCE . . . . 249 ACCEPTANCE . . . . T
ACCEPTED
   SO IT WOULD BE ACCEPTED BY TWO CLASSES, ... 162 NEW HAMPSHIRE . . . 95

ACCEPTED (CONTINUED)
   BEFORE, THAT IS, THEY ARE THEMSELVES ACCEPTED, ... 162 NEW HAMPSHIRE . . . 97
   WHICH I ACCEPTED WITH IMPATIENT SIGHT, ... 295 LOST IN HEAVEN . . . 3
   HIS CAPTORS ACCEPTED IT ALL, ... 310 THE VINDICTIVES . . . 8
   THAT EVER ACCEPTED FATE . . . . 444 THE DRAFT HORSE . . . 14
ACCEPTING
   ACCEPTING ANYTHING BEFORE HE KNOWS . . . . 100 THE SELF-SEEKER . . . 201
ACCESS
   THE THREE STOOD LISTENING TO A FRESH ACCESS . . . . . 143 SNOW 1
ACCIDENT
   "NOW, THE PLACE WHERE THE ACCIDENT OCCURRED----" . . . 100 THE SELF-SEEKER . . . 207
   BUT THE SAD ACCIDENT OF HAVING SEEN . . . . 169 NEW HAMPSHIRE . . . 329
   WHICH SHOWS HOW SAD AN ACCIDENT MAY BE. . . . . 169 NEW HAMPSHIRE . . . 333
ACCIDENTALLY
   TILL ACCIDENTALLY IT HIT ON MIND . . . . 425 ACCIDENTALLY ON PURPOSE 6
   ACCIDENTALLY ON PURPOSE . . . . 425 ACCIDENTALLY ON PURPOSE T
ACCLAIM
   AND A HUSH FALLS FOR ALL ACCLAIM. . . . . 21 THE TRIAL BY EXISTENCE 60
ACCOMMODATE
   AND ACCOMMODATE HER YOUNG LIFE TO HIS. . . . . 66 A SERVANT TO SERVANTS . 128
ACCOMPLISHMENT
   "I KNOW, THAT'S SILAS' ONE ACCOMPLISHMENT. . . . . . 37 DEATH OF THE HIRED MAN 88
   AND GO AHEAD TO ANY ACCOMPLISHMENT. . . . . 521 A MASQUE OF MERCY . . 730
ACCORDED
   WHATEVER I ACCORDED IT OF FATE. . . . . 357 A CONSIDERABLE SPECK . 23
ACCORDING
   ACCORDING AS HE FEARED TO RISK . . . . 138 BROWN'S DESCENT . . 27
   SUCH AS ACCORDING TO BELIEF IN ROME . . . . 315 IRIS BY NIGHT . . . 5
ACCOUNTED
   HAS BEEN THOUGHT OUT AND ACCOUNTED FOR. . . . . . . 306 A TRIAL RUN 12
ACCOUNTING
   THE HARDSHIP OF ACCOUNTING . . . . 309 HARDSHIP OF ACCOUNTING T
ACCOUNTS
   SOMETIMES HE GETS POSSESSED TO KEEP ACCOUNTS . . . . 86 THE HOUSEKEEPER . . . 158
ACCUMULATED
   IN THE FOND FAITH ACCUMULATED FACT . . . . 414 A CABIN IN THE CLEARING 26
ACCURSED
   TO BUILD THE SOIL. FOR WHAT IS MORE ACCURSED . . . . 323 BUILD SOIL 217
   EVEN MORE ACCURSED . . . . 430 KITTY HAWK . . . 76
   ON A LANDSCAPE SO ACCURSED . . . . 466 SOME SCIENCE FICTION . 30
ACHE
   MY INSTEP ARCH NOT ONLY KEEPS THE ACHE, ... 68 AFTER APPLE-PICKING . 21
   I HAD THE SWIRL AND ACHE . . . . 227 TO EARTHWARD . . . 9
   AS IF SHE MADE IT ACHE . . . . 339 THE SUBVERTED FLOWER . 19
ACHIEVE
   ACHIEVE AT TIMES A VERY STARLIKE START. . . . . . . 246 FIREFLIES IN THE GARDEN 5
   AN END YOU CAN'T BY ANY MEANS ACHIEVE, ... 512 A MASQUE OF MERCY . . 509
ACHIEVED
   THE TALE OF THE VOYAGE HE HAD ACHIEVED, ... 347 DISCOVERY OF MADEIRAS . 130
ACHIEVEMENT
   YOU FAILED TO SEE THE WORTH OF YOUR ACHIEVEMENT. . . . 480 A MASQUE OF REASON . . 187
ACHIEVES
   LOUDER THAN ACTIONS, AND SOMETIMES ACHIEVES IT. . . . 171 NEW HAMPSHIRE . . . 402
ACHING
   I DWELL WITH A STRANGELY ACHING HEART . . . . 6 GHOST HOUSE . . . 11
   THE HEART IS STILL ACHING TO SEEK, ... 30 RELUCTANCE . . . 17
A-CHOKING
   I'VE BEEN A-CHOKING LIKE A NURSERY TREE . . . . . . 46 A HUNDRED COLLARS . 56
ACKNOWLEDGE
   I WANTED HIM FORCED TO ACKNOWLEDGE SO MUCH. . . . . . 486 A MASQUE OF REASON . 359
ACKNOWLEDGMENT
   THEN CAME HIS LITTLE ACKNOWLEDGMENT: . . . . 364 TRESPASS 17
   THIS VERSE THAT IN ACKNOWLEDGMENT I BRING . . . . . 422 FOR JOHN F. KENNEDY . 7
A-COMING
   THERE'S A HAY LOAD A-COMING—WHEN IT COMES. . . . . . 49 A HUNDRED COLLARS . . 132
ACQUAINTANCE
   OF AN ACQUAINTANCE MADE ADVENTUROUSLY." . . . . . . 78 THE GENERATIONS OF MEN 153
ACQUAINTED
   I HAVE BEEN ONE ACQUAINTED WITH THE NIGHT. . . . . . 255 ACQUAINTED WITH NIGHT . 1
   ACQUAINTED WITH THE NIGHT . . . . 255 ACQUAINTED WITH NIGHT . T
   I HAVE BEEN ONE ACQUAINTED WITH THE NIGHT. . . . . . 255 ACQUAINTED WITH NIGHT . 14
   IN HER WE MAKE OURSELVES ACQUAINTED . . . . 280 BLUE RIBBON AT AMESBURY 11
ACQUIRE
   AND ACQUIRE A LISTENING AIR. . . . . 156 THE SOUND OF TREES . . 9
ACQUIRED
   ACQUIRED ANCESTRALLY IN JUST SUCH TREES . . . . . . 197 WILD GRAPES . . . 49
ACRE
   AND EVERY ACRE GOOD ENOUGH TO EAT, ... 365 OF STONES OF THE PLACE 7
   HOW MANY THOUSAND OF THEM IN AN ACRE. . . . . 404 FROM PLANE TO PLANE . 17
ACROSS
   ACROSS THE REEDS TO A WINDOW LIGHT. . . . . 15 IN A VALE 5
   ACROSS THE SILL FROM THE OUTER GLOOM. . . . . 15 IN A VALE 9
   ACROSS THE FIELDS BEHIND THE HOUSE . . . . 18 GOING FOR WATER . . . 3
   MY APPLE TREES WILL NEVER GET ACROSS . . . . 33 MENDING WALL . . . 25
   AND A COLD CHILL SHIVERED ACROSS THE LAKE. . . . . . 63 A SERVANT TO SERVANTS . 31
   FLICKERING ACROSS ITS BOSOM. SUDDENLY . . . . 69 THE CODE 6
   BUT NOT COME IN ACROSS THE SACRED SILL----" . . . . 79 THE GENERATIONS OF MEN 170
   SNATCHED RIGHT AND LEFT ACROSS THE SILVER PULLEYS. . . 94 THE SELF-SEEKER . . 39
   ACROSS HIS CHEST TO MAKE AS 'TWERE A BOW. . . . . . 114 IN THE HOME STRETCH . 107
   ACROSS THE LINES OF STRAIGHTER DARKER TREES, ... 121 BIRCHES 2
   BROKEN ACROSS IT, AND ONE EYE IS WEEPING . . . . . 122 BIRCHES 46
   FROM A TWIG'S HAVING LASHED ACROSS IT OPEN. . . . . . 122 BIRCHES 47
   SWEET-SCENTED STUFF WHEN THE BREEZE DREW ACROSS IT. . . 136 "OUT,OUT--" . . . 3
   SO HIGH ACROSS THE PANE OUTSIDE. THERE WHERE . . . . 149 SNOW 191
   THE NEAREST BOUNDARY TO ESCAPE ACROSS. . . . . . . 167 NEW HAMPSHIRE . . . 253
   ACROSS THE ROAR AND CHAOS, AND THE WORDS . . . . . 170 NEW HAMPSHIRE . . . 350
   BEFORE I MADE THE TENTH ACROSS THE THRESHOLD. . . . . 175 THE CENSUS-TAKER . . 33
   STRIKING IT GENTLY ACROSS HER LOWERED EYES . . . . . 181 MAPLE 42

ACROSS (CONTINUED)
ACROSS THE HANDLE'S LONG-DRAWN SERPENTINE, ... 186 THE AX-HELVE 24
LIKE THE TWO STROKES ACROSS A DOLLAR SIGN. . . . . . . 186 THE AX-HELVE 25
OF BENDING LIKE A SWORD ACROSS THE KNEE. . . . . 187 THE AX-HELVE 71
ACROSS THE LOGS LIKE BACKS OF ALLIGATORS, ... 195 PAUL'S WIFE 121
TO OTHER HILLS ACROSS A KETTLE VALLEY. . . . . 195 PAUL'S WIFE 126
FALLING IN LOVE ACROSS THE TWILIGHT MILLPOND. . . . . . 195 PAUL'S WIFE 131
MORE THAN A MILE ACROSS THE WILDERNESS . . . . 195 PAUL'S WIFE 132
THE SISTER HAD NOT COME ACROSS THIS LABAN; . . . . . . 201 PLACE FOR A THIRD . . . 66
ACROSS THE WALL, AS NEAR THE WALL AS THEY. . . . . . . 229 TWO LOOK AT TWO 16
ACROSS THE WALL, AS NEAR THE WALL AS THEY. . . . . . . 229 TWO LOOK AT TWO 28
WHEN SHOEING HOME ACROSS THE WHITE, ... 232 LOOKING FOR SUNSET BIRD   3
FROM NORTH TO SOUTH ACROSS THE BLUE; . . . . 233 LOOKING FOR SUNSET BIRD 19
IN PLACE ACROSS A CLOUD THE SLENDER RAY . . . . . . 235 VALLEY'S SINGING DAY . . 8
ACROSS EACH OTHER AND SIDE BY SIDE THEY LAY. . . . . . 237 A HILLSIDE THAW 29
ON A TREE FALLEN ACROSS THE ROAD . . . . 238 ON A TREE FALLEN ACROSS   T
THE BARN OPPOSED ACROSS THE WAY, ... 241 NEED OF BEING VERSED . . . 5
WAS SOMETHING BRUSHED ACROSS MY MIND . . . . 248 A PASSING GLIMPSE . . . 9
OUR BRIDGE ACROSS IT, AND THE BRIDGE SHALL BE . . . . 258 WEST-RUNNING BROOK . . . 14
SHE GROPES ACROSS THE PEN ALONE . . . . 281 BLUE RIBBON AT AMESBURY 41
ACROSS THE THRESHOLD IN THE TWILIGHT FLED HIM. . . . . 289 OLD BARN AT THE BOTTOM   9
ACROSS THE BARRIER OF ICE: . . . . 327 A MISSIVE MISSILE . . . 6
ACROSS THE ICY BARRIER . . . . 327 A MISSIVE MISSILE . . . 28
ACROSS THE SOUL-FROM-SOUL ABYSS, ... 328 A MISSIVE MISSILE . . . 49
FROM SOME TREE-HIDDEN CLIFF ACROSS THE LAKE. . . . . . 338 THE MOST OF IT 4
ACROSS THE LIGHT SNOW HOMEWARD SMELLING GREEN. . . . . 349 TO A YOUNG WRETCH . . . 6
ACROSS THE LANDSCAPE WITH A WATERING POT . . . . . . 354 THE LESSON FOR TODAY . 129
ACROSS THE GULF OF WELL-NIGH EVERYTHING . . . . . . 356 A MOTH SEEN IN WINTER . 21
SET OFF ACROSS WHAT I HAD WRITTEN THERE. . . . . . . 357 A CONSIDERABLE SPECK . . 3
MAY I IN MY BRIEF BOLT ACROSS THE SCENE . . . . . . 386 THE FEAR OF MAN . . . 15
ACROSS THE TESSELLATION OF THE FLOOR, ... 399 THE INGENUITIES OF DEBT 14
ACROSS THE PAGE TO WHERE WE STARTED FROM. . . . . . 405 FROM PLANE TO PLANE . . 52
ACROSS THE TINTED SNOW. . . . . 470 IN WINTER IN THE WOODS   8
OF OUTRAGE--VIOLENCE--THAT BREAKS ACROSS IT. . . . . 509 A MASQUE OF MERCY . . 431
ACT
YOU ACT AS IF YOU WISHED YOU HADN'T COME. . . . . . 47 A HUNDRED COLLARS . . . 71
BEFORE HE ACTED: HE'S JUST GOT ROUND TO ACT." . . . 70 THE CODE 19
(IN VERSE I THINK) AGAINST THE VOLSTEAD ACT. . . . . 160 NEW HAMPSHIRE 30
WOULD SOMEONE ONLY ACT IN TIME WE YET . . . . . . 290 OLD BARN AT THE BOTTOM   35
SO THE THICK-SKINS NEEDN'T ACT THIN-SKINNED . . . . 295 A RECORD STRIDE . . . 31
WE'RE NATIONAL AND ACT AS NATIONALS. . . . . . . 320 BUILD SOIL 146
WE CAN'T APPRAISE THE TIME IN WHICH WE ACT. . . . . 352 THE LESSON FOR TODAY . 43
THERE IS NO ACT MORE KINGLY THAN TO GIVE?" . . . . 458 HOW HARD TO KEEP FROM 140
I MEAN WE SEEM TO KNOW ENOUGH TO ACT ON. . . . . . 483 A MASQUE OF REASON . . 290
IN WHICH WE ACT IS A SEVERITY, ... 520 A MASQUE OF MERCY . . 711
ACTED
BEFORE HE ACTED: HE'S JUST GOT ROUND TO ACT." . . . 70 THE CODE 19
IT HAS TO SEE THEM ACTED OUT BY ACTORS, ... 481 A MASQUE OF REASON . . 224
ACTION
WITH HIM IT BODED ACTION, DEED. . . . . 274 A LONE STRIKER 49
ACTION IS THE WORD. . . . . 442 KITTY HAWK 450
ACTIONS
LOUDER THAN ACTIONS, AND SOMETIMES ACHIEVES IT. . . . 171 NEW HAMPSHIRE . . . 402
ITS ACTIONS ANY CLOUDLESS NIGHT WILL SHOW IT. . . . 370 THE LITERATE FARMER AND 64
ACTIVE (SEE PAST-ACTIVE)
ACTIVITY
BUT PHYSICAL ACTIVITY, I FIND. . . . . 479 A MASQUE OF REASON . . 154
ACTON
IN ACTON. AND THE MILLER IS SAID TO HAVE LAUGHED-- . . 142 THE VANISHING RED . . . 2
ACTOR
LIKE A LONE ACTOR ON A GLOOMY STAGE-- . . . . . . 160 NEW HAMPSHIRE 46
ACTORS
DON'T MIND A LITTLE THING LIKE THE ACTORS FIGHTING. . . 392 IT BIDS PRETTY FAIR . . 2
IT HAS TO SEE THEM ACTED OUT BY ACTORS, ... 481 A MASQUE OF REASON . . 224
DEVOTED ACTORS AT A SACRIFICE-- . . . . 481 A MASQUE OF REASON . . 225
THE ABLEST ACTORS I CAN LAY MY HANDS ON. . . . . . 481 A MASQUE OF REASON . . 226
ACTRESS
AND LIKE THE ACTRESS EXCLAIM "OH, MY GOD" AT? . . . . 165 NEW HAMPSHIRE . . . 207
ACTS
MAN ACTS MORE LIKE THE POOR BEAR IN A CAGE, ... 269 THE BEAR 13
ACTUAL
OUR ACTUAL MOUNTAINS GIVEN IN A MAP . . . . . . 169 NEW HAMPSHIRE . . . 330
NEVER MIND OF WHAT ACTUAL WORTH, ... 312 THE VINDICTIVES 83
ACTUALLY
THAT THE FLOWERS ACTUALLY KNELT, ... 250 LODGED 4
ACUMEN
BUT THEY'RE BLESSED WITH THE ACUMEN . . . . . . 387 THE COURAGE TO BE NEW . . 9
ACUTE
TRANSFORMED FROM CHRONIC TO ACUTE AND BLOODY? . . . . 317 BUILD SOIL 30
ADAM
LIKE ADAM AND EVE . . . . 413 AWAY! 11
ADAMS
JOHN ADAMS, JEFFERSON, AND MADISON-- . . . . . . 422 FOR JOHN F. KENNEDY . . 26
ADAM'S
LIKE THOSE WHO FURNISHED ADAM'S SONS WITH WIVES; . . . 161 NEW HAMPSHIRE 79
ADAPT
I REFUSE TO ADAPT MYSELF A MITE . . . . 166 NEW HAMPSHIRE . . . 234
ADAPTED
TO GET ADAPTED TO MY KIND OF FOOLING. . . . . . . 470 IT TAKES ALL SORTS.... . 2
ADD
NO CHOICE IS LEFT A POET, YOU MIGHT ADD, ... 352 THE LESSON FOR TODAY . . 61
BUT THAT'S A HARD ONE, FOR I HAVE TO ADD: . . . . . 458 HOW HARD TO KEEP FROM 151
ADDED
HE ADDED, IF YOU REALLY CARE TO KNOW, ... 36 DEATH OF THE HIRED MAN   51
ADDED: "YOU CAN JUDGE BETTER AFTER SEEING.-- . . . . 144 SNOW 35
AND SO BE ADDED TO THE MOON UP THERE. . . . . . . 234 EVENING A SUGAR ORCHARD 10
HAD ADDED TO THEIR OWN AN OVERSOUND, ... 338 NEVER WOULD BIRDS' SONG   4
THEY ADDED CLASPS ABOUT THE NECK . . . . 346 DISCOVERY OF MADEIRAS . 83

ADDED (CONTINUED)
   "HOEING'S TOO MUCH LIKE WORK FOR DICK," HE ADDED. . . . . . 404 FROM PLANE TO PLANE . 27
   THE THOUGHT THAT ADDED CUBITS TO YOUR HEIGHT . . . . . 506 A MASQUE OF MERCY . . 339
ADDING
   WAS ONLY ADDING FROST TO SNOW . . . . 233 LOOKING FOR SUNSET BIRD 15
   AND TRUST IT WON'T BE ADDING TO THE TORTURE. . . . . 484 A MASQUE OF REASON . . 326
ADDITIONAL
   AND SOMEONE ELSE ADDITIONAL TO HIM, ... 338 THE MOST OF IT . . . 15
ADDRESS
   THOSE COLLARS--WHO SHALL I ADDRESS THEM TO, ... 50 A HUNDRED COLLARS . . 163
   WE ALL KNOW HIS ADDRESS, MOUNT HECLA, ICELAND. . . . . 408 FROM PLANE TO PLANE . 143
ADDRESSED
   LOOKED IN A DOOR BEHIND HER AND ADDRESSED . . . . . 110 IN THE HOME STRETCH . 11
ADJECTIVE
   WHEN NO MAN'S NAME AND NO NOUN'S ADJECTIVE . . . . . 461 HOW HARD TO KEEP FROM 239
ADMIRE
   AND SENT HIM TO THE KING TO ADMIRE. . . . . 347 DISCOVERY OF MADEIRAS . 131
   THERE IS A DISTRICT SCHOOLHOUSE I ADMIRE . . . . . . 400 TO THE RIGHT PERSON . 2
ADMIRED
   WOULD KNOW THAT IT WAS THERE TO BE ADMIRED, ... 375 A YOUNG BIRCH . . . 18
   SUFFER YOURSELF TO BE ADMIRED, MY LOVE, ... 474 A MASQUE OF REASON . 30
   AS WALLER SAYS. / OR NOT ADMIRED. GO OVER . . . . . 474 A MASQUE OF REASON . 31
ADMISSION
   GAVE ME IN TRUTH: I LIKE THE FRANK ADMISSION. . . . . 474 A MASQUE OF REASON . 37
ADMIT
   SUCH AS EVEN POETS WOULD ADMIT PERFORCE . . . . . . 173 A STAR IN A STONEBOAT . 28
   IT IS VERY FAR NORTH, WE ADMIT, TO HAVE BROUGHT THE PEACH. . 305 THERE ARE ROUGHLY ZONES 6
   FOR DRAB IT IS ITS FONDEST MUST ADMIT. . . . . . . 411 POD OF THE MILKWEED . 14
ADMITS
   ADMITS NO MEMORY OF CHOICE, ... 21 THE TRIAL BY EXISTENCE 54
   SOMETHING'S THE MATTER, EVERYONE ADMITS. . . . . . 514 A MASQUE OF MERCY . . 562
ADMITTED
   ADMITTED; AND YET, WHAT WAS THAT TO HIM? . . . . . . 186 THE AX-HELVE 28
ADMITTEDLY
   ADMITTEDLY AN ELOQUENCE SO SOFT . . . . 338 NEVER WOULD BIRDS' SONG 6
   THE CITY IS ADMITTEDLY AN EVIL: . . . . 506 A MASQUE OF MERCY . . 336
ADOLESCENCE
   BUT BY OUR BITING OFF OUR ADOLESCENCE . . . . . . 508 A MASQUE OF MERCY . 388
ADOPT
   WITH THE RACE HE CHOSE TO ADOPT: . . . . 314 BEARER OF EVIL TIDINGS 38
ADOPTED
   RAIN WAS THE TEARS ADOPTED BY MY EYES . . . . . . 337 THE WIND AND THE RAIN . 47
ADOPTION
   SO I SPOKE IN TERMS OF ADOPTION THUS: . . . . . . 420 ONE MORE BREVITY . . 27
ADULT
   DEAN, ADULT EDUCATION MAY SEEM SILLY. . . . . . . 393 LUCRETIUS VERSUS POETS 1
ADVANCED
   DARKLY ADVANCED WITH A PERPETUAL DAGGER . . . . . 69 THE CODE 5
   BUT ADVANCED WITH HER AS SHE CROSSED THE GRASS. . . . 91 THE FEAR 60
ADVANCING
   ADVANCING TOWARD HER: "WHAT IS IT YOU SEE . . . . . 51 HOME BURIAL 6
ADVANTAGE
   THEY TAKE ADVANTAGE OF HIM SHAMEFULLY, ... 65 A SERVANT TO SERVANTS . 74
   BUT YOU GIVE HIM THE ADVANTAGE WITH THIS LIGHT. . . . 91 THE FEAR 55
   WHICH GIVES THEM THE ADVANTAGE IN THE TRADE. . . . . 95 THE SELF-SEEKER . . 64
   ONLY YOU HAVE THE ADVANTAGE OF THE GRAPES . . . . . 198 WILD GRAPES 69
   FROM MY ADVANTAGE ON A HILL . . . . 233 LOOKING FOR SUNSET BIRD 13
   THAT THEY MAY BE ABUSED AND TAKEN ADVANTAGE OF . . . 322 BUILD SOIL 189
   BUT HAVE WE THERE THE ADVANTAGE AFTER ALL? . . . . . 352 THE LESSON FOR TODAY . 73
   THEY BOTH WERE HIRED. AND THOUGH PIKE HAD THE ADVANTAGE . 404 FROM PLANE TO PLANE . 2
ADVANTAGE-DISADVANTAGE
   THE ADVANTAGE-DISADVANTAGE OF THESE DOORS . . . . . 289 OLD BARN AT THE BOTTOM 13
ADVANTAGES
   THE ADVANTAGES IT HAS, SO LONG AND NARROW, ... 63 A SERVANT TO SERVANTS . 19
   ADVANTAGES OF GROWING ALMOST WILD . . . . 162 NEW HAMPSHIRE . . . 104
   YOU HAVE HAD YOUR ADVANTAGES. . . . . 381 AN UNSTAMPED LETTER IN 44
ADVENT
   THAT, SILENCED BY MY ADVENT, FINDS ONCE MORE, ... 14 WAITING 20
ADVENTURE
   GOT ME INTO MY DOUBLE ADVENTURE. . . . . 294 A RECORD STRIDE . . . 18
   THE HEIGHT OF THE ADVENTURE IS THE HEIGHT . . . . . 378 DIRECTIVE 33
ADVENTUROUSLY
   OF AN ACQUAINTANCE MADE ADVENTUROUSLY." . . . . . . 78 THE GENERATIONS OF MEN 153
ADVERSE
   WE KNOW ENOUGH TO KNOW IT FOR ADVERSE. . . . . . . 352 THE LESSON FOR TODAY . 45
ADVERTISE
   TO ADVERTISE OUR FARMS TO CITY BUYERS, ... 316 BUILD SOIL 23
ADVERTISED
   BEHIND THE SCENES, ORDAINED AND ADVERTISED . . . . . 497 A MASQUE OF MERCY . . 97
ADVICE
   OH, NEVER BY WAY OF ADVICE! . . . . 134 A GIRL'S GARDEN . . . 46
   PAID HEED TO WOMEN, YOU'D TAKE MY ADVICE . . . . . 150 SNOW 216
   AND THEN TAKE OUR ADVICE NO MORE THAN NOTHING, . . . 155 SNOW 347
ADVISE
   "I DON'T ADVISE YOUR TRYING FROM THIS SIDE. . . . . 41 THE MOUNTAIN 38
   THAT'S WHY I DON'T ADVISE YOUR TRYING THIS SIDE. . . . 43 THE MOUNTAIN 79
   BUT HE WOULDN'T ADVISE A THING TO BLOSSOM. . . . . 276 TWO TRAMPS IN MUD TIME 32
ADVISED (SEE ILL-ADVISED)
   WHO ADVISED MAN TO COME AND LIVE THEREIN? . . . . . 400 THE BROKEN DROUGHT . . 14
ADVOCATE
   I ADVOCATE A SEMI-REVOLUTION. . . . . 363 A SEMI-REVOLUTION . . 1
AEGEAN
   'CROSS THE AEGEAN ISLES, ... 437 KITTY HAWK 289
   ALONG THE AEGEAN COAST. THAT'S ALL THEY TALK OF." . . . 459 HOW HARD TO KEEP FROM 168
AEON-LIMIT
   THERE IS AN AEON-LIMIT SET . . . . 328 A MISSIVE MISSILE . . 50
AEONS
   AEONS OF TIME AND STILL IT'S MOSTLY WOMEN . . . . . 478 A MASQUE OF REASON . 149

AEROPLANE
  WHO GAVE AMERICA THE AEROPLANE . . . . 423 FOR JOHN F. KENNEDY . 47
  AND NOW, O SEA, YOU'RE LOST BY AEROPLANE. . . . . . 446 DOES NO ONE AT ALL EVER 13
AFAR
  AND HE TURNED AND LOOKED AT THE ROAD AFAR . . . . . 7 LOVE AND A QUESTION . 7
  OR PLUNGING HEADLONG WITH FIERCE TWANG AFAR; . . . . 14 WAITING 13
  AT HIDE-AND-SEEK TO GOD AFAR, ... 19 REVELATION 10
  AND SOME EXCLAIMED WHO SAW AFAR . . . . 138 BROWN'S DESCENT . . 30
  WITH SHOUTS AFAR TO PULL THE CABLE TAUT, ... 141 THE LINE-GANG . . . 9
  THE EARTH HAD A SINGLE LIGHT AFAR, ... 291 ON HEART'S BEGINNING TO 6
AFFAIR
  "WELL, ANNE, GO, DEARIE. OUR AFFAIR WILL WAIT. . . . . 98 THE SELF-SEEKER . . . 167
  IT IS NOBODY ELSE'S AFFAIR. . . . . 289 DEPARTMENTAL 41
  A FULL-FLEDGED FAMILY AFFAIR. . . . . 365 A NATURE NOTE . . . 8
  BUT THAT IS NO AFFAIR . . . . 465 MILKY WAY IS A COWPATH 39
AFFAIRS
  MAKE SO MUCH DIFFERENCE IN HIS MAN'S AFFAIRS. . . . . 83 THE HOUSEKEEPER . . . 54
  WERE NOT THE ONE DEAD, TURNED TO THEIR AFFAIRS. . . . 137 "OUT,OUT--" 34
AFFECTION
  AFFECTION OR THE WANT OF IT IN THAT STATE. . . . . . 65 A SERVANT TO SERVANTS . 102
AFFINITY
  THEY CAN COMMAND THE EXACT AFFINITY . . . . 461 HOW HARD TO KEEP FROM 236
AFFIRM
  TO AFFIRM THERE IS SUCH A THING AS EVIL . . . . . . 317 BUILD SOIL 50
AFFLICTED
  YOU WERE AFFLICTED WITH IN THOSE OLD DAYS. . . . . . 475 A MASQUE OF REASON . . 61
AFFLICTING
  WHAT'S MORE, I HATE TO KEEP AFFLICTING WEEDS. . . . . 406 FROM PLANE TO PLANE . 64
AFFORD
  'ALL RIGHT,' I SAY, 'I CAN'T AFFORD TO PAY . . . . . 35 DEATH OF THE HIRED MAN 22
  WAS THE POORHOUSE, AND THOSE WHO COULD AFFORD, ... 65 A SERVANT TO SERVANTS . 94
AFIELD
  AFIELD AT DUSK . . . . 14 WAITING 5
A-FISHING
  ALL DUG TO GO A-FISHING IN." TO PAUL . . . . 193 PAUL'S WIFE 82
AFLOAT
  PARTICLE AFLOAT. . . . . 439 KITTY HAWK 368
AFLUTTER
  AND THE SHALLOW WATERS AFLUTTER WITH WIND . . . . . 27 A LINE-STORM SONG . . 19
A-FORAGING
  A-FORAGING ON STARS, ... 465 MILKY WAY IS A COWPATH 32
AFRAID
  YOU NEEDN'T BE AFRAID HE'LL LEAVE YOU THIS TIME." . . . 38 DEATH OF THE HIRED MAN 112
  THEY SEEM AFRAID. HE WOULDN'T HAVE IT SO: . . . . . 44 A HUNDRED COLLARS . . 11
  "HE WAS AFRAID OF BEING ROBBED OR MURDERED. . . . . 45 A HUNDRED COLLARS . . 31
  "SHOW HIM THIS WAY. I'M NOT AFRAID OF HIM. . . . . . 45 A HUNDRED COLLARS . . 37
  SPEAKING OF WHO'S AFRAID OF WHO, HOWEVER, ... 47 A HUNDRED COLLARS . . 81
  COME, IF YOU'RE NOT AFRAID." / "I'M NOT AFRAID. . . . 47 A HUNDRED COLLARS . . 87
  THERE'S NOTHING I'M AFRAID OF LIKE SCARED PEOPLE. . . . 50 A HUNDRED COLLARS . . 175
  I'M NOT AFRAID OF THEM, THOUGH, IF THEY'RE NOT . . . . 65 A SERVANT TO SERVANTS . 85
  AFRAID OF ME. THERE'S TWO CAN PLAY AT THAT. . . . . 65 A SERVANT TO SERVANTS . 86
  "AREN'T YOU AFRAID OF HIM? WHAT'S THAT GUN FOR?" . . . 83 THE HOUSEKEEPER . . . 65
  LIKE SOME MENFOLK. NO ONE'S AFRAID OF HIM; . . . . . 83 THE HOUSEKEEPER . . . 69
  THAT ISN'T IT. FOLKS AREN'T AFRAID OF US." . . . . 87 THE HOUSEKEEPER . . . 170
  AND THEN THE VOICE AGAIN: "YOU SEEM AFRAID. . . . . 91 THE FEAR 72
  AND MIGHT OUR MEDDLING MAKE HER MORE AFRAID. . . . . 109 THE EXPOSED NEST . . 25
  WAS AFRAID IN AN OFT-REPEATED DREAM . . . . . . 128 THE OFT-REPEATED DREAM 11
  AND HAVE OUR FIRE AND LAUGH AND BE AFRAID." . . . . 133 THE BONFIRE 114
  "I'M HALF AFRAID THAT'S JUST WHAT SHE MIGHT DO." . . . 154 SNOW 306
  I WOULDN'T BE A PRUDE AFRAID OF NATURE. . . . . . 170 NEW HAMPSHIRE . . 366
  I WAS AFRAID, IN BRIGHTENING FIRST ON ME, ... 187 THE AX-HELVE . . . 55
  THE THING THAT MADE ME MORE AND MORE AFRAID . . . . 190 THE GRINDSTONE . . . 65
  DON'T BE AFRAID. A FEW OF THEM WON'T HURT YOU. . . . 198 WILD GRAPES 57
  "I THINK THE LITTLE FELLOW'S AFRAID OF THE SNOW. . . . 223 THE RUNAWAY 9
  IT'S NOT THAT I'M GREATLY AFRAID OF FIRE, ... 232 THE KITCHEN CHIMNEY . 9
  THE TREES ARE ALL I'M AFRAID OF, ... 264 THE LAST MOWING . . 11
  IT'S NO MORE MEN I'M AFRAID OF; . . . . 264 THE LAST MOWING . . 13
  I'M NOT AFRAID TO PROPHESY THE FUTURE, ... 320 BUILD SOIL 134
  THERE IS NO ANSWER, I'M AFRAID, ... 327 A MISSIVE MISSILE . . 27
  SO NONE NEED BE AFRAID OF SIZE. . . . . 333 ALL REVELATION . . . 19
  WOULD BE AFRAID IF WE SHOULD COMPREHEND . . . . . 351 THE LESSON FOR TODAY . 36
  AND AS I WOKE AFRAID TO TURN . . . . 380 AN UNSTAMPED LETTER IN 21
  OR ELSE YOU WERE AFRAID OF BEING MOBBED . . . . . 497 A MASQUE OF MERCY . . 104
  COME ON, OR WE'LL BEGIN TO BE AFRAID. . . . . . . 506 A MASQUE OF MERCY . . 330
  AND I'M AFRAID. (THE BULB LIGHTS SICKEN DOWN. . . . 520 A MASQUE OF MERCY . . 695
  THE FEAR THAT YOU'RE AFRAID WITH IS THE FEAR . . . . 520 A MASQUE OF MERCY . . 697
  BUT I'M TOO MUCH AFRAID OF GOD TO CLAIM . . . . . 520 A MASQUE OF MERCY . . 705
  WE HAVE TO STAY AFRAID DEEP IN OUR SOULS . . . . . 520 A MASQUE OF MERCY . . 717
AFRESH
  TO MAKE IT ROOT AGAIN AND GROW AFRESH. . . . . . 109 THE EXPOSED NEST . . 8
  BY HAVING HIM WHIPPED EVERY DAY AFRESH . . . . . 517 A MASQUE OF MERCY . . 642
AFRICA
  WHERE ASIA WEDGES AFRICA FROM EUROPE. . . . . . 176 THE CENSUS-TAKER . . 53
  YOU COULD LOSE ASIA, AFRICA, AND EUROPE, ... 457 HOW HARD TO KEEP FROM 128
AFRICAN
  SAFELY MADE THE AFRICAN SHORE; . . . . 347 DISCOVERY OF MADEIRAS . 127
AFTER (SEE LONG-AFTER-BEDTIME, LONG-LONG-AFTER-THOUGHT)
  AFTER AN INTERVAL, HIS INSTRUMENT. . . . . . . 15 WAITING 21
  I WENT TO TURN THE GRASS ONCE AFTER ONE . . . . . 22 THE TUFT OF FLOWERS . 1
  AND IT SEEMS LIKE THE TIME WHEN, AFTER DOUBT, ... 27 A LINE-STORM SONG . . 29
  I HAVE COME AFTER THEM AND MADE REPAIR . . . . . 33 MENDING WALL 6
  AND SHUT IT AFTER HER. "BE KIND," SHE SAID. . . . . 34 DEATH OF THE HIRED MAN 7
  AFTER SO MANY YEARS HE STILL KEEPS FINDING . . . . 37 DEATH OF THE HIRED MAN 74
  AFTER THAT ONLY TOPS OF TREES, AND CLIFFS . . . . . 41 THE MOUNTAIN 31
  AFTER ELEVEN O'CLOCK AT NIGHT. TOO TIRED . . . . . 45 A HUNDRED COLLARS . . 17
  ANYTHING IN HER AFTER ALL THE YEARS. . . . . . 56 THE BLACK COTTAGE . . 30
  (NOTHING COULD DRAW HER AFTER THOSE TWO SONS. . . . 56 THE BLACK COTTAGE . . 40
  SHE HAD AT SOME COST TAUGHT THEM AFTER YEARS.) . . . 56 THE BLACK COTTAGE . . 42

```
                                                      PAGE TITLE              LINE
AFTER (CONTINUED)
    AND AFTER ALL, REALLY THEY'RE EBONY SKINNED:  . . . . . 60 BLUEBERRIES . . . . 24
    "I'VE TOLD YOU HOW ONCE, NOT LONG AFTER WE CAME, . . . . 61 BLUEBERRIES . . . . 67
    AND WASHING DISHES AFTER THEM--FROM DOING   . . . . . . 64 A SERVANT TO SERVANTS . 51
    AROUND HIM TO LOOK AFTER THAT MAKE WASTE.  . . . . . . 65 A SERVANT TO SERVANTS . 73
    AFTER APPLE-PICKING . . . . . . . . . . . . . . . . . 68 AFTER APPLE-PICKING . T
    AFTER A WHILE PICKING PEAS IN HIS GARDEN:   . . . . . . 73 THE CODE . . . . . 108
    HE'S GROPING IN THE CELLAR AFTER JAM--   . . . . . . . 77 THE GENERATIONS OF MEN 101
    SHE'S AFTER CIDER, THE OLD GIRL, SHE'S THIRSTY;  . . . . 77 THE GENERATIONS OF MEN 108
    "AND AFTER ALL WHY SHOULD THEY? JOHN'S BEEN FAIR  . . . 84 THE HOUSEKEEPER . . 92
    "HOW ARE YOU, NEIGHBOR? JUST THE MAN I'M AFTER.  . . . . 88 THE HOUSEKEEPER . . 206
    TO THE DARK HOUSE AFTER SO LONG AN ABSENCE,  . . . . . 89 THE FEAR . . . . 18
    HE THOUGHT THAT I WAS AFTER HIM FOR A FEATHER--   . . . 101 THE WOOD-PILE . . . 14
    NIGHT AFTER NIGHT AND STRONGER EVERY NIGHT,  . . . . . 113 IN THE HOME STRETCH . 73
    THE FIRST NIGHT AFTER GUESTS HAVE GONE, THE HOUSE  . . . 115 IN THE HOME STRETCH . 132
    SOUGHT FOR MUCH AFTER THAT, IT WILL BE FOUND  . . . . . 119 HYLA BROOK . . . . 2
    AFTER A RAIN. THEY CLICK UPON THEMSELVES   . . . . . . 121 BIRCHES . . . . . 7
    I WALKED DOWN ALONE SUNDAY AFTER CHURCH  . . . . . . . 123 PEA BRUSH . . . . 1
    IN WINTER AFTER HALF-PAST THREE.  . . . . . . . . . . 137 BROWN'S DESCENT . . 4
    AFTER THE MANNER OF OUR STOCK;   . . . . . . . . . . . 139 BROWN'S DESCENT . . 62
    ADDED: "YOU CAN JUDGE BETTER AFTER SEEING.--   . . . . . 144 SNOW . . . . . 35
    AFTER A DOWNY STORM, HE PASSED OUR PLACE.   . . . . . . 149 SNOW . . . . . 176
    YOU DIDN'T THINK YOU'D KEEP HIM AFTER ALL.  . . . . . . 152 SNOW . . . . . 255
    WE MUST HAVE BEEN ASLEEP: IT'S THREE AND AFTER."  . . . 152 SNOW . . . . . 274
    "FRED, AFTER ALL I SAID! YOU SHAN'T MAKE OUT  . . . . . 153 SNOW . . . . . 285
    ONE OF MY CHILDREN RANGING AFTER ROCKS   . . . . . . . 162 NEW HAMPSHIRE . . 116
    RAKING UP AFTER WINTER, AND I SAID,  . . . . . . . . . 164 NEW HAMPSHIRE . . 153
    AFTER HE'D PICKED THE LOCK AND GOT IT STARTED,  . . . . 170 NEW HAMPSHIRE . . 346
    AFTER HOURS' OVERLOOKING FROM THE CLIFFS   . . . . . . 174 THE CENSUS-TAKER . . 13
    OR BRANCH TO WHISTLE AFTER WHAT WAS SPENT.  . . . . . . 175 THE CENSUS-TAKER . . 24
    AFTER THE GROUND IS FROZEN, I SHOULD HAVE DONE  . . . . 176 THE STAR-SPLITTER . . 6
    AFTER SUCH LOOSE TALK IT WAS NO SURPRISE.   . . . . . . 177 THE STAR-SPLITTER . . 38
    WE'VE LOOKED AND LOOKED, BUT AFTER ALL WHERE ARE WE?  . . 179 THE STAR-SPLITTER . . 95
    WELL, YOU WERE NAMED AFTER A MAPLE TREE.   . . . . . . 180 MAPLE . . . . . 9
    SO AFTER WORK THAT EVENING HE CAME BACK  . . . . . . . 194 PAUL'S WIFE . . . 88
    PAUL TAKING AFTER HER AROUND THE POND.   . . . . . . . 195 PAUL'S WIFE . . . 122
    AND THERE, WELL AFTER DARK, LET MURPHY TELL IT,  . . . . 195 PAUL'S WIFE . . . 127
    AND WAS COME AFTER LIKE EURYDICE   . . . . . . . . . . 196 WILD GRAPES . . . 17
    HE'S AFTER AN OPEN DOOR TO GET OUTDOORS.   . . . . . . 205 THE WITCH OF COOS . 112
    HE NEVER SAID MUCH AFTER WE WERE MARRIED,   . . . . . . 209 PAUPER WITCH OF GRAFTON 73
    STEER STRAIGHT OFF AFTER SOMETHING INTO SPACE.  . . . . 238 ON A TREE FALLEN ACROSS 14
    LIKE A PISTIL AFTER THE PETALS GO.   . . . . . . . . . 241 NEED OF BEING VERSED . 4
    I FLUSHED BIRDS OUT OF HOLE AFTER HOLE,  . . . . . . . 253 THE THATCH . . . . 19
    AND AFTER THAT HER NEXT JOY  . . . . . . . . . . . . 256 THE LOVELY BE CHOOSERS 25
    YET, AFTER ALL, 'TWAS NOT DIVINE,  . . . . . . . . . . 274 A LONE STRIKER . . . 52
    THAT WILL STEAL FORTH AFTER THE SUN IS SET   . . . . . 276 TWO TRAMPS IN MUD TIME 39
    HE'S AFTER THE DOMESTICATED FLY.   . . . . . . . . . . 278 THE WHITE-TAILED HORNET 30
    AND IF AFTER THE HUNT GOES PAST.  . . . . . . . . . . 282 A DRUMLIN WOODCHUCK . 21
    AND AFTER HAVING ENTERTAINED THE BEE,  . . . . . . . . 283 THE GOLD HESPERIDEE . 3
    WELL, THE MOON AFTER THAT, CAME ONE AT LAST  . . . . . 289 OLD BARN AT THE BOTTOM 6
    AND ANOTHER STUMBLING AFTER A HALTING CART.  . . . . . 299 STRONG SAYING NOTHING . 8
    I CAN TELL BETTER AFTER I GET HOME,  . . . . . . . . . 325 BUILD SOIL . . . . 286
    BUT AFTER A TIME ALLOWED FOR IT TO SWIM,   . . . . . . 338 THE MOST OF IT . . . 13
    WHEN AFTER TALK WITH OTHER MEN   . . . . . . . . . . . 346 DISCOVERY OF MADEIRAS . 86
    BUT HAVE WE THERE THE ADVANTAGE AFTER ALL?  . . . . . . 352 THE LESSON FOR TODAY . 73
    AROUND BEND AFTER BEND.  . . . . . . . . . . . . . . 366 NOT OF SCHOOL AGE . . 1
    FOR FAMILY AFTER FAMILY NAME.   . . . . . . . . . . . 367 A SERIOUS STEP LIGHTLY 15
    IS AFTER EXPLOSION GOING AWAY SO FAST.   . . . . . . . 389 SKEPTIC . . . . . 8
    AS AFTER ONE-OF-THEM'S PROVERBIAL FAILURE   . . . . . . 412 POD OF THE MILKWEED . 37
    AFTER HAVING CRAWLED  . . . . . . . . . . . . . . . 434 KITTY HAWK . . . . 203
    IN BIRTH AFTER BIRTH   . . . . . . . . . . . . . . . 436 KITTY HAWK . . . . 249
    AND MEASURED, BUT NOT TAKEN AFTER ALL,   . . . . . . . 443 AUSPEX . . . . . . 3
    IT WILL COME ROLLING AFTER US LIKE A HOOP."  . . . . . 454 HOW HARD TO KEEP FROM 27
    AND SO IT WENT WITH TRIUMPH AFTER TRIUMPH   . . . . . . 456 HOW HARD TO KEEP FROM 93
    WELL, AFTER ALL THESE YEARS! / THIS IS MY WIFE.  . . . . 476 A MASQUE OF REASON . 83
    COME, AFTER ALL THESE YEARS--TO SATISFY ME. . .  . . . 482 A MASQUE OF REASON . 254
    NOW AFTER ALL THESE YEARS YOU MIGHT INDULGE ME.  . . . . 483 A MASQUE OF REASON . 267
    WORTH GOING AFTER. GET DOWN INTO THINGS,   . . . . . . 483 A MASQUE OF REASON . 281
    OF HAVING CHILDREN--AFTER HAVING HAD THEM,  . . . . . . 483 A MASQUE OF REASON . 292
    GOD'S AFTER ME! / YOU MEAN THE DEVIL IS.  . . . . . . . 493 A MASQUE OF MERCY . 19
    WHY IS GOD AFTER YOU?--TO SAVE YOUR SOUL?   . . . . . . 494 A MASQUE OF MERCY . 40
    AFTER THE FIGHT'S SO DEFINITELY DONE  . . . . . . . . 507 A MASQUE OF MERCY . 366
    THE GOSPELS TO IT. AFTER DOING JUSTICE JUSTICE  . . . . 508 A MASQUE OF MERCY . 379
AFTERFLAKES
    AFTERFLAKES  . . . . . . . . . . . . . . . . . . . 303 AFTERFLAKES . . . . T
AFTERGLOW
    AND IN THE ANTIPHONY OF AFTERGLOW  . . . . . . . . . 14 WAITING . . . . . 5
    AND IN THE AFTERGLOW   . . . . . . . . . . . . . . . 470 IN WINTER IN THE WOODS 6
AFTERMARK
    OF TEARS, THE AFTERMARK   . . . . . . . . . . . . . 227 TO EARTHWARD . . . 21
AFTERMATH
    THE HEADLESS AFTERMATH,   . . . . . . . . . . . . . 8 A LATE WALK . . . . 2
AFTERNOON
    WE CHANCED IN PASSING BY THAT AFTERNOON  . . . . . . . 55 THE BLACK COTTAGE . 1
    AS WE ALMOST GOT BY THIS AFTERNOON.   . . . . . . . . 56 THE BLACK COTTAGE . 44
    HE KEPT AWAY FROM US ALL AFTERNOON.  . . . . . . . . 73 THE CODE . . . . . 106
    A BETTER WAY TO PASS THE AFTERNOON   . . . . . . . . . 190 THE GRINDSTONE . . . 53
AFTERTHOUGHT
    AN AFTERTHOUGHT, A LONG-LONG-AFTER-THOUGHT.  . . . . . 482 A MASQUE OF REASON . 246
AFTERWARD
    THEY TOLD ME AFTERWARD. FIRST THEY FORKED HAY,  . . . . 72 THE CODE . . . . . 89
    I'LL TALK TO YOU, OLD WOMAN, AFTERWARD.--   . . . . . . 88 THE HOUSEKEEPER . . 209
    AFTERWARD I WENT PAST WHAT YOU HAD PASSED   . . . . . . 119 MEETING AND PASSING . 13
    WELL, THERE'S--" SHE TOLD FRED AFTERWARD THAT IN  . . . 151 SNOW . . . . . . 237
    HE STUNG ME FIRST AND STUNG ME AFTERWARD.   . . . . . . 278 THE WHITE-TAILED HORNET 19
AFTERWARDS
    YEARS AFTERWARDS, TRAILING THEIR LEAVES ON THE GROUND  . 121 BIRCHES . . . . . 18
```

AFTERWORD
  "AN AFTERWORD" FROM COMPLETE POEMS . . . . 401 AFTERWORD FROM COMPLETE   T
AGAIN
  TO CARRY AGAIN TO YOU. . . . . 9 A LATE WALK 16
  TO COME AGAIN AT DARK. . . . . 10 WIND AND WINDOW FLOWER   12
  IF TIRED OF TREES I SEEK AGAIN MANKIND, ... 17 THE VANTAGE POINT . . . 1
  AN SO THE CHOICE MUST BE AGAIN, ... 21 THE TRIAL BY EXISTENCE 57
  THE SAME LEAVES OVER AND OVER AGAIN! . . . . 25 IN HARDWOOD GROVES . . . 1
  BEFORE THE LEAVES CAN MOUNT AGAIN. . . . . 26 IN HARDWOOD GROVES . . . 5
  AND SET THE WALL BETWEEN US ONCE AGAIN. . . . . 33 MENDING WALL 14
  HE SAYS AGAIN, "GOOD FENCES MAKE GOOD NEIGHBORS." . . . 34 MENDING WALL 45
  TO RAISE HERSELF AND LOOK AGAIN. HE SPOKE . . . . 51 HOME BURIAL 5
  BUT AT LAST HE MURMURED, "OH," AND AGAIN, "OH." . . . . 51 HOME BURIAL 17
  TO LOOK AGAIN, AND STILL YOUR SPADE KEPT LIFTING. . . . 53 HOME BURIAL 80
  IT WILL TURN TRUE AGAIN, FOR SO IT GOES. . . . . 58 THE BLACK COTTAGE . . 108
  "WHERE SHALL WE MEET AGAIN?" / "NOWHERE BUT HERE . . . . 80 THE GENERATIONS OF MEN 208
  NO ONE WILL EVER LIVE ON IT AGAIN. . . . . 83 THE HOUSEKEEPER . . . 49
  AND THEN THE VOICE AGAIN: "YOU SEEM AFRAID. . . . . . . 91 THE FEAR 72
  THE DOCTOR'S SURE YOU'RE GOING TO WALK AGAIN?" . . . . . 93 THE SELF-SEEKER . . . 15
  WHETHER HE'S EVER GOING TO WALK AGAIN. . . . . 100 THE SELF-SEEKER . . . 202
  HE PROVED TO BE THE CITY COME AGAIN . . . . 106 CHRISTMAS TREES . . . 9
  IN CLOMPING HERE, HE SCARED IT ONCE AGAIN . . . . 108 OLD MAN'S WINTER NIGHT 10
  TO MAKE IT ROOT AGAIN AND GROW AFRESH. . . . . 109 THE EXPOSED NEST . . . 8
  OF EVER COMING TO THE PLACE AGAIN . . . . 110 THE EXPOSED NEST . . . 34
  AND OIL ARE BURIED OUT OF REACH?" / AGAIN . . . . 113 IN THE HOME STRETCH . . 81
  NOT OFFERING A LADY----" / "THERE AGAIN, JOE! . . . . . 116 IN THE HOME STRETCH . . 157
  WHO MAKES THE SOLID TREE TRUNKS SOUND AGAIN. . . . . . 119 THE OVEN BIRD 3
  BY RIDING THEM DOWN OVER AND OVER AGAIN . . . . 122 BIRCHES 29
  BUT DIPPED ITS TOP AND SET ME DOWN AGAIN. . . . . 122 BIRCHES 57
  A TREE THAT HAD BEEN DOWN AND RAISED AGAIN-- . . . . . . 125 AN ENCOUNTER 13
  OF GETTING HOME AGAIN BECAUSE . . . . 139 BROWN'S DESCENT . . . 55
  GULPED SNOW, AND THEN BLEW FREE AGAIN--THE COLES, . . . 143 SNOW 3
  I'M HERE--SO FAR--AND STARTING ON AGAIN. . . . . 143 SNOW 12
  TO THEIRS. I'M GOING TO CALL HIS WIFE AGAIN." . . . . . 145 SNOW 75
  LET'S SEE IF HE WILL THINK OF HER AGAIN. . . . . 145 SNOW 77
  AND LET YOU GET TO BED AGAIN. GOOD-NIGHT, ... 150 SNOW 211
  "AND LEAVE THE CHILDREN?" / "WAIT AND CALL AGAIN. . . . 154 SNOW 307
  WHAT'LL YOU BET HE EVER CALLS AGAIN?" . . . . 156 SNOW 350
  TO DRY, FROM POOR TO RICH, OR BACK AGAIN. . . . . 166 NEW HAMPSHIRE . . . 236
  AGAIN AS IN THE DAYS WHEN AHAZ SINNED . . . . 171 NEW HAMPSHIRE . . . 388
  THAT WHEN IT WOKE AND CAME TO LIFE AGAIN . . . . 181 MAPLE 38
  AND LOST THE PLACE NEVER TO READ AGAIN. . . . . 181 MAPLE 68
  AS WELL AS COULD A MOTHER. AND AGAIN . . . . 183 MAPLE 119
  AS FAR AGAIN AS FROM BEING BORN TO BEARING." . . . . . 184 MAPLE 130
  AND THEN LAND SAFELY RIGHT SIDE UP AGAIN, ... 192 PAUL'S WIFE 52
  TO SLAM END-ON AGAIN AGAINST THE SAW TEETH. . . . . . . 193 PAUL'S WIFE 64
  UP ATTIC THAT WE'D EVER WANT AGAIN. . . . . 206 THE WITCH OF COOS . . 122
  I GUESS THEY'D BETTER DRAG IT THROUGH AGAIN. . . . . . 208 PAUPER WITCH OF GRAFTON 29
  AND NOW HE COMES AGAIN WITH CLATTER OF STONE, ... 223 THE RUNAWAY 15
  AND MOUNTS THE WALL AGAIN WITH WHITED EYES . . . . . . 223 THE RUNAWAY 16
  IT SHALL NOT MAKE AGAIN ALL WINTER LONG . . . . 226 THE ONSET 4
  CAN CURE ME OF TO GO AGAIN." THE SAME . . . . 230 NOT TO KEEP 17
  AGAIN AND AGAIN . . . . 235 GATHERING LEAVES . . . 14
  BUT THE KNOCK CAME AGAIN. . . . . 241 THE LOCKLESS DOOR . . 9
  THE HOUSE HAD GONE TO BRING AGAIN . . . . 241 NEED OF BEING VERSED . 1
  IF HEAVEN WERE TO DO AGAIN, ... 252 THE PEACEFUL SHEPHERD . 1
  OF THEIR NEST AGAIN, NOR FIND A PERCH. . . . . 253 THE THATCH 24
  WE NEVER SHALL MOW IN AGAIN, ... 264 THE LAST MOWING . . . 2
  AGAIN COME TO LIFE AND CRAWL OFF, ... 266 SITTING BY A BUSH . . 11
  THEN ONCE AGAIN THE SANDBANK LAY SERENE. . . . . 270 THE EGG AND THE MACHINE 16
  HERE COMMON WITH THE FLOCK AGAIN, ... 280 BLUE RIBBON AT AMESBURY 13
  AND SET THEM UP AGAIN FOR PROPPING SHUT, ... 289 OLD BARN AT THE BOTTOM 11
  CAME DRYLY FORWARD TO THE BARS AGAIN . . . . 294 AT WOODWARD'S GARDENS . 32
  WE THINK OF THE TREE. IF IT NEVER AGAIN HAS LEAVES, . . 305 THERE ARE ROUGHLY ZONES 4
  THE TREE HAS NO LEAVES AND MAY NEVER HAVE THEM AGAIN. . 305 THERE ARE ROUGHLY ZONES 18
  BUT IF IT IS DESTINED NEVER AGAIN TO GROW, ... 305 THERE ARE ROUGHLY ZONES 20
  OUR EVER GETTING INSIDE IN AGAIN. . . . . 320 BUILD SOIL 140
  YOU'LL BE A DEMOCRAT AGAIN. . . . . 326 TO A THINKER 20
  NEVER AGAIN WOULD BIRDS' SONG BE THE SAME . . . . 338 NEVER WOULD BIRDS' SONG T
  NEVER AGAIN WOULD BIRDS' SONG BE THE SAME. . . . . . . 339 NEVER WOULD BIRDS' SONG 13
  A MAN COMES BACK TO A WOMAN AGAIN . . . . 346 DISCOVERY OF MADEIRAS . 87
  TILL THE SPONGY SOIL AGAIN WAS NATAL WET. . . . . 349 OUR HOLD ON THE PLANET 10
  OUR MUSCLES NEVER COULD AGAIN CONTRACT: . . . . 351 THE LESSON FOR TODAY . 38
  AND THEN CAME RACING WILDLY ON AGAIN . . . . 357 A CONSIDERABLE SPECK . 11
  THEN PAUSED AGAIN AND EITHER DRANK OR SMELT-- . . . . . 357 A CONSIDERABLE SPECK . 13
  WITH LOATHING, FOR AGAIN IT TURNED TO FLY. . . . . . . 357 A CONSIDERABLE SPECK . 14
  FIRST UNDER UP AND THEN AGAIN DOWN UNDER, ... 362 SYMPATHY WITH UNDER DOG 1
  THAT MADE ME LOOK AGAIN AT THE CLOCK. . . . . 364 TRESPASS 16
  AND READY AGAIN FOR THE GRASS TO OWN. . . . . 376 SOMETHING FOR HOPE . . 16
  DRINK AND BE WHOLE AGAIN BEYOND CONFUSION. . . . . . . 379 DIRECTIVE 62
  I NEVER SHOULD AGAIN BE WARMED, ... 381 AN UNSTAMPED LETTER IN 24
  THEY WILL NEVER HAVE AGAIN. . . . . 387 THE COURAGE TO BE NEW . 4
  AND STARTED HIS MARCH BACK AGAIN DISCOURSING: . . . . . 406 FROM PLANE TO PLANE . 60
  IN CASE THE ROCKS SHOULD MELT AND RUN AGAIN. . . . . . 407 FROM PLANE TO PLANE . 95
  HERE IT WAS AGAIN . . . . 433 KITTY HAWK 176
  I SAID THE INCENSE TREE'S ON FIRE AGAIN. . . . . 473 A MASQUE OF REASON . . 5
  THAT STRAIN AGAIN! GIVE ME EXCESS OF IT! . . . . 488 A MASQUE OF REASON . . 418
  THERE MAY BE THERE AND GET SPIT OUT AGAIN. . . . . . . 500 A MASQUE OF MERCY . . 189
  (HE STARTS TO SPEAK, BUT STOPS AGAIN TO LISTEN. . . . . 502 A MASQUE OF MERCY . . 244
  AND MEND THE OTHERS UP TO GO AGAIN. . . . . 508 A MASQUE OF MERCY . . 371
  SO THAT THE CREAM COULD NEVER RISE AGAIN . . . . 509 A MASQUE OF MERCY . . 421
  I ASK YOU ALL TO READ IT ONCE AGAIN. . . . . 511 A MASQUE OF MERCY . . 488
  I CAN COUNT ON MY SOURCE TO SPRING AGAIN. . . . . 514 A MASQUE OF MERCY . . 541
  THEY FAIL ME. NOW I'M TEASING YOU AGAIN. . . . . 516 A MASQUE OF MERCY . . 608
  THE CELLAR DOOR SWINGS WIDE AND SLAMS AGAIN.) . . . . . 520 A MASQUE OF MERCY . . 696
AGAINST
  WHEN THE WIND WORKS AGAINST US IN THE DARK, ... 9 STORM FEAR 1
  AGAINST THE UTTERMOST OF EARTH. . . . . 21 THE TRIAL BY EXISTENCE 44

AGAINST (CONTINUED)
THEREAFTER I SAT ME AGAINST A TREE. . . . . 25 THE DEMIURGE'S LAUGH . 18
AGAINST MY LIFE-- . . . . 29 MY BUTTERFLY 33
HUDDLED AGAINST THE BARN DOOR FAST ASLEEP, ... 35 DEATH OF THE HIRED MAN . 35
AND PROPPED HIMSELF AT BAY AGAINST A PILLOW. . . . . 47 A HUNDRED COLLARS . . 74
YOU HAD STOOD THE SPADE UP AGAINST THE WALL . . . . 54 HOME BURIAL 87
AGAINST THE LOUNGE BESIDE IT, THOUGH I DOUBT . . . . 56 THE BLACK COTTAGE . . 28
AND HELD AGAINST THE WORLD OF HOARY GRASS. . . . . . 68 AFTER APPLE-PICKING . 12
AGAINST THE STOVE, THE HOTTEST DAY THAT SUMMER. . . . 72 THE CODE 98
SHE RAISED HER VOICE AGAINST THE CLOSING DOOR: . . . 89 THE HOUSEKEEPER . . 213
THAT HUNG IN BOTH HANDS, HOT AGAINST HER SKIRT. . . . 91 THE FEAR 63
SHE STOOD HER GROUND AGAINST THE NOISY STEPS . . . . 92 THE FEAR 76
BUT MY LEGS GOT THEIR KNOCKS AGAINST THE CEILING." . 93 THE SELF-SEEKER . . 29
IT GOES AGAINST ME NOT TO FINISH IT . . . . 95 THE SELF-SEEKER . . 83
IF THAT WAS YOUR IDEA, AGAINST THE BREEZE, ... 109 THE EXPOSED NEST . . 6
SHE STOOD AGAINST THE KITCHEN SINK, AND LOOKED . . . 110 IN THE HOME STRETCH . 1
WHEN LEANING WITH MY HEAD AGAINST A FLOWER . . . . . 118 THE TELEPHONE . . . 5
EVEN AGAINST THE WAY ITS WATERS WENT. . . . . 119 HYLA BROOK 9
SHE BELLOWS ON A KNOLL AGAINST THE SKY. . . . . . . 125 THE COW IN APPLE TIME . 10
LOOKED UP TOWARD HEAVEN, AND THERE AGAINST THE BLUE, . 125 AN ENCOUNTER . . . 11
THROWN FROM SOMEWHERE AGAINST THEIR WALLPAPER. . . . 129 THE BONFIRE 12
THEY STRING AN INSTRUMENT AGAINST THE SKY . . . . . 141 THE LINE-GANG . . . 5
OF WIND THAT CAUGHT AGAINST THE HOUSE A MOMENT, . . . 143 SNOW 2
AND SHOW YOU HOW IT'S PILING UP AGAINST YOU. . . . . 148 SNOW 156
SHORT OFF, AND DIED AGAINST THE WINDOWPANE." . . . . 149 SNOW 166
THE SNOW AGAINST THE WINDOW CAUGHT HIS EYE. . . . . 149 SNOW 180
IT BURSTS AGAINST US AT THE CHIMNEY MOUTH, ... 150 SNOW 207
(IN VERSE I THINK) AGAINST THE VOLSTEAD ACT. . . . . 160 NEW HAMPSHIRE . . . 30
HE'S YOUR ONE CHANCE TO SCORE AGAINST THE STATE.) . . 161 NEW HAMPSHIRE . . . 66
OF SEVERAL BOOKS AGAINST THE WORLD IN GENERAL. . . . 166 NEW HAMPSHIRE . . . 229
TO TAKE THEM AS AGAINST A SPECIAL STATE . . . . . . 166 NEW HAMPSHIRE . . . 230
TO SAY SO OR BE STOOD AGAINST THE WALL . . . . . . 168 NEW HAMPSHIRE . . . 281
WE'VE HEARD AGAINST THE MID-VICTORIANS . . . . . . 168 NEW HAMPSHIRE . . . 295
AGAINST THE SKY TO BREAK HIS BACK FOR HIM, ... 170 NEW HAMPSHIRE . . . 348
AND WENT ALONE AGAINST A GROVE OF TREES; . . . . . . 170 NEW HAMPSHIRE . . . 368
I ARMED MYSELF AGAINST SUCH BONES AS MIGHT BE . . . 175 THE CENSUS-TAKER . . 43
WITH BOTH HIS FEET AT ONCE AGAINST THE CEILING, . . . 192 PAUL'S WIFE . . . 51
TO SLAM END-ON AGAIN AGAINST THE SAW TEETH. . . . . 193 PAUL'S WIFE . . . 64
WHERE THE LOG DRIVE LAY PRESSED AGAINST THE BOOM, . . 194 PAUL'S WIFE . . . 107
AGAINST HER NECK, AN ORNAMENT OF GRAPES. . . . . . . 197 WILD GRAPES . . . 23
AND SHUT MY EYES AGAINST THE SUN, MY EARS . . . . . 198 WILD GRAPES . . . 74
AGAINST MY BROTHER'S NONSENSE. "DROP," HE SAID, . . . 198 WILD GRAPES . . . 75
AGAINST THE ATTIC DOOR: THE DOOR IS NAILED. . . . . 203 THE WITCH OF COOS . 22
AND PUSH THE HEADBOARD OF THE BED AGAINST IT. . . . 206 THE WITCH OF COOS . 120
"THE OUTSIDE DOORS AS YET HAVE HELD AGAINST US. . . . 215 A FOUNTAIN, A BOTTLE . 74
LIKE A SHADOW AGAINST THE CURTAIN OF FALLING FLAKES. . 223 THE RUNAWAY 8
ONCE, WHEN TRYING WITH CHIN AGAINST A WELL-CURB, . . 225 FOR ONCE SOMETHING . 7
AS MEASURED AGAINST MAPLE, BIRCH, AND OAK, ... 226 THE ONSET 16
(WE MADE IT SECURE AGAINST BEING, I HOPE, ... 228 GOOD-BY AND KEEP COLD . 13
HE STOOD THERE BRINGING MARCH AGAINST HIS THOUGHT, . . 233 A BOUNDLESS MOMENT . 3
ONE LUMINARY CLOCK AGAINST THE SKY . . . . 255 ACQUAINTED WITH NIGHT . 12
IN A WHITE SCARF AGAINST THE FAR-SHORE ALDERS.) . . . 258 WEST-RUNNING BROOK . 26
AGAINST THE STREAM, THAT MOST WE SEE OURSELVES IN, . . 260 WEST-RUNNING BROOK . 69
HE RAISED AGAINST THE GODS IN THE MACHINE. . . . . . 270 THE EGG AND THE MACHINE 15
THAT FLOATS AGAINST THE CEILING OF THE WOODSHED. . . 277 THE WHITE-TAILED HORNET 2
HE LEANS AGAINST THE DUSTY WALL, ... 280 BLUE RIBBON AT AMESBURY 21
AGAINST THE DARK AND WIND AND COLD . . . . 281 BLUE RIBBON AT AMESBURY 54
AS MEASURED AGAINST THE ALL, ... 282 A DRUMLIN WOODCHUCK . 30
AGAINST HIS UNACQUAINTANCES THE RICH . . . . 290 OLD BARN AT THE BOTTOM 30
THAT WAS MAINTAINED AGAINST THE NIGHT, ... 291 ON HEART'S BEGINNING TO 8
AGAINST THE DAY OF PRISONERS' ENNUI. . . . . 293 AT WOODWARD'S GARDENS . 31
TO LEAN AGAINST AND HEAR IN THE DARK. . . . . 297 LEAVES COMPARED WITH . 18
AGAINST THE SHAPELESS SHADOW OF STORM. . . . . 303 AFTERFLAKES 9
WORKS IN THE DARK AS MUCH AGAINST AS FOR US. . . . . 319 BUILD SOIL 106
DON'T LET THE THINGS I SAY AGAINST MYSELF . . . . . 320 BUILD SOIL 131
BETRAY YOU INTO TAKING SIDES AGAINST ME, ... 320 BUILD SOIL 132
WE'RE SO MUCH OUT THAT THE ODDS ARE AGAINST . . . . 320 BUILD SOIL 139
TO SET HIMSELF AGAINST THE PEAKS OF SNOW . . . . . . 334 I COULD GIVE ALL . . 2
TO WARN AGAINST THE DANGER . . . . 335 CARPE DIEM 14
OR FROM HER OWN SELF AGAINST HER WILL . . . . 343 DISCOVERY OF MADEIRAS . 3
AND WENT TO LEAN AGAINST THE RAIL, ... 345 DISCOVERY OF MADEIRAS . 50
THERE IS MUCH IN NATURE AGAINST US. BUT WE FORGET: . 349 OUR HOLD ON THE PLANET 12
IT IS YOUR CHRISTMASES AGAINST MY WOODS. . . . . . . 350 TO A YOUNG WRETCH . . 13
THE SYMBOL STAR IT LIFTS AGAINST YOUR CEILING . . . 350 TO A YOUNG WRETCH . . 23
AGAINST THE ANCIENT SOVEREIGNTY OF NIGHT. . . . . . 361 A LOOSE MOUNTAIN . . 8
I WAS BEING TRESPASSED ON AND AGAINST. . . . . 364 TRESPASS 4
THAT BRACED HIS FEET AGAINST THE ARCTIC POLE. . . . 377 DIRECTIVE 17
BE IT SAID AGAINST OR FOR ME, ... 388 ASTROMETAPHYSICAL . 2
TO FEEL IT CLOSE IN TIGHT AGAINST MY SENSE . . . . . 390 SKEPTIC 11
BUT RAN AGAINST HIM WITH A STAYING HAND. . . . . . . 394 HAEC FABULA DOCET . 10
TO REAR AGAINST THE INSCRIPTION ON THE WALL. . . . . 399 THE INGENUITIES OF DEBT 18
AGAINST THE WRONG SIDE OF A WINDOWPANE. . . . . . . 412 POD OF THE MILKWEED . 39
AGAINST THE TREES I GO. . . . . 470 IN WINTER IN THE WOODS . 2
A MAN SITS LEANING BACK AGAINST A PALM. . . . . . . 473 A MASQUE OF REASON . 2
AGAINST YOUR COMFORTERS IN THEIR CONTENTION . . . . 486 A MASQUE OF REASON . 363
TO PROPHESY AGAINST THE CITY EVIL. . . . . 495 A MASQUE OF MERCY . 64
WHAT HAVE YOU GOT AGAINST THE CITY? / HE KNOWS. . . . 496 A MASQUE OF MERCY . 65
WE HAVE ENOUGH AGAINST IT, HAVEN'T WE? . . . . 496 A MASQUE OF MERCY . 66
IS IT JUST ANY CITY YOU'RE AGAINST? . . . . 496 A MASQUE OF MERCY . 90
THE THREATS HE MAKES AGAINST THE CITY EVIL. . . . . 497 A MASQUE OF MERCY . 115
THE MERCY ON THE SIN AGAINST THE SERMON. . . . . . . 511 A MASQUE OF MERCY . 477
BEYOND THIS GREAT DOOR YOU HAVE LOCKED AGAINST ME, . 513 A MASQUE OF MERCY . 532
AGAPE
BUT MUST LIVE LIVES OUT MENTALLY AGAPE . . . . . . 351 THE LESSON FOR TODAY . 40
AGE
BEFORE THE AGE OF THE FERN; . . . . 27 A LINE-STORM SONG . . 28
AT HIS AGE FOR THE LITTLE HE CAN DO? . . . . 35 DEATH OF THE HIRED MAN 16
EACH AGE WILL HAVE TO RECONSIDER IT. . . . . 57 THE BLACK COTTAGE . . 70

AGE (CONTINUED)
    THAT'S NO WAY FOR A MAN TO DO AT HIS AGE: . . . . . . 83 THE HOUSEKEEPER   63
    THAT BROUGHT HIM TO THAT CREAKING ROOM WAS AGE. . . . . 108 OLD MAN'S WINTER NIGHT .   7
    IT SEEMS A NARROW CHOICE THE AGE INSISTS ON. . . . . . 171 NEW HAMPSHIRE 403
    ABOUT HIS TELESCOPE. BEYOND THE AGE . . . . 178 THE STAR-SPLITTER . . .   54
    BUT ITS AGE KEPT THEM FROM CONSIDERING THIS ONE. . . . . 184 MAPLE 148
    SAID THAT I TOOK HIM OUT IN HIS OLD AGE . . . . . . 208 PAUPER WITCH OF GRAFTON   46
    AND ALTER WITH AGE. . . . . 241 THE LOCKLESS DOOR . . .   20
    WAS COMING, AND NOT ONLY A NIGHT, AN AGE. . . . . . . 250 ONCE BY THE PACIFIC . .   11
    I WENT TO SCHOOL TO AGE TO LEARN THE PAST. . . . . . . 267 WHAT FIFTY SAID . . .   4
    BEGAN TO BLOSSOM AT THE AGE OF FIVE; . . . . 283 THE GOLD HESPERIDEE . .   2
    A GIRL OF HIS AGE HE MET . . . . 313 BEARER OF EVIL TIDINGS   14
    AGE SAW TWO QUIET CHILDREN . . . . 335 CARPE DIEM   1
    'TWAS AGE IMPOSED ON POEMS . . . . 335 CARPE DIEM   12
    IF GOD WOULD SPARE THEM TO DIE OF AGE. . . . . . . 344 DISCOVERY OF MADEIRAS .   26
    IF THIS UNCERTAIN AGE IN WHICH WE DWELL . . . . . . 350 THE LESSON FOR TODAY .   1
    THE AGE MAY VERY WELL HAVE BEEN TO BLAME . . . . . . 351 THE LESSON FOR TODAY .   26
    THE AGE WHEN FULL UPON YOU. THAT'S MY POINT. . . . . 351 THE LESSON FOR TODAY .   30
    THE PRESENT AGE OR YOUR AGE. YOU AND I . . . . . . 352 THE LESSON FOR TODAY .   49
    AS TO WHOSE AGE DESERVES THE LOWER MARK, ... 352 THE LESSON FOR TODAY .   52
    ONE AGE IS LIKE ANOTHER FOR THE SOUL. . . . . . . 354 THE LESSON FOR TODAY . 113
    HAS FAILED TO BRING--I MEAN THE GOLDEN AGE. . . . . . 358 THE LOST FOLLOWER . .   16
    WE HAD ONE AGE OF GOLD . . . . 361 ALMOST TWO THOUSAND .   2
    NOT OF SCHOOL AGE . . . . 366 NOT OF SCHOOL AGE . . .   T
    THE GLORY OF A NEXT AUGUSTAN AGE . . . . 424 FOR JOHN F. KENNEDY .   71
    A GOLDEN AGE OF POETRY AND POWER . . . . 424 FOR JOHN F. KENNEDY .   76
    BUT NO, A WOMAN HAS TO BE HER AGE, ... 458 HOW HARD TO KEEP FROM 157
    WHAT AN EXCITING AGE IT IS WE LIVE IN-- . . . . . 462 HOW HARD TO KEEP FROM 256
    I SHOULD HAVE SAID. YOU GOT YOUR AGE REVERSED . . . . 479 A MASQUE OF REASON . 159
AGED
    ONE AGED MAN--ONE MAN--CAN'T KEEP A HOUSE, ... 108 OLD MAN'S WINTER NIGHT   26
    AND THE AGED ELM, THOUGH TOUCHED WITH FIRE; . . . . . 242 NEED OF BEING VERSED .   18
    THEY SLOWLY AND SILENTLY AGED. . . . . 312 THE VINDICTIVES . . .   53
AGE-LONG
    OUR AGE-LONG THEME, FOR THE UNCERTAINTY . . . . . . 317 BUILD SOIL   37
    THE AGE-LONG THEME IS AGE'S. . . . . 335 CARPE DIEM   11
AGENDA
    THAT'S ONE THING MORE TO PUT ON YOUR AGENDA. . . . . 478 A MASQUE OF REASON . 126
AGENT (SEE UNDER-TICKET-AGENT)
AGES
    FOR THE AGES OF A DAY? . . . . 13 FLOWER-GATHERING . . .   12
    SOMEWHERE AGES AND AGES HENCE: . . . . 105 THE ROAD NOT TAKEN . .   17
    I WONDERED WHAT MACHINE OF AGES GONE . . . . . . 189 THE GRINDSTONE . . .   35
    AND GIVE MYSELF OUT AS TWO DIFFERENT AGES, ... 196 WILD GRAPES   17
    HOW, AGES AND AGES SINCE, ... 313 BEARER OF EVIL TIDINGS   18
    TO THE WORLD'S UNDEBATABLY DARK AGES, ... 350 THE LESSON FOR TODAY .   7
    IN HAVING GRANTED YOU ALL AGES SHINE . . . . . . 354 THE LESSON FOR TODAY . 118
    THE AGES RANGING ALL THE WAY FROM HOURS . . . . . 355 THE LESSON FOR TODAY . 138
    NOW CAME ON A NEW ORDER OF THE AGES . . . . . . 422 FOR JOHN F. KENNEDY .   19
    "NEW ORDER OF THE AGES" DID WE SAY? . . . . . . 423 FOR JOHN F. KENNEDY .   39
AGE'S
    THE AGE-LONG THEME IS AGE'S. . . . . 335 CARPE DIEM   11
AGGRANDIZEMENT (SEE SELF-AGGRANDIZEMENT)
AGGRIEVED
    IN SILENCE, IF IN THIS HE IS AGGRIEVED, ... 176 THE CENSUS-TAKER . .   58
AGITATED
    BUT OH, THE AGITATED HEART . . . . 19 REVELATION   3
AGLITTER
    IN THE CONFUSION OF THEM ALL AGLITTER, ... 237 A HILLSIDE THAW . . .   14
AGLOW
    THE SUNBURNED HILLSIDE SETS MY FACE AGLOW, ... 17 THE VANTAGE POINT . .   11
AGO
    THAT VANISHED MANY A SUMMER AGO, ...   5 GHOST HOUSE   2
    BUT IT IS LONG AGO-- . . . . 28 MY BUTTERFLY   10
    IT WAS TWO YEARS AGO--OR NO!--CAN IT BE . . . . . . 59 BLUEBERRIES   10
    I SAID THAT MORE THAN HALF AN HOUR AGO. . . . . . . 70 THE CODE   13
    THAT SHOUTED IN THE MIST A MONTH AGO, ... 119 HYLA BROOK   5
    "SHE KNEW HE HAD, POOR THING, TWO HOURS AGO." . . . . 153 SNOW 278
    WHEN I LEFT MASSACHUSETTS YEARS AGO . . . . 167 NEW HAMPSHIRE . . . 248
    ONCE LONG AGO HER FATHER HAD PUT HIMSELF OFF.) . . . . 183 MAPLE 111
    TWENTY-FIVE YEARS AGO AT MAPLE'S NAMING . . . . . . 184 MAPLE 149
    IT LEFT THE CELLAR FORTY YEARS AGO . . . . 203 THE WITCH OF COOS . .   28
    IN EIGHTY-FIVE." / "AS LONG AGO AS THAT?" . . . . . 213 A FOUNTAIN, A BOTTLE .   23
    HERE ON THIS VERY CAMPUS YEARS AGO. . . . . 316 BUILD SOIL   4
    HE GAVE UP SLEEP HIMSELF SOME TIME AGO, ... 371 THE LITERATE FARMER AND 104
    WHERE WERE THEY ALL NOT TWENTY YEARS AGO? . . . . . 378 DIRECTIVE   26
    OH, YEARS AGO--TEN THOUSAND YEARS. . . . . 392 A CLIFF DWELLING . .   13
    AS FIFTY MILLION YEARS AGO WE CAME-- . . . . . . 395 WHY WAIT FOR SCIENCE .   12
    SIXTY YEARS AGO. . . . . 428 KITTY HAWK   9
AGONY
    "ONE THOUGHT IN AGONY OF STRIFE . . . . 21 THE TRIAL BY EXISTENCE   50
AGRARIAN
    COME, COME, YOU TALK LIKE AN AGRARIAN. . . . . . . 496 A MASQUE OF MERCY . .   68
    WHEN HE GETS TOO AGRARIAN FOR ME . . . . 496 A MASQUE OF MERCY . .   82
AGREE
    AND I AGREE TO THAT, OR IN SO FAR . . . . 64 A SERVANT TO SERVANTS .   57
    WHY, I AGREE WITH YOU. BUT LET'S FORGIVE HIM. . . . . 156 SNOW 348
    MY LIFE-TRAIN LOGIC. I AGREE WITH YOU . . . . . . 325 BUILD SOIL 290
    THEN A NUMBER OF US AGREE . . . . 348 TRIPLE BRONZE . . .   9
    AS TO WHAT REASONS I AGREE TO WAIVE. . . . . 479 A MASQUE OF REASON . 167
AGREED
    HAVE YOU AGREED TO ANY PRICE?" / "FIVE HUNDRED. . . . . 94 THE SELF-SEEKER . . .   58
    LUCKILY TERMS ARE ALL AGREED UPON. . . . . 99 THE SELF-SEEKER . . . 182
    AGREED IN FROWNING ON THESE IMPROVISED . . . . . . 171 NEW HAMPSHIRE . . . 386
    TOFFILE AGREED TO THAT, AND SURE ENOUGH, ... 206 THE WITCH OF COOS . . 114
    THEIRS WAS THE BETTER RIGHT--AGREED. . . . . . . 277 TWO TRAMPS IN MUD TIME   64
    WAS THE ONE I MEANT. OUR DETAILS AGREED. . . . . . 289 OLD BARN AT THE BOTTOM   21
    FROM ONE ANOTHER ONCE YOU ARE AGREED . . . . . . 300 THE MASTER SPEED . .   12

```
                                                  PAGE TITLE                    LINE
AGREED (CONTINUED)
   WE'VE JUST AGREED I DIDN'T HAVE TO GIVE.--  . . . .  . 477 A MASQUE OF REASON .  . 106
   YOU THOUGHT IT WAS AGREED YOU NEEDN'T GIVE THEM. . . . . 478 A MASQUE OF REASON .  . 144
   YOU THOUGHT TO SUIT YOURSELF. I'VE NOT AGREED  . . . . 478 A MASQUE OF REASON .  . 145
   GIVE ME A HAND UP, IF WE ARE AGREED.  . . . .  . 520 A MASQUE OF MERCY .  . 715
AGREEING
   AT ONE EXTREME AGREEING WITH ONE GREEK,  . . . . . . 269 THE BEAR . . . . .  . 30
   AT THE OTHER AGREEING WITH ANOTHER GREEK,  . . . . . 269 THE BEAR . . . . .  . 31
AGREES
   THE OTHER WITHOUT DEMUR AGREES.  . . . . . . . . 291 ON HEART'S BEGINNING TO  23
AGRICOLAM
   BUT SPES ALIT AGRICOLAM 'TIS SAID. . . . . . . . 376 SOMETHING FOR HOPE .  . 24
AH
   AH, NO!  . . . . . . . . . . . . .  . 10 STORM FEAR . . . .  . 8
   AH! I REMEMBER ME  . . . . . . . . . . 29 MY BUTTERFLY . . . .  . 31
   AH, WHEN TO THE HEART OF MAN . . . . . . . .  . 30 RELUCTANCE . . . .  . 19
   "OH--AH--FOURTEEN--FOURTEEN." / "FOURTEEN! YOU SAY SO! . 46 A HUNDRED COLLARS .  . 63
   "AH," HE SAID, "QUI VIVE,  . . . . . . . . . 468 A REFLEX . . . . .  . 8
   AH, JONAH, JONAH--TWICE--REPROACHFULLY.  . . . . . 495 A MASQUE OF MERCY .  . 57
AHAZ
   AGAIN AS IN THE DAYS WHEN AHAZ SINNED  . . . . . . 171 NEW HAMPSHIRE . . .  . 388
   THIS WAS THE SIN THAT AHAZ WAS FORBID  . . . . . . 284 THE GOLD HESPERIDEE .  . 51
AHAZ'
   COMES TOO NEAR TO AHAZ' SIN FOR SAFETY.  . . . . . 171 NEW HAMPSHIRE . . .  . 393
AHEAD
   THE POLISHED TRAFFIC PASSED WITH A MIND AHEAD,  . . . . 286 A ROADSIDE STAND .  . 7
   PUSHING THE CRUMPLED WATER UP AHEAD,  . . . . .  . 338 THE MOST OF IT . .  . 17
   BUT THE BLIZZARD BLINDS HIM TO ANY HOUSE AHEAD.  . . . 341 WILLFUL HOMING . .  . 2
   PATIENCE AND LOOKING AWAY AHEAD,  . . . . . .  . 376 SOMETHING FOR HOPE .  . 21
   WHO MAY BE JUST AHEAD OF YOU ON FOOT  . . . . .  . 378 DIRECTIVE . . . .  . 31
   WHO HAVE, AS I SUPPOSE, AHEAD  . . . . . . .  . 383 THE NIGHT LIGHT . .  . 7
   NOW JUST AHEAD OF HIM WAS SEEN TO YAWN  . . . . .  . 394 HAEC FABULA DOCET .  . 5
   THEY MUST HAVE SEEN AHEAD WHAT NOW APPEARS:  . . . . 423 FOR JOHN F. KENNEDY  . 28
   (MY WIFE GETS IN AHEAD OF ME WITH HERS.)  . . . . . 479 A MASQUE OF REASON .  . 164
   OH, WE KNOW WELL ENOUGH TO GO AHEAD WITH.  . . . . . 483 A MASQUE OF REASON .  . 289
   AND GO AHEAD TO ANY ACCOMPLISHMENT.  . . . . .  . 521 A MASQUE OF MERCY .  . 730
AHMED
   TO AHMED S. BOKHARI . . . . . . . . . .  . 468 FROM IRON . . . . .  . 0
AID
   BUT GLAD WITH HIM, I WORKED AS WITH HIS AID,  . . . . . 23 THE TUFT OF FLOWERS  . 35
   BY WAY OF TRAVELER'S AID,  . . . . . . . . . 391 A ROGERS GROUP . .  . 10
   IT GIVES US STRANGELY LITTLE AID,  . . . . . .  . 403 SOMETHING LIKE A STAR  . 16
AIDS
   A PRUDENT GRIEF WILL NOT DESPISE SUCH AIDS.  . . . . . 200 PLACE FOR A THIRD .  . 30
AILED
   BUT WHEN I ASKED TO KNOW WHAT AILED NEW HAMPSHIRE,  . . . 166 NEW HAMPSHIRE . . .  . 223
   AND WHEN I ASKED TO KNOW WHAT AILED THE PEOPLE,  . . . 166 NEW HAMPSHIRE . . .  . 226
AILS
   SPACE AILS US MODERNS: WE ARE SICK WITH SPACE.  . . . . 352 THE LESSON FOR TODAY  . 68
   WHAT AILS ME? TELL ME, WHY AM I UNHAPPY?"  . . . . . 457 HOW HARD TO KEEP FROM  . 101
   SATAN, WHAT AILS YOU? WHERE'S THE FAMOUS TONGUE,  . . . 488 A MASQUE OF REASON .  . 405
AIM
   THE AIM WAS SONG  . . . . . . . . . . . 223 THE AIM WAS SONG .  . 1
   IT BLEW TOO HARD--THE AIM WAS SONG.  . . . . .  . 224 THE AIM WAS SONG .  . 7
   THE AIM WAS SONG--THE WIND COULD SEE.  . . . . .  . 224 THE AIM WAS SONG .  . 16
   AND ONE OF THEM PUT ME OFF MY AIM  . . . . . .  . 275 TWO TRAMPS IN MUD TIME  . 3
   AND HAVING POWER TO CHANGE HIS AIM IN FLIGHT,  . . . . 277 THE WHITE-TAILED HORNET  5
   FAR AS WE AIM OUR SIGNS TO REACH,  . . . . . .  . 328 A MISSIVE MISSILE .  . 47
   ALTHOUGH SO COMPROMISED OF AIM AND RATE  . . . . . 341 WILLFUL HOMING . . .  . 10
   NO REVOLUTION I BROUGHT ON WOULD AIM  . . . . .  . 510 A MASQUE OF MERCY .  . 457
AIMED
   IS NO PROOF THAT I AIMED THEM AT NEW HAMPSHIRE.  . . . . 166 NEW HAMPSHIRE . . .  . 247
AIMLESS
   THAN THE MEREST AIMLESS BREATH OF AIR.  . . . . .  . 24 PAN WITH US . . . .  . 25
   AND, TIRED OF AIMLESS CIRCLING IN ONE PLACE,  . . . . 238 ON A TREE FALLEN ACROSS  13
AIN'T
   BUT WORK AIN'T ALL. LEN UNDERTAKES TOO MUCH.  . . . .  . 64 A SERVANT TO SERVANTS  . 70
   THERE AIN'T NO NAMES QUITE LIKE THE OLD ONES, THOUGH,  . . . 80 THE GENERATIONS OF MEN  186
   "MA FRIEND, YOU AIN'T KNOW WHAT IT IS YOU'RE ASK."  . . . 114 IN THE HOME STRETCH  . 105
   "SHE AIN'T SPICK TOO MUCH HENGLISH--DAT'S TOO BAD."  . . . 187 THE AX-HELVE . . .  . 54
   GNAWS IN THE STABLE AIN'T NO PROOF TO ME .  . . . . . 209 PAUPER WITCH OF GRAFTON  66
   LIKE, "NO, SHE AIN'T COME BACK FROM KITING YET.  . . . . 209 PAUPER WITCH OF GRAFTON  80
   ("YOU COULDN'T CALL IT LIVING, FOR IT AIN'T"),  . . . . 263 THE INVESTMENT . .  . 2
   AIN'T IT A CAUTION TO US NOT TO FIX  . . . . .  . 372 THE LITERATE FARMER AND 137
AIR (SEE MID-AIR)
   AND THE AIR WAS STIFLING SWEET . . . . . . .  . 13 ROSE POGONIAS . . .  . 6
   AND FRESHEN IN THIS AIR OF WITHERING SWEETNESS;  . . . . 15 WAITING . . . . .  . 25
   THAN THE MEREST AIMLESS BREATH OF AIR.  . . . . .  . 24 PAN WITH US . . . .  . 25
   I MUST GET OUT OF HERE. I MUST GET AIR.--  . . . .  . 52 HOME BURIAL . . . .  . 37
   MAKING THE GRAVEL LEAP AND LEAP IN AIR,  . . . . .  . 53 HOME BURIAL . . . .  . 75
   AND THE AIR OF THE YOUNGSTERS! NOT ONE OF THEM TURNED,  . . . 61 BLUEBERRIES . . . .  . 58
   KICKING HIS WAY DOWN THROUGH THE AIR TO THE GROUND.  . . . 122 BIRCHES . . . . .  . 40
   A MOMENT SOUGHT IN AIR HIS FLOWER OF REST,  . . . .  . 126 RANGE-FINDING . . .  . 7
   I WALKED SO LIGHT ON AIR IN HEAVY SHOES  . . . .  . 132 THE BONFIRE . . . .  . 92
   YOU MAKE A LITTLE FOURSQUARE BLOCK OF AIR,  . . . .  . 148 SNOW . . . . . .  . 142
   TO BREATHE THE AIR ONE WINTER--HAD A ROOM  . . . .  . 149 SNOW . . . . . .  . 174
   AND ACQUIRE A LISTENING AIR.  . . . . . . .  . 156 THE SOUND OF TREES .  . 9
   OF FROSTY NIGHT AIR ON THE VALE BELOW . .  . . . . 169 NEW HAMPSHIRE . . .  . 341
   TO PENETRATE THE AIR IN WHICH WE ROLL.  . . . . .  . 172 A STAR IN A STONEBOAT  . 12
   NOT A BREEZE STIRRED, BUT JUST THE BREATH OF AIR  . . . 194 PAUL'S WIFE . . . .  . 98
   I LIVED ON AIR  . . . . . . . . . . .  . 226 TO EARTHWARD . . . .  . 4
   OF CASTLES I USED TO BUILD IN AIR. . . . . . .  . 232 THE KITCHEN CHIMNEY  . 20
   THE BREATH OF AIR HAD DIED OF COLD,  . . . . .  . 232 LOOKING FOR SUNSET BIRD  2
   MADE QUICK ASIDES, BUT HAVING DONE IN AIR  . . . .  . 240 OUR SINGING STRENGTH  . 40
   THE BIRDS THAT CAME TO IT THROUGH THE AIR  . . . .  . 242 NEED OF BEING VERSED  . 13
   I'VE TRIED THE NEW MOON TILTED IN THE AIR  . . . .  . 245 THE FREEDOM OF THE MOON  1
   THAT SPREADING IN THE EVENING AIR BOTH WAYS  . . . .  . 247 THE COCOON . . . .  . 2
   AND NOW THE VERY AIR, OF WHAT WE RIDE.--  . . . .  . 267 RIDERS . . . . .  . 4
```

AIR (CONTINUED)
   THE AIR WAS FULL OF DUST OF WOOL. . . . . 273 A LONE STRIKER . . . 18
   AND HEAVING HIM HIGH IN AIR, ... 289 DEPARTMENTAL 38
   IT WILL START HAIR-RAISING CURRENTS OF AIR . . . . . 306 A TRIAL RUN . . . 2
   I SHALL WILL TO THE COMMON STOCK OF AIR MY BREATH . . 307 NOT QUITE SOCIAL . . 15
   AND STILL THE AIR WAS SATURATED TOO, ... 315 IRIS BY NIGHT . . . 15
   IN THE CAPRICIOUSNESS OF SUMMER AIR . . . . 332 THE SILKEN TENT . . 13
   AND ROLLING IT INLAND ON ROLLER AIR, ... 337 THE WIND AND THE RAIN . 31
   THERE STOOD THE PURPLE SPIRES WITH NO BREATH OF AIR . 343 QUEST OF PURPLE-FRINGED 17
   IT WAS THE OBSTINATELY GENTLE AIR . . . . 356 TIME OUT 12
   AND I HAD IDLY POISED MY PEN IN AIR . . . . 357 A CONSIDERABLE SPECK . 4
   RELYING ON ITS BEAUTY, TO THE AIR. . . . . 375 A YOUNG BIRCH . . 9
   WITH AN AIR THAT SAID, "I HAVE PAID MY CALL. . . . . 420 ONE MORE BREVITY . . 46
   COURAGE IS IN THE AIR IN BRACING WHIFFS . . . . . 423 FOR JOHN F. KENNEDY . 58
   SO THE STILLY AIR . . . . 434 KITTY HAWK 209
   THOUGH OUR LEAP IN AIR . . . . 439 KITTY HAWK . . . 357
   AND ALL THE AIR RUSHED TO THE SPOT. . . . . 452 A-WISHING WELL . . 46
   PROSE MADE OF, GIVEN AN AIR BY CHURCH INTONING. . . . 461 HOW HARD TO KEEP FROM 222
   AND LET GO AT THE AIR . . . . 464 MILKY WAY IS A COWPATH 7
   WITH A CAN OF CONDENSED AIR . . . . 466 SOME SCIENCE FICTION . 25
   PRECIPITATED FROM THE DESERT AIR.-- . . . . 487 A MASQUE OF REASON . 385
AIRS
   ONLY YOU WOMEN HAVE TO PUT THESE AIRS ON . . . . . 146 SNOW 98
   MURPHY TOLD ME PAUL PUT ON ALL THOSE AIRS . . . . . 195 PAUL'S WIFE 148
AIRSHIP
   AN AIRSHIP LABORING WITH UNSHIPLIKE MOTION . . . . . 182 MAPLE 82
AIRY
   IN AIRY DALLIANCE, ... 28 MY BUTTERFLY 14
   SO MUCH TOO LIGHT AND AIRY FOR THEIR STRENGTH . . . 113 IN THE HOME STRETCH . 87
   WERE BUT FROST KNOTS ON AN AIRY GAUZE, ... 303 AFTERFLAKES 14
   ITS AIRY PRESSURE TURNED TO WATER WEIGHT. . . . . 315 IRIS BY NIGHT . . . 16
   YOU MAKE A LABOR OF FLIGHT FOR ONE SO AIRY, ... 356 A MOTH SEEN IN WINTER . 11
AISLE (SEE MIDDLE-AISLE)
   THEY EMPTIED THE AISLE . . . . 448 THE BAD ISLAND--EASTER 41
AJAR
   THROUGH THE INTERSTICES OF THINGS AJAR . . . . . 303 A BIRD SINGING IN SLEEP 10
   BUT SCARCELY WAS MY DOOR AJAR, ... 419 ONE MORE BREVITY . . 7
AKIMBO
   A LEG AKIMBO WITH WHICH HE CAN SING, ... 309 ONE GUESS 2
AKIN
   BY THOUSANDS MADE THE BAD WEATHER MADE AKIN. . . . . 240 OUR SINGING STRENGTH . 32
   AND MORE THAN ONE, TO THEIRS AKIN, ... 292 ON HEART'S BEGINNING TO 39
A-KNOWN
   ALL IS, IF I'D A-KNOWN WHEN I WAS YOUNG . . . . . 210 PAUPER WITCH OF GRAFTON 104
ALARM
   AS FISH DO WITH THE LINE IN FIRST ALARM. . . . . 174 A STAR IN A STONEBOAT . 54
   AND FLASH, AT THE LEAST ALARM . . . . 282 A DRUMLIN WOODCHUCK . 15
   I MEAN THEY COULD BE TRUSTED TO GIVE THE ALARM . . . 317 BUILD SOIL . . . 57
ALAS
   COME LEARN THE LATIN EHEU FOR ALAS. . . . . . . 353 THE LESSON FOR TODAY . 85
   ONE MORE FOND ALAS . . . . 431 KITTY HAWK 90
ALASTOR
   AS A YOUNG ALASTOR . . . . 430 KITTY HAWK 53
ALBEIT
   (AND WAS A TEXT ALBEIT DONE IN PLANT). . . . . . 355 TIME OUT 4
   ALBEIT THROUGH A RUSTY SCREEN, ... 381 AN UNSTAMPED LETTER IN 41
   ALBEIT NOT WITHOUT SOME SHAME OF FACE, ... 396 ANY SIZE WE PLEASE . 4
ALBINO
   IN AN ALBINO MONKEY IN A JUNGLE, ... 425 ACCIDENTALLY ON PURPOSE 7
ALDEBARAN
   ALDEBARAN, CAPELLA, SIRIUS . . . . 462 HOW HARD TO KEEP FROM 268
ALDER
   PINE, ALDER, PASTURE, MOWING, WELL, AND BROOK. . . . 117 IN THE HOME STRETCH . 197
   OF BLACK ALDER. . . . . 129 THE IMPULSE 14
   AND ALDER AND GRAPE VINE ENTANGLEMENT, ... 131 THE BONFIRE 63
   OF ALDER CATCH MY LIFTED AX BEHIND ME. . . . . . 185 THE AX-HELVE 2
   AND THAT WAS, AS I SAY, AN ALDER BRANCH. . . . . 185 THE AX-HELVE 5
   A WINTER GARDEN IN AN ALDER SWAMP, ... 254 A WINTER EDEN . . . 1
   'NEATH THE ALDER TREE. . . . . 343 QUEST OF PURPLE-FRINGED 20
   THE ALDER SWAMPS . . . . 360 THE RABBIT-HUNTER . . 5
ALDERS
   IN A WHITE SCARF AGAINST THE FAR-SHORE ALDERS.) . . 258 WEST-RUNNING BROOK . 26
   I SKIRTED THE MARGIN ALDERS FOR MILES AND MILES . . 342 QUEST OF PURPLE-FRINGED 5
ALDER'S
   FROM STRIKING AT ANOTHER ALDER'S ROOTS, ... 185 THE AX-HELVE 4
ALEC
   LATELY IN CONVERSE WITH A NEW YORK ALEC . . . . . 170 NEW HAMPSHIRE . . . 358
ALEXANDER
   EVER SINCE ALEXANDER GREECED THE WORLD. . . . . 511 A MASQUE OF MERCY . . 473
ALEXIUS
   MADE FOR THE EMPEROR ALEXIUS, ... 473 A MASQUE OF REASON . 11
   DEVISED THEM FOR ALEXIUS COMNENUS. . . . . . . 490 A MASQUE OF REASON . 461
ALFRED
   FOR ALFRED EDWARDS . . . . 413 A CABIN IN THE CLEARING 0
ALIAS
   ALIAS JOHN, ... 211 AN EMPTY THREAT . . . 13
ALIGHT
   I THOUGHT I SAW A BIRD ALIGHT. . . . . 232 LOOKING FOR SUNSET BIRD 4
   A BLUEBIRD COMES TENDERLY UP TO ALIGHT . . . . . 275 TWO TRAMPS IN MUD TIME 25
ALIGHTS
   HERE, TAKE MY HAND. / (HE TAKES IT AND ALIGHTS . . 489 A MASQUE OF REASON . 451
ALIKE
   AND LOSE MYSELF AMID SO MANY ALIKE. . . . . . 14 WAITING 8
   TOO MUCH ALIKE TO MARK OR NAME A PLACE BY . . . . 101 THE WOOD-PILE . . . 7
   WHO IN PARTICULAR, WHEN ALL ALIKE . . . . . . 317 BUILD SOIL 39
ALIQUID
   SOMEWHAT (ALIQUID). . . . . 434 KITTY HAWK 199

ALIT
    BUT SPES ALIT AGRICOLAM 'TIS SAID. . . . . 376 SOMETHING FOR HOPE . . 24
ALIVE
    OF ALL THE YOUNG CHATTERING LORENS ALIVE, ... 60 BLUEBERRIES 38
    LIVING. THEY GAVE HIM BACK TO HER ALIVE-- . . . . . . 230 NOT TO KEEP 5
    IT SET ITSELF TO KEEP THOSE THREE ALIVE; . . . . 283 THE GOLD HESPERIDEE . . 5
    AND LATE IN HIS LAST HOUR ALIVE, ... 311 THE VINDICTIVES . . . 42
    "THROW HIM OVER ALIVE," THEY SAID, ... 345 DISCOVERY OF MADEIRAS . 60
ALL (SEE HEAL-ALL, WHERE-ALL)
    ONLY MORE SURE OF ALL I THOUGHT WAS TRUE. . . . . . . 5 INTO MY OWN 14
    AND, FOR ALL BURDEN, CARE. . . . . 7 LOVE AND A QUESTION . 4
    AS WITNESS ALL WITHIN . . . . 11 WIND AND WINDOW FLOWER 19
    ALL SIMPLY IN THE SPRINGING OF THE YEAR. . . . . . . 12 A PRAYER IN SPRING . 4
    ALL FOR ME? AND NOT A QUESTION . . . . 13 FLOWER-GATHERING . . 9
    OR IF NOT ALL SO FAVORED,. . . . . 14 ROSE POGONIAS . . . 21
    BY A MISTY FEN THAT RANG ALL NIGHT, ... 15 IN A VALE 2
    BUT ALL CAME EVERY NIGHT WITH THE MIST; . . . . 15 IN A VALE 11
    NOR VAINLY LISTEN ALL THE NIGHT LONG. . . . . 16 IN A VALE 25
    NOT FAR, BUT NEAR, I STOOD AND SAW IT ALL, ... 16 A DREAM PANG . . . 9
    BUT SO WITH ALL, FROM BABES THAT PLAY . . . . 19 REVELATION 9
    SO ALL WHO HIDE TO WELL AWAY . . . . 19 REVELATION 11
    AND BINDING ALL IS THE HUSHED SNOW . . . . 20 THE TRIAL BY EXISTENCE 15
    AND A HUSH FALLS FOR ALL ACCLAIM. . . . . 21 THE TRIAL BY EXISTENCE 60
    THE LASTING MEMORY AT ALL CLEAR, ... 21 THE TRIAL BY EXISTENCE 67
    BUT HE HAD GONE HIS WAY, THE GRASS ALL MOWN, ... 22 THE TUFT OF FLOWERS . 7
    "AS ALL MUST BE," I SAID WITHIN MY HEART, ... 22 THE TUFT OF FLOWERS . 9
    IN ALL THE COUNTRY HE DID COMMAND . . . . 23 PAN WITH US 8
    THAT I SUDDENLY HEARD--ALL I NEEDED TO HEAR: . . . . 24 THE DEMIURGE'S LAUGH . 5
    NOW CLOSE THE WINDOWS AND HUSH ALL THE FIELDS: . . . 25 NOW CLOSE THE WINDOWS . 1
    BUT SEE ALL WIND-STIRRED. . . . . 25 NOW CLOSE THE WINDOWS . 8
    THE ROAD IS FORLORN ALL DAY, ... 26 A LINE-STORM SONG . 2
    ALL SONG OF THE WOODS IS CRUSHED LIKE SOME . . . . . 26 A LINE-STORM SONG . 13
    SHOULD WASTE THEM ALL. . . . . 27 OCTOBER 4
    FOR THE GRAPES' SAKE, IF THEY WERE ALL, ... 28 OCTOBER 18
    WITH ALL THY DAZZLING OTHER ONES, ... 28 MY BUTTERFLY . . . 13
    OF MY REGRET HUNG NOT ON ALL THE LAND, ... 28 MY BUTTERFLY 19
    THE LEAVES ARE ALL DEAD ON THE GROUND, ... 30 RELUCTANCE 7
    HE IS ALL PINE AND I AM APPLE ORCHARD. . . . . . . 33 MENDING WALL . . . 24
    'ALL RIGHT,' I SAY, 'I CAN'T AFFORD TO PAY . . . . . 35 DEATH OF THE HIRED MAN 22
    ALL THROUGH JULY UNDER THE BLAZING SUN, ... 36 DEATH OF THE HIRED MAN 67
    HE WANTED TO GO OVER THAT. BUT MOST OF ALL . . . . . 37 DEATH OF THE HIRED MAN 85
    IT ALL DEPENDS ON WHAT YOU MEAN BY HOME." . . . . . 38 DEATH OF THE HIRED MAN 114
    HE'D KEEP SO STILL ABOUT HIM ALL THIS TIME?" . . . . 39 DEATH OF THE HIRED MAN 138
    "WARREN?" SHE QUESTIONED. / "DEAD," WAS ALL HE ANSWERED. 40 DEATH OF THE HIRED MAN 166
    THAT THING TAKES ALL THE ROOM!" HE MOVED HIS GOAD. . . 41 THE MOUNTAIN 27
    UNTIL THE BUSHES ALL ALONG ITS BANKS . . . . 42 THE MOUNTAIN 52
    YOU'VE WORKED AROUND THE FOOT OF ALL YOUR LIFE. . . . 43 THE MOUNTAIN 83
    "I DON'T SUPPOSE THE WATER'S CHANGED AT ALL. . . . . 44 THE MOUNTAIN 101
    BUT ALL THE FUN'S IN HOW YOU SAY A THING." . . . . . 44 THE MOUNTAIN 104
    "YOU'VE LIVED HERE ALL YOUR LIFE?" / "EVER SINCE HOR . 44 THE MOUNTAIN 105
    "I KNOW HIM: HE'S ALL RIGHT. A MAN'S A MAN. . . . . 45 A HUNDRED COLLARS . 26
    TOO BAD TO WASTE THEM ALL. YOU OUGHT TO HAVE THEM. . . 47 A HUNDRED COLLARS . 67
    THERE'S FIVE: THAT'S ALL I CARRY." / "I CAN SEARCH YOU? 47 A HUNDRED COLLARS . 88
    ALL ROUND THE COUNTRY FOR THE WEEKLY NEWS, ... 48 A HUNDRED COLLARS . 98
    A GOOD DEAL COMES ON ME WHEN ALL IS SAID. . . . . . 48 A HUNDRED COLLARS . 107
    "YOU SEE I'M IN WITH EVERYBODY, KNOW 'EM ALL. . . . . 49 A HUNDRED COLLARS . 120
    THE FAMILY'S ALL AWAY IN SOME BACK MEADOW. . . . . . 49 A HUNDRED COLLARS . 131
    AND LATER STILL THEY ALL GET DRIVEN IN: . . . . . . 49 A HUNDRED COLLARS . 133
    ALL IN A FAMILY ROW DOWN TO THE YOUNGEST." . . . . . 49 A HUNDRED COLLARS . 148
    HER FINGERS MOVED THE LATCH FOR ALL REPLY. . . . . . 52 HOME BURIAL 44
    THEY MIGHT AS WELL NOT TRY TO GO AT ALL. . . . . . 54 HOME BURIAL 99
    "THERE, YOU HAVE SAID IT ALL AND YOU FEEL BETTER. . . 54 HOME BURIAL 108
    "YOU--OH, YOU THINK THE TALK IS ALL. I MUST GO-- . . 54 HOME BURIAL 112
    ANYTHING IN HER AFTER ALL THE YEARS. . . . . 56 THE BLACK COTTAGE . 30
    TO HAVE GIVEN OUTRIGHT FOR THEM ALL SHE GAVE. . . . . 57 THE BLACK COTTAGE . 59
    THAT ALL MEN ARE CREATED FREE AND EQUAL. . . . . . 57 THE BLACK COTTAGE . 61
    FROM THE WORLD'S VIEW TODAY OF ALL THOSE THINGS. . . . 57 THE BLACK COTTAGE . 63
    WHOM WE ALL HAVE TO THINK OF NOWADAYS, ... 57 THE BLACK COTTAGE . 87
    AND ALL RIPE TOGETHER, NOT SOME OF THEM GREEN . . . . 59 BLUEBERRIES 6
    THE FIRE RAN AND BURNED IT ALL UP BUT THE WALL." . . . 59 BLUEBERRIES 12
    THE PASTURE ALL OVER UNTIL NOT A FERN . . . . 59 BLUEBERRIES 18
    AND PRESTO, THEY'RE UP ALL AROUND YOU AS THICK . . . . 59 BLUEBERRIES 20
    AND AFTER ALL, REALLY THEY'RE EBONY SKINNED: . . . . 60 BLUEBERRIES 24
    OF ALL THE YOUNG CHATTERING LORENS ALIVE, ... 60 BLUEBERRIES 38
    WITH THE MOUTHS OF ALL THOSE YOUNG LORENS TO FEED? . . 60 BLUEBERRIES 49
    HE HAS BROUGHT THEM ALL UP ON WILD BERRIES, THEY SAY, . 60 BLUEBERRIES 50
    OF WHERE ALL THE BERRIES AND OTHER THINGS GROW, . . . 61 BLUEBERRIES 61
    BY GOING TO HIM OF ALL PEOPLE ON EARTH . . . . . . 61 BLUEBERRIES 69
    THERE HAD BEEN SOME BERRIES--BUT THOSE WERE ALL GONE. . 61 BLUEBERRIES 73
    IT WAS ALL HE COULD DO TO KEEP A STRAIGHT FACE." . . . 61 BLUEBERRIES 78
    "IF HE THINKS ALL THE FRUIT THAT GROWS WILD IS FOR HIM, 61 BLUEBERRIES 79
    NOT LIKELY, WHEN ALL THE YOUNG LORENS DEPLOY. . . . . 62 BLUEBERRIES 98
    AND WOULD FEEL IF I WASN'T ALL GONE WRONG. . . . . . 63 A SERVANT TO SERVANTS . 15
    AND ALL OUR STORMS COME UP TOWARD THE HOUSE, ... 63 A SERVANT TO SERVANTS . 24
    INCLUDING ME. HE THINKS I'LL BE ALL RIGHT . . . . . 64 A SERVANT TO SERVANTS . 46
    (WOMEN AND MEN WILL MAKE THEM ALL THE SAME.) . . . . 64 A SERVANT TO SERVANTS . 69
    BUT WORK AIN'T ALL. LEN UNDERTAKES TOO MUCH. . . . . 64 A SERVANT TO SERVANTS . 70
    THAN IF I WASN'T IN THE ROOM AT ALL. . . . . 65 A SERVANT TO SERVANTS . 80
    COMING AND GOING ALL THE TIME, THEY ARE: . . . . . 65 A SERVANT TO SERVANTS . 81
    ANYWAY ALL HE TALKED ABOUT WAS LOVE. . . . . 66 A SERVANT TO SERVANTS . 110
    A NARROW PASSAGE ALL THE WAY AROUND. . . . . 66 A SERVANT TO SERVANTS . 116
    WITH HIS CLOTHES ON HIS ARM--ALL OF HIS CLOTHES. . . . 66 A SERVANT TO SERVANTS . 123
    FOR ALL . . . . 69 AFTER APPLE-PICKING . 32
    WHAT WAS IN ALL OUR MINDS, AND YOU WEREN'T HINTING. . . 70 THE CODE 28
    ALL WIRY ARMS AND LEGS THAT SPREAD OUT WAVY. . . . . 70 THE CODE 34
    I'VE HEARD HIM POUNDING IN THE BARN ALL NIGHT. . . . . 71 THE CODE 42
    HE KEPT AWAY FROM US ALL AFTERNOON. . . . . 73 THE CODE 106
    WHEN ALL WHO WOULD COME SEEKING IN NEW HAMPSHIRE . . . 73 THE GENERATIONS OF MEN 2

PAGE TITLE   LINE

ALL (CONTINUED)

THE ORIGIN OF ALL THE FAMILY THERE.	73	THE GENERATIONS OF MEN	9
THAT NOW NOT ALL THE HOUSES LEFT IN TOWN.	73	THE GENERATIONS OF MEN	11
BUT RAIN SPOILED ALL. THE DAY BEGAN UNCERTAIN,	74	THE GENERATIONS OF MEN	19
ALL CLAIMING SOME PRIORITY IN STARKNESS.	75	THE GENERATIONS OF MEN	49
WITH ALL THIS PRIDE OF ANCESTRY, WE YANKEES?	76	THE GENERATIONS OF MEN	87
I THINK WE'RE ALL MAD. TELL ME WHY WE'RE HERE,	76	THE GENERATIONS OF MEN	88
THE MEANING OF IT ALL IS OUT OF YOU;	78	THE GENERATIONS OF MEN	136
THE LIFE IS NOT YET ALL GONE OUT OF IT.	79	THE GENERATIONS OF MEN	165
I LET YOU SAY ALL THAT. BUT I MUST GO NOW."	80	THE GENERATIONS OF MEN	202
MY FINGERS ARE ABOUT ALL I'VE THE USE OF	81	THE HOUSEKEEPER	6
"YES, WHAT'S IT ALL ABOUT? WHEN DID SHE GO?"	82	THE HOUSEKEEPER	21
ALL IS, HE'S MADE UP HIS MIND NOT TO STAND	83	THE HOUSEKEEPER	70
"THE STRAIN'S BEEN TOO MUCH FOR HER ALL THESE YEARS:	84	THE HOUSEKEEPER	77
I KNOW THE WAY HE'S FELT--BUT ALL THE SAME!"	84	THE HOUSEKEEPER	83
"AND AFTER ALL WHY SHOULD THEY? JOHN'S BEEN FAIR	84	THE HOUSEKEEPER	92
YOU SEE OUR PRETTY THINGS ARE ALL OUTDOORS.	85	THE HOUSEKEEPER	110
ALL WE CAN HOLD TOGETHER BY THE LEGS.	85	THE HOUSEKEEPER	128
BLESS YOU, IT'S ALL EXPENSE, THOUGH. REACH ME DOWN	86	THE HOUSEKEEPER	142
"AND LIKE IT, TOO. IT MAKES IT ALL THE WORSE."	86	THE HOUSEKEEPER	155
"IT SEEMS AS IF. AND THAT'S NOT ALL: HE'S HELPLESS	86	THE HOUSEKEEPER	156
TO SEE WHERE ALL THE MONEY GOES SO FAST.	86	THE HOUSEKEEPER	159
"IT MAKES IT ALL THE WORSE. YOU MUST BE BLIND."	87	THE HOUSEKEEPER	163
"IT'S AS I SAY: SHE'S TURNED FROM HIM, THAT'S ALL."	87	THE HOUSEKEEPER	167
SO THAT WAS WHAT WAS BACK. SHE'S BAD, THAT'S ALL!"	88	THE HOUSEKEEPER	183
"THEN IT'S ALL UP. I THINK I'LL GET AWAY.	88	THE HOUSEKEEPER	190
AND TURN DOLL OUT TO PASTURE, RIG AND ALL.	88	THE HOUSEKEEPER	201
NEARBY, ALL DARK IN EVERY GLOSSY WINDOW.	89	THE FEAR	4
WHAT IF I'M RIGHT, AND SOMEONE ALL THE TIME--	90	THE FEAR	22
HE HAS SEEN ALL THERE WAS TO SEE AND GONE."	91	THE FEAR	58
"WHAT DO YOU WANT?" SHE CRIED TO ALL THE DARK.	91	THE FEAR	61
"BUT IF THAT'S ALL--JOEL--YOU REALIZE--	92	THE FEAR	87
AS THEY BOTH BITE THE WOOD. IT'S ALL OUR MUSIC.	94	THE SELF-SEEKER	43
"YES, THAT'S ONE WAY TO PUT IT--ALL THE FLOWERS	95	THE SELF-SEEKER	67
PROMISE ME ALL THE SHOOKS I WANT TO NAIL."	95	THE SELF-SEEKER	79
I KNEW, ANNE, YOU WOULDN'T LET ME PICK THEM ALL."	97	THE SELF-SEEKER	120
BUT, ANNE, I'M TROUBLED; HAVE YOU TOLD ME ALL?	97	THE SELF-SEEKER	131
OVER STONE WALLS AND ALL ALONG A WOOD	98	THE SELF-SEEKER	152
OF LITTLE FINGERS ALL KEPT DOWN BUT ONE,	98	THE SELF-SEEKER	156
LUCKILY TERMS ARE ALL AGREED UPON.	99	THE SELF-SEEKER	182
"YES, BUT ALL THAT TAKES TIME, AND I'M AS MUCH .	99	THE SELF-SEEKER	191
ONE FOOT WENT THROUGH. THE VIEW WAS ALL IN LINES	101	THE WOOD-PILE	5
NO ONE AT ALL WITH WHOM TO TALK,	102	GOOD HOURS	2
AND THAT HAS MADE ALL THE DIFFERENCE.	105	THE ROAD NOT TAKEN	20
WHERE HOUSES ALL ARE CHURCHES AND HAVE SPIRES.	106	CHRISTMAS TREES	14
AND LEAVE THE SLOPE BEHIND THE HOUSE ALL BARE,	106	CHRISTMAS TREES	18
ALL ROUND AND ROUND. THE LATTER HE NODDED "YES" TO,	107	CHRISTMAS TREES	36
(FOR THAT WAS ALL THEY FIGURED OUT APIECE)--	107	CHRISTMAS TREES	49
ALL OUT-OF-DOORS LOOKED DARKLY IN AT HIM	108	OLD MAN'S WINTER NIGHT	1
ALL THIS TO PROVE WE CARED. WHY IS THERE THEN	109	THE EXPOSED NEST	31
THAT END ALL. AND IT'S SCARCE ENOUGH TO CALL	111	IN THE HOME STRETCH	34
AND THEN THEY ALL TURNED TO WITH DEAFENING BOOTS	114	IN THE HOME STRETCH	109
ALL THEY COULD SAY WAS 'GOD!' WHEN YOU PROPOSED	114	IN THE HOME STRETCH	120
THEY ALMOST SHOOK ME." / "IT'S ALL SO MUCH	114	IN THE HOME STRETCH	126
AND ALL AT ONCE. HE'LL PLAN FOR US AND PLAN	115	IN THE HOME STRETCH	152
TO EMPTY ONE HOUSE OF ALL HOUSEHOLD GOODS	116	IN THE HOME STRETCH	160
"IT'S ALL SO MUCH WHAT I HAVE ALWAYS WANTED,	116	IN THE HOME STRETCH	164
ALL THAT'S NOT NEW IN WHERE WE FIND OURSELVES.	117	IN THE HOME STRETCH	182
ALL OF A FARM IT IS." / " I KNOW THIS MUCH:	117	IN THE HOME STRETCH	198
ALL STILL	118	THE TELEPHONE	4
AS YOU CAME UP THE HILL. WE MET. BUT ALL	118	MEETING AND PASSING	4
AND ALL THE TIME WE TALKED YOU SEEMED TO SEE	119	MEETING AND PASSING	10
(AND TAKEN WITH IT ALL THE HYLA BREED	119	HYLA BROOK	4
HE SAYS THE HIGHWAY DUST IS OVER ALL.	120	THE OVEN BIRD	10
THE QUESTION THAT HE FRAMES IN ALL BUT WORDS	120	THE OVEN BIRD	13
AND SITS IN SIRIUS' DISC ALL NIGHT,	120	BOND AND FREE	12
AND SIMPLY STAYING POSSESSES ALL	120	BOND AND FREE	18
WITH ALL HER MATTER OF FACT ABOUT THE ICE STORM,	121	BIRCHES	22
FOR HIM TO CONQUER. HE LEARNED ALL THERE WAS	122	BIRCHES	32
ALL FRESH AND SOUND FROM THE RECENT AX.	123	PEA BRUSH	14
ON ALL THE HILLS I HAVEN'T HOED,	124	A TIME TO TALK	4
ME? I'M NOT OFF FOR ANYWHERE AT ALL.	125	AN ENCOUNTER	22
BY SETTING FIRE TO ALL THE BRUSH WE PILED	129	THE BONFIRE	3
ROUSE THEM ALL, BOTH THE FREE AND NOT SO FREE	130	THE BONFIRE	13
LET'S ALL BUT BRING TO LIFE THIS OLD VOLCANO,	130	THE BONFIRE	16
THE BLACK WAS ALMOST ALL THERE WAS BY DAYLIGHT,	131	THE BONFIRE	49
AND HEAT SO CLOSE IN; BUT THE THOUGHT OF ALL	131	THE BONFIRE	71
THE WOODS AND TOWN ON FIRE BY ME, AND ALL	131	THE BONFIRE	72
WHERE ALL MY WEARINESS HAD GONE AND WHY	132	THE BONFIRE	91
MY DEARS, MY DEARS, YOU THOUGHT THAT--WE ALL THOUGHT IT.	132	THE BONFIRE	102
FURTHER O'ERHEAD THAN ALL BUT STARS AND ANGELS--	132	THE BONFIRE	107
SO SHE HAD TO WORK IT ALL BY HAND,	133	A GIRL'S GARDEN	19
OF ALL THINGS BUT WEED.	134	A GIRL'S GARDEN	28
WHEN ALL WAS SAID AND DONE,	134	A GIRL'S GARDEN	38
AND NOTHING HAPPENED: DAY WAS ALL BUT DONE.	136	"OUT,OUT--"	9
THE LIFE FROM SPILLING. THEN THE BOY SAW ALL--	137	"OUT,OUT--"	22
HE SAW ALL SPOILED. "DON'T LET HIM CUT MY HAND OFF--	137	"OUT,OUT--"	25
WALLS WERE ALL BURIED, TREES WERE FEW:	137	BROWN'S DESCENT	13
"WELL--I--BE--" THAT WAS ALL HE SAID,	139	BROWN'S DESCENT	45
THAT ALL YOUR DAYS ARE DIM BENEATH,	141	THE GUM-GATHERER	36
OH, YES, HE SHOWED JOHN THE WHEEL PIT ALL RIGHT.	142	THE VANISHING RED	29
LONG ENOUGH FOR RECORDING ALL OUR NAMES ON.--	143	SNOW	10
THREE HOURS TO HERE! BUT THAT WAS ALL UPHILL;	143	SNOW	22
THAT'S ALL YOU EVER HEARD HIM CALLED ROUND HERE.	144	SNOW	46
TRY TO THINK WHAT HE DID WITH ALL THAT TIME.	145	SNOW	61
THAT SORT OF MAN TALKS STRAIGHT-ON ALL HIS LIFE	145	SNOW	64
BUT KEEP STILL IF HE FAILS." / "KEEP STILL ALL OVER.	146	SNOW	87
HE'S HERE. I LEAVE HIM ALL TO YOU. GO IN	146	SNOW	103

ALL (CONTINUED)
    AND SAVE HIS LIFE.--ALL RIGHT, COME IN, MESERVE. . . . . 147 SNOW 104
    QUIET AND LIGHT AND WARM, IN SPITE OF ALL . . . . . 148 SNOW 143
    THOUGH FOR ALL ANYONE CAN TELL, REPOSE . . . . . . 148 SNOW 147
    THOSE WERE HIS WORDS, AND HE WENT HOME AND ALL . . . . 149 SNOW 185
    THIS HOUSE IS FROZEN BRITTLE, ALL EXCEPT . . . . . . 150 SNOW 202
    YOU'RE FURTHER UNDER IN THE SNOW--THAT'S ALL-- . . . . 150 SNOW 205
    UNDER IT ALL, HIS DOOR SEALED UP AND LOST, ... 150 SNOW 224
    YOU DIDN'T THINK YOU'D KEEP HIM AFTER ALL. . . . . . 152 SNOW 255
    I WANT TO SPEAK TO HER." / "ALL SHE SAID WAS, ... 152 SNOW 276
    "FRED, AFTER ALL I SAID! YOU SHAN'T MAKE OUT . . . . 153 SNOW 285
    TILL WE LOSE ALL MEASURE OF PACE, ... 156 THE SOUND OF TREES . . . 7
    MUCH MATTERS. YOU MAY WORK FOR ALL OF ME. . . . . . 159 NEW HAMPSHIRE 5
    HIS FARM WAS "GROUNDS," AND NOT A FARM AT ALL; . . . . 160 NEW HAMPSHIRE 51
    JUST SPECIMENS IS ALL NEW HAMPSHIRE HAS, ... 161 NEW HAMPSHIRE 61
    SHE HAD ONE DANIEL WEBSTER. HE WAS ALL . . . . . . 161 NEW HAMPSHIRE 67
    THE PLACE IS SILENT ALL DAY LONG, NOR YET . . . . . 165 NEW HAMPSHIRE 189
    FOR ALL HER MOUNTAINS FALL A LITTLE SHORT, ... 170 NEW HAMPSHIRE 355
    NEVER TELL ME THAT NOT ONE STAR OF ALL . . . . . . 172 A STAR IN A STONEBOAT . . 1
    FLOWERS FANNED AND NOT PUT OUT BY ALL THE RAIN . . . . 173 A STAR IN A STONEBOAT . . 23
    IS EXTREME WHERE THEY SHRINK TO NONE AT ALL. . . . . 176 THE CENSUS-TAKER . . . 63
    TO FIND HIMSELF IN ONE. WELL, ALL WE SAID WAS . . . . 178 THE STAR-SPLITTER . . . 57
    WE'VE LOOKED AND LOOKED, BUT AFTER ALL WHERE ARE WE? . . 179 THE STAR-SPLITTER . . . 95
    BY AND BY I WILL TELL YOU ALL I KNOW . . . . 180 MAPLE 26
    LUCKILY ALL SHE WANTED OF HER NAME THEN . . . . . . 180 MAPLE 30
    SHE WOULD FORGET IT. SHE ALL BUT FORGOT IT. . . . . . 180 MAPLE 35
    IN THE BIG BIBLE,-AND ALL SHE REMEMBERED . . . . . . 183 MAPLE 105
    NOT MEANT FOR US AT ALL." / "NOT MEANT FOR ME? . . . . 183 MAPLE 114
    WHEN ALL MY STRENGTH PUT FORTH WAS IN HIS FAVOR, . . . 185 THE AX-HELVE 11
    WHAT IT WAS ALL ABOUT. THERE MIGHT BE SOMETHING . . . 185 THE AX-HELVE 15
    BUT ALL HE HAD TO TELL ME IN FRENCH-ENGLISH . . . . . 185 THE AX-HELVE 18
    AND CAUGHT HERSELF UP BODILY, CHAIR AND ALL, ... 187 THE AX-HELVE 52
    NOT ALL THE MOTION, THOUGH, THEY EVER LENT, ... 188 THE GRINDSTONE . . . 5
    NOT ALL THE MILES IT MAY HAVE THOUGHT IT WENT, ... 188 THE GRINDSTONE . . . 6
    ALL OTHER FARM MACHINERY'S GONE IN, ... 189 THE GRINDSTONE . . . 11
    ONE SUMMER DAY, ALL DAY I DROVE IT HARD, ... 189 THE GRINDSTONE . . . 23
    FOR ALL I KNEW IT MAY HAVE SHARPENED SPEARS . . . . . 189 THE GRINDSTONE . . . 37
    WHAT IF IT WASN'T ALL IT SHOULD BE? I'D . . . . . . 191 THE GRINDSTONE . . . 76
    ALL THAT WAS NEEDED WAS TO SAY TO HIM, ... 191 PAUL'S WIFE 2
    HE WAS ALL DUTY TO HER IN A MINUTE: . . . . 191 PAUL'S WIFE 12
    PAUL TOLD THE BOSS THE LOAD WOULD BE ALL RIGHT, ... 192 PAUL'S WIFE 46
    IT WASN'T GREASE AT ALL, BUT A LONG SLOT. . . . . . 193 PAUL'S WIFE 73
    ALL DUG TO GO A-FISHING IN." TO PAUL . . . . 193 PAUL'S WIFE 82
    (MURPHY HAD BEEN THERE WATCHING ALL THE TIME, ... 194 PAUL'S WIFE 114
    PAUL DARKLY, LIKE HER SHADOW. ALL THE LIGHT . . . . . 195 PAUL'S WIFE 136
    ALL THOSE GREAT RUFFIANS PUT THEIR THROATS TOGETHER, . . 195 PAUL'S WIFE 139
    SHE WENT OUT LIKE A FIREFLY, AND THAT WAS ALL. . . . . 195 PAUL'S WIFE 144
    MURPHY TOLD ME PAUL PUT ON ALL THOSE AIRS . . . . . 196 PAUL'S WIFE 148
    IT'S ALL YOU KNOW THE GRAPE, OR KNOW THE BIRCH. . . . . 196 WILD GRAPES 3
    BUNCHES ALL ROUND ME GROWING IN WHITE BIRCHES, ... 197 WILD GRAPES 26
    HOLD ON WITH ALL YOUR MIGHT WHEN I LET GO." . . . . . 197 WILD GRAPES 40
    NOTHING TO SAY TO ALL THOSE MARRIAGES! . . . . . . 199 PLACE FOR A THIRD . . 1
    AND ANXIOUS TO MAKE ALL HE COULD OF IT . . . . . . 200 PLACE FOR A THIRD . . 17
    FELL ALL IN WRINKLES OF RESPONSIBILITY. . . . . . . 201 PLACE FOR A THIRD . . 48
    SHE AND ELIZA HAD BEEN FRIENDS THROUGH ALL. . . . . . 201 PLACE FOR A THIRD . . 63
    TWO OLD-BELIEVERS. THEY DID ALL THE TALKING. . . . . 202 THE WITCH OF COOS . . 3
    THE FAINTEST RESTLESS RUSTLING RAN ALL THROUGH THEM. . . 204 THE WITCH OF COOS . . 64
    AND ALL BUT LOST HIMSELF. (A TONGUE OF FIRE . . . . . 204 THE WITCH OF COOS . . 72
    THE FINGER-PIECES SLID IN ALL DIRECTIONS. . . . . . 204 THE WITCH OF COOS . . 79
    WE'D KEPT UP ALL THESE YEARS BETWEEN OURSELVES . . . . 207 THE WITCH OF COOS . . 146
    AND RODE ALL OVER EVERYTHING ON HIM . . . . 208 PAUPER WITCH OF GRAFTON 47
    THE POOR OLD MAN. IT WOULD HAVE BEEN ALL RIGHT . . . . 209 PAUPER WITCH OF GRAFTON 53
    ALL FOUR OF THEM TO SPLINTERS. WHAT DID THAT PROVE? . . 209 PAUPER WITCH OF GRAFTON 63
    WITH ALL THE RAIN AND SNOW OF SEVEN YEARS; . . . . . 210 PAUPER WITCH OF GRAFTON 92
    ALL IS, IF I'D A-KNOWN WHEN I WAS YOUNG . . . . . . 210 PAUPER WITCH OF GRAFTON 104
    YET DOES PERHAPS FOR ALL THREE. . . . . 212 AN EMPTY THREAT . . . 37
    AND NOTHING CAME OF ALL HE SAILED. . . . . 212 AN EMPTY THREAT . . . 47
    I'LL FIND THAT FOUNTAIN IF IT TAKES ALL SUMMER, ... 213 A FOUNTAIN, A BOTTLE . 18
    BE DRAGGED BY YOU ALL OVER EVERYWHERE----" . . . . . 214 A FOUNTAIN, A BOTTLE . 30
    YOU DON'T LIKE NATURE. ALL YOU LIKE IS BOOKS. . . . . 215 A FOUNTAIN, A BOTTLE . 57
    AND HAD IT PUBLISHED. IT WAS ALL ABOUT . . . . . . 215 A FOUNTAIN, A BOTTLE . 79
    UNFORTUNATELY ALL OF ONE KIND, THOUGH. . . . . . . 216 A FOUNTAIN, A BOTTLE . 99
    BUT ALL THE BURDEN OF ITS BODY SONG), ... 216 A FOUNTAIN, A BOTTLE . 114
    HERE WERE ALL THOSE THE POETESS'S LIFE . . . . . . 217 A FOUNTAIN, A BOTTLE . 121
    "WHY NOT TAKE TWO OR THREE?" / "TAKE ALL YOU WANT. . . . 217 A FOUNTAIN, A BOTTLE . 124
    ALL THE WAY HOME I KEPT REMEMBERING . . . . 217 A FOUNTAIN, A BOTTLE . 132
    IN TIME SHE WOULD BE RID OF ALL HER BOOKS. . . . . . 217 A FOUNTAIN, A BOTTLE . 138
    YET CAN'T HELP MARKING ALL THE TIME . . . . 221 IN A DISUSED GRAVEYARD 10
    WITH THE LITTLE FELLOW AT ALL. HE'S RUNNING AWAY. . . . 223 THE RUNAWAY 11
    AND ALL HIS TAIL THAT ISN'T HAIR UP STRAIGHT. . . . . 223 THE RUNAWAY 17
    BUT THESE ARE FLOWERS THAT FLY AND ALL BUT SING: . . . 225 BLUE-BUTTERFLY DAY . . 5
    IT SHALL NOT MAKE AGAIN ALL WINTER LONG . . . . . . 226 THE ONSET 4
    YET ALL THE PRECEDENT IS ON MY SIDE: . . . . 226 THE ONSET 12
    AND I SHALL SEE THE SNOW ALL GO DOWNHILL . . . . . . 226 THE ONSET 18
    TO ALL MY LENGTH. . . . . 227 TO EARTHWARD 32
    REMINDS ME OF ALL THAT CAN HAPPEN TO HARM . . . . . 228 GOOD-BY AND KEEP COLD . 3
    ALL WINTER, CUT OFF BY A HILL FROM THE HOUSE. . . . . 228 GOOD-BY AND KEEP COLD . 5
    NO FOOTSTEP MOVED IT. "THIS IS ALL," THEY SIGHED, . . . 229 TWO LOOK AT TWO . . . 13
    "THIS, THEN, IS ALL. WHAT MORE IS THERE TO ASK?" . . . 229 TWO LOOK AT TWO . . . 25
    "THIS MUST BE ALL." IT WAS ALL. STILL THEY STOOD, . . . 230 TWO LOOK AT TWO . . . 39
    "WHAT IS IT, DEAR?" AND SHE HAD GIVEN ALL . . . . . 230 NOT TO KEEP 9
    AND STILL SHE HAD ALL--THEY HAD--THEY THE LUCKY! . . . 230 NOT TO KEEP 10
    AND ALL THE REST FOR THEM PERMISSIBLE EASE. . . . . . 230 NOT TO KEEP 12
    AND ALL FOR NOTHING IT HAD EVER DONE, ... 231 A BROOK IN THE CITY . 18
    AND THAT WAS ALL THERE WAS TO SEE . . . . 233 LOOKING FOR SUNSET BIRD 11
    OF RUSTLING ALL DAY . . . . 234 GATHERING LEAVES . . 6
    THE SOUND OF THE CLOSING OUTSIDE DOOR WAS ALL. . . . . 235 VALLEY'S SINGING DAY . 1
    THE FIRST SONGBIRD THAT AWAKENED ALL THE REST. . . . . 235 VALLEY'S SINGING DAY . 5

ALL (CONTINUED)
ALL CRYING, "WE WILL GO WITH YOU, O WIND!" . . . . . . 236 MISGIVING 1
IN THE CONFUSION OF THEM ALL AGLITTER, ... 237 A HILLSIDE THAW . . 14
BY ALL I TELL; BUT SO'S THE MOON A WITCH. . . . . . 237 A HILLSIDE THAW . . 19
AND ALL GO BACK TO WINTER BUT THE ROAD. . . . . . 239 OUR SINGING STRENGTH . 10
THEY'D SOON EXHAUSTED ALL THERE WAS IN FLYING; . . . . 239 OUR SINGING STRENGTH . 27
A TALKING TWITTER ALL THEY HAD TO SING. . . . . . 240 OUR SINGING STRENGTH . 38
WHERE ONE FALSE WING BEAT WOULD HAVE BROUGHT DOWN ALL, . . 240 OUR SINGING STRENGTH . 43
NOW THE CHIMNEY WAS ALL OF THE HOUSE THAT STOOD, . . . 241 NEED OF BEING VERSED . 3
NO MORE IT OPENED WITH ALL ONE END . . . . . . 241 NEED OF BEING VERSED . 9
THE COLOR RUN, ALL SORTS OF WONDER FOLLOW. . . . . . 245 THE FREEDOM OF THE MOON 12
AND HAS NO LEAVES AT ALL OF ITS OWN; . . . . . . 247 ON GOING UNNOTICED . . 7
IS ALL THE SMOKE FROM ONE POOR HOUSE ALONE, ... 248 THE COCOON 5
I WANT TO TELL THEM THAT WITH ALL THIS SMOKE . . . . 248 THE COCOON 12
I NAME ALL THE FLOWERS I AM SURE THEY WEREN'T: . . . . 248 A PASSING GLIMPSE . . 5
ALL THE DUST THE WIND BLEW HIGH . . . . 249 A PECK OF GOLD . . . 5
GOLD DUSTED ALL WE DRANK AND ATE, ... 249 A PECK OF GOLD . . . 10
"WE ALL MUST EAT OUR PECK OF GOLD." . . . . . . 249 A PECK OF GOLD . . . 12
NOW LET THE NIGHT BE DARK FOR ALL CF ME. . . . . . 249 ACCEPTANCE 12
AND NOT SING BY MY HOUSE ALL DAY; . . . . 250 A MINOR BIRD 2
NOT ALL YOUR LIGHT TONGUES TALKING ALOUD . . . . . 252 TREE AT MY WINDOW . . 7
AND ALL BUT LOST. . . . . 252 TREE AT MY WINDOW . . 12
THE CROSS, THE CROWN, THE SCALES MAY ALL . . . . . 252 THE PEACEFUL SHEPHERD . 11
THE LIGHT WAS WHAT IT WAS ALL ABOUT: . . . . . . 253 THE THATCH 5
SO NEAR TO PARADISE ALL PAIRING ENDS: . . . . . . 254 A WINTER EDEN . . . 13
YOU KNOW THEM—SEVEN IN ALL." . . . . 257 THE LOVELY BE CHOOSERS 52
WHEN ALL THE OTHER COUNTRY BROOKS FLOW EAST . . . . 258 WEST-RUNNING BROOK . . 5
ALL THE WAY TO THE WEST . . . . 261 CANIS MAJOR 6
NO SHIP OF ALL THAT UNDER SAIL OR STEAM . . . . . 262 IMMIGRANTS 1
THAT ALL THEY ASK IS ROUGHER WEATHER, ... 262 THE FLOWER BOAT . . . 10
ALL THAT PIANO AND NEW PAINT BACK THERE, ... 264 THE INVESTMENT . . . 9
THE TREES ARE ALL I'M AFRAID OF, ... 264 THE LAST MOWING . . . 11
ALL SHAPES AND COLORS OF FLOWERS, ... 264 THE LAST MOWING . . . 18
ALL CREATURES STILL WARMLY SUSPIRE. . . . . . . 266 SITTING BY A BUSH . . 8
WITH ALL I HAVE TO HOLD WITH, HAND AND MIND . . . . 267 THE ARMFUL 6
THEN SIT DOWN IN THE MIDDLE OF THEM ALL. . . . . . 267 THE ARMFUL 10
AND ALL OUR BLANDISHMENTS WOULD SEEM DEFIED, ... 268 RIDERS 11
THAT ALL DAY FIGHTS A NERVOUS INWARD RAGE, ... 269 THE BEAR 14
HIS MOOD REJECTING ALL HIS MIND SUGGESTS. . . . . . 269 THE BEAR 15
THEN FOR A MOMENT ALL THERE WAS SIZE, ... 270 THE EGG AND THE MACHINE 13
ALL PACKED IN SAND TO WAIT THE TRUMP TOGETHER. . . . . 270 THE EGG AND THE MACHINE 26
ALL DAY FROM SPOOL TO LESSER SPOOL, ... 273 A LONE STRIKER . . . 21
HE WISHED IT ALL THE MODERN SPEED. . . . . . . 274 A LONE STRIKER . . . 51
YET, AFTER ALL, 'TWAS NOT DIVINE, ... 274 A LONE STRIKER . . . 52
THEY THOUGHT ALL CHOPPING WAS THEIRS OF RIGHT. . . . . 276 TWO TRAMPS IN MUD TIME 52
AND ALL THEIR LOGIC WOULD FILL MY HEAD: . . . . . . 277 TWO TRAMPS IN MUD TIME 59
ALL COIFFURED TO A WINTER SHOW, ... 279 BLUE RIBBON AT AMESBURY 2
AND COME WITH ALL HER HONORS HOME. . . . . . . 280 BLUE RIBBON AT AMESBURY 5
HER STYLE, WERE ALL THE FANCY'S TALK. . . . . . . 280 BLUE RIBBON AT AMESBURY 8
HIS CHORES FOR ALL THE WINTRY NIGHT. . . . . . . 280 BLUE RIBBON AT AMESBURY 20
THAT SHALL ALL LIVING THINGS DISPLACE. . . . . . . 280 BLUE RIBBON AT AMESBURY 28
ALL WE WHO PREFER TO LIVE . . . . 282 A DRUMLIN WOODCHUCK . 13
AS MEASURED AGAINST THE ALL, ... 282 A DRUMLIN WOODCHUCK . 30
AND CAST ITS FLOWERS AND ALL THE STEMS BUT THREE, . . . 283 THE GOLD HESPERIDEE . 4
AND TWO WAS ALL HE COUNTED (ONE HE MISSED); . . . . 283 THE GOLD HESPERIDEE . 11
BUT ONE DAY WHEN THE FOLIAGE ALL WENT SWISH . . . . 284 THE GOLD HESPERIDEE . 32
FOR WHEN ALL THAT WAS ROTTED RICH . . . . 285 IN TIME OF CLOUDBURST . 10
THEN ALL I NEED DO IS RUN . . . . 285 IN TIME OF CLOUDBURST . 17
BEGIN ALL OVER TO HOPE. . . . . 285 IN TIME OF CLOUDBURST . 20
IT IS IN THE NEWS THAT ALL THESE PITIFUL KIN . . . . 286 A ROADSIDE STAND . . 23
AND BY TEACHING THEM HOW TO SLEEP THE SLEEP ALL DAY, . . 287 A ROADSIDE STAND . . 30
THAT WAITS ALL DAY IN ALMOST OPEN PRAYER . . . . . 287 A ROADSIDE STAND . . 35
OF ALL THE THOUSAND SELFISH CARS THAT PASS, ... 287 A ROADSIDE STAND . . 37
ALL UP AND DOWN IT. SO THAT WAKING THERE . . . . . 290 OLD BARN AT THE BOTTOM 25
AND THAT WERE ALL THE FINDING TO ANNOUNCE . . . . . 293 AT WOODWARD'S GARDENS . 20
AND I ASK ALL TO TRY TO FORGIVE ME . . . . 295 A RECORD STRIDE . . 33
ALL ANIMALS ARE SMOTHERED IN THEIR LAIRS. . . . . . 296 DESERT PLACES . . . 6
THEY MIGHT AS WELL HAVE NONE AT ALL. . . . . . . 297 LEAVES COMPARED WITH . 10
LEAVES ARE ALL MY DARKER MOOD. . . . . 297 LEAVES COMPARED WITH . 20
I HAVE BEEN TREADING ON LEAVES ALL DAY UNTIL I AM
  AUTUMN—TIRED. . . . . 297 A LEAF-TREADER . . . 1
GOD KNOWS ALL THE COLOR AND FORM OF LEAVES I HAVE TRODDEN
  ON AND MIRED. . . . . 297 A LEAF-TREADER . . . 2
ALL SUMMER LONG THEY WERE OVERHEAD, MORE LIFTED UP THAN I. . 297 A LEAF-TREADER . . . 5
ALL SUMMER LONG I THOUGHT I HEARD THEM THREATENING UNDER
  THEIR BREATH. . . . . 297 A LEAF-TREADER . . . 7
NO, IT TOOK ALL THE SNOWS THAT CLUNG . . . . . . 299 WELCOME TO THEIR BELIEF 5
ALL TURN AND LOOK ONE WAY. . . . . 301 NEITHER OUT FAR NOR IN 2
THEY LOOK AT THE SEA ALL DAY. . . . . 301 NEITHER OUT FAR NOR IN 4
PARTLY BECAUSE IT SANG BUT ONCE ALL NIGHT . . . . . 302 A BIRD SINGING IN SLEEP 3
(ALL MY EYE AND COTTON MATHER!), ... 304 CLEAR AND COLDER . . 18
AND OF ALL BUT ITS TRIVIAL FOLIAGE FREE, ... 304 UNHARVESTED . . . 6
THAN NONE AT ALL. PROVIDE, PROVIDE! . . . . . . 307 PROVIDE, PROVIDE . . 21
NOT ALL THERE . . . . 309 NOT ALL THERE . . . T
HIS CAPTORS ACCEPTED IT ALL, ... 310 THE VINDICTIVES . . . 8
AND HIS SUBJECTS WRUNG ALL THEY COULD WRING . . . . 310 THE VINDICTIVES . . 12
ALL JOINED IN THE GAME OF HIDE-GOLD. . . . . . . 311 THE VINDICTIVES . . 28
THEY SWORE ALL THE GOLD SHOULD GO BACK . . . . . 311 THE VINDICTIVES . . 29
ALL JOINED IN THE MADDENING GAME. . . . . . . 311 THE VINDICTIVES . . 32
AND BE ALL PLUNDERERS CURST. . . . . 312 THE VINDICTIVES . . 80
HAD TAKEN ALL THE WATER IT COULD AS DEW, ... 315 IRIS BY NIGHT . . . 14
FROM ALL DIVISION TIME OR FOE CAN BRING . . . . . 315 IRIS BY NIGHT . . . 30
ALL WOODS AND PASTURE ONLY FIT FOR SHEEP. . . . . . 316 BUILD SOIL 9
WHO IN PARTICULAR, WHEN ALL ALIKE . . . . 317 BUILD SOIL 39
THEY'RE IN THE BEST POSITION OF US ALL . . . . . 317 BUILD SOIL 55
AS LONG AS LIGHTLY ALL THEIR LIVELONG SESSIONS, ... 317 BUILD SOIL 60
I HAVE NO DOUBT LIKE ALL THE LOVES WHEN . . . . . 318 BUILD SOIL 78
MADE SO WE ALL SHOULD GET THE GOOD OF THEM— . . . . 319 BUILD SOIL 95

```
                                                        PAGE  TITLE                      LINE
ALL (CONTINUED)
  ALL, NOT JUST GREAT EXPLOITING BUSINESSES.  . . . . . . . 319  BUILD SOIL        . . . .   96
  BUT THE WORST ONE OF ALL TO LEAVE UNCURBED,  . . . . . . 319  BUILD SOIL        . . . .  101
  MY FRIENDS ALL KNOW I'M INTERPERSONAL.  . . . . . . . . . 320  BUILD SOIL        . . . .  142
  OR BETTER ON DISH PLATES ALL AROUND THE ROOM,  . . . . . 320  BUILD SOIL        . . . .  148
  WHO FALL ALL OVER EACH OTHER TO BRING SOIL  . . . . . . . 321  BUILD SOIL        . . . .  177
  BECAUSE ALL REASONING IS IN A CIRCLE.  . . . . . . . . . 322  BUILD SOIL        . . . .  202
  OR MENDING FENCE IT ALL COMES BACK TO ME  . . . . . . . . 325  BUILD SOIL        . . . .  288
  ALL MODERN, NOTHING ANCIENT IN'T,  . . . . . . . . . . . 328  A MISSIVE MISSILE . . . .   45
  HAS DRIED THE DEW AND ALL ITS ROPES RELENT,  . . . . . . 331  THE SILKEN TENT   . . . .    3
  ALL REVELATION  . . . . . . . . . . . . . . . . . . . . . 332  ALL REVELATION    . . . .    T
  ALL REVELATION HAS BEEN OURS.  . . . . . . . . . . . . . 333  ALL REVELATION    . . . .   20
  WAS NOT IN PART OR ALL IT SAID.  . . . . . . . . . . . . 333  HAPPINESS MAKES UP . . .    6
  BE ALL FROM THAT ONE DAY  . . . . . . . . . . . . . . . . 333  HAPPINESS MAKES UP . . .   20
  I COULD GIVE ALL TO TIME  . . . . . . . . . . . . . . . . 334  I COULD GIVE ALL  . . . .    T
  I COULD GIVE ALL TO TIME EXCEPT--EXCEPT  . . . . . . . . 335  I COULD GIVE ALL  . . . .   11
  I WOULD PICK UP ALL OCEAN LESS ITS SALT,  . . . . . . . . 337  THE WIND AND THE RAIN  .   28
  AND ALL THE MORE THE MIGHTIER THE SHOWER  . . . . . . . . 337  THE WIND AND THE RAIN  .   35
  IN ALL THE PASSION OF A BROKEN DROUTH.  . . . . . . . . . 337  THE WIND AND THE RAIN  .   39
  FOR ALL THE VOICE IN ANSWER HE COULD WAKE  . . . . . . . 338  THE MOST OF IT    . . . .    2
  AND FORCED THE UNDERBRUSH--AND THAT WAS ALL.  . . . . . . 338  THE MOST OF IT    . . . .   20
  THAT THE BIRDS THERE IN ALL THE GARDEN ROUND  . . . . . . 338  NEVER WOULD BIRDS' SONG    2
  AND WOULD POUNCE TO END IT ALL  . . . . . . . . . . . . . 340  THE SUBVERTED FLOWER  .   39
  COUNTED THEM ALL TO THE BUDS IN THE COPSE'S DEPTH  . . . 343  QUEST OF PURPLE-FRINGED .  23
  A STOLEN LADY WAS ALL IT SAID.  . . . . . . . . . . . . . 343  DISCOVERY OF MADEIRAS  .    5
  FOR ALL THE CREW WERE LET TO KNOW.  . . . . . . . . . . . 344  DISCOVERY OF MADEIRAS  .   34
  WHERE ALL DAY LONG SHE LAY AND DOZED.  . . . . . . . . . 344  DISCOVERY OF MADEIRAS  .   37
  HE THOUGHT, ALL RIGHT, IF YOU WANT THE TRUTH!  . . . . . 346  DISCOVERY OF MADEIRAS  .   97
  BUT DARED NOT TELL HER ALL ONE DAY.  . . . . . . . . . . 347  DISCOVERY OF MADEIRAS  .  115
  (BY ALL THAT'S LIBERAL--I SHOULD, I SHOULD)  . . . . . . 350  THE LESSON FOR TODAY  .   10
  THE GROUNDWORK OF ALL FAITH IS HUMAN WOE.  . . . . . . . 352  THE LESSON FOR TODAY  .   58
  BUT HAVE WE THERE THE ADVANTAGE AFTER ALL?  . . . . . . . 352  THE LESSON FOR TODAY  .   73
  SO AUTOMATICALLY WE ALL WERE SAVED,  . . . . . . . . . . 353  THE LESSON FOR TODAY  .  100
  IN HAVING GRANTED YOU ALL AGES SHINE  . . . . . . . . . . 354  THE LESSON FOR TODAY  .  118
  THE AGES RANGING ALL THE WAY FROM HOURS  . . . . . . . . 355  THE LESSON FOR TODAY  .  138
  BUT THOUGH WE ALL MAY BE INCLINED TO WAIT  . . . . . . . 355  THE LESSON FOR TODAY  .  141
  WE ALL ARE DOOMED TO BROKEN-OFF CAREERS,  . . . . . . . . 355  THE LESSON FOR TODAY  .  145
  ONLY BEGETTER OF ALL ILLS THAT ARE.  . . . . . . . . . . 356  A MOTH SEEN IN WINTER  .   16
  THAT POETRY WITH ALL ITS GOLDEN RAGE  . . . . . . . . . . 358  THE LOST FOLLOWER  . . .   14
  IF ALL THE SOUL-AND-BODY SCARS  . . . . . . . . . . . . . 362  A QUESTION        . . . .    3
  ALL OUT OF TIME PELL-MELL!  . . . . . . . . . . . . . . . 365  A NATURE NOTE     . . . .    9
  IF NOT, A GLASS OF MILK WILL BE ALL RIGHT."  . . . . . . 368  THE LITERATE FARMER AND    22
  YOU'LL HEAR ALL SORTS OF THINGS. YOU'LL MEET WITH THEM . 369  THE LITERATE FARMER AND    33
  BETWEEN US TWO IT'S NOT A STAR AT ALL.  . . . . . . . . . 369  THE LITERATE FARMER AND    38
  OF THE LAST FIFTY YEARS ARE ALL A LIBEL,  . . . . . . . . 369  THE LITERATE FARMER AND    45
  HAVE IT FOR ALL OF ME AND HAVE IT DENSE.  . . . . . . . . 371  THE LITERATE FARMER AND    89
  YOU TAKE THE UGLINESS ALL SO MUCH DREAD,  . . . . . . . . 371  THE LITERATE FARMER AND   106
  THEN ALL THERE IS TO DO IS WAIT .  . . . . . . . . . . . 376  SOMETHING FOR HOPE . . .    5
  AND THERE'S YOUR PRISTINE EARTH ALL FREED  . . . . . . . 376  SOMETHING FOR HOPE . . .   14
  A VIRTUE IN WHICH WE ALL MAY SHARE .  . . . . . . . . . . 376  SOMETHING FOR HOPE . . .   19
  BACK OUT OF ALL THIS NOW TOO MUCH FOR US,  . . . . . . . 377  DIRECTIVE         . . . .    1
  WHERE WERE THEY ALL NOT TWENTY YEARS AGO?  . . . . . . . 378  DIRECTIVE         . . . .   26
  AND PUT A SIGN UP CLOSED TO ALL BUT ME.  . . . . . . . . 378  DIRECTIVE         . . . .   38
  'TWAS SOMETHING WE KNEW ALL ABOUT TO BEGIN WITH  . . . . 380  TOO ANXIOUS FOR RIVERS     24
  LAST NIGHT YOUR WATCHDOG BARKED ALL NIGHT,  . . . . . . . 380  AN UNSTAMPED LETTER IN     1
  ALL NIGHT WITH UNIVERSAL SPACE.  . . . . . . . . . . . . 380  AN UNSTAMPED LETTER IN    17
  AND FOR A MOMENT ALL WAS PLAIN  . . . . . . . . . . . . . 381  AN UNSTAMPED LETTER IN    36
  IT MIGHT TAKE ME ALL NIGHT.  . . . . . . . . . . . . . . 384  MAKING CERTAIN ANYTHING    16
  AND ENOUGH DRINK OIL FOR ALL.  . . . . . . . . . . . . . 384  IN THE LONG NIGHT . . .    12
  THERE SCARCELY IS A LIGHT IN ALL ITS WALLS,  . . . . . . 386  THE FEAR OF MAN   . . . .    8
  IF I HAVE IN ME ANY I AT ALL,  . . . . . . . . . . . . . 387  IOTA SUBSCRIPT    . . . .    3
  THE MOON FOR ALL HER LIGHT AND GRACE  . . . . . . . . . . 390  TWO LEADING LIGHTS . . .   12
  ALL I SAW WAS THE LID  . . . . . . . . . . . . . . . . . 392  A WISH TO COMPLY  . . . .   10
  ALL I SAW WAS A WINK.  . . . . . . . . . . . . . . . . . 392  A WISH TO COMPLY  . . . .   13
  WE'LL BE ALL RIGHT IF NOTHING GOES WRONG WITH THE LIGHTING. 392  IT BIDS PRETTY FAIR  . .    4
  BUT WANTS IT ALL MADE OVER NEW.  . . . . . . . . . . . . 393  A CASE FOR JEFFERSON  .    2
  BLOWING IT ALL TO SMITHEREENS  . . . . . . . . . . . . . 393  A CASE FOR JEFFERSON  .   10
  AND HAVING IT ALL MADE OVER NEW.  . . . . . . . . . . . . 393  A CASE FOR JEFFERSON  .   11
  THE WORKMEN ALL TURNED TO AND BURIED HIM.  . . . . . . . 394  HAEC FABULA DOCET . . .    16
  ALL THOSE WHO TRY TO GO IT SOLE ALONE,  . . . . . . . . . 394  HAEC FABULA DOCET . . .    18
  AND BRAIN IS ALL THAT'S LEFT OF MORTAL STUFF,  . . . . . 395  ETHEREALIZING     . . . .    6
  HE THOUGHT IF HE COULD HAVE HIS SPACE ALL CURVED,  . . . 396  ANY SIZE WE PLEASE . . .    9
  HE HAD BEEN TOO ALL OUT, TOO MUCH EXTENDED.  . . . . . . 396  ANY SIZE WE PLEASE . . .   12
  AND HUGGED HIMSELF FOR ALL HIS UNIVERSE.  . . . . . . . . 396  ANY SIZE WE PLEASE . . .   14
  MOST OF ALL THE MASS PRODUCTION .  . . . . . . . . . . . 396  AN IMPORTER       . . . .   11
  WHAT YOU COMPLAIN OF, ALL THE NATIONS SHARE.  . . . . . . 398  BURSTING RAPTURE  . . . .   10
  AND ALL THE GREAT CONVENTION WAS ABOUT.  . . . . . . . . 400  THE BROKEN DROUGHT . . .    5
  BUT ALL HE DID SAY WAS, "WHAT IS THE SUBJECT?"  . . . . . 404  FROM PLANE TO PLANE . .    10
  WERE LOOSE ALL ROUND THEIR LEGS--YOU COULDN'T SAY  . . . 404  FROM PLANE TO PLANE . .    16
  FOR ALL HUMANITY A COMPLETE REST  . . . . . . . . . . . . 405  FROM PLANE TO PLANE . .    30
  FROM ALL THIS WAGERY. BUT WHAT'S THE USE  . . . . . . . . 405  FROM PLANE TO PLANE . .    31
  "ALL RIGHT, LET'S HARMONIZE ABOUT THE DOCTOR.  . . . . . 407  FROM PLANE TO PLANE . .   102
  TO THEIR SURPRISE RANG ONCE ON STONE ALL DAY  . . . . . . 407  FROM PLANE TO PLANE . .   116
  WE ALL KNOW HIS ADDRESS, MOUNT HECLA, ICELAND.  . . . . . 408  FROM PLANE TO PLANE . .   143
  CALLING ALL BUTTERFLIES OF EVERY RACE  . . . . . . . . . 411  POD OF THE MILKWEED . .     1
  THEY EVER WILL RETURN TO ALL THEIR LIVES,  . . . . . . . 411  POD OF THE MILKWEED . .     3
  FROM HAVING BEATEN ALL DAY LONG IN VAIN  . . . . . . . . 412  POD OF THE MILKWEED . .    38
  AND ALL THE GOOD THEY DID FOR MAN OR GOD  . . . . . . . . 412  POD OF THE MILKWEED . .    41
  TO ALL THOSE FLOWERS THEY PASSIONATELY TROD .  . . . . . 412  POD OF THE MILKWEED . .    42
  WHERE HAVE THOSE FLOWERS AND BUTTERFLIES ALL GONE  . . . 412  POD OF THE MILKWEED . .    51
  ALL THEY MAINTAIN THE PATH FOR IS THE COMFORT  . . . . . 414  A CABIN IN THE CLEARING     7
  BUT ALL HE DID WAS SPREAD THE ROOM .  . . . . . . . . . . 417  AMERICA IS HARD TO SEE     37
  TO ALL THE MODERN WORKS OF MAN  . . . . . . . . . . . . . 418  AMERICA IS HARD TO SEE     59
  AND ALL WE CALL AMERICAN.  . . . . . . . . . . . . . . . 418  AMERICA IS HARD TO SEE     60
  ALL HE OWES TO THE ARTIFICE .  . . . . . . . . . . . . . 418  AMERICA IS HARD TO SEE     68
  ALL THAT CAN WAIT FOR THE LIGHT OF DAY.  . . . . . . . . 420  ONE MORE BREVITY  . . . .   33
  I BROKE OFF BAFFLED. BUT ALL THE SAME,  . . . . . . . . . 420  ONE MORE BREVITY  . . . .   38
  YOU MUSTN'T FEEL HURT IF NOW I'M ALL  . . . . . . . . . . 420  ONE MORE BREVITY  . . . .   47
```

ALL (CONTINUED)
    ALL IS AN INTERMINABLE CHAIN OF LONGING. . . . . 421 ESCAPIST--NEVER . . . 12
    A SYMBOL WAS ALL HE COULD HOPE TO CONVEY, ... 421 ONE MORE BREVITY . . . 66
    BETTER THAN ALL THE STALEMATE AN'S AND IFS. . . . . . 423 FOR JOHN F. KENNEDY . 59
    IT MAKES THE PROPHET IN US ALL PRESAGE . . . . 424 FOR JOHN F. KENNEDY . 70
    THE THINGS BUT BALLS ALL GOING ROUND IN RINGS. . . . . 425 ACCIDENTALLY ON PURPOSE 2
    ALL OF THEM RADIANT AND MIGHTY SHINY. . . . . 425 ACCIDENTALLY ON PURPOSE 4
    THEY MEAN TO TELL US ALL WAS ROLLING BLIND . . . . . . 425 ACCIDENTALLY ON PURPOSE 5
    AND YET FOR ALL THIS HELP OF HEAD AND BRAIN . . . . . 425 ACCIDENTALLY ON PURPOSE 21
    ALL THE WAY TO MEN. . . . . 426 A NEVER NAUGHT SONG . 16
    IT IS ALL THE TREE . . . . 426 A NEVER NAUGHT SONG . 17
    AND THIS GIST OF ALL . . . . 426 A NEVER NAUGHT SONG . 21
    TO SAY GOD'S EITHER ALL OR OVER ALL? . . . . 427 CONCEPT SELF-CONCEIVED 7
    LOVE IS ALL ABOUT. . . . . 429 KITTY HAWK 31
    TO BE FIRST OF ALL? . . . . 430 KITTY HAWK 63
    OF ALL CRIMES THE WORST . . . . 430 KITTY HAWK 73
    THAT IS ALL MY TONGUE. . . . . 430 KITTY HAWK 84
    ALL CONCERN TO TAKE . . . . 432 KITTY HAWK 120
    SHOULD AT ALL EVENTS . . . . 432 KITTY HAWK 122
    MADE ALL BEING FULL. . . . . 433 KITTY HAWK 174
    THEN I SAW IT ALL. . . . . 434 KITTY HAWK 212
    ALL THE SCIENCE ZEST . . . . 435 KITTY HAWK 230
    WHAT IS ALL THE FUSS . . . . 435 KITTY HAWK 242
    AND FOR ALL IT'S WORTH . . . . 436 KITTY HAWK 247
    ALL THERE WAS TO THOUGHT . . . . 438 KITTY HAWK 322
    ALL WE DO'S REFLECT . . . . 440 KITTY HAWK 384
    TO KEEP ALL THINGS STIRRED . . . . 442 KITTY HAWK 444
    AND MEASURED, BUT NOT TAKEN AFTER ALL, ... 443 AUSPEX 3
    BY A GREAT EAGLE BIRD IN ALL ITS TERROR. . . . . . . 443 AUSPEX 4
    OF ALL THE THINGS HE MIGHT HAVE SAID, ... 444 ENDS 5
    OH, SOME AS SOON WOULD THROW IT ALL . . . . 445 ENDS 9
    AND SOME WILL SAY ALL SORTS OF THINGS, ... 445 ENDS 11
    O OCEAN SEA, FOR ALL YOUR BEING VAST, ... 446 DOES NO ONE AT ALL EVER 1
    DOES NO ONE AT ALL EVER FEEL THIS WAY IN THE LEAST? . 446 DOES NO ONE AT ALL EVER T
    FOR ALL THE USE YOU ARE ALONG THE STRAND. . . . . . . 446 DOES NO ONE AT ALL EVER 20
    I CRY, "DO WORK FOR WOMEN--ALL THE HELP . . . . 447 DOES NO ONE AT ALL EVER 28
    ALL WAS IN VAIN, ... 449 THE BAD ISLAND--EASTER 47
    ALL THERE IS TO IT IS DIFFUSION-- . . . . 450 OUR DOOM TO BLOOM . . 8
    OF COATS, OATS, VOTES, TO ALL MANKIND. . . . . 450 OUR DOOM TO BLOOM . . 9
    BUT ALL I ASK'S AN EXTRA ONE. . . . . 451 A-WISHING WELL . . . 26
    ALL THE SEA WATER IN ONE TIDE . . . . 452 A-WISHING WELL . . . 45
    AND ALL THE AIR RUSHED TO THE SPOT. . . . . 452 A-WISHING WELL . . . 46
    ONE HAS BEEN LATELY ALL THE TALK . . . . 452 A-WISHING WELL . . . 62
    TO START THE WORLD ALL OVER AT. . . . . 453 A-WISHING WELL . . . 81
    THIS LARRIKIN? ALL RIGHT. YOU COME ALONG. . . . . . . 455 HOW HARD TO KEEP FROM 47
    YOU'D HAVE REWARDED ME FOR ALL I'VE DONE . . . . . . 457 HOW HARD TO KEEP FROM 119
    BUT ALL YOU THOUGHT OF GIVING ME WAS FOOD. . . . . . 457 HOW HARD TO KEEP FROM 122
    FROM ALL THE FIGHTS YOU HAD A MIND TO LOSE. . . . . . 457 HOW HARD TO KEEP FROM 126
    I'LL BET YOU ANYTHING THAT'S ALL AS KING . . . . . . 458 HOW HARD TO KEEP FROM 137
    ALONG THE AEGEAN COAST. THAT'S ALL THEY TALK OF." . . 459 HOW HARD TO KEEP FROM 168
    "ALL THIS FACILITY DISHEARTENS ME. . . . . 460 HOW HARD TO KEEP FROM 203
    OUR DAYS ALL PASS AWAITING ITS RETURN. . . . . 461 HOW HARD TO KEEP FROM 248
    WITH ALL THIS TALK ABOUT THE HOPE OF YOUTH . . . . . 462 HOW HARD TO KEEP FROM 257
    ALL SHE'D BEEN HAVING WAS CLOVER. . . . . 463 LINES IN DEJECTION . . 4
    AND ALL TANKED UP WITH MINERAL JUICE, ... 463 LINES IN DEJECTION . . 7
    FOR ALL THE FUSS . . . . 469 BUT OUTER SPACE... . . 3
    IT TAKES ALL SORTS OF IN- AND OUTDOOR SCHOOLING . . . 470 IT TAKES ALL SORTS... 1
    IT TAKES ALL SORTS... . . . . 470 IT TAKES ALL SORTS... T
    THE BIRDS, SEEM ALL ON FIRE WITH PARADISE. . . . . . 473 A MASQUE OF REASON . 13
    IF THAT IS ALL THERE IS TO BE OF HEAVEN, ... 475 A MASQUE OF REASON . 42
    ESTABLISH ONCE FOR ALL THE PRINCIPLE . . . . 475 A MASQUE OF REASON . 49
    AND IT CAME OUT ALL RIGHT. I HAVE NO DOUBT . . . . . 475 A MASQUE OF REASON . 65
    YOU CHANGED ALL THAT. YOU SET ME FREE TO REIGN. . . . 476 A MASQUE OF REASON . 77
    WELL, AFTER ALL THESE YEARS! / THIS IS MY WIFE. . . . 476 A MASQUE OF REASON . 83
    HIS TENTS BLEW ALL TO PIECES, I PICKED UP . . . . . . 478 A MASQUE OF REASON . 131
    ALL YOU CAN SEEM TO DO IS LOSE YOUR TEMPER . . . . . 478 A MASQUE OF REASON . 135
    OF ALL ORIGINALITY, THE SIN . . . . 481 A MASQUE OF REASON . 205
    ALL VERY SPLENDID. I AM FLATTERED PROUD . . . . 481 A MASQUE OF REASON . 217
    BUT ALL THE TIME IT'S WHAT WE'RE MOST CONCERNED WITH. 481 A MASQUE OF REASON . 229
    THAN ALL THE JUSTIFYING EX-POST-FACTO . . . . 482 A MASQUE OF REASON . 248
    HAS ALL GONE HOME TO BED. THE PLAY'S PLAYED OUT. . . 482 A MASQUE OF REASON . 253
    COME, AFTER ALL THESE YEARS--TO SATISFY ME. . . . . . 482 A MASQUE OF REASON . 254
    ALL YOUR EFFECTS WERE MERELY LUCKY BLUNDERS. . . . . 482 A MASQUE OF REASON . 259
    NOW AFTER ALL THESE YEARS YOU MIGHT INDULGE ME. . . . 483 A MASQUE OF REASON . 267
    I'D TELL YOU, JOB---- / ALL RIGHT, DON'T TELL ME, THEN, 483 A MASQUE OF REASON . 270
    BUT WHAT IS ALL THIS SECRECY ABOUT? . . . . 483 A MASQUE OF REASON . 272
    OF ALL THE DEAD AND BURIED FROM THEIR GRAVES. . . . . 484 A MASQUE OF REASON . 307
    AND ALSO OF THE WAY ALL THINGS COME ROUND, ... 485 A MASQUE OF REASON . 342
    JOB'S WIFE SITS UP.) / WELL, IF WE AREN'T ALL HERE, . 487 A MASQUE OF REASON . 392
    THE CITY IS ALL RIGHT. TO LIVE IN ONE . . . . 496 A MASQUE OF MERCY . 69
    OR SING AND DANCE ALL NIGHT AND SEE SUNRISE . . . . . 496 A MASQUE OF MERCY . 71
    THIS VERY NIGHT. I HAD THE HALL ALL HIRED, ... 497 A MASQUE OF MERCY . 95
    I'M IN THE BIBLE, ALL DONE OUT IN STORY. . . . . . . 497 A MASQUE OF MERCY . 113
    THINKS WHY NOT TAPER OFF TO NONE AT ALL, ... 498 A MASQUE OF MERCY . 122
    ONCE AND FOR ALL. I'M GOING TO MAKE YOU SEE . . . . . 498 A MASQUE OF MERCY . 145
    THERE YOU HAVE THE BEGINNING OF ALL WISDOM. . . . . . 501 A MASQUE OF MERCY . 215
    IN NATURE WOULD WIPE OUT ALL HUMAN FAULT. . . . . . . 502 A MASQUE OF MERCY . 232
    ALL LANGUAGE IN A ONE-MAN TONGUE-CONFUSION. . . . . . 502 A MASQUE OF MERCY . 243
    WE CAN ALL SEE WHAT'S PASSING IN YOUR MIND. . . . . . 503 A MASQUE OF MERCY . 255
    AND HERE COME ALL YOUR GREAT BOOKS TUMBLING DOWN! . . 504 A MASQUE OF MERCY . 288
    TO TAKE THE PUNISHMENT OUT OF ALL FAILURE . . . . . . 505 A MASQUE OF MERCY . 313
    TRYING TO FLUSH ME OUT. THAT'S ALL IT IS. . . . . . . 507 A MASQUE OF MERCY . 350
    ALL SECONDHAND. DON'T GET EXCITED, FOLKS; . . . . . . 507 A MASQUE OF MERCY . 352
    JUST, I WOULD HAVE HIM JUST BEFORE ALL ELSE, ... 507 A MASQUE OF MERCY . 363
    I THOUGHT AS MUCH. YOU HAVE IT ALL ARRANGED. . . . . 508 A MASQUE OF MERCY . 372
    ALL WEALTH AND POWER IN TOO FEW HANDS? . . . . 509 A MASQUE OF MERCY . 411
    DON'T YOU BE MADE FEEL SMALL BY ALL THIS POSING. . . 511 A MASQUE OF MERCY . 461
    'TWERE NOTHING NEW IF THAT WERE ALL CHRIST BROUGHT. . 511 A MASQUE OF MERCY . 474

ALL (CONTINUED)
  THAT MADE ALL OTHER OUTRAGE SEEM AS CHILD'S PLAY: . . . . 511 A MASQUE OF MERCY . . 476
  OF ALL OF US, SO ALL OF US WILL BE . . . . 511 A MASQUE OF MERCY . . 484
  YOU ALL HAVE READ THE SERMON ON THE MOUNT. . . . . . 511 A MASQUE OF MERCY . . 487
  I ASK YOU ALL TO READ IT ONCE AGAIN. . . . . 511 A MASQUE OF MERCY . . 488
  BUT SUCH WE ALL ARE MADE IN THE SIGHT OF GOD. . . . . 512 A MASQUE OF MERCY . . 501
  HERE ALL STARVE TOGETHER, ... 512 A MASQUE OF MERCY . . 504
  ALL DWARFED AND POOR." . . . . 512 A MASQUE OF MERCY . . 505
  HERE WE ALL FAIL TOGETHER, DWARFED AND POOR. . . . . 512 A MASQUE OF MERCY . . 506
  NO TRUE SOURCE CAN BE POISONED. / THEN THAT'S ALL. . . 514 A MASQUE OF MERCY . . 543
  I'M ALL TURNED ROUND. / THERE IS YOUR WAY PREPARED. . . 514 A MASQUE OF MERCY . . 547
  FOR ALL THE LIGHT AT ONCE THE SOURCE OF LIGHT-- . . . 515 A MASQUE OF MERCY . . 587
  NERVOUS IS ALL THE GREAT THINGS EVER MADE YOU. . . . 516 A MASQUE OF MERCY . . 599
  WE HAVE ALL THE BELIEF THAT'S GOOD FOR US. . . . . . 516 A MASQUE OF MERCY . . 601
  WHAT'S ALL THIS TALK OF SLAYING DOWN IN CELLARS-- . . 516 A MASQUE OF MERCY . . 605
  OUR MAKING ALL THIS EFFORT MORTALS MAKE? . . . . . 517 A MASQUE OF MERCY . . 635
  YOU'LL TELL ME SOMETIME. ALL YOU SAY HAS GREATNESS. . . 517 A MASQUE OF MERCY . . 637
  ALL OF US GET EACH OTHER PRETTY WRONG. . . . . . . 518 A MASQUE OF MERCY . . 655
  WAS ABOUT ALL THERE EVER WAS TO ME. . . . . 518 A MASQUE OF MERCY . . 658
  (STILL STANDING OFF) WE'VE ALL GROWN FOND OF YOU. . . 518 A MASQUE OF MERCY . . 666
  WE'VE ALL GROWN FOND OF YOU. (PAUL SAYS IT LOUDER, . . 518 A MASQUE OF MERCY . . 667
  ALL PAUL MEANS, AND I WISH THE DEAD COULD HEAR ME-- . . 519 A MASQUE OF MERCY . . 674
  ALL YOU MEAN, PAUL, I THINK---- / WILL YOU STAND THERE . 519 A MASQUE OF MERCY . . 675
ALL-DISTURBING
  AND A VAGUE ALL-DISTURBING ROAR ABOVE THE RIVER . . . 182 MAPLE 83
ALLEGE
  TO WHERE AS SOME ALLEGE . . . . 465 MILKY WAY IS A COWPATH 34
ALL-FIRED
  TOO MUCH ALL-FIRED BELIEF AND WE'D BE BACK . . . . 516 A MASQUE OF MERCY . . 602
ALLIANCE
  TO WATCH A WAR IN NOMINAL ALLIANCE, ... 398 NO HOLY WARS FOR THEM . 6
ALLIGATORS
  ACROSS THE LOGS LIKE BACKS OF ALLIGATORS, ... 195 PAUL'S WIFE 121
ALL-NIGHT
  THIS TIME AN ALL-NIGHT BANQUET, TO BE SURE, ... 458 HOW HARD TO KEEP FROM 133
ALL-OUT-DOORS
  FOR NOTHING DOWN, ALL-OUT-DOORS OF A PLACE, ... 316 BUILD SOIL 8
ALLOW
  SUCH IS THE INSTINCT OF IT I ALLOW. . . . . 277 THE WHITE-TAILED HORNET 11
  WE ALLOW SOME TIME FOR GUILE . . . . 282 A DRUMLIN WOODCHUCK . 17
ALLOWANCE
  MAKING ALLOWANCE, MAKING DUE ALLOWANCE." . . . . . 77 THE GENERATIONS OF MEN 115
ALLOWED
  WE'RE NOT ALLOWED TO TAKE THEM UPSIDE DOWN, ... 85 THE HOUSEKEEPER . . . 127
  BUT AFTER A TIME ALLOWED FOR IT TO SWIM, ... 338 THE MOST OF IT . . . 13
  YOU'LL SEE IT BE ALLOWED UP JUST SO HIGH, ... 370 THE LITERATE FARMER AND 65
  IN YOUR RESERVE IS NOT ALLOWED. . . . . 403 SOMETHING LIKE A STAR . 8
ALL'S
  ALL'S EVER I HEARD OF IT, WHICH ISN'T MUCH. . . . . 144 SNOW 54
  IN WENTWORTH FROM NOW ON; AND WHEN ALL'S SAID, . . . 208 PAUPER WITCH OF GRAFTON 32
  AND LEAPFROG IN EACH OTHER'S WAY--ALL'S WELL. . . . . 318 BUILD SOIL 64
  IS THAT THE ALL'S A CONCEPT SELF-CONCEIVED, ... 427 CONCEPT SELF-CONCEIVED 3
  AND THE MOST SACRED THING OF ALL'S ABRUPTION. . . . 510 A MASQUE OF MERCY . . 435
ALLUVIUM
  ALLUVIUM SO PURE THAT WHEN A BLADE . . . . 407 FROM PLANE TO PLANE . 115
ALL-WISE
  BUT THOUGH ALMOST ALL-WISE, HE MAKES MISTAKES. . . . 460 HOW HARD TO KEEP FROM 208
ALMOST
  THAT THE STARS WERE ALMOST FADED AWAY . . . . . . 15 IN A VALE 15
  RIGHT ON THE SUMMIT, ALMOST LIKE A FOUNTAIN. . . . . 42 THE MOUNTAIN 64
  I ALMOST KNOW THEIR FARMS AS WELL AS THEY DO." . . . 49 A HUNDRED COLLARS . . 121
  AS WE ALMOST GOT BY THIS AFTERNOON. . . . . 56 THE BLACK COTTAGE . . 44
  I ALMOST PROVOKED POOR LOREN TO MIRTH . . . . . . 61 BLUEBERRIES 68
  IT'S SO LONG SINCE I PICKED I ALMOST FORGET . . . . 62 BLUEBERRIES 84
  I ALMOST THINK IF I COULD DO LIKE YOU, ... 67 A SERVANT TO SERVANTS . 161
  JOHN'S ALMOST HERE. I'VE HAD MY EYE ON SOMEONE . . . 88 THE HOUSEKEEPER . . . 196
  THROUGH THE THIN FROST, ALMOST IN SEPARATE STARS, . . 108 OLD MAN'S WINTER NIGHT 2
  YOU CAN TONIGHT, AND GO. IT'S ALMOST DARK; . . . . 111 IN THE HOME STRETCH . 16
  IT ALMOST SEEMED TO COME BALLOONING UP, ... 113 IN THE HOME STRETCH . 88
  THEY ALMOST SHOOK ME." / "IT'S ALL SO MUCH . . . . 114 IN THE HOME STRETCH . 126
  THE BLACK WAS ALMOST ALL THERE WAS BY DAYLIGHT, . . . 131 THE BONFIRE 49
  "NOW WE ARE DIGGING ALMOST DOWN TO CHINA. . . . . . 132 THE BONFIRE 101
  ALMOST MADE HIM COUGH . . . . 135 LAST WORD OF A BLUEBIRD 12
  ADVANTAGES OF GROWING ALMOST WILD . . . . 162 NEW HAMPSHIRE . . . 104
  WILL SERVE ALMOST AS WELL ABOUT VERMONT, ... 165 NEW HAMPSHIRE . . . 211
  FOR ART'S SAKE ONE COULD ALMOST WISH THEM WORSE . . . 167 NEW HAMPSHIRE . . . 266
  I HAD TO MAKE AN ALMOST FUNNY CHOICE. . . . . . . 170 NEW HAMPSHIRE . . . 361
  SHE ALMOST WROTE THE WORDS DOWN ON HER KNEE, ... 182 MAPLE 86
  AND WHEN IT ALMOST GAILY JUMPED AND FLOWED, ... 189 THE GRINDSTONE . . . 28
  ONCE WHEN THE GRINDSTONE ALMOST JUMPED ITS BEARING . . 190 THE GRINDSTONE . . . 57
  A MAN YOU COULD SAY ALMOST ANYTHING TO . . . . . . 192 PAUL'S WIFE 33
  BLEW IT ONCE OFF HIS HANDS AND ALMOST BROKE IT. . . . 194 PAUL'S WIFE 100
  I LISTENED TILL IT ALMOST CLIMBED THE STAIRS . . . . 205 THE WITCH OF COOS . . 90
  ALMOST THE MOMENT HE WAS GIVEN AN OPENING, ... 206 THE WITCH OF COOS . . 115
  AND, "BETTER DEFEAT ALMOST, ... 212 AN EMPTY THREAT . . . 53
  BE READY, I THOUGHT, FOR ALMOST ANYTHING. . . . . . 215 A FOUNTAIN, A BOTTLE . 64
  I ALMOST STUMBLE LOOKING UP AND ROUND, ... 226 THE ONSET 6
  OF ALMOST TOO MUCH LOVE, ... 227 TO EARTHWARD . . . 22
  THUS TILL HE HAD THEM ALMOST FEELING DARED . . . . 230 TWO LOOK AT TWO . . . 35
  TRANSFIXED ON MOUNTAIN SLOPES ALMOST ERECT. . . . . 237 A HILLSIDE THAW . . . 28
  TO ALMOST STRIPS AND TAPES OF RAGGED WHITE . . . . 239 OUR SINGING STRENGTH . 8
  BORNE DOWN UNTIL THE END ALMOST TOOK ROOT, ... 239 OUR SINGING STRENGTH . 13
  THAT KEPT THE GROUND, ALMOST DISPUTING RIGHT . . . . 240 OUR SINGING STRENGTH . 36
  THE TOTAL SKY ALMOST WITHOUT DEFECT, ... 245 SPRING POOLS . . . 2
  WITH ONE FIRST-WATER STAR ALMOST AS SHINING. . . . . 245 THE FREEDOM OF THE MOON 6
  SO THAT SHE ALMOST SPEAKS. . . . . 257 THE LOVELY BE CHOOSERS 51
  (HE ALMOST LOOKS RELIGIOUS BUT HE'S NOT), ... 269 THE BEAR 28
  WON'T ALMOST ANY THEORY BEAR REVISION? . . . . . . 279 THE WHITE-TAILED HORNET 51

ALMOST (CONTINUED)
SHE SCORED AN ALMOST PERFECT BIRD. . . . . 280 BLUE RIBBON AT AMESBURY 10
IMMURED ALMOST BEYOND RECALL, ... 280 BLUE RIBBON AT AMESBURY 22
IS WHERE TWO ROCKS ALMOST MEET, ... 282 A DRUMLIN WOODCHUCK . .   6
THAT WAITS ALL DAY IN ALMOST OPEN PRAYER . . . . 287 A ROADSIDE STAND . . . 35
AND IT HAD ALMOST GIVEN HIM TROUBLED DREAMS . . . . . 290 OLD BARN AT THE BOTTOM 42
AND THE GROUND ALMOST COVERED SMOOTH IN SNOW, ... 296 DESERT PLACES   3
ALMOST BEFORE THE PRICK OF HOSTILE EARS, ... 302 A BIRD SINGING IN SLEEP 7
I SAID TO MYSELF ALMOST IN PRAYER, ... 306 A TRIAL RUN   1
MAY SEEM ALMOST EXCLUSIVELY DESIGNED. . . . . 321 BUILD SOIL 150
SO BACK AND FORTH. IT ALMOST SCARES . . . . 326 TO A THINKER 13
SO ALMOST CLEAR AND YET OBSCURE. . . . . 327 A MISSIVE MISSILE . . 19
ALMOST LIKE A CALL TO COME IN . . . . 334 COME IN 15
TILL HER HEART ALMOST CEASED TO BEAT. . . . . 346 DISCOVERY OF MADEIRAS . 102
THEN ALMOST MIGRATORY . . . . 359 NOVEMBER   2
IT IS ALMOST THE YEAR TWO THOUSAND . . . . 361 ALMOST TWO THOUSAND .   T
I STOPPED MY SONG AND ALMOST HEART, ... 385 A MOOD APART   6
BUT HAVE ALMOST NOTHING TO DO . . . . 388 MIDDLENESS OF THE ROAD 13
THE PLAY SEEMS OUT FOR AN ALMOST INFINITE RUN. . . . . 392 IT BIDS PRETTY FAIR .   1
HE ALMOST HAS IT IN HIS TALON CLUTCH. . . . . 412 POD OF THE MILKWEED . 50
ALMOST NEXT TO NAUGHT . . . . 426 A NEVER NAUGHT SONG . 30
ALMOST PULLED OUR HAIR . . . . 434 KITTY HAWK 210
BUT THOUGH ALMOST ALL-WISE, HE MAKES MISTAKES. . . . . 460 HOW HARD TO KEEP FROM 208
I COULD GO ALMOST ANYWHERE, ... 466 SOME SCIENCE FICTION . 26
GET BURNED FOR PROPHECY, MEN ALMOST NEVER. . . . . . . 478 A MASQUE OF REASON . 150
IS ALMOST LESS THAN I CAN UNDERSTAND. . . . . 485 A MASQUE OF REASON . 333
CHRIST ALMOST OUT OF CHRISTIANITY. . . . . 498 A MASQUE OF MERCY . 129
PAUL ALMOST HAD POOR KEEPER IN A CORNER . . . . 508 A MASQUE OF MERCY . 401
AND I REPLY I ALMOST THINK I DO, ... 513 A MASQUE OF MERCY . 531
ALOFT
THE WEIGHT OF AN AX-HEAD POISED ALOFT, ... 276 TWO TRAMPS IN MUD TIME 45
WHEN CALL OR LAUGHTER CARRIED IT ALOFT. . . . . 339 NEVER WOULD BIRDS' SONG   8
TALK ALOFT . . . . 438 KITTY HAWK 2P
ALONE
WITHIN, THE BRIDE IN THE DUSK ALONE . . . .   8 LOVE AND A QUESTION . 17
I ENTER ALONE UPON THE STUBBLE FIELD, ... 14 WAITING   3
AND I MUST BE, AS HE HAD BEEN--ALONE, ... 22 THE TUFT OF FLOWERS .   8
SO THAT HENCEFORTH I WORKED NO MORE ALONE; . . . . . . 23 THE TUFT OF FLOWERS . 34
ONE IS ALONE, AND HE DIES MORE ALONE. . . . . 54 HOME BURIAL 101
THEN THE TWO SONS, TILL SHE WAS LEFT ALONE. . . . . . 56 THE BLACK COTTAGE . . 39
I DON'T LEARN WHAT THEIR NAMES ARE, LET ALONE . . . . 65 A SERVANT TO SERVANTS 82
OF SUCH A LITTLE HOUSE. ONCE LEFT ALONE, ... 111 IN THE HOME STRETCH . 40
SUMMER OR WINTER, AND COULD PLAY ALONE. . . . . 121 BIRCHES 27
I WALKED DOWN ALONE SUNDAY AFTER CHURCH . . . . 123 PEA BRUSH   1
AND CAME UPSTAIRS ALONE--AND GAVE THAT LAUGH, ... 142 THE VANISHING RED . . 26
WHO HAVE TO GO OUT INTO IT ALONE." . . . . 149 SNOW 170
AND WENT ALONE AGAINST A GROVE OF TREES; . . . . 170 NEW HAMPSHIRE . . . 368
LET ALONE GROVE OF TREES FOR SUGAR ORCHARD. . . . . . 183 MAPLE 103
STANDING ALONE WITH SMOOTH ARMS LIFTED UP, ... 184 MAPLE 145
WHERE A WHITE BIRCH HE KNEW OF STOOD ALONE, ... 196 WILD GRAPES 20
THE MINUTE IT WAS LEFT WITH ME ALONE, ... 197 WILD GRAPES 43
TO BUY ELIZA A PLOT TO LIE ALONE IN: . . . . 202 PLACE FOR A THIRD . . 80
TOFFILE HAD GONE TO BED ALONE AND LEFT ME, ... 203 THE WITCH OF COOS . . 41
UTTERED ALONE . . . . 219 I WILL SING YOU ONE-O 61
WHERE IS HIS MOTHER? HE CAN'T BE OUT ALONE." . . . . . 223 THE RUNAWAY 14
THE ROAD ALONE MAINTAINED ITSELF IN MUD, ... 239 OUR SINGING STRENGTH 16
NONE FLEW BEHIND ME TO BE LEFT ALONE. . . . . 240 OUR SINGING STRENGTH 48
ALONE, OR IN ONE ORNAMENT COMBINING . . . . 245 THE FREEDOM OF THE MOON   5
IS ALL THE SMOKE FROM ONE POOR HOUSE ALONE, ... 248 THE COCOON   5
WORD I WAS IN THE HOUSE ALONE . . . . 251 BEREFT 13
WORD I WAS IN MY LIFE ALONE, ... 251 BEREFT 15
OUT ALONE IN THE WINTER RAIN, ... 252 THE THATCH   1
HE WISHED WHEN HE HAD HAD THE TRACK ALONE . . . . . . 270 THE EGG AND THE MACHINE   5
SHE GROPES ACROSS THE PEN ALONE . . . . 281 BLUE RIBBON AT AMESBURY 41
MEN WORK ALONE, THEIR LOTS PLOWED FAR APART, ... 299 STRONG SAYING NOTHING   6
AND I ALONE OF US HAVE LIVED TO TELL. . . . . 315 IRIS BY NIGHT 22
TO SELL THE HAY OFF, LET ALONE THE SOIL, ... 321 BUILD SOIL 179
TO LET THE HALF OF LIFE ALONE . . . . 336 THE WIND AND THE RAIN. 16
HE THOUGHT HE KEPT THE UNIVERSE ALONE; . . . . 338 THE MOST OF IT . . .   1
AND NOT TO ME ALONE----" . . . . 340 THE SUBVERTED FLOWER . 24
AND WHEN HER LOVER WAS LEFT ALONE . . . . 347 DISCOVERY OF MADEIRAS . 120
FACING ALONE . . . . 360 THE RABBIT-HUNTER . .   4
AND LIKELY TO HAVE BEEN ENOUGH ALONE. . . . . 382 TO AN ANCIENT . . . 15
AND MADE FEEL LESS ALONE THAN I RIGHTLY SHOULD, . . . 383 WERE I IN TROUBLE . .   8
ALL THOSE WHO TRY TO GO IT SOLE ALONE, ... 394 HAEC FABULA DOCET . . 18
BY HEART AND WHEN ALONE REPEAT. . . . . 403 SOMETHING LIKE A STAR 10
IN THE EARTH ALONE, ... 428 KITTY HAWK 13
FOR ONE THING ALONE, ... 447 THE BAD ISLAND--EASTER   7
IN WINTER IN THE WOODS ALONE . . . . 470 IN WINTER IN THE WOODS   1
LET ME ALONE. / I'M SICK. JOE'S SICK. THE WORLD'S SICK. . . 500 A MASQUE OF MERCY . 167
ALONG
FOR THE GRAPES' SAKE ALONG THE WALL. . . . . 28 OCTOBER 21
HAROLD ALONG BESIDE TO PITCH IT ON." . . . . 37 DEATH OF THE HIRED MAN 69
UNTIL THE BUSHES ALL ALONG ITS BANKS . . . . 42 THE MOUNTAIN 52
I DIDN'T RELISH IT ALONG AT FIRST. . . . . 87 THE HOUSEKEEPER . . 173
"DO GO ALONG WITH HIM AND STOP HIS SHOUTING." . . . . 89 THE HOUSEKEEPER . . 212
ALONG THE BUSHES AT THE ROADSIDE--A MAN'S FACE. . . . 89 THE FEAR 11
"NOTHING." IT CAME FROM WELL ALONG THE ROAD. . . . . . 91 THE FEAR 67
OVER STONE WALLS AND ALL ALONG A WOOD . . . . 98 THE SELF-SEEKER . . 152
HIS ICICLES ALONG THE WALL TO KEEP; . . . . 108 OLD MAN'S WINTER NIGHT 22
AS I WENT DOWN THE HILL ALONG THE WALL . . . . 118 MEETING AND PASSING .   1
AND GO ALONG WITH YOU ERE YOU LOSE SIGHT . . . . 124 PUTTING IN THE SEED .   7
ALONG A STRETCH OF ROAD; . . . . 134 A GIRL'S GARDEN . . 22
OF WATER WE WALKED ALONG BESIDE. . . . . 140 THE GUM-GATHERER . .   8
WE SAW HIM SAY ALONG THE ZIGZAG JOURNEY . . . . 170 NEW HAMPSHIRE . . . 351
A GOOD OLD-TIMER DATING BACK ALONG; . . . . 178 THE STAR-SPLITTER . . 60
FLASHED OUT AND LICKED ALONG HIS UPPER TEETH. . . . . 204 THE WITCH OF COOS . . 73
HE ALWAYS USED TO SING ALONG THE TOTE ROAD. . . . . . 205 THE WITCH OF COOS . . 111

ALONG (CONTINUED)
   SHE SIGHED AND PASSED UNSCARED ALONG THE WALL. . . . . . . 229 TWO LOOK AT TWO . . . 24
   THEN HE TOO PASSED UNSCARED ALONG THE WALL. . . . . . . 230 TWO LOOK AT TWO . . . 37
   AND AS I PASSED ALONG THE EAVES. . . . . 253 THE THATCH 17
   IF WE WHO SIGHT ALONG IT ROUND THE WORLD, ... 261 A SOLDIER 4
   SHE MAKES THE WHOLE FLOCK MOVE ALONG. . . . . 281 BLUE RIBBON AT AMESBURY 48
   WHY, KEEP YOUR MONEY (THIS CROSSLY) AND GO ALONG. . . . 286 A ROADSIDE STAND . . . 15
   THE CHEAPEST TRAMP THAT CAME ALONG THAT WAY . . . . . 290 OLD BARN AT THE BOTTOM 44
   THE PEOPLE ALONG THE SAND . . . . 301 NEITHER OUT FAR NOR IN 1
   AND NATURALLY YOU COULDN'T GO ALONG . . . . 369 THE LITERATE FARMER AND 25
   WHEN MAN FIRST LIVED IN CAVES ALONG THE CREEKS?" . . . 372 THE LITERATE FARMER AND 140
   HOW ONCE IN CUTTING BRUSH ALONG THE WALL. . . . . . 375 A YOUNG BIRCH . . . 12
   THAT ROW OF ICICLES ALONG THE GUTTER . . . . 393 BEYOND WORDS 1
   WITH EVERY COAST HE TRIED ALONG. . . . . 416 AMERICA IS HARD TO SEE 14
   OUT AND DOWN ALONG . . . . 428 KITTY HAWK 7
   FOR ALL THE USE YOU ARE ALONG THE STRAND. . . . . . 446 DOES NO ONE AT ALL EVER 20
   AND JOLLIED ALONG? . . . . 448 THE BAD ISLAND--EASTER 30
   "WE SHOULD HAVE BROUGHT THE CROWN ALONG TO PAWN." . . 454 HOW HARD TO KEEP FROM 29
   THIS LARRIKIN? ALL RIGHT. YOU COME ALONG. . . . . . 455 HOW HARD TO KEEP FROM 47
   ALONG THE AEGEAN COAST. THAT'S ALL THEY TALK OF." . . 459 HOW HARD TO KEEP FROM 168
   ALONG THE MILKY WAY . . . . 465 MILKY WAY IS A COWPATH 31
   I'M APT TO STRING ALONG WITH THYATIRA. . . . . . . 479 A MASQUE OF REASON . 168
   TOGETHER WE WILL GO WITH YOU ALONG. . . . . 489 A MASQUE OF REASON . 437
ALOOF
   BUT 'TIS NOT TRUE THAT THUS I DWELT ALOOF, ... 16 A DREAM PANG . . . 13
   ALOOF YET NOT ALOOF, ... 367 A SERIOUS STEP LIGHTLY 18
ALOUD
   "I MAY HAVE THOUGHT AS MUCH, BUT NOT ALOUD." . . . . 118 THE TELEPHONE . . . 18
   AS SHE STOOD SAYING HER NAME OVER ALOUD, ... 181 MAPLE 41
   NO VOICE IN NATURE IS HEARD TO CRY ALOUD . . . . . 249 ACCEPTANCE 3
   NOT ALL YOUR LIGHT TONGUES TALKING ALOUD . . . . . 252 TREE AT MY WINDOW . 7
ALPHA
   IS NEITHER ALPHA, ETA, NOR OMEGA, ... 388 IOTA SUBSCRIPT . . . 7
ALPHABET
   IN THE ALPHABET, ... 436 KITTY HAWK 272
ALPS
   CAN IT BE FOREIGN TRAVEL IN THE ALPS? . . . . . . 169 NEW HAMPSHIRE . . . 320
ALREADY
   WHOSE LEAVES ALREADY ARE BURNT WITH FROST, ... 28 OCTOBER 19
   THE LAWYER WAS ALREADY IN HIS SATCHEL . . . . . . 96 THE SELF-SEEKER . . . 97
   SO. BUT THE HAND WAS GONE ALREADY. . . . . 137 "OUT,OUT--" 27
   AT THAT DATE WITH A WHARF ALREADY BUILT, ... 161 NEW HAMPSHIRE . . . 84
   THE PEOPLE OR THE ALREADY LOFTY MOUNTAINS, ... 168 NEW HAMPSHIRE . . . 308
   I'D ELEVATE THE ALREADY LOFTY MOUNTAINS. . . . . . 168 NEW HAMPSHIRE . . . 309
   AND CUTTING NOTHING NOT CUT DOWN ALREADY. . . . . . 185 THE AX-HELVE . . . 9
   "HOW OFTEN ALREADY YOU'VE HAD TO BE TOLD, ... 228 GOOD-BY AND KEEP COLD. 17
   ALREADY DETERMINED DAWN BEGAN TO LAY . . . . . . 235 VALLEY'S SINGING DAY . 7
   THE ALREADY KNOWN HAD ONCE MORE BEEN CONFIRMED. . . 293 AT WOODWARD'S GARDENS . 18
   PREACH ON. I THOUGHT YOU WERE ALREADY PREACHING. . . 322 BUILD SOIL . . . 183
   BEGAN ALREADY TO SEEM FORLORN. . . . . 344 DISCOVERY OF MADEIRAS . 18
   BEING ALREADY MORE THAN PROVED IN FIGHT, ... 353 THE LESSON FOR TODAY . 91
   "DON'T LET HIM FOOL YOU: HE'S A KING ALREADY. . . . 460 HOW HARD TO KEEP FROM 207
   PUT THAT IN IF IT ISN'T IN ALREADY: . . . . . . 486 A MASQUE OF REASON . 372
   HAVEN'T YOU HEARD THE NEWS? WE ALREADY HAVE ONE, . . 515 A MASQUE OF MERCY . 577
ALSO
   IS ALSO GREAT . . . . 220 FIRE AND ICE . . . 8
   HIS LITTLE MATTHEW, ALSO FIVE YEARS OLD, ... 283 THE GOLD HESPERIDEE . 13
   SO DO THEY ALSO ASK PHILOSOPHERS . . . . 414 A CABIN IN THE CLEARING 23
   AND ALSO PROVED THE WORLD A BALL, ... 416 AMERICA IS HARD TO SEE 3
   SEE THAT OUR SLAVE IS ALSO. HE'S IN FAVOR. . . . . 455 HOW HARD TO KEEP FROM 64
   AND ALSO OF THE WAY ALL THINGS COME ROUND, ... 485 A MASQUE OF REASON . 342
ALTARS
   ALTARS THE WOODS ARE FULL OF NOWADAYS, ... 171 NEW HAMPSHIRE . . . 387
ALTER
   AND ALTER WITH AGE. . . . . 241 THE LOCKLESS DOOR . 20
ALTERED
   SOMETHING HAS ALTERED IN THE OUTER DOOR.) . . . . 507 A MASQUE OF MERCY . 344
ALTERNATION
   IN ALTERNATION WITH THE WEEDS, THE FIELD, ... 112 IN THE HOME STRETCH . 48
ALTERNATIONS
   LEAVING LOVE'S ALTERNATIONS, JOY AND GRIEF, ... 317 BUILD SOIL . . . 35
   THE WEATHER'S ALTERNATIONS, SUMMER AND WINTER, . . . 317 BUILD SOIL . . . 36
ALTHOUGH---NOT INDEXED
ALTOGETHER
   IT SEEMED NO HARM TO STOP HIM ALTOGETHER. . . . . 41 THE MOUNTAIN . . . 18
   I DON'T MEAN ALTOGETHER BY THE LIVES . . . . . . 56 THE BLACK COTTAGE . 37
   IT MAY BE ALTOGETHER . . . . 333 HAPPINESS MAKES UP . 13
   TAKE NATURE ALTOGETHER SINCE TIME BEGAN, ... 349 OUR HOLD ON THE PLANET 13
ALTRUISTICALLY
   I MEAN SO ALTRUISTICALLY MORAL . . . . 354 THE LESSON FOR TODAY . 122
ALTRURIAN
   WHAT HEIGHTS OF ALTRURIAN THOUGHT TO ATTAIN, . . . 449 THE BAD ISLAND--EASTER 57/8
ALWAY
   WAS SWALLOWED UP IN LEAVES THAT BLEW ALWAY; . . . . 16 A DREAM PANG . . . 2
ALWAYS
   BUT ALWAYS GOD SPEAKS AT THE END: . . . . 21 THE TRIAL BY EXISTENCE 49
   OFF HE GOES ALWAYS WHEN I NEED HIM MOST. . . . . . 35 DEATH OF THE HIRED MAN 18
   IT'S ALWAYS COLD IN SUMMER, WARM IN WINTER. . . . . 42 THE MOUNTAIN . . . 49
   HE TRIED THIS SIDE. I'VE ALWAYS MEANT TO GO . . . . 43 THE MOUNTAIN . . . 80
   AND SLEEP ON IT, THE WAY I ALWAYS DO . . . . . . 48 A HUNDRED COLLARS . 91
   THE NEWS HAS ALWAYS BEEN REPUBLICAN. . . . . . . 48 A HUNDRED COLLARS . 111
   FROM UP THERE ALWAYS?--FOR I WANT TO KNOW." . . . . 51 HOME BURIAL . . . 7
   "MY WORDS ARE NEARLY ALWAYS AN OFFENSE. . . . . . 52 HOME BURIAL . . . 45
   SHE ALWAYS, WHEN SHE TALKED ABOUT THE WAR, ... 56 THE BLACK COTTAGE . 26
   A LITTLE COTTAGE THIS HAS ALWAYS SEEMED; . . . . . 56 THE BLACK COTTAGE . 35
   IT ALWAYS SEEMS TO ME A SORT OF MARK . . . . . . 56 THE BLACK COTTAGE . 45
   THAT'S ALWAYS THE WAY WITH THE BLUEBERRIES, THOUGH: . 59 BLUEBERRIES 14
   YOU KNOW HOW POLITELY HE ALWAYS GOES BY. . . . . . 60 BLUEBERRIES 42

ALWAYS (CONTINUED)
HE SAYS THE BEST WAY OUT IS ALWAYS THROUGH. . . . . 64 A SERVANT TO SERVANTS . 56
THERE'S WORK ENOUGH TO DO--THERE'S ALWAYS THAT; . . . . . 68 A SERVANT TO SERVANTS . 173
WITH AN EYE ALWAYS LIFTED TOWARD THE WEST . . . . 69 THE CODE 3
"IT RESTS WITH US ALWAYS TO CUT HER OFF." . . . . 80 THE GENERATIONS OF MEN 183
AS MARRIED--THAT'S WHAT HE HAS ALWAYS SAID. . . . . . . 84 THE HOUSEKEEPER . . . 82
I TAKE IT. WHAT WAS HIS WAS ALWAYS HERS. . . . . 84 THE HOUSEKEEPER . . . 93
"I MEAN ESTELLE HAS ALWAYS HELD THE PURSE." . . . . . . 84 THE HOUSEKEEPER . . . 98
OUR HENS AND COWS AND PIGS ARE ALWAYS BETTER . . . . . . 85 THE HOUSEKEEPER . . . 111
AND YOU'RE HER MOTHER." / "BUT I DIDN'T ALWAYS. . . . . 87 THE HOUSEKEEPER . . . 172
I ALWAYS HAVE FELT STRANGE WHEN WE CAME HCME . . . . . 89 THE FEAR 17
HER BACK. SHE ALWAYS ANSWERED WITHOUT TURNING. . . . . 110 IN THE HOME STRETCH . 12
WHAT WE HAVE ALWAYS WANTED, I CONFESS . . . . 115 IN THE HOME STRETCH . 127
SEEMS HAUNTED OR EXPOSED. I ALWAYS TAKE . . . . 115 IN THE HOME STRETCH . 133
"IT'S ALL SO MUCH WHAT I HAVE ALWAYS WANTED, ... 116 IN THE HOME STRETCH . 164
AS MUCH AT HOME AS IF THEY'D ALWAYS DANCED THERE. . . . 117 IN THE HOME STRETCH . 204
CLEAR TO THE GROUND. HE ALWAYS KEPT HIS POISE . . . . . 122 BIRCHES 35
ALWAYS--I TELL YOU THIS THEY LEARNED-- . . . . 127 HOUSE FEAR 1
ALWAYS AT NIGHT WHEN THEY RETURNED . . . . 127 HOUSE FEAR 2
BUT SHE ALWAYS RAN AWAY AND LEFT . . . . 134 A GIRL'S GARDEN . . 23
WE ALWAYS LOCKED THE FLOWERS OUTSIDE . . . . 135 LOCKED OUT 2
I ALWAYS THOUGHT IT MUST HAVE BEEN . . . . 135 LOCKED OUT 11
YANKEES ARE WHAT THEY ALWAYS WERE. . . . . 139 BROWN'S DESCENT . . 53
SO FALSE, THAT WHAT WE ALWAYS SAY IS TRUE. . . . . . 148 SNOW 150
I WAS NOT ALWAYS SO; I'VE COME TO BE SO. . . . . . . 169 NEW HAMPSHIRE . . . 312
"YOU KNOW ORION ALWAYS COMES UP SIDEWAYS. . . . . . 176 THE STAR-SPLITTER . 1
THEY ALWAYS TOOK THEIR HOLIDAYS IN AUTUMN. . . . . . 184 MAPLE 143
"HOW IS THE WIFE, PAUL?" AND HE ALWAYS WENT. . . . . 192 PAUL'S WIFE . . . 24
MY BROTHER COULD NOT ALWAYS LEAVE AT HOME. . . . . . 196 WILD GRAPES 9
HE ALWAYS USED TO SING ALONG THE TOTE ROAD. . . . . 205 THE WITCH OF COOS . 111
ALWAYS THE WITCH'S MOTTO ANYWAY. . . . . 207 PAUPER WITCH OF GRAFTON 8
HAS ALWAYS BEEN TOO MUCH FOR ME, IT HAS. . . . . . 208 PAUPER WITCH OF GRAFTON 35
THERE WASN'T ALWAYS HUDSON'S BAY . . . . 210 AN EMPTY THREAT . . 3
EXCEPT ALWAYS JOHN-JOE, ... 211 AN EMPTY THREAT . . 26
ALWAYS WRONG TO THE LIGHT, SO NEVER SEEING . . . . . 225 FOR ONCE SOMETHING . 2
ALWAYS THE SAME, WHEN ON A FATED NIGHT . . . . . . 226 THE ONSET 1
THAT THERE ALWAYS IS ON THE PAPERED WALLS, ... 232 THE KITCHEN CHIMNEY . 14
THAT THERE ALWAYS IS WHEN THE CHIMNEY'S FALSE. . . . 232 THE KITCHEN CHIMNEY . 16
INSISTING ALWAYS ON OUR OWN WAY SO. . . . . . . 238 ON A TREE FALLEN ACROSS 5
AND WAS ALWAYS A ROSE. . . . . 246 THE ROSE FAMILY . . 2
BUT WERE ALWAYS A ROSE. . . . . 246 THE ROSE FAMILY . . 10
DUST ALWAYS BLOWING ABOUT THE TOWN, ... 249 A PECK OF GOLD . . 1
"DO IT BY JOYS, AND LEAVE HER ALWAYS BLAMELESS. . . . 256 THE LOVELY BE CHOOSERS 21
SO THAT THE FALL OF MOST OF IT IS ALWAYS . . . . . 259 WEST-RUNNING BROOK . 62
OUR MISSILES ALWAYS MAKE TOO SHORT AN ARC. . . . . 261 A SOLDIER 8
THAT'S WHAT I ALWAYS TELL MY WIFE . . . . 263 THE TIMES TABLE . . 11
WITH ALWAYS SOMETHING IN HER SMILE. . . . . . . 265 THE BIRTHPLACE . . 10
THE GATHERER CAN ALWAYS TELL . . . . 280 BLUE RIBBON AT AMESBURY 33
MAY SOMETHING GO ALWAYS UNHARVESTED! . . . . . . 305 UNHARVESTED . . . 11
WE'RE ALWAYS TOO MUCH OUT OR TOO MUCH IN. . . . . 320 BUILD SOIL 137
THAN IN THE FUTURE ALWAYS, ... 336 CARPE DIEM . . . 21
AND THERE IS ALWAYS MORE THAN SHOULD BE SAID. . . . 337 THE WIND AND THE RAIN . 40
FOR ALWAYS FIGHTING ON BOTH SIDES AT ONCE. . . . . 350 TO A YOUNG WRETCH . 18
THERE'S ALWAYS SOMETHING TO BE SORRY FOR, ... 352 THE LESSON FOR TODAY . 55
HIS MIND TO THINKING ALWAYS OF THE END. . . . . . 353 THE LESSON FOR TODAY . 95
IS ALWAYS IN THE OPPOSITE DIRECTION. . . . . . . 358 THE LOST FOLLOWER . 10
SHE ALWAYS HAD TO BURN A LIGHT . . . . 382 THE NIGHT LIGHT . . 1
THERE WAS ALWAYS THOUGHT. . . . . 426 A NEVER NAUGHT SONG . 2
ALWAYS WEST-NORTHWEST, ... 437 KITTY HAWK . . . 291
I'M ALWAYS FOR A BETTER SKY. . . . . 451 A-WISHING WELL . . 13
THERE'S ALWAYS BEEN AN ARARAT . . . . 453 A-WISHING WELL . . 79
WE ALWAYS SAY--NOT WHO WON IT, ... 463 LINES IN DEJECTION . 27
THE TEST IS ALWAYS HOW WE TREAT THE POOR. . . . . 477 A MASQUE OF REASON . 123
FOR THIS I THINK. I FIND IT ALWAYS BEST . . . . . 487 A MASQUE OF REASON . 387
SHE ALWAYS CLAIMS SHE HASN'T BEEN ASLEEP.-- . . . . 487 A MASQUE OF REASON . 398
AND ALWAYS WILL BE.--PLEASE DON'T GO. STAY, STAY . . . 489 A MASQUE OF REASON . 435
WE CAN'T BE ALWAYS SELLING PEOPLE THINGS. . . . . 493 A MASQUE OF MERCY . 10
ALWAYS THE SAME WHEN I SET OUT IN FLIGHT. . . . . 500 A MASQUE OF MERCY . 179
SO THAT BECAUSE WE'RE ALWAYS STARTING FRESH . . . . 510 A MASQUE OF MERCY . 433
AM---NOT INDEXED
AMAIN
OUR LOVE CAME BACK AMAIN. . . . . 27 A LINE-STORM SONG . . 30
AMASS
TIME HAD SEEN AMASS . . . . 429 KITTY HAWK 48
AMATEUR
WHEN ANY AMATEUR CAN TELL IT NOW? . . . . 395 WHY WAIT FOR SCIENCE . 10
AMAZE
WHAT SHE BROUGHT BACK WOULD AMAZE YE. . . . . . . 396 AN IMPORTER 2
AMAZONS
AS'T WERE THE COUNTRY OF THE AMAZONS . . . . . . 259 WEST-RUNNING BROOK . . 33
AMBASSADORS
TILL THE AMBASSADORS FROM PUNT OR SOMEWHERE . . . . . 456 HOW HARD TO KEEP FROM 72
AMBITION
YOU WOULD SAY HIS AMBITION WAS TO EXTEND TO REACH . . . 305 THERE ARE ROUGHLY ZONES 9
GET CALLED AS MUCH IN CLASHES OF AMBITION. . . . . . 317 BUILD SOIL 40
IN YOUR SENSE OF THE WORD AMBITION HAS . . . . . . 319 BUILD SOIL 98
POLITICAL AMBITION HAS BEEN TAUGHT, ... 319 BUILD SOIL 114
OF YOUNG AMBITION EAGER TO BE TRIED, ... 424 FOR JOHN F. KENNEDY . 73
AMBITIOUS
FOR--I FORGET--THE LAST AMBITIOUS SAWYER . . . . . 193 PAUL'S WIFE 59
NONE SHALL BE AS AMBITIOUS AS HE CAN. . . . . . 320 BUILD SOIL 121
AMBITIOUSLY
SO AMBITIOUSLY VAST, ... 447 THE BAD ISLAND--EASTER 2
AMBULANCE
AS RED CROSS AMBULANCE COMMANDER-IN-CHIEF . . . . . 507 A MASQUE OF MERCY . 369
WHICH SPOILS YOUR FIGURE OF THE AMBULANCE. . . . . 508 A MASQUE OF MERCY . 383
AMERICA
THE RUSSIAN NOVEL IN AMERICA . . . . 167 NEW HAMPSHIRE . . . 268

AMERICA (CONTINUED)
    AMERICA IS HARD TO SEE . . . . 416 AMERICA IS HARD TO SEE   T
    AMERICA IS HARD TO SEE. . . . . 418 AMERICA IS HARD TO SEE   61
    WHO GAVE AMERICA THE AEROPLANE . . . . 423 FOR JOHN F. KENNEDY . 47
AMERICAN
    'GAINST AMERICAN INVENTION-- . . . . 396 AN IMPORTER 10
    AND ALL WE CALL AMERICAN. . . . . 418 AMERICA IS HARD TO SEE   60
AMESBURY
    A BLUE RIBBON AT AMESBURY . . . . 279 BLUE RIBBON AT AMESBURY   T
AMETHYST
    ENCHANT THE LAND WITH AMETHYST. . . . . 28 OCTOBER 16
AMID
    AND LOSE MYSELF AMID SO MANY ALIKE. . . . . 14 WAITING   8
    THERE AMID LOLLING JUNIPER RECLINED, ... 17 THE VANTAGE POINT .   4
    AMID THE WRECKAGE OF A FORMER HOME? . . . . 116 IN THE HOME STRETCH . 177
A-MIND
    ANYTHING SPECIAL YOU'RE A-MIND TO NAME. . . . . . 53 HOME BURIAL 52
AMONG
    WITH NONE AMONG THEM THAT EVER SINGS, ...   6 GHOST HOUSE 28
    MOVING AMONG TALL HAYCOCKS LIGHTLY PILED, ... 14 WAITING   2
    IT WAS SOMETHING AMONG THE LEAVES I SOUGHT . . . . 25 THE DEMIURGE'S LAUGH . 16
    AMONG THE HARPLIKE MORNING-GLORY STRINGS, ... 38 DEATH OF THE HIRED MAN 107
    IMPERFECTLY CONCEALED AMONG THE LEAVES. . . . . . 41 THE MOUNTAIN 32
    AMONG TAR-BANDED ANCIENT CHERRY TREES, ... 55 THE BLACK COTTAGE .   3
    AND DANGLE FEET AMONG THE RASPBERRY VINES?" . . . 75 THE GENERATIONS OF MEN 64
    I'VE NEVER LISTENED IN AMONG THE SOUNDS . . . . . 78 THE GENERATIONS OF MEN 132
    AMONG THE RASPBERRIES, AND HEW AND SHAPE IT . . . 79 THE GENERATIONS OF MEN 162
    THE LAWYER GAVE A LAUGH AMONG HIS PAPERS . . . . . 98 THE SELF-SEEKER . . 145
    HIS HOUSE AMONG THE LOCAL SHEDS AND SHANTIES . . . 160 NEW HAMPSHIRE . . . 52
    AMONG US: IT WAS JUST A WARREN FARMER . . . . . . 168 NEW HAMPSHIRE . . . 288
    ABOUT OUR PLACE AMONG THE INFINITIES. . . . . . . 168 NEW HAMPSHIRE . . . 305
    ABOUT OUR PLACE AMONG THE INFINITIES. . . . . . . 177 THE STAR-SPLITTER . 19
    AMONG THE BUTTONS POURED OUT IN HER LAP. . . . . . 207 THE WITCH OF COOS . 153
    AMONG BARE MAPLE BOUGHS, AND IN THE RARE . . . . . 234 EVENING AT A SUGAR ORCHARD 8
    A WHIR AMONG WHITE BRANCHES GREAT AND SMALL, . . . 240 OUR SINGING STRENGTH . 41
    MAKE HER AMONG THE HUMBLEST EVEN . . . . 257 THE LOVELY BE CHOOSERS 39
    AMONG UNEARTHED POTATOES STANDING STILL, ... 263 THE INVESTMENT . .   6
    AMONG THE HARPLIKE SPREAD OF STRINGS. . . . . . . 274 A LONE STRIKER . . 29
    'TWOULD BE AMONG THE TOPS OF TREES, ... 274 A LONE STRIKER . . 39
    AND RAISED AMONG THE LEAVES AND DULY TOLD, ... 283 THE GOLD HESPERIDEE 15
    WE'RE TOO UNSEPARATE OUT AMONG EACH OTHER-- . . . 324 BUILD SOIL 268
    THE MAN WAS AMONG THE FIRST IT TOOK. . . . . 345 DISCOVERY OF MADEIRAS 59
    NO PLOW AMONG THESE ROCKS WOULD PAY. . . . . 376 SOMETHING FOR HOPE .   9
    GET PARCELED OUT AMONG THE WINNING GIANTS. . . . . 398 NO HOLY WARS FOR THEM . 8
    I FELL IN AMONG . . . . 431 KITTY HAWK 100
AMOUNTING
    A CRUELTY, AMOUNTING TO INJUSTICE . . . . 520 A MASQUE OF MERCY . 712
AMY
    "AMY! DON'T GO TO SOMEONE ELSE THIS TIME. . . . . 52 HOME BURIAL 39
    AMY! THERE'S SOMEONE COMING DOWN THE ROAD!" . . . 54 HOME BURIAL 111
    THE ARTHUR AMY I WAS MARRIED TO . . . . 207 PAUPER WITCH OF GRAFTON 16
    THE ARTHUR AMY I WAS MARRIED TO . . . . 208 PAUPER WITCH OF GRAFTON 20
    THEIR ARTHUR AMY WAS THE FATHER OF MINE. . . . . . 208 PAUPER WITCH OF GRAFTON 27
    WAS ARTHUR AMY. YOU KNOW WHO HE WAS. . . . . 209 PAUPER WITCH OF GRAFTON 71
    WELL, I SHOWED ARTHUR AMY SIGNS ENOUGH . . . . . . 210 PAUPER WITCH OF GRAFTON 89
AMY'S
    OF ARTHUR AMY'S HAVING ONCE BEEN UP . . . . 207 PAUPER WITCH OF GRAFTON 13
AN---NOT INDEXED
ANALOGIZE
    WHY WILL I NOT ANALOGIZE? . . . . 327 A MISSIVE MISSILE . 36
ANALOGY
    PARDON THE ANALOGY, MY MELIBOEUS, ... 318 BUILD SOIL 90
ANALYST
    HE IS OUR ANALYST. / YOUR ANALYST? . . . . 499 A MASQUE OF MERCY . 151
ANALYST'S
    AN ANALYST'S THE LATEST THING IN DOCTORS. . . . . 499 A MASQUE OF MERCY . 153
ANCESTRAL
    ANCESTRAL MEMORIES MIGHT COME TOGETHER. . . . . . 73 THE GENERATIONS OF MEN   3
ANCESTRALLY
    ACQUIRED ANCESTRALLY IN JUST SUCH TREES . . . . . 197 WILD GRAPES 49
ANCESTRY
    WITH ALL THIS PRIDE OF ANCESTRY, WE YANKEES? . . . 76 THE GENERATIONS OF MEN 87
ANCHOR
    AT ANCHOR SHE RIDES THE SUNNY SOD, ... 262 THE FLOWER BOAT . .   5
ANCHORING
    AND ANCHORING IT TO AN EARTH AND MOON . . . . . . 248 THE COCOON 14
ANCIENT
    TO THE ANCIENT LANDS WHERE IT LEFT THE SHELLS . . 27 A LINE-STORM SONG . 27
    AMONG TAR-BANDED ANCIENT CHERRY TREES, ... 55 THE BLACK COTTAGE .   3
    IN A NEW COTTAGE ON THE ANCIENT SPOT. . . . . . . 79 THE GENERATIONS OF MEN 164
    NO ONE WOULD KNOW EXCEPT FOR ANCIENT MAPS . . . . 231 A BROOK IN THE CITY . 20
    DESTROY THEIR SLEEPING AT NIGHT THE ANCIENT WAY. . 287 A ROADSIDE STAND . 31
    SOMEONE IN ANCIENT MAS D'AZIL . . . . 326 A MISSIVE MISSILE .   1
    ALL MODERN, NOTHING ANCIENT IN'T, ... 328 A MISSIVE MISSILE . 45
    AND TO FORGET THE ANCIENT LENGTHS OF TIME, ... 351 THE LESSON FOR TODAY 17
    AGAINST THE ANCIENT SOVEREIGNTY OF NIGHT. . . . . 361 A LOOSE MOUNTAIN .   8
    COMING ON SUCH AN ANCIENT HUMAN TRACE . . . . . . 382 TO AN ANCIENT . . .   7
    TO AN ANCIENT . . . . 382 TO AN ANCIENT . . .   T
    THE MISTAKES OF ANCIENT MEN, ... 387 THE COURAGE TO BE NEW . 2
AND---NOT INDEXED
ANDEAN
    OR AT MOST SOME ANDEAN QUAKE, ... 418 AMERICA IS HARD TO SEE 71
ANDOVER
    LATELY BROUGHT HOME FROM ANDOVER OR CANAAN . . . . 162 NEW HAMPSHIRE . . . 117
ANDREW
    THE ANDREW JACKSON SLOGAN OF VAE VICTIS . . . . . 510 A MASQUE OF MERCY . 459
ANEW
    COULD CONCENTRATE ANEW AND RISE AS ONE. . . . . . 315 IRIS BY NIGHT . . .   8

ANGEL
    THE ANGEL HOSTS WITH FRESHNESS GO, ... 20 THE TRIAL BY EXISTENCE   13
ANGELIC
    A BIRD WITH AN ANGELIC GIFT . . . . 233 LOOKING FOR SUNSET BIRD   7
ANGELS
    FURTHER O'ERHEAD THAN ALL BUT STARS AND ANGELS-- . . . . 132 THE BONFIRE 107
    WITH GODS AND ANGELS, WE WERE MEN AT LEAST, ... 279 THE WHITE-TAILED HORNET 61
    BUT LITTLE LOWER THAN THE GODS AND ANGELS. . . . . . . 279 THE WHITE-TAILED HORNET 62
    THAT FELLED THE ANGELS, WOLSEY SHOULD HAVE SAID. . . . . 481 A MASQUE OF REASON . . 206
ANGELS'
    I HAVE BEEN FIGHTING ON THE ANGELS' SIDE. . . . . . 520 A MASQUE OF MERCY . . 706
ANGLE
    AND HERE IN THE ANGLE OF HOUSE AND BARN . . . . . . 262 THE FLOWER BOAT . . . 3
ANGRILY
    ANGRILY TRIED TO MAKE ME WRITE A PROTEST . . . . . . 160 NEW HAMPSHIRE 29
ANGRY
    YOU MAKE ME ANGRY. I'LL COME DOWN TO YOU. . . . . . 53 HOME BURIAL 68
    IT WAS EASY TO BE ANGRY AT; . . . . 345 DISCOVERY OF MADEIRAS . 65
ANIMAL
    TO ERR IS HUMAN, NOT TO, ANIMAL. . . . . 279 THE WHITE-TAILED HORNET 52
ANIMALS
    WE WERE LOST PIECEMEAL TO THE ANIMALS, ... 279 THE WHITE-TAILED HORNET 67
    ALL ANIMALS ARE SMOTHERED IN THEIR LAIRS. . . . . . 296 DESERT PLACES 6
ANIMI
    THE MENS ANIMI. . . . . 440 KITTY HAWK 390
ANIMUS
    WITH ANIMUS APPROACHING HATE, ... 418 AMERICA IS HARD TO SEE 51
ANKLE-BAND
    THE ONE WHO GAVE HER ANKLE-BAND, ... 280 BLUE RIBBON AT AMESBURY 17
ANKLES
    BUT THOUGHT HAS SHAKEN HIS ANKLES FREE. . . . . . . 120 BOND AND FREE . . . 10
ANNALS
    WHO KEEPS OUR BOOKSTORE ANNALS. / STOP IT, KEEPER.-- . . 499 A MASQUE OF MERCY . . 152
ANNE
    THE BROKEN ONE SAW ANNE. "WHY, HERE IS ANNE. . . . . 96 THE SELF-SEEKER . . 103
    TELL ME WHAT IS IT?" / ANNE JUST WAGGED HER DRESS, . . . 96 THE SELF-SEEKER . . 105
    ANNE LOOKED AT THE LARGE LAWYER AT HER SIDE, ... 97 THE SELF-SEEKER . . 117
    YOU SEE ANNE HAS HER LESSON LEARNED BY HEART." . . . . 97 THE SELF-SEEKER . . 122
    BUT, ANNE, I'M TROUBLED; HAVE YOU TOLD ME ALL? . . . . 97 THE SELF-SEEKER . . 131
    NOTHING IS HIDDEN FROM SOME PEOPLE, ANNE. . . . . . 97 THE SELF-SEEKER . . 135
    "I'VE BROKEN ANNE OF GATHERING BOUQUETS. . . . . . . 98 THE SELF-SEEKER . . 147
    ANNE HAS A WAY WITH FLOWERS TO TAKE THE PLACE . . . . 98 THE SELF-SEEKER . . 159
    "WELL, ANNE, GO, DEARIE. OUR AFFAIR WILL WAIT. . . . . 98 THE SELF-SEEKER . . 167
    I HAVE TO KEEP ON THE GOOD SIDE OF ANNE. . . . . . . 99 THE SELF-SEEKER . . 176
    I'LL PUT YOU OUT WITH ANNE. BE GOOD OR GO." . . . . 99 THE SELF-SEEKER . . 186
    "WILLIS, BRING ANNE BACK WITH YOU WHEN YOU COME. . . . 100 THE SELF-SEEKER . . 223
ANNOTATING
    AND ANNOTATING BOOKS . . . . 361 ALMOST TWO THOUSAND . 12
ANNOUNCE
    AND THAT WERE ALL THE FINDING TO ANNOUNCE . . . . . 293 AT WOODWARD'S GARDENS . 20
ANNOUNCING
    BY ANNOUNCING A STAR DOWN . . . . 384 MAKING CERTAIN ANYTHING 11
ANNUNCIATION
    IT WAS TO ME--IN AN ANNUNCIATION." . . . . 258 WEST-RUNNING BROOK . . 31
ANOTHER---NOT INDEXED
ANOTHER'S---NOT INDEXED
AN'S
    BETTER THAN ALL THE STALEMATE AN'S AND IFS. . . . . . 423 FOR JOHN F. KENNEDY . 59
ANSWER
    FOR WHEN YOU MADE ANSWER, YOUR VOICE WAS AS LOW . . . 62 BLUEBERRIES 95
    WAS STARTLED WHEN AN ANSWER REALLY CAME. . . . . . 91 THE FEAR 66
    AND DIDN'T ANSWER--DIDN'T SPEAK-- . . . . 129 THE IMPULSE 17
    IF YOU CAN COMFORT ME BY ANY ANSWER." . . . . 132 THE BONFIRE 99
    AND GONE TO SLEEP, SHE NEEDN'T WAKE TO ANSWER." . . . 143 SNOW 14
    GETTING NO ANSWER, CLOSED THE TELEPHONE. . . . . . 143 SNOW 30
    STICK TO HIM, HELEN. MAKE HIM ANSWER YOU. . . . . . 145 SNOW 63
    RECURRING TILL WE ANSWER FROM WITHIN. . . . . . . 147 SNOW 133
    GOOD! WHY I ASKED--SHE DIDN'T SEEM TO ANSWER.-- . . . 155 SNOW 330
    TO MEET HIM WITH HIS ANSWER AT THE DOOR. . . . . . 201 PLACE FOR A THIRD . . 72
    AND NOW THEY ANSWER HIS SUMMONING BLAST . . . . . . 236 MISGIVING 9
    THE ANSWER IS THIS ONE HAS BEEN-- . . . . 279 BLUE RIBBON AT AMESBURY 4
    TO ANSWER FOR THEMSELVES: WHO SAID IT MATTERED . . . 294 AT WOODWARD'S GARDENS . 33
    THERE IS NO ANSWER, I'M AFRAID. . . . . 327 A MISSIVE MISSILE . . 27
    IN ANSWER TO THE MENTAL THRUST. . . . . 332 ALL REVELATION . . . 15
    FOR ALL THE VOICE IN ANSWER HE COULD WAKE . . . . . 338 THE MOST OF IT . . . 2
    AN ANSWER . . . . 363 AN ANSWER . . . . . T
    BUT THE PHYSICIAN'S ANSWER WAS, "THERE, THERE, . . . 398 BURSTING RAPTURE . . 9
    OF AN ANSWER BACK . . . . 429 KITTY HAWK 34
    MOCKED ME FOR AN ANSWER. . . . . 429 KITTY HAWK 39
    WE ARE IMPATIENT FOR YOUR ROYAL ANSWER." . . . . . 456 HOW HARD TO KEEP FROM 76
    I ANSWER FLATLY: THAT'S THE WAY IT IS, ... 477 A MASQUE OF REASON . 111
    IS THAT YOUR ANSWER? / NO, FOR I HAVE YET . . . . . 481 A MASQUE OF REASON . 227
    ONE AT A TIME, PLEASE. I WILL ANSWER JOB FIRST. . . . 484 A MASQUE OF REASON . 324
    BUT YOU--WHAT IS YOUR ANSWER, JONAS DOVE? . . . . . 513 A MASQUE OF MERCY . . 529
ANSWERABLE
    TO RULE FIRST ANSWERABLE TO HIGH DESIGN. . . . . . 424 FOR JOHN F. KENNEDY . 65
    THE FRONT OF BEING ANSWERABLE TO NO ONE . . . . . . 482 A MASQUE OF REASON . 250
ANSWERED
    "WARREN?" SHE QUESTIONED. / "DEAD," WAS ALL HE ANSWERED. . 40 DEATH OF THE HIRED MAN 166
    HER BACK. SHE ALWAYS ANSWERED WITHOUT TURNING. . . . 110 IN THE HOME STRETCH . 12
    I ASKED HIM, ON MY GUARD. "OH, YES," HE ANSWERED, . . 159 NEW HAMPSHIRE . . . 13
    AND THE PRINCE ANSWERED, PICKING UP THE PIECES, . . . 453 HOW HARD TO KEEP FROM 7
    HE ANSWERED HER BACK, "WELL, WHO BEGUN IT?" . . . . 463 LINES IN DEJECTION . . 25
ANSWERING
    NOT ANSWERING YOUR KNOCK. I CAN NO MORE . . . . . . 81 THE HOUSEKEEPER . . 3
    FROM FAR AWAY THERE CAME AN ANSWERING TICK, ... 269 THE EGG AND THE MACHINE 2
ANSWERS
    SHORT OF A FIGHTING WORD. YOU HAVE THE ANSWERS. . . . 192 PAUL'S WIFE 34

```
                                                    PAGE TITLE                    LINE
ANSWERS (CONTINUED)
      YOU WON'T GET ANY ANSWERS OUT OF GOD. . . . . . .  . . . 484 A MASQUE OF REASON .  . 301
      MY DUNGEONEERS, COME FETCH US.--NO ONE ANSWERS. . . . . . 514 A MASQUE OF MERCY .  . 556
ANT
      I LOOK INTO THE CRATER OF THE ANT. . . . . . . . . . . .  17 THE VANTAGE POINT .   . 14
      IT BROODED ANT EGGS, AND HAD ONE LARGE WING, . . . . . .  172 A STAR IN A STONEBOAT . 14
      AN ANT ON THE TABLECLOTH . . . . . . . . . . . . . . . .  287 DEPARTMENTAL . . . .   1
ANTENNAE
      WITH WHOM HE CROSSES ANTENNAE, . . . . . . . . . . . . .  288 DEPARTMENTAL . . . . 19
ANTICIPATED
      THE RANGEY BOUGH ANTICIPATED FRUIT . . . . . . . . . . .  239 OUR SINGING STRENGTH . 14
ANTICS
      AND ON THE BAT'S MUTE ANTICS, WHO WOULD SEEM . . . . . .  14 WAITING  . . . . . 14
ANTI-DARK
      A GOOD CHEAP ANTI-DARK IS NOW THE NEED. . . . . . . . .  371 THE LITERATE FARMER AND 99
ANTI-LURE
      THIS HAS BEEN POETRY'S GREAT ANTI-LURE. . . . . . . . .  358 THE LOST FOLLOWER .  . 20
ANTIOCH
      IN THE MUSEUM OF ANTIOCH. . . . . . . . . . . . . . . .  452 A-WISHING WELL . . .  63
ANTIPHONY
      AND IN THE ANTIPHONY OF AFTERGLOW . . . . . . . . . . .  14 WAITING  . . . . .  5
ANTIQUES
      THAT IS YOUR ANTIQUES RATTLING ON A SHELF. . . . . . .  504 A MASQUE OF MERCY . . 283
ANTLERED
      THIS WAS AN ANTLERED BUCK OF LUSTY NOSTRIL, . . . . . .  229 TWO LOOK AT TWO . . . 29
ANTS
      ANTS ARE A CURIOUS RACE; . . . . . . . . . . . . . . .  288 DEPARTMENTAL . . . . 13
ANXIOUS
      BAPTISTE WAS ANXIOUS FOR HER; BUT NO MORE . . . . . . .  187 THE AX-HELVE . . . .  58
      NO ONE WAS ANXIOUS TO GET RID OF PAUL. . . . . . . . . .  191 PAUL'S WIFE . . . .  16
      AND ANXIOUS TO MAKE ALL HE COULD OF IT . . . . . . . . .  200 PLACE FOR A THIRD .  . 17
      HAS BEEN HER ANXIOUS CONVOY IN TO SHORE. . . . . . . . .  262 IMMIGRANTS . . . . .  4
      OH, I HAVE BEEN OFTEN TOO ANXIOUS FOR RIVERS . . . . . .  379 TOO ANXIOUS FOR RIVERS 6
      TOO ANXIOUS FOR RIVERS . . . . . . . . . . . . . . . .  379 TOO ANXIOUS FOR RIVERS  T
ANXIOUSLY
      (GOD EYES HIM ANXIOUSLY.) / NO. NO, I MUSTN'T. . . . . .  485 A MASQUE OF REASON .  . 330
ANY
      IS SADDER THAN ANY WORDS. . . . . . . . . . . . . . . .  8 A LATE WALK . . . . .  8
      ANY FIXED WAGES, THOUGH I WISH I COULD.' . . . . . . . .  35 DEATH OF THE HIRED MAN  23
      IN HAYING TIME, WHEN ANY HELP IS SCARCE. . . . . . . . .  35 DEATH OF THE HIRED MAN  29
      SO NOW AND NEVER ANY DIFFERENT." . . . . . . . . . . . .  38 DEATH OF THE HIRED MAN 102
      OF COURSE HE'S NOTHING TO US, ANY MORE . . . . . . . . .  38 DEATH OF THE HIRED MAN 115
      IF HE HAD ANY PRIDE IN CLAIMING KIN . . . . . . . . . .  39 DEATH OF THE HIRED MAN 136
      SHE, IN HER PLACE, REFUSED HIM ANY HELP, . . . . . . . .  51 HOME BURIAL . . . . . 13
      I DON'T KNOW RIGHTLY WHETHER ANY MAN CAN." . . . . . . .  52 HOME BURIAL . . . . . 38
      IF YOU HAD ANY FEELINGS, YOU THAT DUG . . . . . . . . .  53 HOME BURIAL . . . . . 72
      TO ASK IF HE KNEW ANY FRUIT TO BE HAD . . . . . . . . .  61 BLUEBERRIES . . . . . 70
      MAME, WE DON'T KNOW ANY GOOD BERRYING PLACE?' . . . . .  61 BLUEBERRIES . . . . . 77
      I CAN'T EXPRESS MY FEELINGS, ANY MORE . . . . . . . . .  63 A SERVANT TO SERVANTS   7
      HIS HANDS HAD WORN THEM SMOOTH AS ANY OXBOW. . . . . . .  66 A SERVANT TO SERVANTS 136
      THAT HE KEPT ANY HOURS--NOT FOR HIMSELF. . . . . . . . .  71 THE CODE . . . . . . 40
      SO'S TO TAKE ANY COMFORT. I CAN SEW: . . . . . . . . . .  81 THE HOUSEKEEPER . . .  7
      I CAN'T EXPLAIN IT ANY OTHER WAY. . . . . . . . . . . .  84 THE HOUSEKEEPER . . . 78
      THAN FOLKS LIKE US HAVE ANY BUSINESS WITH. . . . . . . .  85 THE HOUSEKEEPER . . . 112
      HAVE YOU AGREED TO ANY PRICE?" / "FIVE HUNDRED. . . . .  94 THE SELF-SEEKER . . . 58
      I CAN'T GET BACK THE FEET IN ANY CASE." . . . . . . . .  95 THE SELF-SEEKER . . . 65
      OUT WITH IT IF YOU'VE ANY REAL OBJECTION." . . . . . . .  99 THE SELF-SEEKER . . . 197
      AS BETTER THAN THE SUN IN ANY CASE . . . . . . . . . . .  108 OLD MAN'S WINTER NIGHT 20
      I HAVEN'T ANY MEMORY--HAVE YOU?-- . . . . . . . . . . .  110 THE EXPOSED NEST . . . 33
      YOU'LL NOT HAVE ANY OTHER COMPANY . . . . . . . . . . .  115 IN THE HOME STRETCH  . 147
      IF YOU CAN COMFORT ME BY ANY ANSWER." . . . . . . . . .  132 THE BONFIRE . . . . . 99
      ASK ANY MAN." / HE THREW HER THAT AS SOMETHING . . . . .  151 SNOW . . . . . . . . 242
      WE CAN'T BE ANY HELP BY SITTING HERE . . . . . . . . . .  152 SNOW . . . . . . . . 268
      THAT IT WAS ANY WAY BUT WHAT IT WAS. . . . . . . . . . .  153 SNOW . . . . . . . . 286
      DID SHE LET ON BY ANY WORD SHE SAID . . . . . . . . . .  153 SNOW . . . . . . . . 287
      WHOSE DUTY WAS AT ANY HOUR OF NIGHT . . . . . . . . . .  163 NEW HAMPSHIRE . . .  . 140
      POEMS PRODUCED THAN ANY OTHER THING? . . . . . . . . . .  164 NEW HAMPSHIRE . . .  . 171
      TO ANY CHANGE FROM HOT TO COLD, FROM WET . . . . . . . .  166 NEW HAMPSHIRE . . .  . 235
      OR ANY MOUNTAINS? CAN IT BE SOME STRENGTH . . . . . . .  169 NEW HAMPSHIRE . . .  . 317
      HE KNEW TOO WELL FOR ANY EARTHLY USE . . . . . . . . . .  171 NEW HAMPSHIRE . . .  . 378
      OF THE ONE WORLD COMPLETE IN ANY SIZE . . . . . . . . .  174 A STAR IN A STONEBOAT . 56
      DO WE KNOW ANY BETTER WHERE WE ARE, . . . . . . . . . .  179 THE STAR-SPLITTER .  . 96
      UNSCORCHED, UNBLACKENED, EVEN, BY ANY SMOKE. . . . . . .  184 MAPLE . . . . . . . . 142
      WE ARE NOT LOOKING FOR IT ANY MORE." . . . . . . . . . .  185 MAPLE . . . . . . . . 162
      TONIGHT?" / AS WELL TONIGHT AS ANY NIGHT. . . . . . . .  186 THE AX-HELVE . . . . 34
      HAS NOTHING ANY MORE TO DO WITH ME, . . . . . . . . . .  189 THE GRINDSTONE . . . 21
      AS ANY OTHER BOYHOOD ENEMY . . . . . . . . . . . . . . .  190 THE GRINDSTONE . . . 43
      I'D WELCOME ANY MODERATE DISASTER . . . . . . . . . . .  190 THE GRINDSTONE . . . 62
      TO DRIVE PAUL OUT OF ANY LUMBER CAMP . . . . . . . . . .  191 PAUL'S WIFE . . . . .  1
      IN ANY WAY THE WORLD KNEW HOW TO SPEAK. . . . . . . . .  196 PAUL'S WIFE . . . . . 157
      TO SPARE THEM ANY TROUBLE. DOUBLE TROUBLE'S . . . . . .  207 PAUPER WITCH OF GRAFTON 7
      I COULD HAVE TOLD THEM ANY TIME THIS TWELVEMONTH . . . .  207 PAUPER WITCH OF GRAFTON 15
      YOU WON'T SEE ANY MORMON SWIMMING IN IT. . . . . . . . .  213 A FOUNTAIN, A BOTTLE  . 27
      IN ANY ROUGH PLACE WHERE IT CAUGHT. . . . . . . . . . .  223 THE AIM WAS SONG .  .  4
      THEY MUST HAVE HALTED SOON IN ANY CASE . . . . . . . . .  229 TWO LOOK AT TWO . . .  4
      AND STILL THEY FAILED OF ANY LASTING HOLD. . . . . . . .  239 OUR SINGING STRENGTH .  4
      TO ANY ONE PLACE COVER US WITH SONG. . . . . . . . . . .  239 OUR SINGING STRENGTH . 20
      AND YET NOT OUT BY ANY BROOK OR RIVER, . . . . . . . . .  245 SPRING POOLS . . . .  5
      IN WANTING TO SILENCE ANY SONG. . . . . . . . . . . . .  251 A MINOR BIRD . . . .  8
      LONG, LONG BEFORE WE WERE FROM ANY CREATURE. . . . . . .  259 WEST-RUNNING BROOK .  . 41
      IF BY ANY CHANGE OF SHAPE . . . . . . . . . . . . . . .  260 SAND DUNES . . . . . 11
      THAN THERE WAS EVER ANY HOPE, . . . . . . . . . . . . .  264 THE BIRTHPLACE . . .  2
      WITH LIFTED SNOUT AND EYES (IF ANY) SHUT . . . . . . . .  269 THE BEAR . . . . . . 27
      AND IF ONE BROKE BY ANY CHANCE, . . . . . . . . . . . .  273 A LONE STRIKER . . . 24
      BE ANY INSTITUTION'S NEED. . . . . . . . . . . . . . . .  274 A LONE STRIKER . . . 55
      WON'T ALMOST ANY THEORY BEAR REVISION? . . . . . . . . .  279 THE WHITE-TAILED HORNET 51
      DEARER TO HIM THAN ANY BARNYARD BRUTE, . . . . . . . . .  283 THE GOLD HESPERIDEE  . 22
      BUT HE NO DOUBT REPORTS TO ANY . . . . . . . . . . . . .  288 DEPARTMENTAL . . . . 18
```

- 26 -

ANY (CONTINUED)
THAT KEPT THE OAKS FROM GETTING ANY GIRTH. . . . . . 292 FIGURE IN THE DOORWAY . 4
AND SMALL REGARD TO THE FUTURE OF ANY WEED. . . . . . 299 STRONG SAYING NOTHING . 2
OFF ANY STILL OR MOVING THING YOU SAY. . . . . 300 THE MASTER SPEED . . 9
TO ANY WATCH THEY KEEP? . . . . 301 NEITHER OUT FAR NOR IN 16
THAN WHEN ITS WALLS ROSE HIGHER THAN ANY ROOF. . . . . 306 NOT QUITE SOCIAL . . 8
AN ELEMENT IN ANY GOVERNMENT. . . . . 318 BUILD SOIL 69
I FIGURE THAT LIKE ANY BANDYING . . . . 321 BUILD SOIL . . . 169
SEDUCED BACK TO THE LAND BY ANY CLAIM . . . . 322 BUILD SOIL . . . 207
DON'T JOIN TOO MANY GANGS. JOIN FEW IF ANY. . . . . . 325 BUILD SOIL . . . 280
SEEMS TO OWE NAUGHT TO ANY SINGLE CORD, ... 332 THE SILKEN TENT . . 8
THAT ANY SONG IN WHICH HE MOURNED . . . . 336 THE WIND AND THE RAIN . 13
BUT THE BLIZZARD BLINDS HIM TO ANY HOUSE AHEAD. . . . 341 WILLFUL HOMING . . 2
THEY COULD ONLY SAY LIKE ANY TWO, ... 345 DISCOVERY OF MADEIRAS . 46
TO ANY ONE TIME, PLACE, OR HUMAN KIND. . . . . . . 353 THE LESSON FOR TODAY . 105
AS UNORIGINAL AS ANY RABBIT. . . . . 354 THE LESSON FOR TODAY . 112
I MAY HAVE WEPT THAT ANY SHOULD HAVE DIED . . . . . 355 THE LESSON FOR TODAY . 151
ON ME AS MUCH AS ANY IS THE JEST. . . . . 355 THE LESSON FOR TODAY . 154
ON ANY BUT A PAPER SHEET SO WHITE . . . . 357 A CONSIDERABLE SPECK . 2
MIND WHEN I MEET WITH IT IN ANY GUISE. . . . . . . 358 A CONSIDERABLE SPECK . 31
ON ANY SHEET THE LEAST DISPLAY OF MIND. . . . . . . 358 A CONSIDERABLE SPECK . 33
(ASK ANY REPUTABLE ROSICRUCIAN) . . . . 363 A SEMI-REVOLUTION . 3
TO ANY DEMONSTRABLY BETTER RACE, ... 369 THE LITERATE FARMER AND 50
ITS ACTIONS ANY CLOUDLESS NIGHT WILL SHOW IT. . . . . 370 THE LITERATE FARMER AND 64
ARE MORE DIVINE THAN ANY BULB OR ARC, ... 370 THE LITERATE FARMER AND 77
IT DOESN'T DO YOU ANY GOOD TO TALK. . . . . 370 THE LITERATE FARMER AND 85
OF EITHER MURDER OR WAR IN ANY LAND. . . . . 371 THE LITERATE FARMER AND 111
WHAT STAR IF ANY FELL. . . . . 383 MAKING CERTAIN ANYTHING 4
FOR ANY EYE IS AN EVIL EYE . . . . 385 A MOOD APART . . . 7
IF I HAVE IN ME ANY I AT ALL, ... 387 IOTA SUBSCRIPT . . 3
HE NEVER HAS IN ANY PHASE . . . . 390 TWO LEADING LIGHTS . 5
WHEN ANY AMATEUR CAN TELL IT NOW? . . . . 395 WHY WAIT FOR SCIENCE . 10
ANY SIZE WE PLEASE . . . . 396 ANY SIZE WE PLEASE . T
BUT NOW 'TWAS THERE AS ELSEWHERE, ANY GAIN . . . . . 398 BURSTING RAPTURE . 4
OF ASKING ANY SYMPATHY OF HIM? . . . . 405 FROM PLANE TO PLANE . 32
AS ANY GUATEMALAN PARAKEET. . . . . 412 POD OF THE MILKWEED . 47
ANY WHO SEEK HIM SEEK IN HIM THE SEEKER. . . . . . 421 ESCAPIST--NEVER . . 9
IN ANY GAME THE NATIONS WANT TO PLAY. . . . . . . 424 FOR JOHN F. KENNEDY . 75
I HAD ANY CLAIM . . . . 430 KITTY HAWK . . . 81
ANY MELANCHOLY . . . . 431 KITTY HAWK . . . 97
WHEN ANY BUT MYSELF PRESUMED TO SAY . . . . 443 AUSPEX 11
ANY MORE THAN WE HAD TO TO HATE, ... 444 THE DRAFT HORSE . . 16
BUT AT ANY COST . . . . 445 PERIL OF HOPE . . . 10
I AM ASSURED AT ANY RATE, ... 453 A-WISHING WELL . . 76
AS ANY MIGHT OBSERVE, ... 464 MILKY WAY IS A COWPATH 23
FOR THERE TO HAVE BEEN ANY GOOD. . . . . 467 QUANDARY 4
THERE ISN'T ANY UNIVERSAL REASON; . . . . 478 A MASQUE OF REASON . 138
THAT COULD, LIKE ANY SPACE, BE TURNED AROUND IN? . . . 479 A MASQUE OF REASON . 161
ANY ORIGINALITY IT SHOWED . . . . 480 A MASQUE OF REASON . 189
ANY ORIGINALITY IT SHOWED . . . . 480 A MASQUE OF REASON . 202
WHETHER THERE'S ANY PART OF MAN IMMORTAL. . . . . . 483 A MASQUE OF REASON . 297
YOU WON'T GET ANY ANSWERS OUT OF GOD. . . . . . . 484 A MASQUE OF REASON . 301
AND FIND OUT WHETHER HE IS ANY GOOD, ... 484 A MASQUE OF REASON . 320
AND EARS ARE LENT TO ANY SOPHISTRY . . . . 488 A MASQUE OF REASON . 409
BY ANY CHANCE A LADY APPLE ON YOU? . . . . 488 A MASQUE OF REASON . 421
I'M JONAS DOVE--IF THAT IS ANY HELP. . . . . 495 A MASQUE OF MERCY . 55
IS IT JUST ANY CITY YOU'RE AGAINST? . . . . 496 A MASQUE OF MERCY . 90
FOR ME TO DISAGREE WITH ANY SCIENCE . . . . 500 A MASQUE OF MERCY . 188
WAS WHAT I THOUGHT OF. / HAVE YOU ANY GROUNDS, . . . 502 A MASQUE OF MERCY . 226
FOR ANY BUT THE RAPIDEST EYE READERS.) . . . . . . 502 A MASQUE OF MERCY . 246
DON'T ANY OF YOU HEAR A SOUND? / THE STORM! . . . . 504 A MASQUE OF MERCY . 279
AN END YOU CAN'T BY ANY MEANS ACHIEVE . . . . . . 512 A MASQUE OF MERCY . 509
ANY EQUALITY THEY MAY EXHIBIT'S . . . . 513 A MASQUE OF MERCY . 527
I DON'T SEE ANY STAIRCASE. / THERE ARE STAIRS. . . . 517 A MASQUE OF MERCY . 631
AND GO AHEAD TO ANY ACCOMPLISHMENT. . . . . 521 A MASQUE OF MERCY . 730
ANYBODY
AS ANYBODY. WORTHLESS THOUGH HE IS, ... 39 DEATH OF THE HIRED MAN 144
"I'LL BE THE ONE, IF ANYBODY GOES! . . . . 91 THE FEAR 54
SHE WASN'T ANYBODY ELSE'S BUSINESS, ... 196 PAUL'S WIFE . . . 152
BUT HE'S AS GOOD AS ANYBODY GOING. . . . . 309 WASPISH 6
(DON'T ANYBODY LAUGH); . . . . 309 NOT ALL THERE . . 6
AND THOUGH THEY'RE NOTHING ANYBODY BEGS, ... 365 OF STONES OF THE PLACE 3
WILL ANYBODY SWEAR THAT ISN'T IT? . . . . 368 THE LITERATE FARMER AND 20
"I WOULDN'T HOE BOTH WAYS FOR ANYBODY!" . . . . . 405 FROM PLANE TO PLANE . 48
BUT ANYBODY COULD HAVE GUESSED IN THIS CASE, . . . 456 HOW HARD TO KEEP FROM 89
ANYBODY'S
YOU WERE NOT CHARLES' NOR ANYBODY'S FOOL: . . . . 351 THE LESSON FOR TODAY . 20
OF ANYBODY'S BUT-- . . . . 465 MILKY WAY IS A COWPATH 40
ABOUT OUR OWN OR ANYBODY'S END. . . . . 507 A MASQUE OF MERCY . 354
ANYMORE
TO NO ONE ANYMORE SINCE TOFFILE DIED. . . . . . . 206 THE WITCH OF COOS . 131
BUT NEVER ANYMORE THE DEAD. . . . . 221 IN A DISUSED GRAVEYARD 4
SO PEOPLE AND THINGS DON'T PAIR ANYMORE . . . . . 265 THE DOOR IN THE DARK . 8
"YOU'D BETTER NOT DISTURB ME ANYMORE," . . . . . 270 THE EGG AND THE MACHINE 27
WHERE THEY WON'T HAVE TO THINK FOR THEMSELVES ANYMORE; . 287 A ROADSIDE STAND . 26
KING'S X--NO FAIRS TO USE IT ANYMORE! . . . . . 399 U.S. 1946 KING'S X . 4
AND THIS SCHOOL WASN'T KEEPING ANYMORE, ... 400 TO THE RIGHT PERSON . 11
TO ANYTHING THAT HAPPENED ANYMORE. . . . . . . 501 A MASQUE OF MERCY . 203
ANYONE
"I CAN'T THINK SI EVER HURT ANYONE." . . . . . . 39 DEATH OF THE HIRED MAN 146
BY ANYONE WHO'D COME A LONG WAY UP. . . . . . . 43 THE MOUNTAIN . . . 72
WITH ANYONE TO DEATH, COMES SO FAR SHORT . . . . 54 HOME BURIAL . . . 98
I WOULDN'T HAVE SENT ANYONE OF MINE THERE; . . . 65 A SERVANT TO SERVANTS . 92
I'M AS PARTICULAR AS ANYONE: . . . . 70 THE CODE 24
ANYONE ELSE, BUT OUT OF IDLENESS. . . . . 74 THE GENERATIONS OF MEN 27
ANYONE UPON EARTH AND STILL HER CHILDREN . . . . 75 THE GENERATIONS OF MEN 51
THOUGH WHAT GOOD YOU CAN BE, OR ANYONE-- . . . . 81 THE HOUSEKEEPER . . 19
HE CAN'T FIND ANYONE TO TAKE HER PLACE." . . . . 82 THE HOUSEKEEPER . . 29

PAGE TITLE | LINE

ANYONE (CONTINUED)
DID HE LOOK LIKE----?" / "HE LOOKED LIKE ANYONE. . . . . 90 THE FEAR 31
AND HID FROM ANYONE PASSING. . . . . 134 A GIRL'S GARDEN . . 25
TO ANYTHING ANYONE ELSE MAY SAY. . . . . 145 SNOW 66
YOU LIKE YOUR FUN AS WELL AS ANYONE; . . . . 146 SNOW 97
THOUGH FOR ALL ANYONE CAN TELL, REPOSE . . . . 148 SNOW 147
THE TIME WAS AUTUMN, BUT HOW ANYONE . . . . 175 THE CENSUS-TAKER . . 17
HE NEVER STOPPED TO MURDER ANYONE . . . . 192 PAUL'S WIFE . . . 25
TO SEE IF IT WAS ANYONE BEHIND HIM . . . . 194 PAUL'S WIFE . . . 112
IT WAS THE ONLY GLIMPSE THAT ANYONE . . . . 195 PAUL'S WIFE . . . 129
AND NOT TO ANYONE TO BE ASHAMED OF. . . . . 195 PAUL'S WIFE . . . 146
I WAS BORN, I SUPPOSE, LIKE ANYONE, ... 196 WILD GRAPES . . . 7
WITH ANYONE BUT THAT SHE HAD A MIND TO, ... 200 PLACE FOR A THIRD . 13
IT WASN'T ANYONE WHO COULD BE THERE. . . . . 204 THE WITCH OF COOS . 54
IF ANYONE HAD SEEN ME COMING HOME . . . . 210 PAUPER WITCH OF GRAFTON 85
AND ANYONE IS FREE TO CONDEMN ME TO DEATH-- . . . . 307 NOT QUITE SOCIAL . . 13
IF ONLY ANYONE WERE SURE . . . . 327 A MISSIVE MISSILE . . 20
HOW ANYONE CAN FAIL TO SEE . . . . 327 A MISSIVE MISSILE . . 33
IF ANYONE REMEMBERS HOW THAT WAS. . . . . 395 WHY WAIT FOR SCIENCE . 13
AND ANYONE MIGHT ASK THEM WHO WERE THEY. . . . . . . 397 THE PLANNERS . . . 9
THE TIME HAD BEEN WHEN ANYONE COULD TURN . . . . . . 398 BURSTING RAPTURE . . 2
BY THE CONNECTICUT COULD ANYONE . . . . 404 FROM PLANE TO PLANE . 22
SO ANYONE CAN WRITE TO HIM WHO HAS TO; . . . . 408 FROM PLANE TO PLANE . 144
AS ANYONE WHO EVER BROKE ITS STEM . . . . 411 POD OF THE MILKWEED . 17
THEY WILL ASK ANYONE THERE IS TO ASK-- . . . . 414 A CABIN IN THE CLEARING 25
I HAVE TO WAIT FOR WORDS LIKE ANYONE. . . . . 475 A MASQUE OF REASON . 58
TO ANYTHING WITH ANYONE. / THERE, THERE, ... 478 A MASQUE OF REASON . 146
TO ANYONE AROUND WHEN SHE IS DRINKING. . . . . 496 A MASQUE OF MERCY . . 88
ANYONE'S
WHERE WAS MY SUPPER? WHERE WAS ANYONE'S? . . . . . . 175 THE CENSUS-TAKER . . 34
ANYTHING
ANYTHING MORE THAN THE TRUTH WOULD HAVE SEEMED TOO WEAK . 17 MOWING 9
"WHEN WAS I EVER ANYTHING BUT KIND TO HIM? . . . . . 34 DEATH OF THE HIRED MAN 11
"WHAT DID HE SAY? DID HE SAY ANYTHING?" . . . . . . 36 DEATH OF THE HIRED MAN 44
"BUT LITTLE." / "ANYTHING? MARY, CONFESS . . . . . . 36 DEATH OF THE HIRED MAN 45
OR ANYTHING HE LOOKED FOR FROM HIS BROTHER, ... 39 DEATH OF THE HIRED MAN 137
MAN THAT KNEW ANYTHING I HAPPENED IN WITH. . . . . . 46 A HUNDRED COLLARS . . 47
IF ANYTHING SHOULD HAPPEN TO BE WRONG. . . . . 47 A HUNDRED COLLARS . . 83
ANYTHING THEY'VE NOT GOT. I NEVER DUN. . . . . 50 A HUNDRED COLLARS . . 152
I DON'T KNOW HOW TO SPEAK OF ANYTHING . . . . 52 HOME BURIAL . . . 46
ANYTHING SPECIAL YOU'RE A-MIND TO NAME. . . . . . . 53 HOME BURIAL . . . 52
ANYTHING IN HER AFTER ALL THE YEARS. . . . . 56 THE BLACK COTTAGE . 30
WHETHER I AM GLAD, SORRY, OR ANYTHING. . . . . 63 A SERVANT TO SERVANTS . 12
ANYTHING THEY PUT IN FOR FURNITURE . . . . 66 A SERVANT TO SERVANTS . 117
"STRANGELY, IT'S ANYTHING THEY WISH TO GIVE." . . . . 78 THE GENERATIONS OF MEN 138
ANYTHING SHE MAY SAY. BUT LET ME WARN YOU, ... 79 THE GENERATIONS OF MEN 180
YOU WON'T THINK ANYTHING. YOU UNDERSTAND? . . . . . 92 THE FEAR 88
WELL, YES." / "HEAR ANYTHING THAT MIGHT PROVE USEFUL?" . 96 THE SELF-SEEKER . . 102
ACCEPTING ANYTHING BEFORE HE KNOWS . . . . 100 THE SELF-SEEKER . . 201
SMALL GOOD TO ANYTHING GROWING WILD, ... 123 PEA BRUSH . . . 21
TO ANYTHING ANYONE ELSE MAY SAY. . . . . 145 SNOW 66
HE DOESN'T LOOK ON IT AS ANYTHING." . . . . 145 SNOW 79
THE HAVING ANYTHING TO SELL IS WHAT . . . . 159 NEW HAMPSHIRE . . 7
OF RADIUM OR ANYTHING TO SELL. . . . . 163 NEW HAMPSHIRE . . 123
AND SO NOT GOOD FOR ANYTHING BUT CIDER. . . . . . . 164 NEW HAMPSHIRE . . 162
ANYTHING I CAN SAY ABOUT NEW HAMPSHIRE . . . . 165 NEW HAMPSHIRE . . 210
OF ANYTHING MORE SOCIABLE TO SAY: . . . . 168 NEW HAMPSHIRE . . 292
AND WHEN HE CAN'T DO ANYTHING, FALLS BACK . . . . . . 171 NEW HAMPSHIRE . . 400
"DON'T CALL IT BLAMED; THERE ISN'T ANYTHING . . . . . 177 THE STAR-SPLITTER . . 22
DIDN'T FEEL ANYTHING. AND IF IT DID, ... 178 THE STAR-SPLITTER . . 62
ANYTHING FURTHER HAD BEEN WASTED ON HER, ... 180 MAPLE 33
BUT LACKING FAITH IN ANYTHING TO MEAN . . . . 184 MAPLE 155
A MAN YOU COULD SAY ALMOST ANYTHING TO . . . . 192 PAUL'S WIFE . . . 33
SHE WASN'T ANYTHING TO BE ASHAMED OF. . . . . 192 PAUL'S WIFE . . . 41
PAUL WORKED AT ANYTHING IN LUMBERING. . . . . 193 PAUL'S WIFE . . . 57
DON'T YOU KNOW ANYTHING, YOU GIRL? LET GO!" . . . . . 197 WILD GRAPES . . . 47
MUCH DANGER OF MY PICKING ANYTHING! . . . . 198 WILD GRAPES . . . 59
MY BROTHER SAID: "DON'T YOU WEIGH ANYTHING? . . . . . 199 WILD GRAPES . . . 89
IT WASN'T MY NOT WEIGHING ANYTHING . . . . 199 WILD GRAPES . . . 92
SO MUCH AS MY NOT KNOWING ANYTHING-- . . . . 199 WILD GRAPES . . . 93
BEFORE I GOT UP TO DO ANYTHING; . . . . 205 THE WITCH OF COOS . 92
THEN WE ASKED WAS THERE ANYTHING . . . . 206 THE WITCH OF COOS . 121
BE READY, I THOUGHT, FOR ALMOST ANYTHING. . . . . . . 215 A FOUNTAIN, A BOTTLE . 64
SHE NEVER TENDED ANYTHING HERSELF. . . . . 215 A FOUNTAIN, A BOTTLE . 83
TO BLOW THE EARTH OR ANYTHING SELF-CLEAR: . . . . . . 246 ATMOSPHERE . . . 4
MAKES THE NEW MOON LOOK ANYTHING BUT NEW . . . . . . 247 THE COCOON . . . 3
YOU'LL WAIT A LONG, LONG TIME FOR ANYTHING MUCH . . . 268 ON LOOKING UP BY CHANCE 1
TO KNOW IF ANYTHING IS VERY WRONG. . . . . 317 BUILD SOIL . . . 56
WOULD I GAIN ANYTHING BY USING RHYME? . . . . 382 TO AN ANCIENT . . 17
ON MAKING CERTAIN ANYTHING HAS HAPPENED . . . . . . 383 MAKING CERTAIN ANYTHING T
IF ANYTHING SHOULD PUT AN END TO THIS, ... 397 THE PLANNERS . . . 1
AS MUCH AS ANYTHING FOR SITUATION. . . . . 400 TO THE RIGHT PERSON . 3
ANYTHING TO SLAY . . . . 431 KITTY HAWK . . . 112
ANYTHING WE SAW . . . . 438 KITTY HAWK . . . 327
THAT THERE WAS ANYTHING I COULDN'T BE. . . . . 443 AUSPEX 12
IF IT SHOULD NOT DO ANYTHING FORETOLD . . . . 446 DOES NO ONE AT ALL EVER 5
I WOULD GIVE ANYTHING TO LEARN . . . . 451 A-WISHING WELL . . 8
I'LL BET YOU ANYTHING THAT'S ALL AS KING . . . . . . 458 HOW HARD TO KEEP FROM 137
I WANT HIM TO BE ANYTHING HE HAS TO. . . . . 459 HOW HARD TO KEEP FROM 181
OF ANYTHING THEY ARE CONFRONTED WITH. . . . . 461 HOW HARD TO KEEP FROM 237
PREDICTED ANYTHING THAT CAME TO PASS. . . . . 476 A MASQUE OF REASON . 96
OH, LORD, LET'S NOT GO BACK TO ANYTHING. . . . . . . 477 A MASQUE OF REASON . 115
TO ANYTHING WITH ANYONE. / THERE, THERE, ... 478 A MASQUE OF REASON . 146
TO HAVE BEEN IN ON ANYTHING WITH YOU. . . . . 481 A MASQUE OF REASON . 218
PRAY TELL ME WHAT DOES THAT MEAN? ANYTHING? . . . . . 484 A MASQUE OF REASON . 304
I WOULD DO ANYTHING FOR YOU IN REASON. . . . . 486 A MASQUE OF REASON . 374
THAN ANYTHING. / HE'S VERY REAL TO ME . . . . 489 A MASQUE OF REASON . 434
NOW IF YOU THREE HAVE SETTLED ANYTHING . . . . 490 A MASQUE OF REASON . 464

ANYTHING (CONTINUED)
    HAVEN'T YOU NOTICED ANYTHING (HEAR THAT!) . . . . 495 A MASQUE OF MERCY . . 42
    TO ANYTHING THAT HAPPENED ANYMORE. . . . . 501 A MASQUE OF MERCY . . 203
    ANYTHING WE ONCE THOUGHT WE HAD TO BE. . . . . 505 A MASQUE OF MERCY . . 315
    AT ANYTHING BUT CHANGE OF PERSONNEL. . . . . 510 A MASQUE OF MERCY . . 458
ANYTHING'S
    ANYTHING'S FORBIDDEN . . . . 437 KITTY HAWK 282
ANYWAY
    I DOUBT IF I COULD DO IT ANYWAY.'" . . . . 48 A HUNDRED COLLARS . . 118
    ANYWAY THEY WON'T HAVE THE PLACE DISTURBED." . . . . . 55 THE BLACK COTTAGE . . 21
    ANYWAY ALL HE TALKED ABOUT WAS LOVE. . . . . 66 A SERVANT TO SERVANTS 110
    I SHAN'T CATCH UP IN THIS WORLD, ANYWAY. . . . . 68 A SERVANT TO SERVANTS 176
    THE MEALS WE HAVEN'T HAD WERE, ANYWAY. . . . . 115 IN THE HOME STRETCH . 142
    AND ANYWAY IT CAME TOO LATE FOR MAPLE. . . . . 184 MAPLE 159
    AND, ANYWAY, ITS STANDING IN THE YARD . . . . 189 THE GRINDSTONE . . . 19
    ALWAYS THE WITCH'S MOTTO ANYWAY. . . . . 207 PAUPER WITCH OF GRAFTON 8
    AND ANYWAY THIS TELLS ME WHERE I AM." . . . . 214 A FOUNTAIN, A BOTTLE . 46
    ANYWAY. THAT IS MY STYLE OF DICTATOR. . . . . 323 BUILD SOIL 233
    IT CAME FROM WHERE HE CAME FROM ANYWAY." . . . . 366 OF STONES OF THE PLACE 16
    THESE ANYWAY MIGHT THINK IT WAS IMPORTANT . . . . . . 397 THE PLANNERS 13
    WE'RE GOING ANYWAY AND MAY AS WELL . . . . 482 A MASQUE OF REASON . 234
    JUST AS WE WILL BE TALKING ANYWAY . . . . 482 A MASQUE OF REASON . 236
ANYWHERE
    OF THEM ANYWHERE UNDER THE SHADE OF THE PINE, ... 59 BLUEBERRIES 16
    WE USED TO LIVE--TEN MILES FROM ANYWHERE. . . . . 64 A SERVANT TO SERVANTS 63
    ME? I'M NOT OFF FOR ANYWHERE AT ALL. . . . . 125 AN ENCOUNTER 22
    TO GET IT ANYWHERE THAT I CAN SEE. . . . . 188 THE GRINDSTONE . . .   3
    WHOSE PRIDE HAS FAILED TO GET HIM ANYWHERE). . . . . . 190 THE GRINDSTONE . . . 44
    I PUT IT SHINING ANYWHERE I PLEASE. . . . . 245 THE FREEDOM OF THE MOON 7
    UNDER OR ON THE TREE, OR ANYWHERE. . . . . 284 THE GOLD HESPERIDEE . 39
    THE MILES AND MILES HE LIVED FROM ANYWHERE . . . . . . 292 FIGURE IN THE DOORWAY 11
    I DON'T BELIEVE YOU'RE ANYWHERE NEAR THE LAST, ... 389 SKEPTIC   6
    SHORT OF ANYWHERE, ... 439 KITTY HAWK 356
    ANYWHERE IN SPACE. . . . . 440 KITTY HAWK 394
    I COULD GO ALMOST ANYWHERE, ... 466 SOME SCIENCE FICTION 26
    I'D KNOW HIM BY BLAKE'S PICTURE ANYWHERE. . . . . 474 A MASQUE OF REASON . 18
    (I'D KNOW YOU BY BLAKE'S PICTURE ANYWHERE)-- . . . . . 476 A MASQUE OF REASON . 85
    WHERE ARE YOU STAYING--ANYWHERE IN TOWN? . . . . 501 A MASQUE OF MERCY . . 209
APART
    IN THAT VANISHED ABODE THERE FAR APART . . . .   6 GHOST HOUSE 12
    WE MAKE OURSELVES A PLACE APART . . . . 19 REVELATION   1
    "WHETHER THEY WORK TOGETHER OR APART." . . . . 22 THE TUFT OF FLOWERS . 10
    "WHETHER THEY WORK TOGETHER OR APART." . . . . 23 THE TUFT OF FLOWERS . 40
    APART WOULD MAKE ME OUT. GIVE ME MY CHANCE. . . . . . . 53 HOME BURIAL 61
    HE'D PULL HIS BARS APART LIKE BOW AND BOWSTRING, . . . 66 A SERVANT TO SERVANTS 134
    TO LIVE TOGETHER AND THEN PULL APART. . . . . 82 THE HOUSEKEEPER . . . 40
    MEN WORK ALONE, THEIR LOTS PLOWED FAR APART, ... 299 STRONG SAYING NOTHING   6
    THANK GOD OUR PRACTICE HOLDS THE LOVES APART, ... 318 BUILD SOIL 81
    AND WHEN WE GET TOO FAR APART IN WEALTH, ... 363 AN EQUALIZER   5
    THAT LOOKS IN ONTO A MOOD APART. . . . . 385 A MOOD APART   8
    A MOOD APART . . . . 385 A MOOD APART . . . .   T
APATHY
    OF WAY WITH ME FROM APATHY OF WING, ... 240 OUR SINGING STRENGTH . 37
APIECE
    "A THOUSAND CHRISTMAS TREES!--AT WHAT APIECE?" . . . . 107 CHRISTMAS TREES . . 42
    (FOR THAT WAS ALL THEY FIGURED OUT APIECE)-- . . . . . 107 CHRISTMAS TREES . . 49
    WHATEVER THEY COST APIECE OR A POUND, ... 232 THE KITCHEN CHIMNEY .   6
APOGEE
    THE APOGEE OF HUMAN BLIND CONCEIT. . . . . 394 HAEC FABULA DOCET . .   4
APOLOGY
    TOO LONG I'VE OWED YOU THIS APOLOGY . . . . 475 A MASQUE OF REASON . 59
APOSTLE'S
    WHOSE CELLAR IS IT, YOURS OR THE APOSTLE'S? . . . . . 514 A MASQUE OF MERCY . . 554
APPALL
    WHAT BUT DESIGN OF DARKNESS TO APPALL?-- . . . . 302 DESIGN 13
APPARATUS
    THAT ONCE A YEAR BY HAND OR APPARATUS . . . . 360 A LOOSE MOUNTAIN . .   3
APPAREL
    AND USING FOR APPAREL WHAT WAS MEANT . . . . 385 THE FEAR OF GOD . . . 12
APPARENT (SEE NONE-TOO-APPARENT)
    AS WAS APPARENT FROM WHAT HAPPENED NEXT. . . . . 195 PAUL'S WIFE 138
    (WHEN THE DUST SETTLES IT SHOULD BE APPARENT . . . . 507 A MASQUE OF MERCY . . 343
APPARENTLY
    APPARENTLY I HADN'T BURIED HIM . . . . 72 THE CODE 102
    "THIS IS BETWEEN YOU TWO APPARENTLY. . . . . 100 THE SELF-SEEKER . . . 209
    "APPARENTLY THESE TWO OUGHT TO MARRY. . . . . 345 DISCOVERY OF MADEIRAS 69
    FOR THE APPARENTLY UNMEANING SORROW . . . . 475 A MASQUE OF REASON . 60
    HIS SPIRIT HAD TO COME. APPARENTLY. . . . . 477 A MASQUE OF REASON . 100
APPARITION
    STRANGE APPARITION OF THE MIND! . . . . 332 ALL REVELATION . . . 10
APPEAL
    HALF IN APPEAL, BUT HALF AS IF TO KEEP . . . . 137 "OUT,OUT--" 21
    IN INFINITE APPEAL. THEN SAYING "HELL," . . . . 396 ANY SIZE WE PLEASE. .   7
APPEAR
    MAGNIFIED APPLES APPEAR AND DISAPPEAR, ... 68 AFTER APPLE-PICKING . 18
    APPEAR LIKE STANDING . . . . 219 I WILL SING YOU ONE-O 66
    SHE DOESN'T BOTHER TO APPEAR. . . . . 390 TWO LEADING LIGHTS . 17
    HE HAS BUT TO APPEAR. HE'LL COME FOR ME, ... 487 A MASQUE OF REASON . 384
APPEARANCES
    HE MAY BE BETTER THAN APPEARANCES. . . . . 39 DEATH OF THE HIRED MAN 134
APPEARED
    HE APPEARED TO FORGET TO KEEP HIS HOLD, ... 91 THE FEAR 59
    AND I REMEMBER ONE WHOSE NAME APPEARED . . . . 165 NEW HAMPSHIRE 193
    APPEARED LIKE GOLD IN THE SUNSET SKY, ... 249 A PECK OF GOLD . . .   6
    AS A GREAT BUCK IT POWERFULLY APPEARED, ... 338 THE MOST OF IT . . . 16
APPEARING
    APPEARING TO RETURN ME HATE FOR HATE . . . . 190 THE GRINDSTONE . . . 41

APPEARS
   "TWO WEEKS SINCE." / "SHE'S IN EARNEST, IT APPEARS." . . . 82 THE HOUSEKEEPER . . .   22
   APPEARS A SOLEMN MORTICIAN; . . . . 288 DEPARTMENTAL   34
   IT VENTURED LESS IN PERIL THAN APPEARS. . . . . 302 A BIRD SINGING IN SLEEP 8
   BUT WHAT IMPERFECTLY APPEARS . . . . 327 A MISSIVE MISSILE . .   9
   THEY MUST HAVE SEEN AHEAD WHAT NOW APPEARS: . . . . 423 FOR JOHN F. KENNEDY . . 28
APPETITE
   TO A DISCRIMINATING APPETITE, ... 97 THE SELF-SEEKER . . . 128
APPLE (SEE CIDER-APPLE)
   HE IS ALL PINE AND I AM APPLE ORCHARD. . . . . 33 MENDING WALL   24
   MY APPLE TREES WILL NEVER GET ACROSS . . . . 33 MENDING WALL   25
   COME HERE--I'LL SHOW YOU--IN THAT APPLE TREE. . . . . . .   83 THE HOUSEKEEPER . . .   62
   TO GO THE ROUND OF APPLE, CHERRY, PEACH, ...   117 IN THE HOME STRETCH . 196
   SOFT PETALS FALLEN FROM THE APPLE TREE . . . .   124 PUTTING IN THE SEED .   4
   THE COW IN APPLE TIME . . . . 124 THE COW IN APPLE TIME .   T
   IT STANDS BESIDE THE SAME OLD APPLE TREE. . . . . 189 THE GRINDSTONE . . .   8
   THE SHADOW OF THE APPLE TREE IS THIN . . . . 189 THE GRINDSTONE . . .   9
   UNDER A RUINOUS LIVE APPLE TREE . . . . 189 THE GRINDSTONE . . .   20
   THE APPLE TREES ARE SENT TO HEARTHSTONE FLAME. . . . . .   231 A BROOK IN THE CITY . 11
   SQUARE MATTHEW HALE'S YOUNG GRAFTED APPLE TREE . . . . .   283 THE GOLD HESPERIDEE .   1
   THERE SURE ENOUGH WAS AN APPLE TREE . . . . 304 UNHARVESTED   4
   FOR THERE THERE HAD BEEN AN APPLE FALL . . . .   304 UNHARVESTED   8
   AS COMPLETE AS THE APPLE HAD GIVEN MAN. . . . . 305 UNHARVESTED   9
   HIS CHEEK SMEARED WITH APPLE SAND, ...   366 NOT OF SCHOOL AGE .   9
   A PART APPLE IN HIS HAND, ... 366 NOT OF SCHOOL AGE .   10
   A FEW OLD PECKER-FRETTED APPLE TREES. . . . . 378 DIRECTIVE   28
   FROM THE APPLE TREE. . . . .   435 KITTY HAWK   218
   BY ANY CHANCE A LADY APPLE ON YOU? . . . .   488 A MASQUE OF REASON .   421
APPLE-PICKING
   BUT I AM DONE WITH APPLE-PICKING NOW. . . . .   68 AFTER APPLE-PICKING .   6
   AFTER APPLE-PICKING . . . .   68 AFTER APPLE-PICKING .   T
   OF APPLE-PICKING: I AM OVERTIRED . . . .   69 AFTER APPLE-PICKING .   28
APPLES
   APPLES I DIDN'T PICK UPON SOME BOUGH. . . . .   68 AFTER APPLE-PICKING .   5
   THE SCENT OF APPLES: I AM DROWSING OFF. . . . .   68 AFTER APPLE-PICKING .   8
   MAGNIFIED APPLES APPEAR AND DISAPPEAR, ...   68 AFTER APPLE-PICKING .   18
   OF LOAD ON LOAD OF APPLES COMING IN. . . . .   69 AFTER APPLE-PICKING .   26
   FOR DIAMONDS AND APPLES. "DIAMONDS . . . .   159 NEW HAMPSHIRE . . .   11
   AND APPLES IN COMMERCIAL QUANTITIES?" . . . . 159 NEW HAMPSHIRE . . .   12
   APPLES? NEW HAMPSHIRE HAS THEM, BUT UNSPRAYED, ...   164 NEW HAMPSHIRE . . .   159
   BUT WHEN HE CAME TO LOOK, NO APPLES THERE . . . .   284 THE GOLD HESPERIDEE .   38
   AND WORSHIP APPLES. WHAT ELSE COULD IT MEAN? . . . . .   284 THE GOLD HESPERIDEE .   54
   APPLES OR SOMETHING FORGOTTEN AND LEFT, ... 305 UNHARVESTED   13
   HAVE TO SELL YOU MY APPLES AND BUY YOURS? . . . .   321 BUILD SOIL   165
APPLE'S
   THAT THE APPLE'S A ROSE, ...   246 THE ROSE FAMILY . . .   4
APPLE-TREE'S
   ON SOME WILD APPLE-TREE'S YOUNG TENDER BARK, ...   254 A WINTER EDEN . . .   11
APPLICATION
   MAY MY APPLICATION SO CLOSE . . . .   286 IN TIME OF CLOUDBURST .   25
APPLIED
   'TWAS PROVIDENTIAL YOU APPLIED TO LS, ...   369 THE LITERATE FARMER AND 27
APPLY
   SOME FORCE HAS BUT TO APPLY, ...   285 IN TIME OF CLOUDBURST .   13
APPRAISE
   WE CAN'T APPRAISE THE TIME IN WHICH WE ACT. . . . . . .   352 THE LESSON FOR TODAY .   43
   THAN SMOKE AND MIST WHO BETTER COULD APPRAISE . . . . .   415 A CABIN IN THE CLEARING 41
APPROACH
   LIES IN OUR DIFFERENT APPROACH TO CHRIST, ...   513 A MASQUE OF MERCY . . 517
APPROACHING
   WITH ANIMUS APPROACHING HATE, ...   418 AMERICA IS HARD TO SEE   51
APPROPRIATE
   THEY JUDGED ME BY THEIR APPROPRIATE TOOL. . . . .   276 TWO TRAMPS IN MUD TIME   54
APPROVAL
   FOR WANT OF HIS APPROVAL, WHY, ...   275 A LONE STRIKER   61
   THE FINAL FLAT OF THE HOE'S APPROVAL STAMP . . . .   299 STRONG SAYING NOTHING .   3
   GOD NODDED HIS APPROVAL OF AS GOOD. . . . .   422 FOR JOHN F. KENNEDY .   23
APPROVE
   NO ONE OF HONEST FEELING WOULD APPROVE . . . .   423 FOR JOHN F. KENNEDY .   43
   MEANS THAT WE APPROVE . . . .   442 KITTY HAWK   439
APRIL
   AS ONCE IT DID WITH ME UPON AN APRIL. . . . .   130 THE BONFIRE   34
   IN APRIL BY SUBSIDING MEADOW BROOKS. . . . .   191 PAUL'S WIFE   22
   WHERE WHEELS HAVE FRESHLY SLICED THE APRIL MIRE. . . . .   225 BLUE-BUTTERFLY DAY . .   8
   IN WATER OF A SLENDER APRIL RILL . . . .   226 THE ONSET   19
   YOU KNOW HOW IT IS WITH AN APRIL DAY . . . .   275 TWO TRAMPS IN MUD TIME   18
APRON
   AND SPREAD HER APRON TO IT. SHE PUT OUT HER HAND . . . .   38 DEATH OF THE HIRED MAN 106
   HIS SISTER STOOD BESIDE THEM IN HER APRON . . . .   136 "OUT,OUT--"   13
APROPOS
   APROPOS OF SIN, ...   432 KITTY HAWK   145
APT
   AS A MATTER OF FACT THERE ARE TIMES WHEN I AM APT . . .   389 SKEPTIC   10
   I'M APT TO TELL THEM IN NEW YORK . . . .   452 A-WISHING WELL . . .   34
   I'M APT TO STRING ALONG WITH THYATIRA. . . . .   479 A MASQUE OF REASON .   168
APTLY
   AND I APTLY QUOTED. . . . .   433 KITTY HAWK   169
ARARAT
   THERE'S ALWAYS BEEN AN ARARAT . . . .   453 A-WISHING WELL . . .   79
ARBITRARY
   YOU OWE IT TO AN ARBITRARY GOD . . . .   385 THE FEAR OF GOD . .   4
ARBOREAL
   AND THINK OF AN ORCHARD'S ARBOREAL PLIGHT . . . .   228 GOOD-BY AND KEEP COLD .   26
ARC
   AND LIFELESS FROM AN INTERRUPTED ARC. . . . .   172 A STAR IN A STONEBOAT .   9
   OUR MISSILES ALWAYS MAKE TOO SHORT AN ARC. . . . .   261 A SOLDIER   8
   MY FINGERS AND CLOSE MY ARMS IN AN ARC. . . . .   265 THE DOOR IN THE DARK .   4
   THROUGH NINETY-ODD DEGREES OF ARC, IT SEEMS, ...   269 THE BEAR   24

ARC (CONTINUED)
   ARE MORE DIVINE THAN ANY BULB OR ARC, ... 370 THE LITERATE FARMER AND 77
ARCADIANS
   BELIEVE THE ARCADIANS OR NOT, ... 452 A-WISHING WELL . . . 37
   BELIEVE THE ARCADIANS OR NOT, ... 452 A-WISHING WELL . . 47
ARCH
   MY INSTEP ARCH NOT ONLY KEEPS THE ACHE, ... 68 AFTER APPLE-PICKING . 21
   AND BADE HIM LEAVE THE PAN AND STOKE THE ARCH: . . . . 234 EVENING A SUGAR ORCHARD 4
   A CLOUD COMES OVER THE SUNLIT ARCH, ... 275 TWO TRAMPS IN MUD TIME 22
   I HAVE KEPT HIDDEN IN THE INSTEP ARCH . . . . 379 DIRECTIVE 55
ARCHED
   THE STURDY SEEDLING WITH ARCHED BODY COMES . . . . . 124 PUTTING IN THE SEED . 13
ARCHER
   ONCE THERE WAS AN ARCHER, ... 427 VERSION 1
ARCHES
   I FLED HIM, DOWN THE ARCHES OF THE YEARS." . . . . . 494 A MASQUE OF MERCY . . 23
ARCHING
   YOU MAY SEE THEIR TRUNKS ARCHING IN THE WOODS . . . . 121 BIRCHES 17
ARCHITECTURE
   ON PUEBLO INDIANS AND THEIR ARCHITECTURE . . . . . . 369 THE LITERATE FARMER AND 54
ARCTIC
   "ABOUT THE BRITISH ARCTIC. THAT'S WHAT COMES . . . . 159 NEW HAMPSHIRE . . . 23
   CLEAR TO THE ARCTIC OF EVERY LIVING KIND. . . . . . 305 THERE ARE ROUGHLY ZONES 10
   THAT BRACED HIS FEET AGAINST THE ARCTIC POLE. . . . . 377 DIRECTIVE 17
ARE---NOT INDEXED
AREN'T---NOT INDEXED
ARGUE
   SEEMED TO ARGUE PERHAPS SHE WENT . . . . 343 DISCOVERY OF MADEIRAS . 13
   "I'M SAYING IT TO ARGUE HIS IDEA'S . . . . 406 FROM PLANE TO PLANE . 80
ARGUES
   THE OLD MAN ARGUES SCIENCE CHEAPENED SPEED. . . . . . 371 THE LITERATE FARMER AND 98
ARGUMENT
   BECAUSE HE LIKED IT--THAT AN ARGUMENT! . . . . . 37 DEATH OF THE HIRED MAN 81
   NEEDLESS TO SAY TO YOU, MY ARGUMENT . . . . . . 322 BUILD SOIL 185
   FROM SIDE TO SIDE IN ARGUMENT, ... 326 TO A THINKER 34
   I'M HAVING THE WHOLE ARGUMENT MY WAY-- . . . . . . 354 THE LESSON FOR TODAY . 116
   WHEN A GREAT TIDE OF ARGUMENT SWEEPS IN . . . . . . 513 A MASQUE OF MERCY . 538
ARGUMENTS
   GOOD ARGUMENTS HE SEES HE MIGHT HAVE USED. . . . . . 37 DEATH OF THE HIRED MAN 75
   ARGUMENTS TOO STALE TO MENTION . . . . 396 AN IMPORTER 9
ARIES
   ARIES AND TAURUS, ... 429 KITTY HAWK 37
ARIGHT
   FOR THE BEES TO COME AND SERVE ITS BEAUTY ARIGHT. . . . 300 STRONG SAYING NOTHING . 12
ARISE
   WHETHER 'TIS IN US TO ARISE WITH DAY . . . . 10 STORM FEAR 17
ARISEN
   THEN WHAT OF THIS RIVER THAT HAVING ARISEN . . . . . 379 TOO ANXIOUS FOR RIVERS 3
ARISES
   BUT A RESULTANT THAT ARISES FROM THEM. . . . . . . 460 HOW HARD TO KEEP FROM 217
ARISING (SEE LATE-ARISING)
ARISTOCRAT
   I'M LIBERAL. YOU, YOU ARISTOCRAT, ... 354 THE LESSON FOR TODAY . 120
ARISTOCRATIC
   AND THIS IS NO ARISTOCRATIC JOKE . . . . 423 FOR JOHN F. KENNEDY . 32
ARKANSAS
   I MET A TRAVELER FROM ARKANSAS . . . . 159 NEW HAMPSHIRE . . . 9
ARM
   I HAVE BUT TO TURN ON MY ARM, AND LO, ... 17 THE VANTAGE POINT . 10
   SHE WITHDREW, SHRINKING FROM BENEATH HIS ARM . . . . . 52 HOME BURIAL 31
   WITH HIS CLOTHES ON HIS ARM--ALL OF HIS CLOTHES. . . . 66 A SERVANT TO SERVANTS . 123
   TWO AT A TIME'S THE RULE, ONE ON EACH ARM, ... 85 THE HOUSEKEEPER . . 129
   DON'T HOLD MY ARM!" / "I SAY IT'S SOMEONE PASSING." . . 90 THE FEAR 23
   ON YOUR SLIM-JIM ARM." . . . . 133 A GIRL'S GARDEN . . 16
   THE STUBBORN THING, THE WAY IT JARS YOUR ARM!-- . . . 153 SNOW 296
   OF MIND AND STRONG OF ARM SHOULD FIT TOGETHER, ... 164 NEW HAMPSHIRE . . 181
   HE DODGED A LOG THAT LIFTED LIKE AN ARM . . . . . . 170 NEW HAMPSHIRE . . 347
   AND RUN OFF IN STRANGE TANGENTS WITH THE ARM, ... 174 A STAR IN A STONEBOAT . 53
   AND THE DRY PUMP FLUNG UP AN AWKWARD ARM; . . . . . 242 NEED OF BEING VERSED . 19
   OUR ARM THROWN OVER IT ASLEEP BESIDE IT. . . . . . . 258 WEST-RUNNING BROOK . 15
   THERE WAS A SUDDEN FLASH OF ARM, A SNATCH, ... 293 AT WOODWARD'S GARDENS . 22
   HE STRETCHED HER EITHER ARM . . . . 339 THE SUBVERTED FLOWER . 18
   AN ARM WORKED LIKE A SAW . . . . 340 THE SUBVERTED FLOWER . 43
   YOU LINK AN ARM IN ITS ARM AND YOU LEAN . . . . . . 349 TO A YOUNG WRETCH . 5
   WITH AN ARM OF SCRAWNY MAST . . . . 469 FOUR-ROOM SHACK... . 2
ARMED
   IN EACH HAND, LIKE AN OLD-STONE SAVAGE ARMED. . . . . 34 MENDING WALL 40
   I ARMED MYSELF AGAINST SUCH BONES AS MIGHT BE . . . . 175 THE CENSUS-TAKER . . 43
   ARMED WITH A SCYTHE AND SPECTACLES THAT GLOWED. . . . 189 THE GRINDSTONE . . 30
   HE TOLD THE DISTANCE, "I AM ARMED FOR WAR. . . . . . 270 THE EGG AND THE MACHINE 28
ARMFUL
   THE ARMFUL . . . . 266 THE ARMFUL . . . . T
   I HAD TO DROP THE ARMFUL IN THE ROAD . . . . 267 THE ARMFUL 11
ARMORY
   FEELS LIKE MY ARMORY OF HATE; . . . . 393 BEYOND WORDS . . 2
ARMS
   SHE TOOK THE MARKET THINGS FROM WARREN'S ARMS . . . . 34 DEATH OF THE HIRED MAN 8
   A BUTTONED HAIRCLOTH LOUNGE SPREAD SCROLLING ARMS . . . 55 THE BLACK COTTAGE . . 22
   ALL WIRY ARMS AND LEGS THAT SPREAD OUT WAVY . . . . . 70 THE CODE 34
   GOOD-BY." HE FLUNG HIS ARMS AROUND HIS FACE. . . . . 101 THE SELF-SEEKER . . 228
   WITH HILLS AND CIRCLING ARMS ABOUT-- . . . . 120 BOND AND FREE . . . 2
   SOMETIMES HE CAME WITH ARMS OUTSPREAD . . . . . . 138 BROWN'S DESCENT . . . 21
   MEWLING AND PUKING IN THE PUBLIC ARMS." . . . . . . 170 NEW HAMPSHIRE . . 363
   STANDING ALONE WITH SMOOTH ARMS LIFTED UP, ... 184 MAPLE 145
   "I'LL CATCH YOU IN MY ARMS. IT ISN'T FAR." . . . . . 198 WILD GRAPES 76
   WITH OUR ARMS AT THE LEVEL OF OUR KNEES, ... 205 THE WITCH OF COÖS . 106
   FLOWING OVER MY ARMS . . . . 235 GATHERING LEAVES . 11
   MY FINGERS AND CLOSE MY ARMS IN AN ARC. . . . . . . 265 THE DOOR IN THE DARK . 4

ARMS (CONTINUED)
   I LOSE SOME OTHER OFF MY ARMS AND KNEES, ... 266 THE ARMFUL 2
   THE BEAR PUTS BOTH ARMS AROUND THE TREE ABOVE HER . . . 268 THE BEAR 1
   OF WHIRLING HANDS AND ARMS ABOUT THE HEAD . . . . . . 277 THE WHITE-TAILED HORNET 9
   THEY STOOD ARMS LACED TOGETHER AT THE BARS, ... 293 AT WOODWARD'S GARDENS . 12
   WITH BABIES IN THEIR ARMS . . . . 391 A ROGERS GROUP . . . 3
   THEN WHEN THE ARMS AND LEGS HAVE ATROPHIED, ... 395 ETHEREALIZING . . . 5
   HE STRETCHED HIS ARMS OUT TO THE DARK OF SPACE . . . . 396 ANY SIZE WE PLEASE . . 5
ARM'S
   HE MADE AS IF TO HOLD IT AT ARM'S LENGTH . . . . . . 55 THE BLACK COTTAGE . . 9
ARMY
   SHOUTS LIKE AN ARMY CAPTAIN, 'LET HER COME!' . . . . 71 THE CODE 63
   AND KICK WITH TWO LEGS LIKE AN ARMY MULE. . . . . . 202 THE WITCH OF COOS . . 10
   HAD BEEN FOUND WITH CHILD; AND HER ARMY . . . . . . 314 BEARER OF EVIL TIDINGS 21
   YOU LOST YOUR ARMY AT MOSUL. WHAT HAPPENED? . . . . . 458 HOW HARD TO KEEP FROM 130
   SINCE I CAME IN? / HEAR WHAT? THAT ARMY TRUCK? . . . . 495 A MASQUE OF MERCY . . 43
ARNOLD
   AND RAN FOR SHELTER QUOTING MATTHEW ARNOLD: . . . . . 170 NEW HAMPSHIRE . . . 370
ARNOLDISM
   WHICH IS SHEER MATTHEW ARNOLDISM, ... 171 NEW HAMPSHIRE . . . 382
AROSE
   THE DEMON AROSE FROM HIS WALLOW TO LAUGH, ... 25 THE DEMIURGE'S LAUGH . 10
   THEN I AROSE AND SILENTLY WANDERED HOME, ... 343 QUEST OF PURPLE-FRINGED 25
   WE AROSE FROM THERE . . . . 434 KITTY HAWK 207
AROUND (SEE RING-AROUND)
   THAN THE TREES AROUND WERE TALL; . . . . 13 ROSE POGONIAS . . . 4
   THAT MADE ME HEAR THE WAKENING BIRDS AROUND, ... 23 THE TUFT OF FLOWERS . 31
   "THERE OUGHT TO BE A VIEW AROUND THE WORLD . . . . . 42 THE MOUNTAIN . . . 55
   YOU'VE WORKED AROUND THE FOOT OF ALL YOUR LIFE. . . . 43 THE MOUNTAIN . . . 83
   "CAN ONE WALK AROUND IT? WOULD IT BE TOO FAR?" . . . 43 THE MOUNTAIN . . . 92
   IT'S TIME YOU TURNED AROUND AND BOOSTED US. . . . . 48 A HUNDRED COLLARS . . 115
   "YOU DRIVE AROUND? IT MUST BE PLEASANT WORK." . . . . 49 A HUNDRED COLLARS . . 122
   AND PRESTO, THEY'RE UP ALL AROUND YOU AS THICK . . . 59 BLUEBERRIES 20
   AROUND AND AROUND US. AND THEN FOR A WHILE . . . . . 62 BLUEBERRIES 91
   AROUND HIM TO LOOK AFTER THAT MAKE WASTE. . . . . . 65 A SERVANT TO SERVANTS . 73
   A NARROW PASSAGE ALL THE WAY AROUND. . . . . 66 A SERVANT TO SERVANTS . 116
   FARMERS AROUND TWICE AS WELL OFF AS WE . . . . . . 85 THE HOUSEKEEPER . . . 113
   AROUND US, LOOKING OUT OF TREES AND BUSHES . . . . . 90 THE FEAR 46
   CATERWAUL TO THE HILLS AROUND THE VILLAGE . . . . . 94 THE SELF-SEEKER . . . 42
   GOOD-BY." HE FLUNG HIS ARMS AROUND HIS FACE. . . . . 101 THE SELF-SEEKER . . . 228
   I DON'T STAND STILL AND LOOK AROUND . . . . . . 124 A TIME TO TALK . . . 3
   AS I WALKED ONCE AROUND IT IN POSSESSION. . . . . . 130 THE BONFIRE 39
   THAT COMES OF HAVING PAUL AROUND THE PLACE. . . . . 193 PAUL'S WIFE 76
   PAUL TAKING AFTER HER AROUND THE POND. . . . . . . 195 PAUL'S WIFE 122
   NO DOUBT IT'S GROWN UP SOME TO WOODS AROUND IT. . . . 213 A FOUNTAIN, A BOTTLE . 21
   AROUND, AND UNDER . . . . 220 I WILL SING YOU ONE-O . 75
   IN GOING TWICE AROUND THE TREE. . . . . 233 LOOKING FOR SUNSET BIRD 12
   THE BEAR PUTS BOTH ARMS AROUND THE TREE ABOVE HER . . 268 THE BEAR 1
   AS LARGE AROUND AS THE CHOPPING BLOCK; . . . . . . 275 TWO TRAMPS IN MUD TIME 10
   THE WAY A PLAYER CURLS AROUND A FOOTBALL . . . . . 278 THE WHITE-TAILED HORNET 39
   AND LOOKED AROUND TO SEE IF HE WAS SEEN. . . . . . 284 THE GOLD HESPERIDEE . 50
   IN USING THE YARD TO BACK AND TURN AROUND. . . . . . 287 A ROADSIDE STAND . . 40
   THE WOODS AROUND IT HAVE IT--IT IS THEIRS. . . . . . 296 DESERT PLACES . . . 5
   OR BETTER ON DISH PLATES ALL AROUND THE ROOM, ... 320 BUILD SOIL 148
   FRIENDS CROWD AROUND ME WITH THEIR FIVE-YEAR PLANS . . 323 BUILD SOIL 222
   AROUND WITH MIST AND CLOUD, ... 333 HAPPINESS MAKES UP . . 3
   AROUND BEND AFTER BEND, ... 366 NOT OF SCHOOL AGE . . 1
   WRAPPED IN AROUND ITSELF AND SELF-BEFRIENDED, ... 396 ANY SIZE WE PLEASE . . 10
   TO PUSH THE WOODS BACK FROM AROUND THE HOUSE . . . . 414 A CABIN IN THE CLEARING 3
   OUR MOAT AROUND US IS NO MORE A MOAT, ... 446 DOES NO ONE AT ALL EVER 17
   FOR THEM MY LOITERING AROUND . . . . 466 SOME SCIENCE FICTION . 17
   AROUND HIM SO IT WOULDN'T TOUCH AND HURT HIM. . . . . 478 A MASQUE OF REASON . . 133
   THAT COULD, LIKE ANY SPACE, BE TURNED AROUND IN? . . . 479 A MASQUE OF REASON . . 161
   TO ANYONE AROUND WHEN SHE IS DRINKING. . . . . . . 496 A MASQUE OF MERCY . . 88
AROUSED
   (WE KNOW THE VALLEY STREAMS THAT WHEN AROUSED . . . . 378 DIRECTIVE 53
AROUSING (SEE SELF-AROUSING)
ARRANGED
   I THOUGHT AS MUCH. YOU HAVE IT ALL ARRANGED. . . . . 508 A MASQUE OF MERCY . . 372
ARRANGEMENT
   WITH WOMENFOLK. WE COULD HAVE SOME ARRANGEMENT . . . . 52 HOME BURIAL 50
   (THE ARRANGEMENT MADE A PLEASANT SUNNY CELLAR.) . . . 181 MAPLE 59
   MUST HAVE YOU. THERE, THAT'S JUST THE RIGHT ARRANGEMENT. 489 A MASQUE OF REASON . . 457
ARREST
   ISN'T GIVEN A MOMENT'S ARREST-- . . . . 288 DEPARTMENTAL 16
   WHERE MADISON ATTEMPTED TO ARREST IT. . . . . . . 458 HOW HARD TO KEEP FROM 156
ARRIVE
   IT'S RESTFUL TO ARRIVE AT A DECISION, ... 172 NEW HAMPSHIRE . . . 411
ARRIVES
   BEFORE HE ARRIVES TO SAY IT OUT. . . . . 6 GHOST HOUSE 20
ARROWHEADS
   AND ARROWHEADS ITSELF. MUCH USE FOR YEARS . . . . 189 THE GRINDSTONE . . . 38
ARSENATE
   OF VITRIOL OR ARSENATE OF LEAD, ... 164 NEW HAMPSHIRE . . . 161
ART
   FOR THOU ART DEAD, I SAID, ... 29 MY BUTTERFLY 44
   SHE HAD SOME ART OF HEARING AND YET NOT . . . . . 57 THE BLACK COTTAGE . . 73
   PERHAPS YOU HAVE THE ART OF WHAT I MEAN. . . . . 78 THE GENERATIONS OF MEN 131
   HER PEOPLE NOT QUITE SHORT ENOUGH FOR ART, ... 170 NEW HAMPSHIRE . . . 356
   HE MEDITATES THE BREEDER'S ART. . . . . 280 BLUE RIBBON AT AMESBURY 25
   AND MADE FUN OF BY BUSINESS, LAW, AND ART; . . . . 322 BUILD SOIL 190
   ART AND RELIGION LOVE THE SOMBER CHORD. . . . . . 353 THE LESSON FOR TODAY . 97
   "NATURE I LOVED; AND NEXT TO NATURE, ART." . . . . 393 LUCRETIUS VERSUS POETS 5
   WHICH MAKES OPPOSING IT TO ART ABSURD . . . . . 394 LUCRETIUS VERSUS POETS 10
   THE ART OF LIFE IS PASSING LOSSES ON. . . . . . 399 THE INGENUITIES OF DEBT 5
   GLORY IS OUT OF DATE IN LIFE AND ART. . . . . . 423 FOR JOHN F. KENNEDY . 50
   SO BY CRAFT OR ART . . . . 441 KITTY HAWK 426
   YET SO RUDE IN ITS ART, ... 447 THE BAD ISLAND--EASTER 3

ARTHUR
   OF ARTHUR AMY'S HAVING ONCE BEEN UP . . . . 207 PAUPER WITCH OF GRAFTON 13
   THE ARTHUR AMY I WAS MARRIED TO . . . . 207 PAUPER WITCH OF GRAFTON 16
   THE ARTHUR AMY I WAS MARRIED TO . . . . 208 PAUPER WITCH OF GRAFTON 20
   THEIR ARTHUR AMY WAS THE FATHER OF MINE. . . . . 208 PAUPER WITCH OF GRAFTON 27
   WAS ARTHUR AMY. YOU KNOW WHO HE WAS. . . . . 209 PAUPER WITCH OF GRAFTON 71
   WELL, I SHOWED ARTHUR AMY SIGNS ENOUGH . . . . 210 PAUPER WITCH OF GRAFTON 89
ARTIFICE
   ALL HE OWES TO THE ARTIFICE . . . . 418 AMERICA IS HARD TO SEE 68
ARTIFICERS
   THE ORNAMENTS THE GREEK ARTIFICERS . . . . 473 A MASQUE OF REASON . . 10
   I RECOGNIZE THEM. GREEK ARTIFICERS . . . . 490 A MASQUE OF REASON . . 460
ARTIFICIAL
   IN HAVING TAKEN ARTIFICIAL LIGHT . . . . 361 A LOOSE MOUNTAIN . . . 7
   I'M SICK OF THE WHOLE ARTIFICIAL PUZZLE. . . . . . 484 A MASQUE OF REASON . . 300
   AND TURN THE GOLD ENAMELED ARTIFICIAL BIRDS ON. . . 490 A MASQUE OF REASON . . 459
ARTIST
   THE ARTIST IN ME CRIES OUT FOR DESIGN. . . . . . . 482 A MASQUE OF REASON . . 261
ARTISTICALLY
   ON GLOSSY WIRES ARTISTICALLY BENT . . . . 309 WASPISH 1
ARTISTS
   ARTISTS THE MINUTE THEY SET UP AS ARTISTS, ... 162 NEW HAMPSHIRE . . . 96
   SUMMONING ARTISTS TO PARTICIPATE . . . . 422 FOR JOHN F. KENNEDY . 1
   SEEMS SOMETHING ARTISTS OUGHT TO CELEBRATE. . . . 422 FOR JOHN F. KENNEDY . 3
   THE REASON ARTISTS SHOW SO LITTLE INTEREST . . . . 461 HOW HARD TO KEEP FROM 230
ARTLESS
   AT HAVING THE LANDSCAPE MARRED WITH THE ARTLESS PAINT . 286 A ROADSIDE STAND . . 9
   BUT STILL UNSTORIED, ARTLESS, UNENHANCED, ... 348 THE GIFT OUTRIGHT . . 15
   BUT STILL UNSTORIED, ARTLESS, UNENHANCED, ... 425 THE GIFT OUTRIGHT . . 15
ART'S
   FOR ART'S SAKE ONE COULD ALMOST WISH THEM WORSE . . . 167 NEW HAMPSHIRE . . . 266
AS
   WERE NOT, AS 'TWERE, THE MEREST MASK OF GLOOM, ... 5 INTO MY OWN . . . 3
   AS SWEET COMPANIONS AS MIGHT BE HAD. . . . . 6 GHOST HOUSE . . . 30
   ARE BEAUTIFUL AS DAYS CAN BE; . . . . 6 MY NOVEMBER GUEST . . 3
   WHICH FLOWS IN SHAPES AS TALL AS TREES . . . . . . 9 STARS 3
   AS IF WITH KEENNESS FOR OUR FATE, ... 9 STARS 5
   HOW THE COLD CREEPS AS THE FIRE DIES AT LENGTH-- . . 10 STORM FEAR . . . 12
   AS WITNESS ALL WITHIN . . . . 11 WIND AND WINDOW FLOWER 19
   MELT IT AS THE ICE WILL GO; . . . . 11 TO THE THAWING WIND . 8
   AS THE UNCERTAIN HARVEST; KEEP US HERE . . . . . . 12 A PRAYER IN SPRING . 3
   AS THE SUN'S RIGHT WORSHIP IS, ... 13 ROSE POGONIAS . . 10
   YOU SHOOK YOUR PENSIVE HEAD AS WHO SHOULD SAY, . . . 16 A DREAM PANG . . . 6
   AS TWO IN WHOM THEY WERE PROVED MISTAKEN, ... 16 IN NEGLECT . . . 2
   WE RAN AS IF TO MEET THE MOON . . . . 18 GOING FOR WATER . . 9
   A NOTE AS FROM A SINGLE PLACE, ... 18 GOING FOR WATER . . 21
   EVEN AS ON EARTH, IN PARADISE; . . . . 19 THE TRIAL BY EXISTENCE 4
   AND I MUST BE, AS HE HAD BEEN--ALONE, ... 22 THE TUFT OF FLOWERS . 8
   "AS ALL MUST BE," I SAID WITHIN MY HEART, ... 22 THE TUFT OF FLOWERS . 9
   BUT AS I SAID IT, SWIFT THERE PASSED ME BY . . . . 22 THE TUFT OF FLOWERS . 11
   AS WHERE SOME FLOWER LAY WITHERING ON THE GROUND. . . 22 THE TUFT OF FLOWERS . 16
   AND THEN HE FLEW AS FAR AS EYE COULD SEE, ... 22 THE TUFT OF FLOWERS . 17
   BUT GLAD WITH HIM, I WORKED AS WITH HIS AID, ... 23 THE TUFT OF FLOWERS . 35
   AND DREAMING, AS IT WERE, HELD BROTHERLY SPEECH . . . 23 THE TUFT OF FLOWERS . 37
   IT WAS JUST AS THE LIGHT WAS BEGINNING TO FAIL . . . 24 THE DEMIURGE'S LAUGH . 4
   AS OF ONE WHO UTTERLY COULDN'T CARE, ... 25 THE DEMIURGE'S LAUGH . 9
   BRUSHING THE DIRT FROM HIS EYE AS HE WENT; . . . . . 25 THE DEMIURGE'S LAUGH . 11
   I FELT AS A FOOL TO HAVE BEEN SO CAUGHT, ... 25 THE DEMIURGE'S LAUGH . 14
   WE KEEP THE WALL BETWEEN US AS WE GO. . . . . . . 33 MENDING WALL . . . 15
   HE MOVES IN DARKNESS AS IT SEEMS TO ME, ... 34 MENDING WALL . . . 41
   BETWEEN THEM THEY WILL LAY THIS FARM AS SMOOTH! . . . 36 DEATH OF THE HIRED MAN 63
   AS IF SHE PLAYED UNHEARD SOME TENDERNESS . . . . . . 38 DEATH OF THE HIRED MAN 109
   AS THE ROAD WINDS WOULD BRING HIM TO HIS DOOR. . . . 38 DEATH OF THE HIRED MAN 126
   HE DON'T KNOW WHY HE ISN'T QUITE AS GOOD . . . . . 39 DEATH OF THE HIRED MAN 143
   AS ANYBODY. WORTHLESS THOUGH HE IS, ... 39 DEATH OF THE HIRED MAN 144
   THE MOUNTAIN HELD THE TOWN AS IN A SHADOW. . . . . . 40 THE MOUNTAIN . . . 1
   "AS TO THAT I CAN'T SAY. BUT THERE'S THE SPRING, . . 42 THE MOUNTAIN . . . 63
   WITH A BIG STICK, THE SAME AS WHEN THE COWS . . . . 43 THE MOUNTAIN . . . 85
   BUT IT'S AS MUCH AS EVER YOU CAN DO, ... 43 THE MOUNTAIN . . . 94
   RIFLING A PRINTED LETTER AS HE TALKS. . . . . . . 44 A HUNDRED COLLARS . 10
   YOU ACT AS IF YOU WISHED YOU HADN'T COME. . . . . . 47 A HUNDRED COLLARS . 71
   "JUST AS YOU SAY. HAVE IT YOUR OWN WAY, THEN. . . . 47 A HUNDRED COLLARS . 79
   LET'S HAVE A SHOWDOWN AS AN EVIDENCE . . . . 47 A HUNDRED COLLARS . 85
   I ALMOST KNOW THEIR FARMS AS WELL AS THEY DO." . . . 49 A HUNDRED COLLARS . 121
   AS IF SHE HAD SOME SORT OF CURVATURE, ... 49 A HUNDRED COLLARS . 143
   "ONE WOULD SUPPOSE THEY MIGHT NOT BE AS GLAD . . . . 49 A HUNDRED COLLARS . 149
   TO SEE US AS YOU ARE TO SEE THEM." / "OH, ... 49 A HUNDRED COLLARS . 150
   "JUST AS YOU SAY. HERE'S LOOKING AT YOU, THEN.-- . . 50 A HUNDRED COLLARS . 158
   BUT YOU'RE THE DOCTOR, AS THE SAYING IS. . . . . . 50 A HUNDRED COLLARS . 170
   SO AS TO PLEASE YOU. BUT I MIGHT BE TAUGHT, ... 52 HOME BURIAL . . . 47
   UNLIKE OTHER FOLKS AS YOUR STANDING THERE . . . . . 53 HOME BURIAL . . . 60
   THEY MIGHT AS WELL NOT TRY TO GO AT ALL. . . . . . 54 HOME BURIAL . . . 99
   HE MADE AS IF TO HOLD IT AT ARM'S LENGTH . . . . . 55 THE BLACK COTTAGE . 9
   "EVERYTHING'S AS SHE LEFT IT WHEN SHE DIED. . . . . 55 THE BLACK COTTAGE . 15
   "THAT WAS THE FATHER AS HE WENT TO WAR. . . . . . . 55 THE BLACK COTTAGE . 25
   AS WE ALMOST GOT BY THIS AFTERNOON. . . . . 56 THE BLACK COTTAGE . 44
   IT NEVER GOT SO FAR AS THAT; BUT THE BARE THOUGHT . . 57 THE BLACK COTTAGE . 90
   AS A CHILD MISSES THE UNSAID GOOD-NIGHT . . . . . . 58 THE BLACK COTTAGE . 102
   I'M JUST AS GLAD SHE MADE ME KEEP HANDS OFF, ... 58 THE BLACK COTTAGE . 104
   AS I SIT HERE, AND OFTENTIMES, I WISH . . . . . . 58 THE BLACK COTTAGE . 111
   BLUEBERRIES AS BIG AS THE END OF YOUR THUMB, ... 59 BLUEBERRIES . . . 3
   AND PRESTO, THEY'RE UP ALL AROUND YOU AS THICK . . . 59 BLUEBERRIES . . . 20
   AND HARD TO EXPLAIN AS A CONJUROR'S TRICK." . . . . 59 BLUEBERRIES . . . 21
   STUCK INTO HIS BERRIES AS FRESH AS A SHOWER; . . . . 61 BLUEBERRIES . . . 65
   'I'M SURE--I'M SURE'--AS POLITE AS COULD BE. . . . . 61 BLUEBERRIES . . . 75
   FOR WHEN YOU MADE ANSWER, YOUR VOICE WAS AS LOW . . . 62 BLUEBERRIES . . . 95
   AS TALKING--YOU STOOD UP BESIDE ME, YOU KNOW." . . . 62 BLUEBERRIES . . . 96
   TO PEOPLE THEY LOOK ON AS HAVING NO RIGHT . . . . . 62 BLUEBERRIES . . . 101

```
                                                          PAGE TITLE                          LINE
AS (CONTINUED)
     FOR THEN THERE WOULD BE BUSINESS. AS IT IS,  . . . . .  64 A SERVANT TO SERVANTS .  40
     BUT I DON'T COUNT ON IT AS MUCH AS LEN. . . . . . . .  64 A SERVANT TO SERVANTS .  44
     AS THAT I CAN SEE NO WAY OUT BUT THROUGH-- . . . . . .  64 A SERVANT TO SERVANTS .  58
     BUT HE WORKS WHEN HE WORKS AS HARD AS I DO-- . . . . .  64 A SERVANT TO SERVANTS .  67
     HIS HANDS HAD WORN THEM SMOOTH AS ANY OXBOW. . . . . .  66 A SERVANT TO SERVANTS . 136
     AND THEN HE'D CROW AS IF HE THOUGHT THAT CHILD'S PLAY--  66 A SERVANT TO SERVANTS . 137
     BUT THE PEN STAYED EXACTLY AS IT WAS, . . . . . . . .  67 A SERVANT TO SERVANTS . 141
     JUST AS YOU WILL TILL IT BECOMES A HABIT. . . . . . .  67 A SERVANT TO SERVANTS . 147
     AS I SAID, FOR A WHILE--BUT I DON'T KNOW! . . . . . .  67 A SERVANT TO SERVANTS . 153
     FROM OVER YOU AS YOU LAY IN YOUR BEDS. . . . . . . .  67 A SERVANT TO SERVANTS . 169
     I FEEL THE LADDER SWAY AS THE BOUGHS BEND. . . . . . .  68 AFTER APPLE-PICKING .  23
     AS OF NO WORTH. . . . . . . . . . . . . . . . . . . .  69 AFTER APPLE-PICKING .  36
     LONG SLEEP, AS I DESCRIBE ITS COMING ON, . . . . . . .  69 AFTER APPLE-PICKING .  41
     I SAID IT TO MYSELF AS MUCH AS YOU." . . . . . . . . .  70 THE CODE . . . . .  14
     I'M AS PARTICULAR AS ANYONE: . . . . . . . . . . . . .  70 THE CODE . . . . .  24
     FROM A HUMPED BODY NIGH AS BIG'S A BISCUIT. . . . . .  70 THE CODE . . . . .  35
     NOT IF HE VALUES WHAT HE IS. GOD, I'D AS SOON . . . .  71 THE CODE . . . . .  69
     MURDERED HIM AS LEFT OUT HIS MIDDLE NAME. . . . . . .  71 THE CODE . . . . .  70
     AS I SAT MOPPING HAYSEED FROM MY NECK, . . . . . . . .  72 THE CODE . . . . .  81
     AS ONE WHO CLASPS HER HEART. THEY LAUGHED TOGETHER. . .  74 THE GENERATIONS OF MEN  44
     AS PALE AND DIM AS A MATCH FLAME IN THE SUN; . . . . .  77 THE GENERATIONS OF MEN 100
     "IT'S AS YOU THROW A PICTURE ON A SCREEN: . . . . . .  78 THE GENERATIONS OF MEN 135
     YOU WILL BE LIKELY TO REGARD AS SACRED . . . . . . . .  79 THE GENERATIONS OF MEN 179
     MEBBE I'M WRONG TO TAKE IT AS I DO. . . . . . . . . .  80 THE GENERATIONS OF MEN 185
     SON, YOU DO AS YOU'RE TOLD! YOU TAKE THE TIMBER-- . . .  80 THE GENERATIONS OF MEN 192
     IT'S AS SOUND AS THE DAY WHEN IT WAS CUT-- . . . . . .  80 THE GENERATIONS OF MEN 193
     BETTER THAN MARRIED OUGHT TO BE AS GOOD . . . . . . .  84 THE HOUSEKEEPER . . .  81
     AS MARRIED--THAT'S WHAT HE HAS ALWAYS SAID. . . . . .  84 THE HOUSEKEEPER . . .  82
     A FRIEND OR TWO AS GOOD AS OWN THE FARM, . . . . . . .  84 THE HOUSEKEEPER . . .  96
     SUCH AS IT IS. IT ISN'T WORTH THE MORTGAGE." . . . . .  84 THE HOUSEKEEPER . . .  97
     HALF OF THE OUTDOOR WORK, THOUGH AS FOR THAT, . . . .  85 THE HOUSEKEEPER . . . 108
     FARMERS AROUND TWICE AS WELL OFF AS WE . . . . . . . .  85 THE HOUSEKEEPER . . . 113
     HAVEN'T AS GOOD. THEY DON'T GO WITH THE FARM. . . . .  85 THE HOUSEKEEPER . . . 114
     ON HIS OWN FARM. HE'S BOSS. BUT AS TO HENS: . . . . .  86 THE HOUSEKEEPER . . . 135
     THAT MUCH TO SELL, THEY'RE WORTH AS MUCH TO KEEP. . . .  86 THE HOUSEKEEPER . . . 141
     HE'S BEEN IN A GLASS CASE, AS YOU MAY SAY, . . . . . .  86 THE HOUSEKEEPER . . . 150
     "IT SEEMS AS IF. AND THAT'S NOT ALL: HE'S HELPLESS . .  86 THE HOUSEKEEPER . . . 156
     "IT'S AS I SAY: SHE'S TURNED FROM HIM, THAT'S ALL." . .  87 THE HOUSEKEEPER . . . 167
     MY, BUT HE LOOKS AS IF HE MUST HAVE HEARD! . . . . . .  88 THE HOUSEKEEPER . . . 204
     I SAW IT JUST AS PLAIN AS A WHITE PLATE," . . . . . .  89 THE FEAR . . . . .   9
     SHE SAID, "AS THE LIGHT ON THE DASHBOARD RAN . . . . .  89 THE FEAR . . . . .  10
     AT ONE DOOR AS WE ENTERED AT ANOTHER. . . . . . . . .  89 THE FEAR . . . . .  21
     "YOU SPEAK AS IF THIS WERE A TRAVELED ROAD. . . . . .  90 THE FEAR . . . . .  24
     BUT ADVANCED WITH HER AS SHE CROSSED THE GRASS. . . . .  91 THE FEAR . . . . .  60
     SOMEWHERE TO WALK----" / "THE HIGHWAY, AS IT HAPPENS--  92 THE FEAR . . . . .  85
     JOEL!" SHE SPOKE AS IF SHE COULDN'T TURN. . . . . . .  92 THE FEAR . . . . .  91
     AS THEY BOTH BITE THE WOOD. IT'S ALL OUR MUSIC. . . . .  94 THE SELF-SEEKER . . .  43
     ONE OUGHT AS A GOOD VILLAGER TO LIKE IT. . . . . . . .  94 THE SELF-SEEKER . . .  44
     "YOU MAKE THAT SOUND AS IF IT WASN'T SO . . . . . . .  94 THE SELF-SEEKER . . .  47
     THEY NEVER EARNED ME SO MUCH AS ONE CENT: . . . . . .  95 THE SELF-SEEKER . . .  71
     SUCH AS IT'S GOING TO BE, AND KNOW THE WORST, . . . .  95 THE SELF-SEEKER . . .  77
     AS IF FOR PAPERS THAT MIGHT BEAR THE NAME . . . . . .  96 THE SELF-SEEKER . . .  98
     YOU'RE HIDING SOMETHING. THAT'S AS BAD AS LYING. . . .  97 THE SELF-SEEKER . . . 132
     AS IF WITH SOME IDEA THAT SHE HAD SCORED. . . . . . .  98 THE SELF-SEEKER . . . 146
     AS IF TO SAY, 'YOU! YOU'RE THE HEART'S DESIRE.' . . . .  98 THE SELF-SEEKER . . . 158
     AT SUCH A TIME AS THIS. HE SNAPPED IT NOW. . . . . . .  98 THE SELF-SEEKER . . . 166
     "YES, BUT ALL THAT TAKES TIME, AND I'M AS MUCH . . . .  99 THE SELF-SEEKER . . . 191
     IN HASTE TO GET IT OVER WITH AS YOU.-- . . . . . . . .  99 THE SELF-SEEKER . . . 192
     SO AS TO SAY FOR CERTAIN I WERE HERE . . . . . . . . . 101 THE WOOD-PILE . . .   8
     WHO WAS SO FOOLISH AS TO THINK WHAT HE THOUGHT. . . . . 101 THE WOOD-PILE . . .  13
     EVERYTHING SAID AS PERSONAL TO HIMSELF. . . . . . . . 101 THE WOOD-PILE . . .  16
     WITHOUT SO MUCH AS WISHING HIM GOOD-NIGHT. . . . . . . 101 THE WOOD-PILE . . .  21
     TO WARM THE FROZEN SWAMP AS BEST IT COULD . . . . . . 102 THE WOOD-PILE . . .  39
     AND LOOKED DOWN ONE AS FAR AS I COULD . . . . . . . . 105 THE ROAD NOT TAKEN .   4
     THEN TOOK THE OTHER, AS JUST AS FAIR, . . . . . . . . 105 THE ROAD NOT TAKEN .   6
     THOUGH AS FOR THAT, THE PASSING THERE . . . . . . . . 105 THE ROAD NOT TAKEN .   9
     I HADN'T THOUGHT OF THEM AS CHRISTMAS TREES. . . . . . 106 CHRISTMAS TREES . .  15
     AS OTHERS HOLD THEIRS OR REFUSE FOR THEM, . . . . . . 106 CHRISTMAS TREES . .  22
     AS MAY BE SHOWN BY A SIMPLE CALCULATION. . . . . . . . 107 CHRISTMAS TREES . .  57
     HE CONSIGNED TO THE MOON--SUCH AS SHE WAS, . . . . . . 108 OLD MAN'S WINTER NIGHT 18
     AS BETTER THAN THE SUN IN ANY CASE . . . . . . . . . . 108 OLD MAN'S WINTER NIGHT 20
     STOOD UP TO US AS TO A MOTHER-BIRD . . . . . . . . . . 109 THE EXPOSED NEST .  21
     IT IS SPECKLED WITH GRIME AS IF . . . . . . . . . . . 110 A PATCH OF OLD SNOW .  5
     TO COME AS HERE I STAND AND GO THE ROUND . . . . . . . 111 IN THE HOME STRETCH  27
     AS GREAT AS THOSE IS SHATTERING TO THE FRAME . . . . . 111 IN THE HOME STRETCH  39
     IT SOUNDS AS IF IT WERE THE MEN WENT DOWN, . . . . . . 112 IN THE HOME STRETCH  56
     AT THE FLAME BURNING DOWNWARD AS HE SUCKS IT." . . . . 112 IN THE HOME STRETCH  65
     A WIRE SHE IS OF SILVER, AS NEW AS WE . . . . . . . . 113 IN THE HOME STRETCH  70
     FOR EVERYBODY AS IT IS IN THERE." . . . . . . . . . . 114 IN THE HOME STRETCH  98
     FOOL-LIKE, AND ROLLED HIS EYES AS IF TO SAY . . . . . 114 IN THE HOME STRETCH 102
     ACROSS HIS CHEST TO MAKE AS 'TWERE A BOW." . . . . . . 114 IN THE HOME STRETCH 107
     AS IN THE GAME 'TEN-STEP' THE CHILDREN PLAY." . . . . 114 IN THE HOME STRETCH 118
     AS TO OUR FATE, LIKE FOOLS PAST REASONING WITH. . . . 114 IN THE HOME STRETCH 125
     AS CERTAIN AS THE MEALS WE'VE HAD. I WISH . . . . . . 115 IN THE HOME STRETCH 141
     MUST GET SOMEWHERE. I'VE HEARD YOU SAY AS MUCH. . . . 117 IN THE HOME STRETCH 185
     THE NEIGHBORS MAY NOT HAVE TAKEN AS THEIR RIGHT . . . 117 IN THE HOME STRETCH 191
     AS MUCH AT HOME AS IF THEY'D ALWAYS DANCED THERE. . . 117 IN THE HOME STRETCH 204
     "WHEN I WAS JUST AS FAR AS I COULD WALK . . . . . . . 118 THE TELEPHONE . . .   1
     SOMEONE SAID 'COME'--I HEARD IT AS I BOWED." . . . . . 118 THE TELEPHONE . . .  17
     "I MAY HAVE THOUGHT AS MUCH, BUT NOT ALOUD." . . . . . 118 THE TELEPHONE . . .  18
     AS I WENT DOWN THE HILL ALONG THE WALL . . . . . . . . 118 MEETING AND PASSING .  1
     AS YOU CAME UP THE HILL. WE MET. BUT ALL . . . . . . . 118 MEETING AND PASSING .  4
     FOOTPRINTS IN SUMMER DUST AS IF WE DREW . . . . . . . 118 MEETING AND PASSING .  6
     BUT MORE THAN ONE AS YET. YOUR PARASOL . . . . . . . . 119 MEETING AND PASSING .  8
     THIS AS IT WILL BE SEEN IS OTHER FAR . . . . . . . . . 119 HYLA BROOK . . .  13
     MID-SUMMER IS TO SPRING AS ONE TO TEN. . . . . . . . . 120 THE OVEN BIRD . . .   5
     THE BIRD WOULD CEASE AND BE AS OTHER BIRDS . . . . . . 120 THE OVEN BIRD . . .  11
```

		PAGE	TITLE	LINE

AS (CONTINUED)

	PAGE	TITLE	LINE
AS ICE STORMS DO. OFTEN YOU MUST HAVE SEEN THEM	121	BIRCHES	5
AS THE BREEZE RISES, AND TURN MANY-COLORED	121	BIRCHES	8
AS THE STIR CRACKS AND CRAZES THEIR ENAMEL.	121	BIRCHES	9
AS HE WENT OUT AND IN TO FETCH THE COWS--	121	BIRCHES	24
THE SAME AS YOU SEIZE CAT'S-CRADLE STRINGS,	123	PEA BRUSH	19
WHEN, JUST AS THE SOIL TARNISHES WITH WEED,	124	PUTTING IN THE SEED	12
NO, NOT AS THERE IS A TIME TO TALK.	124	A TIME TO TALK	6
THAT HAD ME BY THE COAT AS GOOD AS SEATED,	125	AN ENCOUNTER	9
AS IF FOR FEAR OF TREADING UPON ME.	125	AN ENCOUNTER	15
SO MUCH AS YOU AND I	126	LONELINESS	2
THE TRUTH BEING WE ARE AS MUCH	126	LONELINESS	7
AS WE ARE TOO SAD FOR THE OTHER HERE--	126	LONELINESS	9
OF SEIZING FROM US AS HE MIGHT HAVE SEIZED.	127	THE SMILE	7
HE'S WATCHING FROM THE WOODS AS LIKE AS NOT.	127	THE SMILE	12
MADE THE GREAT TREE SEEM AS A LITTLE BIRD	128	THE OFT-REPEATED DREAM	7
SUDDEN AND SWIFT AND LIGHT AS THAT	129	THE IMPULSE	25
AS RECKLESS AS THE BEST OF THEM TONIGHT,	129	THE BONFIRE	2
DIVIDE IT? NO! BUT BURN IT AS ONE PILE	129	THE BONFIRE	9
AS ONCE IT DID WITH ME UPON AN APRIL.	130	THE BONFIRE	34
AS I WALKED ONCE AROUND IT IN POSSESSION.	130	THE BONFIRE	39
AND A FLAME SLENDER AS THE HEPATICAS,	131	THE BONFIRE	51
BY LEANING BACK MYSELF, AS IF THE REINS	132	THE BONFIRE	79
"IT'S AS WHEN I WAS A FARMER...."	134	A GIRL'S GARDEN	45
AS TOLD TO A CHILD	135	LOCKED OUT	S
SOME FLOWER I PLAYED WITH AS I SAT	135	LOCKED OUT	12
AS I WENT OUT A CROW	135	LAST WORD OF A BLUEBIRD	1
AS TOLD TO A CHILD	135	LAST WORD OF A BLUEBIRD	S
AS IT RAN LIGHT, OR HAD TO BEAR A LOAD.	136	"OUT,OUT--"	8
AS IF TO PROVE SAWS KNEW WHAT SUPPER MEANT,	136	"OUT,OUT--"	15
AS HE SWUNG TOWARD THEM HOLDING UP THE HAND,	136	"OUT,OUT--"	20
HALF IN APPEAL, BUT HALF AS IF TO KEEP	137	"OUT,OUT--"	21
FASTER OR SLOWER AS HE CHANCED,	138	BROWN'S DESCENT	25
SITTING OR STANDING AS HE CHOSE,	138	BROWN'S DESCENT	26
ACCORDING AS HE FEARED TO RISK	138	BROWN'S DESCENT	27
AS STANDING IN THE RIVER ROAD	139	BROWN'S DESCENT	46
SOMETIMES AS AN AUTHORITY	139	BROWN'S DESCENT	49
IT MUST HAVE LOOKED AS IF THE COURSE	139	BROWN'S DESCENT	65
WILL RUN AS HUSHED AS WHEN THEY WERE A THOUGHT.	141	THE LINE-GANG	7
FOR HE TURNED SUDDENLY GRAVE AS IF TO SAY,	142	THE VANISHING RED	5
YOU CAN'T GET BACK AND SEE IT AS HE SAW IT.	142	THE VANISHING RED	9
THEN YOU WOULDN'T HAVE LOOKED ON IT AS JUST A MATTER	142	THE VANISHING RED	12
DISGUSTED THE MILLER PHYSICALLY AS COMING	142	THE VANISHING RED	17
AS IF A MAN COULD MOVE THAT SLOW AND MOVE.	145	SNOW	60
HE DOESN'T LOOK ON IT AS ANYTHING."	145	SNOW	79
YOU LIKE YOUR FUN AS WELL AS ANYONE;	146	SNOW	97
A THING AS THAT. IT COULDN'T REACH THE LAMP	148	SNOW	139
SINCE LAST WE READ THE GAUGE." / "IT LOOKS AS IF	148	SNOW	159
IN GOING ON." / "OUR SNOWSTORMS AS A RULE	150	SNOW	221
AREN'T LOOKED ON AS MAN-KILLERS, AND ALTHOUGH	150	SNOW	222
AS IF NOT KNOWING WHAT YOU MEANT BY THE WORD STORM."	151	SNOW	232
THAT WANTS ME AS A WAR MIGHT IF IT CAME.	151	SNOW	241
ASK ANY MAN." / HE THREW HER THAT AS SOMETHING	151	SNOW	242
MUCH SAY IN THE MATTER, AND I'M JUST AS GLAD	152	SNOW	257
IT'S QUIET AS AN EMPTY CHURCH WITHOUT HIM."	152	SNOW	260
"BUT HOW MUCH BETTER OFF ARE WE AS IT IS?	152	SNOW	261
AS IT GROWS WISER AND OLDER,	156	THE SOUND OF TREES	13
AND TOSSING SO AS TO SCARE	156	THE SOUND OF TREES	22
WHO BOASTED OF HIS STATE AS BEAUTIFUL	159	NEW HAMPSHIRE	10
AS IF TO PUT FOREVER OUT OF MIND	160	NEW HAMPSHIRE	42
THE HOPE OF BEING, AS WE SAY, RECEIVED.	160	NEW HAMPSHIRE	43
AS AN OLD BOYHOOD FRIEND, AND ONCE INDEED	160	NEW HAMPSHIRE	49
OH, IT WAS TERRIBLE AS WELL COULD BE.	160	NEW HAMPSHIRE	59
ONE EACH OF EVERYTHING AS IN A SHOWCASE.	161	NEW HAMPSHIRE	62
JOHN SMITH REMARKED THEM AS HE COASTED BY,	161	NEW HAMPSHIRE	74
AS FOR WHAT THEY WERE UP TO MORE THAN FISHING--	161	NEW HAMPSHIRE	87
ARTISTS THE MINUTE THEY SET UP AS ARTISTS,	162	NEW HAMPSHIRE	96
ONE EACH OF EVERYTHING AS IN A SHOWCASE.	163	NEW HAMPSHIRE	144
WILL SERVE ALMOST AS WELL ABOUT VERMONT,	165	NEW HAMPSHIRE	211
I MAY AS WELL CONFESS MYSELF THE AUTHOR	166	NEW HAMPSHIRE	228
TO TAKE THEM AS AGAINST A SPECIAL STATE	166	NEW HAMPSHIRE	230
AS HALL OF WINDHAM, GAY OF ATKINSON,	167	NEW HAMPSHIRE	259
AS LONG AS LIFE GOES SO UNTERRIBLY?	167	NEW HAMPSHIRE	269
AND RECOGNIZED AS SUCH IN RUSSIA ITSELF	167	NEW HAMPSHIRE	278
I KNEW A MAN WHO FAILING AS A FARMER	168	NEW HAMPSHIRE	301
I FEEL, AS OF AN EARTHQUAKE IN MY BACK,	169	NEW HAMPSHIRE	318
OR SOME SUCH SENSE AS SAYS HOW HIGH SHALL JET	169	NEW HAMPSHIRE	325
OF EARLY TIMES AS TWICE THE HEIGHT THEY ARE--	169	NEW HAMPSHIRE	331
DOWN FROM THE STARS TO FREEZE THE DEW AS STARRY.	169	NEW HAMPSHIRE	342
WERE DOUBTLESS AS THE WORDS WE HEARD HIM SAY	170	NEW HAMPSHIRE	352
AGAIN AS IN THE DAYS WHEN AHAZ SINNED	171	NEW HAMPSHIRE	388
AND NOT, AS YOU MIGHT THINK, A FLYING CAR,	173	A STAR IN A STONEBOAT	27
SUCH AS EVEN POETS WOULD ADMIT PERFORCE	173	A STAR IN A STONEBOAT	28
IT WENT FOR BUILDING STONE, AND I, AS THOUGH	173	A STAR IN A STONEBOAT	34
YET ASK WHERE ELSE IT COULD HAVE GONE AS WELL,	173	A STAR IN A STONEBOAT	37
TO SUCH RESORTS OF LIFE AS MARS AND EARTH--	174	A STAR IN A STONEBOAT	48
AS FISH DO WITH THE LINE IN FIRST ALARM.	174	A STAR IN A STONEBOAT	54
SUCH AS IT IS, IT PROMISES THE PRIZE	174	A STAR IN A STONEBOAT	55
I CAME AS CENSUS-TAKER TO THE WASTE	174	THE CENSUS-TAKER	9
FOREVER OFF THE LATCH, AS IF RUDE MEN	175	THE CENSUS-TAKER	28
I ARMED MYSELF AGAINST SUCH BONES AS MIGHT BE	175	THE CENSUS-TAKER	43
IN LITTLETON IT MAY AS WELL BE ME."	177	THE STAR-SPLITTER	37
WHY NOT REGARD IT AS A SACRIFICE.	178	THE STAR-SPLITTER	63
AS UNDER-TICKET-AGENT AT A STATION	178	THE STAR-SPLITTER	69
AS ON A FARM, BUT PLANETS, EVENING STARS	178	THE STAR-SPLITTER	72
WE SPREAD OUR TWO LEGS AS WE SPREAD ITS THREE,	179	THE STAR-SPLITTER	83
THERE'S NO SUCH NAME." / "TEACHERS DON'T KNOW AS MUCH	179	MAPLE	5
AS FATHERS ABOUT CHILDREN, YOU TELL TEACHER.	180	MAPLE	6

AS (CONTINUED)

	PAGE TITLE	LINE
AND GIVE THE TEACHER A SCARE AS FROM HER FATHER.	180 MAPLE	32
AS SHE STOOD SAYING HER NAME OVER ALOUD,	181 MAPLE	41
AS LESLEY, CAROL, IRMA, MARJORIE,	181 MAPLE	46
BUT HADN'T AS IT WENT. (SHE KNEW A ROSE.)	181 MAPLE	48
AS IF IT WAS HER MOTHER SPEAKING TO HER.	181 MAPLE	66
SO SHE LOOKED FOR HERSELF, AS EVERYONE	182 MAPLE	70
IT MADE IT SEEM AS IF THERE MUST BE SOMETHING	182 MAPLE	94
NOT SO MUCH AS A SINGLE TREE FOR SHADE,	183 MAPLE	102
AS WELL AS COULD A MOTHER. AND AGAIN	183 MAPLE	119
AS IF HE DIDN'T KNOW WHAT LITTLE THING	183 MAPLE	125
IT WAS AS PERSONAL AS HE COULD BE	183 MAPLE	127
AS FAR AGAIN AS FROM BEING BORN TO BEARING."	184 MAPLE	130
AS LEAVING MORE TO NATURE AND HAPPY CHANCE.	185 MAPLE	169
AND THAT WAS, AS I SAY, AN ALDER BRANCH.	185 THE AX-HELVE	5
ME ONLY AS I TOOK MY AX TO HEART.	186 THE AX-HELVE	20
TONAGHT?" / AS WELL TONIGHT AS ANY NIGHT.	186 THE AX-HELVE	34
SO LONG AS HE WOULD LEAVE ENOUGH UNSAID,	186 THE AX-HELVE	38
THAT HAD AS MANY MOTIONS AS THE WORLD:	186 THE AX-HELVE	47
THEN ON BAPTISTE, AS IF SHE UNDERSTOOD	187 THE AX-HELVE	56
HE LIKED TO HAVE IT SLENDER AS A WHIPSTOCK,	187 THE AX-HELVE	69
WAS I DESIRED IN FRIENDSHIP, PARTLY AS SOMEONE	188 THE AX-HELVE	90
ERECT, BUT NOT WITHOUT ITS WAVES, AS WHEN	188 THE AX-HELVE	96
(BUT I FORGIVE IT NOW AS EASILY	190 THE GRINDSTONE	42
AS ANY OTHER BOYHOOD ENEMY	190 THE GRINDSTONE	43
IT LOOKED AS IF HE MIGHT BE BADLY THROWN	190 THE GRINDSTONE	58
(IT RAN AS IF IT WASN'T GREASED BUT GLUED);	190 THE GRINDSTONE	61
AS IF TO SAY, "THAT'S SO, HOW IS MY WIFE?	191 PAUL'S WIFE	14
AS CLEAN AS BOYS DO OFF A WILLOW TWIG.	191 PAUL'S WIFE	20
AND, AS YOU MIGHT SAY, SAW THE LADY BORN.	193 PAUL'S WIFE	56
(THEY TREATED IT AS HIS.) "YOU TAKE A JACKKNIFE,	193 PAUL'S WIFE	80
BRIGHTLY, AS IF A STAR PLAYED ON THE PLACE,	195 PAUL'S WIFE	135
AS WAS APPARENT FROM WHAT HAPPENED NEXT.	195 PAUL'S WIFE	138
AS A BRUTE TRIBUTE OF RESPECT TO BEAUTY.	195 PAUL'S WIFE	141
EITHER TO PRAISE HER OR SO MUCH AS NAME HER,	196 PAUL'S WIFE	153
AS A GIRL GATHERED FROM THE BIRCH MYSELF	196 WILD GRAPES	4
I CAN WASTE AS I PLEASE ON WHOM I PLEASE.	196 WILD GRAPES	15
AND GIVE MYSELF OUT AS TWO DIFFERENT AGES,	196 WILD GRAPES	17
MOSTLY AS MUCH BEYOND MY LIFTED HANDS, THOUGH,	197 WILD GRAPES	28
AS THE MOON USED TO SEEM WHEN I WAS YOUNGER,	197 WILD GRAPES	29
BUT NOT SO MUCH, PERHAPS, AS A BOY NEEDED.	197 WILD GRAPES	35
IT CAUGHT ME UP AS IF I WERE THE FISH	197 WILD GRAPES	62
"TO BE A BUNCH OF FOX GRAPES, AS THEY CALL THEM,	198 WILD GRAPES	63
GRIM SILENCE ON MY PART AS I SANK LOWER,	198 WILD GRAPES	79
SO MUCH AS MY NOT KNOWING ANYTHING--	199 WILD GRAPES	93
AS STILL I HAVE NOT LEARNED TO WITH THE HEART,	199 WILD GRAPES	97
I MAY YET LIVE, AS I KNOW OTHERS LIVE,	199 WILD GRAPES	100
TO DO, AS SHE HAD PUT IT, WHAT WAS RIGHT.	201 PLACE FOR A THIRD	75
MIGHT JUST AS WELL BE ICE AND THE CLOTHES SNOW.	203 THE WITCH OF COOS	39
SO AS TO SORT OF TURN ME OUT OF IT.	203 THE WITCH OF COOS	43
SO AS TO HAVE IT READY FOR OUTSIDERS.	207 THE WITCH OF COOS	147
THAT AS A WITCH I'D OFTEN MILK A BAT	208 PAUPER WITCH OF GRAFTON	40
THE CRIB HE SLEPT IN--AND AS SURE'S YOU'RE BORN	209 PAUPER WITCH OF GRAFTON	61
SHE MIGHT AS WELL HERSELF." BUT HE LIKED BEST	209 PAUPER WITCH OF GRAFTON	83
AS OFTEN AS HE HAD IN THE TAIL OF THE NIGHT,	210 PAUPER WITCH OF GRAFTON	87
OFF FROM THE HOUSE AS FAR AS WE COULD KEEP	210 PAUPER WITCH OF GRAFTON	90
IT DOESN'T SEEM AS IF I'D HAD THE COURAGE	210 PAUPER WITCH OF GRAFTON	106
I MIGHT HAVE, BUT IT DOESN'T SEEM AS IF.	210 PAUPER WITCH OF GRAFTON	108
BUT IT ISN'T AS IF	210 AN EMPTY THREAT	2
THE MICA SHEETS WERE BIG AS PLATE-GLASS WINDOWS.	213 A FOUNTAIN, A BOTTLE	5
IN EIGHTY-FIVE." / "AS LONG AGO AS THAT?"	213 A FOUNTAIN, A BOTTLE	23
OLD AS I AM, I'M GOING TO LET MYSELF	214 A FOUNTAIN, A BOTTLE	29
"I GUESS YOU'D FIND THE FOUNTAIN JUST AS EMPTY.	214 A FOUNTAIN, A BOTTLE	45
WE MAY AS WELL SEE THAT AND SAVE THE DAY."	214 A FOUNTAIN, A BOTTLE	54
COME STRAIGHT DOWN OFF THIS MOUNTAIN JUST AS FAST	215 A FOUNTAIN, A BOTTLE	61
AS WE CAN FALL AND KEEP A-BOUNCING ON OUR FEET.	215 A FOUNTAIN, A BOTTLE	62
"THE OUTSIDE DOORS AS YET HAVE HELD AGAINST US.	215 A FOUNTAIN, A BOTTLE	74
AS WINDS MIGHT ROUSE	218 I WILL SING YOU ONE-O	31
SINCE EARTH IS EARTH, PERHAPS, NOT HEAVEN (AS YET)--	220 FRAGMENTARY BLUE	5
SPREAD OPEN AS I DROPPED THEM HALF-READ THROUGH	222 THE RUNAWAY	2
HE SHUDDERS HIS COAT AS IF TO THROW OFF FLIES.	223 THE RUNAWAY	18
I DISCERNED, AS I THOUGHT, BEYOND THE PICTURE,	225 FOR ONCE SOMETHING	8
AT LAST THE GATHERED SNOW LETS DOWN AS WHITE	226 THE ONSET	2
AS MAY BE IN DARK WOODS, AND WITH A SONG	226 THE ONSET	3
AS ONE WHO OVERTAKEN BY THE END	226 THE ONSET	7
AS MEASURED AGAINST MAPLE, BIRCH, AND OAK,	226 THE ONSET	16
AS SWEET AS I COULD BEAR;	226 TO EARTHWARD	2
TO FEEL THE EARTH AS ROUGH	227 TO EARTHWARD	31
AND SUCH AS IS DONE TO THEIR WOOD WITH AN AX--	228 GOOD-BY AND KEEP COLD	23
ACROSS THE WALL, AS NEAR THE WALL AS THEY.	229 TWO LOOK AT TWO	16
THEN, AS IF THEY WERE SOMETHING THAT, THOUGH STRANGE,	229 TWO LOOK AT TWO	22
ACROSS THE WALL, AS NEAR THE WALL AS THEY.	229 TWO LOOK AT TWO	28
AS IF TO ASK, "WHY DON'T YOU MAKE SOME MOTION?"	230 TWO LOOK AT TWO	32
I DOUBT IF YOU'RE AS LIVING AS YOU LOOK."	230 TWO LOOK AT TWO	34
AS IF THE EARTH IN ONE UNLOOKED-FOR FAVOR	230 TWO LOOK AT TWO	41
THAT HELD THE HOUSE AS IN AN ELBOW-CROOK?	231 A BROOK IN THE CITY	4
I ASK AS ONE WHO KNEW THE BROOK, ITS STRENGTH	231 A BROOK IN THE CITY	5
AS GILT TO GOLD THAT WOULDN'T SHOW.	233 LOOKING FOR SUNSET BIRD	16
MYSELF AS ONE HIS OWN PRETENSE DECEIVES;	233 A BOUNDLESS MOMENT	10
I THOUGHT A FEW MIGHT TANGLE, AS THEY DID,	234 EVENING A SUGAR ORCHARD	7
AS LEO, ORION, AND THE PLEIADES,	234 EVENING A SUGAR ORCHARD	16
ARE LIGHT AS BALLOONS.	234 GATHERING LEAVES	4
AS FAR AS YOU WENT FROM THE DOOR, WHICH WAS NOT FAR;	235 VALLEY'S SINGING DAY	3
BUT A SLEEP OPPRESSES THEM AS THEY GO,	236 MISGIVING	3
AS THEY ARE FREE, TO GO IN QUEST	236 MISGIVING	14
AS OFTEN AS I'VE SEEN IT DONE BEFORE	237 A HILLSIDE THAW	4
IT LOOKS AS IF SOME MAGIC OF THE SUN	237 A HILLSIDE THAW	6
THE SWARM STILL RAN AND SCUTTLED JUST AS FAST.	237 A HILLSIDE THAW	24

AS (CONTINUED)
THE SPELL THAT SO COULD HOLD THEM AS THEY WERE . . . . . . 237 A HILLSIDE THAW 30
THEY DISAPPEARED AS IF EARTH SENT THEM BACK. . . . . . . 239 OUR SINGING STRENGTH . 6
AS IN SOME TOO MUCH CARVEN MARBLE HALL . . . . 240 OUR SINGING STRENGTH . 42
AS YOU MIGHT TRY A JEWEL IN YOUR HAIR. . . . . 245 THE FREEDOM OF THE MOON . 3
WITH ONE FIRST-WATER STAR ALMOST AS SHINING. . . . . . . 245 THE FREEDOM OF THE MOON . 6
AS VAIN TO RAISE A VOICE AS A SIGH . . . . 247 ON GOING UNNOTICED . . 1
YOU TOOK AS A TROPHY OF THE HOUR. . . . . 247 ON GOING UNNOTICED . . 16
AS FAR AS I CAN SEE, THIS AUTUMN HAZE . . . . 247 THE COCOON 1
SO MUCH AS TO TAKE CARE OF EVENING CHORES. . . . . . . 248 THE COCOON 10
YOU COULD NOT TELL, AND YET IT LOOKED AS IF . . . . . . 250 ONCE BY THE PACIFIC . 7
IT LOOKED AS IF A NIGHT OF DARK INTENT . . . . 250 ONCE BY THE PACIFIC . 10
WHEN IT SEEMED AS IF I COULD BEAR NO MORE. . . . . . . 250 A MINOR BIRD 4
AS HARDLY WORTH RENEWAL. . . . . 252 THE PEACEFUL SHEPHERD . 8
AS WELL HAVE BEEN THE SWORD. . . . . 252 THE PEACEFUL SHEPHERD . 12
AND AS I PASSED ALONG THE EAVES . . . . 253 THE THATCH 17
AS I THOUGHT OF THEM WITHOUT NEST OR ROOST. . . . . . . 253 THE THATCH 29
AS NEAR A PARADISE AS IT CAN BE . . . . 254 A WINTER EDEN 3
HERE LOVELESS BIRDS NOW FLOCK AS WINTER FRIENDS, ... 254 A WINTER EDEN 14
AS YOU AND I ARE MARRIED TO EACH OTHER, ... 258 WEST-RUNNING BROOK . . 12
AS IF REGRET WERE IN IT AND WERE SACRED. . . . . 259 WEST-RUNNING BROOK . . 60
THEY CAN LEAVE HER A HUT AS WELL; . . . . 260 SAND DUNES 14
HE IS THAT FALLEN LANCE THAT LIES AS HURLED, ... 261 A SOLDIER 1
BUT STILL LIES POINTED AS IT PLOWED THE DUST. . . . . . . 261 A SOLDIER 3
FORGETTING THAT AS FITTED TO THE SPHERE, ... 261 A SOLDIER 7
AS FULL TO THE GUNNEL OF FLOWERS GROWING . . . . 262 THE FLOWER BOAT . . . 6
AS EVER SHE TURNED HER HOME WITH COD . . . . 262 THE FLOWER BOAT . . . 7
OVER BACK WHERE THEY SPEAK OF LIFE AS STAYING . . . . . . 263 THE INVESTMENT . . . 1
IF, AS THEY SAY, SOME DUST THROWN IN MY EYES . . . . . . 265 DUST IN THE EYES . . 1
ONE IMPULSE PERSISTS AS OUR BREATH; . . . . 266 SITTING BY A BUSH . . 19
THE OTHER PERSISTS AS OUR FAITH. . . . . 266 SITTING BY A BUSH . . 20
I CROUCH DOWN TO PREVENT THEM AS THEY FALL; . . . . . . 267 THE ARMFUL 9
WE MAY AS WELL GO PATIENTLY ON WITH OUR LIFE, ... 268 ON LOOKING UP BY CHANCE 8
AND DRAWS IT DOWN AS IF IT WERE A LOVER . . . . 268 THE BEAR 2
AS SHE FLINGS OVER AND OFF DOWN THROUGH THE MAPLES, ... 269 THE BEAR 6
SO AS TO WRECK THE ENGINE IN THE DITCH. . . . . 270 THE EGG AND THE MACHINE 8
NOT SO MUCH TIED AS MADE THEM BLEND. . . . . 274 A LONE STRIKER . . . 32
AND IN IT, TALL AS TREES, WERE CLIFFS; . . . . 274 A LONE STRIKER . . . 37
AS LARGE AROUND AS THE CHOPPING BLOCK; . . . . 275 TWO TRAMPS IN MUD TIME 10
FELL SPLINTERLESS AS A CLOVEN ROCK. . . . . 275 TWO TRAMPS IN MUD TIME 12
BUT IF YOU SO MUCH AS DARE TO SPEAK, ... 275 TWO TRAMPS IN MUD TIME 21
HIS SONG SO PITCHED AS NOT TO EXCITE . . . . 276 TWO TRAMPS IN MUD TIME 27
A SINGLE FLOWER AS YET TO BLOOM. . . . . 276 TWO TRAMPS IN MUD TIME 28
EXCEPT AS A FELLOW HANDLED AN AX . . . . 276 TWO TRAMPS IN MUD TIME 55
AS THAT I HAD NO RIGHT TO PLAY . . . . 277 TWO TRAMPS IN MUD TIME 60
AS MY TWO EYES MAKE ONE IN SIGHT. . . . . 277 TWO TRAMPS IN MUD TIME 68
AS NOT TO RECOGNIZE IN ME THE EXCEPTION . . . . 278 THE WHITE-TAILED HORNET 15
THAT'S WHEN I WENT AS VISITOR TO HIS HOUSE. . . . . . . 278 THE WHITE-TAILED HORNET 22
AS VISITOR AT MY HOUSE HE IS BETTER. . . . . 278 THE WHITE-TAILED HORNET 23
TO FEED HIS THUMPING GRUBS AS BIG AS HE IS. . . . . . . 278 THE WHITE-TAILED HORNET 31
DOWNWARD COMPARISONS. AS LONG ON EARTH . . . . 279 THE WHITE-TAILED HORNET 59
AS OUR COMPARISONS WERE STOUTLY UPWARD . . . . 279 THE WHITE-TAILED HORNET 60
HER FLUFF OF PLUMAGE, WHITE AS CHALK, ... 280 BLUE RIBBON AT AMESBURY 7
IT SEEMS AS IF YOU MUST HAVE HEARD. . . . . 280 BLUE RIBBON AT AMESBURY 9
AS SAFE A VEHICLE OF SEED . . . . 281 BLUE RIBBON AT AMESBURY 35
AS IS VOUCHSAFED TO FEATHERED BREED. . . . . 281 BLUE RIBBON AT AMESBURY 36
AS ONE WHO SHREWDLY PRETENDS . . . . 282 A DRUMLIN WOODCHUCK . 11
AS MEASURED AGAINST THE ALL, ... 282 A DRUMLIN WOODCHUCK . 30
AS REGULARLY AS HE WENT TO FEED THE PIG . . . . 283 THE GOLD HESPERIDEE . 19
LONG SINCE THEY SWUNG AS THREE INSTEAD OF TWO-- . . . . . 283 THE GOLD HESPERIDEE . 25
JUST AS HE WAS, WITHOUT AN UTTERED SOUND . . . . 284 THE GOLD HESPERIDEE . 43
AT THOSE WHO'D DONE HIM SUCH A WRONG AS THAT, ... 284 THE GOLD HESPERIDEE . 44
BUT AS READY TO WIELD AS NOW. . . . . 285 IN TIME OF CLOUDBURST . 24
SO MUCH AS THE TRUSTING SORROW OF WHAT IS UNSAID: . . . . 286 A ROADSIDE STAND . . 17
AND THEN NEXT DAY AS I COME BACK INTO THE SANE, ... 287 A ROADSIDE STAND . . 49
AS RELIC OF A VANISHED RACE OF TREES-- . . . . 290 OLD BARN AT THE BOTTOM 39
THE PEOPLE CAN BURN IT AS LONG AS THEY PLEASE; . . . . . 291 ON HEART'S BEGINNING TO 16
THEY CAN KEEP IT BURNING AS LONG AS THEY PLEASE; . . . . . 291 ON HEART'S BEGINNING TO 24
BUT AS THROUGH THE MONOTONY WE RAN, ... 292 FIGURE IN THE DOORWAY . 5
AS IF REMINDED--OR AS IF PERHAPS . . . . 293 AT WOODWARD'S GARDENS . 15
FOR BEING AS OVERELATED . . . . 295 A RECORD STRIDE . . . 34
AS IF I HAD MEASURED THE COUNTRY . . . . 295 A RECORD STRIDE . . . 35
AND LONELY AS IT IS, THAT LONELINESS . . . . 296 DESERT PLACES . . . 9
THEY MIGHT AS WELL HAVE NONE AT ALL. . . . . 297 LEAVES COMPARED WITH . 10
THEY SPOKE TO THE FUGITIVE IN MY HEART AS IF IT WERE LEAF
    TO LEAF. . . . . 298 A LEAF-TREADER . . . 9
TWO SUCH AS YOU WITH SUCH A MASTER SPEED . . . . 300 THE MASTER SPEED . . 10
AS IF THE FINAL ESTIMATE WERE HERS; . . . . 301 MOON COMPASSES . . . 5
AND AS IT MEASURED IN HER CALIPERS, ... 301 MOON COMPASSES . . . 6
AS LONG AS IT TAKES TO PASS . . . . 301 NEITHER OUT FAR NOR IN 6
NOW BREATHED AS LIGHT AS A LADY'S FAN. . . . . 304 UNHARVESTED 7
AS COMPLETE AS THE APPLE HAD GIVEN MAN. . . . . 305 UNHARVESTED 9
AS THEY SAY IN WAR. . . . . 306 A TRIAL RUN 9
YOU HAVE ME THERE, BUT LOOSELY, AS I WOULD BE HELD. . . . 306 NOT QUITE SOCIAL . . 10
I WOULD NOT BE TAKEN AS EVER HAVING REBELLED. . . . . . 306 NOT QUITE SOCIAL . . 12
BUT HE'S AS GOOD AS ANYBODY GOING. . . . . 309 WASPISH 6
AS FULL AS THE ROOM COULD HOLD . . . . 310 THE VINDICTIVES . . . 3
AS LONG AS THE DECLARATION GUARDS . . . . 310 IN DIVES' DIVE . . . 3
HAD SERVED AS A PALACE GATE. . . . . 312 THE VINDICTIVES . . . 68
AS FOR HIS EVIL TIDINGS, ... 314 BEARER OF EVIL TIDINGS 41
SUCH AS ACCORDING TO BELIEF IN ROME . . . . 315 IRIS BY NIGHT 5
COULD CONCENTRATE ANEW AND RISE AS ONE. . . . . 315 IRIS BY NIGHT 8
SO WATERY AS TO SEEM SUBMARINE; . . . . 315 IRIS BY NIGHT 11
HAD TAKEN ALL THE WATER IT COULD AS DEW, ... 315 IRIS BY NIGHT 14
I WONDER! BOW AND RAINBOW AS II BENT, ... 315 IRIS BY NIGHT 23
INSTEAD OF MOVING WITH US AS WE WENT . . . . 315 IRIS BY NIGHT 24
WHY DON'T YOU USE YOUR TALENTS AS A WRITER . . . . . . 316 BUILD SOIL 22
GET CALLED AS MUCH IN CLASHES OF AMBITION. . . . . . . 317 BUILD SOIL 40

	PAGE	TITLE	LINE

AS (CONTINUED)
TO AFFIRM THERE IS SUCH A THING AS EVIL . . . . 317 BUILD SOIL 50
AS LONG AS LIGHTLY ALL THEIR LIVELONG SESSIONS, ... 317 BUILD SOIL 60
THERE'S NO SUCH THING AS SOCIALISM PURE-- . . . . . . 318 BUILD SOIL 70
EXCEPT AS AN ABSTRACTION OF THE MIND. . . . . 318 BUILD SOIL 71
(IN THIS IT IS AS MUCH LIKE HATE AS LOVE), ... 319 BUILD SOIL 105
WORKS IN THE DARK AS MUCH AGAINST AS FOR US. . . . . . 319 BUILD SOIL 106
NONE SHALL BE AS AMBITIOUS AS HE CAN. . . . . 320 BUILD SOIL 121
NONE SHOULD BE AS INGENIOUS AS HE COULD, ... 320 BUILD SOIL 122
WE'RE NATIONAL AND ACT AS NATIONALS. . . . . 320 BUILD SOIL 146
BUT MUCH AS IN THE END WE BRING FOR SALE THERE, ... 321 BUILD SOIL 173
I ONLY SPEAK TO YOU AS ONE OF THEM. . . . . 323 BUILD SOIL 210
AND BE AS UNSOCIAL WITH IT AS I CAN. . . . . 323 BUILD SOIL 238
AS THE MORE ECONOMICAL PRODUCER, ... 324 BUILD SOIL 253
AS MUCH AS LOVE, AND TOO CLOSE IN TO STRIKE . . . . . 325 BUILD SOIL 277
A REASONER AND GOOD AS SUCH, ... 326 TO A THINKER . . . 21
SO VIVID AS TO SEEM TO SPEAK. . . . . 327 A MISSIVE MISSILE . . 8
FAR AS WE AIM OUR SIGNS TO REACH, ... 328 A MISSIVE MISSILE . . 47
FAR AS WE OFTEN MAKE THEM REACH, ... 328 A MISSIVE MISSILE . . 48
IT CANNOT SPEAK AS FAR AS THIS. . . . . 328 A MISSIVE MISSILE . . 55
HAS BEEN IMPRESSED AS WITNESS TREE . . . . 331 BEECH 7
SHE IS AS IN A FIELD A SILKEN TENT . . . . 331 THE SILKEN TENT . . 1
A HEAD THRUSTS IN AS FOR THE VIEW, ... 332 ALL REVELATION . . 1
OR WRAPPED AS IN A SHROUD, ... 333 HAPPINESS MAKES UP . 4
AS THROUGH ITS BLAZING FLOWERS . . . . 333 HAPPINESS MAKES UP . 22
AS I CAME TO THE EDGE OF THE WOODS, ... 334 COME IN 1
THAT, AS IT DID THE FOREST STREW, ... 336 THE WIND AND THE RAIN . 4
WOULD BE AS IF HE PROPHESIED? . . . . 336 THE WIND AND THE RAIN . 14
AND THOUGH IT WERE AS MUCH AS CLOUD COULD BEAR . . . . 337 THE WIND AND THE RAIN . 29
AS STRONG IS RAIN WITHOUT AS WINE WITHIN, ... 337 THE WIND AND THE RAIN . 41
AS MAGICAL AS SUNLIGHT ON THE SKIN. . . . . 337 THE WIND AND THE RAIN . 42
AS A GREAT BUCK IT POWERFULLY APPEARED, ... 338 THE MOST OF IT . . . 16
BE THAT AS MAY BE, SHE WAS IN THEIR SONG. . . . . . 339 NEVER WOULD BIRDS' SONG 9
AS IF SHE MADE IT ACHE . . . . 339 THE SUBVERTED FLOWER . 19
AS IF HE COULD NOT SPARE . . . . 339 THE SUBVERTED FLOWER . 21
AS IF TO BE PERSUASIVE, ... 340 THE SUBVERTED FLOWER . 44
THAT WERE PALE AS A GHOST. . . . . 343 QUEST OF PURPLE-FRINGED 24
THEY LAUGHED AS IF THEY HAD TURNED A TRICK. . . . . . 344 DISCOVERY OF MADEIRAS . 30
HE TELLS HER AS MUCH OF BLOOD AND DIRT . . . . 346 DISCOVERY OF MADEIRAS . 88
AS HE THINKS WILL DO HER NOT TOO MUCH HURT. . . . . . 346 DISCOVERY OF MADEIRAS . 89
HER SPIRIT FADED AS FAR AWAY . . . . 346 DISCOVERY OF MADEIRAS . 103
AS THE LIVING EVER GO YET STAY. . . . . 346 DISCOVERY OF MADEIRAS . 104
SUCH AS WE WERE WE GAVE OURSELVES OUTRIGHT . . . . . 348 THE GIFT OUTRIGHT . . 12
SUCH AS SHE WAS, SUCH AS SHE WOULD BECOME. . . . . . 348 THE GIFT OUTRIGHT . . 16
AS GAY FOR YOU TO TAKE YOUR FATHER'S AX . . . . . . 349 TO A YOUNG WRETCH . . 1
AS TAKE HIS GUN--ROD--TO GO HUNTING--FISHING. . . . . 349 TO A YOUNG WRETCH . . 2
I COULD HAVE BOUGHT YOU JUST AS GOOD A TREE . . . . . 350 TO A YOUNG WRETCH . . 7
AS TREE BY ENTERPRISE AND EXPEDITION. . . . . 350 TO A YOUNG WRETCH . . 11
THEY ARE TO BE THOUGHT OF AS OPPOSING GOODS . . . . . 350 TO A YOUNG WRETCH . . 15
OFTENER THAN AS CONFLICTING GOOD AND ILL; . . . . . . 350 TO A YOUNG WRETCH . . 16
WERE REALLY AS DARK AS I HEAR SAGES TELL, ... 350 THE LESSON FOR TODAY . 2
TELL ME AS PEDAGOGUE TO PEDAGOGUE? . . . . 351 THE LESSON FOR TODAY . 21
YOUR LIGHT WAS SPENT PERHAPS AS IN A FOG . . . . . . 351 THE LESSON FOR TODAY . 24
AS SCHOOLMEN OF REPUTE SHOULD QUALIFY . . . . 352 THE LESSON FOR TODAY . 50
AS TO WHOSE AGE DESERVES THE LOWER MARK, ... 352 THE LESSON FOR TODAY . 52
ITS CONTEMPLATION MAKES US OUT AS SMALL . . . . . . 352 THE LESSON FOR TODAY . 69
AS A BRIEF EPIDEMIC OF MICROBES. . . . . 352 THE LESSON FOR TODAY . 70
ONE AS COMPARED WITH GOD AND ONE WITH SPACE. . . . . 353 THE LESSON FOR TODAY . 78
IT MIGHT AS WELL AT ONCE BE KINGDOM-COME. . . . . . 353 THE LESSON FOR TODAY . 102
AS EVER WHEN PHILOSOPHERS ARE MET, ... 354 THE LESSON FOR TODAY . 107
AS UNORIGINAL AS ANY RABBIT. . . . . 354 THE LESSON FOR TODAY . 112
WITH EQUAL DARKNESS, YOURS AS DARK AS MINE. . . . . . 354 THE LESSON FOR TODAY . 119
ON ME AS MUCH AS ANY IS THE JEST. . . . . 355 THE LESSON FOR TODAY . 154
AS OF A BOOK HELD UP BEFORE HIS EYES . . . . 355 TIME OUT 3
HE FOLLOWINGLY FINGERED AS HE READ, ... 356 TIME OUT 6
THE SAME FOR READING AS IT WAS FOR THOUGHT, ... 356 TIME OUT 9
IF I HAD MOTHS TO FRIEND AS I HAVE FLOWERS?) . . . . 356 A MOTH SEEN IN WINTER . 6
IT PAUSED AS WITH SUSPICION OF MY PEN, ... 357 A CONSIDERABLE SPECK . 10
AS I HAVE KNOWN THEM PASSIONATE AND FINE, ... 358 THE LOST FOLLOWER . . 1
AS GRAVE AS HE ABOUT THE WORLD'S DEFEAT . . . . . . 359 THE LOST FOLLOWER . . 24
WITH SUCH IT HAS PROVED DANGEROUS AS FRIEND . . . . . 359 THE LOST FOLLOWER . . 25
(AS YET UNBROUGHT TO EARTH) HE MEANS TO TRY. . . . . 359 THE LOST FOLLOWER . . 36
TO SEE THE STAR SHOWER KNOWN AS LEONID . . . . . . 360 A LOOSE MOUNTAIN . . 2
NO DOUBT DIRECTED AT OUR HEADS AS REBELS . . . . . . 361 A LOOSE MOUNTAIN . . 6
IT NEVER REACHES EARTH EXCEPT AS NEWS . . . . 361 A LOOSE MOUNTAIN . . 10
AS SURELY AS IT KEEPS THE STROKE AND TIME . . . . . 362 IN A POEM 3
IT IS AS TRUE AS CAESAR'S NAME WAS KAISER . . . . . 363 AN EQUALIZER 1
AS TOUCHING AS A BASKETFUL OF EGGS, ... 365 OF STONES OF THE PLACE 2
AS FINE AS FLOUR PUT THROUGH A BAKER'S SIEVE. . . . . 365 OF STONES OF THE PLACE 8
AS ONE HAVING WAR-COMMAND. . . . . 366 NOT OF SCHOOL AGE . . 12
SO SMALL AS TO BE VIRTUALLY GONE, ... 368 THE LITERATE FARMER AND 15
WHAT'S A STAR DOING BIG AS A BASEBALL? . . . . . . 369 THE LITERATE FARMER AND 37
"AS LIBERALS WE'RE WILLING TO GIVE PLACE . . . . . . 369 THE LITERATE FARMER AND 49
SO FAR AS HE, THE SPEAKER, WAS CONCERNED . . . . . . 370 THE LITERATE FARMER AND 57
BUT COME, ENLIGHTENED AS IN TALK YOU SEEM, ... 370 THE LITERATE FARMER AND 61
AS I SUSPECT YOU HAVE. A TOWN DEBARS . . . . 370 THE LITERATE FARMER AND 69
SOME IGNORANCE TAKES RANK AS INNOCENCE. . . . . . . 371 THE LITERATE FARMER AND 88
AS WHOSOEVER LIKES THE YOUNG AND SLIGHT . . . . . . 375 A YOUNG BIRCH . . . 3
TO LIVE ITS LIFE OUT AS AN ORNAMENT. . . . . 375 A YOUNG BIRCH . . . 22
MAY SEEM AS IF IT SHOULD HAVE BEEN A QUARRY-- . . . . 377 DIRECTIVE 10
AS IF BY EYE PAIRS OUT OF FORTY FIRKINS. . . . . . 378 DIRECTIVE 22
AS FOR THE WOODS' EXCITEMENT OVER YOU . . . . 378 DIRECTIVE 23
COLD AS A SPRING AS YET SO NEAR ITS SOURCE, ... 378 DIRECTIVE 51
SO CAN'T GET SAVED, AS SAINT MARK SAYS THEY MUSTN'T. . . 379 DIRECTIVE 59
AS SOONER OR LATER WE HAVE TO CEASE SOMEWHERE. . . . . 379 TOO ANXIOUS FOR RIVERS 10
THE WORLD AS WE KNOW IS AN ELEPHANT'S HOWDAH; . . . . 379 TOO ANXIOUS FOR RIVERS 14
AND AS I WOKE AFRAID TO TURN . . . . 380 AN UNSTAMPED LETTER IN 21
OR SO MUCH AS UNCROSS MY FEET, ... 381 AN UNSTAMPED LETTER IN 22

	PAGE	TITLE	LINE
AS (CONTINUED)			
TO SAY AS MUCH I WRITE YOU THIS.	381	AN UNSTAMPED LETTER IN	52
SEEMS AS EXPRESSIVE OF THE HUMAN RACE	382	TO AN ANCIENT	8
AS MEETING SOMEONE LIVING, FACE TO FACE.	382	TO AN ANCIENT	9
WHO HAVE, AS I SUPPOSE, AHEAD	383	THE NIGHT LIGHT	7
THAN AS WATCHER OF THE VOID,	383	MAKING CERTAIN ANYTHING	2
AS ONE RANKLY WARM INSIDER	384	IN THE LONG NIGHT	13
AS A GIRL NO ONE GALLANTLY ATTENDS	386	THE FEAR OF MAN	1
AS IN THOSE BUOYANT BIRD BONES THIN AS PAPER,	387	INNATE HELIUM	4
THEY WILL TELL YOU MORE AS SOON AS	387	THE COURAGE TO BE NEW	13
SO SMALL AM I AS AN ATTENTION BEGGAR.	388	IOTA SUBSCRIPT	5
AS LONG THE TREES HAVE STOOD.	388	MIDDLENESS OF THE ROAD	7
AS A MATTER OF FACT THERE ARE TIMES WHEN I AM APT	389	SKEPTIC	10
AS SHEBA CAME TO SOLOMON.	390	TWO LEADING LIGHTS	21
AND SEE AS I'M BID.	392	A WISH TO COMPLY	8
AND LONG ENOUGH GETS RATED AS A CREED:	394	ETHEREALIZING	2
SUCH AS THAT FLESH IS SOMETHING WE CAN SLOUGH	395	ETHEREALIZING	3
THERE ONCE WE LAY AS BLOBS OF JELLYFISH	395	ETHEREALIZING	9
BUT NOW AS BLOBS OF BRAIN WE'LL LIE AND DREAM,	395	ETHEREALIZING	11
AS FIFTY MILLION YEARS AGO WE CAME--	395	WHY WAIT FOR SCIENCE	12
AND AS PICTURESQUE MACHINERY	397	AN IMPORTER	21
BUT NOW 'TWAS THERE AS ELSEWHERE, ANY GAIN.	398	BURSTING RAPTURE	4
IT SEEMED AS IF I COULDN'T STAND THE STRAIN.	398	BURSTING RAPTURE	8
HE DID AS SHAKESPEARE SAYS, YOU MAY RECALL,	400	THE BROKEN DROUGHT	7
BE UNINHABITABLE AS THE MOON.	400	THE BROKEN DROUGHT	12
AS MUCH AS ANYTHING FOR SITUATION.	400	TO THE RIGHT PERSON	3
AS IF TO SAY MERE LEARNING WAS THE DEVIL	400	TO THE RIGHT PERSON	10
UPON ITS DOORSTEPS AS AT MERCY'S FEET	400	TO THE RIGHT PERSON	13
AND STEADFAST AS KEATS' EREMITE,	403	SOMETHING LIKE A STAR	18
HAVE STAYED IN SIGHT SO LONG AS AN EXAMPLE.	404	FROM PLANE TO PLANE	23
"--TAKING HIS OWN SWEET TIME AS IF TO SHOW	404	FROM PLANE TO PLANE	24
THE MORAL KIND'S AS BRAVE AS FACING BULLETS."	405	FROM PLANE TO PLANE	35
AS A SMALL SELF-CONFERRED REWARD OF VIRTUE.	405	FROM PLANE TO PLANE	39
KNOWN AS BOUSTROPHEDON, WAS FOUND TOO AWKWARD."	405	FROM PLANE TO PLANE	54
AS IF HE DIDN'T CARE WHO UNDERSTOOD HIM,	405	FROM PLANE TO PLANE	59
YOU'VE GOT NO SOCIAL CONSCIENCE, AS THEY SAY,	406	FROM PLANE TO PLANE	77
THE SAME AS YOUR IDEA, ONLY MORE SO.	406	FROM PLANE TO PLANE	81
MAY AS EXPECTED WAS A DISAPPOINTMENT,	406	FROM PLANE TO PLANE	88
AND AVOID BEING WORSHIPED AS A GOD.	408	FROM PLANE TO PLANE	131
THE THANKS AND LET HIM CATCH IT AS A SCAPEGOAT.	408	FROM PLANE TO PLANE	140
AS IT HAS NEVER BEEN TO ME BEFORE.	411	POD OF THE MILKWEED	7
AS ANYONE WHO EVER BROKE ITS STEM	411	POD OF THE MILKWEED	17
IT TASTES AS IF IT MIGHT BE OPIATE.	411	POD OF THE MILKWEED	19
MANY SHALL COME AWAY AS STRUGGLE-WORN	412	POD OF THE MILKWEED	34
AS AFTER ONE-OF-THEM'S PROVERBIAL FAILURE	412	POD OF THE MILKWEED	37
WAS LEAVE AS THEIR POSTERITY ONE POD	412	POD OF THE MILKWEED	43
AS ANY GUATEMALAN PARAKEET.	412	POD OF THE MILKWEED	47
MUCH AS I OWN I OWE	415	CLOSED FOR GOOD	1
TO COME AS A FOOT PRINTER,	416	CLOSED FOR GOOD	27
STILL PRINT THERE AS MY PROXY.	416	CLOSED FOR GOOD	30
AS A GOD WHO HAD GIVEN US	417	AMERICA IS HARD TO SEE	35
A HOLIDAY) AS, WHERE HE IS,	418	AMERICA IS HARD TO SEE	47
HIS EYES AS GOOD (OR BAD) AS SHUT	418	AMERICA IS HARD TO SEE	58
COLUMBUS, AS I SAY, WILL MISS	418	AMERICA IS HARD TO SEE	67
EXCEPT AS IT DENIED HIM WAY	419	AMERICA IS HARD TO SEE	77
AS CORTEZ ON THE AZTECS MADE.	419	AMERICA IS HARD TO SEE	84
BUT NEVER SO MUCH AS LIFTED CHIN.	420	ONE MORE BREVITY	22
AS IF BESEECHING ME, "PLEASE, NO MORE;	420	ONE MORE BREVITY	24
AS LONG AS THE GREAT ISSUE WAS TO SEE	422	FOR JOHN F. KENNEDY	12
GOD NODDED HIS APPROVAL OF AS GOOD.	422	FOR JOHN F. KENNEDY	23
SO MUCH THEY KNEW AS CONSECRATED SEERS	422	FOR JOHN F. KENNEDY	27
SUCH AS WE WERE WE GAVE OURSELVES OUTRIGHT	424	THE GIFT OUTRIGHT	12
SUCH AS SHE WAS, SUCH AS SHE WOULD BECOME.	425	THE GIFT OUTRIGHT	16
TO PRODUCE PURPOSE AS THE FITTER BRED:	425	ACCIDENTALLY ON PURPOSE	15
PASSIONATE PREFERENCE SUCH AS LOVE AT SIGHT.	425	ACCIDENTALLY ON PURPOSE	24
AS TO BLIND OUR EYES	426	A NEVER NAUGHT SONG	23
AS A YOUNG ALASTOR	430	KITTY HAWK	53
AND AS FOR MY JEST	430	KITTY HAWK	80
AS SO OFTEN, ENDED	431	KITTY HAWK	96
WHO AS OF A SECT	432	KITTY HAWK	142
AS THE POET SAID	433	KITTY HAWK	168
AS A FIGURE OF SPEECH	434	KITTY HAWK	186
AS A DEMONSTRATION	435	KITTY HAWK	221
AS IT WERE FROM SCRATCH,	436	KITTY HAWK	259
AS HAVE I NOT WRITTEN,	437	KITTY HAWK	292
WE'D HAVE GOT AS FAR	439	KITTY HAWK	348
PROVE AS VAIN A HOP	439	KITTY HAWK	358
AS THE HOP FROM GRASS	439	KITTY HAWK	359
MADE IT, AS IT WERE,	439	KITTY HAWK	364
AS A FACT OF WASTE	439	KITTY HAWK	371
AS THE CAPITAL	440	KITTY HAWK	376
AS TOO NEW TO MENTION.	440	KITTY HAWK	383
(SO AS NOT TO SINK),	440	KITTY HAWK	399
AS ONE WHO WOULD NOT MAKE A GANYMEDE.	443	AUSPEX	8
OH, SOME AS SOON WOULD THROW IT ALL	445	ENDS	9
AS THROW A PART AWAY.	445	ENDS	10
IS AS EASILY READ	447	THE BAD ISLAND--EASTER	4
AS A CLINICAL CHART.	447	THE BAD ISLAND--EASTER	6
OF THEMSELVES AS A RACE	448	THE BAD ISLAND--EASTER	22
AS A VILE RESIDUE,	449	THE BAD ISLAND--EASTER	44
EXCEPT AS A GAIN.	449	THE BAD ISLAND--EASTER	53
AS A CONFIRMED ASTRONOMER	451	A-WISHING WELL	12
AND FILL THE SKY AS FULL OF MOONS	451	A-WISHING WELL	17
AS CIRCUS DAY OF TOY BALLOONS	451	A-WISHING WELL	18
IT COST THE EARTH AS FIERCE A PANG	452	A-WISHING WELL	40
AS KEATS (OR WAS IT MILTON?) SANG	452	A-WISHING WELL	41
THE KINGDOM'S YOURS TO FINISH AS YOU PLEASE.	453	HOW HARD TO KEEP FROM	2
AS COMING FROM A LESSER OCEAN.	453	A-WISHING WELL	68

	PAGE	TITLE	LINE

AS (CONTINUED)
```
THE KING SAID GRANDLY, "EVEN AS WE ARE FED  . . .  . . .  455  HOW HARD TO KEEP FROM    63
SHUFFLED THEIR FEET AS IF TO HINT RESPECTFULLY,  . . . .  456  HOW HARD TO KEEP FROM    73
BUT BETWEEN PEACE AND WAR AS WE CONCEIVE IT.  . . . .  456  HOW HARD TO KEEP FROM    75
AS WELL AS OF YOUR HUNDRED OTHER THINGS. . . . . . .  456  HOW HARD TO KEEP FROM    99
I'LL BET YOU ANYTHING THAT'S ALL AS KING  . . . . . .  458  HOW HARD TO KEEP FROM   137
"MAKE THEM AS HAPPY AS IS GOOD FOR THEM. . . . . . .  458  HOW HARD TO KEEP FROM   150
I LOOKED ON IT AS A CARNEGIE GRANT. . . . . . . . .  459  HOW HARD TO KEEP FROM   174
HIS NAME IS OMAR. I AS A RHODES SCHOLAR  . . . . . .  459  HOW HARD TO KEEP FROM   188
AS FLY THE ATOMIC SMITHEREENS TO NOTHING.  . . . . .  460  HOW HARD TO KEEP FROM   197
I WRITE REAL VERSE IN NUMBERS, AS THEY SAY.  . . . .  460  HOW HARD TO KEEP FROM   211
BUT THAT IS AS DARIUS SEEMS TO WANT IT.  . . . . . .  462  HOW HARD TO KEEP FROM   264
(AS I REMEMBER THEY WERE SUMMER STARS .  . . . . . .  462  HOW HARD TO KEEP FROM   269
THAT WAS HEARD AS FAR AWAY AS NEW YORK  . . . . . .  463  LINES IN DEJECTION . .    23
REPLIED SHE HAD AS SOON  . . . . . . . . . . . . .  464  MILKY WAY IS A COWPATH    18
AS ANY MIGHT OBSERVE, . . . . . . . . . . . . . .  464  MILKY WAY IS A COWPATH    23
PERENNIAL AS FLOWERS,  . . . . . . . . . . . . . .  465  MILKY WAY IS A COWPATH    33
TO WHERE AS SOME ALLEGE  . . . . . . . . . . . . .  465  MILKY WAY IS A COWPATH    34
THOUGH AS YET THEY ONLY SMILE  . . . . . . . . . .  465  SOME SCIENCE FICTION .     9
FOR ME AS AN OLD SLOW COACH. . . . . . . . . . . .  466  SOME SCIENCE FICTION .    12
AS THEY GET MORE NUCLEAR  . . . . . . . . . . . . .  466  SOME SCIENCE FICTION .    14
AS A NOBLE EXPERIMENT. . . . . . . . . . . . . . .  466  SOME SCIENCE FICTION .    28
THAT THERE WAS SUCH A THING AS BAD.  . . . . . . . .  467  QUANDARY . . . . .     2
LOVE THOU THY NEIGHBOR AS THYSELF, AYE, . . . . . .  467  QUANDARY . . . . .    12
AND HATE HIM AS THYSELF THOU HATEST. . . . . . . .  467  QUANDARY . . . . .    13
AS WALLER SAYS. / OR NOT ADMIRED. GO OVER  . . . . .  474  A MASQUE OF REASON .    31
WHO COULD DO GOOD OR EVIL AS HE CHOSE. . . . . . .  475  A MASQUE OF REASON .    72
AND AS SUCH I PROMOTE YOU TO A SAINT. . . . . . . .  476  A MASQUE OF REASON . -   79
THAT WOMEN PROPHETS SHOULD BE BURNED AS WITCHES,  . .  476  A MASQUE OF REASON .    89
WE MAY AS WELL GO BACK TO THE BEGINNING  . . . . . .  477  A MASQUE OF REASON .   113
IN SOME WAY NOT SO PENAL AS THE POORHOUSE. . . . . .  478  A MASQUE OF REASON .   125
DON'T SCRATCH! AND WHEN, AS ROTTEN AS HIS SKIN,  . .  478  A MASQUE OF REASON .   130
AS WELL AS WORDS. / I'M SERIOUS. GOD'S HAD  . . . .  478  A MASQUE OF REASON .   148
GOD NEEDS TIME JUST AS MUCH AS YOU OR I  . . . . . .  478  A MASQUE OF REASON .   151
AS TO WHAT REASONS I AGREE TO WAIVE. . . . . . . .  479  A MASQUE OF REASON .   167
KIPLING INVOKES YOU AS LORD GOD OF HOSTS.  . . . . .  479  A MASQUE OF REASON .   179
IS JUST AS GOOD AS WHEN I UTTERED IT. . . . . . . .  480  A MASQUE OF REASON .   196
AS FOR THE EARTH, WE GROPED THAT OUT TOGETHER,  . . .  481  A MASQUE OF REASON .   207
MUCH AS YOUR HUSBAND, JOB, AND I TOGETHER  . . . . .  481  A MASQUE OF REASON .   208
AND THAT FOR MAN'S OWN SAKE AS WELL AS MINE, . . . .  481  A MASQUE OF REASON .   211
THERE'S WILL AS MOTOR AND THERE'S WILL AS BRAKES.  . .  481  A MASQUE OF REASON .   230
THE WILL AS BRAKES CAN'T STOP THE WILL AS MOTOR  . .  481  A MASQUE OF REASON .   232
WE'RE GOING ANYWAY AND MAY AS WELL . . . . . . . .  482  A MASQUE OF REASON .   234
HAVE SOME SAY AS TO WHERE WE'RE HEADED FOR;  . . . .  482  A MASQUE OF REASON .   235
JUST AS WE WILL BE TALKING ANYWAY  . . . . . . . .  482  A MASQUE OF REASON .   236
AND MAY AS WELL THROW IN A LITTLE SENSE. . . . . .  482  A MASQUE OF REASON .   237
IT SOUNDS TO ME AS IF YOU THOUGHT IT OUT,  . . . . .  482  A MASQUE OF REASON .   244
I DID NOT ASK THEN, BUT IT SEEMS AS IF  . . . . . .  482  A MASQUE OF REASON .   266
FOR INSTANCE, IS THERE SUCH A THING AS PROGRESS?  . .  484  A MASQUE OF REASON .   315
JOB SAYS THERE'S NO SUCH THING AS EARTH'S BECOMING  .  484  A MASQUE OF REASON .   316
EXCEPT AS A HARD PLACE TO SAVE HIS SOUL IN,  . . . .  484  A MASQUE OF REASON .   318
IT WOULD BE MEANINGLESS. IT MIGHT AS WELL  . . . . .  484  A MASQUE OF REASON .   321
AS IS SET FORTH IN CHAPTERS ONE AND TWO. . . . . .  485  A MASQUE OF REASON .   328
BUT I DON'T MIND. LET'S LEAVE IT AS IT STOOD.  . . .  485  A MASQUE OF REASON .   334
JUST AS IF NOTHING MATTERED BUT OUR MANNERS. . . . .  488  A MASQUE OF REASON .   410
YOU LOOK AS IF YOU EITHER HOPED OR FEARED  . . . . .  488  A MASQUE OF REASON .   411
AS DULCET AS A PAGAN TEMPLE GONG!  . . . . . . . .  488  A MASQUE OF REASON .   419
IN THREE QUICK STEPS AS OFF AN ESCALATOR  . . . . .  489  A MASQUE OF REASON .   452
YOU'D AS WELL SMILE AS FROWN ON THE OCCASION. . . . .  490  A MASQUE OF REASON .   465
IT MAKES HER MOVE AS IF TO REINFORCE IT. . . . . .  493  A MASQUE OF MERCY .     7
WHICH IS THE SAME AS SAYING JONAH, JONAH--  . . . .  495  A MASQUE OF MERCY .    56
THE COUNTRY'S ONLY USEFUL AS A PLACE . . . . . . .  496  A MASQUE OF MERCY .    73
YES, BUT NEW YORK WILL DO AS AN EXAMPLE. . . . . .  496  A MASQUE OF MERCY .    91
WELL, YOU'RE AS GOOD AS IN NEW YORK THIS MINUTE--  . .  497  A MASQUE OF MERCY .    92
OR BAD AS IN NEW YORK. / I KNOW I AM.  . . . . . .  497  A MASQUE OF MERCY .    93
EXCEPT AS FATHER PUTATIVE TO SORT OF . . . . . . .  498  A MASQUE OF MERCY .   123
ESCAPIST, AS WE SAY--THOUGH YOU ARE NOT  . . . . .  498  A MASQUE OF MERCY .   138
OF THERAPY. / I DON'T LOVE PAUL--AS YET. . . . . .  499  A MASQUE OF MERCY .   163
OR, AS YOU MIGHT SAY, THROW ME TO THE WHALE--  . . .  500  A MASQUE OF MERCY .   183
I AM SICK, AS SHE SAYS. NOTHING EXHAUSTS ME . . . .  501  A MASQUE OF MERCY .   197
IS THROWN IN SCRIPT, AS AT BELSHAZZAR'S FEAST,  . . .  502  A MASQUE OF MERCY .   238
AS IN A SMUGGLER'S AT THE DIAMOND FIELDS,  . . . . .  503  A MASQUE OF MERCY .   253
A MISSION AS TO HAVE TO TELL NEW YORK . . . . . .  503  A MASQUE OF MERCY .   272
MY TONGUE'S MY OWN, AS TRUE THOMAS USED TO SAY.  . .  505  A MASQUE OF MERCY .   296
AS RED CROSS AMBULANCE COMMANDER-IN-CHIEF  . . . .  507  A MASQUE OF MERCY .   369
I THOUGHT AS MUCH. YOU HAVE IT ALL ARRANGED. . . .  508  A MASQUE OF MERCY .   372
THERE IS SOME JUSTICE, EVEN AS KEEPER SAYS. . . . .  509  A MASQUE OF MERCY .   429
I CHOOSE THE STAR-CROSSED AS A STAR-CROSSED LOVER.  . .  510  A MASQUE OF MERCY .   441
WHO IN HIS FAVORITE POSE AS POET-THINKER  . . . . .  511  A MASQUE OF MERCY .   463
THAT MADE ALL OTHER OUTRAGE SEEM AS CHILD'S PLAY:  . .  511  A MASQUE OF MERCY .   476
YES, CALL ME PAGAN, PAUL, AS IF YOU MEANT IT.  . . .  513  A MASQUE OF MERCY .   524
BUT WHEN THE BRINE GOES BACK, AS GO IT MUST,  . . . .  513  A MASQUE OF MERCY .   540
SO AS TO JUSTIFY THE ORTHODOX  . . . . . . . . . .  515  A MASQUE OF MERCY .   571
AND BED OF WORLD-FLOWERS SO AS NOT TO BLIND ME.  . .  515  A MASQUE OF MERCY .   582
THESE TWO ARE STUBBORN CHILDREN, AS YOU SEE. . . . .  517  A MASQUE OF MERCY .   619
DOES IT TO YOU AS GREATLY AS IT DID? . . . . . . .  517  A MASQUE OF MERCY .   624
THE SAME WITH GOD AS LOSING, HOW EXPLAIN  . . . . .  517  A MASQUE OF MERCY .   634
AS ONCE THE PHARAOH DID IT OUT OF SEKHTI  . . . . .  517  A MASQUE OF MERCY .   641
(JONAH STEPS ON THE THRESHOLD AS THE DOOR  . . . . .  518  A MASQUE OF MERCY .   649
AS IF TO COME, BUT KEEPER WAVES HER OFF.)  . . . . .  518  A MASQUE OF MERCY .   653
AS IF I ASKED FOR ONE MORE CHANCE MYSELF . . . . .  521  A MASQUE OF MERCY .   736
```
ASCENDING
```
ASCENDING TO DESCEND TO REASCEND.  . . . . . . . .  214  A FOUNTAIN, A BOTTLE .    34
```
ASCENT
```
SO I COULD CATCH A BUBBLE IN ASCENT. . . . . . . .  468  IN A GLASS OF CIDER  .     3
```
ASCRIBE
```
WILL HE ASCRIBE THIS LUCKY BREAK. . . . . . . . .  418  AMERICA IS HARD TO SEE    72
AND THE LEAST DISPOSED TO ASCRIBE  . . . . . . . .  444  THE DRAFT HORSE . . .    15
```

ASH
  WHERE UNDER DEEP ASH AND CHARCOAL . . . . 312 THE VINDICTIVES . . . 58
ASHAMED
  HE WON'T BE MADE ASHAMED TO PLEASE HIS BROTHER." . . . . 39 DEATH OF THE HIRED MAN 145
  TO IMPRESS MEN. YOU'VE GOT US SO ASHAMED . . . . . . 146 SNOW 99
  WAS SOMEONE WHO HAD JUST COME BACK ASHAMED . . . . . 160 NEW HAMPSHIRE . . . 37
  PAUL WAS ASHAMED OF HER. TO MATCH A HERO . . . . . . 192 PAUL'S WIFE 37
  SHE WASN'T ANYTHING TO BE ASHAMED OF. . . . . 192 PAUL'S WIFE 41
  AND NOT TO ANYONE TO BE ASHAMED OF. . . . . 195 PAUL'S WIFE 146
ASHES
  IT NEVER REACHES EARTH EXCEPT AS ASHES . . . . 361 A LOOSE MOUNTAIN . . 10
ASHORE
  THE WATER COMES ASHORE, ... 301 NEITHER OUT FAR NOR IN 11
ASIA
  WHERE ASIA WEDGES AFRICA FROM EUROPE. . . . . 176 THE CENSUS-TAKER . . 53
  MRS. SOMEONE'S BEEN TO ASIA. . . . . 396 AN IMPORTER 1
  YOU COULD LOSE ASIA, AFRICA, AND EUROPE, ... 457 HOW HARD TO KEEP FROM 128
  A DARKNESS OUT OF ASIA THAT HAD CROSSED . . . . 511 A MASQUE OF MERCY . . 466
ASIAN
  OF THE TRUTHS WE OWE AN ASIAN? . . . . 397 AN IMPORTER 16
ASIANS
  TEACH THOSE ASIANS MASS PRODUCTION? . . . . 397 AN IMPORTER 25
ASIATIC
  HE'LL FIND THAT ASIATIC STATE . . . . 419 AMERICA IS HARD TO SEE 80
  TO LEAD HIM OFF THE ASIATIC WAY . . . . 462 HOW HARD TO KEEP FROM 262
  NO FATHOMING THE ASIATIC MIND. . . . . 462 HOW HARD TO KEEP FROM 265
ASIDE
  BUT THE FLOWER LEANED ASIDE . . . . 11 WIND AND WINDOW FLOWER 25
  OR PUT THE LEAVES ASIDE THAT FRAMED IT IN. . . . . . 55 THE BLACK COTTAGE . . 10
  OR IF EVER ASIDE A MOMENT, THEN OUT OF SORTS . . . . . 286 A ROADSIDE STAND . . 8
  I ONLY KNELT AND PUTTING THE BOUGHS ASIDE . . . . . . 343 QUEST OF PURPLE-FRINGED 21
  HAVE SET THE DARK ASIDE FOR HERS. . . . . 390 TWO LEADING LIGHTS . . 15
  I TRUST IT IS. HERE'S WHERE I LAY ASIDE . . . . 474 A MASQUE OF REASON . . 27
ASIDES
  MADE QUICK ASIDES, BUT HAVING DONE IN AIR . . . . . . 240 OUR SINGING STRENGTH . 40
ASK
  YOU HAVE ONLY TO ASK ME, AND I CAN TELL. . . . . . . 16 IN A VALE 23
  BEFORE I BUILT A WALL I'D ASK TO KNOW . . . . 34 MENDING WALL 32
  THAT I HAD ON MY MIND TO ASK THE FIRST . . . . 46 A HUNDRED COLLARS . . 46
  I'LL ASK YOU LATER--DON'T LET ME FORGET IT." . . . . . 46 A HUNDRED COLLARS . . 48
  BUT FIRST--LET'S SEE--WHAT WAS I GOING TO ASK YOU? . . . 50 A HUNDRED COLLARS . . 162
  "THERE'S SOMETHING I SHOULD LIKE TO ASK YOU, DEAR." . . . 52 HOME BURIAL 42
  "YOU DON'T KNOW HOW TO ASK IT." / "HELP ME, THEN." . . . 52 HOME BURIAL 43
  NOT THAT SHE EVER HAD TO ASK ME NOT TO; . . . . 57 THE BLACK COTTAGE . . 89
  TO ASK IF HE KNEW ANY FRUIT TO BE HAD . . . . 61 BLUEBERRIES 70
  AND I WON'T ASK HIM--IT'S NOT SURE ENOUGH. . . . . . 67 A SERVANT TO SERVANTS 158
  "OH, IF YOU ASK ME THAT, WHAT WILL HE DO? . . . . . . 82 THE HOUSEKEEPER . . . 30
  THIS IS A GOOD HOME: I DON'T ASK FOR BETTER. . . . . . 84 THE HOUSEKEEPER . . . 89
  YOU ASK THIS LAWYER MAN. AND IT'S NOT SAFE . . . . . . 97 THE SELF-SEEKER . . . 133
  A-BUTTONING COATS, TO ASK HIM WHO HE WAS. . . . . . . 106 CHRISTMAS TREES . . . 8
  MADE ME ASK WOULD THE MOTHER-BIRD RETURN . . . . . . 109 THE EXPOSED NEST . . 23
  IN COMMON LAW, I WONDER." / "BUT I ASK, ... 111 IN THE HOME STRETCH . 24
  ASK THEM TO HELP YOU GET IT ON ITS FEET. . . . . . . 113 IN THE HOME STRETCH . 76
  "MA FRIEND, YOU AIN'T KNOW WHAT IT IS YOU'RE ASK." . . . 114 IN THE HOME STRETCH . 105
  CALL YOU TO ASK YOU TO INVITE ME HOME.--" . . . . . . 143 SNOW 27
  ASK HELEN HOW FAR UP THE SASH IT'S CLIMBED . . . . . . 148 SNOW 158
  ASK ANY MAN." / HE THREW HER THAT AS SOMETHING . . . . 151 SNOW 242
  YOU LET ME THERE. I'LL ASK HER WHY SHE LET HIM. . . . . 153 SNOW 292
  PITY HE DIDN'T ASK WHAT THEY WERE UP TO . . . . 161 NEW HAMPSHIRE . . . 83
  YET ASK WHERE ELSE IT COULD HAVE GONE AS WELL, ... 173 A STAR IN A STONEBOAT . 37
  HAS A MAN, I SHOULD LIKE TO ASK, NO RIGHTS . . . . . . 176 THE STAR-SPLITTER . . 11
  BUT WHAT WE MISS WE GO TO HIM AND ASK FOR. . . . . . 178 THE STAR-SPLITTER . . 50
  YOU ASK HER IF SHE KNOWS A MAPLE TREE. . . . . 180 MAPLE 8
  NOT FOR ME TO ASK WHICH, WHEN WHAT HE TOOK . . . . . . 187 THE AX-HELVE 66
  THEY SEEMED TO ASK HIM JUST TO SEE HIM GO, ... 191 PAUL'S WIFE 23
  (YOU'LL HAVE TO ASK AN EVOLUTIONIST)-- . . . . 197 WILD GRAPES 53
  THE DEAD WAS BOUND TO SILENCE: ASK THE SISTER. . . . . 200 PLACE FOR A THIRD . . 43
  DON'T ASK JOE . . . . 212 AN EMPTY THREAT . . . 38
  "EXCUSE ME IF I ASK YOU IN A WINDOW . . . . 215 A FOUNTAIN, A BOTTLE . 72
  TO ASK IF THERE IS SOME MISTAKE. . . . . 224 STOPPING BY WOODS . . 10
  "THIS, THEN, IS ALL. WHAT MORE IS THERE TO ASK?" . . . . 229 TWO LOOK AT TWO . . . 25
  AS IF TO ASK, "WHY DON'T YOU MAKE SOME MOTION? . . . . 230 TWO LOOK AT TWO . . . 32
  HIS HANDS? SHE HAD TO LOOK, TO LOOK AND ASK, ... 230 NOT TO KEEP 8
  SHE HAD TO ASK, "WHAT WAS IT, DEAR?" / "ENOUGH, ... 230 NOT TO KEEP 13
  I ASK AS ONE WHO KNEW THE BROOK, ITS STRENGTH . . . . 231 A BROOK IN THE CITY . 5
  SHE DARED NO MORE THAN ASK HIM WITH HER EYES . . . . . 231 NOT TO KEEP 19
  AND WITH HIS EYES HE ASKED HER NOT TO ASK. . . . . . 231 NOT TO KEEP 21
  BUT JUST TO ASK US WHO WE THINK WE ARE . . . . 238 ON A TREE FALLEN ACROSS 4
  THAT ALL THEY ASK IS ROUGHER WEATHER. . . . . 262 THE FLOWER BOAT . . . 10
  BY COMING WITH WHAT THEY CAME TO ASK. . . . . 276 TWO TRAMPS IN MUD TIME 43
  AND ASK FOR SOME CITY MONEY TO FEEL IN HAND . . . . . 286 A ROADSIDE STAND . . 19
  AND ANOTHER TO ASK THE WAY TO WHERE IT WAS BOUND; . . . 287 A ROADSIDE STAND . . 41
  AND ANOTHER TO ASK COULD THEY SELL IT A GALLON OF GAS . . 287 A ROADSIDE STAND . . 42
  TO ASK ME A THING OR TWO . . . . 294 A RECORD STRIDE . . . 10
  AND I ASK ALL TO TRY TO FORGIVE ME . . . . 295 A RECORD STRIDE . . . 33
  WHERE WE STILL LOOK TO ASK THE WHY . . . . 303 AFTERFLAKES 4
  NEVER ASK OF MONEY SPENT . . . . 309 HARDSHIP OF ACCOUNTING 1
  PERSONIFIED, BUT ASK TO BE EXCUSED . . . . 317 BUILD SOIL 51
  TO ASK ME IF I THINK IT WORTH THE PAINS . . . . 324 BUILD SOIL 271
  (ASK ANY REPUTABLE ROSICRUCIAN) . . . . 363 A SEMI-REVOLUTION . . 3
  AND ASK US IF OUR PREMISES ARE RIGHT." . . . . 370 THE LITERATE FARMER AND 83
  YOU MAKE ME ASK IF I WOULD GO TO TIME . . . . 382 TO AN ANCIENT . . . 16
  AND ANYONE MIGHT ASK THEM WHO WERE THEY. . . . . . . 397 THE PLANNERS 9
  LET'S HOLLER AND ASK HIM IF HE WON'T PRESCRIBE . . . . 405 FROM PLANE TO PLANE . 29
  WHY DON'T THEY ASK THE RED MAN WHERE THEY ARE? . . . . 414 A CABIN IN THE CLEARING 21
  SO DO THEY ALSO ASK PHILOSOPHERS . . . . 414 A CABIN IN THE CLEARING 23
  THEY WILL ASK ANYONE THERE IS TO ASK-- . . . . 414 A CABIN IN THE CLEARING 25
  (NEED A BODY ASK . . . . 431 KITTY HAWK 106

ASK (CONTINUED)
I ASK OF YOU. GRIND THIS I THROW YOU BACK . . . . . . 447 DOES NO ONE AT ALL EVER 29
WHEN CLEVER PEOPLE ASK ME WHERE . . . . 452 A-WISHING WELL . . . 32
"YOU DIE FOR THAT." / "NO, YOU GO ASK YOUR MOTHER." . . 457 HOW HARD TO KEEP FROM 104
I WANT TO ASK YOU IF IT STANDS TO REASON. . . . . . . 476 A MASQUE OF REASON . 88
WHEN REASON-HUNGRY MORTALS ASK FOR REASONS. . . . . . 478 A MASQUE OF REASON . 136
I HAVE A QUESTION EVEN THERE TO ASK-- . . . . 479 A MASQUE OF REASON . 171
TO ASK MY QUESTION. WE DISPARAGE REASON. . . . . . . 481 A MASQUE OF REASON . 228
I DID NOT ASK THEN, BUT IT SEEMS AS IF . . . . 482 A MASQUE OF REASON . 266
I ASK YOU ALL TO READ IT ONCE AGAIN. . . . . 511 A MASQUE OF MERCY . 488
YOU ASK IF I SEE YONDER SHINING GATE, ... 513 A MASQUE OF MERCY . 530
ASKED
HE ASKED WITH THE EYES MORE THAN THE LIPS . . . . . .   7 LOVE AND A QUESTION .   5
BUT WHETHER OR NOT A MAN WAS ASKED . . . .   8 LOVE AND A QUESTION . 29
HE ASKED ME WHAT I THOUGHT OF HAROLD'S SAYING . . . . 37 DEATH OF THE HIRED MAN 79
"WHAT TOWN IS THIS?" I ASKED. / "THIS? LUNENBURG." . . 41 THE MOUNTAIN 19
ONE TIME I ASKED A FELLOW CLIMBING IT . . . . 43 THE MOUNTAIN 73
I ASKED OUT LOUD, SO'S THERE'D BE NO MISTAKE, ... 71 THE CODE 65
AND SORT OF WAITING TO BE ASKED ABOUT IT, ... 72 THE CODE 82
HE ASKED IF I WOULD SELL MY CHRISTMAS TREES; . . . . 106 CHRISTMAS TREES . . 12
AND, IF YOU ASKED ME, EVEN HELP PRETEND . . . . . . 109 THE EXPOSED NEST . .   7
AND HE ASKED AT HER MOTHER'S HOUSE . . . . 129 THE IMPULSE 23
ONE DAY SHE ASKED HER FATHER . . . . 133 A GIRL'S GARDEN . .   5
ON MOTORCARS, I'M ASKED IF I . . . . 139 BROWN'S DESCENT . . 50
WHY DID YOU LET HIM GO?'" / "ASKED WHY WE LET HIM? . . 153 SNOW 291
GOOD! WHY I ASKED--SHE DIDN'T SEEM TO ANSWER.-- . . . 155 SNOW 330
I ASKED HIM, ON MY GUARD. "OH, YES," HE ANSWERED, . . 159 NEW HAMPSHIRE . . 13
UNTIL I ASKED FOR ONE TO STEADY HIM. . . . . 160 NEW HAMPSHIRE . . 32
WHAT GOLD MORE INNOCENT COULD ONE HAVE ASKED FOR? . . 162 NEW HAMPSHIRE . . 115
BUT WHEN I ASKED TO KNOW WHAT AILED NEW HAMPSHIRE, . . 166 NEW HAMPSHIRE . . 223
AND WHEN I ASKED TO KNOW WHAT AILED THE PEOPLE, . . . 166 NEW HAMPSHIRE . . 226
I ASKED HIM WELL BEFOREHAND. "DON'T YOU GET ONE!" . . 177 THE STAR-SPLITTER . 21
SHE ASKED HER FATHER AND HE TOLD HER, "MAPLE-- . . . 179 MAPLE   3
HER PROBLEM WAS TO FIND OUT WHAT IT ASKED . . . . . 181 MAPLE 52
"YOU'VE NEVER ASKED YOUR FATHER OUTRIGHT, HAVE YOU?" . 183 MAPLE 108
WHO ASKED THE QUESTION. HE JUST DISAPPEARED-- . . . . 192 PAUL'S WIFE . . . 26
OBJECT TO BEING ASKED A CIVIL QUESTION-- . . . . . . 192 PAUL'S WIFE . . . 32
HE SAID THE DEAD HAD SOULS, BUT WHEN I ASKED HIM . . 202 THE WITCH OF COOS . 14
THEN WE ASKED WAS THERE ANYTHING . . . . 206 THE WITCH OF COOS . 121
AND WITH HIS EYES HE ASKED HER NOT TO ASK. . . . . . 231 NOT TO KEEP . . 21
THE VOICE ASKED, "YOU CAN LET HER CHOOSE?" . . . . . 256 THE LOVELY BE CHOOSERS 19
I MEANT NOT EVEN IF ASKED, ... 334 COME IN 19
THE MOST HE ASKED HER EYES TO GRANT . . . . 344 DISCOVERY OF MADEIRAS 41
WE ASKED FOR RAIN. IT DIDN'T FLASH AND ROAR. . . . . 349 OUR HOLD ON THE PLANET   1
HE ASKED FOR A DRINK AT THE KITCHEN DOOR. . . . . . 364 TRESPASS 18
"TRAVELER, I'M GLAD YOU ASKED ABOUT THAT LIGHT. . . . 368 THE LITERATE FARMER AND 23
OR BE WIPED OUT. WILL SHE BE ASKED TO SHOW . . . . . 395 WHY WAIT FOR SCIENCE .   5
NOW ASKED ASYLUM--AND I WAS STIRRED . . . . 419 ONE MORE BREVITY . . 13
ASKED ABOUT MY SOUL . . . . 432 KITTY HAWK . . 143
TO THE FIRST BUYER COMING BY WHO ASKED . . . . 454 HOW HARD TO KEEP FROM 39
A SMALLER PEARL HE ASKED A THOUSAND FOR, ... 455 HOW HARD TO KEEP FROM 67
A LARGER ONE HE ASKED FIVE HUNDRED FOR. . . . . . . 455 HOW HARD TO KEEP FROM 68
YOU! WHO ARE YOU? I ASKED YOU ONCE BEFORE. . . . . . 499 A MASQUE OF MERCY . 150
HE'S MINE. THAT'S WHAT HE IS (YOU ASKED)--MY DOCTOR. . 499 A MASQUE OF MERCY . 154
SOMEONE ELSE READ IT. / NO. YOU ASKED FOR IT. . . . 506 A MASQUE OF MERCY . 329
MERCY ON HIM FOR HAVING ASKED FOR JUSTICE. . . . . . 518 A MASQUE OF MERCY . 662
AS IF I ASKED FOR ONE MORE CHANCE MYSELF . . . . . . 521 A MASQUE OF MERCY . 736
ASKING
I COULDN'T KEEP FROM ASKING IMPOLITELY, ... 160 NEW HAMPSHIRE . . 55
A MOMENT AND STILL ASKING GONE. . . . . 332 ALL REVELATION . .   9
OF ASKING ANY SYMPATHY OF HIM? . . . . 405 FROM PLANE TO PLANE . 32
THERE YOU GO ASKING FOR THE VERY THING . . . . 477 A MASQUE OF REASON . 105
TO ASKING FLATLY FOR THE REASON--OUTRIGHT. . . . . . 483 A MASQUE OF REASON . 269
ARE FREEDOMS FROM THE NEED OF ASKING QUESTIONS. . . . 484 A MASQUE OF REASON . 313
ASKS
EVERYONE ASKS FOR FREEDOM FOR HIMSELF, ... 319 BUILD SOIL . . . 111
IT ASKS A LITTLE OF US HERE. . . . . 403 SOMETHING LIKE A STAR . 20
IT ASKS OF US A CERTAIN HEIGHT, ... 403 SOMETHING LIKE A STAR . 21
ASKS OF HIMSELF ONCE IN SO OFTEN . . . . 453 A-WISHING WELL . . . 74
ASK'S
BUT ALL I ASK'S AN EXTRA ONE. . . . . 451 A-WISHING WELL . . 26
ASLEEP
THOSE OF US NOT ASLEEP SUBDUED TO MARK . . . . . . 10 STORM FEAR . . . 11
"HE'S WORN OUT. HE'S ASLEEP BESIDE THE STOVE. . . . . 35 DEATH OF THE HIRED MAN 33
HUDDLED AGAINST THE BARN DOOR FAST ASLEEP, ... 35 DEATH OF THE HIRED MAN 35
AND OF HER HALF ASLEEP, WAS TOO MUCH FOR ME. . . . . 58 THE BLACK COTTAGE . . 92
AND FALLS ASLEEP WITH HEARTACHE--HOW SHOULD I FEEL? . . 58 THE BLACK COTTAGE . . 103
WE MUST HAVE BEEN ASLEEP: IT'S THREE AND AFTER." . . 152 SNOW 274
I WAS ASLEEP STILL UNDER THE DRIPPING ROOF, ... 236 VALLEY'S SINGING DAY . 16
OUR ARM THROWN OVER IT ASLEEP BESIDE IT. . . . . . . 258 WEST-RUNNING BROOK . 15
YOU'RE NOT ASLEEP? / NO, I CAN HEAR YOU. WHY? . . . 473 A MASQUE OF REASON .   4
WE'VE WAKED HER UP. / I HAVEN'T BEEN ASLEEP. . . . . 487 A MASQUE OF REASON . 395
SHE ALWAYS CLAIMS SHE HASN'T BEEN ASLEEP.-- . . . . 487 A MASQUE OF REASON . 398
ASPASIA
PERICLES SENT ASPASIA IN ABSENTIA: . . . . 461 HOW HARD TO KEEP FROM 250
ASPERGIT
AND VER ASPERGIT TERRAM FLORIBUS . . . . 351 THE LESSON FOR TODAY . 15
ASPHODEL
WIDE FIELDS OF ASPHODEL FORE'ER, ... 19 THE TRIAL BY EXISTENCE   6
ASPIRING
FOUR-ROOM SHACK ASPIRING HIGH . . . . 469 FOUR-ROOM SHACK.... .   1
ASPREAD
AND HER WINGS STRAINING SUDDENLY ASPREAD . . . . . . 445 QUESTIONING FACES . .   3
ASSAULTER (SEE SUN-ASSAULTER)
ASSEMBLE
HAVE NEVER MADE THE FIRST MOVE TO ASSEMBLE, ... 291 ON HEART'S BEGINNING TO 30
ASSEMBLED
THE AUDIENCE ASSEMBLED. THERE I WAS . . . . 497 A MASQUE OF MERCY . . 96

ASSENTING
  TO WHICH YOU GIVE THE ASSENTING VOICE." . . . . 21 THE TRIAL BY EXISTENCE   56
ASSOCIATED
  HAROLD'S ASSOCIATED IN HIS MIND WITH LATIN. . . . . . . 37 DEATH OF THE HIRED MAN   78
ASSORTED
  ASSORTED CHARACTERS OF DEATH AND BLIGHT . . . . 302 DESIGN   4
ASSUAGE
  THAT NOTHING BUT GOD'S MERCY CAN ASSUAGE. . . . . . . 520 A MASQUE OF MERCY . 713
ASSUME
  HAD WE BUT IN US TO ASSUME IN MARCH . . . . 233 A BOUNDLESS MOMENT . .   7
  HE NEVER WOULD ASSUME THAT HE'D . . . . 274 A LONE STRIKER . . . 54
  THAT I ASSUME WAS WHAT OUR PASSING TRAIN MEANT. . . . . 292 FIGURE IN THE DOORWAY . 20
  LET NONE ASSUME TO TILL THE LAND BUT FARMERS. . . . . 322 BUILD SOIL 209
  THESE I ASSUME WERE WORDS SO DEEPLY MEANT . . . . . . 399 THE INGENUITIES OF DEBT   1
  IF YOU'RE THE DEITY I ASSUME YOU ARE . . . . 476 A MASQUE OF REASON . 84
  FROM TELLING ME YOUR REASON, DON'T ASSUME . . . . . . 482 A MASQUE OF REASON . 239
  (FOR RUIN I ASSUME WAS WHAT IT WAS) . . . . 502 A MASQUE OF MERCY . 223
ASSUMED
  WE ASSUMED THAT THE MAN HIMSELF . . . . 444 THE DRAFT HORSE . . . 17
ASSUMING
  THAT IS, ASSUMING--THAT SHE HAS GONE OUT. . . . . . . 155 SNOW 323
ASSURANCE (SEE SELF-ASSURANCE)
  HAROLD'S YOUNG COLLEGE-BOY'S ASSURANCE PIQUED HIM. . . . 37 DEATH OF THE HIRED MAN   73
  ON MOUNTAINS? WHAT HAS GIVEN ME ASSURANCE . . . . . . 169 NEW HAMPSHIRE . . . 315
  ASSURANCE . . . . 363 ASSURANCE . . . . .   T
  (FOR WHICH ASSURANCE MAMMON IS TO THANK). . . . . . . 386 THE FEAR OF MAN . . 10
ASSURED
  WE CAN REST ASSURED ON EIDER . . . . 385 IN THE LONG NIGHT . . 15
  I AM ASSURED AT ANY RATE . . . . 453 A-WISHING WELL . . . 76
AS'T
  AS'T WERE THE COUNTRY OF THE AMAZONS . . . . 259 WEST-RUNNING BROOK . . 33
ASTER
  OF THE LAST REMAINING ASTER FLOWER . . . .   9 A LATE WALK 15
  THE LAST LONE ASTER IS GONE; . . . . 30 RELUCTANCE 15
ASTRAY
  FOR A SON ASTRAY . . . . 433 KITTY HAWK 181
  AND GONE RIGHT ON ASTRAY . . . . 465 MILKY WAY IS A COWPATH 29
ASTRIDE
  WE CAN JUST SEE THE INFANT UP ASTRIDE, ... 267 RIDERS   7
  DOWNWARD TO MAKE HIM SIT ASTRIDE A DRIFT, ... 341 WILLFUL HOMING . . .   6
ASTROLOGER
  AND THEN YOUR TRAMP ASTROLOGER . . . . 381 AN UNSTAMPED LETTER IN 28
ASTROMETAPHYSICAL
  ASTROMETAPHYSICAL . . . . 388 ASTROMETAPHYSICAL . .   T
ASTRONOMER
  AS A CONFIRMED ASTRONOMER . . . . 451 A-WISHING WELL . . . 12
ASTRONOMERS
  THE NOTEDEST ASTRONOMERS . . . . 390 TWO LEADING LIGHTS . . 14
ASTRONOMY
  OF HIS ASTRONOMY. (HE'D HAVE TO TAKE . . . . 407 FROM PLANE TO PLANE . 111
ASUNDER
  NO SENATOR DARES IN TO KICK ASUNDER, ... 362 SYMPATHY WITH UNDER DOG   3
ASYLUM
  THE STATE ASYLUM. I WAS PREJUDICED; . . . . 65 A SERVANT TO SERVANTS . 91
  YOU KNOW THE OLD IDEA--THE ONLY ASYLUM . . . . 65 A SERVANT TO SERVANTS . 93
  BUT IT'S NOT SO: THE PLACE IS THE ASYLUM. . . . . . . 65 A SERVANT TO SERVANTS . 97
  NOW ASKED ASYLUM--AND I WAS STIRRED . . . . 419 ONE MORE BREVITY . . 13
  WILL BE SOME SOULLESS LUNATIC ASYLUM-- . . . . 500 A MASQUE OF MERCY . 187
  THAN BY THE FEAR OF THE ASYLUM, JAIL, OR POORHOUSE, . . 520 A MASQUE OF MERCY . 703
AT---NOT INDEXED
ATE
  GOLD DUSTED ALL WE DRANK AND ATE, ... 249 A PECK OF GOLD . . . 10
  SOME QUAINT DISSATISFACTION ATE HIM. . . . . 451 A-WISHING WELL . . .   7
ATHEISM
  THAT WOULD BE UNBELIEF AND ATHEISM. . . . . 482 A MASQUE OF REASON . 260
ATHENS
  THAT WISDOM NEED NOT BE OF ATHENS ATTIC, ... 362 BOEOTIAN   2
  ATHENS, ROME, FRANCE, BRITAIN, ... 437 KITTY HAWK 290
ATKINSON
  AS HALL OF WINDHAM, GAY OF ATKINSON, ... 167 NEW HAMPSHIRE . . . 259
ATLANTIC
  ON ONE I CAN TASTE ATLANTIC, ... 295 A RECORD STRIDE . . 23
  OF THE ATLANTIC POUNDED. . . . . 432 KITTY HAWK 138
  TO GET ANOTHER FROM THE ATLANTIC. . . . . 453 A-WISHING WELL . . . 66
ATMOSPHERE
  THAT TINGED THE ATMOSPHERE. . . . . 13 ROSE POGONIAS . . . 16
  HILL ATMOSPHERE NOT CEASE TO GLOW, ... 234 EVENING A SUGAR ORCHARD   9
  THE HOURS OF DAYLIGHT GATHER ATMOSPHERE. . . . . 246 ATMOSPHERE   6
  ATMOSPHERE . . . . 246 ATMOSPHERE . . . .   T
ATOLL
  HERE BY OUR ATOLL. / SOMETHING BYZANTINE. . . . . . . 474 A MASQUE OF REASON . 20
ATOMIC
  OF ATOMIC ONE. . . . . 426 A NEVER NAUGHT SONG .   7
  AS FLY THE ATOMIC SMITHEREENS TO NOTHING. . . . . . . 460 HOW HARD TO KEEP FROM 197
ATOMS
  AND FRIES A COUPLE OF EBON ATOMS WHITE, ... 389 SKEPTIC   2
ATONES
  ATONES FOR LATER DISREGARD . . . . 307 PROVIDE, PROVIDE . . 17
ATROPHIED
  THEN WHEN THE ARMS AND LEGS HAVE ATROPHIED, ... 395 ETHEREALIZING . . .   5
ATTACK
  I CAN SIT FORTH EXPOSED TO ATTACK, ... 282 A DRUMLIN WOODCHUCK . 10
ATTACKED
  HE HAD ATTACKED IT WITH A CLUB OR STONE . . . . 270 THE EGG AND THE MACHINE   6
ATTAIN
  WE HAVE IT HIDDEN IN US TO ATTAIN, ... 238 ON A TREE FALLEN ACROSS 11
  IAN THOUGHT TO ATTAIN, ... 449 THE BAD ISLAND--EASTER 58
  NO ONE CAN GIVE THEM--THEY CAN SCARCE ATTAIN-- . . . . 461 HOW HARD TO KEEP FROM 233

ATTAINED
HOW, TO MY SORROW, HOW HAVE I ATTAINED . . . . 169 NEW HAMPSHIRE . . . 313
ATTEMPT
THE SPARKS MADE NO ATTEMPT TO BE THE MOON. . . . . . 234 EVENING A SUGAR ORCHARD 14
ATTEMPTED
TO BE ATTEMPTED. GREED MAY WELL COME NEXT. . . . . . 319 BUILD SOIL 100
WHERE MADISON ATTEMPTED TO ARREST IT. . . . . 458 HOW HARD TO KEEP FROM 156
ATTEMPTING
THE THOUGHT OF MY ATTEMPTING SUCH A STAY! . . . . . 238 A HILLSIDE THAW . . . 35
ATTEMPTS
IN THEIR ATTEMPTS AT SOVEREIGNTY AND FORM. . . . . 423 FOR JOHN F. KENNEDY . 35
ATTEND
SHE SAID HE MIGHT ATTEND TO IN THE VILLAGE, ... 201 PLACE FOR A THIRD . . 54
ATTENDS
AS A GIRL NO ONE GALLANTLY ATTENDS . . . . 386 THE FEAR OF MAN . . 1
ATTENTION
TO EASE ATTENTION OFF WHEN OVERTIGHT, ... 370 THE LITERATE FARMER AND 81
SO SMALL AM I AS AN ATTENTION BEGGAR. . . . . 388 IOTA SUBSCRIPT . . . 5
KEEPER, BE STILL.--PAY NO ATTENTION TO HIM. . . . . 494 A MASQUE OF MERCY . 33
LIGHTS OUT, I SAY, SO'S TO ESCAPE ATTENTION. . . . . 508 A MASQUE OF MERCY . 392
ATTIC
A SORT OF CATCHALL FULL OF ATTIC CLUTTER. . . . . 67 A SERVANT TO SERVANTS . 143
UP ATTIC, MOTHER? / BONES--A SKELETON. . . . . . 203 THE WITCH OF COOS . 20
AGAINST THE ATTIC DOOR: THE DOOR IS NAILED. . . . . 203 THE WITCH OF COOS . 22
ANOTHER FROM THE BEDROOM TO THE ATTIC, ... 203 THE WITCH OF COOS . 32
LET'S TRAP HIM WITH AN OPEN DOOR UP ATTIC." . . . . 206 THE WITCH OF COOS . 113
THE STEPS BEGAN TO CLIMB THE ATTIC STAIRS. . . . . 206 THE WITCH OF COOS . 116
UP ATTIC THAT WE'D EVER WANT AGAIN. . . . . . . 206 THE WITCH OF COOS . 122
THE ATTIC WAS LESS TO US THAN THE CELLAR. . . . . . 206 THE WITCH OF COOS . 123
IF THE BONES LIKED THE ATTIC, LET THEM HAVE IT. . . . 206 THE WITCH OF COOS . 124
LET THEM STAY IN THE ATTIC. WHEN THEY SOMETIMES . . . 206 THE WITCH OF COOS . 125
LET THEM STAY IN THE ATTIC SINCE THEY WENT THERE. . . 206 THE WITCH OF COOS . 132
OUR BUSINESS FIRST'S UP ATTIC WITH HER BOOKS." . . . 216 A FOUNTAIN, A BOTTLE . 88
TO SEND IT SAILING OUT THE ATTIC WINDOW . . . . . . 216 A FOUNTAIN, A BOTTLE . 110
THE ATTIC WASPS WENT MISSING BY LIKE BULLETS. . . . 217 A FOUNTAIN, A BOTTLE . 130
THAT WISDOM NEED NOT BE OF ATHENS ATTIC, ... 362 BOEOTIAN 2
BESIDE HER ATTIC BED AT NIGHT. . . . . 382 THE NIGHT LIGHT . . . 2
OLD ATTIC GRACE AND SPARTAN DISCIPLINE . . . . . 511 A MASQUE OF MERCY . 467
ATTRACTION
STILL, NOVELTY HAS DOUBTLESS AN ATTRACTION. . . . . 480 A MASQUE OF REASON . 197
ATTRIBUTE
WHICH HAS FOR ITS GREAT ATTRIBUTE . . . . 452 A-WISHING WELL . . . 50
ATTRIBUTES
OF MORE THAN ROYAL ATTRIBUTES BETRAYED HIM. . . . . 462 HOW HARD TO KEEP FROM 274
ATWIDDLE
WITH FEELERS CALMLY ATWIDDLE, ... 288 DEPARTMENTAL . . . 36
AUCTION
INSTEAD OF A NEW-FASHIONED ONE AT AUCTION? . . . . 178 THE STAR-SPLITTER . 65
TO THE SLAVE AUCTION IN SOME MARKETPLACE . . . . . 454 HOW HARD TO KEEP FROM 32
AUDIENCE
BUT, LORD, WE SHOWED THEM WHAT. THE AUDIENCE . . . . 482 A MASQUE OF REASON . 252
THE AUDIENCE ASSEMBLED. THERE I WAS . . . . . . 497 A MASQUE OF MERCY . 96
AUGHT
THAT AUGHT WE CHERISH . . . . 469 WE VAINLY WRESTLE... . 2
AUGUST
IN THE AUGUST OCCASIONS OF THE STATE . . . . . . 422 FOR JOHN F. KENNEDY . 2
AUGUSTAN
THE GLORY OF A NEXT AUGUSTAN AGE . . . . 424 FOR JOHN F. KENNEDY . 71
AUK
WITH THE DEAD RACE OF THE GREAT AUK!" . . . . . . 212 AN EMPTY THREAT . . . 52
AUSPEX
AUSPEX . . . . 443 AUSPEX . . . . T
AUSPICES
SUCH AUSPICES ARE VERY HARD TO READ. . . . . . . 443 AUSPEX 5
AUTHENTIC
THE AUTHENTIC SHOES IT WAS MADE IN . . . . 295 A RECORD STRIDE . . . 27
AUTHOR
I MAY AS WELL CONFESS MYSELF THE AUTHOR . . . . . 166 NEW HAMPSHIRE . . . 228
TO BE THE AUTHOR OF THE SEVEN FREEDOMS: . . . . . 459 HOW HARD TO KEEP FROM 185
THE AUTHOR OF THESE WORDS, ... 465 MILKY WAY IS A COWPATH 41
AUTHORITY
SOMETIMES AS AN AUTHORITY . . . . 139 BROWN'S DESCENT . . . 49
YOU SHOULD BE AN AUTHORITY ON MERCY. . . . . . . 508 A MASQUE OF MERCY . 374
AUTHOR'S
I'M A GREAT STICKLER FOR THE AUTHOR'S NAME. . . . . 480 A MASQUE OF REASON . 199
AUTOMATICALLY
SO AUTOMATICALLY WE ALL WERE SAVED, ... 353 THE LESSON FOR TODAY . 100
AUTUMN
THINKS THESE DARK DAYS OF AUTUMN RAIN . . . . . . 6 MY NOVEMBER GUEST . . 2
AUTUMN, YES, WINTER WAS IN THE WIND; . . . . . . 8 LOVE AND A QUESTION . 15
BECAUSE THE AUTUMN EVE WAS FAIR . . . . 18 GOING FOR WATER . . 6
THE TIME WAS AUTUMN, BUT HOW ANYONE . . . . . . 175 THE CENSUS-TAKER . 17
WITHOUT A SINGLE LEAF TO SPEND ON AUTUMN, ... 175 THE CENSUS-TAKER . 23
IT WAS THE TREE THE AUTUMN FIRE RAN THROUGH . . . . 184 MAPLE 140
THEY ALWAYS TOOK THEIR HOLIDAYS IN AUTUMN. . . . . 184 MAPLE 143
EQUALLY WITH MY WEIGHT IN GRAPES, ONE AUTUMN, . . . 196 WILD GRAPES . . . 5
AS FAR AS I CAN SEE, THIS AUTUMN HAZE . . . . . . 247 THE COCOON . . . 1
WITH AUTUMN AND THE FRUIT WAS RUDELY TOSSED, ... 284 THE GOLD HESPERIDEE . 33
AUTUMN-TIRED
I HAVE BEEN TREADING ON LEAVES ALL DAY UNTIL I AM
AUTUMN-TIRED. . . . . 297 A LEAF-TREADER . . . 1
AVAIL
AND PUT MY FOOT ON ONE WITHOUT AVAIL, ... 237 A HILLSIDE THAW . . . 11
AVAILED
HAS NEVER AVAILED THE CUMBERSOME GRINDSTONE . . . . 188 THE GRINDSTONE . . . 2
AVALANCHE
YOUR LAST GOOD AVALANCHE . . . . 298 ON TAKING FROM THE TOP 3

AVALANCHES
  THE TWO CONVERGING SLIDES, THE AVALANCHES, ... 214 A FOUNTAIN, A BOTTLE . 52
AVALANCHING
  SHATTERING AND AVALANCHING ON THE SNOW CRUST-- . . . . 121 BIRCHES 11
AVATAR
  NOT A METEORITE, BUT AN AVATAR-- . . . . 421 ONE MORE BREVITY . . 61
AVENUE
  BY THAT CYB'LAEAN AVENUE, ... 332 ALL REVELATION . . . 4
AVERAGE
  THAT'S WHAT THE AVERAGE FARMER WOULD HAVE MEANT. . . . . 70 THE CODE 17
AVERRED
  MY PARENTS WHEN I RAN TO THEM AVERRED . . . . 443 AUSPEX 6
AVERSE
  HEARTS NOT AVERSE TO BEING BEGUILED, ... 27 OCTOBER 10
  THE FARMHOUSE LINGERS, THOUGH AVERSE TO SQUARE . . . . 231 A BROOK IN THE CITY . 1
  HE LINGERS TOO, AVERSE TO SLIGHT . . . . 280 BLUE RIBBON AT AMESBURY 19
AVERYS'
  DOWN AT THE AVERYS'? WELL, ONE SUNNY MORNING . . . . 149 SNOW 175
AVERY'S
  BUT BANKED THE DAYLIGHT OUT OF AVERY'S WINDOWS. . . . 149 SNOW 186
AVOCATION
  MY AVOCATION AND MY VOCATION . . . . 277 TWO TRAMPS IN MUD TIME 67
AVOID
  OR SO HE TRIED TO THINK TO AVOID BLAME. . . . . . . 180 MAPLE 34
  DIE EARLY AND AVOID THE FATE. . . . . 307 PROVIDE, PROVIDE . . 7
  AND AVOID BEING WORSHIPED AS A GOD. . . . . 408 FROM PLANE TO PLANE . 131
  UP CHIMNEY TO AVOID THE WORST OF IT. . . . . . . 408 FROM PLANE TO PLANE . 142
  TO AVOID MISTAKE, ... 438 KITTY HAWK . . . 317
  TO AVOID WHAT HE WASN'T SURE HE WANTED. . . . . . 453 HOW HARD TO KEEP FROM 5
AVOIDING
  YOU SAID YOURSELF YOU WEREN'T AVOIDING WORK. . . . . 405 FROM PLANE TO PLANE . 45
AVOUCH
  AND BID MY WILL AVOUCH IT LIKE MACBETH. . . . . . 477 A MASQUE OF REASON . 112
AWAIT
  YOU GO TO SLEEP. GOD MUST AWAIT EVENTS, ... 478 A MASQUE OF REASON . 147
AWAITING
  OUR DAYS ALL PASS AWAITING ITS RETURN. . . . . . 461 HOW HARD TO KEEP FROM 248
AWAKE
  WHO LAY THAT NIGHT AWAKE. . . . . 11 WIND AND WINDOW FLOWER 20
  SUPPOSE YOU AREN'T AWAKE WHEN I COME BACK?" . . . . 50 A HUNDRED COLLARS . . 164
  I'VE LAIN AWAKE THINKING OF YOU, I'LL WARRANT, . . . 67 A SERVANT TO SERVANTS 166
  I SHALL NOT LACK FOR PAIN TO KEEP ME AWAKE. . . . . 166 NEW HAMPSHIRE . . 241
  AWAKE THAT NIGHT . . . . 217 I WILL SING YOU ONE-O . 1
  BUT I SHOULD AWAKE TO CONFIRM YOUR STORY YET; . . . . 236 VALLEY'S SINGING DAY . 18
  STILL IT WOULDN'T REWARD THE WATCHER TO STAY AWAKE . . 268 ON LOOKING UP BY CHANCE 13
  AND SIMPLY MUST EVOLVE TO STAY AWAKE. . . . . . . 372 THE LITERATE FARMER AND 127
  BUT TO STAY AWAKE . . . . 438 KITTY HAWK . . . 314
  SHE'LL GO TO SLEEP. NOTHING KEEPS HER AWAKE . . . . 478 A MASQUE OF REASON . 153
  GOD, WHO INVENTED EARTH? / WHAT, STILL AWAKE? . . . . 480 A MASQUE OF REASON . 201
AWAKENED
  BUT YOU HAD AWAKENED UNDER THE MORNING STAR . . . . 235 VALLEY'S SINGING DAY . 4
  THE FIRST SONGBIRD THAT AWAKENED ALL THE REST. . . . 235 VALLEY'S SINGING DAY . 5
AWARE
  IS OF THE SLIGHTEST BONDAGE MADE AWARE. . . . . . 332 THE SILKEN TENT . . 14
  BUT BECOMING AWARE OF SOME BOYS FROM SCHOOL . . . . 385 A MOOD APART . . . 4
AWAY (SEE BLOW-AWAY)
  I'LL ONLY STOP TO RAKE THE LEAVES AWAY . . . . . . 1 THE PASTURE . . . 2
  BUT STRETCHED AWAY UNTO THE EDGE OF DOOM. . . . . . 5 INTO MY OWN . . 4
  INTO THEIR VASTNESS I SHOULD STEAL AWAY, ... 5 INTO MY OWN . . 6
  I HEAR HIM BEGIN FAR ENOUGH AWAY . . . . 6 GHOST HOUSE . . . 18
  SHE'S GLAD THE BIRDS ARE GONE AWAY, ... 7 MY NOVEMBER GUEST . 8
  TILL EVEN THE COMFORTING BARN GROWS FAR AWAY, ... 10 STORM FEAR . . . 15
  A HUNDRED MILES AWAY. . . . . 11 WIND AND WINDOW FLOWER 28
  AND GIVE US NOT TO THINK SO FAR AWAY . . . . . . 12 A PRAYER IN SPRING . 2
  THAT I'VE BEEN LONG AWAY. . . . . 13 FLOWER-GATHERING . 16
  THAT THE STARS WERE ALMOST FADED AWAY . . . . . . 15 IN A VALE . . . 15
  SO ALL WHO HIDE TO WELL AWAY . . . . 19 REVELATION . . . 11
  AND RAVELED A FLOWER AND LOOKED AWAY. . . . . . . 24 PAN WITH US . . . 29
  AND THE HOOFPRINTS VANISH AWAY. . . . . 26 A LINE-STORM SONG . 4
  ONE FROM OUR TREES, ONE FAR AWAY. . . . . 27 OCTOBER . . . 14
  THE RIVER AT THE TIME WAS FALLEN AWAY, ... 40 THE MOUNTAIN . . . 10
  THE DOCTOR LOOKED AT LAFE AND LOOKED AWAY. . . . . 46 A HUNDRED COLLARS . 49
  THE FAMILY'S ALL AWAY IN SOME BACK MEADOW. . . . . 49 A HUNDRED COLLARS . 131
  THEY LIVE SO FAR AWAY--ONE IS OUT WEST-- . . . . . 55 THE BLACK COTTAGE . 19
  LIKE BIRDS. THEY STORE A GREAT MANY AWAY. . . . . 60 BLUEBERRIES . . . 51
  AWAY FROM ITS NEST, AND I SAID IT WAS YOU. . . . . 62 BLUEBERRIES . . . 89
  I'VE BEEN AWAY ONCE--YES, I'VE BEEN AWAY. . . . . 65 A SERVANT TO SERVANTS 90
  NO WONDER I WAS GLAD TO GET AWAY. . . . . 67 A SERVANT TO SERVANTS 148
  THE WONDER WAS THE TENTS WEREN'T SNATCHED AWAY . . . 67 A SERVANT TO SERVANTS 168
  HE KEPT AWAY FROM US ALL AFTERNOON. . . . . . . 73 THE CODE . . . 106
  HE COULDN'T KEEP AWAY FROM DOING SOMETHING." . . . . 73 THE CODE . . . 109
  ONLY ONE FROM A FARM NOT FAR AWAY . . . . 74 THE GENERATIONS OF MEN 25
  HE'LL SORT OF SWEAR THE TIME AWAY. HE'S AWFUL! . . . 83 THE HOUSEKEEPER . . 52
  "THEN IT'S ALL UP. I THINK I'LL GET AWAY. . . . . 88 THE HOUSEKEEPER . . 190
  "YOU NEEDN'T THINK YOU'RE GOING TO GET AWAY. . . . 88 THE HOUSEKEEPER . . 195
  HERE HE IS NOW. THIS BOX! PUT IT AWAY. . . . . . 88 THE HOUSEKEEPER . . 198
  I DIDN'T TRY TOO LONG TO PULL AWAY, ... 93 THE SELF-SEEKER . . 24
  OR FUMBLE FOR MY KNIFE TO CUT AWAY, ... 93 THE SELF-SEEKER . . 25
  WORTH THREE CENTS MORE TO GIVE AWAY THAN SELL, . . . 107 CHRISTMAS TREES . . 56
  I LIKE IT.--BANG GOES SOMETHING BIG AWAY . . . . . 111 IN THE HOME STRETCH . 37
  AND BANG GOES SOMETHING ELSE AWAY OFF THERE. . . . 112 IN THE HOME STRETCH . 55
  AND FILL ANOTHER WITH 'EM FIFTEEN MILES AWAY, . . . 116 IN THE HOME STRETCH . 161
  "HAVING FOUND THE FLOWER AND DRIVEN A BEE AWAY, . . . 118 THE TELEPHONE . . 11
  SUCH HEAPS OF BROKEN GLASS TO SWEEP AWAY . . . . . 121 BIRCHES . . . 12
  AND SO NOT CARRYING THE TREE AWAY . . . . . . 122 BIRCHES . . . 34
  I'D LIKE TO GET AWAY FROM EARTH AWHILE . . . . . 122 BIRCHES . . . 48
  AND HALF GRANT WHAT I WISH AND SNATCH ME AWAY . . . 122 BIRCHES . . . 51
  FROM STUMPS STILL BLEEDING THEIR LIFE AWAY. . . . . 123 PEA BRUSH . . . 8

AWAY (CONTINUED)
```
TO THE LONELY HOUSE FROM FAR AWAY, . . . . . . . . . . 127 HOUSE FEAR . . . .    3
I DIDN'T LIKE THE WAY HE WENT AWAY. . . . . . . . . . . 127 THE SMILE . . . .    1
AND THRUST HANDS IN AND HELD MY FACE AWAY. . . . . . . 131 THE BONFIRE . . . .   66
BUT SHE ALWAYS RAN AWAY AND LEFT . . . . . . . . . . . 134 A GIRL'S GARDEN . .   23
HE STEERED WAS REALLY STRAIGHT AWAY . . . . . . . . . . 139 BROWN'S DESCENT . . .  66
TO EASE AWAY--THEY HAVE IT. WITH A LAUGH, . . . . . . 141 THE LINE-GANG . . . .   11
BUT NEVER GETS AWAY; . . . . . . . . . . . . . . . . . 156 THE SOUND OF TREES .   11
RATHER OF WHAT TO FACE OR RUN AWAY FROM. . . . . . . . 171 NEW HAMPSHIRE . . . . 396
THEY KEPT THEIR THOUGHTS AWAY FROM WHEN THE MAPLES . . 184 MAPLE . . . . . . . 136
HARD IF, THOUGH CAST AWAY FOR LIFE WITH YANKEES, . . . 186 THE AX-HELVE . . . .   44
WHO'D RUN AWAY WITH SOMEONE ELSE AND LEFT HIM; . . . . 191 PAUL'S WIFE . . . .    9
HE'D BEEN HARD AT IT TAKING BOARDS AWAY . . . . . . . . 193 PAUL'S WIFE . . . .   58
HE FOUND THE GRAVE A TOWN OR TWO AWAY, . . . . . . . . 200 PLACE FOR A THIRD .   38
THROWN AWAY . . . . . . . . . . . . . . . . . . . . . 211 AN EMPTY THREAT . .   32
HAD BEEN TOO SHORT TO SELL OR GIVE AWAY. . . . . . . . 217 A FOUNTAIN, A BOTTLE . 122
TO READ THE STONES AND GO AWAY . . . . . . . . . . . . 221 IN A DISUSED GRAVEYARD  7
WITH THE LITTLE FELLOW AT ALL. HE'S RUNNING AWAY. . . 223 THE RUNAWAY . . . .   11
I TAKE AWAY MY HAND . . . . . . . . . . . . . . . . . 227 TO EARTHWARD . . . .   26
AN ORCHARD AWAY AT THE END OF THE FARM . . . . . . . . 228 GOOD-BY AND KEEP COLD .  4
AND WARN THEM AWAY WITH A STICK FOR A GUN.) . . . . . 228 GOOD-BY AND KEEP COLD . 11
RUNNING AWAY. . . . . . . . . . . . . . . . . . . . . 235 GATHERING LEAVES . .    8
SOME THAT HAVE COME TOO FAR NORTH BACK AWAY, . . . . . 239 OUR SINGING STRENGTH .  23
TO BLOT OUT AND DRINK UP AND SWEEP AWAY . . . . . . . 245 SPRING POOLS . . . .   10
I HAVE WISHED A BIRD WOULD FLY AWAY, . . . . . . . . . 250 A MINOR BIRD . . . .    1
IT BREAKS AWAY IN SOME NEW KIND OF SLAUGHTER. . . . . 254 THE FLOOD . . . .      4
WHEN FAR AWAY AN INTERRUPTED CRY . . . . . . . . . . . 255 ACQUAINTED WITH NIGHT .  8
THE STREAM OF EVERYTHING THAT RUNS AWAY. . . . . . . . 259 WEST-RUNNING BROOK .   44
STANDS STILL AND DANCES, BUT IT RUNS AWAY; . . . . . . 259 WEST-RUNNING BROOK .   47
IT SERIOUSLY, SADLY, RUNS AWAY . . . . . . . . . . . . 259 WEST-RUNNING BROOK .   48
FROM FAR AWAY THERE CAME AN ANSWERING TICK, . . . . . 269 THE EGG AND THE MACHINE  2
THAT REALLY TAKES AWAY INSTEAD OF GIVES. . . . . . . . 279 THE WHITE-TAILED HORNET 55
THAT BLINKING COULD NOT SEEM TO BLINK AWAY. . . . . . 293 AT WOODWARD'S GARDENS . 11
CANNOT BE PARTED NOR BE SWEPT AWAY . . . . . . . . . . 300 THE MASTER SPEED . .   11
LET THEIR TRAPPINGS BE TAKEN AWAY. . . . . . . . . . . 313 THE VINDICTIVES . . .  89
FOR SWEEPING ME AWAY. LET'S SEE, WHERE WAS I? . . . . 319 BUILD SOIL . . . .    91
AWAY 'WAY DOWN INSIDE I'M PERSONAL. . . . . . . . . . 320 BUILD SOIL . . . .   144
AND BE SO VERY STRIKING. STEAL AWAY, . . . . . . . . . 325 BUILD SOIL . . . .   278
THE SONG SAYS. STEAL AWAY AND STAY AWAY. . . . . . . . 325 BUILD SOIL . . . .   279
SHE HAD TO LEAN AWAY. . . . . . . . . . . . . . . . . 340 THE SUBVERTED FLOWER .  30
HER SPIRIT FADED AS FAR AWAY . . . . . . . . . . . . . 346 DISCOVERY OF MADEIRAS . 103
HER LOVER SAW THEM SAIL AWAY, . . . . . . . . . . . . 347 DISCOVERY OF MADEIRAS . 114
THE ONLY OTHER THERE WAS FAR AWAY . . . . . . . . . . 354 THE LESSON FOR TODAY . 128
BUT NOT TO TAKE AWAY THE PRECIOUS DARK. . . . . . . . 370 THE LITERATE FARMER AND 79
ON FIRE TO SCARE AWAY THE PTERODIX . . . . . . . . . . 372 THE LITERATE FARMER AND 139
PATIENCE AND LOOKING AWAY AHEAD, . . . . . . . . . . . 376 SOMETHING FOR HOPE .   21
GOOD GLOOM ON HER WAS THROWN AWAY. . . . . . . . . . . 383 THE NIGHT LIGHT . .    5
AWAY ON THE MOUNTAIN UP FAR TOO HIGH, . . . . . . . . 383 WERE I IN TROUBLE . .   2
AND I AWAY IN MY OPPOSITE WOOD . . . . . . . . . . . . 383 WERE I IN TROUBLE . .   6
IS AFTER EXPLOSION GOING AWAY SO FAST. . . . . . . . . 389 SKEPTIC . . . . .      8
HOW WE PROPOSE TO GET AWAY FROM HERE . . . . . . . . . 395 WHY WAIT FOR SCIENCE .  3
THE WAY TO GO AWAY SHOULD BE THE SAME . . . . . . . . 395 WHY WAIT FOR SCIENCE . 11
MANY SHALL COME AWAY AS STRUGGLE-WORN . . . . . . . . 412 POD OF THE MILKWEED .  34
AWAY! . . . . . . . . . . . . . . . . . . . . . . . . 412 AWAY! . . . . . .      T
"I'M--BOUND--AWAY!" . . . . . . . . . . . . . . . . . 413 AWAY! . . . . . .     20
BECAUSE THEY'VE GONE AWAY . . . . . . . . . . . . . . 415 CLOSED FOR GOOD . .    6
OR THE SORROW OF HAVING RUN AWAY. . . . . . . . . . . 420 ONE MORE BREVITY . .   32
AS THROW A PART AWAY. . . . . . . . . . . . . . . . . 445 ENDS . . . . . .      10
BUT THE PRINCE DREW AWAY HIS HAND IN TIME . . . . . . 453 HOW HARD TO KEEP FROM   4
AND FATHER'S IN FOR WHAT WE RAN AWAY FROM. . . . . . . 462 HOW HARD TO KEEP FROM 266
THE NIGHT WE RAN AWAY FROM CTESIPHON) . . . . . . . . 462 HOW HARD TO KEEP FROM 270
THAT WAS HEARD AS FAR AWAY AS NEW YORK . . . . . . . . 463 LINES IN DEJECTION .   23
THE DEVIL'S NEVER VERY FAR AWAY. . . . . . . . . . . . 487 A MASQUE OF REASON . 382
TO BRUSH AWAY A DISRESPECTFUL SMILE. . . . . . . . . . 487 A MASQUE OF REASON . 391
DON'T LET IT CARRY YOU AWAY. I HATE . . . . . . . . . 489 A MASQUE OF REASON . 448
THE KEEPER'S WIFE HAS HARDLY TURNED AWAY . . . . . . . 493 A MASQUE OF MERCY .    5
TO FIND OUT HOW TO GET AWAY FROM GOD? . . . . . . . . 494 A MASQUE OF MERCY .   28
RUNNING AWAY FROM HIM YOU THINK YOU ARE, . . . . . . . 498 A MASQUE OF MERCY .  139
"I'M--BOUND--AWAY!" (HE QUOTES IT TO THE TUNE.) . . . 500 A MASQUE OF MERCY .  172
(HE LEANS AWAY IN TOLERANT DISTASTE.) . . . . . . . . 504 A MASQUE OF MERCY .  287
YET NO ONE TURN AWAY FROM OR IGNORE-- . . . . . . . . 513 A MASQUE OF MERCY .  522
I SIMPLY TURN AWAY FROM IT. / YOU PAGAN! . . . . . . . 513 A MASQUE OF MERCY .  523
```
AWE
```
AND THE AWE PASSES WONDER THEN, . . . . . . . . . . .  21 THE TRIAL BY EXISTENCE  59
```
AWES
```
WHITTIER'S LUCK WITH SKIPPER IRESON AWES ME-- . . . . 317 BUILD SOIL . . . .    44
```
AWFUL
```
HE'LL SORT OF SWEAR THE TIME AWAY. HE'S AWFUL! . . . .  83 THE HOUSEKEEPER . .   52
"AWFUL. WHY DIDN'T THEY THROW OFF THE BELT . . . . . .  93 THE SELF-SEEKER . .   30
OF THE ONE AWFUL GOD. JUST SO THE SAINTS . . . . . . 516 A MASQUE OF MERCY .  596
```
AWH
```
LIGHT, BRING A LIGHT! / AWH, THERE'S NO LACK OF LIGHT, YOU-- 515 A MASQUE OF MERCY . 579
```
AWHILE
```
BLIND CREATURE; AND AWHILE HE DIDN'T SEE. . . . . . .  51 HOME BURIAL . . . .   16
I'C LIKE TO GET AWAY FROM EARTH AWHILE . . . . . . . . 122 BIRCHES . . . . .     48
WHAT'S LAS' AWHILE--GOOD HICK'RY WHAT'S GROW CROOKED, . 186 THE AX-HELVE . . . .  30
HOLD TIGHT AWHILE TILL I THINK WHAT TO DO. . . . . . . 198 WILD GRAPES . . . .   82
THE FLOWERS WILL GO ON WITH GRIEF AWHILE, . . . . . . 200 PLACE FOR A THIRD .   28
AND OFFERED HER A HOME TO REST AWHILE . . . . . . . . 201 PLACE FOR A THIRD .   60
MY BUSINESS AWHILE IS WITH DIFFERENT TREES, . . . . . 228 GOOD-BY AND KEEP COLD . 21
HE LEFT HER TO HER THOUGHTS AWHILE . . . . . . . . . . 345 DISCOVERY OF MADEIRAS . 49
```
A-WISHING
```
A POET WOULD A-WISHING GO, . . . . . . . . . . . . . . 451 A-WISHING WELL . .     1
A-WISHING WELL . . . . . . . . . . . . . . . . . . . . 451 A-WISHING WELL . .     T
```
AWKWARD
```
"YOU TOOK AN AWKWARD WAY. DID HE DISCHARGE YOU?" . . .  73 THE CODE . . . . .   113
AND THE DRY PUMP FLUNG UP AN AWKWARD ARM; . . . . . . 242 NEED OF BEING VERSED . 19
KNOWN AS BOUSTROPHEDON, WAS FOUND TOO AWKWARD." . . . 405 FROM PLANE TO PLANE .  54
```

AX
    AND SPROUT-LANDS FLOURISH WHERE THE AX HAS GONE. . . . . . . 73 THE GENERATIONS OF MEN   6
    HE SPENT HIMSELF, THE LABOR OF HIS AX, ... 102 THE WOOD-PILE . . . 37
    ALL FRESH AND SOUND FROM THE RECENT AX. . . . . . . 123 PEA BRUSH . . . 14
    IN THE SNOW WITH AN AX-- . . . . 136 LAST WORD OF A BLUEBIRD 19
    I KNOW A MAN WHO TOOK A DOUBLE AX . . . . . . 170 NEW HAMPSHIRE . . . 367
    BUT HIS HEART FAILING HIM, HE DROPPED THE AX . . . . 170 NEW HAMPSHIRE . . . 369
    OF ALDER CATCH MY LIFTED AX BEHIND ME. . . . . . 185 THE AX-HELVE 2
    HE CAUGHT MY AX EXPERTLY ON THE RISE, ... 185 THE AX-HELVE 10
    WAS WHAT HE THOUGHT OF--NOT ME, BUT MY AX, ... 185 THE AX-HELVE 19
    ME ONLY AS I TOOK MY AX TO HEART. . . . . . . 186 THE AX-HELVE 20
    WHERE I MUST JUDGE IF WHAT HE KNEW ABOUT AN AX . . . 186 THE AX-HELVE 41
    AND STOOD THE AX THERE ON ITS HORSE'S HOOF, ... 188 THE AX-HELVE 95
    AND SUCH AS IS DONE TO THEIR WOOD WITH AN AX-- . . . 228 GOOD-BY AND KEEP COLD . 23
    DEBATING WHAT TO DO WITHOUT AN AX. . . . . 238 ON A TREE FALLEN ACROSS 8
    EXCEPT AS A FELLOW HANDLED AN AX . . . . . . 276 TWO TRAMPS IN MUD TIME 55
    AS GAY FOR YOU TO TAKE YOUR FATHER'S AX . . . . . 349 TO A YOUNG WRETCH . . 1
    AT FOUR O'CLOCK I SHOULDER AX, ... 470 IN WINTER IN THE WOODS 5
AX-HANDLE
    WITH THE PITCH-BLACKENED STUB OF AN AX-HANDLE . . . . 175 THE CENSUS-TAKER . . 44
AX-HEAD
    HE TRIED IT AT THE EYEHOLE IN THE AX-HEAD. . . . . 187 THE AX-HELVE 78
    THE WEIGHT OF AN AX-HEAD POISED ALOFT, ... 276 TWO TRAMPS IN MUD TIME 45
AX-HELVE
    THE AX-HELVE . . . . 185 THE AX-HELVE . . . . T
    IT WAS THE BAD AX-HELVE SOMEONE HAD SOLD ME-- . . . 186 THE AX-HELVE 21
AX-HELVES
    NEEDLESSLY SOON HE HAD HIS AX-HELVES OUT, ... 187 THE AX-HELVE 63
    WITH THE CURVES OF HIS AX-HELVES AND HIS HAVING . . . 188 THE AX-HELVE 87
AXIS
    UPON HIS LONGER AXIS, AND . . . . 138 BROWN'S DESCENT . . . 23
    IF EARTH WERE THOUGHT ABOUT TO CHANGE ITS AXIS, . . . 317 BUILD SOIL 58
AYE
    LOVE THOU THY NEIGHBOR AS THYSELF, AYE, ... 467 QUANDARY 12
AZTEC
    BY A RELIGIOUS AZTEC INDIAN. . . . . 516 A MASQUE OF MERCY . . 616
AZTECS
    AS CORTEZ ON THE AZTECS MADE. . . . . 419 AMERICA IS HARD TO SEE 84

B

B (SEE A-B-C)
BABE
    THE BABE BORN TO THE DESERT, THE SANDSTORM . . . . . 58 THE BLACK COTTAGE . . 123
BABEL
    --WAS BABEL: EVERYONE DEVELOPING . . . . 502 A MASQUE OF MERCY . . 240
BABES
    BUT SO WITH ALL, FROM BABES THAT PLAY . . . . . . 19 REVELATION 9
BABIES
    HUNG BABIES OUT ON BRANCHES BY THE HANDS . . . . . 197 WILD GRAPES 51
    WITH BABIES IN THEIR ARMS . . . . 391 A ROGERS GROUP . . . 3
BABY
    BUT I, WITH SOMETHING OF THE BABY GRIP . . . . . 197 WILD GRAPES 48
    I WAS A BABY: I DON'T KNOW WHERE I WAS. . . . . . 203 THE WITCH OF COOS . . 35
    OF BABY GREEN AND SHOW THE WHITE BENEATH, ... 375 A YOUNG BIRCH . . . 2
BABY'S
    OF THE FRESH EARTH FROM YOUR OWN BABY'S GRAVE . . . 54 HOME BURIAL 85
    "WHAT DO YOU SAY IT IS?" / "A BABY'S CRYING! . . . 154 SNOW 318
BABY-SCHOOL
    GOES MENTIONLESS EXCEPT IN BABY-SCHOOL . . . . . 447 DOES NO ONE AT ALL EVER 38
BACK (SEE CHAIR-BACK)
    I DO NOT SEE WHY I SHOULD E'ER TURN BACK, ... 5 INTO MY OWN 9
    THE WOODS COME BACK TO THE MOWING FIELD; . . . . . 5 GHOST HOUSE 7
    IN THE ABYSS OF ODOR AND RUSTLE AT MY BACK, ... 14 WAITING 19
    BACK TO THE PLACE FROM WHICH SHE CAME-- . . . . . 15 IN A VALE 17
    AND THEN ON TREMULOUS WING CAME BACK TO ME. . . . . 22 THE TUFT OF FLOWERS . 18
    OUR LOVE CAME BACK AMAIN. . . . . 27 A LINE-STORM SONG . . 30
    AND PUT HIM ON HIS GUARD. "SILAS IS BACK." . . . . 34 DEATH OF THE HIRED MAN 5
    BUT I'LL NOT HAVE THE FELLOW BACK," HE SAID. . . . 35 DEATH OF THE HIRED MAN 12
    IN WINTER HE COMES BACK TO US. I'M DONE." . . . . 35 DEATH OF THE HIRED MAN 30
    SILAS DECLARES YOU'LL HAVE TO GET HIM BACK. . . . . 36 DEATH OF THE HIRED MAN 61
    PICKED UP A LITTLE STICK, AND BROUGHT IT BACK . . . 38 DEATH OF THE HIRED MAN 122
    I MUST BE GETTING BACK TO BREAKFAST NOW." . . . . 41 THE MOUNTAIN 37
    THAT'S FIVE MILES BACK. YOU CAN'T MISTAKE THE PLACE: . 41 THE MOUNTAIN 41
    'TWAS NOTHING BUT MY FOOLISH HANGING BACK, ... 46 A HUNDRED COLLARS . . 59
    AND COME TO THINK I MUST HAVE BACK AT HOME . . . . 47 A HUNDRED COLLARS . . 65
    THE FAMILY'S ALL AWAY IN SOME BACK MEADOW. . . . . 49 A HUNDRED COLLARS . . 131
    AND I LIE BACK AND RIDE. I TAKE THE REINS . . . . 49 A HUNDRED COLLARS . . 138
    SUPPOSE YOU AREN'T AWAKE WHEN I COME BACK?" . . . . 50 A HUNDRED COLLARS . . 164
    WHEN I COME BACK, SO YOU'LL KNOW WHO IT IS. . . . . 50 A HUNDRED COLLARS . . 174
    LOOKING BACK OVER HER SHOULDER AT SOME FEAR. . . . . 51 HOME BURIAL 3
    AND ROLL BACK DOWN THE MOUND BESIDE THE HOLE. . . . 53 HOME BURIAL 77
    AND MAKING THE BEST OF THEIR WAY BACK TO LIFE . . . 54 HOME BURIAL 104
    I'LL FOLLOW AND BRING YOU BACK BY FORCE. I WILL!--" . 55 HOME BURIAL 116
    SET WELL BACK FROM THE ROAD IN RANK LODGED GRASS, . . 55 THE BLACK COTTAGE . . 4
    TO THE TRUTHS WE KEEP COMING BACK AND BACK TO. . . . 58 THE BLACK COTTAGE . . 114
    LOCKED UP FOR YEARS BACK THERE AT THE OLD FARM. . . 65 A SERVANT TO SERVANTS . 89
    IS SET ME BACK A LITTLE MORE BEHIND. . . . . . . 68 A SERVANT TO SERVANTS . 175
    NO MORE THAN BROUGHT US BACK INTO THE NAME. . . . . 75 THE GENERATIONS OF MEN 57
    "I'M SURE SHE WON'T COME BACK. SHE'S HIDING SOMEWHERE. . 82 THE HOUSEKEEPER . . . 23
    AND SHE'LL COME BACK. BUT, BLESS YOU, I'M HER MOTHER-- . 82 THE HOUSEKEEPER . . . 26
    SHE WON'T COME BACK--IT'S WORSE THAN THAT--SHE CAN'T." . 87 THE HOUSEKEEPER . . . 177
    SO THAT WAS WHAT WAS BACK. SHE'S BAD, THAT'S ALL!" . 88 THE HOUSEKEEPER . . . 183
    AND THE BACK OF THE GIG THEY STOOD BESIDE . . . . 89 THE FEAR 6
    AND LET YOU SEE." / "YES, DO.--JOEL, GO BACK!" . . . 92 THE FEAR 75
    I CAN'T GET BACK THE FEET IN ANY CASE." . . . . . 95 THE SELF-SEEKER . . . 65

BACK (CONTINUED)
WHEN YOU COME BACK, I'LL HAVE THE PAPERS SIGNED. . . . . 100 THE SELF-SEEKER . . . 213
I'LL GO OUTDOORS, BY GAD, AND WON'T COME BACK." . . . . 100 THE SELF-SEEKER . . . 222
"WILLIS, BRING ANNE BACK WITH YOU WHEN YOU COME. . . . . 100 THE SELF-SEEKER . . . 223
I PAUSED AND SAID, "I WILL TURN BACK FROM HERE. . . . . 101 THE WOOD-PILE 2
I TURNED AND REPENTED, BUT COMING BACK . . . . 102 GOOD HOURS 11
I DOUBTED IF I SHOULD EVER COME BACK. . . . . 105 THE ROAD NOT TAKEN . 15
WHAT KEPT HIS EYES FROM GIVING BACK THE GAZE . . . . . 108 OLD MAN'S WINTER NIGHT 4
YOU HAD BEGUN, AND GAVE THEM BACK THEIR SHADE. . . . . 109 THE EXPOSED NEST . . 30
HER BACK. SHE ALWAYS ANSWERED WITHOUT TURNING. . . . . 110 IN THE HOME STRETCH . 12
YOU MUST BE GETTING STARTED BACK TO TOWN." . . . . . 111 IN THE HOME STRETCH . 17
WE STAND HERE DREAMING. HURRY! CALL THEM BACK!" . . . . 113 IN THE HOME STRETCH . 77
THE BACK SOME FARM PRESENTS US; AND YOUR WOODS . . . . 114 IN THE HOME STRETCH . 114
BACK PAST THE SUN TO AN EARTHLY ROOM. . . . . 120 BOND AND FREE . . . 15
AND SO I DREAM OF GOING BACK TO BE. . . . . 122 BIRCHES 42
AND THEN COME BACK TO IT AND BEGIN OVER. . . . . . . 122 BIRCHES 49
THAT WOULD BE GOOD BOTH GOING AND COMING BACK. . . . . 122 BIRCHES 58
OR CARE SO MUCH WHEN THEY COME BACK . . . . 126 LONELINESS 5
MADE THE DIM TREES STAND BACK IN WIDER CIRCLE-- . . . . 130 THE BONFIRE 29
THAT BROUGHT ME TO MY FEET TO HOLD IT BACK . . . . . 132 THE BONFIRE 78
BY LEANING BACK MYSELF, AS IF THE REINS . . . . . . 132 THE BONFIRE 79
HE WOULD COME BACK AND SING." . . . . 136 LAST WORD OF A BLUEBIRD 22
HE LOOKED BACK UP THE SLIPPERY SLOPE . . . . 139 BROWN'S DESCENT . . . 47
YOU CAN'T GET BACK AND SEE IT AS HE SAW IT. . . . . . 142 THE VANISHING RED . . 9
TO PLAY----" / "YOU TEND YOUR HORSES AND COME BACK.-- . . 144 SNOW 42
HE WON'T COME BACK, AND IF HE TELEPHONES, ... 152 SNOW 266
YOU'D BETTER DRESS: YOU WON'T GO BACK TO BED. . . . . 152 SNOW 273
WAS SOMEONE WHO HAD JUST COME BACK ASHAMED . . . . . 160 NEW HAMPSHIRE . . . 37
TO DRY, FROM POOR TO RICH, OR BACK AGAIN. . . . . . 166 NEW HAMPSHIRE . . . 236
I FEEL, AS OF AN EARTHQUAKE IN MY BACK, ... 169 NEW HAMPSHIRE . . . 318
AGAINST THE SKY TO BREAK HIS BACK FOR HIM, ... 170 NEW HAMPSHIRE . . . 348
AND WHEN HE CAN'T DO ANYTHING, FALLS BACK . . . . . 171 NEW HAMPSHIRE . . . 400
IT DREW BACK IN ITS BODY LIKE A SNAIL; . . . . . . 172 A STAR IN A STONEBOAT . 18
IF IT COULD PUT A STAR BACK IN ITS COURSE. . . . . . 173 A STAR IN A STONEBOAT . 30
HE PROMPTLY GIVES IT BACK, THAT IS IF STILL . . . . . 178 THE STAR-SPLITTER . . 51
A GOOD OLD-TIMER DATING BACK ALONG; . . . . 178 THE STAR-SPLITTER . . 60
IT CAME BACK VAGUELY AT THE GLASS ONE DAY, ... 181 MAPLE 40
BUT FORGOT TO PUT THE LEAF BACK IN CLOSING . . . . . 181 MAPLE 67
ONE BACK AND FORWARD, IN AND OUT OF SHADOW, ... 186 THE AX-HELVE 48
AND SET HERSELF BACK WHERE SHE STARTED FROM. . . . . 187 THE AX-HELVE 53
BAPTISTE DREW BACK AND SQUINTED AT IT, PLEASED: . . . . 188 THE AX-HELVE 101
THE ONE WHO HELD THE WHEEL BACK OR THE ONE . . . . . 190 THE GRINDSTONE . . . 46
BACK ON THE FLOOR, IS FACT OR PRETTY NEAR FACT. . . . . 192 PAUL'S WIFE 53
AND THE SAWYER HAD SLAMMED THE CARRIAGE BACK . . . . . 193 PAUL'S WIFE 63
SO AFTER WORK THAT EVENING HE CAME BACK . . . . . . 194 PAUL'S WIFE 88
WHO, LEANING ON A LOG, LOOKED BACK AT PAUL. . . . . . 194 PAUL'S WIFE 110
AND THAT MADE PAUL IN TURN LOOK BACK . . . . 194 PAUL'S WIFE 111
AND STILL I CLUNG. I LET MY HEAD FALL BACK, ... 198 WILD GRAPES 73
AND THE WORLD CAME REVOLVING BACK TO ME, ... 198 WILD GRAPES 86
LABAN WAS FORCED TO FALL BACK ON HIS PLAN . . . . . . 202 PLACE FOR A THIRD . . 79
THAT THERE'S SOMETHING THE DEAD ARE KEEPING BACK? . . . 202 THE WITCH OF COOS . . 17
YES, THERE'S SOMETHING THE DEAD ARE KEEPING BACK. . . . 202 THE WITCH OF COOS . . 18
IS BACK INTO THE CELLAR WHERE IT CAME FROM. . . . . . 203 THE WITCH OF COOS . . 26
AND FELL BACK FROM HIM ON THE FLOOR MYSELF. . . . . . 204 THE WITCH OF COOS . . 78
LIKE, "NO, SHE AIN'T COME BACK FROM KITING YET. . . . . 209 PAUPER WITCH OF GRAFTON 80
THE FOE THRUST UNSAFE BEYOND THE RHINE, ... 222 TO E.T. 18
GIVES ME BACK IN A SHINING SURFACE PICTURE . . . . . 225 FOR ONCE SOMETHING . . 4
WITH THOUGHTS OF THE PATH BACK, HOW ROUGH IT WAS . . . 229 TWO LOOK AT TWO . . . 5
NOT THE SAME DOE COME BACK INTO HER PLACE. . . . . . 229 TWO LOOK AT TWO . . . 30
THEY SENT HIM BACK TO HER. THE LETTER CAME . . . . . 230 NOT TO KEEP 1
LIVING. THEY GAVE HIM BACK TO HER ALIVE-- . . . . . 230 NOT TO KEEP 5
THEY HAD GIVEN HIM BACK TO HER, BUT NOT TO KEEP. . . . 231 NOT TO KEEP 22
THEY DISAPPEARED AS IF EARTH SENT THEM BACK. . . . . 239 OUR SINGING STRENGTH . 6
AND ALL GO BACK TO WINTER BUT THE ROAD. . . . . . . 239 OUR SINGING STRENGTH . 10
SOME THAT HAVE COME TOO FAR NORTH BACK AWAY, ... 239 OUR SINGING STRENGTH . 23
CAME TAMELY BACK IN FRONT OF ME, THE DROVER, ... 240 OUR SINGING STRENGTH . 44
THAT BACK BEHIND PURSUIT IT COULDN'T REACH THEM; . . . 240 OUR SINGING STRENGTH . 47
BACK OVER THE SILL . . . . 241 THE LOCKLESS DOOR . . 13
I WANT TO GET OUT OF THE TRAIN AND GO BACK . . . . . 248 A PASSING GLIMPSE . . 3
BLOOD HAS BEEN HARDER TO DAM BACK THAN WATER. . . . . 254 THE FLOOD 1
I HAVE WALKED OUT IN RAIN--AND BACK IN RAIN. . . . . . 255 ACQUAINTED WITH NIGHT . 2
BUT NOT TO CALL ME BACK OR SAY GOOD-BY; . . . . . . 255 ACQUAINTED WITH NIGHT . 10
GET BACK TO THE BEGINNING OF BEGINNINGS, ... 259 WEST-RUNNING BROOK . . 43
NOT JUST A SWERVING, BUT A THROWING BACK, ... 259 WEST-RUNNING BROOK . . 59
AND BRING BACK NATURE IN PEOPLE'S PLACE. . . . . . . 263 THE TIMES TABLE . . . 20
OVER BACK WHERE THEY SPEAK OF LIFE AS STAYING . . . . 263 THE INVESTMENT . . . 1
ALL THAT PIANO AND NEW PAINT BACK THERE, ... 264 THE INVESTMENT . . . 9
THEN LETS IT SNAP BACK UPRIGHT IN THE SKY. . . . . . 268 THE BEAR 4
HE PACES BACK AND FORTH AND NEVER RESTS . . . . . . 269 THE BEAR 16
'TIS ONLY TO SIT BACK AND SWAY HIS HEAD . . . . . . 269 THE BEAR 23
HE SITS BACK ON HIS FUNDAMENTAL BUTT . . . . 269 THE BEAR 26
AND BACK AND FORTH HE SWAYS FROM CHEEK TO CHEEK, . . . 269 THE BEAR 29
(HE STOOD WELL BACK FOR FEAR OF SCALDING SQUIRTS.) . . . 270 THE EGG AND THE MACHINE 12
AND YOU'RE TWO MONTHS BACK IN THE MIDDLE OF MARCH. . . . 275 TWO TRAMPS IN MUD TIME 24
WITH THOSE IN MIND AT MY BACK . . . . 282 A DRUMLIN WOODCHUCK . 9
IN USING THE YARD TO BACK AND TURN AROUND; . . . . . 287 A ROADSIDE STAND . . 40
AND THEN NEXT DAY AS I COME BACK INTO THE SANE, ... 287 A ROADSIDE STAND . . 49
COME BACK THAT WAY A SUMMER HENCE, ... 291 ON HEART'S BEGINNING TO 19
AND FOR BACK WALL A CRUMBLING OLD CHIMNEY . . . . . 294 A RECORD STRIDE . . . 3
BACK UP A STREAM OF RADIANCE TO THE SKY, ... 300 THE MASTER SPEED . . 3
AND BACK THROUGH HISTORY UP THE STREAM OF TIME. . . . . 300 THE MASTER SPEED . . 3
THEY TURN THEIR BACK ON THE LAND. . . . . 301 NEITHER OUT FAR NOR IN 3
I TURNED AND LOOKED BACK UP AT THE SKY, ... 303 AFTERFLAKES 3
I TURNED AND LOOKED BACK UPWARD. . . . . 303 AFTERFLAKES 11
THEY SWORE ALL THE GOLD SHOULD GO BACK . . . . . . 311 THE VINDICTIVES . . 29
AND LOOPED TEN TIMES BACK AND FORTH, ... 312 THE VINDICTIVES . . . 67
AND NEITHER GO ON NOR BACK. . . . . 314 BEARER OF EVIL TIDINGS 26
POETRY, ITSELF ONCE MORE, IS BACK IN LOVE. . . . . . 318 BUILD SOIL 89

BACK (CONTINUED)
   BY BEING PUNISHED BACK, IT IS NOT FREE: . . . . . . 319 BUILD SOIL 115
   MORE THAT SHOULD BE KEPT BACK--THE SOIL FOR INSTANCE, . . . 321 BUILD SOIL 175
   SEDUCED BACK TO THE LAND BY ANY CLAIM . . . . . . 322 BUILD SOIL 207
   OR MENDING FENCE IT ALL COMES BACK TO ME . . . . . . 325 BUILD SOIL 288
   FROM FORCE TO MATTER AND BACK TO FORCE, ... 325 TO A THINKER 8
   FROM FORM TO CONTENT AND BACK TO FORM, ... 325 TO A THINKER 9
   FROM NORM TO CRAZY AND BACK TO NORM, ... 325 TO A THINKER 10
   FROM BOUND TO FREE AND BACK TO BOUND, ... 325 TO A THINKER 11
   FROM SOUND TO SENSE AND BACK TO SOUND. . . . . . . 326 TO A THINKER 12
   SO BACK AND FORTH. IT ALMOST SCARES . . . . . . 326 TO A THINKER 13
   IS NOT ITS OWN LOVE BACK IN COPY SPEECH, ... 338 THE MOST OF IT . . . 7
   SHE DREW BACK; HE WAS CALM: . . . . . . 339 THE SUBVERTED FLOWER . 1
   A MAN COMES BACK TO A WOMAN AGAIN . . . . . . 346 DISCOVERY OF MADEIRAS . 87
   SHE WITHDREW BACK IN SELF-RETREAT . . . . . . 346 DISCOVERY OF MADEIRAS . 101
   I SHOULD BETAKE ME BACK TEN THOUSAND PAGES . . . . . 350 THE LESSON FOR TODAY . 6
   LEAN BACK AND HAVE MY CONFIDENTIAL LAUGH, ... 354 THE LESSON FOR TODAY . 125
   BUT FROM IRRESOLUTION IN HIS BACK . . . . . . 361 A LOOSE MOUNTAIN . . 19
   WHO DREW BACK AT FIRST IN DOUBT, ... 366 NOT OF SCHOOL AGE . . 6
   TO TAKE THE MAYFLOWER BACK WHERE HE BELONGED, ... 370 THE LITERATE FARMER AND 59
   AND THEN GET SLOWLY, SLOWLY PULLED BACK DOWN. . . . . 370 THE LITERATE FARMER AND 67
   BACK OUT OF ALL THIS NOW TOO MUCH FOR US, ... 377 DIRECTIVE 1
   BACK IN A TIME MADE SIMPLE BY THE LOSS . . . . . . 377 DIRECTIVE 2
   THE ELEPHANT STANDS ON THE BACK OF A TURTLE; . . . . 379 TOO ANXIOUS FOR RIVERS 15
   THE WAVE SUCKS BACK AND WITH THE LAST OF WATER . . . . 391 ON BEING IDOLIZED . . 1
   WHAT SHE BROUGHT BACK WOULD AMAZE YE. . . . . . . 396 AN IMPORTER 2
   AND TAKE YOUR WALK OF RECREATION BACK . . . . . . 405 FROM PLANE TO PLANE . 42
   PICK UP OUR EYES AND CARRY THEM BACK IDLE . . . . . 405 FROM PLANE TO PLANE . 51
   THE OTHER WAY OF READING BACK AND FORTH, ... 405 FROM PLANE TO PLANE . 53
   AND STARTED HIS MARCH BACK AGAIN DISCOURSING: . . . . 406 FROM PLANE TO PLANE . 60
   HE LIKES TO TURN HIS BACK ON GRATITUDE . . . . . . 408 FROM PLANE TO PLANE . 130
   TO PUSH THE WOODS BACK FROM AROUND THE HOUSE . . . . 414 A CABIN IN THE CLEARING 3
   AND COME NOT BACK WITH STEED . . . . . . 415 CLOSED FOR GOOD . . 7
   FOR GETTING BACK SOMEWHERE OR FURTHER ON." . . . . . 420 ONE MORE BREVITY . . 48
   NO ONE HAS SEEN HIM STUMBLE LOOKING BACK. . . . . . 421 ESCAPIST--NEVER . . . 2
   GOES BACK TO THE BEGINNING OF THE END . . . . . . 422 FOR JOHN F. KENNEDY . 8
   BACK THERE IN 1953 WITH THE HUNTINGTON CAIRNSES . . . . 428 KITTY HAWK . . . . D
   OF AN ANSWER BACK . . . . . . 429 KITTY HAWK 34
   AND REACHING BACK TO HIS RIBS . . . . . . 444 THE DRAFT HORSE . . . 7
   I ASK OF YOU. GRIND THIS I THROW YOU BACK . . . . . 447 DOES NO ONE AT ALL EVER 29
   THE SIBYL SAID, "GO BACK TO ROME . . . . . . 449 OUR DOOM TO BLOOM . . 5
   BUT HASTENED BACK TO REASSURE HIS SLAVE . . . . . . 457 HOW HARD TO KEEP FROM 112
   THAT WAS BACK IN THE DAYS OF MY GODMOTHER GOOSE. . . . 463 LINES IN DEJECTION . 5
   SO HE LEAPT ON HER HAIRY BACK AND BIT HER . . . . . 463 LINES IN DEJECTION . 19
   HE ANSWERED HER BACK, "WELL, WHO BEGUN IT?" . . . . . 463 LINES IN DEJECTION . 25
   MIGHT NEVER BRING HER BACK. . . . . . 464 MILKY WAY IS A COWPATH 24
   MY STAYING BACK BEHIND . . . . . . 465 SOME SCIENCE FICTION . 6
   AND WHEN THAT LEFT ME TO SINK BACK REVERSED . . . . . 468 IN A GLASS OF CIDER . 5
   A MAN SITS LEANING BACK AGAINST A PALM. . . . . . 473 A MASQUE OF REASON . 2
   WE MAY AS WELL GO BACK TO THE BEGINNING . . . . . 477 A MASQUE OF REASON . 113
   OH, LORD, LET'S NOT GO BACK TO ANYTHING. . . . . . 477 A MASQUE OF REASON . 115
   I THOUGHT YOU HAD NONE. SOMEWHERE BACK . . . . . 482 A MASQUE OF REASON . 240
   SHOW YOURSELF, SON.--I'LL GET BACK ON MY THRONE . . . 487 A MASQUE OF MERCY . 386
   WE DON'T GO BACK ON GRAPES WE COULDN'T REACH. . . . . 496 A MASQUE OF MERCY . 77
   RIGHT BACK IN THE SAME TROUBLE I WAS IN. . . . . . 500 A MASQUE OF MERCY . 185
   WE CAN GO BACK TO WHERE WE STARTED FROM. . . . . . 507 A MASQUE OF MERCY . 359
   AND YET CAN'T TURN YOUR BACK ON OR IGNORE, ... 512 A MASQUE OF MERCY . 510
   BUT WHEN THE BRINE GOES BACK, AS GO IT MUST, ... 513 A MASQUE OF MERCY . 540
   TO BRING FAITH BACK. I'M ONLY LANGUIDLY . . . . . 515 A MASQUE OF MERCY . 566
   TOO MUCH ALL-FIRED BELIEF AND WE'D BE BACK . . . . . 516 A MASQUE OF MERCY . 602
   SOME LINGERING OBJECTION HOLDS YOU BACK. . . . . . 517 A MASQUE OF MERCY . 632
   (STILL ON HIS KNEES, HE SITS BACK ON HIS HEELS.) . . . 519 A MASQUE OF MERCY . 671
BACK-CAGE
   PRECIPITATELY THEY RETIRED BACK-CAGE . . . . . . 293 AT WOODWARD'S GARDENS . 24
BACKED
   THE SHORE WAS LUCKY IN BEING BACKED BY CLIFF, ... 250 ONCE BY THE PACIFIC . 8
   THE CLIFF IN BEING BACKED BY CONTINENT; . . . . . 250 ONCE BY THE PACIFIC . 9
   HAD THE QUEEN BACKED HIM TO A CRUISE. . . . . . 416 AMERICA IS HARD TO SEE 6
BACKS
   "STAY WHERE YOU ARE UNTIL OUR BACKS ARE TURNED!" . . . 33 MENDING WALL . . . 19
   AND COT THEM OFF THE WILD FLOWERS' BACKS. . . . . . 123 PEA BRUSH 16
   WHILE THEY HAD BACKS TURNED, THAT IT HADN'T BEEN THERE . 132 THE BONFIRE 86
   ACROSS THE LOGS LIKE BACKS OF ALLIGATORS, ... 195 PAUL'S WIFE 121
   ON THE BACKS OF A SINGLE-FILE HOST, ... 312 THE VINDICTIVES . . . 72
BACKWARD
   AND NOTHING TO LOOK BACKWARD TO WITH PRIDE, ... 38 DEATH OF THE HIRED MAN 100
   MESERVE WAS FIRST TO SPEAK. HE POINTED BACKWARD . . . 143 SNOW 6
   TRYING TO TURN ITSELF BACKWARD OR FORWARD, ... 147 SNOW 119
   IT WANTS TO SEE HOW YOU WILL TAKE; IF BACKWARD, . . . 147 SNOW 123
   FLUNG BACKWARD ON ITSELF IN ONE WHITE WAVE, ... 258 WEST-RUNNING BROOK . 20
   IT HAS THIS THROWING BACKWARD ON ITSELF . . . . . 259 WEST-RUNNING BROOK . 61
   IT IS THIS BACKWARD MOTION TOWARD THE SOURCE, ... 260 WEST-RUNNING BROOK . 68
   THE OLD DOG BARKS BACKWARD WITHOUT GETTING UP. . . . 308 THE SPAN OF LIFE . . 1
   AND DREW HER BACKWARD HOME. . . . . . 341 THE SUBVERTED FLOWER . 73
   ONE STEP BACKWARD TAKEN . . . . . . 376 ONE STEP BACKWARD TAKEN T
   BUT WITH ONE STEP BACKWARD TAKEN . . . . . . 377 ONE STEP BACKWARD TAKEN 10
BACKWOODS
   AND FOR THE BACKWOODS WOODCHUCK. YOU'RE THE GIRL! . . 97 THE SELF-SEEKER . . . 125
BACKYARD
   IN HIS OWN BACKYARD . . . . . . 441 KITTY HAWK 407
BACON
   WHILE I FRY THEIR BACON. MUCH THEY CARE! . . . . . 65 A SERVANT TO SERVANTS . 78
BAD
   HE NEVER DID A THING SO VERY BAD. . . . . . 39 DEATH OF THE HIRED MAN 142
   TOO BAD TO WASTE THEM ALL. YOU OUGHT TO HAVE THEM. . . 47 A HUNDRED COLLARS . . 67
   TO TELL IF HE KNEW. BUT THE YEAR HAD BEEN BAD. . . . 61 BLUEBERRIES 72
   SHE THINKS IF IT WAS BAD TO LIVE WITH HIM, ... 83 THE HOUSEKEEPER . . . 74
   JOHN'S A BAD FARMER. I'M NOT BLAMING HIM. . . . . 85 THE HOUSEKEEPER . . . 102

BAD (CONTINUED)
    SO THAT WAS WHAT WAS BACK. SHE'S BAD, THAT'S ALL!" . . . . 88 THE HOUSEKEEPER . . . 183
    "BAD TO GET MARRIED WHEN SHE HAD THE CHANCE?" . . . . . 88 THE HOUSEKEEPER . . . 184
    YOU'RE BAD ENOUGH TO MANAGE, WITHOUT HER." . . . . . . 94 THE SELF-SEEKER . . . 55
    OR BEST--IT MAY NOT BE SO BAD. THE FIRM . . . . 95 THE SELF-SEEKER . . . 78
    YOU'RE HIDING SOMETHING. THAT'S AS BAD AS LYING. . . . . 97 THE SELF-SEEKER . . . 132
    TOO BAD I COULDN'T LAY ONE IN A LETTER. . . . . 107 CHRISTMAS TREES . . . 58
    IT'S NOT SO BAD IN THE COUNTRY, SETTLED DOWN, ... 113 IN THE HOME STRETCH . 93
    ITS SEEMING BAD FOR A MOMENT MAKES IT SEEM . . . . . . 115 IN THE HOME STRETCH . 128
    INCREDULOUS OF HIS OWN BAD LUCK. . . . . 138 BROWN'S DESCENT . . . 41
    SO BAD.--GIVE ME AN HOUR FOR IT.--HO, HO, ... 143 SNOW 21
    BUT IN THE BEST STYLE OF BAD SALESMANSHIP, ... 160 NEW HAMPSHIRE . . . 28
    'TWOULD BE TOO BAD TO MAKE HIM SORRY FOR . . . . . . 183 MAPLE 121
    HE HAD IN MIND TO SAY TO A BAD NEIGHBOR . . . . . . 185 THE AX-HELVE 16
    IT WAS THE BAD AX-HELVE. SOMEONE HAD SOLD ME-- . . . . 186 THE AX-HELVE 21
    "SHE AIN'T SPICK TOO MUCH HENGLISH--DAT'S TOO BAD." . . . 187 THE AX-HELVE 54
    CAN DO A GOOD DEAL TO BAD MASONRY. . . . . 213 A FOUNTAIN, A BOTTLE . 26
    BOYS AND BAD HUNTERS HAD KNOWN WHAT TO DO . . . . . . 216 A FOUNTAIN, A BOTTLE . 102
    BY THOUSANDS THE BAD WEATHER MADE AKIN. . . . . 240 OUR SINGING STRENGTH . 32
    BUT TWO FOR A BEGINNING WASN'T BAD. . . . . 283 THE GOLD HESPERIDEE . 12
    BUT TO MAKE BAD MATTERS WORSE . . . . 309 NOT ALL THERE . . .   3
    THE TIMES SEEM REVOLUTIONARY BAD. . . . . 317 BUILD SOIL 32
    LIFE MAY BE TRAGICALLY BAD, AND I . . . . 317 BUILD SOIL 41
    I DOUBT IF YOU'RE CONVINCED THE TIMES ARE BAD. . . . . . 317 BUILD SOIL 53
    WE SOMETIMES ONLY GET THE BAD OF THEM. . . . . 319 BUILD SOIL 97
    AND GET OUTSIDE OF TOO MUCH BAD STATISTICS, ... 351 THE LESSON FOR TODAY . 37
    AND STILL IT'S BAD ENOUGH TO BADLY WOUND, ... 372 THE LITERATE FARMER AND 119
    IT GAVE BAD DREAMS AND BROKEN SLEEP, ... 382 THE NIGHT LIGHT . . .   3
    HIS EYES AS GOOD (OR BAD) AS SHUT . . . . 418 AMERICA IS HARD TO SEE 58
    THE BAD ISLAND--EASTER . . . . 447 THE BAD ISLAND--EASTER   T
    THAT THERE WAS SUCH A THING AS BAD. . . . . 467 QUANDARY   2
    THAT GOOD AND BAD SO LONG HAD LASTED. . . . . 467 QUANDARY   6
    IT WOULD BE TOO BAD IF COLUMBUS-LIKE . . . . 480 A MASQUE OF REASON . 186
    WHERE GOOD AND BAD ARE MINGLED EVERY WHICH WAY, ... 488 A MASQUE OF REASON . 408
    THEY WON'T SHOW IN THE PICTURE. THAT'S TOO BAD. . . . . . 490 A MASQUE OF REASON . 462
    NEITHER WILL I SHOW. THAT'S TOO BAD MOREOVER. . . . . . 490 A MASQUE OF REASON . 463
    OR BAD AS IN NEW YORK. / I KNOW I AM. . . . . 497 A MASQUE OF MERCY . 93
    TO A BAD START IT SEEMS IN THE WRONG SCHOOL . . . . . . 499 A MASQUE OF MERCY . 162
BADE
    "TAKE ONE," OLD DAVIS BADE ME GRACIOUSLY. . . . . . . 217 A FOUNTAIN, A BOTTLE . 123
    AND BADE HIM LEAVE THE PAN AND STOKE THE ARCH: . . . . . 234 EVENING A SUGAR ORCHARD   4
    I BADE A "COME IN" . . . . 241 THE LOCKLESS DOOR . . 14
    I BADE MEN TELL ME WHICH IN BRIEF, ... 297 LEAVES COMPARED WITH . 13
BADGE
    (YOUR BADGE OF OFFICE IS A SPADE). . . . . 327 A MISSIVE MISSILE . . 24
BADLY
    IT LOOKED AS IF HE MIGHT BE BADLY THROWN . . . . 190 THE GRINDSTONE . . . 58
    AND STILL IT'S BAD ENOUGH TO BADLY WOUND, ... 372 THE LITERATE FARMER AND 119
    YOU WOULDN'T SAY SHE FARED SO VERY BADLY. . . . . . . 477 A MASQUE OF REASON . 98
    A GOD CAN FIND IN LAUGHING AT HOW BADLY . . . . 483 A MASQUE OF REASON . 274
BADNESS
    (WE'RE RIVALS IN THE BADNESS OF OUR CASE, ... 352 THE LESSON FOR TODAY . 66
BAFFLED
    I BROKE OFF BAFFLED. BUT ALL THE SAME, ... 420 ONE MORE BREVITY . . 38
    BY BEING BAFFLED FOR THE SAKE OF BEING. . . . . 484 A MASQUE OF REASON . 299
BAG
    A MAN WITH A SWINGING BAG FOR LOAD . . . . 140 THE GUM-GATHERER .   5
    AND HALF THE BAG WOUND ROUND HIS HAND. . . . . 140 THE GUM-GATHERER .   6
    HE DUMPED HIMSELF LIKE A BAG OF BONES. . . . . 419 ONE MORE BREVITY . 15
BAGGAGE
    AND BAGGAGE AT THEIR FEET. . . . . 391 A ROGERS GROUP . . .   4
BAGGY
    A BAGGY FIGURE, EQUALLY PATHETIC . . . . 269 THE BEAR 33
BAGS
    AND BAGS FULL OF LEAVES . . . . 234 GATHERING LEAVES . .   3
BAILEYS
    THE TOWN IS FULL OF CHASES, LOWES, AND BAILEYS, ... 75 THE GENERATIONS OF MEN 48
BAIT
    ENOUGH TO BAIT THE TRAP OF THE IDEAL . . . . 508 A MASQUE OF MERCY . . 386
BAKER'S
    AS FINE AS FLOUR PUT THROUGH A BAKER'S SIEVE. . . . . . 365 OF STONES OF THE PLACE   8
BAKESHOP
    HE GETS SOME SORT OF BAKESHOP MEALS TOGETHER, ... 82 THE HOUSEKEEPER . . . 31
BALANCE
    WE HAVE TO USE A SPELL TO MAKE THEM BALANCE: . . . . . 33 MENDING WALL 18
    GREAT BOULDERS OFF THEIR BALANCE . . . . 376 ONE STEP BACKWARD TAKEN   4
BALANCED
    WHILE YOU SIT WARM AND READ UP BALANCED RATIONS. . . . . 149 SNOW 183
    TO KEEP THEIR BUILDING BALANCED AT MY BREAST. . . . . . 267 THE ARMFUL   8
BALANCING
    A MOMENT HE STOOD BALANCING WITH EMOTION, ... 204 THE WITCH OF COOS . . 71
BALEARIC
    IS SOMETHING IN A BALEARIC SLING . . . . 361 A LOOSE MOUNTAIN . . 16
BALL
    AND THE SUN'S BRILLIANT BALL . . . . 333 HAPPINESS MAKES UP .   5
    AND ALSO PROVED THE WORLD A BALL, ... 416 AMERICA IS HARD TO SEE   3
    FROM THIS BALL OF STONE, ... 440 KITTY HAWK 381
BALLOON
    THE WHITE-TAILED HORNET LIVES IN A BALLOON . . . . . . 277 THE WHITE-TAILED HORNET   1
BALLOONING
    IT ALMOST SEEMED TO COME BALLOONING UP, ... 113 IN THE HOME STRETCH . 88
BALLOONS
    ARE LIGHT AS BALLOONS. . . . . 234 GATHERING LEAVES . .   4
    AS CIRCUS DAY OF TOY BALLOONS. . . . . 451 A-WISHING WELL . . . 18
BALLS
    AND SOME ARE LOAVES AND SOME SO NEARLY BALLS . . . . . 33 MENDING WALL 17
    HE'D BUILT A NOBLE MANSARD ROOF WITH BALLS . . . . . . 160 NEW HAMPSHIRE . . . 39
    THAN HAS THE UNIVERSE'S. WE ARE BALLS, ... 322 BUILD SOIL 199

PAGE TITLE LINE

BALLS (CONTINUED)
THE THINGS BUT BALLS ALL GOING ROUND IN RINGS. . . . . . 425 ACCIDENTALLY ON PURPOSE 2
BALSAMS
MY WOODS--THE YOUNG FIR BALSAMS LIKE A PLACE . . . . . 106 CHRISTMAS TREES . . . 13
BAMBOOS
BAMBOOS, IVORIES, JADES, AND LACQUERS, ... 396 AN IMPORTER 3
BAND (SEE ANKLE-BAND)
WHEN IT OUTGROWS THE WIRE BAND OF ITS NAME TAG. . . . . 46 A HUNDRED COLLARS . . 57
BANDED (SEE TAR-BANDED)
BAND-MUSIC
SPEAKING OR SINGING, AND THE BAND-MUSIC PLAYING. . . . . 78 THE GENERATIONS OF MEN 130
BANDSTAND
UNDER THE BANDSTAND IN SUBURBAN PARK. . . . . 501 A MASQUE OF MERCY . . 210
BANDYING
I FIGURE THAT LIKE ANY BANDYING . . . . 321 BUILD SOIL 169
BANG
I LIKE IT.--BANG GOES SOMETHING BIG AWAY . . . . . . 111 IN THE HOME STRETCH . 37
AND BANG GOES SOMETHING ELSE AWAY OFF THERE. . . . . 112 IN THE HOME STRETCH . 55
BANGED
"A FIT!" SAID ONE, AND BANGED A STOVEPIPE SHOULDER. . . . 113 IN THE HOME STRETCH . 90
BANISHING
THEY MAY END BY BANISHING ME . . . . 466 SOME SCIENCE FICTION . 21
BANISTER
THAT RESTED ON THE BANISTER, AND SLID DOWNSTAIRS; . . . . 52 HOME BURIAL 32
BANJO
MY SMALL WRISTS STRETCHING TILL THEY SHOWED THE BANJO
STRINGS. . . . . 198 WILD GRAPES 80
BANK
A SOMEBODY--DIRECTOR IN THE BANK." . . . . 39 DEATH OF THE HIRED MAN 129
AND BY A RIVER BANK FOR WATER FLOWERS, ... 98 THE SELF-SEEKER . . 153
FROM GEORGES BANK WHEN WINDS WERE BLOWING. . . . . . 262 THE FLOWER BOAT . . . 8
ONE THING HAS A SHELVING BANK, ... 281 A DRUMLIN WOODCHUCK . 1
EXCEPT BESIDE A SAFE INSIDE A BANK . . . . 386 THE FEAR OF MAN . . . 9
THE RIVER BANK, QUIT WORK DEFIANTLY, ... 405 FROM PLANE TO PLANE . 58
BEFORE THEY SAT DOWN WEARY ON A BANK . . . . 454 HOW HARD TO KEEP FROM 13
BANKED
BUT BANKED THE DAYLIGHT OUT OF AVERY'S WINDOWS. . . . 149 SNOW 186
THE CELLAR WINDOWS WERE BANKED UP WITH SAWDUST . . . 204 THE WITCH OF COOS . . 57
THE WINTER OWL BANKED JUST IN TIME TO PASS . . . . 445 QUESTIONING FACES . . 1
BANKING
AND FOUND ME BANKING UP THE HOUSE WITH SNOW. . . . . 149 SNOW 177
BANKS
ITS TWO BANKS HAVE NOT SHUT UPON THE RIVER; . . . . 28 MY BUTTERFLY 9
UNTIL THE BUSHES ALL ALONG ITS BANKS . . . . . . 42 THE MOUNTAIN . . . 52
TO LINK A CHAIN OF MONEY-METAL BANKS. . . . . . . 358 THE LOST FOLLOWER . . 8
BANNERS
WITH THE INTENTION BLAZONED ON THEIR BANNERS . . . . 397 THE PLANNERS 11
BANQUET
THIS TIME AN ALL-NIGHT BANQUET, TO BE SURE, ... 458 HOW HARD TO KEEP FROM 133
BANQUETERS
AND THE MEAL MADE THE BANQUETERS EXCLAIM . . . . . 455 HOW HARD TO KEEP FROM 58
BAPTISMAL
AND BUILT A STONE BAPTISMAL FONT OUTDOORS-- . . . . 213 A FOUNTAIN, A BOTTLE . 10
YOU SAID YOU'D SEEN THE STONE BAPTISMAL FONT. . . . 213 A FOUNTAIN, A BOTTLE . 13
BAPTISTE
THIS WAS A MAN, BAPTISTE, WHO STOLE ONE DAY . . . . 185 THE AX-HELVE . . . 6
BAPTISTE KNEW BEST WHY I WAS WHERE I WAS. . . . . 186 THE AX-HELVE . . . 37
MRS. BAPTISTE CAME IN AND ROCKED A CHAIR . . . . 186 THE AX-HELVE . . . 46
THEN ON BAPTISTE, AS IF SHE UNDERSTOOD . . . . . 187 THE AX-HELVE . . . 56
BAPTISTE WAS ANXIOUS FOR HER; BUT NO MORE . . . . 187 THE AX-HELVE . . . 58
BAPTISTE KNEW HOW TO MAKE A SHORT JOB LONG . . . 187 THE AX-HELVE . . . 80
BAPTISTE ON HIS DEFENSE ABOUT THE CHILDREN . . . 188 THE AX-HELVE . . . 83
BAPTISTE DREW BACK AND SQUINTED AT IT, PLEASED: . . 188 THE AX-HELVE . . . 101
BAR
THE CUTTER BAR HAD JUST GONE CHAMPING OVER . . . . 109 THE EXPOSED NEST . . 14
HE MOVED IT ROUGHLY WITH AN IRON BAR, ... 173 A STAR IN A STONEBOAT . 25
THROWS DOWN IN FRONT OF US IS NOT TO BAR . . . . 238 ON A TREE FALLEN ACROSS 2
BY CRAMPING THE WHEEL ON A WATER BAR, ... 263 THE TIMES TABLE . . 5
BUT WHEN WAS THAT EVER A BAR . . . . 301 NEITHER OUT FAR NOR IN 15
WHEN PAST THE LEG I THRUST FOR BAR . . . . . . 419 ONE MORE BREVITY . . 8
BARB
WILL LEAVE THEIR TATTERS HUNG ON BARB AND THORN.) . . . 379 DIRECTIVE 54
BARBED
HER GREAT WEIGHT CREAKS THE BARBED WIRE IN ITS STAPLES . 269 THE BEAR 7
BARBED-WIRE
WITH BARBED-WIRE BINDING. THEY STOOD FACING THIS, . . . 229 TWO LOOK AT TWO . . . 8
BARBER
UNDER THE HAND OF THE VILLAGE BARBER, ... 262 THE FLOWER BOAT . . . 2
BARD
BUT TRUST MY INSTINCT--I'M A BARD. . . . . 326 TO A THINKER 36
BREATHES THERE A BARD WHO ISN'T MOVED . . . . . . 469 CHOSEN POET OF VERMONT 1
BARDS
THE GLORIOUS BARDS OF MASSACHUSETTS SEEM . . . . . 167 NEW HAMPSHIRE . . . 262
BARE
SHE LOVES THE BARE, THE WITHERED TREE; . . . . . 6 MY NOVEMBER GUEST . . 4
THE LOVE OF BARE NOVEMBER DAYS . . . . 7 MY NOVEMBER GUEST . . 17
A TREE BESIDE THE WALL STANDS BARE, ... 9 A LATE WALK . . . 9
STRIPPED TO BARE GROUND, THE MAPLE TREES . . . . 49 A HUNDRED COLLARS . 135
IT NEVER GOT SO FAR AS THAT; BUT THE BARE THOUGHT . . 57 THE BLACK COTTAGE . . 90
AND LEAVE THE SLOPE BEHIND THE HOUSE ALL BARE, . . . 106 CHRISTMAS TREES . . . 18
ON THE BARE UPLAND PASTURE THERE HAD SPREAD . . . 126 RANGE-FINDING . . 9
FROM THE BARE TOP OF WHICH THERE IS A VIEW . . . 195 PAUL'S WIFE . . . 125
THAT MADE HIM THROW HIS BARE LEGS CUT OF BED . . . 205 THE WITCH OF COOS . . 102
AMONG BARE MAPLE BOUGHS, AND IN THE RARE . . . . 234 EVENING A SUGAR ORCHARD 8
THE ORCHARD BARE . . . . 445 PERIL OF HOPE . . 3
BAREBACK
BUT BEING MOUNTED BAREBACK ON THE EARTH? . . . . . 267 RIDERS 6

BARED
    BESIDE A REEDY BROOK THE SCYTHE HAD BARED. . . . . . . 22 THE TUFT OF FLOWERS . 24
BAREFOOT
    A LITTLE BAREFOOT GIRL, WHO IN THE NOISE . . . . 96 THE SELF-SEEKER . . . 92
    SO UNDERMINES MY BAREFOOT STAND I TOTTER, ... 391 ON BEING IDOLIZED . .   4
BARELY
    THREE TIMES HE BARELY STIRRED THE BELL, THEN LISTENED. . . 143 SNOW 15
    BUT BARELY GETS FROM THEM OR HER . . . . 281 BLUE RIBBON AT AMESBURY 51
BARGAIN
    TO TRY TO HELP ME DRIVE A BETTER BARGAIN." . . . . . . 93 THE SELF-SEEKER . . .   9
    US OF OUR BARGAIN. BUT THEY LEFT US SO . . . . 114 IN THE HOME STRETCH . 124
    TO KEEP HIS BARGAIN OF THE MORNING WITH ME . . . . . . 187 THE AX-HELVE 60
    IS IT A BARGAIN, SHEPHERD MELIBOEUS? . . . . 325 BUILD SOIL 283
BARGAINED
    AND GIVE US MORE THAN OUR SPOKESMAN BARGAINED FOR; . . . 349 OUR HOLD ON THE PLANET 4
BARITONE
    AND BARITONE IMPORTANCE OF THE LAWYER, ... 96 THE SELF-SEEKER . . . 94
BARK
    AND WHISPERS WITH A SORT OF STIFLED BARK, ...   9 STORM FEAR   4
    RIDGES OF SAND, AND DRIFTWOOD STRIPPED OF BARK. . . . . 40 THE MOUNTAIN 14
    THE WOOD WAS GRAY AND THE BARK WARPING OFF IT . . . . 102 THE WOOD-PILE 29
    TO SET YOUR BREAST TO THE BARK OF TREES . . . . 141 THE GUM-GATHERER . . 35
    AND SWEPT OF LEATHERN LEAVES, BUT LEFT THE BARK . . . . 184 MAPLE 141
    THE BARK OF A WHOLE TAMARACK OFF WHOLE, ... 191 PAUL'S WIFE 19
    BEFORE I STRAIGHTENED THEM AND BRUSHED THE BARK OFF. . . 199 WILD GRAPES 88
    THE SWEET OF BITTER BARK . . . . 227 TO EARTHWARD 23
    AND THE COLD TO AN ORCHARD SO YOUNG IN THE BARK . . . . 228 GOOD-BY AND KEEP COLD . 2
    YOU GRASP THE BARK BY A RUGGED PLEAT, ... 247 ON GOING UNNOTICED .   9
    ON SOME WILD APPLE-TREE'S YOUNG TENDER BARK, ... 254 A WINTER EDEN . . . 11
    BUT TONIGHT I WILL BARK . . . . 261 CANIS MAJOR 10
    SO MAY ITS BARK, SO MAY ITS WOOD; . . . . 296 LEAVES COMPARED WITH . 2
    LEAVES FOR SMOOTH AND BARK FOR ROUGH, ... 297 LEAVES COMPARED WITH . 7
    LEAVES AND BARK MAY BE TREE ENOUGH. . . . . 297 LEAVES COMPARED WITH . 8
    LEAVES AND BARK, LEAVES AND BARK, ... 297 LEAVES COMPARED WITH . 17
    SHE HEARD HIM BARK OUTRIGHT. . . . . 341 THE SUBVERTED FLOWER . 64
    IT WILL STAND FORTH, ENTIRELY WHITE IN BARK, ... 375 A YOUNG BIRCH . . .   6
BARKED
    LAST NIGHT YOUR WATCHDOG BARKED ALL NIGHT, ... 380 AN UNSTAMPED LETTER IN 1
BARKEEP
    NOT FIND A BARKEEP UNTO JOVE IN ME? . . . . 443 AUSPEX   9
BARKING
    WE TALKED LIKE BARKING ABOVE THE DIN . . . . 140 THE GUM-GATHERER . .   7
BARKLESS
    A BARKLESS SPECTER. HE HAD HALTED TOO, ... 125 AN ENCOUNTER 14
BARKS
    THE OLD DOG BARKS BACKWARD WITHOUT GETTING UP. . . . . 308 THE SPAN OF LIFE . .   1
BARN
    TILL EVEN THE COMFORTING BARN GROWS FAR AWAY, ... 10 STORM FEAR 15
    HUDDLED AGAINST THE BARN DOOR FAST ASLEEP, ... 35 DEATH OF THE HIRED MAN 35
    EVERYTHING'S SHUT SOMETIMES EXCEPT THE BARN; . . . . . 49 A HUNDRED COLLARS . 130
    LIKE STANCHIONS IN THE BARN, FROM FLOOR TO CEILING-- . . 66 A SERVANT TO SERVANTS 115
    I'VE HEARD HIM POUNDING IN THE BARN ALL NIGHT. . . . . 71 THE CODE 42
    EVERYTHING WENT WELL TILL WE REACHED THE BARN . . . . 71 THE CODE 53
    'I LEFT HIM IN THE BARN UNDER THE HAY. . . . . 72 THE CODE 84
    THEY HEADED FOR THE BARN; I STAYED WHERE I WAS. . . . . 72 THE CODE 88
    A LOT OF IT, OUT INTO THE BARN FLOOR. . . . . 72 THE CODE 90
    OUT OF THE BARN.' SOMEONE LOOKED IN A WINDOW, ... 72 THE CODE 95
    A LANTERN-LIGHT FROM DEEPER IN THE BARN . . . . 89 THE FEAR   1
    BETWEEN THE HOUSE AND BARN THE GALE . . . . 137 BROWN'S DESCENT . .   9
    WHOSE BUSINESS--BUT WHY TALK ROUND THE BARN?-- . . . . 142 THE VANISHING RED .   7
    LIKE DARLINGS, BOTH OF THEM. THEY'RE IN THE BARN.-- . . 143 SNOW 25
    HE HAD COLE WITH HIM TO THE BARN TO SEE HIM OFF. . . . 151 SNOW 244
    HE SAYS SHE WENT TO LET HIM IN THE BARN.-- . . . . . 155 SNOW 331
    INSIDE THE THRESHOLD OF THIS OPEN BARN, ... 160 NEW HAMPSHIRE . . . 45
    AND FROM BARN SMELLS YOU CAN'T WASH OUT OF PLOWED GROUND . 210 PAUPER WITCH OF GRAFTON 91
    THE BARN OPPOSED ACROSS THE WAY, ... 241 NEED OF BEING VERSED . 5
    AND HERE IN THE ANGLE OF HOUSE AND BARN . . . . 262 THE FLOWER BOAT . .   3
    TO CLOSE THIS OUTPOST BARN AND CLOSE THE SEASON. . . . 289 OLD BARN AT THE BOTTOM 7
    THE OLD BARN AT THE BOTTOM OF THE FOGS. . . . . 289 OLD BARN AT THE BOTTOM T
    ONE NIGHT (HE TOLD ME). AND THE BARN HE MEANT . . . . 289 OLD BARN AT THE BOTTOM 20
    THE OLD BARN AT THE BOTTOM OF THE FOGS. . . . . 290 OLD BARN AT THE BOTTOM 23
BARN'S
    WHERE'S THIS BARN'S HOUSE? IT NEVER HAD A HOUSE, . . . 289 OLD BARN AT THE BOTTOM 1
BARNYARD
    DEARER TO HIM THAN ANY BARNYARD BRUTE, ... 283 THE GOLD HESPERIDEE . 22
BARREL
    AND THERE'S A BARREL THAT I DIDN'T FILL . . . . 68 AFTER APPLE-PICKING . 3
    HE CAN EAT OFF A BARREL FROM THE GROUND. . . . . 86 THE HOUSEKEEPER . . 149
    UP THE BRASS BARREL, VELVET BLACK INSIDE, ... 179 THE STAR-SPLITTER . 77
    FAILED TO CRUSH THEIR BARREL STAVES . . . . 344 DISCOVERY OF MADEIRAS . 28
BARRELED (SEE DOUBLE-BARRELED)
BARRELS
    HE STOOD WITH BARRELS ROUND HIM--AT A LOSS. . . . . . 108 OLD MAN'S WINTER NIGHT 8
BARREN
    THE BARREN BOUGHS WITHOUT THE LEAVES, ... 18 GOING FOR WATER . . 11
    (SOFT PETALS, YES, BUT NOT SO BARREN QUITE, ... 124 PUTTING IN THE SEED . 5
BARRENER
    HE COULD IMAGINE NOTHING BARRENER. . . . . 417 AMERICA IS HARD TO SEE 15
BARRIER
    I TRUSTED THE BROOK BARRIER, BUT FEARED . . . . 131 THE BONFIRE 74
    HALTING PERPLEXED BEHIND THE BARRIER . . . . 203 THE WITCH OF COOS . 24
    BEHIND NEW BARRIER WALLS (AND LET IT CHAFE!), ... 254 THE FLOOD   3
    ACROSS THE BARRIER OF ICE: . . . . 327 A MISSIVE MISSILE .   6
    ACROSS THE ICY BARRIER . . . . 327 A MISSIVE MISSILE . 28
BARRING
    AT WHICH RATE BARRING BROODINESS . . . . 280 BLUE RIBBON AT AMESBURY 31
BARS
    HAVEN'T COME DOWN TO THE BARS AT MILKING TIME? . . . . 43 THE MOUNTAIN 86

PAGE TITLE LINE

BARS (CONTINUED)
HE'D PULL HIS BARS APART LIKE BOW AND BOWSTRING, ... 66 A SERVANT TO SERVANTS . 134
I OFTEN THINK OF THE SMOOTH HICKORY BARS. . . . . 67 A SERVANT TO SERVANTS . 144
AND ON THE PASTURE BARS . . . . 252 THE PEACEFUL SHEPHERD . 2
LIKE WAKING IN A CAGE OF SILVER BARS. . . . . 290 OLD BARN AT THE BOTTOM 27
THEY STOOD ARMS LACED TOGETHER AT THE BARS, ... 293 AT WOODWARD'S GARDENS . 12
CAME DRYLY FORWARD TO THE BARS AGAIN . . . . 294 AT WOODWARD'S GARDENS . 32
THROUGH LET-DOWN PASTURE BARS . . . . 465 MILKY WAY IS A COWPATH 30
BARTLETT
BARTLETT OF RAYMOND (NOW OF COLORADO), ... 167 NEW HAMPSHIRE . . . 260
BASALT
OF (WE'LL SAY) BASALT . . . . 436 KITTY HAWK 261
BASE
YOUR BASE HAS SPREAD TOO WIDE, ... 298 ON TAKING FROM THE TOP 6
ON TAKING FROM THE TOP TO BROADEN THE BASE . . . . . 298 ON TAKING FROM THE TOP T
TO BROADEN ITS BASE. . . . . 298 ON TAKING FROM THE TOP 20
OTHER THAN BASE AND FETID: . . . . 340 THE SUBVERTED FLOWER . 52
TO BASE HIS CAMPAIGN ON TO SAVE THE WORLD. . . . . . 514 A MASQUE OF MERCY . 561
BASEBALL
SOME BOY TOO FAR FROM TOWN TO LEARN BASEBALL, ... 121 BIRCHES 25
WHAT'S A STAR DOING BIG AS A BASEBALL? . . . . 369 THE LITERATE FARMER AND 37
BASEST
WAS NOT THE BASEST HUMAN . . . . 387 THE COURAGE TO BE NEW . 11
BASHFUL
IF YOU HAVE LEARNED YOUR LESSON. DON'T BE BASHFUL. . . . 511 A MASQUE OF MERCY . 481
BASIC
THE BASIC THREE THE STATE IS FOUNDED ON. . . . . . . 520 A MASQUE OF MERCY . 704
BASIN
THE FOUNTAIN IN PROPORTION TO THE BASIN? . . . . . . 169 NEW HAMPSHIRE . . . 326
BASKET
OR A BASKET OF EGGS BETWEEN THEIR FEET; . . . . 141 THE GUM-GATHERER . . 27
BASKETFUL
AS TOUCHING AS A BASKETFUL OF EGGS, ... 365 OF STONES OF THE PLACE 2
BASS
AND SEE IF WE CAN TELL THE BASS FROM THE SOPRANO. . . . 415 A CABIN IN THE CLEARING 40
BAT
THAT AS A WITCH I'D OFTEN MILK A BAT . . . . 208 PAUPER WITCH OF GRAFTON 40
OR SOON WE'D BAT EACH OTHER OUT OF TOUCH, ... 371 THE LITERATE FARMER AND 117
BATCH
UNLEAVENED BATCH. . . . . 298 ON TAKING FROM THE TOP 16
BATH (SEE DUST-BATH)
BATHE
BATHE MY WINDOW, MAKE IT FLOW, ... 11 TO THE THAWING WIND . 7
BATHS
AND TAKE OUR DAILY TIDE BATHS SMOOTH AND ROUGH. . . . 395 ETHEREALIZING . . . 8
BATHTUB
"HUH, THAT OLD BATHTUB, WHAT IS THAT TO SEE? . . . . . 213 A FOUNTAIN, A BOTTLE . 15
BATON (SEE SCEPTER-BATON)
BATS
NIGHT COMES; THE BLACK BATS TUMBLE AND DART; . . . . . 6 GHOST HOUSE . . . 15
BAT'S
AND ON THE BAT'S MUTE ANTICS, WHO WOULD SEEM . . . . 14 WAITING 14
BATTLE
THE BATTLE RENT A COBWEB DIAMOND-STRUNG . . . . . . 126 RANGE-FINDING . . . 1
SO HALFWAY DOWN HE FOUGHT THE BATTLE, ... 138 BROWN'S DESCENT . . 40
BATTLEFIELD
NOT ON THE BATTLEFIELD, BUT DOWN IN CELLARS. . . . . 515 A MASQUE OF MERCY . 573
BATTLES
OF ENEMIES DEFIED AND BATTLES FOUGHT. . . . . . . 356 TIME OUT 11
YOU COULD LOSE BATTLES, YOU COULD LOSE WHOLE WARS, . . 457 HOW HARD TO KEEP FROM 127
BAY
AND PROPPED HIMSELF AT BAY AGAINST A PILLOW. . . . . 47 A HUNDRED COLLARS . 74
WITH A BIG JAG TO EMPTY IN A BAY. . . . . . . 71 THE CODE . . . 54
THERE WASN'T ALWAYS HUDSON'S BAY . . . . 210 AN EMPTY THREAT . 3
OVER SO MUCH BAY . . . . 211 AN EMPTY THREAT . . 31
SOME TO GO FURTHER NORTH TO HUDSON'S BAY, ... 239 OUR SINGING STRENGTH . 22
AND THE SHIP LAY IN THE BAY FOR A WHILE . . . . . 347 DISCOVERY OF MADEIRAS . 111
AND THE BAY WHERE HIS STOLEN LADY DIED . . . . . 347 DISCOVERY OF MADEIRAS . 134
MY TREE, A CAPTIVE IN YOUR WINDOW BAY, ... 350 TO A YOUNG WRETCH . . 20
BE---NOT INDEXED
BEACH
HE MADE IN WALKING SLOWLY TO THE BEACH . . . . . 194 PAUL'S WIFE . . . 99
THAT SAD-WITH-DISTANCE RIVER BEACH . . . . . . 328 A MISSIVE MISSILE . . 53
SOME MORNING FROM THE BOULDER-BROKEN BEACH . . . . 338 THE MOST OF IT . . . 5
WE CAN LIE ON THE BEACH WITH THE SEAWEED . . . . . 395 ETHEREALIZING . . . 7
FROM THIS RUNWAY BEACH . . . . 434 KITTY HAWK . . . 185
BEACHES
BEACHES WHERE THE WHOLE . . . . 432 KITTY HAWK . . . 137
BEAD
A BEAD OF SILVER WATER MORE OR LESS, ... 77 THE GENERATIONS OF MEN 122
ON THE LONG BEAD CHAIN OF REPEATED BIRTH, ... 303 A BIRD SINGING IN SLEEP 11
BEADED
LIKE A BEADED FUR. . . . . 218 I WILL SING YOU ONE-O . 37
BEADING
"THAT'S A SMART PAIR OF PUMPS YOU'RE BEADING THERE. . . 81 THE HOUSEKEEPER . . . 9
BEADS
JOHN BOUGHT HIM, AND WE PAID THE BILL WITH BEADS-- . . 86 THE HOUSEKEEPER . . . 152
BEADWORK
I HELP OUT WITH THIS BEADWORK WHAT I CAN." . . . . 81 THE HOUSEKEEPER . . . 8
BEAN
MINGLED WITH THESE, SMOOTH BEAN AND WRINKLED PEA), . . 124 PUTTING IN THE SEED . 6
BEANS
SOUNDS SOMETHING LIKE. BETTER THAN FARMER'S BEANS . . . 97 THE SELF-SEEKER . . 127
TOMATOES, BEETS, BEANS, PUMPKINS, CORN, ... 134 A GIRL'S GARDEN . . 31
HE DOTES ON SATURDAY PORK AND BEANS. . . . . . . 393 A CASE FOR JEFFERSON . 7
BEAR
DOUBTLESS BEAR NAMES THAT THE MOSSES MAR. . . . . . 6 GHOST HOUSE . . . 25
OR WITH A SHOTGUN FOR A STRAY BLACK BEAR? . . . . . 43 THE MOUNTAIN 87

BEAR (CONTINUED)
    ONE MUSTN'T BEAR TOO HARD ON THE NEWCOMERS, ... 80 THE GENERATIONS OF MEN   188
    AND THOSE WILL BEAR SOME KEEPING STILL ABOUT." . . . . . 80 THE GENERATIONS OF MEN   198
    AS IF FOR PAPERS THAT MIGHT BEAR THE NAME . . . . 96 THE SELF-SEEKER . . .   98
    TOWARD HEAVEN, TILL THE TREE COULD BEAR NO MORE, ... 122 BIRCHES   56
    AS IT RAN LIGHT, OR HAD TO BEAR A LOAD. . . . . 136 "OUT,OUT--"   8
    WHY DO WE WISH TO BEAR . . . . 156 THE SOUND OF TREES . .   2
    AS SWEET AS I COULD BEAR; . . . . 226 TO EARTHWARD   2
    BUT I DON'T SEE WHY IT SHOULD HAVE TO BEAR . . . . 232 THE KITCHEN CHIMNEY .   18
    TO BEAR FORSAKEN THE PLACE'S NAME. . . . . 241 NEED OF BEING VERSED .   8
    WHEN IT SEEMED AS IF I COULD BEAR NO MORE. . . . . 250 A MINOR BIRD   4
    THE BEAR PUTS BOTH ARMS AROUND THE TREE ABOVE HER . . . 268 THE BEAR   1
    THE BEAR . . . . 268 THE BEAR . . . . . .   T
    SUCH IS THE UNCAGED PROGRESS OF THE BEAR. . . . . 269 THE BEAR   10
    THE WORLD HAS ROOM TO MAKE A BEAR FEEL FREE; . . . . . . 269 THE BEAR   11
    MAN ACTS MORE LIKE THE POOR BEAR IN A CAGE, ... 269 THE BEAR   13
    WON'T THIS WHOLE INSTINCT MATTER BEAR REVISION? . . . . 279 THE WHITE-TAILED HORNET   50
    WON'T ALMOST ANY THEORY BEAR REVISION? . . . . 279 THE WHITE-TAILED HORNET   51
    SOMETIMES I FEEL MYSELF I CAN HARDLY BEAR . . . . 287 A ROADSIDE STAND . .   32
    WERE EVIDENTLY SOMETHING HE COULD BEAR. . . . . 292 FIGURE IN THE DOORWAY .   12
    EVER TO HAVE TREE BLOOM OR BEAR. . . . . 296 LEAVES COMPARED WITH .   6
    WERE A DANGEROUS THING TO BEAR. . . . . 313 BEARER OF EVIL TIDINGS   4
    AND THOUGH IT WERE AS MUCH AS CLOUD COULD BEAR . . . . . 337 THE WIND AND THE RAIN . 29
    WON'T BEAR TOO CRITICAL EXAMINATION. . . . . 385 THE FEAR OF GOD . . .   6
    THAT WHEN IT GETS TOO EXQUISITE TO BEAR . . . . 398 BURSTING RAPTURE . .   12
    BECAUSE YOUR WIFE'S PAST WON'T BEAR LOOKING INTO?-- . . 477 A MASQUE OF REASON . .   116
BEARER
    THE BEARER OF EVIL TIDINGS, ... 313 BEARER OF EVIL TIDINGS   1
    THE BEARER OF EVIL TIDINGS . . . . 313 BEARER OF EVIL TIDINGS   T
    AND THE BEARER OF EVIL TIDINGS . . . . 314 BEARER OF EVIL TIDINGS   35
    TO BE THE BEARER OF AN EMPTY THREAT. . . . . 505 A MASQUE OF MERCY . .   303
BEARING
    BEARING IT CRUSHED AND MYSTIFIED. . . . . 21 THE TRIAL BY EXISTENCE   72
    OF THE ONE BEARING IT DONE IN DETAIL-- . . . . 74 THE GENERATIONS OF MEN   41
    IN BEARING THERE TODAY IS HERS, ... 134 A GIRL'S GARDEN . . .   35
    AS FAR AGAIN AS FROM BEING BORN TO BEARING." . . . . . . 184 MAPLE   130
    ONCE WHEN THE GRINDSTONE ALMOST JUMPED ITS BEARING . . . 190 THE GRINDSTONE . . .   57
BEARINGS
    THE OLD MAN SERIOUSLY TOOK HIS BEARINGS, ... 214 A FOUNTAIN, A BOTTLE .   35
BEAR-SKIN
    AND ON BLACK GROUND A BEAR-SKIN RUG OF SNOW. . . . . . . 234 EVENING A SUGAR ORCHARD 13
BEAST
    THE BEAST, ...   9 STORM FEAR   5
    I'D RATHER BE THE BEAST THAT SLEEPS THE SLEEP . . . . . 150 SNOW   223
    IT LIFTS A GAUNT LUXURIATING BEAST . . . . 254 A WINTER EDEN   9
    THAT HEAVENLY BEAST . . . . 261 CANIS MAJOR   2
    AND CRACKED BONES, HUMAN AND BEAST, ... 312 THE VINDICTIVES . . .   59
    AND ONLY SOME SLIGHT BEAST . . . . 416 CLOSED FOR GOOD . . .   28
    THE PONDEROUS BEAST WENT DOWN . . . . 444 THE DRAFT HORSE . . .   9
BEASTS
    EVER TO HAVE HOUSED BIRDS OR BEASTS OR BEES. . . . . . . 193 PAUL'S WIFE   84
    WHILE GREEDY GOOD-DOERS, BENEFICENT BEASTS OF PREY, . . 287 A ROADSIDE STAND . .   27
BEAST'S
    LIKE A BEAST'S STALL, TO EASE THEIR CONSCIENCES. . . . . 66 A SERVANT TO SERVANTS 120
    FOR GOD, MAN, OR BEAST'S SAKE, ... 212 AN EMPTY THREAT . . .   36
BEAT (SEE THREE-BEAT)
    WHERE ONE FALSE WING BEAT WOULD HAVE BROUGHT DOWN ALL, . 240 OUR SINGING STRENGTH .   43
    I HAVE PASSED BY THE WATCHMAN ON HIS BEAT . . . . 255 ACQUAINTED WITH NIGHT   5
    THE TELESCOPE AT ONE END OF HIS BEAT, ... 269 THE BEAR   18
    TILL HER HEART ALMOST CEASED TO BEAT. . . . . 346 DISCOVERY OF MADEIRAS . 102
    BEAT A SUNDIAL IN THE SCENERY-- . . . . 397 AN IMPORTER   22
    I HAD BEAT HIM TO IT. . . . . 430 KITTY HAWK   58
BEATEN
    SOMETIMES I WANDER OUT OF BEATEN WAYS . . . . 125 AN ENCOUNTER   23
    WHEREIN WORDS WHETHER BEATEN OUT OR SPOKEN . . . . 141 THE LINE-GANG   6
    GET BEATEN DOWN AND PASTED . . . . 359 NOVEMBER   5
    FROM HAVING BEATEN ALL DAY LONG IN VAIN . . . . 412 POD OF THE MILKWEED .   38
    I SAY YOU SHOULD BE PROUD OF HAVING BEATEN . . . . 508 A MASQUE OF MERCY . .   378
BEATING
    BUT NOTHING SO LIKE BEATING ON A BOX. . . . . 108 OLD MAN'S WINTER NIGHT   14
    FIGHT SUCH A FIRE BY RUBBING NOT BY BEATING. . . . . . . 131 THE BONFIRE   67
    AND BEATING INSECTS AT THEIR GRITTY TUNE. . . . . 190 THE GRINDSTONE . . .   55
    THE FINAL SUMMONS INTO CHURCH WAS BEATING. . . . . 284 THE GOLD HESPERIDEE .   42
BEAUTIES
    THE BEAUTIES SHE SO TRULY SEES, ...   7 MY NOVEMBER GUEST . .   13
    HAD BEAUTIES HE HAD TO POINT ME OUT AT LENGTH . . . . . 187 THE AX-HELVE   67
BEAUTIFUL
    ARE BEAUTIFUL AS DAYS CAN BE; . . . .   6 MY NOVEMBER GUEST . .   3
    WHO BOASTED OF HIS STATE AS BEAUTIFUL. . . . . 159 NEW HAMPSHIRE . . .   10
    THE WITCH WAS YOUNG, AND BEAUTIFUL (NEW STYLE), ... 163 NEW HAMPSHIRE . . .   129
    OR BEAUTY REST IN A BEAUTIFUL MOUNTAIN SCENE. . . . . . 286 A ROADSIDE STAND . .   13
    MORE WONDERFUL, MORE BEAUTIFUL PRODUCER? . . . . 324 BUILD SOIL   254
    SHE'S BEAUTIFUL. / YES, SHE WAS JUST REMARKING . . . . . 479 A MASQUE OF REASON . .   156
    A BEAUTIFUL IMPOSSIBILITY. . . . . 512 A MASQUE OF MERCY . .   493
    KEEPER, I'M GLAD YOU THINK IT BEAUTIFUL. . . . . 512 A MASQUE OF MERCY . .   494
BEAUTIFULLY
    AND VERY BEAUTIFULLY GOD LIMNS, ... 20 THE TRIAL BY EXISTENCE   37
BEAUTY
    IN SEVERAL BEAUTY THAT THOUGHT FARES FAR . . . . 121 BOND AND FREE . . .   19
    AS A BRUTE TRIBUTE OF RESPECT TO BEAUTY. . . . . 195 PAUL'S WIFE   141
    OR BEAUTY REST IN A BEAUTIFUL MOUNTAIN SCENE. . . . . . 286 A ROADSIDE STAND . .   13
    FOR THE BEES TO COME AND SERVE ITS BEAUTY ARIGHT. . . . 300 STRONG SAYING NOTHING .   12
    WAS ONCE THE BEAUTY ABISHAG, ... 307 PROVIDE, PROVIDE . .   3
    YOU SEE THE BEAUTY OF MY PROPOSAL IS . . . . 324 BUILD SOIL   264
    FOR BEAUTY ON THE ILLUMINATED PAGE . . . . 358 THE LOST FOLLOWER . .   15
    YOU GET THE BEAUTY OF FROM WHERE YOU ARE. . . . . 368 THE LITERATE FARMER AND 10
    RELYING ON ITS BEAUTY, TO THE AIR. . . . . 375 A YOUNG BIRCH . . .   9
    IT WAS A THING OF BEAUTY AND WAS SENT . . . . 375 A YOUNG BIRCH . . .   21

BEAUTY (CONTINUED)
    IT HAS ITS BEAUTY, ONLY I DON'T WRITE IT. . . . . . . 461 HOW HARD TO KEEP FROM   223
    A LOFTY BEAUTY NO ONE CAN LIVE UP TO, ... 512 A MASQUE OF MERCY . . 496
    HIS LOFTY BEAUTY NO ONE CAN LIVE UP TO, ... 513 A MASQUE OF MERCY . . 521
BECAME
    NO MORE SO THAN BECAME A MAN-- . . . . 139 BROWN'S DESCENT . . . 69
    IT BECAME AN EXPLORER OF THE DEEP . . . . 162 NEW HAMPSHIRE . . . 91
    THE ROAD BECAME A CHANNEL RUNNING FLOCKS . . . . . . 240 OUR SINGING STRENGTH . 33
    THAT'S HOW WE BECAME, ... 439 KITTY HAWK 373
BECAUSE---NOT INDEXED
BECOME
    OF WHAT YOU CAME FOR AND BECOME LIKE ME, ... 124 PUTTING IN THE SEED . 8
    IN CHESTNUT NOW BECOME A PRECIOUS WOOD . . . . . . 290 OLD BARN AT THE BOTTOM 38
    AN EYE BECOME EVASIVE. . . . . 340 THE SUBVERTED FLOWER . 47
    SUCH AS SHE WAS, SUCH AS SHE WOULD BECOME. . . . . . 348 THE GIFT OUTRIGHT . 16
    IF I DECIDED TO BECOME A DOCTOR, ... 406 FROM PLANE TO PLANE . 67
    SUCH AS SHE WAS, SUCH AS SHE WOULD BECOME. . . . . . 425 THE GIFT OUTRIGHT . 16
    YOUR FUGITIVE ESCAPE BECOME A QUEST. . . . . 513 A MASQUE OF MERCY . 535
    YOUR EXIT DOOR'S BECOME A CELLAR DOOR. . . . . . . 514 A MASQUE OF MERCY . 549
BECOMES
    JUST AS YOU WILL TILL IT BECOMES A HABIT. . . . . . 67 A SERVANT TO SERVANTS. 147
    HERE FIRST MY THEME BECOMES EMBARRASSING. . . . . . 166 NEW HAMPSHIRE . . 217
    TO SAY WHAT HEIGHT BECOMES NEW HAMPSHIRE MOUNTAINS, . . 169 NEW HAMPSHIRE . . 316
    SOME MYSTERY BECOMES THE PROUD. . . . . 403 SOMETHING LIKE A STAR . 6
    THAT BECOMES US BEST . . . . 441 KITTY HAWK 430
BECOMING
    AND THEN BECOMING RECONCILED . . . . 138 BROWN'S DESCENT . . . 42
    WHICH IS BECOMING MY CONCERN OF LATE. . . . . . . 354 THE LESSON FOR TODAY . 136
    BUT BECOMING AWARE OF SOME BOYS FROM SCHOOL . . . . . 385 A MOOD APART 4
    THE BECOMING FEAR . . . . 441 KITTY HAWK 429
    JOB SAYS THERE'S NO SUCH THING AS EARTH'S BECOMING . . 484 A MASQUE OF REASON . 316
BED
    TAUT WITH THE DEW FROM GARDEN BED TO EAVES, ... 38 DEATH OF THE HIRED MAN 108
    I MADE THE BED UP FOR HIM THERE TONIGHT. . . . . . 39 DEATH OF THE HIRED MAN 151
    HE TURNED TO THE HOTEL TO FIND A BED. . . . . . . 45 A HUNDRED COLLARS . 19
    WHAT DO YOU SAY?" / "I'LL HAVE TO HAVE A BED." . . . . 45 A HUNDRED COLLARS . 32
    "NOT THAT WAY, WITH YOUR SHOES ON KIKE'S WHITE BED. . . 47 A HUNDRED COLLARS . 75
    I'LL NOT BE PUT TO BED BY YOU, MY MAN." . . . . . 47 A HUNDRED COLLARS . 78
    HE'D TEAR TO PIECES, EVEN A BED TO LIE ON. . . . . . 66 A SERVANT TO SERVANTS . 118
    THROUGH THE BED BLANKETS I REMIND MYSELF . . . . . 93 THE SELF-SEEKER . . 19
    WHAT DO YOU WANT, DEAR? COME, STAND BY THE BED; . . . 96 THE SELF-SEEKER . . 104
    THE BROKEN ONE WAS TWISTED IN HIS BED. . . . . . . 100 THE SELF-SEEKER . . 208
    WILLIS FLUNG OFF THE BED. "I WASH MY HANDS-- . . . . 100 THE SELF-SEEKER . . 216
    I'M GOING TO PUT YOU IN YOUR BED, IF FIRST . . . . . 117 IN THE HOME STRETCH . 199
    ITS BED IS LEFT A FADED PAPER SHEET . . . . 119 HYLA BROOK 10
    AND LET YOU GET TO BED AGAIN. GOOD-NIGHT, ... 150 SNOW 211
    GET INTO BED I SAY, AND GET SOME REST. . . . . . . 152 SNOW 265
    YOU'D BETTER DRESS: YOU WON'T GO BACK TO BED. . . . . 152 SNOW 273
    "ONE OF TWO THINGS, EITHER SHE'S GONE TO BED . . . . 154 SNOW 311
    "I SEE THE PORTER'S MADE YOUR BED," I TOLD HIM. . . . 159 NEW HAMPSHIRE . . 15
    BUT THE HEADBOARD OF MOTHER'S BED IS PUSHED . . . . 203 THE WITCH OF COOS . 21
    I WENT TO SLEEP BEFORE I WENT TO BED, ... 203 THE WITCH OF COOS . 37
    ESPECIALLY IN WINTER WHEN THE BED . . . . 203 THE WITCH OF COOS . 38
    TOFFILE HAD GONE TO BED ALONE AND LEFT ME, ... 203 THE WITCH OF COOS . 41
    "DON'T MAKE ME GET UP; I'M TOO WARM IN BED." . . . . 205 THE WITCH OF COOS . 95
    THAT MADE HIM THROW HIS BARE LEGS OUT OF BED . . . . 205 THE WITCH OF COOS . 102
    AND PUSH THE HEADBOARD OF THE BED AGAINST IT. . . . . 206 THE WITCH OF COOS . 120
    BEHIND THE DOOR AND HEADBOARD OF THE BED, ... 206 THE WITCH OF COOS . 127
    THEY FOUND HE'D GNAWED THE FOUR POSTS OF HIS BED, . . . 209 PAUPER WITCH OF GRAFTON 62
    LIFE LONG IN BED, AND WROTE HER THINGS IN BED. . . . 215 A FOUNTAIN, A BOTTLE . 85
    THEY SO SMOTE THE GARDEN BED . . . . 250 LODGED 3
    BUT EARLIER FOR BED TONIGHT, ... 292 ON HEART'S BEGINNING TO 40
    TO THE LOW ROOF OVER HIS BED, ... 299 WELCOME TO THEIR BELIEF 6
    IS RESERVED FOR THE BED OF A FEW SELECTED SEED. . . . 299 STRONG SAYING NOTHING . 4
    THAT SUCKS HIS BREATH LIKE A WICKED CAT IN BED. . . . 341 WILLFUL HOMING . . . 4
    OF THE OCEAN BED FOR A MARRIAGE BED. . . . . . . 345 DISCOVERY OF MADEIRAS . 67
    CALLED GETTING OUT OF THE WRONG SIDE OF BED. . . . . 371 THE LITERATE FARMER AND 107
    ON THE RIGHT SIDE OF BED WOULD END THE FRAY, ... 372 THE LITERATE FARMER AND 121
    AND FOUND, HE SAYS, A BED HAS NO RIGHT SIDE. . . . . 372 THE LITERATE FARMER AND 123
    BESIDE HER ATTIC BED AT NIGHT. . . . . 382 THE NIGHT LIGHT . . . 2
    HAS ALL GONE HOME TO BED. THE PLAY'S PLAYED OUT. . . . 482 A MASQUE OF REASON . 253
    AND BED OF WORLD-FLOWERS SO AS NOT TO BLIND ME. . . . 515 A MASQUE OF MERCY . 582
BEDDED
    IT IS COTTER-PINNED, IT IS BEDDED TRUE. . . . . . 306 A TRIAL RUN 10
BEDDING
    AND HAVING HID IT IN THEIR BEDDING STRAW . . . . . 293 AT WOODWARD'S GARDENS . 30
BEDEVILED
    BUT IT'S JUST FUN THE WAY HE GETS BEDEVILED-- . . . . 87 THE HOUSEKEEPER . . . 161
BEDROOM
    NOT SO MUCH LARGER THAN A BEDROOM, IS IT? . . . . . 51 HOME BURIAL 25
    FOR EVERY ROOM A HOUSE HAS--PARLOR, BEDROOM, ... 110 IN THE HOME STRETCH . 8
    HER MOTHER'S BEDROOM WAS HER FATHER'S STILL, ... 181 MAPLE 60
    ANOTHER FROM THE KITCHEN TO THE BEDROOM, ... 203 THE WITCH OF COOS . 31
    ANOTHER FROM THE BEDROOM TO THE ATTIC, ... 203 THE WITCH OF COOS . 32
    WHEN I HEARD TOFFILE UPSTAIRS IN THE BEDROOM . . . . 203 THE WITCH OF COOS . 46
    FROM THE HALL TO THE ONLY FINISHED BEDROOM, ... 205 THE WITCH OF COOS . 91
    THEN RAN AND SHOUTED, "SHUT THE BEDROOM DOOR, ... 205 THE WITCH OF COOS . 93
    IN A VERMONT BEDROOM CLOSET . . . . 294 A RECORD STRIDE . . . 1
    THEY LISTEN FOR ME IN THE BEDROOM . . . . 294 A RECORD STRIDE . . . 9
BEDS
    SEPARATE BEDS, OF COURSE, YOU UNDERSTAND." . . . . 45 A HUNDRED COLLARS . 27
    FROM OVER YOU AS YOU LAY IN YOUR BEDS. . . . . . . 67 A SERVANT TO SERVANTS . 169
    FROM WEEDING GARDEN BEDS . . . . 361 ALMOST TWO THOUSAND . 11
    BUT BEDS--IN LESS THAN FIFTY YEARS HE'S SURE . . . . 372 THE LITERATE FARMER AND 129
    HE'S SURELY GOT IT IN FOR COTS AND BEDS. . . . . . 372 THE LITERATE FARMER AND 131
BED'S
    A BED'S GOT NO RIGHT SIDE TO GET OUT OF. . . . . . 372 THE LITERATE FARMER AND 125

BEDSTEAD
    THE NIGHT CLERK CLAPPED A BEDSTEAD ON THE FOOT. .   .   .   . 46 A HUNDRED COLLARS . . 39
BEDTIME (SEE LONG-AFTER-BEDTIME)
    AT BEDTIME; BUT THE STRANGENESS SOON WEARS OFF." .   .   . 115 IN THE HOME STRETCH . 135
BEE
    THE ROADSIDE FLOWERS, TOO WET FOR THE BEE, ... 26 A LINE-STORM SONG . . 5
    "HAVING FOUND THE FLOWER AND DRIVEN A BEE AWAY, . . . 118 THE TELEPHONE . . 11
    AND AFTER HAVING ENTERTAINED THE BEE, ... 283 THE GOLD HESPERIDEE . 3
    NOR HEADLONG BEE . . . . 343 QUEST OF PURPLE-FRINGED 18
BEECH
    UNDER WHAT BEECH TREE, ON WHAT WOODCHUCK'S KNOLL?" . . 97 THE SELF-SEEKER . . 116
    A YOUNG BEECH CLINGING TO ITS LAST YEAR'S LEAVES. . . 234 A BOUNDLESS MOMENT . 12
    BEECH . . . . 331 BEECH . . . . . T
BEEN---NOT INDEXED
BEES
    AND MAKE US HAPPY IN THE HAPPY BEES, ... 12 A PRAYER IN SPRING . . 7
    THAT SUDDENLY ABOVE THE BEES IS HEARD, ... 12 A PRAYER IN SPRING . 10
    "THERE ARE BEES IN THIS WALL." HE STRUCK THE CLAPBOARDS, . 59 THE BLACK COTTAGE . 125
    EVER TO HAVE HOUSED BIRDS OR BEASTS OR BEES. . . . . 193 PAUL'S WIFE . . . 84
    FOR THE BEES TO COME AND SERVE ITS BEAUTY ARIGHT. . . 300 STRONG SAYING NOTHING . 12
    BECAUSE UNLIKE THE BEES THEY HAVE NO HIVES, ... 411 POD OF THE MILKWEED . 4
BEETS
    TOMATOES, BEETS, BEANS, PUMPKINS, CORN, ... 134 A GIRL'S GARDEN . . . 31
BEFELL
    THAT NEVER YET TO OTHER TWO BEFELL . . . . 315 IRIS BY NIGHT . . . 21
BEFORE
    BEFORE HE ARRIVES TO SAY IT OUT. . . . . 6 GHOST HOUSE . . . 20
    BEFORE THE COMING OF THE SNOW, ... 7 MY NOVEMBER GUEST . . 18
    BEFORE WE LEFT THE SPOT, ... 14 ROSE POGONIAS . . 18
    BEFORE THE LAST WENT, HEAVY WITH DEW, ... 15 IN A VALE 16
    WHERE THE BIRD WAS BEFORE IT FLEW, ... 15 IN A VALE 18
    WHERE THE FLOWER WAS BEFORE IT GREW, ... 15 IN A VALE 19
    WHO MOWED IT IN THE DEW BEFORE THE SUN. . . . . . 22 THE TUFT OF FLOWERS . 2
    BEFORE I CAME TO VIEW THE LEVELED SCENE. . . . . 22 THE TUFT OF FLOWERS . 4
    THE SOUND WAS BEHIND ME INSTEAD OF BEFORE, ... 25 THE DEMIURGE'S LAUGH . 7
    BEFORE THE LEAVES CAN MOUNT AGAIN . . . . . . 26 IN HARDWOOD GROVES . . 5
    BEFORE THE AGE OF THE FERN; . . . . 27 A LINE-STORM SONG . . 28
    BEFORE I BUILT A WALL I'D ASK TO KNOW . . . . . 34 MENDING WALL . . . 32
    THAT SOUNDS LIKE SOMETHING YOU HAVE HEARD BEFORE? . . 36 DEATH OF THE HIRED MAN 53
    I SAW SO MUCH BEFORE I SLEPT THERE ONCE: . . . . 40 THE MOUNTAIN . . . 2
    BEFORE SHE SAW HIM. SHE WAS STARTING DOWN, ... 51 HOME BURIAL . . . 2
    I NEVER NOTICED IT FROM HERE BEFORE. . . . . . . 51 HOME BURIAL . . . 21
    HE SAID TWICE OVER BEFORE HE KNEW HIMSELF: . . . . 52 HOME BURIAL . . . 34
    BUT BEFORE ONE IS IN IT, THEIR MINDS ARE TURNED . . 54 HOME BURIAL . . 103
    SINCE SHE WENT, MORE THAN EVER, BUT BEFORE-- . . . 56 THE BLACK COTTAGE . 36
    HE WAS BEFORE MY TIME--I NEVER SAW HIM; . . . . 67 A SERVANT TO SERVANTS 140
    UPON MY WAY TO SLEEP BEFORE IT FELL," . . . . . 68 AFTER APPLE-PICKING . 15
    BEFORE HE ACTED: HE'S JUST GOT ROUND TO ACT." . . 70 THE CODE 19
    BEFORE I BURIED HIM, OR I COULDN'T HAVE MANAGED. . . 72 THE CODE . . . 93
    YOU NEVER SAW BEFORE. WHAT WILL WE COME TO . . . 76 THE GENERATIONS OF MEN 86
    LIKE WILD GEESE ON A LAKE BEFORE A STORM? . . . . 76 THE GENERATIONS OF MEN 90
    AND SIT BEFORE YOU IN THE OPEN DOOR . . . . . 79 THE GENERATIONS OF MEN 168
    ONCE MORE BEFORE WE MEET ELSEWHERE." / "IN RAIN?" . 81 THE GENERATIONS OF MEN 209
    YOU NEVER SAW THIS ROOM BEFORE A SHOW, ... 85 THE HOUSEKEEPER . . 119
    SHE WON'T GET FAR BEFORE THE WHEELS HANG UP . . . 88 THE HOUSEKEEPER . . 202
    BEFORE HE GOES, BECAUSE I HURT MYSELF, ... 98 THE SELF-SEEKER . . 170
    ISN'T IT SOMETHING I HAVE SEEN BEFORE?" . . . . . 99 THE SELF-SEEKER . . 189
    ACCEPTING ANYTHING BEFORE HE KNOWS . . . . . . 100 THE SELF-SEEKER . . 201
    A SMALL BIRD FLEW BEFORE ME. HE WAS CAREFUL . . . 101 THE WOOD-PILE . . 10
    OR EVEN LAST YEAR'S OR THE YEAR'S BEFORE. . . . . 101 THE WOOD-PILE . . 28
    "NEVER WAS I BELADIED SO BEFORE. . . . . . . 111 IN THE HOME STRETCH . 21
    THE STOVE! BEFORE THEY GO! KNOCK ON THE WINDOW; . . 113 IN THE HOME STRETCH . 75
    BEFORE WE SET OURSELVES TO RIGHT THE HOUSE, . . . 117 IN THE HOME STRETCH . 194
    BEFORE WE MET, AND YOU WHAT I HAD PASSED. . . . . 119 MEETING AND PASSING . 14
    BEFORE THEM OVER THEIR HEADS TO DRY IN THE SUN. . . 121 BIRCHES 20
    THAT HAD BUDDED BEFORE THE BOUGHS WERE PILED . . . 123 PEA BRUSH . . . 23
    BEFORE IT STAINED A SINGLE HUMAN BREAST. . . . . 126 RANGE-FINDING . . 3
    BEFORE THE MYSTERY OF GLASS! . . . . 128 THE OFT-REPEATED DREAM 8
    BY BURNING OUT, AND BEFORE IT BURNS OUT . . . . 130 THE BONFIRE . . . 26
    WHEN THEY HAD PASSED AN HOUR OR SO BEFORE . . . . 132 THE BONFIRE . . . 87
    BEFORE I WENT TO SAY GOOD-MORNING THERE,-- . . . . 143 SNOW 18
    THAT VARIES WITH THE THINGS--BEFORE WE SEE THEM. . . 147 SNOW 128
    EVER PRESENTS ITSELF BEFORE US TWICE. . . . . . 147 SNOW 130
    "BEFORE YOU DROP THE CURTAIN--I'M REMINDED: . . . 149 SNOW 172
    BEFORE THE ERA OF COLONIZATION, ... 161 NEW HAMPSHIRE . . 72
    AND BEFORE THAT OF EXPLORATION EVEN. . . . . . 161 NEW HAMPSHIRE . . 73
    BEFORE, THAT IS, THEY ARE THEMSELVES ACCEPTED, . . 162 NEW HAMPSHIRE . . 97
    BEFORE I MADE THE TENTH ACROSS THE THRESHOLD. . . 175 THE CENSUS-TAKER . . 33
    BEFORE IT FROZE, AND A GUST FLINGS A HANDFUL . . . 176 THE STAR-SPLITTER . . 7
    WERE NATIVE TO THE GRAIN BEFORE THE KNIFE . . . . 187 THE AX-HELVE . . . 73
    BEFORE THEY HEARD OF HIM IN SOME NEW CAMP, . . . 192 PAUL'S WIFE . . . 29
    BEFORE SHE CAUGHT HER FIRST BREATH WITH A GASP . . 194 PAUL'S WIFE . . . 118
    BEFORE I STRAIGHTENED THEM AND BRUSHED THE BARK OFF. . 199 WILD GRAPES . . . 88
    MY BROTHER HAD BEEN NEARER RIGHT BEFORE. . . . . 199 WILD GRAPES . . . 94
    BEFORE SHE WENT THE POOR MAN'S WIDOW'S WAY, . . . 201 PLACE FOR A THIRD . 61
    I WENT TO SLEEP BEFORE I WENT TO BED, ... 203 THE WITCH OF COOS . 37
    BEFORE I GOT UP TO DO ANYTHING; . . . . 205 THE WITCH OF COOS . 92
    BEFORE ITS FACE. . . . . 218 I WILL SING YOU ONE-O . 22
    BEFORE MAN CAME TO BLOW IT RIGHT . . . . . . 223 THE AIM WAS SONG . . 1
    AND MILES TO GO BEFORE I SLEEP, ... 225 STOPPING BY WOODS . 15
    AND MILES TO GO BEFORE I SLEEP. . . . . 225 STOPPING BY WOODS . 16
    SAYING....AND SHE COULD HAVE HIM. AND BEFORE . . . 230 NOT TO KEEP . . . 2
    BEFORE IT CHANGES TO DIAMONDS IN THE SUN), . . . 236 VALLEY'S SINGING DAY . 13
    AS OFTEN AS I'VE SEEN IT DONE BEFORE . . . . . 237 A HILLSIDE THAW . . 4
    LET THEM THINK TWICE BEFORE THEY USE THEIR POWERS. . 245 SPRING POOLS . . . 9
    THAT ARE GONE BEFORE I CAN TELL WHAT THEY ARE. . . 248 A PASSING GLIMPSE . 2
    THAT WATER NEVER DID TO LAND BEFORE. . . . . . 250 ONCE BY THE PACIFIC . 4
    BEFORE GOD'S LAST PUT OUT THE LIGHT WAS SPOKEN. . . 250 ONCE BY THE PACIFIC . 14

BEFORE (CONTINUED)
WHERE HAD I HEARD THIS WIND BEFORE . . . . 251 BEREFT 1
LONG, LONG BEFORE WE WERE FROM ANY CREATURE. . . . . . 259 WEST-RUNNING BROOK . . 41
BEFORE THE NOT MOWING BRINGS TREES ON, ... 264 THE LAST MOWING . . . 8
BEFORE TREES, SEEING THE OPENING, ... 264 THE LAST MOWING . . . 9
WITH WHAT THEY USED TO PAIR WITH BEFORE. . . . . . . 265 THE DOOR IN THE DARK . 9
YOU'D THINK I NEVER HAD FELT BEFORE . . . . 276 TWO TRAMPS IN MUD TIME 44
BEFORE THEIR PANIC HANDS . . . . 298 ON TAKING FROM THE TOP 13
ALMOST BEFORE THE PRICK OF HOSTILE EARS, ... 302 A BIRD SINGING IN SLEEP 7
BEFORE THE FRAGMENTS OF A FORMER SUN . . . . 315 IRIS BY NIGHT 7
BEFORE NOW POETRY HAS TAKEN NOTICE . . . . 316 BUILD SOIL 28
BEFORE THEIR PLAYS AND GAMES WERE ORGANIZED, ... 318 BUILD SOIL 62
AND SHALL BE MORE BEFORE WE'RE DONE WITH IT. . . . . . 319 BUILD SOIL 118
BUT LONG BEFORE I'M INTERPERSONAL, ... 320 BUILD SOIL 143
JUST SO BEFORE WE'RE INTERNATIONAL, ... 320 BUILD SOIL 145
BEFORE HE CAME TO MEET HIS OWN! . . . . 336 THE WIND AND THE RAIN . 11
BEFORE I THOUGHT THE WILTED TO EXALT . . . . 337 THE WIND AND THE RAIN . 26
BEFORE HER MOTHER CAME. . . . . 340 THE SUBVERTED FLOWER . 40
YET FURTHER I WENT TO BE BEFORE THE SCYTHE, ... 342 QUEST OF PURPLE-FRINGED 9
"BEFORE THE THING HAS TIME TO SPREAD. . . . . 345 DISCOVERY OF MADEIRAS . 61
BEFORE THEY WERE HURLED FROM THE SLAVER'S DECK. . . . . 346 DISCOVERY OF MADEIRAS . 82
THE LAND WAS OURS BEFORE WE WERE THE LAND'S. . . . . . 348 THE GIFT OUTRIGHT . . 1
BEFORE WE WERE HER PEOPLE. SHE WAS OURS . . . . 348 THE GIFT OUTRIGHT . . 3
AS OF A BOOK HELD UP BEFORE HIS EYES . . . . 355 TIME OUT 3
BEFORE THE INDIAN RACE WAS FURTHER WRONGED. . . . . . 370 THE LITERATE FARMER AND 60
BEFORE SHE MUST PUT OUT THE LIGHT ON THE CHILDREN . . . 379 TOO ANXIOUS FOR RIVERS 18
(IT WILL BE TAKEN DOWN BEFORE IT FALLS.) . . . . . . 386 THE FEAR OF MAN . . . 7
BEFORE THEY GUESSED THE CORNER . . . . 391 A ROGERS GROUP . . . 7
TAKE CARE TO SELL YOUR HORSE BEFORE HE DIES . . . . . 399 THE INGENUITIES OF DEBT 4
BEFORE THEY TURNED FROM EVERYTHING TO HAY. . . . . . . 404 FROM PLANE TO PLANE . 14
BEFORE OUR REALIZING WHAT WE HAVE . . . . 408 FROM PLANE TO PLANE . 128
AS IT HAS NEVER BEEN TO ME BEFORE. . . . . 411 POD OF THE MILKWEED . 7
BEFORE I GAVE UP SEEING AND SLEPT . . . . 419 ONE MORE BREVITY . . 3
THE LAND WAS OURS BEFORE WE WERE THE LAND'S. . . . . . 424 THE GIFT OUTRIGHT . . 1
BEFORE WE WERE HER PEOPLE. SHE WAS OURS . . . . 424 THE GIFT OUTRIGHT . . 3
LONG BEFORE HE FLEW IT. . . . . 430 KITTY HAWK 56
THE OCEAN HAD BEEN SPOKEN TO BEFORE. . . . . 447 DOES NO ONE AT ALL EVER 31
BEFORE THEY GAVE WAY AT THE FIST. . . . . 452 A-WISHING WELL . . . 57
BEFORE THEY SAT DOWN WEARY ON A BANK . . . . 454 HOW HARD TO KEEP FROM 13
I AM ABJECT BEFORE YOU," SAID DARIUS. . . . . 458 HOW HARD TO KEEP FROM 145
BEFORE THEY MAKE IT A STATE. . . . . 466 SOME SCIENCE FICTION . 32
AND SPEAK TO HIM BEFORE THE OTHERS COME. . . . . . . 474 A MASQUE OF REASON . . 32
BEFORE I AM TOO LATE TO BE GOT RIGHT . . . . 479 A MASQUE OF REASON . 166
I TOOK CARE OF YOU. AND BEFORE YOU DIED . . . . 486 A MASQUE OF REASON . 361
BEFORE THE DOOR'S SO VIOLENTLY TRIED . . . . 493 A MASQUE OF MERCY . . 6
YOU! WHO ARE YOU? I ASKED YOU ONCE BEFORE. . . . . . 499 A MASQUE OF MERCY . . 150
I HAD BEFORE. THAT'S WHY I CHANGED TO PAUL-- . . . . . 499 A MASQUE OF MERCY . . 158
ONE MINUTE, MAY I, PAUL?--BEFORE WE LEAVE . . . . . . 501 A MASQUE OF MERCY . . 216
BEFORE I UNDERTOOK SO DELICATE . . . . 503 A MASQUE OF MERCY . . 271
JUST, I WOULD HAVE HIM JUST BEFORE ALL ELSE, ... 507 A MASQUE OF MERCY . . 363
STRANGE NO ONE EVER THOUGHT OF IT BEFORE HIM. . . . . 511 A MASQUE OF MERCY . . 478
ON THE WET FLAGS BEFORE A CRUCIFIX . . . . 516 A MASQUE OF MERCY . . 614
EVEN BEFORE I CAME IN HERE TONIGHT. . . . . 517 A MASQUE OF MERCY . . 626
BUT ONE THING MORE BEFORE THE CURTAIN FALLS.-- . . . . 519 A MASQUE OF MERCY . . 672
BEFORE THE CROSS, IT IS FROM FELLOW-FEELING, ... 521 A MASQUE OF MERCY . . 735
BEFOREHAND
I ASKED HIM WELL BEFOREHAND. "DON'T YOU GET ONE!" . . . 177 THE STAR-SPLITTER . . 21
I'D GIVE MORE FOR ONE LEAST BEFOREHAND REASON . . . . 482 A MASQUE OF REASON . 247
BEFRIENDED (SEE SELF-BEFRIENDED)
GETTING TOO BEFRIENDED, ... 431 KITTY HAWK 95
BEG
SO HE WON'T HAVE TO BEG AND BE BEHOLDEN. . . . . . . 35 DEATH OF THE HIRED MAN 21
BEGAN
BUT RAIN SPOILED ALL. THE DAY BEGAN UNCERTAIN, ... 74 THE GENERATIONS OF MEN 19
OF WHO BEGAN IT BETWEEN THE TWO RACES. . . . . 142 THE VANISHING RED . . 13
"HOLD ON." THE DOUBLE BELL BEGAN TO CHIRP. . . . . . 155 SNOW 327
ONE BUNCH OF THEM, AND THERE BEGAN TO BE . . . . . . 197 WILD GRAPES 25
BEGAN THE STAIRS, TWO FOOTSTEPS FOR EACH STEP, ... 204 THE WITCH OF COOS . . 51
THE STEPS BEGAN TO CLIMB THE ATTIC STAIRS. . . . . . 206 THE WITCH OF COOS . . 116
SINCE MAN BEGAN . . . . 220 I WILL SING YOU ONE-O . 77
ALREADY DETERMINED DAWN BEGAN TO LAY . . . . 235 VALLEY'S SINGING DAY . 7
THE STRAINING MILL BEGAN TO SHAKE. . . . . 273 A LONE STRIKER . . . 10
ONCE WE BEGAN TO SEE OUR IMAGES . . . . 279 THE WHITE-TAILED HORNET 64
BEGAN TO BLOSSOM AT THE AGE OF FIVE; . . . . 283 THE GOLD HESPERIDEE . 2
AND DOWNY WAX THE THREE BEGAN TO THRIVE. . . . . . . 283 THE GOLD HESPERIDEE . 6
AND WHAT THE FLOWER BEGAN . . . . 340 THE SUBVERTED FLOWER . 54
AND BEGAN TO FLUTTER THE LEAVES TO LOOK . . . . 342 A CLOUD SHADOW . . . 2
BEGAN ALREADY TO SEEM FORLORN. . . . . 344 DISCOVERY OF MADEIRAS 18
TAKE NATURE ALTOGETHER SINCE TIME BEGAN, ... 349 OUR HOLD ON THE PLANET 13
AND SO BEGAN THE MODERN WORLD FOR US. . . . . 351 THE LESSON FOR TODAY . 18
AND BEGAN TO BOUNCE DOWN A GRANITE STAIR, ... 383 WERE I IN TROUBLE . . 4
BEGAT
WHERE SOMEONE SOMEONE ELSE BEGAT . . . . 453 A-WISHING WELL . . . 80
BEGETTER
ONLY BEGETTER OF ALL ILLS THAT ARE. . . . . 356 A MOTH SEEN IN WINTER . 16
BEGGAR
SO SMALL AM I AS AN ATTENTION BEGGAR. . . . . 388 IOTA SUBSCRIPT . . . 5
HAVE MARRIED BEGGAR MAIDS FROM OFF THE STREETS. . . . 457 HOW HARD TO KEEP FROM 110
BEGGED
AND THEN SHE BEGGED THE SEED. . . . . 134 A GIRL'S GARDEN . . . 26
THE LUMBER ON PAUL TILL PAUL BEGGED FOR MERCY. . . . . 193 PAUL'S WIFE 61
BEGGED SIMPLY FOR THE GRAVE. THE SISTER'S FACE . . . . 201 PLACE FOR A THIRD . . 47
WHERE HOMER BEGGED. HE'LL TELL YOU ABOUT FREEDOM. . . 459 HOW HARD TO KEEP FROM 183
BEGGING
HE HAS BEEN BEGGING THROUGH THE SEVEN CITIES . . . . 459 HOW HARD TO KEEP FROM 182
BEGIN
I HEAR HIM BEGIN FAR ENOUGH AWAY . . . . 6 GHOST HOUSE 18
BEGIN THE HOURS OF THIS DAY SLOW. . . . . 27 OCTOBER 8

BEGIN (CONTINUED)
  AND BEGIN OVER----' THERE, SHE'D BETTER STOP. . . . . . . 80 THE GENERATIONS OF MEN 194
  "IT'S GOOD LUCK WHEN YOU MOVE IN TO BEGIN . . . . . . 113 IN THE HOME STRETCH . 91
  AND THEN COME BACK TO IT AND BEGIN OVER. . . . . 122 BIRCHES 49
  BEGIN IN SMUDGE WITH ROPY SMOKE, AND KNOW . . . . . 130 THE BONFIRE 21
  "DON'T BEGIN THAT. YOU DID THE BEST YOU COULD . . . . 153 SNOW 281
  TO SHOW ITS WORLDLY NATURE AND BEGIN . . . . 174 A STAR IN A STONEBOAT . 51
  BUT DAWN WAS NOT TO BEGIN THEIR "PEARLY-PEARLY" . . . . 236 VALLEY'S SINGING DAY 11
  BEGIN ALL OVER TO HOPE. . . . . 285 IN TIME OF CLOUDBURST 20
  MIXED READY TO BEGIN THE MORNING RIGHT, ... 302 DESIGN 5
  'TWAS SOMETHING WE KNEW ALL ABOUT TO BEGIN WITH . . . . 380 TOO ANXIOUS FOR RIVERS 24
  AND I BEGIN TO FEAR THEY NEVER WILL. . . . . . . 414 A CABIN IN THE CLEARING 6
  COME ON, OR WE'LL BEGIN TO BE AFRAID. . . . . 506 A MASQUE OF MERCY . 330
BEGINNING   (SEE NEW-BEGINNING)
  IT WAS JUST AS THE LIGHT WAS BEGINNING TO FAIL . . . . 24 THE DEMIURGE'S LAUGH . 4
  NO, THIS IS NO BEGINNING." / "THEN AN END?" . . . . 117 IN THE HOME STRETCH . 186
  BUT THAT BEGINNING WAS WIPED OUT IN FEAR . . . . . . 196 WILD GRAPES 10
  ONCE WHEN THE SNOW OF THE YEAR WAS BEGINNING TO FALL, . . . 223 THE RUNAWAY 1
  GET BACK TO THE BEGINNING OF BEGINNINGS, ... 259 WEST-RUNNING BROOK . 43
  BUT TWO FOR A BEGINNING WASN'T BAD. . . . . 283 THE GOLD HESPERIDEE 12
  ON THE HEART'S BEGINNING TO CLOUD THE MIND . . . . . 290 ON HEART'S BEGINNING TO T
  BUT MY HEART WAS BEGINNING TO CLOUD MY MIND. . . . . 291 ON HEART'S BEGINNING TO 13
  BEGINNING WHEN HE WAS YOUNG, ... 299 WELCOME TO THEIR BELIEF 7
  GOES BACK TO THE BEGINNING OF THE END . . . . . . 422 FOR JOHN F. KENNEDY . 8
  OF WHICH THIS NOONDAY'S THE BEGINNING HOUR. . . . . 424 FOR JOHN F. KENNEDY . 77
  ONE WHO IN THE BEGINNING WAS THE WORD . . . . . 475 A MASQUE OF REASON . 56
  WE MAY AS WELL GO BACK TO THE BEGINNING . . . . . 477 A MASQUE OF REASON . 113
  THERE YOU HAVE THE BEGINNING OF ALL WISDOM. . . . . 501 A MASQUE OF MERCY . 215
BEGINNINGS
  FOR THINGS THAT DON'T EXIST; I MEAN BEGINNINGS. . . . . 116 IN THE HOME STRETCH . 173
  ENDS AND BEGINNINGS--THERE ARE NO SUCH THINGS. . . . . 116 IN THE HOME STRETCH . 174
  GET BACK TO THE BEGINNING OF BEGINNINGS, ... 259 WEST-RUNNING BROOK . 43
BEGINS
  WHEN HE BEGINS LIKE THAT, THERE'S SOMEONE AT HIM . . . . 35 DEATH OF THE HIRED MAN 27
  TILL ED BEGINS TO GET OUT ON A SUNDAY . . . . . 115 IN THE HOME STRETCH . 148
  ONE BIRD BEGINS TO CLOSE A FADED EYE: . . . . . . 249 ACCEPTANCE 7
  THE BIRCH BEGINS TO CRACK ITS OUTER SHEATH . . . . 375 A YOUNG BIRCH . . . 1
BEGS
  AND THOUGH THEY'RE NOTHING ANYBODY BEGS, ... 365 OF STONES OF THE PLACE 3
BEGUILE
  BEGUILE US IN THE WAY YOU KNOW. . . . . 27 OCTOBER 11
  I MADE THIS YOU TO BEGUILE . . . . 466 SOME SCIENCE FICTION . 33
BEGUILED
  HEARTS NOT AVERSE TO BEING BEGUILED, ... 27 OCTOBER 10
BEGUN   (SEE SELF-BEGUN)
  I'VE JUST BEGUN THE NIGHT. YOU GET SOME SLEEP. . . . . 50 A HUNDRED COLLARS . 172
  YOU HAD BEGUN, AND GAVE THEM BACK THEIR SHADE. . . . . 109 THE EXPOSED NEST . . 30
  MORE THAN IF LIFE HAD NEVER BEEN BEGUN. . . . . . 226 THE ONSET 11
  YOU HAD BEGUN IT, AND IF THERE NEEDED PROOF-- . . . . 236 VALLEY'S SINGING DAY 15
  A RAIN, THOUGH STINGY, HAD BEGUN TO FALL . . . . . 399 THE BROKEN DROUGHT . 3
  MATTER WAS BEGUN-- . . . . 426 A NEVER NAUGHT SONG 8
  HE ANSWERED HER BACK, "WELL, WHO BEGUN IT?" . . . . 463 LINES IN DEJECTION . 25
BEHAVE
  OURS IS TO BEHAVE . . . . 442 KITTY HAWK 441
BEHAVING
  SUPPOSE THEY WEREN'T BEHAVING PURITANLY, ... 161 NEW HAMPSHIRE . . . 88
BEHIND
  BEHIND LOW BOUGHS THE TREES LET DOWN OUTSIDE; . . . . 16 A DREAM PANG . . . 10
  ACROSS THE FIELDS BEHIND THE HOUSE . . . . . . 18 GOING FOR WATER . . 3
  THAT SLOWLY DAWNED BEHIND THE TREES, ... 18 GOING FOR WATER . . 10
  BEHIND LIGHT WORDS THAT TEASE AND FLOUT, ... 19 REVELATION 2
  I LOOKED FOR HIM BEHIND AN ISLE OF TREES; . . . . 22 THE TUFT OF FLOWERS . 5
  THE SOUND WAS BEHIND ME INSTEAD OF BEFORE, ... 25 THE DEMIURGE'S LAUGH . 7
  THERE IS THE GALE TO URGE BEHIND . . . . . . 26 A LINE-STORM SONG . . 17
  HE WILL NOT GO BEHIND HIS FATHER'S SAYING, ... 34 MENDING WALL 43
  BEHIND WHICH I WAS SHELTERED FROM A WIND. . . . . 40 THE MOUNTAIN 6
  WITH DEPTHS BEHIND HIM SHEER A HUNDRED FEET-- . . . . 42 THE MOUNTAIN 60
  BUT BEHIND'S BEHIND. THE WORST THAT YOU CAN DO . . . . 68 A SERVANT TO SERVANTS . 174
  IS SET ME BACK A LITTLE MORE BEHIND. . . . . . 68 A SERVANT TO SERVANTS . 175
  THEM THAT HE COULDN'T LEAD HE'D GET BEHIND . . . . 71 THE CODE 44
  HE LOOKED SO CLEAN DISGUSTED FROM BEHIND . . . . 72 THE CODE 99
  SHYLY BEHIND HER. / "WELL, AND HOW IS MISTER...?" . . . 96 THE SELF-SEEKER . . 96
  WITH BOTH HANDS HELD BEHIND HER. "GUESS," SHE SAID. . . . 96 THE SELF-SEEKER . . 106
  HE WENT BEHIND IT TO MAKE HIS LAST STAND. . . . . 101 THE WOOD-PILE . . . 22
  TO LOOK FOR SOMETHING IT HAD LEFT BEHIND . . . . 106 CHRISTMAS TREES . . 10
  AND LEAVE THE SLOPE BEHIND THE HOUSE ALL BARE, ... 106 CHRISTMAS TREES . . 18
  BEHIND HER WAS CONFUSION IN THE ROOM, ... 110 IN THE HOME STRETCH . 5
  LOOKED IN A DOOR BEHIND HER AND ADDRESSED . . . . 110 IN THE HOME STRETCH . 11
  HE FETCHED A DINGY LANTERN FROM BEHIND . . . . . 115 IN THE HOME STRETCH . 136
  FIVE MOUNTAIN RANGES ONE BEHIND THE OTHER . . . . 136 "OUT,OUT--" 5
  THAN THOSE I LEFT BEHIND. I THOUGHT THEY WEREN'T. . . . 167 NEW HAMPSHIRE . . . 256
  BEHIND THE PITIFUL REALITY . . . . 169 NEW HAMPSHIRE . . . 323
  PASSED IN AND SLAMMED IT SHUT EACH ONE BEHIND HIM . . . 175 THE CENSUS-TAKER . . 29
  OF ALDER CATCH MY LIFTED AX BEHIND ME. . . . . 185 THE AX-HELVE . . . 2
  BEHIND ME ON THE SNOW IN MY OWN YARD . . . . . 185 THE AX-HELVE . . . 11
  TO SEE IF IT WAS ANYONE BEHIND HIM . . . . . 194 PAUL'S WIFE 112
  AND HEAVY ON HER HEAVY HAIR BEHIND, ... 196 WILD GRAPES 22
  BEHIND THE MOUNTAIN, WITH A MOTHER AND SON, ... 202 THE WITCH OF COOS . . 2
  HALTING PERPLEXED BEHIND THE BARRIER . . . . . 203 THE WITCH OF COOS . . 24
  BEHIND THE DOOR AND HEADBOARD OF THE BED, ... 206 THE WITCH OF COOS . . 127
  THAT BACK BEHIND PURSUIT IT COULDN'T REACH THEM; . . . . 240 OUR SINGING STRENGTH . 47
  NONE FLEW BEHIND ME TO BE LEFT ALONE. . . . . 240 OUR SINGING STRENGTH . 48
  BEHIND NEW BARRIER WALLS (AND LET IT CHAFE!), ... 254 THE FLOOD 3
  YET NOTHING I SHOULD CARE TO LEAVE BEHIND. . . . . 266 THE ARMFUL 5
  I KNEW PRETTY WELL WHY HE DROPPED BEHIND . . . . 275 TWO TRAMPS IN MUD TIME 5
  AND WHAT TAKE HENCE OR LEAVE BEHIND, ... 332 ALL REVELATION . . . 7
  TO LEAVE THE ENGLISH LAW BEHIND . . . . . . 344 DISCOVERY OF MADEIRAS . 16
  BEHIND THE PORTHOLE'S SLAB OF GLASS . . . . . 363 ASSURANCE 2

BEHIND (CONTINUED)
    BY NOW, PULL IN YOUR LADDER ROAD BEHIND YOU . . . . . . 378 DIRECTIVE 37
    BEHIND HER AT THE DASHBOARD OF HIS PUNG." . . . . . . 407 FROM PLANE TO PLANE . 108
    I LEAVE BEHIND . . . . 413 AWAY! 5
    THE SORROW OF HAVING BEEN LEFT BEHIND, ... 420 ONE MORE BREVITY . . 31
    HIS FEAR IS NOT BEHIND HIM BUT BESIDE HIM . . . . . . 421 ESCAPIST--NEVER . . . 3
    BEHIND TOO HEAVY A HORSE . . . . 443 THE DRAFT HORSE . . 3
    LEFT TRIVIA BEHIND; . . . . 464 MILKY WAY IS A COWPATH 28
    MY STAYING BACK BEHIND . . . . 465 SOME SCIENCE FICTION . 6
    OF GENESIS BEHIND. THE WISDOM THERE, THOUGH, ... 480 A MASQUE OF REASON . . 195
    BUT THERE IS NOTHING YOU ARE NOT BEHIND. . . . . . . 482 A MASQUE OF REASON . . 265
    BEHIND THE SCENES, ORDAINED AND ADVERTISED . . . . . . 497 A MASQUE OF MERCY . . 97
    AND LEAVING IT BEHIND US IN THE TRAP. . . . . 508 A MASQUE OF MERCY . . 389
BEHIND'S
    BUT BEHIND'S BEHIND. THE WORST THAT YOU CAN DO . . . . 68 A SERVANT TO SERVANTS . 174
BEHOLD
    HE HAD BEEN GIVEN TO BEHOLD . . . . 417 AMERICA IS HARD TO SEE 28
    "BEHOLD MY SON IN RAGS HERE WITH HIS LYRE," . . . . . 459 HOW HARD TO KEEP FROM 169
BEHOLDEN
    SO HE WON'T HAVE TO BEG AND BE BEHOLDEN. . . . . . . 35 DEATH OF THE HIRED MAN 21
    TOO PROUD TO BE BEHOLDEN FOR RELIEF, ... 394 HAEC FABULA DOCET . . 19
BEING (SEE WELL-BEING)
    HEARTS NOT AVERSE TO BEING BEGUILED, ... 27 OCTOBER 10
    ABOUT ITS BEING THERE. I NEVER SAW IT. . . . . 42 THE MOUNTAIN . . . 67
    HIS TRAIN BEING LATE, HE MISSED ANOTHER TRAIN . . . . . 44 A HUNDRED COLLARS . . 15
    "HE WAS AFRAID OF BEING ROBBED OR MURDERED. . . . . . 45 A HUNDRED COLLARS . . 31
    A MAN MUST PARTLY GIVE UP BEING A MAN . . . . 52 HOME BURIAL . . . 49
    IS DUE TO TRUTHS BEING IN AND OUT OF FAVOR. . . . . . 58 THE BLACK COTTAGE . . 110
    WHICH BEING EXPRESSED, MIGHT BE THIS IN EFFECT: . . . . 60 BLUEBERRIES . . . 44
    OR LET HIM KNOW THAT HE WAS BEING LOOKED AT. . . . . . 72 THE CODE 101
    I BLAME HIS BEING BROUGHT UP BY HIS MOTHER. . . . . . 83 THE HOUSEKEEPER . . 56
    YOU SPOKE OF JOHN'S NOT BEING SAFE TO STAY WITH. . . . . 85 THE HOUSEKEEPER . . 123
    BEING CUT OFF FROM FRIENDS?" / "WE HAVE OUR FRIENDS. . . 87 THE HOUSEKEEPER . . 169
    THE FIGURE OF OUR BEING LESS THAN TWO . . . . 118 MEETING AND PASSING . 7
    YET SOME SAY LOVE BY BEING THRALL . . . . 120 BOND AND FREE . . 17
    THE TRUTH BEING WE ARE AS MUCH . . . . 126 LONELINESS . . . 7
    THAT SMILE! IT NEVER CAME OF BEING GAY. . . . . 127 THE SMILE . . . 2
    PERHAPS HE MOCKED AT US FOR BEING WELL. . . . . 127 THE SMILE . . . 8
    OR BEING VERY YOUNG (AND HE WAS PLEASED . . . . 127 THE SMILE . . . 9
    "SCARE YOU. BUT IF YOU SHRINK FROM BEING SCARED, . . . 132 THE BONFIRE . . . 96
    OF BEING MEN WE CAN'T LOOK AT A GOOD FIGHT . . . . . . 146 SNOW 100
    AND BEING WHERE YOU ARE. YOU WANT TO STAY." . . . . . 150 SNOW 200
    "SAVE US FROM BEING CORNERED BY A WOMAN. . . . . . . 151 SNOW 236
    OF BEING IN THE MARKET WITH A CLIMATE." . . . . 159 NEW HAMPSHIRE . . 24
    THE HOPE OF BEING, AS WE SAY, RECEIVED. . . . . 160 NEW HAMPSHIRE . . 43
    WHOSE CLAIM IS GOOD TO BEING SETTLED HERE . . . . . . 161 NEW HAMPSHIRE . . 71
    IN BEING THERE SO EARLY IN OUR HISTORY. . . . . 161 NEW HAMPSHIRE . . 81
    THE HOUR HAD NOT YET STRUCK FOR BEING GOOD, ... 161 NEW HAMPSHIRE . . 89
    BEING THE CREATURE OF LITERATURE I AM, ... 166 NEW HAMPSHIRE . . 240
    ABOUT THE PEOPLE BEING BETTER THERE . . . . 167 NEW HAMPSHIRE . . 255
    HOW ABOUT BEING A GOOD GREEK, FOR INSTANCE? . . . . . . 171 NEW HAMPSHIRE . . 404
    MORE BLAMELESS IN THE SENSE OF BEING LESS . . . . . . 177 THE STAR-SPLITTER . 23
    OF BEING GIVEN ONE FOR CHRISTMAS GIFT, ... 178 THE STAR-SPLITTER . 55
    AS FAR AGAIN AS FROM BEING BORN TO BEARING." . . . . . 184 MAPLE 130
    I SHOULDN'T MIND HIS BEING OVERJOYED . . . . 186 THE AX-HELVE . . 39
    TO INSURE THEIR NOT BEING WASTED ON ME. . . . . 187 THE AX-HELVE . . 68
    OBJECT TO BEING ASKED A CIVIL QUESTION-- . . . . 192 PAUL'S WIFE . . 32
    BY BEING INVISIBLE FOR WHAT IT WAS, ... 216 A FOUNTAIN, A BOTTLE . 106
    I WAS SOON SATISFIED FOR THE TIME BEING. . . . . 217 A FOUNTAIN, A BOTTLE . 131
    (WE MADE IT SECURE AGAINST BEING, I HOPE), ... 228 GOOD-BY AND KEEP COLD . 13
    IF FROM ITS BEING KEPT FOREVER UNDER, ... 231 A BROOK IN THE CITY . 22
    THE NEED OF BEING VERSED IN COUNTRY THINGS . . . . . . 241 NEED OF BEING VERSED . T
    GREATER THAN BEING SHORE TO THE OCEAN-- . . . . 247 DEVOTION 2
    THE SHORE WAS LUCKY IN BEING BACKED BY CLIFF, ... 250 ONCE BY THE PACIFIC . 8
    THE CLIFF IN BEING BACKED BY CONTINENT; . . . . 250 ONCE BY THE PACIFIC . 9
    IT GOES BY MIGHT OF BEING SUCH A FLOOD . . . . 255 THE FLOOD . . . 7
    HOPELESS OF BEING KNOWN FOR WHAT SHE HAS BEEN, ... 257 THE LOVELY BE CHOOSERS 41
    FAILING OF BEING LOVED FOR WHAT SHE IS, ... 257 THE LOVELY BE CHOOSERS 42
    NOT TO SINK UNDER BEING MAN AND WIFE, ... 264 THE INVESTMENT . . 13
    I SUFFERED LIKE A METAL BEING CAST. . . . . 267 WHAT FIFTY SAID . . 3
    BUT BEING MOUNTED BAREBACK ON THE EARTH? . . . . 267 RIDERS 6
    AND TURNED FROM LOOKING UP AND BEING KISSED . . . . . . 283 THE GOLD HESPERIDEE . 8
    TO LOOKING DOWN AND YET NOT BEING SAD, ... 283 THE GOLD HESPERIDEE . 9
    TO TRY IF IT WILL NOT MAKE OUR BEING EXPAND, ... 286 A ROADSIDE STAND . . 20
    ABOUT BEING PAST-ACTIVE SHOES. . . . . 295 A RECORD STRIDE . . 32
    FOR BEING AS OVERELATED . . . . 295 A RECORD STRIDE . . 34
    WHAT HAD THAT FLOWER TO DO WITH BEING WHITE, ... 302 DESIGN 9
    YOU MAY TAUNT ME WITH NOT BEING ABLE TO FLEE THE EARTH. . 306 NOT QUITE SOCIAL . . 9
    OTHERS ON BEING SIMPLY TRUE. . . . . 307 PROVIDE, PROVIDE . . 14
    OR KEEPS THE END FROM BEING HARD." . . . . 307 PROVIDE, PROVIDE . . 18
    OF BEING BROUGHT DOWN TO THE REAL." . . . . 313 THE VINDICTIVES . . 91
    (TO KEEP THE POTS OF GOLD FROM BEING FOUND), ... 315 IRIS BY NIGHT . . 25
    THE LAST BEING WHAT THEY SEEM TO HAVE IN RUSSIA. . . . . 318 BUILD SOIL . . . 74
    BY BEING PUNISHED BACK, IT IS NOT FREE: . . . . 319 BUILD SOIL . . . 115
    TO INGENUITY FOR BEING SO CRUEL . . . . 320 BUILD SOIL . . . 124
    DO I SUBMIT TO BEING SUPPLIED BY HIM . . . . 324 BUILD SOIL . . . 252
    ONE TREE, BY BEING DEEPLY WOUNDED, ... 331 BEECH 6
    MY PROOF OF BEING NOT UNBOUNDED. . . . . 331 BEECH 9
    FROM BEING OVERFLOODED . . . . 335 CARPE DIEM . . . 16
    THE INFINITE'S BEING SO WIDE . . . . 348 TRIPLE BRONZE . . 1
    OF BEING BORN AT ONCE TOO EARLY AND LATE, ... 351 THE LESSON FOR TODAY . 12
    AND FOR THESE REASONS KEPT FROM BEING GREAT. . . . . . 351 THE LESSON FOR TODAY . 13
    BEING ALREADY MORE THAN PROVED IN FIGHT, ... 353 THE LESSON FOR TODAY . 91
    (MAKE NO MISTAKE ABOUT ITS BEING BONES); . . . . . . 354 THE LESSON FOR TODAY . 132
    OF MEANINGLESSLY BEING BROKEN OFF. . . . . 355 THE LESSON FOR TODAY . 148
    WITH WHICH THE MODERN WORLD IS BEING SWEPT. . . . . . 357 A CONSIDERABLE SPECK . 26
    I WAS BEING TRESPASSED ON AND AGAINST. . . . . 364 TRESPASS 4
    WHAT NOW WAS BEING DONE. . . . . 366 NOT OF SCHOOL AGE . . 16

BEING (CONTINUED)
```
    BUT RIGHT IN HEAVEN WAS SLOWLY BEING SHRUNK . . . . . . . 368 THE LITERATE FARMER AND   14
    SO MUCH IS BEING NOW EXPECTED OF, . . . . . . . . . . 369 THE LITERATE FARMER AND   41
    OF BEING WATCHED FROM FORTY CELLAR HOLES . . . . . . . 378 DIRECTIVE . . . . .   21
    FROM BEING NO ONE UP TO BEING SOMEONE, . . . . . . . 385 THE FEAR OF GOD . . .    2
    HER FEAR IS BEING SPOKEN BY THE RUDE . . . . . . . . 386 THE FEAR OF MAN . .   13
    ON BEING IDOLIZED . . . . . . . . . . . . . . . 391 ON BEING IDOLIZED . .    T
    WHERE WITH A GLEE NO LESS FOR BEING GRIM . . . . . . . 394 HAEC FABULA DOCET . .   15
    TO KEEP OUR ABSTRACT VERSE FROM BEING DRY. . . . . . 395 ETHEREALIZING . .   14
    AND BEING GOOD FOR THESE MEANS STANDING BY . . . . . 398 NO HOLY WARS FOR THEM .    5
    HAVE KEPT FROM BEING CAUGHT WITH THE DECAYED, . . . . 399 THE INGENUITIES OF DEBT    8
    COULD SAVE IT FROM ITS LOSSES BEING MET. . . . . . 399 THE INGENUITIES OF DEBT   12
    DICK HAD OF BEING FRESH AND FULL OF COLLEGE. . . . . 404 FROM PLANE TO PLANE .    4
    AT BEING THUS EXPOUNDED TO HIMSELF . . . . . . . . 405 FROM PLANE TO PLANE .   56
    AND EVERYBODY'S BEING SICK FOR CHRISTMAS. . . . . . 407 FROM PLANE TO PLANE .  106
    AND AVOID BEING WORSHIPED AS A GOD. . . . . . . . 408 FROM PLANE TO PLANE .  131
    IN BEING SWEET TO THESE EPHEMERALS . . . . . . . 412 POD OF THE MILKWEED .   30
    OF BEING IN EACH OTHER'S WAY, . . . . . . . . 417 AMERICA IS HARD TO SEE   39
    IS ABOUT TIRED OF BEING LOOTED . . . . . . . . 419 AMERICA IS HARD TO SEE   81
    THAT COMES OF DOGS' LIVES BEING SO BRIEF, . . . . 420 ONE MORE BREVITY .   51
    FOR THE TIME BEING AND WITH THEIR CONSENT, . . . 423 FOR JOHN F. KENNEDY .   37
    I WAS BEING BLOWN . . . . . . . . . . . . 428 KITTY HAWK . . . .   17
    AND ITS BEING FULL . . . . . . . . . . . . 433 KITTY HAWK . . . .  170
    MADE ALL BEING FULL. . . . . . . . . . . . 433 KITTY HAWK . . . .  174
    BEING WHIRLED AND WHIRLED . . . . . . . . . 440 KITTY HAWK . . . .  396
    WHAT IN BEING STELLAR . . . . . . . . . . 442 KITTY HAWK . . . .  460
    O OCEAN SEA, FOR ALL YOUR BEING VAST, . . . . 446 DOES NO ONE AT ALL EVER    1
    OUR CHANCE OF BEING PEOPLE NEWLY BORN. . . . 446 DOES NO ONE AT ALL EVER   12
    INTO BEING BERULED? . . . . . . . . . . 448 THE BAD ISLAND--EASTER   26
    IN BEING A THIEF . . . . . . . . . . . 449 THE BAD ISLAND--EASTER   63
    THE OBJECTION TO BEING STEPPED ON . . . . . 450 OBJECTION TO BE STEPPED    T
    HOW HARD IT IS TO KEEP FROM BEING KING WHEN IT'S IN YOU AND
       IN THE SITUATION . . . . . . . . . . 453 HOW HARD TO KEEP FROM    T
    FOR HARD IT IS TO KEEP FROM BEING KING . . . . 454 HOW HARD TO KEEP FROM   20
    HE COULDN'T KEEP HIMSELF FROM BEING KING. . . . 454 HOW HARD TO KEEP FROM   23
    TILL ON A DAY THE KING, BEING SICK AT HEART . . 456 HOW HARD TO KEEP FROM   94
    AND PRESS YOUR FATHER INTO BEING KING." . . . 460 HOW HARD TO KEEP FROM  206
    HOW HARD IT IS TO KEEP FROM BEING KING . . . 462 HOW HARD TO KEEP FROM  275
    ON BEING CHOSEN POET OF VERMONT . . . . . 469 CHOSEN POET OF VERMONT    T
    I AM A NAME FOR BEING PUT UPON. . . . . . 474 A MASQUE OF REASON .   38
    THE FRONT OF BEING ANSWERABLE TO NO ONE . . 482 A MASQUE OF REASON .  250
    BY BEING BAFFLED FOR THE SAKE OF BEING. . . 484 A MASQUE OF REASON .  299
    --THE DEVIL'S BEING GOD'S BEST INSPIRATION. . 487 A MASQUE OF REASON .  401
    HE'S BEING A RELIGIOUS SNOB FOR FUN. . . . 494 A MASQUE OF MERCY .   34
    TO REST AT TIMES FROM BEING CIVILIZED. . . 496 A MASQUE OF MERCY .   74
    OR ELSE YOU WERE AFRAID OF BEING MOBBED . . 497 A MASQUE OF MERCY .  104
    I SHRINK FROM BEING PUBLICLY LET DOWN. . . 505 A MASQUE OF MERCY .  305
    YOU KNOW WHAT LETS US OFF FROM BEING CAREFUL? . 505 A MASQUE OF MERCY .  316
    BY BEING SPREAD OUT OVER EVERYBODY, . . . 506 A MASQUE OF MERCY .  322
    IT WAS THEIR JUSTICE BEING MERCY-CROSSED. . 509 A MASQUE OF MERCY .  415
    YOU MEAN I'M BEING SENT DOWN IN THE CELLAR? . 514 A MASQUE OF MERCY .  551
```
BEINGS
```
    HUMAN BEINGS LOVE IT--LOVE IT. . . . . . . 304 CLEAR AND COLDER .   22
    ONE DAY TOO SWEET FOR BEINGS TO SURVIVE. . . . 412 POD OF THE MILKWEED .   33
```
BEL
```
    WE BLAME OURSELVES. WE'RE GOOD SPORTS, AREN'T WE, BEL? . 496 A MASQUE OF MERCY .   78
    BEL IS A SOLITARY SOCIAL DRINKER. . . . . . 496 A MASQUE OF MERCY .   86
    YOU LOCKED THE DOOR, BEL. LET ME HAVE THE KEY. . 500 A MASQUE OF MERCY .  174
    MERCY, FOR MERCY'S SAKE! / BEL WANTS SOME MERCY.-- . 507 A MASQUE OF MERCY .  345
    KNEEL BY HIM. BEL STANDS UP BESIDE HER CHAIR . 518 A MASQUE OF MERCY .  652
    I WON'T PRESUME TO TELL BEL WHERE TO GO. . . 519 A MASQUE OF MERCY .  685
    BUT BEL GETS SOME THINGS RIGHT--AND SHE WAS RIGHT-- . 519 A MASQUE OF MERCY .  690
```
BELADIED
```
    "NEVER WAS I BELADIED SO BEFORE. . . . . . . 111 IN THE HOME STRETCH .   21
```
BELATED
```
    NOW WAS SEEN HOW THESE LIKED BELATED SNOW. . . . 239 OUR SINGING STRENGTH .   25
```
BELFRY
```
    A SPIRE AND BELFRY COMING ON THE ROOF . . . . . 386 A STEEPLE ON THE HOUSE    7
```
BELIEF
```
    AND WHAT THE SOUTH, TO HER SERENE BELIEF. . . . .  57 THE BLACK COTTAGE . .   72
    FOR, DEAR ME, WHY ABANDON A BELIEF . . . . . .  58 THE BLACK COTTAGE . .  105
    THEY WERE WELCOME TO THEIR BELIEF, . . . . . 299 WELCOME TO THEIR BELIEF    3
    THEY WERE WELCOME TO THEIR BELIEF . . . . . 299 WELCOME TO THEIR BELIEF    T
    SUCH AS ACCORDING TO BELIEF IN ROME . . . . 315 IRIS BY NIGHT . . .    5
    INTO A BELIEF . . . . . . . . . . . . 449 THE BAD ISLAND--EASTER   62
    WE VAINLY WRESTLE WITH THE BLIND BELIEF . . 469 WE VAINLY WRESTLE... .    1
    IS THAT IT? SOME UTOPIAN BELIEF-- . . . . 501 A MASQUE OF MERCY .  205
    WE HAVE ALL THE BELIEF THAT'S GOOD FOR US. . 516 A MASQUE OF MERCY .  601
    TOO MUCH ALL-FIRED BELIEF AND WE'D BE BACK . 516 A MASQUE OF MERCY .  602
```
BELIEFS
```
    WHILE HAVING ITS BELIEFS DISPUTED. . . . . 419 AMERICA IS HARD TO SEE   82
    FIRM IN OUR FREE BELIEFS WITHOUT DISMAY, . . 424 FOR JOHN F. KENNEDY .   74
```
BELIEVE (SEE MAKE-BELIEVE)
```
    HE SAID HE COULDN'T MAKE THE BOY BELIEVE . . .  37 DEATH OF THE HIRED MAN   82
    "WILL YOU BELIEVE ME IF I PUT IT THERE . . . .  48 A HUNDRED COLLARS . .   93
    I'M CURSED. GOD, IF I DON'T BELIEVE I'M CURSED." .  54 HOME BURIAL . . . .   90
    OVER DESCENDED FROM HER. I BELIEVE . . . . .  77 THE GENERATIONS OF MEN  112
    "OHO, OHO!" / "YOU DON'T BELIEVE ME." / "YES, I DO, .  87 THE HOUSEKEEPER . .  181
    "IN THE FIRST PLACE YOU CAN'T MAKE ME BELIEVE IT'S----" .  90 THE FEAR . . . . .   41
    YOU NEEDN'T LOOK AT ME." / "I DON'T BELIEVE YOU." .  95 THE SELF-SEEKER . .   60
    I CAN'T BELIEVE IT'S WHAT YOU WANTED, TOO." . . 116 IN THE HOME STRETCH .  165
    COULDN'T BELIEVE THAT SO MUCH BLACK HAD COME THERE . 132 THE BONFIRE . . . .   85
    (YOU WON'T BELIEVE SHE SAID IT, BUT SHE SAID IT): . 159 NEW HAMPSHIRE . .    2
    TOFFILE, IF HE WERE HERE, I DON'T BELIEVE . . 207 THE WITCH OF COOS .  150
    I THINK THEY WOULD BELIEVE THE LIE. . . . . 221 IN A DISUSED GRAVEYARD   16
    AND YET TOO READY TO BELIEVE THE MOST. . . . 233 A BOUNDLESS MOMENT .    4
    NOT TO BELIEVE THE PHOEBES WEPT. . . . . . 242 NEED OF BEING VERSED .   24
    I VERILY BELIEVE . . . . . . . . . . . 333 HAPPINESS MAKES UP .   18
```

BELIEVE (CONTINUED)
HE WOULD DECLARE AND COULD HIMSELF BELIEVE . . . . 338 NEVER WOULD BIRDS' SONG 1
"I DON'T BELIEVE IT! IT ISN'T TRUE! . . . . 346 DISCOVERY OF MADEIRAS . 98
YOU DON'T BELIEVE THAT THAT FIRST-WATER GLEAM . . . . . 370 THE LITERATE FARMER AND 62
IS NOT A STAR?" / "BELIEVE IT? WHY, I KNOW IT. . . . . 370 THE LITERATE FARMER AND 63
I DON'T BELIEVE I BELIEVE A THING YOU STATE. . . . . . 389 SKEPTIC 3
I DON'T BELIEVE I BELIEVE YOU'RE THE LAST IN SPACE, . . . 389 SKEPTIC 5
I DON'T BELIEVE YOU'RE ANYWHERE NEAR THE LAST, ... 389 SKEPTIC 6
I DON'T BELIEVE WHAT MAKES YOU RED IN THE FACE, ... 389 SKEPTIC 7
"SO I HAVE HEARD AND DO IN PART BELIEVE IT," . . . . . 408 FROM PLANE TO PLANE . 147
I DON'T BELIEVE THE SLEEPERS IN THIS HOUSE . . . . . 413 A CABIN IN THE CLEARING 1
BUT WHO THEY ARE IS TOO MUCH TO BELIEVE-- . . . . . 414 A CABIN IN THE CLEARING 31
NEVER BELIEVE IT. AT THE VERY WORST . . . . . . 425 ACCIDENTALLY ON PURPOSE 13
BELIEVE THE ARCADIANS OR NOT, ... 452 A-WISHING WELL . . . 37
BELIEVE THE ARCADIANS OR NOT, ... 452 A-WISHING WELL . . . 47
BELIEVE IT WAS THE COW'S . . . . 464 MILKY WAY IS A COWPATH 19
ARE WE TO BELIEVE? . . . . 468 A REFLEX 10
YOU'D BE THE LAST TO WANT ME TO BELIEVE . . . . . 482 A MASQUE OF REASON . 258
WE DON'T BELIEVE THE COMMON MAN SHOULD READ IT. . . . 494 A MASQUE OF MERCY . 31
SINCE YOU PROPOSED IT, I BELIEVE I WILL. . . . . . 497 A MASQUE OF MERCY . 109
IS SOMETHING TO BELIEVE IN, DON'T WE, PAUL? . . . . 515 A MASQUE OF MERCY . 568
BY SOMETHING TO BELIEVE IN, JESSE MEANS . . . . . 515 A MASQUE OF MERCY . 569
LIVE AND LET LIVE, BELIEVE AND LET BELIEVE. . . . . 516 A MASQUE OF MERCY . 594
BELIEVED
SHE WOULDN'T HAVE BELIEVED THOSE ENDS ENOUGH . . . . 56 THE BLACK COTTAGE . 58
NO ONE BELIEVED. THEY LISTENED AT HIS HEART. . . . . 137 "OUT,OUT--" . . . 31
BUT THE MOOR STRANGELY ENOUGH BELIEVED . . . . . 347 DISCOVERY OF MADEIRAS 129
THE LATEST CREED THAT HAS TO BE BELIEVED . . . . . 427 CONCEPT SELF-CONCEIVED 1
BELIEVERS (SEE OLD-BELIEVERS)
BELIEVES
YOU HAVE IT IN FOR WOMEN, SHE BELIEVES. . . . . . 479 A MASQUE OF REASON . 178
BELILACED
BUT ONLY A BELILACED CELLAR HOLE, ... 378 DIRECTIVE 46
BELITTLED
MESERVE, BELITTLED IN THE GREAT SKIN COAT HE WORE. . . 143 SNOW 5
YOU WERE BELITTLED INTO VILEST WORMS . . . . . . 352 THE LESSON FOR TODAY . 74
WE BOTH ARE THE BELITTLED HUMAN RACE, ... 353 THE LESSON FOR TODAY . 77
BELL
THERE! THERE'S THE BELL. HE'S RUNG. BUT YOU GO DOWN . . 95 THE SELF-SEEKER . . 88
THREE TIMES HE BARELY STIRRED THE BELL, THEN LISTENED. . 143 SNOW 15
"HOLD ON." THE DOUBLE BELL BEGAN TO CHIRP. . . . . 155 SNOW 327
THE SWINGING MILL BELL CHANGED ITS RATE . . . . . 273 A LONE STRIKER . . 1
BELLATRIX
RIGEL, BELLATRIX, OR ELSE BETELGEUSE, ... 454 HOW HARD TO KEEP FROM 16
BELLOW
AND CRIED, "I'LL LARN YOU TO BELLOW." . . . . . 463 LINES IN DEJECTION . 16
BELLOWS
SHE BELLOWS ON A KNOLL AGAINST THE SKY. . . . . 125 THE COW IN APPLE TIME . 10
BELLS
LIKE GHOST OF SLEIGH BELLS IN A GHOST OF SNOW)-- . . . 119 HYLA BROOK 6
HE GIVES HIS HARNESS BELLS A SHAKE . . . . . . 224 STOPPING BY WOODS . 9
BELONG
IN SPRING MORE MORTAL SINGERS THAN BELONG . . . . 239 OUR SINGING STRENGTH . 19
"YOU'RE NOT WHERE YOU BELONG. YOU'RE NOT A KING . . . 457 HOW HARD TO KEEP FROM 102
BELONGED
TO TAKE THE MAYFLOWER BACK WHERE HE BELONGED, . . . 370 THE LITERATE FARMER AND 59
IT BELONGED TO US, ... 437 KITTY HAWK 298
BELOVED
THE HEADSTONE CUT WITH JOHN, BELOVED HUSBAND, . . . 200 PLACE FOR A THIRD . . 39
BELOW
AND BELOW ROARED A BROOK HIDDEN IN TREES, ... 76 THE GENERATIONS OF MEN 75
WITH THE BROOK GOING BY BELOW THE YARD, ... 82 THE HOUSEKEEPER . . 46
HE TOOK HIM DOWN BELOW A CRAMPING RAFTER, ... 142 THE VANISHING RED . 20
TO BE BELOW THE THRESHOLD OF COMMERCIAL; . . . . 162 NEW HAMPSHIRE . . 121
OF FROSTY NIGHT AIR ON THE VALE BELOW . . . . . 169 NEW HAMPSHIRE . . 341
DREAD FIFTY ABOVE MORE THAN FIFTY BELOW." . . . . 228 GOOD-BY AND KEEP COLD . 19
AND GOES DOWN BURNING INTO THE GULF BELOW, ... 249 ACCEPTANCE . . . 2
ONE LEVEL HIGHER THAN THE EARTH BELOW, ... 254 A WINTER EDEN . . 6
BELOW THE POINT, AND WERE AT LAST DRIVEN WRINKLED . . 258 WEST-RUNNING BROOK . 25
THE HEAD IN THE DARK BELOW . . . . 299 WELCOME TO THEIR BELIEF 10
OF EVERYTHING BELOW. . . . . 303 AFTERFLAKES . . . 5
JUST WHEN THE COLD WENT DOWN SO MANY BELOW. . . . 305 THERE ARE ROUGHLY ZONES 17
AND MIGHT BE ROLLING DEAD BELOW . . . . . . 344 DISCOVERY OF MADEIRAS . 33
BEL'S
TO TRY ANOTHER. / JESSE BEL'S A GIRL . . . . . 499 A MASQUE OF MERCY . 159
BOTH OF THEM CAUGHT IT FROM BEL'S FAVORITE POET, . . 511 A MASQUE OF MERCY . 462
BELSHAZZAR
WHY HURRY TO TELL BELSHAZZAR . . . . 314 BEARER OF EVIL TIDINGS 43
BELSHAZZAR'S
BELSHAZZAR'S OVERTHROW, ... 314 BEARER OF EVIL TIDINGS 42
IS THROWN IN SCRIPT, AS AT BELSHAZZAR'S FEAST, . . . 502 A MASQUE OF MERCY . 238
BELT
"AWFUL. WHY DIDN'T THEY THROW OFF THE BELT . . . . 93 THE SELF-SEEKER . . 30
"THEY SAY SOME TIME WAS WASTED ON THE BELT-- . . . 94 THE SELF-SEEKER . . 32
THE HEADSMAN HAS DARIUS BY THE BELT . . . . . 462 HOW HARD TO KEEP FROM 261
BEMUSE
YET YOU DON'T SPEAK. LET FOOLS BEMUSE THEMSELVES . . . 484 A MASQUE OF REASON . 298
BEN
THE WAY BEN FRANKLIN USED TO MAKE THE KITE STRING. . . 94 THE SELF-SEEKER . . 35
BEND
I FEEL THE LADDER SWAY AS THE BOUGHS BEND. . . . . 68 AFTER APPLE-PICKING . 23
WHEN I SEE BIRCHES BEND TO LEFT AND RIGHT . . . . 121 BIRCHES 1
BUT SWINGING DOESN'T BEND THEM DOWN TO STAY . . . . 121 BIRCHES 4
I SHOULD PREFER TO HAVE SOME BOY BEND THEM . . . . 121 BIRCHES 23
I'LL BEND THE TREE DOWN AND LET YOU DOWN BY IT." . . . 198 WILD GRAPES 83
YET LIKE A CHRISTIAN DISCIPLINED TO BEND . . . . . 353 THE LESSON FOR TODAY . 94
THAT THE MILLENNIUM TO WHICH YOU BEND . . . . . 359 THE LOST FOLLOWER . 27
AROUND BEND AFTER BEND, ... 366 NOT OF SCHOOL AGE . 1

BEND (CONTINUED)
    SO AT THE DISTANT BEND . . . . 388 MIDDLENESS OF THE ROAD   4
BENDING
    OF BENDING LIKE A SWORD ACROSS THE KNEE. . . . . . . 187 THE AX-HELVE 71
BENDS
    BENDS SQUARE IN WOODS, AN IRON SPINE . . . . 331 BEECH 2
BENEATH
    FIND THE BROWN BENEATH THE WHITE; . . . . 11 TO THE THAWING WIND . . 5
    BENEATH THE FEET OF DANCING FLOWERS. . . . . 26 IN HARDWOOD GROVES . . 10
    SHE WITHDREW, SHRINKING FROM BENEATH HIS ARM . . . . 52 HOME BURIAL 31
    OR PAUSED TO SAY BENEATH SOME LOVELIER ONE, ... 107 CHRISTMAS TREES . . 37
    THAT ALL YOUR DAYS ARE DIM BENEATH, ... 141 THE GUM-GATHERER . . 36
    FOR PRYING BENEATH AND FORCING THE LIDS OF SIGHT, . . . 235 VALLEY'S SINGING DAY . 9
    THE LURKING FROST IN THE EARTH BENEATH . . . . 276 TWO TRAMPS IN MUD TIME 38
    A SPECK THAT WOULD HAVE BEEN BENEATH MY SIGHT . . . . 357 A CONSIDERABLE SPECK . 1
    OF BABY GREEN AND SHOW THE WHITE BENEATH, ... 375 A YOUNG BIRCH . . . 2
    BENEATH A LOW-SLUNG JUNIPER . . . . 380 AN UNSTAMPED LETTER IN 13
    BENEATH THE BRUSH OF SNOW." . . . . 416 CLOSED FOR GOOD . . 24
    A FRACTURE IN THE ROCKS BENEATH NEW YORK . . . . . . 502 A MASQUE OF MERCY . . 229
BENEFICENT
    WHILE GREEDY GOOD-DOERS, BENEFICENT BEASTS OF PREY, . . 287 A ROADSIDE STAND . . 27
BENEFITS
    SWARM OVER THEIR LIVES ENFORCING BENEFITS . . . . . 287 A ROADSIDE STAND . . 28
BENIGHTED
    A BLANKER WHITENESS OF BENIGHTED SNOW . . . . 296 DESERT PLACES . . . 11
BENT
    BENT OVER THE OPEN FIRE, ... 8 LOVE AND A QUESTION . 18
    TO WHERE IT BENT IN THE UNDERGROWTH; . . . . 105 THE ROAD NOT TAKEN . . 5
    WEAK FOLIAGE THAT IS BLOWN UPON AND BENT, ... 119 HYLA BROOK 8
    THE STRICKEN FLOWER BENT DOUBLE AND SO HUNG. . . . . 126 RANGE-FINDING . . . 4
    HE CLIMBED STILL HIGHER AND BENT THE TREE TO EARTH . . 197 WILD GRAPES 37
    AND BENT SOME RAIL WIDE OPEN LIKE A SWITCH, ... 270 THE EGG AND THE MACHINE 7
    ON GLOSSY WIRES ARTISTICALLY BENT . . . . 309 WASPISH 1
    I WONDER! BOW AND RAINBOW AS IT BENT, ... 315 IRIS BY NIGHT . . . 23
    THEY WERE BOTH BENT ON SCUFFLING UP . . . . 407 FROM PLANE TO PLANE . 114
    OR MAKING VERSE IF THAT IS WHAT YOU'RE BENT ON. . . . 454 HOW HARD TO KEEP FROM 35
BEREFT
    BEREFT . . . . 251 BEREFT . . . . . . T
BERLIN
    OFFERED ME NOT LONG SINCE UP BERLIN WAY . . . . . . 162 NEW HAMPSHIRE . . . 110
BERRIES
    THE WOODBINE BERRIES WERE BLUE, ... 8 LOVE AND A QUESTION . 14
    'I HAVE LEFT THOSE THERE BERRIES, I SHREWDLY SUSPECT, . . 60 BLUEBERRIES 45
    HE HAS BROUGHT THEM ALL UP ON WILD BERRIES, THEY SAY, . 60 BLUEBERRIES 50
    OF WHERE ALL THE BERRIES AND OTHER THINGS GROW, . . . 61 BLUEBERRIES 61
    STUCK INTO HIS BERRIES AS FRESH AS A SHOWER; . . . . 61 BLUEBERRIES 65
    THERE HAD BEEN SOME BERRIES--BUT THOSE WERE ALL GONE. . 61 BLUEBERRIES 73
    HOW WE USED TO PICK BERRIES: WE TOOK ONE LOOK ROUND, . 62 BLUEBERRIES 85
    BRING BERRIES UNDER THE WAGON SEAT, ... 141 THE GUM-GATHERER . . 26
    AND LAST YEAR'S BERRIES SHINING SCARLET RED. . . . . 254 A WINTER EDEN . . . 8
    OFFERED FOR SALE WILD BERRIES IN WOODEN QUARTS, . . . 286 A ROADSIDE STAND . . 11
BERRYING
    MAME, WE DON'T KNOW ANY GOOD BERRYING PLACE?' . . . 61 BLUEBERRIES 77
BERTH
    LOOKING OUT OF MY LOWER BERTH . . . . 290 ON HEART'S BEGINNING TO 3
BERULED
    INTO BEING BERULED? . . . . 448 THE BAD ISLAND--EASTER 26
BERYL
    A SPECIMEN OF BERYL WITH A TRACE . . . . 162 NEW HAMPSHIRE . . . 118
BESEECH
    WITH MORTAL LONGING MAY BESEECH; . . . . 328 A MISSIVE MISSILE . . 54
BESEECHING
    AS IF BESEECHING ME, "PLEASE, NO MORE; . . . . . . 420 ONE MORE BREVITY . . 24
BESETTING
    TO REST FROM HIS BESETTING FEARS. . . . . 392 A CLIFF DWELLING . . 9
BESIDE
    A TREE BESIDE THE WALL STANDS BARE, ... 9 A LATE WALK 9
    YOU WALKED A WAY BESIDE ME . . . . 12 FLOWER-GATHERING . . 3
    THAT COULD TAKE ME FROM BESIDE YOU . . . . 13 FLOWER-GATHERING . . 11
    THERE WAS NEVER A SOUND BESIDE THE WOOD BUT ONE, . . . 17 MOWING 1
    THE WELL WAS DRY BESIDE THE DOOR, ... 18 GOING FOR WATER . . 1
    AT A TALL TUFT OF FLOWERS BESIDE A BROOK, ... 22 THE TUFT OF FLOWERS . 22
    BESIDE A REEDY BROOK THE SCYTHE HAD BARED. . . . . . 22 THE TUFT OF FLOWERS . 24
    AND THE WHIMPER OF HAWKS BESIDE THE SUN . . . . . . 24 PAN WITH US 19
    TO SIT BESIDE HER ON THE WOODEN STEPS. . . . . . . 34 DEATH OF THE HIRED MAN 10
    "HE'S WORN OUT. HE'S ASLEEP BESIDE THE STOVE. . . . . 35 DEATH OF THE HIRED MAN 33
    HAROLD ALONG BESIDE TO PITCH IT ON." . . . . 37 DEATH OF THE HIRED MAN 69
    THAT WROUGHT ON HIM BESIDE HER IN THE NIGHT. . . . . 38 DEATH OF THE HIRED MAN 110
    AND ROLL BACK DOWN THE MOUND BESIDE THE HOLE. . . . . 53 HOME BURIAL 77
    AGAINST THE LOUNGE BESIDE IT, THOUGH I DOUBT . . . . 56 THE BLACK COTTAGE . . 28
    AS TALKING--YOU STOOD UP BESIDE ME, YOU KNOW." . . . 62 BLUEBERRIES 96
    BESIDE THE LAKE FROM WHERE THAT DAY I SHOWED YOU . . . 64 A SERVANT TO SERVANTS . 62
    BESIDE IT, AND THERE MAY BE TWO OR THREE . . . . . . 68 AFTER APPLE-PICKING . 4
    AND THE BACK OF THE GIG THEY STOOD BESIDE . . . . . 89 THE FEAR 6
    BUT THIRTY DOLLARS SEEMED SO SMALL BESIDE . . . . . 107 CHRISTMAS TREES . . 47
    THREE CENTS SO SMALL BESIDE THE DOLLAR FRIENDS . . . . 107 CHRISTMAS TREES . . 50
    AND CUT A FLOWER BESIDE A GROUNDBIRD'S NEST . . . . . 126 RANGE-FINDING . . . 2
    I TOOK WHAT FRONT THERE WAS BESIDE. I KNELT . . . . 131 THE BONFIRE 65
    HIS SISTER STOOD BESIDE THEM IN HER APRON . . . . . 136 "OUT, OUT--" 13
    OF WATER WE WALKED ALONG BESIDE. . . . . 140 THE GUM-GATHERER . . 8
    BESIDE THE TABLE, NEAR THE OPEN BOOK, ... 151 SNOW 246
    IT STANDS BESIDE THE SAME OLD APPLE TREE. . . . . . 189 THE GRINDSTONE . . . 8
    BESIDE IT ROOM RESERVED; THE SAY A SISTER'S, ... 200 PLACE FOR A THIRD . . 40
    HE STOOD BESIDE AND LEAVE HIS TRADEMARK ON THEM, . . . 209 PAUPER WITCH OF GRAFTON 55
    ON SLIPPERY ROCKS BESIDE A WATERFALL. . . . . 210 PAUPER WITCH OF GRAFTON 98
    AND LIKE THE FLOWERS BESIDE THEM, CHILL AND SHIVER, . . 245 SPRING POOLS 3
    WILL LIKE THE FLOWERS BESIDE THEM SOON BE GONE, . . . 245 SPRING POOLS 4
    TO SEE WHAT THEY WERE BESIDE THE TRACK. . . . . . . 248 A PASSING GLIMPSE . . 4

BESIDE (CONTINUED)
   OUR ARM THROWN OVER IT ASLEEP BESIDE IT. . . . . . . 258 WEST-RUNNING BROOK . . 15
   IT FLOWS BESIDE US IN THIS WATER BROOK, ... 259 WEST-RUNNING BROOK . . 50
   SHE WAS CARRIED OUT BESIDE THE MAST, ... 344 DISCOVERY OF MADEIRAS . 36
   BUT RIGHT BESIDE YOU BOOKLIKE ON A SHELF, ... 359 THE LOST FOLLOWER . . 31
   BESIDE HER ATTIC BED AT NIGHT. . . . . 382 THE NIGHT LIGHT . . . 2
   EXCEPT BESIDE A SAFE INSIDE A BANK . . . . 386 THE FEAR OF MAN . . . 9
   TO SET HERSELF BESIDE THE SUN, ... 390 TWO LEADING LIGHTS . . 20
   HIS FEAR IS NOT BEHIND HIM BUT BESIDE HIM . . . . . . 421 ESCAPIST--NEVER . . . 3
   AND STANDS BESIDE, SUPPORTING IT IN PLACE.) . . . . . 474 A MASQUE OF REASON . . 23
   I WANT YOU IN MY GROUP BESIDE THE THRONE-- . . . . . 489 A MASQUE OF REASON . 456
   KNEEL BY HIM. BEL STANDS UP BESIDE HER CHAIR . . . . 518 A MASQUE OF MERCY . 652
BESIDES
   SHE SEEMS TO HAVE THE HOUSEWORK, AND BESIDES, ... 85 THE HOUSEKEEPER . . . 107
   BUT I GOT WONTED TO IT. AND BESIDES-- . . . . 87 THE HOUSEKEEPER . . . 174
   WILLIS BROUGHT UP BESIDES THE BOSTON LAWYER . . . . . 96 THE SELF-SEEKER . . . 91
   "NO; FOR BESIDES THE THINGS I TELL YOU OF, ... 112 IN THE HOME STRETCH . 46
   BESIDES THE GRAVE. . . . . 129 THE IMPULSE . . . 28
   THE ONE THING PALPABLE BESIDES THE SOUL . . . . . . 172 A STAR IN A STONEBOAT . 11
   HE SAID HE HAD, BESIDES. BECAUSE A HORSE . . . . . 209 PAUPER WITCH OF GRAFTON 65
   BESIDES THE WEAR OF IRON WAGON WHEELS . . . . 377 DIRECTIVE 14
   A HALF COURSE IN IT NEXT YEAR.) AND BESIDES, ... 407 FROM PLANE TO PLANE . 112
BEST
   WILL ROT THE BEST BIRCH FENCE A MAN CAN BUILD.' . . . . 54 HOME BURIAL 93
   AND MAKING THE BEST OF THEIR WAY BACK TO LIFE . . . . 54 HOME BURIAL . . . 104
   "THE BEST OF IT WAS THAT I DID. DO YOU KNOW, ... 60 BLUEBERRIES 34
   HE SAYS THE BEST WAY OUT IS ALWAYS THROUGH. . . . . 64 A SERVANT TO SERVANTS . 56
   IT'S NOT THAT LEN DON'T WANT THE BEST FOR ME. . . . . 64 A SERVANT TO SERVANTS . 60
   CRUEL--IT SOUNDS. I S'POSE THEY DID THE BEST . . . . 66 A SERVANT TO SERVANTS . 124
   THEY HAVE BEST RIGHT TO BE HEARD IN THIS PLACE." . . . 79 THE GENERATIONS OF MEN 176
   YOU THINK YOU'D BEST TEMPT HER AT SUCH A TIME?" . . . 79 THE GENERATIONS OF MEN 182
   SHE WANTS OUR HENS TO BE THE BEST THERE ARE. . . . . 85 THE HOUSEKEEPER . . . 118
   OR BEST--IT MAY NOT BE SO BAD. THE FIRM . . . . . 95 THE SELF-SEEKER . . . 78
   TO WARM THE FROZEN SWAMP AS BEST IT COULD . . . . . 102 THE WOOD-PILE . . . 39
   BUT DARED NOT SPARE TO DO THE BEST WE COULD . . . . . 109 THE EXPOSED NEST . . 28
   AS RECKLESS AS THE BEST OF THEM TONIGHT, ... 129 THE BONFIRE 2
   A BOARD IS THE BEST WEAPON IF YOU HAVE IT. . . . . 131 THE BONFIRE . . . 68
   THE BEST WAY IS TO COME UPHILL WITH ME . . . . . . 133 THE BONFIRE . . . 113
   "DON'T BEGIN THAT. YOU DID THE BEGIN YOU COULD . . . . 153 SNOW 281
   BUT IN THE BEST STYLE OF BAD SALESMANSHIP, ... 160 NEW HAMPSHIRE . . . 28
   SHE'S ONE OF THE TWO BEST STATES IN THE UNION. . . . . 164 NEW HAMPSHIRE . . . 175
   "THE BEST THING THAT WE'RE PUT HERE FOR'S TO SEE; . . . 177 THE STAR-SPLITTER . . 33
   HE HAD TO TAKE THE BEST WAY HE KNEW HOW . . . . . . 178 THE STAR-SPLITTER . . 56
   SAID SOME OF THE BEST THINGS WE EVER SAID. . . . . 179 THE STAR-SPLITTER . . 86
   BAPTISTE KNEW BEST WHY I WAS WHERE I WAS. . . . . . 186 THE AX-HELVE . . . 37
   TO HAVE THE BEST HE HAD, OR HAD TO SPARE-- . . . . . 187 THE AX-HELVE . . . 65
   HE KEPT FROM SCHOOL, OR DID HIS BEST TO KEEP-- . . . . 188 THE AX-HELVE . . . 84
   SHE MIGHT AS WELL HERSELF." BUT HE LIKED BEST . . . . 209 PAUPER WITCH OF GRAFTON 83
   HE COULD HAVE SLEPT BUT A MOMENT MORE AT BEST. . . . . 235 VALLEY'S SINGING DAY . 6
   AND HEART, IF NEED BE, I WILL DO MY BEST . . . . . 267 THE ARMFUL . . . 7
   WITH WHICH HE PENETRATES MY BEST DEFENSE . . . . . 277 THE WHITE-TAILED HORNET 8
   HERE HE IS AT HIS BEST, BUT EVEN HERE-- . . . . . 278 THE WHITE-TAILED HORNET 32
   "THE BEST WAY TO HATE IS THE WORST. . . . . . . 312 THE VINDICTIVES . . 81
   THEY'RE IN THE BEST POSITION OF US ALL . . . . . . 317 BUILD SOIL . . . 55
   OR MISSED THEIR CHANCE, OR NOT HAVE BEEN THEIR BEST, . . . 355 THE LESSON FOR TODAY . 152
   ABOUT WHEN BEST TO HAVE US IN OUR ORBIT, ... 361 A LOOSE MOUNTAIN . . 20
   IT BEST BE LEFT TO GREAT MEN OF HIS KIND . . . . . 372 THE LITERATE FARMER AND 134
   EACH KNOWS HIS OWN DISCERNMENT BEST. . . . . . . 381 AN UNSTAMPED LETTER IN 43
   BUT THE BEST OF HER EXHIBIT . . . . 397 AN IMPORTER . . . 17
   OUR BEST GUIDE UPWARD FURTHER TO THE LIGHT, ... 425 ACCIDENTALLY ON PURPOSE 23
   PILOT, THOUGH AT BEST YOUR . . . . 440 KITTY HAWK 402
   THAT BECOMES US BEST . . . . 441 KITTY HAWK 430
   THE BEST, I'M TOLD, I EVER HAVE HAD TAKEN. . . . . 476 A MASQUE OF REASON . 86
   FOR THIS I THINK. I FIND IT ALWAYS BEST . . . . . 487 A MASQUE OF REASON . 387
   --THE DEVIL'S BEING GOD'S BEST INSPIRATION. . . . . 487 A MASQUE OF REASON . 401
   IS THAT THE BEST THING IN IT SHOULD BE COURAGE. . . . . 497 A MASQUE OF MERCY . 107
   THE BEST MINDS ARE THE BEST AT PREMISES. . . . . . 510 A MASQUE OF MERCY . 434
   OUR SACRIFICE--THE BEST WE HAVE TO OFFER, ... 520 A MASQUE OF MERCY . 718
   AND NOT OUR WORST NOR SECOND BEST, OUR BEST, ... 520 A MASQUE OF MERCY . 719
   OUR VERY BEST, OUR LIVES LAID DOWN LIKE JONAH'S, . . . 520 A MASQUE OF MERCY . 720
BESTIAL
   OBEYING BESTIAL LAWS, ... 341 THE SUBVERTED FLOWER . 59
BESTOWS
   HE BESTOWS SUMMER ON US AND ESCAPES . . . . . . 408 FROM PLANE TO PLANE . 127
BEST'S
   WHAT I LIKE BEST'S THE LAY OF DIFFERENT FARMS, ... 49 A HUNDRED COLLARS . . 124
BET
   WHAT'LL YOU BET HE EVER CALLS AGAIN?" . . . . . . 156 SNOW 350
   SON-OF-A-BITCH! YOU BET SHE WAS AN I-DEAL." . . . . 170 NEW HAMPSHIRE . . . 354
   HE'D BET HUSE WAS A CRIBBER AND HAD GNAWED . . . . . 209 PAUPER WITCH OF GRAFTON 60
   HE BET IT WAS OUT TODAY, ... 367 NOT OF SCHOOL AGE . . 27
   YOU'D BET YOU GOT MORE WORK DONE IN A DAY, ... 405 FROM PLANE TO PLANE . 46
   I'LL BET YOU ANYTHING THAT'S ALL AS KING . . . . . 458 HOW HARD TO KEEP FROM 137
   I'LL BET SHE'D HAVE MADE A MELODIOUS LOW . . . . . 463 LINES IN DEJECTION . 11
   YOU'RE SPORTING THERE. I'LL BET YOU'RE GOOD AT IT. . . . 502 A MASQUE OF MERCY . 219
BETAKE
   I SHOULD BETAKE ME BACK TEN THOUSAND PAGES . . . . . 350 THE LESSON FOR TODAY . 6
BETELGEUSE
   RIGEL, BELLATRIX, OR ELSE BETELGEUSE. . . . . . . 454 HOW HARD TO KEEP FROM 16
BETHLEHEM
   HARRIS OF DERRY, AND LYNCH OF BETHLEHEM. . . . . . 167 NEW HAMPSHIRE . . . 261
   WILL TELL YOU IT'S THE STAR OF BETHLEHEM . . . . . 369 THE LITERATE FARMER AND 34
   THE STAR OF BETHLEHEM, THE POMEGRANATES, ... 473 A MASQUE OF REASON . . 12
BETRAY
   MUST LEAVE THEM UNLOCKED TO BETRAY HIS PRESENCE. . . . 289 OLD BARN AT THE BOTTOM 15
   BETRAY YOU INTO TAKING SIDES AGAINST ME, ... 320 BUILD SOIL 132
BETRAYED
   BUT WE CAN'T HELP FEELING MORE THAN A LITTLE BETRAYED . . 305 THERE ARE ROUGHLY ZONES 15

BETRAYED (CONTINUED)
  OF MORE THAN ROYAL ATTRIBUTES BETRAYED HIM. . . . . 462 HOW HARD TO KEEP FROM   274
BETTER
  AND THEY ARE BETTER FOR HER PRAISE. . . . . 7 MY NOVEMBER GUEST . . . 20
  "SILAS HAS BETTER CLAIM ON US YOU THINK . . . . 38 DEATH OF THE HIRED MAN 124
  HE MAY BE BETTER THAN APPEARANCES. . . . . 39 DEATH OF THE HIRED MAN 134
  YOU'D BETTER TUCK YOUR MONEY UNDER YOU . . . . 47 A HUNDRED COLLARS . . 90
  "THERE, YOU HAVE SAID IT ALL AND YOU FEEL BETTER. . . . . 54 HOME BURIAL 108
  TO DO WORK BETTER OR FASTER--THOSE TWO THINGS. . . . . . 70 THE CODE 23
  AND BEGIN OVER----' THERE, SHE'D BETTER STOP. . . . . . 80 THE GENERATIONS OF MEN 194
  BETTER THAN MARRIED OUGHT TO BE AS GOOD . . . . . . 84 THE HOUSEKEEPER . . . 81
  THIS IS A GOOD HOME: I DON'T ASK FOR BETTER. . . . . . 84 THE HOUSEKEEPER . . . 89
  OUR HENS AND COWS AND PIGS ARE ALWAYS BETTER . . . . . 85 THE HOUSEKEEPER . . . 111
  THE MAN WAS FOUND. I'D BETTER NAME NO NAMES. . . . . . 88 THE HOUSEKEEPER . . . 188
  TO TRY TO HELP ME DRIVE A BETTER BARGAIN." . . . . . . 93 THE SELF-SEEKER . . . 9
  "I'M GOING TO BE WORSE INSTEAD OF BETTER. . . . . . 94 THE SELF-SEEKER . . . 56
  SOUNDS SOMETHING LIKE. BETTER THAN FARMER'S BEANS . . . 97 THE SELF-SEEKER . . . 127
  AND HAVING PERHAPS THE BETTER CLAIM, ... 105 THE ROAD NOT TAKEN . . 7
  AS BETTER THAN THE SUN IN ANY CASE . . . . . . 108 OLD MAN'S WINTER NIGHT 20
  I DON'T KNOW WHERE IT'S LIKELY TO GO BETTER. . . . . 122 BIRCHES 53
  FOR WHAT THEY'D BETTER WAIT TILL WE HAVE DONE. . . . 130 THE BONFIRE 15
  BETTER THAN IF HE HAD HAD ME RIDE. . . . . . 140 THE GUM-GATHERER . . 4
  ADDED: "YOU CAN JUDGE BETTER AFTER SEEING.-- . . . . 144 SNOW 35
  OR NOT MUCH BETTER. WHY, IT DOESN'T SEEM . . . . 145 SNOW 59
  "BUT HOW MUCH BETTER OFF ARE WE AS IT IS? . . . . . 152 SNOW 261
  YOU'D BETTER DRESS: YOU WON'T GO BACK TO BED. . . . . 152 SNOW 273
  AND MAKE THE MOST OF IT FOR BETTER OR WORSE. . . . . 161 NEW HAMPSHIRE . . . 65
  "I LIKE THIS BETTER." IT WAS REALLY BETTER. . . . . 164 NEW HAMPSHIRE . . . 158
  ABOUT THE PEOPLE BEING BETTER THERE . . . . . 167 NEW HAMPSHIRE . . . 255
  RATHER THAN BETTER. HOW ARE WE TO WRITE . . . . . 167 NEW HAMPSHIRE . . . 267
  DO WE KNOW ANY BETTER WHERE WE ARE, ... 179 THE STAR-SPLITTER . . 96
  BETTER A MEANINGLESS NAME, I SHOULD SAY, ... 185 MAPLE 168
  A BETTER WAY TO PASS THE AFTERNOON . . . . . 190 THE GRINDSTONE . . . 53
  MIGHTN'T WE MAKE IT WORSE INSTEAD OF BETTER? . . . . 191 THE GRINDSTONE . . . 74
  HE THOUGH HE'D BETTER TAKE HIS JACKKNIFE TO. . . . . 193 PAUL'S WIFE 87
  I GUESS THEY'D BETTER DRAG IT THROUGH AGAIN. . . . . 208 PAUPER WITCH OF GRAFTON 29
  AND, "BETTER DEFEAT ALMOST, ... 212 AN EMPTY THREAT . . . 53
  NO BETTER THAN SPOONS, ... 234 GATHERING LEAVES . . 2
  IT MAY NOT SEEM BETTER TO ME TO REST. . . . . . 236 MISGIVING 16
  SOMEONE HAD BETTER BE PREPARED FOR RAGE. . . . . 250 ONCE BY THE PACIFIC . 12
  AND THEN I KNOW OF NO BETTER WAY . . . . . 263 THE TIMES TABLE . . . 17
  AND TRY TO STACK THEM IN A BETTER LOAD. . . . . 267 THE ARMFUL 12
  "YOU'D BETTER NOT DISTURB ME ANYMORE," . . . . 270 THE EGG AND THE MACHINE 27
  THEIRS WAS THE BETTER RIGHT--AGREED. . . . . . 277 TWO TRAMPS IN MUD TIME 64
  AS VISITOR AT MY HOUSE HE IS BETTER. . . . . . 278 THE WHITE-TAILED HORNET 23
  I KNEW A TALE OF A BETTER KIND. . . . . . . 291 ON HEART'S BEGINNING TO 14
  BETTER TO GO DOWN DIGNIFIED . . . . 307 PROVIDE, PROVIDE . . 19
  ITS NAME MIGHT BETTER BE FIRST MOTOR KITE. . . . . 308 THE WRIGHTS' BIPLANE . 2
  OR BETTER ON DISH PLATES ALL AROUND THE ROOM, ... 320 BUILD SOIL 148
  OF SPEECH AND THINKING IS SO MUCH MY BETTER . . . . 324 BUILD SOIL 250
  I CAN TELL BETTER AFTER I GET HOME, ... 325 BUILD SOIL 286
  BETTER A MONTH FROM NOW WHEN CUTTING POSTS . . . . 325 BUILD SOIL 287
  TO BETTER ITS PERCH FOR THE NIGHT, ... 334 COME IN 7
  OR EVEN BETTER GODLIKE IN YOURSELF. . . . . . 359 THE LOST FOLLOWER . . 32
  TO ANY DEMONSTRABLY BETTER RACE, ... 369 THE LITERATE FARMER AND 50
  NEITHER OF THEM WAS BETTER THAN THE OTHER. . . . . 404 FROM PLANE TO PLANE . 1
  AND JUNE WAS NOT MUCH BETTER, COLD AND RAINY. . . . . 407 FROM PLANE TO PLANE . 89
  THEY ARE, THEY MAY KNOW BETTER WHERE THEY ARE. . . . 414 A CABIN IN THE CLEARING 30
  THAN SMOKE AND MIST WHO BETTER COULD APPRAISE . . . . 415 A CABIN IN THE CLEARING 41
  A NEW AND BETTER WAY TO IND . . . . . . 416 AMERICA IS HARD TO SEE 2
  THAT BETTER THAN DA GAMA'S GOLD . . . . . . 417 AMERICA IS HARD TO SEE 27
  A TURBULENCE HE HAD THE BETTER OF. . . . . . 423 FOR JOHN F. KENNEDY . 45
  BETTER THAN ALL THE STALEMATE AN'S AND IFS. . . . . 423 FOR JOHN F. KENNEDY . 59
  AND THE BETTER PART . . . . 440 KITTY HAWK 387
  I'M ALWAYS FOR A BETTER SKY. . . . . . . 451 A-WISHING WELL . . . 13
  I CLAIM TO BE NO BETTER THAN I AM. . . . . . 460 HOW HARD TO KEEP FROM 210
  WOULD BETTER HAVE BEEN TAKEN TO YOUR DEPTH." . . . . 506 A MASQUE OF MERCY . . 340
  THERE IS NO BETTER WAY OF HAVING IT. . . . . 512 A MASQUE OF MERCY . . 508
  SUFFER A FRIEND TO TRY TO WORD YOU BETTER. . . . . 519 A MASQUE OF MERCY . . 677
BETTERING
  I SHOULDN'T MIND HIS BETTERING HIMSELF . . . . . . 35 DEATH OF THE HIRED MAN 25
BETTER-LEFT-UNWRITTEN
  LIKE THE CRUMPLED, BETTER-/LEFT-UNWRITTEN LETTER . . . . 428 KITTY HAWK . . . 19/20
BETWEEN
  AND SET THE WALL BETWEEN US ONCE AGAIN. . . . . . 33 MENDING WALL 14
  WE KEEP THE WALL BETWEEN US AS WE GO. . . . . . 33 MENDING WALL 15
  BETWEEN THEM THEY WILL LAY THIS FARM AS SMOOTH! . . . 36 DEATH OF THE HIRED MAN 63
  "I WONDER WHAT'S BETWEEN THEM." / "I CAN TELL YOU. . . . 39 DEATH OF THE HIRED MAN 139
  AND YET BETWEEN THE TOWN AND IT I FOUND, ... 40 THE MOUNTAIN 7
  HE SAT AND FIXED HIS CHIN BETWEEN HIS FISTS. . . . . 52 HOME BURIAL 41
  A FRONT WITH JUST A DOOR BETWEEN TWO WINDOWS, ... 55 THE BLACK COTTAGE . . 6
  THOUGH WHAT A NAME SHOULD MATTER BETWEEN US----" . . . 79 THE GENERATIONS OF MEN 158
  "THIS IS BETWEEN YOU TWO APPARENTLY. . . . . 100 THE SELF-SEEKER . . . 209
  TO PUT A TREE BETWEEN US WHEN HE LIGHTED, ... 101 THE WOOD-PILE . . . 11
  WHEN BETWEEN WHIRLS OF SNOW NOT COME TO LIE . . . . 106 CHRISTMAS TREES . . . 3
  OF SOMETHING INTERPOSED BETWEEN THEIR SIGHT . . . . 109 THE EXPOSED NEST . . 18
  DOWN DARK CONVERGING PATHS BETWEEN THE PINES. . . . 129 THE BONFIRE 7
  BETWEEN THE HOUSE AND BARN THE GALE . . . . . 137 BROWN'S DESCENT . . . 9
  OR A BASKET OF EGGS BETWEEN THEIR FEET; . . . . 141 THE GUM-GATHERER . . 27
  BUT TURNS TO PINK BETWEEN THE TEETH. . . . . 141 THE GUM-GATHERER . . 33
  OF WHO BEGAN IT BETWEEN THE TWO RACES. . . . . 142 THE VANISHING RED . . 13
  BETWEEN TWO BOYS AND NOT FEEL BOUND TO STOP IT. . . . 146 SNOW 101
  BETWEEN THE PICTURES ON A MOVIE SCREEN . . . . 165 NEW HAMPSHIRE . . . 194
  BETWEEN TWO DAYS, THE REASON WHY I SOUGHT . . . . 167 NEW HAMPSHIRE . . . 249
  AND PLOWED BETWEEN THE ROCKS HE COULDN'T MOVE, ... 177 THE STAR-SPLITTER . . 27
  AND HOW IT STANDS BETWEEN THE NIGHT TONIGHT, ... 179 THE STAR-SPLITTER . . 97
  OF THE TWO PAGES IT WAS PRESSED BETWEEN, ... 181 MAPLE 65
  SOMETHING BETWEEN YOUR FATHER AND YOUR MOTHER . . . . 183 MAPLE 113

BETWEEN (CONTINUED)
   WHAT PASSED BETWEEN US, SHE WAS ONLY FEIGNING. . . . . . 187 THE AX-HELVE 57
   AND HE AND I BETWEEN US GROUND A BLADE. . . . . 189 THE GRINDSTONE . . . 25
   AND SOMETIMES LAUGHED AT WHAT IT WAS BETWEEN THEM. . . . 200 PLACE FOR A THIRD . . 35
   BETWEEN THE DEATH DAY AND THE FUNERAL DAY. . . . . . . 201 PLACE FOR A THIRD . . 69
   SHE GAVE IT THROUGH THE SCREEN DOOR CLOSED BETWEEN THEM: . . 201 PLACE FOR A THIRD . . 76
   WE'D KEPT UP ALL THESE YEARS BETWEEN OURSELVES . . . . . 207 THE WITCH OF COOS . . 146
   AND BETWEEN WHAT HE DOESN'T KNOW . . . . 211 AN EMPTY THREAT . . 14
   BETWEEN ME AND THE NORTH POLE-- . . . . 211 AN EMPTY THREAT . . 25
   UNSAID BETWEEN US, BROTHER, AND THIS REMAINED-- . . . . 222 TO E.T. 10
   BETWEEN THE WOODS AND FROZEN LAKE . . . . 224 STOPPING BY WOODS . . 7
   BETWEEN YOU AND ME. . . . . 251 TREE AT MY WINDOW . . 4
   BETWEEN THE DOTTED STARS, ... 252 THE PEACEFUL SHEPHERD . 4
   BUT IT FLOWS OVER US. IT FLOWS BETWEEN US . . . . . . 259 WEST-RUNNING BROOK . . 51
   IT FLOWS BETWEEN US, OVER US, AND WITH US. . . . . . . 259 WEST-RUNNING BROOK . . 53
   TO FEEL OF BETWEEN THUMB AND FINGERS; . . . . 266 SITTING BY A BUSH . . 3
   BETWEEN TWO METAPHYSICAL EXTREMES. . . . . 269 THE BEAR 25
   BETWEEN THE DOTTED FEET A STREAK OF TAIL, ... 270 THE EGG AND THE MACHINE 18
   BETWEEN STARS--ON STARS WHERE NO HUMAN RACE IS. . . . . 296 DESERT PLACES . . . 14
   BETWEEN TWO DOWNPOURS TO SEE WHAT THERE WAS. . . . . . 300 MOON COMPASSES . . . 2
   SO LOVE WILL TAKE BETWEEN THE HANDS A FACE.... . . . . 301 MOON COMPASSES . . . 8
   THAT THOUGH THERE IS NO FIXED LINE BETWEEN WRONG AND RIGHT, 305 THERE ARE ROUGHLY ZONES 12
   THAT ONCE BETWEEN POST AND POST . . . . 312 THE VINDICTIVES . . . 65
   BUT NOT MUCH IN BETWEEN UNLESS A COLLEGE. . . . . . . 325 BUILD SOIL 282
   SOME STANDING JEST BETWEEN YOU MEN? . . . . 346 DISCOVERY OF MADEIRAS . 94
   BETWEEN TOO MUCH AND ME. . . . . 349 TRIPLE BRONZE . . . 12
   BETWEEN TWO BURRS ON THE MAP . . . . 367 A SERIOUS STEP LIGHTLY 1
   BETWEEN US TWO IT'S NOT A STAR AT ALL. . . . . 369 THE LITERATE FARMER AND 38
   BETWIXT AND BETWEEN . . . . 445 PERIL OF HOPE . . . 2
   "THE CHOICE IS NOT BETWEEN TWO PEARLS, O KING, ... 456 HOW HARD TO KEEP FROM 74
   BUT BETWEEN PEACE AND WAR AS WE CONCEIVE IT. . . . . . 456 HOW HARD TO KEEP FROM 75
   BETWEEN HIS JUST DESERTS AND WHAT HE GETS. . . . . . 475 A MASQUE OF REASON . 51
   BETWEEN US, YOU AND I. / I MAKE YOU SEE? . . . . . . 480 A MASQUE OF REASON . 185
BETWIXT
   BETWIXT AND BETWEEN . . . . 445 PERIL OF HOPE . . . 2
BEWARE
   BEWARE OF COMING TOO MUCH TO THE SURFACE . . . . . . 385 THE FEAR OF GOD . . . 11
BEWHISKERED
   AND LOOKING UP BEWHISKERED OUT OF THE PIT, ... 71 THE CODE 62
BEWILDERED
   ON NOISELESS WING A BEWILDERED BUTTERFLY, ... 22 THE TUFT OF FLOWERS . 12
   OF VISITING WITH THE EQUALLY BEWILDERED. . . . . . . 414 A CABIN IN THE CLEARING 8
BEWITCHED
   ONLY BEWITCHED SO I WOULD LAST HIM LONGER. . . . . . . 210 PAUPER WITCH OF GRAFTON 95
BEYOND
   BEYOND THE SHADOW OF A DOUBT; . . . . 20 THE TRIAL BY EXISTENCE 36
   TOO FAR BEYOND HIM TO BE GATHERED IN, ... 29 MY BUTTERFLY . . . 29
   I LET MY NEIGHBOR KNOW BEYOND THE HILL; . . . . . . 33 MENDING WALL . . . 12
   WERE FIELDS, A RIVER, AND BEYOND, MORE FIELDS. . . . . 40 THE MOUNTAIN . . . 9
   BEYOND THE BRIDGE, WAS NOT THAT OF THE MOUNTAIN, . . . 41 THE MOUNTAIN . . . 21
   BEYOND WHERE THEY WERE WAS A SHATTERED SEEDPOD. . . . . 76 THE GENERATIONS OF MEN 74
   YOU FORGET WHERE WE ARE. WHAT IS BEYOND . . . . . . 90 THE FEAR 25
   BEYOND THE TIME OF PROFITABLE GROWTH-- . . . . 106 CHRISTMAS TREES . . 23
   ABOUT HIS TELESCOPE. BEYOND THE AGE . . . . 178 THE STAR-SPLITTER . . 54
   BEYOND THE HIGHEST CITY BUILT WITH HANDS. . . . . . 182 MAPLE 84
   BEYOND AN OVER-WARMTH OF KITCHEN STOVE . . . . . . 186 THE AX-HELVE . . . 35
   AND THEN BEYOND THE OPEN WATER, DIM WITH MIDGES, . . . 194 PAUL'S WIFE . . . 106
   MOSTLY AS MUCH BEYOND MY LIFTED HANDS, THOUGH, ... 197 WILD GRAPES . . . 28
   BEYOND WHICH GOD IS; . . . . 219 I WILL SING YOU ONE-O . 52
   THE FOE THRUST BACK UNSAFE BEYOND THE RHINE, ... 222 TO E.T. 18
   I DISCERNED, AS I THOUGHT, BEYOND THE PICTURE, ... 225 FOR ONCE SOMETHING . 8
   OF THE KNOWLEDGE BEYOND THE BOUNDS OF LIFE . . . . . 236 MISGIVING 15
   TO THINK THEIR CASE WAS BEYOND RELIEF-- . . . . . . 253 THE THATCH . . . 22
   TAKE UP THE TASK BEYOND HER CHOOSING." . . . . . . 256 THE LOVELY BE CHOOSERS 11
   TO HAPPEN IN HEAVEN BEYOND THE FLOATS OF CLOUD . . . . 268 ON LOOKING UP BY CHANCE 2
   IMMURED ALMOST BEYOND RECALL, ... 280 BLUE RIBBON AT AMESBURY 15
   THERE MAY BE LITTLE OR MUCH BEYOND THE GRAVE, ... 300 STRONG SAYING NOTHING . 15
   BEYOND EMBARRASSING SELF-CONSCIOUSNESS . . . . . . 318 BUILD SOIL 82
   BEYOND WHICH THEY ARE DOOMED TO MISS. . . . . . . 328 A MISSIVE MISSILE . . 51
   DRINK AND BE WHOLE AGAIN BEYOND CONFUSION. . . . . . 379 DIRECTIVE 62
   BEYOND WORDS . . . . 393 BEYOND WORDS . . . T
   BEYOND THIS GREAT DOOR YOU HAVE LOCKED AGAINST ME, . . . 513 A MASQUE OF MERCY . 532
   BEYOND THE STORM, BEYOND THE UNIVERSE. . . . . . . 513 A MASQUE OF MERCY . 533
   TOWARD WHAT YOU MAKE ME SEE BEYOND THE WORLD. . . . . 514 A MASQUE OF MERCY . 545
BIBLE
   ONCE SHE FOUND FOR A BOOKMARK IN THE BIBLE . . . . . 181 MAPLE 62
   IN THE BIG BIBLE, AND ALL SHE REMEMBERED . . . . . . 183 MAPLE 105
   AND DARWIN'S PROVED MISTAKEN, NOT THE BIBLE. . . . . 369 THE LITERATE FARMER AND 46
   WELL, I COULD USE A BOOK. / WHAT BOOK? / A BIBLE. . . . 494 A MASQUE OF MERCY . 27
   LOOK, I DON'T NEED THE BIBLE TO CONSULT. . . . . . 495 A MASQUE OF MERCY . 44
   HE SAID THE BIBLE. / I SHOULD HATE TO SCARE YOU . . . . 495 A MASQUE OF MERCY . 52
   I'M IN THE BIBLE, ALL DONE OUT IN STORY. . . . . . 497 A MASQUE OF MERCY . 113
   YOU DON'T KNOW PAUL: HE'S IN THE BIBLE TOO. . . . . . 498 A MASQUE OF MERCY . 127
   A PROPHET WITH THE BIBLE FOR CREDENTIALS. . . . . . 498 A MASQUE OF MERCY . 135
BIBLE'S
   WHOSE BIBLE'S SO CONFUSED IN MARRIAGE COUNSEL? . . . . 201 PLACE FOR A THIRD . . 65
BID
   OFTEN HE BID ME COME AND HAVE A LOOK . . . . 178 THE STAR-SPLITTER . . 76
   BUT IT SEEMS LIKE SOME WORD SHE LEFT TO BID YOU . . . . 180 MAPLE 21
   BUT NO, NOT YET. A SNORT TO BID THEM WAIT. . . . . . 229 TWO LOOK AT TWO . . 26
   I BID YOU TO A ONE-MAN REVOLUTION-- . . . . 324 BUILD SOIL 266
   TO BID THEM BOTH BE HAPPY. . . . . 335 CARPE DIEM . . . 8
   BUT BID LIFE SEIZE THE PRESENT? . . . . 335 CARPE DIEM . . . 19
   SEND US A FLOOD AND BID US BE DAMNED AND DROWN. . . . . 349 OUR HOLD ON THE PLANET 6
   TO BID US A MOCK FAREWELL. . . . . 365 A NATURE NOTE . . . 12
   AND SEE AS I'M BID. . . . . 392 A WISH TO COMPLY . . 8
   AND BID MY WILL AVOUCH IT LIKE MACBETH. . . . . . . 477 A MASQUE OF REASON . 112
BIDDING
   AND THEY END BY BIDDING HIM STAY WITH THEM. . . . . . 236 MISGIVING 4

BIDE
    AND SAID OUT LOUD, I COULDN'T BIDE THE SMOTHER . . . . . 131 THE BONFIRE 70
BIDS
    IT BIDS PRETTY FAIR . . . . 392 IT BIDS PRETTY FAIR . . T
BIG
    HE TAKES IT OUT IN BUNCHES LIKE BIG BIRDS' NESTS. . . . . 37 DEATH OF THE HIRED MAN   93
    WITH A BIG STICK, THE SAME AS WHEN THE COWS . . . . . 43 THE MOUNTAIN 85
    BLUEBERRIES AS BIG AS THE END OF YOUR THUMB, ... 59 BLUEBERRIES 3
    BUT HE THOUGHT A BIG THOUGHT--I COULD TELL BY HIS EYE-- . 60 BLUEBERRIES 43
    "YOU DIDN'T KNOW. BUT JAMES IS ONE BIG FOOL. . . . . . 70 THE CODE 15
    WITH A BIG JAG TO EMPTY IN A BAY. . . . . 71 THE CODE 54
    I'VE BEEN BUILT IN HERE LIKE A BIG CHURCH ORGAN. . . . . 82 THE HOUSEKEEPER . . . 38
    YOU CAN HEAR THE SMALL BUZZ SAWS WHINE, THE BIG SAW . . . 94 THE SELF-SEEKER . . . 41
    I LIKE IT.--BANG GOES SOMETHING BIG AWAY . . . . . . 111 IN THE HOME STRETCH . . 37
    JOE SAID: "YOU BIG BOYS OUGHT TO FIND A FARM, ... 113 IN THE HOME STRETCH . . 95
    SINCE HE WAS OLD ENOUGH TO KNOW, BIG BOY . . . . . . 137 "OUT,OUT--" 23
    OVER THE GREAT BIG THUMPING, SHUFFLING MILLSTONE, . . . 142 THE VANISHING RED . . 16
    LAUGHED THE LOUD LAUGH THE BIG LAUGH AT THE LITTLE. . . . 165 NEW HAMPSHIRE 200
    IN THE BIG BIBLE, AND ALL SHE REMEMBERED . . . . . . 183 MAPLE 105
    THEY'D SLICED THE FIRST SLAB OFF A BIG BUTT LOG, ... 193 PAUL'S WIFE 62
    THE MICA SHEETS WERE BIG AS PLATE-GLASS WINDOWS, ... 213 A FOUNTAIN, A BOTTLE . 5
    TO FEED HIS THUMPING GRUBS AS BIG AS HE IS. . . . . . 278 THE WHITE-TAILED HORNET 31
    A BUBBLE ON A PIPESTEM, GROWING BIG. . . . . 283 THE GOLD HESPERIDEE . 24
    AND THE BIG FLAG THEY HAD--YOU KNOW . . . . 366 NOT OF SCHOOL AGE . . 24
    THE BIG FLAG: THE RED--WHITE-- . . . . 367 NOT OF SCHOOL AGE . . 25
    WHAT'S A STAR DOING BIG AS A BASEBALL? . . . . 369 THE LITERATE FARMER AND 37
    OF LIGHTING THE WHOLE NIGHT WITH ONE BIG BLOB . . . . . 370 THE LITERATE FARMER AND 72
    SEEK NOT IN ME THE BIG I CAPITAL, ... 387 IOTA SUBSCRIPT . . . 1
    AND I'LL FORGIVE THY GREAT BIG ONE ON ME. . . . . . . 428 FORGIVE, O LORD.... . 2
    BUT THE BIG ONE IS WORTHLESS. BREAK IT OPEN. . . . . . 456 HOW HARD TO KEEP FROM . 82
    MY HEAD FOR IT--YOU'LL FIND THE BIG ONE HOLLOW. . . . . 456 HOW HARD TO KEEP FROM . 83
    LIKE A BIG EGG AND HATCH A HEAVEN OUT . . . . 484 A MASQUE OF REASON . . 306
    IT'S TOO BIG FOR HIM. HELP HIM HOLD IT UP. . . . . . 506 A MASQUE OF MERCY . . 328
BIG-CITY
    BIG-CITY TALK. I'M GETTING OUT OF HERE. . . . . . . 500 A MASQUE OF MERCY . . 171
BIGGER
    WAS NO BIGGER THAN A----" WHAT, I DID NOT HEAR. . . . . 44 THE MOUNTAIN 106
    AT FIRST TO BE NO BIGGER THAN A CANE, ... 375 A YOUNG BIRCH 14
    AND THEN NO BIGGER THAN A FISHING POLE, ... 375 A YOUNG BIRCH 15
    NOW LEFT'S NO BIGGER THAN A HARNESS GALL. . . . . . . 378 DIRECTIVE 40
BIGNESS
    THE KING SAT FAVORING ONE PEARL FOR ITS BIGNESS, ... 455 HOW HARD TO KEEP FROM   69
BIGOTED
    AND MORE BIGOTED IN RELIANCE . . . . 466 SOME SCIENCE FICTION . 15
BIG'S
    FROM A HUMPED BODY NIGH AS BIG'S A BISCUIT. . . . . . 70 THE CODE 35
BILL
    THE METEOR THAT THRUSTS IN WITH NEEDLE BILL, ... 12 A PRAYER IN SPRING . . 11
    IF I'M EXPECTED TO ELECT BILL TAFT. . . . . 48 A HUNDRED COLLARS . . 117
    I'LL SHOW YOU. HERE YOU ARE." / "WHAT'S THIS?" / "A BILL-- . 86 THE HOUSEKEEPER . . . 145
    JOHN BOUGHT HIM, AND WE PAID THE BILL WITH BEADS-- . . . 86 THE HOUSEKEEPER . . . 152
    AND THIS BILL." / "WHAT'S THE HURRY? HE'LL UNHITCH." . . 88 THE HOUSEKEEPER . . . 199
    TO PAY THE DOCTOR'S BILL AND TIDE ME OVER. . . . . . 95 THE SELF-SEEKER . . . 74
    SHE WHETS A SLEEPY SATED BILL. . . . . 281 BLUE RIBBON AT AMESBURY 40
    WAS NOT SET FORTH IN THE LADING BILL. . . . . 343 DISCOVERY OF MADEIRAS . 4
    IN READING, DON'T YOU, BILL?--AT EVERY LINE END . . . . 405 FROM PLANE TO PLANE . 50
    TO WORK WITH, BILL. BUT YOU WON'T HAVE MY THANKS. . . . 408 FROM PLANE TO PLANE . 123
    (IS IT NOT WRITTEN ON THE DOLLAR BILL . . . . 422 FOR JOHN F. KENNEDY . 21
BILLS
    TO GIVE US A PIECE OF THEIR BILLS. . . . . 364 A NATURE NOTE 4
BIN
    AND I KEEP HEARING FROM THE CELLAR BIN . . . . 69 AFTER APPLE-PICKING . 24
    WHEN OTHER CREATURES HAVE GONE TO STALL AND BIN, ... 223 THE RUNAWAY 20
BIND
    THE MYSTIC LINK TO BIND AND HOLD . . . . 21 THE TRIAL BY EXISTENCE 63
    BY WHICH I'D BIND MYSELF TO KEEP HANDS OFF . . . . . 52 HOME BURIAL 51
    I MEAN IT SHALL NOT DO IF I CAN BIND IT. . . . . . . 130 THE BONFIRE 31
BINDING
    AND BINDING ALL IS THE HUSHED SNOW . . . . 20 THE TRIAL BY EXISTENCE 15
    WITH BARBED-WIRE BINDING. THEY STOOD FACING THIS, . . . 229 TWO LOOK AT TWO . . . 8
    THEY BROKE THE HANDLE AND THE BINDING OFF IT. . . . . 293 AT WOODWARD'S GARDENS . 28
BIPLANE
    THIS BIPLANE IS THE SHAPE OF HUMAN FLIGHT. . . . . . 308 THE WRIGHTS' BIPLANE . 1
    THE WRIGHTS' BIPLANE . . . . 308 THE WRIGHTS' BIPLANE . T
BIRCH
    WILL ROT THE BEST BIRCH FENCE A MAN CAN BUILD.' . . . . 54 HOME BURIAL 93
    WHAT HAD HOW LONG IT TAKES A BIRCH TO ROT . . . . . . 54 HOME BURIAL 95
    I'D LIKE TO GO BY CLIMBING A BIRCH TREE, ... 122 BIRCHES 54
    TO SEE FOR MYSELF ABOUT THE BIRCH . . . . 123 PEA BRUSH 3
    BIRCH BOUGHS ENOUGH PILED EVERYWHERE!-- . . . . . . 123 PEA BRUSH 13
    THE GRAPE MAY NOT BE DIFFERENT FROM THE BIRCH? . . . . 196 WILD GRAPES 2
    IT'S ALL YOU KNOW THE GRAPE, OR KNOW THE BIRCH. . . . . 196 WILD GRAPES 3
    AS A GIRL GATHERED FROM THE BIRCH MYSELF . . . . . . 196 WILD GRAPES 4
    WHERE A WHITE BIRCH HE KNEW OF STOOD ALONE, ... 196 WILD GRAPES 20
    BY GROWING WHERE IT SHOULDN'T--ON A BIRCH, ... 198 WILD GRAPES 65
    BE RUN OFF WITH BY BIRCH TREES INTO SPACE." . . . . . 199 WILD GRAPES 91
    AS MEASURED AGAINST MAPLE, BIRCH, AND OAK, ... 226 THE ONSET 16
    NOTHING WILL BE LEFT WHITE BUT HERE A BIRCH, ... 226 THE ONSET 22
    THE BIRCH BEGINS TO CRACK ITS OUTER SHEATH . . . . . 375 A YOUNG BIRCH 1
    A YOUNG BIRCH . . . . 375 A YOUNG BIRCH . . . . T
    FOR MAPLE, BIRCH, AND SPRUCE TO PUSH . . . . 376 SOMETHING FOR HOPE . . 6
BIRCHES
    WHEN I SEE BIRCHES BEND TO LEFT AND RIGHT . . . . . . 121 BIRCHES 1
    BIRCHES . . . . 121 BIRCHES . . . . . . T
    SO WAS I ONCE MYSELF A SWINGER OF BIRCHES. . . . . . 122 BIRCHES 41
    ONE COULD DO WORSE THAN BE A SWINGER OF BIRCHES. . . . . 122 BIRCHES 59
    FAR UP THE BIRCHES OUT OF REACH OF MAN. . . . . . . 164 NEW HAMPSHIRE 164
    BUNCHES ALL ROUND ME GROWING IN WHITE BIRCHES, ... 197 WILD GRAPES 26

BIRCHES (CONTINUED)
    MAPLES AND BIRCHES AND TAMARACKS. . . . . 228 GOOD-BY AND KEEP COLD . 24
BIRD (SEE MOTHER-BIRD)
    AND THE CAGED YELLOW BIRD . . . . 10 WIND AND WINDOW FLOWER 7
    AND MAKE US HAPPY IN THE DARTING BIRD . . . . 12 A PRAYER IN SPRING . . 9
    WHERE THE BIRD WAS BEFORE IT FLEW, ... 15 IN A VALE 18
    WHERE BIRD AND FLOWER WERE ONE AND THE SAME. . . . . . 15 IN A VALE 20
    WHY THE FLOWER HAS ODOR, THE BIRD HAS SONG. . . . . . 16 IN A VALE 22
    NO BIRD IS SINGING NOW, AND IF THERE IS, ... 25 NOW CLOSE THE WINDOWS . 3
    IT WILL BE LONG ERE THE EARLIEST BIRD: . . . . 25 NOW CLOSE THE WINDOWS . 6
    UNLESS WHEN YOU SAID I WAS KEEPING A BIRD . . . . . . 62 BLUEBERRIES 88
    A SMALL BIRD FLEW BEFORE ME. HE WAS CAREFUL . . . . . 101 THE WOOD-PILE 10
    LOUD, A MID-SUMMER AND A MID-WOOD BIRD, ... 119 THE OVEN BIRD 2
    THE OVEN BIRD . . . . 119 THE OVEN BIRD . . . . T
    THE BIRD WOULD CEASE AND BE AS OTHER BIRDS . . . . . . 120 THE OVEN BIRD 11
    AND STILL THE BIRD REVISITED HER YOUNG. . . . . 126 RANGE-FINDING 5
    MADE THE GREAT TREE SEEM AS A LITTLE BIRD . . . . . . 128 THE OFT-REPEATED DREAM 7
    AND A LONG BIRD OF PARADISE'S TAIL . . . . 172 A STAR IN A STONEBOAT . 16
    BY FLYING LIKE A BIRD (SILENT IN FLIGHT), ... 216 A FOUNTAIN, A BOTTLE . 113
    ONLY TO TUMBLE LIKE A STRICKEN BIRD, ... 216 A FOUNTAIN, A BOTTLE . 115
    IN HERE AND THERE A BIRD, OR BUTTERFLY, ... 220 FRAGMENTARY BLUE . . . 2
    I THOUGHT I SAW A BIRD ALIGHT. . . . . 232 LOOKING FOR SUNSET BIRD 4
    LOOKING FOR A SUNSET BIRD IN WINTER . . . . 232 LOOKING FOR SUNSET BIRD T
    A BIRD WITH AN ANGELIC GIFT . . . . 233 LOOKING FOR SUNSET BIRD 7
    NO BIRD WAS SINGING IN IT NOW. . . . . 233 LOOKING FOR SUNSET BIRD 9
    ONE BIRD BEGINS TO CLOSE A FADED EYE; . . . . 249 ACCEPTANCE 7
    I HAVE WISHED A BIRD WOULD FLY AWAY, ... 250 A MINOR BIRD 1
    A MINOR BIRD . . . . 250 A MINOR BIRD . . . . T
    THE BIRD WAS NOT TO BLAME FOR HIS KEY. . . . . 251 A MINOR BIRD 6
    NOT GAINING BUT NOT LOSING, LIKE A BIRD . . . . 258 WEST-RUNNING BROOK . . 22
    SHE SCORED AN ALMOST PERFECT BIRD. . . . . 280 BLUE RIBBON AT AMESBURY 10
    A BIRD HALF WAKENED IN THE LUNAR NOON . . . . 302 A BIRD SINGING IN SLEEP 1
    ON A BIRD SINGING IN ITS SLEEP . . . . 302 A BIRD SINGING IN SLEEP T
    TO BE A BIRD WHILE WE ARE MEN ON EARTH, ... 303 A BIRD SINGING IN SLEEP 12
    TOO DARK IN THE WOODS FOR A BIRD . . . . 334 COME IN 5
    AS IN THOSE BUOYANT BIRD BONES THIN AS PAPER, ... 387 INNATE HELIUM 4
    BY A GREAT EAGLE BIRD IN ALL ITS TERROR. . . . . . . 443 AUSPEX 4
    I WAS REJECTED BY THE ROYAL BIRD . . . . 443 AUSPEX 7
BIRDS
    SHE'S GLAD THE BIRDS ARE GONE AWAY, ... 7 MY NOVEMBER GUEST . . 8
    THE WHIR OF SOBER BIRDS . . . . 8 A LATE WALK 6
    DEAD WEEDS AND UNMATED BIRDS, ... 11 WIND AND WINDOW FLOWER 15
    WITHOUT THE BIRDS, WITHOUT THE BREEZE. . . . . 18 GOING FOR WATER . . . 12
    THAT MADE ME HEAR THE WAKENING BIRDS AROUND, ... 23 THE TUFT OF FLOWERS . 31
    THE BIRDS HAVE LESS TO SAY FOR THEMSELVES . . . . . . 26 A LINE-STORM SONG . . 9
    AND THE STRANGE BIRDS SAY. . . . . 29 MY BUTTERFLY 45
    LIKE BIRDS. THEY STORE A GREAT MANY AWAY. . . . . . . 60 BLUEBERRIES 51
    FULL OF LANK, SHIVERY, HALF-DROWNED BIRDS . . . . . . 85 THE HOUSEKEEPER . . . 120
    'TWAS A NEST FULL OF YOUNG BIRDS ON THE GROUND . . . 109 THE EXPOSED NEST . . 13
    TO SEE IF THE BIRDS LIVED THE FIRST NIGHT THROUGH, . . 110 THE EXPOSED NEST . . 35
    THE BIRD WOULD CEASE AND BE AS OTHER BIRDS . . . . . 120 THE OVEN BIRD . . . 11
    CARE WHEN THE BIRDS COME ROUND THE HOUSE . . . . . . 126 LONELINESS 3
    WITH BIRDS THAT FILL THEIR BREASTS . . . . 126 LONELINESS 10
    YET THINK OF THE SMALL BIRDS AT ROOST AND NOT . . . . 151 SNOW 226
    EVER TO HAVE HOUSED BIRDS OR BEASTS OR BEES. . . . . 193 PAUL'S WIFE 84
    AND THE BIRDS ON HER OUTER WINDOWSILL, ... 215 A FOUNTAIN, A BOTTLE . 81
    TO ENTERTAIN THE BIRDS AND HOLD THE FLOWERS. . . . . 216 A FOUNTAIN, A BOTTLE 87
    AND BIRDS THAT JOINED IN THE EXCITED FUN . . . . . . 237 A HILLSIDE THAW . . . 15
    OF GLOSSY BIRDS LIKE RIPPLES OVER ROCKS. . . . . . . 240 OUR SINGING STRENGTH . 34
    THE BIRDS THAT CAME TO IT THROUGH THE AIR . . . . . . 242 NEED OF BEING VERSED . 13
    AT WHAT HAS HAPPENED. BIRDS, AT LEAST, MUST KNOW . . 249 ACCEPTANCE 4
    WHERE SUMMER BIRDS HAD BEEN GIVEN HATCH, ... 253 THE THATCH 14
    I FLUSHED BIRDS OUT OF HOLE AFTER HOLE, ... 253 THE THATCH 19
    HERE LOVELESS BIRDS NOW FLOCK AS WINTER FRIENDS, . . . 254 A WINTER EDEN . . . 14
    THAT THE BIRDS THERE IN ALL THE GARDEN ROUND . . . . 338 NEVER WOULD BIRDS' SONG 2
    COULD ONLY HAVE HAD AN INFLUENCE ON BIRDS . . . . . . 338 NEVER WOULD BIRDS' SONG 7
    AND TO DO THAT TO BIRDS WAS WHY SHE CAME. . . . . . . 339 NEVER WOULD BIRDS' SONG 14
    LIKE A THOUSAND BIRDS. . . . . 434 KITTY HAWK 191
    THE BIRDS, SEEM ALL ON FIRE WITH PARADISE. . . . . . 473 A MASQUE OF REASON . . 13
    AND TURN THE GOLD ENAMELED ARTIFICIAL BIRDS ON. . . . 490 A MASQUE OF REASON . . 459
BIRDS'
    HE TAKES IT OUT IN BUNCHES LIKE BIG BIRDS' NESTS. . . . 37 DEATH OF THE HIRED MAN 93
    NEVER AGAIN WOULD BIRDS' SONG BE THE SAME . . . . . . 338 NEVER WOULD BIRDS' SONG T
    NEVER AGAIN WOULD BIRDS' SONG BE THE SAME. . . . . . . 339 NEVER WOULD BIRDS' SONG 13
EIRNAM
    REMEMBER BIRNAM WOOD! THE WOOD'S IN FLUX!" . . . . . 170 NEW HAMPSHIRE 373
BIRTH
    THE GATHERING OF THE SOULS FOR BIRTH, ... 20 THE TRIAL BY EXISTENCE 18
    ON THROUGH THE WATCHING FOR THAT EARLY BIRTH . . . . 124 PUTTING IN THE SEED . 11
    SURE THAT THOUGH NOT A STAR OF DEATH AND BIRTH, . . . 174 A STAR IN A STONEBOAT . 46
    THERE WAS A MOMENT OF SUSPENSE IN BIRTH . . . . 194 PAUL'S WIFE 116
    WHAT IS THIS TALKED-OF MYSTERY OF BIRTH . . . . 267 RIDERS 5
    ON THE LONG BEAD CHAIN OF REPEATED BIRTH, ... 303 A BIRD SINGING IN SLEEP 11
    WERE NOT TOO MUCH TO PAY FOR BIRTH. . . . . 362 A QUESTION 4
    IN BIRTH AFTER BIRTH . . . . 436 KITTY HAWK 249
    HOW DID YOU KNOW THE SECRET OF MY BIRTH?" . . . . . . 457 HOW HARD TO KEEP FROM 117
BIRTHDAYS
    SO IF YOU SEE ME CELEBRATE TWO BIRTHDAYS, ... 196 WILD GRAPES 16
BIRTHPLACE
    THE BIRTHPLACE . . . . 264 THE BIRTHPLACE . . . T
BIRTHS
    REDUCE THE BIRTHS OF THE HUMAN RACE, ... 263 THE TIMES TABLE . . . 19
BISCUIT
    IT TOOK MY MIND OFF DOUGHNUTS AND SODA BISCUIT . . . . 63 A SERVANT TO SERVANTS . 26
    FROM A HUMPED BODY NIGH AS BIG'S A BISCUIT. . . . . . 70 THE CODE 35
BIT
    HE THOUGHT OF AN IDLE BIT . . . . 133 A GIRL'S GARDEN . . . 10
    A LITTLE BIT OF EVERYTHING, ... 134 A GIRL'S GARDEN . . . 39

BIT (CONTINUED)
    A THING THE LEAST BIT DOUBTFULLY PERSCENTED . . . . . . 163 NEW HAMPSHIRE   . . . 142
    THEY BIT THE GLASS AND LISTENED FOR THE FLAVOR. . . . . 293 AT WOODWARD'S GARDENS . 27
    LIKE SOME TENACIOUS BIT . . . . 341 THE SUBVERTED FLOWER . 67
    SO HE LEAPT ON HER HAIRY BACK AND BIT HER . . . . . . 463 LINES IN DEJECTION . . 19
    AND HE GOT IT BIT. . . . . 468 A REFLEX   4
BITCH (SEE SON-OF-A-BITCH)
BITE
    AS THEY BOTH BITE THE WOOD. IT'S ALL OUR MUSIC. . . . . 94 THE SELF-SEEKER . . . 43
    WOULD KEEP HIM NOW FROM PROVING WITH A BITE . . . . . 283 THE GOLD HESPERIDEE . 29
    LEST BOTH SHOULD BITE HIM IN THE TOGA-TOGS. . . . . . 362 SYMPATHY WITH UNDER DOG   4
BITING
    BUT BY OUR BITING OFF OUR ADOLESCENCE . . . . 508 A MASQUE OF MERCY . . 388
BITS
    I DROVE THEM UNDERFOOT IN BITS OF FLIGHT . . . . . . 240 OUR SINGING STRENGTH . 35
BITTEN
    SOME THOUGHT HE HAD BEEN BITTEN BY A DOG, ... 65 A SERVANT TO SERVANTS . 105
    SHE LEAVES THEM BITTEN WHEN SHE HAS TO FLY. . . . . . 125 THE COW IN APPLE TIME .   9
    UPON THE STEPS WITH BITTEN STEM. . . . . 135 LOCKED OUT   9
BITTER
    SUCH WERE THE BITTER THOUGHTS TO WHICH I TURNED. . . . 190 THE GRINDSTONE 50
    THE SWEET OF BITTER BARK . . . . 227 TO EARTHWARD 23
    TRUST HIM TO HAVE HIS BITTER POLITICS . . . . 290 OLD BARN AT THE BOTTOM 29
    THE BITTER WORDS SHE SPIT . . . . 341 THE SUBVERTED FLOWER . 66
    WHICH OFTEN MAKES THE MANUMITTER BITTER." . . . . . . 371 THE LITERATE FARMER AND 91
    WITH MILK AND HONEY, IT IS BITTER MILK, ... 411 POD OF THE MILKWEED . 16
    DON'T YOU BE BITTER ABOUT IT. I'M NOT BITTER. . . . . 494 A MASQUE OF MERCY . . 26
BITTERNESS
    UNLESS IN BITTERNESS TO MOCK . . . . 238 PLOWMEN   3
BLACK (SEE BRIGHT-BLACK-EYED, COAL-BLACK)
    NIGHT COMES; THE BLACK BATS TUMBLE AND DART; . . . . .   6 GHOST HOUSE 15
    WHERE ITS BLACK BODY CUT INTO THE SKY. . . . . 40 THE MOUNTAIN   4
    OR WITH A SHOTGUN FOR A STRAY BLACK BEAR? . . . . . . 43 THE MOUNTAIN 87
    FRESH PAINTED BY THE SHOWER A VELVET BLACK. . . . . . 55 THE BLACK COTTAGE . .   7
    THE BLACK COTTAGE . . . . 55 THE BLACK COTTAGE . .   T
    BLACK SHE HAD SCARCELY SEEN, AND YELLOW NEVER. . . . . 57 THE BLACK COTTAGE . . 76
    I SAW NO WINDOW BUT THAT WAS BLACK. . . . . 102 GOOD HOURS 12
    IN LEAVES NO STEP HAD TRODDEN BLACK. . . . . 105 THE ROAD NOT TAKEN . 12
    AND CLIMB BLACK BRANCHES UP A SNOW-WHITE TRUNK . . . . 122 BIRCHES 55
    OF BLACK ALDER. . . . . 129 THE IMPULSE 14
    THE BLACK WAS ALMOST ALL THERE WAS BY DAYLIGHT, . . . 131 THE BONFIRE 49
    BUT THE BLACK SPREAD LIKE BLACK DEATH ON THE GROUND, . . 131 THE BONFIRE 53
    COULDN'T BELIEVE THAT SO MUCH BLACK HAD COME THERE . . 132 THE BONFIRE 85
    VISIONS OF HALF THE WORLD BURNED BLACK . . . . 140 THE GUM-GATHERER . . 23
    TO GET A PUFF OF BLACK SMOKE FROM THE FLAME, ... 148 SNOW 140
    UP THE BRASS BARREL, VELVET BLACK INSIDE, ... 179 THE STAR-SPLITTER . . 77
    SOMETHING HAD LEFT A BROAD BLACK STREAK OF GREASE . . . 193 PAUL'S WIFE 69
    AND ON BLACK GROUND A BEAR-SKIN RUG OF SNOW. . . . . 234 EVENING A SUGAR ORCHARD 13
    THEY MADE NO WHITE IMPRESSION ON THE BLACK. . . . . . 239 OUR SINGING STRENGTH .   5
    THE WORLD WAS A BLACK INVISIBLE FIELD. . . . . . . 253 THE THATCH 10
    (THE BLACK STREAM, CATCHING ON A SUNKEN ROCK, ... 258 WEST-RUNNING BROOK . 19
    AND THE WHITE WATER RODE THE BLACK FOREVER, ... 258 WEST-RUNNING BROOK . 21
    TO THE FRESH AND BLACK OF THE SQUARES OF EARLY MOLD . . 299 STRONG SAYING NOTHING .   9
    THAT VANISHED INTO THE BLACK . . . . 311 THE VINDICTIVES . . . 35
    THE HEARTLESS AND ENORMOUS OUTER BLACK . . . . 361 A LOOSE MOUNTAIN . . 17
    THAT SPOT OF BLACK IS NOT A STAIN . . . . 392 A CLIFF DWELLING . .   6
    LIES IN A WINDROW, BRITTLE-DRY AND BLACK, ... 446 DOES NO ONE AT ALL EVER 26
BLACKBIRD
    THRUSH, BLUEBIRD, BLACKBIRD, SPARROW, AND ROBIN THRONG; . 239 OUR SINGING STRENGTH . 21
BLACK-CHEEKED
    A BLACK-CHEEKED STONE AND STICK OF RAIN-WASHED CHARCOAL. . 171 NEW HAMPSHIRE . . . 391
BLACKENED (SEE PITCH-BLACKENED)
    ANOTHER BLACKENED FACE THRUST IN AND LOOKED . . . . . 111 IN THE HOME STRETCH . . 18
    THE PLACE IT REACHED TO BLACKENED INSTANTLY. . . . . 131 THE BONFIRE 48
BLACKENING
    STEEL-BRIGHT JUNE-GRASS, AND BLACKENING HEADS OF CLOVER. . 109 THE EXPOSED NEST . . 12
BLACK-PAPER-COVERED
    TO A SLAB-BUILT, BLACK-PAPER-COVERED HOUSE . . . . . . 174 THE CENSUS-TAKER . .   2
BLADE (SEE GRASS-BLADE)
    LIKE PEARLS, AND NOW A SILVER BLADE. . . . . 18 GOING FOR WATER . . . 24
    THE DEW WAS GONE THAT MADE HIS BLADE SO KEEN . . . . . 22 THE TUFT OF FLOWERS .   3
    AND HE AND I BETWEEN US GROUND A BLADE. . . . . . . 189 THE GRINDSTONE . . . 25
    AND WOUNDED ON HIS BLADE. SO FAR FROM CARING, ... 190 THE GRINDSTONE . . . 59
    AND NOW WERE ONLY WASTING PRECIOUS BLADE. . . . . . 190 THE GRINDSTONE . . . 67
    AND A PADDLE BLADE. . . . . 211 AN EMPTY THREAT . . .   6
    THE LINE MUST BE A JAGGED BLADE. . . . . 327 A MISSIVE MISSILE . . 15
    ALLUVIUM SO PURE THAT WHEN A BLADE . . . . 407 FROM PLANE TO PLANE . 115
BLADE-END
    BLADE-END UP AND FIVE FEET TALL, ... 124 A TIME TO TALK . . .   8
BLAKE'S
    I'D KNOW HIM BY BLAKE'S PICTURE ANYWHERE. . . . . . 474 A MASQUE OF REASON . . 18
    (I'D KNOW YOU BY BLAKE'S PICTURE ANYWHERE)-- . . . . . 476 A MASQUE OF REASON . 85
BLAME
    TO RIPEN TOO LONG. I AM GREATLY TO BLAME.'" . . . . . 60 BLUEBERRIES 46
    I DIDN'T WANT THE BLAME IF THINGS WENT WRONG. . . . . 67 A SERVANT TO SERVANTS . 150
    I BLAME HIS BEING BROUGHT UP BY HIS MOTHER. . . . . . 83 THE HOUSEKEEPER . . . 56
    AND YOU CAN'T BLAME ME IN THE PLACE I'M IN. . . . . . 99 THE SELF-SEEKER . . . 178
    I MAY HAVE BEEN TO BLAME FOR THAT: . . . . 135 LOCKED OUT 10
    "WHAT DO YOU WANT WITH ONE OF THOSE BLAME THINGS?" . . . 177 THE STAR-SPLITTER . . 20
    OR SO HE TRIED TO THINK TO AVOID BLAME. . . . . . . 180 MAPLE 34
    THE BIRD WAS NOT TO BLAME FOR HIS KEY. . . . . . . 251 A MINOR BIRD   6
    IT CAN BLAME THIS LIMITLESS TRAIT IN THE HEARTS OF MEN. . 305 THERE ARE ROUGHLY ZONES 21
    OH, I DON'T BLAME YOU. I SAY TAKE LIFE EASY. . . . . 316 BUILD SOIL 19
    THE AGE MAY VERY WELL HAVE BEEN TO BLAME . . . . . . 351 THE LESSON FOR TODAY . 26
    TO CARRY PRAISE OR BLAME TOO FAR, ... 403 SOMETHING LIKE A STAR . 23
    YOU'D BE TO BLAME FOR FURNISHING THE REASONS." . . . . 406 FROM PLANE TO PLANE . 68
    IT WASN'T TO BLAME . . . . 450 OBJECTION TO BE STEPPED   7
    THE NAME HIS MOTHER GAVE HIM IS TO BLAME . . . . . . 494 A MASQUE OF MERCY . . 35

BLAME (CONTINUED)
   WE BLAME OURSELVES. WE'RE GOOD SPORTS, AREN'T WE, BEL?   . . 496 A MASQUE OF MERCY . . 78
BLAMED
   I BLAMED IT ON THE HOT SPELL WE'VE BEEN HAVING. . . . . 46 A HUNDRED COLLARS . . 58
   "DON'T CALL IT BLAMED; THERE ISN'T ANYTHING . . . . . 177 THE STAR-SPLITTER . . 22
BLAMELESS
   MORE BLAMELESS IN THE SENSE OF BEING LESS . . . . . 177 THE STAR-SPLITTER . . 23
   "DO IT BY JOYS, AND LEAVE HER ALWAYS BLAMELESS. . . 256 THE LOVELY BE CHOOSERS 21
BLAMES
   AND SUPERSTITION WINS. HE BLAMES THE STARS, ... 462 HOW HARD TO KEEP FROM 267
BLAMING
   JOHN'S A BAD FARMER. I'M NOT BLAMING HIM. . . . . 85 THE HOUSEKEEPER . . . 102
   OH, I'M NOT BLAMING YOU. HE DIDN'T LEAVE YOU . . 152 SNOW 256
BLANDISHMENTS
   AND ALL OUR BLANDISHMENTS WOULD SEEM DEFIED, ... 268 RIDERS 11
BLANK
   I'M TALKING NOT FREE VERSE BUT BLANK VERSE NOW. . . 460 HOW HARD TO KEEP FROM 212
   ON THE BLANK CURTAIN ON THE OUTER DOOR.) . . . . 502 A MASQUE OF MERCY . . 239
BLANKER
   A BLANKER WHITENESS OF BENIGHTED SNOW . . . . . 296 DESERT PLACES . . 11
BLANKET
   SOME CRIED SHAME ON ME NOT TO BLANKET HIM, ... 209 PAUPER WITCH OF GRAFTON 52
   THAT LIKE A BLANKET TO MY CHIN . . . . . . 380 AN UNSTAMPED LETTER IN 14
BLANKETS
   THROUGH THE BED BLANKETS I REMIND MYSELF . . . . 93 THE SELF-SEEKER . . . 19
BLANKS
   A FUSILLADE OF BLANKS AND EMPTY FLASHES, ... 361 A LOOSE MOUNTAIN . . 9
BLAST
   AND NOW THEY ANSWER HIS SUMMONING BLAST . . . . 236 MISGIVING 9
   AND THE DOUBLE-BARRELED BLAST . . . . . 282 A DRUMLIN WOODCHUCK . 22
BLAZED
   WE ROSE TO GO. SUNSET BLAZED ON THE WINDOWS. . . . 59 THE BLACK COTTAGE . . 127
BLAZING
   ALL THROUGH JULY UNDER THE BLAZING SUN, ... 36 DEATH OF THE HIRED MAN 67
   AS THROUGH ITS BLAZING FLOWERS . . . . . 333 HAPPINESS MAKES UP . . 22
BLAZONED
   WITH THE INTENTION BLAZONED ON THEIR BANNERS . . . . 397 THE PLANNERS . . . 11
BLEAK
   WINDS BLOW THE OPEN GRASSY PLACES BLEAK; . . . . 246 ATMOSPHERE . . . 1
BLEEDING
   FROM STUMPS STILL BLEEDING THEIR LIFE AWAY. . . . . 123 PEA BRUSH . . . 8
BLEND
   NOT SO MUCH TIED AS MADE THEM BLEND. . . . . 274 A LONE STRIKER . . 32
   TELL US WHAT ELEMENTS YOU BLEND. . . . . 403 SOMETHING LIKE A STAR . 15
   IN A BLEND MECHANIC, ... 442 KITTY HAWK . . . 445
BLESS
   BLESS YOU, OF COURSE YOU'RE KEEPING ME FROM WORK, . . 67 A SERVANT TO SERVANTS 171
   BLESS YOU, IT ISN'T GRANDSIR STARK, IT'S GRANNY; . . 77 THE GENERATIONS OF MEN 106
   AND SHE'LL COME BACK. BUT, BLESS YOU, I'M HER MOTHER-- . 82 THE HOUSEKEEPER . . 26
   BLESS YOU, IT'S ALL EXPENSE, THOUGH. REACH ME DOWN . 86 THE HOUSEKEEPER . . 142
   GOD BLESS HIMSELF CAN NO ONE ELSE BE BLESSED. . . 355 THE LESSON FOR TODAY . 156
   BUT ISLANDS OF THE BLESSED, BLESS YOU, SON, . . . 363 AN ANSWER . . . 1
   GOD BLESS THE DEAN AND MAKE HIS DEANSHIP PLENARY. . . 394 LUCRETIUS VERSUS POETS 12
BLESSED
   WHAT DOES HE THINK?--HOW ARE THE BLESSED FEET? . . 93 THE SELF-SEEKER . . 14
   TALK CALIFORNIA--A STATE SO BLESSED, . . . 159 NEW HAMPSHIRE . . 17
   GOD BLESS HIMSELF CAN NO ELSE BE BLESSED. . . 355 THE LESSON FOR TODAY . 156
   BUT ISLANDS OF THE BLESSED, BLESS YOU, SON, . . . 363 AN ANSWER . . . 1
   I NEVER CAME UPON A BLESSED ONE. . . . . 363 AN ANSWER . . . 2
   BUT THEY'RE BLESSED WITH THE ACUMEN . . . . 387 THE COURAGE TO BE NEW . 9
BLEW
   WAS SWALLOWED UP IN LEAVES THAT BLEW ALWAY; . . . 16 A DREAM PANG . . . 2
   AND BLEW HIM OUT ON THE ICY CRUST . . . . 137 BROWN'S DESCENT . . . 11
   GULPED SNOW, AND THEN BLEW FREE AGAIN--THE COLES, . . 143 SNOW 3
   BLEW IT ONCE OFF HIS HANDS AND ALMOST BROKE IT. . . 194 PAUL'S WIFE . . . 100
   THE WIND ONCE BLEW ITSELF UNTAUGHT, ... 223 THE AIM WAS SONG . . 2
   IT BLEW TOO HARD--THE AIM WAS SONG. . . . . 224 THE AIM WAS SONG . . 7
   AND THEN BY MEASURE BLEW IT FORTH. . . . . 224 THE AIM WAS SONG . . 12
   I BLEW OUT THE LIGHT, ... 240 THE LOCKLESS DOOR . . 5
   ALL THE DUST THE WIND BLEW HIGH . . . . 249 A PECK OF GOLD . . 5
   A SEASON-ENDING WIND THERE BLEW . . . . 336 THE WIND AND THE RAIN . 3
   THAT BLEW SO HE HAD TO SHOUT. . . . . 366 NOT OF SCHOOL AGE . . 8
   HIS TENTS BLEW ALL TO PIECES, I PICKED UP . . . 478 A MASQUE OF REASON . . 131
BLIGHT
   ASSORTED CHARACTERS OF DEATH AND BLIGHT . . . . 302 DESIGN 4
   WILL THE BLIGHT END THE CHESTNUT? . . . . 308 EVIL TENDENCIES CANCEL 1
   SHALL COME TO END THE BLIGHT. . . . . 308 EVIL TENDENCIES CANCEL 6
BLIND
   BLIND CREATURE; AND AWHILE HE DIDN'T SEE. . . . 51 HOME BURIAL . . . 16
   "IT MAKES IT ALL THE WORSE. YOU MUST BE BLIND." . . 87 THE HOUSEKEEPER . . 163
   AND BLIND ME TO A STANDSTILL IF IT MUST. . . . 265 DUST IN THE EYES . . 6
   FOR NOTHING BUT ITS OWN BLIND SATISFACTION . . . 319 BUILD SOIL . . . 104
   BUT SHE WAS EITHER BLIND . . . . . 339 THE SUBVERTED FLOWER . . 6
   THE APOGEE OF HUMAN BLIND CONCEIT. . . . . 394 HAEC FABULA DOCET . . 4
   THEY MEAN TO TELL US ALL WAS ROLLING BLIND . . . 425 ACCIDENTALLY ON PURPOSE 5
   AS TO BLIND OUR EYES . . . . . 426 A NEVER NAUGHT SONG . . 23
   WE VAINLY WRESTLE WITH THE BLIND BELIEF . . . 469 WE VAINLY WRESTLE... . . 1
   AND BED OF WORLD-FLOWERS SO AS NOT TO BLIND ME. . . 515 A MASQUE OF MERCY . . 582
BLINDING
   A BLINDING HEADLIGHT SHIFTED GLARE . . . . . 383 WERE I IN TROUBLE . . 3
BLINDLY
   BLINDLY STRUCK AT MY KNEE AND MISSED. . . . . 251 BEREFT 10
   I REACHED OUT BLINDLY TO SAVE MY FACE, ... 265 THE DOOR IN THE DARK . . 2
   SHE CAME DOWN WEAKLY AND BLINDLY LED . . . . 343 DISCOVERY OF MADEIRAS . 6
   THAT GO BLINDLY POURING PAST. . . . . 469 FOUR-ROOM SHACK... . . 4
BLINDMAN
   A BLINDMAN BY THE NAME OF LA FONTAINE, ... 394 HAEC FABULA DOCET . . 1
   THE BLINDMAN MIGHT HAVE FOUND IT WITH HIS FERRULE, . . 394 HAEC FABULA DOCET . . 7

BLINDMAN (CONTINUED)
    THE BLINDMAN MISSED HIM WITH A BLOW SO VICIOUS . . . . . 394 HAEC FABULA DOCET . . 12
BLINDNESS
    ABOUT HIS BLINDNESS. / OH, HE SPEAKS! HE CAN SPEAK! . . . 488 A MASQUE OF REASON . . 417
BLINDS
    BUT THE BLIZZARD BLINDS HIM TO ANY HOUSE AHEAD. . . . . 341 WILLFUL HOMING . . . 2
BLINK
    THAT BLINKING COULD NOT SEEM TO BLINK AWAY. . . . . . 293 AT WOODWARD'S GARDENS . 11
BLINKED
    THE NIGHT CLERK BLINKED HIS EYES AND DARED HIM ON. . . . 45 A HUNDRED COLLARS . . 28
BLINKING
    THAT BLINKING COULD NOT SEEM TO BLINK AWAY. . . . . . 293 AT WOODWARD'S GARDENS . 11
BLISS
    WHAT THEY HAD NEVER HAD OF VITAL BLISS. . . . . . . 397 THE PLANNERS 3
BLITHELY
    THE SENTENCING GOES BLITHELY ON ITS WAY . . . . . . 362 IN A POEM 1
BLIZZARD
    AND ROUND A CORNER, BLIZZARD SNOW FOR DUST, ... 265 DUST IN THE EYES . . 5
    BUT THE BLIZZARD BLINDS HIM TO ANY HOUSE AHEAD. . . . . 341 WILLFUL HOMING . . . 2
BLOB
    OF LIGHTING THE WHOLE NIGHT WITH ONE BIG BLOB . . . . . 370 THE LITERATE FARMER AND 72
BLOBS
    THERE ONCE WE LAY AS BLOBS OF JELLYFISH . . . . . . 395 ETHEREALIZING . . . 9
    BUT NOW AS BLOBS OF BRAIN WE'LL LIE AND DREAM, ... 395 ETHEREALIZING . . . 11
BLOCK
    YOU MAKE A LITTLE FOURSQUARE BLOCK OF AIR, ... 148 SNOW 142
    WHERE I WAS WORKING AT THE CHOPPING BLOCK, ... 185 THE AX-HELVE 8
    AS LARGE AROUND AS THE CHOPPING BLOCK; . . . . . . 275 TWO TRAMPS IN MUD TIME 10
BLOCKS
    IS BLOCKS SPLIT OFF THE MOUNTAIN MASS-- . . . . . 140 THE GUM-GATHERER . . 15
    GOOD BLOCKS OF OAK IT WAS I SPLIT, ... 275 TWO TRAMPS IN MUD TIME 9
BLOOD
    "'NATURE IS CRUEL, MAN IS SICK OF BLOOD': . . . . . 170 NEW HAMPSHIRE . . 371
    BLOOD HAS BEEN HARDER TO DAM BACK THAN WATER. . . . . 254 THE FLOOD 1
    BUT POWER OF BLOOD ITSELF RELEASES BLOOD. . . . . . 254 THE FLOOD 6
    OH, BLOOD WILL OUT. IT CANNOT BE CONTAINED. . . . . 255 THE FLOOD 14
    NOT TEARS BUT DROPS OF BLOOD INSTEAD. . . . . . . 327 A MISSIVE MISSILE . . 14
    HE TELLS HER AS MUCH OF BLOOD AND DIRT . . . . . . 346 DISCOVERY OF MADEIRAS . 88
    OF ROYAL BLOOD. YOUR FATHER WAS A COOK." . . . . . 457 HOW HARD TO KEEP FROM 103
    "IF YOU HAD BEEN A KING OF ROYAL BLOOD, ... 457 HOW HARD TO KEEP FROM 118
BLOODROOT
    BLOODROOT, AND VIOLETS SO SOON TO BE NOW. . . . . . 131 THE BONFIRE 52
BLOODY
    TRANSFORMED FROM CHRONIC TO ACUTE AND BLOODY? . . . . 317 BUILD SOIL 30
BLOOM (SEE PARADISE-IN-BLOOM)
    THE FEN HAD EVERY KIND OF BLOOM, ... 15 IN A VALE 6
    A LEAPING TONGUE OF BLOOM THE SCYTHE HAD SPARED . . . . 22 THE TUFT OF FLOWERS . 23
    EXPEND THEIR BLOOM IN VAIN. . . . . 26 A LINE-STORM SONG . . 6
    WHEN PEAR AND CHERRY BLOOM WENT DOWN IN SHOWERS . . . . 120 THE OVEN BIRD . . . 7
    TO SAY WHICH BUDS ARE LEAF AND WHICH ARE BLOOM. . . . . 254 A WINTER EDEN . . . 16
    THAT FLOWERS CAN'T BLOOM IN THE SHADE OF; . . . . . 264 THE LAST MOWING . . . 12
    A SINGLE FLOWER AS YET TO BLOOM. . . . . 276 TWO TRAMPS IN MUD TIME 28
    EVER TO HAVE TREE BLOOM OR BEAR. . . . . 296 LEAVES COMPARED WITH . 6
    SOME GIANT TREES HAVE BLOOM SO SMALL . . . . . . 297 LEAVES COMPARED WITH . 9
    THE LEAFLESS BLOOM OF A PLUM IS FRESH AND WHITE; . . . . 300 STRONG SAYING NOTHING . 10
    CONTRIVE TO BLOOM . . . . 337 THE WIND AND THE RAIN . 22
    OUR DOOM TO BLOOM . . . . 449 OUR DOOM TO BLOOM . . 1
    THE BUD MUST BLOOM TILL BLOWSY BLOWN . . . . . . 450 OUR DOOM TO BLOOM . . 13
BLOOMING
    FROM LOVELY BLOOMING BUT WASTEFUL WEED . . . . . . 376 SOMETHING FOR HOPE . . 15
BLOOMS
    THE DAY WAS THE DAY BY EVERY FLOWER THAT BLOOMS, ... 342 QUEST OF PURPLE-FRINGED 7
BLOSSOM
    AND OFF A BLOSSOM IN MID-AIR STANDS STILL. . . . . . 12 A PRAYER IN SPRING . . 12
    STEM END AND BLOSSOM END, ... 68 AFTER APPLE-PICKING . 19
    AND THAT THRUST UP TO BLOSSOM IN THE SUN . . . . . 98 THE SELF-SEEKER . . . 157
    WITH NO SUSPICION IN STEM END OR BLOSSOM END . . . . . 164 NEW HAMPSHIRE . . 160
    BUT HE WOULDN'T ADVISE A THING TO BLOSSOM. . . . . . 276 TWO TRAMPS IN MUD TIME 32
    BEGAN TO BLOSSOM AT THE AGE OF FIVE; . . . . . . 283 THE GOLD HESPERIDEE . 2
BLOT
    TO BLOT OUT AND DRINK AND SWEEP AWAY . . . . . . 245 SPRING POOLS 10
BLOTTED
    BLURRED IT, BLOTTED IT OUT. WHAT WAS THAT WHITENESS? . . . 225 FOR ONCE SOMETHING . . 14
BLOW
    WHEN WINTRY WINDS DO BLOW!-- . . . . 9 STARS 4
    A WIND TO BLOW IN EARNEST FROM SOME QUARTER, ... 130 THE BONFIRE 33
    IT BLOW BUT THAT YOU SAW THE TREES IN MOTION.) . . . . 130 THE BONFIRE 43
    OR BLOW A RUMPLE IN THE COLLIE'S COAT. . . . . . 148 SNOW 141
    BEFORE MAN CAME TO BLOW IT RIGHT . . . . 223 THE AIM WAS SONG . . 1
    IT HADN'T FOUND THE PLACE TO BLOW; . . . . . . 224 THE AIM WAS SONG . . 6
    WINDS BLOW THE OPEN GRASSY PLACES BLEAK; . . . . . 246 ATMOSPHERE 1
    TO BLOW THE EARTH OR ANYTHING SELF-CLEAR; . . . . . 246 ATMOSPHERE 4
    FROM WHICH NO WINTER GALE CAN HOPE TO BLOW IT-- . . . . 248 THE COCOON 15
    AND HIT ME A BLOW IN THE HEAD SO HARD . . . . . . 265 THE DOOR IN THE DARK . 6
    THE NIGHT IS SETTING IN TO BLOW. . . . . 281 BLUE RIBBON AT AMESBURY 49
    AND BLOW A GALE. IT DIDN'T MISUNDERSTAND . . . . . 349 OUR HOLD ON THE PLANET 3
    THE BLOW CAN BE NO STRONGER THAN THE CLUTCH, ... 371 THE LITERATE FARMER AND 116
    THE BLINDMAN MISSED HIM WITH A BLOW SO VICIOUS . . . . 394 HAEC FABULA DOCET . . 12
    NOR BE REMINDED OF THEM IN A BLOW-- . . . . . . 447 DOES NO ONE AT ALL EVER 36
    AND STRUCK ME A BLOW . . . . 450 OBJECTION TO BE STEPPED 5
    ME A BLOW THAT I FELT . . . . 450 OBJECTION TO BE STEPPED 10
    FOR YET ANOTHER BLOW. . . . . 470 IN WINTER IN THE WOODS 12
    SLAMS IN HIS FACE. THE BLOW AND THE REPULSE . . . . 518 A MASQUE OF MERCY . . 650
BLOW-AWAY
    WAS A BLOW-AWAY PAPER THE RAIN . . . . 110 A PATCH OF OLD SNOW . 3
BLOWING (SEE CLOUD-BLOWING)
    AND NO ONE HERE BUT HENS BLOWING ABOUT. . . . . . 83 THE HOUSEKEEPER . . . 47
    THE BREEZES WERE SO SPENT WITH WINTER BLOWING . . . . 130 THE BONFIRE 35

BLOWING (CONTINUED)
    DUST ALWAYS BLOWING ABOUT THE TOWN, ... 249 A PECK OF GOLD . . . 1
    SOME OF THE BLOWING DUST WAS GOLD. . . . . 249 A PECK OF GOLD . . . 4
    FROM GEORGES BANK WHEN WINDS WERE BLOWING. . . . . . 262 THE FLOWER BOAT . . . 8
    THEN THE RAIN STOPPED AND THE BLOWING, ... 377 ONE STEP BACKWARD TAKEN 13
    BLOWING IT ALL TO SMITHEREENS . . . . 393 A CASE FOR JEFFERSON . 10
BLOWN
    NO LONGER BLOWN HITHER AND THITHER; . . . . 30 RELUCTANCE 14
    BLOWN OVER AND OVER THEMSELVES IN IDLENESS. . . . . . 58 THE BLACK COTTAGE . 121
    WEAK FOLIAGE THAT IS BLOWN UPON AND BENT, ... 119 HYLA BROOK 8
    BLOWN IN THE WIND. I LIKE THAT--I LIKE THAT. . . . . 150 SNOW 196
    WIDE OPEN AND THE WIND'S BLOWN OUT THE LAMP. . . . . 154 SNOW 309
    LIKE LOCKS BLOWN FORWARD IN THE GLEAM OF EYES.. . . . 250 ONCE BY THE PACIFIC . 6
    HIS LIPS WERE SUCKED AND BLOWN . . . . 340 THE SUBVERTED FLOWER . 27
    THIS WAS NO DUST SPECK BY MY BREATHING BLOWN, ... 357 A CONSIDERABLE SPECK . 7
    IT WAS BLOWN WOODS AND NO END. . . . . 366 NOT OF SCHOOL AGE . . 2
    I WAS BEING BLOWN . . . . 428 KITTY HAWK . . . 17
    THE BUD MUST BLOOM TILL BLOWSY BLOWN . . . . 450 OUR DOOM TO BLOOM . 13
BLOWS
    WHERE THE BOUGHS RAIN WHEN IT BLOWS. . . . . 26 A LINE-STORM SONG . 16
    THE BLOWS THAT A LIFE OF SELF-CONTROL . . . . 275 TWO TRAMPS IN MUD TIME 13
    THE SNOW BLOWS ON HIM AND OFF HIM, EXERTING FORCE . . 341 WILLFUL HOMING . . . 5
BLOWSY
    THE BUD MUST BLOOM TILL BLOWSY BLOWN . . . . 450 OUR DOOM TO BLOOM . 13
BLUE (SEE SKY-BLUE, STEEL-BLUE)
    THE WOODBINE BERRIES WERE BLUE, ... 8 LOVE AND A QUESTION . 14
    BY PICKING THE FADED BLUE . . . . 9 A LATE WALK 14
    FOR A SYLVAN SIGN THAT THE BLUE JAY'S SCREECH . . . . 24 PAN WITH US . . . 18
    LOOKED UP TOWARD HEAVEN, AND THERE AGAINST THE BLUE, . 125 AN ENCOUNTER . . . 11
    WHY MAKE SO MUCH OF FRAGMENTARY BLUE . . . . 220 FRAGMENTARY BLUE . 1
    AND BLUE SO FAR ABOVE US COMES SO HIGH, ... 220 FRAGMENTARY BLUE . 7
    IT ONLY GIVES OUR WISH FOR BLUE A WHET. . . . . . . 220 FRAGMENTARY BLUE . 8
    FRAGMENTARY BLUE . . . . 220 FRAGMENTARY BLUE . T
    FROM NORTH TO SOUTH ACROSS THE BLUE; . . . . 233 LOOKING FOR SUNSET BIRD 19
    AND POURS THE ELM-TREE MEADOW FULL OF BLUE, ... 248 THE COCOON . . . 4
    EXCEPT IN COLOR HE ISN'T BLUE, ... 276 TWO TRAMPS IN MUD TIME 31
    A BLUE RIBBON AT AMESBURY . . . . 279 BLUE RIBBON AT AMESBURY T
    LOOKING FOR MY OLD SKY-MARKS IN THE BLUE. . . . . . 295 LOST IN HEAVEN . . 4
    THE WAYSIDE BLUE AND INNOCENT HEAL-ALL? . . . . . . 302 DESIGN 10
    THE WHOLE SKY WAS BLUE; . . . . 303 AFTERFLAKES . . . 12
    AND BLUE FLAG, THE GREAT SIGHT-- . . . . 367 NOT OF SCHOOL AGE . 26
    THE UNIVERSAL BLUE . . . . 388 MIDDLENESS OF THE ROAD 15
BLUEBELLS
    NOT BLUEBELLS GRACING A TUNNEL MOUTH-- . . . . . . 248 A PASSING GLIMPSE . . 7
BLUEBERRIES
    BLUEBERRIES AS BIG AS THE END OF YOUR THUMB, ... 59 BLUEBERRIES 3
    BLUEBERRIES . . . . 59 BLUEBERRIES . . . . T
    THAT'S ALWAYS THE WAY WITH THE BLUEBERRIES, THOUGH: . . 59 BLUEBERRIES 14
BLUEBIRD
    THAT HER LITTLE BLUEBIRD . . . . 135 LAST WORD OF A BLUEBIRD 7
    THE LAST WORD OF A BLUEBIRD . . . . 135 LAST WORD OF A BLUEBIRD T
    THRUSH, BLUEBIRD, BLACKBIRD, SPARROW, AND ROBIN THRONG; . 239 OUR SINGING STRENGTH . 21
    A BLUEBIRD COMES TENDERLY UP TO ALIGHT . . . . . . 275 TWO TRAMPS IN MUD TIME 25
BLUEBIRDS
    THEY SEEMED TO FAIL THE BLUEBIRDS UNDER THEM . . . . 130 THE BONFIRE . . . 36
BLUE-BUTTERFLY
    IT IS BLUE-BUTTERFLY DAY HERE IN SPRING, ... 225 BLUE-BUTTERFLY DAY . 1
    BLUE-BUTTERFLY DAY . . . . 225 BLUE-BUTTERFLY DAY . T
BLUE'S
    THE BLUE'S BUT A MIST FROM THE BREATH OF THE WIND, . . 60 BLUEBERRIES 25
BLUET
    MY BREATHING SHAKES THE BLUET LIKE A BREEZE, ... 17 THE VANTAGE POINT . 12
BLUETS
    AND THE FRAGILE BLUETS CLUSTERED THERE . . . . . . 24 PAN WITH US 24
BLUFF
    HE MIGHT HAVE BOLDLY MADE THE BLUFF . . . . 417 AMERICA IS HARD TO SEE 26
BLUNDERS
    ALL YOUR EFFECTS WERE MERELY LUCKY BLUNDERS. . . . . 482 A MASQUE OF REASON . 259
BLUNTED
    AND THE SHAFT GOT BLUNTED . . . . 427 VERSION 11
BLUR
    WHAT'S THAT SULPHUR BLUR . . . . 438 KITTY HAWK 340
BLURRED
    BLURRED IT, BLOTTED IT OUT. WHAT WAS THAT WHITENESS? . . 225 FOR ONCE SOMETHING . 14
BLUSH
    WHAT DID I TELL YOU? WHAT? I'D BLUSH, I WOULD. . . . . 97 THE SELF-SEEKER . . 138
BOARD (SEE BROAD-BOARD)
    WE HAVE FOUR HERE TO BOARD, GREAT GOOD-FOR-NOTHINGS, . . 65 A SERVANT TO SERVANTS . 76
    ESTELLE TO DO THE HOUSEWORK FOR THE BOARD . . . . . 85 THE HOUSEKEEPER . . 105
    A BOARD IS THE BEST WEAPON IF YOU HAVE IT. . . . . . 131 THE BONFIRE . . . 68
    THE BOARD WE HAD LAID DOWN TO WALK DRY-SHOD ON . . . 204 THE WITCH OF COOS . 48
    A STOLEN LADY WAS COMING ON BOARD, ... 343 DISCOVERY OF MADEIRAS . 1
BOARDED
    I'VE BOARDED HERE SO LONG, SHE THINKS SHE OWNS ME. . . 94 THE SELF-SEEKER . . 54
BOARDS
    THE WARPING BOARDS PULL OUT THEIR OWN OLD NAILS . . . 56 THE BLACK COTTAGE . 49
    AND EDUCATED INTO BOARDS, HE SAID. . . . . 171 NEW HAMPSHIRE . . 377
    HE'D BEEN HARD AT IT TAKING BOARDS AWAY . . . . . . 193 PAUL'S WIFE . . . 58
    WITH A DOOR OF TWO BROAD BOARDS . . . . 294 A RECORD STRIDE . . 2
BOAST
    THAN THE GRINDSTONE CAN BOAST TO STAND OR GO. . . . . 189 THE GRINDSTONE . . 13
    OH, WE MAKE A BOAST OF STORING, ... 359 NOVEMBER . . . 9
    FORGIVE ME IF I SEEM TO BOAST. . . . . 381 AN UNSTAMPED LETTER IN 39
    OH, BUT NOT TO BOAST, ... 429 KITTY HAWK . . . 22
BOASTED
    WHO BOASTED OF HIS STATE AS BEAUTIFUL . . . . . . 159 NEW HAMPSHIRE . . 10
BOASTINGLY
    THE TALE IS STILL BOASTINGLY TOLD . . . . 311 THE VINDICTIVES . . 33

BOASTS
    BECAUSE IT BOASTS A WHISKY STILL--BECAUSE   .   .   .   .   .   . 165 NEW HAMPSHIRE   . . 190
BOAT
    THE FLOWER BOAT . . . . 262 THE FLOWER BOAT . . T
    OUR SAILORS RIDE A BULLET FOR A BOAT. . . . . . 446 DOES NO ONE AT ALL EVER 14
    I TAKE THE FIRST BOAT. GOD PUTS UP A STORM . . . . . 500 A MASQUE OF MERCY . 180
BOBBED
    HE REELED, HE LURCHED, HE BOBBED, HE CHECKED; . . . . . 138 BROWN'S DESCENT . . . 37
BODED
    WITH HIM IT BODED ACTION, DEED. . . . . 274 A LONE STRIKER . . . 49
BODICE
    SHE MADE A SUDDEN MOVEMENT TOWARD HER BODICE, ... 74 THE GENERATIONS OF MEN 43
BODIES
    FIERCE HEADS LOOKED OUT; SMALL BODIES PIVOTED. . . . . 59 THE BLACK COTTAGE . 126
    WITH THE FURTHEST BODIES . . . . 219 I WILL SING YOU ONE-O . 49
    MEN'S LEGS AND BODIES IN THE GALE . . . . 452 A-WISHING WELL . . . 52
BODILY
    AND PUT EACH OTHER BODILY OUT OF THE HOUSE. . . . . . 114 IN THE HOME STRETCH . 110
    AND CAUGHT HERSELF UP BODILY, CHAIR AND ALL, ... 187 THE AX-HELVE . . . 52
BODY (SEE SOUL-AND-BODY)
    WHERE ITS BLACK BODY CUT INTO THE SKY. . . . . . . 40 THE MOUNTAIN 4
    ABOUT MY FACE AND BODY AND THROUGH MY WRAPPER, . . . 63 A SERVANT TO SERVANTS . 29
    FROM A HUMPED BODY NIGH AS BIG'S A BISCUIT. . . . . 70 THE CODE 35
    THAT CAME ON, BUT HER BODY ROCKED A LITTLE. . . . . 92 THE FEAR 77
    THE STURDY SEEDLING WITH ARCHED BODY COMES . . . . 124 PUTTING IN THE SEED . 13
    IT DREW BACK IN ITS BODY LIKE A SNAIL); . . . . . 172 A STAR IN A STONEBOAT . 18
    FOR THE HARD WORK. HE CHAFED ITS LONG WHITE BODY . . 187 THE AX-HELVE . . . 76
    BUT ALL THE BURDEN OF ITS BODY SONG), ... 216 A FOUNTAIN, A BOTTLE . 114
    AND TRIPPED THE BODY, SHOT THE SPIRIT ON . . . . . 262 A SOLDIER 13
    THE BODY OF ONE OF THEIR DEAD . . . . 288 DEPARTMENTAL . . . 15
    ONE SICKNESS OF THE BODY AND THE SOUL. . . . . . 318 BUILD SOIL . . . 80
    IN BODY AND IN MIND, ... 387 THE COURAGE TO BE NEW . 6
    (NEED A BODY ASK . . . . 431 KITTY HAWK . . . 106
    POSSIBLY JUST WELL-BEING IN THE BODY, ... 461 HOW HARD TO KEEP FROM 243
BOEOTIAN
    BUT WELL MAY BE LACONIC, EVEN BOEOTIAN. . . . . 362 BOEOTIAN 3
    BOEOTIAN . . . . 362 BOEOTIAN . . . . . T
BOETHIAN
    (BOETHIAN) . . . . 349 TO A YOUNG WRETCH . . S
BOGGED
    THE IMPORTANT THING IS NOT TO GET BOGGED DOWN . . . . 406 FROM PLANE TO PLANE . 62
BOGS
    CRANBERRIES IN BOGS AND RASPBERRIES ON TOP . . . . . 61 BLUEBERRIES 62
BOHNING
    SO YOU'VE BEEN BOHNING UP ON THOMISM TOO. . . . . . 505 A MASQUE OF MERCY . 297
BOILING
    WE LEFT OUR BOILING CAR . . . . 367 A SERIOUS STEP LIGHTLY 10
BOILS
    JOB SCRATCHED HIS BOILS AND TRIED TO THINK WHAT HE . . . 477 A MASQUE OF REASON . 121
BOKHARI
    TO AHMED S. BOKHARI . . . . 468 FROM IRON . . . . D
BOLD
    MAKE BOLD TO SING IT SO, BUT DO I DARE . . . . . 317 BUILD SOIL 42
BOLDLY
    HE MIGHT HAVE BOLDLY MADE THE BLUFF . . . . . 417 AMERICA IS HARD TO SEE 26
    WHAT GOOD HE WAS HE BOLDLY SAID, "I'LL TELL YOU: . . 454 HOW HARD TO KEEP FROM 40
BOLE
    BUT NOW AT LAST SO OBVIOUS A BOLE . . . . . . 375 A YOUNG BIRCH . . . 16
    BOLE AND BRANCH AND ROOT . . . . 426 A NEVER NAUGHT SONG . 19
BOLT
    AND SNORTED AT US. AND THEN HE HAD TO BOLT. . . . . 223 THE RUNAWAY 5
    MAY I IN MY BRIEF BOLT ACROSS THE SCENE . . . . . 386 THE FEAR OF MAN . . 15
    THAN A BOLT OF LEVIN, ... 441 KITTY HAWK . . . 409
BOMB
    THAT'S WHAT A CERTAIN BOMB WAS SENT TO BE." . . . . 398 BURSTING RAPTURE . 14
BOMBS
    AND FEEL IT LESS. HEAR THE SOFT BOMBS OF DUST . . . . 150 SNOW 206
BOND
    BOND AND FREE . . . . 120 BOND AND FREE . . . T
BONDAGE
    IS OF THE SLIGHTEST BONDAGE MADE AWARE. . . . . . 332 THE SILKEN TENT . . 14
    FROM MORAL BONDAGE TO THE HUMAN RACE. . . . . . 475 A MASQUE OF REASON . 70
BONE (SEE FINGER-BONE)
    LIKE A TIGER AT A BONE. . . . . 340 THE SUBVERTED FLOWER . 29
    YOU MADE THE EOLITH, YOU GREW THE BONE, ... 382 TO AN ANCIENT . . 13
BONES
    I SAW NO MEN THERE AND NO BONES OF MEN THERE. . . . . 175 THE CENSUS-TAKER . . 42
    I ARMED MYSELF AGAINST SUCH BONES AS MIGHT BE . . . . 175 THE CENSUS-TAKER . . 43
    NOT BONES, BUT THE ILL-FITTED WINDOW RATTLED. . . . . 175 THE CENSUS-TAKER . . 46
    UP ATTIC, MOTHER? / BONES--A SKELETON. . . . . 203 THE WITCH OF COOS . 20
    THE NIGHT THE BONES CAME UP THE CELLAR STAIRS . . . . 203 THE WITCH OF COOS . 40
    IT WAS THE BONES. I KNEW THEM--AND GOOD REASON. . . . 204 THE WITCH OF COOS . 59
    AND HOLD THE DOOR. BUT THE BONES DIDN'T TRY . . . . 204 THE WITCH OF COOS . 61
    IT'S WITH US IN THE ROOM, THOUGH. IT'S THE BONES." . 205 THE WITCH OF COOS . 100
    "WHAT BONES?" "THE CELLAR BONES--OUT OF THE GRAVE." . 205 THE WITCH OF COOS . 101
    IF THE BONES LIKED THE ATTIC, LET THEM HAVE IT. . . . 206 THE WITCH OF COOS . 124
    WE NEVER COULD FIND OUT WHOSE BONES THEY WERE. . . . . 206 THE WITCH OF COOS . 137
    UNTIL I'D HAD HIM WORN TO SKIN AND BONES, ... 208 PAUPER WITCH OF GRAFTON 48
    AND CRACKED BONES, HUMAN AND BEAST, ... 312 THE VINDICTIVES . . 59
    (MAKE NO MISTAKE ABOUT ITS BEING BONES); . . . . . 354 THE LESSON FOR TODAY . 132
    OR AREN'T THE BONES ENOUGH I LIVE TO LIME? . . . . 382 TO AN ANCIENT . . 18
    AS IN THOSE BUOYANT BIRD BONES THIN AS PAPER, ... 387 INNATE HELIUM . . . 4
    HE DUMPED HIMSELF LIKE A BAG OF BONES, ... 419 ONE MORE BREVITY . 15
BONFIRE
    THE BONFIRE . . . . 129 THE BONFIRE . . . T
BONNET
    OF HER OLD TREMULOUS BONNET IN THE PEW, ... 57 THE BLACK COTTAGE . . 91
    ONLY--THERE WAS THE BONNET IN THE PEW. . . . . . 58 THE BLACK COTTAGE . . 99

BCO
    SMALL TOWNS--LOST NATION, BUNGEY, MUDDY BOO, ... 165 NEW HAMPSHIRE . . . 187
BOCK
    AND ON THE WORN BOOK OF OLD-GOLDEN SONG . . . . 15 WAITING 23
    IN A BOOK ABOUT FERNS? LISTEN TO THAT! . . . . 63 A SERVANT TO SERVANTS . 35
    "THAT LEAF THERE IN YOUR OPEN BOOK! IT MOVED . . . . . 147 SNOW 116
    BESIDE THE TABLE, NEAR THE OPEN BOOK, ... 151 SNOW 246
    THE POETESS WHO WROTE THE BOOK OF VERSES . . . . 215 A FOUNTAIN, A BOTTLE . 78
    YET OH! THE TEMPTING FLATNESS OF A BOOK, ... 216 A FOUNTAIN, A BOTTLE . 109
    THE SMALL BOOK IN MY POCKET. IT WAS THERE. . . . . . . 217 A FOUNTAIN, A BOTTLE . 133
    A BREEZE DISCOVERED MY OPEN BOOK . . . . 342 A CLOUD SHADOW . . . 1
    AS OF A BOOK HELD UP BEFORE HIS EYES . . . . 355 TIME OUT 3
    THE PICTURE BOOK OF THE TRILOBITE, ... 364 TRESPASS 10
    AND THERE'S A STORY IN A BOOK ABOUT IT: . . . . 377 DIRECTIVE 13
    IN BOOK ON BOOK HAVE TESTIFIED . . . . 418 AMERICA IS HARD TO SEE 63
    SHOULD BE TAKEN OUTSIDE A HOUSE AND BOOK. . . . . . . 419 ONE MORE BREVITY . . 2
    THERE WAS THE BOOK OF PROFILE TALES DECLARING . . . . 423 FOR JOHN F. KENNEDY . 60
    NO BOOK CAN EXPLAIN, ... 449 THE BAD ISLAND--EASTER 50
    IN THE SURVIVING BOOK WE FIND . . . . 450 OUR DOOM TO BLOOM . 10
    THEN BY A SCIENTIFIC BOOK. . . . . 467 QUANDARY 24
    OF RECORD IN MY NOTE BOOK. / WELL, SHE WAS. . . . . . 477 A MASQUE OF REASON . 103
    FOR THE REVISION OF THE BOOK OF PRAYER . . . . 486 A MASQUE OF REASON . 371
    WELL, I COULD USE A BOOK. / WHAT BOOK? / A BIBLE. . . . 494 A MASQUE OF MERCY . 27
    TRUST ME TO HELP YOU FIND THE BOOK YOU WANT. . . . . . 495 A MASQUE OF MERCY . 50
    KEEPER, BE STILL. HE KNOWS WHAT BOOK HE WANTS. . . . . 495 A MASQUE OF MERCY . 51
    A LANGUAGE OF HIS OWN TO WRITE HIS BOOK IN, ... 502 A MASQUE OF MERCY . 241
    HE WROTE ONE BOOK. LET THERE BE NO MORE WRITTEN. . . . 504 A MASQUE OF MERCY . 290
    CAN BE MADE NEGLIGIBLE. / WHAT'S YOUR BOOK? . . . . . 506 A MASQUE OF MERCY . 323
    THAT BOOK OF YOURS IN THE OLD TESTAMENT . . . . . . 508 A MASQUE OF MERCY . 375
    (THEY PUT THEIR HANDS TOGETHER LIKE A BOOK . . . . . 512 A MASQUE OF MERCY . 489
BOOKCASE
    ONE WHO WOULD NEVER HANG ABOVE A BOOKCASE . . . . . 278 THE WHITE-TAILED HORNET 17
BOOKFUL
    UNTIL THE SCRIBES HAD TAKEN DOWN A BOOKFUL . . . . . 518 A MASQUE OF MERCY . 644
BOOK-LEAF
    AND BOOK-LEAF, THAT KEEP NEAR YOU, THEIR REPOSE; . . . 148 SNOW 146
BOOKLIKE
    BUT RIGHT BESIDE YOU BOOKLIKE ON A SHELF, ... 359 THE LOST FOLLOWER . . 31
BOOKMARK
    ONCE SHE FOUND FOR A BOOKMARK IN THE BIBLE . . . . . 181 MAPLE 62
    SHE TOLD HIM OF THE BOOKMARK MAPLE LEAF . . . . . . 183 MAPLE 104
BOOKS
    HE HATES TO SEE A BOY THE FOOL OF BOOKS. . . . . . . 37 DEATH OF THE HIRED MAN 98
    SHE SAID, "GO READ YOUR OWN BOOKS AND FIND OUT." . . . 166 NEW HAMPSHIRE . . . 227
    OF SEVERAL BOOKS AGAINST THE WORLD IN GENERAL. . . . 166 NEW HAMPSHIRE . . . 229
    A FOUNTAIN, A BOTTLE, A DONKEY'S EARS, AND SOME BOOKS . 212 A FOUNTAIN, A BOTTLE . T
    YOU DON'T LIKE NATURE. ALL YOU LIKE IS BOOKS. . . . . 215 A FOUNTAIN, A BOTTLE . 57
    HOWEVER NATURAL? GIVE YOUR BOOKS! . . . . 215 A FOUNTAIN, A BOTTLE . 59
    WELL THEN, RIGHT HERE IS WHERE I SHOW YOU BOOKS. . . . 215 A FOUNTAIN, A BOTTLE . 60
    OUR BUSINESS FIRST'S UP ATTIC WITH HER BOOKS." . . . 216 A FOUNTAIN, A BOTTLE . 88
    BOOKS, I SHOULD SAY!--IF BOOKS ARE WHAT IS NEEDED. . . 216 A FOUNTAIN, A BOTTLE . 92
    BOOKS WERE NOT THROWN IRREVERENTLY ABOUT. . . . . . 216 A FOUNTAIN, A BOTTLE . 117
    GOOD-LOOKING BOOKS LIKE THAT." HE PICKED ONE FRESH . . 217 A FOUNTAIN, A BOTTLE . 125
    IN TIME SHE WOULD BE RID OF ALL HER BOOKS. . . . . 217 A FOUNTAIN, A BOTTLE . 138
    AND ANNOTATING BOOKS . . . . 361 ALMOST TWO THOUSAND . 12
    WHEN YOU WERE READING BOOKS OR OUT OF TOWN. . . . . 375 A YOUNG BIRCH . . . 20
    AND FOR WANT OF BOOKS RECITE. . . . . 384 IN THE LONG NIGHT . 6
    AND HERE COME ALL YOUR GREAT BOOKS TUMBLING DOWN! . . 504 A MASQUE OF MERCY . 288
BOOKSTORE
    A BOOKSTORE LATE AT NIGHT. THE KEEPER'S WIFE . . . . 493 A MASQUE OF MERCY . 1
    THIS IS A BOOKSTORE--NOT A SANCTUARY. . . . . . . 494 A MASQUE OF MERCY . 24
    WHO KEEPS OUR BOOKSTORE ANNALS. / STOP IT, KEEPER.-- . 499 A MASQUE OF MERCY . 152
BOOM
    WHERE THE LOG DRIVE LAY PRESSED AGAINST THE BOOM, . . . 194 PAUL'S WIFE . . . 107
BOOR
    AND WHAT IS A BOOR? . . . . 512 A MASQUE OF MERCY . 503
BOOST
    YOU COULD DO WORSE THAN BOOST ME UP TO SEE." . . . . 406 FROM PLANE TO PLANE . 84
BOOSTED
    IT'S TIME YOU TURNED AROUND AND BOOSTED US. . . . . 48 A HUNDRED COLLARS . 115
BOOT
    THE DEW OF NIGHT AND MORNING ON HIS BOOT. . . . . . 283 THE GOLD HESPERIDEE . 21
    NAMING STARS TO BOOT . . . . 438 KITTY HAWK . . . 316
BOOTS
    AND THEN THEY ALL TURNED TO WITH DEAFENING BOOTS . . . 114 IN THE HOME STRETCH . 109
BORDERED (SEE SUN-BORDERED)
BORE
    HE BORE A GREEN-WHITE STICK IN HIS HAND, ... 7 LOVE AND A QUESTION . 3
    LANCASTER BORE HIM--SUCH A LITTLE TOWN, ... 44 A HUNDRED COLLARS . 1
    I NEVER BORE IT WELL WHEN PEOPLE WENT. . . . . . . 115 IN THE HOME STRETCH . 131
    IN DRESS OR MANNER OF THE GIRL WHO BORE IT. . . . . 181 MAPLE 53
BORING
    I WAS HALF BORING THROUGH, HALF CLIMBING THROUGH . . . 125 AN ENCOUNTER 4
BORN
    THE BABE BORN TO THE DESERT, THE SANDSTORM . . . . . 58 THE BLACK COTTAGE . 123
    AS FAR AGAIN AS FROM BEING BORN TO BEARING." . . . . 184 MAPLE 130
    AND, AS YOU MIGHT SAY, SAW THE LADY BORN. . . . . . 193 PAUL'S WIFE . . . 56
    I WAS BORN, I SUPPOSE, LIKE ANYONE, ... 196 WILD GRAPES . . . 7
    THE CRIB HE SLEPT IN--AND AS SURE'S YOU'RE BORN . . . 209 PAUPER WITCH OF GRAFTON 61
    BECAUSE HE WAS BORN DIVINE. . . . . 314 BEARER OF EVIL TIDINGS . 32
    OF BEING BORN AT ONCE TOO EARLY AND LATE, ... 351 THE LESSON FOR TODAY . 12
    LIKE A CAUL IN WHICH I WAS BORN AND STILL AM WRAPPED. . 390 SKEPTIC 12
    TO WHICH AT DAYBREAK THEY WERE FRESHLY BORN, ... 412 POD OF THE MILKWEED . 36
    OUR CHANCE OF BEING PEOPLE NEWLY BORN. . . . . . . 446 DOES NO ONE AT ALL EVER 12
    FOR HAVING BEEN BORN? . . . . 448 THE BAD ISLAND--EASTER . 23
    WHEN UNTO EARTH HER FIRST WAS BORN. . . . . 452 A-WISHING WELL . . . 39
    THAN THE DAY SHE WAS BORN / THAT'S ABOUT RIGHT, . . . 479 A MASQUE OF REASON . 158

BORNE
    BORNE DOWN UNTIL THE END ALMOST TOOK ROOT, ... 239 OUR SINGING STRENGTH . 13
    THUS TRUTH'S ESTABLISHED AND BORNE OUT, ... 331 BEECH 10
BOSOM
    FLICKERING ACROSS ITS BOSOM. SUDDENLY . . . . 69 THE CODE 6
    SPRING WATER IN OUR MOUNTAIN BOSOM SWELLS . . . . . 446 DOES NO ONE AT ALL EVER 22
BOSS (SEE GANG-BOSS)
    DOING THE HAYING. NO ONE LIKED THE BOSS. . . . . . 70 THE CODE 32
    ON HIS OWN FARM. HE'S BOSS. BUT AS TO HENS: . . . . 86 THE HOUSEKEEPER . . . 135
    PAUL TOLD THE BOSS THE LOAD WOULD BE ALL RIGHT, . . . 192 PAUL'S WIFE . . . 46
BOSTON
    NORTH OF BOSTON . . . . 31 NORTH OF BOSTON . . . T
    WILLIS BROUGHT UP BESIDES THE BOSTON LAWYER . . . . . 96 THE SELF-SEEKER . . 91
    "WHO'S WE?--SOME STOCKHOLDERS IN BOSTON? . . . . . . 100 THE SELF-SEEKER . . 221
    WAS LATELY AT A CUT-GLASS DINNER IN BOSTON. . . . . . 163 NEW HAMPSHIRE . . 127
    THERE'D BEEN SOME BOSTON PEOPLE OUT TO SEE IT: . . . . 212 A FOUNTAIN, A BOTTLE . 3
BOTH
    NOR JUST TO FREE THE SLAVES, THOUGH IT DID BOTH. . . . . 56 THE BLACK COTTAGE . . 57
    CUT SHORT OFF AT BOTH ENDS. IT LIES FIVE MILES . . . . . 63 A SERVANT TO SERVANTS . 21
    BUT THE OLD FOOL SEIZES HIS FORK IN BOTH HANDS, ... 71 THE CODE 61
    SLUMPED WAY DOWN IN A CHAIR, WITH BOTH HIS FEET . . . . 72 THE CODE 97
    SKY-HIGH WITH BOTH HANDS. I CAN SEE IT NOW-- . . . . . 83 THE HOUSEKEEPER . . 61
    OF BOTH OF US. BUT LOOK HOW IT TURNS OUT: . . . . . . 85 THE HOUSEKEEPER . . 106
    THAT HUNG IN BOTH HANDS, HOT AGAINST HER SKIRT. . . . . 91 THE FEAR 63
    "HE THINKS I'LL HOBBLE. IT'S BOTH LEGS AND FEET." . . . . 93 THE SELF-SEEKER . . 16
    AS THEY BOTH BITE THE WOOD. IT'S ALL OUR MUSIC. . . . . 94 THE SELF-SEEKER . . 43
    WITH BOTH HANDS HELD BEHIND HER. "GUESS," SHE SAID. . . . 96 THE SELF-SEEKER . . 106
    TO YOU--TO YOU I MEAN--THEY'RE BOTH TOO COMMON." . . . . 98 THE SELF-SEEKER . . 144
    AND SORRY I COULD NOT TRAVEL BOTH . . . . 105 THE ROAD NOT TAKEN . 2
    AND BOTH THAT MORNING EQUALLY LAY . . . . 105 THE ROAD NOT TAKEN . 11
    HE DOFFED HIS CAP AND HELD IT WITH BOTH HANDS . . . . 114 IN THE HOME STRETCH . 106
    THAT WOULD BE GOOD BOTH GOING AND COMING BACK. . . . . 122 BIRCHES 58
    ROUSE THEM ALL, BOTH THE FREE AND NOT SO FREE . . . . 130 THE BONFIRE . . . 13
    LIKE DARLINGS, BOTH OF THEM. THEY'RE IN THE BARN.-- . . . 143 SNOW 25
    BOTH THE COLES SAID TOGETHER. MRS. COLE . . . . . 144 SNOW 34
    OR GONE OUTDOORS." / "IN WHICH CASE BOTH ARE LOST. . . . 154 SNOW 312
    OF COURSE SHE HASN'T, THOUGH." THEY BOTH SAT DOWN . . . 155 SNOW 324
    WE BOTH OF US TURNED OVER IN OUR GRAVES. . . . . . 161 NEW HAMPSHIRE . . 60
    BOTH ARE DELIGHTFUL STATES FOR THEIR ABSURDLY . . . . 165 NEW HAMPSHIRE . . 186
    THEY WERE BOTH STIRRED THAT HE SHOULD HAVE DIVINED . . . 182 MAPLE 92
    WITH BOTH HIS FEET AT ONCE AGAINST THE CEILING, . . . 192 PAUL'S WIFE . . . 51
    MORE CUTTING AND HE HAD THIS IN BOTH HANDS, ... 194 PAUL'S WIFE . . . 95
    RIGHT PAST BOTH FATHER AND MOTHER, AND NEITHER STOPPED IT. . 203 THE WITCH OF COOS . . 33
    I'LL DOUBLE THEIRS FOR BOTH OF THEM--YOU WATCH ME. . . . 207 PAUPER WITCH OF GRAFTON 9
    WENTWORTH AND WARREN'S BOTH GOOD TOWNS TO LIVE IN, . . . 208 PAUPER WITCH OF GRAFTON 30
    AND BOTH OF OUR UNITED STRENGTHS, TO DO IT." . . . . 213 A FOUNTAIN, A BOTTLE . 19
    AND HOW SHE TENDED BOTH, OR HAD THEM TENDED: . . . . 215 A FOUNTAIN, A BOTTLE . 82
    BOTH EITHER LOOKING FOR OR FINDING SOMETHING. . . . . 217 A FOUNTAIN, A BOTTLE . 129
    FIRST SOLDIER, AND THEN POET, AND THEN BOTH, ... 222 TO E.T. 7
    THIS NEW-BUILT CITY FROM BOTH WORK AND SLEEP. . . . . 231 A BROOK IN THE CITY . 24
    GRIM GIVING TO DO OVER FOR THEM BOTH. . . . . . . 231 NOT TO KEEP . . . 18
    AND RAISED BOTH HANDS . . . . 241 THE LOCKLESS DOOR . . 7
    THAT SPREADING IN THE EVENING AIR BOTH WAYS . . . . 247 THE COCOON 2
    WE'LL BOTH BE MARRIED TO THE BROOK. WE'LL BUILD . . . . 258 WEST-RUNNING BROOK . 13
    "TODAY WILL BE THE DAY OF WHAT WE BOTH SAID." . . . . 260 WEST-RUNNING BROOK . 75
    THE BEAR PUTS BOTH ARMS AROUND THE TREE ABOVE HER . . . 268 THE BEAR 1
    THEY HAD BOTH OF THEM HAD THEIR REASONS . . . . . 314 BEARER OF EVIL TIDINGS 39
    IN MY OPINION--THOUGH WE BOTH KNOW POETS . . . . . 321 BUILD SOIL 176
    WE ARE BOTH ROUND BECAUSE THE MIND IS ROUND, ... 322 BUILD SOIL 201
    TO BID THEM BOTH BE HAPPY. . . . . 335 CARPE DIEM 8
    AND LESS IN BOTH TOGETHER . . . . 336 CARPE DIEM 22
    FOR ALWAYS FIGHTING ON BOTH SIDES AT ONCE. . . . . 350 TO A YOUNG WRETCH . . 18
    WE BOTH ARE THE BELITTLED HUMAN RACE. . . . . . . 353 THE LESSON FOR TODAY . 77
    LEST BOTH SHOULD BITE HIM IN THE TOGA-TOGS. . . . . 362 SYMPATHY WITH UNDER DOG 4
    INTO EACH OTHER. BOTH OF THEM ARE LOST. . . . . . 378 DIRECTIVE 35
    THEY BOTH WERE HIRED. AND THOUGH PIKE HAD THE ADVANTAGE . 404 FROM PLANE TO PLANE . 2
    "I WOULDN'T HOE BOTH WAYS FOR ANYBODY!" . . . . . 405 FROM PLANE TO PLANE . 48
    THEY WERE BOTH BENT ON SCUFFLING UP . . . . . . 407 FROM PLANE TO PLANE . 114
    A RIVALRY THAT MADE THEM BOTH FEEL KINDER. . . . . 408 FROM PLANE TO PLANE . 119
    YES, BOTH OF US: WE SAW TO THAT AT ONCE. . . . . . 479 A MASQUE OF REASON . 162
    FROM WHAT IT IS WITH HIS. BOTH SERVE FOR PAY. . . . . 485 A MASQUE OF REASON . 353
    BOTH OF THEM CAUGHT IT FROM BEL'S FAVORITE POET, . . . 511 A MASQUE OF MERCY . 462
    WE BOTH HAVE LACKED THE COURAGE IN THE HEART . . . . 521 A MASQUE OF MERCY . 728
BOTHER
    "DON'T LET IT BOTHER YOU. YOU'VE FOUND OUT SOMETHING. . . 70 THE CODE 21
    DON'T LET IT BOTHER YOU TOO MUCH . . . . 326 TO A THINKER . . . 22
    SHE DOESN'T BOTHER TO APPEAR. . . . . 390 TWO LEADING LIGHTS . 17
    TO BOTHER ME BY SIDING WITH THE DOCTOR. . . . . . 406 FROM PLANE TO PLANE . 76
BOTHERS
    "ANOTHER WORD THAT BOTHERS ME IS FREEDOM. . . . . . 459 HOW HARD TO KEEP FROM 163
BOTTLE
    I DRINK OUT OF THE BOTTLE--NOT YOUR STYLE. . . . . . 50 A HUNDRED COLLARS . 156
    WHAT AM I DOING CARRYING OFF THIS BOTTLE?-- . . . . . 50 A HUNDRED COLLARS . 177
    AND LET OUT A LOUD YELL, AND THREW A BOTTLE, ... 195 PAUL'S WIFE . . . 140
    OF COURSE THE BOTTLE FELL SHORT BY A MILE. . . . . 195 PAUL'S WIFE . . . 142
    A FOUNTAIN, A BOTTLE, A DONKEY'S EARS, AND SOME BOOKS . . 212 A FOUNTAIN, A BOTTLE . T
    A CLIFF, AND ON THE CLIFF A BOTTLE PAINTED, ... 214 A FOUNTAIN, A BOTTLE . 38
    AT LEAST I'VE BROUGHT YOU TO THE FAMOUS BOTTLE." . . . 214 A FOUNTAIN, A BOTTLE . 42
    WHAT SIGNIFY A DONKEY'S EARS AND BOTTLE? . . . . . 215 A FOUNTAIN, A BOTTLE . 58
BOTTLES
    AND THE WHOLE PILE IS SLIPPING, BOTTLES, BUNS-- . . . . 266 THE ARMFUL 3
BOTTOM
    HE SAW HER FROM THE BOTTOM OF THE STAIRS. . . . . . 51 HOME BURIAL . . . 1
    STRUCK THE HARD CELLAR BOTTOM. AND THEN SOMEONE . . . 204 THE WITCH OF COOS . 50
    SHOOK WHATEVER IT WAS LAY THERE AT BOTTOM, ... 225 FOR ONCE SOMETHING . 13
    THE BOTTOM OF SEAS RAISED DRY-- . . . . 285 IN TIME OF CLOUDBURST . 15
    THE OLD BARN AT THE BOTTOM OF THE FOGS . . . . . . 289 OLD BARN AT THE BOTTOM T
    THE OLD BARN AT THE BOTTOM OF THE FOGS. . . . . . 290 OLD BARN AT THE BOTTOM 23

BOTTOM (CONTINUED)
THAT WAITED FOR THE BOTTOM TO FERMENT . . . . 468 IN A GLASS OF CIDER . 2
BOUGH
THE FRUITED BOUGH OF THE JUNIPER . . . . 24 PAN WITH US . . . 23
APPLES I DIDN'T PICK UPON SOME BOUGH. . . . . 68 AFTER APPLE-PICKING . 5
AND ONCE SHE WENT TO BREAK A BOUGH . . . . 129 THE IMPULSE 13
THE PILE IS OURS: WE DRAGGED IT BOUGH ON BOUGH . . . 129 THE BONFIRE . . . 6
A SINGLE LEAF WAS ON A BOUGH, ... 233 LOOKING FOR SUNSET BIRD 10
THE RANGEY BOUGH ANTICIPATED FRUIT . . . . 239 OUR SINGING STRENGTH . 14
BOUGHS
BEHIND LOW BOUGHS THE TREES LET DOWN OUTSIDE; . . . . 16 A DREAM PANG . . . 10
THE BARREN BOUGHS WITHOUT THE LEAVES, ... 18 GOING FOR WATER . . 11
WHERE THE BOUGHS RAIN WHEN IT BLOWS, ... 26 A LINE-STORM SONG . . 16
A DRY RAVINE EMERGED FROM UNDER BOUGHS . . . . . . 41 THE MOUNTAIN 33
I FEEL THE LADDER SWAY AS THE BOUGHS BEND. . . . . . 68 AFTER APPLE-PICKING . 23
THAT LOP EACH OTHER OF BOUGHS, BUT NOT A FEW . . . . 107 CHRISTMAS TREES . . 34
QUITE SOLITARY AND HAVING EQUAL BOUGHS . . . . . . 107 CHRISTMAS TREES . . . 35
BIRCH BOUGHS ENOUGH PILED EVERYWHERE!-- . . . . . 123 PEA BRUSH 13
THAT HAD BUDDED BEFORE THE BOUGHS WERE PILED . . . . 123 PEA BRUSH 23
THEY WILL COME BUDDING BOUGHS FROM TREE TO TREE, . . . 151 SNOW 230
AMONG BARE MAPLE BOUGHS, AND IN THE RARE . . . . . 234 EVENING A SUGAR ORCHARD 8
AND THAT WAS WHAT THE BOUGHS WERE FULL OF SOON. . . . 234 EVENING A SUGAR ORCHARD 17
I ONLY KNELT AND PUTTING THE BOUGHS ASIDE . . . . 343 QUEST OF PURPLE-FRINGED 21
WHEN THE BOUGHS ARE RIGHT . . . . 445 PERIL OF HOPE . . 5
BOUGHT
JOHN BOUGHT HIM, AND WE PAID THE BILL WITH BEADS-- . . 86 THE HOUSEKEEPER . . . 152
"THE BREAD WE BOUGHT IN PASSING AT THE STORE. . . . . 115 IN THE HOME STRETCH . 144
AND BOUGHT THE TELESCOPE WITH WHAT IT CAME TO. . . . . 177 THE STAR-SPLITTER . . 31
ARE TO BE BOUGHT OUT AND MERCIFULLY GATHERED IN . . . 286 A ROADSIDE STAND . . 24
FOR INTEREST, AND I'VE BOUGHT A MOUNTAIN FARM . . . . 316 BUILD SOIL 7
I COULD HAVE BOUGHT YOU JUST AS GOOD A TREE . . . . . 350 TO A YOUNG WRETCH . . 7
HE HAD HIS TICKET BOUGHT, HIS PASSAGE EARNED, ... 370 THE LITERATE FARMER AND 58
BOUGHTEN (SEE NEW-BOUGHTEN)
WITH BOUGHTEN FRIENDSHIP AT YOUR SIDE . . . . 307 PROVIDE, PROVIDE . . 20
BOULDER
LIKE SOME UP-ENDED BOULDER SPLIT IN TWO, ... 229 TWO LOOK AT TWO . . . 19
HER NEXT STEP ROCKS A BOULDER ON THE WALL . . . . . 268 THE BEAR 5
BOULDER-BROKEN
SOME MORNING FROM THE BOULDER-BROKEN BEACH . . . . 338 THE MOST OF IT . . . 5
BOULDERS
AND SPILLS THE UPPER BOULDERS IN THE SUN, ... 33 MENDING WALL 3
TO EACH THE BOULDERS THAT HAVE FALLEN TO EACH. . . . . 33 MENDING WALL . . . 16
LIKE BOULDERS BROKEN OFF THE UPPER CLIFF, ... 44 THE MOUNTAIN . . . 98
I FARM A PASTURE WHERE THE BOULDERS LIE . . . . . . 365 OF STONES OF THE PLACE 1
GREAT BOULDERS OFF THEIR BALANCE . . . . 376 ONE STEP BACKWARD TAKEN 4
BOULDER-STREWN
OF THE BOULDER-STREWN MOUNTAIN, AND WHEN THEY WILL CROP. . 61 BLUEBERRIES 63
BOUNCE
AND BEGAN TO BOUNCE DOWN A GRANITE STAIR, ... 383 WERE I IN TROUBLE . . 4
BOUNCING (SEE A-BOUNCING)
BOUND
I'D TAKE YOU, BUT I'M BOUND THE OTHER WAY." . . . . . 42 THE MOUNTAIN . . . 43
I HAD SUCH COMPANY OUTWARD BOUND. . . . . 102 GOOD HOURS 9
BETWEEN TWO BOYS AND NOT FEEL BOUND TO STOP IT. . . . . 146 SNOW 101
THE DEAD WAS BOUND TO SILENCE: ASK THE SISTER. . . . 200 PLACE FOR A THIRD . . 43
AND LEAPING ON IT WITH A SOLEMN BOUND, ... 284 THE GOLD HESPERIDEE . 47
AND ANOTHER TO ASK THE WAY TO WHERE IT WAS BOUND; . . . 287 A ROADSIDE STAND . . 41
FROM BOUND TO FREE AND BACK TO BOUND, ... 325 TO A THINKER 11
BUT STRICTLY HELD BY NONE, IS LOOSELY BOUND . . . . . 332 THE SILKEN TENT . . . 9
THEY BOUND THEM NAKED SO THEY FACED . . . . . . 345 DISCOVERY OF MADEIRAS . 76
"I'M--BOUND--AWAY!" . . . . 413 AWAY! 20
"I'M--BOUND--AWAY!" (HE QUOTES IT TO THE TUNE.) . . . 500 A MASQUE OF MERCY . . 172
BOUNDARY
, THE BOUNDARY LINES KEEP IN SO CLOSE TO IT. . . . . . 43 THE MOUNTAIN 95
THE NEAREST BOUNDARY TO ESCAPE ACROSS. . . . . . . 167 NEW HAMPSHIRE . . . 253
ON A NATIONAL BOUNDARY. . . . . 348 TRIPLE BRONZE . . . 10
BOUNDLESS
A BOUNDLESS MOMENT . . . . 233 A BOUNDLESS MOMENT . . T
BOUNDS
OF THE KNOWLEDGE BEYOND THE BOUNDS OF LIFE . . . . . 236 MISGIVING 15
THAT TO NO LIMITS AND BOUNDS HE CAN STAY CONFINED? . . 305 THERE ARE ROUGHLY ZONES 8
NOT IF I HAD MY SAY. BOUNDS SHOULD BE SET . . . . . 320 BUILD SOIL 123
BOUQUETS
"I'VE BROKEN ANNE OF GATHERING BOUQUETS. . . . . . . 98 THE SELF-SEEKER . . . 147
BOURN
AND SAIL FOR SOME VAGUE PAPHIAN BOURN . . . . 344 DISCOVERY OF MADEIRAS . 17
BOUSTROPHEDON
KNOWN AS BOUSTROPHEDON, WAS FOUND TOO AWKWARD." . . . . 405 FROM PLANE TO PLANE . 54
'BOUT
'BOUT OUT!" AND TOOK THE LONG WAY HOME . . . . . . 140 BROWN'S DESCENT . . . 75
BOW
AND BOW AND ACCEPT THE END . . . . 30 RELUCTANCE 23
PUBLISHED IN BOW. YOU KNOW THE WEEKLY NEWS?" . . . . 48 A HUNDRED COLLARS . . 99
"I WISH YOU HAD SEEN HIS PERPETUAL BOW-- . . . . . . 61 BLUEBERRIES . . . 57
HE'D PULL HIS BARS APART LIKE BOW AND BOWSTRING, . . . 66 A SERVANT TO SERVANTS . 134
AND THOSE OF THE NAME STARK GATHERED IN BOW, ... 73 THE GENERATIONS OF MEN 4
THEY WERE AT BOW, BUT THAT WAS NOT ENOUGH: . . . . . 73 THE GENERATIONS OF MEN 14
ACROSS HIS CHEST TO MAKE AS 'TWERE A BOW: . . . . . 114 IN THE HOME STRETCH . 107
A VERY SMALL MOON-MADE PRISMATIC BOW, ... 315 IRIS BY NIGHT . . . 18
I WONDER! BOW AND RAINBOW AS IT BENT, ... 315 IRIS BY NIGHT . . . 23
BOWED (SEE WATER-BOWED)
THERE WE BOWED US IN THE BURNING, ... 13 ROSE POGONIAS . . . 9
BOWED OUTWARD ON THE MOUNTAIN HALFWAY UP, ... 75 THE GENERATIONS OF MEN 71
SOMEONE SAID 'COME'--I HEARD IT AS I BOWED." . . . . 118 THE TELEPHONE . . . 17
AND THEY SEEM NOT TO BREAK; THOUGH ONCE THEY ARE BOWED . 121 BIRCHES 15
HE BOWED WITH GRACE TO NATURAL LAW, ... 139 BROWN'S DESCENT . . . 60
BOWER
TOOK HIM HOME TO HER BOWER, ... 313 BEARER OF EVIL TIDINGS 15

BOWSTRING
   HE'D PULL HIS BARS APART LIKE BOW AND BOWSTRING, ... 66 A SERVANT TO SERVANTS . 134
BOX
   THE LITTLE TIN BOX ON THE CUPBOARD SHELF-- . . . . . . 86 THE HOUSEKEEPER . . . 143
   THE UPPER SHELF, THE TIN BOX. THAT'S THE ONE. . . . . . 86 THE HOUSEKEEPER . . . 144
   HERE HE IS NOW. THIS BOX! PUT IT AWAY. . . . . 88 THE HOUSEKEEPER . . . 198
   BUT NOTHING SO LIKE BEATING ON A BOX. . . . . 108 OLD MAN'S WINTER NIGHT . 14
   HAND ME MY BUTTON BOX--IT MUST BE THERE.) . . . . . 205 THE WITCH OF COOS . . 81
   THE RURAL LETTER BOX SAID TOFFILE LAJWAY. . . . . . 207 THE WITCH OF COOS . . 155
   IN VIRGIN WRAPPER FROM DEEP IN THE BOX, ... 217 A FOUNTAIN, A BOTTLE . 126
   NO, IN YOUR RURAL LETTER BOX . . . . 380 AN UNSTAMPED LETTER IN . 4
   AN UNSTAMPED LETTER IN OUR RURAL LETTER BOX . . . . . 380 AN UNSTAMPED LETTER IN . T
BOXES
   HER GIFT FOR READING LETTERS LOCKED IN BOXES. . . . . 163 NEW HAMPSHIRE . . . 131
   WHY WAS IT SO MUCH GREATER WHEN THE BOXES . . . . . 163 NEW HAMPSHIRE . . . 132
BOXFUL
   I SAW A BOXFUL IN THE CHRISTMAS MARKET. . . . . . . 488 A MASQUE OF REASON . . 422
BOY
   THE BOY YOU HAD IN HAYING FOUR YEARS SINCE. . . . . . 36 DEATH OF THE HIRED MAN . 59
   HE SAID HE COULDN'T MAKE THE BOY BELIEVE . . . . . . 37 DEATH OF THE HIRED MAN . 82
   HE HATES TO SEE A BOY THE FOOL OF BOOKS. . . . . . . 37 DEATH OF THE HIRED MAN . 98
   WHAT I SEE. IT'S A LITTLE, LITTLE BOY, ... 77 THE GENERATIONS OF MEN . 99
   I'M A GREAT BOY TO THINK OF NUMBER ONE. . . . . . . 99 THE SELF-SEEKER . . . 177
   HE SAW HIMSELF A FARMER. THEN THERE WAS A FRENCH BOY . . 114 IN THE HOME STRETCH . 103
   I SHOULD PREFER TO HAVE SOME BOY BEND THEM . . . . . 121 BIRCHES 23
   SOME BOY TOO FAR FROM TOWN TO LEARN BASEBALL, ... 121 BIRCHES 25
   TO PLEASE THE BOY BY GIVING HIM THE HALF HOUR . . . . 136 "OUT,OUT--" . . . 11
   THAT A BOY COUNTS SO MUCH WHEN SAVED FROM WORK. . . . 136 "OUT,OUT--" . . . 12
   THE LIFE FROM SPILLING. THEN THE BOY SAW ALL-- . . . 137 "OUT,OUT--" . . . 22
   SINCE HE WAS OLD ENOUGH TO KNOW, BIG BOY . . . . . 137 "OUT,OUT--" . . . 23
   YOU RECOLLECT THE BOY WHO CAME OUT HERE . . . . . . 149 SNOW 173
   BUT NOT SO MUCH, PERHAPS, AS A BOY NEEDED. . . . . . 197 WILD GRAPES . . . 35
   SOMEWHERE MUST BE THE GRAVE OF THE YOUNG BOY . . . . 200 PLACE FOR A THIRD . . 33
   OF HIS OLD SONG, 'THE WILD COLONIAL BOY,' . . . . . 205 THE WITCH OF COOS . . 110
   A BOY, PRESUMING ON HIS INTELLECT, ... 293 AT WOODWARD'S GARDENS . 1
   HAD THE BOY NOT PRESUMED TOO CLOSE AND LONG. . . . . 293 AT WOODWARD'S GARDENS . 21
   AND MADE OF BY A BOY; THEN HAVING REACHED . . . . . 405 FROM PLANE TO PLANE . 57
   "GUSTIE, OLD BOY, DALMATIAN GUS, ... 420 ONE MORE BREVITY . . 28
   HE'S A GOOD BOY. 'TWAS AT MY INSTIGATION. . . . . . 459 HOW HARD TO KEEP FROM . 173
BOYHOOD
   AS AN OLD BOYHOOD FRIEND, AND ONCE INDEED . . . . . 160 NEW HAMPSHIRE . . . 49
   AS ANY OTHER BOYHOOD ENEMY . . . . 190 THE GRINDSTONE . . . 43
BOYISH
   AND GREW TO BE A LITTLE BOYISH GIRL . . . . 196 WILD GRAPES 8
BOYS
   WHERE THEY WERE BOYS. THEY HAVEN'T COME THIS YEAR. . . . 55 THE BLACK COTTAGE . . 18
   ONE OF THE BOYS SINGS OUT, 'WHERE'S THE OLD MAN?' . . . 72 THE CODE 83
   JOE SAID: "YOU BIG BOYS OUGHT TO FIND A FARM, . . . 113 IN THE HOME STRETCH . 95
   "GOOD BOYS THEY SEEMED, AND LET THEM LOVE THE CITY. . . 114 IN THE HOME STRETCH . 119
   BETWEEN TWO BOYS AND NOT FEEL BOUND TO STOP IT. . . . 146 SNOW 101
   AND BOYS THE MINUTE THEY GET OUT OF COLLEGE. . . . . 162 NEW HAMPSHIRE . . . 98
   AS CLEAN AS BOYS DO OFF A WILLOW TWIG. . . . . . 191 PAUL'S WIFE 20
   BOYS AND BAD HUNTERS HAD KNOWN WHAT TO DO . . . . . 216 A FOUNTAIN, A BOTTLE . 102
   A DOZEN GIRLS AND BOYS WE WERE. . . . . 265 THE BIRTHPLACE . . . 7
   BUT BECOMING AWARE OF SOME BOYS FROM SCHOOL . . . . 385 A MOOD APART . . . 4
   LIKE SMALL BOYS WE GOT MAD . . . . 464 MILKY WAY IS A COWPATH . 6
   LET'S CHANGE THE SUBJECT, BOYS, I'M GETTING NERVOUS. . . 516 A MASQUE OF MERCY . . 598
BOY'S (SEE COLLEGE-BOY'S)
   A BOY'S WILL . . . . 3 A BOY'S WILL . . . . T
   I LIKE TO THINK SOME BOY'S BEEN SWINGING THEM. . . . . 121 BIRCHES 3
   LEAPED OUT AT THE BOY'S HAND, OR SEEMED TO LEAP-- . . . 136 "OUT,OUT--" . . . 16
   THE BOY'S FIRST OUTCRY WAS A RUEFUL LAUGH, ... 136 "OUT,OUT--" . . . 19
   AND THE GLASS WAS THE MONKEYS', NOT THE BOY'S. . . . 293 AT WOODWARD'S GARDENS . 23
BRACED
   THAT BRACED HIS FEET AGAINST THE ARCTIC POLE. . . . . 377 DIRECTIVE 17
BRACING
   COURAGE IS IN THE AIR IN BRACING WHIFFS . . . . . 423 FOR JOHN F. KENNEDY . 58
BRACKEN
   THEY ARE DRAGGED TO THE WITHERED BRACKEN BY THE LOAD, . . 121 BIRCHES 14
BRACKISH
   NOT EVEN BRACKISH FROM ITS SALT EXPERIENCE. . . . . 514 A MASQUE OF MERCY . . 542
BRAD
   SO BRAD MCLAUGHLIN MINGLED RECKLESS TALK . . . . . 176 THE STAR-SPLITTER . . 13
   IT WOULDN'T DO TO BE TOO HARD ON BRAD . . . . . 178 THE STAR-SPLITTER . . 53
   AT ONE STROKE (OF A MATCH), BRAD HAD TO TURN . . . . 178 THE STAR-SPLITTER . . 67
BRADFORD
   BRADFORD AND I HAD OUT THE TELESCOPE. . . . . . 179 THE STAR-SPLITTER . . 82
   NOWHERE BUT ON THE BRADFORD INTERVAL . . . . . . 404 FROM PLANE TO PLANE . 21
BRAIN
   ONLY WITHIN. INSIDE THE BRAIN . . . . 381 AN UNSTAMPED LETTER IN . 32
   AND BRAIN IS ALL THAT'S LEFT OF MORTAL STUFF, ... 395 ETHEREALIZING . . . 6
   BUT NOW AS BLOBS OF BRAIN WE'LL LIE AND DREAM, ... 395 ETHEREALIZING . . . 11
   WAS MADE BY GETTING SCIENCE ON THE BRAIN: . . . . 398 BURSTING RAPTURE . . 5
   AND YET FOR ALL THIS HELP OF HEAD AND BRAIN . . . . 425 ACCIDENTALLY ON PURPOSE 21
BRAINS
   FROM OUR BRAINS NO LESS. . . . . 440 KITTY HAWK 386
   THAT'S WHY WE NEED A LOT OF BRAINS . . . . . . 467 QUANDARY 8
   FOR BRAINS THERE IS NO SUBSTITUTE. . . . . . . 467 QUANDARY 16
   THAT BRAINS AND SWEETBREADS WERE THE SAME, ... 467 QUANDARY 21
BRAKE
   THEY MIGHT FIND FUEL THERE, IN WITHERED BRAKE, ... 131 THE BONFIRE 61
   THAT FLASHES TAIL THROUGH LAST YEAR'S WITHERED BRAKE . . 226 THE ONSET 20
   IN GOLDENROD AND BRAKE, ... 339 THE SUBVERTED FLOWER . 16
BRAKES
   FOR THE SQUEAL OF BRAKES, THE SOUND OF A STOPPING CAR, . . 287 A ROADSIDE STAND . . 36
   THERE'S WILL AS MOTOR AND THERE'S WILL AS BRAKES. . . . 481 A MASQUE OF REASON . . 230
   THE WILL AS BRAKES CAN'T STOP THE WILL AS MOTOR . . . 481 A MASQUE OF REASON . . 232

BRANCH
```
    DRAWN ON A SORT OF PASSPORT WITH THE BRANCH  .   .   .   .   .  .  74 THE GENERATIONS OF MEN    40
    "FOUR CARDS: ONE YOURS, THREE MINE (ONE FOR EACH BRANCH .  .  76 THE GENERATIONS OF MEN    80
    OR BRANCH TO WHISTLE AFTER WHAT WAS SPENT.  .   .   .   .   .  . 175 THE CENSUS-TAKER  .   .   . 24
    I'VE KNOWN ERE NOW AN INTERFERING BRANCH.   .   .   .   .   .  . 185 THE AX-HELVE  .   .   .   .   1
    AND THAT WAS, AS I SAY, AN ALDER BRANCH.   .   .   .   .   .   . 185 THE AX-HELVE  .   .   .   .   5
    BOLE AND BRANCH AND ROOT  .   .   .   .   .   .   .   .   .   .  . 426 A NEVER NAUGHT SONG      19
BRANCHES
    OF TREES AND CRACK OF BRANCHES, COMMON THINGS,  .   .   .   .  . 108 OLD MAN'S WINTER NIGHT   13
    TO THE TOP BRANCHES, CLIMBING CAREFULLY  .   .   .   .   .   .  . 122 BIRCHES  .   .   .   .   .  36
    AND CLIMB BLACK BRANCHES UP A SNOW-WHITE TRUNK  .   .   .   .  . 122 BIRCHES  .   .   .   .   .  55
    HUNG BABIES OUT ON BRANCHES BY THE HANDS  .   .   .   .   .   .  . 197 WILD GRAPES  .   .   .   .  51
    A WHIR AMONG WHITE BRANCHES GREAT AND SMALL,  .   .   .   .   . 240 OUR SINGING STRENGTH   41
    THEIR UPPER BRANCHES ROUND HIM WREATHING,   .   .   .   .   .  . 274 A LONE STRIKER  .   .   . 40
    LEAVES TO STRIP AND BRANCHES SPLINTER,   .   .   .   .   .   .  . 304 CLEAR AND COLDER  .   . 12
    AND WITH LONG-SLEEVED BRANCHES HOLD THEIR SWAY.  .   .   .   . 376 SOMETHING FOR HOPE  .   . 12
    IN BRANCHES OF THE SILPHION  .   .   .   .   .   .   .   .   .  . 452 A-WISHING WELL  .   .   . 58
    SOMEONE'S CAUGHT IN THE BRANCHES. / SO THERE IS.  .   .   .   . 473 A MASQUE OF REASON  .   . 16
BRASS
    UP THE BRASS BARREL, VELVET BLACK INSIDE,   .   .   .   .   .  . 179 THE STAR-SPLITTER  .   .  77
    AND DOUBLE RING OF FITTED BRASS  .   .   .   .   .   .   .   .  . 363 ASSURANCE  .   .   .   .   .   3
BRAVADO
    BRAVADO  .   .   .   .   .   .   .   .   .   .   .   .   .   .  . 383 BRAVADO  .   .   .   .   .   .   T
BRAVE
    AND SEEK WITH LAUGHTER WHAT TO BRAVE--  .   .   .   .   .   .  .  20 THE TRIAL BY EXISTENCE   14
    IT WILL HAVE OUTLET, BRAVE AND NOT SO BRAVE.  .   .   .   .   . 255 THE FLOOD  .   .   .   .   9
    MATTER OF FACT HAS MADE THEM BRAVE.  .   .   .   .   .   .   .  . 291 ON HEART'S BEGINNING TO 35
    TO TIME IT NEVER SEEMS THAT HE IS BRAVE  .   .   .   .   .   .  . 334 I COULD GIVE ALL  .   .   1
    (LESS BRAVE PERHAPS THAN TRUSTING ARE THE FAIR.)  .   .   .   . 375 A YOUNG BIRCH  .   .   . 10
    THE MORAL KIND'S AS BRAVE AS FACING BULLETS."  .   .   .   .  . 405 FROM PLANE TO PLANE  .   . 35
    FROM THE GREAT AND BRAVE,  .   .   .   .   .   .   .   .   .   . 430 KITTY HAWK  .   .   .   .  75
BRAVER
    AND BRAVER FOR THE EARNER, LEARNER, YEARNER.  .   .   .   .   . 424 FOR JOHN F. KENNEDY  .   . 67
BRAVEST
    EVEN THE BRAVEST THAT ARE SLAIN  .   .   .   .   .   .   .   .  .  19 THE TRIAL BY EXISTENCE    1
    THE BRAVEST WOULD HAVE BY FOR FRIEND,  .   .   .   .   .   .   .  21 THE TRIAL BY EXISTENCE   51
BRAWL
    AND MADE A WIDESPREAD BRAWL ON COBBLESTONES;  .   .   .   .   .  40 THE MOUNTAIN  .   .   .  . 11
    CAN EVER GIVE US IS A NUISANCE BRAWL.  .   .   .   .   .   .   . 398 NO HOLY WARS FOR THEM .  14
BRAZIL
    THEY SEARCHED FOR INTO BRAZIL,  .   .   .   .   .   .   .   .  . 311 THE VINDICTIVES  .   .   . 50
BREACH
    EITHER TO BREACH OR CLIMB.  .   .   .   .   .   .   .   .   .  . 348 TRIPLE BRONZE  .   .   .   8
BREAD
    A DOLE OF BREAD, A PURSE,   .   .   .   .   .   .   .   .   .  .   8 LOVE AND A QUESTION  .  26
    "THE BREAD WE BOUGHT IN PASSING AT THE STORE.  .   .   .   .  . 115 IN THE HOME STRETCH  . 144
    THERE'S BUTTER SOMEWHERE, TOO." / "LET'S REND THE BREAD.  .   . 115 IN THE HOME STRETCH  . 145
    PERHAPS BECAUSE WE GAVE HIM ONLY BREAD  .   .   .   .   .   .  . 127 THE SMILE  .   .   .   .   4
    IT WOULD NOT BE FAIR TO SAY FOR A DOLE OF BREAD,  .   .   .   . 286 A ROADSIDE STAND  .   .   4
BREADTH
    I'VE TRIED IT FINE WITH LITTLE BREADTH OF LUSTER,  .   .   .   . 245 THE FREEDOM OF THE MOON   4
BREAK
    RELEASE ONE LEAF AT BREAK OF DAY;  .   .   .   .   .   .   .   .  27 OCTOBER  .   .   .   .   .  12
    IT MELTED, AND I LET IT FALL AND BREAK.  .   .   .   .   .   .  .  68 AFTER APPLE-PICKING  .   . 13
    TO BREAK IT TO HIM. YOU MAY HAVE THE JOB."  .   .   .   .   .  .  88 THE HOUSEKEEPER  .   . 194
    AND THEY SEEM NOT TO BREAK; THOUGH ONCE THEY ARE BOWED  .   .  . 121 BIRCHES  .   .   .   .  15
    AND ONCE SHE WENT TO BREAK A BOUGH .   .   .   .   .   .   .   . 129 THE IMPULSE  .   .   .  13
    SORRY I HAD TO BREAK IN ON YOUR SLEEP."  .   .   .   .   .   .  . 150 SNOW  .   .   .   .   .  212
    AGAINST THE SKY TO BREAK HIS BACK FOR HIM,  .   .   .   .   .  . 170 NEW HAMPSHIRE  .   .  348
    BREAK SILENCE NOW OR BE FOREVER SILENT.  .   .   .   .   .   .  . 176 THE CENSUS-TAKER  .   . 59
    THE CURVE OF EARTH, AND STRIKING, BREAK THEIR OWN;  .   .   .  . 261 A SOLDIER  .   .   .   .  12
    IN HOPES OF SEEING THE CALM OF HEAVEN BREAK  .   .   .   .   .  . 268 ON LOOKING UP BY CHANCE 14
    (HE COULDN'T HOPE ITS HEART WOULD BREAK.)  .   .   .   .   .  . 273 A LONE STRIKER  .   .  . 16
    TO BREAK OUR LOGIC IN TOO LONG A FLIGHT,   .   .   .   .   .   . 370 THE LITERATE FARMER AND 82
    WILL HE ASCRIBE THIS LUCKY BREAK.  .   .   .   .   .   .   .   . 418 AMERICA IS HARD TO SEE  72
    TO BREAK WITH FOLLOWERS WHEN IN THE WRONG,  .   .   .   .   .  . 424 FOR JOHN F. KENNEDY  .  62
    FOR ME TO BREAK LOOSE  .   .   .   .   .   .   .   .   .   .   . 432 KITTY HAWK  .   .   .  . 130
    BUT THE BIG ONE IS WORTHLESS. BREAK IT OPEN.  .   .   .   .   . 456 HOW HARD TO KEEP FROM   82
    HOW DID YOU KNOW THAT WAY TO BREAK MY HEART?  .   .   .   .   . 495 A MASQUE OF MERCY  .   . 59
    AND HELP YOU'RE GOING TO GET. / I'LL BREAK YOUR DOOR DOWN.  . 500 A MASQUE OF MERCY  .  178
    CHRIST CAME TO INTRODUCE A BREAK WITH LOGIC  .   .   .   .   .  . 511 A MASQUE OF MERCY  .  475
BREAKFAST
    I MUST BE GETTING BACK TO BREAKFAST NOW."  .   .   .   .   .  .  41 THE MOUNTAIN  .   .   .  . 37
BREAKING  (SEE SPELL-BREAKING)
    OF THE FAR-DISTANT BREAKING WAVE.  .   .   .   .   .   .   .   .  20 THE TRIAL BY EXISTENCE   16
    HAS BEEN TO KEEP THE THING FROM BREAKING UP.  .   .   .   .   .  84 THE HOUSEKEEPER  .   .  . 88
    OF WHAT WANTS PRUNING, SHINGLING, BREAKING UP.  .   .   .   .  . 115 IN THE HOME STRETCH  . 150
    AND THE LIGHT BREAKING ON THEM MADE THEM RUN.  .   .   .   .  . 237 A HILLSIDE THAW  .   .   . 8
    WITH BREAKING STEP I STABBED THE DUST,  .   .   .   .   .   .  . 336 THE WIND AND THE RAIN .   7
    WITH THEIR EVER BREAKING NEWNESS  .   .   .   .   .   .   .   .  . 387 THE COURAGE TO BE NEW .  15
    AND SAVE HERSELF FROM BREAKING WINDOW GLASS.  .   .   .   .   . 445 QUESTIONING FACES  .   .   2
BREAKS
    IT BREAKS AWAY IN SOME NEW KIND OF SLAUGHTER.  .   .   .   .  . 254 THE FLOOD  .   .   .   .   4
    OF OUTRAGE--VIOLENCE--THAT BREAKS ACROSS IT.  .   .   .   .   . 509 A MASQUE OF MERCY  .  431
BREAST
    FOR WILDING BROOCH, SHALL WET YOUR BREAST  .   .   .   .   .  .  27 A LINE-STORM SONG  .   . 23
    BEFORE IT STAINED A SINGLE HUMAN BREAST.  .   .   .   .   .   . 126 RANGE-FINDING  .   .   .   3
    TO SET YOUR BREAST TO THE BARK OF TREES  .   .   .   .   .   .  . 141 THE GUM-GATHERER  .   . 35
    I SLUMBERED WITH YOUR POEMS ON MY BREAST,  .   .   .   .   .  . 222 TO E.T.  .   .   .   .   .   1
    THE OTHER CURLED AT HIS BREAST. HE DIPPED HIS HEAD  .   .   .  . 223 THE RUNAWAY  .   .   .   4
    HIGH IN THE BREAST. NOTHING BUT WHAT GOOD CARE  .   .   .   .  . 230 NOT TO KEEP  .   .   .   15
    MURMURING SOMETHING QUIET IN HER BREAST,  .   .   .   .   .   . 249 ACCEPTANCE  .   .   .   .   6
    WHITE FEATHERS FROM THE STRUGGLE OF WHOSE BREAST  .   .   .   . 258 WEST-RUNNING BROOK  .  23
    TO KEEP THEIR BUILDING BALANCED AT MY BREAST.  .   .   .   .  . 267 THE ARMFUL  .   .   .   .   8
    IN A THRUSH'S BREAST.  .   .   .   .   .   .   .   .   .   .   . 334 COME IN  .   .   .   .  . 12
    HE SLAPPED HIS BREAST TO VERIFY HIS PURSE  .   .   .   .   .  . 396 ANY SIZE WE PLEASE  .  . 13
BREASTING
    HERE IT CAME BREASTING LIKE A HORSE IN SKIRTS.  .   .   .   .  . 270 THE EGG AND THE MACHINE  11
```

BREASTS
    WITH BIRDS THAT FILL THEIR BREASTS . . . . 126 LONELINESS 10
BREATH
    WITH THE BREATH OF MANY FLOWERS-- . . . . 13 ROSE POGONIAS . . . 7
    THAN THE MEREST AIMLESS BREATH OF AIR. . . . . 24 PAN WITH US . . . 25
    IT STEAM IN WINTER LIKE AN OX'S BREATH, ... 42 THE MOUNTAIN . . . 51
    THE BLUE'S BUT A MIST FROM THE BREATH OF THE WIND, . . . 60 BLUEBERRIES . . . 25
    HE LAY AND PUFFED HIS LIPS OUT WITH HIS BREATH. . . . 137 "OUT,OUT--" . . . 29
    NOT A BREEZE STIRRED, BUT JUST THE BREATH OF AIR . . . 194 PAUL'S WIFE . . . 98
    BEFORE SHE CAUGHT HER FIRST BREATH WITH A GASP . . . . 194 PAUL'S WIFE . . . 118
    THE BREATH OF AIR HAD DIED OF COLD, ... 232 LOOKING FOR SUNSET BIRD 2
    WAS WROUGHT THROUGH TREES WITHOUT A BREATH OF STORM . . 238 A HILLSIDE THAW . . 31
    "A SIGH FOR EVERY SO MANY BREATH, ... 263 THE TIMES TABLE . . 9
    ONE IMPULSE PERSISTS AS OUR BREATH; . . . . 266 SITTING BY A BUSH . 19
    ALL SUMMER LONG I THOUGHT I HEARD THEM THREATENING UNDER
        THEIR BREATH. . . . . 297 A LEAF-TREADER . . 7
    I SHALL WILL TO THE COMMON STOCK OF AIR MY BREATH . . 307 NOT QUITE SOCIAL . 15
    THAT SUCKS HIS BREATH LIKE A WICKED CAT IN BED. . . . 341 WILLFUL HOMING . . 4
    THERE STOOD THE PURPLE SPIRES WITH NO BREATH OF AIR . 343 QUEST OF PURPLE-FRINGED 17
    TO KISS AND DRINK EACH OTHER'S BREATH . . . . 346 DISCOVERY OF MADEIRAS . 81
    SHE TRIES TO MAKE IT IN ONE CATCH OF BREATH, ... 386 THE FEAR OF MAN . . 3
    TILL IT CAN MUSTER BREATH INSIDE A HALL . . . . . . 399 THE INGENUITIES OF DEBT 17
BREATHE
    "I'LL HARDLY BREATHE." / "THE VOICES SEEM TO SAY----" . 78 THE GENERATIONS OF MEN 150
    TO BREATHE THE AIR ONE WINTER--HAD A ROOM . . . . . 149 SNOW 174
BREATHED
    NOW BREATHED AS LIGHT AS A LADY'S FAN. . . . . . . 304 UNHARVESTED 7
BREATHES
    BREATHES THERE A BARD WHO ISN'T MOVED . . . . 469 CHOSEN POET OF VERMONT 1
BREATHING
    MY BREATHING SHAKES THE BLUET LIKE A BREEZE, ... 17 THE VANTAGE POINT . 12
    AND EASED HIS HEAVY BREATHING, BUT STILL SLEPT. . . . 108 OLD MAN'S WINTER NIGHT 25
    OF BREATHING TREES SAID SOMETHING OF THE TIME . . . . 175 THE CENSUS-TAKER . . 26
    THEIR BREATHING MINGLED WITH HIS BREATHING. . . . . 274 A LONE STRIKER . . 41
    THIS WAS NO DUST SPECK BY MY BREATHING BLOWN, ... 357 A CONSIDERABLE SPECK . 7
BRED (SEE TOWN-BRED)
    LIFTED THE RUG THAT BRED THEM ON THE FLOOR . . . . . 237 A HILLSIDE THAW . . . 7
    TO PRODUCE PURPOSE AS THE FITTER BRED: . . . . . . 425 ACCIDENTALLY ON PURPOSE 15
BREED (SEE HALF-BREED)
    (AND TAKEN WITH IT ALL THE HYLA BREED . . . . 119 HYLA BROOK 4
    AS IS VOUCHSAFED TO FEATHERED BREED. . . . . 281 BLUE RIBBON AT AMESBURY 36
    NOT FOR A LONG, LONG TIME. PLANT, BREED, PRODUCE, . . 323 BUILD SOIL . . . 214
    BUT AN EARTHLY DOG OF THE CARRIAGE BREED; . . . . . 419 ONE MORE BREVITY . 11
BREEDER
    ONCE ON THE KIND OF DAY CALLED "WEATHER BREEDER," . . 125 AN ENCOUNTER 1
BREEDER'S
    HE MEDITATES THE BREEDER'S ART. . . . . 280 BLUE RIBBON AT AMESBURY 25
BREEDS
    WITH A GREAT FLOCK OF CHICKENS OF RARE BREEDS . . . . 162 NEW HAMPSHIRE . . . 102
BREEZE
    SO OLD AND FIRM THEY SCARCELY SHOW THE BREEZE, . . . 5 INTO MY OWN 2
    AND HE A WINTER BREEZE. . . . . 10 WIND AND WINDOW FLOWER 4
    AND MORNING FOUND THE BREEZE . . . . 11 WIND AND WINDOW FLOWER 27
    MY BREATHING SHAKES THE BLUET LIKE A BREEZE, ... 17 THE VANTAGE POINT . . 12
    WITHOUT THE BIRDS, WITHOUT THE BREEZE. . . . . . . 18 GOING FOR WATER . . 12
    I LISTENED FOR HIS WHETSTONE ON THE BREEZE. . . . . 22 THE TUFT OF FLOWERS . 6
    THE BREEZE THREE ODORS BROUGHT, ... 29 MY BUTTERFLY . . . 36
    IF THAT WAS YOUR IDEA, AGAINST THE BREEZE, ... 109 THE EXPOSED NEST . . 6
    AS THE BREEZE RISES, AND TURN MANY-COLORED . . . . 121 BIRCHES 8
    SWEET-SCENTED STUFF WHEN THE BREEZE DREW ACROSS IT. . 136 "OUT,OUT--" . . . 3
    NOT A BREEZE STIRRED, BUT JUST THE BREATH OF AIR . . 194 PAUL'S WIFE . . . 98
    ENGAGED UP THERE WITH THE LIGHT AND BREEZE? . . . . 247 ON GOING UNNOTICED . 4
    AT MIDDAY WHEN A SUNNY SUMMER BREEZE . . . . 331 THE SILKEN TENT . . 2
    A BREEZE DISCOVERED MY OPEN BOOK . . . . 342 A CLOUD SHADOW . . 1
    THE BREEZE DISDAINED TO MAKE REPLY; . . . . 342 A CLOUD SHADOW . . 6
BREEZES
    THE BREEZES WERE SO SPENT WITH WINTER BLOWING . . . . 130 THE BONFIRE . . . 35
BREVITY
    ONE MORE BREVITY . . . . 419 ONE MORE BREVITY . T
BREWS
    WIND SHE BREWS A HEADY KETTLE. . . . . 304 CLEAR AND COLDER . 21
BRIBED
    THEY WERE PUNISHED AND BRIBED; . . . . 449 THE BAD ISLAND--EASTER 46
BRICKS
    HOWEVER FAR YOU MUST GO FOR BRICKS, ... 232 THE KITCHEN CHIMNEY . 5
BRIDAL
    BY HARBORING WOE IN THE BRIDAL HOUSE, ... 8 LOVE AND A QUESTION . 31
    FROM THINKING IT COULD BE A THING SO BRIDAL. . . . . 184 MAPLE 158
BRIDE
    WITHIN, THE BRIDE IN THE DUSK ALONE . . . . . . 8 LOVE AND A QUESTION . 17
    A BRIDE, TO HELP TAKE CARE OF SUCH A CREATURE, . . . 66 A SERVANT TO SERVANTS 127
    THE BRIDE WHO SHARED THE CRUST HE BROKE TO EAT, . . . 359 THE LOST FOLLOWER . 23
BRIDEGROOM
    AND HE SPOKE THE BRIDEGROOM FAIR. . . . . 7 LOVE AND A QUESTION . 2
    THE BRIDEGROOM CAME FORTH INTO THE PORCH . . . . . 7 LOVE AND A QUESTION . 9
    THE BRIDEGROOM LOOKED AT THE WEARY ROAD, ... 8 LOVE AND A QUESTION . 21
    THE BRIDEGROOM THOUGHT IT LITTLE TO GIVE . . . . . 8 LOVE AND A QUESTION . 25
    THE BRIDEGROOM WISHED HE KNEW. . . . . 8 LOVE AND A QUESTION . 32
BRIDGE
    BEYOND THE BRIDGE, WAS NOT THAT OF THE MOUNTAIN, . . 41 THE MOUNTAIN . . . 21
    OUR BRIDGE ACROSS IT, AND THE BRIDGE SHALL BE . . . 258 WEST-RUNNING BROOK . 14
BRIEF
    MAKE THE DAY SEEM TO US LESS BRIEF. . . . . 27 OCTOBER 9
    I BADE MEN TELL ME WHICH IN BRIEF, ... 297 LEAVES COMPARED WITH . 13
    AS A BRIEF EPIDEMIC OF MICROBES . . . . 352 THE LESSON FOR TODAY . 70
    MAY I IN MY BRIEF BOLT ACROSS THE SCENE . . . . . 386 THE FEAR OF MAN . . 15
    THAT COMES OF DOGS' LIVES BEING SO BRIEF, ... 420 ONE MORE BREVITY . 51

BRIGHT (SEE STEEL-BRIGHT)
  (PALE ORCHISES), AND SCARED A BRIGHT GREEN SNAKE. . . . . . 17 MOWING 12
  HE LOOKS ON THE BRIGHT SIDE OF EVERYTHING, ... 64 A SERVANT TO SERVANTS . 45
  "SEE HOW IT MAKES HIS NOSE-SIDE BRIGHT, A PROOF . . . . 112 IN THE HOME STRETCH . 66
  THAT MADE THE STARS BRIGHT . . . . 135 LAST WORD OF A BLUEBIRD 10
  NO ONE WAS BRIGHT ENOUGH TO IDENTIFY; . . . . . . 295 LOST IN HEAVEN 7
  THE STARS ARE BROUGHT OUT BRIGHT. . . . . 301 VOICE WAYS 5
  THERE BRIGHT IN THE FILTH IT LAY . . . . 312 THE VINDICTIVES . . . 78
  TO SEE IT SO, THE BRIGHT AND ONLY ONE . . . . . 368 THE LITERATE FARMER AND 11
  DON'T LET HIM MAKE YOU SEE TOO BRIGHT A GATE . . . . 513 A MASQUE OF MERCY . 536
  IF EVEN THE FACE OF MAN'S TOO BRIGHT A LIGHT . . . . 515 A MASQUE OF MERCY . 583
BRIGHT-BLACK-EYED
  BRIGHT-BLACK-EYED SILVERY CREATURE, BRUSHED WITH BROWN, . . 356 A MOTH SEEN IN WINTER . 3
BRIGHTENING
  I WAS AFRAID, IN BRIGHTENING FIRST ON ME, ... 187 THE AX-HELVE 55
BRIGHTEST
  BUT MERCY FIRST AND LAST SHALL BRIGHTEST SHINE-- . . . 508 A MASQUE OF MERCY . 381
BRIGHTLY
  BRIGHTLY, AS IF A STAR PLAYED ON THE PLACE, ... 195 PAUL'S WIFE 135
BRIGHTNESS
  HOW ONCE SHE WALKED IN BRIGHTNESS, ... 257 THE LOVELY BE CHOOSERS 33
BRIGHTON
  A DROVER WITH ME ON THE ROAD TO BRIGHTON. . . . . 160 NEW HAMPSHIRE . . . 50
BRILLIANT
  AND THE SUN'S BRILLIANT BALL . . . . 333 HAPPINESS MAKES UP . . 5
BRIM
  BUT FROM SHEER MORNING GLADNESS AT THE BRIM. . . . 23 THE TUFT OF FLOWERS . 28
  UP TO THE BRIM, AND EVEN ABOVE THE BRIM. . . . . 122 BIRCHES 38
ERINE
  BUT WHEN THE BRINE GOES BACK, AS GO IT MUST, ... 513 A MASQUE OF MERCY . 540
BRING
  BRING THE SINGER, BRING THE NESTER; . . . . . . 11 TO THE THAWING WIND . 2
  AS THE ROAD WINDS WOULD BRING HIM TO HIS DOOR. . . . 38 DEATH OF THE HIRED MAN 126
  I'LL FOLLOW AND BRING YOU BACK BY FORCE. I WILL!--" . . 55 HOME BURIAL 116
  FOR THE FRIENDS IT MIGHT BRING ME. BY THE WAY, . . . 95 THE SELF-SEEKER . . 84
  AND BRING HIM UP, AND DON'T LET MRS. CORBIN.-- . . . 96 THE SELF-SEEKER . . 89
  "I DIDN'T BRING A PURPLE LADY'S SLIPPER. . . . . 98 THE SELF-SEEKER . . 143
  "WILLIS, BRING ANNE BACK WITH YOU WHEN YOU COME. . . 100 THE SELF-SEEKER . . 223
  LET'S ALL BUT BRING TO LIFE THIS OLD VOLCANO, . . . 130 THE BONFIRE 16
  WELL IF IT DOESN'T WITH ITS DRAFT BRING ON . . . . 130 THE BONFIRE 32
  WANTED ME TO BRING WORD . . . . 135 LAST WORD OF A BLUEBIRD 8
  BRING BERRIES UNDER THE WAGON SEAT, ... 141 THE GUM-GATHERER . . 26
  AND BRING IT TO MARKET WHEN YOU PLEASE. . . . . 141 THE GUM-GATHERER . . 39
  THEY BRING THE TELEPHONE AND TELEGRAPH. . . . . 141 THE LINE-GANG . . 13
  A NAME WITH MEANING COULD BRING UP A CHILD, . . . 185 MAPLE 166
  USED THESE UNSCRUPULOUSLY TO BRING ME . . . . . 188 THE AX-HELVE . . 88
  "THE SUN WILL BRING YOUR LOAD IN"--AND IT DID-- . . 192 PAUL'S WIFE . . . 47
  AND BRING THE CHALK-PILE DOWN. "I'LL TELL YOU WHAT-- . 205 THE WITCH OF COOS . 107
  TO BRING ME TO FOR BROAD-BOARD PANELING. . . . . 215 A FOUNTAIN, A BOTTLE . 70
  THE HOUSE HAD GONE TO BRING AGAIN . . . . . . 241 NEED OF BEING VERSED . 1
  BUT UP BY ROOTS TO BRING DARK FOLIAGE ON. . . . . 245 SPRING POOLS . . . 6
  AND BRING BACK NATURE IN PEOPLE'S PLACE. . . . . 263 THE TIMES TABLE . . 20
  GO BRING HIM HOME TO HIS PEOPLE. . . . . . . 288 DEPARTMENTAL . . . 28
  BRING ON WIND. BRING RAIN IN TORRENTS-- . . . . 304 CLEAR AND COLDER . 13
  BUT WHEN THERE SEEMED NO MORE TO BRING, ... 310 THE VINDICTIVES . . 14
  FROM ALL DIVISION TIME OR FOE CAN BRING . . . . 315 IRIS BY NIGHT . . . 30
  BUT MUST BRING TO THE MEETING THE MATUREST, . . . 321 BUILD SOIL . . . 160
  WE HAVE STRENGTH OF RESERVE IN US TO BRING. . . . 321 BUILD SOIL . . . 162
  BUT MUCH AS IN THE END WE BRING FOR SALE THERE, . . 321 BUILD SOIL . . . 173
  THERE IS STILL MORE WE NEVER BRING OR SHOULD BRING; . 321 BUILD SOIL . . . 174
  WHO FALL ALL OVER EACH OTHER TO BRING SOIL . . . 321 BUILD SOIL . . . 177
  O YOU WHO BRING THIS TO MY HAND, ... 327 A MISSIVE MISSILE . 22
  BRING OUT THE STARS, BRING OUT THE FLOWERS, . . . 332 ALL REVELATION . . 17
  AND BRING US TO THE NEAREST LAND; . . . . . 346 DISCOVERY OF MADEIRAS 107
  HAS FAILED TO BRING--I MEAN THE GOLDEN AGE. . . . 358 THE LOST FOLLOWER . 16
  WILL BRING HER OUT, DIMINISHED DIM, ... 390 TWO LEADING LIGHTS . 19
  SINCE YOU BRING UP THE SUBJECT OF THE SUN. . . . 408 FROM PLANE TO PLANE . 125
  THIS VERSE THAT IN ACKNOWLEDGMENT I BRING . . . 422 FOR JOHN F. KENNEDY . 7
  THEY WOULD BRING EMPIRES DOWN ABOUT OUR EARS . . 423 FOR JOHN F. KENNEDY . 29
  WAITING WAS TO BRING, ... 426 A NEVER NAUGHT SONG . 14
  MIGHT NEVER BRING HER BACK. . . . . 464 MILKY WAY IS A COWPATH 24
  YET COULD NOT BRING MYSELF TO SAY A WORD. . . . 497 A MASQUE OF MERCY . 99
  TO BRING FAITH BACK. I'M ONLY LANGUIDLY . . . . 515 A MASQUE OF MERCY . 566
  LIGHT, BRING A LIGHT! / AWH, THERE'S NO LACK OF LIGHT, YOU-- 515 A MASQUE OF MERCY . 579
BRINGING
  BRINGING A STONE GRASPED FIRMLY BY THE TOP . . . 34 MENDING WALL . . . 39
  NOW BRINGING OUT ITS RINGS IN SUGAR OF PITCH; . . 175 THE CENSUS-TAKER . 21
  BY BRINGING IT UP TO HIM WHEN HE WAS TOO OLD. . . 183 MAPLE 122
  HE STOOD THERE BRINGING MARCH AGAINST HIS THOUGHT, . 233 A BOUNDLESS MOMENT . 3
  IN BRINGING CHANGE UNHERALDED ON THE UNREADY. . . 320 BUILD SOIL . . 125
  BRINGING HIM ON . . . . 360 THE RABBIT-HUNTER . 12
  THE REVOLUTION KEEPER'S BRINGING ON . . . . . 509 A MASQUE OF MERCY . 416
BRINGS
  BEFORE THE NOT MOWING BRINGS TREES ON, . . . 264 THE LAST MOWING . 8
  IS THAT IT BRINGS THE SAME CLASS UP ON TOP. . . 363 A SEMI-REVOLUTION . 4
  SINCE DARK IS WHAT BRINGS OUT YOUR LIGHT. . . 403 SOMETHING LIKE A STAR . 5
  THE MILKWEED BRINGS UP TO MY VERY DOOR . . . 411 POD OF THE MILKWEED . 5
BRISK
  THE CHIMNEY, THOUGH, KEEPS UP A GOOD BRISK SMOKING. . . 49 A HUNDRED COLLARS . 137
BRISKLY
  AND SET OFF BRISKLY FOR SO SLOW A THING, ... 205 THE WITCH OF COOS . 86
BRISTLES
  ARE INCH-DEEP WITH THE FROSTY SPINES AND BRISTLES-- . . 42 THE MOUNTAIN . . . 53
BRITAIN
  ATHENS, ROME, FRANCE, BRITAIN, ... 437 KITTY HAWK . . . 290
BRITISH
  "ABOUT THE BRITISH ARCTIC. THAT'S WHAT COMES . . . 159 NEW HAMPSHIRE . . 23

BRITTLE
    THIS HOUSE IS FROZEN BRITTLE, ALL EXCEPT . . . . . . 150 SNOW 202
    I STRUCK THE HAND OFF BRITTLE ON THE FLOOR, ... 204 THE WITCH OF COOS . . 77
BRITTLE-DRY
    LIES IN A WINDROW, BRITTLE-DRY AND BLACK, ... 446 DOES NO ONE AT ALL EVER 26
BROAD
    SOMETHING HAD LEFT A BROAD BLACK STREAK OF GREASE . . 193 PAUL'S WIFE 69
    IN BROAD ROUND EARRINGS, GOLD AND JET WITH PEARLS, . . 256 THE LOVELY BE CHOOSERS 15
    AND BROAD ROUND SUCHLIKE BROOCH, ... 256 THE LOVELY BE CHOOSERS 16
    SITTING BY A BUSH IN BROAD SUNLIGHT . . . . 266 SITTING BY A BUSH . . T
    WITH A DOOR OF TWO BROAD BOARDS . . . . 294 A RECORD STRIDE . . 2
BROAD-BOARD
    TO BRING ME TO FOR BROAD-BOARD PANELING. . . . . . 215 A FOUNTAIN, A BOTTLE . 70
BROADEN
    ON TAKING FROM THE TOP TO BROADEN THE BASE . . . . . 298 ON TAKING FROM THE TOP T
    TO BROADEN ITS BASE. . . . . 298 ON TAKING FROM THE TOP 20
BROAD-SHOULDERED
    BROAD-SHOULDERED LITTLE SLABS THERE IN THE SUNLIGHT . . . 52 HOME BURIAL 27
BROKE
    AND BROKE IT IN HIS HAND AND TOSSED IT BY. . . . . . 38 DEATH OF THE HIRED MAN 123
    BUT I WAS GOING TO SAY WHEN TRUTH BROKE IN . . . . . 121 BIRCHES 21
    AND STANDING AT OUR LEISURE TILL THE DAY BROKE, . . . 179 THE STAR-SPLITTER . . 85
    BLEW IT ONCE OFF HIS HANDS AND ALMOST BROKE IT. . . . 194 PAUL'S WIFE 100
    HE BROKE MY TRANCE. DON'T THAT MAKE YOU SUSPICIOUS . . 202 THE WITCH OF COOS . . 16
    AND IF ONE BROKE BY ANY CHANCE, ... 273 A LONE STRIKER . . 24
    THEY BROKE THE HANDLE AND THE BINDING OFF IT. . . . . 293 AT WOODWARD'S GARDENS . 28
    THE BRIDE WHO SHARED THE CRUST HE BROKE TO EAT, . . . 359 THE LOST FOLLOWER . 23
    AS ANYONE WHO EVER BROKE ITS STEM . . . . 411 POD OF THE MILKWEED . 17
    I BROKE OFF BAFFLED. BUT ALL THE SAME, ... 420 ONE MORE BREVITY . 38
BROKEN (SEE BOULDER-BROKEN, WINTER-BROKEN)
    AND BROKEN IT, AND USED THEREFROM . . . . 21 THE TRIAL BY EXISTENCE 62
    I FOUND THAT WING BROKEN TODAY! . . . . 29 MY BUTTERFLY 43
    YOU'LL BE SURPRISED AT HIM--HOW MUCH HE'S BROKEN. . . . 39 DEATH OF THE HIRED MAN 152
    LIKE BOULDERS BROKEN OFF THE UPPER CLIFF. . . . . . 44 THE MOUNTAIN . . . 98
    THE BROKEN ONE SAW ANNE. "WHY, HERE IS ANNE. . . . . 96 THE SELF-SEEKER . . 103
    "I'VE BROKEN ANNE OF GATHERING BOUQUETS. . . . . . 98 THE SELF-SEEKER . . 147
    THE BROKEN ONE WAS TWISTED IN HIS BED. . . . . . . 100 THE SELF-SEEKER . . 208
    SO LATE-ARISING--TO THE BROKEN MOON, ... 108 OLD MAN'S WINTER NIGHT 19
    SUCH HEAPS OF BROKEN GLASS TO SWEEP AWAY . . . . . 121 BIRCHES 12
    BROKEN ACROSS IT, AND ONE EYE IS WEEPING . . . . . 122 BIRCHES 46
    THEY THROW A FOREST DOWN LESS CUT THAN BROKEN. . . . 141 THE LINE-GANG . . . 2
    OR BROKEN ITS WHITE NECK OF MUSHROOM STUFF . . . . . 149 SNOW 165
    I RECOLLECT A NIGHT OF BROKEN CLOUDS . . . . . . 179 THE STAR-SPLITTER . . 79
    THAT HAPPENS TO BE BROKEN," DAVIS SAID. . . . . . 215 A FOUNTAIN, A BOTTLE . 73
    AT BROKEN WINDOWS FLEW OUT AND IN, ... 242 NEED OF BEING VERSED . 14
    THERE WOULD BE MORE THAN OCEAN-WATER BROKEN . . . . 250 ONCE BY THE PACIFIC . 13
    WAS A SPRING WITH A BROKEN DRINKING GLASS, ... 263 THE TIMES TABLE . . 2
    IN ALL THE PASSION OF A BROKEN DROUTH. . . . . . . 337 THE WIND AND THE RAIN . 39
    OF MEANINGLESSLY BEING BROKEN OFF. . . . . 355 THE LESSON FOR TODAY . 148
    OF DETAIL, BURNED, DISSOLVED, AND BROKEN OFF . . . . 377 DIRECTIVE 3
    A BROKEN DRINKING GOBLET LIKE THE GRAIL . . . . . . 379 DIRECTIVE 57
    IT GAVE BAD DREAMS AND BROKEN SLEEP, ... 382 THE NIGHT LIGHT . . 3
    INFIRM, WORN-OUT, AND BROKEN ON ITS HANDS; . . . . . 399 THE INGENUITIES OF DEBT 9
    THE BROKEN DROUGHT . . . . 399 THE BROKEN DROUGHT . . T
    WITH A CRACK OF A BROKEN SHAFT. . . . . 444 THE DRAFT HORSE . . 10
BROKEN-OFF
    WE ALL ARE DOOMED TO BROKEN-OFF CAREERS, ... 355 THE LESSON FOR TODAY . 145
BRONZE
    TRIPLE BRONZE . . . . 348 TRIPLE BRONZE . . . T
BROOCH
    FOR WILDING BROOCH, SHALL WET YOUR BREAST . . . . . 27 A LINE-STORM SONG . . 23
    AND BROAD ROUND SUCHLIKE BROOCH, ... 256 THE LOVELY BE CHOOSERS 16
BROOD
    THEY MUST BROOD WHERE THEY FELL IN MULCH AND MIRE, . . 253 THE THATCH 25
BROODED
    IT BROODED ANT EGGS, AND HAD ONE LARGE WING, ... 172 A STAR IN A STONEBOAT . 14
BROODINESS
    AT WHICH RATE BARRING BROODINESS . . . . 280 BLUE RIBBON AT AMESBURY 31
BROODINGLY
    SO BROODINGLY SOON IN EVERY DIRECTION. . . . . . . 379 TOO ANXIOUS FOR RIVERS 13
BROOK
    TO SEEK THE BROOK IF STILL IT RAN; . . . . 18 GOING FOR WATER . . . 4
    AND BY THE BROOK OUR WOODS WERE THERE. . . . . . . 18 GOING FOR WATER . . 8
    WE HEARD, WE KNEW WE HEARD THE BROOK. . . . . . . 18 GOING FOR WATER . . 20
    AT A TALL TUFT OF FLOWERS BESIDE A BROOK, ... 22 THE TUFT OF FLOWERS . 22
    BESIDE A REEDY BROOK THE SCYTHE HAD BARED. . . . . . 22 THE TUFT OF FLOWERS . 24
    DEER-HUNTING AND TROUT-FISHING. THERE'S A BROOK . . . 42 THE MOUNTAIN . . . 45
    BUT WHAT WOULD INTEREST YOU ABOUT THE BROOK, ... 42 THE MOUNTAIN . . . 48
    THERE WERE THREE IN THE MEADOW BY THE BROOK . . . . 69 THE CODE 1
    AND BELOW ROARED A BROOK HIDDEN IN TREES, ... 76 THE GENERATIONS OF MEN 75
    THAT THE BROOK RAISES IN THE EMPTY VALLEY. . . . . . 77 THE GENERATIONS OF MEN 125
    THAT A BROOK MAKES IN SUCH A WILD DESCENT. . . . . . 78 THE GENERATIONS OF MEN 133
    WITH THE BROOK GOING BY BELOW THE YARD. . . . . . 82 THE HOUSEKEEPER . . 46
    PINE, ALDER, PASTURE, MOWING, WELL, AND BROOK. . . . . 117 IN THE HOME STRETCH . 197
    HYLA BROOK . . . . 119 HYLA BROOK . . . . T
    A BROOK TO NONE BUT WHO REMEMBER LONG. . . . . . . 119 HYLA BROOK 12
    AND SETTING SUN TO HYLA BROOK, I GAVE IT . . . . . 131 THE BONFIRE . . . 58
    I TRUSTED THE BROOK BARRIER, BUT FEARED . . . . . . 131 THE BONFIRE 74
    A NUMBER IN. BUT WHAT ABOUT THE BROOK . . . . . . 231 A BROOK IN THE CITY . 3
    I ASK AS ONE WHO KNEW THE BROOK, ITS STRENGTH . . . . 231 A BROOK IN THE CITY . 5
    A BROOK IN THE CITY . . . . 231 A BROOK IN THE CITY . T
    IS WATER WOOD TO SERVE A BROOK THE SAME? .. . . . . 231 A BROOK IN THE CITY . 12
    WITH CINDER LOADS DUMPED DOWN? A BROOK WAS THROWN . . 231 A BROOK IN THE CITY . 15
    THAT SUCH A BROOK RAN WATER. BUT I WONDER . . . . . 231 A BROOK IN THE CITY . 21
    WEST-RUNNING BROOK . . . . 243 WEST-RUNNING BROOK . T
    AND YET NOT OUT BY ANY BROOK OR RIVER, ... 245 SPRING POOLS . . . 5
    THE BROOK RUNS WEST." / "WEST-RUNNING BROOK THEN CALL IT." . 257 WEST-RUNNING BROOK . 2
    (WEST-RUNNING BROOK MEN CALL IT TO THIS DAY.) . . . . 257 WEST-RUNNING BROOK . 3

```
                                                          PAGE  TITLE                    LINE
BROOK (CONTINUED)
    WEST-RUNNING BROOK . . . . . . . . . . . . . . .      257  WEST-RUNNING BROOK  . .    1
    TO REACH THE OCEAN? IT MUST BE THE BROOK . . . .      258  WEST-RUNNING BROOK  . .    6
    WE'LL BOTH BE MARRIED TO THE BROOK. WE'LL BUILD  . .  258  WEST-RUNNING BROOK  . .   13
    IT IS YOUR BROOK! I HAVE NO MORE TO SAY." . . . .     259  WEST-RUNNING BROOK  . .   36
    "SPEAKING OF CONTRARIES, SEE HOW THE BROOK . . . .    259  WEST-RUNNING BROOK  . .   38
    IT FLOWS BESIDE US IN THIS WATER BROOK, . . . . .     259  WEST-RUNNING BROOK  . .   50
    THE BROOK RUNS DOWN IN SENDING UP OUR LIFE. . . .     260  WEST-RUNNING BROOK  . .   65
    THE SUN RUNS DOWN IN SENDING UP THE BROOK. . . .      260  WEST-RUNNING BROOK  . .   66
    YOU SAID THE BROOK WAS CALLED WEST-RUNNING BROOK."    260  WEST-RUNNING BROOK  . .   74
    IN EVERY WHEELRUT'S NOW A BROOK, . . . . . . . .      276  TWO TRAMPS IN MUD TIME    35
    BUSYING BY MY WOODS AND BROOK . . . . . . . . .       364  TRESPASS . . . . . .       7
    A BROOK THAT WAS THE WATER OF THE HOUSE, . . . . .    378  DIRECTIVE . . . . .       50
    BUT FOUND ONE IN THE DELTA OF A BROOK, . . . . . .    382  TO AN ANCIENT . . . .      5
    THAT BY BROOK POWER IN THE GARDEN . . . . . . .       397  AN IMPORTER . . . .       19
    SHE WAS LEFT OVER FROM THE BROOK FARM VENTURE. . .    494  A MASQUE OF MERCY . .     39
BROOKS
    THAN WITH BROOKS TAKEN OTHERWHERE IN SONG. . . . .    119  HYLA BROOK . . . . .      14
    WHERE THE GRIST OF THE NEW-BEGINNING BROOKS . . .     140  THE GUM-GATHERER  . .     14
    IN APRIL BY SUBSIDING MEADOW BROOKS. . . . . . .      191  PAUL'S WIFE . . . .       22
    WHEN ALL THE OTHER COUNTRY BROOKS FLOW EAST . . .     258  WEST-RUNNING BROOK. .      5
BROOK'S
    BY JUNE OUR BROOK'S RUN OUT OF SONG AND SPEED. . .    119  HYLA BROOK . . . . .       1
BROOMSTICK
    OVER THE RIDGEPOLE, 'STRIDE OF A BROOMSTICK, . . .    210  PAUPER WITCH OF GRAFTON   86
BROTH
    LIKE THE INGREDIENTS OF A WITCHES' BROTH-- . . . .    302  DESIGN . . . . . .         6
BROTHER
    THAN ON HIS BROTHER? THIRTEEN LITTLE MILES . . . .     38  DEATH OF THE HIRED MAN   125
    "I THINK HIS BROTHER OUGHT TO HELP, OF COURSE. . .     39  DEATH OF THE HIRED MAN   131
    OR ANYTHING HE LOOKED FOR FROM HIS BROTHER. . . .      39  DEATH OF THE HIRED MAN   137
    HE WON'T BE MADE ASHAMED TO PLEASE HIS BROTHER."       39  DEATH OF THE HIRED MAN   145
    MY FATHER'S BROTHER WASN'T RIGHT. THEY KEPT HIM        65  A SERVANT TO SERVANTS     88
    MY FATHER'S BROTHER, HE WENT MAD QUITE YOUNG. . .      65  A SERVANT TO SERVANTS    104
    BROTHER MESERVE.  YOU KNOW TO FIND YOUR WAY . . .     144  SNOW . . . . . .          37
    HOW CAN YOU HELP YOURSELF? / "I CALLED HIM BROTHER.   144  SNOW . . . . . .          44
    "BROTHER MESERVE, TAKE CARE, YOU'LL SCARE YOURSELF    149  SNOW . . . . . .         167
    MY BROTHER COULD NOT ALWAYS LEAVE AT HOME. . . .      196  WILD GRAPES . . . .        9
    ONE DAY MY BROTHER LED ME TO A GLADE . . . . . .      196  WILD GRAPES . . . .       19
    MY BROTHER DID THE CLIMBING; AND AT FIRST . . . .     197  WILD GRAPES . . . .       31
    TO LOUD CRIES FROM MY BROTHER OF "LET GO! . . . .     197  WILD GRAPES . . . .       46
    MY BROTHER TRIED TO MAKE ME LAUGH TO HELP ME. . .     197  WILD GRAPES . . . .       55
    "NOW YOU KNOW HOW IT FEELS," MY BROTHER SAID, . .     198  WILD GRAPES . . . .       62
    MY BROTHER SAID: "DON'T YOU WEIGH ANYTHING? . . .     199  WILD GRAPES . . . .       89
    MY BROTHER HAD BEEN NEARER RIGHT BEFORE. . . . .      199  WILD GRAPES . . . .       94
    UNSAID BETWEEN US, BROTHER, AND THIS REMAINED-- . .   222  TO E.T. . . . . .         10
    LIKE A LITTLE BROTHER . . . . . . . . . . . .         432  KITTY HAWK . . . .       118
BROTHERHOOD
    SEEK CONVERSE COMMON CAUSE AND BROTHERHOOD . . . .    350  THE LESSON FOR TODAY      9
    LEGITIMIZE THE BROTHERHOOD OF MAN, . . . . . . .      498  A MASQUE OF MERCY .      124
BROTHERLY
    AND DREAMING, AS IT WERE, HELD BROTHERLY SPEECH . .    23  THE TUFT OF FLOWERS      37
BROTHERS
    TO THE BROTHERS WRIGHT, . . . . . . . . . . .         443  KITTY HAWK . . . .       468
BROTHER'S
    WHY DOESN'T HE GO THERE? HIS BROTHER'S RICH, . . .     39  DEATH OF THE HIRED MAN   128
    AGAINST MY BROTHER'S NONSENSE. "DROP," HE SAID, . .   198  WILD GRAPES . . . .       75
    FOR KEEPER'S LEVITY: MY BROTHER'S KEEPER. . . . .     494  A MASQUE OF MERCY .       36
    WHAT DO YOU SAY TO IT, MY BROTHER'S KEEPER? . . .     512  A MASQUE OF MERCY .      513
BROUGHT
    I BROUGHT NOT HERE TO READ, IT SEEMS, BUT HOLD . .     15  WAITING . . . . .         24
    AND OFTEN THEY BROUGHT SO MUCH TO SAY . . . . . .      15  IN A VALE . . . . .       12
    THE BREEZE THREE ODORS BROUGHT, . . . . . . . .        29  MY BUTTERFLY . . . .      36
    PICKED UP A LITTLE STICK, AND BROUGHT IT BACK . .      38  DEATH OF THE HIRED MAN   122
    WHAT WAS IT BROUGHT YOU UP TO THINK IT THE THING       53  HOME BURIAL . . . .       63
    TO MEASURE HOW FAR FIFTY YEARS HAVE BROUGHT US. .      56  THE BLACK COTTAGE . .     46
    HE HAS BROUGHT THEM ALL UP ON WILD BERRIES, THEY SAY,  60  BLUEBERRIES . . . .       50
    NO MORE THAN BROUGHT US BACK INTO THE NAME." . . .     75  THE GENERATIONS OF MEN    57
    I BLAME HIS BEING BROUGHT UP BY HIS MOTHER. . . .      83  THE HOUSEKEEPER . . .     56
    WILLIS BROUGHT UP BESIDES THE BOSTON LAWYER. . . .     96  THE SELF-SEEKER . . .     91
    THAT BROUGHT HIM TO THAT CREAKING ROOM WAS AGE. .     108  OLD MAN'S WINTER NIGHT     7
    HAD BROUGHT TO REST. . . . . . . . . . . . .          110  A PATCH OF OLD SNOW        4
    OF PEOPLE BROUGHT TO WINDOWS BY A LIGHT . . . . .     129  THE BONFIRE . . . .       11
    THAT BROUGHT ME TO MY FEET TO HOLD IT BACK . . .      132  THE BONFIRE . . . .       78
    WHAT THIS MAN BROUGHT IN A COTTON SACK . . . . .      141  THE GUM-GATHERER  . .     28
    LATELY BROUGHT HOME FROM ANDOVER OR CANAAN . . . .    162  NEW HAMPSHIRE . . .      117
    FOR THE NAME MAPLE TO HAVE BROUGHT HER TO, . . . .    182  MAPLE . . . . . .         78
    AND BROUGHT DOWN SAFELY FROM THE UPPER REGIONS; .     196  WILD GRAPES . . . .       13
    "WELL, IF I HAVEN'T BROUGHT YOU TO THE FOUNTAIN, .    214  A FOUNTAIN, A BOTTLE      41
    AT LEAST I'VE BROUGHT YOU TO THE FAMOUS BOTTLE." .    214  A FOUNTAIN, A BOTTLE      42
    THEY HAD BEEN BROUGHT HOME FROM SOME PUBLISHER . .    216  A FOUNTAIN, A BOTTLE     100
    TO SEE IF IN A DREAM THEY BROUGHT OF YOU . . . . .    222  TO E.T. . . . . .          4
    WHERE ONE FALSE WING BEAT WOULD HAVE BROUGHT DOWN ALL,240  OUR SINGING STRENGTH      43
    THE COUNTRY'S SINGING STRENGTH THUS BROUGHT TOGETHER, 240  OUR SINGING STRENGTH      50
    AND BROUGHT IT OVER GLOSSY WATER, GREATER, . . . .    245  THE FREEDOM OF THE MOON   10
    AND BROUGHT OUR VARIOUS LIVES TO PASS. . . . . .      265  THE BIRTHPLACE . . .       6
    AND SO HE BROUGHT THEM TO THE VERGE OF FROST. . .     284  THE GOLD HESPERIDEE       31
    OF FIRST ONE, THEN THE OTHER, TILL IT BROUGHT . .     293  AT WOODWARD'S GARDENS      9
    THE MOUNTAINS ARE BROUGHT UP NEAR, . . . . . . .      301  VOICE WAYS . . . .         4
    THE STARS ARE BROUGHT OUT BRIGHT. . . . . . . .       301  VOICE WAYS . . . .         5
    WHAT BROUGHT THE KINDRED SPIDER TO THAT HEIGHT, . .   302  DESIGN . . . . . .        11
    IT IS VERY FAR NORTH, WE ADMIT, TO HAVE BROUGHT THE PEACH. 305  THERE ARE ROUGHLY ZONES  6
    OF BEING BROUGHT DOWN TO THE REAL." . . . . . . .     313  THE VINDICTIVES . .       91
    WE SHALL BE DRIVEN IN. I WAS BROUGHT UP . . . . .     324  BUILD SOIL . . . .       244
    I AM BROUGHT GUARANTEED YOUNG PRATTLE POEMS . . .     324  BUILD SOIL . . . .       273
    THEY BROUGHT HER TO A NAMELESS ISLE. . . . . . .      347  DISCOVERY OF MADEIRAS    110
    AND COULD IT BE BROUGHT UNDER STATE CONTROL, . . .    353  THE LESSON FOR TODAY      99
    HAS BROUGHT HER MERELY VISITING, . . . . . . . .      390  TWO LEADING LIGHTS .      26
```

BROUGHT (CONTINUED)
    WHAT SHE BROUGHT BACK WOULD AMAZE YE. . . . . 396 AN IMPORTER   2
    BEEN BROUGHT IN A SHIP . . . . 447 THE BAD ISLAND--EASTER   11
    "WE SHOULD HAVE BROUGHT THE CROWN ALONG TO PAWN." . . . 454 HOW HARD TO KEEP FROM   29
    NOTHING HAS BEEN BROUGHT OUT THAT FOR MY PART . . . . . 488 A MASQUE OF REASON . 413
    JOB MENTIONED HIM, AND SO I BROUGHT HIM IN, ... 489 A MASQUE OF REASON . 432
    IT'S NOTHING I BROUGHT ON BY WORDS OF MINE. . . . . . . 507 A MASQUE OF MERCY . 355
    NO REVOLUTION I BROUGHT ON WOULD AIM . . . . 510 A MASQUE OF MERCY . 457
    ONCE CHARGED THE NAZARENE WITH HAVING BROUGHT . . . 511 A MASQUE OF MERCY . 465
    'TWERE NOTHING NEW IF THAT WERE ALL CHRIST BROUGHT. . . 511 A MASQUE OF MERCY . 474
BROW
    LIKE TROUBLE IN THE BROW ABOVE THE EYES: . . . . . . 399 THE INGENUITIES OF DEBT   3
    HIS BROW WAS PERCEPTIBLY TROUBLE-CREASED. . . . . . 420 ONE MORE BREVITY   . . 26
BROWN
    BUT A LEAF THAT LINGERED BROWN, ...   9 A LATE WALK 10
    FIND THE BROWN BENEATH THE WHITE; . . . . 11 TO THE THAWING WIND .   5
    TO MAKE ONE TEXTURE OF FADED BROWN . . . . 25 IN HARDWOOD GROVES . .   3
    WITH HIS PIPE IN HIS MOUTH AND HIS BROWN JUG-- . . . . 77 THE GENERATIONS OF MEN 105
    BROWN LIVED AT SUCH A LOFTY FARM . . . . 137 BROWN'S DESCENT . . .   1
    "BROWN MAKES AT SUCH AN HOUR OF NIGHT! . . . . . . 138 BROWN'S DESCENT . . 33
    DON'T THINK BROWN EVER GAVE UP HOPE . . . . 139 BROWN'S DESCENT . . 54
    I'VE KEPT BROWN STANDING IN THE COLD . . . . 140 BROWN'S DESCENT . . 71
    IT COMES TO MARKET GOLDEN BROWN; . . . . 141 THE GUM-GATHERER . . 32
    AND THOSE ARE BROWN AND DRY. . . . . 260 SAND DUNES   4
    HER WELL-TURNED EGG'S BROWN STURDY SHELL, ... 281 BLUE RIBBON AT AMESBURY 34
    BRIGHT-BLACK-EYED SILVERY CREATURE, BRUSHED WITH BROWN, . 356 A MOTH SEEN IN WINTER .   3
BROWNING
    THAT'S BROWNING AND SHEER CHAPEL NON-CONFORMISM. . . . 486 A MASQUE OF REASON . 365
BROWN'S
    BROWN'S DESCENT . . . . 137 BROWN'S DESCENT . . .   T
BROWSE
    I DON'T WANT IT DREAMILY NIBBLED FOR BROWSE . . . . . 228 GOOD-BY AND KEEP COLD .   7
BRUISED
    I SMELL THE EARTH, I SMELL THE BRUISED PLANT, ... 17 THE VANTAGE POINT . 13
    NO MATTER IF NOT BRUISED OR SPIKED WITH STUBBLE, . . . 69 AFTER APPLE-PICKING . 34
BRUIT
    AND BRUIT OUR SINGING DOWN, ... 26 A LINE-STORM SONG . 18
BRUSH
    PEA BRUSH . . . . 123 PEA BRUSH . . . . .   T
    BY SETTING FIRE TO ALL THE BRUSH WE PILED . . . . . 129 THE BONFIRE   3
    A BRUSH HAD LEFT A CROOKED STROKE . . . . 233 LOOKING FOR SUNSET BIRD 17
    FROM INWARD FIRES OR BRUSH OF PASSING FEET. . . . . . 239 OUR SINGING STRENGTH . 18
    AND BRUSH THE MOW WITH THE SUMMER LOAD. . . . . . 242 NEED OF BEING VERSED . 12
    HOW ONCE IN CUTTING BRUSH ALONG THE WALL . . . . . 375 A YOUNG BIRCH . . . 12
    BENEATH THE BRUSH OF SNOW." . . . . 416 CLOSED FOR GOOD . . 24
    TO BRUSH AWAY A DISRESPECTFUL SMILE. . . . . . . 487 A MASQUE OF REASON . 391
BRUSHED
    AND BRUSHED WITH BUTTONS UPON SLEEVES, ... 135 LOCKED OUT   5
    BUT NOW HE BRUSHED THE SHAVINGS FROM HIS KNEE . . . . 188 THE AX-HELVE 94
    BEFORE I STRAIGHTENED THEM AND BRUSHED THE BARK OFF. . . 199 WILD GRAPES 88
    WAS SOMETHING BRUSHED ACROSS MY MIND . . . . 248 A PASSING GLIMPSE . .   9
    SO LOW I BRUSHED THE STRAW WITH MY SLEEVES, ... 253 THE THATCH 18
    BRIGHT-BLACK-EYED SILVERY CREATURE, BRUSHED WITH BROWN, . 356 A MOTH SEEN IN WINTER .   3
BRUSHING
    BRUSHING THE DIRT FROM HIS EYE AS HE WENT; . . . . . 25 THE DEMIURGE'S LAUGH . 11
    BRUSHING THEIR CHALKY SKULL WITH CHALKY FINGERS, . . . 206 THE WITCH OF COOS . . 128
BRUTALITY
    THE BRUTALITY AND FIGHTING . . . . 387 THE COURAGE TO BE NEW .   3
BRUTALIZES
    IT PUFFS THE FACE AND BRUTALIZES SO. . . . . 371 THE LITERATE FARMER AND 105
BRUTE
    A MAN? A BRUTE. NAKED ABOVE THE WAIST, ... 46 A HUNDRED COLLARS . . 50
    AS A BRUTE TRIBUTE OF RESPECT TO BEAUTY. . . . . . 195 PAUL'S WIFE 141
    DEARER TO HIM THAN ANY BARNYARD BRUTE, ... 283 THE GOLD HESPERIDEE . 22
    WITH A GODFORSAKEN BRUTE DESPAIR. . . . . 291 ON HEART'S BEGINNING TO 10
    SELF-TAUGHT. BUT OUR BRUTE SNARLING AND LASHING TAUGHT IT. . 320 BUILD SOIL 120
    THAT SLUMBERS IN A BRUTE. . . . . 340 THE SUBVERTED FLOWER . 34
    YOUR PROBABLE BRUTE NATURE IS DISCUSSED. . . . . . 382 TO AN ANCIENT . . . 11
BRUTUS
    HE HAD TO BE STOPPED BY THE SWORD OF BRUTUS. . . . . 454 HOW HARD TO KEEP FROM   24
BRYAN
    AND NEVER RIGHTLY UNDERSTOOD TILL BRYAN . . . . . 168 NEW HAMPSHIRE . . . 296
BUBBLE
    A BUBBLE ON A PIPESTEM, GROWING BIG. . . . . . . 283 THE GOLD HESPERIDEE . 24
    SO I COULD CATCH A BUBBLE IN ASCENT. . . . . . . 468 IN A GLASS OF CIDER .   3
    I RODE UP ON ONE TILL THE BUBBLE BURST, ... 468 IN A GLASS OF CIDER .   4
    I'D CATCH ANOTHER BUBBLE IF I WAITED. . . . . . . 468 IN A GLASS OF CIDER .   7
BUCK
    A BUCK FROM ROUND THE SPRUCE STOOD LOOKING AT THEM . 229 TWO LOOK AT TWO . . 27
    THIS WAS AN ANTLERED BUCK OF LUSTY NOSTRIL, ... 229 TWO LOOK AT TWO . . 29
    AS A GREAT BUCK IT POWERFULLY APPEARED, ... 338 THE MOST OF IT . . . 16
BUCKET
    ON EVERY TREE A BUCKET WITH A LID, ... 234 EVENING A SUGAR ORCHARD 12
BUCKETS
    STOOD UNIFORM IN BUCKETS, AND THE STEAM . . . . . 184 MAPLE 137
BUCOLIC
    "YOUR TROUBLE IS BUCOLIC LACK OF LOGIC," . . . . . 404 FROM PLANE TO PLANE .   9
BUD
    WITH SNOWBALLS CUPPED IN EVERY OPENING BUD. . . . . 239 OUR SINGING STRENGTH . 15
    (WHO CARES BUT FOR THE FUTURE OF THE BUD?), ... 337 THE WIND AND THE RAIN . 34
    THE BUD MUST BLOOM TILL BLOWSY BLOWN . . . . . 450 OUR DOOM TO BLOOM . 13
BUDDED
    THAT HAD BUDDED BEFORE THE BOUGHS WERE PILED . . . . 123 PEA BRUSH 23
    BY DEER, AND I DON'T WANT IT BUDDED BY GROUSE. . . . . 228 GOOD-BY AND KEEP COLD .   8
BUDDING
    THEY WILL COME BUDDING BOUGHS FROM TREE TO TREE, . . . 151 SNOW 230
BUDGE
    THAT WOULDN'T BUDGE, UNTIL THEY SIMPLY STRETCHED . . . 192 PAUL'S WIFE 44

BUD-INSPECTING
    CONTENT WITH BUD-INSPECTING. THEY PRESUME . . . . . . 254 A WINTER EDEN . . . 15
BUDS
    THE TREES THAT HAVE IT IN THEIR PENT-UP BUDS . . . . 245 SPRING POOLS 7
    TO SAY WHICH BUDS ARE LEAF AND WHICH ARE BLOOM. . . . 254 A WINTER EDEN . . . 16
    COUNTED THEM ALL TO THE BUDS IN THE COPSE'S DEPTH . . 343 QUEST OF PURPLE-FRINGED 23
BUGGY
    OR CREAKING WITH A BUGGY LOAD OF GRAIN. . . . . . . 378 DIRECTIVE 32
    WITH ONE FOOT ON THE DASHBOARD OF HIS BUGGY . . . . . 404 FROM PLANE TO PLANE . 19
    IN TOO FRAIL A BUGGY WE DROVE . . . . 443 THE DRAFT HORSE . . . 2
BUILD
    SILAS UP ON THE CART TO BUILD THE LOAD, ... 36 DEATH OF THE HIRED MAN 68
    TO TEACH HIM HOW TO BUILD A LOAD OF HAY----" . . . . 37 DEATH OF THE HIRED MAN 87
    WILL ROT THE BEST BIRCH FENCE A MAN CAN BUILD.' . . . 54 HOME BURIAL 93
    I HAVE TO MAKE YOU BUILD IT. COME, THE LIGHT." . . . 117 IN THE HOME STRETCH . 200
    NO MORE TO BUILD ON THERE. AND THEY, SINCE THEY . . 137 "OUT,OUT--" 33
    AND VERY SENSIBLE. NO STATE CAN BUILD . . . . 168 NEW HAMPSHIRE . . . 284
    HAS BEEN PICKED UP WITH STONES TO BUILD A WALL. . . . 172 A STAR IN A STONEBOAT . 3
    DON'T BUILD ME A CHIMNEY UPON A SHELF. . . . . . . 232 THE KITCHEN CHIMNEY . 4
    AND BUILD THE CHIMNEY CLEAR FROM THE GROUND. . . . . 232 THE KITCHEN CHIMNEY . 8
    OF CASTLES I USED TO BUILD IN AIR. . . . . 232 THE KITCHEN CHIMNEY . 20
    REALLY A VERY FEW TO BUILD AND STAY. . . . . 239 OUR SINGING STRENGTH . 24
    WE'LL BOTH BE MARRIED TO THE BROOK. WE'LL BUILD . . . 258 WEST-RUNNING BROOK . . 13
    BUILD SOIL . . . . 316 BUILD SOIL . . . . . T
    TO BUILD THE SOIL. FOR WHAT IS MORE ACCURSED . . . . 323 BUILD SOIL 217
    BUILD SOIL. TURN THE FARM IN UPON ITSELF . . . . . . 323 BUILD SOIL 234
    I WOULD BUILD MY HOUSE OF CRYSTAL, ... 384 IN THE LONG NIGHT . . 1
    ENOUGH TO BUILD HIM EVERY NIGHT A PUP TENT . . . . . 478 A MASQUE OF REASON . 132
BUILDER
    BUILDER, IN BUILDING THE LITTLE HOUSE, ... 232 THE KITCHEN CHIMNEY . 1
BUILDERS (SEE WALL-BUILDERS)
BUILDING
    IN FATHER'S BUILDING HIM A SORT OF CAGE, ... 66 A SERVANT TO SERVANTS . 113
    IT WENT FOR BUILDING STONE, AND I, AS THOUGH . . . 173 A STAR IN A STONEBOAT . 34
    BUILDER, IN BUILDING THE LITTLE HOUSE, ... 232 THE KITCHEN CHIMNEY . 1
    TO KEEP THEIR BUILDING BALANCED AT MY BREAST. . . . 267 THE ARMFUL 8
BUILT (SEE NEW-BUILT, SLAB-BUILT)
    BEFORE I BUILT A WALL I'D ASK TO KNOW . . . . . . 34 MENDING WALL 32
    THE COTTAGES LEN BUILT, SOMETIMES WE RENT THEM, . . 64 A SERVANT TO SERVANTS . 41
    I BUILT THE LOAD AND TOPPED IT OFF; OLD SANDERS . . 71 THE CODE 51
    I'D BUILT THE LOAD AND KNEW RIGHT WHERE TO FIND IT. . 71 THE CODE 71
    I'VE BEEN BUILT IN HERE LIKE A BIG CHURCH ORGAN. . . 82 THE HOUSEKEEPER . . . 38
    THOUGH HARM SHOULD COME OF IT; SO BUILT THE SCREEN . 109 THE EXPOSED NEST . . 29
    AND THEIR BUILT OR DRIVEN NESTS. . . . . 127 LONELINESS 12
    THERE HE HAD BUILT HIS STOLEN SHACK. . . . . . . 140 THE GUM-GATHERER . . 19
    HE'D BUILT A NOBLE MANSARD ROOF WITH BALLS . . . . . 160 NEW HAMPSHIRE . . . 39
    AT THAT DATE WITH A WHARF ALREADY BUILT, ... 161 NEW HAMPSHIRE . . . 84
    NOTHING NOT BUILT WITH HANDS OF COURSE IS SACRED. . . 171 NEW HAMPSHIRE . . . 394
    BEYOND THE HIGHEST CITY BUILT WITH HANDS. . . . . . 182 MAPLE 84
    AND BUILT A STONE BAPTISMAL FONT OUTDOORS-- . . . . 213 A FOUNTAIN, A BOTTLE . 10
    MY FATHER BUILT, ENCLOSED A SPRING, ... 265 THE BIRTHPLACE . . . 3
BULB
    ARE MORE DIVINE THAN ANY BULB OR ARC, ... 370 THE LITERATE FARMER AND 77
    (HE SNAPS ONE BULB OFF. PAUL SNAPS ON ANOTHER.) . . 508 A MASQUE OF MERCY . 393
    AND I'M AFRAID. (THE BULB LIGHTS SICKEN DOWN. . . . 520 A MASQUE OF MERCY . 695
BULGING
    NOW STOOD UPON ITS BULGING PROW . . . . 344 DISCOVERY OF MADEIRAS . 23
BULK
    THEIR BULK IN WATER WOULD BE FROZEN ROCK . . . . . 151 SNOW 228
    OF ELECTRICITY IN BULK THE WAY . . . . 370 THE LITERATE FARMER AND 73
BULKHEAD
    THE BULKHEAD DOUBLE DOORS WERE DOUBLE-LOCKED . . . . 204 THE WITCH OF COOS . . 55
BULLET
    A SUDDEN PASSING BULLET SHOOK IT DRY. . . . . . . 126 RANGE-FINDING . . . 12
    YET NOT ENOUGH. A BULLET THROUGH AND THROUGH, . . . 230 NOT TO KEEP 14
    THE EXIT HE COMES OUT AT LIKE A BULLET . . . . . . 277 THE WHITE-TAILED HORNET 3
    HE COMES OUT MORE UNERRING THAN A BULLET. . . . . . 277 THE WHITE-TAILED HORNET 6
    LIKE A DUM-DUM BULLET-- . . . . 427 VERSION 13
    OUR SAILORS RIDE A BULLET FOR A BOAT. . . . . . . 446 DOES NO ONE AT ALL EVER 14
BULLETS
    THE ATTIC WASPS WENT MISSING BY LIKE BULLETS. . . . 217 A FOUNTAIN, A BOTTLE . 130
    THE MORAL KIND'S AS BRAVE AS FACING BULLETS." . . . 405 FROM PLANE TO PLANE . 35
BULLING
    I'D SEEN ABOUT ENOUGH OF HIS BULLING TRICKS . . . . 71 THE CODE 47
    (WE CALL THAT BULLING). I'D BEEN WATCHING HIM. . . . 71 THE CODE 48
BUMPED
    BUMPED HEADS TOGETHER DULLY . . . . 376 ONE STEP BACKWARD TAKEN 5
BUNCH
    ONE BUNCH OF THEM, AND THERE BEGAN TO BE . . . . . 197 WILD GRAPES 25
    "TO BE A BUNCH OF FOX GRAPES, AS THEY CALL THEM, . . 198 WILD GRAPES 63
    A BUNCH OF SMALL-TIME REVOLUTIONARIES.-- . . . . . 509 A MASQUE OF MERCY . 406
BUNCHES
    HE TAKES IT OUT IN BUNCHES LIKE BIG BIRDS' NESTS. . . 37 DEATH OF THE HIRED MAN 93
    BUNCHES ALL ROUND ME GROWING IN WHITE BIRCHES, . . . 197 WILD GRAPES 26
BUNDLE
    HAD WOUND STRINGS ROUND AND ROUND IT LIKE A BUNDLE. . . 102 THE WOOD-PILE . . . 31
BUNDLES
    HE BUNDLES EVERY FORKFUL IN ITS PLACE, ... 37 DEATH OF THE HIRED MAN 89
BUNGEY
    SMALL TOWNS--LOST NATION, BUNGEY, MUDDY BOO, ... 165 NEW HAMPSHIRE . . . 187
    THERE'S BUNGEY; AND FOR BUNGEY THERE ARE TOWNS, . . . 165 NEW HAMPSHIRE . . . 208
BUNGLE
    AND EVEN THEN IT HAD TO GROPE AND BUNGLE, ... 425 ACCIDENTALLY ON PURPOSE 8
BUNKS
    THEY WERE NOT SLEEPING IN THE SHELVES OF BUNKS. . . . 175 THE CENSUS-TAKER . . 41
BUNS
    AND THE WHOLE PILE IS SLIPPING, BOTTLES, BUNS-- . . . 266 THE ARMFUL 3

BUOYANCY
  TO GIVE THEM STILL MORE BUOYANCY IN FLIGHT. . . . . 387 INNATE HELIUM . . . 5
BUOYANT
  AS IN THOSE BUOYANT BIRD BONES THIN AS PAPER, ... 387 INNATE HELIUM . . . 4
BURDEN
  AND, FOR ALL BURDEN, CARE. . . . . 7 LOVE AND A QUESTION . 4
  BUT ALL THE BURDEN OF ITS BODY SONG), ... 216 A FOUNTAIN, A BOTTLE . 114
  THEIR GATHER-ROSES BURDEN . . . . 335 CARPE DIEM 13
BUREAU
  "WHERE WILL I PUT THIS WALNUT BUREAU, LADY?" . . . . . 110 IN THE HOME STRETCH . 13
BUREAUCRATS
  FOR DISTRIBUTION TO HIS BUREAUCRATS. . . . . 518 A MASQUE OF MERCY . 645
BURIAL
  HOME BURIAL . . . . 51 HOME BURIAL . . . T
  SHE THOUGHT OF CHILDREN IN A BURIAL ROW; . . . . . . 199 PLACE FOR A THIRD . 5
  THREE CHILDREN IN A BURIAL ROW WERE SAD. . . . . . . 199 PLACE FOR A THIRD . 6
  ONE MAN'S THREE WOMEN IN A BURIAL ROW . . . . 199 PLACE FOR A THIRD . 7
  ONE KNEW OF A BURIAL HOLE . . . . 312 THE VINDICTIVES . . 56
BURIED
  GIVE THE BURIED FLOWER A DREAM; . . . . 11 TO THE THAWING WIND . 3
  BEFORE I BURIED HIM, OR I COULDN'T HAVE MANAGED. . . . 72 THE CODE 93
  APPARENTLY I HADN'T BURIED HIM . . . . 72 THE CODE 102
  AND OIL ARE BURIED OUT OF REACH?" / AGAIN . . . . . 113 IN THE HOME STRETCH . 81
  WALLS WERE ALL BURIED, TREES WERE FEW: . . . . . . 137 BROWN'S DESCENT . . 13
  HE'LL BE DEAD--DEAD AND BURIED." / "SUCH A TROUBLE! . . 146 SNOW 88
  AND SWOLLEN TIGHT AND BURIED UNDER SNOW. . . . . . 204 THE WITCH OF COOS . 56
  AND SWOLLEN TIGHT AND BURIED UNDER SNOW. . . . . . 204 THE WITCH OF COOS . 58
  HIS SMALL FIST BURIED IN THE BUSHY HIDE. . . . . . 267 RIDERS 8
  BUT CERTAIN SIGNS OF BURIED TURTLE'S EGG; . . . . . 270 THE EGG AND THE MACHINE 20
  THE WORKMEN ALL TURNED TO AND BURIED HIM. . . . . . 394 HAEC FABULA DOCET . 16
  OF ALL THE DEAD AND BURIED FROM THEIR GRAVES. . . . 484 A MASQUE OF REASON . 307
BURN
  BUT GET THE PINE OUT OF THE WAY, YOU MAY BURN . . . . 59 BLUEBERRIES . . . 17
  DIVIDE IT? NO! BUT BURN IT AS ONE PILE . . . . . 129 THE BONFIRE . . . 9
  THE PEOPLE CAN BURN IT AS LONG AS THEY PLEASE; . . . 291 ON HEART'S BEGINNING TO 16
  SHE ALWAYS HAD TO BURN A LIGHT . . . . 382 THE NIGHT LIGHT . . 1
  SAY SOMETHING! AND IT SAYS, "I BURN." . . . . . . 403 SOMETHING LIKE A STAR . 11
  WITH A LANTERN THAT WOULDN'T BURN . . . . 443 THE DRAFT HORSE . . 1
BURNED
  THE FIRE RAN AND BURNED IT ALL UP BUT THE WALL." . . . 59 BLUEBERRIES . . . 12
  VISIONS OF HALF THE WORLD BURNED BLACK . . . . . . 140 THE GUM-GATHERER . 23
  BURNED DOWN HIS FARMHOUSE FOR THE FIRE INSURANCE, . . 168 NEW HAMPSHIRE . . 302
  HE BURNED HIS HOUSE DOWN FOR THE FIRE INSURANCE . . . 177 THE STAR-SPLITTER . 16
  HE BURNED HIS HOUSE DOWN FOR THE FIRE INSURANCE . . . 177 THE STAR-SPLITTER . 30
  WHEN HE DID WHAT HE DID AND BURNED HIS HOUSE DOWN. . . 177 THE STAR-SPLITTER . 39
  BUT WON'T, SHOULD BE BURNED AT THE STAKE OR SOMETHING. . 202 THE WITCH OF COOS . 6
  OF DETAIL, BURNED, DISSOLVED, AND BROKEN OFF . . . . 377 DIRECTIVE . . . 3
  THAT WOMEN PROPHETS SHOULD BE BURNED AS WITCHES, . . 476 A MASQUE OF REASON . 89
  BUT SHE WAS BURNED FOR WITCHCRAFT. / THAT IS NOT . . 477 A MASQUE OF REASON . 102
  GET BURNED FOR PROPHECY, MEN ALMOST NEVER. . . . . 478 A MASQUE OF REASON . 150
BURNING
  THERE WE BOWED US IN THE BURNING, ... 13 ROSE POGONIAS . . 9
  WITH THE SLOW SMOKELESS BURNING OF DECAY. . . . . 102 THE WOOD-PILE . . 40
  AT THE FLAME BURNING DOWNWARD AS HE SUCKS IT." . . . 112 IN THE HOME STRETCH . 65
  WITH SMELL OF BURNING ON EVERY PLUME, ... 120 BOND AND FREE . . 14
  OF BURNING FATNESS, AND THEN NOTHING BUT . . . . . 130 THE BONFIRE . . . 24
  BY BURNING OUT, AND BEFORE IT BURNS OUT . . . . . 130 THE BONFIRE . . . 26
  AND BURNING TO YIELD FLOWERS INSTEAD OF GRAIN, . . . 173 A STAR IN A STONEBOAT . 22
  AND BURNING CLOVE. . . . . 227 TO EARTHWARD . . . 24
  AND GOES DOWN BURNING INTO THE GULF BELOW, ... 249 ACCEPTANCE . . . 2
  THEY CAN KEEP IT BURNING AS LONG AS THEY PLEASE; . . 291 ON HEART'S BEGINNING TO 24
  THAT AT ONCE KEPT YOU BURNING LOW AND HID YOU. . . . 351 THE LESSON FOR TODAY . 25
  YOU MEAN THE BURNING BUSH? / THE CHRISTMAS TREE. . . 473 A MASQUE OF REASON . 6
  THE MYRRH TREE GIVES IT. SMELL THE ROSIN BURNING? . . 473 A MASQUE OF REASON . 9
  NOW SOMEONE CAN LIGHT UP THE BURNING BUSH . . . . 490 A MASQUE OF REASON . 458
  DOWN BURNING SKEPTICS IN THE CELLAR FURNACE . . . 516 A MASQUE OF MERCY . 603
BURNING-GLASS
  A BURNING-GLASS THEY COULD NOT UNDERSTAND . . . . 293 AT WOODWARD'S GARDENS . 3
  THEY MIGHT NOT UNDERSTAND A BURNING-GLASS. . . . . 294 AT WOODWARD'S GARDENS . 35
BURNS
  WHERE YOUR FACE BURNS AND TICKLES WITH THE COBWEBS . . 122 BIRCHES 45
  HOW LOVE BURNS THROUGH THE PUTTING IN THE SEED . . . 124 PUTTING IN THE SEED . 10
  BY BURNING OUT, AND BEFORE IT BURNS OUT . . . . . 130 THE BONFIRE . . . 26
  BUT WHERE THIS OLD WALL BURNS A SUNNY CHEEK, . . . 246 ATMOSPHERE . . . 2
  CONTEMPLATE TRUTH UNTIL IT BURNS YOUR EYES OUT. . . 517 A MASQUE OF MERCY . 630
BURNT
  WHOSE LEAVES ALREADY ARE BURNT WITH FROST, ... 28 OCTOBER 19
  NOT FIREWEED LOVING WHERE WOODS HAVE BURNT-- . . . 248 A PASSING GLIMPSE . 6
BURR
  THEODOSIA BURR . . . . 432 KITTY HAWK . . . 148
  BURR HAD FOR HIS DAUGHTER: . . . . 433 KITTY HAWK . . . 160
BURROUGHS
  I HAD A LETTER FROM BURROUGHS--DID I TELL YOU?-- . . 95 THE SELF-SEEKER . . 85
BURROW
  A TWO-DOOR BURROW I DUG. . . . . 282 A DRUMLIN WOODCHUCK . 8
  ABOUT MY CREVICE AND BURROW. . . . . 282 A DRUMLIN WOODCHUCK . 32
BURROWING
  AND I WAS BURROWING IN DEEP FOR WARMTH, ... 149 SNOW 178
BURRS
  BETWEEN TWO BURRS ON THE MAP . . . . 367 A SERIOUS STEP LIGHTLY 1
  THE BURRS WERE HILLS, THE SNAKE WAS A STREAM, . . . 367 A SERIOUS STEP LIGHTLY 3
BURST
  BURST INTO MY NARROW STALL; . . . . 11 TO THE THAWING WIND . 11
  DOOR-FILLING MEN BURST IN AND SEIZED THE STOVE. . . . 113 IN THE HOME STRETCH . 83
  AND COULD IN ONE BURST OVERWHELM . . . . 390 TWO LEADING LIGHTS . 8
  NO BURST OF NUCLEAR PHENOMENON . . . . 397 THE PLANNERS . . . 4
  WILL FIND RELIEF IN ONE BURST. YOU SHALL SEE. . . . 398 BURSTING RAPTURE . 13
  IT WAS FAIRLY BURST . . . . 426 A NEVER NAUGHT SONG . 4

```
                                                     PAGE TITLE              LINE
BURST (CONTINUED)
    IN A FLOWERY BURST . . . . . . . . . . . . . . . 445 PERIL OF HOPE  . . .   6
    I RODE UP ON ONE TILL THE BUBBLE BURST, . . . . . 468 IN A GLASS OF CIDER .   4
BURSTING
    BURSTING RAPTURE . . . . . . . . . . . . . . . . 398 BURSTING RAPTURE   . . T
BURSTS
    IT BURSTS AGAINST US AT THE CHIMNEY MOUTH, . . . . 150 SNOW  . . . . .  . 207
BURY
    TO BURY HIM HAD HURT HIS DIGNITY. . . . . . . . .  72 THE CODE  . . . . . 104
    AND BURY IN SOLID SAND . . . . . . . . . . . . . 260 SAND DUNES  . . . .   7
    WHOSE OFFICE IT IS TO BURY . . . . . . . . . . . 288 DEPARTMENTAL . . . .  26
BURYING
    IF I CAN LEAVÉ OFF BURYING THE WHITE . . . . . . 124 PUTTING IN THE SEED .   3
BUSH
    HE SAID I COULD HAVE TO BUSH MY PEAS. . . . . . . 123 PEA BRUSH . . . . .   4
    SITTING BY A BUSH IN BROAD SUNLIGHT . . . . . . . 266 SITTING BY A BUSH  . T
    THEN DESCENDED OF OLD ON THE BUSH. . . . . . . . 266 SITTING BY A BUSH  .  16
    OR RUSTLE IN A BUSH OR TREE. . . . . . . . . . . 328 A MISSIVE MISSILE  .  40
    STEEPLE BUSH . . . . . . . . . . . . . . . . . . 373 STEEPLE BUSH . . . .  T
    AND STEEPLE BUSH, NOT GOOD TO EAT, . . . . . . . 376 SOMETHING FOR HOPE .   3
    THROUGH MEADOWSWEET AND STEEPLE BUSH . . . . . . 376 SOMETHING FOR HOPE .   7
    YOU MEAN THE BURNING BUSH? / THE CHRISTMAS TREE. . 473 A MASQUE OF REASON .   6
    NOW SOMEONE CAN LIGHT UP THE BURNING BUSH . . . . 490 A MASQUE OF REASON . 458
BUSHEL
    IN BUSHEL LOTS--DOESN'T COME ON THE MARKET. . . .  97 THE SELF-SEEKER . . 130
    AT THIRTY CENTS A BUSHEL. GIVE ME SHEEP. . . . . 316 BUILD SOIL  . . . .  12
BUSHES
    UNTIL THE BUSHES ALL ALONG ITS BANKS . . . . . .  42 THE MOUNTAIN . . . .  52
    "WHY, THERE HASN'T BEEN TIME FOR THE BUSHES TO GROW. . .  59 BLUEBERRIES . . . .  13
    ALONG THE BUSHES AT THE ROADSIDE--A MAN'S FACE. . .  89 THE FEAR . . . . .  11
    WHAT WAS HE STANDING STILL FOR IN THE BUSHES?" . . .  90 THE FEAR . . . . .  28
    AROUND US, LOOKING OUT OF TREES AND BUSHES . . . .  90 THE FEAR . . . . .  46
    AND LIE IN STONES AND BUSHES UNRETRIEVED. . . . . 216 A FOUNTAIN, A BOTTLE . 116
BUSH'S
    AND THAT FROM NO ESPECIAL BUSH'S HEIGHT, . . . . . 302 A BIRD SINGING IN SLEEP   4
BUSHY
    HIS SMALL FIST BURIED IN THE BUSHY HIDE. . . . . . 267 RIDERS . . . . . .   8
BUSINESS
    MY BUSINESS IS TO FIND WHAT PEOPLE WANT: . . . . .  48 A HUNDRED COLLARS . 103
    "IT'S BUSINESS, BUT I CAN'T SAY IT'S NOT FUN. . . .  49 A HUNDRED COLLARS . 123
    FOR THEN THERE WOULD BE BUSINESS. AS IT IS, . . . .  64 A SERVANT TO SERVANTS  40
    THE HAND THAT KNOWS HIS BUSINESS WON'T BE TOLD . . .  70 THE CODE  . . . .  22
    THAN FOLKS LIKE US HAVE ANY BUSINESS WITH. . . . .  85 THE HOUSEKEEPER . . 112
    "YOU'RE NOT TO COME," SHE SAID. "THIS IS MY BUSINESS. . .  90 THE FEAR . . . . .  35
    "WHOSE BUSINESS--IF I TAKE IT ON MYSELF, . . . . . 142 THE VANISHING RED .   6
    WHOSE BUSINESS--BUT WHY TALK ROUND THE BARN?-- . . 142 THE VANISHING RED .   7
    NOT TO EXPLORE TOO DEEP IN OTHERS' BUSINESS. . . . 162 NEW HAMPSHIRE  . . .  92
    SHE WASN'T ANYBODY ELSE'S BUSINESS, . . . . . . . 196 PAUL'S WIFE  . . . 152
    OF HAVING INTERFERED IN THE HUSE BUSINESS. . . . . 209 PAUPER WITCH OF GRAFTON  75
    OUR BUSINESS FIRST'S UP ATTIC WITH HER BOOKS." . . 216 A FOUNTAIN, A BOTTLE  88
    MY BUSINESS AWHILE IS WITH DIFFERENT TREES, . . . 228 GOOD-BY AND KEEP COLD . 21
    HIS BUSINESS WASN'T WITH SUCH. . . . . . . . . . 288 DEPARTMENTAL . . . .   5
    AND MADE FUN OF BY BUSINESS, LAW, AND ART; . . . . 322 BUILD SOIL . . . . 190
    SHOULD BE ENOUGH TO SET YOU UP IN BUSINESS-- . . . 454 HOW HARD TO KEEP FROM  34
    HE HAS HIS BUSINESS HE MUST BE ABOUT. . . . . . . 489 A MASQUE OF REASON . 431
    OF BUSINESS, MIGHT INCREASE INTO A MADNESS. . . . 503 A MASQUE OF MERCY . 249
BUSINESSES
    ALL, NOT JUST GREAT EXPLOITING BUSINESSES. . . . . 319 BUILD SOIL . . . .  96
BUSINESSLIKE
    SO MUCH MORE BUSINESSLIKE THAN BUSINESSMEN. . . . 164 NEW HAMPSHIRE  . . 173
BUSINESSMAN
    THE MAN FREE LOVE, THE BUSINESSMAN FREE TRADE, . . 319 BUILD SOIL . . . . 112
BUSINESSMEN
    SO MUCH MORE BUSINESSLIKE THAN BUSINESSMEN. . . . 164 NEW HAMPSHIRE  . . 173
BUSY
    IN THE MEADOW, BUSY WITH THE NEW-CUT HAY, . . . . 109 THE EXPOSED NEST . .   3
    BUSY OUTDOORS BY LANTERN-LIGHT WITH SOMETHING . . . 176 THE STAR-SPLITTER .   4
    SO BUSY YOURSELF WITH OTHER THINGS . . . . . . . 376 SOMETHING FOR HOPE .  10
    I OWN HE DOES LOOK BUSY WHEN THE SUN . . . . . . 407 FROM PLANE TO PLANE  104
BUSYING
    BUSYING BY MY WOODS AND BROOK  . . . . . . . . . 364 TRESPASS . . . . . .   7
BUT---NOT INDEXED
BUTCHER
    FIRST BY A BUTCHER, THEN A COOK,  . . . . . . . . 467 QUANDARY . . . . .  23
BUTT
    THEY'D SLICED THE FIRST SLAB OFF A BIG BUTT LOG, . . . 193 PAUL'S WIFE  . . . .  62
    HE SITS BACK ON HIS FUNDAMENTAL BUTT . . . . . . 269 THE BEAR . . . . .  26
    BUT IN A BUTT OF MALMSEY I WAS DROWNED. . . . . . 510 A MASQUE OF MERCY . 449
BUTTER
    THERE'S BUTTER SOMEWHERE, TOO." / "LET'S REND THE BREAD. . 115 IN THE HOME STRETCH  . 145
    RECIPES FOR TEA WITH BUTTER, . . . . . . . . . . 396 AN IMPORTER  . . . .   5
BUTTERFLIES
    CALLING ALL BUTTERFLIES OF EVERY RACE . . . . . . 411 POD OF THE MILKWEED .   1
    IT MAKES THE BUTTERFLIES INTEMPERATE. . . . . . . 411 POD OF THE MILKWEED .  22
    WHERE HAVE THOSE FLOWERS AND BUTTERFLIES ALL GONE . . 412 POD OF THE MILKWEED .  51
BUTTERFLY (SEE BLUE-BUTTERFLY)
    ON NOISELESS WING A BEWILDERED BUTTERFLY, . . . . .  22 THE TUFT OF FLOWERS  12
    THE BUTTERFLY AND I HAD LIT UPON, . . . . . . . .  23 THE TUFT OF FLOWERS  29
    MY BUTTERFLY . . . . . . . . . . . . . . . . . .  28 MY BUTTERFLY . . . .  T
    A BUTTERFLY ITS FALL HAD DISPOSSESSED, . . . . . . 126 RANGE-FINDING  . . .   6
    IN HERE AND THERE A BIRD, OR BUTTERFLY, . . . . . 220 FRAGMENTARY BLUE . .   2
    OF MINGLED BUTTERFLY AND FLOWER DUST . . . . . . 412 POD OF THE MILKWEED .  28
BUTTON
    SUMMONING SPIRTS ISN'T "BUTTON, BUTTON, . . . . . 202 THE WITCH OF COOS  .   7
    WHO'S GOT THE BUTTON," I WOULD HAVE THEM KNOW. . . 202 THE WITCH OF COOS  .   8
    HAND ME MY BUTTON BOX--IT MUST BE THERE.) . . . . 205 THE WITCH OF COOS  .  81
BUTTONED
    A BUTTONED HAIRCLOTH LOUNGE SPREAD SCROLLING ARMS . . . .  55 THE BLACK COTTAGE . .  22
```

BUTTONING (SEE A-BUTTONING)
BUTTONS
     FUMBLING THE BUTTONS IN A WELL-STARCHED SHIRT. . . . . 46 A HUNDRED COLLARS . . 52
     AND BRUSHED WITH BUTTONS UPON SLEEVES, ... 135 LOCKED OUT 5
     AMONG THE BUTTONS POURED OUT IN HER LAP. . . . . 207 THE WITCH OF COOS . . 153
BUY
     ENOUGH AT LEAST TO BUY TOBACCO WITH, ... 35 DEATH OF THE HIRED MAN 20
     THEY SELL IN THE STORE AND BUY SHOES FOR THEIR FEET." . . 61 BLUEBERRIES 53
     I HAD TO TAKE BY FORCE RATHER THAN BUY. . . . . 163 NEW HAMPSHIRE . . 151
     "I'LL HAVE ONE IF I SELL MY FARM TO BUY IT." . . . . . 177 THE STAR-SPLITTER . . 25
     TO BUY ELIZA A PLOT TO LIE ALONE IN: . . . . 202 PLACE FOR A THIRD . . 80
     BUY ME ENOUGH FOR A FULL-LENGTH CHIMNEY, ... 232 THE KITCHEN CHIMNEY . 7
     'TWAS TO BUY HIMSELF OFF HIS DOOM. . . . . 310 THE VINDICTIVES . . . 6
     HAVE TO SELL YOU MY APPLES AND BUY YOURS? . . . . 321 BUILD SOIL . . . 165
     AND THERE MIGHT BE A HOUSE WE COULD BUY . . . . 367 A SERIOUS STEP LIGHTLY 7
     WHAT YOU GET IS WHAT TO BUY. . . . . 469 FOUR-ROOM SHACK... . . 6
BUYER
     TO THE FIRST BUYER COMING BY WHO ASKED . . . . 454 HOW HARD TO KEEP FROM 39
BUYERS
     TO ADVERTISE OUR FARMS TO CITY BUYERS, ... 316 BUILD SOIL . . . 23
BUYER'S
     WITH A BUYER'S MODERATION, "THAT WOULD DO." . . . . . . 107 CHRISTMAS TREES . . . 38
BUYING
     THE LAWYER DON'T KNOW WHAT IT IS HE'S BUYING: . . . . . 93 THE SELF-SEEKER . . . 11
BUYS
     CONTROL OF WHAT IT SELLS OR WHAT IT BUYS. . . . . 324 BUILD SOIL . . . 248
BUZZ
     YOU CAN HEAR THE SMALL BUZZ SAWS WHINE, THE BIG SAW . . 94 THE SELF-SEEKER . . . 41
     THE BUZZ SAW SNARLED AND RATTLED IN THE YARD . . . . . 136 "OUT,OUT--" 1
BY---NOT INDEXED
BYROAD
     IN AN OLD CELLAR HOLE IN A BYROAD . . . . 73 THE GENERATIONS OF MEN 8
BYZANTINE
     HERE BY OUR ATOLL. / SOMETHING BYZANTINE. . . . . . . 474 A MASQUE OF REASON . . 20

C

C (SEE A-B-C)
CABIN
     HIS GREAT GAUNT FIGURE FILLED HIS CABIN DOOR, ... 292 FIGURE IN THE DOORWAY . 7
     A CABIN IN THE CLEARING . . . . 413 A CABIN IN THE CLEARING T
CABLE
     WITH SHOUTS AFAR TO PULL THE CABLE TAUT, ... 141 THE LINE-GANG . . . 9
CABLES
     AND STRAINING CABLES WET WITH SILVER DEW. . . . . . . 126 RANGE-FINDING . . . 11
CAESAR
     WITNESS HOW HARD IT WAS FOR JULIUS CAESAR. . . . . . . 454 HOW HARD TO KEEP FROM 22
CAESAR'S
     IT IS AS TRUE AS CAESAR'S NAME WAS KAISER . . . . . . 363 AN EQUALIZER 1
CAF
     IT COST HER FOR ENORMOUS CAF. . . . . 452 A-WISHING WELL . . . 42
CAGE (SEE BACK-CAGE)
     IN FATHER'S BUILDING HIM A SORT OF CAGE, ... 66 A SERVANT TO SERVANTS . 113
     I EMPTIED MY CAGE . . . . 241 THE LOCKLESS DOOR . . 18
     MAN ACTS MORE LIKE THE POOR BEAR IN A CAGE, ... 269 THE BEAR 13
     LIKE WAKING IN A CAGE OF SILVER BARS. . . . . 290 OLD BARN AT THE BOTTOM 27
     ONCE SHOWED TWO LITTLE MONKEYS IN A CAGE . . . . 293 AT WOODWARD'S GARDENS . 2
CAGED
     AND THE CAGED YELLOW BIRD . . . . 10 WIND AND WINDOW FLOWER 7
CAIRNSES
     BACK THERE IN 1953 WITH THE HUNTINGTON CAIRNSES . . . . 428 KITTY HAWK 0
CAJOLED
     BEEN CAJOLED AND COERCED . . . . 448 THE BAD ISLAND--EASTER 25
CAKE
     ON AN ICE CAKE. . . . . 211 AN EMPTY THREAT . . . 20
     AND CAKE THEIR CONCRETE DIRT OFF IN THE STREETS." . . . 506 A MASQUE OF MERCY . . 334
CAKED
     WHOLE CAPES CAKED OFF IN SLICES. . . . . 377 ONE STEP BACKWARD TAKEN 7
CALCULATE
     BUT I DON'T CALCULATE TO SELL MY WOOL. . . . . 316 BUILD SOIL 14
CALCULATED
     THAT MIGHT BE CALCULATED TO POSTPONE . . . . 190 THE GRINDSTONE . . . 63
     THAT ARE CALCULATED TO SOOTHE THEM OUT OF THEIR WITS, . . 287 A ROADSIDE STAND . . 29
     IT GIVES A SENSE OF LETUP CALCULATED . . . . 475 A MASQUE OF REASON . . 44
CALCULATION
     AS MAY BE SHOWN BY A SIMPLE CALCULATION. . . . . 107 CHRISTMAS TREES . . . 57
CALF
     I'M GOING OUT TO FETCH THE LITTLE CALF . . . . 1 THE PASTURE 5
CALIFORNIA
     TALK CALIFORNIA--A STATE SO BLESSED, ... 159 NEW HAMPSHIRE . . . 17
     FROM SELLING THINGS IN CALIFORNIA. . . . . 160 NEW HAMPSHIRE . . . 38
     ONCE IN A CALIFORNIA SIERRA . . . . 443 AUSPEX 1
CALIFORNIAN
     I MET A CALIFORNIAN WHO WOULD . . . . 159 NEW HAMPSHIRE . . . 16
CALIPERS
     AND AS IT MEASURED IN HER CALIPERS, ... 301 MOON COMPASSES . . . 6
CALL
     AND THE SWEET PANG IT COST ME NOT TO CALL . . . . . . 16 A DREAM PANG 11
     THE CROWS ABOVE THE FOREST CALL; . . . . 27 OCTOBER 5
     "WE CALL IT HOR: I DON'T KNOW IF THAT'S RIGHT." . . . . 43 THE MOUNTAIN . . . 91
     HE WAS ONE OF THE KIND SPORTS CALL A SPIDER, ... 70 THE CODE 33
     (WE CALL THAT BULLING). I'D BEEN WATCHING HIM. . . . . 71 THE CODE 48
     CALL HER NAUSICAA, THE UNAFRAID . . . . 78 THE GENERATIONS OF MEN 152
     CALL HER NAUSICAA, AND TAKE A TIMBER . . . . 79 THE GENERATIONS OF MEN 160
     NOR GRANNY'S, SURELY. CALL UP ONE OF THEM. . . . . . . 79 THE GENERATIONS OF MEN 175
     WAMPUM, I CALL IT. MIND, WE DON'T COMPLAIN. . . . . . . 86 THE HOUSEKEEPER . . 153

	PAGE	TITLE	LINE

CALL (CONTINUED)

FOR THE NEXT FORTY SUMMERS--CALL IT FORTY.	95	THE SELF-SEEKER	69
THAT END ALL. AND IT'S SCARCE ENOUGH TO CALL	111	IN THE HOME STRETCH	34
WE STAND HERE DREAMING. HURRY! CALL THEM BACK!"	113	IN THE HOME STRETCH	77
TO DRAG YOU OUT FOR JUST A GOOD-NIGHT CALL	117	IN THE HOME STRETCH	188
WHAT WAS IT? DID YOU CALL ME BY MY NAME?	118	THE TELEPHONE	15
CALL IT A DAY, I WISH THEY MIGHT HAVE SAID	136	"OUT,OUT--"	10
IF YOU LIKE TO CALL SUCH A SOUND A LAUGH.	142	THE VANISHING RED	3
I THINK I'LL JUST CALL UP MY WIFE AND TELL HER	143	SNOW	11
I'LL CALL HER SOFTLY SO THAT IF SHE'S WISE	143	SNOW	13
CALL YOU TO ASK YOU TO INVITE ME HOME.--"	143	SNOW	27
WHY DID I CALL HIM THAT?" / "IT'S RIGHT ENOUGH.	144	SNOW	45
"CHRISTIAN ENOUGH I SHOULD CALL THAT MYSELF.	144	SNOW	48
TO THEIRS. I'M GOING TO CALL HIS WIFE AGAIN."	145	SNOW	75
DO YOU CALL THAT?" SHE SAID. / "HE HAD THE GIFT	151	SNOW	248
"DID SHE CALL YOU OR YOU CALL HER?" / "SHE ME.	152	SNOW	272
"AND LEAVE THE CHILDREN?" / "WAIT AND CALL AGAIN.	154	SNOW	307
THOUGHT HE'D JUST CALL TO TELL US IT WAS SNOWING.	155	SNOW	340
I CALL HER OLD. SHE HAS ONE FAMILY	161	NEW HAMPSHIRE	70
AND SHE HAS ONE I DON'T KNOW WHAT TO CALL HIM,	162	NEW HAMPSHIRE	100
"DON'T CALL IT BLAMED; THERE ISN'T ANYTHING	177	THE STAR-SPLITTER	22
"NO DOUBT YOU'VE HEARD THE OFFICE CALL ME MABEL.	182	MAPLE	90
I HAVE TO LET THEM CALL ME WHAT THEY LIKE."	182	MAPLE	91
"TO BE A BUNCH OF FOX GRAPES, AS THEY CALL THEM,	198	WILD GRAPES	63
SHE COULD CALL UP TO PASS A WINTER EVENING,	202	THE WITCH OF COOS	5
TO CALL IT DAY	218	I WILL SING YOU ONE-O	6
THROUGH SOME DELAY, AND CALL YOU TO YOUR FACE	222	TO E.T.	6
(IF CERTAIN IT WOULDN'T BE IDLE TO CALL	228	GOOD-BY AND KEEP COLD	9
WITH BUT ONE CHIMNEY IT CAN CALL ITS OWN;	248	THE COCOON	6
BUT NOT TO CALL ME BACK OR SAY GOOD-BY;	255	ACQUAINTED WITH NIGHT	10
THE BROOK RUNS WEST." / "WEST-RUNNING BROOK THEN CALL IT."	257	WEST-RUNNING BROOK	2
(WEST-RUNNING BROOK MEN CALL IT TO THIS DAY.)	257	WEST-RUNNING BROOK	3
("YOU COULDN'T CALL IT LIVING, FOR IT AIN'T"),	263	THE INVESTMENT	2
I NEEDN'T CALL YOU BY NAME.	264	THE LAST MOWING	19
WHERE NOBODY CAN CALL YOU CRONE.	307	PROVIDE, PROVIDE	12
THEY MADE HIM SEND OUT A CALL	310	THE VINDICTIVES	10
YOUR POEMS ON A FARM AND CALL THAT FARMING.	316	BUILD SOIL	18
A FIVE-YEAR PLAN I CALL SO NOT BECAUSE	323	BUILD SOIL	225
YOU CALL THIS THINKING, BUT IT'S WALKING.	325	TO A THINKER	5
ALMOST LIKE A CALL TO COME IN	334	COME IN	15
WHEN CALL OR LAUGHTER CARRIED IT ALOFT.	339	NEVER WOULD BIRDS' SONG	8
IT WAS THEN HER MOTHER'S CALL	340	THE SUBVERTED FLOWER	35
WE HAVE TODAY AND I COULD CALL THEIR NAME	351	THE LESSON FOR TODAY	31
I CAN JUST HEAR YOU CALL YOUR PALACE CLASS:	353	THE LESSON FOR TODAY	84
WITH INCLINATIONS IT COULD CALL ITS OWN.	357	A CONSIDERABLE SPECK	9
THE ESQUIMAUX SHOULD CALL,	384	IN THE LONG NIGHT	10
AND ALL WE CALL AMERICAN.	418	AMERICA IS HARD TO SEE	60
WITH AN AIR THAT SAID, "I HAVE PAID MY CALL.	420	ONE MORE BREVITY	46
(THINK OF PRESUMING TO CALL HIM GUS),	421	ONE MORE BREVITY	59
THERE IS A CALL TO LIFE A LITTLE STERNER,	424	FOR JOHN F. KENNEDY	66
INTO WHAT THEY CALL	435	KITTY HAWK	215
WE CAN CALL OUR OWN	440	KITTY HAWK	380
IT SEEMED TO COMFORT US TO CALL IT CORN.	446	DOES NO ONE AT ALL EVER	9
YOU MAY CALL ME A FOOL,	450	OBJECTION TO BE STEPPED	12
IT SEEMS YOU CALL QUINTESSENCE QUINTESSENCE."	455	HOW HARD TO KEEP FROM	51
YOU CALL IT MINE. / WE GROPED IT OUT TOGETHER.	480	A MASQUE OF REASON	188
WHY DO YOU CALL YOURSELF A STAR-CROSSED LOVER?	510	A MASQUE OF MERCY	450
YES, CALL ME PAGAN, PAUL, AS IF YOU MEANT IT.	513	A MASQUE OF MERCY	524

CALLED (SEE SO-CALLED)

THEY HAVE TO TAKE YOU IN." / "I SHOULD HAVE CALLED IT	38	DEATH OF THE HIRED MAN	119
WOULD EVIDENCE OF HAVING BEEN CALLED LADY	111	IN THE HOME STRETCH	22
ONCE ON THE KIND OF DAY CALLED "WEATHER BREEDER,"	125	AN ENCOUNTER	1
WHEN HE CALLED HER--	129	THE IMPULSE	16
I CALLED YOU UP TO SAY GOOD-NIGHT FROM HERE	143	SNOW	17
HOW CAN YOU HELP YOURSELF? / "I CALLED HIM BROTHER.	144	SNOW	44
THAT'S ALL YOU EVER HEARD HIM CALLED ROUND HERE.	144	SNOW	46
THIS IS CALLED HAVING AN IDEA TO SELL.	160	NEW HAMPSHIRE	33
A COMPANY WE CALLED THE WHITE CORPUSCLES,	163	NEW HAMPSHIRE	139
POPLIN, STILL CORNERS (SO CALLED NOT BECAUSE	165	NEW HAMPSHIRE	188
I'M WHAT IS CALLED A SENSIBILITIST,	166	NEW HAMPSHIRE	232
THAT'S WHAT IS CALLED A STRETCHER. BUT I GUESS	192	PAUL'S WIFE	49
PAUL WAS WHAT'S CALLED A TERRIBLE POSSESSOR.	195	PAUL'S WIFE	150
BUT SMITH, OR SOMEONE, CALLED THEM OFF THE MOUNTAIN	213	A FOUNTAIN, A BOTTLE	11
I CALLED THE FIREMAN WITH A CAREFUL VOICE	234	EVENING A SUGAR ORCHARD	3
YOU SAID THE BROOK WAS CALLED WEST-RUNNING BROOK."	260	WEST-RUNNING BROOK	74
THERE'S A PLACE CALLED FARAWAY MEADOW	264	THE LAST MOWING	1
THEIR NAME WAS CALLED THE GOLD HESPERIDEE.	283	THE GOLD HESPERIDEE	18
IT COULDN'T BE CALLED UNGENTLE.	289	DEPARTMENTAL	42
GET CALLED AS MUCH IN CLASHES OF AMBITION.	317	BUILD SOIL	40
CALLED GETTING OUT OF THE WRONG SIDE OF BED.	371	THE LITERATE FARMER AND	107
WHAT CATULLUS CALLED	434	KITTY HAWK	198
(PERHAPS SO CALLED BECAUSE IT MAY HAVE RISEN ONCE)	447	THE BAD ISLAND--EASTER	5
BUT I CALLED IT A NAME.	450	OBJECTION TO BE STEPPED	8
TO A PLANT CALLED THE SILPHION,	452	A-WISHING WELL	49
I PICKED YOU OUT A HORSE CALLED SAFETY THIRD,	457	HOW HARD TO KEEP FROM	123
FREE VERSE, SO CALLED, IS REALLY CHERISHED PROSE,	460	HOW HARD TO KEEP FROM	221
I NOTICED WHEN SHE CALLED UP SAMUEL	477	A MASQUE OF REASON	99
(I HOPE YOU KNOW THE GAME CALLED TWENTY QUESTIONS.)	484	A MASQUE OF REASON	314
I'D WANT TO BE MORE CERTAIN I WAS CALLED,	503	A MASQUE OF MERCY	270

CALLING

OF CAPITAL, AND CALLING THRIFT A MISER).	363	AN EQUALIZER	4
CALLING ALL BUTTERFLIES OF EVERY RACE	411	POD OF THE MILKWEED	1
OF WHAT IT IS BY CALLING IT A POOL	447	DOES NO ONE AT ALL EVER	41
(I WON'T HAVE KEEPER CALLING IT RELIGION.)	503	A MASQUE OF MERCY	256

CALLOUSED

TO CHAFE AND SHUFFLE IN MY CALLOUSED PALM	174	A STAR IN A STONEBOAT	52

CALLS

WHEN A FRIEND CALLS TO ME FROM THE ROAD	124	A TIME TO TALK	1

CALLS (CONTINUED)
    WHAT'LL YOU BET HE EVER CALLS AGAIN?" . . . . 156 SNOW 350
CALLUS
    I SEE THE CALLUS ON HIS SOLE, ... 392 A CLIFF DWELLING . . 10
CALM
    HELD IT A MOMENT WHERE IT WAS, TO CALM ME, ... 185 THE AX-HELVE . . . 12
    IN HOPES OF SEEING THE CALM OF HEAVEN BREAK . . . . 268 ON LOOKING UP BY CHANCE 14
    THAT CALM SEEMS CERTAINLY SAFE TO LAST TONIGHT. . . . 268 ON LOOKING UP BY CHANCE 16
    SHE DREW BACK; HE WAS CALM: . . . . 339 THE SUBVERTED FLOWER . 1
    AND CALM YOURSELF. BE SANE! I HEREBY HOLD . . . . . 501 A MASQUE OF MERCY . . 192
CALMLY
    WITH FEELERS CALMLY ATWIDDLE, ... 288 DEPARTMENTAL 36
    IMPRINT A SADDLE, AND CALMLY CONSIDER A COURSE. . . . 341 WILLFUL HOMING . . . 7
    WITH POETS WHO COULD CALMLY TAKE THE FATE . . . . . 351 THE LESSON FOR TODAY . 11
CALYPSO
    HALF LOOKING FOR THE ORCHID CALYPSO." . . . . 125 AN ENCOUNTER 24
CAME
    A STRANGER CAME TO THE DOOR AT EVE, ...   7 LOVE AND A QUESTION . 1
    THE BRIDEGROOM CAME FORTH INTO THE PORCH . . . . . .   7 LOVE AND A QUESTION . 9
    EACH CAME SINGLY UNTO HER PLACE, ... 15 IN A VALE 10
    BUT ALL CAME EVERY NIGHT WITH THE MIST: . . . . . . 15 IN A VALE 11
    BACK TO THE PLACE FROM WHICH SHE CAME-- . . . . . . 15 IN A VALE 17
    AND TO THE FOREST EDGE YOU CAME ONE DAY . . . . . . 16 A DREAM PANG . . . 3
    BEFORE I CAME TO VIEW THE LEVELED SCENE. . . . . . 22 THE TUFT OF FLOWERS . 4
    AND THEN ON TREMULOUS WING CAME BACK TO ME. . . . . 22 THE TUFT OF FLOWERS . 18
    PAN CAME OUT OF THE WOODS ONE DAY-- . . . . 23 PAN WITH US 1
    HIS HEART KNEW PEACE, FOR NONE CAME HERE . . . . . 24 PAN WITH US 11
    OUR LOVE CAME BACK AGAIN. . . . . 27 A LINE-STORM SONG . . 30
    WHEN I CAME UP FROM ROWE'S I FOUND HIM HERE, ... 35 DEATH OF THE HIRED MAN 34
    THAN WAS THE HOUND THAT CAME A STRANGER TO US . . . . 38 DEATH OF THE HIRED MAN 116
    THEN CAME THE IN. I HEARD YOUR RUMBLING VOICE . . . . 53 HOME BURIAL 81
    SOONER OR LATER CAME AND LEANED, HALF KNELT, ... 56 THE BLACK COTTAGE . . 27
    "I'VE TOLD YOU HOW ONCE, NOT LONG AFTER WE CAME, . . . 61 BLUEBERRIES 67
    IT WOULD BE DIFFERENT IF MORE PEOPLE CAME, ... 63 A SERVANT TO SERVANTS 39
    FATHER AND MOTHER MARRIED, AND MOTHER CAME, ... 66 A SERVANT TO SERVANTS 126
    WHICH MEANS THE-SEVEN-CAVES-THAT-WE-CAME-OUT-OF. . . . 76 THE GENERATIONS OF MEN 93
    WE CAME HERE FOR A HOME FOR HER, YOU KNOW, ... 85 THE HOUSEKEEPER . . . 104
    I ALWAYS HAVE FELT STRANGE WHEN WE CAME HOME . . . . 89 THE FEAR 17
    WAS STARTLED WHEN AN ANSWER REALLY CAME. . . . . . 91 THE FEAR 66
    "NOTHING." IT CAME FROM WELL ALONG THE ROAD. . . . . 91 THE FEAR 67
    THAT CAME ON, BUT HER BODY ROCKED A LITTLE. . . . . 92 THE FEAR 77
    "I HALF SUSPECT YOU KNEW, AND CAME ON PURPOSE . . . . 93 THE SELF-SEEKER . . . 8
    "I TOLD YOU, WILLIS, WHEN YOU FIRST CAME IN. . . . . 95 THE SELF-SEEKER . . . 61
    AND CAME DOWN ON THE NORTH. / HE SAID, "A THOUSAND." . . 107 CHRISTMAS TREES . . . 41
    CAME UP THE JOINTED STOVEPIPE IN THEIR HANDS, ... 113 IN THE HOME STRETCH . 86
    "WELL, SO I CAME." . . . . 118 THE TELEPHONE . . . 19
    AS YOU CAME UP THE HILL. WE MET. BUT ALL . . . . . 118 MEETING AND PASSING . 4
    TO WATCH ME AND SEE WHAT I CAME TO GET. . . . . . 123 PEA BRUSH 12
    TIME SOMEONE CAME WITH CART AND PAIR . . . . . . 123 PEA BRUSH 15
    OF WHAT YOU CAME FOR AND BECOME LIKE ME, ... 124 PUTTING IN THE SEED . 8
    THAT SMILE! IT NEVER CAME OF BEING GAY. . . . . . 127 THE SMILE 2
    THERE CAME A GUST. (YOU USED TO THINK THE TREES . . . 130 THE BONFIRE 41
    I JUST CAME TO TELL YOU . . . . 135 LAST WORD OF A BLUEBIRD 5
    SOMETIMES HE CAME WITH ARMS OUTSPREAD . . . . . . 138 BROWN'S DESCENT . . . 21
    AND CAME DOWN LIKE A COASTING CHILD. . . . . . . 139 BROWN'S DESCENT . . . 44
    HE CAME FROM HIGHER UP IN THE PASS . . . . 140 THE GUM-GATHERER . . 13
    AND CAME UPSTAIRS ALONE--AND GAVE THAT LAUGH, ... 142 THE VANISHING RED . . 26
    THERE ON THE TABLE, EVER SINCE I CAME, ... 147 SNOW 118
    YOU RECOLLECT THE BOY WHO CAME OUT HERE . . . . . 149 SNOW 173
    THAT WANTS ME AS A WAR MIGHT IF IT CAME. . . . . . 151 SNOW 241
    MRS. COLE'S VOICE CAME FROM AN INNER ROOM: . . . . 152 SNOW 271
    AND THEN HER VOICE CAME SCRAPING SLOW: 'OH, YOU, . . . 153 SNOW 290
    THEN CAME IN DANCING, SKIPPING WITH HIS LIFE . . . . 170 NEW HAMPSHIRE . . . 349
    I CAME AN ERRAND ONE CLOUD-BLOWING EVENING . . . . 174 THE CENSUS-TAKER . . 1
    I CAME AS CENSUS-TAKER TO THE WASTE . . . . . . 174 THE CENSUS-TAKER . . 9
    WHERE I CAME LAST WITH SOME HOPE, BUT NOT MUCH, . . . 174 THE CENSUS-TAKER . . 12
    AND BOUGHT THE TELESCOPE WITH WHAT IT CAME TO. . . . 177 THE STAR-SPLITTER . . 31
    AND CAME SO NEAR DEATH IN THE DARK OF YEARS, ... 180 MAPLE 37
    THAT WHEN IT WOKE AND CAME TO LIFE AGAIN . . . . . 181 MAPLE 38
    IT CAME BACK VAGUELY AT THE GLASS ONE DAY, ... 181 MAPLE 40
    AND I GIVE UP"; WHICH LAST LOOK CAME TO NOTHING. . . . 184 MAPLE 132
    ONCE THEY CAME ON A MAPLE IN A GLADE, ... 184 MAPLE 144
    AND ANYWAY IT CAME TOO LATE FOR MAPLE. . . . . . 184 MAPLE 159
    MRS. BAPTISTE CAME IN AND ROCKED A CHAIR . . . . . 186 THE AX-HELVE . . . 46
    SO AFTER WORK THAT EVENING HE CAME BACK . . . . . 194 PAUL'S WIFE . . . 88
    AND THE WORLD CAME REVOLVING BACK TO ME, ... 198 WILD GRAPES . . . 86
    (SHE MADE SHREWD EYES TO SEE WHERE HE CAME IN.) . . . 201 PLACE FOR A THIRD . . 57
    IS BACK INTO THE CELLAR WHERE IT CAME FROM. . . . . 203 THE WITCH OF COOS . . 26
    THE NIGHT THE BONES CAME UP THE CELLAR STAIRS . . . . 203 THE WITCH OF COOS . . 40
    THEN HE CAME AT ME WITH ONE HAND OUTSTRETCHED, ... 204 THE WITCH OF COOS . . 75
    AND NOTHING CAME OF ALL HE SAILED. . . . . 212 AN EMPTY THREAT . . . 47
    WE CAME OUT ON A LOOK-OFF WHERE WE FACED . . . . . 214 A FOUNTAIN, A BOTTLE . 37
    THEN CAME ONE KNOCK! . . . . 218 I WILL SING YOU ONE-O . 23
    BEFORE MAN CAME TO BLOW IT RIGHT . . . . 223 THE AIM WAS SONG . . 1
    MAN CAME TO TELL IT WHAT WAS WRONG: . . . . . . 224 THE AIM WAS SONG . . 5
    WATER CAME TO REBUKE THE TOO CLEAR WATER. . . . . 225 FOR ONCE SOMETHING . . 11
    THEY SENT HIM BACK TO HER. THE LETTER CAME . . . . 230 NOT TO KEEP 1
    CAME TAMELY BACK IN FRONT OF ME, THE DROVER, ... 240 OUR SINGING STRENGTH . 44
    BUT AT LAST CAME A KNOCK, ... 240 THE LOCKLESS DOOR . . 2
    BUT THE KNOCK CAME AGAIN. . . . . 241 THE LOCKLESS DOOR . . 9
    FOR TEAMS THAT CAME BY THE STONY ROAD . . . . . . 241 NEED OF BEING VERSED . 10
    THE BIRDS THAT CAME TO IT THROUGH THE AIR . . . . . 242 NEED OF BEING VERSED . 13
    IT WOULD NOT GO OUT TILL I CAME IN. . . . . . . 253 THE THATCH 7
    CAME OVER HOUSES FROM ANOTHER STREET, ... 255 ACQUAINTED WITH NIGHT . 9
    SHE CAME TO FROM TOO HIGH TOO LATE TO LEARN. . . . . 257 THE LOVELY BE CHOOSERS 45
    AND WORDS TO WONDER IN HER HEARING HOW SHE CAME THERE, . 257 THE LOVELY BE CHOOSERS 48
    FROM FAR AWAY THERE CAME AN ANSWERING TICK. . . . . 269 THE EGG AND THE MACHINE 2
    HERE IT CAME BREASTING LIKE A HORSE IN SKIRTS. . . . 270 THE EGG AND THE MACHINE 11

CAME (CONTINUED)
   THAT ON THE ONE WHO CAME TOO LATE . . . . 273 A LONE STRIKER . . . 6
   THAT'S WHERE THE HUMAN STILL CAME IN. . . . . 273 A LONE STRIKER . . . 27
   OUT OF THE MUD TWO STRANGERS CAME . . . . 275 TWO TRAMPS IN MUD TIME 1
   BY COMING WITH WHAT THEY CAME TO ASK. . . . . 276 TWO TRAMPS IN MUD TIME 43
   WHEN CAME SQUARE HALE WITH LET'S SEE WHAT WE HAD; . . . 283 THE GOLD HESPERIDEE . 10
   BUT WHEN HE CAME TO LOOK, NO APPLES THERE . . . . . . 284 THE GOLD HESPERIDEE . 38
   WELL, THE MOON AFTER THAT, CAME ONE AT LAST . . . . . 289 OLD BARN AT THE BOTTOM 6
   THE CHEAPEST TRAMP THAT CAME ALONG THAT WAY . . . . . 290 OLD BARN AT THE BOTTOM 44
   WE CAME TO WHERE THERE WAS A LIVING MAN. . . . . 292 FIGURE IN THE DOORWAY . 6
   CAME DRYLY FORWARD TO THE BARS AGAIN . . . . 294 AT WOODWARD'S GARDENS . 32
   AND WHEN THEY CAME IT SEEMED WITH A WILL TO CARRY ME WITH
      THEM TO DEATH. . . . . 297 A LEAF-TREADER . . . 8
   THE MUD CAME IN ONE COLD . . . . 298 ON TAKING FROM THE TOP 15
   BUT WHENEVER THE ROOF CAME WHITE . . . . 299 WELCOME TO THEIR BELIEF 9
   THE WITCH THAT CAME (THE WITHERED HAG) . . . . 307 PROVIDE, PROVIDE . . 1
   DEEP INTO THE EARTH WHENCE IT CAME. . . . . 311 THE VINDICTIVES . . . 30
   SO WHEN HE CAME TO THE PARTING . . . . 313 BEARER OF EVIL TIDINGS 5
   TILL HE CAME TO THE LAND OF PAMIR. . . . . 313 BEARER OF EVIL TIDINGS 12
   AND THE CHILD THAT CAME OF THE PRINCESS . . . . 314 BEARER OF EVIL TIDINGS 29
   THERE CAME A MOMENT OF CONFUSING LIGHTS, ... 315 IRIS BY NIGHT . . . 4
   AS I CAME TO THE EDGE OF THE WOODS, ... 334 COME IN 1
   BEFORE HE CAME TO MEET HIS OWN! . . . . 336 THE WIND AND THE RAIN . 11
   AND NOTHING EVER CAME OF WHAT HE CRIED . . . . 338 THE MOST OF IT . . . 9
   AND TO DO THAT TO BIRDS WAS WHY SHE CAME. . . . . . . 339 NEVER WOULD BIRDS' SONG 14
   BEFORE HER MOTHER CAME. . . . . 340 THE SUBVERTED FLOWER . 40
   SHE CAME DOWN WEAKLY AND BLINDLY LED . . . . 343 DISCOVERY OF MADEIRAS . 6
   HE CAME AT LAST TO HIS NATIVE SHIRE. . . . . 347 DISCOVERY OF MADEIRAS . 132
   AND THEN CAME RACING WILDLY ON AGAIN . . . . 357 A CONSIDERABLE SPECK . 11
   I NEVER CAME UPON A BLESSED ONE. . . . . 363 AN ANSWER 2
   THEN CAME HIS LITTLE ACKNOWLEDGMENT: . . . . 364 TRESPASS 17
   IT CAME FROM WHERE HE CAME FROM ANYWAY." . . . . . . 366 NOT OF STONES OF THE PLACE 16
   I CAME TO BUT ONE HOUSE, ... 366 NOT OF SCHOOL AGE . . 3
   HE AND A LOT OF CHILDREN CAME OUTSIDE, ... 368 THE LITERATE FARMER AND 6
   WHO WERE JUST ON THE SUBJECT WHEN YOU CAME. . . . . . 369 THE LITERATE FARMER AND 28
   AND THE SUN CAME OUT TO DRY ME. . . . . 377 ONE STEP BACKWARD TAKEN 14
   AS SHEBA CAME TO SOLOMON. . . . . 390 TWO LEADING LIGHTS . . 21
   CAME TAP-TAP-TAPPING DOWN THE VILLAGE STREET, ... 394 HAEC FABULA DOCET . . 3
   AS FIFTY MILLION YEARS AGO WE CAME-- . . . . 395 WHY WAIT FOR SCIENCE . 12
   CAME JUST THEN SAILING INTO PORT . . . . 417 AMERICA IS HARD TO SEE 21
   NOW CAME ON A NEW ORDER OF THE AGES . . . . 422 FOR JOHN F. KENNEDY . 19
   TILL DARWIN CAME TO EARTH UPON A YEAR . . . . 425 ACCIDENTALLY ON PURPOSE 9
   WHEN I CAME HERE YOUNG. . . . . 428 KITTY HAWK 6
   CAME UPON THEIR PITY, ... 433 KITTY HAWK 179
   TILL WE CAME TO BE . . . . 440 KITTY HAWK 391
   AND A MAN CAME OUT OF THE TREES . . . . 444 THE DRAFT HORSE . . . 5
   IT CAME NEAR SPLITTING HER IN HALF. . . . . 452 A-WISHING WELL . . . 43
   THERE CAME TO COURT A MERCHANT SELLING PEARLS, ... 455 HOW HARD TO KEEP FROM 66
   YOU CAME COMPANIONLESS, BUT YOU CAME HOME. . . . . . . 458 HOW HARD TO KEEP FROM 131
   AND IT CAME OUT ALL RIGHT. I HAVE NO DOUBT . . . . . 475 A MASQUE OF REASON . 65
   PREDICTED ANYTHING THAT CAME TO PASS. . . . . 476 A MASQUE OF REASON . 96
   SINCE I CAME IN? / HEAR WHAT? THAT ARMY TRUCK? . . . . 495 A MASQUE OF MERCY . 43
   WHEN YOU CAME IN. WE'RE REVOLUTIONISTS. . . . . . . 508 A MASQUE OF MERCY . 399
   CHRIST CAME TO INTRODUCE A BREAK WITH LOGIC . . . . . 511 A MASQUE OF MERCY . 475
   EVEN BEFORE I CAME IN HERE TONIGHT. . . . . 517 A MASQUE OF MERCY . 626
CAMP
   TO HAVE YOU COME AND CAMP HERE ON OUR LAND. . . . . . 62 A SERVANT TO SERVANTS . 2
   TO DRIVE PAUL OUT OF ANY LUMBER CAMP . . . . 191 PAUL'S WIFE 1
   BEFORE THEY HEARD OF HIM IN SOME NEW CAMP, ... 192 PAUL'S WIFE 29
   THEIR RAWHIDE HARNESS FROM THE LOAD TO CAMP. . . . . . 192 PAUL'S WIFE 45
   WHO USED YOUR PASTURE FOR A CAMP. . . . . 380 AN UNSTAMPED LETTER IN 7
CAMPAIGN
   TO BASE HIS CAMPAIGN ON TO SAVE THE WORLD. . . . . . 514 A MASQUE OF MERCY . . 561
CAMPS
   HE'D BEEN THE HERO OF THE MOUNTAIN CAMPS . . . . . . 191 PAUL'S WIFE 17
   BUT NOT LONG SINCE IN THE LUMBER CAMPS). . . . . . . 276 TWO TRAMPS IN MUD TIME 51
CAMPUS
   HERE ON THIS VERY CAMPUS YEARS AGO. . . . . 316 BUILD SOIL 4
CAN---NOT INDEXED--EXCEPT FOR:
   AND SO WE WENT WITH PAIL AND CAN . . . . 18 GOING FOR WATER . . . 2
   WITH A CAN OF CONDENSED AIR . . . . 466 SOME SCIENCE FICTION . 25
CANAAN
   LATELY BROUGHT HOME FROM ANDOVER OR CANAAN . . . . . 162 NEW HAMPSHIRE . . 117
CANADA
   IN A TROUT HATCHERY NEAR CANADA, ... 165 NEW HAMPSHIRE . . 184
CANCEL
   EVIL TENDENCIES CANCEL . . . . 308 EVIL TENDENCIES CANCEL T
CANCELING
   OF MY INCENTIVE--CANCELING MY MISSION. . . . . 499 A MASQUE OF MERCY . . 148
CANCER
   GEMINI AND CANCER . . . . 429 KITTY HAWK 38
CANDIDATES
   VOICES CONFLICTING LIKE THE CANDIDATES. . . . . 368 THE LITERATE FARMER AND 4
CANDLE
   HAVE WE A PIECE OF CANDLE IF THE LAMP . . . . 113 IN THE HOME STRETCH . 80
   TO FRIZZLE RESIN IN A CANDLE FLAME, ... 350 TO A YOUNG WRETCH . 8
CANDLES
   THERE WERE FOUR CANDLES AND FOUR PEOPLE PRESENT. . . . 163 NEW HAMPSHIRE . . 128
CANDLESTICKS
   AND TOOK THE GOLD CANDLESTICKS HOME. . . . . 311 THE VINDICTIVES . . . 40
CANE
   AT FIRST TO BE NO BIGGER THAN A CANE, ... 375 A YOUNG BIRCH . . . 14
   RELYING ON HIMSELF AND ON HIS CANE, ... 394 HAEC FABULA DOCET . . 2
CANIS
   CANIS MAJOR . . . . 261 CANIS MAJOR . . . . T
CANNON-MOUTH-LIKE
   A CANNON-MOUTH-LIKE HOLE WAS IN THE WALL, ... 113 IN THE HOME STRETCH . 84

CANNOT---NOT INDEXED
CAN'T---NOT INDEXED
CANVAS
    SO THE EFFECT WHEN THEY ARE MIXED ON CANVAS . . . . . . 321 BUILD SOIL 149
CANYON
    THE TRUTH IS THE RIVER FLOWS INTO THE CANYON . . . . . 379 TOO ANXIOUS FOR RIVERS   8
CAP
    HE DOFFED HIS CAP AND HELD IT WITH BOTH HANDS . . . . . 114 IN THE HOME STRETCH . 106
    AND ONE TO CAP THE CLIMAX BY COMBINING . . . . 502 A MASQUE OF MERCY . . 242
CAPE
    SHE WORE HER CAPE; HER HAT WAS IN HER HAND. . . . . . . 110 IN THE HOME STRETCH .   4
    SHE MAY KNOW COVE AND CAPE, ... 260 SAND DUNES   9
CAPELLA
    ALDEBARAN, CAPELLA, SIRIUS . . . . 462 HOW HARD TO KEEP FROM   268
CAPES
    WHOLE CAPES CAKED OFF IN SLICES. . . . . 377 ONE STEP BACKWARD TAKEN   7
CAPITAL
    OF CAPITAL, AND CALLING THRIFT A MISER). . . . . . . 363 AN EQUALIZER   4
    SEEK NOT IN ME THE BIG I CAPITAL, ... 387 IOTA SUBSCRIPT . . .   1
    AS THE CAPITAL . . . . 440 KITTY HAWK 376
CAPPED
    THE LAWYER GRAVELY CAPPED HIS FOUNTAIN PEN. . . . . . 100 THE SELF-SEEKER . . . 218
CAPRICIOUSNESS
    IN THE CAPRICIOUSNESS OF SUMMER AIR . . . . 332 THE SILKEN TENT . . . 13
CAPS
    TO RUSH IN SHEETS AND FOOL'S CAPS WHERE THEY SMELLED . . 163 NEW HAMPSHIRE . . . 141
CAPTAIN
    SHOUTS LIKE AN ARMY CAPTAIN, 'LET HER COME!' . . . . . 71 THE CODE 63
    AND LET THE CAPTAIN TELL HIM A TALE. . . . . 345 DISCOVERY OF MADEIRAS . 51
    HE SAID TO THE CAPTAIN, "GIVE COMMAND, ... 346 DISCOVERY OF MADEIRAS . 106
CAPTAIN'S
    IT'S THE OLD CAPTAIN'S DARK FATE . . . . 212 AN EMPTY THREAT . . . 43
    (HE HAD TO KEEP THE CAPTAIN'S FAVOR.) . . . . 345 DISCOVERY OF MADEIRAS . 52
    "WHAT WAS THE PIRATE CAPTAIN'S CHAFF? . . . . 346 DISCOVERY OF MADEIRAS . 90
CAPTIVE
    AND ONCE THEY HAD SHIPPED A CAPTIVE PAIR . . . . . . 345 DISCOVERY OF MADEIRAS . 54
    MY TREE, A CAPTIVE IN YOUR WINDOW BAY, ... 350 TO A YOUNG WRETCH . . 20
    SHALL IT BE TOLD WE HAD A PROPHET CAPTIVE . . . . 502 A MASQUE OF MERCY . . 220
CAPTORS
    HIS CAPTORS ACCEPTED IT ALL, ... 310 THE VINDICTIVES . . . 8
    HIS CAPTORS CONVICTED THE KING . . . . 310 THE VINDICTIVES . . . 15
CAR
    AND NOT, AS YOU MIGHT THINK, A FLYING CAR, ... 173 A STAR IN A STONEBOAT . 27
    I OFTEN SEE FLOWERS FROM A PASSING CAR . . . . . . 248 A PASSING GLIMPSE . . 1
    FOR THE SQUEAL OF BRAKES, THE SOUND OF A STOPPING CAR, . 287 A ROADSIDE STAND . . 36
    WE LEFT OUR BOILING CAR . . . . 367 A SERIOUS STEP LIGHTLY 10
    TO DRIVE MY TON OF CAR . . . . 388 MIDDLENESS OF THE ROAD 10
    A TROLLEY CAR THEY HAILED . . . . 391 A ROGERS GROUP . . . 5
CARAVANS
    RETARD MID-WASTE MY COWERING CARAVANS-- . . . . . . 59 THE BLACK COTTAGE . . 124
CARD
    YOU TAKE MY CARD--YOU SEEM SO GOOD AT SUCH THINGS-- . . 75 THE GENERATIONS OF MEN   61
CARDS
    "DON'T BE TOO TECHNICAL.--YOU HAVE THREE CARDS." . . . 76 THE GENERATIONS OF MEN   79
    "FOUR CARDS: ONE YOURS, THREE MINE (ONE FOR EACH BRANCH . 76 THE GENERATIONS OF MEN   80
    MY RIGHT TO BE EQUAL IN NUMBER OF CARDS, ... 310 IN DIVES' DIVE . . . 4
CARE
    AND, FOR ALL BURDEN, CARE. . . . . 7 LOVE AND A QUESTION .   4
    WHICH GOD MAKES HIS ESPECIAL CARE. . . . . 20 THE TRIAL BY EXISTENCE 32
    AS OF ONE WHO UTTERLY COULDN'T CARE. . . . . 25 THE DEMIURGE'S LAUGH . 9
    HE ADDED, IF YOU REALLY CARE TO KNOW, ... 36 DEATH OF THE HIRED MAN 51
    "YES, I TOOK CARE TO KEEP WELL OUT OF EARSHOT." . . . 37 DEATH OF THE HIRED MAN 70
    I'M NOT SO DRUNK I CAN'T TAKE CARE OF MYSELF." . . . . 45 A HUNDRED COLLARS . . 38
    YOU COULDN'T CARE! THE NEAREST FRIENDS CAN GO . . . . 54 HOME BURIAL 97
    "PRETTY," HE SAID. "COME IN. NO ONE WILL CARE." . . . 55 THE BLACK COTTAGE . . 11
    "HE MAY AND NOT CARE, AND SO LEAVE THE CHEWINK . . . . 60 BLUEBERRIES 29
    WHILE I FRY THEIR BACON. MUCH THEY CARE! . . . . . 65 A SERVANT TO SERVANTS 78
    A BRIDE, TO HELP TAKE CARE OF SUCH A CREATURE, ... 66 A SERVANT TO SERVANTS 127
    BUT YOU SEE, DON'T YOU, WE TAKE CARE OF HIM." . . . . 86 THE HOUSEKEEPER . . . 154
    "BUT IT'S NONSENSE TO THINK HE'D CARE ENOUGH." . . . . 91 THE FEAR 49
    WHO WILL TAKE CARE OF MY NECESSITIES . . . . 99 THE SELF-SEEKER . . . 179
    AND CARE FOR THEM IN SUCH A CHANGE OF SCENE, ... 109 THE EXPOSED NEST . . 24
    WE'D CARE TO KNOW, FOR WE ARE NOT YOUNG NOW.-- . . . . 112 IN THE HOME STRETCH . 54
    ONE OUGHT NOT TO HAVE TO CARE . . . . 126 LONELINESS 1
    CARE WHEN THE BIRDS COME ROUND THE HOUSE . . . . . . 126 LONELINESS 3
    OR CARE SO MUCH WHEN THEY COME BACK . . . . 126 LONELINESS 5
    LET'S NOT CARE WHAT WE DO WITH IT TONIGHT. . . . . . 129 THE BONFIRE 8
    NOT BUT I'VE EVERY REASON NOT TO CARE . . . . 146 SNOW 89
    "BROTHER MESERVE, TAKE CARE, YOU'LL SCARE YOURSELF . . . 149 SNOW 167
    WHICH NATURALLY SHE DOESN'T CARE TO SELL. . . . . . 161 NEW HAMPSHIRE . . . 63
    UNDER HE DIDN'T CARE HOW GREAT A STONE: . . . . . . 200 PLACE FOR A THIRD . . 24
    LABAN WAS OLD AND POOR, YET SEEMED TO CARE; . . . . . 201 PLACE FOR A THIRD . . 50
    BUT TONIGHT I DON'T CARE ENOUGH TO LIE-- . . . . . 207 THE WITCH OF COOS . . 148
    HIGH IN THE BREAST. NOTHING BUT WHAT GOOD CARE . . . . 230 NOT TO KEEP 15
    SO MUCH AS TO TAKE CARE OF EVENING CHORES. . . . . . 248 THE COCOON 10
    TO THINK MUCH OR MUCH CARE. . . . . 256 THE LOVELY BE CHOOSERS 30
    OR OLD LOVE ON AN IMPULSE NOT TO CARE-- . . . . . . 264 THE INVESTMENT . . . 12
    YET NOTHING I SHOULD CARE TO LEAVE BEHIND. . . . . . 266 THE ARMFUL 5
    AND THE LIGHT-NATURED TREE SEEMED NOT TO CARE! . . . . 284 THE GOLD HESPERIDEE . 40
    BUT I MAY BE ONE WHO DOES NOT CARE . . . . 296 LEAVES COMPARED WITH . 5
    CARE MAY HAVE THOUGHT IT WAS CARE. . . . . 299 WELCOME TO THEIR BELIEF 2
    CARE MAY HAVE THOUGHT IT WAS CARE. . . . . 299 WELCOME TO THEIR BELIEF 14
    THE MUSE TAKES CARE OF YOU. YOU LIVE BY WRITING . . . 316 BUILD SOIL 17
    AND DO WHAT I COMMAND YOU. I TAKE CARE . . . . . . 323 BUILD SOIL 231
    WHOSE LOVE WAS SUCH THEY DIDN'T CARE . . . . 345 DISCOVERY OF MADEIRAS . 55
    TAKE CARE TO SELL YOUR HORSE BEFORE HE DIES . . . . . 399 THE INGENUITIES OF DEBT 4
    AS IF HE DIDN'T CARE WHO UNDERSTOOD HIM, ... 405 FROM PLANE TO PLANE . 59
    SPIRITED TO CARE . . . . 428 KITTY HAWK 15

CARE (CONTINUED)
CARE MY INNOCENCE . . . . 432 KITTY HAWK 121
(I DON'T CARE HOW THE WORLD GETS BY.) . . . . . . 451 A-WISHING WELL . . . 14
AND IF SHE DON'T TAKE CARE . . . . 465 MILKY WAY IS A COWPATH . 37
NO, LET'S NOT LIVE THINGS OVER. I DON'T CARE. . . . 477 A MASQUE OF REASON . . 119
AND, TOO, TAKE CARE OF TWENTY OF THE FOUR . . . . 484 A MASQUE OF REASON . . 310
I TOOK CARE OF YOU. AND BEFORE YOU DIED . . . . . 486 A MASQUE OF REASON . . 361
WON'T FIND A FORMULA FOR TAKING CARE OF. . . . . . 488 A MASQUE OF REASON . . 415
I SHOULD DARE SAY SHE WOULD BE TAKEN CARE OF. . . . 519 A MASQUE OF MERCY . . 687
CARED
ALL THIS TO PROVE WE CARED. WHY IS THERE THEN . . . 109 THE EXPOSED NEST . . 31
BUT COME TO DIE SHE FOUND SHE CARED SO MUCH: . . . 199 PLACE FOR A THIRD . . 4
AND SHE WAS OLD AND POOR--BUT SHE CARED, TOO. . . . 201 PLACE FOR A THIRD . . 51
WHILE SHE MADE UP HER MIND HOW MUCH SHE CARED-- . . 201 PLACE FOR A THIRD . . 55
AND HOW MUCH LABAN CARED--AND WHY HE CARED. . . . . 201 PLACE FOR A THIRD . . 56
I DON'T REMEMBER WHY I EVER CARED. . . . . 207 THE WITCH OF COOS . . 149
COULD TELL YOU WHY HE EVER CARED HIMSELF.... . . . 207 THE WITCH OF COOS . . 151
CAREERS
WE ALL ARE DOOMED TO BROKEN-OFF CAREERS, ... 355 THE LESSON FOR TODAY . 145
CAREFUL
YOU UNDERSTAND THAT WE HAVE TO BE CAREFUL. . . . . 92 THE FEAR 89
A SMALL BIRD FLEW BEFORE ME. HE WAS CAREFUL . . . . 101 THE WOOD-PILE . . . 10
I CALLED THE FIREMAN WITH A CAREFUL VOICE . . . . . 234 EVENING A SUGAR ORCHARD . 3
"BE CAREFUL HOW YOU USE YOUR INFLUENCE. . . . . . 406 FROM PLANE TO PLANE . 66
BE CAREFUL NOT TO LOSE THE PLACE. BE CAREFUL. . . . 505 A MASQUE OF MERCY . . 293
TO BE STRONG, CAREFUL, THRIFTY, DILIGENT, ... 505 A MASQUE OF MERCY . . 314
YOU KNOW WHAT LETS US OFF FROM BEING CAREFUL? . . . 505 A MASQUE OF MERCY . . 316
CAREFULLY
TO THE TOP BRANCHES, CLIMBING CAREFULLY . . . . . 122 BIRCHES 36
LESS CAREFULLY NURTURED, LESS FRUITFUL THAN THESE, . . 228 GOOD-BY AND KEEP COLD . 22
CARELESS
WITH THOSE GREAT CARELESS WINGS, ... 29 MY BUTTERFLY 24
CARELESS AND STILL . . . . 360 THE RABBIT-HUNTER . . 1
CARES
"WHO CARES WHAT THEY SAY? IT'S A NICE WAY TO LIVE, . . 61 BLUEBERRIES 54
IT WON'T LIE DOWN. THEN LET IT STAND. WHO CARES?" . . 148 SNOW 152
WHO CARES NOT WHAT HE DOES IN COMPANY, ... 171 NEW HAMPSHIRE . . . 399
OF CARES, AT NIGHT, TO SLEEP; BUT NOTHING TELLS ME . . 199 WILD GRAPES 102
(WHO CARES BUT FOR THE FUTURE OF THE BUD?), ... 337 THE WIND AND THE RAIN . 34
CARING
"YOU MEAN YOU COULDN'T UNDERSTAND HIS CARING. . . . 91 THE FEAR 50
YES. THANKS FOR CARING.--DON'T MIND WILL: HE'S SAVAGE. . 100 THE SELF-SEEKER . . 224
AND WOUNDED ON HIS BLADE. SO FAR FROM CARING, . . . 190 THE GRINDSTONE . . . 59
CARNEGIE
I LOOKED ON IT AS A CARNEGIE GRANT . . . . 459 HOW HARD TO KEEP FROM 174
CAROL
AS LESLEY, CAROL, IRMA, MARJORIE, ... 181 MAPLE 46
CARPE
CARPE DIEM . . . . 335 CARPE DIEM . . . . T
CARPET
OF MIDDLE-AISLE CHURCH CARPET, SISAL HEMP, ... 489 A MASQUE OF REASON . . 454
CARRIAGE
AND THE SAWYER HAD SLAMMED THE CARRIAGE BACK . . . . 193 PAUL'S WIFE 63
BUT AN EARTHLY DOG OF THE CARRIAGE BREED; . . . . . 419 ONE MORE BREVITY . . 11
CARRIED
AND CARRIED ITSELF LIKE A PILE OF DISHES . . . . . 203 THE WITCH OF COOS . . 29
LOVE AND FORGETTING MIGHT HAVE CARRIED THEM . . . . 229 TWO LOOK AT TWO . . . 1
AND THE FENCE POST CARRIED A STRAND OF WIRE. . . . . 242 NEED OF BEING VERSED . 20
AND DEAD WINGS CARRIED LIKE A PAPER KITE. . . . . . 302 DESIGN 8
WHEN CALL OR LAUGHTER CARRIED IT ALOFT. . . . . . 339 NEVER WOULD BIRDS' SONG . 8
SHE WAS CARRIED OUT BESIDE THE MAST, ... 344 DISCOVERY OF MADEIRAS . 36
CARRIES
CARRIES HIM OUT OF THERE. . . . . 289 DEPARTMENTAL 39
BUT CARRIES NO CRY OF WHAT IS HOPED TO BE. . . . . 300 STRONG SAYING NOTHING . 14
CARRY
TO CARRY AGAIN TO YOU. . . . . 9 A LATE WALK 16
THERE'S FIVE: THAT'S ALL I CARRY." / "I CAN SEARCH YOU? . . 47 A HUNDRED COLLARS . . 88
DON'T CARRY IT TO SOMEONE ELSE THIS TIME. . . . . . 53 HOME BURIAL 57
CARRY HIM OFF THE WAY I MIGHT HAVE GONE, ... 101 THE WOOD-PILE . . . 20
AND WHAT'S THE NEWS YOU CARRY--IF YOU KNOW? . . . . 125 AN ENCOUNTER 20
A NAME TO CARRY FOR LIFE AND NEVER KNOW . . . . . 183 MAPLE 116
IS CARRY SOME GARDEN SOIL . . . . 285 IN TIME OF CLOUDBURST . 3
AND WHEN THEY CAME IT SEEMED WITH A WILL TO CARRY ME WITH
THEM TO DEATH. . . . . 297 A LEAF-TREADER . . . 8
IF HE LEAVES IT TO NATURE TO CARRY OUT THE SENTENCE. . . 307 NOT QUITE SOCIAL . . 14
IT TAKES TEN YEARS OR SO TO CARRY OUT, ... 323 BUILD SOIL 226
TO CARRY PRAISE OR BLAME TOO FAR, ... 403 SOMETHING LIKE A STAR . 23
PICK UP OUR EYES AND CARRY THEM BACK IDLE . . . . . 405 FROM PLANE TO PLANE . 51
WE CARRY IN OUR PURSE AND POCKET STILL?) . . . . . 422 FOR JOHN F. KENNEDY . 22
DON'T LET IT CARRY YOU AWAY. I HATE . . . . . . 489 A MASQUE OF REASON . . 448
I'VE LOST MY FAITH IN GOD TO CARRY OUT . . . . . . 497 A MASQUE OF MERCY . . 114
CARRYING
WHAT AM I DOING CARRYING OFF THIS BOTTLE?-- . . . . 50 A HUNDRED COLLARS . . 177
OF CARRYING HIS PILLOW IN HIS TEETH; . . . . . . 66 A SERVANT TO SERVANTS . 107
AND SO NOT CARRYING THE TREE AWAY . . . . 122 BIRCHES 34
CARS
AND CARS THAT SHOCK AND RATTLE--AND ONE HOTEL. . . . 45 A HUNDRED COLLARS . . 22
TO SELL THEM OFF THEIR FEET TO GO IN CARS . . . . . 106 CHRISTMAS TREES . . . 17
OF ALL THE THOUSAND SELFISH CARS THAT PASS, ... 287 A ROADSIDE STAND . . 37
JUST LIKE PULLMAN CARS, ... 438 KITTY HAWK 319
CART
SILAS UP ON THE CART TO BUILD THE LOAD, ... 36 DEATH OF THE HIRED MAN 68
WITH WHITE-FACED OXEN, IN A HEAVY CART, ... 41 THE MOUNTAIN 17
TIME SOMEONE CAME WITH CART AND PAIR . . . . . . 123 PEA BRUSH 15
AND ANOTHER STUMBLING AFTER A HALTING CART. . . . . 299 STRONG SAYING NOTHING . 8
CARVE
HE STAYED LONG ENOUGH TO CARVE ON STONE . . . . . 347 DISCOVERY OF MADEIRAS . 121
CARVE NOTHING ON IT. YOU CAN SIMPLY SAY . . . . . 365 OF STONES OF THE PLACE 13

CARVED
   CARVED IN THE SHED TO TELL ME WHO I AM . . . . 144 SNOW 40
   AND CARVED THEM ROUND WITH A SCROLL OF VINES. . . . . 347 DISCOVERY OF MADEIRAS . 124
CARVEN
   AS IN SOME TOO MUCH CARVEN MARBLE HALL . . . . . . 240 OUR SINGING STRENGTH . 42
CASCADES
   (A WHOLE SHELF CASCADES DOWN.) HERE COME SOME MORE. . . . 506 A MASQUE OF MERCY . . 341
CASE
   AND WISHED HER HEART IN A CASE OF GOLD . . . . 8 LOVE AND A QUESTION . 23
   'TIS PITY IF THE CASE REQUIRE . . . . 19 REVELATION 5
   HOW SHALL WE SAY GOOD-BY IN SUCH A CASE?" . . . . . 80 THE GENERATIONS OF MEN 204
   HE WON'T BE LONG IN THAT CASE. YOU CAN WAIT. . . . . 81 THE HOUSEKEEPER . . 18
   "NOT IN A GLASS CASE, THEN?" / "HE'D NEED A TALL ONE: . . 86 THE HOUSEKEEPER . . . 148
   HE'S BEEN IN A GLASS CASE, AS YOU MAY SAY, ... 86 THE HOUSEKEEPER . . . 150
   I CAN'T GET BACK THE FEET IN ANY CASE." . . . . . . 95 THE SELF-SEEKER . . . 65
   THE LAWYER WORE A WATCH THE CASE OF WHICH . . . . . 98 THE SELF-SEEKER . . . 163
   AS BETTER THAN THE SUN IN ANY CASE . . . . 108 OLD MAN'S WINTER NIGHT 20
   "HE DON'T CONSIDER IT A CASE FOR GOD." . . . . . . 146 SNOW 82
   HE'LL MAKE A CASE OF IT IF HE SUCCEEDS, ... 146 SNOW 86
   OR GONE OUTDOORS." / "IN WHICH CASE BOTH ARE LOST. . . 154 SNOW 312
   A WHOLE EDITION IN A PACKING CASE . . . . 216 A FOUNTAIN, A BOTTLE . 93
   THEY MUST HAVE HALTED SOON IN ANY CASE . . . . . . 229 TWO LOOK AT TWO . . 4
   TO THINK THEIR CASE WAS BEYOND RELIEF-- . . . . . . 253 THE THATCH 22
   HE WOULD PUT HIM ONTO THE CASE. . . . . 288 DEPARTMENTAL 12
   OF AN OLD MOUNTAIN'S CASE . . . . 298 ON TAKING FROM THE TOP 18
   AND SEE IF IT WILL HELP HER CASE." . . . . 347 DISCOVERY OF MADEIRAS . 109
   (WE'RE RIVALS IN THE BADNESS OF OUR CASE, ... 352 THE LESSON FOR TODAY . 66
   A CASE FOR JEFFERSON . . . . 393 A CASE FOR JEFFERSON . T
   NO ONE WAS LOOKING AT HIS LONELY CASE; . . . . . . 396 ANY SIZE WE PLEASE . . 1
   HE DON'T MIND HAVING LOST A CASE," PIKE SAID; . . . . 404 FROM PLANE TO PLANE . 25
   IN CASE THE ROCKS SHOULD MELT AND RUN AGAIN. . . . . 407 FROM PLANE TO PLANE . 95
   BUT ANYBODY COULD HAVE GUESSED IN THIS CASE, ... 456 HOW HARD TO KEEP FROM 89
   IN CASE I SHOULD DECIDE TO REIGN SOME MORE. . . . . 458 HOW HARD TO KEEP FROM 148
   SALVATION IN OUR CASE IS RETROACTIVE. . . . . . . 476 A MASQUE OF REASON . . 81
   AND LOOK FOR JUSTICE IN THE CASE OF SEGUB. . . . . 477 A MASQUE OF REASON . . 114
   OUR SECOND SECOND-CHILDHOOD CASE TONIGHT. . . . . . 493 A MASQUE OF MERCY . . 14
   IT'S A HARD CASE. IT'S GOT SO PROPHECY . . . . . . 503 A MASQUE OF MERCY . 257
   THEIR CASE IS NOT SO SIMPLE. YOU ARE GOOD. . . . . 517 A MASQUE OF MERCY . 620
CASED
   THAT CASED THE WORLD, AND HE WAS GONE! . . . . . . 137 BROWN'S DESCENT . . 12
CASES
   BUT LET'S GO ON TO WHERE OUR CASES PART, ... 352 THE LESSON FOR TODAY . 64
CASH
   WITH AN INCOME IN CASH OF, SAY, A THOUSAND . . . . . 172 NEW HAMPSHIRE . . . 409
   BUT FOR SOME OF THE MONEY, THE CASH, WHOSE FLOW SUPPORTS . 286 A ROADSIDE STAND . . 5
CASHMERE
   HE RAN THROUGH THE VALE OF CASHMERE, ... 313 BEARER OF EVIL TIDINGS 10
CAST
   HARD IF, THOUGH CAST AWAY FOR LIFE WITH YANKEES, . . . 186 THE AX-HELVE 44
   IT MIGHT HAVE BEEN THE SKIN A SNAKE HAD CAST . . . . 194 PAUL'S WIFE 92
   THEY SAT. SHE CAST ONE DULL, OLD LOOK AT HIM, ... 201 PLACE FOR A THIRD . . 52
   FROM THE HIGH WEST SHE MAKES A GENTLE CAST . . . . . 237 A HILLSIDE THAW . . . 20
   I SUFFERED LIKE A METAL BEING CAST. . . . . 267 WHAT FIFTY SAID . . . 3
   AND CAST ITS FLOWERS AND ALL THE STEMS BUT THREE, . . . 283 THE GOLD HESPERIDEE . 4
   IT WILL SHAKE ITS CAST STONE REEF OF FLOOR. . . . . 306 A TRIAL RUN 5
   THE TWO IN THE CELESTIAL CAST . . . . 390 TWO LEADING LIGHTS . . 2
   THE GREATEST VOTE A PEOPLE EVER CAST, ... 423 FOR JOHN F. KENNEDY . 55
CASTAWAY
   POOR CASTAWAY OF COMMERCE, AND SO LIVE . . . . . . 323 BUILD SOIL 212
   ENVOI TO HYDE THE CASTAWAY OF CROW ISLAND . . . . . 466 SOME SCIENCE FICTION . D
CASTING
   IN CASTING ABOUT FOR A CORNER . . . . 133 A GIRL'S GARDEN . . . 9
CASTLE
   OUR CONTINENT NO MORE A MOATED CASTLE. . . . . . . 446 DOES NO ONE AT ALL EVER 18
CASTLES
   OF CASTLES I USED TO BUILD IN AIR. . . . . 232 THE KITCHEN CHIMNEY . 20
CAST-OFF
   FOR THE ONE MORE CAST-OFF SHELL. . . . . 261 SAND DUNES 16
CAT
   THAT SUCKS HIS BREATH LIKE A WICKED CAT IN BED. . . . 341 WILLFUL HOMING . . . 4
   SHE WAS A SAVAGE JUNGLE CAT . . . . 345 DISCOVERY OF MADEIRAS . 64
CATALOGUES
   HIS FAVORITE READING IS SEED CATALOGUES. . . . . . 496 A MASQUE OF MERCY . . 81
CATAMOUNT
   GOT DRUNK, AND TRACKED THE PAIR UP CATAMOUNT, ... 195 PAUL'S WIFE 124
CATARACT
   THE UNIVERSAL CATARACT OF DEATH . . . . 259 WEST-RUNNING BROOK . . 56
CATCH
   TO CATCH IT IN A SORT OF SPECIAL PICTURE . . . . . 55 THE BLACK COTTAGE . . 2
   I SHAN'T CATCH UP IN THIS WORLD, ANYWAY. . . . . . 68 A SERVANT TO SERVANTS . 176
   THAT THE MAN WITH THE MEAL SACK DIDN'T CATCH--THEN. . . 142 THE VANISHING RED . . 28
   OF ALDER CATCH MY LIFTED AX BEHIND ME. . . . . . . 185 THE AX-HELVE 2
   "I'LL CATCH YOU IN MY ARMS. IT ISN'T FAR." . . . . . 198 WILD GRAPES 76
   I CATCH NO MORE THAN A RAY . . . . 266 SITTING BY A BUSH . . 2
   HE HAD A WELL, HE HAD THE RAIN TO CATCH. . . . . . 292 FIGURE IN THE DOORWAY . 17
   TO CATCH THEM AND TAKE TOLL OF THEM IN TRANSIT. . . . 321 BUILD SOIL 167
   SHE TRIES TO MAKE IT IN ONE CATCH OF BREATH, ... 386 THE FEAR OF MAN . . 3
   THE THANKS AND LET HIM CATCH IT AS A SCAPEGOAT. . . . 408 FROM PLANE TO PLANE . 140
   TO CATCH UP WITH US? . . . . 435 KITTY HAWK 243
   SO I COULD CATCH A BUBBLE IN ASCENT. . . . . . . 468 IN A GLASS OF CIDER . 3
   I'D CATCH ANOTHER BUBBLE IF I WAITED. . . . . . . 468 IN A GLASS OF CIDER . 7
   YOU DON'T CATCH WOMEN TRYING TO BE PLATO. . . . . . 478 A MASQUE OF REASON . . 140
CATCHALL
   A SORT OF CATCHALL FULL OF ATTIC CLUTTER. . . . . . 67 A SERVANT TO SERVANTS . 143
CATCHING
   (THE BLACK STREAM, CATCHING ON A SUNKEN ROCK, ... 258 WEST-RUNNING BROOK . . 19
CATECHISM
   AND ENTERED IN OUR CHILDISH CATECHISM . . . . . . 427 CONCEPT SELF-CONCEIVED 2

CATERWAUL
    CATERWAUL TO THE HILLS AROUND THE VILLAGE . . . . . . 94 THE SELF-SEEKER 42
CATHAY
    TO FORTUNE-HUNTING IN CATHAY. . . . . 419 AMERICA IS HARD TO SEE 78
CATHODE
    OF CRYSTALS WITH A RAY CATHODE . . . . 332 ALL REVELATION . . . 13
CAT'S-CRADLE
    THE SAME AS YOU SEIZE CAT'S-CRADLE STRINGS, ... 123 PEA BRUSH 19
CATTLE
    TO A SLOPE WHERE THE CATTLE KEEP THE LAWN. . . . . . 17 THE VANTAGE POINT . . 3
CATULLUS
    WHAT CATULLUS CALLED . . . . 434 KITTY HAWK 198
CAUGHT
    I FELT AS A FOOL TO HAVE BEEN SO CAUGHT, ... 25 THE DEMIURGE'S LAUGH . 14
    SLIPPED TO HER SIDE, CAUGHT UP HER HAND AND WAITED. . . 40 DEATH OF THE HIRED MAN 165
    THE DOCTOR CAUGHT HIS THROAT CONVULSIVELY. . . . . . 46 A HUNDRED COLLARS . . 62
    AND CAUGHT SIGHT OF HIM TREADING-WATER-LIKE, ... 72 THE CODE 76
    I LISTENED AND I THOUGHT I CAUGHT THE WORD-- . . . . 118 THE TELEPHONE 14
    OF WIND THAT CAUGHT AGAINST THE HOUSE A MOMENT, . . . 143 SNOW 2
    THE SNOW AGAINST THE WINDOW CAUGHT HIS EYE. . . . . 149 SNOW 180
    I CAUGHT THE OWNER OUTDOORS BY HIMSELF . . . . . 164 NEW HAMPSHIRE . . . 152
    OR ELSE FUN OF ORION'S HAVING CAUGHT ME. . . . . . 176 THE STAR-SPLITTER . . 10
    HE CAUGHT MY AX EXPERTLY ON THE RISE, ... 185 THE AX-HELVE . . . 10
    AND CAUGHT HERSELF UP BODILY, CHAIR AND ALL, ... 187 THE AX-HELVE . . . 52
    TO JUDGE THEM BY THE WAY THEY CAUGHT THEMSELVES . . . 193 PAUL'S WIFE 65
    BEFORE SHE CAUGHT HER FIRST BREATH WITH A GASP . . . 194 PAUL'S WIFE 118
    IT CAUGHT ME UP AS IF I WERE THE FISH . . . . . . 197 WILD GRAPES 44
    SHE WENT HER WAY. BUT LABAN HAVING CAUGHT . . . . . 200 PLACE FOR A THIRD . . 15
    TILL IT CAUGHT WIND AND, OPENING OUT ITS COVERS, . . . 216 A FOUNTAIN, A BOTTLE . 111
    IN ANY ROUGH PLACE WHERE IT CAUGHT. . . . . . . 223 THE AIM WAS SONG . . 4
    AND CAUGHT ONE SILVER LIZARD BY THE TAIL, ... 237 A HILLSIDE THAW . . . 10
    SHE CAUGHT THE PIECES END TO END . . . . 274 A LONE STRIKER . . . 30
    AND CAUGHT ME SPLITTING WOOD IN THE YARD. . . . . 275 TWO TRAMPS IN MUD TIME 2
    CAUGHT UP LIKE FINGERTIPS . . . . 339 THE SUBVERTED FLOWER . 12
    IT'S GONE SO FAR SHE'S PROBABLY CAUGHT . . . . . 345 DISCOVERY OF MADEIRAS . 74
    HAVE KEPT FROM BEING CAUGHT WITH THE DECAYED, . . . 399 THE INGENUITIES OF DEBT 8
    AND WHEN HE CAUGHT DICK LOOKING ONCE TOO OFTEN, . . . 404 FROM PLANE TO PLANE . 26
    SO THE PICTURE'S CAUGHT . . . . 426 A NEVER NAUGHT SONG . 29
    CAUGHT COLOR FROM THE LAST OF EVENING RED . . . . . 445 QUESTIONING FACES . . 4
    WE HAVEN'T CAUGHT UP WITH MY COW. . . . . 463 LINES IN DEJECTION . 8
    AND HAD CAUGHT MY COW BY THE TAIL, ... 463 LINES IN DEJECTION . 10
    TILL I WAS CAUGHT AND PUT TO SHAME, ... 467 QUANDARY 22
    SOMEONE'S CAUGHT IN THE BRANCHES. / SO THERE IS. . . 473 A MASQUE OF REASON . 16
    BOTH OF THEM CAUGHT IT FROM BEL'S FAVORITE POET, . . . 511 A MASQUE OF MERCY . 462
CAUL
    LIKE A CAUL IN WHICH I WAS BORN AND STILL AM WRAPPED. . 390 SKEPTIC 12
CAUSE
    OUT OF NOT HAVING CAUSE FOR MISERY. . . . . . . 167 NEW HAMPSHIRE . . . 273
    WAS THERE EVER A CAUSE TOO LOST, ... 262 HANNIBAL 1
    EVER A CAUSE THAT WAS LOST TOO LONG, ... 262 HANNIBAL 2
    SEEK CONVERSE COMMON CAUSE AND BROTHERHOOD . . . . 350 THE LESSON FOR TODAY . 9
    THAT MAY BE CLAMORED AT BY CAUSE AND SECT, ... 356 TIME OUT 13
    TODAY IS FOR MY CAUSE A DAY OF DAYS. . . . . . . 422 FOR JOHN F. KENNEDY . 4
CAUTION
    AIN'T IT A CAUTION TO US NOT TO FIX . . . . . . 372 THE LITERATE FARMER AND 137
    OF CAUTION UNDER STARS THAT VERY WELL . . . . . . 383 BRAVADO 2
CAVE
    IN THE FLOOR OF A TRIBAL CAVE, ... 312 THE VINDICTIVES . . . 57
CAVERN
    ONE IN A CAVERN WHERE YOU USED TO COOK. . . . . . 382 TO AN ANCIENT . . . 6
    OR SHADOW, BUT A CAVERN HOLE, ... 392 A CLIFF DWELLING . . 7
CAVERNOUS
    IN THE CAVERNOUS PAIL OF THE FIRST ONE TO COME! . . . 59 BLUEBERRIES 5
CAVES
    WHICH MEANS THE-SEVEN-CAVES-THAT-WE-CAME-OUT-OF. . . . 76 THE GENERATIONS OF MEN 93
    WHEN MAN FIRST LIVED IN CAVES ALONG THE CREEKS?" . . . 372 THE LITERATE FARMER AND 140
CEASE
    THE BIRD WOULD CEASE AND BE AS OTHER BIRDS . . . . 120 THE OVEN BIRD . . . 11
    HILL ATMOSPHERE NOT CEASE TO GLOW, ... 234 EVENING IN A SUGAR ORCHARD 9
    AS SOONER OR LATER WE HAVE TO CEASE SOMEWHERE. . . . 379 TOO ANXIOUS FOR RIVERS 10
CEASED
    THE KING HAD SCARCE CEASED TO WRITHE, ... 311 THE VINDICTIVES . . . 21
    TILL HER HEART ALMOST CEASED TO BEAT. . . . . . . 346 DISCOVERY OF MADEIRAS . 102
    THE PROPHET OF DISASTER CEASED TO SHOUT. . . . . . 399 THE BROKEN DROUGHT . . 1
    TILL EVEN I HAVE CEASED . . . . 416 CLOSED FOR GOOD . . . 26
    SEEMINGLY HAS CEASED . . . . 435 KITTY HAWK 239
CEASES
    MERELY BECAUSE IT CEASES TO BE TRUE. . . . . . . 58 THE BLACK COTTAGE . 106
CEASING
    OF CEASING-TO-QUESTION-WHAT-DOESN'T-CONCERN-US, . . . 379 TOO ANXIOUS FOR RIVERS 9
CEDAR
    A SWAMP OF CEDAR. CHOKED WITH OIL OF CEDAR . . . . 125 AN ENCOUNTER 5
    THAT MIGHT BE PEOPLE AND ARE BUT CEDAR, ... 291 ON HEART'S BEGINNING TO 28
    AND ITS SUPPORTING CENTRAL CEDAR POLE, ... 332 THE SILKEN TENT . . 5
    OF AN OLD CEDAR AT THE WATERSIDE . . . . 379 DIRECTIVE 56
CEILING
    LIKE STANCHIONS IN THE BARN, FROM FLOOR TO CEILING-- . 66 A SERVANT TO SERVANTS 115
    BUT MY LEGS GOT THEIR KNOCKS AGAINST THE CEILING." . . 93 THE SELF-SEEKER . . 29
    SLIPPING FROM CLUMSY CLUTCHES TOWARD THE CEILING. . . 113 IN THE HOME STRETCH . 89
    AND DANCED IN YELLOW WRIGGLERS ON THE CEILING, . . . 117 IN THE HOME STRETCH . 203
    WITH BOTH HIS FEET AT ONCE AGAINST THE CEILING, . . . 192 PAUL'S WIFE 51
    THAT FLOATS AGAINST THE CEILING OF THE WOODSHED. . . 277 THE WHITE-TAILED HORNET 2
    THE SYMBOL STAR IT LIFTS AGAINST YOUR CEILING . . . 350 TO A YOUNG WRETCH . . 23
CELEBRATE
    SO IF YOU SEE ME CELEBRATE TWO BIRTHDAYS, ... 196 WILD GRAPES 16
    LET'S CELEBRATE THE EVENT, MY DISTANT FRIEND, . . . 352 THE LESSON FOR TODAY . 47
    SEEMS SOMETHING ARTISTS OUGHT TO CELEBRATE. . . . . 422 FOR JOHN F. KENNEDY . 3

CELEBRATING
    HE'S CELEBRATING SOMETHING STRANGE. . . . . 138 BROWN'S DESCENT . . . 34
CELEBRATION
    A GOOD OLD GET-TOGETHER CELEBRATION. . . . . 487 A MASQUE OF REASON . . 380
CELESTIAL
    THE TWO IN THE CELESTIAL CAST . . . . 390 TWO LEADING LIGHTS . . . 2
    OF HER CELESTIAL TRACK, ... 464 MILKY WAY IS A COWPATH   22
CELLAR
    AND LEFT NO TRACE BUT THE CELLAR WALLS, ... 5 GHOST HOUSE 3
    AND A CELLAR IN WHICH THE DAYLIGHT FALLS . . . . 5 GHOST HOUSE 4
    AND I KEEP HEARING FROM THE CELLAR BIN . . . . 69 AFTER APPLE-PICKING . 24
    IN AN OLD CELLAR HOLE IN A BYROAD . . . . 73 THE GENERATIONS OF MEN   8
    WHY NOT TAKE SEATS HERE ON THE CELLAR WALL . . . . . . 75 THE GENERATIONS OF MEN 63
    DRAWN INTO TOWN ABOUT THIS CELLAR HOLE . . . . 76 THE GENERATIONS OF MEN 89
    HE'S GROPING IN THE CELLAR AFTER JAM-- . . . . 77 THE GENERATIONS OF MEN 101
    THAT YOU SHALL FIND LIES IN THE CELLAR, CHARRED . . . . 79 THE GENERATIONS OF MEN 161
    AND HAVING SCARED THE CELLAR UNDER HIM . . . . . . 108 OLD MAN'S WINTER NIGHT   9
    (THE ARRANGEMENT MADE A PLEASANT SUNNY CELLAR.) . . . 181 MAPLE 59
    IS BACK INTO THE CELLAR WHERE IT CAME FROM. . . . . 203 THE WITCH OF COOS . . 26
    IT LEFT THE CELLAR FORTY YEARS AGO . . . . 203 THE WITCH OF COOS . . 28
    UP ONE FLIGHT FROM THE CELLAR TO THE KITCHEN, ... 203 THE WITCH OF COOS . . 30
    THE NIGHT THE BONES CAME UP THE CELLAR STAIRS . . . . 203 THE WITCH OF COOS . . 40
    AND THOUGHT I HEARD HIM DOWNSTAIRS IN THE CELLAR. . . . 203 THE WITCH OF COOS . . 47
    WHEN THERE WAS WATER IN THE CELLAR IN SPRING . . . . 204 THE WITCH OF COOS . . 49
    STRUCK THE HARD CELLAR BOTTOM. AND THEN SOMEONE . . . 204 THE WITCH OF COOS . . 50
    THE CELLAR WINDOWS WERE BANKED UP WITH SAWDUST . . . . 204 THE WITCH OF COOS . . 57
    OF THE DOOR TO THE CELLAR OR THE HALL. . . . . . . 205 THE WITCH OF COOS . . 84
    "WHAT BONES?" "THE CELLAR BONES--OUT OF THE GRAVE." . . 205 THE WITCH OF COOS . . 101
    THE ATTIC WAS LESS TO US THAN THE CELLAR. . . . . . 206 THE WITCH OF COOS . . 123
    WE THINK THEY HAD A GRAVE DOWN IN THE CELLAR. . . . . 206 THE WITCH OF COOS . . 135
    WE KNOW THEY HAD A GRAVE DOWN IN THE CELLAR. . . . . 206 THE WITCH OF COOS . . 136
    WE WERE ABOUT IT ONE NIGHT IN THE CELLAR. . . . . . 206 THE WITCH OF COOS . . 142
    OF BEING WATCHED FROM FORTY CELLAR HOLES . . . . . 378 DIRECTIVE 21
    BUT ONLY A BELILACED CELLAR HOLE, ... 378 DIRECTIVE 46
    YOUR EXIT DOOR'S BECOME A CELLAR DOOR. . . . . . . 514 A MASQUE OF MERCY . . 549
    YOU MEAN I'M BEING SENT DOWN IN THE CELLAR? . . . . . 514 A MASQUE OF MERCY . . 551
    WHOSE CELLAR IS IT, YOURS OR THE APOSTLE'S? . . . . . 514 A MASQUE OF MERCY . . 554
    IT IS THE CELLAR TO MY STORE.--WHAT HO, DOWN THERE! . . 514 A MASQUE OF MERCY . . 555
    IT IS THE CELLAR TO MY STORE, BUT NOT MY CELLAR. . . . 514 A MASQUE OF MERCY . . 559
    I HAVE CONTRIBUTED THE EMPTY CELLAR . . . . 515 A MASQUE OF MERCY . . 564
    DOWN BURNING SKEPTICS IN THE CELLAR FURNACE . . . . . 516 A MASQUE OF MERCY . . 603
    I HAVE HAD PAINTED ON THE CELLAR WALL . . . . . . 516 A MASQUE OF MERCY . . 615
    THE CELLAR DOOR SWINGS WIDE AND SLAMS AGAIN.) . . . . 520 A MASQUE OF MERCY . . 696
CELLARS
    NOT ON THE BATTLEFIELD, BUT DOWN IN CELLARS. . . . . 515 A MASQUE OF MERCY . . 573
    WHAT'S ALL THIS TALK OF SLAYING DOWN IN CELLARS-- . . . 516 A MASQUE OF MERCY . . 605
CEMENTED
    THE MEADOW GRASS COULD BE CEMENTED DOWN . . . . . . 231 A BROOK IN THE CITY . 9
CEMETERY
    AND WEREN'T THERE SPECIAL CEMETERY FLOWERS, ... 200 PLACE FOR A THIRD . . 26
CENSURE
    I HOPE THEY WON'T TAKE IT FOR CENSURE. . . . . . . 294 A RECORD STRIDE . . 20
    TO SAVE THE QUEEN FROM FAMILY CENSURE . . . . . . 416 AMERICA IS HARD TO SEE 11
    PULPITEERS WILL CENSURE . . . . 434 KITTY HAWK 213
CENSUS-TAKER
    I CAME AS CENSUS-TAKER TO THE WASTE . . . . 174 THE CENSUS-TAKER . . 9
    THE CENSUS-TAKER . . . . 174 THE CENSUS-TAKER . . T
CENT
    THEY NEVER EARNED ME SO MUCH AS ONE CENT: . . . . . 95 THE SELF-SEEKER . . . 71
    "A THOUSAND WOULDN'T BE A CENT TOO MUCH; . . . . . . 100 THE SELF-SEEKER . . 199
    WHAT HE DID WITH EVERY CENT. . . . . 309 HARDSHIP OF ACCOUNTING   5
CENTIGRADE
    TALK FAHRENHEIT, TALK CENTIGRADE. . . . . 403 SOMETHING LIKE A STAR . 13
CENTRAL
    AND ITS SUPPORTING CENTRAL CEDAR POLE, ... 332 THE SILKEN TENT . . . 5
CENTS
    THE EXTENT OF PASTURE I SHOULD STRIP, THREE CENTS . . . 107 CHRISTMAS TREES . . . 48
    THREE CENTS SO SMALL BESIDE THE DOLLAR FRIENDS . . . . 107 CHRISTMAS TREES . . . 50
    WORTH THREE CENTS MORE TO GIVE AWAY THAN SELL, ... 107 CHRISTMAS TREES . . . 56
    AT THIRTY CENTS A BUSHEL. GIVE ME SHEEP. . . . . . 316 BUILD SOIL 12
    I KNOW WOOL'S DOWN TO SEVEN CENTS A POUND. . . . . . 316 BUILD SOIL 13
CENTURIES
    OF WHAT HAD BEEN FOR CENTURIES THE TREND; . . . . . 422 FOR JOHN F. KENNEDY . 9
CEREMONIOUSLY
    AND CEREMONIOUSLY LAID IT ON THE GROUND, ... 284 THE GOLD HESPERIDEE . 46
CERTAIN
    IF THAT WAS WHAT IT WAS. YOU CAN BE CERTAIN, ... 35 DEATH OF THE HIRED MAN 26
    I KNEW A LOVELY WAY TO TELL FOR CERTAIN . . . . . . 96 THE SELF-SEEKER . . . 108
    SO AS TO SAY FOR CERTAIN I WAS HERE . . . . 101 THE WOOD-PILE . . . 8
    THEN I WAS CERTAIN I HAD NEVER MEANT . . . . . . 107 CHRISTMAS TREES . . . 45
    AS CERTAIN AS THE MEALS WE'VE HAD. I WISH . . . . . 115 IN THE HOME STRETCH . 141
    AND TUGGED IT FROM HIS FIRST TOO CERTAIN HOLD, ... 172 A STAR IN A STONEBOAT. 6
    (IF CERTAIN IT WOULDN'T BE IDLE TO CALL . . . . . . 228 GOOD-BY AND KEEP COLD . 9
    HAD MADE THEM CERTAIN EARTH RETURNED THEIR LOVE. . . . 230 TWO LOOK AT TWO . . 42
    OF A CERTAIN UPPER-WINDOW LIGHT. . . . . 253 THE THATCH 4
    BUT CERTAIN SIGNS OF BURIED TURTLE'S EGG; . . . . . 270 THE EGG AND THE MACHINE 20
    THREE MADE IT CERTAIN NOTHING FATE COULD DO . . . . . 283 THE GOLD HESPERIDEE . 27
    YOU MUST NOT MIND A CERTAIN COOLNESS FROM HIM . . . . 377 DIRECTIVE 18
    ON MAKING CERTAIN ANYTHING HAS HAPPENED . . . . . . 383 MAKING CERTAIN ANYTHING T
    THAT'S WHAT A CERTAIN BOMB WAS SENT TO BE." . . . . . 398 BURSTING RAPTURE . . 14
    IT ASKS OF US A CERTAIN HEIGHT, ... 403 SOMETHING LIKE A STAR . 21
    ON A CERTAIN SLAB . . . . 436 KITTY HAWK 260
    THE ONLY CERTAIN FREEDOM'S IN DEPARTURE. . . . . . 460 HOW HARD TO KEEP FROM 194
    I'D WANT TO BE MORE CERTAIN I WAS CALLED, ... 503 A MASQUE OF MERCY . . 270
CERTAINLY
    THAT CALM SEEMS CERTAINLY SAFE TO LAST TONIGHT. . . . 268 ON LOOKING UP BY CHANCE 16
CERTAINTY
    HER TEACHER'S CERTAINTY IT MUST BE MABEL . . . . . 179 MAPLE 1

CERTAINTY (CONTINUED)
    VERSE COULD BE WRITTEN ON THE CERTAINTY . . . . . . 277 THE WHITE-TAILED HORNET   7
    YET HOW ABOUT THE INSECT CERTAINTY . . . . 277 THE WHITE-TAILED HORNET 12
CHAFE
    TO CHAFE AND SHUFFLE IN MY CALLOUSED PALM . . . . . 174 A STAR IN A STONEBOAT . 52
    BEHIND NEW BARRIER WALLS (AND LET IT CHAFE!), ... 254 THE FLOOD 3
    I'D SHIP A SMOOTH ONE YOU COULD SLAP AND CHAFE, . . . 365 OF STONES OF THE PLACE 9
CHAFED
    FOR THE HARD WORK. HE CHAFED ITS LONG WHITE BODY . . 187 THE AX-HELVE 76
CHAFF
    "WHAT WAS THE PIRATE CAPTAIN'S CHAFF? . . . . 346 DISCOVERY OF MADEIRAS . 90
CHAIN
    ONE STRINGING A CHAIN OF SEED IN AN OPEN CREASE, . . 299 STRONG SAYING NOTHING . 7
    ON THE LONG BEAD CHAIN OF REPEATED BIRTH, ... 303 A BIRD SINGING IN SLEEP 11
    THE GREAT THOUSAND-LINKED GOLD CHAIN, ... 312 THE VINDICTIVES . . . 63
    AND THOUGH IN TINSEL CHAIN AND POPCORN ROPE . . . . 350 TO A YOUNG WRETCH . . 19
    TO LINK A CHAIN OF MONEY-METAL BANKS. . . . . 358 THE LOST FOLLOWER . . 8
    ALL IS AN INTERMINABLE CHAIN OF LONGING. . . . . . . 421 ESCAPIST--NEVER . . . 12
CHAINS
    STRUNG CHAINS OF WALL ROUND EVERYTHING, ... 265 THE BIRTHPLACE . . . 4
    HE GOT NO MORE THAN DUNGEON CHAINS . . . . 417 AMERICA IS HARD TO SEE 44
CHAIR
    "WHO'S THAT MAN SLEEPING IN THE OFFICE CHAIR? . . . . 45 A HUNDRED COLLARS . . 29
    SLUMPED WAY DOWN IN A CHAIR, WITH BOTH HIS FEET . . . 72 THE CODE 97
    MRS. BAPTISTE CAME IN AND ROCKED A CHAIR . . . . . . 186 THE AX-HELVE 46
    AND CAUGHT HERSELF UP BODILY, CHAIR AND ALL, ... 187 THE AX-HELVE 52
    BUT LEAVING NOT THE CHAIR I LONG HAVE SAT IN . . . . 350 THE LESSON FOR TODAY . 5
    (SHE HAS HER OWN GLASS IN A VACANT CHAIR.) . . . . . 496 A MASQUE OF MERCY . . 84
    KNEEL BY HIM. BEL STANDS UP BESIDE HER CHAIR . . . . 518 A MASQUE OF MERCY . . 652
CHAIR-BACK
    AND ROLLED HIS OLD HEAD ON THAT SHARP-EDGED CHAIR-BACK. . . 39 DEATH OF THE HIRED MAN 148
CHAIRS
    OF CHAIRS TURNED UPSIDE DOWN TO SIT LIKE PEOPLE . . . 110 IN THE HOME STRETCH . 6
    IN OTHER CHAIRS, AND SOMETHING, COME TO LOOK, ... 110 IN THE HOME STRETCH . 7
    I LIKE CHAIRS OCCUPYING OTHER CHAIRS . . . . 115 IN THE HOME STRETCH . 156
    STARTED CHAIRS THUNDERING ON THE KITCHEN FLOOR, . . . 368 THE LITERATE FARMER AND 2
    HE THINKS THAT CHAIRS AND TABLES WILL ENDURE, ... 372 THE LITERATE FARMER AND 128
CHALK
    HER FLUFF OF PLUMAGE, WHITE AS CHALK, ... 280 BLUE RIBBON AT AMESBURY 7
CHALK-PILE
    AND BRING THE CHALK-PILE DOWN. "I'LL TELL YOU WHAT-- . . 205 THE WITCH OF COOS . . 107
CHALKY
    BRUSHING THEIR CHALKY SKULL WITH CHALKY FINGERS, . . . 206 THE WITCH OF COOS . . 128
CHALLENGED
    "YOU DON'T," SHE CHALLENGED. "TELL ME WHAT IT IS." . . 51 HOME BURIAL 19
CHAMBER (SEE LOWER-CHAMBER)
    THERE IN THE UPPER CHAMBER IN THE ELL, ... 67 A SERVANT TO SERVANTS . 142
    IN ONTO THE UPPER CHAMBER FLOORS. . . . . 253 THE THATCH 35
CHAMPING
    THE CUTTER BAR HAD JUST GONE CHAMPING OVER . . . . . 109 THE EXPOSED NEST . . . 14
CHANCE (SEE OFF-CHANCE)
    HE THINKS IF HE COULD HAVE ANOTHER CHANCE . . . . . 37 DEATH OF THE HIRED MAN 86
    HAS HE HAD THE REFUSAL OF MY CHANCE?" . . . . 45 A HUNDRED COLLARS . . 30
    APART WOULD MAKE ME OUT. GIVE ME MY CHANCE. . . . . 53 HOME BURIAL 61
    "BAD TO GET MARRIED WHEN SHE HAD THE CHANCE?" . . . . 88 THE HOUSEKEEPER . . . 184
    TO GIVE WHATEVER MIGHT CHANCE TO BE, ... 127 HOUSE FEAR 6
    AND GIVE YOU A CHANCE TO PUT SOME STRENGTH . . . . . 133 A GIRL'S GARDEN . . . 15
    HE'S YOUR ONE CHANCE TO SCORE AGAINST THE STATE.) . . 161 NEW HAMPSHIRE 66
    AS LEAVING MORE TO NATURE AND HAPPY CHANCE. . . . . 185 MAPLE 169
    BUT WELCOMED FOR THE CHANCE TO LACE MY SHOES . . . . 215 A FOUNTAIN, A BOTTLE . 66
    I MIGHT NOT HAVE THE CHANCE I MISSED IN LIFE . . . . 222 TO E.T. 5
    THEN NOW IS THE CHANCE FOR THE FLOWERS . . . . . . 264 THE LAST MOWING . . . 5
    ON LOOKING UP BY CHANCE AT THE CONSTELLATIONS . . . . 268 ON LOOKING UP BY CHANCE T
    AND IF ONE BROKE BY ANY CHANCE, ... 273 A LONE STRIKER . . . 24
    IT CAN'T BE JUST TO GIVE THE ROBBER A CHANCE . . . . 321 BUILD SOIL 166
    YOU HAD NO CHANCE BUT TO BE MINOR, DID YOU? . . . . 351 THE LESSON FOR TODAY . 23
    OR MISSED THEIR CHANCE, OR NOT HAVE BEEN THEIR BEST, . . 355 THE LESSON FOR TODAY . 152
    OF GETTING ONE MORE CHANCE TO CHANGE OUR MANNERS? . . 397 THE PLANNERS 12
    IF I HAD HAD MY CHANCE WHEN YOUNG . . . . 417 AMERICA IS HARD TO SEE 33
    WHEN THE CHANCE WENT BY . . . . 434 KITTY HAWK 183
    OUR CHANCE OF BEING PEOPLE NEWLY BORN. . . . . . . 446 DOES NO ONE AT ALL EVER 12
    HE GOT HIS FIRST CHANCE TO PREPARE A MEAL . . . . . 455 HOW HARD TO KEEP FROM 55
    THE CHANCE IS THE REMOTEST . . . . 465 SOME SCIENCE FICTION . 1
    BY ANY CHANCE A LADY APPLE ON YOU? . . . . 488 A MASQUE OF REASON . . 421
    AS IF I ASKED FOR ONE MORE CHANCE MYSELF . . . . . . 521 A MASQUE OF MERCY . . 736
CHANCED
    WE CHANCED IN PASSING BY THAT AFTERNOON . . . . . . 55 THE BLACK COTTAGE . . 1
    FASTER OR SLOWER AS HE CHANCED, ... 138 BROWN'S DESCENT . . . 25
CHANCES
    "WE'RE GIVING YOU OUR CHANCES ON DE FARM." . . . . . 114 IN THE HOME STRETCH . 108
    THE CHANCES ARE WHEN THERE'S SO MUCH PRETENSE . . . . 483 A MASQUE OF REASON . . 277
CHANDELIER
    NOT LIKE A MAN, BUT LIKE A CHANDELIER. . . . . . . 204 THE WITCH OF COOS . . 69
CHANGE
    IF I CAN CHANGE IT. OH, I WON'T, I WON'T!" . . . . . 54 HOME BURIAL 107
    MOST OF THE CHANGE WE THINK WE SEE IN LIFE . . . . . 58 THE BLACK COTTAGE . . 109
    THE PAINS OF CONQUERING TO FORCE CHANGE ON. . . . . 58 THE BLACK COTTAGE . . 118
    WE DIDN'T CHANGE WITHOUT SOME SACRIFICE, ... 64 A SERVANT TO SERVANTS . 64
    SOMEHOW THE CHANGE WORE OUT LIKE A PRESCRIPTION. . . . 67 A SERVANT TO SERVANTS . 154
    COME, HOLD IT OUT. DON'T CHANGE.--A RAM'S HORN ORCHID! . 96 THE SELF-SEEKER . . . 112
    AND CARE FOR THEM IN SUCH A CHANGE OF SCENE, ... 109 THE EXPOSED NEST . . . 24
    ONE REAL REFORMER WHO WOULD CHANGE THE WORLD . . . . 162 NEW HAMPSHIRE 94
    TO ANY CHANGE FROM HOT TO COLD, FROM WET . . . . . 166 NEW HAMPSHIRE 235
    A CHANGE OF MOOD . . . . 221 DUST OF SNOW 6
    IT IS THE CHANGE TO DARKNESS IN THE SKY. . . . . . . 249 ACCEPTANCE 5
    CHANGE LIKE THIS TO A DEEPER ROAR? . . . . 251 BEREFT 2
    WE'VE SAID WE TWO. LET'S CHANGE THAT TO WE THREE. . . 258 WEST-RUNNING BROOK . . 11
    IF BY ANY CHANGE OF SHAPE . . . . 260 SAND DUNES 11

CHANGE (CONTINUED)
AND HAVING POWER TO CHANGE HIS AIM IN FLIGHT, ... 277 THE WHITE-TAILED HORNET   5
IF EARTH WERE THOUGHT ABOUT TO CHANGE ITS AXIS, . . . 317 BUILD SOIL 58
IN BRINGING CHANGE UNHERALDED ON THE UNREADY. . . . . 320 BUILD SOIL 125
FOR CHANGE OF SOLITUDE. . . . . 333 HAPPINESS MAKES UP . . 24
AT SUCH A PLANETARY CHANGE OF STYLE. . . . . . . 335 I COULD GIVE ALL . . . 10
HOW FOR A CHANGE WOULD A WEDDING BE?-- . . . . . . 345 DISCOVERY OF MADEIRAS . 71
OF GETTING ONE MORE CHANCE TO CHANGE OUR MANNERS? . . 397 THE PLANNERS 12
"I THINK I'LL CHANGE MY MIND." / "YOU'RE SAYING THAT . . 406 FROM PLANE TO PLANE . 75
SOME CHANGE IN THE LAW . . . . 449 THE BAD ISLAND--EASTER 51
AND CHANGE THE TENOR OF RELIGIOUS THOUGHT. . . . . 475 A MASQUE OF REASON . . 68
THE WRITING ON THE SCREEN MUST CHANGE TOO FAST . . . 502 A MASQUE OF MERCY . . 245
AT ANYTHING BUT CHANGE OF PERSONNEL. . . . . . . 510 A MASQUE OF MERCY . . 458
LET'S CHANGE THE SUBJECT, BOYS, I'M GETTING NERVOUS. . . 516 A MASQUE OF MERCY . . 598
CHANGED
THEY WOULD NOT FIND ME CHANGED FROM HIM THEY KNEW-- . . 5 INTO MY OWN 13
TIMES WERE CHANGED FROM WHAT THEY WERE: . . . . . . 24 PAN WITH US 21
I WASN'T LOOKING FOR HIM--AND HE'S CHANGED. . . . . . 35 DEATH OF THE HIRED MAN 38
"I DON'T SUPPOSE THE WATER'S CHANGED AT ALL. . . . . 44 THE MOUNTAIN 101
AND HER FACE CHANGED FROM TERRIFIED TO DULL. . . . . 51 HOME BURIAL 9
I WOULD HAVE CHANGED THE CREED A VERY LITTLE? . . . . 57 THE BLACK COTTAGE . . 88
HE MUST HAVE CHANGED HIS MIND AND GONE TO GARLAND'S. . . 81 THE HOUSEKEEPER . . . 17
FEW FARMS CHANGED HANDS; SO RATHER THAN SPEND YEARS . . 177 THE STAR-SPLITTER . . 28
I CHANGED FROM HAND TO HAND IN DESPERATION. . . . . 189 THE GRINDSTONE . . . 34
IT HAS NOT CHANGED . . . . 220 I WILL SING YOU ONE-O . 72
NOT TILL FROM SEPARATE FLAKES THEY CHANGED AT NIGHT . . 239 OUR SINGING STRENGTH . 7
THE SWINGING MILL BELL CHANGED ITS RATE . . . . . . 273 A LONE STRIKER . . . 1
THE WOOD OF IT CHANGED TO STONE, ... 285 IN TIME OF CLOUDBURST . 23
AND CHANGED IT TO THE ENGLISH NAME FOR WHEAT. . . . . 446 DOES NO ONE AT ALL EVER 8
YOU CHANGED ALL THAT. YOU SET ME FREE TO REIGN. . . . 476 A MASQUE OF REASON . . 77
I HAD BEFORE. THAT'S WHY I CHANGED TO PAUL-- . . . . 499 A MASQUE OF MERCY . . 158
CHANGES
BEFORE IT CHANGES TO DIAMONDS IN THE SUN), ... 236 VALLEY'S SINGING DAY . 13
FOR THE SHOCKS AND CHANGES WE NEED TO KEEP US SANE. . . 268 ON LOOKING UP BY CHANCE 10
THAT CHANGES WINTER INTO SPRING . . . . 390 TWO LEADING LIGHTS . . 25
CHANGING
CHANGING AN OLD KING FOR ANOTHER OLD ONE. . . . . . 462 HOW HARD TO KEEP FROM   255
CHANNEL
THE ROAD BECAME A CHANNEL RUNNING FLOCKS . . . . . 240 OUR SINGING STRENGTH . 33
CHANTS
IN TIME WITH A MEDLEY OF SOTTO CHANTS; . . . . . . 385 A MOOD APART 3
CHAOS
ACROSS THE ROAR AND CHAOS, AND THE WORDS . . . . . 170 NEW HAMPSHIRE . . . 350
LET CHAOS STORM! . . . . 308 PERTINAX 1
PERSISTING FROM OLD CHAOS IN THEIR MYTH, ... 511 A MASQUE OF MERCY . . 470
CHAPEL
THAT'S BROWNING AND SHEER CHAPEL NON-CONFORMISM. . . . 486 A MASQUE OF REASON . . 365
CHAPTER
(HERE ENDETH CHAPTER FORTY-THREE OF JOB.) . . . . . 490 A MASQUE OF REASON . . 466
IT SEEMS TO BE A CHAPTER HEAD IN METER. . . . . . 506 A MASQUE OF MERCY . . 327
CHAPTERS
AS IS SET FORTH IN CHAPTERS ONE AND TWO. . . . . . 485 A MASQUE OF REASON . . 328
CHARACTER
"HERE COME MORE STARS TO CHARACTER THE SKIES, ... 370 THE LITERATE FARMER AND 75
BY CHARACTER, BY TONGUE, BY NATIVE TRAIT, ... 422 FOR JOHN F. KENNEDY . 14
"YES, BUT GIVE CHARACTER AND NOT JUST FOOD. . . . . 458 HOW HARD TO KEEP FROM 141
A KING MUST GIVE HIS PEOPLE CHARACTER." . . . . . 458 HOW HARD TO KEEP FROM 142
"THEY CAN'T HAVE CHARACTER UNLESS THEY'RE FED." . . . 458 HOW HARD TO KEEP FROM 143
HOW SHALL I GIVE A PEOPLE CHARACTER?" . . . . . . 458 HOW HARD TO KEEP FROM 149
WHAT HAS IT GOT TO DO WITH CHARACTER? . . . . . . 459 HOW HARD TO KEEP FROM 165
CHARACTERS
THEIR CHARACTERS, OR WHETHER THEY ARE SAFE . . . . . 65 A SERVANT TO SERVANTS . 83
ASSORTED CHARACTERS OF DEATH AND BLIGHT . . . . . 302 DESIGN 4
CHARADES
OF SOME KIND. WE COULD HAVE CHARADES. . . . . . . 489 A MASQUE OF REASON . . 430
CHARCOAL
"IT MUST BE ON CHARCOAL THEY FATTEN THEIR FRUIT. . . . 59 BLUEBERRIES 22
A BLACK-CHEEKED STONE AND STICK OF RAIN-WASHED CHARCOAL. . 171 NEW HAMPSHIRE . . . 391
WHERE UNDER DEEP ASH AND CHARCOAL . . . . 312 THE VINDICTIVES . . 58
CHARGE
FOR SUCH A CHARGE, HIS SNOW UPON THE ROOF, ... 108 OLD MAN'S WINTER NIGHT 21
CHARGE THAT TO UPSTART INEXPERIENCE. . . . . . . 378 DIRECTIVE 25
WAS ONE MIGHTY CHARGE . . . . 436 KITTY HAWK 254
CHARGED
ONCE CHARGED THE NAZARENE WITH HAVING BROUGHT . . . 511 A MASQUE OF MERCY . . 465
CHARGES
CHARGES INTO EARTH . . . . 436 KITTY HAWK 248
CHARIOT
AND CHARIOT TO CHIDE . . . . 415 CLOSED FOR GOOD . . . 8
CHARITABLY
IT MAY BE CHARITABLY GUESSED . . . . 390 TWO LEADING LIGHTS . . 22
CHARITY
BUT TREE BY CHARITY IS NOT THE SAME . . . . . . 350 TO A YOUNG WRETCH . . 10
CHARLES
YOU DID NOT KNOW THAT SINCE KING CHARLES DID RULE . . . 351 THE LESSON FOR TODAY . 22
CHARLES'
YOU WERE NOT CHARLES' NOR ANYBODY'S FOOL: . . . . . 351 THE LESSON FOR TODAY . 20
CHARM
THE THOUSANDTH TIME MAY PROVE THE CHARM.--THAT LEAF! . . 148 SNOW 134
CHARMED
I'M CHARMED WITH HER. / YES, I COULD SEE YOU WERE. . . 480 A MASQUE OF REASON . . 182
CHARMING
CUMAEAN SIBYL, CHARMING OGRESS, ... 449 OUR DOOM TO BLOOM . . 1
CHARRED
THAT YOU SHALL FIND LIES IN THE CELLAR, CHARRED . . . 79 THE GENERATIONS OF MEN 161
CHART
AS A CLINICAL CHART. . . . . 447 THE BAD ISLAND--EASTER 6

CHARTED
   WHERE SHOWERS OF CHARTED METEORS LET FLY. . . . . . . 173 A STAR IN A STONEBOAT . 42
CHASES
   THE TOWN IS FULL OF CHASES, LOWES, AND BAILEYS, ... 75 THE GENERATIONS OF MEN . 48
CHATTER
   WE KNOW THE LITERARY CHATTER. . . . . 418 AMERICA IS HARD TO SEE . 66
CHATTERING
   OF ALL THE YOUNG CHATTERING LORENS ALIVE, ... 60 BLUEBERRIES 38
CHAUCER
   DORKINGS BECAUSE THEY'RE SPOKEN OF BY CHAUCER, . . . 162 NEW HAMPSHIRE . . . 106
CHEAP
   A GOOD CHEAP ANTI-DARK IS NOW THE NEED. . . . . . 371 THE LITERATE FARMER AND 99
   GIVE US A GOOD CHEAP TWENTY-FOUR-HOUR DAY, ... 371 THE LITERATE FARMER AND 100
CHEAPENED
   THE OLD MAN ARGUES SCIENCE CHEAPENED SPEED. . . . . 371 THE LITERATE FARMER AND 98
CHEAPEST
   THE CHEAPEST TRAMP THAT CAME ALONG THAT WAY . . . . . 290 OLD BARN AT THE BOTTOM 44
CHEATING
   OF PLAGIARISM AND HELP OF CHEATING PARENTS. . . . . . 325 BUILD SOIL 275
CHECK
   IT CANNOT CHECK THE PEEPER'S SILVER CROAK; . . . . . 226 THE ONSET 17
   I SHOULD HAVE TO CHECK ON MY LIST . . . . 384 MAKING CERTAIN ANYTHING 14
CHECKED
   AND CHECKED MY STEPS TO MAKE PRETENSE . . . . . . 25 THE DEMIURGE'S LAUGH . 15
   HE REELED, HE LURCHED, HE BOBBED, HE CHECKED; . . . . 138 BROWN'S DESCENT . . . 37
   HAD CHECKED THE PACE . . . . 218 I WILL SING YOU ONE-O . 18
   BUT THIS WE KNOW, THE OBSTACLE THAT CHECKED . . . 261 A SOLDIER 12
CHEEK
   SIDELONG, FULL ON MY CHEEK, ... 29 MY BUTTERFLY 40
   SHE PUT HER FINGER IN YOUR CHEEK SO HARD . . . . 180 MAPLE 16
   BUT WHERE THIS OLD WALL BURNS A SUNNY CHEEK, ... 246 ATMOSPHERE 2
   AND BACK AND FORTH HE SWAYS FROM CHEEK TO CHEEK, . . . 269 THE BEAR 29
   HIS CHEEK SMEARED WITH APPLE SAND, ... 366 NOT OF SCHOOL AGE . . 9
CHEEKED (SEE BLACK-CHEEKED)
CHEEKS
   HER CHEEKS HIGH-COLORED, ... 256 THE LOVELY BE CHOOSERS 17
CHEER
   A CHEER WENT UP THAT SHOOK THE MOTTOED WALL. . . . 400 THE BROKEN DROUGHT . . 6
CHEERILY
   BY HAILING CHEERILY "HIT THEM HARD!" . . . . . . 275 TWO TRAMPS IN MUD TIME 4
CHEERING
   MAKE YOURSELF UP A CHEERING SONG OF HOW . . . . . 378 DIRECTIVE 29
CHEMIST
   EVEN WHILE WE TALK SOME CHEMIST AT COLUMBIA . . . . . 319 BUILD SOIL 107
CHERISH
   CHERISH IN HAND, LIFT DOWN, AND NOT LET FALL. . . . 69 AFTER APPLE-PICKING . 31
   THAT AUGHT WE CHERISH . . . . 469 WE VAINLY WRESTLE... . 2
CHERISHED
   FREE VERSE, SO CALLED, IS REALLY CHERISHED PROSE, . . 460 HOW HARD TO KEEP FROM 221
CHERRY
   AMONG TAR-BANDED ANCIENT CHERRY TREES, ... 55 THE BLACK COTTAGE . . 3
   TO GO THE ROUND OF APPLE, CHERRY, PEACH, ... 117 IN THE HOME STRETCH . 196
   WHEN PEAR AND CHERRY BLOOM WENT DOWN IN SHOWERS . . 120 THE OVEN BIRD . . . 7
CHEST
   ACROSS HIS CHEST TO MAKE AS 'TWERE A BOW: . . . . 114 IN THE HOME STRETCH . 107
CHESTNUT
   IN CHESTNUT NOW BECOME A PRECIOUS WOOD . . . . . 290 OLD BARN AT THE BOTTOM 38
   WILL THE BLIGHT END THE CHESTNUT? . . . . 308 EVIL TENDENCIES CANCEL 1
CHEW
   JAMES WOULD TAKE TIME, OF COURSE, TO CHEW IT OVER . . . 70 THE CODE 18
CHEWINK
   "HE MAY AND NOT CARE, AND SO LEAVE THE CHEWINK . . . . 60 BLUEBERRIES 29
CHICAMOZTOC
   "THE INDIANS HAD A MYTH OF CHICAMOZTOC, ... 76 THE GENERATIONS OF MEN 92
CHICKADEE
   FLIRTING THEIR WINGS AND SAYING CHICKADEE, ... 151 SNOW 231
CHICKENS
   WITH A GREAT FLOCK OF CHICKENS OF RARE BREEDS . . . . 162 NEW HAMPSHIRE . . . 102
CHICKEN-TIME
   "OH, THAT'S BEEN THERE FOR HAWKS SINCE CHICKEN-TIME. . . . 83 THE HOUSEKEEPER . . . 66
CHIDE
   AND CHARIOT TO CHIDE . . . . 415 CLOSED FOR GOOD . . . 8
CHIEF (SEE COMMANDER-IN-CHIEF)
   "I THOUGHT YOU MEANT TO BE AN INDIAN CHIEF-- . . . . 406 FROM PLANE TO PLANE . 69
   ONE DAY WHEN THE CHIEF COOK WAS SICK AT HEART. . . . 455 HOW HARD TO KEEP FROM 56
CHIEFLY
   (I'M THINKING CHIEFLY OF THE WHEELBARROW.) . . . . . 189 THE GRINDSTONE . . . 14
   NOR CHIEFLY THAT YOU MAY GO WHERE YOU WILL, ... 300 THE MASTER SPEED . . 6
CHILD
   TWO AND A CHILD, ... 10 STORM FEAR 10
   "CAN'T A MAN SPEAK OF HIS OWN CHILD HE'S LOST?" . . . 52 HOME BURIAL 35
   TO TAKE YOUR MOTHER-LOSS OF A FIRST CHILD . . . . . 53 HOME BURIAL 64
   A MAN CAN'T SPEAK OF HIS OWN CHILD THAT'S DEAD." . . . 53 HOME BURIAL 70
   AS A CHILD MISSES THE UNSAID GOOD-NIGHT . . . . . 58 THE BLACK COTTAGE . . 102
   HE'S JUST DROPPED EVERYTHING. HE'S LIKE A CHILD. . . . 83 THE HOUSEKEEPER . . . 55
   "YOU DON'T SEE--I'VE A CHILD HERE BY THE HAND. . . . 92 THE FEAR 79
   "WHAT'S A CHILD DOING AT THIS TIME OF NIGHT----?" . . . 92 THE FEAR 81
   "OUT WALKING. EVERY CHILD SHOULD HAVE THE MEMORY . . . 92 THE FEAR 82
   IT'S NOT FAIR TO THE CHILD. IT CAN'T BE HELPED, THOUGH: . . 98 THE SELF-SEEKER . . . 148
   AND NO CHILD, ... 128 THE IMPULSE 4
   AS TOLD TO A CHILD . . . . 135 LOCKED OUT 5
   AS TOLD TO A CHILD . . . . 135 LAST WORD OF A BLUEBIRD 5
   DOING A MAN'S WORK, THOUGH A CHILD AT HEART-- . . . . 137 "OUT,OUT--" 24
   AND CAME DOWN LIKE A COASTING CHILD. . . . . . 139 BROWN'S DESCENT . . . 44
   A NAME WITH MEANING COULD BRING UP A CHILD, ... 185 MAPLE 166
   TAKING THE CHILD OUT OF THE PARENTS' HANDS. . . . . 185 MAPLE 167
   OR A LITTLE CHILD, COMES UP. IT WASN'T TOFFILE: . . . 204 THE WITCH OF COOS . . 53
   GIVE HER A CHILD AT EITHER KNEE FOR FOURTH JOY . . . . 256 THE LOVELY BE CHOOSERS 31

CHILD (CONTINUED)
     HAD BEEN FOUND WITH CHILD; AND HER ARMY . . . . 314 BEARER OF EVIL TIDINGS   21
     AND THE CHILD THAT CAME OF THE PRINCESS . . . . 314 BEARER OF EVIL TIDINGS   29
     OH, SHOULD A CHILD BE LEFT UNWARNED . . . . 336 THE WIND AND THE RAIN .   12
     AT THE ONE HOUSE A CHILD WAS OUT . . . . 366 NOT OF SCHOOL AGE . .   5
     THE RULE IS, NEVER GIVE A CHILD A CHOICE. . . . . . 427 CONCEPT SELF-CONCEIVED   8
     I'M NOT A CHILD FOR YOU TO PUT ME OFF . . . . . . 482 A MASQUE OF REASON . . 256
     OR CHILD, AND THIS IS MOTHERLY RESENTMENT? . . . . 501 A MASQUE OF MERCY . . 206
CHILDHOOD (SEE SECOND-CHILDHOOD)
     THIS WAS HER MOTHER'S CHILDHOOD HOME; . . . . . . 181 MAPLE   56
     FROM CHILDHOOD HAS MY HEART BEEN SET. . . . . . . 451 A-WISHING WELL . . .   22
CHILDISH
     THE THOUGHT OF SO MUCH CHILDISH LONGING IN VAIN, . . . 287 A ROADSIDE STAND . .   33
     AND ENTERED IN OUR CHILDISH CATECHISM . . . . 427 CONCEPT SELF-CONCEIVED   2
CHILDISHNESS
     WHAT CHILDISHNESS HE WOULDN'T GIVE WAY TO. . . . . . 86 THE HOUSEKEEPER . . . 133
CHILDLIKE
     A CHILDLIKE THING. . . . . 133 A GIRL'S GARDEN . . .   4
CHILDREN
     OR HOMESPUN CHILDREN WITH CLICKING PAILS . . . . . 24 PAN WITH US   14
     AND SENDS THE CHILDREN DOWN THERE WITH THEIR MOTHER . . . 44 A HUNDRED COLLARS . .   4
     ANYONE UPON EARTH AND STILL HER CHILDREN . . . . . 75 THE GENERATIONS OF MEN   51
     AS IN THE GAME 'TEN-STEP' THE CHILDREN PLAY." . . . . 114 IN THE HOME STRETCH . 118
     "AND SCARE YOU TOO?" THE CHILDREN SAID TOGETHER. . . . 130 THE BONFIRE   19
     "OH, BUT WAR'S NOT FOR CHILDREN--IT'S FOR MEN." . . . 132 THE BONFIRE 100
     AND CHILDREN IN THE SHIPS AND IN THE TOWNS? . . . . 132 THE BONFIRE 108
     WAR IS FOR EVERYONE, FOR CHILDREN TOO. . . . . . . 133 THE BONFIRE 111
     WITH HIS TEN CHILDREN UNDER TEN YEARS OLD. . . . . 144 SNOW   52
     "AND LEAVE THE CHILDREN?" / "WAIT AND CALL AGAIN. . . . 154 SNOW 307
     MAYBE SHE ONLY WANTS HIM FOR THE CHILDREN." . . . . 155 SNOW 336
     ONE OF MY CHILDREN RANGING AFTER ROCKS . . . . . 162 NEW HAMPSHIRE . . . 116
     AS FATHERS ABOUT CHILDREN, YOU TELL TEACHER. . . . 180 MAPLE   6
     NAME CHILDREN SOME NAMES AND SEE WHAT YOU DO. . . . 185 MAPLE 170
     BAPTISTE ON HIS DEFENSE ABOUT THE CHILDREN . . . . 188 THE AX-HELVE   83
     WHATEVER SCHOOL AND CHILDREN AND OUR DOUBTS . . . . 188 THE AX-HELVE   85
     SHE THOUGHT OF CHILDREN IN A BURIAL ROW; . . . . 199 PLACE FOR A THIRD . .   5
     THREE CHILDREN IN A BURIAL ROW WERE SAD. . . . . 199 PLACE FOR A THIRD . .   6
     AND I WAS ONE OF THE CHILDREN TOLD . . . . 249 A PECK OF GOLD . . .   3
     BUT I WAS ONE OF THE CHILDREN TOLD . . . . 249 A PECK OF GOLD . . .   7
     AND I WAS ONE OF THE CHILDREN TOLD, ... 249 A PECK OF GOLD . . .   11
     THAT IN THE NEIGHBORHOOD OF HOME AND CHILDREN . . . . 277 THE WHITE-TAILED HORNET 13
     OF CHILDREN, LOVE OF FRIENDS, OF MEN, OF GOD: . . . . 318 BUILD SOIL   86
     AGE SAW TWO QUIET CHILDREN . . . . 335 CARPE DIEM   1
     HE AND A LOT OF CHILDREN CAME OUTSIDE, ... 368 THE LITERATE FARMER AND   6
     THE PLAYTHINGS IN THE PLAYHOUSE OF THE CHILDREN. . . . 378 DIRECTIVE   43
     BEFORE SHE MUST PUT OUT THE LIGHT ON THE CHILDREN . . . 379 TOO ANXIOUS FOR RIVERS   18
     "YOU CHILDREN MAY DREAM IT AND TELL IT TOMORROW." . . . 379 TOO ANXIOUS FOR RIVERS   20
     TO GLASSED-IN CHILDREN AT THE WINDOWSILL. . . . . 445 QUESTIONING FACES . .   6
     OF HAVING CHILDREN--AFTER HAVING HAD THEM, ... 483 A MASQUE OF REASON . 292
     BUT WARN THE CHILDREN THEY PERHAPS SHOULD HAVE NONE. . . 483 A MASQUE OF REASON . 294
     THESE TWO ARE STUBBORN CHILDREN, AS YOU SEE. . . . 517 A MASQUE OF MERCY . 619
CHILDREN'S
     FIRST THERE'S THE CHILDREN'S HOUSE OF MAKE-BELIEVE, . . 378 DIRECTIVE   41
     (I STOLE THE GOBLET FROM THE CHILDREN'S PLAYHOUSE.) . . 379 DIRECTIVE   60
CHILD'S
     BUT THE CHILD'S MOUND----" / "DON'T, DON'T, DON'T, DON'T,"
       SHE CRIED. . . . . 52 HOME BURIAL   30
     AND THEN HE'D CROW AS IF HE THOUGHT THAT CHILD'S PLAY-- . 66 A SERVANT TO SERVANTS . 137
     THAT MADE ALL OTHER OUTRAGE SEEM AS CHILD'S PLAY: . . . 511 A MASQUE OF MERCY . 476
CHILL
     (THOUGH CHILL), BECAUSE THE FIELDS WERE OURS, ... 18 GOING FOR WATER . .   7
     AND A COLD CHILL SHIVERED ACROSS THE LAKE. . . . . 63 A SERVANT TO SERVANTS . 31
     I JUDGED THAT SUCH A CRYSTAL CHILL . . . . 233 LOOKING FOR SUNSET BIRD 14
     THE MOON WAS WAITING FOR HER CHILL EFFECT. . . . . 237 A HILLSIDE THAW . .   25
     AND LIKE THE FLOWERS BESIDE THEM, CHILL AND SHIVER, . . 245 SPRING POOLS . . .   3
     THE SUN WAS WARM BUT THE WIND WAS CHILL. . . . . 275 TWO TRAMPS IN MUD TIME   17
     I FELT THE CHILL OF THE MEADOW UNDERFOOT, ... 342 QUEST OF PURPLE-FRINGED   1
CHIMES
     OR (CHIMES WERE RINGING) CHURCHWARD. . . . . . 335 CARPE DIEM   5
CHIMNEY
     THE CHIMNEY, THOUGH, KEEPS UP A GOOD BRISK SMOKING. . . 49 A HUNDRED COLLARS . . 137
     IT BURSTS AGAINST US AT THE CHIMNEY MOUTH, ... 150 SNOW 207
     THE STOVE WAS COLD--THE STOVE WAS OFF THE CHIMNEY-- . . 175 THE CENSUS-TAKER . .   36
     OF WASTE LEAVES AT MY SMOKY LANTERN CHIMNEY . . . . 176 THE STAR-SPLITTER . .   8
     AND A MAN WITH A SMOKY LANTERN CHIMNEY? . . . . . 179 THE STAR-SPLITTER . .   98
     BUT PLEASE PLEASE ME IN THE KITCHEN CHIMNEY: . . . . 232 THE KITCHEN CHIMNEY .   3
     DON'T BUILD ME A LANTERN UPON A SHELF. . . . . . 232 THE KITCHEN CHIMNEY .   4
     BUY ME ENOUGH FOR A FULL-LENGTH CHIMNEY, ... 232 THE KITCHEN CHIMNEY .   7
     AND BUILD THE CHIMNEY CLEAR FROM THE GROUND. . . . 232 THE KITCHEN CHIMNEY .   8
     THE KITCHEN CHIMNEY . . . . 232 THE KITCHEN CHIMNEY .   T
     WHERE THE CHIMNEY STARTED ABOVE THE STOVE. . . . . 232 THE KITCHEN CHIMNEY .   12
     A CHIMNEY THAT ONLY WOULD SERVE TO REMIND ME . . . . 232 THE KITCHEN CHIMNEY .   19
     AND SEND MORE SPARKS UP CHIMNEY WITH THE SMOKE." . . . 234 EVENING A SUGAR ORCHARD   6
     NOW THE CHIMNEY WAS ALL OF THE HOUSE THAT STOOD, . . . 241 NEED OF BEING VERSED   3
     WITH BUT ONE CHIMNEY IT CAN CALL ITS OWN; . . . . 248 THE COCOON   6
     AND FOR BACK WALL A CRUMBLING OLD CHIMNEY . . . . 294 A RECORD STRIDE . .   3
     UP CHIMNEY TO AVOID THE WORST OF IT. . . . . . 408 FROM PLANE TO PLANE . 142
     THAT LEANS OUT THIS AND THAT WAY FROM THEIR CHIMNEY. . . 414 A CABIN IN THE CLEARING 11
     FROM SOME EXTINCT OLD CHIMNEY POT. . . . . . . 452 A-WISHING WELL . . .   36
CHIMNEY'S
     THAT THERE ALWAYS IS WHEN THE CHIMNEY'S FALSE. . . . 232 THE KITCHEN CHIMNEY .   16
CHIN
     HE SAT AND FIXED HIS CHIN BETWEEN HIS FISTS. . . . . 52 HOME BURIAL   41
     THE NOSE IS JUST THE SAME, AND SO'S THE CHIN-- . . . 77 THE GENERATIONS OF MEN 114
     AND LIFTS THEIR FACES BY THE CHIN TO HERS . . . . . 98 THE SELF-SEEKER . . . 161
     THICK HAND MADE LIGHT OF, STEEL-BLUE CHIN DRAWN DOWN . . 188 THE AX-HELVE   99
     ONCE, WHEN TRYING WITH CHIN AGAINST A WELL-CURB, . . . 225 FOR ONCE SOMETHING .   7
     FROM HER CHIN, PICKED UP HER COMB, ... 341 THE SUBVERTED FLOWER .   72

CHIN (CONTINUED)
   THAT LIKE A BLANKET TO MY CHIN . . . . 380 AN UNSTAMPED LETTER IN   14
   AND ONLY RESTS, A SERPENT ON ITS CHIN, ... 399 THE INGENUITIES OF DEBT 15
   BUT NEVER SO MUCH AS LIFTED CHIN. . . . . 420 ONE MORE BREVITY . . 22
CHINA
   "NOW WE ARE DIGGING ALMOST DOWN TO CHINA. . . . . . 132 THE BONFIRE 101
   THE LONGEST PEACE IN CHINA WILL END IN STRIFE. . . . 268 ON LOOKING UP BY CHANCE 12
   A PRINCESS EN ROUTE FROM CHINA . . . . 313 BEARER OF EVIL TIDINGS 19
CHIPS
   THE FRESH CHIPS, ... 128 THE IMPULSE 10
   PROVE BUT FLYING CHIPS . . . . 439 KITTY HAWK 352
CHIRP
   "HOLD ON." THE DOUBLE BELL BEGAN TO CHIRP. . . . . 155 SNOW 327
CHIRR
   FOR COMMENT A COMPLACENT CHIRR. . . . . 281 BLUE RIBBON AT AMESBURY 52
CHISEL
   THE CHISEL WORK OF AN ENORMOUS GLACIER . . . . . 377 DIRECTIVE 16
CHOICE
   ADMITS NO MEMORY OF CHOICE, ... 21 THE TRIAL BY EXISTENCE 54
   AN SO THE CHOICE MUST BE AGAIN, ... 21 THE TRIAL BY EXISTENCE 57
   BUT THE LAST CHOICE IS STILL THE SAME; . . . . . . 21 THE TRIAL BY EXISTENCE 58
   I SHALL MAKE THE RECKLESS CHOICE . . . . 156 THE SOUND OF TREES . . 20
   I HAD TO MAKE AN ALMOST FUNNY CHOICE. . . . . . . 170 NEW HAMPSHIRE . . .361
   IT SEEMS A NARROW CHOICE THE AGE INSISTS ON. . . . . 171 NEW HAMPSHIRE . . .403
   WHICH GIVES HIM FOR HIMSELF A CHOICE OF LOTS . . . . 202 PLACE FOR A THIRD . . 81
   IT'S COMING UP TO YOU." IT HAD ITS CHOICE . . . . . 205 THE WITCH OF COOS . . 83
   OUTSIDE THE SUGARHOUSE ONE NIGHT FOR CHOICE, ... 234 EVENING A SUGAR ORCHARD   2
   FATE HAS NO CHOICE BUT TO FULFILL. . . . . 336 THE WIND AND THE RAIN . 20
   NO CHOICE IS LEFT A POET, YOU MIGHT ADD, ... 352 THE LESSON FOR TODAY . 61
   AND VERY WIDE THE CHOICE THEY SEEMED TO GIVE; . . . . 354 THE LESSON FOR TODAY .137
   THE RULE IS, NEVER GIVE A CHILD A CHOICE. . . . . . 427 CONCEPT SELF-CONCEIVED   8
   "THE CHOICE IS NOT BETWEEN TWO PEARLS, O KING, ... 456 HOW HARD TO KEEP FROM 74
   I HAD NO CHOICE BUT I MUST FOLLOW HIM . . . . . . 475 A MASQUE OF REASON . . 73
CHOKE
   AND THE EFFORT MADE HIM CHOKE . . . . 340 THE SUBVERTED FLOWER . 28
CHOKECHERRIES
   AND ITS CHOKECHERRIES LIPS TO KISS GOOD-BY, ... 268 THE BEAR   3
CHOKED
   A SWAMP OF CEDAR. CHOKED WITH OIL OF CEDAR . . . . . 125 AN ENCOUNTER   5
CHOKING (SEE A-CHOKING)
CHOOSE
   THOUGH WE CHOOSE GREATLY, STILL TO LACK . . . . . . 21 THE TRIAL BY EXISTENCE 66
   IF I MUST CHOOSE WHICH I WOULD ELEVATE-- . . . . . 168 NEW HAMPSHIRE . . .307
   "CHOOSE YOU WHICH YOU WILL BE--A PRUDE, OR PUKE, . . . 170 NEW HAMPSHIRE . . .362
   "ME FOR THE HILLS WHERE I DON'T HAVE TO CHOOSE." . . . 170 NEW HAMPSHIRE . . .364
   "BUT IF YOU HAD TO CHOOSE, WHICH WOULD YOU BE?" . . . 170 NEW HAMPSHIRE . . .365
   AND NEITHER WOULD I CHOOSE TO BE A PUKE . . . . . 171 NEW HAMPSHIRE . . .398
   WELL, IF I HAVE TO CHOOSE ONE OR THE OTHER, ... 172 NEW HAMPSHIRE . . .407
   I CHOOSE TO BE A PLAIN NEW HAMPSHIRE FARMER . . . . 172 NEW HAMPSHIRE . . .408
   A QUIVERFUL TO CHOOSE FROM, SINCE HE WISHED ME . . . 187 THE AX-HELVE . . . 64
   WE CHOOSE TO SAY IT IS LET LOOSE BY THE DEVIL; . . . 254 THE FLOOD   5
   THEN LET THEM CHOOSE!" . . . . 256 THE LOVELY BE CHOOSERS   8
   "THEN WE SHALL LET HER CHOOSE?" . . . . 256 THE LOVELY BE CHOOSERS   9
   "YES, LET HER CHOOSE. . . . . 256 THE LOVELY BE CHOOSERS 10
   THE VOICE ASKED, "YOU CAN LET HER CHOOSE?" . . . . 256 THE LOVELY BE CHOOSERS 19
   I CHOOSE THE STAR-CROSSED AS A STAR-CROSSED LOVER. . . 510 A MASQUE OF MERCY . .441
CHOOSERS
   THE LOVELY SHALL BE CHOOSERS . . . . 255 THE LOVELY BE CHOOSERS   T
   THE LOVELY SHALL BE CHOOSERS, SHALL THEY? . . . . . 256 THE LOVELY BE CHOOSERS   7
CHOOSING
   "COME, BUT THIS ISN'T CHOOSING--PUKE OR PRUDE?" . . . 171 NEW HAMPSHIRE . . .406
   TAKE UP THE TASK BEYOND HER CHOOSING." . . . . . 256 THE LOVELY BE CHOOSERS 11
CHOPPING
   WHERE I WAS WORKING AT THE CHOPPING BLOCK, ... 185 THE AX-HELVE   8
   AS LARGE AROUND AS THE CHOPPING BLOCK; . . . . . 275 TWO TRAMPS IN MUD TIME 10
   THEY THOUGHT ALL CHOPPING WAS THEIRS OF RIGHT. . . . 276 TWO TRAMPS IN MUD TIME 52
CHOPS
   OF NEW WOOD AND OLD WHERE THE WOODPECKER CHOPS; . . . 6 GHOST HOUSE   9
CHORD
   ART AND RELIGION LOVE THE SOMBER CHORD. . . . . . 353 THE LESSON FOR TODAY . 97
CHORES
   HIS LANTERN WHEN HE DID HIS CHORES . . . . . . 137 BROWN'S DESCENT . . .   3
   SO MUCH AS TO TAKE CARE OF EVENING CHORES. . . . . 248 THE COCOON 10
   HIS CHORES FOR ALL THE WINTRY NIGHT. . . . . . . 280 BLUE RIBBON AT AMESBURY 20
CHORUS
   RETIRED FROM POLITICS AND JOINED THE CHORUS. . . . . 168 NEW HAMPSHIRE . . .297
   HAD FED IN CHORUS, AND LIVED TO FLEDGE, ... 253 THE THATCH 15
   WHEN IN HEARTLESS CHORUS . . . . 429 KITTY HAWK 36
CHOSE
   THE MEMORY THAT HE CHOSE THE LIFE; . . . . . . 21 THE TRIAL BY EXISTENCE 52
   NOTHING BUT WHAT WE SOMEHOW CHOSE; . . . . 21 THE TRIAL BY EXISTENCE 69
   SITTING OR STANDING AS HE CHOSE, ... 138 BROWN'S DESCENT . . . 26
   WITH THE RACE HE CHOSE TO ADOPT: . . . . 314 BEARER OF EVIL TIDINGS 38
   WHO COULD DO GOOD OR EVIL AS HE CHOSE. . . . . . 475 A MASQUE OF REASON . . 72
CHOSEN
   IF I HAD CHOSEN LEFT. HOLD OUT THE LEFT. . . . . . 97 THE SELF-SEEKER . .114
   ON BEING CHOSEN POET OF VERMONT . . . . 469 CHOSEN POET OF VERMONT   T
CHOWDER
   IF THIS SEEMS A WITCHES' CHOWDER . . . . 304 CLEAR AND COLDER . . 17
CHRIST
   CHRIST ALMOST OUT OF CHRISTIANITY. . . . . . . 498 A MASQUE OF MERCY . .129
   'TWERE NOTHING NEW IF THAT WERE ALL CHRIST BROUGHT. . . 511 A MASQUE OF MERCY . .474
   CHRIST CAME TO INTRODUCE A BREAK WITH LOGIC . . . . 511 A MASQUE OF MERCY . .475
   LIES IN OUR DIFFERENT APPROACH TO CHRIST, ... 513 A MASQUE OF MERCY . .517
CHRISTENED
   THAT TELESCOPE WAS CHRISTENED THE STAR-SPLITTER, . . . 179 THE STAR-SPLITTER . . 87
CHRISTIAN
   HE SEEMS TO HAVE LOST OFF HIS CHRISTIAN NAME." . . . . 144 SNOW 47

CHRISTIAN (CONTINUED)
    "CHRISTIAN ENOUGH I SHOULD CALL THAT MYSELF. . . . . . . 144 SNOW 48
    YET LIKE A CHRISTIAN DISCIPLINED TC BEND . . . . 353 THE LESSON FOR TODAY . 94
    OR BE A CHRISTIAN.--PAUL, I WISH YOU'D SAY . . . . . 509 A MASQUE OF MERCY . . 403
CHRISTIANITY
    CHRIST ALMOST OUT OF CHRISTIANITY. . . . . 498 A MASQUE OF MERCY . . 129
CHRISTIANS
    PAUL MAKES IT COME OUT SO THEY LOOK LIKE CHRISTIANS.. . . 509 A MASQUE OF MERCY . . 407
CHRISTMAS
    A CHRISTMAS CIRCULAR LETTER . . . . 105 CHRISTMAS TREES . . . S
    CHRISTMAS TREES . . . . 105 CHRISTMAS TREES . . . T
    AND COULD NOT DO WITHOUT AND KEEP ITS CHRISTMAS. . . . 106 CHRISTMAS TREES . . . 11
    HE ASKED IF I WOULD SELL MY CHRISTMAS TREES; . . . . 106 CHRISTMAS TREES . . . 12
    I HADN'T THOUGHT OF THEM AS CHRISTMAS TREES. . . . . 106 CHRISTMAS TREES . . . 15
    "A THOUSAND CHRISTMAS TREES!--AT WHAT APIECE?" . . . . 107 CHRISTMAS TREES . . . 42
    A THOUSAND CHRISTMAS TREES I DIDN'T KNOW I HAD! . . . 107 CHRISTMAS TREES . . . 55
    IN WISHING YOU HEREWITH A MERRY CHRISTMAS. . . . . . 107 CHRISTMAS TREES . . . 60
    OF BEING GIVEN ONE FOR CHRISTMAS GIFT, ... 178 THE STAR-SPLITTER . . 55
    I MUST NOT SPOIL YOUR CHRISTMAS WITH CONTRITION. . . . 350 TO A YOUNG WRETCH . . 12
    HELP ME ACCEPT ITS FATE WITH CHRISTMAS FEELING. . . . 350 TO A YOUNG WRETCH . . 24
    AND EVERYBODY'S BEING SICK FOR CHRISTMAS. . . . . . 407 FROM PLANE TO PLANE . 106
    IN CHRISTMAS GIVING, SO THEY CAN ESCAPE . . . . . . 408 FROM PLANE TO PLANE . 139
    WITH SOME OPTIMISM FOR CHRISTMAS . . . . 466 SOME SCIENCE FICTION . 34
    YOU MEAN THE BURNING BUSH? / THE CHRISTMAS TREE. . . . 473 A MASQUE OF REASON . . 6
    I SAW A BOXFUL IN THE CHRISTMAS MARKET. . . . . . . 488 A MASQUE OF REASON . . 422
CHRISTMASES
    IT IS YOUR CHRISTMASES AGAINST MY WOODS. . . . . . . 350 TO A YOUNG WRETCH . . 13
CHRISTOPHER
    THE NEW WORLD CHRISTOPHER COLUMBUS FOUND. . . . . . 422 FOR JOHN F. KENNEDY . 15
CHRIST'S
    CHRIST'S OR KARL MARX', AND IT WILL SET YOU FREE. . . . 460 HOW HARD TO KEEP FROM 192
CHRONIC
    TRANSFORMED FROM CHRONIC TO ACUTE AND BLOODY? . . . . 317 BUILD SOIL 30
CHUNKS
    OF PELTING HEAVEN WITH CHUNKS . . . . 464 MILKY WAY IS A COWPATH 11
CHURCH
    WHEN, TO PLEASE YOUNGER MEMBERS OF THE CHURCH, ... 57 THE BLACK COTTAGE . . 85
    OR RATHER SAY NON-MEMBERS IN THE CHURCH, ... 57 THE BLACK COTTAGE . . 86
    I'VE BEEN BUILT IN HERE LIKE A BIG CHURCH ORGAN. . . . 82 THE HOUSEKEEPER . . . 38
    I WALKED DOWN ALONE SUNDAY AFTER CHURCH . . . . . . 123 PEA BRUSH 1
    IT'S QUIET AS AN EMPTY CHURCH WITHOUT HIM." . . . . . 152 SNOW 260
    SOME MAY KNOW WHAT THEY SEEK IN SCHOOL AND CHURCH, . . 173 A STAR IN A STONEBOAT . 43
    WE DON'T CUT OFF FROM COMING TO CHURCH SUPPERS, . . . 178 THE STAR-SPLITTER . . 49
    AND THERE A CLUMP OF HOUSES WITH A CHURCH. . . . . . 226 THE ONSET 23
    THAT IS TO SAY, 'TWAS NOT A CHURCH. . . . . 274 A LONE STRIKER . . . 53
    THE FINAL SUMMONS INTO CHURCH WAS BEATING. . . . . . 284 THE GOLD HESPERIDEE . 42
    TO FRIGHTEN CHURCH OR STATE . . . . 384 MAKING CERTAIN ANYTHING 10
    FOR THE DEFICIENCY BY CHURCH INTONING. . . . . . . 460 HOW HARD TO KEEP FROM 220
    PROSE MADE OF, GIVEN AN AIR BY CHURCH INTONING. . . . 461 HOW HARD TO KEEP FROM 222
    DON'T YOU TWIT. HE'S UNHAPPY. CHURCH NEGLECT . . . . 488 A MASQUE OF REASON . . 424
    OF MIDDLE-AISLE CHURCH CARPET, SISAL HEMP, ... 489 A MASQUE OF REASON . . 454
    LET HIM SEEK HIS RELIGION IN THE CHURCH. . . . . . . 494 A MASQUE OF MERCY . . 32
    THAN FOUND IN CHURCH. / THAT DOESN'T HELP ME MUCH. . . 513 A MASQUE OF MERCY . . 515
    HIS CHURCH ON EARTH A ROMAN PANTHEON; . . . . 516 A MASQUE OF MERCY . . 592
CHURCHES
    WHERE HOUSES ALL ARE CHURCHES AND HAVE SPIRES. . . . . 106 CHRISTMAS TREES . . . 14
CHURCHWARD
    OR (CHIMES WERE RINGING) CHURCHWARD. . . . . 335 CARPE DIEM 5
CIDER
    SHE'S AFTER CIDER, THE OLD GIRL, SHE'S THIRSTY; . . . . 77 THE GENERATIONS OF MEN 108
    A CIDER SYRUP. HAVING TASTED FRUIT, ... 124 THE COW IN APPLE TIME . 5
    AND SO NOT GOOD FOR ANYTHING BUT CIDER. . . . . . . 164 NEW HAMPSHIRE . . . 162
    IN A GLASS OF CIDER . . . . 468 IN A GLASS OF CIDER . T
CIDER-APPLE
    WENT SURELY TO THE CIDER-APPLE HEAP . . . . 69 AFTER APPLE-PICKING . 35
    THAT A CIDER-APPLE TREE . . . . 134 A GIRL'S GARDEN . . . 34
CIGARETTE
    THAT AND THE MEREST CURL OF CIGARETTE SMOKE-- . . . . 131 THE BONFIRE 50
CINDER
    WITH CINDER LOADS DUMPED DOWN? THE BROOK WAS THROWN . . 231 A BROOK IN THE CITY . 15
CIRCLE
    A CIRCLE SCARCELY WIDER . . . . 13 ROSE POGONIAS . . . 3
    "PROFESSOR SQUARE-THE-CIRCLE-TILL-YOU'RE-TIRED? . . . . 46 A HUNDRED COLLARS . . 44
    MADE THE DIM TREES STAND BACK IN WIDER CIRCLE-- . . . 130 THE BONFIRE 29
    THE GROUND WAS ONE CIRCLE OF SOLID RED. . . . . . . 305 UNHARVESTED 10
    BECAUSE ALL REASONING IS IN A CIRCLE. . . . . 322 BUILD SOIL 202
CIRCLED
    AND THE FLY CIRCLED ROUND HIM IN DERISION. . . . . . 278 THE WHITE-TAILED HORNET 43
    AND WE STOOD IN IT SOFTLY CIRCLED ROUND . . . . . . 315 IRIS BY NIGHT . . . 29
CIRCLES
    REASON IN CIRCLES? / NO, REFUSE TO BE . . . . . . 322 BUILD SOIL 206
    OF PROGRESS ROUND AND ROUND IN CIRCLES . . . . . . 459 HOW HARD TO KEEP FROM 159
CIRCLING
    EACH CIRCLING EACH WITH VAGUE UNEARTHLY CRY, ... 14 WAITING 12
    WITH HILLS AND CIRCLING ARMS ABOUT-- . . . . 120 BOND AND FREE . . . 2
    AND, TIRED OF AIMLESS CIRCLING IN ONE PLACE, ... 238 ON A TREE FALLEN ACROSS 13
CIRCUITOUS
    CIRCUITOUS WANDERER," AND "TOOK DEJECTEDLY . . . . . 171 NEW HAMPSHIRE . . . 384
CIRCULAR
    A CHRISTMAS CIRCULAR LETTER . . . . 105 CHRISTMAS TREES . . . S
CIRCUMAMBIENT
    HE TOO IS PRETTY CIRCUMAMBIENT. . . . . 487 A MASQUE OF REASON . . 383
CIRCUMSTANCED
    THOUGH CIRCUMSTANCED WITH DARK AND DOUBT-- . . . . . 331 BEECH 11
CIRCUMSTANCES
    UNDER THOSE CIRCUMSTANCES, WOULD YCU NOW? . . . . . 71 THE CODE 60
CIRCUS
    WE WATCH A CIRCUS OF REVOLVING DOGS . . . . 362 SYMPATHY WITH UNCER DOG 2

CIRCUS (CONTINUED)
    AS CIRCUS DAY OF TOY BALLOONS. . . . . 451 A-WISHING WELL . . . 18
CISATLANTIC
    ON OUR CISATLANTIC SHORE . . . . 367 A SERIOUS STEP LIGHTLY 14
CITIES
    WOULD PAY IN CITIES FOR GOOD TREES LIKE THOSE, ... 107 CHRISTMAS TREES . . . 52
    THE FLOWER OF CITIES FROM SINKING AND WITHERING FAINT. . . 286 A ROADSIDE STAND . . 6
    OF TROUBLE WITH IT IN HIS GRECIAN CITIES . . . . . 459 HOW HARD TO KEEP FROM 167
    HE HAS BEEN BEGGING THROUGH THE SEVEN CITIES . . . . 459 HOW HARD TO KEEP FROM 182
CITY (SEE BIG-CITY)
    THE CITY HAD WITHDRAWN INTO ITSELF . . . . 105 CHRISTMAS TREES . . . 1
    A STRANGER TO OUR YARD, WHO LOOKED THE CITY, ... 106 CHRISTMAS TREES . . 5
    HE PROVED TO BE THE CITY COME AGAIN . . . . 106 CHRISTMAS TREES . . 9
    TO LIGHTED CITY STREETS WE, TOO, HAVE KNOWN, ... 112 IN THE HOME STRETCH . 58
    THE CITY WORK TO DO. THERE'S NOT ENOUGH . . . . . 114 IN THE HOME STRETCH . 97
    "GOOD BOYS THEY SEEMED, AND LET THEM LOVE THE CITY. . . . 114 IN THE HOME STRETCH . 119
    IT SET OUT ONCE TO BE A CITY AND STILL . . . . . . 165 NEW HAMPSHIRE . . 191
    (FROM, SAY, A PUBLISHER IN NEW YORK CITY). . . . . . 172 NEW HAMPSHIRE . . 410
    AND THINK A LITTLE, AND GET SOME CITY SCHOOLING. . . . 182 MAPLE 74
    BEYOND THE HIGHEST CITY BUILT WITH HANDS. . . . . . 182 MAPLE 84
    WITH THE NEW CITY STREET IT HAS TO WEAR . . . . . . 231 A BROOK IN THE CITY . 2
    A BROOK IN THE CITY . . . . 231 A BROOK IN THE CITY . T
    THIS NEW-BUILT CITY FROM BOTH WORK AND SLEEP. . . . . 231 A BROOK IN THE CITY . 24
    I HAVE OUTWALKED THE FURTHEST CITY LIGHT. . . . . . 255 ACQUAINTED WITH NIGHT . 3
    I HAVE LOOKED DOWN THE SADDEST CITY LANE. . . . . . 255 ACQUAINTED WITH NIGHT . 4
    HERE FAR FROM THE CITY WE MAKE OUR ROADSIDE STAND . . . 286 A ROADSIDE STAND . . 18
    AND ASK FOR SOME CITY MONEY TO FEEL IN HAND . . . . . 286 A ROADSIDE STAND . . 19
    TO ADVERTISE OUR FARMS TO CITY BUYERS, ... 316 BUILD SOIL . . . 23
    IS NOT TO LURE THE CITY TO THE COUNTRY. . . . . . 322 BUILD SOIL . . . 186
    LONG SINCE IN SOME ABYSMAL CITY STREET, ... 359 THE LOST FOLLOWER . 22
    THE PLACE WAS LIKE A CITY PARK. . . . . 380 AN UNSTAMPED LETTER IN 11
    THE CITY SEEMS IN-TOPPLING FROM A HEIGHT, ... 386 THE FEAR OF MAN . . 5
    THE CITY SAYING IT WAS CTESIPHON, ... 399 THE INGENUITIES OF DEBT 6
    PAST ELIZABETH CITY . . . . 428 KITTY HAWK . . . 8
    FROM ELIZABETH CITY, ... 431 KITTY HAWK . . . 102
    TO PROPHESY AGAINST THE CITY EVIL. . . . . 495 A MASQUE OF MERCY . 64
    WHAT HAVE YOU GOT AGAINST THE CITY? / HE KNOWS. . . . 496 A MASQUE OF MERCY . 65
    THE CITY IS ALL RIGHT. TO LIVE IN ONE . . . . . . 496 A MASQUE OF MERCY . 69
    SO LOSERS IN THE CITY, BUT WE'RE GAME: . . . . . . 496 A MASQUE OF MERCY . 76
    IS IT JUST ANY CITY YOU'RE AGAINST? . . . . 496 A MASQUE OF MERCY . 90
    THE THREATS HE MAKES AGAINST THE CITY EVIL. . . . . 497 A MASQUE OF MERCY . 115
    HAD YOU IN MIND TO VISIT ON THE CITY, ... 502 A MASQUE OF MERCY . 224
    GOD COMES ON ME TO DOOM A CITY FOR HIM. . . . . . 505 A MASQUE OF MERCY . 301
    THE CITY IS ADMITTEDLY AN EVIL: . . . . 506 A MASQUE OF MERCY . 336
    "O CITY ON INSECURE ROCK PEDESTAL, ... 506 A MASQUE OF MERCY . 337
CITY'S
    THAT THE CITY'S HOLD ON A MAN IS NO MORE TIGHT . . . . 306 NOT QUITE SOCIAL . . 7
    "THE CITY'S GROTESQUE IRON SKELETONS . . . . 506 A MASQUE OF MERCY . 332
CIVIL
    WHATEVER ELSE THE CIVIL WAR WAS FOR, ... 56 THE BLACK COTTAGE . . 55
    "OR DISREGARDING PEOPLE'S CIVIL QUESTIONS-- . . . . . 151 SNOW 251
    OBJECT TO BEING ASKED A CIVIL QUESTION-- . . . . . 192 PAUL'S WIFE 32
CIVILIZED
    IS TO BE CIVILIZED, STAY UP AND READ . . . . . . 496 A MASQUE OF MERCY . 70
    TO REST AT TIMES FROM BEING CIVILIZED. . . . . . . 496 A MASQUE OF MERCY . 74
CLAIM
    "SILAS HAS BETTER CLAIM ON US YOU THINK . . . . . 38 DEATH OF THE HIRED MAN 124
    AND HAVING PERHAPS THE BETTER CLAIM, ... 105 THE ROAD NOT TAKEN . . 7
    WHOSE CLAIM IS GOOD TO BEING SETTLED HERE . . . . . 161 NEW HAMPSHIRE . . 71
    MARCH INTO A SHADOWY CLAIM. . . . . 264 THE LAST MOWING . . 10
    AND THEN I'D CLAIM THE CREDIT FOR THE OUTCOME. . . . 320 BUILD SOIL . . . 129
    SEDUCED BACK TO THE LAND BY ANY CLAIM . . . . . . 322 BUILD SOIL . . . 207
    BUT NO ONE EVER HEARD YOU MAKE THE CLAIM. . . . . . 351 THE LESSON FOR TODAY . 28
    MORE THAN THEY KNOW WHAT COURAGE IS THAT CLAIM . . . . 405 FROM PLANE TO PLANE . 34
    YOU CAN'T CLAIM YOU'RE A SOCIAL VISIONARY." . . . . 406 FROM PLANE TO PLANE . 79
    HIS CLAIM IT WAS ANOTHER OPHIR. . . . . 417 AMERICA IS HARD TO SEE 24
    I MIGHT EVEN CLAIM, HE WAS SIRIUS . . . . 421 ONE MORE BREVITY . 58
    NOT TO CLAIM ELATE, ... 429 KITTY HAWK . . . 25
    I HAD ANY CLAIM . . . . 430 KITTY HAWK . . . 81
    THEY CLAIM THEY RECOLLECT THE MORN . . . . 452 A-WISHING WELL . . 38
    I CLAIM TO BE NO BETTER THAN I AM. . . . . 460 HOW HARD TO KEEP FROM 210
    BUT I'M TOO MUCH AFRAID OF GOD TO CLAIM . . . . . 520 A MASQUE OF MERCY . 705
CLAIMING
    IF HE HAD ANY PRIDE IN CLAIMING KIN . . . . . . 39 DEATH OF THE HIRED MAN 136
    ALL CLAIMING SOME PRIORITY IN STARKNESS. . . . . . . 75 THE GENERATIONS OF MEN 49
CLAIMS
    YOUR CLAIMS TO IMMORTALITY WERE TWO. . . . . . . 382 TO AN ANCIENT . . 1
    "A MAN'S OUT THERE WHO CLAIMS HE KNOWS THE SECRET, . . . 455 HOW HARD TO KEEP FROM 60
    SHE ALWAYS CLAIMS SHE HASN'T BEEN ASLEEP.-- . . . . . 487 A MASQUE OF REASON . 398
    COULD MOCK AT RICHES IN THE RIGHT IT CLAIMS . . . . . 509 A MASQUE OF MERCY . 424
CLAMORED
    THAT MAY BE CLAMORED AT BY CAUSE AND SECT, ... 356 TIME OUT 13
CLAMORING
    FOR CLAMORING FOR JUSTICE AT THE GATE, ... 518 A MASQUE OF MERCY . 643
CLANGING
    WENT BY WITH CLANGING GONG . . . . 391 A ROGERS GROUP . . . 6
CLANK
    ITS CLICK WAS RISING TO A NEARER CLANK. . . . . . 270 THE EGG AND THE MACHINE 10
CLAP
    WHEN THE CLAP OF TWO CONVERGING WAVES . . . . 344 DISCOVERY OF MADEIRAS . 27
CLAPBOARDS
    "THERE ARE BEES IN THIS WALL." HE STRUCK THE CLAPBOARDS, . 59 THE BLACK COTTAGE . . 125
CLAPPED
    THE NIGHT CLERK CLAPPED A BEDSTEAD ON THE FOOT. . . . . 46 A HUNDRED COLLARS . . 39
    HAVE CLAPPED MY HANDS AT HIM FROM THE DOOR . . . . 250 A MINOR BIRD . . . 3
CLARA
    YOU MUST HAVE HEARD OF CLARA ROBINSON, ... 215 A FOUNTAIN, A BOTTLE . 77

CLASHES
    GET CALLED AS MUCH IN CLASHES OF AMBITION. . . . . . . 317 BUILD SOIL 40
CLASP
    IT SEEMED GOD LET THEE FLUTTER FROM HIS GENTLE CLASP, . . 29 MY BUTTERFLY . . . 27
    TO CLASP HER--NOT TO HARM; . . . . 339 THE SUBVERTED FLOWER . 20
CLASPS
    AS ONE WHO CLASPS HER HEART. THEY LAUGHED TOGETHER. . . . 74 THE GENERATIONS OF MEN 44
    THEY ADDED CLASPS ABOUT THE NECK . . . . 346 DISCOVERY OF MADEIRAS . 83
CLASS
    I CAN JUST HEAR YOU CALL YOUR PALACE CLASS: . . . . . 353 THE LESSON FOR TODAY . 84
    IS THAT IT BRINGS THE SAME CLASS UP ON TOP. . . . . . 363 A SEMI-REVOLUTION . 4
    THAT CLASS OF PEOPLE DON'T KNOW WHAT WORK IS-- . . . . 405 FROM PLANE TO PLANE . 33
    AND SHE CAN ONLY GIVE THE CLASS A NOTION . . . . . 447 DOES NO ONE AT ALL EVER 40
CLASSES
    SO IT WOULD BE ACCEPTED BY TWO CLASSES, ... 162 NEW HAMPSHIRE . . 95
    OR YOU'D FEEL DIFFERENTLY ABOUT THE CLASSES. . . . . 406 FROM PLANE TO PLANE . 78
CLATTER
    AND NOW HE COMES AGAIN WITH CLATTER OF STONE, ... 223 THE RUNAWAY 15
CLATTERED
    IT TOUCHED, IT STRUCK, IT CLATTERED AND WENT OUT. . . . 92 THE FEAR 93
CLAUS
    "THAT'S WHERE I RECKON SANTA CLAUS COMES IN-- . . . . 408 FROM PLANE TO PLANE . 137
    A SANTA CLAUS WAS NEEDED. AND THERE IS ONE." . . . . 408 FROM PLANE TO PLANE . 146
CLEAN
    I'M GOING OUT TO CLEAN THE PASTURE SPRING; . . . . . 1 THE PASTURE 1
    HE LOOKED SO CLEAN DISGUSTED FROM BEHIND . . . . . . 72 THE CODE 99
    AS CLEAN AS BOYS DO OFF A WILLOW TWIG . . . . 191 PAUL'S WIFE 20
    THE HOLLOW LOOKED TOO SOUND AND CLEAN AND EMPTY . . . 193 PAUL'S WIFE 83
    YOU'VE GOT TO KEEP THE QUARTERS CLEAN." . . . . . 345 DISCOVERY OF MADEIRAS . 62
CLEANED
    I CLEANED THE RACK AND DROVE OUT TO COOL OFF. . . . . 72 THE CODE 80
CLEAR (SEE SELF-CLEAR)
    (AND WAIT TO WATCH THE WATER CLEAR, I MAY): . . . . . 1 THE PASTURE 3
    THE LASTING MEMORY AT ALL CLEAR, ... 21 THE TRIAL BY EXISTENCE 67
    WHAT MATTER IF WE GO CLEAR TO THE WEST, ... 27 A LINE-STORM SONG . 21
    HE MEANT TO CLEAR THE UPPER PASTURE, TOO. . . . . . 36 DEATH OF THE HIRED MAN 52
    CLEAR TO THE TOP." I SAW THROUGH LEAFY SCREENS . . . . 42 THE MOUNTAIN 57
    WE'LL GO IN THE MORNING, THAT IS, IF IT'S CLEAR, . . . 61 BLUEBERRIES 82
    AND EVERY FLECK OF RUSSET SHOWING CLEAR. . . . . . 68 AFTER APPLE-PICKING . 20
    INSTEAD OF GOING CLEAR DOWN IN THE WHEEL PIT?" . . . 93 THE SELF-SEEKER . . . 31
    CLEAR TO THE GROUND. HE ALWAYS KEPT HIS POISE . . . . 122 BIRCHES 35
    NO MATTER THAT THE MEANING WAS NOT CLEAR. . . . . . 185 MAPLE 165
    IF SEEN CLEAR, ... 212 AN EMPTY THREAT . . 54
    WATER CAME TO REBUKE THE TOO CLEAR WATER. . . . . . 225 FOR ONCE SOMETHING . 11
    AND BUILD THE CHIMNEY CLEAR FROM THE GROUND. . . . . 232 THE KITCHEN CHIMNEY . 8
    SOME THINGS ARE NEVER CLEAR. . . . . 301 VOICE WAYS 1
    BUT THE WEATHER IS CLEAR TONIGHT, ... 301 VOICE WAYS 2
    "SO WE WON'T SAY NOTHING IS CLEAR." . . . . 302 VOICE WAYS 8
    CLEAR AND COLDER . . . . 303 CLEAR AND COLDER . . T
    CLEAR TO THE ARCTIC OF EVERY LIVING KIND. . . . . . 305 THERE ARE ROUGHLY ZONES 10
    SO ALMOST CLEAR AND YET OBSCURE. . . . . 327 A MISSIVE MISSILE . . 19
    WHEN STARTING CLEAR AT DAWN . . . . 333 HAPPINESS MAKES UP . 15
    TO FINISH CLEAR AT EVE. . . . . 333 HAPPINESS MAKES UP . 17
    HAVE LOVED IT CLEAR AND HIGH, ... 388 ASTROMETAPHYSICAL . 3
    BUT THERE ARE MANY NIGHTS, THOUGH CLEAR, ... 390 TWO LEADING LIGHTS . 16
    CLEAR FROM HYDROGEN . . . . 426 A NEVER NAUGHT SONG . 15
    CLEAR INTO HER MARROW SPINE. . . . . 463 LINES IN DEJECTION . 20
    I TRUST I MADE IT CLEAR I TOOK YOUR SIDE . . . . . 486 A MASQUE OF REASON . 362
    OR CLEAR OFF WHAT WE KNOW HIS INTERESTS ARE. . . . . 509 A MASQUE OF MERCY . 427
CLEARING
    THE TOTE ROAD TO OUR CLEARING WHERE WE LIVED. . . . . 208 PAUPER WITCH OF GRAFTON 25
    THANKS TO A CLEARING RAIN. . . . . 301 VOICE WAYS 3
    IN THE CLEARING . . . . 409 IN THE CLEARING . . . T
    A CABIN IN THE CLEARING . . . . 413 A CABIN IN THE CLEARING T
CLEARLY
    YET WASN'T ENJOINED AND WASN'T EXPECTED, CLEARLY. . . . 306 NOT QUITE SOCIAL . . 4
    THE DAY SWEPT CLEARLY ON . . . . 333 HAPPINESS MAKES UP . 16
CLEAVES
    THOUGHT CLEAVES THE INTERSTELLAR GLOOM . . . . . . 120 BOND AND FREE . . . 11
CLEMATIS
    AND THE PILE SOMEWHAT SUNKEN. CLEMATIS . . . . . . 102 THE WOOD-PILE . . . 30
CLERK
    "NO ROOM," THE NIGHT CLERK SAID, "UNLESS----" . . . . 45 A HUNDRED COLLARS . . 20
    THE NIGHT CLERK BLINKED HIS EYES AND DARED HIM ON. . . 45 A HUNDRED COLLARS . . 28
    THE NIGHT CLERK LED HIM UP THREE FLIGHTS OF STAIRS . . 45 A HUNDRED COLLARS . . 33
    THE NIGHT CLERK CLAPPED A BEDSTEAD ON THE FOOT. . . . 46 A HUNDRED COLLARS . . 39
CLEVER
    IT WOULD BE EASY TO BE CLEVER . . . . 221 IN A DISUSED GRAVEYARD 13
    WHEN CLEVER PEOPLE ASK ME WHERE . . . . 452 A-WISHING WELL . . 32
CLICK
    AFTER A RAIN. THEY CLICK UPON THEMSELVES . . . . . 121 BIRCHES 7
    THE TOENAIL CLICK AND SHUFFLE OF HIS FEET, ... 269 THE BEAR 17
    ITS CLICK WAS RISING TO A NEARER CLANK. . . . . . 270 THE EGG AND THE MACHINE 10
CLICKING
    OR HOMESPUN CHILDREN WITH CLICKING PAILS . . . . . 24 PAN WITH US 14
CLIENTELE
    AND TELL YOUR CLIENTELE AT HOME . . . . 450 OUR DOOM TO BLOOM . . 6
CLIENTS
    IN CONSULTATION WITH MY CLIENTS? . . . . 449 OUR DOOM TO BLOOM . 4
CLIFF
    AND FROM A CLIFF TOP IS PROCLAIMED . . . . 20 THE TRIAL BY EXISTENCE 17
    LIKE BOULDERS BROKEN OFF THE UPPER CLIFF, ... 44 THE MOUNTAIN 98
    THEY SAT TOGETHER HALFWAY UP A CLIFF . . . . . . 195 PAUL'S WIFE . . . 133
    A CLIFF, AND ON THE CLIFF A BOTTLE PAINTED, ... 214 A FOUNTAIN, A BOTTLE . 38
    THE SHORE WAS LUCKY IN BEING BACKED BY CLIFF, . . . 250 ONCE BY THE PACIFIC . 8
    THE CLIFF IN BEING BACKED BY CONTINENT; . . . . . 250 ONCE BY THE PACIFIC . 9
    THE OTHER I WET AT THE CLIFF HOUSE . . . . . . 294 A RECORD STRIDE . . . 15
    FROM SOME TREE-HIDDEN CLIFF ACROSS THE LAKE. . . . . 338 THE MOST OF IT . . . 4

PAGE TITLE LINE

CLIFF (CONTINUED)
A CLIFF DWELLING . . . . 392 A CLIFF DWELLING . . T
ON A CLIFF FOR A THRONE. . . . . 448 THE BAD ISLAND--EASTER 19
CLIFFS
AFTER THAT ONLY TOPS OF TREES, AND CLIFFS . . . . . 41 THE MOUNTAIN . . . 31
AFTER HOURS' OVERLOOKING FROM THE CLIFFS . . . . . 174 THE CENSUS-TAKER . . 13
AND DECLARE TO THE CLIFFS TOO FAR FOR ECHO, ... 176 THE CENSUS-TAKER . . 56
AND IN IT, TALL AS TREES, WERE CLIFFS; . . . . . . 274 A LONE STRIKER . . . 37
CLIFF'S
IN THE CLIFF'S TALUS ON THE OTHER SIDE, ... 338 THE MOST OF IT . . . 11
CLIMATE (SEE SEASON-CLIMATE)
HE SAID, IN CLIMATE, NONE HAD EVER DIED THERE . . . 159 NEW HAMPSHIRE . . . 18
OF BEING IN THE MARKET WITH A CLIMATE." . . . . . . 159 NEW HAMPSHIRE . . . 24
CLIMAX
AND ONE TO CAP THE CLIMAX BY COMBINING . . . . . . 502 A MASQUE OF MERCY . 242
CLIMB
IT DOESN'T SEEM SO MUCH TO CLIMB A MOUNTAIN . . . . 43 THE MOUNTAIN . . . 82
'TWOULDN'T SEEM REAL TO CLIMB FOR CLIMBING IT." . . 43 THE MOUNTAIN . . . 88
"I SHOULDN'T CLIMB IT IF I DIDN'T WANT TO-- . . . . 43 THE MOUNTAIN . . . 89
AND CLIMB BLACK BRANCHES UP A SNOW-WHITE TRUNK . . 122 BIRCHES 55
HE COULDN'T CLIMB THAT SLIPPERY SLOPE; . . . . . . 139 BROWN'S DESCENT . . 56
THE STEPS BEGAN TO CLIMB THE ATTIC STAIRS. . . . . 206 THE WITCH OF COOS . 116
BUT YOU HAVE SPEED FAR GREATER. YOU CAN CLIMB . . 300 THE MASTER SPEED . . 2
DID CLIMB THE TREE . . . . 331 SYCAMORE 2
EITHER TO BREACH OR CLIMB. . . . . 348 TRIPLE BRONZE . . . 8
WHERE SOMEONE USED TO CLIMB AND CRAWL . . . . . . 392 A CLIFF DWELLING . . 8
CLIMBED
I HAVE CLIMBED THE HILLS OF VIEW . . . . 30 RELUCTANCE 3
BEEN UP, I UNDERSTAND, HAVE CLIMBED FROM LADD'S. . . 41 THE MOUNTAIN . . . 40
"YOU'VE NEVER CLIMBED IT?" / "I'VE BEEN ON THE SIDES, . 42 THE MOUNTAIN . . . 44
WE CLIMBED THE PASTURE ON THE SOUTH, CROSSED OVER, . 107 CHRISTMAS TREES . . 40
ASK HELEN HOW FAR UP THE SASH IT'S CLIMBED . . . . 148 SNOW 158
AND LAUGHED. THEN SHE CLIMBED SLOWLY TO HER FEET, . 194 PAUL'S WIFE 119
HE CLIMBED STILL HIGHER AND BENT THE TREE TO EARTH . 197 WILD GRAPES . . . 37
I LISTENED TILL IT ALMOST CLIMBED THE STAIRS . . . 205 THE WITCH OF COOS . 90
I CLIMBED ON THE SILL . . . . 241 THE LOCKLESS DOOR . 11
CLIMBING
ONE TIME I ASKED A FELLOW CLIMBING IT . . . . 43 THE MOUNTAIN . . . 73
'TWOULDN'T SEEM REAL TO CLIMB FOR CLIMBING IT." . . 43 THE MOUNTAIN . . . 88
NOT FOR THE SAKE OF CLIMBING. WHAT'S ITS NAME?" . . 43 THE MOUNTAIN . . . 90
TO THE TOP BRANCHES, CLIMBING CAREFULLY . . . . . 122 BIRCHES 36
I'D LIKE TO GO BY CLIMBING A BIRCH TREE, ... 122 BIRCHES 54
I WAS HALF BORING THROUGH, HALF CLIMBING THROUGH . 125 AN ENCOUNTER . . . 4
AND ONLY FREELY TO BE HAD FOR CLIMBING. . . . . . 197 WILD GRAPES . . . 30
MY BROTHER DID THE CLIMBING; AND AT FIRST . . . . 197 WILD GRAPES . . . 31
THE MOUNTAIN HE WAS CLIMBING HAD THE SLANT . . . . 355 TIME OUT 2
CLIME
FOR THERE'S NOT A CLIME . . . . 445 PERIL OF HOPE . . . 9
CLING
CLING TO IT LONG ENOUGH, AND NOT A DOUBT . . . . . 58 THE BLACK COTTAGE . 107
IN ONE WAY: YOU HAVE ONE MORE STEM TO CLING BY, . . 198 WILD GRAPES . . . 70
THEY LIE CLOSED OVER IN THE WIND AND CLING . . . . 225 BLUE-BUTTERFLY DAY . 7
CLINGING
IS SILVER NOW WITH CLINGING MIST. . . . . 7 MY NOVEMBER GUEST . 10
A YOUNG BEECH CLINGING TO ITS LAST YEAR'S LEAVES. . 234 A BOUNDLESS MOMENT . 12
RESTS ON THE WORLD, AND CLINGING SLOWLY ROLLS. . . 322 BUILD SOIL . . . 196
CLINGS
LOVE HAS EARTH TO WHICH SHE CLINGS . . . . 120 BOND AND FREE . . . 1
ONE KNOCKS ANOTHER OFF FROM WHERE HE CLINGS. . . . 411 POD OF THE MILKWEED 24
CLINICAL
AS A CLINICAL CHART. . . . . 447 THE BAD ISLAND--EASTER 6
CLOAK
RALEIGH OF THE CLOAK, ... 431 KITTY HAWK 93
CLOCK
I THINK I HEAR A CLOCK--AND WINDOWS RATTLING. . . . 153 SNOW 301
"A CLOCK MAYBE." / "DON'T YOU HEAR SOMETHING ELSE?" . 154 SNOW 316
OF THE TOWER CLOCK . . . . 218 I WILL SING YOU ONE-O 19
THEY SPOKE FOR THE CLOCK . . . . 219 I WILL SING YOU ONE-O 57
A SHELF'S FOR A CLOCK OR VASE OR PICTURE, ... 232 THE KITCHEN CHIMNEY 17
ONE LUMINARY CLOCK AGAINST THE SKY . . . . 255 ACQUAINTED WITH NIGHT 12
OUR LIFE RUNS DOWN IN SENDING UP THE CLOCK. . . . 259 WEST-RUNNING BROOK . 64
THAT MADE ME LOOK AGAIN AT THE CLOCK. . . . . . . 364 TRESPASS 16
CLOISTER
THE CLOISTER AND THE OBSERVATORY SAINT . . . . . . 353 THE LESSON FOR TODAY 81
CLOMPING
IN CLOMPING HERE, HE SCARED IT ONCE AGAIN . . . . 108 OLD MAN'S WINTER NIGHT 10
IN CLOMPING OFF--AND SCARED THE OUTER NIGHT, . . . 108 OLD MAN'S WINTER NIGHT 11
CLOSE
IN THE PAIN THAT HAS BUT ONE CLOSE, ... 21 THE TRIAL BY EXISTENCE 71
NOW CLOSE THE WINDOWS AND HUSH ALL THE FIELDS: . . 25 NOW CLOSE THE WINDOWS 1
SO CLOSE THE WINDOWS AND NOT HEAR THE WIND, . . . 25 NOW CLOSE THE WINDOWS 7
NOW CLOSE THE WINDOWS . . . . 25 NOW CLOSE THE WINDOWS T
THE BOUNDARY LINES KEEP IN SO CLOSE TO IT. . . . . 43 THE MOUNTAIN . . . 95
YOU WON'T GO NOW. YOU'RE CRYING. CLOSE THE DOOR. . 54 HOME BURIAL . . . 109
PASTURE THEY SPRING IN, SOME IN CLUMPS TOO CLOSE . 107 CHRISTMAS TREES . . 33
AND HEAT SO CLOSE IN; BUT THE THOUGHT OF ALL . . . 131 THE BONFIRE . . . 71
SO CLOSE TO OUR DWELLING PLACE? . . . . 156 THE SOUND OF TREES . 5
I FOUND HIM STANDING AT THE CLOSE OF DAY . . . . . 160 NEW HAMPSHIRE . . 44
I FOUND MYSELF IN A CLOSE CORNER WHERE . . . . . . 170 NEW HAMPSHIRE . . 360
SO CLOSE IT WILL NOT LIGHT AN EARLY LIGHT, ... 248 THE COCOON . . . 7
KEEPING ITS LIFE SO CLOSE AND OUT OF SIGHT . . . . 248 THE COCOON . . . 8
NOT IN POSITION TO LOOK TOO CLOSE. . . . . 248 A PASSING GLIMPSE . 12
ONE BIRD BEGINS TO CLOSE A FADED EYE; . . . . . . 249 ACCEPTANCE . . . 7
TO CLOSE A ROAD, ABANDON A FARM, ... 263 THE TIMES TABLE . . 18
MY FINGERS AND CLOSE MY ARMS IN AN ARC. . . . . . 265 THE DOOR IN THE DARK 4
MAY MY APPLICATION SO CLOSE . . . . 286 IN TIME OF CLOUDBURST 25
TO CLOSE THIS OUTPOST BARN AND CLOSE THE SEASON. . 289 OLD BARN AT THE BOTTOM 7
HAD THE BOY NOT PRESUMED TOO CLOSE AND LONG. . . . 293 AT WOODWARD'S GARDENS 21

CLOSE (CONTINUED)
    TO THINK IT OUT. COME CLOSE, LET US CONSPIRE-- . . . . . 323 BUILD SOIL   228
    AS MUCH AS LOVE, AND TOO CLOSE IN TO STRIKE . . . . 325 BUILD SOIL   277
    TO FEEL IT CLOSE IN TIGHT AGAINST MY SENSE . . . . 390 SKEPTIC   11
    SO CLOSE YET SURE TO BE ABIDED BY, ... 423 FOR JOHN F. KENNEDY   . 56
CLOSED
    GETTING NO ANSWER, CLOSED THE TELEPHONE. . . . . 143 SNOW 30
    SHE GAVE IT THROUGH THE SCREEN DOOR CLOSED BETWEEN THEM: . 201 PLACE FOR A THIRD . 76
    THEY LIE CLOSED OVER IN THE WIND AND CLING . . . . 225 BLUE-BUTTERFLY DAY .   7
    AND PUT A SIGN UP CLOSED TO ALL BUT ME. . . . . 378 DIRECTIVE 38
    CLOSED FOR GOOD . . . . 415 CLOSED FOR GOOD . .   T
    YOU CAN'T COME IN! (KNOCK, KNOCK) THE STORE IS CLOSED! . 493 A MASQUE OF MERCY .   8
CLOSE-KEEPING
    THOUGH TWO, CLOSE-KEEPING, ARE LASS AND LAD-- . . . . . .   6 GHOST HOUSE 27
CLOSELY
    STOOD CLOSELY OVER US THROUGH WHICH TO GO. . . . . 315 IRIS BY NIGHT . . . 19
CLOSER
    WOULD YOU TWO PLEASE DRAW IN A LITTLE CLOSER? . . . . . . 488 A MASQUE OF REASON . 403
CLOSES
    HALF CLOSES THE GARDEN PATH. . . . .   8 A LATE WALK   4
    IT MAY BE A MERCY THE DARK CLOSES ROUND US . . . . 379 TOO ANXIOUS FOR RIVERS 12
CLOSET
    IN A VERMONT BEDROOM CLOSET . . . . 294 A RECORD STRIDE . . . 1
CLOSING
    SHE RAISED HER VOICE AGAINST THE CLOSING DOOR: . . . . . 89 THE HOUSEKEEPER . . . 213
    BUT FORGOT TO PUT THE LEAF BACK IN CLOSING . . . . 181 MAPLE 67
    THE SOUND OF THE CLOSING OUTSIDE DOOR WAS ALL. . . . . . 235 VALLEY'S SINGING DAY . 1
    ONE FAILED TO MAKE THE CLOSING GATE. . . . . 273 A LONE STRIKER 4
    NOW SLOWLY CLOSING LIKE A DENT IN DOUGH. . . . . 378 DIRECTIVE 47
CLOTH
    LIKE A WHITE PIECE OF RIGID SATIN CLOTH--   . . . . 302 DESIGN   3
CLOTHED
    THEY TRIED TO KEEP HIM CLOTHED, BUT HE PARADED . . . . . 66 A SERVANT TO SERVANTS . 122
CLOTHES
    WITH HIS CLOTHES ON HIS ARM--ALL OF HIS CLOTHES. . . . . 66 A SERVANT TO SERVANTS . 123
    HIS NECK, OR THOUGHT TO SPARE HIS CLOTHES. . . . . 138 BROWN'S DESCENT . . 28
    MIGHT JUST AS WELL BE ICE AND THE CLOTHES SNOW. . . . . . 203 THE WITCH OF COOS . 39
    AND TEAR HIS CLOTHES OFF TO EXAMINE HIM . . . . 503 A MASQUE OF MERCY . 251
CLOTHING
    I'LL DRESS UP IN SHEEP'S CLOTHING AND EAT SHEEP. . . . . . 316 BUILD SOIL   . . . 16
CLOUD
    I'LL SIT AND SEE IF THAT SMALL SAILING CLOUD . . . . . . 40 DEATH OF THE HIRED MAN 160
    THE MOON, THE LITTLE SILVER CLOUD, AND SHE. . . . . 40 DEATH OF THE HIRED MAN 163
    WHERE AN IRREGULAR SUN-BORDERED CLOUD . . . . 69 THE CODE   4
    AND I THINK THE SKY DARKENED WITH A CLOUD   . . . . 131 THE BONFIRE 54
    THE SOLID MOLDING OF VAST PEAKS OF CLOUD . . . . 169 NEW HAMPSHIRE . . . 322
    LOOKING OUT OF A WREATH OF FERN AND CLOUD PUFFS. . . . . . 225 FOR ONCE SOMETHING . . 6
    OF WHAT WAS EITHER CLOUD OR SMOKE . . . . 233 LOOKING FOR SUNSET BIRD 18
    IN PLACE ACROSS A CLOUD THE SLENDER RAY . . . . 235 VALLEY'S SINGING DAY . 8
    WHEN THE SPENT SUN THROWS UP ITS RAYS ON CLOUD . . . . . 249 ACCEPTANCE   1
    AND THING NEXT MOST DIFFUSE TO CLOUD, ... 251 TREE AT MY WINDOW .   6
    TO HAPPEN IN HEAVEN BEYOND THE FLOATS OF CLOUD . . . . . 268 ON LOOKING UP BY CHANCE 2
    A CLOUD COMES OVER THE SUNLIT ARCH. . . . . 275 TWO TRAMPS IN MUD TIME 22
    ON THE HEART'S BEGINNING TO CLOUD THE MIND . . . . 290 ON HEART'S BEGINNING TO T
    BUT MY HEART WAS BEGINNING TO CLOUD MY MIND. . . . . . . 291 ON HEART'S BEGINNING TO 13
    LET CLOUD SHAPES SWARM! . . . . 308 PERTINAX   2
    AROUND WITH MIST AND CLOUD, ... 333 HAPPINESS MAKES UP . . 3
    AND THOUGH IT WERE AS MUCH AS CLOUD COULD BEAR . . . . . 337 THE WIND AND THE RAIN . 29
    WOULD LOAD IT ONTO CLOUD, ... 337 THE WIND AND THE RAIN . 30
    AND A CLOUD SHADOW CROSSED HER FACE . . . . 342 A CLOUD SHADOW . .   7
    A CLOUD SHADOW . . . . 342 A CLOUD SHADOW . .   T
    TO SOME OBSCURITY OF CLOUD-- . . . . 403 SOMETHING LIKE A STAR . 3
    THEY RAISE IN THEIR INTEMPERANCE A CLOUD . . . . 411 POD OF THE MILKWEED . 27
CLOUD-BLOWING
    I CAME AN ERRAND ONE CLOUD-BLOWING EVENING . . . . 174 THE CENSUS-TAKER . . 1
CLOUDBURST
    IN TIME OF CLOUDBURST . . . . 285 IN TIME OF CLOUDBURST . T
CLOUDED
    WAS IN HER CLOUDED EYES: THEY SAW NO FEAR THERE. . . . . . 229 TWO LOOK AT TWO . . 20
CLOUDLESS
    ITS ACTIONS ANY CLOUDLESS NIGHT WILL SHOW IT. . . . . . . 370 THE LITERATE FARMER AND 64
    I NEVER SAW SO MUCH SWIFT WATER RUN CLOUDLESS. . . . . . 379 TOO ANXIOUS FOR RIVERS 5
CLOUDS
    THE LINE-STORM CLOUDS FLY TATTERED AND SWIFT. . . . . . . 26 A LINE-STORM SONG . . 1
    WITH CLOUDS LOW-TRAILING AND MOMENTS OF RAIN THAT MISTED. . 74 THE GENERATIONS OF MEN 20
    THROUGH OPENING CLOUDS AT NIGHT WITH DRONING SPEED . . . 132 THE BONFIRE 106
    THE WHITE CLOUDS OVER THEM ON. . . . . 156 THE SOUND OF TREES . 23
    I RECOLLECT A NIGHT OF BROKEN CLOUDS . . . . 179 THE STAR-SPLITTER . 79
    THE CLOUDS WERE LOW AND HAIRY IN THE SKIES, ... 250 ONCE BY THE PACIFIC . 5
    SOMBER CLOUDS IN THE WEST WERE MASSED. . . . . 251 BEREFT   7
    THE CLOUDS, THE SOURCE OF RAIN, ONE STORMY NIGHT . . . . 295 LOST IN HEAVEN . . . 1
    O OPENING CLOUDS, BY OPENING ON ME WIDE. . . . . 296 LOST IN HEAVEN . . . 11
CLOUDY
    NOR FIND IN DEW THE SLIGHTEST CLOUDY TRACE. . . . . 361 A LOOSE MOUNTAIN . 12
CLOVE
    AND BURNING CLOVE. 227 TO EARTHWARD 24
CLOVEN
    FELL SPLINTERLESS AS A CLOVEN ROCK. . . . . 275 TWO TRAMPS IN MUD TIME 12
CLOVER
    STEEL-BRIGHT JUNE-GRASS, AND BLACKENING HEADS OF CLOVER. . 109 THE EXPOSED NEST . . 12
    ALL SHE'D BEEN HAVING WAS CLOVER. . . . . 463 LINES IN DEJECTION .   4
CLOVER-MINGLED
    THE CLOVER-MINGLED ROWAN ON THE GROUND . . . . 315 IRIS BY NIGHT . . . 13
CLUB
    HE HAD ATTACKED IT WITH A CLUB OR STONE . . . . 270 THE EGG AND THE MACHINE 6
CLUBS
    YOU WOULDN'T WANT THE NIGHT CLUBS LAUGHING AT YOU. . . . . 504 A MASQUE OF MERCY . 275

CLUCK
    AND HUSH AND CLUCK AND FLUTTER ABOUT: . . . . 6 GHOST HOUSE 17
CLUMP
    AND THERE A CLUMP OF HOUSES WITH A CHURCH. . . . . . . 226 THE ONSET 23
CLUMPS
    PASTURE THEY SPRING IN, SOME IN CLUMPS TOO CLOSE . . . . 107 CHRISTMAS TREES . . . 33
CLUMSY
    SLIPPING FROM CLUMSY CLUTCHES TOWARD THE CEILING. . . . 113 IN THE HOME STRETCH . 89
    THEN HE GOUGED A CLUMSY SAILING TROUGH . . . . . . 347 DISCOVERY OF MADEIRAS . 125
CLUNG
    THEN LIGHTLY STOOPED TO IT AND FLUTTERING CLUNG. . . . 126 RANGE-FINDING . . . 8
    THEY CLUNG TO WHAT ONE HAD SEEN IN THE OTHER . . . . 184 MAPLE 134
    AND STILL I CLUNG. I LET MY HEAD FALL BACK, ... 198 WILD GRAPES . . . 73
    NO, IT TOOK ALL THE SNOWS THAT CLUNG . . . . 299 WELCOME TO THEIR BELIEF 5
    AND STILL THE HORROR CLUNG. . . . . 341 THE SUBVERTED FLOWER . 70
    THE WAY SHE CLUNG TO HIM THE MORE . . . . 343 DISCOVERY OF MADEIRAS . 12
CLUSTER
    ABOVE A HAZY TREE-AND-FARMHOUSE CLUSTER . . . . . . 245 THE FREEDOM OF THE MOON 2
    SOME CLUSTER ONE STAR SHORT. . . . . 384 MAKING CERTAIN ANYTHING 8
CLUSTERED
    AND THE FRAGILE BLUETS CLUSTERED THERE . . . . . . 24 PAN WITH US 24
    WHOSE CLUSTERED FRUIT MUST ELSE BE LOST-- . . . . . 28 OCTOBER 20
CLUTCH
    THE BLOW CAN BE NO STRONGER THAN THE CLUTCH, . . . 371 THE LITERATE FARMER AND 116
    HE ALMOST HAS IT IN HIS TALON CLUTCH. . . . . . . 412 POD OF THE MILKWEED . 50
    NOT TO MENTION CLUTCH. . . . . 438 KITTY HAWK . . . 332
CLUTCHES
    SLIPPING FROM CLUMSY CLUTCHES TOWARD THE CEILING. . . . 113 IN THE HOME STRETCH . 89
CLUTCHING
    OF DESPERATELY CLUTCHING HAND . . . . 452 A-WISHING WELL . . . 60
CLUTTER
    A SORT OF CATCHALL FULL OF ATTIC CLUTTER. . . . . . 67 A SERVANT TO SERVANTS . 143
COACH
    FOR ME AS AN OLD SLOW COACH. . . . . 466 SOME SCIENCE FICTION . 12
COAL
    HER FACE ROSE-RED WITH THE GLOWING COAL . . . . . . 8 LOVE AND A QUESTION . 19
    HE DID NOT RECOGNIZE IN THAT SMOOTH COAL . . . . . 172 A STAR IN A STONEBOAT . 10
    ONE LEAST GERM OR COAL. . . . . 441 KITTY HAWK . . . 418
COAL-BLACK
    THAT I SPREAD COAL-BLACK OVER IN THE TIME . . . . . 132 THE BONFIRE . . . 83
COALESCED
    FROM TWO STARS' HAVING COALESCED . . . . 381 AN UNSTAMPED LETTER IN 26
COAST
    IN ITS TWO-THOUSAND-MILE COAST; . . . . 212 AN EMPTY THREAT . . . 45
    SOME SAID IT HAD GONE TO THE COAST, ... 312 THE VINDICTIVES . . . 69
    WITH EVERY COAST HE TRIED ALONG. . . . . 416 AMERICA IS HARD TO SEE 14
    STILL PROBES AND DENTS OUR ROCKY COAST . . . . . . 418 AMERICA IS HARD TO SEE 50
    WITH A LONE COAST GUARD . . . . 432 KITTY HAWK . . . 140
    ALONG THE AEGEAN COAST. THAT'S ALL THEY TALK OF." . . . 459 HOW HARD TO KEEP FROM 168
COASTED
    JOHN SMITH REMARKED THEM AS HE COASTED BY, ... 161 NEW HAMPSHIRE . . . 74
COASTING
    AND CAME DOWN LIKE A COASTING CHILD. . . . . . . 139 BROWN'S DESCENT . . . 44
COAT
    WHEN I SAW THE SHAFT HAD ME BY THE COAT, ... 93 THE SELF-SEEKER . . . 23
    THAT HAD ME BY THE COAT AS GOOD AS SEATED, ... 125 AN ENCOUNTER . . . 9
    I HAD MY COAT. AND OH, I KNEW, I KNEW, ... 131 THE BONFIRE . . . 69
    MESERVE, BELITTLED IN THE GREAT SKIN COAT HE WORE. . . 143 SNOW 5
    OR BLOW A RUMPLE IN THE COLLIE'S COAT. . . . . . 148 SNOW 141
    HE SHUDDERS HIS COAT AS IF TO THROW OFF FLIES. . . . 223 THE RUNAWAY . . . 18
    A PRIMING COAT OF LEAVES. . . . . 416 CLOSED FOR GOOD . . 18
    BUT WITH A COAT SO LIGHT . . . . 416 CLOSED FOR GOOD . . 22
    THAT'S THE RIGHT STYLE OF COAT FOR PROPHECY . . . . 501 A MASQUE OF MERCY . 218
COATS
    A-BUTTONING COATS, TO ASK HIM WHO HE WAS. . . . . 106 CHRISTMAS TREES . . . 8
    OF COATS, OATS, VOTES, TO ALL MANKIND. . . . . . 450 OUR DOOM TO BLOOM . . 9
COAX
    TRYING TO COAX HIM OFF WITH POCKET MONEY-- . . . . 35 DEATH OF THE HIRED MAN 28
    THAT DAY A WOMAN COULDN'T COAX HIM OFF. . . . . . 94 THE SELF-SEEKER . . . 37
COBBLESTONES
    AND MADE A WIDESPREAD BRAWL ON COBBLESTONES; . . . . 40 THE MOUNTAIN 11
COBWEB
    THE BATTLE RENT A COBWEB DIAMOND-STRUNG . . . . . 126 RANGE-FINDING . . . 1
COBWEBS
    WHERE YOUR FACE BURNS AND TICKLES WITH THE COBWEBS . . 122 BIRCHES 45
COCK
    "TO COCK THE HAY?--BECAUSE IT'S GOING TO SHOWER? . . . 70 THE CODE 12
    TWENTY FOR THIS COCK, TWENTY-FIVE FOR THAT. . . . . 86 THE HOUSEKEEPER . . . 139
    FOR FIFTY DOLLARS FOR ONE LANGSHANG COCK-- . . . . 86 THE HOUSEKEEPER . . . 146
    RECEIPTED. AND THE COCK IS IN THE YARD." . . . . . 86 THE HOUSEKEEPER . . . 147
    "SEE HOW SHE'S COCK HER HEAD!" . . . . 188 THE AX-HELVE . . . 102
COCKNEY
    PRONOUNCE IT HOMER WITH A COCKNEY ROUGH. . . . . . 459 HOW HARD TO KEEP FROM 189
COCKS
    GATHERING UP WINDROWS, PILING COCKS OF HAY, ... 69 THE CODE 2
    YOU STAND UP TO IT LIKE A PAIR OF COCKS. . . . . . 100 THE SELF-SEEKER . . . 211
COCKTAIL-PARTY
    IT'S GREENWICH VILLAGE COCKTAIL-PARTY TALK-- . . . . 500 A MASQUE OF MERCY . . 170
COCOON
    THE COCOON . . . . 247 THE COCOON . . . . T
    THEY PRUDENTLY ARE SPINNING THEIR COCOON . . . . . 248 THE COCOON 13
    SPINNING THEIR OWN COCOON DID THEY BUT KNOW IT. . . . 248 THE COCOON 16
COD
    AS EVER SHE TURNED HER HOME WITH COD . . . . . . 262 THE FLOWER BOAT . . . 7
CODE
    THE CODE . . . . 69 THE CODE . . . . . T
    AND THEN ANOTHER TICK. HE KNEW THE CODE: . . . . . 270 THE EGG AND THE MACHINE 3

COOLIN
   WITH COOLIN MOTH OR RUSTY PARASITE . . . . 283 THE GOLD HESPERIDEE . 28
COEDUCATION
   IT HAS TWO ENTRIES FOR COEDUCATION. . . . . 400 TO THE RIGHT PERSON . 7
COERCED
   BEEN CAJOLED AND COERCED . . . . 448 THE BAD ISLAND--EASTER 25
COFFEE
   A HALFWAY COFFEE HOUSE 'TWIXT TOWN AND NOWHERE----" . . 155 SNOW 342
COGNIZANCE
   GOD, HAVE YOU TAKEN COGNIZANCE OF THIS? . . . . . . 398 NO HOLY WARS FOR THEM . 9
COGNIZANT
   WAS COGNIZANT. HER HUSBAND WAS WORTH MILLIONS. . . . . 163 NEW HAMPSHIRE . . . 136
COIFFURED
   ALL COIFFURED TO A WINTER SHOW, ... 279 BLUE RIBBON AT AMESBURY 2
COIL
   NEW HAMPSHIRE MOUNTAINS CURL UP IN A COIL. . . . . . 165 NEW HAMPSHIRE . . . 214
   LEAVES GOT UP IN A COIL AND HISSED, ... 251 BEREFT 9
COILED
   WAS COILED IN ITS LAST RESTING GRAVE . . . . 312 THE VINDICTIVES . . . 61
COIN
   YOU POOR OLD SAPE, IF I MAY COIN THE SLANG. . . . . . 518 A MASQUE OF MERCY . 664
COINAGE
   FREE WILL, TRADE, VERSE, THOUGHT, LOVE, SPEECH, COINAGE. . 459 HOW HARD TO KEEP FROM 186
COINCIDENCE
   IT'S A COINCIDENCE, BUT WE WERE ON . . . . 508 A MASQUE OF MERCY . 397
COINS
   (YOU OUGHT TO SEE THE COINS DONE IN COS.) . . . . . . 459 HOW HARD TO KEEP FROM 187
COLD (SEE STONE-COLD)
   HOW THE COLD CREEPS AS THE FIRE DIES AT LENGTH-- . . . 10 STORM FEAR 12
   IT'S ALWAYS COLD IN SUMMER, WARM IN WINTER. . . . . . 42 THE MOUNTAIN . . . 49
   "WARM IN DECEMBER, COLD IN JUNE, YOU SAY?" . . . . . 44 THE MOUNTAIN . . . 100
   COMPARED WITH COLD, AND COLD COMPARED WITH WARM. . . . 44 THE MOUNTAIN . . . 103
   AND A COLD CHILL SHIVERED ACROSS THE LAKE. . . . . . 63 A SERVANT TO SERVANTS . 31
   I'VE KEPT BROWN STANDING IN THE COLD . . . . 140 BROWN'S DESCENT . . 71
   THE ILLIMITABLE DARK AND COLD AND STORM, ... 148 SNOW 144
   "I'LL OWN IT'S COLD FOR SUCH A FALL OF SNOW. . . . . . 150 SNOW 201
   AND THE FIRE'S DIED AND THE ROOM'S DARK AND COLD?" . . . 154 SNOW 310
   TO ANY CHANGE FROM HOT TO COLD, FRCM WET . . . . . . 166 NEW HAMPSHIRE . . 235
   THE STOVE WAS COLD--THE STOVE WAS OFF THE CHIMNEY-- . . 175 THE CENSUS-TAKER . 36
   BUT STANDING OUTDOORS HUNGRY, IN THE COLD, ... 189 THE GRINDSTONE . . 17
   TO WONDER WHERE THE COLD WAS COMING FROM, ... 203 THE WITCH OF COOS . 45
   BUT FEARED THE COLD . . . . 218 I WILL SING YOU ONE-O . 17
   AND THE COLD TO AN ORCHARD SO YOUNG IN THE BARK . . . 228 GOOD-BY AND KEEP COLD . 2
   GOOD-BY AND KEEP COLD . . . . 228 GOOD-BY AND KEEP COLD . T
   KEEP COLD, YOUNG ORCHARD. GOOD-BY AND KEEP COLD. . . . 228 GOOD-BY AND KEEP COLD . 18
   THE BREATH OF AIR HAD DIED OF COLD, ... 232 LOOKING FOR SUNSET BIRD . 3
   HORDES SPENT THEMSELVES TO MAKE IT WET AND COLD, . . . 239 OUR SINGING STRENGTH . 3
   THE RAIN BY RIGHTS WAS SNOW FOR COLD. . . . . 253 THE THATCH 11
   OUT IN THE PLOWED GROUND IN THE COLD A DIGGER, ... 263 THE INVESTMENT . . . 5
   I GAVE UP FIRE FOR FORM TILL I WAS COLD. . . . . . . 267 WHAT FIFTY SAID . . 2
   AGAINST THE DARK AND WIND AND COLD . . . . 281 BLUE RIBBON AT AMESBURY 54
   THE MUD CAME IN ONE COLD . . . . 298 ON TAKING FROM THE TOP 15
   THOUGH THERE'S MORE THAN A DOUBT IF THE WEATHER IS NOT TOO
     COLD . . . . 300 STRONG SAYING NOTHING . 11
   WE SIT INDOORS AND TALK OF THE COLD OUTSIDE. . . . . 305 THERE ARE ROUGHLY ZONES 1
   JUST WHEN THE COLD WENT DOWN SO MANY BELOW. . . . . 305 THERE ARE ROUGHLY ZONES 17
   AND WENT EMBRACED TO THE COLD AND DARK . . . . . . 346 DISCOVERY OF MADEIRAS . 84
   COLD AS A SPRING AS YET SO NEAR ITS SOURCE, ... 378 DIRECTIVE 51
   WHERE THE COLD CRACKS LIKE A PISTOL . . . . 384 IN THE LONG NIGHT . . 3
   AND JUNE WAS NOT MUCH BETTER, COLD AND RAINY. . . . . 407 FROM PLANE TO PLANE . 89
COLDER
   CLEAR AND COLDER . . . . 303 CLEAR AND COLDER . . T
   COLDER THAN THE SEASON WARRANTS. . . . . 304 CLEAR AND COLDER . 14
   WERE LETTING IN THE COLDER LIGHT. . . . . 336 THE WIND AND THE RAIN . 2
COLE
   BOTH THE COLES SAID TOGETHER. MRS. COLE . . . . . . 144 SNOW 34
   FRED COLE, YOU'RE GOING TO LET HIM!" / "WELL, AREN'T YOU? . 144 SNOW 43
   BUT THAT'S NOT SAYING--LOOK, FRED COLE, IT'S TWELVE, . . 144 SNOW 55
   HE HAD COLE WITH HIM TO THE BARN TO SEE HIM OFF. . . . 151 SNOW 244
   WHEN COLE RETURNED HE FOUND HIS WIFE STILL STANDING . . 151 SNOW 245
   COLE HAD BEEN TELEPHONING IN THE DARK. . . . . . . 152 SNOW 270
COLEBROOK
   SHE HAS ONE WITCH--OLD STYLE. SHE LIVES IN COLEBROOK. . . 163 NEW HAMPSHIRE . . . 125
COLES
   GULPED SNOW, AND THEN BLEW FREE AGAIN--THE COLES, . . . 143 SNOW 3
   BOTH THE COLES SAID TOGETHER. MRS. COLE . . . . . . 144 SNOW 34
COLE'S
   "WHY, LETT, STILL UP? LETT, I'M AT COLE'S. I'M LATE. . . 143 SNOW 16
   MRS. COLE'S VOICE CAME FROM AN INNER ROOM: . . . . . 152 SNOW 271
COLLAPSE (SEE SELF-COLLAPSE)
COLLAPSES
   (THE THRONE COLLAPSES. BUT HE PICKS IT UP . . . . . 477 A MASQUE OF REASON . 107
COLLARS
   A HUNDRED COLLARS . . . . 44 A HUNDRED COLLARS . . T
   MORE THAN A HUNDRED COLLARS, SIZE FOURTEEN. . . . . . 47 A HUNDRED COLLARS . . 66
   THOSE COLLARS--WHO SHALL I ADDRESS THEM TO, ... 50 A HUNDRED COLLARS . 163
   "BUT REALLY I--I HAVE SO MANY COLLARS." . . . . . . 50 A HUNDRED COLLARS . 167
COLLECTIVISTIC
   COLLECTIVISTIC REGIMENTING LOVE . . . . 357 A CONSIDERABLE SPECK . 25
COLLECTOR
   "YOU'D SAY SO, MISTER MAN.--I'M A COLLECTOR. . . . . 48 A HUNDRED COLLARS . 95
COLLEGE
   HE'S FINISHED SCHOOL, AND TEACHING IN HIS COLLEGE. . . 36 DEATH OF THE HIRED MAN 60
   AND BOYS THE MINUTE THEY GET OUT OF COLLEGE. . . . . 162 NEW HAMPSHIRE . . . 98
   I THINK HE OWNED SOME SHARES IN HARVARD COLLEGE.) . . . 163 NEW HAMPSHIRE . . . 137
   BUT NOT MUCH IN BETWEEN UNLESS A CCLLEGE . . . . . 325 BUILD SOIL 282
   THE OTHER EVENING AT YOUR COLLEGE DEANERY. . . . . . 393 LUCRETIUS VERSUS POETS 3
   BUT YOU SAY THAT IN COLLEGE NOMENCLATURE . . . . . 393 LUCRETIUS VERSUS POETS 7

COLLEGE (CONTINUED)
      DICK HAD OF BEING FRESH AND FULL OF COLLEGE.   .   .   .   .   . 404 FROM PLANE TO PLANE   .   4
      ON A COLLEGE GATE." .   .   .   . 436 KITTY HAWK   .   .   . 276
      I WAS AT COLLEGE IN THE ISLE OF RHODES." .   .   .   .   .   . 455 HOW HARD TO KEEP FROM   53
COLLEGE-BOY'S
      HAROLD'S YOUNG COLLEGE-BOY'S ASSURANCE PIQUED HIM.   .   .   .   37 DEATH OF THE HIRED MAN   73
COLLIE'S
      OR BLOW A RUMPLE IN THE COLLIE'S COAT.   .   .   .   .   .   . 148 SNOW   141
COLONIAL
      OF HIS OLD SONG, 'THE WILD COLONIAL BOY,'   .   .   .   .   . 205 THE WITCH OF COOS   . . 110
      COLONIAL HAD BEEN THE THING TO BE   .   .   .   . 422 FOR JOHN F. KENNEDY   . 11
COLONIALS
      BUT WE WERE ENGLAND'S, STILL COLONIALS, ... 348 THE GIFT OUTRIGHT   .   .   5
      BUT WE WERE ENGLAND'S, STILL COLONIALS, ... 424 THE GIFT OUTRIGHT   .   .   5
COLONIZATION
      BEFORE THE ERA OF COLONIZATION, ... 161 NEW HAMPSHIRE   .   .   . 72
COLONY
      TO THE PENAL COLONY .   .   .   . 466 SOME SCIENCE FICTION . 22
COLOR
      SEEMED TIPPED WITH WINGS OF COLOR   .   .   .   .   13 ROSE POGONIAS   .   .   . 15
      ANOTHER COLOR OVER A TENTH THE SPACE   .   .   .   .   .   .   132 THE BONFIRE   82
      THERE IS MORE UNMIXED COLOR ON THE WING   .   .   .   .   .   . 225 BLUE-BUTTERFLY DAY   .   .   3
      NEXT TO NOTHING FOR COLOR.   .   .   .   . 235 GATHERING LEAVES   .   . 20
      THE COLOR RUN, ALL SORTS OF WONDER FOLLOW.   .   .   .   .   . 245 THE FREEDOM OF THE MOON 12
      MOISTURE AND COLOR AND ODOR THICKEN HERE.   .   .   .   .   . 246 ATMOSPHERE   5
      BUT GET SOME COLOR AND MUSIC OUT OF LIFE?   .   .   .   .   . 264 THE INVESTMENT   .   .   . 14
      EXCEPT IN COLOR HE ISN'T BLUE, ... 276 TWO TRAMPS IN MUD TIME   31
      "WRONG SHAPE, WRONG COLOR, AND WRONG SCENT," I SAID.   .   . 278 THE WHITE-TAILED HORNET 40
      GOD KNOWS ALL THE COLOR AND FORM OF LEAVES I HAVE TRODDEN
           ON AND MIRED.   .   .   .   . 297 A LEAF-TREADER   .   .   .   2
      WAS A SHADE LESS THE COLOR OF NIGHT, ... 299 WELCOME TO THEIR BELIEF 11
      A SHADE MORE THE COLOR OF SNOW.   .   .   .   . 299 WELCOME TO THEIR BELIEF 12
      OF HIS RAVEN COLOR OF HAIR.   .   .   .   . 299 WELCOME TO THEIR BELIEF 16
      BUT NO, THE COLOR USED IS RED.   .   .   .   . 327 A MISSIVE MISSILE   .   . 13
      WHEN THE COLOR FLUSHED TO THE PETALS IT MUST HAVE BEEN--   . 343 QUEST OF PURPLE-FRINGED 15
      NO MATTER WHAT THE COLOR OF ITS SKIN.   .   .   .   .   .   . 369 THE LITERATE FARMER AND 51
      DO NO DOUBT WITH THEIR COLOR COMPENSATE   .   .   .   .   .   411 POD OF THE MILKWEED   . 12
      CAUGHT COLOR FROM THE LAST OF EVENING RED   .   .   .   .   . 445 QUESTIONING FACES   .   .   4
COLORADO
      BARTLETT OF RAYMOND (NOW OF COLORADO), ... 167 NEW HAMPSHIRE   .   .   . 260
COLORED (SEE HIGH-COLORED, MANY-COLORED)
COLORS
      ALL SHAPES AND COLORS OF FLOWERS, ... 264 THE LAST MOWING   .   .   . 18
      THE COLORS ARE KEPT UNMIXED ON THE PALETTE.   .   .   .   . 320 BUILD SOIL   147
      ARE GOD'S WHITE LIGHT REFRACTED INTO COLORS.   .   .   .   . 516 A MASQUE OF MERCY   .   . 597
COLT
      WE STOPPED BY A MOUNTAIN PASTURE TO SAY, "WHOSE COLT?"   .   . 223 THE RUNAWAY   2
COLUMBIA
      EVEN WHILE WE TALK SOME CHEMIST AT COLUMBIA   .   .   .   .   319 BUILD SOIL   107
COLUMBUS
      COLUMBUS MAY HAVE WORKED THE WIND   .   .   .   . 416 AMERICA IS HARD TO SEE   1
      HAD BUT COLUMBUS KNOWN ENOUGH   .   .   .   . 417 AMERICA IS HARD TO SEE   25
      I SHOULD HAVE HAD COLUMBUS SUNG   .   .   .   .   417 AMERICA IS HARD TO SEE   34
      COLUMBUS, AS I SAY, WILL MISS   .   .   .   . 418 AMERICA IS HARD TO SEE   67
      THE NEW WORLD CHRISTOPHER COLUMBUS FOUND.   .   .   .   .   . 422 FOR JOHN F. KENNEDY   . 15
COLUMBUS-LIKE
      IT WOULD BE TOO BAD IF COLUMBUS-LIKE   .   .   .   .   .   . 480 A MASQUE OF REASON   . . 186
COMB
      HER GOLDEN LEG, HER CORAL COMB, ...   280 BLUE RIBBON AT AMESBURY   6
      FROM HER CHIN, PICKED UP HER COMB, ... 341 THE SUBVERTED FLOWER   . 72
COMBED
      COMBED IT DOWN WITH A RAKE AND SAYS, 'O.K.'   .   .   .   .   . 71 THE CODE   52
COMBINATION
      OR A COMBINATION OF THE TWO, ... 345 DISCOVERY OF MADEIRAS   72
COMBINED
      RIVALRY COMBINED)--   .   .   .   . 436 KITTY HAWK   269
COMBINING
      ALONE, OR IN ONE ORNAMENT COMBINING   .   .   .   .   .   .   245 THE FREEDOM OF THE MOON   5
      AND ONE TO CAP THE CLIMAX BY COMBINING   .   .   .   .   .   . 502 A MASQUE OF MERCY   .   . 242
COME (SEE KINGDOM-COME)
      I SHAN'T BE GONE LONG.--YOU COME TOO.   .   .   .   .   .   .   1 THE PASTURE   4
      I SHAN'T BE GONE LONG.--YOU COME TOO.   .   .   .   .   .   .   1 THE PASTURE   8
      THE WOODS COME BACK TO THE MOWING FIELD;   .   .   .   .   .   5 GHOST HOUSE   7
      AND WHEN I COME TO THE GARDEN GROUND, ...   8 A LATE WALK   5
      "COME OUT! COME OUT!"--   .   .   .   .   10 STORM FEAR   6
      TO COME AGAIN AT DARK.   .   .   .   .   10 WIND AND WINDOW FLOWER   12
      COME WITH RAIN, O LOUD SOUTHWESTER!   .   .   .   . 11 TO THE THAWING WIND   .   1
      SPIRIT TO MATTER TILL DEATH COME.   .   .   .   .   21 THE TRIAL BY EXISTENCE   64
      COME OVER THE HILLS AND FAR WITH ME, ...   26 A LINE-STORM SONG   .   .   7
      COME, BE MY LOVE IN THE WET WOODS, COME, ...   26 A LINE-STORM SONG   .   . 15
      AND COME NOT THROUGH DRY-SHOD?   .   .   .   . 27 A LINE-STORM SONG   .   . 22
      OH, COME FORTH INTO THE STORM AND ROUT   .   .   .   .   .   . 27 A LINE-STORM SONG   .   . 31
      I HAVE COME BY THE HIGHWAY HOME, ...   30 RELUCTANCE   5
      I HAVE COME AFTER THEM AND MADE REPAIR   .   .   .   .   .   . 33 MENDING WALL   6
      HE SAID HE'D COME TO DITCH THE MEADOW FOR ME."   .   .   .   . 36 DEATH OF THE HIRED MAN   46
      "WARREN," SHE SAID, "HE HAS COME HOME TO DIE: .   .   .   . 38 DEATH OF THE HIRED MAN 111
      HE'S COME TO HELP YOU DITCH THE MEADOW.   .   .   .   .   .   40 DEATH OF THE HIRED MAN 157
      BY ANYONE WHO'D COME A LONG WAY UP.   .   .   .   . 43 THE MOUNTAIN   .   .   . 72
      HAVEN'T COME DOWN TO THE BARS AT MILKING TIME?   .   .   .   . 43 THE MOUNTAIN   .   .   . 86
      AND COME TO THINK I MUST HAVE BACK AT HOME   .   .   .   .   . 47 A HUNDRED COLLARS   .   . 65
      YOU ACT AS IF YOU WISHED YOU HADN'T COME.   .   .   .   .   .   47 A HUNDRED COLLARS   .   . 71
      COME, IF YOU'RE NOT AFRAID." / "I'M NOT AFRAID.   .   .   .   . 47 A HUNDRED COLLARS   .   . 87
      SUPPOSE YOU AREN'T AWAKE WHEN I COME BACK?   .   .   .   .   . 50 A HUNDRED COLLARS   .   . 164
      WHEN I COME BACK, SO YOU'LL KNOW WHO IT IS.   .   .   .   .   . 50 A HUNDRED COLLARS   .   . 174
      LISTEN TO ME. I WON'T COME DOWN THE STAIRS."   .   .   .   .   52 HOME BURIAL   40
      YOU MAKE ME ANGRY. I'LL COME DOWN TO YOU.   .   .   .   .   .   53 HOME BURIAL   68
      GOD, WHAT A WOMAN! AND IT'S COME TO THIS, ...   53 HOME BURIAL   69
      "PRETTY," HE SAID. "COME IN. NO ONE WILL CARE."   .   .   .   . 55 THE BLACK COTTAGE   .   . 11

COME (CONTINUED)
    THEY SAY THEY MEAN TO COME AND SUMMER HERE . . . . 55 THE BLACK COTTAGE . . . 17
    WHERE THEY WERE BOYS. THEY HAVEN'T COME THIS YEAR. . . . . 55 THE BLACK COTTAGE . . . 18
    IN THE CAVERNOUS PAIL OF THE FIRST ONE TO COME! . . . . . 59 BLUEBERRIES 5
    WHEN WHO SHOULD COME BY, WITH A DEMOCRAT-LOAD . . . . . . 60 BLUEBERRIES 37
    TO HAVE YOU COME AND CAMP HERE ON OUR LAND. . . . . 62 A SERVANT TO SERVANTS . 2
    AND ALL OUR STORMS COME UP TOWARD THE HOUSE, ... 63 A SERVANT TO SERVANTS . 24
    BUT IT MIGHT BE, COME NIGHT, I SHOULDN'T LIKE IT, ... 67 A SERVANT TO SERVANTS . 163
    SHOUTS LIKE AN ARMY CAPTAIN, 'LET HER COME!' . . . . . . 71 THE CODE 63
    'DID YOU SAY, "LET HER COME"?' 'YES, LET HER COME.' . . . 71 THE CODE 66
    WHEN ALL WHO WOULD COME SEEKING IN NEW HAMPSHIRE . . . . . 73 THE GENERATIONS OF MEN . 2
    ANCESTRAL MEMORIES MIGHT COME TOGETHER. . . . . 73 THE GENERATIONS OF MEN . 3
    YOU NEVER SAW BEFORE. WHAT WILL WE COME TO . . . . 76 THE GENERATIONS OF MEN . 86
    AND COME AND MAKE YOUR SUMMER DWELLING HERE, ... 79 THE GENERATIONS OF MEN . 166
    AND PERHAPS SHE WILL COME, STILL UNAFRAID, ... 79 THE GENERATIONS OF MEN . 167
    BUT NOT COME IN ACROSS THE SACRED SILL----". . . . . . . 79 THE GENERATIONS OF MEN . 170
    TO COME TO HIS HOUSE WHEN HE'S GONE TO YOURS. . . . . . . 81 THE HOUSEKEEPER . . . 15
    "I'M SURE SHE WON'T COME BACK. SHE'S HIDING SOMEWHERE. . . 82 THE HOUSEKEEPER . . . 23
    AND SHE'LL COME BACK. BUT, BLESS YOU, I'M HER MOTHER-- . . 82 THE HOUSEKEEPER . . . 26
    COME HERE--I'LL SHOW YOU--IN THAT APPLE TREE. . . . . . . 83 THE HOUSEKEEPER . . . 62
    SHE WON'T COME BACK--IT'S WORSE THAN THAT--SHE CAN'T." . . 87 THE HOUSEKEEPER . . . 177
    COME OUT HERE IF YOU WANT TO HEAR ME TALK.-- . . . . . . 88 THE HOUSEKEEPER . . . 208
    "YOU'RE NOT TO COME," SHE SAID. "THIS IS MY BUSINESS. . . 90 THE FEAR 35
    IF THE TIME'S COME TO FACE IT, I'M THE ONE . . . . 90 THE FEAR 36
    I'LL JUST COME FORWARD IN THE LANTERN-LIGHT . . . . 91 THE FEAR 74
    WHAT DO YOU WANT, DEAR? COME, STAND BY THE BED; . . . . . 96 THE SELF-SEEKER . . . 104
    COME, HOLD IT OUT. DON'T CHANGE.--A RAM'S HORN ORCHID! . . 96 THE SELF-SEEKER . . . 112
    IN BUSHEL LOTS--DOESN'T COME ON THE MARKET. . . . . 97 THE SELF-SEEKER . . . 130
    "YOU, WILL, STOP MAKING FACES. COME ROUND HERE . . . . . 99 THE SELF-SEEKER . . . 184
    WHERE I COME IN IS WHAT I WANT TO KNOW. . . . . 100 THE SELF-SEEKER . . . 210
    WHEN YOU COME BACK, I'LL HAVE THE PAPERS SIGNED. . . . . . 100 THE SELF-SEEKER . . . 213
    I'LL GO OUTDOORS, BY GAD, AND WON'T COME BACK." . . . . . 100 THE SELF-SEEKER . . . 222
    "WILLIS, BRING ANNE BACK WITH YOU WHEN YOU COME. . . . . . 100 THE SELF-SEEKER . . . 223
    I DOUBTED IF I SHOULD EVER COME BACK. . . . . 105 THE ROAD NOT TAKEN . . 15
    WHEN BETWEEN WHIRLS OF SNOW NOT COME TO LIE . . . . 106 CHRISTMAS TREES . . . 3
    HE PROVED TO BE THE CITY COME AGAIN . . . . 106 CHRISTMAS TREES . . . 9
    THE TRIAL BY MARKET EVERYTHING MUST COME TO. . . . . . . 106 CHRISTMAS TREES . . . 24
    "A THOUSAND TREES WOULD COME TO THIRTY DOLLARS." . . . . . 107 CHRISTMAS TREES . . . 44
    THOUGH HARM SHOULD COME OF IT; SO BUILT THE SCREEN . . . . 109 THE EXPOSED NEST . . . 29
    IN OTHER CHAIRS, AND SOMETHING, COME TO LOOK, ... 110 IN THE HOME STRETCH . . 7
    TO COME AS HERE I STAND AND GO THE ROUND . . . . 111 IN THE HOME STRETCH . . 27
    NOT MUCH OF THAT UNTIL I COME TO WOODS . . . . 111 IN THE HOME STRETCH . . 33
    I ONLY SEE THE YEARS. THEY COME AND GO . . . . 112 IN THE HOME STRETCH . . 47
    "COME FROM THAT WINDOW WHERE YOU SEE TOO MUCH, ... 112 IN THE HOME STRETCH . . 60
    IT ALMOST SEEMED TO COME BALLOONING UP, ... 113 IN THE HOME STRETCH . . 88
    BUT WHO FIRST SAID THE WORD TO COME?" / "MY DEAR, ... 116 IN THE HOME STRETCH . . 171
    I HAVE TO MAKE YOU BUILD IT. COME, THE LIGHT. . . . . . . 117 IN THE HOME STRETCH . . 200
    SOMEONE SAID 'COME'--I HEARD IT AS I BOWED." . . . . . . 118 THE TELEPHONE 17
    OR FLOURISHED AND COME UP IN JEWELWEED, ... 119 HYLA BROOK 7
    AND THEN COME BACK TO IT AND BEGIN OVER. . . . . 122 BIRCHES 49
    AND SINCE IT WAS COMING UP HAD TO COME. . . . . 123 PEA BRUSH 24
    YOU COME TO FETCH ME FROM MY WORK TONIGHT . . . . 123 PUTTING IN THE SEED . . 1
    CARE WHEN THE BIRDS COME ROUND THE HOUSE . . . . 126 LONELINESS 3
    OR CARE SO MUCH WHEN THEY COME BACK . . . . 126 LONELINESS 5
    COULDN'T BELIEVE THAT SO MUCH BLACK HAD COME THERE . . . . 132 THE BONFIRE 85
    WHAT WOULD YOU SAY TO WAR IF IT SHOULD COME? . . . . . . 132 THE BONFIRE 97
    AT SEA, ABOUT THE TOWNS WHERE WAR HAS COME . . . . 132 THE BONFIRE 105
    THE BEST WAY IS TO COME UPHILL WITH ME . . . . 133 THE BONFIRE 113
    JUST WHEN IT SEEMS TO COME IN RIGHT, ... 134 A GIRL'S GARDEN . . . 43
    HE WOULD COME BACK AND SING." . . . . 136 LAST WORD OF A BLUEBIRD . 12
    WE KNOW WHO WHEN THEY COME TO TOWN . . . . 141 THE GUM-GATHERER . . . 25
    HERE COME THE LINE-GANG PIONEERING BY. . . . . 141 THE LINE-GANG 1
    "COME, JOHN," HE SAID, "YOU WANT TO SEE THE WHEEL PIT?" . . 142 THE VANISHING RED . . . 19
    TO PLAY---" / "YOU TEND YOUR HORSES AND COME BACK.-- . . . 144 SNOW 42
    AND SAVE HIS LIFE.--ALL RIGHT, COME IN, MESERVE. . . . . . 147 SNOW 104
    THINGS MUST EXPECT TO COME IN FRONT OF US . . . . 147 SNOW 126
    WELL, NOW I LEAVE YOU, PEOPLE." / "COME, MESERVE, ... 150 SNOW 197
    THEY WILL COME BUDDING BOUGHS FROM TREE TO TREE, ... 151 SNOW 230
    HE WON'T COME BACK, AND IF HE TELEPHONES, ... 152 SNOW 266
    HE HADN'T COME AND HAD HE REALLY STARTED." . . . . 152 SNOW 277
    "FRED, SEE IF YOU CAN HEAR WHAT I HEAR. COME." . . . . . 154 SNOW 315
    WHAT DID HE COME IN FOR?--TO TALK AND VISIT? . . . . . . 155 SNOW 339
    WAS SOMEONE WHO HAD JUST COME BACK ASHAMED . . . . 160 NEW HAMPSHIRE 37
    IN LITERATURE TO DATE IS HEARD TO COME. . . . . 167 NEW HAMPSHIRE 271
    I WAS NOT ALWAYS SO; I'VE COME TO BE SO. . . . . 169 NEW HAMPSHIRE 312
    SCARCELY A MILE BUT THAT I COME ON ONE, ... 171 NEW HAMPSHIRE 390
    "COME, BUT THIS ISN'T CHOOSING--PUKE OR PRUDE?" . . . . . 171 NEW HAMPSHIRE 406
    OFTEN HE BID ME COME AND HAVE A LOOK . . . . 178 THE STAR-SPLITTER . . 76
    "COME ON MY HOUSE AND I PUT YOU ONE IN . . . . 186 THE AX-HELVE 29
    "DEN WHEN YOU SAY YOU COME? IT'S CCST YOU NOTHING. . . . . 186 THE AX-HELVE 33
    OTHERS BECAUSE HE'D COME WITHIN A DAY . . . . 191 PAUL'S WIFE 6
    AND WAS COME AFTER LIKE EURYDICE . . . . 196 WILD GRAPES 12
    JUST THEN COME YOU AND I TO GATHER IT. . . . . 198 WILD GRAPES 68
    BUT COME TO DIE SHE FOUND SHE CARED SO MUCH: . . . . . . 199 PLACE FOR A THIRD . . 4
    THE SISTER HAD NOT COME ACROSS THIS LABAN; . . . . 201 PLACE FOR A THIRD . . 66
    COME DOWN THE STAIRS AT NIGHT AND STAND PERPLEXED . . . . 206 THE WITCH OF COOS . . 126
    TO TELL THE TRUTH, SUPPOSE THE TIME HAD COME. . . . . . . 207 THE WITCH OF COOS . . 144
    LIKE, "NO, SHE AIN'T COME BACK FROM KITING YET. . . . . . 209 PAUPER WITCH OF GRAFTON 80
    HE'S SO FAR OFF HE CAN'T SEE WHAT I'VE COME TO. . . . . . 210 PAUPER WITCH OF GRAFTON 102
    YOU CAN COME DOWN FROM EVERYTHING TO NOTHING. . . . . . . 210 PAUPER WITCH OF GRAFTON 103
    COME STRAIGHT DOWN OFF THIS MOUNTAIN JUST AS FAST . . . . 215 A FOUNTAIN, A BOTTLE . 61
    THE LIVING COME WITH GRASSY TREAD . . . . 221 IN A DISUSED GRAVEYARD 1
    "THE ONES WHO LIVING COME TODAY . . . . 221 IN A DISUSED GRAVEYARD 6
    TOMORROW DEAD WILL COME TO STAY." . . . . 221 IN A DISUSED GRAVEYARD 8
    HOW NO ONE DEAD WILL SEEM TO COME. . . . . 221 IN A DISUSED GRAVEYARD 11
    OUGHT TO BE TOLD TO COME AND TAKE HIM IN." . . . . 223 THE RUNAWAY 21
    NOT THE SAME DOE COME BACK INTO HER PLACE. . . . . 229 TWO LOOK AT TWO . . . 30
    SOME THAT HAVE COME TOO FAR NORTH BACK AWAY, ... 239 OUR SINGING STRENGTH . 23

COME (CONTINUED)
    I BADE A "COME IN" . . . . 241 THE LOCKLESS DOOR . . .   14
    HERE COME REAL STARS TO FILL THE UPPER SKIES, ... 246 FIREFLIES IN THE GARDEN . 1
    AND HERE ON EARTH COME EMULATING FLIES . . . . 246 FIREFLIES IN THE GARDEN . 2
    WHERE CONIES NOW COME OUT TO SUN AND ROMP, ... 254 A WINTER EDEN . . .   2
    TO COME AT THE FISHER TOWN . . . . 260 SAND DUNES   6
    THAT LIES UNLIFTED NOW, COME DEW, COME RUST, ... 261 A SOLDIER   2
    WAS IT SOME MONEY SUDDENLY COME INTO? . . . . 264 THE INVESTMENT . . .   10
    AGAIN COME TO LIFE AND CRAWL OFF, ... 266 SITTING BY A BUSH . .   11
    IF THERE SHOULD EVER COME A DAY . . . . 274 A LONE STRIKER . . .   57
    COME GET HIM--THEY KNEW WHERE TO SEARCH. . . . . . . 275 A LONE STRIKER . . .   62
    AND COME WITH ALL HER HONORS HOME. . . . . 280 BLUE RIBBON AT AMESBURY . 5
    AND DON'T COME OUT FOR A WHILE, ... 282 A DRUMLIN WOODCHUCK . .   18
    AND THEN NEXT DAY AS I COME BACK INTO THE SANE, ... 287 A ROADSIDE STAND . .   49
    I WONDER HOW I SHOULD LIKE YOU TO COME TO ME . . . . . 287 A ROADSIDE STAND . .   50
    "DEATH'S COME TO JERRY MCCORMIC, ... 288 DEPARTMENTAL   23
    COME BACK THAT WAY A SUMMER HENCE, ... 291 ON HEART'S BEGINNING TO . 19
    LATE IN LIFE I HAVE COME ON FERN. . . . . 297 LEAVES COMPARED WITH .   11
    TO COME TO THEIR FINAL PLACE IN EARTH THEY HAD TO PASS ME
      BY. . . . . 297 A LEAF-TREADER . . .   6
    FOR THE BEES TO COME AND SERVE ITS BEAUTY ARIGHT. . . . 300 STRONG SAYING NOTHING .   12
    WOULD COME IN LIKE YOU HERE: . . . . 302 VOICE WAYS   7
    IT COULD NOT HAVE COME DOWN TO US SO FAR, ... 302 A BIRD SINGING IN SLEEP . 9
    AND COME TO LEAVE THE ROUTINE ROAD . . . . 304 UNHARVESTED   2
    SHALL COME TO END THE BLIGHT. . . . . 308 EVIL TENDENCIES CANCEL .   6
    HAD COME TO A TROUBLED HALT. . . . . 314 BEARER OF EVIL TIDINGS .   22
    TO BE ATTEMPTED. GREED MAY WELL COME NEXT. . . . . . 319 BUILD SOIL   100
    COME LOOK AT MY SIGNIFICANT MUD PIE." . . . . 321 BUILD SOIL   154
    THAT NONE SHALL EVER SEE YOU COME TO MARKET-- . . . . . 323 BUILD SOIL   213
    YOU COME TO ME AND I'LL UNFOLD TO YOU . . . . 323 BUILD SOIL   224
    TO THINK IT OUT. COME CLOSE, LET US CONSPIRE-- . . . . 323 BUILD SOIL   228
    A MAN THE WAY THINGS COME IN PAIRS. . . . . 326 TO A THINKER . . .   14
    AND WHAT CAN OF ITS COMING COME, ... 332 ALL REVELATION . . .   5
    COME IN . . . . 334 COME IN   1
    ALMOST LIKE A CALL TO COME IN . . . . 334 COME IN   15
    I WOULD NOT COME IN. . . . . 334 COME IN   18
    "IF THIS HAS COME TO US . . . . 339 THE SUBVERTED FLOWER .   23
    SINCE HE MEANS TO COME TO A DOOR HE WILL COME TO A DOOR, . 341 WILLFUL HOMING . . .   9
    TILL I SAW THE PATH WHERE THE SLENDER FOX HAD COME , . . 342 QUEST OF PURPLE-FRINGED . 11
    SAID THAT THE FALL MIGHT COME AND WHIRL OF LEAVES, . . . 343 QUEST OF PURPLE-FRINGED . 27
    COME LEARN THE LATIN EHEU FOR ALAS. . . . . 353 THE LESSON FOR TODAY .   85
    THE FLOWERS FADING ON THE SEED TO COME; . . . . . . 356 TIME OUT   7
    THE SECOND SUCH HAS COME, ... 361 ALMOST TWO THOUSAND .   5
    HAVE COME DOWN FROM THEIR NATIVE LEDGE . . . . 364 A NATURE NOTE . . .   2
    BUT COME, ENLIGHTENED AS IN TALK YOU SEEM, ... 370 THE LITERATE FARMER AND . 61
    "HERE COME MORE STARS TO CHARACTER THE SKIES, ... 370 THE LITERATE FARMER AND . 75
    AT THE PRESENT RATE IT MUST COME TO PASS, ... 375 SOMETHING FOR HOPE .   1
    THERE WILL COME ANOTHER DAY. . . . . 385 IN THE LONG NIGHT . .   16
    SEEMS TO COME TO AN END . . . . 388 MIDDLENESS OF THE ROAD .   2
    ARE ABSOLUTELY SURE TO COME TO GRIEF. . . . . 394 HAEC FABULA DOCET . .   20
    WHO ADVISED MAN TO COME AND LIVE THEREIN? . . . . . . 400 THE BROKEN DROUGHT .   14
    MANY SHALL COME AWAY AS STRUGGLE-WORN . . . . 412 POD OF THE MILKWEED .   34
    SHOULD COME TO NOTHING MUST BE FAIRLY FACED. . . . . . 412 POD OF THE MILKWEED .   54
    WHO COME TO LOOK IN ON THEM FROM THE PULPIT. . . . . . 414 A CABIN IN THE CLEARING . 24
    AND COME NOT BACK WITH STEED . . . . 415 CLOSED FOR GOOD . .   7
    TO COME AS A FOOT PRINTER, ... 416 CLOSED FOR GOOD . . .   27
    COME FRESH FROM AN ELECTION LIKE THE LAST, ... 423 FOR JOHN F. KENNEDY .   54
    BUT IT MUST COME DOWN." . . . . 437 KITTY HAWK   307
    WE COME NOWHERE NEAR . . . . 442 KITTY HAWK   435
    WE TWO COME IN FLIGHT . . . . 442 KITTY HAWK   455
    WHERE WOULD WE GET ANOTHER? COME, ... 451 A-WISHING WELL . . .   30
    IT WILL COME ROLLING AFTER US LIKE A HOOP." . . . . . 454 HOW HARD TO KEEP FROM .   27
    THIS LARRIKIN? ALL RIGHT. YOU COME ALONG. . . . . . 455 HOW HARD TO KEEP FROM .   47
    GUARANTEED TO COME SAFELY OFF WITH YOU . . . . 457 HOW HARD TO KEEP FROM .   125
    NO ONE COULD GET YOU: YOU WOULD COME THROUGH SMILING. . 458 HOW HARD TO KEEP FROM .   129
    THEY'VE COME TO FEEL THE NEED OF IS A KIND . . . . . 461 HOW HARD TO KEEP FROM .   232
    WE WOULD SEE WHAT WOULD COME . . . . 464 MILKY WAY IS A COWPATH .   10
    AND COME TO REST IN AN OFFICIAL VERDICT. . . . . . . 474 A MASQUE OF REASON .   29
    AND SPEAK TO HIM BEFORE THE OTHERS COME. . . . . . . 474 A MASQUE OF REASON .   32
    HIS SPIRIT HAD TO COME. APPARENTLY . . . . 477 A MASQUE OF REASON .   100
    COME, AFTER ALL THESE YEARS--TO SATISFY ME. . . . . . 482 A MASQUE OF REASON .   254
    I'VE COME TO THINK NO SO-CALLED HIDDEN VALUE'S . . . . 483 A MASQUE OF REASON .   280
    YOUR KINGDOM, YES, YOUR KINGDOM COME ON EARTH. . . . . 484 A MASQUE OF REASON .   303
    AND ALSO OF THE WAY ALL THINGS COME ROUND, ... 485 A MASQUE OF REASON .   342
    HE HAS BUT TO APPEAR. HE'LL COME FOR ME, ... 487 A MASQUE OF REASON .   384
    OH, YES, THAT TENDENCY!--OH, DO COME OFF IT. . . . . 489 A MASQUE OF REASON .   447
    YOU CAN'T COME IN! (KNOCK, KNOCK) THE STORE IS CLOSED! . 493 A MASQUE OF MERCY . .   8
    KEEPER, YOU COME AND SEE. OR YOU COME, PAUL. . . . . 493 A MASQUE OF MERCY . .   13
    MORE THAN IT TOUCHES ME. / YOU MAY COME IN. . . . . 493 A MASQUE OF MERCY . .   17
    COME, COME, YOU TALK LIKE AN AGRARIAN. . . . . . . 496 A MASQUE OF MERCY . .   68
    AND HERE COME ALL YOUR GREAT BOOKS TUMBLING DOWN! . . . 504 A MASQUE OF MERCY . .   288
    COME ON, OR WE'LL BEGIN TO BE AFRAID. . . . . 506 A MASQUE OF MERCY . .   330
    (A WHOLE SHELF CASCADES DOWN.) HERE COME SOME MORE. . . 506 A MASQUE OF MERCY . .   341
    TO SOME OF KEEPER'S FRIENDS THAT COME IN HERE, ... 509 A MASQUE OF MERCY . .   405
    PAUL MAKES IT COME OUT SO THEY LOOK LIKE CHRISTIANS. . . 509 A MASQUE OF MERCY . .   407
    STILL, NOT SO FAR OFF, COME TO THINK OF IT. . . . . . 509 A MASQUE OF MERCY . .   428
    OR YOU WILL COME TO WITH A FOOLISH FEELING. . . . . . 513 A MASQUE OF MERCY . .   537
    MY DUNGEONEERS, COME FETCH US.--NO ONE ANSWERS. . . . 514 A MASQUE OF MERCY . .   556
    AS IF TO COME, BUT KEEPER WAVES HER OFF.) . . . . . 518 A MASQUE OF MERCY . .   653
COMEDY
    COMEDY WAS IN IT. . . . . 427 VERSION   6
COMES
    NIGHT COMES; THE BLACK BATS TUMBLE AND DART; . . . . .   6 GHOST HOUSE   15
    COMES SOFTLY RATTLING DOWN. . . . .   9 A LATE WALK   12
    ONE ON A SIDE. IT COMES TO LITTLE MORE: . . . . . . 33 MENDING WALL . . .   22
    IN WINTER HE COMES BACK TO US. I'M DONE." . . . . . 35 DEATH OF THE HIRED MAN   30
    A GOOD DEAL COMES ON ME WHEN ALL IS SAID. . . . . . 48 A HUNDRED COLLARS . .   107
    THERE'S A HAY LOAD A-COMING--WHEN IT COMES. . . . . . 49 A HUNDRED COLLARS . .   132

COMES (CONTINUED)
WITH ANYONE TO DEATH, COMES SO FAR SHORT . . . . 54 HOME BURIAL 98
AND COMES THAT OTHER FALL WE NAME THE FALL. . . . . . 120 THE OVEN BIRD . . . 9
THE STURDY SEEDLING WITH ARCHED BODY COMES . . . . . 124 PUTTING IN THE SEED . 13
THE DOCTOR, WHEN HE COMES. DON'T LET HIM, SISTER!" . . 137 "OUT,OUT--" 26
IT COMES TO MARKET GOLDEN BROWN; . . . . 141 THE GUM-GATHERER . . 32
"ABOUT THE BRITISH ARCTIC. THAT'S WHAT COMES . . . . 159 NEW HAMPSHIRE . . . 23
WHO COMES FROM PHILADELPHIA EVERY YEAR . . . . . . 162 NEW HAMPSHIRE . . . 101
COMES TOO NEAR TO AHAZ' SIN FOR SAFETY. . . . . . . 171 NEW HAMPSHIRE . . . 393
"YOU KNOW ORION ALWAYS COMES UP SIDEWAYS. . . . . . 176 THE STAR-SPLITTER . . 1
THAT COMES OF HAVING PAUL AROUND THE PLACE. . . . . 193 PAUL'S WIFE 76
WHEN HIS TIME COMES TO DIE AND SETTLE DOWN. . . . . 202 PLACE FOR A THIRD . . 82
OR A LITTLE CHILD, COMES UP. IT WASN'T TOFFILE: . . . 204 THE WITCH OF COOS . . 53
AND BLUE SO FAR ABOVE US COMES SO HIGH, ... 220 FRAGMENTARY BLUE . . 7
AND NOW HE COMES AGAIN WITH CLATTER OF STONE, . . . 223 THE RUNAWAY 15
WHEN SLOWLY (AND NOBODY COMES WITH A LIGHT) . . . . 228 GOOD-BY AND KEEP COLD . 27
MY SASH IS LOWERED WHEN NIGHT COMES ON; . . . . . . 251 TREE AT MY WINDOW . . 2
A CLOUD COMES OVER THE SUNLIT ARCH, ... 275 TWO TRAMPS IN MUD TIME 22
A WIND COMES OFF A FROZEN PEAK, ... 275 TWO TRAMPS IN MUD TIME 23
A BLUEBIRD COMES TENDERLY UP TO ALIGHT . . . . . . 275 TWO TRAMPS IN MUD TIME 25
THE EXIT HE COMES OUT AT LIKE A BULLET . . . . . . 277 THE WHITE-TAILED HORNET 3
HE COMES OUT MORE UNERRING THAN A BULLET. . . . . . 277 THE WHITE-TAILED HORNET 6
WHEN IT COMES TO A MOUNTAIN FARM . . . . 285 IN TIME OF CLOUDBURST . 6
THE WATER COMES ASHORE, ... 301 NEITHER OUT FAR NOR IN 11
WHAT COMES OVER A MAN, IS IT SOUL OR MIND-- . . . . 305 THERE ARE ROUGHLY ZONES 7
SUPPOSE SOMEONE COMES NEAR ME WHO IN RATE . . . . . 324 BUILD SOIL 249
A YOUNGSTER COMES TO ME WITH HALF A QUATRAIN . . . . 324 BUILD SOIL 270
OR MENDING FENCE IT ALL COMES BACK TO ME . . . . . 325 BUILD SOIL 288
A MAN COMES BACK TO A WOMAN AGAIN . . . . 346 DISCOVERY OF MADEIRAS . 87
WHICH COMES TO THE SAME THING IN DIFFERENT TERMS. . . 353 THE LESSON FOR TODAY . 76
OR SEE WHAT COMES OF SCIENCE AND INVENTION, ... 355 THE LESSON FOR TODAY . 143
"THAT'S WHERE I RECKON SANTA CLAUS COMES IN— . . . 408 FROM PLANE TO PLANE . 137
IF THE DAY EVER COMES WHEN THEY KNOW WHO . . . . . 414 A CABIN IN THE CLEARING 29
THAT COMES OF DOGS' LIVES BEING SO BRIEF, ... 420 ONE MORE BREVITY . . 51
FROM THAT STRAIN COMES THE EXPRESSION STRAINS OF MUSIC. . 460 HOW HARD TO KEEP FROM 215
IT COMES DOWN TO A DOUBT ABOUT THE WISDOM . . . . . 483 A MASQUE OF REASON . 291
THE TEMPTER COMES TO ME AND I AM TEMPTED. . . . . . 485 A MASQUE OF REASON . 348
GOD COMES ON ME TO DOOM A CITY FOR HIM. . . . . . 505 A MASQUE OF MERCY . 301
COMFORT
BUT THERE'S A DITE TOO MANY OF THEM FOR COMFORT. . . . 80 THE GENERATIONS OF MEN 189
SO'S TO TAKE ANY COMFORT. I CAN SEW: . . . . . . 81 THE HOUSEKEEPER . . . 7
IF YOU CAN COMFORT ME BY ANY ANSWER." . . . . . . 132 THE BONFIRE 99
THE WAYS YOU FOUND TO SAY THE PRAISE OF COMFORT . . . 150 SNOW 199
AND DEMOCRATS WERE SORE IN NEED OF COMFORT: . . . . 165 NEW HAMPSHIRE . . . 197
ON NOTHING WORSE THAN TOO MUCH LUCK AND COMFORT. . . 167 NEW HAMPSHIRE . . . 276
GIVE HER THE COMFORT FOR HER SIXTH OF KNOWING . . . 257 THE LOVELY BE CHOOSERS 43
TOO MEAN A THOUGHT TO GET MUCH COMFORT OUT OF. . . . 321 BUILD SOIL 168
TAKE COMFORT IN ABOUT THE SAME COMPLAINT. . . . . . 353 THE LESSON FOR TODAY . 82
ALL THEY MAINTAIN THE PATH FOR IS THE COMFORT . . . 414 A CABIN IN THE CLEARING 7
BUT THE COMFORT IS . . . . 441 KITTY HAWK 420
IT SEEMED TO COMFORT US TO CALL IT CORN. . . . . . 446 DOES NO ONE AT ALL EVER 9
COMFORTABLE
SO THEY MADE THE PLACE COMFORTABLE WITH STRAW, . . . 66 A SERVANT TO SERVANTS . 119
COMFORTERS
AGAINST YOUR COMFORTERS IN THEIR CONTENTION . . . . 486 A MASQUE OF REASON . 363
YOUR COMFORTERS WERE WRONG. / OH, THAT COMMITTEE! . . 486 A MASQUE OF REASON . 368
CCMFORTING
TILL EVEN THE COMFORTING BARN GROWS FAR AWAY, . . . 10 STORM FEAR 15
COMIC
BUT HOW TO TAKE THE CURSE, TRAGIC OR COMIC. . . . . 352 THE LESSON FOR TODAY . 62
COMING (SEE A-COMING)
THE WHIPPOORWILL IS COMING TO SHOUT . . . . . . 6 GHOST HOUSE 16
BEFORE THE COMING OF THE SNOW, ... 7 MY NOVEMBER GUEST . . 18
THEY MUST GO DOWN PAST THINGS COMING UP. . . . . . 26 IN HARDWOOD GROVES . . 7
LATELY WHEN COMING UP TO LANCASTER, ... 44 A HUNDRED COLLARS . . 14
COMING OUT ON THEM FROM A STRETCH OF WOODS, ... 49 A HUNDRED COLLARS . . 125
ONLY WHEN SOMEONE'S COMING, AND THE MARE . . . . . 49 A HUNDRED COLLARS . . 139
AMY! THERE'S SOMEONE COMING DOWN THE ROAD!" . . . . 54 HOME BURIAL 111
TO THE TRUTHS WE KEEP COMING BACK AND BACK TO. . . . 58 THE BLACK COTTAGE . . 114
YOUR GOING AND COMING. AND YOU LIKE IT HERE? . . . . 63 A SERVANT TO SERVANTS . 37
COMING AND GOING ALL THE TIME, THEY ARE: . . . . . 65 A SERVANT TO SERVANTS . 81
OF LOAD ON LOAD OF APPLES COMING IN. . . . . . . 69 AFTER APPLE-PICKING . 26
LONG SLEEP, AS I DESCRIBE ITS COMING ON, ... 69 AFTER APPLE-PICKING . 41
COMING DOWN RYAN'S HILL. I THOUGHT 'TWAS HIM. . . . 88 THE HOUSEKEEPER . . . 197
THAT HE'D BE GOING TO OR COMING FROM . . . . . . 90 THE FEAR 26
HE'S COMING TOWARDS US. JOEL, GO IN--PLEASE. . . . 90 THE FEAR 39
THE LAWYER'S COMING FOR THE COMPANY. . . . . . . 92 THE SELF-SEEKER . . . 2
I WANT TO SEE YOU DO IT. WHEN'S HE COMING?" . . . . 93 THE SELF-SEEKER . . . 7
I TURNED AND REPENTED, BUT COMING BACK . . . . . . 102 GOOD HOURS 11
WHOSE COMING HOME HAS BEEN TOO LONG DEFERRED, . . . 109 THE EXPOSED NEST . . 22
OF EVER COMING TO THE PLACE AGAIN . . . . 110 THE EXPOSED NEST . . 34
THEIR COMING OUT AND MAKING USEFUL FARMERS." . . . . 114 IN THE HOME STRETCH . 121
THAT WOULD BE GOOD BOTH GOING AND COMING BACK. . . . 122 BIRCHES 58
AND SINCE IT WAS COMING UP HAD TO COME. . . . . . 123 PEA BRUSH 24
LIKE WINTER AND EVENING COMING ON TOGETHER. . . . . 131 THE BONFIRE 55
IT TOOK ME. NEIGHBORS COMING HOME FROM TOWN . . . . 132 THE BONFIRE 84
TO BE COMING HOME THE WAY I WAS, ... 140 THE GUM-GATHERER . . 11
DISGUSTED THE MILLER PHYSICALLY AS COMING . . . . . 142 THE VANISHING RED . . 17
MY DEAR, I'M COMING JUST THE SAME. I DIDN'T . . . . 143 SNOW 26
WAS COMING. "GOD." BUT NO, HE ONLY SAID, ... 151 SNOW 239
I HAD BEEN COMING TO NEW HAMPSHIRE MOUNTAINS. . . . 166 NEW HAMPSHIRE . . . 215
ON COMING NEARER: "WASN'T SHE AN I-DEAL . . . . . 170 NEW HAMPSHIRE . . . 353
WE DON'T CUT OFF FROM COMING TO CHURCH SUPPERS, . . . 178 THE STAR-SPLITTER . . 49
ONE COMING THIS WAY INTO LIFE, AND ONE . . . . . . 180 MAPLE 12
LIKE A SUDDEN RAILROAD STATION. . . . . 189 THE GRINDSTONE . . . 33
SO WHEN SHE SAW HIM COMING IN THE STREET . . . . . 201 PLACE FOR A THIRD . . 70
I WAS JUST COMING TO MYSELF ENOUGH . . . . 203 THE WITCH OF COOS . . 44
TO WONDER WHERE THE COLD WAS COMING FROM, ... 203 THE WITCH OF COOS . . 45

COMING (CONTINUED)
 IT'S COMING UP TO YOU." IT HAD ITS CHOICE . . . . . 205 THE WITCH OF COOS . . 83
 IF ANYONE HAD SEEN ME COMING HOME . . . . 210 PAUPER WITCH OF GRAFTON 85
 GREAT WAVES LOOKED OVER OTHERS COMING IN, ... 250 ONCE BY THE PACIFIC . 2
 WAS COMING, AND NOT ONLY A NIGHT, AN AGE. . . . . . . 250 ONCE BY THE PACIFIC . 11
 BY COMING WITH WHAT THEY CAME TO ASK. . . . . 276 TWO TRAMPS IN MUD TIME 43
 OR A STAR COMING TO DILATE THE SUN. . . . . 317 BUILD SOIL 59
 THE ONLY REVOLUTION THAT IS COMING. . . . . 324 BUILD SOIL 267
 FROM COMPANY MEANS COMING TO OUR SENSES. . . . . 325 BUILD SOIL 292
 AND WHAT CAN OF ITS COMING COME, ... 332 ALL REVELATION . . . 5
 A STOLEN LADY WAS COMING ON BOARD, ... 343 DISCOVERY OF MADEIRAS . 1
 UNLESS IT WAS COMING TO FOLK . . . . 365 A NATURE NOTE . . . 11
 YET THERE TO WATCH THE DARKNESS COMING ON-- . . . . . 368 THE LITERATE FARMER AND 16
 COMING ON SUCH AN ANCIENT HUMAN TRACE . . . . 382 TO AN ANCIENT . . . 7
 BEWARE OF COMING TOO MUCH TO THE SURFACE. . . . . . . 385 THE FEAR OF GOD . . . 11
 A SPIRE AND BELFRY COMING ON THE ROOF . . . . 386 A STEEPLE ON THE HOUSE 7
 MEANS THAT A SOUL IS COMING ON THE FLESH. . . . . . . 386 A STEEPLE ON THE HOUSE 8
 YOU SAID THE SECOND COMING OF TECUMSEH. . . . . 406 FROM PLANE TO PLANE . 70
 AND SO IT SEEMS A FLOWER'S COMING OUT . . . . 411 POD OF THE MILKWEED . 8
 WE WERE JUST PURPOSE COMING TO A HEAD. . . . . 425 ACCIDENTALLY ON PURPOSE 16
 AS COMING FROM A LESSER OCEAN. . . . . 453 A-WISHING WELL . . . 68
 TO THE FIRST BUYER COMING BY WHO ASKED . . . . 454 HOW HARD TO KEEP FROM 39
 YOU COULD END THIS BY SIMPLY COMING OUT . . . . 483 A MASQUE OF REASON . 295
 A REVOLUTION'S COMING DOWN THE STREET! . . . . 508 A MASQUE OF MERCY . 391
 THERE'S NOTHING COMING ON US, IS THERE, PAUL? . . . . 508 A MASQUE OF MERCY . 395
 WE KNOW WHAT'S COMING NOW. / YOU SAY IT, KEEPER, . . . 511 A MASQUE OF MERCY . 480
COMING-IN
 OUT OF COMING-IN . . . . 426 A NEVER NAUGHT SONG . 27
COMMAND (SEE WAR-COMMAND)
 IN ALL THE COUNTRY HE DID COMMAND . . . . 23 PAN WITH US 8
 HE HADN'T AT COMMAND. "YOU MUST EXCUSE ME, ... 96 THE SELF-SEEKER . . 99
 AND DO WHAT I COMMAND YOU. I TAKE CARE . . . . 323 BUILD SOIL 231
 TO COMMAND ONLY WHAT YOU MEANT TO DO . . . . 323 BUILD SOIL 232
 HE SAID TO THE CAPTAIN, "GIVE COMMAND, ... 346 DISCOVERY OF MADEIRAS 106
 NOT ONLY WARNED HIM WITH A LOUD COMMAND . . . . 394 HAEC FABULA DOCET . 9
 THEY CAN COMMAND THE EXACT AFFINITY . . . . 461 HOW HARD TO KEEP FROM 236
 WOULD BE IN A POSITION TO COMMAND IT. . . . . 475 A MASQUE OF REASON . 57
COMMANDED
 COMMANDED IN A DREAM, FOREVER GO . . . . 173 A STAR IN A STONEBOAT . 35
 COMMANDED BY ONE SUN-PRIEST, ... 312 THE VINDICTIVES . . . 73
COMMANDER-IN-CHIEF
 AS RED CROSS AMBULANCE COMMANDER-IN-CHIEF . . . . . 507 A MASQUE OF MERCY . 369
COMMENT
 FOR COMMENT A COMPLACENT CHIRR. . . . . 281 BLUE RIBBON AT AMESBURY 52
COMMERCE
 TO FIND THE GOOD OF COMMERCE. WHY SHOULD I . . . . . 321 BUILD SOIL 164
 POOR CASTAWAY OF COMMERCE, AND SO LIVE . . . . 323 BUILD SOIL 212
COMMERCIAL
 AND APPLES IN COMMERCIAL QUANTITIES?" . . . . 159 NEW HAMPSHIRE . . 12
 BUT NOT GOLD IN COMMERCIAL QUANTITIES, ... 162 NEW HAMPSHIRE . . 112
 TO BE BELOW THE THRESHOLD OF COMMERCIAL; . . . . . . 162 NEW HAMPSHIRE . . 121
COMMISSARY
 THE DEAD OF THE COMMISSARY . . . . 288 DEPARTMENTAL 27
COMMIT
 AND MADE COMMIT TO MEMORY . . . . 331 BEECH 8
COMMITTEE
 SOME KIND OF COMMITTEE . . . . 431 KITTY HAWK . . . 101
 YOUR COMFORTERS WERE WRONG. / OH, THAT COMMITTEE! . . 486 A MASQUE OF REASON . 368
COMMITTEES
 A NATURAL DEATH, AND VIGILANCE COMMITTEES . . . . . 159 NEW HAMPSHIRE . . 19
 I SAW YOU HAD NO FONDNESS FOR COMMITTEES. . . . . . 486 A MASQUE OF REASON . 369
 DELIVER US FROM COMMITTEES. 'TWILL REMIND ME. . . . . 486 A MASQUE OF REASON . 373
COMMON
 "WELL, IF IT'S TRUE! YOURS ARE NO COMMON FEET. . . . 93 THE SELF-SEEKER . 10
 "WELL, WAIT--IT'S COMMON--IT'S TOO COMMON." / "COMMON? . 97 THE SELF-SEEKER . 141
 TO YOU--TO YOU I MEAN--THEY'RE BOTH TOO COMMON." . . . 98 THE SELF-SEEKER . 144
 OF TREES AND CRACK OF BRANCHES, COMMON THINGS, ... 108 OLD MAN'S WINTER NIGHT 13
 IN COMMON LAW, I WONDER." / "BUT I ASK, ... 111 IN THE HOME STRETCH . 24
 MOTHER CAN MAKE A COMMON TABLE REAR . . . . 202 THE WITCH OF COOS . 9
 SPARES TO STRIKE FOR THE COMMON GOOD, ... 275 TWO TRAMPS IN MUD TIME 14
 HERE COMMON WITH THE FLOCK AGAIN, ... 280 BLUE RIBBON AT AMESBURY 13
 AND THE LOSS OF COMMON SENSE). . . . . 282 A DRUMLIN WOODCHUCK . 24
 WE SAID WELL TWICE TO WHAT WE HAD IN COMMON, ... 290 OLD BARN AT THE BOTTOM 22
 NOR DID HE LACK FOR COMMON ENTERTAINMENT. . . . . . 292 FIGURE IN THE DOORWAY . 19
 I SHALL WILL TO THE COMMON STOCK OF AIR MY BREATH . . . 307 NOT QUITE SOCIAL . . 15
 AT LEAST HE HAD THIS IN COMMON . . . . 314 BEARER OF EVIL TIDINGS 37
 YOU ARE NO COMMON MESSENGER . . . . 327 A MISSIVE MISSILE . 23
 SEEK CONVERSE COMMON CAUSE AND BROTHERHOOD . . . . . 350 THE LESSON FOR TODAY . 9
 NO NEED FOR US TO RACK OUR COMMON HEADS . . . . . . 372 THE LITERATE FARMER AND 132
 WE DON'T BELIEVE THE COMMON MAN SHOULD READ IT. . . . 494 A MASQUE OF MERCY . 31
COMMONER
 THE PURPLE LADY'S SLIPPER'S COMMONER." . . . . . . 98 THE SELF-SEEKER . . 142
COMMONPLACE
 OF INFLUENCE. IT'S BEEN A COMMONPLACE. . . . . . . 511 A MASQUE OF MERCY . 472
COMNENUS
 DEVISED THEM FOR ALEXIUS COMNENUS. . . . . 490 A MASQUE OF REASON . 461
COMPACT
 I'LL MAKE A COMPACT WITH YOU, MELIBOEUS, ... 323 BUILD SOIL . . . 220
COMPANION
 BUT WITH NO COMPANION OF WOMANKIND . . . . 344 DISCOVERY OF MADEIRAS 15
COMPANIONLESS
 YOU CAME COMPANIONLESS, BUT YOU CAME HOME. . . . . . 458 HOW HARD TO KEEP FROM 131
COMPANIONS
 AS SWEET COMPANIONS AS MIGHT BE HAD. . . . . 6 GHOST HOUSE . . . 30
COMPANY
 THE LAWYER'S COMING FOR THE COMPANY. . . . . 92 THE SELF-SEEKER . . 2
 I HAD SUCH COMPANY OUTWARD BOUND. . . . . 102 GOOD HOURS 9

	PAGE TITLE	LINE

COMPANY (CONTINUED)
    I'LL LIGHT THE FIRE FOR COMPANY FOR YOU; . . . . 115 IN THE HOME STRETCH . 146
    YOU'LL NOT HAVE ANY OTHER COMPANY . . . . 115 IN THE HOME STRETCH . 147
    A COMPANY WE CALLED THE WHITE CORPUSCLES, ... 163 NEW HAMPSHIRE . . 139
    WHO CARES NOT WHAT HE DOES IN COMPANY, ... 171 NEW HAMPSHIRE . . 399
    TOFFILE, FOR MY SAKE!" "COMPANY?" HE SAID, ... 205 THE WITCH OF COOS . . 94
    FROM COMPANY MEANS COMING TO OUR SENSES. . . . . . . 325 BUILD SOIL . . . 292
COMPARED
    COMPARED WITH COLD, AND COLD COMPARED WITH WARM. . . . . 44 THE MOUNTAIN . . . 103
    SO NOT TO BE COMPARED, PERHAPS, IN WORTH . . . . . . 174 A STAR IN A STONEBOAT . 47
    'SA THING TO BE COMPARED WITH SPLITTING WOOD. . . . . . 179 THE STAR-SPLITTER . . 94
    LEAVES COMPARED WITH FLOWERS . . . . 296 LEAVES COMPARED WITH . T
    NOTHING COMPARED TO THE PRODUCING OF THEM. . . . . . 324 BUILD SOIL . . . 258
    ONE AS COMPARED WITH GOD AND ONE WITH SPACE. . . . . . 353 THE LESSON FOR TODAY . 78
COMPARING
    HE HAD BEEN AT HIS POETRY, COMPARING . . . . 278 THE WHITE-TAILED HORNET 45
COMPARISON
    COMPARISON IS NOT HER QUEST. . . . . 390 TWO LEADING LIGHTS . . 23
COMPARISONS
    THOUGH THERE'S SMALL PROFIT IN COMPARISONS. . . . . . 64 A SERVANT TO SERVANTS . 68
    DOWNWARD COMPARISONS. AS LONG ON EARTH . . . . . . 279 THE WHITE-TAILED HORNET 59
    AS OUR COMPARISONS WERE STOUTLY UPWARD . . . . . . 279 THE WHITE-TAILED HORNET 60
    BUT ONCE COMPARISONS WERE YIELDED DOWNWARD, ... 279 THE WHITE-TAILED HORNET 63
COMPASS
    THAT I AM LIKE TO COMPASS, FOOL OR WISE. . . . . . . 174 A STAR IN A STONEBOAT . 57
    AND A MASKED MOON HAD SPREAD DOWN COMPASS RAYS . . . 300 MOON COMPASSES . . . 3
    TO EVERYTHING ON EARTH THE COMPASS ROUND, ... 332 THE SILKEN TENT . . 11
COMPASSES
    MOON COMPASSES . . . . 300 MOON COMPASSES . . T
COMPEL
    THAT A KING MIGHT HAVE HOPED TO COMPEL-- . . . . . . 310 THE VINDICTIVES . . . 19
    AND IT IS PARTLY TO COMPEL . . . . 381 AN UNSTAMPED LETTER IN 50
COMPENSATE
    DO NO DOUBT WITH THEIR COLOR COMPENSATE . . . . . 411 POD OF THE MILKWEED . 12
COMPLACENT
    FOR COMMENT A COMPLACENT CHIRR. . . . . 281 BLUE RIBBON AT AMESBURY 52
    IN HER COMPLACENT MINISTRY OF FEAR, ... 395 WHY WAIT FOR SCIENCE . 2
COMPLAIN
    TO PICK WHERE THEY'RE PICKING. BUT WE WON'T COMPLAIN. . . 62 BLUEBERRIES . . . 102
    BUT ESTELLE DON'T COMPLAIN: SHE'S LIKE HIM THERE. . . . 85 THE HOUSEKEEPER . . 117
    WAMPUM, I CALL IT. MIND, WE DON'T COMPLAIN. . . . . 86 THE HOUSEKEEPER . . 153
    SAMOA, RUSSIA, IRELAND I COMPLAIN OF, ... 166 NEW HAMPSHIRE . . 244
    OR SO THE VOICE OF THE COUNTRY SEEMS TO COMPLAIN. . . . 287 A ROADSIDE STAND . 46
    I WENT TO THE PHYSICIAN TO COMPLAIN, ... 398 BURSTING RAPTURE . 1
    WHAT YOU COMPLAIN OF, ALL THE NATIONS SHARE. . . . . 398 BURSTING RAPTURE . 10
COMPLAINING
    'WELL, ONE OF US IS.' FOR COMPLAINING IT FLEW . . . . 62 BLUEBERRIES . . . 90
COMPLAINT
    THE HURT TO THE SCENERY WOULDN'T BE MY COMPLAINT . . . 286 A ROADSIDE STAND . 16
    TAKE COMFORT IN ABOUT THE SAME COMPLAINT. . . . . 353 THE LESSON FOR TODAY . 82
COMPLETE
    OF THE ONE WORLD COMPLETE IN ANY SIZE . . . . . . 174 A STAR IN A STONEBOAT . 56
    AS COMPLETE AS THE APPLE HAD GIVEN MAN. . . . . . 305 UNHARVESTED . . 9
    WE DON'T PRETEND TO COMPLETE OCCUPANCY. . . . . . 322 BUILD SOIL . . . 193
    YET MUST HAVE HAD A SET OF THEM COMPLETE . . . . . 357 A CONSIDERABLE SPECK . 17
    "AN AFTERWORD" FROM COMPLETE POEMS . . . . . . 401 AFTERWORD FROM COMPLETE T
    FOR ALL HUMANITY A COMPLETE REST . . . . . . 405 FROM PLANE TO PLANE . 30
    AND IN FACT COMPLETE, ... 426 A NEVER NAUGHT SONG . 9
COMPLETED
    HAD TERRIBLY COMPLETED. . . . . 341 THE SUBVERTED FLOWER . 56
COMPLIMENT
    OR SO WE PAY THE COMPLIMENT TO INSTINCT, ... 279 THE WHITE-TAILED HORNET 53
    ONLY TOO LIBERAL OF OUR COMPLIMENT . . . . . . 279 THE WHITE-TAILED HORNET 54
    "I STOPPED TO COMPLIMENT YOU ON THIS STAR . . . . . 368 THE LITERATE FARMER AND 9
COMPLY
    A WISH TO COMPLY . . . . 391 A WISH TO COMPLY . . T
    IT'S A WISH TO COMPLY . . . . 392 A WISH TO COMPLY . . 7
COMPOSITE
    OF TYPES, COMPOSITE AND IMAGINED PEOPLE: . . . . . 317 BUILD SOIL . . . 49
COMPREHEND
    EXTREMES TOO HARD TO COMPREHEND AT ONCE, ... 266 THE ARMFUL . . 4
    WOULD BE AFRAID IF WE SHOULD COMPREHEND . . . . . 351 THE LESSON FOR TODAY . 36
    TO COMPREHEND. . . . . 360 THE RABBIT-HUNTER . 18
    USE LANGUAGE WE CAN COMPREHEND. . . . . . . 403 SOMETHING LIKE A STAR . 14
COMPRESSION
    COMPRESSION TO UPLIFT US OUT OF WEIGHT-- . . . . . 387 INNATE HELIUM . . . 3
COMPROMISED
    ALTHOUGH SO COMPROMISED OF AIM AND RATE . . . . . 341 WILLFUL HOMING . . 10
CONCEAL
    CONCEAL A WISH TO SEE HIM SHOW THE SPUNK . . . . . 153 SNOW 283
CONCEALED
    IMPERFECTLY CONCEALED AMONG THE LEAVES. . . . . . 41 THE MOUNTAIN . . . 32
CONCEIT
    SOME OF THE SANCTIMONIOUS CONCEIT . . . . . . 146 SNOW 91
    BUT DOUBTLESS THIS WAS ONLY MY CONCEIT. . . . . . 353 THE LESSON FOR TODAY . 80
    THE APOGEE OF HUMAN BLIND CONCEIT. . . . . . . 394 HAEC FABULA DOCET . 4
CONCEIVE
    BUT BETWEEN PEACE AND WAR AS WE CONCEIVE IT. . . . . 456 HOW HARD TO KEEP FROM 75
CONCEIVED (SEE SELF-CONCEIVED)
CONCENTRATE
    COULD CONCENTRATE ANEW AND RISE AS ONE. . . . . . 315 IRIS BY NIGHT . . . 8
CONCENTRATES
    AND HOW BY ITS OWN LOGIC IT CONCENTRATES . . . . . 509 A MASQUE OF MERCY . . 410
CONCENTRATING
    THUS CONCENTRATING EARTH AND SKIES . . . . . . 333 ALL REVELATION . . . 18
CONCEPT
    IS THAT THE ALL'S A CONCEPT SELF-CONCEIVED, ... 427 CONCEPT SELF-CONCEIVED 3
    A CONCEPT SELF-CONCEIVED . . . . 427 CONCEPT SELF-CONCEIVED T

- 112 -

CONCERN
    NOR WAS THE GRASS ITSELF YOUR REAL CONCERN, ... 109 THE EXPOSED NEST . . 10
    WHICH IS BECOMING MY CONCERN OF LATE. . . . . 354 THE LESSON FOR TODAY . 136
    OF CEASING-TO-QUESTION-WHAT-DOESN'T-CONCERN-US, ... 379 TOO ANXIOUS FOR RIVERS 9
    TO WHAT WAS NEVER HIS CONCERN . . . . 419 AMERICA IS HARD TO SEE 76
    ALL CONCERN TO TAKE . . . . 432 KITTY HAWK 120
    THE ONE THING MORE OF HIS CONCERN. . . . . 451 A-WISHING WELL . . . 9
    THE POINT WAS IT WAS NONE OF MY CONCERN. . . . . . . 485 A MASQUE OF REASON . 335
CONCERNED
    CONCERNED WITH ICE AND SNOW, ... 10 WIND AND WINDOW FLOWER 14
    POOR SILAS, SO CONCERNED FOR OTHER FOLK, ... 37 DEATH OF THE HIRED MAN 99
    AND THEY LOOKED SO SOLEMN-ABSURDLY CONCERNED." . . . . 61 BLUEBERRIES 59
    WHERE NOW HE SAT, CONCERNED WITH HE KNEW WHAT, ... 108 OLD MAN'S WINTER NIGHT 16
    "THAT'S WHAT YOU'RE SO CONCERNED TO KNOW! YOU HOPE . . . 111 IN THE HOME STRETCH . 36
    NOT MUCH CONCERNED FOR THOSE TO WHOM, ... 139 BROWN'S DESCENT . . . 63
    NOT MUCH CONCERNED FOR THEM, I SAY; . . . . 139 BROWN'S DESCENT . . . 68
    "I THOUGHT YOU'D FEEL YOU'D BEEN TOO MUCH CONCERNED." . . 155 SNOW 343
    "YOU THINK YOU HAVEN'T BEEN CONCERNED YOURSELF." . . . . 155 SNOW 344
    NOT FOR MYSELF WAS I SO MUCH CONCERNED. . . . . . . 190 THE GRINDSTONE . . . 51
    NOR WAS I FOR THE MAN SO MUCH CONCERNED. . . . . . . 190 THE GRINDSTONE . . . 56
    YOUR HEAD SO MUCH CONCERNED WITH OUTER, ... 252 TREE AT MY WINDOW . 15
    AND TO THOSE CONCERNED HE MAY SEEM A LITTLE LATE. . . . 342 WILLFUL HOMING . . . 12
    SO FAR AS HE, THE SPEAKER, WAS CONCERNED . . . . . . 370 THE LITERATE FARMER AND 57
    BUT ALL THE TIME IT'S WHAT WE'RE MOST CONCERNED WITH. . . 481 A MASQUE OF REASON . 229
CONCERNS
    AND TALK ABOUT YOUR EVERYDAY CONCERNS. . . . . . . 54 HOME BURIAL 86
CONCLUDE
    WHAT EVIDENTLY NOTHING COULD CONCLUDE. . . . . . . 190 THE GRINDSTONE . . . 64
CONCLUSION
    A SANDBURG. BUT PERMIT ME IN CONCLUSION: . . . . . . 461 HOW HARD TO KEEP FROM 226
CONCORD
    TO EARN A LIVING ON THE CONCORD RAILROAD, ... 178 THE STAR-SPLITTER . . 68
CONCOURSE
    AND A WHITE SHIMMERING CONCOURSE ROLLS . . . . . . 20 THE TRIAL BY EXISTENCE 29
CONCRETE
    AND CAKE THEIR CONCRETE DIRT OFF IN THE STREETS." . . . 506 A MASQUE OF MERCY . 334
CONDEMN
    AND ANYONE IS FREE TO CONDEMN ME TO DEATH-- . . . . . 307 NOT QUITE SOCIAL . 13
CONDEMNED
    THE CONDEMNED WORLD THE LEGACY WAS MERITED. . . . . . 370 THE LITERATE FARMER AND 56
CONDENSED
    WITH A CAN OF CONDENSED AIR . . . . 466 SOME SCIENCE FICTION . 25
CONDITION
    TO YOU IN YOUR CONDITION; YOU CAN'T KNOW . . . . . . 65 A SERVANT TO SERVANTS . 101
    AND RESENTFUL OF MAN'S CONDITION. . . . . 286 IN TIME OF CLOUDBURST . 28
CONDUCT
    IF WHAT YOU'RE PREACHING IS A LINE OF CONDUCT, ... 322 BUILD SOIL 204
CONE
    TO A CONE MOUNTAIN IN THE MIDNIGHT HAZE, ... 300 MOON COMPASSES . . . 4
CONES
    AND EAT THE CONES UNDER HIS PINES, I TELL HIM. . . . . 33 MENDING WALL 26
CONFERRED (SEE SELF-CONFERRED)
CONFESS
    "BUT LITTLE." / "ANYTHING? MARY, CONFESS . . . . . . 36 DEATH OF THE HIRED MAN 45
    WHAT WE HAVE ALWAYS WANTED, I CONFESS . . . . 115 IN THE HOME STRETCH . 127
    I MAY AS WELL CONFESS MYSELF THE AUTHOR . . . . . . 166 NEW HAMPSHIRE . . 228
    DID GRASS AND GARDEN GROUND CONFESS IT SNOWED, ... 239 OUR SINGING STRENGTH . 9
    YOU DRIVE ME TO CONFESS IN INK: . . . . 467 QUANDARY 19
CONFESSION
    THERE WAS NO CONFESSION. . . . . 433 KITTY HAWK 153
CONFIDE
    NOBODY HAS TO CONFIDE IN ME." . . . . 420 ONE MORE BREVITY . 35
CONFIDENCE
    IF I CAN WITH CONFIDENCE SAY . . . . 282 A DRUMLIN WOODCHUCK . 25
    IN CONFIDENCE. THERE'S NO ONE HERE BUT HER, ... 479 A MASQUE OF REASON . 172
    THAT I MIGHT BE A CONFIDENCE IMPOSTOR. . . . . . . 495 A MASQUE OF MERCY . 54
    OR UNDERGROUNDS, FOR CONFIDENCE IN EARTHQUAKE? . . . . 502 A MASQUE OF MERCY . 227
CONFIDENTIAL
    LEAN BACK AND HAVE MY CONFIDENTIAL LAUGH, ... 354 THE LESSON FOR TODAY . 125
CONFINED
    THAT TO NO LIMITS AND BOUNDS HE CAN STAY CONFINED? . . 305 THERE ARE ROUGHLY ZONES 8
    BUT THESE ARE UNIVERSALS, NOT CONFINED . . . . . . 353 THE LESSON FOR TODAY . 104
    TO STAY TOO CONFINED. . . . . 434 KITTY HAWK . . . 202
CONFINES
    WE MEN MUST SEE YOU TO THE CONFINES OF . . . . . . 259 WEST-RUNNING BROOK . 34
CONFIRM
    BUT I SHOULD AWAKE TO CONFIRM YOUR STORY YET; . . . . 236 VALLEY'S SINGING DAY . 18
CONFIRMED
    THE ALREADY KNOWN HAD ONCE MORE BEEN CONFIRMED . . . . 293 AT WOODWARD'S GARDENS . 18
    AS A CONFIRMED ASTRONOMER . . . . 451 A-WISHING WELL . . . 12
    HUMOR HER THERE OR SHE WILL BE CONFIRMED . . . . . . 479 A MASQUE OF REASON . 176
CONFLICT
    TO CONFLICT AND PAIR. . . . . 426 A NEVER NAUGHT SONG . 11
CONFLICTING
    OFTENER THAN AS CONFLICTING GOOD AND ILL; . . . . . 350 TO A YOUNG WRETCH . 16
    VOICES CONFLICTING LIKE THE CANDIDATES. . . . . . . 368 THE LITERATE FARMER AND 4
CONFORMISM (SEE NON-CONFORMISM)
CONFOUNDED
    SOME MINDS ARE SO CONFOUNDED INTERMENTAL . . . . . . 321 BUILD SOIL 151
CONFRONTED
    OF ANYTHING THEY ARE CONFRONTED WITH. . . . . . . 461 HOW HARD TO KEEP FROM 237
CONFUSE
    TWO PITCHING ON LIKE THIS TEND TO CONFUSE ME. . . . . 484 A MASQUE OF REASON . 323
CONFUSED
    WHILE SO CONFUSED WITH FLOWERS. . . . . 14 ROSE POGONIAS . . 24
    WHOSE BIBLE'S SO CONFUSED IN MARRIAGE COUNSEL? . . . . 201 PLACE FOR A THIRD . . 65
CONFUSING
    THERE CAME A MOMENT OF CONFUSING LIGHTS, ... 315 IRIS BY NIGHT . . . 4

CONFUSING (CONTINUED)
    TOO CROWDING, TOO CONFUSING-- . . . . 336 CARPE DIEM 25
    WHY GO ON FURTHER WITH CONFUSING VOICE . . . . . . 427 CONCEPT SELF-CONCEIVED 6
CONFUSION (SEE TONGUE-CONFUSION)
    "ONE OUGHT NOT TO BE THROWN INTO CONFUSION . . . . . 75 THE GENERATIONS OF MEN 58
    BEHIND HER WAS CONFUSION IN THE ROOM, ... 110 IN THE HOME STRETCH .   5
    IN THE CONFUSION OF THEM ALL AGLITTER, ... 237 A HILLSIDE THAW . . . 14
    CONFUSION, AND A ROAR THAT DROWNED THE CRIES . . . . 270 THE EGG AND THE MACHINE 14
    DRINK AND BE WHOLE AGAIN BEYOND CONFUSION. . . . . . 379 DIRECTIVE 62
    'TIS A CONFUSION IT WAS OURS TO START . . . . 423 FOR JOHN F. KENNEDY . 41
    I STICK TO THAT. BUT TALK ABOUT CONFUSION!-- . . . . 485 A MASQUE OF REASON . 336
    YET I SUPPOSE WHAT SEEMS TO US CONFUSION . . . . . . 485 A MASQUE OF REASON . 338
    IS NOT CONFUSION, BUT THE FORM OF FORMS, ... 485 A MASQUE OF REASON . 339
CONGESTED
    CURSED BE THE ERA THAT CONGESTED IT. . . . . 496 A MASQUE OF MERCY . 67
CONGREGATE
    HOW COUNTLESSLY THEY CONGREGATE . . . .   9 STARS   1
    WE CONGREGATE EMBRACING FROM DISTRUST . . . . 325 BUILD SOIL 276
CONGRESS
    I KEEP MY EYE ON CONGRESS, MELIBOEUS. . . . . 317 BUILD SOIL 54
CONIES
    WHERE CONIES NOW COME OUT TO SUN AND ROMP, ... 254 A WINTER EDEN . . .   2
CONJUNCTION
    AND IN CONJUNCTION GIVING QUITE A SPREAD. . . . . . 269 THE BEAR 21
CONJUROR'S
    AND HARD TO EXPLAIN AS A CONJUROR'S TRICK." . . . . 59 BLUEBERRIES 21
CONNECTICUT
    NEW HAMPSHIRE RAISES THE CONNECTICUT . . . . 165 NEW HAMPSHIRE . . . 183
    NEW HAMPSHIRE, NOT CONNECTICUT, ... 167 NEW HAMPSHIRE . . . 250
    BY THE CONNECTICUT COULD ANYONE . . . . 404 FROM PLANE TO PLANE . 22
CONNECTION
    BUT NOBODY HAD NOTICED THE CONNECTION), ... 456 HOW HARD TO KEEP FROM 96
    THERE'S NO CONNECTION MAN CAN REASON OUT . . . . . . 475 A MASQUE OF REASON . 50
CONNECTIONS
    FREEDOM TO FLASH OFF INTO WILD CONNECTIONS. . . . . 461 HOW HARD TO KEEP FROM 246
CONNECTS
    THAT SOMEONE IN THE CREW CONNECTS WITH ME. . . . . . 500 A MASQUE OF MERCY . 181
CONQUER
    FOR HIM TO CONQUER. HE LEARNED ALL THERE WAS . . . . 122 BIRCHES 32
CONQUERED
    BUT THE CONQUERED GREW MEEK AND STILL. . . . . . . 312 THE VINDICTIVES . . 52
CONQUERING
    THE PAINS OF CONQUERING TO FORCE CHANGE ON. . . . . 58 THE BLACK COTTAGE . 118
    THE WHOLE FIERCE CONQUERING PACK . . . . 311 THE VINDICTIVES . . 47
CONQUEROR
    IF GOLD PLEASED THE CONQUEROR, WELL, ... 311 THE VINDICTIVES . . 24
    THE CONQUEROR HENCEFORTH SHOULD LACK. . . . . 311 THE VINDICTIVES . . 26
CONSCIENCE
    YOU WANTED IT FOR ME." / "A TROUBLED CONSCIENCE! . . . 116 IN THE HOME STRETCH . 168
    YOU'VE GOT NO SOCIAL CONSCIENCE, AS THEY SAY, ... 406 FROM PLANE TO PLANE . 77
CONSCIENCES
    LIKE A BEAST'S STALL, TO EASE THEIR CONSCIENCES. . . . 66 A SERVANT TO SERVANTS . 120
CONSCIENTIOUSNESS
    OUR WORSHIP, HUMOR, CONSCIENTIOUSNESS . . . . 279 THE WHITE-TAILED HORNET 56
CONSCIOUSNESS (SEE SELF-CONSCIOUSNESS)
CONSECRATED
    SO MUCH THEY KNEW AS CONSECRATED SEERS . . . . . . 422 FOR JOHN F. KENNEDY . 27
CONSENT
    IF I WAS TO CONSENT TO GIVE SOME SIGN . . . . 208 PAUPER WITCH OF GRAFTON 43
    NOT ENTIRELY WITHOUT CONSENT. . . . . 344 DISCOVERY OF MADEIRAS . 14
    FOR THE TIME BEING AND WITH THEIR CONSENT, ... 423 FOR JOHN F. KENNEDY . 37
CONSERVATIVE
    FOR FEAR IT WOULD MAKE ME CONSERVATIVE WHEN OLD. . . . 308 PRECAUTION   2
    THAT LIBERAL, OR CONSERVATIVE, ... 450 OUR DOOM TO BLOOM . 11
CONSERVATIVES
    CONSERVATIVES, THEY DON'T KNOW WHAT TO SAVE. . . . . 290 OLD BARN AT THE BOTTOM 32
    HOW THEY'LL LIKE THAT. PAUL SAID CONSERVATIVES-- . . . 509 A MASQUE OF MERCY . 408
CONSIDER
    "HE DON'T CONSIDER IT A CASE FOR GOD." . . . . . . 146 SNOW 82
    CONSIDER WHAT THEY TREASURE UNDER GLASS, ... 290 OLD BARN AT THE BOTTOM 33
    IMPRINT A SADDLE, AND CALMLY CONSIDER A COURSE. . . . 341 WILLFUL HOMING . . .   7
    AND NOTHING MADE OF YOUTH. CONSIDER ME, ... 462 HOW HARD TO KEEP FROM 258
    THE THING THAT DID WHAT YOU CONSIDER MISCHIEF, ... 505 A MASQUE OF MERCY . 317
CONSIDERABLE
    A CONSIDERABLE SPECK . . . . 357 A CONSIDERABLE SPECK .   T
CONSIDERATE
    SHE VALUED THE CONSIDERATE NEGLECT . . . . 56 THE BLACK COTTAGE . 41
CONSIDERATION
    "I LET YOU SAY THAT--ON CONSIDERATION." . . . . . . 79 THE GENERATIONS OF MEN 154
    "YOU LET ME SAY IT? ON CONSIDERATION? . . . . 80 THE GENERATIONS OF MEN 203
CONSIDERATIONS
    IT'S WHEN I'M WEARY OF CONSIDERATIONS, ... 122 BIRCHES 43
CONSIDERED
    ONCE CONSIDERED CRANKS . . . . 443 KITTY HAWK 469
CONSIDERING
    CONSIDERING THE MARKET, THERE ARE MORE . . . . . . 164 NEW HAMPSHIRE . . . 170
    BUT ITS AGE KEPT THEM FROM CONSIDERING THIS ONE. . . . 184 MAPLE 148
CONSIGNED
    HE CONSIGNED TO THE MOON--SUCH AS SHE WAS, ... 108 OLD MAN'S WINTER NIGHT 18
CONSISTENCE
    TILL ABOUT THE RIGHT CONSISTENCE. . . . . 304 CLEAR AND COLDER . .   6
CONSPIRACY
    HOW ONCE CONSPIRACY WAS RIFE . . . . 29 MY BUTTERFLY 32
CONSPIRE
    TO THINK IT OUT. COME CLOSE, LET US CONSPIRE-- . . . . 323 BUILD SOIL 228
CONSTANT
    PAUL'S CONSTANT THEME. THE SERMON ON THE MOUNT . . . . 511 A MASQUE OF MERCY . 482

CONSTANTINOPLE
     ON TURRETS, LIKE CONSTANTINOPLE, DEEP . . . . 160 NEW HAMPSHIRE . . . 40
CONSTELLATED
     BE CONSTELLATED. . . . . 389 ASTROMETAPHYSICAL . . 16
CONSTELLATION
     AND NO TWO WERE OF THE SAME CONSTELLATION-- . . . . . 295 LOST IN HEAVEN . . . 6
CONSTELLATIONS
     OF CONSTELLATIONS. . . . . 219 I WILL SING YOU ONE-O . 47
     ON LOOKING UP BY CHANCE AT THE CONSTELLATIONS . . . . . 268 ON LOOKING UP BY CHANCE   T
CONSTERNATION
     SO 'TWAS WITH NOT UNGRATEFUL CONSTERNATION, ... 295 LOST IN HEAVEN . . . 8
CONSTITUTES
     NEVERTHELESS IT CONSTITUTES A HINT . . . . 361 A LOOSE MOUNTAIN . . 13
CONSTITUTION
     EQUALLY FOR THE NATION'S CONSTITUTION). . . . . 317 BUILD SOIL 47
CONSULT
     WE HAVE SEEN VISIONS--NOW CONSULT THE VOICES. . . . . . 77 THE GENERATIONS OF MEN 126
     GO CONSULT THE LOG. . . . . 438 KITTY HAWK 342
     LOOK, I DON'T NEED THE BIBLE TO CONSULT. . . . . . . 495 A MASQUE OF MERCY . . 44
CONSULTATION
     IN CONSULTATION WITH MY CLIENTS? . . . . 449 OUR DOOM TO BLOOM . . 4
     NOT WITHOUT CONSULTATION WITH THEIR WISHES; . . . . . 458 HOW HARD TO KEEP FROM 152
CONSUMED
     I DIDN'T MY POTATOES. I CONSUMED THEM. . . . . 316 BUILD SOIL 15
CONTACT
     FROM CONTACT WITH EARTH, ... 235 GATHERING LEAVES . . 19
CONTAIN
     UNTIL IT CAN CONTAIN ITSELF NO MORE, ... 323 BUILD SOIL 235
     I HAVE BEEN ONE NO DWELLING COULD CONTAIN . . . . . . 337 THE WIND AND THE RAIN . 43
CONTAINED
     OH, BLOOD WILL OUT. IT CANNOT BE CONTAINED. . . . . . 255 THE FLOOD 14
     AND SHOWED THEM IT CONTAINED A LIVE TEREDO. . . . . . 456 HOW HARD TO KEEP FROM 85
CONTEMPLATE
     MEDITATE NOTHING. LEARN TO CONTEMPLATE. . . . . . . 517 A MASQUE OF MERCY . 628
     CONTEMPLATE GLORY. THERE WILL BE A LIGHT. . . . . . 517 A MASQUE OF MERCY . 629
     CONTEMPLATE TRUTH UNTIL IT BURNS YOUR EYES OUT. . . . 517 A MASQUE OF MERCY . 630
CONTEMPLATING
     CONTENT WITH CONTEMPLATING, TAKING IN, ... 399 THE INGENUITIES OF DEBT 16
CONTEMPLATION
     ITS CONTEMPLATION MAKES US OUT AS SMALL . . . . . . 352 THE LESSON FOR TODAY . 69
CONTEMPLATIVE
     BUT ONLY GRAVE, CONTEMPLATIVE AND GRAVE. . . . . . . 334 I COULD GIVE ALL . . 5
CONTEMPORARY
     OF JUDGING WHO IS A CONTEMPORARY LIAR-- . . . . . . 317 BUILD SOIL 38
CONTEND
     EVEN IN A PLAYFUL MOMENT TO CONTEND . . . . 359 THE LOST FOLLOWER . . 26
CONTENT
     THEY WERE CONTENT TO FIGURE IN THE TREES . . . . . . 234 EVENING IN A SUGAR ORCHARD 15
     THAT IS CONTENT WITH THE DAYLIGHT LOW, ... 247 ON GOING UNNOTICED . . 6
     CONTENT WITH BUD-INSPECTING. THEY PRESUME . . . . . 254 A WINTER EDEN . . . 15
     FROM FORM TO CONTENT AND BACK TO FORM, ... 325 TO A THINKER 9
     CONTENT WITH CONTEMPLATING, TAKING IN, ... 399 THE INGENUITIES OF DEBT 16
CONTENTION
     TO WAGE A FINE SCHOLASTICAL CONTENTION . . . . . . 352 THE LESSON FOR TODAY . 51
     AGAINST YOUR COMFORTERS IN THEIR CONTENTION . . . . . 486 A MASQUE OF REASON . 363
CONTINENT
     THE CLIFF IN BEING BACKED BY CONTINENT; . . . . . . 250 ONCE BY THE PACIFIC . 9
     OUR CONTINENT NO MORE A MOATED CASTLE. . . . . . . 446 DOES NO ONE AT ALL EVER 18
CONTINUE
     I DON'T SEE BUT YOU MUST CONTINUE . . . . 326 TO A THINKER 26
CONTINUED
     ON WHAT SHOULD BE THEIR DAYLONG THEME CONTINUED. . . . 415 A CABIN IN THE CLEARING 35
CONTRACT
     OUR MUSCLES NEVER COULD AGAIN CONTRACT: . . . . . . 351 THE LESSON FOR TODAY . 38
CONTRADICTION
     BUT FROM HIS MERCY-JUSTICE CONTRADICTION. . . . . . 498 A MASQUE OF MERCY . 140
     MERCY AND JUSTICE ARE A CONTRADICTION. . . . . . . 498 A MASQUE OF MERCY . 141
CONTRARIES
     CAN TRUST ITSELF TO GO BY CONTRARIES . . . . 258 WEST-RUNNING BROOK . . 7
     "SPEAKING OF CONTRARIES, SEE HOW THE BROOK . . . . . 259 WEST-RUNNING BROOK . . 38
CONTRAST
     I NEVER HAPPENED TO CONTRAST . . . . 390 TWO LEADING LIGHTS . . 1
CONTRASTED
     IT WAS BY HAVING BEEN CONTRASTED . . . . 467 QUANDARY 5
CONTRIBUTED
     I HAVE CONTRIBUTED THE EMPTY CELLAR . . . . 515 A MASQUE OF MERCY . 564
CONTRITION
     I MUST NOT SPOIL YOUR CHRISTMAS WITH CONTRITION. . . . 350 TO A YOUNG WRETCH . . 12
CONTRIVE
     CONTRIVE TO BLOOM . . . . 337 THE WIND AND THE RAIN . 22
     THE SOBER WEED HAS MANAGED TO CONTRIVE . . . . . . 412 POD OF THE MILKWEED . 31
CONTRIVING
     IS STEALTHILY CONTRIVING WOOL FROM JUTE . . . . . . 319 BUILD SOIL 108
CONTROL   (SEE SELF-CONTROL)
     TELL YOU WHAT RALLE THE SIOUX CONTROL ONCE TOLD ME. . . 202 THE WITCH OF COOS . 13
     CONTROL OF WHAT IT SELLS OR WHAT IT BUYS. . . . . . 324 BUILD SOIL 248
     AND COULD IT BE BROUGHT UNDER STATE CONTROL, ... 353 THE LESSON FOR TODAY . 99
     WE MAY GET CONTROL, ... 441 KITTY HAWK 422
CONTROVERSY
     WHY GIVE THE CONTROVERSY A RELAPSE? . . . . 407 FROM PLANE TO PLANE . 113
CONVENTION
     YES, YES, OF COURSE. WE HAVE THE SAME CONVENTION. . . . 352 THE LESSON FOR TODAY . 57
     AND ALL THE GREAT CONVENTION WAS ABOUT. . . . . . . 400 THE BROKEN DROUGHT . . 5
     TOO LONG PENT UP IN RIGOROUS CONVENTION-- . . . . . 509 A MASQUE OF MERCY . 418
CONVERGING
     DOWN DARK CONVERGING PATHS BETWEEN THE PINES. . . . . 129 THE BONFIRE 7
     THE TWO CONVERGING SLIDES, THE AVALANCHES, ... 214 A FOUNTAIN, A BOTTLE . 52
     WHEN THE CLAP OF TWO CONVERGING WAVES . . . . . . 344 DISCOVERY OF MADEIRAS . 27

CONVERSATIONISTS
    THOU ONETIME PRINCE OF CONVERSATIONISTS? . . . . 488 A MASQUE OF REASON . . 406
CONVERSE
    LATELY IN CONVERSE WITH A NEW YORK ALEC . . . . 170 NEW HAMPSHIRE 358
    SEEK CONVERSE COMMON CAUSE AND BROTHERHOOD . . . . . 350 THE LESSON FOR TODAY .   9
CONVERSION
    AND YET CONVERSION HAS ITS PLACE . . . . 326 TO A THINKER   31
CONVERT
    I AM YOUR CONVERT. TELL ME WHAT I THINK. . . . . . . 517 A MASQUE OF MERCY . . 621
CONVERTED
    TO BE CONVERTED INTO SOUTH, ... 224 THE AIM WAS SONG . . .   11
CONVEY
    TO CONVEY MY RESPECT FOR YOUR POSITION?" . . . . . . 408 FROM PLANE TO PLANE . 135
    A SYMBOL WAS ALL HE COULD HOPE TO CONVEY, ... 421 ONE MORE BREVITY . .   66
CONVEYED
    AND BE SUCCESSFULLY CONVEYED. . . . . 327 A MISSIVE MISSILE . .   32
CONVICTED
    HIS CAPTORS CONVICTED THE KING . . . . 310 THE VINDICTIVES . . .   15
CONVINCE
    I WOULDN'T BE TOO HARD TO CONVINCE, ... 421 ONE MORE BREVITY . .   57
    HE THINKS HE'S SMART. HE THINKS HE CAN CONVINCE ME . . 485 A MASQUE OF REASON . . 351
CONVINCED
    LEASTWAYS FOR ME--AND THEN THEY'LL BE CONVINCED. . . . 64 A SERVANT TO SERVANTS . 59
    I DOUBT IF YOU'RE CONVINCED THE TIMES ARE BAD. . . . 317 BUILD SOIL   53
    AND I CONVINCED THAT THEY WERE REALLY SAGES, ... 350 THE LESSON FOR TODAY .   3
CONVOY
    HAS BEEN HER ANXIOUS CONVOY IN TO SHORE. . . . . . . 262 IMMIGRANTS   4
CONVULSIVELY
    THE DOCTOR CAUGHT HIS THROAT CONVULSIVELY. . . . . . 46 A HUNDRED COLLARS . .   62
COOK
    ONE IN A CAVERN WHERE YOU USED TO COOK. . . . . . . 382 TO AN ANCIENT   6
    YOU'RE OFF TO XANADU TO HELP THE COOK. . . . . . . 455 HOW HARD TO KEEP FROM   48
    ONE DAY WHEN THE CHIEF COOK WAS SICK AT HEART. . . . 455 HOW HARD TO KEEP FROM   56
    (THE COOK WAS TEMPERAMENTAL LIKE THE KING.) . . . . 455 HOW HARD TO KEEP FROM   57
    (THE KING WAS TEMPERAMENTAL LIKE HIS COOK, ... 456 HOW HARD TO KEEP FROM   95
    OF ROYAL BLOOD. YOUR FATHER WAS A COOK." . . . . . 457 HOW HARD TO KEEP FROM 103
    I KNEW YOUR FATHER MUST HAVE BEEN A COOK. . . . . . 458 HOW HARD TO KEEP FROM 136
    FIRST BY A BUTCHER, THEN A COOK, ... 467 QUANDARY   23
COOKED
    THERE WOULD BE FISH RAW AND COOKED TOO . . . . . . 384 IN THE LONG NIGHT . .   11
COOKING
    FROM COOKING MEALS FOR HUNGRY HIRED MEN . . . . . . 64 A SERVANT TO SERVANTS   50
COOK'S
    NONE BUT A COOK'S SON COULD BE SO FOOD-MINDED. . . . 458 HOW HARD TO KEEP FROM 135
COOL
    I CLEANED THE RACK AND DROVE OUT TO COOL OFF. . . . . 72 THE CODE   80
    DOES THE RAIN SEEM TO YOU TO COOL THE EYES?" . . . . 75 THE GENERATIONS OF MEN 69
    BUT LEFT AN OPEN DOOR TO COOL THE ROOM OFF . . . . . 203 THE WITCH OF COOS . .   42
COOLNESS
    YOU MUST NOT MIND A CERTAIN COOLNESS FROM HIM . . . . 377 DIRECTIVE   18
COOPS
    IN SEPARATE COOPS, HAVING THEIR PLUMAGE DONE. . . . . 85 THE HOUSEKEEPER . . . 121
COOS
    THE WITCH OF COOS . . . . 202 THE WITCH OF COOS . .   T
COPE
    MY SCALP WILL IN THE COPE . . . . 389 ASTROMETAPHYSICAL . .   15
COPSE
    THE ORCHARD TREE HAS GROWN ONE COPSE . . . .   5 GHOST HOUSE   8
COPSE'S
    COUNTED THEM ALL TO THE BUDS IN THE COPSE'S DEPTH . . 343 QUEST OF PURPLE-FRINGED 23
COPY
    AT HAVING EASED HER HEART OF ONE MORE COPY-- . . . . 217 A FOUNTAIN, A BOTTLE . 135
    IS NOT ITS OWN LOVE BACK IN COPY SPEECH, ... 338 THE MOST OF IT . . .   7
    I JUST THOUGHT IF YOU HAD A COPY HANDY, ... 495 A MASQUE OF MERCY . .   45
CORAL
    HER GOLDEN LEG, HER CORAL COMB, ... 280 BLUE RIBBON AT AMESBURY   6
CORALROOT
    LESS THAN THE CORALROOT, YOU KNOW. . . . . 247 ON GOING UNNOTICED .   5
    NOT EVEN MISSING THE CORALROOT FLOWER . . . . . . 247 ON GOING UNNOTICED .   15
CORBIN
    I'D RATHER MRS. CORBIN DIDN'T KNOW; . . . . 94 THE SELF-SEEKER . . .   53
    AND BRING HIM UP, AND DON'T LET MRS. CORBIN.-- . . . 96 THE SELF-SEEKER . . .   89
CORD
    IT WAS A CORD OF MAPLE, CUT AND SPLIT . . . . . . 101 THE WOOD-PILE   23
    SEEMS TO OWE NAUGHT TO ANY SINGLE CORD, ... 332 THE SILKEN TENT . . .   8
CORDAGE
    WITH A LENGTH OF CORDAGE ABOUT THE WAIST. . . . . . 346 DISCOVERY OF MADEIRAS   77
CORN
    TOMATOES, BEETS, BEANS, PUMPKINS, CORN, ... 134 A GIRL'S GARDEN . . .   31
    NOW TAKE THE DOCTOR--" / THEY WERE GIVING CORN . . . 404 FROM PLANE TO PLANE .   12
    THE WAVY UPFLUNG PENNONS OF THE CORN . . . . . . 404 FROM PLANE TO PLANE .   15
    IT SEEMED TO COMFORT US TO CALL IT CORN. . . . . . 446 DOES NO ONE AT ALL EVER 9
CORNEL
    DWARF CORNEL, GOLDTHREAD, AND MAIANTHEMUM, ... 355 TIME OUT   5
CORNER
    OR OVER A HILL OR ROUND A SUDDEN CORNER. . . . . . 49 A HUNDRED COLLARS . . 126
    FOR A DOORSILL OR OTHER CORNER PIECE . . . . 79 THE GENERATIONS OF MEN 163
    THERE'S A PATCH OF OLD SNOW IN A CORNER, ... 110 A PATCH OF OLD SNOW .   1
    IN CASTING ABOUT FOR A CORNER . . . . 133 A GIRL'S GARDEN . . .   9
    I FOUND MYSELF IN A CLOSE CORNER WHERE . . . . . . 170 NEW HAMPSHIRE 360
    AND ROUND A CORNER, BLIZZARD SNOW FOR DUST, ... 265 DUST IN THE EYES . .   5
    AND OFF THIS CORNER IN THE WILD, ... 331 BEECH   4
    LIKE THE CURL AT THE CORNER OF A SMILE; . . . . . 335 I COULD GIVE ALL . .   8
    BEFORE THEY GUESSED THE CORNER . . . . 391 A ROGERS GROUP . . .   7
    PAUL ALMOST HAD POOR KEEPER IN A CORNER . . . . . 508 A MASQUE OF MERCY . . 401
CORNERED
    "SAVE US FROM BEING CORNERED BY A WOMAN. . . . . . 151 SNOW 236

CORNERS
    POPLIN. STILL CORNERS (SO CALLED NOT BECAUSE . . . . . 165 NEW HAMPSHIRE . . . 188
    IS ONLY CORNERS, CROSSROADS IN A WOOD). . . . . 165 NEW HAMPSHIRE . . . 192
    THE CORNERS OF HIS LIPS . . . . 339 THE SUBVERTED FLOWER . 13
CORPUSCLES
    A COMPANY WE CALLED THE WHITE CORPUSCLES, ... 163 NEW HAMPSHIRE . . . 139
CORRECT
    (NINE TIMES REMOVED. CORRECT ME IF I ERR.) . . . . . 79 THE GENERATIONS OF MEN 178
CORRECTED
    OF THE WORD LOVE CORRECTED. SHE GOT OFF . . . . . . 499 A MASQUE OF MERCY . . 161
CORTEZ
    AS CORTEZ ON THE AZTECS MADE. . . . . 419 AMERICA IS HARD TO SEE   84
COS
    (YOU OUGHT TO SEE THE COINS DONE IN COS.) . . . . . 459 HOW HARD TO KEEP FROM 187
COSMIC
    THE COSMIC MOTES . . . . 219 I WILL SING YOU ONE-O . 53
COSMICAL
    AT PRESENT FROM A COSMICAL DILATION . . . . 320 BUILD SOIL 138
COST
    AND THE SWEET PANG IT COST ME NOT TO CALL . . . . . 16 A DREAM PANG 11
    SHE HAD AT SOME COST TAUGHT THEM AFTER YEARS.) . . . . 56 THE BLACK COTTAGE . . 42
    "DEN WHEN YOU SAY YOU COME? IT'S COST YOU NOTHING. . . . 186 THE AX-HELVE 33
    WHATEVER THEY COST APIECE OR A POUND, ... 232 THE KITCHEN CHIMNEY . 6
    BUT AT ANY COST . . . . 445 PERIL OF HOPE . . . 10
    IT COST THE EARTH AS FIERCE A PANG . . . . 452 A-WISHING WELL . . . 40
    IT COST HER FOR ENORMOUS CAF. . . . . 452 A-WISHING WELL . . . 42
COSTLINESS
    AND THEN THE OTHER FOR ITS COSTLINESS . . . . 455 HOW HARD TO KEEP FROM 70
COSTS
    IT COSTS NO INWARD STRUGGLE NOT TO GO, ... 10 STORM FEAR 7
COTS
    HE'S SURELY GOT IT IN FOR COTS AND BEDS. . . . . . 372 THE LITERATE FARMER AND 131
COTTAGE
    THE LITTLE COTTAGE WE WERE SPEAKING OF, ... 55 THE BLACK COTTAGE . . 5
    THE BLACK COTTAGE . . . . 55 THE BLACK COTTAGE . . T
    A LITTLE COTTAGE THIS HAS ALWAYS SEEMED; . . . . . . 56 THE BLACK COTTAGE . . 35
    IN A NEW COTTAGE ON THE ANCIENT SPOT. . . . . 79 THE GENERATIONS OF MEN 164
    THEY TELL ME THE COTTAGE WHERE WE DWELT, ... 253 THE THATCH 31
COTTAGES
    THE COTTAGES LEN BUILT, SOMETIMES WE RENT THEM, ... 64 A SERVANT TO SERVANTS . 41
    BUT I HAD THE COTTAGES IN A ROW . . . . 102 GOOD HOURS 3
    I WENT TILL THERE WERE NO COTTAGES FOUND. . . . . . 102 GOOD HOURS 10
COTTER-PINNED
    IT IS COTTER-PINNED, IT IS BEDDED TRUE. . . . . . . 306 A TRIAL RUN 10
COTTON
    WHAT THIS MAN BROUGHT IN A COTTON SACK . . . . . . 141 THE GUM-GATHERER . . 28
    (ALL MY EYE AND COTTON MATHER!), ... 304 CLEAR AND COLDER . . 18
    I COTTON TO THEIR LANDSCAPE. THAT'S WHO I AM. . . . . 414 A CABIN IN THE CLEARING 18
COUGH
    ALMOST MADE HIM COUGH . . . . 135 LAST WORD OF A BLUEBIRD 12
COULD---NOT INDEXED
COULDLOOKTOO
    IF ETOOKASHOO AND COULDLOOKTOO . . . . 384 IN THE LONG NIGHT . . 9
COULDN'T---NOT INDEXED
COUNSEL
    WHOSE BIBLE'S SO CONFUSED IN MARRIAGE COUNSEL? . . . . 201 PLACE FOR A THIRD . . 65
COUNT
    I COUNT OUR STRENGTH, ... 10 STORM FEAR 9
    BUT I DON'T COUNT ON IT AS MUCH AS LEN. . . . . . . 64 A SERVANT TO SERVANTS . 44
    YOU DIDN'T COUNT THEM?" / "NO, THE FURTHER OFF . . . . 112 IN THE HOME STRETCH . 51
    AND FROM THERE THOSE THAT LIFTED EYES COULD COUNT . . . 136 "OUT,OUT--" 4
    TO COUNT THE PEOPLE IN IT AND FOUND NONE, ... 174 THE CENSUS-TAKER . . 10
    I COUNTED NINE I HAD NO RIGHT TO COUNT . . . . . . 175 THE CENSUS-TAKER . . 31
    THE MELANCHOLY OF HAVING TO COUNT SOULS . . . . . . 176 THE CENSUS-TAKER . . 61
    THAT NOT EVERYBODY ELSE KNEW WAS TO COUNT . . . . . 186 THE AX-HELVE 42
    TO TOLLING LIKE THE COUNT OF FATE, ... 273 A LONE STRIKER . . . 2
    I AM TOO ABSENT-SPIRITED TO COUNT; . . . . 296 DESERT PLACES . . . 7
    IT'S ON THE INCREASE. HE COULD COUNT ON NO ONE: . . . 485 A MASQUE OF REASON . . 357
    THAT WAS HIS LOOKOUT. I COULD COUNT ON YOU. . . . . 485 A MASQUE OF REASON . . 358
    TO COUNT ON JUSTICE TO BE MERELY JUST. . . . . . . 509 A MASQUE OF MERCY . . 425
    I CAN COUNT ON MY SOURCE TO SPRING AGAIN, ... 514 A MASQUE OF MERCY . . 541
COUNTED
    IN NESTS. SHALL I BE COUNTED LESS THAN THEY ARE? . . . 151 SNOW 227
    I COUNTED NINE I HAD NO RIGHT TO COUNT . . . . . . 175 THE CENSUS-TAKER . . 31
    IF ONE BY ONE WE COUNTED PEOPLE OUT . . . . 177 THE STAR-SPLITTER . . 11
    AND TWO WAS ALL HE COUNTED (ONE HE MISSED); . . . . 283 THE GOLD HESPERIDEE . 11
    COUNTED THEM ALL TO THE BUDS IN THE COPSE'S DEPTH . . . 343 QUEST OF PURPLE-FRINGED 23
    AND COUNTED OUT. HEROIC DEEDS WERE DONE. . . . . . 422 FOR JOHN F. KENNEDY . 17
COUNTER
    IN THAT WHITE WAVE RUNS COUNTER TO ITSELF. . . . . . 259 WEST-RUNNING BROOK . . 39
COUNTER-LOVE
    BUT COUNTER-LOVE, ORIGINAL RESPONSE. . . . . 338 THE MOST OF IT . . . 8
COUNTERPANE
    RIGHT ON THE COUNTERPANE--THAT I DO TRUST YOU?" . . . . 48 A HUNDRED COLLARS . . 94
COUNTERPART
    I AM THE DAMPER COUNTERPART OF SMOKE, ... 414 A CABIN IN THE CLEARING 15
COUNTER-STREAMS
    IN STREAMS AND CROSS- AND COUNTER-STREAMS . . . . . 20 THE TRIAL BY EXISTENCE 22
COUNTERWISDOM
    FOR WISDOM THAT CAN HAVE NO COUNTERWISDOM. . . . . . 515 A MASQUE OF MERCY . . 588
COUNTING
    (BUT THIS WAS DREAMY UNOFFICIAL COUNTING) . . . . . 175 THE CENSUS-TAKER . . 32
    COUNTING AN ENDLESS REPETITION. . . . . 247 DEVOTION 4
    WAS COUNTING WINTER DINNERS, ONE A HILL, ... 263 THE INVESTMENT . . . 7
    WE WERE COUNTING STARS, ... 437 KITTY HAWK 312
COUNTLESS
    BY COUNTLESS SILKEN TIES OF LOVE AND THOUGHT . . . . 332 THE SILKEN TENT . . . 10
    THE COUNTLESS WINGS THAT FROM THE INFINITE . . . . . 411 POD OF THE MILKWEED . 10

COUNTLESSLY
    HOW COUNTLESSLY THEY CONGREGATE . . . . 9 STARS 1
COUNTRY (SEE CROSS-COUNTRY)
    IN ALL THE COUNTRY HE DID COMMAND . . . . 23 PAN WITH US 8
    ALL ROUND THE COUNTRY FOR THE WEEKLY NEWS, ... 48 A HUNDRED COLLARS . . 98
    AND LEFT AT LAST THE COUNTRY TO THE COUNTRY; . . . . 105 CHRISTMAS TREES . . 2
    YET DID IN COUNTRY FASHION IN THAT THERE . . . . . . 106 CHRISTMAS TREES . . 6
    BUT NOW ARE GIVING UP FOR COUNTRY DARKNESS." . . . . 112 IN THE HOME STRETCH . 59
    IT'S NOT SO BAD IN THE COUNTRY, SETTLED DOWN, ... 113 IN THE HOME STRETCH . 93
    TO THINK TO KNOW THE COUNTRY AND NCT KNOW . . . . . 237 A HILLSIDE THAW . . . 1
    THE NEED OF BEING VERSED IN COUNTRY THINGS . . . . . 241 NEED OF BEING VERSED . T
    ONE HAD TO BE VERSED IN COUNTRY THINGS . . . . . . 242 NEED OF BEING VERSED . 23
    WHEN ALL THE OTHER COUNTRY BROOKS FLOW EAST . . . . 258 WEST-RUNNING BROOK . 5
    AS'T WERE THE COUNTRY OF THE AMAZONS . . . . 259 WEST-RUNNING BROOK . 33
    NO, IN COUNTRY MONEY, THE COUNTRY SCALE OF GAIN, . . 287 A ROADSIDE STAND . . 44
    OR SO THE VOICE OF THE COUNTRY SEEMS TO COMPLAIN. . . 287 A ROADSIDE STAND . . 46
    AS IF I HAD MEASURED THE COUNTRY . . . . 295 A RECORD STRIDE . . . 35
    SOME INTO THE COUNTRY NORTH, ... 312 THE VINDICTIVES . . 71
    IS NOT TO LURE THE CITY TO THE COUNTRY. . . . . . . 322 BUILD SOIL 186
    TO THE OPEN COUNTRY EDGE . . . . 364 A NATURE NOTE . . . 3
    OF COUNTRY WHERE TWO VILLAGE CULTURES FADED . . . . 378 DIRECTIVE 34
    HARRISON LOVES MY COUNTRY TOO, ... 393 A CASE FOR JEFFERSON . 1
    WITH HIM THE LOVE OF COUNTRY MEANS . . . . 393 A CASE FOR JEFFERSON . 9
    (A COUNTRY NAMED FOR HIM, A TOWN, ... 418 AMERICA IS HARD TO SEE 46
    BY HIS COUNTRY AND HIS NEIGHBORHOOD? . . . . 469 CHOSEN POET OF VERMONT 4
    EXCEPT IN THEIR OWN COUNTRY, THYATIRA. . . . . . . 476 A MASQUE OF REASON . 91
COUNTRY'D
    WHAT COUNTRY'D BE THE ONE TO DOMINATE . . . . 422 FOR JOHN F. KENNEDY . 13
COUNTRY'S
    THE COUNTRY'S SINGING STRENGTH THUS BROUGHT TOGETHER, . 240 OUR SINGING STRENGTH . 50
    THE COUNTRY'S ONLY USEFUL AS A PLACE . . . . 496 A MASQUE OF MERCY . 73
COUNTRYSIDE
    A FARM, A COUNTRYSIDE, OR IF HE CAN, ... 108 OLD MAN'S WINTER NIGHT 27
COUNTS
    OF THE OLD STOCK? WHAT COUNTS IS THE IDEALS, ... 80 THE GENERATIONS OF MEN 197
    THAT A BOY COUNTS SO MUCH WHEN SAVED FROM WORK. . . . 136 "OUT,OUT--" . . . 12
    IT'S KNOWING WHAT TO DO WITH THINGS THAT COUNTS. . . . 294 AT WOODWARD'S GARDENS . 37
    THE THING THAT REALLY CCUNTS, THOUGH, IS THE FORM . . 509 A MASQUE OF MERCY . 430
COUNTY
    IN FRONT OF EVERY ONE IN GRAFTON COUNTY. . . . . . . 209 PAUPER WITCH OF GRAFTON 51
COUPLE
    AND FRIES A COUPLE OF EBON ATOMS WHITE, ... 389 SKEPTIC 2
    HE SIGHED HIMSELF A COUPLE OF GROANS, ... 419 ONE MORE BREVITY . . 16
COURAGE
    I HAVEN'T COURAGE FOR A RISK LIKE THAT. . . . . . . 67 A SERVANT TO SERVANTS . 170
    IT DOESN'T SEEM AS IF I'D HAD THE COURAGE . . . . . 210 PAUPER WITCH OF GRAFTON 106
    THE COURAGE TO BE NEW . . . . 387 THE COURAGE TO BE NEW . T
    AND THEIR COURAGE TO BE NEW. . . . . 387 THE COURAGE TO BE NEW . 16
    MORE THAN THEY KNOW WHAT COURAGE IS THAT CLAIM . . . 405 FROM PLANE TO PLANE . 34
    COURAGE IS IN THE AIR IN BRACING WHIFFS . . . . . . 423 FOR JOHN F. KENNEDY . 58
    YOUR COURAGE FAILED. THE SADDEST THING IN LIFE . . . 497 A MASQUE OF MERCY . 106
    IS THAT THE BEST THING IN IT SHOULD BE COURAGE. . . . 497 A MASQUE OF MERCY . 107
    I AM RIGHT, THEN? / --IN GLORIFYING COURAGE. . . . . 519 A MASQUE OF MERCY . 692
    COURAGE IS OF THE HEART BY DERIVATION, ... 519 A MASQUE OF MERCY . 693
    WE BOTH HAVE LACKED THE COURAGE IN THE HEART . . . . 521 A MASQUE OF MERCY . 728
    COURAGE IS WHAT IT TAKES AND TAKES THE MORE OF . . . 521 A MASQUE OF MERCY . 731
COURAGEOUS
    SO IN IT HAVE TO TAKE COURAGEOUS PART. . . . . . . 423 FOR JOHN F. KENNEDY . 42
COURSE
    "OF COURSE HE DID. WHAT WOULD YOU HAVE HIM SAY? . . . 36 DEATH OF THE HIRED MAN 48
    OF COURSE HE'S NOTHING TO US, ANY MORE . . . . . . 38 DEATH OF THE HIRED MAN 115
    "I THINK HIS BROTHER OUGHT TO HELP, OF COURSE. . . . 39 DEATH OF THE HIRED MAN 131
    SEPARATE BEDS, OF COURSE, YOU UNDERSTAND." . . . . . 45 A HUNDRED COLLARS . 27
    FREDERICKSBURG WASN'T GETTYSBURG, OF COURSE. . . . . 56 THE BLACK COTTAGE . 33
    WHAT DID HE MEAN? OF COURSE THE EASY WAY . . . . . 57 THE BLACK COTTAGE . 65
    HIS WORK'S A MAN'S, OF COURSE, FROM SUN TO SUN, . . . 64 A SERVANT TO SERVANTS . 66
    OF COURSE THEY HAD TO FEED HIM WITHOUT DISHES. . . . 66 A SERVANT TO SERVANTS . 121
    BLESS YCU, OF COURSE YOU'RE KEEPING ME FROM WORK, . . 67 A SERVANT TO SERVANTS . 171
    JAMES WOULD TAKE TIME, OF COURSE, TO CHEW IT OVER . . 70 THE CODE 18
    BUT WHEN I'M GONE--OF COURSE I CAN'T STAY HERE: . . . 82 THE HOUSEKEEPER . . 34
    "OF COURSE YOU DID. YOU LEFT THE REST FOR SEED, . . . 97 THE SELF-SEEKER . . 124
    IT MUST HAVE LOOKED AS IF THE COURSE . . . . 139 BROWN'S DESCENT . . 65
    OF COURSE SHE HASN'T, THOUGH." THEY BOTH SAT DOWN . . 155 SNOW 324
    NOTHING NOT BUILT WITH HANDS OF COURSE IS SACRED. . . 171 NEW HAMPSHIRE . . 394
    THAT COURSE, THEY TELL ME, ISN'T OFFERED THIS YEAR. . 171 NEW HAMPSHIRE . . 405
    IF IT COULD PUT A STAR BACK IN ITS COURSE. . . . . . 173 A STAR IN A STONEBOAT . 30
    OH NO!--ALTHOUGH, OF COURSE, I COULD HAVE FOUND . . . 190 THE GRINDSTONE . . 52
    OF COURSE THE BOTTLE FELL SHORT BY A MILE, ... 195 PAUL'S WIFE . . . 142
    IF THAT HOW SHE FELT, OF COURSE, HE SAID. . . . . . 200 PLACE FOR A THIRD . 14
    YOU, OF COURSE, ARE A ROSE-- . . . . 246 THE ROSE FAMILY . . 9
    ONLY, OF COURSE, THEY CAN'T SUSTAIN THE PART. . . . . 246 FIREFLIES IN THE GARDEN 6
    AND OF COURSE THERE MUST BE SOMETHING WRONG . . . . 251 A MINOR BIRD . . 7
    (NO GIRL'S, OF COURSE, HAS STAYED THE SAME.) . . . . 265 THE BIRTHPLACE . . 12
    BUT THOUGH IT RUNS UNBRIDLED OFF ITS COURSE, ... 268 RIDERS 10
    WHAT SHOULD YOU DO? / I'D LET THINGS TAKE THEIR COURSE . 320 BUILD SOIL . . . 128
    IMPRINT A SADDLE, AND CALMLY CONSIDER A COURSE. . . . 341 WILLFUL HOMING . . 7
    YES, YES, OF COURSE. WE HAVE THE SAME CONVENTION. . . 352 THE LESSON FOR TODAY . 57
    AND LEAVING SOME THINGS TO TAKE THEIR COURSE. . . . 376 SOMETHING FOR HOPE . 22
    A HALF COURSE IN IT NEXT YEAR.) AND BESIDES, ... 407 FROM PLANE TO PLANE . 112
    ON EITHER HAND TO MAKE HIS COURSE PERHAPS . . . . . 421 ESCAPIST--NEVER . . 4
    A NATION HAS TO TAKE ITS NATURAL COURSE . . . . . . 459 HOW HARD TO KEEP FROM 158
    OF COURSE, IN THE ABSTRACT HIGH SINGULAR . . . . . 478 A MASQUE OF REASON . 137
    A REVOLUTIONARY--WHICH OF COURSE YOU CAN'T BE. . . . 510 A MASQUE OF MERCY . 455
    MY SMALL FRESH-WATER SPRING GETS DROWNED OF COURSE. . 513 A MASQUE OF MERCY . 539
COURT
    TO THE HIGHER-UP AT COURT. . . . . 288 DEPARTMENTAL . . . 21
    LESS CRITICISM OF THE FIELD AND COURT . . . . 424 FOR JOHN F. KENNEDY . 68
    THERE CAME TO COURT A MERCHANT SELLING PEARLS, . . . 455 HOW HARD TO KEEP FROM 66

COURT (CONTINUED)
   OR COURT OF LOVE. / MORE LIKELY ROYAL COURT-- . . . . . 474 A MASQUE OF REASON . . 25
   OR COURT OF LAW, AND THIS IS JUDGMENT DAY. . . . . . . 474 A MASQUE OF REASON . . 26
COURTESY
   THEN WHETHER FROM MISTAKEN COURTESY . . . . 106 CHRISTMAS TREES . . . 26
COURTING
   THAT WAS THE WAY HE STARTED COURTING ME. . . . . . . 209 PAUPER WITCH OF GRAFTON 72
COURTS
   SO NOW THEY'VE DRAGGED IT THROUGH THE LAW COURTS ONCE, . . 208 PAUPER WITCH OF GRAFTON 28
   WITH THE IDEA OF JUSTICE IN THE COURTS, ... 509 A MASQUE OF MERCY . . 423
COUSINS (SEE STRANGER-COUSINS)
   "YOU KNOW WE MIGHT NOT BE AND STILL BE COUSINS: . . . . 75 THE GENERATIONS OF MEN 47
COUSINSHIP
   AND SEE IF YOU CAN RECKON OUR COUSINSHIP. . . . . . 75 THE GENERATIONS OF MEN 62
COVE
   SHE MAY KNOW COVE AND CAPE, ... 260 SAND DUNES 9
COVENANT
   IN THE COVENANT . . . . 441 KITTY HAWK 421
COVER
   SHE USED HER HANDS TO COVER UP HER EYES. . . . . . 184 MAPLE 160
   TO ANY ONE PLACE COVER US WITH SONG. . . . . . . 239 OUR SINGING STRENGTH . 20
   THE OBSCURITY'S A FRAUD TO COVER NOTHING. . . . . 483 A MASQUE OF REASON . 279
COVERAGE
   OUR COVERAGE OF DISTANCE IS SO FACILE . . . . . 446 DOES NO ONE AT ALL EVER 15
COVERED (SEE BLACK-PAPER-COVERED, STRAW-DUST-COVERED)
   AND THE GROUND ALMOST COVERED SMOOTH IN SNOW, . . . 296 DESERT PLACES . . . 3
   LONG SINCE GAVE UP PRETENSE OF KEEPING COVERED. . . . 377 DIRECTIVE 12
COVERS
   TILL IT CAUGHT WIND AND, OPENING OUT ITS COVERS, . . . 216 A FOUNTAIN, A BOTTLE . 111
COVET
   NO ONE WOULD COVET IT OR THINK IT WORTH . . . . . 58 THE BLACK COTTAGE . 117
COW
   SOMETHING INSPIRES THE ONLY COW OF LATE . . . . . 124 THE COW IN APPLE TIME . 1
   THE COW IN APPLE TIME . . . . 124 THE COW IN APPLE TIME . T
   THE NEXT COW MIGHT HAVE LICKED UP OUT AT PASTURE. . . 184 MAPLE 151
   OR MILK THE COW, HE VISITED THE FRUIT, ... 283 THE GOLD HESPERIDEE . 20
   HOPE MAY NOT NOURISH A COW OR HORSE, ... 376 SOMETHING FOR HOPE . 23
   I ONCE HAD A COW THAT JUMPED OVER THE MOON, ... 462 LINES IN DEJECTION . 1
   WE HAVEN'T CAUGHT UP WITH MY COW. . . . . . . 463 LINES IN DEJECTION . 8
   AND HAD CAUGHT MY COW BY THE TAIL, ... 463 LINES IN DEJECTION . 10
   A COW DID THAT ONCE TO A FELLOW . . . . 463 LINES IN DEJECTION . 14
COWARD
   A COWARD SAVE AT NIGHT, ... 341 THE SUBVERTED FLOWER . 60
COWER
   COWER DOWN IN DESPERATION TO ACCEPT . . . . . . 357 A CONSIDERABLE SPECK . 22
COWERED
   MOUNTING UNTIL SHE COWERED UNDER HIM. . . . . . . 51 HOME BURIAL 11
COWERING
   RETARD MID-WASTE MY COWERING CARAVANS-- . . . . . 59 THE BLACK COTTAGE . 124
COWPATH
   THE MILKY WAY IS A COWPATH . . . . 464 MILKY WAY IS A COWPATH T
COWS
   WHERE THERE ARE COWS? BUT HERE THERE ARE NO COWS. . . 34 MENDING WALL . . . 31
   WITH A BIG STICK, THE SAME AS WHEN THE COWS . . . 43 THE MOUNTAIN . . . 85
   OUR HENS AND COWS AND PIGS ARE ALWAYS BETTER . . . 85 THE HOUSEKEEPER . . 111
   AS HE WENT OUT AND IN TO FETCH THE COWS-- . . . 121 BIRCHES 24
COW'S
   BELIEVE IT WAS THE COW'S . . . . 464 MILKY WAY IS A COWPATH 19
COZENED
   SO COZENED AND FOOLED . . . . 448 THE BAD ISLAND--EASTER 29
COZIER
   TO GIVE IT COZIER SKIES . . . . 281 A DRUMLIN WOODCHUCK . 3
CRAB
   IN SPECIMEN CRAB IN SPECIMEN ROCK, ... 364 TRESPASS 14
CRACK
   OF TREES AND CRACK OF BRANCHES, COMMON THINGS, . . . 108 OLD MAN'S WINTER NIGHT 13
   "YOU GIVE HER ONE GOOD CRACK, SHE'S SNAP RAGHT OFF. . . 186 THE AX-HELVE . . . 26
   THEIR MINDS RAN ON CRANNY AND CRACK. . . . . . . 311 THE VINDICTIVES . . 31
   THE BIRCH BEGINS TO CRACK ITS OUTER SHEATH . . . . 375 A YOUNG BIRCH . . . 1
   WITH A CRACK OF A BROKEN SHAFT. . . . . 444 THE DRAFT HORSE . . 10
   PERHAPS THAT EARTH IS GOING TO CRACK SOMEDAY . . . 484 A MASQUE OF REASON . 305
CRACKED
   WHAT CAN'T BE MOLDED MUST BE CRACKED AND SPRUNG. . . 267 WHAT FIFTY SAID . . 6
   AND CRACKED BONES, HUMAN AND BEAST, ... 312 THE VINDICTIVES . . 59
   AND CRACKED HIS RAGGED MUZZLE. . . . . 339 THE SUBVERTED FLOWER . 14
   NOW STANDING CRACKED ITS SAIL AND SPUN; . . . . . 344 DISCOVERY OF MADEIRAS . 22
CRACKLING
   DIED NOT WITHOUT A NOISE OF CRACKLING WOOD-- . . . 131 THE BONFIRE 76
CRACKS
   AS THE STIR CRACKS AND CRAZES THEIR ENAMEL. . . . 121 BIRCHES 9
   YOU NICK MY SPRUCE UNTIL ITS FIBER CRACKS, ... 349 TO A YOUNG WRETCH . . 3
   WHERE THE COLD CRACKS LIKE A PISTOL . . . . . . 384 IN THE LONG NIGHT . . 3
CRADLE (SEE CAT'S-CRADLE)
CRAFT
   SO BY CRAFT OR ART . . . . 441 KITTY HAWK 426
CRAMPED
   THE UNIVERSE SEEMS CRAMPED TO YOU AND ME. . . . . 269 THE BEAR 12
CRAMPING
   HE TOOK HIM DOWN BELOW A CRAMPING RAFTER, ... 142 THE VANISHING RED . . 20
   BY CRAMPING THE WHEEL ON A WATER BAR, ... 263 THE TIMES TABLE . . 5
CRANBERRIES
   CRANBERRIES IN BOGS AND RASPBERRIES ON TOP . . . . 61 BLUEBERRIES 62
CRANKED
   I LAUGHED INSIDE, AND ONLY CRANKED THE FASTER . . . 190 THE GRINDSTONE . . . 60
CRANKS
   ONCE CONSIDERED CRANKS . . . . 443 KITTY HAWK 469
CRANNIES
   THE FIRE GOT OUT THROUGH CRANNIES IN THE STOVE . . . 117 IN THE HOME STRETCH . 202

CRANNY
   THEIR MINDS RAN ON CRANNY AND CRACK. . . . . 311 THE VINDICTIVES 31
CRASH
   AND EVERY CRASH MEANT ONE LESS TO RETURN . . . . . . 112 IN THE HOME STRETCH . 57
   THE TREE THE TEMPEST WITH A CRASH OF WOOD . . . . . . 238 ON A TREE FALLEN ACROSS . 1
   NOR STRIKE OUT FIRE FROM EACH OTHER, NOR CRASH OUT LOUD. . 268 ON LOOKING UP BY CHANCE 5
   DON'T YOU CRASH ME DOWN. . . . . 439 KITTY HAWK 350
CRASHED
   UNLESS IT WAS THE EMBODIMENT THAT CRASHED . . . . . . 338 THE MOST OF IT . . . 10
CRASHES
   THE FOLLY CRASHES AND THE DUST GOES UP. . . . . . . 506 A MASQUE OF MERCY . . 342
CRATE
   I'VE PULLED IT FROM A CRATE OF CROOKED TREES, ... 245 THE FREEDOM OF THE MOON 9
CRATER
   I LOOK INTO THE CRATER OF THE ANT. . . . . 17 THE VANTAGE POINT . . 14
CRATER'S
   TO STAND TOGETHER ON THE CRATER'S VERGE . . . . . . 73 THE GENERATIONS OF MEN 16
CRAVE
   I CRAVE THE STAIN . . . . 227 TO EARTHWARD 20
CRAVED
   I CRAVED STRONG SWEETS, BUT THOSE . . . . 227 TO EARTHWARD 13
CRAWL
   AGAIN COME TO LIFE AND CRAWL OFF, ... 266 SITTING BY A BUSH . . 11
   THAT IN A GOOD GLASS MAY BE SEEN TO CRAWL . . . . . 352 THE LESSON FOR TODAY . 71
   WE WOULD CRAWL OUT FILING SINGLE . . . . 384 IN THE LONG NIGHT . . 7
   WHERE SOMEONE USED TO CLIMB AND CRAWL . . . . 392 A CLIFF DWELLING . . 8
CRAWLED
   AFTER HAVING CRAWLED . . . . 434 KITTY HAWK 203
CRAYON
   UNDER A CRAYON PORTRAIT ON THE WALL, ... 55 THE BLACK COTTAGE . . 23
CRAZES
   AS THE STIR CRACKS AND CRAZES THEIR ENAMEL. . . . . . 121 BIRCHES 9
CRAZY
   FROM NORM TO CRAZY AND BACK TO NORM, ... 325 TO A THINKER 10
CREAKING
   OVER THE SNOW MY CREAKING FEET . . . . 102 GOOD HOURS 13
   THAT BROUGHT HIM TO THAT CREAKING ROOM WAS AGE. . . . . 108 MAN'S WINTER NIGHT 7
   OR CREAKING WITH A BUGGY LOAD OF GRAIN. . . . . . . 378 DIRECTIVE 32
CREAKS
   HER GREAT WEIGHT CREAKS THE BARBED WIRE IN ITS STAPLES . 269 THE BEAR 7
CREAM
   SO THAT THE CREAM COULD NEVER RISE AGAIN . . . . . . 509 A MASQUE OF MERCY . . 421
CREASE
   ONE STRINGING A CHAIN OF SEED IN AN OPEN CREASE, . . . 299 STRONG SAYING NOTHING . 7
CREASED (SEE TROUBLE-CREASED)
   HE SAT THERE CREASED AND SHINING IN THE LIGHT, ... 46 A HUNDRED COLLARS . . 51
CREATE
   EVER TO CREATE . . . . 441 KITTY HAWK 417
CREATED
   THAT ALL MEN ARE CREATED FREE AND EQUAL. . . . . . . 57 THE BLACK COTTAGE . . 61
CREATES
   IT IS THE FUTURE THAT CREATES HIS PRESENT. . . . . . 421 ESCAPIST--NEVER . . . 11
CREATION
   IT IN CREATION . . . . 220 I WILL SING YOU ONE-O . 76
CREATURE
   BLIND CREATURE; AND AWHILE HE DIDN'T SEE. . . . . . 51 HOME BURIAL 16
   A BRIDE, TO HELP TAKE CARE OF SUCH A CREATURE, . . . 66 A SERVANT TO SERVANTS . 127
   BEING THE CREATURE OF LITERATURE I AM, ... 166 NEW HAMPSHIRE . . . 240
   THEY SAW PAUL AND HIS CREATURE KEEPING HOUSE. . . . . 195 PAUL'S WIFE 128
   LONG, LONG BEFORE WE WERE FROM ANY CREATURE. . . . . 259 WEST-RUNNING BROOK . . 41
   BRIGHT-BLACK-EYED SILVERY CREATURE, BRUSHED WITH BROWN, . 356 A MOTH SEEN IN WINTER . 3
   WITH ONLY ONE VESTIGIAL CREATURE WISH: . . . . . . 395 ETHEREALIZING . . . 12
CREATURES
   WHEN OTHER CREATURES HAVE GONE TO STALL AND BIN, . . . 223 THE RUNAWAY 20
   ALL CREATURES STILL WARMLY SUSPIRE. . . . . 266 SITTING BY A BUSH . . 8
CREDENTIALS
   A PROPHET WITH THE BIBLE FOR CREDENTIALS. . . . . . 498 A MASQUE OF MERCY . . 135
CREDIBLE
   THEY ARE TOO SUDDEN TO BE CREDIBLE. . . . . 415 A CABIN IN THE CLEARING 33
CREDIT
   AND THEN I'D CLAIM THE CREDIT FOR THE OUTCOME. . . . . 320 BUILD SOIL 129
   I GIVE YOU CREDIT FOR. MY FORTE IS TRUTH, ... 480 A MASQUE OF REASON . . 190
CREDITED
   OR HAVING SEEN AND CREDITED A MOMENT . . . . 169 NEW HAMPSHIRE . . . 321
CREED
   I WOULD HAVE CHANGED THE CREED A VERY LITTLE? . . . . 57 THE BLACK COTTAGE . . 88
   BUT SUPPOSE SHE HAD MISSED IT FROM THE CREED, ... 58 THE BLACK COTTAGE . . 101
   AND LONG ENOUGH GETS RATED AS A CREED: . . . . . . 394 ETHEREALIZING . . . 2
   THE LATEST CREED THAT HAS TO BE BELIEVED . . . . . . 427 CONCEPT SELF-CONCEIVED 1
CREEKS
   WHEN MAN FIRST LIVED IN CAVES ALONG THE CREEKS?" . . . 372 THE LITERATE FARMER AND 140
CREEPING
   AND LET THEM GO SCRAPING AND CREEPING . . . . . . 30 RELUCTANCE 10
CREEPS
   HOW THE COLD CREEPS AS THE FIRE DIES AT LENGTH-- . . . 10 STORM FEAR 12
CREEPY
   THE CREEPY EDGE OF IT WITH WARY TOUCH, ... 190 THE GRINDSTONE . . . 69
CREPE-PAPER
   HIS JAPANESE CREPE-PAPER GLOBE FOR TROPHY? . . . . . 278 THE WHITE-TAILED HORNET 18
CREPT
   AND I CREPT DOWN THE STAIRS AND UP THE STAIRS . . . . 53 HOME BURIAL 79
   IT RAN WITH TERROR AND WITH CUNNING CREPT. . . . . . 357 A CONSIDERABLE SPECK . 19
CREVICE
   ABOUT MY CREVICE AND BURROW. . . . . 282 A DRUMLIN WOODCHUCK . 32
   WHICH IS THE CREVICE THAT LETS PROGRESS IN. . . . . . 458 HOW HARD TO KEEP FROM 153
CREVICES
   WITH LITTLE FERNS IN CREVICES AT HIS ELBOW. . . . . . 42 THE MOUNTAIN 62
   ITS ONLY WINDOWS WERE THE CREVICES . . . . 290 OLD BARN AT THE BOTTOM 24

CREW
    AND HIS CREW LEFT HIM WHERE HE FAILED, ... 212 AN EMPTY THREAT . . . 46
    FOR ALL THE CREW WERE LET TO KNOW. . . . . 344 DISCOVERY OF MADEIRAS . 34
    THAT SOMEONE IN THE CREW CONNECTS WITH ME. . . . . . 500 A MASQUE OF MERCY . . 181
CRIB
    THE CRIB HE SLEPT IN--AND AS SURE'S YOU'RE BORN . . . 209 PAUPER WITCH OF GRAFTON 61
CRIBBER
    HE'D BET HUSE WAS A CRIBBER AND HAD GNAWED . . . . . 209 PAUPER WITCH OF GRAFTON 60
CRIED
    BUT THE CHILD'S MOUND----" / "DON'T, DON'T, DON'T, DON'T,"
      SHE CRIED. . . . . 52 HOME BURIAL 30
    "WHAT DO YOU WANT?" SHE CRIED TO ALL THE DARK. . . . . 91 THE FEAR 61
    WHAT DO YOU WANT?" SHE CRIED, AND THEN HERSELF . . . . 91 THE FEAR 65
    IT NEEDED A TURN MORE, I COULD HAVE CRIED . . . . . 191 THE GRINDSTONE . . . 72
    SOME CRIED SHAME ON ME NOT TO BLANKET HIM, ... 209 PAUPER WITCH OF GRAFTON 52
    AND NOTHING EVER CAME OF WHAT HE CRIED . . . . . . 338 THE MOST OF IT . . . 9
    CRIED, "THE LEAP--THE LEAP!" . . . . 437 KITTY HAWK 297
    "BUT TELL US HOW YOU KNEW," DARIUS CRIED. . . . . . 456 HOW HARD TO KEEP FROM 86
    AND CRIED, "I'LL LARN YOU TO BELLOW." . . . . . . 463 LINES IN DEJECTION . . 16
CRIES
    TO LOUD CRIES FROM MY BROTHER OF "LET GO! . . . . . 197 WILD GRAPES 46
    CONFUSION, AND A ROAR THAT DROWNED THE CRIES . . . . 270 THE EGG AND THE MACHINE 14
    WHAT CRIES MORE TO OUR KIND FOR SYMPATHY? . . . . . 323 BUILD SOIL 219
    THE ARTIST IN ME CRIES OUT FOR DESIGN. . . . . . . 482 A MASQUE OF REASON . .261
CRIME
    A WALL TOO HARD FOR CRIME . . . . 348 TRIPLE BRONZE 7
    IN SLEEP OR SLOWNESS IS THE DEADLY CRIME. . . . . . 371 THE LITERATE FARMER AND 103
CRIMES
    OF ALL CRIMES THE WORST . . . . 430 KITTY HAWK 73
CRINGE
    THEY MAKE US CRINGE FOR METAL-POINT ON STONE. . . . 261 A SOLDIER 11
CRISIS
    IN THE UNIVERSAL CRISIS. . . . . 377 ONE STEP BACKWARD TAKEN 9
CRISISES
    I THINK MY TROUBLE'S WITH THE CRISISES . . . . . . 510 A MASQUE OF MERCY . .442
CRITICAL
    A HEIGHT FROM WHICH TO LOOK DOWN CRITICAL . . . . . 169 NEW HAMPSHIRE 314
    WON'T BEAR TOO CRITICAL EXAMINATION. . . . . 385 THE FEAR OF GOD . . . 6
CRITICISM
    LESS CRITICISM OF THE FIELD AND COURT . . . . . . 424 FOR JOHN F. KENNEDY . 68
CROAK
    IT CANNOT CHECK THE PEEPER'S SILVER CROAK; . . . . . 226 THE ONSET 17
CRONE
    WHERE NOBODY CAN CALL YOU CRONE. . . . . 307 PROVIDE, PROVIDE . . 12
CROOK (SEE ELBOW-CROOK)
CROOKED
    WHAT'S LAS' AWHILE--GOOD HICK'RY WHAT'S GROW CROOKED, . 186 THE AX-HELVE 30
    A BRUSH HAD LEFT A CROOKED STROKE . . . . 233 LOOKING FOR SUNSET BIRD 17
    I'VE PULLED IT FROM A CRATE OF CROOKED TREES, ... 245 THE FREEDOM OF THE MOON 9
    A CROOKED STRAIGHTNESS YET NO LESS A STRAIGHTNESS. . . 421 ESCAPIST--NEVER . . . 5
CROOKING
    THEY WERE CROOKING MANY A TRILLIUM . . . . 123 PEA BRUSH 22
CROOK-NECKED
    OR CROOK-NECKED GOLDEN SQUASH WITH SILVER WARTS, . . . 286 A ROADSIDE STAND . . 12
CROP
    OF THE BOULDER-STREWN MOUNTAIN, AND WHEN THEY WILL CROP. 61 BLUEBERRIES 63
    HER CROP WAS A MISCELLANY . . . . 134 A GIRL'S GARDEN . . . 37
    BUT A CROP IS A CROP, ... 235 GATHERING LEAVES . . 22
CROPS
    I'M DONE FOREVER WITH POTATO CROPS . . . . 316 BUILD SOIL 11
CROSS
    IN STREAMS AND CROSS- AND COUNTER-STREAMS . . . . . 20 THE TRIAL BY EXISTENCE 22
    THE SCALES OF TRADE, THE CROSS OF FAITH, ... 252 THE PEACEFUL SHEPHERD . 7
    THE CROSS, THE CROWN, THE SCALES MAY ALL . . . . . 252 THE PEACEFUL SHEPHERD . 11
    WHEREAT IN A MOMENT OF CROSS UNRUTH . . . . 346 DISCOVERY OF MADEIRAS . 96
    FROM, SAY, THE CROSS OR CROWN. . . . . 384 MAKING CERTAIN ANYTHING 12
    YOUR FOREARMS IN THE FIGURE OF A CROSS . . . . . . 501 A MASQUE OF MERCY . .193
    AS RED CROSS AMBULANCE COMMANDER-IN-CHIEF . . . . . 507 A MASQUE OF MERCY . .369
    BEFORE THE CROSS, IT IS FROM FELLOW-FEELING, ... 521 A MASQUE OF MERCY . .735
'CROSS
    'CROSS LOTS, 'CROSS WALLS, 'CROSS EVERYTHING, ... 137 BROWN'S DESCENT . . . 7
    'CROSS THE AEGEAN ISLES, ... 437 KITTY HAWK 289
CROSS-COUNTRY
    (SHE'S MAKING HER CROSS-COUNTRY IN THE FALL). . . . 268 THE BEAR 6
CROSSED (SEE EVIL-CROSSED, MERCY-CROSSED, STAR-CROSSED)
    I CROSSED THE RIVER AND SWUNG ROUND THE MOUNTAIN, . . 41 THE MOUNTAIN 15
    BUT IT'S MORE LIKELY HE WAS CROSSED IN LOVE, ... 66 A SERVANT TO SERVANTS .108
    BUT ADVANCED WITH HER AS SHE CROSSED THE GRASS. . . . 91 THE FEAR 60
    WE CLIMBED THE PASTURE ON THE SOUTH, CROSSED OVER, . . 107 CHRISTMAS TREES . . . 40
    THAT CROSSED ME FROM SWEET THINGS, ... 227 TO EARTHWARD 5
    A FLOWER TO TRY ITS CURRENTS WHERE THEY CROSSED. . . . 231 A BROOK IN THE CITY . 8
    THE SUN AND MOON GET CROSSED, BUT THEY NEVER TOUCH, . . 268 ON LOOKING UP BY CHANCE 4
    NO SHADOW CROSSED BUT OURS . . . . 333 HAPPINESS MAKES UP . 21
    I HAVE CROSSED TO SAFETY WITH? FOR I AM THERE, . . . 335 I COULD GIVE ALL . . 14
    MOREOVER HER VOICE UPON THEIR VOICES CROSSED . . . . 339 NEVER WOULD BIRDS' SONG 10
    AND A CLOUD SHADOW CROSSED HER FACE . . . . 342 A CLOUD SHADOW . . . 7
    HOW THEY MAKE HASTE TO CRY WITH FINGERS CROSSED, . . . 399 U.S. 1946 KING'S X . 3
    AND IF YOU'VE GOT TO SEE YOUR JUSTICE CROSSED . . . . 510 A MASQUE OF MERCY . .436
    A DARKNESS OUT OF ASIA THAT HAD CROSSED . . . . . . 511 A MASQUE OF MERCY . .466
CROSSES
    WITH WHOM HE CROSSES ANTENNAE, ... 288 DEPARTMENTAL 19
CROSSING
    ONE CROSSING WITH HURRIED TREAD . . . . 288 DEPARTMENTAL 14
CROSS-LEGGED
    CROSS-LEGGED. . . . . 211 AN EMPTY THREAT . . . 9
CROSSLY
    WHY, KEEP YOUR MONEY (THIS CROSSLY) AND GO ALONG. . . . 286 A ROADSIDE STAND . . 15
    THEY COULDN'T (THIS CROSSLY): THEY HAD NONE, DIDN'T IT SEE? 287 A ROADSIDE STAND . . 43

CROSSROADS
    IS ONLY CORNERS, CROSSROADS IN A WOOD). . . . . 165 NEW HAMPSHIRE . . . 192
CROUCH
    I CROUCH DOWN TO PREVENT THEM AS THEY FALL; . . . . . 267 THE ARMFUL 9
CROW
    AND THEN HE'D CROW AS IF HE THOUGHT THAT CHILD'S PLAY-- . . 66 A SERVANT TO SERVANTS . 137
    AS I WENT OUT A CROW . . . . 135 LAST WORD OF A BLUEBIRD 1
    THE WAY A CROW . . . . 221 DUST OF SNOW . . . 1
    ENVOI TO HYDE THE CASTAWAY OF CROW ISLAND . . . . . 466 SOME SCIENCE FICTION . 0
CROWD
    BUT MERCIFULLY KEPT THE PASSING CROWD . . . . 284 THE GOLD HESPERIDEE . 56
    FRIENDS CROWD AROUND ME WITH THEIR FIVE-YEAR PLANS . . 323 BUILD SOIL . . . 222
    BUT THIS WAS A FAMILY CROWD, ... 365 A NATURE NOTE . . . 7
    AND CROWD THEM OUT AT A SIMILAR RATE. . . . . 376 SOMETHING FOR HOPE . 8
    ON HOW TO CROWD BUT STILL BE KIND. . . . . 417 AMERICA IS HARD TO SEE 42
CROWDED
    INVISIBLE HANDS CROWDED ON HER SHOULDER . . . . . 256 THE LOVELY BE CHOOSERS 12
    WILL HAVE CROWDED OUT THE EDIBLE GRASS. . . . . . . 376 SOMETHING FOR HOPE . 4
CROWDING
    TOO CROWDING, TOO CONFUSING-- . . . . 336 CARPE DIEM . . . 25
CROWN
    I FEAR, THE CROWN OF RULE, ... 252 THE PEACEFUL SHEPHERD . 6
    THE CROSS, THE CROWN, THE SCALES MAY ALL . . . . . 252 THE PEACEFUL SHEPHERD . 11
    FROM, SAY, THE CROSS OR CROWN. . . . . 384 MAKING CERTAIN ANYTHING 12
    AND HAVE WON THE CROWN, ... 437 KITTY HAWK 302
    I'M GETTING OUT TONIGHT. HERE, TAKE THE CROWN." . . 453 HOW HARD TO KEEP FROM 3
    SO THE CROWN FELL AND THE CROWN JEWELS SCATTERED. . . 453 HOW HARD TO KEEP FROM 6
    MY CROWN SHALL OVERTAKE ME, YOU WILL SEE; . . . . . 454 HOW HARD TO KEEP FROM 26
    "WE SHOULD HAVE BROUGHT THE CROWN ALONG TO PAWN." . . 454 HOW HARD TO KEEP FROM 29
CROWS
    THE CROWS ABOVE THE FOREST CALL; . . . . 27 OCTOBER 5
CRUCIFIX
    LIKE A HERMIT'S CRUCIFIX; . . . . 11 TO THE THAWING WIND . 10
    ON THE WET FLAGS BEFORE A CRUCIFIX . . . . 516 A MASQUE OF MERCY . 614
CRUDE
    OF CRUDE URANIUM. . . . . 464 MILKY WAY IS A COWPATH 12
CRUDELY
    WE SOUGHT HOWEVER CRUDELY TO DEFEAT . . . . . . 446 DOES NO ONE AT ALL EVER 11
CRUEL
    CRUEL--IT SOUNDS. I S'POSE THEY DID THE BEST . . . 66 A SERVANT TO SERVANTS . 124
    "'NATURE IS CRUEL, MAN IS SICK OF BLOOD': . . . . 170 NEW HAMPSHIRE . . . 371
    I PROMISED TOFFILE TO BE CRUEL TO THEM . . . . . 206 THE WITCH OF COOS . 133
    FOR HELPING THEM BE CRUEL ONCE TO HIM. . . . . . 206 THE WITCH OF COOS . 134
    TO INGENUITY FOR BEING SO CRUEL . . . . 320 BUILD SOIL . . . 124
CRUELTY
    A CRUELTY, AMOUNTING TO INJUSTICE . . . . 520 A MASQUE OF MERCY . 712
CRUISE
    HAD THE QUEEN BACKED HIM TO A CRUISE. . . . . . 416 AMERICA IS HARD TO SEE 6
CRUMBLING
    AND FOR BACK WALL A CRUMBLING OLD CHIMNEY . . . . 294 A RECORD STRIDE . . 3
CRUMBS
    SHOULDERING ITS WAY AND SHEDDING THE EARTH CRUMBS. . . 124 PUTTING IN THE SEED . 14
CRUMPLE
    CRUMPLE HIM ON THE FLOOR. KEEPER AND PAUL . . . . 518 A MASQUE OF MERCY . 651
CRUMPLED
    LIKE A WHITE CRUMPLED SPIDER ON HIS KNEE: . . . . 147 SNOW 115
    PUSHING THE CRUMPLED WATER UP AHEAD, ... 338 THE MOST OF IT . . . 17
    LIKE THE CRUMPLED, BETTER- . . . . 428 KITTY HAWK . . . 19
CRUMPLING
    YOU, CRUMPLING FOLKS'S LEGAL DOCUMENTS. . . . . . 99 THE SELF-SEEKER . . . 196
CRUNCHING
    WE TROD UNCOMFORTABLY ON CRUNCHING GLASS . . . . . 216 A FOUNTAIN, A BOTTLE . 89
CRUSH
    FAILED TO CRUSH THEIR BARREL STAVES . . . . . . 344 DISCOVERY OF MADEIRAS . 28
CRUSHED
    BEARING IT CRUSHED AND MYSTIFIED. . . . . 21 THE TRIAL BY EXISTENCE 72
    ALL SONG OF THE WOODS IS CRUSHED LIKE SOME . . . . 26 A LINE-STORM SONG . 13
    PERMIT ME." AND HE CRUSHED IT UNDER HIS HEEL . . . . 456 HOW HARD TO KEEP FROM 84
CRUST
    SHATTERING AND AVALANCHING ON THE SNOW CRUST-- . . . 121 BIRCHES 11
    AND BLEW HIM OUT ON THE ICY CRUST . . . . 137 BROWN'S DESCENT . . 11
    SHOULD TAKE THE POLISH OFF THE CRUST. . . . . . . 139 BROWN'S DESCENT . . 59
    WAS ENTERED, AND ITS INNER CRUST . . . . 332 ALL REVELATION . . . 12
    THE BRIDE WHO SHARED THE CRUST HE BROKE TO EAT, . . . 359 THE LOST FOLLOWER . . 23
CRUSTED
    OUT OVER THE CRUSTED SNOW, ... 30 RELUCTANCE . . . 11
CRUTCH
    THE WAY A MAN WITH ONE LEG AND A CRUTCH, ... 204 THE WITCH OF COOS . 52
    TO WEAR A CRUTCH. . . . . 389 ASTROMETAPHYSICAL . . 8
CRY
    EACH CIRCLING EACH WITH VAGUE UNEARTHLY CRY, ... 14 WAITING 12
    CAN BUT GIVE EAR TO THAT SWEET CRY . . . . 20 THE TRIAL BY EXISTENCE 23
    ITS MOTHER WOULDN'T LET IT CRY LIKE THAT, ... 154 SNOW 320
    WELL, THEY REMIND ME OF THE HUE AND CRY . . . . . 168 NEW HAMPSHIRE . . . 294
    NO VOICE IN NATURE IS HEARD TO CRY ALOUD . . . . . 249 ACCEPTANCE . . . 3
    WHEN FAR AWAY AN INTERRUPTED CRY . . . . 255 ACQUAINTED WITH NIGHT . 8
    BUT CARRIES NO CRY OF WHAT IS HOPED TO BE. . . . . 300 STRONG SAYING NOTHING . 14
    HE WOULD CRY OUT ON LIFE, THAT WHAT IT WANTS . . . 338 THE MOST OF IT . . 6
    HOW THEY MAKE HASTE TO CRY WITH FINGERS CROSSED, . . 399 U.S. 1946 KING'S X . 3
    A SUPERSTITIOUS CRY FOR FARMERS' LUCK-- . . . . . 407 FROM PLANE TO PLANE . 118
    I CRY, "DO WORK FOR WOMEN--ALL THE HELP . . . . . 447 DOES NO ONE AT ALL EVER 28
CRYING
    YOU WON'T GO NOW. YOU'RE CRYING. CLOSE THE DOOR. . . 54 HOME BURIAL 109
    "WHAT DO YOU SAY IT IS?" / "A BABY'S CRYING! . . . 154 SNOW 318
    ALL CRYING, "WE WILL GO WITH YOU, O WIND!" . . . . 236 MISGIVING 1
    THE WORLD SEEMS CRYING OUT FOR A MESSIAH. . . . . 515 A MASQUE OF MERCY . 576
CRYPT
    THE CRYPT WAS LONG SINCE RIFLED BY THE GREEKS. . . . 483 A MASQUE OF REASON . 284

CRYSTAL
     THE CRYSTAL PALACE, LONDON. HE'S IMPORTED. . . . . .   86 THE HOUSEKEEPER . . . 151
     SOON THE SUN'S WARMTH MAKES THEM SHED CRYSTAL SHELLS . . 121 BIRCHES   10
     I JUDGED THAT SUCH A CRYSTAL CHILL . . . .   233 LOOKING FOR SUNSET BIRD 14
     AND SHOW ON THE WATER ITS CRYSTAL TEETH. . . . . . .   276 TWO TRAMPS IN MUD TIME   40
     I WOULD BUILD MY HOUSE OF CRYSTAL, ...   384 IN THE LONG NIGHT . .   1
CRYSTALS
     OF CRYSTALS WITH A RAY CATHODE . . . .   332 ALL REVELATION . . .   13
CTESIPHON
     THE CITY SAYING IT WAS CTESIPHON, ...   399 THE INGENUITIES OF DEBT   6
     THE NIGHT WE RAN AWAY FROM CTESIPHON), ...   462 HOW HARD TO KEEP FROM   270
CUBAN
     THAT NATIONS LIKE THE CUBAN AND THE SWISS . . . . .   398 NO HOLY WARS FOR THEM . 11
CUBITS
     THE THOUGHT THAT ADDED CUBITS TO YOUR HEIGHT . . . .   506 A MASQUE OF MERCY . . 339
CULEBRA
     AND LOCK HIM THROUGH CULEBRA CUT, ...   418 AMERICA IS HARD TO SEE 57
CULT
     THE CULT OF ONE WHO OWNED HIMSELF "A FOILED . . . . .   171 NEW HAMPSHIRE . . . 383
CULTIVATED
     AT HAVING CULTIVATED ROCK. . . . .   238 PLOWMEN   4
CULTURES
     OF COUNTRY WHERE TWO VILLAGE CULTURES FADED . . . .   378 DIRECTIVE   34
CUMAEAN
     CUMAEAN SIBYL, CHARMING OGRESS, ...   449 OUR DOOM TO BLOOM . .   1
CUMBERSOME
     HAS NEVER AVAILED THE CUMBERSOME GRINDSTONE . . . . .   188 THE GRINDSTONE . . .   2
CUNNING
     IT RAN WITH TERROR AND WITH CUNNING CREPT. . . . . .   357 A CONSIDERABLE SPECK . 19
CUNNINGLY
     WAS CUNNINGLY DEVISED TO MAKE A NOISE . . . .   98 THE SELF-SEEKER . . 164
     YOU KNOW HOW CUNNINGLY MANKIND IS PLANNED: . . . . .   371 THE LITERATE FARMER AND 112
     CUNNINGLY MINUTE. . . . .   426 A NEVER NAUGHT SONG .   20
CUP
     SORRY THERE IS NO CUP TO GIVE YOU A DRINK. . . . . .   50 A HUNDRED COLLARS . 155
     THE PITCHER'S TOO FULL FOR HER.--THERE'S NO CUP? . . .   99 THE SELF-SEEKER . . 173
     WITH THE SAME PAINS YOU USE TO FILL A CUP . . . . .   122 BIRCHES   37
     OR LET'S SAY THE CUP, ...   437 KITTY HAWK . . . 303
CUPBOARD
     THE LITTLE TIN BOX ON THE CUPBOARD SHELF-- . . . . .   86 THE HOUSEKEEPER . . 143
CUPPED
     WITH SNOWBALLS CUPPED IN EVERY OPENING BUD. . . . . .   239 OUR SINGING STRENGTH . 15
CURB (SEE WELL-CURB)
     I ELECT YOU TO PUT THE CURB ON IT. . . . .   320 BUILD SOIL . . . 126
CURBS (SEE WELL-CURBS)
CURD
     MATTER MUSTN'T CURD, ...   442 KITTY HAWK 448
CURE
     CAN CURE ME OF TO GO AGAIN." THE SAME . . . . . .   230 NOT TO KEEP   17
     PUT UP TO CURE THE WORLD BY MR. EDISON." . . . . .   371 THE LITERATE FARMER AND 93
     THE DROUGHT WAS ONE NO SPIT OF RAIN COULD CURE. . . .   400 THE BROKEN DROUGHT .   10
     WHOSE CURE WILL LIE IN GETTING HER IDEA . . . . . .   499 A MASQUE OF MERCY . 160
CURIOSITY
     TO SATISFY A LIFELONG CURIOSITY . . . .   168 NEW HAMPSHIRE . . 304
     TO SATISFY A LIFELONG CURIOSITY . . . .   177 THE STAR-SPLITTER . . 18
CURIOUS
     RIGHT ON THE TOP, TIP-TOP--A CURIOUS THING. . . . . .   42 THE MOUNTAIN   47
     ANTS ARE A CURIOUS RACE; . . . .   288 DEPARTMENTAL . . .   13
     I'M CURIOUS. AND I'M A GROWN-UP MAN: . . . .   482 A MASQUE OF REASON . 255
CURL
     TO CURL A LITTLE FINGER ROUND, ...   123 PEA BRUSH   18
     THAT AND THE MEREST CURL OF CIGARETTE SMOKE-- . . . .   131 THE BONFIRE   50
     NEW HAMPSHIRE MOUNTAINS CURL UP IN A COIL. . . . . .   165 NEW HAMPSHIRE . . 214
     LIKE THE CURL AT THE CORNER OF A SMILE; . . . . . .   335 I COULD GIVE ALL . .   8
CURLED
     THE OTHER CURLED AT HIS BREAST. HE DIPPED HIS HEAD . .   223 THE RUNAWAY   4
     AND HEAD TO TAIL THEN FIRMLY CURLED . . . .   419 ONE MORE BREVITY . .   17
     SO SCORNFULLY CURLED, ...   447 THE BAD ISLAND--EASTER   9
CURLED-UP
     I KNOW I LOOKED LONG AT MY CURLED-UP FINGERS, ...   198 WILD GRAPES   87
CURLS
     THE WAY A PLAYER CURLS AROUND A FOOTBALL. . . . . .   278 THE WHITE-TAILED HORNET 39
CURRENT
     THE TRIBUTE OF THE CURRENT TO THE SOURCE. . . . . .   260 WEST-RUNNING BROOK .   70
     LOOK AT HOW FAR WE'VE LEFT THE CURRENT SCIENCE . . .   480 A MASQUE OF REASON . 194
CURRENTS
     A FLOWER TO TRY ITS CURRENTS WHERE THEY CROSSED. . . . 231 A BROOK IN THE CITY .   8
     IT WILL START HAIR-RAISING CURRENTS OF AIR . . . . .   306 A TRIAL RUN   2
CURRITUCK
     OVER CURRITUCK. . . . .   431 KITTY HAWK . . . 110
CURRY
     TO CURRY FAVOR WITH THE DIRT SOME MORE. . . . . . .   405 FROM PLANE TO PLANE .   43
CURSE
     OR FOR THE RICH A CURSE; . . . .   8 LOVE AND A QUESTION .   28
     AND CURSE ME IF HE WASN'T IN THE KITCHEN . . . . . .   72 THE CODE   96
     I SHOULD NOT CURSE MYSELF WITH IT TO HELL, ...   350 THE LESSON FOR TODAY .   4
     BUT HOW TO TAKE THE CURSE, TRAGIC OR COMIC. . . . . . 352 THE LESSON FOR TODAY . 62
     WHO ROSE FROM THE MILKING STOOL WITH A CURSE . . . .   463 LINES IN DEJECTION .   15
CURSED
     I'M CURSED. GOD, IF I DON'T BELIEVE I'M CURSED." . . .   54 HOME BURIAL   90
     HE HAS CURSED EVERY RIVER MOUTH . . . .   418 AMERICA IS HARD TO SEE 53
     CURSED BE THE ERA THAT CONGESTED IT. . . . .   496 A MASQUE OF MERCY . . 67
CURST
     AND BE ALL PLUNDERERS CURST. . . . .   312 THE VINDICTIVES . . . 80
CURTAIN
     BUT READ IT, READ IT.--THAT'S RIGHT, DRAW THE CURTAIN: . . 99 THE SELF-SEEKER . . 193
     I HAD A GLIMPSE THROUGH CURTAIN LACES . . . .   102 GOOD HOURS   7
     BUT LET ME RAISE THIS CURTAIN ON A SCENE. . . . . .   148 SNOW 155

CURTAIN (CONTINUED)
    "BEFORE YOU DROP THE CURTAIN--I'M REMINDED: . . . . . . 149 SNOW 172
    LIKE A SHADOW AGAINST THE CURTAIN OF FALLING FLAKES. . . . 223 THE RUNAWAY . . . 8
    MY WINDOW CURTAIN HUNG OVER THE SILL TO WET; . . . . . 236 VALLEY'S SINGING DAY . 17
    BUT LET THERE NEVER BE ANY CURTAIN DRAWN . . . . 251 TREE AT MY WINDOW . 3
    TO BE THE CURTAIN OF THE INMOST SOUL. . . . . 385 THE FEAR OF GOD . . 13
    PULLS DOWN THE WINDOW CURTAIN ON THE DOOR . . . . 493 A MASQUE OF MERCY . 2
    ON THE BLANK CURTAIN ON THE OUTER DOOR.) . . . . 502 A MASQUE OF MERCY . 239
    BUT ONE THING MORE BEFORE THE CURTAIN FALLS.-- . . . . 519 A MASQUE OF MERCY . 672
    (THE CURTAIN STARTS TO FALL.) PLEASE HOLD THE CURTAIN.-- 519 A MASQUE OF MERCY . 673
    CURTAIN . . . . 521 A MASQUE OF MERCY . 739
CURTAINS
    DOORS LOCKED AND CURTAINS DRAWN WILL MAKE NO DIFFERENCE. . 89 THE FEAR 16
CURVATURE
    AS IF SHE HAD SOME SORT OF CURVATURE, ... 49 A HUNDRED COLLARS . 143
CURVE
    HOLDING THE CURVE OF ONE POSITION, ... 247 DEVOTION 3
    THE CURVE OF EARTH, AND STRIKING, BREAK THEIR OWN; . . . 261 A SOLDIER 10
    THE PARABOLIC CURVE . . . . 464 MILKY WAY IS A COWPATH 21
CURVED
    HE THOUGHT IF HE COULD HAVE HIS SPACE ALL CURVED, . . . 396 ANY SIZE WE PLEASE . 9
    SOMEONE TOOK CURVED NAIL-SCISSORS AND SNIPPED OFF . . . 501 A MASQUE OF MERCY . 201
CURVES
    EXPRESSED THEM, AND ITS CURVES WERE NO FALSE CURVES . . . 187 THE AX-HELVE . . . 74
    WITH THE CURVES OF HIS AX-HELVES AND HIS HAVING . . . . 188 THE AX-HELVE . . . 87
    THE PLANETS SEEM TO INTERFERE IN THEIR CURVES, ... 268 ON LOOKING UP BY CHANCE 6
CURVING
    THE SECOND ROUND THE CURVING HILLSIDE ROAD . . . . . . 74 THE GENERATIONS OF MEN 29
CUSTOMER
    AND LOCKS THE DOOR. ONE CUSTOMER, LOCKED IN, ... 493 A MASQUE OF MERCY . 3
CUSTOMS
    THE THINGS FORBIDDEN THAT WHILE THE CUSTOMS SLEPT . . . 335 I COULD GIVE ALL . 13
CUT (SEE NEW-CUT)
    WHERE ITS BLACK BODY CUT INTO THE SKY. . . . . 40 THE MOUNTAIN . . . 4
    WHO WANTS TO CUT YOUR NUMBER FOURTEEN THROAT! . . . . 47 A HUNDRED COLLARS . 84
    "YOU KNOW WHERE THEY CUT OFF THE WOODS--LET ME SEE-- . 59 BLUEBERRIES . . . 9
    CUT SHORT OFF AT BOTH ENDS. IT LIES FIVE MILES . . . . 63 A SERVANT TO SERVANTS 21
    "IT RESTS WITH US ALWAYS TO CUT HER OFF." . . . . . . 80 THE GENERATIONS OF MEN 183
    IT'S AS SOUND AS THE DAY WHEN IT WAS CUT-- . . . . . 80 THE GENERATIONS OF MEN 193
    BEING CUT OFF FROM FRIENDS?" / "WE HAVE OUR FRIENDS. . . 87 THE HOUSEKEEPER . . 169
    OR FUMBLE FOR MY KNIFE TO CUT AWAY, ... 93 THE SELF-SEEKER . . 25
    IT WAS A CORD OF MAPLE, CUT AND SPLIT . . . . 101 THE WOOD-PILE . . 23
    "I COULD SOON TELL HOW MANY THEY WOULD CUT, ... 106 CHRISTMAS TREES . . 30
    AND CUT A FLOWER BESIDE A GROUNDBIRD'S NEST . . . . . 126 RANGE-FINDING . . 2
    AND CUT THEM OFF FROM WINDOW LIGHT. . . . . 135 LOCKED OUT . . . 3
    HE SAW ALL SPOILED. "DON'T LET HIM CUT MY HAND OFF-- . 137 "OUT,OUT--" . . . 25
    THEY THROW A FOREST DOWN LESS CUT THAN BROKEN. . . . . 141 THE LINE-GANG . . 2
    THE ONLY DWELLING IN A WASTE CUT OVER . . . . 174 THE CENSUS-TAKER . 4
    WE DON'T CUT OFF FROM COMING TO CHURCH SUPPERS, . . . 178 THE STAR-SPLITTER . 49
    AND CUTTING NOTHING NOT CUT DOWN ALREADY. . . . . . . 185 THE AX-HELVE . . . 9
    DE SECOND GROWT' I CUT MYSELF--TOUGH, TOUGH!" . . . . 186 THE AX-HELVE . . . 31
    THE HEADSTONE CUT WITH JOHN, BELOVED HUSBAND, ... 200 PLACE FOR A THIRD . 39
    ALL WINTER, CUT OFF BY A HILL FROM THE HOUSE. . . . . 228 GOOD-BY AND KEEP COLD . 5
    SHE HOPES TO CUT OFF MIND. . . . . 260 SAND DUNES . . . 12
    THAT CUT THE SNOUT IN HALF, ... 340 THE SUBVERTED FLOWER . 46
    TO DOUBLE DAY AND CUT IN HALF THE DARK . . . . 375 A YOUNG BIRCH . . 5
    AND ZEAL WOULD NOT BE THANKED THAT CUT IT DOWN . . . . 375 A YOUNG BIRCH . . 19
    THEN CUT DOWN THE TREES WHEN LUMBER GROWN, ... 376 SOMETHING FOR HOPE . 13
    THEY CUT THEMSELVES IN STONE FOR PERMANENT . . . . . 399 THE INGENUITIES OF DEBT 2
    HAS CUT THIS ROAD TO LAST, ... 415 CLOSED FOR GOOD . . 4
    AND LOCK HIM THROUGH CULEBRA CUT, ... 418 AMERICA IS HARD TO SEE 57
    SHE'LL GET HER GULLET CUT, ... 465 MILKY WAY IS A COWPATH 38
CUT-GLASS
    WAS LATELY AT A CUT-GLASS DINNER IN BOSTON. . . . . . 163 NEW HAMPSHIRE . . . 127
CUTTER
    THE CUTTER BAR HAD JUST GONE CHAMPING OVER . . . . . 109 THE EXPOSED NEST . 14
CUTTING
    AND IT WAS OLDER SURE THAN THIS YEAR'S CUTTING, . . . 101 THE WOOD-PILE . . 27
    TO THE PLACE WHERE JOHN HAS BEEN CUTTING TREES, . . . 123 PEA BRUSH 2
    AND CUTTING NOTHING NOT CUT DOWN ALREADY. . . . . . . 185 THE AX-HELVE . . . 9
    AND LET ENOUGH LIGHT INTO IT BY CUTTING . . . . . . 194 PAUL'S WIFE . . . 89
    MORE CUTTING AND HE HAD THIS IN BOTH HANDS, ... 194 PAUL'S WIFE . . . 95
    BETTER A MONTH FROM NOW WHEN CUTTING POSTS . . . . . 325 BUILD SOIL . . . 287
    HOW ONCE IN CUTTING BRUSH ALONG THE WALL . . . . . . 375 A YOUNG BIRCH . . 12
CYB'LAEAN
    BY THAT CYB'LAEAN AVENUE, ... 332 ALL REVELATION . . 4
CYCLE
    A CYCLE WE'LL SAY OF A HUNDRED YEARS. . . . . 376 SOMETHING FOR HOPE . 17
CYGNUS
    "BUT CYGNUS ISN'T IN THE ZODIAC," . . . . 407 FROM PLANE TO PLANE . 109
CYNICAL (SEE SWEET-CYNICAL)
    WAS THEIR CYNICAL THRONG . . . . 448 THE BAD ISLAND--EASTER 28
    WITH CYNICAL DARING. . . . . 449 THE BAD ISLAND--EASTER 65
CYPRIPEDIUM
    ABOUT MY CYPRIPEDIUM REGINAE; . . . . 95 THE SELF-SEEKER . . 86

D

DA
    ANOTHER MARINER, DA GAMA, ... 417 AMERICA IS HARD TO SEE 20
    THAT BETTER THAN DA GAMA'S GOLD . . . . 417 AMERICA IS HARD TO SEE 27
DABBED
    IT PUT THE FLAME TIP-DOWN AND DABBED THE GRASS . . . 131 THE BONFIRE 45
DAFT
    AND THE DAFT SUN-ASSAULTER, HE . . . . 28 MY BUTTERFLY . . . 2
    HE THINKS YOUNG WILSON A LIKELY LAD, THOUGH DAFT . . . 36 DEATH OF THE HIRED MAN 65

DAGGER
    DARKLY ADVANCED WITH A PERPETUAL DAGGER . . . . 69 THE CODE 5
DAGUERREOTYPE
    DONE SADLY FROM AN OLD DAGUERREOTYPE. . . . . 55 THE BLACK COTTAGE . . 24
DAILY
    AND TAKE OUR DAILY TIDE BATHS SMOOTH AND ROUGH. . . . . 395 ETHEREALIZING . . . 8
DALLIANCE
    IN AIRY DALLIANCE, ... 28 MY BUTTERFLY 14
DALLIED
    I DALLIED SO MUCH WITH THE THOUGHT OF SELLING. . . . . 106 CHRISTMAS TREES . . . 25
DALMATIAN
    "GUSTIE, OLD BOY, DALMATIAN GUS, ... 420 ONE MORE BREVITY . . 28
    GUSTIE--DALMATIAN GUS, THAT IS-- . . . . 420 ONE MORE BREVITY . . 40
DALTON
    IN DALTON THAT WOULD SOME DAY MAKE HIS FORTUNE. . . . 212 A FOUNTAIN, A BOTTLE . 2
DAM
    BLOOD HAS BEEN HARDER TO DAM BACK THAN WATER. . . . . 254 THE FLOOD 1
DAMN
    KEEPING HIS HEAD ABOVE. 'DAMN YE,' I SAYS, ... 72 THE CODE 77
DAMNED
    SEND US A FLOOD AND BID US BE DAMNED AND DROWN. . . . 349 OUR HOLD ON THE PLANET 6
DAMP
    THE SOIL NOW GETS A RUMPLING SOFT AND DAMP, ... 299 STRONG SAYING NOTHING. 1
DAMPER
    I AM THE DAMPER COUNTERPART OF SMOKE, ... 414 A CABIN IN THE CLEARING 15
DANA
    WHAT'S THIS? / DON'T LOSE THE PLACE. / OLD DANA LYLE, . 506 A MASQUE OF MERCY . 324
DANCE
    LIKE A LIMP ROSE-WREATH IN A FAIRY DANCE. . . . . . 28 MY BUTTERFLY 17
    WHOSE SHOES I PRIMPED TO DANCE IN!" / "AND WHERE'S JOHN?" . 81 THE HOUSEKEEPER . . 13
    WE DANCE ROUND IN A RING AND SUPPOSE, ... 362 THE SECRET SITS . . 1
    OR SING AND DANCE ALL NIGHT AND SEE SUNRISE . . . . . 496 A MASQUE OF MERCY . 71
DANCED
    AND DANCED IN YELLOW WRIGGLERS ON THE CEILING, ... 117 IN THE HOME STRETCH . 203
    AS MUCH AT HOME AS IF THEY'D ALWAYS DANCED THERE. . . . 117 IN THE HOME STRETCH . 204
    DANCED SLOWLY ON IT TILL HE TROD IT FLAT. . . . . . . 284 THE GOLD HESPERIDEE . 48
DANCES
    STANDS STILL AND DANCES, BUT IT RUNS AWAY; . . . . . 259 WEST-RUNNING BROOK . 47
    HE DANCES UPRIGHT . . . . 261 CANIS MAJOR 5
DANCING
    BENEATH THE FEET OF DANCING FLOWERS. . . . . 26 IN HARDWOOD GROVES . 10
    THEN CAME IN DANCING, SKIPPING WITH HIS LIFE . . . . 170 NEW HAMPSHIRE . . . 349
    GOD SAW HIM DANCING IN THE ORCHARD PATH, ... 284 THE GOLD HESPERIDEE . 55
DANGER
    IN TIME, HAD SHE NOT REALIZED HER DANGER . . . . . . 187 THE AX-HELVE 51
    WASN'T THERE DANGER OF A TURN TOO MUCH? . . . . . . 191 THE GRINDSTONE . . . 73
    MUCH DANGER OF MY PICKING ANYTHING! . . . . 198 WILD GRAPES 59
    EACH SWUNG IN DANGER ON ITS SLENDER TWIG, ... 283 THE GOLD HESPERIDEE . 23
    TO WARN AGAINST THE DANGER . . . . 335 CARPE DIEM 14
    THE LOSS TO SONG, THE DANGER OF DEFECTION . . . . . 358 THE LOST FOLLOWER . 9
    THE DANGER NOT AN INCH OUTSIDE . . . . 363 ASSURANCE 1
DANGEROUS
    DANGEROUS SELF-AROUSING WORDS TO SOW. . . . . 180 MAPLE 29
    WERE A DANGEROUS THING TO BEAR. . . . . 313 BEARER OF EVIL TIDINGS 4
    WITH SUCH IT HAS PROVED DANGEROUS AS FRIEND . . . . . 359 THE LOST FOLLOWER . 25
DANGEROUSLY
    THE MISSED FLY MADE ME DANGEROUSLY SKEPTIC. . . . . . 279 THE WHITE-TAILED HORNET 49
DANGLE
    AND DANGLE FEET AMONG THE RASPBERRY VINES?" . . . . . 75 THE GENERATIONS OF MEN 64
DANGLING
    DANGLING THEIR LEGS AND FISHING OFF A WHARF . . . . . 161 NEW HAMPSHIRE . . . 75
DANIEL
    SHE HAD ONE DANIEL WEBSTER. HE WAS ALL . . . . . . 161 NEW HAMPSHIRE . . . 67
    THE DANIEL WEBSTER EVER WAS OR SHALL BE. . . . . . . 161 NEW HAMPSHIRE . . . 68
DAPPLED
    THE GRAY GRASS IS SCARCE DAPPLED WITH THE SNOW; . . . 28 MY BUTTERFLY 8
DARE
    "I DARE NOT--TOO FAR IN HIS FOOTSTEPS STRAY-- . . . . 16 A DREAM PANG . . . 7
    OF DARING SHOULD BE STILL TO DARE. . . . . 19 THE TRIAL BY EXISTENCE 8
    TO PUT IT THE RIGHT WAY. HE'D NEVER DARE-- . . . . . 90 THE FEAR 37
    TILL I SHAN'T DARE TO SET A FOOT OUTDOORS. . . . . . 90 THE FEAR 47
    SHE DIDN'T DARE TO SPEAK WHEN HE WAS HERE. . . . . . 153 SNOW 293
    BUT GIVE HER FRIENDS, FOR THEN SHE DARE NOT TELL . . . 257 THE LOVELY BE CHOOSERS 35
    BUT IF YOU SO MUCH AS DARE TO SPEAK, ... 275 TWO TRAMPS IN MUD TIME 21
    MAKE BOLD TO SING IT SO, BUT DO I DARE . . . . . . 317 BUILD SOIL 42
    DARE TO SPEAK OUT AND TELL ME ABOUT MYSELF. . . . . . 456 HOW HARD TO KEEP FROM 100
    I SHOULD DARE SAY SHE WOULD BE TAKEN CARE OF. . . . . 519 A MASQUE OF MERCY . 687
DARED
    TO LISTEN ERE WE DARED TO LOOK, ... 18 GOING FOR WATER . . 18
    THE NIGHT CLERK BLINKED HIS EYES AND DARED HIM ON. . . 45 A HUNDRED COLLARS . . 28
    LOWE IS THE ONLY DOCTOR'S DARED TO SAY SO-- . . . . . 64 A SERVANT TO SERVANTS 48
    THERE WAS NO ONE THAT DARED TO STIR HIM UP-- . . . . 72 THE CODE 100
    "I HAVEN'T DARED TO LOOK AT THEM UNCOVERED. . . . . . 93 THE SELF-SEEKER . . 18
    BUT DARED NOT SPARE TO DO THE BEST WE COULD . . . . . 109 THE EXPOSED NEST . . 28
    I FOUND NO PEOPLE THAT DARED SHOW THEMSELVES, ... 174 THE CENSUS-TAKER . . 15
    THUS TILL HE HAD THEM ALMOST FEELING DARED . . . . . 230 TWO LOOK AT TWO . . 35
    SHE DARED NO MORE THAN ASK HIM WITH HER EYES . . . . 231 NOT TO KEEP . . . 19
    I NEVER DARED BE RADICAL WHEN YOUNG . . . . 308 PRECAUTION 1
    SHE DARED NOT STIR A FOOT, ... 340 THE SUBVERTED FLOWER . 31
    BUT DARED NOT TELL HER ALL ONE DAY. . . . . 347 DISCOVERY OF MADEIRAS . 115
    AND DARED TO TASTE THE WOUND A LITTLE KNOWS. . . . . 411 POD OF THE MILKWEED . 18
DARES
    NO SENATOR DARES IN TO KICK ASUNDER. . . . . 362 SYMPATHY WITH UNDER DOG 3
    THE ONLY NATIVE TREE THAT DARES TO LEAN, ... 375 A YOUNG BIRCH . . . 8
DARING
    OF DARING SHOULD BE STILL TO DARE. . . . . 19 THE TRIAL BY EXISTENCE 8
    AND A SHOUT GREETS THE DARING ONE. . . . . 21 THE TRIAL BY EXISTENCE 48
    FOR THE EMBOLDENED POLITICIANS DARING . . . . 424 FOR JOHN F. KENNEDY . 61

DARING (CONTINUED)
  WITH CYNICAL DARING. . . . . 449 THE BAD ISLAND--EASTER   65
DARIUS
  LIKE DARIUS GREEN . . . . 443 KITTY HAWK 470
  "BUT TELL US HOW YOU KNEW," DARIUS CRIED. . . . . . 456 HOW HARD TO KEEP FROM   86
  I AM ABJECT BEFORE YOU," SAID DARIUS. . . . . 458 HOW HARD TO KEEP FROM   145
  "SO MUCH FOR PROGRESS," SAID DARIUS MEEKLY. . . . . 459 HOW HARD TO KEEP FROM   162
  THE HEADSMAN HAS DARIUS BY THE BELT . . . . 462 HOW HARD TO KEEP FROM   261
  BUT THAT IS AS DARIUS SEEMS TO WANT IT. . . . . . . 462 HOW HARD TO KEEP FROM   264
DARK (SEE ANTI-DARK, PITCH-DARK)
  ONE OF MY WISHES IS THAT THOSE DARK TREES, ...   5 INTO MY OWN   1
  THINKS THESE DARK DAYS OF AUTUMN RAIN . . . .   6 MY NOVEMBER GUEST . . .   2
  WHEN THE WIND WORKS AGAINST US IN THE DARK, ...   9 STORM FEAR   1
  TO COME AGAIN AT DARK. . . . . 10 WIND AND WINDOW FLOWER   12
  THEY MUST GO DOWN INTO THE DARK DECAYED. . . . . . 26 IN HARDWOOD GROVES . .   8
  HE THINKS IT'S DARK, AND IT'S FLOODED WITH DAYLIGHT." 77 THE GENERATIONS OF MEN 102
  NEARBY, ALL DARK IN EVERY GLOSSY WINDOW. . . . . . 89 THE FEAR   4
  TO THE DARK HOUSE AFTER SO LONG AN ABSENCE, ... 89 THE FEAR   18
  "IT'S NOT SO VERY LATE--IT'S ONLY DARK. . . . . . . 90 THE FEAR   29
  "WHAT DO YOU WANT?" SHE CRIED TO ALL THE DARK. . . 91 THE FEAR   61
  YOU CAN TONIGHT, AND GO. IT'S ALMOST DARK; . . . . 111 IN THE HOME STRETCH   16
  HOW DARK IT'S GETTING. CAN YOU TELL WHAT TIME . . . 113 IN THE HOME STRETCH   67
  THE HOUSE WAS FULL OF TRAMPING, AND THE DARK, . . . 113 IN THE HOME STRETCH   82
  SHE HAD NO SAYING DARK ENOUGH . . . . 128 THE OFT-REPEATED DREAM   1
  FOR THE DARK PINE THAT KEPT . . . . 128 THE OFT-REPEATED DREAM   2
  DOWN DARK CONVERGING PATHS BETWEEN THE PINES. . . . 129 THE BONFIRE   7
  THE DOCTOR PUT HIM IN THE DARK OF ETHER. . . . . . 137 "OUT,OUT--"   28
  THE ILLIMITABLE DARK AND COLD AND STORM, ... 148 SNOW   144
  COLE HAD BEEN TELEPHONING IN THE DARK. . . . . . . 152 SNOW   270
  AND THE FIRE'S DIED AND THE ROOM'S DARK AND COLD?" 154 SNOW   310
  HE WAS NOT USED TO HANDLING STARS THROWN DARK . . . 172 A STAR IN A STONEBOAT .   8
  AND CAME SO NEAR DEATH IN THE DARK OF YEARS, . . . 180 MAPLE   37
  AND THERE, WELL AFTER DARK, LET MURPHY TELL IT, . . 195 PAUL'S WIFE   127
  (THE KITCHEN HAD BEEN DARK) I HAD TO OWN . . . . . 205 THE WITCH OF COOS . .   98
  THAT'S WHAT I SIT UP IN THE DARK TO SAY-- . . . . . 206 THE WITCH OF COOS . .   130
  I MADE HIM DO IT FOR ME IN THE DARK. . . . . 210 PAUPER WITCH OF GRAFTON   99
  IT'S THE OLD CAPTAIN'S DARK FATE . . . . 212 AN EMPTY THREAT . . .   43
  THE WOODS ARE LOVELY, DARK, AND DEEP, ... 224 STOPPING BY WOODS . .   13
  AS MAY BE IN DARK WOODS, AND WITH A SONG . . . . . 226 THE ONSET   3
  THIS SAYING GOOD-BY ON THE EDGE OF THE DARK . . . . 228 GOOD-BY AND KEEP COLD .   1
  BUT UP BY ROOTS TO BRING DARK FOLIAGE ON. . . . . . 245 SPRING POOLS   6
  NOW LET THE NIGHT BE DARK FOR ALL OF ME.. . . . . . 249 ACCEPTANCE   12
  LET THE NIGHT BE TOO DARK FOR ME TO SEE . . . . . . 249 ACCEPTANCE   13
  IT LOOKED AS IF A NIGHT OF DARK INTENT . . . . . . 250 ONCE BY THE PACIFIC .   10
  FLECKED THE DARK STREAM AND FLECKED THE DARKER POOL 258 WEST-RUNNING BROOK .   24
  THAT ROMPS THROUGH THE DARK. . . . . 261 CANIS MAJOR   12
  IN GOING FROM ROOM TO ROOM IN THE DARK . . . . . . 265 THE DOOR IN THE DARK .   1
  THE DOOR IN THE DARK . . . . 265 THE DOOR IN THE DARK .   T
  AGAINST THE DARK AND WIND AND COLD . . . . 281 BLUE RIBBON AT AMESBURY   54
  TO LEAN AGAINST AND HEAR IN THE DARK. . . . . 297 LEAVES COMPARED WITH .   18
  THE HEAD IN THE DARK BELOW . . . . 299 WELCOME TO THEIR BELIEF   10
  WORKS IN THE DARK AS MUCH AGAINST AS FOR US. . . . 319 BUILD SOIL   106
  THOUGH CIRCUMSTANCED WITH DARK AND DOUBT-- . . . . . 331 BEECH   11
  INSIDE IT WAS DARK. . . . . 334 COME IN   4
  TOO DARK IN THE WOODS FOR A BIRD . . . . 334 COME IN   5
  FAR IN THE PILLARED DARK . . . . 334 COME IN   13
  TO THE DARK AND LAMENT. . . . . 334 COME IN   16
  IT IS GETTING DARK AND TIME HE DREW TO A HOUSE, . . 341 WILLFUL HOMING . . .   1
  AND WENT EMBRACED TO THE COLD AND DARK . . . . . . 346 DISCOVERY OF MADEIRAS .   84
  WERE REALLY AS DARK AS I HEAR SAGES TELL, ... 350 THE LESSON FOR TODAY .   2
  TO THE WORLD'S UNDEBATABLY DARK AGES, ... 350 THE LESSON FOR TODAY .   7
  OR SHOULD I SAY THE HIGHER ONE, FOR DARK. . . . . . 352 THE LESSON FOR TODAY .   53
  WITH EQUAL DARKNESS, YOURS AS DARK AS MINE.. . . . . 354 THE LESSON FOR TODAY . 119
  BUT NOT TO TAKE AWAY THE PRECIOUS DARK. . . . . . . 370 THE LITERATE FARMER AND   79
  TO DOUBLE DAY AND CUT IN HALF THE DARK . . . . . . 375 A YOUNG BIRCH   5
  IT MAY BE A MERCY THE DARK CLOSES ROUND US . . . . 379 TOO ANXIOUS FOR RIVERS   12
  SO REGULAR THAT IN THE DARK . . . . 380 AN UNSTAMPED LETTER IN   10
  HAVE SET THE DARK ASIDE FOR HERS. . . . . 390 TWO LEADING LIGHTS . .   15
  HE STRETCHED HIS ARMS OUT TO THE DARK OF SPACE . . 396 ANY SIZE WE PLEASE . .   5
  SINCE DARK IS WHAT BRINGS OUT YOUR LIGHT. . . . . . 403 SOMETHING LIKE A STAR .   5
  FOR THE OUTER DARK . . . . 413 AWAY!   10
  LISTEN, THEY MURMUR TALKING IN THE DARK . . . . . . 415 A CABIN IN THE CLEARING   34
  OF DARK HATTERAS . . . . 431 KITTY HAWK   88
  LET THE LOST MILLIONS PRAY IT IN THE DARK! . . . . 521 A MASQUE OF MERCY . .   726
DARKEN
  TO DARKEN NATURE AND BE SUMMER WOODS-- . . . . 245 SPRING POOLS   8
DARKENED
  SHE RAN ON TIPTOE DOWN THE DARKENED PASSAGE . . . . 34 DEATH OF THE HIRED MAN   3
  TO DO WITH WHAT WAS IN THE DARKENED PARLOR? . . . . 54 HOME BURIAL   96
  AND I THINK THE SKY DARKENED WITH A CLOUD . . . . . 131 THE BONFIRE   54
  ONE LOOKS OUT LAST FROM THE DARKENED ROOM . . . . . 291 ON HEART'S BEGINNING TO   26
DARKENING
  AND YOU AREN'T DARKENING OTHER PEOPLE'S LIVES-- . . . 65 A SERVANT TO SERVANTS .   99
  TO THE DARKENING, WINDY VILLAGE SLIP. . . . . 343 DISCOVERY OF MADEIRAS .   7
DARKER
  ACROSS THE LINES OF STRAIGHTER DARKER TREES, . . . 121 BIRCHES   2
  FLECKED THE DARK STREAM AND FLECKED THE DARKER POOL 258 WEST-RUNNING BROOK .   24
  LEAVES ARE ALL MY DARKER MOOD. . . . . 297 LEAVES COMPARED WITH .   20
DARKEST
  THE DARKEST EVENING OF THE YEAR. . . . . 224 STOPPING BY WOODS . .   8
  THE DARKEST OF IT STILL TO DREAD. . . . . 383 THE NIGHT LIGHT . . .   8
  AND DAYIFY THE DARKEST REALM. . . . . 390 TWO LEADING LIGHTS . .   9
DARKLY
  DARKLY ADVANCED WITH A PERPETUAL DAGGER . . . . . . 69 THE CODE   5
  ALL OUT-OF-DOORS LOOKED DARKLY IN AT HIM . . . . . 108 OLD MAN'S WINTER NIGHT   1
  PAUL DARKLY, LIKE HER SHADOW. ALL THE LIGHT . . . . 195 PAUL'S WIFE   136
  AND DARKLY DRINK EACH OTHER'S EYES . . . . 344 DISCOVERY OF MADEIRAS .   39
  (THE DOOR HERE OPENS DARKLY OF ITSELF.) . . . . . . 514 A MASQUE OF MERCY . .   550

DARKNESS
  HE MOVES IN DARKNESS AS IT SEEMS TO ME, ... 34 MENDING WALL 41
  BUT NOW ARE GIVING UP FOR COUNTRY DARKNESS." . . . . . 112 IN THE HOME STRETCH . 59
  WITH ROCK AND WASHOUT, AND UNSAFE IN DARKNESS; . . . . . 229 TWO LOOK AT TWO . . . 6
  IN FETID DARKNESS STILL TO LIVE AND RUN-- . . . . 231 A BROOK IN THE CITY . 17
  IT IS THE CHANGE TO DARKNESS IN THE SKY. . . . . 249 ACCEPTANCE 5
  INTO THE DARKNESS. IT GRIEVED MY SOUL, ... 253 THE THATCH 20
  WHAT BUT DESIGN OF DARKNESS TO APPALL?-- . . . . 302 DESIGN 13
  IF I SHED SUCH A DARKNESS, ... 303 AFTERFLAKES 6
  WITH EQUAL DARKNESS, YOURS AS DARK AS MINE. . . . . . . 354 THE LESSON FOR TODAY . 119
  NEVER THE GOLD OF DARKNESS FROM A MINE. . . . . 358 THE LOST FOLLOWER . 4
  YET THERE TO WATCH THE DARKNESS COMING ON-- . . . . . . 368 THE LITERATE FARMER AND 16
  A DARKNESS OUT OF ASIA THAT HAD CROSSED . . . . 511 A MASQUE OF MERCY . . 466
DARLINGS
  LIKE DARLINGS, BOTH OF THEM. THEY'RE IN THE BARN.-- . . 143 SNOW 25
DART
  NIGHT COMES; THE BLACK BATS TUMBLE AND DART; . . . . . 6 GHOST HOUSE 15
  IS THE RAY WE DART . . . . 440 KITTY HAWK 388
DARTING
  AND MAKE US HAPPY IN THE DARTING BIRD . . . . 12 A PRAYER IN SPRING . . 9
DARTMOUTH
  SHE HAD THE DARTMOUTH NEEDED TO PRODUCE HIM. . . . . . 161 NEW HAMPSHIRE . . . 69
DARWIN
  SEEMS TO HAVE BEEN A MAN NAMED JOHN L. DARWIN." . . . . 168 NEW HAMPSHIRE . . . 299
  TILL DARWIN CAME TO EARTH UPON A YEAR . . . . 425 ACCIDENTALLY ON PURPOSE 9
DARWIN'S
  AND DARWIN'S PROVED MISTAKEN, NOT THE BIBLE. . . . . . 369 THE LITERATE FARMER AND 46
DASH
  THE DOCTOR MADE A SUBDUED DASH FOR IT, ... 47 A HUNDRED COLLARS . . 73
  DASH IT WITH SOME SNOW FOR POWDER. . . . . 304 CLEAR AND COLDER . . 15
DASHBOARD
  SHE SAID, "AS THE LIGHT ON THE DASHBOARD RAN . . . . . 89 THE FEAR 10
  WITH ONE FOOT ON THE DASHBOARD OF HIS BUGGY . . . . . 404 FROM PLANE TO PLANE . 19
  FULL OF SUCCESS, WITH THAT FOOT ON THE DASHBOARD, . . . 405 FROM PLANE TO PLANE . 38
  BEHIND HER AT THE DASHBOARD OF HIS PUNG." . . . . . . 407 FROM PLANE TO PLANE . 108
DASHED
  THAT IS NOT DASHED WITH PAIN . . . . 227 TO EARTHWARD 18
DATE
  AT THAT DATE WITH A WHARF ALREADY BUILT, ... 161 NEW HAMPSHIRE . . . 84
  IN LITERATURE TO DATE IS HEARD TO COME. . . . . 167 NEW HAMPSHIRE . . . 271
  WE DATE YOU BY YOUR DEPTH IN SILT AND DUST . . . . . . 382 TO AN ANCIENT . . . 10
  GLORY IS OUT OF DATE IN LIFE AND ART. . . . . 423 FOR JOHN F. KENNEDY . 50
  ON WHICH WITH A DATE . . . . 437 KITTY HAWK 304
DATED
  A DATED POPULAR-SCIENCE MEDLEY ON A MYSTERIOUS LIGHT... 368 THE LITERATE FARMER AND 5
DATING
  A GOOD OLD-TIMER DATING BACK ALONG; . . . . 178 THE STAR-SPLITTER . . 60
DAT'S
  "SHE AIN'T SPICK TOO MUCH HENGLISH--DAT'S TOO BAD." . . 187 THE AX-HELVE 54
DAUGHTER
  SOMETHING A FATHER COULDN'T TELL A DAUGHTER . . . . . 183 MAPLE 118
  BURR HAD FOR HIS DAUGHTER: . . . . 433 KITTY HAWK 160
  AND A DAUGHTER DROWNED. . . . . 433 KITTY HAWK 182
DAUGHTERS
  I CAN'T KEEP TRACK OF OTHER PEOPLE'S DAUGHTERS. . . . 81 THE HOUSEKEEPER . . . 11
DAUNTING
  AND TURNED ON HIM WITH SUCH A DAUNTING LOOK, ... 52 HOME BURIAL 33
DAUNTLESS
  FOR THOUGHT HAS A PAIR OF DAUNTLESS WINGS. . . . . . . 120 BOND AND FREE . . . 5
DAVIS
  OLD DAVIS OWNED A SOLID MICA MOUNTAIN . . . . 212 A FOUNTAIN, A BOTTLE . 1
  THAT HAPPENS TO BE BROKEN," DAVIS SAID. . . . . 215 A FOUNTAIN, A BOTTLE . 73
  "TAKE ONE," OLD DAVIS BADE ME GRACIOUSLY. . . . . . . 217 A FOUNTAIN, A BOTTLE . 123
DAWN
  INVISIBLE AT DAWN-- . . . . 9 STARS 8
  WELL I KNOW WHERE TO HIE ME--IN THE DAWN, ... 17 THE VANTAGE POINT . . 2
  NEVERTHELESS, A MESSAGE FROM THE DAWN, ... 23 THE TUFT OF FLOWERS . 30
  WHEN I WALKED FORTH AT DAWN TO SEE NEW THINGS, ... 40 THE MOUNTAIN 8
  PRE-PRIMITIVES OF THE WHITE RACE, DAWN PEOPLE, ... 161 NEW HAMPSHIRE . . . 78
  SO DAWN GOES DOWN TO DAY. . . . . 223 NOTHING GOLD CAN STAY . 7
  ALREADY DETERMINED DAWN BEGAN TO LAY . . . . 235 VALLEY'S SINGING DAY . 7
  BUT DAWN WAS NOT TO BEGIN THEIR "PEARLY-PEARLY" . . . 236 VALLEY'S SINGING DAY . 11
  WHEN STARTING CLEAR AT DAWN . . . . 333 HAPPINESS MAKES UP . . 15
DAWNED
  THAT SLOWLY DAWNED BEHIND THE TREES, ... 18 GOING FOR WATER . . . 10
DAY
  I SHOULD NOT BE WITHHELD BUT THAT SOME DAY . . . . . 5 INTO MY OWN 5
  WHETHER 'TIS IN US TO ARISE WITH DAY . . . . 10 STORM FEAR 17
  LIKE NOTHING ELSE BY DAY, LIKE GHOSTS BY NIGHT; . . . 12 A PRAYER IN SPRING . . 6
  FOR THE AGES OF A DAY? . . . . 13 FLOWER-GATHERING . . 12
  AND TO THE FOREST EDGE YOU CAME ONE DAY . . . . 16 A DREAM PANG 3
  PAN CAME OUT OF THE WOODS ONE DAY-- . . . . 23 PAN WITH US 1
  THE ROAD IS FORLORN ALL DAY, ... 26 A LINE-STORM SONG . . 2
  BEGIN THE HOURS OF THIS DAY SLOW. . . . . 27 OCTOBER 8
  MAKE THE DAY SEEM TO US LESS BRIEF. . . . . 27 OCTOBER 9
  RELEASE ONE LEAF AT BREAK OF DAY; . . . . 27 OCTOBER 12
  AND ON A DAY WE MEET TO WALK THE LINE . . . . 33 MENDING WALL 13
  SOMETIMES HE JOINS THEM FOR A DAY OR TWO . . . . . . 44 A HUNDRED COLLARS . . 6
  'THREE FOGGY MORNINGS AND ONE RAINY DAY . . . . 54 HOME BURIAL 92
  I MET THEM ONE DAY AND EACH HAD A FLOWER . . . . . . 61 BLUEBERRIES 64
  I PROMISED MYSELF TO GET DOWN SOME DAY . . . . 62 A SERVANT TO SERVANTS . 3
  BESIDE THE LAKE FROM WHERE THAT DAY I SHOWED YOU . . 64 A SERVANT TO SERVANTS . 62
  AGAINST THE STOVE, THE HOTTEST DAY THAT SUMMER. . . . 72 THE CODE 98
  NOTHING WOULD DO BUT THEY MUST FIX A DAY . . . . . . 73 THE GENERATIONS OF MEN 15
  BUT RAIN SPOILED ALL. THE DAY BEGAN UNCERTAIN, . . . 74 THE GENERATIONS OF MEN 19
  FOLKS IN HER DAY WERE GIVEN TO PLAIN SPEAKING. . . . 79 THE GENERATIONS OF MEN 181
  IT'S AS SOUND AS THE DAY WHEN IT WAS CUT-- . . . . . 80 THE GENERATIONS OF MEN 193

DAY (CONTINUED)

HE'S FIFTY-FIVE, YOU KNOW, IF HE'S A DAY." . . . . . 83 THE HOUSEKEEPER . . . 64
THAT DAY A WOMAN COULDN'T COAX HIM OFF. . . . . . . 94 THE SELF-SEEKER . . . 37
OUT WALKING IN THE FROZEN SWAMP ONE GRAY DAY, ... 101 THE WOOD-PILE . . . 1
OH, I KEPT THE FIRST FOR ANOTHER DAY! . . . . 105 THE ROAD NOT TAKEN . . 13
THE NEWS OF A DAY I'VE FORGOTTEN-- . . . . 110 A PATCH OF OLD SNOW . . 7
WE DID THAT DAY WAS MINGLE GREAT AND SMALL . . . . . 118 MEETING AND PASSING . . 5
TILL DAY MAKES HIM RETRACE HIS FLIGHT, ... 120 BOND AND FREE . . . 13
ONCE ON THE KIND OF DAY CALLED "WEATHER BREEDER," . . 125 AN ENCOUNTER . . . 1
ONE DAY SHE ASKED HER FATHER . . . . 133 A GIRL'S GARDEN . . . 5
AND NOTHING HAPPENED: DAY WAS ALL BUT DONE. . . . . 136 "OUT,OUT--" 9
CALL IT A DAY, I WISH THEY MIGHT HAVE SAID . . . . . 136 "OUT,OUT--" 10
WE SUFFER THEM BY THE DAY . . . . 156 THE SOUND OF TREES . . 6
SOME DAY WHEN THEY ARE IN VOICE . . . . 156 THE SOUND OF TREES . . 21
I FOUND HIM STANDING AT THE CLOSE OF DAY . . . . . . 160 NEW HAMPSHIRE . . . 44
THE PLACE IS SILENT ALL DAY LONG, NOR YET . . . . . 165 NEW HAMPSHIRE . . . 189
AND CANNOT REST FROM PLANNING DAY OR NIGHT . . . . . 169 NEW HAMPSHIRE . . . 338
OF YEAR OR DAY THE WAY IT SWUNG A DOOR . . . . . . 175 THE CENSUS-TAKER . . 27
MEAN LAUGHTER WENT AROUND THE TOWN THAT DAY . . . . . 177 THE STAR-SPLITTER . . 40
AND STANDING AT OUR LEISURE TILL THE DAY BROKE, . . . 179 THE STAR-SPLITTER . . 85
WAS TO REBUKE HER TEACHER WITH IT NEXT DAY, ... 180 MAPLE 31
IT CAME BACK VAGUELY AT THE GLASS ONE DAY, ... 181 MAPLE 40
THIS WAS A MAN, BAPTISTE, WHO STOLE ONE DAY . . . . . 185 THE AX-HELVE . . . 6
ONE SUMMER DAY, ALL DAY I DROVE IT HARD, ... 189 THE GRINDSTONE . . . 23
OTHERS BECAUSE HE'D COME WITHIN A DAY . . . . 191 PAUL'S WIFE 6
THE DAY I SWUNG SUSPENDED WITH THE GRAPES, ... 196 WILD GRAPES 11
ONE DAY MY BROTHER LED ME TO A GLADE . . . . 196 WILD GRAPES 19
BETWEEN THE DEATH DAY AND THE FUNERAL DAY. . . . . . 201 PLACE FOR A THIRD . . 69
WE MADE A DAY OF IT OUT OF THE WORLD, ... 214 A FOUNTAIN, A BOTTLE . . 33
WE MAY AS WELL SEE THAT AND SAVE THE DAY." . . . . . 214 A FOUNTAIN, A BOTTLE . . 54
TO CALL IT DAY . . . . 218 I WILL SING YOU ONE-O . 6
OF A DAY I HAD RUED. . . . . 221 DUST OF SNOW . . . 8
ON VIMY RIDGE; AND WHEN YOU FELL THAT DAY . . . . . 222 TO E.T. 14
AND DID ITS LOUDEST DAY AND NIGHT . . . . 223 THE AIM WAS SONG . . 3
SO DAWN GOES DOWN TO DAY. . . . . 223 NOTHING GOLD CAN STAY . 7
IT IS BLUE-BUTTERFLY DAY HERE IN SPRING, ... 225 BLUE-BUTTERFLY DAY . . 1
BLUE-BUTTERFLY DAY . . . . 225 BLUE-BUTTERFLY DAY . . T
OF RUSTLING ALL DAY . . . . 234 GATHERING LEAVES . . 6
THE VALLEY'S SINGING DAY . . . . 235 VALLEY'S SINGING DAY . . T
NEITHER WAS SONG THAT DAY TO BE SELF-BEGUN. . . . . 236 VALLEY'S SINGING DAY . 14
THAT ONCE YOU HAD OPENED THE VALLEY'S SINGING DAY. . . 236 VALLEY'S SINGING DAY . 20
THE HILLSIDE ON THE DAY THE SUN LETS GO . . . . . . 237 A HILLSIDE THAW . . . 2
IT WAS THE MOON'S: SHE HELD THEM UNTIL DAY, ... 238 A HILLSIDE THAW . . . 33
NEXT DAY THE SCENE WAS PILED AND PUFFED AND DEAD. . . 239 OUR SINGING STRENGTH . 11
AND NOT SING BY MY HOUSE ALL DAY; . . . . 250 A MINOR BIRD . . . 2
SUMMER WAS PAST AND DAY WAS PAST. . . . . 251 BEREFT 6
THAT DAY SHE PUT OUR HEADS TOGETHER, ... 252 TREE AT MY WINDOW . . 13
THIS EDEN DAY IS DONE AT TWO O'CLOCK. . . . . . . 254 A WINTER EDEN . . . 18
AN HOUR OF WINTER DAY MIGHT SEEM TOO SHORT . . . . . 254 A WINTER EDEN . . . 19
(WEST-RUNNING BROOK MEN CALL IT THIS DAY.) . . . . . 257 WEST-RUNNING BROOK . 3
IT IS MOST US." / "TODAY WILL BE THE DAY . . . . . 260 WEST-RUNNING BROOK . 72
YOU SAID SO." / "NO, TODAY WILL BE THE DAY . . . . . 260 WEST-RUNNING BROOK . 73
"TODAY WILL BE THE DAY OF WHAT WE BOTH SAID." . . . . 260 WEST-RUNNING BROOK . 75
THAT ALL DAY FIGHTS A NERVOUS INWARD RAGE, ... 269 THE BEAR 14
ALL DAY FROM SPOOL TO LESSER SPOOL, ... 273 A LONE STRIKER . . . 21
IF THERE SHOULD EVER COME A DAY . . . . 274 A LONE STRIKER . . . 57
THAT DAY, GIVING A LOOSE TO MY SOUL, ... 275 TWO TRAMPS IN MUD TIME . 15
YOU KNOW HOW IT IS WITH AN APRIL DAY . . . . 275 TWO TRAMPS IN MUD TIME . 18
THE FULL SIX DAYS. THEN REST A DAY; . . . . 280 BLUE RIBBON AT AMESBURY 30
THAT STILL FOR ANOTHER DAY, ... 282 A DRUMLIN WOODCHUCK . . 26
BUT ONE DAY WHEN THE FOLIAGE ALL WENT SWISH . . . . 284 THE GOLD HESPERIDEE . . 32
AND BY TEACHING THEM HOW TO SLEEP THE SLEEP ALL DAY, . 287 A ROADSIDE STAND . . 30
THAT WAITS ALL DAY IN ALMOST OPEN PRAYER . . . . . . 287 A ROADSIDE STAND . . 35
AND THEN NEXT DAY AS I COME BACK INTO THE SANE, . . . 287 A ROADSIDE STAND . . 49
NEXT MORNING TO THE LIGHT OF DAY WAS MORE . . . . . 290 OLD BARN AT THE BOTTOM 26
AGAINST THE DAY OF PRISONERS' ENNUI, ... 293 AT WOODWARD'S GARDENS . 31
LEAVES BY NIGHT AND FLOWERS BY DAY. . . . . 297 LEAVES COMPARED WITH . 16
I HAVE BEEN TREADING ON LEAVES ALL DAY UNTIL I AM
    AUTUMN-TIRED. . . . . 297 A LEAF-TREADER . . . 1
THEY LOOK AT THE SEA ALL DAY. . . . . 301 NEITHER OUT FAR NOR IN 4
THE DAY SWEPT CLEARLY ON . . . . 333 HAPPINESS MAKES UP . 16
BE ALL FROM THAT ONE DAY . . . . 333 HAPPINESS MAKES UP . 20
AND SEIZE THE DAY OF PLEASURE." . . . . 335 CARPE DIEM 10
THAT FAR-OFF DAY THE LEAVES IN FLIGHT . . . . 336 THE WIND AND THE RAIN . 1
BUT I MUST FORTH AT DUSK, MY TIME OF DAY, ... 337 THE WIND AND THE RAIN . 45
THE DAY WAS THE DAY BY EVERY FLOWER THAT BLOOMS, . . . 342 QUEST OF PURPLE-FRINGED 7
TO DISTURB THEIR PERFECT POISE THE LIVELONG DAY . . . 343 QUEST OF PURPLE-FRINGED 19
WHERE ALL DAY LONG SHE LAY AND DOZED. . . . . . . 344 DISCOVERY OF MADEIRAS . 37
BUT DARED NOT TELL HER ALL ONE DAY. . . . . 347 DISCOVERY OF MADEIRAS . 115
IT SENT ME TO THE GRAVES THE OTHER DAY. . . . . . . 354 THE LESSON FOR TODAY . 127
IN ONE WILD DAY OF RAIN. . . . . 359 NOVEMBER 6
GAVE ME A STRANGELY RESTLESS DAY. . . . . 364 TRESPASS 8
THE SUN SETS THE EXAMPLE IN THE DAY." . . . . . . 370 THE LITERATE FARMER AND 74
GIVE US A GOOD CHEAP TWENTY-FOUR-HOUR DAY, ... 371 THE LITERATE FARMER AND 100
AND IF OUR GETTING UP TO START THE DAY . . . . . . 372 THE LITERATE FARMER AND 120
TO DOUBLE DAY AND CUT IN HALF THE DARK . . . . . . 375 A YOUNG BIRCH . . . 5
IT IS ON ME BY NIGHT OR DAY, ... 383 THE NIGHT LIGHT . . . 6
THERE WILL COME ANOTHER DAY. . . . . 385 IN THE LONG NIGHT . . 16
WE DO NOT GO UP THERE TO LIVE BY DAY. . . . . . . 386 A STEEPLE ON THE HOUSE 5
BY DAY HE'S MARXIAN MUSCOVITE. . . . . 393 A CASE FOR JEFFERSON . 4
ONLY A FEW OF THOSE EVEN IN WHOSE DAY . . . . 397 THE PLANNERS . . . 7
THERE WAS SO MUCH MORE EVERY DAY TO LEARN, ... 398 BURSTING RAPTURE . . 6
YOU'D BET YOU GOT MORE WORK DONE IN A DAY, ... 405 FROM PLANE TO PLANE . 46
THE SUN THEN HAD HIS LONGEST DAY IN HEAVEN, ... 407 FROM PLANE TO PLANE . 90
TO THEIR SURPRISE RANG ONCE ON STONE ALL DAY . . . . 407 FROM PLANE TO PLANE . 116
ONE DAY TOO SWEET FOR BEINGS TO SURVIVE. . . . . . 412 POD OF THE MILKWEED . 33

- 128 -

DAY (CONTINUED)
  FROM HAVING BEATEN ALL DAY LONG IN VAIN . . . . 412 POD OF THE MILKWEED .   38
  IF THE DAY EVER COMES WHEN THEY KNOW WHO . . . . 414 A CABIN IN THE CLEARING 29
  AND SO PUT OFF THE WEARY DAY . . . . 417 AMERICA IS HARD TO SEE   40
  ALL THAT CAN WAIT FOR THE LIGHT OF DAY. . . . . 420 ONE MORE BREVITY   .   33
  TODAY IS FOR MY CAUSE A DAY OF DAYS. . . . . 422 FOR JOHN F. KENNEDY .   4
  THIS WAS NOT THEIR DAY . . . . 431 KITTY HAWK   111
  IN THE SELFSAME DAY, ... 433 KITTY HAWK   177
  I HAVE REMAINED RESENTFUL TO THIS DAY . . . . 443 AUSPEX   10
  AS CIRCUS DAY OF TOY BALLOONS. . . . . 451 A-WISHING WELL . . .   18
  ONE DAY WHEN THE CHIEF COOK WAS SICK AT HEART. . . . . 455 HOW HARD TO KEEP FROM   56
  TILL ON A DAY THE KING, BEING SICK AT HEART . . . . . 456 HOW HARD TO KEEP FROM   94
  OR COURT OF LAW, AND THIS IS JUDGMENT DAY. . . . . . . 474 A MASQUE OF REASON . .   26
  THAN THE DAY SHE WAS BORN / THAT'S ABOUT RIGHT, ... 479 A MASQUE OF REASON . . 158
  ONLY TO SEE IT SHATTERED EVERY DAY. . . . . 508 A MASQUE OF MERCY . 373
  BY HAVING HIM WHIPPED EVERY DAY AFRESH . . . . 517 A MASQUE OF MERCY . 642
DAYBREAK
  TO WHICH AT DAYBREAK THEY WERE FRESHLY BORN, ... 412 POD OF THE MILKWEED .   36
DAYFULS
  I COULD STAND WHOLE DAYFULS OF IT. . . . . 304 CLEAR AND COLDER . .   20
DAYIFY
  AND DAYIFY THE DARKEST REALM . . . . 390 TWO LEADING LIGHTS . .   9
DAYLIGHT
  AND A CELLAR IN WHICH THE DAYLIGHT FALLS . . . .   5 GHOST HOUSE   4
  DAYLIGHT AND LANTERN-LIGHT WERE ONE TO HIM: . . . . . 71 THE CODE   41
  HE THINKS IT'S DARK, AND IT'S FLOODED WITH DAYLIGHT." . . 77 THE GENERATIONS OF MEN 102
  THE BLACK WAS ALMOST ALL THERE WAS BY DAYLIGHT, ... 131 THE BONFIRE   49
  BUT BANKED THE DAYLIGHT OUT OF AVERY'S WINDOWS. . . . . 149 SNOW 186
  I SHOULD HAVE DONE BY DAYLIGHT, AND INDEED, ... 176 THE STAR-SPLITTER . .   5
  THE HOURS OF DAYLIGHT GATHER ATMOSPHERE. . . . . 246 ATMOSPHERE   6
  THAT IS CONTENT WITH THE DAYLIGHT LOW, ... 247 ON GOING UNNOTICED . .   6
  TILL DAYLIGHT MADE IT SAFE FOR A FLYER. . . . . 253 THE THATCH   27
DAYLONG
  FROM HAVING HEARD THE DAYLONG VOICE OF EVE . . . . . . 338 NEVER WOULD BIRDS' SONG   3
  ON WHAT SHOULD BE THEIR DAYLONG THEME CONTINUED. . . . 415 A CABIN IN THE CLEARING 35
DAYS
  THINKS THESE DARK DAYS OF AUTUMN RAIN . . . .   6 MY NOVEMBER GUEST . .   2
  ARE BEAUTIFUL AS DAYS CAN BE; . . . .   6 MY NOVEMBER GUEST . .   3
  THE LOVE OF BARE NOVEMBER DAYS . . . .   7 MY NOVEMBER GUEST . .   17
  "WELL, THOSE DAYS TROUBLE SILAS LIKE A DREAM. . . . . . 37 DEATH OF THE HIRED MAN   71
  HIS WORKING DAYS ARE DONE; I'M SURE OF IT." . . . . . . 39 DEATH OF THE HIRED MAN 153
  THAT MUST BE IT. SOME DAYS HE WON'T STAY ON. . . . . . 94 THE SELF-SEEKER . . .   36
  ON SUNNY DAYS A MOMENT OVERCAST; . . . . 120 THE OVEN BIRD   8
  THAT ALL YOUR DAYS ARE DIM BENEATH, ... 141 THE GUM-GATHERER . .   36
  BETWEEN TWO DAYS, THE REASON WHY I SOUGHT . . . . . . 167 NEW HAMPSHIRE . . . 249
  AGAIN AS IN THE DAYS WHEN AHAZ SINNED . . . . 171 NEW HAMPSHIRE . . . 388
  AND THAT'D BE ENOUGH TO LAST FOR DAYS. . . . . 208 PAUPER WITCH OF GRAFTON 41
  THAN FLOWERS WILL SHOW FOR DAYS UNLESS THEY HURRY. . . . 225 BLUE-BUTTERFLY DAY . .   4
  THE FULL SIX DAYS. THEN REST A DAY; . . . . 280 BLUE RIBBON AT AMESBURY 30
  THE DAYS YOU WERE NOT SWIRLED . . . . 333 HAPPINESS MAKES UP . .   2
  WERE DAYS SO VERY FEW . . . . 333 HAPPINESS MAKES UP . .   8
  A HUNDRED THOUSAND DAYS . . . . 367 A SERIOUS STEP LIGHTLY   21
  THE SUN IS SATISFIED WITH DAYS. . . . . 390 TWO LEADING LIGHTS . .   4
  IN THE OLD DAYS IN PERSIA AND PERU. . . . . 408 FROM PLANE TO PLANE . 133
  IN OUR THREE HUNDRED DAYS AND SIXTY-FIVE . . . . 412 POD OF THE MILKWEED .   32
  TODAY IS FOR MY CAUSE A DAY OF DAYS. . . . . 422 FOR JOHN F. KENNEDY .   4
  THEY WERE DAYS ON THAT STONE. . . . . 448 THE BAD ISLAND--EASTER   13
  OUR DAYS ALL PASS AWAITING ITS RETURN. . . . . 461 HOW HARD TO KEEP FROM 248
  THAT WAS BACK IN THE DAYS OF MY GODMOTHER GOOSE. . . . . 463 LINES IN DEJECTION .   5
  YOU WERE AFFLICTED WITH IN THOSE OLD DAYS. . . . . . . 475 A MASQUE OF REASON . .   61
  "I FLED HIM, DOWN THE NIGHTS AND DOWN THE DAYS; . . . . 494 A MASQUE OF MERCY . .   22
DAY'S
  DON'T MIND A WORD I SAY. IT'S A DAY'S WORK . . . . . . 116 IN THE HOME STRETCH . 159
  AND THIS DAY'S WORK MADE EVEN THAT SEEM DOUBTFUL. . . . . 279 THE WHITE-TAILED HORNET 70
  FROM ONE DAY'S PERFECT WEATHER, ... 333 HAPPINESS MAKES UP . .   14
DAYTON
  IN THEIR HOMETOWN, DAYTON. . . . . 443 KITTY HAWK   . . . 471
DAZED
  (WHO HAS BEEN STANDING DAZED WITH NEW IDEAS) . . . . . 489 A MASQUE OF REASON . 441
D'AZIL
  SOMEONE IN ANCIENT MAS D'AZIL . . . . 326 A MISSIVE MISSILE . .   1
DAZZLE
  TO STEP OUTDOORS AND TAKE THE WATER DAZZLE . . . . . . 63 A SERVANT TO SERVANTS . 27
DAZZLING
  WITH ALL THY DAZZLING OTHER ONES, ... 28 MY BUTTERFLY   13
DE
  "WE'RE GIVING YOU OUR CHANCES ON DE FARM." . . . . . . 114 IN THE HOME STRETCH . 108
  DEN WHERE'S YOUR HAX-EAD FLYING T'ROUGH DE HAIR?" . . . 186 THE AX-HELVE . . .   27
  DE SECOND GROWT' I CUT MYSELF--TOUGH, TOUGH!" . . . . . 186 THE AX-HELVE . . .   31
DEAD
  DEAD WEEDS AND UNMATED BIRDS, ... 11 WIND AND WINDOW FLOWER   15
  LIVING OR DEAD, WHICHEVER ARE TO MIND. . . . . 17 THE VANTAGE POINT . .   8
  THINE EMULOUS FOND FLOWERS ARE DEAD, TOO, ... 28 MY BUTTERFLY   1
  THAT FRIGHTED THEE SO OFT, IS FLED OR DEAD: . . . . . . 28 MY BUTTERFLY   3
  FOR THOU ART DEAD, I SAID, ... 29 MY BUTTERFLY   44
  THE LEAVES ARE ALL DEAD ON THE GROUND, ... 30 RELUCTANCE   7
  AND THE DEAD LEAVES LIE HUDDLED AND STILL, ... 30 RELUCTANCE   13
  "WARREN?" SHE QUESTIONED. / "DEAD," WAS ALL HE ANSWERED. . 40 DEATH OF THE HIRED MAN 166
  A MAN CAN'T SPEAK OF HIS OWN CHILD THAT'S DEAD." . . . . 53 HOME BURIAL   70
  "WEREN'T YOU RELIEVED TO FIND HE WASN'T DEAD?" . . . . . 73 THE CODE 110
  OF DEAD LEAVES STUCK TOGETHER BY THE HEAT-- . . . . . . 119 HYLA BROOK   11
  TO HAVE A VISION OF US OLD AND DEAD). . . . . 127 THE SMILE   10
  WERE NOT THE ONE DEAD, TURNED TO THEIR AFFAIRS. . . . . 137 "OUT,OUT--"   34
  THEY PAINT DEAD TREES FOR LIVING, AND THE DEAD . . . . 141 THE LINE-GANG . . .   3
  HE'LL BE DEAD--DEAD AND BURIED." / "SUCH A TROUBLE! . . . 146 SNOW   88
  AND GIVE GOOD MEASURE TO THE DEAD, THOUGH THANKLESS. . . 200 PLACE FOR A THIRD . .   20

DEAD (CONTINUED)
   THE DEAD WAS BOUND TO SILENCE: ASK THE SISTER. . . . . . 200 PLACE FOR A THIRD . . 43
   HE SAID THE DEAD HAD SOULS, BUT WHEN I ASKED HIM . . . . 202 THE WITCH OF COOS . . 14
   HOW COULD THAT BE--I THOUGHT THE DEAD WERE SOULS-- . . . 202 THE WITCH OF COOS . . 15
   THAT THERE'S SOMETHING THE DEAD ARE KEEPING BACK? . . . . 202 THE WITCH OF COOS . . 17
   YES, THERE'S SOMETHING THE DEAD ARE KEEPING BACK. . . . . 202 THE WITCH OF COOS . . 18
   WITH THE DEAD RACE OF THE GREAT AUK!" . . . . 212 AN EMPTY THREAT . . . 52
   BUT NEVER ANYMORE THE DEAD. . . . . 221 IN A DISUSED GRAVEYARD . 4
   TOMORROW DEAD WILL COME TO STAY." . . . . 221 IN A DISUSED GRAVEYARD . 8
   HOW NO ONE DEAD WILL SEEM TO COME. . . . . 221 IN A DISUSED GRAVEYARD . 11
   AND DEAD WEEDS, LIKE A DISAPPEARING SNAKE. . . . . 226 THE ONSET 21
   HOW ELSE? THEY ARE NOT KNOWN TO SEND THE DEAD.-- . . . . 230 NOT TO KEEP 6
   NEXT DAY THE SCENE WAS PILED AND PUFFED AND DEAD. . . . . 239 OUR SINGING STRENGTH . 11
   AND LAY LODGED--THOUGH NOT DEAD. . . . . 250 LODGED 5
   THE BODY OF ONE OF THEIR DEAD . . . . 288 DEPARTMENTAL 15
   THE DEAD OF THE COMMISSARY . . . . 288 DEPARTMENTAL 27
   SEIZES THE DEAD BY THE MIDDLE, ... 289 DEPARTMENTAL 37
   AND DEAD WINGS CARRIED LIKE A PAPER KITE. . . . . 302 DESIGN 8
   AND MIGHT BE ROLLING DEAD BELOW . . . . 344 DISCOVERY OF MADEIRAS . 33
   LIKE SOMEONE DEAD PERMITTED TO EXIST . . . . 368 THE LITERATE FARMER AND 17
   COULD MAKE MUCH DIFFERENCE TO THE DEAD AND GONE. . . . . 397 THE PLANNERS 6
   DELIBERATELY STABBED HIM DEAD. . . . . 444 THE DRAFT HORSE . . . 8
   I PICK A DEAD SHELL UP FROM WHERE THE KELP . . . . 446 DOES NO ONE AT ALL EVER 25
   OF ALL THE DEAD AND BURIED FROM THEIR GRAVES. . . . . . . 484 A MASQUE OF REASON . . 307
   ALL PAUL MEANS, AND I WISH THE DEAD COULD HEAR ME-- . . . 519 A MASQUE OF MERCY . . 674
DEADFALL
   TO SPRING IT LIKE A DEADFALL AND THE FAULT . . . . 502 A MASQUE OF MERCY . . 231
DEADLINE
   TO LEAP THE DUSTY DEADLINE. FOR MY OWN . . . . 131 THE BONFIRE 64
DEADLY
   IN SLEEP OR SLOWNESS IS THE DEADLY CRIME. . . . . 371 THE LITERATE FARMER AND 103
DEAF
   FROM THE LAST THING HE SAID HIMSELF, STONE DEAF . . . . 145 SNOW 65
DEAFENING
   AND THEN THEY ALL TURNED TO WITH DEAFENING BOOTS . . . 114 IN THE HOME STRETCH . 109
DEAL (SEE I-DEAL)
   A GOOD DEAL COMES ON ME WHEN ALL IS SAID. . . . . . . 48 A HUNDRED COLLARS . . 107
   A GREAT DEAL OF NONE. . . . . 134 A GIRL'S GARDEN . . . 40
   A GOOD DEAL RIGHT; DON'T DO THE LAST THING WRONG. . . . 199 PLACE FOR A THIRD . . 10
   CAN DO A GOOD DEAL TO BAD MASONRY. . . . . 213 A FOUNTAIN, A BOTTLE . 26
   AND DEAL A DEATH . . . . 360 THE RABBIT-HUNTER . . 15
   THEY DEAL WITH NEAR AND FAR, ... 388 MIDDLENESS OF THE ROAD 12
DEALING
   IN DEALING IN "OLD RAGS" IN SAN FRANCISCO. . . . . . . 160 NEW HAMPSHIRE . . . 58
DEALT
   PLAINLY WITH AN INTELLIGENCE I DEALT. . . . . 357 A CONSIDERABLE SPECK . 15
   AND I MUST SAY IT DEALT . . . . 450 OBJECTION TO BE STEPPED 9
DEAN
   DEAN, ADULT EDUCATION MAY SEEM SILLY. . . . . 393 LUCRETIUS VERSUS POETS 1
   GOD BLESS THE DEAN AND MAKE HIS DEANSHIP PLENARY. . . . 394 LUCRETIUS VERSUS POETS 12
DEANERY
   THE OTHER EVENING AT YOUR COLLEGE DEANERY. . . . . . . 393 LUCRETIUS VERSUS POETS 3
DEAN'S
   WE'RE STOPPING FOR THE FORTNIGHT DOWN AT DEAN'S." . . . 92 THE FEAR 86
DEANSHIP
   GOD BLESS THE DEAN AND MAKE HIS DEANSHIP PLENARY. . . . 394 LUCRETIUS VERSUS POETS 12
DEAR
   AND LONG TO KNOW IF STILL I HELD THEM DEAR. . . . . . . 5 INTO MY OWN 12
   "I WILL FIND OUT NOW--YOU MUST TELL ME, DEAR." . . . . 51 HOME BURIAL 12
   "THERE'S SOMETHING I SHOULD LIKE TO ASK YOU, DEAR." . . 52 HOME BURIAL 42
   FOR, DEAR ME, WHY ABANDON A BELIEF . . . . 58 THE BLACK COTTAGE . . 105
   "YOU POOR, DEAR, GREAT, GREAT, GREAT, GREAT GRANNY!" . . 77 THE GENERATIONS OF MEN 116
   THAT'S HIS MISTAKE. THE DEAR KNOWS MY INTEREST . . . . 84 THE HOUSEKEEPER . . . 87
   WHAT DO YOU WANT, DEAR? COME, STAND BY THE BED; . . . . 96 THE SELF-SEEKER . . . 104
   A VIEW." / "AND YET YOU THINK YOU LIKE IT, DEAR?" . . . 111 IN THE HOME STRETCH . 35
   YOU AND I, DEAR, WILL GO WITH SOFTER STEPS . . . . . . 111 IN THE HOME STRETCH . 41
   BUT WHO FIRST SAID THE WORD TO COME?" / "MY DEAR, . . . 116 IN THE HOME STRETCH . 171
   MY DEAR, I'M COMING JUST THE SAME. I DIDN'T . . . . . 143 SNOW 26
   THE DEAR KNOWS. I DETEST THE THOUGHT OF HIM-- . . . . 144 SNOW 51
   "HE SHAN'T GO--THERE! / "IT IS A NIGHT, MY DEAR." . . . 145 SNOW 80
   "WHAT IS IT, DEAR? AND SHE HAD GIVEN ALL . . . . 230 NOT TO KEEP 9
   SHE HAD TO ASK, "WHAT WAS IT, DEAR?" / "ENOUGH, ... 230 NOT TO KEEP 13
   THE DEAR ONLY KNOWS . . . . 246 THE ROSE FAMILY . . . 7
   TO LET US KNOW IT HEARS ME." / "WHY, MY DEAR, ... 258 WEST-RUNNING BROOK . 17
   I WILL BE THERE FOR YOU, MY DEAR, ... 282 A DRUMLIN WOODCHUCK . 28
   AND HADN'T BEEN HIS DEAR. . . . . 444 ENDS 8
   "BUT YES," SHE SAID, "SOME DAY I'LL TELL YOU, DEAR. . . 457 HOW HARD TO KEEP FROM 106
DEARER
   DEARER TO HIM THAN ANY BARNYARD BRUTE, ... 283 THE GOLD HESPERIDEE . 22
DEAREST
   LISTEN AND I WILL TAKE MY DEAREST RISK. . . . . 320 BUILD SOIL 136
DEARIE
   "WELL, ANNE, GO, DEARIE. OUR AFFAIR WILL WAIT. . . . . 98 THE SELF-SEEKER . . . 167
DEARS
   MY DEARS, MY DEARS, YOU THOUGHT THAT--WE ALL THOUGHT IT. 132 THE BONFIRE 102
DEATH
   SPIRIT TO MATTER TILL DEATH COME. . . . . 21 THE TRIAL BY EXISTENCE 64
   THE DEATH OF THE HIRED MAN . . . . 34 DEATH OF THE HIRED MAN T
   WITH ANYONE TO DEATH, COMES SO FAR SHORT . . . . 54 HOME BURIAL 98
   NO, FROM THE TIME WHEN ONE IS SICK TO DEATH, ... 54 HOME BURIAL 100
   AND IT'S OUR LIFE." / "YES, WHEN IT'S NOT OUR DEATH." . 94 THE SELF-SEEKER . . . 46
   BUT THE BLACK SPREAD LIKE BLACK DEATH ON THE GROUND, . . 131 THE BONFIRE 53
   A NATURAL DEATH, AND VIGILANCE COMMITTEES . . . . 159 NEW HAMPSHIRE . . . 19
   AND SHOT. IT'S POLLYANNA NOW OR DEATH. . . . . 168 NEW HAMPSHIRE . . . 282
   SURE THAT THOUGH NOT A STAR OF DEATH AND BIRTH, ... 174 A STAR IN A STONEBOAT . 46
   THOUGH NOT, I SAY, A STAR OF DEATH AND SIN, ... 174 A STAR IN A STONEBOAT . 49
   AND CAME SO NEAR DEATH IN THE DARK OF YEARS, ... 180 MAPLE 37

DEATH (CONTINUED)
   THUS HAD A NAME WITH MEANING, GIVEN IN DEATH, ... 185 MAPLE 163
   BETWEEN THE DEATH DAY AND THE FUNERAL DAY. . . . . . . 201 PLACE FOR A THIRD . . 69
   TO LET ON HE WAS PLAGUED TO DEATH WITH ME: . . . . . . 210 PAUPER WITCH OF GRAFTON 84
   SO SURE OF DEATH THE MARBLES RHYME, ... 221 IN A DISUSED GRAVEYARD 9
   GIVES UP HIS ERRAND, AND LETS DEATH DESCEND . . . . . 226 THE ONSET 8
   I KNOW THAT WINTER DEATH HAS NEVER TRIED . . . . 226 THE ONSET 13
   THE UNIVERSAL CATARACT OF DEATH . . . . 259 WEST-RUNNING BROOK . . 56
   AND FOR EVERY SO MANY SIGH A DEATH. . . . . 263 THE TIMES TABLE . . . 10
   AND WHEN THEY CAME IT SEEMED WITH A WILL TO CARRY ME WITH
     THEM TO DEATH. . . . . 297 A LEAF-TREADER . . . 8
   ASSORTED CHARACTERS OF DEATH AND BLIGHT . . . . 302 DESIGN 4
   AND ANYONE IS FREE TO CONDEMN ME TO DEATH-- . . . . . 307 NOT QUITE SOCIAL . . 13
   AND PAY A DEATH TAX OF FAIRLY POLITE REPENTANCE. . . . 307 NOT QUITE SOCIAL . . 16
   HIS DEATH WAS SACRIFICIAL-VOTIVE. . . . . 327 A MISSIVE MISSILE . . 18
   I SANG OF DEATH--BUT HAD I KNOWN . . . . 336 THE WIND AND THE RAIN . 9
   BUT PRESENCE OF LOVE THESE HAD IN DEATH . . . . 346 DISCOVERY OF MADEIRAS . 80
   AND DEAL A DEATH . . . . 360 THE RABBIT-HUNTER . . 15
   AND THIS IS NOT BECAUSE SHE THINKS OF DEATH. . . . . . 386 THE FEAR OF MAN . . . 4
DEATHS
   THE MANY DEATHS ONE MUST HAVE DIED . . . . 336 THE WIND AND THE RAIN . 10
DEATH'S
   "DEATH'S COME TO JERRY MCCORMIC, ... 288 DEPARTMENTAL 23
DEATHWARD
   AND LET IT DRIVE ME DEATHWARD TOO. . . . . 336 THE WIND AND THE RAIN . 6
DEBARS
   AS I SUSPECT YOU HAVE. A TOWN DEBARS . . . . 370 THE LITERATE FARMER AND 69
DEBATING
   DEBATING WHAT TO DO WITHOUT AN AX. . . . . 238 ON A TREE FALLEN ACROSS 8
DEBT
   THE INGENUITIES OF DEBT . . . . 399 THE INGENUITIES OF DEBT T
   NOT EVEN THE INGENUITIES OF DEBT . . . . 399 THE INGENUITIES OF DEBT 11
DECAY
   WITH THE SLOW SMOKELESS BURNING OF DECAY. . . . . . 102 THE WOOD-PILE . . . 40
   THIS HOUSE IN ONE YEAR FALLEN TO DECAY . . . . 176 THE CENSUS-TAKER . . 50
   UNTARNISHED BY RUST AND DECAY. . . . . 312 THE VINDICTIVES . . . 79
DECAYED
   THEY MUST GO DOWN INTO THE DARK DECAYED. . . . . . . 26 IN HARDWOOD GROVES . . 8
   HAVE KEPT FROM BEING CAUGHT WITH THE DECAYED, ... 399 THE INGENUITIES OF DEBT 8
   AND THAT HAS DECAYED . . . . 449 THE BAD ISLAND--EASTER 61
DECEIVE
   I WON'T DECEIVE MYSELF ABOUT SUCCESS . . . . 513 A MASQUE OF MERCY . . 525
DECEIVED
   I WAS DECEIVED BY WHAT HE DID. . . . . 417 AMERICA IS HARD TO SEE 32
DECEIVES
   MYSELF AS ONE HIS OWN PRETENSE DECEIVES; . . . . . . 233 A BOUNDLESS MOMENT . . 10
DECEMBER
   "WARM IN DECEMBER, COLD IN JUNE, YOU SAY?" . . . . . 44 THE MOUNTAIN 100
DECENT
   THE ONLY DECENT TREE HAD BEEN TO MILL . . . . 171 NEW HAMPSHIRE . . . 376
   A DECENT PRODUCT OF LIFE'S IRONING-OUT; . . . . . . 201 PLACE FOR A THIRD . . 67
DECENTLY
   AND THAT'S WHY I CAN'T DECENTLY REFUSE YOU." . . . . 214 A FOUNTAIN, A BOTTLE . 32
DECIDE
   IS TO DECIDE IT SIMPLY ISN'T TRUE. . . . . 57 THE BLACK COTTAGE . . 66
   ONLY DISINTERESTEDLY TO DECIDE . . . . 191 THE GRINDSTONE . . . 71
   IN CASE I SHOULD DECIDE TO REIGN SOME MORE. . . . . 458 HOW HARD TO KEEP FROM 148
DECIDED
   SHE HAD SUPPOSED THE WAR DECIDED THAT. . . . . . . 57 THE BLACK COTTAGE . . 79
   DECIDED TO STAY THERE HIMSELF. . . . . 314 BEARER OF EVIL TIDINGS 36
   IF I DECIDED TO BECOME A DOCTOR, ... 406 FROM PLANE TO PLANE . 67
DECIDEDLY
   DECIDEDLY UPON THE LEFT. . . . . 325 TO A THINKER 2
DECIDING
   WE THOUGHT YOU WERE DECIDING NOT TO GO-- . . . . . . 150 SNOW 198
DECIMAL
   POINTED THE DECIMAL OFF WITH ONE DEEP THRUST. . . . . 119 MEETING AND PASSING . 9
DECISION
   IT'S RESTFUL TO ARRIVE AT A DECISION, ... 172 NEW HAMPSHIRE . . . 411
   SHE HURRIED HER DECISION TO BE READY . . . . 201 PLACE FOR A THIRD . . 71
   OF GOD'S DECISION LASTLY ON YOUR DEEDS. . . . . . . 520 A MASQUE OF MERCY . . 698
DECK
   BEFORE THEY WERE HURLED FROM THE SLAVER'S DECK. . . . 346 DISCOVERY OF MADEIRAS . 82
DECLARATION
   AS LONG AS THE DECLARATION GUARDS . . . . 310 IN DIVES' DIVE . . . 3
   AND BY THE EXAMPLE OF OUR DECLARATION . . . . 423 FOR JOHN F. KENNEDY . 30
DECLARE
   AND DECLARE TO THE CLIFFS TOO FAR FOR ECHO, ... 176 THE CENSUS-TAKER . . 56
   WHAT I MYSELF HAVE HELD. BUT WHY DECLARE . . . . . . 335 I COULD GIVE ALL . . 12
   HE WOULD DECLARE AND COULD HIMSELF BELIEVE . . . . . 338 NEVER WOULD BIRDS' SONG 1
   DECLARE THAT IF SUCH INDIANS INHERITED . . . . . . 369 THE LITERATE FARMER AND 55
DECLARED
   LET HIM SAY WHY IT SHOULD NOT BE DECLARED SO." . . . 176 THE CENSUS-TAKER . . 60
   GOD ONCE DECLARED HE WAS TRUE . . . . 266 SITTING BY A BUSH . . 13
   SO THEY STAYED AND DECLARED A VILLAGE . . . . 314 BEARER OF EVIL TIDINGS 27
DECLARES
   SILAS DECLARES YOU'LL HAVE TO GET HIM BACK. . . . . . 36 DEATH OF THE HIRED MAN 61
DECLARING
   THERE WAS THE BOOK OF PROFILE TALES DECLARING . . . . 423 FOR JOHN F. KENNEDY . 60
DEDICATE
   I COULD DEVOTE AND DEDICATE FOREVER . . . . 58 THE BLACK COTTAGE . . 113
DEED
   WITH HIM IT BODED ACTION, DEED. . . . . 274 A LONE STRIKER . . . 49
   IS THE DEED EVER REALLY DONE . . . . 277 TWO TRAMPS IN MUD TIME 71
   TO MATCH YOU DEED FOR DEED AND PLAN FOR PLAN. . . . . 323 BUILD SOIL 221
   (THE DEED OF GIFT WAS MANY DEEDS OF WAR) . . . . . . 348 THE GIFT OUTRIGHT . . 13
   (THE DEED OF GIFT WAS MANY DEEDS OF WAR) . . . . . . 424 THE GIFT OUTRIGHT . . 13

DEEDS
    (THE DEED OF GIFT WAS MANY DEEDS OF WAR) . . . . 348 THE GIFT OUTRIGHT . . 13
    TO SHOW BY DEEDS HE DIDN'T RESENT . . . . 421 ONE MORE BREVITY . . 63
    AND COUNTED OUT. HEROIC DEEDS WERE DONE. . . . . 422 FOR JOHN F. KENNEDY . 17
    (THE DEED OF GIFT WAS MANY DEEDS OF WAR) . . . . 424 THE GIFT OUTRIGHT . . 13
    OF GOD'S DECISION LASTLY ON YOUR DEEDS. . . . . 520 A MASQUE OF MERCY . . 698
DEEP (SEE INCH-DEEP)
    LIKE A DEEP PIECE OF SOME OLD RUNNING RIVER . . . . 63 A SERVANT TO SERVANTS . 20
    POINTED THE DECIMAL OFF WITH ONE DEEP THRUST. . . . . . . 119 MEETING AND PASSING . 9
    AND I WAS BURROWING IN DEEP FOR WARMTH, ... 149 SNOW 178
    'SO YOU CAN THINK IT'S SIX FEET DEEP OUTSIDE, ... 149 SNOW 182
    ON TURRETS, LIKE CONSTANTINOPLE, DEEP . . . . 160 NEW HAMPSHIRE . . . 40
    IT BECAME AN EXPLORER OF THE DEEP . . . . 162 NEW HAMPSHIRE . . . 91
    NOT TO EXPLORE TOO DEEP IN OTHERS' BUSINESS. . . . . . . 162 NEW HAMPSHIRE . . . 92
    THE UNCOMMONLY DEEP SNOW HAS MADE HIM THINK . . . . 205 THE WITCH OF COÖS . . 109
    AND EXPERTS SAID THAT DEEP DOWN IN THE MOUNTAIN . . . . . 212 A FOUNTAIN, A BOTTLE . 4
    IN VIRGIN WRAPPER FROM DEEP IN THE BOX, ... 217 A FOUNTAIN, A BOTTLE . 126
    THE SNOW FELL DEEP . . . . 218 I WILL SING YOU ONE-O . 9
    THE WOODS ARE LOVELY, DARK, AND DEEP, ... 224 STOPPING BY WOODS . . 13
    IN LONG STORMS AN UNDRIFTED FOUR FEET DEEP . . . . 226 THE ONSET 15
    DEEP IN A SEWER DUNGEON UNDER STONE . . . . 231 A BROOK IN THE CITY . 16
    NEITHER OUT FAR NOR IN DEEP . . . . 301 NEITHER OUT FAR NOR IN . T
    THEY CANNOT LOOK IN DEEP. . . . . 301 NEITHER OUT FAR NOR IN . 14
    DEEP INTO THE EARTH WHENCE IT CAME. . . . . 311 THE VINDICTIVES . . . 30
    WHERE UNDER DEEP ASH AND CHARCOAL . . . . 312 THE VINDICTIVES . . . 58
    KNOWS THE OLD MAN, AND NOBODY'S SO DEEP . . . . 371 THE LITERATE FARMER AND 96
    I HEARD A DEEP GROAN--MAYBE OUT OF HIM. . . . . 516 A MASQUE OF MERCY . . 611
    WE HAVE TO STAY AFRAID DEEP IN OUR SOULS . . . . 520 A MASQUE OF MERCY . . 717
DEEPER
    A LANTERN-LIGHT FROM DEEPER IN THE BARN . . . . 89 THE FEAR 1
    DEEPER DOWN IN THE WELL THAN WHERE THE WATER . . . . . . 225 FOR ONCE SOMETHING . . 3
    CHANGE LIKE THIS TO A DEEPER ROAR? . . . . 251 BEREFT 2
    DEEPER INTO MATTER-- . . . . 435 KITTY HAWK 227
    BECAUSE THE DEEPER FEAR IS SO ETERNAL. . . . . 521 A MASQUE OF MERCY . . 732
DEEPLY
    ONE TREE, BY BEING DEEPLY WOUNDED, ... 331 BEECH 6
    THESE I ASSUME WERE WORDS SO DEEPLY MEANT . . . . 399 THE INGENUITIES OF DEBT 1
DEEP-SEA
    HIS DEEP-SEA DORY HAS FOUND A HARBOR. . . . . 262 THE FLOWER BOAT . . . 4
DEER
    BY DEER, AND I DON'T WANT IT BUDDED BY GROUSE. . . . . . 228 GOOD-BY AND KEEP COLD . 8
    I'D SUMMON GROUSE, RABBIT, AND DEER TO THE WALL . . . . . 228 GOOD-BY AND KEEP COLD . 10
    LIKE RABBIT AND DEER . . . . 235 GATHERING LEAVES . . 7
DEER-HUNTING
    DEER-HUNTING AND TROUT-FISHING. THERE'S A BROOK . . . . . 42 THE MOUNTAIN 45
DEFEAT
    AND, "BETTER DEFEAT ALMOST, ... 212 AN EMPTY THREAT . . . 53
    AS GRAVE AS HE ABOUT THE WORLD'S DEFEAT. . . . . 359 THE LOST FOLLOWER . . 24
    WE SOUGHT HOWEVER CRUDELY TO DEFEAT . . . . 446 DOES NO ONE AT ALL EVER 11
    I SEE FOR NATURE NO DEFEAT . . . . 470 IN WINTER IN THE WOODS 9
DEFECT
    THE TOTAL SKY ALMOST WITHOUT DEFECT, ... 245 SPRING POOLS 2
    IF I HAVE A DEFECT . . . . 392 A WISH TO COMPLY . . 6
DEFECTION
    THE LOSS TO SONG, THE DANGER OF DEFECTION . . . . 358 THE LOST FOLLOWER . . 9
DEFEND
    DON'T YOU DEFEND YOURSELF. IF IT WAS THERE, ... 97 THE SELF-SEEKER . . . 139
DEFENSE (SEE SELF-DEFENSE)
    BAPTISTE ON HIS DEFENSE ABOUT THE CHILDREN . . . . 188 THE AX-HELVE 83
    WITH WHICH HE PENETRATES MY BEST DEFENSE . . . . 277 THE WHITE-TAILED HORNET 8
    FOR INNER DEFENSE MY HIDE. . . . . 348 TRIPLE BRONZE . . . 3
    FOR NEXT DEFENSE OUTSIDE . . . . 348 TRIPLE BRONZE . . . 4
    AND THAT DEFENSE MAKES THREE . . . . 349 TRIPLE BRONZE . . . 11
DEFENSELESS
    AND LEFT DEFENSELESS TO THE HEAT AND LIGHT. . . . . 109 THE EXPOSED NEST . . 16
DEFERRED
    WHOSE COMING HOME HAS BEEN TOO LONG DEFERRED, ... 109 THE EXPOSED NEST . . 22
DEFIANTLY
    THE RIVER BANK, QUIT WORK DEFIANTLY, ... 405 FROM PLANE TO PLANE . 58
DEFICIENCY
    FOR THE DEFICIENCY BY CHURCH INTONING. . . . . 460 HOW HARD TO KEEP FROM 220
DEFIED
    OR ELSE BY SOME REMOTENESS THAT DEFIED THEM . . . . . . 216 A FOUNTAIN, A BOTTLE . 107
    AND ALL OUR BLANDISHMENTS WOULD SEEM DEFIED, ... 268 RIDERS 11
    OF ENEMIES DEFIED AND BATTLES FOUGHT. . . . . 356 TIME OUT 11
    I TRUST FEELS PROPERLY DEFIED. . . . . 363 ASSURANCE 4
DEFINED
    MYSELF UNSEEN, I SEE IN WHITE DEFINED . . . . 17 THE VANTAGE POINT . . 5
DEFINITELY
    WHILE WE KNOW DEFINITELY WHERE HE IS. . . . . 90 THE FEAR 44
    AFTER THE FIGHT'S SO DEFINITELY DONE . . . . 507 A MASQUE OF MERCY . . 366
DEFT
    HER DEFT HAND SHOWED WITH FINGER RINGS . . . . 273 A LONE STRIKER . . . 28
DEGREE
    BUT SAY WITH WHAT DEGREE OF HEAT. . . . . 403 SOMETHING LIKE A STAR . 12
    HE WASN'T OFF A MERE DEGREE; . . . . 417 AMERICA IS HARD TO SEE 17
DEGREES
    THROUGH NINETY-ODD DEGREES OF ARC, IT SEEMS, ... 269 THE BEAR 24
DEIGN
    HE TRUSTS MY LOVE TOO WELL TO DEIGN REPLY. . . . . 359 THE LOST FOLLOWER . . 33
DEIGNED
    HER NEVER HAVING DEIGNED TO TELL THEM. . . . . 257 THE LOVELY BE CHOOSERS 38
DEITY
    IF YOU'RE THE DEITY I ASSUME YOU ARE . . . . 476 A MASQUE OF REASON . . 84
DEJECTEDLY
    CIRCUITOUS WANDERER," AND "TOOK DEJECTEDLY . . . . 171 NEW HAMPSHIRE . . . 384
DEJECTION
    SOME TURN IN SHEER, IN SHELLEYAN DEJECTION . . . . 358 THE LOST FOLLOWER . . 11

```
                                                       PAGE TITLE                    LINE
DEJECTION (CONTINUED)
    LINES WRITTEN IN DEJECTION ON THE EVE OF GREAT SUCCESS  .  . 462 LINES IN DEJECTION  .  .   T
DELAY
    THROUGH SOME DELAY, AND CALL YOU TO YOUR FACE  .  .  .  .  . 222 TO E.T.  .  .  .  .  .  .   6
    LIKE PEOPLE THROWN OUT TO DELAY THE WOLVES.  .  .  .  .  .  . 279 THE WHITE-TAILED HORNET  68
DELIBERATELY
    DELIBERATELY STABBED HIM DEAD.  .  .  .  .  .  .  .  .  .  . 444 THE DRAFT HORSE  .  .  .   8
DELICATE
    BEFORE I UNDERTOOK SO DELICATE  .  .  .  .  .  .  .  .  .  . 503 A MASQUE OF MERCY  .  . 271
DELIGHT
    SOME RESTING FLOWER OF YESTERDAY'S DELIGHT.  .  .  .  .  .  .  22 THE TUFT OF FLOWERS  .  14
    AND YELPS DELIGHT  .  .  .  .  .  .  .  .  .  .  .  .  .  .  . 360 THE RABBIT-HUNTER  .  10
DELIGHTFUL
    BOTH ARE DELIGHTFUL STATES FOR THEIR ABSURDLY  .  .  .  .  . 165 NEW HAMPSHIRE  .  .  . 186
DELIVER
    DELIVER US FROM COMMITTEES. 'TWILL REMIND ME.  .  .  .  .  . 486 A MASQUE OF REASON  . 373
DELPHI
    TO QUOTE THE ORACLE OF DELPHI,  .  .  .  .  .  .  .  .  .  . 467 QUANDARY  .  .  .  .  .  11
DELTA
    BUT FOUND ONE IN THE DELTA OF A BROOK,  .  .  .  .  .  .  . 382 TO AN ANCIENT  .  .  .   5
DELUXE
    TO WATCH THIS END DELUXE.  .  .  .  .  .  .  .  .  .  .  .  . 361 ALMOST TWO THOUSAND  .  13
DEMAND
    LEGITIMATELY. MY DEMAND UPON HER,  .  .  .  .  .  .  .  .  . 217 A FOUNTAIN, A BOTTLE  . 136
    THOUGH SLIGHT, WAS A DEMAND. SHE FELT THE TUG.  .  .  .  .  . 217 A FOUNTAIN, A BOTTLE  . 137
    IT DIDN'T LOSE ITS TEMPER AT OUR DEMAND  .  .  .  .  .  .  . 349 OUR HOLD ON THE PLANET   2
DEMANDING
    DEMANDING PROOF.  .  .  .  .  .  .  .  .  .  .  .  .  .  .  . 298 ON TAKING FROM THE TOP  12
DEMIJOHN
    OR A DEMIJOHN.  .  .  .  .  .  .  .  .  .  .  .  .  .  .  .  . 431 KITTY HAWK  .  .  .  . 105
DEMIURGE
    THAT THE JUST-PAUSING DEMIURGE  .  .  .  .  .  .  .  .  .  . 453 A-WISHING WELL  .  .  .  73
DEMIURGE'S
    THE DEMIURGE'S LAUGH  .  .  .  .  .  .  .  .  .  .  .  .  .  .  24 THE DEMIURGE'S LAUGH  .   T
DEMOCRACY
    LEAST IN DEMOCRACY. IN PRACTICE, PURE,  .  .  .  .  .  .  . 318 BUILD SOIL  .  .  .  .  .  76
    JUST NOW YOU'RE OFF DEMOCRACY  .  .  .  .  .  .  .  .  .  . 326 TO A THINKER  .  .  .  .  15
    TO TEACH THEM HOW DEMOCRACY IS MEANT.  .  .  .  .  .  .  . 423 FOR JOHN F. KENNEDY  .  38
DEMOCRAT
    THOUGH A GREAT SCHOLAR, HE'S A DEMOCRAT,  .  .  .  .  .  .  .  44 A HUNDRED COLLARS  .  12
    IN POLITICS: I'M VERMONT DEMOCRAT--  .  .  .  .  .  .  .  .  .  48 A HUNDRED COLLARS  . 109
    A STATE-RIGHTS FREE-TRADE DEMOCRAT. WHAT'S THAT?  .  .  .  . 324 BUILD SOIL  .  .  .  . 245
    YOU'LL BE A DEMOCRAT AGAIN.  .  .  .  .  .  .  .  .  .  .  . 326 TO A THINKER  .  .  .  .  20
DEMOCRATIC
    EASTON GOES DEMOCRATIC, WILSON 4  .  .  .  .  .  .  .  .  . 165 NEW HAMPSHIRE  .  .  . 198
    THERE'S ONLY DEMOCRATIC SOCIALISM,  .  .  .  .  .  .  .  .  . 318 BUILD SOIL  .  .  .  .  72
    A DEMOCRATIC FORM OF RIGHT DIVINE  .  .  .  .  .  .  .  .  . 424 FOR JOHN F. KENNEDY  .  64
DEMOCRAT-LOAD
    WHEN WHO SHOULD COME BY, WITH A DEMOCRAT-LOAD  .  .  .  .  .  60 BLUEBERRIES  .  .  .  .  37
DEMOCRATS
    AND DEMOCRATS WERE SORE IN NEED OF COMFORT:  .  .  .  .  .  . 165 NEW HAMPSHIRE  .  .  . 197
DEMON
    THE DEMON AROSE FROM HIS WALLOW TO LAUGH,  .  .  .  .  .  .  25 THE DEMIURGE'S LAUGH  .  10
    AND WELL I KNEW WHAT THE DEMON MEANT.  .  .  .  .  .  .  .  .  25 THE DEMIURGE'S LAUGH  .  12
    THE DEMON OF PURSUIT  .  .  .  .  .  .  .  .  .  .  .  .  . 340 THE SUBVERTED FLOWER  .  33
DEMON'S
    I WAS RUNNING WITH JOY ON THE DEMON'S TRAIL,  .  .  .  .  .  24 THE DEMIURGE'S LAUGH  .   2
DEMONSTRABLY
    TO ANY DEMONSTRABLY BETTER RACE,  .  .  .  .  .  .  .  .  . 369 THE LITERATE FARMER AND  50
DEMONSTRATION
    AS A DEMONSTRATION  .  .  .  .  .  .  .  .  .  .  .  .  .  . 435 KITTY HAWK  .  .  .  .  . 221
    'TWAS A GREAT DEMONSTRATION WE PUT ON.  .  .  .  .  .  .  . 475 A MASQUE OF REASON  .  53
    'TWAS A GREAT DEMONSTRATION IF YOU SAY SO.  .  .  .  .  .  . 481 A MASQUE OF REASON  . 219
DEMUR
    THE OTHER WITHOUT DEMUR AGREES.  .  .  .  .  .  .  .  .  .  . 291 ON HEART'S BEGINNING TO  23
    THERE I ELECTED TO DEMUR  .  .  .  .  .  .  .  .  .  .  .  . 380 AN UNSTAMPED LETTER IN  12
DEN
    WHEN A STORM THREATENED FROM THE DRAGON'S DEN,  .  .  .  .  .  63 A SERVANT TO SERVANTS  .  30
    DEN WHERE'S YOUR HAX-EAD FLYING T'ROUGH DE HAIR?"  .  .  . 186 THE AX-HELVE  .  .  .  .  27
    "DEN WHEN YOU SAY YOU COME? IT'S COST YOU NOTHING.  .  .  . 186 THE AX-HELVE  .  .  .  .  33
DENDROPHOBIA
    THAT SHOWED ITSELF IN DENDROPHOBIA.  .  .  .  .  .  .  .  . 171 NEW HAMPSHIRE  .  .  . 375
DENIED
    OR BEEN THEIR RICHES, FAME, OR LOVE DENIED;  .  .  .  .  . 355 THE LESSON FOR TODAY  . 153
    EXCEPT AS IT DENIED HIM WAY  .  .  .  .  .  .  .  .  .  .  . 419 AMERICA IS HARD TO SEE   77
DENSE
    HAVE IT FOR ALL OF ME AND HAVE IT DENSE.  .  .  .  .  .  .  . 371 THE LITERATE FARMER AND  89
DENT
    NOW SLOWLY CLOSING LIKE A DENT IN DOUGH.  .  .  .  .  .  .  . 378 DIRECTIVE  .  .  .  .  .  47
DENTS
    STILL PROBES AND DENTS OUR ROCKY COAST  .  .  .  .  .  .  . 418 AMERICA IS HARD TO SEE   50
DENY
    YOU WON'T DENY THE LANTERN ISN'T NEW.  .  .  .  .  .  .  . 116 IN THE HOME STRETCH  . 178
    AT THE SAME TIME YOU CAN'T DENY IT MAKES .  .  .  .  .  .  . 149 SNOW  .  .  .  .  .  . 188
    THERE'S SOME SUCH THING AND NO ONE WILL DENY IT--  .  .  .  . 508 A MASQUE OF MERCY  . 385
DENYING
    OUT OF HIS HIRED HELP. I'M NOT DENYING  .  .  .  .  .  .  .  70 THE CODE  .  .  .  .  .  38
    BY DENYING AND IGNORING  .  .  .  .  .  .  .  .  .  .  .  . 360 NOVEMBER  .  .  .  .  .  14
DEPART
    WE FEEL IT IN THE MOMENT WE DEPART  .  .  .  .  .  .  .  . 460 HOW HARD TO KEEP FROM  196
DEPARTMENTAL
    DEPARTMENTAL  .  .  .  .  .  .  .  .  .  .  .  .  .  .  .  . 287 DEPARTMENTAL  .  .  .  .   T
    BUT HOW THOROUGHLY DEPARTMENTAL.  .  .  .  .  .  .  .  .  . 289 DEPARTMENTAL  .  .  .  .  43
DEPARTURE
    ON A NEW DEPARTURE.  .  .  .  .  .  .  .  .  .  .  .  .  .  . 427 VERSION  .  .  .  .  .  .   4
    THE ONLY CERTAIN FREEDOM'S IN DEPARTURE.  .  .  .  .  .  . 460 HOW HARD TO KEEP FROM  194
    TO INSURE A JET DEPARTURE OF OUR GOING  .  .  .  .  .  .  . 460 HOW HARD TO KEEP FROM  201
    IT'S WHAT MY FATHER MUST MEAN BY DEPARTURE,  .  .  .  .  . 461 HOW HARD TO KEEP FROM  245
```

DEPEND
   SUCH DOUBTS OF EDUCATION SHOULD DEPEND   . . . . 188 THE AX-HELVE   92
   WAS STILL IN SIGHT LIKE SOMEONE TO DEPEND ON. . . . . 404 FROM PLANE TO PLANE .   20
DEPENDED
   MY HAVING DEPENDED ON HIM SO LONG, ... 421 ONE MORE BREVITY . .   64
DEPENDING
   WHAT HELP HE IS THERE'S NO DEPENDING ON. . . . . . .   35 DEATH OF THE HIRED MAN 17
CEPENCS
   IT ALL DEPENDS ON WHAT YOU MEAN BY HOME. . . . . . .   38 DEATH OF THE HIRED MAN 114
   OUR VERY LIFE DEPENDS ON EVERYTHING'S . . . . 147 SNOW   132
DEPLOY
   NOT LIKELY, WHEN ALL THE YOUNG LORENS DEPLOY. . . . .   62 BLUEBERRIES   98
DEPRESSED
   WITH GUN DEPRESSED, ... 360 THE RABBIT-HUNTER . .   3
DEPTH
   A DEPTH PAST MANY SWINGING DOORS   . . . . 280 BLUE RIBBON AT AMESBURY 23
   THE QUESTION IS WHETHER THEY'VE REACHED A DEPTH . . . 317 BUILD SOIL   33
   COUNTED THEM ALL TO THE BUDS IN THE COPSE'S DEPTH   . . 343 QUEST OF PURPLE-FRINGED 23
   IN WIND-SOIL TO A DEPTH OF THIRTY FEET, ... 365 OF STONES OF THE PLACE 6
   WE DATE YOU BY YOUR DEPTH IN SILT AND DUST . . . . . 382 TO AN ANCIENT . . .   10
   WOULD BETTER HAVE BEEN TAKEN TO YOUR DEPTH." . . . . . 506 A MASQUE OF MERCY . . 340
DEPTHS
   WITH DEPTHS BEHIND HIM SHEER A HUNDRED FEET-- . . . .   42 THE MOUNTAIN   60
   SOMETHING MORE OF THE DEPTHS--AND THEN I LOST IT. . . . 225 FOR ONCE SOMETHING .   10
DERELICT
   WILL TAKE IN TOW THIS DERELICT . . . . 418 AMERICA IS HARD TO SEE 56
DERISION
   AND THE FLY CIRCLED ROUND HIM IN DERISION. . . . . . . 278 THE WHITE-TAILED HORNET 43
   I'D HAD ABOUT ENOUGH OF HIS DERISION . . . . 485 A MASQUE OF REASON . . 349
DERIVATION
   COURAGE IS OF THE HEART BY DERIVATION, ... 519 A MASQUE OF MERCY . . 693
DERRING-DO
   THAT ITS DERRING-DO . . . . 436 KITTY HAWK   252
DERRY
   HARRIS OF DERRY, AND LYNCH OF BETHLEHEM. . . . . 167 NEW HAMPSHIRE . . . 261
DESCEND
   ASCENDING TO DESCEND TO REASCEND. . . . . 214 A FOUNTAIN, A BOTTLE . 34
   GIVES UP HIS ERRAND, AND LETS DEATH DESCEND . . . . . 226 THE ONSET   8
DESCENDED
   AND LOOKED AT THE WORLD, AND DESCENDED; . . . . 30 RELUCTANCE   4
   IT WAS THE WORDS 'DESCENDED INTO HADES'   . . . . . .   58 THE BLACK COTTAGE . . 94
   OVER DESCENDED FROM HER. I BELIEVE . . . .   77 THE GENERATIONS OF MEN 112
   AND DESCENDED OUTSIDE. . . . . 241 THE LOCKLESS DOOR .   12
   THEN DESCENDED OF OLD ON THE BUSH. . . . . 266 SITTING BY A BUSH .   16
   YOU'RE WELL DESCENDED ON YOUR MOTHER'S SIDE, ... 457 HOW HARD TO KEEP FROM 108
DESCENT
   THAT A BROOK MAKES IN SUCH A WILD DESCENT. . . . . . . 78 THE GENERATIONS OF MEN 133
   HIS WILD DESCENT FROM THERE ONE NIGHT, ... 137 BROWN'S DESCENT . . .   6
   BROWN'S DESCENT . . . . 137 BROWN'S DESCENT . . .   T
   WHO HAD MADE AN OVERNIGHT DESCENT . . . . 421 ONE MORE BREVITY . .   62
   BUT GOD'S OWN DESCENT . . . . 435 KITTY HAWK   219
   YOU MUST MAKE YOUR DESCENT LIKE EVERYONE. . . . . . . 514 A MASQUE OF MERCY . . 552
DESCRIBE
   LONG SLEEP, AS I DESCRIBE ITS COMING ON, ... 69 AFTER APPLE-PICKING . 41
DESCRIBED
   THE FIGURES HE DESCRIBED WITH IT, ... 138 BROWN'S DESCENT . . . 31
   THAT CAN BUT BE DESCRIBED . . . . 448 THE BAD ISLAND--EASTER 43
DESCRIBING
   DESCRIBING RINGS OF LANTERN-LIGHT. . . . . 137 BROWN'S DESCENT . . .   8
DESERT
   I COULD BE MONARCH OF A DESERT LAND . . . . 58 THE BLACK COTTAGE . . 112
   SO DESERT IT WOULD HAVE TO BE, SO WALLED . . . . 58 THE BLACK COTTAGE . . 115
   THE BABE BORN TO THE DESERT, THE SANDSTORM . . . . . . 58 THE BLACK COTTAGE . . 123
   "THE PLACE IS DESERT, AND LET WHOSO LURKS . . . . . . 176 THE CENSUS-TAKER . . 57
   TO GO WEST TO A WORSE FIGHT WITH THE DESERT. . . . . . 213 A FOUNTAIN, A BOTTLE . 12
   IN THE DESERT AT MIDNIGHT IN UTAH, ... 290 ON HEART'S BEGINNING TO 2
   AT THE SHINY DESERT WITH SPOTS OF GLOOM . . . . 291 ON HEART'S BEGINNING TO 27
   DESERT PLACES . . . . 296 DESERT PLACES . . .   T
   TO SCARE MYSELF WITH MY OWN DESERT PLACES. . . . . . . 296 DESERT PLACES . . .   16
   FLOWERS IN THE DESERT HEAT . . . . 337 THE WIND AND THE RAIN 21
   THE WORLD DESERT, ... 412 AWAY!   2
   A FAIR OASIS IN THE PUREST DESERT. . . . . 473 A MASQUE OF REASON .   1
   PRECIPITATED FROM THE DESERT AIR.-- . . . . 487 A MASQUE OF REASON . . 385
   FROM THE SURROUNDING DESERT; JUST TODAY . . . . 489 A MASQUE OF REASON . . 445
DESERTED
   THE DESOLATE, DESERTED TREES, ...   7 MY NOVEMBER GUEST . . 11
   I NEVER SAW SO GOOD A HOUSE DESERTED. . . . . 215 A FOUNTAIN, A BOTTLE . 71
DESERTS
   IT WAS THE DROUGHT OF DESERTS. EARTH WOULD SOON   . . 400 THE BROKEN DROUGHT .   11
   BETWEEN HIS JUST DESERTS AND WHAT HE GETS. . . . . . . 475 A MASQUE OF REASON .   51
DESERVE
   SOMETHING YOU SOMEHOW HAVEN'T TO DESERVE." . . . . . 38 DEATH OF THE HIRED MAN 120
   YOU MUST BE WICKED TO DESERVE SUCH PAIN. . . . . 486 A MASQUE OF REASON . . 364
DESERVES
   I SUPPOSE SHE DESERVES SOME PITY, TOO. . . . . 88 THE HOUSEKEEPER . . 192
   AS TO WHOSE AGE DESERVES THE LOWER MARK, ... 352 THE LESSON FOR TODAY . 52
DESIGN
   DESIGN . . . . 302 DESIGN . . . .   T
   WHAT BUT DESIGN OF DARKNESS TO APPALL?-- . . . . 302 DESIGN   13
   IF DESIGN GOVERN IN A THING SO SMALL. . . . . 302 DESIGN   14
   TO RULE FIRST ANSWERABLE TO HIGH DESIGN. . . . . 424 FOR JOHN F. KENNEDY   65
   GRANT ME INTENTION, PURPOSE, AND DESIGN-- . . . . . . 425 ACCIDENTALLY ON PURPOSE 19
   A DESIGN FOR LIVING . . . . 435 KITTY HAWK   226
   IN HER VAGUE DESIGN . . . . 442 KITTY HAWK   453
   THE ARTIST IN ME CRIES OUT FOR DESIGN.   . . . . 482 A MASQUE OF REASON . . 261
DESIGNED
   MAY SEEM ALMOST EXCLUSIVELY DESIGNED. . . . . 321 BUILD SOIL 150

	PAGE TITLE	LINE

DESIRE
ANC THE THOUGHT OF THE HEART'S DESIRE. . . . . 8 LOVE AND A QUESTION . 20
AS IF TO SAY, 'YOU! YOU'RE THE HEART'S DESIRE.' . . . . 98 THE SELF-SEEKER . . . 158
FROM WHAT I'VE TASTED OF DESIRE . . . . 220 FIRE AND ICE 3
AND NOW FROM HAVING RIDDEN OUT DESIRE . . . . 225 BLUE-BUTTERFLY DAY . . 6
DESIRED
OF THE GREAT HARVEST I MYSELF DESIRED. . . . . 69 AFTER APPLE-PICKING . 29
WAS I DESIRED IN FRIENDSHIP, PARTLY AS SOMEONE . . . . 188 THE AX-HELVE 90
DESIST
ANC HAD THE INSPIRATION TO DESIST . . . . 302 A BIRD SINGING IN SLEEP 6
DESOLATE
THE DESOLATE, DESERTED TREES, ... 7 MY NOVEMBER GUEST . . 11
DESPAIR
IN THE WOOD-WORLD'S TORN DESPAIR . . . . 26 A LINE-STORM SONG . 10
A FEW I MUST HAVE DRIVEN TO DESPAIR . . . . 240 OUR SINGING STRENGTH . 39
WITH A GODFORSAKEN BRUTE DESPAIR. . . . . 291 ON HEART'S BEGINNING TO 10
ABOUT THE WORLD'S DESPAIR; . . . . 309 NOT ALL THERE . . . 2
I GET A POEM, I DESPAIR. . . . . 452 A-WISHING WELL . . . 33
DESPAIRED
I WILL NOT HAVE THEIR HAPPINESS DESPAIRED OF. . . . . 414 A CABIN IN THE CLEARING 12
DESPERATE
THE WATER IN DESPERATE STRAITS LIKE FRANTIC FISH, . . . 142 THE VANISHING RED . . 22
DESPERATELY
OF DESPERATELY CLUTCHING HAND . . . . 452 A-WISHING WELL . . . 60
DESPERATION
I CHANGED FROM HAND TO HAND IN DESPERATION. . . . . . 189 THE GRINDSTONE . . . 34
OF DESPERATION THAT WOULD WARRANT POETRY'S . . . . . 317 BUILD SOIL 34
COWER DOWN IN DESPERATION TO ACCEPT . . . . 357 A CONSIDERABLE SPECK . 22
DESPISE
A PRUDENT GRIEF WILL NOT DESPISE SUCH AIDS. . . . . . 200 PLACE FOR A THIRD . . 30
DESPISER
(THOUGH PRODIGAL HIMSELF AND A DESPISER . . . . . . 363 AN EQUALIZER 3
DESTINATION
YOUR DESTINATION AND YOUR DESTINY'S . . . . 378 DIRECTIVE 49
DESTINED
BUT IF IT IS DESTINED NEVER AGAIN TO GROW, ... 305 THERE ARE ROUGHLY ZONES 20
DESTINED TO PROVE OUR DESTRUCTION. . . . . 396 AN IMPORTER 12
DESTINY
TO MARKET 'TIS OUR DESTINY TO GO. . . . . 321 BUILD SOIL 172
DESTINY'S
YOUR DESTINATION AND YOUR DESTINY'S . . . . 378 DIRECTIVE 49
DESTROY
DESTROY THEIR SLEEPING AT NIGHT THE ANCIENT WAY. . . . 287 A ROADSIDE STAND . 31
DESTRUCTION
TO SAY THAT FOR DESTRUCTION ICE . . . . 220 FIRE AND ICE 7
DESTINED TO PROVE OUR DESTRUCTION. . . . . 396 AN IMPORTER 12
DETACHMENT
(WHY ARE WE SO RESENTFUL OF DETACHMENT?) . . . . . 462 HOW HARD TO KEEP FROM 272
DETAIL
OF THE ONE BEARING IT DONE IN DETAIL-- . . . . . 74 THE GENERATIONS OF MEN 41
OF DETAIL, BURNED, DISSOLVED, AND BROKEN OFF . . . . 377 DIRECTIVE 3
DETAILS
WAS THE ONE I MEANT. OUR DETAILS AGREED. . . . . . 289 OLD BARN AT THE BOTTOM 21
DETAINED
I DROPPED IN AT THE MILL AND WAS DETAINED." . . . . . 96 THE SELF-SEEKER . . . 100
DETERIORATE
THOUGH I HOLD RAYS DETERIORATE TO NOTHING: . . . . . 485 A MASQUE OF REASON . . 345
DETERIORATED
MIGHT HAVE DETERIORATED HAD NOT SOMEONE . . . . . . 456 HOW HARD TO KEEP FROM 78
DETERMINED
ALREADY DETERMINED DAWN BEGAN TO LAY . . . . 235 VALLEY'S SINGING DAY . 7
DETEST
THE DEAR KNOWS. I DETEST THE THOUGHT OF HIM-- . . . . 144 SNOW 51
WITH INNUENDO I DETEST. . . . . 467 QUANDARY 18
DEUTERONOMIST
TO STULTIFY THE DEUTERONOMIST . . . . 475 A MASQUE OF REASON . . 67
DEVELOPED
DEVELOPED IN THE GRASS AND FERN, ... 380 AN UNSTAMPED LETTER IN 20
A DEVELOPED TASTE IN VASES, ... 396 AN IMPORTER 8
DEVELOPING
--WAS BABEL: EVERYONE DEVELOPING . . . . 502 A MASQUE OF MERCY . . 240
DEVELOPMENT
AND FOLLOW SOME DEVELOPMENT OF STATE, ... 355 THE LESSON FOR TODAY . 142
DEVELOPMENTS
TO GIVE DEVELOPMENTS THE FINAL SHOVE . . . . 369 THE LITERATE FARMER AND 42
DEVICE
SOME ZEALOUS ONE'S LABORIOUS DEVICE. . . . . 74 THE GENERATIONS OF MEN 42
DEVIL
AND IF YOU'RE GOING TO SELL THEM TO THE DEVIL, ... 93 THE SELF-SEEKER . . . 6
WE CHOOSE TO SAY IT IS LET LOOSE BY THE DEVIL; . . . . 254 THE FLOOD 5
AS IF TO SAY MERE LEARNING WAS THE DEVIL . . . . . . 400 TO THE RIGHT PERSON . 10
WAS OF THE DEVIL. HE INVENTED HELL, ... 480 A MASQUE OF REASON . . 203
I WAS JUST SHOWING OFF TO THE DEVIL, JOB, ... 484 A MASQUE OF REASON . . 327
YOU'RE PENSIVE. / OH, I'M THINKING OF THE DEVIL. . . . 486 A MASQUE OF REASON . . 376
WHY NOT RIGHT NOW? / WE CAN'T WITHOUT THE DEVIL. . . . 487 A MASQUE OF REASON . . 381
(THE DEVIL ENTERS LIKE A SAPPHIRE WASP . . . . . . 487 A MASQUE OF REASON . . 389
GOD'S AFTER ME! / YOU MEAN THE DEVIL IS. . . . . . . 493 A MASQUE OF MERCY . . 19
DEVILISH
SUCH DEVILISH INGENUITY OF TORTURE . . . . 482 A MASQUE OF REASON . . 262
DEVIL'S
THE DEVIL'S NEVER VERY FAR AWAY. . . . . 487 A MASQUE OF REASON . . 382
WHAT DID WE SAY? / YOU SAID THE DEVIL'S IN IT. . . . . 487 A MASQUE OF REASON . . 397
--THE DEVIL'S BEING GOD'S BEST INSPIRATION. . . . . . 487 A MASQUE OF REASON . . 401
DEVIL-SCARING
DEVIL-SCARING FIRECRACKERS, ... 396 AN IMPORTER 4
DEVISED
WAS CUNNINGLY DEVISED TO MAKE A NOISE . . . . 98 THE SELF-SEEKER . . . 164
DEVISED THEM FOR ALEXIUS COMNENUS. . . . . 490 A MASQUE OF REASON . . 461

- 135 -

DEVOTE
    I COULD DEVOTE AND DEDICATE FOREVER . . . . 58 THE BLACK COTTAGE . . 113
    BUT INSTEAD I PROUDLY DEVOTE THEM . . . . 295 A RECORD STRIDE . . . 29
DEVOTED
    THE SPEEDING OF DEVOTED SOULS . . . . 20 THE TRIAL BY EXISTENCE 31
    HE WAS TOO DEVOTED. . . . . 433 KITTY HAWK 161
    DEVOTED ACTORS AT A SACRIFICE-- . . . . 481 A MASQUE OF REASON . 225
DEVOTION
    THE HEART CAN THINK OF NO DEVOTION . . . . 247 DEVOTION 1
    DEVOTION . . . . 247 DEVOTION . . . . . T
    OF THE STRANGE DEVOTION . . . . 433 KITTY HAWK 159
DEVOTIONS
    AT HIS DEVOTIONS IN A SPECIAL PLOT. . . . . 354 THE LESSON FOR TODAY . 130
DEW
    SMOOTH-LAID LIKE THATCH WITH THE HEAVY DEW, ... 8 A LATE WALK 3
    BEFORE THE LAST WENT, HEAVY WITH DEW, ... 15 IN A VALE 16
    WHO MOWED IT IN THE DEW BEFORE THE SUN. . . . . . . 22 THE TUFT OF FLOWERS . 2
    THE DEW WAS GONE THAT MADE HIS BLADE SO KEEN . . . . 22 THE TUFT OF FLOWERS . 3
    THE MOWER IN THE DEW HAD LOVED THEM THUS, ... 23 THE TUFT OF FLOWERS . 25
    TAUT WITH THE DEW FROM GARDEN BED TO EAVES, ... 38 DEATH OF THE HIRED MAN 108
    SAND GRAINS SHOULD SUGAR IN THE NATAL DEW . . . . . 58 THE BLACK COTTAGE . . 122
    AND STRAINING CABLES WET WITH SILVER DEW. . . . . . 126 RANGE-FINDING . . . 11
    DOWN FROM THE STARS TO FREEZE THE DEW AS STARRY. . . . 169 NEW HAMPSHIRE . . . 342
    DEW ON THE KNUCKLE. . . . . 227 TO EARTHWARD 12
    THAT LIES UNLIFTED NOW, COME DEW, COME RUST, ... 261 A SOLDIER 2
    THE DEW OF NIGHT AND MORNING ON HIS BOOT. . . . . . 283 THE GOLD HESPERIDEE . 21
    OFFERED AN OPENING TO THE SOURCE OF DEW; . . . . . . 295 LOST IN HEAVEN . . . 2
    HAD TAKEN ALL THE WATER IT COULD AS DEW, ... 315 IRIS BY NIGHT . . . 14
    HAS DRIED THE DEW AND ALL ITS ROPES RELENT, ... 331 THE SILKEN TENT . . . 3
    NOR FIND IN DEW THE SLIGHTEST CLOUDY TRACE. . . . . . 361 A LOOSE MOUNTAIN . . 12
    KEPT SOME DEW OUT AND SOME HEAT IN, ... 380 AN UNSTAMPED LETTER IN 15
DEWDROPS
    LET US PRETEND THE DEWDROPS FROM THE EAVES . . . . . 415 A CABIN IN THE CLEARING 37
DEWY
    IT LIFTED FROM ITS DEWY PEDIMENT . . . . 315 IRIS BY NIGHT . . . 26
DIALECT
    OR IT WOULD SPEAK IN DIALECT. WHOSE VOICE . . . . . 79 THE GENERATIONS OF MEN 173
DIALOGUE
    'TWAS TOO ONE-SIDED A DIALOGUE, ... 420 ONE MORE BREVITY . . 36
DIAMOND
    AS IN A SMUGGLER'S AT THE DIAMOND FIELDS, ... 503 A MASQUE OF MERCY . . 253
DIAMONDS
    FOR DIAMONDS AND APPLES. "DIAMONDS . . . . 159 NEW HAMPSHIRE . . . 11
    BEFORE IT CHANGES TO DIAMONDS IN THE SUN), ... 236 VALLEY'S SINGING DAY . 13
DIAMOND-STRING
    THE BATTLE RENT A COBWEB DIAMOND-STRUNG . . . . . . 126 RANGE-FINDING . . . 1
DIAPHANOUS
    THAT EXPLAINS WHY HE'S SO DIAPHANOUS . . . . 488 A MASQUE OF REASON . 427
DICK
    SOME TOM SAID TO DICK OR HARRY: . . . . 345 DISCOVERY OF MADEIRAS . 68
    DICK HAD OF BEING FRESH AND FULL OF COLLEGE. . . . . 404 FROM PLANE TO PLANE . 4
    PIKE SAID WITH TEMPER. AND DICK LONGED TO SAY, . . . 404 FROM PLANE TO PLANE . 8
    EVERY TIME DICK OR PIKE LOOKED UP, THE DOCTOR . . . . 404 FROM PLANE TO PLANE . 18
    AND WHEN HE CAUGHT DICK LOOKING ONCE TOO OFTEN, . . . 404 FROM PLANE TO PLANE . 26
    "HOEING'S TOO MUCH LIKE WORK FOR DICK," HE ADDED. . . 404 FROM PLANE TO PLANE . 27
    "DICK WISHES HE COULD SWAP JOBS WITH THE DOCTOR. . . . 404 FROM PLANE TO PLANE . 28
    DICK TOLD HIM TO BE FAIRER TO THE DOCTOR: . . . . . 405 FROM PLANE TO PLANE . 36
    DICK LONGED TO SAY, BUT WASN'T SURE ENOUGH . . . . . 407 FROM PLANE TO PLANE . 110
    DICK SAID, "YOU'VE BEEN A LESSON IN WORK WISDOM . . . 408 FROM PLANE TO PLANE . 122
    DICK SAID, TO OLD PIKE INNOCENT OF SHAKESPEARE. . . . 408 FROM PLANE TO PLANE . 148
    ABOUT A WHALE. / OH, YOU MEAN MOBY DICK . . . . . . 495 A MASQUE OF MERCY . . 48
DICK'S
    (HE TRIED TO IMITATE DICK'S TONE OF VOICE.) . . . . . 406 FROM PLANE TO PLANE . 73
DICTATION
    TAKING DICTATION ON A PAPER PAD . . . . 182 MAPLE 79
DICTATOR
    WERE I DICTATOR, I'LL TELL YOU WHAT I'D DO. . . . . . 320 BUILD SOIL 127
    YOU'D MAKE A SORT OF SAFETY-FIRST DICTATOR. . . . . . 320 BUILD SOIL 130
    ANYWAY. THAT IS MY STYLE OF DICTATOR. . . . . 323 BUILD SOIL 233
DICTATORSHIP
    AND LEANING ON DICTATORSHIP; . . . . 326 TO A THINKER . . . 17
DID---NOT INDEXED
DIDN'T---NOT INDEXED
DIDST
    THOU DIDST NOT KNOW, WHO TOTTERED, WANDERING ON HIGH, . 28 MY BUTTERFLY . . . 22
DIE
    "WARREN," SHE SAID, "HE HAS COME HOME TO DIE: . . . . 38 DEATH OF THE HIRED MAN 111
    WITH EVERYTHING. WHAT WE LIVE BY WE DIE BY.— . . . . 94 THE SELF-SEEKER . . . 48
    BUT COME TO DIE SHE FOUND SHE CARED SO MUCH: . . . . 199 PLACE FOR A THIRD . . 4
    WHEN HIS TIME COMES TO DIE AND SETTLE DOWN. . . . . . 202 PLACE FOR A THIRD . . 82
    AND TELL THE STONES: MEN HATE TO DIE . . . . 221 IN A DISUSED GRAVEYARD 14
    BUT UP FROM WHERE THEY DIE . . . . 260 SAND DUNES 2
    WHEN INDUSTRY SEEMED LIKE TO DIE . . . . 274 A LONE STRIKER . . . 58
    DIE EARLY AND AVOID THE FATE. . . . . 307 PROVIDE, PROVIDE . . 7
    OR IF PREDESTINED TO DIE LATE, ... 307 PROVIDE, PROVIDE . . 8
    MAKE UP YOUR MIND TO DIE IN STATE. . . . . 307 PROVIDE, PROVIDE . . 9
    LET THEM DIE OF UNSATISFIED GREED, ... 313 THE VINDICTIVES . . . 85
    LET THEM SUFFER STARVATION AND DIE . . . . 313 THE VINDICTIVES . . . 90
    THE SENDER MUST HAVE HAD TO DIE, ... 327 A MISSIVE MISSILE . . 16
    IF GOD WOULD SPARE THEM TO DIE OF AGE. . . . . 344 DISCOVERY OF MADEIRAS . 26
    OR DIE OF PHILOSOPHICAL DISTENTION. . . . . 351 THE LESSON FOR TODAY . 41
    TO EXPRESS HOW MUCH IT DIDN'T WANT TO DIE. . . . . . 357 A CONSIDERABLE SPECK . 18
    "YOU DIE FOR THAT." / "NO, YOU GO ASK YOUR MOTHER." . . 457 HOW HARD TO KEEP FROM 104
    "AT LEAST YOU OUGHT TO DIE FOR WIZARDRY." . . . . . 457 HOW HARD TO KEEP FROM 115
    DIE SAYING THAT, OLD-FASHIONED SAPIENT, ... 518 A MASQUE OF MERCY . . 663
DIED
    FROM WHICH THE LABORERS' VOICES LATE HAVE DIED, . . . 14 WAITING 4
    "EVERYTHING'S AS SHE LEFT IT WHEN SHE DIED. . . . . . 55 THE BLACK COTTAGE . . 15

DIED (CONTINUED)
    AND HIS VOICE DIED DOWN SLOWLY FROM EXHAUSTION.   .   .   .   . 66 A SERVANT TO SERVANTS . 133
    DIED NOT WITHOUT A NOISE OF CRACKLING WOOD--   .   .   .   .   . 131 THE BONFIRE 76
    SHORT OFF, AND DIED AGAINST THE WINDOWPANE."   .   .   .   .   . 149 SNOW   166
    AND THE FIRE'S DIED AND THE ROOM'S DARK AND COLD?"   .   .   . 154 SNOW   310
    HE SAID, IN CLIMATE, NONE HAD EVER DIED THERE .   .   .   .   . 159 NEW HAMPSHIRE   .   .   . 18
    TO NO ONE ANYMORE SINCE TOFFILE DIED. .   .   .   . 206 THE WITCH OF COOS .   . 131
    WHO DIED A SOLDIER-POET OF YOUR RACE. .   .   .   . 222 TO E.T.   8
    THE BREATH OF AIR HAD DIED OF COLD, ... 232 LOOKING FOR SUNSET BIRD   2
    WE'LL KNOW, WE SAY, THAT THIS WAS THE NIGHT IT DIED.   .   .   . 305 THERE ARE ROUGHLY ZONES   5
    THEY KEPT THEIR SECRETS AND DIED, ... 312 THE VINDICTIVES .   .   . 54
    THAT HAD DIED IN THE WEST.   .   .   .   .   334 COME IN   10
    THE MANY DEATHS ONE MUST HAVE DIED .   .   .   . 336 THE WIND AND THE RAIN . 10
    THE STORY IS SHE DIED OF THOUGHT. .   .   .   . 347 DISCOVERY OF MADEIRAS . 119
    AND THE BAY WHERE HIS STOLEN LADY DIED   .   .   .   .   .   . 347 DISCOVERY OF MADEIRAS . 134
    I MAY HAVE WEPT THAT ANY SHOULD HAVE DIED .   .   .   .   .   . 355 THE LESSON FOR TODAY   . 151
    FROM HAVING DIED. .   .   .   . 413 AWAY!   24
    I TOOK CARE OF YOU. AND BEFORE YOU DIED .   .   .   .   .   . 486 A MASQUE OF REASON .   . 361
DIEM
    CARPE DIEM .   .   .   . 335 CARPE DIEM   .   .   .   .   T
DIES
    HOW THE COLD CREEPS AS THE FIRE DIES AT LENGTH--   .   .   .   . 10 STORM FEAR   12
    ONE IS ALONE, AND HE DIES MORE ALONE. .   .   .   . 54 HOME BURIAL 101
    TAKE CARE TO SELL YOUR HORSE BEFORE HE DIES .   .   .   .   . 399 THE INGENUITIES OF DEBT   4
DIFFER
    EXCEPTING THAT THEY DIFFER IN THEIR MOUNTAINS.   .   .   .   . 165 NEW HAMPSHIRE   .   .   . 212
DIFFERED
    MY WELCOME DIFFERED FROM NO OTHER WELCOME.   .   .   .   .   . 186 THE AX-HELVE 36
DIFFERENCE
    I OUGHT TO KNOW--IT MAKES A DIFFERENCE WHICH: .   .   .   .   . 56 THE BLACK COTTAGE   .   . 32
    MAKE SO MUCH DIFFERENCE IN HIS MAN'S AFFAIRS. .   .   .   .   . 83 THE HOUSEKEEPER .   .   . 54
    DOORS LOCKED AND CURTAINS DRAWN WILL MAKE NO DIFFERENCE.   .   . 89 THE FEAR 16
    AND THAT HAS MADE ALL THE DIFFERENCE. .   .   .   . 105 THE ROAD NOT TAKEN .   . 20
    THIS DIFFERENCE FROM OTHER NAMES IT WAS .   .   .   .   .   . 181 MAPLE   49
    BUT PREACH AND SEE IF I CAN TELL THE DIFFERENCE.   .   .   .   . 322 BUILD SOIL   184
    COULD MAKE MUCH DIFFERENCE TO THE DEAD AND GONE.   .   .   .   . 397 THE PLANNERS   6
DIFFERENT
    SO NOW AND NEVER ANY DIFFERENT."   .   .   .   . 38 DEATH OF THE HIRED MAN 102
    "BUT A LAKE'S DIFFERENT. WHAT ABOUT THE SPRING?"   .   .   .   . 43 THE MOUNTAIN 77
    WHAT I LIKE BEST'S THE LAY OF DIFFERENT FARMS, ... 49 A HUNDRED COLLARS   .   . 124
    IT WOULD BE DIFFERENT IF MORE PEOPLE CAME, ... 63 A SERVANT TO SERVANTS . 39
    IT'S DIFFERENT WITH A MAN, AT LEAST WITH JOHN: .   .   .   .   . 84 THE HOUSEKEEPER .   .   . 79
    DIFFERENT FROM EARLY YEARS." / "I SEE THEM, TOO. .   .   .   . 112 IN THE HOME STRETCH .   . 50
    HOW DIFFERENT FROM THE WAY IT EVER STOOD? .   .   .   .   .   . 179 THE STAR-SPLITTER .   . 99
    ABOUT THE DIFFERENT TREES, AND SOMETHING, TOO, ... 180 MAPLE   27
    THE FLOWER WAS DIFFERENT FROM THE PARENT SEED. .   .   .   .   . 181 MAPLE   39
    THE SAME AT DIFFERENT TIMES TO DIFFERENT PEOPLE. .   .   .   . 184 MAPLE   156
    AND GIVE MYSELF OUT AS TWO DIFFERENT AGES, ... 196 WILD GRAPES 17
    MY BUSINESS AWHILE IS WITH DIFFERENT TREES, ... 228 GOOD-BY AND KEEP COLD . 21
    TWO ENTIRELY DIFFERENT GRANDCHILDREN   .   .   .   . 294 A RECORD STRIDE .   .   . 17
    WHICH COMES TO THE SAME THING IN DIFFERENT TERMS. .   .   .   . 353 THE LESSON FOR TODAY   . 76
    SO DIFFERENT FROM THE HARD AND LEVEL STARE   .   .   .   .   . 356 TIME OUT 10
    TO MAKE US DIFFERENT IN A SINGLE TRAIT. .   .   .   .   .   . 446 DOES NO ONE AT ALL EVER   6
    IT IS NO DIFFERENT WITH MY FOLLOWERS .   .   .   . 485 A MASQUE OF REASON .   . 352
    IT HAS A RATE DISTINCTLY DIFFERENT .   .   .   . 489 A MASQUE OF REASON .   . 444
    LIES IN OUR DIFFERENT APPROACH TO CHRIST, ... 513 A MASQUE OF MERCY   .   . 517
    MY FAILURE IS NO DIFFERENT FROM JONAH'S.   .   .   .   .   .   . 521 A MASQUE OF MERCY   .   . 727
DIFFERENTLY
    OR YOU'D FEEL DIFFERENTLY ABOUT THE CLASSES.   .   .   .   .   . 406 FROM PLANE TO PLANE .   . 78
DIFFICULTY
    THE DIFFICULTY OF SEEING WHAT STOOD STILL, ... 229 TWO LOOK AT TWO .   .   . 18
DIFFIDENCE
    PERHAPS A FILIAL DIFFIDENCE PARTLY KEPT THEM   .   .   .   .   . 184 MAPLE   157
DIFFUSE
    AND THING NEXT MOST DIFFUSE TO CLOUD, ... 251 TREE AT MY WINDOW   .   .   6
DIFFUSED
    A LIGHT THAT FALLS DIFFUSED OVER MY SHOULDER   .   .   .   .   . 515 A MASQUE OF MERCY   .   . 580
DIFFUSION
    ALL THERE IS TO IT IS DIFFUSION-- .   .   .   . 450 OUR DOOM TO BLOOM   .   .   8
DIG
    IF YE WANT HIM, YE CAN GO AND DIG HIM OUT.' .   .   .   .   .   72 THE CODE 85
    THE LEAST I COULD DO WAS HELP DIG THEIR GRAVE. .   .   .   .   . 206 THE WITCH OF COOS .   . 141
DIGGED
    THIS IS THE PIT FROM WHICH WE STARKS WERE DIGGED." .   .   .   76 THE GENERATIONS OF MEN   94
DIGGER
    OUT IN THE PLOWED GROUND IN THE COLD A DIGGER, ... 263 THE INVESTMENT   .   .   .   5
DIGGING
    "NOW WE ARE DIGGING ALMOST DOWN TO CHINA. .   .   .   .   .   . 132 THE BONFIRE 101
DIGNIFIED
    BETTER TO GO DOWN DIGNIFIED .   .   .   . 307 PROVIDE, PROVIDE .   .   . 19
DIGNITY
    TO BURY HIM HAD HURT HIS DIGNITY. .   .   .   . 72 THE CODE 104
    WITH NO SMALL DIGNITY OF MIEN. .   .   .   . 138 BROWN'S DESCENT .   .   . 24
    TO BE UPON MY DIGNITY WITH HIM. .   .   .   . 487 A MASQUE OF REASON .   . 388
DILATE
    OR A STAR COMING TO DILATE THE SUN. .   .   .   . 317 BUILD SOIL   59
DILATING
    THE SWARM DILATING ROUND THE PERFECT TREES. .   .   .   .   .   12 A PRAYER IN SPRING .   .   8
DILATION
    AT PRESENT FROM A COSMICAL DILATION .   .   .   . 320 BUILD SOIL   138
DILIGENT
    TO BE STRONG, CAREFUL, THRIFTY, DILIGENT, ... 505 A MASQUE OF MERCY   .   . 314
DIM
    IT IS UNDER THE SMALL, DIM, SUMMER STAR.   .   .   .   .   .   .   6 GHOST HOUSE 21
    SEEKING WITH MEMORIES GROWN DIM O'ER NIGHT .   .   .   .   .   . 22 THE TUFT OF FLOWERS .   . 13
    THEN THERE WERE THREE THERE, MAKING A DIM ROW, ... 40 DEATH OF THE HIRED MAN 162
    AS PALE AND DIM AS A MATCH FLAME IN THE SUN;   .   .   .   .   . 77 THE GENERATIONS OF MEN 100
    MADE THE DIM TREES STAND BACK IN WIDER CIRCLE-- .   .   .   . 130 THE BONFIRE 29

```
                                                          PAGE TITLE                        LINE
DIM (CONTINUED)
     THAT ALL YOUR DAYS ARE DIM BENEATH,       . . . . . . .  141 THE GUM-GATHERER      . .  36
     AND THEN BEYOND THE OPEN WATER, DIM WITH MIDGES,  . . . .  194 PAUL'S WIFE    . . .     106
     IT'S SOMETIMES DIM   . . . . . . . . . . . . . . . .  212 AN EMPTY THREAT    . .      40
     AND WE SAW HIM, OR THOUGHT WE SAW HIM, DIM AND GRAY,  . .  223 THE RUNAWAY   . . . .      7
     AND LOVE ITSELF WERE GROWING DIM.   . . . . . . . . .  347 DISCOVERY OF MADEIRAS .   117
     WILL BRING HER OUT, DIMINISHED DIM,  . . . . . . . .  390 TWO LEADING LIGHTS . .      19
     OR SOME DIM SECRET OF THE GOOD OF WASTE?   . . . . . .  412 POD OF THE MILKWEED   .   49
DIMENSION
     WHEN TIME WAS FOUND TO BE A SPACE DIMENSION  . . . . .  479 A MASQUE OF REASON . .  160
DIMINISHED
     IS WHAT TO MAKE OF A DIMINISHED THING.   . . . . . .  120 THE OVEN BIRD    . . .   14
     WILL BRING HER OUT, DIMINISHED DIM,   . . . . . . . .  390 TWO LEADING LIGHTS . .   19
DIMLY
     DIMLY TO HAVE MADE OUT MY SECRET PLACE,   . . . . . .   14 WAITING . . . . . . .   15
     I STOLE FORTH DIMLY IN THE DRIPPING PAUSE   . . . . .  300 MOON COMPASSES   . . .    1
DIMNESS
     A LOOK OF PUZZLED DIMNESS TO THEIR EYES  . . . . . .  293 AT WOODWARD'S GARDENS .   10
DIMPLE
     IT MUST HAVE MADE YOUR DIMPLE THERE, AND SAID,  . . . .  180 MAPLE  . . . . . . .   17
DIMPLED
     I FOUND A DIMPLED SPIDER, FAT AND WHITE,  . . . . . .  302 DESIGN . . . . . . .    1
DIMS
     BUT NAUGHT EXTENUATES OR DIMS,   . . . . . . . . . .   20 THE TRIAL BY EXISTENCE   39
DIN
     WE TALKED LIKE BARKING ABOVE THE DIN  . . . . . . . .  140 THE GUM-GATHERER   . .    7
     THE SHATTERED WATER MADE A MISTY DIN.   . . . . . . .  250 ONCE BY THE PACIFIC   .    1
DINER
     HE COULD LOOK AT US IN OUR DINER EATING,  . . . . . .  292 FIGURE IN THE DOORWAY .   21
DINGY
     HE FETCHED A DINGY LANTERN FROM BEHIND   . . . . . .  115 IN THE HOME STRETCH   .  136
DINING
     AND DINING ROOM--THROWN PELL-MELL IN THE KITCHEN.  . . .  110 IN THE HOME STRETCH   .    9
DINNER
     WAS LATELY AT A CUT-GLASS DINNER IN BOSTON.   . . . . .  163 NEW HAMPSHIRE    . . .  127
DINNERS
     WAS COUNTING WINTER DINNERS, ONE A HILL,  . . . . . .  263 THE INVESTMENT   . . .    7
DIONE
     YET SINGING BUT DIONE IN THE WOOD  . . . . . . . .  351 THE LESSON FOR TODAY .   14
DIPPED
     BUT DIPPED ITS TOP AND SET ME DOWN AGAIN.   . . . . .  122 BIRCHES  . . . . . .   57
     THE OTHER CURLED AT HIS BREAST. HE DIPPED HIS HEAD  . . .  223 THE RUNAWAY   . . . .    4
     AND IMPULSE, HAVING DIPPED A FINGER LENGTH   . . . .  231 A BROOK IN THE CITY   .    6
DIRECT
     THE ROAD THERE, IF YOU'LL LET A GUIDE DIRECT YOU   . . .  377 DIRECTIVE . . . . . .    8
DIRECTED
     NO DOUBT DIRECTED AT OUR HEADS AS REBELS  . . . . . .  361 A LOOSE MOUNTAIN   . .    6
DIRECTION
     NOBODY KNEW IN WHAT DIRECTION,   . . . . . . . . . .  192 PAUL'S WIFE    . . . .   27
     SUPPOSE YOU'VE NO DIRECTION IN YOU,   . . . . . . . .  326 TO A THINKER    . . .   25
     IS ALWAYS IN THE OPPOSITE DIRECTION.  . . . . . . . .  358 THE LOST FOLLOWER   . .   10
     SO BROODINGLY SOON IN EVERY DIRECTION.   . . . . . .  379 TOO ANXIOUS FOR RIVERS   13
DIRECTIONS
     THE FINGER-PIECES SLID IN ALL DIRECTIONS.   . . . . .  204 THE WITCH OF COOS   . .   79
DIRECTIVE
     DIRECTIVE  . . . . . . . . . . . . . . . . . .  377 DIRECTIVE . . . . . .    T
DIRECTLY
     TO LOOK AT LONG DIRECTLY (LIKE THE SUN),  . . . . . .  515 A MASQUE OF MERCY   .  584
DIRECTOR
     A SOMEBODY--DIRECTOR IN THE BANK."   . . . . . . . .   39 DEATH OF THE HIRED MAN  129
DIRT
     BRUSHING THE DIRT FROM HIS EYE AS HE WENT;  . . . . .   25 THE DEMIURGE'S LAUGH  .   11
     HE TELLS HER AS MUCH OF BLOOD AND DIRT   . . . . . .  346 DISCOVERY OF MADEIRAS .   88
     TO CURRY FAVOR WITH THE DIRT SOME MORE.   . . . . . .  405 FROM PLANE TO PLANE   .   43
     AND CAKE THEIR CONCRETE DIRT OFF IN THE STREETS."  . . .  506 A MASQUE OF MERCY   .  334
DISABLED
     HEARTBROKEN AND DISABLED  . . . . . . . . . . . .  387 THE COURAGE TO BE NEW .    5
DISADVANTAGE  (SEE ADVANTAGE-DISADVANTAGE)
DISAGREE
     THE ONLY TROUBLE IS WE DISAGREE   . . . . . . . . .   48 A HUNDRED COLLARS   .  108
     FOR ME TO DISAGREE WITH HIM AND GET SPIT OUT   . . . .  500 A MASQUE OF MERCY   .  184
     FOR ME TO DISAGREE WITH ANY SCIENCE   . . . . . . .  500 A MASQUE OF MERCY   .  188
     OUR DISAGREEMENT WHEN WE DISAGREE, PAUL,  . . . . . .  513 A MASQUE OF MERCY   .  516
DISAGREEABLE
     IF WHAT YOU HAD TO SAY WAS DISAGREEABLE.  . . . . . .  497 A MASQUE OF MERCY   .  105
DISAGREEMENT
     OUR DISAGREEMENT WHEN WE DISAGREE, PAUL,  . . . . . .  513 A MASQUE OF MERCY   .  516
DISAPPEAR
     MAGNIFIED APPLES APPEAR AND DISAPPEAR,   . . . . . .   68 AFTER APPLE-PICKING   .   18
     "HOW IS THE WIFE, PAUL?"--AND HE'D DISAPPEAR.  . . . .  191 PAUL'S WIFE    . . . .    3
     FOR LONG THE LADY WOULD DISAPPEAR,   . . . . . . . .  344 DISCOVERY OF MADEIRAS .   32
DISAPPEARED
     AND DISAPPEARED AND ENDED NOT FAR OFF.   . . . . . .   75 THE GENERATIONS OF MEN   72
     WHO ASKED THE QUESTION. HE JUST DISAPPEARED--  . . . .  192 PAUL'S WIFE    . . . .   26
     THEY DISAPPEARED AS IF EARTH SENT THEM BACK.  . . . .  239 OUR SINGING STRENGTH  .    6
DISAPPEARING
     AND DEAD WEEDS, LIKE A DISAPPEARING SNAKE.  . . . . .  226 THE ONSET   . . . . .   21
     THE DISAPPEARING LAST OF HIM.   . . . . . . . . . .  392 A CLIFF DWELLING   . .   11
DISAPPEARS
     ALTHOUGH AT TIMES WE THINK IT DISAPPEARS.   . . . . .  369 THE LITERATE FARMER AND  32
DISAPPOINT
     WOULD ONLY DISAPPOINT US AT THE LAST  . . . . . . .  446 DOES NO ONE AT ALL EVER    4
DISAPPOINTMENT
     MAY AS EXPECTED WAS A DISAPPOINTMENT,   . . . . . . .  406 FROM PLANE TO PLANE   .   88
DISAPPROVED
     AND NOT ENTIRELY DISAPPROVED   . . . . . . . . . .  469 CHOSEN POET OF VERMONT    3
DISARMED
     HE MIGHT PREFER TO SAY TO HIM DISARMED.   . . . . . .  185 THE AX-HELVE    . . . .   17
```

DISASTER
   I'D WELCOME ANY MODERATE DISASTER . . . . 190 THE GRINDSTONE 62
   THE PROPHET OF DISASTER CEASED TO SHOUT. . . . . . . 399 THE BROKEN DROUGHT . . . 1
DISC
   AND SITS IN SIRIUS' DISC ALL NIGHT, ... 120 BOND AND FREE . . . 12
DISCERNED
   OF THOSE WHO FOR SOME GOOD DISCERNED . . . . 20 THE TRIAL BY EXISTENCE 27
   I DISCERNED, AS I THOUGHT, BEYOND THE PICTURE, ... 225 FOR ONCE SOMETHING . . . 8
DISCERNMENT
   EACH KNOWS HIS OWN DISCERNMENT BEST. . . . . 381 AN UNSTAMPED LETTER IN 43
DISCHARGE
   "YOU TOOK AN AWKWARD WAY. DID HE DISCHARGE YOU?" . . . . 73 THE CODE 113
   "DISCHARGE ME? NO! HE KNEW I DID JUST RIGHT." . . . . 73 THE CODE 114
DISCIPLINE
   THE DISCIPLINE OF FARMING WAS SO STERN, ... 398 BURSTING RAPTURE . . 7
   AND DISCIPLINE SHOULD BE IN SCHOOL AND STATE . . . . . 460 HOW HARD TO KEEP FROM 200
   FOUND OUT THE DISCIPLINE MAN NEEDED MOST . . . . . . 481 A MASQUE OF REASON . 209
   OLD ATTIC GRACE AND SPARTAN DISCIPLINE . . . . . . 511 A MASQUE OF MERCY . 467
DISCIPLINED
   YET LIKE A CHRISTIAN DISCIPLINED TO BEND . . . . . . 353 THE LESSON FOR TODAY . 94
DISCONCERTED
   THEN DISCONCERTED AND NOT UNANNOYED, ... 278 THE WHITE-TAILED HORNET 37
DISCORD
   THAN GRINDING DISCORD OUT OF A GRINDSTONE, ... 190 THE GRINDSTONE . . . 54
DISCOUNT
   DON'T DISCOUNT OUR POWERS; . . . . 439 KITTY HAWK 361
DISCOURAGED
   I AM IMPOSED ON, SILENCED AND DISCOURAGED. . . . . . 324 BUILD SOIL . . . 251
   YOU'RE WORKING IT, OLD MAN. DON'T BE DISCOURAGED. . . . 507 A MASQUE OF MERCY . 347
DISCOURSING
   AND STARTED HIS MARCH BACK AGAIN DISCOURSING: . . . . 406 FROM PLANE TO PLANE . 60
DISCOVERED
   A BREEZE DISCOVERED MY OPEN BOOK . . . . 342 A CLOUD SHADOW . . . 1
DISCOVERY
   MIGHT LEAD US ON TO A DISCOVERY. . . . . 183 MAPLE 126
   THEY HOVERED FOR A MOMENT NEAR DISCOVERY, ... 184 MAPLE 153
   THE DISCOVERY OF THE MADEIRAS . . . . 343 DISCOVERY OF MADEIRAS . T
   WAS THE DISCOVERY OF FIRE INSURANCE. . . . . 506 A MASQUE OF MERCY . 319
   FROM THE DISCOVERY THAT LOSS FROM FAILURE, ... 506 A MASQUE OF MERCY . 321
DISCREET
   IT HAD SEEMED DISCREET TO REMAIN THERE . . . . . . 314 BEARER OF EVIL TIDINGS 25
DISCRETE
   ONE AND YET DISCRETE . . . . 426 A NEVER NAUGHT SONG . 10
DISCRIMINATE
   IF ONLY TO DISCRIMINATE . . . . 467 QUANDARY 9
DISCRIMINATED
   ROUGHLY DISCRIMINATED FOR THE ROUGH. . . . . 318 BUILD SOIL 88
DISCRIMINATING
   TO A DISCRIMINATING APPETITE, ... 97 THE SELF-SEEKER . . . 128
DISCRIMINATION
   THAT'S WHY DISCRIMINATION REIGNS. . . . . 467 QUANDARY 7
DISCUSS
   YOU'RE RIGHT, THERE'S NOTHING TO DISCUSS. . . . . . 420 ONE MORE BREVITY . . 29
DISCUSSED
   YOUR PROBABLE BRUTE NATURE IS DISCUSSED. . . . . . . 382 TO AN ANCIENT . . . 11
DISDAINED
   THE BREEZE DISDAINED TO MAKE REPLY; . . . . 342 A CLOUD SHADOW . . . 6
DISEASE
   IS A DISEASE OF YOUR IMAGINATION. . . . . 503 A MASQUE OF MERCY . 258
DISFIGURED
   AND NOT DISFIGURED VISIBLY. HIS FACE? . . . . 230 NOT TO KEEP 7
DISGRACE
   IS THE DISGRACE IN MAN OR STATE OR NATION. . . . . . 159 NEW HAMPSHIRE . . . 8
   I HAD THOUGHT OURS THE MORE PROFOUND DISGRACE; . . . . 353 THE LESSON FOR TODAY . 79
DISGUSTED
   HE LOOKED SO CLEAN DISGUSTED FROM BEHIND . . . . . . 72 THE CODE 99
   DISGUSTED THE MILLER PHYSICALLY AS COMING . . . . . 142 THE VANISHING RED . . 17
DISH
   AND SAW THEM PICKED UNBRUISED AND IN A DISH, ... 284 THE GOLD HESPERIDEE . 36
   OR BETTER ON DISH PLATES ALL AROUND THE ROOM, ... 320 BUILD SOIL 148
DISHEARTENS
   "ALL THIS FACILITY DISHEARTENS ME. . . . . 460 HOW HARD TO KEEP FROM 203
DISHES
   AND WASHING DISHES AFTER THEM--FROM DOING . . . . . 64 A SERVANT TO SERVANTS . 51
   OF COURSE THEY HAD TO FEED HIM WITHOUT DISHES. . . . . 66 A SERVANT TO SERVANTS . 121
   AND CARRIED ITSELF LIKE A PILE OF DISHES . . . . . . 203 THE WITCH OF COOS . . 29
   SOME SHATTERED DISHES UNDERNEATH A PINE, ... 378 DIRECTIVE 42
DISHEVELED
   DRESSED, BUT DISHEVELED FROM SOME HOURS OF SLEEP; . . . 143 SNOW 4
DISHONEST
   IT SMELLS TO ME LIKE A DISHONEST TRICK." . . . . . . 100 THE SELF-SEEKER . . . 203
DISHPAN
   "RANK WEEDS THAT LOVE THE WATER FROM THE DISHPAN . . . 111 IN THE HOME STRETCH . 30
   MORE THAN SOME WOMEN LIKE THE DISHPAN, JOE; . . . . . 111 IN THE HOME STRETCH . 31
DISHWASHING
   THE SLAVE SERVED HIS NOVITIATE DISHWASHING. . . . . . 455 HOW HARD TO KEEP FROM 54
DISILLUSION
   'TWAS DISILLUSION UPON DISILLUSION. . . . . 279 THE WHITE-TAILED HORNET 66
DISILLUSIONMENT
   FROM DISILLUSIONMENT. YOU'VE HAD TO TAKE IT. . . . . 518 A MASQUE OF MERCY . 648
DISINTERESTEDLY
   ONLY DISINTERESTEDLY TO DECIDE . . . . 191 THE GRINDSTONE . . . 71
DISINTERESTEDNESS
   DISINTERESTEDNESS NEVER DID EXIST, ... 485 A MASQUE OF REASON . 354
DISLODGE
   SO HE CAN FIND AND EASILY DISLODGE IT . . . . 37 DEATH OF THE HIRED MAN 91
DISMAY
   FIRM IN OUR FREE BELIEFS WITHOUT DISMAY, ... 424 FOR JOHN F. KENNEDY . 74

	PAGE TITLE	LINE

DISMISSED
YOU'VE FINISHED. I'M DISMISSED. I WANT TO RUN . . . . . 514 A MASQUE OF MERCY . . 544
DISOBEY
TO DISOBEY YOU. MUCH HIS WIFE'LL THANK YOU." . . . . . 153 SNOW 284
DISPARAGE
TO ASK MY QUESTION. WE DISPARAGE REASON. . . . . 481 A MASQUE OF REASON . 228
DISPENSES
KNEEL TO YOUR DOCTOR. HE DISPENSES MERCY.-- . . . . . 507 A MASQUE OF MERCY . . 346
DISPLACE
THAT SHALL ALL LIVING THINGS DISPLACE. . . . . . . 280 BLUE RIBBON AT AMESBURY 28
DISPLACED
HER SHINING HAIR DISPLACED. . . . . 339 THE SUBVERTED FLOWER . 17
DISPLAY
OF UNSATISFIED LOVE OF DISPLAY, ... 313 THE VINDICTIVES . . . 86
ON ANY SHEET THE LEAST DISPLAY OF MIND. . . . . . . 358 A CONSIDERABLE SPECK . 33
IN A DISPLAY OF UNDERDOWN AND QUILL . . . . 445 QUESTIONING FACES . . 5
BUT DON'T TELL ME IT WASN'T HIS DISPLAY . . . . . 462 HOW HARD TO KEEP FROM 273
DISPOSE
THEY DON'T DISPOSE ME, EITHER ONE OF THEM, ... 207 PAUPER WITCH OF GRAFTON 6
HOW ELSE DISPOSE OF AN IMMORTAL FORCE . . . . . . 231 A BROOK IN THE CITY . 13
DISPOSED
AND FINDING, WASN'T DISPOSED TO SPEAK. . . . . . . 421 ONE MORE BREVITY . . 69
AND THE LEAST DISPOSED TO ASCRIBE . . . . 444 THE DRAFT HORSE . . . 15
DISPOSING
ABOUT DISPOSING OF IT. DO YOU KNOW, ... 164 NEW HAMPSHIRE . . . 169
DISPOSSESSED
A BUTTERFLY ITS FALL HAD DISPOSSESSED, ... 126 RANGE-FINDING . . . 6
DISPUTED
WHILE HAVING ITS BELIEFS DISPUTED. . . . . 419 AMERICA IS HARD TO SEE 82
DISPUTING
THAT KEPT THE GROUND, ALMOST DISPUTING RIGHT . . . . 240 OUR SINGING STRENGTH . 36
IN PUBLICLY DISPUTING WHICH IS WORSE, ... 352 THE LESSON FOR TODAY . 48
THERE CAN BE NO DISPUTING WHO HAS WON-- . . . . . 507 A MASQUE OF MERCY . . 367
DISREGARD
ATONES FOR LATER DISREGARD . . . . 307 PROVIDE, PROVIDE . . 17
DISREGARDED
YET YOUR FRIEND HERE CAN'T BE QUITE DISREGARDED. . . . 517 A MASQUE OF MERCY . . 638
DISREGARDING
"OR DISREGARDING PEOPLE'S CIVIL QUESTIONS-- . . . . 151 SNOW 251
DISRESPECTFUL
TO BRUSH AWAY A DISRESPECTFUL SMILE. . . . . . . 487 A MASQUE OF REASON . 391
DISSATISFACTION
OF INTELLECTUAL DISSATISFACTION, ... 169 NEW HAMPSHIRE . . . 328
SOME QUAINT DISSATISFACTION ATE HIM. . . . . . . 451 A-WISHING WELL . . . 7
DISSATISFIED
IF DISSATISFIED . . . . 413 AWAY! 22
DISSEMBLE
SHALL NOT DISSEMBLE THEIR SURPRISE . . . . 19 THE TRIAL BY EXISTENCE 2
DISSOLVED
OF DETAIL, BURNED, DISSOLVED, AND BROKEN OFF . . . . 377 DIRECTIVE 3
DISTANCE (SEE SAD-WITH-DISTANCE)
AND A GOOD DISTANCE DOWN MIGHT NOT BE NOTICED . . . . 43 THE MOUNTAIN 71
TOO LOUD FOR THE DISTANCE YOU WERE, IT TURNED OUT, . . . 62 BLUEBERRIES 94
HE TOLD THE DISTANCE, "I AM ARMED FOR WAR. . . . . 270 THE EGG AND THE MACHINE 28
IT DID MORE DISTANCE UP AND DOWN, ... 344 DISCOVERY OF MADEIRAS . 19
NO PLACE TO GET LOST LIKE TOO FAR IN THE DISTANCE. . . . 379 TOO ANXIOUS FOR RIVERS 11
NEARER IN PLIGHT THEIR NEIGHBORS ARE THAN DISTANCE. . . . 414 A CABIN IN THE CLEARING 9
ANOTHER STILL, LOST FAR INTO THE DISTANCE. . . . . 421 ESCAPIST--NEVER . . 8
OUR COVERAGE OF DISTANCE IS SO FACILE . . . . . . 446 DOES NO ONE AT ALL EVER 15
DISTANT (SEE FAR-DISTANT)
LET'S CELEBRATE THE EVENT, MY DISTANT FRIEND, ... 352 THE LESSON FOR TODAY . 47
SO AT THE DISTANT BEND . . . . 388 MIDDLENESS OF THE ROAD 4
DISTASTE
(HE LEANS AWAY IN TOLERANT DISTASTE.) . . . . . . 504 A MASQUE OF MERCY . . 287
DISTENTION
OR DIE OF PHILOSOPHICAL DISTENTION. . . . . . . 351 THE LESSON FOR TODAY . 41
DISTILLED
ITS FLOWERS' DISTILLED HONEY IS SO SWEET . . . . . 411 POD OF THE MILKWEED . 21
DISTINCTLY
I CAN MAKE OUT OLD GRANDSIR STARK DISTINCTLY-- . . . . 77 THE GENERATIONS OF MEN 104
IT HAS A RATE DISTINCTLY DIFFERENT . . . . 489 A MASQUE OF REASON . 444
DISTRAUGHT
THEN WHEN I WAS DISTRAUGHT . . . . 29 MY BUTTERFLY 38
DISTRESSED
(TAKING A WALK OFF DOWN THE STORE DISTRESSED) . . . . 503 A MASQUE OF MERCY . . 267
DISTRIBUTION
FOR DISTRIBUTION TO HIS BUREAUCRATS. . . . . . . 518 A MASQUE OF MERCY . . 645
DISTRICT
THERE IS A DISTRICT SCHOOLHOUSE I ADMIRE . . . . . 400 TO THE RIGHT PERSON . 2
DISTRUST
WE CONGREGATE EMBRACING FROM DISTRUST . . . . . . 325 BUILD SOIL 276
DISTURB
"YOU'D BETTER NOT DISTURB ME ANYMORE," . . . . 270 THE EGG AND THE MACHINE 27
TO DISTURB THEIR PERFECT POISE THE LIVELONG DAY . . . 343 QUEST OF PURPLE-FRINGED 19
DISTURBED
DISTURBED, I DOUBT NOT, BY MY THOUGHT, ... 9 A LATE WALK . . . 11
ANYWAY THEY WON'T HAVE THE PLACE DISTURBED." . . . 55 THE BLACK COTTAGE . . 21
DISTURBED THE SLUMBERING VILLAGE STREET . . . . . 102 GOOD HOURS 14
ONCE IN THE STOVE, DISTURBED HIM AND HE SHIFTED, . . . 108 OLD MAN'S WINTER NIGHT 24
DISTURBING (SEE ALL-DISTURBING)
DISUSED
ON THAT DISUSED AND FORGOTTEN ROAD . . . . 6 GHOST HOUSE . . . 13
IN A DISUSED GRAVEYARD . . . . 221 IN A DISUSED GRAVEYARD T
DITCH
HE SAID HE'D COME TO DITCH THE MEADOW FOR ME." . . . . 36 DEATH OF THE HIRED MAN 46
HE'S COME TO HELP YOU DITCH THE MEADOW. . . . . . . 40 DEATH OF THE HIRED MAN 157
SO AS TO WRECK THE ENGINE IN THE DITCH. . . . . . . 270 THE EGG AND THE MACHINE 8
WHEN MY GARDEN HAS GONE DOWN DITCH, ... 285 IN TIME OF CLOUDBURST . 12

DITCH (CONTINUED)
    WITH TWO WHEELS LOW IN THE DITCH . . . . 367 A SERIOUS STEP LIGHTLY   9
DITE
    BUT THERE'S A DITE TOO MANY OF THEM FOR COMFORT. . . . . 80 THE GENERATIONS OF MEN 189
DITTY
    EMBLEMATIC DITTY, ... 428 KITTY HAWK 4
DIVE
    WE DIVE DOWN UNDER THE FARM. . . . . 282 A DRUMLIN WOODCHUCK . 16
    IT IS NOTHING TO ME WHO RUNS THE DIVE. . . . . 310 IN DIVES' DIVE . . . 5
    IN DIVES' DIVE . . . . 310 IN DIVES' DIVE . . . T
    TOLD THEM IN WHAT LAKE TO DIVE . . . . 311 THE VINDICTIVES . . . 43
    HE TOLD THEM TO DIVE TILL THEY DROWNED. . . . . . . 311 THE VINDICTIVES . . . 46
DIVED
    THEY DIVED AND NOTHING WAS FOUND. . . . . 311 THE VINDICTIVES . . . 45
DIVERGED
    TWO ROADS DIVERGED IN A YELLOW WOOD, ... 105 THE ROAD NOT TAKEN . 1
    TWO ROADS DIVERGED IN A WOOD, AND I-- . . . . 105 THE ROAD NOT TAKEN . . 18
DIVES'
    IN DIVES' DIVE . . . . 310 IN DIVES' DIVE . . . T
DIVIDE
    DIVIDE IT? NO! BUT BURN IT AS ONE PILE . . . . . . 129 THE BONFIRE 9
DIVIDES
    BUT SOON DIVIDES THE RIVER WITH VERMONT. . . . . . . 165 NEW HAMPSHIRE . . . 185
    NATURE WITHIN HER INMOST SELF DIVIDES . . . . 468 FROM IRON 1
DIVINE
    YET, AFTER ALL, 'TWAS NOT DIVINE, ... 274 A LONE STRIKER . . . 52
    BECAUSE HE WAS BORN DIVINE. . . . . 314 BEARER OF EVIL TIDINGS 32
    DIVINE LOVE, HUMAN LOVE, PARENTAL LOVE, ... 318 BUILD SOIL 87
    OF LYRIC IS A GOLDEN LIGHT DIVINE, ... 358 THE LOST FOLLOWER . . 3
    ARE MORE DIVINE THAN ANY BULB OR ARC, ... 370 THE LITERATE FARMER AND 77
    AND WHAT ON THIS IS YOUR DIVINE POSITION? . . . . . . 398 NO HOLY WARS FOR THEM . 10
    A DEMOCRATIC FORM OF RIGHT DIVINE . . . . 424 FOR JOHN F. KENNEDY . 64
    THAT'S NEAR ENOUGH FOR ME TO THE DIVINE. . . . . . . 425 ACCIDENTALLY ON PURPOSE 20
    AND BY RIGHT DIVINE, ... 442 KITTY HAWK 457
DIVINED
    THEY WERE BOTH STIRRED THAT HE SHOULD HAVE DIVINED . . 182 MAPLE 92
DIVINITY
    AN IRRESPONSIBLE DIVINITY . . . . 390 TWO LEADING LIGHTS . . 27
DIVISION
    FROM ALL DIVISION TIME OR FOE CAN BRING . . . . . . 315 IRIS BY NIGHT . . . 30
DIVORCED
    MANY LOVERS HAVE BEEN DIVORCED . . . . 346 DISCOVERY OF MADEIRAS . 78
DIZZIED
    SURGING, THE GRASSES DIZZIED ME OF THOUGHT, ... 29 MY BUTTERFLY 35
DO---NOT INDEXED
DOCET
    HAEC FABULA DOCET . . . . 394 HAEC FABULA DOCET . . T
DOCKED
    HIS TIME BE LOST, HIS PITTANCE DOCKED. . . . . . . 273 A LONE STRIKER . . . 8
DOCKET
    AND TWENTY FREEDOMS ON THE PARTY DOCKET. . . . . . . 484 A MASQUE OF REASON . 311
DOCTOR
    DOCTOR MAGOON." / "A DOCTOR?" / "WELL, A TEACHER." . . 46 A HUNDRED COLLARS . 43
    THE DOCTOR LOOKED AT LAFE AND LOOKED AWAY. . . . . . 46 A HUNDRED COLLARS . 49
    THE DOCTOR CAUGHT HIS THROAT CONVULSIVELY. . . . . . 46 A HUNDRED COLLARS . 62
    THE DOCTOR MADE A SUBDUED DASH FOR IT, ... 47 A HUNDRED COLLARS . 73
    BUT YOU'RE THE DOCTOR, AS THE SAYING IS. . . . . . . 50 A HUNDRED COLLARS . 170
    THE DOCTOR SLID A LITTLE DOWN THE PILLOW. . . . . . 51 A HUNDRED COLLARS . 179
    THE DOCTOR, WHEN HE COMES. DON'T LET HIM, SISTER!" . . 137 "OUT, OUT--" 26
    THE DOCTOR PUT HIM IN THE DARK OF ETHER. . . . . . . 137 "OUT, OUT--" 28
    NOW TAKE THE DOCTOR--" / THEY WERE GIVING CORN . . . 404 FROM PLANE TO PLANE . 12
    EVERY TIME DICK OR PIKE LOOKED UP, THE DOCTOR . . . . 404 FROM PLANE TO PLANE . 18
    "DICK WISHES HE COULD SWAP JOBS WITH THE DOCTOR. . . . 404 FROM PLANE TO PLANE . 28
    DICK TOLD HIM TO BE FAIRER TO THE DOCTOR: . . . . . 405 FROM PLANE TO PLANE . 36
    IF I DECIDED TO BECOME A DOCTOR, ... 406 FROM PLANE TO PLANE . 67
    TO BOTHER ME BY SIDING WITH THE DOCTOR. . . . . . . 406 FROM PLANE TO PLANE . 76
    YET YOU REFUSE TO SEE IT IN THE DOCTOR." . . . . . . 407 FROM PLANE TO PLANE . 101
    "ALL RIGHT, LET'S HARMONIZE ABOUT THE DOCTOR. . . . . 407 FROM PLANE TO PLANE . 102
    HE'S MINE. THAT'S WHAT HE IS (YOU ASKED)--MY DOCTOR. . 499 A MASQUE OF MERCY . 154
    I'M NOT IN LOVE. I DIDN'T LOVE THE DOCTOR . . . . . 499 A MASQUE OF MERCY . 157
    KNEEL TO YOUR DOCTOR. HE DISPENSES MERCY.-- . . . . 507 A MASQUE OF MERCY . 346
    FOR WHAT YOU THINK YOUR DOCTOR THINKS, WHY DON'T YOU? . 519 A MASQUE OF MERCY . 680
DOCTORING
    WITH DOCTORING. BUT IT'S NOT MEDICINE-- . . . . . . 64 A SERVANT TO SERVANTS . 47
DOCTORS
    AN ANALYST'S THE LATEST THING IN DOCTORS. . . . . . 499 A MASQUE OF MERCY . 153
    THE DOCTORS SAY THE TROUBLE WITH ME IS . . . . . . 499 A MASQUE OF MERCY . 156
DOCTOR'S
    LOWE IS THE ONLY DOCTOR'S DARED TO SAY SO-- . . . . 64 A SERVANT TO SERVANTS . 48
    THE DOCTOR'S SURE YOU'RE GOING TO WALK AGAIN?" . . . 93 THE SELF-SEEKER . . 15
    TO PAY THE DOCTOR'S BILL AND TIDE ME OVER. . . . . . 95 THE SELF-SEEKER . . 74
    "THAT'S WHAT THE DOCTOR'S DOING, KEEPING HIS. . . . . 407 FROM PLANE TO PLANE . 97
DOCTRINE
    I HOLD YOUR DOCTRINE OF MEMENTO MORI. . . . . 355 THE LESSON FOR TODAY . 157
    NEITHER WOULD FAIRNESS. YOU HAVE HEARD THE DOCTRINE. . 485 A MASQUE OF REASON . 356
    (HIS WAS THE DOCTRINE OF THE SEVEN POSES) . . . . . 511 A MASQUE OF MERCY . 464
DOCUMENTS
    NOW RUN.--GET OUT YOUR DOCUMENTS! YOU SEE . . . . . 99 THE SELF-SEEKER . . . 175
    YOU, CRUMPLING FOLKS'S LEGAL DOCUMENTS. . . . . . . 99 THE SELF-SEEKER . . . 196
DODGED
    HE DODGED A LOG THAT LIFTED LIKE AN ARM . . . . . . 170 NEW HAMPSHIRE . . . 347
DODGES
    AND EVEN HE, YOU'LL NOTICE, DODGES OFF . . . . . . 408 FROM PLANE TO PLANE . 141
DOE
    A DOE FROM ROUND A SPRUCE STOOD LOOKING AT THEM . . . 229 TWO LOOK AT TWO . . . 15
    NOT THE SAME DOE COME BACK INTO HER PLACE. . . . . . 229 TWO LOOK AT TWO . . . 30
DOERS (SEE GOOD-DOERS)

DOES---NOT INDEXED
DOESN'T---NOT INDEXED
DOFFED
    HE DOFFED HIS CAP AND HELD IT WITH BOTH HANDS . . . . . 114 IN THE HOME STRETCH . 106
DOG
    SOME THOUGHT HE HAD BEEN BITTEN BY A DOG, ... 65 A SERVANT TO SERVANTS . 105
    AND BY SO DOING GIVE THESE THREE, LAMP, DOG, ... 148 SNOW 145
    THE OLD DOG BARKS BACKWARD WITHOUT GETTING UP. . . . . 308 THE SPAN OF LIFE . . 1
    AND THE DOG OR WHAT IT WAS, ... 341 THE SUBVERTED FLOWER . 58
    ON OUR SYMPATHY WITH THE UNDER DOG . . . . 362 SYMPATHY WITH UNDER DOG . T
    NOT A HEAVENLY DOG MADE MANIFEST, ... 419 ONE MORE BREVITY . . 10
    BUT AN EARTHLY DOG OF THE CARRIAGE BREED; . . . . . 419 ONE MORE BREVITY . . 11
    AND I WASN'T SURE I WAS TALKING DOG. . . . . . . 420 ONE MORE BREVITY . . 37
DOG-PREFERRED
    TO BE THE ONE SO DOG-PREFERRED. . . . . 419 ONE MORE BREVITY . . 14
DOGS
    TO PLEASE THE YELPING DOGS. THE GAPS I MEAN, ... 33 MENDING WALL . . . 9
    "YOU HEAR THOSE HOUND DOGS SING ON MOOSILAUKE? . . . . 168 NEW HAMPSHIRE . . . 293
    WENT LONG SINCE TO THE DOGS UNDER THE TABLE. . . . . 279 THE WHITE-TAILED HORNET 57
    WHERE NATURAL FRIENDS ARE MET, WHERE DOGS ARE KEPT, . . 318 BUILD SOIL 83
    WE WATCH A CIRCUS OF REVOLVING DOGS . . . . . . 362 SYMPATHY WITH UNDER DOG 2
DOGS'
    THAT COMES OF DOGS' LIVES BEING SO BRIEF, ... 420 ONE MORE BREVITY . . 51
DOING
    WHAT AM I DOING CARRYING OFF THIS BOTTLE?-- . . . . . 50 A HUNDRED COLLARS . . 177
    AND WASHING DISHES AFTER THEM--FROM DOING . . . . . 64 A SERVANT TO SERVANTS . 51
    AND PROUD, TOO, OF THEMSELVES FOR DOING SO. . . . . . 65 A SERVANT TO SERVANTS . 75
    DOING THE HAYING. NO ONE LIKED THE BOSS. . . . . . 70 THE CODE 32
    IF BY SO DOING HE COULD GET MORE WORK . . . . . . 70 THE CODE 37
    HE COULDN'T KEEP AWAY FROM DOING SOMETHING." . . . . . 73 THE CODE 109
    "WHAT ARE YOU DOING ROUND THIS HOUSE AT NIGHT?" . . . . 91 THE FEAR 70
    "WHAT'S A CHILD DOING AT THIS TIME OF NIGHT----?" . . . 92 THE FEAR 81
    "YOU'RE DOING THE WISE THING: YOU WON'T REGRET IT. . . . 100 THE SELF-SEEKER . . 219
    WE SAW THE RISK WE TOOK IN DOING GOOD, ... 109 THE EXPOSED NEST . . 27
    DOING A MAN'S WORK, THOUGH A CHILD AT HEART-- . . . . 137 "OUT,OUT--" . . . 24
    "WHAT IS HE DOING OUT A NIGHT LIKE THIS? . . . . . 145 SNOW 68
    I DON'T LIKE WHAT HE'S DOING, WHICH IS WHAT . . . . . 146 SNOW 95
    AND BY SO DOING GIVE THESE THREE, LAMP, DOG, ... 148 SNOW 145
    WHERE HAD HE BEEN AND WHAT HAD HE BEEN DOING? . . . . 160 NEW HAMPSHIRE . . . 56
    TO MAKE FUN OF MY WAY OF DOING THINGS, ... 176 THE STAR-SPLITTER . . 9
    "WHAT ARE YOU DOING UP THERE IN THOSE GRAPES? . . . . 198 WILD GRAPES 56
    WHEN I CAN HURT SOMEONE BY DOING IT . . . . . . 208 PAUPER WITCH OF GRAFTON 34
    AND THOUGHT OF DOING SOMETHING TO THE SHORE . . . . . 250 ONCE BY THE PACIFIC . 3
    "WHAT DOES IT THINK IT'S DOING RUNNING WEST . . . . . 257 WEST-RUNNING BROOK . . 4
    UNLESS OUR PURPOSE IS DOING HARM, ... 263 THE TIMES TABLE . . 16
    TO SAVE HIM THE EXPENSE OF DOING. . . . . . . 274 A LONE STRIKER . . 48
    WHAT'S A STAR DOING BIG AS A BASEBALL? . . . . . 369 THE LITERATE FARMER AND 37
    "THAT'S WHAT THE DOCTOR'S DOING, KEEPING HIS. . . . . 407 FROM PLANE TO PLANE . 97
    NOW WHAT'S HE DOING? / PITCHING THRONE, I GUESS, . . . 474 A MASQUE OF REASON . . 19
    YOU'RE DOING IT. / I'M NOT. HOW COULD I BE? . . . . 504 A MASQUE OF MERCY . . 284
    YOU'RE DOING SOMETHING TO OUR MINDS. / I'M NOT.-- . . . 504 A MASQUE OF MERCY . . 285
    THE GOSPELS TO IT. AFTER DOING JUSTICE JUSTICE . . . . 508 A MASQUE OF MERCY . . 379
DOLE
    A DOLE OF BREAD, A PURSE, ... 8 LOVE AND A QUESTION . 26
    IT WOULD NOT BE FAIR TO SAY FOR A DOLE OF BREAD, . . . 286 A ROADSIDE STAND . . 4
DOLL
    AND TURN DOLL OUT TO PASTURE, RIG AND ALL. . . . . . 88 THE HOUSEKEEPER . . 201
DOLLAR
    I PICK IT UP A DOLLAR AT A TIME . . . . 48 A HUNDRED COLLARS . . 97
    BECAUSE I WANT THEIR DOLLAR? I DON'T WANT . . . . . 50 A HUNDRED COLLARS . . 151
    THREE CENTS SO SMALL BESIDE THE DOLLAR FRIENDS . . . . 107 CHRISTMAS TREES . . 50
    LIKE THE TWO STROKES ACROSS A DOLLAR SIGN. . . . . . 186 THE AX-HELVE . . . 25
    FOR ONLY A DOLLAR DOWN. . . . . 367 A SERIOUS STEP LIGHTLY 8
    (IS IT NOT WRITTEN ON THE DOLLAR BILL . . . . . . 422 FOR JOHN F. KENNEDY . 21
DOLLARS
    OF GOOD FAITH. THERE IS NINETY DOLLARS. . . . . . 47 A HUNDRED COLLARS . . 86
    FOR FIFTY DOLLARS FOR ONE LANGSHANG COCK-- . . . . . 86 THE HOUSEKEEPER . . 146
    FIVE HUNDRED DOLLARS FOR THE PAIR, YOU KNOW. . . . . 93 THE SELF-SEEKER . . 4
    "FIVE HUNDRED DOLLARS!" / "WHAT WOULD YOU THINK RIGHT?" . 99 THE SELF-SEEKER . . 198
    "A THOUSAND TREES WOULD COME TO THIRTY DOLLARS." . . . 107 CHRISTMAS TREES . . 44
    BUT THIRTY DOLLARS SEEMED SO SMALL BESIDE . . . . . 107 CHRISTMAS TREES . . 47
    HE GOT A GOOD GLASS FOR SIX HUNDRED DOLLARS. . . . . 178 THE STAR-SPLITTER . . 74
DOLLARS'
    AND TRIED TO LOOK TEN THOUSAND DOLLARS' WORTH. . . . . 454 HOW HARD TO KEEP FROM 38
DOMAIN
    BY RIGHT OF EMINENT DOMAIN. . . . . 390 TWO LEADING LIGHTS . . 10
DOME
    YOU'D THINK THE INNER DOME OF HEAVEN HAD FALLEN. . . . 121 BIRCHES 13
DOMESTICATED
    HE'S AFTER THE DOMESTICATED FLY . . . . 278 THE WHITE-TAILED HORNET 30
DOMINATE
    WHAT COUNTRY'D BE THE ONE TO DOMINATE . . . . . . 422 FOR JOHN F. KENNEDY . 13
DONE
    IN WINTER HE COMES BACK TO US. I'M DONE." . . . . . 35 DEATH OF THE HIRED MAN 30
    WHICH SHOWED HOW MUCH GOOD SCHOOL HAD EVER DONE HIM. . . 37 DEATH OF THE HIRED MAN 84
    HIS WORKING DAYS ARE DONE; I'M SURE OF IT." . . . . 39 DEATH OF THE HIRED MAN 153
    BUT THE SIGNS SHOWED WHAT IT HAD DONE IN SPRING: . . . 40 THE MOUNTAIN . . . 12
    DONE SADLY FROM AN OLD DAGUERREOTYPE. . . . . . . 55 THE BLACK COTTAGE . . 24
    THINGS OVER AND OVER THAT JUST WON'T STAY DONE. . . . . 64 A SERVANT TO SERVANTS . 52
    BUT I AM DONE WITH APPLE-PICKING NOW. . . . . . . 68 AFTER APPLE-PICKING . 6
    OF THE ONE BEARING IT DONE IN DETAIL-- . . . . . 74 THE GENERATIONS OF MEN 41
    IN SEPARATE COOPS, HAVING THEIR PLUMAGE DONE. . . . . 85 THE HOUSEKEEPER . . 121
    BUT WHAT'S THE USE OF TALKING WHEN IT'S DONE? . . . . 87 THE HOUSEKEEPER . . 176
    WHAT DO YOU MEAN?--SHE'S DONE HARM TO HERSELF?" . . . 87 THE HOUSEKEEPER . . 179
    "NONSENSE! SEE WHAT SHE'S DONE! BUT WHO, BUT WHO----?" . 88 THE HOUSEKEEPER . . 185
    FOR WHAT THEY'D BETTER WAIT TILL WE HAVE DONE. . . . . 130 THE BONFIRE . . . 15
    DONE SO MUCH AND I KNOW NOT HOW MUCH MORE . . . . . 130 THE BONFIRE . . . 30
    THEY LOOKED ABOUT FOR SOMEONE TO HAVE DONE IT. . . . . 132 THE BONFIRE . . . 89

DONE (CONTINUED)
WHEN ALL WAS SAID AND DONE, ... 134 A GIRL'S GARDEN . . . 38
AND NOTHING HAPPENED: DAY WAS ALL BUT DONE. . . . . . . 136 "OUT, OUT--" 9
WHEN IT'S JUST THAT I HOLD WITH GETTING A THING DONE WITH." . 142 THE VANISHING RED . . 8
YOU'VE DONE MORE THAN YOU HAD A RIGHT TO THINK . . . . 150 SNOW 219
THE HARM WAS DONE: FROM HAVING BEEN STAR-SHOT . . . . 173 A STAR IN A STONEBOAT . 20
WHILE I THOUGHT WHAT TO DO THAT COULD BE DONE-- . . . 175 THE CENSUS-TAKER . . 48
I SHOULD HAVE DONE BY DAYLIGHT, AND INDEED, ... 176 THE STAR-SPLITTER . . 5
AFTER THE GROUND IS FROZEN, I SHOULD HAVE DONE . . . . 176 THE STAR-SPLITTER . . 6
FOR HIM TO HAVE THE SAY WHEN WE WERE DONE. . . . . . 190 THE GRINDSTONE . . 49
AND SO SHE SAID TO LABAN, "YOU HAVE DONE . . . . . 199 PLACE FOR A THIRD . . 9
AND WHEN I'VE DONE IT, WHAT GOOD HAVE I DONE? . . . . 202 THE WITCH OF COOS . 11
I NEVER COULD HAVE DONE THE THING I DID . . . . . 204 THE WITCH OF COOS . . 65
TO UNDO WHAT HE'D DONE AND MAKE IT RIGHT, ... 209 PAUPER WITCH OF GRAFTON 79
IT'S HELL FOR KNEES UNLESS DONE HELL-FOR-LEATHER." . . . 215 A FOUNTAIN, A BOTTLE . 63
UPON HIM WHERE HE IS, WITH NOTHING DONE . . . . . 226 THE ONSET 9
AND SUCH AS IS DONE TO THEIR WOOD WITH AN AX-- . . . 228 GOOD-BY AND KEEP COLD . 23
AND ALL FOR NOTHING IT HAD EVER DONE, ... 231 A BROOK IN THE CITY . 18
AS OFTEN AS I'VE SEEN IT DONE BEFORE . . . . . . 237 A HILLSIDE THAW . . 4
I CAN'T PRETEND TO TELL THE WAY IT'S DONE. . . . . 237 A HILLSIDE THAW . . 5
MADE QUICK ASIDES, BUT HAVING DONE IN AIR . . . . . 240 OUR SINGING STRENGTH . 40
THIS EDEN DAY IS DONE AT TWO O'CLOCK. . . . . . 254 A WINTER EDEN . . . 18
THE MEADOW IS DONE WITH THE TAME. . . . . . . 264 THE LAST MOWING . . 14
BUT NOTHING EVER HAPPENS, NO HARM IS DONE. . . . . 268 ON LOOKING UP BY CHANCE 7
IS THE DEED EVER REALLY DONE . . . . 277 TWO TRAMPS IN MUD TIME 71
AT THOSE WHO'D DONE HIM SUCH A WRONG AS THAT, ... 284 THE GOLD HESPERIDEE . 44
(THE SAYING IS NEVER DONE.) . . . . 312 THE VINDICTIVES . . 77
I'M DONE FOREVER WITH POTATO CROPS . . . . . . 316 BUILD SOIL . . . 11
AND SHALL BE MORE BEFORE WE'RE DONE WITH IT. . . . . 319 BUILD SOIL . . . 118
TO DO WHAT IS DONE-- . . . . 324 BUILD SOIL . . . 261
THAT THE FLOWER HAD DONE BUT PART, ... 340 THE SUBVERTED FLOWER . 53
FOR SUMMER WAS DONE. . . . . 343 QUEST OF PURPLE-FRINGED 28
(AND WAS A TEXT ALBEIT DONE IN PLANT). . . . . . 355 TIME OUT 4
BUT THEY'RE ONE THING THAT SHOULD BE DONE BY HALVES. . . 363 A SEMI-REVOLUTION . . 8
WHAT NOW WAS BEING DONE. . . . . 366 NOT OF SCHOOL AGE . . 16
YOU'D BET YOU GOT MORE WORK DONE IN A DAY, ... 405 FROM PLANE TO PLANE . 46
IT WILL BE FURTHER DONE, ... 416 CLOSED FOR GOOD . . 21
AND YET DONE NOTHING ABOUT IT IN SONG. . . . . . 421 ONE MORE BREVITY . . 65
AND COUNTED OUT. HEROIC DEEDS WERE DONE. . . . . . 422 FOR JOHN F. KENNEDY . 17
AND DONE YEOMAN SHARE . . . . 434 KITTY HAWK . . . 205
YOU'D HAVE REWARDED ME FOR ALL I'VE DONE . . . . . 457 HOW HARD TO KEEP FROM 119
(YOU OUGHT TO SEE THE COINS DONE IN COS.) . . . . . 459 HOW HARD TO KEEP FROM 187
HAD DONE OR NOT DONE TO OR FOR THE POOR. . . . . . 477 A MASQUE OF REASON . 122
JOB HADN'T DONE A THING, POOR INNOCENT. . . . . . 478 A MASQUE OF REASON . 127
TO GET THINGS DONE. REFORMERS FAIL TO SEE THAT.-- . . . 478 A MASQUE OF REASON . 152
I'M IN THE BIBLE, ALL DONE OUT IN STORY. . . . . . 497 A MASQUE OF MERCY . 113
AFTER THE FIGHT'S SO DEFINITELY DONE . . . . . . 507 A MASQUE OF MERCY . 366
NOW WE HAVE DONE IT, PAUL. WHAT DID HE SAY? . . . . 518 A MASQUE OF MERCY . 656
DONKEY'S
A FOUNTAIN, A BOTTLE, A DONKEY'S EARS, AND SOME BOOKS . . 212 A FOUNTAIN, A BOTTLE . T
ON MARSHALL, LOOK LIKE DONKEY'S EARS. . . . . . 214 A FOUNTAIN, A BOTTLE . 53
"DON'T DONKEY'S EARS SUGGEST WE SHAKE OUR OWN?" . . . 215 A FOUNTAIN, A BOTTLE . 55
WHAT SIGNIFY A DONKEY'S EARS AND BOTTLE, ... 215 A FOUNTAIN, A BOTTLE . 58
DON'T---NOT INDEXED
DOOM
BUT STRETCHED AWAY UNTO THE EDGE OF DOOM. . . . . 5 INTO MY OWN . . . 4
'TWAS TO BUY HIMSELF OFF HIS DOOM. . . . . . . 310 THE VINDICTIVES . . 6
OF OUR ENACTING OUT THE DOOM . . . . 417 AMERICA IS HARD TO SEE 38
OUR DOOM TO BLOOM . . . . 449 OUR DOOM TO BLOOM . T
GOD COMES ON ME TO DOOM A CITY FOR HIM. . . . . . 505 A MASQUE OF MERCY . 301
DOOMED
BEYOND WHICH THEY ARE DOOMED TO MISS. . . . . . 328 A MISSIVE MISSILE . . 51
WE ALL ARE DOOMED TO BROKEN-OFF CAREERS, ... 355 THE LESSON FOR TODAY . 145
DOOR (SEE TWO-DOOR)
A STRANGER CAME TO THE DOOR AT EVE, ... 7 LOVE AND A QUESTION . 1
TURN THE POET OUT OF DOOR. . . . . 12 TO THE THAWING WIND . 15
THE WELL WAS DRY BESIDE THE DOOR, ... 18 GOING FOR WATER . . 1
SHE PUSHED HIM OUTWARD WITH HER THROUGH THE DOOR . . . 34 DEATH OF THE HIRED MAN 6
HUDDLED AGAINST THE BARN DOOR FAST ASLEEP, ... 35 DEATH OF THE HIRED MAN 35
AS THE ROAD WINDS WOULD BRING HIM TO HIS DOOR. . . . 38 DEATH OF THE HIRED MAN 126
I'LL KNOCK SO-FASHION AND PEEP THROUGH THE DOOR . . . 50 A HUNDRED COLLARS . 173
THERE NOW, YOU GET SOME SLEEP." / HE SHUT THE DOOR. . . 50 A HUNDRED COLLARS . 178
YOU WON'T GO NOW. YOU'RE CRYING. CLOSE THE DOOR. . . . 54 HOME BURIAL . . . 109
"IF--YOU--DO!" SHE WAS OPENING THE DOOR WIDER. . . . 55 HOME BURIAL . . . 114
A FRONT WITH JUST A DOOR BETWEEN TWO WINDOWS, ... 55 THE BLACK COTTAGE . 6
HE SPOKE TO HIS WIFE IN THE DOOR, 'LET ME SEE, ... 61 BLUEBERRIES . . . 79
AND SIT BEFORE YOU IN THE OPEN DOOR . . . . . . 79 THE GENERATIONS OF MEN 168
I LET MYSELF IN AT THE KITCHEN DOOR. . . . . . 81 THE HOUSEKEEPER . . 1
I TELL THEM THEY CAN'T GET ME THROUGH THE DOOR, THOUGH: . 82 THE HOUSEKEEPER . . 37
JOHN THREW THE DOOR WIDE BUT HE DIDN'T ENTER. . . . . 88 THE HOUSEKEEPER . . 205
SHE RAISED HER VOICE AGAINST THE CLOSING DOOR: . . . 89 THE HOUSEKEEPER . . 213
SHONE ON A MAN AND WOMAN IN THE DOOR . . . . . 89 THE FEAR . . . 2
AT ONE DOOR AS WE ENTERED AT ANOTHER. . . . . . 89 THE FEAR . . . 21
LOOKED IN A DOOR BEHIND HER AND ADDRESSED . . . . . 110 IN THE HOME STRETCH . 11
A DOOR. "THERE'S THAT WE DIDN'T LOSE! AND THESE!"-- . . 115 IN THE HOME STRETCH . 137
THEY LEARNED TO LEAVE THE HOUSE DOOR WIDE . . . . . 127 HOUSE FEAR . . . 9
THE TIME I DREAMED THE DOOR WAS TRIED . . . . . 135 LOCKED OUT . . . 4
THEN HE SHUT DOWN THE TRAP DOOR WITH A RING IN IT . . . 142 THE VANISHING RED . . 24
UNDER IT ALL, HIS DOOR SEALED UP AND LOST, ... 150 SNOW 224
TO LAST HER TILL HE GOT OUTSIDE THE DOOR, ... 151 SNOW 243
YOU CAN'T HEAR WHETHER SHE HAS LEFT THE DOOR . . . . 154 SNOW 308
FROM THE WINDOW OR THE DOOR. . . . . 156 THE SOUND OF TREES . 18
OF ONE ROOM AND ONE WINDOW AND ONE DOOR, ... 174 THE CENSUS-TAKER . . 3
OF YEAR OR DAY THE WAY IT SWUNG A DOOR . . . . . 175 THE CENSUS-TAKER . . 27
THE PEOPLE THAT HAD LOUDLY PASSED THE DOOR . . . . 175 THE CENSUS-TAKER . . 38
THE DOOR WAS STILL BECAUSE I HELD IT SHUT . . . . . 175 THE CENSUS-TAKER . . 47
TO MEET HIM WITH HIS ANSWER AT THE DOOR. . . . . . 201 PLACE FOR A THIRD . . 72
SHE GAVE IT THROUGH THE SCREEN DOOR CLOSED BETWEEN THEM: . 201 PLACE FOR A THIRD . . 76

PAGE TITLE   LINE

DOOR (CONTINUED)
    AGAINST THE ATTIC DOOR: THE DOOR IS NAILED. . . . . . . 203 THE WITCH OF COOS . . 22
    OF DOOR AND HEADBOARD. WHERE IT WANTS TO GET . . . . . 203 THE WITCH OF COOS . . 25
    BUT LEFT AN OPEN DOOR TO COOL THE ROOM OFF . . . . . 203 THE WITCH OF COOS . . 42
    AND HOLD THE DOOR. BUT THE BONES DIDN'T TRY . . . . . 204 THE WITCH OF COOS . . 61
    THE DOOR; THEY HALTED HELPLESS ON THE LANDING, ... 204 THE WITCH OF COOS . . 62
    SO SUDDENLY I FLUNG THE DOOR WIDE ON HIM. . . . . . 204 THE WITCH OF COOS . . 70
    OF THE DOOR TO THE CELLAR OR THE HALL. . . . . . . 205 THE WITCH OF COOS . . 84
    IT TOOK THE HALL DOOR FOR THE NOVELTY, ... 205 THE WITCH OF COOS . . 85
    THEN RAN AND SHOUTED, "SHUT THE BEDROOM DOOR, ... 205 THE WITCH OF COOS . . 93
    IT'S LOOKING FOR ANOTHER DOOR TO TRY. . . . . . . 205 THE WITCH OF COOS . . 108
    HE'S AFTER AN OPEN DOOR TO GET OUTDOORS. . . . . . 205 THE WITCH OF COOS . . 112
    LET'S TRAP HIM WITH AN OPEN DOOR UP ATTIC." . . . . . 206 THE WITCH OF COOS . . 113
    "QUICK!" I SLAMMED TO THE DOOR AND HELD THE KNOB. . . . 206 THE WITCH OF COOS . . 118
    "TOFFILE, GET NAILS." I MADE HIM NAIL THE DOOR SHUT . . . 206 THE WITCH OF COOS . . 119
    BEHIND THE DOOR AND HEADBOARD OF THE BED, ... 206 THE WITCH OF COOS . . 127
    AND A TRAPPER LOOKING IN AT THE DOOR . . . . 211 AN EMPTY THREAT . . . 10
    THE SOUND OF THE CLOSING OUTSIDE DOOR WAS ALL. . . . . 235 VALLEY'S SINGING DAY . 1
    AS FAR AS YOU WENT FROM THE DOOR, WHICH WAS NOT FAR: . . . 235 VALLEY'S SINGING DAY . 3
    AND I THOUGHT OF THE DOOR . . . . 240 THE LOCKLESS DOOR . . 3
    THE LOCKLESS DOOR . . . . 240 THE LOCKLESS DOOR . . T
    IN PRAYER TO THE DOOR. . . . . 241 THE LOCKLESS DOOR . . 8
    AT THE DOOR MAY HAVE BEEN. . . . . 241 THE LOCKLESS DOOR . . 16
    HAVE CLAPPED MY HANDS AT HIM FROM THE DOOR . . . . . 250 A MINOR BIRD 3
    HOLDING OPEN A RESTIVE DOOR, ... 251 BEREFT 4
    A SLIM DOOR GOT IN PAST MY GUARD, ... 265 THE DOOR IN THE DARK . 5
    THE DOOR IN THE DARK . . . . 265 THE DOOR IN THE DARK . T
    HAWKING FOR FLIES ABOUT THE KITCHEN DOOR, ... 278 THE WHITE-TAILED HORNET 24
    IN AT ONE DOOR PERHAPS AND OUT ANOTHER, ... 278 THE WHITE-TAILED HORNET 25
    HIS GREAT GAUNT FIGURE FILLED HIS CABIN DOOR, ... 292 FIGURE IN THE DOORWAY . 7
    WITH A DOOR OF TWO BROAD BOARDS . . . . 294 A RECORD STRIDE . . . 2
    SINCE HE MEANS TO COME TO A DOOR HE WILL COME TO A DOOR, . . 341 WILLFUL HOMING . . . 9
    HE ASKED FOR A DRINK AT THE KITCHEN DOOR, ... 364 TRESPASS 18
    AND KNOCKED AT THE DOOR OF A HOUSE WE FOUND, ... 367 A SERIOUS STEP LIGHTLY 11
    MY UNEXPECTED KNOCKING AT THE DOOR . . . . 368 THE LITERATE FARMER AND 1
    A MIGHTY FARMER FLUNG THE HOUSE DOOR WIDE, ... 368 THE LITERATE FARMER AND 5
    THAT'S THE TIME KNOCKING AT A DOOR DID GOOD. . . . . . 368 THE LITERATE FARMER AND 8
    SAND HAS BEEN THRUSTING IN THE SQUARE OF DOOR . . . . . 399 THE INGENUITIES OF DEBT 13
    BUT THERE'S A TIGHT-SHUT LOOK TO EITHER DOOR . . . . . 400 TO THE RIGHT PERSON . 8
    THE MILKWEED BRINGS UP TO MY VERY DOOR . . . . . . 411 POD OF THE MILKWEED . 5
    I OPENED THE DOOR SO MY LAST LOOK . . . . 419 ONE MORE BREVITY . . 1
    BUT SCARCELY WAS MY DOOR AJAR, ... 419 ONE MORE BREVITY . . 7
    HE WAS AT THE DOOR TO BE LET OUT . . . . 420 ONE MORE BREVITY . . 45
    I OPENED THE DOOR AND HE WAS GONE. . . . . 420 ONE MORE BREVITY . . 49
    PULLS DOWN THE WINDOW CURTAIN ON THE DOOR . . . . . 493 A MASQUE OF MERCY . . 2
    AND LOCKS THE DOOR. ONE CUSTOMER, LOCKED IN, ... 493 A MASQUE OF MERCY . . 3
    YOU LOCKED THE DOOR, BEL. LET ME HAVE THE KEY. . . . . 500 A MASQUE OF MERCY . . 174
    (HE GOES AND TAKES IT FROM THE DOOR HIMSELF.) . . . . . 500 A MASQUE OF MERCY . . 175
    AND HELP YOU'RE GOING TO GET. / I'LL BREAK YOUR DOOR DOWN. . 500 A MASQUE OF MERCY . . 178
    ON THE BLANK CURTAIN ON THE OUTER DOOR.) . . . . . . 502 A MASQUE OF MERCY . . 239
    SOMETHING HAS ALTERED IN THE OUTER DOOR.) . . . . . 507 A MASQUE OF MERCY . . 344
    BEYOND THIS GREAT DOOR YOU HAVE LOCKED AGAINST ME, . . . 513 A MASQUE OF MERCY . . 532
    UNLOCK THE DOOR FOR ME. / NOT THAT WAY OUT. . . . . . 514 A MASQUE OF MERCY . . 546
    THAT'S NOT MY DOOR. / NO, THAT'S ANOTHER DOOR. . . . . 514 A MASQUE OF MERCY . . 548
    YOUR EXIT DOOR'S BECOME A CELLAR DOOR. . . . . . . 514 A MASQUE OF MERCY . . 549
    (THE DOOR HERE OPENS DARKLY OF ITSELF.) . . . . . . 514 A MASQUE OF MERCY . . 550
    (JONAH STEPS ON THE THRESHOLD AS THE DOOR . . . . . . 518 A MASQUE OF MERCY . . 649
    THE CELLAR DOOR SWINGS WIDE AND SLAMS AGAIN.) . . . . 520 A MASQUE OF MERCY . . 696
DOOR-FILLING
    DOOR-FILLING MEN BURST IN AND SEIZED THE STOVE. . . . . 113 IN THE HOME STRETCH . 83
DOOR'S
    BEFORE THE DOOR'S SO VIOLENTLY TRIED . . . . 493 A MASQUE OF MERCY . . 6
    YOUR EXIT DOOR'S BECOME A CELLAR DOOR. . . . . . . 514 A MASQUE OF MERCY . . 549
DOORS   (SEE ALL-OUT-DOORS, OUT-OF-DOORS)
    AND DOWN A NARROW PASSAGE FULL OF DOORS, ... 45 A HUNDRED COLLARS . . 34
    TO HAVE INSIDE THE HOUSE WITH DOORS UNLOCKED. . . . . . 65 A SERVANT TO SERVANTS . 84
    DOORS LOCKED AND CURTAINS DRAWN WILL MAKE NO DIFFERENCE. . . 89 THE FEAR 16
    WILL EVER SLAM THE DOORS." / "I THINK YOU SEE . . . . . 112 IN THE HOME STRETCH . 44
    THE BULKHEAD DOUBLE DOORS WERE DOUBLE-LOCKED. . . . . 204 THE WITCH OF COOS . . 55
    "THE OUTSIDE DOORS AS YET HAVE HELD AGAINST US. . . . . 215 A FOUNTAIN, A BOTTLE . 74
    A DEPTH PAST MANY SWINGING DOORS . . . . 280 BLUE RIBBON AT AMESBURY 23
    THE WIDESPREAD DOUBLE DOORS TWO STORIES HIGH. . . . . 289 OLD BARN AT THE BOTTOM 12
    THE ADVANTAGE-DISADVANTAGE OF THESE DOORS . . . . . 289 OLD BARN AT THE BOTTOM 13
DOORSILL
    FOR A DOORSILL OR OTHER CORNER PIECE . . . . 79 THE GENERATIONS OF MEN 163
DOORSTEP
    FOLKS ENTERTAIN ME FROM THE KITCHEN DOORSTEP, ... 49 A HUNDRED COLLARS . . 147
DOORSTEPS
    THESE DOORSTEPS SELDOM HAVE A VISITOR. . . . . . . 56 THE BLACK COTTAGE . . 48
    UPON ITS DOORSTEPS AS AT MERCY'S FEET . . . . 400 TO THE RIGHT PERSON . 13
DOORWAY
    TO MEET HIM IN THE DOORWAY WITH THE NEWS . . . . . . 34 DEATH OF THE HIRED MAN 4
    THE FIGURE IN THE DOORWAY . . . . 292 FIGURE IN THE DOORWAY . T
DOORYARD
    DOORYARD AND ROAD UNGRADED, ... 10 STORM FEAR 14
    RAKING THE DOORYARD, WORKING NEAR THE HOUSE. . . . . . 49 A HUNDRED COLLARS . . 128
    OR JOINED WITH SHEDS IN RING-AROUND A DOORYARD. . . . . 289 OLD BARN AT THE BOTTOM 2
DORKINGS
    DORKINGS BECAUSE THEY'RE SPOKEN OF BY CHAUCER, ... 162 NEW HAMPSHIRE . . . 106
DORMANT
    AND NOT MELT SNOW OR START A DORMANT TREE. . . . . . 254 A WINTER EDEN . . . 4
    RAN INTO A DORMANT MOTH . . . . 287 DEPARTMENTAL 2
DORY
    HIS DEEP-SEA DORY HAS FOUND A HARBOR. . . . . . . 262 THE FLOWER BOAT . . . 4
    AND DORY AND MASTER WILL SAIL BY FATE . . . . 262 THE FLOWER BOAT . . . 11
DO'S
    ALL WE DO'S REFLECT . . . . 440 KITTY HAWK 384

DOSTOIEVSKIS
  TO BE EXPECTED TO BE DOSTOIEVSKIS . . . . 167 NEW HAMPSHIRE . . . 275
DOT
  AND THE DOT IN FRONT OF A NAME . . . . 367 A SERIOUS STEP LIGHTLY . 5
DOTES
  HE DOTES ON SATURDAY PORK AND BEANS. . . . . 393 A CASE FOR JEFFERSON . 7
DOTS
  TWO ROUND DOTS AND A RIPPLE STREAK, ... 327 A MISSIVE MISSILE . . 7
  IS WHETHER THE TWO DOTS WERE TEARS, ... 327 A MISSIVE MISSILE . . 10
  THE TWO DOTS AND THE RIPPLE LINE. . . . . 328 A MISSIVE MISSILE . . 42
DOTTED
  BETWEEN THE DOTTED STARS, ... 252 THE PEACEFUL SHEPHERD . 4
  BETWEEN THE DOTTED FEET A STREAK OF TAIL, ... 270 THE EGG AND THE MACHINE 18
  AND DOTTED IT WITH RED FOR ME, ... 326 A MISSIVE MISSILE . . 3
  NOR YET THE LITTLE DOTTED IN ME SEEK. . . . . 387 IOTA SUBSCRIPT . . . 2
DOUBLE
  THE STRICKEN FLOWER BENT DOUBLE AND SO HUNG. . . . . . 126 RANGE-FINDING . . . 4
  "HOLD ON." THE DOUBLE BELL BEGAN TO CHIRP. . . . . . . 155 SNOW 327
  I KNOW A MAN WHO TOOK A DOUBLE AX . . . . 170 NEW HAMPSHIRE . . 367
  THE BULKHEAD DOUBLE DOORS WERE DOUBLE-LOCKED . . . . . 204 THE WITCH OF COOS . 55
  TO SPARE THEM ANY TROUBLE. DOUBLE TROUBLE'S . . . . . 207 PAUPER WITCH OF GRAFTON 7
  I'LL DOUBLE THEIRS FOR BOTH OF THEM--YOU WATCH ME. . . 207 PAUPER WITCH OF GRAFTON 9
  A FEATHER-HAMMER GIVES A DOUBLE KNOCK. . . . . 254 A WINTER EDEN . . . 17
  THE WIDESPREAD DOUBLE DOORS TWO STORIES HIGH. . . . . 289 OLD BARN AT THE BOTTOM 12
  GOT ME INTO MY DOUBLE ADVENTURE. . . . . 294 A RECORD STRIDE . . 18
  AND DOUBLE RING OF FITTED BRASS . . . . 363 ASSURANCE 3
  TO DOUBLE DAY AND CUT IN HALF THE DARK . . . . 375 A YOUNG BIRCH . . . 5
DOUBLE-BARRELED
  AND THE DOUBLE-BARRELED BLAST . . . . 282 A DRUMLIN WOODCHUCK . 22
DOUBLE-DYED
  YOU KNOW WHAT THAT IS, SORT OF DOUBLE-DYED; . . . . . 48 A HUNDRED COLLARS . 110
DOUBLE-LOCKED
  THE BULKHEAD DOUBLE DOORS WERE DOUBLE-LOCKED . . . . . 204 THE WITCH OF COOS . 55
DOUBLING
  BY DOUBLING AND REDOUBLING SONG AND TWITTER-- . . . . 237 A HILLSIDE THAW . . . 16
DOUBLY
  FOR IT WAS WRIT IN HEAVEN DOUBLY WRIGHT. . . . . . . 308 THE WRIGHTS' BIPLANE . 4
DOUBT
  DISTURBED, I DOUBT NOT, BY MY THOUGHT, ... 9 A LATE WALK 11
  AND MY HEART OWNS A DOUBT . . . . 10 STORM FEAR 16
  BEYOND THE SHADOW OF A DOUBT. . . . . 20 THE TRIAL BY EXISTENCE 36
  AND IT SEEMS LIKE THE TIME WHEN, AFTER DOUBT, ... 27 A LINE-STORM SONG . 29
  SILAS HAS WALKED THAT FAR NO DOUBT TODAY. . . . . . . 38 DEATH OF THE HIRED MAN 127
  YOU NEVER SAW IT?" / "I GUESS THERE'S NO DOUBT . . . 42 THE MOUNTAIN . . . 66
  I DOUBT IF I COULD DO IT ANYWAY.'" . . . . 48 A HUNDRED COLLARS . 118
  AGAINST THE LOUNGE BESIDE IT, THOUGH I DOUBT . . . . 56 THE BLACK COTTAGE . 28
  CLING TO IT LONG ENOUGH, AND NOT A DOUBT . . . . . . 58 THE BLACK COTTAGE . 107
  NO DOUBT IT HAS A SORT OF PROSPEROUS SOUND, ... 94 THE SELF-SEEKER . . 45
  I DOUBT IF I WAS TEMPTED FOR A MOMENT . . . . 106 CHRISTMAS TREES . . 16
  I DOUBT IF THEY HAVE LEFT US MANY GRAPES. . . . . . . 117 IN THE HOME STRETCH . 193
  BUT THEN, I DOUBT HE'S THINKING OF HIMSELF. . . . . . 145 SNOW 78
  "NO DOUBT YOU'VE HEARD THE OFFICE CALL ME MABEL. . . . 182 MAPLE 90
  THAN LIFE'S VICTORIES OF DOUBT . . . . 212 AN EMPTY THREAT . . 55
  NO DOUBT IT'S GROWN UP SOME TO WOODS AROUND IT. . . . 213 A FOUNTAIN, A BOTTLE . 21
  I DOUBT IF EVEN HIS MOTHER COULD TELL HIM, 'SAKES, . . 223 THE RUNAWAY . . . 12
  I DOUBT IF YOU'RE AS LIVING AS YOU LOOK." . . . . . 230 TWO LOOK AT TWO . . 34
  I HAVE NO DOUBT I'D END BY HOLDING NONE. . . . . . . 237 A HILLSIDE THAW . . 17
  BUT HE NO DOUBT REPORTS TO ANY . . . . 288 DEPARTMENTAL . . . 18
  AND THEY NO DOUBT REPORT . . . . 288 DEPARTMENTAL . . . 20
  I PASS, BUT SCARCELY PASS NO DOUBT, ... 291 ON HEART'S BEGINNING TO 21
  THOUGH THERE'S MORE THAN A DOUBT IF THE WEATHER IS NOT TOO
    COLD . . . . 300 STRONG SAYING NOTHING . 11
  FOR YOU TO DOUBT THE LIKELIHOOD. . . . . 307 PROVIDE, PROVIDE . . 6
  I DOUBT IF YOU'RE CONVINCED THE TIMES ARE BAD. . . . 317 BUILD SOIL 53
  I HAVE NO DOUBT LIKE ALL THE LOVES WHEN . . . . . . 318 BUILD SOIL 78
  THOUGH CIRCUMSTANCED WITH DARK AND DOUBT-- . . . . . 331 BEECH 11
  THOUGH BY A WORLD OF DOUBT SURROUNDED. . . . . 331 BEECH 12
  WE MAY DOUBT THE JUST PROPORTION OF GOOD TO ILL. . . . 349 OUR HOLD ON THE PLANET 11
  NO DOUBT DIRECTED AT OUR HEADS AS REBELS . . . . . . 361 A LOOSE MOUNTAIN . . 6
  WHO DREW BACK AT FIRST IN DOUBT, ... 366 NOT OF SCHOOL AGE . . 6
  THE IDEA IS NO DOUBT TO MAKE ONE JOB . . . . 370 THE LITERATE FARMER AND 71
  AND HAVE OCCURRED TO YOU NO DOUBT, ... 381 AN UNSTAMPED LETTER IN 46
  DO NO DOUBT WITH THEIR COLOR COMPENSATE . . . . . . 411 POD OF THE MILKWEED . 12
  AND STILL I DOUBT IF THEY KNOW WHERE THEY ARE. . . . 414 A CABIN IN THE CLEARING 5
  NO DOUBT SHE WOULD HAVE PREFERRED THE FORK. . . . . 463 LINES IN DEJECTION . 21
  AND IT CAME OUT ALL RIGHT. I HAVE NO DOUBT . . . . . 475 A MASQUE OF REASON . 65
  IT COMES DOWN TO A DOUBT ABOUT THE WISDOM . . . . . 483 A MASQUE OF REASON . 291
DOUBTED
  I DOUBTED IF I SHOULD EVER COME BACK. . . . . 105 THE ROAD NOT TAKEN . 15
DOUBTFUL
  (THOUGH DOUBTFUL WHETHER HE STAYED TO SEE). . . . . . 25 THE DEMIURGE'S LAUGH . 17
  SHE TOOK A DOUBTFUL STEP AND THEN UNDID IT . . . . . 51 HOME BURIAL 4
  AND THIS DAY'S WORK MADE EVEN THAT SEEM DOUBTFUL. . . 279 THE WHITE-TAILED HORNET 70
DOUBTFULLY
  A THING THE LEAST BIT DOUBTFULLY PERSCENTED . . . . . 163 NEW HAMPSHIRE . . . 142
DOUBTLESS
  DOUBTLESS BEAR NAMES THAT THE MOSSES MAR. . . . . . . 6 GHOST HOUSE 25
  WOULD HAVE BEEN STARKS, AND DOUBTLESS HERE TODAY." . . 75 THE GENERATIONS OF MEN 52
  WERE DOUBTLESS AS THE WORDS WE HEARD HIM SAY . . . . 170 NEW HAMPSHIRE . . . 352
  BUT DOUBTLESS THIS WAS ONLY MY CONCEIT. . . . . . . 353 THE LESSON FOR TODAY . 80
  STILL, NOVELTY HAS DOUBTLESS AN ATTRACTION. . . . . . 480 A MASQUE OF REASON . 197
DOUBTS
  WHATEVER SCHOOL AND CHILDREN AND OUR DOUBTS . . . . . 188 THE AX-HELVE . . . 85
  SUCH DOUBTS OF EDUCATION SHOULD DEPEND . . . . 188 THE AX-HELVE . . . 92
  AND SPOKE HIS DOUBTS IN EVERY OPEN PLACE. . . . . . . 214 A FOUNTAIN, A BOTTLE . 36
DOUGH
  NOW SLOWLY CLOSING LIKE A DENT IN DOUGH. . . . . . . 378 DIRECTIVE 47

DOUGHNUTS
    IT TOOK MY MIND OFF DOUGHNUTS AND SODA BISCUIT . . . . . 63 A SERVANT TO SERVANTS . 26
DOVE
    LIKE DOVE WINGS ON A FIGURE ON A TOMB, ... 222 TO E.T.   3
    I'M JONAS DOVE--IF THAT IS ANY HELP. . . . . 495 A MASQUE OF MERCY . . 55
    I'M GOING TO TELL YOU SOMETHING, JONAS DOVE. . . . . . . 498 A MASQUE OF MERCY . . 131
    DO YOU ACCEPT IT, MASTER JONAS DOVE? . . . . 512 A MASQUE OF MERCY . . 512
    BUT YOU--WHAT IS YOUR ANSWER, JONAS DOVE? . . . . 513 A MASQUE OF MERCY . . 529
DOWN (SEE LET-DOWN, TIP-DOWN)
    THE FOOTPATH DOWN TO THE WELL IS HEALED. . . . .   6 GHOST HOUSE 10
    COMES SOFTLY RATTLING DOWN. . . . .   9 A LATE WALK 12
    WAS MELTED DOWN AT NOON, ...   10 WIND AND WINDOW FLOWER 6
    AND RISING FULL MOON, SIT ME DOWN . . . . 14 WAITING   6
    BEHIND LOW BOUGHS THE TREES LET DOWN OUTSIDE; . . . . .   16 A DREAM PANG 10
    HE LAID HIM DOWN ON THE SUNBURNED EARTH . . . . 24 PAN WITH US 28
    THEY MUST GO DOWN PAST THINGS COMING UP. . . . . 26 IN HARDWOOD GROVES . . 7
    THEY MUST GO DOWN INTO THE DARK DECAYED. . . . . 26 IN HARDWOOD GROVES . . 8
    AND BRUIT OUR SINGING DOWN, ...   26 A LINE-STORM SONG . . 18
    THAT WANTS IT DOWN." I COULD SAY "ELVES" TO HIM, ... 34 MENDING WALL 36
    SHE RAN ON TIPTOE DOWN THE DARKENED PASSAGE . . . . . . 34 DEATH OF THE HIRED MAN   3
    AND SET THEM ON THE PORCH, THEN DREW HIM DOWN . . . . . 34 DEATH OF THE HIRED MAN   9
    PART OF A MOON WAS FALLING DOWN THE WEST, ...   38 DEATH OF THE HIRED MAN 103
    OR TURN AND SIT ON AND LOOK OUT AND DOWN . . . .   42 THE MOUNTAIN 61
    IT WOULDN'T HAVE TO BE A LONG WAY DOWN . . . .   42 THE MOUNTAIN 69
    AND A GOOD DISTANCE DOWN MIGHT NOT BE NOTICED . . . . . 43 THE MOUNTAIN 71
    HAVEN'T COME DOWN TO THE BARS AT MILKING TIME? . . . . . 43 THE MOUNTAIN 86
    AND SENDS THE CHILDREN DOWN THERE WITH THEIR MOTHER . . 44 A HUNDRED COLLARS . .   4
    AND DOWN A NARROW PASSAGE FULL OF DOORS, ... 45 A HUNDRED COLLARS . . 34
    SIT DOWN OR LIE DOWN, FRIEND; YOU MAKE ME NERVOUS." . .   47 A HUNDRED COLLARS . . 72
    IT'S SELDOM I GET DOWN EXCEPT FOR MEALS, THOUGH. . . . . 49 A HUNDRED COLLARS . . 146
    ALL IN A FAMILY ROW DOWN TO THE YOUNGEST." . . . . 49 A HUNDRED COLLARS . . 148
    LIE DOWN--LET YOURSELF GO AND GET SOME SLEEP. . . . . .   50 A HUNDRED COLLARS . . 161
    THE DOCTOR SLID A LITTLE DOWN THE PILLOW. . . . .   51 A HUNDRED COLLARS . . 179
    BEFORE SHE SAW HIM. SHE WAS STARTING DOWN, ... 51 HOME BURIAL   2
    LISTEN TO ME. I WON'T COME DOWN THE STAIRS." . . . . . . 52 HOME BURIAL 40
    YOU MAKE ME ANGRY. I'LL COME DOWN TO YOU. . . . .   53 HOME BURIAL 68
    AND ROLL BACK DOWN THE MOUND BESIDE THE HOLE. . . . . .   53 HOME BURIAL 77
    AND I CREPT DOWN THE STAIRS AND UP THE STAIRS . . . . . 53 HOME BURIAL 79
    AMY! THERE'S SOMEONE COMING DOWN THE ROAD!" . . . . . .   54 HOME BURIAL 111
    WHY NOT SIT DOWN IF YOU ARE IN NO HASTE? . . . . 56 THE BLACK COTTAGE . . 47
    "HE JUST KEPT NODDING HIS HEAD UP AND DOWN. . . . . . .   60 BLUEBERRIES 41
    I PROMISED MYSELF TO GET DOWN SOME DAY . . . .   62 A SERVANT TO SERVANTS . 3
    AND HIS VOICE DIED DOWN SLOWLY FROM EXHAUSTION. . . . .   66 A SERVANT TO SERVANTS 133
    CHERISH IN HAND, LIFT DOWN, AND NOT LET FALL. . . . . .   69 AFTER APPLE-PICKING . 31
    COMBED IT DOWN WITH A RAKE AND SAYS, 'O.K.' . . . . . .   71 THE CODE   52
    FOR THE MAN UP ON TOP, OF THROWING DOWN . . . . 71 THE CODE   56
    SLUMPED WAY DOWN IN A CHAIR, WITH BOTH HIS FEET . . . . 72 THE CODE   97
    (I MAY HAVE KNOCKED HIM DOWN); BUT MY JUST TRYING . . .   72 THE CODE 103
    TILL WELL TOWARD NOON, WHEN THE STORM SETTLED DOWN . .   74 THE GENERATIONS OF MEN 22
    "I ONLY IDLED DOWN." / "I IDLED DOWN." . . . . 74 THE GENERATIONS OF MEN 37
    ESTELLE'S TO TAKE ME WHEN SHE'S SETTLED DOWN. . . . . .   82 THE HOUSEKEEPER . . . 35
    IT'S TOO RUN DOWN. THIS IS THE LAST OF IT. . . . . 83 THE HOUSEKEEPER . . . 50
    HE'S GOT HAY DOWN THAT'S BEEN RAINED ON THREE TIMES. . . 83 THE HOUSEKEEPER . . . 57
    WE'RE NOT ALLOWED TO TAKE THEM UPSIDE DOWN, ...   85 THE HOUSEKEEPER . . . 127
    BLESS YOU, IT'S ALL EXPENSE, THOUGH. REACH ME DOWN . .   86 THE HOUSEKEEPER . . . 142
    COMING DOWN RYAN'S HILL. I THOUGHT 'TWAS HIM. . . . . .   88 THE HOUSEKEEPER . . . 197
    WE'RE STOPPING FOR THE FORTNIGHT DOWN AT DEAN'S." . . .   92 THE FEAR   86
    YOU HAVEN'T RUN YOUR FORTY ORCHIDS DOWN. . . . . 93 THE SELF-SEEKER . . . 13
    INSTEAD OF GOING CLEAR DOWN IN THE WHEEL PIT?" . . . . . 93 THE SELF-SEEKER . . . 31
    THERE! THERE'S THE BELL. HE'S RUNG. BUT YOU GO DOWN . . 95 THE SELF-SEEKER . . . 88
    OF LITTLE FINGERS ALL KEPT DOWN BUT ONE, ... 98 THE SELF-SEEKER . . . 156
    OF WHAT SHE'S LOST: SHE GOES DOWN ON ONE KNEE . . . . . 98 THE SELF-SEEKER . . . 160
    STRAIGHT UP AND DOWN OF TALL SLIM TREES . . . . 101 THE WOOD-PILE   6
    AND LOOKED DOWN ONE AS FAR AS I COULD . . . . 105 THE ROAD NOT TAKEN . . 4
    AND CAME DOWN ON THE NORTH. / HE SAID, "A THOUSAND." . . 107 CHRISTMAS TREES . . . 41
    SO WHEN I SAW YOU DOWN ON HANDS AND KNEES . . . . 109 THE EXPOSED NEST . . . 2
    OF CHAIRS TURNED UPSIDE DOWN TO SIT LIKE PEOPLE . . . . 110 IN THE HOME STRETCH .   6
    UP AND DOWN STAIRS AND THROUGH THE ROOMS, AND NONE . . . 112 IN THE HOME STRETCH . 42
    IT SOUNDS AS IF IT WERE THE MEN WENT DOWN, ... 112 IN THE HOME STRETCH . 56
    LIGHTING HIS PIPE NOW, SQUINTING DOWN HIS NOSE . . . . . 112 IN THE HOME STRETCH . 64
    IT'S NOT SO BAD IN THE COUNTRY, SETTLED DOWN, ... 113 IN THE HOME STRETCH . 93
    EVEN WORSE STILL, AND SO ON DOWN, DOWN, DOWN. . . . . . 115 IN THE HOME STRETCH . 129
    ALTHOUGH YOU DO NO MORE THAN DUMP THEM DOWN." . . . . . 116 IN THE HOME STRETCH . 162
    "DUMPED DOWN IN PARADISE WE ARE AND HAPPY." . . . . . . 116 IN THE HOME STRETCH . 163
    AS I WENT DOWN THE HILL ALONG THE WALL . . . . 118 MEETING AND PASSING .   1
    SOMETHING DOWN THERE TO SMILE AT IN THE DUST. . . . . . 119 MEETING AND PASSING . 11
    WHEN PEAR AND CHERRY BLOOM WENT DOWN IN SHOWERS . . . . 120 THE OVEN BIRD   7
    BUT SWINGING DOESN'T BEND THEM DOWN TO STAY . . . . . . 121 BIRCHES   4
    BY RIDING THEM DOWN OVER AND OVER AGAIN . . . . 122 BIRCHES   29
    KICKING HIS WAY DOWN THROUGH THE AIR TO THE GROUND. . . 122 BIRCHES   40
    BUT DIPPED ITS TOP AND SET ME DOWN AGAIN. . . . . 122 BIRCHES   57
    I WALKED DOWN ALONE SUNDAY AFTER CHURCH . . . . 123 PEA BRUSH   1
    A TREE THAT HAD BEEN DOWN AND RAISED AGAIN-- . . . . . . 125 AN ENCOUNTER 13
    I WONDER HOW FAR DOWN THE ROAD HE'S GOT. . . . . 127 THE SMILE 11
    DOWN DARK CONVERGING PATHS BETWEEN THE PINES. . . . . . 129 THE BONFIRE   7
    "NOW WE ARE DIGGING ALMOST DOWN TO CHINA. . . . . 132 THE BONFIRE 101
    AT DUSK TO WATCH THE MOON DOWN EARLY. . . . . 135 LOCKED OUT 13
    HIS JOURNEY DOWN FROM FIELD TO FIELD. . . . . 138 BROWN'S DESCENT . . . 20
    SO HALFWAY DOWN HE FOUGHT THE BATTLE, ... 138 BROWN'S DESCENT . . . 40
    AND CAME DOWN LIKE A COASTING CHILD. . . . . 139 BROWN'S DESCENT . . . 44
    TO LOOSE THE RESIN AND TAKE IT DOWN . . . . 141 THE GUM-GATHERER . . . 38
    THEY THROW A FOREST DOWN LESS CUT THAN BROKEN. . . . . . 141 THE LINE-GANG   2
    HE TOOK HIM DOWN BELOW A CRAMPING RAFTER, ... 142 THE VANISHING RED . . 20
    THEN HE SHUT DOWN THE TRAP DOOR WITH A RING IN IT . . . 142 THE VANISHING RED . . 24
    THE REST IS DOWN.--WHY NO, NO, NOT A WALLOW: . . . . . . 143 SNOW   23
    SIT DOWN, SIT DOWN. HOW DID YOU FIND THE HORSES?" . . . 147 SNOW   105
    IT WON'T LIE DOWN. THEN LET IT STAND. WHO CARES?" . . . 148 SNOW   152
    DOWN AT THE AVERYS'? WELL, ONE SUNNY MORNING . . . . . . 149 SNOW   175

DOWN (CONTINUED)
```
                                                      PAGE TITLE                      LINE
MORE LIKE A TUNNEL THAN A HOLE--WAY DOWN . . . . .  .  149 SNOW      . . . . . . 193
SOMEONE'S RECEIVER'S DOWN. THE HANDLE STUMBLES. .   .  153 SNOW      . . . . . . 295
NO STEP, THOUGH. IF SHE'S THERE SHE'S SITTING DOWN." .  153 SNOW      . . . . . . 302
OF COURSE SHE HASN'T, THOUGH." THEY BOTH SAT DOWN .  .  155 SNOW      . . . . . . 324
BURNED DOWN HIS FARMHOUSE FOR THE FIRE INSURANCE, . .  168 NEW HAMPSHIRE   . . 302
A HEIGHT FROM WHICH TO LOOK DOWN CRITICAL  . . . .  .  169 NEW HAMPSHIRE   . . 314
DOWN FROM THE STARS TO FREEZE THE DEW AS STARRY. .  .  169 NEW HAMPSHIRE   . . 342
THAT COULD HAVE DROPPED A LEAF DOWN UPON ITSELF . . .  175 THE CENSUS-TAKER  .  19
AND DOWN BY ONE SIDE WHERE IT LACKED A LEG. . . . .  .  175 THE CENSUS-TAKER  .  37
HE BURNED HIS HOUSE DOWN FOR THE FIRE INSURANCE . .  .  177 THE STAR-SPLITTER .  16
HE BURNED HIS HOUSE DOWN FOR THE FIRE INSURANCE . .  .  177 THE STAR-SPLITTER .  30
WHEN HE DID WHAT HE DID AND BURNED HIS HOUSE DOWN. .  .  177 THE STAR-SPLITTER .  39
WAS SETTING OUT, UP TRACK AND DOWN, NOT PLANTS . .  .  178 THE STAR-SPLITTER .  71
AND UNDERFOOT SNOW MELTED DOWN TO ICE, . . . . . .  .  179 THE STAR-SPLITTER .  80
SHE ALMOST WROTE THE WORDS DOWN ON HER KNEE, . . . .  182 MAPLE     . . . . . . 86
AND CUTTING NOTHING NOT CUT DOWN ALREADY. . . . . .  .  185 THE AX-HELVE   . . .  9
"HAHN, HAHN," HE MUSED, "DON'T NEED MUCH TAKING DOWN." 187 THE AX-HELVE   . . . 79
THICK HAND MADE LIGHT OF, STEEL-BLUE CHIN DRAWN DOWN   188 THE AX-HELVE   . . . 99
WASHED DOWN WITH RUSTY WATER IN A TIN. . . . . . .  .  189 THE GRINDSTONE  . .  16
AND SLOW ME DOWN--AND I ABRUPTLY SLOWED. . . . . .  .  189 THE GRINDSTONE  . .  32
AND BROUGHT DOWN SAFELY FROM THE UPPER REGIONS; . .  .  196 WILD GRAPES    . . . 13
THREW ME DOWN GRAPES TO MISS AND SCATTER . . . . .  .  197 WILD GRAPES    . . . 32
"HERE, TAKE A TREETOP, I'LL GET DOWN ANOTHER. . . .  .  197 WILD GRAPES    . . . 39
"DROP OR I'LL SHAKE THE TREE AND SHAKE YOU DOWN." .  .  198 WILD GRAPES    . . . 78
I'LL BEND THE TREE DOWN AND LET YOU DOWN BY IT." .  .  198 WILD GRAPES    . . . 83
I DON'T KNOW MUCH ABOUT THE LETTING DOWN; . . . . .  .  198 WILD GRAPES    . . . 84
WHEN HIS TIME COMES TO DIE AND SETTLE DOWN. . . . .  .  202 PLACE FOR A THIRD  . 82
THE BOARD WE HAD LAID DOWN TO WALK DRY-SHOD ON . . .  204 THE WITCH OF COOS  . 48
AND BRING THE CHALK-PILE DOWN. "I'LL TELL YOU WHAT-- . 205 THE WITCH OF COOS  . 107
COME DOWN THE STAIRS AT NIGHT AND STAND PERPLEXED . .  206 THE WITCH OF COOS  . 126
WE THINK THEY HAD A GRAVE DOWN IN THE CELLAR. . . .  .  206 THE WITCH OF COOS  . 135
WE KNOW THEY HAD A GRAVE DOWN IN THE CELLAR. . . .  .  206 THE WITCH OF COOS  . 136
YOU CAN COME DOWN FROM EVERYTHING TO NOTHING. . . .  .  210 PAUPER WITCH OF GRAFTON 103
AND EXPERTS SAID THAT DEEP DOWN IN THE MOUNTAIN . .  .  212 A FOUNTAIN, A BOTTLE .  4
COME STRAIGHT DOWN OFF THIS MOUNTAIN JUST AS FAST .  .  215 A FOUNTAIN, A BOTTLE . 61
ONE DOWN ONE STREET, . . . . . . . . . . . . . . .  .  218 I WILL SING YOU ONE-O . 12
ONE DOWN ANOTHER, . . . . . . . . . . . . . . . . .  .  218 I WILL SING YOU ONE-O . 13
TO DRAG DOWN MAN . . . . . . . . . . . . . . . . .  .  220 I WILL SING YOU ONE-O . 78
SHOOK DOWN ON ME . . . . . . . . . . . . . . . . .  .  221 DUST OF SNOW   . . .  2
SO DAWN GOES DOWN TO DAY. . . . . . . . . . . . . .  .  223 NOTHING GOLD CAN STAY  7
DEEPER DOWN IN THE WELL THAN WHERE THE WATER . . . .  225 FOR ONCE SOMETHING .  3
AND WITH THESE SKY-FLAKES DOWN IN FLURRY ON FLURRY .  225 BLUE-BUTTERFLY DAY .  2
AT LAST THE GATHERED SNOW LETS DOWN AS WHITE . . . .  226 THE ONSET   . . . .  2
THE MEADOW GRASS COULD BE CEMENTED DOWN . . . . . .  .  231 A BROOK IN THE CITY .  9
WITH CINDER LOADS DUMPED DOWN? THE BROOK WAS THROWN .  231 A BROOK IN THE CITY . 15
THROWS DOWN IN FRONT OF US IS NOT TO BAR . . . . .  .  238 ON A TREE FALLEN ACROSS 2
AND MAKE US GET DOWN IN A FOOT OF SNOW . . . . . .  .  238 ON A TREE FALLEN ACROSS 7
BORNE DOWN UNTIL THE END ALMOST TOOK ROOT, . . . .  .  239 OUR SINGING STRENGTH  13
WHERE ONE FALSE WING BEAT WOULD HAVE BROUGHT DOWN ALL, 240 OUR SINGING STRENGTH  43
WHOSE SPOTTED FLOWERS HANG MEANLY DOWN. . . . . . .  .  247 ON GOING UNNOTICED  .  8
EXCEPT WHEN SEA FOG LAID IT DOWN, . . . . . . . . .  .  249 A PECK OF GOLD   . .  2
AND GOES DOWN BURNING INTO THE GULF BELOW, . . . .  .  249 ACCEPTANCE    . . .  2
I HAVE LOOKED DOWN THE SADDEST CITY LANE. . . . . .  .  255 ACQUAINTED WITH NIGHT  4
THE VOICE SAID, "HURL HER DOWN!" . . . . . . . . .  .  255 THE LOVELY BE CHOOSERS 1
THE VOICES, "HOW FAR DOWN?" . . . . . . . . . . . .  .  255 THE LOVELY BE CHOOSERS 2
OUR LIFE RUNS DOWN IN SENDING UP THE CLOCK. . . . .  .  259 WEST-RUNNING BROOK . 64
THE BROOK RUNS DOWN IN SENDING UP OUR LIFE. . . . .  .  260 WEST-RUNNING BROOK . 65
THE SUN RUNS DOWN IN SENDING UP THE BROOK. . . . .  .  260 WEST-RUNNING BROOK . 66
FOR EVERY PARCEL I STOOP DOWN TO SEIZE . . . . . .  .  266 THE ARMFUL    . . .  1
I CROUCH DOWN TO PREVENT THEM AS THEY FALL; . . . .  .  267 THE ARMFUL    . . .  9
THEN SIT DOWN IN THE MIDDLE OF THEM ALL. . . . . .  .  267 THE ARMFUL    . . . 10
AND DRAWS IT DOWN AS IF IT WERE A LOVER . . . . . .  .  268 THE BEAR    . . . .  2
AS SHE FLINGS OVER AND OFF DOWN THROUGH THE MAPLES, .  269 THE BEAR    . . . .  8
"THOSE ARE JUST NAILHEADS. THOSE ARE FASTENED DOWN." . 278 THE WHITE-TAILED HORNET 36
WE DIVE DOWN UNDER THE FARM. . . . . . . . . . . .  .  282 A DRUMLIN WOODCHUCK . 16
TO LOOKING DOWN AND YET NOT BEING SAD, . . . . . .  .  283 THE GOLD HESPERIDEE .  9
WHEN MY GARDEN HAS GONE DOWN DITCH, . . . . . . . .  .  285 IN TIME OF CLOUDBURST . 12
HE TOOK THE PROPS DOWN USED FOR PROPPING OPEN, . .  .  289 OLD BARN AT THE BOTTOM 10
OR DOWN A MINE OR AT THE MILL (I MET HIM) . . . . .  .  289 OLD BARN AT THE BOTTOM 18
ALL UP AND DOWN IT. SO THAT WALKING THERE . . . . .  .  290 OLD BARN AT THE BOTTOM 25
ROLL STONES DOWN ON OUR HEAD! . . . . . . . . . . .  .  298 ON TAKING FROM THE TOP  2
DOWN IF YOU TRIED. . . . . . . . . . . . . . . . .  .  298 ON TAKING FROM THE TOP  8
AND A MASKED MOON HAD SPREAD DOWN COMPASS RAYS . .  .  300 MOON COMPASSES   . .  3
IT COULD NOT HAVE COME DOWN TO US SO FAR, . . . . .  .  302 A BIRD SINGING IN SLEEP 9
JUST WHEN THE COLD WENT DOWN SO MANY BELOW. . . . .  .  305 THERE ARE ROUGHLY ZONES 17
BETTER TO GO DOWN DIGNIFIED . . . . . . . . . . . .  .  307 PROVIDE, PROVIDE  . . 19
OF BEING BROUGHT DOWN TO THE REAL." . . . . . . . .  .  313 THE VINDICTIVES  . . 91
WE TWO WERE GROPING DOWN A MALVERN SIDE . . . . . .  .  315 IRIS BY NIGHT    . .  2
FOR NOTHING DOWN, ALL-OUT-DOORS OF A PLACE, . . . .  .  316 BUILD SOIL    . . .  8
I KNOW WOOL'S DOWN TO SEVEN CENTS A POUND. . . . .  .  316 BUILD SOIL    . . . 13
AWAY 'WAY DOWN INSIDE I'M PERSONAL. . . . . . . . .  .  320 BUILD SOIL    . . . 144
NOT HALFWAY DOWN THE SCALE OF GRACE. . . . . . . .  .  326 TO A THINKER   . . . 32
THE STORM GETS DOWN HIS NECK IN AN ICY SOUSE . . . .  341 WILLFUL HOMING   . .  3
SHE CAME DOWN WEAKLY AND BLINDLY LED . . . . . . .  .  343 DISCOVERY OF MADEIRAS  6
IT DID MORE DISTANCE UP AND DOWN, . . . . . . . . .  .  344 DISCOVERY OF MADEIRAS  19
IT GENTLY THREW US A GLITTERING SHOWER DOWN. . . .  .  349 OUR HOLD ON THE PLANET  7
IT GIVES UP STANDING STRAIGHT AND GOES DOWN SWISHING. . 349 TO A YOUNG WRETCH .  4
SITS DOWN IN SCHOOL TO TRY IF HE CAN WRITE . . . .  .  353 THE LESSON FOR TODAY  92
COWER DOWN IN DESPERATION TO ACCEPT . . . . . . . .  .  357 A CONSIDERABLE SPECK  22
GO PART WAY DOWN THE LANE. . . . . . . . . . . . .  .  359 NOVEMBER    . . . .  3
GET BEATEN DOWN AND PASTED . . . . . . . . . . . .  .  359 NOVEMBER    . . . .  5
FIRST UNDER UP AND THEN AGAIN DOWN UNDER, . . . . .  .  362 SYMPATHY WITH UNDER DOG 1
HAVE COME DOWN FROM THEIR NATIVE LEDGE . . . . . .  .  364 A NATURE NOTE    . .  6
FOR ONLY A DOLLAR DOWN. . . . . . . . . . . . . . .  .  367 A SERIOUS STEP LIGHTLY  8
BUT PUT THAT DOWN TO SUPERSTITION, STRANGER. . . .  .  369 THE LITERATE FARMER AND 36
AND THEN GET SLOWLY, SLOWLY PULLED BACK DOWN. . . .  .  370 THE LITERATE FARMER AND 67
AND ZEAL WOULD NOT BE THANKED THAT CUT IT DOWN . .  .  375 A YOUNG BIRCH    . . 19
```

DOWN (CONTINUED)
THEN CUT DOWN THE TREES WHEN LUMBER GROWN, ... 376 SOMETHING FOR HOPE . . 13
AND STARTED DOWN THE GULLY. . . . . 377 ONE STEP BACKWARD TAKEN 6
LOOK DOWN THE LONG VALLEY AND THERE STANDS A MOUNTAIN . 379 TOO ANXIOUS FOR RIVERS 1
WENT STREAKING MOLTEN DOWN THE WEST. . . . . 381 AN UNSTAMPED LETTER IN 27
AND BEGAN TO BOUNCE DOWN A GRANITE STAIR, ... 383 WERE I IN TROUBLE . . 4
BY ANNOUNCING A STAR DOWN . . . . 384 MAKING CERTAIN ANYTHING 11
ONCE DOWN ON MY KNEES TO GROWING PLANTS . . . . 385 A MOOD APART 1
(IT WILL BE TAKEN DOWN BEFORE IT FALLS.) . . . . . . 386 THE FEAR OF MAN . . . 7
ME UP, NOT DOWN. . . . . 389 ASTROMETAPHYSICAL . . 20
CAME TAP-TAP-TAPPING DOWN THE VILLAGE STREET, ... 394 HAEC FABULA DOCET . . 3
THE IMPORTANT THING IS NOT TO GET BOGGED DOWN . . . . 406 FROM PLANE TO PLANE . 62
HE HANGS ON UPSIDE DOWN WITH TALON FEET . . . . 412 POD OF THE MILKWEED . 45
AND GO LIE DOWN. . . . . 413 AWAY! 8
THEY WOULD BRING EMPIRES DOWN ABOUT OUR EARS . . . . . 423 FOR JOHN F. KENNEDY . 29
RIGHT DOWN TO NOW IN GLORY UPON GLORY. . . . . 423 FOR JOHN F. KENNEDY . 53
OUT AND DOWN ALONG . . . . 428 KITTY HAWK 7
BUT IT MUST COME DOWN." . . . . 437 KITTY HAWK 307
DON'T YOU CRASH ME DOWN. . . . . 439 KITTY HAWK 350
I WAS SWOOPED DOWN UPON WHEN I WAS SMALL, ... 443 AUSPEX 2
THE PONDEROUS BEAST WENT DOWN . . . . 444 THE DRAFT HORSE . . 9
WANTED US TO GET DOWN . . . . 444 THE DRAFT HORSE . . 19
BEFORE THEY SAT DOWN WEARY ON A BANK . . . . 454 HOW HARD TO KEEP FROM 13
DOWN A LIKELY HOLE . . . . 468 A REFLEX 3
WORTH GOING AFTER. GET DOWN INTO THINGS, ... 483 A MASQUE OF REASON . 281
IT COMES DOWN TO A DOUBT ABOUT THE WISDOM . . . . . . 483 A MASQUE OF REASON . 291
THE SERPENT'S TAIL STUCK DOWN THE SERPENT'S THROAT, . . 485 A MASQUE OF REASON . 340
PULLS DOWN THE WINDOW CURTAIN ON THE DOOR . . . . . . 493 A MASQUE OF MERCY . 2
"I FLED HIM, DOWN THE NIGHTS AND DOWN THE DAYS; . . . . 494 A MASQUE OF MERCY . 22
I FLED HIM, DOWN THE ARCHES OF THE YEARS." . . . . . 494 A MASQUE OF MERCY . 23
AND HELP YOU'RE GOING TO GET. / I'LL BREAK YOUR DOOR DOWN. 500 A MASQUE OF MERCY . 178
AND THEN NOT PROPHESYING. (HE SITS DOWN.) . . . . . . 501 A MASQUE OF MERCY . 199
(TAKING A WALK OFF DOWN THE STORE DISTRESSED) . . . . 503 A MASQUE OF MERCY . 267
'TWAS IN FOR AN OLD-FASHIONED SHAKING DOWN . . . . . . 503 A MASQUE OF MERCY . 273
AND HERE COME ALL YOUR GREAT BOOKS TUMBLING DOWN! . . . 504 A MASQUE OF MERCY . 288
I SHRINK FROM BEING PUBLICLY LET DOWN. . . . . 505 A MASQUE OF MERCY . 305
THEN FURTHER DOWN IT SEEMS TO START FROM WHERE . . . . 506 A MASQUE OF MERCY . 335
(A WHOLE SHELF CASCADES DOWN.) HERE COME SOME MORE. . . 506 A MASQUE OF MERCY . 341
A REVOLUTION'S COMING DOWN THE STREET! . . . . 508 A MASQUE OF MERCY . 391
THEY TOOK MY LOVE AND THREW HER DOWN A WELL. . . . . . 510 A MASQUE OF MERCY . 446
HE'S THINKING OF, IT WASN'T DOWN A WELL, ... 510 A MASQUE OF MERCY . 448
YOU MEAN I'M BEING SENT DOWN IN THE CELLAR? . . . . . 514 A MASQUE OF MERCY . 551
IT IS THE CELLAR TO MY STORE.--WHAT HO, DOWN THERE! . . 514 A MASQUE OF MERCY . 555
NOT ON THE BATTLEFIELD, BUT DOWN IN CELLARS. . . . . . 515 A MASQUE OF MERCY . 573
DOWN BURNING SKEPTICS IN THE CELLAR FURNACE . . . . . 516 A MASQUE OF MERCY . 603
WHAT'S ALL THIS TALK OF SLAYING DOWN IN CELLARS-- . . . 516 A MASQUE OF MERCY . 605
SO SINISTER? YOU SPOKE TO SOMEONE DOWN THERE. . . . . 516 A MASQUE OF MERCY . 606
THERE'S NO ONE DOWN THERE GETTING TORTURED, SAVE . . . 516 A MASQUE OF MERCY . 609
WHAT'S REALLY DOWN THERE? / JUST AN OUBLIETTE, ... 516 A MASQUE OF MERCY . 612
HAVE THEY BEEN DOWN? / NOT IN THE PROPER SPIRIT. . . . 516 A MASQUE OF MERCY . 618
UNTIL THE SCRIBES HAD TAKEN DOWN A BOOKFUL . . . . . . 518 A MASQUE OF MERCY . 644
AND I'M AFRAID. (THE BULB LIGHTS SICKEN DOWN. . . . . 520 A MASQUE OF MERCY . 695
OUR VERY BEST, OUR LIVES LAID DOWN LIKE JONAH'S, . . . 520 A MASQUE OF MERCY . 720
OUR LIVES LAID DOWN IN WAR AND PEACE--MAY NOT . . . . 520 A MASQUE OF MERCY . 721
DOWNED
THE FRENCH, THE SPANISH, AND THE DUTCH WERE DOWNED . . . 422 FOR JOHN F. KENNEDY . 16
DOWNHILL
TO HIS DOWNHILL, EARLY-MORNING STRIDE, ... 140 THE GUM-GATHERER . . 2
AND I SHALL SEE THE SNOW ALL GO DOWNHILL . . . . . . 226 THE ONSET 18
DOWNHILL AT DUSK? . . . . 227 TO EARTHWARD 8
LOCKING DOWNHILL TO A FROTHY SHORE? . . . . 251 BEREFT 5
DOWNPOUR
LET THE DOWNPOUR ROIL AND TOIL! . . . . 285 IN TIME OF CLOUDBURST 1
DOWNPOURS
BETWEEN TWO DOWNPOURS TO SEE WHAT THERE WAS. . . . . . 300 MOON COMPASSES . . . 2
DOWNSTAIRS
THAT RESTED ON THE BANISTER, AND SLID DOWNSTAIRS; . . . 52 HOME BURIAL 32
FATHER HAD GONE UPSTAIRS; MOTHER WAS DOWNSTAIRS. . . . 203 THE WITCH OF COOS . 34
AND THOUGHT I HEARD HIM DOWNSTAIRS IN THE CELLAR. . . . 203 THE WITCH OF COOS . 47
DOWNWARD
AT THE FLAME BURNING DOWNWARD AS HE SUCKS IT." . . . . 112 IN THE HOME STRETCH . 65
DOWNWARD COMPARISONS. AS LONG ON EARTH . . . . 279 THE WHITE-TAILED HORNET 59
BUT ONCE COMPARISONS WERE YIELDED DOWNWARD, ... 279 THE WHITE-TAILED HORNET 63
DOWNWARD TO MAKE HIM SIT ASTRIDE A DRIFT, ... 341 WILLFUL HOMING . . . 6
DOWNY
AFTER A DOWNY STORM, HE PASSED OUR PLACE . . . . . . 149 SNOW 176
OF EASY WIND AND DOWNY FLAKE. . . . . 224 STOPPING BY WOODS . 12
AND DOWNY WAX THE THREE BEGAN TO THRIVE. . . . . . . 283 THE GOLD HESPERIDEE . 6
DOZED
WHERE ALL DAY LONG SHE LAY AND DOZED. . . . . 344 DISCOVERY OF MADEIRAS 37
DOZEN
A DOZEN GIRLS AND BOYS WE WERE. . . . . 265 THE BIRTHPLACE . . . 7
A HALF A DOZEN MAJOR WARS, ... 368 A SERIOUS STEP LIGHTLY 23
DRAB
FOR WHAT THE DRAB WEED LACKS OF THE ORNATE. . . . . . 411 POD OF THE MILKWEED . 13
FOR DRAB IT IS ITS FONDEST MUST ADMIT. . . . . 411 POD OF THE MILKWEED . 14
DRAFT
WELL IF IT DOESN'T WITH ITS DRAFT BRING ON . . . . . 130 THE BONFIRE 32
THE DRAFT HORSE . . . . 443 THE DRAFT HORSE . . T
IN ONE LONG INVIDIOUS DRAFT. . . . . 444 THE DRAFT HORSE . . 12
DRAG
TO DRAG YOU OUT FOR JUST A GOOD-NIGHT CALL . . . . . 117 IN THE HOME STRETCH . 188
"ONE THING: HE DIDN'T DRAG GOD INTO IT." . . . . . . 146 SNOW 81
I GUESS THEY'D BETTER DRAG IT THROUGH AGAIN. . . . . . 208 PAUPER WITCH OF GRAFTON 29
TO DRAG DOWN MAN . . . . 220 I WILL SING YOU ONE-O 78
DRAGGED
"HE DIDN'T SAY. I DRAGGED HIM TO THE HOUSE, ... 35 DEATH OF THE HIRED MAN 40
THEY ARE DRAGGED TO THE WITHERED BRACKEN BY THE LOAD, . 121 BIRCHES 14

PAGE TITLE LINE

DRAGGED (CONTINUED)
THE PILE IS OURS: WE DRAGGED IT BOUGH ON BOUGH . . . . . 129 THE BONFIRE 6
HE DRAGGED IT THROUGH THE PLOWED GROUND AT A PACE . . . . 173 A STAR IN A STONEBOAT . 31
PAUL DRAGGED THE SHALLOWS FOR IT WITH HIS FINGERS, ... 194 PAUL'S WIFE . . . 104
SO NOW THEY'VE DRAGGED IT THROUGH THE LAW COURTS ONCE, . . 208 PAUPER WITCH OF GRAFTON 28
BE DRAGGED BY YOU ALL OVER EVERYWHERE----" . . . . . . 214 A FOUNTAIN, A BOTTLE . 30
DRAGGING
DRAGGING THE WHOLE SKY WITH IT TO THE HILLS. . . . . . 38 DEATH OF THE HIRED MAN 104
UP AT HIS SHOULDERS, DRAGGING YELLOW STRANDS . . . . 125 AN ENCOUNTER . . . 17
DRAGON'S
WHEN A STORM THREATENED FROM THE DRAGON'S DEN, ... 63 A SERVANT TO SERVANTS . 30
DRAMA
AND TO INTENSIFY THE DRAMA . . . . 417 AMERICA IS HARD TO SEE 19
DRAMATIC
INDULGING AN ABSURD DRAMATIC SPELL, ... 396 ANY SIZE WE PLEASE . . 3
DRAMATIS
INCLUDING ME, THE ONLY DRAMATIS . . . . 487 A MASQUE OF REASON . . 393
DRANK
GOLD DUSTED ALL WE DRANK AND ATE, ... 249 A PECK OF GOLD . . 10
AND WHETHER THE FARMER DRANK OR NOT . . . . . . 263 THE TIMES TABLE . . 3
THEN PAUSED AGAIN AND EITHER DRANK OR SMELT-- . . . . 357 A CONSIDERABLE SPECK 13
ONE DRANK TO HIS MOTHER . . . . 432 KITTY HAWK . . . 127
DRAW
NOR YET TO DRAW ONE THOUGHT OF OURS TO HIM, ... 23 THE TUFT OF FLOWERS . 27
(NOTHING COULD DRAW HER AFTER THOSE TWO SONS. . . . . 56 THE BLACK COTTAGE . 40
BUT READ IT, READ IT.--THAT'S RIGHT, DRAW THE CURTAIN: . . 99 THE SELF-SEEKER . . 193
TO TAP THE UPPER SKY AND DRAW A FLOW . . . . . . 169 NEW HAMPSHIRE . . 340
WE ARE TOO MUCH OUT, AND IF WE WON'T DRAW IN . . . 324 BUILD SOIL . . . 243
WOULD YOU TWO PLEASE DRAW IN A LITTLE CLOSER? . . . . 488 A MASQUE OF REASON . 403
DRAWING
DRAWING THE SLOW WAVES WHITER AND WHITER AND WHITER. . . . 63 A SERVANT TO SERVANTS . 25
DRAWN (SEE LONG-DRAWN)
DRAWN ON A SORT OF PASSPORT WITH THE BRANCH . . . . . 74 THE GENERATIONS OF MEN 40
DRAWN INTO TOWN ABOUT THIS CELLAR HOLE . . . . . 76 THE GENERATIONS OF MEN 89
DOORS LOCKED AND CURTAINS DRAWN WILL MAKE NO DIFFERENCE. . 89 THE FEAR 16
THICK HAND MADE LIGHT OF, STEEL-BLUE CHIN DRAWN DOWN . . 188 THE AX-HELVE . . . 99
BUT LET THERE NEVER BE CURTAIN DRAWN . . . . . 251 TREE AT MY WINDOW . . 3
DRAWS
THE GRAVEYARD DRAWS THE LIVING STILL, ... 221 IN A DISUSED GRAVEYARD 3
AND DRAWS IT DOWN AS IF IT WERE A LOVER . . . . 268 THE BEAR 2
HE DRAWS HIMSELF UP TO HIS FULL EXTENT. . . . . . 309 WASPISH 2
DREAD
DREAD FIFTY ABOVE MORE THAN FIFTY BELOW." . . . . . 228 GOOD-BY AND KEEP COLD . 19
AND I DREAD THE OMINOUS STAIN OF TAR . . . . . 232 THE KITCHEN CHIMNEY . 13
YOU TAKE THE UGLINESS ALL SO MUCH DREAD, ... 371 THE LITERATE FARMER AND 106
THE DARKEST OF IT STILL TO DREAD. . . . . . . 383 THE NIGHT LIGHT . . . 8
DREADED
THE PAUSE RIGHT THERE, SHE THOUGHT THE DREADED WORD . . 151 SNOW 238
DREADFUL
SHE HAD TO LIE AND HEAR LOVE THINGS MADE DREADFUL . . . 66 A SERVANT TO SERVANTS . 130
"WHO WANTS TO HEAR YOUR NEWS, YOU--DREADFUL FOOL?" . . . 89 THE HOUSEKEEPER . . . 214
DREAM
GIVE THE BURIED FLOWER A DREAM; . . . . 11 TO THE THAWING WIND . 3
WHAT THINGS FOR DREAM THERE ARE WHEN SPECTER-LIKE, . . . 14 WAITING 1
I DREAM UPON THE OPPOSING LIGHTS OF THE HOUR, ... 14 WAITING 9
I DREAM UPON THE NIGHTHAWKS PEOPLING HEAVEN, ... 14 WAITING 11
(THIS WAS MY DREAM) AND LOOKED AND PONDERED LONG, . . . 16 A DREAM PANG . . . 4
A DREAM PANG . . . . 16 A DREAM PANG . . . T
IT WAS NO DREAM OF THE GIFT OF IDLE HOURS, ... 17 MOWING 7
THE FACT IS THE SWEETEST DREAM THAT LABOR KNOWS. . . . 17 MOWING 13
AND TENDERLY, LIFE'S LITTLE DREAM, ... 20 THE TRIAL BY EXISTENCE 38
"WELL, THOSE DAYS TROUBLE SILAS LIKE A DREAM. . . . . 37 DEATH OF THE HIRED MAN 71
LORD, IF I WERE TO DREAM OF EVERYONE . . . . . 81 THE HOUSEKEEPER . . 12
AND SO I DREAM OF GOING BACK TO BE. . . . . . 122 BIRCHES 42
THE OFT-REPEATED DREAM . . . . 128 THE OFT-REPEATED DREAM T
WAS AFRAID IN AN OFT-REPEATED DREAM . . . . . 128 THE OFT-REPEATED DREAM 11
COMMANDED IN A DREAM, FOREVER GO . . . . . 173 A STAR IN A STONEBOAT . 35
TO SEE IF IN A DREAM THEY BROUGHT OF YOU . . . . 222 TO E.T. 4
BUT, PILGRIM-MANNED, THE MAYFLOWER IN A DREAM . . . 262 IMMIGRANTS . . . 3
IF SINGING OUT OF SLEEP AND DREAM THAT WAY . . . 303 A BIRD SINGING IN SLEEP 13
"YOU CHILDREN MAY DREAM IT AND TELL IT TOMORROW." . . 379 TOO ANXIOUS FOR RIVERS 20
BUT NOW AS BLOBS OF BRAIN WE'LL LIE AND DREAM, . . . 395 ETHEREALIZING . . 11
WITH AN INHERITANCE OF RESTLESS DREAM. . . . . 412 POD OF THE MILKWEED . 44
HE MIGHT HAVE BEEN THE DREAM OF A GHOST . . . . 421 ONE MORE BREVITY . 53
MIGHT HAVE BEEN A DREAM . . . . 431 KITTY HAWK . . . 87
DREAMED
THE TIME I DREAMED THE DOOR WAS TRIED . . . . . 135 LOCKED OUT . . . 4
CAN YOU INTERPRET DREAMS? I DREAMED LAST NIGHT . . . 501 A MASQUE OF MERCY . 200
DREAM-HEAD
VAGUE DREAM-HEAD LIFTED OUT OF THE GROUND, ... 251 TREE AT MY WINDOW . 5
DREAMILY
I DON'T WANT IT DREAMILY NIBBLED FOR BROWSE . . . . 228 GOOD-BY AND KEEP COLD . 7
DREAMING
AND DREAMING, AS IT WERE, HELD BROTHERLY SPEECH . . . 23 THE TUFT OF FLOWERS 37
THE LANGUOR OF IT AND THE DREAMING FOND; . . . . 29 MY BUTTERFLY . . 34
WHAT FORM MY DREAMING WAS ABOUT TO TAKE. . . . . 68 AFTER APPLE-PICKING . 17
WE STAND HERE DREAMING. HURRY! CALL THEM BACK!" . . . 113 IN THE HOME STRETCH 77
AND TELL THEM THE REST OF THE STORY IS DREAMING? . . . 379 TOO ANXIOUS FOR RIVERS 19
DREAMS
FOR ITS SUGGESTION OF WHAT DREAMS! . . . . . 20 THE TRIAL BY EXISTENCE 24
AND NEVER OVERSTEPPED IT SAVE IN DREAMS. . . . . 171 NEW HAMPSHIRE . . 380
AND IT HAD ALMOST GIVEN HIM TROUBLED DREAMS . . . . 290 OLD BARN AT THE BOTTOM 42
IT GAVE BAD DREAMS AND BROKEN SLEEP, ... 382 THE NIGHT LIGHT . . 3
CAN YOU INTERPRET DREAMS? I DREAMED LAST NIGHT . . . 501 A MASQUE OF MERCY . 200
DREAMY
(BUT THIS WAS DREAMY UNOFFICIAL COUNTING) . . . . 175 THE CENSUS-TAKER . . 32
DREARY
TO THE DREARY WAIL . . . . 429 KITTY HAWK . . . 29

DREGS
    AND WITH THE SWIFT RUSH OF ITS SANDY DREGS . . . . . 391 ON BEING IDOLIZED . .   3
DRESS
    TELL ME WHAT IS IT?" / ANNE JUST WAGGED HER DRESS, . . . 96 THE SELF-SEEKER . . 105
    STYLE UPON STYLE IN DRESS AND THOUGHT AT LAST . . . . 117 IN THE HOME STRETCH . 184
    YOU'D BETTER DRESS: YOU WON'T GO BACK TO BED. . . . . . 152 SNOW 273
    IN DRESS OR MANNER OF THE GIRL WHO BORE IT. . . . . . . 181 MAPLE 53
    I'LL DRESS UP IN SHEEP'S CLOTHING AND EAT SHEEP. . . . 316 BUILD SOIL 16
DRESSED
    DRESSED, BUT DISHEVELED FROM SOME HOURS OF SLEEP; . . . 143 SNOW 4
    'TWAS SUNDAY AND SQUARE HALE WAS DRESSED FOR MEETING. . 284 THE GOLD HESPERIDEE . 41
DREW
    AND SET THEM ON THE PORCH, THEN DREW HIM DOWN . . . . 34 DEATH OF THE HIRED MAN 9
    HE DREW THE OXEN TOWARD HIM WITH LIGHT TOUCHES . . . . . 44 THE MOUNTAIN 107
    "YES, STARK. AND YOU?" / "I'M STARK." HE DREW HIS PASSPORT. 74 THE GENERATIONS OF MEN 46
    HE SAT AND WAITED TILL HE DREW US OUT, ... 106 CHRISTMAS TREES . . . 7
    FOOTPRINTS IN SUMMER DUST AS IF WE DREW . . . . . . 118 MEETING AND PASSING . 6
    SWEET-SCENTED STUFF WHEN THE BREEZE DREW ACROSS IT. . . 136 "OUT,OUT--" 3
    THERE OVERTOOK ME AND DREW ME IN . . . . 140 THE GUM-GATHERER . . 1
    IT DREW BACK IN ITS BODY LIKE A SNAIL); . . . . . . 172 A STAR IN A STONEBOAT . 18
    BAPTISTE DREW BACK AND SQUINTED AT IT, PLEASED: . . . . 188 THE AX-HELVE 101
    SHE DREW BACK; HE WAS CALM: . . . . . . 339 THE SUBVERTED FLOWER . 1
    AND DREW HER BACKWARD HOME. . . . . 341 THE SUBVERTED FLOWER . 73
    IT IS GETTING DARK AND TIME HE DREW TO A HOUSE, ... 341 WILLFUL HOMING . . . 1
    HE NO MORE DREW THE SMILE HE SOUGHT. . . . . 347 DISCOVERY OF MADEIRAS . 118
    WHO DREW BACK AT FIRST IN DOUBT, ... 366 NOT OF SCHOOL AGE . . 6
    HE DREW THEM IN FOR WARMTH OF SELF-EMBRACE. . . . . . 396 ANY SIZE WE PLEASE . . 8
    AND THE NIGHT DREW THROUGH THE TREES . . . . 444 THE DRAFT HORSE . . . 11
    BUT THE PRINCE DREW AWAY HIS HAND IN TIME . . . . . 453 HOW HARD TO KEEP FROM 4
DRIED
    HAS DRIED THE DEW AND ALL ITS ROPES RELENT, ... 331 THE SILKEN TENT . . . 3
DRIFT
    TO GO WITH THE DRIFT OF THINGS, ... 30 RELUCTANCE 21
    AND QUIVER LIKE THE FRAYED EDGE OF THE DRIFT . . . . . 149 SNOW 195
    DOWNWARD TO MAKE HIM SIT ASTRIDE A DRIFT, ... 341 WILLFUL HOMING . . . 6
DRIFTS
    HOW DRIFTS ARE PILED, ... 10 STORM FEAR 13
DRIFTWOOD
    RIDGES OF SAND, AND DRIFTWOOD STRIPPED OF BARK. . . . . 40 THE MOUNTAIN 14
DRILL (SEE MOTOR-DRILL)
DRINK
    SORRY THERE IS NO CUP TO GIVE YOU A DRINK. . . . . . 50 A HUNDRED COLLARS . . 155
    I DRINK OUT OF THE BOTTLE--NOT YOUR STYLE. . . . . . 50 A HUNDRED COLLARS . . 156
    HERE'S HOPING SHE GETS HER DRINK AND GETS OUT SAFELY." 77 THE GENERATIONS OF MEN 109
    HE DIDN'T EVEN OFFER ME A DRINK . . . . 160 NEW HAMPSHIRE . . . 31
    HE LAID IT AT THE EDGE, WHERE IT COULD DRINK. . . . . 194 PAUL'S WIFE 101
    AT THE FIRST DRINK IT RUSTLED AND GREW LIMP. . . . . . 194 PAUL'S WIFE 102
    AT THE NEXT DRINK IT GREW INVISIBLE. . . . . . . 194 PAUL'S WIFE 103
    TO BLOT OUT AND DRINK UP AND SWEEP AWAY . . . . . 245 SPRING POOLS 10
    EITHER TO EAT OR DRINK. . . . . 282 A DRUMLIN WOODCHUCK . 19
    AND DARKLY DRINK EACH OTHER'S EYES . . . . 344 DISCOVERY OF MADEIRAS . 39
    TO KISS AND DRINK EACH OTHER'S BREATH . . . . 346 DISCOVERY OF MADEIRAS . 81
    HE ASKED FOR A DRINK AT THE KITCHEN DOOR, ... 364 TRESPASS 18
    DRINK AND BE WHOLE AGAIN BEYOND CONFUSION. . . . . . 379 DIRECTIVE 62
    AND ENOUGH DRINK OIL FOR ALL. . . . . 384 IN THE LONG NIGHT . . 12
    OF DUSTY WEEDS TO TAKE A DRINK OF STARS. . . . . . 454 HOW HARD TO KEEP FROM 14
    I TAKE TO DRINK--AT LEAST I TAKE A DRINK. . . . . . 496 A MASQUE OF MERCY . . 83
    SHE'LL TAKE TO DRINK AND SEE HOW WE LIKE THAT. . . . . 496 A MASQUE OF MERCY . . 85
    SHE DOESN'T MIND NOT OFFERING A DRINK . . . . . . 496 A MASQUE OF MERCY . . 87
    I'LL TAKE TO DRINK--AT LEAST I'LL TAKE A DRINK. . . . . 500 A MASQUE OF MERCY . . 168
DRINKER
    BEL IS A SOLITARY SOCIAL DRINKER. . . . . 496 A MASQUE OF MERCY . . 86
DRINKING
    I SKIMMED THIS MORNING FROM THE DRINKING TROUGH . . . . 68 AFTER APPLE-PICKING . 11
    WAS A SPRING WITH A BROKEN DRINKING GLASS, ... 263 THE TIMES TABLE . . . 2
    HE KNEW A SPRING THAT WANTED DRINKING; . . . . . . 274 A LONE STRIKER . . . 44
    A BROKEN DRINKING GOBLET LIKE THE GRAIL . . . . . . 379 DIRECTIVE 57
    TO ANYONE AROUND WHEN SHE IS DRINKING. . . . . . . 496 A MASQUE OF MERCY . . 88
DRIPPING
    AND WHEN HE RAISED IT DRIPPING ONCE AND TRIED . . . . 190 THE GRINDSTONE . . . 68
    I WAS ASLEEP STILL UNDER THE DRIPPING ROOF, ... 236 VALLEY'S SINGING DAY . 16
    I STOLE FORTH DIMLY IN THE DRIPPING PAUSE . . . . . 300 MOON COMPASSES . . . 1
    THE LAST WET FIELDS AND DRIPPING HEDGES HOME. . . . . 315 IRIS BY NIGHT . . . 3
DRIPS
    BUT SWEATING-FULL, DRIPS WINE AND OIL A LITTLE. . . . . 323 BUILD SOIL 236
DRIVE
    "YOU CAN DRIVE ROUND AND KEEP IN LUNENBURG, ... 43 THE MOUNTAIN 93
    "YOU DRIVE AROUND? IT MUST BE PLEASANT WORK." . . . . 49 A HUNDRED COLLARS . . 122
    BUT LOREN, THE FATHERLY, OUT FOR A DRIVE." . . . . . 60 BLUEBERRIES 39
    AND DRIVE, THE WAY YOU CAN, YOU KNOW, IN MOWING-- . . . 71 THE CODE 45
    TO TRY TO HELP ME DRIVE A BETTER BARGAIN." . . . . . 93 THE SELF-SEEKER . . . 9
    TO DRIVE PAUL OUT OF ANY LUMBER CAMP . . . . . . 191 PAUL'S WIFE 1
    WHERE THE LOG DRIVE LAY PRESSED AGAINST THE BOOM, . . . 194 PAUL'S WIFE 107
    THE LAST TO LET NIGHT DRIVE HER OFF. . . . . . . 280 BLUE RIBBON AT AMESBURY 16
    AND LET IT DRIVE ME DEATHWARD TOO. . . . . . . 336 THE WIND AND THE RAIN . 6
    TO DRIVE MY TON OF CAR . . . . 388 MIDDLENESS OF THE ROAD 10
    YOU DRIVE ME TO CONFESS IN INK: . . . . 467 QUANDARY 19
DRIVEN
    AND LATER STILL THEY ALL GET DRIVEN IN: . . . . . 49 A HUNDRED COLLARS . . 133
    "HAVING FOUND THE FLOWER AND DRIVEN A BEE AWAY, ... 118 THE TELEPHONE . . . 11
    AND THEIR BUILT OR DRIVEN NESTS. . . . . 127 LONELINESS 12
    WHERE DRIVEN RAIN HAD WET AND SWOLLEN THEM. . . . . . 216 A FOUNTAIN, A BOTTLE . 97
    A FEW I MUST HAVE DRIVEN TO DESPAIR . . . . . . 240 OUR SINGING STRENGTH . 39
    TO SUFFER THE SAME DRIVEN NIGHTMARE OVER. . . . . . 240 OUR SINGING STRENGTH . 45
    BELOW THE POINT, AND WERE AT LAST DRIVEN WRINKLED . . . 258 WEST-RUNNING BROOK . . 25
    WE SHALL BE DRIVEN IN. I WAS BROUGHT UP . . . . . 324 BUILD SOIL 244
    WHERE THESE ARE DRIVEN IN AND PILED, ... 331 BEECH 5

DRONING
   THROUGH OPENING CLOUDS AT NIGHT WITH DRONING SPEED . . . 132 THE BONFIRE 106
DROOLS
   HER FACE IS FLECKED WITH POMACE AND SHE DROOLS . . . . . 124 THE COW IN APPLE TIME . 4
DROP (SEE SNOW-DROP)
   SAYING THEM LIKE THE HEATHEN? WE COULD DROP THEM. . . . . 58 THE BLACK COTTAGE . . 98
   DROP EVERYTHING AND LIVE OUT ON THE GROUND-- . . . . . 67 A SERVANT TO SERVANTS . 162
   "NO, HE WON'T, EITHER. HE'LL JUST DROP THE REINS . . . . 88 THE HOUSEKEEPER . . . 200
   WE DROP OUR EYES OR TURN TO OTHER THINGS, ... 114 IN THE HOME STRETCH . 117
   HE NEVER LET THE LANTERN DROP. . . . . 138 BROWN'S DESCENT . . 29
   "BEFORE YOU DROP THE CURTAIN--I'M REMINDED: . . . . 149 SNOW 172
   DROP IN AND SEE US WHEN YOU'RE PASSING." / "WELL, . . . 155 SNOW 333
   AGAINST MY BROTHER'S NONSENSE. "DROP," HE SAID, . . . 198 WILD GRAPES . . . 75
   "DROP OR I'LL SHAKE THE TREE AND SHAKE YOU DOWN." . . . 198 WILD GRAPES . . . 78
   ONE DROP FELL FROM A FERN, AND LO, A RIPPLE . . . . 225 FOR ONCE SOMETHING . 12
   I HAD TO DROP THE ARMFUL IN THE ROAD . . . . . . 267 THE ARMFUL . . 11
   THEY MAY HAVE TO DROP . . . . 439 KITTY HAWK . . . 355
DROPPED
   HE'S JUST DROPPED EVERYTHING. HE'S LIKE A CHILD. . . . 83 THE HOUSEKEEPER . . 55
   I DROPPED IN AT THE MILL AND WAS DETAINED." . . . . 96 THE SELF-SEEKER . . 100
   AND MADE DUST AND DROPPED STOVE-LENGTH STICKS OF WOOD, . . 136 "OUT, OUT--" . . . 2
   IT'S THEIRS. SHE'S DROPPED IT FROM HER HAND AND GONE." . . 153 SNOW 297
   BUT HIS HEART FAILING HIM, HE DROPPED THE AX . . . . 170 NEW HAMPSHIRE . . 369
   THAT COULD HAVE DROPPED A LEAF WAS DOWN ITSELF . . . 175 THE CENSUS-TAKER . . 19
   HAVING TRIED ONE, HAD DROPPED IT AT HIS FEET . . . . 217 A FOUNTAIN, A BOTTLE . 119
   SPREAD OPEN AS I DROPPED THEM HALF-READ THROUGH . . . 222 TO E.T. . . . 2
   AND DROPPED IT IN, AND SEEN THE IMAGE WALLOW, . . . 245 THE FREEDOM OF THE MOON 11
   AND DROPPED MY EYES, UNWILLING TO EXPLAIN. . . . . 255 ACQUAINTED WITH NIGHT . 6
   I KNEW PRETTY WELL WHY HE DROPPED BEHIND . . . . 275 TWO TRAMPS IN MUD TIME 5
DROPS
   NOW DROPS THAT FLOATED ON THE POOL . . . . 18 GOING FOR WATER . . 23
   THAT DROPS THEM NO FURTHER THAN WHERE THEY WERE. . . . 236 MISGIVING . . . 12
   THE ONLY LEAF IT DROPS GOES WIDE, ... 247 ON GOING UNNOTICED . 11
   AND NEVER ONCE DROPS . . . . 261 CANIS MAJOR . . . 7
   NOT TEARS BUT DROPS OF BLOOD INSTEAD. . . . . . 327 A MISSIVE MISSILE . 14
   THE MINERAL DROPS THAT EXPLODE . . . . . . 388 MIDDLENESS OF THE ROAD 9
   TRY TO READ TO HER AND SHE DROPS RIGHT OFF. . . . . 479 A MASQUE OF REASON . 155
DROUGHT
   THE BROKEN DROUGHT . . . . 399 THE BROKEN DROUGHT . T
   THAT RATHER HURT HIS THEORY OF THE DROUGHT . . . . 400 THE BROKEN DROUGHT . 4
   THE DROUGHT WAS ONE NO SPIT OF RAIN COULD CURE. . . . 400 THE BROKEN DROUGHT . 10
   IT WAS THE DROUGHT OF DESERTS. EARTH WOULD SOON . . . 400 THE BROKEN DROUGHT . 11
DROUTH
   NOT LUPINE LIVING ON SAND AND DROUTH. . . . . . 248 A PASSING GLIMPSE . 8
   IT IS TRUE THE LONGEST DROUTH WILL END IN RAIN, . . . 268 ON LOOKING UP BY CHANCE 11
   IN ALL THE PASSION OF A BROKEN DROUTH. . . . . 337 THE WIND AND THE RAIN . 39
DROVE
   I CLEANED THE RACK AND DROVE OUT TO COOL OFF. . . . . 72 THE CODE 80
   AND WHIRLS OF FOLIAGE NOT YET LAID, THERE DROVE . . . 106 CHRISTMAS TREES . . . 4
   ONE SUMMER DAY, ALL DAY I DROVE IT HARD, ... 189 THE GRINDSTONE . . 23
   I DROVE THEM UNDERFOOT IN BITS OF FLIGHT . . . . . 240 OUR SINGING STRENGTH . 35
   IN TOO FRAIL A BUGGY WE DROVE . . . . 443 THE DRAFT HORSE . . 2
DROVER
   A DROVER WITH ME ON THE ROAD TO BRIGHTON. . . . . 160 NEW HAMPSHIRE . . 50
   CAME TAMELY BACK IN FRONT OF ME, THE DROVER, ... 240 OUR SINGING STRENGTH . 44
DROWN
   THE MEN SHE COULD NOT DROWN. . . . . 260 SAND DUNES . . . 8
   SEND US A FLOOD AND BID US BE DAMNED AND DROWN. . . . 349 OUR HOLD ON THE PLANET 6
DROWNED (SEE HALF-DROWNED)
   AND THE SMELL OF FIRE DROWNED IN RAIN . . . . . 232 THE KITCHEN CHIMNEY . 15
   CONFUSION, AND A ROAR THAT DROWNED THE CRIES . . . . 270 THE EGG AND THE MACHINE 14
   HE TOLD THEM TO DIVE TILL THEY DROWNED. . . . . 311 THE VINDICTIVES . 46
   IN WHICH WE TWO STOOD SATURATED, DROWNED. . . . . 315 IRIS BY NIGHT . . 12
   AND A DAUGHTER DROWNED. . . . . 433 KITTY HAWK . . . 182
   BUT IN A BUTT OF MALMSEY I WAS DROWNED. . . . . . 510 A MASQUE OF MERCY . 449
   MY SMALL FRESH-WATER SPRING GETS DROWNED OF COURSE. . . 513 A MASQUE OF MERCY . 539
DROWSING
   THE SCENT OF APPLES: I AM DROWSING OFF. . . . . . . 68 AFTER APPLE-PICKING . 8
DRUM
   REAL SKY-BLUE, AND HEAVY, AND READY TO DRUM . . . . 59 BLUEBERRIES 4
   TO DRUM ON THE FLOOR WITH SCURRYING HOOFS . . . . 241 NEED OF BEING VERSED . 11
DRUMLIN
   A DRUMLIN WOODCHUCK . . . . 281 A DRUMLIN WOODCHUCK . T
DRUNK
   I'M NOT SO DRUNK I CAN'T TAKE CARE OF MYSELF." . . . . 45 A HUNDRED COLLARS . . 38
   GOT DRUNK, AND TRACKED THE PAIR UP CATAMOUNT, ... 195 PAUL'S WIFE 124
DRUNKEN
   WOULD KNOCK THEIR DRUNKEN PENTHOUSE HEADS TOGETHER . . 506 A MASQUE OF MERCY . 333
DRUNK-NONSENSICAL
   YOU'RE TIRED." / "I'M DRUNK-NONSENSICAL TIRED OUT; . . . 116 IN THE HOME STRETCH . 158
DRY (SEE BRITTLE-DRY)
   THE WELL WAS DRY BESIDE THE DOOR, ... 18 GOING FOR WATER . . 1
   AND WOULD HAVE TURNED TO TOSS THE GRASS TO DRY; . . . 22 THE TUFT OF FLOWERS . 20
   A DRY RAVINE EMERGED FROM UNDER BOUGHS . . . . . 41 THE MOUNTAIN . . 33
   BEFORE THEM OVER THEIR HEADS TO DRY IN THE SUN. . . . 121 BIRCHES . . . 20
   HER UDDER SHRIVELS AND THE MILK GOES DRY. . . . . 125 THE COW IN APPLE TIME . 11
   A SUDDEN PASSING BULLET SHOOK IT DRY. . . . . . 126 RANGE-FINDING . . . 12
   TO DRY, FROM POOR TO RICH, OR BACK AGAIN. . . . . 166 NEW HAMPSHIRE . . 236
   TO DRY OR WASH OR TAN, I DON'T KNOW WHICH . . . . 197 WILD GRAPES . . . 52
   WITH SOUNDS LIKE THE DRY RATTLING OF A SHUTTER, . . . 206 THE WITCH OF COOS . 129
   IT SNOWED IN SPRING ON EARTH SO DRY AND WARM . . . 239 OUR SINGING STRENGTH . 1
   AND THE DRY PUMP FLUNG UP AN AWKWARD ARM; . . . . 242 NEED OF BEING VERSED . 19
   AND THOSE ARE BROWN AND DRY. . . . . 260 SAND DUNES . . . 4
   THE BOTTOM OF SEAS RAISED DRY-- . . . . . . 285 IN TIME OF CLOUDBURST . 15
   TO WHERE MY MANUSCRIPT WAS NOT YET DRY; . . . . 357 A CONSIDERABLE SPECK . 12
   AND THE SUN CAME OUT TO DRY ME. . . . . . . 377 ONE STEP BACKWARD TAKEN 14
   TO KEEP OUR ABSTRACT VERSE FROM BEING DRY. . . . . 395 ETHEREALIZING . . 14

DRYLY
    CAME DRYLY FORWARD TO THE BARS AGAIN . . . . 294 AT WOODWARD'S GARDENS . 32
DRY-SHOD
    AND COME NOT THROUGH DRY-SHOD? . . . . 27 A LINE-STORM SONG . . 22
    THE BOARD WE HAD LAID DOWN TO WALK DRY-SHOD ON . . . . 204 THE WITCH OF COOS . . 48
DUBLIN
    I'VE GIVEN UP MY SUMMER PLACE IN DUBLIN." . . . . . 166 NEW HAMPSHIRE . . . 222
DUCK
    OUT TO KILL A DUCK . . . . 431 KITTY HAWK 108
DUE
    IS DUE TO TRUTHS BEING IN AND OUT OF FAVOR. . . . . . 58 THE BLACK COTTAGE . 110
    MAKING ALLOWANCE, MAKING DUE ALLOWANCE." . . . . . . 77 THE GENERATIONS OF MEN 115
    LOOK HERE, YOU TREAT YOUR GUIDE WITH DUE RESPECT . . . 214 A FOUNTAIN, A BOTTLE . 49
    NOW LICHENS ARE DUE TO HAVE THEIR TURN. . . . . . . 297 LEAVES COMPARED WITH . 12
    NOT WITHOUT DUE PATTER . . . . 435 KITTY HAWK 228
    MORE TO GIVE HIS REALITY ITS DUE . . . . 489 A MASQUE OF REASON . 433
DUG
    IF YOU HAD ANY FEELINGS, YOU THAT DUG . . . . 53 HOME BURIAL 72
    LIKE MEDITATING, AND THEN I JUST DUG IN . . . . . . 72 THE CODE 73
    ALL DUG TO GO A-FISHING IN." TO PAUL . . . . 193 PAUL'S WIFE 82
    A TWO-DOOR BURROW I DUG. . . . . 282 A DRUMLIN WOODCHUCK . 8
DUGOUT .
    AND SPREAD THE OPENING, AND YOU'VE GOT A DUGOUT . . . . 193 PAUL'S WIFE 81
DULCET
    AS DULCET AS A PAGAN TEMPLE GONG! . . . . 488 A MASQUE OF REASON . 419
DULL
    AND HER FACE CHANGED FROM TERRIFIED TO DULL. . . . . 51 HOME BURIAL 9
    LIKE UNCUT JEWELS, DULL AND ROUGH. . . . . 141 THE GUM-GATHERER . . 31
    THEY SAT. SHE CAST ONE DULL, OLD LOOK AT HIM, ... 201 PLACE FOR A THIRD . . 52
DULLER
    AND SINCE THEY GREW DULLER . . . . 235 GATHERING LEAVES . . 18
DULLY
    BUMPED HEADS TOGETHER DULLY . . . . 376 ONE STEP BACKWARD TAKEN 5
DULY
    AND RAISED AMONG THE LEAVES AND DULY TOLD, ... 283 THE GOLD HESPERIDEE . 15
DUM (SEE DUM-DUM)
DUMB
    ARE YOU DUMB BECAUSE YOU KNOW ME NOT, ... 13 FLOWER-GATHERING . . 7
    OR DUMB BECAUSE YOU KNOW? . . . . 13 FLOWER-GATHERING . . 8
DUM-DUM
    LIKE A DUM-DUM BULLET-- . . . . 427 VERSION 13
DUMP
    ALTHOUGH YOU DO NO MORE THAN DUMP THEM DOWN." . . . 116 IN THE HOME STRETCH . 162
    OF OUR DUMP OF EARNING . . . . 441 KITTY HAWK 433
    AND OUR DUMP OF LEARNING . . . . 441 KITTY HAWK 434
DUMPED
    AND DUMPED THE RACKFUL ON HIM IN TEN LOTS. . . . . . 72 THE CODE 74
    "DUMPED DOWN IN PARADISE WE ARE AND HAPPY." . . . . 116 IN THE HOME STRETCH . 163
    WITH CINDER LOADS DUMPED DOWN? THE BROOK WAS THROWN . 231 A BROOK IN THE CITY . 15
    HE DUMPED HIMSELF LIKE A BAG OF BONES, ... 419 ONE MORE BREVITY . . 15
DUN
    ANYTHING THEY'VE NOT GOT. I NEVER DUN. . . . . . . 50 A HUNDRED COLLARS . . 152
DUNCE
    WHICH MAKES THE WAR GOD SEEM NO SPECIAL DUNCE . . . . 350 TO A YOUNG WRETCH . . 17
DUNES
    SAND DUNES HELD LOOSELY IN TAMARISK . . . . 58 THE BLACK COTTAGE . 120
    SAND DUNES . . . . 260 SAND DUNES . . . . T
DUNG
    SHE WHEELED THE DUNG IN THE WHEELBARROW . . . . . . 134 A GIRL'S GARDEN . . . 21
DUNGEON
    DEEP IN A SEWER DUNGEON UNDER STONE . . . . 231 A BROOK IN THE CITY . 16
    HE GOT NO MORE THAN DUNGEON CHAINS . . . . 417 AMERICA IS HARD TO SEE 44
DUNGEONEERS
    MY DUNGEONEERS, COME FETCH US.--NO ONE ANSWERS. . . . 514 A MASQUE OF MERCY . . 556
DUNNOW
    "WELL THEN, IT'S GRANNY SPEAKING: 'I DUNNOW! . . . . 80 THE GENERATIONS OF MEN 184
DUSK
    WITHIN, THE BRIDE IN THE DUSK ALONE . . . . 8 LOVE AND A QUESTION . 17
    AFIELD AT DUSK . . . . 14 WAITING 5
    IT'S NOTHING; IT'S THEIR LEAVING US AT DUSK. . . . . 115 IN THE HOME STRETCH . 130
    AT DUSK TO WATCH THE MOON DOWN EARLY. . . . . . . 135 LOCKED OUT 13
    DOWNHILL AT DUSK? . . . . 227 TO EARTHWARD 8
    THE HUNTER SCUFFLING LEAVES GOES BY AT DUSK, ... 289 OLD BARN AT THE BOTTOM 3
    NOW IF IT WAS DUSK OUTSIDE, ... 334 COME IN 3
    BUT I MUST FORTH AT DUSK, MY TIME OF DAY, ... 337 THE WIND AND THE RAIN . 45
DUST (SEE STRAW-DUST-COVERED)
    I LOOKED OVER THE SIDE ONCE IN THE DUST . . . . . . 72 THE CODE 75
    FOOTPRINTS IN SUMMER DUST AS IF WE DREW . . . . . 118 MEETING AND PASSING . 6
    SOMETHING DOWN THERE TO SMILE AT IN THE DUST. . . . . 119 MEETING AND PASSING . 11
    HE SAYS THE HIGHWAY DUST IS OVER ALL. . . . . . . 120 THE OVEN BIRD . . . 10
    AND MADE DUST AND DROPPED STOVE-LENGTH STICKS OF WOOD, . 136 "OUT,OUT--" 2
    AND FEEL IT LESS. HEAR THE SOFT BOMBS OF DUST . . . . 150 SNOW 206
    IN DUST ONCE MORE. WE FOLLOWED THIS A MILE, ... 215 A FOUNTAIN, A BOTTLE . 67
    OF DUST AND FEATHER. . . . . 218 I WILL SING YOU ONE-O . 15
    THE DUST OF SNOW . . . . 221 DUST OF SNOW 3
    DUST OF SNOW . . . . 221 DUST OF SNOW . . . . T
    DUST ALWAYS BLOWING ABOUT THE TOWN, ... 249 A PECK OF GOLD . . . 1
    SOME OF THE BLOWING DUST WAS GOLD. . . . . 249 A PECK OF GOLD . . . 4
    ALL THE DUST THE WIND BLEW HIGH . . . . 249 A PECK OF GOLD . . . 5
    SOME OF THE DUST WAS REALLY GOLD. . . . . 249 A PECK OF GOLD . . . 8
    BUT STILL LIES POINTED AS IT PLOWED THE DUST. . . . . 261 A SOLDIER 3
    IF, AS THEY SAY, SOME DUST THROWN IN MY EYES . . . . 265 DUST IN THE EYES . . 1
    AND ROUND A CORNER, BLIZZARD SNOW FOR DUST, ... 265 DUST IN THE EYES . . 5
    DUST IN THE EYES . . . . 265 DUST IN THE EYES . . T
    WHEN DUST REALLY TOOK IN THE SUN; . . . . 266 SITTING BY A BUSH . . 6
    THE AIR WAS FULL OF DUST OF WOOL, ... 273 A LONE STRIKER . . . 18
    REFLECTED IN THE MUD AND EVEN DUST, ... 279 THE WHITE-TAILED HORNET 65
    HE HAS DUST IN HIS EYES AND A FAN FOR A WING, ... 309 ONE GUESS 1

DUST (CONTINUED)
```
    AND RAISING A DUST WITH A TRAIN . . . . . . . . .   312 THE VINDICTIVES . . .   74
    WITH BREAKING STEP I STABBED THE DUST, . . . . . .   336 THE WIND AND THE RAIN .    7
    THIS WAS NO DUST SPECK BY MY BREATHING BLOWN, . . .   357 A CONSIDERABLE SPECK .    7
    IT IS BUT FIERY PUFFS OF DUST AND PEBBLES, . . . .   360 A LOOSE MOUNTAIN . .     5
    WE DATE YOU BY YOUR DEPTH IN SILT AND DUST . . . .   382 TO AN ANCIENT . . .     10
    SO JEWEL-STEADY IN THE WIND AND DUST. . . . . . .   386 THE FEAR OF MAN . . .   12
    OF MINGLED BUTTERFLY AND FLOWER DUST . . . . . . .   412 POD OF THE MILKWEED .   28
    THE FOLLY CRASHES AND THE DUST GOES UP. . . . . .   506 A MASQUE OF MERCY . .  342
    (WHEN THE DUST SETTLES IT SHOULD BE APPARENT . . .   507 A MASQUE OF MERCY . .  343
```
DUST-BATH
```
    THAT HAS NO DUST-BATH NOW FOR THE TOAD. . . . . .     6 GHOST HOUSE . . . .     14
```
DUSTED
```
    GOLD DUSTED ALL WE DRANK AND ATE, . . . . . . . .   249 A PECK OF GOLD . . .    10
    AND SPENT AND DUSTED OFF OF THEIR REGALIA, . . . .   412 POD OF THE MILKWEED .   35
```
DUSTY (SEE DYE-DUSTY)
```
    GAUNT AND DUSTY GRAY WITH ROAMING? . . . . . . . .    13 FLOWER-GATHERING . .     6
    OVER THE SINK OUT THROUGH A DUSTY WINDOW . . . . .   110 IN THE HOME STRETCH .    2
    TO LEAP THE DUSTY DEADLINE. FOR MY OWN . . . . . .   131 THE BONFIRE . . . .     64
    HE LEANS AGAINST THE DUSTY WALL, . . . . . . . .    280 BLUE RIBBON AT AMESBURY 21
    OF DUSTY WEEDS TO TAKE A DRINK OF STARS. . . . . .   454 HOW HARD TO KEEP FROM   14
```
DUTCH
```
    THE FRENCH, THE SPANISH, AND THE DUTCH WERE DOWNED   422 FOR JOHN F. KENNEDY .    16
```
DUTY
```
    WHOSE DUTY WAS AT ANY HOUR OF NIGHT . . . . . . .   163 NEW HAMPSHIRE . . .    140
    HE WAS ALL DUTY TO HER IN A MINUTE: . . . . . . .   191 PAUL'S WIFE . . . .     12
    AND WAS OFF ON HIS DUTY RUN. . . . . . . . . . .    288 DEPARTMENTAL . . . .     7
    I NEEDN'T THINK I HAVE ESCAPED MY DUTY, . . . . .    454 HOW HARD TO KEEP FROM   19
    I DID MY WIFELY DUTY. I SHOULD TREMBLE! . . . . .    478 A MASQUE OF REASON .   134
```
DWARF
```
    DWARF CORNEL, GOLDTHREAD, AND MAIANTHEMUM, . . . .   355 TIME OUT . . . . .      5
```
DWARFED
```
    ALL DWARFED AND POOR." . . . . . . . . . . . .      512 A MASQUE OF MERCY . .  505
    HERE WE ALL FAIL TOGETHER, DWARFED AND POOR. . . .   512 A MASQUE OF MERCY . .  506
```
DWELL
```
    I DWELL IN A LONELY HOUSE I KNOW . . . . . . . .      5 GHOST HOUSE . . . .      1
    I DWELL WITH A STRANGELY ACHING HEART . . . . . .     6 GHOST HOUSE . . . .     11
    NO, NOT VAINLY THERE DID I DWELL, . . . . . . . .    16 IN A VALE . . . . .     24
    IF THIS UNCERTAIN AGE IN WHICH WE DWELL . . . . .    350 THE LESSON FOR TODAY .    1
```
DWELLING
```
    AND COME AND MAKE YOUR SUMMER DWELLING HERE, . . .    79 THE GENERATIONS OF MEN 166
    SO CLOSE TO OUR DWELLING PLACE? . . . . . . . .     156 THE SOUND OF TREES .     5
    THE ONLY DWELLING IN A WASTE CUT OVER . . . . . .   174 THE CENSUS-TAKER . .     4
    FROM TOO MUCH DWELLING ON WHAT HAS BEEN. . . . . .   242 NEED OF BEING VERSED .   16
    I HAVE BEEN ONE NO DWELLING COULD CONTAIN . . . .   337 THE WIND AND THE RAIN .  43
    A CLIFF DWELLING . . . . . . . . . . . . . .       392 A CLIFF DWELLING . .      T
```
DWELT
```
    WHEN I WAS YOUNG, WE DWELT IN A VALE . . . . . .     15 IN A VALE . . . . .      1
    BUT 'TIS NOT TRUE THAT THUS I DWELT ALOOF, . . . .    16 A DREAM PANG . . . .    13
    SCATTERED OASES WHERE MEN DWELT, BUT MOSTLY . . .    58 THE BLACK COTTAGE . .  119
    AND THAT NOT DWELT IN NOW BY MEN OR WOMEN. . . . .   174 THE CENSUS-TAKER . .     6
    (IT NEVER HAD BEEN DWELT IN, THOUGH, BY WOMEN, . .   174 THE CENSUS-TAKER . .     7
    THEY TELL ME THE COTTAGE WHERE WE DWELT, . . . . .   253 THE THATCH . . . .     31
```
D'YE
```
    THINKS I, D'YE MEAN IT? 'WHAT WAS THAT YOU SAID?' .    71 THE CODE . . . . .     64
```
DYED (SEE DOUBLE-DYED)
DYE-DUSTY
```
    BUT THE WILD TOUCH OF THY DYE-DUSTY WING! . . . .    29 MY BUTTERFLY . . . .    42
```
DYES
```
    AND IS NOT SHATTERED INTO DYES, . . . . . . . .     19 THE TRIAL BY EXISTENCE  10
```
DYESTUFF
```
    AND A MOUTHFUL OF DYESTUFF INSTEAD OF A STING. . .   309 ONE GUESS . . . . .      3
    THEY KNOCK THE DYESTUFF OFF EACH OTHER'S WINGS-- .   411 POD OF THE MILKWEED .   25
```
DYING
```
    SOUNDS FURTHER OFF, IT'S NOT BECAUSE IT'S DYING; .   150 SNOW . . . . . . .     204
    AND HAVE STOPPED DYING NOW FOREVER. . . . . . . .   221 IN A DISUSED GRAVEYARD  15
```
D'YOU
```
    "D'YOU KNOW A PERSON SO RELATED TO HERSELF . . . .    76 THE GENERATIONS OF MEN  82
```

E

EACH
```
    EACH CIRCLING EACH WITH VAGUE UNEARTHLY CRY, . . .    14 WAITING . . . . .       12
    EACH CAME SINGLY UNTO HER PLACE, . . . . . . . .     15 IN A VALE . . . . .     10
    EACH LAID ON EACH A STAYING HAND . . . . . . . .     18 GOING FOR WATER . .     17
    TO EACH THE BOULDERS THAT HAVE FALLEN TO EACH. . .    33 MENDING WALL . . . .    16
    IN EACH HAND, LIKE AN OLD-STONE SAVAGE ARMED. . .    34 MENDING WALL . . . .    40
    EACH AGE WILL HAVE TO RECONSIDER IT. . . . . . .     57 THE BLACK COTTAGE . .   70
    I MET THEM ONE DAY AND EACH HAD A FLOWER . . . . .    61 BLUEBERRIES . . . .     64
    AND SAW NOTHING MORE OF EACH OTHER, OR HEARD, . .    62 BLUEBERRIES . . . .     87
    THE YOUNG FOLK HELD SOME HOPE OUT TO EACH OTHER . .    74 THE GENERATIONS OF MEN  21
    "FOUR CARDS: ONE YOURS, THREE MINE (ONE FOR EACH BRANCH .  76 THE GENERATIONS OF MEN  80
    YOU CAN'T HAVE PASSED EACH OTHER. I KNOW WHAT: . .    81 THE HOUSEKEEPER . .     16
    TWO AT A TIME'S THE RULE, ONE ON EACH ARM, . . . .    85 THE HOUSEKEEPER . .    129
    THAT LOP EACH OTHER OF BOUGHS, BUT NOT A FEW . . .   107 CHRISTMAS TREES . .     34
    AND PUT EACH OTHER BODILY OUT OF THE HOUSE. . . .   114 IN THE HOME STRETCH .  110
    BUT WITH EACH OTHER AND THEMSELVES . . . . . . .    127 LONELINESS . . . .     11
    A HILL EACH OF POTATOES, . . . . . . . . . . .      134 A GIRL'S GARDEN . .     29
    ONE EACH OF EVERYTHING AS IN A SHOWCASE, . . . . .   161 NEW HAMPSHIRE . . .     62
    ONE EACH OF EVERYTHING AS IN A SHOWCASE. . . . . .   163 NEW HAMPSHIRE . . .    144
    PASSED IN AND SLAMMED IT SHUT EACH ONE BEHIND HIM .   175 THE CENSUS-TAKER . .    29
    EACH OTHER IN PASSING IN THE ROOM UPSTAIRS, . . .   180 MAPLE . . . . . .      11
    BEGAN THE STAIRS, TWO FOOTSTEPS FOR EACH STEP, . .   204 THE WITCH OF COOS . .   51
    TO MAKE A PRESENT OF ME TO EACH OTHER. . . . . .    207 PAUPER WITCH OF GRAFTON  5
    ACROSS EACH OTHER AND SIDE BY SIDE THEY LAY. . . .   237 A HILLSIDE THAW . . .   29
```

EACH (CONTINUED)
      AS YOU AND I ARE MARRIED TO EACH OTHER, ... 258 WEST-RUNNING BROOK .   12
      NOR STRIKE OUT FIRE FROM EACH OTHER, NOR CRASH OUT LOUD. . 268 ON LOOKING UP BY CHANCE   5
      EACH SWUNG IN DANGER ON ITS SLENDER TWIG, ... 283 THE GOLD HESPERIDEE . 23
      WHO ONCE KEPT SURPASSING EACH OTHER, ... 294 A RECORD STRIDE . . .   7
      ONE FOOT IN EACH GREAT OCEAN. . . . . 295 A RECORD STRIDE . . . 25
      EACH LINK OF A HUNDREDWEIGHT, ... 312 THE VINDICTIVES . . . 64
      AND LEAPFROG IN EACH OTHER'S WAY--ALL'S WELL. . . . . . 318 BUILD SOIL 64
      WHO FALL ALL OVER EACH OTHER TO BRING SOIL. . . . . . . 321 BUILD SOIL 177
      KEEP OFF EACH OTHER AND KEEP EACH OTHER OFF. . . . . . . 324 BUILD SOIL 263
      WE'RE TOO UNSEPARATE OUT AMONG EACH OTHER-- . . . . . . 324 BUILD SOIL 268
      UNSATISFYING TO US EACH. . . . . 328 A MISSIVE MISSILE . . 46
      AND DARKLY DRINK EACH OTHER'S EYES . . . . 344 DISCOVERY OF MADEIRAS . 39
      TO KISS AND DRINK EACH OTHER'S BREATH . . . . 346 DISCOVERY OF MADEIRAS . 81
      THE LOVING'S MADE TO HOLD EACH OTHER LIKE, ... 371 THE LITERATE FARMER AND 114
      OR SOON WE'D BAT EACH OTHER OUT OF TOUCH, ... 371 THE LITERATE FARMER AND 117
      INTO EACH OTHER. BOTH OF THEM ARE LOST. . . . . 378 DIRECTIVE 35
      NOW QUIVERED TOWARD EACH OTHER, LIPPED . . . . 381 AN UNSTAMPED LETTER IN 34
      EACH KNOWS HIS OWN DISCERNMENT BEST. . . . . 381 AN UNSTAMPED LETTER IN 43
      EACH TRIED TO BE THE FIRST AT GETTING IN . . . . . . 407 FROM PLANE TO PLANE . 117
      THEY KNOCK THE DYESTUFF OFF EACH OTHER'S WINGS-- . . . 411 POD OF THE MILKWEED . 25
      OF BEING IN EACH OTHER'S WAY, ... 417 AMERICA IS HARD TO SEE 39
      EACH AND EVERY ONE . . . . 431 KITTY HAWK 103
      ALL OF US GET EACH OTHER PRETTY WRONG. . . . . 518 A MASQUE OF MERCY . . 655
EAD (SEE HAX-EAD)
EAGER
      OF YOUNG AMBITION EAGER TO BE TRIED, ... 424 FOR JOHN F. KENNEDY   73
EAGLE
      UNDER THE WATCHFUL EYE OF HAWK AND EAGLE-- . . . . . . 162 NEW HAMPSHIRE   . . . 105
      BY A GREAT EAGLE BIRD IN ALL ITS TERROR. . . . . 443 AUSPEX   4
EAR
      CAN BUT GIVE EAR TO THAT SWEET CRY . . . . 20 THE TRIAL BY EXISTENCE 23
      LET THE MAN FREEZE AN EAR OR TWO, I SAY.-- . . . . . . 146 SNOW 102
      WERE PEOPLE TO THE EAR BUT NOT THE EYE. . . . . 175 THE CENSUS-TAKER . . 39
      WITH HALF AN EAR TO THE PIANO'S VIGOR. . . . . 263 THE INVESTMENT . . .   8
      IN THE EAR AND IN THE EYE . . . . 469 FOUR-ROOM SHACK.... .   5
EARLIER
      BUT EARLIER OUT FOR BED TONIGHT, ... 292 ON HEART'S BEGINNING TO 40
EARLIEST
      IT WILL BE LONG ERE THE EARLIEST BIRD: . . . . 25 NOW CLOSE THE WINDOWS .   6
EARLY
      DIFFERENT FROM EARLY YEARS." / "I SEE THEM, TOO. . . . . 112 IN THE HOME STRETCH . 50
      HE SAYS THE EARLY PETAL-FALL IS PAST, ... 120 THE OVEN BIRD . . .   6
      ON THROUGH THE WATCHING FOR THAT EARLY BIRTH . . . . . 124 PUTTING IN THE SEED . 11
      AT DUSK TO WATCH THE MOON DOWN EARLY. . . . . 135 LOCKED OUT 13
      IN BEING THERE SO EARLY IN OUR HISTORY. . . . . 161 NEW HAMPSHIRE . . . 81
      OF EARLY TIMES AS TWICE THE HEIGHT THEY ARE-- . . . . . 169 NEW HAMPSHIRE . . . 331
      THE EARLY MORMONS MADE A SETTLEMENT . . . . 213 A FOUNTAIN, A BOTTLE .   9
      HER EARLY LEAF'S A FLOWER; . . . . 222 NOTHING GOLD CAN STAY .   3
      (BY WHICH THEY MEAN THE RAIN IS PEARLS SO EARLY, ... 236 VALLEY'S SINGING DAY . 12
      SO CLOSE IT WILL NOT LIGHT AN EARLY LIGHT, ... 248 THE COCOON   7
      TO THE FRESH AND BLACK OF THE SQUARES OF EARLY MOLD . . 299 STRONG SAYING NOTHING .   9
      DIE EARLY AND AVOID THE FATE. . . . . 307 PROVIDE, PROVIDE . .   7
      OF BEING BORN AT ONCE TOO EARLY AND LATE, ... 351 THE LESSON FOR TODAY   12
EARLY-MORNING
      TO HIS DOWNHILL, EARLY-MORNING STRIDE, ... 140 THE GUM-GATHERER   .   2
EARN
      HE THINKS HE OUGHT TO EARN A LITTLE PAY, ... 35 DEATH OF THE HIRED MAN 19
      TO EARN A LIVING ON THE CONCORD RAILROAD, ... 178 THE STAR-SPLITTER . 68
      TO FARMING FOR A SIMPLE WAY TO EARN; . . . . 398 BURSTING RAPTURE . .   3
      IN WHAT HE HAS TO DO TO EARN A LIVING. . . . . 406 FROM PLANE TO PLANE . 63
      TO EARN A LIVING. I DON'T INTERFERE. . . . . 459 HOW HARD TO KEEP FROM 180
      FOR WHAT THEY DIDN'T EARN. . . . . 465 MILKY WAY IS A COWPATH 44
      WE'RE POOR--THAT'S WHY. MY MAN CAN'T EARN A LIVING. . . . 496 A MASQUE OF MERCY . . 89
EARNED
      THEY NEVER EARNED ME SO MUCH AS ONE CENT: . . . . . . 95 THE SELF-SEEKER . . 71
      HE HAD HIS TICKET BOUGHT, HIS PASSAGE EARNED. . . . . . 370 THE LITERATE FARMER AND 58
EARNER
      AND BRAVER FOR THE EARNER, LEARNER, YEARNER. . . . . . 424 FOR JOHN F. KENNEDY . 67
EARNEST
      TO THE EARNEST LOVE THAT LAID THE SWALE IN ROWS, ... 17 MOWING 10
      "TWO WEEKS SINCE." / "SHE'S IN EARNEST, IT APPEARS." . . . 82 THE HOUSEKEEPER . . 22
      A WIND TO BLOW IN EARNEST FROM SOME QUARTER, ... 130 THE BONFIRE 33
      THIS WAS NO PLAYHOUSE BUT A HOUSE IN EARNEST. . . . . . 378 DIRECTIVE 48
EARNING
      OF OUR DUMP OF EARNING . . . . 441 KITTY HAWK 433
EARRINGS
      IN BROAD ROUND EARRINGS, GOLD AND JET WITH PEARLS, . . . 256 THE LOVELY BE CHOOSERS 15
EARS
      BY LOOKING IN THE EARS. BUT I FORGET IT. . . . . . . 96 THE SELF-SEEKER . . 109
      AND SHUT MY EYES AGAINST THE SUN, MY EARS . . . . . . 198 WILD GRAPES 74
      A FOUNTAIN, A BOTTLE, A DONKEY'S EARS, AND SOME BOOKS . . 212 A FOUNTAIN, A BOTTLE .   T
      ON MARSHALL, LOOK LIKE DONKEY'S EARS. . . . . 214 A FOUNTAIN, A BOTTLE . 53
      "DON'T DONKEY'S EARS SUGGEST WE SHAKE OUR OWN?" . . . . 215 A FOUNTAIN, A BOTTLE . 55
      WHAT SIGNIFY A DONKEY'S EARS AND BOTTLE, ... 215 A FOUNTAIN, A BOTTLE . 58
      ALMOST BEFORE THE PRICK OF HOSTILE EARS, ... 302 A BIRD SINGING IN SLEEP   7
      THEY WOULD BRING EMPIRES DOWN ABOUT OUR EARS . . . . . 423 FOR JOHN F. KENNEDY . 29
      AND EARS ARE LENT TO ANY SOPHISTRY . . . . 488 A MASQUE OF REASON . 409
EARSHOT
      "YES, I TOOK CARE TO KEEP WELL OUT OF EARSHOT." . . . . 37 DEATH OF THE HIRED MAN 70
EARTH
      THE FADED EARTH, THE HEAVY SKY, ... 7 MY NOVEMBER GUEST . . 12
      I SMELL THE EARTH, I SMELL THE BRUISED PLANT, ... 17 THE VANTAGE POINT . 13
      EVEN AS ON EARTH, IN PARADISE; . . . . 19 THE TRIAL BY EXISTENCE   4
      THE OBSCURATION UPON EARTH. . . . . 20 THE TRIAL BY EXISTENCE 20
      AGAINST THE UTTERMOST OF EARTH. . . . . 21 THE TRIAL BY EXISTENCE 44
      HE LAID HIM DOWN ON THE SUNBURNED EARTH . . . . 24 PAN WITH US 28
      AND FIT THE EARTH LIKE A LEATHER GLOVE. . . . . 26 IN HARDWOOD GROVES . .   4

EARTH (CONTINUED)
    OF THE FRESH EARTH FROM YOUR OWN BABY'S GRAVE . . . . . 54 HOME BURIAL 85
    BY GOING TO HIM OF ALL PEOPLE ON EARTH . . . . . . 61 BLUEBERRIES 69
    THAT STRUCK THE EARTH, ... 69 AFTER APPLE-PICKING . 33
    SOMEONE HAD LITERALLY RUN TO EARTH . . . . . . 73 THE GENERATIONS OF MEN 7
    ANYONE UPON EARTH AND STILL HER CHILDREN . . . . . . 75 THE GENERATIONS OF MEN 51
    I WISH THAT EVERYTHING ON EARTH WERE JUST . . . . . . 115 IN THE HOME STRETCH . 140
    LOVE HAS EARTH TO WHICH SHE CLINGS . . . . 120 BOND AND FREE . . . 1
    I'D LIKE TO GET AWAY FROM EARTH AWHILE . . . . . . 122 BIRCHES 48
    SLAVE TO A SPRINGTIME PASSION FOR THE EARTH. . . . . 124 PUTTING IN THE SEED . 9
    SHOULDERING ITS WAY AND SHEDDING THE EARTH CRUMBS. . . 124 PUTTING IN THE SEED . 14
    TO SUCH RESORTS OF LIFE AS MARS AND EARTH-- . . . . 174 A STAR IN A STONEBOAT . 48
    HE CLIMBED STILL HIGHER AND BENT THE TREE TO EARTH . . 197 WILD GRAPES . . . 37
    SINCE EARTH IS EARTH, PERHAPS, NOT HEAVEN (AS YET)-- . . 220 FRAGMENTARY BLUE . . 5
    THOUGH SOME SAVANTS MAKE EARTH INCLUDE THE SKY; . . . . 220 FRAGMENTARY BLUE . . 6
    THE EARTH BUT IT HAS FAILED: THE SNOW MAY HEAP . . . . 226 THE ONSET 14
    TO FEEL THE EARTH AS ROUGH . . . . 227 TO EARTHWARD 31
    AS IF THE EARTH IN ONE UNLOOKED-FOR FAVOR . . . . . 230 TWO LOOK AT TWO . . 41
    HAD MADE THEM CERTAIN EARTH RETURNED THEIR LOVE. . . . 230 TWO LOOK AT TWO . . 42
    FROM CONTACT WITH EARTH, ... 235 GATHERING LEAVES . . 19
    NOT THOUGH WE HAVE TO SEIZE EARTH BY THE POLE . . . . 238 ON A TREE FALLEN ACROSS 12
    IT SNOWED IN SPRING ON EARTH SO DRY AND WARM . . . . 239 OUR SINGING STRENGTH . 1
    THEY DISAPPEARED AS IF EARTH SENT THEM BACK. . . . . 239 OUR SINGING STRENGTH . 6
    AND HERE ON EARTH COME EMULATING FLIES . . . . . . 246 FIREFLIES IN THE GARDEN 2
    TO BLOW THE EARTH OR ANYTHING SELF-CLEAR; . . . . . 246 ATMOSPHERE 4
    AND ANCHORING IT TO AN EARTH AND MOON . . . . . . 248 THE COCOON 14
    THAT NO ONE ON EARTH WILL EVER FIND? . . . . . . 248 A PASSING GLIMPSE . . 10
    ONE LEVEL HIGHER THAN THE EARTH BELOW, ... 254 A WINTER EDEN . . . 6
    THE CURVE OF EARTH, AND STRIKING, BREAK THEIR OWN; . . 261 A SOLDIER 10
    SUBDUED THE GROWTH OF EARTH TO GRASS, ... 265 THE BIRTHPLACE . . . 5
    BUT BEING MOUNTED BAREBACK ON THE EARTH? . . . . . . 267 RIDERS 6
    THE LURKING FROST IN THE EARTH BENEATH . . . . . . 276 TWO TRAMPS IN MUD TIME 38
    THE GRIP ON EARTH OF OUTSPREAD FEET, ... 276 TWO TRAMPS IN MUD TIME 46
    DOWNWARD COMPARISONS. AS LONG ON EARTH . . . . . . 279 THE WHITE-TAILED HORNET 59
    THE SLOPE OF THE EARTH REVERSED. . . . . . . 285 IN TIME OF CLOUDBURST . 16
    AT MOONLIT SKY AND MOONLIT EARTH. . . . . . . 290 ON HEART'S BEGINNING TO 4
    THE EARTH HAD A SINGLE LIGHT AFAR, ... 291 ON HEART'S BEGINNING TO 6
    BUT SCRUB OAK, SCRUB OAK AND LACK OF EARTH . . . . . 292 FIGURE IN THE DOORWAY . 3
    TO COME TO THEIR FINAL PLACE IN EARTH THEY HAD TO PASS ME
       BY. . . . . 297 A LEAF-TREADER . . . 6
    TO BE A BIRD WHILE WE ARE MEN ON EARTH, ... 303 A BIRD SINGING IN SLEEP 12
    YOU MAY TAUNT ME WITH NOT BEING ABLE TO FLEE THE EARTH. . 306 NOT QUITE SOCIAL . . 9
    DEEP INTO THE EARTH WHENCE IT CAME. . . . . . . 311 THE VINDICTIVES . . . 30
    AND WIPE THAT OUT OF THE EARTH. . . . . 313 THE VINDICTIVES . . . 84
    IF EARTH WERE THOUGHT ABOUT TO CHANGE ITS AXIS, . . . 317 BUILD SOIL 58
    TO EVERYTHING ON EARTH THE COMPASS ROUND, ... 332 THE SILKEN TENT . . . 11
    THUS CONCENTRATING EARTH AND SKIES . . . . . . 333 ALL REVELATION . . . 18
    THE EARTH ITSELF IS LIABLE TO THE FATE . . . . . . 355 THE LESSON FOR TODAY . 147
    (AS YET UNBROUGHT TO EARTH) HE MEANS TO TRY. . . . . 359 THE LOST FOLLOWER . . 36
    IT NEVER REACHES EARTH EXCEPT AS ASHES . . . . . . 361 A LOOSE MOUNTAIN . . 10
    AND TELL ME TRULY, MEN OF EARTH, ... 362 A QUESTION 2
    AND THERE'S YOUR PRISTINE EARTH ALL FREED . . . . . 376 SOMETHING FOR HOPE . . 14
    I PRODDED THE EARTH WITH A LAZY TOOL . . . . . . 385 A MOOD APART 2
    IT WAS THE DROUGHT OF DESERTS. EARTH WOULD SOON . . . 400 THE BROKEN DROUGHT . . 11
    TILL DARWIN CAME TO EARTH UPON A YEAR . . . . . . 425 ACCIDENTALLY ON PURPOSE 9
    IN THE EARTH ALONE, ... 428 KITTY HAWK 13
    INTO EARTH AND SKIES . . . . 435 KITTY HAWK 233
    CHARGES INTO EARTH . . . . 436 KITTY HAWK 248
    EARTH IS STILL OUR FATE. . . . . 437 KITTY HAWK 308
    THOUGH AN EARTH SO SMALL, ... 440 KITTY HAWK 374
    GIVE EARTH ANOTHER SATELLITE. . . . . 451 A-WISHING WELL . . . 29
    WHEN UNTO EARTH HER FIRST WAS BORN. . . . . . . 452 A-WISHING WELL . . . 39
    IT COST THE EARTH AS FIERCE A PANG . . . . . . 452 A-WISHING WELL . . . 40
    ESCAPE FROM SO GREAT PAINS OF LIFE ON EARTH . . . . 475 A MASQUE OF REASON . . 43
    GOD, WHO INVENTED EARTH? / WHAT, STILL AWAKE? . . . 480 A MASQUE OF REASON . . 201
    AS FOR THE EARTH, WE GROPED THAT OUT TOGETHER, . . . 481 A MASQUE OF REASON . . 207
    YOUR KINGDOM, YES, YOUR KINGDOM COME ON EARTH. . . . 484 A MASQUE OF REASON . . 303
    PERHAPS THAT EARTH IS GOING TO CRACK SOMEDAY . . . . 484 A MASQUE OF REASON . . 305
    HIS CHURCH ON EARTH A ROMAN PANTHEON; . . . . . . 516 A MASQUE OF MERCY . . 592
EARTHLY
    OR THE WOE WERE NOT EARTHLY WOE . . . . 21 THE TRIAL BY EXISTENCE 55
    BACK PAST THE SUN TO AN EARTHLY ROOM. . . . . . 120 BOND AND FREE . . . 15
    HE KNEW TOO WELL FOR ANY EARTHLY USE . . . . . . 171 NEW HAMPSHIRE . . . 378
    OF EARTHLY WEATHER, ... 218 I WILL SING YOU ONE-O . 25
    BUT AN EARTHLY DOG OF THE CARRIAGE BREED; . . . . . 419 ONE MORE BREVITY . . 11
EARTHQUAKE
    I FEEL, AS OF AN EARTHQUAKE IN MY BACK, ... 169 NEW HAMPSHIRE . . . 318
    REBELLION, PESTILENCE, INVASION? / EARTHQUAKE . . . 502 A MASQUE OF MERCY . . 225
    OR UNDERGROUNDS, FOR CONFIDENCE IN EARTHQUAKE? . . . 502 A MASQUE OF MERCY . . 227
    AND WE ARE SHAKEN. BUT IT ISN'T EARTHQUAKE. . . . . 502 A MASQUE OF MERCY . . 234
    YOU STICK TO EARTHQUAKE, YOU HAVE SOMETHING THERE-- . 503 A MASQUE OF MERCY . . 265
EARTH'S
    THE TALE OF EARTH'S UNHONORED THINGS . . . . . . 21 THE TRIAL BY EXISTENCE 45
    NOT TO RETURN. EARTH'S THE RIGHT PLACE FOR LOVE: . . 122 BIRCHES 52
    THEY STILL HANG ON. THAT SO MUCH OF THE EARTH'S . . 322 BUILD SOIL 191
    EARTH'S A HARD PLACE IN WHICH TO SAVE THE SOUL, . . 353 THE LESSON FOR TODAY . 98
    JOB SAYS THERE'S NO SUCH THING AS EARTH'S BECOMING . 484 A MASQUE OF REASON . . 316
EARTHSLIDE
    OR EARTHSLIDE MOVED AT NIGHT, IT MOVED ITSELF; . . . 229 TWO LOOK AT TWO . . . 12
EARTHWARD
    THAT OPENS EARTHWARD, GOOD AND ILL, ... 20 THE TRIAL BY EXISTENCE 35
    TO EARTHWARD . . . . 226 TO EARTHWARD . . . . T
EASE
    LIKE A BEAST'S STALL, TO EASE THEIR CONSCIENCES. . . . 66 A SERVANT TO SERVANTS . 120
    TO EASE AWAY--THEY HAVE IT. WITH A LAUGH, ... 141 THE LINE-GANG . . . 11
    AND ALL THE REST FOR THEM PERMISSIBLE EASE. . . . . 230 NOT TO KEEP 12
    SO THAT IN GUYS IT GENTLY SWAYS AT EASE, ... 331 THE SILKEN TENT . . . 4
    TO EASE ATTENTION OFF WHEN OVERTIGHT, ... 370 THE LITERATE FARMER AND 81

EASE (CONTINUED)
    TO EASE THE MORE EXTREMELY WOUNDED OUT . . . . 507 A MASQUE OF MERCY . . 370
EASED
    AND EASED HIS HEAVY BREATHING, BUT STILL SLEPT. . . . . 108 OLD MAN'S WINTER NIGHT   25
    AT HAVING EASED HER HEART OF ONE MORE COPY-- . . . . . 217 A FOUNTAIN, A BOTTLE . 135
    THAT HAD EASED ITSELF OF ITS SUMMER LOAD, ... 304 UNHARVESTED   5
EASIER
    YOU'LL REST EASIER WHEN I'M GONE, PERHAPS-- . . . . . 50 A HUNDRED COLLARS . . 160
    I SHOULD FEEL EASIER IF I COULD SEE . . . . 80 THE GENERATIONS OF MEN 190
    AND MUCH, MUCH EASIER TO GET, ... 451 A-WISHING WELL . . . 21
    AN EASIER PLACE FOR MAN TO SAVE HIS SOUL IN. . . . . 484 A MASQUE OF REASON . 317
EASILY
    WILD, EASILY SHATTERED ROSE. . . . . 26 A LINE-STORM SONG . . 14
    SO HE CAN FIND AND EASILY DISLODGE IT . . . . . . 37 DEATH OF THE HIRED MAN 91
    (BUT I FORGIVE IT NOW AS EASILY . . . . 190 THE GRINDSTONE . . . 42
    HAD MADE IT MUCH MORE EASILY A PREY. . . . . . . 303 A BIRD SINGING IN SLEEP 14
    IS AS EASILY READ . . . . 447 THE BAD ISLAND--EASTER   4
EAST
    THE LOWER-CHAMBER WINDOW ON THE EAST, ...   9 STORM FEAR   3
    OH, NEVER THIS WHELMING EAST WIND SWELLS . . . . . 27 A LINE-STORM SONG . . 25
    WHEN ALL THE OTHER COUNTRY BROOKS FLOW EAST . . . . 258 WEST-RUNNING BROOK .   5
    GIVES A LEAP IN THE EAST. . . . . 261 CANIS MAJOR   4
    SOME OVER THE MOUNTAINS EAST, ... 312 THE VINDICTIVES . . . 70
    FINDING THE EAST BY SAILING WEST. . . . . 416 AMERICA IS HARD TO SEE   8
    TELL ME WHY THE EAST . . . . 435 KITTY HAWK 238
EASTER
    THE BAD ISLAND--EASTER . . . . 447 THE BAD ISLAND--EASTER   T
EASTON
    EASTON GOES DEMOCRATIC, WILSON 4 . . . . 165 NEW HAMPSHIRE . . . 198
    AT EASTON. WHAT HAS EASTON LEFT TO LAUGH AT, ... 165 NEW HAMPSHIRE . . . 206
EASY
    OR EASY GOLD AT THE HAND OF FAY OR ELF: . . . . . 17 MOWING   8
    WHAT DID HE MEAN? OF COURSE THE EASY WAY . . . . . 57 THE BLACK COTTAGE . . 65
    YOU UNDERSTAND THAT MEANT THE EASY JOB . . . . . 71 THE CODE 55
    IT WOULD BE EASY TO BE CLEVER . . . . 221 IN A DISUSED GRAVEYARD 13
    OF EASY WIND AND DOWNY FLAKE. . . . . 224 STOPPING BY WOODS . . 12
    YET FOUND IT EASY TO RESIST. . . . . 274 A LONE STRIKER . . . 35
    OH, I DON'T BLAME YOU. I SAY TAKE LIFE EASY. . . . . 316 BUILD SOIL 19
    IT WAS EASY TO BE ANGRY AT; . . . . 345 DISCOVERY OF MADEIRAS . 65
    HIS CAN BE NO SUCH EASY RAID . . . . 419 AMERICA IS HARD TO SEE 83
    AND EASY TO SEE THROUGH. BUT WHERE'S HE OFF TO? . . . 488 A MASQUE OF REASON . 428
    WHAT DON'T I UNDERSTAND? IT'S EASY ENOUGH. . . . . . 497 A MASQUE OF MERCY . 112
EAT
    AND EAT THE CONES UNDER HIS PINES, I TELL HIM. . . . . 33 MENDING WALL . . . 26
    THEY EAT THEM THE YEAR ROUND, AND THOSE THEY DON'T EAT . 60 BLUEBERRIES 52
    HE CAN EAT OFF A BARREL FRUM THE GROUND. . . . . . 86 THE HOUSEKEEPER . . 149
    WHICH GAVE HIM SOME TIME TO HIMSELF TO EAT, ... 197 WILD GRAPES 34
    "WE ALL MUST EAT OUR PECK OF GOLD." . . . . . . 249 A PECK OF GOLD . . . 12
    EITHER TO EAT OR DRINK. . . . . 282 A DRUMLIN WOODCHUCK . 19
    I'LL DRESS UP IN SHEEP'S CLOTHING AND EAT SHEEP. . . . 316 BUILD SOIL 16
    EAT IT OR PLOW IT UNDER WHERE IT STANDS, ... 323 BUILD SOIL 216
    THE BRIDE WHO SHARED THE CRUST HE BROKE TO EAT, . . . 359 THE LOST FOLLOWER . 23
    AND EVERY ACRE GOOD ENOUGH TO EAT, ... 365 OF STONES OF THE PLACE   7
    AND STEEPLE BUSH, NOT GOOD TO EAT, ... 376 SOMETHING FOR HOPE .   3
    SOMETHING ELUDES HIM. IS IT FOOD TO EAT? . . . . . 412 POD OF THE MILKWEED . 48
EATEN (SEE WORM-EATEN)
EATING
    WHERE THEY COULD RIPEN SAFELY TO THE EATING. . . . . 284 THE GOLD HESPERIDEE . 37
    HE COULD LOOK AT US IN OUR DINER EATING, ... 292 FIGURE IN THE DOORWAY 21
EAVES
    UNDER THE EAVES. . . . . 29 MY BUTTERFLY 47
    TAUT WITH THE DEW FROM GARDEN BED TO EAVES, ... 38 DEATH OF THE HIRED MAN 108
    AND AT THE EAVES. I LIKE IT FROM INSIDE . . . . . 150 SNOW 208
    AND AS I PASSED ALONG THE EAVES . . . . 253 THE THATCH 17
    LET US PRETEND THE DEWDROPS FROM THE EAVES . . . . 415 A CABIN IN THE CLEARING 37
EAVESDROPPING
    ARE YOU AND I EAVESDROPPING ON THEIR UNREST-- . . . . 415 A CABIN IN THE CLEARING 38
    A MIST AND SMOKE EAVESDROPPING ON A HAZE-- . . . . . 415 A CABIN IN THE CLEARING 39
EBON
    AND FRIES A COUPLE OF EBON ATOMS WHITE, ... 389 SKEPTIC   2
EBONY
    AND AFTER ALL, REALLY THEY'RE EBONY SKINNED: . . . . 60 BLUEBERRIES 24
ECHO
    AND DECLARE TO THE CLIFFS TOO FAR FOR ECHO, ... 176 THE CENSUS-TAKER . . 56
    WAS BUT THE MOCKING ECHO OF HIS OWN . . . . . . 338 THE MOST OF IT . . .   3
ECONOMICAL
    AS THE MORE ECONOMICAL PRODUCER, ... 324 BUILD SOIL 253
ECONOMIST
    THAT NO ECONOMIST WAS EVER WISER . . . . 363 AN EQUALIZER   2
ECSTASY
    THEIR EFFORT IS A MOUNTING ECSTASY . . . . 398 BURSTING RAPTURE . . 11
ED
    TILL ED BEGINS TO GET OUT ON A SUNDAY . . . . . . 115 IN THE HOME STRETCH . 148
EDDIES
    THEN EDDIES PLAYING ROUND A SUNKEN REEF . . . . . 335 I COULD GIVE ALL . .   7
    UNTIL THE EDDY OF IT EDDIES OUT." . . . . 459 HOW HARD TO KEEP FROM 161
EDDY
    THEY EDDY OVER IT TOO TOPPLING WEAK . . . . . . 246 ATMOSPHERE   3
    UNTIL THE EDDY OF IT EDDIES OUT." . . . . 459 HOW HARD TO KEEP FROM 161
EDEN
    SO EDEN SANK TO GRIEF, ... 222 NOTHING GOLD CAN STAY .   6
    A WINTER EDEN . . . . 254 A WINTER EDEN . . .   T
    THIS EDEN DAY IS DONE AT TWO O'CLOCK. . . . . . . 254 A WINTER EDEN . . . 18
EDGE
    BUT STRETCHED AWAY UNTO THE EDGE OF DOOM. . . . . .   5 INTO MY OWN   4
    AND TO THE FOREST EDGE YOU CAME ONE DAY . . . . . 16 A DREAM PANG   3
    AND QUIVER LIKE THE FRAYED EDGE OF THE DRIFT . . . . 149 SNOW 195
    THE CREEPY EDGE OF IT WITH WARY TOUCH, ... 190 THE GRINDSTONE . . . 69

EDGE (CONTINUED)
     HE LAID IT AT THE EDGE, WHERE IT COULD DRINK. . . . . . 194 PAUL'S WIFE 101
     THIS SAYING GOOD-BY ON THE EDGE OF THE DARK . . . . . . 228 GOOD-BY AND KEEP COLD .   1
     IN FRONT AT THE EDGE OF THE ROAD WHERE THE TRAFFIC SPED, . . 286 A ROADSIDE STAND . . .   2
     AS I CAME TO THE EDGE OF THE WOODS, ... 334 COME IN   1
     TO THE OPEN COUNTRY EDGE . . . . 364 A NATURE NOTE   3
     HAS GOT A RAZOR EDGE; . . . . 465 MILKY WAY IS A COWPATH 36
EDGED (SEE SHARP-EDGED)
EDIBLE
     WILL HAVE CROWDED OUT THE EDIBLE GRASS. . . . . 376 SOMETHING FOR HOPE . .   4
EDISON
     PUT UP TO CURE THE WORLD BY MR. EDISON." . . . . 371 THE LITERATE FARMER AND 93
EDITION
     A WHOLE EDITION IN A PACKING CASE . . . . 216 A FOUNTAIN, A BOTTLE . 93
EDITOR
     FAIRBANKS, HE SAYS TO ME--HE'S EDITOR-- . . . . 48 A HUNDRED DOLLARS . . 105
EDUCATED
     AND EDUCATED INTO BOARDS, HE SAID. . . . . 171 NEW HAMPSHIRE . . . 377
EDUCATION
     ON EDUCATION--YOU KNOW HOW THEY FOUGHT . . . . 36 DEATH OF THE HIRED MAN 66
     OF LAID-ON EDUCATION HAD TO DO . . . . 188 THE AX-HELVE 86
     SUCH DOUBTS OF EDUCATION SHOULD DEPEND . . . . 188 THE AX-HELVE 92
     UPON THE EDUCATION OF THOSE WHO HELD THEM? . . . . . . 188 THE AX-HELVE 93
     DEAN, ADULT EDUCATION MAY SEEM SILLY. . . . . 393 LUCRETIUS VERSUS POETS   1
EDUCATIONAL
     HE WANTS TO GIVE THE EDUCATIONAL . . . . 162 NEW HAMPSHIRE . . . 103
EDWARDS
     FOR ALFRED EDWARDS . . . . 413 A CABIN IN THE CLEARING   D
E'ER
     I DO NOT SEE WHY I SHOULD E'ER TURN BACK, ...   5 INTO MY OWN   9
EFFECT
     WHICH BEING EXPRESSED, MIGHT BE THIS IN EFFECT: . . . . 60 BLUEBERRIES 44
     THE MOON WAS WAITING FOR HER CHILL EFFECT. . . . . . . 237 A HILLSIDE THAW . . . 25
     NO LASTING EFFECT OF IT LINGERS. . . . . 266 SITTING BY A BUSH . .   4
     SO THE EFFECT WHEN THEY ARE MIXED ON CANVAS . . . . . . 321 BUILD SOIL 149
EFFECTS
     AND FEEL NO ILL EFFECTS FROM WHAT I GAVE YOU. . . . . . 474 A MASQUE OF REASON . 36
     ALL YOUR EFFECTS WERE MERELY LUCKY BLUNDERS. . . . . . 482 A MASQUE OF REASON . 259
EFFICIENT
     THE MOST EFFICIENT HELP YOU EVER HIRED . . . . 375 A YOUNG BIRCH . . . 17
EFFORT
     AND THE EFFORT MADE HIM CHOKE . . . . 340 THE SUBVERTED FLOWER . 28
     TO FIND 'TWAS THE EFFORT, THE ESSAY OF LOVE. . . . . . 380 TOO ANXIOUS FOR RIVERS 26
     THEIR EFFORT IS A MOUNTING ECSTASY . . . . 398 BURSTING RAPTURE . . 11
     OUR MAKING ALL THIS EFFORT MORTALS MAKE? . . . . 517 A MASQUE OF MERCY . . 635
EGG
     THE EGG AND THE MACHINE . . . . 269 THE EGG AND THE MACHINE T
     BUT CERTAIN SIGNS OF BURIED TURTLE'S EGG; . . . . . . 270 THE EGG AND THE MACHINE 20
     IF THERE WAS ONE EGG IN IT THERE WERE NINE, ... 270 THE EGG AND THE MACHINE 24
     TEACH YOUR GRANDMOTHER EGG SUCTION. . . . . 397 AN IMPORTER 26
     LIKE A BIG EGG AND HATCH A HEAVEN OUT . . . . 484 A MASQUE OF REASON . 306
EGGS
     OR A BASKET OF EGGS BETWEEN THEIR FEET; . . . . 141 THE GUM-GATHERER . . 27
     IT BROODED ANT EGGS, AND HAD ONE LARGE WING, ... 172 A STAR IN A STOAT . 14
     AS TOUCHING AS A BASKETFUL OF EGGS, ... 365 OF STONES OF THE PLACE   2
EGG'S
     HER WELL-TURNED EGG'S BROWN STURDY SHELL, ... 281 BLUE RIBBON AT AMESBURY 34
EGG-SUCCESS
     SHE WELL MAY SCORE AN EGG-SUCCESS. . . . . 280 BLUE RIBBON AT AMESBURY 32
EGOTIST
     POOR EGOTIST, HE HAS NO WAY OF KNOWING . . . . 309 WASPISH   5
EHEU
     COME LEARN THE LATIN EHEU FOR ALAS. . . . . 353 THE LESSON FOR TODAY . 85
EIDER
     WE CAN REST ASSURED ON EIDER . . . . 385 IN THE LONG NIGHT . . 15
EIGHT
     AND PILED--AND MEASURED, FOUR BY FOUR BY EIGHT. . . . . 101 THE WOOD-PILE . . . 24
     ONE MAN HAD LIVED ONE HUNDRED YEARS AND EIGHT. . . . . 355 THE LESSON FOR TODAY . 140
EIGHTEEN
     NUMBER EIGHTEEN THIS IS. WHAT SIZE DO YOU WEAR?" . . . . 46 A HUNDRED DOLLARS . . 61
EIGHTY-FIVE
     IN EIGHTY-FIVE." / "AS LONG AGO AS THAT?" . . . . . . 213 A FOUNTAIN, A BOTTLE . 23
EITHER
     "NO, HE WON'T, EITHER. HE'LL JUST DROP THE REINS . . . . 88 THE HOUSEKEEPER . . . 200
     WE MUSTN'T SAY HARD THINGS. YOU MUSTN'T EITHER." . . . . 91 THE FEAR 53
     EITHER TO HAVE GONE GROPING UNDERGROUND . . . . 119 HYLA BROOK   3
     IT CAN'T TURN EITHER WAY. IT NEEDS THE WIND'S HELP. . . 148 SNOW 135
     "ONE OF TWO THINGS, EITHER SHE'S GONE TO BED . . . . . 154 SNOW 311
     (THEY EITHER NOTICED IT, OR GOT IT WRONG.) . . . . . . 181 MAPLE 51
     FOR LOVE OF IT, AND YET NOT WASTE TIME EITHER. . . . . 188 THE AX-HELVE 81
     EXCEPT, PERHAPS, A FOOT AT EITHER END. . . . . 193 PAUL'S WIFE 71
     EITHER TO PRAISE HER OR SO MUCH AS NAME HER, ... 196 PAUL'S WIFE 153
     THEY DON'T DISPOSE ME, EITHER ONE OF THEM, ... 207 PAUPER WITCH OF GRAFTON 6
     BOTH EITHER LOOKING FOR OR FINDING SOMETHING. . . . . . 217 A FOUNTAIN, A BOTTLE . 129
     OF WHAT WAS EITHER CLOUD OR SMOKE . . . . 233 LOOKING FOR SUNSET BIRD 18
     YOUR NAME NOT WRITTEN ON EITHER SIDE. . . . . 247 ON GOING UNNOTICED . . 12
     GIVE HER A CHILD AT EITHER KNEE FOR FOURTH JOY . . . . . 256 THE LOVELY BE CHOOSERS 31
     NOTHING ON EITHER SIDE WAS SAID. . . . . 277 TWO TRAMPS IN MUD TIME 57
     EITHER TO EAT OR DRINK. . . . . 282 A DRUMLIN WOODCHUCK . 19
     TWO TEARDROPS, ONE FOR EITHER EYE, ... 327 A MISSIVE MISSILE . . 11
     BUT SHE WAS EITHER BLIND . . . . 339 THE SUBVERTED FLOWER .   6
     HE STRETCHED HER EITHER ARM . . . . 339 THE SUBVERTED FLOWER . 18
     EITHER TO BREACH OR CLIMB. . . . . 348 TRIPLE BRONZE . . .   8
     WE'RE EITHER NOTHING OR A GOD'S REGRET. . . . . 353 THE LESSON FOR TODAY . 106
     NOR WILL YOU FIND LOVE EITHER, NOR LOVE YOU. . . . . . 356 A MOTH SEEN IN WINTER . 13
     THEN PAUSED AGAIN AND EITHER DRANK OR SMELT-- . . . . . 357 A CONSIDERABLE SPECK . 13
     OF EITHER MURDER OR WAR IN ANY LAND. . . . . 371 THE LITERATE FARMER AND 111
     BUT THERE'S A TIGHT-SHUT LOOK TO EITHER DOOR . . . . . 400 TO THE RIGHT PERSON .   8

EITHER (CONTINUED)
    EITHER FOR THEM OR THE ONLOOKING WORLD. . . . . 415 A CABIN IN THE CLEARING 32
    OR INSIDE EITHER FOR THAT MATTER. . . . . 418 AMERICA IS HARD TO SEE   65
    ON EITHER HAND TO MAKE HIS COURSE PERHAPS . . . . . 421 ESCAPIST--NEVER . . . 4
    TO SAY GOD'S EITHER ALL OR OVER ALL? . . . . 427 CONCEPT SELF-CONCEIVED 7
    YOU LOOK AS IF YOU EITHER HOPED OR FEARED . . . . . 488 A MASQUE OF REASON . . 411
    AND I DON'T LOVE YOU EITHER, DO I, KEEPER? . . . . . 499 A MASQUE OF MERCY . . 165
ELATE
    NOT TO CLAIM ELATE, ... 429 KITTY HAWK 25
ELATED
    THE THING WAS TO GET NOW AND THEN ELATED. . . . . . 468 IN A GLASS OF CIDER . 8
ELBOW
    WITH LITTLE FERNS IN CREVICES AT HIS ELBOW. . . . . . 42 THE MOUNTAIN 62
ELBOW-CROOK
    THAT HELD THE HOUSE AS IN AN ELBOW-CROOK? . . . . . 231 A BROOK IN THE CITY . 4
ELBOWED (SEE WET-ELBOWED)
ELBOWS
    THEY WERE NOT ON THE TABLE WITH THEIR ELBOWS. . . . . 175 THE CENSUS-TAKER . . 40
ELECT
    IF I'M EXPECTED TO ELECT BILL TAFT. . . . . 48 A HUNDRED COLLARS . 117
    I ELECT YOU TO PUT THE CURB ON IT. . . . . 320 BUILD SOIL 126
ELECTED
    IN A RELATION OF ELECTED FRIENDS. . . . . 315 IRIS BY NIGHT . . . 31
    THERE I ELECTED TO DEMUR . . . . 380 AN UNSTAMPED LETTER IN 12
ELECTION
    WE WERE BUT SIXTY VOTERS LAST ELECTION. . . . . . . 41 THE MOUNTAIN . . . 25
    ELECTION NIGHT ONCE IN FRANCONIA, ... 165 NEW HAMPSHIRE . . . 195
    GET IN A POEM TOWARD THE NEXT ELECTION. . . . . . . 316 BUILD SOIL 25
    TO TRY IF ONE MORE POPULAR ELECTION . . . . 358 THE LOST FOLLOWER . 12
    COME FRESH FROM AN ELECTION LIKE THE LAST, ... 423 FOR JOHN F. KENNEDY . 54
ELECTRIC
    IT'S A NEW PATENTED ELECTRIC LIGHT, ... 369 THE LITERATE FARMER AND 39
ELECTRICITY
    OF ELECTRICITY IN BULK THE WAY . . . . 370 THE LITERATE FARMER AND 73
ELEMENT
    AN ELEMENT IN ANY GOVERNMENT. . . . . 318 BUILD SOIL 69
ELEMENTS
    TELL US WHAT ELEMENTS YOU BLEND. . . . . 403 SOMETHING LIKE A STAR . 15
ELEPHANT
    THE ELEPHANT STANDS ON THE BACK OF A TURTLE; . . . . 379 TOO ANXIOUS FOR RIVERS 15
ELEPHANT'S
    THE WORLD AS WE KNOW IS AN ELEPHANT'S HOWDAH; . . . . 379 TOO ANXIOUS FOR RIVERS 14
ELEVATE
    IF I MUST CHOOSE WHICH I WOULD ELEVATE-- . . . . . 168 NEW HAMPSHIRE . . . 307
    I'D ELEVATE THE ALREADY LOFTY MOUNTAINS. . . . . . . 168 NEW HAMPSHIRE . . . 309
ELEVATING
    KEEP ON ELEVATING. . . . . 441 KITTY HAWK 411
ELEVEN
    AFTER ELEVEN O'CLOCK AT NIGHT. TOO TIRED . . . . . . 45 A HUNDRED COLLARS . 17
ELF
    OR EASY GOLD AT THE HAND OF FAY OR ELF: . . . . . . 17 MOWING 8
ELIMINATION
    WHO HAVING BY ELIMINATION GOT . . . . 498 A MASQUE OF MERCY . 120
ELIXIR
    SAYS, TO MAKE THIS FALL ELIXIR . . . . 303 CLEAR AND COLDER . 3
ELIZA
    THIS GLIMPSE OF LINGERING PERSON IN ELIZA, ... 200 PLACE FOR A THIRD . 16
    WHETHER ELIZA WOULD BE WELCOME THERE. . . . . 200 PLACE FOR A THIRD . 42
    OF WHERE ELIZA WANTED NOT TO LIE, ... 201 PLACE FOR A THIRD . 45
    SHE'D LOOKED ELIZA UP HER SECOND TIME, ... 201 PLACE FOR A THIRD . 58
    SHE AND ELIZA HAD BEEN FRIENDS THROUGH ALL. . . . . . 201 PLACE FOR A THIRD . 63
    TO BUY ELIZA A PLOT TO LIE ALONE IN: . . . . . . 202 PLACE FOR A THIRD . 80
ELIZABETH
    ELIZABETH THE FIRST AND ENGLAND WON. . . . . . . 422 FOR JOHN F. KENNEDY . 18
    PAST ELIZABETH CITY . . . . 428 KITTY HAWK 8
    FROM ELIZABETH CITY, ... 431 KITTY HAWK . . . 102
ELIZA'S
    ELIZA'S HAD TOO MANY OTHER MEN." . . . . 202 PLACE FOR A THIRD . 78
ELL
    THERE IN THE UPPER CHAMBER IN THE ELL, ... 67 A SERVANT TO SERVANTS . 142
ELM
    AND THE AGED ELM, THOUGH TOUCHED WITH FIRE; . . . . . 242 NEED OF BEING VERSED . 18
ELM-TREE
    AND POURS THE ELM-TREE MEADOW FULL OF BLUE, ... 248 THE COCOON . . . 4
ELOQUENCE
    ADMITTEDLY AN ELOQUENCE SO SOFT . . . . 338 NEVER WOULD BIRDS' SONG 6
ELSE
    LIKE NOTHING ELSE BY DAY, LIKE GHOSTS BY NIGHT; . . . 12 A PRAYER IN SPRING . . 6
    FOR THIS IS LOVE AND NOTHING ELSE IS LOVE, ... 12 A PRAYER IN SPRING . . 13
    WHOSE CLUSTERED FRUIT MUST ELSE BE LOST-- . . . . . 28 OCTOBER 20
    WHAT GOOD IS HE? WHO ELSE WILL HARBOR HIM . . . . . 35 DEATH OF THE HIRED MAN 15
    'SOMEONE ELSE CAN.' 'THEN SOMEONE ELSE WILL HAVE TO.' . 35 DEATH OF THE HIRED MAN 24
    "HOME," HE MOCKED GENTLY. / "YES, WHAT ELSE BUT HOME? . 38 DEATH OF THE HIRED MAN 113
    SHARING A ROOM WITH SOMEONE ELSE." / "WHO IS IT?" . . . 45 A HUNDRED COLLARS . . 24
    "AMY! DON'T GO TO SOMEONE ELSE THIS TIME. . . . . . . 52 HOME BURIAL . . . 39
    DON'T CARRY IT TO SOMEONE ELSE THIS TIME. . . . . . . 53 HOME BURIAL . . . 57
    WHATEVER ELSE THE CIVIL WAR WAS FOR, ... 56 THE BLACK COTTAGE . . 55
    ANYONE ELSE, BUT OUT OF IDLENESS. . . . . 74 THE GENERATIONS OF MEN 27
    HE'S GIVEN HER TIME TO THINK OF SOMETHING ELSE. . . . 84 THE HOUSEKEEPER . . 86
    "I MEAN SHE'S MARRIED--MARRIED SOMEONE ELSE." . . . . 87 THE HOUSEKEEPER . . 180
    "IT IS--OR SOMEONE ELSE HE'S SENT TO WATCH." . . . . 90 THE FEAR 42
    OR SOMEWHERE ELSE: I WAS JUST FAR FROM HOME. . . . . 101 THE WOOD-PILE . . 9
    OF SOMETHING ELSE," SHE LAUGHED. "OH, PUT IT WHERE . . 111 IN THE HOME STRETCH . 15
    AND BANG GOES SOMETHING ELSE AWAY OFF THERE. . . . . 112 IN THE HOME STRETCH . 55
    WHATEVER ELSE WE WANT FOR. AND A LIGHT. . . . . . . 113 IN THE HOME STRETCH . 79
    BUT HE GAVE NO ONE ELSE A LAUGHER'S LICENSE. . . . . 142 THE VANISHING RED . . 4
    TO ANYTHING ANYONE ELSE MAY SAY. . . . . 145 SNOW 66
    I'LL HAVE TO TURN THE LEAF IF NO ONE ELSE WILL. . . . 148 SNOW 151

ELSE (CONTINUED)
    AND YOU YOURSELF DON'T WANT TO. WHO ELSE IS THERE?" . . . 151 SNOW 235
    "A CLOCK MAYBE." / "DON'T YOU HEAR SOMETHING ELSE?" . . . 154 SNOW 316
    SOMETHING ELSE TO PROTECT HER FROM HERSELF. . . . . . . 163 NEW HAMPSHIRE . . . 147
    YET ASK WHERE ELSE IT COULD HAVE GONE AS WELL, ... 173 A STAR IN A STONEBOAT . 37
    OR ELSE FUN OF ORION'S HAVING CAUGHT ME. . . . . 176 THE STAR-SPLITTER . . 10
    THAT NOT EVERYBODY ELSE KNEW WAS TO COUNT . . . . 186 THE AX-HELVE 42
    WHO'D RUN AWAY WITH SOMEONE ELSE AND LEFT HIM; . . . . . 191 PAUL'S WIFE 9
    IF I COULD SEE IT, OR ELSE MOW THE ROOM, ... 205 THE WITCH OF COOS . 105
    OR ELSE BY SOME REMOTENESS THAT DEFIED THEM . . . . . . 216 A FOUNTAIN, A BOTTLE . 107
    HOW ELSE? THEY ARE NOT KNOWN TO SEND THE DEAD.-- . . . . 230 NOT TO KEEP . . . 6
    HOW ELSE DISPOSE OF AN IMMORTAL FORCE . . . . 231 A BROOK IN THE CITY . 13
    NOR I NOR NOBODY ELSE MAY SAY, ... 263 THE TIMES TABLE . . 15
    AND WORSHIP APPLES. WHAT ELSE COULD IT MEAN? . . . . . 284 THE GOLD HESPERIDEE . 54
    THEY CAN LEAVE IT TO SOMEONE ELSE TO TEND. . . . . . . 291 ON HEART'S BEGINNING TO 18
    AND NOBODY ELSE AT FAULT, ... 314 BEARER OF EVIL TIDINGS 24
    OR ELSE WRITE SOMETHING TO IMPROVE FOOD PRICES. . . . . 316 BUILD SOIL 24
    OR ELSE I FEAR ENTIRELY MINE, ... 328 A MISSIVE MISSILE . . 44
    AND SOMEONE ELSE ADDITIONAL TO HIM, ... 338 THE MOST OF IT . . . 15
    GOD BLESS HIMSELF CAN NO ONE ELSE BE BLESSED. . . . . . 355 THE LESSON FOR TODAY . 156
    BUT WHATSOEVER ELSE IT MAY SECRETE, ... 411 POD OF THE MILKWEED . 20
    WHERE SOMEONE SOMEONE ELSE BEGAT . . . . 453 A-WISHING WELL . . . 80
    RIGEL, BELLATRIX, OR ELSE BETELGEUSE, ... 454 HOW HARD TO KEEP FROM 16
    AND HE MAY HAVE TO TURN TO SOMETHING ELSE . . . . . . 459 HOW HARD TO KEEP FROM 179
    ONCE TO HAVE KNOWN IT, NOTHING ELSE WILL DO. . . . . . 461 HOW HARD TO KEEP FROM 247
    WE'RE SAVED, WE'RE SAVED, WHATEVER ELSE IT MEANS. . . . 476 A MASQUE OF REASON . . 82
    AND WHAT ELSE DID WE SAY? / WELL, WHAT LED UP-- . . . . 487 A MASQUE OF REASON . 399
    OR ELSE YOU WERE AFRAID OF BEING MOBBED . . . . 497 A MASQUE OF MERCY . 104
    SOMEONE ELSE READ IT. / NO, YOU READ IT TO US. . . . . 505 A MASQUE OF MERCY . 298
    SOMEONE ELSE READ IT. / NO. YOU ASKED FOR IT. . . . . 506 A MASQUE OF MERCY . 329
    JUST, I WOULD HAVE HIM JUST BEFORE ALL ELSE, ... 507 A MASQUE OF MERCY . 363
ELSE'S
    SHE WASN'T ANYBODY ELSE'S BUSINESS, ... 196 PAUL'S WIFE 152
    IT IS NOBODY ELSE'S AFFAIR. . . . . 289 DEPARTMENTAL 41
ELSEWHERE
    ONCE MORE BEFORE WE MEET ELSEWHERE." / "IN RAIN?" . . . 81 THE GENERATIONS OF MEN 209
    AND LOOK ELSEWHERE THAN TO STARS AND MOON AND SUN . . . 268 ON LOOKING UP BY CHANCE 9
    BUT NOW 'TWAS THERE AS ELSEWHERE, ANY GAIN . . . . . 398 BURSTING RAPTURE . . 4
ELUDE
    ELUDE MY EMBRACE, ... 235 GATHERING LEAVES . . 10
ELUDES
    SOMETHING ELUDES HIM. IS IT FOOD TO EAT? . . . . . . 412 POD OF THE MILKWEED . 48
ELVES
    THAN NOW THESE NUMBERLESS YEARS THE ELVES, ... 26 A LINE-STORM SONG . . 11
    THAT WANTS IT DOWN." I COULD SAY "ELVES" TO HIM, . . . 34 MENDING WALL 36
    BUT IT'S NOT ELVES EXACTLY, AND I'D RATHER . . . . . 34 MENDING WALL 37
ELYSIAN
    AND I JUDGE FROM THAT ELYSIAN FREIGHT . . . . 262 THE FLOWER BOAT . . . 9
'EM
    "YOU SEE I'M IN WITH EVERYBODY, KNOW 'EM ALL. . . . . 49 A HUNDRED COLLARS . 120
    AND FILL ANOTHER WITH 'EM FIFTEEN MILES AWAY, ... 116 IN THE HOME STRETCH . 161
EMANCIPATOR
    YOU ARE THE EMANCIPATOR OF YOUR GOD, ... 476 A MASQUE OF REASON . 78
EMBALM
    EMBALM HIM WITH ICHOR OF NETTLE. . . . . 288 DEPARTMENTAL 31
EMBARRASSING
    HERE FIRST MY THEME BECOMES EMBARRASSING. . . . . . . 166 NEW HAMPSHIRE . . . 217
    BEYOND EMBARRASSING SELF-CONSCIOUSNESS . . . . 318 BUILD SOIL 82
EMBARRASSMENT
    FROM NOTHING BUT EMBARRASSMENT AND WANT . . . . . . 168 NEW HAMPSHIRE . . . 291
EMBLEMATIC
    EMBLEMATIC DITTY, ... 428 KITTY HAWK 4
EMBODIMENT
    UNLESS IT WAS THE EMBODIMENT THAT CRASHED . . . . . 338 THE MOST OF IT . . . 10
EMBOLDENED
    FOR THE EMBOLDENED POLITICIANS DARING . . . . 424 FOR JOHN F. KENNEDY . 61
EMBRACE (SEE SELF-EMBRACE)
    WITH STRAINING IN THE WORLD'S EMBRACE. . . . . . . 120 BOND AND FREE . . . 8
    YOU WENT TO MEET THE SHELL'S EMBRACE OF FIRE . . . . 222 TO E.T. 13
    ELUDE MY EMBRACE, ... 235 GATHERING LEAVES . . 10
EMBRACED
    I JUST EMBRACED THE SHAFT AND RODE IT OUT-- . . . . . 93 THE SELF-SEEKER . . . 26
    AND WENT EMBRACED TO THE COLD AND DARK . . . . . . 346 DISCOVERY OF MADEIRAS . 84
EMBRACING
    WE CONGREGATE EMBRACING FROM DISTRUST . . . . 325 BUILD SOIL 276
EMBROIL
    TO EMBROIL THE VERY GODS ABOUT THEIR SPHERES . . . . 511 A MASQUE OF MERCY . 471
EMERGED
    A DRY RAVINE EMERGED FROM UNDER BOUGHS . . . . . . 41 THE MOUNTAIN 33
EMERSON
    EMERSON SAID, "THE GOD WHO MADE NEW HAMPSHIRE . . . . 166 NEW HAMPSHIRE . . . 218
EMINENT
    BY RIGHT OF EMINENT DOMAIN. . . . . 390 TWO LEADING LIGHTS . 10
EMOTION
    A MOMENT HE STOOD BALANCING WITH EMOTION, ... 204 THE WITCH OF COOS . . 71
EMPEROR
    MADE FOR THE EMPEROR ALEXIUS, ... 473 A MASQUE OF REASON . 11
EMPIRE
    THE LOOKS OF EMPIRE HERE. I'M LEAVING WITH YOU." . . . 453 HOW HARD TO KEEP FROM 9
EMPIRES
    THEY WOULD BRING EMPIRES DOWN ABOUT OUR EARS . . . . 423 FOR JOHN F. KENNEDY . 29
EMPLOYED
    I COULD BE WORSE EMPLOYED . . . . 383 MAKING CERTAIN ANYTHING 1
EMPOWERED
    I AM EMPOWERED TO EXCUSE YOU FROM IT. . . . . 499 A MASQUE OF MERCY . 149
EMPTIED
    A LEAK AND EMPTIED THEN. AND FORTY YEARS . . . . . 213 A FOUNTAIN, A BOTTLE . 25
    I EMPTIED MY CAGE . . . . 241 THE LOCKLESS DOOR . . 18

EMPTIED (CONTINUED)
    THEY EMPTIED THE AISLE . . . . 448 THE BAD ISLAND--EASTER   41
EMPTINESS
    AN EMPTINESS FLAYED TO THE VERY STONE. . . . . . . 174 THE CENSUS-TAKER   . . 14
    TO FILL THE ABYSS'S VOID WITH EMPTINESS. . . . . . 259 WEST-RUNNING BROOK . . 49
EMPTY
    WITH A BIG JAG TO EMPTY IN A BAY. . . . . 71 THE CODE   54
    THAT THE BROOK RAISES IN THE EMPTY VALLEY. . . . . 77 THE GENERATIONS OF MEN 125
    TWO OF YOU OUT WILL LEAVE AN EMPTY HOUSE." . . . . 82 THE HOUSEKEEPER . . . 42
    THAT GATHERS ON THE PANE IN EMPTY ROOMS. . . . . . 108 OLD MAN'S WINTER NIGHT   3
    TO EMPTY ONE HOUSE OF ALL HOUSEHOLD GOODS . . . . 116 IN THE HOME STRETCH . 160
    IT'S QUIET AS AN EMPTY CHURCH WITHOUT HIM." . . . 152 SNOW   260
    "WHAT DO YOU HEAR?" / "I HEAR AN EMPTY ROOM-- . . 153 SNOW   299
    THE HOLLOW LOOKED TOO SOUND AND CLEAN AND EMPTY . 193 PAUL'S WIFE 83
    TO SEE IF IT WAS EMPTY. HE MADE OUT IN THERE . . . 194 PAUL'S WIFE 90
    AN EMPTY THREAT . . . . 210 AN EMPTY THREAT . . . . T
    "I WON'T ACCEPT THE SUBSTITUTE. IT'S EMPTY." . . . 214 A FOUNTAIN, A BOTTLE . 43
    "I GUESS YOU'D FIND THE FOUNTAIN JUST AS EMPTY. . 214 A FOUNTAIN, A BOTTLE . 45
    HER KEEPER, EMPTY PAIL IN HAND, ... 280 BLUE RIBBON AT AMESBURY 18
    THEY CANNOT SCARE ME WITH THEIR EMPTY SPACES . . . 296 DESERT PLACES 13
    WOULD EMPTY IT UNSPARING ON THE FLOWER . . . . . . 337 THE WIND AND THE RAIN . 32
    A FUSILLADE OF BLANKS AND EMPTY FLASHES, ... 361 A LOOSE MOUNTAIN . . . 9
    MUST FIND WHERE TO POUR ITSELF INTO AND EMPTY? . . 379 TOO ANXIOUS FOR RIVERS   4
    GRIND SHELLS, O FUTILE SEA, GRIND EMPTY SHELLS . . 446 DOES NO ONE AT ALL EVER 19
    I LEFT LIGHT SHINING ON AN EMPTY STAGE . . . . . . 497 A MASQUE OF MERCY . . 100
    TO BE THE BEARER OF AN EMPTY THREAT. . . . . 505 A MASQUE OF MERCY . . 303
    I HAVE CONTRIBUTED THE EMPTY CELLAR . . . . 515 A MASQUE OF MERCY . . 564
EMPTY-IDLE
    MY SHARE AT LEAST, LEST I BE EMPTY-IDLE. . . . . . 324 BUILD SOIL   262
EMULATING
    AND HERE ON EARTH COME EMULATING FLIES . . . . . . 246 FIREFLIES IN THE GARDEN 2
EMULATION
    US WITH EMULATION? . . . . 435 KITTY HAWK   245
EMULOUS
    THINE EMULOUS FOND FLOWERS ARE DEAD, TOO, ... 28 MY BUTTERFLY 1
EN
    THAT STRUCK EN MASSE . . . . 218 I WILL SING YOU ONE-O. 35
    A PRINCESS EN ROUTE FROM CHINA . . . . 313 BEARER OF EVIL TIDINGS 19
ENACT
    PERSONAE NEEDED TO ENACT THE PROBLEM. . . . . . . 487 A MASQUE OF REASON . . 394
ENACTING
    OF OUR ENACTING OUT THE DOOM . . . . 417 AMERICA IS HARD TO SEE   38
ENAMEL
    AS THE STIR CRACKS AND CRAZES THEIR ENAMEL. . . . 121 BIRCHES   9
ENAMELED
    AND HARK, THE GOLD ENAMELED NIGHTINGALES . . . . . 473 A MASQUE OF REASON . . 14
    AND TURN THE GOLD ENAMELED ARTIFICIAL BIRDS ON. . 490 A MASQUE OF REASON . . 459
ENCHANT
    ENCHANT THE LAND WITH AMETHYST. . . . . 28 OCTOBER   16
ENCLOSED
    MY FATHER BUILT, ENCLOSED A SPRING, ... 265 THE BIRTHPLACE 3
ENCOUNTER
    AN ENCOUNTER . . . . 125 AN ENCOUNTER . . . . . T
    DON'T LET ME SEEM TO SAY THE EXCHANGE, THE ENCOUNTER, . 321 BUILD SOIL   157
ENCOUNTERED
    YET IF HE ENCOUNTERED ONE . . . . 288 DEPARTMENTAL 8
ENCOURAGE
    BUT WHAT HE LIKED WAS SOMEONE TO ENCOURAGE. . . . . 71 THE CODE 43
ENCROACH
    TRESPASS AND ENCROACH . . . . 437 KITTY HAWK   284
END (SEE BLADE-END, PROGRESS-END)
    I END NOT FAR FROM MY GOING FORTH, ...   9 A LATE WALK 13
    (OR SO WE SAY) THAT IN THE END . . . . 19 REVELATION 6
    BUT ALWAYS GOD SPEAKS AT THE END: . . . . 21 THE TRIAL BY EXISTENCE 49
    AND BOW AND ACCEPT THE END . . . . 30 RELUCTANCE 23
    BLUEBERRIES AS BIG AS THE END OF YOUR THUMB, . . . 59 BLUEBERRIES 3
    I WAS GLAD THOUGH, NO END, WHEN WE MOVED OUT, . . 67 A SERVANT TO SERVANTS . 151
    STEM END AND BLOSSOM END, ... 68 AFTER APPLE-PICKING . 19
    AND END IT." / "TOO LATE NOW: SHE WOULDN'T HAVE HIM. . 84 THE HOUSEKEEPER . . . 85
    TRYING, I THOUGHT, TO SET IT UP ON END, ... 109 THE EXPOSED NEST . . . 4
    THAT END ALL. AND IT'S SCARCE ENOUGH TO CALL . . . 111 IN THE HOME STRETCH . 34
    NO, THIS IS NO BEGINNING." / "THEN AN END?" . . . 117 IN THE HOME STRETCH . 186
    "END IS A GLOOMY WORD." / "IS IT TOO LATE . . . . 117 IN THE HOME STRETCH . 187
    AT THE FAR END OF IT YOU SEE A STIR . . . . 149 SNOW   194
    WITH NO SUSPICION IN STEM END OR BLOSSOM END . . . 164 NEW HAMPSHIRE 160
    THICK END TO THIN END AND THIN END TO THICK END, . 164 NEW HAMPSHIRE 179
    AT A STAR QUAKING IN THE OTHER END. . . . . 179 THE STAR-SPLITTER . . 78
    ON THE END IT PRESENTED TO THE ROAD. . . . . 181 MAPLE   58
    FROM END TO END WITH HIS ROUGH HAND SHUT ROUND IT. . 187 THE AX-HELVE 77
    EXCEPT, PERHAPS, A FOOT AT EITHER END. . . . . . . 193 PAUL'S WIFE 71
    AND LEFT STOOD UP ON END INSIDE THE TREE . . . . . 194 PAUL'S WIFE 93
    SON LOOKS SURPRISED TO SEE ME END A LIE . . . . . 207 THE WITCH OF COOS . . 145
    AND FULL OF IT, THAT THIS WOULD BE THE END, . . . 210 PAUPER WITCH OF GRAFTON 105
    SOME SAY THE WORLD WILL END IN FIRE, ... 220 FIRE AND ICE 1
    AS ONE WHO OVERTAKEN BY THE END . . . . 226 THE ONSET 7
    AN ORCHARD AWAY AT THE END OF THE FARM . . . . . . 228 GOOD-BY AND KEEP COLD . 4
    AND THEY END BY BIDDING HIM STAY WITH THEM. . . . 236 MISGIVING 4
    I HAVE NO DOUBT I'D END BY HOLDING NONE. . . . . . 237 A HILLSIDE THAW . . . 17
    ONE LIZARD AT THE END OF EVERY RAY. . . . . 238 A HILLSIDE THAW . . . 34
    OUR PASSAGE TO OUR JOURNEY'S END FOR GOOD, ... 238 ON A TREE FALLEN ACROSS 3
    BORNE DOWN UNTIL THE END ALMOST TOOK ROOT, ... 239 OUR SINGING STRENGTH . 13
    NO MORE IT OPENED WITH ALL ONE END . . . . 241 NEED OF BEING VERSED . 9
    IT IS TRUE THE LONGEST DROUTH WILL END IN RAIN, . 268 ON LOOKING UP BY CHANCE 11
    THE LONGEST PEACE IN CHINA WILL END IN STRIFE. . . 268 ON LOOKING UP BY CHANCE 12
    THE TELESCOPE AT ONE END OF HIS BEAT, ... 269 THE BEAR   18
    AND AT THE OTHER END THE MICROSCOPE. . . . . 269 THE BEAR   19
    SHE CAUGHT THE PIECES END TO END . . . . 274 A LONE STRIKER . . . 30
    SHALL BE IN THE END SCOURED POOR, ... 285 IN TIME OF CLOUDBURST . 11

END (CONTINUED)
    TO THE OTHER END OF THE SLOPE, ... 285 IN TIME OF CLOUDBURST .   18
    AND WHEN THEIR INTERESTS IN IT END, ... 291 ON HEART'S BEGINNING TO   17
    OR KEEPS THE END FROM BEING HARD. . . . . 307 PROVIDE, PROVIDE . .   18
    WILL THE BLIGHT END THE CHESTNUT? . . . . 308 EVIL TENDENCIES CANCEL   1
    SHALL COME TO END THE BLIGHT. . . . . 308 EVIL TENDENCIES CANCEL   6
    BUT MUCH AS IN THE END WE BRING FOR SALE THERE, . . 321 BUILD SOIL   173
    AND WOULD POUNCE TO END IT ALL . . . . 340 THE SUBVERTED FLOWER .   39
    BUT SAILED AND LEFT THEM IN THE END. . . . . 347 DISCOVERY OF MADEIRAS . 113
    ONE MORE MILLENNIUM'S ABOUT TO END. . . . . 352 THE LESSON FOR TODAY .   46
    HIS MIND TO THINKING ALWAYS OF THE END. . . . . . . 353 THE LESSON FOR TODAY .   95
    THEY END UP IN THE UNIVERSAL WHOLE . . . . 354 THE LESSON FOR TODAY . 111
    AND THEN TO END THE STORY . . . . 359 NOVEMBER   4
    TO END IT. AND IF SO . . . . 361 ALMOST TWO THOUSAND   .   8
    TO WATCH THIS END DELUXE. . . . . 361 ALMOST TWO THOUSAND   .   13
    IT WAS BLOWN WOODS AND NO END. . . . . 366 NOT OF SCHOOL AGE . .   2
    ON THE RIGHT SIDE OF BED WOULD END THE FRAY, ... 372 THE LITERATE FARMER AND 121
    THAT SOMEONE HAS SAID IS THE END OF THE WORLD. . . . 379 TOO ANXIOUS FOR RIVERS   2
    AND THE NEEDLE STANDS ON END. . . . . 384 IN THE LONG NIGHT . .   4
    SEEMS TO COME TO AN END . . . . 388 MIDDLENESS OF THE ROAD   2
    IF ANYTHING SHOULD PUT AN END TO THIS, ... 397 THE PLANNERS   1
    THAT PUT AN END TO WHAT WAS GOING ON . . . . 397 THE PLANNERS   5
    BUT DOES TELL SOMETHING IN THE END. . . . . 403 SOMETHING LIKE A STAR .   17
    IN READING, DON'T YOU, BILL?--AT EVERY LINE END . . 405 FROM PLANE TO PLANE   .   50
    GOES BACK TO THE BEGINNING OF THE END . . . . 422 FOR JOHN F. KENNEDY .   8
    'TWAS AN END FOREGONE . . . . 438 KITTY HAWK   326
    AT THE END OF THE ROW . . . . 450 OBJECTION TO BE STEPPED   1
    TO PUT AN END TO THE KING'S VACILLATION. . . . . . . 456 HOW HARD TO KEEP FROM   80
    MY SATRAP TISSAPHERNES HAS NO END . . . . 459 HOW HARD TO KEEP FROM   166
    THAT'S WHAT AT THE END OF A WAR . . . . 463 LINES IN DEJECTION .   26
    THEY MAY END BY BANISHING ME . . . . 466 SOME SCIENCE FICTION .   21
    YOU COULD END THIS BY SIMPLY COMING OUT . . . . . . 483 A MASQUE OF REASON .   295
    WOULD PUT AN END TO SUCH FANTASTIC NONSENSE; . . . . 484 A MASQUE OF REASON .   309
    BUT HERE'S WHERE YOUR EVASION HAS AN END. . . . . . 498 A MASQUE OF MERCY .   142
    ABOUT OUR OWN OR ANYBODY'S END. . . . . 507 A MASQUE OF MERCY .   354
    AN END YOU CAN'T BY ANY MEANS ACHIEVE, ... 512 A MASQUE OF MERCY .   509
ENDEARING
    HIS VERY WEAKNESS FOR MANKIND'S ENDEARING. . . . . . 505 A MASQUE OF MERCY .   309
ENDED (SEE UP-ENDED)
    AND LO, IT IS ENDED. . . . . 30 RELUCTANCE   6
    IF HE LEFT THEN, I SAID, THAT ENDED IT. . . . . . . 35 DEATH OF THE HIRED MAN   14
    IF HE WA'N'T KEPT STRICT WATCH OF, AND IT ENDED . . 66 A SERVANT TO SERVANTS . 112
    AND DISAPPEARED AND ENDED NOT FAR OFF. . . . . 75 THE GENERATIONS OF MEN   72
    LITTLE--LESS--NOTHING!--AND THAT ENDED IT. . . . . . 137 "OUT,OUT--"   32
    PERHAPS, TO WHERE IT ENDED AT A HOUSE . . . . 215 A FOUNTAIN, A BOTTLE .   68
    ITS LIFE OF HUNDREDS OF YEARS HAS ENDED . . . . . . 253 THE THATCH   33
    AS SO OFTEN, ENDED . . . . 431 KITTY HAWK   96
ENDETH
    (HERE ENDETH CHAPTER FORTY-THREE OF JOB.) . . . . . 490 A MASQUE OF REASON .   466
ENDING (SEE SEASON-ENDING)
    IN INCANDESCENT LAMPS AND ENDING SLEEP. . . . . . . 371 THE LITERATE FARMER AND 97
ENDLESS
    THAT NEED ENDLESS TALK-TALK . . . . 212 AN EMPTY THREAT . . .   56
    COUNTING AN ENDLESS REPETITION. . . . . 247 DEVOTION   4
    TO SO ENDLESS A REPETITION . . . . 286 IN TIME OF CLOUDBURST .   26
ENDLESSLY
    AND SEEK IT ENDLESSLY WITH PURBLIND HASTE; . . . . . 14 WAITING   17
END-ON
    TO SLAM END-ON AGAIN AGAINST THE SAW TEETH. . . . . 193 PAUL'S WIFE   64
ENDOR
    THE WITCH OF ENDOR WAS A FRIEND OF MINE. . . . . . . 476 A MASQUE OF REASON .   97
ENDS
    TO SANCTIFY TO WHAT FAR ENDS HE WILL, ... 12 A PRAYER IN SPRING . .   15
    SHE WOULDN'T HAVE BELIEVED THOSE ENDS ENOUGH . . . . 56 THE BLACK COTTAGE . .   58
    CUT SHORT OFF AT BOTH ENDS. IT LIES FIVE MILES . . . 63 A SERVANT TO SERVANTS .   21
    ENDS AND BEGINNINGS--THERE ARE NO SUCH THINGS. . . . 116 IN THE HOME STRETCH . 174
    SO NEAR TO PARADISE ALL PAIRING ENDS: . . . . 254 A WINTER EDEN   . . .   13
    ITS TWO MOTE-SWIMMING MANY-COLORED ENDS . . . . . . 315 IRIS BY NIGHT   . . .   27
    ENDS . . . . 444 ENDS . . . . . .   T
ENDURE
    ENDURING WHAT THE UNGOLDEN MUST ENDURE. . . . . . . 358 THE LOST FOLLOWER . .   19
    HE THINKS THAT CHAIRS AND TABLES WILL ENDURE, ... 372 THE LITERATE FARMER AND 128
ENDURING
    ENDURING WHAT THE UNGOLDEN MUST ENDURE. . . . . . . 358 THE LOST FOLLOWER . .   19
ENEMIES
    OF ENEMIES DEFIED AND BATTLES FOUGHT. . . . . 356 TIME OUT   11
    I LIKE TO GIVE MY ENEMIES A TRUCE." . . . . 406 FROM PLANE TO PLANE   .   65
    WE SEND OUR WICKED ENEMIES TO HELL, ... 519 A MASQUE OF MERCY .   688
ENEMY
    AS ANY OTHER BOYHOOD ENEMY . . . . 190 THE GRINDSTONE . . .   43
ENFORCED
    BY HAVING WHAT IS FREE ENFORCED. . . . . 346 DISCOVERY OF MADEIRAS .   79
ENFORCING
    SWARM OVER THEIR LIVES ENFORCING BENEFITS . . . . . 287 A ROADSIDE STAND   .   28
ENGAGED
    ENGAGED UP THERE WITH THE LIGHT AND BREEZE? . . . . 247 ON GOING UNNOTICED . .   4
ENGAGEMENT
    JUST ENOUGH GOLD TO MAKE THE ENGAGEMENT RINGS . . . 162 NEW HAMPSHIRE   . .   113
    THAT WAS WHERE MY ENGAGEMENT WAS TO SPEAK . . . . . 497 A MASQUE OF MERCY .   94
ENGINE
    HIS HATE HAD ROUSED AN ENGINE UP THE ROAD. . . . . 270 THE EGG AND THE MACHINE   4
    SO AS TO WRECK THE ENGINE IN THE DITCH. . . . . . . 270 THE EGG AND THE MACHINE   8
    LOOKING THROUGH WREATHS OF ENGINE SMOKE . . . . . . 292 ON HEART'S BEGINNING TO 44
ENGINES
    THE MOST PRIMITIVE OF ENGINES . . . . 397 AN IMPORTER   23
ENGLAND
    NO LESS THAN ENGLAND, FRANCE, AND ITALY. . . . . . . 166 NEW HAMPSHIRE   . . .   245
    --THE NEW ENGLAND PRIMER . . . . 331 SYCAMORE   4

```
                                                    PAGE TITLE              LINE
ENGLAND (CONTINUED)
   ELIZABETH THE FIRST AND ENGLAND WON. . . . . . . . 422 FOR JOHN F. KENNEDY  .  18
ENGLAND'S
   BUT WE WERE ENGLAND'S, STILL COLONIALS, . . . . . . 348 THE GIFT OUTRIGHT  . .  5
   BUT WE WERE ENGLAND'S, STILL COLONIALS, . . . . . . 424 THE GIFT OUTRIGHT  . .  5
ENGLISH  (SEE FRENCH-ENGLISH)
   TO LEAVE THE ENGLISH LAW BEHIND . . . . . . . . . 344 DISCOVERY OF MADEIRAS .  16
   AND CHANGED IT TO THE ENGLISH NAME FOR WHEAT. . . . . 446 DOES NO ONE AT ALL EVER  8
ENJOINED
   YET WASN'T ENJOINED AND WASN'T EXPECTED, CLEARLY. . . . 306 NOT QUITE SOCIAL  . .  4
ENJOY
   "WE SHAN'T HAVE THE PLACE TO OURSELVES TO ENJOY-- . . .  62 BLUEBERRIES  . . . .  97
ENJOYED
   WE ENJOYED AT NIGHT . . . . . . . . . . . . 437 KITTY HAWK  . . . . 310
   WHERE HE WAS HOARDING MORE THAN THEY ENJOYED. . . . . 503 A MASQUE OF MERCY  . . 254
ENLIGHTENED
   BUT COME, ENLIGHTENED AS IN TALK YOU SEEM, . . . . . 370 THE LITERATE FARMER AND 61
ENNUI
   AGAINST THE DAY OF PRISONERS' ENNUI, . . . . . . . 293 AT WOODWARD'S GARDENS . 31
ENORMOUS
   THE HEARTLESS AND ENORMOUS OUTER BLACK   . . . . . . 361 A LOOSE MOUNTAIN  . . 17
   THE CHISEL WORK OF AN ENORMOUS GLACIER . . . . . . 377 DIRECTIVE . . . . . 16
   IT COST HER FOR ENORMOUS CAF. . . . . . . . . . 452 A-WISHING WELL  . . . 42
ENOUGH
   I HEAR HIM BEGIN FAR ENOUGH AWAY . . . . . . . .   6 GHOST HOUSE  . . . . 18
   WERE MUSIC ENOUGH FOR HIM, FOR ONE. . . . . . . .  24 PAN WITH US  . . . . 20
   ENOUGH AT LEAST TO BUY TOBACCO WITH, . . . . . . .  35 DEATH OF THE HIRED MAN 20
   "HE NEVER GOT UP HIGH ENOUGH TO SEE. . . . . . . .  43 THE MOUNTAIN . . . . 78
   YOU AND I KNOW ENOUGH TO KNOW IT'S WARM . . . . . .  44 THE MOUNTAIN . . . . 102
   'I CAN'T AND WON'T. YOU'VE BEEN IN LONG ENOUGH: . . .  48 A HUNDRED COLLARS  . 114
   SHE WOULDN'T HAVE BELIEVED THOSE ENDS ENOUGH . . . .  56 THE BLACK COTTAGE  . 58
   CLING TO IT LONG ENOUGH, AND NOT A DOUBT . . . . .  58 THE BLACK COTTAGE  . 107
   AND I WON'T ASK HIM--IT'S NOT SURE ENOUGH. . . . . .  67 A SERVANT TO SERVANTS . 158
   OR A LONG RAIN. I SHOULD SOON GET ENOUGH, . . . . .  67 A SERVANT TO SERVANTS . 164
   THERE'S WORK ENOUGH TO DO--THERE'S ALWAYS THAT; . . .  68 A SERVANT TO SERVANTS . 173
   I'D SEEN ABOUT ENOUGH OF HIS BULLING TRICKS . . . . .  71 THE CODE . . . . . 47
   I WENT ABOUT TO KILL HIM FAIR ENOUGH." . . . . . .  73 THE CODE . . . . . 112
   THEY WERE AT BOW, BUT THAT WAS NOT ENOUGH: . . . . .  73 THE GENERATIONS OF MEN 14
   "JUST SO--THAT OUGHT TO BE ENOUGH PROTECTION." . . . .  75 THE GENERATIONS OF MEN 66
   "THEN I DON'T KNOW. IT MUST BE STRANGE ENOUGH. . . . .  78 THE GENERATIONS OF MEN 139
   "NO, I DON'T TRUST YOUR EYES. YOU'VE SAID ENOUGH. . . .  80 THE GENERATIONS OF MEN 206
   "REASON ENOUGH, THERE WAS NO PROPERTY. . . . . . .  84 THE HOUSEKEEPER  . . 95
   "BUT IT'S NONSENSE TO THINK HE'D CARE ENOUGH." . . . .  91 THE FEAR . . . . . 49
   OH, BUT YOU SEE HE HADN'T HAD ENOUGH-- . . . . . .  91 THE FEAR . . . . . 51
   YOU'RE BAD ENOUGH TO MANAGE, WITHOUT HER." . . . . .  94 THE SELF-SEEKER  . . 55
   I SAID, "THERE AREN'T ENOUGH TO BE WORTH WHILE." . . . 106 CHRISTMAS TREES  . . 29
   COULD HANG ENOUGH ON TO PICK OFF ENOUGH. . . . . . 107 CHRISTMAS TREES  . . 54
   THAT END ALL. AND IT'S SCARCE ENOUGH TO CALL . . . . 111 IN THE HOME STRETCH  . 34
   THE CITY WORK TO DO. THERE'S NOT ENOUGH . . . . . . 114 IN THE HOME STRETCH  . 97
   WAS HOT ENOUGH FOR THE FIRST OF MAY, . . . . . . . 123 PEA BRUSH  . . . . 6
   BIRCH BOUGHS ENOUGH PILED EVERYWHERE!-- . . . . . . 123 PEA BRUSH  . . . . 13
   SHE HAD NO SAYING DARK ENOUGH . . . . . . . . . 128 THE OFT-REPEATED DREAM 1
   THERE WERE ENOUGH THINGS TO BE THOUGHT OF THEN. . . . 131 THE BONFIRE  . . . . 56
   IT WAS NOT ENOUGH OF A GARDEN, . . . . . . . . . 133 A GIRL'S GARDEN  . . 17
   SINCE HE WAS OLD ENOUGH TO KNOW, BIG BOY . . . . . 137 "OUT,OUT--"  . . . . 23
   AND HOPELESS GRIST ENOUGH IT LOOKS . . . . . . . 140 THE GUM-GATHERER  . . 16
   LONG ENOUGH FOR RECORDING ALL OUR NAMES ON.-- . . . . 143 SNOW . . . . . . 10
   WHY DID I CALL HIM THAT?" / "IT'S RIGHT ENOUGH. . . . 144 SNOW . . . . . . 45
   "CHRISTIAN ENOUGH I SHOULD CALL THAT MYSELF. . . . . 144 SNOW . . . . . . 48
   JUST ENOUGH GOLD TO MAKE THE ENGAGEMENT RINGS . . . . 162 NEW HAMPSHIRE  . . . 113
   BUT TRUST NEW HAMPSHIRE NOT TO HAVE ENOUGH . . . . . 163 NEW HAMPSHIRE  . . . 122
   MORE THAN ENOUGH LAND FOR A SPECIMEN . . . . . . . 163 NEW HAMPSHIRE  . . . 145
   IS THAT HER MOUNTAINS AREN'T QUITE HIGH ENOUGH. . . . 169 NEW HAMPSHIRE  . . . 311
   FIVE THOUSAND IS NO LONGER HIGH ENOUGH. . . . . . . 169 NEW HAMPSHIRE  . . . 334
   HER PEOPLE NOT QUITE SHORT ENOUGH FOR ART, . . . . . 170 NEW HAMPSHIRE  . . . 356
   THERE'S BEEN ENOUGH SHED WITHOUT SHEDDING MINE. . . . 170 NEW HAMPSHIRE  . . . 372
   FIGURATIVE ENOUGH TO SEE THE SYMBOL, . . . . . . . 184 MAPLE  . . . . . 154
   I DIDN'T KNOW HIM WELL ENOUGH TO KNOW . . . . . . . 185 THE AX-HELVE . . . . 14
   SO LONG AS HE WOULD LEAVE ENOUGH UNSAID, . . . . . 186 THE AX-HELVE . . . . 38
   AND LET ENOUGH LIGHT INTO IT BY CUTTING . . . . . . 194 PAUL'S WIFE  . . . . 89
   I WAS JUST COMING TO MYSELF ENOUGH . . . . . . . 203 THE WITCH OF COOS  . 44
   TOFFILE AGREED TO THAT, AND SURE ENOUGH, . . . . . 206 THE WITCH OF COOS  . 114
   BUT TONIGHT I DON'T CARE ENOUGH TO LIE-- . . . . . 207 THE WITCH OF COOS  . 148
   AND THAT'D BE ENOUGH TO LAST FOR DAYS. . . . . . . 208 PAUPER WITCH OF GRAFTON 41
   WELL, I SHOWED ARTHUR AMY SIGNS ENOUGH . . . . . . 210 PAUPER WITCH OF GRAFTON 89
   ENOUGH TO STOCK A VILLAGE LIBRARY-- . . . . . . . 216 A FOUNTAIN, A BOTTLE . 98
   I THINK I KNOW ENOUGH OF HATE . . . . . . . . . 220 FIRE AND ICE . . . . 6
   AND HELD IT LONG ENOUGH FOR NORTH . . . . . . . . 224 THE AIM WAS SONG . . 10
   THE HURT IS NOT ENOUGH: . . . . . . . . . . . 227 TO EARTHWARD . . . . 29
   SHE HAD TO ASK, "WHAT WAS IT, DEAR?" / "ENOUGH, . . . 230 NOT TO KEEP  . . . . 13
   YET NOT ENOUGH. A BULLET THROUGH AND THROUGH, . . . 230 NOT TO KEEP  . . . . 14
   BUY ME ENOUGH FOR A FULL-LENGTH CHIMNEY, . . . . . 232 THE KITCHEN CHIMNEY  7
   AND TRULY IT WAS FAIR ENOUGH FOR FLOWERS . . . . . 233 A BOUNDLESS MOMENT . 6
   THE MOON, THOUGH SLIGHT, WAS MOON ENOUGH TO SHOW . . . 234 EVENING A SUGAR ORCHARD 11
   THE TREES THEY'D HAD ENOUGH OF WITH ONCE TRYING . . . 239 OUR SINGING STRENGTH . 28
   HE FOUND SUSPICIOUS SAND, AND SURE ENOUGH, . . . . . 270 THE EGG AND THE MACHINE 22
   IF--IF HE STOOD! ENOUGH OF IFS! . . . . . . . . . 274 A LONE STRIKER . . . 42
   NO ONE WAS BRIGHT ENOUGH TO IDENTIFY; . . . . . . . 295 LOST IN HEAVEN . . . 7
   LEAVES AND BARK MAY BE TREE ENOUGH. . . . . . . . 297 LEAVES COMPARED WITH . 8
   THERE SURE ENOUGH WAS AN APPLE TREE . . . . . . . 304 UNHARVESTED  . . . . 4
   BUT IT WASN'T RANSOM ENOUGH. . . . . . . . . . 310 THE VINDICTIVES  . . 7
   WHAT SOON ENOUGH HE WOULD KNOW? . . . . . . . . . 314 BEARER OF EVIL TIDINGS 44
   IT IS JUST FOOL ENOUGH TO THINK ITSELF . . . . . . 319 BUILD SOIL  . . . . 119
   FAR ENOUGH FOR MY THOUGHT-FLOW TO RESUME. . . . . . 324 BUILD SOIL  . . . . 256
   ENOUGH TO MAKE A SPIRIT MOAN . . . . . . . . . 328 A MISSIVE MISSILE  . 39
   'TIS NOT ENOUGH ON ROOTS AND IN THE MOUTH, . . . . . 337 THE WIND AND THE RAIN . 37
   HE STAYED LONG ENOUGH TO CARVE ON STONE . . . . . . 347 DISCOVERY OF MADEIRAS . 121
   BUT THE MOOR STRANGELY ENOUGH BELIEVED . . . . . . 347 DISCOVERY OF MADEIRAS . 129
```

ENOUGH (CONTINUED)
   YOU WOULD NOT THINK YOU KNEW ENOUGH TO JUDGE . . . . . 351 THE LESSON FOR TODAY . 29
   WE KNOW ENOUGH TO KNOW IT FOR ADVERSE. . . . . . . 352 THE LESSON FOR TODAY . 45
   AND EVERY ACRE GOOD ENOUGH TO EAT, ... 365 OF STONES OF THE PLACE   7
   ENOUGH TO SEE IF HE WAS GREATLY MISSED. . . . . . . 368 THE LITERATE FARMER AND 18
   AND STILL IT'S BAD ENOUGH TO BADLY WOUND, ... 372 THE LITERATE FARMER AND 119
   AND IF YOU'RE LOST ENOUGH TO FIND YOURSELF . . . . . 378 DIRECTIVE 36
   AND LIKELY TO HAVE BEEN ENOUGH ALONE. . . . . . . 382 TO AN ANCIENT . . . 15
   OR AREN'T THE BONES ENOUGH I LIVE TC LIME? . . . . . 382 TO AN ANCIENT . . . 18
   AND ENOUGH DRINK OIL FOR ALL. . . . . 384 IN THE LONG NIGHT . . 12
   A THEORY IF YOU HOLD IT HARD ENOUGH . . . . 394 ETHEREALIZING . . . 1
   AND LONG ENOUGH GETS RATED AS A CREED: . . . . . . 394 ETHEREALIZING . . . 2
   OH, MAY THE TIDE BE SOON ENOUGH AT HIGH . . . . . . 395 ETHEREALIZING . . . 13
   STATES STRONG ENOUGH TO DO GOOD ARE BUT FEW. . . . . 398 NO HOLY WARS FOR THEM . 1
   DICK LONGED TO SAY, BUT WASN'T SURE ENOUGH . . . . . 407 FROM PLANE TO PLANE . 110
   SHALL I GO ON OR HAVE I SAID ENOUGH-- . . . . . . 408 FROM PLANE TO PLANE . 134
   KNOW WHERE THEY ARE. / THEY'VE BEEN HERE LONG ENOUGH . 413 A CABIN IN THE CLEARING 2
   HAD BUT COLUMBUS KNOWN ENOUGH . . . . 417 AMERICA IS HARD TO SEE 25
   THAT'S NEAR ENOUGH FOR ME TO THE DIVINE. . . . . . 425 ACCIDENTALLY ON PURPOSE 20
   THIS WORLD WERE GOOD ENOUGH FOR ME." . . . . 451 A-WISHING WELL . . . 5
   THE KING SAID TO HIS SON: "ENOUGH OF THIS! . . . . . 453 HOW HARD TO KEEP FROM 1
   SHOULD BE ENOUGH TO SET YOU UP IN BUSINESS-- . . . . 454 HOW HARD TO KEEP FROM 34
   UNLUCKILY IT WASN'T MONEY ENOUGH . . . . 459 HOW HARD TO KEEP FROM 177
   ONCE I WAS FOOL ENOUGH TO THINK . . . . 467 QUANDARY 20
   ENOUGH TO BUILD HIM EVERY NIGHT A PUP TENT . . . . . 478 A MASQUE OF REASON . 132
   OH, WE KNOW WELL ENOUGH TO GO AHEAD WITH. . . . . . 483 A MASQUE OF REASON . 289
   I MEAN WE SEEM TO KNOW ENOUGH TO ACT ON. . . . . . 483 A MASQUE OF REASON . 290
   I'D HAD ABOUT ENOUGH OF HIS DERISION . . . . 485 A MASQUE OF REASON . 349
   GOD, PLEASE, ENOUGH FOR NOW. I'M IN NO MOOD . . . . 486 A MASQUE OF REASON . 366
   THERE ARE WHO WON'T HAVE HAD ENOUGH OF YOU . . . . . 489 A MASQUE OF REASON . 438
   OPEN ENOUGH TO FIND OUT WHO IT IS. . . . . 493 A MASQUE OF MERCY . 12
   WE HAVE ENOUGH AGAINST IT, HAVEN'T WE? . . . . . . 496 A MASQUE OF MERCY . 66
   WHAT DON'T I UNDERSTAND? IT'S EASY ENOUGH. . . . . . 497 A MASQUE OF MERCY . 112
   NOW IF WE'VE HAD ENOUGH OF SACRILEGE, ... 507 A MASQUE OF MERCY . 358
   ENOUGH TO BAIT THE TRAP OF THE IDEAL . . . . 508 A MASQUE OF MERCY . 386
   WE'VE HAD ABOUT ENOUGH OF THESE SENSATIONS. . . . . 508 A MASQUE OF MERCY . 396
ENQUIRY (SEE ALSO INQUIRY)
   OF THE HIVE'S ENQUIRY SQUAD . . . . 288 DEPARTMENTAL 9
ENRAGED
   ENRAGED AT WHAT HE COULD BUT THINK OFFICIOUS, ... 394 HAEC FABULA DOCET . . 11
ENRICHING
   ENRICHING SOIL AND INCREASING STOCK, ... 367 A SERIOUS STEP LIGHTLY 19
ENSLAVE
   ENSLAVE YOURSELF TO THE RIGHT LEADER'S TRUTH, ... 460 HOW HARD TO KEEP FROM 191
ENTAIL
   IT MERELY WOULD ENTAIL THE PURGE . . . . 453 A-WISHING WELL . . . 72
ENTANGLEMENT
   AND ALDER AND GRAPE VINE ENTANGLEMENT, ... 131 THE BONFIRE 63
ENTENTE
   NO ESTIMATING HOW FAR THE ENTENTE . . . . 456 HOW HARD TO KEEP FROM 77
ENTER
   I ENTER ALONE UPON THE STUBBLE FIELD, ... 14 WAITING 3
   BUT DID NOT ENTER, THOUGH THE WISH WAS STRONG: . . . 16 A DREAM PANG . . . 5
   JOHN THREW THE DOOR WIDE BUT HE DIDN'T ENTER. . . . . 88 THE HOUSEKEEPER . . 205
   AND LEAVE YOU THERE, OURSELVES FORBID TO ENTER-- . . . 259 WEST-RUNNING BROOK . 35
   LATE, LATE, TOO LATE, YOU CANNOT ENTER NOW. . . . . 493 A MASQUE OF MERCY . 9
   THEN HE COULD ENTER ON THE STRICKEN FIELD . . . . . 507 A MASQUE OF MERCY . 365
   THEN HE COULD ENTER ON THE STRICKEN FIELD . . . . . 507 A MASQUE OF MERCY . 368
   WHO SAID, "TOO LATE, YOU CANNOT ENTER NOW"? . . . . 519 A MASQUE OF MERCY . 669
ENTERED
   AT THE LAST ONE OF WHICH HE KNOCKED AND ENTERED. . . . 45 A HUNDRED COLLARS . . 35
   AT ONE DOOR AS WE ENTERED AT ANOTHER. . . . . . . 89 THE FEAR 21
   WAS ENTERED, AND ITS INNER CRUST . . . . 332 ALL REVELATION . . 12
   AND ENTERED IN OUR CHILDISH CATECHISM . . . . . . 427 CONCEPT SELF-CONCEIVED 2
ENTERING
   (ENTERING HATLESS IN A WHIRL OF SNOW) . . . . . . 493 A MASQUE OF MERCY . 18
ENTERPRISE
   AS TREE BY ENTERPRISE AND EXPEDITION. . . . . . . 350 TO A YOUNG WRETCH . 11
ENTERS
   YOU'LL SAY SHE HAS, BUT THERE THERE ENTERS IN . . . . 163 NEW HAMPSHIRE . . . 146
   SPIRIT ENTERS FLESH . . . . 435 KITTY HAWK . . . 246
   (THE DEVIL ENTERS LIKE A SAPPHIRE WASP . . . . . . 487 A MASQUE OF REASON . 389
ENTERTAIN
   FOLKS ENTERTAIN ME FROM THE KITCHEN DOORSTEP, ... 49 A HUNDRED COLLARS . 147
   TO ENTERTAIN THE BIRDS AND HOLD THE FLOWERS. . . . . 216 A FOUNTAIN, A BOTTLE . 87
ENTERTAINED
   AND AFTER HAVING ENTERTAINED THE BEE, ... 283 THE GOLD HESPERIDEE . 3
ENTERTAINMENT
   NOR DID HE LACK FOR COMMON ENTERTAINMENT. . . . . . 292 FIGURE IN THE DOORWAY . 19
ENTIRELY
   TWO ENTIRELY DIFFERENT GRANDCHILDREN . . . . . . 294 A RECORD STRIDE . . 17
   OR ELSE I FEAR ENTIRELY MINE, ... 328 A MISSIVE MISSILE . 44
   NOT ENTIRELY WITHOUT CONSENT. . . . . 344 DISCOVERY OF MADEIRAS . 14
   MAY WELL HAVE NOTICED. SOON ENTIRELY WHITE . . . . . 375 A YOUNG BIRCH . . . 4
   IT WILL STAND FORTH, ENTIRELY WHITE IN BARK, ... 375 A YOUNG BIRCH . . . 6
   SO THAT THE MIND CAN BE ENTIRELY FREED. . . . . . 395 ETHEREALIZING . . . 4
   AND NOT ENTIRELY DISAPPROVED . . . . 469 CHOSEN POET OF VERMONT 3
   THESE OTHERS DON'T. / YOU DON'T YOURSELF ENTIRELY. . . 497 A MASQUE OF MERCY . 111
   I THINK I MAY HAVE GOT GOD WRONG ENTIRELY. . . . . 518 A MASQUE OF MERCY . 654
ENTRANCE
   THERE WAS NO ENTRANCE FOR THEM TO GET IN BY. . . . . 193 PAUL'S WIFE 85
ENTRIES
   IT HAS TWO ENTRIES FOR COEDUCATION. . . . . . . 400 TO THE RIGHT PERSON . 7
ENTRY
   OUTSIDE THERE IN THE ENTRY, FOR I SAW IT." . . . . 54 HOME BURIAL 88
ENVIED
   REMEMBER HOW YOU ENVIED GENERAL SHERMAN. . . . . . 406 FROM PLANE TO PLANE . 71

ENVIRONMENTALIST
    OR OTHERWISE AN ENVIRONMENTALIST. . . . . 166 NEW HAMPSHIRE . . . 233
ENVOI
    ENVOI TO HYDE THE CASTAWAY OF CROW ISLAND . . . . . 466 SOME SCIENCE FICTION . D
EOLITH
    AN EOLITH PALLADIUM TO GUARD . . . . 365 OF STONES OF THE PLACE 11
    YOU MADE THE EOLITH, YOU GREW THE BONE, ... 382 TO AN ANCIENT . . . 13
EPHEMERALS
    IN BEING SWEET TO THESE EPHEMERALS . . . . 412 POD OF THE MILKWEED . 30
EPICUREAN
    LUCRETIUS THE EPICUREAN MIGHT TELL US . . . . . . 380 TOO ANXIOUS FOR RIVERS 23
EPICURUS
    FOR I THOUGHT EPICURUS AND LUCRETIUS . . . . . . 393 LUCRETIUS VERSUS POETS 5
EPIDEMIC
    AS A BRIEF EPIDEMIC OF MICROBES . . . . 352 THE LESSON FOR TODAY . 70
EPITAPH
    AND TELL HIM I HAD READ HIS EPITAPH. . . . . . . 354 THE LESSON FOR TODAY . 126
    AND WERE AN EPITAPH TO BE MY STORY . . . . 355 THE LESSON FOR TODAY . 158
EPITHET
    WITH AN EPITHET, ... 438 KITTY HAWK 329
EQUAL
    THAT ALL MEN ARE CREATED FREE AND EQUAL. . . . . . 57 THE BLACK COTTAGE . . 61
    QUITE SOLITARY AND HAVING EQUAL BOUGHS . . . . . 107 CHRISTMAS TREES . . . 35
    FREE FROM THE LEAST KNOT, EQUAL TO THE STRAIN . . . 187 THE AX-HELVE . . . 70
    THAT PAUL HAD MARRIED A WIFE NOT HIS EQUAL. . . . . 192 PAUL'S WIFE 36
    THAT, THOUGH THEY NEVER EQUAL STARS IN SIZE . . . . 246 FIREFLIES IN THE GARDEN 3
    TWO INSTRUMENTS OF NEARLY EQUAL HOPE, ... 269 THE BEAR 20
    MY RIGHT TO BE EQUAL IN NUMBER OF CARDS, ... 310 IN DIVES' DIVE . . . 4
    WITH EQUAL DARKNESS, YOURS AS DARK AS MINE. . . . . 354 THE LESSON FOR TODAY . 119
    BY MAKING FAILURE OUT OF EQUAL VALUE. . . . . . . 513 A MASQUE OF MERCY . 526
EQUALITY
    AND THERE ON AN EQUALITY WE STOOD. . . . . 368 THE LITERATE FARMER AND 7
    SO IF THEY FOUGHT ABOUT EQUALITY . . . . 404 FROM PLANE TO PLANE . 5
    IT WAS ON AN EQUALITY THEY FOUGHT. . . . . . . 404 FROM PLANE TO PLANE . 6
    ANY EQUALITY THEY MAY EXHIBIT'S . . . . 513 A MASQUE OF MERCY . 527
EQUALIZER
    WE NOW AND THEN SHOULD TAKE AN EQUALIZER. . . . . . 363 AN EQUALIZER 8
    AN EQUALIZER . . . . 363 AN EQUALIZER . . . . T
EQUALLY
    AND BOTH THAT MORNING EQUALLY LAY . . . . 105 THE ROAD NOT TAKEN . 11
    EQUALLY WITH MY WEIGHT IN GRAPES, ONE AUTUMN, . . . 196 WILD GRAPES 5
    A BAGGY FIGURE, EQUALLY PATHETIC . . . . 269 THE BEAR 33
    EQUALLY FOR THE NATION'S CONSTITUTION). . . . . . 317 BUILD SOIL 47
    OF VISITING WITH THE EQUALLY BEWILDERED. . . . . . 414 A CABIN IN THE CLEARING 8
    EQUALLY PROFOUND . . . . 433 KITTY HAWK 180
    IN MAKING FOOLS OF PEOPLE EQUALLY. . . . . . . 513 A MASQUE OF MERCY . 528
EQUIVALENT
    HIMSELF HAD THE EQUIVALENT, ... 381 AN UNSTAMPED LETTER IN 31
ER
    ER, LET ME SEE. I THINK I'LL TAKE THE RIGHT. . . . . 96 THE SELF-SEEKER . . . 110
ERA
    BEFORE THE ERA OF COLONIZATION. . . . . 161 NEW HAMPSHIRE . . . 72
    CURSED BE THE ERA THAT CONGESTED IT. . . . . . . 496 A MASQUE OF MERCY . 67
ERE
    TO LISTEN ERE WE DARED TO LOOK, ... 18 GOING FOR WATER . . . 18
    IT WILL BE LONG ERE THE MARSHES RESUME, ... 25 NOW CLOSE THE WINDOWS . 5
    IT WILL BE LONG ERE THE EARLIEST BIRD: . . . . . 25 NOW CLOSE THE WINDOWS . 6
    AND GO ALONG WITH YOU ERE YOU LOSE SIGHT . . . . . 124 PUTTING IN THE SEED . 7
    I'VE KNOWN ERE NOW AN INTERFERING BRANCH . . . . . 185 THE AX-HELVE . . . 1
    WILL BE MORE LONELY ERE IT WILL BE LESS-- . . . . . 296 DESERT PLACES . . . 10
ERECT
    JUST THEN, I THOUGHT. IT'S STOOD ERECT LIKE THAT, . . 147 SNOW 117
    ERECT, BUT NOT WITHOUT ITS WAVES, AS WHEN . . . . . 188 THE AX-HELVE . . . 96
    TRANSFIXED ON MOUNTAIN SLOPES ALMOST ERECT. . . . . 237 A HILLSIDE THAW . . . 28
EREMITE
    AND STEADFAST AS KEATS' EREMITE, ... 403 SOMETHING LIKE A STAR . 18
ERR
    (NINE TIMES REMOVED. CORRECT ME IF I ERR.) . . . . 79 THE GENERATIONS OF MEN 178
    TO ERR IS HUMAN, NOT TO, ANIMAL. . . . . 279 THE WHITE-TAILED HORNET 52
    BUT SO IS HISTORY LIKE TO ERR. . . . . 347 DISCOVERY OF MADEIRAS 136
ERRAND
    NO MATTER IF I HAVE NO ERRAND THERE. . . . . . . 49 A HUNDRED COLLARS . . 144
    I CAME AN ERRAND ONE CLOUD-BLOWING EVENING . . . . 174 THE CENSUS-TAKER . . 1
    GIVES UP HIS ERRAND, AND LETS DEATH DESCEND . . . . 226 THE ONSET 8
    AN ERRAND HE MAY HAVE HAD TO INVENT, ... 364 TRESPASS 19
ERRANDS
    THEN TURNED HIM OUT TO GO ON OTHER ERRANDS . . . . 201 PLACE FOR A THIRD . . 53
ERRED
    SURE SHE HASN'T ERRED . . . . 442 KITTY HAWK 452
ESCALATOR
    IN THREE QUICK STEPS AS OFF AN ESCALATOR. . . . . . 489 A MASQUE OF REASON . 452
ESCAPE
    THE NEAREST BOUNDARY TO ESCAPE ACROSS. . . . . . 167 NEW HAMPSHIRE . . . 253
    IN CHRISTMAS GIVING, SO THEY CAN ESCAPE . . . . . 408 FROM PLANE TO PLANE . 139
    ESCAPE FROM SO GREAT PAINS OF LIFE ON EARTH . . . . 475 A MASQUE OF REASON . 43
    WHERE DO THESE SENILE RUNAWAYS ESCAPE FROM? . . . . 493 A MASQUE OF MERCY . 15
    FROM WHICH THERE CAN BE NO ESCAPE FOR US . . . . . 508 A MASQUE OF MERCY . 387
    LIGHTS OUT, I SAY, SO'S TO ESCAPE ATTENTION. . . . . 508 A MASQUE OF MERCY . 392
    YOUR FUGITIVE ESCAPE BECOME A QUEST. . . . . . . 513 A MASQUE OF MERCY . 535
ESCAPED
    THAT WHEN IT THINKS IT HAS ESCAPED THE FOX . . . . 198 WILD GRAPES 64
    HOW HAD THE TENDER VERSE ESCAPED THEIR OUTRAGE? . . . 216 A FOUNTAIN, A BOTTLE . 105
    HE IS NO FUGITIVE--ESCAPED, ESCAPING. . . . . . . 421 ESCAPIST--NEVER . . 1
    I NEEDN'T THINK I HAVE ESCAPED MY DUTY. . . . . . 454 HOW HARD TO KEEP FROM 19
ESCAPES
    HE BESTOWS SUMMER ON US AND ESCAPES . . . . . . 408 FROM PLANE TO PLANE . 127
ESCAPING
    HE IS NO FUGITIVE--ESCAPED, ESCAPING. . . . . . . 421 ESCAPIST--NEVER . . . 1

	PAGE TITLE	LINE

ESCAPIST
    ESCAPIST--NEVER . . . . 421 ESCAPIST--NEVER . . . T
    ESCAPIST, AS WE SAY--THOUGH YOU ARE NOT . . . . . . 498 A MASQUE OF MERCY . 138
ESPECIAL
    WHICH GOD MAKES HIS ESPECIAL CARE. . . . . 20 THE TRIAL BY EXISTENCE 32
    AND THAT FROM NO ESPECIAL BUSH'S HEIGHT, ... 302 A BIRD SINGING IN SLEEP 4
ESPECIALLY
    BUT WORK! THAT MAN COULD WORK, ESPECIALLY . . . . . 70 THE CODE . . . 36
    ESPECIALLY IN WINTER WHEN THE BED . . . . 203 THE WITCH OF COOS . . 38
    IN PEACE AND WAR--ESPECIALLY IN WAR. . . . . 481 A MASQUE OF REASON . 214
ESQUIMAUX
    MY FRENCH INDIAN ESQUIMAUX, ... 211 AN EMPTY THREAT . . 27
    THE ESQUIMAUX SHOULD CALL, ... 384 IN THE LONG NIGHT . . 10
ESSAY
    TO FIND 'TWAS THE EFFORT, THE ESSAY OF LOVE. . . . . 380 TOO ANXIOUS FOR RIVERS 26
ESSENCE
    'TIS OF THE ESSENCE OF LIFE HERE, ... 21 THE TRIAL BY EXISTENCE 65
    ESSENCE OF WINTER SLEEP IS ON THE NIGHT, ... 68 AFTER APPLE-PICKING . 7
    BUT WASTE WAS OF THE ESSENCE OF THE SCHEME. . . . . 412 POD OF THE MILKWEED . 40
    BUT IT WAS OF THE ESSENCE OF THE TRIAL . . . . . 475 A MASQUE OF REASON . . 62
ESTABLISH
    ESTABLISH ONCE FOR ALL THE PRINCIPLE . . . . . . 475 A MASQUE OF REASON . . 49
ESTABLISHED
    ESTABLISHED A ROYAL LINE, ... 314 BEARER OF EVIL TIDINGS 30
    THUS TRUTH'S ESTABLISHED AND BORNE OUT, ... 331 BEECH . . . 10
    WITH WHAT YOU SAY WE HAVE ESTABLISHED, ... 480 A MASQUE OF REASON . 184
ESTABLISHING
    ESTABLISHING ON THE MOON. . . . . 466 SOME SCIENCE FICTION . 24
ESTATE
    OR GIVING ME A NOBLEMAN'S ESTATE. . . . . 457 HOW HARD TO KEEP FROM 121
ESTELLE
    WHAT HE HAS GOT TO STAND." / "WHERE IS ESTELLE? . . . 83 THE HOUSEKEEPER . . . 71
    "I MEAN ESTELLE HAS ALWAYS HELD THE PURSE." . . . . 84 THE HOUSEKEEPER . . . 98
    I GUESS ESTELLE AND I HAVE FILLED THE PURSE. . . . . 84 THE HOUSEKEEPER . . . 100
    ESTELLE TO DO THE HOUSEWORK FOR THE BOARD . . . . 85 THE HOUSEKEEPER . . . 105
    BUT ESTELLE DON'T COMPLAIN: SHE'S LIKE HIM THERE. . . . 85 THE HOUSEKEEPER . . . 117
    YOU'LL BE EXPECTING JOHN. I PITY ESTELLE; . . . . 88 THE HOUSEKEEPER . . . 191
ESTELLE'S
    IT'S GONE SO FAR. YOU'VE HEARD? ESTELLE'S RUN OFF." . . 82 THE HOUSEKEEPER . . . 20
    ESTELLE'S TO TAKE ME WHEN SHE'S SETTLED DOWN. . . . . 82 THE HOUSEKEEPER . . . 35
    "ESTELLE'S THE ONE. YOU NEEDN'T TALK TO ME." . . . . 87 THE HOUSEKEEPER . . . 164
ESTIMATE
    AS IF THE FINAL ESTIMATE WERE HERS; . . . . 301 MOON COMPASSES . . . 5
ESTIMATING
    NO ESTIMATING HOW FAR THE ENTENTE . . . . 456 HOW HARD TO KEEP FROM 77
ESTIMATION
    AND THEY IN THE ESTIMATION OF THE WISE . . . . . 370 THE LITERATE FARMER AND 76
    THIS SIDE THE ROCKIES IN MY ESTIMATION-- . . . . . 400 TO THE RIGHT PERSON . 5
E.T.
    TO E.T. . . . . 222 TO E.T. . . . . . T
ETA
    IS NEITHER ALPHA, ETA, NOR OMEGA, ... 388 IOTA SUBSCRIPT . . . 7
ETERNAL
    BECAUSE THE DEEPER FEAR IS SO ETERNAL. . . . . . . 521 A MASQUE OF MERCY . . 732
ETERNITY
    TO MAKE THE VENTURE OF ETERNITY . . . . 356 A MOTH SEEN IN WINTER . 8
    WHAT IF IT SHOULD TURN OUT ETERNITY . . . . . . 386 A STEEPLE ON THE HOUSE 1
    TO LAST A FELLOW TO ETERNITY . . . . 475 A MASQUE OF REASON . 45
    WHICH IS THE SYMBOL OF ETERNITY . . . . 485 A MASQUE OF REASON . 341
ETHER
    THE DOCTOR PUT HIM IN THE DARK OF ETHER. . . . . . 137 "OUT, OUT--" . . . 28
ETHEREAL
    OF THE SOUL'S ETHEREAL . . . . 436 KITTY HAWK 256
ETHEREALIZING
    ETHEREALIZING . . . . 394 ETHEREALIZING . . . T
ETOOKASHOO
    IF ETOOKASHOO AND COULDLOOKTOO . . . . 384 IN THE LONG NIGHT . . 9
EUNUCH
    THE EUNUCH LAUGHED: "WELL, THAT'S A LOT TO KNOW. . . . 455 HOW HARD TO KEEP FROM 45
EUROPE
    WHERE ASIA WEDGES AFRICA FROM EUROPE. . . . . . . 176 THE CENSUS-TAKER . 53
    YOU COULD LOSE ASIA, AFRICA, AND EUROPE, ... 457 HOW HARD TO KEEP FROM 128
EURYDICE
    AND WAS COME AFTER LIKE EURYDICE . . . . . . 196 WILD GRAPES . . . 12
EVADE
    AND THAT'S A FATE IT CAN'T EVADE . . . . . . 450 OUR DOOM TO BLOOM . 15
EVASION
    BUT THE SILLIEST EVASION . . . . 397 AN IMPORTER 15
    BUT HERE'S WHERE YOUR EVASION HAS AN END. . . . . 498 A MASQUE OF MERCY . 142
EVASIVE
    AN EYE BECOME EVASIVE. . . . . 340 THE SUBVERTED FLOWER . 47
EVE
    A STRANGER CAME TO THE DOOR AT EVE, ... 7 LOVE AND A QUESTION . 1
    BECAUSE THE AUTUMN EVE WAS FAIR . . . . 18 GOING FOR WATER . . 6
    AT TEN O'CLOCK OF A WINTER EVE. . . . . 102 GOOD HOURS 16
    WITH HER FOR MOTHER EVE, A RACE . . . . 280 BLUE RIBBON AT AMESBURY 27
    TO FINISH CLEAR AT EVE. . . . . 333 HAPPINESS MAKES UP . 17
    FROM HAVING HEARD THE DAYLONG VOICE OF EVE . . . . 338 NEVER WOULD BIRDS' SONG 3
    LIKE ADAM AND EVE . . . . 413 AWAY! 11
    LINES WRITTEN IN DEJECTION ON THE EVE OF GREAT SUCCESS . 462 LINES IN DEJECTION . . T
EVEN
    TILL EVEN THE COMFORTING BARN GROWS FAR AWAY, . . . 10 STORM FEAR . . . 15
    EVEN THE BRAVEST THAT ARE SLAIN . . . . . . 19 THE TRIAL BY EXISTENCE 1
    EVEN AS ON EARTH, IN PARADISE; . . . . . . 19 THE TRIAL BY EXISTENCE 4
    AND MAKES GAPS EVEN TWO CAN PASS ABREAST. . . . . 33 MENDING WALL . . . 4
    THEY'LL BE THERE TOMORROW, OR EVEN TONIGHT. . . . . 62 BLUEBERRIES . . . 99
    IT'S GOT SO I DON'T EVEN KNOW FOR SURE . . . . . 63 A SERVANT TO SERVANTS 11
    HE'D TEAR TO PIECES, EVEN A BED TO LIE ON. . . . . 66 A SERVANT TO SERVANTS . 118

EVEN (CONTINUED)
    THAT'S SURE TO BE RIGHT, EVEN IF IT'S WRONG. . . . . . 96 THE SELF-SEEKER . . . 111
    OR EVEN LAST YEAR'S OR THE YEAR'S BEFORE. . . . . . . 101 THE WOOD-PILE 28
    A QUIET LIGHT, AND THEN NOT EVEN THAT. . . . . . . 108 OLD MAN'S WINTER NIGHT 17
    AND, IF YOU ASKED ME, EVEN HELP PRETEND . . . . . . 109 THE EXPOSED NEST . . . 7
    EVEN WORSE STILL, AND SO ON DOWN, DOWN, DOWN. . . . 115 IN THE HOME STRETCH . 129
    EVEN AGAINST THE WAY ITS WATERS WENT. . . . . . . 119 HYLA BROOK 9
    UP TO THE BRIM, AND EVEN ABOVE THE BRIM. . . . . . 122 BIRCHES 38
    AND EVEN FRUIT TREES. . . . . 134 A GIRL'S GARDEN . . . 32
    OR EVEN THOUGHT OF STANDING THERE . . . . 139 BROWN'S DESCENT . . . 57
    THAT JANGLED EVEN ABOVE THE GENERAL NOISE, ... 142 THE VANISHING RED . . 25
    HE DIDN'T EVEN OFFER ME A DRINK . . . . 160 NEW HAMPSHIRE . . . 31
    AND BEFORE THAT OF EXPLORATION EVEN. . . . . . . 161 NEW HAMPSHIRE . . . 73
    NOT EVEN NEW HAMPSHIRE FARMS ARE MUCH FOR SALE. . . . 163 NEW HAMPSHIRE . . . 149
    OR EVEN NATION'S TO RESTRICT MY MEANING. . . . . . 166 NEW HAMPSHIRE . . . 231
    EVEN TO SAY THE GROVES WERE GOD'S FIRST TEMPLES . . . . 171 NEW HAMPSHIRE . . . 392
    SUCH AS EVEN POETS WOULD ADMIT PERFORCE . . . . . 173 A STAR IN A STONEBOAT . 28
    UNSCORCHED, UNBLACKENED, EVEN, BY ANY SMOKE. . . . . 184 MAPLE 142
    THESE HANDS HAVE HELPED IT GO, AND EVEN RACE; . . . . 188 THE GRINDSTONE . . . 4
    THE SCORE WAS EVEN FOR THEM, THREE TO THREE. . . . . 199 PLACE FOR A THIRD . . 3
    THAT EVEN I WOULD BE. THEY OUGHT TO KNOW . . . . . 208 PAUPER WITCH OF GRAFTON 39
    HOW OVER, THOUGH, FOR EVEN HE WHO KNEW . . . . . . 222 TO E.T. 17
    I DOUBT IF EVEN HIS MOTHER COULD TELL HIM, 'SAKES, . . . 223 THE RUNAWAY 12
    NOT EVEN MISSING THE CORALROOT FLOWER . . . . . . 247 ON GOING UNNOTICED . . 15
    MAKE HER AMONG THE HUMBLEST EVEN . . . . 257 THE LOVELY BE CHOOSERS 39
    AND EVEN SUBSTANCE LAPSING UNSUBSTANTIAL; . . . . . 259 WEST-RUNNING BROOK . 55
    OR EVEN MERELY SEEMED TO PINE . . . . 275 A LONE STRIKER . . . 60
    HERE HE IS AT HIS BEST, BUT EVEN HERE-- . . . . . 278 THE WHITE-TAILED HORNET 32
    REFLECTED IN THE MUD AND EVEN DUST. . . . . . . 279 THE WHITE-TAILED HORNET 65
    AND THIS DAY'S WORK MADE EVEN THAT SEEM DOUBTFUL. . . . 279 THE WHITE-TAILED HORNET 70
    OR EVEN ANOTHER YEAR, ... 282 A DRUMLIN WOODCHUCK . 27
    SEEMS NOT EVEN IMPRESSED. . . . . 288 DEPARTMENTAL 17
    BUT NOW LIVE EVEN TOGETHER. . . . . 294 A RECORD STRIDE . . . 8
    BUT EVEN AT THE WORD . . . . 298 ON TAKING FROM THE TOP 9
    EVEN WHILE WE TALK SOME CHEMIST AT COLUMBIA . . . . 319 BUILD SOIL 107
    AND EVEN SUBSOIL AND HARDPAN TO MARKET. . . . . . 321 BUILD SOIL 178
    NOT EVEN THAT, IT'S ONLY ROCKING, ... 325 TO A THINKER 6
    I MEANT NOT EVEN IF ASKED, ... 334 COME IN 19
    FOR SLOWLY EVEN HER SENSE OF HIM . . . . 347 DISCOVERY OF MADEIRAS 116
    BUT EVEN WHERE, THUS, OPPOSING INTERESTS KILL, ... 350 TO A YOUNG WRETCH . . 14
    EVEN IN A PLAYFUL MOMENT TO CONTEND . . . . . . 359 THE LOST FOLLOWER . . 26
    OR EVEN BETTER GODLIKE IN YOURSELF. . . . . . . 359 THE LOST FOLLOWER . . 32
    BUT WELL MAY BE LACONIC, EVEN BOEOTIAN. . . . . . 362 BOEOTIAN 3
    ONLY A FEW OF THOSE EVEN IN WHOSE DAY . . . . . . 397 THE PLANNERS 7
    NOT EVEN THE INGENUITIES OF DEBT . . . . 399 THE INGENUITIES OF DEBT 11
    NOT EVEN STOOPING FROM ITS SPHERE, ... 403 SOMETHING LIKE A STAR . 19
    AND EVEN HE, YOU'LL NOTICE, DODGES OFF . . . . . . 408 FROM PLANE TO PLANE . 141
    TILL EVEN I HAVE CEASED . . . . 416 CLOSED FOR GOOD . . . 26
    I MIGHT EVEN CLAIM, HE WAS SIRIUS . . . . 421 ONE MORE BREVITY . . . 58
    AND EVEN THEN IT HAD TO GROPE AND BUNGLE, ... 425 ACCIDENTALLY ON PURPOSE 8
    EVEN MORE ACCURSED . . . . 430 KITTY HAWK 76
    EVEN AT A WALK. . . . . 439 KITTY HAWK 349
    THE KING SAID GRANDLY, "EVEN AS WE ARE FED . . . . 455 HOW HARD TO KEEP FROM 63
    OR EVEN THE SPEED OF LIGHT . . . . 466 SOME SCIENCE FICTION . 19
    I HAVE A QUESTION EVEN THERE TO ASK-- . . . . . . 479 A MASQUE OF REASON . 171
    THE FUTURE STATE IS SPRINGING EVEN NOW . . . . . . 506 A MASQUE OF MERCY . . 320
    THERE IS SOME JUSTICE, EVEN AS KEEPER SAYS. . . . . 509 A MASQUE OF MERCY . . 429
    NOT EVEN BRACKISH FROM ITS SALT EXPERIENCE. . . . . 514 A MASQUE OF MERCY . . 542
    IF EVEN THE FACE OF MAN'S TOO BRIGHT A LIGHT . . . . 515 A MASQUE OF MERCY . . 583
    EVEN BEFORE I CAME IN HERE TONIGHT. . . . . . . 517 A MASQUE OF MERCY . . 626
EVENING
    I HAD FOR MY WINTER EVENING WALK-- . . . . 102 GOOD HOURS 1
    LIKE WINTER AND EVENING COMING ON TOGETHER. . . . . 131 THE BONFIRE 55
    OFF HIS. THE TIME WAS EVENING IN THE PULLMAN. . . . 159 NEW HAMPSHIRE . . . 14
    I CAME AN ERRAND ONE CLOUD-BLOWING EVENING . . . . 174 THE CENSUS-TAKER . . 1
    AS ON A FARM, BUT PLANETS, EVENING STARS . . . . . 178 THE STAR-SPLITTER . . 72
    SO AFTER WORK THAT EVENING HE CAME BACK . . . . . 194 PAUL'S WIFE 88
    NEXT EVENING MURPHY AND SOME OTHER FELLOWS . . . . 195 PAUL'S WIFE 123
    SHE COULD CALL UP TO PASS A WINTER EVENING, ... 202 THE WITCH OF COOS . . 5
    THE DARKEST EVENING OF THE YEAR. . . . . 224 STOPPING BY WOODS . . 8
    STOPPING BY WOODS ON A SNOWY EVENING . . . . . . 224 STOPPING BY WOODS . . T
    EVENING IN A SUGAR ORCHARD . . . . 234 EVENING A SUGAR ORCHARD T
    BY WALKING SLOWLY ON SOME EVENING LATER . . . . . 245 THE FREEDOM OF THE MOON 8
    THAT SPREADING IN THE EVENING AIR BOTH WAYS . . . . 247 THE COCOON 2
    SO MUCH AS TO TAKE CARE OF EVENING CHORES. . . . . 248 THE COCOON 10
    ONE MISTY EVENING, ONE ANOTHER'S GUIDE, ... 315 IRIS BY NIGHT . . . 1
    ...RECENTLY OBSERVED IN THE WESTERN SKY AT EVENING . . 368 THE LITERATE FARMER AND S
    THE OTHER EVENING AT YOUR COLLEGE DEANERY. . . . . 393 LUCRETIUS VERSUS POETS 3
    CAUGHT COLOR FROM THE LAST OF EVENING RED . . . . . 445 QUESTIONING FACES . . 4
EVENSONG
    BUT TO THE EVENSONG, AND HAVING PLAYED . . . . . 489 A MASQUE OF REASON . 436
EVENT
    LET'S CELEBRATE THE EVENT, MY DISTANT FRIEND, ... 352 THE LESSON FOR TODAY . 47
    TO HAVE RUN THE EVENT . . . . 437 KITTY HAWK 300
EVENTS
    OF FRONT-PAGE PAPER EVENTS, ... 367 A SERIOUS STEP LIGHTLY 22
    SHOULD AT ALL EVENTS . . . . 432 KITTY HAWK 122
    YOU GO TO SLEEP. GOD MUST AWAIT EVENTS, ... 478 A MASQUE OF REASON . 147
EVER
    FEARLESS OF EVER FINDING OPEN LAND, ... 5 INTO MY OWN 7
    WITH NONE AMONG THEM THAT EVER SINGS, ... 6 GHOST HOUSE 28
    WAS IT EVER LESS THAN A TREASON . . . . 30 RELUCTANCE 20
    "WHEN WAS I EVER ANYTHING BUT KIND TO HIM? . . . . 34 DEATH OF THE HIRED MAN 11
    WHICH SHOWED HOW MUCH GOOD SCHOOL HAD EVER DONE HIM. . . 37 DEATH OF THE HIRED MAN 84
    "I CAN'T THINK SI EVER HURT ANYONE." . . . . . . 39 DEATH OF THE HIRED MAN 146
    BUT IT'S AS MUCH AS EVER YOU CAN DO, ... 43 THE MOUNTAIN 94
    "YOU'VE LIVED HERE ALL YOUR LIFE?" / "EVER SINCE HOR . . 44 THE MOUNTAIN 105
    "I SHALL LAUGH THE WORST LAUGH I EVER LAUGHED. . . . 54 HOME BURIAL 89

                                                PAGE TITLE   LINE
EVER (CONTINUED)
    SINCE SHE WENT, MORE THAN EVER, BUT BEFORE-- . . . . . 56 THE BLACK COTTAGE . . 36
    WHITE WAS THE ONLY RACE SHE EVER KNEW. . . . . 57 THE BLACK COTTAGE . . 75
    NOT THAT SHE EVER HAD TO ASK ME NOT TO; . . . . 57 THE BLACK COTTAGE . . 89
    DID EVER YOU FEEL SO? I HOPE YOU NEVER. . . . . 63 A SERVANT TO SERVANTS . 10
    NO ONE WILL EVER LIVE ON IT AGAIN. . . . . 83 THE HOUSEKEEPER . . . 49
    WHETHER HE'S EVER GOING TO WALK AGAIN. . . . . 100 THE SELF-SEEKER . . . 202
    I DOUBTED IF I SHOULD EVER COME BACK. . . . . 105 THE ROAD NOT TAKEN . . 15
    OF EVER COMING TO THE PLACE AGAIN . . . . 110 THE EXPOSED NEST . . . 34
    IF I EVER READ IT. . . . . 110 A PATCH OF OLD SNOW . . 8
    WILL EVER SLAM THE DOORS." / "I THINK YOU SEE . . . . 112 IN THE HOME STRETCH . . 44
    AND SORRY I EVER LEFT THE ROAD I KNEW, ... 125 AN ENCOUNTER 7
    IF THAT IS WHAT THE MOUNTAIN EVER WAS-- . . . . 130 THE BONFIRE 17
    I WON! BUT I'M SURE NO ONE EVER SPREAD . . . . 132 THE BONFIRE 81
    DON'T THINK BROWN EVER GAVE UP HOPE . . . . 139 BROWN'S DESCENT . . 54
    EVER TO GRIND TO SOIL FOR GRASS. . . . . 140 THE GUM-GATHERER . . 17
    THAT'S ALL YOU EVER HEARD HIM CALLED ROUND HERE. . . 144 SNOW 46
    ALL'S EVER I HEARD OF IT, WHICH ISN'T MUCH. . . . . 144 SNOW 54
    THERE ON THE TABLE, EVER SINCE I CAME, ... 147 SNOW 118
    EVER PRESENTS ITSELF BEFORE US TWICE. . . . . 147 SNOW 130
    "WAS EVER SUCH A MAN FOR SEEING LIKENESS?" . . . . . 151 SNOW 250
    "WHY DID I EVER LET HIM LEAVE THIS HOUSE!" . . . . . 153 SNOW 280
    DO YOU KNOW WHAT SHE'S LIKE? HAVE YOU EVER MET HER? . 154 SNOW 313
    WHAT'LL YOU BET HE EVER CALLS AGAIN?" . . . . . . 156 SNOW 350
    "NONE OF MY FAMILY EVER WORKED, OR HAD . . . . . . 159 NEW HAMPSHIRE . . 3
    HE SAID, IN CLIMATE, NONE HAD EVER DIED THERE . . . 159 NEW HAMPSHIRE . . 18
    I EVER STUMBLED ON IN OLD NEW HAMPSHIRE . . . . . 160 NEW HAMPSHIRE . . 36
    THE DANIEL WEBSTER EVER WAS OR SHALL BE. . . . . . 161 NEW HAMPSHIRE . . 68
    (THE ONLY OTHER WITCH I EVER MET . . . . 163 NEW HAMPSHIRE . . 126
    SAID SOME OF THE BEST THINGS WE EVER SAID. . . . . 179 THE STAR-SPLITTER . . 86
    IT'S A STAR-SPLITTER IF THERE EVER WAS ONE, ... 179 THE STAR-SPLITTER . . 92
    HOW DIFFERENT FROM THE WAY IT EVER STOOD? . . . . . 179 THE STAR-SPLITTER . . 99
    NOT ALL THE MOTION, THOUGH, THEY EVER LENT, ... 188 THE GRINDSTONE . . 5
    EVER SINCE, JUST TO SHOW THEM, HE HAD SLIPPED . . . 191 PAUL'S WIFE . . . 18
    "FIRST TIME I EVER SAW A HOLLOW PINE. . . . . . . 193 PAUL'S WIFE . . . 75
    EVER TO HAVE HOUSED BIRDS OR BEASTS OR BEES. . . . 193 PAUL'S WIFE . . . 84
    UP ATTIC THAT WE'D EVER WANT AGAIN. . . . . . . 206 THE WITCH OF COOS . . 122
    I DON'T REMEMBER WHY I EVER CARED. . . . . 207 THE WITCH OF COOS . . 149
    COULD TELL YOU WHY HE EVER CARED HIMSELF.... . . . 207 THE WITCH OF COOS . . 151
    VOTED THE ONLY TIMES HE EVER VOTED, ... 208 PAUPER WITCH OF GRAFTON 21
    AND ALL FOR NOTHING IT HAD EVER DONE, ... 231 A BROOK IN THE CITY . . 18
    SINCE EVER THEY FLUNG ABROAD IN SPRING . . . . . 236 MISGIVING 5
    WITH AN EVER VAGUER AND VAGUER STIR, ... 236 MISGIVING 10
    THAT NO ONE ON EARTH WILL EVER FIND? . . . . . 248 A PASSING GLIMPSE . . 10
    EVER SINCE RIVERS, I WAS GOING TO SAY, ... 258 WEST-RUNNING BROOK . . 28
    WAS THERE EVER A CAUSE TOO LOST, ... 262 HANNIBAL 1
    EVER A CAUSE THAT WAS LOST TOO LONG, ... 262 HANNIBAL 2
    AS EVER SHE TURNED HER HOME WITH COD . . . . . 262 THE FLOWER BOAT . . 7
    FURTHER THAN TARGET EVER SHOWED OR SHONE. . . . 262 A SOLDIER 14
    THE SAYING MAY BE EVER SO TRUE; . . . . 263 THE TIMES TABLE . . 13
    THAN THERE WAS EVER ANY HOPE, ... 264 THE BIRTHPLACE . . 2
    BUT NOTHING EVER HAPPENS, NO HARM IS DONE. . . 268 ON LOOKING UP BY CHANCE 7
    IF THERE SHOULD EVER COME A DAY . . . . 274 A LONE STRIKER . . 57
    IS THE DEED EVER REALLY DONE . . . . 277 TWO TRAMPS IN MUD TIME 71
    OR IF EVER ASIDE A MOMENT, THEN OUT OF SORTS . 286 A ROADSIDE STAND . . 8
    A TREE'S LEAVES MAY BE EVER SO GOOD, ... 296 LEAVES COMPARED WITH . 1
    EVER TO HAVE TREE BLOOM OR BEAR. . . . . . . 296 LEAVES COMPARED WITH . 6
    BUT WHEN WAS THAT EVER A BAR . . . . 301 NEITHER OUT FAR NOR IN 15
    I WOULD NOT BE TAKEN AS EVER HAVING REBELLED. . 306 NOT QUITE SOCIAL . . 12
    NOBODY WAS EVER MEANT . . . . 309 HARDSHIP OF ACCOUNTING 3
    OUR EVER GETTING INSIDE IN AGAIN. . . . . . 320 BUILD SOIL 140
    THAT NONE SHALL EVER SEE YOU COME TO MARKET-- . 323 BUILD SOIL 213
    AND NOTHING EVER CAME OF WHAT HE CRIED . . . 338 THE MOST OF IT . . 9
    AS THE LIVING EVER GO YET STAY. . . . . . . 346 DISCOVERY OF MADEIRAS . 104
    BUT NO ONE EVER HEARD YOU MAKE THE CLAIM. . . 351 THE LESSON FOR TODAY . 28
    AS EVER WHEN PHILOSOPHERS ARE MET, ... 354 THE LESSON FOR TODAY . 107
    NO ONE HAS EVER FAILED THE POET RANKS . . . . 358 THE LOST FOLLOWER . . 7
    THAT NO ECONOMIST WAS EVER WISER . . . . . . 363 AN EQUALIZER 2
    THE MOST EFFICIENT HELP YOU EVER HIRED . . . 375 A YOUNG BIRCH . . . 17
    THE LARGEST FIREDROP EVER FORMED . . . . . . 381 AN UNSTAMPED LETTER IN 25
    NOR NEED WE EVER GO UP THERE TO LIVE. . . . 386 A STEEPLE ON THE HOUSE 6
    WITH THEIR EVER BREAKING NEWNESS . . . . . . 387 THE COURAGE TO BE NEW . 15
    CAN EVER GIVE US IS A NUISANCE BRAWL. . . . 398 NO HOLY WARS FOR THEM . 14
    WHAT FOR THAT MATTER HAD IT EVER BEEN? . . . 400 THE BROKEN DROUGHT . . 13
    THEY EVER WILL RETURN TO ALL THEIR LIVES, . . 411 POD OF THE MILKWEED . 3
    AS ANYONE WHO EVER BROKE ITS STEM . . . . . 411 POD OF THE MILKWEED . 17
    IF THE DAY EVER COMES WHEN THEY KNOW WHO . . 414 A CABIN IN THE CLEARING 29
    THE GREATEST VOTE A PEOPLE EVER CAST, . . . 423 FOR JOHN F. KENNEDY . 55
    IT WILL EVER BE, ... 426 A NEVER NAUGHT SONG . 18
    EVER SINCE NAG'S HEAD . . . . 429 KITTY HAWK 23
    EVER THOUGHT TO FLY. . . . . 434 KITTY HAWK . . . 193
    EVER FRESH AND FRESH. . . . . 436 KITTY HAWK . . . 250
    EVER TO CREATE . . . . 441 KITTY HAWK . . . 417
    THAT EVER ACCEPTED FATE . . . . 444 THE DRAFT HORSE . . 14
    DOES NO ONE AT ALL EVER FEEL THIS WAY IN THE LEAST? . 446 DOES NO ONE AT ALL EVER T
    CAN EVER QUITE PASS OUT OF UTTER GRIEF . . . 469 WE VAINLY WRESTLE... . 3
    THE BEST, I'M TOLD, I EVER HAVE HAD TAKEN. . 476 A MASQUE OF REASON . 86
    YOU'RE NOT A WITCH? / NO. / HAVE YOU EVER BEEN ONE? . 476 A MASQUE OF REASON . 92
    THAN ON THE SURFACE. IF THERE EVER WAS, . . 483 A MASQUE OF REASON . 283
    EVER SINCE ALEXANDER GREECED THE WORLD. . . 511 A MASQUE OF MERCY . 473
    STRANGE NO ONE EVER THOUGHT OF IT BEFORE HIM. . 511 A MASQUE OF MERCY . 478
    NERVOUS IS ALL THE GREAT THINGS EVER MADE YOU. . 516 A MASQUE OF MERCY . 599
    WAS ABOUT ALL THERE EVER WAS TO ME. . . . . 518 A MASQUE OF MERCY . 658
EVERGREEN
    HE THOUGHT OF EVERGREEN AND EVERLASTING. . . . . . . 200 PLACE FOR A THIRD . . 31
EVERLASTING
    HE THOUGHT OF EVERGREEN AND EVERLASTING. . . . . . . 200 PLACE FOR A THIRD . . 31

EVERY
    YET EVERY SECOND SPEAR . . . . 13 ROSE POGONIAS . . . 14
    THE FEN HAD EVERY KIND OF BLOOM, ... 15 IN A VALE 6
    AND FOR EVERY KIND THERE WAS A FACE, ... 15 IN A VALE 7
    BUT ALL CAME EVERY NIGHT WITH THE MIST; . . . . 15 IN A VALE 11
    HE BUNDLES EVERY FORKFUL IN ITS PLACE, ... 37 DEATH OF THE HIRED MAN . 89
    SHE'S GOT SO SHE TURNS IN AT EVERY HOUSE . . . 49 A HUNDRED COLLARS . . 142
    THERE THEY HAVE EVERY MEANS PROPER TO DO WITH, . 65 A SERVANT TO SERVANTS . 98
    AND EVERY FLECK OF RUSSET SHOWING CLEAR. . . . 68 AFTER APPLE-PICKING . . 20
    NEARBY, ALL DARK IN EVERY GLOSSY WINDOW. . . . 89 THE FEAR 4
    "OUT WALKING. EVERY CHILD SHOULD HAVE THE MEMORY . 92 THE FEAR 82
    OF EVERY KIND EVERYWHERE IN THIS REGION . . . 95 THE SELF-SEEKER . . . 68
    THE WAY THE NEST-FULL EVERY TIME WE STIRRED . . 109 THE EXPOSED NEST . . 20
    FOR EVERY ROOM A HOUSE HAS--PARLOR, BEDROOM, . . 110 IN THE HOME STRETCH . 8
    AND EVERY CRASH MEANT ONE LESS TO RETURN . . . 112 IN THE HOME STRETCH . 57
    NIGHT AFTER NIGHT AND STRONGER EVERY NIGHT . . 113 IN THE HOME STRETCH . 73
    WITH SMELL OF BURNING ON EVERY PLUME, ... 120 BOND AND FREE . . . 14
    THAT WITH EVERY FUTILE PASS . . . . 128 THE OFT-REPEATED DREAM . 6
    NOT BUT I'VE EVERY REASON NOT TO CARE . . . . 146 SNOW 89
    WHO COMES FROM PHILADELPHIA EVERY YEAR . . . . 162 NEW HAMPSHIRE . . . 101
    COULD TELL THE TIME OF YEAR WHEN EVERY TREE . . 175 THE CENSUS-TAKER . . 18
    AND EVERY TREE UP STOOD A ROTTING TRUNK . . . 175 THE CENSUS-TAKER . . 22
    WHERE THEY GROW FEWER AND FEWER EVERY YEAR . . 176 THE CENSUS-TAKER . . 62
    A TELESCOPE. SOMEONE IN EVERY TOWN . . . . . 177 THE STAR-SPLITTER . . 35
    IN WAIT FOR HER THERE. SHE READ EVERY WORD . . 181 MAPLE 64
    AND EVERY LEAF OF FOLIAGE SHE'D WORN . . . . . 184 MAPLE 146
    STILL GOING EVERY WHICH WAY IN THE JOINTS, THOUGH, . 205 THE WITCH OF COOS . . 87
    IN FRONT OF EVERY ONE IN GRAFTON COUNTY. . . . 209 PAUPER WITCH OF GRAFTON . 51
    AND SPOKE HIS DOUBTS IN EVERY OPEN PLACE. . . . 214 A FOUNTAIN, A BOTTLE . 36
    IN EVERY WAY YOU MAY PLEASE YOURSELF; . . . . 232 THE KITCHEN CHIMNEY . 2
    ON EVERY TREE A BUCKET WITH A LID, ... 234 EVENING A SUGAR ORCHARD 12
    SHE HAS HER SPELL ON EVERY SINGLE LIZARD. . . . 237 A HILLSIDE THAW . . 22
    IN EVERY LIFELIKE POSTURE OF THE SWARM, . . . 237 A HILLSIDE THAW . . 27
    ONE LIZARD AT THE END OF EVERY RAY, ... 238 A HILLSIDE THAW . . 34
    WITH SNOWBALLS CUPPED IN EVERY OPENING BUD. . . 239 OUR SINGING STRENGTH . 15
    "A SIGH FOR EVERY SO MANY BREATH, ... 263 THE TIMES TABLE . . 9
    AND FOR EVERY SO MANY SIGH A DEATH. . . . . . 263 THE TIMES TABLE . . 10
    FOR EVERY PARCEL I STOOP DOWN TO SEIZE . . . . 266 THE ARMFUL 1
    AND EVERY PIECE I SQUARELY HIT . . . . 275 TWO TRAMPS IN MUD TIME . 11
    IN EVERY WHEELRUT'S NOW A BROOK, ... 276 TWO TRAMPS IN MUD TIME . 35
    IN EVERY PRINT OF A HOOF A POND. . . . . . . 276 TWO TRAMPS IN MUD TIME . 36
    AND EVERY GUST THAT GATHERS STRENGTH AND HEAVES . 305 THERE ARE ROUGHLY ZONES . 2
    CLEAR TO THE ARCTIC OF EVERY LIVING KIND. . . . 305 THERE ARE ROUGHLY ZONES 10
    WHAT HE DID WITH EVERY CENT. . . . . 309 HARDSHIP OF ACCOUNTING . 5
    WITH EVERY KNOWN SHAPE OF THE STUFF. . . . . 310 THE VINDICTIVES . . . 5
    AT EVERY POINT AND FACET GLOWED . . . . 332 ALL REVELATION . . . 14
    THOUGH WITH EVERY WORD HE SPOKE . . . . 340 THE SUBVERTED FLOWER . 26
    THE DAY WAS THE DAY BY EVERY FLOWER THAT BLOOMS, . 342 QUEST OF PURPLE-FRINGED . 7
    AND EVERY SHEEPISH PALADIN AND PEER, ... 353 THE LESSON FOR TODAY . 90
    AND EVERY ACRE GOOD ENOUGH TO EAT, ... 365 OF STONES OF THE PLACE . 7
    SO BROODINGLY SOON IN EVERY DIRECTION. . . . . 379 TOO ANXIOUS FOR RIVERS 13
    EVERY STAR IN SIGHT. . . . . 384 MAKING CERTAIN ANYTHING 15
    MY LOVE FOR EVERY HEAVEN . . . . 389 ASTROMETAPHYSICAL . . 9
    THERE WAS SO MUCH MORE EVERY DAY TO LEARN, . . 398 BURSTING RAPTURE . . 6
    EVERY TIME DICK OR PIKE LOOKED UP, THE DOCTOR . 404 FROM PLANE TO PLANE . 18
    IN READING, DON'T YOU, BILL?--AT EVERY LINE END . 405 FROM PLANE TO PLANE . 50
    CALLING ALL BUTTERFLIES OF EVERY RACE . . . . 411 POD OF THE MILKWEED . 1
    WITH EVERY COAST HE TRIED ALONG. . . . . . . 416 AMERICA IS HARD TO SEE 14
    HE HAS CURSED EVERY RIVER MOUTH . . . . 418 AMERICA IS HARD TO SEE 53
    EVERY SINGLE THING . . . . 426 A NEVER NAUGHT SONG . 13
    TO ITS EVERY GUISE . . . . 426 A NEVER NAUGHT SONG . 24
    EACH AND EVERY ONE . . . . 431 KITTY HAWK 103
    ENOUGH TO BUILD HIM EVERY NIGHT A PUP TENT . . 478 A MASQUE OF REASON . 132
    I'VE HEARD WHAT YOU WERE SAYING--EVERY WORD. . . 487 A MASQUE OF REASON . 396
    WHERE GOOD AND BAD ARE MINGLED EVERY WHICH WAY, . 488 A MASQUE OF REASON . 408
    AT EVERY STATION BUT THE FINAL ONE. . . . . . 501 A MASQUE OF MERCY . 195
    ONLY TO SEE IT SHATTERED EVERY DAY. . . . . . 508 A MASQUE OF MERCY . 373
    BY HAVING HIM WHIPPED EVERY DAY AFRESH . . . . 517 A MASQUE OF MERCY . 642
    WHEN THAT FADES I FADE--EVERY TIME I FADE. . . . 518 A MASQUE OF MERCY . 659
EVERYBODY
    "YOU SEE I'M IN WITH EVERYBODY, KNOW 'EM ALL. . . 49 A HUNDRED COLLARS . 120
    FOR EVERYBODY AS IT IS IN THERE." . . . . . . 114 IN THE HOME STRETCH . 98
    HUGHES 2. AND EVERYBODY TO THE SADDEST . . . . 165 NEW HAMPSHIRE . . . 199
    THAT NOT EVERYBODY ELSE KNEW WAS TO COUNT . . . 186 THE AX-HELVE . . . 42
    BUT EVERYBODY TOOK IT FOR A PROOF. . . . . . 209 PAUPER WITCH OF GRAFTON 68
    MAKE EVERYBODY WANT TO BE A NATION. . . . . . 423 FOR JOHN F. KENNEDY . 31
    BY BEING SPREAD OUT OVER EVERYBODY, ... 506 A MASQUE OF MERCY . 322
EVERYBODY'S
    AND EVERYBODY'S BEING SICK FOR CHRISTMAS. . . . 407 FROM PLANE TO PLANE . 106
    BY ROCKWELL KENT THAT EVERYBODY'S READING. . . . 495 A MASQUE OF MERCY . 49
EVERYDAY
    AND TALK ABOUT YOUR EVERYDAY CONCERNS. . . . . 54 HOME BURIAL 86
EVERYONE
    LORD, IF I WERE TO DREAM OF EVERYONE . . . . . 81 THE HOUSEKEEPER . . 12
    THERE IS A SINGER EVERYONE HAS HEARD, ... 119 THE OVEN BIRD . . . 1
    WAR IS FOR EVERYONE, FOR CHILDREN TOO. . . . . 133 THE BONFIRE . . . 111
    THAT EVERYONE FOR MILES COULD SEE . . . . . . 137 BROWN'S DESCENT . . 2
    SO SHE LOOKED FOR HERSELF, AS EVERYONE . . . . 182 MAPLE 70
    EVERYONE HAD TO HAVE A LOOK AT IT, ... 193 PAUL'S WIFE . . . 78
    EVERYONE HAD BEEN WRONG IN JUDGING PAUL. . . . 195 PAUL'S WIFE . . . 147
    MADE GOOD FOR EVERYONE--THINGS LIKE INVENTIONS-- . 319 BUILD SOIL . . . 94
    EVERYONE ASKS FOR FREEDOM FOR HIMSELF. . . . . 319 BUILD SOIL . . . 111
    EVERYONE HAS TO KEEP HIS EXTRICATION." . . . . 407 FROM PLANE TO PLANE . 96
    EVERYONE KNOWS THE GLORY OF THE TWAIN . . . . 423 FOR JOHN F. KENNEDY . 46
    --WAS BABEL: EVERYONE DEVELOPING . . . . . . 502 A MASQUE OF MERCY . 240
    YOU MUST MAKE YOUR DESCENT LIKE EVERYONE. . . . 514 A MASQUE OF MERCY . 552
    SOMETHING'S THE MATTER, EVERYONE ADMITS. . . . 514 A MASQUE OF MERCY . 562

EVERYONE'S
    I EXPECT, THOUGH, EVERYONE'S HEARD OF IT. . . . . . . 63 A SERVANT TO SERVANTS . 34
    YOU KNOW PAUL COULD DO WONDERS. EVERYONE'S . . . . . 192 PAUL'S WIFE 42
EVERYTHING
    HE JUMBLED EVERYTHING. I STOPPED TO LOOK . . . . 36 DEATH OF THE HIRED MAN   55
    HE LOOKS ON THE BRIGHT SIDE OF EVERYTHING, ... 64 A SERVANT TO SERVANTS . 45
    HE'S INTO EVERYTHING IN TOWN. THIS YEAR . . . . 64 A SERVANT TO SERVANTS . 71
    DROP EVERYTHING AND LIVE OUT ON THE GROUND-- . . . . . 67 A SERVANT TO SERVANTS . 162
    EVERYTHING WENT WELL TILL WE REACHED THE BARN . . . . 71 THE CODE 53
    WITH ME TO SIT AND TELL HIM EVERYTHING, ... 82 THE HOUSEKEEPER . . . 32
    HE'S JUST DROPPED EVERYTHING. HE'S LIKE A CHILD. . . . 83 THE HOUSEKEEPER . . . 55
    EVERYTHING GOES THE SAME WITHOUT ME THERE. . . . . . . 94 THE SELF-SEEKER . . . 40
    WITH EVERYTHING. WHAT WE LIVE BY WE DIE BY-- . . . . . 94 THE SELF-SEEKER . . . 48
    EVERYTHING SAID AS PERSONAL TO HIMSELF. . . . . 101 THE WOOD-PILE 16
    THE TRIAL BY MARKET EVERYTHING MUST COME TO. . . . . . 106 CHRISTMAS TREES . . . 24
    TO EVERYTHING. HER LIGHT WON'T LAST US LONG. . . . . . 113 IN THE HOME STRETCH . 71
    I WISH THAT EVERYTHING ON EARTH WERE JUST . . . . . . 115 IN THE HOME STRETCH . 140
    A LITTLE BIT OF EVERYTHING, ... 134 A GIRL'S GARDEN . . . 39
    AND DO EVERYTHING! . . . . 136 LAST WORD OF A BLUEBIRD 20
    'CROSS LOTS, 'CROSS WALLS, 'CROSS EVERYTHING, ... 137 BROWN'S DESCENT . . . 7
    TO EVERYTHING, HE GAVE IT UP . . . . 139 BROWN'S DESCENT . . . 43
    ONE EACH OF EVERYTHING AS IN A SHOWCASE, ... 161 NEW HAMPSHIRE 62
    A SPECIMEN OF EVERYTHING, I SAID. . . . . 163 NEW HAMPSHIRE' . . . 124
    ONE EACH OF EVERYTHING AS IN A SHOWCASE. . . . . . . 163 NEW HAMPSHIRE 144
    WHEN EVERYTHING HAD GONE REPUBLICAN . . . . 165 NEW HAMPSHIRE 196
    FROM NEARLY EVERYTHING THAT GOES ON ROUND ME. . . . . 166 NEW HAMPSHIRE 238
    AND RODE ALL OVER EVERYTHING ON HIM . . . . 208 PAUPER WITCH OF GRAFTON 47
    THE SMARTY SOMEONE WHO SPOILED EVERYTHING . . . . . . 209 PAUPER WITCH OF GRAFTON 70
    AND HE LIKED EVERYTHING I MADE HIM DO. . . . . 210 PAUPER WITCH OF GRAFTON 100
    YOU CAN COME DOWN FROM EVERYTHING TO NOTHING. . . . . 210 PAUPER WITCH OF GRAFTON 103
    "SO'S EVERYTHING." / "I WANT MY FOUNTAIN." . . . . . 214 A FOUNTAIN, A BOTTLE . 44
    THROUGH A HOUSE STRIPPED OF EVERYTHING . . . . 216 A FOUNTAIN, A BOTTLE . 90
    WASN'T SHE GLAD NOW? EVERYTHING SEEMED WON, ... 230 NOT TO KEEP 11
    THE STREAM OF EVERYTHING THAT RUNS AWAY. . . . . . . 259 WEST-RUNNING BROOK . . 44
    STRUNG CHAINS OF WALL ROUND EVERYTHING, ... 265 THE BIRTHPLACE 4
    THROUGH EVERYTHING PRESENTED, LAND AND TIDE . . . . . 267 RIDERS 3
    I LIKE TO THINK I AM IN EVERYTHING-- . . . . 278 THE WHITE-TAILED HORNET 16
    BUT IN THE RUSH OF EVERYTHING TO WASTE, ... 300 THE MASTER SPEED . . . 7
    OF EVERYTHING BELOW. . . . . 303 AFTERFLAKES 5
    EVERYTHING ITS PARTS CAN DO . . . . 306 A TRIAL RUN 11
    TO EVERYTHING ON EARTH THE COMPASS ROUND, ... 332 THE SILKEN TENT . . . 11
    ACROSS THE GULF OF WELL-NIGH EVERYTHING . . . . 356 A MOTH SEEN IN WINTER . 21
    BEFORE THEY TURNED FROM EVERYTHING TO HAY. . . . . . 404 FROM PLANE TO PLANE . 14
    EVERYTHING WAS THERE, ... 426 A NEVER NAUGHT SONG . 12
    NOT OF FOOD ONLY BUT OF EVERYTHING, ... 455 HOW HARD TO KEEP FROM . 61
    WITH EVERYTHING WE HAD. . . . . 464 MILKY WAY IS A COWPATH   8
    THERE'S A STRANGE LIGHT ON EVERYTHING TODAY. . . . . 473 A MASQUE OF REASON . . 8
    I'M SICK. / OF WHAT? / OH, EVERYTHING, I GUESS. . . . 499 A MASQUE OF MERCY . . 155
    NOT EVERYTHING I SAY IS SAID IN SCORN. . . . . 510 A MASQUE OF MERCY . . 451
EVERYTHING'S
    EVERYTHING'S SHUT SOMETIMES EXCEPT THE BARN; . . . . . 49 A HUNDRED COLLARS . . 130
    "EVERYTHING'S AS SHE LEFT IT WHEN SHE DIED. . . . . . 55 THE BLACK COTTAGE . . 15
    OUR EVERY LIFE DEPENDS ON EVERYTHING'S . . . . 147 SNOW 132
EVERYWHERE
    LET HIM GET OFF AND HE'LL BE EVERYWHERE . . . . 90 THE FEAR 45
    OF EVERY KIND EVERYWHERE IN THIS REGION . . . . 95 THE SELF-SEEKER . . . 68
    BIRCH BOUGHS ENOUGH PILED EVERYWHERE!-- . . . . 123 PEA BRUSH 13
    EVERYWHERE, ... 129 THE IMPULSE 22
    THE QUESTION EVERYWHERE WAS WHY SHOULD PAUL . . . . . 192 PAUL'S WIFE 31
    BE DRAGGED BY YOU ALL OVER EVERYWHERE----" . . . . . 214 A FOUNTAIN, A BOTTLE . 30
EVIDENCE
    LET'S HAVE A SHOWDOWN AS AN EVIDENCE . . . . 47 A HUNDRED COLLARS . . 85
    WOULD EVIDENCE OF HAVING BEEN CALLED LADY . . . . . 111 IN THE HOME STRETCH . 22
EVIDENTLY
    WHAT EVIDENTLY NOTHING COULD CONCLUDE. . . . . 190 THE GRINDSTONE . . . 64
    WERE EVIDENTLY SOMETHING HE COULD BEAR. . . . . . . 292 FIGURE IN THE DOORWAY . 12
EVIL
    BUT THE WORLD'S EVIL. I WON'T HAVE GRIEF SO . . . . . 54 HOME BURIAL 106
    THE SNAKE STOOD UP FOR EVIL IN THE GARDEN-- . . . . 188 THE AX-HELVE 97
    TO EVIL, NO IMPORTANT TRIUMPH WON, ... 226 THE ONSET 10
    EVIL TENDENCIES CANCEL . . . . 308 EVIL TENDENCIES CANCEL   T
    THE BEARER OF EVIL TIDINGS, ... 313 BEARER OF EVIL TIDINGS   1
    REMEMBERED THAT EVIL TIDINGS . . . . 313 BEARER OF EVIL TIDINGS   3
    THE BEARER OF EVIL TIDINGS . . . . 313 BEARER OF EVIL TIDINGS   T
    AND THE BEARER OF EVIL TIDINGS . . . . 314 BEARER OF EVIL TIDINGS   35
    AS FOR HIS EVIL TIDINGS, ... 314 BEARER OF EVIL TIDINGS   41
    TO AFFIRM THERE IS SUCH A THING AS EVIL . . . . . . 317 BUILD SOIL 50
    SINCE IT WAS NOTHING I KNEW EVIL OF . . . . 358 A CONSIDERABLE SPECK . 28
    FOR ANY EYE IS AN EVIL EYE . . . . 385 A MOOD APART 7
    WHO COULD DO GOOD OR EVIL AS HE CHOSE. . . . . 475 A MASQUE OF REASON . . 72
    I HAD TO PROSPER GOOD AND PUNISH EVIL. . . . . 476 A MASQUE OF REASON . . 76
    TO PROPHESY AGAINST THE CITY EVIL. . . . . 495 A MASQUE OF MERCY . . 64
    THE THREATS HE MAKES AGAINST THE CITY EVIL. . . . . 497 A MASQUE OF MERCY . . 115
    THE CITY IS ADMITTEDLY AN EVIL: . . . . 506 A MASQUE OF MERCY . . 336
EVIL-CROSSED
    TO SEE IT, EVIL-CROSSED OR MERCY-CROSSED? . . . . . 510 A MASQUE OF MERCY . . 438
    OF STAR-CROSSED, MERCY-CROSSED, OR EVIL-CROSSED . . . 510 A MASQUE OF MERCY . . 440
    WHERE MERCY-CROSSED TO ME SEEMED EVIL-CROSSED. . . . 510 A MASQUE OF MERCY . . 443
EVOLUTION
    TO SHOW THE EVOLUTION HOW TO STEER. . . . . 425 ACCIDENTALLY ON PURPOSE 10
EVOLUTIONIST
    (YOU'LL HAVE TO ASK AN EVOLUTIONIST)-- . . . . 197 WILD GRAPES 53
EVOLUTION'S
    AT EVOLUTION'S OPPOSITE EXTREME. . . . . 395 ETHEREALIZING 10
EVOLVE
    AND SIMPLY MUST EVOLVE TO STAY AWAKE. . . . . 372 THE LITERATE FARMER AND 127
EXACT
    TO EXACT FOR A PRESENT GAIN . . . . 285 IN TIME OF CLOUDBURST . 7

EXACT (CONTINUED)
    THEY CAN COMMAND THE EXACT AFFINITY . . . . 461 HOW HARD TO KEEP FROM   236
EXACTLY
    BUT IT'S NOT ELVES EXACTLY, AND I'D RATHER . . . . . 34 MENDING WALL 37
    BUT THE PEN STAYED EXACTLY AS IT WAS, ... 67 A SERVANT TO SERVANTS . 141
    WHO KNOW EXACTLY WHAT IS OUT OF JOINT . . . . 351 THE LESSON FOR TODAY . 32
    WON'T KNOW EXACTLY WHAT I MEAN BY THAT. . . . . . . 354 THE LESSON FOR TODAY . 121
    "YOU SAID IT—THAT'S EXACTLY WHAT IT IS. . . . . . . 371 THE LITERATE FARMER AND 94
    WE NEVER KNEW EXACTLY WHERE TO LOOK, ... 382 TO AN ANCIENT . . . 4
EXALT
    BEFORE I THOUGHT THE WILTED TO EXALT . . . . 337 THE WIND AND THE RAIN . 26
EXALTED
    THE MOUNTAIN STOOD EXALTED IN ITS PLACE. . . . . . . 301 MOON COMPASSES . . . 7
EXAMINATION
    WON'T BEAR TOO CRITICAL EXAMINATION. . . . . 385 THE FEAR OF GOD . . . 6
EXAMINE
    AND TEAR HIS CLOTHES OFF TO EXAMINE HIM . . . . . . 503 A MASQUE OF MERCY . . 251
EXAMPLE
    THE SUN SETS THE EXAMPLE IN THE DAY." . . . . 370 THE LITERATE FARMER AND 74
    HAVE STAYED IN SIGHT SO LONG AS AN EXAMPLE. . . . . 404 FROM PLANE TO PLANE . 23
    AND BY THE EXAMPLE OF OUR DECLARATION . . . . 423 FOR JOHN F. KENNEDY . 30
    YES, BUT NEW YORK WILL DO AS AN EXAMPLE. . . . . . . 496 A MASQUE OF MERCY . . 91
    THE VERY SLEEP WE SLEEP IS AN EXAMPLE. . . . . . . 509 A MASQUE OF MERCY . . 432
EXCAVATED
    THEY EXCAVATED MORE. 'GO KEEP HIS WIFE . . . . 72 THE CODE 94
EXCEED
    TRIED TO THINK HOW HE COULD EXCEED HIS PROMISE, ... 200 PLACE FOR A THIRD . . 19
EXCEPT
    EVERYTHING'S SHUT SOMETIMES EXCEPT THE BARN; . . . . 49 A HUNDRED COLLARS . . 130
    IT'S SELDOM I GET DOWN EXCEPT FOR MEALS, THOUGH. . . . 49 A HUNDRED COLLARS . . 146
    YET MORE I'D HATE TO HOLD MY TREES, EXCEPT . . . . . 106 CHRISTMAS TREES . . . 21
    THIS HOUSE IS FROZEN BRITTLE, ALL EXCEPT . . . . . . 150 SNOW 202
    AND—WRITING; NONE OF THESE EXCEPT PERHAPS . . . . . 164 NEW HAMPSHIRE . . . 166
    EXCEPT AT NIGHT TO PLACES IN THE SKY . . . . 173 A STAR IN A STONEBOAT . 41
    EXCEPT IN TOWNS AT NIGHT, IS NOT A SIN. . . . . . . 189 THE GRINDSTONE . . . 18
    EXCEPT THAT I REMEMBER HOW OF OLD . . . . 189 THE GRINDSTONE . . . 22
    EXCEPT, PERHAPS, A FOOT AT EITHER END. . . . . . . 193 PAUL'S WIFE 71
    EXCEPT ALWAYS JOHN-JOE, ... 211 AN EMPTY THREAT . . . 26
    EXCEPT, IT SEEMED, THE POETESS'S POEMS. . . . . . . 216 A FOUNTAIN, A BOTTLE . 91
    EXCEPT FORGET TO GO IN FEAR PERHAPS. . . . . 231 A BROOK IN THE CITY . 19
    NO ONE WOULD KNOW EXCEPT FOR ANCIENT MAPS . . . . . 231 A BROOK IN THE CITY . 20
    EXCEPT WHEN SEA FOG LAID IT DOWN, ... 249 A PECK OF GOLD . . . 2
    EXCEPT IN COLOR HE ISN'T BLUE, ... 276 TWO TRAMPS IN MUD TIME 31
    EXCEPT AS A FELLOW HANDLED AN AX . . . . 276 TWO TRAMPS IN MUD TIME 55
    EXCEPT AS AN ABSTRACTION OF THE MIND. . . . . 318 BUILD SOIL 71
    I COULD GIVE ALL TO TIME EXCEPT—EXCEPT . . . . . . 335 I COULD GIVE ALL . . 11
    IT NEVER REACHES EARTH EXCEPT AS ASHES . . . . . . 361 A LOOSE MOUNTAIN . . 10
    EXCEPT BESIDE A SAFE INSIDE A BANK . . . . 386 THE FEAR OF MAN . . . 9
    EXCEPT AS IT DENIED HIM WAY . . . . 419 AMERICA IS HARD TO SEE 77
    GOES MENTIONLESS EXCEPT IN BABY-SCHOOL . . . . . . 447 DOES NO ONE AT ALL EVER 38
    EXCEPT FOR A FEW . . . . 448 THE BAD ISLAND—EASTER 42
    EXCEPT AS A GAIN. . . . . 449 THE BAD ISLAND—EASTER 53
    BUT, YES, I'M FINE, EXCEPT FOR NOW AND THEN . . . . 474 A MASQUE OF REASON . 39
    EXCEPT IN THEIR OWN COUNTRY, THYATIRA. . . . . . . 476 A MASQUE OF REASON . 91
    EXCEPT AS A HARD PLACE TO SAVE HIS SOUL IN, ... 484 A MASQUE OF REASON . 318
    EXCEPT AS FATHER PUTATIVE TO SORT OF . . . . 498 A MASQUE OF MERCY . 123
EXCEPTING
    EXCEPTING THAT THEY DIFFER IN THEIR MOUNTAINS. . . . . 165 NEW HAMPSHIRE . . . 212
EXCEPTION
    AS NOT TO RECOGNIZE IN ME THE EXCEPTION . . . . . . 278 THE WHITE-TAILED HORNET 15
EXCESS
    THAT STRAIN AGAIN! GIVE ME EXCESS OF IT! . . . . . 488 A MASQUE OF REASON . 418
EXCHANGE
    MAKE THE WHOLE STOCK EXCHANGE YOUR OWN! . . . . . . 307 PROVIDE, PROVIDE . . 10
    DON'T LET ME SEEM TO SAY THE EXCHANGE, THE ENCOUNTER, . . 321 BUILD SOIL 157
EXCHANGED
    AND EXCHANGED TROUBLED GLANCES OVER LIFE. . . . . . 293 AT WOODWARD'S GARDENS . 13
EXCITE
    HIS SONG SO PITCHED AS NOT TO EXCITE . . . . 276 TWO TRAMPS IN MUD TIME 27
EXCITED
    AND BIRDS THAT JOINED IN THE EXCITED FUN . . . . . . 237 A HILLSIDE THAW . . . 15
    I SEE WHAT YOU ARE: CAN'T GET YOU EXCITED . . . . . 370 THE LITERATE FARMER AND 86
    ALL SECONDHAND. DON'T GET EXCITED, FOLKS; . . . . . 507 A MASQUE OF MERCY . . 352
EXCITEMENT
    AS FOR THE WOODS' EXCITEMENT OVER YOU . . . . 378 DIRECTIVE 23
EXCITING
    WHAT AN EXCITING AGE IT IS WE LIVE IN— . . . . . . 462 HOW HARD TO KEEP FROM 256
EXCLAIM
    AND LIKE THE ACTRESS EXCLAIM "OH, MY GOD" AT? . . . . 165 NEW HAMPSHIRE . . . 207
    AND THE MEAL MADE THE BANQUETERS EXCLAIM . . . . . . 455 HOW HARD TO KEEP FROM 58
EXCLAIMED
    AND SOME EXCLAIMED WHO SAW AFAR . . . . 138 BROWN'S DESCENT . . . 30
EXCLAMATION
    SOME GUTTURAL EXCLAMATION OF SURPRISE . . . . 142 THE VANISHING RED . . 14
EXCLUDED
    WHERE WINDS WERE QUITE EXCLUDED, ... 13 ROSE POGONIAS . . . 5
EXCLUSIVELY
    MAY SEEM ALMOST EXCLUSIVELY DESIGNED. . . . . 321 BUILD SOIL 150
EXCUSE
    NOT LOTH TO HAVE EXCUSE TO GO, ... 18 GOING FOR WATER . . . 5
    AN EXCUSE FOR KEEPING US OTHER FOLK OUT." . . . . . 60 BLUEBERRIES 32
    HE HADN'T AT COMMAND. "YOU MUST EXCUSE ME, ... 96 THE SELF-SEEKER . . . 99
    "EXCUSE ME IF I ASK YOU IN A WINDOW . . . . 215 A FOUNTAIN, A BOTTLE . 72
    I AM EMPOWERED TO EXCUSE YOU FROM IT. . . . . 499 A MASQUE OF MERCY . . 149
EXCUSED
    PERSONIFIED, BUT ASK TO BE EXCUSED . . . . 317 BUILD SOIL 51
EXCUSES
    TO MAKE THEIR VERSE AND THEIR EXCUSES LAME. . . . . . 351 THE LESSON FOR TODAY . 33

EXCUSES (CONTINUED)
   EXCUSES TRUMPED UP BY YOU FOR THEOLOGISTS. . . . . . . 482 A MASQUE OF REASON . . 249
   FOR MORE EXCUSES. / WHAT I MEAN TO SAY: . . . . . . 486 A MASQUE OF REASON . . 367
EXECRABLE
   IS SUCH AN EXECRABLE JUDGE OF MOTIVES . . . . 278 THE WHITE-TAILED HORNET 14
EXECUTE
   I GUESS I'LL HAVE THE HEADSMAN EXECUTE ME . . . . . 460 HOW HARD TO KEEP FROM   205
EXECUTION
   EXECUTIVES OF SKILLFUL EXECUTION . . . . 363 A SEMI-REVOLUTION . .   5
EXECUTIVE
   BY EXECUTIVE GUILE, ... 448 THE BAD ISLAND--EASTER   35
EXECUTIVES
   EXECUTIVES OF SKILLFUL EXECUTION . . . . 363 A SEMI-REVOLUTION . .   5
EXEGETE
   NOW WE ARE HEARING FROM THE EXEGETE. . . . . 498 A MASQUE OF MERCY . . 126
EXERCISE
   AND SHARING HIS MILES OF EXERCISE. . . . . 420 ONE MORE BREVITY . . 43
EXERTING
   THE SNOW BLOWS ON HIM AND OFF HIM, EXERTING FORCE . . . 341 WILLFUL HOMING . . .   5
EXHAUSTED
   THEY'D SOON EXHAUSTED ALL THERE WAS IN FLYING; . . . . 239 OUR SINGING STRENGTH . 27
EXHAUSTION
   AND HIS VOICE DIED DOWN SLOWLY FROM EXHAUSTION. . . . . 66 A SERVANT TO SERVANTS . 133
EXHAUSTS
   I AM SICK, AS SHE SAYS. NOTHING EXHAUSTS ME . . . . . 501 A MASQUE OF MERCY . . 197
EXHIBIT
   BUT THE BEST OF HER EXHIBIT . . . . 397 AN IMPORTER 17
EXHIBITED
   AND BE EXHIBITED, AND WIN. . . . . 279 BLUE RIBBON AT AMESBURY   3
EXHIBIT'S
   ANY EQUALITY THEY MAY EXHIBIT'S . . . . 513 A MASQUE OF MERCY . . 527
EXIST
   FOR THINGS THAT DON'T EXIST; I MEAN BEGINNINGS. . . . 116 IN THE HOME STRETCH . 173
   THAT DOESN'T EXIST, ... 211 AN EMPTY THREAT . . 34
   AND WHERE THE TWO EXIST IN TWAIN . . . . 277 TWO TRAMPS IN MUD TIME 63
   LIKE SOMEONE DEAD PERMITTED TO EXIST . . . . 368 THE LITERATE FARMER AND 17
   DISINTERESTEDNESS NEVER DID EXIST, ... 485 A MASQUE OF REASON . . 354
EXISTENCE (SEE NON-EXISTENCE)
   THE TRIAL BY EXISTENCE . . . . 19 THE TRIAL BY EXISTENCE   T
   THE TRIAL BY EXISTENCE NAMED, ... 20 THE TRIAL BY EXISTENCE 19
   IT LIFTS EXISTENCE ON A PLANE OF SNOW . . . . . . 254 A WINTER EDEN . . .   5
   SOME SAY EXISTENCE LIKE A PIROUOT . . . . 259 WEST-RUNNING BROOK . . 45
   NONE REMAINING IN EXISTENCE . . . . 304 CLEAR AND COLDER . .   8
EXIT
   THE EXIT HE COMES OUT AT LIKE A BULLET . . . . . . 277 THE WHITE-TAILED HORNET   3
   YOUR EXIT DOOR'S BECOME A CELLAR DOOR. . . . . . . 514 A MASQUE OF MERCY . . 549
EX-KING
   THE EX-KING SAID, "YON STAR'S INDIFFERENCE . . . . . 454 HOW HARD TO KEEP FROM   17
   "YOU'RE RIGHT," THE EX-KING SAID, "WE'LL NEED SOME MONEY. . 454 HOW HARD TO KEEP FROM   30
   THE EX-KING STOOD UP IN THE MARKETPLACE . . . . . . 454 HOW HARD TO KEEP FROM   37
   SENT FOR THE EX-KING IN A PRIVATE MATTER. . . . . . 456 HOW HARD TO KEEP FROM   97
   THE EX-KING SAID. "WE'RE IN THIS THING TOGETHER. . . . 459 HOW HARD TO KEEP FROM 170
EXODUS
   A MORE THAN MOSES' EXODUS. . . . . 417 AMERICA IS HARD TO SEE 36
EXPAND
   TO TRY IF IT WILL NOT MAKE OUR BEING EXPAND, ... 286 A ROADSIDE STAND . . 20
EXPANDING
   OF ONCE EXPANDING . . . . 219 I WILL SING YOU ONE-O . 70
EXPECT
   I EXPECT, THOUGH, EVERYONE'S HEARD OF IT. . . . . . 63 A SERVANT TO SERVANTS . 34
   BUT DON'T EXPECT I'M GOING TO LET YOU HAVE THEM." . . . 106 CHRISTMAS TREES . . . 32
   THINGS MUST EXPECT TO COME IN FRONT OF US . . . . . 147 SNOW 126
EXPECTATION
   THEY MUST HAVE HAD A GUILTY EXPECTATION . . . . . . 193 PAUL'S WIFE 67
EXPECTED
   IF I'M EXPECTED TO ELECT BILL TAFT. . . . . 48 A HUNDRED COLLARS . . 117
   TO BE EXPECTED TO BE DOSTOIEVSKIS . . . . 167 NEW HAMPSHIRE . . . 275
   YET WASN'T ENJOINED AND WASN'T EXPECTED, CLEARLY. . . . 306 NOT QUITE SOCIAL . .   4
   SO MUCH IS BEING NOW EXPECTED OF, ... 369 THE LITERATE FARMER AND 41
   MAY AS EXPECTED WAS A DISAPPOINTMENT, ... 406 FROM PLANE TO PLANE . 88
   'TWAS HUMAN OF YOU. I EXPECTED MORE . . . . 485 A MASQUE OF REASON . . 331
EXPECTING
   STROLLED THITHER, NOT EXPECTING HE WOULD FIND . . . . 74 THE GENERATIONS OF MEN 26
   YOU'LL BE EXPECTING JOHN. I PITY ESTELLE; . . . . . 88 THE HOUSEKEEPER . . . 191
EXPEDITION
   AS TREE BY ENTERPRISE AND EXPEDITION. . . . . . . 350 TO A YOUNG WRETCH . . 11
EXPEND
   EXPEND THEIR BLOOM IN VAIN. . . . . 26 A LINE-STORM SONG . .   6
EXPENSE
   BLESS YOU, IT'S ALL EXPENSE, THOUGH. REACH ME DOWN . . 86 THE HOUSEKEEPER . . . 142
   BUT MOST WOULD HAVE TO THINK OF THE EXPENSE . . . . 208 PAUPER WITCH OF GRAFTON 38
   TO SAVE HIM THE EXPENSE OF DOING. . . . . 274 A LONE STRIKER . . 48
   AT THE EXPENSE OF NEGLIGIBLE FOLK. . . . . 423 FOR JOHN F. KENNEDY . 33
   WHY IT HAD HAD TO BE AT MY EXPENSE. . . . . 481 A MASQUE OF REASON . . 221
   IT HAD TO BE AT SOMEBODY'S EXPENSE. . . . . 481 A MASQUE OF REASON . . 222
EXPERIENCE
   NOT EVEN BRACKISH FROM ITS SALT EXPERIENCE. . . . . 514 A MASQUE OF MERCY . . 542
EXPERIENCES
   WHEN TEACHER'S OWN EXPERIENCES FAIL HER . . . . . . 447 DOES NO ONE AT ALL EVER 39
EXPERIMENT
   BY PSYCHOLOGICAL EXPERIMENT, ... 293 AT WOODWARD'S GARDENS . 19
   AS A NOBLE EXPERIMENT. . . . . 466 SOME SCIENCE FICTION . 28
EXPERTLY
   HE CAUGHT MY AX EXPERTLY ON THE RISE, ... 185 THE AX-HELVE . . . 10
EXPERTS
   AND EXPERTS SAID THAT DEEP DOWN IN THE MOUNTAIN . . . 212 A FOUNTAIN, A BOTTLE .   4
EXPLAIN
   AND HARD TO EXPLAIN AS A CONJUROR'S TRICK." . . . . . 59 BLUEBERRIES 21

EXPLAIN (CONTINUED)
    I CAN'T EXPLAIN IT ANY OTHER WAY. . . . . 84 THE HOUSEKEEPER . . . 78
    AND DROPPED MY EYES, UNWILLING TO EXPLAIN. . . . . . 255 ACQUAINTED WITH NIGHT . 6
    I CAN'T EXPLAIN--TONIGHT AT LEAST." . . . . 420 ONE MORE BREVITY . . 25
    NO BOOK CAN EXPLAIN, ... 449 THE BAD ISLAND--EASTER 50
    THE SAME WITH GOD AS LOSING, HOW EXPLAIN . . . . . 517 A MASQUE OF MERCY . . 634
EXPLAINED
    TO BE GONE INTO IF NOT EXPLAINED. . . . . 419 ONE MORE BREVITY . . 6
EXPLAINS
    THAT EXPLAINS WHY HE'S SO DIAPHANOUS . . . . 488 A MASQUE OF REASON . . 427
EXPLANATIONS
    AND WOULD NOT LISTEN TO MY EXPLANATIONS. . . . . . 278 THE WHITE-TAILED HORNET 21
EXPLICITLY
    WHERE MERCY IS EXPLICITLY THE SUBJECT. . . . . . . 508 A MASQUE OF MERCY . . 377
EXPLODE
    THE MINERAL DROPS THAT EXPLODE . . . . 388 MIDDLENESS OF THE ROAD 9
EXPLOITING
    ALL, NOT JUST GREAT EXPLOITING BUSINESSES. . . . . . 319 BUILD SOIL 96
EXPLORATION
    AND BEFORE THAT OF EXPLORATION EVEN. . . . . 161 NEW HAMPSHIRE . . . 73
EXPLORE
    NOT TO EXPLORE TOO DEEP IN OTHERS' BUSINESS. . . . . 162 NEW HAMPSHIRE . . . 92
EXPLORER
    IT BECAME AN EXPLORER OF THE DEEP . . . . 162 NEW HAMPSHIRE . . . 91
EXPLOSION
    IS AFTER EXPLOSION GOING AWAY SO FAST. . . . . . . 389 SKEPTIC 8
EXPOSED
    THE EXPOSED NEST . . . . 109 THE EXPOSED NEST . . T
    SEEMS HAUNTED OR EXPOSED. I ALWAYS TAKE . . . . . 115 IN THE HOME STRETCH . 133
    I CAN SIT FORTH EXPOSED TO ATTACK, ... 282 A DRUMLIN WOODCHUCK . 10
EX-POST-FACTO
    THAN ALL THE JUSTIFYING EX-POST-FACTO . . . . 482 A MASQUE OF REASON . . 248
EXPOSURE
    AND HAVING HER EXPOSURE MISCONSTRUED. . . . . . . 386 THE FEAR OF MAN . . . 14
EXPOUNDED
    AT BEING THUS EXPOUNDED TO HIMSELF . . . . 405 FROM PLANE TO PLANE . 56
EXPRESS
    I CAN'T EXPRESS MY FEELINGS, ANY MORE . . . . . . 63 A SERVANT TO SERVANTS . 7
    WITH NO EXPRESSION, NOTHING TO EXPRESS. . . . . . 296 DESERT PLACES . . . 12
    TO EXPRESS HOW MUCH IT DIDN'T WANT TO DIE. . . . . . 357 A CONSIDERABLE SPECK . 18
EXPRESSED
    WHICH BEING EXPRESSED, MIGHT BE THIS IN EFFECT: . . . 60 BLUEBERRIES 44
    EXPRESSED THEM, AND ITS CURVES WERE NO FALSE CURVES . . 187 THE AX-HELVE 74
    PURPOSE WAS EXPRESSED . . . . 437 KITTY HAWK 294
    GETTING THOUGHT EXPRESSED. . . . . 442 KITTY HAWK 436
EXPRESSION
    WITH NO EXPRESSION, NOTHING TO EXPRESS. . . . . . . 296 DESERT PLACES . . . 12
    FROM THAT STRAIN COMES THE EXPRESSION STRAINS OF MUSIC. . 460 HOW HARD TO KEEP FROM 215
EXPRESSIVE
    SEEMS AS EXPRESSIVE OF THE HUMAN RACE . . . . . . 382 TO AN ANCIENT . . . 8
EXQUISITE
    THAT WHEN IT GETS TOO EXQUISITE TO BEAR . . . . . . 398 BURSTING RAPTURE . . 12
EXTEND
    YOU WOULD SAY HIS AMBITION WAS TO EXTEND TO REACH . . . 305 THERE ARE ROUGHLY ZONES 9
EXTENDED
    THE VERMONT MOUNTAINS STRETCH EXTENDED STRAIGHT; . . . 165 NEW HAMPSHIRE . . . 213
    I'LL SHOW YOU HOW SHE HAD HER SILLS EXTENDED . . . . 216 A FOUNTAIN, A BOTTLE . 86
    HE HAD BEEN TOO ALL OUT, TOO MUCH EXTENDED.. . . . . 396 ANY SIZE WE PLEASE . . 12
EXTENSION
    THERE IS A LIMIT TO OUR TIME EXTENSION. . . . . . . 355 THE LESSON FOR TODAY . 144
EXTENT
    THE EXTENT OF PASTURE I SHOULD STRIP, THREE CENTS . . . 107 CHRISTMAS TREES . . 48
    THE ROOST IS HER EXTENT OF FLIGHT. . . . . 281 BLUE RIBBON AT AMESBURY 45
    HE DRAWS HIMSELF UP TO HIS FULL EXTENT. . . . . . . 309 WASPISH 2
    THEY ARE OUR WARDS WE THINK TO SOME EXTENT . . . . . 423 FOR JOHN F. KENNEDY . 36
    TO ITS FULL EXTENT . . . . 437 KITTY HAWK 301
EXTENUATES
    BUT NAUGHT EXTENUATES OR DIMS, ... 20 THE TRIAL BY EXISTENCE 39
EXTINCT
    FROM SOME EXTINCT OLD CHIMNEY POT. . . . . 452 A-WISHING WELL . . . 36
EXTRA
    AND THE LIFE I LIVE NOW'S AN EXTRA LIFE . . . . . . 196 WILD GRAPES 14
    BUT ALL I ASK'S AN EXTRA ONE. . . . . 451 A-WISHING WELL . . . 26
    OR IS IT ONLY FOUR? MY EXTRA TWENTY . . . . 484 A MASQUE OF REASON . . 312
EXTRAVAGANCE
    OR SOME EXTRAVAGANCE YOUNG LOVE HAD BEEN TO? . . . . 264 THE INVESTMENT . . . 11
EXTRA-VAGANT
    IN AN EXTRA-VAGANT WAVE. . . . . 294 A RECORD STRIDE . . . 16
EXTREME
    IS EXTREME WHERE THEY SHRINK TO NONE AT ALL. . . . . 176 THE CENSUS-TAKER . . 63
    AT ONE EXTREME AGREEING WITH ONE GREEK, ... 269 THE BEAR 30
    AT EVOLUTION'S OPPOSITE EXTREME. . . . . 395 ETHEREALIZING . . . 10
EXTREMELY
    TO EASE THE MORE EXTREMELY WOUNDED OUT . . . . . . 507 A MASQUE OF MERCY . . 370
EXTREMES
    EXTREMES TOO HARD TO COMPREHEND AT ONCE, ... 266 THE ARMFUL 4
    BETWEEN TWO METAPHYSICAL EXTREMES. . . . . 269 THE BEAR 25
EXTRICATION
    "A MAN HAS GOT TO KEEP HIS EXTRICATION. . . . . . . 406 FROM PLANE TO PLANE . 61
    EVERYONE HAS TO KEEP HIS EXTRICATION." . . . . . . 407 FROM PLANE TO PLANE . 96
EXULT
    WE STARTED TO EXULT . . . . 464 MILKY WAY IS A COWPATH 2
EYE
    SHE THINKS I HAVE NO EYE FOR THESE, ... 7 MY NOVEMBER GUEST . . 14
    FOR WHOM THESE LINES WHEN THEY SHALL GREET HER EYE. . . 15 WAITING 27
    AND THEN HE FLEW AS FAR AS EYE COULD SEE, ... 22 THE TUFT OF FLOWERS . 17
    BUT HE TURNED FIRST, AND LED MY EYE TO LOOK . . . . . 22 THE TUFT OF FLOWERS . 21
    BRUSHING THE DIRT FROM HIS EYE AS HE WENT; . . . . . 25 THE DEMIURGE'S LAUGH . 11

EYE (CONTINUED)
BUT HE THOUGHT A BIG THOUGHT--I COULD TELL BY HIS EYE-- . . 60 BLUEBERRIES 43
WITH AN EYE ALWAYS LIFTED TOWARD THE WEST . . . . 69 THE CODE 3
JOHN'S ALMOST HERE. I'VE HAD MY EYE ON SOMEONE . . . . . 88 THE HOUSEKEEPER . . . 196
TO WHICH THEY SET IT TRUE BY EYE; AND THEN . . . . . . 113 IN THE HOME STRETCH . 85
BROKEN ACROSS IT, AND ONE EYE IS WEEPING . . . . 122 BIRCHES 46
I'VE HAD MY EYE ON IT TO MAKE OUT WHICH: . . . . 147 SNOW 120
THE SNOW AGAINST THE WINDOW CAUGHT HIS EYE. . . . . . . 149 SNOW 180
UNDER THE WATCHFUL EYE OF HAWK AND EAGLE-- . . . . . . 162 NEW HAMPSHIRE . . . 105
FROM FOLLOWING WALLS I NEVER LIFT MY EYE, ... 173 A STAR IN A STONEBOAT . 40
NONE NOT IN HIDING FROM THE OUTWARD EYE. . . . . 174 THE CENSUS-TAKER . . 16
WERE PEOPLE TO THE EAR BUT NOT THE EYE. . . . . 175 THE CENSUS-TAKER . . 39
TO THE EYE OF MAN . . . . 220 I WILL SING YOU ONE-O . 73
OR FLOWER, OR WEARING-STONE, OR OPEN EYE, ... 220 FRAGMENTARY BLUE . . 3
ONE BIRD BEGINS TO CLOSE A FADED EYE; . . . . 249 ACCEPTANCE 7
WITH A STAR IN ONE EYE, ... 261 CANIS MAJOR 3
THE TRAVELER'S EYE PICKED UP A TURTLE TRAIL, ... 270 THE EGG AND THE MACHINE 17
THROUGH LEVEL MOUNTAINS NOTHING TO THE EYE . . . . . . 292 FIGURE IN THE DOORWAY . 2
(ALL MY EYE AND COTTON MATHER!), ... 304 CLEAR AND COLDER . . 18
I KEEP MY EYE ON CONGRESS, MELIBOEUS. . . . . 317 BUILD SOIL 54
TWO TEARDROPS, ONE FOR EITHER EYE, ... 327 A MISSIVE MISSILE . . 11
AN EYE BECOME EVASIVE. . . . . 340 THE SUBVERTED FLOWER . 47
BUT THERE IS IN THE SADNESS OF HIS EYE . . . . 359 THE LOST FOLLOWER . . 34
AS IF BY EYE PAIRS OUT OF FORTY FIRKINS. . . . . 378 DIRECTIVE 22
FOR ANY EYE IS AN EVIL EYE . . . . 385 A MOOD APART 7
GOING OVER MY EYE. . . . . 392 A WISH TO COMPLY . . 11
NO HABITATION MEETS THE EYE . . . . 392 A CLIFF DWELLING . . 3
HIS WATCHDOG EYE ON WHAT REMAINED . . . . 419 ONE MORE BREVITY . . 5
HE ROLLED AN EYE WITH GRATITUDE . . . . 420 ONE MORE BREVITY . . 20
IN THE EAR AND IN THE EYE . . . . 469 FOUR-ROOM SHACK.... . 5
FOR ANY BUT THE RAPIDEST EYE READERS.) . . . . 502 A MASQUE OF MERCY . . 246
EYED (SEE BRIGHT-BLACK-EYED, FUNNY-EYED, MANY-MANY-EYED)
HE EYED HER FOR A WHILE . . . . 339 THE SUBVERTED FLOWER . 8
EYEHOLE
HE TRIED IT AT THE EYEHOLE IN THE AX-HEAD. . . . . . . 187 THE AX-HELVE 78
EYEING
AND EYEING ONE HE ONLY WISHED WERE HIS, ... 454 HOW HARD TO KEEP FROM 15
EYELIDS
THEY TAPPED AT MY EYELIDS AND TOUCHED MY LIPS WITH AN
    INVITATION TO GRIEF. . . . . 298 A LEAF-TREADER . . . 10
MY EYELIDS SO I COULDN'T SHUT MY EYES . . . . 501 A MASQUE OF MERCY . . 202
EYES
HE ASKED WITH THE EYES MORE THAN THE LIPS . . . . . . 7 LOVE AND A QUESTION . 5
MINERVA'S SNOW-WHITE MARBLE EYES . . . . 9 STARS 11
HIS SKIN AND HIS HAIR AND HIS EYES WERE GRAY, ... 23 PAN WITH US 2
THE NIGHT CLERK BLINKED HIS EYES AND DARED HIM ON. . . 45 A HUNDRED COLLARS . . 28
BUT I WENT NEAR TO SEE WITH MY OWN EYES. . . . . 54 HOME BURIAL 83
DOES THE RAIN SEEM TO YOU TO COOL THE EYES?" . . . . . 75 THE GENERATIONS OF MEN 69
"OH, IF YOU'RE GOING TO USE YOUR EYES, JUST HEAR . . . 76 THE GENERATIONS OF MEN 98
"NO, I DON'T TRUST YOUR EYES. YOU'VE SAID ENOUGH. . . 80 THE GENERATIONS OF MEN 206
UP TO THEIR SHINING EYES IN SNOW. . . . . 102 GOOD HOURS 4
WHAT KEPT HIS EYES FROM GIVING BACK THE GAZE . . . . 108 OLD MAN'S WINTER NIGHT 4
FOOL-LIKE, AND ROLLED HIS EYES AS IF TO SAY . . . . . 114 IN THE HOME STRETCH . 102
WE DROP OUR EYES OR TURN TO OTHER THINGS, ... 114 IN THE HOME STRETCH . 117
AND FROM THERE THOSE THAT LIFTED EYES COULD COUNT . . 136 "OUT, OUT--" 4
BUT NOW HE SNAPPED HIS EYES THREE TIMES; . . . . . . 140 BROWN'S DESCENT . . 73
WITH LOWERED EYES A MOMENT TILL HE SAID, ... 144 SNOW 32
AND ITS EYES SHUT WITH OVEREAGERNESS . . . . 148 SNOW 161
IN WHICH HIS FACE WAS MUFFLED TO THE EYES, ... 160 NEW HAMPSHIRE . . . 48
STRIKING IT GENTLY ACROSS HER LOWERED EYES, ... 181 MAPLE 42
AND, IN THE PAUSES WHEN SHE RAISED HER EYES, ... 182 MAPLE 80
SHE USED HER HANDS TO COVER UP HER EYES. . . . . . . 184 MAPLE 160
AND SHUT MY EYES AGAINST THE SUN, MY EARS . . . . . 198 WILD GRAPES . . . 74
(SHE MADE SHREWD EYES TO SEE WHERE HE CAME IN.) . . . 201 PLACE FOR A THIRD . . 57
SMOKE ROLLED INSIDE THE SOCKETS OF HIS EYES.) . . . . 204 THE WITCH OF COOS . . 74
AND MOUNTS THE WALL AGAIN WITH WHITED EYES . . . . . 223 THE RUNAWAY . . . 16
WAS IN HER CLOUDED EYES: THEY SAW NO FEAR THERE. . . 229 TWO LOOK AT TWO . . 20
SHE DARED NO MORE THAN ASK HIM WITH HER EYES . . . . 231 NOT TO KEEP . . . 19
AND WITH HIS EYES HE ASKED HER NOT TO ASK. . . . . . 231 NOT TO KEEP . . . 21
LIKE LOCKS BLOWN FORWARD IN THE GLEAM OF EYES.. . . . 250 ONCE BY THE PACIFIC . 6
AND DROPPED MY EYES, UNWILLING TO EXPLAIN. . . . . . 255 ACQUAINTED WITH NIGHT . 6
THEN SEND SOME ONE WITH EYES TO SEE . . . . 257 THE LOVELY BE CHOOSERS 46
IF, AS THEY SAY, SOME DUST THROWN IN MY EYES . . . . 265 DUST IN THE EYES . . 1
DUST IN THE EYES . . . . 265 DUST IN THE EYES . . 1
WITH LIFTED SNOUT AND EYES (IF ANY) SHUT . . . . . . 269 THE BEAR 27
HAD EYES INSCRUTABLY OPAQUE; . . . . 273 A LONE STRIKER . . 12
AS MY TWO EYES MAKE ONE IN SIGHT. . . . . 277 TWO TRAMPS IN MUD TIME 68
A LOOK OF PUZZLED DIMNESS TO THEIR EYES . . . . . . 293 AT WOODWARD'S GARDENS . 10
HE HAS DUST IN HIS EYES AND A FAN FOR A WING, ... 309 ONE GUESS 1
LIGHT WAS A PASTE OF PIGMENT IN OUR EYES. . . . . . 315 IRIS BY NIGHT . . . 9
(I DO TOO MUCH IN SOME MEN'S EYES.) . . . . 327 A MISSIVE MISSILE . . 37
EYES SEEKING THE RESPONSE OF EYES . . . . 332 ALL REVELATION . . 16
RAIN WAS THE TEARS ADOPTED BY MY EYES . . . . 337 THE WIND AND THE RAIN . 47
AND DARKLY DRINK EACH OTHER'S EYES . . . . 344 DISCOVERY OF MADEIRAS . 39
THE MOST HE ASKED HER EYES TO GRANT . . . . 344 DISCOVERY OF MADEIRAS . 41
AS OF A BOOK HELD UP BEFORE HIS EYES . . . . 355 TIME OUT 3
LIKE TROUBLE IN THE BROW ABOVE THE EYES: . . . . . 399 THE INGENUITIES OF DEBT 3
PICK UP OUR EYES AND CARRY THEM BACK IDLE . . . . . 405 FROM PLANE TO PLANE . 51
HIS EYES AS GOOD (OR BAD) AS SHUT . . . . 418 AMERICA IS HARD TO SEE 58
AS TO BLIND OUR EYES . . . . 426 A NEVER NAUGHT SONG . 23
(GOD EYES HIM ANXIOUSLY.) / NO. NO, I MUSTN'T. . . . 485 A MASQUE OF REASON . 330
MY EYELIDS SO I COULDN'T SHUT MY EYES . . . . 501 A MASQUE OF MERCY . . 202
PROJECTED FROM THE LANTERN OF HIS EYES, ... 502 A MASQUE OF MERCY . . 237
WHERE SHALL I START IN? WHERE MY EYES FELL FIRST? . . 506 A MASQUE OF MERCY . . 326
WE WERE NOT GIVEN EYES OR INTELLECT . . . . 515 A MASQUE OF MERCY . . 586
CONTEMPLATE TRUTH UNTIL IT BURNS YOUR EYES OUT. . . . 517 A MASQUE OF MERCY . . 630

F
  FOR JOHN F. KENNEDY HIS INAUGURATION . . . . 422 FOR JOHN F. KENNEDY . T
FABLED
  THEY RENEW TALK OF THE FABLED . . . . 387 THE COURAGE TO BE NEW . 7
FABULA
  HAEC FABULA DOCET . . . . 394 HAEC FABULA DOCET . . T
FACE
  HER FACE ROSE-RED WITH THE GLOWING COAL . . . . 8 LOVE AND A QUESTION . 19
  AND FOR EVERY KIND THERE WAS A FACE, ... 15 IN A VALE 7
  THE SUNBURNED HILLSIDE SETS MY FACE AGLOW, ... 17 THE VANTAGE POINT . . 11
  AND HER FACE CHANGED FROM TERRIFIED TO DULL. . . . . . 51 HOME BURIAL 9
  SO INCONSOLABLY--IN THE FACE OF LOVE. . . . . 53 HOME BURIAL 65
  IT WAS ALL HE COULD DO TO KEEP A STRAIGHT FACE." . . . . 61 BLUEBERRIES 78
  ABOUT MY FACE AND BODY AND THROUGH MY WRAPPER, ... 63 A SERVANT TO SERVANTS . 29
  ALONG THE BUSHES AT THE ROADSIDE--A MAN'S FACE. . . . . 89 THE FEAR 11
  ARE YOU SURE----" / "YES, I'M SURE!" / "--IT WAS A FACE?" . . 89 THE FEAR 13
  IF THE TIME'S COME TO FACE IT, I'M THE ONE . . . . . 90 THE FEAR 36
  GOOD-BY." HE FLUNG HIS ARMS AROUND HIS FACE. . . . . . 101 THE SELF-SEEKER . . 228
  AND NOW AND THEN A SMUDGED, INFERNAL FACE . . . . . . 110 IN THE HOME STRETCH . 10
  ANOTHER BLACKENED FACE THRUST IN AND LOOKED . . . . . 111 IN THE HOME STRETCH . 18
  WHERE YOUR FACE BURNS AND TICKLES WITH THE COBWEBS . . . 122 BIRCHES 45
  HER FACE IS FLECKED WITH POMACE AND SHE DROOLS . . . . 124 THE COW IN APPLE TIME . 4
  AND THRUST HANDS IN AND HELD MY FACE AWAY. . . . . . 131 THE BONFIRE 66
  IN WHICH HIS FACE WAS MUFFLED TO THE EYES, ... 160 NEW HAMPSHIRE . . 48
  RATHER OF WHAT TO FACE OR RUN AWAY FROM. . . . . . 171 NEW HAMPSHIRE . . 396
  BEGGED SIMPLY FOR THE GRAVE. THE SISTER'S FACE . . . . 201 PLACE FOR A THIRD . 47
  BEFORE ITS FACE. . . . . 218 I WILL SING YOU ONE-O . 22
  THROUGH SOME DELAY, AND CALL YOU TO YOUR FACE . . . . 222 TO E.T. 6
  AND NOT DISFIGURED VISIBLY. HIS FACE? . . . . . . 230 NOT TO KEEP 7
  I HAD TO STOP AND LIFT MY FACE; . . . . 233 LOOKING FOR SUNSET BIRD 6
  AND INTO MY FACE. . . . . 235 GATHERING LEAVES . 12
  I REACHED OUT BLINDLY TO SAVE MY FACE, ... 265 THE DOOR IN THE DARK . 2
  SO LOVE WILL TAKE BETWEEN THE HANDS A FACE.... . . . . 301 MOON COMPASSES . . 8
  AND A CLOUD SHADOW CROSSED HER FACE . . . . 342 A CLOUD SHADOW . . 7
  REMEMBER, AND MUST KEEP A SOLEMN FACE.) . . . . . . 352 THE LESSON FOR TODAY . 67
  OF WHICH YOU FEEL NO LEAST TOUCH ON YOUR FACE . . . . 361 A LOOSE MOUNTAIN . 11
  IT PUFFS THE FACE AND BRUTALIZES SO. . . . . . . 371 THE LITERATE FARMER AND 105
  YET LEFT ME FREELY FACE TO FACE, ... 380 AN UNSTAMPED LETTER IN 16
  AS MEETING SOMEONE LIVING, FACE TO FACE. . . . . . 382 TO AN ANCIENT . . 9
  I DON'T BELIEVE WHAT MAKES YOU RED IN THE FACE . . . . 389 SKEPTIC 7
  ALBEIT NOT WITHOUT SOME SHAME OF FACE, ... 396 ANY SIZE WE PLEASE . 4
  HE RUNS FACE FORWARD. HE IS A PURSUER. . . . . . . 421 ESCAPIST--NEVER . . 6
  THEN THEY GAVE IT A FACE. . . . . 448 THE BAD ISLAND--EASTER 16
  THEY GAVE IT A FACE . . . . 448 THE BAD ISLAND--EASTER 20
  THAT'S SOMETHING I'M PREPARED TO FACE. . . . . . . 453 A-WISHING WELL . . 71
  IF EVEN THE FACE OF MAN'S TOO BRIGHT A LIGHT . . . . 515 A MASQUE OF MERCY . 583
  THEN HOW MUCH MORE THE FACE OF TRUTH MUST BE. . . . . 515 A MASQUE OF MERCY . 585
  SLAMS THE BLOW, THE BLOW AND THE REPULSE . . . . . 518 A MASQUE OF MERCY . 650
FACED (SEE WHITE-FACED)
  WE CAME OUT ON A LOOK-OFF WHERE WE FACED . . . . . 214 A FOUNTAIN, A BOTTLE . 37
  THEY BOUND THEM NAKED SO THEY FACED . . . . . . 345 DISCOVERY OF MADEIRAS . 76
  SHOULD COME TO NOTHING MUST BE FAIRLY FACED. . . . . 412 POD OF THE MILKWEED . 54
  WHAT HAD LONG BEEN FACED . . . . 439 KITTY HAWK . . . 370
FACES
  WE PRESSED OUR FACES TO THE PANE. "YOU SEE," HE SAID, . . 55 THE BLACK COTTAGE . 14
  AND LIFTS THEIR FACES BY THE CHIN TO HERS . . . . . 98 THE SELF-SEEKER . . 161
  "YOU, WILL, STOP MAKING FACES. COME ROUND HERE . . . . 99 THE SELF-SEEKER . . 184
  OF YOUTHFUL FORMS AND YOUTHFUL FACES. . . . . . . 102 GOOD HOURS . . . 8
  TO MAKE SO FREE AND KICK UP IN FOLKS' FACES. . . . . 210 PAUPER WITCH OF GRAFTON 107
  SUBTERFUGE FOR SAVING FACES. . . . . 396 AN IMPORTER . . . 7
  QUESTIONING FACES . . . . 445 QUESTIONING FACES . T
FACET
  AT EVERY POINT AND FACET GLOWED . . . . 332 ALL REVELATION . . 14
FACETIOUS
  AND GRATEFUL FOR IT (LET'S NOT BE FACETIOUS!) . . . . 393 LUCRETIUS VERSUS POETS 4
FACILE
  OUR COVERAGE OF DISTANCE IS SO FACILE . . . . . . 446 DOES NO ONE AT ALL EVER 15
FACILITY
  "ALL THIS FACILITY DISHEARTENS ME. . . . . 460 HOW HARD TO KEEP FROM 203
FACING
  WITH BARBED-WIRE BINDING. THEY STOOD FACING THIS, . . . 229 TWO LOOK AT TWO . . 8
  FACING ALONE . . . . 360 THE RABBIT-HUNTER . 4
  THE MORAL KIND'S AS BRAVE AS FACING BULLETS." . . . . 405 FROM PLANE TO PLANE . 35
FACT (SEE MATTER-OF-FACT)
  THE FACT IS THE SWEETEST DREAM THAT LABOR KNOWS. . . . 17 MOWING 13
  HE WON'T MAKE THE FACT THAT THEY'RE RIGHTFULLY HIS . . . 60 BLUEBERRIES . . . 31
  WITH ALL HER MATTER OF FACT ABOUT THE ICE STORM, . . . 121 BIRCHES . . . 22
  BACK ON THE FLOOR, IS FACT OR PRETTY NEAR FACT. . . . 192 PAUL'S WIFE . . . 53
  MATTER OF FACT HAS MADE THEM BRAVE. . . . . . . 291 ON HEART'S BEGINNING TO 35
  THEY'VE TRIED TO GRASP WITH TOO MUCH SOCIAL FACT . . . 351 THE LESSON FOR TODAY . 34
  AS A MATTER OF FACT THERE ARE TIMES WHEN I AM APT . . . 389 SKEPTIC . . . 10
  IN THE FOND FAITH ACCUMULATED FACT . . . . . . 414 A CABIN IN THE CLEARING 26
  AND IN FACT COMPLETE, ... 426 A NEVER NAUGHT SONG . 9
  DID IN FACT GET SPLATTERED . . . . 427 VERSION . . . 14
  AS A FACT OF WASTE . . . . 439 KITTY HAWK . . . 371
FACTO (SEE EX-POST-FACTO)
FACTOR'S
  ROSE LIKE A FACTOR'S AT A TRADING STATION. . . . . 160 NEW HAMPSHIRE . . 53
FACTORY
  THE FACTORY WAS VERY FINE; . . . . 274 A LONE STRIKER . . 50
FACTS
  THAT IS, IF FACTS IS WHAT THEY WANT TO GO BY. . . . 207 PAUPER WITCH OF GRAFTON 11
  I PUT NO FAITH IN THE SEEMING FACTS OF LIGHT. . . . 389 SKEPTIC . . . 4
  WHAT ARE THE SIMPLE FACTS OF PROGRESS . . . . . 449 OUR DOOM TO BLOOM . 2
FADE
  WITH FLOWERS IN HER LAP UNTIL THEY FADE, ... 79 THE GENERATIONS OF MEN 169
  UNLESS 'TWOULD RATHER WILT THAN FADE." . . . . . 450 OUR DOOM TO BLOOM . 16
  WHEN THAT FADES I FADE--EVERY TIME I FADE. . . . . 518 A MASQUE OF MERCY . 659

FADED
    THE FADED EARTH, THE HEAVY SKY, ...   7 MY NOVEMBER GUEST . . 12
    BY PICKING THE FADED BLUE . . . .   9 A LATE WALK 14
    FOR THE FADED FLOWERS GAY . . . .   13 FLOWER-GATHERING . . 10
    THAT THE STARS WERE ALMOST FADED AWAY. . . . . . .   15 IN A VALE 15
    TO MAKE ONE TEXTURE OF FADED BROWN . . . .   25 IN HARDWOOD GROVES . . 3
    ITS BED IS LEFT A FADED PAPER SHEET . . . .   119 HYLA BROOK 10
    SOME LABORER FOUND ONE FADED AND STONE-COLD, ... 172 A STAR IN A STONEBOAT . 4
    (THIS WAS HER FADED MEMORY OF THE WAY . . . . . .   183 MAPLE 110
    ONE BIRD BEGINS TO CLOSE A FADED EYE; . . . . . .   249 ACCEPTANCE 7
    HER SPIRIT FADED AS FAR AWAY . . . .   346 DISCOVERY OF MADEIRAS . 103
    OF COUNTRY WHERE TWO VILLAGE CULTURES FADED . . . .   378 DIRECTIVE 34
    I OWN THE NEED OF IT HAD SOMEWHAT FADED . . . . .   517 A MASQUE OF MERCY . . 625
FADES
    WHEN THAT FADES I FADE--EVERY TIME I FADE. . . . .   518 A MASQUE OF MERCY . . 659
FADING
    WHERE SHE COULD WATCH HER MOTHER'S PICTURE FADING. . . 181 MAPLE 61
    THE FLOWERS FADING ON THE SEED TO COME; . . . . . .   356 TIME OUT 7
FAHRENHEIT
    TALK FAHRENHEIT, TALK CENTIGRADE. . . . .   403 SOMETHING LIKE A STAR . 13
FAIL
    IT WAS JUST AS THE LIGHT WAS BEGINNING TO FAIL . . . . 24 THE DEMIURGE'S LAUGH . 4
    THEY SEEMED TO FAIL THE BLUEBIRDS UNDER THEM . . . . 130 THE BONFIRE 36
    THE ROAD WOULD FAIL; AND ON THAT SIDE THE FIRE . . . 131 THE BONFIRE 75
    HOW ANYONE CAN FAIL TO SEE . . . .   327 A MISSIVE MISSILE . . 33
    NEVER DID I FAIL . . . .   429 KITTY HAWK 33
    WHEN TEACHER'S OWN EXPERIENCES FAIL HER . . . . . .   447 DOES NO ONE AT ALL EVER 39
    VIRTUE MAY FAIL AND WICKEDNESS SUCCEED. . . . . .   475 A MASQUE OF REASON . 52
    TO GET THINGS DONE. REFORMERS FAIL TO SEE THAT.-- . . 478 A MASQUE OF REASON . 152
    I FAIL TO SEE WHAT FUN, WHAT SATISFACTION . . . .   483 A MASQUE OF REASON . 273
    HERE WE ALL FAIL TOGETHER, DWARFED AND POOR. . . . . 512 A MASQUE OF MERCY . 506
    THEY FAIL ME. NOW I'M TEASING YOU AGAIN. . . . . .   516 A MASQUE OF MERCY . 608
FAILED
    THE TOWN-BRED FARMER FAILED TO UNDERSTAND. . . . .   69 THE CODE 9
    AND FAILED TO SEE THE GOOD OF. NEVER MIND, ...   147 SNOW 125
    TILL HAVING FAILED AT HUGGER-MUGGER FARMING . . . .   177 THE STAR-SPLITTER . 15
    WHOSE PRIDE HAS FAILED TO GET HIM ANYWHERE). . . .   190 THE GRINDSTONE . . 44
    WHO FAILED TO FIND OR FORCE A STRAIT . . . . . .   212 AN EMPTY THREAT . . 44
    AND HIS CREW LEFT HIM WHERE HE FAILED, ...   212 AN EMPTY THREAT . . 46
    THE EARTH BUT IT HAS FAILED: THE SNOW MAY HEAP . . . 226 THE ONSET 14
    AND STILL THEY FAILED OF ANY LASTING HOLD. . . . .   239 OUR SINGING STRENGTH . 4
    ONE FAILED TO MAKE THE CLOSING GATE. . . . . . .   273 A LONE STRIKER . . 4
    FAILED TO CRUSH THEIR BARREL STAVES . . . .   344 DISCOVERY OF MADEIRAS . 28
    NO ONE HAS EVER FAILED THE POET RANKS . . . . . .   358 THE LOST FOLLOWER . 7
    HAS FAILED TO BRING--I MEAN THE GOLDEN AGE. . . . . 358 THE LOST FOLLOWER . 16
    WHO, HAVING FAILED OF THE MODERN SPEED, ...   419 ONE MORE BREVITY . 12
    SCIENCE HAS FAILED TO UNDERSTAND. . . . .   452 A-WISHING WELL . . 61
    YOU FAILED TO SEE THE WORTH OF YOUR ACHIEVEMENT. . . 480 A MASQUE OF REASON . 187
    YOUR COURAGE FAILED. THE SADDEST THING IN LIFE . . . 497 A MASQUE OF MERCY . 106
FAILING
    I KNEW A MAN WHO FAILING AS A FARMER . . . . . .   168 NEW HAMPSHIRE . . 301
    BUT HIS HEART FAILING HIM, HE DROPPED THE AX . . . . 170 NEW HAMPSHIRE . . 369
    ON UP THE FAILING PATH, WHERE, IF A STONE . . . . . 229 TWO LOOK AT TWO . . 11
    FAILING OF BEING LOVED FOR WHAT SHE IS, ...   257 THE LOVELY BE CHOOSERS 42
FAILS
    BUT KEEP STILL IF HE FAILS." / "KEEP STILL ALL OVER. . 146 SNOW 87
    SHE FAILS FROM STRANGENESS TO A WAY OF LIFE . . . . 257 THE LOVELY BE CHOOSERS 44
FAILURE
    AS AFTER ONE-OF-THEM'S PROVERBIAL FAILURE . . . .   412 POD OF THE MILKWEED . 37
    TO TAKE THE PUNISHMENT OUT OF ALL FAILURE . . . .   505 A MASQUE OF MERCY . 313
    FROM THE DISCOVERY THAT LOSS FROM FAILURE, ...   506 A MASQUE OF MERCY . 321
    IS JUST A FRAME-UP TO INSURE THE FAILURE . . . . .   511 A MASQUE OF MERCY . 483
    FAILURE IS FAILURE, BUT SUCCESS IS FAILURE. . . .   512 A MASQUE OF MERCY . 507
    BY MAKING FAILURE OUT OF EQUAL VALUE. . . . . . .   513 A MASQUE OF MERCY . 526
    MY FAILURE IS NO DIFFERENT FROM JONAH'S. . . . . .   521 A MASQUE OF MERCY . 727
FAIN
    SHE TALKS AND I AM FAIN TO LIST: . . . .   7 MY NOVEMBER GUEST . 7
    ONE SO LONELY WAS FAIN TO LIST, ...   15 IN A VALE 14
    WHO NOW WOULD FAIN SEEK SHELTERING WALL, ...   236 MISGIVING 7
FAINT
    THE SMELL OF SCORCHING WOOLEN MADE HER FAINT. . . .   91 THE FEAR 69
    THE FLOWER OF CITIES FROM SINKING AND WITHERING FAINT. . 286 A ROADSIDE STAND . 6
    WITH FAINT HEADSHAKINGS, NO MORE WISE. . . . . . .   344 DISCOVERY OF MADEIRAS . 40
    I WAS SUPPORTING YOU FOR FEAR YOU'D FAINT . . . . . 518 A MASQUE OF MERCY . 647
FAINTEST
    THE FAINTEST RESTLESS RUSTLING RAN ALL THROUGH THEM. . . 204 THE WITCH OF COOS . . 64
FAINTLY
    BUT FAINTLY REMINISCENT OF THE RACE . . . .   173 A STAR IN A STONEBOAT . 32
FAIR
    AND HE SPOKE THE BRIDEGROOM FAIR. . . . .   7 LOVE AND A QUESTION . 2
    BECAUSE THE AUTUMN EVE WAS FAIR . . . .   18 GOING FOR WATER . . 6
    I SEE IT'S A FAIR, PRETTY SHEET OF WATER. . . . .   63 A SERVANT TO SERVANTS . 17
    I SEE IT'S A FAIR, PRETTY SHEET OF WATER, ...   63 A SERVANT TO SERVANTS . 32
    I WENT ABOUT TO KILL HIM FAIR ENOUGH." . . . . .   73 THE CODE 112
    "IT'S RAINING." / "NO, IT'S MISTING; LET'S BE FAIR. . . 75 THE GENERATIONS OF MEN 68
    "AND AFTER ALL WHY SHOULD THEY? JOHN'S BEEN FAIR . . . 84 THE HOUSEKEEPER . . 92
    IT'S NOT FAIR TO THE CHILD. IT CAN'T BE HELPED, THOUGH: . 98 THE SELF-SEEKER . . 148
    THEN TOOK THE OTHER, AS JUST AS FAIR, ...   105 THE ROAD NOT TAKEN . 6
    I WONDERED IF HE REALLY THOUGHT IT FAIR . . . . .   190 THE GRINDSTONE . . 48
    AND THERE WAS ONE MORE NOT SO FAIR TO PAUL: . . .   192 PAUL'S WIFE . . . 35
    AND TRULY IT WAS FAIR ENOUGH FOR FLOWERS . . . . .   233 A BOUNDLESS MOMENT . 6
    IT WOULD NOT BE FAIR TO SAY FOR A DOLE OF BREAD, . . 286 A ROADSIDE STAND . 4
    MY FAIR IMPRESSION MAY . . . .   333 HAPPINESS MAKES UP . 19
    WHETHER TIME'S REWARDS ARE FAIR OR UNFAIR. . . . .   347 DISCOVERY OF MADEIRAS . 138
    (LESS BRAVE PERHAPS THAN TRUSTING ARE THE FAIR.) . . 375 A YOUNG BIRCH . . 10
    IT BIDS PRETTY FAIR . . . .   392 IT BIDS PRETTY FAIR . T
    A FAIR OASIS IN THE PUREST DESERT. . . . .   473 A MASQUE OF REASON . . 1
    IT'S ONLY FAIR TO KEEPER TO INFORM YOU . . . . .   496 A MASQUE OF MERCY . . 80

FAIR (CONTINUED)
    TO SEE THAT THE FAIR FIGHT IS REALLY FAIR. . . . . . . 507 A MASQUE OF MERCY . 364
FAIRBANKS
    FAIRBANKS, HE SAYS TO ME--HE'S EDITOR-- . . . . 48 A HUNDRED COLLARS . 105
    FAIRBANKS, HE SAYS TO ME, 'HELP US THIS YEAR,' . . . . 48 A HUNDRED COLLARS . 112
FAIRE (SEE LAISSEZ-FAIRE)
FAIRER
    WHICH IS FAIRER, FLOWER OR LEAF. . . . . 297 LEAVES COMPARED WITH . 14
    DICK TOLD HIM TO BE FAIRER TO THE DOCTOR: . . . . . 405 FROM PLANE TO PLANE . 36
FAIREST
    O STAR (THE FAIREST ONE IN SIGHT), ... 403 SOMETHING LIKE A STAR . 1
FAIRLY
    AND PAY A DEATH TAX OF FAIRLY POLITE REPENTANCE. . . . 307 NOT QUITE SOCIAL . 16
    SHOULD COME TO NOTHING MUST BE FAIRLY FACED. . . . . 412 POD OF THE MILKWEED . 54
    IT WAS FAIRLY BURST. . . . . 426 A NEVER NAUGHT SONG . 4
FAIRNESS
    WHERE WOULD THE FAIRNESS BE IN GIVING ME . . . . . 183 MAPLE 115
    NEITHER WOULD FAIRNESS. YOU HAVE HEARD THE DOCTRINE. . . 485 A MASQUE OF REASON . 356
FAIRS
    KING'S X--NO FAIRS TO USE IT ANYMORE! . . . . . . 399 U.S. 1946 KING'S X . 4
FAIRY
    LIKE A LIMP ROSE-WREATH IN A FAIRY DANCE. . . . . . 28 MY BUTTERFLY . . . 17
FAITH
    OF GOOD FAITH. THERE IS NINETY DOLLARS. . . . . . 47 A HUNDRED COLLARS . 86
    BUT LACKING FAITH IN ANYTHING TO MEAN . . . . . . 184 MAPLE 155
    THE SCALES OF TRADE, THE CROSS OF FAITH, ... 252 THE PEACEFUL SHEPHERD . 7
    THE OTHER PERSISTS AS OUR FAITH. . . . . 266 SITTING BY A BUSH . 20
    THE GROUNDWORK OF ALL FAITH IS HUMAN WOE. . . . . 352 THE LESSON FOR TODAY . 58
    RELIGIOUS FAITH IS A MOST FILLING VAPOR. . . . . . 386 INNATE HELIUM . . 1
    I PUT NO FAITH IN THE SEEMING FACTS OF LIGHT. . . . . 389 SKEPTIC 4
    IN THE FOND FAITH ACCUMULATED FACT . . . . 414 A CABIN IN THE CLEARING 26
    I'VE LOST MY FAITH IN GOD TO CARRY OUT . . . . . 497 A MASQUE OF MERCY . 114
    YOU'VE LOST YOUR FAITH IN GOD? HOW WICKED OF YOU. . . . 497 A MASQUE OF MERCY . 117
    ON THE OFF-CHANCE IT MAY BE LACK OF FAITH, ... 515 A MASQUE OF MERCY . 563
    TO BRING FAITH BACK. I'M ONLY LANGUIDLY . . . . . 515 A MASQUE OF MERCY . 566
FAITHFUL
    IT WOULDN'T HURT YOU TO VOUCHSAFE THE FAITHFUL. . . . 478 A MASQUE OF REASON . 143
FALL (SEE PETAL-FALL)
    A SLENDER TINKLING FALL THAT MADE . . . . 18 GOING FOR WATER . . 22
    THEY FALL FROM GIVING SHADE ABOVE, ... 25 IN HARDWOOD GROVES . 2
    THY LEAVES HAVE RIPENED TO THE FALL; . . . . . . 27 OCTOBER 2
    NO LONGER THAN THAT?--AND THE FOLLOWING FALL . . . . 59 BLUEBERRIES . . . 11
    IT MELTED, AND I LET IT FALL AND BREAK. . . . . . 68 AFTER APPLE-PICKING . 13
    CHERISH IN HAND, LIFT DOWN, AND NOT LET FALL. . . . . 69 AFTER APPLE-PICKING . 31
    THESE LATTER ABOUT TO FALL. I THOUGHT THAT ONLY . . . 102 THE WOOD-PILE . . 34
    AND COMES THAT OTHER FALL WE NAME THE FALL. . . . . 120 THE OVEN BIRD . . 9
    A BUTTERFLY ITS FALL HAD DISPOSSESSED, ... 126 RANGE-FINDING . . 6
    "I'LL OWN IT'S COLD FOR SUCH A FALL OF SNOW. . . . . 150 SNOW 201
    FOR ALL HER MOUNTAINS FALL A LITTLE SHORT, ... 170 NEW HAMPSHIRE . . 355
    THAT SLIP FROM HEAVEN AT NIGHT AND SOFTLY FALL . . . 172 A STAR IN A STONEBOAT . 2
    AND STILL I CLUNG. I LET MY HEAD FALL BACK, ... 198 WILD GRAPES . . . 73
    LABAN WAS FORCED TO FALL BACK ON HIS PLAN . . . . 202 PLACE FOR A THIRD . 79
    AS WE CAN FALL AND KEEP A-BOUNCING ON OUR FEET. . . . 215 A FOUNTAIN, A BOTTLE . 62
    ONCE WHEN THE SNOW OF THE YEAR WAS BEGINNING TO FALL, . 223 WEST-RUNNING BROOK . 1
    SO THAT THE FALL OF MOST OF IT IS ALWAYS . . . . . 259 WEST-RUNNING BROOK . 62
    THEY FALL, THEY RIP THE GRASS, THEY INTERSECT . . . 261 A SOLDIER 9
    I CROUCH DOWN TO PREVENT THEM AS THEY FALL; . . . . 267 THE ARMFUL . . . 9
    (SHE'S MAKING HER CROSS-COUNTRY IN THE FALL). . . . 268 THE BEAR 6
    IT WOULD FLUTTER AND FALL IN HALF AN HOUR . . . . 291 ON HEART'S BEGINNING TO 11
    BUT WE WHO PASSED WERE NOT TO SEE HIM FALL. . . . . 292 FIGURE IN THE DOORWAY . 10
    SAYS, TO MAKE THIS FALL ELIXIR . . . . 303 CLEAR AND COLDER . 3
    FOR THERE THERE HAD BEEN AN APPLE FALL . . . . . 304 UNHARVESTED . . . 8
    TOO MANY FALL FROM GREAT AND GOOD . . . . 307 PROVIDE, PROVIDE . 5
    WHO FALL ALL OVER EACH OTHER TO BRING SOIL . . . . 321 BUILD SOIL . . . 177
    SAID THAT THE FALL MIGHT COME AND WHIRL OF LEAVES, . . 343 QUEST OF PURPLE-FRINGED 27
    BUT SHE CAN TRUST IT NOT TO FALL TONIGHT. . . . . 386 THE FEAR OF MAN . . 6
    A RAIN, THOUGH STINGY, HAD BEGUN TO FALL . . . . . 399 THE BROKEN DROUGHT . 3
    WHEN WE TOOK THAT FALL . . . . 435 KITTY HAWK . . . 217
    (THE CURTAIN STARTS TO FALL.) PLEASE HOLD THE CURTAIN.-- . 519 A MASQUE OF MERCY . 673
FALLEN
    TO EACH THE BOULDERS THAT HAVE FALLEN TO EACH. . . . . 33 MENDING WALL . . . 16
    THE RIVER AT THE TIME WAS FALLEN AWAY, ... 40 THE MOUNTAIN . . . 10
    A ROCK-STREWN TOWN WHERE FARMING HAS FALLEN OFF, . . . 73 THE GENERATIONS OF MEN 5
    YOU'D THINK THE INNER DOME OF HEAVEN HAD FALLEN. . . . 121 BIRCHES 13
    SOFT PETALS FALLEN FROM THE APPLE TREE . . . . . 124 PUTTING IN THE SEED . 4
    THIS HOUSE IN ONE YEAR FALLEN TO DECAY . . . . . 176 THE CENSUS-TAKER . 50
    FALLEN TO RUIN IN TEN THOUSAND YEARS . . . . . . 176 THE CENSUS-TAKER . 52
    ON A TREE FALLEN ACROSS THE ROAD . . . . 238 ON A TREE FALLEN ACROSS T
    HE IS THAT FALLEN LANCE THAT LIES AS HURLED, ... 261 A SOLDIER 1
    AND HAD HE FALLEN INWARD ON THE FLOOR, ... 292 FIGURE IN THE DOORWAY . 8
    FROM A FALLEN TREE AND PUSHING OFF . . . . 347 DISCOVERY OF MADEIRAS . 126
    LIKE A STAR FRESH FALLEN OUT OF THE SKY. . . . . . 383 WERE I IN TROUBLE . 5
    AND FALLEN AND BEEN HUMBLED . . . . 389 ASTROMETAPHYSICAL . 7
    HOW ARE THEIR VOLUMES FALLEN! / ONLY ONE! . . . . . 504 A MASQUE OF MERCY . 291
FALLIBILITY
    NOTHING BUT FALLIBILITY WAS LEFT US, ... 279 THE WHITE-TAILED HORNET 69
FALLING
    PART OF A MOON WAS FALLING DOWN THE WEST, ... 38 DEATH OF THE HIRED MAN 103
    FALLING IN LOVE ACROSS THE TWILIGHT MILLPOND. . . . 195 PAUL'S WIFE . . . 131
    LIKE A SHADOW AGAINST THE CURTAIN OF FALLING FLAKES. . . 223 THE RUNAWAY . . . 8
    SNOW FALLING AND NIGHT FALLING FAST, OH, FAST . . . 296 DESERT PLACES . . 1
FALLS
    AND A CELLAR IN WHICH THE DAYLIGHT FALLS . . . . . 5 GHOST HOUSE . . . 4
    THE LIGHT OF HEAVEN FALLS WHOLE AND WHITE . . . . 19 THE TRIAL BY EXISTENCE 9
    AND A HUSH FALLS FOR ALL ACCLAIM. . . . . 21 THE TRIAL BY EXISTENCE 60
    AND FALLS ASLEEP WITH HEARTACHE--HOW SHOULD I FEEL? . . 58 THE BLACK COTTAGE . 103
    AND WHEN HE CAN'T DO ANYTHING, FALLS BACK . . . . 171 NEW HAMPSHIRE . . 400
    (IT WILL BE TAKEN DOWN BEFORE IT FALLS.) . . . . 386 THE FEAR OF MAN . . 7

PAGE TITLE   LINE

FALLS (CONTINUED)
    A LIGHT THAT FALLS DIFFUSED OVER MY SHOULDER . . . . . 515 A MASQUE OF MERCY . 580
    BUT ONE THING MORE BEFORE THE CURTAIN FALLS.-- . . . . . 519 A MASQUE OF MERCY . 672
FALSE
    SO FALSE IT IS THAT WHAT WE HAVEN'T WE CAN'T GIVE; . . . 148 SNOW 149
    SO FALSE, THAT WHAT WE ALWAYS SAY IS TRUE. . . . . . . 148 SNOW 150
    EXPRESSED THEM, AND ITS CURVES WERE NO FALSE CURVES . . . 187 THE AX-HELVE . . 74
    THAT THERE ALWAYS IS WHEN THE CHIMNEY'S FALSE. . . . . . 232 THE KITCHEN CHIMNEY . 16
    WHERE ONE FALSE WING BEAT WOULD HAVE BROUGHT DOWN ALL, . 240 OUR SINGING STRENGTH . 43
    AND NOW PRAY TELL WHAT LURED YOU WITH FALSE HOPE . . . 356 A MOTH SEEN IN WINTER . 7
    FALSE PREMISES THAT ARE THE ORIGINAL . . . . 480 A MASQUE OF REASON . 204
FALTERED
    IT FALTERED: I COULD SEE IT HESITATE; . . . . 357 A CONSIDERABLE SPECK . 20
FALTERING
    OUR FALTERING FEW STEPS ON . . . . 9 STARS 6
FAME
    FOR YOUR NOT HAVING WON TO VIRGIL'S FAME. . . . . . 351 THE LESSON FOR TODAY . 27
    OR BEEN THEIR RICHES, FAME, OR LOVE DENIED; . . . . . 355 THE LESSON FOR TODAY . 153
    TO THE RUNWAY'S FAME . . . . 430 KITTY HAWK . . 82
    JUSTLY KNOWN TO FAME . . . . 440 KITTY HAWK . . . 375
FAMILIAR
    WHICH HAS ITS SOUNDS, FAMILIAR, LIKE THE ROAR . . . . 108 OLD MAN'S WINTER NIGHT 12
    FOLKS THINK A WITCH WHO HAS FAMILIAR SPIRITS . . . . 202 THE WITCH OF COOS . . 4
FAMILY
    ALL IN A FAMILY ROW DOWN TO THE YOUNGEST." . . . . . 49 A HUNDRED COLLARS . 148
    I HAVE MY FANCIES: IT RUNS IN THE FAMILY. . . . . . 65 A SERVANT TO SERVANTS . 87
    THE ORIGIN OF ALL THE FAMILY THERE. . . . . . . 73 THE GENERATIONS OF MEN 9
    OF STRANGER-COUSINS, IN A FAMILY TREE . . . . . . 74 THE GENERATIONS OF MEN 39
    "UNDER THE SHELTER OF THE FAMILY TREE." . . . . . . 75 THE GENERATIONS OF MEN 65
    OF THE STARK FAMILY I'M A MEMBER OF)." . . . . . . 76 THE GENERATIONS OF MEN 81
    I NEVER SAW A MAN LET FAMILY TROUBLES . . . . . . 83 THE HOUSEKEEPER . . 53
    A ROBBER WOULDN'T HAVE HIS FAMILY WITH HIM." . . . . 92 THE FEAR 80
    "NONE OF MY FAMILY EVER WORKED, OR HAD . . . . . 159 NEW HAMPSHIRE . . 3
    I CALL HER OLD. SHE HAS ONE FAMILY . . . . . . 161 NEW HAMPSHIRE . . 70
    AND TAKEN THUS INTO THE FAMILY. . . . . . . 216 A FOUNTAIN, A BOTTLE . 101
    THE ROSE FAMILY . . . . 246 THE ROSE FAMILY . . T
    JOIN THE UNITED STATES AND JOIN THE FAMILY-- . . . 325 BUILD SOIL . . 281
    BUT THIS WAS A FAMILY CROWD, ... 365 A NATURE NOTE . . 7
    A FULL-FLEDGED FAMILY AFFAIR. . . . . . . 365 A NATURE NOTE . . 8
    FOR FAMILY AFTER FAMILY NAME. . . . . . . 367 A SERIOUS STEP LIGHTLY 15
    TO SAVE THE QUEEN FROM FAMILY CENSURE . . . . 416 AMERICA IS HARD TO SEE 11
FAMILY'S
    THE FAMILY'S ALL AWAY IN SOME BACK MEADOW. . . . 49 A HUNDRED COLLARS . 131
    AND FOR YOUR FAMILY'S SAKE STAY WHERE YOU ARE. . . . 150 SNOW . . . 217
FAMOUS
    AT LEAST I'VE BROUGHT YOU TO THE FAMOUS BOTTLE." . . 214 A FOUNTAIN, A BOTTLE . 42
    MIGHT SEE THEM ON A RACK LIKE FAMOUS OARS, ... 290 OLD BARN AT THE BOTTOM 36
    YOU MUST HAVE READ THE FAMOUS VALENTINE . . . . 461 HOW HARD TO KEEP FROM 249
    THE FAMOUS FOSTER NURSE . . . . 464 MILKY WAY IS A COWPATH 25
    SATAN, WHAT AILS YOU? WHERE'S THE FAMOUS TONGUE, . . 488 A MASQUE OF REASON . 405
FAN
    NOW BREATHED AS LIGHT AS A LADY'S FAN. . . . . . 304 UNHARVESTED 7
    HE HAS DUST IN HIS EYES AND A FAN FOR A WING, . . . 309 ONE GUESS 1
FANATICAL
    SOMETHING TO BE FANATICAL ABOUT, ... 515 A MASQUE OF MERCY . 570
FANCIED
    I FANCIED WHEN I LOOKED AT SIX O'CLOCK . . . . . 237 A HILLSIDE THAW . . 23
FANCIES
    I HAVE MY FANCIES: IT RUNS IN THE FAMILY. . . . . 65 A SERVANT TO SERVANTS . 87
FANCY
    PLAYING OUR FANCY, TO HAVE THE SNOW-LINE RUN . . . 149 SNOW 190
    AND TOOK THE FANCY HOME WITH THEM TO LIVE BY. . . . 182 MAPLE 96
    IT MAY HAVE BEEN THEIR ONE LAPSE INTO FANCY . . . 183 MAPLE . . . 120
    BUT SAY WHAT FANCY WILL, ... 388 MIDDLENESS OF THE ROAD 8
    IN FANCY I RATIFIED HIS NAME, ... 420 ONE MORE BREVITY . . 39
FANCY'S
    HER STYLE, WERE ALL THE FANCY'S TALK. . . . . . 280 BLUE RIBBON AT AMESBURY 8
FANNED
    FLOWERS FANNED AND NOT PUT OUT BY ALL THE RAIN . . . 173 A STAR IN A STONEBOAT . 23
FANNING
    MADE WIND BY FANNING, SINCE YOU NEVER KNEW . . . 130 THE BONFIRE . . . 42
FANTASTIC
    WOULD PUT AN END TO SUCH FANTASTIC NONSENSE; . . . 484 A MASQUE OF REASON . 309
FAR
    IN THAT VANISHED ABODE THERE FAR APART . . . . 6 GHOST HOUSE . . 12
    I HEAR HIM BEGIN FAR ENOUGH AWAY . . . . . . 6 GHOST HOUSE . . 18
    I END NOT FAR FROM MY GOING FORTH, ... 9 A LATE WALK . . . 13
    TILL EVEN THE COMFORTING BARN GROWS FAR AWAY, . . . 10 STORM FEAR . . . 15
    AND GIVE US NOT TO THINK SO FAR AWAY . . . . 12 A PRAYER IN SPRING . 2
    TO SANCTIFY TO WHAT FAR ENDS HE WILL, ... 12 A PRAYER IN SPRING . 15
    "I DARE NOT--TOO FAR IN HIS FOOTSTEPS STRAY-- . . . 16 A DREAM PANG . . 7
    NOT FAR, BUT NEAR, I STOOD AND SAW IT ALL, . . . 16 A DREAM PANG . . 9
    FAR OFF THE HOMES OF MEN, AND FARTHER STILL, . . . 17 THE VANTAGE POINT . . 6
    AND THEN HE FLEW AS FAR AS EYE COULD SEE, . . . 22 THE TUFT OF FLOWERS . 17
    A NEW-WORLD SONG, FAR OUT OF REACH, ... 24 PAN WITH US . . . 17
    IT WAS FAR IN THE SAMENESS OF THE WOOD; . . . 24 THE DEMIURGE'S LAUGH . 1
    COME OVER THE HILLS AND FAR WITH ME, ... 26 A LINE-STORM SONG . 7
    ONE FROM OUR TREES, ONE FAR AWAY. . . . . 27 OCTOBER . . . 14
    TOO FAR BEYOND HIM TO BE GATHERED IN, . . . 29 MY BUTTERFLY . . . 29
    SILAS HAS WALKED THAT FAR NO DOUBT TODAY. . . . 38 DEATH OF THE HIRED MAN 127
    "WHERE IS YOUR VILLAGE? VERY FAR FROM HERE?" . . . 41 THE MOUNTAIN . . 23
    "CAN YOU WALK AROUND IT? WOULD IT BE TOO FAR?" . . 43 THE MOUNTAIN . . 92
    WITH ANYONE TO DEATH, COMES SO FAR SHORT . . . 54 HOME BURIAL . . . 98
    THEY LIVE SO FAR AWAY--ONE IS OUT WEST-- . . . 55 THE BLACK COTTAGE . 19
    TO MEASURE HOW FAR FIFTY YEARS HAVE BROUGHT US. . . 56 THE BLACK COTTAGE . 46
    IT NEVER GOT SO FAR AS THAT; BUT THE BARE THOUGHT . 57 THE BLACK COTTAGE . 90
    AND I AGREE TO THAT, OR IN SO FAR . . . . 64 A SERVANT TO SERVANTS . 57
    ONLY ONE FROM A FARM NOT FAR AWAY . . . . . 74 THE GENERATIONS OF MEN 25

FAR (CONTINUED)
AND DISAPPEARED AND ENDED NOT FAR OFF. . . . . 75 THE GENERATIONS OF MEN   72
IT'S GONE SO FAR. YOU'VE HEARD? ESTELLE'S RUN OFF." . . . 82 THE HOUSEKEEPER . . .   20
NO MATTER HOW FAR AND HOW MANY TIMES . . . . 85 THE HOUSEKEEPER . . .   130
SHE WON'T GET FAR BEFORE THE WHEELS HANG UP . . . . 88 THE HOUSEKEEPER . . .   202
YOU'VE GOT TO TELL ME HOW FAR THIS IS GONE: . . . . 94 THE SELF-SEEKER . . .   57
HE SAYS IT'S NOT REPORTED SO FAR NORTH.-- . . . . 95 THE SELF-SEEKER . . .   87
OR SOMEWHERE ELSE: I WAS JUST FAR FROM HOME. . . . . . . 101 THE WOOD-PILE   9
AND LEAVE IT THERE FAR FROM A USEFUL FIREPLACE . . . . . 102 THE WOOD-PILE   38
AND LOOKED DOWN ONE AS FAR AS I COULD . . . . 105 THE ROAD NOT TAKEN . .   4
"WHEN I WAS JUST AS FAR AS I COULD WALK . . . . 118 THE TELEPHONE   1
THIS AS IT WILL BE SEEN IS OTHER FAR . . . . 119 HYLA BROOK   13
IN SEVERAL BEAUTY THAT THOUGHT FARES FAR . . . . 121 BOND AND FREE   19
SOME BOY TOO FAR FROM TOWN TO LEARN BASEBALL, ... 121 BIRCHES   25
TO THE LONELY HOUSE FROM FAR AWAY, ... 127 HOUSE FEAR   3
I WONDER HOW FAR DOWN THE ROAD HE'S GOT. . . . . 127 THE SMILE   11
SHE STRAYED SO FAR SHE SCARCELY HEARD . . . . 129 THE IMPULSE   15
UNDER THE SUNSET FAR INTO VERMONT. . . . . 136 "OUT, OUT--"   6
I'M HERE--SO FAR--AND STARTING ON AGAIN. . . . . 143 SNOW   12
OR SOMETHING NOT FAR FROM IT ON THE TABLE. . . . . 147 SNOW   112
ASK HELEN HOW FAR UP THE SASH IT'S CLIMBED . . . . 148 SNOW   158
AT THE FAR END OF IT YOU SEE A STIR . . . . 149 SNOW   194
FRANTIC IT SOUNDS, THOUGH MUFFLED AND FAR OFF. . . . . . 154 SNOW   319
FAR UP THE BIRCHES OUT OF REACH OF MAN. . . . . 164 NEW HAMPSHIRE   164
AND DECLARE TO THE CLIFFS TOO FAR FOR ECHO, ... 176 THE CENSUS-TAKER . .   56
AS FAR AGAIN AS FROM BEING BORN TO BEARING." . . . . . . 184 MAPLE   130
AND WOUNDED ON HIS BLADE. SO FAR FROM CARING, ... 190 THE GRINDSTONE . . .   59
"I'LL CATCH YOU IN MY ARMS. IT ISN'T FAR." . . . . 198 WILD GRAPES   76
OFF FROM THE HOUSE AS FAR AS WE COULD KEEP . . . . 210 PAUPER WITCH OF GRAFTON   90
HE'S SO FAR OFF HE CAN'T SEE WHAT I'VE COME TO. . . . . 210 PAUPER WITCH OF GRAFTON 102
THOUGH SET SO FAR . . . . 219 I WILL SING YOU ONE-O .   64
AND BLUE SO FAR ABOVE US COMES SO HIGH, ... 220 FRAGMENTARY BLUE . .   7
HOWEVER FAR YOU MUST GO FOR BRICKS, ... 232 THE KITCHEN CHIMNEY .   5
FAR IN THE MAPLES, PALE, BUT NOT A GHOST? . . . . 233 A BOUNDLESS MOMENT . .   2
AS FAR AS YOU WENT FROM THE DOOR, WHICH WAS NOT FAR; . . 235 VALLEY'S SINGING DAY .   3
SOME THAT HAVE COME TOO FAR NORTH BACK AWAY, ... 239 OUR SINGING STRENGTH .   23
AS FAR AS I CAN SEE, THIS AUTUMN HAZE . . . . 247 THE COCOON   1
OR OVERTAKEN TOO FAR FROM HIS NEST, ... 249 ACCEPTANCE   8
BUT NEVER WAS I FAR OUT OF SIGHT . . . . 253 THE THATCH   3
WHEN FAR AWAY AN INTERRUPTED CRY . . . . 253 ACQUAINTED WITH NIGHT .   8
THE VOICES, "HOW FAR DOWN?" . . . . 255 THE LOVELY BE CHOOSERS   2
THEY MOVE IN PLEASURE TOO FAR OFF . . . . 256 THE LOVELY BE CHOOSERS   29
FROM FAR AWAY THERE CAME AN ANSWERING TICK, ... 269 THE EGG AND THE MACHINE   2
HERE FAR FROM THE CITY WE MAKE OUR ROADSIDE STAND . . . 286 A ROADSIDE STAND . .   18
THAT FAR LIGHT FLICKERS BECAUSE OF TREES. . . . . 291 ON HEART'S BEGINNING TO   15
FAR INTO THE LIVES OF OTHER FOLK. . . . . 292 ON HEART'S BEGINNING TO   45
MEN WORK ALONE, THEIR LOTS PLOWED FAR APART, ... 299 STRONG SAYING NOTHING .   6
BUT YOU HAVE SPEED FAR GREATER. YOU CAN CLIMB . . . . . 300 THE MASTER SPEED . .   2
NEITHER OUT FAR NOR IN DEEP . . . . 301 NEITHER OUT FAR NOR IN   T
THEY CANNOT LOOK OUT FAR. . . . . 301 NEITHER OUT FAR NOR IN   13
IT COULD NOT HAVE COME DOWN TO US SO FAR, ... 302 A BIRD SINGING IN SLEEP   9
FAR TO NORTH OF THE ST. LAWRENCE. . . . . 304 CLEAR AND COLDER . .   11
IT IS VERY FAR NORTH, WE ADMIT, TO HAVE BROUGHT THE PEACH. . 305 THERE ARE ROUGHLY ZONES 6
FAR ENOUGH FOR MY THOUGHT-FLOW TO RESUME. . . . . 324 BUILD SOIL   256
PROBABLY, BUT YOU'RE FAR TOO FAST AND STRONG . . . . . 325 BUILD SOIL   284
FAR AS WE AIM OUR SIGNS TO REACH, ... 328 A MISSIVE MISSILE . .   47
FAR AS WE OFTEN MAKE THEM REACH, ... 328 A MISSIVE MISSILE . .   48
IT CANNOT SPEAK AS FAR AS THIS. . . . . 328 A MISSIVE MISSILE . .   55
FAR IN THE PILLARED DARK . . . . 334 COME IN   13
IT'S GONE SO FAR SHE'S PROBABLY CAUGHT . . . . 345 DISCOVERY OF MADEIRAS   74
HER SPIRIT FADED AS FAR AWAY . . . . 346 DISCOVERY OF MADEIRAS   103
THE ONLY OTHER THERE WAS FAR AWAY . . . . 354 THE LESSON FOR TODAY .   128
AND WHEN WE GET TOO FAR APART IN WEALTH, ... 363 AN EQUALIZER   5
SO FAR AS HE, THE SPEAKER, WAS CONCERNED . . . . 370 THE LITERATE FARMER AND   57
NO PLACE TO GET LOST LIKE TOO FAR IN THE DISTANCE. . . 379 TOO ANXIOUS FOR RIVERS   11
AWAY ON THE MOUNTAIN UP FAR TOO HIGH, ... 383 WERE I IN TROUBLE . .   2
THEY DEAL WITH NEAR AND FAR, ... 388 MIDDLENESS OF THE ROAD   12
FAR STAR THAT TICKLES FOR ME MY SENSITIVE PLATE . . . . 389 SKEPTIC   1
NO ONE WAS SO FAR TOUCHED . . . . 391 A ROGERS GROUP . . .   11
TO CARRY PRAISE OR BLAME TOO FAR, ... 403 SOMETHING LIKE A STAR .   23
ANOTHER STILL, LOST FAR INTO THE DISTANCE. . . . . . . 421 ESCAPIST--NEVER . . .   8
WE'RE NOT VERY FAR . . . . 439 KITTY HAWK   345
WE'D HAVE GOT AS FAR . . . . 439 KITTY HAWK   348
AND HOLDING IT FAR FORWARD FOR A SYMBOL . . . . 446 DOES NO ONE AT ALL EVER   27
SO FAR INLAND THE VERY NAME OF OCEAN . . . . 447 DOES NO ONE AT ALL EVER   37
BUT THEY HAD NOT WALKED FAR INTO THE NIGHT . . . . . . 454 HOW HARD TO KEEP FROM   12
NO ESTIMATING HOW FAR THE ENTENTE . . . . 456 HOW HARD TO KEEP FROM   77
THAT WAS HEARD AS FAR AWAY AS NEW YORK . . . . 463 LINES IN DEJECTION . .   23
AT LEAST THIS FAR, ... 469 BUT OUTER SPACE... .   2
LOOK AT HOW FAR WE'VE LEFT THE CURRENT SCIENCE . . . . 480 A MASQUE OF REASON .   194
THE DEVIL'S NEVER VERY FAR AWAY. . . . . 487 A MASQUE OF REASON .   382
STILL, NOT SO FAR OFF, COME TO THINK OF IT. . . . . . . 509 A MASQUE OF MERCY .   428
FARAWAY
THERE'S A PLACE CALLED FARAWAY MEADOW . . . . 264 THE LAST MOWING . . .   1
FAR-DISTANT
OF THE FAR-DISTANT BREAKING WAVE. . . . . 20 THE TRIAL BY EXISTENCE   16
AND THEN IN THE FAR-DISTANT WATER SPLASHED, ... 338 THE MOST OF IT . . .   12
FARED
AND NEEDN'T HAVE FARED INTO SPACE LIKE HIS MASTER . . . 380 TOO ANXIOUS FOR RIVERS   25
YOU WOULDN'T SAY SHE FARED SO VERY BADLY. . . . . 477 A MASQUE OF REASON .   98
FARES
IN SEVERAL BEAUTY THAT THOUGHT FARES FAR . . . . 121 BOND AND FREE   19
FAREWELL
AND FORCE HER FAREWELL STEP OFF SHORE. . . . . 343 DISCOVERY OF MADEIRAS   11
TO BID US A MOCK FAREWELL. . . . . 365 A NATURE NOTE   12
FARM
BETWEEN THEM THEY WILL LAY THIS FARM AS SMOOTH! . . . . 36 DEATH OF THE HIRED MAN   63
LOCKED UP FOR YEARS BACK THERE AT THE OLD FARM. . . . . 65 A SERVANT TO SERVANTS .   89

FARM (CONTINUED)

PAGE TITLE — LINE

ONLY ONE FROM A FARM NOT FAR AWAY . . . . 74 THE GENERATIONS OF MEN . 25
A FRIEND OR TWO AS GOOD AS OWN THE FARM, ... 84 THE HOUSEKEEPER . . . 96
HAVEN'T AS GOOD. THEY DON'T GO WITH THE FARM. . . . . 85 THE HOUSEKEEPER . . . 114
ON HIS OWN FARM. HE'S BOSS. BUT AS TO HENS: . . . . . 86 THE HOUSEKEEPER . . . 135
A FARM, A COUNTRYSIDE, OR IF HE CAN, ... 108 OLD MAN'S WINTER NIGHT . 27
JOE SAID: "YOU BIG BOYS OUGHT TO FIND A FARM, ... 113 IN THE HOME STRETCH . 95
"SAY THAT TO JIMMY HERE. HE NEEDS A FARM." . . . . 114 IN THE HOME STRETCH . 100
"WE'RE GIVING YOU OUR CHANCES ON DE FARM." . . . . 114 IN THE HOME STRETCH . 108
THE BACK SOME FARM PRESENTS US; AND YOUR WOODS . . . 114 IN THE HOME STRETCH . 114
ALL OF A FARM IT IS." / " I KNOW THIS MUCH: . . . . 117 IN THE HOME STRETCH . 198
WHEN SHE WAS A GIRL ON THE FARM, SHE DID . . . . . 133 A GIRL'S GARDEN . . . 3
AN IDEAL ONE-GIRL FARM, ... 133 A GIRL'S GARDEN . . . 14
BROWN LIVED AT SUCH A LOFTY FARM . . . . . . 137 BROWN'S DESCENT . . . 1
I WONDER IF HE'S SOLD HIS FARM, ... 138 BROWN'S DESCENT . . . 35
HIS FARM WAS "GROUNDS," AND NOT A FARM AT ALL; . . . 160 NEW HAMPSHIRE . . . 51
YOU MAY HAVE HEARD OF IT. I HAD A FARM . . . . . 162 NEW HAMPSHIRE . . . 109
AND MARRIAGE RINGS OF THOSE WHO OWNED THE FARM. . . . 162 NEW HAMPSHIRE . . . 114
THE FARM I MADE MY HOME ON IN THE MOUNTAINS . . . . 163 NEW HAMPSHIRE . . . 150
"I'M GOING TO PUT YOU OFF THIS FARM: I WANT IT." . . 164 NEW HAMPSHIRE . . . 154
"I'M GOING TO PUT YOU ON THE FARM NEXT TO IT." . . . 164 NEW HAMPSHIRE . . . 156
"WHY WON'T THE FARM NEXT TO IT DO FOR YOU?" . . . . 164 NEW HAMPSHIRE . . . 157
"I'LL HAVE ONE IF I SELL MY FARM TO BUY IT." . . . 177 THE STAR-SPLITTER . . 25
TRYING TO SELL HIS FARM AND THEN NOT SELLING, . . . 177 THE STAR-SPLITTER . . 29
OUT OF A HOUSE AND SO OUT OF A FARM . . . . . . 178 THE STAR-SPLITTER . . 66
AS ON A FARM, BUT PLANETS, EVENING STARS . . . . . 178 THE STAR-SPLITTER . . 72
ALL OTHER FARM MACHINERY'S GONE IN, ... 189 THE GRINDSTONE . . . 11
I STAYED THE NIGHT FOR SHELTER AT A FARM . . . . . 202 THE WITCH OF COOS . . 1
AN ORCHARD AWAY AT THE END OF THE FARM . . . . . 228 GOOD-BY AND KEEP COLD . 4
TO CLOSE A ROAD, ABANDON A FARM, ... 263 THE TIMES TABLE . . . 18
WE DIVE DOWN UNDER THE FARM. . . . . 282 A DRUMLIN WOODCHUCK . 16
WHEN IT COMES TO A MOUNTAIN FARM . . . . . . 285 IN TIME OF CLOUDBURST . 6
WIND GOES FROM FARM TO FARM IN WAVE ON WAVE, . . . 300 STRONG SAYING NOTHING . 13
I'VE HAD TO GIVE MY INTERVAL FARM UP . . . . . 316 BUILD SOIL 6
FOR INTEREST, AND I'VE BOUGHT A MOUNTAIN FARM . . . 316 BUILD SOIL 7
YOUR POEMS ON A FARM AND CALL THAT FARMING. . . . 316 BUILD SOIL 18
YOU SHALL GO TO YOUR RUN-OUT MOUNTAIN FARM, . . . 323 BUILD SOIL 211
YOU WILL GO TO YOUR RUN-OUT MOUNTAIN FARM . . . . 323 BUILD SOIL 230
BUILD SOIL. TURN THE FARM IN UPON ITSELF . . . . 323 BUILD SOIL 234
I FARM A PASTURE WHERE THE BOULDERS LIE . . . . 365 OF STONES OF THE PLACE . 1
UPON A FARM THAT IS NO MORE A FARM . . . . . 377 DIRECTIVE 6
SHE WAS LEFT OVER FROM THE BROOK FARM VENTURE. . . . 494 A MASQUE OF MERCY . . 39

FARMER

THE TOWN-BRED FARMER FAILED TO UNDERSTAND. . . . . 69 THE CODE 9
THAT'S WHAT THE AVERAGE FARMER WOULD HAVE MEANT. . . 70 THE CODE 17
JOHN'S A BAD FARMER. I'M NOT BLAMING HIM. . . . . 85 THE HOUSEKEEPER . . . 102
HE SAW HIMSELF A FARMER. THEN THERE WAS A FRENCH BOY . 114 IN THE HOME STRETCH . 103
"IT'S AS WHEN I WAS A FARMER...." . . . . . . 134 A GIRL'S GARDEN . . . 45
AMONG US: IT WAS JUST A WARREN FARMER . . . . . 168 NEW HAMPSHIRE . . . 288
I KNEW A MAN WHO FAILING AS A FARMER . . . . . 168 NEW HAMPSHIRE . . . 301
I CHOOSE TO BE A PLAIN NEW HAMPSHIRE FARMER . . . . 172 NEW HAMPSHIRE . . . 408
AND WHETHER THE FARMER DRANK OR NOT . . . . . 263 THE TIMES TABLE . . . 3
TO WHICH THE FARMER WOULD MAKE REPLY, ... 263 THE TIMES TABLE . . . 8
A MIGHTY FARMER FLUNG THE HOUSE DOOR WIDE, ... 368 THE LITERATE FARMER AND 5
THE LITERATE FARMER AND THE PLANET VENUS . . . . . 368 THE LITERATE FARMER AND T

FARMERS

FARMERS AROUND TWICE AS WELL OFF AS WE . . . . 85 THE HOUSEKEEPER . . . 113
AND MAKE GOOD FARMERS, AND LEAVE OTHER FELLOWS." . . 114 IN THE HOME STRETCH . 96
THEIR COMING OUT AND MAKING USEFUL FARMERS. . . . 114 IN THE HOME STRETCH . 121
THE FARMERS RATHER GUESS NOT. . . . . . . 308 EVIL TENDENCIES CANCEL . 2
WILL PUT TEN THOUSAND FARMERS OUT OF SHEEP. . . . 319 BUILD SOIL 110
LET NONE ASSUME TO TILL THE LAND BUT FARMERS. . . . 322 BUILD SOIL 209

FARMERS'

A SUPERSTITIOUS CRY FOR FARMERS' LUCK-- . . . . . 407 FROM PLANE TO PLANE . 118

FARMER'S

SOUNDS SOMETHING LIKE. BETTER THAN FARMER'S BEANS . . 97 THE SELF-SEEKER . . . 127
JUST ONE TO INQUIRE WHAT A FARMER'S PRICES ARE. . . 287 A ROADSIDE STAND . . 38

FARMHOUSE (SEE TREE-AND-FARMHOUSE)

BURNED DOWN HIS FARMHOUSE FOR THE FIRE INSURANCE, . . 168 NEW HAMPSHIRE . . . 302
TO STOP WITHOUT A FARMHOUSE NEAR . . . . . . 224 STOPPING BY WOODS . . 6
THE FARMHOUSE LINGERS, THOUGH AVERSE TO SQUARE . . . 231 A BROOK IN THE CITY . 1
OR SUCH IS THE TALK AT THE FARMHOUSE: . . . . . 264 THE LAST MOWING . . 3

FARMING

A ROCK-STREWN TOWN WHERE FARMING HAS FALLEN OFF, . . 73 THE GENERATIONS OF MEN . 5
OF HEAVENLY STARS WITH HUGGER-MUGGER FARMING. . . . 176 THE STAR-SPLITTER . . 14
TILL HAVING FAILED AT HUGGER-MUGGER FARMING . . . 177 THE STAR-SPLITTER . . 15
YOUR POEMS ON A FARM AND CALL THAT FARMING. . . . 316 BUILD SOIL 18
IS AN UNPARDONABLE SIN IN FARMING. . . . . . 322 BUILD SOIL 180
FOR OUR NAME FARMING HERE, ... 367 A SERIOUS STEP LIGHTLY . 17
IN FARMING WELL--OR PRETTY WELL. . . . . . 381 AN UNSTAMPED LETTER IN . 49
TO FARMING FOR A SIMPLE WAY TO EARN; . . . . . 398 BURSTING RAPTURE . . 3
THE DISCIPLINE OF FARMING WAS SO STERN, ... 398 BURSTING RAPTURE . . 7

FARMS

"THERE IS NO VILLAGE--ONLY SCATTERED FARMS. . . . 41 THE MOUNTAIN 24
I ALMOST KNOW THEIR FARMS AS WELL AS THEY DO." . . 49 A HUNDRED COLLARS . . 121
WHAT I LIKE BEST'S THE LAY OF DIFFERENT FARMS, . . 49 A HUNDRED COLLARS . . 124
NOT EVEN NEW HAMPSHIRE FARMS ARE MUCH FOR SALE. . . 163 NEW HAMPSHIRE . . . 149
FEW FARMS CHANGED HANDS; SO RATHER THAN SPEND YEARS . 177 THE STAR-SPLITTER . . 28
TO ADVERTISE OUR FARMS TO CITY BUYERS, ... 316 BUILD SOIL 23

FAR-OFF

THAT FAR-OFF DAY THE LEAVES IN FLIGHT . . . . . 336 THE WIND AND THE RAIN . 1

FAR-SHORE

IN A WHITE SCARF AGAINST THE FAR-SHORE ALDERS.) . . . 258 WEST-RUNNING BROOK . . 26

FAR-SOUGHT

THE FAR-SOUGHT FLOWER. . . . . 343 QUEST OF PURPLE-FRINGED 16

FARTHER

FAR OFF THE HOMES OF MEN, AND FARTHER STILL, . . . 17 THE VANTAGE POINT . . 6
ROLLED OUT A LITTLE FARTHER THAN THE REST." . . . 44 THE MOUNTAIN 99

FARTHER (CONTINUED)
  NO, I WILL GO ON FARTHER--AND WE SHALL SEE." . . . . . 101 THE WOOD-PILE . . . 3
FASHION (SEE SO-FASHION)
  YET DID IN COUNTRY FASHION IN THAT THERE . . . . . . 106 CHRISTMAS TREES . . . 6
FASHIONABLE
  THAT SOVIET RUSSIA HAS MADE FASHIONABLE. . . . . . . 323 BUILD SOIL 223
FASHIONED (SEE NEW-FASHIONED, OLD-FASHIONED)
FAST
  HUDDLED AGAINST THE BARN DOOR FAST ASLEEP, ... 35 DEATH OF THE HIRED MAN 35
  TO SEE WHERE ALL THE MONEY GOES SO FAST. . . . . . . 86 THE HOUSEKEEPER . . . 159
  TO HOLD IT HARD UNTIL THEY MAKE IT FAST, ... 141 THE LINE-GANG . . . 10
  UPON IT NOW; ITS FEET ARE FAST IN SNOW. . . . . . . 189 THE GRINDSTONE . . . 10
  COME STRAIGHT DOWN OFF THIS MOUNTAIN JUST AS FAST . . 215 A FOUNTAIN, A BOTTLE . 61
  THE SWARM STILL RAN AND SCUTTLED JUST AS FAST. . . . 237 A HILLSIDE THAW . . . 24
  SNOW FALLING AND NIGHT FALLING FAST, OH, FAST . . . . 296 DESERT PLACES . . . 1
  PROBABLY, BUT YOU'RE FAR TOO FAST AND STRONG . . . . 325 BUILD SOIL 284
  IS AFTER EXPLOSION GOING AWAY SO FAST. . . . . 389 SKEPTIC 8
  THE WRITING ON THE SCREEN MUST CHANGE TOO FAST . . . 502 A MASQUE OF MERCY . 245
FASTENED
  "THOSE ARE JUST NAILHEADS. THOSE ARE FASTENED DOWN." . 278 THE WHITE-TAILED HORNET 36
  AND THUS FASTENED ON . . . . 438 KITTY HAWK 328
FASTER
  TO DO WORK BETTER OR FASTER--THOSE TWO THINGS. . . . 70 THE CODE 23
  FASTER OR SLOWER AS HE CHANCED, ... 138 BROWN'S DESCENT . . . 25
  I LAUGHED INSIDE, AND ONLY CRANKED THE FASTER . . . 190 THE GRINDSTONE . . . 60
  FASTER THAN MY TREAD-- . . . . 428 KITTY HAWK . . . 18
FAT
  I FOUND A DIMPLED SPIDER, FAT AND WHITE, ... 302 DESIGN 1
FATE
  AS IF WITH KEENNESS FOR OUR FATE, ... 9 STARS 5
  BUT THE PURE FATE TO WHICH YOU GO . . . . 21 THE TRIAL BY EXISTENCE 53
  THAT FATE HAD MADE THEE FOR THE PLEASURE OF THE WIND, . 29 MY BUTTERFLY 23
  AS TO OUR FATE, LIKE FOOLS PAST REASONING WITH. . . 114 IN THE HOME STRETCH . 125
  MAY NO FATE WILLFULLY MISUNDERSTAND ME . . . . . 122 BIRCHES 50
  IT'S THE OLD CAPTAIN'S DARK FATE . . . . 212 AN EMPTY THREAT . . 43
  FATE HAD HER IMAGINATION ABOUT HER, ... 252 TREE AT MY WINDOW . 14
  AND DORY AND MASTER WILL SAIL BY FATE . . . . . 262 THE FLOWER BOAT . . 11
  TO TOLLING LIKE THE COUNT OF FATE, ... 273 A LONE STRIKER . . 2
  THREE MADE IT CERTAIN NOTHING FATE COULD DO . . . 283 THE GOLD HESPERIDEE . 27
  (THIS LIKE FATE BY STARS IS RECKONED, ... 304 CLEAR AND COLDER . 7
  DIE EARLY AND AVOID THE FATE. . . . . 307 PROVIDE, PROVIDE . 7
  FATE HAS NO CHOICE BUT TO FULFILL. . . . . . . 336 THE WIND AND THE RAIN 20
  HELP ME ACCEPT ITS FATE WITH CHRISTMAS FEELING. . . 350 TO A YOUNG WRETCH . 24
  WITH POETS WHO COULD CALMLY TAKE THE FATE . . . 351 THE LESSON FOR TODAY . 11
  THE EARTH ITSELF IS LIABLE TO THE FATE . . . . 355 THE LESSON FOR TODAY . 147
  MAY REACH TO YOU, BUT CANNOT TOUCH YOUR FATE. . . 357 A MOTH SEEN IN WINTER . 22
  WHATEVER I ACCORDED IT OF FATE, ... 357 A CONSIDERABLE SPECK . 23
  I AM NO FURTHER FROM THEIR FATE THAN YOU ARE, . . 414 A CABIN IN THE CLEARING 19
  OUT OF SORTS WITH FATE, ... 428 KITTY HAWK 11
  EARTH IS STILL OUR FATE. . . . . 437 KITTY HAWK 308
  THAT EVER ACCEPTED FATE . . . . 444 THE DRAFT HORSE . . 14
  AND THAT'S A FATE IT CAN'T EVADE . . . . 450 OUR DOOM TO BLOOM . 15
  FILLS ME WITH FEAR I'LL BE LEFT TO MY FATE: . . . 454 HOW HARD TO KEEP FROM 18
  SPARE ME THE SETTING OF MY FATE TO MUSIC. . . . 495 A MASQUE OF MERCY . 58
FATED
  ALWAYS THE SAME, WHEN ON A FATED NIGHT . . . . . 226 THE ONSET 1
FATEFUL
  SHE WOULD NOT LOOK AT THE FATEFUL SHIP. . . . . . 343 DISCOVERY OF MADEIRAS . 8
FATHER
  "THAT WAS THE FATHER AS HE WENT TO WAR. . . . . 55 THE BLACK COTTAGE . 25
  THAT HAD GONE OUT OF IT, THE FATHER FIRST, . . . 56 THE BLACK COTTAGE . 38
  FATHER AND MOTHER MARRIED, AND MOTHER CAME, . . . 66 A SERVANT TO SERVANTS . 126
  THAT WAS WHAT MARRYING FATHER MEANT TO HER. . . . 66 A SERVANT TO SERVANTS . 129
  SEVERAL TIMES OVER, AND BY MARRYING FATHER . . . 75 THE GENERATIONS OF MEN 56
  ONE DAY SHE ASKED HER FATHER . . . . 133 A GIRL'S GARDEN . . 5
  HER FATHER SAID; TO PLOW; . . . . 133 A GIRL'S GARDEN . . 18
  SHE ASKED HER FATHER AND HE TOLD HER, "MAPLE-- . . 179 MAPLE 3
  AND GIVE THE TEACHER A SCARE AS FROM HER FATHER. . 180 MAPLE 32
  "YOU'VE NEVER ASKED YOUR FATHER OUTRIGHT, HAVE YOU?" . 183 MAPLE 108
  ONCE LONG AGO HER FATHER HAD PUT HIMSELF OFF.) . . 183 MAPLE 111
  SOMETHING BETWEEN YOUR FATHER AND YOUR MOTHER . . 183 MAPLE 113
  SOMETHING A FATHER COULDN'T TELL A DAUGHTER . . . 183 MAPLE 118
  YOUR FATHER FEELS US ROUND HIM WITH OUR QUESTING, . 183 MAPLE 123
  RIGHT PAST BOTH FATHER AND MOTHER, AND NEITHER STOPPED IT. . 203 THE WITCH OF COOS . 33
  FATHER HAD GONE UPSTAIRS; MOTHER WAS DOWNSTAIRS. . 203 THE WITCH OF COOS . 34
  THEY WERE A MAN'S HIS FATHER KILLED FOR ME. . . . 206 THE WITCH OF COOS . 139
  THEIR ARTHUR AMY WAS THE FATHER OF MINE. . . . . 208 PAUPER WITCH OF GRAFTON 27
  MY FATHER BUILT, ENCLOSED A SPRING, ... 265 THE BIRTHPLACE . . 3
  AND THOUGH A GOD WAS THE FATHER . . . . 314 BEARER OF EVIL TIDINGS 23
  BUT HER FATHER MORE-- . . . . 433 KITTY HAWK 151
  HOW WOULD IT BE FOR YOU TO TAKE YOUR FATHER . . . 454 HOW HARD TO KEEP FROM 31
  DON'T LET YOUR FATHER TELL YOU WHAT TO BE." . . . 454 HOW HARD TO KEEP FROM 36
  OF ROYAL BLOOD. YOUR FATHER WAS A COOK." . . . . 457 HOW HARD TO KEEP FROM 103
  I KNEW YOUR FATHER MUST HAVE BEEN A COOK. . . . . 458 HOW HARD TO KEEP FROM 136
  AND PRESS YOUR FATHER INTO BEING KING." . . . . 460 HOW HARD TO KEEP FROM 206
  IT'S WHAT MY FATHER MUST MEAN BY DEPARTURE, . . . 461 HOW HARD TO KEEP FROM 245
  EXCEPT AS FATHER PUTATIVE TO SORT OF . . . . . 498 A MASQUE OF MERCY . 123
FATHERLY
  BUT LOREN, THE FATHERLY, OUT FOR A DRIVE." . . . . 60 BLUEBERRIES 39
FATHERS
  AS FATHERS ABOUT CHILDREN, YOU TELL TEACHER. . . . 180 MAPLE 6
FATHER'S
  HE WILL NOT GO BEHIND HIS FATHER'S SAYING, . . . 34 MENDING WALL . . . 43
  MY FATHER'S BROTHER WASN'T RIGHT. THEY KEPT HIM . . 65 A SERVANT TO SERVANTS . 88
  MY FATHER'S BROTHER, HE WENT MAD QUITE YOUNG. . . 65 A SERVANT TO SERVANTS . 104
  IN FATHER'S BUILDING HIM A SORT OF CAGE, ... 66 A SERVANT TO SERVANTS . 113
  "ON FATHER'S SIDE, IT SEEMS, WE'RE--LET ME SEE----" . 76 THE GENERATIONS OF MEN 78
  ONE BY ONE HE SUBDUED HIS FATHER'S TREES . . . . 122 BIRCHES 28

FATHER'S (CONTINUED)
    HER MOTHER'S BEDROOM WAS HER FATHER'S STILL, ... 181 MAPLE   60
    THEY WENT ON PILGRIMAGE ONCE TO HER FATHER'S   .   .   .   .   . 182 MAPLE   97
    AS GAY FOR YOU TO TAKE YOUR FATHER'S AX .   .   .   .   .   . 349 TO A YOUNG WRETCH .   .   1
    AND FATHER'S IN FOR WHAT WE RAN AWAY FROM.   .   .   .   .   . 462 HOW HARD TO KEEP FROM 266
FATHER-TIME-LIKE
    A FATHER-TIME-LIKE MAN GOT ON AND RODE, ... 189 THE GRINDSTONE .   .   .   29
FATHOM
    THAT TURNED THEM ON THE WORLD, AND TRY TO FATHOM   .   .   .   . 73 THE GENERATIONS OF MEN   17
FATHOMING
    NO FATHOMING THE ASIATIC MIND.   .   .   .   . 462 HOW HARD TO KEEP FROM 265
FATNESS
    OF BURNING FATNESS, AND THEN NOTHING BUT .   .   .   .   .   . 130 THE BONFIRE   24
FATTEN
    "IT MUST BE ON CHARCOAL THEY FATTEN THEIR FRUIT.   .   .   .   . 59 BLUEBERRIES   22
FAULT
    HE THOUGHT YOU MEANT TO FIND FAULT WITH HIS WORK.   .   .   .   . 70 THE CODE   16
    THE ONLY FAULT I FIND WITH OLD NEW HAMPSHIRE   .   .   .   . 168 NEW HAMPSHIRE .   .   . 310
    THE ONLY FAULT MY HUSBAND FOUND WITH ME-- .   .   .   .   . 203 THE WITCH OF COOS .   36
    AND WEARINESS AND FAULT;   .   .   .   . 227 TO EARTHWARD .   .   .   19
    THE FAULT MUST PARTLY HAVE BEEN IN ME.   .   .   .   .   .   . 251 A MINOR BIRD .   .   .   5
    FROM WITNESSING THE FAULT OF ONE SO PROUD.   .   .   .   .   . 284 THE GOLD HESPERIDEE .   57
    AND UNLESS MY SENSE IS AT FAULT, ... 295 A RECORD STRIDE .   .   22
    AND NOBODY ELSE AT FAULT, ... 314 BEARER OF EVIL TIDINGS   24
    I CANNOT HOLD YOU INNOCENT OF FAULT.   .   .   .   .   .   . 446 DOES NO ONE AT ALL EVER   21
    IT'S GOOD GEOLOGY--THE FUNDAY FAULT.   .   .   .   .   .   . 502 A MASQUE OF MERCY . 228
    TO SPRING IT LIKE A DEADFALL AND THE FAULT   .   .   .   .   . 502 A MASQUE OF MERCY . 231
    IN NATURE WOULD WIPE OUT ALL HUMAN FAULT.   .   .   .   .   . 502 A MASQUE OF MERCY . 232
FAVOR
    IS DUE TO TRUTHS BEING IN AND OUT OF FAVOR.   .   .   .   .   . 58 THE BLACK COTTAGE . 110
    WHEN ALL MY STRENGTH PUT FORTH WAS IN HIS FAVOR, ... 185 THE AX-HELVE .   .   .   11
    WAITING FOR THINGS TO HAPPEN IN THEIR FAVOR.   .   .   .   . 204 THE WITCH OF COOS .   63
    I HOLD WITH THOSE WHO FAVOR FIRE.   .   .   .   . 220 FIRE AND ICE .   .   .   4
    AS IF THE EARTH IN ONE UNLOOKED-FOR FAVOR   .   .   .   .   . 230 TWO LOOK AT TWO .   .   41
    (HE HAD TO KEEP THE CAPTAIN'S FAVOR.)   .   .   .   .   .   . 345 DISCOVERY OF MADEIRAS .   52
    AND IT MUST BE A LITTLE MORE IN FAVOR OF MAN, ... 349 OUR HOLD ON THE PLANET   15
    BUT IN YOUR FAVOR--PLEASE TO TELL YOUR KING--   .   .   .   . 354 THE LESSON FOR TODAY . 117
    TO CURRY FAVOR WITH THE DIRT SOME MORE.   .   .   .   .   . 405 FROM PLANE TO PLANE .   43
    SEE THAT OUR SLAVE IS ALSO. HE'S IN FAVOR.   .   .   .   .   . 455 HOW HARD TO KEEP FROM   64
    TAKE NOTICE, HAMAN, HE'S IN FAVOR WITH US."   .   .   .   .   . 455 HOW HARD TO KEEP FROM   65
FAVORED
    OR IF NOT ALL SO FAVORED, ... 14 ROSE POGONIAS .   .   .   21
FAVORING
    THE KING SAT FAVORING ONE PEARL FOR ITS BIGNESS, ... 455 HOW HARD TO KEEP FROM   69
FAVORITE
    HIS FAVORITE READING IS SEED CATALOGUES.   .   .   .   .   . 496 A MASQUE OF MERCY .   81
    BOTH OF THEM CAUGHT IT FROM BEL'S FAVORITE POET,   .   .   . 511 A MASQUE OF MERCY . 462
    WHO IN HIS FAVORITE POSE AS POET-THINKER   .   .   .   .   . 511 A MASQUE OF MERCY . 463
FAY
    OR EASY GOLD AT THE HAND OF FAY OR ELF: .   .   .   .   .   . 17 MOWING   8
FEAR
    STORM FEAR .   .   .   . 9 STORM FEAR .   .   .   .   T
    LOOKING BACK OVER HER SHOULDER AT SOME FEAR.   .   .   .   . 51 HOME BURIAL   3
    THE FEAR .   .   .   . 89 THE FEAR .   .   .   .   .   T
    I FORGOT HIM AND LET HIS LITTLE FEAR   .   .   .   .   .   . 101 THE WOOD-PILE .   .   .   19
    AND FEAR OF SEEMING SHORT OF SPEECH, OR WHETHER   .   .   . 106 CHRISTMAS TREES .   .   27
    WALL WITHIN WALL TO SHUT FEAR OUT.   .   .   .   . 120 BOND AND FREE .   .   .   3
    AS IF FOR FEAR OF TREADING UPON ME.   .   .   .   . 125 AN ENCOUNTER .   .   .   15
    HOUSE FEAR .   .   .   . 127 HOUSE FEAR .   .   .   .   T
    UPON THE ROAD, TO FLAMES TOO, THOUGH IN FEAR   .   .   .   . 131 THE BONFIRE   60
    FRANCONIA LAUGHS, I FEAR--DID LAUGH THAT NIGHT--   .   .   . 165 NEW HAMPSHIRE .   .   . 205
    BUT THAT BEGINNING WAS WIPED OUT IN FEAR .   .   .   .   .   . 196 WILD GRAPES .   .   .   10
    WAS IN HER CLOUDED EYES: THEY SAW NO FEAR THERE.   .   .   . 229 TWO LOOK AT TWO .   .   20
    EXCEPT FORGET TO GO IN FEAR PERHAPS.   .   .   .   .   .   . 231 A BROOK IN THE CITY .   19
    I FEAR, THE CROWN OF RULE, ... 252 THE PEACEFUL SHEPHERD .   6
    (HE STOOD WELL BACK FOR FEAR OF SCALDING SQUIRTS.)   .   .   . 270 THE EGG AND THE MACHINE 12
    SHE FEARS NOT HIM, THEY FEAR NOT LIFE.   .   .   .   .   .   . 291 ON HEART'S BEGINNING TO 37
    PERHAPS I HAVE PUT FORTH TOO MUCH STRENGTH AND BEEN TOO
        FIERCE FROM FEAR.   .   .   .   . 297 A LEAF-TREADER .   .   .   3
    FOR FEAR IT WOULD MAKE ME CONSERVATIVE WHEN OLD.   .   .   . 308 PRECAUTION   2
    LET NEWSPAPERS PROFESS TO FEAR THE WORST!   .   .   .   .   . 318 BUILD SOIL   65
    OR ELSE I FEAR ENTIRELY MINE, ... 328 A MISSIVE MISSILE .   .   44
    MADE HER STEAL A LOOK OF FEAR .   .   .   . 340 THE SUBVERTED FLOWER .   37
    FOR FEAR I WOULD MAKE HER MISS THE PLACE.   .   .   .   .   . 342 A CLOUD SHADOW .   .   .   8
    THE FEAR OF GOD .   .   .   . 385 THE FEAR OF GOD .   .   .   T
    THE FEAR OF MAN .   .   .   . 386 THE FEAR OF MAN .   .   .   T
    HER FEAR IS BEING SPOKEN BY THE RUDE   .   .   .   .   .   . 386 THE FEAR OF MAN .   .   .   13
    IN HER COMPLACENT MINISTRY OF FEAR, ... 395 WHY WAIT FOR SCIENCE .   2
    THEN FLED FOR FEAR OF GETTING STUCK IN LAVA   .   .   .   . 407 FROM PLANE TO PLANE .   94
    AND I BEGIN TO FEAR THEY NEVER WILL.   .   .   .   .   .   . 414 A CABIN IN THE CLEARING   6
    HIS FEAR IS NOT BEHIND HIM BUT BESIDE HIM   .   .   .   .   . 421 ESCAPIST--NEVER .   .   . 429
    THE BECOMING FEAR .   .   .   . 441 KITTY HAWK 429
    THAT WE FEAR THE WORST.   .   .   .   . 445 PERIL OF HOPE .   .   .   8
    FILLS ME WITH FEAR I'LL BE LEFT TO MY FATE: .   .   .   .   . 454 HOW HARD TO KEEP FROM   18
    I LOVE AND FEAR HIM. YES, BUT I FEAR FOR HIM. .   .   .   . 505 A MASQUE OF MERCY . 310
    I WAS SUPPORTING YOU FOR FEAR YOU'D FAINT   .   .   .   .   . 518 A MASQUE OF MERCY . 647
    AND GREAT IT IS. BUT FEAR IS OF THE SOUL.   .   .   .   .   . 519 A MASQUE OF MERCY . 694
    THE FEAR THAT YOU'RE AFRAID WITH IS THE FEAR   .   .   .   . 520 A MASQUE OF MERCY . 697
    THAT IS THE FEAR OF GOD WHEREOF 'TIS WRITTEN.   .   .   .   . 520 A MASQUE OF MERCY . 699
    BUT NOT THE FEAR OF PUNISHMENT FOR SIN   .   .   .   .   .   . 520 A MASQUE OF MERCY . 700
    I'M NO MORE GOVERNED BY THE FEAR OF HELL .   .   .   .   .   . 520 A MASQUE OF MERCY . 702
    THAN   THE FEAR OF THE ASYLUM, JAIL, OR POORHOUSE,   .   .   . 520 A MASQUE OF MERCY . 703
    T   ME THE FEAR WITHIN THE SOUL .   .   .   . 521 A MASQUE OF MERCY . 729
           HE DEEPER FEAR IS SO ETERNAL.   .   .   .   .   .   . 521 A MASQUE OF MERCY . 732

           TILL I FEARED YOU HAD WANDERED A MILE, ... 62 BLUEBERRIES   92
         E BROOK BARRIER, BUT FEARED   .   .   .   . 131 THE BONFIRE   74
           HE FEARED TO RISK .   .   .   . 138 BROWN'S DESCENT .   .   .   27

PAGE TITLE   LINE

FEARED (CONTINUED)
    BUT FEARED THE COLD . . . . 218 I WILL SING YOU ONE-O . 17
    YOU LOOK AS IF YOU EITHER HOPED OR FEARED . . . . . . 488 A MASQUE OF REASON . . 411
FEARFUL
    THEN FEARFUL HE HAD LET THEE WIN . . . . 29 MY BUTTERFLY 28
FEARLESS
    FEARLESS OF EVER FINDING OPEN LAND, ... 5 INTO MY OWN 7
FEARS
    BECAUSE OF THE FEARS OF FIRE AND LOSS . . . . 140 THE GUM-GATHERER . . . 21
    SHE FEARS NOT HIM, THEY FEAR NOT LIFE. . . . . 291 ON HEART'S BEGINNING TO 37
    TO 'REST FROM HIS BESETTING FEARS. . . . . 392 A CLIFF DWELLING . . . 9
    HAVE NO HALLOWING FEARS . . . . 437 KITTY HAWK 281
FEAST
    WHERE HE CAN STRETCH AND HOLD HIS HIGHEST FEAST . . . 254 A WINTER EDEN 10
    NO HUMAN SPECTER AT THE FEAST . . . . 281 BLUE RIBBON AT AMESBURY 37
    THE MIDDEN OF FEAST UPON FEAST, ... 312 THE VINDICTIVES . . . 60
    TO BE THEIR OWN MARRIAGE FEAST FOR THE SHARK. . . . . 346 DISCOVERY OF MADEIRAS . 85
    "FEED HIM ANOTHER FEAST OF RECOGNITION." . . . . . . 456 HOW HARD TO KEEP FROM 92
    IS THROWN IN SCRIPT, AS AT BELSHAZZAR'S FEAST, . . . 502 A MASQUE OF MERCY . . 238
FEATHER
    HE THOUGHT THAT I WAS AFTER HIM FOR A FEATHER-- . . . 101 THE WOOD-PILE 14
    OF DUST AND FEATHER. . . . . 218 I WILL SING YOU ONE-O . 15
FEATHERED
    AS IS VOUCHSAFED TO FEATHERED BREED. . . . . 281 BLUE RIBBON AT AMESBURY 36
FEATHER-HAMMER
    A FEATHER-HAMMER GIVES A DOUBLE KNOCK. . . . . 254 A WINTER EDEN 17
FEATHERS
    YOU LET THINGS MORE LIKE FEATHERS REGULATE . . . . . 63 A SERVANT TO SERVANTS . 36
    THE SMELL OF THE WET FEATHERS IN THE HEAT! . . . . . 85 THE HOUSEKEEPER . . . 122
    HIS TAIL FEATHERS OFF. . . . . 135 LAST WORD OF A BLUEBIRD 13
    TRUSTING FEATHERS AND INWARD FIRE . . . . 253 THE THATCH 26
    WHITE FEATHERS FROM THE STRUGGLE OF WHOSE BREAST . . 258 WEST-RUNNING BROOK . . 23
FEATS
    THE SAME PAUL AT THE SAME OLD FEATS OF LOGGING. . . . 192 PAUL'S WIFE 30
FEATURES
    SOME PALLID THING HAD SQUASHED ITS FEATURES FLAT . . 148 SNOW 160
FED
    HAD FED IN CHORUS, AND LIVED TO FLEDGE, ... 253 THE THATCH 15
    THE KING SAID GRANDLY, "EVEN AS WE ARE FED . . . . . 455 HOW HARD TO KEEP FROM 63
    "THEY CAN'T HAVE CHARACTER UNLESS THEY'RE FED." . . . 458 HOW HARD TO KEEP FROM 143
FEDERATION
    FEDERATION OF MANKIND. . . . . 387 THE COURAGE TO BE NEW . 8
FEEBLE-POINTED
    NOT WITHOUT FEEBLE-POINTED SPIKES OF FLOWERS . . . . 17 MOWING 11
FEFD
    WITH THE MOUTHS OF ALL THOSE YOUNG LORENS TO FEED? . 60 BLUEBERRIES 49
    WITH A HOUSEFUL OF HUNGRY MEN TO FEED . . . . 62 A SERVANT TO SERVANTS . 5
    OF COURSE THEY HAD TO FEED HIM WITHOUT DISHES. . . . 66 A SERVANT TO SERVANTS . 121
    TO FEED HIS THUMPING GRUBS AS BIG AS HE IS. . . . . 278 THE WHITE-TAILED HORNET 31
    AS REGULARLY AS HE WENT TO FEED THE PIG . . . . . . 283 THE GOLD HESPERIDEE . 19
    BUT WHAT YOU RAISE OR GROW, WHY, FEED IT OUT, . . . 323 BUILD SOIL 215
    "FEED HIM ANOTHER FEAST OF RECOGNITION." . . . . . . 456 HOW HARD TO KEEP FROM 92
FEEDING
    TO THIS LEAN FEEDING, SAVE ONCE A YEAR . . . . 24 PAN WITH US 12
    SHE LINGERS FEEDING AT THE TROUGH, ... 280 BLUE RIBBON AT AMESBURY 15
    YOU THINK OF FOR YOUR PEOPLE--FEEDING THEM." . . . . 458 HOW HARD TO KEEP FROM 138
FEEL
    AND TRY IF WE CANNOT FEEL FORSAKEN. . . . . 16 IN NEGLECT 5
    AND FEEL A SPIRIT KINDRED TO MY OWN; . . . . 23 THE TUFT OF FLOWERS . 33
    TWO OR THREE TIMES--HE MADE ME FEEL SO QUEER-- . . . 36 DEATH OF THE HIRED MAN 56
    'FEEL OUT THE PUBLIC SENTIMENT'--HE SAYS. . . . . . 48 A HUNDRED COLLARS . . 106
    "THERE, YOU HAVE SAID IT ALL AND YOU FEEL BETTER. . 54 HOME BURIAL 108
    AND FALLS ASLEEP WITH HEARTACHE--HOW SHOULD I FEEL? . 58 THE BLACK COTTAGE . . 103
    DID EVER YOU FEEL SO? I HOPE YOU NEVER. . . . . . . 63 A SERVANT TO SERVANTS . 10
    THAT SEEMS TO TELL ME HOW I OUGHT TO FEEL, ... 63 A SERVANT TO SERVANTS . 14
    AND WOULD FEEL IF I WASN'T ALL GONE WRONG. . . . . . 63 A SERVANT TO SERVANTS . 15
    I FEEL THE LADDER SWAY AS THE BOUGHS BEND. . . . . . 68 AFTER APPLE-PICKING . 23
    A LITTLE LONGER. I MUSTN'T FEEL TOO HURRIED, ... 78 THE GENERATIONS OF MEN 146
    I SHOULD FEEL EASIER IF I COULD SEE . . . . 80 THE GENERATIONS OF MEN 190
    BETWEEN TWO BOYS AND NOT FEEL BOUND TO STOP IT. . . 146 SNOW 101
    AND FEEL IT LESS. HEAR THE SOFT BOMBS OF DUST . . . 150 SNOW 206
    "I THOUGHT YOU'D FEEL YOU'D BEEN TOO MUCH CONCERNED." 155 SNOW 343
    IF WELL IT IS WITH RUSSIA, THEN FEEL FREE . . . . . 168 NEW HAMPSHIRE 280
    I FEEL, AS OF AN EARTHQUAKE IN MY BACK, ... 169 NEW HAMPSHIRE 318
    DIDN'T FEEL ANYTHING, AND IF IT DID, ... 178 THE STAR-SPLITTER . . 62
    TO FEEL THE EARTH AS ROUGH . . . . 227 TO EARTHWARD 31
    TO FEEL OF BETWEEN THUMB AND FINGERS; . . . . 266 SITTING BY A BUSH . . 3
    THE WORLD HAS ROOM TO MAKE A BEAR FEEL FREE; . . . . 269 THE BEAR 11
    AND ASK FOR SOME CITY MONEY TO FEEL IN HAND . . . . 286 A ROADSIDE STAND . . 19
    SOMETIMES I FEEL MYSELF I CAN HARDLY BEAR . . . . . 287 A ROADSIDE STAND . . 32
    THAT'S HOW WE FEEL--AND WE'RE NO SPECIAL MYSTICS. . 351 THE LESSON FOR TODAY . 42
    OF WHICH YOU FEEL NO LEAST TOUCH ON YOUR FACE . . . 361 A LOOSE MOUNTAIN . . 11
    AND MADE FEEL LESS ALONE THAN I RIGHTLY SHOULD, . . 383 WERE I IN TROUBLE . . 8
    TO FEEL IT CLOSE IN TIGHT AGAINST MY SENSE . . . . . 390 SKEPTIC 11
    OR YOU'D FEEL DIFFERENTLY ABOUT THE CLASSES. . . . . 406 FROM PLANE TO PLANE . 78
    A RIVALRY THAT MADE THEM BOTH FEEL KINDER. . . . . . 408 FROM PLANE TO PLANE . 119
    MEANWHILE FEEL OBLIGATION-FREE. . . . . 420 ONE MORE BREVITY . . 34
    YOU MUSTN'T FEEL HURT IF NOW I'M ALL . . . . 420 ONE MORE BREVITY . . 47
    DOES NO ONE AT ALL EVER FEEL THIS WAY IN THE LEAST? . 446 DOES NO ONE AT ALL EVER T
    WE FEEL IT IN THE MOMENT WE DEPART . . . . 460 HOW HARD TO KEEP FROM 196
    THEY'VE COME TO FEEL THE NEED OF IS A KIND . . . . . 461 HOW HARD TO KEEP FROM 232
    AND FEEL NO ILL EFFECTS FROM WHAT I GAVE YOU. . . . 474 A MASQUE OF REASON . . 36
    DON'T YOU FEEL SOMETHING? / LEAVE ME OUT OF THIS. . 504 A MASQUE OF MERCY . . 286
    DON'T YOU BE MADE FEEL SMALL BY ALL THIS POSING. . . 511 A MASQUE OF MERCY . . 461
FEELERS
    WITH FEELERS CALMLY ATWIDDLE, ... 288 DEPARTMENTAL 36
FEELING (SEE FELLOW-FEELING)
    IN SPITE OF A SCORCHED FOURTH-OF-JULY FEELING. . . . 132 THE BONFIRE 93

FEELING (CONTINUED)
    THUS TILL HE HAD THEM ALMOST FEELING DARED . . . . . . 230 TWO LOOK AT TWO   35
    BUT WE CAN'T HELP FEELING MORE THAN A LITTLE BETRAYED . . 305 THERE ARE ROUGHLY ZONES   15
    HELP ME ACCEPT ITS FATE WITH CHRISTMAS FEELING. . . . . 350 TO A YOUNG WRETCH . . .   24
    BUT NO ONE FROM THE FEELING WOULD HAVE GUESSED . . . . . 407 FROM PLANE TO PLANE . .   91
    NO ONE OF HONEST FEELING WOULD APPROVE . . . . 423 FOR JOHN F. KENNEDY . .   43
    FOR GOD HIMSELF THE HEIGHT OF FEELING FREE . . . . 461 HOW HARD TO KEEP FROM   251
    OR YOU WILL COME TO WITH A FOOLISH FEELING. . . . . . . 513 A MASQUE OF MERCY . .   537
FEELINGS
    IF YOU HAD ANY FEELINGS, YOU THAT DUG . . . .   53 HOME BURIAL   72
    I CAN'T EXPRESS MY FEELINGS, ANY MORE . . . .   63 A SERVANT TO SERVANTS .   7
FEELS
    I SYMPATHIZE. I KNOW JUST HOW IT FEELS . . . .   37 DEATH OF THE HIRED MAN   76
    YOUR FATHER FEELS US ROUND HIM WITH OUR QUESTING, ... 183 MAPLE   123
    "NOW YOU KNOW HOW IT FEELS," MY BROTHER SAID, ...   198 WILD GRAPES   62
    I TRUST FEELS PROPERLY DEFIED. . . . . 363 ASSURANCE   4
    FEELS LIKE MY ARMORY OF HATE; . . . . 393 BEYOND WORDS   2
FEET
    BENEATH THE FEET OF DANCING FLOWERS. . . . .   26 IN HARDWOOD GROVES . .   10
    BUT THE FEET QUESTION "WHITHER?" . . . .   30 RELUCTANCE   18
    WITH DEPTHS BEHIND HIM SHEER A HUNDRED FEET-- . . . . .   42 THE MOUNTAIN   60
    THEY SELL IN THE STORE AND BUY SHOES FOR THEIR FEET." . .   61 BLUEBERRIES   53
    SLUMPED WAY DOWN IN A CHAIR, WITH BOTH HIS FEET . . . .   72 THE CODE   97
    AND DANGLE FEET AMONG THE RASPBERRY VINES?" . . . . . .   75 THE GENERATIONS OF MEN   64
    I'M GOING TO SELL MY SOUL, OR RATHER, FEET. . . . . .   92 THE SELF-SEEKER . . .   3
    "WITH YOU THE FEET HAVE NEARLY BEEN THE SOUL; . . . . .   93 THE SELF-SEEKER . . .   5
    "WELL, IF IT'S TRUE! YOURS ARE NO COMMON FEET. . . . .   93 THE SELF-SEEKER . . .   10
    WHAT DOES HE THINK?--HOW ARE THE BLESSED FEET? . . . .   93 THE SELF-SEEKER . . .   14
    "HE THINKS I'LL HOBBLE. IT'S BOTH LEGS AND FEET." . . .   93 THE SELF-SEEKER . . .   16
    WHAT I CAN GET. YOU SEE THEY HAVE THE FEET, ...   95 THE SELF-SEEKER . . .   63
    I CAN'T GET BACK THE FEET IN ANY CASE." . . . .   95 THE SELF-SEEKER . . .   65
    OVER THE SNOW MY CREAKING FEET . . . . 102 GOOD HOURS   13
    TO SELL THEM OFF THEIR FEET TO GO IN CARS . . . .   106 CHRISTMAS TREES . . .   17
    ASK THEM TO HELP YOU GET IT ON ITS FEET. . . . .   113 IN THE HOME STRETCH .   76
    THEN HE FLUNG OUTWARD, FEET FIRST, WITH A SWISH, ... 122 BIRCHES   39
    BLADE-END UP AND FIVE FEET TALL, ...   124 A TIME TO TALK . . .   8
    THAT BROUGHT ME TO MY FEET TO HOLD IT BACK . . . . . .   132 THE BONFIRE   78
    AND THEN WENT ROUND IT ON HIS FEET, ...   139 BROWN'S DESCENT . . .   61
    OR A BASKET OF EGGS BETWEEN THEIR FEET; . . . .   141 THE GUM-GATHERER . .   27
    'SO YOU CAN THINK IT'S SIX FEET DEEP OUTSIDE, ...   149 SNOW   182
    MY FEET TUG AT THE FLOOR . . . .   156 THE SOUND OF TREES . .   15
    TEN THOUSAND FEET INSTEAD OF ONLY FIVE-- . . . . 169 NEW HAMPSHIRE   332
    LAID SCARLET AND PALE PINK ABOUT HER FEET. . . . . . . 184 MAPLE   147
    UPON IT NOW; ITS FEET ARE FAST IN SNOW. . . . .   189 THE GRINDSTONE . . .   10
    WITH BOTH HIS FEET AT ONCE AGAINST THE CEILING, ...   192 PAUL'S WIFE   51
    AND LAUGHED. THEN SHE CLIMBED SLOWLY TO HER FEET, . . .   194 PAUL'S WIFE   119
    BUT ONCE I FELT GROUND WITH MY STOCKING FEET . . . . .   198 WILD GRAPES   85
    AS WE CAN FALL AND KEEP A-BOUNCING ON OUR FEET. . . . .   215 A FOUNTAIN, A BOTTLE .   62
    HAVING TRIED ONE, HAD DROPPED IT AT HIS FEET . . . . .   217 A FOUNTAIN, A BOTTLE .   119
    IN LONG STORMS AN UNDRIFTED FOUR FEET DEEP . . . . . .   226 THE ONSET   15
    FROM INWARD FIRES OR BRUSH OF PASSING FEET. . . . . . .   239 OUR SINGING STRENGTH .   18
    AND LOOK UP SMALL FROM THE FOREST'S FEET. . . . .   247 ON GOING UNNOTICED . .   10
    I HAVE STOOD STILL AND STOPPED THE SOUND OF FEET . . . . 255 ACQUAINTED WITH NIGHT .   7
    THE TOENAIL CLICK AND SHUFFLE OF HIS FEET. . . . . . .   269 THE BEAR   17
    BETWEEN THE DOTTED FEET A STREAK OF TAIL, ...   270 THE EGG AND THE MACHINE 18
    THE GRIP ON EARTH OF OUTSPREAD FEET, ...   276 TWO TRAMPS IN MUD TIME   46
    SO MANY PRICKLY GRAPPLING FEET AT ONCE. . . . . 278 THE WHITE-TAILED HORNET 29
    TO WET THEIR FEET. . . . .   337 THE WIND AND THE RAIN .   24
    SEEING NO HELP IN WINGS OR FEET . . . .   346 DISCOVERY OF MADEIRAS . 100
    GOD HARDLY TOLERATED WITH HIS FEET; . . . .   352 THE LESSON FOR TODAY .   75
    IT SEEMED TOO TINY TO HAVE ROOM FOR FEET, ...   357 A CONSIDERABLE SPECK .   16
    IN WIND-SOIL TO A DEPTH OF THIRTY FEET, ... 365 OF STONES OF THE PLACE   6
    THAT BRACED HIS FEET AGAINST THE ARCTIC POLE. . . . . .   377 DIRECTIVE   17
    OR SO MUCH AS UNCROSS MY FEET, ...   381 AN UNSTAMPED LETTER IN   22
    AND BAGGAGE AT THEIR FEET. . . . .   391 A ROGERS GROUP . . .   4
    TWO THOUSAND FEET ABOVE THE OCEAN LEVEL. . . . .   400 TO THE RIGHT PERSON .   6
    UPON ITS DOORSTEPS AS AT MERCY'S FEET . . . .   400 TO THE RIGHT PERSON .   13
    HE HANGS ON UPSIDE DOWN WITH TALON FEET . . . .   412 POD OF THE MILKWEED .   45
    SHUFFLED THEIR FEET AS IF TO HINT RESPECTFULLY, ...   456 HOW HARD TO KEEP FROM   73
    TO LEARN TO SAY (HE MOVES TO JONAH'S FEET.) . . . . . .   521 A MASQUE OF MERCY . .   737
FEIGNING
    WHAT PASSED BETWEEN US, SHE WAS ONLY FEIGNING. . . . . . 187 THE AX-HELVE   57
FELL
    HE FELL AT GETTYSBURG OR FREDERICKSBURG, ...   56 THE BLACK COTTAGE . .   31
    UPON MY WAY TO SLEEP BEFORE IT FELL, ...   68 AFTER APPLE-PICKING .   15
    HE FELL AND MADE THE LANTERN RATTLE . . . .   138 BROWN'S DESCENT . . .   38
    HE MIGHT HAVE LEFT IT LYING WHERE IT FELL. . . . . . .   173 A STAR IN A STONEBOAT   39
    OF COURSE THE BOTTLE FELL SHORT BY A MILE. . . . . . .   195 PAUL'S WIFE   142
    FELL ALL IN WRINKLES OF RESPONSIBILITY. . . . .   201 PLACE FOR A THIRD . .   48
    AND FELL BACK FROM HIM ON THE FLOOR MYSELF. . . . . . .   204 THE WITCH OF COOS . .   78
    AND LEFT IT LYING WHERE IT FELL REJECTED. . . . .   217 A FOUNTAIN, A BOTTLE .   120
    THE SNOW FELL DEEP . . . .   218 I WILL SING YOU ONE-O   9
    ON VIMY RIDGE; AND WHEN YOU FELL THAT DAY . . . . . .   222 TO E.T.   14
    ONE DROP FELL FROM A FERN, AND LO, A RIPPLE . . . . . .   225 FOR ONCE SOMETHING .   12
    THEY MUST BROOD WHERE THEY FELL IN MULCH AND MIRE, . . . 253 THE THATCH   25
    FELL SPLINTERLESS AS A CLOVEN ROCK. . . . .   275 TWO TRAMPS IN MUD TIME   12
    WHERE HE FELL A PRISONER TO THE MOOR. . . . .   347 DISCOVERY OF MADEIRAS . 128
    MIGHT NOT HAVE MISSED ME WHEN THEY SHOT AND FELL? . . .   383 BRAVADO   3
    WHAT STAR IF ANY FELL. . . . .   383 MAKING CERTAIN ANYTHING   4
    I FELL IN AMONG . . . .   431 KITTY HAWK   100
    THERE I NEXT FELL IN . . . .   432 KITTY HAWK   139
    SO THE CROWN FELL AND THE CROWN JEWELS SCATTERED. . . .   453 HOW HARD TO KEEP FROM   6
    WHERE SHALL I START IN? WHERE MY EYES FELL FIRST? . . .   506 A MASQUE OF MERCY . .   326
    BUT IF THIS PROPHET'S MANTLE FELL ON ME . . . .   519 A MASQUE OF MERCY . .   686
FELLED
    OR FELLED TREE. . . . .   128 THE IMPULSE   8
    THAT FELLED THE ANGELS, WOLSEY SHOULD HAVE SAID. . . . . 481 A MASQUE OF REASON . .   206

FELLOW
    BUT I'LL NOT HAVE THE FELLOW BACK," HE SAID. . . . . . 35 DEATH OF THE HIRED MAN   12
    ONE TIME I ASKED A FELLOW CLIMBING IT . . . . 43 THE MOUNTAIN   73
    "LAFE, HERE'S A FELLOW WANTS TO SHARE YOUR ROOM." . . . 45 A HUNDRED COLLARS . .   36
    IT MAY NOT BE. I HEARD A FELLOW SAY SO. . . . . 57 THE BLACK COTTAGE . .   67
    WITH THE LITTLE FELLOW AT ALL. HE'S RUNNING AWAY. . . . 223 THE RUNAWAY   11
    EXCEPT AS A FELLOW HANDLED AN AX . . . . 276 TWO TRAMPS IN MUD TIME   55
    THERE IS A FELLOW ON THE OCEAN NOW . . . . 289 OLD BARN AT THE BOTTOM   17
    I HEARD A FELLOW IN A PUBLIC LECTURE . . . . 369 THE LITERATE FARMER AND   53
    A COW DID THAT ONCE TO A FELLOW . . . . 463 LINES IN DEJECTION . .   14
    TO LAST A FELLOW TO ETERNITY. . . . . 475 A MASQUE OF REASON . .   45
    HE IS THE FELLOW WHO THEOLOGIZED . . . . 498 A MASQUE OF MERCY . .   128
FELLOW'D
    YOU WOULDN'T THINK A FELLOW'D NEED MUCH URGING . . . . 71 THE CODE   59
FELLOW-FEELING
    BEFORE THE CROSS, IT IS FROM FELLOW-FEELING, ... 521 A MASQUE OF MERCY . .   735
FELLOWS
    AND MAKE GOOD FARMERS, AND LEAVE OTHER FELLOWS . . . . 114 IN THE HOME STRETCH .   96
    NEXT EVENING MURPHY AND SOME OTHER FELLOWS . . . . . . 195 PAUL'S WIFE   123
FELLOW'S
    "I THINK THE LITTLE FELLOW'S AFRAID OF THE SNOW. . . . . 223 THE RUNAWAY   9
FELT
    I FELT AS A FOOL TO HAVE BEEN SO CAUGHT, ... 25 THE DEMIURGE'S LAUGH .   14
    NEAR ME IT SEEMED: I FELT IT LIKE A WALL. . . . . 40 THE MOUNTAIN   5
    BUT ONLY FELT AT NIGHT ITS SHADOWY PRESENCE. . . . . . 41 THE MOUNTAIN   22
    I'VE FELT MEAN LATELY; MEAN'S NO NAME FOR IT. . . . . . 46 A HUNDRED COLLARS . .   54
    I KNOW THE WAY HE'S FELT--BUT ALL THE SAME!" . . . . . 84 THE HOUSEKEEPER . . .   83
    I ALWAYS HAVE FELT STRANGE WHEN WE CAME HOME . . . . . 89 THE FEAR   17
    HE FELT SOME NEED OF SOFTENING THAT TO ME: . . . . . . 107 CHRISTMAS TREES . . .   43
    BUT ONCE I FELT GROUND WITH MY STOCKING FEET . . . . . 198 WILD GRAPES   85
    IF THAT WAS HOW SHE FELT, OF COURSE, HE SAID. . . . . . 200 PLACE FOR A THIRD . .   14
    IF THAT WAS HOW SHE FELT, HE KEPT REPEATING. . . . . . 200 PLACE FOR A THIRD . .   21
    THOUGH SLIGHT, WAS A DEMAND. SHE FELT THE TUG. . . . . 217 A FOUNTAIN, A BOTTLE .   137
    I KNOW HOW THE FLOWERS FELT. . . . . 250 LODGED   6
    YOU'D THINK I NEVER HAD FELT BEFORE . . . . 276 TWO TRAMPS IN MUD TIME   44
    I FELT THE CHILL OF THE MEADOW UNDERFOOT, ... 342 QUEST OF PURPLE-FRINGED   1
    I FELT MY STANDPOINT SHAKEN . . . . 377 ONE STEP BACKWARD TAKEN   8
    ME A BLOW THAT I FELT . . . . 450 OBJECTION TO BE STEPPED   10
    (HE SEEMS TO HAVE FELT LIMITED TO ONE), ... 456 HOW HARD TO KEEP FROM   71
    SHE NOW FELT YOUNGER BY A THOUSAND YEARS . . . . 479 A MASQUE OF REASON . .   157
FEMININITY
    PRESUMING ON HER FEMININITY. . . . . 390 TWO LEADING LIGHTS . .   28
FEMINIST
    IN HER SUSPICION YOU'RE NO FEMINIST. . . . . 479 A MASQUE OF REASON . .   177
FEN
    BY A MISTY FEN THAT RANG ALL NIGHT, ... 15 IN A VALE   2
    THE FEN HAD EVERY KIND OF BLOOM, ... 15 IN A VALE   6
FENCE
    WILL ROT THE BEST BIRCH FENCE A MAN CAN BUILD.' . . . . 54 HOME BURIAL   93
    WE FENCE OUR FLOWERS IN AND THE HENS RANGE. . . . . . . 86 THE HOUSEKEEPER . . .   136
    THROWING A LEG UP OVER OUR FENCE OF MOUNTAINS, ... 176 THE STAR-SPLITTER . .   2
    AND THE FENCE POST CARRIED A STRAND OF WIRE. . . . . . 242 NEED OF BEING VERSED .   20
    OR MENDING FENCE IT ALL COMES BACK TO ME . . . . 325 BUILD SOIL   288
    REPAIRING FENCE AND ROOF; . . . . 367 A SERIOUS STEP LIGHTLY   20
    WHO HAD STOPPED OUTSIDE THE FENCE TO SPY, ... 385 A MOOD APART   5
FENCED
    AND YES, MY LAND WAS HARDLY FENCED. . . . . 364 TRESPASS   2
FENCES
    O'ER RUINED FENCES THE GRAPEVINES SHIELD . . . .   5 GHOST HOUSE   6
    HE ONLY SAYS, "GOOD FENCES MAKE GOOD NEIGHBORS." . . . . 33 MENDING WALL   27
    HE SAYS AGAIN, "GOOD FENCES MAKE GOOD NEIGHBORS." . . . 34 MENDING WALL   45
    HE DON'T GNAW TREES AND POSTS AND FENCES TOO. . . . . . 209 PAUPER WITCH OF GRAFTON   67
FENESTRATION
    AND TO THE WINDOWS OF ITS FENESTRATION, ... 400 TO THE RIGHT PERSON .   9
FERMENT
    THAT WAITED FOR THE BOTTOM TO FERMENT . . . . 468 IN A GLASS OF CIDER .   2
FERN
    BEFORE THE AGE OF THE FERN; . . . . 27 A LINE-STORM SONG . .   28
    THE PASTURE ALL OVER UNTIL NOT A FERN . . . . 59 BLUEBERRIES   18
    THOUGH I FOUND YOUR HAND FULL OF WILTED FERN, ... 109 THE EXPOSED NEST . . .   11
    IN THE FERN. . . . . 129 THE IMPULSE   20
    AND HAVE TO HUNT FOR IN SWEET FERN AND HARDHACK; . . . 197 WILD GRAPES   33
    LOOKING OUT OF A WREATH OF FERN AND CLOUD PUFFS. . . . . 225 FOR ONCE SOMETHING . .   6
    ONE DROP FELL FROM A FERN, AND LO, A RIPPLE . . . . . . 225 FOR ONCE SOMETHING . .   12
    LATE IN LIFE I HAVE COME ON FERN. . . . . 297 LEAVES COMPARED WITH .   11
    DEVELOPED IN THE GRASS AND FERN, ... 380 AN UNSTAMPED LETTER IN   20
FERNS
    WITH LITTLE FERNS IN CREVICES AT HIS ELBOW. . . . . . . 42 THE MOUNTAIN   62
    IN A BOOK ABOUT FERNS? LISTEN TO THAT! . . . . 63 A SERVANT TO SERVANTS .   35
FERRULE
    THE BLINDMAN MIGHT HAVE FOUND IT WITH HIS FERRULE, . . 394 HAEC FABULA DOCET . .   7
FESTIVITIES
    I THOUGHT THERE WERE TO BE FESTIVITIES . . . . 488 A MASQUE OF REASON . .   429
FETCH
    I'M GOING OUT TO FETCH THE LITTLE CALF . . . .   1 THE PASTURE   5
    AS HE WENT OUT AND IN TO FETCH THE COWS-- . . . . 121 BIRCHES   24
    YOU COME TO FETCH ME FROM MY WORK TONIGHT . . . . 123 PUTTING IN THE SEED .   1
    I SHOULD SELL FOR WHAT THEY WOULD FETCH. . . . . 295 A RECORD STRIDE . . .   28
    MY DUNGEONEERS, COME FETCH US.--NO ONE ANSWERS. . . . . 514 A MASQUE OF MERCY . .   556
FETCHED
    HE FETCHED A DINGY LANTERN FROM BEHIND . . . . 115 IN THE HOME STRETCH .   136
FETE
    "NO FETE TODAY," HE SAID. / "IT LOOKS THAT WAY." . . . 74 THE GENERATIONS OF MEN   35
FETID
    IN FETID DARKNESS STILL TO LIVE AND RUN-- . . . . 231 A BROOK IN THE CITY .   17
    OTHER THAN BASE AND FETID: . . . . 340 THE SUBVERTED FLOWER .   52
FEVER
    WELL, WHEN AT LENGTH THE FEVER STRUCK . . . . 345 DISCOVERY OF MADEIRAS   57

PAGE TITLE   LINE

FEW
  OUR FALTERING FEW STEPS ON . . . .   9 STARS   6
  AND A FEW HOUSES SPRINKLED ROUND THE FOOT, ... 43 THE MOUNTAIN   97
  THAT LOP EACH OTHER OF BOUGHS, BUT NOT A FEW . . . . 107 CHRISTMAS TREES . . .   34
  WALLS WERE ALL BURIED, TREES WERE FEW: . . . . . . 137 BROWN'S DESCENT . . .   13
  FEW FARMS CHANGED HANDS; SO RATHER THAN SPEND YEARS . . 177 THE STAR-SPLITTER . .   28
  DON'T BE AFRAID. A FEW OF THEM WON'T HURT YOU. . . . . 198 WILD GRAPES   57
  AND SUCH FEW PEOPLE . . . . 218 I WILL SING YOU ONE-O .   30
  I THOUGHT A FEW MIGHT TANGLE, AS THEY DID, ... 234 EVENING A SUGAR ORCHARD   7
  REALLY A VERY FEW TO BUILD AND STAY. . . . . . . 239 OUR SINGING STRENGTH .   24
  A FEW I MUST HAVE DRIVEN TO DESPAIR . . . . 240 OUR SINGING STRENGTH .   39
  BUT A FEW WEEDS AND STUBBLE SHOWING LAST. . . . . . 296 DESERT PLACES . . .   4
  IS RESERVED FOR THE BED OF A FEW SELECTED SEED. . . . 299 STRONG SAYING NOTHING .   4
  DON'T JOIN TOO MANY GANGS. JOIN FEW IF ANY. . . . . 325 BUILD SOIL   280
  WERE DAYS SO VERY FEW . . . . 333 HAPPINESS MAKES UP . .   8
  A FEW OLD PECKER-FRETTED APPLE TREES. . . . . . . 378 DIRECTIVE   28
  ONLY A FEW OF THOSE EVEN IN WHOSE DAY . . . . . . 397 THE PLANNERS   7
  STATES STRONG ENOUGH TO DO GOOD ARE BUT FEW. . . . . 398 NO HOLY WARS FOR THEM .   1
  THERE ARE FEW INSTITUTIONS STANDING HIGHER . . . . 400 TO THE RIGHT PERSON .   4
  EXCEPT FOR A FEW . . . . 448 THE BAD ISLAND--EASTER   42
  (JOB TAKES A FEW STEPS PACING.) DO YOU MIND? . . . . 485 A MASQUE OF REASON .   329
  ALL WEALTH AND POWER IN TOO FEW HANDS? . . . . . . 509 A MASQUE OF MERCY .   411
FEWER
  WHERE THEY GROW FEWER AND FEWER EVERY YEAR . . . . . 176 THE CENSUS-TAKER . .   62
FIBER
  YOU NICK MY SPRUCE UNTIL ITS FIBER CRACKS, ... 349 TO A YOUNG WRETCH . .   3
FICTION
  SOME SCIENCE FICTION . . . . 465 SOME SCIENCE FICTION .   1
FIELD
  THE WOODS COME BACK TO THE MOWING FIELD; . . . . . .   5 GHOST HOUSE   7
  WHEN I GO UP THROUGH THE MOWING FIELD, ...   8 A LATE WALK   1
  I ENTER ALONE UPON THE STUBBLE FIELD, ... 14 WAITING   3
  I WAS JUST GETTING THROUGH WHAT THE FIELD HAD TO SHOW . . 60 BLUEBERRIES   35
  MARCHED HIMSELF OFF THE FIELD AND HOME. ONE STAYED. . . 69 THE CODE   8
  SHE'S GOING TO DO MY SCOUTING IN THE FIELD, ... 98 THE SELF-SEEKER . .   151
  A LITTLE STRETCH OF MOWING FIELD FOR YOU; . . . . . 111 IN THE HOME STRETCH .   32
  IN ALTERNATION WITH THE WEEDS, THE FIELD, ... 112 IN THE HOME STRETCH .   48
  AND FOLLOWED WHERE HE FURROWED FIELD, ... 128 THE IMPULSE   7
  WHERE THE FIELD STRETCHES TOWARD THE NORTH . . . . . 131 THE BONFIRE   57
  HIS JOURNEY DOWN FROM FIELD TO FIELD. . . . . . . 138 BROWN'S DESCENT . . .   20
  SHE SAW THEM IN THEIR FIELD, THEY HER IN HERS. . . . . 229 TWO LOOK AT TWO . .   17
  THE WORLD WAS A BLACK INVISIBLE FIELD. . . . . . . 253 THE THATCH   10
  HE ROLLED ME OFF THE FIELD HEAD OVER HEELS . . . . . 278 THE WHITE-TAILED HORNET 20
  IN A FIELD I LOOKED INTO GOING PAST, ... 296 DESERT PLACES . . .   2
  SHE IS AS IN A FIELD A SILKEN TENT . . . . 331 THE SILKEN TENT . . .   1
  THEN MAKE YOURSELF AT HOME. THE ONLY FIELD . . . . . 378 DIRECTIVE   39
  LESS CRITICISM OF THE FIELD AND COURT . . . . . . 424 FOR JOHN F. KENNEDY .   68
  THEN HE COULD ENTER ON THE STRICKEN FIELD . . . . . 507 A MASQUE OF MERCY .   365
  THEN HE COULD ENTER ON THE STRICKEN FIELD . . . . . 507 A MASQUE OF MERCY .   368
FIELDS
  ACROSS THE FIELDS BEHIND THE HOUSE . . . . 18 GOING FOR WATER . . .   3
  (THOUGH CHILL), BECAUSE THE FIELDS WERE OURS, ... 18 GOING FOR WATER . . .   7
  WIDE FIELDS OF ASPHODEL FORE'ER, ... 19 THE TRIAL BY EXISTENCE   6
  NOW CLOSE THE WINDOWS AND HUSH ALL THE FIELDS: . . . . 25 NOW CLOSE THE WINDOWS .   1
  THERE IS NONE LEFT TO MOURN THEE IN THE FIELDS. . . . . 28 MY BUTTERFLY   7
  OUT THROUGH THE FIELDS AND THE WOODS . . . . 29 RELUCTANCE   1
  WERE FIELDS, A RIVER, AND BEYOND, MORE FIELDS. . . . . 40 THE MOUNTAIN   9
  LATER THEY GET OUT FURTHER IN THE FIELDS. . . . . . 49 A HUNDRED COLLARS .   129
  THE FIELDS ARE STRIPPED TO LAWN, THE GARDEN PATCHES . . 49 A HUNDRED COLLARS .   134
  THE FIELDS HAD NOWHERE LEFT FOR THEM TO GO; . . . . . 239 OUR SINGING STRENGTH .   26
  THE LAST WET FIELDS AND DRIPPING HEDGES HOME. . . . . 315 IRIS BY NIGHT . . .   3
  AS IN A SMUGGLER'S AT THE DIAMOND FIELD. . . . . . 503 A MASQUE OF MERCY .   253
FIERCE
  OR PLUNGING HEADLONG WITH FIERCE TWANG AFAR; . . . . . 14 WAITING   13
  FIERCE HEADS LOOKED OUT; SMALL BODIES PIVOTED. . . . . 59 THE BLACK COTTAGE .   126
  PERHAPS I HAVE PUT FORTH TOO MUCH STRENGTH AND BEEN TOO
      FIERCE FROM FEAR. . . . . 297 A LEAF-TREADER . . .   3
  THE WHOLE FIERCE CONQUERING PACK . . . . 311 THE VINDICTIVES . . .   47
  IT COST THE EARTH AS FIERCE A PANG . . . . 452 A-WISHING WELL . . .   40
FIERY
  IT IS BUT FIERY PUFFS OF DUST AND PEBBLES, ... 360 A LOOSE MOUNTAIN . .   5
FIFTEEN
  WE'VE BEEN HERE FIFTEEN YEARS." / "THAT'S A LONG TIME . . 82 THE HOUSEKEEPER . . .   39
  AND FILL ANOTHER WITH 'EM FIFTEEN MILES AWAY, ... 116 IN THE HOME STRETCH .   161
  HE WA'N'T BUT FIFTEEN AT THE TIME THEY SAY. . . . . 208 PAUPER WITCH OF GRAFTON 19
FIFTY (SEE NINETEEN-FIFTY-THREE)
  TO MEASURE HOW FAR FIFTY YEARS HAVE BROUGHT US. . . . . 56 THE BLACK COTTAGE . .   46
  FOR FIFTY DOLLARS FOR ONE LANGSHANG COCK-- . . . . . 86 THE HOUSEKEEPER . .   146
  DREAD FIFTY ABOVE MORE THAN FIFTY BELOW." . . . . . 228 GOOD-BY AND KEEP COLD .   19
  WHAT FIFTY SAID . . . . 267 WHAT FIFTY SAID . . .   1
  OF THE LAST FIFTY YEARS ARE ALL A LIBEL, ... 369 THE LITERATE FARMER AND 45
  BUT BEDS--IN LESS THAN FIFTY YEARS HE'S SURE . . . . 372 THE LITERATE FARMER AND 129
  AS FIFTY MILLION YEARS AGO WE CAME-- . . . . . . 395 WHY WAIT FOR SCIENCE .   12
  OF HAVING HOED AND MOWED FOR FIFTY YEARS, ... 404 FROM PLANE TO PLANE .   3
  FROM FIFTY NORTH TO FIFTY SOUTH. . . . . 418 AMERICA IS HARD TO SEE   54
FIFTY-FIVE
  HE'S FIFTY-FIVE, YOU KNOW, IF HE'S A DAY." . . . . . 83 THE HOUSEKEEPER . . .   64
FIG
  WHAT TREE MAY NOT THE FIG BE GATHERED FROM? . . . . . 196 WILD GRAPES   1
FIGHT
  IT'S THAT OR FIGHT, AND I DON'T WANT TO FIGHT-- . . . . 95 THE SELF-SEEKER . .   75
  GO OUTDOORS IF YOU WANT TO FIGHT. SPARE ME. . . . . 100 THE SELF-SEEKER . .   212
  FIGHT SUCH A FIRE BY RUBBING NOT BY BEATING. . . . . 131 THE BONFIRE   67
  THE TOWN TURNED OUT TO FIGHT FOR ME--THAT HELD ME. . . 131 THE BONFIRE   73
  OF BEING MEN WE CAN'T LOOK AT A GOOD FIGHT . . . . . 146 SNOW   100
  AND LIVING HIS FIGHT THROUGH WITH HIM, I SUPPOSE." . . 152 SNOW   269
  "HE HAD THE SHOVEL. HE'LL HAVE MADE A FIGHT." . . . . 153 SNOW   279
  A WEAPON IN OUR HUMAN FIGHT," HE SAID. . . . . . . 177 THE STAR-SPLITTER . .   24

FIGHT (CONTINUED)
     TO GO WEST TO A WORSE FIGHT WITH THE DESERT. . . . . . . 213 A FOUNTAIN, A BOTTLE . 12
     AND FIGHT IN A SMOTHER . . . . 218 I WILL SING YOU ONE-O . 14
     BEING ALREADY MORE THAN PROVED IN FIGHT, ... 353 THE LESSON FOR TODAY . 91
     TO SEE THAT THE FAIR FIGHT IS REALLY FAIR. . . . . . . 507 A MASQUE OF MERCY . 364
FIGHTING
     THAN THE MAN FIGHTING IT TO KEEP ABOVE IT, ... 151 SNOW 225
     SHORT OF A FIGHTING WORD. YOU HAVE THE ANSWERS. . . . . 192 PAUL'S WIFE 34
     FLATTERED I MUST BE TO HAVE TWO TOWNS FIGHTING . . . . . 207 PAUPER WITCH OF GRAFTON 4
     WERE FIGHTING FOR THE LATCH, ... 298 ON TAKING FROM THE TOP 14
     FOR ALWAYS FIGHTING ON BOTH SIDES AT ONCE. . . . . . . 350 TO A YOUNG WRETCH . 18
     THE BRUTALITY AND FIGHTING . . . . 387 THE COURAGE TO BE NEW . 3
     DON'T MIND A LITTLE THING LIKE THE ACTORS FIGHTING. . . . 392 IT BIDS PRETTY FAIR . 2
     I HAVE BEEN FIGHTING ON THE ANGELS' SIDE. . . . . . . 520 A MASQUE OF MERCY . 706
FIGHTS
     THAT ALL DAY FIGHTS A NERVOUS INWARD RAGE, ... 269 THE BEAR 14
     FROM ALL THE FIGHTS YOU HAD A MIND TO LOSE. . . . . . . 457 HOW HARD TO KEEP FROM 126
FIGHT'S
     AFTER THE FIGHT'S SO DEFINITELY DONE . . . . 507 A MASQUE OF MERCY . 366
FIGURATIVE
     FIGURATIVE ENOUGH TO SEE THE SYMBOL, ... 184 MAPLE 154
     AND FIGURATIVE USE HAVE PRETTY WELL . . . . 488 A MASQUE OF REASON . 425
FIGURE
     THE FIGURE OF OUR BEING LESS THAN TWO . . . . 118 MEETING AND PASSING . 7
     AND ARE A FIGURE OF THE WAY THE STRONG . . . . 164 NEW HAMPSHIRE . . 180
     LIKE DOVE WINGS ON A FIGURE ON A TOMB, ... 222 TO E.T. 3
     THEY WERE CONTENT TO FIGURE IN THE TREES . . . . 234 EVENING A SUGAR ORCHARD 15
     A BAGGY FIGURE, EQUALLY PATHETIC . . . . 269 THE BEAR 33
     HIS GREAT GAUNT FIGURE FILLED HIS CABIN DOOR, ... 292 FIGURE IN THE DOORWAY . 7
     THE FIGURE IN THE DOORWAY . . . . 292 FIGURE IN THE DOORWAY . T
     I FIGURE THAT LIKE ANY BANDYING . . . . 321 BUILD SOIL 169
     AS A FIGURE OF SPEECH . . . . 434 KITTY HAWK 186
     YOUR FOREARMS IN THE FIGURE OF A CROSS . . . . 501 A MASQUE OF MERCY . 193
     WHICH SPOILS YOUR FIGURE OF THE AMBULANCE. . . . . . . 508 A MASQUE OF MERCY . 383
FIGURED
     (FOR THAT WAS ALL THEY FIGURED OUT APIECE)-- . . . . . 107 CHRISTMAS TREES . . 49
FIGURES
     THE FIGURES HE DESCRIBED WITH IT, ... 138 BROWN'S DESCENT . . 31
     I LEANED TO LINE THE FIGURES IN . . . . 252 THE PEACEFUL SHEPHERD . 3
FILE (SEE SINGLE-FILE)
FILIAL
     PERHAPS A FILIAL DIFFIDENCE PARTLY KEPT THEM . . . . . 184 MAPLE 157
FILING
     WE WOULD CRAWL OUT FILING SINGLE . . . . 384 IN THE LONG NIGHT . . 7
FILL
     AND STOOD IN THE SUN AND LOOKED HIS FILL . . . . . . 23 PAN WITH US . . . 4
     TO FILL THE TREES WITH ANOTHER SHADE, ... 26 IN HARDWOOD GROVES . . 6
     AND THERE'S A BARREL THAT I DIDN'T FILL . . . . 68 AFTER APPLE-PICKING . 3
     AND FILL ANOTHER WITH 'EM FIFTEEN MILES AWAY, ... 116 IN THE HOME STRETCH . 161
     WITH THE SAME PAINS YOU USE TO FILL A CUP . . . . . . 122 BIRCHES 37
     WITH BIRDS THAT FILL THEIR BREASTS . . . . 126 LONELINESS 10
     TO WATCH HIS WOODS FILL UP WITH SNOW. . . . . 224 STOPPING BY WOODS . 4
     TILL I FILL THE WHOLE SHED, ... 235 GATHERING LEAVES . . 15
     HERE COME REAL STARS TO FILL THE UPPER SKIES, ... 246 FIREFLIES IN THE GARDEN 1
     TO FILL THE ABYSS'S VOID WITH EMPTINESS. . . . . . . 259 WEST-RUNNING BROOK . 49
     AND ALL THEIR LOGIC WOULD FILL MY HEAD: . . . . 277 TWO TRAMPS IN MUD TIME 59
     SHE TAKES HER TIME TO TAKE HER FILL. . . . . 281 BLUE RIBBON AT AMESBURY 39
     AND FILL THE SKY AS FULL OF MOONS . . . . 451 A-WISHING WELL . . . 17
FILLED
     I GUESS ESTELLE AND I HAVE FILLED THE PURSE. . . . . . 84 THE HOUSEKEEPER . . 100
     FILLED ME WITH NO LESS SORROW THAN THE HOUSES . . . . . 176 THE CENSUS-TAKER . 51
     THEY FILLED THEIR THROATS . . . . 219 I WILL SING YOU ONE-O . 48
     HIS GREAT GAUNT FIGURE FILLED HIS CABIN DOOR, ... 292 FIGURE IN THE DOORWAY . 7
     A KING FILLED HIS PRISON ROOM . . . . 310 THE VINDICTIVES . . 2
     FILLED ME WITH TO SHOUT . . . . 429 KITTY HAWK 27
FILLING (SEE DOOR-FILLING)
     RELIGIOUS FAITH IS A MOST FILLING VAPOR. . . . . . . 386 INNATE HELIUM . . . 1
FILLS
     FILLS ME WITH FEAR I'LL BE LEFT TO MY FATE: . . . . . 454 HOW HARD TO KEEP FROM 18
FILTH
     THERE BRIGHT IN THE FILTH IT LAY . . . . 312 THE VINDICTIVES . . . 78
FINAL
     WE WILL NOT BE PUT OFF THE FINAL GOAL . . . . 238 ON A TREE FALLEN ACROSS 10
     AND REMEMBER HOW FINAL A HUSH . . . . 266 SITTING BY A BUSH . . 15
     THE FINAL SUMMONS INTO CHURCH WAS BEATING. . . . . . . 284 THE GOLD HESPERIDEE . 42
     TO COME TO THEIR FINAL PLACE IN EARTH THEY HAD TO PASS ME
         BY. . . . . 297 A LEAF-TREADER . . 6
     THE FINAL FLAT OF THE HOE'S APPROVAL STAMP . . . . . . 299 STRONG SAYING NOTHING . 3
     AS IF THE FINAL ESTIMATE WERE HERS; . . . . 301 MOON COMPASSES . . 5
     HAD TO GIVE HER THE FINAL LIFT . . . . 343 DISCOVERY OF MADEIRAS . 10
     WILL GIVE US BY SHORTCUT THE FINAL STAGE . . . . 358 THE LOST FOLLOWER . 13
     THE FINAL GOLDEN GLOW . . . . 361 ALMOST TWO THOUSAND . 7
     TO GIVE DEVELOPMENTS THE FINAL SHOVE . . . . 369 THE LITERATE FARMER AND 42
     A FINAL GOING OVER WITH THE HOE . . . . 404 FROM PLANE TO PLANE . 13
     AT EVERY STATION BUT THE FINAL ONE. . . . . 501 A MASQUE OF MERCY . 195
FINALITIES
     AND HE LEARNED OF FINALITIES . . . . 129 THE IMPULSE 27
FIND
     THEY WOULD NOT FIND ME CHANGED FROM HIM THEY KNEW-- . . . 5 INTO MY OWN . . . 13
     FIND THE BROWN BENEATH THE WHITE; . . . . 11 TO THE THAWING WIND . 5
     TILL SOMEONE REALLY FIND US OUT. . . . . 19 REVELATION . . . 4
     ON WAKING TO FIND VALOR REIGN, ... 19 THE TRIAL BY EXISTENCE 3
     TO FIND THAT THE UTMOST REWARD . . . . 19 THE TRIAL BY EXISTENCE 7
     BUT AT SPRING MENDING-TIME WE FIND THEM THERE. . . . . . 33 MENDING WALL . . . 11
     HE COULD FIND WATER WITH A HAZEL PRONG-- . . . . 37 DEATH OF THE HIRED MAN 83
     SO HE CAN FIND AND EASILY DISLODGE IT . . . . 37 DEATH OF THE HIRED MAN 91
     HE TURNED TO THE HOTEL TO FIND A BED. . . . . 45 A HUNDRED COLLARS . 19
     MY BUSINESS IS TO FIND WHAT PEOPLE WANT: . . . . 48 A HUNDRED COLLARS . 103

FIND (CONTINUED)
    I LIKE TO FIND FOLKS GETTING OUT IN SPRING. . . . . 49 A HUNDRED COLLARS . . 127
    "I WILL FIND OUT NOW--YOU MUST TELL ME, DEAR." . . . . . 51 HOME BURIAL 12
    HE'LL FIND HE'S MISTAKEN. SEE HERE, FOR A WHIM, ... 61 BLUEBERRIES 80
    I GUESS YOU'D FIND... IT SEEMS TO ME . . . . 62 A SERVANT TO SERVANTS . 6
    HE THOUGHT YOU MEANT TO FIND FAULT WITH HIS WORK. . . . . 70 THE CODE 16
    HE WAS HARD ON HIMSELF. I COULDN'T FIND . . . . 71 THE CODE 39
    I'D BUILT THE LOAD AND KNEW RIGHT WHERE TO FIND IT. . . . 71 THE CODE 71
    "WEREN'T YOU RELIEVED TO FIND HE WASN'T DEAD?" . . . . . . 73 THE CODE 110
    STROLLED THITHER, NOT EXPECTING HE WOULD FIND . . . . . . 74 THE GENERATIONS OF MEN 26
    THAT YOU SHALL FIND LIES IN THE CELLAR, CHARRED . . . . . 79 THE GENERATIONS OF MEN 161
    HE CAN'T FIND ANYONE TO TAKE HER PLACE." . . . . 82 THE HOUSEKEEPER . . . 29
    WHAT, SON?" / "THEN I SHOULD THINK YOU'D TRY TO FIND . . . 92 THE FEAR 84
    ANOTHER RAM'S HORN! WHERE DID YOU FIND THOSE, ... 97 THE SELF-SEEKER . . . 115
    WITH A LAWYER AT HAND TO FIND YOU OUT. . . . . 97 THE SELF-SEEKER . . . 134
    YOU DIDN'T FIND A YELLOW LADY'S SLIPPER. . . . . 97 THE SELF-SEEKER . . . 137
    "YOU'LL FIND IT IS. LET YOUR FRIEND LOOK AT IT." . . . . . 99 THE SELF-SEEKER . . . 190
    JOE SAID: "YOU BIG BOYS OUGHT TO FIND A FARM, ... 113 IN THE HOME STRETCH . 95
    LET'S SEE YOU FIND YOUR LOAF. I'LL LIGHT THE FIRE. . . . . 115 IN THE HOME STRETCH . 155
    "I DON'T WANT TO FIND OUT WHAT CAN'T BE KNOWN. . . . . . . 116 IN THE HOME STRETCH . 170
    ALL THAT'S NOT NEW IN WHERE WE FIND OURSELVES. . . . . . . 117 IN THE HOME STRETCH . 182
    TO FIND FUSED IN ANOTHER STAR. . . . . 121 BOND AND FREE 20
    THEY MIGHT FIND FUEL THERE, IN WITHERED BRAKE, ... 131 THE BONFIRE 61
    WE DID FIND ONE NASTURTIUM . . . . 135 LOCKED OUT 8
    BROTHER MESERVE. YOU KNOW TO FIND YOUR WAY . . . . 144 SNOW 37
    I GUESS I KNOW WHERE I CAN FIND MY NAME . . . . 144 SNOW 39
    SIT DOWN, SIT DOWN. HOW DID YOU FIND THE HORSES?" . . . . 147 SNOW 105
    SHE SAID, "GO READ YOUR OWN BOOKS AND FIND OUT." . . . . . 166 NEW HAMPSHIRE 227
    THE ONLY FAULT I FIND WITH OLD NEW HAMPSHIRE . . . . 168 NEW HAMPSHIRE 310
    UNLESS TO FIND THAT THERE WAS NO ONE THERE . . . . 176 THE CENSUS-TAKER . . . 55
    TO FIND HIMSELF IN ONE. WELL, ALL WE SAID WAS . . . . . . 178 THE STAR-SPLITTER . . 57
    HER PROBLEM WAS TO FIND OUT WHAT IT ASKED . . . . 181 MAPLE 52
    SHE MIGHT HAVE OVERLOOKED. THEY COULD FIND NONE, ... 183 MAPLE 101
    TO WANT TO FIND OUT IF HE COULDN'T PILE . . . . 193 PAUL'S WIFE 60
    WE NEVER COULD FIND OUT WHOSE BONES THEY WERE. . . . . . . 206 THE WITCH OF COÖS . . 137
    THEY'LL FIND THEY'VE GOT THE WHOLE THING TO DO OVER, . . . 207 PAUPER WITCH OF GRAFTON 10
    WHO FAILED TO FIND OR FORCE A STRAIT . . . . 212 AN EMPTY THREAT . . . 44
    I'LL FIND THAT FOUNTAIN IF IT TAKES ALL SUMMER, ... 213 A FOUNTAIN, A BOTTLE . 18
    "YOU'VE LOST IT, THEN?" / "NOT SO BUT I CAN FIND IT. . . . 213 A FOUNTAIN, A BOTTLE . 20
    BUT YOU HAVE SAID IT, AND WE'RE OFF TO FIND IT. . . . . . 213 A FOUNTAIN, A BOTTLE . 28
    "I GUESS YOU'D FIND THE FOUNTAIN JUST AS EMPTY. . . . . . 214 A FOUNTAIN, A BOTTLE . 45
    TO FIND OUT WHAT TO DO TO HURT A POEM. . . . . 216 A FOUNTAIN, A BOTTLE . 108
    THE FLAKES COULD FIND NO LANDING PLACE TO FORM. . . . . . 239 OUR SINGING STRENGTH . 2
    THEY COULD FIND NOTHING OPEN BUT THE ROAD. . . . . 239 OUR SINGING STRENGTH . 30
    THAT NO ONE ON EARTH WILL EVER FIND? . . . . 248 A PASSING GLIMPSE . . 10
    OF THEIR NEST AGAIN, NOR FIND A PERCH. . . . . 253 THE THATCH 24
    WHOSE WORK IS TO FIND OUT GOD . . . . 288 DEPARTMENTAL 10
    I SHOULD FIND IT NO MORE NO LESS INTENSE. . . . . 291 ON HEART'S BEGINNING TO 20
    'TIS TO FIND WHAT THE HATED NEED, ... 312 THE VINDICTIVES . . . 82
    TO FIND THE GOOD OF COMMERCE. WHY SHOULD I . . . . 321 BUILD SOIL 164
    SO IF YOU FIND YOU MUST REPENT . . . . 326 TO A THINKER 33
    NOR WILL YOU FIND LOVE EITHER, NOR LOVE YOU. . . . . 356 A MOTH SEEN IN WINTER . 13
    NO ONE CAN KNOW HOW GLAD I AM TO FIND . . . . 358 A CONSIDERABLE SPECK . 32
    NOR FIND IN DEW THE SLIGHTEST CLOUDY TRACE. . . . . 361 A LOOSE MOUNTAIN . . . 12
    AND IF YOU'RE LOST ENOUGH TO FIND YOURSELF . . . . 378 DIRECTIVE 36
    UNDER A SPELL SO THE WRONG ONES CAN'T FIND IT, ... 379 DIRECTIVE 58
    MUST FIND WHERE TO POUR ITSELF INTO AND EMPTY? . . . . . . 379 TOO ANXIOUS FOR RIVERS 4
    TO FIND 'TWAS THE EFFORT, THE ESSAY OF LOVE. . . . . 380 TOO ANXIOUS FOR RIVERS 26
    THE LETTER YOU WILL FIND ME SUBSCRIPT TO . . . . 388 IOTA SUBSCRIPT 6
    WILL FIND RELIEF IN ONE BURST. YOU SHALL SEE. . . . . . . 398 BURSTING RAPTURE . . . 13
    HE'LL FIND THAT ASIATIC STATE . . . . 419 AMERICA IS HARD TO SEE 80
    NOT FIND A BARKEEP UNTO JOVE IN ME? . . . . 443 AUSPEX 9
    IN THE SURVIVING BOOK WE FIND . . . . 450 OUR DOOM TO BLOOM . . 10
    MY HEAD FOR IT--YOU'LL FIND THE BIG ONE HOLLOW. . . . . . 456 HOW HARD TO KEEP FROM 83
    BUT PHYSICAL ACTIVITY, I FIND. . . . . 479 A MASQUE OF REASON . 154
    BY PROPER NAMES I FIND I DO MY THINKING. . . . . 480 A MASQUE OF REASON . 200
    SO HE WON'T FIND IT HARD TO TAKE HIS ORDERS . . . . 481 A MASQUE OF REASON . 212
    SO HE WON'T FIND IT HARD TO TAKE HIS WAR. . . . . 481 A MASQUE OF REASON . 215
    A GOD CAN FIND IN LAUGHING AT HOW BADLY . . . . 483 A MASQUE OF REASON . 274
    AND FIND OUT WHETHER HE IS ANY GOOD, ... 484 A MASQUE OF REASON . 320
    NEXT TIME YOU FIND YOURSELF PRESSED ONTO ONE . . . . 486 A MASQUE OF REASON . 370
    FOR THIS I THINK. I FIND IT ALWAYS BEST . . . . 487 A MASQUE OF REASON . 387
    WON'T FIND A FORMULA FOR TAKING CARE OF. . . . . 488 A MASQUE OF REASON . 415
    OPEN ENOUGH TO FIND OUT WHO IT IS. . . . . 493 A MASQUE OF MERCY . . 12
    TO FIND OUT HOW TO GET AWAY FROM GOD? . . . . 494 A MASQUE OF MERCY . . 28
    TRUST ME TO HELP YOU FIND THE BOOK YOU WANT. . . . . 495 A MASQUE OF MERCY . . 50
    TO FIND IF THERE WERE POCKETS IN HIS SKIN, ... 503 A MASQUE OF MERCY . . 252
    THIS MODERN TENDENCY I FIND IN HIM . . . . 505 A MASQUE OF MERCY . . 312
FINDING (SEE RANGE-FINDING)
    FEARLESS OF EVER FINDING OPEN LAND, ...   5 INTO MY OWN 7
    AFTER SO MANY YEARS HE STILL KEEPS FINDING . . . . 37 DEATH OF THE HIRED MAN 74
    YOU WERE FOREVER FINDING SOME NEW PLAY. . . . . 109 THE EXPOSED NEST . . . 1
    BUT FINDING NOTHING, SULLENLY WITHDREW. . . . . 126 RANGE-FINDING 14
    BOTH EITHER LOOKING FOR OR FINDING SOMETHING. . . . . . . 217 A FOUNTAIN, A BOTTLE . 129
    AND THAT WERE ALL THE FINDING TO ANNOUNCE . . . . 293 AT WOODWARD'S GARDENS . 20
    FOR FINDING A THING TO DO THAT THOUGH NOT FORBID . . . . . 306 NOT QUITE SOCIAL . . . 3
    FINDING THE EAST BY SAILING WEST. . . . . 416 AMERICA IS HARD TO SEE 8
    FINDING HIM IN HIS RIGHT SUPPLIES . . . . 420 ONE MORE BREVITY . . . 42
    AND FINDING, WASN'T DISPOSED TO SPEAK. . . . . 421 ONE MORE BREVITY . . . 69
FINDS
    THAT, SILENCED BY MY ADVENT, FINDS ONCE MORE, ... 14 WAITING 20
    ARE BUT THE POINTS AT WHICH IT FINDS RELEASE. . . . . . . 255 THE FLOOD 11
    WHEN HE FINDS HIS VERSE IS UNDERSTOOD . . . . 469 CHOSEN POET OF VERMONT 2
FINE
    "FINE, FINE." / "AND READY FOR SOME MORE? MY WIFE HERE . . 147 SNOW 106
    I'VE TRIED IT FINE WITH LITTLE BREADTH OF LUSTER, ... 245 THE FREEDOM OF THE MOON 4
    THE FACTORY WAS VERY FINE; . . . . 274 A LONE STRIKER 50
    SUCH A FINE PULLET OUGHT TO GO . . . . 279 BLUE RIBBON AT AMESBURY 1

FINE (CONTINUED)
     TO WAGE A FINE SCHOLASTICAL CONTENTION . . . . 352 THE LESSON FOR TODAY . 51
     AS I HAVE KNOWN THEM PASSIONATE AND FINE, ... 358 THE LOST FOLLOWER . . 1
     AS FINE AS FLOUR PUT THROUGH A BAKER'S SIEVE. . . . . 365 OF STONES OF THE PLACE 8
     TILL ON SOME FINE NIGHT . . . . 442 KITTY HAWK 454
     BUT, YES, I'M FINE, EXCEPT FOR NOW AND THEN . . . . . 474 A MASQUE OF REASON . 39
FINGER
     TO CURL A LITTLE FINGER ROUND, ... 123 PEA BRUSH 18
     WITH ONE STROKE OF YOUR FINGER IN THE MIDDLE. . . . . 179 THE STAR-SPLITTER . 91
     SHE PUT HER FINGER IN YOUR CHEEK SO HARD . . . . . . 180 MAPLE 16
     BUT WHEN PAUL PUT HIS FINGER IN THE GREASE, ... 193 PAUL'S WIFE . . . 72
     AND IMPULSE, HAVING DIPPED A FINGER LENGTH . . . . . 231 A BROOK IN THE CITY 6
     AND PROBING WITH ONE FINGER NOT TOO ROUGH, ... 270 THE EGG AND THE MACHINE 21
     HER DEFT HAND SHOWED WITH FINGER RINGS . . . . 273 A LONE STRIKER . . 28
     INTO A LADY'S FINGER RING OR THIMBLE." . . . . 447 DOES NO ONE AT ALL EVER 30
     THAT ONLY NEEDS A FINGER TOUCH FROM GOD . . . . . . 502 A MASQUE OF MERCY . . 230
FINGER-BONE
     SHE HADN'T FOUND THE FINGER-BONE SHE WANTED . . . . . 207 THE WITCH OF COOS . 152
FINGERED
     HE FOLLOWINGLY FINGERED AS HE READ, ... 356 TIME OUT 6
FINGER-PIECES
     THE FINGER-PIECES SLID IN ALL DIRECTIONS. . . . . . 204 THE WITCH OF COOS . 79
FINGERS
     WE WEAR OUR FINGERS ROUGH WITH HANDLING THEM. . . . . 33 MENDING WALL 20
     HER FINGERS MOVED THE LATCH FOR ALL REPLY. . . . . . 52 HOME BURIAL 44
     MY FINGERS ARE ABOUT ALL I'VE THE USE OF . . . . . . 81 THE HOUSEKEEPER . . 6
     OF LITTLE FINGERS ALL KEPT DOWN BUT ONE, ... 98 THE SELF-SEEKER . . 156
     PAUL DRAGGED THE SHALLOWS FOR IT WITH HIS FINGERS, . 194 PAUL'S WIFE 104
     I KNOW I LOOKED LONG AT MY CURLED-UP FINGERS, ... 198 WILD GRAPES 87
     BRUSHING THEIR CHALKY SKULL WITH CHALKY FINGERS, . . 206 THE WITCH OF COOS . 128
     MY FINGERS AND CLOSE MY ARMS IN AN ARC. . . . . . . 265 THE DOOR IN THE DARK . 4
     TO FEEL OF BETWEEN THUMB AND FINGERS; . . . . 266 SITTING BY A BUSH . 3
     HOW THEY MAKE HASTE TO CRY WITH FINGERS CROSSED, . . 399 U.S. 1946 KING'S X . 3
     LIKE A PIP SHOT FROM 'TWIXT OUR PINCHING FINGERS." . 460 HOW HARD TO KEEP FROM 202
FINGERTIPS
     CAUGHT UP LIKE FINGERTIPS . . . . 339 THE SUBVERTED FLOWER . 12
FINISH
     IT GOES AGAINST ME NOT TO FINISH IT . . . . 95 THE SELF-SEEKER . . 83
     TO FINISH CLEAR AT EVE. . . . . 333 HAPPINESS MAKES UP . . 17
     THE KINGDOM'S YOURS TO FINISH AS YOU PLEASE. . . . . 453 HOW HARD TO KEEP FROM 2
FINISHED
     HE'S FINISHED SCHOOL, AND TEACHING IN HIS COLLEGE. . 36 DEATH OF THE HIRED MAN 60
     FROM THE HALL TO THE ONLY FINISHED BEDROOM, ... 205 THE WITCH OF COOS . 91
     THE MEADOW IS FINISHED WITH MEN. . . . . 264 THE LAST MOWING . . 4
     YOU'VE FINISHED. I'M DISMISSED. I WANT TO RUN . . . . 514 A MASQUE OF MERCY . 544
FIR
     MY WOODS--THE YOUNG FIR BALSAMS LIKE A PLACE . . . . 106 CHRISTMAS TREES . . . 13
FIRE
     BENT OVER THE OPEN FIRE, ... 8 LOVE AND A QUESTION . 18
     HOW THE COLD CREEPS AS THE FIRE DIES AT LENGTH-- . . 10 STORM FEAR 12
     THE FIRE RAN AND BURNED IT ALL UP BUT THE WALL." . . 59 BLUEBERRIES 12
     BECAUSE I MAKE HIM SPIT FIRE AT MY KNUCKLES, ... 94 THE SELF-SEEKER . . 34
     I'LL LIGHT THE FIRE FOR COMPANY FOR YOU; . . . . . . 115 IN THE HOME STRETCH . 146
     LET'S SEE YOU FIND YOUR LOAF. I'LL LIGHT THE FIRE. . 115 IN THE HOME STRETCH . 155
     THE FIRE GOT OUT THROUGH CRANNIES IN THE STOVE . . . 117 IN THE HOME STRETCH . 202
     TO LAMPS UNLIGHTED AND FIRE GONE GRAY, ... 127 HOUSE FEAR 4
     BY SETTING FIRE TO ALL THE BRUSH WE PILED . . . . . 129 THE BONFIRE 3
     AND SCARE OURSELVES. LET WILD FIRE LOOSE WE WILL----" 130 THE BONFIRE 18
     "WHY WOULDN'T IT SCARE ME TO HAVE A FIRE . . . . . . 130 THE BONFIRE 20
     THE FIRE ITSELF CAN PUT IT OUT, AND THAT . . . . . . 130 THE BONFIRE 25
     FIGHT SUCH A FIRE BY RUBBING NOT BY BEATING, ... 131 THE BONFIRE 67
     THE WOODS AND TOWN ON FIRE BY ME, AND ALL . . . . . 131 THE BONFIRE 72
     THE ROAD WOULD FAIL; AND ON THAT SIDE THE FIRE . . . 131 THE BONFIRE 75
     AND HAVE OUR FIRE AND LAUGH AND BE AFRAID." . . . . 133 THE BONFIRE 114
     BECAUSE OF THE FEARS OF FIRE AND LOSS . . . . 140 THE GUM-GATHERER . 21
     BURNED DOWN HIS FARMHOUSE FOR THE FIRE INSURANCE, . 168 NEW HAMPSHIRE . . . 302
     HE BURNED HIS HOUSE DOWN FOR THE FIRE INSURANCE . . 177 THE STAR-SPLITTER . 16
     HE BURNED HIS HOUSE DOWN FOR THE FIRE INSURANCE . . 177 THE STAR-SPLITTER . 30
     AND AN OLD-FASHIONED SACRIFICE BY FIRE, ... 178 THE STAR-SPLITTER . 64
     IT WAS THE TREE THE AUTUMN FIRE RAN THROUGH . . . . 184 MAPLE 140
     AND ALL BUT LOST HIMSELF. (A TONGUE OF FIRE . . . . 204 THE WITCH OF COOS . 72
     SOME SAY THE WORLD WILL END IN FIRE, ... 220 FIRE AND ICE . . . 1
     I HOLD WITH THOSE WHO FAVOR FIRE. . . . . 220 FIRE AND ICE . . . 4
     FIRE AND ICE . . . . 220 FIRE AND ICE . . . T
     YOU WENT TO MEET THE SHELL'S EMBRACE OF FIRE . . . . 222 TO E.T. 13
     IT'S NOT THAT I'M GREATLY AFRAID OF FIRE, ... 232 THE KITCHEN CHIMNEY 9
     AND THE SMELL OF FIRE DROWNED IN RAIN . . . . 232 THE KITCHEN CHIMNEY 15
     "O FIREMAN, GIVE THE FIRE ANOTHER STOKE, ... 234 EVENING A SUGAR ORCHARD 5
     AND THE AGED ELM, THOUGH TOUCHED WITH FIRE; . . . . 242 NEED OF BEING VERSED . 18
     TRUSTING FEATHERS AND INWARD FIRE . . . . 253 THE THATCH 26
     AND FROM THAT ONE INTAKE OF FIRE . . . . 266 SITTING BY A BUSH . 7
     I GAVE UP FIRE FOR FORM TILL I WAS COLD. . . . . . . 267 WHAT FIFTY SAID . . 2
     NOR STRIKE OUT FIRE FROM EACH OTHER, NOR CRASH OUT LOUD. 268 ON LOOKING UP BY CHANCE 5
     ON FIRE TO SCARE AWAY THE PTERODIX . . . . 372 THE LITERATE FARMER AND 139
     WHAT SET US ON FIRE AND WHAT SET US REVOLVING, . . . 380 TOO ANXIOUS FOR RIVERS 22
     HE ONLY STAYED TO SET THE SUMMER ON FIRE, ... 407 FROM PLANE TO PLANE . 93
     WILL OF ITSELF TAKE FIRE AND LIGHT THE WORLD UP. . . 414 A CABIN IN THE CLEARING 27
     I SAID THE INCENSE TREE'S ON FIRE AGAIN. . . . . . . 473 A MASQUE OF REASON . 5
     THE BIRDS, SEEM ALL ON FIRE WITH PARADISE. . . . . . 473 A MASQUE OF REASON . 13
     WAS THE DISCOVERY OF FIRE INSURANCE. . . . . 506 A MASQUE OF MERCY . 319
FIRECRACKERS
     DEVIL-SCARING FIRECRACKERS, ... 396 AN IMPORTER 4
FIRED (SEE ALL-FIRED)
FIREDROP
     THE LARGEST FIREDROP EVER FORMED . . . . 381 AN UNSTAMPED LETTER IN 25
FIREFLIES
     FIREFLIES IN THE GARDEN . . . . 246 FIREFLIES IN THE GARDEN T

                                                    PAGE TITLE   LINE
FIREFLY
     SHE WENT OUT LIKE A FIREFLY, AND THAT WAS ALL. . . . . . 195 PAUL'S WIFE 144
FIRELIGHT
     AND MAKE THEM SEE IT IN THE WINTER FIRELIGHT. . . . . . 257 THE LOVELY BE CHOOSERS   34
FIRELIT
     FROM THE FIRELIT LOOKING-GLASS . . . . 11 WIND AND WINDOW FLOWER   23
FIREMAN
     I CALLED THE FIREMAN WITH A CAREFUL VOICE . . . . . . 234 EVENING A SUGAR ORCHARD   3
     "O FIREMAN, GIVE THE FIRE ANOTHER STOKE, ... 234 EVENING A SUGAR ORCHARD   5
FIREPLACE
     AND LEAVE IT THERE FAR FROM A USEFUL FIREPLACE . . . . 102 THE WOOD-PILE 38
FIRES
     FROM INWARD FIRES OR BRUSH OF PASSING FEET. . . . . . 239 OUR SINGING STRENGTH . 18
FIRE'S
     AND THE FIRE'S DIED AND THE ROOM'S DARK AND COLD?" . . . 154 SNOW 310
FIREWEED
     NOT FIREWEED LOVING WHERE WOODS HAVE BURNT-- . . . . 248 A PASSING GLIMPSE . . 6
FIRKINS
     AS IF BY EYE PAIRS OUT OF FORTY FIRKINS. . . . . . . 378 DIRECTIVE 22
FIRM
     SO OLD AND FIRM THEY SCARCELY SHOW THE BREEZE, ... 5 INTO MY OWN . . . 2
     OR BEST--IT MAY NOT BE SO BAD. THE FIRM . . . . . . 95 THE SELF-SEEKER . . 78
     FIRM IN OUR FREE BELIEFS WITHOUT DISMAY, ... 424 FOR JOHN F. KENNEDY . 74
     SO THE FIRM FIRMAMENT WON'T SOFTEN. . . . . 453 A-WISHING WELL . . 75
FIRMAMENT
     IN HEAVEN'S FIRM-SET FIRMAMENT, ... 381 AN UNSTAMPED LETTER IN 30
     SO THE FIRM FIRMAMENT WON'T SOFTEN. . . . . 453 A-WISHING WELL . . 75
FIRMLY
     BRINGING A STONE GRASPED FIRMLY BY THE TOP . . . . . 34 MENDING WALL . . . 39
     AND HEAD TO TAIL THEN FIRMLY CURLED . . . . . . 419 ONE MORE BREVITY . . 17
FIRM-SET
     IN HEAVEN'S FIRM-SET FIRMAMENT, ... 381 AN UNSTAMPED LETTER IN 30
FIRST (SEE SAFETY-FIRST)
     UPON THE FULL MOON'S SIDE OF THE FIRST HAYCOCK . . . 14 WAITING 7
     HAVING FIRST HEARD THE LIFE READ OUT . . . . . 20 THE TRIAL BY EXISTENCE 34
     BUT HE TURNED FIRST, AND LED MY EYE TO LOOK . . . . 22 THE TUFT OF FLOWERS . 21
     SINCE FIRST I SAW THEE GLANCE, ... 28 MY BUTTERFLY . . . 12
     YOU GOT IT THE FIRST TIME. AND YOURS?" / "MAGOON. . . 46 A HUNDRED COLLARS . . 42
     THAT I HAD ON MY MIND TO ASK THE FIRST . . . . 46 A HUNDRED COLLARS . . 46
     BUT FIRST--LET'S SEE--WHAT WAS I GOING TO ASK YOU? . . 50 A HUNDRED COLLARS . . 162
     TO TAKE YOUR MOTHER-LOSS OF A FIRST CHILD . . . . 53 HOME BURIAL . . . 64
     "WHERE DO YOU MEAN TO GO? FIRST TELL ME THAT. . . . 55 HOME BURIAL . . . 115
     THAT HAD GONE OUT OF IT, THE FATHER FIRST, ... 56 THE BLACK COTTAGE . . 38
     IN THE CAVERNOUS PAIL OF THE FIRST ONE TO COME! . . . 59 BLUEBERRIES 5
     THEY TOLD ME AFTERWARD. FIRST THEY FORKED HAY, . . . 72 THE CODE 89
     FIRST LET ME LOOK. I SEE RASPBERRY VINES----" . . . . 76 THE GENERATIONS OF MEN 97
     I DIDN'T RELISH IT ALONG AT FIRST. . . . . . . 87 THE HOUSEKEEPER . . 173
     "IN THE FIRST PLACE YOU CAN'T MAKE ME BELIEVE IT'S----" . . 90 THE FEAR 41
     "I TOLD YOU, WILLIS, WHEN YOU FIRST CAME IN. . . . 95 THE SELF-SEEKER . . 61
     BUT PUT OUR FLOWERS IN WATER FIRST.--WILL, HELP HER: . . 99 THE SELF-SEEKER . . 172
     OH, I KEPT THE FIRST FOR ANOTHER DAY! . . . . . 105 THE ROAD NOT TAKEN . 13
     TO SEE IF THE BIRDS LIVED THE FIRST NIGHT THROUGH, . . 110 THE EXPOSED NEST . . 35
     TO SEE US THROUGH OUR FIRST TWO WEEKS. BUT, JOE, . . . 113 IN THE HOME STRETCH . 74
     THE FIRST NIGHT AFTER GUESTS HAVE GONE, THE HOUSE . . . 115 IN THE HOME STRETCH . 132
     BUT WHO FIRST SAID THE WORD TO COME?" / "MY DEAR, . . . 116 IN THE HOME STRETCH . 171
     IT'S WHO FIRST THOUGHT THE THOUGHT. YOU'RE SEARCHING, JOE, . 116 IN THE HOME STRETCH . 172
     THE FIRST THING IN THE MORNING, OUT WE GO . . . . 117 IN THE HOME STRETCH . 195
     I'M GOING TO PUT YOU IN YOUR BED, IF FIRST . . . . 117 IN THE HOME STRETCH . 199
     "FIRST TELL ME WHAT IT WAS YOU THOUGHT YOU HEARD." . . 118 THE TELEPHONE . . 10
     AND HAD JUST TURNED FROM WHEN I FIRST SAW YOU . . . 118 MEETING AND PASSING . 3
     THEN HE FLUNG OUTWARD, FEET FIRST, WITH A SWISH, . . . 122 BIRCHES 39
     WAS HOT ENOUGH FOR THE FIRST OF MAY, ... 123 PEA BRUSH . . . 6
     IT WILL HAVE ROARED FIRST AND MIXED SPARKS WITH STARS, . . 130 THE BONFIRE . . . 27
     THE BOY'S FIRST OUTCRY WAS A RUEFUL LAUGH, ... 136 "OUT, OUT--" . . . 19
     MESERVE WAS FIRST TO SPEAK. HE POINTED BACKWARD . . . 143 SNOW 6
     HERE FIRST MY THEME BECOMES EMBARRASSING. . . . . 166 NEW HAMPSHIRE . . . 217
     EVEN TO SAY THE GROVES WERE GOD'S FIRST TEMPLES . . . 171 NEW HAMPSHIRE . . . 392
     AND TUGGED IT FROM HIS FIRST TOO CERTAIN HOLD, . . . 172 A STAR IN A STONEBOAT . 6
     AS FISH DO WITH THE LINE IN FIRST ALARM. . . . . 174 A STAR IN A STONEBOAT . 54
     BUT THE FIRST THING NEXT MORNING WE REFLECTED . . . 177 THE STAR-SPLITTER . . 43
     MADE MAPLE FIRST TAKE NOTICE OF HER NAME. . . . . 179 MAPLE 2
     I WAS AFRAID, IN BRIGHTENING FIRST ON ME, ... 187 THE AX-HELVE . . . 55
     THEY'D SLICED THE FIRST SLAB OFF A BIG BUTT LOG, . . . 193 PAUL'S WIFE . . . 62
     "FIRST TIME I EVER SAW A HOLLOW PINE, ... 193 PAUL'S WIFE . . . 75
     AT THE FIRST DRINK IT RUSTLED AND GREW LIMP. . . . 194 PAUL'S WIFE . . . 102
     BEFORE SHE CAUGHT HER FIRST BREATH WITH A GASP . . . 194 PAUL'S WIFE . . . 118
     MY BROTHER DID THE CLIMBING; AND AT FIRST . . . . 197 WILD GRAPES . . . 31
     I HAD NOT TAKEN THE FIRST STEP IN KNOWLEDGE; . . . 199 WILD GRAPES . . . 95
     HIS FIRST THOUGHT UNDER PRESSURE WAS A GRAVE . . . 200 PLACE FOR A THIRD . . 22
     AND WHO HAD THOUGHT TO LAY HER WITH HER FIRST LOVE, . . 201 PLACE FOR A THIRD . . 46
     MY FIRST IMPULSE WAS TO GET TO THE KNOB . . . . 204 THE WITCH OF COOS . . 60
     FIRST SOLDIER, AND THEN POET, AND THEN BOTH, . . . 222 TO E.T. 7
     NATURE'S FIRST GREEN IS GOLD, ... 222 NOTHING GOLD CAN STAY . 1
     THE FIRST SONGBIRD THAT AWAKENED ALL THE REST. . . . 235 VALLEY'S SINGING DAY . 5
     WE SHOULD SEE WHICH ONE WOULD BE FIRST TO YIELD. . . 253 THE THATCH . . . 9
     BE HER FIRST JOY HER WEDDING, ... 256 THE LOVELY BE CHOOSERS 22
     HE STUNG ME FIRST AND STUNG ME AFTERWARD. . . . . 278 THE WHITE-TAILED HORNET 19
     HAVE NEVER MADE THE FIRST MOVE TO ASSEMBLE, ... 291 ON HEART'S BEGINNING TO 30
     OF FIRST ONE, THEN THE OTHER, TILL IT BROUGHT . . . 293 AT WOODWARD'S GARDENS . 9
     FIRST YOU LET THE SUMMER SIMMER, ... 303 CLEAR AND COLDER . . 4
     ITS NAME MIGHT BETTER BE FIRST MOTOR KITE. . . . . 308 THE WRIGHTS' BIPLANE . 2
     BEEN SOCIALIZED--THE FIRST PROPENSITY . . . . . 319 BUILD SOIL . . . 99
     THE THOUGHT I HAVE, AND MY FIRST IMPULSE IS . . . . 323 BUILD SOIL . . . 239
     SHE HEARD HIM STUMBLE FIRST . . . . 341 THE SUBVERTED FLOWER . 62
     THE MAN WAS AMONG THE FIRST I TOOK. . . . . . 345 DISCOVERY OF MADEIRAS . 59
     HERE'S FIRST A GLOVELESS HAND WARM FROM MY POCKET, . . 356 A MOTH SEEN IN WINTER . 1
     FIRST UNDER UP AND THEN AGAIN DOWN UNDER, ... 362 SYMPATHY WITH UNDER DOG 1
     WHO DREW BACK AT FIRST IN DOUBT, ... 366 NOT OF SCHOOL AGE . . 6

FIRST (CONTINUED)
WHEN MAN FIRST LIVED IN CAVES ALONG THE CREEKS?" . . . . . 372 THE LITERATE FARMER AND 140
AT FIRST TO BE NO BIGGER THAN A CANE, ... 375 A YOUNG BIRCH . . . 14
FIRST THERE'S THE CHILDREN'S HOUSE OF MAKE-BELIEVE, . . . 378 DIRECTIVE 41
AND BEEN THE FIRST WITH IT TO WIN A WAR, ... 399 U.S. 1946 KING'S X . . 2
EACH TRIED TO BE THE FIRST AT GETTING IN . . . . . . 407 FROM PLANE TO PLANE . 117
WHO WAS THE FIRST TO THINK OF SUCH A THING. . . . . . 422 FOR JOHN F. KENNEDY . 6
ELIZABETH THE FIRST AND ENGLAND WON. . . . . 422 FOR JOHN F. KENNEDY . 18
TO RULE FIRST ANSWERABLE TO HIGH DESIGN. . . . . . . 424 FOR JOHN F. KENNEDY . 65
IT MUST HAVE HAD THE PURPOSE FROM THE FIRST . . . . . 425 ACCIDENTALLY ON PURPOSE 14
BUT WHEN NOTICED FIRST . . . . 426 A NEVER NAUGHT SONG . 3
TO BE FIRST OF ALL? . . . . 430 KITTY HAWK 63
THAT HE WASN'T FIRST? . . . . 430 KITTY HAWK 65
OH, THERE HAD ONCE BEEN NIGHT THE FIRST, ... 444 ENDS 3
AND THEN HAVING FIRST . . . . 448 THE BAD ISLAND--EASTER 24
THE FIRST TOOL I STEP ON . . . . 450 OBJECTION TO BE STEPPED 17
WHEN UNTO EARTH HER FIRST WAS BORN. . . . . 452 A-WISHING WELL . . . 39
TO THE FIRST BUYER COMING BY WHO ASKED . . . . . . 454 HOW HARD TO KEEP FROM 39
I'LL TRY YOU IN THE KITCHEN FIRST ON FOOD . . . . . 455 HOW HARD TO KEEP FROM 49
SINCE YOU PUT FOOD FIRST IN YOUR REPERTORY. . . . . 455 HOW HARD TO KEEP FROM 50
HE GOT HIS FIRST CHANCE TO PREPARE A MEAL . . . . . 455 HOW HARD TO KEEP FROM 55
BY SAFETY SECOND OUT OF SAFETY FIRST, ... 457 HOW HARD TO KEEP FROM 124
THEY SHOULD TRY ONE WASTREL FIRST . . . . . . 466 SOME SCIENCE FICTION . 29
FIRST BY A BUTCHER, THEN A COOK, ... 467 QUANDARY 23
I WAS NO WORSE OFF THAN I WAS AT FIRST. . . . . . 468 IN A GLASS OF CIDER . 6
YES, BY AND BY. BUT FIRST A LARGER MATTER. . . . . 475 A MASQUE OF REASON . . 46
THE ONLY FREE WILL THERE AT FIRST WAS MAN'S, . . . 475 A MASQUE OF REASON . . 71
SO IT'S IMPORTANT WHO FIRST THINKS OF THINGS? . . . 480 A MASQUE OF REASON . . 198
ONE AT A TIME, PLEASE. I WILL ANSWER JOB FIRST. . . 484 A MASQUE OF REASON . . 324
FIRST WHITE, THEN RED, THEN ULTRARED, THEN OUT. . . 485 A MASQUE OF REASON . . 346
I TAKE THE FIRST BOAT. GOD PUTS UP A STORM . . . 500 A MASQUE OF MERCY . . 180
WHERE SHALL I START IN? WHERE MY EYES FELL FIRST? . 506 A MASQUE OF MERCY . . 326
IS THE FIRST PLACE IN LITERATURE, I THINK, . . . 508 A MASQUE OF MERCY . . 376
BUT MERCY FIRST AND LAST SHALL BRIGHTEST SHINE-- . 508 A MASQUE OF MERCY . . 381
NOT ONLY LAST, BUT FIRST, YOU WILL OBSERVE; . . . 508 A MASQUE OF MERCY . . 382
FIRST'S
OUR BUSINESS FIRST'S UP ATTIC WITH HER BOOKS." . . . . . 216 A FOUNTAIN, A BOTTLE . 88
FIRST-WATER
WITH ONE FIRST-WATER STAR ALMOST AS SHINING. . . . . . 245 THE FREEDOM OF THE MOON 6
YOU DON'T BELIEVE THAT THAT FIRST-WATER GLEAM . . . . 370 THE LITERATE FARMER AND 62
FISH
THE WATER IN DESPERATE STRAITS LIKE FRANTIC FISH, ... 142 THE VANISHING RED . . 22
AS FISH DO WITH THE LINE IN FIRST ALARM. . . . . . 174 A STAR IN A STONEBOAT . 54
IT CAUGHT ME UP AS IF I WERE THE FISH . . . . . . 197 WILD GRAPES . . . 44
THERE WOULD BE FISH RAW AND COOKED TOO . . . . . 384 IN THE LONG NIGHT . . 11
NOR TASTE ITS SALT, NOR SMELL ITS FISH AND WEED, . . . 447 DOES NO ONE AT ALL EVER 35
FISHER
TO COME AT THE FISHER TOWN . . . . 260 SAND DUNES 6
FISHERMAN'S
THE FISHERMAN'S SWAPPING A YARN FOR A YARN . . . . . 262 THE FLOWER BOAT . . . 1
FISHING (SEE A-FISHING, TROUT-FISHING)
DANGLING THEIR LEGS AND FISHING OFF A WHARF . . . . 161 NEW HAMPSHIRE . . . 75
AS FOR WHAT THEY WERE UP TO MORE THAN FISHING-- . . . 161 NEW HAMPSHIRE . . . 87
AS TAKE HIS GUN--ROD--TO GO HUNTING--FISHING. . . . 349 TO A YOUNG WRETCH . . 2
AND THEN NO BIGGER THAN A FISHING POLE . . . . . 375 A YOUNG BIRCH . . . 15
FISHPOLE
AND IT THE FISHPOLE. SO I WAS TRANSLATED, ... 197 WILD GRAPES . . . 45
FIST
AND AT THE SINUS UNDER WATER A FIST . . . . . . 98 THE SELF-SEEKER . . 155
HIS SMALL FIST BURIED IN THE BUSHY HIDE. . . . . . 267 RIDERS 8
BEFORE THEY GAVE WAY AT THE FIST. . . . . . . 452 A-WISHING WELL . . . 57
FISTS
HE SAT AND FIXED HIS CHIN BETWEEN HIS FISTS. . . . . 52 HOME BURIAL . . . 41
FIT
AND FIT THE EARTH LIKE A LEATHER GLOVE. . . . . . 26 IN HARDWOOD GROVES . 4
"A FIT!" SAID ONE, AND BANGED A STOVEPIPE SHOULDER. . . 113 IN THE HOME STRETCH . 90
OF MIND AND STRONG OF ARM SHOULD FIT TOGETHER, . . . 164 NEW HAMPSHIRE . . . 181
I STRAIN AT LESSONS FIT TO START A SUTURE. . . . . 267 WHAT FIFTY SAID . . . 7
ALL WOODS AND PASTURE ONLY FIT FOR SHEEP. . . . . 316 BUILD SOIL 9
FITFUL
AND HER SELF-SEEKING, FITFUL THOUGH IT WAS, ... 182 MAPLE 72
NOW IT TOOK A FITFUL RUN; . . . . 344 DISCOVERY OF MADEIRAS . 21
FITTED (SEE ILL-FITTED)
FORGETTING THAT AS FITTED TO THE SPHERE, ... 261 A SOLDIER 7
AND DOUBLE RING OF FITTED BRASS . . . . . . 363 ASSURANCE . . . 3
FITTER
TO PRODUCE PURPOSE AS THE FITTER BRED: . . . . . 425 ACCIDENTALLY ON PURPOSE 15
FIVE (SEE EIGHTY-FIVE, FIFTY-FIVE, FORTY-FIVE, SIXTY-FIVE, TWENTY-FIVE)
THAT'S FIVE MILES BACK. YOU CAN'T MISTAKE THE PLACE: . . 41 THE MOUNTAIN . . . 41
THERE'S FIVE: THAT'S ALL I CARRY." / "I CAN SEARCH YOU? . 47 A HUNDRED COLLARS . . 88
CUT SHORT OFF AT BOTH ENDS. IT LIES FIVE MILES . . . 63 A SERVANT TO SERVANTS . 21
NAMED SANDERS, WITH A GANG OF FOUR OR FIVE . . . . 70 THE CODE 31
FIVE HUNDRED DOLLARS FOR THE PAIR, YOU KNOW." . . . 93 THE SELF-SEEKER . . 4
HAVE YOU AGREED TO ANY PRICE?" / "FIVE HUNDRED. . . . 94 THE SELF-SEEKER . . 58
FIVE HUNDRED--FIVE--FIVE! ONE, TWO, THREE, FOUR,FIVE. . . 94 THE SELF-SEEKER . . 59
NO, THE FIVE HUNDRED WAS THE SUM THEY NAMED. . . . 95 THE SELF-SEEKER . . 73
"WERE THERE NO OTHERS?" / "THERE WERE FOUR OR FIVE. . . 97 THE SELF-SEEKER . . 119
"FIVE HUNDRED DOLLARS!" / "WHAT WOULD YOU THINK RIGHT?" . 99 THE SELF-SEEKER . . 198
BLADE-END UP AND FIVE FEET TALL, ... 124 A TIME TO TALK . . . 8
FIVE MOUNTAIN RANGES ONE BEHIND THE OTHER . . . . 136 "OUT,OUT--" . . . 5
AND SET ME FIVE MILES ON MY ROAD . . . . . . 140 THE GUM-GATHERER . . 3
NEW YORK (FIVE MILLION) LAUGHS AT MANCHESTER, . . . 165 NEW HAMPSHIRE . . . 201
TEN THOUSAND FEET INSTEAD OF ONLY FIVE-- . . . . 169 NEW HAMPSHIRE . . . 332
FIVE THOUSAND IS NO LONGER HIGH ENOUGH. . . . . 169 NEW HAMPSHIRE . . . 334
ONE OF THEM FIVE YEARS YOUNGER THAN I LOOK-- . . . 196 WILD GRAPES . . . 18
BEGAN TO BLOSSOM AT THE AGE OF FIVE; . . . . . 283 THE GOLD HESPERIDEE . 2
HIS LITTLE MATTHEW, ALSO FIVE YEARS OLD, ... 283 THE GOLD HESPERIDEE . 13
LET'S HAVE A LOOK AT ANOTHER FIVE. . . . . . . 310 IN DIVES' DIVE . . . 6

FIVE (CONTINUED)
RATHER BECAUSE IT TOOK FIVE YEARS AT LEAST . . . . . . 323 BUILD SOIL 227
FOUR OR FIVE WHIPPOORWILLS . . . . 364 A NATURE NOTE . . . 1
FIVE NOCTURNES . . . . 382 FIVE NOCTURNES . . . T
A LARGER ONE HE ASKED FIVE HUNDRED FOR. . . . . . 455 HOW HARD TO KEEP FROM 68
FIVE-YEAR
FRIENDS CROWD AROUND ME WITH THEIR FIVE-YEAR PLANS . . 323 BUILD SOIL 222
A FIVE-YEAR PLAN I CALL SO NOT BECAUSE . . . . . 323 BUILD SOIL 225
FIX
NOTHING WOULD DO BUT THEY MUST FIX A DAY . . . . . . 73 THE GENERATIONS OF MEN 15
AIN'T IT A CAUTION TO US NOT TO FIX . . . . . . 372 THE LITERATE FARMER AND 137
FIXED
ANY FIXED WAGES, THOUGH I WISH I COULD.' . . . . . 35 DEATH OF THE HIRED MAN 23
HE SAT AND FIXED HIS CHIN BETWEEN HIS FISTS. . . . . 52 HOME BURIAL 41
THAT THOUGH THERE IS NO FIXED LINE BETWEEN WRONG AND RIGHT, 305 THERE ARE ROUGHLY ZONES 12
FIXITY
AND FIXITY IN OUR JOYS, ... 156 THE SOUND OF TREES . . 8
FIZZLED
YOUR RIGHTEOUS INDIGNATION FIZZLED OUT, ... 497 A MASQUE OF MERCY . . 103
FLAG
AND THE BIG FLAG THEY HAD--YOU KNOW . . . . . 366 NOT OF SCHOOL AGE . . 24
THE BIG FLAG: THE RED--WHITE-- . . . . 367 NOT OF SCHOOL AGE . . 25
AND BLUE FLAG, THE GREAT SIGHT-- . . . . 367 NOT OF SCHOOL AGE . . 26
FLAGS
ON THE WET FLAGS BEFORE A CRUCIFIX . . . . 516 A MASQUE OF MERCY . . 614
FLAGSHIP'S
THEY SAY HIS FLAGSHIP'S UNLAID GHOST . . . . 418 AMERICA IS HARD TO SEE 49
FLAKE
OF EASY WIND AND DOWNY FLAKE. . . . . 224 STOPPING BY WOODS . . 12
IT IS SNOWING A FLAKE: AND HE HALF KNEW . . . . . . 276 TWO TRAMPS IN MUD TIME 29
FLAKED
TILL IT FLAKED FROM THE LEDGE. . . . . 448 THE BAD ISLAND--EASTER 15
FLAKES (SEE SKY-FLAKES)
LIKE A SHADOW AGAINST THE CURTAIN OF FALLING FLAKES. . . 223 THE RUNAWAY 8
THE FLAKES COULD FIND NO LANDING PLACE TO FORM. . . . 239 OUR SINGING STRENGTH . 2
NOT TILL FROM SEPARATE FLAKES THEY CHANGED AT NIGHT . . 239 OUR SINGING STRENGTH . 7
AND THE THICK FLAKES FLOATING AT A PAUSE . . . . . 303 AFTERFLAKES 13
FLAME (SEE LAMP-FLAME)
AS PALE AND DIM AS A MATCH FLAME IN THE SUN; . . . . 77 THE GENERATIONS OF MEN 100
AT THE FLAME BURNING DOWNWARD AS HE SUCKS IT." . . . . 112 IN THE HOME STRETCH . 65
AND MY FLAME MADE A PINNACLE TO HEAVEN . . . . . 130 THE BONFIRE 38
IT PUT THE FLAME TIP-DOWN AND DABBED THE GRASS . . . . 131 THE BONFIRE 45
AND A FLAME SLENDER AS THE HEPATICAS, ... 131 THE BONFIRE 51
TO GET A PUFF OF BLACK SMOKE FROM THE FLAME, ... 148 SNOW 140
THE APPLE TREES BE SENT TO HEARTHSTONE FLAME. . . . . 231 A BROOK IN THE CITY . 11
THAT WOULD HAVE JOINED THE HOUSE IN FLAME . . . . . 241 NEED OF BEING VERSED . 6
THE SUN ONCE IMPARTED ITS FLAME. . . . . 266 SITTING BY A BUSH . . 18
TO FRIZZLE RESIN IN A CANDLE FLAME, ... 350 TO A YOUNG WRETCH . . 8
FLAMES
TO FLAMES WITHOUT TWICE THINKING, WHERE IT VERGES . . . 131 THE BONFIRE 59
UPON THE ROAD, TO FLAMES TOO, THOUGH IN FEAR . . . . 131 THE BONFIRE 60
FLAMING
AND SWEEPING ROUND IT WITH A FLAMING SWORD, ... 130 THE BONFIRE 28
FLANK
OF HIS SLIM GOAD ON NOSE AND OFFSIDE FLANK, ... 44 THE MOUNTAIN 108
FLAP
ON WINGS TOO STIFF TO FLAP . . . . 464 MILKY WAY IS A COWPATH 1
FLASH
AND FLASH, AT THE LEAST ALARM . . . . 282 A DRUMLIN WOODCHUCK . 15
THERE WAS A SUDDEN FLASH OF ARM, A SNATCH, ... 293 AT WOODWARD'S GARDENS . 22
WE ASKED FOR RAIN. IT DIDN'T FLASH AND ROAR. . . . . 349 OUR HOLD ON THE PLANET 1
BECAUSE THEIR PURPOSE IS TO FLASH AND SPARK, ... 370 THE LITERATE FARMER AND 78
FREEDOM TO FLASH OFF INTO WILD CONNECTIONS. . . . . . 461 HOW HARD TO KEEP FROM 246
FLASHED
FLASHED OUT AND LICKED ALONG HIS UPPER TEETH. . . . . 204 THE WITCH OF COOS . . 73
FLASHES
THAT FLASHES TAIL THROUGH LAST YEAR'S WITHERED BRAKE . . 226 THE ONSET 20
A FUSILLADE OF BLANKS AND EMPTY FLASHES, ... 361 A LOOSE MOUNTAIN . . 9
FLASHING
OF FLASHING LINKS IN THE SUN. . . . . 312 THE VINDICTIVES . . . 75
FLASK
IF IT WAS A FLASK?) . . . . 431 KITTY HAWK 107
FLAT
SOME PALLID THING HAD SQUASHED ITS FEATURES FLAT . . . 148 SNOW 160
DANCED SLOWLY ON IT TILL HE TROD IT FLAT. . . . . . 284 THE GOLD HESPERIDEE . 48
THE FINAL FLAT OF THE HOE'S APPROVAL STAMP . . . . . 299 STRONG SAYING NOTHING . 3
(THE THRONE'S A PLYWOOD FLAT, PREFABRICATED, ... 474 A MASQUE OF REASON . . 21
FLATLY
I ANSWER FLATLY: THAT'S THE WAY IT IS, ... 477 A MASQUE OF REASON . . 111
TO ASKING FLATLY FOR THE REASON--OUTRIGHT. . . . . . 483 A MASQUE OF REASON . . 269
FLATNESS
YET OH! THE TEMPTING FLATNESS OF A BOOK, ... 216 A FOUNTAIN, A BOTTLE . 109
FLATTENED
THE GRASS LAY FLATTENED UNDER ONE GREAT TREAD. . . . . 239 OUR SINGING STRENGTH . 12
. ANOTHER SOFTER GLOBE THAT SLIGHTLY FLATTENED . . . . 322 BUILD SOIL 195
FLATTER
CAN IT BE TO FLATTER . . . . 435 KITTY HAWK 244
FLATTERED
FLATTERED I MUST BE TO HAVE TWO TOWNS FIGHTING . . . . 207 PAUPER WITCH OF GRAFTON 4
ALL VERY SPLENDID. I AM FLATTERED PROUD . . . . . . 481 A MASQUE OF REASON . . 217
FLAVOR
I TASTE IN THEM SOMETIMES THE FLAVOR OF SOOT. . . . . 59 BLUEBERRIES 23
THEY BIT THE GLASS AND LISTENED FOR THE FLAVOR. . . . 293 AT WOODWARD'S GARDENS . 27
FLAYED
AN EMPTINESS FLAYED TO THE VERY STONE. . . . . . . 174 THE CENSUS-TAKER . . 14
FLECK
AND EVERY FLECK OF RUSSET SHOWING CLEAR. . . . . . . 68 AFTER APPLE-PICKING . 20

FLECKED
   HER FACE IS FLECKED WITH POMACE AND SHE DROOLS . . . . . 124 THE COW IN APPLE TIME . 4
   FLECKED THE DARK STREAM AND FLECKED THE DARKER POOL . . . 258 WEST-RUNNING BROOK . . 24
FLED
   THAT FRIGHTED THEE SO OFT, IS FLED OR DEAD: . . . . . . 28 MY BUTTERFLY 3
   WE HEARD THE MINIATURE THUNDER WHERE HE FLED, ... 223 THE RUNAWAY 6
   ACROSS THE THRESHOLD IN THE TWILIGHT FLED HIM. . . . . . 289 OLD BARN AT THE BOTTOM 9
   THEN FLED FOR FEAR OF GETTING STUCK IN LAVA . . . . . . 407 FROM PLANE TO PLANE . 94
   FLED FROM THE PALACE IN THE GUISE OF MEN. . . . . 454 HOW HARD TO KEEP FROM 11
   "I FLED HIM, DOWN THE NIGHTS AND DOWN THE DAYS; . . . . 494 A MASQUE OF MERCY . . 22
   I FLED HIM, DOWN THE ARCHES OF THE YEARS." . . . . . . 494 A MASQUE OF MERCY . . 23
   AND FLED TO YOU. BUT YOU RECEIVE ME NOT. . . . . 497 A MASQUE OF MERCY . . 101
FLEDGE
   HAD FED IN CHORUS, AND LIVED TO FLEDGE, ... 253 THE THATCH 15
FLEDGED (SEE FULL-FLEDGED)
FLEE
   YOU MAY TAUNT ME WITH NOT BEING ABLE TO FLEE THE EARTH. . 306 NOT QUITE SOCIAL . . 9
FLESH
   (MIRACULOUSLY WITHOUT TASTING FLESH) . . . . 109 THE EXPOSED NEST . . 4
   MEANS THAT A SOUL IS COMING ON THE FLESH. . . . . . . 386 A STEEPLE ON THE HOUSE 8
   SUCH AS THAT FLESH IS SOMETHING WE CAN SLOUGH . . . . 395 ETHEREALIZING . . . 3
   INTO FLESH WAS MEANT . . . . 435 KITTY HAWK 220
   SPIRIT ENTERS FLESH . . . . 435 KITTY HAWK 246
   LIKE FLESH, THERE MUST BE SOMETHING LIVING IN IT." . . 456 HOW HARD TO KEEP FROM 91
FLEW
   WHERE THE BIRD WAS BEFORE IT FLEW, ... 15 IN A VALE 18
   AND THEN HE FLEW AS FAR AS EYE COULD SEE, ... 22 THE TUFT OF FLOWERS . 17
   'WELL, ONE OF US IS.' FOR COMPLAINING IT FLEW . . . . 62 BLUEBERRIES 90
   A SMALL BIRD FLEW BEFORE ME. HE WAS CAREFUL . . . . . 101 THE WOOD-PILE . . . 10
   NONE FLEW BEHIND ME TO BE LEFT ALONE. . . . . 240 OUR SINGING STRENGTH 48
   AT BROKEN WINDOWS FLEW OUT AND IN, ... 242 NEED OF BEING VERSED 14
   LONG BEFORE HE FLEW IT. . . . . 430 KITTY HAWK 56
FLICKED
   HE FLICKED AND FLUNG THE FLOWER, ... 339 THE SUBVERTED FLOWER 10
FLICKERING
   FLICKERING ACROSS ITS BOSOM. SUDDENLY . . . . 69 THE CODE 6
   A FLICKERING, HUMAN PATHETIC LIGHT, ... 291 ON HEART'S BEGINNING TO 7
FLICKERS
   THAT FAR LIGHT FLICKERS BECAUSE OF TREES. . . . . . 291 ON HEART'S BEGINNING TO 15
   THAT FLICKERS MICA WINGS. HE LIFTS A HAND . . . . . 487 A MASQUE OF REASON . 390
FLIES
   HE SHUDDERS HIS COAT AS IF TO THROW OFF FLIES. . . . 223 THE RUNAWAY 18
   AND HERE ON EARTH COME EMULATING FLIES . . . . . . 246 FIREFLIES IN THE GARDEN 2
   HAWKING FOR FLIES ABOUT THE KITCHEN DOOR, ... 278 THE WHITE-TAILED HORNET 24
FLIGHT
   TO WIN HER FOR THE FLIGHT . . . . 11 WIND AND WINDOW FLOWER 22
   AND ONCE I MARKED HIS FLIGHT GO ROUND AND ROUND, . . 22 THE TUFT OF FLOWERS . 15
   ONE FLIGHT OUT SIDEWAYS WOULD HAVE UNDECEIVED HIM. . 101 THE WOOD-PILE . . . 17
   TILL DAY MAKES HIM RETRACE HIS FLIGHT, ... 120 BOND AND FREE . . . 13
   WARNING AND TIME TO BE OFF IN FLIGHT: . . . . 127 HOUSE FEAR 7
   SHORT OF THE PERCH THEIR LANGUID FLIGHT WAS TOWARD; . 130 THE BONFIRE 37
   UP ONE FLIGHT FROM THE CELLAR TO THE KITCHEN, . . . 203 THE WITCH OF COOS . 30
   BY FLYING LIKE A BIRD (SILENT IN FLIGHT, ... 216 A FOUNTAIN, A BOTTLE . 113
   THE LEAVES HAD PROMISED THEMSELVES THIS FLIGHT, . . 236 MISGIVING 6
   I DROVE THEM UNDERFOOT IN BITS OF FLIGHT. . . . . . 240 OUR SINGING STRENGTH 35
   AND HAVING POWER TO CHANGE HIS AIM IN FLIGHT, . . . 277 THE WHITE-TAILED HORNET 5
   THE ROOST IS HER EXTENT OF FLIGHT. . . . . 281 BLUE RIBBON AT AMESBURY 45
   SO LOST ON ME IN MY SURFACE FLIGHT. . . . . 292 ON HEART'S BEGINNING TO 41
   THIS BIPLANE IS THE SHAPE OF HUMAN FLIGHT. . . . . 308 THE WRIGHTS' BIPLANE . 1
   THAT FAR-OFF DAY THE LEAVES IN FLIGHT . . . . 336 THE WIND AND THE RAIN . 1
   AND USE HIS HANDS IN FLIGHT. . . . . 341 THE SUBVERTED FLOWER . 63
   YOU MAKE A LABOR OF FLIGHT FOR ONE SO AIRY, ... 356 A MOTH SEEN IN WINTER . 11
   TO BREAK OUR LOGIC IN TOO LONG A FLIGHT, ... 370 THE LITERATE FARMER AND 82
   TO GIVE THEM STILL MORE BUOYANCY IN FLIGHT. . . . . 387 INNATE HELIUM . . . 5
   WITH THE ABSOLUTE FLIGHT AND REST . . . . 388 MIDDLENESS OF THE ROAD 14
   THE INITIAL FLIGHT . . . . 429 KITTY HAWK 42
   FOR SOME KIND OF FLIGHT . . . . 430 KITTY HAWK 55
   IN A FLIGHT OF WORDS, ... 434 KITTY HAWK 187
   FLIGHT IS BUT A GESTURE, ... 441 KITTY HAWK 403
   THIS WIDE FLIGHT WE WAVE . . . . 442 KITTY HAWK 437
   WE TWO COME IN FLIGHT . . . . 442 KITTY HAWK 455
   FOR THIS TOKEN FLIGHT, ... 443 KITTY HAWK 466
   ALWAYS THE SAME WHEN I SET OUT IN FLIGHT. . . . . . 500 A MASQUE OF MERCY . 179
FLIGHTS
   THE NIGHT CLERK LED HIM UP THREE FLIGHTS OF STAIRS . . 45 A HUNDRED COLLARS . 33
FLING
   WHAT SHOULD THAT RECKLESS ZEPHYR FLING . . . . 29 MY BUTTERFLY 41
FLINGS
   BEFORE IT FROZE, AND A GUST FLINGS A HANDFUL . . . . 176 THE STAR-SPLITTER . . 7
   AS SHE FLINGS OVER AND OFF DOWN THROUGH THE MAPLES, . 269 THE BEAR 8
FLINT
   I HAVE THE OCHER-WRITTEN FLINT, ... 328 A MISSIVE MISSILE . 41
FLIRTING
   FLIRTING THEIR WINGS AND SAYING CHICKADEE, ... 151 SNOW 231
FLOATED
   NOW DROPS THAT FLOATED ON THE POOL . . . . 18 GOING FOR WATER . . 23
FLOATING
   THE FLOATING HEART, WITH SMALL LEAF LIKE A HEART, . . 98 THE SELF-SEEKER . . 154
   AND THE THICK FLAKES FLOATING AT A PAUSE . . . . . 303 AFTERFLAKES . . . 13
FLOATS
   TO HAPPEN IN HEAVEN BEYOND THE FLOATS OF CLOUD . . . 268 ON LOCKING UP BY CHANCE 2
   THAT FLOATS AGAINST THE CEILING OF THE WOODSHED. . . 277 THE WHITE-TAILED HORNET 2
FLOCK
   "I WISH I KNEW HALF WHAT THE FLOCK OF THEM KNOW . . . 61 BLUEBERRIES 60
   MOVING A FLOCK OF HENS FROM PLACE TO PLACE. . . . . 85 THE HOUSEKEEPER . . 126
   WITH A GREAT FLOCK OF CHICKENS OF RARE BREEDS . . . 162 NEW HAMPSHIRE . . . 102
   HERE LOVELESS BIRDS NOW FLOCK AS WINTER FRIENDS, . . 254 A WINTER EDEN . . . 14
   HERE COMMON WITH THE FLOCK AGAIN, ... 280 BLUE RIBBON AT AMESBURY 13

```
                                                     PAGE TITLE                      LINE

FLOCK (CONTINUED)
    SHE MAKES THE WHOLE FLOCK MOVE ALONG. . . . . . . .  . 281 BLUE RIBBON AT AMESBURY  48
FLOCKS
    THE ROAD BECAME A CHANNEL RUNNING FLOCKS . . . . . .  . 240 OUR SINGING STRENGTH  .  33
    HAS BEEN WITH FLOCKS AND HERDS . . . . . . . . .  .  . 465 MILKY WAY IS A COWPATH   43
FLOOD
    THE FLOOD . . . . . . . . . . . . . . . . . .  . .  . 254 THE FLOOD . . . . . .      T
    IT GOES BY MIGHT OF BEING SUCH A FLOOD . . . . . .  . 255 THE FLOOD . . . . . .      7
    THAT PAST ITS PRIME LOST PETALS IN THE FLOOD . . .  . 337 THE WIND AND THE RAIN .  33
    SEND US A FLOOD AND BID US BE DAMNED AND DROWN. . .  . 349 OUR HOLD ON THE PLANET    6
    THEM IS MY SENTIMENTS, AND, MR. FLOOD, . . . . . .  . 497 A MASQUE OF MERCY . . . 108
FLOODED
    HE THINKS IT'S DARK, AND IT'S FLOODED WITH DAYLIGHT." . .  77 THE GENERATIONS OF MEN 102
FLOOR
    SCATTER POEMS ON THE FLOOR; . . . . . . . . . . .  .  12 TO THE THAWING WIND  .  14
    LIKE STANCHIONS IN THE BARN, FROM FLOOR TO CEILING-- . .  66 A SERVANT TO SERVANTS . 115
    A LOT OF IT, OUT INTO THE BARN FLOOR. . . . . . . .  .  72 THE CODE . . . . . .    90
    A HORSE'S HOOF PAWED ONCE THE HOLLOW FLOOR, . . . .  .  89 THE FEAR . . . . . .     5
    AND SHOWED HIM, THROUGH A MANHOLE IN THE FLOOR, . .  . 142 THE VANISHING RED . .   21
    MY FEET TUG AT THE FLOOR . . . . . . . . . . . .  . 156 THE SOUND OF TREES . .   15
    I PICKED UP OFF THE STRAW-DUST-COVERED FLOOR. . . .  . 175 THE CENSUS-TAKER . .   45
    BACK ON THE FLOOR, IS FACT OR PRETTY NEAR FACT. . .  . 192 PAUL'S WIFE . . . .   53
    I STRUCK THE HAND OFF BRITTLE ON THE FLOOR, . . . .  . 204 THE WITCH OF COOS . .   77
    AND FELL BACK FROM HIM ON THE FLOOR MYSELF. . . . .  . 204 THE WITCH OF COOS . .   78
    I SAT UP ON THE FLOOR AND SHOUTED, "TOFFILE, . . .  . 205 THE WITCH OF COOS . .   82
    AND ME ON THE FLOOR, . . . . . . . . . . . . .  . 211 AN EMPTY THREAT . .     8
    LIFTED THE RUG THAT BRED THEM ON THE FLOOR . . . .  . 237 A HILLSIDE THAW . .      7
    I TIPTOED THE FLOOR, . . . . . . . . . . . . .  . 240 THE LOCKLESS DOOR . .     6
    TO DRUM ON THE FLOOR WITH SCURRYING HOOFS . . . . .  . 241 NEED OF BEING VERSED .  11
    OUT IN THE PORCH'S SAGGING FLOOR . . . . . . . .  . 251 BEREFT . . . . . .       8
    AND HAD HE FALLEN INWARD ON THE FLOOR, . . . . . .  . 292 FIGURE IN THE DOORWAY   8
    IT WILL SHAKE ITS CAST STONE REEF OF FLOOR. . . . .  . 306 A TRIAL RUN . . . .     5
    IN THE FLOOR OF A TRIBAL CAVE, . . . . . . . . .  . 312 THE VINDICTIVES . . .  57
    STARTED CHAIRS THUNDERING ON THE KITCHEN FLOOR, . .  . 368 THE LITERATE FARMER AND  2
    ACROSS THE TESSELLATION OF THE FLOOR, . . . . . . .  . 399 THE INGENUITIES OF DEBT 14
    HIS HARD TAIL LOUDLY SMACKED THE FLOOR . . . . . .  . 420 ONE MORE BREVITY . .  23
    MY FLOOR SO HARD AND MATTER-OF-FACT. . . . . . . .  . 421 ONE MORE BREVITY . .  55
    CRUMPLE HIM ON THE FLOOR. KEEPER AND PAUL . . . . .  . 518 A MASQUE OF MERCY . . 651
    AND IF I SAY WE LIFT HIM FROM THE FLOOR . . . . . .  . 521 A MASQUE OF MERCY . . 733
FLOORS
    SHATTER IT INWARD ON THE UNSWEPT FLOORS. . . . . .  . 216 A FOUNTAIN, A BOTTLE . 104
    IN ONTO THE UPPER CHAMBER FLOORS. . . . . . . . .  . 253 THE THATCH . . . .     35
    AND MANY LITTER-MUFFLED FLOORS. . . . . . . . . .  . 280 BLUE RIBBON AT AMESBURY 24
FLORA
    "BUT WHAT ABOUT YOUR FLORA OF THE VALLEY?" . . . .  .  95 THE SELF-SEEKER . . .   80
FLORIBUS
    AND VER ASPERGIT TERRAM FLORIBUS . . . . . . . .  . 351 THE LESSON FOR TODAY .  15
FLOUR
    AS FINE AS FLOUR PUT THROUGH A BAKER'S SIEVE. . . .  . 365 OF STONES OF THE PLACE   8
FLOURISH
    BY LEAVING THEM TO FLOURISH, NOT FOR US, . . . . .  .  23 THE TUFT OF FLOWERS .   26
    AND SPROUT-LANDS FLOURISH WHERE THE AX HAS GONE. .  .  73 THE GENERATIONS OF MEN   6
FLOURISHED
    OR FLOURISHED AND COME UP IN JEWELWEED, . . . . . .  . 119 HYLA BROOK . . . .      7
    WELL THEY FLOURISHED AND WAXED . . . . . . . . .  . 448 THE BAD ISLAND--EASTER  34
    TO THE IDEA OF VIOLENCE. IT FLOURISHED, . . . . . .  . 511 A MASQUE OF MERCY . . 469
FLOUT
    BEHIND LIGHT WORDS THAT TEASE AND FLOUT, . . . . .  .  19 REVELATION . . . .      2
FLOW  (SEE THOUGHT-FLOW)
    BATHE MY WINDOW, MAKE IT FLOW, . . . . . . . . .  .  11 TO THE THAWING WIND .    7
    TO TAP THE UPPER SKY AND DRAW A FLOW . . . . . . .  . 169 NEW HAMPSHIRE . . . . 340
    THE FLOW OF--WAS IT MUSK . . . . . . . . . . . .  . 227 TO EARTHWARD . . . .    6
    WHEN ALL THE OTHER COUNTRY BROOKS FLOW EAST . . . .  . 258 WEST-RUNNING BROOK . .   5
    BUT FOR SOME OF THE MONEY, THE CASH, WHOSE FLOW SUPPORTS . 286 A ROADSIDE STAND . .    5
FLOWED
    AND WHEN IT ALMOST GAILY JUMPED AND FLOWED, . . . .  . 189 THE GRINDSTONE . . .   28
FLOWER  (SEE GEM-FLOWER)
    OF THE LAST REMAINING ASTER FLOWER . . . . . . . .  .   9 A LATE WALK . . . .    15
    SHE A WINDOW FLOWER, . . . . . . . . . . . . .  .  10 WIND AND WINDOW FLOWER   3
    WIND AND WINDOW FLOWER . . . . . . . . . . . .  .  10 WIND AND WINDOW FLOWER   T
    BUT THE FLOWER LEANED ASIDE . . . . . . . . . . .  .  11 WIND AND WINDOW FLOWER  25
    GIVE THE BURIED FLOWER A DREAM; . . . . . . . . .  .  11 TO THE THAWING WIND .    3
    WHERE THE FLOWER WAS BEFORE IT GREW, . . . . . . .  .  15 IN A VALE . . . . .    19
    WHERE BIRD AND FLOWER WERE ONE AND THE SAME. . . .  .  15 IN A VALE . . . . .    20
    WHY THE FLOWER HAS ODOR, THE BIRD HAS SONG. . . . .  .  16 IN A VALE . . . . .    22
    AND GOD HAS TAKEN A FLOWER OF GOLD . . . . . . . .  .  21 THE TRIAL BY EXISTENCE  61
    SOME RESTING FLOWER OF YESTERDAY'S DELIGHT. . . . .  .  22 THE TUFT OF FLOWERS .   14
    AS WHERE SOME FLOWER LAY WITHERING ON THE GROUND. .  .  22 THE TUFT OF FLOWERS .   16
    AND RAVELED A FLOWER AND LOOKED AWAY. . . . . . . .  .  24 PAN WITH US . . . .    29
    I MET THEM ONE DAY AND EACH HAD A FLOWER . . . . .  .  61 BLUEBERRIES . . . .    64
    NOW GIVE ME YOUR HAND UP.--PICK ME THAT FLOWER." .  .  80 THE GENERATIONS OF MEN 207
    WHEN LEANING WITH MY HEAD AGAINST A FLOWER . . . .  . 118 THE TELEPHONE . . .     5
    YOU SPOKE FROM THAT FLOWER ON THE WINDOWSILL-- . .  . 118 THE TELEPHONE . . .     8
    "HAVING FOUND THE FLOWER AND DRIVEN A BEE AWAY, . .  . 118 THE TELEPHONE . . .    11
    AND CUT A FLOWER BESIDE A GROUNDBIRD'S NEST . . . .  . 126 RANGE-FINDING . . .     2
    THE STRICKEN FLOWER BENT DOUBLE AND SO HUNG. . . .  . 126 RANGE-FINDING . . .     4
    A MOMENT SOUGHT IN AIR HIS FLOWER OF REST, . . . .  . 126 RANGE-FINDING . . .     7
    SOME FLOWER I PLAYED WITH AS I SAT . . . . . . . .  . 135 LOCKED OUT . . . .     12
    THE FLOWER WAS DIFFERENT FROM THE PARENT SEED. . .  . 181 MAPLE . . . . . .      39
    OR FLOWER, OR WEARING-STONE, OR OPEN EYE, . . . . .  . 220 FRAGMENTARY BLUE . .    3
    HER EARLY LEAF'S A FLOWER; . . . . . . . . . . .  . 222 NOTHING GOLD CAN STAY .  3
    A FLOWER TO TRY ITS CURRENTS WHERE THEY CROSSED. .  . 231 A BROOK IN THE CITY .   8
    NOT EVEN MISSING THE CORALROOT FLOWER . . . . . . .  . 247 ON GOING UNNOTICED .   15
    THE FLOWER BOAT . . . . . . . . . . . . . . .  . 262 THE FLOWER BOAT . . .    T
    A SINGLE FLOWER AS YET TO BLOOM. . . . . . . . .  . 276 TWO TRAMPS IN MUD TIME  28
    THE FLOWER OF CITIES FROM SINKING AND WITHERING FAINT. . 286 A ROADSIDE STAND . .    6
    LIKE THE LAST PETAL OFF A FLOWER. . . . . . . . .  . 291 ON HEART'S BEGINNING TO 12
    IT NEVER WILL SHOW MUCH FLOWER OR FRUIT. . . . . .  . 296 LEAVES COMPARED WITH .  4
```

FLOWER (CONTINUED)
    WHICH IS FAIRER, FLOWER OR LEAF. . . . . 297 LEAVES COMPARED WITH . 14
    A SNOW-DROP SPIDER, A FLOWER LIKE A FROTH, ... 302 DESIGN 7
    WHAT HAD THAT FLOWER TO DO WITH BEING WHITE, ... 302 DESIGN 9
    WOULD EMPTY IT UNSPARING ON THE FLOWER . . . . 337 THE WIND AND THE RAIN . 32
    WITH THE TENDER-HEADED FLOWER. . . . . 339 THE SUBVERTED FLOWER . 4
    THE SUBVERTED FLOWER . . . . 339 THE SUBVERTED FLOWER . T
    HE FLICKED AND FLUNG THE FLOWER, ... 339 THE SUBVERTED FLOWER . 10
    THAT A FLOWER HAD MARRED A MAN, ... 340 THE SUBVERTED FLOWER . 49
    WAS THAT THE FLOWER MIGHT BE . . . . 340 THE SUBVERTED FLOWER . 51
    THAT THE FLOWER HAD DONE BUT PART, ... 340 THE SUBVERTED FLOWER . 53
    AND WHAT THE FLOWER BEGAN . . . . 340 THE SUBVERTED FLOWER . 54
    THE DAY WAS THE DAY BY EVERY FLOWER THAT BLOOMS, ... 342 QUEST OF PURPLE-FRINGED 7
    THE FAR-SOUGHT FLOWER. . . . . 343 QUEST OF PURPLE-FRINGED 16
    AND YES, ALTHOUGH IT IS A FLOWER THAT FLOWS . . . . . 411 POD OF THE MILKWEED . 15
    OF MINGLED BUTTERFLY AND FLOWER DUST . . . . 412 POD OF THE MILKWEED . 28
FLOWER-GATHERING
    FLOWER-GATHERING . . . . 12 FLOWER-GATHERING . . T
FLOWER'S
    AND SO IT SEEMS A FLOWER'S COMING OUT . . . . 411 POD OF THE MILKWEED . 8
FLOWERS (SEE WORLD-FLOWERS)
    OH, GIVE US PLEASURE IN THE FLOWERS TODAY; . . . . . . 12 A PRAYER IN SPRING . . 1
    FOR THE FADED FLOWERS GAY. . . . . 13 FLOWER-GATHERING . . 10
    WITH THE BREATH OF MANY FLOWERS-- . . . . 13 ROSE POGONIAS . . . 7
    WHILE SO CONFUSED WITH FLOWERS. . . . . 14 ROSE POGONIAS . . . 24
    NOT WITHOUT FEEBLE-POINTED SPIKES OF FLOWERS . . . . . 17 MOWING 11
    THE TUFT OF FLOWERS . . . . 22 THE TUFT OF FLOWERS . T
    AT A TALL TUFT OF FLOWERS BESIDE A BROOK, ... 22 THE TUFT OF FLOWERS . 22
    THEY MUST BE PIERCED BY FLOWERS AND PUT . . . . 26 IN HARDWOOD GROVES . 9
    BENEATH THE FEET OF DANCING FLOWERS. . . . . 26 IN HARDWOOD GROVES . 10
    THE ROADSIDE FLOWERS, TOO WET FOR THE BEE, ... 26 A LINE-STORM SONG . . 5
    THINE EMULOUS FOND FLOWERS ARE DEAD, TOO, ... 28 MY BUTTERFLY 1
    THE FLOWERS OF THE WITCH HAZEL WITHER; . . . . 30 RELUCTANCE 16
    WITH FLOWERS IN HER LAP UNTIL THEY FADE, ... 79 THE GENERATIONS OF MEN 169
    WE FENCE OUR FLOWERS IN AND THE HENS RANGE. . . . . . 86 THE HOUSEKEEPER . . 136
    "BUT YOUR FLOWERS, MAN, YOU'RE SELLING OUT YOUR FLOWERS." . 95 THE SELF-SEEKER . . 66
    "YES, THAT'S ONE WAY TO PUT IT--ALL THE FLOWERS . . . . 95 THE SELF-SEEKER . . 67
    AND BY A RIVER BANK FOR WATER FLOWERS, ... 98 THE SELF-SEEKER . . 153
    ANNE HAS A WAY WITH FLOWERS TO TAKE THE PLACE . . . . 98 THE SELF-SEEKER . . 159
    BUT PUT OUR FLOWERS IN WATER FIRST.--WILL, HELP HER: . . 99 THE SELF-SEEKER . . 172
    HE THINKS YOU OUGHT TO PAY ME FOR MY FLOWERS. . . . . 100 THE SELF-SEEKER . . 225
    YOU DON'T KNOW WHAT I MEAN ABOUT THE FLOWERS. . . . . 100 THE SELF-SEEKER . . 226
    HE SAYS THAT LEAVES ARE OLD AND THAT FOR FLOWERS . . . 119 THE OVEN BIRD . . . 4
    WE ALWAYS LOCKED THE FLOWERS OUTSIDE . . . . 135 LOCKED OUT 2
    THE FLOWERS WERE OUT THERE WITH THE THIEVES. . . . . . 135 LOCKED OUT 6
    AND BURNING TO YIELD FLOWERS INSTEAD OF GRAIN, ... 173 A STAR IN A STONEBOAT . 22
    FLOWERS FANNED AND NOT PUT OUT BY ALL THE RAIN . . . . 173 A STAR IN A STONEBOAT . 23
    AND WEREN'T THERE SPECIAL CEMETERY FLOWERS, ... 200 PLACE FOR A THIRD . . 26
    THE FLOWERS WILL GO ON WITH GRIEF AWHILE, ... 200 PLACE FOR A THIRD . . 28
    TO ENTERTAIN THE BIRDS AND HOLD THE FLOWERS. . . . . . 216 A FOUNTAIN, A BOTTLE . 87
    THAN FLOWERS WILL SHOW FOR DAYS UNLESS THEY HURRY. . . . 225 BLUE-BUTTERFLY DAY . . 4
    BUT THESE ARE FLOWERS THAT FLY AND ALL BUT SING: . . . 225 BLUE-BUTTERFLY DAY . . 5
    AND TRULY IT WAS FAIR ENOUGH FOR FLOWERS . . . . . . 233 A BOUNDLESS MOMENT . . 6
    AND SING THE WILD FLOWERS UP FROM ROOT AND SEED. . . . 240 OUR SINGING STRENGTH . 53
    AND LIKE THE FLOWERS BESIDE THEM, CHILL AND SHIVER, . . 245 SPRING POOLS . . . 3
    WILL LIKE THE FLOWERS BESIDE THEM SOON BE GONE, ... 245 SPRING POOLS . . . 4
    THESE FLOWERY WATERS AND THESE WATERY FLOWERS . . . . 245 SPRING POOLS . . . 11
    WHOSE SPOTTED FLOWERS HANG MEANLY DOWN. . . . . . . 247 ON GOING UNNOTICED . . 8
    I OFTEN SEE FLOWERS FROM A PASSING CAR . . . . 248 A PASSING GLIMPSE . . 1
    I NAME ALL THE FLOWERS I AM SURE THEY WEREN'T: . . . . 248 A PASSING GLIMPSE . . 5
    THAT THE FLOWERS ACTUALLY KNELT, ... 250 LODGED 4
    I KNOW HOW THE FLOWERS FELT. . . . . 250 LODGED 6
    AS FULL TO THE GUNNEL OF FLOWERS GROWING . . . . . . 262 THE FLOWER BOAT . . . 6
    THEN NOW IS THE CHANCE FOR THE FLOWERS . . . . 264 THE LAST MOWING . . . 5
    THAT FLOWERS CAN'T BLOOM IN THE SHADE OF; . . . . . . 264 THE LAST MOWING . . . 12
    FOR YOU, O TUMULTUOUS FLOWERS, ... 264 THE LAST MOWING . . . 16
    ALL SHAPES AND COLORS OF FLOWERS, ... 264 THE LAST MOWING . . . 18
    AND CAST ITS FLOWERS AND ALL THE STEMS BUT THREE, . . . 283 THE GOLD HESPERIDEE . 4
    LEAVES COMPARED WITH FLOWERS . . . . 296 LEAVES COMPARED WITH . T
    LEAVES BY NIGHT AND FLOWERS BY DAY. . . . . 297 LEAVES COMPARED WITH . 16
    BRING OUT THE STARS, BRING OUT THE FLOWERS, ... 332 ALL REVELATION . . . 17
    AS THROUGH ITS BLAZING FLOWERS . . . . 333 HAPPINESS MAKES UP . . 22
    FLOWERS IN THE DESERT HEAT . . . . 337 THE WIND AND THE RAIN . 21
    AND HE WAS THERE RESUSCITATING FLOWERS . . . . 354 THE LESSON FOR TODAY . 131
    THE FLOWERS FADING ON THE SEED TO COME; . . . . . . 356 TIME OUT 7
    IF I HAD MOTHS TO FRIEND AS I HAVE FLOWERS?) . . . . . 356 A MOTH SEEN IN WINTER . 6
    TO ALL THOSE FLOWERS THEY PASSIONATELY TROD . . . . . 412 POD OF THE MILKWEED . 42
    WHERE HAVE THOSE FLOWERS AND BUTTERFLIES ALL GONE . . . 412 POD OF THE MILKWEED . 51
    PERENNIAL AS FLOWERS, ... 465 MILKY WAY IS A COWPATH 33
FLOWERS'
    AND GOT THEM OFF THE WILD FLOWERS' BACKS. . . . . . . 123 PEA BRUSH 16
    ITS FLOWERS' DISTILLED HONEY IS SO SWEET . . . . . . 411 POD OF THE MILKWEED . 21
FLOWERY
    THESE FLOWERY WATERS AND THESE WATERY FLOWERS . . . . 245 SPRING POOLS 11
    IN A FLOWERY BURST . . . . 445 PERIL OF HOPE . . . 6
FLOWING
    FLOWING OVER MY ARMS . . . . 235 GATHERING LEAVES . . 11
FLOWS
    WHICH FLOWS IN SHAPES AS TALL AS TREES . . . . 9 STARS 3
    IT FLOWS BESIDE US IN THIS WATER BROOK, ... 259 WEST-RUNNING BROOK . . 50
    BUT IT FLOWS OVER US. IT FLOWS BETWEEN US . . . . . . 259 WEST-RUNNING BROOK . . 51
    IT FLOWS BETWEEN US, OVER US, AND WITH US. . . . . . 259 WEST-RUNNING BROOK . . 53
    THE TRUTH IS THE RIVER FLOWS INTO THE CANYON . . . . . 379 TOO ANXIOUS FOR RIVERS . 8
    AND YES, ALTHOUGH IT IS A FLOWER THAT FLOWS . . . . . 411 POD OF THE MILKWEED . 15
FLUFF
    HER FLUFF OF PLUMAGE, WHITE AS CHALK, ... 280 BLUE RIBBON AT AMESBURY 7
FLUID
    A ZEALOT FULL OF FLUID INSPIRATION, ... 159 NEW HAMPSHIRE . . . 26

FLUID (CONTINUED)
  WHO IN THE NAME OF FLUID INSPIRATION, ... 159 NEW HAMPSHIRE . . . 27
FLUME
  ON MELTED MOUNTAIN WATER LED BY FLUME . . . . 337 THE WIND AND THE RAIN . 23
FLUNG
  WILLIS FLUNG OFF THE BED. "I WASH MY HANDS-- . . . . 100 THE SELF-SEEKER . . . 216
  GOOD-BY." HE FLUNG HIS ARMS AROUND HIS FACE. . . . . 101 THE SELF-SEEKER . . . 228
  THEN HE FLUNG OUTWARD, FEET FIRST, WITH A SWISH, . . . 122 BIRCHES 39
  HER UNPRUNED GRAPES ARE FLUNG LIKE LARIATS . . . . . 164 NEW HAMPSHIRE . . . 163
  SO SUDDENLY I FLUNG THE DOOR WIDE ON HIM. . . . . . 204 THE WITCH OF COOS . . 70
  SINCE EVER THEY FLUNG ABROAD IN SPRING . . . . . . 236 MISGIVING 5
  AND THE DRY PUMP FLUNG UP AN AWKWARD ARM; . . . . . 242 NEED OF BEING VERSED . 19
  FLUNG BACKWARD ON ITSELF IN ONE WHITE WAVE, ... 258 WEST-RUNNING BROOK . . 20
  HE FLICKED AND FLUNG THE FLOWER, ... 339 THE SUBVERTED FLOWER . 10
  A MIGHTY FARMER FLUNG THE HOUSE DOOR WIDE, ... 368 THE LITERATE FARMER AND 5
FLURRY
  AND WITH THESE SKY-FLAKES DOWN IN FLURRY ON FLURRY . . . 225 BLUE-BUTTERFLY DAY . . 2
FLUSH
  TRYING TO FLUSH ME OUT. THAT'S ALL IT IS. . . . . . 507 A MASQUE OF MERCY . . 350
FLUSHED
  I FLUSHED BIRDS OUT OF HOLE AFTER HOLE, ... 253 THE THATCH 19
  WHEN THE COLOR FLUSHED TO THE PETALS IT MUST HAVE BEEN-- . 343 QUEST OF PURPLE-FRINGED 15
FLUTTER
  AND HUSH AND CLUCK AND FLUTTER ABOUT: . . . . 6 GHOST HOUSE 17
  IT SEEMED GOD LET THEE FLUTTER FROM HIS GENTLE CLASP, . 29 MY BUTTERFLY 27
  IT WOULD FLUTTER AND FALL IN HALF AN HOUR . . . . . 291 ON HEART'S BEGINNING TO 11
  AND BEGAN TO FLUTTER THE LEAVES TO LOOK . . . . . . 342 A CLOUD SHADOW . . . 2
FLUTTERING
  THEN LIGHTLY STOOPED TO IT AND FLUTTERING CLUNG. . . . 126 RANGE-FINDING . . . 8
FLUX
  REMEMBER BIRNAM WOOD! THE WOOD'S IN FLUX!" . . . . . 170 NEW HAMPSHIRE . . . 373
  HE HAD A SPECIAL TERROR OF THE FLUX . . . . 171 NEW HAMPSHIRE . . . 374
FLY
  THE LINE-STORM CLOUDS FLY TATTERED AND SWIFT. . . . . 26 A LINE-STORM SONG . . 1
  SHE LEAVES THEM BITTEN WHEN SHE HAS TO FLY, ... 125 THE COW IN APPLE TIME . 9
  THE INDWELLING SPIDER RAN TO GREET THE FLY, ... 126 RANGE-FINDING . . . 13
  HE JUST HAD TO FLY! . . . . 136 LAST WORD OF A BLUEBIRD 14
  (THOUGH THESE WHEN NOT IN USE TO FLY AND TRAIL . . . . 172 A STAR IN A STONEBOAT . 17
  WHERE SHOWERS OF CHARTED METEORS LET FLY. . . . . . 173 A STAR IN A STONEBOAT . 42
  BUT THESE ARE FLOWERS THAT FLY AND ALL BUT SING: . . . 225 BLUE-BUTTERFLY DAY . . 5
  I HAVE WISHED A BIRD WOULD FLY AWAY, ... 250 A MINOR BIRD 1
  HE'S AFTER THE DOMESTICATED FLY . . . . 278 THE WHITE-TAILED HORNET 30
  AT LAST IT WAS A FLY. HE SHOT AND MISSED; . . . . . 278 THE WHITE-TAILED HORNET 42
  AND THE FLY CIRCLED ROUND HIM IN DERISION. . . . . . 278 THE WHITE-TAILED HORNET 43
  BUT FOR THE FLY HE MIGHT HAVE MADE ME THINK . . . . . 278 THE WHITE-TAILED HORNET 44
  NAILHEAD WITH FLY AND FLY WITH HUCKLEBERRY: . . . . . 279 THE WHITE-TAILED HORNET 46
  HOW LIKE A FLY, HOW VERY LIKE A FLY. . . . . 279 THE WHITE-TAILED HORNET 47
  BUT THE REAL FLY HE MISSED WOULD NEVER DO; . . . . . 279 THE WHITE-TAILED HORNET 48
  THE MISSED FLY MADE ME DANGEROUSLY SKEPTIC. . . . . . 279 THE WHITE-TAILED HORNET 49
  WITH LOATHING, FOR AGAIN IT TURNED TO FLY. . . . . . 357 A CONSIDERABLE SPECK . 14
  FOR MY MUSE TO FLY . . . . 434 KITTY HAWK 184
  EVER THOUGHT TO FLY. . . . . 434 KITTY HAWK 193
  OH, BUT FLY WE DID, ... 434 KITTY HAWK 194
  LITERALLY FLY. . . . . 434 KITTY HAWK 195
  AS FLY THE ATOMIC SMITHEREENS TO NOTHING. . . . . . 460 HOW HARD TO KEEP FROM 197
FLYER
  TILL DAYLIGHT MADE IT SAFE FOR A FLYER. . . . . . . 253 THE THATCH 27
FLYING
  HE DID NOT SEE HOW LIKE A FLYING THING . . . . . . 172 A STAR IN A STONEBOAT . 13
  ONE NOT SO LARGE FOR FLYING IN A RING, ... 172 A STAR IN A STONEBOAT . 15
  AND NOT, AS YOU MIGHT THINK, A FLYING CAR, ... 173 A STAR IN A STONEBOAT . 27
  DEN WHERE'S YOUR HAX-EAD FLYING T'ROUGH DE HAIR?" . . . 186 THE AX-HELVE 27
  BY FLYING LIKE A BIRD (SILENT IN FLIGHT), ... 216 A FOUNTAIN, A BOTTLE . 113
  THEY'D SOON EXHAUSTED ALL THERE WAS IN FLYING; . . . . 239 OUR SINGING STRENGTH . 27
  THEY COULD NOT GO FLYING ABOUT IN SEARCH . . . . . . 253 THE THATCH 23
  PROVE BUT FLYING CHIPS . . . . 439 KITTY HAWK 352
FOAM
  HER MOTHER WIPED THE FOAM . . . . 341 THE SUBVERTED FLOWER . 71
FOE
  THE FOE THRUST BACK UNSAFE BEYOND THE RHINE, ... 222 TO E.T. 18
  AND PUT OUT ITS LIGHT FOR THE FOE. . . . . 311 THE VINDICTIVES . . . 36
  FROM ALL DIVISION TIME OR FOE CAN BRING . . . . . . 315 IRIS BY NIGHT . . . 30
FOG
  EXCEPT WHEN SEA FOG LAID IT DOWN, ... 249 A PECK OF GOLD . . . 2
  YOUR LIGHT WAS SPENT PERHAPS AS IN A FOG . . . . . . 351 THE LESSON FOR TODAY . 24
  OFF THERE IN THE FOG? . . . . 438 KITTY HAWK 341
FOGGY
  'THREE FOGGY MORNINGS AND ONE RAINY DAY . . . . . . 54 HOME BURIAL 92
FOGS
  THE OLD BARN AT THE BOTTOM OF THE FOGS . . . . . . 289 OLD BARN AT THE BOTTOM T
  THE OLD BARN AT THE BOTTOM OF THE FOGS. . . . . . . 290 OLD BARN AT THE BOTTOM 23
FOILED
  THE CULT OF ONE WHO OWNED HIMSELF "A FOILED . . . . . 171 NEW HAMPSHIRE . . . 383
FOLDED
  THE WINGS NOT FOLDED IN REPOSE, BUT SPREAD. . . . . 356 A MOTH SEEN IN WINTER . 4
FOLIAGE
  AND WHIRLS OF FOLIAGE NOT YET LAID, THERE DROVE . . . 106 CHRISTMAS TREES . . . 4
  WEAK FOLIAGE THAT IS BLOWN UPON AND BENT, ... 119 HYLA BROOK 8
  AND EVERY LEAF OF FOLIAGE SHE'D WORN . . . . 184 MAPLE 146
  THE FOLIAGE FOLLOW HIM, LEAF AND STEM; . . . . . . 236 MISGIVING 2
  BUT UP BY ROOTS TO BRING DARK FOLIAGE ON. . . . . . 245 SPRING POOLS 6
  BUT ONE DAY WHEN THE FOLIAGE ALL WENT SWISH . . . . . 284 THE GOLD HESPERIDEE . 32
  AND OF ALL BUT ITS TRIVIAL FOLIAGE FREE, ... 304 UNHARVESTED 6
FOLK
  I KNOW NOT WHO THESE MUTE FOLK ARE . . . . 6 GHOST HOUSE 22
  THEY ARE TIRELESS FOLK, BUT SLOW AND SAD-- . . . . . 6 GHOST HOUSE 26
  POOR SILAS, SO CONCERNED FOR OTHER FOLK, ... 37 DEATH OF THE HIRED MAN 99
  AN EXCUSE FOR KEEPING US OTHER FOLK OUT." . . . . . 60 BLUEBERRIES 32

FOLK (CONTINUED)
   THE YOUNG FOLK HELD SOME HOPE OUT TO EACH OTHER . . . . 74 THE GENERATIONS OF MEN   21
   AND I THOUGHT I HAD THE FOLK WITHIN: . . . . 102 GOOD HOURS 5
   THAT TROUBLE THE SLEEP OF LUMBER FOLK: . . . . . . 140 THE GUM-GATHERER . . 22
   FAR INTO THE LIVES OF OTHER FOLK. . . . . 292 ON HEART'S BEGINNING TO 45
   UNLESS IT WAS COMING TO FOLK . . . . 365 A NATURE NOTE . . . 11
   AT THE EXPENSE OF NEGLIGIBLE FOLK. . . . . 423 FOR JOHN F. KENNEDY . 33
   FOR THE SEED OF FOLK . . . . 431 KITTY HAWK 91
FOLKS
   I LIKE TO FIND FOLKS GETTING OUT IN SPRING. . . . . . 49 A HUNDRED COLLARS . . 127
   FOLKS ENTERTAIN ME FROM THE KITCHEN DOORSTEP, ... 49 A HUNDRED COLLARS . . 147
   UNLIKE OTHER FOLKS AS YOUR STANDING THERE . . . . . 53 HOME BURIAL 60
   RATHER THAN SEND THEIR FOLKS TO SUCH A PLACE, ... 65 A SERVANT TO SERVANTS 95
   OTHER FOLKS HAVE TO, AND WHY SHOULDN'T I? . . . . . 67 A SERVANT TO SERVANTS 160
   FOLKS IN HER DAY WERE GIVEN TO PLAIN SPEAKING. . . . 79 THE GENERATIONS OF MEN 181
   THAN FOLKS LIKE US HAVE ANY BUSINESS WITH. . . . . 85 THE HOUSEKEEPER . . 112
   THAT ISN'T IT. FOLKS AREN'T AFRAID OF US." . . . . 87 THE HOUSEKEEPER . . 170
   FOLKS THINK A WITCH WHO HAS FAMILIAR SPIRITS . . . . 202 THE WITCH OF COOS . . 4
   I KNOW OF SOME FOLKS THAT'D BE SET UP . . . . . . 208 PAUPER WITCH OF GRAFTON 36
   AND TURN US INTO THE NEXT SPECIE FOLKS . . . . . . 369 THE LITERATE FARMER AND 43
   YOUR MOTHER'S FOLKS----" / HE STAYED TO HEAR NO MORE, . . 457 HOW HARD TO KEEP FROM 111
   ALL SECONDHAND. DON'T GET EXCITED, FOLKS; . . . . . 507 A MASQUE OF MERCY . . 352
FOLKS'
   TO MAKE SO FREE AND KICK UP IN FOLKS' FACES. . . . . 210 PAUPER WITCH OF GRAFTON 107
FOLKS'S
   YOU, CRUMPLING FOLKS'S LEGAL DOCUMENTS. . . . . . . 99 THE SELF-SEEKER . . . 196
FOLLOW
   I'LL FOLLOW AND BRING YOU BACK BY FORCE. I WILL!--" . . 55 HOME BURIAL 116
   LIKE A VIOLA. I DON'T FOLLOW YOU." . . . . 75 THE GENERATIONS OF MEN 54
   THE FOLIAGE FOLLOW HIM, LEAF AND STEM; . . . . . . 236 MISGIVING 2
   THE COLOR RUN, ALL SORTS OF WONDER FOLLOW. . . . . 245 THE FREEDOM OF THE MOON 12
   AND FOLLOW SOME DEVELOPMENT OF STATE. . . . . . . 355 THE LESSON FOR TODAY . 142
   I HAD NO CHOICE BUT I MUST FOLLOW HIM . . . . . . 475 A MASQUE OF REASON . . 73
FOLLOWED
   AND FOLLOWED WHERE HE FURROWED FIELD, ... 128 THE IMPULSE 7
   IN DUST ONCE MORE. WE FOLLOWED THIS A MILE, ... 215 A FOUNTAIN, A BOTTLE . 67
   AND FOLLOWED IT TO WHERE HE MADE OUT VAGUE . . . . 270 THE EGG AND THE MACHINE 19
FOLLOWER
   THE LOST FOLLOWER . . . . 358 THE LOST FOLLOWER . . T
FOLLOWERS
   TO BREAK WITH FOLLOWERS WHEN IN THE WRONG, ... 424 FOR JOHN F. KENNEDY . 62
   IT IS NO DIFFERENT WITH MY FOLLOWERS . . . . 485 A MASQUE OF REASON . . 352
FOLLOWING
   FRIENDS MAKE PRETENSE OF FOLLOWING TO THE GRAVE, . . . 54 HOME BURIAL 102
   NO LONGER THAN THAT?--AND THE FOLLOWING FALL . . . . 59 BLUEBERRIES 11
   FROM FOLLOWING WALLS I NEVER LIFT MY EYE, ... 173 A STAR IN A STONEBOAT . 40
   THEN AT LAST AND FOLLOWING HIM I FOUND-- . . . . . 342 QUEST OF PURPLE-FRINGED 13
FOLLOWINGLY
   HE FOLLOWINGLY FINGERED AS HE READ, ... 356 TIME OUT 6
FOLLY
   BUT FOR THE FOLLY OF IT, LET'S PRETEND . . . . . . 352 THE LESSON FOR TODAY . 44
   AND SOME OTHER FOLLY. . . . . 431 KITTY HAWK 94
   THE FOLLY CRASHES AND THE DUST GOES UP. . . . . . 506 A MASQUE OF MERCY . . 342
FOND
   THINE EMULOUS FOND FLOWERS ARE DEAD, TOO, ... 28 MY BUTTERFLY 1
   THE LANGUOR OF IT AND THE DREAMING FOND; . . . . . 29 MY BUTTERFLY 34
   HE'S FOND OF NICE THINGS--TOO FOND, SOME WOULD SAY. . . 85 THE HOUSEKEEPER . . . 116
   "FOR GOD'S SAKE, AREN'T YOU FOND OF VIEWING NATURE? . . 215 A FOUNTAIN, A BOTTLE . 56
   IN THE FOND FAITH ACCUMULATED FACT . . . . 414 A CABIN IN THE CLEARING 26
   ONE MORE FOND ALAS . . . . 431 KITTY HAWK 90
   (STILL STANDING OFF) WE'VE ALL GROWN FOND OF YOU. . . 518 A MASQUE OF MERCY . . 666
   WE'VE ALL GROWN FOND OF YOU. (PAUL SAYS IT LOUDER, . . 518 A MASQUE OF MERCY . . 667
FONDEST
   FOR DRAB IT IS ITS FONDEST MUST ADMIT. . . . . . . 411 POD OF THE MILKWEED . 14
FONDNESS
   I SAW YOU HAD NO FONDNESS FOR COMMITTEES. . . . . . 486 A MASQUE OF REASON . . 369
FONT
   AND BUILT A STONE BAPTISMAL FONT OUTDOORS-- . . . . 213 A FOUNTAIN, A BOTTLE . 10
   YOU SAID YOU'D SEEN THE STONE BAPTISMAL FONT. . . . . 213 A FOUNTAIN, A BOTTLE . 13
FONTAINE
   A BLINDMAN BY THE NAME OF LA FONTAINE, ... 394 HAEC FABULA DOCET . . 1
FOOD
   SOME MATCHES HE UNPOCKETED. "FOR FOOD-- . . . . . 115 IN THE HOME STRETCH . 138
   OR ELSE WRITE SOMETHING TO IMPROVE FOOD PRICES. . . . 316 BUILD SOIL 24
   THOUGHT PRODUCT AND FOOD PRODUCT ARE TO ME . . . . . 324 BUILD SOIL 257
   SOMETHING ELUDES HIM. IS IT FOOD TO EAT? . . . . . 412 POD OF THE MILKWEED . 48
   I SET HIM WATER, I SET HIM FOOD. . . . . 419 ONE MORE BREVITY . . 19
   I KNOW THE QUINTESSENCE OF FOOD, I KNOW . . . . . . 455 HOW HARD TO KEEP FROM 42
   I'LL TRY YOU IN THE KITCHEN FIRST ON FOOD . . . . . 455 HOW HARD TO KEEP FROM 49
   SINCE YOU PUT FOOD FIRST IN YOUR REPERTORY. . . . . 455 HOW HARD TO KEEP FROM 50
   NOT OF FOOD ONLY BUT OF EVERYTHING, ... 455 HOW HARD TO KEEP FROM 61
   BUT ALL YOU THOUGHT OF GIVING ME WAS FOOD. . . . . 457 HOW HARD TO KEEP FROM 122
   BUT STILL FOOD, FOOD. YOUR ONE IDEA WAS FOOD. . . . 458 HOW HARD TO KEEP FROM 134
   "YES, BUT GIVE CHARACTER AND NOT JUST FOOD. . . . . 458 HOW HARD TO KEEP FROM 141
FOOD-MINDED
   NONE BUT A COOK'S SON COULD BE SO FOOD-MINDED. . . . 458 HOW HARD TO KEEP FROM 135
FOOL
   I FELT AS A FOOL TO HAVE BEEN SO CAUGHT, ... 25 THE DEMIURGE'S LAUGH . 14
   HE HATES TO SEE A BOY THE FOOL OF BOOKS. . . . . . 37 DEATH OF THE HIRED MAN 98
   "YOU DIDN'T KNOW. BUT JAMES IS ONE BIG FOOL. . . . . 70 THE CODE 15
   "HE IS A FOOL IF THAT'S THE WAY HE TAKES ME." . . . . 70 THE CODE 20
   BUT THE OLD FOOL SEIZES HIS FORK IN BOTH HANDS, . . . 71 THE CODE 61
   "WHO WANTS TO HEAR YOUR NEWS, YOU--DREADFUL FOOL?" . . 89 THE HOUSEKEEPER . . . 214
   WHAT DO YOU SAY, WILL? DON'T YOU BE A FOOL, ... 99 THE SELF-SEEKER . . . 195
   THAT I AM LIKE TO COMPASS, FOOL OR WISE. . . . . . 174 A STAR IN A STONEBOAT . 57
   THEY HAD NO WAY OF KNOWING A FOOL. . . . . 276 TWO TRAMPS IN MUD TIME 56
   IT IS JUST FOOL ENOUGH TO THINK ITSELF . . . . . . 319 BUILD SOIL 119
   YOU WERE NOT CHARLES' NOR ANYBODY'S FOOL: . . . . . 351 THE LESSON FOR TODAY . 20

	PAGE TITLE	LINE

FOOL (CONTINUED)
SOME POOR FOOL HAS BEEN SAYING IN HIS HEART . . . . . . 423 FOR JOHN F. KENNEDY . 49
YOU MAY CALL ME A FOOL, ... 450 OBJECTION TO BE STEPPED 12
"DON'T LET HIM FOOL YOU: HE'S A KING ALREADY. . . . . 460 HOW HARD TO KEEP FROM 207
ONCE I WAS FOOL ENOUGH TO THINK . . . . 467 QUANDARY 20
LIKE THE ONE MILTON FOUND TO FOOL HIMSELF . . . . . 488 A MASQUE OF REASON . 416
FOOLED
OR WAS THE INSTINCT IN HIM FOOLED? . . . . 344 DISCOVERY OF MADEIRAS . 44
HE MIGHT HAVE FOOLED VALLADOLID. . . . . 417 AMERICA IS HARD TO SEE 31
SO COZENED AND FOOLED . . . . 448 THE BAD ISLAND--EASTER 29
FOOLING
IT GOT SO I WOULD SAY--YOU KNOW, HALF FOOLING-- . . . 67 A SERVANT TO SERVANTS . 145
TO GET ADAPTED TO MY KIND OF FOOLING. . . . . . 470 IT TAKES ALL SORTS... . 2
FOOLISH
'TWAS NOTHING BUT MY FOOLISH HANGING BACK, ... 46 A HUNDRED COLLARS . . 59
"YOU'RE GETTING READY TO DO SOMETHING FOOLISH." . . . 94 THE SELF-SEEKER . . . 51
WHO WAS SO FOOLISH AS TO THINK WHAT HE THOUGHT. . . . 101 THE WOOD-PILE . . . 13
OR YOU WILL COME TO WITH A FOOLISH FEELING. . . . . 513 A MASQUE OF MERCY . 537
FOOL-LIKE
FOOL-LIKE, AND ROLLED HIS EYES AS IF TO SAY . . . . . 114 IN THE HOME STRETCH . 102
FOOLS
AS TO OUR FATE, LIKE FOOLS PAST REASONING WITH. . . . 114 IN THE HOME STRETCH . 125
NEW IS A WORD FOR FOOLS IN TOWNS WHO THINK . . . . 117 IN THE HOME STRETCH . 183
AND THINK NO MORE OF WALL-BUILDERS THAN FOOLS. . . . 124 THE COW IN APPLE TIME . 3
YET YOU DON'T SPEAK. LET FOOLS BEMUSE THEMSELVES . . . 484 A MASQUE OF REASON . 298
IN MAKING FOOLS OF PEOPLE EQUALLY. . . . . 513 A MASQUE OF MERCY . 528
FOOL'S
TO RUSH IN SHEETS AND FOOL'S CAPS WHERE THEY SMELLED . . 163 NEW HAMPSHIRE . . . 141
FOOT
YOU'VE WORKED AROUND THE FOOT OF ALL YOUR LIFE. . . . . 43 THE MOUNTAIN 83
AND A FEW HOUSES SPRINKLED ROUND THE FOOT, ... 43 THE MOUNTAIN 97
THE NIGHT CLERK CLAPPED A BEDSTEAD ON THE FOOT. . . . 46 A HUNDRED COLLARS . . 39
AT SUCH AN HOUR OF NIGHT, AND ON FOOT TOO? . . . . 90 THE FEAR 27
TILL I SHAN'T DARE TO SET A FOOT OUTDOORS. . . . . 90 THE FEAR 47
ONE FOOT WENT THROUGH. THE VIEW WAS ALL IN LINES . . . 101 THE WOOD-PILE . . . 5
EXCEPT, PERHAPS, A FOOT AT EITHER END. . . . . . . 193 PAUL'S WIFE . . . 71
AND PUT MY FOOT ON ONE WITHOUT AVAIL, ... 237 A HILLSIDE THAW . . . 11
AND MAKE US GET DOWN IN A FOOT OF SNOW . . . . . 238 ON A TREE FALLEN ACROSS 7
NO ONE FOR HOURS HAS SET A FOOT OUTDOORS . . . . . 248 THE COCOON 9
ONE FOOT IN EACH GREAT OCEAN . . . . 295 A RECORD STRIDE . . 25
SHE DARED NOT STIR A FOOT, ... 340 THE SUBVERTED FLOWER . 31
WHO MAY BE JUST AHEAD OF YOU ON FOOT . . . . . . 378 DIRECTIVE 31
WITH ONE FOOT ON THE DASHBOARD OF HIS BUGGY . . . . . 404 FROM PLANE TO PLANE . 19
FULL OF SUCCESS, WITH THAT FOOT ON THE DASHBOARD, . . . 405 FROM PLANE TO PLANE . 38
TO COME AS A FOOT PRINTER, ... 416 CLOSED FOR GOOD . . 27
ROUND THE PLACE ON FOOT . . . . 434 KITTY HAWK . . . 204
AND PUT HER FOOT IN THE PAIL; . . . . 463 LINES IN DEJECTION . 12
FOOTBALL
THE WAY A PLAYER CURLS AROUND A FOOTBALL. . . . . . 278 THE WHITE-TAILED HORNET 39
FOOTFALL
YOU MADE NO SOUND IN THE GRASS WITH YOUR FOOTFALL, . . . 235 VALLEY'S SINGING DAY . 2
FOOTHOLD
HE GAINED NO FOOTHOLD, BUT PURSUED . . . . 138 BROWN'S DESCENT . . . 19
FOOTING
HAS LOST ITS FOOTING ON MY MOUNTAIN SLOPE . . . . . 350 TO A YOUNG WRETCH . . 21
FOOTPATH
THE FOOTPATH DOWN TO THE WELL IS HEALED. . . . . . 6 GHOST HOUSE 10
FOOTPRINT
THERE'S NOT A FOOTPRINT TO IT IN THE SNOW. . . . . 501 A MASQUE OF MERCY . 212
FOOTPRINTS
FOOTPRINTS IN SUMMER DUST AS IF WE DREW . . . . . 118 MEETING AND PASSING . 6
FOOTSTEP
NO FOOTSTEP MOVED IT. "THIS IS ALL," THEY SIGHED, . . . 229 TWO LOOK AT TWO . . . 13
FOOTSTEPS
"I DARE NOT--TOO FAR IN HIS FOOTSTEPS STRAY-- . . . . 16 A DREAM PANG 7
OF HEAVY FOOTSTEPS IN THE OLD FRAME HOUSE, ... 96 THE SELF-SEEKER . . . 93
BEGAN THE STAIRS, TWO FOOTSTEPS FOR EACH STEP, ... 204 THE WITCH OF COOS . . 51
FOR---NOT INDEXED
FORAGER
OUR SELFLESS FORAGER JERRY. . . . . 288 DEPARTMENTAL 24
FORAGING (SEE A-FORAGING)
FORBID
AND LEAVE YOU THERE, OURSELVES FORBID TO ENTER— . . . 259 WEST-RUNNING BROOK . 35
THIS WAS THE SIN THAT AHAZ WAS FORBID . . . . . 284 THE GOLD HESPERIDEE . 51
FOR FINDING A THING TO DO THAT THOUGH NOT FORBID . . . 306 NOT QUITE SOCIAL . 3
FORBIDDEN
UNDER THE NEW REGIME, AND SO FORBIDDEN. . . . . . 167 NEW HAMPSHIRE . 279
THE THINGS FORBIDDEN THAT WHILE THE CUSTOMS SLEPT . . . 335 I COULD GIVE ALL . 13
ANYTHING'S FORBIDDEN . . . . 437 KITTY HAWK . 282
WE LEARNED FROM THE FORBIDDEN FRUIT . . . . . 467 QUANDARY . 15
FORCE
I'LL FOLLOW AND BRING YOU BACK BY FORCE. I WILL!--" . . 55 HOME BURIAL . . . 116
IT WERE THE FORCE THAT WOULD AT LAST PREVAIL. . . . . 57 THE BLACK COTTAGE . 83
THE PAINS OF CONQUERING TO FORCE CHANGE ON. . . . . 58 THE BLACK COTTAGE . 118
I HAD TO TAKE BY FORCE RATHER THAN BUY. . . . . . 163 NEW HAMPSHIRE . 151
WHO FAILED TO FIND OR FORCE A STRAIT . . . . . 212 AN EMPTY THREAT . 44
HOW ELSE DISPOSE OF AN IMMORTAL FORCE . . . . . 231 A BROOK IN THE CITY . 13
SOME FORCE HAS BUT TO APPLY, ... 285 IN TIME OF CLOUDBURST . 13
FROM FORCE TO MATTER AND BACK TO FORCE, ... 325 TO A THINKER . . . 8
THE SNOW BLOWS ON HIM AND OFF HIM, EXERTING FORCE . . . 341 WILLFUL HOMING . . . 5
AND FORCE HER FAREWELL STEP OFF SHORE. . . . . . 343 DISCOVERY OF MADEIRAS . 11
TO NAUGHT BUT HIS OWN FORCE OF WILL. . . . . . 418 AMERICA IS HARD TO SEE 70
BUT THE FORCE OF THOUGHT. . . . . 426 A NEVER NAUGHT SONG . 31
BY FRAUD AND BY FORCE, ... 448 THE BAD ISLAND--EASTER 36
FORCED
LABAN WAS FORCED TO FALL BACK ON HIS PLAN . . . . . 202 PLACE FOR A THIRD . . 79
AND FORCED THE UNDERBRUSH--AND THAT WAS ALL. . . . . 338 THE MOST OF IT . . . 20
I WANTED HIM FORCED TO ACKNOWLEDGE SO MUCH. . . . . 486 A MASQUE OF REASON . 359

FORCES
    THESE FORCES ARE OBLIGED TO PAY RESPECT TO?" . . . . . 176 THE STAR-SPLITTER . . 12
FORCING
    NOT FORCING HER HAND WITH HARROW AND PLOW." . . . . . 61 BLUEBERRIES 56
    FOR PRYING BENEATH AND FORCING THE LIDS OF SIGHT, ... 235 VALLEY'S SINGING DAY . 9
FOREARMS
    YOUR FOREARMS IN THE FIGURE OF A CROSS . . . . . . 501 A MASQUE OF MERCY . . 193
FORE'ER
    WIDE FIELDS OF ASPHODEL FORE'ER, ... 19 THE TRIAL BY EXISTENCE   6
FOREFEET
    ON HIS FOREFEET TO REST. . . . . 261 CANIS MAJOR 8
FOREFINGER
    BY STRAIGHTENING OUT AND LIFTING A FOREFINGER, ... 147 SNOW 113
FOREFOOT
    A LITTLE MORGAN HAD ONE FOREFOOT ON THE WALL, ... 223 THE RUNAWAY 3
FOREGONE
    FOR THEIR FOREGONE INCREDULOUSNESS. . . . . 257 THE LOVELY BE CHOOSERS 36
    'TWAS AN END FOREGONE . . . . 438 KITTY HAWK 326
FOREHEAD
    TURNING HER FOREHEAD WITH A STAR, ... 263 THE TIMES TABLE . . . 6
FOREIGN
    CAN IT BE FOREIGN TRAVEL IN THE ALPS? . . . . . . 169 NEW HAMPSHIRE . . . 320
FOREMOST
    AND PLUNGED HIMSELF HEAD FOREMOST IN THE TRENCH: . . . . 394 HAEC FABULA DOCET . . 14
FORESIGHT
    THUS FORESIGHT DOES IT AND LAISSEZ-FAIRE, ... 376 SOMETHING FOR HOPE . . 18
FOREST
    I HAD WITHDRAWN IN FOREST, AND MY SONG . . . . . . 16 A DREAM PANG 1
    AND TO THE FOREST EDGE YOU CAME ONE DAY . . . . . . 16 A DREAM PANG 3
    THE CROWS ABOVE THE FOREST CALL; . . . . 27 OCTOBER 5
    THEY THROW A FOREST DOWN LESS CUT THAN BROKEN. . . . . 141 THE LINE-GANG . . . 2
    SINCE THE FOREST GERMANS SACKED ROME . . . . . . 311 THE VINDICTIVES . . . 39
    THAT, AS IT DID THE FOREST STREW, ... 336 THE WIND AND THE RAIN . 4
FORESTER
    --THE MOODIE FORESTER . . . . 331 BEECH 13
FORESTS
    THESE POOLS THAT, THOUGH IN FORESTS, STILL REFLECT . . . 245 SPRING POOLS 1
FOREST'S
    AND LOOK UP SMALL FROM THE FOREST'S FEET. . . . . . 247 ON GOING UNNOTICED . . 10
FORETOLD
    IF IT SHOULD NOT DO ANYTHING FORETOLD . . . . . . 446 DOES NO ONE AT ALL EVER 5
FOREVER
    THE LIGHT FOREVER IS MORNING LIGHT; . . . . . . 19 THE TRIAL BY EXISTENCE 11
    IT SEEMS FOREVER-- . . . . 28 MY BUTTERFLY 11
    I COULD DEVOTE AND DEDICATE FOREVER . . . . 58 THE BLACK COTTAGE . . 113
    "YES, YOU MUST GO; WE CAN'T STAY HERE FOREVER. . . . . 77 THE GENERATIONS OF MEN 120
    YOU WERE FOREVER FINDING SOME NEW PLAY. . . . . . 109 THE EXPOSED NEST . . 1
    "IT WOULD TAKE ME FOREVER TO RECITE . . . . . . 117 IN THE HOME STRETCH . 181
    FOREVER TRYING THE WINDOW LATCH . . . . 128 THE OFT-REPEATED DREAM 3
    FOREVER THE NOISE OF THESE . . . . 156 THE SOUND OF TREES . . 3
    AS IF TO PUT FOREVER OUT OF MIND . . . . 160 NEW HAMPSHIRE . . . 42
    COMMANDED IN A DREAM, FOREVER GO . . . . 173 A STAR IN A STONEBOAT . 35
    FOREVER OFF THE LATCH, AS IF RUDE MEN . . . . . . 175 THE CENSUS-TAKER . . 28
    BREAK SILENCE NOW OR BE FOREVER SILENT. . . . . . 176 THE CENSUS-TAKER . . 59
    BUT THOUGH THEY NOW GAVE UP THE SEARCH FOREVER, ... 184 MAPLE 133
    AND HAVE STOPPED DYING NOW FOREVER. . . . . . . 221 IN A DISUSED GRAVEYARD 15
    IF FROM ITS BEING KEPT FOREVER UNDER, ... 231 A BROOK IN THE CITY . 22
    AND THE WHITE WATER RODE THE BLACK FOREVER, ... 258 WEST-RUNNING BROOK . 21
    AND PIROUETTE, FOREVER IN ONE PLACE, ... 259 WEST-RUNNING BROOK . 46
    WHY IS HIS NATURE FOREVER SO HARD TO TEACH . . . . . 305 THERE ARE ROUGHLY ZONES 11
    I'M DONE FOREVER WITH POTATO CROPS . . . . 316 BUILD SOIL 11
    HIS LIFE IS A PURSUIT OF A PURSUIT FOREVER. . . . . . 421 ESCAPIST--NEVER . . 10
    FOREVER VOTING AND HARANGUING FOR IT. . . . . . . 461 HOW HARD TO KEEP FROM 229
    FOR STANDING STILL IN ONE PLACE TRUE FOREVER; . . . . 480 A MASQUE OF REASON . 192
    WHEN LEFT TO GUESS FOREVER FOR THEMSELVES. . . . . 483 A MASQUE OF REASON . 276
FOREVERMORE
    THAT LIFE IS ONLY LIFE FOREVERMORE . . . . 300 THE MASTER SPEED . . 13
FORFEITS
    WITH FORFEITS AND REWARDS HE UNDERSTOOD-- . . . . . 476 A MASQUE OF REASON . 74
FORGET
    LOVERS, FORGET YOUR LOVE, ... 10 WIND AND WINDOW FLOWER 1
    I SHALL NOT FORGET HOW HIS LAUGH RANG OUT. . . . . 25 THE DEMIURGE'S LAUGH . 13
    I'LL ASK YOU LATER--DON'T LET ME FORGET IT." . . . . 46 A HUNDRED COLLARS . . 48
    IT'S SO LONG SINCE I PICKED I ALMOST FORGET . . . . . 62 BLUEBERRIES 84
    YOU FORGET WHERE WE ARE. WHAT IS BEYOND . . . . . 90 THE FEAR 25
    HE APPEARED TO FORGET TO KEEP HIS HOLD, ... 91 THE FEAR 59
    BY LOOKING IN THE EARS. BUT I FORGET IT. . . . . . 96 THE SELF-SEEKER . . . 109
    COULD SO FORGET HIS HANDIWORK ON WHICH . . . . . . 102 THE WOOD-PILE . . . 36
    SHE WOULD FORGET IT. SHE ALL BUT FORGOT IT. . . . . 180 MAPLE 35
    FOR--I FORGET--THE LAST AMBITIOUS SAWYER . . . . . 193 PAUL'S WIFE 59
    EXCEPT FORGET TO GO IN FEAR PERHAPS. . . . . . . 231 A BROOK IN THE CITY . 19
    I SHOULD BE TEMPTED TO FORGET, ... 252 THE PEACEFUL SHEPHERD . 5
    TO TELL ONCE AND ONCE ONLY, FOR THEM NEVER TO FORGET, . . 257 THE LOVELY BE CHOOSERS 32
    BE GLAD OF WATER, BUT DON'T FORGET . . . . . . 276 TWO TRAMPS IN MUD TIME 37
    THERE IS MUCH IN NATURE AGAINST US. BUT WE FORGET: . . . 349 OUR HOLD ON THE PLANET 12
    AND TO FORGET THE ANCIENT LENGTHS OF TIME, ... 351 THE LESSON FOR TODAY . 17
    FORGET THE MYTH. . . . . 413 AWAY! 13
    (DON'T FORGET THE LATTER . . . . 435 KITTY HAWK 234
FORGETFULNESS (SEE SELF-FORGETFULNESS)
FORGETTING
    LOVE AND FORGETTING MIGHT HAVE CARRIED THEM . . . . . 229 TWO LOOK AT TWO . . . 1
    FORGETTING THAT AS FITTED TO THE SPHERE, ... 261 A SOLDIER 7
FORGIVE
    "IT'S YOU," SHE SAID. "I CAN'T GET UP. FORGIVE ME . . . 81 THE HOUSEKEEPER . . . 2
    WHY, I AGREE WITH YOU. BUT LET'S FORGIVE HIM. . . . . 156 SNOW 348
    (BUT I FORGIVE IT NOW AS EASILY . . . . 190 THE GRINDSTONE . . . 42
    AND I ASK ALL TO TRY TO FORGIVE ME . . . . 295 A RECORD STRIDE . . . 33
    FORGIVE ME IF I SEEM TO BOAST. . . . . 381 AN UNSTAMPED LETTER IN 39

FORGIVE (CONTINUED)
    FORGIVE, O LORD, MY LITTLE JOKES ON THEE . . . . 428 FORGIVE, O LORD... . . 1
    AND I'LL FORGIVE THY GREAT BIG ONE ON ME. . . . . . . 428 FORGIVE, O LORD... . . 2
    FORGIVE, O LORD... . . . . 428 FORGIVE, O LORD... . . T
    GOD KNOWS--OR RATHER, YOU KNOW (GOD FORGIVE ME) . . . 479 A MASQUE OF REASON . 169
    BUT IF YOU WILL FORGIVE ME THE IRREVERENCE, ... 482 A MASQUE OF REASON . 243
FORGIVING
    FOR TO BE SOCIAL IS TO BE FORGIVING. . . . . 178 THE STAR-SPLITTER . . 47
FORGOT
    THAT PLACE MIGHT BE FORGOT; . . . . 14 ROSE POGONIAS . . . 20
    I FORGOT HIM AND LET HIS LITTLE FEAR . . . . 101 THE WOOD-PILE . . . 19
    SHE WOULD FORGET IT. SHE ALL BUT FORGOT IT. . . . . . 180 MAPLE 35
    BUT FORGOT TO PUT THE LEAF BACK IN CLOSING . . . . . 181 MAPLE 67
FORGOTTEN
    ON THAT DISUSED AND FORGOTTEN ROAD . . . . 6 GHOST HOUSE . . . 13
    THE NEWS OF A DAY I'VE FORGOTTEN-- . . . . 110 A PATCH OF OLD SNOW . 7
    NOTHING SO NEW--SOMETHING WE HAD FORGOTTEN: . . . . . 133 THE BONFIRE . . . 110
    APPLES OR SOMETHING FORGOTTEN AND LEFT, ... 305 UNHARVESTED . . . 13
    WHY, TITYRUS! BUT YOU'VE FORGOTTEN ME. . . . . . . 316 BUILD SOIL . . . 1
    THERE IS A STORY YOU MAY HAVE FORGOTTEN . . . . . . 495 A MASQUE OF MERCY . 47
    OF GETTING UP GOOD RUINS, YOU'VE FORGOTTEN . . . . . 503 A MASQUE OF MERCY . 260
FORK
    BUT THE OLD FOOL SEIZES HIS FORK IN BOTH HANDS, . . . 71 THE CODE 61
    NO DOUBT SHE WOULD HAVE PREFERRED THE FORK. . . . . 463 LINES IN DEJECTION . 21
FORKED
    THEY TOLD ME AFTERWARD. FIRST THEY FORKED HAY, . . . 72 THE CODE 89
FORKFUL
    HE BUNDLES EVERY FORKFUL IN ITS PLACE, ... 37 DEATH OF THE HIRED MAN 89
FORKFULS
    TWO OR THREE FORKFULS I PICKED LIGHTLY ROUND FOR . . . 72 THE CODE 72
FORKS
    KNIVES AND FORKS RINGING ON THE SUPPER PLATES, ... 368 THE LITERATE FARMER AND 3
FORLORN
    THE ROAD IS FORLORN ALL DAY, ... 26 A LINE-STORM SONG . 2
    TO SEE IF SOME FORLORN MACHINE . . . . 273 A LONE STRIKER . . . 14
    BEGAN ALREADY TO SEEM FORLORN. . . . . 344 DISCOVERY OF MADEIRAS . 18
FORM
    TOMORROW THEY MAY FORM AND GO. . . . . 27 OCTOBER 6
    BECAUSE HIS VIOLENCE TOOK ON THE FORM . . . . 66 A SERVANT TO SERVANTS . 106
    WHAT FORM MY DREAMING WAS ABOUT TO TAKE. . . . . . . 68 AFTER APPLE-PICKING . 17
    IF SHE COULD FORM SOME NOTION OF HER MOTHER-- . . . . 181 MAPLE 54
    THE FLAKES COULD FIND NO LANDING PLACE TO FORM. . . . 239 OUR SINGING STRENGTH . 2
    I GAVE UP FIRE FOR FORM TILL I WAS COLD. . . . . . . 267 WHAT FIFTY SAID . . . 2
    GOD KNOWS ALL THE COLOR AND FORM OF LEAVES I HAVE TRODDEN
      ON AND MIRED. . . . . 297 A LEAF-TREADER . . . 2
    THAT SHADOW OF MINE SHOULD SHOW IN FORM . . . . . . 303 AFTERFLAKES . . . 8
    I WAIT FOR FORM. . . . . 308 PERTINAX 3
    FROM FORM TO CONTENT AND BACK TO FORM, ... 325 TO A THINKER . . . 9
    WHERE PERFECTLY IN FORM AND TINT . . . . 327 A MISSIVE MISSILE . . 34
    IN THEIR ATTEMPTS AT SOVEREIGNTY AND FORM. . . . . . 423 FOR JOHN F. KENNEDY . 35
    A DEMOCRATIC FORM OF RIGHT DIVINE . . . . 424 FOR JOHN F. KENNEDY . 64
    IS NOT CONFUSION, BUT THE FORM OF FORMS, ... 485 A MASQUE OF REASON . 339
    INDULGENCE IN YOUR FORM OF MELANCHOLY . . . . 498 A MASQUE OF MERCY . 144
    LET'S HAVE SOME PROPHECY. WHAT FORM OF RUIN . . . . 502 A MASQUE OF MERCY . 222
    THE THING THAT REALLY COUNTS, THOUGH, IS THE FORM . . 509 A MASQUE OF MERCY . 430
FORMA
    MYSELF, IN FORMA PAUPERIS, ... 381 AN UNSTAMPED LETTER IN 51
FORMAL
    UNDER THE FORMAL WRITING, HE WAS THERE, ... 230 NOT TO KEEP . . . 4
    AND TAKING FORMAL POSITION, ... 288 DEPARTMENTAL . . . 35
    WITH GRACE AND NOT TOO FORMAL A SURRENDER . . . . . 408 FROM PLANE TO PLANE . 121
FORMED
    THE LARGEST FIREDROP EVER FORMED . . . . 381 AN UNSTAMPED LETTER IN 25
FORMER
    AMID THE WRECKAGE OF A FORMER HOME? . . . . 116 IN THE HOME STRETCH . 177
    BEFORE THE FRAGMENTS OF A FORMER SUN . . . . 315 IRIS BY NIGHT . . . 7
    GREAT MONOLITHIC KNEES THE FORMER TOWN . . . . . . 377 DIRECTIVE 11
FORMIC
    THEN WORD GOES FORTH IN FORMIC: . . . . 288 DEPARTMENTAL . . . 22
FORMIDABLE
    PREOCCUPIED WITH FORMIDABLE MAIL, ... 44 A HUNDRED COLLARS . . 9
FORMS
    OF YOUTHFUL FORMS AND YOUTHFUL FACES. . . . . . . 102 GOOD HOURS . . . 8
    IS NOT CONFUSION, BUT THE FORM OF FORMS, ... 485 A MASQUE OF REASON . 339
FORMULA
    WON'T FIND A FORMULA FOR TAKING CARE OF. . . . . . 488 A MASQUE OF REASON . 415
FOR'S
    "THE BEST THING THAT WE'RE PUT HERE FOR'S TO SEE; . . . 177 THE STAR-SPLITTER . . 33
FORSAKEN
    AND TRY IF WE CANNOT FEEL FORSAKEN. . . . . 16 IN NEGLECT 5
    BUT WHAT I'M GETTING TO IS HOW FORSAKEN . . . . . . 56 THE BLACK COTTAGE . 34
    TO BEAR FORSAKEN THE PLACE'S NAME. . . . . 241 NEED OF BEING VERSED . 8
FORTE
    I GIVE YOU CREDIT FOR. MY FORTE IS TRUTH, ... 480 A MASQUE OF REASON . 190
FORTH
    OR THOSE SHOULD NOT SET FORTH UPON MY TRACK . . . . 5 INTO MY OWN 10
    THE BRIDEGROOM CAME FORTH INTO THE PORCH . . . . . 7 LOVE AND A QUESTION . 9
    I END NOT FAR FROM MY GOING FORTH, ... 9 A LATE WALK 13
    SOME SPIRIT TO STAND SIMPLY FORTH, ... 20 THE TRIAL BY EXISTENCE 42
    OH, COME FORTH INTO THE STORM AND ROUT . . . . . . 27 A LINE-STORM SONG . 31
    WHEN I WALKED FORTH AT DAWN TO SEE NEW THINGS, . . . 40 THE MOUNTAIN . . . 8
    I SHALL SET FORTH FOR SOMEWHERE, ... 156 THE SOUND OF TREES . 19
    WHEN ALL MY STRENGTH PUT FORTH WAS IN HIS FAVOR, . . . 185 THE AX-HELVE . . . 11
    AND THEN BY MEASURE BLEW IT FORTH. . . . . 224 THE AIM WAS SONG . . 12
    HE PACES BACK AND FORTH AND NEVER RESTS . . . . . . 269 THE BEAR 16
    AND BACK AND FORTH HE SWAYS FROM CHEEK TO CHEEK, . . . 269 THE BEAR 29
    THAT WILL STEAL FORTH AFTER THE SUN IS SET . . . . 276 TWO TRAMPS IN MUD TIME 39
    I CAN SIT FORTH EXPOSED TO ATTACK, ... 282 A DRUMLIN WOODCHUCK . 10

```
                                                      PAGE  TITLE                 LINE
FORTH (CONTINUED)
    THEN WORD GOES FORTH IN FORMIC: . . . . . . . . . . 288 DEPARTMENTAL . . . .   22
    PERHAPS I HAVE PUT FORTH TOO MUCH STRENGTH AND BEEN TOO
        FIERCE FROM FEAR. . . . . . . . . . . . . . . . 297 A LEAF-TREADER . . .    3
    I STOLE FORTH DIMLY IN THE DRIPPING PAUSE . . . . . 300 MOON COMPASSES . . .    1
    AND LOOPED TEN TIMES BACK AND FORTH, . . . . . . . 312 THE VINDICTIVES . . .   67
    SO BACK AND FORTH. IT ALMOST SCARES . . . . . . . . 326 TO A THINKER . . . .   13
    BUT I MUST FORTH AT DUSK, MY TIME OF DAY, . . . . . 337 THE WIND AND THE RAIN  45
    WAS NOT SET FORTH IN THE LADING BILL. . . . . . . . 343 DISCOVERY OF MADEIRAS   4
    LOOKED FORTH ON HER SMALL SON . . . . . . . . . . . 366 NOT OF SCHOOL AGE . .  14
    IT WILL STAND FORTH, ENTIRELY WHITE IN BARK, . . . 375 A YOUNG BIRCH . . . .    6
    SETS FORTH FOR HOME AT MIDNIGHT FROM A FRIEND'S-- . 386 THE FEAR OF MAN . . .   2
    THE OTHER WAY OF READING BACK AND FORTH, . . . . . 405 FROM PLANE TO PLANE .   53
    FROM HOLDING FORTH ON FREEDOM LIKE A WHITMAN-- . . 461 HOW HARD TO KEEP FROM 225
    AS IS SET FORTH IN CHAPTERS ONE AND TWO. . . . . . 485 A MASQUE OF REASON .  328
FORTHWITH
    AND FORTHWITH FOUND SALVATION IN SURRENDER. . . . . 348 THE GIFT OUTRIGHT . .  11
    AND FORTHWITH FOUND SALVATION IN SURRENDER. . . . . 424 THE GIFT OUTRIGHT . .  11
FORTNIGHT
    WE'RE STOPPING FOR THE FORTNIGHT DOWN AT DEAN'S." .  92 THE FEAR . . . . .     86
FORTUNE
    IN DALTON THAT WOULD SOME DAY MAKE HIS FORTUNE. . . 212 A FOUNTAIN, A BOTTLE .  2
FORTUNE-HUNTING
    TO FORTUNE-HUNTING IN CATHAY. . . . . . . . . . . . 419 AMERICA IS HARD TO SEE 78
FORTY
    YOU HAVEN'T RUN YOUR FORTY ORCHIDS DOWN. . . . . .   93 THE SELF-SEEKER . . .  13
    FOR THE NEXT FORTY SUMMERS--CALL IT FORTY. . . . .   95 THE SELF-SEEKER . . .  69
    IT LEFT THE CELLAR FORTY YEARS AGO . . . . . . . . 203 THE WITCH OF COOS . .  28
    A LEAK AND EMPTIED THEN. AND FORTY YEARS . . . . . 213 A FOUNTAIN, A BOTTLE .  25
    OF BEING WATCHED FROM FORTY CELLAR HOLES . . . . . 378 DIRECTIVE . . . . . .  21
    AS IF BY EYE PAIRS OUT OF FORTY FIRKINS. . . . . . 378 DIRECTIVE . . . . . .  22
FORTY-FIVE
    AND FORTY-FIVE PRESIDENTS. . . . . . . . . . . . . 368 A SERIOUS STEP LIGHTLY 24
FORTY-SIX (SEE NINETEEN-FORTY-SIX)
FORTY-THREE
    (HERE ENDETH CHAPTER FORTY-THREE OF JOB.) . . . . . 490 A MASQUE OF REASON . 466
FORWARD
    AND NOTHING TO LOOK FORWARD TO WITH HOPE, . . . . .  38 DEATH OF THE HIRED MAN 101
    I'LL JUST COME FORWARD IN THE LANTERN-LIGHT . . . .  91 THE FEAR . . . . . .   74
    TRYING TO TURN ITSELF BACKWARD OR FORWARD, . . . . 147 SNOW . . . . . . . . 119
    IF FORWARD, THEN IT'S WITH A FRIEND'S IMPATIENCE-- 147 SNOW . . . . . . . . 121
    ONE BACK AND FORWARD, IN AND OUT OF SHADOW, . . . 186 THE AX-HELVE . . . .   48
    SO LYING FORWARD WEAKLY ON THE HANDRAIL . . . . . 205 THE WITCH OF COOS . .  96
    LIKE LOCKS BLOWN FORWARD IN THE GLEAM OF EYES. . . 250 ONCE BY THE PACIFIC .   6
    CAME DRYLY FORWARD TO THE BARS AGAIN . . . . . . . 294 AT WOODWARD'S GARDENS  32
    HE RUNS FACE FORWARD. HE IS A PURSUER. . . . . . . 421 ESCAPIST--NEVER . .     6
    AND HOLDING IT FAR FORWARD FOR A SYMBOL . . . . . 446 DOES NO ONE AT ALL EVER 27
FOSTER
    THE FAMOUS FOSTER NURSE . . . . . . . . . . . . . 464 MILKY WAY IS A COWPATH  25
FOSTERED
    FOSTERED OVERLONG . . . . . . . . . . . . . . . . 430 KITTY HAWK . . . . .   69
FOUGHT
    ON EDUCATION--YOU KNOW HOW THEY FOUGHT . . . . . .  36 DEATH OF THE HIRED MAN  66
    SO HALFWAY DOWN HE FOUGHT THE BATTLE, . . . . . . 138 BROWN'S DESCENT . .    40
    BUT THE GIRL FOUGHT THEM AND MADE A SCENE. . . . . 345 DISCOVERY OF MADEIRAS  63
    OF ENEMIES DEFIED AND BATTLES FOUGHT. . . . . . . 356 TIME OUT . . . . . .   11
    SO IF THEY FOUGHT ABOUT EQUALITY . . . . . . . . . 404 FROM PLANE TO PLANE .   5
    IT WAS ON AN EQUALITY THEY FOUGHT. . . . . . . . . 404 FROM PLANE TO PLANE .   6
FOUGHTEN
    OR WHAT IT WAS FOUGHTEN FOR. . . . . . . . . . . . 463 LINES IN DEJECTION .  28
FOUND
    AND MORNING FOUND THE BREEZE . . . . . . . . . . .  11 WIND AND WINDOW FLOWER 27
    WITH LAUGHTER WHEN SHE FOUND US SOON. . . . . . .   18 GOING FOR WATER . . .  16
    AND THE WORLD HAD FOUND NEW TERMS OF WORTH. . . .   24 PAN WITH US . . . .    27
    I FOUND THAT WING BROKEN TODAY! . . . . . . . . .   29 MY BUTTERFLY . . . .   43
    I FOUND IT WITH THE WITHERED LEAVES . . . . . . .   29 MY BUTTERFLY . . . .   46
    WHEN I CAME UP FROM ROWE'S I FOUND HIM HERE, . . .  35 DEATH OF THE HIRED MAN 34
    AND YET BETWEEN THE TOWN AND IT I FOUND, . . . . .  40 THE MOUNTAIN . . . .    7
    I JUST FOUND WHAT THE MATTER WAS TONIGHT: . . . .   46 A HUNDRED COLLARS . .  55
    THEY FOUND A WAY TO PUT A STOP TO IT. . . . . . .   67 A SERVANT TO SERVANTS 139
    "DON'T LET IT BOTHER YOU. YOU'VE FOUND OUT SOMETHING. 70 THE CODE . . . . .   21
    THE MAN WAS FOUND. I'D BETTER NAME NO NAMES. . . .  88 THE HOUSEKEEPER . . . 188
    YOU DON'T TELL ME THAT WHERE YOU FOUND A RAM'S HORN  97 THE SELF-SEEKER . . . 136
    I WENT TILL THERE WERE NO COTTAGES FOUND. . . . . 102 GOOD HOURS . . . . .   10
    THOUGH I FOUND YOUR HAND FULL OF WILTED FERN, . . 109 THE EXPOSED NEST . .   11
    AND TOO MUCH WORLD AT ONCE--COULD MEANS BE FOUND. 109 THE EXPOSED NEST . .   19
    "HAVING FOUND THE FLOWER AND DRIVEN A BEE AWAY, . 118 THE TELEPHONE . . .    11
    SOUGHT FOR MUCH AFTER THAT, IT WILL BE FOUND . . . 119 HYLA BROOK . . . . .    2
    WHOSE ONLY PLAY WAS WHAT HE FOUND HIMSELF, . . . . 121 BIRCHES . . . . . .    26
    HE NEVER FOUND HER, THOUGH HE LOOKED . . . . . . . 129 THE IMPULSE . . . .    21
    ABOUT THE SHIPS WHERE WAR HAS FOUND THEM OUT . . . 132 THE BONFIRE . . . .   104
    TO SEE WHAT PEOPLE FOUND SO INTERESTING . . . . . 148 SNOW . . . . . . . . 162
    AND FOUND ME BANKING UP THE HOUSE WITH SNOW. . . . 149 SNOW . . . . . . . . 177
    THE WAYS YOU FOUND TO SAY THE PRAISE OF COMFORT . 150 SNOW . . . . . . . . 199
    WHEN COLE RETURNED HE FOUND HIS WIFE STILL STANDING 151 SNOW . . . . . . .  245
    WHAT? WE'VE FOUND OUT IN ONE HOUR MORE ABOUT HIM . 152 SNOW . . . . . . . . 252
    I FOUND HIM STANDING AT THE CLOSE OF DAY . . . . . 160 NEW HAMPSHIRE . . .   44
    I FOUND MYSELF IN A CLOSE CORNER WHERE . . . . . . 170 NEW HAMPSHIRE . . .  360
    SOME LABORER FOUND ONE FADED AND STONE-COLD, . . . 172 A STAR IN A STONEBOAT  4
    TO COUNT THE PEOPLE IN IT AND FOUND NONE, . . . . 174 THE CENSUS-TAKER . .   10
    I FOUND NO PEOPLE THAT DARED SHOW THEMSELVES, . . 174 THE CENSUS-TAKER . .   15
    ONCE SHE FOUND FOR A BOOKMARK IN THE BIBLE . . . . 181 MAPLE . . . . . . .   62
    SO, TILL SHE FOUND HERSELF IN A STRANGE PLACE . . 182 MAPLE . . . . . . .    77
    OH NO!--ALTHOUGH, OF COURSE, I COULD HAVE FOUND . 190 THE GRINDSTONE . . .   52
    AND IF HE LOOKED AND FOUND IT, COULDN'T FOUND IT-- 198 WILD GRAPES . . . .   67
    BUT COME TO DIE SHE FOUND SHE CARED SO MUCH: . . . 199 PLACE FOR A THIRD .     4
    HE FOUND THE GRAVE A TOWN OR TWO AWAY, . . . . . . 200 PLACE FOR A THIRD .    38
    THE ONLY FAULT MY HUSBAND FOUND WITH ME-- . . . . 203 THE WITCH OF COOS .    36
    SHE HADN'T FOUND THE FINGER-BONE SHE WANTED . . . 207 THE WITCH OF COOS .   152
```

FOUND (CONTINUED)
```
THEY FOUND HE'D GNAWED THE FOUR POSTS OF HIS BED, . . . . . 209 PAUPER WITCH OF GRAFTON  62
I GUESS HE FOUND HE GOT MORE OUT OF ME  . . . . . . . . . . 209 PAUPER WITCH OF GRAFTON  76
IT HADN'T FOUND THE PLACE TO BLOW; . . . . . . . . . . . . . 224 THE AIM WAS SONG  . .  6
HIS DEEP-SEA DORY HAS FOUND A HARBOR. . . . . . . . . . . . 262 THE FLOWER BOAT . . .  4
HE FOUND SUSPICIOUS SAND, AND SURE ENOUGH, . . . . . . . . . 270 THE EGG AND THE MACHINE  22
YET FOUND IT EASY TO RESIST. . . . . . . . . . . . . . . . . 274 A LONE STRIKER  . . .  35
BUT WHAT HE FOUND HE HAD WAS JUST A NAILHEAD. . . . . . . . . 278 THE WHITE-TAILED HORNET  34
THE REQUISITE LIFT OF SPIRIT HAS NEVER BEEN FOUND, . . . . . 287 A ROADSIDE STAND . . .  45
I FOUND A DIMPLED SPIDER, FAT AND WHITE, . . . . . . . . . . 302 DESIGN . . . . . . .  1
I FOUND GOD WASN'T THERE. . . . . . . . . . . . . . . . . . 309 NOT ALL THERE . . . .  4
GOD FOUND I WASN'T THERE-- . . . . . . . . . . . . . . . . . 309 NOT ALL THERE . . . .  7
THEY DIVED AND NOTHING WAS FOUND. . . . . . . . . . . . . . 311 THE VINDICTIVES . . . .  45
HAD BEEN FOUND WITH CHILD; AND HER ARMY . . . . . . . . . . 314 BEARER OF EVIL TIDINGS  21
(TO KEEP THE POTS OF GOLD FROM BEING FOUND), . . . . . . . . 315 IRIS BY NIGHT . . . .  25
THE LAST STEP TAKEN FOUND YOUR HEFT . . . . . . . . . . . . 325 TO A THINKER . . . . .  1
THEN AT LAST AND FOLLOWING HIM I FOUND-- . . . . . . . . . . 342 QUEST OF PURPLE-FRINGED  13
THE ISLAND HE FOUND WAS VERIFIED. . . . . . . . . . . . . . 347 DISCOVERY OF MADEIRAS . .  133
UNTIL WE FOUND OUT THAT IT WAS OURSELVES . . . . . . . . . . 348 THE GIFT OUTRIGHT . .  9
AND FORTHWITH FOUND SALVATION IN SURRENDER. . . . . . . . . 348 THE GIFT OUTRIGHT . .  11
AND KNOCKED AT THE DOOR OF A HOUSE WE FOUND, . . . . . . . . 367 A SERIOUS STEP LIGHTLY  11
AND FOUND, HE SAYS, A BED HAS NO RIGHT SIDE. . . . . . . . . 372 THE LITERATE FARMER AND  123
BUT FOUND ONE IN THE DELTA OF A BROOK, . . . . . . . . . . . 382 TO AN ANCIENT . . . .  5
THE BLINDMAN MIGHT HAVE FOUND IT WITH HIS FERRULE, . . . . . 394 HAEC FABULA DOCET . .  7
KNOWN AS BOUSTROPHEDON, WAS FOUND TOO AWKWARD." . . . . . . 405 FROM PLANE TO PLANE . .  54
THEY HAVE FOUND OTHER SCENES . . . . . . . . . . . . . . . . 415 CLOSED FOR GOOD . . .  11
BUT HAD HE FOUND IT? HERE HE WAS . . . . . . . . . . . . . . 416 AMERICA IS HARD TO SEE  9
THE NEW WORLD CHRISTOPHER COLUMBUS FOUND. . . . . . . . . . 422 FOR JOHN F. KENNEDY . .  15
UNTIL WE FOUND OUT THAT IT WAS OURSELVES . . . . . . . . . . 424 THE GIFT OUTRIGHT . .  9
AND FORTHWITH FOUND SALVATION IN SURRENDER. . . . . . . . . 424 THE GIFT OUTRIGHT . .  11
IS SOMETIMES FOUND A SKELETON . . . . . . . . . . . . . . . 452 A-WISHING WELL . . . .  59
I SHOULD HAVE SPOKEN SOONER HAD I FOUND . . . . . . . . . . 475 A MASQUE OF REASON . .  54
WHEN TIME WAS FOUND TO BE A SPACE DIMENSION . . . . . . . . 479 A MASQUE OF REASON . .  160
FOUND OUT THE DISCIPLINE MAN NEEDED MOST . . . . . . . . . . 481 A MASQUE OF REASON . .  209
IT WILL BE FOUND THERE'S NO MORE GIVEN THERE . . . . . . . . 483 A MASQUE OF REASON . .  282
LIKE THE ONE MILTON FOUND TO FOOL HIMSELF . . . . . . . . . 488 A MASQUE OF REASON . .  416
THAN FOUND IN CHURCH. / THAT DOESN'T HELP ME MUCH. . . . . . 513 A MASQUE OF MERCY . .  515
BE FOUND ACCEPTABLE IN HEAVEN'S SIGHT. . . . . . . . . . . . 520 A MASQUE OF MERCY . .  722
BE FOUND ACCEPTABLE IN HEAVEN'S SIGHT. . . . . . . . . . . . 520 A MASQUE OF MERCY . .  725
```
FOUNDATION
```
AND SAD ON A FOUNDATION OF WELL-BEING. . . . . . . . . . . . 168 NEW HAMPSHIRE . . . .  286
```
FOUNDED
```
AND PILE OF REAL ROCKS HAVE BEEN FOUNDED. . . . . . . . . . 331 BEECH . . . . . . .  3
THE BASIC THREE THE STATE IS FOUNDED ON. . . . . . . . . . . 520 A MASQUE OF MERCY . .  704
```
FOUNDING
```
THAT IN THE LATIN OF OUR FOUNDING SAGES . . . . . . . . . . 422 FOR JOHN F. KENNEDY . .  20
```
FOUNT
```
SHE WATERS AT THE PATENT FOUNT. . . . . . . . . . . . . . . 281 BLUE RIBBON AT AMESBURY  43
```
FOUNTAIN
```
RIGHT ON THE SUMMIT, ALMOST LIKE A FOUNTAIN. . . . . . . . .  42 THE MOUNTAIN . . . .  64
WILL PENCIL DO? THEN, PLEASE, YOUR FOUNTAIN PEN. . . . . . . 100 THE SELF-SEEKER . . .  214
THE LAWYER GRAVELY CAPPED HIS FOUNTAIN PEN. . . . . . . . . 100 THE SELF-SEEKER . . .  218
THE FOUNTAIN IN PROPORTION TO THE BASIN? . . . . . . . . . . 169 NEW HAMPSHIRE . . . .  326
A FOUNTAIN, A BOTTLE, A DONKEY'S EARS, AND SOME BOOKS . . . 212 A FOUNTAIN, A BOTTLE . .  T
I'LL FIND THAT FOUNTAIN IF IT TAKES ALL SUMMER, . . . . . . 213 A FOUNTAIN, A BOTTLE . .  18
"WELL, IF I HAVEN'T BROUGHT YOU TO THE FOUNTAIN, . . . . . . 214 A FOUNTAIN, A BOTTLE . .  41
"SO'S EVERYTHING." / "I WANT MY FOUNTAIN." . . . . . . . . . 214 A FOUNTAIN, A BOTTLE . .  44
"I GUESS YOU'D FIND THE FOUNTAIN JUST AS EMPTY. . . . . . . 214 A FOUNTAIN, A BOTTLE . .  45
```
FOUR (SEE TWENTY-FOUR-HOUR)
```
THE BOY YOU HAD IN HAYING FOUR YEARS SINCE. . . . . . . . .  36 DEATH OF THE HIRED MAN  59
AND HAD FOUR HOURS TO WAIT AT WOODSVILLE JUNCTION . . . . . .  45 A HUNDRED COLLARS . .  16
WE HAVE FOUR HERE TO BOARD, GREAT GOOD-FOR-NOTHINGS, . . . .  65 A SERVANT TO SERVANTS .  76
NAMED SANDERS, WITH A GANG OF FOUR OR FIVE . . . . . . . . .  70 THE CODE . . . . . .  31
"FOUR CARDS: ONE YOURS, THREE MINE (ONE FOR EACH BRANCH . .  76 THE GENERATIONS OF MEN  80
FIVE HUNDRED--FIVE--FIVE! ONE, TWO, THREE, FOUR,FIVE. . . .  94 THE SELF-SEEKER . . .  59
"WERE THERE NO OTHERS?" / "THERE WERE FOUR OR FIVE. . . . .  97 THE SELF-SEEKER . . .  119
AND PILED--AND MEASURED, FOUR BY FOUR BY EIGHT. . . . . . . 101 THE WOOD-PILE . . . .  24
THREE HOURS TO DO FOUR MILES--A MILE AN HOUR . . . . . . . . 145 SNOW . . . . . . . .  58
THERE WERE FOUR CANDLES AND FOUR PEOPLE PRESENT. . . . . . . 163 NEW HAMPSHIRE . . . .  128
EASTON GOES DEMOCRATIC, WILSON 4 . . . . . . . . . . . . . . 165 NEW HAMPSHIRE . . . .  198
AT LITTLETON (FOUR THOUSAND), LITTLETON . . . . . . . . . . 165 NEW HAMPSHIRE . . . .  203
HAVING A WHEEL AND FOUR LEGS OF ITS OWN . . . . . . . . . . 188 THE GRINDSTONE . . . .  1
THEY FOUND HE'D GNAWED THE FOUR POSTS OF HIS BED, . . . . . 209 PAUPER WITCH OF GRAFTON  62
ALL FOUR OF THEM TO SPLINTERS. WHAT DID THAT PROVE? . . . . 209 PAUPER WITCH OF GRAFTON  63
IN LONG STORMS AN UNDRIFTED FOUR FEET DEEP . . . . . . . . . 226 THE ONSET . . . . .  15
FOUR OR FIVE WHIPPOORWILLS . . . . . . . . . . . . . . . . . 364 A NATURE NOTE . . . .  1
NOT OVER FOUR OR SO. . . . . . . . . . . . . . . . . . . . . 366 NOT OF SCHOOL AGE . .  22
I MEAN THE GREAT FOUR, WASHINGTON, . . . . . . . . . . . . . 422 FOR JOHN F. KENNEDY . .  25
SOME PLANETS, THE UNBLINKING FOUR, . . . . . . . . . . . . . 451 A-WISHING WELL . . . .  23
AT FOUR O'CLOCK I SHOULDER AX, . . . . . . . . . . . . . . . 470 IN WINTER IN THE WOODS  5
AND, TOO, TAKE CARE OF TWENTY OF THE FOUR . . . . . . . . . 484 A MASQUE OF REASON . .  310
OR IS IT ONLY FOUR? MY EXTRA TWENTY . . . . . . . . . . . . 484 A MASQUE OF REASON . .  312
```
FOUR-ROOM
```
FOUR-ROOM SHACK ASPIRING HIGH . . . . . . . . . . . . . . . 469 FOUR-ROOM SHACK... . .  1
FOUR-ROOM SHACK... . . . . . . . . . . . . . . . . . . . . . 469 FOUR-ROOM SHACK... . .  T
```
FOURSQUARE
```
YOU MAKE A LITTLE FOURSQUARE BLOCK OF AIR, . . . . . . . . . 148 SNOW . . . . . . . .  142
```
FOURTEEN
```
"OH--AH--FOURTEEN--FOURTEEN." / "FOURTEEN! YOU SAY SO! . . .  46 A HUNDRED COLLARS . .  63
I CAN REMEMBER WHEN I WORE FOURTEEN. . . . . . . . . . . . .  47 A HUNDRED COLLARS . .  64
MORE THAN A HUNDRED COLLARS, SIZE FOURTEEN. . . . . . . . .  47 A HUNDRED COLLARS . .  66
WHO WANTS TO CUT YOUR NUMBER FOURTEEN THROAT! . . . . . . . .  47 A HUNDRED COLLARS . .  84
```
FOURTH
```
GIVE HER A CHILD AT EITHER KNEE FOR FOURTH JOY . . . . . . . 256 THE LOVELY BE CHOOSERS  31
```
FOURTH-OF-JULY
```
IN SPITE OF A SCORCHED FOURTH-OF-JULY FEELING. . . . . . . . 132 THE BONFIRE . . . . .  93
```
FOX
```
"TO BE A BUNCH OF FOX GRAPES, AS THEY CALL THEM, . . . . . . 198 WILD GRAPES . . . . .  63
THAT WHEN IT THINKS IT HAS ESCAPED THE FOX . . . . . . . . . 198 WILD GRAPES . . . . .  64
```

FOX (CONTINUED)
   WHERE A FOX WOULDN'T THINK TO LOOK FOR IT-- . . . . 198 WILD GRAPES 66
   TILL I SAW THE PATH WHERE THE SLENDER FOX HAD COME . . . 342 QUEST OF PURPLE-FRINGED 11
FOXY
   SO MOUSY OR SO FOXY . . . . 416 CLOSED FOR GOOD 29
FRACTION
   SAY A FRACTION OF ONE PERCENT AT THE VERY LEAST, ... 349 OUR HOLD ON THE PLANET   16
   ONLY A FRACTION OF OURS AT MOST. . . . . 421 ONE MORE BREVITY   . . 52
FRACTURE
   A FRACTURE IN THE ROCKS BENEATH NEW YORK . . . . . . 502 A MASQUE OF MERCY . . 229
FRAGILE
   AND THE FRAGILE BLUETS CLUSTERED THERE . . . . 24 PAN WITH US 24
FRAGMENTARY
   WHY MAKE SO MUCH OF FRAGMENTARY BLUE . . . . 220 FRAGMENTARY BLUE   . . 1
   FRAGMENTARY BLUE . . . . 220 FRAGMENTARY BLUE   . . T
FRAGMENTS
   BEFORE THE FRAGMENTS OF A FORMER SUN . . . . 315 IRIS BY NIGHT . . . 7
FRAIL
   IN TOO FRAIL A BUGGY WE DROVE . . . . 443 THE DRAFT HORSE . . . 2
FRAME
   OF HEAVY FOOTSTEPS IN THE OLD FRAME HOUSE, ... 96 THE SELF-SEEKER . . . 93
   AS GREAT AS THOSE IS SHATTERING TO THE FRAME . . . . 111 IN THE HOME STRETCH . 39
FRAMED
   OR PUT THE LEAVES ASIDE THAT FRAMED IT IN. . . . . 55 THE BLACK COTTAGE . . 10
FRAMES
   SO SMALL THE WINDOW FRAMES THE WHOLE OF IT. . . . . 51 HOME BURIAL 24
   THE QUESTION THAT HE FRAMES IN ALL BUT WORDS . . . . 120 THE OVEN BIRD . . . 13
FRAME-UP
   IS JUST A FRAME-UP TO INSURE THE FAILURE . . . . . . 511 A MASQUE OF MERCY . . 483
FRANCE
   NO LESS THAN ENGLAND, FRANCE, AND ITALY. . . . . . . 166 NEW HAMPSHIRE   . . 245
   ATHENS, ROME, FRANCE, BRITAIN, ... 437 KITTY HAWK 290
FRANCISCO
   IN DEALING IN "OLD RAGS" IN SAN FRANCISCO. . . . . . 160 NEW HAMPSHIRE   . . 58
FRANCONIA
   ELECTION NIGHT ONCE IN FRANCONIA, ... 165 NEW HAMPSHIRE   . . 195
   LAUGHS AT FRANCONIA (SEVEN HUNDRED), AND . . . . . . 165 NEW HAMPSHIRE   . . 204
   FRANCONIA LAUGHS, I FEAR--DID LAUGH THAT NIGHT-- . . . 165 NEW HAMPSHIRE   . . 205
FRANK
   GAVE ME IN TRUTH: I LIKE THE FRANK ADMISSION. . . . . 474 A MASQUE OF REASON . . 37
FRANKLIN
   THE WAY BEN FRANKLIN USED TO MAKE THE KITE STRING. . . 94 THE SELF-SEEKER . . . 35
FRANKLY
   THEN NONE THE WISER, FRANKLY GAVE IT UP, ... 293 AT WOODWARD'S GARDENS . 29
FRANTIC
   THE WATER IN DESPERATE STRAITS LIKE FRANTIC FISH, . . . 142 THE VANISHING RED . . 22
   FRANTIC IT SOUNDS, THOUGH MUFFLED AND FAR OFF. . . . . 154 SNOW 319
FRAUD
   BY FRAUD AND BY FORCE, ... 448 THE BAD ISLAND--EASTER   36
   THE OBSCURITY'S A FRAUD TO COVER NOTHING. . . . . . 483 A MASQUE OF REASON . . 279
FRAY
   AND THE FRAY WOULDN'T LAST A SINGLE ROUND. . . . . . 371 THE LITERATE FARMER AND 118
   ON THE RIGHT SIDE OF BED WOULD END THE FRAY, ... 372 THE LITERATE FARMER AND 121
FRAYED
   AND QUIVER LIKE THE FRAYED EDGE OF THE DRIFT . . . . 149 SNOW 195
FRED
   I WANT YOU HERE WITH ME, FRED.--LEAVE HIM HERE, . . . 144 SNOW 36
   FRED COLE, YOU'RE GOING TO LET HIM!" / "WELL, AREN'T YOU? 144 SNOW 43
   BUT THAT'S NOT SAYING--LOOK, FRED COLE, IT'S TWELVE, . . 144 SNOW 55
   WELL, THERE'S--" SHE TOLD FRED AFTERWARD THAT IN . . . 151 SNOW 237
   "FRED, AFTER ALL I SAID! YOU SHAN'T MAKE OUT . . . . 153 SNOW 285
   "FRED, SEE IF YOU CAN HEAR WHAT I HEAR. COME." . . . 154 SNOW 315
   "FRED, I SHAN'T LET YOU THINK OF GOING OUT." . . . . 155 SNOW 326
   THEY STARTED UP. FRED TOOK THE TELEPHONE. . . . . . 155 SNOW 328
   "FRED, WHERE IS NORTH?" / "NORTH? NORTH IS THERE, MY LOVE. 257 WEST-RUNNING BROOK . . 1
FREDERICKSBURG
   HE FELL AT GETTYSBURG OR FREDERICKSBURG, ... 56 THE BLACK COTTAGE . . 31
   FREDERICKSBURG WASN'T GETTYSBURG, OF COURSE. . . . . 56 THE BLACK COTTAGE . . 33
FREE   (SEE OBLIGATION-FREE)
   NOR JUST TO FREE THE SLAVES, THOUGH IT DID BOTH. . . . 56 THE BLACK COTTAGE . . 57
   THAT ALL MEN ARE CREATED FREE AND EQUAL. . . . . . . 57 THE BLACK COTTAGE . . 61
   BOND AND FREE . . . . 120 BOND AND FREE . . . T
   BUT THOUGHT HAS SHAKEN HIS ANKLES FREE. . . . . . . 120 BOND AND FREE . . . 10
   SHE WAS FREE, ... 128 THE IMPULSE 6
   ROUSE THEM ALL, BOTH THE FREE AND NOT SO FREE . . . . 130 THE BONFIRE 13
   GULPED SNOW, AND THEN BLEW FREE AGAIN--THE COLES, . . . 143 SNOW 3
   AND OPEN-MINDED. SHE WAS FREE TO QUESTION . . . . . 163 NEW HAMPSHIRE   . . 130
   IF WELL IT IS WITH RUSSIA, THEN FEEL FREE . . . . . 168 NEW HAMPSHIRE   . . 280
   FREE FROM THE LEAST KNOT, EQUAL TO THE STRAIN . . . . 187 THE AX-HELVE 70
   TO MAKE SO FREE AND KICK UP IN FOLKS' FACES. . . . . 210 PAUPER WITCH OF GRAFTON 107
   I ONLY HOPE THAT WHEN I AM FREE, ... 236 MISGIVING 13
   AS THEY ARE FREE, TO GO IN QUEST . . . . 236 MISGIVING 14
   IN THE TUMULT OF FREE LEAVES ON HIGH. . . . . 247 ON GOING UNNOTICED . . 2
   AND BE BUT MORE FREE TO THINK . . . . 261 SAND DUNES 15
   THE WORLD HAS ROOM TO MAKE A BEAR FEEL FREE; . . . . 269 THE BEAR 11
   AND OF ALL BUT ITS TRIVIAL FOLIAGE FREE; . . . . . . 304 UNHARVESTED 6
   AND ANYONE IS FREE TO CONDEMN ME TO DEATH-- . . . . 307 NOT QUITE SOCIAL . . 13
   THE MAN FREE LOVE, THE BUSINESSMAN FREE TRADE, ... 319 BUILD SOIL 112
   THE WRITER AND TALKER FREE SPEECH AND FREE PRESS. . . . 319 BUILD SOIL 113
   BY BEING PUNISHED BACK, IT IS NOT FREE: . . . . . . 319 BUILD SOIL 115
   FROM BOUND TO FREE AND BACK TO BOUND, ... 325 TO A THINKER . . . 11
   BY HAVING WHAT IS FREE ENFORCED. . . . . 346 DISCOVERY OF MADEIRAS . 79
   FIRM IN OUR FREE BELIEFS WITHOUT DISMAY, ... 424 FOR JOHN F. KENNEDY . 74
   WERE THEY TOLD THEY WERE FREE . . . . 448 THE BAD ISLAND--EASTER   31
   HE WRITES FREE VERSE, I'M TOLD, AND HE IS THOUGHT . . . 459 HOW HARD TO KEEP FROM   184
   FREE WILL, TRADE, VERSE, THOUGHT, LOVE, SPEECH, COINAGE, . 459 HOW HARD TO KEEP FROM   186
   CHRIST'S OR KARL MARX', AND IT WILL SET YOU FREE. . . . 460 HOW HARD TO KEEP FROM   192
   I'M TALKING NOT FREE VERSE BUT BLANK VERSE NOW. . . . . 460 HOW HARD TO KEEP FROM   212

                                                              PAGE TITLE   LINE
FREE (CONTINUED)
    FREE VERSE LEAVES OUT THE METER AND MAKES UP . . . . . 460 HOW HARD TO KEEP FROM   219
    FREE VERSE, SO CALLED, IS REALLY CHERISHED PROSE, ... 460 HOW HARD TO KEEP FROM   221
    FOR GOD HIMSELF THE HEIGHT OF FEELING FREE . . . . . . 461 HOW HARD TO KEEP FROM   251
    THE ONLY FREE WILL THERE AT FIRST WAS MAN'S, ... 475 A MASQUE OF REASON . .   71
    YOU CHANGED ALL THAT. YOU SET ME FREE TO REIGN. . . . . 476 A MASQUE OF REASON . .   77
FREED
    WAS NONETHELESS THERE READY TO BE FREED . . . . . . 240 OUR SINGING STRENGTH .   52
    AND THERE'S YOUR PRISTINE EARTH ALL FREED . . . . . 376 SOMETHING FOR HOPE . .   14
    SO THAT THE MIND CAN BE ENTIRELY FREED. . . . . . . 395 ETHEREALIZING   4
FREEDOM
    THIS, THEN, IS THE NEW FREEDOM WE HEAR TELL OF; . . . . 168 NEW HAMPSHIRE 283
    THE FREEDOM OF THE MOON . . . . 245 THE FREEDOM OF THE MOON   T
    EVERYONE ASKS FOR FREEDOM FOR HIMSELF, ... 319 BUILD SOIL 111
    WHOEVER THE SURLY FREEDOM TOOK . . . . 364 TRESPASS   5
    "ANOTHER WORD THAT BOTHERS ME IS FREEDOM. . . . . . 459 HOW HARD TO KEEP FROM   163
    YOU'RE GOOD AT MAXIMS. SAY ME ONE ON FREEDOM. . . . . 459 HOW HARD TO KEEP FROM   164
    WHERE HOMER BEGGED. HE'LL TELL YOU ABOUT FREEDOM. . . . 459 HOW HARD TO KEEP FROM   183
    FREEDOM IS SLAVERY SOME POETS TELL US. . . . . . . 460 HOW HARD TO KEEP FROM   190
    FROM HOLDING FORTH ON FREEDOM LIKE A WHITMAN-- . . . . 461 HOW HARD TO KEEP FROM   225
    THE FREEDOM THEY SEEK IS BY POLITICS, ... 461 HOW HARD TO KEEP FROM   228
    IN PUBLIC FREEDOM IS BECAUSE THE FREEDOM . . . . . 461 HOW HARD TO KEEP FROM   231
    THE FREEDOM OF THEIR OWN MATERIAL: . . . . 461 HOW HARD TO KEEP FROM   234
    FREEDOM TO FLASH OFF INTO WILD CONNECTIONS. . . . . . 461 HOW HARD TO KEEP FROM   246
FREEDOMS
    TO BE THE AUTHOR OF THE SEVEN FREEDOMS: . . . . . . 459 HOW HARD TO KEEP FROM   185
    AND TWENTY FREEDOMS ON THE PARTY DOCKET. . . . . . 484 A MASQUE OF REASON . . 311
    ARE FREEDOMS FROM THE NEED OF ASKING QUESTIONS. . . . . 484 A MASQUE OF REASON . . 313
FREEDOM'S
    HAS JUSTIFIED ITSELF IN FREEDOM'S STORY . . . . . . 423 FOR JOHN F. KENNEDY .   52
    THE ONLY CERTAIN FREEDOM'S IN DEPARTURE. . . . . . 460 HOW HARD TO KEEP FROM   194
FREELY
    AND ONLY FREELY TO BE HAD FOR CLIMBING. . . . . . . 197 WILD GRAPES   30
    YET LEFT ME FREELY FACE TO FACE . . . . 380 AN UNSTAMPED LETTER IN   16
FREEST
    HE WON'T MISUNDERSTAND YOUR FREEST MOVEMENTS. . . . . . 278 THE WHITE-TAILED HORNET 27
FREE-TRADE
    A STATE-RIGHTS FREE-TRADE DEMOCRAT. WHAT'S THAT? . . . 324 BUILD SOIL 245
FREE-VERSE
    I'M NOT A FREE-VERSE SINGER. HE WAS WRONG THERE. . . . 460 HOW HARD TO KEEP FROM   209
FREEZE
    LET THE MAN FREEZE AN EAR OR TWO, I SAY.-- . . . . . 146 SNOW 102
    DOWN FROM THE STARS TO FREEZE THE DEW AS STARRY. . . . 169 NEW HAMPSHIRE . . . 342
FREIGHT
    AND I JUDGE FROM THAT ELYSIAN FREIGHT . . . . 262 THE FLOWER BOAT . . .   9
FRENCH
    HE SAW HIMSELF A FARMER. THEN THERE WAS A FRENCH BOY . . 114 IN THE HOME STRETCH . 103
    AND IN A LITTLE--A FRENCH TOUCH IN THAT. . . . . . 188 THE AX-HELVE 100
    MY FRENCH INDIAN ESQUIMAUX, ... 211 AN EMPTY THREAT . . .   27
    THE FRENCH, THE SPANISH, AND THE DUTCH WERE DOWNED . . 422 FOR JOHN F. KENNEDY .   16
FRENCH-ENGLISH
    BUT ALL HE HAD TO TELL ME IN FRENCH-ENGLISH . . . . . 185 THE AX-HELVE   18
FRENCHMAN
    A FRENCHMAN COULDN'T GET HIS HUMAN RATING! . . . . . 186 THE AX-HELVE   45
FRENZIES
    ITS WHIRLING FRENZIES . . . . 219 I WILL SING YOU ONE-O .   65
FRESH (SEE RAIN-FRESH)
    OF THE FRESH EARTH FROM YOUR OWN BABY'S GRAVE . . . . .   54 HOME BURIAL   85
    FRESH PAINTED BY THE SHOWER A VELVET BLACK. . . . . .   55 THE BLACK COTTAGE . .   7
    STUCK INTO HIS BERRIES AS FRESH AS A SHOWER; . . . . .   61 BLUEBERRIES   65
    SOMEONE WHO LIVED IN TURNING TO FRESH TASKS . . . . . 102 THE WOOD-PILE   35
    ALL FRESH AND SOUND FROM THE RECENT AX. . . . . . . 123 PEA BRUSH   14
    THE FRESH CHIPS, ... 128 THE IMPULSE   10
    THE THREE STOOD LISTENING TO A FRESH ACCESS . . . . . 143 SNOW   1
    GOOD-LOOKING BOOKS LIKE THAT." HE PICKED ONE FRESH . . . 217 A FOUNTAIN, A BOTTLE . 125
    TO THE FRESH AND BLACK OF THE SQUARES OF EARLY MOLD . . 299 STRONG SAYING NOTHING .   9
    THE LEAFLESS BLOOM OF A PLUM IS FRESH AND WHITE; . . . 300 STRONG SAYING NOTHING .   10
    LIKE A STAR FRESH FALLEN OUT OF THE SKY. . . . . . 383 WERE I IN TROUBLE . .   5
    DICK HAD OF BEING FRESH AND FULL OF COLLEGE. . . . . . 404 FROM PLANE TO PLANE .   4
    A FRESH START FOR THE HUMAN RACE. . . . . 417 AMERICA IS HARD TO SEE   30
    COME FRESH FROM AN ELECTION LIKE THE LAST, ... 423 FOR JOHN F. KENNEDY .   54
    EVER FRESH AND FRESH. . . . . 436 KITTY HAWK 250
    TO POUR FRESH RIVERS ON YOU FROM THE LAND, ... 446 DOES NO ONE AT ALL EVER   23
    SO THAT BECAUSE WE'RE ALWAYS STARTING FRESH . . . . . 510 A MASQUE OF MERCY . . 433
FRESHEN
    AND FRESHEN IN THIS AIR OF WITHERING SWEETNESS; . . . .   15 WAITING   25
FRESHLY
    WHERE WHEELS HAVE FRESHLY SLICED THE APRIL MIRE. . . . 225 BLUE-BUTTERFLY DAY . .   8
    TO WHICH AT DAYBREAK THEY WERE FRESHLY BORN, ... 412 POD OF THE MILKWEED .   36
FRESHNESS
    THE ANGEL HOSTS WITH FRESHNESS GO, ...   20 THE TRIAL BY EXISTENCE   13
FRESH-WATER
    MY SMALL FRESH-WATER SPRING GETS DROWNED OF COURSE. . . 513 A MASQUE OF MERCY . . 539
FRETTED (SEE PECKER-FRETTED)
FREUDIAN
    HE'S FREUDIAN VIENNESE BY NIGHT. . . . . 393 A CASE FOR JEFFERSON .   3
FRIEND
    THE UNDERSTANDING OF A FRIEND. . . . .   19 REVELATION   8
    THE BRAVEST WOULD HAVE BY FOR FRIEND, ...   21 THE TRIAL BY EXISTENCE   51
    SIT DOWN OR LIE DOWN, FRIEND; YOU MAKE ME NERVOUS." . .   47 A HUNDRED COLLARS . .   72
    "REALLY, FRIEND, I CAN'T LET YOU. YOU--MAY NEED THEM." . .   50 A HUNDRED COLLARS . . 165
    A FRIEND OR TWO AS GOOD AS OWN THE FARM, ...   84 THE HOUSEKEEPER . . .   96
    "YOU'LL FIND IT IS. LET YOUR FRIEND LOOK AT IT." . . .   99 THE SELF-SEEKER . . . 190
    "MA FRIEND, YOU AIN'T KNOW WHAT IT IS YOU'RE ASK." . . . 114 IN THE HOME STRETCH . 105
    WHEN A FRIEND CALLS TO ME FROM THE ROAD . . . . . . 124 A TIME TO TALK . . .   1
    AS AN OLD BOYHOOD FRIEND, AND ONCE INDEED . . . . . 160 NEW HAMPSHIRE . . .   49
    LET'S CELEBRATE THE EVENT, MY DISTANT FRIEND, ... 352 THE LESSON FOR TODAY .   47
    IF I HAD MOTHS TO FRIEND AS I HAVE FLOWERS?) . . . . . 356 A MOTH SEEN IN WINTER .   6

FRIEND (CONTINUED)
   WITH SUCH IT HAS PROVED DANGEROUS AS FRIEND . . . . 359 THE LOST FOLLOWER . . 25
   I MADE BUT THE ONE FRIEND. . . . . 366 NOT OF SCHOOL AGE . . 4
   MY SON IN JERSEY SAYS A FRIEND OF HIS . . . . 371 THE LITERATE FARMER AND 95
   WITH A SOLITARY FRIEND, ... 384 IN THE LONG NIGHT . . 2
   THE WITCH OF ENDOR WAS A FRIEND OF MINE. . . . . 476 A MASQUE OF REASON . . 97
   YES, WE DO TOO, WITH SYMPATHY, MY FRIEND. . . . . 497 A MASQUE OF MERCY . . 102
   YET YOUR FRIEND HERE CAN'T BE QUITE DISREGARDED. . . . . . 517 A MASQUE OF MERCY . . 638
   SUFFER A FRIEND TO TRY TO WORD YOU BETTER. . . . . 519 A MASQUE OF MERCY . . 677
FRIENDLY
   THEY WON'T BE TOO FRIENDLY--THEY MAY BE POLITE-- . . . . . 62 BLUEBERRIES 100
   FOR A FRIENDLY VISIT. . . . . 124 A TIME TO TALK . . . 10
FRIENDS
   AND SEES OLD FRIENDS HE SOMEHOW CAN'T GET NEAR. . . . . . 44 A HUNDRED COLLARS . . 7
   YOU COULDN'T CARE! THE NEAREST FRIENDS CAN GO . . . . . . 54 HOME BURIAL 97
   FRIENDS MAKE PRETENSE OF FOLLOWING TO THE GRAVE, ... 54 HOME BURIAL 102
   "I CAN SEE WE ARE GOING TO BE GOOD FRIENDS." . . . . 80 THE GENERATIONS OF MEN 199
   JOHN HALL TOUCH ME! NOT IF HE KNOWS HIS FRIENDS. . . . . . 83 THE HOUSEKEEPER . . 67
   BEING CUT OFF FROM FRIENDS?" / "WE HAVE OUR FRIENDS. . . . 87 THE HOUSEKEEPER . . 169
   FOR THE FRIENDS IT MIGHT BRING ME. BY THE WAY, ... 95 THE SELF-SEEKER . . 84
   THREE CENTS SO SMALL BESIDE THE DOLLAR FRIENDS . . . . . . 107 CHRISTMAS TREES . . 50
   I'D SURE HAD NO SUCH FRIENDS IN MASSACHUSETTS . . . . . . 167 NEW HAMPSHIRE . . . 258
   SHE AND ELIZA HAD BEEN FRIENDS THROUGH ALL. . . . . 201 PLACE FOR A THIRD . . 63
   HERE LOVELESS BIRDS NOW FLOCK AS WINTER FRIENDS, ... 254 A WINTER EDEN . . . 14
   PROUD AND THE PRIDE OF FRIENDS. . . . . 256 THE LOVELY BE CHOOSERS 18
   THOSE FRIENDS KNOW NOTHING OF HER GRIEF TO MAKE IT SHAMEFUL. 256 THE LOVELY BE CHOOSERS 27
   BUT GIVE HER FRIENDS, FOR THEN SHE DARE NOT TELL . . . . . 257 THE LOVELY BE CHOOSERS 35
   THAT HE AND THE WORLD ARE FRIENDS. . . . . 282 A DRUMLIN WOODCHUCK . 12
   IN A RELATION OF ELECTED FRIENDS. . . . . 315 IRIS BY NIGHT . . . 31
   WHERE NATURAL FRIENDS ARE MET, WHERE DOGS ARE KEPT, . . . 318 BUILD SOIL 83
   OF CHILDREN, LOVE OF FRIENDS, OF MEN, OF GOD: . . . . . . 318 BUILD SOIL 86
   MY FRIENDS ALL KNOW I'M INTERPERSONAL. . . . . 320 BUILD SOIL 142
   FRIENDS CROWD AROUND ME WITH THEIR FIVE-YEAR PLANS . . . . 323 BUILD SOIL 222
   GOOD FRIENDS IN TOWN. . . . . 413 AWAY! 6
   NOT OUR FRIENDS THE RUSS, ... 437 KITTY HAWK 299
   TO SOME OF KEEPER'S FRIENDS THAT COME IN HERE, ... 509 A MASQUE OF MERCY . . 405
   MY FRIENDS AND STOKERS, JEFFERS AND O'NEILL. . . . . 516 A MASQUE OF MERCY . . 607
   OUR WICKED FRIENDS WE SEND TO PURGATORY. . . . . 519 A MASQUE OF MERCY . . 689
FRIEND'S
   IF FORWARD, THEN IT'S WITH A FRIEND'S IMPATIENCE-- . . . . 147 SNOW 121
   SETS FORTH FOR HOME AT MIDNIGHT FROM A FRIEND'S-- . . . . 386 THE FEAR OF MAN . . 2
FRIENDSHIP
   WAS I DESIRED IN FRIENDSHIP, PARTLY AS SOMEONE . . . . . . 188 THE AX-HELVE . . . 90
   WITH BOUGHTEN FRIENDSHIP AT YOUR SIDE . . . . 307 PROVIDE, PROVIDE . . 20
FRIES
   AND FRIES A COUPLE OF EBON ATOMS WHITE, ... 389 SKEPTIC 2
FRIGHT
   AND THEN--THE WATCHER AT HIS PULSE TOOK FRIGHT. . . . . . 137 "OUT,OUT--" 30
FRIGHTED
   THAT FRIGHTED THEE SO OFT, IS FLED OR DEAD: . . . . 28 MY BUTTERFLY . . . 3
FRIGHTEN
   TO FRIGHTEN CHURCH OR STATE . . . . 384 MAKING CERTAIN ANYTHING 10
FRIGHTENING
   A MISERABLE SIGHT, AND FRIGHTENING, TOO-- . . . . 35 DEATH OF THE HIRED MAN 36
FRIGHTENS
   WRETCHEDNESS IN A STRANGER FRIGHTENS ME . . . . 493 A MASQUE OF MERCY . . 16
FRINGED (SEE PURPLE-FRINGED)
FRIZZLE
   TO FRIZZLE RESIN IN A CANDLE FLAME, ... 350 TO A YOUNG WRETCH . . 8
FRO
   BECAUSE THEIR TO AND FRO . . . . 415 CLOSED FOR GOOD . . 3
   WANDERING TO AND FRO . . . . 428 KITTY HAWK 12
FROGS
   THE FROGS THAT WERE PEEPING A THOUSAND SHRILL . . . . . . 123 PEA BRUSH 9
FROM---NOT INDEXED
FRONT
   I'M SORT OF SOMETHING FOR IT AT THE FRONT. . . . . 48 A HUNDRED COLLARS . . 102
   A FRONT WITH JUST A DOOR BETWEEN TWO WINDOWS, ... 55 THE BLACK COTTAGE . . 6
   I TOOK WHAT FRONT THERE WAS BESIDE. I KNELT . . . . 131 THE BONFIRE 65
   THINGS MUST EXPECT TO COME IN FRONT OF US . . . . 147 SNOW 126
   THE HOUSE ONE STORY HIGH IN FRONT, THREE STORIES . . . . 181 MAPLE 57
   (THE HOUSE ONE STORY HIGH IN FRONT, THREE STORIES . . . . 182 MAPLE 98
   IN FRONT OF ONE TOWN HALL, I'D LEFT HIM HITCHED . . . . . 208 PAUPER WITCH OF GRAFTON 50
   IN FRONT OF EVERY ONE IN GRAFTON COUNTY. . . . . 209 PAUPER WITCH OF GRAFTON 51
   IN FRONT OF TWENTY OTHERS' WRIGGLING SPEED-- . . . . . . 237 A HILLSIDE THAW . . 13
   THROWS DOWN IN FRONT OF US IS NOT TO BAR . . . . 238 ON A TREE FALLEN ACROSS 2
   CAME TAMELY BACK IN FRONT OF ME, THE DROVER, ... 240 OUR SINGING STRENGTH . 44
   IN FRONT AT THE EDGE OF THE ROAD WHERE THE TRAFFIC SPED, . 286 A ROADSIDE STAND . . 2
   AND THE DOT IN FRONT OF A NAME . . . . 367 A SERIOUS STEP LIGHTLY 5
   AND MADE THE PAPERS' FRONT PAGE. . . . . 463 LINES IN DEJECTION . 24
   THE FRONT OF BEING ANSWERABLE TO NO ONE . . . . 482 A MASQUE OF REASON . . 250
FRONT-PAGE
   OF FRONT-PAGE PAPER EVENTS, ... 367 A SERIOUS STEP LIGHTLY 22
FROST
   WHOSE LEAVES ALREADY ARE BURNT WITH FROST, ... 28 OCTOBER 19
   THROUGH THE THIN FROST, ALMOST IN SEPARATE STARS, ... 108 OLD MAN'S WINTER NIGHT 2
   YOU SEE THE SNOW-WHITE THROUGH THE WHITE OF FROST? . . . . 148 SNOW 157
   THERE IS A SORT OF TUNNEL IN THE FROST-- . . . . 149 SNOW 192
   WAS ONLY ADDING FROST TO SNOW . . . . 233 LOOKING FOR SUNSET BIRD 15
   THE LURKING FROST IN THE EARTH BENEATH . . . . 276 TWO TRAMPS IN MUD TIME 38
   AND SO HE BROUGHT THEM TO THE VERGE OF FROST. . . . . . . 284 THE GOLD HESPERIDEE . 31
   WERE BUT FROST KNOTS ON AN AIRY GAUZE. . . . . 303 AFTERFLAKES 14
   FOR A NIGHT OF FROST. . . . . 445 PERIL OF HOPE . . . 12
FROSTY
   WHEN THE FROSTY WINDOW VEIL . . . . 10 WIND AND WINDOW FLOWER 5
   ARE INCH-DEEP WITH THE FROSTY SPINES AND BRISTLES-- . . . 42 THE MOUNTAIN . . . 53
   OF FROSTY NIGHT AIR ON THE VALE BELOW . . . . 169 NEW HAMPSHIRE . . . 341

PAGE TITLE   LINE

FROTH
  A SNOW-DROP SPIDER, A FLOWER LIKE A FROTH, ... 302 DESIGN 7
FROTHY
  LOOKING DOWNHILL TO A FROTHY SHORE? . . . . 251 BEREFT 5
FROWN
  "HE SAW YOU, THEN? WHAT DID HE DO? DID HE FROWN?" . . . . 60 BLUEBERRIES 40
  YOU'D AS WELL SMILE AS FROWN ON THE OCCASION. . . . . 490 A MASQUE OF REASON . . 465
FROWNING
  AGREED IN FROWNING ON THESE IMPROVISED . . . . 171 NEW HAMPSHIRE 386
FROZE
  BEFORE IT FROZE, AND A GUST FLINGS A HANDFUL . . . . . 176 THE STAR-SPLITTER . . 7
FROZEN
  OUT WALKING IN THE FROZEN SWAMP ONE GRAY DAY, ... 101 THE WOOD-PILE 1
  TO WARM THE FROZEN SWAMP AS BEST IT COULD . . . . . 102 THE WOOD-PILE 39
  THIS HOUSE IS FROZEN BRITTLE, ALL EXCEPT . . . . . . 150 SNOW 202
  THEIR BULK IN WATER WOULD BE FROZEN ROCK . . . . . . 151 SNOW 228
  AFTER THE GROUND IS FROZEN, I SHOULD HAVE DONE . . . . 176 THE STAR-SPLITTER . . 6
  BETWEEN THE WOODS AND FROZEN LAKE . . . . 224 STOPPING BY WOODS . . 7
  A WIND COMES OFF A FROZEN PEAK, ... 275 TWO TRAMPS IN MUD TIME 23
FROZEN-GROUND-SWELL
  THAT SENDS THE FROZEN-GROUND-SWELL UNDER IT . . . . . 33 MENDING WALL 2
FRUIT
  WHOSE CLUSTERED FRUIT MUST ELSE BE LOST-- . . . . . . 28 OCTOBER 20
  "IT MUST BE ON CHARCOAL THEY FATTEN THEIR FRUIT. . . . 59 BLUEBERRIES 22
  TO ASK IF HE KNEW ANY FRUIT TO BE HAD . . . . 61 BLUEBERRIES 70
  "IF HE THINKS ALL THE FRUIT THAT GROWS WILD IS FOR HIM, . . 61 BLUEBERRIES 79
  THE FRUIT MIXED WITH WATER IN LAYERS OF LEAVES, ... 62 BLUEBERRIES 104
  THERE WERE TEN THOUSAND THOUSAND FRUIT TO TOUCH, . . . 69 AFTER APPLE-PICKING . 30
  A CIDER SYRUP. HAVING TASTED FRUIT, ... 124 THE COW IN APPLE TIME . 5
  AND EVEN FRUIT TREES. . . . . 134 A GIRL'S GARDEN . . . 32
  I OUGHT TO KNOW WHAT TREE THE GRAPE IS FRUIT OF. . . . 196 WILD GRAPES 6
  THE RANGEY BOUGH ANTICIPATED FRUIT . . . . 239 OUR SINGING STRENGTH . 14
  OR MILK THE COW, HE VISITED THE FRUIT, ... 283 THE GOLD HESPERIDEE . 20
  WITH AUTUMN AND THE FRUIT WAS RUDELY TOSSED, ... 284 THE GOLD HESPERIDEE . 33
  IT NEVER WILL SHOW MUCH FLOWER OR FRUIT. . . . . . 296 LEAVES COMPARED WITH . 4
  WE LEARNED FROM THE FORBIDDEN FRUIT . . . . 467 QUANDARY 15
FRUITED
  THE FRUITED BOUGH OF THE JUNIPER . . . . 24 PAN WITH US 23
FRUITFUL
  LESS CAREFULLY NURTURED, LESS FRUITFUL THAN THESE, . . . 228 GOOD-BY AND KEEP COLD . 22
FRY
  WHILE I FRY THEIR BACON. MUCH THEY CARE! . . . . . . 65 A SERVANT TO SERVANTS . 78
FUEL
  THEY MIGHT FIND FUEL THERE, IN WITHERED BRAKE, ... 131 THE BONFIRE 61
FUGITIVE
  THEY SPOKE TO THE FUGITIVE IN MY HEART AS IF IT WERE LEAF
    TO LEAF. . . . . 298 A LEAF-TREADER . . . 9
  HE IS NO FUGITIVE--ESCAPED, ESCAPING. . . . . 421 ESCAPIST—NEVER . . . 1
  YOU ARE THE UNIVERSAL FUGITIVE-- . . . . 498 A MASQUE OF MERCY . . 137
  YOUR FUGITIVE ESCAPE BECOME A QUEST. . . . . 513 A MASQUE OF MERCY . . 535
FULFILL
  BUT WHICH IT ONLY NEEDS THAT WE FULFILL. . . . . . . 12 A PRAYER IN SPRING . . 16
  FATE HAS NO CHOICE BUT TO FULFILL. . . . . 336 THE WIND AND THE RAIN . 20
FULFILLED
  IF HE FULFILLED AT LAST HIS SUMMER WISH, ... 284 THE GOLD HESPERIDEE . 35
FULL (SEE NEST-FULL, SWEATING-FULL)
  FULL MANY A TIME TO SAY HIS SAY . . . . 6 GHOST HOUSE 19
  AND RISING FULL MOON, SIT ME DOWN . . . . 14 WAITING 6
  UPON THE FULL MOON'S SIDE OF THE FIRST HAYCOCK . . . . 14 WAITING 7
  SIDELONG, FULL ON MY CHEEK, ... 29 MY BUTTERFLY 40
  AND DOWN A NARROW PASSAGE FULL OF DOORS, ... 45 A HUNDRED COLLARS . . 34
  A SORT OF CATCHALL FULL OF ATTIC CLUTTER. . . . . . 67 A SERVANT TO SERVANTS . 143
  THE TOWN IS FULL OF CHASES, LOWES, AND BAILEYS, . . . 75 THE GENERATIONS OF MEN 48
  FULL OF LANK, SHIVERY, HALF-DROWNED BIRDS . . . . . 85 THE HOUSEKEEPER . . . 120
  THE PITCHER'S TOO FULL FOR HER.--THERE'S NO CUP? . . . 99 THE SELF-SEEKER . . . 173
  THOUGH I FOUND YOUR HAND FULL OF WILTED FERN, ... 109 THE EXPOSED NEST . . 11
  'TWAS A NEST FULL OF YOUNG BIRDS ON THE GROUND . . . . 109 THE EXPOSED NEST . . 13
  THE HOUSE WAS FULL OF TRAMPING, AND THE DARK, ... 113 IN THE HOME STRETCH . 82
  GRASS IS FULL LENGTH, OLD SILVER GOLDENROD, ... 131 THE BONFIRE 62
  A ZEALOT FULL OF FLUID INSPIRATION, ... 159 NEW HAMPSHIRE . . . 26
  ALTARS THE WOODS ARE FULL OF NOWADAYS, ... 171 NEW HAMPSHIRE . . . 387
  AND FULL OF IT, THAT THIS WOULD BE THE END, ... 210 PAUPER WITCH OF GRAFTON 105
  AND THAT WAS WHAT THE BOUGHS WERE FULL OF SOON. . . . 234 EVENING A SUGAR ORCHARD 17
  AND BAGS FULL OF LEAVES . . . . 234 GATHERING LEAVES . . 3
  AND POURS THE ELM-TREE MEADOW FULL OF BLUE, ... 248 THE COCOON 4
  AS FULL TO THE GUNNEL OF FLOWERS GROWING . . . . . 262 THE FLOWER BOAT . . . 6
  AND NOW HER LAP IS FULL OF TREES. . . . . 265 THE BIRTHPLACE . . . 14
  THE AIR WAS FULL OF DUST OF WOOL. . . . . 273 A LONE STRIKER . . . 18
  THE FULL SIX DAYS. THEN REST A DAY: . . . . 280 BLUE RIBBON AT AMESBURY 30
  HE DRAWS HIMSELF UP TO HIS FULL EXTENT. . . . . . 309 WASPISH 2
  AS FULL AS THE ROOM COULD HOLD . . . . 310 THE VINDICTIVES . . . 3
  THE AGE WHEN FULL UPON YOU. THAT'S MY POINT. . . . . 351 THE LESSON FOR TODAY . 30
  DICK HAD OF BEING FRESH AND FULL OF COLLEGE. . . . . 404 FROM PLANE TO PLANE . 4
  FULL OF SUCCESS, WITH THAT FOOT ON THE DASHBOARD, . . . 405 FROM PLANE TO PLANE . 38
  "AND THE MOON WAS FULL," . . . . 433 KITTY HAWK 167
  AND ITS BEING FULL . . . . 433 KITTY HAWK 170
  MADE ALL BEING FULL. . . . . 433 KITTY HAWK 174
  TO ITS FULL EXTENT . . . . 437 KITTY HAWK 301
  AND FILL THE SKY AS FULL OF MOONS . . . . 451 A-WISHING WELL . . . 17
  TO PROPHESY, AND FULL OF PROPHECY. . . . . 497 A MASQUE OF MERCY . . 98
FULL-FLEDGED
  A FULL-FLEDGED FAMILY AFFAIR. . . . . 365 A NATURE NOTE . . . 8
FULL-LENGTH
  BUY ME ENOUGH FOR A FULL-LENGTH CHIMNEY, ... 232 THE KITCHEN CHIMNEY . 7
FUMBLE
  OR FUMBLE FOR MY KNIFE TO CUT AWAY, ... 93 THE SELF-SEEKER . . . 25
  HE MAY FUMBLE WIDE OF THE KNOB A YARD OR MORE, ... 342 WILLFUL HOMING . . . 11
  MEN FUMBLE AT THE POSSIBILITIES . . . . 483 A MASQUE OF REASON . . 275

- 205 -

FUMBLING
    FUMBLING THE BUTTONS IN A WELL-STARCHED SHIRT. . . . . . . 46 A HUNDRED COLLARS . . 52
FUN
    "IT'S BUSINESS, BUT I CAN'T SAY IT'S NOT FUN. . . . . 49 A HUNDRED COLLARS . . 123
    THE ONLY FUN HE HAD. I'VE HEARD THEM SAY, THOUGH, ... 66 A SERVANT TO SERVANTS 138
    BUT IT'S JUST FUN THE WAY HE GETS BEDEVILED-- . . . . 87 THE HOUSEKEEPER . . . 161
    YOU LIKE YOUR FUN AS WELL AS ANYONE; . . . . 146 SNOW 97
    WHAT SPOILED OUR NIGHT WAS TO HIM JUST HIS FUN. . . . . . . 155 SNOW 338
    TO MAKE FUN OF MY WAY OF DOING THINGS, ... 176 THE STAR-SPLITTER . . 9
    OR ELSE FUN OF ORION'S HAVING CAUGHT ME. . . . . 176 THE STAR-SPLITTER . . 10
    AND BIRDS THAT JOINED IN THE EXCITED FUN . . . . 237 A HILLSIDE THAW . . . 15
    AND MADE FUN OF BY BUSINESS, LAW, AND ART; . . . . 322 BUILD SOIL 190
    A LOT WOULD BE A LOT OF FUN. . . . . 451 A-WISHING WELL . . . 25
    I FAIL TO SEE WHAT FUN, WHAT SATISFACTION . . . . 483 A MASQUE OF REASON . 273
    HE'S BEING A RELIGIOUS SNOB FOR FUN. . . . . 494 A MASQUE OF MERCY . . 34
FUNCTION
    THE STATE'S ONE FUNCTION IS TO GIVE. . . . . 450 OUR DOOM TO BLOOM . . 12
FUNDAMENTAL
    HE SITS BACK ON HIS FUNDAMENTAL BUTT . . . . 269 THE BEAR 26
FUNDAY
    IT'S GOOD GEOLOGY--THE FUNDAY FAULT. . . . . 502 A MASQUE OF MERCY . . 228
FUNERAL
    BETWEEN THE DEATH DAY AND THE FUNERAL DAY. . . . . 201 PLACE FOR A THIRD . . 69
    OH, THERE'S TO BE A FUNERAL ORATION. . . . . 519 A MASQUE OF MERCY . . 678
FUNERALS
    WE GET PLENTY FUNERALS AT SEA. . . . . 345 DISCOVERY OF MADEIRAS . 70
FUNERAL-WEDDING
    HOW WOULD A FUNERAL-WEDDING DO? . . . . 345 DISCOVERY OF MADEIRAS . 73
FUNNY
    I HAD TO MAKE AN ALMOST FUNNY CHOICE. . . . . 170 NEW HAMPSHIRE . . . 361
FUNNY-EYED
    AND VIEWED IT OVER HIS GLASSES FUNNY-EYED, ... 190 THE GRINDSTONE . . . 70
FUN'S
    BUT ALL THE FUN'S IN HOW YOU SAY A THING." . . . . 44 THE MOUNTAIN 104
FUR
    AND THE FUR TRADE, ... 210 AN EMPTY THREAT . . . 4
    LIKE A BEADED FUR. . . . . 218 I WILL SING YOU ONE-O . 37
FURNACE
    DOWN BURNING SKEPTICS IN THE CELLAR FURNACE . . . . 516 A MASQUE OF MERCY . . 603
FURNISHED
    LIKE THOSE WHO FURNISHED ADAM'S SONS WITH WIVES; . . . . . 161 NEW HAMPSHIRE . . . 79
FURNISHING
    YOU'D BE TO BLAME FOR FURNISHING THE REASONS." . . . . . . 406 FROM PLANE TO PLANE . 68
FURNITURE
    ANYTHING THEY PUT IN FOR FURNITURE . . . . 66 A SERVANT TO SERVANTS 117
    LEFT HERE WITH NOTHING BUT THE FURNITURE. . . . . 82 THE HOUSEKEEPER . . . 44
    THERE WILL BE NO SUCH PIECE OF FURNITURE. . . . . 372 THE LITERATE FARMER AND 130
FURROWED
    AND FOLLOWED WHERE HE FURROWED FIELD, ... 128 THE IMPULSE 7
FURS
    WITH FURS TO SELL. . . . . 211 AN EMPTY THREAT . . . 11
FURTHER
    LATER THEY GET OUT FURTHER IN THE FIELDS. . . . . 49 A HUNDRED COLLARS . . 129
    YOU DIDN'T COUNT THEM?" / "NO, THE FURTHER OFF . . . . . . 112 IN THE HOME STRETCH . 51
    FURTHER O'ERHEAD THAN ALL BUT STARS AND ANGELS-- . . . . . 132 THE BONFIRE 107
    SOUNDS FURTHER OFF, IT'S NOT BECAUSE IT'S DYING; . . . . . 150 SNOW 204
    YOU'RE FURTHER UNDER IN THE SNOW--THAT'S ALL-- . . . . . . 150 SNOW 205
    AND MELTING FURTHER IN THE WIND TO MUD. . . . . 179 THE STAR-SPLITTER . . 81
    ANYTHING FURTHER HAD BEEN WASTED ON HER, ... 180 MAPLE 33
    A LITTLE FURTHER UP THE MOUNTAINSIDE . . . . 229 TWO LOOK AT TWO . . . 2
    WITH NIGHT SO NEAR, BUT NOT MUCH FURTHER UP. . . . . 229 TWO LOOK AT TWO . . . 3
    THAT DROPS THEM NO FURTHER THAN WHERE THEY WERE. . . . . . 236 MISGIVING 12
    SOME TO GO FURTHER NORTH TO HUDSON'S BAY, ... 239 OUR SINGING STRENGTH . 22
    AND FURTHER STILL AT AN UNEARTHLY HEIGHT . . . . 255 ACQUAINTED WITH NIGHT . 11
    FURTHER THAN TARGET EVER SHOWED OR SHONE. . . . . 262 A SOLDIER 14
    HERE FURTHER UP THE MOUNTAIN SLOPE . . . . 264 THE BIRTHPLACE . . . 1
    A FURTHER RANGE . . . . 271 A FURTHER RANGE . . . T
    A THOUGHT THAT WANTED FURTHER THINKING; . . . . 274 A LONE STRIKER . . . 45
    HE MUST HAVE MEASURED TO THE FURTHER WALL. . . . . 292 FIGURE IN THE DOORWAY 9
    YET FURTHER I WENT TO BE BEFORE THE SCYTHE, ... 342 QUEST OF PURPLE-FRINGED 9
    BEFORE THE INDIAN RACE WAS FURTHER WRONGED. . . . . 370 THE LITERATE FARMER AND 60
    THE FURTHER UP THE SCALE OF WORK YOU GO. . . . . 406 FROM PLANE TO PLANE . 83
    I AM NO FURTHER FROM THEIR FATE THAN YOU ARE. . . . . 414 A CABIN IN THE CLEARING 19
    IT WILL BE FURTHER DONE, ... 416 CLOSED FOR GOOD . . . 21
    FOR GETTING BACK SOMEWHERE OR FURTHER ON." . . . . 420 ONE MORE BREVITY . . 48
    OUR BEST GUIDE UPWARD FURTHER TO THE LIGHT, ... 425 ACCIDENTALLY ON PURPOSE 23
    WHY GO ON FURTHER WITH CONFUSING VOICE . . . . 427 CONCEPT SELF-CONCEIVED 6
    IS BUT FURTHER MATTER) . . . . 435 KITTY HAWK 235
    "YOU KNOW SO MUCH, GO ON, INSTRUCT ME FURTHER. . . . . . . 458 HOW HARD TO KEEP FROM 146
    THEN FURTHER DOWN IT SEEMS TO START FROM WHERE . . . . . . 506 A MASQUE OF MERCY . . 335
FURTHERER
    YOU'RE NOT MUCH FURTHERER THAN WHERE KIKE LEFT YOU. . . . . 47 A HUNDRED COLLARS . . 70
FURTHEST
    WITH THE FURTHEST BODIES . . . . 219 I WILL SING YOU ONE-O . 49
    I HAVE OUTWALKED THE FURTHEST CITY LIGHT. . . . . 255 ACQUAINTED WITH NIGHT . 3
FUR-THING
    THE FUR-THING, MUFF-THING, ROCKING IN AND OUT . . . . 289 OLD BARN AT THE BOTTOM 8
FUSED
    TO FIND FUSED IN ANOTHER STAR. . . . . 121 BOND AND FREE . . . 20
FUSILLADE
    A FUSILLADE OF BLANKS AND EMPTY FLASHES, ... 361 A LOOSE MOUNTAIN . . 9
FUSS
    WHAT IS ALL THE FUSS . . . . 435 KITTY HAWK 242
    FOR ALL THE FUSS . . . . 469 BUT OUTER SPACE... . 3
    THE ONE INDECENCY'S TO MAKE A FUSS . . . . 507 A MASQUE OF MERCY . . 353
FUTILE
    THAT WITH EVERY FUTILE PASS . . . . 128 THE OFT-REPEATED DREAM 6
    GRIND SHELLS, O FUTILE SEA, GRIND EMPTY SHELLS . . . . . . 446 DOES NO ONE AT ALL EVER 19

FUTURE
    AND TAGS AND NUMBERS IT FOR FUTURE REFERENCE, ... 37 DEATH OF THE HIRED MAN   90
    INTO THE FUTURE. LET WHAT WILL BE, BE." . . . . 249 ACCEPTANCE 14
    I GO TO SCHOOL TO YOUTH TO LEARN THE FUTURE. . . . . . 267 WHAT FIFTY SAID . . . 8
    A LITTLE OF FUTURE HARM. . . . . 285 IN TIME OF CLOUDBURST . 8
    AND SMALL REGARD TO THE FUTURE OF ANY WEED. . . . . . 299 STRONG SAYING NOTHING . 2
    I'M NOT AFRAID TO PROPHESY THE FUTURE, ... 320 BUILD SOIL 134
    THAN IN THE FUTURE ALWAYS, ... 336 CARPE DIEM 21
    (WHO CARES BUT FOR THE FUTURE OF THE BUD?), ... 337 THE WIND AND THE RAIN . 34
    THAT SCIENCE MAY HAVE STAKED THE FUTURE ON? . . . . . 412 POD OF THE MILKWEED . 52
    THE RACE'S FUTURE TRIAL PLACE, ... 417 AMERICA IS HARD TO SEE 29
    IT IS THE FUTURE THAT CREATES HIS PRESENT. . . . . . 421 ESCAPIST--NEVER . . . 11
    THE FUTURE STATE IS SPRINGING EVEN NOW . . . . . . 506 A MASQUE OF MERCY . . 320
FUTURE'S
    FOR HEAVEN AND THE FUTURE'S SAKES. . . . . 277 TWO TRAMPS IN MUD TIME   72

G

GAD
    I'LL GO OUTDOORS, BY GAD, AND WON'T COME BACK." . . . . 100 THE SELF-SEEKER . . . 222
GAILY
    AND WHEN IT ALMOST GAILY JUMPED AND FLOWED, ... 189 THE GRINDSTONE . . . 28
GAIN
    HE SAID TO GAIN TIME: "WHAT IS IT YOU SEE?" . . . . . 51 HOME BURIAL 10
    WITH WHAT WAS ANOTHER MAN'S WORK FOR GAIN. . . . . . 277 TWO TRAMPS IN MUD TIME 61
    TO EXACT FOR A PRESENT GAIN . . . . 285 IN TIME OF CLOUDBURST . 7
    NO, IN COUNTRY MONEY, THE COUNTRY SCALE OF GAIN, . . . 287 A ROADSIDE STAND . . 44
    WOULD I GAIN ANYTHING BY USING RHYME? . . . . . . 382 TO AN ANCIENT . . . 17
    BUT NOW 'TWAS THERE AS ELSEWHERE, ANY GAIN . . . . . 398 BURSTING RAPTURE . . 4
    EXCEPT AS A GAIN. . . . . 449 THE BAD ISLAND--EASTER 53
GAINED
    HE GAINED NO FOOTHOLD, BUT PURSUED . . . . 138 BROWN'S DESCENT . . . 19
    THE VICTORY FOR WHAT IT LOST AND GAINED. . . . . . 222 TO E.T. 12
GAINING
    NOT GAINING BUT NOT LOSING, LIKE A BIRD . . . . . . 258 WEST-RUNNING BROOK . . 22
GAINS
    HIS GAINS IN HEAVEN ARE WHAT THEY ARE. . . . . . . 120 BOND AND FREE . . . 16
    FOR THESE NONE-TOO-APPARENT GAINS . . . . 417 AMERICA IS HARD TO SEE 43
'GAINST
    'GAINST AMERICAN INVENTION-- . . . . 396 AN IMPORTER . . . 10
GAIT
    SPHEROID THAT KICKED AND STRUGGLED IN ITS GAIT, . . . 190 THE GRINDSTONE . . . 40
GALE
    THERE IS THE GALE TO URGE BEHIND . . . . 26 A LINE-STORM SONG . . 17
    BETWEEN THE HOUSE AND BARN THE GALE . . . . . . 137 BROWN'S DESCENT . . . 9
    FROM WHICH NO WINTER GALE CAN HOPE TO BLOW IT-- . . . 248 THE COCOON 15
    AND BLOW A GALE. IT DIDN'T MISUNDERSTAND . . . . . 349 OUR HOLD ON THE PLANET 3
    BUT SPOKE TO ME IN A GALE . . . . 366 NOT OF SCHOOL AGE . . 7
    WITH A NEED THE GALE . . . . 429 KITTY HAWK 26
    MEN'S LEGS AND BODIES IN THE GALE . . . . 452 A-WISHING WELL . . . 52
GALL
    NOW LEFT'S NO BIGGER THAN A HARNESS GALL. . . . . . 378 DIRECTIVE 40
GALLANTLY
    AS A GIRL NO ONE GALLANTLY ATTENDS . . . . 386 THE FEAR OF MAN . . 1
GALLON
    AND ANOTHER TO ASK COULD THEY SELL IT A GALLON OF GAS . 287 A ROADSIDE STAND . . 42
GALLONS
    BUT GULPING MUDDY GALLONS . . . . 376 ONE STEP BACKWARD TAKEN 3
GALORE
    ARE SEEN TO JUGGLE MOONS GALORE. . . . . 451 A-WISHING WELL . . . 24
GAMA
    ANOTHER MARINER, DA GAMA, ... 417 AMERICA IS HARD TO SEE 20
GAMA'S
    THAT BETTER THAN DA GAMA'S GOLD . . . . 417 AMERICA IS HARD TO SEE 27
GAME
    OH, JUST ANOTHER KIND OF OUTDOOR GAME, ... 33 MENDING WALL . . . 21
    AS IN THE GAME 'TEN-STEP' THE CHILDREN PLAY." . . . . 114 IN THE HOME STRETCH . 118
    ALL JOINED IN THE GAME OF HIDE-GOLD. . . . . . . 311 THE VINDICTIVES . . . 28
    ALL JOINED IN THE MADDENING GAME. . . . . 311 THE VINDICTIVES . . . 32
    IN ANY GAME THE NATIONS WANT TO PLAY. . . . . . . 424 FOR JOHN F. KENNEDY . 75
    FOR THE GAME HE HUNTED . . . . 427 VERSION 7
    (I HOPE YOU KNOW THE GAME CALLED TWENTY QUESTIONS.) . . 484 A MASQUE OF REASON . . 314
    SO LOSERS IN THE CITY, BUT WE'RE GAME: . . . . . . 496 A MASQUE OF MERCY . . 76
GAMES
    BEFORE THEIR PLAYS AND GAMES WERE ORGANIZED, ... 318 BUILD SOIL 62
GANG   (SEE LINE-GANG)
    NAMED SANDERS, WITH A GANG OF FOUR OR FIVE . . . . . 70 THE CODE 31
GANG-BOSS
    THE WAY THE WIRY GANG-BOSS LIKED THE LOGJAM. . . . . 170 NEW HAMPSHIRE . . . 345
GANGS
    DON'T JOIN TOO MANY GANGS. JOIN FEW IF ANY. . . . . 325 BUILD SOIL 280
GANYMEDE
    AS ONE WHO WOULD NOT MAKE A GANYMEDE. . . . . . . 443 AUSPEX 8
GAP
    THE SUN IN THE NEW-CUT NARROW GAP . . . . 123 PEA BRUSH 5
GAPS
    AND MAKES GAPS EVEN TWO CAN PASS ABREAST. . . . . . 33 MENDING WALL . . . 4
    TO PLEASE THE YELPING DOGS. THE GAPS I MEAN, ... 33 MENDING WALL . . . 9
GARDEN
    HALF CLOSES THE GARDEN PATH. . . . . 8 A LATE WALK . . . 4
    AND WHEN I COME TO THE GARDEN GROUND, ... 8 A LATE WALK . . . 5
    TAUT WITH THE DEW FROM GARDEN BED TO EAVES, ... 38 DEATH OF THE HIRED MAN 108
    THE FIELDS ARE STRIPPED TO STUBBLE, THE GARDEN PATCHES . 49 A HUNDRED COLLARS . 134
    AFTER A WHILE PICKING PEAS IN HIS GARDEN: . . . . . 73 THE CODE 108
    THEY MIGHT BE GOOD FOR GARDEN THINGS . . . . . . 123 PEA BRUSH 17
    TO GIVE HER A GARDEN PLOT . . . . 133 A GIRL'S GARDEN . . . 6

GARDEN (CONTINUED)
    A GIRL'S GARDEN . . . . 133 A GIRL'S GARDEN . . .   T
    IT WAS NOT ENOUGH OF A GARDEN, ... 133 A GIRL'S GARDEN . . .   17
    THE SNAKE STOOD UP FOR EVIL IN THE GARDEN-- . . . 188 THE AX-HELVE . . .   97
    DID GRASS AND GARDEN GROUND CONFESS IT SNOWED, . . . 239 OUR SINGING STRENGTH .   9
    FIREFLIES IN THE GARDEN . . . . 246 FIREFLIES IN THE GARDEN   T
    INSCRIPTION FOR A GARDEN WALL . . . . 246 ATMOSPHERE . . . . .   S
    THEY SO SMOTE THE GARDEN BED . . . . 250 LODGED   3
    A WINTER GARDEN IN AN ALDER SWAMP, ... 254 A WINTER EDEN . . .   1
    IS CARRY SOME GARDEN SOIL . . . . 285 IN TIME OF CLOUDBURST .   3
    WHEN MY GARDEN HAS GONE DOWN DITCH, ... 285 IN TIME OF CLOUDBURST .   12
    HE HAD A TEN-BY-TWENTY GARDEN PATCH. . . . . . . 292 FIGURE IN THE DOORWAY .   18
    THAT THE BIRDS THERE IN ALL THE GARDEN ROUND . . . 338 NEVER WOULD BIRDS' SONG   2
    FROM INSIDE THE GARDEN WALL . . . . 340 THE SUBVERTED FLOWER .   36
    FROM WEEDING GARDEN BEDS . . . . 361 ALMOST TWO THOUSAND .   11
    THAT BY BROOK POWER IN THE GARDEN . . . . 397 AN IMPORTER . . .   19
    THAT GIVES OFF FROM A GARDEN GROUND AT NIGHT . . . 414 A CABIN IN THE CLEARING   16
    BUT LIFTS NO HIGHER THAN A GARDEN GROWS. . . . . . 414 A CABIN IN THE CLEARING   17
GARDENS
    AT WOODWARD'S GARDENS . . . . 293 AT WOODWARD'S GARDENS .   T
GARLAND'S
    HE MUST HAVE CHANGED HIS MIND AND GONE TO GARLAND'S. . . . 81 THE HOUSEKEEPER . . .   17
GARMENTS
    I KNEW SO WELL, WHOSE GARMENTS TRAIL . . . . 15 IN A VALE   4
GARRISON
    AND SHE LIKED TALK. SHE HAD SEEN GARRISON . . . . . 56 THE BLACK COTTAGE . .   52
GARRULOUS
    AND A GARRULOUS TOO. . . . . 449 THE BAD ISLAND--EASTER   45
GAS
    AND ANOTHER TO ASK COULD THEY SELL IT A GALLON OF GAS . . 287 A ROADSIDE STAND . .   42
    SOME GAS LIKE HELIUM MUST BE INNATE. . . . . . . 387 INNATE HELIUM . . .   6
GASP
    BEFORE SHE CAUGHT HER FIRST BREATH WITH A GASP . . . . 194 PAUL'S WIFE . . . 118
GATE
    THERE WAS A GATE I HAD LEANED AT FOR THE VIEW . . . . 118 MEETING AND PASSING .   2
    TO MAKE NO MORE OF A WALL THAN AN OPEN GATE . . . . 124 THE COW IN APPLE TIME .   2
    SUCH WAS LIFE IN THE GOLDEN GATE: . . . . 249 A PECK OF GOLD . . .   9
    ONE FAILED TO MAKE THE CLOSING GATE. . . . . . . 273 A LONE STRIKER . . .   4
    THE GATE FOR HALF AN HOUR BE LOCKED, ... 273 A LONE STRIKER . . .   7
    HAD SERVED AS A PALACE GATE. . . . . 312 THE VINDICTIVES . . .   68
    THEN A SMALL RAINBOW LIKE A TRELLIS GATE, ... 315 IRIS BY NIGHT . . .   17
    ON A COLLEGE GATE." . . . . 436 KITTY HAWK . . . 276
    YOU ASK IF I SEE YONDER SHINING GATE, ... 513 A MASQUE OF MERCY . . 530
    DON'T LET HIM MAKE YOU SEE TOO BRIGHT A GATE . . . . 513 A MASQUE OF MERCY . . 536
    FOR CLAMORING FOR JUSTICE AT THE GATE, ... 518 A MASQUE OF MERCY . . 643
GATH
    AND SO THE STORY WASN'T TOLD IN GATH; . . . . . . 284 THE GOLD HESPERIDEE .   58
GATHER
    FROM WHICH TO GATHER YOUR GOWN. . . . . 27 A LINE-STORM SONG . .   20
    TO GATHER THEM FOR HIM--YOU KNOW WHAT HE IS. . . . . 60 BLUEBERRIES   30
    JUST THEN COME YOU AND I TO GATHER IT. . . . . . . 198 WILD GRAPES   68
    I MADE HIM GATHER ME WET SNOWBERRIES . . . . . . 210 PAUPER WITCH OF GRAFTON   97
    THE HOURS OF DAYLIGHT GATHER ATMOSPHERE. . . . . . 246 ATMOSPHERE   6
    IT WILL GATHER SPEED TILL YOUR NERVES PREPARE . . . . 306 A TRIAL RUN   6
    TO HIS SUBJECTS TO GATHER THEM MORE. . . . . . . 310 THE VINDICTIVES . . .   11
GATHERED
    TOO FAR BEYOND HIM TO BE GATHERED IN, ... 29 MY BUTTERFLY   29
    AND THOSE OF THE NAME STARK GATHERED IN BOW, ... 73 THE GENERATIONS OF MEN   4
    WHAT TREE MAY NOT THE FIG BE GATHERED FROM? . . . . 196 WILD GRAPES   1
    THE GRAPE MAY NOT BE GATHERED FROM THE BIRCH? . . . . 196 WILD GRAPES   2
    AS A GIRL GATHERED FROM THE BIRCH MYSELF . . . . . 196 WILD GRAPES   4
    AT LAST THE GATHERED SNOW LETS DOWN AS WHITE . . . . 226 THE ONSET   2
    THAT WHEN THEY'RE GATHERED SHAKE . . . . 227 TO EARTHWARD   11
    HAVE GATHERED PEOPLE TO US MORE AND MORE . . . . . 262 IMMIGRANTS   2
    ARE TO BE BOUGHT OUT AND MERCIFULLY GATHERED IN . . . 286 A ROADSIDE STAND . .   24
    AND GATHERED THEM TOGETHER IN A RING. . . . . . . 315 IRIS BY NIGHT . . .   28
GATHERER (SEE GUM-GATHERER)
    THE GATHERER CAN ALWAYS TELL . . . . 280 BLUE RIBBON AT AMESBURY   33
GATHERING (SEE FLOWER-GATHERING)
    THE GATHERING OF THE SOULS FOR BIRTH, ... 20 THE TRIAL BY EXISTENCE   18
    GATHERING UP WINDROWS, PILING COCKS OF HAY, ... 69 THE CODE   2
    "I'VE BROKEN ANNE OF GATHERING BOUQUETS. . . . . . 98 THE SELF-SEEKER . . 147
    GATHERING LEAVES . . . . 234 GATHERING LEAVES . .   T
    FOR GATHERING SOLAR RAYS WOULD NOT HAVE HELPED. . . . 293 AT WOODWARD'S GARDENS .   6
GATHER-ROSES
    THEIR GATHER-ROSES BURDEN . . . . 335 CARPE DIEM . . .   13
GATHERS
    THAT GATHERS ON THE PANE IN EMPTY ROOMS. . . . . . 108 OLD MAN'S WINTER NIGHT   3
    AND EVERY GUST THAT GATHERS STRENGTH AND HEAVES . . . . 305 THERE ARE ROUGHLY ZONES   2
GAUGE
    SINCE LAST WE READ THE GAUGE." / "IT LOOKS AS IF . . . 148 SNOW 159
GAUNT
    GAUNT AND DUSTY GRAY WITH ROAMING? . . . . 13 FLOWER-GATHERING . .   6
    IT LIFTS A GAUNT LUXURIATING BEAST . . . . 254 A WINTER EDEN . . .   9
    HIS GREAT GAUNT FIGURE FILLED HIS CABIN DOOR, ... 292 FIGURE IN THE DOORWAY .   7
    HE STOOD UNSHAKEN, AND IF GRIM AND GAUNT, ... 292 FIGURE IN THE DOORWAY .   13
GAUZE
    WERE BUT FROST KNOTS ON AN AIRY GAUZE, ... 303 AFTERFLAKES   14
GAVE
    HE GAVE THE SASH A SHAKE, ... 11 WIND AND WINDOW FLOWER   18
    AND GAVE HIM TEA AND TRIED TO MAKE HIM SMOKE. . . . . 36 DEATH OF THE HIRED MAN   41
    GAVE THEM THEIR MARCHING ORDERS AND WAS MOVING. . . . 44 THE MOUNTAIN . . . 109
    TO HAVE GIVEN OUTRIGHT FOR THEM ALL SHE GAVE. . . . . 57 THE BLACK COTTAGE . .   59
    THIS HE SAT LISTENING TO TILL SHE GAVE JUDGMENT. . . . 76 THE GENERATIONS OF MEN   77
    THE LAWYER GAVE A LAUGH AMONG HIS PAPERS . . . . . 98 THE SELF-SEEKER . . 145
    YOU HAD BEGUN, AND GAVE THEM BACK THEIR SHADE. . . . . 109 THE EXPOSED NEST . .   30
    PERHAPS BECAUSE WE GAVE HIM ONLY BREAD . . . . . . 127 THE SMILE   4
    THE TIES GAVE, ... 129 THE IMPULSE . . .   26

PAGE TITLE   LINE
GAVE (CONTINUED)
    AND SETTING SUN TO HYLA BROOK, I GAVE IT . . . . 131 THE BONFIRE 58
    TO EVERYTHING, HE GAVE IT UP . . . . 139 BROWN'S DESCENT . . . 43
    DON'T THINK BROWN EVER GAVE UP HOPE . . . . 139 BROWN'S DESCENT . . . 54
    BUT HE GAVE NO ONE ELSE A LAUGHER'S LICENSE. . . . . . 142 THE VANISHING RED . . 4
    THE RED MAN GAVE IN POKING ABOUT THE MILL, ... 142 THE VANISHING RED . . 15
    AND CAME UPSTAIRS ALONE--AND GAVE THAT LAUGH, ... 142 THE VANISHING RED . . 26
    HIS NEW JOB GAVE HIM LEISURE FOR STARGAZING. . . . . . 178 THE STAR-SPLITTER . . 75
    BUT THOUGH THEY NOW GAVE UP THE SEARCH FOREVER, ... 184 MAPLE 133
    I GAVE IT THE PRELIMINARY SPIN, ... 189 THE GRINDSTONE . . . 26
    WHO GAVE HIS LIFE TO KEEP IT GOING ROUND? . . . . 190 THE GRINDSTONE . . . 47
    WHICH GAVE HIM SOME TIME TO HIMSELF TO EAT, ... 197 WILD GRAPES 34
    SHE GAVE IT THROUGH THE SCREEN DOOR CLOSED BETWEEN THEM: . 201 PLACE FOR A THIRD . . 76
    LIVING. THEY GAVE HIM BACK TO HER ALIVE-- . . . . . . 230 NOT TO KEEP 5
    I GAVE UP FIRE FOR FORM TILL I WAS COLD. . . . . 267 WHAT FIFTY SAID . . . 2
    HE GAVE THE SOLID RAIL A HATEFUL KICK. . . . . 269 THE EGG AND THE MACHINE 1
    THE ONE WHO GAVE HER ANKLE-BAND, ... 280 BLUE RIBBON AT AMESBURY 17
    HE GAVE IT SCARCELY A TOUCH, ... 288 DEPARTMENTAL 6
    THEN NONE THE WISER, FRANKLY GAVE IT UP, ... 293 AT WOODWARD'S GARDENS . 29
    WHEN HATE GAVE A TERRIBLE LAUGH, ... 311 THE VINDICTIVES . . . 22
    THEY GAVE NO MORE THOUGHT TO THE KING. . . . . 311 THE VINDICTIVES . . . 27
    SUCH AS WE WERE WE GAVE OURSELVES OUTRIGHT . . . . . . 348 THE GIFT OUTRIGHT . . 12
    BUT THE THING WAS THE SLOPE IT GAVE HIS HEAD: . . . . . 356 TIME OUT 8
    GAVE ME A STRANGELY RESTLESS DAY. . . . . 364 TRESPASS 8
    HE GAVE UP SLEEP HIMSELF SOME TIME AGO, ... 371 THE LITERATE FARMER AND 104
    LONG SINCE GAVE UP PRETENSE OF KEEPING COVERED. . . . . 377 DIRECTIVE 12
    IT GAVE BAD DREAMS AND BROKEN SLEEP, ... 382 THE NIGHT LIGHT . . . 3
    HE GAVE HIS OWN POOR ILIAC A WRENCH . . . . 394 HAEC FABULA DOCET . . 13
    BEFORE I GAVE UP SEEING AND SLEPT . . . . 419 ONE MORE BREVITY . . 3
    WHO GAVE AMERICA THE AEROPLANE . . . . 423 FOR JOHN F. KENNEDY . 47
    SUCH AS WE WERE WE GAVE OURSELVES OUTRIGHT . . . . . . 424 THE GIFT OUTRIGHT . . 12
    THEY GAVE IT THE WEDGE . . . . 448 THE BAD ISLAND--EASTER 14
    THEN THEY GAVE IT A FACE. . . . . 448 THE BAD ISLAND--EASTER 16
    THEY GAVE IT A FACE . . . . 448 THE BAD ISLAND--EASTER 20
    SOME OF THEM GAVE WAY AT THE WRIST . . . . 452 A-WISHING WELL . . . 56
    BEFORE THEY GAVE WAY AT THE FIST. . . . . 452 A-WISHING WELL . . . 57
    SCIENCE GAVE A STAB . . . . 468 A REFLEX 5
    AND FEEL NO ILL EFFECTS FROM WHAT I GAVE YOU. . . . . . 474 A MASQUE OF REASON . 36
    GAVE ME IN TRUTH: I LIKE THE FRANK ADMISSION. . . . . . 474 A MASQUE OF REASON . 37
    I GAVE YOU OVER TO HIM, BUT WITH SAFEGUARDS. . . . . . 486 A MASQUE OF REASON . 360
    THE NAME HIS MOTHER GAVE HIM IS TO BLAME . . . . 494 A MASQUE OF MERCY . . 35
    LIKE THE ONE JOSHUA GAVE JERICHO. . . . . 504 A MASQUE OF MERCY . . 274
GAY
    FOR THE FADED FLOWERS GAY . . . . 13 FLOWER-GATHERING . . 10
    THAT SMILE! IT NEVER CAME OF BEING GAY . . . . 127 THE SMILE 2
    AS HALL OF WINDHAM, GAY OF ATKINSON, ... 167 NEW HAMPSHIRE . . . 259
    AS GAY FOR YOU TO TAKE YOUR FATHER'S AX . . . . 349 TO A YOUNG WRETCH . . 1
    MADE THEM NO LESS GAY, ... 431 KITTY HAWK 115
GAZE
    WHAT KEPT HIS EYES FROM GIVING BACK THE GAZE . . . . . 108 OLD MAN'S WINTER NIGHT 4
GEAR
    REASON IS, I SUPPOSED, THE STEERING GEAR. . . . . . . 481 A MASQUE OF REASON . 231
GEESE
    LIKE WILD GEESE ON A LAKE BEFORE A STORM? . . . . . . 76 THE GENERATIONS OF MEN 90
GEM-FLOWER
    AND A GEM-FLOWER WAVED IN A WAND! . . . . 29 MY BUTTERFLY 37
GEMINI
    GEMINI AND CANCER . . . . 429 KITTY HAWK 38
GENEALOGY
    "YOU RIDDLE WITH YOUR GENEALOGY, ... 75 THE GENERATIONS OF MEN 53
    STUDYING GENEALOGY WITH ME . . . . 76 THE GENERATIONS OF MEN 85
GENERAL
    THAT IN THE GENERAL MOWING . . . . 14 ROSE POGONIAS . . . 19
    THEY MEET HIM IN THE GENERAL STORE AT NIGHT, ... 44 A HUNDRED COLLARS . . 8
    YOU KNOW THEY SUFFERED FROM A GENERAL ONSLAUGHT. . . . 58 THE BLACK COTTAGE . . 96
    THAT JANGLED EVEN ABOVE THE GENERAL NOISE, ... 142 THE VANISHING RED . . 25
    OF SEVERAL BOOKS AGAINST THE WORLD IN GENERAL. . . . . 166 NEW HAMPSHIRE . . . 229
    IT NEEDN'T WAIT ON GENERAL REVOLUTION. . . . . 324 BUILD SOIL 265
    REMEMBER HOW YOU ENVIED GENERAL SHERMAN. . . . . 406 FROM PLANE TO PLANE . 71
    FROM THE SAME GENERAL RESORT, ... 417 AMERICA IS HARD TO SEE 22
    IN GENERAL IDEAS AND PRINCIPLES. . . . . 479 A MASQUE OF REASON . 174
GENERATIONS
    THE GENERATIONS OF MEN . . . . 73 THE GENERATIONS OF MEN T
GENEROUS
    FOR THE GENEROUS TEARS OF YOUTH AND SONG? . . . . . . 262 HANNIBAL 4
GENESIS
    OF GENESIS BEHIND. THE WISDOM THERE, THOUGH, ... 480 A MASQUE OF REASON . 195
GENTLE
    RETARD THE SUN WITH GENTLE MIST; . . . . 27 OCTOBER 15
    IT SEEMED GOD LET THEE FLUTTER FROM HIS GENTLE CLASP, . 29 MY BUTTERFLY 27
    YOU DON'T KNOW WHAT A GENTLE LOT WE ARE: . . . . 85 THE HOUSEKEEPER . . 124
    FROM THE HIGH WEST SHE MAKES A GENTLE CAST . . . . . . 237 A HILLSIDE THAW . . 20
    FOR MERELY GIVING YOU ONCE MORE GENTLE PROOF . . . . . 306 NOT QUITE SOCIAL . . 6
    IT WAS THE OBSTINATELY GENTLE AIR . . . . 356 TIME OUT 12
    AND IF THEY WERE GENTLE . . . . 432 KITTY HAWK 125
GENTLER
    A PARENT, HIS GENTLER ONE, ... 366 NOT OF SCHOOL AGE . . 13
GENTLY
    "HOME," HE MOCKED GENTLY. / "YES, WHAT ELSE BUT HOME? . 38 DEATH OF THE HIRED MAN 113
    AND SMILED, AND WHEN SHE DID NOT TURN, SPOKE GENTLY, . 111 IN THE HOME STRETCH . 19
    STRIKING IT GENTLY ACROSS HER LOWERED EYES . . . . . . 181 MAPLE 42
    AND OFFER TO PUT ME GENTLY OUT OF MY PAIN. . . . . . . 287 A ROADSIDE STAND . . 51
    SO THAT IN GUYS IT GENTLY SWAYS AT EASE, ... 331 THE SILKEN TENT . . 4
    IT GENTLY THREW US A GLITTERING SHOWER DOWN. . . . . . 349 OUR HOLD ON THE PLANET 7
GEODE
    BUT THE IMPERVIOUS GEODE . . . . 332 ALL REVELATION . . . 11
GEOLOGY
    IT'S GOOD GEOLOGY--THE FUNDAY FAULT. . . . . 502 A MASQUE OF MERCY . 228

GEORGES
    FROM GEORGES BANK WHEN WINDS WERE BLOWING. . . . . . . 262 THE FLOWER BOAT . . . 8
GERM
    ONE LEAST GERM OR COAL. . . . . 441 KITTY HAWK 418
GERMAN
    THE WAY THEY GREW ROUND LEIF THE LUCKY'S GERMAN; . . . . 197 WILD GRAPES 27
GERMANS
    SINCE THE FOREST GERMANS SACKED ROME . . . . 311 THE VINDICTIVES . . . 39
GESTURE
    FLIGHT IS BUT A GESTURE, ... 441 KITTY HAWK 403
GET
    MY APPLE TREES WILL NEVER GET ACROSS . . . . 33 MENDING WALL 25
    SILAS DECLARES YOU'LL HAVE TO GET HIM BACK. . . . . . 36 DEATH OF THE HIRED MAN 61
    AND SEES OLD FRIENDS HE SOMEHOW CAN'T GET NEAR. . . . . 44 A HUNDRED COLLARS . . 7
    LATER THEY GET OUT FURTHER IN THE FIELDS. . . . . . . 49 A HUNDRED COLLARS . . 129
    AND LATER STILL THEY ALL GET DRIVEN IN: . . . . 49 A HUNDRED COLLARS . . 133
    IT'S SELDOM I GET DOWN EXCEPT FOR MEALS, THOUGH. . . . 49 A HUNDRED COLLARS . . 146
    LIE DOWN--LET YOURSELF GO AND GET SOME SLEEP. . . . . 50 A HUNDRED COLLARS . . 161
    I'VE JUST BEGUN THE NIGHT. YOU GET SOME SLEEP. . . . . 50 A HUNDRED COLLARS . . 172
    THERE NOW, YOU GET SOME SLEEP." / HE SHUT THE DOOR. . . 50 A HUNDRED COLLARS . . 178
    I MUST GET OUT OF HERE. I MUST GET AIR.-- . . . . . . 52 HOME BURIAL 37
    BUT GET THE PINE OUT OF THE WAY, YOU MAY BURN . . . . 59 BLUEBERRIES 17
    I PROMISED MYSELF TO GET DOWN SOME DAY . . . . 62 A SERVANT TO SERVANTS . 3
    NO WONDER I WAS GLAD TO GET AWAY. . . . . 67 A SERVANT TO SERVANTS . 148
    OR A LONG RAIN. I SHOULD SOON GET ENOUGH, ... 67 A SERVANT TO SERVANTS . 164
    IF BY SO DOING HE COULD GET MORE WORK . . . . 70 THE CODE 37
    THEM THAT HE COULDN'T LEAD HE'D GET BEHIND . . . . . . 71 THE CODE 44
    THE PAST AND GET SOME STRANGENESS OUT OF IT. . . . . . 73 THE GENERATIONS OF MEN 18
    "SEE THAT YOU GET HER GREATNESS RIGHT. DON'T STINT HER." . 77 THE GENERATIONS OF MEN 117
    "IT'S YOU," SHE SAID. "I CAN'T GET UP. FORGIVE ME . . . 81 THE HOUSEKEEPER . . . 2
    I TELL THEM THEY CAN'T GET ME THROUGH THE DOOR, THOUGH: . 82 THE HOUSEKEEPER . . . 37
    "THE RIGHTS OF THAT ARE HARDER TO GET AT. . . . . . . 84 THE HOUSEKEEPER . . . 99
    "CAN'T YOU AND I GET TO THE ROOT OF IT? . . . . 87 THE HOUSEKEEPER . . . 165
    "BAD TO GET MARRIED WHEN SHE HAD THE CHANCE?" . . . . 88 THE HOUSEKEEPER . . . 184
    "THEN IT'S ALL UP. I THINK I'LL GET AWAY. . . . . . . 88 THE HOUSEKEEPER . . . 190
    "YOU NEEDN'T THINK YOU'RE GOING TO GET AWAY. . . . . . 88 THE HOUSEKEEPER . . . 195
    SHE WON'T GET FAR BEFORE THE WHEELS HANG UP . . . . . 88 THE HOUSEKEEPER . . . 202
    LET HIM GET OFF AND HE'LL BE EVERYWHERE . . . . 90 THE FEAR 45
    WHAT I CAN GET. YOU SEE THEY HAVE THE FEET, ... 95 THE SELF-SEEKER . . . 63
    I CAN'T GET BACK THE FEET IN ANY CASE." . . . . 95 THE SELF-SEEKER . . . 65
    I JUST WANT TO GET SETTLED IN MY LIFE, ... 95 THE SELF-SEEKER . . . 76
    NOW RUN.--GET OUT YOUR DOCUMENTS! YOU SEE . . . . . . 99 THE SELF-SEEKER . . . 175
    IN HASTE TO GET IT OVER WITH AS YOU.-- . . . . 99 THE SELF-SEEKER . . . 192
    ASK THEM TO HELP YOU GET IT ON ITS FEET. . . . . . . 113 IN THE HOME STRETCH . 76
    TILL ED BEGINS TO GET OUT ON A SUNDAY. . . . . 115 IN THE HOME STRETCH . 148
    MUST GET SOMEWHERE. I'VE HEARD YOU SAY AS MUCH. . . . 117 IN THE HOME STRETCH . 185
    I'D LIKE TO GET AWAY FROM EARTH AWHILE . . . . 122 BIRCHES 48
    TO WATCH ME AND SEE WHAT I CAME TO GET. . . . . 123 PEA BRUSH 12
    YOU CAN'T GET BACK AND SEE IT AS HE SAW IT. . . . . . 142 THE VANISHING RED . . 9
    YOU SEE I KNOW--TO GET YOU ON TO FOLLOWS . . . . . . 147 SNOW 122
    TO GET A PUFF OF BLACK SMOKE FROM THE FLAME, ... 148 SNOW 140
    YOU CAN'T GET TOO MUCH WINTER IN THE WINTER.' . . . . 149 SNOW 184
    AND LET YOU GET TO BED AGAIN. GOOD-NIGHT, ... 150 SNOW 211
    GET INTO BED I SAY, AND GET SOME REST. . . . . 152 SNOW 265
    "HAD SHE BEEN RINGING LONG? I'LL GET MY WRAPPER. . . . 152 SNOW 275
    HOW DID HE GET SO? (RICH WAS UNDERSTOOD.) . . . . . . 160 NEW HAMPSHIRE . . . 57
    AND BOYS THE MINUTE THEY GET OUT OF COLLEGE. . . . . . 162 NEW HAMPSHIRE . . . 98
    THEIR WARES ARE SO MUCH HARDER TO GET RID OF. . . . . 164 NEW HAMPSHIRE . . . 174
    WE GET WHAT LITTLE MISERY WE CAN . . . . 167 NEW HAMPSHIRE . . . 272
    I ASKED HIM WELL BEFOREHAND. "DON'T YOU GET ONE!" . . . 177 THE STAR-SPLITTER . . 21
    TO GET SO WE HAD NO ONE LEFT TO LIVE WITH. . . . . . 178 THE STAR-SPLITTER . . 46
    AND THINK A LITTLE, AND GET SOME CITY SCHOOLING. . . . 182 MAPLE 74
    A FRENCHMAN COULDN'T GET HIS HUMAN RATING! . . . . . . 186 THE AX-HELVE 45
    TO GET IT ANYWHERE THAT I CAN SEE. . . . . 188 THE GRINDSTONE . . . 3
    WHOSE PRIDE HAS FAILED TO GET HIM ANYWHERE). . . . . . 190 THE GRINDSTONE . . . 44
    NO ONE WAS ANXIOUS TO GET RID OF PAUL. . . . . 191 PAUL'S WIFE 16
    THERE WAS NO ENTRANCE FOR THEM TO GET IN BY. . . . . . 193 PAUL'S WIFE 85
    "HERE, TAKE A TREETOP, I'LL GET DOWN ANOTHER. . . . . 197 WILD GRAPES 39
    OF DOOR AND HEADBOARD. WHERE IT WANTS TO GET . . . . . 203 THE WITCH OF COOS . . 25
    MY FIRST IMPULSE WAS TO GET TO THE KNOB . . . . 204 THE WITCH OF COOS . . 60
    "DON'T MAKE ME GET UP; I'M TOO WARM IN BED." . . . . . 205 THE WITCH OF COOS . . 95
    HE'S AFTER AN OPEN DOOR TO GET OUTDOORS. . . . . . . 205 THE WITCH OF COOS . . 112
    "TOFFILE, GET NAILS." I MADE HIM NAIL THE DOOR SHUT . . 206 THE WITCH OF COOS . . 119
    BUT WE GET ON. . . . . 211 AN EMPTY THREAT . . . 18
    BUT ONE THING ABOUT IT, IT MUSTN'T GET WARM. . . . . . 228 GOOD-BY AND KEEP COLD . 16
    AND MAKE US GET DOWN IN A FOOT OF SNOW . . . . 238 ON A TREE FALLEN ACROSS 7
    I WANT TO GET OUT OF THE TRAIN AND GO BACK . . . . . . 248 A PASSING GLIMPSE . . 3
    GET BACK TO THE BEGINNING OF BEGINNINGS, ... 259 WEST-RUNNING BROOK . . 43
    BUT GET SOME COLOR AND MUSIC OUT OF LIFE? . . . . . . 264 THE INVESTMENT . . . 14
    THE SUN AND MOON GET CROSSED, BUT THEY NEVER TOUCH, . . 268 ON LOOKING UP BY CHANCE 4
    WILL GET THIS PLASM IN ITS GOGGLE GLASS." . . . . . . 270 THE EGG AND THE MACHINE 30
    COME GET HIM--THEY KNEW WHERE TO SEARCH. . . . . . . 275 A LONE STRIKER . . . 62
    ITS MAKERS' NAME--TIME CANNOT GET THAT WRONG, ... 308 THE WRIGHTS' BIPLANE . 3
    GET IN A POEM TOWARD THE NEXT ELECTION. . . . . 316 BUILD SOIL 25
    GET CALLED AS MUCH IN CLASHES OF AMBITION. . . . . . . 317 BUILD SOIL 40
    YOU OFTEN GET IT MOST IN MONARCHY. . . . . 318 BUILD SOIL 75
    MADE SO WE ALL SHOULD GET THE GOOD OF THEM-- . . . . . 319 BUILD SOIL 95
    WE SOMETIMES ONLY GET THE BAD OF THEM. . . . . 319 BUILD SOIL 97
    OR IT MIGHT GET YOU INTO TROUBLE WITH ME. . . . . . . 320 BUILD SOIL 133
    BUT INSIDE IN IS WHERE WE'VE GOT TO GET. . . . . . . 320 BUILD SOIL 141
    TOO MEAN A THOUGHT TO GET MUCH COMFORT OUT OF. . . . . 321 BUILD SOIL 168
    I CAN TELL BETTER AFTER I GET HOME, ... 325 BUILD SOIL 286
    I GET THE LASTING SENSE . . . . 333 HAPPINESS MAKES UP . . 10
    WOULD RUN IN UNDER IT TO GET MY SHARE. . . . . 337 THE WIND AND THE RAIN . 36
    WE GET PLENTY FUNERALS AT SEA. . . . . 345 DISCOVERY OF MADEIRAS . 70
    AND GET OUTSIDE OF TOO MUCH BAD STATISTICS, ... 351 THE LESSON FOR TODAY . 37
    NO MATTER WHERE THEY STOUTLY MEAN TO GET, ... 354 THE LESSON FOR TODAY . 108
    GET BEATEN DOWN AND PASTED . . . . 359 NOVEMBER 5

GET (CONTINUED)

	PAGE	TITLE	LINE
AND WHEN WE GET TOO FAR APART IN WEALTH,	363	AN EQUALIZER	5
YOU GET THE BEAUTY OF FROM WHERE YOU ARE.	368	THE LITERATE FARMER AND	10
AND THEN GET SLOWLY, SLOWLY PULLED BACK DOWN.	370	THE LITERATE FARMER AND	67
I SEE WHAT YOU ARE: CAN'T GET YOU EXCITED	370	THE LITERATE FARMER AND	86
AND WHO KNOWS WHERE WE CAN'T GET! WASTING TIME	371	THE LITERATE FARMER AND	102
GET RID OF THAT AND THERE'D BE LEFT NO GREAT	371	THE LITERATE FARMER AND	110
A BED'S GOT NO RIGHT SIDE TO GET OUT OF.	372	THE LITERATE FARMER AND	125
SO LET'S GET SAVED, AS SAINT MARK SAYS THEY MUSTN'T.	379	DIRECTIVE	59
TO LEAVE IT TO THEM TO GET OUT OF THEIR VALLEYS.	379	TOO ANXIOUS FOR RIVERS	7
NO PLACE TO GET LOST LIKE TOO FAR IN THE DISTANCE.	379	TOO ANXIOUS FOR RIVERS	11
HOW WE PROPOSE TO GET AWAY FROM HERE	395	WHY WAIT FOR SCIENCE	3
HIS SCIENCE NEEDN'T GET HIM SO UNNERVED.	396	ANY SIZE WE PLEASE	11
GET PARCELED OUT AMONG THE WINNING GIANTS.	398	NO HOLY WARS FOR THEM	8
I GET YOU WHEN YOU HOE OUT TO THE RIVER,	405	FROM PLANE TO PLANE	40
THE IMPORTANT THING IS NOT TO GET BOGGED DOWN	406	FROM PLANE TO PLANE	62
LET THEM GET WELL-WINED	413	AWAY!	7
DID IN FACT GET SPLATTERED	427	VERSION	14
VOICE THAT SAID, "GET SET	436	KITTY HAWK	271
WE MAY GET CONTROL,	441	KITTY HAWK	422
WANTED US TO GET DOWN	444	THE DRAFT HORSE	19
AND MUCH, MUCH EASIER TO GET,	451	A-WISHING WELL	21
LET'S GET MY INCANTATION RIGHT:	451	A-WISHING WELL	27
WHERE WOULD WE GET ANOTHER? COME,	451	A-WISHING WELL	30
I GET A POEM, I DESPAIR.	452	A-WISHING WELL	33
I THINK I GET IT VIA STORK	452	A-WISHING WELL	35
TO GET ANOTHER FROM THE ATLANTIC.	453	A-WISHING WELL	66
"LET'S NOT GET SUPERSTITIOUS, SIRE," THE PRINCE SAID.	454	HOW HARD TO KEEP FROM	28
NO ONE COULD GET YOU: YOU WOULD COME THROUGH SMILING.	458	HOW HARD TO KEEP FROM	129
SHE'LL GET HER GULLET CUT,	465	MILKY WAY IS A COWPATH	38
AS THEY GET MORE NUCLEAR	466	SOME SCIENCE FICTION	14
THE THING WAS TO GET NOW AND THEN ELATED.	468	IN A GLASS OF CIDER	8
WHAT YOU GET IS WHAT TO BUY.	469	FOUR-ROOM SHACK...	6
TO GET ADAPTED TO MY KIND OF FOOLING.	470	IT TAKES ALL SORTS...	2
HE CAN'T GET OUT. / HE'S LOOSE! HE'S OUT! / IT'S GOD.	473	A MASQUE OF REASON	17
GET BURNED FOR PROPHECY, MEN ALMOST NEVER.	478	A MASQUE OF REASON	150
TO GET THINGS DONE. REFORMERS FAIL TO SEE THAT.--	478	A MASQUE OF REASON	152
WORTH GOING AFTER. GET DOWN INTO THINGS,	483	A MASQUE OF REASON	281
YOU WON'T GET ANY ANSWERS OUT OF GOD.	484	A MASQUE OF REASON	301
THAN I COULD UNDERSTAND AND WHAT I GET	485	A MASQUE OF REASON	332
SHOW YOURSELF, SON.--I'LL GET BACK ON MY THRONE	487	A MASQUE OF REASON	386
GOOD, PRETTY GOOD. / WAIT TILL I GET MY KODAK.--	488	A MASQUE OF REASON	402
A TENDENCY. THE MINUTE YOU GET ON ONE	489	A MASQUE OF REASON	449
TO FIND OUT HOW TO GET AWAY FROM GOD?	494	A MASQUE OF MERCY	28
AND HELP YOU'RE GOING TO GET. / I'LL BREAK YOUR DOOR DOWN.	500	A MASQUE OF MERCY	178
FOR ME TO DISAGREE WITH HIM AND GET SPIT OUT	500	A MASQUE OF MERCY	184
THERE MAY BE THERE AND GET SPIT OUT AGAIN.	500	A MASQUE OF MERCY	189
AND LET HIM GET OFF WITHOUT PROPHESYING?	502	A MASQUE OF MERCY	221
SOMETHING WE'LL KNOW WE'RE GETTING WHEN WE GET IT.	503	A MASQUE OF MERCY	266
ALL SECONDHAND. DON'T GET EXCITED, FOLKS;	507	A MASQUE OF MERCY	352
BUT TO REPEAT AND GET IT THROUGH YOUR HEAD:	516	A MASQUE OF MERCY	600
THEN IT'S NOT LETHAL--TO GET RID OF ME?	516	A MASQUE OF MERCY	617
ALL OF US GET EACH OTHER PRETTY WRONG.	518	A MASQUE OF MERCY	655
AND WE'RE AN ORATOR. GET UP. STAND UP.	519	A MASQUE OF MERCY	679

GETS

	PAGE	TITLE	LINE
STRANGE HOW SUCH INNOCENCE GETS ITS OWN WAY.	57	THE BLACK COTTAGE	81
'THAT GETS YE!' HE SQUEAKED LIKE A SQUEEZED RAT.	72	THE CODE	78
HERE'S HOPING SHE GETS HER DRINK AND GETS OUT SAFELY."	77	THE GENERATIONS OF MEN	109
HE GETS SOME SORT OF BAKESHOP MEALS TOGETHER,	82	THE HOUSEKEEPER	31
SOMETIMES HE GETS POSSESSED TO KEEP ACCOUNTS	86	THE HOUSEKEEPER	158
BUT IT'S JUST FUN THE WAY HE GETS BEDEVILED--	87	THE HOUSEKEEPER	161
BUT NEVER GETS AWAY;	156	THE SOUND OF TREES	11
BUT BARELY GETS FROM THEM OR HER	281	BLUE RIBBON AT AMESBURY	51
THE SOIL NOW GETS A RUMPLING SOFT AND DAMP,	299	STRONG SAYING NOTHING	1
THE STORM GETS DOWN HIS NECK IN AN ICY SOUSE	341	WILLFUL HOMING	3
AND LONG ENOUGH GETS RATED AS A CREED;	394	ETHEREALIZING	2
THAT WHEN IT GETS TOO EXQUISITE TO BEAR	398	BURSTING RAPTURE	12
(I DON'T CARE HOW THE WORLD GETS BY.)	451	A-WISHING WELL	14
BETWEEN HIS JUST DESERTS AND WHAT HE GETS.	475	A MASQUE OF REASON	51
SOMETIMES SHE THINKS SHE HAS AND GETS HERSELF	476	A MASQUE OF REASON	93
(MY WIFE GETS IN AHEAD OF ME WITH HERS.)	479	A MASQUE OF REASON	164
WHEN HE GETS TOO AGRARIAN FOR ME	496	A MASQUE OF MERCY	82
MY SMALL FRESH-WATER SPRING GETS DROWNED OF COURSE.	513	A MASQUE OF MERCY	539
THERE'S NOT MUCH WE CAN DO TILL MARTIN GETS HERE.--	514	A MASQUE OF MERCY	557
BUT BEL GETS SOME THINGS GROWN--AND SHE WAS RIGHT--	519	A MASQUE OF MERCY	690

GETTING

	PAGE	TITLE	LINE
I MUST BE GETTING BACK TO BREAKFAST NOW."	41	THE MOUNTAIN	37
SHELVES ONE COULD REST A KNEE ON GETTING UP--	42	THE MOUNTAIN	59
NOW WE ARE GETTING ON TOGETHER--TALKING.	48	A HUNDRED COLLARS	101
I LIKE TO FIND FOLKS GETTING OUT IN SPRING.	49	A HUNDRED COLLARS	127
BUT WHAT I'M GETTING TO IS HOW FORSAKEN	56	THE BLACK COTTAGE	34
I WAS JUST GETTING THROUGH WHAT THE FIELD HAD TO SHOW	60	BLUEBERRIES	35
I'M GETTING TOO OLD FOR MY SIZE, I TELL THEM.	81	THE HOUSEKEEPER	5
SEEMED TO WARN SOMEONE TO BE GETTING OUT	89	THE FEAR	20
"YOU'RE GETTING READY TO DO SOMETHING FOOLISH."	94	THE SELF-SEEKER	51
YOU MUST BE GETTING STARTED BACK TO TOWN."	111	IN THE HOME STRETCH	17
HOW DARK IT'S GETTING. CAN YOU TELL WHAT TIME	113	IN THE HOME STRETCH	67
WHEN PEOPLE'RE GETTING ON IN LIFE. YOU'LL LIKE IT."	113	IN THE HOME STRETCH	94
OF GETTING HOME AGAIN BECAUSE	139	BROWN'S DESCENT	55
WHEN IT'S JUST THAT I HOLD WITH GETTING A THING DONE WITH."	142	THE VANISHING RED	8
GETTING NO ANSWER, CLOSED THE TELEPHONE.	143	SNOW	30
HE'S GETTING UP A MIRACLE THIS MINUTE.	146	SNOW	84
I HOPE SHE ISN'T GETTING INTO MISCHIEF."	191	PAUL'S WIFE	15
THE WEST WAS GETTING OUT OF GOLD,	232	LOOKING FOR SUNSET BIRD	1
WILL KEEP MY TALK FROM GETTING OVERWISE,	265	DUST IN THE EYES	2
THAT KEPT THE OAKS FROM GETTING ANY GIRTH.	292	FIGURE IN THE DOORWAY	4
THE OLD DOG BARKS BACKWARD WITHOUT GETTING UP.	308	THE SPAN OF LIFE	1
OUR EVER GETTING INSIDE IN AGAIN.	320	BUILD SOIL	140

                                                          PAGE TITLE   LINE
GETTING (CONTINUED)
    IT IS GETTING DARK AND TIME HE DREW TO A HOUSE, ... 341 WILLFUL HOMING   . . .   1
    AND GETTING UP MY MEDIEVAL LATIN, ... 350 THE LESSON FOR TODAY .   8
    WITH HOPES OF GETTING MANKIND UNBENIGHTED. . . . . 371 THE LITERATE FARMER AND 87
    CALLED GETTING OUT OF THE WRONG SIDE OF BED. . . . . 371 THE LITERATE FARMER AND 107
    AND IF OUR GETTING UP TO START THE DAY . . . . 372 THE LITERATE FARMER AND 120
    WHO ONLY HAS AT HEART YOUR GETTING LOST, ... 377 DIRECTIVE   9
    OF GETTING ONE MORE CHANCE TO CHANGE OUR MANNERS? . . . . 397 THE PLANNERS . . . 12
    WAS MADE BY GETTING SCIENCE ON THE BRAIN; . . . . 398 BURSTING RAPTURE . .   5
    THEN FLED FOR FEAR OF GETTING STUCK IN LAVA. . . . . 407 FROM PLANE TO PLANE 94
    EACH TRIED TO BE THE FIRST AT GETTING IN. . . . . 407 FROM PLANE TO PLANE 117
    FOR GETTING BACK SOMEWHERE OR FURTHER ON." . . . . 420 ONE MORE BREVITY . . 48
    GETTING TOO BEFRIENDED, ... 431 KITTY HAWK 95
    GETTING THOUGHT EXPRESSED. . . . . 442 KITTY HAWK 436
    I'M GETTING OUT TONIGHT. HERE, TAKE THE CROWN." . . . . . 453 HOW HARD TO KEEP FROM   3
    BY WAITING UP INSTEAD OF GETTING UP. . . . . 496 A MASQUE OF MERCY . . 72
    WHOSE CURE WILL LIE IN GETTING HER IDEA . . . . 499 A MASQUE OF MERCY . . 160
    BIG-CITY TALK. I'M GETTING OUT OF HERE. . . . . 500 A MASQUE OF MERCY . . 171
    A QUESTION WHO WAS GETTING THE MOST OUT . . . . 503 A MASQUE OF MERCY . . 248
    OF GETTING UP GOOD RUINS, YOU'VE FORGOTTEN . . . . 503 A MASQUE OF MERCY . . 260
    SOMETHING WE'LL KNOW WE'RE GETTING WHEN WE GET IT. . . . . 503 A MASQUE OF MERCY . . 266
    LET'S CHANGE THE SUBJECT, BOYS, I'M GETTING NERVOUS. . . . 516 A MASQUE OF MERCY . . 598
    THERE'S NO ONE DOWN THERE GETTING TORTURED, SAVE . . . . . 516 A MASQUE OF MERCY . . 609
GET-TOGETHER
    A GOOD OLD GET-TOGETHER CELEBRATION. . . . . 487 A MASQUE OF REASON . 380
GETTYSBURG
    HE FELL AT GETTYSBURG OR FREDERICKSBURG, ... 56 THE BLACK COTTAGE . . 31
    FREDERICKSBURG WASN'T GETTYSBURG, OF COURSE. . . . . . . 56 THE BLACK COTTAGE . . 33
GHASTLY
    GHASTLY SNOW-WHITE. . . . . 360 THE RABBIT-HUNTER . .   6
GHIBELLINE
    OR POLITICS OF GHIBELLINE OR GUELPH, ... 359 THE LOST FOLLOWER . . 30
GHOST
    GHOST HOUSE . . . .   5 GHOST HOUSE . . . .   T
    THERE MAY NOT HAVE BEEN THE GHOST OF A SIGN . . . . 59 BLUEBERRIES 15
    LIKE GHOST OF SLEIGH BELLS IN A GHOST OF SNOW)-- . . . . 119 HYLA BROOK   6
    TO SUCH A GHOST-- . . . . 212 AN EMPTY THREAT . . 49
    FAR IN THE MAPLES, PALE, BUT NOT A GHOST? . . . . 233 A BOUNDLESS MOMENT . .   2
    SUPPOSE HIS GHOST IS STANDING BY . . . . 327 A MISSIVE MISSILE . . 30
    THAT WERE PALE AS A GHOST. . . . . 343 QUEST OF PURPLE-FRINGED 24
    THEY SAY HIS FLAGSHIP'S UNLAID GHOST . . . . 418 AMERICA IS HARD TO SEE 49
    HE MIGHT HAVE BEEN THE DREAM OF A GHOST . . . . 421 ONE MORE BREVITY . . 53
GHOSTS
    LIKE NOTHING ELSE BY DAY, LIKE GHOSTS BY NIGHT; . . . . . 12 A PRAYER IN SPRING . .   6
GIANT
    SOME GIANT TREES HAVE BLOOM SO SMALL . . . . 297 LEAVES COMPARED WITH .   9
GIANTS
    GET PARCELED OUT AMONG THE WINNING GIANTS. . . . . 398 NO HOLY WARS FOR THEM . 8
GIFT
    WITHOUT THE GIFT OF SIGHT. . . . .   9 STARS 12
    IT WAS NO DREAM OF THE GIFT OF IDLE HOURS, ... 17 MOWING   7
    DO YOU CALL THAT?" SHE SAID. / "HE HAD THE GIFT . . . . . 151 SNOW 248
    HER GIFT FOR READING LETTERS LOCKED IN BOXES. . . . . . . 163 NEW HAMPSHIRE . . . 131
    OF BEING GIVEN FOR CHRISTMAS GIFT, ... 178 THE STAR-SPLITTER . . 55
    A BIRD WITH AN ANGELIC GIFT . . . . 233 LOOKING FOR SUNSET BIRD 7
    TO USE THE GIFT YOU DO POSSESS, ... 326 TO A THINKER . . . 27
    THE GIFT OUTRIGHT . . . . 348 THE GIFT OUTRIGHT . .   T
    (THE DEED OF GIFT WAS MANY DEEDS OF WAR) . . . . 348 THE GIFT OUTRIGHT . . 13
    GIFT OUTRIGHT OF "THE GIFT OUTRIGHT" . . . . 422 FOR JOHN F. KENNEDY .   S
    THE GIFT OUTRIGHT . . . . 424 THE GIFT OUTRIGHT . .   T
    (THE DEED OF GIFT WAS MANY DEEDS OF WAR) . . . . 424 THE GIFT OUTRIGHT . . 13
    I THOUGHT YOU JUST NOW SAID IT WAS A GIFT SHOP. . . . . . 494 A MASQUE OF MERCY . . 25
GIG
    AND THE BACK OF THE GIG THEY STOOD BESIDE . . . . 89 THE FEAR   6
GIGANTIC
    IT NEEDN'T BE QUITE SO GIGANTIC . . . . 453 A-WISHING WELL . . . 67
GILT
    AS GILT TO GOLD THAT WOULDN'T SHOW. . . . . 233 LOOKING FOR SUNSET BIRD 16
GIRDLE
    WHAT WELL MAY PROVE THE YEAR'S HIGH GIRDLE MARK. . . . . . 254 A WINTER EDEN . . . 12
GIRDLED
    I DON'T WANT IT GIRDLED BY RABBIT AND MOUSE, ... 228 GOOD-BY AND KEEP COLD . 6
GIRL (SEE ONE-GIRL)
    OR SO THE STORY GOES. IT WAS SOME GIRL. . . . . 66 A SERVANT TO SERVANTS . 109
    WAS A GIRL; AND SHE HALTED SOME WAY OFF . . . . 74 THE GENERATIONS OF MEN 30
    SHE'S AFTER CIDER, THE OLD GIRL, SHE'S THIRSTY; . . . . . 77 THE GENERATIONS OF MEN 108
    A LITTLE BAREFOOT GIRL, WHO IN THE NOISE . . . . 96 THE SELF-SEEKER . . 92
    "I WOULDN'T--SO I WOULDN'T. YOU'RE THE GIRL! . . . . . . 97 THE SELF-SEEKER . . 121
    AND FOR THE BACKWOODS WOODCHUCK. YOU'RE THE GIRL! . . . . 97 THE SELF-SEEKER . . 125
    WHEN SHE WAS A GIRL ON THE FARM, SHE DID . . . . 133 A GIRL'S GARDEN . .   3
    BE A GOOD GIRL--BE LIKE A MAPLE TREE. . . . . 180 MAPLE 22
    OR FOR A LITTLE GIRL TO GUESS SOMETIME. . . . . 180 MAPLE 24
    IN DRESS OR MANNER OF THE GIRL WHO BORE IT. . . . . 181 MAPLE 53
    IT SLOWLY ROSE A PERSON, ROSE A GIRL, ... 194 PAUL'S WIFE . . . 108
    WHEN THE GIRL SEEMED TOO WATERLOGGED TO LIVE, ... 194 PAUL'S WIFE . . . 117
    IN A SMALL NICHE LET INTO IT, THE GIRL . . . . 195 PAUL'S WIFE . . . 134
    WAS FROM THE GIRL HERSELF, THOUGH, NOT FROM A STAR, . . . 195 PAUL'S WIFE . . . 137
    BUT THE SHOUT REACHED THE GIRL AND PUT HER LIGHT OUT. . . 195 PAUL'S WIFE . . . 143
    AS A GIRL GATHERED FROM THE BIRCH MYSELF . . . . 196 WILD GRAPES . . .   4
    AND GREW TO BE A LITTLE BOYISH GIRL . . . . 196 WILD GRAPES . . .   8
    DON'T YOU KNOW ANYTHING, YOU GIRL? LET GO!" . . . . 197 WILD GRAPES . . . 47
    I WAS A STRAPPING GIRL OF TWENTY THEN. . . . . 209 PAUPER WITCH OF GRAFTON 69
    A GIRL OF HIS AGE HE MET . . . . 313 BEARER OF EVIL TIDINGS 14
    A GIRL COULD ONLY SEE . . . . 340 THE SUBVERTED FLOWER . 48
    BUT THE GIRL FOUGHT THEM AND MADE A SCENE. . . . . 345 DISCOVERY OF MADEIRAS . 63
    AS A GIRL NO ONE GALLANTLY ATTENDS . . . . 386 THE FEAR OF MAN . .   1
    TO TRY ANOTHER. / JESSE BEL'S A GIRL . . . . 499 A MASQUE OF MERCY . . 159

GIRLS
   LIKE GIRLS ON HANDS AND KNEES THAT THROW THEIR HAIR . . . 121 BIRCHES 19
   A DOZEN GIRLS AND BOYS WE WERE. . . . . 265 THE BIRTHPLACE . . . 7
GIRL'S
   A GIRL'S GARDEN . . . . 133 A GIRL'S GARDEN . . . T
   MADE A GIRL'S MARRIAGE, AND RULED IN HER LIFE. . . . . 185 MAPLE 164
   (NO GIRL'S, OF COURSE, HAS STAYED THE SAME.) . . . . 265 THE BIRTHPLACE . . . 12
GIRTH
   THAT KEPT THE OAKS FROM GETTING ANY GIRTH. . . . . . 292 FIGURE IN THE DOORWAY . 4
GIST
   AND THIS GIST OF ALL . . . . 426 A NEVER NAUGHT SONG . 21
GIVE
   THE BRIDEGROOM THOUGHT IT LITTLE TO GIVE . . . . . . 8 LOVE AND A QUESTION . 25
   GIVE THE BURIED FLOWER A DREAM; . . . . 11 TO THE THAWING WIND . 3
   OH, GIVE US PLEASURE IN THE FLOWERS TODAY; . . . . . 12 A PRAYER IN SPRING . 1
   AND GIVE US NOT TO THINK SO FAR AWAY . . . . 12 A PRAYER IN SPRING . 2
   OH, GIVE US PLEASURE IN THE ORCHARD WHITE, ... 12 A PRAYER IN SPRING . 5
   CAN BUT GIVE EAR TO THAT SWEET CRY . . . . 20 THE TRIAL BY EXISTENCE 23
   WILL GLADLY GIVE UP PARADISE. . . . . 20 THE TRIAL BY EXISTENCE 28
   TO WHICH YOU GIVE THE ASSENTING VOICE." . . . . . . 21 THE TRIAL BY EXISTENCE 56
   AND TO WHOM I WAS LIKE TO GIVE OFFENSE. . . . . . . 34 MENDING WALL . . . 34
   SORRY THERE IS NO CUP TO GIVE YOU A DRINK. . . . . . 50 A HUNDRED COLLARS . . . 155
   A MAN MUST PARTLY GIVE UP BEING A MAN . . . . 52 HOME BURIAL 49
   APART WOULD MAKE ME OUT. GIVE ME MY CHANCE. . . . . 53 HOME BURIAL 61
   JUST TAKING WHAT NATURE IS WILLING TO GIVE, ... 61 BLUEBERRIES 55
   BUT WAIT UNTIL I GIVE YOU A HAND UP. . . . . 77 THE GENERATIONS OF MEN 121
   IT OUGHT TO GIVE A PURER ORACLE." . . . . 78 THE GENERATIONS OF MEN 134
   THE VOICES GIVE YOU WHAT YOU WISH TO HEAR." . . . . 78 THE GENERATIONS OF MEN 137
   "STRANGELY, IT'S ANYTHING THEY WISH TO GIVE." . . . . 78 THE GENERATIONS OF MEN 138
   OR I CAN'T GIVE MYSELF TO HEAR THE VOICES." . . . . 78 THE GENERATIONS OF MEN 147
   NOW GIVE ME YOUR HAND UP.--PICK ME THAT FLOWER." . . . 80 THE GENERATIONS OF MEN 207
   WHAT CHILDISHNESS HE WOULDN'T GIVE WAY TO. . . . . 86 THE HOUSEKEEPER . . . 133
   GIVE ME THE LANTERN." / "YOU DON'T WANT THE LANTERN." . 90 THE FEAR 33
   BUT YOU GIVE HIM THE ADVANTAGE WITH THIS LIGHT. . . . 91 THE FEAR 55
   HE WANTS TO GIVE ME LOTS AND LOTS OF MONEY . . . . . 98 THE SELF-SEEKER . . . 169
   WORTH THREE CENTS MORE TO GIVE AWAY THAN SELL, . . . 107 CHRISTMAS TREES . . . 56
   TO LOOK US OVER AND GIVE US HIS IDEA . . . . 115 IN THE HOME STRETCH . 149
   TO GIVE WHATEVER MIGHT CHANCE TO BE, ... 127 HOUSE FEAR 6
   PERHAPS BECAUSE HE LET US GIVE INSTEAD . . . . . . 127 THE SMILE 6
   TO GIVE HER A GARDEN PLOT . . . . 133 A GIRL'S GARDEN . . . 6
   AND GIVE YOU A CHANCE TO PUT SOME STRENGTH . . . . 133 A GIRL'S GARDEN . . . 15
   SO BAD.--GIVE ME AN HOUR FOR IT.--FO, HO, ... 143 SNOW 21
   SAYS IT WON'T DO. YOU'VE GOT TO GIVE IT UP." . . . . 147 SNOW 107
   AND BY SO DOING GIVE THESE THREE, LAMP, DOG, ... 148 SNOW 145
   MAY BE THE THING YOU HAVEN'T, YET YOU GIVE IT. . . . 148 SNOW 148
   SO FALSE IT IS THAT WHAT WE HAVEN'T WE CAN'T GIVE; . . 148 SNOW 149
   HE WANTS TO GIVE THE EDUCATIONAL . . . . 162 NEW HAMPSHIRE . . . 103
   AND GIVE SOMEONE THE SKIPPER IRESON'S RIDE. . . . . 163 NEW HAMPSHIRE . . . 143
   AND GIVE THE TEACHER A SCARE AS FROM HER FATHER. . . 180 MAPLE 32
   AND I GIVE UP"; WHICH LAST LOOK CAME TO NOTHING. . . 184 MAPLE 132
   "YOU GIVE HER ONE GOOD CRACK, SHE'S SNAP RAGHT OFF. . 186 THE AX-HELVE 26
   AND GIVE MYSELF OUT AS TWO DIFFERENT AGES, ... 196 WILD GRAPES 17
   AND GIVE GOOD MEASURE TO THE DEAD, THOUGH THANKLESS. . 200 PLACE FOR A THIRD . . 20
   IF I WAS TO CONSENT TO GIVE SOME SIGN . . . . . . 208 PAUPER WITCH OF GRAFTON 43
   GIVE A HEADSHAKE . . . . 211 AN EMPTY THREAT . . . 30
   HOWEVER NATURAL? GIVE YOU YOUR BOOKS! . . . . . . 215 A FOUNTAIN, A BOTTLE . 59
   HAD BEEN TOO SHORT TO SELL OR GIVE AWAY. . . . . . 217 A FOUNTAIN, A BOTTLE . 122
   AND GIVE UP SLEEP. . . . . 218 I WILL SING YOU ONE-O . 8
   OR GIVE SOME SIGN OF LIFE? BECAUSE YOU CAN'T. . . . 230 TWO LOOK AT TWO . . . 33
   "O FIREMAN, GIVE THE FIRE ANOTHER STOKE, ... 234 EVENING A SUGAR ORCHARD 5
   GIVE HER A CHILD AT EITHER KNEE FOR FOURTH JOY . . . 256 THE LOVELY BE CHOOSERS 31
   BUT GIVE HER FRIENDS, FOR THEN SHE DARE NOT TELL . . 257 THE LOVELY BE CHOOSERS 35
   GIVE HER THE COMFORT FOR HER SIXTH OF KNOWING . . . 257 THE LOVELY BE CHOOSERS 43
   TO GIVE IT COZIER SKIES . . . . 281 A DRUMLIN WOODCHUCK . 3
   TO GIVE A PROSPECT TO A PLAN . . . . 281 BLUE RIBBON AT AMESBURY 55
   HAVE A LITTLE WHISTLE WE GIVE, ... 282 A DRUMLIN WOODCHUCK . 14
   AND GIVE US THE LIFE OF THE MOVING-PICTURES' PROMISE . 286 A ROADSIDE STAND . . . 21
   WHEN YOU GIVE IT THE LIVID METAL-SAP. . . . . . . 306 A TRIAL RUN 3
   I'VE HAD TO GIVE MY INTERVAL FARM UP . . . . . . 316 BUILD SOIL 6
   AT THIRTY CENTS A BUSHEL. GIVE ME SHEEP. . . . . . 316 BUILD SOIL 12
   I MEAN THEY COULD BE TRUSTED TO GIVE THE ALARM . . . 317 BUILD SOIL 57
   IT CAN'T BE JUST TO GIVE THE ROBBER A CHANCE . . . 321 BUILD SOIL 166
   IMPORTUNATE TO GIVE THE HINT . . . . 327 A MISSIVE MISSILE . . 31
   I COULD GIVE ALL TO TIME . . . . 334 I COULD GIVE ALL . . . T
   I COULD GIVE ALL TO TIME EXCEPT--EXCEPT . . . . . 335 I COULD GIVE ALL . . . 11
   BUT GIVE ME WATER HEAVY ON THE HEAD . . . . . . 337 THE WIND AND THE RAIN . 38
   HAD TO GIVE HER THE FINAL LIFT . . . . 343 DISCOVERY OF MADEIRAS . 10
   HE SAID TO THE CAPTAIN, "GIVE COMMAND, ... 346 DISCOVERY OF MADEIRAS . 106
   AND GIVE US MORE THAN OUR SPOKESMAN BARGAINED FOR; . 349 OUR HOLD ON THE PLANET 4
   AND VERY WIDE THE CHOICE THEY SEEMED TO GIVE; . . . 354 THE LESSON FOR TODAY . 137
   WILL GIVE US BY SHORTCUT THE FINAL STAGE . . . . . 358 THE LOST FOLLOWER . . 13
   TO GIVE US A PIECE OF THEIR BILLS. . . . . . . 364 A NATURE NOTE 4
   AND WILL YOU GIVE ME SHELTER FOR THE NIGHT? . . . . 368 THE LITERATE FARMER AND 21
   TO GIVE DEVELOPMENTS THE FINAL SHOVE . . . . . . 369 THE LITERATE FARMER AND 42
   "AS LIBERALS WE'RE WILLING TO GIVE PLACE . . . . . 369 THE LITERATE FARMER AND 49
   GIVE US A GOOD CHEAP TWENTY-FOUR-HOUR DAY, ... 371 THE LITERATE FARMER AND 100
   TO GIVE THEM STILL MORE BUOYANCY IN FLIGHT. . . . . 387 INNATE HELIUM 5
   IT MAY NOT GIVE ME HOPE . . . . 389 ASTROMETAPHYSICAL . . 13
   CAN EVER GIVE US IS A NUISANCE BRAWL. . . . . . . 398 NO HOLY WARS FOR THEM . 14
   I LIKE TO GIVE MY ENEMIES A TRUCE." . . . . . . 406 FROM PLANE TO PLANE . 65
   WHY GIVE THE CONTROVERSY A RELAPSE? . . . . . . 407 FROM PLANE TO PLANE . 113
   NO ONE--NOT I--WOULD GIVE THEM UP FOR LOST . . . . 414 A CABIN IN THE CLEARING 13
   THE RULE IS, NEVER GIVE A CHILD A CHOICE. . . . . . 427 CONCEPT SELF-CONCEIVED 8
   WE CAN GIVE THE PART . . . . 441 KITTY HAWK 427
   AND SHE CAN ONLY GIVE THE CLASS A NOTION . . . . . 447 DOES NO ONE AT ALL EVER 40
   THE STATE'S ONE FUNCTION IS TO GIVE. . . . . . . 450 OUR DOOM TO BLOOM . . . 12
   I WOULD GIVE ANYTHING TO LEARN . . . . 451 A-WISHING WELL . . . 8
   GIVE EARTH ANOTHER SATELLITE. . . . . 451 A-WISHING WELL . . . 29

GIVE (CONTINUED)
    THERE IS NO ACT MORE KINGLY THAN TO GIVE?" . . . . . .   458 HOW HARD TO KEEP FROM   140
    "YES, BUT GIVE CHARACTER AND NOT JUST FOOD. . . . . . .   458 HOW HARD TO KEEP FROM   141
    A KING MUST GIVE HIS PEOPLE CHARACTER. " . . . .   458 HOW HARD TO KEEP FROM   142
    HOW SHALL I GIVE A PEOPLE CHARACTER?" . . . .   458 HOW HARD TO KEEP FROM   149
    NO ONE CAN GIVE THEM--THEY CAN SCARCE ATTAIN-- . . . . .   461 HOW HARD TO KEEP FROM   233
    OR GIVE HER A STAB OF THE TINE. . . . .   463 LINES IN DEJECTION .   . 18
    WE'VE JUST AGREED I DIDN'T HAVE TO GIVE.-- . . . . . .   477 A MASQUE OF REASON .   106
    YOU THOUGHT IT WAS AGREED YOU NEEDN'T GIVE THEM. . . . .   478 A MASQUE OF REASON .   144
    I GIVE YOU CREDIT FOR. MY FORTE IS TRUTH, ...   480 A MASQUE OF REASON .   190
    I'D GIVE MORE FOR ONE LEAST BEFOREHAND REASON . . . . .   482 A MASQUE OF REASON .   247
    THAT STRAIN AGAIN! GIVE ME EXCESS OF IT! . . . .   488 A MASQUE OF REASON .   418
    MORE TO GIVE HIS REALITY ITS DUE . . . .   489 A MASQUE OF REASON .   433
    AND GIVE YOU REST, POOR WANDERING JEW. / I'M NOT . . . .   498 A MASQUE OF MERCY .   133
    GIVE ME A HAND UP, IF WE ARE AGREED. . . . .   520 A MASQUE OF MERCY .   715
GIVEN
    TO HAVE GIVEN OUTRIGHT FOR THEM ALL SHE GAVE. . . . . .   57 THE BLACK COTTAGE .   . 59
    FOLKS IN HER DAY WERE GIVEN TO PLAIN SPEAKING. . . . . .   79 THE GENERATIONS OF MEN 181
    HE'S GIVEN HER TIME TO THINK OF SOMETHING ELSE. . . . .   84 THE HOUSEKEEPER . .   . 86
    HE MUST HAVE GIVEN THE HAND. HOWEVER IT WAS, ...   136 "OUT,OUT--"   17
    I'VE GIVEN UP MY SUMMER PLACE IN DUBLIN." . . . . . .   166 NEW HAMPSHIRE . . .   222
    ON MOUNTAINS? WHAT HAS GIVEN ME ASSURANCE . . . . . .   169 NEW HAMPSHIRE . . .   315
    OUR ACTUAL MOUNTAINS GIVEN IN A MAP . . . .   169 NEW HAMPSHIRE . . .   330
    THE STRONGEST THING THAT'S GIVEN US TO SEE WITH'S . . .   177 THE STAR-SPLITTER .   . 34
    OF BEING GIVEN ONE FOR CHRISTMAS GIFT, ...   178 THE STAR-SPLITTER .   . 55
    THUS HAD A NAME WITH MEANING, GIVEN IN DEATH, ...   185 MAPLE   163
    FROM THE SLAP I HAD JUST NOW GIVEN ITS HAND. . . . . .   205 THE WITCH OF COOS .   . 89
    ALMOST THE MOMENT HE WAS GIVEN AN OPENING, ...   206 THE WITCH OF COOS .   115
    HAS GIVEN MY HEART . . . .   221 DUST OF SNOW 5
    "WHAT IS IT, DEAR?" AND SHE HAD GIVEN ALL . . . . . .   230 NOT TO KEEP 9
    THEY HAD GIVEN HIM BACK TO HER, BUT NOT TO KEEP. . . . .   231 NOT TO KEEP   22
    WHERE SUMMER BIRDS HAD BEEN GIVEN HATCH, ...   253 THE THATCH 14
    THEY HAD JUST GIVEN THEMSELVES A LITTLE TWIST . . . . .   283 THE GOLD HESPERIDEE .   . 7
    ISN'T GIVEN A MOMENT'S ARREST-- . . . .   288 DEPARTMENTAL . . .   16
    AND IT HAD ALMOST GIVEN HIM TROUBLED DREAMS . . . . . .   290 OLD BARN AT THE BOTTOM   42
    AND YOU WERE GIVEN THIS SWIFTNESS, NOT FOR HASTE . . . .   300 THE MASTER SPEED . .   . 5
    AS COMPLETE AS THE APPLE HAD GIVEN MAN. . . . .   305 UNHARVESTED 9
    AND HIS MANDATES WERE GIVEN HEED TO . . . .   314 BEARER OF EVIL TIDINGS   31
    HE HAD BEEN GIVEN TO BEHOLD . . . .   417 AMERICA IS HARD TO SEE   28
    AS A GOD WHO HAD GIVEN US . . . .   417 AMERICA IS HARD TO SEE   35
    PROSE MADE OF, GIVEN AN AIR BY CHURCH INTONING. . . . .   461 HOW HARD TO KEEP FROM   222
    IT WILL BE FOUND THERE'S NO MORE GIVEN THERE . . . . .   483 A MASQUE OF REASON .   282
    JESSE HAS GIVEN PAUL THE RENT OF IT . . . .   514 A MASQUE OF MERCY .   560
    WE WERE NOT GIVEN EYES OR INTELLECT . . . .   515 A MASQUE OF MERCY .   586
GIVES
    WHICH GIVES THEM THE ADVANTAGE IN THE TRADE. . . . . .   95 THE SELF-SEEKER . .   . 64
    YOUR TONGUE GIVES SALT OR SUGAR IN YOUR HAND. . . . . .   131 THE BONFIRE   47
    HE PROMPTLY GIVES IT BACK, THAT IS IF STILL . . . . .   178 THE STAR-SPLITTER .   . 51
    WHICH GIVES HIM FOR HIMSELF A CHOICE OF LOTS . . . . .   202 PLACE FOR A THIRD .   . 81
    IT ONLY GIVES OUR WISH FOR BLUE A WHET. . . . .   220 FRAGMENTARY BLUE . .   . 8
    HE GIVES HIS HARNESS BELLS A SHAKE . . . .   224 STOPPING BY WOODS .   . 9
    GIVES ME BACK IN A SHINING SURFACE PICTURE . . . . . .   225 FOR ONCE SOMETHING .   . 4
    GIVES UP HIS ERRAND, AND LETS DEATH DESCEND . . . . . .   226 THE ONSET 8
    HEAVEN GIVES ITS GLIMPSES ONLY TO THOSE . . . .   248 A PASSING GLIMPSE .   . 11
    A FEATHER-HAMMER GIVES A DOUBLE KNOCK. . . . .   254 A WINTER EDEN 17
    GIVES A LEAP IN THE EAST. . . . .   261 CANIS MAJOR 4
    THAT REALLY TAKES AWAY INSTEAD OF GIVES. . . . .   279 THE WHITE-TAILED HORNET 55
    IT GIVES UP STANDING STRAIGHT AND GOES DOWN SWISHING. . .   349 TO A YOUNG WRETCH .   . 4
    IT GIVES US STRANGELY LITTLE AID, ...   403 SOMETHING LIKE A STAR .   16
    THAT GIVES OFF FROM A GARDEN GROUND AT NIGHT . . . . .   414 A CABIN IN THE CLEARING 16
    THE MYRRH TREE GIVES IT. SMELL THE ROSIN BURNING? . . .   473 A MASQUE OF REASON .   . 9
    IT GIVES A SENSE OF LETUP CALCULATED . . . .   475 A MASQUE OF REASON .   . 44
    BUT JONAH GIVES NO SIGN OF HAVING HEARD.) . . . . . .   518 A MASQUE OF MERCY .   668
GIVING
    THEY FALL FROM GIVING SHADE ABOVE, ...   25 IN HARDWOOD GROVES .   . 2
    HER GIVING SOMEHOW TOUCHED THE PRINCIPLE . . . .   57 THE BLACK COTTAGE .   . 60
    BUT I'M NOT SELLING THOSE, I'M GIVING THEM; . . . . .   95 THE SELF-SEEKER . .   . 70
    WHAT KEPT HIS EYES FROM GIVING BACK THE GAZE . . . . .   108 OLD MAN'S WINTER NIGHT   4
    BUT NOW ARE GIVING UP FOR COUNTRY DARKNESS." . . . . .   112 IN THE HOME STRETCH .   59
    "WE'RE GIVING YOU OUR CHANCES ON DE FARM." . . . . . .   114 IN THE HOME STRETCH .   108
    TO PLEASE THE BOY BY GIVING HIM THE HALF HOUR . . . . .   136 "OUT,OUT--"   11
    WHERE WOULD THE FAIRNESS BE IN GIVING ME . . . . . .   183 MAPLE   115
    GRIM GIVING TO DO OVER FOR THEM BOTH. . . . .   231 NOT TO KEEP   18
    INTENT ON GIVING AND TAKING PAIN. . . . .   252 THE THATCH 2
    AND IN CONJUNCTION GIVING QUITE A SPREAD. . . . . . .   269 THE BEAR   21
    THAT DAY, GIVING A LOOSE TO MY SOUL, ...   275 TWO TRAMPS IN MUD TIME   15
    FOR MERELY GIVING YOU ONCE MORE GENTLE PROOF . . . . .   306 NOT QUITE SOCIAL . .   . 6
    NOW TAKE THE DOCTOR--" / THEY WERE GIVING CORN . . . .   404 FROM PLANE TO PLANE .   12
    IN CHRISTMAS GIVING, SO THEY CAN ESCAPE . . . .   408 FROM PLANE TO PLANE .   139
    OR GIVING ME A NOBLEMAN'S ESTATE. . . . .   457 HOW HARD TO KEEP FROM   121
    BUT ALL YOU THOUGHT OF GIVING ME WAS FOOD. . . . . . .   457 HOW HARD TO KEEP FROM   122
    YOU'RE GIVING ME. YOU SAY WE GROPED THIS OUT. . . . . .   482 A MASQUE OF REASON .   242
GLACIER
    THE CHISEL WORK OF AN ENORMOUS GLACIER . . . .   377 DIRECTIVE   16
GLAD
    SHE'S GLAD THE BIRDS ARE GONE AWAY, ...   7 MY NOVEMBER GUEST .   . 8
    SHE'S GLAD HER SIMPLE WORSTED GRAY . . . .   7 MY NOVEMBER GUEST .   . 9
    BUT GLAD WITH HIM, I WORKED AS WITH HIS AID, ...   23 THE TUFT OF FLOWERS .   35
    AND I WAS GLAD FOR THEE, ...   28 MY BUTTERFLY . . .   20
    AND GLAD FOR ME, I WIST. . . . .   28 MY BUTTERFLY . . .   21
    "ONE WOULD SUPPOSE THEY MIGHT NOT BE AS GLAD . . . . .   49 A HUNDRED COLLARS .   149
    I'M JUST AS GLAD SHE MADE ME KEEP HANDS OFF, ...   58 THE BLACK COTTAGE .   104
    FOR THE PICKING. THE RASCAL, HE SAID HE'D BE GLAD . . .   61 BLUEBERRIES   71
    I DIDN'T MAKE YOU KNOW HOW GLAD I WAS . . . .   62 A SERVANT TO SERVANTS . 1
    WHETHER I AM GLAD, SORRY, OR ANYTHING. . . . .   63 A SERVANT TO SERVANTS . 12
    NO WONDER I WAS GLAD TO GET AWAY. . . . .   67 A SERVANT TO SERVANTS . 148
    I WAS GLAD THOUGH, NO END, WHEN WE MOVED OUT, ...   67 A SERVANT TO SERVANTS . 151
    AND BE GLAD OF A GOOD ROOF OVERHEAD. . . . .   67 A SERVANT TO SERVANTS . 165

GLAD (CONTINUED)
    AND SUCH IS LOVE AND GLAD TO BE. . . . . 120 BOND AND FREE . . .   9
    TOO GLAD FOR THE ONE THING . . . . 126 LONELINESS   8
    MUCH SAY IN THE MATTER, AND I'M JUST AS GLAD . . . . 152 SNOW 257
    WE'RE GLAD. OH, SAY NO MORE ABOUT IT, MAN. . . . . . 155 SNOW 332
    WASN'T SHE GLAD NOW? EVERYTHING SEEMED WON, ... 230 NOT TO KEEP 11
    BE GLAD OF WATER, BUT DON'T FORGET. . . . . 276 TWO TRAMPS IN MUD TIME 37
    SOME OF YOU WILL BE GLAD I DID WHAT I DID, ... 306 NOT QUITE SOCIAL .   1
    NO ONE CAN KNOW HOW GLAD I AM TO FIND . . . . 358 A CONSIDERABLE SPECK . 32
    "TRAVELER, I'M GLAD YOU ASKED ABOUT THAT LIGHT. . . . 368 THE LITERATE FARMER AND 23
    WEEP FOR WHAT LITTLE THINGS COULD MAKE THEM GLAD. . . 378 DIRECTIVE 44
    I WAS GLAD HE LAUGHED. . . . . 430 KITTY HAWK 66
    TO MAKE THEMSELVES GLAD . . . . 432 KITTY HAWK 132
    NEVER HAVE I BEEN SAD OR GLAD . . . . 467 QUANDARY   1
    JONAH, I'M GLAD, NOT SAD, TO HEAR YOU SAY . . . . . 501 A MASQUE OF MERCY . 213
    LET ME REPEAT: I'M GLAD TO HEAR YOU SAY . . . . . . 507 A MASQUE OF MERCY . 360
    KEEPER, I'M GLAD YOU THINK IT BEAUTIFUL. . . . . . . 512 A MASQUE OF MERCY . 494
GLADE
    ONCE THEY CAME ON A MAPLE IN A GLADE, ... 184 MAPLE 144
    ONE DAY MY BROTHER LED ME TO A GLADE . . . . 196 WILD GRAPES 19
GLADES
    THE YOUNG SPRUCE MADE A SUITE OF GLADES . . . . . . 380 AN UNSTAMPED LETTER IN   9
GLADLY
    WILL GLADLY GIVE UP PARADISE. . . . . 20 THE TRIAL BY EXISTENCE 28
GLADNESS
    BUT FROM SHEER MORNING GLADNESS AT THE BRIM. . . . . 23 THE TUFT OF FLOWERS . 28
GLANCE
    SINCE FIRST I SAW THEE GLANCE, ... 28 MY BUTTERFLY 12
    THE SPINNER SAW IT AT A GLANCE. . . . . 273 A LONE STRIKER . . . 25
GLANCES
    AND EXCHANGED TROUBLED GLANCES OVER LIFE. . . . . . 293 AT WOODWARD'S GARDENS . 13
GLANCING
    "YOU CAN JUST SEE IT GLANCING OFF THE ROOF . . . . . 143 SNOW   8
GLARE
    A BLINDING HEADLIGHT SHIFTED GLARE . . . . 383 WERE I IN TROUBLE . .   3
GLASS (SEE BURNING-GLASS, CUT-GLASS, LOOKING-GLASS, PLATE-GLASS)
    MELT THE GLASS AND LEAVE THE STICKS . . . . 11 TO THE THAWING WIND .   9
    I GOT FROM LOOKING THROUGH A PANE OF GLASS . . . . . 68 AFTER APPLE-PICKING . 10
    "NOT IN A GLASS CASE, THEN?" / "HE'D NEED A TALL ONE: . 86 THE HOUSEKEEPER . . . 148
    HE'S BEEN IN A GLASS CASE, AS YOU MAY SAY, ... 86 THE HOUSEKEEPER . . . 150
    SUCH HEAPS OF BROKEN GLASS TO SWEEP AWAY . . . . . . 121 BIRCHES 12
    BEFORE THE MYSTERY OF GLASS!. . . . . 128 THE OFT-REPEATED DREAM   8
    HE GOT A GOOD GLASS FOR SIX HUNDRED DOLLARS. . . . . 178 THE STAR-SPLITTER . . 74
    IT CAME BACK VAGUELY AT THE GLASS ONE DAY, ... 181 MAPLE 40
    WE TROD UNCOMFORTABLY ON CRUNCHING GLASS . . . . . . 216 A FOUNTAIN, A BOTTLE . 89
    WITH STONE AND LEAD TO UNPROTECTED GLASS: . . . . . 216 A FOUNTAIN, A BOTTLE . 103
    MY WINDOW GLASS . . . . 218 I WILL SING YOU ONE-O . 36
    WAS A SPRING WITH A BROKEN DRINKING GLASS, ... 263 THE TIMES TABLE . . .   2
    WILL GET THIS PLASM IN ITS GOGGLE GLASS." . . . . . . 270 THE EGG AND THE MACHINE 30
    CONSIDER WHAT THEY TREASURE UNDER GLASS, ... 290 OLD BARN AT THE BOTTOM   33
    AND THE GLASS WAS THE MONKEYS', NOT THE BOY'S. . . . 293 AT WOODWARD'S GARDENS . 23
    THEY BIT THE GLASS AND LISTENED FOR THE FLAVOR. . . 293 AT WOODWARD'S GARDENS . 27
    ANOTHER SHOT THROUGH GLASS, ... 298 ON TAKING FROM THE TOP   11
    THE WETTER GROUND LIKE GLASS . . . . 301 NEITHER OUT FAR NOR IN   7
    THAT IN A GOOD GLASS MAY BE SEEN TO CRAWL . . . . . 352 THE LESSON FOR TODAY . 71
    BEHIND THE PORTHOLE'S SLAB OF GLASS . . . . 363 ASSURANCE   2
    IF NOT, A GLASS OF MILK WILL BE ALL RIGHT." . . . . . 368 THE LITERATE FARMER AND 22
    AND SAVE HERSELF FROM BREAKING WINDOW GLASS. . . . . 445 QUESTIONING FACES . .   2
    IN A GLASS OF CIDER . . . . 468 IN A GLASS OF CIDER .   T
    (SHE HAS HER OWN GLASS IN A VACANT CHAIR.) . . . . . 496 A MASQUE OF MERCY . . 84
GLASSED-IN
    TO GLASSED-IN CHILDREN AT THE WINDOWSILL. . . . . . 445 QUESTIONING FACES . .   6
GLASSES
    AND VIEWED IT OVER HIS GLASSES FUNNY-EYED, ... 190 THE GRINDSTONE . . . 70
GLEAM
    LIKE LOCKS BLOWN FORWARD IN THE GLEAM OF EYES, . . . 250 ONCE BY THE PACIFIC .   6
    YOU DON'T BELIEVE THAT THAT FIRST-WATER GLEAM . . . 370 THE LITERATE FARMER AND 62
GLEE
    WHERE WITH A GLEE NO LESS FOR BEING GRIM . . . . . . 394 HAEC FABULA DOCET . . 15
GLIMPSE
    I HAD A GLIMPSE THROUGH CURTAIN LACES . . . . 102 GOOD HOURS   7
    IT WAS THE ONLY GLIMPSE THAT ANYONE . . . . 195 PAUL'S WIFE 129
    THIS GLIMPSE OF LINGERING PERSON IN ELIZA, ... 200 PLACE FOR A THIRD . . 16
    A PASSING GLIMPSE . . . . 248 A PASSING GLIMPSE . .   T
GLIMPSES
    HEAVEN GIVES ITS GLIMPSES ONLY TO THOSE . . . . . . 248 A PASSING GLIMPSE . . 11
GLINT
    THAT THE LOOSE MOUNTAIN LATELY SEEN TO GLINT . . . . 361 A LOOSE MOUNTAIN . . 14
GLITTERING
    IT GENTLY THREW US A GLITTERING SHOWER DOWN. . . . . 349 OUR HOLD ON THE PLANET   7
GLOAMING
    DO YOU KNOW ME IN THE GLOAMING, ... 12 FLOWER-GATHERING . .   5
GLOBAL
    CAN NEVER HOPE TO WAGE A GLOBAL MISSION. . . . . . . 398 NO HOLY WARS FOR THEM . 12
GLOBE
    HIS JAPANESE CREPE-PAPER GLOBE FOR TROPHY? . . . . . 278 THE WHITE-TAILED HORNET 18
    THE WORLD'S ONE GLOBE, HUMAN SOCIETY . . . . 322 BUILD SOIL 194
    ANOTHER SOFTER GLOBE THAT SLIGHTLY FLATTENED . . . . 322 BUILD SOIL 195
GLOBES
    THE PATINA OF THIS THE LEAST OF GLOBES. . . . . . . 352 THE LESSON FOR TODAY . 72
GLOBULE
    A GLOBULE OF QUICKSILVER IN YOUR HAND . . . . 179 THE STAR-SPLITTER . . 90
GLOOM
    WERE NOT, AS 'TWERE, THE MEREST MASK OF GLOOM, . . .   5 INTO MY OWN   3
    ACROSS THE SILL FROM THE OUTER GLOOM. . . . . 15 IN A VALE   9
    THOUGHT CLEAVES THE INTERSTELLAR GLOOM . . . . 120 BOND AND FREE . . . 11
    AT THE SHINY DESERT WITH SPOTS OF GLOOM . . . . . . 291 ON HEART'S BEGINNING TO 27
    GOOD GLOOM ON HER WAS THROWN AWAY. . . . . 383 THE NIGHT LIGHT . . .   5

GLOOMY
      "END IS A GLOOMY WORD." / "IS IT TOO LATE . . . . 117 IN THE HOME STRETCH . 187
      LIKE A LONE ACTOR ON A GLOOMY STAGE-- . . . . 160 NEW HAMPSHIRE   . . . 46
GLORIFYING
      I AM RIGHT, THEN? / --IN GLORIFYING COURAGE. . . . . . 519 A MASQUE OF MERCY . . 692
GLORIOUS
      THE GLORIOUS BARDS OF MASSACHUSETTS SEEM . . . . 167 NEW HAMPSHIRE   . . . 262
GLORY   (SEE MORNING-GLORY)
      WE SAW LEAVES GO TO GLORY, ... 359 NOVEMBER   1
      EVERYONE KNOWS THE GLORY OF THE TWAIN . . . . 423 FOR JOHN F. KENNEDY . 46
      GLORY IS OUT OF DATE IN LIFE AND ART. . . . . 423 FOR JOHN F. KENNEDY . 50
      RIGHT DOWN TO NOW IN GLORY UPON GLORY. . . . . 423 FOR JOHN F. KENNEDY . 53
      THE GLORY OF A NEXT AUGUSTAN AGE . . . . 424 FOR JOHN F. KENNEDY . 71
      IS TO STEAL THE GLORY . . . . 430 KITTY HAWK   74
      CONTEMPLATE GLORY. THERE WILL BE A LIGHT. . . . . 517 A MASQUE OF MERCY . . 629
GLOSSY
      NEARBY, ALL DARK IN EVERY GLOSSY WINDOW. . . . . 89 THE FEAR   4
      OF GLOSSY BIRDS LIKE RIPPLES OVER ROCKS. . . . . 240 OUR SINGING STRENGTH . 34
      AND BROUGHT IT OVER GLOSSY WATER, GREATER, ... 245 THE FREEDOM OF THE MOON 10
      ON GLOSSY WIRES ARTISTICALLY BENT . . . . 309 WASPISH   1
GLOVE
      AND FIT THE EARTH LIKE A LEATHER GLOVE. . . . . 26 IN HARDWOOD GROVES . . 4
GLOVELESS
      HERE'S FIRST A GLOVELESS HAND WARM FROM MY POCKET, . . . 356 A MOTH SEEN IN WINTER . 1
GLOW
      AND IN THE MORNING GLOW . . . . 12 FLOWER-GATHERING   . . 2
      HILL ATMOSPHERE NOT CEASE TO GLOW, ... 234 EVENING A SUGAR ORCHARD 9
      TO THE MIDNIGHT SKY A SUNSET GLOW. . . . . 241 NEED OF BEING VERSED . 2
      THE FINAL GOLDEN GLOW . . . . 361 ALMOST TWO THOUSAND . 7
GLOWED
      ARMED WITH A SCYTHE AND SPECTACLES THAT GLOWED. . . . . 189 THE GRINDSTONE   . . 30
      AT EVERY POINT AND FACET GLOWED . . . . 332 ALL REVELATION   . . . 14
GLOWING
      HER FACE ROSE-RED WITH THE GLOWING COAL . . . .   8 LOVE AND A QUESTION . 19
GLUED
      (IT RAN AS IF IT WASN'T GREASED BUT GLUED); . . . . . . 190 THE GRINDSTONE   . . . 61
GNAW
      IF SOMEONE HADN'T SAID TO GNAW THE POSTS . . . . 209 PAUPER WITCH OF GRAFTON 54
      HE DON'T GNAW TREES AND POSTS AND FENCES TOO. . . . . . 209 PAUPER WITCH OF GRAFTON 67
GNAWED
      HE'D BET HUSE WAS A CRIBBER AND HAD GNAWED . . . . . . 209 PAUPER WITCH OF GRAFTON 60
      THEY FOUND HE'D GNAWED THE FOUR POSTS OF HIS BED, ... 209 PAUPER WITCH OF GRAFTON 62
      NOT THAT HE HADN'T GNAWED THE HITCHING POSTS . . . . . . 209 PAUPER WITCH OF GRAFTON 64
GNAWING
      THEY MADE HIM KEEP ON GNAWING TILL HE WHINED. . . . . . 209 PAUPER WITCH OF GRAFTON 58
GNAWS
      GNAWS IN THE STABLE AIN'T NO PROOF TO ME . . . . 209 PAUPER WITCH OF GRAFTON 66
GNOMES
      LIKE GNOMES THAT HID US FROM THE MOON, ... 18 GOING FOR WATER . . . 14
GO
      WHEN I GO UP THROUGH THE MOWING FIELD, ...   8 A LATE WALK 1
      IT COSTS NO INWARD STRUGGLE NOT TO GO, ... 10 STORM FEAR   7
      MELT IT AS THE ICE WILL GO; . . . . 11 TO THE THAWING WIND . 8
      TO MAKE ME SAD TO GO. . . . . 12 FLOWER-GATHERING   . . 4
      NOT LOTH TO HAVE EXCUSE TO GO, ... 18 GOING FOR WATER . . . 5
      THE ANGEL HOSTS WITH FRESHNESS GO, ... 20 THE TRIAL BY EXISTENCE 13
      BUT THE PURE FATE TO WHICH YOU GO . . . . 21 THE TRIAL BY EXISTENCE 53
      AND ONCE I MARKED HIS FLIGHT GO ROUND AND ROUND, ... 22 THE TUFT OF FLOWERS . 15
      THEY MUST GO DOWN PAST THINGS COMING UP. . . . . 26 IN HARDWOOD GROVES . . 7
      THEY MUST GO DOWN INTO THE DARK DECAYED. . . . . 26 IN HARDWOOD GROVES . . 8
      WHAT MATTER IF WE GO CLEAR TO THE WEST, ... 27 A LINE-STORM SONG . . 21
      TOMORROW THEY MAY FORM AND GO. . . . . 27 OCTOBER 6
      AND LET THEM GO SCRAPING AND CREEPING . . . . 30 RELUCTANCE   10
      TO GO WITH THE DRIFT OF THINGS, ... 30 RELUCTANCE   21
      WE KEEP THE WALL BETWEEN US AS WE GO. . . . . 33 MENDING WALL   . . . 15
      HE WILL NOT GO BEHIND HIS FATHER'S SAYING, ... 34 MENDING WALL   . . . 43
      HE WANTED TO GO OVER THAT. BUT MOST OF ALL . . . . . . 37 DEATH OF THE HIRED MAN 85
      "HOME IS THE PLACE WHERE, WHEN YOU HAVE TO GO THERE, . . 38 DEATH OF THE HIRED MAN 118
      WHY DOESN'T HE GO THERE? HIS BROTHER'S RICH, ... 39 DEATH OF THE HIRED MAN 128
      YOU MUST GO IN AND SEE WHAT YOU CAN DO. . . . . 39 DEATH OF THE HIRED MAN 150
      "I HAVEN'T BEEN. GO, LOOK, SEE FOR YOURSELF. . . . . . . 40 DEATH OF THE HIRED MAN 155
      HE TRIED THIS SIDE. I'VE ALWAYS MEANT TO GO . . . . . . 43 THE MOUNTAIN   . . . 80
      WHAT WOULD I DO? GO IN MY OVERALLS. . . . . 43 THE MOUNTAIN   . . . 84
      STOPS WHEN SHE LIKES: I TELL HER WHEN TO GO. . . . . . . 49 A HUNDRED COLLARS . 140
      I GO NOWHERE ON PURPOSE: I HAPPEN BY.-- . . . . 50 A HUNDRED COLLARS . 154
      LIE DOWN--LET YOURSELF GO AND GET SOME SLEEP. . . . . . 50 A HUNDRED COLLARS . 161
      "AMY' DON'T GO TO SOMEONE ELSE THIS TIME. . . . . 52 HOME BURIAL 39
      SHE MOVED THE LATCH A LITTLE. "DON'T--DON'T GO. . . . . 53 HOME BURIAL 56
      "THERE YOU GO SNEERING NOW'" / "I'M NOT, I'M NOT' . . . . 53 HOME BURIAL 67
      YOU COULDN'T CARE' THE NEAREST FRIENDS CAN GO . . . . . 54 HOME BURIAL 97
      THEY MIGHT AS WELL NOT TRY TO GO AT ALL. . . . . 54 HOME BURIAL 99
      YOU WON'T GO NOW. YOU'RE CRYING. CLOSE THE DOOR. . . . . 54 HOME BURIAL 109
      "YOU--OH, YOU THINK THE TALK IS ALL. I MUST GO-- . . . . 54 HOME BURIAL 112
      "WHERE DO YOU MEAN TO GO? FIRST TELL ME THAT. . . . . . 55 HOME BURIAL 115
      WE ROSE TO GO. SUNSET BLAZED ON THE WINDOWS. . . . . . . 59 THE BLACK COTTAGE . 127
      WE'LL GO IN THE MORNING, THAT IS, IF IT'S CLEAR, ... 61 BLUEBERRIES 82
      AND LET THEM GO AND MAKE THEM TWANG, UNTIL . . . . 66 A SERVANT TO SERVANTS .135
      I S'POSE I'VE GOT TO GO THE ROAD I'M GOING: . . . . . . 67 A SERVANT TO SERVANTS .159
      I'D RATHER YOU'D NOT GO UNLESS YOU MUST. . . . . 68 A SERVANT TO SERVANTS .177
      IF YE WANT HIM, YE CAN GO AND DIG HIM OUT.' . . . . . . 72 THE CODE   85
      THEY EXCAVATED MORE. 'GO KEEP HIS WIFE . . . . 72 THE CODE   94
      "YES, YOU MUST GO; WE CAN'T STAY HERE FOREVER. . . . . . 77 THE GENERATIONS OF MEN 120
      I LET YOU SAY ALL THAT. BUT I MUST GO NOW." . . . . . . 80 THE GENERATIONS OF MEN 202
      "YES, WHAT'S IT ALL ABOUT? WHEN DID SHE GO?" . . . . . . 82 THE HOUSEKEEPER . . 21
      "IT WILL GO HARD WITH JOHN. WHAT WILL HE DO? . . . . . . 82 THE HOUSEKEEPER . . 28
      HAVEN'T AS GOOD. THEY DON'T GO WITH THE FARM. . . . . . 85 THE HOUSEKEEPER . . 114
      WE HAVE TO GO." / "YOU MEAN THAT'S JOHN'S IDEA." . . . . 85 THE HOUSEKEEPER . . 131
      "DO GO ALONG WITH HIM AND STOP HIS SHOUTING." . . . . . 89 THE HOUSEKEEPER . . 212

	PAGE	TITLE	LINE

GO (CONTINUED)
```
"JOEL, I'LL HAVE TO LOOK. I CAN'T GO IN, . . . . . .  .  89 THE FEAR . . . . .  . 14
HE'S COMING TOWARDS US. JOEL, GO IN--PLEASE.  .  .  .  .  90 THE FEAR . . . . .  . 39
HARK!--I DON'T HEAR HIM NOW. BUT PLEASE GO IN."  .  .  .  90 THE FEAR . . . . .  . 40
AND I CAN'T STAND IT. JOEL, LET ME GO!"  .  .  .  .  .  .  91 THE FEAR . . . . .  . 48
AND LET YOU SEE." / "YES, DO.--JOEL, GO BACK!"  .  .  .  .  92 THE FEAR . . . . .  . 75
THERE! THERE'S THE BELL. HE'S RUNG. BUT YOU GO DOWN  .  .  95 THE SELF-SEEKER . . .  . 88
"WELL, ANNE, GO, DEARIE. OUR AFFAIR WILL WAIT.  .  .  .  .  98 THE SELF-SEEKER . . . 167
I'LL PUT YOU OUT WITH ANNE. BE GOOD OR GO."  .  .  .  .  .  99 THE SELF-SEEKER . . . 186
GO OUTDOORS IF YOU WANT TO FIGHT. SPARE ME.  .  .  .  .  . 100 THE SELF-SEEKER . . . 212
I'LL GO OUTDOORS, BY GAD, AND WON'T COME BACK."  .  .  .  . 100 THE SELF-SEEKER . . . 222
NO, I WILL GO ON FARTHER--AND WE SHALL SEE."  .  .  .  .  . 101 THE WOOD-PILE . . .  .  3
TO SELL THEM OFF THEIR FEET TO GO IN CARS  .  .  .  .  .  . 106 CHRISTMAS TREES . .  . 17
YOU CAN TONIGHT, AND GO. IT'S ALMOST DARK;  .  .  .  .  .  . 111 IN THE HOME STRETCH . 16
TO COME AS HERE I STAND AND GO THE ROUND  .  .  .  .  .  .  . 111 IN THE HOME STRETCH . 27
YOU AND I, DEAR, WILL GO WITH SOFTER STEPS  .  .  .  .  .  . 111 IN THE HOME STRETCH . 41
I ONLY SEE THE YEARS. THEY COME AND GO  .  .  .  .  .  .  .  . 112 IN THE HOME STRETCH . 47
THE STOVE! BEFORE THEY GO! KNOCK ON THE WINDOW;  .  .  .  . 113 IN THE HOME STRETCH . 75
"DID THEY MAKE SOMETHING LONESOME GO THROUGH YOU?  .  .  . 114 IN THE HOME STRETCH . 122
THE FIRST THING IN THE MORNING, OUT WE GO  .  .  .  .  .  . 117 IN THE HOME STRETCH . 195
TO GO THE ROUND OF APPLE, CHERRY, PEACH,  .  .  .  .  .  .  . 117 IN THE HOME STRETCH . 196
I DON'T KNOW WHERE IT'S LIKELY TO GO BETTER.  .  .  .  .  . 122 BIRCHES . . . . .  . 53
I'D LIKE TO GO BY CLIMBING A BIRCH TREE,  .  .  .  .  .  .  . 122 BIRCHES . . . . .  . 54
AND GO ALONG WITH YOU ERE YOU LOSE SIGHT  .  .  .  .  .  .  . 124 PUTTING IN THE SEED .  7
AND PLOD: I GO UP TO THE STONE WALL  .  .  .  .  .  .  .  .  . 124 A TIME TO TALK . .  .  9
"OH, LET'S GO UP THE HILL AND SCARE OURSELVES,  .  .  .  .  . 129 THE BONFIRE . . .  .  1
HOW VILLAGE THINGS GO,  .  .  .  .  .  .  .  .  .  .  .  .  . 134 A GIRL'S GARDEN .  . 42
BUT IN NO HUSH THEY STRING IT: THEY GO PAST  .  .  .  .  .  . 141 THE LINE-GANG . .  .  8
IT'S TOO LONG A STORY TO GO INTO NOW.  .  .  .  .  .  .  .  . 142 THE VANISHING RED .  . 10
AND THREE MILES MORE TO GO!" / "DON'T LET HIM GO.  .  .  .  . 145 SNOW . . . . .  . 62
"HE SHAN'T GO--THERE!" / "IT IS A NIGHT, MY DEAR."  .  .  . 145 SNOW . . . . .  . 80
HE'S HERE. I LEAVE HIM ALL TO YOU. GO IN .  .  .  .  .  .  . 146 SNOW . . . . .  . 103
WHO HAVE TO GO OUT INTO IT ALONE."  .  .  .  .  .  .  .  .  . 149 SNOW . . . . .  . 170
NOW YOU AND I WOULD GO TO NO SUCH LENGTH.  .  .  .  .  .  .  . 149 SNOW . . . . .  . 187
WE THOUGHT YOU WERE DECIDING NOT TO GO--  .  .  .  .  .  .  . 150 SNOW . . . . .  . 198
"BUT WHY, WHEN NO ONE WANTS YOU TO, GO ON?  .  .  .  .  .  . 151 SNOW . . . . .  . 233
"WELL, THERE'S--THE STORM. THAT SAYS I MUST GO ON.  .  .  . 151 SNOW . . . . .  . 240
YOU'D BETTER DRESS: YOU WON'T GO BACK TO BED.  .  .  .  .  . 152 SNOW . . . . .  . 273
WHY DID YOU LET HIM GO?'" / "ASKED WHY WE LET HIM?  .  .  . 153 SNOW . . . . .  . 291
YOU DON'T SUPPOSE?--SHE WOULDN'T GO OUTDOORS?"  .  .  .  .  . 154 SNOW . . . . .  . 305
I CAN'T HELP THINKING THOSE ARE TESTS TO GO BY.  .  .  .  . 162 NEW HAMPSHIRE . .  . 99
"I GO NO MORE TO SUMMER IN NEW HAMPSHIRE.  .  .  .  .  .  .  . 166 NEW HAMPSHIRE . . . 221
SHE SAID, "GO READ YOUR OWN BOOKS AND FIND OUT."  .  .  .  . 166 NEW HAMPSHIRE . . . 227
"GO 'LONG," I SAID TO HIM, HE TO HIS HORSE.  .  .  .  .  .  . 168 NEW HAMPSHIRE . . . 300
COMMANDED IN A DREAM, FOREVER GO  .  .  .  .  .  .  .  .  .  . 173 A STAR IN A STONEBOAT . 35
I MUST GO MEASURING STONE WALLS, PERCH ON PERCH;  .  .  .  . 173 A STAR IN A STONEBOAT . 45
IT MUST BE I WANT LIFE TO GO ON LIVING.  .  .  .  .  .  .  . 176 THE CENSUS-TAKER .  . 64
BUT WHAT WE MISS WE GO TO HIM AND ASK FOR.  .  .  .  .  .  . 178 THE STAR-SPLITTER .  . 50
TO MAKE IT GO WELL WITH THE WAY SHE LOOKED.  .  .  .  .  .  . 181 MAPLE . . . . .  . 43
THESE HANDS HAVE HELPED IT GO, AND EVEN RACE;  .  .  .  .  . 188 THE GRINDSTONE . .  .  4
THAN THE GRINDSTONE CAN BOAST TO STAND OR GO.  .  .  .  .  . 189 THE GRINDSTONE . .  . 13
THEY SEEMED TO ASK HIM JUST TO SEE HIM GO,  .  .  .  .  .  . 191 PAUL'S WIFE . . .  . 23
SOMETHING WAS GOING TO GO WITH THEIR SLAMBANGING.  .  .  .  . 193 PAUL'S WIFE . . .  . 68
ALL DUG TO GO A-FISHING IN." TO PAUL  .  .  .  .  .  .  .  . 193 PAUL'S WIFE . . .  . 82
HOLD ON WITH ALL YOUR MIGHT WHEN I LET GO."  .  .  .  .  .  . 197 WILD GRAPES . . .  . 40
TO LOUD CRIES FROM MY BROTHER OF "LET GO!  .  .  .  .  .  .  . 197 WILD GRAPES . . .  . 46
DON'T YOU KNOW ANYTHING, YOU GIRL? LET GO!"  .  .  .  .  .  . 197 WILD GRAPES . . .  . 47
I HAD NOT LEARNED TO LET GO WITH THE HANDS,  .  .  .  .  .  . 199 WILD GRAPES . . .  . 96
TO WISH IN VAIN TO LET GO WITH THE MIND--  .  .  .  .  .  .  . 199 WILD GRAPES . . . 101
THAT I NEED LEARN TO LET GO WITH THE HEART.  .  .  .  .  .  . 199 WILD GRAPES . . . 103
THE FLOWERS WILL GO ON WITH GRIEF AWHILE,  .  .  .  .  .  .  . 200 PLACE FOR A THIRD .  . 28
THEN TURNED HIM OUT TO GO ON OTHER ERRANDS  .  .  .  .  .  . 201 PLACE FOR A THIRD .  . 53
THAT IS, IF FACTS IS WHAT THEY WANT TO GO BY.  .  .  .  .  . 207 PAUPER WITCH OF GRAFTON 11
TO GO WEST TO A WORSE FIGHT WITH THE DESERT.  .  .  .  .  .  . 213 A FOUNTAIN, A BOTTLE . 12
LET'S TALK ABOUT IT." / "LET'S GO SEE THE PLACE."  .  .  .  . 213 A FOUNTAIN, A BOTTLE . 16
TO READ THE STONES AND GO AWAY  .  .  .  .  .  .  .  .  .  . 221 IN A DISUSED GRAVEYARD 7
AND LISTEN--HOW IT OUGHT TO GO!  .  .  .  .  .  .  .  .  .  . 224 THE AIM WAS SONG .  .  8
AND MILES TO GO BEFORE I SLEEP,  .  .  .  .  .  .  .  .  .  . 225 STOPPING BY WOODS .  . 15
AND MILES TO GO BEFORE I SLEEP.  .  .  .  .  .  .  .  .  .  . 225 STOPPING BY WOODS .  . 16
AND I SHALL SEE THE SNOW ALL GO DOWNHILL  .  .  .  .  .  .  . 226 THE ONSET . . .  . 18
IN ONE LAST LOOK THE WAY THEY MUST NOT GO,  .  .  .  .  .  . 229 TWO LOOK AT TWO .  . 10
CAN CURE ME OF TO GO AGAIN." THE SAME .  .  .  .  .  .  .  . 230 NOT TO KEEP . .  . 17
EXCEPT FORGET TO GO IN FEAR PERHAPS.  .  .  .  .  .  .  .  . 231 A BROOK IN THE CITY . 19
HOWEVER FAR YOU MUST GO FOR BRICKS,  .  .  .  .  .  .  .  .  . 232 THE KITCHEN CHIMNEY .  5
ALL CRYING, "WE WILL GO WITH YOU, O WIND!"  .  .  .  .  .  . 236 MISGIVING . . . .  .  1
BUT A SLEEP OPPRESSES THEM AS THEY GO,  .  .  .  .  .  .  .  . 236 MISGIVING . . . .  .  3
AS THEY ARE FREE, TO GO IN QUEST  .  .  .  .  .  .  .  .  .  . 236 MISGIVING . . . .  . 14
THE HILLSIDE ON THE DAY THE SUN LETS GO  .  .  .  .  .  .  . 237 A HILLSIDE THAW . .  .  2
AND ALL GO BACK TO WINTER BUT THE ROAD.  .  .  .  .  .  .  . 239 OUR SINGING STRENGTH . 10
SOME TO GO FURTHER NORTH TO HUDSON'S BAY,  .  .  .  .  .  .  . 239 OUR SINGING STRENGTH . 22
THE FIELDS HAD NOWHERE LEFT FOR THEM TO GO;  .  .  .  .  .  . 239 OUR SINGING STRENGTH . 26
LIKE A PISTIL AFTER THE PETALS GO.  .  .  .  .  .  .  .  .  . 241 NEED OF BEING VERSED .  4
I WANT TO GET OUT OF THE TRAIN AND GO BACK  .  .  .  .  .  . 248 A PASSING GLIMPSE .  .  3
I WOULD NOT GO IN TILL THE LIGHT WENT OUT;  .  .  .  .  .  . 253 THE THATCH . . .  .  6
IT WOULD NOT GO OUT TILL I CAME IN.  .  .  .  .  .  .  .  .  . 253 THE THATCH . . .  .  7
THEY COULD NOT GO FLYING ABOUT IN SEARCH  .  .  .  .  .  .  . 253 THE THATCH . . .  . 23
CAN TRUST ITSELF TO GO BY CONTRARIES  .  .  .  .  .  .  .  . 258 WEST-RUNNING BROOK .  .  7
"YES, YOU HAVE, TOO. GO ON. YOU THOUGHT OF SOMETHING."  .  . 259 WEST-RUNNING BROOK .  . 37
TO GO TO WASTE AND GO WILD IN,  .  .  .  .  .  .  .  .  .  . 264 THE LAST MOWING .  . 17
I GO TO SCHOOL TO YOUTH TO LEARN THE FUTURE.  .  .  .  .  .  . 267 WHAT FIFTY SAID .  .  8
WE MAY AS WELL GO PATIENTLY ON WITH OUR LIFE,  .  .  .  .  . 268 ON LOOKING UP BY CHANCE 8
AND LET THE OTHER GO ON A WAY.  .  .  .  .  .  .  .  .  .  . 275 TWO TRAMPS IN MUD TIME  6
SUCH A PULLET OUGHT TO GO  .  .  .  .  .  .  .  .  .  .  .  . 279 BLUE RIBBON AT AMESBURY 1
WHY, KEEP YOUR MONEY (THIS CROSSLY) AND GO ALONG.  .  .  .  . 286 A ROADSIDE STAND . .  . 15
GO BRING HIM HOME TO HIS PEOPLE.  .  .  .  .  .  .  .  .  .  . 288 DEPARTMENTAL . . .  . 28
WHEN THESE GO THERE WILL BE NONE TO REPLACE THEM.  .  .  .  . 290 OLD BARN AT THE BOTTOM 40
ABOUT WHO IS TOO OLD TO GO WALKING,  .  .  .  .  .  .  .  .  . 294 A RECORD STRIDE . .  . 11
BUT IT WAS NO REASON I HAD TO GO BECAUSE THEY HAD TO GO.  .  . 298 A LEAF-TREADER . .  . 11
```

GO (CONTINUED)
  NOR CHIEFLY THAT YOU MAY GO WHERE YOU WILL, ... 300 THE MASTER SPEED . . 6
  MAY SOMETHING GO ALWAYS UNHARVESTED! . . . . 305 UNHARVESTED . . . 11
  BETTER TO GO DOWN DIGNIFIED . . . . 307 PROVIDE, PROVIDE . . 19
  BUT DIDN'T LET GO OF THE KING. . . . . 310 THE VINDICTIVES . . 9
  THEY SWORE ALL THE GOLD SHOULD GO BACK . . . . . 311 THE VINDICTIVES . . . 29
  AND NEITHER GO ON NOR BACK. . . . . 314 BEARER OF EVIL TIDINGS 26
  STOOD CLOSELY OVER US THROUGH WHICH TO GO. . . . . 315 IRIS BY NIGHT . . 19
  TO MARKET 'TIS OUR DESTINY TO GO. . . . . 321 BUILD SOIL . . . 172
  YOU SHALL GO TO YOUR RUN-OUT MOUNTAIN FARM, ... 323 BUILD SOIL . . . 211
  YOU WILL GO TO YOUR RUN-OUT MOUNTAIN FARM . . . . 323 BUILD SOIL . . . 230
  I WILL GO TO MY RUN-OUT SOCIAL MIND . . . . . 323 BUILD SOIL . . . 237
  GO LOVING BY AT TWILIGHT, ... 335 CARPE DIEM . . . 2
  OF WHERE THEY WOULD GO ON PILGRIMAGE . . . . . 344 DISCOVERY OF MADEIRAS . 25
  AS THE LIVING EVER GO YET STAY. . . . . 346 DISCOVERY OF MADEIRAS . 104
  AS TAKE HIS GUN--ROD--TO GO HUNTING--FISHING. . . . 349 TO A YOUNG WRETCH . 2
  I CAN JUST HEAR THE WAY YOU MAKE IT GO: . . . . 352 THE LESSON FOR TODAY . 54
  BUT LET'S GO ON TO WHERE OUR CASES PART. . . . 352 THE LESSON FOR TODAY . 64
  BUT GO. YOU ARE RIGHT. MY PITY CANNOT HELP. . . . 356 A MOTH SEEN IN WINTER . 17
  GO TILL YOU WET YOUR PINIONS AND ARE QUENCHED. . . . 356 A MOTH SEEN IN WINTER . 18
  WE SAW LEAVES GO TO GLORY, ... 359 NOVEMBER 1
  GO PART WAY DOWN THE LANE, ... 359 NOVEMBER 3
  WILL THEREFORE PLAN TO GO HALFWAY AND STOP. . . . 363 A SEMI-REVOLUTION . 6
  SOMETHING WHERE I COULD GO-- . . . . 366 NOT OF SCHOOL AGE . 19
  HE WAS TOO YOUNG TO GO, ... 366 NOT OF SCHOOL AGE . 21
  WELL, WOULD I PLEASE GO TO SCHOOL, ... 366 NOT OF SCHOOL AGE . 23
  AND NATURALLY YOU COULDN'T GO ALONG . . . . . 369 THE LITERATE FARMER AND 25
  YOU MAKE ME ASK IF I WOULD GO TO TIME . . . . 382 TO AN ANCIENT . . 16
  WE DO NOT GO UP THERE TO SLEEP AT NIGHT. . . . 386 A STEEPLE ON THE HOUSE . 4
  WE DO NOT GO UP THERE TO LIVE BY DAY. . . . . 386 A STEEPLE ON THE HOUSE . 5
  NOR NEED WE EVER GO UP THERE TO LIVE. . . . . 386 A STEEPLE ON THE HOUSE . 6
  IT SEEMS TO GO INTO A WOOD, ... 388 MIDDLENESS OF THE ROAD . 5
  DID I SEE IT GO BY, ... 391 A WISH TO COMPLY . 1
  ALL THOSE WHO TRY TO GO IT SOLE ALONE, ... 394 HAEC FABULA DOCET . 18
  WHEN SHE HAS MADE THINGS SO WE HAVE TO GO . . . 395 WHY WAIT FOR SCIENCE . 4
  THE WAY TO GO AWAY SHOULD BE THE SAME . . . . 395 WHY WAIT FOR SCIENCE . 11
  THE FURTHER UP THE SCALE OF WORK YOU GO. . . . 406 FROM PLANE TO PLANE . 83
  SHALL I GO ON OR HAVE I SAID ENOUGH-- . . . . 408 FROM PLANE TO PLANE . 134
  AND GO LIE DOWN. . . . . 413 AWAY! 8
  WHY GO ON FURTHER WITH CONFUSING VOICE . . . . 427 CONCEPT SELF-CONCEIVED 6
  REGION VOICE SAID, "GO, ... 436 KITTY HAWK . . . 278
  GO YOU ON TO KNOW . . . . 436 KITTY HAWK . . . 279
  "NOTHING CAN GO UP . . . . 437 KITTY HAWK . . . 306
  NOT TO GO TO SLEEP, ... 438 KITTY HAWK . . . 313
  GO CONSULT THE LOG. . . . . 438 KITTY HAWK . . . 342
  TO TAUNT OF MINE I KNEW A PLACE TO GO . . . . 447 DOES NO ONE AT ALL EVER 33
  THE SIBYL SAID, "GO BACK TO ROME . . . . . . 449 OUR DOOM TO BLOOM . 5
  A POET WOULD A-WISHING GO, ... 451 A-WISHING WELL . . 1
  I'M TEMPTED TO LET GO RESTRAINT, ... 451 A-WISHING WELL . . 15
  MOST OF THEM LET GO AND WERE GONE. . . . . . 452 A-WISHING WELL . . 54
  SOMEDAY I MUST GO INTO THAT. . . . . 453 A-WISHING WELL . . 78
  "YOU DIE FOR THAT." / "NO, YOU GO ASK YOUR MOTHER." . 457 HOW HARD TO KEEP FROM . 104
  "YOU KNOW SO MUCH, GO ON, INSTRUCT ME FURTHER. . . 458 HOW HARD TO KEEP FROM . 146
  BUT IF OVER THE MOON I HAD WANTED TO GO . . . 463 LINES IN DEJECTION . 9
  AND LET GO AT THE AIR . . . . 464 MILKY WAY IS A COWPATH 7
  I COULD GO ALMOST ANYWHERE, ... 466 SOME SCIENCE FICTION . 26
  THAT GO BLINDLY POURING PAST. . . . . 469 FOUR-ROOM SHACK. . . 4
  AGAINST THE TREES I GO. . . . . 470 IN WINTER IN THE WOODS 2
  AS WALLER SAYS. / OR NOT ADMIRED. GO OVER . . . 474 A MASQUE OF REASON . 31
  THERE YOU GO ASKING FOR THE VERY THING . . . . 477 A MASQUE OF REASON . 105
  WE MAY AS WELL GO BACK TO THE BEGINNING . . . 477 A MASQUE OF REASON . 113
  OH, LORD, LET'S NOT GO BACK TO ANYTHING. . . . 477 A MASQUE OF REASON . 115
  YOU GO TO SLEEP. GOD MUST AWAIT EVENTS, ... 478 A MASQUE OF REASON . 147
  SHE'LL GO TO SLEEP. NOTHING KEEPS HER AWAKE . . . 478 A MASQUE OF REASON . 153
  FOR VERY LONG. WE'RE PLAINLY MADE TO GO. . . . 481 A MASQUE OF REASON . 233
  OH, WE KNOW WELL ENOUGH TO GO AHEAD WITH. . . . 483 A MASQUE OF REASON . 289
  AND ALWAYS WILL BE.--PLEASE DON'T GO. STAY, STAY . 489 A MASQUE OF REASON . 435
  TOGETHER WE WILL GO WITH YOU ALONG. . . . . . 489 A MASQUE OF REASON . 437
  IF YOU GO NOW.--LOOK HOW HE TAKES NO STEPS! . . . 489 A MASQUE OF REASON . 439
  HE DOESN'T GO. / YOU NEEDN'T BE SO STERN. . . . 493 A MASQUE OF MERCY . 11
  WE DON'T GO BACK ON GRAPES WE COULDN'T REACH. . . 496 A MASQUE OF MERCY . 77
  TO GO STRAIGHT HOME, WE WOULDN'T KEEP HIM, WOULD WE?-- 501 A MASQUE OF MERCY . 208
  WE CAN GO BACK TO WHERE WE STARTED FROM. . . . 507 A MASQUE OF MERCY . 359
  AND MEND THE OTHERS UP TO GO AGAIN. . . . . . 508 A MASQUE OF MERCY . 371
  MILTON'S PENTAMETERS ON TO SAY, ... 508 A MASQUE OF MERCY . 380
  BUT WHEN THE BRINE GOES BACK, AS GO IT MUST, . . 513 A MASQUE OF MERCY . 540
  GO IF YOU'RE GOING. / WHO IS SENDING ME? . . . 514 A MASQUE OF MERCY . 553
  I WON'T PRESUME TO TELL BEL WHERE TO GO. . . . 519 A MASQUE OF MERCY . 685
  AND GO AHEAD TO ANY ACCOMPLISHMENT. . . . . . 521 A MASQUE OF MERCY . 730
GOAD
  THAT THING TAKES ALL THE ROOM!" HE MOVED HIS GOAD. . . 41 THE MOUNTAIN . . . 27
  OF HIS SLIM GOAD ON NOSE AND OFFSIDE FLANK, ... 44 THE MOUNTAIN . . . 108
GOAL
  WE WILL NOT BE PUT OFF THE FINAL GOAL . . . . . 238 ON A TREE FALLEN ACROSS 10
GOBLET
  A BROKEN DRINKING GOBLET LIKE THE GRAIL . . . . 379 DIRECTIVE 57
  (I STOLE THE GOBLET FROM THE CHILDREN'S PLAYHOUSE.) . 379 DIRECTIVE 60
GOD
  A HEARTFELT PRAYER FOR THE POOR OF GOD, ... 8 LOVE AND A QUESTION . 27
  THE WHICH IT IS RESERVED FOR GOD ABOVE . . . . 12 A PRAYER IN SPRING . 14
  AT HIDE-AND-SEEK TO GOD AFAR, ... 19 REVELATION . . . 10
  WHICH GOD MAKES HIS ESPECIAL CARE. . . . . . . 20 THE TRIAL BY EXISTENCE 32
  AND VERY BEAUTIFULLY GOD LIMNS, ... 20 THE TRIAL BY EXISTENCE 37
  BUT ALWAYS GOD SPEAKS AT THE END: . . . . . . 21 THE TRIAL BY EXISTENCE 49
  AND GOD HAS TAKEN A FLOWER OF GOLD . . . . . 21 THE TRIAL BY EXISTENCE 61
  THOUGH I KNEW WHAT I HUNTED WAS NO TRUE GOD. . . 24 THE DEMIURGE'S LAUGH . 3
  IT SEEMED GOD LET THEE FLUTTER FROM HIS GENTLE CLASP, . 29 MY BUTTERFLY . . . 27
  GOD, WHAT A WOMAN! AND IT'S COME TO THIS, ... 53 HOME BURIAL . . . 69

PAGE TITLE   LINE

GOD (CONTINUED)
I'M CURSED. GOD, IF I DON'T BELIEVE I'M CURSED."   . . . . 54 HOME BURIAL 90
NOT IF HE VALUES WHAT HE IS. GOD, I'D AS SOON . . . . . 71 THE CODE 69
"GOD!" ONE SAID WILDLY, AND, WHEN NO ONE SPOKE: . . . . 114 IN THE HOME STRETCH . 99
ALL THEY COULD SAY WAS 'GOD!' WHEN YOU PROPOSED . . . . 114 IN THE HOME STRETCH . 120
"ONE THING: HE DIDN'T DRAG GOD INTO IT." . . . . 146 SNOW 81
"HE DON'T CONSIDER IT A CASE FOR GOD." . . . . 146 SNOW 82
WAS COMING. "GOD." BUT NO, HE ONLY SAID, ... 151 SNOW 239
AND LIKE THE ACTRESS EXCLAIM "OH, MY GOD" AT? . . . . 165 NEW HAMPSHIRE . . . 207
EMERSON SAID, "THE GOD WHO MADE NEW HAMPSHIRE . . . . 166 NEW HAMPSHIRE . . . 218
FOR GOD, MAN, OR BEAST'S SAKE, ... 212 AN EMPTY THREAT . . 36
BEYOND WHICH GOD IS; . . . . 219 I WILL SING YOU ONE-O . 52
BUT SOMETHING HAS TO BE LEFT TO GOD. . . . . 228 GOOD-BY AND KEEP COLD . 29
WORD I HAD NO ONE LEFT BUT GOD. . . . . 251 BEREFT 16
GOD ONCE DECLARED HE WAS TRUE . . . . 266 SITTING BY A BUSH . . 13
GOD ONCE SPOKE TO PEOPLE BY NAME. . . . . 266 SITTING BY A BUSH . . 17
THERE WAS A LAW OF GOD OR MAN . . . . 273 A LONE STRIKER . . . 5
(FROM SLEEPING GOD KNOWS WHERE LAST NIGHT, ... 276 TWO TRAMPS IN MUD TIME 50
GOD SAW HIM DANCING IN THE ORCHARD PATH, ... 284 THE GOLD HESPERIDEE . 55
WHOSE WORK IS TO FIND OUT GOD . . . . 288 DEPARTMENTAL 10
GOD KNOWS ALL THE COLOR AND FORM OF LEAVES I HAVE TRODDEN
  ON AND MIRED. . . . . 297 A LEAF-TREADER . . . 2
I TURNED TO SPEAK TO GOD . . . . 309 NOT ALL THERE . . . 1
I FOUND GOD WASN'T THERE. . . . . 309 NOT ALL THERE . . . 4
GOD TURNED TO SPEAK TO ME . . . . 309 NOT ALL THERE . . . 5
GOD FOUND I WASN'T THERE-- . . . . 309 NOT ALL THERE . . . 7
AND THOUGH A GOD WAS THE FATHER . . . . 314 BEARER OF EVIL TIDINGS 23
THANK GOD OUR PRACTICE HOLDS THE LOVES APART, ... 318 BUILD SOIL 81
OF CHILDREN, LOVE OF FRIENDS, OF MEN, OF GOD: . . . . 318 BUILD SOIL 86
"LOOK AT WHAT HAPPENED. SURELY SOME GOD PINXIT. . . . 321 BUILD SOIL 153
IF GOD WOULD SPARE THEM TO DIE OF AGE. . . . . . . 344 DISCOVERY OF MADEIRAS . 26
WHICH MAKES THE WAR GOD SEEM NO SPECIAL DUNCE . . . . 350 TO A YOUNG WRETCH . . 17
GOD HARDLY TOLERATED WITH HIS FEET; . . . . 352 THE LESSON FOR TODAY . 75
ONE AS COMPARED WITH GOD AND ONE WITH SPACE. . . . . 353 THE LESSON FOR TODAY . 78
GOD BLESS HIMSELF CAN NO ONE ELSE BE BLESSED. . . . . 355 THE LESSON FOR TODAY . 156
TO WHATSOEVER GOD WE OWE THE THANKS. . . . . . . 358 THE LOST FOLLOWER . . 6
YOU OWE IT TO AN ARBITRARY GOD . . . . 385 THE FEAR OF GOD . . 4
THE FEAR OF GOD . . . . 385 THE FEAR OF GOD . . T
GOD BLESS THE DEAN AND MAKE HIS DEANSHIP PLENARY. . . . 394 LUCRETIUS VERSUS POETS 12
GOD, HAVE YOU TAKEN COGNIZANCE OF THIS? . . . . . . 398 NO HOLY WARS FOR THEM . 9
AND AVOID BEING WORSHIPED AS A GOD. . . . . 408 FROM PLANE TO PLANE . 131
AND ALL THE GOOD THEY DID FOR MAN OR GOD . . . . . 412 POD OF THE MILKWEED . 41
AS A GOD WHO HAD GIVEN US . . . . 417 AMERICA IS HARD TO SEE 35
GOD NODDED HIS APPROVAL OF AS GOOD. . . . . 422 FOR JOHN F. KENNEDY . 23
WHERE GOD SAYS IT, THOUGH. . . . . 438 KITTY HAWK 337
GOD OF THE MACHINE, ... 442 KITTY HAWK 462
FOR GOD HIMSELF THE HEIGHT OF FEELING FREE . . . . . 461 HOW HARD TO KEEP FROM 251
HE CAN'T GET OUT. / HE'S LOOSE! HE'S OUT! / IT'S GOD. . 473 A MASQUE OF REASON . . 17
THAT GOD PULLS LIGHTLY UPRIGHT ON ITS HINGES . . . . 474 A MASQUE OF REASON . . 22
YOU ARE THE EMANCIPATOR OF YOUR GOD, ... 476 A MASQUE OF REASON . . 78
YOU GO TO SLEEP. GOD MUST AWAIT EVENTS, ... 478 A MASQUE OF REASON . . 147
GOD NEEDS TIME JUST AS MUCH AS YOU OR I . . . . . . 478 A MASQUE OF REASON . . 151
BUT, GOD, I HAVE A QUESTION TOO TO RAISE. . . . . . 479 A MASQUE OF REASON . . 163
GOD KNOWS--OR RATHER, YOU KNOW (GOD FORGIVE ME) . . . 479 A MASQUE OF REASON . . 169
KIPLING INVOKES YOU AS LORD GOD OF HOSTS. . . . . . 479 A MASQUE OF REASON . . 179
THAT STARTED OFF LORD GOD OF HOSTESSES. . . . . . . 480 A MASQUE OF REASON . . 181
GOD, WHO INVENTED EARTH? / WHAT, STILL AWAKE? . . . . 480 A MASQUE OF REASON . . 201
A GOD CAN FIND IN LAUGHING AT HOW BADLY . . . . . . 483 A MASQUE OF REASON . . 274
YOU WON'T GET ANY ANSWERS OUT OF GOD. . . . . . . 484 A MASQUE OF REASON . . 301
(GOD EYES HIM ANXIOUSLY.) / NO. NO, I MUSTN'T. . . . 485 A MASQUE OF REASON . . 330
GOD, PLEASE, ENOUGH FOR NOW. I'M IN NO MOOD . . . . 486 A MASQUE OF REASON . . 366
NO, GOD. / I NEVER HEARD OF SUCH A THING. . . . . . 493 A MASQUE OF MERCY . . 20
TO FIND OUT HOW TO GET AWAY FROM GOD? . . . . . . 494 A MASQUE OF MERCY . . 28
WHY IS GOD AFTER YOU?--TO SAVE YOUR SOUL? . . . . . 494 A MASQUE OF MERCY . . 40
I'VE LOST MY FAITH IN GOD TO CARRY OUT . . . . . . 497 A MASQUE OF MERCY . . 114
I CAN'T TRUST GOD TO BE UNMERCIFUL. . . . . 497 A MASQUE OF MERCY . . 116
YOU'VE LOST YOUR FAITH IN GOD? HOW WICKED OF YOU. . . 497 A MASQUE OF MERCY . . 117
HOW ABOUT LOVING GOD? / YOU MAKE ME SHRUG.-- . . . . 499 A MASQUE OF MERCY . . 164
I TAKE THE FIRST BOAT. GOD PUTS UP A STORM . . . . . 500 A MASQUE OF MERCY . . 180
SHE'S HAD SOME LOSS SHE CAN'T ACCEPT FROM GOD-- . . . 501 A MASQUE OF MERCY . . 204
YOU CAN'T TRUST GOD TO BE UNMERCIFUL. . . . . . . 501 A MASQUE OF MERCY . . 214
THAT ONLY NEEDS A FINGER TOUCH FROM GOD . . . . . . 502 A MASQUE OF MERCY . . 230
YOU HEARD FROM GOD--I MEAN HAD ORDERS FROM HIM? . . . 504 A MASQUE OF MERCY . . 277
YOU SEE THE LORD GOD IS A JEALOUS GOD! . . . . . . 504 A MASQUE OF MERCY . . 289
LOOK, WILL YOU LOOK! GOD CAN'T PUT WORDS IN MY MOUTH. . 505 A MASQUE OF MERCY . . 295
GOD COMES ON ME TO DOOM A CITY FOR HIM. . . . . . . 505 A MASQUE OF MERCY . . 301
HE MAY BE GOD, BUT ME, I'M ONLY HUMAN: . . . . . . 505 A MASQUE OF MERCY . . 304
IS THIS THE LOVE OF GOD YOU PREACHED TO ME? . . . . 505 A MASQUE OF MERCY . . 306
THERE'S NOT THE LEAST LACK OF THE LOVE OF GOD . . . . 505 A MASQUE OF MERCY . . 307
THIS IS GOD AT ME IN MY SKULKING PLACE, ... 507 A MASQUE OF MERCY . . 349
YOU CAN'T TRUST GOD TO BE UNMERCIFUL. . . . . . . 507 A MASQUE OF MERCY . . 361
WHAT WOULD YOU HAVE GOD IF NOT MERCIFUL? . . . . . 507 A MASQUE OF MERCY . . 362
BUT SUCH WE ALL ARE MADE IN THE SIGHT OF GOD. . . . . 512 A MASQUE OF MERCY . . 501
OF ONE GOD, WE PROVIDE HE SHALL BE ONE . . . . . . 515 A MASQUE OF MERCY . . 590
OF THE ONE AWFUL GOD. JUST SO THE SAINTS . . . . . 516 A MASQUE OF MERCY . . 596
THE SAME WITH GOD AS LOSING, HOW EXPLAIN . . . . . 517 A MASQUE OF MERCY . . 634
I THINK I MAY HAVE GOT GOD WRONG ENTIRELY. . . . . . 518 A MASQUE OF MERCY . . 654
THAT IS THE FEAR OF GOD WHEREOF 'TIS WRITTEN. . . . . 520 A MASQUE OF MERCY . . 699
BUT I'M TOO MUCH AFRAID OF GOD TO CLAIM . . . . . . 520 A MASQUE OF MERCY . . 705
GODDAM
BY NATURE MEANT THE WHOLE GODDAM MACHINERY. . . . . . 393 LUCRETIUS VERSUS POETS 6
GODFORSAKEN
WITH A GODFORSAKEN BRUTE DESPAIR. . . . . 291 ON HEART'S BEGINNING TO 10
GODLIKE
ME MYSELF IN THE SUMMER HEAVEN, GODLIKE, ... 225 FOR ONCE SOMETHING . . 5
OR EVEN BETTER GODLIKE IN YOURSELF. . . . . 359 THE LOST FOLLOWER . . 32
GODMOTHER
THAT WAS BACK IN THE DAYS OF MY GODMOTHER GOOSE. . . . 463 LINES IN DEJECTION . . 5

- 219 -

GODS
HE RAISED AGAINST THE GODS IN THE MACHINE. . . . . . . 270 THE EGG AND THE MACHINE   15
WITH GODS AND ANGELS, WE WERE MEN AT LEAST, ... 279 THE WHITE-TAILED HORNET   61
BUT LITTLE LOWER THAN THE GODS AND ANGELS. . . . . . . 279 THE WHITE-TAILED HORNET   62
GODS ABOVE ARE NOT ABOVE IT. . . . . 304 CLEAR AND COLDER .   23
FROM MANY GODS TO THREE, AND THREE TO ONE, ... 498 A MASQUE OF MERCY . 121
TO EMBROIL THE VERY GODS ABOUT THEIR SPHERES . . . . . 511 A MASQUE OF MERCY . 471
WHO CAN BE MANY GODS TO MANY MEN, ... 516 A MASQUE OF MERCY . 591
'TWAS SAID THE LESSER GODS WERE ONLY TRAITS . . . . . . 516 A MASQUE OF MERCY . 595
GOD'S
EVEN TO SAY THE GROVES WERE GOD'S FIRST TEMPLES . . . . 171 NEW HAMPSHIRE . . . 392
"FOR GOD'S SAKE, AREN'T YOU FOND OF VIEWING NATURE? . . 215 A FOUNTAIN, A BOTTLE . 56
BEFORE GOD'S LAST PUT OUT THE LIGHT WAS SPOKEN. . . . . 250 ONCE BY THE PACIFIC . 14
WE'RE EITHER NOTHING OR A GOD'S REGRET. . . . . 353 THE LESSON FOR TODAY . 106
TO SAY GOD'S EITHER ALL OR OVER ALL? . . . . 427 CONCEPT SELF-CONCEIVED   7
BUT GOD'S OWN DESCENT . . . . 435 KITTY HAWK 219
AS WELL AS WORDS. / I'M SERIOUS. GOD'S HAD . . . . . . 478 A MASQUE OF REASON . 148
--THE DEVIL'S BEING GOD'S BEST INSPIRATION. . . . . . 487 A MASQUE OF REASON . 401
GOD'S AFTER ME! / YOU MEAN THE DEVIL IS. . . . . 493 A MASQUE OF MERCY . 19
ARE GOD'S WHITE LIGHT REFRACTED INTO COLORS. . . . . . 516 A MASQUE OF MERCY . 597
OF GOD'S DECISION LASTLY ON YOUR DEEDS. . . . . 520 A MASQUE OF MERCY . 698
THAT NOTHING BUT GOD'S MERCY CAN ASSUAGE. . . . . 520 A MASQUE OF MERCY . 713
GOES
OFF HE GOES ALWAYS WHEN I NEED HIM MOST. . . . . 35 DEATH OF THE HIRED MAN   18
IT WILL TURN TRUE AGAIN, FOR SO IT GOES. . . . . 58 THE BLACK COTTAGE . 108
A TARNISH THAT GOES AT A TOUCH OF THE HAND, ... 60 BLUEBERRIES 26
YOU KNOW HOW POLITELY HE ALWAYS GOES BY. . . . . 60 BLUEBERRIES 42
OR SO THE STORY GOES. IT WAS SOME GIRL. . . . . 66 A SERVANT TO SERVANTS . 109
TO SEE WHERE ALL THE MONEY GOES SO FAST. . . . . 86 THE HOUSEKEEPER . . 159
"I'LL BE THE ONE, IF ANYBODY GOES! . . . . 91 THE FEAR 54
EVERYTHING GOES THE SAME WITHOUT ME THERE. . . . . . . 94 THE SELF-SEEKER . . 40
IT GOES AGAINST ME NOT TO FINISH IT . . . . 95 THE SELF-SEEKER . . 83
OF WHAT SHE'S LOST: SHE GOES DOWN ON ONE KNEE . . . . . 98 THE SELF-SEEKER . . 160
BEFORE HE GOES, BECAUSE I HURT MYSELF, ... 98 THE SELF-SEEKER . . 170
I LIKE IT.--BANG GOES SOMETHING BIG AWAY . . . . 111 IN THE HOME STRETCH . 37
AND BANG GOES SOMETHING ELSE AWAY OFF THERE. . . . . . 112 IN THE HOME STRETCH . 55
HER UDDER SHRIVELS AND THE MILK GOES DRY. . . . . 125 THE COW IN APPLE TIME . 11
EASTON GOES DEMOCRATIC, WILSON 4 . . . . 165 NEW HAMPSHIRE . . . 198
FROM NEARLY EVERYTHING THAT GOES ON ROUND ME. . . . . . 166 NEW HAMPSHIRE . . . 238
AS LONG AS LIFE GOES SO UNTERRIBLY? . . . . 167 NEW HAMPSHIRE . . . 269
SO DAWN GOES DOWN TO DAY. . . . . 223 NOTHING GOLD CAN STAY .   7
BUT THE THEORY NOW GOES . . . . 246 THE ROSE FAMILY . .   3
THE ONLY LEAF IT DROPS GOES WIDE, ... 247 ON GOING UNNOTICED . 11
AND GOES DOWN BURNING INTO THE GULF BELOW, ... 249 ACCEPTANCE   2
ITS WIND-TORN THATCH GOES NOW UNMENDED; . . . . 253 THE THATCH 32
IT GOES BY MIGHT OF BEING SUCH A FLOOD . . . . 255 THE FLOOD   7
AND IF AFTER THE HUNT GOES PAST . . . . 282 A DRUMLIN WOODCHUCK . 21
THEN WORD GOES FORTH IN FORMIC: . . . . 288 DEPARTMENTAL . . . 22
THE HUNTER SCUFFLING LEAVES GOES BY AT DUSK, ... 289 OLD BARN AT THE BOTTOM   3
WIND GOES FROM FARM TO FARM IN WAVE ON WAVE, ... 300 STRONG SAYING NOTHING . 13
IT GIVES UP STANDING STRAIGHT AND GOES DOWN SWISHING. . 349 TO A YOUNG WRETCH .   4
THE SENTENCING GOES BLITHELY ON ITS WAY . . . . 362 IN A POEM   1
WE'LL BE ALL RIGHT IF NOTHING GOES WRONG WITH THE LIGHTING. 392 IT BIDS PRETTY FAIR .   4
GOES BACK TO THE BEGINNING OF THE END . . . . 422 FOR JOHN F. KENNEDY .   8
GOES MENTIONLESS EXCEPT IN BABY-SCHOOL . . . . 447 DOES NO ONE AT ALL EVER 38
WHO GOES THERE, AND WHAT . . . . 468 A REFLEX   9
WHILE SCIENCE GOES SELF-SUPERSEDING ON. . . . . 480 A MASQUE OF REASON . 193
(HE GOES AND TAKES IT FROM THE DOOR HIMSELF.) . . . . . 500 A MASQUE OF MERCY . 175
THERE HE GOES OFF INTO ANOTHER TRANCE. . . . . 503 A MASQUE OF MERCY . 264
THE FOLLY CRASHES AND THE DUST GOES UP. . . . . 506 A MASQUE OF MERCY . 342
BUT WHEN THE BRINE GOES BACK, AS GO IT MUST, ... 513 A MASQUE OF MERCY . 540
GOGGLE
WILL GET THIS PLASM IN ITS GOGGLE GLASS." . . . . . . 270 THE EGG AND THE MACHINE   30
GOING
I'M GOING OUT TO CLEAN THE PASTURE SPRING; . . . . . .   1 THE PASTURE   1
I'M GOING OUT TO FETCH THE LITTLE CALF . . . .   1 THE PASTURE   5
I END NOT FAR FROM MY GOING FORTH, ...   9 A LATE WALK 13
GOING FOR WATER . . . . 18 GOING FOR WATER . .   T
ONE OF THE GREAT SIGHTS GOING IS TO SEE . . . . 42 THE MOUNTAIN . . . 50
BUT FIRST--LET'S SEE--WHAT WAS I GOING TO ASK YOU? . . 50 A HUNDRED COLLARS . 162
WHAT ARE YOU GOING TO DO WITH SUCH A PERSON? . . . . . 57 THE BLACK COTTAGE . 80
BY GOING TO HIM OF ALL PEOPLE ON EARTH . . . . 61 BLUEBERRIES 69
YOUR GOING AND COMING. AND YOU LIKE IT HERE? . . . . . 63 A SERVANT TO SERVANTS . 37
COMING AND GOING ALL THE TIME, THEY ARE: . . . . 65 A SERVANT TO SERVANTS . 81
I S'POSE I'VE GOT TO GO THE ROAD I'M GOING: . . . . . . 67 A SERVANT TO SERVANTS . 159
"TO COCK THE HAY?--BECAUSE IT'S GOING TO SHOWER? . . . 70 THE CODE 12
ARE THERE," THEY SAID. "IT ISN'T GOING TO RAIN." . . . 74 THE GENERATIONS OF MEN   24
"NOT FROM THE RAIN. I THINK IT'S GOING TO RAIN." . . . 75 THE GENERATIONS OF MEN   67
"OH, IF YOU'RE GOING TO USE YOUR EYES, JUST HEAR . . . 76 THE GENERATIONS OF MEN   98
"I CAN SEE WE ARE GOING TO BE GOOD FRIENDS." . . . . . 80 THE GENERATIONS OF MEN 199
"I LIKE YOUR 'GOING TO BE.' YOU SAID JUST NOW . . . . . 80 THE GENERATIONS OF MEN 200
IT'S GOING TO RAIN." / "I KNOW, AND IT WAS RAINING. . . 80 THE GENERATIONS OF MEN 201
WITH THE BROOK GOING BY BELOW THE YARD, ... 82 THE HOUSEKEEPER . . 46
"YOU NEEDN'T THINK YOU'RE GOING TO GET AWAY. . . . . . 88 THE HOUSEKEEPER . . 195
THAT HE'D BE GOING TO OR COMING FROM . . . . 90 THE FEAR 26
I'M GOING TO SELL MY SOUL, OR RATHER, FEET. . . . . . . 92 THE SELF-SEEKER . .   3
AND IF YOU'RE GOING TO SELL THEM TO THE DEVIL, ... 93 THE SELF-SEEKER . .   6
THE DOCTOR'S SURE YOU'RE GOING TO WALK AGAIN?" . . . . 93 THE SELF-SEEKER . . 15
INSTEAD OF GOING CLEAR DOWN IN THE WHEEL PIT?" . . . . 93 THE SELF-SEEKER . . 31
"I'M GOING TO BE WORSE INSTEAD OF BETTER. . . . . 94 THE SELF-SEEKER . . 56
SUCH AS IT'S GOING TO BE, AND KNOW THE WORST, ... 95 THE SELF-SEEKER . . 77
SHE'S GOING TO DO MY SCOUTING IN THE FIELD, ... 98 THE SELF-SEEKER . . 151
WHETHER HE'S EVER GOING TO WALK AGAIN. . . . . 100 THE SELF-SEEKER . . 202
BUT DON'T EXPECT I'M GOING TO LET YOU HAVE THEM." . . . 106 CHRISTMAS TREES . . 32
THEY'RE GOING. WATCH THIS HUSKY SWARMING UP . . . . . . 112 IN THE HOME STRETCH . 62
IT'S SOMETHING, THOUGH, TO KNOW WE'RE GOING TO HAVE HER 113 IN THE HOME STRETCH . 72
I'M GOING TO PUT YOU IN YOUR BED, IF FIRST . . . . . . 117 IN THE HOME STRETCH . 199
BUT I WAS GOING TO SAY WHEN TRUTH BROKE IN . . . . . . 121 BIRCHES 21

GOING (CONTINUED)
AND SO I DREAM OF GOING BACK TO BE. . . . . 122 BIRCHES 42
THAT WOULD BE GOOD BOTH GOING AND COMING BACK. . . . . 122 BIRCHES 58
GOING THE OTHER WAY AND THEY NOT SEEN IT. . . . . . . 132 THE BONFIRE 88
I WASN'T GOING TO TELL YOU AND I MUSTN'T. . . . . . . 133 THE BONFIRE 112
(BUT SAVED THE LIGHT FROM GOING OUT). . . . . 138 BROWN'S DESCENT . . 39
FRED COLE, YOU'RE GOING TO LET HIM!" / "WELL, AREN'T YOU? . 144 SNOW 43
TO THEIRS. I'M GOING TO CALL HIS WIFE AGAIN." . . . . . 145 SNOW 75
BUT IF YOU'RE GOING--SAY YOU'LL STAY, YOU KNOW. . . . . 148 SNOW 154
IN GOING ON." / "OUR SNOWSTORMS AS A RULE . . . . . . 150 SNOW 221
IF HE HAD STAYED. THE LEAST THING SET HIM GOING. . . . 152 SNOW 259
"FRED, I SHAN'T LET YOU THINK OF GOING OUT." . . . . . 155 SNOW 326
IF HE THINKS HE IS GOING TO MAKE OUR HOUSE . . . . . . 155 SNOW 341
THEY ARE THAT THAT TALKS OF GOING . . . . 156 THE SOUND OF TREES . . 10
"I'M GOING TO PUT YOU OFF THIS FARM: I WANT IT." . . . 164 NEW HAMPSHIRE . . 154
"WHERE ARE YOU GOING TO PUT ME? IN THE ROAD?" . . . . 164 NEW HAMPSHIRE . . 155
"I'M GOING TO PUT YOU ON THE FARM NEXT TO IT." . . . . 164 NEW HAMPSHIRE . . 156
GOING THE OTHER OUT OF LIFE--YOU KNOW? . . . . 180 MAPLE 13
WHO GAVE HIS LIFE TO KEEP IT GOING ROUND? . . . . . . 190 THE GRINDSTONE . . 47
SOMETHING WAS GOING TO GO WITH THEIR SLAMBANGING. . . . 193 PAUL'S WIFE . . . 68
STILL GOING EVERY WHICH WAY IN THE JOINTS, THOUGH, . . . 205 THE WITCH OF COOS . . 87
I'M GOING TO TELL THEM SOMETHING THEY WON'T LIKE: . . . 207 PAUPER WITCH OF GRAFTON 2
I WAS GOING TO SAY, ... 212 AN EMPTY THREAT . . . 35
OLD AS I AM, I'M GOING TO LET MYSELF . . . . 214 A FOUNTAIN, A BOTTLE . 29
A GREAT WAVE FROM IT GOING OVER THEM, ... 230 TWO LOOK AT TWO . . . 40
IN GOING TWICE AROUND THE TREE. . . . . 233 LOOKING FOR SUNSET BIRD 12
ON GOING UNNOTICED . . . . 247 ON GOING UNNOTICED . . T
BE HER LAST JOY HER HEART'S GOING OUT TO THIS ONE . . . 257 THE LOVELY BE CHOOSERS 50
EVER SINCE RIVERS, I WAS GOING TO SAY, ... 258 WEST-RUNNING BROOK . . 28
IN GOING FROM ROOM TO ROOM IN THE DARK . . . . 265 THE DOOR IN THE DARK . 1
GOING BY AT A RAILROAD RATE, ... 292 ON HEART'S BEGINNING TO 43
IN A FIELD I LOOKED INTO GOING PAST, ... 296 DESERT PLACES . . . 2
YOUR LEAST TOUCH SETS IT GOING ROUND, ... 306 A TRIAL RUN . . . 13
BUT HE'S AS GOOD AS ANYBODY GOING. . . . . 309 WASPISH 6
BUT SHEEP IS WHAT I'M GOING INTO NEXT. . . . . 316 BUILD SOIL . . . 10
WE'RE TOO UNSEPARATE. AND GOING HOME . . . . 325 BUILD SOIL . . . 291
AND ONLY BY ONE'S GOING SLIGHTLY TAUT . . . . 332 THE SILKEN TENT . . . 12
THIS LIGHT'S BEEN GOING ON FOR SEVERAL YEARS, ... 369 THE LITERATE FARMER AND 31
ARE GOING TO BE, UNLESS THESE MONKEY JOKES . . . . . . 369 THE LITERATE FARMER AND 44
MUCH NOTICE OF WHAT'S GOING ON IN STARS. . . . . . . 370 THE LITERATE FARMER AND 70
I SAVED MYSELF FROM GOING. . . . . 377 ONE STEP BACKWARD TAKEN 11
IS AFTER EXPLOSION GOING AWAY SO FAST. . . . . 389 SKEPTIC 8
GOING OVER MY EYE. . . . . 392 A WISH TO COMPLY . . 11
THAT PUT AN END TO WHAT WAS GOING ON . . . . 397 THE PLANNERS . . . 5
SOMETHING WAS GOING RIGHT OUTSIDE THE HALL. . . . . . 399 THE BROKEN DROUGHT . . 2
A FINAL GOING OVER WITH THE HOE . . . . 404 FROM PLANE TO PLANE . 13
"HE LOOKS TO ME LIKE GOING HOME SUCCESSFUL, ... 405 FROM PLANE TO PLANE . 37
AND THINGS HAVE BEEN GOING SO STRANGELY SINCE, ... 421 ONE MORE BREVITY . 56
THE THINGS BUT BALLS ALL GOING ROUND IN RINGS. . . . . 425 ACCIDENTALLY ON PURPOSE 2
TO INSURE A JET DEPARTURE OF OUR GOING . . . . 460 HOW HARD TO KEEP FROM 201
OF ITS GOING MUCH LONGER UNNOTICED . . . . 465 SOME SCIENCE FICTION . 2
WE'RE GOING ANYWAY AND MAY AS WELL . . . . 482 A MASQUE OF REASON . 234
WORTH GOING AFTER. GET DOWN INTO THINGS. . . . . . . 483 A MASQUE OF REASON . 281
PERHAPS THAT EARTH IS GOING TO CRACK SOMEDAY . . . . . 484 A MASQUE OF REASON . 305
I'M GOING TO TELL JOB WHY I TORTURED HIM, ... 484 A MASQUE OF REASON . 325
HE ISN'T REALLY GOING, YET HE'S LEAVING. . . . . . . 489 A MASQUE OF REASON . 440
I'M GOING TO TELL YOU SOMETHING, JONAS DOVE. . . . . . 498 A MASQUE OF MERCY . 131
I'M GOING TO TAKE THE NONSENSE OUT OF YOU . . . . . . 498 A MASQUE OF MERCY . 132
ONCE AND FOR ALL. I'M GOING TO MAKE YOU SEE . . . . . 498 A MASQUE OF MERCY . 145
AND HELP YOU'RE GOING TO GET. / I'LL BREAK YOUR DOOR DOWN. 500 A MASQUE OF MERCY . 178
TRUCKS GOING BY TO WAR. A WAR IS ON. . . . . 504 A MASQUE OF MERCY . 281
GO IF YOU'RE GOING. / WHO IS SENDING ME? . . . . . . 514 A MASQUE OF MERCY . 553
I'M GOING NOW. BUT DON'T YOU PUSH ME OFF. . . . . . . 518 A MASQUE OF MERCY . 646
GOLD (SEE HIDE-GOLD)
AND WISHED HER HEART IN A CASE OF GOLD . . . . 8 LOVE AND A QUESTION . 23
OR EASY GOLD AT THE HAND OF FAY OR ELF: . . . . 17 MOWING 8
AND GOD HAS TAKEN A FLOWER OF GOLD . . . . 21 THE TRIAL BY EXISTENCE 61
SHE HAS A TOUCH OF GOLD. NEW HAMPSHIRE GOLD-- . . . . 162 NEW HAMPSHIRE . . 108
WITH A MINE ON IT THAT WAS WORKED FOR GOLD; . . . . . 162 NEW HAMPSHIRE . . 111
BUT NOT GOLD IN COMMERCIAL QUANTITIES, ... 162 NEW HAMPSHIRE . . 112
JUST ENOUGH GOLD TO MAKE THE ENGAGEMENT RINGS . . . . 162 NEW HAMPSHIRE . . 113
WHAT GOLD MORE INNOCENT COULD ONE HAVE ASKED FOR? . . . 162 NEW HAMPSHIRE . . 115
AND SAVING THAT ITS WEIGHT SUGGESTED GOLD . . . . . . 172 A STAR IN A STONEBOAT . 5
ITS HANDS OF GOLD . . . . 218 I WILL SING YOU ONE-O . 21
NATURE'S FIRST GREEN IS GOLD, ... 222 NOTHING GOLD CAN STAY . 1
NOTHING GOLD CAN STAY . . . . 222 NOTHING GOLD CAN STAY . T
NOTHING GOLD CAN STAY. . . . . 223 NOTHING GOLD CAN STAY . 8
THE WEST WAS GETTING OUT OF GOLD, ... 232 LOOKING FOR SUNSET BIRD 1
AS GILT TO GOLD THAT WOULDN'T SHOW. . . . . 233 LOOKING FOR SUNSET BIRD 16
SOME OF THE BLOWING DUST WAS GOLD. . . . . 249 A PECK OF GOLD . . . 4
APPEARED LIKE GOLD IN THE SUNSET SKY, ... 249 A PECK OF GOLD . . . 6
SOME OF THE DUST WAS REALLY GOLD. . . . . 249 A PECK OF GOLD . . . 8
A PECK OF GOLD . . . . 249 A PECK OF GOLD . . . T
GOLD DUSTED ALL WE DRANK AND ATE, ... 249 A PECK OF GOLD . . . 10
"WE ALL MUST EAT OUR PECK OF GOLD." . . . . 249 A PECK OF GOLD . . . 12
IN BROAD ROUND EARRINGS, GOLD AND JET WITH PEARLS, . . . 256 THE LOVELY BE CHOOSERS 15
THE GOLD HESPERIDEE . . . . 283 THE GOLD HESPERIDEE . T
AND WHAT WAS GREEN WOULD BY AND BY BE GOLD. . . . . . 283 THE GOLD HESPERIDEE . 17
THEIR NAME WAS CALLED THE GOLD HESPERIDEE. . . . . . 283 THE GOLD HESPERIDEE . 18
THAT THE NAME GOLD HESPERIDEE WAS RIGHT. . . . . . . 284 THE GOLD HESPERIDEE . 30
YOU LIKE TO HEAR ABOUT GOLD. . . . . 310 THE VINDICTIVES . . 1
BUT REALLY THAT GOLD WAS NOT HALF . . . . 310 THE VINDICTIVES . . 18
IF GOLD PLEASED THE CONQUEROR, WELL, ... 311 THE VINDICTIVES . . 24
THAT GOLD SHOULD BE THE ONE THING . . . . 311 THE VINDICTIVES . . 25
THEY SWORE ALL THE GOLD SHOULD GO BACK . . . . 311 THE VINDICTIVES . . 29
AND TOOK THE GOLD CANDLESTICKS HOME. . . . . 311 THE VINDICTIVES . . 40
THE GREAT THOUSAND-LINKED GOLD CHAIN, ... 312 THE VINDICTIVES . . 63
(TO KEEP THE POTS OF GOLD FROM BEING FOUND), ... 315 IRIS BY NIGHT . . 25

GOLD (CONTINUED)
    THE GOLD FOR WHICH THEY LEAVE THE GOLDEN LINE . . . . . 358 THE LOST FOLLOWER . .   2
    NEVER THE GOLD OF DARKNESS FROM A MINE. . . . . 358 THE LOST FOLLOWER . .   4
    WE HAD ONE AGE OF GOLD . . . . 361 ALMOST TWO THOUSAND .   2
    AND WITH THE GOLD IN HAND TO SHOW FOR . . . . 417 AMERICA IS HARD TO SEE   23
    THAT BETTER THAN DA GAMA'S GOLD . . . . 417 AMERICA IS HARD TO SEE   27
    AND HARK, THE GOLD ENAMELED NIGHTINGALES . . . . 473 A MASQUE OF REASON . .   14
    AND TURN THE GOLD ENAMELED ARTIFICIAL BIRDS ON. . . . . 490 A MASQUE OF REASON . . 459
GOLDEN (SEE OLD-GOLDEN)
    IT COMES TO MARKET GOLDEN BROWN: . . . . 141 THE GUM-GATHERER . . .   32
    SUCH WAS LIFE IN THE GOLDEN GATE: . . . . 249 A PECK OF GOLD . . .   9
    HER GOLDEN LEG, HER CORAL COMB, ... 280 BLUE RIBBON AT AMESBURY 6
    OR CROOK-NECKED GOLDEN SQUASH WITH SILVER WARTS, . . . 286 A ROADSIDE STAND . .   12
    THE GOLD FOR WHICH THEY LEAVE THE GOLDEN LINE . . . . . 358 THE LOST FOLLOWER . .   2
    OF LYRIC IS A GOLDEN LIGHT DIVINE, ... 358 THE LOST FOLLOWER . .   3
    THAT POETRY WITH ALL ITS GOLDEN RAGE . . . . 358 THE LOST FOLLOWER . .   14
    HAS FAILED TO BRING--I MEAN THE GOLDEN AGE. . . . . . . 358 THE LOST FOLLOWER . .   16
    THE FINAL GOLDEN GLOW . . . . 361 ALMOST TWO THOUSAND   7
    THERE SANDY SEEMS THE GOLDEN SKY . . . . 392 A CLIFF DWELLING . .   1
    AND GOLDEN SEEMS THE SANDY PLAIN. . . . . 392 A CLIFF DWELLING . .   2
    A GOLDEN AGE OF POETRY AND POWER . . . . 424 FOR JOHN F. KENNEDY .   76
GOLDENROD
    THE RAIN-FRESH GOLDENROD. . . . . 27 A LINE-STORM SONG . .   24
    GRASS ITS FULL LENGTH, OLD SILVER GOLDENROD, ... 131 THE BONFIRE   62
    IN GOLDENROD AND BRAKE, ... 339 THE SUBVERTED FLOWER . 16
GOLDTHREAD
    DWARF CORNEL, GOLDTHREAD, AND MAIANTHEMUM, ... 355 TIME OUT   5
GONE
    I SHAN'T BE GONE LONG.--YOU COME TOO. . . . .   1 THE PASTURE   4
    I SHAN'T BE GONE LONG.--YOU COME TOO. . . . .   1 THE PASTURE   8
    SHE'S GLAD THE BIRDS ARE GONE AWAY, ...   7 MY NOVEMBER GUEST . .   8
    THE DEW WAS GONE THAT MADE HIS BLADE SO KEEN . . . . .   22 THE TUFT OF FLOWERS   3
    BUT HE HAD GONE HIS WAY, THE GRASS ALL MOWN, ...   22 THE TUFT OF FLOWERS   7
    THE LAST LONE ASTER IS GONE; . . . .   30 RELUCTANCE   15
    YOU'LL REST EASIER WHEN I'M GONE, PERHAPS-- . . . . . . 50 A HUNDRED COLLARS . . 160
    THE HEART'S GONE OUT OF IT: WHY KEEP IT UP? . . . . . . 54 HOME BURIAL   110
    THAT HAD GONE OUT OF IT, THE FATHER FIRST, ...   56 THE BLACK COTTAGE . .   38
    THERE HAD BEEN SOME BERRIES--BUT THOSE WERE ALL GONE. . 61 BLUEBERRIES   73
    AND WOULD FEEL IF I WASN'T ALL GONE WRONG. . . . . . .   63 A SERVANT TO SERVANTS   15
    WERE HE NOT GONE, ... 69 AFTER APPLE-PICKING .   39
    HE HAD GONE TO THE HOUSE SO'S NOT TO MEET ME. . . . . . 73 THE CODE   105
    AND SPROUT-LANDS FLOURISH WHERE THE AX HAS GONE. . . .   73 THE GENERATIONS OF MEN   6
    THE LIFE IS NOT YET ALL GONE OUT OF IT. . . . . 79 THE GENERATIONS OF MEN 165
    TO COME TO HIS HOUSE WHEN HE'S GONE TO YOURS. . . . . . 81 THE HOUSEKEEPER . .   15
    HE MUST HAVE CHANGED HIS MIND AND GONE TO GARLAND'S. .   81 THE HOUSEKEEPER . .   17
    IT'S GONE SO FAR. YOU'VE HEARD? ESTELLE'S RUN OFF." . . 82 THE HOUSEKEEPER . .   20
    BUT WHEN I'M GONE--OF COURSE I CAN'T STAY HERE: . . . . 82 THE HOUSEKEEPER . .   34
    HOW DO YOU SEE HIM LIVING WHEN YOU'RE GONE? . . . . . . 82 THE HOUSEKEEPER . .   41
    I HATE TO THINK OF THE OLD PLACE WHEN WE'RE GONE, . . . 82 THE HOUSEKEEPER . .   45
    HE HAS SEEN ALL THERE WAS TO SEE AND GONE." . . . . . . 91 THE FEAR   58
    YOU'VE GOT TO TELL ME HOW FAR THIS IS GONE: . . . . . . 94 THE SELF-SEEKER . .   57
    CARRY HIM OFF THE WAY I MIGHT HAVE GONE, ... 101 THE WOOD-PILE . . .   20
    THE CUTTER BAR HAD JUST GONE CHAMPING OVER . . . . . . 109 THE EXPOSED NEST . .   14
    "THEY'RE NOT GONE YET." / "WE'VE GOT TO HAVE THE STOVE, 113 IN THE HOME STRETCH   78
    THE FIRST NIGHT AFTER GUESTS HAVE GONE, THE HOUSE . . . 115 IN THE HOME STRETCH   132
    EITHER TO HAVE GONE GROPING UNDERGROUND . . . . 119 HYLA BROOK   3
    TO LAMPS UNLIGHTED AND FIRE GONE GRAY, ... 127 HOUSE FEAR   4
    WHERE ALL MY WEARINESS HAD GONE AND WHY . . . . 132 THE BONFIRE   91
    SO. BUT THE HAND WAS GONE ALREADY. . . . . 137 "OUT,OUT--"   27
    THAT CASED THE WORLD, AND HE WAS GONE! . . . . 137 BROWN'S DESCENT . .   12
    AND GONE TO SLEEP, SHE NEEDN'T WAKE TO ANSWER." . . . . 143 SNOW   14
    IN ONE ANOTHER, AND HAD GONE TO SLEEP . . . . 148 SNOW   163
    SHE DIDN'T THANK ME?" / "WHEN I TOLD HER 'GONE,' . . . 153 SNOW   288
    IT'S THEIRS. SHE'S DROPPED IT FROM HER HAND AND GONE." 153 SNOW   297
    "ONE OF TWO THINGS, EITHER SHE'S GONE TO BED . . . . . 154 SNOW   311
    OR GONE OUTDOORS." / "IN WHICH CASE BOTH ARE LOST. . . 154 SNOW   312
    THAT IS, ASSUMING--THAT SHE HAS GONE OUT. . . . . 155 SNOW   323
    BUT I SHALL BE GONE. . . . . 156 THE SOUND OF TREES .   25
    MANKIND HAD NOT YET GONE ON THE SABBATICAL. . . . . . . 161 NEW HAMPSHIRE . . .   90
    WHEN EVERYTHING HAD GONE REPUBLICAN . . . . 165 NEW HAMPSHIRE . . .   196
    YET ASK WHERE ELSE IT COULD HAVE GONE AS WELL, ... 173 A STAR IN A STONEBOAT . 37
    ALL OTHER FARM MACHINERY'S GONE IN, ... 189 THE GRINDSTONE . .   11
    I WONDERED WHAT MACHINE OF AGES GONE . . . . 189 THE GRINDSTONE . .   35
    AND THOUGHT IT MUST HAVE MELTED. IT WAS GONE. . . . . . 194 PAUL'S WIFE   105
    FATHER HAD GONE UPSTAIRS; MOTHER WAS DOWNSTAIRS. . . . 203 THE WITCH OF COOS .   34
    TOFFILE HAD GONE TO BED ALONE AND LEFT ME, ... 203 THE WITCH OF COOS .   41
    ABOUT WHERE HENRY HUDSON'S GONE, ... 211 AN EMPTY THREAT . .   16
    WHEN OTHER CREATURES HAVE GONE TO STALL AND BIN, . . . 223 THE RUNAWAY   20
    I HAVE TO BE GONE FOR A SEASON OR SO. . . . . 228 GOOD-BY AND KEEP COLD   20
    THE HOUSE HAD GONE TO BRING AGAIN . . . . 241 NEED OF BEING VERSED   1
    WILL LIKE THE FLOWERS BESIDE THEM SOON BE GONE, ... 245 SPRING POOLS . . .   4
    YOU LINGER YOUR LITTLE HOUR AND ARE GONE, ... 247 ON GOING UNNOTICED .   13
    THAT ARE GONE BEFORE I CAN TELL WHAT THEY ARE. . . . . 248 A PASSING GLIMPSE .   2
    WHEN MY GARDEN HAS GONE DOWN DITCH, ... 285 IN TIME OF CLOUDBURST   69
    SOME SAID IT HAD GONE TO THE COAST, ... 312 THE VINDICTIVES . .   9
    A MOMENT AND STILL ASKING GONE. . . . . 332 ALL REVELATION . .   12
    AND GONE PANTING BY. . . . . 342 QUEST OF PURPLE-FRINGED 74
    IT'S GONE SO FAR SHE'S PROBABLY CAUGHT . . . . 345 DISCOVERY OF MADEIRAS . 15
    SO SMALL AS TO BE VIRTUALLY GONE, ... 368 THE LITERATE FARMER AND 6
    COULD MAKE MUCH DIFFERENCE TO THE DEAD AND GONE. . . . 397 THE PLANNERS . . .   51
    WHERE HAVE THOSE FLOWERS AND BUTTERFLIES ALL GONE . . . 412 POD OF THE MILKWEED   6
    BECAUSE THEY'VE GONE AWAY . . . . 415 CLOSED FOR GOOD . .   6
    TO BE GONE INTO IF NOT EXPLAINED. . . . . 419 ONE MORE BREVITY . .   49
    I OPENED THE DOOR AND HE WAS GONE. . . . . 420 ONE MORE BREVITY . .   54
    MOST OF THEM LET GO AND WERE GONE. . . . . 452 A-WISHING WELL . .   29
    AND GONE RIGHT ON ASTRAY . . . . 465 MILKY WAY IS A COWPATH 253
    HAS ALL GONE HOME TO BED. THE PLAY'S PLAYED OUT. . . . 482 A MASQUE OF REASON .   253

GONG
  WENT BY WITH CLANGING GONG . . . . 391 A ROGERS GROUP 6
  AS DULCET AS A PAGAN TEMPLE GONG! . . . . 488 A MASQUE OF REASON . . 419
GOOD
  OF THOSE WHO FOR SOME GOOD DISCERNED . . . . . 20 THE TRIAL BY EXISTENCE   27
  THAT OPENS EARTHWARD, GOOD AND ILL. . . . . . . 20 THE TRIAL BY EXISTENCE   35
  HE ONLY SAYS, "GOOD FENCES MAKE GOOD NEIGHBORS." . . 33 MENDING WALL 27
  "WHY DO THEY MAKE GOOD NEIGHBORS? ISN'T IT . . . . 34 MENDING WALL 30
  HE SAYS AGAIN, "GOOD FENCES MAKE GOOD NEIGHBORS." . . 34 MENDING WALL 45
  WHAT GOOD IS HE? WHO ELSE WILL HARBOR HIM . . . . 35 DEATH OF THE HIRED MAN   15
  GOOD ARGUMENTS HE SEES HE MIGHT HAVE USED. . . . 37 DEATH OF THE HIRED MAN   75
  WHICH SHOWED HOW MUCH GOOD SCHOOL HAD EVER DONE HIM. . 37 DEATH OF THE HIRED MAN   84
  SOME GOOD PERHAPS TO SOMEONE IN THE WORLD. . . . . 37 DEATH OF THE HIRED MAN   97
  HE DON'T KNOW WHY HE ISN'T QUITE AS GOOD . . . . 39 DEATH OF THE HIRED MAN 143
  GOOD GRASSLAND GULLIED OUT, AND IN THE GRASS . . . 40 THE MOUNTAIN 13
  AND A GOOD DISTANCE DOWN MIGHT NOT BE NOTICED . . . 43 THE MOUNTAIN 71
  OF GOOD FAITH. THERE IS NINETY DOLLARS. . . . . . 47 A HUNDRED COLLARS . . . 86
  A GOOD DEAL COMES ON ME WHEN ALL IS SAID. . . . . 48 A HUNDRED COLLARS . . . 107
  THE CHIMNEY, THOUGH, KEEPS UP A GOOD BRISK SMOKING. . 49 A HUNDRED COLLARS . . . 137
  MAME, WE DON'T KNOW ANY GOOD BERRYING PLACE?' . . . 61 BLUEBERRIES 77
  SOMETIMES WE DON'T. WE'VE A GOOD PIECE OF SHORE . . 64 A SERVANT TO SERVANTS . 42
  BY GOOD RIGHTS I OUGHT NOT TO HAVE SO MUCH . . . 64 A SERVANT TO SERVANTS . 53
  WORSE THAN NO GOOD TO THEM, AND THEY NO GOOD . . . 65 A SERVANT TO SERVANTS . 100
  AND BE GLAD OF A GOOD ROOF OVERHEAD. . . . . . . 67 A SERVANT TO SERVANTS . 165
  YOU TAKE MY CARD--YOU SEEM SO GOOD AT SUCH THINGS-- . 75 THE GENERATIONS OF MEN   61
  "I SHALL SUSPECT----" / "BE GOOD. THE VOICES SAY: . 79 THE GENERATIONS OF MEN 159
  "I CAN SEE WE ARE GOING TO BE GOOD FRIENDS." . . . 80 THE GENERATIONS OF MEN 199
  THOUGH WHAT GOOD YOU CAN BE, OR ANYONE-- . . . . 81 THE HOUSEKEEPER 19
  I THOUGHT THE GROWING THINGS WOULD DO HIM GOOD. . . 83 THE HOUSEKEEPER 59
  BETTER THAN MARRIED OUGHT TO BE AS GOOD . . . . . 84 THE HOUSEKEEPER 81
  THIS IS A GOOD HOME: I DON'T ASK FOR BETTER. . . . 84 THE HOUSEKEEPER 89
  A FRIEND OR TWO AS GOOD AS OWN THE FARM. . . . . 84 THE HOUSEKEEPER 96
  HAVEN'T AS GOOD. THEY DON'T GO WITH THE FARM. . . . 85 THE HOUSEKEEPER 114
  NOTHING'S TOO GOOD FOR THEM. WE SAY IT PAYS. . . . 86 THE HOUSEKEEPER 137
  ONE OUGHT AS A GOOD VILLAGER TO LIKE IT. . . . . 94 THE SELF-SEEKER 44
  I HAVE TO KEEP ON THE GOOD SIDE OF ANNE. . . . . 99 THE SELF-SEEKER 176
  I'LL PUT YOU OUT WITH ANNE. BE GOOD OR GO." . . . 99 THE SELF-SEEKER 186
  GOOD HOURS . . . . 102 GOOD HOURS . . . . . . T
  FROM HOPE OF HEARING GOOD OF WHAT WAS MINE, . . . 106 CHRISTMAS TREES 28
  WOULD PAY IN CITIES FOR GOOD TREES LIKE THOSE, . . 107 CHRISTMAS TREES 52
  WE SAW THE RISK WE TOOK IN DOING GOOD, ... 109 THE EXPOSED NEST 27
  "IT'S GOOD LUCK WHEN YOU MOVE IN TO BEGIN . . . . 113 IN THE HOME STRETCH . . 91
  WITH GOOD LUCK WITH YOUR STOVEPIPE. NEVER MIND, . . 113 IN THE HOME STRETCH . . 92
  AND MAKE GOOD FARMERS, AND LEAVE OTHER FELLOWS . . 114 IN THE HOME STRETCH . . 96
  "GOOD BOYS THEY SEEMED, AND LET THEM LOVE THE CITY. . 114 IN THE HOME STRETCH . . 119
  THAT WOULD BE GOOD BOTH GOING AND COMING BACK. . . 122 BIRCHES 58
  THEY MIGHT BE GOOD FOR GARDEN THINGS . . . . . . 123 PEA BRUSH 17
  SMALL GOOD TO ANYTHING GROWING WILD, ... 123 PEA BRUSH 21
  THAT HAD ME BY THE COAT AS GOOD AS SEATED, . . . 125 AN ENCOUNTER 9
  AND SAID TO BE GOOD, ... 136 LAST WORD OF A BLUEBIRD 16
  HE MAY BE GOOD, BUT ONE THING'S SURE, HE'S TOUGH." . 145 SNOW 71
  OF BEING MEN WE CAN'T LOOK AT A GOOD FIGHT . . . 146 SNOW 100
  AND FAILED TO SEE THE GOOD OF. NEVER MIND, . . . 147 SNOW 125
  BUT WHAT GOOD IS MY SAYING IT OVER AND OVER? . . . 150 SNOW 218
  "SHOUT, SHE MAY HEAR YOU." / "SHOUTING IS NO GOOD." . 154 SNOW 303
  GOOD! WHY I ASKED--SHE DIDN'T SEEM TO ANSWER.-- . . 155 SNOW 330
  WHOSE CLAIM IS GOOD TO BEING SETTLED HERE . . . . 161 NEW HAMPSHIRE 71
  THE HOUR HAD NOT YET STRUCK FOR BEING GOOD, . . . 161 NEW HAMPSHIRE 89
  AND SO NOT GOOD FOR ANYTHING BUT CIDER. . . . . . 164 NEW HAMPSHIRE 162
  WHEREAS I NEVER HAD A GOOD IDEA . . . . 169 NEW HAMPSHIRE 335
  HOW ABOUT BEING A GOOD GREEK, FOR INSTANCE? . . . 171 NEW HAMPSHIRE 404
  A GOOD OLD-TIMER DATING BACK ALONG; . . . . . . 178 THE STAR-SPLITTER . . . 60
  HE GOT A GOOD GLASS FOR SIX HUNDRED DOLLARS. . . . 178 THE STAR-SPLITTER . . . 74
  AND OUGHT TO DO SOME GOOD IF SPLITTING STARS . . . 179 THE STAR-SPLITTER . . . 93
  BE A GOOD GIRL--BE LIKE A MAPLE TREE. . . . . . 180 MAPLE 22
  WHAT SHE HAD THOUGHT WAS LOVELY, AND WHAT GOOD. . . 181 MAPLE 55
  "YOU GIVE HER ONE GOOD CRACK, SHE'S SNAP RAGHT OFF. . 186 THE AX-HELVE 26
  WHAT'S LAS' AWHILE--GOOD HICK'RY WHAT'S GROW CROOKED, . 186 THE AX-HELVE 30
  HE SHOWED ME THAT THE LINES OF A GOOD HELVE . . . 187 THE AX-HELVE 72
  OTHERS BECAUSE HE'D HAD ONE ONCE, A GOOD ONE, . . 191 PAUL'S WIFE 8
  A GOOD DEAL RIGHT; DON'T DO THE LAST THING WRONG. . 199 PLACE FOR A THIRD . . . 10
  AND GIVE GOOD MEASURE TO THE DEAD, THOUGH THANKLESS. . 200 PLACE FOR A THIRD . . . 20
  AND WHEN I'VE DONE IT, WHAT GOOD HAVE I DONE? . . 202 THE WITCH OF COÖS . . . 11
  IT WAS THE BONES. I KNEW THEM--AND GOOD REASON. . 204 THE WITCH OF COÖS . . . 59
  WENTWORTH AND WARREN'S BOTH GOOD TOWNS TO LIVE IN, . 208 PAUPER WITCH OF GRAFTON 30
  CAN DO A GOOD DEAL TO BAD MASONRY. . . . . . . 213 A FOUNTAIN, A BOTTLE . . 26
  I NEVER SAW SO GOOD A HOUSE DESERTED. . . . . . 215 A FOUNTAIN, A BOTTLE . . 71
  HIGH IN THE BREAST. NOTHING BUT WHAT GOOD CARE . . 230 NOT TO KEEP 15
  OUR PASSAGE TO OUR JOURNEY'S END FOR GOOD, . . . 238 ON A TREE FALLEN ACROSS 3
  MAN'S INGENUITY WAS GOOD. . . . . 274 A LONE STRIKER 33
  GOOD BLOCKS OF OAK IT WAS I SPLIT, ... 275 TWO TRAMPS IN MUD TIME   9
  SPARES TO STRIKE FOR THE COMMON GOOD, ... 275 TWO TRAMPS IN MUD TIME   14
  WORDS ARE NO GOOD: TO SAY IT WAS A LENS . . . . 293 AT WOODWARD'S GARDENS . 5
  A TREE'S LEAVES MAY BE EVER SO GOOD, ... 296 LEAVES COMPARED WITH . . 1
  YOUR LAST GOOD AVALANCHE . . . . 298 ON TAKING FROM THE TOP   3
  TOO MANY FALL FROM GREAT AND GOOD . . . . 307 PROVIDE, PROVIDE . . . 5
  BUT HE'S AS GOOD AS ANYBODY GOING. . . . . . . 309 WASPISH 6
  MADE GOOD FOR EVERYONE--THINGS LIKE INVENTIONS-- . 319 BUILD SOIL 94
  MADE SO WE ALL SHOULD GET THE GOOD OF THEM-- . . 319 BUILD SOIL 95
  TO FIND THE GOOD OF COMMERCE. WHY SHOULD I . . . 321 BUILD SOIL 164
  A REASONER AND GOOD AS SUCH, ... 326 TO A THINKER 21
  AND PLAY THE GOOD WITHOUT THE ILL. . . . . . . 336 THE WIND AND THE RAIN   17
  WE MAY DOUBT THE JUST PROPORTION OF GOOD TO ILL. . 349 OUR HOLD ON THE PLANET   11
  I COULD HAVE BOUGHT YOU JUST AS GOOD A TREE . . . 350 TO A YOUNG WRETCH . . . 7
  OFTENER THAN AS CONFLICTING GOOD AND ILL; . . . . 350 TO A YOUNG WRETCH . . . 16
  THAT IN A GOOD GLASS MAY BE SEEN TO CRAWL . . . . 352 THE LESSON FOR TODAY . . 71
  AND EVERY ACRE GOOD ENOUGH TO EAT, ... 365 OF STONES OF THE PLACE   7
  HIS ACCENT WAS NOT GOOD. . . . . 366 NOT OF SCHOOL AGE . . . 17

GOOD (CONTINUED)
    THAT'S THE TIME KNOCKING AT A DOOR DID GOOD. . . . . . 368 THE LITERATE FARMER AND   8
    IT DOESN'T DO YOU ANY GOOD TO TALK. . . . . 370 THE LITERATE FARMER AND   85
    A GOOD CHEAP ANTI-DARK IS NOW THE NEED. . . . . 371 THE LITERATE FARMER AND   99
    GIVE US A GOOD CHEAP TWENTY-FOUR-HOUR DAY, ... 371 THE LITERATE FARMER AND 100
    WHO HAVE NO OTHER OBJECT THAN OUR GOOD. . . . . 372 THE LITERATE FARMER AND 135
    AND STEEPLE BUSH, NOT GOOD TO EAT. . . . . 376 SOMETHING FOR HOPE . . .   3
    GOOD GLOOM ON HER WAS THROWN AWAY. . . . . 383 THE NIGHT LIGHT . . .   5
    FOR TRAVELER THERE COULD DO ME NO GOOD . . . . 383 WERE I IN TROUBLE . .   9
    I MADE A GOOD TRY. . . . . 391 A WISH TO COMPLY . .   4
    STATES STRONG ENOUGH TO DO GOOD ARE BUT FEW. . . . . . 398 NO HOLY WARS FOR THEM .   1
    GOOD IS A THING THAT THEY, THE GREAT, CAN DO, ... 398 NO HOLY WARS FOR THEM .   3
    AND BEING GOOD FOR THESE MEANS STANDING BY . . . . . . 398 NO HOLY WARS FOR THEM .   5
    GOOD ORATORS WILL DO WHEN THEY ARE OUT. . . . . 400 THE BROKEN DROUGHT . .   8
    HE MAY BE SOME GOOD, IN A MANNER OF SPEAKING. . . . . 407 FROM PLANE TO PLANE . 103
    AND ALL THE GOOD THEY DID FOR MAN CR GOD. . . . . . . 412 POD OF THE MILKWEED . 41
    OR SOME DIM SECRET OF THE GOOD OF WASTE? . . . . 412 POD OF THE MILKWEED . 49
    GOOD FRIENDS IN TOWN. . . . . 413 AWAY!   6
    CLOSED FOR GOOD . . . . 415 CLOSED FOR GOOD . . .   T
    HIS EYES AS GOOD (OR BAD) AS SHUT . . . . 418 AMERICA IS HARD TO SEE   58
    GOD NODDED HIS APPROVAL OF AS GOOD. . . . . 422 FOR JOHN F. KENNEDY . 23
    WHICH IS NO MORE THAN GOOD OLD PANTHEISM. . . . . . . 427 CONCEPT SELF-CONCEIVED   4
    FOR GOOD GRACIOUS' SAKE. . . . . 432 KITTY HAWK 124
    FOR GOOD GRACIOUS' SAKE. . . . . 438 KITTY HAWK 315
    THIS WORLD WERE GOOD ENOUGH FOR ME." . . . . 451 A-WISHING WELL . . .   5
    GOOD LIBERALS WILL OBJECT MY NOTION . . . . 453 A-WISHING WELL . . .   69
    SO THE TWO MAKING GOOD THEIR ABDICATION . . . . 454 HOW HARD TO KEEP FROM   10
    WHAT GOOD HE WAS HE BOLDLY SAID, "I'LL TELL YOU: . . . 454 HOW HARD TO KEEP FROM   40
    "MAKE THEM AS HAPPY AS IS GOOD FOR THEM. . . . . 458 HOW HARD TO KEEP FROM   150
    AT A GOOD POINT FOR PLIANT PERMANENCE, ... 458 HOW HARD TO KEEP FROM   155
    YOU'RE GOOD AT MAXIMS. SAY ME ONE ON FREEDOM. . . . . 459 HOW HARD TO KEEP FROM   164
    HE'S A GOOD BOY. 'TWAS AT MY INSTIGATION. . . . . . . 459 HOW HARD TO KEEP FROM   173
    FOR THERE TO HAVE BEEN ANY GOOD. . . . . 467 QUANDARY   4
    THAT GOOD AND BAD SO LONG HAD LASTED. . . . . 467 QUANDARY   6
    WHO COULD DO GOOD OR EVIL AS HE CHOSE. . . . . 475 A MASQUE OF REASON .   72
    I HAD TO PROSPER GOOD AND PUNISH EVIL. . . . . 476 A MASQUE OF REASON .   76
    IS JUST AS GOOD AS WHEN I UTTERED IT. . . . . 480 A MASQUE OF REASON .   196
    AND FIND OUT WHETHER HE IS ANY GOOD, ... 484 A MASQUE OF REASON .   320
    A GOOD OLD GET-TOGETHER CELEBRATION. . . . . 487 A MASQUE OF REASON .   380
    GOOD, PRETTY GOOD. / WAIT TILL I GET MY KODAK.-- . . . 488 A MASQUE OF REASON .   402
    WHERE GOOD AND BAD ARE MINGLED EVERY WHICH WAY, . . . 488 A MASQUE OF REASON .   408
    WE BLAME OURSELVES. WE'RE GOOD SPORTS, AREN'T WE, BEL? . 496 A MASQUE OF MERCY .   78
    WELL, YOU'RE AS GOOD AS IN NEW YORK THIS MINUTE-- . . 497 A MASQUE OF MERCY .   92
    WHAT GOOD IS THAT? / I'LL MAKE YOU SEE WHAT GOOD. . . 501 A MASQUE OF MERCY .   196
    YOU'RE SPORTING THERE. I'LL BET YOU'RE GOOD AT IT. . . 502 A MASQUE OF MERCY .   219
    IT'S GOOD GEOLOGY--THE FUNDAY FAULT. . . . . 502 A MASQUE OF MERCY .   228
    OF GETTING UP GOOD RUINS, YOU'VE FORGOTTEN . . . . . . 503 A MASQUE OF MERCY .   260
    GOOD FOR YOU, JONAH. THAT'S WHAT I'VE BEEN SAYING. . . 510 A MASQUE OF MERCY .   444
    WE HAVE ALL THE BELIEF THAT'S GOOD FOR US. . . . . . . 516 A MASQUE OF MERCY .   601
    THEIR CASE IS NOT SO SIMPLE. YOU ARE GOOD. . . . . . . 517 A MASQUE OF MERCY .   620
    GOOD FOR YOU, JONAH. THAT'S WHAT I'VE BEEN SAYING. . . 517 A MASQUE OF MERCY .   636
GOOD-BY
    HOW SHALL WE SAY GOOD-BY IN SUCH A CASE?" . . . . . . 80 THE GENERATIONS OF MEN 204
    GOOD-BY." HE FLUNG HIS ARMS AROUND HIS FACE. . . . . . 101 THE SELF-SEEKER . .   228
    "GOOD-BY TO THEM! WE PUZZLE THEM. THEY THINK-- . . . . 114 IN THE HOME STRETCH . 111
    TO SEEM TO SAY GOOD-BY; . . . . 126 LONELINESS   4
    BUT HE SENT HER GOOD-BY, ... 136 LAST WORD OF A BLUEBIRD 15
    THIS SAYING GOOD-BY ON THE EDGE OF THE DARK . . . . . 228 GOOD-BY AND KEEP COLD .   1
    GOOD-BY AND KEEP COLD. . . . . 228 GOOD-BY AND KEEP COLD .   T
    KEEP COLD, YOUNG ORCHARD. GOOD-BY AND KEEP COLD. . . . 228 GOOD-BY AND KEEP COLD .   18
    BUT NOT TO CALL ME BACK OR SAY GOOD-BY; . . . . 255 ACQUAINTED WITH NIGHT .   10
    AND ITS CHOKECHERRIES LIPS TO KISS GOOD-BY, ... 268 THE BEAR   3
GOOD-DOERS
    WHILE GREEDY GOOD-DOERS, BENEFICENT BEASTS OF PREY, . 287 A ROADSIDE STAND . .   27
GOOD-FOR-NOTHINGS
    WE HAVE FOUR HERE TO BOARD, GREAT GOOD-FOR-NOTHINGS, . 65 A SERVANT TO SERVANTS .   76
GOOD-LOOKING
    GOOD-LOOKING BOOKS LIKE THAT." HE PICKED ONE FRESH . . 217 A FOUNTAIN, A BOTTLE . 125
GOOD-MORNING
    BEFORE I WENT TO SAY GOOD-MORNING THERE.-- . . . . . . 143 SNOW   18
GOODNESS
    HE THOUGHT NO SPECIAL GOODNESS COULD BE LOST . . . . . 284 THE GOLD HESPERIDEE .   34
GOOD-NIGHT
    "THIS WILL BE YOURS, GOOD-NIGHT," HE SAID, AND WENT. . 46 A HUNDRED COLLARS . .   40
    AS A CHILD MISSES THE UNSAID GOOD-NIGHT. . . . . 58 THE BLACK COTTAGE . .   102
    WITHOUT SO MUCH AS WISHING HIM GOOD-NIGHT. . . . . . . 101 THE WOOD-PILE . . .   21
    TO DRAG YOU OUT FOR JUST A GOOD-NIGHT CALL . . . . . . 117 IN THE HOME STRETCH . 188
    I CALLED YOU UP TO SAY GOOD-NIGHT FROM HERE . . . . . 143 SNOW   17
    SAID IT AT LAST HIMSELF, "GOOD-NIGHT," AND THEN, . . . 143 SNOW   29
    ARE RESTED AND IT'S TIME TO SAY GOOD-NIGHT. . . . . . 150 SNOW   210
    AND LET YOU GET TO BED AGAIN. GOOD-NIGHT, ... 150 SNOW   211
    "GOOD-NIGHT TO WOODS." BUT NOT SO; THERE WAS MORE. . . 229 TWO LOOK AT TWO . .   14
GOODS
    TO EMPTY ONE HOUSE OF ALL HOUSEHOLD GOODS . . . . . . 116 IN THE HOME STRETCH . 160
    WITH GOODS TO SELL AND NOTIONS TO IMPART. . . . . . . 324 BUILD SOIL   269
    THEY ARE TO BE THOUGHT OF AS OPPOSING GOODS . . . . . 350 TO A YOUNG WRETCH . .   15
GOOSE
    THAT WAS BACK IN THE DAYS OF MY GODMOTHER GOOSE. . . . 463 LINES IN DEJECTION . .   5
GOOSIER
    BUT THOUGH WE ARE GOOSIER NOW, ... 463 LINES IN DEJECTION . .   6
GOSPEL
    BUT THE GOSPEL OF SHARING, ... 449 THE BAD ISLAND--EASTER   60
    ON THE GOSPEL OF MODERN SCIENCE, ... 466 SOME SCIENCE FICTION .   16
GOSPELS
    THE GOSPELS TO IT. AFTER DOING JUSTICE JUSTICE . . . . 508 A MASQUE OF MERCY .   379
GOT
    "HE NEVER GOT UP HIGH ENOUGH TO SEE. . . . . 43 THE MOUNTAIN   78

	PAGE	TITLE	LINE

GOT (CONTINUED)
```
    YOU GOT IT THE FIRST TIME. AND YOURS?" / "MAGOON. . . . .   46  A HUNDRED COLLARS . .  42
    SHE'S GOT SO SHE TURNS IN AT EVERY HOUSE . . . . . .         49  A HUNDRED COLLARS . . 142
    ANYTHING THEY'VE NOT GOT. I NEVER DUN. . . . . . . .         50  A HUNDRED COLLARS . . 152
    AS WE ALMOST GOT BY THIS AFTERNOON. . . . . . . . .          56  THE BLACK COTTAGE . .  44
    BUT NEVER MIND, THE WELSHMAN GOT IT PLANTED . . . . .        57  THE BLACK COTTAGE . .  68
    IT NEVER GOT SO FAR AS THAT; BUT THE BARE THOUGHT . . .      57  THE BLACK COTTAGE . .  90
    IT'S GOT SO I DON'T EVEN KNOW FOR SURE . . . . . .           63  A SERVANT TO SERVANTS  11
    IT'S HIGHWAYS, AND HE'S GOT TOO MANY MEN . . . . . .         64  A SERVANT TO SERVANTS  72
    IT GOT SO I WOULD SAY--YOU KNOW, HALF FOOLING-- . . .        67  A SERVANT TO SERVANTS 145
    I S'POSE I'VE GOT TO GO THE ROAD I'M GOING: . . . . .        67  A SERVANT TO SERVANTS 159
    I GOT FROM LOOKING THROUGH A PANE OF GLASS . . . . .         68  AFTER APPLE-PICKING .  10
    BEFORE HE ACTED: HE'S JUST GOT ROUND TO ACT." . . . .        70  THE CODE . . . . .  19
    HE'S GOT HAY DOWN THAT'S BEEN RAINED ON THREE TIMES. .       83  THE HOUSEKEEPER . . .  57
    WHAT HE HAS GOT TO STAND." / "WHERE IS ESTELLE? . . .        83  THE HOUSEKEEPER . . .  71
    BUT I GOT WONTED TO IT. AND BESIDES-- . . . . . . .          87  THE HOUSEKEEPER . . . 174
    I'VE GOT SOME NEWS THAT MAYBE ISN'T NEWS. . . . . .          88  THE HOUSEKEEPER . . . 210
    SHE PUSHED PAST HIM AND GOT IT FOR HERSELF. . . . . .        90  THE FEAR . . . . .  34
    BUT MY LEGS GOT THEIR KNOCKS AGAINST THE CEILING." . .       93  THE SELF-SEEKER . .  29
    YOU'VE GOT TO TELL ME HOW FAR THIS IS GONE: . . . . .        94  THE SELF-SEEKER . .  57
    A RAM'S HORN! WHAT WOULD I HAVE GOT, I WONDER, . . . .       96  THE SELF-SEEKER . . . 113
    "THEY'RE NOT GONE YET." / "WE'VE GOT TO HAVE THE STOVE, . . 113  IN THE HOME STRETCH .  78
    THE FIRE GOT OUT THROUGH CRANNIES IN THE STOVE . . . .      117  IN THE HOME STRETCH . 202
    AND GOT THEM OFF THE WILD FLOWERS' BACKS. . . . . .         123  PEA BRUSH . . . .  16
    I WONDER HOW FAR DOWN THE ROAD HE'S GOT. . . . . . .        127  THE SMILE . . . . .  11
    GOT HIM BY SOMETHING HE HAD ON . . . . . . . . .           137  BROWN'S DESCENT . . .  10
    TO IMPRESS MEN. YOU'VE GOT US SO ASHAMED . . . . . .       146  SNOW . . . . . .  99
    SAYS IT WON'T DO. YOU'VE GOT TO GIVE IT UP." . . . . .      147  SNOW . . . . . . 107
    TO LAST HER TILL HE GOT OUTSIDE THE DOOR, . . . . .         151  SNOW . . . . . . 243
    AFTER HE'D PICKED THE LOCK AND GOT IT STARTED, . . . .      170  NEW HAMPSHIRE . . . 346
    HE GOT A GOOD GLASS FOR SIX HUNDRED DOLLARS. . . . .        178  THE STAR-SPLITTER . .  74
    (THEY EITHER NOTICED IT, OR GOT IT WRONG.) . . . . .        181  MAPLE . . . . . .  51
    (IF OVERJOYED HE WAS) AT HAVING GOT ME . . . . . . .        186  THE AX-HELVE . . .  40
    THAT GOT HER NOWHERE; ONE MORE GRADUAL, . . . . . .         187  THE AX-HELVE . . .  49
    HAVE GOT IT ONE STEP FROM THE STARTING PLACE. . . . .       189  THE GRINDSTONE . . .   7
    A FATHER-TIME-LIKE MAN GOT ON AND RODE, . . . . . .         189  THE GRINDSTONE . . .  29
    AND SPREAD THE OPENING, AND YOU'VE GOT A DUGOUT . . .       193  PAUL'S WIFE . . . .  81
    GOT DRUNK, AND TRACKED THE PAIR UP CATAMOUNT, . . . .       195  PAUL'S WIFE . . . . 124
    WHO'S GOT THE BUTTON," I WOULD HAVE THEM KNOW. . . . .      202  THE WITCH OF COOS . .   8
    BEFORE I GOT UP TO DO ANYTHING; . . . . . . . . .          205  THE WITCH OF COOS . .  92
    NOW THAT THEY'VE GOT IT SETTLED WHOSE I BE, . . . . .       207  PAUPER WITCH OF GRAFTON  1
    THEY'VE GOT IT SETTLED WRONG, AND I CAN PROVE IT. . .       207  PAUPER WITCH OF GRAFTON  3
    THEY'LL FIND THEY'VE GOT THE WHOLE THING TO DO OVER, .      207  PAUPER WITCH OF GRAFTON 10
    I GUESS HE FOUND HE GOT MORE OUT OF ME . . . . . .         209  PAUPER WITCH OF GRAFTON 76
    TO TURN HIM ROUND. HE GOT TO SAYING THINGS . . . . .       209  PAUPER WITCH OF GRAFTON 78
    LEAVES GOT UP IN A COIL AND HISSED, . . . . . . . .        251  BEREFT . . . . . .   9
    A SLIM DOOR GOT IN PAST MY GUARD, . . . . . . . .         265  THE DOOR IN THE DARK .   5
    HE GOT HIS PURPLE LITTLE KNUCKLES STUNG. . . . . . .       293  AT WOODWARD'S GARDENS . 17
    GOT ME INTO MY DOUBLE ADVENTURE. . . . . . . . .          294  A RECORD STRIDE . .  18
    AND GOT THE UNITED STATES STATED. . . . . . . . .         295  A RECORD STRIDE . .  36
    BUT INSIDE IN IS WHERE WE'VE GOT TO GET. . . . . .         320  BUILD SOIL . . . . 141
    YOU'VE GOT TO KEEP THE QUARTERS CLEAN." . . . . . .        345  DISCOVERY OF MADEIRAS . 62
    WHATEVER IT IS THE NIGGER'S GOT." . . . . . . . .         345  DISCOVERY OF MADEIRAS . 75
    A BED'S GOT NO RIGHT SIDE TO GET OUT OF. . . . . .         372  THE LITERATE FARMER AND 125
    HE'S SURELY GOT IT IN FOR COTS AND BEDS. . . . . .        372  THE LITERATE FARMER AND 131
    ABOUT IT, THOUGH. WE HAVEN'T GOT THE MIND. . . . . .       372  THE LITERATE FARMER AND 133
    WHAT OF IT, THOUGH? I GOT SOME WILLY-NILLY . . . . .       393  LUCRETIUS VERSUS POETS   2
    YOU'D BET YOU GOT MORE WORK DONE IN A DAY, . . . . .       405  FROM PLANE TO PLANE .  46
    "A MAN HAS GOT TO KEEP HIS EXTRICATION. . . . . . .        406  FROM PLANE TO PLANE .  61
    YOU'VE GOT NO SOCIAL CONSCIENCE, AS THEY SAY, . . . .       406  FROM PLANE TO PLANE .  77
    HE GOT NO MORE THAN DUNGEON CHAINS . . . . . . . .        417  AMERICA IS HARD TO SEE  44
    HAD NO REAL PURPOSE TILL IT GOT TO US. . . . . . .        425  ACCIDENTALLY ON PURPOSE 12
    AND THE SHAFT GOT BLUNTED . . . . . . . . . .            427  VERSION . . . . .  11
    WE'D HAVE GOT AS FAR . . . . . . . . . . . .            439  KITTY HAWK . . . . 348
    HE GOT HIS FIRST CHANCE TO PREPARE A MEAL . . . . .        455  HOW HARD TO KEEP FROM  55
    WHAT HAS IT GOT TO DO WITH CHARACTER? . . . . . .         459  HOW HARD TO KEEP FROM 165
    BUT SINCE WE GOT NOWHERE, . . . . . . . . . .            464  MILKY WAY IS A COWPATH   5
    LIKE SMALL BOYS WE GOT MAD . . . . . . . . . .           464  MILKY WAY IS A COWPATH   6
    HAS GOT A RAZOR EDGE; . . . . . . . . . . .             465  MILKY WAY IS A COWPATH  36
    AND HE GOT IT BIT. . . . . . . . . . . . .             468  A REFLEX . . . . .   4
    AND HE GOT A GRAB. . . . . . . . . . . . .             468  A REFLEX . . . . .   6
    THAT WAS WHAT HE GOT. . . . . . . . . . . .            468  A REFLEX . . . . .   7
    I SHOULD HAVE SAID. YOU GOT YOUR AGE REVERSED . . . .       479  A MASQUE OF REASON . . 159
    BEFORE I AM TOO LATE TO BE GOT RIGHT . . . . . .          479  A MASQUE OF REASON . . 166
    WHO SAYS WE DON'T? WHO GOT UP THESE MISGIVINGS? . . .       483  A MASQUE OF REASON . . 288
    I STUMBLED OVER IT AND GOT TRIPPED UP. . . . . . .        489  A MASQUE OF REASON . . 446
    WHAT HAVE YOU GOT AGAINST THE CITY? / HE KNOWS. . . .       496  A MASQUE OF MERCY . .  65
    WHO HAVING BY ELIMINATION GOT . . . . . . . . .          498  A MASQUE OF MERCY . . 120
    OF THE WORD LOVE CORRECTED. SHE GOT OFF . . . . . .        499  A MASQUE OF MERCY . . 161
    IT'S A HARD CASE. IT'S GOT SO PROPHECY . . . . . .        503  A MASQUE OF MERCY . . 257
    AND IF YOU'VE GOT TO SEE YOUR JUSTICE CROSSED . . . .       510  A MASQUE OF MERCY . . 436
    (AND YOU'VE GOT TO), WHICH WILL YOU PREFER . . . . .       510  A MASQUE OF MERCY . . 437
    WE'RE READING IT. / WELL, NOW YOU'VE GOT IT READ, . .       512  A MASQUE OF MERCY . . 491
    I THINK I MAY HAVE GOT GOD WRONG ENTIRELY. . . . .        518  A MASQUE OF MERCY . . 654
```
GOTTEN
```
    SOMEHOW MUST HAVE GOTTEN ABROAD, . . . . . . . .         251  BEREFT . . . . . .  14
```
GOTTERDAMMERUNG
```
    GOTTERDAMMERUNG . . . . . . . . . . . . .             431  KITTY HAWK . . . .  98
```
GOUGED
```
    THEN HE GOUGED A CLUMSY SAILING TROUGH . . . . . .        347  DISCOVERY OF MADEIRAS . 125
```
GOVERN
```
    IF DESIGN GOVERN IN A THING SO SMALL. . . . . . .        302  DESIGN . . . . . .  14
```
GOVERNED
```
    FOR THESE HAVE GOVERNED IN OUR LIVES, . . . . . .        252  THE PEACEFUL SHEPHERD .   9
    I'M NO MORE GOVERNED BY THE FEAR OF HELL . . . . .        520  A MASQUE OF MERCY . . 702
```
GOVERNMENT
```
    AN ELEMENT IN ANY GOVERNMENT. . . . . . . . . .          318  BUILD SOIL . . . .  69
    UNLESS A GOVERNMENT INTERFERES. . . . . . . . .          376  SOMETHING FOR HOPE . .  20
```

GOVERNOR
    A GOVERNOR IT WAS PROCLAIMED THIS TIME, ... 73 THE GENERATIONS OF MEN   1
GOWN
    FROM WHICH TO GATHER YOUR GOWN. . . . . 27 A LINE-STORM SONG . . 20
GRAB
    AND HE GOT A GRAB. . . . . 468 A REFLEX 6
GRACE
    OBTAIN SUCH GRACE OF HOURS . . . . 14 ROSE POGONIAS . . . 22
    TO YIELD WITH A GRACE TO REASON, ... 30 RELUCTANCE . . . 22
    HE BOWED WITH GRACE TO NATURAL LAW, ... 139 BROWN'S DESCENT . . . 60
    NOT HALFWAY DOWN THE SCALE OF GRACE. . . . . . . 326 TO A THINKER . . . 32
    BY GRACE OF STATE-MANIPULATED PELF, ... 359 THE LOST FOLLOWER . . 29
    THE MOON FOR ALL HER LIGHT AND GRACE . . . . . 390 TWO LEADING LIGHTS . 12
    WITH GRACE AND NOT TOO FORMAL A SURRENDER . . . . 408 FROM PLANE TO PLANE . 121
    OLD ATTIC GRACE AND SPARTAN DISCIPLINE . . . . . 511 A MASQUE OF MERCY . . 467
GRACEFULLY
    IT MUST AT SOME POINT GRACEFULLY REFRAIN. . . . . 319 BUILD SOIL . . . 116
GRACING
    NOT BLUEBELLS GRACING A TUNNEL MOUTH-- . . . . . 248 A PASSING GLIMPSE . . 7
GRACIOUS'
    FOR GOOD GRACIOUS' SAKE. . . . . 432 KITTY HAWK . . . 124
    FOR GOOD GRACIOUS' SAKE, ... 438 KITTY HAWK . . . 315
GRACIOUSLY
    "TAKE ONE," OLD DAVIS BADE ME GRACIOUSLY. . . . . 217 A FOUNTAIN, A BOTTLE . 123
GRADE
    THE GRADE SURMOUNTED, WE WERE RIDING HIGH . . . . 292 FIGURE IN THE DOORWAY . 1
GRADUAL
    THAT GOT HER NOWHERE; ONE MORE GRADUAL, ... 187 THE AX-HELVE . . . 49
GRADUALLY
    HAD GRADUALLY WORN IT AN OBLATE . . . . 190 THE GRINDSTONE . . . 39
GRAFTED
    SQUARE MATTHEW HALE'S YOUNG GRAFTED APPLE TREE . . . . 283 THE GOLD HESPERIDEE . 1
GRAFTON
    THE PAUPER WITCH OF GRAFTON . . . . 207 PAUPER WITCH OF GRAFTON   T
    IN FRONT OF EVERY ONE IN GRAFTON COUNTY. . . . . . 209 PAUPER WITCH OF GRAFTON   51
GRAIL
    A BROKEN DRINKING GOBLET LIKE THE GRAIL . . . . . 379 DIRECTIVE 57
GRAIN
    AND BURNING TO YIELD FLOWERS INSTEAD OF GRAIN, ... 173 A STAR IN A STONEBOAT . 22
    "MADE ON MACHINE," HE SAID, PLOWING THE GRAIN . . . . 186 THE AX-HELVE . . . 22
    WERE NATIVE TO THE GRAIN BEFORE THE KNIFE . . . . 187 THE AX-HELVE . . . 73
    AND WHEN WE HAD TAKEN THAT INTO THE ROOTS OF GRAIN, . . 349 OUR HOLD ON THE PLANET . 8
    OR CREAKING WITH A BUGGY LOAD OF GRAIN. . . . . . 378 DIRECTIVE 32
GRAINS
    SAND GRAINS SHOULD SUGAR IN THE NATAL DEW . . . . . 58 THE BLACK COTTAGE . . 122
GRANDCHILDREN
    JOHN SAID I WAS TOO OLD TO HAVE GRANDCHILDREN. . . . . 87 THE HOUSEKEEPER . . . 175
    TWO ENTIRELY DIFFERENT GRANDCHILDREN . . . . . . 294 A RECORD STRIDE . . . 17
GRANDLY
    THE KING SAID GRANDLY, "EVEN AS WE ARE FED . . . . 455 HOW HARD TO KEEP FROM   63
GRANDMOTHER (SEE GREAT-GRANDMOTHER)
    TEACH YOUR GRANDMOTHER EGG SUCTION. . . . . . . 397 AN IMPORTER 26
GRANDSIR
    I CAN MAKE OUT OLD GRANDSIR STARK DISTINCTLY-- . . . . 77 THE GENERATIONS OF MEN   104
    BLESS YOU, IT ISN'T GRANDSIR STARK, IT'S GRANNY; . . . 77 THE GENERATIONS OF MEN   106
GRANDSIR'S
    DOES IT PURPORT TO SPEAK IN? NOT OLD GRANDSIR'S . . . 79 THE GENERATIONS OF MEN   174
GRANGE
    OR BEEN MADE MASTER OF THE GRANGE." . . . . . . 138 BROWN'S DESCENT . . . 36
GRANITE
    GREAT GRANITE TERRACES IN SUN AND SHADOW, ... 42 THE MOUNTAIN . . . 58
    OF WOOD OR GRANITE OR LIME . . . . 348 TRIPLE BRONZE . . . 6
    AND BEGAN TO BOUNCE DOWN A GRANITE STAIR, ... 383 WERE I IN TROUBLE . . 4
GRANNY
    BLESS YOU, IT ISN'T GRANDSIR STARK, IT'S GRANNY; . . . 77 THE GENERATIONS OF MEN   106
    "YOU POOR, DEAR, GREAT, GREAT, GREAT, GREAT GRANNY!" . . 77 THE GENERATIONS OF MEN   116
    "WELL THEN, IT'S GRANNY SPEAKING: 'I DUNNOW! . . . . 80 THE GENERATIONS OF MEN   184
    YOU CAN SEE WHAT IS TROUBLING GRANNY, THOUGH. . . . . 80 THE GENERATIONS OF MEN   195
GRANNY'S
    NOR GRANNY'S, SURELY. CALL UP ONE OF THEM. . . . . 79 THE GENERATIONS OF MEN   175
GRANSIR
    "THE PORTRAIT OF THE SOUL OF MY GRANSIR IRA. . . . . 366 OF STONES OF THE PLACE   15
GRANT
    AND HALF GRANT WHAT I WISH AND SNATCH ME AWAY . . . . 122 BIRCHES 51
    THE MOST HE ASKED HER EYES TO GRANT . . . . . . 344 DISCOVERY OF MADEIRAS . 41
    I GRANT YOU--IF YOU'RE SURE ABOUT THE WORD. . . . . 394 LUCRETIUS VERSUS POETS . 11
    WE GRANT YOUR LOFTINESS THE RIGHT . . . . . . 403 SOMETHING LIKE A STAR . 2
    GRANT ME INTENTION, PURPOSE, AND DESIGN-- . . . . . 425 ACCIDENTALLY ON PURPOSE 19
    I LOOKED ON IT AS A CARNEGIE GRANT . . . . . . 459 HOW HARD TO KEEP FROM   174
GRANTED
    IN HAVING GRANTED YOU ALL AGES SHINE . . . . . . 354 THE LESSON FOR TODAY . 118
GRAPE
    AND ALDER AND GRAPE VINE ENTANGLEMENT, ... 131 THE BONFIRE . . . 63
    THE GRAPE MAY NOT BE GATHERED FROM THE BIRCH? . . . . 196 WILD GRAPES . . . 2
    IT'S ALL YOU KNOW THE GRAPE, OR KNOW THE BIRCH. . . . 196 WILD GRAPES . . . 3
    I OUGHT TO KNOW WHAT TREE THE GRAPE IS FRUIT OF. . . . 196 WILD GRAPES . . . 6
GRAPES
    I DOUBT IF THEY HAVE LEFT US MANY GRAPES. . . . . . 117 IN THE HOME STRETCH . 193
    HER UNPRUNED GRAPES ARE FLUNG LIKE LARIATS . . . . 164 NEW HAMPSHIRE . . . 163
    EQUALLY WITH MY WEIGHT IN GRAPES, ONE AUTUMN, ... 196 WILD GRAPES . . . 5
    WILD GRAPES . . . . 196 WILD GRAPES . . . T
    THE DAY I SWUNG SUSPENDED WITH THE GRAPES, ... 196 WILD GRAPES . . . 11
    AGAINST HER NECK, AN ORNAMENT OF GRAPES. . . . . . 197 WILD GRAPES . . . 23
    GRAPES, I KNEW GRAPES FROM HAVING SEEN THEM LAST YEAR. . 197 WILD GRAPES . . . 24
    THREW ME DOWN GRAPES TO MISS AND SCATTER . . . . . 197 WILD GRAPES . . . 32
    AND PUT IT IN MY HANDS TO PICK MY OWN GRAPES. . . . . 197 WILD GRAPES . . . 38
    "WHAT ARE YOU DOING UP THERE IN THOSE GRAPES? . . . . 198 WILD GRAPES . . . 56
    "TO BE A BUNCH OF FOX GRAPES, AS THEY CALL THEM, . . . 198 WILD GRAPES . . . 63

GRAPES (CONTINUED)
    ONLY YOU HAVE THE ADVANTAGE OF THE GRAPES . . . . . . 198 WILD GRAPES 69
    WE DON'T GO BACK ON GRAPES WE COULDN'T REACH. . . . . . 496 A MASQUE OF MERCY . . . 77
GRAPES'
    FOR THE GRAPES' SAKE, IF THEY WERE ALL, ... 28 OCTOBER 18
    FOR THE GRAPES' SAKE ALONG THE WALL. . . . . 28 OCTOBER 21
GRAPEVINE
    FROM HIDDEN GRAPEVINE SPRINGS . . . . 227 TO EARTHWARD 7
GRAPEVINES
    O'ER RUINED FENCES THE GRAPEVINES SHIELD . . . . 5 GHOST HOUSE 6
GRAPPLING
    SO MANY PRICKLY GRAPPLING FEET AT ONCE. . . . . 278 THE WHITE-TAILED HORNET 29
GRASP
    SNATCHED THEE, O'EREAGER, WITH UNGENTLE GRASP. . . . . . 29 MY BUTTERFLY 30
    YOU GRASP THE BARK BY A RUGGED PLEAT, ... 247 ON GOING UNNOTICED . . . 9
    THEY'VE TRIED TO GRASP WITH TOO MUCH SOCIAL FACT . . . . 351 THE LESSON FOR TODAY . 34
GRASPED
    BRINGING A STONE GRASPED FIRMLY BY THE TOP . . . . . . 34 MENDING WALL 39
    MOVED IN A LITTLE. THE MAN GRASPED A WHEEL. . . . . . . 89 THE FEAR 7
GRASS (SEE JUNE-GRASS, TINDER-GRASS)
    FOR THOUGH THE GRASS WAS SCATTERED, ... 13 ROSE POGONIAS 13
    THAT NONE SHOULD MOW THE GRASS THERE . . . . 14 ROSE POGONIAS 23
    I WENT TO TURN THE GRASS ONCE AFTER ONE . . . . 22 THE TUFT OF FLOWERS . 1
    BUT HE HAD GONE HIS WAY, THE GRASS ALL MOWN, ... 22 THE TUFT OF FLOWERS . 7
    AND WOULD HAVE TURNED TO TOSS THE GRASS TO DRY; . . . . 22 THE TUFT OF FLOWERS . 20
    THE GRAY GRASS IS SCARCE DAPPLED WITH THE SNOW; . . . . 28 MY BUTTERFLY 8
    GOOD GRASSLAND GULLIED OUT, AND IN THE GRASS . . . . . 40 THE MOUNTAIN 13
    SET WELL BACK FROM THE ROAD IN RANK LODGED GRASS, . . . 55 THE BLACK COTTAGE . 4
    THE PATH WAS A VAGUE PARTING IN THE GRASS . . . . . . 55 THE BLACK COTTAGE . 12
    AND HELD AGAINST THE WORLD OF HOARY GRASS. . . . . . . 68 AFTER APPLE-PICKING . 12
    WITH A SWISH IN THE GRASS. "WHAT IF THE OTHERS . . . . 74 THE GENERATIONS OF MEN 23
    BUT ADVANCED WITH HER AS SHE CROSSED THE GRASS. . . . . 91 THE FEAR 60
    NOR WAS THE GRASS ITSELF YOUR REAL CONCERN, ... 109 THE EXPOSED NEST . . . 10
    BY STARLIGHT IN THE GRASS FOR A LAST PEACH . . . . . . 117 IN THE HOME STRETCH . 190
    IT PUT THE FLAME TIP-DOWN AND DABBED THE GRASS . . . . 131 THE BONFIRE 45
    GRASS ITS FULL LENGTH, OLD SILVER GOLDENROD, ... 131 THE BONFIRE 62
    EVER TO GRIND TO SOIL FOR GRASS. . . . . 140 THE GUM-GATHERER . . . 17
    IN GRASS AND SAND, ... 227 TO EARTHWARD 28
    THE MEADOW GRASS COULD BE CEMENTED DOWN . . . . 231 A BROOK IN THE CITY . 9
    YOU MADE NO SOUND IN THE GRASS WITH YOUR FOOTFALL, . . . 235 VALLEY'S SINGING DAY . 2
    DID GRASS AND GARDEN GROUND CONFESS IT SNOWED, ... 239 OUR SINGING STRENGTH . 9
    THE GRASS LAY FLATTENED UNDER ONE GREAT TREAD. . . . . 239 OUR SINGING STRENGTH . 12
    THEY FALL, THEY RIP THE GRASS, THEY INTERSECT . . . . 261 A SOLDIER 9
    SUBDUED THE GROWTH OF EARTH TO GRASS, ... 265 THE BIRTHPLACE 5
    AND ONE DID STOP, BUT ONLY TO PLOW UP GRASS . . . . . 287 A ROADSIDE STAND . . . 39
    FOR THE GRASS WAS HIGH; . . . . 342 QUEST OF PURPLE-FRINGED 10
    WILL HAVE CROWDED OUT THE EDIBLE GRASS. . . . . 376 SOMETHING FOR HOPE . . . 4
    AND READY AGAIN FOR THE GRASS TO OWN. . . . . 376 SOMETHING FOR HOPE . . . 16
    DEVELOPED IN THE GRASS AND FERN, ... 380 AN UNSTAMPED LETTER IN . 20
    AS THE HOP FROM GRASS . . . . 439 KITTY HAWK 359
GRASS-BLADE
    OR GRASS-BLADE IS LEFT, NOT TO MENTION A STICK, ... 59 BLUEBERRIES 19
GRASSES
    SURGING, THE GRASSES DIZZIED ME OF THOUGHT, ... 29 MY BUTTERFLY 35
GRASSHOPPER
    OF A GRASSHOPPER, ... 439 KITTY HAWK 360
GRASSLAND
    GOOD GRASSLAND GULLIED OUT, AND IN THE GRASS . . . . . 40 THE MOUNTAIN 13
GRASSY
    BECAUSE IT WAS GRASSY AND WANTED WEAR; . . . . 105 THE ROAD NOT TAKEN . . . 8
    THE LIVING COME WITH GRASSY TREAD. . . . . 221 IN A DISUSED GRAVEYARD . 1
    WINDS BLOW THE OPEN GRASSY PLACES BLEAK; . . . . 246 ATMOSPHERE 1
GRATEFUL
    AND GRATEFUL FOR IT (LET'S NOT BE FACETIOUS!) . . . . . 393 LUCRETIUS VERSUS POETS 4
GRATITUDE
    IN GRATITUDE FOR WHICH SQUARE MATTHEW VOWED . . . . . . 285 THE GOLD HESPERIDEE . 59
    HE LIKES TO TURN HIS BACK ON GRATITUDE . . . . 408 FROM PLANE TO PLANE . 130
    HE WILL NOT STOP FOR GRATITUDE . . . . 418 AMERICA IS HARD TO SEE 74
    HE ROLLED AN EYE WITH GRATITUDE. . . . . 420 ONE MORE BREVITY . . . 20
GRAVE (SEE SINISTER-GRAVE)
    WITH YOUR OWN HAND--HOW COULD YOU?--HIS LITTLE GRAVE; . . 53 HOME BURIAL 73
    OF THE FRESH EARTH FROM YOUR OWN BABY'S GRAVE . . . . . 54 HOME BURIAL 85
    FRIENDS MAKE PRETENSE OF FOLLOWING TO THE GRAVE, ... 54 HOME BURIAL 102
    BESIDES THE GRAVE. . . . . 129 THE IMPULSE 28
    FOR HE TURNED SUDDENLY GRAVE AS IF TO SAY, ... 142 THE VANISHING RED . 5
    HIS FIRST THOUGHT UNDER PRESSURE WAS A GRAVE . . . . . 200 PLACE FOR A THIRD . 22
    IN A NEW-BOUGHTEN GRAVE PLOT BY HERSELF, ... 200 PLACE FOR A THIRD . 23
    SOMEWHERE MUST BE THE GRAVE OF THE YOUNG BOY . . . . . 200 PLACE FOR A THIRD . 33
    WHERE WAS HIS GRAVE? DID LABAN KNOW HIS NAME? . . . . . 200 PLACE FOR A THIRD . 37
    HE FOUND THE GRAVE A TOWN OR TWO AWAY, ... 200 PLACE FOR A THIRD . 38
    BEGGED SIMPLY FOR THE GRAVE. THE SISTER'S FACE . . . . 201 PLACE FOR A THIRD . 47
    A WIDOW AT HER SECOND HUSBAND'S GRAVE, ... 201 PLACE FOR A THIRD . 59
    "WHAT BONES?" "THE CELLAR BONES--OUT OF THE GRAVE." . . 205 THE WITCH OF COOS . 101
    WE THINK THEY HAD A GRAVE DOWN IN THE CELLAR. . . . . . 206 THE WITCH OF COOS . 135
    WE KNOW THEY HAD A GRAVE DOWN IN THE CELLAR. . . . . . 206 THE WITCH OF COOS . 136
    THE LEAST I COULD DO WAS HELP DIG THEIR GRAVE. . . . . 206 THE WITCH OF COOS . 141
    IN THAT GRAVE ONE . . . . 219 I WILL SING YOU ONE-O . 38
    IN THAT GRAVE WORD . . . . 219 I WILL SING YOU ONE-O . 60
    THERE MAY BE LITTLE OR MUCH BEYOND THE GRAVE, ... 300 STRONG SAYING NOTHING . 15
    WAS COILED IN ITS LAST RESTING GRAVE. . . . . 312 THE VINDICTIVES 61
    BUT ONLY GRAVE, CONTEMPLATIVE AND GRAVE. . . . . . . 334 I COULD GIVE ALL . . . 5
    AS GRAVE AS HE ABOUT THE WORLD'S DEFEAT. . . . . . . 359 THE LOST FOLLOWER . 24
    THAN TO ROB THE GRAVE. . . . . 430 KITTY HAWK 77
GRAVEL
    MAKING THE GRAVEL LEAP AND LEAP IN AIR, ... 53 HOME BURIAL 75
GRAVELS
    NOT ONLY SANDS AND GRAVELS . . . . 376 ONE STEP BACKWARD TAKEN 1

                                                          PAGE TITLE   LINE
GRAVELY
    THE LAWYER GRAVELY CAPPED HIS FOUNTAIN PEN. . . . . . . 100 THE SELF-SEEKER . . . 218
GRAVER
    TO WALK A GRAVER MAN RESTRAINED IN WRATH. . . . . . . 285 THE GOLD HESPERIDEE . . 60
GRAVES
    THE GRAVES OF MEN ON AN OPPOSING HILL, ... 17 THE VANTAGE POINT . . 7
    WE BOTH OF US TURNED OVER IN OUR GRAVES. . . . . 161 NEW HAMPSHIRE . . . 60
    IT SENT ME TO THE GRAVES THE OTHER DAY. . . . . 354 THE LESSON FOR TODAY . 127
    OF ALL THE DEAD AND BURIED FROM THEIR GRAVES. . . . . . 484 A MASQUE OF REASON . . 307
GRAVESTONES
    TO READ THE GRAVESTONES ON THE HILL; . . . . 221 IN A DISUSED GRAVEYARD 2
GRAVEYARD
    THE LITTLE GRAVEYARD WHERE MY PEOPLE ARE! . . . . . . 51 HOME BURIAL 23
    THE GRAVEYARD DRAWS THE LIVING STILL, ... 221 IN A DISUSED GRAVEYARD 3
    IN A DISUSED GRAVEYARD . . . . 221 IN A DISUSED GRAVEYARD T
    LIKE GRAVEYARD MARBLE SCULPTURE IN THE WEATHER, ... 377 DIRECTIVE 4
GRAVEYARDS
    HAD HAD TO ORGANIZE TO STOCK THE GRAVEYARDS . . . . . . 159 NEW HAMPSHIRE . . . 20
GRAY
    SHE'S GLAD HER SIMPLE WORSTED GRAY . . . . 7 MY NOVEMBER GUEST . . 9
    GAUNT AND DUSTY GRAY WITH ROAMING? . . . . 13 FLOWER-GATHERING . . 6
    HIS SKIN AND HIS HAIR AND HIS EYES WERE GRAY, ... 23 PAN WITH US 2
    THE GRAY OF THE MOSS OF WALLS WERE THEY-- . . . . 23 PAN WITH US 3
    THE GRAY GRASS IS SCARCE DAPPLED WITH THE SNOW; . . . . 28 MY BUTTERFLY 8
    OUT WALKING IN THE FROZEN SWAMP ONE GRAY DAY, ... 101 THE WOOD-PILE . . . 1
    THE WOOD WAS GRAY AND THE BARK WARPING OFF IT . . . . . 102 THE WOOD-PILE . . . 29
    TO LAMPS UNLIGHTED AND FIRE GONE GRAY, ... 127 HOUSE FEAR 4
    AND RECOGNIZED HIM, THROUGH THE IRON GRAY . . . . 160 NEW HAMPSHIRE . . . 47
    AND WE SAW HIM, OR THOUGHT WE SAW HIM, DIM AND GRAY, . . 223 THE RUNAWAY 7
GRAZING
    THAT WHEN LET LOOSE UPON THE GRAZING WORLD . . . . . . 319 BUILD SOIL 109
GREASE
    SOMETHING HAD LEFT A BROAD BLACK STREAK OF GREASE . . . 193 PAUL'S WIFE 69
    BUT WHEN PAUL PUT HIS FINGER IN THE GREASE, ... 193 PAUL'S WIFE 72
    IT WASN'T GREASE AT ALL, BUT A LONG SLOT. . . . . . . 193 PAUL'S WIFE 73
GREASED
    (IT RAN AS IF IT WASN'T GREASED BUT GLUED); . . . . . . 190 THE GRINDSTONE . . . 61
GREAT
    WITH THOSE GREAT CARELESS WINGS, ... 29 MY BUTTERFLY 24
    ONE OF THE GREAT SIGHTS GOING IS TO SEE . . . . 42 THE MOUNTAIN . . . 50
    GREAT GRANITE TERRACES IN SUN AND SHADOW, ... 42 THE MOUNTAIN . . . 58
    SUCH A GREAT MAN. IT DOESN'T SEE HIM OFTEN . . . . . . 44 A HUNDRED COLLARS . . 2
    THOUGH A GREAT SCHOLAR, HE'S A DEMOCRAT, ... 44 A HUNDRED COLLARS . . 12
    LIKE BIRDS. THEY STORE A GREAT MANY AWAY. . . . . . . 60 BLUEBERRIES 51
    WE HAVE FOUR HERE TO BOARD, GREAT GOOD-FOR-NOTHINGS, . . 65 A SERVANT TO SERVANTS . 76
    OF THE GREAT HARVEST I MYSELF DESIRED. . . . . 69 AFTER APPLE-PICKING . 29
    "YOU POOR, DEAR, GREAT, GREAT, GREAT, GREAT GRANNY!" . . 77 THE GENERATIONS OF MEN 116
    I'M A GREAT BOY TO THINK OF NUMBER ONE. . . . . 99 THE SELF-SEEKER . . 177
    AS GREAT AS THOSE IS SHATTERING TO THE FRAME . . . . . 111 IN THE HOME STRETCH . 39
    WE DID THAT DAY WAS MINGLE GREAT AND SMALL . . . . . . 118 MEETING AND PASSING . 5
    MADE THE GREAT TREE SEEM AS A LITTLE BIRD . . . . 128 THE OFT-REPEATED DREAM 7
    A GREAT DEAL OF NONE. . . . . 134 A GIRL'S GARDEN . . . 40
    OVER THE GREAT BIG THUMPING, SHUFFLING MILLSTONE, . . . 142 THE VANISHING RED . . 16
    MESERVE, BELITTLED IN THE GREAT SKIN COAT HE WORE. . . . 143 SNOW 5
    MAKING A GREAT SCROLL UPWARD TOWARD THE SKY, ... 143 SNOW 9
    WITH A GREAT FLOCK OF CHICKENS OF RARE BREEDS . . . . . 162 NEW HAMPSHIRE . . . 102
    ALL THOSE GREAT RUFFIANS PUT THEIR THROATS TOGETHER, . . 195 PAUL'S WIFE 139
    UNDER HE DIDN'T CARE HOW GREAT A STONE: . . . . 200 PLACE FOR A THIRD . . 24
    WITH THE DEAD RACE OF THE GREAT AUK!" . . . . 212 AN EMPTY THREAT . . . 52
    IS ALSO GREAT . . . . 220 FIRE AND ICE . . . 8
    A GREAT WAVE FROM IT GOING OVER THEM, ... 230 TWO LOOK AT TWO . . 40
    I MAKE A GREAT NOISE . . . . 234 GATHERING LEAVES . . 5
    THE GRASS LAY FLATTENED UNDER ONE GREAT TREAD. . . . . 239 OUR SINGING STRENGTH . 12
    A WHIR AMONG WHITE BRANCHES GREAT AND SMALL, ... 240 OUR SINGING STRENGTH . 41
    GREAT WAVES LOOKED OVER OTHERS COMING IN, ... 250 ONCE BY THE PACIFIC . 2
    THE GREAT OVERDOG, ... 261 CANIS MAJOR . . . 1
    WITH THE GREAT OVERDOG . . . . 261 CANIS MAJOR . . . 11
    HER GREAT WEIGHT CREAKS THE BARBED WIRE IN ITS STAPLES . 269 THE BEAR 7
    I CAN'T HELP OWNING THE GREAT RELIEF IT WOULD BE . . . . 287 A ROADSIDE STAND . . 47
    HIS GREAT GAUNT FIGURE FILLED HIS CABIN DOOR, ... 292 FIGURE IN THE DOORWAY . 7
    ONE FOOT IN EACH GREAT OCEAN . . . . 295 A RECORD STRIDE . . 25
    TOO MANY FALL FROM GREAT AND GOOD . . . . 307 PROVIDE, PROVIDE . . 5
    THE GREAT TREASURE WANTED THE MOST, ... 312 THE VINDICTIVES . . 62
    THE GREAT THOUSAND-LINKED GOLD CHAIN, ... 312 THE VINDICTIVES . . 63
    ALL, NOT JUST GREAT EXPLOITING BUSINESSES. . . . . . . 319 BUILD SOIL 96
    AS A GREAT BUCK IT POWERFULLY APPEARED, ... 338 THE MOST OF IT . . . 16
    AND FOR THESE REASONS KEPT FROM BEING GREAT. . . . . . 351 THE LESSON FOR TODAY . 13
    THIS HAS BEEN POETRY'S GREAT ANTI-LURE. . . . . 358 THE LOST FOLLOWER . 20
    AND BLUE FLAG, THE GREAT SIGHT-- . . . . 367 NOT OF SCHOOL AGE . . 26
    GET RID OF THAT AND THERE'D BE LEFT NO GREAT . . . . . 371 THE LITERATE FARMER AND 110
    IT BEST BE LEFT TO GREAT MEN OF HIS KIND . . . . 372 THE LITERATE FARMER AND 134
    GREAT BOULDERS OFF THEIR BALANCE . . . . 376 ONE STEP BACKWARD TAKEN 4
    GREAT MONOLITHIC KNEES THE FORMER TOWN . . . . 377 DIRECTIVE 11
    GOOD IS A THING THAT THEY, THE GREAT, CAN DO, ... 398 NO HOLY WARS FOR THEM . 3
    AND ALL THE GREAT CONVENTION WAS ABOUT. . . . . 400 THE BROKEN DROUGHT . . 5
    AS LONG AS THE GREAT ISSUE WAS TO SEE . . . . 422 FOR JOHN F. KENNEDY . 12
    I MEAN THE GREAT FOUR, WASHINGTON, ... 422 FOR JOHN F. KENNEDY . 25
    GREAT IS THE REASSURANCE OF RECALL. . . . . 427 CONCEPT SELF-CONCEIVED 5
    WHO KNOWS BUT A GREAT . . . . 428 KITTY HAWK 3
    AND I'LL FORGIVE THY GREAT BIG ONE ON ME. . . . . . . 428 FORGIVE, O LORD.... . 2
    HAD MY HEART BEEN GREAT, ... 429 KITTY HAWK 24
    FROM THE GREAT AND BRAVE, ... 430 KITTY HAWK 75
    OF A GREAT MISGIVING. . . . . 435 KITTY HAWK 229
    BY A GREAT EAGLE BIRD IN ALL ITS TERROR. . . . . 443 AUSPEX 4
    THAT SHOULD HAVE MADE THE NEW WORLD NEWLY GREAT . . . . 446 DOES NO ONE AT ALL EVER 3
    WHICH HAS FOR ITS GREAT ATTRIBUTE . . . . 452 A-WISHING WELL . . . 50
    AND THE GREAT KING INQUIRE WHOSE WORK IT WAS. . . . . . 455 HOW HARD TO KEEP FROM . 59
    LINES WRITTEN IN DEJECTION ON THE EVE OF GREAT SUCCESS . 462 LINES IN DEJECTION . . T

GREAT (CONTINUED)
    ESCAPE FROM SO GREAT PAINS OF LIFE ON EARTH . . . . . . 475 A MASQUE OF REASON . . 43
    'TWAS A GREAT DEMONSTRATION WE PUT ON. . . . . 475 A MASQUE OF REASON . . 53
    IN OUR GREAT MOMENT WHAT DID YOU DO, MADAM? . . . . . . 477 A MASQUE OF REASON . . 117
    I'M A GREAT STICKLER FOR THE AUTHOR'S NAME. . . . . . . 480 A MASQUE OF REASON . . 199
    'TWAS A GREAT DEMONSTRATION IF YOU SAY SO. . . . . . . 481 A MASQUE OF REASON . . 219
    AND HERE COME ALL YOUR GREAT BOOKS TUMBLING DOWN! . . . . 504 A MASQUE OF MERCY . . 288
    BEYOND THIS GREAT DOOR YOU HAVE LOCKED AGAINST ME, . . . 513 A MASQUE OF MERCY . . 532
    WHEN A GREAT TIDE OF ARGUMENT SWEEPS IN . . . . . . 513 A MASQUE OF MERCY . . 538
    NERVOUS IS ALL THE GREAT THINGS EVER MADE YOU. . . . . 516 A MASQUE OF MERCY . . 599
    AND GREAT IT IS. BUT FEAR IS OF THE SOUL. . . . . . 519 A MASQUE OF MERCY . . 694
GREATER
    WHY WAS IT SO MUCH GREATER WHEN THE BOXES . . . . . 163 NEW HAMPSHIRE . . . 132
    WHATEVER ITS SECRET WAS OF GREATER HEAT . . . . . 239 OUR SINGING STRENGTH . 17
    AND BROUGHT IT OVER GLOSSY WATER, GREATER, ... 245 THE FREEDOM OF THE MOON 10
    GREATER THAN BEING SHORE TO THE OCEAN-- . . . . . 247 DEVOTION 2
    MY GREATER GRIEF WAS BY SO MUCH REDUCED . . . . . . 253 THE THATCH 28
    BUT YOU HAVE SPEED FAR GREATER. YOU CAN CLIMB . . . . 300 THE MASTER SPEED . . 2
GREATEST
    MANY MEN'S LUCK WITH GREATEST WASHINGTON . . . . . 317 BUILD SOIL 45
    THE STAR ITSELF--HEAVEN'S GREATEST STAR, ... 421 ONE MORE BREVITY . . 60
    THE GREATEST VOTE A PEOPLE EVER CAST, ... 423 FOR JOHN F. KENNEDY . 55
    THERE QUANDARY IS AT ITS GREATEST. . . . . . . 467 QUANDARY 14
    TO QUOTE THE GREATEST WESTERN POEM YET. . . . . . 485 A MASQUE OF REASON . 344
    WHICH IS OUR GREATEST HOPE OF REST FROM WAR. . . . 516 A MASQUE OF MERCY . 593
GREAT-GRANDMOTHER
    "YOU SEEM SO PARTIAL TO OUR GREAT-GRANDMOTHER . . . . 79 THE GENERATIONS OF MEN 177
GREATLY
    THOUGH WE CHOOSE GREATLY, STILL TO LACK . . . . . 21 THE TRIAL BY EXISTENCE 66
    TO RIPEN TOO LONG. I AM GREATLY TO BLAME.'" . . . . 60 BLUEBERRIES . . . 46
    IT'S NOT THAT I'M GREATLY AFRAID OF FIRE, ... 232 THE KITCHEN CHIMNEY . 9
    ENOUGH TO SEE IF HE WAS GREATLY MISSED. . . . . . 368 THE LITERATE FARMER AND 18
    DOES IT TO YOU AS GREATLY AS IT DID? . . . . . . 517 A MASQUE OF MERCY . 624
GREATNESS
    "SEE THAT YOU GET HER GREATNESS RIGHT. DON'T STINT HER." . 77 THE GENERATIONS OF MEN 117
    HE HAS THE GREATNESS TO REFRAIN. . . . . . . 390 TWO LEADING LIGHTS . . 11
    YOU'LL TELL ME SOMETIME. ALL YOU SAY HAS GREATNESS. . . 517 A MASQUE OF MERCY . 637
GRECIAN
    OF TROUBLE WITH IT IN HIS GRECIAN CITIES . . . . . 459 HOW HARD TO KEEP FROM 167
GREECED
    EVER SINCE ALEXANDER GREECED THE WORLD. . . . . . 511 A MASQUE OF MERCY . . 473
GREED
    LET THEM DIE OF UNSATISFIED GREED, ... 313 THE VINDICTIVES . . 85
    TO BE ATTEMPTED. GREED MAY WELL COME NEXT. . . . . 319 BUILD SOIL 100
    GREED HAS BEEN TAUGHT A LITTLE ABNEGATION . . . . 319 BUILD SOIL 117
GREEDY
    WHILE GREEDY GOOD-DOERS, BENEFICENT BEASTS OF PREY, . . . 287 A ROADSIDE STAND . . 27
GREEK
    HOW ABOUT BEING A GOOD GREEK, FOR INSTANCE? . . . . . 171 NEW HAMPSHIRE . . . 404
    AT ONE EXTREME AGREEING WITH ONE GREEK, ... 269 THE BEAR 30
    AT THE OTHER AGREEING WITH ANOTHER GREEK, ... 269 THE BEAR 31
    'TIS THE IOTA SUBSCRIPT OF THE GREEK. . . . . . . 387 IOTA SUBSCRIPT . . 4
    BUT UPSILON WHICH IS THE GREEK FOR YOU. . . . . . 388 IOTA SUBSCRIPT . . 8
    THE ORNAMENTS THE GREEK ARTIFICERS . . . . . . 473 A MASQUE OF REASON . 10
    I RECOGNIZE THEM. GREEK ARTIFICERS . . . . . . 490 A MASQUE OF REASON . 460
GREEKS
    TELL TISSAPHERNES NOT TO MIND THE GREEKS. . . . . 461 HOW HARD TO KEEP FROM 227
    THE CRYPT WAS LONG SINCE RIFLED BY THE GREEKS. . . . 483 A MASQUE OF REASON . 284
    WITH VIOLENCE. THE GREEKS WERE HARDLY STRANGERS . . . 511 A MASQUE OF MERCY . 468
GREEN
    (PALE ORCHISES), AND SCARED A BRIGHT GREEN SNAKE. . . 17 MOWING 12
    AND ALL RIPE TOGETHER, NOT SOME OF THEM GREEN . . . 59 BLUEBERRIES . . . 6
    BY WORSHIP UNDER GREEN TREES IN THE OPEN. . . . . 171 NEW HAMPSHIRE . . 389
    THAT VARIED IN THEIR HUE FROM RED TO GREEN. . . . . 178 THE STAR-SPLITTER . 73
    NATURE'S FIRST GREEN IS GOLD, ... 222 NOTHING GOLD CAN STAY . 1
    SEA WAVES ARE GREEN AND WET, ... 260 SAND DUNES . . . 1
    AND WHAT WAS GREEN WOULD BY AND BY BE GOLD. . . . 283 THE GOLD HESPERIDEE . 17
    TO LOOK UPON THE TREE WHEN IT WAS GREEN . . . . 284 THE GOLD HESPERIDEE . 53
    ACROSS THE LIGHT SNOW HOMEWARD SMELLING GREEN. . . . 349 TO A YOUNG WRETCH . . 6
    OF BABY GREEN AND SHOW THE WHITE BENEATH, . . . 375 A YOUNG BIRCH . . 2
    AND NOTHING BUT THE TOP A LEAFY GREEN-- . . . . 375 A YOUNG BIRCH . . 7
    AND LOCAL GREEN SUGGEST. . . . . 388 MIDDLENESS OF THE ROAD 16
    LIKE DARIUS GREEN . . . . 443 KITTY HAWK . . . 470
    AND THE ORCHARD GREEN, ... 445 PERIL OF HOPE . . 4
GREEN-WHITE
    HE BORE A GREEN-WHITE STICK IN HIS HAND, ... 7 LOVE AND A QUESTION . 3
GREENWICH
    IT'S GREENWICH VILLAGE COCKTAIL-PARTY TALK-- . . . 500 A MASQUE OF MERCY . . 170
GREET
    FOR WHOM THESE LINES WHEN THEY SHALL GREET HER EYE. . . 15 WAITING 27
    THE INDWELLING SPIDER RAN TO GREET THE FLY, ... 126 RANGE-FINDING . . . 13
GREETING
    AND IF SO MOVED UNCURL A HAND IN GREETING. . . . . . 292 FIGURE IN THE DOORWAY . 22
GREETS
    AND A SHOUT GREETS THE DARING ONE. . . . . . . 21 THE TRIAL BY EXISTENCE 48
GREW
    WHERE THE FLOWER WAS BEFORE IT GREW, ... 15 IN A VALE 19
    AT THE FIRST DRINK IT RUSTLED AND GREW LIMP. . . . 194 PAUL'S WIFE . . . 102
    AT THE NEXT DRINK IT GREW INVISIBLE. . . . . 194 PAUL'S WIFE . . . 103
    AND GREW TO BE A LITTLE BOYISH GIRL . . . . . 196 WILD GRAPES . . . 8
    THE WAY THEY GREW ROUND LEIF THE LUCKY'S GERMAN; . . 197 WILD GRAPES . . . 27
    AND SINCE THEY GREW DULLER . . . . . . 235 GATHERING LEAVES . . 18
    THEY SAFELY GREW IN SLENDER LENGTH. . . . . 273 A LONE STRIKER . . 23
    BUT THE CONQUERED GREW MEEK AND STILL. . . . . 312 THE VINDICTIVES . . 52
    THE ONE YOU MADE, THE OTHER ONE YOU GREW. . . . 382 TO AN ANCIENT . . 2
    YOU MADE THE EOLITH, YOU GREW THE BONE, ... 382 TO AN ANCIENT . . 13
GRIEF
    LET ME INTO YOUR GRIEF. I'M NOT SO MUCH . . . . . 53 HOME BURIAL 59

GRIEF (CONTINUED)
BUT THE WORLD'S EVIL. I WON'T HAVE GRIEF SO . . . . . . 54 HOME BURIAL . . . 106
THAT, ONCE GRIEF SETS TO GROWING, GRIEF MAY REST: . . . 200 PLACE FOR A THIRD . . 27
THE FLOWERS WILL GO ON WITH GRIEF AWHILE, ... 200 PLACE FOR A THIRD . . 28
A PRUDENT GRIEF WILL NOT DESPISE SUCH AIDS. . . . . . 200 PLACE FOR A THIRD . . 30
SO EDEN SANK TO GRIEF, ... 222 NOTHING GOLD CAN STAY . 6
IT STARTED A GRIEF WITHIN A GRIEF, ... 253 THE THATCH . . . 21
MY GREATER GRIEF WAS BY SO MUCH REDUCED . . . . . . 253 THE THATCH . . . 28
THAT WAS HOW THAT GRIEF STARTED TO MELT. . . . . . . 253 THE THATCH . . . 30
THAT THOUGH SHE GRIEVES, HER GRIEF IS SECRET: . . . . 256 THE LOVELY BE CHOOSERS 26
THOSE FRIENDS KNOW NOTHING OF HER GRIEF TO MAKE IT SHAMEFUL. 256 THE LOVELY BE CHOOSERS 27
THEY TAPPED AT MY EYELIDS AND TOUCHED MY LIPS WITH AN
 INVITATION TO GRIEF. . . . . 298 A LEAF-TREADER . . . 10
GRIEF MAY HAVE THOUGHT IT WAS GRIEF. . . . . 299 WELCOME TO THEIR BELIEF 1
GRIEF MAY HAVE THOUGHT IT WAS GRIEF. . . . . 299 WELCOME TO THEIR BELIEF 13
LEAVING LOVE'S ALTERNATIONS, JOY AND GRIEF, ... 317 BUILD SOIL 35
AND I COULD SHARE TIME'S LACK OF JOY OR GRIEF . . . . 335 I COULD GIVE ALL . . 9
ARE ABSOLUTELY SURE TO COME TO GRIEF. . . . . 394 HAEC FABULA DOCET . . 20
I WAS TO TASTE IN LITTLE THE GRIEF . . . . 420 ONE MORE BREVITY . . 50
CAN EVER QUITE PASS OUT OF UTTER GRIEF . . . . . . 469 WE VAINLY WRESTLE... . 3
GRIEVED
INTO THE DARKNESS. IT GRIEVED MY SOUL, ... 253 THE THATCH . . . 20
GRIEVES
THAT THOUGH SHE GRIEVES, HER GRIEF IS SECRET: . . . . 256 THE LOVELY BE CHOOSERS 26
IT GRIEVES ME TO HAVE HAD YOU STAND . . . . 327 A MISSIVE MISSILE . . 25
GRIM
GRIM SILENCE ON MY PART AS I SANK LOWER, ... 198 WILD GRAPES 79
GRIM GIVING TO DO OVER FOR THEM BOTH. . . . . . . 231 NOT TO KEEP . . . 18
HE STOOD UNSHAKEN, AND IF GRIM AND GAUNT, ... 292 FIGURE IN THE DOORWAY . 13
WHERE WITH A GLEE NO LESS FOR BEING GRIM . . . . . 394 HAEC FABULA DOCET . . 15
GRIME
IT IS SPECKLED WITH GRIME AS IF . . . . 110 A PATCH OF OLD SNOW . 5
GRIMLY
PIKE GRUNTED RATHER GRIMLY WITH MISGIVING . . . . . 405 FROM PLANE TO PLANE . 55
GRIN
NO--NO, THAT'S NOT A SMILE THERE. THAT'S A GRIN. . . . 488 A MASQUE OF REASON . 404
GRIND
EVER TO GRIND TO SOIL FOR GRASS. . . . . 140 THE GUM-GATHERER . . 17
GRIND SHELLS, O FUTILE SEA, GRIND EMPTY SHELLS . . . . 446 DOES NO ONE AT ALL EVER 19
I ASK OF YOU. GRIND THIS I THROW YOU BACK . . . . . 447 DOES NO ONE AT ALL EVER 29
GRINDING
THAN GRINDING DISCORD OUT OF A GRINDSTONE, ... 190 THE GRINDSTONE . . . 54
GRINDSTONE
HAS NEVER AVAILED THE CUMBERSOME GRINDSTONE . . . . . 188 THE GRINDSTONE . . . 2
THE GRINDSTONE . . . . 188 THE GRINDSTONE . . . 1
THAN THE GRINDSTONE CAN BOAST TO STAND OR GO. . . . . 189 THE GRINDSTONE . . . 13
THAN GRINDING DISCORD OUT OF A GRINDSTONE, ... 190 THE GRINDSTONE . . . 54
ONCE WHEN THE GRINDSTONE ALMOST JUMPED ITS BEARING . . 190 THE GRINDSTONE . . . 57
GRIP
BUT I, WITH SOMETHING OF THE BABY GRIP . . . . . . 197 WILD GRAPES . . . 48
THE GRIP ON EARTH OF OUTSPREAD FEET, ... 276 TWO TRAMPS IN MUD TIME 46
GRIST
WHERE THE GRIST OF THE NEW-BEGINNING BROOKS . . . . . 140 THE GUM-GATHERER . . 14
AND HOPELESS GRIST ENOUGH IT LOOKS . . . . 140 THE GUM-GATHERER . . 16
GRITTY
AND BEATING INSECTS AT THEIR GRITTY TUNE. . . . . . 190 THE GRINDSTONE . . . 55
TORPEDO-LIKE, WITH SHELL OF GRITTY LEATHER, ... 270 THE EGG AND THE MACHINE 25
GROAN
I HEARD A DEEP GROAN--MAYBE OUT OF HIM. . . . . . . 516 A MASQUE OF MERCY . . 611
GROANS
HE SIGHED HIMSELF A COUPLE OF GROANS, ... 419 ONE MORE BREVITY . . 16
GROPE
ON THE OLD PEACH TREES ON THE KNOLL, TO GROPE . . . . 117 IN THE HOME STRETCH . 189
AND EVEN THEN IT HAD TO GROPE AND BUNGLE, ... 425 ACCIDENTALLY ON PURPOSE 8
GROPED
YOU CALL IT MINE. / WE GROPED IT OUT TOGETHER. . . . 480 A MASQUE OF REASON . 188
AS FOR THE EARTH, WE GROPED THAT OUT TOGETHER, . . . 481 A MASQUE OF REASON . 207
YOU'RE GIVING ME. YOU SAY WE GROPED THIS OUT. . . . 482 A MASQUE OF REASON . 242
GROPES
SHE GROPES ACROSS THE PEN ALONE . . . . 281 BLUE RIBBON AT AMESBURY 41
GROPING
HE'S GROPING IN THE CELLAR AFTER JAM-- . . . . . . 77 THE GENERATIONS OF MEN 101
EITHER TO HAVE GONE GROPING UNDERGROUND . . . . . . 119 HYLA BROOK 3
WE TWO WERE GROPING DOWN A MALVERN SIDE . . . . . . 315 IRIS BY NIGHT . . . 2
GROTESQUE
"THE CITY'S GROTESQUE IRON SKELETONS . . . . 506 A MASQUE OF MERCY . . 332
GROUND (SEE FROZEN-GROUND-SWELL)
AND WHEN I COME TO THE GARDEN GROUND, ... 8 A LATE WALK 5
AND THAT WAS MY LONG SCYTHE WHISPERING TO THE GROUND. . 17 MOWING 2
AS WHERE SOME FLOWER LAY WITHERING ON THE GROUND. . . 22 THE TUFT OF FLOWERS . 16
AND HEAR HIS LONG SCYTHE WHISPERING TO THE GROUND, . . 23 THE TUFT OF FLOWERS . 32
THE LEAVES ARE ALL DEAD ON THE GROUND, ... 30 RELUCTANCE 7
STRIPPED TO BARE GROUND, THE MAPLE TREES . . . . . 49 A HUNDRED COLLARS . . 135
DROP EVERYTHING AND LIVE OUT ON THE GROUND-- . . . . 67 A SERVANT TO SERVANTS . 162
ONE HELPER, THRUSTING PITCHFORK IN THE GROUND, . . . 69 THE CODE 7
HE CAN EAT OFF A BARREL FROM THE GROUND. . . . . . 86 THE HOUSEKEEPER . . . 149
SHE STOOD HER GROUND AGAINST THE NOISY STEPS . . . . 92 THE FEAR 76
THE SWINGING LANTERN LENGTHENED TO THE GROUND, . . . 92 THE FEAR 92
'TWAS A NEST FULL OF YOUNG BIRDS ON THE GROUND . . . 109 THE EXPOSED NEST . . 13
YEARS AFTERWARDS, TRAILING THEIR LEAVES ON THE GROUND . 121 BIRCHES 18
CLEAR TO THE GROUND. HE ALWAYS KEPT HIS POISE . . . 122 BIRCHES 35
KICKING HIS WAY DOWN THROUGH THE AIR TO THE GROUND. . 122 BIRCHES 40
WHEREVER THE GROUND WAS LOW AND WET, ... 123 PEA BRUSH 10
AND LIFT THEMSELVES UP OFF THE GROUND. . . . . . . 123 PEA BRUSH 20
I THRUST MY HOE IN THE MELLOW GROUND, ... 124 A TIME TO TALK . . . 7
BUT THE BLACK SPREAD LIKE BLACK DEATH ON THE GROUND, . 131 THE BONFIRE . . . 53
OF WALLED-OFF GROUND WHERE A SHOP HAD STOOD, ... 133 A GIRL'S GARDEN . . . 11
HE DRAGGED IT THROUGH THE PLOWED GROUND AT A PACE . . 173 A STAR IN A STONEBOAT . 31

GROUND (CONTINUED)
    AFTER THE GROUND IS FROZEN, I SHOULD HAVE DONE . . . . . 176 THE STAR-SPLITTER . . . 6
    THERE WHERE HE MOVED THE ROCKS TO PLOW THE GROUND . . . . 177 THE STAR-SPLITTER . . . 26
    AND HE AND I BETWEEN US GROUND A BLADE. . . . . . . 189 THE GRINDSTONE . . . 25
    I WONDERED WHO IT WAS THE MAN THOUGHT GROUND-- . . . . . 190 THE GRINDSTONE . . . 45
    WAS THAT WE'D GROUND IT SHARP AND HADN'T KNOWN, ... 190 THE GRINDSTONE . . . 66
    BUT ONCE I FELT GROUND WITH MY STOCKING FEET . . . . . 198 WILD GRAPES . . . 85
    AND FROM BARN SMELLS YOU CAN'T WASH OUT OF PLOWED GROUND . . 210 PAUPER WITCH OF GRAFTON 91
    OF HISSING ON THE YET UNCOVERED GROUND, ... 226 THE ONSET 5
    AND BUILD THE CHIMNEY CLEAR FROM THE GROUND. . . . . . 232 THE KITCHEN CHIMNEY . 8
    AND ON BLACK GROUND A BEAR-SKIN RUG OF SNOW. . . . . . 234 EVENING A SUGAR ORCHARD 13
    DID GRASS AND GARDEN GROUND CONFESS IT SNOWED, ... 239 OUR SINGING STRENGTH . 9
    THAT KEPT THE GROUND, ALMOST DISPUTING RIGHT . . . . . 240 OUR SINGING STRENGTH . 36
    VAGUE DREAM-HEAD LIFTED OUT OF THE GROUND, ... 251 TREE AT MY WINDOW . . 5
    OUT IN THE PLOWED GROUND IN THE COLD A DIGGER, ... 263 THE INVESTMENT . . . 5
    AND CEREMONIOUSLY LAID IT ON THE GROUND, ... 284 THE GOLD HESPERIDEE . 46
    AND THE GROUND ALMOST COVERED SMOOTH IN SNOW, ... 296 DESERT PLACES . . . 3
    THE WETTER GROUND LIKE GLASS . . . . 301 NEITHER OUT FAR NOR IN 7
    THE GROUND WAS ONE CIRCLE OF SOLID RED. . . . . . . 305 UNHARVESTED . . . 10
    BUT STAND YOUR GROUND, ... 306 A TRIAL RUN 8
    THE CLOVER-MINGLED ROWAN ON THE GROUND . . . . . . 315 IRIS BY NIGHT . . . 13
    THAT GIVES OFF FROM A GARDEN GROUND AT NIGHT . . . . 414 A CABIN IN THE CLEARING 16
    A TRIAL GROUND WHERE HE CAN TRY HIMSELF . . . . . . 484 A MASQUE OF REASON . 319
    THE WAY IT RESTED TWO POINTS ON THE GROUND . . . . . 501 A MASQUE OF MERCY . 194
GROUNDBIRD'S
    AND CUT A FLOWER BESIDE A GROUNDBIRD'S NEST . . . . . 126 RANGE-FINDING . . . 2
GROUNDS
    HIS FARM WAS "GROUNDS," AND NOT A FARM AT ALL; . . . . 160 NEW HAMPSHIRE . . . 51
    WAS WHAT I THOUGHT OF. / HAVE YOU ANY GROUNDS, ... 502 A MASQUE OF MERCY . 226
GROUNDWORK
    THE GROUNDWORK OF ALL FAITH IS HUMAN WOE. . . . . . 352 THE LESSON FOR TODAY . 58
GROUP
    A ROGERS GROUP . . . . 391 A ROGERS GROUP . . . T
    BY THE ROGERS GROUP THEY MADE. . . . . 391 A ROGERS GROUP . . . 12
    I WANT YOU IN MY GROUP BESIDE THE THRONE-- . . . . . 489 A MASQUE OF REASON . 456
GROUSE
    BY DEER, AND I DON'T WANT IT BUDDED BY GROUSE. . . . . 228 GOOD-BY AND KEEP COLD . 8
    I'D SUMMON GROUSE, RABBIT, AND DEER TO THE WALL . . . . 228 GOOD-BY AND KEEP COLD . 10
GROVE
    OF HERE AND THERE A TENT IN GROVE AND ORCHARD. . . . . 73 THE GENERATIONS OF MEN 13
    AND WENT ALONE AGAINST A GROVE OF TREES; . . . . . 170 NEW HAMPSHIRE . . . 368
    LET ALONE GROVE OF TREES FOR SUGAR ORCHARD. . . . . 183 MAPLE 103
    HURRYING LOW ABOVE THE GROVE, SOME WAIF . . . . . . 249 ACCEPTANCE 9
    THROUGH A PITCH-DARK LIMITLESS GROVE. . . . . . . 443 THE DRAFT HORSE . . . 4
GROVES
    IN HARDWOOD GROVES . . . . 25 IN HARDWOOD GROVES . . T
    EVEN TO SAY THE GROVES WERE GOD'S FIRST TEMPLES . . . 171 NEW HAMPSHIRE . . . 392
GROW
    AND THE PURPLE-STEMMED WILD RASPBERRIES GROW. . . . . 5 GHOST HOUSE . . . 5
    WE CAN'T IN NATURE GROW TO MANY MORE: . . . . . . 41 THE MOUNTAIN . . . 26
    "WHY, THERE HASN'T BEEN TIME FOR THE BUSHES TO GROW. . . 59 BLUEBERRIES 13
    OF WHERE ALL THE BERRIES AND OTHER THINGS GROW, . . . 61 BLUEBERRIES 61
    TO MAKE IT ROOT AGAIN AND GROW AFRESH. . . . . . . 109 THE EXPOSED NEST . . 8
    WHERE THEY GROW FEWER AND FEWER EVERY YEAR . . . . . 176 THE CENSUS-TAKER . . 62
    WHAT'S LAS' AWHILE--GOOD HICK'RY WHAT'S GROW CROOKED, . . 186 THE AX-HELVE . . . 30
    UP WHERE THE TREES GROW SHORT, THE MOSSES TALL, . . . 210 PAUPER WITCH OF GRAFTON 96
    BUT WHEN THEY GROW UP AND CAN READ THIS . . . . . 294 A RECORD STRIDE . . . 19
    BUT IF IT IS DESTINED NEVER AGAIN TO GROW, ... 305 THERE ARE ROUGHLY ZONES 20
    BUT WHAT YOU RAISE OR GROW, WHY, FEED IT OUT, ... 323 BUILD SOIL 215
GROWING
    I THOUGHT THE GROWING THINGS WOULD DO HIM GOOD. . . . 83 THE HOUSEKEEPER . . . 59
    STILL GROWING, AND ON ONE A STAKE AND PROP, ... 102 THE WOOD-PILE . . . 33
    SMALL GOOD TO ANYTHING GROWING WILD, ... 123 PEA BRUSH 21
    ADVANTAGES OF GROWING ALMOST WILD . . . . 162 NEW HAMPSHIRE . . . 104
    THE HUNDRED YEARS THE TREE MUST HAVE BEEN GROWING. . . 194 PAUL'S WIFE 94
    BUNCHES ALL ROUND ME GROWING IN WHITE BIRCHES, ... 197 WILD GRAPES . . . 26
    BY GROWING WHERE IT SHOULDN'T--ON A BIRCH, ... 198 WILD GRAPES . . . 65
    THAT, ONCE GRIEF SETS TO GROWING, GRIEF MAY REST: . . . 200 PLACE FOR A THIRD . . 27
    FROM GROWING UNDER PAVEMENTS OF A TOWN; . . . . . 231 A BROOK IN THE CITY . 10
    AS FULL TO THE GUNNEL OF FLOWERS GROWING . . . . . 262 THE FLOWER BOAT . . . 6
    A BUBBLE ON A PIPESTEM, GROWING BIG. . . . . . . 283 THE GOLD HESPERIDEE . 24
    AND LOVE ITSELF WERE GROWING DIM. . . . . 347 DISCOVERY OF MADEIRAS 117
    ONCE DOWN ON MY KNEES TO GROWING PLANTS . . . . . 385 A MOOD APART . . . 1
GROWN
    THE ORCHARD TREE HAS GROWN ONE COPSE . . . . . . 5 GHOST HOUSE . . . 8
    SEEKING WITH MEMORIES GROWN DIM O'ER NIGHT . . . . . 22 THE TUFT OF FLOWERS . 13
    NOT LIKING TO OWN UP I'D GROWN A SIZE. . . . . . . 46 A HUNDRED COLLARS . . 60
    NO DOUBT IT'S GROWN UP SOME TO WOODS AROUND IT. . . . 213 A FOUNTAIN, A BOTTLE . 21
    THEN CUT DOWN THE TREES WHEN LUMBER GROWN, ... 376 SOMETHING FOR HOPE . . 13
    (STILL STANDING OFF) WE'VE ALL GROWN FOND OF YOU. . . . 518 A MASQUE OF MERCY . 666
    WE'VE ALL GROWN FOND OF YOU. (PAUL SAYS IT LOUDER, . . . 518 A MASQUE OF MERCY . 667
GROWN-UP
    I'M CURIOUS. AND I'M A GROWN-UP MAN: . . . . . . 482 A MASQUE OF REASON . 255
GROWS
    TILL EVEN THE COMFORTING BARN GROWS FAR AWAY, ... 10 STORM FEAR 15
    "IF HE THINKS ALL THE FRUIT THAT GROWS WILD IS FOR HIM, . . 61 BLUEBERRIES 79
    AS IT GROWS WISER AND OLDER, ... 156 THE SOUND OF TREES . 13
    BUT LIFTS NO HIGHER THAN A GARDEN GROWS. . . . . . 414 A CABIN IN THE CLEARING 17
GROWT'
    DE SECOND GROWT' I CUT MYSELF--TOUGH, TOUGH!" . . . . 186 THE AX-HELVE . . . 31
GROWTH
    BEYOND THE TIME OF PROFITABLE GROWTH-- . . . . . 106 CHRISTMAS TREES . . 23
    SUBDUED THE GROWTH OF EARTH TO GRASS, ... 265 THE BIRTHPLACE . . . 5
GRUBS
    TO FEED HIS THUMPING GRUBS AS BIG AS HE IS. . . . . 278 THE WHITE-TAILED HORNET 31
GRUDGE
    SURELY YOU WOULDN'T GRUDGE THE POOR OLD MAN . . . . 36 DEATH OF THE HIRED MAN 49

GRUNTED
    PIKE GRUNTED RATHER GRIMLY WITH MISGIVING . . . . . . 405 FROM PLANE TO PLANE . 55
GUARANTEED
    I AM BROUGHT GUARANTEED YOUNG PRATTLE POEMS . . . . . 324 BUILD SOIL 273
    GUARANTEED TO COME SAFELY OFF WITH YOU . . . . . . 457 HOW HARD TO KEEP FROM 125
GUARD
    AND PUT HIM ON HIS GUARD. "SILAS IS BACK." . . . . 34 DEATH OF THE HIRED MAN 5
    I ASKED HIM, ON MY GUARD. "OH, YES," HE ANSWERED, . . . 159 NEW HAMPSHIRE . . 13
    A SLIM DOOR GOT IN PAST MY GUARD, ... 265 THE DOOR IN THE DARK . 5
    AN EOLITH PALLADIUM TO GUARD. . . . . 365 OF STONES OF THE PLACE 11
    WITH A LONE COAST GUARD . . . . 432 KITTY HAWK 140
GUARDIAN
    I AM THE GUARDIAN WRAITH OF STARLIT SMOKE . . . . . 414 A CABIN IN THE CLEARING 10
GUARDS
    AS LONG AS THE DECLARATION GUARDS . . . . 310 IN DIVES' DIVE . . . 3
GUATEMALAN
    AS ANY GUATEMALAN PARAKEET. . . . . 412 POD OF THE MILKWEED . 47
GUELPH
    OR POLITICS OF GHIBELLINE OR GUELPH, ... 359 THE LOST FOLLOWER . . 30
GUESS
    YOU NEVER SAW IT?" / "I GUESS THERE'S NO DOUBT . . . . 42 THE MOUNTAIN . . . 66
    I GUESS YOU'D FIND... IT SEEMS TO ME . . . . . . 62 A SERVANT TO SERVANTS 6
    I GUESS THEY THOUGHT I'D SPIKED HIM IN THE TEMPLE . . . 72 THE CODE 92
    I GUESS ESTELLE AND I HAVE FILLED THE PURSE. . . . . 84 THE HOUSEKEEPER . . 100
    WITH BOTH HANDS HELD BEHIND HER. "GUESS," SHE SAID. . . 96 THE SELF-SEEKER . . 106
    "OH, GUESS WHICH HAND? MY, MY! ONCE ON A TIME . . . 96 THE SELF-SEEKER . . 107
    OUT THROUGH THE SHED." / "I GUESS I KNOW MY WAY. . . . 144 SNOW 38
    I GUESS I KNOW WHERE I CAN FIND MY NAME . . . . 144 SNOW 39
    HOW LIKE A MAPLE TREE'S FOR US TO GUESS. . . . . . 180 MAPLE 23
    OR FOR A LITTLE GIRL TO GUESS SOMETIME. . . . . . 180 MAPLE 24
    THAT'S WHAT IS CALLED A STRETCHER. BUT I GUESS . . . 192 PAUL'S WIFE . . . 49
    I GUESS THEY'D BETTER DRAG IT THROUGH AGAIN. . . . 208 PAUPER WITCH OF GRAFTON 29
    I GUESS HE FOUND HE GOT MORE OUT OF ME . . . . . 209 PAUPER WITCH OF GRAFTON 76
    "I GUESS YOU'D FIND THE FOUNTAIN JUST AS EMPTY. . . . 214 A FOUNTAIN, A BOTTLE . 45
    THE FARMERS RATHER GUESS NOT. . . . . 308 EVIL TENDENCIES CANCEL 2
    ONE GUESS . . . . 309 ONE GUESS . . . . T
    "I GUESS SO," PIKE SAID, INNOCENT OF MILTON. . . . . 408 FROM PLANE TO PLANE . 136
    "YOU'RE HOPELESS," SAID THE SLAVE. / "I GUESS I AM; . . 458 HOW HARD TO KEEP FROM 144
    I GUESS I'LL HAVE THE HEADSMAN EXECUTE ME . . . . 460 HOW HARD TO KEEP FROM 205
    NOW WHAT'S HE DOING? / PITCHING THRONE, I GUESS, . . . 474 A MASQUE OF REASON . 19
    WHEN LEFT TO GUESS FOREVER FOR THEMSELVES. . . . . 483 A MASQUE OF REASON . 276
    I'M SICK. / OF WHAT? / OH, EVERYTHING, I GUESS. . . . 499 A MASQUE OF MERCY . 155
GUESSED
    THAT I SHOULD HAVE GUESSED . . . . 110 A PATCH OF OLD SNOW . 2
    HE GUESSED THEY'D KNOW WHAT HE HAD TO PUT UP WITH. . . 210 PAUPER WITCH OF GRAFTON 88
    IT MAY BE CHARITABLY GUESSED . . . . 390 TWO LEADING LIGHTS . 22
    BEFORE THEY GUESSED THE CORNER . . . . 391 A ROGERS GROUP . . 7
    BUT NO ONE FROM THE FEELING WOULD HAVE GUESSED . . . 407 FROM PLANE TO PLANE . 91
    BUT ANYBODY COULD HAVE GUESSED IN THIS CASE, ... 456 HOW HARD TO KEEP FROM 89
GUEST
    MY NOVEMBER GUEST . . . . 6 MY NOVEMBER GUEST . . T
    THE SAME SIGN HEAVEN SHOWED YOUR GUEST. . . . . . 381 AN UNSTAMPED LETTER IN 42
    SLIPPED IN TO BE MY PROBLEM GUEST, ... 419 ONE MORE BREVITY . . 9
GUESTS
    THE FIRST NIGHT AFTER GUESTS HAVE GONE, THE HOUSE . . . 115 IN THE HOME STRETCH . 132
GUIDE
    "I THOUGHT YOU WERE A GUIDE." / "I AM A GUIDE, ... 214 A FOUNTAIN, A BOTTLE . 31
    LOOK HERE, YOU TREAT YOUR GUIDE WITH DUE RESPECT . . . 214 A FOUNTAIN, A BOTTLE . 49
    ONE MISTY EVENING, ONE ANOTHER'S GUIDE, ... 315 IRIS BY NIGHT . . . 1
    THE ROAD THERE, IF YOU'LL LET A GUIDE DIRECT YOU . . . 377 DIRECTIVE 8
    OUR BEST GUIDE UPWARD FURTHER TO THE LIGHT, ... 425 ACCIDENTALLY ON PURPOSE 23
GUIDERS
    AND THOUGH NONE TOO SUCCESSFUL AT IT, GUIDERS, . . . 267 RIDERS 2
GUILD
    IT MAKES THE GUILD OF NOVEL WRITERS SICK . . . . . 167 NEW HAMPSHIRE . . . 274
    WHO WOULD THEY BE? THE GUILD OF SOCIAL PLANNERS . . . 397 THE PLANNERS . . . 10
GUILE
    WE ALLOW SOME TIME FOR GUILE . . . . 282 A DRUMLIN WOODCHUCK . 17
    BY EXECUTIVE GUILE, ... 448 THE BAD ISLAND--EASTER 35
GUILTY
    THEY MUST HAVE HAD A GUILTY EXPECTATION . . . . . 193 PAUL'S WIFE . . . 67
    FROM SAYING ON A JURY "HERE'S THE GUILTY." . . . . 317 BUILD SOIL . . . 52
    YOU WERE MORE GUILTY OF MISCHIEF THAN YOU ARE. . . . 488 A MASQUE OF REASON . 412
GUISE
    MIND WHEN I MEET WITH IT IN ANY GUISE. . . . . . 358 A CONSIDERABLE SPECK . 31
    TO ITS EVERY GUISE . . . . 426 A NEVER NAUGHT SONG . 24
    FLED FROM THE PALACE IN THE GUISE OF MEN. . . . . 454 HOW HARD TO KEEP FROM 11
GULF
    AND GOES DOWN BURNING INTO THE GULF BELOW, ... 249 ACCEPTANCE . . . 2
    ACROSS THE GULF OF WELL-NIGH EVERYTHING . . . . . 356 A MOTH SEEN IN WINTER . 21
    HE'S ON THAT TENDENCY THAT LIKE THE GULF STREAM, . . . 489 A MASQUE OF REASON . 442
GULL
    REFLECTS A STANDING GULL. . . . . 301 NEITHER OUT FAR NOR IN 8
GULLET
    SHE'LL GET HER GULLET CUT, ... 465 MILKY WAY IS A COWPATH 38
GULLIED
    GOOD GRASSLAND GULLIED OUT, AND IN THE GRASS . . . . 40 THE MOUNTAIN . . . 13
GULLY
    AND STARTED DOWN THE GULLY. . . . . 377 ONE STEP BACKWARD TAKEN 6
GULPED
    GULPED SNOW, AND THEN BLEW FREE AGAIN--THE COLES, . . . 143 SNOW 3
GULPING
    BUT GULPING MUDDY GALLONS . . . . 376 ONE STEP BACKWARD TAKEN 3
GUM
    WAS GUM, THE GUM OF THE MOUNTAIN SPRUCE. . . . . . 141 THE GUM-GATHERER . . 29
GUM-GATHERER
    THE GUM-GATHERER . . . . 140 THE GUM-GATHERER . . T

GUN
    "AREN'T YOU AFRAID OF HIM? WHAT'S THAT GUN FOR?" . . . . 83 THE HOUSEKEEPER . . . 65
    AND WARN THEM AWAY WITH A STICK FOR A GUN.) . . . . . . 228 GOOD-BY AND KEEP COLD . 11
    IS LIKE THE PUPIL OF A POINTED GUN. . . . . 277 THE WHITE-TAILED HORNET . 4
    THE GUN REVERSED THAT HE WENT OUT WITH SHOULDERED. . . . 289 OLD BARN AT THE BOTTOM . 4
    AS TAKE HIS GUN--ROD--TO GO HUNTING--FISHING. . . . . 349 TO A YOUNG WRETCH . . 2
    WITH GUN DEPRESSED, ... 360 THE RABBIT-HUNTER . . 3
    LOADED WITH A GUN . . . . 431 KITTY HAWK 104
GUNNEL
    AS FULL TO THE GUNNEL OF FLOWERS GROWING . . . . . . 262 THE FLOWER BOAT . . . 6
GUS
    "GUSTIE, OLD BOY, DALMATIAN GUS, ... 420 ONE MORE BREVITY . . 28
    GUSTIE--DALMATIAN GUS, THAT IS-- . . . . 420 ONE MORE BREVITY . . 40
    (THINK OF PRESUMING TO CALL HIM GUS), ... 421 ONE MORE BREVITY . . 59
GUST
    THERE CAME A GUST. (YOU USED TO THINK THE TREES . . . 130 THE BONFIRE 41
    SOMETHING OR SOMEONE WATCHING MADE THAT GUST. . . . . 130 THE BONFIRE 44
    BEFORE IT FROZE, AND A GUST FLINGS A HANDFUL . . . . 176 THE STAR-SPLITTER . . 7
    AND EVERY GUST THAT GATHERS STRENGTH AND HEAVES . . . 305 THERE ARE ROUGHLY ZONES 2
GUSTIE
    "GUSTIE, OLD BOY, DALMATIAN GUS, ... 420 ONE MORE BREVITY . . 28
    GUSTIE--DALMATIAN GUS, THAT IS-- . . . . 420 ONE MORE BREVITY . . 40
GUTTER
    THAT ROW OF ICICLES ALONG THE GUTTER . . . . 393 BEYOND WORDS 1
GUTTURAL
    SOME GUTTURAL EXCLAMATION OF SURPRISE . . . . 142 THE VANISHING RED . . 14
GUYS
    SO THAT IN GUYS IT GENTLY SWAYS AT EASE, ... 331 THE SILKEN TENT . . . 4

H

HABIT
    JUST AS YOU WILL TILL IT BECOMES A HABIT. . . . . . . 67 A SERVANT TO SERVANTS . 147
    THEY ARE PHILOSOPHERS, AND FROM OLD HABIT . . . . . 354 THE LESSON FOR TODAY . 110
HABITATION
    NO HABITATION MEETS THE EYE . . . . 392 A CLIFF DWELLING . . 3
HABIT-RIDDEN
    IS LEST HABIT-RIDDEN . . . . 441 KITTY HAWK 431
HAD---NOT INDEXED
HADES
    IT WAS THE WORDS 'DESCENDED INTO HADES' . . . . . . 58 THE BLACK COTTAGE . . 94
HADN'T---NOT INDEXED
HAEC
    HAEC FABULA DOCET . . . . 394 HAEC FABULA DOCET . . T
HAG
    THE WITCH THAT CAME (THE WITHERED HAG) . . . . . . 307 PROVIDE, PROVIDE . . 1
HAHN
    "HAHN, HAHN," HE MUSED, "DON'T NEED MUCH TAKING DOWN." . 187 THE AX-HELVE . . . 79
HAIL
    WE'D HAIL THE REMEDY. BUT IT'S BEEN TRIED . . . . . 372 THE LITERATE FARMER AND 122
HAILED
    A TROLLEY CAR THEY HAILED . . . . 391 A ROGERS GROUP . . . 5
HAILING
    BY HAILING CHEERILY "HIT THEM HARD!" . . . . 275 TWO TRAMPS IN MUD TIME 4
HAIR
    HIS SKIN AND HIS HAIR AND HIS EYES WERE GRAY, ... 23 PAN WITH US 2
    STRUNG ON YOUR HAIR, WON'T HURT YOUR SUMMER LOOKS. . . 77 THE GENERATIONS OF MEN 123
    LIKE GIRLS ON HANDS AND KNEES THAT THROW THEIR HAIR . . 121 BIRCHES 19
    DEN WHERE'S YOUR HAX-EAD FLYING T'ROUGH DE HAIR?" . . 186 THE AX-HELVE . . . 27
    HER WET HAIR HEAVY ON HER LIKE A HELMET, ... 194 PAUL'S WIFE . . . 109
    AND HEAVY ON HER HEAVY HAIR BEHIND, ... 196 WILD GRAPES . . . 22
    AND ALL HIS TAIL THAT ISN'T HAIR UP STRAIGHT. . . . . 223 THE RUNAWAY 17
    AS YOU MIGHT TRY A JEWEL IN YOUR HAIR. . . . . . . 245 THE FREEDOM OF THE MOON 3
    LEAVING ON ONE WIRE TOOTH A LOCK OF HAIR. . . . . . 269 THE BEAR 9
    OF HIS RAVEN COLOR OF HAIR. . . . . 299 WELCOME TO THEIR BELIEF 16
    HER SHINING HAIR DISPLACED. . . . . 339 THE SUBVERTED FLOWER . 17
    TO TOUCH HER NECK AND HAIR. . . . . 339 THE SUBVERTED FLOWER . 22
    ALMOST PULLED OUR HAIR . . . . 434 KITTY HAWK . . . 210
    IF YOU WOULD TAKE THE HANDS OUT OF YOUR HAIR . . . . 500 A MASQUE OF MERCY . . 191
HAIRCLOTH
    A BUTTONED HAIRCLOTH LOUNGE SPREAD SCROLLING ARMS . . . 55 THE BLACK COTTAGE . . 22
HAIR-RAISING
    IT WILL START HAIR-RAISING CURRENTS OF AIR . . . . . 306 A TRIAL RUN . . . 2
HAIRY
    THE CLOUDS WERE LOW AND HAIRY IN THE SKIES, ... 250 ONCE BY THE PACIFIC . 5
    SO HE LEAPT ON HER HAIRY BACK AND BIT HER . . . . . 463 LINES IN DEJECTION . . 19
HAKLUYT
    A RHYME OF HAKLUYT . . . . 343 DISCOVERY OF MADEIRAS . S
HALE
    WHEN CAME SQUARE HALE WITH LET'S SEE WHAT WE HAD; . . . 283 THE GOLD HESPERIDEE . 10
    'TWAS SUNDAY AND SQUARE HALE WAS DRESSED FOR MEETING. . 284 THE GOLD HESPERIDEE . 41
    SQUARE MATTHEW HALE TOOK OFF HIS SUNDAY HAT . . . . . 284 THE GOLD HESPERIDEE . 45
HALE'S
    SQUARE MATTHEW HALE'S YOUNG GRAFTED APPLE TREE . . . . 283 THE GOLD HESPERIDEE . 1
HALF
    HALF CLOSES THE GARDEN PATH. . . . . 8 A LATE WALK 4
    PERCHANCE HE HALF PREVAILED . . . . 11 WIND AND WINDOW FLOWER 21
    A SLEEPY SOUND, BUT MOCKING HALF, ... 25 THE DEMIURGE'S LAUGH . 8
    SOONER OR LATER CAME AND LEANED, HALF KNELT, ... 56 THE BLACK COTTAGE . . 27
    AND OF HER HALF ASLEEP, WAS TOO MUCH FOR ME. . . . . 58 THE BLACK COTTAGE . . 92
    BY MOUNTAIN RANGES HALF IN SUMMER SNOW, ... 58 THE BLACK COTTAGE . . 116
    "I WISH I KNEW HALF WHAT THE FLOCK OF THEM KNOW . . . 61 BLUEBERRIES 60
    IT GOT SO I WOULD SAY--YOU KNOW, HALF FOOLING-- . . . 67 A SERVANT TO SERVANTS . 145
    I SAID THAT MORE THAN HALF AN HOUR AGO. . . . . . . 70 THE CODE 13
    HALF OF THE OUTDOOR WORK, THOUGH AS FOR THAT, ... 85 THE HOUSEKEEPER . . . 108
    "I HALF SUSPECT YOU KNEW, AND CAME ON PURPOSE . . . . 93 THE SELF-SEEKER . . . 8

HALF (CONTINUED)
    HALF THE TIME I DON'T KNOW WHAT'S TROUBLING ME.-- . . . . 99 THE SELF-SEEKER . . . 194
    AND HALF GRANT WHAT I WISH AND SNATCH ME AWAY . . . . . 122 BIRCHES 51
    I WAS HALF BORING THROUGH, HALF CLIMBING THROUGH . . . 125 AN ENCOUNTER 4
    HALF LOOKING FOR THE ORCHID CALYPSO." . . . . 125 AN ENCOUNTER 24
    TO PLEASE THE BOY BY GIVING HIM THE HALF HOUR . . . . . 136 "OUT,OUT--" 11
    HALF IN APPEAL, BUT HALF AS IF TO KEEP . . . . 137 "OUT,OUT--" 21
    AND HALF THE BAG WOUND ROUND HIS HAND. . . . . 140 THE GUM-GATHERER . . 6
    VISIONS OF HALF THE WORLD BURNED BLACK . . . . 140 THE GUM-GATHERER . . 23
    ISN'T IT, NOW? HE'S BEEN HERE HALF AN HOUR. . . . . . . 145 SNOW 56
    "I'M HALF AFRAID THAT'S JUST WHAT SHE MIGHT DO." . . . 154 SNOW 306
    WITH HALF AN EAR TO THE PIANO'S VIGOR. . . . . 263 THE INVESTMENT . . . 8
    THE GATE FOR HALF AN HOUR BE LOCKED, ... 273 A LONE STRIKER . . . 7
    IT IS SNOWING A FLAKE: AND HE HALF KNEW . . . . 276 TWO TRAMPS IN MUD TIME 29
    HE HAS A HALF A MIND TO START, ... 280 BLUE RIBBON AT AMESBURY 26
    IT WOULD FLUTTER AND FALL IN HALF AN HOUR . . . . 291 ON HEART'S BEGINNING TO 11
    A BIRD HALF WAKENED IN THE LUNAR NOON . . . . 302 A BIRD SINGING IN SLEEP 1
    AT LEAST NOT OVER HALF. . . . . 309 NOT ALL THERE 8
    BUT REALLY THAT GOLD WAS NOT HALF . . . . 310 THE VINDICTIVES . . . 18
    NOT A HALF, NOT A THIRD, NOT A TITHE. . . . . 310 THE VINDICTIVES . . . 20
    OH, MELIBOEUS, I HAVE HALF A MIND . . . . 316 BUILD SOIL 26
    A YOUNGSTER COMES TO ME WITH HALF A QUATRAIN . . . . . . 324 BUILD SOIL 270
    OF WORKING OUT THE REST, THE OTHER HALF. . . . . 324 BUILD SOIL 272
    TO LET THE HALF OF LIFE ALONE . . . . 336 THE WIND AND THE RAIN . 16
    THAT CUT THE SNOUT IN HALF, ... 340 THE SUBVERTED FLOWER . 46
    A HALF A DOZEN MAJOR WARS, ... 368 A SERIOUS STEP LIGHTLY 23
    TO DOUBLE DAY AND CUT IN HALF THE DARK . . . . 375 A YOUNG BIRCH . . . 5
    TO SOME STAR OFF THERE, SAY, A HALF LIGHT-YEAR . . . . . 395 WHY WAIT FOR SCIENCE . 7
    A HALF COURSE IN IT NEXT YEAR.) AND BESIDES, ... 407 FROM PLANE TO PLANE . 112
    IT CAME NEAR SPLITTING HER IN HALF. . . . . 452 A-WISHING WELL . . . 43
    AND THAT IS HALF THE TROUBLE WITH THE WORLD. . . . . . . 462 HOW HARD TO KEEP FROM 277
    (OR MORE THAN HALF I'M HALF INCLINED TO SAY)." . . . . . 462 HOW HARD TO KEEP FROM 278
    WHERE HAS SHE BEEN THE LAST HALF HOUR OR SO? . . . . . . 477 A MASQUE OF REASON . . 109
HALF-BREED
    INSTEAD OF WHICH SHE WAS SOME HALF-BREED SQUAW. . . . . 192 PAUL'S WIFE 39
HALF-DROWNED
    FULL OF LANK, SHIVERY, HALF-DROWNED BIRDS . . . . . . 85 THE HOUSEKEEPER . . . 120
HALF-MAD
    SO, LIKE A HALF-MAD OUTPOST SENTINEL, ... 396 ANY SIZE WE PLEASE . . 2
HALF-PAST
    IN WINTER AFTER HALF-PAST THREE. . . . . 137 BROWN'S DESCENT . . . 4
HALF-READ
    SPREAD OPEN AS I DROPPED THEM HALF-READ THROUGH . . . . 222 TO E.T. 2
HALFWAY
    BOWED OUTWARD ON THE MOUNTAIN HALFWAY UP, ... 75 THE GENERATIONS OF MEN 71
    SO HALFWAY DOWN HE FOUGHT THE BATTLE, ... 138 BROWN'S DESCENT . . . 40
    YOU HAD US FOR A HALFWAY STATION . . . . 150 SNOW 214
    A HALFWAY COFFEE HOUSE 'TWIXT TOWN AND NOWHERE----" . . 155 SNOW 342
    THEY SAT TOGETHER HALFWAY UP A CLIFF . . . . 195 PAUL'S WIFE . . . 133
    MORE THAN HALFWAY UP THE PASS . . . . 263 THE TIMES TABLE . . 1
    SANG HALFWAY THROUGH ITS LITTLE INBORN TUNE. . . . . . 302 A BIRD SINGING IN SLEEP 2
    WHEN HE WAS HALFWAY THERE, ... 313 BEARER OF EVIL TIDINGS 2
    NOT HALFWAY DOWN THE SCALE OF GRACE. . . . . 326 TO A THINKER . . . 32
    WILL THEREFORE PLAN TO GO HALFWAY AND STOP. . . . . . . 363 A SEMI-REVOLUTION . . 6
    SAY ABOUT HALFWAY UP THE WESTERN SKY, ... 370 THE LITERATE FARMER AND 66
    SOME HALFWAY UP THE LIMESTONE WALL, ... 392 A CLIFF DWELLING . . 5
    HALFWAY ROUND THE WORLD. . . . . 448 THE BAD ISLAND--EASTER 12
HALF-WILD
    SOMEONE TO SALT THE HALF-WILD STEER, ... 24 PAN WITH US 13
HALL
    JOHN HALL TOUCH ME! NOT IF HE KNOWS HIS FRIENDS. . . . . 83 THE HOUSEKEEPER . . . 67
    AS HALL OF WINDHAM, GAY OF ATKINSON, ... 167 NEW HAMPSHIRE . . . 259
    OF THE DOOR TO THE CELLAR OR THE HALL. . . . . 205 THE WITCH OF COOS . . 84
    IT TOOK THE HALL DOOR FOR THE NOVELTY, ... 205 THE WITCH OF COOS . . 85
    FROM THE HALL TO THE ONLY FINISHED BEDROOM, ... 205 THE WITCH OF COOS . . 91
    IN FRONT OF ONE TOWN HALL, I'D LEFT HIM HITCHED . . . . 208 PAUPER WITCH OF GRAFTON 50
    AS IN SOME TOO MUCH CARVEN MARBLE HALL . . . . 240 OUR SINGING STRENGTH . 42
    TILL IT CAN MUSTER BREATH INSIDE A HALL . . . . 399 THE INGENUITIES OF DEBT 17
    SOMETHING WAS GOING RIGHT OUTSIDE THE HALL. . . . . . . 399 THE BROKEN DROUGHT . . 2
    THIS VERY NIGHT. I HAD THE HALL ALL HIRED, ... 497 A MASQUE OF MERCY . . 95
HALLOWING
    HAVE NO HALLOWING FEARS . . . . 437 KITTY HAWK 281
HALT
    SHE LIKES TO HALT US IN OUR RUNNER TRACKS, ... 238 ON A TREE FALLEN ACROSS 6
    HAD COME TO A TROUBLED HALT. . . . . 314 BEARER OF EVIL TIDINGS 22
HALTED
    WAS A GIRL; AND SHE HALTED SOME WAY OFF . . . . 74 THE GENERATIONS OF MEN 30
    A BARKLESS SPECTER. HE HAD HALTED TOO, ... 125 AN ENCOUNTER 14
    THE DOOR; THEY HALTED HELPLESS ON THE LANDING, ... 204 THE WITCH OF COOS . . 62
    THEY MUST HAVE HALTED SOON IN ANY CASE . . . . 229 TWO LOOK AT TWO . . . 4
    WHEN THEY WERE HALTED BY A TUMBLED WALL . . . . 229 TWO LOOK AT TWO . . . 7
    HE HALTED IN THE WIND, AND--WHAT WAS THAT . . . . 233 A BOUNDLESS MOMENT . . 1
HALTING
    HALTING PERPLEXED BEHIND THE BARRIER . . . . 203 THE WITCH OF COOS . . 24
    AND ANOTHER STUMBLING AFTER A HALTING CART. . . . . . . 299 STRONG SAYING NOTHING . 8
HALVES
    BUT THEY'RE ONE THING THAT SHOULD BE DONE BY HALVES. . . 363 A SEMI-REVOLUTION . . 8
HAMAN
    TAKE NOTICE, HAMAN, HE'S IN FAVOR WITH US." . . . . . . 455 HOW HARD TO KEEP FROM 65
HAMMER (SEE FEATHER-HAMMER)
HAMPSHIRE
    WHEN ALL WHO WOULD COME SEEKING IN NEW HAMPSHIRE . . . 73 THE GENERATIONS OF MEN 2
    NEW HAMPSHIRE . . . . 157 NEW HAMPSHIRE . . . T
    NEW HAMPSHIRE . . . . 159 NEW HAMPSHIRE . . . T
    IT NEVER COULD HAVE HAPPENED IN NEW HAMPSHIRE. . . . . . 160 NEW HAMPSHIRE . . . 34
    I EVER STUMBLED ON IN OLD NEW HAMPSHIRE . . . . 160 NEW HAMPSHIRE . . . 36
    JUST SPECIMENS IS ALL NEW HAMPSHIRE HAS, ... 161 NEW HAMPSHIRE . . . 61
    DID YOU BUT KNOW OF HIM, NEW HAMPSHIRE HAS . . . . 162 NEW HAMPSHIRE . . . 93

HAMPSHIRE (CONTINUED)
    SHE HAS A TOUCH OF GOLD. NEW HAMPSHIRE GOLD-- . . . . . 162 NEW HAMPSHIRE   . . .108
    BUT TRUST NEW HAMPSHIRE NOT TO HAVE ENOUGH . . . . . . 163 NEW HAMPSHIRE   . . .122
    NEW HAMPSHIRE USED TO HAVE AT SALEM . . . . 163 NEW HAMPSHIRE   . . .138
    NOT EVEN NEW HAMPSHIRE FARMS ARE MUCH FOR SALE. . . . . 163 NEW HAMPSHIRE   . . .149
    APPLES? NEW HAMPSHIRE HAS THEM, BUT UNSPRAYED, ... 164 NEW HAMPSHIRE   . . .159
    NEW HAMPSHIRE RAISES THE CONNECTICUT . . . . 165 NEW HAMPSHIRE   . . .183
    ANYTHING I CAN SAY ABOUT NEW HAMPSHIRE . . . . 165 NEW HAMPSHIRE   . . .210
    NEW HAMPSHIRE MOUNTAINS CURL UP IN A COIL. . . . . . . 165 NEW HAMPSHIRE   . . .214
    I HAD BEEN COMING TO NEW HAMPSHIRE MOUNTAINS. . . . . . 166 NEW HAMPSHIRE   . . .215
    EMERSON SAID, "THE GOD WHO MADE NEW HAMPSHIRE . . . . . 166 NEW HAMPSHIRE   . . .218
    "I GO NO MORE TO SUMMER IN NEW HAMPSHIRE. . . . . 166 NEW HAMPSHIRE   . . .221
    BUT WHEN I ASKED TO KNOW WHAT AILED NEW HAMPSHIRE, . . . 166 NEW HAMPSHIRE   . . .223
    BECAUSE I WROTE MY NOVELS IN NEW HAMPSHIRE . . . . . . 166 NEW HAMPSHIRE   . . .246
    IS NO PROOF THAT I AIMED THEM AT NEW HAMPSHIRE. . . . . 166 NEW HAMPSHIRE   . . .247
    NEW HAMPSHIRE, NOT CONNECTICUT, ... 167 NEW HAMPSHIRE   . . .250
    WHERE I WAS LIVING THEN, NEW HAMPSHIRE OFFERED . . . . . 167 NEW HAMPSHIRE   . . .252
    TO WANT TO MAKE NEW HAMPSHIRE PEOPLE OVER. . . . . . . 167 NEW HAMPSHIRE   . . .263
    THE ONLY FAULT I FIND WITH OLD NEW HAMPSHIRE . . . . . 168 NEW HAMPSHIRE   . . .310
    TO SAY WHAT HEIGHT BECOMES NEW HAMPSHIRE MOUNTAINS, . . . 169 NEW HAMPSHIRE   . . .316
    SHE'S STILL NEW HAMPSHIRE, A MOST RESTFUL STATE. . . . . 170 NEW HAMPSHIRE   . . .357
    I CHOOSE TO BE A PLAIN NEW HAMPSHIRE FARMER . . . . . . 172 NEW HAMPSHIRE   . . .408
    AND RESTFUL JUST TO THINK ABOUT NEW HAMPSHIRE. . . . . . 172 NEW HAMPSHIRE   . . .412
HAND
    HE BORE A GREEN-WHITE STICK IN HIS HAND, ...   7 LOVE AND A QUESTION .   3
    OR EASY GOLD AT THE HAND OF FAY OR ELF: . . . . 17 MOWING   8
    EACH LAID ON OTHER A STAYING HAND . . . . 18 GOING FOR WATER . . . 17
    HE STOOD IN THE ZEPHYR, PIPES IN HAND, ... 23 PAN WITH US   6
    IN EACH HAND, LIKE AN OLD-STONE SAVAGE ARMED. . . . . . 34 MENDING WALL 40
    AND SPREAD HER APRON TO IT. SHE PUT OUT HER HAND . . . . 38 DEATH OF THE HIRED MAN 106
    AND BROKE IT IN HIS HAND AND TOSSED IT BY. . . . . . . 38 DEATH OF THE HIRED MAN 123
    SLIPPED TO HER SIDE, CAUGHT UP HER HAND AND WAITED. . . . 40 DEATH OF THE HIRED MAN 165
    WITH YOUR OWN HAND--HOW COULD YOU?--HIS LITTLE GRAVE; . . . 53 HOME BURIAL 73
    BY THE SAME HAND WORKING IN THE SAME STUFF? . . . . . . 57 THE BLACK COTTAGE . . 78
    A TARNISH THAT GOES AT A TOUCH OF THE HAND, ... 60 BLUEBERRIES 26
    NOT FORCING HER HAND WITH HARROW AND PLOW." . . . . . . 61 BLUEBERRIES 56
    MY HAND (OH, I CAN LIFT IT WHEN I HAVE TO). . . . . . . 63 A SERVANT TO SERVANTS .   9
    CHERISH IN HAND, LIFT DOWN, AND NOT LET FALL. . . . . . 69 AFTER APPLE-PICKING . 31
    THE HAND THAT KNOWS HIS BUSINESS WON'T BE TOLD . . . . . 70 THE CODE 22
    BUT WAIT UNTIL I GIVE YOU A HAND UP. . . . . 77 THE GENERATIONS OF MEN 121
    NOW GIVE ME YOUR HAND UP.--PICK ME THAT FLOWER." . . . . 80 THE GENERATIONS OF MEN 207
    HE MANAGES TO KEEP THE UPPER HAND . . . . 86 THE HOUSEKEEPER . . . 134
    SHE REACHED A HAND TO JOEL FOR SUPPORT: . . . . 91 THE FEAR 68
    "YOU DON'T SEE--I'VE A CHILD HERE BY THE HAND. . . . . . 92 THE FEAR 79
    "OH, GUESS WHICH HAND? MY, MY! ONCE ON A TIME . . . . . 96 THE SELF-SEEKER . . . 107
    WITH A LAWYER AT HAND TO FIND YOU OUT. . . . . 97 THE SELF-SEEKER . . . 134
    WAS THE LAMP TILTED NEAR THEM IN HIS HAND. . . . . . . 108 OLD MAN'S WINTER NIGHT   5
    THOUGH I FOUND YOUR HAND FULL OF WILTED FERN, ... 109 THE EXPOSED NEST . . 11
    SHE WORE HER CAPE; HER HAT WAS IN HER HAND. . . . . . . 110 IN THE HOME STRETCH .   4
    YOUR TONGUE GIVES SALT OR SUGAR IN YOUR HAND. . . . . . 131 THE BONFIRE 47
    SO SHE HAD TO WORK IT ALL BY HAND. . . . . 133 A GIRL'S GARDEN . . . 19
    LEAPED OUT AT THE BOY'S HAND, OR SEEMED TO LEAP-- . . . . 136 "OUT,OUT--" 16
    HE MUST HAVE GIVEN THE HAND. HOWEVER IT WAS, ... 136 "OUT,OUT--" 17
    NEITHER REFUSED THE MEETING. BUT THE HAND! . . . . . . 136 "OUT,OUT--" 18
    AS HE SWUNG TOWARD THEM HOLDING UP THE HAND, ... 136 "OUT,OUT--" 20
    HE SAW ALL SPOILED. "DON'T LET HIM CUT MY HAND OFF-- . . 137 "OUT,OUT--" 25
    SO. BUT THE HAND WAS GONE ALREADY. . . . . 137 "OUT,OUT--" 27
    AND HALF THE BAG WOUND ROUND HIS HAND. . . . . 140 THE GUM-GATHERER . .   6
    HE POINTED WITH HIS HAND FROM WHERE IT LAY . . . . . . 147 SNOW 114
    IT'S THEIRS. SHE'S DROPPED IT FROM HER HAND AND GONE." . . 153 SNOW 297
    A GLOBULE OF QUICKSILVER IN YOUR HAND . . . . 179 THE STAR-SPLITTER . . 90
    BUT THAT WAS IN THE WOODS, TO HOLD MY HAND . . . . . . 185 THE AX-HELVE   3
    FROM END TO END WITH HIS ROUGH HAND SHUT ROUND IT. . . . 187 THE AX-HELVE 77
    THICK HAND MADE LIGHT OF, STEEL-BLUE CHIN DRAWN DOWN . . . 188 THE AX-HELVE 99
    I CHANGED FROM HAND TO HAND IN DESPERATION. . . . . . . 189 THE GRINDSTONE . . . 34
    THEN HE CAME AT ME WITH ONE HAND OUTSTRETCHED, ... 204 THE WITCH OF COOS . . 75
    I STRUCK THE HAND OFF BRITTLE ON THE FLOOR, ... 204 THE WITCH OF COOS . . 77
    HAND ME MY BUTTON BOX--IT MUST BE THERE.) . . . . . . 205 THE WITCH OF COOS . . 81
    FROM THE SLAP I HAD JUST NOW GIVEN ITS HAND. . . . . . 205 THE WITCH OF COOS . . 89
    I TAKE AWAY MY HAND . . . . 227 TO EARTHWARD 26
    TO STRETCH A PROFFERING HAND--AND A SPELL-BREAKING. . . . 230 TWO LOOK AT TWO . . . 36
    UNDER THE HAND OF THE VILLAGE BARBER, ... 262 THE FLOWER BOAT . . .   2
    WHEN I SPREAD OUT MY HAND HERE TODAY, ... 266 SITTING BY A BUSH . .   1
    WITH ALL I HAVE TO HOLD WITH, HAND AND MIND . . . . . . 267 THE ARMFUL   6
    HER DEFT HAND SHOWED WITH FINGER RINGS . . . . 273 A LONE STRIKER . . . 28
    HER KEEPER, EMPTY PAIL IN HAND, ... 280 BLUE RIBBON AT AMESBURY 18
    AND ASK FOR SOME CITY MONEY TO FEEL IN HAND . . . . . . 286 A ROADSIDE STAND . . 19
    AND IF SO MOVED UNCURL A HAND IN GREETING. . . . . . . 292 FIGURE IN THE DOORWAY 22
    ONE PUT A THOUGHTFUL HAND UP TO HIS NOSE . . . . 293 AT WOODWARD'S GARDENS 14
    TO TAKE A WRITING HAND IN POLITICS. . . . . 316 BUILD SOIL 27
    O YOU WHO BRING THIS TO MY HAND, ... 327 A MISSIVE MISSILE . . 22
    A HAND HUNG LIKE A PAW, ... 340 THE SUBVERTED FLOWER 42
    I'D LAY MY HAND ON HIS HAND ON HIS STAFF, ... 354 THE LESSON FOR TODAY 124
    HERE'S FIRST A GLOVELESS HAND WARM FROM MY POCKET, ... 356 A MOTH SEEN IN WINTER .   1
    TO KNOW THE HAND I STRETCH IMPULSIVELY . . . . 356 A MOTH SEEN IN WINTER 20
    THAT ONCE A YEAR BY HAND OR APPARATUS . . . . 360 A LOOSE MOUNTAIN . .   3
    A PART APPLE IN HIS HAND, ... 366 NOT OF SCHOOL AGE . . 10
    WE HAVE ONE LOVING AND ONE HATING HAND. . . . . 371 THE LITERATE FARMER AND 113
    WHILE WITH THE HATING OTHER HAND WE STRIKE. . . . . . . 371 THE LITERATE FARMER AND 115
    BUT RAN AGAINST HIM WITH A STAYING HAND. . . . . 394 HAEC FABULA DOCET . . 10
    AND WITH THE GOLD IN HAND TO SHOW FOR . . . . 417 AMERICA IS HARD TO SEE 23
    ON EITHER HAND TO MAKE HIS COURSE PERHAPS . . . . 421 ESCAPIST--NEVER . . .   4
    OF DESPERATELY CLUTCHING HAND . . . . 452 A-WISHING WELL . . . 60
    BUT THE PRINCE DREW AWAY HIS HAND IN TIME . . . . 453 HOW HARD TO KEEP FROM   4
    THAT FLICKERS MICA WINGS. HE LIFTS A HAND . . . . 487 A MASQUE OF REASON . . 390
    HERE, TAKE MY HAND. / (HE TAKES IT AND ALIGHTS . . . . 489 A MASQUE OF REASON . . 451
    DON'T LAY YOUR HAND ON ME TO SAY IT, SHAMELESS. . . . . . 500 A MASQUE OF MERCY . . 166
    GIVE ME A HAND UP, IF WE ARE AGREED. . . . . 520 A MASQUE OF MERCY . . 715

HANDBAG
    I HADN'T AN ILLUSION IN MY HANDBAG . . . . 167 NEW HAMPSHIRE   . . . 254
HANDED (SEE HORNY-HANDED)
HANDFUL
    BEFORE IT FROZE, AND A GUST FLINGS A HANDFUL   . . . . 176 THE STAR-SPLITTER . . 7
HANDIWORK
    COULD SO FORGET HIS HANDIWORK ON WHICH   . . . . . . 102 THE WOOD-PILE   . . . 36
HANDLE (SEE AX-HANDLE)
    SOMEONE'S RECEIVER'S DOWN. THE HANDLE STUMBLES.   . . . . 153 SNOW 295
    THEY BROKE THE HANDLE AND THE BINDING OFF IT.   . . . . 293 AT WOODWARD'S GARDENS . 28
HANDLED
    EXCEPT AS A FELLOW HANDLED AN AX   . . . . 276 TWO TRAMPS IN MUD TIME 55
HANDLE'S
    ACROSS THE HANDLE'S LONG-DRAWN SERPENTINE, ... 186 THE AX-HELVE   . . . 24
HANDLING
    WE WEAR OUR FINGERS ROUGH WITH HANDLING THEM.   . . . . 33 MENDING WALL . . . 20
    HE WAS NOT USED TO HANDLING STARS THROWN DARK   . . . . 172 A STAR IN A STONEBOAT . 8
HANDRAIL
    SO LYING FORWARD WEAKLY ON THE HANDRAIL   . . . . . . 205 THE WITCH OF COOS . 96
HANDS
    BY WHICH I'D BIND MYSELF TO KEEP HANDS OFF   . . . . . 52 HOME BURIAL . . . 51
    I'M JUST AS GLAD SHE MADE ME KEEP HANDS OFF, ... 58 THE BLACK COTTAGE . 104
    HIS HANDS HAD WORN THEM SMOOTH AS ANY OXBOW.   . . . . . 66 A SERVANT TO SERVANTS . 136
    BUT THE OLD FOOL SEIZES HIS FORK IN BOTH HANDS, ... 71 THE CODE . . . 61
    SKY-HIGH WITH BOTH HANDS. I CAN SEE IT NOW--   . . . . . 83 THE HOUSEKEEPER . 61
    THAT HUNG IN BOTH HANDS, HOT AGAINST HER SKIRT.   . . . . 91 THE FEAR . . . 63
    STOOD FOR A WHILE UNNOTICED, WITH HER HANDS .   . . . . . 96 THE SELF-SEEKER . 95
    WITH BOTH HANDS HELD BEHIND HER. "GUESS," SHE SAID.   . . . 96 THE SELF-SEEKER . 106
    WILLIS FLUNG OFF THE BED. "I WASH MY HANDS--   . . . . . 100 THE SELF-SEEKER . 216
    SO WHEN I SAW YOU DOWN ON HANDS AND KNEES   . . . . . 109 THE EXPOSED NEST . 2
    BUT SUDDEN WINDS THAT SNATCH THEM FROM OUR HANDS   . . . . 112 IN THE HOME STRETCH 43
    CAME UP THE JOINTED STOVEPIPE IN THEIR HANDS, ... 113 IN THE HOME STRETCH 86
    HE DOFFED HIS CAP AND HELD IT WITH BOTH HANDS   . . . . . 114 IN THE HOME STRETCH 106
    WHAT HAVE YOU YOU KNOW WHERE TO LAY YOUR HANDS ON?"   . . . 115 IN THE HOME STRETCH 143
    LIKE GIRLS ON HANDS AND KNEES THAT THROW THEIR HAIR   . . . 121 BIRCHES 19
    I SAW THE STRANGE POSITION OF HIS HANDS--   . . . . . . 125 AN ENCOUNTER . . 16
    THE TIRELESS BUT INEFFECTUAL HANDS .   . . . 128 THE OFT-REPEATED DREAM 5
    WITH PITCHY HANDS TO WAIT FOR RAIN OR SNOW.   . . . . . 129 THE BONFIRE . . . 4
    AND THRUST HANDS IN AND HELD MY FACE AWAY.   . . . . . 131 THE BONFIRE . . . 66
    NOTHING NOT BUILT WITH HANDS OF COURSE IS SACRED.   . . . . 171 NEW HAMPSHIRE . . 394
    AND RISING ON HIS HANDS, HE LOOKS IN ON ME .   . . . . . 176 THE STAR-SPLITTER . 3
    FEW FARMS CHANGED HANDS; SO RATHER THAN SPEND YEARS   . . . 177 THE STAR-SPLITTER . 28
    BEYOND THE HIGHEST CITY BUILT WITH HANDS.   . . . . . . 182 MAPLE 84
    SHE USED HER HANDS TO COVER UP HER EYES.   . . . . . . 184 MAPLE 160
    TAKING THE CHILD OUT OF THE PARENTS' HANDS.   . . . . . 185 MAPLE 167
    THESE HANDS HAVE HELPED IT GO, AND EVEN RACE;   . . . . . 188 THE GRINDSTONE . . 4
    MORE CUTTING AND HE HAD THIS IN BOTH HANDS, ... 194 PAUL'S WIFE . . . 95
    BLEW IT ONCE OFF HIS HANDS AND ALMOST BROKE IT.   . . . . 194 PAUL'S WIFE . . . 100
    MOSTLY AS MUCH BEYOND MY LIFTED HANDS, THOUGH, ... 197 WILD GRAPES . . . 28
    AND PUT IT IN MY HANDS TO PICK MY OWN GRAPES.   . . . . . 197 WILD GRAPES . . . 38
    HUNG BABIES OUT ON BRANCHES BY THE HANDS .   . . . 197 WILD GRAPES . . . 51
    I HAD NOT LEARNED TO LET GO WITH THE HANDS, ... 199 WILD GRAPES . . . 96
    ITS HANDS OF GOLD   . . . . 218 I WILL SING YOU ONE-O . 21
    HIS HANDS? SHE HAD TO LOOK, TO LOOK AND ASK, ... 230 NOT TO KEEP . . . 8
    AND RAISED BOTH HANDS   . . . . 241 THE LOCKLESS DOOR . 7
    HAVE CLAPPED MY HANDS AT HIM FROM THE DOOR   . . . . . 250 A MINOR BIRD . . 3
    INVISIBLE HANDS CROWDED ON HER SHOULDER   . . . . . . 256 THE LOVELY BE CHOOSERS 12
    OF WHIRLING HANDS AND ARMS ABOUT THE HEAD   . . . . . . 277 THE WHITE-TAILED HORNET 9
    BEFORE THEIR PANIC HANDS   . . . . 298 ON TAKING FROM THE TOP 13
    SO LOVE WILL TAKE BETWEEN THE HANDS A FACE....   . . . . 301 MOON COMPASSES . . 8
    AND USE HIS HANDS IN FLIGHT.   . . . . 341 THE SUBVERTED FLOWER . 63
    INFIRM, WORN-OUT, AND BROKEN ON ITS HANDS;   . . . . . 399 THE INGENUITIES OF DEBT 9
    HE COULDN'T LAY HANDS ON A PITCHFORK TO HIT HER   . . . . 463 LINES IN DEJECTION . 17
    THE ABLEST ACTORS I CAN LAY MY HANDS ON.   . . . . . . 481 A MASQUE OF REASON . 226
    IS WORKED BY HANDS INVISIBLE, OFFSTAGE.)   . . . . . . 489 A MASQUE OF REASON . 455
    IF YOU WOULD TAKE THE HANDS OUT OF YOUR HAIR   . . . . . 500 A MASQUE OF MERCY . 191
    ALL WEALTH AND POWER IN TOO FEW HANDS?   . . . . . . 509 A MASQUE OF MERCY . 411
    (THEY PUT THEIR HANDS TOGETHER LIKE A BOOK   . . . . . 512 A MASQUE OF MERCY . 489
HANDY
    I JUST THOUGHT IF YOU HAD A COPY HANDY, ... 495 A MASQUE OF MERCY . 45
HANG (SEE HANG-AND-LET-HANG)
    SHE WON'T GET FAR BEFORE THE WHEELS HANG UP   . . . . . 88 THE HOUSEKEEPER . . 202
    COULD HANG ENOUGH ON TO PICK OFF ENOUGH.   . . . . . . 107 CHRISTMAS TREES . . 54
    WHOSE SPOTTED FLOWERS HANG MEANLY DOWN.   . . . . . . 247 ON GOING UNNOTICED . . 8
    ONE WHO WOULD NEVER HANG ABOVE A BOOKCASE   . . . . . . 278 THE WHITE-TAILED HORNET 17
    THEY HANG ON. THAT SO MUCH OF THE EARTH'S   . . . . . . 322 BUILD SOIL . . . 191
    SO WE CAN HANG TOGETHER IN A STRIKE.   . . . . 498 A MASQUE OF MERCY . 125
HANG-AND-LET-HANG
    TO A PHILOSOPHY OF HANG-AND-LET-HANG.   . . . . 198 WILD GRAPES . . . 61
HANGING
    'TWAS NOTHING BUT MY FOOLISH HANGING BACK, ... 46 A HUNDRED COLLARS . 59
    THEIR TONGUES HANGING OUT UNASSUAGED.   . . . . 311 THE VINDICTIVES . . 51
    THEY SAVED THEMSELVES BY HANGING ON   . . . . 452 A-WISHING WELL . . 48
HANGS
    THAT HANGS PERCEPTIBLY ABOVE THE SCENE.   . . . . . . 412 POD OF THE MILKWEED . 29
    HE HANGS ON UPSIDE DOWN WITH TALON FEET   . . . . . . 412 POD OF THE MILKWEED . 45
HANNIBAL
    HANNIBAL   . . . . 262 HANNIBAL   . . . . T
HAPPEN
    IF ANYTHING SHOULD HAPPEN TO BE WRONG.   . . . . . . 47 A HUNDRED COLLARS . 83
    I GO NOWHERE ON PURPOSE: I HAPPEN BY.--   . . . . . . 50 A HUNDRED COLLARS . 154
    WAITING FOR THINGS TO HAPPEN IN THEIR FAVOR.   . . . . . 204 THE WITCH OF COOS . 63
    ONLY I HAPPEN TO PREFER TO LIVE .   . . . 208 PAUPER WITCH OF GRAFTON 31
    REMINDS ME OF ALL THAT CAN HAPPEN TO HARM   . . . . . . 228 GOOD-BY AND KEEP COLD . 3
    TO HAPPEN IN HEAVEN BEYOND THE FLOATS OF CLOUD   . . . . 268 ON LOOKING UP BY CHANCE 2
    NOTHING WOULD HAPPEN. THAT'S THE THING OF IT.   . . . . 505 A MASQUE OF MERCY . 300
HAPPENED
    MAN THAT KNEW ANYTHING I HAPPENED IN WITH.   . . . . . 46 A HUNDRED COLLARS . 47

| | PAGE TITLE | LINE |

HAPPENED (CONTINUED)

TELL YOU A STORY OF WHAT HAPPENED CNCE: . . . . 70 THE CODE 29
AND NOTHING HAPPENED: DAY WAS ALL BUT DONE. . . . . . . 136 "OUT,OUT--" 9
IT NEVER COULD HAVE HAPPENED IN NEW HAMPSHIRE. . . . . . 160 NEW HAMPSHIRE . . . 34
WHEN THEY SAW WHAT HAD HAPPENED TO THE LOG, ... 193 PAUL'S WIFE 66
AS WAS APPARENT FROM WHAT HAPPENED NEXT. . . . . 195 PAUL'S WIFE 138
BY HAVING ME A WITCH. OR SOMETHING HAPPENED . . . . . 209 PAUPER WITCH OF GRAFTON 77
AT WHAT HAS HAPPENED. BIRDS, AT LEAST, MUST KNOW . . . 249 ACCEPTANCE 4
"LOOK AT WHAT HAPPENED. SURELY SOME GOD PINXIT. . . . . 321 BUILD SOIL 153
IT NEVER HAPPENED! DID IT, YOU?" . . . . 346 DISCOVERY OF MADEIRAS . 99
THINGS MUST HAVE HAPPENED TO YOU, YES, ... 381 AN UNSTAMPED LETTER IN 45
ON MAKING CERTAIN ANYTHING HAS HAPPENED . . . . 383 MAKING CERTAIN ANYTHING T
I NEVER HAPPENED TO CONTRAST . . . . 390 TWO LEADING LIGHTS . . 1
IT HAPPENED WOULD HAVE VERY MUCH TO SAY. . . . . . . 397 THE PLANNERS 8
YOU LOST YOUR ARMY AT MOSUL. WHAT HAPPENED? . . . . . 458 HOW HARD TO KEEP FROM 130
TO ANYTHING THAT HAPPENED ANYMORE. . . . . 501 A MASQUE OF MERCY . . 203

HAPPENS

SOMEWHERE TO WALK----" / "THE HIGHWAY, AS IT HAPPENS-- . . 92 THE FEAR 85
WHAT HAPPENS TO HIM IF IT ONLY TAKES . . . . 146 SNOW 90
THAT HAPPENS TO BE BROKEN," DAVIS SAID. . . . . . . 215 A FOUNTAIN, A BOTTLE . 73
BUT NOTHING EVER HAPPENS, NO HARM IS DONE. . . . . . 268 ON LOOKING UP BY CHANCE 7
AND IF IT'S PROPHECY, WE'LL SEE WHAT HAPPENS. . . . . 505 A MASQUE OF MERCY . . 299

HAPPILY

HOW HAPPILY INSTINCTIVE WE REMAIN, ... 425 ACCIDENTALLY ON PURPOSE 22

HAPPINESS

HAPPINESS MAKES UP IN HEIGHT FOR WHAT IT LACKS IN LENGTH . 333 HAPPINESS MAKES UP . . T
WITH HAPPINESS SHOULD HAVE IT . . . . 335 CARPE DIEM 17
I WILL NOT HAVE THEIR HAPPINESS DESPAIRED OF. . . . . 414 A CABIN IN THE CLEARING 12

HAPPY

AND MAKE US HAPPY IN THE HAPPY BEES, ... 12 A PRAYER IN SPRING . . 7
AND MAKE US HAPPY IN THE DARTING BIRD . . . . 12 A PRAYER IN SPRING . . 9
AND I LOOKED TO BE HAPPY, AND I WAS, ... 67 A SERVANT TO SERVANTS . 152
"DUMPED DOWN IN PARADISE WE ARE AND HAPPY." . . . . . 116 IN THE HOME STRETCH . 163
AS LEAVING MORE TO NATURE AND HAPPY CHANCE. . . . . . 185 MAPLE 169
TO SEEK FOR THE HAPPY ISLES TOGETHER. . . . . 262 THE FLOWER BOAT . . . 12
TO BID THEM BOTH BE HAPPY. . . . . 335 CARPE DIEM 8
"BE HAPPY, HAPPY, HAPPY, ... 335 CARPE DIEM 9
IN HAPPY SADNESS BY THE YOUNG, ... 336 THE WIND AND THE RAIN . 19
"MAKE THEM AS HAPPY AS IS GOOD FOR THEM. . . . . . . 458 HOW HARD TO KEEP FROM 150

HARANGUING

FOREVER VOTING AND HARANGUING FOR IT. . . . . 461 HOW HARD TO KEEP FROM 229

HARBOR

WHAT GOOD IS HE? WHO ELSE WILL HARBOR HIM . . . . . 35 DEATH OF THE HIRED MAN 15
HIS DEEP-SEA DORY HAS FOUND A HARBOR. . . . . 262 THE FLOWER BOAT . . . 4

HARBORING

BY HARBORING WOE IN THE BRIDAL HOUSE, ... 8 LOVE AND A QUESTION . 31

HARD

HE TOSSED HIS PIPES, TOO HARD TO TEACH . . . . . . 24 PAN WITH US 16
IT WILL BE HARD FOR THEM TO KEEP THEIR WORD. . . . . . 55 THE BLACK COTTAGE . . 20
THAT'S A HARD MYSTERY OF JEFFERSON'S. . . . . 57 THE BLACK COTTAGE . . 64
AND HARD TO EXPLAIN AS A CONJUROR'S TRICK." . . . . . 59 BLUEBERRIES 21
BUT HE WORKS WHEN HE WORKS AS HARD AS I DO-- . . . . . 64 A SERVANT TO SERVANTS . 67
HE WAS HARD ON HIMSELF. I COULDN'T FIND . . . . . . 71 THE CODE 39
"NO! AND YET I DON'T KNOW--IT'S HARD TO SAY. . . . . . 73 THE CODE 111
ONE MUSTN'T BEAR TOO HARD ON THE NEWCOMERS, ... 80 THE GENERATIONS OF MEN 188
"IT WILL GO HARD WITH JOHN. WHAT WILL HE DO? . . . . . 82 THE HOUSEKEEPER . . . 28
WE MUSTN'T SAY HARD THINGS, YOU MUSTN'T EITHER." . . . . 91 THE FEAR 53
"IT'S HARD TO TELL YOU HOW I MANAGED IT. . . . . . . 93 THE SELF-SEEKER . . . 22
DON'T YOU BE HARD ON ME. I HAVE TO TAKE . . . . . . 95 THE SELF-SEEKER . . . 62
THE HARD SNOW HELD ME, SAVE WHERE NOW AND THEN . . . . 101 THE WOOD-PILE . . . 4
TO HOLD IT HARD UNTIL THEY MAKE IT FAST, ... 141 THE LINE-GANG . . . 10
IT WOULDN'T DO TO BE TOO HARD ON BRAD . . . . 178 THE STAR-SPLITTER . . 53
SHE PUT HER FINGER IN YOUR CHEEK SO HARD . . . . . . 180 MAPLE 16
NOT NOW--AT LEAST I SHOULDN'T TRY TOO HARD NOW. . . . . 180 MAPLE 25
HARD IF, THOUGH CAST AWAY FOR LIFE WITH YANKEES, ... 186 THE AX-HELVE 44
FOR THE HARD WORK. HE CHAFED ITS LONG WHITE BODY . . . . 187 THE AX-HELVE 76
ONE SUMMER DAY, ALL DAY I DROVE IT HARD, ... 189 THE GRINDSTONE . . . 23
AND SOMEONE MOUNTED ON IT RODE IT HARD, ... 189 THE GRINDSTONE . . . 24
HE'D BEEN HARD AT IT TAKING BOARDS AWAY . . . . . . 193 PAUL'S WIFE 58
STRUCK THE HARD CELLAR BOTTOM. AND THEN SOMEONE . . . . 204 THE WITCH OF COOS . . 50
IT BLEW TOO HARD--THE AIM WAS SONG. . . . . 224 THE AIM WAS SONG . . 7
FROM LEANING ON IT HARD . . . . 227 TO EARTHWARD 27
AND HIT ME A BLOW IN THE HEAD SO HARD . . . . 265 THE DOOR IN THE DARK . 6
EXTREMES TOO HARD TO COMPREHEND AT ONCE, ... 266 THE ARMFUL 4
BY HAILING CHEERILY "HIT THEM HARD!" . . . . 275 TWO TRAMPS IN MUD TIME 4
WHY IS HIS NATURE FOREVER SO HARD TO TEACH . . . . . 305 THERE ARE ROUGHLY ZONES 11
OR KEEPS THE END FROM BEING HARD. . . . . 307 PROVIDE, PROVIDE . . 18
HARD TIMES HAVE STRUCK ME AND I'M ON THE MOVE. . . . . 316 BUILD SOIL 5
IT'S HARD TO TELL WHICH IS THE WORSE ABHORRENCE, ... 321 BUILD SOIL 155
AT LEAST DON'T USE YOUR MIND TOO HARD, ... 326 TO A THINKER 35
A WALL TOO HARD FOR CRIME . . . . 348 TRIPLE BRONZE . . . 7
EARTH'S A HARD PLACE IN WHICH TO SAVE THE SOUL, ... 353 THE LESSON FOR TODAY . 98
SO DIFFERENT FROM THE HARD AND LEVEL STARE . . . . . 356 TIME OUT 10
A THEORY IF YOU HOLD IT HARD ENOUGH . . . . 394 ETHEREALIZING 1
AMERICA IS HARD TO SEE . . . . 416 AMERICA IS HARD TO SEE T
AMERICA IS HARD TO SEE. . . . . 418 AMERICA IS HARD TO SEE 61
HIS HARD TAIL LOUDLY SMACKED THE FLOOR . . . . . . 420 ONE MORE BREVITY . . 23
MY FLOOR SO HARD AND MATTER-OF-FACT. . . . . 421 ONE MORE BREVITY . . 55
I WOULDN'T BE TOO HARD TO CONVINCE, ... 421 ONE MORE BREVITY . . 57
MANNERS MADE IT HARD, ... 432 KITTY HAWK 134
LANDS ON SOMEONE HARD . . . . 441 KITTY HAWK 406
SUCH AUSPICES ARE VERY HARD TO READ. . . . . 443 AUSPEX 5
HOW HARD IT IS TO KEEP FROM BEING KING WHEN IT'S IN YOU AND
    IN THE SITUATION . . . . 453 HOW HARD TO KEEP FROM T
IS TOO HARD ON THE HUMAN RACE. . . . . 453 A-WISHING WELL . . . 70
FOR HARD IT IS TO KEEP FROM BEING KING . . . . . . 454 HOW HARD TO KEEP FROM 20
WITNESS HOW HARD IT WAS FOR JULIUS CAESAR. . . . . . 454 HOW HARD TO KEEP FROM 22
ONLY LESS HARD WAS IT FOR WASHINGTON. . . . . . . 454 HOW HARD TO KEEP FROM 25

		PAGE	TITLE	LINE
HARD (CONTINUED)				
BUT THAT'S A HARD ONE, FOR I HAVE TO ADD:		458	HOW HARD TO KEEP FROM	151
HOW HARD IT IS TO KEEP FROM BEING KING		462	HOW HARD TO KEEP FROM	275
SO HE WON'T FIND IT HARD TO TAKE HIS ORDERS		481	A MASQUE OF REASON	212
SO HE WON'T FIND IT HARD TO TAKE HIS WAR.		481	A MASQUE OF REASON	215
EXCEPT AS A HARD PLACE TO SAVE HIS SOUL IN,		484	A MASQUE OF REASON	318
IT'S A HARD CASE. IT'S GOT SO PROPHECY		503	A MASQUE OF MERCY	257
HARDER				
"THE RIGHTS OF THAT ARE HARDER TO GET AT.		84	THE HOUSEKEEPER	99
THEIR WARES ARE SO MUCH HARDER TO GET RID OF.		164	NEW HAMPSHIRE	174
BLOOD HAS BEEN HARDER TO DAM BACK THAN WATER.		254	THE FLOOD	1
HARDEST				
HER HARDEST HUE TO HOLD.		222	NOTHING GOLD CAN STAY	2
HARDHACK				
AND HAVE TO HUNT FOR IN SWEET FERN AND HARDHACK;		197	WILD GRAPES	33
HARDLY				
"I'LL HARDLY BREATHE." / "THE VOICES SEEM TO SAY----"		78	THE GENERATIONS OF MEN	150
IN WAYS THAT I CAN HARDLY TELL YOU OF.		86	THE HOUSEKEEPER	157
IT HARDLY COULD HAVE BEEN A TWO-LEAVED SEEDLING		184	MAPLE	150
AS HARDLY WORTH RENEWAL.		252	THE PEACEFUL SHEPHERD	8
SOMETIMES I FEEL MYSELF I CAN HARDLY BEAR		287	A ROADSIDE STAND	32
GOD HARDLY TOLERATED WITH HIS FEET;		352	THE LESSON FOR TODAY	75
AND YES, MY LAND WAS HARDLY FENCED.		364	TRESPASS	2
BUT HIS MIND IS HARDLY OUT OF HIS TEENS:		393	A CASE FOR JEFFERSON	8
THE MORAL IS, IT HARDLY NEED BE SHOWN,		394	HAEC FABULA DOCET	17
I HAVE A THEORY, BUT IT HARDLY DOES.		395	WHY WAIT FOR SCIENCE	14
THE KEEPER'S WIFE HAS HARDLY TURNED AWAY		493	A MASQUE OF MERCY	5
WITH VIOLENCE. THE GREEKS WERE HARDLY STRANGERS		511	A MASQUE OF MERCY	468
HARDPAN				
AND EVEN SUBSOIL AND HARDPAN TO MARKET.		321	BUILD SOIL	178
HARDSHIP				
THE HARDSHIP OF ACCOUNTING		309	HARDSHIP OF ACCOUNTING	T
HARDWOOD				
IN HARDWOOD GROVES		25	IN HARDWOOD GROVES	T
HARE				
THE SHADOWY HARE		360	THE RABBIT-HUNTER	13
HARK				
HARK!--I DON'T HEAR HIM NOW. BUT PLEASE GO IN."		90	THE FEAR	40
THRUSH MUSIC--HARK!		334	COME IN	2
AND HARK, THE GOLD ENAMELED NIGHTINGALES		473	A MASQUE OF REASON	14
HARM				
IT SEEMED NO HARM TO STOP HIM ALTOGETHER.		41	THE MOUNTAIN	18
WHAT DO YOU MEAN?--SHE'S DONE HARM TO HERSELF?"		87	THE HOUSEKEEPER	179
ON SOMETHING--THERE'S NO HARM. SEE, THERE HE IS!		88	THE HOUSEKEEPER	203
THOUGH HARM SHOULD COME OF IT; SO BUILT THE SCREEN		109	THE EXPOSED NEST	29
THE HARM WAS DONE: FROM HAVING BEEN STAR-SHOT		173	A STAR IN A STONEBOAT	20
REMINDS ME OF ALL THAT CAN HAPPEN TO HARM		228	GOOD-BY AND KEEP COLD	3
UNLESS OUR PURPOSE IS DOING HARM,		263	THE TIMES TABLE	16
BUT NOTHING EVER HAPPENS, NO HARM IS DONE.		268	ON LOOKING UP BY CHANCE	7
A LITTLE OF FUTURE HARM.		285	IN TIME OF CLOUDBURST	8
AND THE HARM IS NONE TOO SURE,		285	IN TIME OF CLOUDBURST	9
TO CLASP HER--NOT TO HARM;		339	THE SUBVERTED FLOWER	20
HARMLESS				
IT'S HARMLESS. MOTHER HEARS IT IN THE NIGHT,		203	THE WITCH OF COOS	23
HARMONIZE				
"ALL RIGHT, LET'S HARMONIZE ABOUT THE DOCTOR.		407	FROM PLANE TO PLANE	102
HARNESS				
THEIR RAWHIDE HARNESS FROM THE LOAD TO CAMP.		192	PAUL'S WIFE	45
HE GIVES HIS HARNESS BELLS A SHAKE.		224	STOPPING BY WOODS	9
NOW LEFT'S NO BIGGER THAN A HARNESS GALL.		378	DIRECTIVE	40
HAROLD				
HE RAN ON HAROLD WILSON--YOU REMEMBER--		36	DEATH OF THE HIRED MAN	58
HAROLD ALONG BESIDE TO PITCH IT ON."		37	DEATH OF THE HIRED MAN	69
HAROLD'S				
HAROLD'S YOUNG COLLEGE-BOY'S ASSURANCE PIQUED HIM.		37	DEATH OF THE HIRED MAN	73
HAROLD'S ASSOCIATED IN HIS MIND WITH LATIN.		37	DEATH OF THE HIRED MAN	78
HE ASKED ME WHAT I THOUGHT OF HAROLD'S SAYING		37	DEATH OF THE HIRED MAN	79
HARPLIKE				
AMONG THE HARPLIKE MORNING-GLORY STRINGS,		38	DEATH OF THE HIRED MAN	107
AMONG THE HARPLIKE SPREAD OF STRINGS.		274	A LONE STRIKER	29
HARRIS				
HARRIS OF DERRY, AND LYNCH OF BETHLEHEM.		167	NEW HAMPSHIRE	261
HARRISON				
HARRISON LOVES MY COUNTRY TOO,		393	A CASE FOR JEFFERSON	1
HARROW				
NOT FORCING HER HAND WITH HARROW AND PLOW."		61	BLUEBERRIES	56
HARROWED				
THERE IS SELDOM MORE THAN A MAN TO A HARROWED PIECE.		299	STRONG SAYING NOTHING	5
HARRY				
SOME TOM SAID TO DICK OR HARRY:		345	DISCOVERY OF MADEIRAS	68
HARVARD				
I THINK HE OWNED SOME SHARES IN HARVARD COLLEGE.)		163	NEW HAMPSHIRE	137
HARVEST				
AS THE UNCERTAIN HARVEST; KEEP US HERE		12	A PRAYER IN SPRING	3
OF THE GREAT HARVEST I MYSELF DESIRED.		69	AFTER APPLE-PICKING	29
THE HARVEST SHALL STOP?		235	GATHERING LEAVES	24
THE HARVEST MOON AND THEN THE HUNTER'S MOON.		289	OLD BARN AT THE BOTTOM	5
HAS---NOT INDEXED				
HASN'T---NOT INDEXED				
HASTE				
AND SEEK IT ENDLESSLY WITH PURBLIND HASTE;		14	WAITING	17
WHY NOT SIT DOWN IF YOU ARE IN NO HASTE?		56	THE BLACK COTTAGE	47
IN HASTE TO GET IT OVER WITH AS YOU.--		99	THE SELF-SEEKER	192
AND YOU WERE GIVEN THIS SWIFTNESS, NOT FOR HASTE		300	THE MASTER SPEED	5
HOW THEY MAKE HASTE TO CRY WITH FINGERS CROSSED,		399	U.S. 1946 KING'S X	3
FOR HASTE AND OTHER MEANS.		415	CLOSED FOR GOOD	12
HASTENED				
BUT HASTENED BACK TO REASSURE HIS SLAVE		457	HOW HARD TO KEEP FROM	112

```
                                                            PAGE  TITLE                      LINE
HAT
     "NOT YOU!--OH, WHERE'S MY HAT? OH, I DON'T NEED IT"  .  .  .  . 52 HOME BURIAL  .  .  .  .     36
     SHE WORE HER CAPE; HER HAT WAS IN HER HAND.  .  .  .  .  .  .  110 IN THE HOME STRETCH  .     4
     ONE BY ONE I LOST OFF MY HAT AND SHOES,  .  .  .  .  .  .  .  198 WILD GRAPES  .  .  .  .    72
     SQUARE MATTHEW HALE TOOK OFF HIS SUNDAY HAT  .  .  .  .  .  284 THE GOLD HESPERIDEE  .    45
     FOR A HAT I HAD TO SAVE.  .  .  .  .  .  .  .  .  .  .  .  .  294 A RECORD STRIDE  .  .  .    14
HATCH
     WHERE SUMMER BIRDS HAD BEEN GIVEN HATCH,  .  .  .  .  .  .  .  253 THE THATCH  .  .  .  .     14
     LIKE A BIG EGG AND HATCH A HEAVEN OUT  .  .  .  .  .  .  .  484 A MASQUE OF REASON  .  306
HATCHERY
     IN A TROUT HATCHERY NEAR CANADA,  .  .  .  .  .  .  .  .  .  165 NEW HAMPSHIRE  .  .  .  184
HATE
     AND YET WITH NEITHER LOVE NOR HATE,  .  .  .  .  .  .  .  .  .   9 STARS  .  .  .  .  .  .    9
     I HATE TO THINK OF THE OLD PLACE WHEN WE'RE GONE,  .  .  .  .  82 THE HOUSEKEEPER  .  .  .   45
     I'D HATE TO HAVE THEM KNOW IT IF I WAS.  .  .  .  .  .  .  106 CHRISTMAS TREES  .  .  .    20
     YET MORE I'D HATE TO HOLD MY TREES, EXCEPT  .  .  .  .  .  106 CHRISTMAS TREES  .  .  .    21
     I HATE HIS WRETCHED LITTLE RACKER SECT,  .  .  .  .  .  .  .  144 SNOW  .  .  .  .  .  .  .   53
     I'D HATE TO BE A RUNAWAY FROM NATURE.  .  .  .  .  .  .  .  171 NEW HAMPSHIRE  .  .  .  397
     APPEARING TO RETURN ME HATE FOR HATE  .  .  .  .  .  .  .  .  190 THE GRINDSTONE  .  .  .    41
     I THINK I KNOW ENOUGH OF HATE  .  .  .  .  .  .  .  .  .  .  220 FIRE AND ICE  .  .  .  .    6
     AND TELL THE STONES: MEN HATE TO DIE  .  .  .  .  .  .  .  .  221 IN A DISUSED GRAVEYARD    14
     HIS HATE HAD ROUSED AN ENGINE UP THE ROAD.  .  .  .  .  .  270 THE EGG AND THE MACHINE    4
     WHEN HATE GAVE A TERRIBLE LAUGH,  .  .  .  .  .  .  .  .  .  311 THE VINDICTIVES  .  .  .   22
     "THE BEST WAY TO HATE IS THE WORST.  .  .  .  .  .  .  .  .  312 THE VINDICTIVES  .  .  .   81
     (IN THIS IT IS AS MUCH LIKE HATE AS LOVE),  .  .  .  .  .  .  319 BUILD SOIL  .  .  .  .  105
     THAT IS THE SOURCE PERHAPS OF HUMAN HATE  .  .  .  .  .  .  371 THE LITERATE FARMER AND 108
     FEELS LIKE MY ARMORY OF HATE;  .  .  .  .  .  .  .  .  .  .  393 BEYOND WORDS  .  .  .  .    2
     WHAT'S MORE, I HATE TO KEEP AFFLICTING WEEDS.  .  .  .  .  406 FROM PLANE TO PLANE  .   64
     WITH ANIMUS APPROACHING HATE,  .  .  .  .  .  .  .  .  .  .  418 AMERICA IS HARD TO SEE    51
     IN A LOVE AND HATE  .  .  .  .  .  .  .  .  .  .  .  .  .  .  436 KITTY HAWK  .  .  .  .  268
     ANY MORE THAN WE HAD TO TO HATE,  .  .  .  .  .  .  .  .  .  444 THE DRAFT HORSE  .  .  .   16
     'TWIXT WHAT TO LOVE AND WHAT TO HATE.  .  .  .  .  .  .  .  467 QUANDARY  .  .  .  .  .  .   10
     AND HATE HIM AS THYSELF THOU HATEST.  .  .  .  .  .  .  .  467 QUANDARY  .  .  .  .  .  .   13
     DON'T LET IT CARRY YOU AWAY. I HATE  .  .  .  .  .  .  .  489 A MASQUE OF REASON  .  448
     HE SAID THE BIBLE. / I SHOULD HATE TO SCARE YOU  .  .  .  495 A MASQUE OF MERCY  .  .   52
HATED
     AND HATED TO BE TWITTED ON THE SUBJECT;  .  .  .  .  .  .  191 PAUL'S WIFE  .  .  .  .  .    5
     'TIS TO FIND WHAT THE HATED NEED,  .  .  .  .  .  .  .  .  312 THE VINDICTIVES  .  .  .   82
HATEFUL
     HE GAVE THE SOLID RAIL A HATEFUL KICK.  .  .  .  .  .  .  .  269 THE EGG AND THE MACHINE    1
HATES
     HE HATES TO SEE A BOY THE FOOL OF BOOKS.  .  .  .  .  .  .   37 DEATH OF THE HIRED MAN    98
HATEST
     AND HATE HIM AS THYSELF THOU HATEST.  .  .  .  .  .  .  .  467 QUANDARY  .  .  .  .  .  .   13
HATING
     WE HAVE ONE LOVING AND ONE HATING HAND.  .  .  .  .  .  .  371 THE LITERATE FARMER AND 113
     WHILE WITH THE HATING OTHER HAND WE STRIKE.  .  .  .  .  .  371 THE LITERATE FARMER AND 115
HATLESS
     (ENTERING HATLESS IN A WHIRL OF SNOW)  .  .  .  .  .  .  .  493 A MASQUE OF MERCY  .  .   18
HATTERAS
     OF DARK HATTERAS  .  .  .  .  .  .  .  .  .  .  .  .  .  .  .  431 KITTY HAWK  .  .  .  .   88
HAUGHTY
     BUT LET HIM SHOW HIS HAUGHTY STERN  .  .  .  .  .  .  .  .  419 AMERICA IS HARD TO SEE    75
HAUNT
     STILL SAID TO HAUNT THIS SIDE OF PANTHER MOUNTAIN.  .  .  377 DIRECTIVE  .  .  .  .  .  .   19
HAUNTED
     SEEMS HAUNTED OR EXPOSED. I ALWAYS TAKE  .  .  .  .  .  .  115 IN THE HOME STRETCH  .  133
HAVE---NOT INDEXED
HAVEN'T---NOT INDEXED
HAVING
     HAVING FIRST HEARD THE LIFE READ OUT  .  .  .  .  .  .  .   20 THE TRIAL BY EXISTENCE    34
     AND HE LIKES HAVING THOUGHT OF IT SO WELL  .  .  .  .  .   34 MENDING WALL  .  .  .  .    44
     I BLAMED IT ON THE HOT SPELL WE'VE BEEN HAVING.  .  .  .   46 A HUNDRED COLLARS  .  .    58
     I MEAN BY THE WORLD'S HAVING PASSED IT BY--  .  .  .  .   56 THE BLACK COTTAGE  .  .    43
     TO PEOPLE THEY LOOK ON AS HAVING NO RIGHT  .  .  .  .  .   62 BLUEBERRIES  .  .  .  .  101
     "FROM THE SENSE OF OUR HAVING BEEN TOGETHER--  .  .  .  .   78 THE GENERATIONS OF MEN  142
     IN SEPARATE COOPS, HAVING THEIR PLUMAGE DONE.  .  .  .  .   85 THE HOUSEKEEPER  .  .  .  121
     AND HAVING PERHAPS THE BETTER CLAIM,  .  .  .  .  .  .  .  105 THE ROAD NOT TAKEN  .  .    7
     QUITE SOLITARY AND HAVING EQUAL BOUGHS  .  .  .  .  .  .  107 CHRISTMAS TREES  .  .  .   35
     AND HAVING SCARED THE CELLAR UNDER HIM  .  .  .  .  .  .  108 OLD MAN'S WINTER NIGHT    9
     WOULD EVIDENCE OF HAVING BEEN CALLED LADY  .  .  .  .  .  111 IN THE HOME STRETCH  .   22
     "HAVING FOUND THE FLOWER AND DRIVEN A BEE AWAY,  .  .  .  118 THE TELEPHONE  .  .  .  .   11
     FROM A TWIG'S HAVING LASHED ACROSS IT OPEN.  .  .  .  .  .  122 BIRCHES  .  .  .  .  .  .   47
     A CIDER SYRUP. HAVING TASTED FRUIT,  .  .  .  .  .  .  .  124 THE COW IN APPLE TIME  .    5
     THE HAVING ANYTHING TO SELL IS WHAT  .  .  .  .  .  .  .  159 NEW HAMPSHIRE  .  .  .  .    7
     THIS IS CALLED HAVING AN IDEA TO SELL.  .  .  .  .  .  .  160 NEW HAMPSHIRE  .  .  .  .   33
     OUT OF NOT HAVING CAUSE FOR MISERY.  .  .  .  .  .  .  .  167 NEW HAMPSHIRE  .  .  .  273
     OR HAVING SEEN AND CREDITED A MOMENT  .  .  .  .  .  .  .  169 NEW HAMPSHIRE  .  .  .  321
     BUT THE SAD ACCIDENT OF HAVING SEEN  .  .  .  .  .  .  .  169 NEW HAMPSHIRE  .  .  .  329
     THE HARM WAS DONE: FROM HAVING BEEN STAR-SHOT  .  .  .  .  173 A STAR IN A STONEBOAT  .   20
     THE MELANCHOLY OF HAVING TO COUNT SOULS  .  .  .  .  .  .  176 THE CENSUS-TAKER  .  .  .   61
     OR ELSE FUN OF ORION'S HAVING CAUGHT ME.  .  .  .  .  .  .  176 THE STAR-SPLITTER  .  .   10
     TILL HAVING FAILED AT HUGGER-MUGGER FARMING  .  .  .  .  177 THE STAR-SPLITTER  .  .   15
     SHE HAD BEEN HAVING A LONG LOOK AT YOU.  .  .  .  .  .  .  180 MAPLE  .  .  .  .  .  .  .   15
     IN HAVING TOO MUCH MEANING. OTHER NAMES,  .  .  .  .  .  181 MAPLE  .  .  .  .  .  .  .   45
     (IF OVERJOYED HE WAS) AT HAVING GOT ME  .  .  .  .  .  .  186 THE AX-HELVE  .  .  .  .   40
     OF REALLY NEVER HAVING MEANT TO KEEP IT.  .  .  .  .  .  .  187 THE AX-HELVE  .  .  .  .   62
     WITH THE CURVES OF HIS AX-HELVES AND HIS HAVING  .  .  .  188 THE AX-HELVE  .  .  .  .   87
     HAVING A WHEEL AND FOUR LEGS OF ITS OWN  .  .  .  .  .  .  188 THE GRINDSTONE  .  .  .  .    1
     OR SO OF HAVING ONE, AND THEN BEEN JILTED;  .  .  .  .  .  191 PAUL'S WIFE  .  .  .  .  .    7
     THAT COMES OF HAVING PAUL AROUND THE PLACE.  .  .  .  .  193 PAUL'S WIFE  .  .  .  .  .   76
     GRAPES, I KNEW GRAPES FROM HAVING SEEN THEM LAST YEAR.  .  .  197 WILD GRAPES  .  .  .  .   24
     SHE WENT HER WAY. BUT LABAN HAVING CAUGHT  .  .  .  .  .  200 PLACE FOR A THIRD  .  .   15
     OF ARTHUR AMY'S HAVING ONCE BEEN UP  .  .  .  .  .  .  .  207 PAUPER WITCH OF GRAFTON   13
     AT HAVING IN THEIR TOWN A NOTED WITCH:  .  .  .  .  .  .  208 PAUPER WITCH OF GRAFTON   37
     OF HAVING INTERFERED IN THE HOUSE BUSINESS.  .  .  .  .  .  209 PAUPER WITCH OF GRAFTON   75
     BY HAVING ME A WITCH. OR SOMETHING HAPPENED  .  .  .  .  209 PAUPER WITCH OF GRAFTON   77
     HAVING TRIED ONE, HAD DROPPED IT AT HIS FEET  .  .  .  .  217 A FOUNTAIN, A BOTTLE  . 119
```

HAVING (CONTINUED)
    AT HAVING EASED HER HEART OF ONE MORE COPY--   . . . . . 217 A FOUNTAIN, A BOTTLE . 135
    OTHERS TAUNT ME WITH HAVING KNELT AT WELL-CURBS   . . . 225 FOR ONCE SOMETHING . .   1
    AND NOW FROM HAVING RIDDEN OUT DESIRE . . . . 225 BLUE-BUTTERFLY DAY . .   6
    AND IMPULSE, HAVING DIPPED A FINGER LENGTH   . . . . . 231 A BROOK IN THE CITY .   6
    AND MADE IT LEAP MY KNUCKLE, HAVING TOSSED   . . . . . 231 A BROOK IN THE CITY .   7
    AT HAVING CULTIVATED ROCK. . . . . 238 PLOWMEN   4
    MADE QUICK ASIDES, BUT HAVING DONE IN AIR   . . . . . 240 OUR SINGING STRENGTH . 40
    HER NEVER HAVING DEIGNED TO TELL THEM. . . . . 257 THE LOVELY BE CHOOSERS 38
    AND HAVING POWER TO CHANGE HIS AIM IN FLIGHT, ... 277 THE WHITE-TAILED HORNET 5
    AND SERVED US RIGHT FOR HAVING INSTITUTED   . . . . . 279 THE WHITE-TAILED HORNET 58
    AND AFTER HAVING ENTERTAINED THE BEE, ... 283 THE GOLD HESPERIDEE .   3
    AT HAVING THE LANDSCAPE MARRED WITH THE ARTLESS PAINT . 286 A ROADSIDE STAND . .   9
    AND HAVING HID IT IN THEIR BEDDING STRAW . . . . 293 AT WOODWARD'S GARDENS . 30
    I WOULD NOT BE TAKEN AS EVER HAVING REBELLED. . . . . . 306 NOT QUITE SOCIAL . .   12
    NO MEMORY OF HAVING STARRED . . . . 307 PROVIDE, PROVIDE . .   16
    OF ONCE HAVING STARTED A WAR, ... 310 THE VINDICTIVES . .   16
    FROM HAVING HEARD THE DAYLONG VOICE OF EVE   . . . . . 338 NEVER WOULD BIRDS' SONG 3
    BY HAVING WHAT IS FREE ENFORCED. . . . . 346 DISCOVERY OF MADEIRAS . 79
    FOR YOUR NOT HAVING WON TO VIRGIL'S FAME. . . . . 351 THE LESSON FOR TODAY . 27
    I'M HAVING THE WHOLE ARGUMENT MY WAY--   . . . . 354 THE LESSON FOR TODAY . 116
    IN HAVING GRANTED YOU ALL AGES SHINE   . . . . 354 THE LESSON FOR TODAY . 118
    IN HAVING TAKEN ARTIFICIAL LIGHT   . . . . 361 A LOOSE MOUNTAIN . .   7
    IN HAVING ITS UNDEVIABLE SAY. . . . . 362 IN A POEM   4
    AS ONE HAVING WAR-COMMAND. . . . . 366 NOT OF SCHOOL AGE . .   12
    THEY THINK TOO MUCH OF HAVING SHADED OUT . . . . 378 DIRECTIVE   27
    THEN WHAT OF THIS RIVER THAT HAVING ARISEN   . . . . . 379 TOO ANXIOUS FOR RIVERS   3
    LEST HAVING WASTED PRECIOUS HEAT   . . . . 381 AN UNSTAMPED LETTER IN 23
    FROM TWO STARS' HAVING COALESCED   . . . . 381 AN UNSTAMPED LETTER IN 26
    AND HAVING HER EXPOSURE MISCONSTRUED. . . . . 386 THE FEAR OF MAN . .   14
    AND HAVING IT ALL MADE OVER NEW. . . . . 393 A CASE FOR JEFFERSON . 11
    HAVING INVENTED A NEW HOLOCAUST, ... 399 U.S. 1946 KING'S X .   1
    OF HAVING HOED AND MOWED FOR FIFTY YEARS, ... 404 FROM PLANE TO PLANE .   3
    HE DON'T MIND HAVING LOST A CASE," PIKE SAID; . . . . . 404 FROM PLANE TO PLANE .   25
    AND MADE OF BY A BOY; THEN HAVING REACHED   . . . . . 405 FROM PLANE TO PLANE .   57
    FROM HAVING BEATEN ALL DAY LONG IN VAIN   . . . . . . 412 POD OF THE MILKWEED .   38
    FROM HAVING DIED. . . . . 413 AWAY!   24
    WHILE HAVING ITS BELIEFS DISPUTED. . . . . 419 AMERICA IS HARD TO SEE 82
    WHO, HAVING FAILED OF THE MODERN SPEED, ... 419 ONE MORE BREVITY . .   12
    THE SORROW OF HAVING BEEN LEFT BEHIND, ... 420 ONE MORE BREVITY . .   31
    OR THE SORROW OF HAVING RUN AWAY. . . . . 420 ONE MORE BREVITY . .   32
    MY HAVING DEPENDED ON HIM SO LONG, ... 421 ONE MORE BREVITY . .   64
    INTO HAVING WEIGHT. . . . . 426 A NEVER NAUGHT SONG .   5
    INTO HAVING BEEN! . . . . 426 A NEVER NAUGHT SONG .   28
    AFTER HAVING CRAWLED   . . . . 434 KITTY HAWK   203
    FOR HAVING BEEN BORN? . . . . 448 THE BAD ISLAND--EASTER 23
    AND THEN HAVING FIRST   . . . . 448 THE BAD ISLAND--EASTER 24
    FROM THE PEARL'S HAVING ITS OWN NATIVE WARMTH, ... 456 HOW HARD TO KEEP FROM   90
    FOR HAVING LIED BUT HAVING TOLD THE TRUTH. . . . . . . 457 HOW HARD TO KEEP FROM 114
    ALL SHE'D BEEN HAVING WAS CLOVER. . . . . 463 LINES IN DEJECTION .   4
    IN HAVING LEFT THE MAP . . . . 464 MILKY WAY IS A COWPATH   3
    IT WAS BY HAVING BEEN CONTRASTED   . . . . 467 QUANDARY   5
    TO TROUBLE MEN WITH HAVING TO TAKE SIDES. . . . . 468 FROM IRON   2
    NOT IN THE SENSE OF HAVING TO MY KNOWLEDGE   . . . . . 476 A MASQUE OF REASON .   95
    OF HAVING CHILDREN--AFTER HAVING HAD THEM, ... 483 A MASQUE OF REASON .   292
    BUT TO THE EVENSONG, AND HAVING PLAYED   . . . . . . 489 A MASQUE OF REASON .   436
    WHO HAVING BY ELIMINATION GOT   . . . . 498 A MASQUE OF MERCY .   120
    I SAY YOU SHOULD BE PROUD OF HAVING BEATEN   . . . . . 508 A MASQUE OF MERCY .   378
    ONCE CHARGED THE NAZARENE WITH HAVING BROUGHT   . . . . 511 A MASQUE OF MERCY .   465
    THERE IS NO BETTER WAY OF HAVING IT. . . . . 512 A MASQUE OF MERCY .   508
    BY HAVING HIM WHIPPED EVERY DAY AFRESH   . . . . . . 517 A MASQUE OF MERCY .   642
    MERCY ON ME FOR HAVING THOUGHT I KNEW. . . . . 518 A MASQUE OF MERCY .   660
    MERCY ON HIM FOR HAVING ASKED FOR JUSTICE. . . . . . . 518 A MASQUE OF MERCY .   662
    BUT JONAH GIVES NO SIGN OF HAVING HEARD.) . . . . 518 A MASQUE OF MERCY .   668
HAWK
    UNDER THE WATCHFUL EYE OF HAWK AND EAGLE--   . . . . . 162 NEW HAMPSHIRE . . .   105
    KITTY HAWK, O KITTY. . . . . 428 KITTY HAWK . . .   1
    KITTY HAWK . . . . 428 KITTY HAWK . . .   T
    HERE AT KITTY HAWK. . . . . 433 KITTY HAWK . . .   157
    KITTY HAWK, O KITTY. . . . . 433 KITTY HAWK . . .   175
    IT'S STILL KITTY HAWK. . . . . 439 KITTY HAWK . . .   347
HAWKING
    HAWKING FOR FLIES ABOUT THE KITCHEN DOOR, ... 278 THE WHITE-TAILED HORNET 24
HAWKS
    AND THE WHIMPER OF HAWKS BESIDE THE SUN   . . . . . . 24 PAN WITH US . . .   19
    "OH, THAT'S BEEN THERE FOR HAWKS SINCE CHICKEN-TIME. . . 83 THE HOUSEKEEPER . . .   66
HAX-EAD
    DEN WHERE'S YOUR HAX-EAD FLYING T'ROUGH DE HAIR?" . . . 186 THE AX-HELVE   27
HAY
    MY LONG SCYTHE WHISPERED AND LEFT THE HAY TO MAKE. . . 17 MOWING   14
    TO TEACH HIM HOW TO BUILD A LOAD OF HAY----" . . . . . 37 DEATH OF THE HIRED MAN 87
    YOU NEVER SEE HIM STANDING ON THE HAY . . . . 37 DEATH OF THE HIRED MAN 94
    THERE'S A HAY LOAD A-COMING--WHEN IT COMES. . . . . . . 49 A HUNDRED COLLARS . . 132
    GATHERING UP WINDROWS, PILING COCKS OF HAY, ... 69 THE CODE   2
    "TO COCK THE HAY?--BECAUSE IT'S GOING TO SHOWER? . . . . 70 THE CODE   12
    THE HAY AND ROLLING IT OFF WHOLESALE, ... 71 THE CODE   57
    'I LEFT HIM IN THE BARN UNDER THE HAY. . . . . 72 THE CODE   84
    THEY TOLD ME AFTERWARD. FIRST THEY FORKED HAY, ... 72 THE CODE   89
    WE TENDED TO HIS HAY. WE SAW HIM OUT . . . . 73 THE CODE   107
    HE'S GOT HAY DOWN THAT'S BEEN RAINED ON THREE TIMES. . . 83 THE HOUSEKEEPER . . .   57
    IN THE MEADOW, BUSY WITH THE NEW-CUT HAY, ... 109 THE EXPOSED NEST . .   3
    WHO SLEPT THERE IN A MOW OF MEADOW HAY   . . . . . . 289 OLD BARN AT THE BOTTOM 19
    TO SELL THE HAY OFF, LET ALONE THE SOIL, ... 321 BUILD SOIL   179
    BEFORE THEY TURNED FROM EVERYTHING TO HAY. . . . . . . 404 FROM PLANE TO PLANE .   14
HAYCOCK
    UPON THE FULL MOON'S SIDE OF THE FIRST HAYCOCK   . . . 14 WAITING   7
HAYCOCKS
    MOVING AMONG TALL HAYCOCKS LIGHTLY PILED, ... 14 WAITING   2

HAYFIELD
   SO WHEN HE PAIRED OFF WITH ME IN THE HAYFIELD . . . . . . 71 THE CODE 49
HAYING
   "I TOLD HIM SO LAST HAYING, DIDN'T I? . . . . 35 DEATH OF THE HIRED MAN 13
   IN HAYING TIME, WHEN ANY HELP IS SCARCE. . . . . . . 35 DEATH OF THE HIRED MAN 29
   THE BOY YOU HAD IN HAYING FOUR YEARS SINCE. . . . . . 36 DEATH OF THE HIRED MAN 59
   DOING THE HAYING. NO ONE LIKED THE BOSS. . . . . . . 70 THE CODE 32
HAYSEED
   AS I SAT MOPPING HAYSEED FROM MY NECK, ... 72 THE CODE 81
HAZE
   AS FAR AS I CAN SEE, THIS AUTUMN HAZE . . . . 247 THE COCOON 1
   TO A CONE MOUNTAIN IN THE MIDNIGHT HAZE, ... 300 MOON COMPASSES . . 4
   A MIST AND SMOKE EAVESDROPPING ON A HAZE-- . . . . . 415 A CABIN IN THE CLEARING 39
   THE KINDRED SPIRIT OF AN INNER HAZE? . . . . 415 A CABIN IN THE CLEARING 42
HAZEL
   THE FLOWERS OF THE WITCH HAZEL WITHER; . . . . 30 RELUCTANCE 16
   HE COULD FIND WATER WITH A HAZEL PRONG-- . . . . . . 37 DEATH OF THE HIRED MAN 83
HAZES
   WHEN THE HEAT SLOWLY HAZES AND THE SUN . . . . . . 125 AN ENCOUNTER 2
HAZY
   ABOVE A HAZY TREE-AND-FARMHOUSE CLUSTER . . . . . . 245 THE FREEDOM OF THE MOON 2
HE---NOT INDEXED
HEAD (SEE AX-HEAD, DREAM-HEAD)
   YOU SHOOK YOUR PENSIVE HEAD AS WHO SHOULD SAY, ... 16 A DREAM PANG . . . 6
   IF I COULD PUT A NOTION IN HIS HEAD: . . . . 34 MENDING WALL 29
   AND ROLLED HIS OLD HEAD ON THAT SHARP-EDGED CHAIR-BACK. . 39 DEATH OF THE HIRED MAN 148
   TO HAVE SOME HEAD OF WATER FROM ABOVE, ... 43 THE MOUNTAIN . . . 70
   I DON'T WANT YOU SHOULD SHOOT ME IN THE HEAD.-- . . . . 50 A HUNDRED COLLARS . 176
   "HE JUST KEPT NODDING HIS HEAD UP AND DOWN. . . . . . 60 BLUEBERRIES 41
   KEEPING HIS HEAD ABOVE. 'DAMN YE,' I SAYS, ... 72 THE CODE 77
   BUT I OWN WHAT YOU SAY MAKES MY HEAD SPIN. . . . . . 75 THE GENERATIONS OF MEN 60
   "THE WONDER IS IT HADN'T BEEN YOUR HEAD." . . . . . 93 THE SELF-SEEKER . . 21
   THAT'S HOW I THINK I DIDN'T LOSE MY HEAD. . . . . . 93 THE SELF-SEEKER . . 28
   ONE OF YOU HOLD MY HEAD UP FROM THE PILLOW." . . . . 100 THE SELF-SEEKER . . 215
   WHEN LEANING WITH MY HEAD AGAINST A FLOWER . . . . . 118 THE TELEPHONE . . . 5
   I LEANED MY HEAD, ... 118 THE TELEPHONE . . . 12
   AND MY HEAD SWAYS TO MY SHOULDER . . . . 156 THE SOUND OF TREES . 16
   "SEE HOW SHE'S COCK HER HEAD!" . . . . 188 THE AX-HELVE . . . 102
   AND STILL I CLUNG. I LET MY HEAD FALL BACK, ... 198 WILD GRAPES 73
   THE OTHER CURLED AT HIS BREAST. HE DIPPED HIS HEAD . . . 223 THE RUNAWAY . . . 4
   HE VIEWED THEM QUIZZICALLY WITH JERKS OF HEAD, ... 229 TWO LOOK AT TWO . . 31
   YOUR HEAD SO MUCH CONCERNED WITH OUTER, ... 252 TREE AT MY WINDOW . 15
   AND HIT ME A BLOW IN THE HEAD SO HARD . . . . . . 265 THE DOOR IN THE DARK . 6
   'TIS ONLY TO SIT BACK AND SWAY HIS HEAD . . . . . . 269 THE BEAR 23
   AND ALL THEIR LOGIC WOULD FILL MY HEAD: . . . . . . 277 TWO TRAMPS IN MUD TIME 59
   OF WHIRLING HANDS AND ARMS ABOUT THE HEAD . . . . . 277 THE WHITE-TAILED HORNET 9
   HE ROLLED ME OFF THE FIELD HEAD OVER HEELS . . . . . 278 THE WHITE-TAILED HORNET 20
   THE HUCKLEBERRY ROLLED HIM ON HIS HEAD. . . . . . . 278 THE WHITE-TAILED HORNET 41
   ROLL STONES DOWN ON OUR HEAD! . . . . 298 ON TAKING FROM THE TOP 1
   TO INDUCE THE ONE SNOW ON HIS HEAD. . . . . 299 WELCOME TO THEIR BELIEF 8
   THE HEAD IN THE DARK BELOW . . . . 299 WELCOME TO THEIR BELIEF 10
   A HEAD THRUSTS IN AS FOR THE VIEW, ... 332 ALL REVELATION . . . 1
   BUT GIVE ME WATER HEAVY ON THE HEAD . . . . 337 THE WIND AND THE RAIN . 38
   WHICH PUT THE THOUGHT INTO SOMEONE'S HEAD . . . . . 345 DISCOVERY OF MADEIRAS . 66
   BUT THE THING WAS THE SLOPE IT GAVE HIS HEAD: . . . . 356 TIME OUT 8
   AND THE HOLLOW HEAD WAS A LAKE. . . . . 367 A SERIOUS STEP LIGHTLY 4
   AND PLUNGED HIMSELF HEAD FOREMOST IN THE TRENCH: . . . 394 HAEC FABULA DOCET . . 14
   AND HEAD TO TAIL THEN FIRMLY CURLED . . . . 419 ONE MORE BREVITY . . 17
   WE WERE JUST PURPOSE COMING TO A HEAD. . . . . . . 425 ACCIDENTALLY ON PURPOSE 16
   AND YET FOR ALL THIS HELP OF HEAD AND BRAIN . . . . . 425 ACCIDENTALLY ON PURPOSE 21
   EVER SINCE NAG'S HEAD . . . . 429 KITTY HAWK 23
   FROM THIS HEAD AND HEART, ... 440 KITTY HAWK 389
   AND TOOK OUR HORSE BY THE HEAD . . . . 444 THE DRAFT HORSE . . 6
   THAT PRIMITIVE HEAD . . . . 447 THE BAD ISLAND--EASTER 1
   MY HEAD FOR IT--YOU'LL FIND THE BIG ONE HOLLOW. . . . 456 HOW HARD TO KEEP FROM 83
   IT SEEMS TO BE A CHAPTER HEAD IN METER. . . . . . . 506 A MASQUE OF MERCY . . 327
   BUT WE ARE TALKING OVER JONAH'S HEAD, ... 509 A MASQUE OF MERCY . . 426
   BUT TO REPEAT AND GET IT THROUGH YOUR HEAD: . . . . . 516 A MASQUE OF MERCY . . 600
HEADBOARD
   BUT THE HEADBOARD OF MOTHER'S BED IS PUSHED . . . . . 203 THE WITCH OF COOS . . 21
   OF DOOR AND HEADBOARD. WHERE IT WANTS TO GET . . . . 203 THE WITCH OF COOS . . 25
   AND PUSH THE HEADBOARD OF THE BED AGAINST IT. . . . . 206 THE WITCH OF COOS . . 120
   BEHIND THE DOOR AND HEADBOARD OF THE BED, ... 206 THE WITCH OF COOS . . 127
HEADDRESS
   WEARING A THIN HEADDRESS OF POINTED LEAVES, ... 196 WILD GRAPES 21
HEADED (SEE HOLLOW-HEADED, TENDER-HEADED)
   THEY HEADED FOR THE BARN; I STAYED WHERE I WAS. . . . 72 THE CODE 88
   FROM THAT WHICH HE WAS HEADED FOR-- . . . . 139 BROWN'S DESCENT . . 67
   HAVE SOME SAY AS TO WHERE WE'RE HEADED FOR; . . . . . 482 A MASQUE OF REASON . 235
HEADLESS
   THE HEADLESS AFTERMATH, ... 8 A LATE WALK 2
   THERE IS OUR WILDEST MOUNT--A HEADLESS HORSE. . . . . 267 RIDERS 9
HEADLIGHT
   A BLINDING HEADLIGHT SHIFTED GLARE . . . . 383 WERE I IN TROUBLE . . 3
HEADLONG
   OR PLUNGING HEADLONG WITH FIERCE TWANG AFAR; . . . . 14 WAITING 13
   NOR HEADLONG BEE . . . . 343 QUEST OF PURPLE-FRINGED 18
   WITH THE HEADLONG HUMAN RACE. . . . . 465 SOME SCIENCE FICTION . 4
HEADS
   FIERCE HEADS LOOKED OUT; SMALL BODIES PIVOTED. . . . . 59 THE BLACK COTTAGE . 126
   STEEL-BRIGHT JUNE-GRASS, AND BLACKENING HEADS OF CLOVER. . 109 THE EXPOSED NEST . . 12
   BEFORE THEM OVER THEIR HEADS TO DRY IN THE SUN. . . . 121 BIRCHES 20
   THEY KEPT THEIR HEADS AND TOOK THEIR TIME TO IT . . . 143 SNOW 24
   THAT DAY SHE PUT OUR HEADS TOGETHER, ... 252 TREE AT MY WINDOW . 13
   NO DOUBT DIRECTED AT OUR HEADS AS REBELS . . . . . 361 A LOOSE MOUNTAIN . . 6
   WE WELL MAY RAISE OUR HEADS . . . . 361 ALMOST TWO THOUSAND . 10
   NO NEED FOR US TO RACK OUR COMMON HEADS . . . . . 372 THE LITERATE FARMER AND 132
   BUMPED HEADS TOGETHER DULLY . . . . 376 ONE STEP BACKWARD TAKEN 5

		PAGE	TITLE	LINE

HEADS (CONTINUED)
    WOULD KNOCK THEIR DRUNKEN PENTHOUSE HEADS TOGETHER . . . 506 A MASQUE OF MERCY . 333
HEADSHAKE
    GIVE A HEADSHAKE . . . . 211 AN EMPTY THREAT . . . 30
HEADSHAKINGS
    WITH FAINT HEADSHAKINGS, NO MORE WISE. . . . . . 344 DISCOVERY OF MADEIRAS . 40
HEADSMAN
    I GUESS I'LL HAVE THE HEADSMAN EXECUTE ME . . . . . 460 HOW HARD TO KEEP FROM 205
    THE HEADSMAN HAS DARIUS BY THE BELT . . . . . . 462 HOW HARD TO KEEP FROM 261
HEADSTONE
    THE HEADSTONE CUT WITH JOHN, BELOVED HUSBAND, ... 200 PLACE FOR A THIRD . . 39
HEADY
    WIND SHE BREWS A HEADY KETTLE. . . . . . . 304 CLEAR AND COLDER . . 21
HEAL-ALL
    ON A WHITE HEAL-ALL, HOLDING UP A MOTH . . . . 302 DESIGN 2
    THE WAYSIDE BLUE AND INNOCENT HEAL-ALL? . . . . . 302 DESIGN 10
HEALED
    THE FOOTPATH DOWN TO THE WELL IS HEALED. . . . . . 6 GHOST HOUSE 10
HEALTH
    OF WORDS OR TOYS, IT MINISTERS TO HEALTH. . . . . 321 BUILD SOIL 170
    'TWAS HIS IDEA THAT FOR THE PUBLIC HEALTH, ... 363 AN EQUALIZER 6
HEALTHY
    A HEALTHY INDEPENDENCE OF THE THRONG, ... 424 FOR JOHN F. KENNEDY . 63
HEAP
    WENT SURELY TO THE CIDER-APPLE HEAP . . . . 69 AFTER APPLE-PICKING . 35
    THE EARTH BUT IT HAS FAILED: THE SNOW MAY HEAP . . . 226 THE ONSET 14
HEAPS
    SUCH HEAPS OF BROKEN GLASS TO SWEEP AWAY . . . . . 121 BIRCHES 12
HEAR
    I HEAR HIM BEGIN FAR ENOUGH AWAY . . . . . . 6 GHOST HOUSE . . . 18
    THAT MADE ME HEAR THE WAKENING BIRDS AROUND, ... 23 THE TUFT OF FLOWERS . 31
    AND HEAR HIS LONG SCYTHE WHISPERING TO THE GROUND, . . 23 THE TUFT OF FLOWERS . 32
    THAT I SUDDENLY HEARD--ALL I NEEDED TO HEAR: . . . . 24 THE DEMIURGE'S LAUGH . 5
    SO CLOSE THE WINDOWS AND NOT HEAR THE WIND, ... 25 NOW CLOSE THE WINDOWS . 7
    "SH! NOT SO LOUD: HE'LL HEAR YOU," MARY SAID. . . . . 35 DEATH OF THE HIRED MAN 31
    WAS NO BIGGER THAN A----" WHAT, I DID NOT HEAR. . . . 44 THE MOUNTAIN 106
    AND TO HEAR HER QUAINT PHRASES--SO REMOVED . . . . 57 THE BLACK COTTAGE . 62
    OUR WILLOUGHBY! HOW DID YOU HEAR OF IT? . . . . 63 A SERVANT TO SERVANTS . 33
    SHE HAD TO LIE AND HEAR LOVE THINGS MADE DREADFUL . . 66 A SERVANT TO SERVANTS . 130
    AND PERHAPS HEAR SOME WORD ABOUT THE WEATHER. . . . 74 THE GENERATIONS OF MEN 33
    "OH, IF YOU'RE GOING TO USE YOUR EYES, JUST HEAR . . 76 THE GENERATIONS OF MEN 98
    THE VOICES GIVE YOU WHAT YOU WISH TO HEAR." . . . 78 THE GENERATIONS OF MEN 137
    WHAT DO YOU THINK YOU'RE LIKE TO HEAR TODAY?" . . . 78 THE GENERATIONS OF MEN 141
    BUT WHY TAKE TIME FOR WHAT I'M LIKE TO HEAR? . . . 78 THE GENERATIONS OF MEN 143
    OR I CAN'T GIVE MYSELF TO HEAR THE VOICES." . . . . 78 THE GENERATIONS OF MEN 147
    COME OUT HERE IF YOU WANT TO HEAR ME TALK.-- . . . 88 THE HOUSEKEEPER . . . 208
    "WHO WANTS TO HEAR YOUR NEWS, YOU--DREADFUL FOOL?" . . 89 THE HOUSEKEEPER . . . 214
    LISTEN! HE KICKED A STONE. HEAR THAT, HEAR THAT! . . 90 THE FEAR 38
    HARK!--I DON'T HEAR HIM NOW. BUT PLEASE GO IN." . . 90 THE FEAR 40
    YOU CAN HEAR THE SMALL BUZZ SAWS WHINE, THE BIG SAW . . 94 THE SELF-SEEKER . . 41
    WELL, YES." / "HEAR ANYTHING THAT MIGHT PROVE USEFUL?" . 96 THE SELF-SEEKER . . 102
    "WHAT DID YOU HEAR, FOR INSTANCE?" WILLIS SAID. . . . 100 THE SELF-SEEKER . . 206
    I SHOULD HAVE THOUGHT, THOUGH, YOU COULD MAKE HIM HEAR YOU." 145 SNOW 67
    AND FEEL IT LESS. HEAR THE SOFT BOMBS OF DUST . . . 150 SNOW 206
    "WHAT DO YOU HEAR?" / "I HEAR AN EMPTY ROOM-- . . . 153 SNOW 299
    YOU KNOW--IT SOUNDS THAT WAY, AND YES, I HEAR-- . . . 153 SNOW 300
    I THINK I HEAR A CLOCK--AND WINDOWS RATTLING. . . . 153 SNOW 301
    "SHOUT, SHE MAY HEAR YOU." / "SHOUTING IS NO GOOD." . . 154 SNOW 303
    YOU CAN'T HEAR WHETHER SHE HAS LEFT THE DOOR . . . 154 SNOW 308
    "FRED, SEE IF YOU CAN HEAR WHAT I HEAR. COME." . . . 154 SNOW 315
    "A CLOCK MAYBE." / "DON'T YOU HEAR SOMETHING ELSE?" . . 154 SNOW 316
    "NOT TALKING." / "NO." / "WHY, YES, I HEAR--WHAT IS IT?" . 154 SNOW 317
    THIS, THEN, IS THE NEW FREEDOM WE HEAR TELL OF; . . . 168 NEW HAMPSHIRE . . . 283
    "YOU HEAR THOSE HOUND DOGS SING ON MOOSILAUKE? . . . 168 NEW HAMPSHIRE . . . 293
    I HEARD THEM. TOFFILE DIDN'T SEEM TO HEAR THEM. . . . 206 THE WITCH OF COOS . . 117
    THAT THEY COULD HEAR TELL OF WAS SCARIFIED. . . . 209 PAUPER WITCH OF GRAFTON 57
    (TO HEAR US TALK) . . . . 238 ON A TREE FALLEN ACROSS 5
    TO LEAN AGAINST AND HEAR IN THE DARK. . . . . . 297 LEAVES COMPARED WITH . 18
    TO HEAR IT WRECK IN A THUNDERCLAP. . . . . . 306 A TRIAL RUN 7
    YOU LIKE TO HEAR ABOUT GOLD. . . . . . . 310 THE VINDICTIVES . . . 1
    TO SEE IF HE COULD HEAR . . . . . . 340 THE SUBVERTED FLOWER . 38
    WERE REALLY AS DARK AS I HEAR SAGES TELL, ... 350 THE LESSON FOR TODAY . 2
    I CAN JUST HEAR THE WAY YOU MAKE IT GO: . . . . . 352 THE LESSON FOR TODAY . 54
    I CAN JUST HEAR YOU CALL YOUR PALACE CLASS: . . . . 353 THE LESSON FOR TODAY . 84
    BUT STAY AND HEAR ME OUT. I SURELY THINK . . . . 356 A MOTH SEEN IN WINTER . 10
    YOU'LL HEAR ALL SORTS OF THINGS. YOU'LL MEET WITH THEM . 369 THE LITERATE FARMER AND 33
    I HEAR THE WORLD RECITING . . . . . . 387 THE COURAGE TO BE NEW . 1
    YOUR MOTHER'S FOLKS----" / HE STAYED TO HEAR NO MORE, . 457 HOW HARD TO KEEP FROM 111
    HEAR MY RIGMAROLE. . . . . 468 A REFLEX 1
    YOU'RE NOT ASLEEP? / NO, I CAN HEAR YOU. WHY? . . . 473 A MASQUE OF REASON . . 4
    YOU HEAR HIM, THYATIRA: WE'RE A SAINT. . . . . 476 A MASQUE OF REASON . . 80
    HAVEN'T YOU NOTICED ANYTHING (HEAR THAT!) . . . . 495 A MASQUE OF MERCY . . 42
    SINCE I CAME IN? / HEAR WHAT? THAT ARMY TRUCK? . . . 495 A MASQUE OF MERCY . . 43
    JONAH, I'M GLAD, NOT SAD, TO HEAR YOU SAY . . . . 501 A MASQUE OF MERCY . . 213
    DON'T ANY OF YOU HEAR A SOUND? / THE STORM! . . . . 504 A MASQUE OF MERCY . . 279
    LET ME REPEAT: I'M GLAD TO HEAR YOU SAY . . . . 507 A MASQUE OF MERCY . . 360
    WHAT DID HE SAY? I CAN'T HEAR WHAT HE SAYS. . . . 518 A MASQUE OF MERCY . . 661
    ALL PAUL MEANS, AND I WISH THE DEAD COULD HEAR ME-- . 519 A MASQUE OF MERCY . . 674
HEARD
    THAT SUDDENLY ABOVE THE BEES IS HEARD, ... 12 A PRAYER IN SPRING . . 10
    WE HEARD, WE KNEW WE HEARD THE BROOK. . . . . . 18 GOING FOR WATER . . . 20
    HAVING FIRST HEARD THE LIFE READ OUT . . . . . 20 THE TRIAL BY EXISTENCE 34
    THAT I SUDDENLY HEARD--ALL I NEEDED TO HEAR: . . . . 24 THE DEMIURGE'S LAUGH . 5
    NO ONE HAS SEEN THEM MADE OR HEARD THEM MADE: . . . 33 MENDING WALL 10
    WAITING FOR WARREN. WHEN SHE HEARD HIS STEP, . . . 34 DEATH OF THE HIRED MAN 2
    THAT SOUNDS LIKE SOMETHING YOU HAVE HEARD BEFORE? . . 36 DEATH OF THE HIRED MAN 53
    WARREN, I WISH YOU COULD HAVE HEARD THE WAY . . . 36 DEATH OF THE HIRED MAN 54
    THAT STARTS UP ON IT SOMEWHERE--I'VE HEARD SAY . . . 42 THE MOUNTAIN 46

- 242 -

HEARD (CONTINUED)
THEN YOU CAME IN. I HEARD YOUR RUMBLING VOICE . . . . . . 53 HOME BURIAL 81
IT MAY NOT BE. I HEARD A FELLOW SAY SO. . . . . 57 THE BLACK COTTAGE . . 67
AND SAW NOTHING MORE OF EACH OTHER, OR HEARD, ... 62 BLUEBERRIES 87
I EXPECT, THOUGH, EVERYONE'S HEARD OF IT. . . . . 63 A SERVANT TO SERVANTS . 34
I'VE HEARD TOO MUCH OF THE OLD-FASHIONED WAY. . . . . . 65 A SERVANT TO SERVANTS . 103
THE ONLY FUN HE HAD. I'VE HEARD THEM SAY, THOUGH, . . . 66 A SERVANT TO SERVANTS . 138
I'VE HEARD HIM POUNDING IN THE BARN ALL NIGHT. . . . . . 71 THE CODE 42
THAT WAS THE LAST I SAW OR HEARD OF HIM. . . . . 72 THE CODE 79
THEY HAVE BEST RIGHT TO BE HEARD IN THIS PLACE." . . . . 79 THE GENERATIONS OF MEN 176
IT'S GONE SO FAR. YOU'VE HEARD? ESTELLE'S RUN OFF." . . . 82 THE HOUSEKEEPER . . . 20
MY, BUT HE LOOKS AS IF HE MUST HAVE HEARD!" . . . . . . 88 THE HOUSEKEEPER . . . 204
"I THINK--I THINK--FROM WHAT I HEARD TODAY-- . . . . . . 100 THE SELF-SEEKER . . . 204
MUST GET SOMEWHERE. I'VE HEARD YOU SAY AS MUCH. . . . . 117 IN THE HOME STRETCH . 185
I HEARD YOU TALK. . . . . 118 THE TELEPHONE . . . 6
DON'T SAY I DIDN'T, FOR I HEARD YOU SAY-- . . . . 118 THE TELEPHONE . . . 7
"FIRST TELL ME WHAT IT WAS YOU THOUGHT YOU HEARD." . . . 118 THE TELEPHONE . . . 10
SOMEONE SAID 'COME'--I HEARD IT AS I BOWED." . . . . . 118 THE TELEPHONE . . . 17
THERE IS A SINGER EVERYONE HAS HEARD, ... 119 THE OVEN BIRD . . . 1
THE MINUTE THEY HEARD MY STEP WENT STILL . . . . 123 PEA BRUSH 11
SHE STRAYED SO FAR SHE SCARCELY HEARD . . . . 129 THE IMPULSE 15
SO YOUR MISTAKE WAS OURS. HAVEN'T YOU HEARD, THOUGH, . . 132 THE BONFIRE 103
HAVEN'T YOU HEARD WHAT WE HAVE LIVED TO LEARN? . . . . 133 THE BONFIRE 109
FROM ONE WHO HAD NO RIGHT TO BE HEARD FROM. . . . . . 142 THE VANISHING RED . . 18
THAT'S ALL YOU EVER HEARD HIM CALLED ROUND HERE. . . . . 144 SNOW 46
ALL'S EVER I HEARD OF IT, WHICH ISN'T MUCH. . . . . . . 144 SNOW 54
YOU MAY HAVE HEARD OF IT. I HAD A FARM . . . . 162 NEW HAMPSHIRE . . . 109
IN LITERATURE TO DATE IS HEARD TO COME. . . . . 167 NEW HAMPSHIRE . . . 271
WE'VE HEARD AGAINST THE MID-VICTORIANS . . . . 168 NEW HAMPSHIRE . . . 295
WERE DOUBTLESS AS THE WORDS WE HEARD HIM SAY . . . . . 170 NEW HAMPSHIRE . . . 352
HE HAD BEEN HEARD TO SAY BY SEVERAL: . . . . 177 THE STAR-SPLITTER . . 32
"NO DOUBT YOU'VE HEARD THE OFFICE CALL ME MABEL. . . . . 182 MAPLE 90
BEFORE THEY HEARD OF HIM IN SOME NEW CAMP, ... 192 PAUL'S WIFE 29
HEARD HOW HE THRASHED THE HORSES ON A LOAD . . . . . . 192 PAUL'S WIFE 43
WHEN I HEARD TOFFILE UPSTAIRS IN THE BEDROOM . . . . . 203 THE WITCH OF COOS . . 46
AND THOUGHT I HEARD HIM DOWNSTAIRS IN THE CELLAR. . . . 203 THE WITCH OF COOS . . 47
I HEARD THEM. TOFFILE DIDN'T SEEM TO HEAR THEM. . . . . 206 THE WITCH OF COOS . . 117
YOU MUST HAVE HEARD OF CLARA ROBINSON, ... 215 A FOUNTAIN, A BOTTLE . 77
WE HEARD THE MINIATURE THUNDER WHERE HE FLED, ... 223 THE RUNAWAY 6
BUT I NEVER HEARD OF A HOUSE THAT THROVE . . . . 232 THE KITCHEN CHIMNEY . 10
NO VOICE IN NATURE IS HEARD TO CRY ALOUD . . . . 249 ACCEPTANCE 3
WHERE HAD I HEARD THIS WIND BEFORE . . . . 251 BEREFT 1
IT SEEMS AS IF YOU MUST HAVE HEARD. . . . . 280 BLUE RIBBON AT AMESBURY 9
ALL SUMMER LONG I THOUGHT I HEARD THEM THREATENING UNDER
   THEIR BREATH. . . . . 297 A LEAF-TREADER . . . 7
FROM HAVING HEARD THE DAYLONG VOICE OF EVE . . . . . . 338 NEVER WOULD BIRDS' SONG 3
SO SHE THOUGHT SHE HEARD HIM SAY; . . . . 340 THE SUBVERTED FLOWER . 25
SHE HEARD HIM STUMBLE FIRST . . . . 341 THE SUBVERTED FLOWER . 62
SHE HEARD HIM BARK OUTRIGHT. . . . . 341 THE SUBVERTED FLOWER . 64
I HEARD HIM SHOUT 'WHAT A THING IT IS!' . . . . 346 DISCOVERY OF MADEIRAS . 93
BUT NO ONE EVER HEARD YOU MAKE THE CLAIM. . . . . . . 351 THE LESSON FOR TODAY . 28
WE HEARD "'TIS OVER" ROARING. . . . . 359 NOVEMBER 7
I HEARD A FELLOW IN A PUBLIC LECTURE . . . . 369 THE LITERATE FARMER AND 53
THAT I HAVE HEARD OF SHONE AT NIGHT. . . . . 390 TWO LEADING LIGHTS . . 6
"SO I HAVE HEARD AND DO IN PART BELIEVE IT," . . . . . 408 FROM PLANE TO PLANE . 147
THAT WAS HEARD AS FAR AWAY AS NEW YORK . . . . 463 LINES IN DEJECTION . . 23
NEITHER WOULD FAIRNESS. YOU HAVE HEARD THE DOCTRINE. . . 485 A MASQUE OF REASON . 356
I'VE HEARD WHAT YOU WERE SAYING--EVERY WORD. . . . . . 487 A MASQUE OF REASON . 396
NO, GOD. / I NEVER HEARD OF SUCH A THING. . . . . . . 493 A MASQUE OF MERCY . . 20
HAVEN'T YOU HEARD OF THOMPSON'S "HOUND OF HEAVEN"? . . . 494 A MASQUE OF MERCY . . 21
YOU HEARD FROM GOD--I MEAN HAD ORDERS FROM HIM? . . . . 504 A MASQUE OF MERCY . . 277
HAVEN'T YOU HEARD THE NEWS? WE ALREADY HAVE ONE, . . . 515 A MASQUE OF MERCY . . 577
I HEARD A DEEP GROAN--MAYBE OUT OF HIM. . . . . 516 A MASQUE OF MERCY . . 611
BUT JONAH GIVES NO SIGN OF HAVING HEARD.) . . . . . . 518 A MASQUE OF MERCY . . 668
HEARING
SHE HAD SOME ART OF HEARING AND YET NOT . . . . 57 THE BLACK COTTAGE . . 73
FEARING THE LATTER WISDOM OF THE WORLD. . . . . 57 THE BLACK COTTAGE . . 74
AND I KEEP HEARING FROM THE CELLAR BIN . . . . 69 AFTER APPLE-PICKING . 24
FROM HOPE OF HEARING GOOD OF WHAT WAS MINE, ... 106 CHRISTMAS TREES . . . 28
AND WORDS TO WONDER IN HER HEARING HOW SHE CAME THERE, . 257 THE LOVELY BE CHOOSERS 48
TILL THEY WERE OUT OF HEARING . . . . 335 CARPE DIEM 7
NOW WE ARE HEARING FROM THE EXEGETE. . . . . 498 A MASQUE OF MERCY . . 126
I'M HEARING FROM HIM NOW, DID YOU BUT NOTICE, ... 504 A MASQUE OF MERCY . . 278
HEARS
IT'S HARMLESS. MOTHER HEARS IT IN THE NIGHT, ... 203 THE WITCH OF COOS . . 23
TO LET US KNOW IT HEARS ME." / "WHY, MY DEAR, ... 258 WEST-RUNNING BROOK . . 17
HEART
I DWELL WITH A STRANGELY ACHING HEART . . . . 6 GHOST HOUSE 11
AND WISHED HER HEART IN A CASE OF GOLD . . . . 8 LOVE AND A QUESTION . 23
AND MY HEART OWNS A DOUBT . . . . 10 STORM FEAR 16
BUT OH, THE AGITATED HEART . . . . 19 REVELATION 3
AND THE MIND WHIRLS AND THE HEART SINGS, ... 21 THE TRIAL BY EXISTENCE 47
"AS ALL MUST BE," I SAID WITHIN MY HEART, ... 22 THE TUFT OF FLOWERS . 9
"MEN WORK TOGETHER," I TOLD HIM FROM THE HEART, ... 23 THE TUFT OF FLOWERS . 39
HIS HEART KNEW PEACE, FOR NONE CAME HERE . . . . . . 24 PAN WITH US 11
THE HEART IS STILL ACHING TO SEEK, ... 30 RELUCTANCE 17
AH, WHEN TO THE HEART OF MAN . . . . 30 RELUCTANCE 19
"NO, BUT HE HURT MY HEART THE WAY HE LAY . . . . . . 39 DEATH OF THE HIRED MAN 147
IF NOT AT HEART, AT LEAST ON PRINCIPLE. . . . . . . 44 A HUNDRED COLLARS . . 13
AS ONE WHO CLASPS HER HEART. THEY LAUGHED TOGETHER. . . 74 THE GENERATIONS OF MEN 44
YOU SEE ANNE HAS HER LESSON LEARNED BY HEART." . . . . 97 THE SELF-SEEKER . . . 122
THE FLOATING HEART, WITH SMALL LEAF LIKE A HEART, . . . 98 THE SELF-SEEKER . . . 154
DOING A MAN'S WORK, THOUGH A CHILD AT HEART-- . . . . 137 "OUT, OUT--" 24
NO ONE BELIEVED. THEY LISTENED AT HIS HEART. . . . . . 137 "OUT, OUT--" 31
BUT HIS HEART FAILING HIM, HE DROPPED THE AX . . . . . 170 NEW HAMPSHIRE . . . 369
ME ONLY AS I TOOK MY AX TO HEART. . . . . 186 THE AX-HELVE 20
AS STILL I HAVE NOT LEARNED TO WITH THE HEART, ... 199 WILD GRAPES 97
AND HAVE NO WISH TO WITH THE HEART--NOR NEED, ... 199 WILD GRAPES 98

HEART (CONTINUED)
   THAT I CAN SEE. THE MIND--IS NOT THE HEART. . . . . . . 199 WILD GRAPES 99
   THAT I NEED LEARN TO LET GO WITH THE HEART. . . . . . 199 WILD GRAPES . . . 103
   OR LIKE THE POETESS'S HEART OF LOVE, ... 216 A FOUNTAIN, A BOTTLE . 95
   AT HAVING EASED HER HEART OF ONE MORE COPY-- . . . . 217 A FOUNTAIN, A BOTTLE . 135
   HAS GIVEN MY HEART . . . . 221 DUST OF SNOW 5
   ITS HEART SINKS LOWER UNDER THE SOD. . . . . 228 GOOD-BY AND KEEP COLD . 28
   (AND THEY WERE NEVER REALLY STARS AT HEART), ... 246 FIREFLIES IN THE GARDEN 4
   THE HEART CAN THINK OF NO DEVOTION . . . . 247 DEVOTION 1
   AND HEART, IF NEED BE, I WILL DO MY BEST . . . . . . 267 THE ARMFUL 7
   (HE COULDN'T HOPE ITS HEART WOULD BREAK.) . . . . . 273 A LONE STRIKER . . . 16
   BUT MY HEART WAS BEGINNING TO CLOUD MY MIND. . . . . 291 ON HEART'S BEGINNING TO 13
   THEY SPOKE TO THE FUGITIVE IN MY HEART AS IF IT WERE LEAF
      TO LEAF. . . . . 298 A LEAF-TREADER . . . 9
   HER OWN TOO MEAGER HEART . . . . 340 THE SUBVERTED FLOWER . 55
   TILL HER HEART ALMOST CEASED TO BEAT. . . . . 346 DISCOVERY OF MADEIRAS . 102
   WHO ONLY HAS AT HEART YOUR GETTING LOST, ... 377 DIRECTIVE 9
   I STOPPED MY SONG AND ALMOST HEART, ... 385 A MOOD APART 6
   YET IN HIS HEART HE WAS UNSHAKEN SURE . . . . 400 THE BROKEN DROUGHT . . 9
   BY HEART AND WHEN ALONE REPEAT. . . . . 403 SOMETHING LIKE A STAR . 10
   SOME POOR FOOL HAS BEEN SAYING IN HIS HEART . . . . . 423 FOR JOHN F. KENNEDY . 49
   HAD MY HEART BEEN GREAT, ... 429 KITTY HAWK 24
   FROM THIS HEAD AND HEART, ... 440 KITTY HAWK 389
   FROM CHILDHOOD HAS MY HEART BEEN SET. . . . . 451 A-WISHING WELL . . . 22
   ONE DAY WHEN THE CHIEF COOK WAS SICK AT HEART. . . . 455 HOW HARD TO KEEP FROM . 56
   TILL ON A DAY THE KING, BEING SICK AT HEART . . . . . 456 HOW HARD TO KEEP FROM . 94
   HOW DID YOU KNOW THAT WAY TO BREAK MY HEART? . . . . 495 A MASQUE OF MERCY . . 59
   COURAGE IS OF THE HEART BY DERIVATION, ... 519 A MASQUE OF MERCY . . 693
   WE BOTH HAVE LACKED THE COURAGE IN THE HEART . . . . 521 A MASQUE OF MERCY . . 728
HEARTACHE
   AND FALLS ASLEEP WITH HEARTACHE--HOW SHOULD I FEEL? . . 58 THE BLACK COTTAGE . . 103
HEARTBROKEN
   HEARTBROKEN AND DISABLED . . . . 387 THE COURAGE TO BE NEW . 5
HEARTFELT
   A HEARTFELT PRAYER FOR THE POOR OF GOD, ... 8 LOVE AND A QUESTION . 27
HEARTHSTONE
   THE APPLE TREES BE SENT TO HEARTHSTONE FLAME. . . . . 231 A BROOK IN THE CITY . 11
HEARTLESS
   THE HEARTLESS AND ENORMOUS OUTER BLACK . . . . . . 361 A LOOSE MOUNTAIN . . 17
   WHEN IN HEARTLESS CHORUS . . . . 429 KITTY HAWK 36
HEARTS
   HEARTS NOT AVERSE TO BEING BEGUILED, ... 27 OCTOBER 10
   IT CAN BLAME THIS LIMITLESS TRAIT IN THE HEARTS OF MEN. . 305 THERE ARE ROUGHLY ZONES 21
HEART'S
   AND THE THOUGHT OF THE HEART'S DESIRE. . . . . 8 LOVE AND A QUESTION . 20
   THE HEART'S GONE OUT OF IT: WHY KEEP IT UP? . . . . . 54 HOME BURIAL 110
   AS IF TO SAY, 'YOU! YOU'RE THE HEART'S DESIRE.' . . . . 98 THE SELF-SEEKER . . . 158
   BE HER LAST JOY HER HEART'S GOING CUT TO THIS ONE . . . 257 THE LOVELY BE CHOOSERS 50
   ON THE HEART'S BEGINNING TO CLOUD THE MIND . . . . . 290 ON HEART'S BEGINNING TO T
HEAT
   A TEMPLE OF THE HEAT. . . . . 13 ROSE POGONIAS . . . 8
   PERHAPS IT WAS SOMETHING ABOUT THE HEAT OF THE SUN, . . 17 MOWING 4
   THE SMELL OF THE WET FEATHERS IN THE HEAT! . . . . . 85 THE HOUSEKEEPER . . . 122
   AND LEFT DEFENSELESS TO THE HEAT AND LIGHT. . . . . . 109 THE EXPOSED NEST . . 16
   OF DEAD LEAVES STUCK TOGETHER BY THE HEAT-- . . . . . 119 HYLA BROOK 11
   WHEN THE HEAT SLOWLY HAZES AND THE SUN . . . . . . 125 AN ENCOUNTER . . . 2
   AND HEAT SO CLOSE IN; BUT THE THOUGHT OF ALL . . . . . 131 THE BONFIRE 71
   I DON'T WANT IT STIRRED BY THE HEAT OF THE SUN. . . . . 228 GOOD-BY AND KEEP COLD . 12
   WHATEVER ITS SECRET WAS OF GREATER HEAT . . . . . . 239 OUR SINGING STRENGTH . 17
   AND SMOOTH AND MOIST IN VERNAL HEAT. . . . . 276 TWO TRAMPS IN MUD TIME 48
   FLOWERS IN THE DESERT HEAT . . . . 337 THE WIND AND THE RAIN . 21
   KEPT SOME DEW OUT AND SOME HEAT IN, ... 380 AN UNSTAMPED LETTER IN 15
   LEST HAVING WASTED PRECIOUS HEAT . . . . 381 AN UNSTAMPED LETTER IN 23
   BUT SAY WITH WHAT DEGREE OF HEAT. . . . . 403 SOMETHING LIKE A STAR . 12
HEATHEN
   SAYING THEM LIKE THE HEATHEN? WE CCULD DROP THEM. . . . 58 THE BLACK COTTAGE . . 98
HEATING
   HE HAD THE OAKS FOR HEATING AND FOR LIGHT. . . . . . 292 FIGURE IN THE DOORWAY . 15
HEAVE
   TO HEAVE THEM HIGHER TO THE MORNING STAR? . . . . . 169 NEW HAMPSHIRE . . . 319
HEAVEN
   I DREAM UPON THE NIGHTHAWKS PEOPLING HEAVEN, ... 14 WAITING 11
   THE LIGHT OF HEAVEN FALLS WHOLE AND WHITE . . . . . 19 THE TRIAL BY EXISTENCE 9
   TOWARD HEAVEN STILL, ... 68 AFTER APPLE-PICKING . 2
   HIS GAINS IN HEAVEN ARE WHAT THEY ARE. . . . . 120 BOND AND FREE . . . 16
   YOU'D THINK THE INNER DOME OF HEAVEN HAD FALLEN. . . . 121 BIRCHES 13
   TOWARD HEAVEN, TILL THE TREE COULD BEAR NO MORE, . . . 122 BIRCHES 56
   LOOKED UP TOWARD HEAVEN, AND THERE AGAINST THE BLUE, . . 125 AN ENCOUNTER . . . 11
   AND MY FLAME MADE A PINNACLE TO HEAVEN . . . . . . 130 THE BONFIRE 38
   THAT SLIP FROM HEAVEN AT NIGHT AND SOFTLY FALL . . . . 172 A STAR IN A STONEBOAT . 2
   THE POETESS HAD SIGHED, I KNEW, IN HEAVEN . . . . . . 217 A FOUNTAIN, A BOTTLE . 134
   WHEN HEAVEN PRESENTS IN SHEETS THE SOLID HUE? . . . . 220 FRAGMENTARY BLUE . . 4
   SINCE EARTH IS EARTH, PERHAPS, NOT HEAVEN (AS YET)-- . . 220 FRAGMENTARY BLUE . . 5
   ME MYSELF IN THE SUMMER HEAVEN, GODLIKE, ... 225 FOR ONCE SOMETHING . . 5
   HEAVEN GIVES ITS GLIMPSES ONLY TO THOSE . . . . . . 248 A PASSING GLIMPSE . . 11
   IF HEAVEN WERE TO DO AGAIN, ... 252 THE PEACEFUL SHEPHERD . 1
   ONE LEVEL NEARER HEAVEN OVERHEAD, ... 254 A WINTER EDEN . . . 7
   WERE MADE IN HEAVEN. IT WASN'T WAVED TO US." . . . . 258 WEST-RUNNING BROOK . . 29
   TO HAPPEN IN HEAVEN BEYOND THE FLOATS OF CLOUD . . . . 268 ON LOCKING UP BY CHANCE 2
   IN HOPES OF SEEING THE CALM OF HEAVEN BREAK . . . . . 268 ON LOOKING UP BY CHANCE 14
   FOR HEAVEN AND THE FUTURE'S SAKES. . . . . 277 TWO TRAMPS IN MUD TIME 72
   LOST IN HEAVEN . . . . 295 LOST IN HEAVEN . . . T
   "WHERE, WHERE IN HEAVEN AM I? BUT DON'T TELL ME! . . . 295 LOST IN HEAVEN . . . 10
   FOR IT WAS WRIT IN HEAVEN DOUBLY WRIGHT. . . . . . . 308 THE WRIGHTS' BIPLANE . 4
   AND LOST THE STARS OF HEAVEN, MAY, OH, MAY . . . . . 350 TO A YOUNG WRETCH . . 22
   ITS SEPARATENESS FROM HEAVEN COULD BE WAIVED; . . . . 353 THE LESSON FOR TODAY . 101
   BUT RIGHT IN HEAVEN WAS SLOWLY BEING SHRUNK . . . . . 368 THE LITERATE FARMER . 14
   THE SAME SIGN HEAVEN SHOWED YOUR GUEST. . . . . . . 381 AN UNSTAMPED LETTER IN 42

HEAVEN (CONTINUED)
   MY LOVE FOR EVERY HEAVEN . . . . 389 ASTROMETAPHYSICAL . . 9
   THE SUN THEN HAD HIS LONGEST DAY IN HEAVEN, ... 407 FROM PLANE TO PLANE . 90
   FROM NO HIGHER HEAVEN . . . . 441 KITTY HAWK 408
   OF PELTING HEAVEN WITH CHUNKS . . . . 464 MILKY WAY IS A COWPATH 11
   IF THAT IS ALL THERE IS TO BE OF HEAVEN, ... 475 A MASQUE OF REASON . . 42
   LIKE A BIG EGG AND HATCH A HEAVEN OUT . . . . . 484 A MASQUE OF REASON . 306
   BE HEAVEN AT ONCE AND HAVE IT OVER WITH. . . . . . 484 A MASQUE OF REASON . 322
   HAVEN'T YOU HEARD OF THOMPSON'S "HOUND OF HEAVEN"? . . 494 A MASQUE OF MERCY . 21
HEAVENLY
   OF HEAVENLY STARS WITH HUGGER-MUGGER FARMING. . . . . 176 THE STAR-SPLITTER . 14
   THAT HEAVENLY BEAST . . . . 261 CANIS MAJOR . . . 2
   LET'S LET MY HEAVENLY LOSTNESS OVERWHELM ME." . . . . 296 LOST IN HEAVEN . . 12
   NOT A HEAVENLY DOG MADE MANIFEST, ... 419 ONE MORE BREVITY . 10
   THE LETUP'S HEAVENLY. YOU PERHAPS WILL TELL US . . . . 474 A MASQUE OF REASON . 41
HEAVENS
   SHE SWEPT THE HEAVENS, TURNING ON HER HEEL. . . . . 74 THE GENERATIONS OF MEN 36
HEAVEN'S
   IN HEAVEN'S FIRM-SET FIRMAMENT, ... 381 AN UNSTAMPED LETTER IN 30
   THE STAR ITSELF--HEAVEN'S GREATEST STAR, ... 421 ONE MORE BREVITY . 60
   BE FOUND ACCEPTABLE IN HEAVEN'S SIGHT. . . . . . 520 A MASQUE OF MERCY . 722
   BE FOUND ACCEPTABLE IN HEAVEN'S SIGHT. . . . . . 520 A MASQUE OF MERCY . 725
HEAVENWARD
   THAT IS ITS PINNACLE TO HEAVENWARD . . . . 332 THE SILKEN TENT . . . 6
HEAVES
   AND EVERY GUST THAT GATHERS STRENGTH AND HEAVES . . . 305 THERE ARE ROUGHLY ZONES 2
HEAVINESS
   TOP-HEAVY WITH A HEAVINESS HIS SHORT, ... 188 THE AX-HELVE 98
HEAVING
   AND HEAVING HIM HIGH IN AIR, ... 289 DEPARTMENTAL . . . 38
HEAVY (SEE TOP-HEAVY)
   THE FADED EARTH, THE HEAVY SKY, ... 7 MY NOVEMBER GUEST . 12
   SMOOTH-LAID LIKE THATCH WITH THE HEAVY DEW, ... 8 A LATE WALK 3
   BEFORE THE LAST WENT, HEAVY WITH DEW, ... 15 IN A VALE 16
   WITH WHITE-FACED OXEN, IN A HEAVY CART, ... 41 THE MOUNTAIN . . . 17
   REAL SKY-BLUE, AND HEAVY, AND READY TO DRUM . . . 59 BLUEBERRIES 4
   OF HEAVY FOOTSTEPS IN THE OLD FRAME HOUSE, . . . 96 THE SELF-SEEKER . . 93
   AND EASED HIS HEAVY BREATHING, BUT STILL SLEPT. . . 108 OLD MAN'S WINTER NIGHT 25
   I WALKED SO LIGHT ON AIR IN HEAVY SHOES . . . . 132 THE BONFIRE . . . 92
   HER WET HAIR HEAVY ON HER LIKE A HELMET, ... 194 PAUL'S WIFE . . . 109
   AND HEAVY ON HER HEAVY HAIR BEHIND, ... 196 WILD GRAPES . . . 22
   AND SETTING OFF THEIR HEAVY POWDER LOAD. . . . . 239 OUR SINGING STRENGTH 29
   BUT GIVE ME WATER HEAVY ON THE HEAD . . . . . . 337 THE WIND AND THE RAIN 38
   BEHIND TOO HEAVY A HORSE . . . . 443 THE DRAFT HORSE . . 3
HECLA
   WE ALL KNOW HIS ADDRESS, MOUNT HECLA, ICELAND. . . . 408 FROM PLANE TO PLANE . 143
HE'D---NOT INDEXED
HEDGES
   THE LAST WET FIELDS AND DRIPPING HEDGES HOME. . . . 315 IRIS BY NIGHT . . . 3
HEED
   MESERVE SEEMED TO HEED NOTHING BUT THE LAMP . . . 147 SNOW 111
   PAID HEED TO WOMEN, YOU'D TAKE MY ADVICE . . . . 150 SNOW 216
   AND HIS MANDATES WERE GIVEN HEED TO . . . . . 314 BEARER OF EVIL TIDINGS 31
   BUT IF IT HAD NO THOUGHT OF PAYING HEED . . . . 447 DOES NO ONE AT ALL EVER 32
HEEL
   SHE SWEPT THE HEAVENS, TURNING ON HER HEEL. . . . . 74 THE GENERATIONS OF MEN 36
   A HOLE IN SOMEWHERE WITH HIS HEEL . . . . . . 138 BROWN'S DESCENT . . 15
   PERMIT ME." AND HE CRUSHED IT UNDER HIS HEEL . . . 456 HOW HARD TO KEEP FROM 84
HEELS
   KEEP AT THEIR HEELS AND THREATEN TO MOW THEIR LEGS OFF. . 71 THE CODE 46
   HE ROLLED ME OFF THE FIELD HEAD OVER HEELS . . . . 278 THE WHITE-TAILED HORNET 20
   (STILL ON HIS KNEES, HE SITS BACK ON HIS HEELS.) . . 519 A MASQUE OF MERCY . 671
HEFT
   THE LAST STEP TAKEN FOUND YOUR HEFT . . . . . 325 TO A THINKER . . . 1
HEIGHT
   ON A HEIGHT OF NAKED PASTURE LAND; . . . . . 23 PAN WITH US . . . 7
   THEY KNEW. AND JUST WHEN HE WAS AT THE HEIGHT, . . 66 A SERVANT TO SERVANTS . 125
   A HEIGHT FROM WHICH TO LOOK DOWN CRITICAL . . . 169 NEW HAMPSHIRE . 314
   TO SAY WHAT HEIGHT BECOMES NEW HAMPSHIRE MOUNTAINS, . 169 NEW HAMPSHIRE . 316
   OF EARLY TIMES AS TWICE THE HEIGHT THEY ARE— . . 169 NEW HAMPSHIRE . 331
   AND FURTHER STILL AT AN UNEARTHLY HEIGHT . . . 255 ACQUAINTED WITH NIGHT . 11
   YET ONCE SHE RISES TO THE HEIGHT, ... 281 BLUE RIBBON AT AMESBURY 46
   WHAT BROUGHT THE KINDRED SPIDER TO THAT HEIGHT, . . 302 DESIGN . . . 11
   AND THAT FROM NO ESPECIAL BUSH'S HEIGHT, . . . 302 A BIRD SINGING IN SLEEP 4
   THAT THE NORTHWEST WIND SHOULD RISE TO SUCH A HEIGHT . . 305 THERE ARE ROUGHLY ZONES 16
   HAPPINESS MAKES UP IN HEIGHT FOR WHAT IT LACKS IN LENGTH 333 HAPPINESS MAKES UP . T
   THE HEIGHT OF THE ADVENTURE IS THE HEIGHT . . . 378 DIRECTIVE . . . 33
   THE CITY SEEMS IN-TOPPLING FROM A HEIGHT, . . . 386 THE FEAR OF MAN . . 5
   IT ASKS OF US A CERTAIN HEIGHT, ... 403 SOMETHING LIKE A STAR . 21
   FOR GOD HIMSELF THE HEIGHT OF FEELING FREE . . . 461 HOW HARD TO KEEP FROM 251
   THE THOUGHT THAT ADDED CUBITS TO YOUR HEIGHT . . . 506 A MASQUE OF MERCY . 339
HEIGHTS
   WERE SEEN OF OLD AT MEMPHIS ON THE HEIGHTS . . . . 315 IRIS BY NIGHT . . . 6
   WHAT HEIGHTS OF ALTRUR- . . . . 449 THE BAD ISLAND--EASTER 57
HELD
   AND LONG TO KNOW IF STILL I HELD THEM DEAR. . . . . 5 INTO MY OWN . . . 12
   AND DREAMING, AS IT WERE, HELD BROTHERLY SPEECH . . 23 THE TUFT OF FLOWERS . 37
   THE MOUNTAIN HELD THE TOWN AS IN A SHADOW. . . . . 40 THE MOUNTAIN . . . 1
   SAND DUNES HELD LOOSELY IN TAMARISK . . . . . 58 THE BLACK COTTAGE . 120
   AND HELD AGAINST THE WORLD OF HOARY GRASS. . . . 68 AFTER APPLE-PICKING . 12
   THE YOUNG FOLK HELD SOME HOPE OUT TO EACH OTHER . . 74 THE GENERATIONS OF MEN 21
   "I MEAN ESTELLE HAS ALWAYS HELD THE PURSE." . . . 84 THE HOUSEKEEPER . . 98
   WITH BOTH HANDS HELD BEHIND HER. "GUESS," SHE SAID. . 96 THE SELF-SEEKER . 106
   THE HARD SNOW HELD ME, SAVE WHERE NOW AND THEN . . 101 THE WOOD-PILE . . 4
   WHAT HELD IT, THOUGH, ON ONE SIDE WAS A TREE . . 102 THE WOOD-PILE . . 32
   HE DOFFED HIS CAP AND HELD IT WITH BOTH HANDS . . 114 IN THE HOME STRETCH . 106
   AND THRUST HANDS IN AND HELD MY FACE AWAY. . . . 131 THE BONFIRE . . . 66
   THE TOWN TURNED OUT TO FIGHT FOR ME—THAT HELD ME. . . 131 THE BONFIRE . . . 73

PAGE TITLE   LINE

HELD (CONTINUED)

THE DOOR WAS STILL BECAUSE I HELD IT SHUT . . . . . 175 THE CENSUS-TAKER . . . 47
HELD IT A MOMENT WHERE IT WAS, TO CALM ME, ... 185 THE AX-HELVE . . . 12
UPON THE EDUCATION OF THOSE WHO HELD THEM? . . . . . 188 THE AX-HELVE . . . 93
THE ONE WHO HELD THE WHEEL BACK OR THE ONE . . . . . 190 THE GRINDSTONE . . . 46
I HELD ON UNCOMPLAININGLY FOR LIFE. . . . . 197 WILD GRAPES . . . 54
"QUICK!" I SLAMMED TO THE DOOR AND HELD THE KNOB. . . 206 THE WITCH OF COOS . . 118
"THE OUTSIDE DOORS AS YET HAVE HELD AGAINST US. . . . 215 A FOUNTAIN, A BOTTLE . 74
AND HELD IT LONG ENOUGH FOR NORTH . . . . 224 THE AIM WAS SONG . . . 10
THAT HELD THE HOUSE AS IN AN ELBOW-CROOK? . . . . . 231 A BROOK IN THE CITY . . 4
IT WAS THE MOON'S: SHE HELD THEM UNTIL DAY, ... 238 A HILLSIDE THAW . . . 33
HELD HIGH AT SO UNNATURAL A LEVEL. . . . . 255 THE FLOOD . . . 8
YOU HAVE ME THERE, BUT LOOSELY, AS I WOULD BE HELD. . 306 NOT QUITE SOCIAL . . 10
BUT STRICTLY HELD BY NONE, IS LOOSELY BOUND . . . . 332 THE SILKEN TENT . . . 9
WHAT I MYSELF HAVE HELD. BUT WHY DECLARE . . . . . . 335 I COULD GIVE ALL . . 12
AS OF A BOOK HELD UP BEFORE HIS EYES . . . . 355 TIME OUT . . . 3
AND HELD THEM ABSOLUTELY PARALLEL . . . . 396 ANY SIZE WE PLEASE . . 6

HELEN

STICK TO HIM, HELEN. MAKE HIM ANSWER YOU. . . . . . 145 SNOW 63
ASK HELEN HOW FAR UP THE SASH IT'S CLIMBED . . . . 148 SNOW 158
"LET HIM TALK, HELEN, AND PERHAPS HE'LL STAY." . . . 149 SNOW 171

HELIUM

INNATE HELIUM . . . . 386 INNATE HELIUM . . . T
SOME GAS LIKE HELIUM MUST BE INNATE. . . . . 387 INNATE HELIUM . . . 6

HELL

ISN'T IT HELL?" HE SAID. "I WANT TO KNOW. . . . . . 88 THE HOUSEKEEPER . . . 207
"WHY, THIS IS HELL," HE SAID. "I'M OUT OF IT." . . . 166 NEW HAMPSHIRE . . . 243
TAKE IT TO HELL FOR ME," THE SAWYER SAID. . . . . . 193 PAUL'S WIFE . . . 77
IT'S HELL FOR KNEES UNLESS DONE HELL-FOR-LEATHER." . 215 A FOUNTAIN, A BOTTLE . 63
LIKE A MANHOLE OPENED TO HELL. . . . . 311 THE VINDICTIVES . . . 23
I SHOULD NOT CURSE MYSELF WITH IT TO HELL, ... 350 THE LESSON FOR TODAY . 4
IN INFINITE APPEAL. THEN SAYING "HELL," . . . . . . 396 ANY SIZE WE PLEASE . . 7
WAS OF THE DEVIL. HE INVENTED HELL, ... 480 A MASQUE OF REASON . . 203
WE SEND OUR WICKED ENEMIES TO HELL, ... 519 A MASQUE OF MERCY . . 688
I'M NO MORE GOVERNED BY THE FEAR OF HELL . . . . . . 520 A MASQUE OF MERCY . . 702

HE'LL---NOT INDEXED

HELL-FOR-LEATHER

IT'S HELL FOR KNEES UNLESS DONE HELL-FOR-LEATHER." . . 215 A FOUNTAIN, A BOTTLE . 63

HELLO

"TRY SPEAKING. SAY 'HELLO!'" / "HELLO. HELLO." . . . 153 SNOW 298
"KEEP SPEAKING, THEN." / "HELLO. HELLO. HELLO.-- . . 154 SNOW 304
"HELLO, MESERVE. YOU'RE THERE, THEN!--AND YOUR WIFE? . 155 SNOW 329

HELMET

HER WET HAIR HEAVY ON HER LIKE A HELMET, ... 194 PAUL'S WIFE . . . 109

HELP

HE COULD NOT HELP BUT MARK, ... 10 WIND AND WINDOW FLOWER 10
WHAT HELP HE IS THERE'S NO DEPENDING ON. . . . . . . 35 DEATH OF THE HIRED MAN 17
IN HAYING TIME, WHEN ANY HELP IS SCARCE. . . . . . . 35 DEATH OF THE HIRED MAN 29
"I THINK HIS BROTHER OUGHT TO HELP, OF COURSE. . . . 39 DEATH OF THE HIRED MAN 131
HE'S COME TO HELP YOU DITCH THE MEADOW. . . . . . . 40 DEATH OF THE HIRED MAN 157
FAIRBANKS, HE SAYS TO ME, 'HELP US THIS YEAR,' . . . 48 A HUNDRED COLLARS . . 112
SHE, IN HER PLACE, REFUSED HIM ANY HELP, ... 51 HOME BURIAL . . . 13
"YOU DON'T KNOW HOW TO ASK IT." / "HELP ME, THEN." . 52 HOME BURIAL . . . 43
A BRIDE, TO HELP TAKE CARE OF SUCH A CREATURE, . . . 66 A SERVANT TO SERVANTS . 127
AND LIVING BY A LAKE. I'M PAST SUCH HELP-- . . . . . 67 A SERVANT TO SERVANTS . 156
OUT OF HIS HIRED HELP. I'M NOT DENYING . . . . 70 THE CODE 38
MADE SHIFT TO SHELTER THEM WITHOUT THE HELP . . . . 73 THE GENERATIONS OF MEN 12
"I DON'T SEE VERY WELL HOW YOU CAN HELP IT. . . . . 79 THE GENERATIONS OF MEN 155
I HELP OUT WITH THIS BEADWORK WHAT I CAN." . . . . . 81 THE HOUSEKEEPER . . . 8
ONE THING YOU CAN'T HELP LIKING ABOUT JOHN, ... 85 THE HOUSEKEEPER . . . 115
TO TRY TO HELP ME DRIVE A BETTER BARGAIN." . . . . . 93 THE SELF-SEEKER . . . 9
BUT PUT OUR FLOWERS IN WATER FIRST.--WILL, HELP HER: . 99 THE SELF-SEEKER . . . 172
I CAN'T HELP WISHING I COULD SEND YOU ONE . . . . . 107 CHRISTMAS TREES . . . 59
AND, IF YOU ASKED ME, EVEN HELP PRETEND . . . . . . 109 THE EXPOSED NEST . . . 7
ASK THEM TO HELP YOU GET IT ON ITS FEET. . . . . . . 113 IN THE HOME STRETCH . . 76
TO HELP US, BUT HE'LL TAKE IT OUT IN PLANNING. . . . 115 IN THE HOME STRETCH . . 153
HOW CAN YOU HELP YOURSELF? / "I CALLED HIM BROTHER. . 144 SNOW 44
IT CAN'T TURN EITHER WAY. IT NEEDS THE WIND'S HELP. . 148 SNOW 135
WE CAN'T BE ANY HELP BY SITTING HERE . . . . 152 SNOW 268
I CAN'T HELP THINKING THOSE ARE TESTS TO GO BY. . . 162 NEW HAMPSHIRE . . . 99
PERHAPS THE WIND THE MORE WITHOUT THE HELP . . . . . 175 THE CENSUS-TAKER . . . 25
ABOUT YOUR MOTHER THAT PERHAPS MAY HELP. . . . . . . 180 MAPLE . . . 28
MY BROTHER TRIED TO MAKE ME LAUGH TO HELP ME. . . . 197 WILD GRAPES . . . 55
THE LEAST I COULD DO WAS HELP DIG THEIR GRAVE. . . . 206 THE WITCH OF COOS . . 141
I CAN'T SAY HE'S MUCH HELP; . . . . 211 AN EMPTY THREAT . . . 17
YET CAN'T HELP MARKING ALL THE TIME . . . . 221 IN A DISUSED GRAVEYARD 10
I SHOULD BE WILLING TO SAY AND HELP YOU SAY . . . . 236 VALLEY'S SINGING DAY . 19
HER THIRD JOY THAT THOUGH NOW THEY CANNOT HELP BUT KNOW, 256 THE LOVELY BE CHOOSERS 28
I CAN'T HELP OWNING THE GREAT RELIEF IT WOULD BE . . 287 A ROADSIDE STAND . . . 47
BUT WE CAN'T HELP FEELING MORE THAN A LITTLE BETRAYED 305 THERE ARE ROUGHLY ZONES 15
OF PLAGIARISM AND HELP OF CHEATING PARENTS. . . . . 325 BUILD SOIL . . . 275
SEEING NO HELP IN WINGS OR FEET . . . . 346 DISCOVERY OF MADEIRAS . 100
AND SEE IF IT WILL HELP HER CASE." . . . . 347 DISCOVERY OF MADEIRAS . 109
HELP ME ACCEPT ITS FATE WITH CHRISTMAS FEELING. . . 350 TO A YOUNG WRETCH . . 24
BUT GO. YOU ARE RIGHT. MY PITY CANNOT HELP. . . . . 356 A MOTH SEEN IN WINTER . 17
THE MOST EFFICIENT HELP YOU EVER HIRED . . . . 375 A YOUNG BIRCH . . . 17
AND YET FOR ALL THIS HELP OF HEAD AND BRAIN . . . . 425 ACCIDENTALLY ON PURPOSE 21
I CRY, "DO WORK FOR WOMEN--ALL THE HELP . . . . . . 447 DOES NO ONE AT ALL EVER 28
YOU'RE OFF TO XANADU TO HELP THE COOK. . . . . . . 455 HOW HARD TO KEEP FROM . 48
I NEED SOME HELP ABOUT THIS REASON PROBLEM . . . . . 479 A MASQUE OF REASON . . 165
TRUST ME TO HELP YOU FIND THE BOOK YOU WANT. . . . . 495 A MASQUE OF MERCY . . 50
I'M JONAS DOVE--IF THAT IS ANY HELP. . . . . 495 A MASQUE OF MERCY . . 55
WE TAKE IT YOU WERE SENT IN HERE FOR HELP. . . . . . 500 A MASQUE OF MERCY . . 177
AND HELP YOU'RE GOING TO GET. / I'LL BREAK YOUR DOOR DOWN. 500 A MASQUE OF MERCY . . 178
IT'S TOO BIG FOR HIM. HELP HIM HOLD IT UP. . . . . 506 A MASQUE OF MERCY . . 328
THAN FOUND IN CHURCH. / THAT DOESN'T HELP ME MUCH. . 513 A MASQUE OF MERCY . . 515

HELPED

IT'S NOT FAIR TO THE CHILD. IT CAN'T BE HELPED, THOUGH: . 98 THE SELF-SEEKER . . . 148

PAGE TITLE   LINE

HELPED (CONTINUED)
    THESE HANDS HAVE HELPED IT GO, AND EVEN RACE; . . . . . 188 THE GRINDSTONE . . .   4
    FOR GATHERING SOLAR RAYS WOULD NOT HAVE HELPED. . . . . 293 AT WOODWARD'S GARDENS . 6
    BUT HELPED THE LORD HER SOUL TO KEEP. . . . . 382 THE NIGHT LIGHT . . .   4
    TO THANK YOU SOMEDAY FOR THE WAY YOU HELPED ME . . . . . 475 A MASQUE OF REASON . . 48
HELPER
    ONE HELPER, THRUSTING PITCHFORK IN THE GROUND, ... 69 THE CODE   7
HELPING
    FOR HELPING THEM BE CRUEL ONCE TO HIM. . . . . 206 THE WITCH OF COOS . . 134
HELPLESS
    "IT SEEMS AS IF. AND THAT'S NOT ALL: HE'S HELPLESS . . . 86 THE HOUSEKEEPER . . . 156
    HELPLESS. "THERE'S NOTHING WE CAN DO TILL MORNING." . . 155 SNOW 325
    THE DOOR; THEY HALTED HELPLESS ON THE LANDING, ... 204 THE WITCH OF COOS . . 62
    IF IT MAKES YOU LOOK HELPLESS, PLEASE, ... 326 TO A THINKER 23
HELPMATE
    WHO MARRIED HER FOR PLAYMATE MORE THAN HELPMATE, ... 200 PLACE FOR A THIRD . . 34
HELVE (SEE AX-HELVE)
    HE SHOWED ME THAT THE LINES OF A GOOD HELVE . . . . . . 187 THE AX-HELVE 72
HELVES (SEE AX-HELVES)
HEMAN
    I'LL TELL YOU WHO'D REMEMBER--HEMAN LAPISH. . . . . . . 208 PAUPER WITCH OF GRAFTON 26
HEMLOCK
    FROM A HEMLOCK TREE . . . . 221 DUST OF SNOW   4
HEMP
    OF MIDDLE-AISLE CHURCH CARPET, SISAL HEMP, ... 489 A MASQUE OF REASON . 454
HEN
    WE WOULDN'T HURT A HEN! YOU OUGHT TO SEE US . . . . . . 85 THE HOUSEKEEPER . . . 125
    HE HAD A HEN, HE HAD A PIG IN SIGHT. . . . . 292 FIGURE IN THE DOORWAY . 16
HENCE
    SOMEWHERE AGES AND AGES HENCE: . . . . 105 THE ROAD NOT TAKEN . . 17
    COME BACK THAT WAY A SUMMER HENCE, ... 291 'ON HEART'S BEGINNING TO 19
    WE MUST WAIT TILL SOME MONTHS HENCE IN THE SPRING TO KNOW. . 305 THERE ARE ROUGHLY ZONES 19
    AND WHAT TAKE HENCE OR LEAVE BEHIND, ... 332 ALL REVELATION . . .   7
    (AND HENCE SO MANY LITERARY TEARS . . . . 355 THE LESSON FOR TODAY . 149
HENCEFORTH
    SO THAT HENCEFORTH I WORKED NO MORE ALONE; . . . . . . 23 THE TUFT OF FLOWERS . 34
    THE CONQUEROR HENCEFORTH SHOULD LACK. . . . . 311 THE VINDICTIVES . . . 26
HENGLISH
    "SHE AIN'T SPICK TOO MUCH HENGLISH--DAT'S TOO BAD." . . 187 THE AX-HELVE 54
HENRY
    ABOUT WHERE HENRY HUDSON'S GONE, ... 211 AN EMPTY THREAT . . . 16
HENS
    AND NO ONE HERE BUT HENS BLOWING ABOUT. . . . . 83 THE HOUSEKEEPER . . . 47
    OUR HENS AND COWS AND PIGS ARE ALWAYS BETTER . . . . . 85 THE HOUSEKEEPER . . . 111
    SHE WANTS OUR HENS TO BE THE BEST THERE ARE. . . . . . 85 THE HOUSEKEEPER . . . 118
    MOVING A FLOCK OF HENS FROM PLACE TO PLACE. . . . . . . 85 THE HOUSEKEEPER . . . 126
    ON HIS OWN FARM. HE'S BOSS. BUT AS TO HENS: . . . . . . 86 THE HOUSEKEEPER . . . 135
    WE FENCE OUR FLOWERS IN AND THE HENS RANGE. . . . . . . 86 THE HOUSEKEEPER . . . 136
HEPATICAS
    AND A FLAME SLENDER AS THE HEPATICAS, ... 131 THE BONFIRE 51
HER---NOT INDEXED
HERBERT
    UNTIL HERBERT HOOVER . . . . 430 KITTY HAWK 70
HERDS
    HAS BEEN WITH FLOCKS AND HERDS . . . . 465 MILKY WAY IS A COWPATH 43
HERE---NOT INDEXED
HEREBY
    AND CALM YOURSELF. BE SANE! I HEREBY HOLD . . . . 501 A MASQUE OF MERCY . . 192
HERE'S---NOT INDEXED
HERETICS
    IN SAVING HERETICS BY SLAYING THEM, ... 515 A MASQUE OF MERCY . . 572
HEREWITH
    IN WISHING YOU HEREWITH A MERRY CHRISTMAS. . . . . 107 CHRISTMAS TREES . . . 60
HERMITAGE
    SOME STILL WERE LIVING IN HERMITAGE. . . . . 253 THE THATCH 16
HERMIT'S
    LIKE A HERMIT'S CRUCIFIX; . . . . 11 TO THE THAWING WIND . 10
HERO
    HE'D BEEN THE HERO OF THE MOUNTAIN CAMPS . . . . 191 PAUL'S WIFE 17
    PAUL WAS ASHAMED OF HER. TO MATCH A HERO . . . . 192 PAUL'S WIFE 37
    HIGH PURPOSE MAKES THE HERO RUDE; . . . . 418 AMERICA IS HARD TO SEE 73
HEROES
    SO MUCH THOSE HEROES KNEW AND UNDERSTOOD-- . . . . . . 422 FOR JOHN F. KENNEDY . 24
HEROIC
    HEROIC IN ITS NAKEDNESS, ... 21 THE TRIAL BY EXISTENCE 43
    AND COUNTED OUT. HEROIC DEEDS WERE DONE. . . . . 422 FOR JOHN F. KENNEDY . 17
HEROINE
    SHE WOULD HAVE HAD TO BE A HEROINE; . . . . 192 PAUL'S WIFE 38
HERRICK
    SUSSEX BECAUSE THEY'RE SPOKEN OF BY HERRICK. . . . . . 162 NEW HAMPSHIRE . . . 107
HERS---NOT INDEXED
HERSELF
    TO RAISE HERSELF AND LOOK AGAIN. HE SPOKE . . . . . . 51 HOME BURIAL   5
    "D'YOU KNOW A PERSON SO RELATED TO HERSELF . . . . . . 76 THE GENERATIONS OF MEN 82
    WHAT DO YOU MEAN?--SHE'S DONE HARM TO HERSELF?" . . . . 87 THE HOUSEKEEPER . . . 179
    SHE PUSHED PAST HIM AND GOT IT FOR HERSELF. . . . . . . 90 THE FEAR 34
    WHAT DO YOU WANT?" SHE CRIED, AND THEN HERSELF . . . . 91 THE FEAR 65
    WITH A SONG ONLY TO HERSELF . . . . 128 THE IMPULSE 11
    TO PLANT AND TEND AND REAP HERSELF, ... 133 A GIRL'S GARDEN . .   7
    I DON'T SEE." / "POSSIBLY NOT FOR HERSELF. . . . . . . 155 SNOW 335
    SOMETHING ELSE TO PROTECT HER FROM HERSELF. . . . . . . 163 NEW HAMPSHIRE . . . 147
    SO SHE LOOKED FOR HERSELF, AS EVERYONE . . . . 182 MAPLE 70
    SO, TILL SHE FOUND HERSELF IN A STRANGE PLACE . . . . . 182 MAPLE 77
    SHE MUST HAVE MISSED HERSELF. SO THEY WERE MARRIED, . . 182 MAPLE 95
    AND CAUGHT HERSELF UP BODILY, CHAIR AND ALL, ... 187 THE AX-HELVE . . . 52
    AND SET HERSELF BACK WHERE SHE STARTED FROM. . . . . . 187 THE AX-HELVE . . . 53
    AND WALKED OFF, TALKING TO HERSELF OR PAUL, ... 195 PAUL'S WIFE 120
    WAS FROM THE GIRL HERSELF, THOUGH, NOT FROM A STAR, . . 195 PAUL'S WIFE 137

HERSELF (CONTINUED)
    SHE HAD MADE THREE HERSELF TO THREE OF HIS. . . . . 199 PLACE FOR A THIRD . . 2
    IN A NEW-BOUGHTEN GRAVE PLOT BY HERSELF, ... 200 PLACE FOR A THIRD . . 23
    SHE MIGHT AS WELL HERSELF." BUT HE LIKED BEST . . . . 209 PAUPER WITCH OF GRAFTON . 83
    SHE NEVER TENDED ANYTHING HERSELF. . . . . 215 A FOUNTAIN, A BOTTLE . 83
    TO PECK HERSELF A PRECIOUS STONE. . . . . 281 BLUE RIBBON AT AMESBURY . 42
    TO SET HERSELF BESIDE THE SUN, ... 390 TWO LEADING LIGHTS . . 20
    AND SAVE HERSELF FROM BREAKING WINDOW GLASS. . . . . 445 QUESTIONING FACES . . 2
    SOMETIMES SHE THINKS SHE HAS AND GETS HERSELF . . . . 476 A MASQUE OF REASON . . 93
HE'S---NOT INDEXED
HESITATE
    IT FALTERED: I COULD SEE IT HESITATE; . . . . 357 A CONSIDERABLE SPECK . 20
    I SHOULD JUSTLY HESITATE . . . . 384 MAKING CERTAIN ANYTHING 9
HESPERIDEE
    THE GOLD HESPERIDEE . . . . 283 THE GOLD HESPERIDEE . T
    THEIR NAME WAS CALLED THE GOLD HESPERIDEE. . . . . . . 283 THE GOLD HESPERIDEE . 18
    THAT THE NAME GOLD HESPERIDEE WAS RIGHT. . . . . 284 THE GOLD HESPERIDEE . 30
HESPERIDES
    TO RIDGELY TORRENCE ON LAST LOOKING INTO HIS "HESPERIDES" . . 248 A PASSING GLIMPSE . . 0
HEW
    AMONG THE RASPBERRIES, AND HEW AND SHAPE IT . . . . 79 THE GENERATIONS OF MEN 162
HEY
    'HEY, THAT'S A PRETTY THOUGHT'--THOSE WERE HIS WORDS-- . . . 149 SNOW 181
HICKORY
    OR ROOM WITHIN A ROOM, OF HICKORY POLES, ... 66 A SERVANT TO SERVANTS . 114
    I OFTEN THINK OF THE SMOOTH HICKORY BARS. . . . . . . 67 A SERVANT TO SERVANTS . 144
HICK'RY
    WHAT'S LAS' AWHILE--GOOD HICK'RY WHAT'S GROW CROOKED, . 186 THE AX-HELVE . . . 30
HID
    LIKE GNOMES THAT HID US FROM THE MOON, ... 18 GOING FOR WATER . . 14
    SHE STOOD, AND THEN SHE RAN AND HID . . . . 129 THE IMPULSE 19
    AND HID FROM ANYONE PASSING. . . . . 134 A GIRL'S GARDEN . . 25
    (THE MEANING OF THE PASSAGE HAD BEEN HID; . . . . . . 284 THE GOLD HESPERIDEE . 52
    AND HAVING HID IT IN THEIR BEDDING STRAW . . . . . . 293 AT WOODWARD'S GARDENS . 30
    THAT AT ONCE KEPT YOU BURNING LOW AND HID YOU. . . . . 351 THE LESSON FOR TODAY . 25
HIDDEN (SEE TREE-HIDDEN)
    AND BELOW ROARED A BROOK HIDDEN IN TREES, ... 76 THE GENERATIONS OF MEN 75
    NOTHING IS HIDDEN FROM SOME PEOPLE, ANNE. . . . . . . 97 THE SELF-SEEKER . . 135
    FROM HIDDEN GRAPEVINE SPRINGS . . . . 227 TO EARTHWARD . . . 7
    SHE COULD BE SURE THERE WAS NO HIDDEN ILL . . . . . . 230 NOT TO KEEP . . . 3
    WE HAVE IT HIDDEN IN US TO ATTAIN, ... 238 ON A TREE FALLEN ACROSS 11
    I HAVE KEPT HIDDEN IN THE INSTEP ARCH . . . . 379 DIRECTIVE 55
    JUST BECAUSE IT'S HIDDEN. . . . . 437 KITTY HAWK . . . 283
    I'VE COME TO THINK NO SO-CALLED HIDDEN VALUE'S . . . . 483 A MASQUE OF REASON . 280
HIDE
    SO ALL WHO HIDE TO WELL AWAY . . . . 19 REVELATION . . . 11
    TO HIDE IN THE WORLD . . . . 241 THE LOCKLESS DOOR . . 19
    HIS SMALL FIST BURIED IN THE BUSHY HIDE. . . . . . . 267 RIDERS 8
    FOR INNER DEFENSE MY HIDE. . . . . 348 TRIPLE BRONZE . . . 3
HIDE-AND-SEEK
    AT HIDE-AND-SEEK TO GOD AFAR, ... 19 REVELATION . . . 10
    THEY YELLING MIX TAG, HIDE-AND-SEEK, HOPSCOTCH, ... 318 BUILD SOIL . . . 63
HIDE-GOLD
    ALL JOINED IN THE GAME OF HIDE-GOLD. . . . . 311 THE VINDICTIVES . . 28
HIDING
    READY TO RUN TO HIDING NEW . . . . 18 GOING FOR WATER . . 15
    BUT THEY WOULD HAVE THE RABBIT OUT OF HIDING, ... 33 MENDING WALL . . . 8
    "I'M SURE SHE WON'T COME BACK. SHE'S HIDING SOMEWHERE. . . 82 THE HOUSEKEEPER . . 23
    YOU'RE HIDING SOMETHING. THAT'S AS BAD AS LYING. . . . . 97 THE SELF-SEEKER . . 132
    NONE NOT IN HIDING FROM THE OUTWARD EYE. . . . . . . 174 THE CENSUS-TAKER . . 16
HIE
    WELL I KNOW WHERE TO HIE ME--IN THE DAWN, ... 17 THE VANTAGE POINT . . 2
HIGH (SEE SKY-HIGH)
    THOU DIDST NOT KNOW, WHO TOTTERED, WANDERING ON HIGH, . . 28 MY BUTTERFLY . . . 22
    "HE NEVER GOT UP HIGH ENOUGH TO SEE. . . . . 43 THE MOUNTAIN . . . 78
    SO HIGH ACROSS THE PANE OUTSIDE. THERE WHERE . . . . . 149 SNOW 191
    IS THAT HER MOUNTAINS AREN'T QUITE HIGH ENOUGH. . . . . 169 NEW HAMPSHIRE . . 311
    OR SOME SUCH SENSE AS SAYS HOW HIGH SHALL JET . . . . . 169 NEW HAMPSHIRE . . 325
    FIVE THOUSAND IS NO LONGER HIGH ENOUGH. . . . . . . 169 NEW HAMPSHIRE . . 334
    HOW HIGH I'D THRUST THE PEAKS IN SUMMER SNOW . . . . . 169 NEW HAMPSHIRE . . 339
    THE HOUSE ONE STORY HIGH IN FRONT, THREE STORIES . . . . 181 MAPLE 57
    (THE HOUSE ONE STORY HIGH IN FRONT, THREE STORIES . . . . 182 MAPLE 98
    AND BLUE SO FAR ABOVE US COMES SO HIGH, ... 220 FRAGMENTARY BLUE . . 7
    HIGH IN THE BREAST. NOTHING BUT WHAT GOOD CARE . . . . 230 NOT TO KEEP . . . 15
    FROM THE HIGH WEST SHE MAKES A GENTLE CAST . . . . . 237 A HILLSIDE THAW . . 20
    IN THE TUMULT OF FREE LEAVES ON HIGH. . . . . 247 ON GOING UNNOTICED . 2
    ALL THE DUST THE WIND BLEW HIGH . . . . 249 A PECK OF GOLD . . 5
    WHAT WELL MAY PROVE THE YEAR'S HIGH GIRDLE MARK. . . . . 254 A WINTER EDEN . . 12
    HELD HIGH AT SO UNNATURAL A LEVEL. . . . . 255 THE FLOOD . . . 8
    SHE CAME TO FROM TOO HIGH TOO LATE TO LEARN. . . . . . 257 THE LOVELY BE CHOOSERS 45
    AND HEAVING HIM HIGH IN AIR, ... 289 DEPARTMENTAL . . . 38
    THE WIDESPREAD DOUBLE DOORS TWO STORIES HIGH. . . . . . 289 OLD BARN AT THE BOTTOM 12
    THE GRADE SURMOUNTED, WE WERE RIDING HIGH . . . . . . 292 FIGURE IN THE DOORWAY . 1
    OF UNSATISFIED LOVE OF THE HIGH, ... 313 THE VINDICTIVES . . 87
    FOR THE GRASS WAS HIGH; . . . . 342 QUEST OF PURPLE-FRINGED 10
    YOU'LL SEE IT BE ALLOWED UP JUST SO HIGH, ... 370 THE LITERATE FARMER AND 65
    AWAY ON THE MOUNTAIN UP FAR TOO HIGH, ... 383 WERE I IN TROUBLE . 2
    HAVE LOVED IT CLEAR AND HIGH, ... 388 ASTROMETAPHYSICAL . 3
    OH, MAY THE TIDE BE SOON ENOUGH AT HIGH . . . . . . 395 ETHEREALIZING . . 13
    HIGH PURPOSE MAKES THE HERO RUDE; . . . . 418 AMERICA IS HARD TO SEE 73
    IT IS NO MIRACLE OUR MOOD IS HIGH. . . . . 423 FOR JOHN F. KENNEDY . 57
    TO RULE FIRST ANSWERABLE TO HIGH DESIGN. . . . . . . 424 FOR JOHN F. KENNEDY . 65
    I PASSED WITH SUCH A HIGH I.Q. . . . . 467 QUANDARY . . . 26
    FOUR-ROOM SHACK ASPIRING HIGH . . . . 469 FOUR-ROOM SHACK... . 1
    OF COURSE, IN THE ABSTRACT HIGH SINGULAR . . . . . . 478 A MASQUE OF REASON . 137
HIGH-COLORED
    HER CHEEKS HIGH-COLORED, ... 256 THE LOVELY BE CHOOSERS 17

HIGHER
   HE CAME FROM HIGHER UP IN THE PASS . . . . 140 THE GUM-GATHERER . . 13
   TO HEAVE THEM HIGHER TO THE MORNING STAR? . . . . . 169 NEW HAMPSHIRE . . . 319
   HE CLIMBED STILL HIGHER AND BENT THE TREE TO EARTH . 197 WILD GRAPES 37
   ONE LEVEL HIGHER THAN THE EARTH BELOW. . . . . . . 254 A WINTER EDEN 6
   THAN WHEN ITS WALLS ROSE HIGHER THAN ANY ROOF. . . 306 NOT QUITE SOCIAL . . 8
   OR SHOULD I SAY THE HIGHER ONE, FOR DARK. . . . . . 352 THE LESSON FOR TODAY . 53
   THERE ARE FEW INSTITUTIONS STANDING HIGHER . . . . 400 TO THE RIGHT PERSON . 4
   BUT LIFTS NO HIGHER THAN A GARDEN GROWS. . . . . . 414 A CABIN IN THE CLEARING 17
   FROM NO HIGHER HEAVEN . . . . 441 KITTY HAWK 408
HIGHER-UP
   TO THE HIGHER-UP AT COURT. . . . . 288 DEPARTMENTAL 21
HIGHEST
   BEYOND THE HIGHEST CITY BUILT WITH HANDS. . . . . . 182 MAPLE 84
   WHERE HE CAN STRETCH AND HOLD HIS HIGHEST FEAST . . 254 A WINTER EDEN . . . 10
HIGHWAY
   OR HIGHWAY WHERE THE SLOW WHEEL POURS THE SAND. . . 5 INTO MY OWN 8
   I HAVE COME BY THE HIGHWAY HOME, ... 30 RELUCTANCE 5
   SOMEWHERE TO WALK----" / "THE HIGHWAY, AS IT HAPPENS-- . 92 THE FEAR 85
   HE SAYS THE HIGHWAY DUST IS OVER ALL. . . . . 120 THE OVEN BIRD . . . 10
HIGHWAYS
   IT'S HIGHWAYS, AND HE'S GOT TOO MANY MEN . . . . . 64 A SERVANT TO SERVANTS . 72
HILL
   THE GRAVES OF MEN ON AN OPPOSING HILL, ... 17 THE VANTAGE POINT . . 7
   AT WOODED VALLEY AND WOODED HILL. . . . . 23 PAN WITH US 5
   I LET MY NEIGHBOR KNOW BEYOND THE HILL; . . . . . . 33 MENDING WALL . . . 12
   OR OVER A HILL OR ROUND A SUDDEN CORNER. . . . . . 49 A HUNDRED COLLARS . . 126
   COMING DOWN RYAN'S HILL. I THOUGHT 'TWAS HIM. . . . 88 THE HOUSEKEEPER . . . 197
   AS I WENT DOWN THE HILL ALONG THE WALL . . . . . . 118 MEETING AND PASSING . 1
   AS YOU CAME UP THE HILL. WE MET. BUT ALL . . . . . 118 MEETING AND PASSING . 4
   THE HILL WIFE . . . . 126 THE HILL WIFE . . . T
   "OH, LET'S GO UP THE HILL AND SCARE OURSELVES, . . . 129 THE BONFIRE . . . 1
   A HILL EACH OF POTATOES, ... 134 A GIRL'S GARDEN . . 29
   TO READ THE GRAVESTONES ON THE HILL; . . . . 221 IN A DISUSED GRAVEYARD 2
   ALL WINTER, CUT OFF BY A HILL FROM THE HOUSE. . . . 228 GOOD-BY AND KEEP COLD . 5
   FROM MY ADVANTAGE ON A HILL . . . . 233 LOOKING FOR SUNSET BIRD 13
   HILL ATMOSPHERE NOT CEASE TO GLOW, ... 234 EVENING A SUGAR ORCHARD 9
   WAS COUNTING WINTER DINNERS, ONE A HILL, ... 263 THE INVESTMENT . . . 7
HILLS
   THE HILLS ARE VERDURED PASTUREWISE; . . . . 19 THE TRIAL BY EXISTENCE 12
   COME OVER THE HILLS AND FAR WITH ME, ... 26 A LINE-STORM SONG . . 7
   I HAVE CLIMBED THE HILLS OF VIEW . . . . 30 RELUCTANCE 3
   DRAGGING THE WHOLE SKY WITH IT TO THE HILLS. . . . 38 DEATH OF THE HIRED MAN 104
   CATERWAUL TO THE HILLS AROUND THE VILLAGE . . . . . 94 THE SELF-SEEKER . . . 42
   WITH HILLS AND CIRCLING ARMS ABOUT-- . . . . 120 BOND AND FREE . . . 2
   ON ALL THE HILLS I HAVEN'T HOED, ... 124 A TIME TO TALK . . . 4
   "ME FOR THE HILLS WHERE I DON'T HAVE TO CHOOSE." . 170 NEW HAMPSHIRE . . . 364
   TO OTHER HILLS ACROSS A KETTLE VALLEY. . . . . . . 195 PAUL'S WIFE . . . 126
   THE BURRS WERE HILLS, THE SNAKE WAS A STREAM, . . . 367 A SERIOUS STEP LIGHTLY 3
HILLSIDE
   THE SUNBURNED HILLSIDE SETS MY FACE AGLOW, ... 17 THE VANTAGE POINT . . 11
   THE SECOND ROUND THE CURVING HILLSIDE ROAD . . . . 74 THE GENERATIONS OF MEN 29
   THE HILLSIDE ON THE DAY THE SUN LETS GO . . . . . . 237 A HILLSIDE THAW . . 2
   A HILLSIDE THAW . . . . 237 A HILLSIDE THAW . . T
HIM---NOT INDEXED
HIMALAYAN
   ON ONE HIMALAYAN SHELF; . . . . 314 BEARER OF EVIL TIDINGS 34
HIMSELF
   HE SAID IT FOR HIMSELF. I SEE HIM THERE, ... 34 MENDING WALL 38
   I SHOULDN'T MIND HIS BETTERING HIMSELF . . . . . . 35 DEATH OF THE HIRED MAN 25
   HE'S TRYING TO LIFT, STRAINING TO LIFT HIMSELF." . 37 DEATH OF THE HIRED MAN 95
   AND PROPPED HIMSELF AT BAY AGAINST A PILLOW. . . . 47 A HUNDRED COLLARS . . 74
   HE SAID TWICE OVER BEFORE HE KNEW HIMSELF: . . . . 52 HOME BURIAL 34
   MARCHED HIMSELF OFF THE FIELD AND HOME. ONE STAYED. 69 THE CODE 8
   HE WAS HARD ON HIMSELF. I COULDN'T FIND . . . . . . 71 THE CODE 39
   THAT HE KEPT ANY HOURS--NOT FOR HIMSELF. . . . . . 71 THE CODE 40
   JOHN HIMSELF WON'T IMAGINE WHO HE IS." . . . . . . 88 THE HOUSEKEEPER . . . 189
   EVERYTHING SAID AS PERSONAL TO HIMSELF. . . . . . . 101 THE WOOD-PILE . . . 16
   HE SPENT HIMSELF, THE LABOR OF HIS AX, ... 102 THE WOOD-PILE . . . 37
   A LIGHT HE WAS TO NO ONE BUT HIMSELF . . . . 108 OLD MAN'S WINTER NIGHT 15
   HE SAW HIMSELF A FARMER. THEN THERE WAS A FRENCH BOY . 114 IN THE HOME STRETCH . 103
   WHOSE ONLY PLAY WAS WHAT HE FOUND HIMSELF, ... 121 BIRCHES 26
   AND STAMPED AND SAID THINGS TO HIMSELF, ... 138 BROWN'S DESCENT . . 17
   HE TOLD ME A LITTLE ABOUT HIMSELF. . . . . 140 THE GUM-GATHERER . . 12
   SAID IT AT LAST HIMSELF, "GOOD-NIGHT," AND THEN, . 143 SNOW 29
   FROM THE LAST THING HE SAID HIMSELF, STONE DEAF . . 145 SNOW 65
   BUT THEN, I DOUBT HE'S THINKING OF HIMSELF. . . . . 145 SNOW 78
   PRIVATELY--TO HIMSELF, RIGHT NOW, HE'S THINKING . . 146 SNOW 85
   AT THE ISLES OF SHOALS, AND SATISFIED HIMSELF . . . 161 NEW HAMPSHIRE . . . 76
   I CAUGHT THE OWNER OUTDOORS BY HIMSELF . . . . . . 164 NEW HAMPSHIRE . . . 152
   THE CULT OF ONE WHO OWNED HIMSELF "A FOILED . . . . 171 NEW HAMPSHIRE . . . 383
   FOR THE NEXT ONE TO OPEN FOR HIMSELF. . . . . 175 THE CENSUS-TAKER . . 30
   TO FIND HIMSELF IN ONE. WELL, ALL WE SAID WAS . . . 178 THE STAR-SPLITTER . . 57
   LOCKS FOR HIMSELF, MORE OR LESS OUTWARDLY. . . . . 182 MAPLE 71
   ONCE LONG AGO HER FATHER HAD PUT HIMSELF OFF.) . . 183 MAPLE 111
   THAN FOR HIMSELF, SO PLACED HE COULDN'T HOPE . . . 187 THE AX-HELVE . . . 59
   ABOUT HIS WIFE TO KEEP HER TO HIMSELF. . . . . . . 195 PAUL'S WIFE . . . 149
   WHICH GAVE HIM SOME TIME TO HIMSELF TO EAT, ... 197 WILD GRAPES . . . 34
   WITH SOMETHING HE REMEMBERED IN HIMSELF, ... 200 PLACE FOR A THIRD . 18
   WHICH GIVES HIM FOR HIMSELF A CHOICE OF LOTS . . . 202 PLACE FOR A THIRD . 81
   AND ALL BUT LOST HIMSELF. (A TONGUE OF FIRE . . . . 204 THE WITCH OF COOS . 72
   COULD TELL YOU WHY HE EVER CARED HIMSELF.... . . . 207 THE WITCH OF COOS . 151
   IN ONE HIMSELF PERHAPS. . . . . 211 AN EMPTY THREAT . . 29
   TOO LATE THOUGH, NOW, HE HAD HIMSELF TO THANK. . . 270 THE EGG AND THE MACHINE 9
   TO THINK THAT THOUGH HE COULD NOT LOCK HIMSELF IN, . 290 OLD BARN AT THE BOTTOM 43
   HE DRAWS HIMSELF UP TO HIS FULL EXTENT. . . . . . . 309 WASPISH 2
   'TWAS TO BUY HIMSELF OFF HIS DOOM. . . . . 310 THE VINDICTIVES . . . 6
   DECIDED TO STAY THERE HIMSELF. . . . . 314 BEARER OF EVIL TIDINGS 36

HIMSELF (CONTINUED)
    EVERYONE ASKS FOR FREEDOM FOR HIMSELF, ... 319 BUILD SOIL 111
    TO SET HIMSELF AGAINST THE PEAKS OF SNOW . . . . 334 I COULD GIVE ALL . . 2
    HE WOULD DECLARE AND COULD HIMSELF BELIEVE . . . . . . 338 NEVER WOULD BIRDS' SONG 1
    GOD BLESS HIMSELF CAN NO ONE ELSE BE BLESSED. . . . . . 355 THE LESSON FOR TODAY . 156
    (THOUGH PRODIGAL HIMSELF AND A DESPISER . . . . 363 AN EQUALIZER 3
    HE GAVE UP SLEEP HIMSELF SOME TIME AGO, ... 371 THE LITERATE FARMER AND 104
    HIMSELF HAD THE EQUIVALENT, ... 381 AN UNSTAMPED LETTER IN 31
    RELYING ON HIMSELF AND ON HIS CANE, ... 394 HAEC FABULA DOCET . . 2
    AND PLUNGED HIMSELF HEAD FOREMOST IN THE TRENCH: . . . . 394 HAEC FABULA DOCET . 14
    AND HUGGED HIMSELF FOR ALL HIS UNIVERSE. . . . . 396 ANY SIZE WE PLEASE . 14
    AT BEING THUS EXPOUNDED TO HIMSELF . . . . 405 FROM PLANE TO PLANE . 56
    HE DUMPED HIMSELF LIKE A BAG OF BONES, ... 419 ONE MORE BREVITY . . 15
    HE SIGHED HIMSELF A COUPLE OF GROANS, ... 419 ONE MORE BREVITY . 16
    WE ASSUMED THAT THE MAN HIMSELF . . . . 444 THE DRAFT HORSE . . . 17
    ASKS OF HIMSELF ONCE IN SO OFTEN . . . . 453 A-WISHING WELL . . . 74
    HE COULDN'T KEEP HIMSELF FROM BEING KING. . . . . 454 HOW HARD TO KEEP FROM 23
    FOR HIM TO MAKE A POET OF HIMSELF ON . . . . 459 HOW HARD TO KEEP FROM 175
    FOR GOD HIMSELF THE HEIGHT OF FEELING FREE . . . . 461 HOW HARD TO KEEP FROM 251
    A TRIAL GROUND WHERE HE CAN TRY HIMSELF . . . . 484 A MASQUE OF REASON . 319
    I'M NOT PREPARED FOR OR THAT JOB HIMSELF . . . . 488 A MASQUE OF REASON . 414
    LIKE THE ONE MILTON FOUND TO FOOL HIMSELF . . . . 488 A MASQUE OF REASON . 416
    REDUCED HIM TO A SHADOW OF HIMSELF. . . . . 488 A MASQUE OF REASON . 426
    (HE GOES AND TAKES IT FROM THE DOOR HIMSELF.) . . . . . 500 A MASQUE OF MERCY . . 175
HINDER
    HE AND I ONLY HINDER ONE ANOTHER. . . . . 82 THE HOUSEKEEPER . . . 36
HINGES
    THAT GOD PULLS LIGHTLY UPRIGHT ON ITS HINGES . . . . . . 474 A MASQUE OF REASON . 22
HINT
    IMPORTUNATE TO GIVE THE HINT . . . . 327 A MISSIVE MISSILE . . 31
    NEVERTHELESS IT CONSTITUTES A HINT . . . . 361 A LOOSE MOUNTAIN . . 13
    SHUFFLED THEIR FEET AS IF TO HINT RESPECTFULLY, ... 456 HOW HARD TO KEEP FROM 73
HINTING
    WHAT WAS IN ALL OUR MINDS, AND YOU WEREN'T HINTING. . . . 70 THE CODE 28
HIRED
    THE DEATH OF THE HIRED MAN . . . . 34 DEATH OF THE HIRED MAN T
    FROM COOKING MEALS FOR HUNGRY HIRED MEN . . . . 64 A SERVANT TO SERVANTS . 50
    OUT OF HIS HIRED HELP. I'M NOT DENYING . . . . 70 THE CODE 38
    THE MOST EFFICIENT HELP YOU EVER HIRED . . . . 375 A YOUNG BIRCH . . . 17
    THEY BOTH WERE HIRED. AND THOUGH PIKE HAD THE ADVANTAGE . 404 FROM PLANE TO PLANE . 2
    THIS VERY NIGHT. I HAD THE HALL ALL HIRED, ... 497 A MASQUE OF MERCY . . 95
HIS---NOT INDEXED
HISS
    WITH THE HISS OF SPRAY; . . . . 218 I WILL SING YOU ONE-O . 10
HISSED
    LEAVES GOT UP IN A COIL AND HISSED, ... 251 BEREFT 9
HISSING
    OF HISSING ON THE YET UNCOVERED GROUND, ... 226 THE ONSET 5
HISTORY
    IN BEING THERE SO EARLY IN OUR HISTORY. . . . . 161 NEW HAMPSHIRE . . . 81
    AND BACK THROUGH HISTORY UP THE STREAM OF TIME. . . . . 300 THE MASTER SPEED . . 4
    BUT SO IS HISTORY LIKE TO ERR. . . . . 347 DISCOVERY OF MADEIRAS 136
    THAT HUMAN HISTORY SHOULD NOT BE SHORTENED. . . . . . . 397 THE PLANNERS . . . 14
    (WITH SOME PRELIMINARY HISTORY IN RHYME) . . . . 422 FOR JOHN F. KENNEDY . 5
    A TURNING POINT IN MODERN HISTORY. . . . . 422 FOR JOHN F. KENNEDY . 10
HIT
    WILL HIT OR MISS THE MOON." / IT HIT THE MOON. . . . . . 40 DEATH OF THE HIRED MAN 161
    AND HIT ME A BLOW IN THE HEAD SO HARD . . . . 265 THE DOOR IN THE DARK . 6
    BY HAILING CHEERILY "HIT THEM HARD!" . . . . 275 TWO TRAMPS IN MUD TIME 4
    AND EVERY PIECE I SQUARELY HIT . . . . 275 TWO TRAMPS IN MUD TIME 11
    A PEBBLE HIT THE ROOF, ... 298 ON TAKING FROM THE TOP 10
    TILL ACCIDENTALLY IT HIT ON MIND . . . . 425 ACCIDENTALLY ON PURPOSE 6
    HE COULDN'T LAY HANDS ON A PITCHFORK TO HIT HER . . . . 463 LINES IN DEJECTION . 17
HITCHED
    AND IF I'D LEFT HIM HITCHED UNBLANKETED . . . . 208 PAUPER WITCH OF GRAFTON 49
    IN FRONT OF ONE TOWN HALL, I'D LEFT HIM HITCHED . . . . 208 PAUPER WITCH OF GRAFTON 50
HITCHING
    NOT THAT HE HADN'T GNAWED THE HITCHING POSTS . . . . . . 209 PAUPER WITCH OF GRAFTON 64
HITHER
    NO LONGER BLOWN HITHER AND THITHER; . . . . 30 RELUCTANCE 14
HIVES
    BECAUSE UNLIKE THE BEES THEY HAVE NO HIVES, ... 411 POD OF THE MILKWEED . 4
HIVE'S
    OF THE HIVE'S ENQUIRY SQUAD . . . . 288 DEPARTMENTAL 9
HO
    SO BAD.--GIVE ME AN HOUR FOR IT.--HO, HO, ... 143 SNOW 21
    IT IS THE CELLAR TO MY STORE.--WHAT HO, DOWN THERE! . . 514 A MASQUE OF MERCY . . 555
HOARDING
    WHERE HE WAS HOARDING MORE THAN THEY ENJOYED. . . . . . 503 A MASQUE OF MERCY . . 254
HOARY
    AND HELD AGAINST THE WORLD OF HOARY GRASS. . . . . 68 AFTER APPLE-PICKING . 12
HOBBLE
    "HE THINKS I'LL HOBBLE. IT'S BOTH LEGS AND FEET." . . . 93 THE SELF-SEEKER . . . 16
HOE
    SOMETHING WENT WRONG. I SAW HIM THROW THE HOE . . . . . 83 THE HOUSEKEEPER . . . 60
    I THRUST MY HOE IN THE MELLOW GROUND, ... 124 A TIME TO TALK . . 7
    A FINAL GOING OVER WITH THE HOE . . . . 404 FROM PLANE TO PLANE . 13
    I GET YOU WHEN YOU HOE OUT TO THE RIVER, ... 405 FROM PLANE TO PLANE . 40
    THEN PICK YOUR HOE UP, MAYBE SHOULDER IT, ... 405 FROM PLANE TO PLANE . 41
    "I WOULDN'T HOE BOTH WAYS FOR ANYBODY!" . . . . 405 FROM PLANE TO PLANE . 48
    OF AN UNEMPLOYED HOE. . . . . 450 OBJECTION TO BE STEPPED 3
HOED
    HE HOED A LITTLE YESTERDAY FOR ME: . . . . 83 THE HOUSEKEEPER . . . 58
    ON ALL THE HILLS I HAVEN'T HOED, ... 124 A TIME TO TALK . . 4
    OF HAVING HOED AND MOWED FOR FIFTY YEARS, ... 404 FROM PLANE TO PLANE . 3
HOEING'S
    "HOEING'S TOO MUCH LIKE WORK FOR DICK," HE ADDED. . . . 404 FROM PLANE TO PLANE . 27

HOE'S
  THE FINAL FLAT OF THE HOE'S APPROVAL STAMP . . . . . . 299 STRONG SAYING NOTHING .   3
HOG
  FOR HOG REEVE IN MARCH MEETING HERE IN WARREN. . . . . . 207 PAUPER WITCH OF GRAFTON 14
HOLD
  I BROUGHT NOT HERE TO READ, IT SEEMS, BUT HOLD . . . . . 15 WAITING   24
  THE MYSTIC LINK TO BIND AND HOLD . . . . 21 THE TRIAL BY EXISTENCE 63
  HOLD ON, THERE'S SOMETHING I DON'T THINK OF NOW . . . . 46 A HUNDRED COLLARS . . 45
  HE MADE AS IF TO HOLD IT AT ARM'S LENGTH . . . . 55 THE BLACK COTTAGE . .   9
  ALL WE CAN HOLD TOGETHER BY THE LEGS. . . . . 85 THE HOUSEKEEPER . . . 128
  DON'T HOLD MY ARM!" / "I SAY IT'S SOMEONE PASSING." . . 90 THE FEAR 23
  HE APPEARED TO FORGET TO KEEP HIS HOLD, ... 91 THE FEAR 59
  COME, HOLD IT OUT. DON'T CHANGE.--A RAM'S HORN ORCHID! . . 96 THE SELF-SEEKER . . . 112
  IF I HAD CHOSEN LEFT. HOLD OUT THE LEFT. . . . . 97 THE SELF-SEEKER . . . 114
  ONE OF YOU HOLD MY HEAD UP FROM THE PILLOW." . . . . . 100 THE SELF-SEEKER . . . 215
  YET MORE I'D HATE TO HOLD MY TREES, EXCEPT . . . . . . 106 CHRISTMAS TREES . . 21
  AS OTHERS HOLD THEIRS OR REFUSE FOR THEM, ... 106 CHRISTMAS TREES . . 22
  THAT BROUGHT ME TO MY FEET TO HOLD IT BACK . . . . . . 132 THE BONFIRE 78
  TO HOLD IT HARD UNTIL THEY MAKE IT FAST, ... 141 THE LINE-GANG . . . 10
  WHEN IT'S JUST THAT I HOLD WITH GETTING A THING DONE WITH." 142 THE VANISHING RED . .   8
  "HOLD ON." THE DOUBLE BELL BEGAN TC CHIRP. . . . . . . 155 SNOW 327
  AND TUGGED IT FROM HIS FIRST TOO CERTAIN HOLD, ... 172 A STAR IN A STONEBOAT . 6
  BUT THAT WAS IN THE WOODS, TO HOLD MY HAND . . . . . . 185 THE AX-HELVE . . .   3
  TO LEAVE IT TO, WHETHER THE RIGHT TO HOLD . . . . . . 188 THE AX-HELVE . . . 91
  HOLD ON WITH ALL YOUR MIGHT WHEN I LET GO." . . . . . . 197 WILD GRAPES 40
  HOLD TIGHT AWHILE TILL I THINK WHAT TO DO. . . . . . . 198 WILD GRAPES 82
  AND HOLD THE DOOR. BUT THE BONES DIDN'T TRY . . . . . . 204 THE WITCH OF COOS . 61
  AND SIT UP BY ME AND TAKE HOLD OF ME. . . . . 205 THE WITCH OF COOS . . 103
  TO ENTERTAIN THE BIRDS AND HOLD THE FLOWERS. . . . . . 216 A FOUNTAIN, A BOTTLE . 87
  I HOLD WITH THOSE WHO FAVOR FIRE. . . . . 220 FIRE AND ICE . . .   4
  HER HARDEST HUE TO HOLD. . . . . 222 NOTHING GOLD CAN STAY . 2
  THE SPELL THAT SO COULD HOLD THEM AS THEY WERE . . . . . 237 A HILLSIDE THAW . . 30
  AND STILL THEY FAILED OF ANY LASTING HOLD. . . . . . . 239 OUR SINGING STRENGTH . 4
  WHERE HE CAN STRETCH AND HOLD HIS HIGHEST FEAST . . . . 254 A WINTER EDEN . . . 10
  WITH ALL I HAVE TO HOLD WITH, HAND AND MIND . . . . . . 267 THE ARMFUL   6
  THE LOWLY PEN IS YET A HOLD . . . . 281 BLUE RIBBON AT AMESBURY 53
  THAT THE CITY'S HOLD ON A MAN IS NC MORE TIGHT . . . . . 306 NOT QUITE SOCIAL . .   7
  AS FULL AS THE ROOM COULD HOLD . . . . 310 THE VINDICTIVES . .   3
  OUR HOLD ON THE PLANET . . . . 349 OUR HOLD ON THE PLANET T
  OUR HOLD ON THE PLANET WOULDN'T HAVE SO INCREASED. . . . 349 OUR HOLD ON THE PLANET 18
  I HOLD YOUR DOCTRINE OF MEMENTO MORI. . . . . 355 THE LESSON FOR TODAY . 157
  THE LOVING'S MADE TO HOLD EACH OTHER LIKE, ... 371 THE LITERATE FARMER AND 114
  AND WITH LONG-SLEEVED BRANCHES HOLD THEIR SWAY. . . . . 376 SOMETHING FOR HOPE . 12
  A THEORY IF YOU HOLD IT HARD ENOUGH . . . . 394 ETHEREALIZING . . .   1
  I CANNOT HOLD YOU INNOCENT OF FAULT. . . . . 446 DOES NO ONE AT ALL EVER 21
  THOUGH I HOLD RAYS DETERIORATE TO NOTHING: . . . . . . 485 A MASQUE OF REASON . 345
  AND CALM YOURSELF. BE SANE! I HEREBY HOLD . . . . . . 501 A MASQUE OF MERCY . 192
  THE MOB MIGHT HOLD A MAN UP IN THE STREETS . . . . . . 503 A MASQUE OF MERCY . 250
  HOLD ON THERE. LEAVE THAT OPEN WHERE IT LIES. . . . . . 504 A MASQUE OF MERCY . 292
  IT'S TOO BIG FOR HIM. HELP HIM HOLD IT UP. . . . . . . 506 A MASQUE OF MERCY . 328
  AND HOLD IT UP NEARSIGHTEDLY TO READ.) . . . . 512 A MASQUE OF MERCY . 490
  (THE CURTAIN STARTS TO FALL.) PLEASE HOLD THE CURTAIN.-- . 519 A MASQUE OF MERCY . 673
HOLDING
  AND HOLDING BY THE STALK, ... 118 THE TELEPHONE . . . 13
  AS HE SWUNG TOWARD THEM HOLDING UP THE HAND, ... 136 "OUT,OUT--" 20
  I HAVE NO DOUBT I'D END BY HOLDING NONE. . . . . . . 237 A HILLSIDE THAW . . . 17
  HOLDING THE CURVE OF ONE POSITION, ... 247 DEVOTION   3
  HOLDING OPEN A RESTIVE DOOR, ... 251 BEREFT   4
  ON A WHITE HEAL-ALL, HOLDING UP A MOTH . . . . 302 DESIGN   2
  AND HOLDING IT FAR FORWARD FOR A SYMBOL . . . . 446 DOES NO ONE AT ALL EVER 27
  FROM HOLDING FORTH ON FREEDOM LIKE A WHITMAN-- . . . . . 461 HOW HARD TO KEEP FROM 225
HOLDS
  AND HOLDS US OFF UNNECESSARILY, ... 183 MAPLE 124
  THANK GOD OUR PRACTICE HOLDS THE LOVES APART, ... 318 BUILD SOIL 81
  SOME LINGERING OBJECTION HOLDS YOU BACK. . . . . . . 517 A MASQUE OF MERCY . 632
HOLE
  AND ROLL BACK DOWN THE MOUND BESIDE THE HOLE. . . . . . 53 HOME BURIAL 77
  IN AN OLD CELLAR HOLE IN A BYROAD . . . . 73 THE GENERATIONS OF MEN   8
  DRAWN INTO TOWN ABOUT THIS CELLAR HOLE . . . . 76 THE GENERATIONS OF MEN 89
  WHAT DO WE SEE IN SUCH A HOLE, I WONDER." . . . . . . 76 THE GENERATIONS OF MEN 91
  A CANNON-MOUTH-LIKE HOLE WAS IN THE WALL, ... 113 IN THE HOME STRETCH . 84
  A HOLE IN SOMEWHERE WITH HIS HEEL. . . . . 138 BROWN'S DESCENT . . 15
  MORE LIKE A TUNNEL THAN A HOLE--WAY DOWN . . . . . . 149 SNOW 193
  I FLUSHED BIRDS OUT OF HOLE AFTER HOLE, ... 253 THE THATCH 19
  ONE KNEW OF A BURIAL HOLE . . . . 312 THE VINDICTIVES . . 56
  BUT ONLY A BELILACED CELLAR HOLE . . . . 378 DIRECTIVE 46
  OR SHADOW, BUT A CAVERN HOLE, ... 392 A CLIFF DWELLING . .   7
  DOWN A LIKELY HOLE . . . . 468 A REFLEX   3
HOLES
  OF BEING WATCHED FROM FORTY CELLAR HOLES . . . . . . 378 DIRECTIVE 21
HOLIDAY
  A HOLIDAY) AS, WHERE HE IS, ... 418 AMERICA IS HARD TO SEE 47
HOLIDAYS
  THEY ALWAYS TOOK THEIR HOLIDAYS IN AUTUMN. . . . . . . 184 MAPLE 143
HOLINESS
  THE HOLINESS OF WHOLENESS . . . . 440 KITTY HAWK 3P
HOLLER
  LET'S HOLLER AND ASK HIM IF HE WON'T PRESCRIBE . . . . . 405 FROM PLANE TO PLANE . 29
HOLLOW
  A HORSE'S HOOF PAWED ONCE THE HOLLOW FLOOR, ... 89 THE FEAR   5
  THE LOG WAS HOLLOW. THEY WERE SAWING PINE. . . . . . . 193 PAUL'S WIFE 74
  "FIRST TIME I EVER SAW A HOLLOW PINE. . . . . 193 PAUL'S WIFE 75
  THE HOLLOW LOOKED TOO SOUND AND CLEAN AND EMPTY . . . . 193 PAUL'S WIFE 83
  IT LOOKED TO HIM LIKE SOME NEW KIND OF HOLLOW . . . . . 193 PAUL'S WIFE 86
  OR THICKET, OR HOLLOW PLACE FOR THE NIGHT. . . . . . . 236 MISGIVING   8
  AND THE HOLLOW HEAD WAS A LAKE. . . . . 367 A SERIOUS STEP LIGHTLY   4
  MY HEAD FOR IT--YOU'LL FIND THE BIG ONE HOLLOW. . . . . 456 HOW HARD TO KEEP FROM 83

HOLLOW-HEADED
   WAS A HOLLOW-HEADED SNAKE. . . . . 367 A SERIOUS STEP LIGHTLY   2
HOLLYWOOD
   THE PICTURE PRIDE OF HOLLYWOOD. . . . . 307 PROVIDE, PROVIDE   . . 4
HOLOCAUST
   HAVING INVENTED A NEW HOLOCAUST, ... 399 U.S. 1946 KING'S X . . 1
HOLY
   NO HOLY WARS FOR THEM . . . . 398 NO HOLY WARS FOR THEM . T
   NO HOLY WARS FOR THEM. THE MOST THE SMALL . . . . 398 NO HOLY WARS FOR THEM . 13
   A HOLY IMPULSE TOWARDS REDISTRIBUTION. . . . . . 509 A MASQUE OF MERCY . . 419
HOME
   I HAVE COME BY THE HIGHWAY HOME, ... 30 RELUCTANCE   5
   "WARREN," SHE SAID, "HE HAS COME HOME TO DIE: . . . 38 DEATH OF THE HIRED MAN 111
   "HOME," HE MOCKED GENTLY. / "YES, WHAT ELSE BUT HOME? . 38 DEATH OF THE HIRED MAN 113
   IT ALL DEPENDS ON WHAT YOU MEAN BY HOME. . . . . 38 DEATH OF THE HIRED MAN 114
   "HOME IS THE PLACE WHERE, WHEN YOU HAVE TO GO THERE, . 38 DEATH OF THE HIRED MAN 118
   AND COME TO THINK I MUST HAVE BACK AT HOME . . . . 47 A HUNDRED COLLARS . . 65
   HOME BURIAL . . . . 51 HOME BURIAL . . . . T
   KEPT THEM AT HOME; AND IT DOES SEEM MORE HUMAN. . . 65 A SERVANT TO SERVANTS . 96
   MARCHED HIMSELF OFF THE FIELD AND HOME. ONE STAYED. . 69 THE CODE   8
   NO ONE WENT HOME THAT WAY, THE ONLY HOUSE . . . . 76 THE GENERATIONS OF MEN 73
   THIS IS A GOOD HOME: I DON'T ASK FOR BETTER. . . . 84 THE HOUSEKEEPER . . 89
   WE CAME HERE FOR A HOME FOR ME, YOU KNOW, ... 85 THE HOUSEKEEPER . . 104
   I ALWAYS HAVE FELT STRANGE WHEN WE CAME HOME . . . 89 THE FEAR   17
   OR SOMEWHERE ELSE: I WAS JUST FAR FROM HOME. . . . 101 THE WOOD-PILE . . . 9
   WHOSE COMING HOME HAS BEEN TOO LONG DEFERRED, . . . 109 THE EXPOSED NEST . 22
   IN THE HOME STRETCH . . . . 110 IN THE HOME STRETCH . T
   AMID THE WRECKAGE OF A FORMER HOME? . . . . . . 116 IN THE HOME STRETCH . 177
   AS MUCH AT HOME AS IF THEY'D ALWAYS DANCED THERE. . . 117 IN THE HOME STRETCH . 204
   IT TOOK ME. NEIGHBORS COMING HOME FROM TOWN . . . 132 THE BONFIRE . . . 84
   OF GETTING HOME AGAIN BECAUSE . . . . 139 BROWN'S DESCENT . . 55
   'BOUT OUT!" AND TOOK THE LONG WAY HOME . . . . . 140 BROWN'S DESCENT . . 75
   TO BE COMING HOME THE WAY I WAS, ... 140 THE GUM-GATHERER . 11
   CALL YOU TO ASK YOU TO INVITE ME HOME.--" . . . . 143 SNOW   27
   WHY CAN'T HE STAY AT HOME?" / "HE HAD TO PREACH." . . 145 SNOW   69
   THOSE WERE HIS WORDS, AND HE WENT HOME AND ALL . . 149 SNOW   185
   LATELY BROUGHT HOME FROM ANDOVER OR CANAAN . . . . 162 NEW HAMPSHIRE . . 117
   THE FARM I MADE MY HOME ON IN THE MOUNTAINS . . . 163 NEW HAMPSHIRE . . 150
   THIS WAS HER MOTHER'S CHILDHOOD HOME; . . . . . 181 MAPLE 56
   AND TOOK THE FANCY HOME WITH THEM TO LIVE BY. . . . 182 MAPLE 96
   MY BROTHER COULD NOT ALWAYS LEAVE AT HOME. . . . . 196 WILD GRAPES . . . 9
   AND OFFERED HER A HOME TO REST AWHILE . . . . . 201 PLACE FOR A THIRD . 60
   IF ANYONE HAD SEEN ME COMING HOME . . . . 210 PAUPER WITCH OF GRAFTON 85
   THEY HAD BEEN BROUGHT HOME FROM SOME PUBLISHER . . . 216 A FOUNTAIN, A BOTTLE . 100
   ALL THE WAY HOME I KEPT REMEMBERING . . . . . . 217 A FOUNTAIN, A BOTTLE . 132
   WHEN SHOEING HOME ACROSS THE WHITE, ... 232 LOOKING FOR SUNSET BIRD 3
   AS EVER SHE TURNED HER HOME WITH GOD . . . . . . 262 THE FLOWER BOAT . . 7
   THAT IN THE NEIGHBORHOOD OF HOME AND CHILDREN . . . 277 THE WHITE-TAILED HORNET 13
   AND COME WITH ALL HER HONORS HOME. . . . . . . 280 BLUE RIBBON AT AMESBURY 5
   AT HOME IN HER ABIDING PEN, ... 280 BLUE RIBBON AT AMESBURY 14
   GO BRING HIM HOME TO HIS PEOPLE. . . . . 288 DEPARTMENTAL . . . 28
   I HAVE IT IN ME SO MUCH NEARER HOME . . . . . . 296 DESERT PLACES . . 15
   AND TOOK THE GOLD CANDLESTICKS HOME. . . . . . . 311 THE VINDICTIVES . . 40
   TOOK HIM HOME TO HER BOWER. . . . . 313 BEARER OF EVIL TIDINGS 15
   THE LAST WET FIELDS AND DRIPPING HEDGES HOME. . . . 315 IRIS BY NIGHT . . 3
   I CAN TELL BETTER AFTER I GET HOME, ... 325 BUILD SOIL   . . . 286
   WE'RE TOO UNSEPARATE. AND GOING HOME . . . . . . 325 BUILD SOIL   . . . 291
   AND DREW HER BACKWARD HOME. . . . . 341 THE SUBVERTED FLOWER . 73
   THEN I AROSE AND SILENTLY WANDERED HOME, ... 343 QUEST OF PURPLE-FRINGED 25
   SOMEONE'S ROAD HOME FROM WORK THIS ONCE WAS, . . . 378 DIRECTIVE 30
   THEN MAKE YOURSELF AT HOME. THE ONLY FIELD . . . . 378 DIRECTIVE 39
   SETS FORTH FOR HOME AT MIDNIGHT FROM A FRIEND'S-- . . 386 THE FEAR OF MAN . . 2
   "HE LOOKS TO ME LIKE GOING HOME SUCCESSFUL, ... 405 FROM PLANE TO PLANE . 37
   AND TELL YOUR CLIENTELE AT HOME . . . . 450 OUR DOOM TO BLOOM . 6
   YOU CAME COMPANIONLESS, BUT YOU CAME HOME. . . . . 458 HOW HARD TO KEEP FROM 131
   HAS ALL GONE HOME TO BED. THE PLAY'S PLAYED OUT. . . 482 A MASQUE OF REASON . 253
   TO GO STRAIGHT HOME, WE WOULDN'T KEEP HIM, WOULD WE?-- . 501 A MASQUE OF MERCY . 208
HOMER
   WHERE HOMER BEGGED. HE'LL TELL YOU ABOUT FREEDOM. . . 459 HOW HARD TO KEEP FROM 183
   PRONOUNCE IT HOMER WITH A COCKNEY ROUGH. . . . . . 459 HOW HARD TO KEEP FROM 189
HOMES
   FAR OFF THE HOMES OF MEN, AND FARTHER STILL, . . . 17 THE VANTAGE POINT . 6
HOMESICKNESS
   AND SO WITH HOMESICKNESS IN MANY WAYS . . . . . . 446 DOES NO ONE AT ALL EVER 10
HOMESPUN
   OR HOMESPUN CHILDREN WITH CLICKING PAILS . . . . . 24 PAN WITH US . . . 14
HOMESTEAD
   OF LATE YEARS, THOUGH HE KEEPS THE OLD HOMESTEAD . . 44 A HUNDRED COLLARS . 3
HOMETOWN
   IN THEIR HOMETOWN, DAYTON. . . . . 443 KITTY HAWK   . . . 471
HOMEWARD
   HE KNEW NOT WHETHER HOMEWARD, ... 335 CARPE DIEM   . . . 3
   ACROSS THE LIGHT SNOW HOMEWARD SMELLING GREEN. . . . 349 TO A YOUNG WRETCH . 6
HOMICIDAL
   IT WILL MAKE A HOMICIDAL ROAR. . . . . 306 A TRIAL RUN . . . 4
HOMING
   WILLFUL HOMING . . . . 341 WILLFUL HOMING   . . T
HOMOGENIZE
   TO SET OUT TO HOMOGENIZE MANKIND . . . . 509 A MASQUE OF MERCY . 420
HONEST
   NO ONE OF HONEST FEELING WOULD APPROVE . . . . . 423 FOR JOHN F. KENNEDY . 43
HONESTLY
   I HONESTLY THINK . . . . 392 A WISH TO COMPLY   . 12
HONEY
   WITH MILK AND HONEY, IT IS BITTER MILK, ... 411 POD OF THE MILKWEED . 16
   ITS FLOWERS' DISTILLED HONEY IS SO SWEET . . . . . 411 POD OF THE MILKWEED . 21
HONEYSUCKLE
   FROM SPRAYS OF HONEYSUCKLE . . . . 227 TO EARTHWARD . . . 10

HONOR
    SHE WOULD REFUSE LOVE SAFE WITH WEALTH AND HONOR! . . . . 256 THE LOVELY BE CHOOSERS   6
    WHEREAS MEN PROPHETS ARE RECEIVED WITH HONOR. . . . . . 476 A MASQUE OF REASON . . 90
HONORED
    TODAY AN HONORED ONE IN NOTTINGHAM. . . . . 161 NEW HAMPSHIRE   . . . 86
HONORS
    AND COME WITH ALL HER HONORS HOME. . . . . 280 BLUE RIBBON AT AMESBURY 5
HOOD
    AND WEAR HER RED HOOD, ... 136 LAST WORD OF A BLUEBIRD 17
HOOF
    THAT WAS WELL! AND HE STAMPED A HOOF. . . . . 24 PAN WITH US 10
    A HORSE'S HOOF PAWED ONCE THE HOLLOW FLOOR, ... 89 THE FEAR 5
    AND STOOD THE AX THERE ON ITS HORSE'S HOOF, ... 188 THE AX-HELVE 95
    IN EVERY PRINT OF A HOOF A POND. . . . . 276 TWO TRAMPS IN MUD TIME 36
HOOFPRINTS
    AND THE HOOFPRINTS VANISH AWAY. . . . . 26 A LINE-STORM SONG . . 4
HOOFS
    TO DRUM ON THE FLOOR WITH SCURRYING HOOFS . . . . . 241 NEED OF BEING VERSED . 11
HOOK
    JUST HOOK THEM ON THE INSIDE OF THE PITCHER. . . . . 99 THE SELF-SEEKER . . . 174
    I PAUSED AND RESTED ON A SORT OF HOOK . . . . . . 125 AN ENCOUNTER 8
HOOP
    IT WILL COME ROLLING AFTER US LIKE A HOOP." . . . . . 454 HOW HARD TO KEEP FROM 27
HOOVER
    UNTIL HERBERT HOOVER . . . . 430 KITTY HAWK 70
HOP
    PROVE AS VAIN A HOP . . . . 439 KITTY HAWK 358
    AS THE HOP FROM GRASS . . . . 439 KITTY HAWK 359
HOPE
    AND NOTHING TO LOOK FORWARD TO WITH HOPE, ... 38 DEATH OF THE HIRED MAN 101
    "A MAN." / "SO I SHOULD HOPE. WHAT KIND OF MAN?" . . . 45 A HUNDRED COLLARS . . 25
    DID EVER YOU FEEL SO? I HOPE YOU NEVER. . . . . . . 63 A SERVANT TO SERVANTS . 10
    THE YOUNG FOLK HELD SOME HOPE OUT TO EACH OTHER . . . 74 THE GENERATIONS OF MEN 21
    FROM HOPE OF HEARING GOOD OF WHAT WAS MINE, ... 106 CHRISTMAS TREES . . . 28
    "THAT'S WHAT YOU'RE SO CONCERNED TO KNOW! YOU HOPE . . 111 IN THE HOME STRETCH . 36
    DON'T THINK BROWN EVER GAVE UP HOPE . . . . 139 BROWN'S DESCENT . . . 54
    THE HOPE OF BEING, AS WE SAY, RECEIVED. . . . . . . 160 NEW HAMPSHIRE . . . 43
    WHERE I CAME LAST WITH SOME HOPE, BUT NOT MUCH, . . . 174 THE CENSUS-TAKER . . 12
    THAN FOR HIMSELF, SO PLACED HE COULDN'T HOPE . . . . 187 THE AX-HELVE 59
    I HOPE SHE ISN'T GETTING INTO MISCHIEF." . . . . . . 191 PAUL'S WIFE 15
    I HOPE IF HE IS WHERE HE SEES ME NOW . . . . 210 PAUPER WITCH OF GRAFTON 101
    (WE MADE IT SECURE AGAINST BEING, I HOPE, ... 228 GOOD-BY AND KEEP COLD . 13
    I ONLY HOPE THAT WHEN I AM FREE, ... 236 MISGIVING 13
    FROM WHICH NO WINTER GALE CAN HOPE TO BLOW IT-- . . . 248 THE COCOON 15
    THAN THERE WAS EVER ANY HOPE, ... 264 THE BIRTHPLACE . . . 2
    TWO INSTRUMENTS OF NEARLY EQUAL HOPE, ... 269 THE BEAR 20
    (HE COULDN'T HOPE ITS HEART WOULD BREAK.) . . . . . 273 A LONE STRIKER . . . 16
    BEGIN ALL OVER TO HOPE. . . . . 285 IN TIME OF CLOUDBURST . 20
    I HOPE THEY WON'T TAKE IT FOR CENSURE. . . . . . . 294 A RECORD STRIDE . . . 20
    AND NOW PRAY TELL WHAT LURED YOU WITH FALSE HOPE . . . 356 A MOTH SEEN IN WINTER . 7
    I LET IT LIE THERE TILL I HOPE IT SLEPT. . . . . . 358 A CONSIDERABLE SPECK . 29
    SOMETHING FOR HOPE . . . . 375 SOMETHING FOR HOPE . . T
    HOPE MAY NOT NOURISH A COW OR HORSE, ... 376 SOMETHING FOR HOPE . . 23
    IT MAY NOT GIVE ME HOPE . . . . 389 ASTROMETAPHYSICAL . . 13
    US HOW BY ROCKET WE MAY HOPE TO STEER . . . . . . 395 WHY WAIT FOR SCIENCE . 6
    CAN NEVER HOPE TO WAGE A GLOBAL MISSION. . . . . . 398 NO HOLY WARS FOR THEM . 12
    A SYMBOL WAS ALL HE COULD HOPE TO CONVEY, ... 421 ONE MORE BREVITY . . 66
    PERIL OF HOPE . . . . 445 PERIL OF HOPE . . . T
    WITH ALL THIS TALK ABOUT THE HOPE OF YOUTH . . . . 462 HOW HARD TO KEEP FROM 257
    HOPE YOU'RE SATISFIED TO LAST. . . . . 469 FOUR-ROOM SHACK.... . 7
    (I HOPE YOU KNOW THE GAME CALLED TWENTY QUESTIONS.) . . 484 A MASQUE OF REASON . . 314
    INCLINED TO HOPE FOR MUCH. STILL WHAT WE NEED . . . 515 A MASQUE OF MERCY . . 567
    WHICH IS OUR GREATEST HOPE OF REST FROM WAR. . . . . 516 A MASQUE OF MERCY . . 593
HOPED
    WITH ONE WHOSE THOUGHT I HAD NOT HOPED TO REACH. . . . 23 THE TUFT OF FLOWERS . 38
    BUT CARRIES NO CRY OF WHAT IS HOPED TO BE. . . . . . 300 STRONG SAYING NOTHING . 14
    THAT A KING MIGHT HAVE HOPED TO COMPEL-- . . . . . 310 THE VINDICTIVES . . . 19
    YOU LOOK AS IF YOU EITHER HOPED OR FEARED . . . . . 488 A MASQUE OF REASON . . 411
HOPELESS
    AND HOPELESS GRIST ENOUGH IT LOOKS . . . . 140 THE GUM-GATHERER . . 16
    HOPELESS OF BEING KNOWN FOR WHAT SHE HAS BEEN, . . . 257 THE LOVELY BE CHOOSERS 41
    "YOU'RE HOPELESS," SAID THE SLAVE. / "I GUESS I AM; . . 458 HOW HARD TO KEEP FROM 144
HOPES
    SHE HOPES TO CUT OFF MIND. . . . . 260 SAND DUNES 12
    IN HOPES OF SEEING THE CALM OF HEAVEN BREAK . . . . 268 ON LOOKING UP BY CHANCE 14
    WITH HOPES OF GETTING MANKIND UNBENIGHTED. . . . . 371 THE LITERATE FARMER AND 87
HOPING
    HERE'S HOPING SHE GETS HER DRINK AND GETS OUT SAFELY." . . 77 THE GENERATIONS OF MEN 109
HOPSCOTCH
    THEY YELLING MIX TAG, HIDE-AND-SEEK, HOPSCOTCH, . . . 318 BUILD SOIL 63
HOR
    "WE CALL IT HOR: I DON'T KNOW IF THAT'S RIGHT." . . . 43 THE MOUNTAIN 91
    HOR IS THE TOWNSHIP, AND THE TOWNSHIP'S HOR-- . . . 43 THE MOUNTAIN 96
    "YOU'VE LIVED HERE ALL YOUR LIFE?" / "EVER SINCE HOR . . 44 THE MOUNTAIN 105
HORACE
    LIKE HORACE IN THE TRUE HORATIAN VEIN, ... 353 THE LESSON FOR TODAY . 93
HORATIAN
    LIKE HORACE IN THE TRUE HORATIAN VEIN, ... 353 THE LESSON FOR TODAY . 93
HORDES
    HORDES SPENT THEMSELVES TO MAKE IT WET AND COLD, . . . 239 OUR SINGING STRENGTH . 3
HORIZON
    UNLESS IN THE HORIZON RIM. . . . . 392 A CLIFF DWELLING . . 4
HORN
    COME, HOLD IT OUT. DON'T CHANGE.--A RAM'S HORN ORCHID! . . 96 THE SELF-SEEKER . . . 112
    A RAM'S HORN! WHAT WOULD I HAVE GOT, I WONDER, . . . 96 THE SELF-SEEKER . . . 113
    ANOTHER RAM'S HORN! WHERE DID YOU FIND THOSE, ... 97 THE SELF-SEEKER . . . 115
    A RAM'S HORN ORCHID SEEDPOD FOR A WOODCHUCK, ... 97 THE SELF-SEEKER . . . 126
    THOUGH THE RAM'S HORN IS SELDOM TO BE HAD . . . . . 97 THE SELF-SEEKER . . . 129

HORN (CONTINUED)
YOU DON'T TELL ME THAT WHERE YOU FOUND A RAM'S HORN . . . 97 THE SELF-SEEKER . . . 136
THAT, OVERFLOWING LIKE A HORN OF PLENTY, ... 216 A FOUNTAIN, A BOTTLE . 94
HORNET
THE WHITE-TAILED HORNET LIVES IN A BALLOON . . . . . . 277 THE WHITE-TAILED HORNET 1
THE WHITE-TAILED HORNET . . . . 277 THE WHITE-TAILED HORNET T
HORNY
AND STUMBLED THROUGH THE ROCKS WITH HORNY TREAD, ... 338 THE MOST OF IT 19
HORNY-HANDED
AND STROKED IT WITH A HORNY-HANDED KINDNESS. . . . . . 217 A FOUNTAIN, A BOTTLE . 127
HORROR
AND STILL THE HORROR CLUNG. . . . . 341 THE SUBVERTED FLOWER . 70
HORSE
I SAW BY THE WAY YOU WHIPPED UP THE HORSE. . . . . . . 91 THE FEAR 73
AND SLOWS HIS HORSE TO A MEANING WALK, ... 124 A TIME TO TALK . . . 2
WHOSE HORSE HAD PULLED HIM SHORT UP IN THE ROAD . . . . 168 NEW HAMPSHIRE . . . 289
"GO 'LONG," I SAID TO HIM, HE TO HIS HORSE. . . . . . 168 NEW HAMPSHIRE . . . 300
MORE PRACTICAL THAN PEGASUS THE HORSE . . . . 173 A STAR IN A STONEBOAT . 29
HE SAID HE HAD, BESIDES. BECAUSE A HORSE . . . . . . 209 PAUPER WITCH OF GRAFTON 65
MY LITTLE HORSE MUST THINK IT QUEER . . . . 224 STOPPING BY WOODS . . 5
THERE IS OUR WILDEST MOUNT--A HEADLESS HORSE. . . . . 267 RIDERS 9
HERE IT CAME BREASTING LIKE A HORSE IN SKIRTS. . . . . 270 THE EGG AND THE MACHINE 11
OR WEAVING LIKE A STABLED HORSE: . . . . 325 TO A THINKER . . . 7
HOPE MAY NOT NOURISH A COW OR HORSE, ... 376 SOMETHING FOR HOPE . . 23
TAKE CARE TO SELL YOUR HORSE BEFORE HE DIES . . . . . 399 THE INGENUITIES OF DEBT 4
BEHIND TOO HEAVY A HORSE . . . . 443 THE DRAFT HORSE . . . 3
THE DRAFT HORSE . . . . 443 THE DRAFT HORSE . . . T
AND TOOK OUR HORSE BY THE HEAD . . . . 444 THE DRAFT HORSE . . . 6
I PICKED YOU OUT A HORSE CALLED SAFETY THIRD, ... 457 HOW HARD TO KEEP FROM 123
HORSES
"I'LL JUST SEE HOW THE HORSES ARE." / "YES, DO," . . . 144 SNOW 33
TO PLAY----" / "YOU TEND YOUR HORSES AND COME BACK.-- . 144 SNOW 42
SIT DOWN, SIT DOWN. HOW DID YOU FIND THE HORSES?" . . . 147 SNOW 105
MORE THAN I SHALL OUT IN IT. BUT THE HORSES . . . . . 150 SNOW 209
HEARD HOW HE THRASHED THE HORSES ON A LOAD . . . . . 192 PAUL'S WIFE . . . 43
THE QUINTESSENCE OF HORSES, MEN, AND WOMEN." . . . . 455 HOW HARD TO KEEP FROM 44
JEWELS AND HORSES, WOMEN, WINE, AND SONG." . . . . . 455 HOW HARD TO KEEP FROM 62
HORSE'S
A HORSE'S HOOF PAWED ONCE THE HOLLOW FLOOR, ... 89 THE FEAR 5
AND STOOD THE AX THERE ON ITS HORSE'S HOOF, ... 188 THE AX-HELVE . . . 95
HOST
ON THE BACKS OF A SINGLE-FILE HOST, ... 312 THE VINDICTIVES . . . 72
PLEASE, MY INVOLUNTARY HOST, ... 381 AN UNSTAMPED LETTER IN 38
HOSTESSES
THAT STARTED OFF LORD GOD OF HOSTESSES. . . . . . . 480 A MASQUE OF REASON . . 181
HOSTILE
ALMOST BEFORE THE PRICK OF HOSTILE EARS, ... 302 A BIRD SINGING IN SLEEP 7
HOSTS
THE ANGEL HOSTS WITH FRESHNESS GO, ... 20 THE TRIAL BY EXISTENCE 13
KIPLING INVOKES YOU AS LORD GOD OF HOSTS. . . . . . 479 A MASQUE OF REASON . . 179
HOT
I BLAMED IT ON THE HOT SPELL WE'VE BEEN HAVING. . . . 46 A HUNDRED COLLARS . . 58
THAT HUNG IN BOTH HANDS, HOT AGAINST HER SKIRT. . . . 91 THE FEAR 63
I WANT THIS OVER WITH; I'M HOT AND TIRED." . . . . . 94 THE SELF-SEEKER . . . 50
WAS HOT ENOUGH FOR THE FIRST OF MAY, ... 123 PEA BRUSH 6
AND STIFLING HOT WITH THE ODOR OF SAP . . . . . . 123 PEA BRUSH 7
TO ANY CHANGE FROM HOT TO COLD, FROM WET . . . . . 166 NEW HAMPSHIRE . . . 235
THE VERY NATURE OF THE SOIL WAS HOT . . . . 173 A STAR IN A STONEBOAT . 21
HOTEL
HE TURNED TO THE HOTEL TO FIND A BED. . . . . . . 45 A HUNDRED COLLARS . . 19
AND CARS THAT SHOCK AND RATTLE--AND ONE HOTEL. . . . 45 A HUNDRED COLLARS . . 22
HOTTEST
AGAINST THE STOVE, THE HOTTEST DAY THAT SUMMER. . . . 72 THE CODE 98
HOUND
THAN WAS THE HOUND THAT CAME A STRANGER TO US . . . . 38 DEATH OF THE HIRED MAN 116
"YOU HEAR THOSE HOUND DOGS SING ON MOOSILAUKE? . . . . 168 NEW HAMPSHIRE . . . 293
AND HIS HOUND WORKS . . . . 360 THE RABBIT-HUNTER . . 7
HAVEN'T YOU HEARD OF THOMPSON'S "HOUND OF HEAVEN"? . . 494 A MASQUE OF MERCY . . 21
HOUR (SEE TWENTY-FOUR-HOUR)
I DREAM UPON THE OPPOSING LIGHTS OF THE HOUR, ... 14 WAITING 9
I SAID THAT MORE THAN HALF AN HOUR AGO, ... 70 THE CODE 13
AT SUCH AN HOUR OF NIGHT, AND ON FOOT TOO? . . . . . 90 THE FEAR 27
I SHOULD BE WRITING TO WITHIN THE HOUR . . . . . . 107 CHRISTMAS TREES . . 51
THERE WAS AN HOUR . . . . 118 THE TELEPHONE . . 3
WHEN THEY HAD PASSED AN HOUR OR SO BEFORE . . . . . 132 THE BONFIRE . . . 87
TO PLEASE THE BOY BY GIVING HIM THE HALF HOUR . . . . 136 "OUT, OUT--" . . . 11
"BROWN MAKES AT SUCH AN HOUR OF NIGHT! . . . . . . 138 BROWN'S DESCENT . . 33
SO BAD.--GIVE ME AN HOUR FOR IT.--HO, HO, ... 143 SNOW 21
ISN'T IT, NOW? HE'S BEEN HERE HALF AN HOUR. . . . . 145 SNOW 56
THREE HOURS TO DO FOUR MILES--A MILE AN HOUR . . . . 145 SNOW 58
WHAT? WE'VE FOUND OUT IN ONE HOUR MORE ABOUT HIM . . . 152 SNOW 252
IT WON'T BE FOR AN HOUR OR TWO." / "WELL THEN-- . . . 152 SNOW 267
THE HOUR HAD NOT YET STRUCK FOR BEING GOOD, ... 161 NEW HAMPSHIRE . . 89
WHOSE DUTY WAS AT ANY HOUR OF NIGHT . . . . . . 163 NEW HAMPSHIRE . . 140
WOULD NAME THE HOUR . . . . 217 I WILL SING YOU ONE-O . 4
BUT ONLY SO AN HOUR. . . . . 222 NOTHING GOLD CAN STAY . 4
YOU LINGER YOUR LITTLE HOUR AND ARE GONE, ... 247 ON GOING UNNOTICED . 13
YOU TOOK AS A TROPHY OF THE HOUR. . . . . 247 ON GOING UNNOTICED . 16
AN HOUR OF WINTER DAY MIGHT SEEM TOO SHORT . . . . . 254 A WINTER EDEN . . 19
THE GATE FOR HALF AN HOUR BE LOCKED, ... 273 A LONE STRIKER . . 7
IT WOULD FLUTTER AND FALL IN HALF AN HOUR . . . . . 291 ON HEART'S BEGINNING TO 11
AND LATE IN HIS LAST HOUR ALIVE, ... 311 THE VINDICTIVES . . 42
IN THE VERY HOUR . . . . 342 QUEST OF PURPLE-FRINGED 14
OF WHICH THIS NOONDAY'S THE BEGINNING HOUR. . . . . 424 FOR JOHN F. KENNEDY . 77
WHERE HAS SHE BEEN THE LAST HOUR OR SO? . . . . . 477 A MASQUE OF REASON . 109
WITH THE SUSPICION AT THIS HOUR OF NIGHT . . . . . 495 A MASQUE OF MERCY . 53
HOURGLASS
FROM HIS HOURGLASS. . . . . 429 KITTY HAWK . . . 49

HOURS
  OBTAIN SUCH GRACE OF HOURS . . . . 14 ROSE POGONIAS . . . 22
  IT WAS NO DREAM OF THE GIFT OF IDLE HOURS, ... 17 MOWING 7
  BEGIN THE HOURS OF THIS DAY SLOW. . . . . 27 OCTOBER 8
  AND HAD FOUR HOURS TO WAIT AT WOODSVILLE JUNCTION . . . 45 A HUNDRED COLLARS . . 16
  THAT HE KEPT ANY HOURS--NOT FOR HIMSELF. . . . . . . 71 THE CODE 40
  GOOD HOURS . . . . 102 GOOD HOURS . . . T
  DRESSED, BUT DISHEVELED FROM SOME HOURS OF SLEEP; . . . 143 SNOW 4
  THREE HOURS TO HERE! BUT THAT WAS ALL UPHILL; . . . . 143 SNOW 22
  THREE HOURS TO DO FOUR MILES--A MILE AN HOUR . . . . 145 SNOW 58
  "SHE KNEW HE HAD, POOR THING, TWO HOURS AGO." . . . . 153 SNOW 278
  THE HOURS OF DAYLIGHT GATHER ATMOSPHERE. . . . . . . 246 ATMOSPHERE 6
  NO ONE FOR HOURS HAS SET A FOOT OUTDOORS . . . . . . 248 THE COCOON . . . 9
  THE AGES RANGING ALL THE WAY FROM HOURS . . . . . . 355 THE LESSON FOR TODAY . 138
HOURS'
  AFTER HOURS' OVERLOOKING FROM THE CLIFFS . . . . . . 174 THE CENSUS-TAKER . . 13
HOUSE
  I DWELL IN A LONELY HOUSE I KNOW . . . . 5 GHOST HOUSE . . . 1
  GHOST HOUSE . . . . 5 GHOST HOUSE . . . T
  BY HARBORING WOE IN THE BRIDAL HOUSE, ... 8 LOVE AND A QUESTION . 31
  ACROSS THE FIELDS BEHIND THE HOUSE . . . . 18 GOING FOR WATER . . 3
  "HE DIDN'T SAY. I DRAGGED HIM TO THE HOUSE, ... 35 DEATH OF THE HIRED MAN 40
  RAKING THE DOORYARD, WORKING NEAR THE HOUSE. . . . . 49 A HUNDRED COLLARS . . 128
  SHE'S GOT SO SHE TURNS IN AT EVERY HOUSE . . . . . . 49 A HUNDRED COLLARS . . 142
  SOMEWHERE OUT OF THIS HOUSE. HOW CAN I MAKE YOU----" . . 55 HOME BURIAL . . . 113
  HER SONS WON'T SELL THE HOUSE OR THE THINGS IN IT. . . 55 THE BLACK COTTAGE . . 16
  AND ALL OUR STORMS COME UP TOWARD THE HOUSE, ... 63 A SERVANT TO SERVANTS . 24
  TO HAVE INSIDE THE HOUSE WITH DOORS UNLOCKED. . . . . 65 A SERVANT TO SERVANTS . 84
  HE HAD GONE TO THE HOUSE SO'S NOT TO MEET ME. . . . . 73 THE CODE 105
  NO ONE WENT HOME THAT WAY, THE ONLY HOUSE . . . . . 76 THE GENERATIONS OF MEN 73
  TO COME TO HIS HOUSE WHEN HE'S GONE TO YOURS. . . . . 81 THE HOUSEKEEPER . . 15
  TWO OF YOU OUT WILL LEAVE AN EMPTY HOUSE." . . . . . 82 THE HOUSEKEEPER . . 42
  AND THREW THEIR LURCHING SHADOWS ON A HOUSE . . . . . 89 THE FEAR 3
  TO THE DARK HOUSE AFTER SO LONG AN ABSENCE, ... 89 THE FEAR 18
  "WHAT ARE YOU DOING ROUND THIS HOUSE AT NIGHT?" . . . 91 THE FEAR 70
  OF HEAVY FOOTSTEPS IN THE OLD FRAME HOUSE, ... 96 THE SELF-SEEKER . . 93
  AND LEAVE THE SLOPE BEHIND THE HOUSE ALL BARE, ... 106 CHRISTMAS TREES . . 18
  ONE AGED MAN--ONE MAN--CAN'T KEEP A HOUSE, ... 108 OLD MAN'S WINTER NIGHT 26
  FOR EVERY ROOM A HOUSE HAS--PARLOR, BEDROOM, ... 110 IN THE HOME STRETCH . 8
  OF SUCH A LITTLE HOUSE. ONCE LEFT ALONE, ... 111 IN THE HOME STRETCH . 40
  THE HOUSE WAS FULL OF TRAMPING, AND THE DARK, ... 113 IN THE HOME STRETCH . 82
  AND PUT EACH OTHER BODILY OUT OF THE HOUSE. . . . . . 114 IN THE HOME STRETCH . 110
  THE FIRST NIGHT AFTER GUESTS HAVE GONE, THE HOUSE . . . 115 IN THE HOME STRETCH . 132
  TO EMPTY ONE HOUSE OF ALL HOUSEHOLD GOODS . . . . . 116 IN THE HOME STRETCH . 160
  WHEN THE HOUSE WASN'T LIVED IN? I'VE BEEN LOOKING: . . 117 IN THE HOME STRETCH . 192
  BEFORE WE SET OURSELVES TO RIGHT THE HOUSE, ... 117 IN THE HOME STRETCH . 194
  CARE WHEN THE BIRDS COME ROUND THE HOUSE . . . . . . 126 LONELINESS . . . 3
  TO THE LONELY HOUSE FROM FAR AWAY, ... 127 HOUSE FEAR . . . 3
  THEY LEARNED TO LEAVE THE HOUSE DOOR WIDE . . . . . 127 HOUSE FEAR . . . 9
  HOUSE FEAR . . . . 127 HOUSE FEAR . . . T
  AND WORK WAS LITTLE IN THE HOUSE, ... 128 THE IMPULSE . . . 5
  AND HE ASKED AT HER MOTHER'S HOUSE . . . . 129 THE IMPULSE . . . 23
  WHEN WE LOCKED UP THE HOUSE AT NIGHT, ... 135 LOCKED OUT . . . 1
  BETWEEN THE HOUSE AND BARN THE GALE . . . . 137 BROWN'S DESCENT . . 9
  OF WIND THAT CAUGHT AGAINST THE HOUSE A MOMENT, . . . 143 SNOW 2
  "YOU ONLY SAY SO. NOT ANOTHER HOUSE . . . . 145 SNOW 73
  AND FOUND ME BANKING UP THE HOUSE WITH SNOW. . . . . 149 SNOW 177
  THIS HOUSE IS FROZEN BRITTLE, ALL EXCEPT . . . . . . 150 SNOW 202
  "WHY DID I EVER LET HIM LEAVE THIS HOUSE!" . . . . . 153 SNOW 280
  IF HE THINKS HE IS GOING TO MAKE OUR HOUSE . . . . . 155 SNOW 341
  A HALFWAY COFFEE HOUSE 'TWIXT TOWN AND NOWHERE----" . . 155 SNOW 342
  HIS HOUSE AMONG THE LOCAL SHEDS AND SHANTIES . . . . 160 NEW HAMPSHIRE . . 52
  TO A SLAB-BUILT, BLACK-PAPER-COVERED HOUSE . . . . . 174 THE CENSUS-TAKER . . 2
  NONE IN THE HUNDRED MILES, NONE IN THE HOUSE, ... 174 THE CENSUS-TAKER . . 11
  ABOUT THE HOUSE--ABOUT THE PEOPLE NOT THERE. . . . . 175 THE CENSUS-TAKER . . 49
  THIS HOUSE IN ONE YEAR FALLEN TO DECAY . . . . . . 176 THE CENSUS-TAKER . . 50
  HE BURNED HIS HOUSE DOWN FOR THE FIRE INSURANCE . . . 177 THE STAR-SPLITTER . . 16
  HE BURNED HIS HOUSE DOWN FOR THE FIRE INSURANCE . . . 177 THE STAR-SPLITTER . . 30
  WHEN HE DID WHAT HE DID AND BURNED HIS HOUSE DOWN. . . 177 THE STAR-SPLITTER . . 39
  SOME SYMPATHY WAS WASTED ON THE HOUSE, ... 178 THE STAR-SPLITTER . . 59
  BUT A HOUSE ISN'T SENTIENT; THE HOUSE . . . . . . 178 THE STAR-SPLITTER . . 61
  OUT OF A HOUSE AND SO OUT OF A FARM . . . . 178 THE STAR-SPLITTER . . 66
  THE HOUSE ONE STORY HIGH IN FRONT, THREE STORIES . . . 181 MAPLE 57
  (THE HOUSE ONE STORY HIGH IN FRONT, THREE STORIES . . . 182 MAPLE 98
  "COME ON MY HOUSE AND I PUT YOU ONE IN . . . . . . 186 THE AX-HELVE . . . 29
  TO SEE FOR ONCE THE INSIDE OF HIS HOUSE. . . . . . . 188 THE AX-HELVE . . . 89
  THEY SAW PAUL AND HIS CREATURE KEEPING HOUSE. . . . . 195 PAUL'S WIFE . . . 128
  OFF FROM THE HOUSE AS FAR AS WE COULD KEEP . . . . . 210 PAUPER WITCH OF GRAFTON 90
  PERHAPS, TO WHERE IT ENDED AT A HOUSE . . . . 215 A FOUNTAIN, A BOTTLE . 68
  I NEVER SAW SO GOOD A HOUSE DESERTED. . . . . 215 A FOUNTAIN, A BOTTLE . 71
  THROUGH A HOUSE STRIPPED OF EVERYTHING . . . . . . 216 A FOUNTAIN, A BOTTLE . 90
  HIS HOUSE IS IN THE VILLAGE, THOUGH; . . . . 224 STOPPING BY WOODS . . 2
  ALL WINTER, CUT OFF BY A HILL FROM THE HOUSE. . . . . 228 GOOD-BY AND KEEP COLD . 5
  THAT HELD THE HOUSE AS IN AN ELBOW-CROOK? . . . . . 231 A BROOK IN THE CITY . 4
  BUILDER, IN BUILDING THE LITTLE HOUSE, ... 232 THE KITCHEN CHIMNEY . 1
  BUT I NEVER HEARD OF A HOUSE THAT THROVE . . . . . . 232 THE KITCHEN CHIMNEY . 10
  THE HOUSE HAD GONE TO BRING AGAIN . . . . 241 NEED OF BEING VERSED . 1
  NOW THE CHIMNEY WAS ALL OF THE HOUSE THAT STOOD, . . . 241 NEED OF BEING VERSED . 3
  THAT WOULD HAVE JOINED THE HOUSE IN FLAME . . . . . 241 NEED OF BEING VERSED . 6
  IS ALL THE SMOKE FROM ONE POOR HOUSE ALONE, ... 248 THE COCOON . . . 5
  AND NOT SING BY MY HOUSE ALL DAY; . . . . 250 A MINOR BIRD . . . 2
  WORD I WAS IN THE HOUSE ALONE . . . . 251 BEREFT 13
  AND HERE IN THE ANGLE OF HOUSE AND BARN . . . . . . 262 THE FLOWER BOAT . . 3
  THERE WAS AN OLD, OLD HOUSE RENEWED WITH PAINT, . . . 263 THE INVESTMENT . . 3
  THAT'S WHEN I WENT AS VISITOR TO HIS HOUSE. . . . . . 278 THE WHITE-TAILED HORNET 22
  AS VISITOR AT MY HOUSE HE IS BETTER. . . . . 278 THE WHITE-TAILED HORNET 23
  THE LITTLE OLD HOUSE WAS OUT WITH A LITTLE NEW SHED . . 286 A ROADSIDE STAND . . 1
  WHERE'S THIS BARN'S HOUSE? IT NEVER HAD A HOUSE, . . . 289 OLD BARN AT THE BOTTOM 1

HOUSE (CONTINUED)
    THE OTHER I WET AT THE CLIFF HOUSE . . . . 294 A RECORD STRIDE . . .   15
    IS A THREAT TO THE HOUSE. BUT THE HOUSE HAS LONG BEEN TRIED. 305 THERE ARE ROUGHLY ZONES   3
    WE WENT FROM HOUSE TO WOOD . . . . 333 HAPPINESS MAKES UP . .   23
    IT IS GETTING DARK AND TIME HE DREW TO A HOUSE, ... 341 WILLFUL HOMING . . .   1
    BUT THE BLIZZARD BLINDS HIM TO ANY HOUSE AHEAD. . . . 341 WILLFUL HOMING . . .   2
    I CAME TO BUT ONE HOUSE. . . . . 366 NOT OF SCHOOL AGE . .   3
    AT THE ONE HOUSE A CHILD WAS OUT . . . . 366 NOT OF SCHOOL AGE . .   5
    AND THERE MIGHT BE A HOUSE WE COULD BUY . . . . . . 367 A SERIOUS STEP LIGHTLY   7
    AND KNOCKED AT THE DOOR OF A HOUSE WE FOUND, ... 367 A SERIOUS STEP LIGHTLY   11
    A MIGHTY FARMER FLUNG THE HOUSE DOOR WIDE, ... 368 THE LITERATE FARMER AND   5
    THERE IS A HOUSE THAT IS NO MORE A HOUSE . . . . . . 377 DIRECTIVE   5
    FIRST THERE'S THE CHILDREN'S HOUSE OF MAKE-BELIEVE, . . 378 DIRECTIVE   41
    THEN FOR THE HOUSE THAT IS NO MORE A HOUSE, ... 378 DIRECTIVE   45
    THIS WAS NO PLAYHOUSE BUT A HOUSE IN EARNEST. . . . . 378 DIRECTIVE   48
    A BROOK THAT WAS THE WATER OF THE HOUSE, ... 378 DIRECTIVE   50
    I WOULD BUILD MY HOUSE OF CRYSTAL, ... 384 IN THE LONG NIGHT . .   1
    WAS BUT THE STEEPLE ON OUR HOUSE OF LIFE . . . . . . 386 A STEEPLE ON THE HOUSE   2
    THAT MADE OUR HOUSE OF LIFE A HOUSE OF WORSHIP? . . . 386 A STEEPLE ON THE HOUSE   3
    A STEEPLE ON THE HOUSE . . . . 386 A STEEPLE ON THE HOUSE   T
    I DON'T BELIEVE THE SLEEPERS IN THIS HOUSE . . . . . 413 A CABIN IN THE CLEARING   1
    TO PUSH THE WOODS BACK FROM AROUND THE HOUSE . . . . 414 A CABIN IN THE CLEARING   3
    SHOULD BE TAKEN OUTSIDE A HOUSE AND BOOK. . . . . . 419 ONE MORE BREVITY . .   2
    LOUD TALK IN THE OVERLIGHTED HOUSE . . . . 444 ENDS   1
HOUSED
    EVER TO HAVE HOUSED BIRDS OR BEASTS OR BEES. . . . . 193 PAUL'S WIFE   84
HOUSEFUL
    WITH A HOUSEFUL OF HUNGRY MEN TO FEED . . . . 62 A SERVANT TO SERVANTS .   5
HOUSEHOLD
    TO EMPTY ONE HOUSE OF ALL HOUSEHOLD GOODS . . . . . 116 IN THE HOME STRETCH . 160
HOUSEKEEPER
    THE HOUSEKEEPER . . . . 81 THE HOUSEKEEPER . . .   T
HOUSEKEEPING
    HOUSEKEEPING FOR THE NEXT MAN OUT OF WEDLOCK. . . . . 201 PLACE FOR A THIRD . .   62
HOUSES
    AND A FEW HOUSES SPRINKLED ROUND THE FOOT, ... 43 THE MOUNTAIN   97
    THAT NOW NOT ALL THE HOUSES LEFT IN TOWN . . . . . . 73 THE GENERATIONS OF MEN   11
    WHERE HOUSES ALL ARE CHURCHES AND HAVE SPIRES. . . . 106 CHRISTMAS TREES . .   14
    FILLED ME WITH NO LESS SORROW THAN THE HOUSES . . . . 176 THE CENSUS-TAKER . .   51
    AND THERE A CLUMP OF HOUSES WITH A CHURCH. . . . . . 226 THE ONSET   23
    CAME OVER HOUSES FROM ANOTHER STREET, ... 255 ACQUAINTED WITH NIGHT .   9
    WHO SLEEP IN HOUSES OF THEIR OWN, THOUGH MORTGAGED. . . 290 OLD BARN AT THE BOTTOM   31
HOUSEWORK
    ESTELLE TO DO THE HOUSEWORK FROM THE BOARD . . . . . 85 THE HOUSEKEEPER . . . 105
    SHE SEEMS TO HAVE THE HOUSEWORK, AND BESIDES, ... 85 THE HOUSEKEEPER . . . 107
HOVERED
    THEY HOVERED FOR A MOMENT NEAR DISCOVERY, ... 184 MAPLE 153
HOW---NOT INDEXED
HOWDAH
    THE WORLD AS WE KNOW IS AN ELEPHANT'S HOWDAH; . . . . 379 TOO ANXIOUS FOR RIVERS   14
HOWEVER
    HOWEVER IT IS IN SOME OTHER WORLD . . . . 26 IN HARDWOOD GROVES . .   11
    SPEAKING OF WHO'S AFRAID OF WHO, HOWEVER, ... 47 A HUNDRED COLLARS . .   81
    HE MUST HAVE GIVEN THE HAND. HOWEVER IT WAS, ... 136 "OUT,OUT--" . . .   17
    HOWEVER UNINNOCENT THEY MAY HAVE BEEN . . . . 161 NEW HAMPSHIRE . . .   80
    HOWEVER NATURAL? GIVE YOU YOUR BOOKS! . . . . 215 A FOUNTAIN, A BOTTLE   59
    HOWEVER FAR YOU MUST GO FOR BRICKS. . . . . 232 THE KITCHEN CHIMNEY .   5
    BUT NEGLECTED, HOWEVER LIGHTLY, TO LACE . . . . . . 265 THE DOOR IN THE DARK .   3
    WE SOUGHT HOWEVER CRUDELY TO DEFEAT . . . . 446 DOES NO ONE AT ALL EVER   11
HOWL
    SHE LET OUT A HOWL OF RAGE . . . . 463 LINES IN DEJECTION .   22
HUCKLEBERRY
    HE STOOPED AND STRUCK A LITTLE HUCKLEBERRY . . . . . 278 THE WHITE-TAILED HORNET   38
    THE HUCKLEBERRY ROLLED HIM ON HIS HEAD. . . . . . . 278 THE WHITE-TAILED HORNET   41
    NAILHEAD WITH FLY AND FLY WITH HUCKLEBERRY: . . . . 279 THE WHITE-TAILED HORNET   46
HUDDLED
    AND THE DEAD LEAVES LIE HUDDLED AND STILL, ... 30 RELUCTANCE   13
    HUDDLED AGAINST THE BARN DOOR FAST ASLEEP, ... 35 DEATH OF THE HIRED MAN   35
HUDSON'S
    THERE WASN'T ALWAYS HUDSON'S BAY . . . . 210 AN EMPTY THREAT . . .   3
    ABOUT WHERE HENRY HUDSON'S GONE, ... 211 AN EMPTY THREAT . . .   16
    SOME TO GO FURTHER NORTH TO HUDSON'S BAY, ... 239 OUR SINGING STRENGTH .   22
HUE
    WELL, THEY REMIND ME OF THE HUE AND CRY . . . . . . 168 NEW HAMPSHIRE . . . 294
    THAT VARIED IN THEIR HUE FROM RED TO GREEN. . . . . 178 THE STAR-SPLITTER . .   73
    WHEN HEAVEN PRESENTS IN SHEETS THE SOLID HUE? . . . . 220 FRAGMENTARY BLUE . .   4
    HER HARDEST HUE TO HOLD. . . . . 222 NOTHING GOLD CAN STAY .   2
HUGE
    SOME OF THEM MIGHTY HUGE, SOME MIGHTY TINY, ... 425 ACCIDENTALLY ON PURPOSE   3
HUGGED
    AND HUGGED HIMSELF FOR ALL HIS UNIVERSE. . . . . . . 396 ANY SIZE WE PLEASE .   14
HUGGER-MUGGER
    OF HEAVENLY STARS WITH HUGGER-MUGGER FARMING. . . . . 176 THE STAR-SPLITTER . .   14
    TILL HAVING FAILED AT HUGGER-MUGGER FARMING . . . . 177 THE STAR-SPLITTER . .   15
HUGHES
    HUGHES 2. AND EVERYBODY TO THE SADDEST . . . . . . 165 NEW HAMPSHIRE . . . 199
HUH
    "HUH, THAT OLD BATHTUB, WHAT IS THAT TO SEE? . . . . 213 A FOUNTAIN, A BOTTLE .   15
HULKING
    OUT OF THE WOODS TWO HULKING TRAMPS . . . . 276 TWO TRAMPS IN MUD TIME   49
HULL
    A SHIP KEEPS RAISING ITS HULL; . . . . 301 NEITHER OUT FAR NOR IN   6
HUMAN
    TELL ME ABOUT IT IF IT'S SOMETHING HUMAN. . . . . . 53 HOME BURIAL   58
    KEPT THEM AT HOME; AND IT DOES SEEM MORE HUMAN. . . . 65 A SERVANT TO SERVANTS .   96
    OR JUST SOME HUMAN SLEEP. . . . . 69 AFTER APPLE-PICKING .   42
    BEFORE IT STAINED A SINGLE HUMAN BREAST. . . . . . . 126 RANGE-FINDING . . .   3
    A WEAPON IN OUR HUMAN FIGHT," HE SAID. . . . . 177 THE STAR-SPLITTER . .   24

HUMAN (CONTINUED)
    A FRENCHMAN COULDN'T GET HIS HUMAN RATING! . . . . . . 186 THE AX-HELVE 45
    REDUCE THE BIRTHS OF THE HUMAN RACE, ... 263 THE TIMES TABLE 19
    THAT'S WHERE THE HUMAN STILL CAME IN. . . . . 273 A LONE STRIKER 27
    TO ERR IS HUMAN, NOT TO, ANIMAL. . . . . 279 THE WHITE-TAILED HORNET 52
    NO HUMAN SPECTER AT THE FEAST . . . . 281 BLUE RIBBON AT AMESBURY 37
    A FLICKERING, HUMAN PATHETIC LIGHT, ... 291 ON HEART'S BEGINNING TO   7
    BETWEEN STARS--ON STARS WHERE NO HUMAN RACE IS. . . . . 296 DESERT PLACES 14
    HUMAN BEINGS LOVE IT--LOVE IT. . . . . 304 CLEAR AND COLDER . . . 22
    THIS BIPLANE IS THE SHAPE OF HUMAN FLIGHT. . . . . . 308 THE WRIGHTS' BIPLANE . .   1
    AND CRACKED BONES, HUMAN AND BEAST, ... 312 THE VINDICTIVES 59
    DIVINE LOVE, HUMAN LOVE, PARENTAL LOVE, ... 318 BUILD SOIL 87
    THE WORLD'S ONE GLOBE, HUMAN SOCIETY . . . . 322 BUILD SOIL 194
    INSTEAD OF PROVING HUMAN WHEN IT NEARED . . . . 338 THE MOST OF IT 14
    INCLUDING HUMAN NATURE, IN PEACE AND WAR, ... 349 OUR HOLD ON THE PLANET 14
    WE NEVER COULD RECOVER HUMAN SHAPE, ... 351 THE LESSON FOR TODAY . 39
    THE GROUNDWORK OF ALL FAITH IS HUMAN WOE. . . . . . . 352 THE LESSON FOR TODAY . 58
    WE BOTH ARE THE BELITTLED HUMAN RACE, ... 353 THE LESSON FOR TODAY . 77
    TO ANY ONE TIME, PLACE, OR. HUMAN KIND. . . . . 353 THE LESSON FOR TODAY . 105
    AND WHAT I PITY IN YOU IS SOMETHING HUMAN, ... 356 A MOTH SEEN IN WINTER   14
    (BUT WHAT A HUMAN RACE THE WHITE HAS BEEN!) . . . . . 369 THE LITERATE FARMER AND 52
    THAT IS THE SOURCE PERHAPS OF HUMAN HATE . . . . . . 371 THE LITERATE FARMER AND 108
    COMING ON SUCH AN ANCIENT HUMAN TRACE . . . . 382 TO AN ANCIENT   7
    SEEMS AS EXPRESSIVE OF THE HUMAN RACE . . . . 382 TO AN ANCIENT   8
    TO SUSPECT THE HUMAN TRAIT . . . . 387 THE COURAGE TO BE NEW . 10
    WAS NOT THE BASEST HUMAN . . . . 387 THE COURAGE TO BE NEW . 11
    THE APOGEE OF HUMAN BLIND CONCEIT. . . . . 394 HAEC FABULA DOCET . . .   4
    THAT HUMAN HISTORY SHOULD NOT BE SHORTENED. . . . . . 397 THE PLANNERS 14
    A FRESH START FOR THE HUMAN RACE. . . . . 417 AMERICA IS HARD TO SEE 30
    ON OUR HUMAN PART . . . . 436 KITTY HAWK 255
    IS TOO HARD ON THE HUMAN RACE. . . . . 453 A-WISHING WELL 70
    WITH THE HEADLONG HUMAN RACE. . . . . 465 SOME SCIENCE FICTION .   4
    FROM MORAL BONDAGE TO THE HUMAN RACE. . . . . 475 A MASQUE OF REASON . . 70
    'TWAS HUMAN OF YOU. I EXPECTED MORE . . . . 485 A MASQUE OF REASON . . 331
    OF WHAT I VALUED MOST IN HUMAN NATURE. . . . . 485 A MASQUE OF REASON . . 350
    IN NATURE WOULD WIPE OUT ALL HUMAN FAULT. . . . . . . 502 A MASQUE OF MERCY . . 232
    HE MAY BE GOD, BUT ME, I'M ONLY HUMAN: . . . . 505 A MASQUE OF MERCY . . 304
HUMANITY
    AND VINDICATE THE STATE'S HUMANITY. . . . . 159 NEW HAMPSHIRE 21
    FOR ALL HUMANITY A COMPLETE REST . . . . 405 FROM PLANE TO PLANE . 30
HUMBLE
    SOME HUMBLE WAY TO SAVE HIS SELF-RESPECT. . . . . . . 36 DEATH OF THE HIRED MAN 50
HUMBLED
    AND FALLEN AND BEEN HUMBLED . . . . 389 ASTROMETAPHYSICAL . .   7
HUMBLEST
    MAKE HER AMONG THE HUMBLEST EVEN . . . . 257 THE LOVELY BE CHOOSERS 39
HUMOR
    OUR WORSHIP, HUMOR, CONSCIENTIOUSNESS . . . . 279 THE WHITE-TAILED HORNET 56
    HUMOR HER THERE OR SHE WILL BE CONFIRMED . . . . . . 479 A MASQUE OF REASON . . 176
HUMPED
    FROM A HUMPED BODY NIGH AS BIG'S A BISCUIT. . . . . . . 70 THE CODE 35
HUNDRED
    A HUNDRED MILES AWAY. . . . . 11 WIND AND WINDOW FLOWER 28
    WITH DEPTHS BEHIND HIM SHEER A HUNDRED FEET-- . . . . 42 THE MOUNTAIN 60
    A HUNDRED COLLARS . . . . 44 A HUNDRED COLLARS . .   T
    MORE THAN A HUNDRED COLLARS, SIZE FOURTEEN. . . . . . 47 A HUNDRED COLLARS . . 66
    FIVE HUNDRED DOLLARS FOR THE PAIR, YOU KNOW." . . . . 93 THE SELF-SEEKER . . .   4
    HAVE YOU AGREED TO ANY PRICE?" / "FIVE HUNDRED. . . . . 94 THE SELF-SEEKER . . . 58
    FIVE HUNDRED--FIVE--FIVE! ONE, TWO, THREE, FOUR,FIVE. . . 94 THE SELF-SEEKER . . . 59
    NO, THE FIVE HUNDRED WAS THE SUM THEY NAMED . . . . . 95 THE SELF-SEEKER . . . 73
    "FIVE HUNDRED DOLLARS!" / "WHAT WOULD YOU THINK RIGHT?" . 99 THE SELF-SEEKER . . . 198
    THEY'D BEEN THERE THEN A HUNDRED YEARS OR MORE. . . . 161 NEW HAMPSHIRE 82
    LAUGHS AT FRANCONIA (SEVEN HUNDRED), AND . . . . . 165 NEW HAMPSHIRE 204
    A HUNDRED SQUARE MILES ROUND IT IN THE MOUNTAINS: . . . 174 THE CENSUS-TAKER . . .   5
    NONE IN THE HUNDRED MILES, NONE IN THE HOUSE, ... 174 THE CENSUS-TAKER . . . 11
    HE GOT A GOOD GLASS FOR SIX HUNDRED DOLLARS. . . . . 178 THE STAR-SPLITTER . . 74
    THE HUNDRED YEARS THE TREE MUST HAVE BEEN GROWING. . . 194 PAUL'S WIFE 94
    SHE WAS OUR LAND MORE THAN A HUNDRED YEARS . . . . . 348 THE GIFT OUTRIGHT . .   2
    ONE MAN HAD LIVED ONE HUNDRED YEARS AND EIGHT. . . . . 355 THE LESSON FOR TODAY . 140
    IT IS TURNING THREE HUNDRED YEARS . . . . 367 A SERIOUS STEP LIGHTLY 13
    WE'LL MAKE IT THREE HUNDRED MORE . . . . 367 A SERIOUS STEP LIGHTLY 16
    A HUNDRED THOUSAND DAYS . . . . 367 A SERIOUS STEP LIGHTLY 21
    A CYCLE WE'LL SAY OF A HUNDRED YEARS. . . . . 376 SOMETHING FOR HOPE . . 17
    IN OUR THREE HUNDRED DAYS AND SIXTY-FIVE . . . . . . 412 POD OF THE MILKWEED . 32
    SHE WAS OUR LAND MORE THAN A HUNDRED YEARS . . . . . 424 THE GIFT OUTRIGHT . .   2
    A LARGER ONE HE ASKED FIVE HUNDRED FOR. . . . . . . 455 HOW HARD TO KEEP FROM 68
    AS WELL AS OF YOUR HUNDRED OTHER THINGS. . . . . . . 456 HOW HARD TO KEEP FROM 99
HUNDREDS
    ITS LIFE OF HUNDREDS OF YEARS HAS ENDED . . . . . . 253 THE THATCH 33
HUNDREDWEIGHT
    EACH LINK OF A HUNDREDWEIGHT, ... 312 THE VINDICTIVES 64
HUNG
    HUNG OVER HER IN TUNE, ... 10 WIND AND WINDOW FLOWER   8
    OF MY REGRET HUNG NOT ON ALL THE LAND, ... 28 MY BUTTERFLY 19
    THAT HUNG IN BOTH HANDS, HOT AGAINST HER SKIRT. . . . . 91 THE FEAR 63
    AND NOT ONE BUT HUNG LIMP, NOT ONE WAS LEFT . . . . . 122 BIRCHES 31
    THE STRICKEN FLOWER BENT DOUBLE AND SO HUNG. . . . . 126 RANGE-FINDING   4
    HUNG BABIES OUT ON BRANCHES BY THE HANDS . . . . . 197 WILD GRAPES 51
    MY WINDOW CURTAIN HUNG OVER THE SILL TO WET; . . . . 236 VALLEY'S SINGING DAY . 17
    A HAND HUNG LIKE A PAW, ... 340 THE SUBVERTED FLOWER . 42
    WILL LEAVE THEIR TATTERS HUNG ON BARB AND THORN.) . . . 379 DIRECTIVE 54
HUNGER
    WITH THIRST ON HUNGER TO THE POINT OF LUST. . . . . . 411 POD OF THE MILKWEED . 26
HUNGRY (SEE REASON-HUNGRY)
    WITH A HOUSEFUL OF HUNGRY MEN TO FEED . . . . 62 A SERVANT TO SERVANTS .   5
    FROM COOKING MEALS FOR HUNGRY HIRED MEN . . . . . . 64 A SERVANT TO SERVANTS . 50
    BUT STANDING OUTDOORS HUNGRY, IN THE COLD, ... 189 THE GRINDSTONE 17

HUNT
AND HAVE TO HUNT FOR IN SWEET FERN AND HARDHACK; . . . . 197 WILD GRAPES 33
AND IF AFTER THE HUNT GOES PAST . . . . 282 A DRUMLIN WOODCHUCK . 21
HUNTED
THOUGH I KNEW WHAT I HUNTED WAS NO TRUE GOD. . . . . . 24 THE DEMIURGE'S LAUGH . 3
HUNTED AND TORTURED AND RAGED. . . . . 311 THE VINDICTIVES . . . 48
FOR THE GAME HE HUNTED . . . . 427 VERSION 7
HUNTER (SEE RABBIT-HUNTER)
THE HUNTER SCUFFLING LEAVES GOES BY AT DUSK, ... 289 OLD BARN AT THE BOTTOM 3
THE HUNTER LURKS . . . . 360 THE RABBIT-HUNTER . . 2
HUNTERS
THE WORK OF HUNTERS IS ANOTHER THING: . . . . . . 33 MENDING WALL 5
BOYS AND BAD HUNTERS HAD KNOWN WHAT TO DO . . . . . 216 A FOUNTAIN, A BOTTLE . 102
HUNTER'S
THE HARVEST MOON AND THEN THE HUNTER'S MOON. . . . . 289 OLD BARN AT THE BOTTOM 5
HUNTING (SEE DEER-HUNTING, FORTUNE-HUNTING)
AS TAKE HIS GUN--ROD--TO GO HUNTING--FISHING. . . . . 349 TO A YOUNG WRETCH . . 2
HUNTINGTON
BACK THERE IN 1953 WITH THE HUNTINGTON CAIRNSES . . . 428 KITTY HAWK 0
HURL
THE VOICE SAID, "HURL HER DOWN!" . . . . 255 THE LOVELY BE CHOOSERS 1
HURLED
HE IS THAT FALLEN LANCE THAT LIES AS HURLED, ... 261 A SOLDIER 1
BEFORE THEY WERE HURLED FROM THE SLAVER'S DECK. . . . 346 DISCOVERY OF MADEIRAS . 82
HURRICANE
TO RIDE THE WHIRLWIND AND THE HURRICANE. . . . . . 423 FOR JOHN F. KENNEDY . 48
LIKE A HURRICANE. . . . . 434 KITTY HAWK . . . 211
HURRIED
A LITTLE LONGER. I MUSTN'T FEEL TOO HURRIED, ... 78 THE GENERATIONS OF MEN 146
SHE HURRIED HER DECISION TO BE READY . . . . 201 PLACE FOR A THIRD . . 71
ONE CROSSING WITH HURRIED TREAD . . . . 288 DEPARTMENTAL 14
HURRY
"I'D NOT BE IN A HURRY TO SAY THAT." . . . . . . 39 DEATH OF THE HIRED MAN 154
AND THIS BILL." / "WHAT'S THE HURRY? HE'LL UNHITCH." . 88 THE HOUSEKEEPER . . . 199
WE STAND HERE DREAMING. HURRY! CALL THEM BACK!" . . 113 IN THE HOME STRETCH . 77
"I SHOULDN'T WANT TO HURRY YOU, MESERVE, ... 148 SNOW 153
THAN FLOWERS WILL SHOW FOR DAYS UNLESS THEY HURRY. . . 225 BLUE-BUTTERFLY DAY . . 4
CAN SCANT OR HURRY HER THE LEAST. . . . . 281 BLUE RIBBON AT AMESBURY 38
WHY HURRY TO TELL BELSHAZZAR . . . . 314 BEARER OF EVIL TIDINGS 43
HURRYING
HURRYING LOW ABOVE THE GROVE, SOME WAIF . . . . . 249 ACCEPTANCE 9
HURT
"I CAN'T THINK SI EVER HURT ANYONE." . . . . . . 39 DEATH OF THE HIRED MAN 146
"NO, BUT HE HURT MY HEART THE WAY HE LAY . . . . . 39 DEATH OF THE HIRED MAN 147
TO BURY HIM HAD HURT HIS DIGNITY. . . . . 72 THE CODE 104
STRUNG ON YOUR HAIR, WON'T HURT YOUR SUMMER LOOKS. . . 77 THE GENERATIONS OF MEN 123
WE WOULDN'T HURT A HEN! YOU OUGHT TO SEE US . . . . 85 THE HOUSEKEEPER . . . 125
BEFORE HE GOES, BECAUSE I HURT MYSELF, ... 98 THE SELF-SEEKER . . . 170
DON'T BE AFRAID. A FEW OF THEM WON'T HURT YOU. . . . 198 WILD GRAPES 57
WHEN I CAN HURT SOMEONE BY DOING IT . . . . . . 208 PAUPER WITCH OF GRAFTON 34
TO FIND OUT WHAT TO DO TO HURT A POEM. . . . . . 216 A FOUNTAIN, A BOTTLE . 108
THE HURT IS NOT ENOUGH: . . . . 227 TO EARTHWARD . . . 29
THE HURT TO THE SCENERY WOULDN'T BE MY COMPLAINT . . 286 A ROADSIDE STAND . . 16
AS HE THINKS WILL DO HER NOT TOO MUCH HURT. . . . . 346 DISCOVERY OF MADEIRAS . 89
THAT RATHER HURT HIS THEORY OF THE DROUGHT . . . . 400 THE BROKEN DROUGHT . . 4
DO ME NO HURT. . . . . 413 AWAY! 4
YOU MUSTN'T FEEL HURT IF NOW I'M ALL . . . . . . 420 ONE MORE BREVITY . . 47
AROUND HIM SO IT WOULDN'T TOUCH AND HURT HIM. . . . 478 A MASQUE OF REASON . . 133
IT WOULDN'T HURT YOU TO VOUCHSAFE THE FAITHFUL. . . . 478 A MASQUE OF REASON . . 143
WHY DID YOU HURT ME SO? I AM REDUCED . . . . . . 483 A MASQUE OF REASON . . 268
HUSBAND
WAS COGNIZANT. HER HUSBAND WAS WORTH MILLIONS. . . . 163 NEW HAMPSHIRE . . . 136
THE HEADSTONE CUT WITH JOHN, BELOVED HUSBAND, . . . 200 PLACE FOR A THIRD . . 39
A NEVER-MARRIED SISTER'S OF THAT HUSBAND, ... 200 PLACE FOR A THIRD . . 41
THE ONLY FAULT MY HUSBAND FOUND WITH ME-- . . . . 203 THE WITCH OF COOS . . 36
HE IS HUSBAND, SHE IS WIFE. . . . . 291 ON HEART'S BEGINNING TO 36
WHAT DID YOU TRY TO MAKE YOUR HUSBAND SAY? . . . . 477 A MASQUE OF REASON . . 118
MUCH AS YOUR HUSBAND, JOB, AND I TOGETHER . . . . 481 A MASQUE OF REASON . . 208
HUSBAND'S
A WIDOW AT HER SECOND HUSBAND'S GRAVE, ... 201 PLACE FOR A THIRD . . 59
HUSE
IT WA'N'T NO SIGN, I S'POSE, WHEN MALLICE HUSE . . . 208 PAUPER WITCH OF GRAFTON 45
HE'D BET HUSE WAS A CRIBBER AND HAD GNAWED . . . . 209 PAUPER WITCH OF GRAFTON 60
OF HAVING INTERFERED IN THE HUSE BUSINESS. . . . . 209 PAUPER WITCH OF GRAFTON 75
HUSH
AND HUSH AND CLUCK AND FLUTTER ABOUT: . . . . . 6 GHOST HOUSE 17
AND IN THE HUSH WE JOINED TO MAKE . . . . . . 18 GOING FOR WATER . . . 19
AND A HUSH FALLS FOR ALL ACCLAIM. . . . . . . 21 THE TRIAL BY EXISTENCE 60
NOW CLOSE THE WINDOWS AND HUSH ALL THE FIELDS: . . . 25 NOW CLOSE THE WINDOWS . 1
BUT IN NO HUSH THEY STRING IT: THEY GO PAST . . . 141 THE LINE-GANG . . . 8
AND REMEMBER HOW FINAL A HUSH . . . . 266 SITTING BY A BUSH . . 15
HUSHED
AND BINDING ALL IS THE HUSHED SNOW . . . . . . 20 THE TRIAL BY EXISTENCE 15
O HUSHED OCTOBER MORNING MILD, ... 27 OCTOBER 1
O HUSHED OCTOBER MORNING MILD, ... 27 OCTOBER 7
WILL RUN AS HUSHED AS WHEN THEY WERE A THOUGHT. . . 141 THE LINE-GANG . . . 7
HUSKY
THEY'RE GOING. WATCH THIS HUSKY SWARMING UP . . . 112 IN THE HOME STRETCH . 62
HUT
THEY CAN LEAVE HER A HUT AS WELL; . . . . . . 260 SAND DUNES 14
HYDE
ENVOI TO HYDE THE CASTAWAY OF CROW ISLAND . . . . 466 SOME SCIENCE FICTION . 0
HYDROGEN
CLEAR FROM HYDROGEN . . . . 426 A NEVER NAUGHT SONG . 15
HYLA
(AND TAKEN WITH IT ALL THE HYLA BREED . . . . . 119 HYLA BROOK 4
HYLA BROOK . . . . 119 HYLA BROOK . . . . T
AND SETTING SUN TO HYLA BROOK, I GAVE IT . . . . . 131 THE BONFIRE 58

I---NOT INDEXED
IAMB
    TELL THEM IAMB, JEHOVAH SAID, AND MEANT IT. . . . . 460 HOW HARD TO KEEP FROM   218
IAMBIC
    UPON A METER, STRICT OR LOOSE IAMBIC. . . . . 460 HOW HARD TO KEEP FROM   214
ICE
    CONCERNED WITH ICE AND SNOW, ...   10 WIND AND WINDOW FLOWER   14
    MELT IT AS THE ICE WILL GO; . . . .   11 TO THE THAWING WIND .   8
    AS ICE STORMS DO. OFTEN YOU MUST HAVE SEEN THEM . . . 121 BIRCHES   5
    LOADED WITH ICE A SUNNY WINTER MORNING . . . . . . 121 BIRCHES   6
    WITH ALL HER MATTER OF FACT ABOUT THE ICE STORM, . . . 121 BIRCHES 22
    AND MADE ICE ON THE TROUGH . . . . 135 LAST WORD OF A BLUEBIRD 11
    AND UNDERFOOT SNOW MELTED DOWN TO ICE, ... 179 THE STAR-SPLITTER . . 80
    MIGHT JUST AS WELL BE ICE AND THE CLOTHES SNOW. . . . . 203 THE WITCH OF COÖS . . 39
    ON AN ICE CAKE. . . . . 211 AN EMPTY THREAT . . . 20
    SOME SAY IN ICE. . . . . 220 FIRE AND ICE   2
    TO SAY THAT FOR DESTRUCTION ICE . . . . 220 FIRE AND ICE   7
    FIRE AND ICE . . . . 220 FIRE AND ICE . . . .   T
    ACROSS THE BARRIER OF ICE: . . . . 327 A MISSIVE MISSILE . .   6
ICELAND
    WE ALL KNOW HIS ADDRESS, MOUNT HECLA, ICELAND. . . . . 408 FROM PLANE TO PLANE . 143
ICHOR
    EMBALM HIM WITH ICHOR OF NETTLE. . . . . 288 DEPARTMENTAL 31
ICICLES
    HIS ICICLES ALONG THE WALL TO KEEP; . . . . 108 OLD MAN'S WINTER NIGHT 22
    THAT ROW OF ICICLES ALONG THE GUTTER . . . . 393 BEYOND WORDS   1
ICY
    AND BLEW HIM OUT ON THE ICY CRUST . . . . 137 BROWN'S DESCENT . . . 11
    ACROSS THE ICY BARRIER . . . . 327 A MISSIVE MISSILE . . 28
    THE STORM GETS DOWN HIS NECK IN AN ICY SOUSE . . . . 341 WILLFUL HOMING . . .   3
I'D---NOT INDEXED
IDEA
    SHE HAD HER OWN IDEA OF THINGS, THE OLD LADY. . . . . .   56 THE BLACK COTTAGE . . 51
    YOU KNOW THE OLD IDEA--THE ONLY ASYLUM . . . . . .   65 A SERVANT TO SERVANTS . 93
    WE HAVE TO GO." / "YOU MEAN THAT'S JOHN'S IDEA." . . . .   85 THE HOUSEKEEPER . . 131
    AS IF WITH SOME IDEA THAT SHE HAD SCORED. . . . . .   98 THE SELF-SEEKER . . 146
    IF THAT WAS YOUR IDEA, AGAINST THE BREEZE, ... 109 THE EXPOSED NEST . .   6
    TO LOOK US OVER AND GIVE US HIS IDEA . . . . 115 IN THE HORN STRETCH . 149
    THIS IS CALLED HAVING AN IDEA TO SELL. . . . . . . 160 NEW HAMPSHIRE . . . 33
    WHEREAS I NEVER HAD A GOOD IDEA . . . . 169 NEW HAMPSHIRE . . . 335
    MURPHY'S IDEA WAS THAT A MAN LIKE PAUL . . . . . . 196 PAUL'S WIFE 155
    WITHIN A MILLION YEARS OF AN IDEA. . . . . 293 AT WOODWARD'S GARDENS . 16
    'TWAS HIS IDEA THAT FOR THE PUBLIC HEALTH, ... 363 AN EQUALIZER   6
    THE IDEA IS NO DOUBT TO MAKE ONE JOB . . . . 370 THE LITERATE FARMER AND 71
    ISN'T IT PRETTY MUCH THE SAME IDEA? . . . . 405 FROM PLANE TO PLANE . 44
    THE SAME AS YOUR IDEA, ONLY MORE SO. . . . . 406 FROM PLANE TO PLANE . 81
    BUT STILL FOOD, FOOD. YOUR ONE IDEA WAS FOOD. . . . . 458 HOW HARD TO KEEP FROM 134
    YOU HAVE THE IDEA. THERE'S NOT MUCH I CAN TELL YOU. . . . 481 A MASQUE OF REASON . 216
    WHOSE CURE WILL LIE IN GETTING HER IDEA . . . . . . 499 A MASQUE OF MERCY . 160
    WITH THE IDEA OF JUSTICE IN THE COURTS, ... 509 A MASQUE OF MERCY . 423
    TO THE IDEA OF VIOLENCE. IT FLOURISHED, ... 511 A MASQUE OF MERCY . 469
IDEAL
    AN IDEAL ONE-GIRL FARM, ... 133 A GIRL'S GARDEN . . 14
    UNVULGAR, UNSOILED, AND IDEAL. . . . . 313 THE VINDICTIVES . . 88
    LIKE THE IDEAL OF SOME MISTAKEN LOVER. . . . . . . 391 ON BEING IDOLIZED .   6
    ENOUGH TO BAIT THE TRAP OF THE IDEAL . . . . 508 A MASQUE OF MERCY . 386
I-DEAL
    ON COMING NEARER: "WASN'T SHE AN I-DEAL . . . . . . 170 NEW HAMPSHIRE . . . 353
    SON-OF-A-BITCH? YOU BET SHE WAS AN I-DEAL." . . . . . 170 NEW HAMPSHIRE . . . 354
IDEALS
    OF THE OLD STOCK? WHAT COUNTS IS THE IDEALS, ...   80 THE GENERATIONS OF MEN 197
IDEAS
    WE HAVE IDEAS YET THAT WE HAVEN'T TRIED. . . . . . . 268 RIDERS 12
    IN GENERAL IDEAS AND PRINCIPLES. . . . . 479 A MASQUE OF REASON . 174
    (WHO HAS BEEN STANDING DAZED WITH NEW IDEAS) . . . . . 489 A MASQUE OF REASON . 441
IDEA'S
    "I'M SAYING IT TO ARGUE HIS IDEA'S . . . . 406 FROM PLANE TO PLANE . 80
IDENTIFY
    NO ONE WAS BRIGHT ENOUGH TO IDENTIFY; . . . . 295 LOST IN HEAVEN . . .   7
IDLE (SEE EMPTY-IDLE)
    IT WAS NO DREAM OF THE GIFT OF IDLE HOURS, ...   17 MOWING   7
    HE THOUGH OF AN IDLE BIT . . . . 133 A GIRL'S GARDEN . . 10
    (IF CERTAIN IT WOULDN'T BE IDLE TO CALL . . . . . . 228 GOOD-BY AND KEEP COLD .   9
    WAS STANDING IDLE FOR HIS SAKE. . . . . 273 A LONE STRIKER . . . 15
    PICK UP OUR EYES AND CARRY THEM BACK IDLE . . . . . 405 FROM PLANE TO PLANE . 51
IDLED
    "I ONLY IDLED DOWN." / "I IDLED DOWN." . . . . . .   74 THE GENERATIONS OF MEN 37
IDLENESS
    BLOWN OVER AND OVER THEMSELVES IN IDLENESS. . . . . .   58 THE BLACK COTTAGE . 121
    ANYONE ELSE, BUT OUT OF IDLENESS. . . . .   74 THE GENERATIONS OF MEN 27
IDLY
    AND I HAD IDLY POISED MY PEN IN AIR . . . . 357 A CONSIDERABLE SPECK .   4
IDOLIZED
    ON BEING IDOLIZED . . . . 391 ON BEING IDOLIZED . .   T
IF---NOT INDEXED
IFS
    IF--IF HE STOOD! ENOUGH OF IFS! . . . . 274 A LONE STRIKER . . . 42
    BETTER THAN ALL THE STALEMATE AN'S AND IFS. . . . . . 423 FOR JOHN F. KENNEDY . 59
IGNORANCE
    SOME IGNORANCE TAKES RANK AS INNOCENCE. . . . . . . 371 THE LITERATE FARMER AND 88
IGNORE
    AND YET CAN'T TURN YOUR BACK ON OR IGNORE, ... 512 A MASQUE OF MERCY . 510
    YET NO ONE TURN AWAY FROM OR IGNORE-- . . . . 513 A MASQUE OF MERCY . 522
IGNORED
    HOW TOTALLY IGNORED I SEEM TO BE. . . . . 462 HOW HARD TO KEEP FROM 259
IGNORING
    BUT ONLY BY IGNORING . . . . 359 NOVEMBER 11
    BY DENYING AND IGNORING . . . . 360 NOVEMBER 14

PAGE TITLE   LINE

IGNORING (CONTINUED)
  BUT HIS IGNORING WHAT WAS WHOSE . . . . 364 TRESPASS 15
ILE'S
  THEN SHOOK HIS LANTERN, SAYING, "ILE'S . . . . . . 140 BROWN'S DESCENT . . . 74
ILIAC
  HE GAVE HIS OWN POOR ILIAC A WRENCH . . . . 394 HAEC FABULA DOCET . . 13
ILL
  THAT OPENS EARTHWARD, GOOD AND ILL, ... 20 THE TRIAL BY EXISTENCE 35
  SHE COULD BE SURE THERE WAS NO HIDDEN ILL . . . . 230 NOT TO KEEP 3
  AND PLAY THE GOOD WITHOUT THE ILL. . . . . 336 THE WIND AND THE RAIN . 17
  WE MAY DOUBT THE JUST PROPORTION OF GOOD TO ILL. . 349 OUR HOLD ON THE PLANET 11
  OFTENER THAN AS CONFLICTING GOOD AND ILL; . . . . 350 TO A YOUNG WRETCH . . 16
  AND FEEL NO ILL EFFECTS FROM WHAT I GAVE YOU. . . 474 A MASQUE OF REASON . . 36
I'LL---NOT INDEXED
ILL-ADVISED
  AND SAW MYSELF--HE WOULD BE ILL-ADVISED----" . . . 100 THE SELF-SEEKER . . . 205
ILL-FITTED
  NOT BONES, BUT THE ILL-FITTED WINDOW RATTLED. . . . 175 THE CENSUS-TAKER . . 46
ILLIMITABLE
  THE ILLIMITABLE DARK AND COLD AND STORM, ... 148 SNOW 144
ILLS
  ONLY BEGETTER OF ALL ILLS THAT ARE. . . . . 356 A MOTH SEEN IN WINTER . 16
ILLUMINATED
  FOR BEAUTY ON THE ILLUMINATED PAGE . . . . 358 THE LOST FOLLOWER . . 15
ILLUSION
  I HADN'T AN ILLUSION IN MY HANDBAG . . . . 167 NEW HAMPSHIRE . . . 254
  THAT IF IT'S NOT A MERE ILLUSION . . . . 450 OUR DOOM TO BLOOM . . 7
I'M---NOT INDEXED
IMAGE
  AND DROPPED IT IN, AND SEEN THE IMAGE WALLOW, . . . 245 THE FREEDOM OF THE MOON 11
IMAGES
  ONCE WE BEGAN TO SEE OUR IMAGES . . . . 279 THE WHITE-TAILED HORNET 64
IMAGINARY
  WHERE MY IMAGINARY LINE . . . . 331 BEECH 1
IMAGINATION
  FATE HAD HER IMAGINATION ABOUT HER, ... 252 TREE AT MY WINDOW . . 14
  IS A DISEASE OF YOUR IMAGINATION. . . . . 503 A MASQUE OF MERCY . . 258
IMAGINE
  JOHN HIMSELF WON'T IMAGINE WHO HE IS." . . . . . . 88 THE HOUSEKEEPER . . . 189
  TOO PRESENT TO IMAGINE. . . . . 336 CARPE DIEM 26
  HE COULD IMAGINE NOTHING BARRENER. . . . . 417 AMERICA IS HARD TO SEE 15
IMAGINED
  OF TYPES, COMPOSITE AND IMAGINED PEOPLE: . . . . . 317 BUILD SOIL 49
  LITTLE I IMAGINED . . . . 434 KITTY HAWK 188
IMITATE
  (HE TRIED TO IMITATE DICK'S TONE OF VOICE.) . . . . 406 FROM PLANE TO PLANE . 73
IMMENSE
  THE UNIVERSE MAY OR MAY NOT BE VERY IMMENSE. . . . 389 SKEPTIC 9
  WHERE NOT TOO IMMENSE, ... 441 KITTY HAWK 425
IMMERSED
  AND SUMMITS SHALL BE IMMERSED, ... 285 IN TIME OF CLOUDBURST . 14
IMMIGRANTS
  IMMIGRANTS . . . . 262 IMMIGRANTS . . . . T
IMMORTAL
  HOW ELSE DISPOSE OF AN IMMORTAL FORCE . . . . . . 231 A BROOK IN THE CITY . 13
  WHETHER THERE'S ANY PART OF MAN IMMORTAL. . . . . 483 A MASQUE OF REASON . 297
IMMORTALITY
  YOUR CLAIMS TO IMMORTALITY WERE TWO. . . . . . . 382 TO AN ANCIENT . . . 1
IMMURED
  IMMURED ALMOST BEYOND RECALL, ... 280 BLUE RIBBON AT AMESBURY 22
IMPART
  WITH GOODS TO SELL AND NOTIONS TO IMPART. . . . . 324 BUILD SOIL 269
IMPARTED
  THE SUN ONCE IMPARTED ITS FLAME. . . . . 266 SITTING BY A BUSH . . 18
IMPATIENCE
  IF FORWARD, THEN IT'S WITH A FRIEND'S IMPATIENCE-- . 147 SNOW 121
  HERE WE, IN OUR IMPATIENCE OF THE STEPS, ... 259 WEST-RUNNING BROOK . . 42
IMPATIENT
  SOMEHOW MADE HER IMPATIENT WITH THE MAN. . . . . . 199 PLACE FOR A THIRD . . 8
  WHICH I ACCEPTED WITH IMPATIENT SIGHT, ... 295 LOST IN HEAVEN . . . 3
  WE ARE IMPATIENT FOR YOUR ROYAL ANSWER." . . . . . 456 HOW HARD TO KEEP FROM 76
IMPERFECTLY
  IMPERFECTLY CONCEALED AMONG THE LEAVES. . . . . . 41 THE MOUNTAIN 32
  BUT WHAT IMPERFECTLY APPEARS . . . . 327 A MISSIVE MISSILE . . 9
IMPERVIOUS
  BUT THE IMPERVIOUS GEODE . . . . 332 ALL REVELATION . . . 11
IMPLEMENTS
  WEAPONS OF WAR AND IMPLEMENTS OF PEACE . . . . . . 255 THE FLOOD 10
IMPOLITELY
  I COULDN'T KEEP FROM ASKING IMPOLITELY, ... 160 NEW HAMPSHIRE . . . 55
IMPORTANCE
  AND BARITONE IMPORTANCE OF THE LAWYER, ... 96 THE SELF-SEEKER . . . 94
IMPORTANT
  "YES, IT'S IMPORTANT, THOUGH YOU THINK IT ISN'T. . . 77 THE GENERATIONS OF MEN 118
  TO EVIL, NO IMPORTANT TRIUMPH WON, ... 226 THE ONSET 10
  MAY NOT BE THE IMPORTANT THING AT LAST. . . . . . 321 BUILD SOIL 158
  THESE ANYWAY MIGHT THINK IT WAS IMPORTANT . . . . 397 THE PLANNERS 13
  THE IMPORTANT THING IS NOT TO GET BOGGED DOWN . . . 406 FROM PLANE TO PLANE . 62
  SO IT'S IMPORTANT WHO FIRST THINKS OF THINGS? . . . 480 A MASQUE OF REASON . 198
IMPORTED
  THE CRYSTAL PALACE, LONDON. HE'S IMPORTED. . . . . 86 THE HOUSEKEEPER . . . 151
IMPORTER
  AN IMPORTER . . . . 396 AN IMPORTER . . . . T
IMPORTUNATE
  IMPORTUNATE TO GIVE THE HINT . . . . 327 A MISSIVE MISSILE . . 31
IMPOSED
  TO LET HIM KNOW WE WEREN'T THE LEAST IMPOSED ON, . . 177 THE STAR-SPLITTER . . 41
  I AM IMPOSED ON, SILENCED AND DISCOURAGED. . . . . 324 BUILD SOIL 251

		PAGE	TITLE	LINE

IMPOSED (CONTINUED)
   'TWAS AGE IMPOSED ON POEMS . . . . 335 CARPE DIEM 12
IMPOSSIBILITY
   A BEAUTIFUL IMPOSSIBILITY. . . . . 512 A MASQUE OF MERCY . . 493
   AN IRRESISTIBLE IMPOSSIBILITY. . . . . 512 A MASQUE OF MERCY . . 495
   HIS IRRESISTIBLE IMPOSSIBILITY, ... 513 A MASQUE OF MERCY . . 520
IMPOSTOR
   THAT I MIGHT BE A CONFIDENCE IMPOSTOR. . . . . . 495 A MASQUE OF MERCY . . 54
IMPOUNDED
   JUST WHEN WE THINK WE HAVE IT IMPOUNDED SAFE . . . . 254 THE FLOOD 2
IMPOVERISHED
   THAN AN IMPOVERISHED SOIL, PALE AND METALLIC? . . . . 323 BUILD SOIL 218
IMPOVERISHMENT
   IN THEIR IMPOVERISHMENT BY REVOLUTION . . . . 509 A MASQUE OF MERCY . . 413
IMPRESS
   TO IMPRESS MEN. YOU'VE GOT US SO ASHAMED . . . . . 146 SNOW 99
IMPRESSED
   SEEMS NOT EVEN IMPRESSED. . . . . 288 DEPARTMENTAL . . . 17
   HAS BEEN IMPRESSED AS WITNESS TREE . . . . 331 BEECH 7
   BUT TO MY QUESTION. I AM MUCH IMPRESSED . . . . . . 480 A MASQUE OF REASON . 183
IMPRESSION
   THEY MADE NO WHITE IMPRESSION ON THE BLACK. . . . . 239 OUR SINGING STRENGTH . 5
   MY FAIR IMPRESSION MAY . . . . 333 HAPPINESS MAKES UP . . 19
IMPRINT
   IMPRINT A SADDLE, AND CALMLY CONSIDER A COURSE. . . . 341 WILLFUL HOMING . . . 7
IMPROVE
   TRIED TO IMPROVE ON SAILING LIKE A TILE . . . . . 216 A FOUNTAIN, A BOTTLE . 112
   OR ELSE WRITE SOMETHING TO IMPROVE FOOD PRICES. . . . 316 BUILD SOIL 24
IMPROVEMENT
   THIS REPRESENTED AN IMPROVEMENT ON. . . . . 189 THE GRINDSTONE . . . 36
IMPROVING
   ABOUT IMPROVING PEOPLE IN THE WORLD, ... 169 NEW HAMPSHIRE . . . 336
IMPROVISED
   AGREED IN FROWNING ON THESE IMPROVISED . . . . . . 171 NEW HAMPSHIRE . . . 386
IMPULSE
   THE IMPULSE . . . . 128 THE IMPULSE . . . . T
   MY FIRST IMPULSE WAS TO GET TO THE KNOB . . . . . 204 THE WITCH OF COOS . . 60
   SPENDING WHAT ONWARD IMPULSE THEY STILL HAD . . . . 229 TWO LOOK AT TWO . . . 9
   AND IMPULSE, HAVING DIPPED A FINGER LENGTH . . . . 231 A BROOK IN THE CITY . 6
   OR OLD LOVE ON AN IMPULSE NOT TO CARE-- . . . . . 264 THE INVESTMENT . . . 12
   ONE IMPULSE PERSISTS AS OUR BREATH; . . . . 266 SITTING BY A BUSH . . 19
   THE THOUGHT I HAVE, AND MY FIRST IMPULSE IS . . . . 323 BUILD SOIL 239
   A HOLY IMPULSE TOWARDS REDISTRIBUTION. . . . . . . 509 A MASQUE OF MERCY . . 419
IMPULSIVELY
   TO KNOW THE HAND I STRETCH IMPULSIVELY . . . . . . 356 A MOTH SEEN IN WINTER . 20
IN---NOT INDEXED
INAUDIBLY
   INAUDIBLY IN THOUGHT, ... 415 CLOSED FOR GOOD . . . 16
INAUGURATION
   FOR JOHN F. KENNEDY HIS INAUGURATION . . . . . . 422 FOR JOHN F. KENNEDY . T
INBORN
   SANG HALFWAY THROUGH ITS LITTLE INBORN TUNE. . . . . 302 A BIRD SINGING IN SLEEP 2
INCA
   ONE INCA PRINCE ON THE RACK, ... 311 THE VINDICTIVES . . . 41
INCANDESCENT
   IN INCANDESCENT LAMPS AND ENDING SLEEP. . . . . . 371 THE LITERATE FARMER AND 97
INCANTATION
   LET'S GET MY INCANTATION RIGHT: . . . . 451 A-WISHING WELL . . . 27
INCARNATION
   IF IT IS ME IN MY LAST INCARNATION . . . . 510 A MASQUE OF MERCY . . 447
INCENSE
   I SAID THE INCENSE TREE'S ON FIRE AGAIN. . . . . . 473 A MASQUE OF REASON . . 5
INCENTIVE
   OF MY INCENTIVE--CANCELING MY MISSION. . . . . . . 499 A MASQUE OF MERCY . . 148
INCH
   THE DANGER NOT AN INCH OUTSIDE . . . . 363 ASSURANCE 1
INCH-DEEP
   ARE INCH-DEEP WITH THE FROSTY SPINES AND BRISTLES-- . . 42 THE MOUNTAIN . . . 53
INCIDENTALLY
   THOUGH INCIDENTALLY I SOMETIMES WONDER . . . . . . 481 A MASQUE OF REASON . . 220
INCLINATION
   AT WHICH MY INCLINATION IS TO SCOFF.) . . . . 355 THE LESSON FOR TODAY . 150
INCLINATIONS
   WITH INCLINATIONS IT COULD CALL ITS OWN. . . . . . 357 A CONSIDERABLE SPECK . 9
INCLINED
   THERE'S MORE IN IT THAN YOU'RE INCLINED TO SAY. . . . 90 THE FEAR 30
   BUT THOUGH WE ALL MAY BE INCLINED TO WAIT . . . . 355 THE LESSON FOR TODAY . 141
   (OR MORE THAN HALF I'M HALF INCLINED TO SAY)." . . . 462 HOW HARD TO KEEP FROM 278
   INCLINED TO HOPE FOR MUCH. STILL WHAT WE NEED . . . 515 A MASQUE OF MERCY . . 567
INCLUDE
   THOUGH SOME SAVANTS MAKE EARTH INCLUDE THE SKY; . . . 220 FRAGMENTARY BLUE . . 6
INCLUDED
   THEY INCLUDED ME . . . . 431 KITTY HAWK 117
INCLUDES
   THE LONELINESS INCLUDES ME UNAWARES. . . . . 296 DESERT PLACES . . . 8
INCLUDING
   INCLUDING ME. HE THINKS I'LL BE ALL RIGHT . . . . . 64 A SERVANT TO SERVANTS . 46
   INCLUDING HUMAN NATURE, IN PEACE AND WAR, ... 349 OUR HOLD ON THE PLANET 14
   INCLUDING ME, THE ONLY DRAMATIS . . . . 487 A MASQUE OF REASON . . 393
INCOME
   WITH AN INCOME IN CASH OF, SAY, A THOUSAND . . . . 172 NEW HAMPSHIRE . . . 409
INCOME-TAX
   SUSPICION OF THE INCOME-TAX RETURNS, ... 503 A MASQUE OF MERCY . . 247
INCOMPLETE
   BUT SOMETHING IN IT STILL IS INCOMPLETE. . . . . . 337 THE WIND AND THE RAIN . 25
INCOMPLETENESS
   I TAKE MY INCOMPLETENESS WITH THE REST. . . . . . 355 THE LESSON FOR TODAY . 155

INCONSIDERATE
 "IF YOU MEAN HE WAS INCONSIDERATE . . . . 155 SNOW 345
INCONSISTENCY
 AN INCONSISTENCY. THE STATE SHALL BE . . . . 324 BUILD SOIL 246
INCONSOLABLY
 SO INCONSOLABLY--IN THE FACE OF LOVE. . . . . 53 HOME BURIAL 65
INCORRIGIBLE
 INCORRIGIBLE QUIDNUNCS, ... 464 MILKY WAY IS A COWPATH 9
INCREASE
 HE TURNED ON WILLPOWER TO INCREASE THE LOAD . . . . 189 THE GRINDSTONE . . . 31
 IT'S ON THE INCREASE. HE COULD COUNT ON NO ONE: . . . . 485 A MASQUE OF REASON . 357
 OF BUSINESS, MIGHT INCREASE INTO A MADNESS. . . . . . 503 A MASQUE OF MERCY . 249
INCREASED
 OUR HOLD ON THE PLANET WOULDN'T HAVE SO INCREASED. . . . 349 OUR HOLD ON THE PLANET 18
INCREASING
 ENRICHING SOIL AND INCREASING STOCK, ... 367 A SERIOUS STEP LIGHTLY 19
INCREDULOUS
 INCREDULOUS OF HIS OWN BAD LUCK. . . . . 138 BROWN'S DESCENT . . 41
INCREDULOUSNESS
 FOR THEIR FOREGONE INCREDULOUSNESS. . . . . 257 THE LOVELY BE CHOOSERS 36
INCURABLE
 THE OLD INCURABLE UNTIMELINESS, ... 356 A MOTH SEEN IN WINTER . 15
IND
 A NEW AND BETTER WAY TO IND . . . . 416 AMERICA IS HARD TO SEE 2
INDECENCY'S
 THE ONE INDECENCY'S TO MAKE A FUSS . . . . 507 A MASQUE OF MERCY . 353
INDEED
 AS AN OLD BOYHOOD FRIEND, AND ONCE INDEED . . . . . 160 NEW HAMPSHIRE . . 49
 I SHOULD HAVE DONE BY DAYLIGHT, AND INDEED, ... 176 THE STAR-SPLITTER . . 5
 IF NOT INDEED FROM SLEEPING OUT, ... 381 AN UNSTAMPED LETTER IN 47
INDEPENDENCE
 A HEALTHY INDEPENDENCE OF THE THRONG, ... 424 FOR JOHN F. KENNEDY . 63
INDIAN
 MY FRENCH INDIAN ESQUIMAUX, ... 211 AN EMPTY THREAT . . 27
 BEFORE THE INDIAN RACE WAS FURTHER WRONGED. . . . . . 370 THE LITERATE FARMER AND 60
 "I THOUGHT YOU MEANT TO BE AN INDIAN CHIEF-- . . . . . 406 FROM PLANE TO PLANE . 69
 THIS THOUGH WE TOOK THE INDIAN NAME FOR MAIZE . . . . 446 DOES NO ONE AT ALL EVER 7
 BY A RELIGIOUS AZTEC INDIAN. . . . . 516 A MASQUE OF MERCY . 616
INDIANS
 "THE INDIANS HAD A MYTH OF CHICAMOZTOC, ... 76 THE GENERATIONS OF MEN 92
 THEY WEREN'T RED INDIANS BUT VERITABLE . . . . . . 161 NEW HAMPSHIRE . . 77
 ON PUEBLO INDIANS AND THEIR ARCHITECTURE . . . . . 369 THE LITERATE FARMER AND 54
 DECLARE THAT IF SUCH INDIANS INHERITED . . . . . . 369 THE LITERATE FARMER AND 55
INDIFFERENCE
 THE EX-KING SAID, "YON STAR'S INDIFFERENCE . . . . . 454 HOW HARD TO KEEP FROM 17
INDIGNATION
 YOUR RIGHTEOUS INDIGNATION FIZZLED OUT, ... 497 A MASQUE OF MERCY . 103
INDIGNITY
 THAN WHICH THERE IS NO INDIGNITY WORSE. . . . . . . 463 LINES IN DEJECTION . . 13
INDOOR
 AND PREFERRING THE OUT- TO THE INDOOR NIGHT, ... 127 HOUSE FEAR . . 8
INDOORS
 WE SIT INDOORS AND TALK OF THE COLD OUTSIDE. . . . . 305 THERE ARE ROUGHLY ZONES 1
INDUCE
 TO INDUCE THE ONE SNOW ON HIS HEAD. . . . . 299 WELCOME TO THEIR BELIEF 8
INDULGE
 NOW AFTER ALL THESE YEARS YOU MIGHT INDULGE ME. . . . 483 A MASQUE OF REASON . 267
INDULGENCE
 INDULGENCE IN YOUR FORM OF MELANCHOLY . . . . . . 498 A MASQUE OF MERCY . 144
INDULGING
 WITHOUT INDULGING A "NOT FOR US!" . . . . 291 ON HEART'S BEGINNING TO 33
 INDULGING AN ABSURD DRAMATIC SPELL, ... 396 ANY SIZE WE PLEASE . 3
INDUSTRY
 WHEN INDUSTRY SEEMED LIKE TO DIE . . . . 274 A LONE STRIKER . 58
INDWELLING
 THE INDWELLING SPIDER RAN TO GREET THE FLY, ... 126 RANGE-FINDING . . . 13
INEFFECTUAL
 THE TIRELESS BUT INEFFECTUAL HANDS . . . . 128 THE OFT-REPEATED DREAM 5
INEXPERIENCE
 CHARGE THAT TO UPSTART INEXPERIENCE. . . . . 378 DIRECTIVE 25
INEXTERMINATE
 MAN'S PRACTICALLY INEXTERMINATE. . . . . 453 A-WISHING WELL . . 77
INFANT
 WE CAN JUST SEE THE INFANT UP ASTRIDE, ... 267 RIDERS 7
INFERIORS
 FROM HIS INFERIORS IN INTELLIGENCE . . . . 481 A MASQUE OF REASON . 213
INFERNAL
 AND NOW AND THEN A SMUDGED, INFERNAL FACE . . . . . 110 IN THE HOME STRETCH . 10
INFINITE
 THE PLAY SEEMS OUT FOR AN ALMOST INFINITE RUN. . . . . 392 IT BIDS PRETTY FAIR . 1
 IN INFINITE APPEAL. THEN SAYING "HELL," . . . . . 396 ANY SIZE WE PLEASE . 7
 THE COUNTLESS WINGS THAT FROM THE INFINITE . . . . . 411 POD OF THE MILKWEED . 10
 AT THE INFINITE, ... 439 KITTY HAWK . . 363
INFINITE'S
 THE INFINITE'S BEING SO WIDE . . . . 348 TRIPLE BRONZE . . . 1
INFINITIES
 ABOUT OUR PLACE AMONG THE INFINITIES. . . . . . . 168 NEW HAMPSHIRE . . 305
 ABOUT OUR PLACE AMONG THE INFINITIES. . . . . . . 177 THE STAR-SPLITTER . 19
INFIRM
 INFIRM, WORN-OUT, AND BROKEN ON ITS HANDS; . . . . . 399 THE INGENUITIES OF DEBT 9
INFLUENCE
 COULD ONLY HAVE HAD AN INFLUENCE ON BIRDS . . . . . 338 NEVER WOULD BIRDS' SONG 7
 "BE CAREFUL HOW YOU USE YOUR INFLUENCE. . . . . . . 406 FROM PLANE TO PLANE . 66
 OF INFLUENCE. IT'S BEEN A COMMONPLACE . . . . . . 511 A MASQUE OF MERCY . 472
INFORM
 IT'S ONLY FAIR TO KEEPER TO INFORM YOU . . . . . . 496 A MASQUE OF MERCY . 80
INFRA-SMALL
 IS SO INFRA-SMALL . . . . 426 A NEVER NAUGHT SONG . 22

INGENIOUS
      NONE SHOULD BE AS INGENIOUS AS HE COULD, ... 320 BUILD SOIL 122
INGENUITIES
      THE INGENUITIES OF DEBT . . . . 399 THE INGENUITIES OF DEBT   T
      NOT EVEN THE INGENUITIES OF DEBT . . . . 399 THE INGENUITIES OF DEBT 11
INGENUITY
      MAN'S INGENUITY WAS GOOD. . . . . 274 A LONE STRIKER . . . 33
      UNSOCIALIZED, IS INGENUITY: . . . . 319 BUILD SOIL 102
      TO INGENUITY FOR BEING SO CRUEL . . . . 320 BUILD SOIL 124
      SUCH DEVILISH INGENUITY OF TORTURE . . . . 482 A MASQUE OF REASON . . 262
INGLE
      WE WOULD POUR OIL ON THE INGLE . . . . 384 IN THE LONG NIGHT . . 5
INGRATIATING
      AN INGRATIATING LAUGH . . . . 340 THE SUBVERTED FLOWER . 45
INGREDIENTS
      LIKE THE INGREDIENTS OF A WITCHES' BROTH-- . . . . . 302 DESIGN 6
INHERIT
      WESTERNERS INHERIT . . . . 435 KITTY HAWK 225
INHERITANCE
      WITH AN INHERITANCE OF RESTLESS DREAM. . . . . . . 412 POD OF THE MILKWEED . 44
INHERITED
      DECLARE THAT IF SUCH INDIANS INHERITED . . . . . 369 THE LITERATE FARMER AND 55
INITIAL
      THE INITIAL FLIGHT . . . . 429 KITTY HAWK 42
INJUSTICE
      THERE'S NOTHING BUT INJUSTICE TO BE HAD, ... 352 THE LESSON FOR TODAY . 60
      SHE WANTS TO KNOW WHY THERE IS STILL INJUSTICE. . . . 477 A MASQUE OF REASON . . 110
      THE RICH IN SEEING NOTHING BUT INJUSTICE . . . . . 509 A MASQUE OF MERCY . . 412
      ARE RIGHT. BUT 'TWAS INTENTIONAL INJUSTICE. . . . . 509 A MASQUE OF MERCY . . 414
      A CRUELTY, AMOUNTING TO INJUSTICE . . . . 520 A MASQUE OF MERCY . . 712
      NOTHING CAN MAKE INJUSTICE JUST BUT MERCY. . . . . 521 A MASQUE OF MERCY . . 738
INK
      TO STOP IT WITH A PERIOD OF INK, ... 357 A CONSIDERABLE SPECK . 5
      YOU DRIVE ME TO CONFESS IN INK: . . . . 467 QUANDARY 19
INLAND
      WHAT NOW IS INLAND SHALL BE OCEAN ISLE, ... 335 I COULD GIVE ALL . . 6
      AND ROLLING IT INLAND ON ROLLER AIR, ... 337 THE WIND AND THE RAIN . 31
      SO FAR INLAND THE VERY NAME OF OCEAN . . . . . . 447 DOES NO ONE AT ALL EVER 37
IN-LEANING
      (IN-LEANING UNDER THE STRAIN), ... 312 THE VINDICTIVES . . . 66
INMATES
      THE INMATES MAY BE LONELY WOMENFOLK. . . . . . . 248 THE COCOON 11
INMOST
      TO BE THE CURTAIN OF THE INMOST SOUL. . . . . . . 385 THE FEAR OF GOD . . . 13
      NATURE WITHIN HER INMOST SELF DIVIDES . . . . . . 468 FROM IRON 1
INNATE
      INNATE HELIUM . . . . 386 INNATE HELIUM . . . T
      SOME GAS LIKE HELIUM MUST BE INNATE. . . . . . . 387 INNATE HELIUM . . . 6
INNER
      YOU'D THINK THE INNER DOME OF HEAVEN HAD FALLEN. . . . 121 BIRCHES 13
      MRS. COLE'S VOICE CAME FROM AN INNER ROOM: . . . . 152 SNOW 271
      THE POSIES ON HER INNER WINDOWSILL, ... 215 A FOUNTAIN, A BOTTLE . 80
      MINE WITH INNER, WEATHER. . . . . 252 TREE AT MY WINDOW . . 16
      WAS ENTERED, AND ITS INNER CRUST . . . . 332 ALL REVELATION . . . 12
      FOR INNER DEFENSE MY HIDE. . . . . 348 TRIPLE BRONZE . . . 3
      THE KINDRED SPIRIT OF AN INNER HAZE? . . . . . . 415 A CABIN IN THE CLEARING 42
      OF THE INNER SOUND; . . . . 433 KITTY HAWK 166
INNOCENCE
      STRANGE HOW SUCH INNOCENCE GETS ITS OWN WAY. . . . . 57 THE BLACK COTTAGE . . 81
      SOME IGNORANCE TAKES RANK AS INNOCENCE. . . . . . 371 THE LITERATE FARMER AND 88
      CARE MY INNOCENCE . . . . 432 KITTY HAWK 121
INNOCENT
      WHAT GOLD MORE INNOCENT COULD ONE HAVE ASKED FOR? . . . 162 NEW HAMPSHIRE . . . 115
      THE WAYSIDE BLUE AND INNOCENT HEAL-ALL? . . . . . 302 DESIGN 10
      "I GUESS SO," PIKE SAID, INNOCENT OF MILTON. . . . . 408 FROM PLANE TO PLANE . 136
      DICK SAID, TO OLD PIKE INNOCENT OF SHAKESPEARE. . . . 408 FROM PLANE TO PLANE . 148
      I CANNOT HOLD YOU INNOCENT OF FAULT. . . . . . . 446 DOES NO ONE AT ALL EVER 21
      JOB HADN'T DONE A THING, POOR INNOCENT. . . . . . 478 A MASQUE OF REASON . . 127
INNUENDO
      WITH INNUENDO I DETEST. . . . . 467 QUANDARY 18
INQUIRE
      JUST ONE TO INQUIRE WHAT A FARMER'S PRICES ARE. . . . 287 A ROADSIDE STAND . . 38
      AND THE GREAT KING INQUIRE WHOSE WORK IT WAS. . . . 455 HOW HARD TO KEEP FROM 59
INQUIRED
      "STARK?" HE INQUIRED. "NO MATTER FOR THE PROOF." . . 74 THE GENERATIONS OF MEN 45
INQUIRING
      WITHOUT INQUIRING IF 'TWAS SERIOUS. . . . . . . 369 THE LITERATE FARMER AND 26
INQUIRY (SEE ALSO ENQUIRY)
      IN SELF-DEFENSE TO QUIZZICAL INQUIRY: . . . . . . 365 OF STONES OF THE PLACE 14
INQUISITIVE
      IN AN INQUISITIVE POSITION ODD . . . . 412 POD OF THE MILKWEED . 46
INSCRIPTION
      INSCRIPTION FOR A GARDEN WALL . . . . 246 ATMOSPHERE . . . . S
      TO REAR AGAINST THE INSCRIPTION ON THE WALL. . . . 399 THE INGENUITIES OF DEBT 18
      IS THE INSCRIPTION, THOUGH, ... 437 KITTY HAWK 305
INSCRUTABLY
      HAD EYES INSCRUTABLY OPAQUE; . . . . 273 A LONE STRIKER . . . 12
INSECT
      YET HOW ABOUT THE INSECT CERTAINTY . . . . . . 277 THE WHITE-TAILED HORNET 12
INSECTS
      AND BEATING INSECTS AT THEIR GRITTY TUNE. . . . . . 190 THE GRINDSTONE . . . 55
INSECURE
      "O CITY ON INSECURE ROCK PEDESTAL, ... 506 A MASQUE OF MERCY . . 337
INSIDE
      THERE'S NOTHING BUT A VOICE-LIKE LEFT INSIDE . . . . 63 A SERVANT TO SERVANTS . 13
      TO HAVE INSIDE THE HOUSE WITH DOORS UNLOCKED. . . . 65 A SERVANT TO SERVANTS . 84
      JUST HOOK THEM ON THE INSIDE OF THE PITCHER. . . . 99 THE SELF-SEEKER . . 174
      UNTIL THEY HAD LIT THE LAMP INSIDE. . . . . . . 127 HOUSE FEAR 10

```
                                                      PAGE TITLE                        LINE
INSIDE (CONTINUED)
   IT NEVER HAD BEEN INSIDE THE ROOM, . . . . . . . .  .  .  128 THE OFT-REPEATED DREAM      9
   AND AT THE EAVES. I LIKE IT FROM INSIDE . . . . . .  .  .  150 SNOW . . . . .  .  .  208
   INSIDE THE THRESHOLD OF HIS OPEN BARN, . . . . . .  .  .   160 NEW HAMPSHIRE  .  .  .   45
   UP THE BRASS BARREL, VELVET BLACK INSIDE, . . . .  .  .    179 THE STAR-SPLITTER  .  .   77
   TO SEE FOR ONCE THE INSIDE OF HIS HOUSE. . . . . .  .  .   188 THE AX-HELVE .  .  .   89
   I LAUGHED INSIDE, AND ONLY CRANKED THE FASTER . . .  .  .  190 THE GRINDSTONE  .  .  .   60
   AND LEFT STOOD UP ON END INSIDE THE TREE . . . . .  .  .   194 PAUL'S WIFE  .  .  .   93
   SMOKE ROLLED INSIDE THE SOCKETS OF HIS EYES.) . . .  .  .  204 THE WITCH OF COOS  .  .   74
   SO THAT HE COULDN'T LOOK INSIDE . . . . . . . . .  .  .    273 A LONE STRIKER  .  .  .   13
   OUR EVER GETTING INSIDE IN AGAIN. . . . . . . . .  .  .    320 BUILD SOIL  .  .  .  140
   BUT INSIDE IN IS WHERE WE'VE GOT TO GET. . . . . .  .  .   320 BUILD SOIL  .  .  .  141
   AWAY 'WAY DOWN INSIDE I'M PERSONAL. . . . . . . .  .  .    320 BUILD SOIL  .  .  .  144
   INSIDE IT WAS DARK. . . . . . . . . . . . . . .  .  .      334 COME IN  .  .  .  .   4
   FROM INSIDE THE GARDEN WALL . . . . . . . . . . .  .  .    340 THE SUBVERTED FLOWER  .   36
   ONLY WITHIN. INSIDE THE BRAIN . . . . . . . . . .  .  .    381 AN UNSTAMPED LETTER IN   32
   EXCEPT BESIDE A SAFE INSIDE A BANK . . . . . . . .  .  .   386 THE FEAR OF MAN .  .  .    9
   TILL IT CAN MUSTER BREATH INSIDE A HALL . . . . .  .  .    399 THE INGENUITIES OF DEBT   17
   OR INSIDE EITHER FOR THAT MATTER. . . . . . . . .  .  .    418 AMERICA IS HARD TO SEE   65
INSIDER
   AS ONE RANKLY WARM INSIDER . . . . . . . . . . .  .  .     384 IN THE LONG NIGHT  .  .   13
INSIGHT
   ON THEIR PART, THOUGH WITHOUT THE NEEDED INSIGHT. . . . .  293 AT WOODWARD'S GARDENS .   26
INSINCERE
   SINCERE OR INSINCERE, . . . . . . . . . . . . .  .  .      444 ENDS . . . . . .   6
INSISTING
   INSISTING ALWAYS ON OUR OWN WAY SO. . . . . . . .  .  .    238 ON A TREE FALLEN ACROSS   5
INSISTS
   IT SEEMS A NARROW CHOICE THE AGE INSISTS ON. . . .  .  .   171 NEW HAMPSHIRE  .  .  403
INSPECTING  (SEE BUD-INSPECTING)
INSPIRATION
   A ZEALOT FULL OF FLUID INSPIRATION, . . . . . . .  .  .    159 NEW HAMPSHIRE  .  .  .   26
   WHO IN THE NAME OF FLUID INSPIRATION, . . . . . .  .  .    159 NEW HAMPSHIRE  .  .  .   27
   BY INSPIRATION. IT PROVED THERE WAS SOMETHING. . .  .  .   184 MAPLE  .  .  .  135
   AND HAD THE INSPIRATION TO DESIST . . . . . . . .  .  .    302 A BIRD SINGING IN SLEEP   6
   --THE DEVIL'S BEING GOD'S BEST INSPIRATION. . . .  .  .    487 A MASQUE OF REASON .  .  401
INSPIRE
   WE SPEAK THE LITERAL TO INSPIRE . . . . . . . . .  .  .     19 REVELATION  .  .  .    7
INSPIRES
   SOMETHING INSPIRES THE ONLY COW OF LATE . . . . .  .  .    124 THE COW IN APPLE TIME .   1
INSTANCE
   "WHAT DID YOU HEAR, FOR INSTANCE?" WILLIS SAID. .  .  .    100 THE SELF-SEEKER  .  .  .  206
   HOW ABOUT BEING A GOOD GREEK, FOR INSTANCE? . . .  .  .    171 NEW HAMPSHIRE  .  .  .  404
   MORE THAT SHOULD BE KEPT BACK--THE SOIL FOR INSTANCE, . .  321 BUILD SOIL  .  .  .  175
   FOR INSTANCE, IS THERE SUCH A THING AS PROGRESS? .  .  .   484 A MASQUE OF REASON .  .  315
   FOR INSTANCE, WHEN TO PURIFY THE ITZAS . . . . .  .  .     510 A MASQUE OF MERCY .  .  445
INSTANTLY
   THE PLACE IT REACHED TO BLACKENED INSTANTLY. . . .  .  .   131 THE BONFIRE .  .  .   48
INSTEAD
   THE SOUND WAS BEHIND ME INSTEAD OF BEFORE, . . . .  .  .    25 THE DEMIURGE'S LAUGH  .    7
   INSTEAD OF GOING CLEAR DOWN IN THE WHEEL PIT?" . .  .  .    93 THE SELF-SEEKER  .  .   31
   "I'M GOING TO BE WORSE INSTEAD OF BETTER. . . . .  .  .     94 THE SELF-SEEKER  .  .   56
   PERHAPS BECAUSE HE LET US GIVE INSTEAD . . . . . .  .  .   127 THE SMILE  .  .  .  .    6
   TEN THOUSAND FEET INSTEAD OF ONLY FIVE-- . . . . .  .  .   169 NEW HAMPSHIRE  .  .  .  332
   AND BURNING TO YIELD FLOWERS INSTEAD OF GRAIN, . .  .  .   173 A STAR IN A STONEBOAT .   22
   INSTEAD OF A NEW-FASHIONED ONE AT AUCTION? . . . .  .  .   178 THE STAR-SPLITTER  .  .   65
   MIGHTN'T WE MAKE IT WORSE INSTEAD OF BETTER? . . .  .  .   191 THE GRINDSTONE  .  .  .   74
   INSTEAD OF WHICH SHE WAS SOME HALF-BREED SQUAW. . .  .  .  192 PAUL'S WIFE  .  .  .   39
   THAT SHE WAS LOOKING AT INSTEAD OF HIM. . . . . .  .  .    194 PAUL'S WIFE  .  .  .  113
   I MEAN A MAN HE KILLED INSTEAD OF ME. . . . . . .  .  .    206 THE WITCH OF COOS  .  .  140
   THAT REALLY TAKES AWAY INSTEAD OF GIVES. . . . . .  .  .   279 THE WHITE-TAILED HORNET  55
   LONG SINCE THEY SWUNG AS THREE INSTEAD OF TWO-- .  .  .    283 THE GOLD HESPERIDEE  .   25
   BUT INSTEAD I PROUDLY DEVOTE THEM . . . . . . . .  .  .    295 A RECORD STRIDE .  .  .   29
   AND A MOUTHFUL OF DYESTUFF INSTEAD OF A STING. . .  .  .   309 ONE GUESS  .  .  .  .    3
   INSTEAD OF MOVING WITH US AS WE WENT . . . . . . .  .  .   315 IRIS BY NIGHT  .  .  .   24
   NOT TEARS BUT DROPS OF BLOOD INSTEAD. . . . . . .  .  .    327 A MISSIVE MISSILE  .  .   14
   INSTEAD OF PROVING HUMAN WHEN IT NEARED . . . . .  .  .    338 THE MOST OF IT  .  .  .   14
   WAS NAMED FOR HIM INSTEAD OF HER. . . . . . . . .  .  .    347 DISCOVERY OF MADEIRAS  135
   WHEN INSTEAD OF SHEEP . . . . . . . . . . . . .  .  .      437 KITTY HAWK  .  .  .  311
   BY WAITING UP INSTEAD OF GETTING UP. . . . . . . .  .  .   496 A MASQUE OF MERCY .  .   72
   YES, PILGRIM NOW INSTEAD OF RUNAWAY, . . . . . . .  .  .   513 A MASQUE OF MERCY .  .  534
INSTEP
   MY INSTEP ARCH NOT ONLY KEEPS THE ACHE, . . . . .  .  .     68 AFTER APPLE-PICKING  .   21
   I HAVE KEPT HIDDEN IN THE INSTEP ARCH . . . . . .  .  .    379 DIRECTIVE .  .  .  .   55
INSTIGATION
   HE'S A GOOD BOY. 'TWAS AT MY INSTIGATION. . . . .  .  .    459 HOW HARD TO KEEP FROM  173
INSTINCT
   SUCH IS THE INSTINCT OF IT I ALLOW. . . . . . . .  .  .    277 THE WHITE-TAILED HORNET  11
   WON'T THIS WHOLE INSTINCT MATTER BEAR REVISION? .  .  .    279 THE WHITE-TAILED HORNET  50
   OR SO WE PAY THE COMPLIMENT TO INSTINCT, . . . . .  .  .   279 THE WHITE-TAILED HORNET  53
   BUT TRUST MY INSTINCT--I'M A BARD. . . . . . . . .  .  .   326 TO A THINKER  .  .  .   36
   OR WAS THE INSTINCT IN HIM FOOLED? . . . . . . . .  .  .   344 DISCOVERY OF MADEIRAS  44
INSTINCTIVE
   HOW HAPPILY INSTINCTIVE WE REMAIN, . . . . . . . .  .  .   425 ACCIDENTALLY ON PURPOSE  22
   OUR INSTINCTIVE VENTURE . . . . . . . . . . . .  .  .      435 KITTY HAWK  .  .  .  214
INSTINCTIVELY
   I HAVE BEEN SO INSTINCTIVELY THOROUGH . . . . . .  .  .    282 A DRUMLIN WOODCHUCK  .   31
INSTITUTED
   AND SERVED US RIGHT FOR HAVING INSTITUTED . . . .  .  .    279 THE WHITE-TAILED HORNET  58
   AND INSTITUTED AN INVESTIGATION . . . . . . . . .  .  .    293 AT WOODWARD'S GARDENS .   25
INSTITUTIONS
   THERE ARE FEW INSTITUTIONS STANDING HIGHER . . . .  .  .   400 TO THE RIGHT PERSON  .    4
INSTITUTION'S
   BE ANY INSTITUTION'S NEED. . . . . . . . . . . .  .  .     274 A LONE STRIKER  .  .  .   55
INSTRUCT
   "YOU KNOW SO MUCH, GO ON, INSTRUCT ME FURTHER. . .  .  .   458 HOW HARD TO KEEP FROM  146
INSTRUMENT
   AFTER AN INTERVAL, HIS INSTRUMENT, . . . . . . . .  .  .    15 WAITING  .  .  .  .   21
```

INSTRUMENT (CONTINUED)
    THEY STRING AN INSTRUMENT AGAINST THE SKY . . . . 141 THE LINE-GANG . . . 5
INSTRUMENTS
    TWO INSTRUMENTS OF NEARLY EQUAL HOPE, ... 269 THE BEAR 20
INSURANCE
    BURNED DOWN HIS FARMHOUSE FOR THE FIRE INSURANCE, ... 168 NEW HAMPSHIRE . . . 302
    HE BURNED HIS HOUSE DOWN FOR THE FIRE INSURANCE . . . . 177 THE STAR-SPLITTER . . 16
    HE BURNED HIS HOUSE DOWN FOR THE FIRE INSURANCE . . . . 177 THE STAR-SPLITTER . . 30
    WAS THE DISCOVERY OF FIRE INSURANCE. . . . . 506 A MASQUE OF MERCY . . 319
INSURE
    TO INSURE THEIR NOT BEING WASTED ON ME. . . . . 187 THE AX-HELVE 68
    TO INSURE A JET DEPARTURE OF OUR GOING . . . . 460 HOW HARD TO KEEP FROM 201
    IS JUST A FRAME-UP TO INSURE THE FAILURE . . . . 511 A MASQUE OF MERCY . . 483
IN'T
    ALL MODERN, NOTHING ANCIENT IN'T, ... 328 A MISSIVE MISSILE . . 45
INTAKE
    AND FROM THAT ONE INTAKE OF FIRE . . . . 266 SITTING BY A BUSH . . 7
INTELLECT
    A BOY, PRESUMING ON HIS INTELLECT, ... 293 AT WOODWARD'S GARDENS . 1
    WE WERE NOT GIVEN EYES OR INTELLECT . . . . 515 A MASQUE OF MERCY . . 586
INTELLECTUAL
    OF INTELLECTUAL DISSATISFACTION, ... 169 NEW HAMPSHIRE . . . 328
    HIS SEAT UPON THE INTELLECTUAL THRONE"-- . . . . 171 NEW HAMPSHIRE . . . 385
INTELLIGENCE
    TO SHOW THE LEVEL OF INTELLIGENCE . . . . 168 NEW HAMPSHIRE . . . 287
    PLAINLY WITH AN INTELLIGENCE I DEALT. . . . . 357 A CONSIDERABLE SPECK . 15
    FROM HIS INFERIORS IN INTELLIGENCE . . . . 481 A MASQUE OF REASON . . 213
INTEMPERANCE
    THEY RAISE IN THEIR INTEMPERANCE A CLOUD . . . . . 411 POD OF THE MILKWEED . 27
INTEMPERATE
    IT MAKES THE BUTTERFLIES INTEMPERATE. . . . . 411 POD OF THE MILKWEED . 22
INTENSE
    I SHOULD FIND IT NO MORE NO LESS INTENSE. . . . . . 291 ON HEART'S BEGINNING TO 20
INTENSIFY
    AND TO INTENSIFY THE DRAMA . . . . 417 AMERICA IS HARD TO SEE 19
INTENT
    IT LOOKED AS IF A NIGHT OF DARK INTENT . . . . . 250 ONCE BY THE PACIFIC . 10
    INTENT ON GIVING AND TAKING PAIN. . . . . 252 THE THATCH 2
    WITH INTENT TO VAULT . . . . 436 KITTY HAWK 263
INTENTION
    WITH THE INTENTION BLAZONED ON THEIR BANNERS . . . . 397 THE PLANNERS 11
    GRANT ME INTENTION, PURPOSE, AND DESIGN-- . . . . 425 ACCIDENTALLY ON PURPOSE 19
INTENTIONAL
    ARE RIGHT. BUT 'TWAS INTENTIONAL INJUSTICE. . . . . 509 A MASQUE OF MERCY . . 414
INTEREST
    BUT WHAT WOULD INTEREST YOU ABOUT THE BROOK, ... 42 THE MOUNTAIN 48
    THAT'S HIS MISTAKE. THE DEAR KNOWS MY INTEREST . . . . 84 THE HOUSEKEEPER . . . 87
    A PERSONAL INTEREST IN THE LOCKING UP . . . . . . 115 IN THE HOME STRETCH . 134
    FOR INTEREST, AND I'VE BOUGHT A MOUNTAIN FARM . . . . 316 BUILD SOIL 7
    THE REASON ARTISTS SHOW SO LITTLE INTEREST . . . . 461 HOW HARD TO KEEP FROM 230
    I DON'T SEE HOW IT CAN BE TO HIS INTEREST, ... 505 A MASQUE OF MERCY . . 311
INTERESTED
    AND SHE'S A WOMAN: SHE'S NOT INTERESTED . . . . . 479 A MASQUE OF REASON . . 173
INTERESTING
    TO SEE WHAT PEOPLE FOUND SO INTERESTING . . . . . 148 SNOW 162
INTERESTS
    AND WHEN THEIR INTERESTS IN IT END, ... 291 ON HEART'S BEGINNING TO 17
    BUT EVEN WHERE, THUS, OPPOSING INTERESTS KILL, ... 350 TO A YOUNG WRETCH . . 14
    WHAT ARE HER INTERESTS, JOB? / WITCH-WOMEN'S RIGHTS. . . 479 A MASQUE OF REASON . . 175
    OR CLEAR OFF WHAT WE KNOW HIS INTERESTS ARE. . . . . 509 A MASQUE OF MERCY . . 427
INTERFERE
    THE PLANETS SEEM TO INTERFERE IN THEIR CURVES, ... 268 ON LOOKING UP BY CHANCE 6
    TO EARN A LIVING. I DON'T INTERFERE. . . . . 459 HOW HARD TO KEEP FROM 180
INTERFERED
    OF HAVING INTERFERED IN THE HUSE BUSINESS. . . . . 209 PAUPER WITCH OF GRAFTON 75
INTERFERES
    UNLESS A GOVERNMENT INTERFERES. . . . . 376 SOMETHING FOR HOPE . . 20
INTERFERING
    I'VE KNOWN ERE NOW AN INTERFERING BRANCH . . . . . 185 THE AX-HELVE 1
INTERLOCK
    THEIRS INTERLOCK. . . . . 219 I WILL SING YOU ONE-O . 59
INTERLUDE
    UNLESS I DO?" / " A PRETTY INTERLUDE," . . . . . . 99 THE SELF-SEEKER . . . 180
INTERMENTAL
    SOME MINDS ARE SO CONFOUNDED INTERMENTAL . . . . . 321 BUILD SOIL 151
INTERMINABLE
    ALL IS AN INTERMINABLE CHAIN OF LONGING. . . . . . 421 ESCAPIST--NEVER . . . 12
INTERNATIONAL
    JUST SO BEFORE WE'RE INTERNATIONAL, ... 320 BUILD SOIL 145
INTERPERSONAL
    MY FRIENDS ALL KNOW I'M INTERPERSONAL. . . . . . . 320 BUILD SOIL 142
    BUT LONG BEFORE I'M INTERPERSONAL, ... 320 BUILD SOIL 143
INTERPOSED
    OF SOMETHING INTERPOSED BETWEEN THEIR SIGHT . . . . . 109 THE EXPOSED NEST . . 18
INTERPRET
    CAN YOU INTERPRET DREAMS? I DREAMED LAST NIGHT . . . . 501 A MASQUE OF MERCY . . 200
INTERPRETATION
    THIS WOULD BE MY INTERPRETATION OF HIM. . . . . . . 408 FROM PLANE TO PLANE . 126
INTERRUPTED
    AND LIFELESS FROM AN INTERRUPTED ARC. . . . . . . 172 A STAR IN A STONEBOAT . 9
    WHEN FAR AWAY AN INTERRUPTED CRY . . . . 255 ACQUAINTED WITH NIGHT . 8
    WHAT I WAS THINKING WHEN YOU INTERRUPTED . . . . . 325 BUILD SOIL 289
INTERRUPTION
    WE NEED THE INTERRUPTION OF THE NIGHT . . . . . . 370 THE LITERATE FARMER AND 80
    PARDON MY INTERRUPTION; I'M UNHAPPY. . . . . 460 HOW HARD TO KEEP FROM 204
INTERSECT
    THEY FALL, THEY RIP THE GRASS, THEY INTERSECT . . . . 261 A SOLDIER 9

INTERSTELLAR
    THOUGHT CLEAVES THE INTERSTELLAR GLOOM . . . . 120 BOND AND FREE . . . 11
    OF JOSTLING ROCK IN INTERSTELLAR SPACE. . . . . 173 A STAR IN A STONEBOAT. 33
INTERSTICES
    THROUGH THE INTERSTICES OF THINGS AJAR . . . . 303 A BIRD SINGING IN SLEEP 10
INTERVAL
    AFTER AN INTERVAL, HIS INSTRUMENT, ... 15 WAITING 21
    MOUNTAIN INTERVAL . . . . 103 MOUNTAIN INTERVAL . . T
    I'VE HAD TO GIVE MY INTERVAL FARM UP . . . . 316 BUILD SOIL 6
    NOWHERE BUT ON THE BRADFORD INTERVAL . . . . 404 FROM PLANE TO PLANE . 21
INTIMATION
    AN INTIMATION, A SHOT OF RAY, ... 421 ONE MORE BREVITY . . 67
INTO---NOT INDEXED
INTONING
    FOR THE DEFICIENCY BY CHURCH INTONING. . . . . . . 460 HOW HARD TO KEEP FROM 220
    PROSE MADE OF, GIVEN AN AIR BY CHURCH INTONING. . . . 461 HOW HARD TO KEEP FROM 222
IN-TOPPLING
    THE CITY SEEMS IN-TOPPLING FROM A HEIGHT, ... 386 THE FEAR OF MAN . . . 5
INTRODUCE
    I WANT TO INTRODUCE YOU TO THE PEOPLE . . . . 215 A FOUNTAIN, A BOTTLE . 75
    CHRIST CAME TO INTRODUCE A BREAK WITH LOGIC . . . . . 511 A MASQUE OF MERCY . . 475
INVASION
    REBELLION, PESTILENCE, INVASION? / EARTHQUAKE . . . . 502 A MASQUE OF MERCY . . 225
INVENT
    TO REMEMBER OR INVENT . . . . 309 HARDSHIP OF ACCOUNTING 4
    AN ERRAND HE MAY HAVE HAD TO INVENT, ... 364 TRESPASS 19
INVENTED
    HAVING INVENTED A NEW HOLOCAUST, ... 399 U.S. 1946 KING'S X . . 1
    GOD, WHO INVENTED EARTH? / WHAT, STILL AWAKE? . . . . 480 A MASQUE OF REASON . . 201
    WAS OF THE DEVIL. HE INVENTED HELL, ... 480 A MASQUE OF REASON . . 203
INVENTION
    OR SEE WHAT COMES OF SCIENCE AND INVENTION, ... 355 THE LESSON FOR TODAY . 143
    'GAINST AMERICAN INVENTION-- . . . . 396 AN IMPORTER 10
INVENTIONS
    MADE GOOD FOR EVERYONE--THINGS LIKE INVENTIONS-- . . . 319 BUILD SOIL 94
INVESTED
    WHILE I INVESTED HIM WITH REASONS; . . . . 140 BROWN'S DESCENT . . . 72
INVESTIGATION
    AND INSTITUTED AN INVESTIGATION . . . . 293 AT WOODWARD'S GARDENS . 25
INVESTMENT
    THE INVESTMENT . . . . 263 THE INVESTMENT . . . T
    FOR HER INVESTMENT IN HIS VENTURE. . . . . 416 AMERICA IS HARD TO SEE 12
INVIDIOUS
    IN ONE LONG INVIDIOUS DRAFT. . . . . 444 THE DRAFT HORSE . . . 12
INVISIBLE
    INVISIBLE AT DAWN-- . . . .   9 STARS 8
    AT THE NEXT DRINK IT GREW INVISIBLE. . . . . 194 PAUL'S WIFE 103
    BY BEING INVISIBLE FOR WHAT IT WAS, ... 216 A FOUNTAIN, A BOTTLE . 106
    THE WORLD WAS A BLACK INVISIBLE FIELD. . . . . . . 253 THE THATCH 10
    INVISIBLE HANDS CROWDED ON HER SHOULDER . . . . . . 256 THE LOVELY BE CHOOSERS 12
    IS WORKED BY HANDS INVISIBLE, OFFSTAGE.) . . . . . . 489 A MASQUE OF REASON . . 455
INVITATION
    THEY TAPPED AT MY EYELIDS AND TOUCHED MY LIPS WITH AN
        INVITATION TO GRIEF. . . . . 298 A LEAF-TREADER . . . 10
INVITE
    CALL YOU TO ASK YOU TO INVITE ME HOME.--" . . . . . 143 SNOW 27
INVOKES
    KIPLING INVOKES YOU AS LORD GOD OF HOSTS. . . . . . 479 A MASQUE OF REASON . . 179
INVOLUNTARY
    PLEASE, MY INVOLUNTARY HOST, ... 381 AN UNSTAMPED LETTER IN 38
INWARD
    IT COSTS NO INWARD STRUGGLE NOT TO GO, ... 10 STORM FEAR 7
    SHATTER IT INWARD ON THE UNSWEPT FLOORS. . . . . . . 216 A FOUNTAIN, A BOTTLE . 104
    FROM INWARD FIRES OR BRUSH OF PASSING FEET. . . . . . 239 OUR SINGING STRENGTH . 18
    TRUSTING FEATHERS AND INWARD FIRE . . . . 253 THE THATCH 26
    THAT ALL DAY FIGHTS A NERVOUS INWARD RAGE, ... 269 THE BEAR 14
    AND HAD HE FALLEN INWARD ON THE FLOOR, ... 292 FIGURE IN THE DOORWAY . 8
INWARDNESS
    "YOU SAY YOU KNOW THE INWARDNESS OF MEN, ... 456 HOW HARD TO KEEP FROM 98
IOTA
    'TIS THE IOTA SUBSCRIPT OF THE GREEK. . . . . 387 IOTA SUBSCRIPT . . . 4
    IOTA SUBSCRIPT . . . . 387 IOTA SUBSCRIPT . . . T
I.Q.
    I PASSED WITH SUCH A HIGH I.Q. . . . . 467 QUANDARY 26
IRA
    "THE PORTRAIT OF THE SOUL OF MY GRANSIR IRA. . . . . 366 OF STONES OF THE PLACE 15
IRELAND
    SOMEWHERE IN IRELAND ON A MOUNTAIN TOP." . . . . . . 43 THE MOUNTAIN 76
    SAMOA, RUSSIA, IRELAND I COMPLAIN OF, ... 166 NEW HAMPSHIRE . . . 244
IRESON
    WHITTIER'S LUCK WITH SKIPPER IRESON AWES ME-- . . . . 317 BUILD SOIL 44
IRESON'S
    AND GIVE SOMEONE THE SKIPPER IRESON'S RIDE. . . . . . 163 NEW HAMPSHIRE . . . 143
IRIS
    IRIS BY NIGHT . . . . 315 IRIS BY NIGHT . . . T
IRMA
    AS LESLEY, CAROL, IRMA, MARJORIE, ... 181 MAPLE 46
IRON
    AND RECOGNIZED HIM, THROUGH THE IRON GRAY . . . . . 160 NEW HAMPSHIRE . . . 47
    HE MOVED IT ROUGHLY WITH AN IRON BAR, ... 173 A STAR IN A STONEBOAT . 25
    BENDS SQUARE IN WOODS, AN IRON SPINE . . . . 331 BEECH 2
    BESIDES THE WEAR OF IRON WAGON WHEELS . . . . 377 DIRECTIVE 14
    FROM IRON . . . . 468 FROM IRON . . . . . T
    "THE CITY'S GROTESQUE IRON SKELETONS . . . . 506 A MASQUE OF MERCY . . 332
IRONING-OUT
    A DECENT PRODUCT OF LIFE'S IRONING-OUT; . . . . . . 201 PLACE FOR A THIRD . . 67
IRREGULAR
    WHERE AN IRREGULAR SUN-BORDERED CLOUD . . . . 69 THE CODE 4

PAGE TITLE   LINE

IRRELIGIOUS
    FOR ME TO SAY IT WOULD BE IRRELIGIOUS. . . . . . . 520 A MASQUE OF MERCY . . 708
IRRESISTIBLE
    AN IRRESISTIBLE IMPOSSIBILITY. . . . . 512 A MASQUE OF MERCY . . 495
    HIS IRRESISTIBLE IMPOSSIBILITY, ... 513 A MASQUE OF MERCY . . 520
IRRESOLUTION
    BUT FROM IRRESOLUTION IN HIS BACK . . . . 361 A LOOSE MOUNTAIN . . 19
IRRESPONSIBLE
    AN IRRESPONSIBLE DIVINITY . . . . 390 TWO LEADING LIGHTS . . 27
IRREVERENCE
    BUT IF YOU WILL FORGIVE ME THE IRREVERENCE, ... 482 A MASQUE OF REASON . . 243
IRREVERENTLY
    BOOKS WERE NOT THROWN IRREVERENTLY ABOUT. . . . . . 216 A FOUNTAIN, A BOTTLE . 117
IS---NOT INDEXED
ISLAND
    RHODE ISLAND, NEW YORK, OR VERMONT WAS THIS: . . . . 167 NEW HAMPSHIRE . . . 251
    THE ISLAND HE FOUND WAS VERIFIED. . . . . 347 DISCOVERY OF MADEIRAS . 133
    THE BAD ISLAND--EASTER . . . . 447 THE BAD ISLAND--EASTER T
    ENVOI TO HYDE THE CASTAWAY OF CROW ISLAND . . . . . 466 SOME SCIENCE FICTION . D
ISLANDS
    BUT ISLANDS OF THE BLESSED, BLESS YOU, SON, ... 363 AN ANSWER 1
ISLE
    I LOOKED FOR HIM BEHIND AN ISLE OF TREES; . . . . . 22 THE TUFT OF FLOWERS . 5
    WHAT NOW IS INLAND SHALL BE OCEAN ISLE, ... 335 I COULD GIVE ALL . . 6
    THEY BROUGHT HER TO A NAMELESS ISLE. . . . . . . 347 DISCOVERY OF MADEIRAS . 110
    I WAS AT COLLEGE IN THE ISLE OF RHODES." . . . . . 455 HOW HARD TO KEEP FROM 53
    ON YOUR ISLE THAT WOULD BE AN ISLE . . . . . . 466 SOME SCIENCE FICTION . 35
ISLES
    AT THE ISLES OF SHOALS, AND SATISFIED HIMSELF . . . . 161 NEW HAMPSHIRE . . . 76
    TO SEEK FOR THE HAPPY ISLES TOGETHER. . . . . . 262 THE FLOWER BOAT . . 12
    'CROSS THE AEGEAN ISLES, ... 437 KITTY HAWK . . . 289
ISN'T---NOT INDEXED
ISSUE
    AS LONG AS THE GREAT ISSUE WAS TO SEE . . . . . . 422 FOR JOHN F. KENNEDY . 12
ISTHMUS
    BUT ISN'T BECAUSE OF AN ISTHMUS. . . . . 466 SOME SCIENCE FICTION . 36
IT---NOT INDEXED
ITALY
    NO LESS THAN ENGLAND, FRANCE, AND ITALY. . . . . . 166 NEW HAMPSHIRE . . . 245
IT'D---NOT INDEXED
ITEM
    BUT THIS POOR MICROSCOPIC ITEM NOW! . . . . . . 358 A CONSIDERABLE SPECK . 27
IT'S---NOT INDEXED
ITS---NOT INDEXED
ITSELF
    THE CITY HAD WITHDRAWN INTO ITSELF . . . . . . 105 CHRISTMAS TREES . . . 1
    NOR WAS THE GRASS ITSELF YOUR REAL CONCERN, ... 109 THE EXPOSED NEST . . 10
    THE FIRE ITSELF CAN PUT IT OUT, AND THAT . . . . . 130 THE BONFIRE . . . 25
    TRYING TO TURN ITSELF BACKWARD OR FORWARD, ... 147 SNOW 119
    EVER PRESENTS ITSELF BEFORE US TWICE. . . . . . 147 SNOW 130
    IT MOVED ITSELF. THE WIND'S AT NAUGHT IN HERE. . . . . 148 SNOW 137
    AND RECOGNIZED AS SUCH IN RUSSIA ITSELF . . . . . 167 NEW HAMPSHIRE . . . 278
    THAT SHOWED ITSELF IN DENDROPHOBIA. . . . . . 171 NEW HAMPSHIRE . . . 375
    THAT COULD HAVE DROPPED A LEAF WAS DOWN ITSELF . . . . 175 THE CENSUS-TAKER . . 19
    AND ARROWHEADS ITSELF. MUCH USE FOR YEARS . . . . . 189 THE GRINDSTONE . . 38
    AND CARRIED ITSELF LIKE A PILE OF DISHES . . . . . 203 THE WITCH OF COOS . 29
    THE WIND ONCE BLEW ITSELF UNTAUGHT, ... 223 THE AIM WAS SONG . 2
    OR EARTHSLIDE MOVED AT NIGHT, IT MOVED ITSELF; . . . . 229 TWO LOOK AT TWO . . 12
    THE ROAD ALONE MAINTAINED ITSELF IN MUD, ... 239 OUR SINGING STRENGTH . 16
    BUT POWER OF BLOOD ITSELF RELEASES BLOOD. . . . . . 254 THE FLOOD 6
    CAN TRUST ITSELF TO GO BY CONTRARIES . . . . . 258 WEST-RUNNING BROOK . . 7
    FLUNG BACKWARD ON ITSELF IN ONE WHITE WAVE, ... 258 WEST-RUNNING BROOK . . 20
    IN THAT WHITE WAVE RUNS COUNTER TO ITSELF. . . . . 259 WEST-RUNNING BROOK . . 39
    SAVE BY SOME STRANGE RESISTANCE IN ITSELF, ... 259 WEST-RUNNING BROOK . . 58
    IT HAS THIS THROWING BACKWARD ON ITSELF . . . . . 259 WEST-RUNNING BROOK . . 61
    IT SET ITSELF TO KEEP THOSE THREE ALIVE; . . . . . 283 THE GOLD HESPERIDEE . 5
    THEY MIGHT NOT UNDERSTAND THE SUN ITSELF. . . . . . 294 AT WOODWARD'S GARDENS . 36
    THAT HAD EASED ITSELF OF ITS SUMMER LOAD, ... 304 UNHARVESTED 5
    POETRY, ITSELF ONCE MORE, IS BACK IN LOVE. . . . . 318 BUILD SOIL . . . 89
    IT IS JUST FOOL ENOUGH TO THINK ITSELF . . . . . 319 BUILD SOIL . . . 119
    BUILD SOIL. TURN THE FARM IN UPON ITSELF . . . . . 323 BUILD SOIL . . . 234
    UNTIL IT CAN CONTAIN ITSELF NO MORE, ... 323 BUILD SOIL . . . 235
    LAWS TO ITSELF, IT SEEMS, AND YET HAVE NO . . . . . 324 BUILD SOIL . . . 247
    AND LOVE ITSELF WERE GROWING DIM. . . . . . 347 DISCOVERY OF MADEIRAS . 117
    THE EARTH ITSELF IS LIABLE TO THE FATE . . . . . 355 THE LESSON FOR TODAY . 147
    MUST FIND WHERE TO POUR ITSELF INTO AND EMPTY? . . . . 379 TOO ANXIOUS FOR RIVERS 4
    WRAPPED IN AROUND ITSELF AND SELF-BEFRIENDED, ... 396 ANY SIZE WE PLEASE . . 10
    WILL OF ITSELF TAKE FIRE AND LIGHT THE WORLD UP. . . . 414 A CABIN IN THE CLEARING 27
    THE STAR ITSELF--HEAVEN'S GREATEST STAR, ... 421 ONE MORE BREVITY . 60
    HAS JUSTIFIED ITSELF IN FREEDOM'S STORY . . . . . 423 FOR JOHN F. KENNEDY . 52
    (THE DOOR HERE OPENS DARKLY OF ITSELF.) . . . . . 514 A MASQUE OF MERCY . 550
ITZAS
    FOR INSTANCE, WHEN TO PURIFY THE ITZAS . . . . . 510 A MASQUE OF MERCY . 445
I'VE---NOT INDEXED
IVORIES
    BAMBOOS, IVORIES, JADES, AND LACQUERS, ... 396 AN IMPORTER 3

J

JACKKNIFE
    (THEY TREATED IT AS HIS.) "YOU TAKE A JACKKNIFE, . . . 193 PAUL'S WIFE . . . 80
    HE THOUGH HE'D BETTER TAKE HIS JACKKNIFE TO. . . . . 193 PAUL'S WIFE . . . 87
JACKSON
    THE ANDREW JACKSON SLOGAN OF VAE VICTIS . . . . . 510 A MASQUE OF MERCY . 459
JADES
    BAMBOOS, IVORIES, JADES, AND LACQUERS, ... 396 AN IMPORTER 3

JAG
   WITH A BIG JAG TO EMPTY IN A BAY. . . . . 71 THE CODE 54
JAGGED
   THE LINE MUST BE A JAGGED BLADE. . . . . 327 A MISSIVE MISSILE . . 15
JAIL
   "IT'S TIME I TOOK MY TURN UPSTAIRS IN JAIL"-- . . . . 67 A SERVANT TO SERVANTS . 146
   THAN BY THE FEAR OF THE ASYLUM, JAIL, OR POORHOUSE, . . 520 A MASQUE OF MERCY . . 703
JAM
   HE'S GROPING IN THE CELLAR AFTER JAM-- . . . . . 77 THE GENERATIONS OF MEN 101
JAMES
   "YOU DIDN'T KNOW. BUT JAMES IS ONE BIG FOOL. . . . . 70 THE CODE 15
   JAMES WOULD TAKE TIME, OF COURSE, TO CHEW IT OVER . . 70 THE CODE 18
JANGLED
   THAT JANGLED EVEN ABOVE THE GENERAL NOISE, ... 142 THE VANISHING RED . . 25
JANIZARY
   WILL THE SPECIAL JANIZARY . . . . 288 DEPARTMENTAL 25
JANUARY
   UNTIL THE JANUARY THAW . . . . 139 BROWN'S DESCENT . . 58
JAPANESE
   HIS JAPANESE CREPE-PAPER GLOBE FOR TROPHY? . . . . . 278 THE WHITE-TAILED HORNET 18
JARRED
   I HAD MY NATIVE SIMILE JARRED. . . . . 265 THE DOOR IN THE DARK . 7
JARS
   THE STUBBORN THING, THE WAY IT JARS YOUR ARM!-- . . . 153 SNOW 296
JAW
   BUT JIMMY ONLY MADE HIS JAW RECEDE . . . . 114 IN THE HOME STRETCH . 101
JAY'S
   FOR A SYLVAN SIGN THAT THE BLUE JAY'S SCREECH . . . . 24 PAN WITH US 18
JEALOUS
   YOU SEE THE LORD GOD IS A JEALOUS GOD! . . . . . 504 A MASQUE OF MERCY . . 289
JEFFERS
   "SHINE, PERISHING REPUBLIC." / ROBINSON JEFFERS . . . 449 OUR DOOM TO BLOOM . . S
   MY FRIENDS AND STOKERS, JEFFERS AND O'NEILL. . . . 516 A MASQUE OF MERCY . . 607
JEFFERSON
   A CASE FOR JEFFERSON . . . . 393 A CASE FOR JEFFERSON . T
   JOHN ADAMS, JEFFERSON, AND MADISON-- . . . . . . 422 FOR JOHN F. KENNEDY . 26
JEFFERSON'S
   THAT'S A HARD MYSTERY OF JEFFERSON'S. . . . . . . 57 THE BLACK COTTAGE . . 64
JEHOVAH
   TELL THEM IAMB, JEHOVAH SAID, AND MEANT IT. . . . . 460 HOW HARD TO KEEP FROM 218
JELLYFISH
   THERE ONCE WE LAY AS BLOBS OF JELLYFISH . . . . . 395 ETHEREALIZING . . . 9
JEMIMA
   I'VE SPOILED JEMIMA IN MORE WAYS THAN ONE. . . . . 49 A HUNDRED COLLARS . . 141
JERICHO
   LIKE THE ONE JOSHUA GAVE JERICHO. . . . . 504 A MASQUE OF MERCY . . 274
JERK
   AND SUDDENLY, WITHOUT A JERK OR TWITCH, ... 237 A HILLSIDE THAW . . . 21
JERKS
   HE VIEWED THEM QUIZZICALLY WITH JERKS OF HEAD, . . . 229 TWO LOOK AT TWO . . . 31
JERRY
   "DEATH'S COME TO JERRY MCCORMIC, ... 288 DEPARTMENTAL 23
   OUR SELFLESS FORAGER JERRY. . . . . 288 DEPARTMENTAL 24
JERSEY
   MY SON IN JERSEY SAYS A FRIEND OF HIS . . . . . . 371 THE LITERATE FARMER AND 95
JERSEYITE
   PUT UP ON TRIAL BY THAT JERSEYITE . . . . 369 THE LITERATE FARMER AND 40
JESSE
   TO TRY ANOTHER. / JESSE BEL'S A GIRL . . . . . . 499 A MASQUE OF MERCY . 159
   JESSE HAS GIVEN PAUL THE RENT OF IT . . . . . . 514 A MASQUE OF MERCY . 560
   BY SOMETHING TO BELIEVE IN, JESSE MEANS . . . . . 515 A MASQUE OF MERCY . 569
JEST
   THE JEST SEEMED HIS AND THE PLAUDITS HIS. . . . . 346 DISCOVERY OF MADEIRAS . 92
   SOME STANDING JEST BETWEEN YOU MEN? . . . . . . 346 DISCOVERY OF MADEIRAS . 94
   ON ME AS MUCH AS ANY IS THE JEST. . . . . 355 THE LESSON FOR TODAY . 154
   AND AS FOR MY JEST . . . . 430 KITTY HAWK 80
JET
   OR SOME SUCH SENSE AS SAYS HOW HIGH SHALL JET . . . 169 NEW HAMPSHIRE . . . 325
   IN BROAD ROUND EARRINGS, GOLD AND JET WITH PEARLS, . . 256 THE LOVELY BE CHOOSERS 15
   TO INSURE A JET DEPARTURE OF OUR GOING . . . . . 460 HOW HARD TO KEEP FROM 201
JEW
   IT ISN'T BECAUSE HE'S RUSSIAN JEW. . . . . . . 393 A CASE FOR JEFFERSON . 5
   AND GIVE YOU REST, POOR WANDERING JEW. / I'M NOT . . 498 A MASQUE OF MERCY . 133
   THE WANDERING JEW--I'M WHO I SAY I AM, ... 498 A MASQUE OF MERCY . 134
JEWEL
   AS YOU MIGHT TRY A JEWEL IN YOUR HAIR. . . . . . 245 THE FREEDOM OF THE MOON 3
JEWELS
   LIKE TWO KINDS OF JEWELS, A VISION FOR THIEVES." . . 62 BLUEBERRIES 105
   LIKE UNCUT JEWELS, DULL AND ROUGH. . . . . . . 141 THE GUM-GATHERER . . 31
   SO THE CROWN FELL AND THE CROWN JEWELS SCATTERED. . . 453 HOW HARD TO KEEP FROM 6
   THE QUINTESSENCE OF JEWELS, AND I KNOW . . . . . 455 HOW HARD TO KEEP FROM 43
   JEWELS AND HORSES, WOMEN, WINE, AND SONG." . . . . 455 HOW HARD TO KEEP FROM 62
   I TOLD YOU I KNEW THE QUINTESSENCE OF JEWELS. . . . 456 HOW HARD TO KEEP FROM 88
JEWEL-SMALL
   SUN-SHAPED AND JEWEL-SMALL, ... 13 ROSE POGONIAS . . . 2
JEWEL-STEADY
   SO JEWEL-STEADY IN THE WIND AND DUST. . . . . . 386 THE FEAR OF MAN . . . 12
JEWELWEED
   OR FLOURISHED AND COME UP IN JEWELWEED, ... 119 HYLA BROOK 7
JILTED
   OR SO OF HAVING ONE, AND THEN BEEN JILTED; . . . . 191 PAUL'S WIFE 7
JIM (SEE SLIM-JIM)
JIMMY
   "SAY THAT TO JIMMY HERE. HE NEEDS A FARM." . . . . 114 IN THE HOME STRETCH . 100
   BUT JIMMY ONLY MADE HIS JAW RECEDE . . . . . . 114 IN THE HOME STRETCH . 101
JINNI
   BUT SUMMONS OUT OF NOWHERE LIKE A JINNI. . . . . . 461 HOW HARD TO KEEP FROM 240

JOB
YOU UNDERSTAND THAT MEANT THE EASY JOB . . . . 71 THE CODE 55
TO BREAK IT TO HIM. YOU MAY HAVE THE JOB." . . . . . 88 THE HOUSEKEEPER . . . 194
WHERE HIS JOB, WHEN HE WASN'T SELLING TICKETS, ... 178 THE STAR-SPLITTER . . 70
HIS NEW JOB GAVE HIM LEISURE FOR STARGAZING. . . . . . 178 THE STAR-SPLITTER . . 75
BAPTISTE KNEW HOW TO MAKE A SHORT JOB LONG . . . . . . 187 THE AX-HELVE 80
HE WANTED TO TAKE MY JOB FOR PAY. . . . . 275 TWO TRAMPS IN MUD TIME . 8
THE IDEA IS NO DOUBT TO MAKE ONE JOB . . . . 370 THE LITERATE FARMER AND 71
TELL HIM HE MAY REMEMBER YOU: YOU'RE JOB. . . . . . . 474 A MASQUE OF REASON . . 33
OH, I REMEMBER WELL: YOU'RE JOB, MY PATIENT. . . . . . 474 A MASQUE OF REASON . . 34
I STOOD BY JOB. I MAY HAVE TURNED ON YOU. . . . . . . 477 A MASQUE OF REASON . . 120
JOB SCRATCHED HIS BOILS AND TRIED TO THINK WHAT HE . . 477 A MASQUE OF REASON . . 121
JOB HADN'T DONE A THING, POOR INNOCENT. . . . . 478 A MASQUE OF REASON . . 127
WHAT ARE HER INTERESTS, JOB? / WITCH-WOMEN'S RIGHTS. . 479 A MASQUE OF REASON . . 175
MUCH AS YOUR HUSBAND, JOB, AND I TOGETHER . . . . . . 481 A MASQUE OF REASON . . 208
I'D TELL YOU, JOB---- / ALL RIGHT, DON'T TELL ME, THEN, 483 A MASQUE OF REASON . . 270
MY KINGDOM, WHAT AN OUTBREAK! / JOB IS RIGHT. . . . . 484 A MASQUE OF REASON . . 302
JOB SAYS THERE'S NO SUCH THING AS EARTH'S BECOMING . . 484 A MASQUE OF REASON . . 316
ONE AT A TIME, PLEASE. I WILL ANSWER JOB FIRST. . . . 484 A MASQUE OF REASON . . 324
I'M GOING TO TELL JOB WHY I TORTURED HIM, ... 484 A MASQUE OF REASON . . 325
I WAS JUST SHOWING OFF TO THE DEVIL, JOB, ... 484 A MASQUE OF REASON . . 327
(JOB TAKES A FEW STEPS PACING.) DO YOU MIND? . . . . 485 A MASQUE OF REASON . . 329
JOB, YOU MUST UNDERSTAND MY PROVOCATION. . . . . . . 485 A MASQUE OF REASON . . 347
I'M NOT PREPARED FOR OR THAT JOB HIMSELF . . . . . . 488 A MASQUE OF REASON . . 414
JOB MENTIONED HIM, AND SO I BROUGHT HIM IN, ... 489 A MASQUE OF REASON . . 432
(HERE ENDETH CHAPTER FORTY-THREE OF JOB.) . . . . . . 490 A MASQUE OF REASON . . 466
JOBS
"DICK WISHES HE COULD SWAP JOBS WITH THE DOCTOR. . . . 404 FROM PLANE TO PLANE . 28
JOB'S
JOB'S WIFE SITS UP.) / WELL, IF WE AREN'T ALL HERE, . . 487 A MASQUE OF REASON . . 392
JOE (SEE JOHN-JOE)
MORE THAN SOME WOMEN LIKE THE DISHPAN, JOE; . . . . . 111 IN THE HOME STRETCH . 31
TO SEE US THROUGH OUR FIRST TWO WEEKS. BUT, JOE, . . . 113 IN THE HOME STRETCH . 74
JOE SAID: "YOU BIG BOYS OUGHT TO FIND A FARM, ... 113 IN THE HOME STRETCH . 95
NOT OFFERING A LADY----" / "THERE AGAIN, JOE! . . . . 116 IN THE HOME STRETCH . 157
IT'S WHO FIRST THOUGHT THE THOUGHT. YOU'RE SEARCHING, JOE, 116 IN THE HOME STRETCH . 172
HIS NAME'S JOE, ... 211 AN EMPTY THREAT . . . 12
DON'T ASK JOE . . . . 212 AN EMPTY THREAT . . . 38
MY NAME'S NOT JOE. I DON'T LIKE WHAT SHE SAYS. . . . . 500 A MASQUE OF MERCY . . 169
JOEL
"JOEL, I'LL HAVE TO LOOK. I CAN'T GO IN, ... 89 THE FEAR 14
HE'S COMING TOWARDS US. JOEL, GO IN--PLEASE. . . . . 90 THE FEAR 39
AND I CAN'T STAND IT. JOEL, LET ME GO!" . . . . . . 91 THE FEAR 48
JOEL, I WON'T--I WON'T--I PROMISE YOU. . . . . . . 91 THE FEAR 52
SHE REACHED A HAND TO JOEL FOR SUPPORT: . . . . . . 91 THE FEAR 68
AND LET YOU SEE." / "YES, DO.--JOEL, GO BACK!" . . . 92 THE FEAR 75
"BUT IF THAT'S ALL--JOEL--YOU REALIZE-- . . . . . . 92 THE FEAR 87
JOEL!" SHE SPOKE AS IF SHE COULDN'T TURN. . . . . . 92 THE FEAR 91
JOE'S
LET ME ALONE. / I'M SICK. JOE'S SICK. THE WORLD'S SICK. . 500 A MASQUE OF MERCY . . 167
JOHN
WHOSE SHOES I PRIMPED TO DANCE IN!" / "AND WHERE'S JOHN?" 81 THE HOUSEKEEPER . . 13
I DON'T KNOW WHERE MYSELF. JOHN THINKS I DO. . . . . 82 THE HOUSEKEEPER . . 24
"IT WILL GO HARD WITH JOHN. WHAT WILL HE DO? . . . . 82 THE HOUSEKEEPER . . 28
JOHN HALL TOUCH ME! NOT IF HE KNOWS HIS FRIENDS. . . . 83 THE HOUSEKEEPER . . 67
IT'S DIFFERENT WITH A MAN, AT LEAST WITH JOHN: . . . . 84 THE HOUSEKEEPER . . 79
ONE THING YOU CAN'T HELP LIKING ABOUT JOHN, ... 85 THE HOUSEKEEPER . . 115
JOHN LIKES TO TELL THE OFFERS HE HAS HAD, ... 86 THE HOUSEKEEPER . . 138
JOHN BOUGHT HIM, AND WE PAID THE BILL WITH BEADS-- . . 86 THE HOUSEKEEPER . . 152
JOHN SAID I WAS TOO OLD TO HAVE GRANDCHILDREN. . . . . 87 THE HOUSEKEEPER . . 175
JOHN HIMSELF WON'T IMAGINE WHO HE IS." . . . . 88 THE HOUSEKEEPER . . 189
YOU'LL BE EXPECTING JOHN. I PITY ESTELLE: . . . . . . 88 THE HOUSEKEEPER . . 191
JOHN THREW THE DOOR WIDE BUT HE DIDN'T ENTER. . . . . 88 THE HOUSEKEEPER . . 205
TO THE PLACE WHERE JOHN HAS BEEN CUTTING TREES, . . . 123 PEA BRUSH 2
"COME, JOHN," HE SAID, "YOU WANT TO SEE THE WHEEL PIT?" 142 THE VANISHING RED . 19
OH, YES, HE SHOWED JOHN THE WHEEL PIT ALL RIGHT. . . . 142 THE VANISHING RED . 29
JOHN SMITH REMARKED THEM AS HE COASTED BY, ... 161 NEW HAMPSHIRE . . 74
SEEMS THERE HAVE BEEN A MAN NAMED JOHN L. DARWIN." . . 168 NEW HAMPSHIRE . . 299
THE HEADSTONE CUT WITH JOHN, BELOVED HUSBAND, ... 200 PLACE FOR A THIRD . 39
"NO, NOT WITH JOHN. THERE WOULDN'T BE NO SENSE. . . . 202 PLACE FOR A THIRD . 77
ALIAS JOHN, ... 211 AN EMPTY THREAT . . 13
FOR JOHN F. KENNEDY HIS INAUGURATION . . . . 422 FOR JOHN F. KENNEDY . T
JOHN ADAMS, JEFFERSON, AND MADISON-- . . . . 422 FOR JOHN F. KENNEDY . 26
JOHN-JOE
EXCEPT ALWAYS JOHN-JOE, ... 211 AN EMPTY THREAT . . 26
JOHN'S
I'LL SAY THAT FOR HIM, JOHN'S NO THREATENER . . . . . 83 THE HOUSEKEEPER . . 68
"AND AFTER ALL WHY SHOULD THEY? JOHN'S BEEN FAIR . . . 84 THE HOUSEKEEPER . . 92
JOHN'S A BAD FARMER. I'M NOT BLAMING HIM. . . . . . . 85 THE HOUSEKEEPER . . 102
YOU SPOKE OF JOHN'S NOT BEING SAFE TO STAY WITH. . . . 85 THE HOUSEKEEPER . . 123
WE HAVE TO GO." / "YOU MEAN THAT'S JOHN'S IDEA." . . . 85 THE HOUSEKEEPER . . 131
JOHN'S ALMOST HERE. I'VE HAD MY EYE ON SOMEONE . . . . 88 THE HOUSEKEEPER . . 196
JOIN
DON'T JOIN TOO MANY GANGS. JOIN FEW IF ANY. . . . . . 325 BUILD SOIL 280
JOIN THE UNITED STATES AND JOIN THE FAMILY-- . . . . 325 BUILD SOIL 281
JOINED
AND IN THE HUSH WE JOINED TO MAKE . . . . 18 GOING FOR WATER . . 19
RETIRED FROM POLITICS AND JOINED THE CHORUS. . . . . 168 NEW HAMPSHIRE . . 297
AND BIRDS THAT JOINED IN THE EXCITED FUN. . . . . . 237 A HILLSIDE THAW . . 15
THAT WOULD HAVE JOINED THE HOUSE IN FLAME . . . . . 241 NEED OF BEING VERSED . 6
OR JOINED WITH SHEDS IN RING-AROUND A DOORYARD. . . . 289 OLD BARN AT THE BOTTOM 2
ALL JOINED IN THE GAME OF HIDE-GOLD. . . . . 311 THE VINDICTIVES . . 28
ALL JOINED IN THE MADDENING GAME. . . . . 311 THE VINDICTIVES . . 32
JOINS
SOMETIMES HE JOINS THEM FOR A DAY OR TWO . . . . . . 44 A HUNDRED COLLARS . . 6
JOINT
WHO KNOW EXACTLY WHAT IS OUT OF JOINT . . . . 351 THE LESSON FOR TODAY . 32

JOINTED
    CAME UP THE JOINTED STOVEPIPE IN THEIR HANDS, ... 113 IN THE HOME STRETCH . 86
JOINTS
    STILL GOING EVERY WHICH WAY IN THE JOINTS, THOUGH, . . . 205 THE WITCH OF COOS . 87
JOKE
    I WASN'T IN ON THE JOKE, ... 365 A NATURE NOTE . . . 10
    AND THIS IS NO ARISTOCRATIC JOKE . . . . 423 FOR JOHN F. KENNEDY . 32
JOKES
    ARE GOING TO BE, UNLESS THESE MONKEY JOKES . . . . . 369 THE LITERATE FARMER AND 44
    FORGIVE, O LORD, MY LITTLE JOKES ON THEE . . . . . . 428 FORGIVE, O LORD.... . 1
JOLLIED
    AND JOLLIED ALONG? . . . . 448 THE BAD ISLAND--EASTER 30
JOLT
    AND SLEPT. THE LOG THAT SHIFTED WITH A JOLT . . . . . 108 OLD MAN'S WINTER NIGHT 23
JONAH
    WHICH IS THE SAME AS SAYING JONAH, JONAH-- . . . . . 495 A MASQUE OF MERCY . 56
    AH, JONAH, JONAH--TWICE--REPROACHFULLY. . . . . . 495 A MASQUE OF MERCY . 57
    JONAH, I'M GLAD, NOT SAD, TO HEAR YOU SAY . . . . . 501 A MASQUE OF MERCY . 213
    BUT OH, NO, NOT FOR JONAH. I REFUSE . . . . . . 505 A MASQUE OF MERCY . 302
    GOOD FOR YOU, JONAH. THAT'S WHAT I'VE BEEN SAYING. . . 510 A MASQUE OF MERCY . 444
    GOOD FOR YOU, JONAH. THAT'S WHAT I'VE BEEN SAYING. . . 517 A MASQUE OF MERCY . 636
    (JONAH STEPS ON THE THRESHOLD AS THE DOOR . . . . . 518 A MASQUE OF MERCY . 649
    BUT JONAH GIVES NO SIGN OF HAVING HEARD.) . . . . . 518 A MASQUE OF MERCY . 668
JONAH'S
    BUT WE ARE TALKING OVER JONAH'S HEAD, ... 509 A MASQUE OF MERCY . 426
    OUR VERY BEST, OUR LIVES LAID DOWN LIKE JONAH'S, . . . 520 A MASQUE OF MERCY . 720
    MY FAILURE IS NO DIFFERENT FROM JONAH'S. . . . . . 521 A MASQUE OF MERCY . 727
    TO LEARN TO SAY (HE MOVES TO JONAH'S FEET.) . . . . 521 A MASQUE OF MERCY . 737
JONAS
    I'M JONAS DOVE--IF THAT IS ANY HELP. . . . . . . 495 A MASQUE OF MERCY . 55
    I'M GOING TO TELL YOU SOMETHING, JONAS DOVE. . . . . 498 A MASQUE OF MERCY . 131
    DO YOU ACCEPT IT, MASTER JONAS DOVE? . . . . . . 512 A MASQUE OF MERCY . 512
    BUT YOU--WHAT IS YOUR ANSWER, JONAS DOVE? . . . . 513 A MASQUE OF MERCY . 529
JOSHUA
    LIKE THE ONE JOSHUA GAVE JERICHO. . . . . . . 504 A MASQUE OF MERCY . 274
JOSTLING
    OF JOSTLING ROCK IN INTERSTELLAR SPACE. . . . . . 173 A STAR IN A STONEBOAT . 33
JOURNEY
    HIS JOURNEY DOWN FROM FIELD TO FIELD. . . . . . 138 BROWN'S DESCENT . 20
    WE SAW HIM SAY ALONG THE ZIGZAG JOURNEY . . . . . 170 NEW HAMPSHIRE . . . 351
    ON JOURNEY THE PENULT. . . . . 464 MILKY WAY IS A COWPATH . 4
JOURNEY'S
    OUR PASSAGE TO OUR JOURNEY'S END FOR GOOD, ... 238 ON A TREE FALLEN ACROSS . 3
JOVE
    NOT FIND A BARKEEP UNTO JOVE IN ME? . . . . . . 443 AUSPEX 9
JOY
    I WAS RUNNING WITH JOY ON THE DEMON'S TRAIL, ... 24 THE DEMIURGE'S LAUGH . 2
    NOW NO JOY BUT LACKS SALT, ... 227 TO EARTHWARD . . . 17
    BE HER FIRST JOY HER WEDDING, ... 256 THE LOVELY BE CHOOSERS 22
    AND AFTER THAT HER NEXT JOY . . . . 256 THE LOVELY BE CHOOSERS 25
    HER THIRD JOY THAT THOUGH NOW THEY CANNOT HELP BUT KNOW, 256 THE LOVELY BE CHOOSERS 28
    GIVE HER A CHILD AT EITHER KNEE FOR FOURTH JOY. . . . 256 THE LOVELY BE CHOOSERS 31
    AND BE HER NEXT JOY THIS: . . . . 257 THE LOVELY BE CHOOSERS 37
    BE HER LAST JOY HER HEART'S GOING OUT TO THIS ONE . . . 257 THE LOVELY BE CHOOSERS 50
    LEAVING LOVE'S ALTERNATIONS, JOY AND GRIEF, ... 317 BUILD SOIL . . . 35
    AND I COULD SHARE TIME'S LACK OF JOY OR GRIEF . . . 335 I COULD GIVE ALL . 9
JOYS
    AND FIXITY IN OUR JOYS, ... 156 THE SOUND OF TREES . . 8
    "DO IT BY JOYS, AND LEAVE HER ALWAYS BLAMELESS. . . . 256 THE LOVELY BE CHOOSERS 21
JUDGE
    ADDED: "YOU CAN JUDGE BETTER AFTER SEEING.-- . . . . 144 SNOW 35
    WHERE I MUST JUDGE IF WHAT HE KNEW ABOUT AN AX . . . . 186 THE AX-HELVE . . 41
    TO JUDGE THEM BY THE WAY THEY CAUGHT THEMSELVES . . . 193 PAUL'S WIFE . . . 65
    WHO WAS SHE TO JUDGE MARRIAGE IN A WORLD . . . . . 201 PLACE FOR A THIRD . 64
    AND I JUDGE FROM THAT ELYSIAN FREIGHT . . . . . . 262 THE FLOWER BOAT . . 9
    IS SUCH AN EXECRABLE JUDGE OF MOTIVES . . . . . . 278 THE WHITE-TAILED HORNET 14
    YOU WOULD NOT THINK YOU KNEW ENOUGH TO JUDGE . . . . 351 THE LESSON FOR TODAY . 29
JUDGED
    I JUDGED THAT SUCH A CRYSTAL CHILL . . . . . . 233 LOOKING FOR SUNSET BIRD 14
    THEY JUDGED ME BY THEIR APPROPRIATE TOOL. . . . . . 276 TWO TRAMPS IN MUD TIME 54
    AND BE JUDGED BY THE OUTCOME, MELIBOEUS. . . . . . 320 BUILD SOIL . . 135
JUDGING
    EVERYONE HAD BEEN WRONG IN JUDGING PAUL. . . . . . 195 PAUL'S WIFE . . . 147
    OF JUDGING WHO IS A CONTEMPORARY LIAR-- . . . . . 317 BUILD SOIL . . 38
    BUT JUDGING BY WHAT LITTLE OF IT STANDS, ... 399 THE INGENUITIES OF DEBT 10
JUDGMENT
    THIS HE SAT LISTENING TO TILL SHE GAVE JUDGMENT. . . . 76 THE GENERATIONS OF MEN 77
    OR COURT OF LAW, AND THIS IS JUDGMENT DAY. . . . . 474 A MASQUE OF REASON . 26
JUG
    WITH HIS PIPE IN HIS MOUTH AND HIS BROWN JUG-- . . . . 77 THE GENERATIONS OF MEN 105
    BUT THE PIPE'S THERE AND SMOKING, AND THE JUG. . . . . 77 THE GENERATIONS OF MEN 107
JUGGLE
    ARE SEEN TO JUGGLE MOONS GALORE. . . . . . . 451 A-WISHING WELL . . . 24
JUICE
    THERE IS NO SLUMBER IN ITS JUICE FOR THEM. . . . . 411 POD OF THE MILKWEED . 23
    AND ALL TANKED UP WITH MINERAL JUICE, ... 463 LINES IN DEJECTION . . 7
JULIUS
    WITNESS HOW HARD IT WAS FOR JULIUS CAESAR. . . . . 454 HOW HARD TO KEEP FROM 22
JULY (SEE FOURTH-OF-JULY)
    ALL THROUGH JULY UNDER THE BLAZING SUN, ... 36 DEATH OF THE HIRED MAN 67
JUMBLED
    HE JUMBLED EVERYTHING. I STOPPED TO LOOK . . . . . 36 DEATH OF THE HIRED MAN 55
JUMPED
    AND WHEN IT ALMOST GAILY JUMPED AND FLOWED, ... 189 THE GRINDSTONE . . 28
    ONCE WHEN THE GRINDSTONE ALMOST JUMPED ITS BEARING . . . 190 THE GRINDSTONE . . . 57
    I ONCE HAD A COW THAT JUMPED OVER THE MOON, ... 462 LINES IN DEJECTION . . 1
JUMPING
    THE ONE ABOUT HIS JUMPING SO'S TO LAND . . . . . . 192 PAUL'S WIFE 50

	PAGE	TITLE	LINE

JUNCTION
AND HAD FOUR HOURS TO WAIT AT WOODSVILLE JUNCTION . . . . 45 A HUNDRED COLLARS . . 16
JUNE
"WARM IN DECEMBER, COLD IN JUNE, YOU SAY?" . . . . . . 44 THE MOUNTAIN 100
BY JUNE OUR BROOK'S RUN OUT OF SONG AND SPEED. . . . . . 119 HYLA BROOK 1
TWO IN JUNE WERE A PAIR-- . . . . 365 A NATURE NOTE 5
AND JUNE WAS NOT MUCH BETTER, COLD AND RAINY. . . . . 407 FROM PLANE TO PLANE . 89
JUNE-GRASS
STEEL-BRIGHT JUNE-GRASS, AND BLACKENING HEADS OF CLOVER. . 109 THE EXPOSED NEST . . 12
JUNGLE
SHE WAS A SAVAGE JUNGLE CAT . . . . 345 DISCOVERY OF MADEIRAS . 64
IN AN ALBINO MONKEY IN A JUNGLE, ... 425 ACCIDENTALLY ON PURPOSE 7
JUNIPER
THERE AMID LOLLING JUNIPER RECLINED, ... 17 THE VANTAGE POINT . . . 4
THE FRUITED BOUGH OF THE JUNIPER . . . . 24 PAN WITH US 23
BENEATH A LOW-SLUNG JUNIPER . . . . 380 AN UNSTAMPED LETTER IN 13
JUPITER
AND JUPITER. . . . . 219 I WILL SING YOU ONE-O . 42
JUPITER AND MARS, ... 438 KITTY HAWK 318
JURY
FROM SAYING ON A JURY "HERE'S THE GUILTY." . . . . . . 317 BUILD SOIL 52
JUST
IT WAS JUST AS THE LIGHT WAS BEGINNING TO FAIL . . . . . 24 THE DEMIURGE'S LAUGH . 4
OH, JUST ANOTHER KIND OF OUTDOOR GAME, ... 33 MENDING WALL . . . 21
NOTHING WOULD DO: HE JUST KEPT NODDING OFF." . . . . . 36 DEATH OF THE HIRED MAN 43
"WARREN!" / "BUT DID HE? I JUST WANT TO KNOW." . . . . . 36 DEATH OF THE HIRED MAN 47
I SYMPATHIZE. I KNOW JUST HOW IT FEELS . . . . 37 DEATH OF THE HIRED MAN 76
BUT JUST THE KIND THAT KINSFOLK CAN'T ABIDE. . . . . . 39 DEATH OF THE HIRED MAN 141
I JUST FOUND WHAT THE MATTER WAS TONIGHT: . . . . . 46 A HUNDRED COLLARS . . 55
"JUST AS YOU SAY. HAVE IT YOUR OWN WAY, THEN. . . . . 47 A HUNDRED COLLARS . . 79
"JUST AS YOU SAY. HERE'S LOOKING AT YOU, THEN.-- . . . . 50 A HUNDRED COLLARS . . 158
I'VE JUST BEGUN THE NIGHT. YOU GET SOME SLEEP. . . . . 50 A HUNDRED COLLARS . . 172
"WHAT IS IT--WHAT?" SHE SAID. / "JUST THAT I SEE." . . . 51 HOME BURIAL 18
A FRONT WITH JUST A DOOR BETWEEN TWO WINDOWS, ... 55 THE BLACK COTTAGE . . 6
IT WASN'T JUST TO KEEP THE STATES TOGETHER, ... 56 THE BLACK COTTAGE . . 56
NOR JUST TO FREE THE SLAVES, THOUGH IT DID BOTH. . . . . 56 THE BLACK COTTAGE . . 57
I'M JUST AS GLAD SHE MADE ME KEEP HANDS OFF, ... 58 THE BLACK COTTAGE . . 104
I WAS JUST GETTING THROUGH WHAT THE FIELD HAD TO SHOW . . 60 BLUEBERRIES 35
"HE JUST KEPT NODDING HIS HEAD UP AND DOWN. . . . . . . 60 BLUEBERRIES 41
JUST TAKING WHAT NATURE IS WILLING TO GIVE, ... 61 BLUEBERRIES 55
THINGS OVER AND OVER THAT JUST WON'T STAY DONE. . . . . 64 A SERVANT TO SERVANTS . 52
THEY KNEW. AND JUST WHEN HE WAS AT THE HEIGHT, ... 66 A SERVANT TO SERVANTS . 125
JUST AS YOU WILL TILL IT BECOMES A HABIT. . . . . . . 67 A SERVANT TO SERVANTS . 147
AND THERE'S MORE TO IT THAN JUST WINDOW VIEWS . . . . . 67 A SERVANT TO SERVANTS . 155
OR JUST SOME HUMAN SLEEP. . . . . 69 AFTER APPLE-PICKING . 42
"WHAT IS THERE WRONG?" / "SOMETHING YOU JUST NOW SAID." . 69 THE CODE 10
BEFORE HE ACTED: HE'S JUST GOT ROUND TO ACT." . . . . 70 THE CODE 19
MOST LIKELY I'D HAVE SERVED YOU JUST THE SAME. . . . . 70 THE CODE 25
YOU WERE JUST TALKING WHAT WAS IN YOUR MIND, ... 70 THE CODE 27
LIKE MEDITATING, AND THEN I JUST DUG IN . . . . . . 72 THE CODE 73
(I MAY HAVE KNOCKED HIM DOWN); BUT MY JUST TRYING . . . 72 THE CODE 103
"DISCHARGE ME? NO! HE KNEW I DID JUST RIGHT." . . . . . 73 THE CODE 114
PROVISION THERE HAD BEEN FOR JUST SUCH MEETING . . . . 74 THE GENERATIONS OF MEN 38
"JUST SO--THAT OUGHT TO BE ENOUGH PROTECTION." . . . . 75 THE GENERATIONS OF MEN 66
"OH, IF YOU'RE GOING TO USE YOUR EYES, JUST HEAR . . . . 76 THE GENERATIONS OF MEN 98
THE NOSE IS JUST THE SAME, AND SO'S THE CHIN-- . . . . 77 THE GENERATIONS OF MEN 114
"I LIKE YOUR 'GOING TO BE.' YOU SAID JUST NOW . . . . . 80 THE GENERATIONS OF MEN 200
"I DON'T JUST SEE HIM LIVING MANY YEARS, ... 82 THE HOUSEKEEPER . . . 43
HE'S JUST DROPPED EVERYTHING. HE'S LIKE A CHILD. . . . . 83 THE HOUSEKEEPER . . . 55
BUT IT'S JUST FUN THE WAY HE GETS BEDEVILED-- . . . . 87 THE HOUSEKEEPER . . . 161
"NO, HE WON'T, EITHER. HE'LL JUST DROP THE REINS . . . . 88 THE HOUSEKEEPER . . . 200
"HOW ARE YOU, NEIGHBOR? JUST THE MAN I'M AFTER. . . . . 88 THE HOUSEKEEPER . . . 206
I SAW IT JUST AS PLAIN AS A WHITE PLATE," . . . . . . 89 THE FEAR 9
I'LL JUST COME FORWARD IN THE LANTERN-LIGHT . . . . . 91 THE FEAR 74
I JUST EMBRACED THE SHAFT AND RODE IT OUT-- . . . . . 93 THE SELF-SEEKER . . . 26
I JUST WANT TO GET SETTLED IN MY LIFE, ... 95 THE SELF-SEEKER . . . 76
TELL ME WHAT IS IT?" / ANNE JUST WAGGED HER DRESS, . . . 96 THE SELF-SEEKER . . . 105
JUST HOOK THEM ON THE INSIDE OF THE PITCHER. . . . . . 99 THE SELF-SEEKER . . . 174
OR SOMEWHERE ELSE: I WAS JUST FAR FROM HOME. . . . . . 101 THE WOOD-PILE . . . 9
THEN TOOK THE OTHER, AS JUST AS FAIR, ... 105 THE ROAD NOT TAKEN . 6
THE CUTTER BAR HAD JUST GONE CHAMPING OVER . . . . . . 109 THE EXPOSED NEST . . 14
I WISH THAT EVERYTHING ON EARTH WERE JUST . . . . . . 115 IN THE HOME STRETCH . 140
TO DRAG YOU OUT FOR JUST A GOOD-NIGHT CALL . . . . . . 117 IN THE HOME STRETCH . 188
"WHEN I WAS JUST AS FAR AS I COULD WALK . . . . 118 THE TELEPHONE . . . 1
AND HAD JUST TURNED FROM WHEN I FIRST SAW YOU . . . . . 118 MEETING AND PASSING . 3
WHEN, JUST AS THE SOIL TARNISHES WITH WEED, ... 124 PUTTING IN THE SEED . 12
AND HE SAID, "JUST IT." . . . . 133 A GIRL'S GARDEN . . . 12
JUST WHEN IT SEEMS TO COME IN RIGHT, ... 134 A GIRL'S GARDEN . . . 43
I JUST CAME TO TELL YOU . . . . 135 LAST WORD OF A BLUEBIRD 5
HE JUST HAD TO FLY! . . . . 136 LAST WORD OF A BLUEBIRD 14
WHEN IT'S JUST THAT I HOLD WITH GETTING A THING DONE WITH." 142 THE VANISHING RED . . 8
THEN YOU WOULDN'T HAVE LOOKED ON IT AS JUST A MATTER . . 142 THE VANISHING RED . . 12
"YOU CAN JUST SEE IT GLANCING OFF THE ROOF . . . . . . 143 SNOW 8
I THINK I'LL JUST CALL UP MY WIFE AND TELL HER . . . . . 143 SNOW 11
MY DEAR, I'M COMING JUST THE SAME. I DIDN'T . . . . . 143 SNOW 26
"I'LL JUST SEE HOW THE HORSES ARE." / "YES, DO," . . . . 144 SNOW 33
JUST THEN, I THOUGHT. IT'S STOOD ERECT LIKE THAT, . . . 147 SNOW 117
A MANY TIMES--I DON'T SAY JUST HOW MANY-- . . . . . 147 SNOW 127
MUCH SAY IN THE MATTER, AND I'M JUST AS GLAD . . . . 152 SNOW 257
"I'M HALF AFRAID THAT'S JUST WHAT SHE MIGHT DO." . . . . 154 SNOW 306
WHAT SPOILED OUR NIGHT WAS TO HIM JUST HIS FUN. . . . . 155 SNOW 338
THOUGHT HE'D JUST CALL TO TELL US IT WAS SNOWING. . . . 155 SNOW 340
"JUST THE WAY STEFANSSON RUNS ON," I MURMURED, ... 159 NEW HAMPSHIRE . . . 22
WAS SOMEONE WHO HAD JUST COME BACK ASHAMED . . . . . 160 NEW HAMPSHIRE . . . 37
JUST SPECIMENS IS ALL NEW HAMPSHIRE HAS, ... 161 NEW HAMPSHIRE . . . 61
JUST ENOUGH GOLD TO MAKE THE ENGAGEMENT RINGS . . . . 162 NEW HAMPSHIRE . . . 113
THIS IS NOT SORROW, THOUGH; IT'S JUST THE VAPORS, . . . 167 NEW HAMPSHIRE . . . 277
AMONG US: IT WAS JUST A WARREN FARMER . . . . 168 NEW HAMPSHIRE . . . 288

	PAGE	TITLE	LINE

JUST (CONTINUED)

AND RESTFUL JUST TO THINK ABOUT NEW HAMPSHIRE.	172	NEW HAMPSHIRE	412
YOUR MOTHER NAMED YOU. YOU AND SHE JUST SAW.	180	MAPLE	10
"JUST ONE LOOK MORE WITH WHAT YOU SAY IN MIND,	184	MAPLE	131
EVER SINCE, JUST TO SHOW THEM, HE HAD SLIPPED	191	PAUL'S WIFE	18
THEY SEEMED TO ASK HIM JUST TO SEE HIM GO,	191	PAUL'S WIFE	23
WHO ASKED THE QUESTION. HE JUST DISAPPEARED--	192	PAUL'S WIFE	26
NOT A BREEZE STIRRED, BUT JUST THE BREATH OF AIR	194	PAUL'S WIFE	98
ACQUIRED ANCESTRALLY IN JUST SUCH TREES	197	WILD GRAPES	49
JUST THEN COME YOU AND I TO GATHER IT.	198	WILD GRAPES	68
MIGHT JUST AS WELL BE ICE AND THE CLOTHES SNOW.	203	THE WITCH OF COOS	39
I WAS JUST COMING TO MYSELF ENOUGH	203	THE WITCH OF COOS	44
FROM THE SLAP I HAD JUST NOW GIVEN ITS HAND.	205	THE WITCH OF COOS	89
AND I DON'T MEAN JUST SKULLS OF ROGERS' RANGERS	210	PAUPER WITCH OF GRAFTON	93
I CAN JUST SEE MY TENT PEGGED,	211	AN EMPTY THREAT	7
"I GUESS YOU'D FIND THE FOUNTAIN JUST AS EMPTY.	214	A FOUNTAIN, A BOTTLE	45
COME STRAIGHT DOWN OFF THIS MOUNTAIN JUST AS FAST	215	A FOUNTAIN, A BOTTLE	61
THE SWARM STILL RAN AND SCUTTLED JUST AS FAST.	237	A HILLSIDE THAW	24
BUT JUST TO ASK US WHO WE THINK WE ARE	238	ON A TREE FALLEN ACROSS	4
SWOOPS JUST IN TIME TO HIS REMEMBERED TREE.	249	ACCEPTANCE	10
JUST WHEN WE THINK WE HAVE IT IMPOUNDED SAFE	254	THE FLOOD	2
NOT JUST A SWERVING, BUT A THROWING BACK,	259	WEST-RUNNING BROOK	59
BUT IT'S JUST THE KIND OF A THING THAT YOU	263	THE TIMES TABLE	14
WE CAN JUST SEE THE INFANT UP ASTRIDE,	267	RIDERS	7
NOR WAS THIS JUST A WAY OF TALKING	274	A LONE STRIKER	47
BUT WHAT HE FOUND HE HAD WAS JUST A NAILHEAD.	278	THE WHITE-TAILED HORNET	34
"THOSE ARE JUST NAILHEADS. THOSE ARE FASTENED DOWN."	278	THE WHITE-TAILED HORNET	36
THEY HAD JUST GIVEN THEMSELVES A LITTLE TWIST	283	THE GOLD HESPERIDEE	7
JUST AS HE WAS, WITHOUT AN UTTERED SOUND	284	THE GOLD HESPERIDEE	43
JUST ONE TO INQUIRE WHAT A FARMER'S PRICES ARE.	287	A ROADSIDE STAND	38
JUST WHEN THE COLD WENT DOWN SO MANY BELOW.	305	THERE ARE ROUGHLY ZONES	17
ALL, NOT JUST GREAT EXPLOITING BUSINESSES.	319	BUILD SOIL	96
IT IS JUST FOOL ENOUGH TO THINK ITSELF	319	BUILD SOIL	119
JUST SO BEFORE WE'RE INTERNATIONAL,	320	BUILD SOIL	145
IT CAN'T BE JUST TO GIVE THE ROBBER A CHANCE	321	BUILD SOIL	166
JUST WHAT AM I SUPPOSED TO DO ABOUT IT?	322	BUILD SOIL	205
JUST NOW YOU'RE OFF DEMOCRACY	326	TO A THINKER	15
AND JUST BECAUSE WE OWNED TO A WISH FOR RAIN,	349	OUR HOLD ON THE PLANET	5
WE MAY DOUBT THE JUST PROPORTION OF GOOD TO ILL.	349	OUR HOLD ON THE PLANET	11
I COULD HAVE BOUGHT YOU JUST AS GOOD A TREE	350	TO A YOUNG WRETCH	7
I CAN JUST HEAR THE WAY YOU MAKE IT GO:	352	THE LESSON FOR TODAY	54
I CAN JUST HEAR YOU CALL YOUR PALACE CLASS:	353	THE LESSON FOR TODAY	84
WHO WERE JUST ON THE SUBJECT WHEN YOU CAME.	369	THE LITERATE FARMER AND	28
YOU'LL SEE IT BE ALLOWED UP JUST SO HIGH,	370	THE LITERATE FARMER AND	65
WHO MAY BE JUST AHEAD OF YOU ON FOOT	378	DIRECTIVE	31
TO TELL YOU IT WAS JUST A TRAMP	380	AN UNSTAMPED LETTER IN	6
NOW JUST AHEAD OF HIM WAS SEEN TO YAWN	394	HAEC FABULA DOCET	5
"IT ISN'T JUST THE SAME, AND SOME DAY, SCHOOLBOY,"	406	FROM PLANE TO PLANE	85
NOT JUST FOR SCIENTIFIC NEWS	416	AMERICA IS HARD TO SEE	5
CAME JUST THEN SAILING INTO PORT	417	AMERICA IS HARD TO SEE	21
WE WERE JUST PURPOSE COMING TO A HEAD.	425	ACCIDENTALLY ON PURPOSE	16
JUST SUPPOSING I--	430	KITTY HAWK	57
OF JUST STAYING PUT,	434	KITTY HAWK	206
JUST BECAUSE IT'S HIDDEN.	437	KITTY HAWK	283
JUST LIKE PULLMAN CARS,	438	KITTY HAWK	319
THE WINTER OWL BANKED JUST IN TIME TO PASS	445	QUESTIONING FACES	1
"YES, BUT GIVE CHARACTER AND NOT JUST FOOD.	458	HOW HARD TO KEEP FROM	141
THE PROBLEM FOR THE KING IS JUST HOW STRICT	460	HOW HARD TO KEEP FROM	198
POSSIBLY JUST WELL-BEING IN THE BODY,	461	HOW HARD TO KEEP FROM	243
BETWEEN HIS JUST DESERTS AND WHAT HE GETS.	475	A MASQUE OF REASON	51
WE'VE JUST AGREED I DIDN'T HAVE TO GIVE.--	477	A MASQUE OF REASON	106
GOD NEEDS TIME JUST AS MUCH AS YOU OR I	478	A MASQUE OF REASON	151
SHE'S BEAUTIFUL. / YES, SHE WAS JUST REMARKING	479	A MASQUE OF REASON	156
IS JUST AS GOOD AS WHEN I UTTERED IT.	480	A MASQUE OF REASON	196
JUST AS WE WILL BE TALKING ANYWAY	482	A MASQUE OF REASON	236
I WAS JUST SHOWING OFF TO THE DEVIL, JOB,	484	A MASQUE OF REASON	327
JUST AS IF NOTHING MATTERED BUT OUR MANNERS.	488	A MASQUE OF REASON	410
FROM THE SURROUNDING DESERT; JUST TODAY	489	A MASQUE OF REASON	445
MUST HAVE YOU. THERE, THAT'S JUST THE RIGHT ARRANGEMENT.	489	A MASQUE OF REASON	457
I THOUGHT YOU JUST NOW SAID IT WAS A GIFT SHOP.	494	A MASQUE OF MERCY	25
NO, MAKE ME PROPHESY. / AND--YOU--JUST--WON'T?	494	A MASQUE OF MERCY	41
I JUST THOUGHT IF YOU HAD A COPY HANDY,	495	A MASQUE OF MERCY	45
IS IT JUST ANY CITY YOU'RE AGAINST?	496	A MASQUE OF MERCY	90
JUST, I WOULD HAVE HIM JUST BEFORE ALL ELSE,	507	A MASQUE OF MERCY	363
TO COUNT ON JUSTICE TO BE MERELY JUST.	509	A MASQUE OF MERCY	425
I NOTICED HOW HE JUST NOW MADE YOU CUT	510	A MASQUE OF MERCY	454
IS JUST A FRAME-UP TO INSURE THE FAILURE	511	A MASQUE OF MERCY	483
OF THE ONE AWFUL GOD. JUST SO THE SAINTS	516	A MASQUE OF MERCY	596
WHAT'S REALLY DOWN THERE? / JUST AN OUBLIETTE,	516	A MASQUE OF MERCY	612
NOTHING CAN MAKE INJUSTICE JUST BUT MERCY.	521	A MASQUE OF MERCY	738

JUSTICE (SEE MERCY-JUSTICE)

AND LOOK FOR JUSTICE IN THE CASE OF SEGUB.	477	A MASQUE OF REASON	114
MERCY AND JUSTICE ARE A CONTRADICTION.	498	A MASQUE OF MERCY	141
HOW RELATIVELY LITTLE JUSTICE MATTERS.	499	A MASQUE OF MERCY	146
THE GOSPELS TO IT. AFTER DOING JUSTICE JUSTICE	508	A MASQUE OF MERCY	379
PAUL ONLY MEANS YOU MAKE TOO MUCH OF JUSTICE.	508	A MASQUE OF MERCY	384
IT WAS THEIR JUSTICE BEING MERCY-CROSSED.	509	A MASQUE OF MERCY	415
WITH THE IDEA OF JUSTICE IN THE COURTS,	509	A MASQUE OF MERCY	423
TO COUNT ON JUSTICE TO BE MERELY JUST.	509	A MASQUE OF MERCY	425
THERE IS SOME JUSTICE, EVEN AS KEEPER SAYS.	509	A MASQUE OF MERCY	429
AND IF YOU'VE GOT TO SEE YOUR JUSTICE CROSSED	510	A MASQUE OF MERCY	436
MY TROUBLE HAS BEEN WITH MY SENSE OF JUSTICE.	517	A MASQUE OF MERCY	622
AND YOU SAY JUSTICE DOESN'T REALLY MATTER.	517	A MASQUE OF MERCY	623
NAIVENESS ABOUT JUSTICE OUT OF HIM,	517	A MASQUE OF MERCY	640
FOR CLAMORING FOR JUSTICE AT THE GATE,	518	A MASQUE OF MERCY	643
I SHOULD HAVE WARNED YOU, THOUGH, MY SENSE OF JUSTICE	518	A MASQUE OF MERCY	657
MERCY ON HIM FOR HAVING ASKED FOR JUSTICE.	518	A MASQUE OF MERCY	662

```
                                                    PAGE TITLE                      LINE
JUSTIFIED
  HAS JUSTIFIED ITSELF IN FREEDOM'S STORY  . . . . . . . 423 FOR JOHN F. KENNEDY  .  52
JUSTIFY
  SO AS TO JUSTIFY THE ORTHODOX  . . . . . . . . . . . 515 A MASQUE OF MERCY  . . 571
JUSTIFYING
  THAN ALL THE JUSTIFYING EX-POST-FACTO  . . . . . . . 482 A MASQUE OF REASON .  248
JUSTLY
  I SHOULD JUSTLY HESITATE  . . . . . . . . . . . 384 MAKING CERTAIN ANYTHING   9
  JUSTLY KNOWN TO FAME  . . . . . . . . . . . . . 440 KITTY HAWK  . . . . . 375
JUST-PAUSING
  THAT THE JUST-PAUSING DEMIURGE  . . . . . . . . . 453 A-WISHING WELL  . . .  73
JUT
  THAT WAVE'S BEEN STANDING OFF THIS JUT OF SHORE--"  . . . 258 WEST-RUNNING BROOK .  18
  "THAT WAVE'S BEEN STANDING OFF THIS JUT OF SHORE  . . . 258 WEST-RUNNING BROOK .  27
JUTE
  IS STEALTHILY CONTRIVING WOOL FROM JUTE  . . . . . . 319 BUILD SOIL  . . . . 108
```

K

```
KAISER
  IT IS AS TRUE AS CAESAR'S NAME WAS KAISER  . . . . . 363 AN EQUALIZER . . . .   1
KARL
  CHRIST'S OR KARL MARX', AND IT WILL SET YOU FREE.  . . . 460 HOW HARD TO KEEP FROM   192
  AND OF THE MESSIANIC RACE, KARL MARX.  . . . . . . . 515 A MASQUE OF MERCY  . 578
KEATS
  AS KEATS (OR WAS IT MILTON?) SANG  . . . . . . . . 452 A-WISHING WELL  . . .  41
KEATS'
  AND STEADFAST AS KEATS' EREMITE,  . . . . . . . 403 SOMETHING LIKE A STAR . 18
KEEN
  THE DEW WAS GONE THAT MADE HIS BLADE SO KEEN  . . . .  22 THE TUFT OF FLOWERS .   3
KEENNESS
  AS IF WITH KEENNESS FOR OUR FATE,  . . . . . . . .   9 STARS . . . . . .   5
KEEP
  AS THE UNCERTAIN HARVEST; KEEP US HERE  . . . . . .  12 A PRAYER IN SPRING . .   3
  TO A SLOPE WHERE THE CATTLE KEEP THE LAWN.  . . . . .  17 THE VANTAGE POINT  .   3
  WE KEEP THE WALL BETWEEN US AS WE GO.  . . . . . . .  33 MENDING WALL . . . .  15
  "YES, I TOOK CARE TO KEEP WELL OUT OF EARSHOT."  . . .  37 DEATH OF THE HIRED MAN  70
  HE'D KEEP SO STILL ABOUT HIM ALL THIS TIME?"  . . . .  39 DEATH OF THE HIRED MAN 138
  "YOU CAN DRIVE ROUND AND KEEP IN LUNENBURG,  . . . . .  43 THE MOUNTAIN . . . .  93
  THE BOUNDARY LINES KEEP IN SO CLOSE TO IT.  . . . . .  43 THE MOUNTAIN . . . .  95
  BY WHICH I'D BIND MYSELF TO KEEP HANDS OFF  . . . . .  52 HOME BURIAL . . . .  51
  THE HEART'S GONE OUT OF IT: WHY KEEP IT UP?  . . . . .  54 HOME BURIAL . . . . 110
  IT WILL BE HARD FOR THEM TO KEEP THEIR WORD.  . . . .  55 THE BLACK COTTAGE  .  20
  IT WASN'T JUST TO KEEP THE STATES TOGETHER,  . . . . .  56 THE BLACK COTTAGE  .  56
  AND WELL, IF THEY WEREN'T TRUE WHY KEEP RIGHT ON  . . .  58 THE BLACK COTTAGE  .  97
  I'M JUST AS GLAD SHE MADE ME KEEP HANDS OFF,  . . . .  58 THE BLACK COTTAGE  . 104
  TO THE TRUTHS WE KEEP COMING BACK AND BACK TO.  . . . .  58 THE BLACK COTTAGE  . 114
  IT WAS ALL HE COULD DO TO KEEP A STRAIGHT FACE."  . . .  61 BLUEBERRIES . . . .  78
  THEY TRIED TO KEEP HIM CLOTHED, BUT HE PARADED  . . . .  66 A SERVANT TO SERVANTS . 122
  AND I KEEP HEARING FROM THE CELLAR BIN  . . . . . .  69 AFTER APPLE-PICKING .  24
  KEEP AT THEIR HEELS AND THREATEN TO MOW THEIR LEGS OFF. .  71 THE CODE . . . . .  46
  THEY EXCAVATED MORE. 'GO KEEP HIS WIFE  . . . . . .  72 THE CODE . . . . .  94
  HE COULDN'T KEEP AWAY FROM DOING SOMETHING."  . . . .  73 THE CODE . . . . . 109
  LET PEOPLE IN THAN I CAN KEEP THEM OUT.  . . . . . .  81 THE HOUSEKEEPER . .   4
  I CAN'T KEEP TRACK OF OTHER PEOPLE'S DAUGHTERS.  . . .  81 THE HOUSEKEEPER . .  11
  HAS BEEN TO KEEP THE THING FROM BREAKING UP.  . . . .  84 THE HOUSEKEEPER . .  88
  HE MANAGES TO KEEP THE UPPER HAND  . . . . . . . .  86 THE HOUSEKEEPER . . 134
  THAT MUCH TO SELL, THEY'RE WORTH AS MUCH TO KEEP.  . . .  86 THE HOUSEKEEPER . . 141
  SOMETIMES HE GETS POSSESSED TO KEEP ACCOUNTS  . . . .  86 THE HOUSEKEEPER . . 158
  HE APPEARED TO FORGET TO KEEP HIS HOLD,  . . . . . .  91 THE FEAR . . . . .  59
  I HAVE TO KEEP ON THE GOOD SIDE OF ANNE.  . . . . .  99 THE SELF-SEEKER . . 176
  AND COULD NOT DO WITHOUT AND KEEP ITS CHRISTMAS.  . . . 106 CHRISTMAS TREES . .  11
  HIS ICICLES ALONG THE WALL TO KEEP;  . . . . . . . 108 OLD MAN'S WINTER NIGHT  22
  ONE AGED MAN--ONE MAN--CAN'T KEEP A HOUSE,  . . . . . 108 OLD MAN'S WINTER NIGHT  26
  HALF IN APPEAL, BUT HALF AS IF TO KEEP  . . . . . . 137 "OUT, OUT--"  . . .  21
  BUT KEEP STILL IF HE FAILS." / "KEEP STILL ALL OVER.  . . 146 SNOW . . . . . .  87
  AND BOOK-LEAF, THAT KEEP NEAR YOU, THEIR REPOSE;  . . . 148 SNOW . . . . . . 146
  THAN THE MAN FIGHTING IT TO KEEP ABOVE IT,  . . . . . 151 SNOW . . . . . . 225
  YOU DIDN'T THINK YOU'D KEEP HIM AFTER ALL.  . . . . . 152 SNOW . . . . . . 255
  TO KEEP HIM--THOUGH PERHAPS YOU DIDN'T QUITE  . . . . 153 SNOW . . . . . . 282
  "KEEP SPEAKING, THEN." / "HELLO. HELLO. HELLO.--  . . . 154 SNOW . . . . . . 304
  I COULDN'T KEEP FROM ASKING IMPOLITELY,  . . . . . . 160 NEW HAMPSHIRE . .  55
  I SHALL NOT LACK FOR PAIN TO KEEP ME AWAKE.  . . . . . 166 NEW HAMPSHIRE . . 241
  SEEMS TO ME OWES IT TO THE TOWN TO KEEP ONE.  . . . . 177 THE STAR-SPLITTER .  36
  TO KEEP HIS BARGAIN OF THE MORNING WITH ME  . . . . . 187 THE AX-HELVE . . .  60
  IN TIME TO KEEP ME FROM SUSPECTING HIM  . . . . . . 187 THE AX-HELVE . . .  61
  OF REALLY NEVER HAVING MEANT TO KEEP IT.  . . . . . . 187 THE AX-HELVE . . .  62
  HE KEPT FROM SCHOOL, OR DID HIS BEST TO KEEP--  . . . . 188 THE AX-HELVE . . .  84
  WHO GAVE HIS LIFE TO KEEP IT GOING ROUND?  . . . . . 190 THE GRINDSTONE . .  47
  ABOUT HIS WIFE TO KEEP HER TO HIMSELF.  . . . . . . 195 PAUL'S WIFE . . . 149
  SHE MUST NOT KEEP HIM WAITING. TIME WOULD PRESS  . . . 201 PLACE FOR A THIRD .  68
  THEY MADE HIM KEEP ON GNAWING TILL HE WHINED.  . . . . 209 PAUPER WITCH OF GRAFTON  58
  OFF FROM THE HOUSE AS FAR AS WE COULD KEEP  . . . . . 210 PAUPER WITCH OF GRAFTON  90
  AS WE CAN FALL AND KEEP A-BOUNCING ON OUR FEET.  . . . 215 A FOUNTAIN, A BOTTLE .  62
  BUT I HAVE PROMISES TO KEEP,  . . . . . . . . . 225 STOPPING BY WOODS .  14
  GOOD-BY AND KEEP COLD  . . . . . . . . . . . . 228 GOOD-BY AND KEEP COLD . T
  KEEP COLD, YOUNG ORCHARD. GOOD-BY AND KEEP COLD.  . . . 228 GOOD-BY AND KEEP COLD . 18
  NOT TO KEEP  . . . . . . . . . . . . . . 230 NOT TO KEEP . . . .   T
  THE THOUGHTS MAY NOT HAVE RISEN THAT SO KEEP  . . . . 231 A BROOK IN THE CITY  23
  THEY HAD GIVEN HIM BACK TO HER, BUT NOT TO KEEP.  . . . 231 NOT TO KEEP . . . .  22
  WILL KEEP MY TALK FROM GETTING OVERWISE,  . . . . . 265 DUST IN THE EYES . .   2
  TO KEEP THEIR BUILDING BALANCED AT MY BREAST.  . . . . 267 THE ARMFUL . . . .   8
  FOR THE SHOCKS AND CHANGES WE NEED TO KEEP US SANE.  . . 268 ON LOOKING UP BY CHANCE 10
  IT SET ITSELF TO KEEP THOSE THREE ALIVE:  . . . . . 283 THE GOLD HESPERIDEE .   5
  WOULD KEEP HIM NOW FROM PROVING WITH A BITE  . . . . . 283 THE GOLD HESPERIDEE .  29
  WHY, KEEP YOUR MONEY (THIS CROSSLY) AND GO ALONG.  . . . 286 A ROADSIDE STAND . .  15
```

KEEP (CONTINUED)
    THEY CAN KEEP IT BURNING AS LONG AS THEY PLEASE; . . . . . 291 ON HEART'S BEGINNING TO   24
    NOW UP, MY KNEE, TO KEEP ON TOP OF ANOTHER YEAR OF SNOW. . . 298 A LEAF-TREADER . . . 12
    TO ANY WATCH THEY KEEP? . . . . 301 NEITHER OUT FAR NOR IN   16
    (TO KEEP THE POTS OF GOLD FROM BEING FOUND), ... 315 IRIS BY NIGHT 25
    I KEEP MY EYE ON CONGRESS, MELIBOEUS. . . . . 317 BUILD SOIL 54
    WE HAVE OUR OWN ROUND SHAPE TO KEEP UNBROKEN. . . . . 322 BUILD SOIL 197
    KEEP OFF EACH OTHER AND KEEP EACH OTHER OFF. . . . . . 324 BUILD SOIL 263
    FOR MY MIND TO KEEP WORKING IN YOUR PRESENCE. . . . . . 325 BUILD SOIL 285
    (HE HAD TO KEEP THE CAPTAIN'S FAVOR.) . . . . 345 DISCOVERY OF MADEIRAS . 52
    YOU'VE GOT TO KEEP THE QUARTERS CLEAN." . . . . . . 345 DISCOVERY OF MADEIRAS . 62
    REMEMBER, AND MUST KEEP A SOLEMN FACE.) . . . . 352 THE LESSON FOR TODAY . 67
    THE WEST AND KEEP THE OLD TRADITION SAFE. . . . . . . 365 OF STONES OF THE PLACE . 12
    BUT HELPED THE LORD HER SOUL TO KEEP. . . . . 382 THE NIGHT LIGHT . . . 4
    BE SURE TO KEEP REPEATING TO YOURSELF . . . . 385 THE FEAR OF GOD . . . 3
    TO KEEP OUR ABSTRACT VERSE FROM BEING DRY. . . . . . . 395 ETHEREALIZING . . . 14
    "A MAN HAS GOT TO KEEP HIS EXTRICATION. . . . . . . 406 FROM PLANE TO PLANE . 61
    WHAT'S MORE, I HATE TO KEEP AFFLICTING WEEDS. . . . . . 406 FROM PLANE TO PLANE . 64
    EVERYONE HAS TO KEEP HIS EXTRICATION." . . . . 407 FROM PLANE TO PLANE . 96
    THAT'S WHAT I HAVE TO DO IN SCHOOL, KEEP MINE . . . . 407 FROM PLANE TO PLANE . 98
    KEEP ON ELEVATING. . . . . 441 KITTY HAWK 411
    LET'S KEEP STARRING MAN . . . . 441 KITTY HAWK 414
    TO KEEP ALL THINGS STIRRED . . . . 442 KITTY HAWK 444
    HOW HARD IT IS TO KEEP FROM BEING KING WHEN IT'S IN YOU AND
        IN THE SITUATION . . . . 453 HOW HARD TO KEEP FROM   T
    FOR HARD IT IS TO KEEP FROM BEING KING . . . . 454 HOW HARD TO KEEP FROM   20
    HE COULDN'T KEEP HIMSELF FROM BEING KING. . . . . . . 454 HOW HARD TO KEEP FROM   23
    HOW HARD IT IS TO KEEP FROM BEING KING . . . . 462 HOW HARD TO KEEP FROM 275
    TO GO STRAIGHT HOME, WE WOULDN'T KEEP HIM, WOULD WE?-- . . 501 A MASQUE OF MERCY . 208
    KEEPER, I'LL TURN ON YOU IF YOU KEEP ON. . . . . . . 503 A MASQUE OF MERCY . 268
    I SAY WE KEEP HIM TILL WE WRING SOME MORE . . . . . . 517 A MASQUE OF MERCY . 639
KEEPER
    HER KEEPER, EMPTY PAIL IN HAND, ... 280 BLUE RIBBON AT AMESBURY 18
    STAYS TALKING WITH THE KEEPER AT A SHOWCASE. . . . . . 493 A MASQUE OF MERCY . . 4
    KEEPER, YOU COME AND SEE. OR YOU COME, PAUL. . . . . . 493 A MASQUE OF MERCY . 13
    KEEPER, BE STILL.--PAY NO ATTENTION TO HIM. . . . . . 494 A MASQUE OF MERCY . 33
    FOR KEEPER'S LEVITY: MY BROTHER'S KEEPER. . . . . . . 494 A MASQUE OF MERCY . 36
    KEEPER, BE STILL. HE KNOWS WHAT BOOK HE WANTS. . . . . 495 A MASQUE OF MERCY . 51
    IT'S ONLY FAIR TO KEEPER TO INFORM YOU . . . . 496 A MASQUE OF MERCY . 80
    WHO KEEPS OUR BOOKSTORE ANNALS. / STOP IT, KEEPER.-- . . 499 A MASQUE OF MERCY . 152
    AND I DON'T LOVE YOU EITHER, DO I, KEEPER? . . . . . . 499 A MASQUE OF MERCY . 165
    (I WON'T HAVE KEEPER CALLING IT RELIGION.) . . . . . . 503 A MASQUE OF MERCY . 256
    KEEPER, I'LL TURN ON YOU IF YOU KEEP ON. . . . . . . 503 A MASQUE OF MERCY . 268
    OR KEEPER IS A REVOLUTIONIST. . . . . 508 A MASQUE OF MERCY . 400
    PAUL ALMOST HAD POOR KEEPER IN A CORNER . . . . 508 A MASQUE OF MERCY . 401
    THERE IS SOME JUSTICE, EVEN AS KEEPER SAYS. . . . . . 509 A MASQUE OF MERCY . 429
    WE KNOW WHAT'S COMING NOW. / YOU SAY IT, KEEPER, . . . 511 A MASQUE OF MERCY . 480
    KEEPER, I'M GLAD YOU THINK IT BEAUTIFUL. . . . . . . 512 A MASQUE OF MERCY . 494
    WHAT DO YOU SAY TO IT, MY BROTHER'S KEEPER? . . . . . 512 A MASQUE OF MERCY . 513
    CRUMPLE HIM ON THE FLOOR. KEEPER AND PAUL . . . . . . 518 A MASQUE OF MERCY . 651
    AS IF TO COME, BUT KEEPER WAVES HER OFF.) . . . . . . 518 A MASQUE OF MERCY . 653
KEEPER'S
    A BOOKSTORE LATE AT NIGHT. THE KEEPER'S WIFE . . . . 493 A MASQUE OF MERCY . . 1
    THE KEEPER'S WIFE HAS HARDLY TURNED AWAY . . . . 493 A MASQUE OF MERCY . . 5
    FOR KEEPER'S LEVITY: MY BROTHER'S KEEPER. . . . . . . 494 A MASQUE OF MERCY . 36
    KEEPER'S THE KIND OF UNITARIAN . . . . 498 A MASQUE OF MERCY . 119
    TO SOME OF KEEPER'S FRIENDS THAT COME IN HERE, ... 509 A MASQUE OF MERCY . 405
    THE REVOLUTION KEEPER'S BRINGING ON . . . . 509 A MASQUE OF MERCY . 416
KEEPING (SEE CLOSE-KEEPING)
    SAVE THOSE THAT THE OAK IS KEEPING . . . . 30 RELUCTANCE 8
    AN EXCUSE FOR KEEPING US OTHER FOLK OUT." . . . . . . 60 BLUEBERRIES . . . 32
    UNLESS WHEN YOU SAID I WAS KEEPING A BIRD . . . . . . 62 BLUEBERRIES . . . 88
    BLESS YOU, OF COURSE YOU'RE KEEPING ME FROM WORK, . . . 67 A SERVANT TO SERVANTS 171
    KEEPING HIS HEAD ABOVE. 'DAMN YE,' I SAYS, ... 72 THE CODE 77
    AND THOSE WILL BEAR SOME KEEPING STILL ABOUT." . . . . 80 THE GENERATIONS OF MEN 198
    THEY SAW PAUL AND HIS CREATURE KEEPING HOUSE. . . . . 195 PAUL'S WIFE . . . 128
    THAT THERE'S SOMETHING THE DEAD ARE KEEPING BACK? . . . 202 THE WITCH OF COOS . 17
    YES, THERE'S SOMETHING THE DEAD ARE KEEPING BACK. . . . 202 THE WITCH OF COOS . 18
    KEEPING ITS LIFE SO CLOSE AND OUT OF SIGHT . . . . . 248 THE COCOON 8
    THAT THE PARTY IN POWER IS SAID TO BE KEEPING FROM US. . 286 A ROADSIDE STAND . 22
    OF SAVING AND OF KEEPING, ... 359 NOVEMBER 10
    LONG SINCE GAVE UP PRETENSE OF KEEPING COVERED. . . . 377 DIRECTIVE 12
    AND THIS SCHOOL WASN'T KEEPING ANYMORE, ... 400 TO THE RIGHT PERSON . 11
    "THAT'S WHAT THE DOCTOR'S DOING, KEEPING HIS. . . . . 407 FROM PLANE TO PLANE . 97
    THAT I'M NOT KEEPING PACE . . . . 465 SOME SCIENCE FICTION . 3
KEEPS
    AFTER SO MANY YEARS HE STILL KEEPS FINDING . . . . . . 37 DEATH OF THE HIRED MAN 74
    OF LATE YEARS, THOUGH HE KEEPS THE OLD HOMESTEAD . . . . 44 A HUNDRED COLLARS . 3
    THE CHIMNEY, THOUGH, KEEPS UP A GOOD BRISK SMOKING. . . 49 A HUNDRED COLLARS . 137
    MY INSTEP ARCH NOT ONLY KEEPS THE ACHE, ... 68 AFTER APPLE-PICKING . 21
    IT KEEPS THE PRESSURE OF A LADDER-ROUND. . . . . 68 AFTER APPLE-PICKING . 22
    A SHIP KEEPS RAISING ITS HULL; . . . . 301 NEITHER OUT FAR NOR IN 6
    OR KEEPS THE END FROM BEING HARD. . . . . 307 PROVIDE, PROVIDE . 18
    IT KEEPS SMOLDERING AT THE ROOTS . . . . 308 EVIL TENDENCIES CANCEL 3
    AS SURELY AS IT KEEPS THE STROKE AND TIME . . . . . . 362 IN A POEM 3
    SHE'LL GO TO SLEEP. NOTHING KEEPS HER AWAKE . . . . . 478 A MASQUE OF REASON . 153
    WHO KEEPS OUR BOOKSTORE ANNALS. / STOP IT, KEEPER.-- . . 499 A MASQUE OF MERCY . 152
KELP
    I PICK A DEAD SHELL UP FROM WHERE THE KELP . . . . . 446 DOES NO ONE AT ALL EVER 25
KENNEDY
    FOR JOHN F. KENNEDY HIS INAUGURATION . . . . 422 FOR JOHN F. KENNEDY . T
KENT
    BY ROCKWELL KENT THAT EVERYBODY'S READING. . . . . . 495 A MASQUE OF MERCY . . 49
KEPT (SEE SO-LONG-KEPT)
    SUCH PIPES KEPT LESS OF POWER TO STIR . . . . 24 PAN WITH US . . . 22
    NOTHING WOULD DO: HE JUST KEPT NODDING OFF." . . . . . 36 DEATH OF THE HIRED MAN 43
    TO LOOK AGAIN, AND STILL YOUR SPADE KEPT LIFTING. . . . 53 HOME BURIAL . . . 80
    IF SUCH UNLIFELIKE LINES KEPT POWER TO STIR . . . . . 56 THE BLACK COTTAGE . 29

KEPT (CONTINUED)
"HE JUST KEPT NODDING HIS HEAD UP AND DOWN. . . . . . . 60 BLUEBERRIES 41
MY FATHER'S BROTHER WASN'T RIGHT. THEY KEPT HIM . . . . 65 A SERVANT TO SERVANTS . 88
KEPT THEM AT HOME; AND IT DOES SEEM MORE HUMAN. . . . . 65 A SERVANT TO SERVANTS . 96
IF HE WA'N'T KEPT STRICT WATCH OF, AND IT ENDED . . . . 66 A SERVANT TO SERVANTS . 112
BUT THE THING OF IT IS, I NEED TO BE KEPT. . . . . . . 68 A SERVANT TO SERVANTS . 172
THAT HE KEPT ANY HOURS--NOT FOR HIMSELF. . . . . 71 THE CODE 40
HE KEPT AWAY FROM US ALL AFTERNOON. . . . . 73 THE CODE 106
OF LITTLE FINGERS ALL KEPT DOWN BUT ONE. . . . . 98 THE SELF-SEEKER . . . 156
OH, I KEPT THE FIRST FOR ANOTHER DAY! . . . . 105 THE ROAD NOT TAKEN . 13
WHAT KEPT HIS EYES FROM GIVING BACK THE GAZE . . . . . 108 OLD MAN'S WINTER NIGHT 4
WHAT KEPT HIM FROM REMEMBERING WHAT IT WAS . . . . . . 108 OLD MAN'S WINTER NIGHT 6
CLEAR TO THE GROUND. HE ALWAYS KEPT HIS POISE . . . . . 122 BIRCHES 35
FOR THE DARK PINE THAT KEPT . . . . 128 THE OFT-REPEATED DREAM 2
I'VE KEPT BROWN STANDING IN THE COLD . . . . 140 BROWN'S DESCENT . . . 71
THEY KEPT THEIR HEADS AND TOOK THEIR TIME TO IT . . . . 143 SNOW 24
THEY KEPT THEIR THOUGHTS AWAY FROM WHEN THE MAPLES . . . 184 MAPLE 136
BUT ITS AGE KEPT THEM FROM CONSIDERING THIS ONE. . . . 184 MAPLE 148
PERHAPS A FILIAL DIFFIDENCE PARTLY KEPT THEM . . . . . 184 MAPLE 157
HE KEPT FROM SCHOOL, OR DID HIS BEST TO KEEP-- . . . . 188 THE AX-HELVE 84
IF THAT WAS HOW SHE FELT, HE KEPT REPEATING. . . . . . 200 PLACE FOR A THIRD . 21
WE'D KEPT UP ALL THESE YEARS BETWEEN OURSELVES . . . . 207 THE WITCH OF COOS . 146
ALL THE WAY HOME I KEPT REMEMBERING . . . . 217 A FOUNTAIN, A BOTTLE . 132
IF FROM ITS BEING KEPT FOREVER UNDER, ... 231 A BROOK IN THE CITY . 22
THAT KEPT THE GROUND, ALMOST DISPUTING RIGHT . . . . . 240 OUR SINGING STRENGTH . 36
BUT THOUGH THEY REJOICED IN THE NEST THEY KEPT, ... 242 NEED OF BEING VERSED . 22
BUT MERCIFULLY KEPT THE PASSING CROWD . . . . 284 THE GOLD HESPERIDEE . 56
THAT KEPT THE OAKS FROM GETTING ANY GIRTH. . . . . . . 292 FIGURE IN THE DOORWAY . 4
WHO ONCE KEPT SURPASSING EACH OTHER, ... 294 A RECORD STRIDE . . . 7
THEY KEPT THEIR SECRETS AND DIED, ... 312 THE VINDICTIVES . . . 54
WHERE NATURAL FRIENDS ARE MET, WHERE DOGS ARE KEPT, . . . 318 BUILD SOIL 83
THE COLORS ARE KEPT UNMIXED ON THE PALETTE, ... 320 BUILD SOIL 147
MORE THAT SHOULD BE KEPT BACK--THE SOIL FOR INSTANCE, . . 321 BUILD SOIL 175
AND WHAT I WOULD NOT PART WITH I HAVE KEPT. . . . . . . 335 I COULD GIVE ALL . . . 15
HE THOUGHT HE KEPT THE UNIVERSE ALONE; . . . . 338 THE MOST OF IT . . . 1
AND FOR THESE REASONS KEPT FROM BEING GREAT. . . . . . 351 THE LESSON FOR TODAY . 13
THAT AT ONCE KEPT YOU BURNING LOW AND HID YOU. . . . . 351 THE LESSON FOR TODAY . 25
I HAVE KEPT HIDDEN IN THE INSTEP ARCH . . . . 379 DIRECTIVE 55
KEPT SOME DEW OUT AND SOME HEAT IN, ... 380 AN UNSTAMPED LETTER IN 15
KEPT REPEATING PARDON, PARDON; . . . . 397 AN IMPORTER 20
HAVE KEPT FROM BEING CAUGHT WITH THE DECAYED, ... 399 THE INGENUITIES OF DEBT 8
I SAID I WOULD SEE HOW SIRIUS KEPT . . . . 419 ONE MORE BREVITY . . . 4
TENDERLY BE KEPT . . . . 432 KITTY HAWK 123
KETTLE
TO OTHER HILLS ACROSS A KETTLE VALLEY. . . . . 195 PAUL'S WIFE 126
WIND SHE BREWS A HEADY KETTLE. . . . . 304 CLEAR AND COLDER . . 21
THAT'S THE PRETTY KETTLE! . . . . 442 KITTY HAWK 447
KEY
AND THE KEY RATTLED LOUDLY INTO PLACE . . . . 89 THE FEAR 19
THEY LEARNED TO RATTLE THE LOCK AND KEY . . . . 127 HOUSE FEAR 5
THE BIRD WAS NOT TO BLAME FOR HIS KEY. . . . . 251 A MINOR BIRD 6
YOU LOCKED THE DOOR, BEL. LET ME HAVE THE KEY. . . . . 500 A MASQUE OF MERCY . . 174
KICK
AND KICK WITH TWO LEGS LIKE AN ARMY MULE. . . . . . . 202 THE WITCH OF COOS . 10
TO MAKE SO FREE AND KICK UP IN FOLKS' FACES. . . . . . 210 PAUPER WITCH OF GRAFTON 107
HE GAVE THE SOLID RAIL A HATEFUL KICK. . . . . 269 THE EGG AND THE MACHINE 1
NO SENATOR DARES IN TO KICK ASUNDER, ... 362 SYMPATHY WITH UNDER DOG 3
KICKED
LISTEN! HE KICKED A STONE. HEAR THAT, HEAR THAT! . . . . 90 THE FEAR 38
SPHEROID THAT KICKED AND STRUGGLED IN ITS GAIT. . . . . 190 THE GRINDSTONE . . . 40
KICKING
KICKING HIS WAY DOWN THROUGH THE AIR TO THE GROUND. . . . 122 BIRCHES 40
KIKE
YOU'RE NOT MUCH FURTHERER THAN WHERE KIKE LEFT YOU. . . . 47 A HUNDRED COLLARS . . 70
KIKE'S
"NOT THAT WAY, WITH YOUR SHOES ON KIKE'S WHITE BED. . . . 47 A HUNDRED COLLARS . . 75
KILL
I WENT ABOUT TO KILL HIM FAIR ENOUGH." . . . . 73 THE CODE 112
BUT EVEN WHERE, THUS, OPPOSING INTERESTS KILL, ... 350 TO A YOUNG WRETCH . . 14
OUT TO KILL A DUCK . . . . 431 KITTY HAWK 108
KILLED
THEY WERE A MAN'S HIS FATHER KILLED FOR ME. . . . . . 206 THE WITCH OF COOS . 139
I MEAN A MAN HE KILLED INSTEAD OF ME. . . . . 206 THE WITCH OF COOS . 140
KILLERS (SEE MAN-KILLERS)
KIN
IF HE HAD ANY PRIDE IN CLAIMING KIN . . . . 39 DEATH OF THE HIRED MAN 136
IT IS IN THE NEWS THAT ALL THESE PITIFUL KIN . . . . . 286 A ROADSIDE STAND . . 23
KIND
THE FEN HAD EVERY KIND OF BLOOM, ... 15 IN A VALE 6
AND FOR EVERY KIND THERE WAS A FACE, ... 15 IN A VALE 7
OH, JUST ANOTHER KIND OF OUTDOOR GAME, ... 33 MENDING WALL . . . 21
AND SHUT IT AFTER HER. "BE KIND," SHE SAID. . . . . . 34 DEATH OF THE HIRED MAN 7
"WHEN WAS I EVER ANYTHING BUT KIND TO HIM? . . . . . 34 DEATH OF THE HIRED MAN 11
BUT JUST THE KIND THAT KINSFOLK CAN'T ABIDE. . . . . . 39 DEATH OF THE HIRED MAN 141
YOU KNOW THE KIND. THEN LET THE SUN SHINE ON IT!" . . . 42 THE MOUNTAIN 54
"A MAN." / "SO I SHOULD HOPE. WHAT KIND OF MAN?" . . . . 45 A HUNDRED COLLARS . . 25
SOME STRANGE KIND--THEY TOLD ME IT HADN'T A NAME." . . . 61 BLUEBERRIES 66
HE WAS ONE OF THE KIND SPORTS CALL A SPIDER, ... 70 THE SELF-SEEKER . . . 33
OF EVERY KIND EVERYWHERE IN THIS REGION . . . . . . 95 THE SELF-SEEKER . . . 68
THE WOOD." / "WHAT KIND OF YEARS?" / "WHY, LATTER YEARS-- . 112 IN THE HOME STRETCH . 49
ONCE ON THE KIND OF DAY CALLED "WEATHER BREEDER," . . . 125 AN ENCOUNTER 1
"YOU THINK SO, DO YOU? YOU DON'T KNOW THE KIND. . . . . 146 SNOW 83
TO STOP AT. IF YOU WERE THE KIND OF MAN . . . . . . 150 SNOW 215
NOT READING IT. / "WELL, WHAT KIND OF A MAN . . . . . 151 SNOW 247
IT LOOKED TO HIM LIKE SOME NEW KIND OF HOLLOW . . . . . 193 PAUL'S WIFE 86
I DIDN'T KNOW WAS THERE. IT WAS THE KIND . . . . . . 215 A FOUNTAIN, A BOTTLE . 69
UNFORTUNATELY ALL OF ONE KIND, THOUGH. . . . . 216 A FOUNTAIN, A BOTTLE . 99
IT BREAKS AWAY IN SOME NEW KIND OF SLAUGHTER. . . . . . 254 THE FLOOD 4

PAGE TITLE   LINE

KIND (CONTINUED)
  BUT IT'S JUST THE KIND OF A THING THAT YOU . . . . 263 THE TIMES TABLE . . . 14
  I KNEW A TALE OF A BETTER KIND. . . . . 291 ON HEART'S BEGINNING TO 14
  CLEAR TO THE ARCTIC OF EVERY LIVING KIND. . . . . 305 THERE ARE ROUGHLY ZONES 10
  WHAT CRIES MORE TO OUR KIND FOR SYMPATHY? . . . . 323 BUILD SOIL 219
  TO ANY ONE TIME, PLACE, OR HUMAN KIND. . . . . 353 THE LESSON FOR TODAY . 105
  AND SEEK THE LOVE OF KIND IN WINTERTIME? . . . . 356 A MOTH SEEN IN WINTER . 9
  IT BEST BE LEFT TO GREAT MEN OF HIS KIND . . . . 372 THE LITERATE FARMER AND 134
  ON HOW TO CROWD BUT STILL BE KIND. . . . . 417 AMERICA IS HARD TO SEE 42
  FOR SOME KIND OF FLIGHT . . . . 430 KITTY HAWK 55
  SOME KIND OF COMMITTEE . . . . 431 KITTY HAWK 101
  WE ARE NOT THE KIND . . . . 434 KITTY HAWK 201
  IT'S SOME KIND OF TOWN, ... 439 KITTY HAWK 343
  THEY'VE COME TO FEEL THE NEED OF IS A KIND . . . . 461 HOW HARD TO KEEP FROM 232
  TO GET ADAPTED TO MY KIND OF FOOLING. . . . . 470 IT TAKES ALL SORTS... . 2
  OF SOME KIND. WE COULD HAVE CHARADES. . . . . 489 A MASQUE OF REASON . . 430
  KEEPER'S THE KIND OF UNITARIAN . . . . 498 A MASQUE OF MERCY . . 119
  OR NOT AT LEAST THE ORDINARY KIND. . . . . 510 A MASQUE OF MERCY . . 456
KINDER
  HE KNOWS HE'S KINDER THAN THE RUN OF MEN. . . . . 84 THE HOUSEKEEPER . . . 80
  A RIVALRY THAT MADE THEM BOTH FEEL KINDER. . . . . . . 408 FROM PLANE TO PLANE . 119
KINDNESS
  AND STROKED IT WITH A HORNY-HANDED KINDNESS. . . . . . 217 A FOUNTAIN, A BOTTLE . 127
  (SHE STARTLES AT THE SUDDEN NOTE OF KINDNESS.) . . . . 519 A MASQUE OF MERCY . 691
KINDRED
  AND FEEL A SPIRIT KINDRED TO MY OWN; . . . . 23 THE TUFT OF FLOWERS . 33
  WHAT BROUGHT THE KINDRED SPIDER TO THAT HEIGHT, ... 302 DESIGN 11
  THE KINDRED SPIRIT OF AN INNER HAZE? . . . . 415 A CABIN IN THE CLEARING 42
KINDS
  LIKE TWO KINDS OF JEWELS, A VISION FOR THIEVES." . . . . 62 BLUEBERRIES 105
KIND'S
  THE MORAL KIND'S AS BRAVE AS FACING BULLETS." . . . . . 405 FROM PLANE TO PLANE . 35
KING (SEE EX-KING)
  A KING FILLED HIS PRISON ROOM . . . . 310 THE VINDICTIVES . . . 2
  BUT DIDN'T LET GO OF THE KING. . . . . 310 THE VINDICTIVES . . . 9
  HIS CAPTORS CONVICTED THE KING . . . . 310 THE VINDICTIVES . . . 15
  THAT A KING MIGHT HAVE HOPED TO COMPEL-- . . . . . . 310 THE VINDICTIVES . . . 19
  THE KING HAD SCARCE CEASED TO WRITHE, ... 311 THE VINDICTIVES . . . 21
  THEY GAVE NO MORE THOUGHT TO THE KING. . . . . 311 THE VINDICTIVES . . . 27
  AND SENT HIM TO THE KING TO ADMIRE. . . . . 347 DISCOVERY OF MADEIRAS 131
  YOU DID NOT KNOW THAT SINCE KING CHARLES DID RULE . . . 351 THE LESSON FOR TODAY . 22
  BUT IN YOUR FAVOR--PLEASE TO TELL YOUR KING-- . . . . 354 THE LESSON FOR TODAY . 117
  LIKE A KING AND QUEEN . . . . 442 KITTY HAWK 456
  THE KING SAID TO HIS SON: "ENOUGH OF THIS! . . . . . 453 HOW HARD TO KEEP FROM 1
  HOW HARD IT IS TO KEEP FROM BEING KING WHEN IT'S IN YOU AND
    IN THE SITUATION . . . . 453 HOW HARD TO KEEP FROM T
  FOR HARD IT IS TO KEEP FROM BEING KING . . . . 454 HOW HARD TO KEEP FROM 20
  HE COULDN'T KEEP HIMSELF FROM BEING KING. . . . . . . 454 HOW HARD TO KEEP FROM 23
  (THE COOK WAS TEMPERAMENTAL LIKE THE KING.) . . . . . 455 HOW HARD TO KEEP FROM 57
  AND THE GREAT KING INQUIRE WHOSE WORK IT WAS. . . . . 455 HOW HARD TO KEEP FROM 59
  THE KING SAID GRANDLY, "EVEN AS WE ARE FED . . . . . 455 HOW HARD TO KEEP FROM 63
  THE KING SAT FAVORING ONE PEARL FOR ITS BIGNESS, . . . 455 HOW HARD TO KEEP FROM 69
  "THE CHOICE IS NOT BETWEEN TWO PEARLS, O KING, ... 456 HOW HARD TO KEEP FROM 74
  TILL ON A DAY THE KING, BEING SICK AT HEART . . . . . 456 HOW HARD TO KEEP FROM 94
  (THE KING WAS TEMPERAMENTAL LIKE HIS COOK, ... 456 HOW HARD TO KEEP FROM 95
  "YOU'RE NOT WHERE YOU BELONG. YOU'RE NOT A KING . . . . 457 HOW HARD TO KEEP FROM 102
  "IF YOU HAD BEEN A KING OF ROYAL BLOOD, ... 457 HOW HARD TO KEEP FROM 118
  I'LL BET YOU ANYTHING THAT'S ALL AS KING . . . . . . 458 HOW HARD TO KEEP FROM 137
  BUT THE KING SAID, "HAVEN'T I READ SOMEWHERE . . . . . 458 HOW HARD TO KEEP FROM 139
  A KING MUST GIVE HIS PEOPLE CHARACTER." . . . . . . 458 HOW HARD TO KEEP FROM 142
  FROM KING TO MOB TO KING TO KING . . . . 459 HOW HARD TO KEEP FROM 160
  THE PROBLEM FOR THE KING IS JUST HOW STRICT . . . . . 460 HOW HARD TO KEEP FROM 198
  AND PRESS YOUR FATHER INTO BEING KING. . . . . 460 HOW HARD TO KEEP FROM 206
  "DON'T LET HIM FOOL YOU: HE'S A KING ALREADY. . . . . 460 HOW HARD TO KEEP FROM 207
  CHANGING AN OLD KING FOR ANOTHER OLD ONE. . . . . . . 462 HOW HARD TO KEEP FROM 255
  NO ONE IS NOMINATING ME FOR KING. . . . . 462 HOW HARD TO KEEP FROM 260
  HOW HARD IT IS TO KEEP FROM BEING KING . . . . 462 HOW HARD TO KEEP FROM 275
  "OH, WHAT IS A KING HERE, ... 512 A MASQUE OF MERCY . . 502
KINGDOM
  SOMETHING ABOUT A KINGDOM IN THE SKY . . . . 359 THE LOST FOLLOWER . . 35
  MY KINGDOM, WHAT AN OUTBREAK! / JOB IS RIGHT. . . . . 484 A MASQUE OF REASON . . 302
  YOUR KINGDOM, YES, YOUR KINGDOM COME ON EARTH. . . . . 484 A MASQUE OF REASON . . 303
KINGDOM-COME
  IT MIGHT AS WELL AT ONCE BE KINGDOM-COME. . . . . . . 353 THE LESSON FOR TODAY . 102
KINGDOM'S
  THE KINGDOM'S YOURS TO FINISH AS YOU PLEASE. . . . . . 453 HOW HARD TO KEEP FROM 2
KINGLY
  THERE IS NO ACT MORE KINGLY THAN TO GIVE?" . . . . . 458 HOW HARD TO KEEP FROM 140
KINGS
  WHICH IS UNUSUAL. SO MANY KINGS . . . . 457 HOW HARD TO KEEP FROM 109
KING'S
  KING'S X--NO FAIRS TO USE IT ANYMORE! . . . . 399 U.S. 1946 KING'S X . . 4
  U.S. 1946 KING'S X . . . . 399 U.S. 1946 KING'S X . . T
  TO PUT AN END TO THE KING'S VACILLATION. . . . . . . 456 HOW HARD TO KEEP FROM 80
KINSFOLK
  BUT JUST THE KIND THAT KINSFOLK CAN'T ABIDE. . . . . . 39 DEATH OF THE HIRED MAN 141
KINSMAN
  YOU SAID YOU KNEW THE PLACE WHERE ONCE, ON KINSMAN, . . 213 A FOUNTAIN, A BOTTLE . 8
KIPLING
  KIPLING INVOKES YOU AS LORD GOD OF HOSTS. . . . . . . 479 A MASQUE OF REASON . . 179
KISS
  AND ITS CHOKECHERRIES LIPS TO KISS GOOD-BY, ... 268 THE BEAR 3
  TO KISS AND DRINK EACH OTHER'S BREATH . . . . 346 DISCOVERY OF MADEIRAS . 81
KISSED
  AND TURNED FROM LOOKING UP AND BEING KISSED . . . . . 283 THE GOLD HESPERIDEE . 8
KIT
  KIT MARLOWE TAUGHT ME HOW TO SAY MY PRAYERS: . . . . . 166 NEW HAMPSHIRE . . . 242

KITCHEN
  FOLKS ENTERTAIN ME FROM THE KITCHEN DOORSTEP, ... 49 A HUNDRED COLLARS . . 147
  OUT IN THE KITCHEN, AND I DON'T KNOW WHY, ... 54 HOME BURIAL 82
  SPRAWLING ABOUT THE KITCHEN WITH THEIR TALK . . . . . 65 A SERVANT TO SERVANTS . 77
  AND CURSE ME IF HE WASN'T IN THE KITCHEN . . . . . . 72 THE CODE 96
  I LET MYSELF IN AT THE KITCHEN DOOR. . . . . 81 THE HOUSEKEEPER . . . 1
  YOU OUGHT TO HAVE THE KITCHEN TO YOURSELF . . . . . . 88 THE HOUSEKEEPER . . . 193
  SHE STOOD AGAINST THE KITCHEN SINK, AND LOOKED . . . . 110 IN THE HOME STRETCH . 1
  AND DINING ROOM--THROWN PELL-MELL IN THE KITCHEN. . . . 110 IN THE HOME STRETCH . 9
  WHEN THERE WAS NO MORE LANTERN IN THE KITCHEN, ... 117 IN THE HOME STRETCH . 201
  BEYOND AN OVER-WARMTH OF KITCHEN STOVE . . . . 186 THE AX-HELVE 35
  UP ONE FLIGHT FROM THE CELLAR TO THE KITCHEN, ... 203 THE WITCH OF COOS . . 30
  ANOTHER FROM THE KITCHEN TO THE BEDROOM, ... 203 THE WITCH OF COOS . . 31
  (THE KITCHEN HAD BEEN DARK) I HAD TO OWN . . . . . . 205 THE WITCH OF COOS . . 98
  BUT PLEASE PLEASE ME IN THE KITCHEN CHIMNEY: . . . . . 232 THE KITCHEN CHIMNEY . 3
  THE KITCHEN CHIMNEY . . . . 232 THE KITCHEN CHIMNEY . T
  HAWKING FOR FLIES ABOUT THE KITCHEN DOOR, ... 278 THE WHITE-TAILED HORNET 24
  HE ASKED FOR A DRINK AT THE KITCHEN DOOR, ... 364 TRESPASS 18
  STARTED CHAIRS THUNDERING ON THE KITCHEN FLOOR, ... 368 THE LITERATE FARMER AND 2
  IN THE KITCHEN MIDDEN . . . . 441 KITTY HAWK 432
  LIKE A KITCHEN SPOON . . . . 442 KITTY HAWK 442
  I'LL TRY YOU IN THE KITCHEN FIRST ON FOOD . . . . . 455 HOW HARD TO KEEP FROM 49
  THOUGHT OF THE KITCHEN SLAVE AND HAD HIM IN . . . . . 456 HOW HARD TO KEEP FROM 79
KITE
  THE WAY BEN FRANKLIN USED TO MAKE THE KITE STRING. . . . 94 THE SELF-SEEKER . . . 35
  AND DEAD WINGS CARRIED LIKE A PAPER KITE. . . . . . . 302 DESIGN 8
  ITS NAME MIGHT BETTER BE FIRST MOTOR KITE. . . . . . 308 THE WRIGHTS' BIPLANE . 2
KITING
  LIKE, "NO, SHE AIN'T COME BACK FROM KITING YET. . . . 209 PAUPER WITCH OF GRAFTON 80
  LAST NIGHT WAS ONE OF HER NIGHTS OUT. SHE'S KITING. . . 209 PAUPER WITCH OF GRAFTON 81
  THOUGH OUR KITING SHIPS . . . . 439 KITTY HAWK 351
KITTEN
  YOU NAUGHTY KITTEN, YOU SHALL HAVE NO PIE. . . . . . 498 A MASQUE OF MERCY . . 118
KITTY
  KITTY HAWK, O KITTY, ... 428 KITTY HAWK 1
  KITTY HAWK. . . . . 428 KITTY HAWK . . . . T
  HERE AT KITTY HAWK. . . . . 433 KITTY HAWK 157
  KITTY HAWK, O KITTY, ... 433 KITTY HAWK 175
  IT'S STILL KITTY HAWK. . . . . 439 KITTY HAWK 347
KNEE
  SHELVES ONE COULD REST A KNEE ON GETTING UP-- . . . . 42 THE MOUNTAIN 59
  OF WHAT SHE'S LOST: SHE GOES DOWN ON ONE KNEE . . . . 98 THE SELF-SEEKER . . . 160
  LIKE A WHITE CRUMPLED SPIDER ON HIS KNEE: . . . . . 147 SNOW 115
  SHE ALMOST WROTE THE WORDS DOWN ON HER KNEE, ... 182 MAPLE 86
  OF BENDING LIKE A SWORD ACROSS THE KNEE. . . . . . 187 THE AX-HELVE 71
  BUT NOW HE BRUSHED THE SHAVINGS FROM HIS KNEE . . . . 188 THE AX-HELVE 94
  BLINDLY STRUCK AT MY KNEE AND MISSED. . . . . . . 251 BEREFT 10
  GIVE HER A CHILD AT EITHER KNEE FOR FOURTH JOY . . . . 256 THE LOVELY BE CHOOSERS 31
  NOW UP, MY KNEE, TO KEEP ON TOP OF ANOTHER YEAR OF SNOW. 298 A LEAF-TREADER . . . 12
KNEED (SEE WET-KNEED)
KNEEL
  KNEEL TO YOUR DOCTOR. HE DISPENSES MERCY.-- . . . . 507 A MASQUE OF MERCY . . 346
  KNEEL BY HIM. BEL STANDS UP BESIDE HER CHAIR . . . . 518 A MASQUE OF MERCY . . 652
KNEES
  SO WHEN I SAW YOU DOWN ON HANDS AND KNEES . . . . . 109 THE EXPOSED NEST . . 2
  LIKE GIRLS ON HANDS AND KNEES THAT THROW THEIR HAIR . . 121 BIRCHES 19
  WITH OUR ARMS AT THE LEVEL OF OUR KNEES, ... 205 THE WITCH OF COOS . . 106
  IT'S HELL FOR KNEES UNLESS DONE HELL-FOR-LEATHER." . . 215 A FOUNTAIN, A BOTTLE . 63
  THE MOUNTAIN PUSHED US OFF HER KNEES. . . . . . . 265 THE BIRTHPLACE . . . 13
  I LOSE SOME OTHER OFF MY ARMS AND KNEES, ... 266 THE ARMFUL 2
  GREAT MONOLITHIC KNEES THE FORMER TOWN . . . . . . 377 DIRECTIVE 11
  ONCE DOWN ON MY KNEES TO GROWING PLANTS . . . . . . 385 A MOOD APART 1
  (STILL ON HIS KNEES, HE SITS BACK ON HIS HEELS.) . . . 519 A MASQUE OF MERCY . . 671
  DON'T WEAR YOUR PANTS OUT PREACHING ON YOUR KNEES. . . 519 A MASQUE OF MERCY . . 681
KNELT
  SOONER OR LATER CAME AND LEANED, HALF KNELT, ... 56 THE BLACK COTTAGE . . 27
  I TOOK WHAT FRONT THERE WAS BESIDE. I KNELT . . . . 131 THE BONFIRE 65
  OTHERS TAUNT ME WITH HAVING KNELT AT WELL-CURBS . . . 225 FOR ONCE SOMETHING . . 1
  THAT THE FLOWERS ACTUALLY KNELT, ... 250 LODGED 4
  I ONLY KNELT AND PUTTING THE BOUGHS ASIDE . . . . . 343 QUEST OF PURPLE-FRINGED 21
KNEW
  THEY WOULD NOT FIND ME CHANGED FROM HIM THEY KNEW-- . . 5 INTO MY OWN 13
  "STRANGER, I WISH I KNEW." . . . . 8 LOVE AND A QUESTION . 16
  THE BRIDEGROOM WISHED HE KNEW. . . . . 8 LOVE AND A QUESTION . 32
  I KNEW SO WELL, WHOSE GARMENTS TRAIL . . . . . . 15 IN A VALE 4
  WHAT WAS IT IT WHISPERED? I KNEW NOT WELL MYSELF; . . 17 MOWING 3
  WE HEARD, WE KNEW WE HEARD THE BROOK. . . . . . . 18 GOING FOR WATER . . . 20
  HIS HEART KNEW PEACE, FOR NONE CAME THERE . . . . . 24 PAN WITH US 11
  THOUGH I KNEW WHAT I HUNTED WAS NO TRUE GOD. . . . . 24 THE DEMIURGE'S LAUGH . 3
  AND WELL I KNEW WHAT THE DEMON MEANT. . . . . . . 25 THE DEMIURGE'S LAUGH . 12
  MAN THAT KNEW ANYTHING I HAPPENED IN WITH. . . . . 46 A HUNDRED COLLARS . . 47
  HE SAID TWICE OVER BEFORE HE KNEW HIMSELF: . . . . . 52 HOME BURIAL 34
  WHITE WAS THE ONLY RACE SHE EVER KNEW. . . . . . . 57 THE BLACK COTTAGE . . 75
  "I WISH I KNEW HALF WHAT THE FLOCK OF THEM KNOW . . . 61 BLUEBERRIES 60
  TO ASK IF HE KNEW ANY FRUIT TO BE HAD . . . . . . 61 BLUEBERRIES 70
  TO TELL IF HE KNEW. BUT THE YEAR HAD BEEN BAD. . . . 61 BLUEBERRIES 72
  THEY KNEW. AND JUST WHEN HE WAS AT THE HEIGHT, . . . 66 A SERVANT TO SERVANTS . 125
  I'D BUILT THE LOAD AND KNEW RIGHT WHERE TO FIND IT. . . 71 THE CODE 71
  "DISCHARGE ME? NO! HE KNEW I DID JUST RIGHT." . . . . 73 THE CODE 114
  ONLY TOO WELL. I KNEW THERE MUST BE SOMETHING! . . . 87 THE HOUSEKEEPER . . . 182
  "I HALF SUSPECT YOU KNEW, AND CAME ON PURPOSE . . . . 93 THE SELF-SEEKER . . . 8
  I KNEW A LOVELY WAY TO TELL FOR CERTAIN . . . . . 96 THE SELF-SEEKER . . . 108
  I KNEW YOU WOULDN'T LET ME PICK THEM ALL." . . . . 97 THE SELF-SEEKER . . . 120
  WHERE NOW HE SAT, CONCERNED WITH THE HE KNEW WHAT, . . 108 OLD MAN'S WINTER NIGHT 16
  AND SORRY I EVER LEFT THE ROAD I KNEW, ... 125 AN ENCOUNTER 7
  AND THE WRETCH KNEW FROM THAT THAT WE WERE POOR. . . . 127 THE SMILE 5
  MADE WIND BY FANNING, SINCE YOU NEVER KNEW . . . . . 130 THE BONFIRE 42
  I HAD MY COAT. AND OH, I KNEW, I KNEW . . . . . . 131 THE BONFIRE 69

KNEW (CONTINUED)

	PAGE	TITLE	LINE
AS IF TO PROVE SAWS KNEW WHAT SUPPER MEANT,	136	"OUT,OUT--"	15
"SHE KNEW HE HAD, POOR THING, TWO HOURS AGO."	153	SNOW	278
I KNEW A MAN WHO FAILING AS A FARMER	168	NEW HAMPSHIRE	301
HE KNEW TOO WELL FOR ANY EARTHLY USE	171	NEW HAMPSHIRE	378
HE HAD TO TAKE THE BEST WAY HE KNEW HOW	178	THE STAR-SPLITTER	56
BUT HADN'T AS IT WENT. (SHE KNEW A ROSE.)	181	MAPLE	48
BAPTISTE KNEW BEST WHY I WAS WHERE I WAS.	186	THE AX-HELVE	37
WHERE I MUST JUDGE IF WHAT HE KNEW ABOUT AN AX	186	THE AX-HELVE	41
THAT NOT EVERYBODY ELSE KNEW WAS TO COUNT	186	THE AX-HELVE	42
BAPTISTE KNEW HOW TO MAKE A SHORT JOB LONG	187	THE AX-HELVE	80
FOR ALL I KNEW IT MAY HAVE SHARPENED SPEARS	189	THE GRINDSTONE	37
NOBODY KNEW IN WHAT DIRECTION,	192	PAUL'S WIFE	27
IN ANY WAY THE WORLD KNEW HOW TO SPEAK.	196	PAUL'S WIFE	157
WHERE A WHITE BIRCH HE KNEW OF STOOD ALONE,	196	WILD GRAPES	20
GRAPES, I KNEW GRAPES FROM HAVING SEEN THEM LAST YEAR.	197	WILD GRAPES	24
IT WAS THE BONES. I KNEW THEM--AND GOOD REASON.	204	THE WITCH OF COOS	59
YOU SAID YOU KNEW THE PLACE WHERE ONCE, ON KINSMAN,	213	A FOUNTAIN, A BOTTLE	8
THE POETESS HAD SIGHED, I KNEW, IN HEAVEN	217	A FOUNTAIN, A BOTTLE	134
HOW OVER, THOUGH, FOR EVEN ME WHO KNEW	222	TO E.T.	17
I ASK AS ONE WHO KNEW THE BROOK, ITS STRENGTH	231	A BROOK IN THE CITY	5
BY LETTING THE RAIN I KNEW OUTDOORS	253	THE THATCH	34
AND THEN ANOTHER TICK. HE KNEW THE CODE:	270	THE EGG AND THE MACHINE	3
HE KNEW ANOTHER PLACE, A WOOD,	274	A LONE STRIKER	36
HE KNEW A PATH THAT WANTED WALKING;	274	A LONE STRIKER	43
HE KNEW A SPRING THAT WANTED DRINKING;	274	A LONE STRIKER	44
COME GET HIM--THEY KNEW WHERE TO SEARCH.	275	A LONE STRIKER	62
I KNEW PRETTY WELL WHY HE DROPPED BEHIND	275	TWO TRAMPS IN MUD TIME	5
I KNEW PRETTY WELL WHAT HE HAD IN MIND:	275	TWO TRAMPS IN MUD TIME	7
IT IS SNOWING A FLAKE: AND HE HALF KNEW	276	TWO TRAMPS IN MUD TIME	29
THEY KNEW THEY HAD BUT TO STAY THEIR STAY	277	TWO TRAMPS IN MUD TIME	58
I KNEW A TALE OF A BETTER KIND.	291	ON HEART'S BEGINNING TO	14
SOME HAVE RELIED ON WHAT THEY KNEW,	307	PROVIDE, PROVIDE	13
ONE KNEW OF A BURIAL HOLE.	312	THE VINDICTIVES	56
HE KNEW NOT WHETHER HOMEWARD,	335	CARPE DIEM	3
HE KNEW NOT, NEITHER OF THEM KNEW.	345	DISCOVERY OF MADEIRAS	45
YOU WOULD NOT THINK YOU KNEW ENOUGH TO JUDGE	351	THE LESSON FOR TODAY	29
SINCE IT WAS NOTHING I KNEW EVIL OF	358	A CONSIDERABLE SPECK	28
'TWAS SOMETHING WE KNEW ALL ABOUT TO BEGIN WITH	380	TOO ANXIOUS FOR RIVERS	24
WE NEVER KNEW EXACTLY WHERE TO LOOK,	382	TO AN ANCIENT	4
SO MUCH THOSE HEROES KNEW AND UNDERSTOOD--	422	FOR JOHN F. KENNEDY	24
SO MUCH THEY KNEW AS CONSECRATED SEERS	422	FOR JOHN F. KENNEDY	27
TO TAUNT OF MINE I KNEW A PLACE TO GO	447	DOES NO ONE AT ALL EVER	33
"BUT TELL US HOW YOU KNEW," DARIUS CRIED.	456	HOW HARD TO KEEP FROM	86
I TOLD YOU I KNEW THE QUINTESSENCE OF JEWELS.	456	HOW HARD TO KEEP FROM	88
I KNEW YOUR FATHER MUST HAVE BEEN A COOK.	458	HOW HARD TO KEEP FROM	136
I KNEW YOU HAD ONE. BUT THIS ISN'T IT	482	A MASQUE OF REASON	241
MERCY ON ME FOR HAVING THOUGHT I KNEW.	518	A MASQUE OF MERCY	660

KNIFE

OR FUMBLE FOR MY KNIFE TO CUT AWAY,	93	THE SELF-SEEKER	25
AND REACHING UP WITH A LITTLE KNIFE,	141	THE GUM-GATHERER	37
WERE NATIVE TO THE GRAIN BEFORE THE KNIFE	187	THE AX-HELVE	73

KNIVES

KNIVES AND FORKS RINGING ON THE SUPPER PLATES,	368	THE LITERATE FARMER AND	3

KNOB

MY FIRST IMPULSE WAS TO GET TO THE KNOB	204	THE WITCH OF COOS	60
"QUICK!" I SLAMMED TO THE DOOR AND HELD THE KNOB.	206	THE WITCH OF COOS	118
HE MAY FUMBLE WIDE OF THE KNOB A YARD OR MORE,	342	WILLFUL HOMING	11

KNOCK

I'LL KNOCK SO-FASHION AND PEEP ROUND THE DOOR	50	A HUNDRED COLLARS	173
NOT ANSWERING YOUR KNOCK. I CAN NO MORE	81	THE HOUSEKEEPER	3
THE STOVE! BEFORE THEY GO! KNOCK ON THE WINDOW;	113	IN THE HOME STRETCH	75
THEN CAME ONE KNOCK!	218	I WILL SING YOU ONE-O	23
BUT AT LAST CAME A KNOCK,	240	THE LOCKLESS DOOR	2
BUT THE KNOCK CAME AGAIN.	241	THE LOCKLESS DOOR	9
TO WHATEVER THE KNOCK	241	THE LOCKLESS DOOR	15
SO AT A KNOCK	241	THE LOCKLESS DOOR	17
A FEATHER-HAMMER GIVES A DOUBLE KNOCK.	254	A WINTER EDEN	17
THEY KNOCK THE DYESTUFF OFF EACH OTHER'S WINGS--	411	POD OF THE MILKWEED	25
YOU CAN'T COME IN! (KNOCK, KNOCK) THE STORE IS CLOSED!	493	A MASQUE OF MERCY	8
WOULD KNOCK THEIR DRUNKEN PENTHOUSE HEADS TOGETHER	506	A MASQUE OF MERCY	333

KNOCKED

AT THE LAST ONE OF WHICH HE KNOCKED AND ENTERED.	45	A HUNDRED COLLARS	35
(I MAY HAVE KNOCKED HIM DOWN); BUT MY JUST TRYING	72	THE CODE	103
AND KNOCKED AT THE DOOR OF A HOUSE WE FOUND,	367	A SERIOUS STEP LIGHTLY	11

KNOCKING

MY UNEXPECTED KNOCKING AT THE DOOR	368	THE LITERATE FARMER AND	1
THAT'S THE TIME KNOCKING AT A DOOR DID GOOD.	368	THE LITERATE FARMER AND	8

KNOCKS

BUT MY LEGS GOT THEIR KNOCKS AGAINST THE CEILING."	93	THE SELF-SEEKER	29
ONE KNOCKS ANOTHER OFF FROM WHERE HE CLINGS.	411	POD OF THE MILKWEED	24

KNOLL

UNDER WHAT BEECH TREE, ON WHAT WOODCHUCK'S KNOLL?"	97	THE SELF-SEEKER	116
ON THE OLD PEACH TREES ON THE KNOLL, TO GROPE	117	IN THE HOME STRETCH	189
SHE BELLOWS ON A KNOLL AGAINST THE SKY.	125	THE COW IN APPLE TIME	10

KNOT

FREE FROM THE LEAST KNOT, EQUAL TO THE STRAIN	187	THE AX-HELVE	70

KNOTS

WERE BUT FROST KNOTS ON AN AIRY GAUZE,	303	AFTERFLAKES	14

KNOW

AND LONG TO KNOW IF STILL I HELD THEM DEAR.	5	INTO MY OWN	12
I DWELL IN A LONELY HOUSE I KNOW	5	GHOST HOUSE	1
I KNOW NOT WHO THESE MUTE FOLK ARE	6	GHOST HOUSE	22
NOT YESTERDAY I LEARNED TO KNOW	7	MY NOVEMBER GUEST	16
AND LITTLE OF LOVE COULD KNOW.	11	WIND AND WINDOW FLOWER	16
DO YOU KNOW ME IN THE GLOAMING,	12	FLOWER-GATHERING	5
ARE YOU DUMB BECAUSE YOU KNOW ME NOT,	13	FLOWER-GATHERING	7
OR DUMB BECAUSE YOU KNOW?	13	FLOWER-GATHERING	8

```
                                                          PAGE TITLE                    LINE
KNOW (CONTINUED)
   AND THUS IT IS I KNOW SO WELL  . . . . . . . .  .  .   16 IN A VALE . . . . .      21
   WELL I KNOW WHERE TO HIE ME--IN THE DAWN,  . . . . .   17 THE VANTAGE POINT . .     2
   I KNOW THAT THIS IS THE WAY IN OURS. . . . . . . .  .  26 IN HARDWOOD GROVES .  .  12
   BEGUILE US IN THE WAY YOU KNOW. . . . . . . . . . . .  27 OCTOBER . . . . . .       11
   THOU DIDST NOT KNOW, WHO TOTTERED, WANDERING ON HIGH,  28 MY BUTTERFLY . . . .      22
   I LET MY NEIGHBOR KNOW BEYOND THE HILL; . . . . . .  . 33 MENDING WALL . . . .      12
   BEFORE I BUILT A WALL I'D ASK TO KNOW . . . . . . .  . 34 MENDING WALL . . . .      32
   "WARREN!" / "BUT DID HE? I JUST WANT TO KNOW." . .  .  36 DEATH OF THE HIRED MAN    47
   HE ADDED, IF YOU REALLY CARE TO KNOW, . . . . . . . .  36 DEATH OF THE HIRED MAN    51
   ON EDUCATION--YOU KNOW HOW THEY FOUGHT . . . . . .  .  36 DEATH OF THE HIRED MAN    66
   I SYMPATHIZE. I KNOW JUST HOW IT FEELS . . . . . .  .  37 DEATH OF THE HIRED MAN    76
   "I KNOW, THAT'S SILAS' ONE ACCOMPLISHMENT. . . . . .   37 DEATH OF THE HIRED MAN    88
   "HE NEVER TOLD US THAT." / "WE KNOW IT, THOUGH." . .   39 DEATH OF THE HIRED MAN   130
   HE DON'T KNOW WHY HE ISN'T QUITE AS GOOD . . . . . .   39 DEATH OF THE HIRED MAN   143
   YOU KNOW THE KIND. THEN LET THE SUN SHINE ON IT!" . .  42 THE MOUNTAIN . . . .      54
   AND LOOK MYSELF, BUT YOU KNOW HOW IT IS: . . . . .  .  43 THE MOUNTAIN . . . .      81
   "WE CALL IT HOR: I DON'T KNOW IF THAT'S RIGHT." . . .  43 THE MOUNTAIN . . . .      91
   YOU AND I KNOW ENOUGH TO KNOW IT'S WARM . . . . . .  . 44 THE MOUNTAIN . . . .     102
   "I KNOW HIM: HE'S ALL RIGHT. A MAN'S A MAN. . . . . .  45 A HUNDRED COLLARS . .     26
   PUBLISHED IN ROW. YOU KNOW THE WEEKLY NEWS?" . . .  .  48 A HUNDRED COLLARS . .     99
   "KNOWN IT SINCE I WAS YOUNG." / "THEN YOU KNOW ME. . . 48 A HUNDRED COLLARS . .    100
   YOU KNOW WHAT THAT IS, SORT OF DOUBLE-DYED; . . . .  . 48 A HUNDRED COLLARS . .    110
   "YOU SEE I'M IN WITH EVERYBODY, KNOW 'EM ALL. . . . .  49 A HUNDRED COLLARS . .    120
   I ALMOST KNOW THEIR FARMS AS WELL AS THEY DO." . . .   49 A HUNDRED COLLARS . .    121
   "I DON'T KNOW WHO I RATHER WOULD HAVE HAVE THEM. . . . 50 A HUNDRED COLLARS . .    168
   WHEN I COME BACK, SO YOU'LL KNOW WHO IT IS. . . . .  . 50 A HUNDRED COLLARS . .    174
   FROM UP THERE ALWAYS?--FOR I WANT TO KNOW." . . . . .  51 HOME BURIAL . . . .        7
   I DON'T KNOW RIGHTLY WHETHER ANY MAN CAN." . . . . .   52 HOME BURIAL . . . .       38
   "YOU DON'T KNOW HOW TO ASK IT." / "HELP ME, THEN." . . 52 HOME BURIAL . . . .       43
   I DON'T KNOW HOW TO SPEAK OF ANYTHING . . . . . . .  . 52 HOME BURIAL . . . .       46
   "YOU CAN'T BECAUSE YOU DON'T KNOW HOW TO SPEAK. . . .  53 HOME BURIAL . . . .       71
   I THOUGHT, WHO IS THAT MAN? I DIDN'T KNOW YOU. . . .   53 HOME BURIAL . . . .       78
   OUT IN THE KITCHEN, AND I DON'T KNOW WHY, . . . . .  . 54 HOME BURIAL . . . .       82
   I OUGHT TO KNOW--IT MAKES A DIFFERENCE WHICH: . . . .  56 THE BLACK COTTAGE . .     32
   DO YOU KNOW BUT FOR HER THERE WAS A TIME . . . . . .   57 THE BLACK COTTAGE . .     84
   YOU KNOW THEY SUFFERED FROM A GENERAL ONSLAUGHT. . . . 58 THE BLACK COTTAGE . .     96
   "I DON'T KNOW WHAT PART OF THE PASTURE YOU MEAN." . .  59 BLUEBERRIES . . . .        8
   "YOU KNOW WHERE THEY CUT OFF THE WOODS--LET ME SEE-- . 59 BLUEBERRIES . . . .        9
   "DOES PATTERSON KNOW WHAT HE HAS, DO YOU THINK?" . .   60 BLUEBERRIES . . . .       28
   TO GATHER THEM FOR HIM--YOU KNOW WHAT HE IS. . . . .   60 BLUEBERRIES . . . .       30
   "THE BEST OF IT WAS THAT I DID. DO YOU KNOW, . . . .   60 BLUEBERRIES . . . .       34
   YOU KNOW HOW POLITELY HE ALWAYS GOES BY. . . . . .  .  60 BLUEBERRIES . . . .       42
   "I WISH I KNEW HALF WHAT THE FLOCK OF THEM KNOW . . .  61 BLUEBERRIES . . . .       60
   MAME, WE DON'T KNOW ANY GOOD BERRYING PLACE?' . . . .  61 BLUEBERRIES . . . .       77
   AS TALKING--YOU STOOD UP BESIDE ME, YOU KNOW." . . .   62 BLUEBERRIES . . . .       96
   I DIDN'T MAKE YOU KNOW HOW GLAD I WAS . . . . . . .  . 62 A SERVANT TO SERVANTS      1
   AND SEE THE WAY YOU LIVED, BUT I DON'T KNOW! . . . .   62 A SERVANT TO SERVANTS      4
   IT'S GOT SO I DON'T EVEN KNOW FOR SURE . . . . . . .   63 A SERVANT TO SERVANTS     11
   I CAN SEE HOW YOU MIGHT. BUT I DON'T KNOW! . . . . .   63 A SERVANT TO SERVANTS     38
   YOU KNOW THE OLD IDEA--THE ONLY ASYLUM . . . . . . .   65 A SERVANT TO SERVANTS     93
   TO YOU IN YOUR CONDITION; YOU CAN'T KNOW . . . . .  .  65 A SERVANT TO SERVANTS    101
   IT GOT SO I WOULD SAY--YOU KNOW, HALF FOOLING-- . . .  67 A SERVANT TO SERVANTS    145
   AS I SAID, FOR A WHILE--BUT I DON'T KNOW. . . . . .  . 67 A SERVANT TO SERVANTS    153
   "YOU DIDN'T KNOW. BUT JAMES IS ONE BIG FOOL. . . . .   70 THE CODE . . . . .        15
   BUT I KNOW YOU DON'T UNDERSTAND OUR WAYS. . . . . .  . 70 THE CODE . . . . .        26
   AND DRIVE, THE WAY YOU CAN, YOU KNOW, IN MOWING-- . .  71 THE CODE . . . . .        45
   OR LET HIM KNOW THAT HE WAS BEING LOOKED AT. . . . .   72 THE CODE . . . . .       101
   "NO! AND YET I DON'T KNOW--IT'S HARD TO SAY. . . . .   73 THE CODE . . . . .       111
   THIS WAS SOME STARK SHE DIDN'T KNOW. HE NODDED. . . .  74 THE GENERATIONS OF MEN    34
   "YOU KNOW WE MIGHT NOT BE AND STILL BE COUSINS? . . .  75 THE GENERATIONS OF MEN    47
   "D'YOU KNOW A PERSON SO RELATED TO HERSELF . . . . .   76 THE GENERATIONS OF MEN    82
   "THEN I DON'T KNOW. IT MUST BE STRANGE ENOUGH. . . .   78 THE GENERATIONS OF MEN   139
   YOU SEE THEY KNOW I HAVEN'T HAD YOUR NAME, . . . . .   79 THE GENERATIONS OF MEN   157
   IT'S GOING TO RAIN." / "I KNOW, AND IT WAS RAINING. .  80 THE GENERATIONS OF MEN   201
   YOU CAN'T HAVE PASSED EACH OTHER. I KNOW WHAT: . . .   81 THE HOUSEKEEPER . . .     16
   I DON'T KNOW WHERE MYSELF. JOHN THINKS I DO. . . . .   82 THE HOUSEKEEPER . . .     24
   HE'S FIFTY-FIVE, YOU KNOW, IF HE'S A DAY." . . . . .   83 THE HOUSEKEEPER . . .     64
   YOU SAY YOU DON'T KNOW WHERE SHE IS." / "NOR WANT TO!  83 THE HOUSEKEEPER . . .     73
   "YES, BUT HE SHOULD HAVE MARRIED HER." / "I KNOW." . . 84 THE HOUSEKEEPER . . .     76
   I KNOW THE WAY HE'S FELT--BUT ALL THE SAME!" . . . .   84 THE HOUSEKEEPER . . .     83
   WE CAME HERE FOR A HOME FOR ME, YOU KNOW, . . . . .  . 85 THE HOUSEKEEPER . . .    104
   YOU DON'T KNOW WHAT A GENTLE LOT WE ARE: . . . . . .   85 THE HOUSEKEEPER . . .    124
   "AND WE LIVE UP TO IT; OR I DON'T KNOW . . . . . . .   85 THE HOUSEKEEPER . . .    132
   YOU KNOW HOW MEN WILL BE RIDICULOUS. . . . . . . .  .  87 THE HOUSEKEEPER . . .    160
   "WHY DO YOU SPEAK LIKE THAT? WHAT DO YOU KNOW? . . .   87 THE HOUSEKEEPER . . .    178
   ISN'T IT HELL?" HE SAID. "I WANT TO KNOW. . . . . .  . 88 THE HOUSEKEEPER . . .    207
   I'LL NEVER REST TONIGHT UNLESS I KNOW. . . . . . .  .  90 THE FEAR . . . . .        32
   WHILE WE KNOW DEFINITELY WHERE HE IS. . . . . . . .  . 90 THE FEAR . . . . .        44
   FIVE HUNDRED DOLLARS FOR THE PAIR, YOU KNOW." . . . .  93 THE SELF-SEEKER . . .      4
   THE LAWYER DON'T KNOW WHAT IT IS HE'S BUYING: . . . .  93 THE SELF-SEEKER . . .     11
   I'D RATHER MRS. CORBIN DIDN'T KNOW; . . . . . . . .  . 94 THE SELF-SEEKER . . .     53
   SUCH AS IT'S GOING TO BE, AND KNOW THE WORST, . . . .  95 THE SELF-SEEKER . . .     77
   AND IT MAY TAKE HIM I DON'T KNOW HOW LONG. . . . .  .  98 THE SELF-SEEKER . . .    171
   HALF THE TIME I DON'T KNOW WHAT'S TROUBLING ME.-- . .  99 THE SELF-SEEKER . . .    194
   YOU KNOW IT, MR. LAWYER. THE SIN IS . . . . . . . .  .100 THE SELF-SEEKER . . .    200
   WHERE I COME IN IS WHAT I WANT TO KNOW. . . . . . .  .100 THE SELF-SEEKER . . .    210
   YOU DON'T KNOW WHAT I MEAN ABOUT THE FLOWERS. . . . .  100 THE SELF-SEEKER . . .    226
   I'D HATE TO HAVE THEM KNOW IT IF I WAS. . . . . . .  .106 CHRISTMAS TREES . .       20
   A THOUSAND CHRISTMAS TREES I DIDN'T KNOW I HAD! . . .  107 CHRISTMAS TREES . .       55
   "THAT'S WHAT YOU'RE SO CONCERNED TO KNOW! YOU HOPE . . 111 IN THE HOME STRETCH       36
   WE'D CARE TO KNOW, FOR WE ARE NOT YOUNG NOW.-- . . .   112 IN THE HOME STRETCH       54
   IT'S SOMETHING, THOUGH, TO KNOW WE'RE GOING TO HAVE HER 113 IN THE HOME STRETCH      72
   "MA FRIEND, YOU AIN'T KNOW WHAT IT IS YOU'RE ASK." . . 114 IN THE HOME STRETCH      105
   I DON'T KNOW WHAT THEY THINK WE SEE IN WHAT . . . .  . 114 IN THE HOME STRETCH      112
   WHAT HAVE YOU YOU KNOW WHERE TO LAY YOUR HANDS ON?" .  115 IN THE HOME STRETCH      143
   HE'LL KNOW WHAT HE WOULD DO IF HE WERE WE, . . . . .   115 IN THE HOME STRETCH      151
   "SHOULDN'T YOU LIKE TO KNOW?" / "I'D LIKE TO KNOW . .  116 IN THE HOME STRETCH      166
```

KNOW (CONTINUED)
YOU DON'T WANT ME TO TELL IF I DON'T KNOW." . . . . . . 116 IN THE HOME STRETCH . 169
ALL OF A FARM IT IS." / " I KNOW THIS MUCH: . . . . . . 117 IN THE HOME STRETCH . 198
I DON'T KNOW WHERE IT'S LIKELY TO GO BETTER. . . . . . . 122 BIRCHES 53
AND WHAT'S THE NEWS YOU CARRY--IF YOU KNOW? . . . . . . 125 AN ENCOUNTER 20
BEGIN IN SMUDGE WITH ROPY SMOKE, AND KNOW . . . . . . 130 THE BONFIRE 21
DONE SO MUCH AND I KNOW NOT HOW MUCH MORE . . . . . . 130 THE BONFIRE 30
BUT THE WIND OUT-OF-DOORS--YOU KNOW THE SAYING. . . . . 130 THE BONFIRE 40
THAT'S WHAT FOR REASONS I SHOULD LIKE TO KNOW-- . . . . 132 THE BONFIRE 98
SHE SAYS, "I KNOW! . . . . 134 A GIRL'S GARDEN . . 44
SINCE HE WAS OLD ENOUGH TO KNOW, BIG BOY . . . . . . 137 "OUT,OUT--" 23
WE KNOW WHO WHEN THEY COME TO TOWN . . . . 141 THE GUM-GATHERER . . 25
I THOUGHT I WOULD.--I KNOW, BUT, LETT--I KNOW-- . . . . 143 SNOW 19
BROTHER MESERVE. YOU KNOW TO FIND YOUR WAY . . . . . 144 SNOW 37
OUT THROUGH THE SHED." / "I GUESS I KNOW MY WAY. . . . 144 SNOW 38
I GUESS I KNOW WHERE I CAN FIND MY NAME . . . . . . 144 SNOW 39
"YOU THINK SO, DO YOU? YOU DON'T KNOW THE KIND. . . . 146 SNOW 83
YOU SEE I KNOW--TO GET YOU ON TO THINGS . . . . . . 147 SNOW 122
BUT IF YOU'RE GOING--SAY YOU'LL STAY, YOU KNOW. . . . . 148 SNOW 154
YOU COULD DO--NOW. YOU KNOW THE RISK YOU TAKE . . . . 150 SNOW 220
WE'LL HAVE TO SIT HERE TILL WE KNOW HE'S SAFE." . . . 152 SNOW 262
YOU KNOW--IT SOUNDS THAT WAY, AND YES, I HEAR-- . . . 153 SNOW 300
DO YOU KNOW WHAT SHE'S LIKE? HAVE YOU EVER MET HER? . . 154 SNOW 313
DID YOU BUT KNOW OF HIM, NEW HAMPSHIRE HAS . . . . . 162 NEW HAMPSHIRE . . 93
AND SHE HAS ONE I DON'T KNOW WHAT TO CALL HIM, ... 162 NEW HAMPSHIRE . . 100
OF RADIUM. I KNOW WITH RADIUM . . . . 162 NEW HAMPSHIRE . . 119
ABOUT DISPOSING OF IT. DO YOU KNOW, ... 164 NEW HAMPSHIRE . . 169
BUT WHEN I ASKED TO KNOW WHAT AILED NEW HAMPSHIRE, . . . 166 NEW HAMPSHIRE . . 223
AND WHEN I ASKED TO KNOW WHAT AILED THE PEOPLE, . . . 166 NEW HAMPSHIRE . . 226
IN OTHER WORDS, I KNOW WHEREVER I AM, ... 166 NEW HAMPSHIRE . . 239
I DON'T KNOW WHAT TO SAY ABOUT THE PEOPLE. . . . . . 167 NEW HAMPSHIRE . . 265
I KNOW A MAN WHO TOOK A DOUBLE AX . . . . 170 NEW HAMPSHIRE . . 367
NOR KNOW THAT HE MIGHT MOVE IT FROM THE SPOT-- . . . . 173 A STAR IN A STONEBOAT . 19
I DO NOT KNOW--I CANNOT STOP TO TELL: . . . . . . 173 A STAR IN A STONEBOAT . 38
SOME MAY KNOW WHAT THEY SEEK IN SCHOOL AND CHURCH, . . . 173 A STAR IN A STONEBOAT . 43
"YOU KNOW ORION ALWAYS COMES UP SIDEWAYS. . . . . . 176 THE STAR-SPLITTER . 1
TO LET HIM KNOW WE WEREN'T THE LEAST IMPOSED ON, . . . 177 THE STAR-SPLITTER . 41
DO WE KNOW ANY BETTER WHERE WE ARE, ... 179 THE STAR-SPLITTER . 96
THERE'S NO SUCH NAME." / "TEACHERS DON'T KNOW AS MUCH . . 179 MAPLE 5
GOING THE OTHER OUT OF LIFE--YOU KNOW? . . . . . . 180 MAPLE 13
I DON'T KNOW WHAT SHE WANTED IT TO MEAN, ... 180 MAPLE 20
BY AND BY I WILL TELL YOU ALL I KNOW . . . . . . 180 MAPLE 26
"DO YOU KNOW YOU REMIND ME OF A TREE-- . . . . . . 182 MAPLE 87
A NAME TO CARRY FOR LIFE AND NEVER KNOW . . . . . . 183 MAPLE 116
AS IF HE DIDN'T KNOW WHAT LITTLE THING . . . . . . 183 MAPLE 125
I DIDN'T KNOW HIM WELL ENOUGH TO KNOW . . . . . . 185 THE AX-HELVE . . 14
DO YOU KNOW, WHAT WE TALKED ABOUT WAS KNOWLEDGE? . . . 188 THE AX-HELVE . . 82
YOU KNOW PAUL COULD DO WONDERS. EVERYONE'S . . . . . 192 PAUL'S WIFE . . . 42
IT'S ALL YOU KNOW THE GRAPE, OR KNOW THE BIRCH. . . . 196 WILD GRAPES . . . 3
I OUGHT TO KNOW WHAT TREE THE GRAPE IS FRUIT OF. . . . 196 WILD GRAPES . . . 6
DON'T YOU KNOW ANYTHING, YOU GIRL? LET GO!" . . . . 197 WILD GRAPES . . . 47
TO DRY OR WASH OR TAN, I DON'T KNOW WHICH . . . . . 197 WILD GRAPES . . . 52
"NOW YOU KNOW HOW IT FEELS," MY BROTHER SAID, ... 198 WILD GRAPES . . . 62
I DON'T KNOW MUCH ABOUT THE LETTING DOWN; . . . . . 198 WILD GRAPES . . . 84
I KNOW I LOOKED LONG AT MY CURLED-UP FINGERS, ... 198 WILD GRAPES . . . 87
I MAY YET LIVE, AS I KNOW OTHERS LIVE, ... 199 WILD GRAPES . . . 100
WHERE WAS HIS GRAVE? DID LABAN KNOW HIS NAME? . . . . 200 PLACE FOR A THIRD . 37
WHO'S GOT THE BUTTON," I WOULD HAVE THEM KNOW. . . . . 202 THE WITCH OF COOS . 8
I WAS A BABY: I DON'T KNOW WHERE I WAS. . . . . . 203 THE WITCH OF COOS . 35
WE KNOW THEY HAD A GRAVE DOWN IN THE CELLAR. . . . . 206 THE WITCH OF COOS . 136
I KNOW OF SOME FOLKS THAT'D BE SET UP . . . . . . 208 PAUPER WITCH OF GRAFTON 36
THAT EVEN I WOULD BE. THEY OUGHT TO KNOW . . . . . 208 PAUPER WITCH OF GRAFTON 39
WAS ARTHUR AMY. YOU KNOW WHO HE WAS. . . . . . . 209 PAUPER WITCH OF GRAFTON 71
HE GUESSED THEY'D KNOW WHAT HE HAD TO PUT UP WITH. . . 210 PAUPER WITCH OF GRAFTON 88
AND BETWEEN WHAT HE DOESN'T KNOW . . . . 211 AN EMPTY THREAT . . 14
I DIDN'T KNOW WAS THERE. IT WAS THE KIND . . . . . 215 A FOUNTAIN, A BOTTLE . 69
I THINK I KNOW ENOUGH OF HATE . . . . 220 FIRE AND ICE . . 6
IT'S ONLY WEATHER.' HE'D THINK SHE DIDN'T KNOW! . . . 223 THE RUNAWAY . . . 13
WHOSE WOODS THESE ARE I THINK I KNOW. . . . . . 224 STOPPING BY WOODS . 1
I KNOW THAT WINTER DEATH HAS NEVER TRIED . . . . . 226 THE ONSET . . . 13
NO ONE WOULD KNOW EXCEPT FOR ANCIENT MAPS . . . . . 231 A BROOK IN THE CITY . 20
(AND I KNOW OF ONE THAT DIDN'T THRIVE) . . . . . 232 THE KITCHEN CHIMNEY . 11
TO THINK TO KNOW THE COUNTRY AND NOT KNOW . . . . . 237 A HILLSIDE THAW . . 1
LESS THAN THE CORALROOT, YOU KNOW, ... 247 ON GOING UNNOTICED . 5
SPINNING THEIR OWN COCOON DID THEY BUT KNOW IT. . . . 248 THE COCOON . . . 16
AT WHAT HAS HAPPENED. BIRDS, AT LEAST, MUST KNOW . . . 249 ACCEPTANCE . . . 4
I KNOW HOW THE FLOWERS FELT. . . . . 250 LODGED 6
IS YET--WELL, SOMETHING THEY KNOW, HE AND SHE. . . . 256 THE LOVELY BE CHOOSERS 24
THOSE FRIENDS KNOW NOTHING OF HER GRIEF TO MAKE IT SHAMEFUL. 256 THE LOVELY BE CHOOSERS 27
HER THIRD JOY THAT THOUGH NOW THEY CANNOT HELP BUT KNOW, . 256 THE LOVELY BE CHOOSERS 28
YOU KNOW THEM--SEVEN IN ALL." . . . . . . 257 THE LOVELY BE CHOOSERS 52
BECAUSE WE'RE--WE'RE--I DON'T KNOW WHAT WE ARE. . . . 258 WEST-RUNNING BROOK . 9
TO LET US KNOW IT HEARS ME." / "WHY, MY DEAR, . . . 258 WEST-RUNNING BROOK . 17
SHE MAY KNOW COVE AND CAPE, ... 260 SAND DUNES . . . 9
BUT SHE DOES NOT KNOW MANKIND . . . . 260 SAND DUNES . . . 10
BUT THIS WE KNOW, THE OBSTACLE THAT CHECKED . . . . 261 A SOLDIER . . . 12
AND THEN I KNOW OF NO BETTER WAY . . . . . . 263 THE TIMES TABLE . . 17
TODAY SHE WOULDN'T KNOW OUR NAME. . . . . . . 265 THE BIRTHPLACE . . 11
YOU KNOW HOW IT IS WITH AN APRIL DAY . . . . . . 275 TWO TRAMPS IN MUD TIME 18
CONSERVATIVES, THEY DON'T KNOW WHAT TO SAVE. . . . . 290 OLD BARN AT THE BOTTOM 32
THEY KNOW WHERE ANOTHER LIGHT HAS BEEN, ... 291 ON HEART'S BEGINNING TO 38
WE'LL KNOW, WE SAY, THAT THIS WAS THE NIGHT IT DIED. . . 305 THERE ARE ROUGHLY ZONES 5
WE MUST WAIT TILL SOME MONTHS HENCE IN THE SPRING TO KNOW. . 305 THERE ARE ROUGHLY ZONES 19
WHAT SOON ENOUGH HE WOULD KNOW? . . . . . . 314 BEARER OF EVIL TIDINGS 44
I KNOW WOOL'S DOWN TO SEVEN CENTS A POUND. . . . . 316 BUILD SOIL . . . 13
I SHOULD MYSELF, ONLY I DON'T KNOW HOW. . . . . . 316 BUILD SOIL . . . 20
TO KNOW IF ANYTHING IS VERY WRONG. . . . . . . 317 BUILD SOIL . . . 56
I DON'T KNOW WHAT IT WOULD BE. NO ONE KNOWS. . . . . 318 BUILD SOIL . . . 77

KNOW (CONTINUED)
MY FRIENDS ALL KNOW I'M INTERPERSONAL. . . . . 320 BUILD SOIL 142
IN MY OPINION--THOUGH WE BOTH KNOW POETS . . . . . . 321 BUILD SOIL 176
AND WANTED SOMEONE NOW TO KNOW . . . . 327 A MISSIVE MISSILE . . 17
AND YET NOT KNOW THEY HAVE IT. . . . . 335 CARPE DIEM 18
FOR ALL THE CREW WERE LET TO KNOW. . . . . 344 DISCOVERY OF MADEIRAS . 34
YOU DID NOT KNOW THAT SINCE KING CHARLES DID RULE . . . 351 THE LESSON FOR TODAY . 22
WHO KNOW, EXACTLY WHAT IS OUT OF JOINT . . . . . . 351 THE LESSON FOR TODAY . 32
WE KNOW ENOUGH TO KNOW IT FOR ADVERSE. . . . . . . 352 THE LESSON FOR TODAY . 45
WON'T KNOW EXACTLY WHAT I MEAN BY THAT. . . . . . . 354 THE LESSON FOR TODAY . 121
TO KNOW THE HAND I STRETCH IMPULSIVELY . . . . . . 356 A MOTH SEEN IN WINTER . 20
NO ONE CAN KNOW HOW GLAD I AM TO FIND . . . . . 358 A CONSIDERABLE SPECK . 32
(AND SCIENCE OUGHT TO KNOW) . . . . 361 ALMOST TWO THOUSAND . 9
AND THE BIG FLAG THEY HAD--YOU KNOW . . . . 366 NOT OF SCHOOL AGE . . 24
IS NOT A STAR?" / "BELIEVE IT? WHY, I KNOW IT. . . . . 370 THE LITERATE FARMER AND 63
YOU KNOW HOW CUNNINGLY MANKIND IS PLANNED: . . . . . 371 THE LITERATE FARMER AND 112
WOULD KNOW THAT IT WAS THERE TO BE ADMIRED, ... 375 A YOUNG BIRCH . . . 18
(WE KNOW THE VALLEY STREAMS THAT WHEN AROUSED . . . . 378 DIRECTIVE 53
THE WORLD AS WE KNOW IS AN ELEPHANT'S HOWDAH; . . . . 379 TOO ANXIOUS FOR RIVERS 14
HAS NEVER LEARNED TO KNOW HER PLACE. . . . . 390 TWO LEADING LIGHTS . 13
SARCASTIC SCIENCE, SHE WOULD LIKE TO KNOW, ... 395 WHY WAIT FOR SCIENCE . 1
THAT CLASS OF PEOPLE DON'T KNOW WHAT WORK IS-- . . . 405 FROM PLANE TO PLANE . 33
MORE THAN THEY KNOW WHAT COURAGE IS THAT CLAIM . . . . 405 FROM PLANE TO PLANE . 34
FROM KNOWING MORE THAN I KNOW HOW TO THINK WITH. . . . 407 FROM PLANE TO PLANE . 99
WE ALL KNOW HIS ADDRESS, MOUNT HECLA, ICELAND. . . . . 408 FROM PLANE TO PLANE . 143
KNOW WHERE THEY ARE. / THEY'VE BEEN HERE LONG ENOUGH . 413 A CABIN IN THE CLEARING 2
AND STILL I DOUBT IF THEY KNOW WHERE THEY ARE. . . . . 414 A CABIN IN THE CLEARING 5
SIMPLY BECAUSE THEY DON'T KNOW WHERE THEY ARE. . . . . 414 A CABIN IN THE CLEARING 14
IF THE DAY EVER COMES WHEN THEY KNOW WHO . . . . . 414 A CABIN IN THE CLEARING 29
THEY ARE, THEY MAY KNOW BETTER WHERE THEY ARE. . . . 414 A CABIN IN THE CLEARING 30
WE KNOW THE LITERARY CHATTER. . . . . 418 AMERICA IS HARD TO SEE 66
POETS KNOW A LOT. . . . . 429 KITTY HAWK 32
WE DON'T KNOW WHAT FOR: . . . . 433 KITTY HAWK 152
GO YOU ON TO KNOW . . . . 436 KITTY HAWK 279
ONE WOULD LIKE TO KNOW . . . . 438 KITTY HAWK 336
WE KNOW OF NO WORLD . . . . 440 KITTY HAWK 395
DON'T YOU KNOW WHERE NEW MOONS ARE FROM? . . . . . 451 A-WISHING WELL . . . 31
I KNOW THE QUINTESSENCE OF MANY THINGS. . . . . . 455 HOW HARD TO KEEP FROM 41
I KNOW THE QUINTESSENCE OF FOOD, I KNOW . . . . . 455 HOW HARD TO KEEP FROM 42
THE QUINTESSENCE OF JEWELS, AND I KNOW . . . . . 455 HOW HARD TO KEEP FROM 43
THE EUNUCH LAUGHED: "WELL, THAT'S A LOT TO KNOW. . . 455 HOW HARD TO KEEP FROM 45
"YOU SAY YOU KNOW THE INWARDNESS OF MEN, ... 456 HOW HARD TO KEEP FROM 98
YOU HAVE A RIGHT TO KNOW YOUR PEDIGREE. . . . . . 457 HOW HARD TO KEEP FROM 107
HOW DID YOU KNOW THE SECRET OF MY BIRTH?" . . . . . 457 HOW HARD TO KEEP FROM 117
"YOU KNOW SO MUCH, GO ON, INSTRUCT ME FURTHER. . . . 458 HOW HARD TO KEEP FROM 146
MY SON AND I HAVE TASTED IT AND KNOW. . . . . . . 460 HOW HARD TO KEEP FROM 195
WE KNOW NOT WHAT WE OWE THIS MOMENT TO. . . . . . 461 HOW HARD TO KEEP FROM 241
I DON'T KNOW WHAT MADE HER SO LUNAR A LOON; . . . . 463 LINES IN DEJECTION . 3
BUT I KNOW THEM WHAT THEY ARE: . . . . 466 SOME SCIENCE FICTION . 13
I'D KNOW HIM BY BLAKE'S PICTURE ANYWHERE. . . . . . 474 A MASQUE OF REASON . 18
(I'D KNOW YOU BY BLAKE'S PICTURE ANYWHERE)-- . . . . 476 A MASQUE OF REASON . 85
AND I SHOULD LIKE TO KNOW THE REASON WHY. . . . . . 477 A MASQUE OF REASON . 104
SHE WANTS TO KNOW WHY THERE IS STILL INJUSTICE. . . . 477 A MASQUE OF REASON . 110
GOD KNOWS--OR RATHER, YOU KNOW (GOD FORGIVE ME) . . . 479 A MASQUE OF REASON . 169
SHE'D LIKE TO KNOW HOW YOU WOULD TAKE A PRAYER . . . 479 A MASQUE OF REASON . 180
IF YOU DON'T WANT TO. I DON'T WANT TO KNOW. . . . . 483 A MASQUE OF REASON . 271
WE DON'T KNOW WHERE WE ARE, OR WHO WE ARE. . . . . 483 A MASQUE OF REASON . 285
WE DON'T KNOW ONE ANOTHER; DON'T KNOW YOU; . . . . 483 A MASQUE OF REASON . 286
DON'T KNOW WHAT TIME IT IS. WE DON'T KNOW, DON'T WE? . 483 A MASQUE OF REASON . 287
OH, WE KNOW WELL ENOUGH TO GO AHEAD WITH. . . . . 483 A MASQUE OF REASON . 289
I MEAN WE SEEM TO KNOW ENOUGH TO ACT ON. . . . . . 483 A MASQUE OF REASON . 290
(I HOPE YOU KNOW THE GAME CALLED TWENTY QUESTIONS.) . . 484 A MASQUE OF REASON . 314
HOW DID YOU KNOW THAT WAY TO BREAK MY HEART? . . . . 495 A MASQUE OF MERCY . 59
WHO ARE YOU? / WHO ARE YOU? / I THINK YOU KNOW, . . . 495 A MASQUE OF MERCY . 60
OR BAD AS IN NEW YORK. / I KNOW I AM. . . . . . . 497 A MASQUE OF MERCY . 93
YOU DON'T KNOW PAUL: HE'S IN THE BIBLE TOO. . . . . 498 A MASQUE OF MERCY . 127
SOMETHING WE'LL KNOW WE'RE GETTING WHEN WE GET IT. . . 503 A MASQUE OF MERCY . 266
YOU KNOW WHAT LETS US OFF FROM BEING CAREFUL? . . . 505 A MASQUE OF MERCY . 316
YOU KNOW, THERE MAY HAVE BEEN A SMALL TEMBLOR. . . . 507 A MASQUE OF MERCY . 356
OR CLEAR OFF WHAT WE KNOW HIS INTERESTS ARE. . . . 509 A MASQUE OF MERCY . 427
WE KNOW WHAT'S COMING NOW. / YOU SAY IT, KEEPER, . . 511 A MASQUE OF MERCY . 480
KNOWING
YET KNOWING HOW WAY LEADS ON TO WAY, ... 105 THE ROAD NOT TAKEN . 14
AS IF NOT KNOWING WHAT YOU MEANT BY THE WORD STORM." . 151 SNOW 232
AND THAT TALKS NO LESS FOR KNOWING, ... 156 THE SOUND OF TREES . 12
SO MUCH AS MY NOT KNOWING ANYTHING-- . . . . . . 199 WILD GRAPES 93
GIVE HER THE COMFORT FOR HER SIXTH OF KNOWING . . . 257 THE LOVELY BE CHOOSERS 43
THEY HAD NO WAY OF KNOWING A FOOL. . . . . 276 TWO TRAMPS IN MUD TIME 56
IT'S KNOWING WHAT TO DO WITH THINGS THAT COUNTS. . . 294 AT WOODWARD'S GARDENS . 37
POOR EGOTIST, HE HAS NO WAY OF KNOWING . . . . . 309 WASPISH 5
FROM KNOWING MORE THAN I KNOW HOW TO THINK WITH. . . 407 FROM PLANE TO PLANE . 99
THERE'S NO KNOWING WHAT . . . . 429 KITTY HAWK 30
SO KNOWING--AND YET NEEDING TO BE TOLD . . . . . 506 A MASQUE OF MERCY . 338
KNOWLEDGE
DO YOU KNOW, WHAT WE TALKED ABOUT WAS KNOWLEDGE? . . . 188 THE AX-HELVE 82
I HAD NOT TAKEN THE FIRST STEP IN KNOWLEDGE; . . . 199 WILD GRAPES 95
OF THE KNOWLEDGE BEYOND THE BOUNDS OF LIFE . . . . 236 MISGIVING 15
"OH, FROM MY KNOWLEDGE OF ITS QUINTESSENCE. . . . . 456 HOW HARD TO KEEP FROM 87
NOT IN THE SENSE OF HAVING TO MY KNOWLEDGE . . . . 476 A MASQUE OF REASON . 95
KNOWN (SEE A-KNOWN)
"KNOWN IT SINCE I WAS YOUNG." / "THEN YOU KNOW ME. . . 48 A HUNDRED COLLARS . 100
TO LIGHTED CITY STREETS WE, TOO, HAVE KNOWN, . . . 112 IN THE HOME STRETCH . 58
"I DON'T WANT TO FIND OUT WHAT CAN'T BE KNOWN. . . . 116 IN THE HOME STRETCH . 170
I'VE KNOWN ERE NOW AN INTERFERING BRANCH . . . . . 185 THE AX-HELVE 1
FOR MONTHS IT HASN'T KNOWN THE TASTE OF STEEL . . . 189 THE GRINDSTONE . . . 15
WAS THAT WE'D GROUND IT SHARP AND HADN'T KNOWN, . . . 190 THE GRINDSTONE . . . 66
LABAN HAD KNOWN ABOUT WHAT IT WOULD BE . . . . . 201 PLACE FOR A THIRD . 73
BOYS AND BAD HUNTERS HAD KNOWN WHAT TO DO . . . . 216 A FOUNTAIN, A BOTTLE . 102

KNOWN (CONTINUED)   PAGE TITLE   LINE

    HOW ELSE? THEY ARE NOT KNOWN TO SEND THE DEAD.-- . . . 230 NOT TO KEEP 6
    TOLD ME MY SECRET MUST BE KNOWN: . . . . 251 BEREFT 12
    HOPELESS OF BEING KNOWN FOR WHAT SHE HAS BEEN, ... 257 THE LOVELY BE CHOOSERS . 41
    THE ALREADY KNOWN HAD ONCE MORE BEEN CONFIRMED . . . . 293 AT WOODWARD'S GARDENS . 18
    WITH EVERY KNOWN SHAPE OF THE STUFF. . . . . 310 THE VINDICTIVES . . . 5
    I SANG OF DEATH--BUT HAD I KNOWN . . . . 336 THE WIND AND THE RAIN . 9
    AS I HAVE KNOWN THEM PASSIONATE AND FINE, ... 358 THE LOST FOLLOWER . . 1
    TO SEE THE STAR SHOWER KNOWN AS LEONID . . . . 360 A LOOSE MOUNTAIN . . . 2
    FOR WHICH THE REGION ROUND WAS KNOWN, ... 364 TRESPASS 11
    KNOWN AS BOUSTROPHEDON, WAS FOUND TOO AWKWARD." . . . 405 FROM PLANE TO PLANE . . 54
    HAD BUT COLUMBUS KNOWN ENOUGH . . . . 417 AMERICA IS HARD TO SEE . 25
    JUSTLY KNOWN TO FAME . . . . 440 KITTY HAWK 375
    ONCE TO HAVE KNOWN IT, NOTHING ELSE WILL DO. . . . . 461 HOW HARD TO KEEP FROM . 247
KNOWS
    THE FACT IS THE SWEETEST DREAM THAT LABOR KNOWS. . . . 17 MOWING 13
    THE HAND THAT KNOWS HIS BUSINESS WON'T BE TOLD. . . . 70 THE CODE 22
    JOHN HALL TOUCH ME! NOT IF HE KNOWS HIS FRIENDS. . . . 83 THE HOUSEKEEPER . . . 67
    HE KNOWS HE'S KINDER THAN THE RUN OF MEN. . . . . . 84 THE HOUSEKEEPER . . . 80
    THAT'S HIS MISTAKE. THE DEAR KNOWS MY INTEREST . . . . 84 THE HOUSEKEEPER . . . 87
    ACCEPTING ANYTHING BEFORE HE KNOWS . . . . 100 THE SELF-SEEKER . . . 201
    BUT THAT HE KNOWS IN SINGING NOT TO SING. . . . . . 120 THE OVEN BIRD . . . 12
    THE DEAR KNOWS. I DETEST THE THOUGHT OF HIM-- . . . . 144 SNOW 51
    HE KNOWS WHAT HE CAN DO, OR HE WOULDN'T TRY. . . . . 152 SNOW 264
    YOU ASK HER IF SHE KNOWS A MAPLE TREE. . . . . . . 180 MAPLE 8
    SON KNOWS THE STORY: BUT 'TWAS NOT FOR HIM . . . . . 206 THE WITCH OF COOS . . 143
    AND YET SHE KNOWS OBSTRUCTION IS IN VAIN: . . . . . 238 ON A TREE FALLEN ACROSS . 9
    THE DEAR ONLY KNOWS . . . . 246 THE ROSE FAMILY . . . 7
    (FROM SLEEPING GOD KNOWS WHERE LAST NIGHT, ... 276 TWO TRAMPS IN MUD TIME . 50
    GOD KNOWS ALL THE COLOR AND FORM OF LEAVES I HAVE TRODDEN
      ON AND MIRED. . . . . 297 A LEAF-TREADER . . . 2
    I DON'T KNOW WHAT IT WOULD BE. NO ONE KNOWS. . . . . 318 BUILD SOIL 77
    BUT THE SECRET SITS IN THE MIDDLE AND KNOWS. . . . . 362 THE SECRET SITS . . . 2
    KNOWS THE OLD MAN, AND NOBODY'S SO DEEP . . . . . . 371 THE LITERATE FARMER AND 96
    AND WHO KNOWS WHERE WE CAN'T GET! WASTING TIME . . . . 371 THE LITERATE FARMER AND 102
    EACH KNOWS HIS OWN DISCERNMENT BEST. . . . . 381 AN UNSTAMPED LETTER IN . 43
    AND DARED TO TASTE THE WOUND A LITTLE KNOWS. . . . . 411 POD OF THE MILKWEED . . 18
    EVERYONE KNOWS THE GLORY OF THE TWAIN . . . . 423 FOR JOHN F. KENNEDY . . 46
    WHO KNOWS BUT A GREAT . . . . 428 KITTY HAWK 3
    "A MAN'S OUT THERE WHO CLAIMS HE KNOWS THE SECRET, . . . 455 HOW HARD TO KEEP FROM . 60
    GOD KNOWS--OR RATHER, YOU KNOW (GOD FORGIVE ME) . . . 479 A MASQUE OF REASON . . 169
    KEEPER, BE STILL. HE KNOWS WHAT BOOK HE WANTS. . . . 495 A MASQUE OF MERCY . . 51
    WHAT HAVE YOU GOT AGAINST THE CITY? / HE KNOWS. . . . 496 A MASQUE OF MERCY . . 65
KNUCKLE
    DEW ON THE KNUCKLE. . . . . 227 TO EARTHWARD 12
    AND MADE IT LEAP MY KNUCKLE, HAVING TOSSED . . . . . 231 A BROOK IN THE CITY . 7
KNUCKLES
    BECAUSE I MAKE HIM SPIT FIRE AT MY KNUCKLES, ... 94 THE SELF-SEEKER . . . 34
    HE GOT HIS PURPLE LITTLE KNUCKLES STUNG. . . . . . 293 AT WOODWARD'S GARDENS . 17
KODAK
    GOOD, PRETTY GOOD. / WAIT TILL I GET MY KODAK.-- . . . 488 A MASQUE OF REASON . . 402
KULTUR
    WHATEVER KULTUR . . . . 449 THE BAD ISLAND--EASTER . 55

L

L
    SEEMS TO HAVE BEEN A MAN NAMED JOHN L. DARWIN." . . . 168 NEW HAMPSHIRE . . . 299
LA
    A BLINDMAN BY THE NAME OF LA FONTAINE, ... 394 HAEC FABULA DOCET . . 1
LABAN
    AND SO SHE SAID TO LABAN, "YOU HAVE DONE . . . . . 199 PLACE FOR A THIRD . . 9
    LABAN SAID, NO, HE WOULD NOT MAKE HER LIE . . . . . 199 PLACE FOR A THIRD . . 12
    SHE WENT HER WAY. BUT LABAN HAVING CAUGHT . . . . . 200 PLACE FOR A THIRD . . 15
    WHERE WAS HIS GRAVE? DID LABAN KNOW HIS NAME? . . . . 200 PLACE FOR A THIRD . . 37
    SO LABAN SAW THE SISTER, AND, SAYING NOTHING . . . . 200 PLACE FOR A THIRD . . 44
    LABAN WAS OLD AND POOR, YET SEEMED TO CARE; . . . . 201 PLACE FOR A THIRD . . 50
    AND HOW MUCH LABAN CARED--AND WHY HE CARED. . . . . 201 PLACE FOR A THIRD . . 56
    THE SISTER HAD NOT COME ACROSS THIS LABAN; . . . . . 201 PLACE FOR A THIRD . . 66
    LABAN HAD KNOWN ABOUT WHAT IT WOULD BE . . . . . . 201 PLACE FOR A THIRD . . 73
    LABAN WAS FORCED TO FALL BACK ON HIS PLAN . . . . . 202 PLACE FOR A THIRD . . 79
LABEL
    THEIR LABEL PROP-LOCKS, ONLY SPECIMENS . . . . . . 290 OLD BARN AT THE BOTTOM 37
LABOR
    THE FACT IS THE SWEETEST DREAM THAT LABOR KNOWS. . . . 17 MOWING 13
    HE SPENT HIMSELF, THE LABOR OF HIS AX, ... 102 THE WOOD-PILE . . . 37
    YOU MAKE A LABOR OF FLIGHT FOR ONE SO AIRY, ... 356 A MOTH SEEN IN WINTER . 11
LABORED
    NOT LABORED OUT OF MINES, ... 361 ALMOST TWO THOUSAND . 3
LABORER
    SOME LABORER FOUND ONE FADED AND STONE-COLD, ... 172 A STAR IN A STONEBOAT . 4
LABORERS'
    FROM WHICH THE LABORERS' VOICES LATE HAVE DIED, . . . 14 WAITING 4
LABORING
    AN AIRSHIP LABORING WITH UNSHIPLIKE MOTION . . . . . 182 MAPLE 82
LABORIOUS
    SOME ZEALOUS ONE'S LABORIOUS DEVICE. . . . . 74 THE GENERATIONS OF MEN 42
LACE
    BUT NEGLECTED, HOWEVER LIGHTLY, TO LACE . . . . . . 265 THE DOOR IN THE DARK . 3
LACED
    THEY STOOD ARMS LACED TOGETHER AT THE BARS, ... 293 AT WOODWARD'S GARDENS . 12
LACES
    I HAD A GLIMPSE THROUGH CURTAIN LACES . . . . . . 102 GOOD HOURS 7
LACK
    SOMETHING, PERHAPS, ABOUT THE LACK OF SOUND-- . . . . 17 MOWING 5
    THOUGH WE CHOOSE GREATLY, STILL TO LACK . . . . . . 21 THE TRIAL BY EXISTENCE 66

```
                                               PAGE TITLE                      LINE
LACK (CONTINUED)
    OF ITS OWN STUPID LACK OF UNDERSTANDING, . . . . . . . 148 SNOW . . . . . . 164
    I SHALL NOT LACK FOR PAIN TO KEEP ME AWAKE. . . . . . . 166 NEW HAMPSHIRE . . . 241
    AND MAKE UP FOR ITS LACK OF SIZE. . . . . . . . . . . 281 A DRUMLIN WOODCHUCK . 4
    BUT SCRUB OAK, SCRUB OAK AND THE LACK OF EARTH . . . . 292 FIGURE IN THE DOORWAY . 3
    NOR DID HE LACK FOR COMMON ENTERTAINMENT. . . . . . . 292 FIGURE IN THE DOORWAY . 19
    THE CONQUEROR HENCEFORTH SHOULD LACK. . . . . . . . . 311 THE VINDICTIVES . . . 26
    AND I COULD SHARE TIME'S LACK OF JOY OR GRIEF . . . . 335 I COULD GIVE ALL . . . 9
    STAY UNASSUMING. IF FOR LACK OF LICENSE . . . . . . . 385 THE FEAR OF GOD . . . 7
    TO MAKE UP FOR A LACK OF MEDITATION. . . . . . . . . 400 TO THE RIGHT PERSON . 14
    "YOUR TROUBLE IS BUCOLIC LACK OF LOGIC," . . . . . . . 404 FROM PLANE TO PLANE . 9
    "AND SOON FOR LACK OF SUN, . . . . . . . . . . . . 416 CLOSED FOR GOOD . . . 19
    BUT THEIR LACK OF LUCK . . . . . . . . . . . . . 431 KITTY HAWK . . . . 114
    THE LACK OF LIBERTY, THE SQUEEZE OF LAW . . . . . . . 460 HOW HARD TO KEEP FROM 199
    THERE'S NOT THE LEAST LACK OF THE LOVE OF GOD . . . . 505 A MASQUE OF MERCY . . 307
    ON THE OFF-CHANCE IT MAY BE LACK OF FAITH, . . . . . 515 A MASQUE OF MERCY . . 563
    LIGHT, BRING A LIGHT! / AWH, THERE'S NO LACK OF LIGHT, YOU-- 515 A MASQUE OF MERCY . . 579
LACKED
    AND DOWN BY ONE SIDE WHERE IT LACKED A LEG. . . . . . 175 THE CENSUS-TAKER . . 37
    WE BOTH HAVE LACKED THE COURAGE IN THE HEART . . . . 521 A MASQUE OF MERCY . . 728
LACKING
    BUT LACKING FAITH IN ANYTHING TO MEAN . . . . . . . 184 MAPLE . . . . . 155
LACKS
    NOW NO JOY BUT LACKS SALT, . . . . . . . . . . . 227 TO EARTHWARD . . . . 17
    HAPPINESS MAKES UP IN HEIGHT FOR WHAT IT LACKS IN LENGTH 333 HAPPINESS MAKES UP . . T
    FOR WHAT THE DRAB WEED LACKS OF THE ORNATE. . . . . . 411 POD OF THE MILKWEED . 13
LACONIC
    BUT WELL MAY BE LACONIC, EVEN BOEOTIAN. . . . . . . 362 BOEOTIAN . . . . . 3
LACQUERS
    BAMBOOS, IVORIES, JADES, AND LACQUERS, . . . . . . 396 AN IMPORTER . . . . 3
LAD
    THOUGH TWO, CLOSE-KEEPING, ARE LASS AND LAD-- . . . . 6 GHOST HOUSE . . . . 27
    HE THINKS YOUNG WILSON A LIKELY LAD, THOUGH DAFT . . . 36 DEATH OF THE HIRED MAN 65
LADDER
    I FEEL THE LADDER SWAY AS THE BOUGHS BEND. . . . . . 68 AFTER APPLE-PICKING . 23
    BY NOW, PULL IN YOUR LADDER ROAD BEHIND YOU . . . . . 378 DIRECTIVE . . . . . 37
LADDER-ROUND
    IT KEEPS THE PRESSURE OF A LADDER-ROUND. . . . . . . 68 AFTER APPLE-PICKING . 22
LADDER'S
    MY LONG TWO-POINTED LADDER'S STICKING THROUGH A TREE . 68 AFTER APPLE-PICKING . 1
LADD'S
    BEEN UP, I UNDERSTAND, HAVE CLIMBED FROM LADD'S. . . . 41 THE MOUNTAIN . . . . 40
LADING
    WAS NOT SET FORTH IN THE LADING BILL. . . . . . . . 343 DISCOVERY OF MADEIRAS . 4
LADY
    SHE HAD HER OWN IDEA OF THINGS, THE OLD LADY. . . . . 56 THE BLACK COTTAGE . . 51
    "WHERE WILL I PUT THIS WALNUT BUREAU, LADY?" . . . . 110 IN THE HOME STRETCH . 13
    "WHAT ARE YOU SEEING OUT THE WINDOW, LADY?" . . . . . 111 IN THE HOME STRETCH . 20
    WOULD EVIDENCE OF HAVING BEEN CALLED LADY . . . . . 111 IN THE HOME STRETCH . 22
    MORE THAN SO MANY TIMES MAKE ME A LADY . . . . . . 111 IN THE HOME STRETCH . 23
    WHAT ARE YOU SEEING OUT THE WINDOW, LADY?" . . . . . 111 IN THE HOME STRETCH . 25
    NOT OFFERING A LADY----" / "THERE AGAIN, JOE! . . . . 116 IN THE HOME STRETCH . 157
    I MET A LADY FROM THE SOUTH WHO SAID . . . . . . . 159 NEW HAMPSHIRE . . . 1
    AND, AS YOU MIGHT SAY, SAW THE LADY BORN. . . . . . 193 PAUL'S WIFE . . . . 56
    A STOLEN LADY WAS COMING ON BOARD, . . . . . . . 343 DISCOVERY OF MADEIRAS . 1
    A STOLEN LADY WAS ALL IT SAID. . . . . . . . . . 343 DISCOVERY OF MADEIRAS . 5
    FOR LONG THE LADY WOULD DISAPPEAR, . . . . . . . 344 DISCOVERY OF MADEIRAS . 32
    THE NAME OF THE LADY WITH HIS OWN . . . . . . . . 347 DISCOVERY OF MADEIRAS . 122
    AND THE BAY WHERE HIS STOLEN LADY DIED . . . . . . 347 DISCOVERY OF MADEIRAS . 134
    BY ANY CHANCE YOU LADY APPLE ON YOU? . . . . . . . 488 A MASQUE OF REASON . . 421
    LADY, AT SUCH A TIME, AND IN THE PRESENCE!-- . . . . 519 A MASQUE OF MERCY . . 684
LADY-LAND
    "OH, IF YOU TAKE IT OFF TO LADY-LAND, . . . . . . 258 WEST-RUNNING BROOK . . 32
LADY'S
    YOU DIDN'T FIND A YELLOW LADY'S SLIPPER. . . . . . 97 THE SELF-SEEKER . . . 137
    WHERE IS IT NOW, THE YELLOW LADY'S SLIPPER?" . . . . 97 THE SELF-SEEKER . . . 140
    THE PURPLE LADY'S SLIPPER'S COMMONER." . . . . . . 98 THE SELF-SEEKER . . . 142
    "I DIDN'T BRING A PURPLE LADY'S SLIPPER. . . . . . 98 THE SELF-SEEKER . . . 143
    NOW BREATHED AS LIGHT AS A LADY'S FAN. . . . . . . 304 UNHARVESTED . . . . 7
    THIS WAS NO LADY'S TIME OF YEAR. . . . . . . . . 344 DISCOVERY OF MADEIRAS . 31
    INTO A LADY'S FINGER RING OR THIMBLE." . . . . . . 447 DOES NO ONE AT ALL EVER 30
LAFAYETTE
    OF LINCOLN, LAFAYETTE, AND LIBERTY? . . . . . . . 169 NEW HAMPSHIRE . . . 324
LAFE
    "LAFE, HERE'S A FELLOW WANTS TO SHARE YOUR ROOM." . . . 45 A HUNDRED COLLARS . . 36
    "LAFE WAS THE NAME, I THINK?" / "YES, LAYFAYETTE. . . . 46 A HUNDRED COLLARS . . 41
    THE DOCTOR LOOKED AT LAFE AND LOOKED AWAY. . . . . . 46 A HUNDRED COLLARS . . 49
LAID (SEE SMOOTH-LAID)
    TO THE EARNEST LOVE THAT LAID THE SWALE IN ROWS, . . . 17 MOWING . . . . . . 10
    EACH LAID ON OTHER A STAYING HAND . . . . . . . . 18 GOING FOR WATER . . . 17
    HE LAID HIM DOWN ON THE SUNBURNED EARTH . . . . . . 24 PAN WITH US . . . . 28
    OF A STARFISH LAID OUT WITH RIGID POINTS." . . . . . 93 THE SELF-SEEKER . . . 20
    AND WHIRLS OF FOLIAGE NOT YET LAID, THERE DROVE . . . 106 CHRISTMAS TREES . . . 4
    A MAPLE LEAF SHE THOUGHT MUST HAVE BEEN LAID . . . . 181 MAPLE . . . . . . 63
    LAID SCARLET AND PALE PINK ABOUT HER FEET. . . . . . 184 MAPLE . . . . . . 147
    HE LAID IT AT THE EDGE, WHERE IT COULD DRINK. . . . . 194 PAUL'S WIFE . . . . 101
    THE BOARD WE HAD LAID DOWN TO WALK DRY-SHOD ON . . . . 204 THE WITCH OF COOS . . 48
    EXCEPT WHEN SEA FOG LAID IT DOWN, . . . . . . . . 249 A PECK OF GOLD . . . 2
    AND CEREMONIOUSLY LAID IT ON THE GROUND, . . . . . . 284 THE GOLD HESPERIDEE . 46
    AND ON TRACTS LAID NEW TO THE SUN, . . . . . . . . 285 IN TIME OF CLOUDBURST . 19
    OUR VERY BEST, OUR LIVES LAID DOWN LIKE JONAH'S, . . . 520 A MASQUE OF MERCY . . 720
    OUR LIVES LAID DOWN IN WAR AND PEACE--MAY NOT . . . . 520 A MASQUE OF MERCY . . 721
LAID-ON
    OF LAID-ON EDUCATION HAD TO DO . . . . . . . . . 188 THE AX-HELVE . . . . 86
LAIN
    I'VE LAIN AWAKE THINKING OF YOU, I'LL WARRANT, . . . . 67 A SERVANT TO SERVANTS . 166
    TWO MEMORIES THAT LONG HAD LAIN . . . . . . . . . 381 AN UNSTAMPED LETTER IN 33
```

LAIRS
    ALL ANIMALS ARE SMOTHERED IN THEIR LAIRS. . . . . . . 296 DESERT PLACES . . . 6
LAISSEZ-FAIRE
    THUS FORESIGHT DOES IT AND LAISSEZ-FAIRE, ... 376 SOMETHING FOR HOPE . . 18
LAJWAY
    THE RURAL LETTER BOX SAID TOFFILE LAJWAY. . . . . . 207 THE WITCH OF COOS . . 155
LAKE
    "WHAT DID HE SAY?" / "HE SAID THERE WAS A LAKE . . . . . 43 THE MOUNTAIN 75
    YOU TAKE THE LAKE. I LOOK AND LOOK AT IT. . . . . . 63 A SERVANT TO SERVANTS . 16
    AND A COLD CHILL SHIVERED ACROSS THE LAKE. . . . . 63 A SERVANT TO SERVANTS . 31
    BESIDE THE LAKE FROM WHERE THAT DAY I SHOWED YOU . . . 64 A SERVANT TO SERVANTS . 62
    AND LIVING BY A LAKE. I'M PAST SUCH HELP-- . . . . 67 A SERVANT TO SERVANTS . 156
    LIKE WILD GEESE ON A LAKE BEFORE A STORM? . . . . . 76 THE GENERATIONS OF MEN . 90
    BETWEEN THE WOODS AND FROZEN LAKE. . . . . 224 STOPPING BY WOODS . . 7
    TOLD THEM IN WHAT LAKE TO DIVE . . . . 311 THE VINDICTIVES . . . 43
    FROM SOME TREE-HIDDEN CLIFF ACROSS THE LAKE. . . . . 338 THE MOST OF IT 4
    AND THE HOLLOW HEAD WAS A LAKE. . . . . 367 A SERIOUS STEP LIGHTLY . 4
    LUCRETIUS VERSUS THE LAKE POETS . . . . 393 LUCRETIUS VERSUS POETS . T
LAKE'S
    "BUT A LAKE'S DIFFERENT. WHAT ABOUT THE SPRING?" . . . . 43 THE MOUNTAIN 77
LAME
    TO MAKE THEIR VERSE AND THEIR EXCUSES LAME. . . . . 351 THE LESSON FOR TODAY . 33
LAMENT
    TO THE DARK AND LAMENT. . . . . 334 COME IN 16
LAMP
    WAS THE LAMP TILTED NEAR THEM IN HIS HAND. . . . . 108 OLD MAN'S WINTER NIGHT . 5
    HAVE WE A PIECE OF CANDLE IF THE LAMP . . . . . . 113 IN THE HOME STRETCH . 80
    UNTIL THEY HAD LIT THE LAMP INSIDE. . . . . . . 127 HOUSE FEAR 10
    MESERVE SEEMED TO HEED NOTHING BUT THE LAMP . . . . 147 SNOW 111
    A THING AS THAT. IT COULDN'T REACH THE LAMP . . . . 148 SNOW 139
    AND BY SO DOING GIVE THESE THREE, LAMP, DOG, ... 148 SNOW 145
    WIDE OPEN AND THE WIND'S BLOWN OUT THE LAMP . . . . 154 SNOW 309
    NO LAMP WAS LIT. NOTHING WAS ON THE TABLE. . . . . 175 THE CENSUS-TAKER . . 35
    PUTTING THE LAMP OUT HAS NOT PUT THEIR THOUGHT OUT. . . 415 A CABIN IN THE CLEARING 36
LAMP-FLAME
    MARY SAT MUSING ON THE LAMP-FLAME AT THE TABLE, ... 34 DEATH OF THE HIRED MAN . 1
LAMPLIGHT
    THE THREE STOOD IN THE LAMPLIGHT ROUND THE TABLE . . . 144 SNOW 31
LAMPS
    WOODSVILLE'S A PLACE OF SHRIEKS AND WANDERING LAMPS . . . 45 A HUNDRED COLLARS . . 21
    TO LAMPS UNLIGHTED AND FIRE GONE GRAY, ... 127 HOUSE FEAR 4
    IN INCANDESCENT LAMPS AND ENDING SLEEP. . . . . . 371 THE LITERATE FARMER AND 97
LANCASTER
    LANCASTER BORE HIM--SUCH A LITTLE TOWN, ... 44 A HUNDRED COLLARS . . 1
    LATELY WHEN COMING UP TO LANCASTER, ... 44 A HUNDRED COLLARS . . 14
LANCE (SEE LADY-LAND)
    HE IS THAT FALLEN LANCE THAT LIES AS HURLED, ... 261 A SOLDIER 1
LAND (SEE LADY-LAND)
    FEARLESS OF EVER FINDING OPEN LAND, ... 5 INTO MY OWN . . . 7
    ON A HEIGHT OF NAKED PASTURE LAND: . . . . . . 23 PAN WITH US . . . 7
    ENCHANT THE LAND WITH AMETHYST. . . . . 28 OCTOBER . . . 16
    OF MY REGRET HUNG NOT ON ALL THE LAND, ... 28 MY BUTTERFLY . . . 19
    LEAP UP, LIKE THAT, LIKE THAT, AND LAND SO LIGHTLY . . . 53 HOME BURIAL . . . 76
    I COULD BE MONARCH OF A DESERT LAND . . . . . . 58 THE BLACK COTTAGE . 112
    TO HAVE YOU COME AND CAMP HERE ON OUR LAND. . . . . 62 A SERVANT TO SERVANTS . 2
    AND WHERE I LIVED IN MOUNTAIN LAND . . . . . . 140 THE GUM-GATHERER . 10
    MORE THAN ENOUGH LAND FOR A SPECIMEN . . . . . . 163 NEW HAMPSHIRE . 145
    TAUNTED THE LOFTY LAND WITH LITTLE MEN." . . . . . 166 NEW HAMPSHIRE . 219
    THEY TAUNT THE LOFTY LAND WITH LITTLE MEN. . . . . 167 NEW HAMPSHIRE . 264
    THE ONE ABOUT HIS JUMPING SO'S TO LAND . . . . . 192 PAUL'S WIFE . . . 50
    AND THEN LAND SAFELY RIGHT SIDE UP AGAIN, ... 192 PAUL'S WIFE . . . 52
    THAT WATER NEVER DID TO LAND BEFORE. . . . . . 250 ONCE BY THE PACIFIC . 4
    THEY ARE THE SEA MADE LAND . . . . 260 SAND DUNES . . . 5
    THROUGH EVERYTHING PRESENTED, LAND AND TIDE . . . . 267 RIDERS 3
    THEY TURN THEIR BACK ON THE LAND. . . . . . . 301 NEITHER OUT FAR NOR IN 3
    THE LAND MAY VARY MORE; . . . . 301 NEITHER OUT FAR NOR IN 9
    TILL HE CAME TO THE LAND OF PAMIR. . . . . . . 313 BEARER OF EVIL TIDINGS 12
    THERE IN THE LAND OF THE YAK. . . . . 314 BEARER OF EVIL TIDINGS 28
    LET THOSE POSSESS THE LAND, AND ONLY THOSE, ... 322 BUILD SOIL . . . 187
    SEDUCED BACK TO THE LAND BY ANY CLAIM . . . . . 322 BUILD SOIL . . . 207
    THE LAND MAY SEEM TO HAVE ON MAN TO USE IT. . . . . 322 BUILD SOIL . . . 208
    LET NONE ASSUME TO TILL THE LAND BUT FARMERS. . . . 322 BUILD SOIL . . . 209
    AND BRING US TO THE NEAREST LAND; . . . . . . 346 DISCOVERY OF MADEIRAS . 107
    THE LAND WAS OURS BEFORE WE WERE THE LAND'S. . . . . 348 THE GIFT OUTRIGHT . 1
    SHE WAS OUR LAND MORE THAN A HUNDRED YEARS . . . . 348 THE GIFT OUTRIGHT . 2
    WE WERE WITHHOLDING FROM OUR LAND OF LIVING, ... 348 THE GIFT OUTRIGHT . 10
    TO THE LAND VAGUELY REALIZING WESTWARD, ... 348 THE GIFT OUTRIGHT . 14
    AND YES, MY LAND WAS HARDLY FENCED. . . . . . 364 TRESPASS 2
    NEVERTHELESS THE LAND WAS MINE: . . . . . . 364 TRESPASS 3
    OF EITHER MURDER OR WAR IN ANY LAND. . . . . . 371 THE LITERATE FARMER AND 111
    THE LAND WAS OURS BEFORE WE WERE THE LAND'S. . . . . 424 THE GIFT OUTRIGHT . 1
    SHE WAS OUR LAND MORE THAN A HUNDRED YEARS . . . . 424 THE GIFT OUTRIGHT . 2
    WE WERE WITHHOLDING FROM OUR LAND OF LIVING, ... 424 THE GIFT OUTRIGHT . 10
    TO THE LAND VAGUELY REALIZING WESTWARD, ... 425 THE GIFT OUTRIGHT . 14
    TO POUR FRESH RIVERS ON YOU FROM THE LAND, ... 446 DOES NO ONE AT ALL EVER 23
LANDED
    AND LANDED POURING LIKE A WATERFALL, ... 338 THE MOST OF IT . . . 18
LANDING
    THE DOOR; THEY HALTED HELPLESS ON THE LANDING. . . . 204 THE WITCH OF COOS . 62
    THE FLAKES COULD FIND NO LANDING PLACE TO FORM. . . . 239 OUR SINGING STRENGTH . 2
LANDOR'S
    IN LANDOR'S QUATRAIN WOULD BE PRETTY SCENERY. . . . . 393 LUCRETIUS VERSUS POETS 9
LAND'S
    THE LAND WAS OURS BEFORE WE WERE THE LAND'S. . . . . 348 THE GIFT OUTRIGHT . 1
    THE LAND WAS OURS BEFORE WE WERE THE LAND'S. . . . . 424 THE GIFT OUTRIGHT . 1
LANDS (SEE SPROUT-LANDS)
    TO THE ANCIENT LANDS WHERE IT LEFT THE SHELLS . . . . 27 A LINE-STORM SONG . 27
    LANDS ON SOMEONE HARD . . . . 441 KITTY HAWK . . . 406

LANDSCAPE
  AT HAVING THE LANDSCAPE MARRED WITH THE ARTLESS PAINT . . . 286 A ROADSIDE STAND . . . 9
  ACROSS THE LANDSCAPE WITH A WATERING POT . . . . . . 354 THE LESSON FOR TODAY . 129
  I COTTON TO THEIR LANDSCAPE. THAT'S WHO I AM. . . . . . 414 A CABIN IN THE CLEARING 18
  ON A LANDSCAPE SO ACCURSED . . . . 466 SOME SCIENCE FICTION . 30
LANE
  SHE WALKS THE SODDEN PASTURE LANE. . . . .   6 MY NOVEMBER GUEST . .   5
  MY MOTHER WAS A LANE, YET MIGHT HAVE MARRIED . . . . .   75 THE GENERATIONS OF MEN 50
  I HAVE LOOKED DOWN THE SADDEST CITY LANE. . . . . . . 255 ACQUAINTED WITH NIGHT . 4
  GO PART WAY DOWN THE LANE. . . . . 359 NOVEMBER   3
LANGSHANG
  FOR FIFTY DOLLARS FOR ONE LANGSHANG COCK-- . . . . . .   86 THE HOUSEKEEPER . . . 146
LANGUAGE
  USE LANGUAGE WE CAN COMPREHEND. . . . . 403 SOMETHING LIKE A STAR . 14
  A LANGUAGE OF HIS OWN TO WRITE HIS BOOK IN, ... 502 A MASQUE OF MERCY . . 241
  ALL LANGUAGE IN A ONE-MAN TONGUE-CONFUSION. . . . . . 502 A MASQUE OF MERCY . . 243
LANGUID
  SHORT OF THE PERCH THEIR LANGUID FLIGHT WAS TOWARD; . . 130 THE BONFIRE 37
LANGUIDLY
  TO BRING FAITH BACK. I'M ONLY LANGUIDLY . . . . . . 515 A MASQUE OF MERCY . . 566
LANGUOR
  THE LANGUOR OF IT AND THE DREAMING FOND; . . . . . .   29 MY BUTTERFLY 34
LANK
  FULL OF LANK, SHIVERY, HALF-DROWNED BIRDS . . . . . .   85 THE HOUSEKEEPER . . . 120
LANTERN
  GIVE ME THE LANTERN." / "YOU DON'T WANT THE LANTERN." .   90 THE FEAR 33
  THE SWINGING LANTERN LENGTHENED TO THE GROUND, ...   92 THE FEAR 92
  HE FETCHED A DINGY LANTERN FROM BEHIND . . . . 115 IN THE HOME STRETCH . 136
  YOU WON'T DENY THE LANTERN ISN'T NEW. . . . . 116 IN THE HOME STRETCH . 178
  WHEN THERE WAS NO MORE LANTERN IN THE KITCHEN, ... 117 IN THE HOME STRETCH . 201
  HIS LANTERN WHEN HE DID HIS CHORES . . . . 137 BROWN'S DESCENT . .   3
  HE NEVER LET THE LANTERN DROP. . . . . 138 BROWN'S DESCENT . . 29
  HE FELL AND MADE THE LANTERN RATTLE . . . . 138 BROWN'S DESCENT . . 38
  THEN SHOOK HIS LANTERN, SAYING, "ILE'S . . . . 140 BROWN'S DESCENT . . 74
  OF WASTE LEAVES AT MY SMOKY LANTERN CHIMNEY . . . . . 176 THE STAR-SPLITTER . . 8
  AND A MAN WITH A SMOKY LANTERN CHIMNEY? . . . . . . 179 THE STAR-SPLITTER . . 98
  WITH A LANTERN THAT WOULDN'T BURN . . . . 443 THE DRAFT HORSE . . . 1
  PROJECTED FROM THE LANTERN OF HIS EYES, ... 502 A MASQUE OF MERCY . . 237
LANTERN-LIGHT
  DAYLIGHT AND LANTERN-LIGHT WERE ONE TO HIM: . . . . .   71 THE CODE 41
  A LANTERN-LIGHT FROM DEEPER IN THE BARN . . . . . .   89 THE FEAR 1
  I'LL JUST COME FORWARD IN THE LANTERN-LIGHT . . . . .   91 THE FEAR 74
  OUR SITTING HERE BY LANTERN-LIGHT TOGETHER . . . . . 116 IN THE HOME STRETCH . 176
  DESCRIBING RINGS OF LANTERN-LIGHT. . . . . 137 BROWN'S DESCENT . .   8
  BUSY OUTDOORS BY LANTERN-LIGHT WITH SOMETHING . . . . 176 THE STAR-SPLITTER . . 4
LAP
  ITS LIGHT POURED SOFTLY IN HER LAP. SHE SAW IT . . . .   38 DEATH OF THE HIRED MAN 105
  WITH FLOWERS IN HER LAP UNTIL THEY FADE. . . . . . .   79 THE GENERATIONS OF MEN 169
  AMONG THE BUTTONS POURED OUT IN HER LAP. . . . . . . 207 THE WITCH OF COOS . . 153
  AND NOW HER LAP IS FULL OF TREES. . . . . 265 THE BIRTHPLACE . . . 14
LAPISH
  I'LL TELL YOU WHO'D REMEMBER--HEMAN LAPISH. . . . . . 208 PAUPER WITCH OF GRAFTON 26
LAPSE
  IT MAY HAVE BEEN THEIR ONE LAPSE INTO FANCY . . . . . 183 MAPLE 120
  OR THAT SHOWED WITH THE LAPSE OF TIME TOO VAIN . . . . 262 HANNIBAL 3
LAPSING
  AND EVEN SUBSTANCE LAPSING UNSUBSTANTIAL; . . . . . . 259 WEST-RUNNING BROOK . . 55
LARGE
  ANNE LOOKED AT THE LARGE LAWYER AT HER SIDE, ...   97 THE SELF-SEEKER . . . 117
  IT BROODED ANT EGGS, AND HAD ONE LARGE WING, ... 172 A STAR IN A STONEBOAT . 14
  ONE NOT SO LARGE FOR FLYING IN A RING, ... 172 A STAR IN A STONEBOAT . 15
  AS LARGE AROUND AS THE CHOPPING BLOCK; . . . . 275 TWO TRAMPS IN MUD TIME 10
  TOO LARGE A SITUATION. YOU AND I . . . . 351 THE LESSON FOR TODAY . 35
  THOUGHT OF IN THE LARGE . . . . 436 KITTY HAWK 253
LARGER (SEE SIZE-LARGER)
  NOT SO MUCH LARGER THAN A BEDROOM, IS IT? . . . . .   51 HOME BURIAL 25
  A LARGER ONE HE ASKED FIVE HUNDRED FOR. . . . . . . 455 HOW HARD TO KEEP FROM 68
  YES, BY AND BY. BUT FIRST A LARGER MATTER. . . . . . 475 A MASQUE OF REASON . . 46
LARGEST
  THE LARGEST FIREDROP EVER FORMED . . . . 381 AN UNSTAMPED LETTER IN 25
LARIATS
  HER UNPRUNED GRAPES ARE FLUNG LIKE LARIATS . . . . . 164 NEW HAMPSHIRE . . . 163
LARN
  AND CRIED, "I'LL LARN YOU TO BELLOW." . . . . 463 LINES IN DEJECTION . . 16
LARRIKIN
  THIS LARRIKIN? ALL RIGHT. YOU COME ALONG. . . . . . 455 HOW HARD TO KEEP FROM 47
LAS'
  WHAT'S LAS' AWHILE--GOOD HICK'RY WHAT'S GROW CROOKED, . 186 THE AX-HELVE 30
LASHED
  FROM A TWIG'S HAVING LASHED ACROSS IT OPEN. . . . . . 122 BIRCHES 47
  AND HE LASHED HIS OPEN PALM . . . . 339 THE SUBVERTED FLOWER . 3
LASHING
  SALMON AND STURGEON, LASHING WITH THEIR TAILS. . . . . 142 THE VANISHING RED . . 23
  SELF-TAUGHT. BUT OUR BRUTE SNARLING AND LASHING TAUGHT IT. 320 BUILD SOIL 120
LASS
  THOUGH TWO, CLOSE-KEEPING, ARE LASS AND LAD-- . . . .   6 GHOST HOUSE 27
LAST
  OF THE LAST REMAINING ASTER FLOWER . . . .   9 A LATE WALK 15
  ON THE LAST SWALLOW'S SWEEP; AND ON THE RASP . . . .   14 WAITING 18
  BEFORE THE LAST WENT, HEAVY WITH DEW, ...   15 IN A VALE 16
  BUT THE LAST CHOICE IS STILL THE SAME; . . . .   21 THE TRIAL BY EXISTENCE 58
  THE LAST LONE ASTER IS GONE; . . . .   30 RELUCTANCE 15
  "I TOLD HIM SO LAST HAYING, DIDN'T I? . . . .   35 DEATH OF THE HIRED MAN 13
  WE WERE BUT SIXTY VOTERS LAST ELECTION. . . . . . .   41 THE MOUNTAIN . . . 25
  THEY LOGGED IT THERE LAST WINTER SOME WAY UP. . . . .   41 THE MOUNTAIN . . . 42
  AT THE LAST ONE OF WHICH HE KNOCKED AND ENTERED. . . .   45 A HUNDRED COLLARS . . 35
  BUT AT LAST HE MURMURED, "OH," AND AGAIN, "OH." . . .   51 HOME BURIAL 17
  IT WERE THE FORCE THAT WOULD AT LAST PREVAIL . . . .   57 THE BLACK COTTAGE . . 83

PAGE TITLE   LINE

LAST (CONTINUED)
		PAGE	TITLE	LINE
THAT WAS THE LAST I SAW OR HEARD OF HIM.		72	THE CODE	79
IT'S TOO RUN DOWN. THIS IS THE LAST OF IT.		83	THE HOUSEKEEPER	50
HE WENT BEHIND IT TO MAKE HIS LAST STAND.		101	THE WOOD-PILE	22
OR EVEN LAST YEAR'S OR THE YEAR'S BEFORE.		101	THE WOOD-PILE	28
AND LEFT AT LAST THE COUNTRY TO THE COUNTRY;		105	CHRISTMAS TREES	2
AND SO AT LAST TO LEARN TO USE THEIR WINGS.		110	THE EXPOSED NEST	36
TO EVERYTHING. HER LIGHT WON'T LAST US LONG.		113	IN THE HOME STRETCH	71
STYLE UPON STYLE IN DRESS AND THOUGHT AT LAST		117	IN THE HOME STRETCH	184
BY STARLIGHT IN THE GRASS FOR A LAST PEACH		117	IN THE HOME STRETCH	190
THAT THE NORTH WIND LAST NIGHT		135	LAST WORD OF A BLUEBIRD	9
THE LAST WORD OF A BLUEBIRD		135	LAST WORD OF A BLUEBIRD	T
HE IS SAID TO HAVE BEEN THE LAST RED MAN		142	THE VANISHING RED	1
SAID IT AT LAST HIMSELF, "GOOD-NIGHT," AND THEN,		143	SNOW	29
FROM THE LAST THING HE SAID HIMSELF, STONE DEAF		145	SNOW	65
WHERE WOULD WE BE AT LAST IF THAT WERE SO?		147	SNOW	131
SINCE LAST WE READ THE GAUGE." / "IT LOOKS AS IF		148	SNOW	159
TO LAST HER TILL HE GOT OUTSIDE THE DOOR,		151	SNOW	243
WHERE I CAME LAST WITH SOME HOPE, BUT NOT MUCH,		174	THE CENSUS-TAKER	12
AND I GIVE UP; WHICH LAST LOOK CAME TO NOTHING.		184	MAPLE	132
FOR--I FORGET--THE LAST AMBITIOUS SAWYER		193	PAUL'S WIFE	59
GRAPES, I KNEW GRAPES FROM HAVING SEEN THEM LAST YEAR.		197	WILD GRAPES	24
A GOOD DEAL RIGHT; DON'T DO THE LAST THING WRONG.		199	PLACE FOR A THIRD	10
HOW WOULD SHE LIKE TO SLEEP HER LAST WITH HIM?		200	PLACE FOR A THIRD	36
AND THAT'D BE ENOUGH TO LAST FOR DAYS.		208	PAUPER WITCH OF GRAFTON	41
LAST NIGHT WAS ONE OF HER NIGHTS OUT. SHE'S KITING.		209	PAUPER WITCH OF GRAFTON	81
ONLY BEWITCHED SO I WOULD LAST HIM LONGER.		210	PAUPER WITCH OF GRAFTON	95
AT LAST THE GATHERED SNOW LETS DOWN AS WHITE		226	THE ONSET	2
THAT FLASHES TAIL THROUGH LAST YEAR'S WITHERED BRAKE		226	THE ONSET	20
IN ONE LAST LOOK THE WAY THEY MUST NOT GO,		229	TWO LOOK AT TWO	10
A YOUNG BEECH CLINGING TO ITS LAST YEAR'S LEAVES.		234	A BOUNDLESS MOMENT	12
BUT AT LAST CAME A KNOCK,		240	THE LOCKLESS DOOR	2
TO RIDGELY TORRENCE ON LAST LOOKING INTO HIS "HESPERIDES"		248	A PASSING GLIMPSE	D
BEFORE GOD'S LAST PUT OUT THE LIGHT WAS SPOKEN.		250	ONCE BY THE PACIFIC	14
AND LAST YEAR'S BERRIES SHINING SCARLET RED.		254	A WINTER EDEN	8
BE HER LAST JOY HER HEART'S GOING OUT TO THIS ONE		257	THE LOVELY BE CHOOSERS	50
BELOW THE POINT, AND WERE AT LAST DRIVEN WRINKLED		258	WEST-RUNNING BROOK	25
THE LAST MOWING		264	THE LAST MOWING	T
THAT CALM SEEMS CERTAINLY SAFE TO LAST TONIGHT.		268	ON LOOKING UP BY CHANCE	16
(FROM SLEEPING GOD KNOWS WHERE LAST NIGHT,		276	TWO TRAMPS IN MUD TIME	50
AT LAST IT WAS A FLY. HE SHOT AND MISSED;		278	THE WHITE-TAILED HORNET	42
THE LAST TO LET NIGHT DRIVE HER OFF.		280	BLUE RIBBON AT AMESBURY	16
AND SO TO ROOST, THE LAST TO MOUNT.		281	BLUE RIBBON AT AMESBURY	44
IF HE FULFILLED AT LAST HIS SUMMER WISH,		284	THE GOLD HESPERIDEE	35
WELL, THE MOON AFTER THAT, CAME ONE AT LAST.		289	OLD BARN AT THE BOTTOM	6
LIKE THE LAST PETAL OFF A FLOWER.		291	ON HEART'S BEGINNING TO	12
ONE LOOKS OUT LAST FROM THE DARKENED ROOM		291	ON HEART'S BEGINNING TO	26
I WET ONE LAST YEAR AT MONTAUK		294	A RECORD STRIDE	13
BUT A FEW WEEDS AND STUBBLE SHOWING LAST.		296	DESERT PLACES	4
YOUR LAST GOOD AVALANCHE		298	ON TAKING FROM THE TOP	3
AND LATE IN HIS LAST HOUR ALIVE,		311	THE VINDICTIVES	42
WAS COILED IN ITS LAST RESTING GRAVE		312	THE VINDICTIVES	61
THE LAST WET FIELDS AND DRIPPING HEDGES HOME.		315	IRIS BY NIGHT	3
THE LAST BEING WHAT THEY SEEM TO HAVE IN RUSSIA.		318	BUILD SOIL	74
MAY NOT BE THE IMPORTANT THING AT LAST.		321	BUILD SOIL	158
THE LAST STEP TAKEN FOUND YOUR HEFT		325	TO A THINKER	1
THE LAST OF THE LIGHT OF THE SUN		334	COME IN	9
THEN AT LAST AND FOLLOWING HIM I FOUND--		342	QUEST OF PURPLE-FRINGED	13
HE CAME AT LAST TO HIS NATIVE SHIRE.		347	DISCOVERY OF MADEIRAS	132
DID YOU STAY UP LAST NIGHT (THE MAGI DID)		360	A LOOSE MOUNTAIN	1
OF THE LAST FIFTY YEARS ARE ALL A LIBEL,		369	THE LITERATE FARMER AND	45
AND THE FRAY WOULDN'T LAST A SINGLE ROUND.		371	THE LITERATE FARMER AND	118
BUT NOW AT LAST SO OBVIOUS A BOLE		375	A YOUNG BIRCH	16
LAST NIGHT YOUR WATCHDOG BARKED ALL NIGHT,		380	AN UNSTAMPED LETTER IN	1
I DON'T BELIEVE I BELIEVE YOU'RE THE LAST IN SPACE,		389	SKEPTIC	5
I DON'T BELIEVE I BELIEVE ANYWHERE NEAR THE LAST,		389	SKEPTIC	6
THE WAVE SUCKS BACK AND WITH THE LAST OF WATER		391	ON BEING IDOLIZED	1
THE DISAPPEARING LAST OF HIM		392	A CLIFF DWELLING	11
HAS CUT THIS ROAD TO LAST,		415	CLOSED FOR GOOD	4
I OPENED THE DOOR SO MY LAST LOOK		419	ONE MORE BREVITY	1
COME FRESH FROM AN ELECTION LIKE THE LAST,		423	FOR JOHN F. KENNEDY	54
BUT THIS WAS NIGHT THE LAST.		444	ENDS	4
CAUGHT COLOR FROM THE LAST OF EVENING RED		445	QUESTIONING FACES	4
WOULD ONLY DISAPPOINT US AT THE LAST		446	DOES NO ONE AT ALL EVER	4
TO BE A TEST. IT DIDN'T LAST HIM OUT.		459	HOW HARD TO KEEP FROM	178
AT LAST IN SELF-COLLAPSE		464	MILKY WAY IS A COWPATH	13
HOPE YOU'RE SATISFIED TO LAST.		469	FOUR-ROOM SHACK...	7
TO LAST A FELLOW TO ETERNITY.		475	A MASQUE OF REASON	45
WHERE HAS SHE BEEN THE LAST HALF HOUR OR SO?		477	A MASQUE OF REASON	109
YOU'D BE THE LAST TO WANT ME TO BELIEVE		482	A MASQUE OF REASON	258
CAN YOU INTERPRET DREAMS? I DREAMED LAST NIGHT		501	A MASQUE OF MERCY	200
OR THE NEW YORKER. / WHEN WAS THE LAST TIME		504	A MASQUE OF MERCY	276
BUT MERCY FIRST AND LAST SHALL BRIGHTEST SHINE--		508	A MASQUE OF MERCY	381
NOT ONLY LAST, BUT FIRST, YOU WILL OBSERVE;		508	A MASQUE OF MERCY	382
IF IT IS ME IN MY LAST INCARNATION .		510	A MASQUE OF MERCY	447

LASTED
IT HAS LASTED ME MANY AND MANY A YEAR.		25	THE DEMIURGE'S LAUGH	6
THAT GOOD AND BAD SO LONG HAD LASTED.		467	QUANDARY	6

LASTING
THE LASTING MEMORY AT ALL CLEAR,		21	THE TRIAL BY EXISTENCE	67
AND STILL THEY FAILED OF ANY LASTING HOLD.		239	OUR SINGING STRENGTH	4
NO LASTING EFFECT OF IT LINGERS.		266	SITTING BY A BUSH	4
I GET THE LASTING SENSE		333	HAPPINESS MAKES UP	10

LASTLY
OF GOD'S DECISION LASTLY ON YOUR DEEDS.		520	A MASQUE OF MERCY	698

LATCH
HER FINGERS MOVED THE LATCH FOR ALL REPLY.		52	HOME BURIAL	44
SHE MOVED THE LATCH A LITTLE. "DON'T--DON'T GO.		53	HOME BURIAL	56

LATCH (CONTINUED)
    FOREVER TRYING THE WINDOW LATCH . . . . 128 THE OFT-REPEATED DREAM   3
    FOREVER OFF THE LATCH, AS IF RUDE MEN . . . . 175 THE CENSUS-TAKER   . .   28
    WERE FIGHTING FOR THE LATCH, ... 298 ON TAKING FROM THE TOP   14
LATE
    A LATE WALK . . . .   8 A LATE WALK . . . .   T
    FROM WHICH THE LABORERS' VOICES LATE HAD DIED, . . . 14 WAITING   4
    "I WANT HIM TO: HE'LL HAVE TO SOON OR LATE." . . . . 35 DEATH OF THE HIRED MAN   32
    TO THINK OF THE RIGHT THING TO SAY TOO LATE. . . . . 37 DEATH OF THE HIRED MAN   77
    OF LATE YEARS, THOUGH HE KEEPS THE OLD HOMESTEAD . . 44 A HUNDRED COLLARS   . .   3
    HIS TRAIN BEING LATE, HE MISSED ANOTHER TRAIN . . . 44 A HUNDRED COLLARS   . .   15
    AND END IT." / "TOO LATE NOW: SHE WOULDN'T HAVE HIM. . 84 THE HOUSEKEEPER . . .   85
    "IT'S NOT SO VERY LATE--IT'S ONLY DARK. . . . . . . 90 THE FEAR   29
    "END IS A GLOOMY WORD." / "IS IT TOO LATE . . . . . 117 IN THE HOME STRETCH . 187
    SOMETHING INSPIRES THE ONLY COW OF LATE . . . . . . 124 THE COW IN APPLE TIME .   1
    "WHY, LETT, STILL UP? LETT, I'M AT COLE'S. I'M LATE. . 143 SNOW   16
    AND ANYWAY IT CAME TOO LATE FOR MAPLE. . . . . 184 MAPLE 159
    "WHOEVER IT IS THAT LEAVES HIM OUT SO LATE, ... 223 THE RUNAWAY   19
    SHE CAME TO FROM TOO HIGH TOO LATE TO LEARN. . . . . 257 THE LOVELY BE CHOOSERS   45
    TOO LATE THOUGH, NOW, HE HAD HIMSELF TO THANK. . . . 270 THE EGG AND THE MACHINE   9
    THAT ON THE ONE WHO CAME TOO LATE . . . . 273 A LONE STRIKER . . .   6
    THIS I SAW WHEN WAKING LATE, ... 292 ON HEART'S BEGINNING TO   42
    LATE IN LIFE I HAVE COME ON FERN. . . . . 297 LEAVES COMPARED WITH . 11
    OR IF PREDESTINED TO DIE LATE, ... 307 PROVIDE, PROVIDE . . .   8
    IT IS LATE AT NIGHT AND STILL I AM LOSING, ... 310 IN DIVES' DIVE . . .   1
    AND LATE IN HIS LAST HOUR ALIVE, ... 311 THE VINDICTIVES . . .   42
    THE MORAL IS, MAKE A LATE START TO MARKET. . . . . . 322 BUILD SOIL 181
    AND TO THOSE CONCERNED HE MAY SEEM A LITTLE LATE. . . 342 WILLFUL HOMING . . .   12
    OF BEING BORN AT ONCE TOO EARLY AND LATE, ... 351 THE LESSON FOR TODAY . 12
    WHICH IS BECOMING MY CONCERN OF LATE. . . . . 354 THE LESSON FOR TODAY . 136
    HE WILL BE STARTING PRETTY LATE. . . . . 419 AMERICA IS HARD TO SEE   79
    BEFORE I AM TOO LATE TO BE GOT RIGHT . . . . 479 A MASQUE OF REASON . 166
    A BOOKSTORE LATE AT NIGHT. THE KEEPER'S WIFE . . . . 493 A MASQUE OF MERCY . .   1
    LATE, LATE, TOO LATE, YOU CANNOT ENTER NOW. . . . . 493 A MASQUE OF MERCY . .   9
    WHO SAID, "TOO LATE, YOU CANNOT ENTER NOW"? . . . . 519 A MASQUE OF MERCY . . 669
LATE-ARISING
    SO LATE-ARISING--TO THE BROKEN MOON, ... 108 OLD MAN'S WINTER NIGHT   19
LATELY
    LATELY WHEN COMING UP TO LANCASTER, ... 44 A HUNDRED COLLARS   . .   14
    I'VE FELT MEAN LATELY; MEAN'S NO NAME FOR IT. . . . . 46 A HUNDRED COLLARS   . .   54
    LATELY BROUGHT HOME FROM ANDOVER OR CANAAN . . . . . 162 NEW HAMPSHIRE . . . 117
    WAS LATELY AT A CUT-GLASS DINNER IN BOSTON. . . . . . 163 NEW HAMPSHIRE . . . 127
    LATELY IN CONVERSE WITH A NEW YORK ALEC . . . . . . 170 NEW HAMPSHIRE . . . 358
    (WHERE DID I SEE ONE OF THOSE PIECES LATELY? . . . . 205 THE WITCH OF COOS . .   80
    THAT THE LOOSE MOUNTAIN LATELY SEEN TO GLINT . . . . 361 A LOOSE MOUNTAIN . .   14
    ONE HAS BEEN LATELY ALL THE TALK . . . . 452 A-WISHING WELL . . .   62
LATER
    TO LOOK AND TELL ME LATER HOW IT WAS." . . . . 43 THE MOUNTAIN   74
    I'LL ASK YOU LATER--DON'T LET ME FORGET IT." . . . . 46 A HUNDRED COLLARS   . .   48
    LATER THEY GET OUT FURTHER IN THE FIELDS. . . . . . . 49 A HUNDRED COLLARS   . . 129
    AND LATER STILL THEY ALL GET DRIVEN IN: . . . . 49 A HUNDRED COLLARS   . . 133
    SOONER OR LATER CAME AND LEANED, HALF KNELT, ... 56 THE BLACK COTTAGE . .   27
    BY WALKING SLOWLY ON SOME EVENING LATER . . . . . . 245 THE FREEDOM OF THE MOON   8
    ATONES FOR LATER DISREGARD . . . . 307 PROVIDE, PROVIDE . . .   17
    AS SOONER OR LATER WE HAVE TO CEASE SOMEWHERE. . . . 379 TOO ANXIOUS FOR RIVERS   10
    LATER WHEN WE MET, ... 429 KITTY HAWK   51
LATEST
    THEIR LATEST THAT I REMEMBER, ... 365 A NATURE NOTE   15
    THE LATEST CREED THAT HAS TO BE BELIEVED . . . . . . 427 CONCEPT SELF-CONCEIVED   1
    AN ANALYST'S THE LATEST THING IN DOCTORS. . . . . . 499 A MASQUE OF MERCY . . 153
LATIN
    HAROLD'S ASSOCIATED IN HIS MIND WITH LATIN. . . . . . 37 DEATH OF THE HIRED MAN   78
    HE STUDIED LATIN, LIKE THE VIOLIN, ... 37 DEATH OF THE HIRED MAN   80
    AND GETTING UP MY MEDIEVAL LATIN, ... 350 THE LESSON FOR TODAY .   8
    THEY SLOWLY LED OLD LATIN VERSE TO RHYME . . . . . . 351 THE LESSON FOR TODAY .   16
    COME LEARN THE LATIN EHEU FOR ALAS. . . . . 353 THE LESSON FOR TODAY .   85
    THAT IN THE LATIN OF OUR FOUNDING SAGES . . . . . . 422 FOR JOHN F. KENNEDY .   20
LATTER
    HEARING THE LATTER WISDOM OF THE WORLD. . . . . 57 THE BLACK COTTAGE . .   74
    THESE LATTER ABOUT TO FALL. I THOUGHT THAT ONLY . . . 102 THE WOOD-PILE . . .   34
    ALL ROUND AND ROUND. THE LATTER HE NODDED "YES" TO, . 107 CHRISTMAS TREES . . .   36
    THE WOOD." / "WHAT KIND OF YEARS?" / "WHY, LATTER YEARS-- 112 IN THE HOME STRETCH .   49
    (DON'T FORGET THE LATTER . . . . 435 KITTY HAWK 234
LAUGH
    THE DEMIURGE'S LAUGH . . . . 24 THE DEMIURGE'S LAUGH .   T
    THE DEMON AROSE FROM HIS WALLOW TO LAUGH, ... 25 THE DEMIURGE'S LAUGH .   10
    I SHALL NOT FORGET HOW HIS LAUGH RANG OUT. . . . . . 25 THE DEMIURGE'S LAUGH .   13
    HE HAS A PLAN. YOU MUSTN'T LAUGH AT HIM. . . . . . . 40 DEATH OF THE HIRED MAN   158
    "I SHALL LAUGH THE WORST LAUGH I EVER LAUGHED. . . . 54 HOME BURIAL   89
    THE LAWYER GAVE A LAUGH AMONG HIS PAPERS . . . . . . 98 THE SELF-SEEKER . . . 145
    WHO SAID WITH SERIOUSNESS THAT MADE THEM LAUGH, . . . 114 IN THE HOME STRETCH . 104
    AND HAVE OUR FIRE AND LAUGH AND BE AFRAID." . . . . 133 THE BONFIRE 114
    THE BOY'S FIRST OUTCRY WAS A RUEFUL LAUGH, ... 136 "OUT,OUT--"   19
    TO EASE AWAY--THEY HAVE IT. WITH A LAUGH, ... 141 THE LINE-GANG . . .   11
    IF YOU LIKE TO CALL SUCH A SOUND A LAUGH. . . . . . 142 THE VANISHING RED . .   3
    AND CAME UPSTAIRS ALONE--AND GAVE THAT LAUGH, ... 142 THE VANISHING RED . .   26
    LAUGHED THE LOUD LAUGH THE BIG LAUGH AT THE LITTLE. . 165 NEW HAMPSHIRE . . . 200
    FRANCONIA LAUGHS, I FEAR--DID LAUGH THAT NIGHT-- . . . 165 NEW HAMPSHIRE . . . 205
    AT EASTON. WHAT HAS EASTON LEFT TO LAUGH AT, ... 165 NEW HAMPSHIRE . . . 206
    MY BROTHER TRIED TO MAKE ME LAUGH TO HELP ME. . . . 197 WILD GRAPES   55
    (DON'T ANYBODY LAUGH); . . . . 309 NOT ALL THERE   6
    WHEN HATE GAVE A TERRIBLE LAUGH, ... 311 THE VINDICTIVES . . .   22
    AN INGRATIATING LAUGH . . . . 340 THE SUBVERTED FLOWER .   45
    HE LAUGHED BUT HE DID NOT MAKE YOU LAUGH. . . . . . 346 DISCOVERY OF MADEIRAS .   91
    LEAN BACK AND HAVE MY CONFIDENTIAL LAUGH, ... 354 THE LESSON FOR TODAY . 125
    SOMETHING ABOUT--(THE THREE MEN LAUGH.) . . . . . . 487 A MASQUE OF REASON . 400
LAUGHED
    "I SHALL LAUGH THE WORST LAUGH I EVER LAUGHED. . . . . 54 HOME BURIAL   89

LAUGHED (CONTINUED)
    AS ONE WHO CLASPS HER HEART. THEY LAUGHED TOGETHER. . . . 74 THE GENERATIONS OF MEN   44
    OF SOMETHING ELSE," SHE LAUGHED. "OH, PUT IT WHERE . . . . 111 IN THE HOME STRETCH   . 15
    IN ACTON. AND THE MILLER IS SAID TO HAVE LAUGHED-- . . . . 142 THE VANISHING RED . .   2
    LAUGHED THE LOUD LAUGH THE BIG LAUGH AT THE LITTLE. . . . . 165 NEW HAMPSHIRE 200
    I LAUGHED INSIDE, AND ONLY CRANKED THE FASTER . . . . . . 190 THE GRINDSTONE   . .   60
    AND LAUGHED. THEN SHE CLIMBED SLOWLY TO HER FEET, ... 194 PAUL'S WIFE 119
    AND SOMETIMES LAUGHED AT WHAT IT WAS BETWEEN THEM. . . . . 200 PLACE FOR A THIRD . . 35
    THEY LAUGHED AS IF THEY HAD TURNED A TRICK. . . . . 344 DISCOVERY OF MADEIRAS . 30
    HE LAUGHED BUT HE DID NOT MAKE YOU LAUGH. . . . . 346 DISCOVERY OF MADEIRAS . 91
    THEN HE MUST HAVE LAUGHED: . . . . 427 VERSION   5
    I WAS GLAD HE LAUGHED. . . . . 430 KITTY HAWK   66
    THE EUNUCH LAUGHED: "WELL, THAT'S A LOT TO KNOW. . . . . . 455 HOW HARD TO KEEP FROM   45
LAUGHER'S
    BUT HE GAVE NO ONE ELSE A LAUGHER'S LICENSE. . . . . . . 142 THE VANISHING RED . .   4
LAUGHING
    A GOD CAN FIND IN LAUGHING AT HOW BADLY . . . . 483 A MASQUE OF REASON . . 274
    YOU WOULDN'T WANT THE NIGHT CLUBS LAUGHING AT YOU. . . . . 504 A MASQUE OF MERCY . . 275
LAUGHINGLY
    REQUIRED SOMEONE WHO LAUGHINGLY COULD PLAY . . . . . . 509 A MASQUE OF MERCY . . 422
LAUGHS
    NEW YORK (FIVE MILLION) LAUGHS AT MANCHESTER, ... 165 NEW HAMPSHIRE . . . 201
    MANCHESTER (SIXTY OR SEVENTY THOUSAND) LAUGHS . . . . . 165 NEW HAMPSHIRE . . . 202
    LAUGHS AT FRANCONIA (SEVEN HUNDRED), AND . . . . . . 165 NEW HAMPSHIRE . . . 204
    FRANCONIA LAUGHS, I FEAR--DID LAUGH THAT NIGHT-- . . . . 165 NEW HAMPSHIRE . . . 205
LAUGHTER
    WITH LAUGHTER WHEN SHE FOUND US SOON. . . . . 18 GOING FOR WATER . . . 16
    AND SEEK WITH LAUGHTER WHAT TO BRAVE-- . . . . 20 THE TRIAL BY EXISTENCE   14
    MEAN LAUGHTER WENT ABOUT THE TOWN THAT DAY . . . . . . 177 THE STAR-SPLITTER . . 40
    WHEN CALL OR LAUGHTER CARRIED IT ALOFT. . . . . 339 NEVER WOULD BIRDS' SONG   8
LAUNCHING
    TO LEARN ABOUT NOT LAUNCHING OUT TOO SOON . . . . . . 122 BIRCHES 33
LAVA
    THEN FLED FOR FEAR OF GETTING STUCK IN LAVA . . . . . 407 FROM PLANE TO PLANE . 94
LAVE
    BUT WELCOMED FOR THE CHANCE TO LAVE MY SHOES . . . . 215 A FOUNTAIN, A BOTTLE . 66
LAW
    IN COMMON LAW, I WONDER." / "BUT I ASK, ... 111 IN THE HOME STRETCH   . 24
    HE BOWED WITH GRACE TO NATURAL LAW, ... 139 BROWN'S DESCENT . . 60
    SO NOW THEY'VE DRAGGED IT THROUGH THE LAW COURTS ONCE, . 208 PAUPER WITCH OF GRAFTON 28
    THERE WAS A LAW OF GOD OR MAN . . . . 273 A LONE STRIKER   . . .   5
    AND MADE FUN OF BY BUSINESS, LAW, AND ART; . . . . . 322 BUILD SOIL   190
    TO LEAVE THE ENGLISH LAW BEHIND . . . . 344 DISCOVERY OF MADEIRAS . 16
    BUT IF NOT A LAW . . . . 438 KITTY HAWK   325
    SOME CHANGE IN THE LAW . . . . 449 THE BAD ISLAND--EASTER   51
    THE LACK OF LIBERTY, THE SQUEEZE OF LAW . . . . . . 460 HOW HARD TO KEEP FROM   199
    OR COURT OF LAW, AND THIS IS JUDGMENT DAY. . . . . . 474 A MASQUE OF REASON . . 26
LAWN
    TO A SLOPE WHERE THE CATTLE KEEP THE LAWN. . . . . . . 17 THE VANTAGE POINT   .   3
    THE FIELDS ARE STRIPPED TO LAWN, THE GARDEN PATCHES . . . 49 A HUNDRED COLLARS . . 134
LAWRENCE
    FAR TO NORTH OF THE ST. LAWRENCE. . . . . 304 CLEAR AND COLDER   . . 11
LAWS
    THERE ARE ROUGHLY ZONES WHOSE LAWS MUST BE OBEYED? . . . 305 THERE ARE ROUGHLY ZONES 13
    LAWS TO ITSELF, IT SEEMS, AND YET HAVE NO . . . . . 324 BUILD SOIL   247
    OBEYING BESTIAL LAWS, ... 341 THE SUBVERTED FLOWER . 59
LAWYER
    THE LAWYER DON'T KNOW WHAT IT IS HE'S BUYING: . . . . . 93 THE SELF-SEEKER . . 11
    I WONDER WHERE MY LAWYER IS. HIS TRAIN'S IN. . . . . . 94 THE SELF-SEEKER . . 49
    WILLIS BROUGHT UP BESIDES THE BOSTON LAWYER . . . . . 96 THE SELF-SEEKER . . 91
    AND BARITONE IMPORTANCE OF THE LAWYER, ... 96 THE SELF-SEEKER . . 94
    THE LAWYER WAS ALREADY IN HIS SATCHEL . . . . 96 THE SELF-SEEKER . . 97
    ANNE LOOKED AT THE LARGE LAWYER AT HER SIDE, ... 97 THE SELF-SEEKER . . 117
    YOU ASK THIS LAWYER MAN. AND IT'S NOT SAFE . . . . . 97 THE SELF-SEEKER . . 133
    WITH A LAWYER AT HAND TO FIND YOU OUT. . . . . 97 THE SELF-SEEKER . . 134
    THE LAWYER GAVE A LAUGH AMONG HIS PAPERS . . . . . . 98 THE SELF-SEEKER . . 145
    THE LAWYER WORE A WATCH THE CASE OF WHICH . . . . . . 98 THE SELF-SEEKER . . 163
    THE LAWYER MAN IS THINKING OF HIS TRAIN. . . . . . . 98 THE SELF-SEEKER . . 168
    THE LAWYER SAID. "I'M SORRY, BUT MY TRAIN-- . . . . . 99 THE SELF-SEEKER . . 181
    YOU KNOW IT, MR. LAWYER. THE SIN IS . . . . 100 THE SELF-SEEKER . . 200
    THE LAWYER GRAVELY CAPPED HIS FOUNTAIN PEN. . . . . . 100 THE SELF-SEEKER . . 218
    INTO OBLIVION WITHOUT A LAWYER. . . . . 462 HOW HARD TO KEEP FROM   263
LAWYER'S
    THE LAWYER'S COMING FOR THE COMPANY. . . . . 92 THE SELF-SEEKER . . .   2
LAY
    WHO LAY THAT NIGHT AWAKE. . . . . 11 WIND AND WINDOW FLOWER   20
    AS WHERE SOME FLOWER LAY WITHERING ON THE GROUND. . . . . 22 THE TUFT OF FLOWERS   . 16
    BETWEEN THEM THEY WILL LAY THIS FARM AS SMOOTH! . . . . 36 DEATH OF THE HIRED MAN   63
    "NO, BUT HE HURT MY HEART THE WAY HE LAY . . . . . . 39 DEATH OF THE HIRED MAN 147
    WHAT I LIKE BEST'S THE LAY OF DIFFERENT FARMS, ... 49 A HUNDRED COLLARS . . 124
    FROM OVER US AS YOU LAY IN YOUR BEDS. . . . . 67 A SERVANT TO SERVANTS . 169
    AND BOTH THAT MORNING EQUALLY LAY . . . . 105 THE ROAD NOT TAKEN . 11
    TOO BAD I COULDN'T LAY ONE IN A LETTER. . . . . . . 107 CHRISTMAS TREES . . 58
    WHAT HAVE YOU YOU KNOW WHERE TO LAY YOUR HANDS ON?" . . . 115 IN THE HOME STRETCH   . 143
    HE LAY AND PUFFED HIS LIPS OUT WITH HIS BREATH. . . . . 137 "OUT,OUT--" 29
    HE POINTED WITH HIS HAND FROM WHERE IT LAY . . . . . 147 SNOW 114
    WHAT WAS IT ABOUT HER NAME? ITS STRANGENESS LAY . . . . 181 MAPLE 44
    PUT ON IT FROM WITHOUT. AND THERE ITS STRENGTH LAY . . . 187 THE AX-HELVE . . . 75
    WHERE THE LOG DRIVE LAY PRESSED AGAINST THE BOOM, . . . 194 PAUL'S WIFE 107
    AND WHO HAD THOUGHT TO LAY HER WITH HER FIRST LOVE, . . . 201 PLACE FOR A THIRD . . 46
    THEY SIMPLY LAY WHERE SOMEONE NOW AND THEN, ... 217 A FOUNTAIN, A BOTTLE . 118
    IT WAS LONG I LAY . . . . 217 I WILL SING YOU ONE-O .   1
    SHOOK WHATEVER IT WAS LAY THERE AT BOTTOM, ... 225 FOR ONCE SOMETHING . 13
    ALREADY DETERMINED DAWN BEGAN TO LAY . . . . 235 VALLEY'S SINGING DAY .   7
    ACROSS EACH OTHER AND SIDE BY SIDE THEY LAY. . . . . . 237 A HILLSIDE THAW . . 29
    THE GRASS LAY FLATTENED UNDER ONE GREAT TREAD. . . . . 239 OUR SINGING STRENGTH . 12
    AND LAY LODGED--THOUGH NOT DEAD. . . . . 250 LODGED   5
    THEN ONCE AGAIN THE SANDBANK LAY SERENE. . . . . . . 270 THE EGG AND THE MACHINE 16

LAY (CONTINUED)
'TIS RITUAL WITH HER TO LAY . . . . 280 BLUE RIBBON AT AMESBURY 29
LAY HIM IN STATE ON A SEPAL. . . . . 288 DEPARTMENTAL 29
THERE BRIGHT IN THE FILTH IT LAY . . . . 312 THE VINDICTIVES . . . 78
TO LAY THEM LEVEL WITH THE RUNNING WAVE, ... 334 I COULD GIVE ALL . . . 3
WHERE ALL DAY LONG SHE LAY AND DOZED. . . . . 344 DISCOVERY OF MADEIRAS . 37
AND THE SHIP LAY IN THE BAY FOR A WHILE . . . . . . 347 DISCOVERY OF MADEIRAS . 111
I'D LAY MY HAND ON HIS HAND ON HIS STAFF, ... 354 THE LESSON FOR TODAY . 124
THERE ONCE WE LAY AS BLOBS OF JELLYFISH . . . . . . 395 ETHEREALIZING 9
LAY IN RISKING SPIRIT . . . . 435 KITTY HAWK 223
HE COULDN'T LAY HANDS ON A PITCHFORK TO HIT HER . . . 463 LINES IN DEJECTION . . 17
AND LAY THE MAPLE LOW. . . . . 470 IN WINTER IN THE WOODS 4
I TRUST IT IS. HERE'S WHERE I LAY ASIDE . . . . . . 474 A MASQUE OF REASON . . 27
THE ABLEST ACTORS I CAN LAY MY HANDS ON. . . . . . . 481 A MASQUE OF REASON . 226
DON'T LAY YOUR HAND ON ME TO SAY IT, SHAMELESS. . . . 500 A MASQUE OF MERCY . 166
AND LAY HIM WHERE YOU ORDERED HIM TO LIE . . . . . . 521 A MASQUE OF MERCY . 734
LAYER
THE WIND WAS ANOTHER LAYER OF MOLD. . . . . 253 THE THATCH 12
LAYERS
THE FRUIT MIXED WITH WATER IN LAYERS OF LEAVES, . . . 62 BLUEBERRIES 104
LAYFAYETTE
"LAFE WAS THE NAME, I THINK?" / "YES, LAYFAYETTE. . . 46 A HUNDRED COLLARS . 41
LAYING
A TRENCH WERE WATER PIPES WERE LAYING ON. . . . . . 394 HAEC FABULA DOCET . . 6
LAZY
I PRODDED THE EARTH WITH A LAZY TOOL . . . . 385 A MOOD APART 2
LEAD
THEM THAT HE COULDN'T LEAD HE'D GET BEHIND . . . . . 71 THE CODE 44
OF VITRIOL OR ARSENATE OF LEAD, ... 164 NEW HAMPSHIRE . . . 161
MIGHT LEAD US ON TO A DISCOVERY. . . . . 183 MAPLE 126
WITH STONE AND LEAD TO UNPROTECTED GLASS: . . . . . 216 A FOUNTAIN, A BOTTLE . 103
TO LEAD HIM OFF THE ASIATIC WAY . . . . 462 HOW HARD TO KEEP FROM 262
LEADER
HAVE NO PURPOSE, HAVE NO LEADER, ... 291 ON HEART'S BEGINNING TO 29
LEADER'S
ENSLAVE YOURSELF TO THE RIGHT LEADER'S TRUTH, ... 460 HOW HARD TO KEEP FROM 191
LEADING
TWO LEADING LIGHTS . . . . 390 TWO LEADING LIGHTS . . T
OF A POWER LEADING FROM ITS STRENGTH AND PRIDE, . . . 424 FOR JOHN F. KENNEDY . 72
LEADS
YET FOLLOWING HOW WAY LEADS ON TO WAY, ... 105 THE ROAD NOT TAKEN . 14
LEAF (SEE BOOK-LEAF)
BUT A LEAF THAT LINGERED BROWN, ... 9 A LATE WALK 10
RELEASE ONE LEAF AT BREAK OF DAY; . . . . 27 OCTOBER 12
AT NOON RELEASE ANOTHER LEAF; . . . . 27 OCTOBER 13
THE FLOATING HEART, WITH SMALL LEAF LIKE A HEART, . . 98 THE SELF-SEEKER . . . 154
"THAT LEAF THERE IN YOUR OPEN BOOK! IT MOVED . . . . 147 SNOW 116
THE THOUSANDTH TIME MAY PROVE THE CHARM.--THAT LEAF! . 148 SNOW 134
I'LL HAVE TO TURN THE LEAF IF NO ONE ELSE WILL. . . . 148 SNOW 151
THAT COULD HAVE DROPPED A LEAF WAS DOWN ITSELF . . . 175 THE CENSUS-TAKER . . 19
WITHOUT A SINGLE LEAF TO SPEND ON AUTUMN, ... 175 THE CENSUS-TAKER . . 23
A MAPLE LEAF SHE THOUGHT MUST HAVE BEEN LAID . . . . 181 MAPLE 63
BUT FORGOT TO PUT THE LEAF BACK IN CLOSING . . . . . 181 MAPLE 67
SHE TOLD HIM OF THE BOOKMARK MAPLE LEAF . . . . . . 183 MAPLE 104
AND EVERY LEAF OF FOLIAGE SHE'D WORN . . . . 184 MAPLE 146
THEN LEAF SUBSIDES TO LEAF. . . . . 222 NOTHING GOLD CAN STAY . 5
A SINGLE LEAF WAS ON A BOUGH, ... 233 LOOKING FOR SUNSET BIRD 10
THE FOLIAGE FOLLOW HIM, LEAF AND STEM; . . . . . . 236 MISGIVING 2
TO MAKE A LEAF, IF THERE HAD BEEN ONE, STIR. . . . . 238 A HILLSIDE THAW . . . 32
YET FOR THEM THE LILAC RENEWED ITS LEAF, ... 242 NEED OF BEING VERSED . 17
THE ONLY LEAF IT DROPS GOES WIDE, ... 247 ON GOING UNNOTICED . 11
TO SAY WHICH BUDS ARE LEAF AND WHICH ARE BLOOM. . . . 254 A WINTER EDEN . . . 16
WHICH IS FAIRER, FLOWER OR LEAF. . . . . 297 LEAVES COMPARED WITH . 14
THEY SPOKE TO THE FUGITIVE IN MY HEART AS IF IT WERE LEAF
TO LEAF. . . . . 298 A LEAF-TREADER . . . 9
LEAFILY
AND STILL THE WOODS SWEEP LEAFILY ON, ... 247 ON GOING UNNOTICED . 14
LEAFLESS
THE LEAFLESS BLOOM OF A PLUM IS FRESH AND WHITE; . . . 300 STRONG SAYING NOTHING . 10
LEAF'S
HER EARLY LEAF'S A FLOWER; . . . . 222 NOTHING GOLD CAN STAY . 3
LEAF-TREADER
A LEAF-TREADER . . . . 297 A LEAF-TREADER . . . T
LEAFY
CLEAR TO THE TOP." I SAW THROUGH LEAFY SCREENS . . . 42 THE MOUNTAIN 57
AND NOTHING BUT THE TOP A LEAFY GREEN-- . . . . . . 375 A YOUNG BIRCH . . . 7
LEAK
A LEAK AND EMPTIED THEN. AND FORTY YEARS . . . . . 213 A FOUNTAIN, A BOTTLE . 25
LEAN
TO THIS LEAN FEEDING, SAVE ONCE A YEAR . . . . . . 24 PAN WITH US 12
"HE'S NOTHING. LISTEN. WHEN I LEAN LIKE THIS . . . . 77 THE GENERATIONS OF MEN 103
TO LEAN AGAINST AND HEAR IN THE DARK. . . . . 297 LEAVES COMPARED WITH . 18
SHE HAD TO LEAN AWAY. . . . . 340 THE SUBVERTED FLOWER . 30
AND WENT TO LEAN AGAINST THE RAIL, ... 345 DISCOVERY OF MADEIRAS . 50
YOU LINK AN ARM IN ITS ARM AND YOU LEAN . . . . . . 349 TO A YOUNG WRETCH . . 5
LEAN BACK AND HAVE MY CONFIDENTIAL LAUGH, ... 354 THE LESSON FOR TODAY . 125
THE ONLY NATIVE TREE THAT DARES TO LEAN, ... 375 A YOUNG BIRCH . . . 8
LEANED
BUT THE FLOWER LEANED ASIDE . . . . 11 WIND AND WINDOW FLOWER 25
WARREN LEANED OUT AND TOOK A STEP OR TWO, ... 38 DEATH OF THE HIRED MAN 121
SOONER OR LATER CAME AND LEANED, HALF KNELT, ... 56 THE BLACK COTTAGE . . 27
I LEANED MY HEAD, ... 118 THE TELEPHONE . . . 12
THERE WAS A GATE I HAD LEANED AT FOR THE VIEW . . . . 118 MEETING AND PASSING . 2
I LEANED TO LINE THE FIGURES IN . . . . 252 THE PEACEFUL SHEPHERD . 3
I LEANED ON WITH A SINGING TRUST . . . . 336 THE WIND AND THE RAIN . 5
LEANING (SEE IN-LEANING)
WHEN LEANING WITH MY HEAD AGAINST A FLOWER . . . . . 118 THE TELEPHONE . . . 5
BY LEANING BACK MYSELF, AS IF THE REINS . . . . . . 132 THE BONFIRE 79

LEANING (CONTINUED)
    WHO, LEANING ON A LOG, LOOKED BACK AT PAUL. . . . . 194 PAUL'S WIFE 110
    FROM LEANING ON IT HARD . . . . 227 TO EARTHWARD 27
    AND LEANING ON DICTATORSHIP; . . . . 326 TO A THINKER 17
    A MAN SITS LEANING BACK AGAINST A PALM. . . . . 473 A MASQUE OF REASON . . . 2
LEANS
    HE LEANS AGAINST THE DUSTY WALL, ... 280 BLUE RIBBON AT AMESBURY 21
    THAT LEANS OUT THIS AND THAT WAY FROM THEIR CHIMNEY. . . 414 A CABIN IN THE CLEARING 11
    (HE LEANS AWAY IN TOLERANT DISTASTE.) . . . . 504 A MASQUE OF MERCY . . 287
LEAP
    MAKING THE GRAVEL LEAP AND LEAP IN AIR, ... 53 HOME BURIAL 75
    LEAP UP, LIKE THAT, LIKE THAT, AND LAND SO LIGHTLY . . 53 HOME BURIAL 76
    TO LEAP THE DUSTY DEADLINE. FOR MY OWN . . . . . . 131 THE BONFIRE 64
    LEAPED OUT AT THE BOY'S HAND, OR SEEMED TO LEAP-- . . 136 "OUT, OUT--" 16
    AND MADE IT LEAP MY KNUCKLE, HAVING TOSSED . . . . . 231 A BROOK IN THE CITY . 7
    GIVES A LEAP IN THE EAST. . . . . 261 CANIS MAJOR 4
    IN THE LEAP WE LEAPT. . . . . 437 KITTY HAWK 295
    CRIED, "THE LEAP--THE LEAP!" . . . . 437 KITTY HAWK 297
    THOUGH OUR LEAP IN AIR . . . . 439 KITTY HAWK 357
LEAPED
    LEAPED OUT AT THE BOY'S HAND, OR SEEMED TO LEAP-- . . . 136 "OUT, OUT--" 16
LEAPFROG
    AND LEAPFROG IN EACH OTHER'S WAY--ALL'S WELL. . . . . 318 BUILD SOIL 64
LEAPING
    A LEAPING TONGUE OF BLOOM THE SCYTHE HAD SPARED . . . 22 THE TUFT OF FLOWERS . 23
    AND LEAPING ON IT WITH A SOLEMN BOUND, ... 284 THE GOLD HESPERIDEE . 47
LEAPT
    IN THE LEAP WE LEAPT. . . . . 437 KITTY HAWK 295
    SO HE LEAPT ON HER HAIRY BACK AND BIT HER . . . . . 463 LINES IN DEJECTION . . 19
LEARN
    I DON'T LEARN WHAT THEIR NAMES ARE, LET ALONE . . . . 65 A SERVANT TO SERVANTS . 82
    THAT WAS A THING WE COULD NOT WAIT TO LEARN. . . . . 109 THE EXPOSED NEST . . . 26
    AND SO AT LAST TO LEARN TO USE THEIR WINGS. . . . . 110 THE EXPOSED NEST . . . 36
    SOME BOY TOO FAR FROM TOWN TO LEARN BASEBALL, . . . 121 BIRCHES 25
    TO LEARN ABOUT NOT LAUNCHING OUT TOO SOON . . . . . 122 BIRCHES 33
    HAVEN'T YOU HEARD WHAT WE HAVE LIVED TO LEARN? . . . 133 THE BONFIRE 109
    THAT I NEED LEARN TO LET GO WITH THE HEART. . . . . 199 WILD GRAPES 103
    SHE CAME TO FROM TOO HIGH TOO LATE TO LEARN. . . . 257 THE LOVELY BE CHOOSERS 45
    I WENT TO SCHOOL TO AGE TO LEARN THE PAST. . . . . 267 WHAT FIFTY SAID . . . 4
    I GO TO SCHOOL TO YOUTH TO LEARN THE FUTURE. . . . 267 WHAT FIFTY SAID . . . 8
    COME LEARN THE LATIN EHEU FOR ALAS. . . . . 353 THE LESSON FOR TODAY . 85
    THERE WAS SO MUCH MORE EVERY DAY TO LEARN, ... 398 BURSTING RAPTURE . . 6
    SAY SOMETHING TO US WE CAN LEARN . . . . 403 SOMETHING LIKE A STAR . 9
    WITH WHAT I LEARN . . . . 413 AWAY! 23
    I WOULD GIVE ANYTHING TO LEARN . . . . 451 A-WISHING WELL . . . 8
    WAS TO LEARN HIS SUBMISSION TO UNREASON; . . . . . 481 A MASQUE OF REASON . 210
    MEDITATE NOTHING. LEARN TO CONTEMPLATE. . . . . . 517 A MASQUE OF MERCY . . 628
    TO LEARN TO SAY (HE MOVES TO JONAH'S FEET.) . . . 521 A MASQUE OF MERCY . . 737
LEARNED
    NOT YESTERDAY I LEARNED TO KNOW . . . . 7 MY NOVEMBER GUEST . . 16
    "YOU MUST BE LEARNED. THAT'S WHAT YOU SEE IN IT?" . . . 76 THE GENERATIONS OF MEN 95
    SOMETHING I MUST HAVE LEARNED RIDING IN TRAINS . . . 77 THE GENERATIONS OF MEN 127
    YOU SEE ANNE HAS HER LESSON LEARNED BY HEART." . . . 97 THE SELF-SEEKER . . . 122
    FOR HIM TO CONQUER. HE LEARNED ALL THERE WAS . . . 122 BIRCHES 32
    ALWAYS--I TELL YOU THIS THEY LEARNED-- . . . . . . 127 HOUSE FEAR 1
    THEY LEARNED TO RATTLE THE LOCK AND KEY . . . . . 127 HOUSE FEAR 5
    THEY LEARNED TO LEAVE THE HOUSE DOOR WIDE . . . . 127 HOUSE FEAR 9
    AND HE LEARNED OF FINALITIES . . . . 129 THE IMPULSE 27
    SHE LEARNED SHORTHAND, WHATEVER SHORTHAND MAY . . 182 MAPLE 75
    I HAD NOT LEARNED TO LET GO WITH THE HANDS, . . . 199 WILD GRAPES 96
    AS STILL I HAVE NOT LEARNED TO WITH THE HEART, . . . 199 WILD GRAPES 97
    HAS NEVER LEARNED TO KNOW HER PLACE. . . . . . . 390 TWO LEADING LIGHTS . 13
    THEY MUST BY NOW HAVE LEARNED THE NATIVE TONGUE. . . 414 A CABIN IN THE CLEARING 20
    WE LEARNED FROM THE FORBIDDEN FRUIT . . . . . . 467 QUANDARY 15
    IF YOU HAVE LEARNED YOUR LESSON. DON'T BE BASHFUL. . . 511 A MASQUE OF MERCY . . 481
LEARNER
    AND BRAVER FOR THE EARNER, LEARNER, YEARNER. . . . . 424 FOR JOHN F. KENNEDY . 67
LEARNING
    ONE WASN'T LONG IN LEARNING THAT SHE THOUGHT, . . . 56 THE BLACK COTTAGE . . 54
    AS IF TO SAY MERE LEARNING WAS THE DEVIL . . . . . 400 TO THE RIGHT PERSON . 10
    LEARNING HAS BEEN A PART OF THEIR RELIGION. . . . . 414 A CABIN IN THE CLEARING 28
    AND OUR DUMP OF LEARNING . . . . 441 KITTY HAWK 434
LEAST
    ENOUGH AT LEAST TO BUY TOBACCO WITH, ... 35 DEATH OF THE HIRED MAN 20
    IF NOT AT HEART, AT LEAST ON PRINCIPLE. . . . . . 44 A HUNDRED COLLARS . . 13
    WITH THE LEAST STIFFENING OF HER NECK AND SILENCE. . 51 HOME BURIAL 14
    AT LEAST TO PASS BY AND SEE WHO HE WAS, ... 74 THE GENERATIONS OF MEN 32
    IT'S DIFFERENT WITH A MAN, AT LEAST WITH JOHN: . . . 84 THE HOUSEKEEPER . . . 79
    OF AT LEAST ONE LONG-AFTER-BEDTIME WALK. . . . . 92 THE FEAR 83
    OF OVER-WINTER WITH THE LEAST TIP-TOUCH . . . . . 131 THE BONFIRE 46
    OR AT LEAST MAY BE. . . . . 134 A GIRL'S GARDEN . . . 36
    HE TOOK NO NOTICE, DID HE? WELL, AT LEAST . . . . 144 SNOW 49
    IF HE HAD STAYED. THE LEAST THING SET HIM GOING. . . 152 SNOW 259
    A THING THE LEAST BIT DOUBTFULLY PERSCENTED . . . . 163 NEW HAMPSHIRE . . . 142
    TO LET HIM KNOW WE WEREN'T THE LEAST IMPOSED ON, . . 177 THE STAR-SPLITTER . . 41
    FOR THE LEAST SIN, IT WOULDN'T TAKE US LONG . . . . 177 THE STAR-SPLITTER . . 45
    NOT NOW--AT LEAST I SHOULDN'T TRY TOO HARD NOW. . . 180 MAPLE 25
    FREE FROM THE LEAST KNOT, EQUAL TO THE STRAIN . . . 187 THE AX-HELVE 70
    THE LEAST I COULD DO WAS HELP DIG THEIR GRAVE. . . . 206 THE WITCH OF COOS . . 141
    AT LEAST I'VE BROUGHT YOU TO THE FAMOUS BOTTLE." . . 214 A FOUNTAIN, A BOTTLE . 42
    AT WHAT HAS HAPPENED. BIRDS, AT LEAST, MUST KNOW . . 249 ACCEPTANCE 4
    WITH GODS AND ANGELS, WE WERE MEN AT LEAST, ... 279 THE WHITE-TAILED HORNET 61
    CAN SCANT OR HURRY HER THE LEAST. . . . . 281 BLUE RIBBON AT AMESBURY 38
    AND FLASH, AT THE LEAST ALARM . . . . 282 A DRUMLIN WOODCHUCK . 15
    HE SHOWED NOT THE LEAST SURPRISE. . . . . 288 DEPARTMENTAL 4
    YOUR LEAST TOUCH SETS IT GOING ROUND, ... 306 A TRIAL RUN 13
    AT LEAST NOT OVER HALF. . . . . 309 NOT ALL THERE . . . 8
    AT LEAST HE HAD THIS IN COMMON . . . . 314 BEARER OF EVIL TIDINGS 37

LEAST (CONTINUED)
    LEAST IN DEMOCRACY. IN PRACTICE, PURE, ... 318 BUILD SOIL 76
    AT LEAST THAT'S WHY THE UNIVERSE IS ROUND. . . . . . 322 BUILD SOIL 203
    RATHER BECAUSE IT TOOK FIVE YEARS AT LEAST . . . . . 323 BUILD SOIL 227
    MY SHARE AT LEAST, LEST I BE EMPTY-IDLE. . . . . . . 324 BUILD SOIL 262
    AT LEAST DON'T USE YOUR MIND TOO HARD, ... 326 TO A THINKER 35
    SAY A FRACTION OF ONE PERCENT AT THE VERY LEAST, . . 349 OUR HOLD ON THE PLANET 16
    THE PATINA OF THIS THE LEAST OF GLOBES. . . . . . . 352 THE LESSON FOR TODAY . 72
    ON ANY SHEET THE LEAST DISPLAY OF MIND. . . . . . . 358 A CONSIDERABLE SPECK . 33
    AT LEAST TO LIVE UNGOLDEN WITH THE POOR, ... 358 THE LOST FOLLOWER . . 18
    OF WHICH YOU FEEL NO LEAST TOUCH ON YOUR FACE . . . . 361 A LOOSE MOUNTAIN . . 11
    AT LEAST I WILL NOT HAVE IT SYSTEMATIC. . . . . . . 362 BOEOTIAN 4
    AT LEAST IT OUGHT TO SEND . . . . 389 ASTROMETAPHYSICAL . . 19
    OR AT LEAST IN A LIFETIME, BY THAT METHOD." . . . . . 405 FROM PLANE TO PLANE . 47
    I CAN'T EXPLAIN--TONIGHT AT LEAST." . . . . 420 ONE MORE BREVITY . . 25
    ONE LEAST GERM OR COAL. . . . . 441 KITTY HAWK 418
    OF AT LEAST SOME PART . . . . 441 KITTY HAWK 424
    AND THE LEAST DISPOSED TO ASCRIBE . . . . 444 THE DRAFT HORSE . . . 15
    DOES NO ONE AT ALL EVER FEEL THIS WAY IN THE LEAST? . 446 DOES NO ONE AT ALL EVER T
    "AT LEAST YOU OUGHT TO DIE FOR WIZARDRY. . . . . . . 457 HOW HARD TO KEEP FROM 115
    AT LEAST THIS FAR, ... 469 BUT OUTER SPACE.... . 2
    I'D GIVE MORE FOR ONE LEAST BEFOREHAND REASON . . . . 482 A MASQUE OF REASON . 247
    I TAKE TO DRINK--AT LEAST I TAKE A DRINK. . . . . . . 496 A MASQUE OF MERCY . . 83
    I'LL TAKE TO DRINK--AT LEAST I'LL TAKE A DRINK. . . . 500 A MASQUE OF MERCY . 168
    THERE'S NOT THE LEAST LACK OF THE LOVE OF GOD . . . . 505 A MASQUE OF MERCY . 307
    OR NOT AT LEAST THE ORDINARY KIND. . . . . 510 A MASQUE OF MERCY . 456
LEASTWAYS
    LEASTWAYS FOR ME--AND THEN THEY'LL BE CONVINCED. . . . 64 A SERVANT TO SERVANTS . 59
LEATHER (SEE HELL-FOR-LEATHER)
    AND FIT THE EARTH LIKE A LEATHER GLOVE. . . . . 26 IN HARDWOOD GROVES . . 4
    OLD STREAK OF LEATHER--DOESN'T LOVE ME MUCH . . . . . 94 THE SELF-SEEKER . . 33
    TORPEDO-LIKE, WITH SHELL OF GRITTY LEATHER, ... 270 THE EGG AND THE MACHINE 25
    OLD RIVALS OF SAGGING LEATHER, ... 294 A RECORD STRIDE . . . 6
LEATHERN
    AND SWEPT OF LEATHERN LEAVES, BUT LEFT THE BARK . . . 184 MAPLE 141
LEAVE
    MELT THE GLASS AND LEAVE THE STICKS . . . . 11 TO THE THAWING WIND . 9
    THEY LEAVE US SO TO THE WAY WE TOOK, ... 16 IN NEGLECT 1
    YOU NEEDN'T BE AFRAID HE'LL LEAVE YOU THIS TIME." . . 38 DEATH OF THE HIRED MAN 112
    "HE MAY AND NOT CARE, AND SO LEAVE THE CHEWINK. . . . 60 BLUEBERRIES . . . 29
    "HOW SHALL WE?" / "WILL YOU LEAVE THE WAY TO ME?" . . 80 THE GENERATIONS OF MEN 205
    TWO OF YOU OUT WILL LEAVE AN EMPTY HOUSE." . . . . . 82 THE HOUSEKEEPER . . . 42
    IT MUST BE RIGHT TO LEAVE HIM." / "WHICH IS WRONG!" . 83 THE HOUSEKEEPER . . . 75
    I CAN'T, AND LEAVE A THING LIKE THAT UNSETTLED. . . . 89 THE FEAR 15
    AND LEAVE IT THERE FAR FROM A USEFUL FIREPLACE . . . . 102 THE WOOD-PILE . . . 38
    LIKE PROFANATION, BY YOUR LEAVE, ... 102 GOOD HOURS 15
    AND LEAVE THE SLOPE BEHIND THE HOUSE ALL BARE, . . . 106 CHRISTMAS TREES . . 18
    AND MAKE GOOD FARMERS, AND LEAVE OTHER FELLOWS . . . . 114 IN THE HOME STRETCH . 96
    THEY LEAVE US TO: THAT PASTURE SLOPE THAT SEEMS . . . 114 IN THE HOME STRETCH . 113
    IF I CAN LEAVE OFF BURYING THE WHITE . . . . 124 PUTTING IN THE SEED . 3
    THEY LEARNED TO LEAVE THE HOUSE DOOR WIDE . . . . . . 127 HOUSE FEAR 9
    I WANT YOU HERE WITH ME, FRED.--LEAVE HIM HERE, . . . 144 SNOW 36
    HE'S HERE. I LEAVE HIM ALL TO YOU. GO IN . . . . . . 146 SNOW 103
    MR. MESERVE, I'LL LEAVE IT TO YOUR WIFE. . . . . . . 147 SNOW 109
    WELL, NOW I LEAVE YOU, PEOPLE." / "COME, MESERVE, . . 150 SNOW 197
    OH, I'M NOT BLAMING YOU. HE DIDN'T LEAVE YOU . . . . 152 SNOW 256
    "WHY DID I EVER LET HIM LEAVE THIS HOUSE!" . . . . . 153 SNOW 280
    "AND LEAVE THE CHILDREN?" / "WAIT AND CALL AGAIN. . . 154 SNOW 307
    SO LONG AS HE WOULD LEAVE ENOUGH UNSAID, ... 186 THE AX-HELVE . . . 38
    TO LEAVE IT TO, WHETHER THE RIGHT TO HOLD . . . . . . 188 THE AX-HELVE . . . 91
    MY BROTHER COULD NOT ALWAYS LEAVE AT HOME. . . . . . 196 WILD GRAPES . . . 9
    HE STOOD BESIDE AND LEAVE HIS TRADEMARK ON THEM, . . 209 PAUPER WITCH OF GRAFTON 55
    AND BADE HIM LEAVE THE PAN AND STOKE THE ARCH: . . . 234 EVENING A SUGAR ORCHARD 4
    "DO IT BY JOYS, AND LEAVE HER ALWAYS BLAMELESS. . . . 256 THE LOVELY BE CHOOSERS 21
    AND LEAVE YOU THERE, OURSELVES FORBID TO ENTER-- . . . 259 WEST-RUNNING BROOK . 35
    THEY CAN LEAVE HER A HUT AS WELL; . . . . 260 SAND DUNES . . . 14
    YET NOTHING I SHOULD CARE TO LEAVE BEHIND. . . . . . 266 THE ARMFUL . . . 5
    MUST LEAVE THEM UNLOCKED TO BETRAY HIS PRESENCE. . . 289 OLD BARN AT THE BOTTOM 15
    YET LEAVE SUCH LOVELY SHAFTS OUTDOORS TO PERISH. . . 290 OLD BARN AT THE BOTTOM 34
    THEY CAN LEAVE IT TO SOMEONE ELSE TO TEND. . . . . . 291 ON HEART'S BEGINNING TO 18
    AND COME TO LEAVE THE ROUTINE ROAD . . . . 304 UNHARVESTED . . . 2
    BUT THE WORST ONE OF ALL TO LEAVE UNCURBED, ... 319 BUILD SOIL 101
    AND WHAT TAKE HENCE OR LEAVE BEHIND, ... 332 ALL REVELATION . . . 7
    THAT WILL NOT LEAVE THE TONGUE. . . . . 341 THE SUBVERTED FLOWER . 68
    TO LEAVE THE ENGLISH LAW BEHIND . . . . 344 DISCOVERY OF MADEIRAS . 16
    THE GOLD FOR WHICH THEY LEAVE THE GOLDEN LINE . . . . 358 THE LOST FOLLOWER . . 2
    WILL LEAVE THEIR TATTERS HUNG ON BARB AND THORN.) . . 379 DIRECTIVE 54
    TO LEAVE IT TO THEM TO GET OUT OF THEIR VALLEYS. . . 379 TOO ANXIOUS FOR RIVERS 7
    I LEAVE THIS NOTE WITHOUT A STAMP . . . . 380 AN UNSTAMPED LETTER IN . 1
    WAS LEAVE AS THEIR POSTERITY ONE POD . . . . 412 POD OF THE MILKWEED . 43
    I LEAVE BEHIND . . . . 413 AWAY! 5
    DON'T THINK I LEAVE . . . . 413 AWAY! 9
    THEY LEAVE THE ROAD TO ME . . . . 415 CLOSED FOR GOOD . . 13
    LET'S LEAVE THAT TO THE SCIENTIFIC WITS. . . . . . . 425 ACCIDENTALLY ON PURPOSE 18
    BUT I DON'T MIND. LET'S LEAVE IT AS IT STOOD. . . . . 485 A MASQUE OF REASON . 334
    WE CAN'T LEAVE HIM OUT. / NO. NO, WE DON'T NEED TO. . 486 A MASQUE OF REASON . 378
    ONE MINUTE, MAY I, PAUL?--BEFORE WE LEAVE . . . . . . 501 A MASQUE OF MERCY . 216
    DON'T YOU FEEL SOMETHING? / LEAVE ME OUT OF THIS. . . 504 A MASQUE OF MERCY . 286
    HOLD ON THERE. LEAVE THAT OPEN WHERE IT LIES. . . . . 504 A MASQUE OF MERCY . 292
LEAVED (SEE TWO-LEAVED)
LEAVES
    I'LL ONLY STOP TO RAKE THE LEAVES AWAY . . . . 1 THE PASTURE . . . 2
    THE WOODBINE LEAVES LITTERED THE YARD, ... 7 LOVE AND A QUESTION . 13
    WAS SWALLOWED UP IN LEAVES THAT BLEW ALWAY; . . . . . 16 A DREAM PANG . . . 2
    THE BARREN BOUGHS WITHOUT THE LEAVES, ... 18 GOING FOR WATER . . 11
    IT WAS SOMETHING AMONG THE LEAVES I SOUGHT . . . . . 25 THE DEMIURGE'S LAUGH . 16
    THE SAME LEAVES OVER AND OVER AGAIN! . . . . 25 IN HARDWOOD GROVES . . 1
    BEFORE THE LEAVES CAN MOUNT AGAIN . . . . 26 IN HARDWOOD GROVES . . 5

LEAVES (CONTINUED)
    THY LEAVES HAVE RIPENED TO THE FALL; . . . . 27 OCTOBER 2
    WHOSE LEAVES ALREADY ARE BURNT WITH FROST, ... 28 OCTOBER 19
    I FOUND IT WITH THE WITHERED LEAVES . . . . 29 MY BUTTERFLY 46
    THE LEAVES ARE ALL DEAD ON THE GROUND, ... 30 RELUCTANCE 7
    AND THE DEAD LEAVES LIE HUDDLED AND STILL, ... 30 RELUCTANCE 13
    IMPERFECTLY CONCEALED AMONG THE LEAVES. . . . . . . 41 THE MOUNTAIN 32
    OR PUT THE LEAVES ASIDE THAT FRAMED IT IN. . . . . . 55 THE BLACK COTTAGE . . 10
    THE FRUIT MIXED WITH WATER IN LAYERS OF LEAVES, . . . 62 BLUEBERRIES 104
    AND SAYS THEIR NAMES, AND LEAVES THEM WHERE THEY ARE." . 98 THE SELF-SEEKER . . . 162
    IN LEAVES NO STEP HAD TRODDEN BLACK. . . . . 105 THE ROAD NOT TAKEN . 12
    OF DEAD LEAVES STUCK TOGETHER BY THE HEAT-- . . . . . 119 HYLA BROOK 11
    HE SAYS THAT LEAVES ARE OLD AND THAT FOR FLOWERS . . . 119 THE OVEN BIRD . . . 4
    YEARS AFTERWARDS, TRAILING THEIR LEAVES ON THE GROUND . 121 BIRCHES 18
    SHE LEAVES THEM BITTEN WHEN SHE HAS TO FLY. . . . . 125 THE COW IN APPLE TIME . 9
    THE LINE WHERE MAN LEAVES OFF AND NATURE STARTS, . . . 171 NEW HAMPSHIRE . . . 379
    OF WASTE LEAVES AT MY SMOKY LANTERN CHIMNEY . . . . 176 THE STAR-SPLITTER . . 8
    AND SWEPT OF LEATHERN LEAVES, BUT LEFT THE BARK . . . 184 MAPLE 141
    WEARING A THIN HEADDRESS OF POINTED LEAVES, ... 196 WILD GRAPES . . . 21
    "WHOEVER IT IS THAT LEAVES HIM OUT SO LATE, ... 223 THE RUNAWAY 19
    A YOUNG BEECH CLINGING TO ITS LAST YEAR'S LEAVES. . . 234 A BOUNDLESS MOMENT . 12
    SPADES TAKE UP LEAVES . . . . 234 GATHERING LEAVES . 1
    AND BAGS FULL OF LEAVES . . . . 234 GATHERING LEAVES . 3
    GATHERING LEAVES . . . . 234 GATHERING LEAVES . T
    THE LEAVES HAD PROMISED THEMSELVES THIS FLIGHT, . . . 236 MISGIVING 6
    IN THE TUMULT OF FREE LEAVES ON HIGH. . . . . . . 247 ON GOING UNNOTICED . 2
    AND HAS NO LEAVES AT ALL OF ITS OWN; . . . . . . 247 ON GOING UNNOTICED . 7
    LEAVES GOT UP IN A COIL AND HISSED, ... 251 BEREFT 9
    THAT WHEN IT HAS SWEPT BY, LEAVES SUMMITS STAINED. . . 255 THE FLOOD 13
    AND RAISED AMONG THE LEAVES AND DULY TOLD, ... 283 THE GOLD HESPERIDEE . 15
    THE HUNTER SCUFFLING LEAVES GOES BY AT DUSK, ... 289 OLD BARN AT THE BOTTOM 3
    A TREE'S LEAVES MAY BE EVER SO GOOD, ... 296 LEAVES COMPARED WITH . 1
    LEAVES COMPARED WITH FLOWERS . . . . 296 LEAVES COMPARED WITH . T
    LEAVES FOR SMOOTH AND BARK FOR ROUGH, ... 297 LEAVES COMPARED WITH . 7
    LEAVES AND BARK MAY BE TREE ENOUGH. . . . . . . 297 LEAVES COMPARED WITH . 8
    LEAVES BY NIGHT AND FLOWERS BY DAY. . . . . . . 297 LEAVES COMPARED WITH . 16
    LEAVES AND BARK, LEAVES AND BARK, ... 297 LEAVES COMPARED WITH . 17
    LEAVES ARE ALL MY DARKER MOOD. . . . . 297 LEAVES COMPARED WITH . 20
    I HAVE BEEN TREADING ON LEAVES ALL DAY UNTIL I AM
      AUTUMN-TIRED. . . . . 297 A LEAF-TREADER . . . 1
    GOD KNOWS ALL THE COLOR AND FORM OF LEAVES I HAVE TRODDEN
      ON AND MIRED. . . . . 297 A LEAF-TREADER . . . 2
    I HAVE SAFELY TRODDEN UNDERFOOT THE LEAVES OF ANOTHER YEAR. 297 A LEAF-TREADER . . . 4
    LEAVES TO STRIP AND BRANCHES SPLINTER, ... 304 CLEAR AND COLDER . . 12
    WE THINK OF THE TREE. IF IT NEVER AGAIN HAS LEAVES, . . 305 THERE ARE ROUGHLY ZONES 4
    THE TREE HAS NO LEAVES AND MAY NEVER HAVE THEM AGAIN. . 305 THERE ARE ROUGHLY ZONES 18
    IF HE LEAVES IT TO NATURE TO CARRY OUT THE SENTENCE. . . 307 NOT QUITE SOCIAL . . 14
    THAT FAR-OFF DAY THE LEAVES IN FLIGHT . . . . . . 336 THE WIND AND THE RAIN . 1
    AND BEGAN TO FLUTTER THE LEAVES TO LOOK . . . . . 342 A CLOUD SHADOW . . . 2
    SAID THAT THE FALL MIGHT COME AND WHIRL OF LEAVES, . . 343 QUEST OF PURPLE-FRINGED 27
    WE SAW LEAVES GO TO GLORY, ... 359 NOVEMBER 1
    A YEAR OF LEAVES WAS WASTED. . . . . 359 NOVEMBER 8
    HE MIGHT BE OPENING LEAVES OF STONE, ... 364 TRESPASS 9
    THAT SENDS LIGHT RUSTLE RUSHES TO THEIR LEAVES, . . . 378 DIRECTIVE 24
    A PRIMING COAT OF LEAVES. . . . . 416 CLOSED FOR GOOD . . 18
    THE SHAPE OF LEAVES WILL SHOW . . . . 416 CLOSED FOR GOOD . . 23
    FREE VERSE LEAVES OUT THE METER AND MAKES UP . . . 460 HOW HARD TO KEEP FROM 219
    AND THIS TIME LOCKS IT UP AND LEAVES IT.) . . . . 477 A MASQUE OF REASON . 108
LEAVING
    BY LEAVING THEM TO FLOURISH, NOT FOR US, ... 23 THE TUFT OF FLOWERS . 26
    AND NOW I'M LEAVING YOU A LITTLE WHILE. . . . . . 50 A HUNDRED COLLARS . . 159
    IT'S NOTHING; IT'S THEIR LEAVING US AT DUSK. . . . . 115 IN THE HOME STRETCH . 130
    AS LEAVING MORE TO NATURE AND HAPPY CHANCE. . . . 185 MAPLE 169
    I WAS FOR LEAVING SOMETHING TO THE WHETTER. . . . . 191 THE GRINDSTONE . . . 75
    LEAVING ON ONE WIRE TOOTH A LOCK OF HAIR. . . . . 269 THE BEAR 9
    LEAVING LOVE'S ALTERNATIONS, JOY AND GRIEF, ... 317 BUILD SOIL 35
    BUT LEAVING NOT THE CHAIR I LONG HAVE SAT IN . . . . 350 THE LESSON FOR TODAY . 5
    AND LEAVING SOME THINGS TO TAKE THEIR COURSE. . . . 376 SOMETHING FOR HOPE . 22
    THE LOOKS OF EMPIRE HERE. I'M LEAVING WITH YOU." . . . 453 HOW HARD TO KEEP FROM 9
    HE ISN'T REALLY GOING, YET HE'S LEAVING. . . . . . 489 A MASQUE OF REASON . 440
    AND LEAVING IT BEHIND US IN THE TRAP. . . . . . 508 A MASQUE OF MERCY . 389
LECTURE
    I HEARD A FELLOW IN A PUBLIC LECTURE . . . . . . 369 THE LITERATE FARMER AND 53
LED
    BUT HE TURNED FIRST, AND LED MY EYE TO LOOK . . . . 22 THE TUFT OF FLOWERS . 21
    THE NIGHT CLERK LED HIM UP THREE FLIGHTS OF STAIRS . . 45 A HUNDRED COLLARS . . 33
    THAT LED US TO A WEATHERED WINDOWSILL. . . . . . 55 THE BLACK COTTAGE . 13
    MAY STILL HAVE BEEN WHAT LED HER ON TO READ, ... 182 MAPLE 73
    ONE DAY MY BROTHER LED ME TO A GLADE . . . . . . 196 WILD GRAPES . . . 19
    WAS LED INTO THE PRESENCE OF THE TREE . . . . . . 283 THE GOLD HESPERIDEE . 14
    WHERE ONE ROAD LED TO THE THRONE . . . . . . 313 BEARER OF EVIL TIDINGS 6
    ON MELTED MOUNTAIN WATER LED BY FLUME . . . . . 337 THE WIND AND THE RAIN . 23
    SHE CAME DOWN WEAKLY AND BLINDLY LED . . . . . 343 DISCOVERY OF MADEIRAS . 6
    THEY SLOWLY LED OLD LATIN VERSE TO RHYME . . . . 351 THE LESSON FOR TODAY . 16
    AND WHAT ELSE DID WE SAY? / WELL, WHAT LED UP-- . . 487 A MASQUE OF REASON . 399
LEDGE
    HAVE COME DOWN FROM THEIR NATIVE LEDGE . . . . . 364 A NATURE NOTE . . . 2
    TILL IT FLAKED FROM THE LEDGE. . . . . 448 THE BAD ISLAND--EASTER 15
LEDGES
    THE LEDGES SHOW LINES RULED SOUTHEAST-NORTHWEST, . . . 377 DIRECTIVE 15
LEFT   (SEE BETTER-LEFT-UNWRITTEN)
    AND LEFT NO TRACE BUT THE CELLAR WALLS, ... 5 GHOST HOUSE 3
    I LEFT YOU IN THE MORNING, ... 12 FLOWER-GATHERING . . 1
    BEFORE WE LEFT THE SPOT, ... 14 ROSE POGONIAS . . . 18
    MY LONG SCYTHE WHISPERED AND LEFT THE HAY TO MAKE. . . 17 MOWING 14
    TO THE ANCIENT LANDS WHERE IT LEFT THE SHELLS . . . 27 A LINE-STORM SONG . . 27
    THERE IS NONE LEFT TO MOURN THEE IN THE FIELDS. . . . 28 MY BUTTERFLY 7
    WHERE THEY HAVE LEFT NOT ONE STONE ON A STONE, . . . 33 MENDING WALL 7

LEFT (CONTINUED)

IF HE LEFT THEN, I SAID, THAT ENDED IT. . . . . 35 DEATH OF THE HIRED MAN   14
YOU'RE NOT MUCH FURTHERER THAN WHERE KIKE LEFT YOU. . . . 47 A HUNDRED COLLARS . . 70
"EVERYTHING'S AS SHE LEFT IT WHEN SHE DIED. . . . . 55 THE BLACK COTTAGE . . 15
THEN THE TWO SONS, TILL SHE WAS LEFT ALONE. . . . . 56 THE BLACK COTTAGE . . 39
OR GRASS-BLADE IS LEFT, NOT TO MENTION A STICK, ... 59 BLUEBERRIES 19
'I HAVE LEFT THOSE THERE BERRIES, I SHREWDLY SUSPECT, . . 60 BLUEBERRIES 45
THERE'S NOTHING BUT A VOICE-LIKE LEFT INSIDE . . . . . . 63 A SERVANT TO SERVANTS 13
MURDERED HIM AS LEFT OUT HIS MIDDLE NAME. . . . . 71 THE CODE 70
'I LEFT HIM IN THE BARN UNDER THE HAY. . . . . 72 THE CODE 84
THAT NOW NOT ALL THE HOUSES LEFT IN TOWN . . . . 73 THE GENERATIONS OF MEN 11
LEFT HERE WITH NOTHING BUT THE FURNITURE. . . . . 82 THE HOUSEKEEPER . . 44
SNATCHED RIGHT AND LEFT ACROSS THE SILVER PULLEYS. . . . 94 THE SELF-SEEKER . . . 39
IF I HAD CHOSEN LEFT. HOLD OUT THE LEFT. . . . . 97 THE SELF-SEEKER . . . 114
"OF COURSE YOU DID. YOU LEFT THE REST FOR SEED, ... 97 THE SELF-SEEKER . . . 124
AND LEFT AT LAST THE COUNTRY TO THE COUNTRY; . . . . . . 105 CHRISTMAS TREES . . . 2
TO LOOK FOR SOMETHING IT HAD LEFT BEHIND . . . . 106 CHRISTMAS TREES . . . 10
AND LEFT DEFENSELESS TO THE HEAT AND LIGHT. . . . . 109 THE EXPOSED NEST . . 16
OF SUCH A LITTLE HOUSE. ONCE LEFT ALONE, ... 111 IN THE HOME STRETCH . 40
US OF OUR BARGAIN. BUT THEY LEFT US SO . . . . 114 IN THE HOME STRETCH . 124
I DOUBT IF THEY HAVE LEFT US MANY GRAPES. . . . . 117 IN THE HOME STRETCH . 193
ITS BED IS LEFT A FADED PAPER SHEET . . . . 119 HYLA BROOK 10
WHERE LOVE HAS LEFT A PRINTED TRACE . . . . 120 BOND AND FREE . . . 7
WHEN I SEE BIRCHES BEND TO LEFT AND RIGHT . . . . 121 BIRCHES 1
AND NOT ONE BUT HUNG LIMP, NOT ONE WAS LEFT . . . . 122 BIRCHES 31
AND SORRY I EVER LEFT THE ROAD I KNEW, ... 125 AN ENCOUNTER 7
BUT SHE ALWAYS RAN AWAY AND LEFT . . . . 134 A GIRL'S GARDEN . . 23
HE SAYS HE LEFT THE VILLAGE STORE AT NINE: . . . . 145 SNOW 5
YOU CAN'T HEAR WHETHER SHE HAS LEFT THE DOOR . . . . . . 154 SNOW 308
AT EASTON. WHAT HAS EASTON LEFT TO LAUGH AT, ... 165 NEW HAMPSHIRE . . . 206
WHEN I LEFT MASSACHUSETTS YEARS AGO . . . . 167 NEW HAMPSHIRE . . . 248
THAN THOSE I LEFT BEHIND. I THOUGHT THEY WEREN'T. . . . . 167 NEW HAMPSHIRE . . . 256
HE MIGHT HAVE LEFT IT LYING WHERE IT FELL. . . . . 173 A STAR IN A STONEBOAT 39
AND NOTHING BUT THE STUMP OF IT WAS LEFT . . . . 175 THE CENSUS-TAKER . . 20
NOTHING WAS LEFT TO DO THAT I COULD SEE . . . . 176 THE CENSUS-TAKER . . 54
TO GET SO WE HAD NO ONE LEFT TO LIVE WITH. . . . . 178 THE STAR-SPLITTER . . 46
BUT IT SEEMS LIKE SOME WORD SHE LEFT TO BID YOU . . . . . 180 MAPLE 21
ANC SWEPT OF LEATHERN LEAVES, BUT LEFT THE BARK . . . . . 184 MAPLE 141
WHO'D RUN AWAY WITH SOMEONE ELSE AND LEFT HIM; . . . . . 191 PAUL'S WIFE 9
SOMETHING HAD LEFT A BROAD BLACK STREAK OF GREASE . . . . 193 PAUL'S WIFE 69
AND LEFT STOOD UP ON END INSIDE THE TREE . . . . 194 PAUL'S WIFE 93
THE MINUTE IT WAS LEFT WITH ME ALONE, ... 197 WILD GRAPES 43
IT LEFT THE CELLAR FORTY YEARS AGO . . . . 203 THE WITCH OF COOS . . 28
TOFFILE HAD GONE TO BED ALONE AND LEFT ME, ... 203 THE WITCH OF COOS . . 41
BUT LEFT AN OPEN DOOR TO COOL THE ROOM OFF . . . . 203 THE WITCH OF COOS . . 42
AND IF I'D LEFT HIM HITCHED UNBLANKETED . . . . 208 PAUPER WITCH OF GRAFTON 49
IN FRONT OF ONE TOWN HALL, I'D LEFT HIM HITCHED . . . . . 208 PAUPER WITCH OF GRAFTON 50
AND HIS CREW LEFT HIM WHERE HE FAILED, ... 212 AN EMPTY THREAT . . . 46
AND LEFT IT LYING WHERE IT FELL REJECTED. . . . . 217 A FOUNTAIN, A BOTTLE . 120
THEY LEFT THE STORM . . . . 218 I WILL SING YOU ONE-O 34
THEY LEFT THE NAMED . . . . 219 I WILL SING YOU ONE-O 44
NOTHING WILL BE LEFT WHITE BUT HERE A BIRCH, ... 226 THE ONSET 22
BUT SOMETHING HAS TO BE LEFT TO GOD. . . . . 228 GOOD-BY AND KEEP COLD 29
A BRUSH HAD LEFT A CROOKED STROKE . . . . 233 LOOKING FOR SUNSET BIRD 17
THE FIELDS HAD NOWHERE LEFT FOR THEM TO GO; . . . . 239 OUR SINGING STRENGTH . 26
NONE FLEW BEHIND ME TO BE LEFT ALONE. . . . . 240 OUR SINGING STRENGTH . 48
HAD IT BEEN THE WILL OF THE WIND, WAS LEFT . . . . 241 NEED OF BEING VERSED . 7
WORD I HAD NO ONE LEFT BUT GOD. . . . . 251 BEREFT 16
MEN LEFT HER A SHIP TO SINK: . . . . 260 SAND DUNES 13
BECAUSE HE LEFT IT IN THE LURCH, ... 274 A LONE STRIKER . . . 59
NOTHING BUT FALLIBILITY WAS LEFT US, ... 279 THE WHITE-TAILED HORNET 69
AND NONE WAS LEFT TO PRATE . . . . 298 ON TAKING FROM THE TOP 17
APPLES OR SOMETHING FORGOTTEN AND LEFT, ... 305 UNHARVESTED 13
DECIDEDLY UPON THE LEFT. . . . . 325 TO A THINKER . . . 2
OH, SHOULD A CHILD BE LEFT UNWARNED . . . . 336 THE WIND AND THE RAIN 12
THAT HAVE NONE LEFT TO STAY. . . . . 337 THE WIND AND THE RAIN 48
HE LEFT HER TO HER THOUGHTS AWHILE . . . . 345 DISCOVERY OF MADEIRAS 49
BUT SAILED AND LEFT THEM IN THE END. . . . . 347 DISCOVERY OF MADEIRAS 113
AND WHEN HER LOVER WAS LEFT ALONE . . . . 347 DISCOVERY OF MADEIRAS 120
NO CHOICE IS LEFT A POET, YOU MIGHT ADD, ... 352 THE LESSON FOR TODAY . 61
WE LEFT OUR BOILING CAR . . . . 367 A SERIOUS STEP LIGHTLY 10
GET RID OF THAT AND THERE'D BE LEFT NO GREAT . . . . . . 371 THE LITERATE FARMER AND 110
IT BEST BE LEFT TO GREAT MEN OF HIS KIND . . . . 372 THE LITERATE FARMER AND 134
YET LEFT ME FREELY FACE TO FACE . . . . 380 AN UNSTAMPED LETTER IN 16
AND BRAIN IS ALL THAT'S LEFT OF MORTAL STUFF, ... 395 ETHEREALIZING . . . 6
THE SORROW OF HAVING BEEN LEFT BEHIND, ... 420 ONE MORE BREVITY . . 31
NOT A TRACE OF IT'S LEFT . . . . 449 THE BAD ISLAND--EASTER 59
FILLS ME WITH FEAR I'LL BE LEFT TO MY FATE: . . . . 454 HOW HARD TO KEEP FROM 18
IN HAVING LEFT THE MAP . . . . 464 MILKY WAY IS A COWPATH 3
LEFT TRIVIA BEHIND; . . . . 464 MILKY WAY IS A COWPATH 28
AND WHEN THAT LEFT ME TO SINK BACK REVERSED . . . . 468 IN A GLASS OF CIDER . 5
LOOK AT HOW FAR WE'VE LEFT THE CURRENT SCIENCE . . . . . 480 A MASQUE OF REASON . 194
WHEN LEFT TO GUESS FOREVER FOR THEMSELVES. . . . . 483 A MASQUE OF REASON . 276
SHE WAS LEFT OVER FROM THE BROOK FARM VENTURE. . . . . . 494 A MASQUE OF MERCY . 39
I LEFT LIGHT SHINING ON AN EMPTY STAGE . . . . 497 A MASQUE OF MERCY . 100
LEFTOVER
THEN TAKE SOME LEFTOVER WINTER . . . . 304 CLEAR AND COLDER . . 10
LEFT'S
NOW LEFT'S NO BIGGER THAN A HARNESS GALL. . . . . 378 DIRECTIVE 40
LEFT-UNWRITTEN
LEFT-UNWRITTEN LETTER . . . . 429 KITTY HAWK 20
LEG
WHAT MAKES YOU STAND THERE ON ONE LEG LIKE THAT? . . . . 47 A HUNDRED COLLARS . . 69
AND DOWN BY ONE SIDE WHERE IT LACKED A LEG. . . . . 175 THE CENSUS-TAKER . . 37
THROWING A LEG UP OVER OUR FENCE OF MOUNTAINS, ... 176 THE STAR-SPLITTER . . 2
THE WAY A MAN WITH ONE LEG AND A CRUTCH, ... 204 THE WITCH OF COOS . . 52
HER GOLDEN LEG, HER CORAL COMB, ... 280 BLUE RIBBON AT AMESBURY 6
A LEG AKIMBO WITH WHICH HE CAN SING, ... 309 ONE GUESS 2

LEG (CONTINUED)
    WHEN PAST THE LEG I THRUST FOR BAR . . . . 419 ONE MORE BREVITY . . 8
LEGACY
    THE CONDEMNED WORLD THE LEGACY WAS MERITED. . . . . . . 370 THE LITERATE FARMER AND 56
LEGAL
    YOU, CRUMPLING FOLKS'S LEGAL DOCUMENTS. . . . . 99 THE SELF-SEEKER . . . 196
LEGGED (SEE CROSS-LEGGED)
LEGITIMATELY
    LEGITIMATELY. MY DEMAND UPON HER, ... 217 A FOUNTAIN, A BOTTLE . 136
LEGITIMIZE
    LEGITIMIZE THE BROTHERHOOD OF MAN, ... 498 A MASQUE OF MERCY . . 124
LEGS
    ALL WIRY ARMS AND LEGS THAT SPREAD OUT WAVY . . . . . . 70 THE CODE 34
    KEEP AT THEIR HEELS AND THREATEN TO MOW THEIR LEGS OFF. . . 71 THE CODE 46
    ALL WE CAN HOLD TOGETHER BY THE LEGS. . . . . 85 THE HOUSEKEEPER . . 128
    "HE THINKS I'LL HOBBLE. IT'S BOTH LEGS AND FEET." . . . 93 THE SELF-SEEKER . . 16
    BUT MY LEGS GOT THEIR KNOCKS AGAINST THE CEILING." . . . 93 THE SELF-SEEKER . . 29
    DANGLING THEIR LEGS AND FISHING OFF A WHARF . . . . . 161 NEW HAMPSHIRE . . 75
    WE SPREAD OUR TWO LEGS AS WE SPREAD ITS THREE, ... 179 THE STAR-SPLITTER . . 83
    HAVING A WHEEL AND FOUR LEGS OF ITS OWN . . . . . . 188 THE GRINDSTONE . . 1
    AND SOME OF IT ON NO MORE LEGS AND WHEEL . . . . . . 189 THE GRINDSTONE . . 12
    AND KICK WITH TWO LEGS LIKE AN ARMY MULE. . . . . . 202 THE WITCH OF COOS . 10
    THAT MADE HIM THROW HIS BARE LEGS OUT OF BED . . . . . 205 THE WITCH OF COOS . 102
    IT WRAPS A WISP OF SEAWEED ROUND MY LEGS, ... 391 ON BEING IDOLIZED . 2
    THEN WHEN THE ARMS AND LEGS HAVE ATROPHIED, ... 395 ETHEREALIZING . . 5
    WERE LOOSE ALL ROUND THEIR LEGS--YOU COULDN'T SAY . . . 404 FROM PLANE TO PLANE . 16
    MEN'S LEGS AND BODIES IN THE GALE . . . . 452 A-WISHING WELL . . 52
LEIF
    THE WAY THEY GREW ROUND LEIF THE LUCKY'S GERMAN; . . . 197 WILD GRAPES . . . 27
LEISURE
    HIS NEW JOB GAVE HIM LEISURE FOR STARGAZING. . . . . 178 THE STAR-SPLITTER . 75
    AND STANDING AT OUR LEISURE TILL THE DAY BROKE, . . . 179 THE STAR-SPLITTER . 85
LEN
    THE COTTAGES LEN BUILT, SOMETIMES WE RENT THEM, . . . 64 A SERVANT TO SERVANTS . 41
    BUT I DON'T COUNT ON IT AS MUCH AS LEN. . . . . 64 A SERVANT TO SERVANTS . 44
    LEN SAYS ONE STEADY PULL MORE OUGHT TO DO IT. . . . 64 A SERVANT TO SERVANTS . 55
    IT'S NOT THAT LEN DON'T WANT THE BEST FOR ME. . . . 64 A SERVANT TO SERVANTS . 60
    BUT LEN WENT AT IT TO MAKE UP THE LOSS. . . . . 64 A SERVANT TO SERVANTS . 65
    BUT WORK AIN'T ALL. LEN UNDERTAKES TOO MUCH. . . . 64 A SERVANT TO SERVANTS . 70
    MIND YOU, I WAITED TILL LEN SAID THE WORD. . . . . 67 A SERVANT TO SERVANTS . 149
    UNLESS LEN TOOK THE NOTION, WHICH HE WON'T, ... 67 A SERVANT TO SERVANTS . 157
LENDING
    IT'S NOTHING BUT THE LENDING LIBRARY. . . . . . . 507 A MASQUE OF MERCY . 351
LENGTH (SEE FULL-LENGTH, STOVE-LENGTH)
    HOW THE COLD CREEPS AS THE FIRE DIES AT LENGTH-- . . . 10 STORM FEAR 12
    HE MADE AS IF TO HOLD IT AT ARM'S LENGTH . . . . . 55 THE BLACK COTTAGE . 9
    GRASS ITS FULL LENGTH, OLD SILVER GOLDENROD, ... 131 THE BONFIRE . . . 62
    NOW YOU AND I WOULD GO TO NO SUCH LENGTH. . . . . 149 SNOW 187
    HAD BEAUTIES HE HAD TO POINT ME OUT AT LENGTH . . . . 187 THE AX-HELVE . . . 67
    BY SHRINKING THE RAWHIDE TO NATURAL LENGTH.. . . . . 192 PAUL'S WIFE . . . 48
    ON THE NEW WOOD THE WHOLE LENGTH OF THE LOG . . . . 193 PAUL'S WIFE . . . 70
    A SLENDER LENGTH OF PITH, OR WAS IT PITH? . . . . 194 PAUL'S WIFE . . . 91
    TO ALL MY LENGTH. . . . . 227 TO EARTHWARD . . . 32
    AND IMPULSE, HAVING DIPPED A FINGER LENGTH . . . . . 231 A BROOK IN THE CITY . 6
    THEY SAFELY GREW IN SLENDER LENGTH. . . . . . . 273 A LONE STRIKER . . 23
    HAPPINESS MAKES UP IN HEIGHT FOR WHAT IT LACKS IN LENGTH . 333 HAPPINESS MAKES UP . T
    WELL, WHEN AT LENGTH THE FEVER STRUCK. . . . . . 345 DISCOVERY OF MADEIRAS . 57
    WITH A LENGTH OF CORDAGE ABOUT THE WAIST. . . . . . 346 DISCOVERY OF MADEIRAS . 77
LENGTHENED
    THE SWINGING LANTERN LENGTHENED TO THE GROUND, ... 92 THE FEAR 92
LENGTHS
    (STATED IN LENGTHS OF HIM IT MIGHT NOT BE.) . . . . 198 WILD GRAPES . . . 77
    AND TO FORGET THE ANCIENT LENGTHS OF TIME, ... 351 THE LESSON FOR TODAY . 17
LENIENCE
    THAT USHERED IN THIS MODERN LENIENCE, ... 505 A MASQUE OF MERCY . 318
LENS
    WORDS ARE NO GOOD: TO SAY IT WAS A LENS . . . . . 293 AT WOODWARD'S GARDENS . 5
LENSES
    OF YAWNING LENSES. . . . . 219 I WILL SING YOU ONE-O . 54
LENT
    NOT ALL THE MOTION, THOUGH, THEY EVER LENT, ... 188 THE GRINDSTONE . . 5
    AND EARS ARE LENT TO ANY SOPHISTRY . . . . . . 488 A MASQUE OF REASON . 409
LEO
    AS LEO, ORION, AND THE PLEIADES. . . . . 234 EVENING A SUGAR ORCHARD 16
LEONID
    TO SEE THE STAR SHOWER KNOWN AS LEONID . . . . . . 360 A LOOSE MOUNTAIN . . 2
LESLEY
    TO TELL LESLEY (WILL YOU?) . . . . 135 LAST WORD OF A BLUEBIRD 6
    AS LESLEY, CAROL, IRMA, MARJORIE, ... 181 MAPLE 46
LESS
    SUCH PIPES KEPT LESS OF POWER TO STIR . . . . . 24 PAN WITH US . . . 22
    THE BIRDS HAVE LESS TO SAY FOR THEMSELVES . . . . 26 A LINE-STORM SONG . 9
    ALTHOUGH THEY ARE NO LESS THERE: . . . . . . 26 A LINE-STORM SONG . 12
    MAKE THE DAY SEEM TO US LESS BRIEF. . . . . . . 27 OCTOBER 9
    WAS IT EVER LESS THAN A TREASON . . . . . . 30 RELUCTANCE . . . 20
    AND LESS THAN THE TAN WITH WHICH PICKERS ARE TANNED." . . 60 BLUEBERRIES . . . 27
    A BEAD OF SILVER WATER MORE OR LESS, ... 77 THE GENERATIONS OF MEN 122
    I TOOK THE ONE LESS TRAVELED BY, ... 105 THE ROAD NOT TAKEN . 19
    AND EVERY CRASH MEANT ONE LESS TO RETURN . . . . . 112 IN THE HOME STRETCH . 57
    THE FIGURE OF OUR BEING LESS THAN TWO . . . . . 118 MEETING AND PASSING . 7
    LITTLE--LESS--NOTHING!--AND THAT ENDED IT. . . . . 137 "OUT, OUT--" . . . 32
    THEY THROW A FOREST DOWN LESS CUT THAN BROKEN. . . . 141 THE LINE-GANG . . 2
    AND FEEL IT LESS. HEAR THE SOFT BOMBS OF DUST . . . 150 SNOW 206
    IN NESTS. SHALL I BE COUNTED LESS THAN THEY ARE? . . . 151 SNOW 227
    AND THAT TALKS NO LESS FOR KNOWING, ... 156 THE SOUND OF TREES . 12
    I SHALL HAVE LESS TO SAY, ... 156 THE SOUND OF TREES . 24
    NO LESS THAN ENGLAND, FRANCE, AND ITALY. . . . . . 166 NEW HAMPSHIRE . . 245
    FILLED ME WITH NO LESS SORROW THAN THE HOUSES . . . . 176 THE CENSUS-TAKER . . 51

LESS (CONTINUED)
   MORE BLAMELESS IN THE SENSE OF BEING LESS . . . . . 177 THE STAR-SPLITTER . . 23
   LOOKS FOR HIMSELF, MORE OR LESS OUTWARDLY. . . . . . 182 MAPLE 71
   THE ATTIC WAS LESS TO US THAN THE CELLAR. . . . . . 206 THE WITCH OF COOS . . 123
   LESS CAREFULLY NURTURED, LESS FRUITFUL THAN THESE, . . 228 GOOD-BY AND KEEP COLD . 22
   LESS THAN THE CORALROOT, YOU KNOW, ... 247 ON GOING UNNOTICED . . 5
   SEEM TO THEM LESS THAN THEY ARE. . . . . 257 THE LOVELY BE CHOOSERS . 40
   I SHOULD FIND IT NO MORE NO LESS INTENSE. . . . . . 291 ON HEART'S BEGINNING TO 20
   WILL BE MORE LONELY ERE IT WILL BE LESS-- . . . . . 296 DESERT PLACES . . . 10
   WAS A SHADE LESS THE COLOR OF NIGHT, ... 299 WELCOME TO THEIR BELIEF 11
   IT VENTURED LESS IN PERIL THAN APPEARS. . . . . . . 302 A BIRD SINGING IN SLEEP 8
   IN LESS THAN NO TIME, TONGUE AND PEN, ... 326 TO A THINKER . . . 19
   AND SWAY WITH REASON MORE OR LESS. . . . . 326 TO A THINKER . . . 28
   IT LIVES LESS IN THE PRESENT . . . . 336 CARPE DIEM 20
   AND LESS IN BOTH TOGETHER . . . . 336 CARPE DIEM 22
   I WOULD PICK UP ALL OCEAN LESS ITS SALT, ... 337 THE WIND AND THE RAIN . 28
   I CANNOT TOUCH YOUR LIFE, MUCH LESS CAN SAVE, . . . 357 A MOTH SEEN IN WINTER . 23
   BUT BEDS--IN LESS THAN FIFTY YEARS HE'S SURE . . . 372 THE LITERATE FARMER AND 129
   (LESS BRAVE PERHAPS THAN TRUSTING ARE THE FAIR.) . . 375 A YOUNG BIRCH . . . 10
   AND MADE FEEL LESS ALONE THAN I RIGHTLY SHOULD, . . 383 WERE I IN TROUBLE . . 8
   WHERE WITH A GLEE NO LESS FOR BEING GRIM . . . . . 394 HAEC FABULA DOCET . . 15
   LESS PARTIAL WITNESSES THAN HE . . . . 418 AMERICA IS HARD TO SEE 62
   A CROOKED STRAIGHTNESS YET NO LESS A STRAIGHTNESS. . 421 ESCAPIST--NEVER . . . 5
   LESS CRITICISM OF THE FIELD AND COURT . . . . . . 424 FOR JOHN F. KENNEDY . 68
   MADE THEM NO LESS GAY, ... 431 KITTY HAWK 115
   NO, NOR LESS POLITE. . . . . 431 KITTY HAWK 116
   FROM OUR BRAINS NO LESS. . . . . 440 KITTY HAWK 386
   BUT THAT'S NOT LIKE ME. ON MUCH LESS . . . . . . 451 A-WISHING WELL . . . 20
   ONLY LESS HARD WAS IT FOR WASHINGTON. . . . . . . 454 HOW HARD TO KEEP FROM 25
   AT LESS THAN THE SPEED OF SOUND . . . . 466 SOME SCIENCE FICTION . 18
   IS ALMOST LESS THAN I CAN UNDERSTAND. . . . . . . 485 A MASQUE OF REASON . 333
LESSER
   ALL DAY FROM SPOOL TO LESSER SPOOL, ... 273 A LONE STRIKER . . . 21
   AS COMING FROM A LESSER OCEAN. . . . . 453 A-WISHING WELL . . . 68
   'TWAS SAID THE LESSER GODS WERE ONLY TRAITS . . . . 516 A MASQUE OF MERCY . 595
LESSON
   YOU SEE ANNE HAS HER LESSON LEARNED BY HEART." . . . 97 THE SELF-SEEKER . . . 122
   THE LESSON FOR TODAY . . . . 350 THE LESSON FOR TODAY . T
   O PALADINS, THE LESSON FOR TODAY . . . . 353 THE LESSON FOR TODAY . 87
   DICK SAID, "YOU'VE BEEN A LESSON IN WORK WISDOM . . 408 FROM PLANE TO PLANE . 122
   IF YOU HAVE LEARNED YOUR LESSON. DON'T BE BASHFUL. . 511 A MASQUE OF MERCY . 481
LESSONS
   I STRAIN AT LESSONS FIT TO START A SUTURE. . . . . 267 WHAT FIFTY SAID . . . 7
LEST
   MY SHARE AT LEAST, LEST I BE EMPTY-IDLE. . . . . . 324 BUILD SOIL . . . 262
   LEST MOVEMENT SHOULD PROVOKE . . . . 340 THE SUBVERTED FLOWER . 32
   LEST BOTH SHOULD BITE HIM IN THE TOGA-TOGS. . . . . 362 SYMPATHY WITH UNDER DOG 4
   LEST HAVING WASTED PRECIOUS HEAT . . . . 381 AN UNSTAMPED LETTER IN 23
   IS LEST HABIT-RIDDEN . . . . 441 KITTY HAWK 431
LET (SEE HANG-AND-LET-HANG)
   HER PLEASURE WILL NOT LET ME STAY. . . . . 7 MY NOVEMBER GUEST . . 6
   WITH, "LET US LOOK AT THE SKY, ... 7 LOVE AND A QUESTION . 10
   BEHIND LOW BOUGHS THE TREES LET DOWN OUTSIDE; . . . 16 A DREAM PANG . . . 10
   IF THE TREES MUST, LET THEM SILENTLY TOSS; . . . . 25 NOW CLOSE THE WINDOWS . 2
   IT SEEMED GOD LET THEE FLUTTER FROM HIS GENTLE CLASP, . 29 MY BUTTERFLY . . . 27
   THEN FEARFUL HE HAD LET THEE WIN . . . . 29 MY BUTTERFLY . . . 28
   AND LET THEM GO SCRAPING AND CREEPING . . . . . . 30 RELUCTANCE 10
   I LET MY NEIGHBOR KNOW BEYOND THE HILL; . . . . . 33 MENDING WALL . . . 12
   HE WOULDN'T LET ME PUT HIM ON THE LOUNGE. . . . . 39 DEATH OF THE HIRED MAN 149
   YOU KNOW THE KIND. THEN LET THE SUN SHINE ON IT!" . . 42 THE MOUNTAIN . . . 54
   I'LL ASK YOU LATER--DON'T LET ME FORGET IT." . . . 46 A HUNDRED COLLARS . . 48
   THEY'RE YOURS AND WELCOME; LET ME SEND THEM TO YOU.-- . 47 A HUNDRED COLLARS . . 68
   YOU CAN'T REST THAT WAY. LET ME PULL YOUR SHOES OFF." . 47 A HUNDRED COLLARS . . 76
   LIE DOWN--LET YOURSELF GO AND GET SOME SLEEP. . . . 50 A HUNDRED COLLARS . . 161
   "REALLY, FRIEND, I CAN'T LET YOU. YOU--MAY NEED THEM." . 50 A HUNDRED COLLARS . . 165
   SHE LET HIM LOOK, SURE THAT HE WOULDN'T SEE, . . . 51 HOME BURIAL . . . 15
   LET ME INTO YOUR GRIEF. I'M NOT SO MUCH . . . . . 53 HOME BURIAL . . . 59
   "YOU KNOW WHERE THEY CUT OFF THE WOODS--LET ME SEE-- . 59 BLUEBERRIES . . . 9
   HE SPOKE TO HIS WIFE IN THE DOOR, 'LET ME SEE, . . . 61 BLUEBERRIES . . . 76
   YOU LET THINGS MORE LIKE FEATHERS REGULATE . . . . 63 A SERVANT TO SERVANTS . 36
   I DON'T LEARN WHAT THEIR NAMES ARE, LET ALONE . . . 65 A SERVANT TO SERVANTS . 82
   AND LET THEM GO AND MAKE THEM TWANG, UNTIL . . . . 66 A SERVANT TO SERVANTS . 135
   IT MELTED, AND I LET IT FALL AND BREAK. . . . . . 68 AFTER APPLE-PICKING . 13
   CHERISH IN HAND, LIFT DOWN, AND NOT LET FALL. . . . 69 AFTER APPLE-PICKING . 31
   "DON'T LET IT BOTHER YOU. YOU'VE FOUND OUT SOMETHING. . 70 THE CODE 21
   SHOUTS LIKE AN ARMY CAPTAIN, 'LET HER COME!' . . . 71 THE CODE 63
   'DID YOU SAY, "LET HER COME"?' 'YES, LET HER COME.' . 71 THE CODE 66
   OR LET HIM KNOW THAT HE WAS BEING LOOKED AT. . . . 72 THE CODE 101
   "ON FATHER'S SIDE, IT SEEMS, WE'RE--LET ME SEE----" . 76 THE GENERATIONS OF MEN 78
   FIRST LET ME LOOK. I SEE RASPBERRY VINES----" . . . 76 THE GENERATIONS OF MEN 97
   "I LET YOU SAY THAT--ON CONSIDERATION." . . . . . 79 THE GENERATIONS OF MEN 154
   ANYTHING SHE MAY SAY. BUT LET ME WARN YOU, ... 79 THE GENERATIONS OF MEN 180
   I LET YOU SAY ALL THAT. BUT I MUST GO NOW." . . . 80 THE GENERATIONS OF MEN 202
   "YOU LET ME SAY IT? ON CONSIDERATION? . . . . . 80 THE GENERATIONS OF MEN 203
   I LET MYSELF IN AT THE KITCHEN DOOR. . . . . . . 81 THE HOUSEKEEPER . . . 1
   LET PEOPLE IN THAN I CAN KEEP THEM OUT. . . . . . 81 THE HOUSEKEEPER . . . 4
   WHAT I THINK HE WILL DO, IS LET THINGS SMASH. . . . 83 THE HOUSEKEEPER . . 51
   I NEVER SAW A MAN LET FAMILY TROUBLES . . . . . . 83 THE HOUSEKEEPER . . 53
   'TWAS WE LET HIM HAVE MONEY, NOT HE US. . . . . . 84 THE HOUSEKEEPER . . 101
   "SHE'S LET IT WORRY HER. YOU STOOD THE STRAIN, . . . 87 THE HOUSEKEEPER . . 171
   LET HIM GET OFF AND HE'LL BE EVERYWHERE . . . . . 90 THE FEAR 45
   AND I CAN'T STAND IT. JOEL, LET ME GO!" . . . . . 91 THE FEAR 48
   AND LET YOU SEE." / "YES, DO.--JOEL, GO BACK!" . . . 92 THE FEAR 75
   "WATCH FOR HIM, WILL YOU, WILL? YOU LET HIM IN. . . 94 THE SELF-SEEKER . . 52
   AND BRING HIM UP, AND DON'T LET MRS. CORBIN.-- . . 96 THE SELF-SEEKER . . 89
   ER, LET ME SEE. I THINK I'LL TAKE THE RIGHT. . . . 96 THE SELF-SEEKER . . 110
   I KNEW YOU WOULDN'T LET ME PICK THEM ALL." . . . . 97 THE SELF-SEEKER . . 120
   "YOU'LL FIND IT IS. LET YOUR FRIEND LOOK AT IT." . . 99 THE SELF-SEEKER . . 190

	PAGE	TITLE	LINE

LET (CONTINUED)

	PAGE	TITLE	LINE
I FORGOT HIM AND LET HIS LITTLE FEAR	101	THE WOOD-PILE	19
YOU LET ME LOOK THEM OVER." / "YOU COULD LOOK.	106	CHRISTMAS TREES	31
BUT DON'T EXPECT I'M GOING TO LET YOU HAVE THEM." . . .	106	CHRISTMAS TREES	32
TO LET HIM HAVE THEM. NEVER SHOW SURPRISE!	107	CHRISTMAS TREES	46
"GOOD BOYS THEY SEEMED, AND LET THEM LOVE THE CITY. . . .	114	IN THE HOME STRETCH	119
PERHAPS BECAUSE HE LET US GIVE INSTEAD	127	THE SMILE	6
AND SCARE OURSELVES. LET WILD FIRE LOOSE WE WILL----" .	130	THE BONFIRE	18
HE SAW ALL SPOILED. "DON'T LET HIM CUT MY HAND OFF-- .	137	"OUT,OUT--"	25
THE DOCTOR, WHEN HE COMES. DON'T LET HIM, SISTER!" . .	137	"OUT,OUT--"	26
HE NEVER LET THE LANTERN DROP.	138	BROWN'S DESCENT	29
FRED COLE, YOU'RE GOING TO LET HIM!" / "WELL, AREN'T YOU?	144	SNOW	43
AND THREE MILES MORE TO GO!" / "DON'T LET HIM GO. . . .	145	SNOW	62
LET THE MAN FREEZE AN EAR OR TWO, I SAY--	146	SNOW	102
IT WON'T LIE DOWN. THEN LET IT STAND. WHO CARES?" . .	148	SNOW	152
BUT LET ME RAISE THIS CURTAIN ON A SCENE, ...	148	SNOW	155
"LET THEM TALK, HELEN, AND PERHAPS HE'LL STAY." . . .	149	SNOW	171
AND LET YOU GET TO BED AGAIN. GOOD-NIGHT, ...	150	SNOW	211
"WHY DID I EVER LET HIM LEAVE THIS HOUSE!"	153	SNOW	280
DID SHE LET ON BY ANY WORD SHE SAID	153	SNOW	287
WHY DID YOU LET HIM GO?'" / "ASKED WHY WE LET HIM? . .	153	SNOW	291
YOU LET ME THERE. I'LL ASK HER WHY SHE LET HIM. . . .	153	SNOW	292
ITS MOTHER WOULDN'T LET IT CRY LIKE THAT, ...	154	SNOW	320
"FRED, I SHAN'T LET YOU THINK OF GOING OUT."	155	SNOW	326
HE SAYS SHE WENT TO LET HIM IN THE BARN.--	155	SNOW	331
WHERE SHOWERS OF CHARTED METEORS LET FLY.	173	A STAR IN A STONEBOAT	42
"THE PLACE IS DESERT, AND LET WHOSO LURKS	176	THE CENSUS-TAKER	57
LET HIM SAY WHY IT SHOULD NOT BE DECLARED SO." . . .	176	THE CENSUS-TAKER	60
TO LET HIM KNOW WE WEREN'T THE LEAST IMPOSED ON, . . .	177	THE STAR-SPLITTER	41
I HAVE TO LET THEM CALL ME WHAT THEY LIKE."	182	MAPLE	91
LET ALONE GROVE OF TREES FOR SUGAR ORCHARD.	183	MAPLE	103
THEN TOOK IT FROM ME--AND I LET HIM TAKE IT.	185	THE AX-HELVE	13
AND LET ENOUGH LIGHT INTO IT BY CUTTING	194	PAUL'S WIFE	89
AND THERE, WELL AFTER DARK, LET MURPHY TELL IT, . . .	195	PAUL'S WIFE	127
IN A SMALL NICHE LET INTO IT, THE GIRL	195	PAUL'S WIFE	134
AND LET OUT A LOUD YELL, AND THREW A BOTTLE, ...	195	PAUL'S WIFE	140
HOLD ON WITH ALL YOUR MIGHT WHEN I LET GO."	197	WILD GRAPES	40
TO LOUD CRIES FROM MY BROTHER OF "LET GO!	197	WILD GRAPES	46
DON'T YOU KNOW ANYTHING, YOU GIRL? LET GO!"	197	WILD GRAPES	47
AND STILL I CLUNG. I LET MY HEAD FALL BACK, ...	198	WILD GRAPES	73
I'LL BEND THE TREE DOWN AND LET YOU DOWN BY IT." . . .	198	WILD GRAPES	83
I HAD NOT LEARNED TO LET GO WITH THE HANDS, ...	199	WILD GRAPES	96
TO WISH IN VAIN TO LET GO WITH THE MIND--	199	WILD GRAPES	101
THAT I NEED LEARN TO LET GO WITH THE HEART.	199	WILD GRAPES	103
RATHER THAN TIP A TABLE FOR YOU, LET ME	202	THE WITCH OF COÖS	12
WE'LL NEVER LET THEM, WILL WE, SON? WE'LL NEVER! . . .	203	THE WITCH OF COÖS	27
IF THE BONES LIKED THE ATTIC, LET THEM HAVE IT. . . .	206	THE WITCH OF COÖS	124
LET THEM STAY IN THE ATTIC. WHEN THEY SOMETIMES . . .	206	THE WITCH OF COÖS	125
LET THEM STAY IN THE ATTIC SINCE THEY WENT THERE. . . .	206	THE WITCH OF COÖS	132
TO LET ON HE WAS PLAGUED TO DEATH WITH ME:	210	PAUPER WITCH OF GRAFTON	84
OLD AS I AM, I'M GOING TO LET MYSELF	214	A FOUNTAIN, A BOTTLE	29
SO THERE THEY LET THEIR LIVES BE NARROWED IN	240	OUR SINGING STRENGTH	31
LET THEM THINK TWICE BEFORE THEY USE THEIR POWERS . . .	245	SPRING POOLS	9
NOW LET THE NIGHT BE DARK FOR ALL OF ME.	249	ACCEPTANCE	12
LET THE NIGHT BE TOO DARK FOR ME TO SEE	249	ACCEPTANCE	13
INTO THE FUTURE. LET WHAT WILL BE, BE."	249	ACCEPTANCE	14
BUT LET THERE NEVER BE CURTAIN DRAWN	251	TREE AT MY WINDOW	3
BEHIND NEW BARRIER WALLS (AND LET IT CHAFE!), ...	254	THE FLOOD	3
WE CHOOSE TO SAY IT IS LET LOOSE BY THE DEVIL; . . .	254	THE FLOOD	5
THEN LET THEM CHOOSE!"	256	THE LOVELY BE CHOOSERS	8
"THEN WE SHALL LET HER CHOOSE?"	256	THE LOVELY BE CHOOSERS	9
"YES, LET HER CHOOSE.	256	THE LOVELY BE CHOOSERS	10
THE VOICE ASKED, "YOU CAN LET HER CHOOSE?"	256	THE LOVELY BE CHOOSERS	19
"YES, WE CAN LET HER AND STILL TRIUMPH."	256	THE LOVELY BE CHOOSERS	20
TO LET US KNOW IT HEARS ME." / "WHY, MY DEAR, . . .	258	WEST-RUNNING BROOK	17
LET IT BE OVERWHELMING, OFF A ROOF	265	DUST IN THE EYES	4
AND LET THE OTHER GO ON A WAY.	275	TWO TRAMPS IN MUD TIME	6
LET HIM LIGHT ON YOUR SKIN UNLESS YOU MIND	278	THE WHITE-TAILED HORNET	28
THE LAST TO LET NIGHT DRIVE HER OFF.	280	BLUE RIBBON AT AMESBURY	16
LET THE DOWNPOUR ROIL AND TOIL!	285	IN TIME OF CLOUDBURST	22
WHEN ONE WILL SAY, "LET US PUT IT OUT."	291	ON HEART'S BEGINNING TO	22
BUT LET HIM SHOW THEM HOW THE WEAPON WORKED.	293	AT WOODWARD'S GARDENS	7
LET'S LET MY HEAVENLY LOSTNESS OVERWHELM ME."	296	LOST IN HEAVEN	12
FIRST YOU LET THE SUMMER SIMMER, ...	303	CLEAR AND COLDER	4
LET CHAOS STORM!	308	PERTINAX	1
LET CLOUD SHAPES SWARM!	308	PERTINAX	2
BUT DIDN'T LET GO OF THE KING.	310	THE VINDICTIVES	9
LET THEM DIE OF UNSATISFIED GREED, ...	313	THE VINDICTIVES	85
LET THEIR TRAPPINGS BE TAKEN AWAY.	313	THE VINDICTIVES	89
LET THEM SUFFER STARVATION AND DIE	313	THE VINDICTIVES	90
LET NEWSPAPERS PROFESS TO FEAR THE WORST!	318	BUILD SOIL	65
THAT WHEN LET LOOSE UPON THE GRAZING WORLD	319	BUILD SOIL	109
WHAT SHOULD YOU DO? / I'D LET THINGS TAKE THEIR COURSE .	320	BUILD SOIL	128
DON'T LET THE THINGS I SAY AGAINST MYSELF	320	BUILD SOIL	131
DON'T LET ME SEEM TO SAY THE EXCHANGE, THE ENCOUNTER, .	321	BUILD SOIL	157
TO SELL THE HAY OFF, LET ALONE THE SOIL, ...	321	BUILD SOIL	179
LET ME PREACH TO YOU, WILL YOU, MELIBOEUS?	322	BUILD SOIL	182
LET THOSE POSSESS THE LAND, AND ONLY THOSE, ...	322	BUILD SOIL	187
LET NONE ASSUME TO TILL THE LAND BUT FARMERS. . . .	322	BUILD SOIL	209
TO THINK IT OUT. COME CLOSE, LET US CONSPIRE-- . . .	323	BUILD SOIL	228
LET ME BE THE ONE	324	BUILD SOIL	260
DON'T LET IT BOTHER YOU TOO MUCH	326	TO A THINKER	22
AND LET IT DRIVE ME DEATHWARD TOO.	336	THE WIND AND THE RAIN	6
TO LET THE HALF OF LIFE ALONE	336	THE WIND AND THE RAIN	16
FOR ALL THE CREW WERE LET TO KNOW.	344	DISCOVERY OF MADEIRAS	34
AND LET THE CAPTAIN TELL HIM A TALE.	345	DISCOVERY OF MADEIRAS	51
AND LET US TRY AN UNTOSSED PLACE	347	DISCOVERY OF MADEIRAS	108
IF PART THEY DO. LET ME PROPOSE A START.	352	THE LESSON FOR TODAY	65

LET (CONTINUED)
    I LET IT LIE THERE TILL I HOPE IT SLEPT. . . . . 358 A CONSIDERABLE SPECK . 29
    THE ROAD THERE, IF YOU'LL LET A GUIDE DIRECT YOU . . . . 377 DIRECTIVE 8
    AND SO TO LET PIKE SEEM TO HAVE THE PALM . . . . 408 FROM PLANE TO PLANE   . 120
    THE THANKS AND LET HIM CATCH IT AS A SCAPEGOAT. . . . . 408 FROM PLANE TO PLANE   . 140
    LET THEM GET WELL-WINED . . . . 413 AWAY! 7
    LET US PRETEND THE DEWDROPS FROM THE EAVES . . . . . . 415 A CABIN IN THE CLEARING 37
    BUT LET HIM SHOW HIS HAUGHTY STERN . . . . 419 AMERICA IS HARD TO SEE   75
    HE WAS AT THE DOOR TO BE LET OUT . . . . 420 ONE MORE BREVITY   . 45
    I'M TEMPTED TO LET GO RESTRAINT, ... 451 A-WISHING WELL . . . 15
    MOST OF THEM LET GO AND WERE GONE. . . . . 452 A-WISHING WELL . . . 54
    DON'T LET YOUR FATHER TELL YOU WHAT TO BE." . . . . . 454 HOW HARD TO KEEP FROM   36
    BUT LET ME INTO IT AND I WILL SPARE YOU. . . . . . . 457 HOW HARD TO KEEP FROM 116
    "DON'T LET HIM FOOL YOU: HE'S A KING ALREADY. . . . . 460 HOW HARD TO KEEP FROM 207
    SHE LET OUT A HOWL OF RAGE . . . . 463 LINES IN DEJECTION . 22
    AND LET GO AT THE AIR . . . . 464 MILKY WAY IS A COWPATH   7
    LET'S DO SO NOW. BECAUSE I LET YOU OFF . . . . . . 482 A MASQUE OF REASON . 238
    YET YOU DON'T SPEAK. LET FOOLS BEMUSE THEMSELVES . . 484 A MASQUE OF REASON . 298
    DON'T LET IT CARRY YOU AWAY. I HATE . . . . 489 A MASQUE OF REASON . 448
    LET HIM SEEK HIS RELIGION IN THE CHURCH. . . . . . 494 A MASQUE OF MERCY   . 32
    LET ME ALONE. / I'M SICK. JOE'S SICK. THE WORLD'S SICK. . 500 A MASQUE OF MERCY   . 167
    YOU LOCKED THE DOOR, BEL. LET ME HAVE THE KEY. . . . 500 A MASQUE OF MERCY   . 174
    AND LET HIM GET OFF WITHOUT PROPHESYING? . . . . . 502 A MASQUE OF MERCY   . 221
    HE WROTE ONE BOOK. LET THERE BE NO MORE WRITTEN. . . 504 A MASQUE OF MERCY   . 290
    PLEASE LET ME HAVE IT. / READ US WHAT IT SAYS. . . . 505 A MASQUE OF MERCY   . 294
    I SHRINK FROM BEING PUBLICLY LET DOWN. . . . . . . 505 A MASQUE OF MERCY   . 305
    LET ME REPEAT: I'M GLAD TO HEAR YOU SAY . . . . . 507 A MASQUE OF MERCY   . 360
    DON'T LET HIM MAKE YOU SEE TOO BRIGHT A GATE . . . 513 A MASQUE OF MERCY   . 536
    DON'T LET ME SCARE YOU. I WAS ONLY TEASING. . . . 514 A MASQUE OF MERCY   . 558
    LIVE AND LET LIVE, BELIEVE AND LET BELIEVE. . . . 516 A MASQUE OF MERCY   . 594
    AND LET THAT TELL YOU WHAT YOU THINK, LIKE THAT? . 519 A MASQUE OF MERCY   . 676
    LET THE LOST MILLIONS PRAY IT IN THE DARK! . . . 521 A MASQUE OF MERCY   . 726
LET-DOWN
    THROUGH LET-DOWN PASTURE BARS . . . . 465 MILKY WAY IS A COWPATH 30
LETHAL
    THEN IT'S NOT LETHAL--TO GET RID OF ME? . . . . . 516 A MASQUE OF MERCY   . 617
LETS
    AT LAST THE GATHERED SNOW LETS DOWN AS WHITE . . 226 THE ONSET 2
    GIVES UP HIS ERRAND, AND LETS DEATH DESCEND . . . 226 THE ONSET 8
    THE HILLSIDE ON THE DAY THE SUN LETS GO . . . . 237 A HILLSIDE THAW 2
    THEN LETS IT SNAP BACK UPRIGHT IN THE SKY. . . . 268 THE BEAR 4
    WHICH IS THE CREVICE THAT LETS PROGRESS IN. . . 458 HOW HARD TO KEEP FROM 153
    YOU KNOW WHAT LETS US OFF FROM BEING CAREFUL? . 505 A MASQUE OF MERCY   . 316
LET'S
    LET'S HAVE A SHOWDOWN AS AN EVIDENCE . . . . . 47 A HUNDRED COLLARS   . 85
    BUT FIRST--LET'S SEE--WHAT WAS I GOING TO ASK YOU? . 50 A HUNDRED COLLARS   . 162
    "IT'S RAINING." / "NO, IT'S MISTING; LET'S BE FAIR. . 75 THE GENERATIONS OF MEN 68
    THERE'S BUTTER SOMEWHERE, TOO." / "LET'S REND THE BREAD. . 115 IN THE HOME STRETCH . 145
    LET'S SEE YOU FIND YOUR LOAF. I'LL LIGHT THE FIRE. . . . 115 IN THE HOME STRETCH . 155
    "OH, LET'S GO UP THE HILL AND SCARE OURSELVES. . . . 129 THE BONFIRE 1
    OH, LET'S NOT WAIT FOR RAIN TO MAKE IT SAFE. . . . . 129 THE BONFIRE 5
    LET'S NOT CARE WHAT WE DO WITH IT TONIGHT. . . . . 129 THE BONFIRE 8
    THE WAY WE PILED IT. AND LET'S BE THE TALK . . . . 129 THE BONFIRE 10
    LET'S ALL BUT BRING TO LIFE THIS OLD VOLCANO, . . . 130 THE BONFIRE 16
    "WAIT AND HE MAY. LET'S SEE WHAT WE WILL DO. . . . 145 SNOW 76
    LET'S SEE IF HE WILL THINK OF HER AGAIN. . . . . . 145 SNOW 77
    WHY, I AGREE WITH YOU. BUT LET'S FORGIVE HIM. . . . 156 SNOW 348
    LET'S TRAP HIM WITH AN OPEN DOOR UP ATTIC." . . . . 206 THE WITCH OF COOS   . 113
    LET'S TALK ABOUT IT." / "LET'S GO SEE THE PLACE." . 213 A FOUNTAIN, A BOTTLE   . 16
    WE'VE SAID WE TWO. LET'S CHANGE THAT TO WE THREE. . 258 WEST-RUNNING BROOK . 11
    WHEN CAME SQUARE HALE WITH LET'S SEE WHAT WE HAD; . 283 THE GOLD HESPERIDEE . 10
    LET'S LET MY HEAVENLY LOSTNESS OVERWHELM ME." . . . 296 LOST IN HEAVEN . . . 12
    LET'S HAVE A LOOK AT ANOTHER FIVE. . . . . 310 IN DIVES' DIVE . . . 6
    FOR SWEEPING ME AWAY. LET'S SEE, WHERE WAS I? . . . 319 BUILD SOIL 91
    BUT FOR THE FOLLY OF IT, LET'S PRETEND . . . . . 352 THE LESSON FOR TODAY . 44
    LET'S CELEBRATE THE EVENT, MY DISTANT FRIEND, . . . 352 THE LESSON FOR TODAY . 47
    BUT LET'S GO ON TO WHERE OUR CASES PART, ... 352 THE LESSON FOR TODAY . 64
    AND GRATEFUL FOR IT (LET'S NOT BE FACETIOUS!) . . . 393 LUCRETIUS VERSUS POETS   4
    LET'S HOLLER AND ASK HIM IF HE WON'T PRESCRIBE . . 405 FROM PLANE TO PLANE   . 29
    "ALL RIGHT, LET'S HARMONIZE ABOUT THE DOCTOR. . . . 407 FROM PLANE TO PLANE   . 102
    LET'S LEAVE THAT TO THE SCIENTIFIC WITS. . . . . . 425 ACCIDENTALLY ON PURPOSE 18
    OR LET'S SAY THE CUP, ... 437 KITTY HAWK 303
    LET'S SEE WHERE WE ARE. . . . . 438 KITTY HAWK 339
    LET'S KEEP STARRING MAN . . . . 441 KITTY HAWK 414
    LET'S GET MY INCANTATION RIGHT: . . . . 451 A-WISHING WELL . . . 27
    "LET'S NOT GET SUPERSTITIOUS, SIRE," THE PRINCE SAID. . 454 HOW HARD TO KEEP FROM   28
    LET'S SEE, WHERE ARE WE? OH, WE'RE IN TRANSITION, . . . 462 HOW HARD TO KEEP FROM 254
    OH, LORD, LET'S NOT GO BACK TO ANYTHING. . . . . . 477 A MASQUE OF REASON . 115
    NO, LET'S NOT LIVE THINGS OVER. I DON'T CARE. . . . 477 A MASQUE OF REASON . 119
    LET'S DO SO NOW. BECAUSE I LET YOU OFF . . . . . 482 A MASQUE OF REASON . 238
    BUT I DON'T MIND. LET'S LEAVE IT AS IT STOOD. . . . 485 A MASQUE OF REASON . 334
    LET'S HAVE SOME PROPHECY. WHAT FORM OF RUIN . . . 502 A MASQUE OF MERCY   . 222
    BUT LET'S BE SERIOUS ABOUT PAUL'S OFFER. . . . . . 513 A MASQUE OF MERCY   . 519
    LET'S CHANGE THE SUBJECT, BOYS, I'M GETTING NERVOUS. . . 516 A MASQUE OF MERCY   . 598
LETT
    "WHY, LETT, STILL UP? LETT, I'M AT COLE'S. I'M LATE. . . . 143 SNOW 16
    I THOUGHT I WOULD.--I KNOW, BUT, LETT--I KNOW-- . . . . 143 SNOW 19
LETTER
    RIFLING A PRINTED LETTER AS HE TALKS. . . . . 44 A HUNDRED COLLARS   . . 10
    I HAD A LETTER FROM BURROUGHS--DID I TELL YOU?-- . . . 95 THE SELF-SEEKER . . 85
    A CHRISTMAS CIRCULAR LETTER . . . . 105 CHRISTMAS TREES . . 5
    TOO BAD I COULDN'T LAY ONE IN A LETTER. . . . . . . 107 CHRISTMAS TREES . . 58
    THE RURAL LETTER BOX SAID TOFFILE LAJWAY. . . . . . 207 THE WITCH OF COOS   . 155
    THEY SENT HIM BACK TO HER. THE LETTER CAME . . . . 230 NOT TO KEEP 1
    NO, IN YOUR RURAL LETTER BOX . . . . 380 AN UNSTAMPED LETTER IN   4
    AN UNSTAMPED LETTER IN OUR RURAL LETTER BOX . . . . 380 AN UNSTAMPED LETTER IN   T
    THE LETTER YOU WILL FIND ME SUBSCRIPT TO . . . . . 388 IOTA SUBSCRIPT . . . 6
    LEFT-UNWRITTEN LETTER . . . . 429 KITTY HAWK 20

LETTERED
    AND SPOKE OF THE LETTERED, ... 219 I WILL SING YOU ONE-O . 45
LETTERS
    HER GIFT FOR READING LETTERS LOCKED IN BOXES. . . . . 163 NEW HAMPSHIRE . . . 131
    THOUGH THEY DO SAY HE DOESN'T OPEN LETTERS. . . . . . 408 FROM PLANE TO PLANE . 145
LETTING
    I DON'T KNOW MUCH ABOUT THE LETTING DOWN; . . . . . 198 WILD GRAPES 84
    BY LETTING THE RAIN I KNEW OUTDOORS . . . . 253 THE THATCH 34
    WERE LETTING IN THE COLDER LIGHT. . . . . 336 THE WIND AND THE RAIN . 2
LETTUCE
    RADISHES, LETTUCE, PEAS, ... 134 A GIRL'S GARDEN . . . 30
LETUP
    IT GIVES A SENSE OF LETUP CALCULATED . . . . 475 A MASQUE OF REASON . 44
LETUP'S
    THE LETUP'S HEAVENLY. YOU PERHAPS WILL TELL US . . . . 474 A MASQUE OF REASON . 41
LEVEL
    TO SHOW THE LEVEL OF INTELLIGENCE . . . . 168 NEW HAMPSHIRE . . . 287
    WITH OUR ARMS AT THE LEVEL OF OUR KNEES, ... 205 THE WITCH OF COOS . . 106
    ONE LEVEL HIGHER THAN THE EARTH BELOW, ... 254 A WINTER EDEN . . . 6
    ONE LEVEL NEARER HEAVEN OVERHEAD, ... 254 A WINTER EDEN . . . 7
    HELD HIGH AT SO UNNATURAL A LEVEL. . . . . 255 THE FLOOD 8
    THROUGH LEVEL MOUNTAINS NOTHING TO THE EYE . . . . . 292 FIGURE IN THE DOORWAY . 2
    TO LAY THEM LEVEL WITH THE RUNNING WAVE, ... 334 I COULD GIVE ALL . . 3
    SO DIFFERENT FROM THE HARD AND LEVEL STARE . . . . . 356 TIME OUT 10
    TWO THOUSAND FEET ABOVE THE OCEAN LEVEL. . . . . . 400 TO THE RIGHT PERSON . 6
LEVELED
    BEFORE I CAME TO VIEW THE LEVELED SCENE. . . . . . . 22 THE TUFT OF FLOWERS . 4
LEVELS
    "SEVEN LEVELS OF THE WORLD." . . . . 256 THE LOVELY BE CHOOSERS 3
LEVIN
    THAN A BOLT OF LEVIN, ... 441 KITTY HAWK 409
LEVITY
    FOR KEEPER'S LEVITY: MY BROTHER'S KEEPER. . . . . . 494 A MASQUE OF MERCY . 36
LIABLE
    THE EARTH ITSELF IS LIABLE TO THE FATE . . . . . . 355 THE LESSON FOR TODAY . 147
LIAR
    OF JUDGING WHO IS A CONTEMPORARY LIAR-- . . . . . . 317 BUILD SOIL 38
LIBEL
    OF THE LAST FIFTY YEARS ARE ALL A LIBEL, ... 369 THE LITERATE FARMER AND 45
LIBERAL
    THAT SEEMED TOO PAGAN TO OUR LIBERAL YOUTH. . . . . . 58 THE BLACK COTTAGE . 95
    ONLY TOO LIBERAL OF OUR COMPLIMENT . . . . 279 THE WHITE-TAILED HORNET 54
    (BY ALL THAT'S LIBERAL--I SHOULD, I SHOULD) . . . . . 350 THE LESSON FOR TODAY . 10
    I'M LIBERAL. YOU, YOU ARISTOCRAT, ... 354 THE LESSON FOR TODAY . 120
    THAT LIBERAL, OR CONSERVATIVE, ... 450 OUR DOOM TO BLOOM . 11
LIBERALS
    "AS LIBERALS WE'RE WILLING TO GIVE PLACE . . . . . . 369 THE LITERATE FARMER AND 49
    GOOD LIBERALS WILL OBJECT MY NOTION . . . . 453 A-WISHING WELL . . . 69
LIBERTY
    OF LINCOLN, LAFAYETTE, AND LIBERTY? . . . . 169 NEW HAMPSHIRE . . . 324
    THE LACK OF LIBERTY, THE SQUEEZE OF LAW . . . . . . 460 HOW HARD TO KEEP FROM 199
LIBRARY
    ENOUGH TO STOCK A VILLAGE LIBRARY-- . . . . 216 A FOUNTAIN, A BOTTLE . 98
    IT'S NOTHING BUT THE LENDING LIBRARY. . . . . 507 A MASQUE OF MERCY . 351
LICENSE
    BUT HE GAVE NO ONE ELSE A LAUGHER'S LICENSE. . . . . 142 THE VANISHING RED . 4
    STAY UNASSUMING. IF FOR LACK OF LICENSE . . . . . . 385 THE FEAR OF GOD . . . 7
LICHENS
    NOW LICHENS ARE DUE TO HAVE THEIR TURN. . . . . . . 297 LEAVES COMPARED WITH . 12
LICKED
    THE NEXT COW MIGHT HAVE LICKED UP OUT AT PASTURE. . . . 184 MAPLE 151
    FLASHED OUT AND LICKED ALONG HIS UPPER TEETH. . . . . 204 THE WITCH OF COOS . . 73
LICKS
    IT TOTTERS WHEN SHE LICKS IT WITH HER TONGUE. . . . . 1 THE PASTURE 7
LID
    ON EVERY TREE A BUCKET WITH A LID, ... 234 EVENING A SUGAR ORCHARD 12
    ALL I SAW WAS THE LID . . . . 392 A WISH TO COMPLY . . 10
LIDS
    FOR PRYING BENEATH AND FORCING THE LIDS OF SIGHT, . . . 235 VALLEY'S SINGING DAY . 9
LIE
    AND THE DEAD LEAVES LIE HUDDLED AND STILL, ... 30 RELUCTANCE 13
    SIT DOWN OR LIE DOWN, FRIEND; YOU MAKE ME NERVOUS." . . 47 A HUNDRED COLLARS . 72
    AND I LIE BACK AND RIDE. I TAKE THE REINS . . . . . 49 A HUNDRED COLLARS . 138
    LIE DOWN--LET YOURSELF GO AND GET SOME SLEEP. . . . . 50 A HUNDRED COLLARS . 161
    HE'D TEAR TO PIECES, EVEN A BED TO LIE ON. . . . . . 66 A SERVANT TO SERVANTS . 118
    SHE HAD TO LIE AND HEAR LOVE THINGS MADE DREADFUL . . . 66 A SERVANT TO SERVANTS . 130
    WHEN BETWEEN WHIRLS OF SNOW NOT COME TO LIE . . . . 106 CHRISTMAS TREES . . . 3
    SHE RUNS FROM TREE TO TREE WHERE LIE AND SWEETEN . . . 125 THE COW IN APPLE TIME . 7
    IT WON'T LIE DOWN. THEN LET IT STAND. WHO CARES?" . . 148 SNOW 152
    IN MANY MARCHES. AND THEY LIE LIKE WEDGES, ... 164 NEW HAMPSHIRE . . . 178
    DON'T MAKE ME LIE WITH THOSE TWO OTHER WOMEN." . . . 199 PLACE FOR A THIRD . 11
    LABAN SAID, NO, HE WOULD NOT MAKE HER LIE . . . . 199 PLACE FOR A THIRD . 12
    OF WHERE ELIZA WANTED NOT TO LIE, ... 201 PLACE FOR A THIRD . 45
    TO BUY ELIZA A PLOT TO LIE ALONE IN: . . . . . . 202 PLACE FOR A THIRD . 80
    SON LOOKS SURPRISED TO SEE ME END A LIE . . . . . 207 THE WITCH OF COOS . 145
    BUT TONIGHT I DON'T CARE ENOUGH TO LIE-- . . . . . 207 THE WITCH OF COOS . 148
    AND LIE IN STONES AND BUSHES UNRETRIEVED. . . . . . 216 A FOUNTAIN, A BOTTLE . 116
    I THINK THEY WOULD BELIEVE THE LIE. . . . . . . 221 IN A DISUSED GRAVEYARD 16
    THEY LIE CLOSED OVER IN THE WIND AND CLING . . . . 225 BLUE-BUTTERFLY DAY . 7
    I WISH I COULD PROMISE TO LIE IN THE NIGHT . . . . 228 GOOD-BY AND KEEP COLD . 25
    NOR IS HE OVERJOYED WHEN THEY LIE LOW, ... 334 I COULD GIVE ALL . . 4
    I LET IT LIE THERE TILL I HOPE IT SLEPT. . . . . . 358 A CONSIDERABLE SPECK . 29
    I FARM A PASTURE WHERE THE BOULDERS LIE . . . . . 365 OF STONES OF THE PLACE 1
    WE CAN LIE ON THE BEACH WITH THE SEAWEED . . . . . 395 ETHEREALIZING . . . 7
    BUT NOW AS BLOBS OF BRAIN WE'LL LIE AND DREAM, . . . 395 ETHEREALIZING . . . 11
    AND GO LIE DOWN. . . . . 413 AWAY! 8
    HOW ABOUT THE LIE . . . . 430 KITTY HAWK 64
    THERE WAS SUCH A LIE . . . . 430 KITTY HAWK 67

LIE (CONTINUED)
    WHOSE CURE WILL LIE IN GETTING HER IDEA . . . . 499 A MASQUE OF MERCY . . 160
    WHERE YOU MUST LIE IN SELF-FORGETFULNESS . . . . 516 A MASQUE OF MERCY . . 613
    AND LAY HIM WHERE YOU ORDERED HIM TO LIE . . . . 521 A MASQUE OF MERCY . . 734
LIED
    FOR HAVING LIED BUT HAVING TOLD THE TRUTH. . . . . 457 HOW HARD TO KEEP FROM 114
LIES
    CUT SHORT OFF AT BOTH ENDS. IT LIES FIVE MILES . . . . . 63 A SERVANT TO SERVANTS . 21
    THAT YOU SHALL FIND LIES IN THE CELLAR, CHARRED . . . . 79 THE GENERATIONS OF MEN 161
    ONE OF THE LIES WOULD MAKE IT OUT THAT NOTHING . . . . . 147 SNOW 129
    HE IS THAT FALLEN LANCE THAT LIES AS HURLED, ... 261 A SOLDIER   1
    THAT LIES UNLIFTED NOW, COME DEW, COME RUST, ... 261 A SOLDIER   2
    BUT STILL LIES POINTED AS IT PLOWED THE DUST. . . . . . 261 A SOLDIER   3
    THE METAPHOR, THE SYMBOL LIES! . . . . 327 A MISSIVE MISSILE . . 35
    LIES IN A WINDROW, BRITTLE-DRY AND BLACK, ... 446 DOES NO ONE AT ALL EVER 26
    HIS WIFE LIES BY HIM LOOKING AT THE SKY. . . . . 473 A MASQUE OF REASON . .   3
    HOLD ON THERE. LEAVE THAT OPEN WHERE IT LIES. . . . . . 504 A MASQUE OF MERCY . . 292
    LIES IN OUR DIFFERENT APPROACH TO CHRIST, ... 513 A MASQUE OF MERCY . . 517
LIFE
    HAVING FIRST HEARD THE LIFE READ OUT . . . . 20 THE TRIAL BY EXISTENCE 34
    THE MEMORY THAT HE CHOSE THE LIFE; . . . . 21 THE TRIAL BY EXISTENCE 52
    'TIS OF THE ESSENCE OF LIFE HERE, ... 21 THE TRIAL BY EXISTENCE 65
    THAT LIFE HAS FOR US ON THE WRACK . . . . 21 THE TRIAL BY EXISTENCE 68
    AGAINST MY LIFE-- . . . . 29 MY BUTTERFLY 33
    YOU'VE WORKED AROUND THE FOOT OF ALL YOUR LIFE. . . . . . 43 THE MOUNTAIN 83
    "YOU'VE LIVED HERE ALL YOUR LIFE?" / "EVER SINCE HOR . 44 THE MOUNTAIN 105
    AND MAKING THE BEST OF THEIR WAY BACK TO LIFE . . . . . 54 HOME BURIAL 104
    MOST OF THE CHANGE WE THINK WE SEE IN LIFE . . . . . . 58 THE BLACK COTTAGE . . 109
    AND ACCOMMODATE HER YOUNG LIFE TO HIS. . . . . 66 A SERVANT TO SERVANTS . 128
    THE LIFE IS NOT YET ALL GONE OUT OF IT. . . . . 79 THE GENERATIONS OF MEN 165
    AND IT'S OUR LIFE." / "YES, WHEN IT'S NOT OUR DEATH." . 94 THE SELF-SEEKER . . . 46
    I JUST WANT TO GET SETTLED IN MY LIFE, ... 95 THE SELF-SEEKER . . . 76
    WHEN PEOPLE'RE GETTING ON IN LIFE. YOU'LL LIKE IT." . . 113 IN THE HOME STRETCH . 94
    THERE ARE ONLY MIDDLES." / "WHAT IS THIS?" / "THIS LIFE? 116 IN THE HOME STRETCH . 175
    AND LIFE IS TOO MUCH LIKE A PATHLESS WOOD . . . . 122 BIRCHES 44
    FROM STUMPS STILL BLEEDING THEIR LIFE AWAY. . . . . . . 123 PEA BRUSH   8
    LET'S ALL BUT BRING TO LIFE THIS OLD VOLCANO, ... 130 THE BONFIRE 16
    THE LIFE FROM SPILLING. THEN THE BOY SAW ALL-- . . . . 137 "OUT,OUT--" 22
    I TOLD HIM THIS IS A PLEASANT LIFE, ... 141 THE GUM-GATHERER . . 34
    THAT SORT OF MAN TALKS STRAIGHT-ON ALL HIS LIFE . . . . 145 SNOW 64
    AND SAVE HIS LIFE.--ALL RIGHT, COME IN, MESERVE. . . . . 147 SNOW 104
    OUR VERY LIFE DEPENDS ON EVERYTHING'S . . . . 147 SNOW 132
    WE'VE HAD A SHARE IN ONE NIGHT OF HIS LIFE. . . . . . . 156 SNOW 349
    AS LONG AS LIFE GOES SO UTTERRIBLY? . . . . 167 NEW HAMPSHIRE . . . 269
    THEN CAME IN DANCING, SKIPPING WITH HIS LIFE . . . . . . 170 NEW HAMPSHIRE . . . 349
    TO SUCH RESORTS OF LIFE AS MARS AND EARTH-- . . . . . . 174 A STAR IN A STONEBOAT . 48
    IT MUST BE I WANT LIFE TO GO ON LIVING. . . . . 176 THE CENSUS-TAKER . . 64
    ONE COMING THIS WAY INTO LIFE, AND ONE . . . . 180 MAPLE 12
    GOING THE OTHER OUT OF LIFE--YOU KNOW? . . . . 180 MAPLE 13
    THAT WHEN IT WOKE AND CAME TO LIFE AGAIN . . . . 181 MAPLE 38
    A NAME TO CARRY FOR LIFE AND NEVER KNOW . . . . 183 MAPLE 116
    MADE A GIRL'S MARRIAGE, AND RULED IN HER LIFE. . . . . . 185 MAPLE 164
    HARD IF, THOUGH CAST AWAY FOR LIFE WITH YANKEES, ... 186 THE AX-HELVE 44
    WHO GAVE HIS LIFE TO KEEP IT GOING ROUND? . . . . 190 THE GRINDSTONE . . . 47
    AND THE LIFE I LIVE NOW'S AN EXTRA LIFE . . . . 196 WILD GRAPES 14
    I HELD ON UNCOMPLAININGLY FOR LIFE. . . . . 197 WILD GRAPES 54
    THE WAY HE DID IN LIFE ONCE; BUT THIS TIME . . . . 204 THE WITCH OF COOS . . 76
    SHE WAS 'SHUT IN' FOR LIFE. SHE LIVED HER WHOLE . . . . 215 A FOUNTAIN, A BOTTLE . 84
    LIFE LONG IN BED, AND WROTE HER THINGS IN BED. . . . . . 215 A FOUNTAIN, A BOTTLE . 85
    HERE WERE ALL THOSE THE POETESS'S LIFE . . . . 217 A FOUNTAIN, A BOTTLE . 121
    I MIGHT NOT HAVE THE CHANCE I MISSED IN LIFE . . . . . . 222 TO E.T.   5
    MORE THAN IF LIFE HAD NEVER BEEN BEGUN. . . . . 226 THE ONSET 11
    OR GIVE SOME SIGN OF LIFE? BECAUSE YOU CAN'T. . . . . . 230 TWO LOOK AT TWO . . 33
    OF THE KNOWLEDGE BEYOND THE BOUNDS OF LIFE . . . . 236 MISGIVING 15
    KEEPING ITS LIFE SO CLOSE AND OUT OF SIGHT . . . . 248 THE COCOON   8
    SUCH WAS LIFE IN THE GOLDEN GATE: . . . . 249 A PECK OF GOLD . . .   9
    WORD I WAS IN MY LIFE ALONE, ... 251 BEREFT 15
    ITS LIFE OF HUNDREDS OF YEARS HAS ENDED . . . . 253 THE THATCH 33
    SHE FAILS FROM STRANGENESS TO A WAY OF LIFE . . . . . . 257 THE LOVELY BE CHOOSERS 44
    AND IT IS TIME, STRENGTH, TONE, LIGHT, LIFE, AND LOVE-- 259 WEST-RUNNING BROOK . 54
    OUR LIFE RUNS DOWN IN SENDING UP THE CLOCK. . . . . . . 259 WEST-RUNNING BROOK . 64
    THE BROOK RUNS DOWN IN SENDING UP OUR LIFE. . . . . . . 260 WEST-RUNNING BROOK . 65
    IS THE MULTIPLICATION TABLE OF LIFE." . . . . 263 THE TIMES TABLE . . 12
    OVER BACK WHERE THEY SPEAK OF LIFE AS STAYING . . . . . 263 THE INVESTMENT . . .   1
    BUT GET SOME COLOR AND MUSIC OUT OF LIFE? . . . . 264 THE INVESTMENT . . . 14
    AGAIN COME TO LIFE AND CRAWL OFF, ... 266 SITTING BY A BUSH . . 11
    WE MAY AS WELL GO PATIENTLY ON WITH OUR LIFE, ... 268 ON LOOKING UP BY CHANCE 8
    THE BLOWS THAT A LIFE OF SELF-CONTROL . . . . 275 TWO TRAMPS IN MUD TIME 13
    THE LIFE OF MUSCLES ROCKING SOFT . . . . 276 TWO TRAMPS IN MUD TIME 47
    AND GIVE US THE LIFE OF THE MOVING-PICTURES' PROMISE . . 286 A ROADSIDE STAND . . 21
    LIFE IS NOT SO SINISTER-GRAVE. . . . . 291 ON HEART'S BEGINNING TO 34
    SHE FEARS NOT HIM, THEY FEAR NOT LIFE. . . . . 291 ON HEART'S BEGINNING TO 37
    AND EXCHANGED TROUBLED GLANCES OVER LIFE. . . . . 293 AT WOODWARD'S GARDENS . 13
    LATE IN LIFE I HAVE COME ON FERN. . . . . 297 LEAVES COMPARED WITH . 11
    THAT LIFE IS ONLY LIFE FOREVERMORE . . . . 300 THE MASTER SPEED . . 13
    THE SPAN OF LIFE . . . . 308 THE SPAN OF LIFE . .   T
    OH, I DON'T BLAME YOU. I SAY LIFE EASY. . . . . 316 BUILD SOIL 19
    LIFE MAY BE TRAGICALLY BAD, AND I . . . . 317 BUILD SOIL 41
    BUT BID LIFE SEIZE THE PRESENT? . . . . 335 CARPE DIEM 19
    TO LET THE HALF OF LIFE ALONE . . . . 336 THE WIND AND THE RAIN 16
    HE WOULD CRY OUT ON LIFE, THAT WHAT IT WANTS . . . . . . 338 THE MOST OF IT . . .   6
    I CANNOT TOUCH YOUR LIFE, MUCH LESS CAN SAVE, ... 357 A MOTH SEEN IN WINTER . 23
    TO LIVE ITS LIFE OUT AS AN ORNAMENT. . . . . 375 A YOUNG BIRCH . . . 22
    WAS BUT THE STEEPLE ON OUR HOUSE OF LIFE . . . . 386 A STEEPLE ON THE HOUSE   2
    THAT MADE OUR HOUSE OF LIFE A HOUSE OF WORSHIP? . . . . 386 A STEEPLE ON THE HOUSE   3
    THE ART OF LIFE IS PASSING LOSSES ON. . . . . 399 THE INGENUITIES OF DEBT 5
    AND STARTED SHAPING MY LIFE TO HIS, ... 420 ONE MORE BREVITY . . 41
    HIS LIFE IS A PURSUIT OF A PURSUIT FOREVER. . . . . . . 421 ESCAPIST--NEVER . . . 10

LIFE (CONTINUED)
```
    GLORY IS OUT OF DATE IN LIFE AND ART. . . . . . . . . . 423 FOR JOHN F. KENNEDY  .  50
    THERE IS A CALL TO LIFE A LITTLE STERNER, . . . . . . . 424 FOR JOHN F. KENNEDY  .  66
    WAS WOMAN'S WAY OF LIFE. . . . . . . . . . . . . . . . . 464 MILKY WAY IS A COWPATH  16
    TO TAKE LIFE AT A WALK . . . . . . . . . . . . . . . . . 465 SOME SCIENCE FICTION .   7
    ESCAPE FROM SO GREAT PAINS OF LIFE ON EARTH . . . . . . 475 A MASQUE OF REASON  .  43
    YOUR COURAGE FAILED. THE SADDEST THING IN LIFE . . . . . 497 A MASQUE OF MERCY  . 106
LIFELESS
    AND LIFELESS FROM AN INTERRUPTED ARC. . . . . . . . . . 172 A STAR IN A STONEBOAT .  9
LIFELIKE
    IN EVERY LIFELIKE POSTURE OF THE SWARM, . . . . . . . . 237 A HILLSIDE THAW  .  .  27
LIFELONG
    TO SATISFY A LIFELONG CURIOSITY . . . . . . . . . . . . 168 NEW HAMPSHIRE  .  .  . 304
    TO SATISFY A LIFELONG CURIOSITY . . . . . . . . . . . . 177 THE STAR-SPLITTER  .  . 18
    WHOSE LIFELONG UNCONCERN . . . . . . . . . . . . . . . . 465 MILKY WAY IS A COWPATH  42
LIFE'S
    AND TENDERLY, LIFE'S LITTLE DREAM, . . . . . . . . . . .  20 THE TRIAL BY EXISTENCE  38
    A DECENT PRODUCT OF LIFE'S IRONING-OUT; . . . . . . . . 201 PLACE FOR A THIRD  .  . 67
    THAN LIFE'S VICTORIES OF DOUBT . . . . . . . . . . . . . 212 AN EMPTY THREAT  .  .  55
    TO MAKE IT WORTH LIFE'S WHILE TO WAKE AND SPORT. . . . . 254 A WINTER EDEN  .  .  .  20
LIFETIME
    ONE SUCH STORM IN A LIFETIME COULDN'T TEACH THEM . . . . 240 OUR SINGING STRENGTH .  46
    OR AT LEAST IN A LIFETIME, BY THAT METHOD." . . . . . . 405 FROM PLANE TO PLANE  .  47
LIFE-TRAIN
    MY LIFE-TRAIN LOGIC. I AGREE WITH YOU . . . . . . . . . 325 BUILD SOIL  .  .  .  . 290
LIFT
    WHERE A MYRIAD SNOWY QUARTZ-STONES LIFT, . . . . . . . .  26 A LINE-STORM SONG  .  .  3
    HE'S TRYING TO LIFT, STRAINING TO LIFT HIMSELF." . . . .  37 DEATH OF THE HIRED MAN  95
    THAN I CAN RAISE MY VOICE OR WANT TO LIFT . . . . . . .  63 A SERVANT TO SERVANTS .  8
    MY HAND (OH, I CAN LIFT IT WHEN I HAVE TO). . . . . . .  63 A SERVANT TO SERVANTS .  9
    CHERISH IN HAND, LIFT DOWN, AND NOT LET FALL. . . . . .  69 AFTER APPLE-PICKING  .  31
    AND LIFT THEMSELVES UP OFF THE GROUND. . . . . . . . . . 123 PEA BRUSH . . . . .  .  20
    FROM FOLLOWING WALLS I NEVER LIFT MY EYE, . . . . . . . 173 A STAR IN A STONEBOAT .  40
    I HAD TO STOP AND LIFT MY FACE; . . . . . . . . . . . . 233 LOOKING FOR SUNSET BIRD  6
    THE REQUISITE LIFT OF SPIRIT HAS NEVER BEEN FOUND, . . . 287 A ROADSIDE STAND  .  .  45
    HAD TO GIVE HER THE FINAL LIFT . . . . . . . . . . . . . 343 DISCOVERY OF MADEIRAS .  10
    AND IF I SAY WE LIFT HIM FROM THE FLOOR . . . . . . . . 521 A MASQUE OF MERCY  . 733
LIFTED
    AND I THOUGHT I HAD LOST YOU. I LIFTED A SHOUT . . . . .  62 BLUEBERRIES  .  .  .  .  93
    WITH AN EYE ALWAYS LIFTED TOWARD THE WEST . . . . . . .  69 THE CODE  .  .  .  .  .   3
    AND FROM THERE THOSE THAT LIFTED EYES COULD COUNT . . . 136 "OUT, OUT--"  .  .  .  .   4
    HE DODGED A LOG THAT LIFTED LIKE AN ARM . . . . . . . . 170 NEW HAMPSHIRE  .  .  . 347
    STANDING ALONE WITH SMOOTH ARMS LIFTED UP, . . . . . . . 184 MAPLE  .  .  .  .  . . 145
    OF ALDER CATCH MY LIFTED AX BEHIND ME. . . . . . . . . . 185 THE AX-HELVE  .  .  .  .  2
    MOSTLY AS MUCH BEYOND MY LIFTED HANDS, THOUGH, . . . . . 197 WILD GRAPES  .  .  .  .  28
    LIFTED THE RUG THAT BRED THEM ON THE FLOOR . . . . . . . 237 A HILLSIDE THAW  .  .  .  7
    VAGUE DREAM-HEAD LIFTED OUT OF THE GROUND, . . . . . . . 251 TREE AT MY WINDOW  .  .  5
    WITH LIFTED SNOUT AND EYES (IF ANY) SHUT . . . . . . . . 269 THE BEAR  .  .  .  .  .  27
    ALL SUMMER LONG THEY WERE OVERHEAD, MORE LIFTED UP THAN I. 297 A LEAF-TREADER  .  .  .  5
    IT LIFTED FROM ITS DEWY PEDIMENT . . . . . . . . . . . . 315 IRIS BY NIGHT  .  .  .  26
    BUT NEVER SO MUCH AS LIFTED CHIN. . . . . . . . . . . . 420 ONE MORE BREVITY  .  .  22
LIFTING
    TO LOOK AGAIN, AND STILL YOUR SPADE KEPT LIFTING. . . .  53 HOME BURIAL  .  .  .  .  80
    WHERE ON A MOW IT WOULD HAVE BEEN SLOW LIFTING. . . . .  71 THE CODE  .  .  .  .  .  58
    BY STRAIGHTENING OUT AND LIFTING A FOREFINGER, . . . . . 147 SNOW  .  .  .  .  . . 113
LIFTS
    AND LIFTS THEIR FACES BY THE CHIN TO HERS . . . . . . .  98 THE SELF-SEEKER  .  . 161
    IT LIFTS EXISTENCE ON A PLANE OF SNOW . . . . . . . . . 254 A WINTER EDEN  .  .  .   5
    IT LIFTS A GAUNT LUXURIATING BEAST . . . . . . . . . . . 254 A WINTER EDEN  .  .  .   9
    THE SYMBOL STAR IT LIFTS AGAINST YOUR CEILING . . . . . 350 TO A YOUNG WRETCH  .  .  23
    BUT LIFTS NO HIGHER THAN A GARDEN GROWS. . . . . . . . . 414 A CABIN IN THE CLEARING  17
    THAT FLICKERS MICA WINGS. HE LIFTS A HAND . . . . . . . 487 A MASQUE OF REASON  . 390
LIGHT   (SEE LANTERN-LIGHT)
    WITHOUT A WINDOW LIGHT. . . . . . . . . . . . . . . . .   7 LOVE AND A QUESTION  .   8
    AND WARM STOVE-WINDOW LIGHT. . . . . . . . . . . . . . .  11 WIND AND WINDOW FLOWER  24
    ACROSS THE REEDS TO A WINDOW LIGHT. . . . . . . . . . .  15 IN A VALE  .  .  .  .  .   5
    BEHIND LIGHT WORDS THAT TEASE AND FLOUT, . . . . . . . .  19 REVELATION  .  .  .  .   2
    THE LIGHT OF HEAVEN FALLS WHOLE AND WHITE . . . . . . .  19 THE TRIAL BY EXISTENCE   9
    THE LIGHT FOREVER IS MORNING LIGHT; . . . . . . . . . .  19 THE TRIAL BY EXISTENCE  11
    IT WAS JUST AS THE LIGHT WAS BEGINNING TO FAIL . . . . .  24 THE DEMIURGE'S LAUGH  .   4
    ITS LIGHT POURED SOFTLY IN HER LAP. SHE SAW IT . . . . .  38 DEATH OF THE HIRED MAN 105
    HE DREW THE OXEN TOWARD HIM WITH LIGHT TOUCHES . . . . .  44 THE MOUNTAIN  .  .  . 107
    HE SAT THERE CREASED AND SHINING IN THE LIGHT, . . . . .  46 A HUNDRED COLLARS  .  .  51
    I'LL PUT THE LIGHT OUT. DON'T YOU WAIT FOR ME: . . . . .  50 A HUNDRED COLLARS  .  . 171
    SHE SAID, "AS THE LIGHT ON THE DASHBOARD RAN . . . . . .  89 THE FEAR  .  .  .  .  .  10
    BUT YOU GIVE HIM THE ADVANTAGE WITH THIS LIGHT. . . . .  91 THE FEAR  .  .  .  .  .  55
    SHE STRETCHED UP TALL TO OVERLOOK THE LIGHT. . . . . . .  91 THE FEAR  .  .  .  .  .  62
    A LIGHT HE WAS TO NO ONE BUT HIMSELF . . . . . . . . . . 108 OLD MAN'S WINTER NIGHT  15
    A QUIET LIGHT, AND THEN NOT EVEN THAT. . . . . . . . . . 108 OLD MAN'S WINTER NIGHT  17
    AND LEFT DEFENSELESS TO THE HEAT AND LIGHT. . . . . . . 109 THE EXPOSED NEST  .  .  16
    TO EVERYTHING. HER LIGHT WON'T LAST US LONG. . . . . . . 113 IN THE HOME STRETCH  .  71
    WHATEVER ELSE WE WANT FOR. AND A LIGHT. . . . . . . . . 113 IN THE HOME STRETCH  .  79
    SO MUCH TOO LIGHT AND AIRY FOR THEIR STRENGTH . . . . . 113 IN THE HOME STRETCH  .  87
    I'LL LIGHT THE FIRE FOR COMPANY FOR YOU; . . . . . . . . 115 IN THE HOME STRETCH  . 146
    LET'S SEE YOU FIND YOUR LOAF. I'LL LIGHT THE FIRE. . . . 115 IN THE HOME STRETCH  . 155
    I HAVE TO MAKE YOU BUILD IT. COME, THE LIGHT." . . . . . 117 IN THE HOME STRETCH  . 200
    SUDDEN AND SWIFT AND LIGHT AS THAT . . . . . . . . . . . 129 THE IMPULSE  .  .  .  .  25
    OF PEOPLE BROUGHT TO WINDOWS BY A LIGHT . . . . . . . . 129 THE BONFIRE  .  .  .  .  11
    I WALKED SO LIGHT ON AIR IN HEAVY SHOES . . . . . . . . 132 THE BONFIRE  .  .  .  .  92
    AND CUT THEM OFF FROM WINDOW LIGHT. . . . . . . . . . . 135 LOCKED OUT  .  .  .  .   3
    AS IT RAN LIGHT, OR HAD TO BEAR A LOAD. . . . . . . . . 136 "OUT, OUT--"  .  .  .  .   8
    (BUT SAVED THE LIGHT FROM GOING OUT). . . . . . . . . . 138 BROWN'S DESCENT  .  .  .  39
    QUIET AND LIGHT AND WARM, IN SPITE OF ALL . . . . . . . 148 SNOW  .  .  .  .  . . 143
    THICK HAND MADE LIGHT OF, STEEL-BLUE CHIN DRAWN DOWN . . 188 THE AX-HELVE  .  .  .  99
    AND LET ENOUGH LIGHT INTO IT BY CUTTING . . . . . . . . 194 PAUL'S WIFE  .  .  .  .  89
    PAUL DARKLY, LIKE HER SHADOW. ALL THE LIGHT . . . . . . 195 PAUL'S WIFE  .  .  .  . 136
    BUT THE SHOUT REACHED THE GIRL AND PUT HER LIGHT OUT. . 195 PAUL'S WIFE  .  .  .  . 143
    I PUSHED MYSELF UPSTAIRS, AND IN THE LIGHT . . . . . . . 205 THE WITCH OF COOS  .  .  97
```

PAGE TITLE   LINE

LIGHT (CONTINUED)
I WANTED TO PUT OUT THE LIGHT AND SEE . . . . 205 THE WITCH OF COOS . . 104
HAD SPILLED THEM NEAR THE WINDOW, TOWARD THE LIGHT, . . . 216 A FOUNTAIN, A BOTTLE . 96
(THOUGH NOT YET LIGHT) . . . . 218 I WILL SING YOU ONE-O . 7
ALWAYS WRONG TO THE LIGHT, SO NEVER SEEING . . . . . 225 FOR ONCE SOMETHING . . 2
WHEN SLOWLY (AND NOBODY COMES WITH A LIGHT) . . . . . 228 GOOD-BY AND KEEP COLD . 27
ARE LIGHT AS BALLOONS. . . . . 234 GATHERING LEAVES . . . 4
AND THE LIGHT BREAKING ON THEM MADE THEM RUN. . . . . 237 A HILLSIDE THAW . . . 8
I BLEW OUT THE LIGHT, ... 240 THE LOCKLESS DOOR . . 5
ENGAGED UP THERE WITH THE LIGHT AND BREEZE? . . . . . 247 ON GOING UNNOTICED . . 4
SO CLOSE IT WILL NOT LIGHT AN EARLY LIGHT, ... 248 THE COCOON 7
BEFORE GOD'S LAST PUT OUT THE LIGHT WAS SPOKEN. . . . . 250 ONCE BY THE PACIFIC . 14
NOT ALL YOUR LIGHT TONGUES TALKING ALOUD . . . . . . 252 TREE AT MY WINDOW . . 7
OF A CERTAIN UPPER-WINDOW LIGHT. . . . . 253 THE THATCH 4
THE LIGHT WAS WHAT IT WAS ALL ABOUT: . . . . 253 THE THATCH 5
I WOULD NOT GO IN TILL THE LIGHT WENT OUT; . . . . . 253 THE THATCH 6
I HAVE OUTWALKED THE FURTHEST CITY LIGHT. . . . . . . 255 ACQUAINTED WITH NIGHT . 3
AND IT IS TIME, STRENGTH, TONE, LIGHT, LIFE, AND LOVE-- . 259 WEST-RUNNING BROOK . . 54
LET HIM LIGHT ON YOUR SKIN UNLESS YOU MIND . . . . . 278 THE WHITE-TAILED HORNET 28
NEXT MORNING TO THE LIGHT OF DAY WAS MORE . . . . . . 290 OLD BARN AT THE BOTTOM 26
THE EARTH HAD A SINGLE LIGHT AFAR, ... 291 ON HEART'S BEGINNING TO 6
A FLICKERING, HUMAN PATHETIC LIGHT, ... 291 ON HEART'S BEGINNING TO 7
THAT FAR LIGHT FLICKERS BECAUSE OF TREES. . . . . . . 291 ON HEART'S BEGINNING TO 15
THEY KNOW WHERE ANOTHER LIGHT HAS BEEN, ... 291 ON HEART'S BEGINNING TO 38
HE HAD THE OAKS FOR HEATING AND FOR LIGHT. . . . . . 292 FIGURE IN THE DOORWAY . 15
NOW BREATHED AS LIGHT AS A LADY'S FAN. . . . . 304 UNHARVESTED 7
AND PUT OUT ITS LIGHT FOR THE FOE. . . . . 311 THE VINDICTIVES . . . 36
LIGHT WAS A PASTE OF PIGMENT IN OUR EYES. . . . . . . 315 IRIS BY NIGHT 9
OF SO MUCH WARMTH AND LIGHT. . . . . 333 HAPPINESS MAKES UP . . 11
THE LAST OF THE LIGHT OF THE SUN . . . . 334 COME IN 9
WERE LETTING IN THE COLDER LIGHT. . . . . 336 THE WIND AND THE RAIN . 2
ACROSS THE LIGHT SNOW HOMEWARD SMELLING GREEN. . . . . 349 TO A YOUNG WRETCH . . 6
YOUR LIGHT WAS SPENT PERHAPS AS IN A FOG. . . . . . . 351 THE LESSON FOR TODAY . 24
OF LYRIC IS A GOLDEN LIGHT DIVINE, ... 358 THE LOST FOLLOWER . . 3
IN HAVING TAKEN ARTIFICIAL LIGHT . . . . 361 A LOOSE MOUNTAIN . . . 7
A DATED POPULAR-SCIENCE MEDLEY ON A MYSTERIOUS LIGHT... . 368 THE LITERATE FARMER AND 5
IN SUNSET LIGHT, YOU'D THINK IT WAS THE SUN . . . . . 368 THE LITERATE FARMER AND 12
"TRAVELER, I'M GLAD YOU ASKED ABOUT THAT LIGHT. . . . . 368 THE LITERATE FARMER AND 23
IT'S A NEW PATENTED ELECTRIC LIGHT, ... 369 THE LITERATE FARMER AND 39
THAT SENDS LIGHT RUSTLE RUSHES TO THEIR LEAVES, ... 378 DIRECTIVE 24
BEFORE SHE MUST PUT OUT THE LIGHT ON THE CHILDREN . . . 379 TOO ANXIOUS FOR RIVERS 18
SO ONCE YOU ROSE AND LIT THE LIGHT. . . . . 380 AN UNSTAMPED LETTER IN 2
SHE ALWAYS HAD TO BURN A LIGHT . . . . 382 THE NIGHT LIGHT . . . 1
THE NIGHT LIGHT . . . . 382 THE NIGHT LIGHT . . . T
AM TOUCHED BY THAT UNINTIMATE LIGHT . . . . 383 WERE I IN TROUBLE . . 7
TO OBSERVE THE NORTHERN LIGHT. . . . . 384 IN THE LONG NIGHT . . 8
THERE SCARCELY IS A LIGHT IN ALL ITS WALLS, ... 386 THE FEAR OF MAN . . . 8
I PUT NO FAITH IN THE SEEMING FACTS OF LIGHT. . . . . 389 SKEPTIC 4
AND YET HE IS A POWER OF LIGHT . . . . 390 TWO LEADING LIGHTS . . 7
THE MOON FOR ALL HER LIGHT AND GRACE . . . . 390 TWO LEADING LIGHTS . . 12
SINCE DARK IS WHAT BRINGS OUT YOUR LIGHT. . . . . . . 403 SOMETHING LIKE A STAR . 5
WILL OF ITSELF TAKE FIRE AND LIGHT THE WORLD UP. . . . 414 A CABIN IN THE CLEARING 27
BUT WITH A COAT SO LIGHT . . . . 416 CLOSED FOR GOOD . . . 22
ALL THAT CAN WAIT FOR THE LIGHT OF DAY. . . . . . . 420 ONE MORE BREVITY . . . 33
OUR BEST GUIDE UPWARD FURTHER TO THE LIGHT, ... 425 ACCIDENTALLY ON PURPOSE 23
OR EVEN THE SPEED OF LIGHT . . . . 466 SOME SCIENCE FICTION . 19
I SHOULDN'T BE SURPRISED. THE STRANGEST LIGHT! . . . . 473 A MASQUE OF REASON . . 7
THERE'S A STRANGE LIGHT ON EVERYTHING TODAY. . . . . . 473 A MASQUE OF REASON . . 8
NOW SOMEONE CAN LIGHT UP THE BURNING BUSH . . . . . . 490 A MASQUE OF REASON . . 458
I LEFT LIGHT SHINING ON AN EMPTY STAGE . . . . 497 A MASQUE OF MERCY . . 100
LIGHT, BRING A LIGHT! / AWH, THERE'S NO LACK OF LIGHT, YOU-- 515 A MASQUE OF MERCY . . 579
A LIGHT THAT FALLS DIFFUSED OVER MY SHOULDER . . . . . 515 A MASQUE OF MERCY . . 580
IF EVEN THE FACE OF MAN'S TOO BRIGHT A LIGHT . . . . . 515 A MASQUE OF MERCY . . 583
FOR ALL THE LIGHT AT ONCE THE SOURCE OF LIGHT-- . . . . 515 A MASQUE OF MERCY . . 587
ARE GOD'S WHITE LIGHT REFRACTED INTO COLORS. . . . . . 516 A MASQUE OF MERCY . . 597
CONTEMPLATE GLORY. THERE WILL BE A LIGHT. . . . . . . 517 A MASQUE OF MERCY . . 629
LIGHTED
TO PUT A TREE BETWEEN US WHEN HE LIGHTED, ... 101 THE WOOD-PILE 11
TO LIGHTED CITY STREETS WE, TOO, HAVE KNOWN, ... 112 IN THE HOME STRETCH . 58
LIGHTING
LIGHTING HIS PIPE NOW, SQUINTING DOWN HIS NOSE . . . . 112 IN THE HOME STRETCH . 64
OF LIGHTING THE WHOLE NIGHT WITH ONE BIG BLOB . . . . 370 THE LITERATE FARMER AND 72
WE'LL BE ALL RIGHT IF NOTHING GOES WRONG WITH THE LIGHTING. 392 IT BIDS PRETTY FAIR . 4
LIGHTLY
MOVING AMONG TALL HAYCOCKS LIGHTLY PILED, ... 14 WAITING 2
LEAP UP, LIKE THAT, LIKE THAT, AND LAND SO LIGHTLY . . 53 HOME BURIAL 76
TWO OR THREE FORKFULS I PICKED LIGHTLY ROUND FOR . . . 72 THE CODE 72
THEN LIGHTLY STOOPED TO IT AND FLUTTERING CLUNG. . . . 126 RANGE-FINDING . . . 8
BUT NEGLECTED, HOWEVER LIGHTLY, TO LACE . . . . . . 265 THE DOOR IN THE DARK . 3
AS LONG AS LIGHTLY ALL THEIR LIVELONG SESSIONS, . . . 317 BUILD SOIL 60
A SERIOUS STEP LIGHTLY TAKEN . . . . 367 A SERIOUS STEP LIGHTLY T
THAT GOD PULLS LIGHTLY UPRIGHT ON ITS HINGES . . . . 474 A MASQUE OF REASON . . 22
LIGHT-NATURED
AND THE LIGHT-NATURED TREE SEEMED NOT TO CARE! . . . . 284 THE GOLD HESPERIDEE . 40
LIGHTNING
SO THAT IT LOOKED LIKE LIGHTNING OR A SCRIBBLE, . . . 205 THE WITCH OF COOS . . 88
LIGHTS
I DREAM UPON THE OPPOSING LIGHTS OF THE HOUR, ... 14 WAITING 9
AND THE NORTHERN LIGHTS THAT RUN LIKE TINGLING NERVES. . 268 ON LOOKING UP BY CHANCE 3
THERE CAME A MOMENT OF CONFUSING LIGHTS, ... 315 IRIS BY NIGHT 4
TWO LEADING LIGHTS . . . . 390 TWO LEADING LIGHTS . . T
THEN'S WHEN HIS MORGAN LIGHTS OUT THROWING SNOWBALLS . . 407 FROM PLANE TO PLANE . 107
LIGHTS OUT, I SAY, SO'S TO ESCAPE ATTENTION. . . . . . 508 A MASQUE OF MERCY . . 392
AND I'M AFRAID. (THE BULB LIGHTS SICKEN DOWN. . . . . 520 A MASQUE OF MERCY . . 695
LIGHT'S
THIS LIGHT'S BEEN GOING ON FOR SEVERAL YEARS, ... 369 THE LITERATE FARMER AND 31
LIGHT-YEAR
TO SOME STAR OFF THERE, SAY, A HALF LIGHT-YEAR . . . . 395 WHY WAIT FOR SCIENCE . 7

```
                                                         PAGE  TITLE                        LINE
LIKE  (SEE CANNON-MOUTH-LIKE, COLUMBUS-LIKE, FATHER-TIME-LIKE, FOOL-LIKE, SPECTER-LIKE,
         TORPEDO-LIKE, TREADING-WATER-LIKE, VOICE-LIKE)
     SMOOTH-LAID LIKE THATCH WITH THE HEAVY DEW, . . . . . .    8  A LATE WALK . . . . .       3
     THOSE STARS LIKE SOME SNOW-WHITE  . . . . . . . . . .      9  STARS . . . . . .          10
     LIKE A HERMIT'S CRUCIFIX; . . . . . . . . . . . . . .     11  TO THE THAWING WIND .      10
     LIKE NOTHING ELSE BY DAY, LIKE GHOSTS BY NIGHT; . . .     12  A PRAYER IN SPRING . .      6
     MY BREATHING SHAKES THE BLUET LIKE A BREEZE, . . . . .    17  THE VANTAGE POINT . .      12
     LIKE GNOMES THAT HID US FROM THE MOON, . . . . . . .      18  GOING FOR WATER . . .      14
     LIKE PEARLS, AND NOW A SILVER BLADE. . . . . . . . .      18  GOING FOR WATER . . .      24
     AND FIT THE EARTH LIKE A LEATHER GLOVE. . . . . . . .     26  IN HARDWOOD GROVES . .      4
     ALL SONG OF THE WOODS IS CRUSHED LIKE SOME . . . . .      26  A LINE-STORM SONG . .      13
     BUT IT SEEMS LIKE THE SEA'S RETURN . . . . . . . .        27  A LINE-STORM SONG . .      26
     ANC IT SEEMS LIKE THE TIME WHEN, AFTER DOUBT, . . . .     27  A LINE-STORM SONG . .      29
     LIKE A LIMP ROSE-WREATH IN A FAIRY DANCE. . . . . . .     28  MY BUTTERFLY . . . .       17
     AND TO WHOM I WAS LIKE TO GIVE OFFENSE. . . . . . .       34  MENDING WALL . . . .       34
     IN EACH HAND, LIKE AN OLD-STONE SAVAGE ARMED. . . . .     34  MENDING WALL . . . .       40
     WHEN HE BEGINS LIKE THAT, THERE'S SOMEONE AT HIM . . .    35  DEATH OF THE HIRED MAN     27
     THAT SOUNDS LIKE SOMETHING YOU HAVE HEARD BEFORE? . . .   36  DEATH OF THE HIRED MAN     53
     "WELL, THOSE DAYS TROUBLE SILAS LIKE A DREAM. . . . .     37  DEATH OF THE HIRED MAN     71
     HE STUDIED LATIN, LIKE THE VIOLIN, . . . . . . .         37  DEATH OF THE HIRED MAN     80
     HE TAKES IT OUT IN BUNCHES LIKE BIG BIRDS' NESTS. . .     37  DEATH OF THE HIRED MAN     93
     NEAR ME IT SEEMED: I FELT IT LIKE A WALL . . . . .       40  THE MOUNTAIN . . . .        5
     INTO THE PASTURE. / "THAT LOOKS LIKE A PATH. . . . .      41  THE MOUNTAIN . . . .       34
     IT STEAM IN WINTER LIKE AN OX'S BREATH, . . . . . .      42  THE MOUNTAIN . . . .       51
     RIGHT ON THE SUMMIT, ALMOST LIKE A FOUNTAIN. . . . .      42  THE MOUNTAIN . . . .       64
     LIKE BOULDERS BROKEN OFF THE UPPER CLIFF. . . . . .      44  THE MOUNTAIN . . . .       98
     I'VE BEEN A-CHOKING LIKE A NURSERY TREE . . . . . .      46  A HUNDRED COLLARS . .      56
     WHAT MAKES YOU STAND THERE ON ONE LEG LIKE THAT? . .     47  A HUNDRED COLLARS . .      69
     'MY MAN' IS IT? YOU TALK LIKE A PROFESSOR. . . . . .     47  A HUNDRED COLLARS . .      80
     WHAT I LIKE BEST'S THE LAY OF DIFFERENT FARMS, . . . .   49  A HUNDRED COLLARS . .     124
     I LIKE TO FIND FOLKS GETTING OUT IN SPRING. . . . .     49  A HUNDRED COLLARS . .     127
     I'M THERE, AND THEY CAN PAY ME IF THEY LIKE. . . . .    50  A HUNDRED COLLARS . .     153
     THERE'S NOTHING I'M AFRAID OF LIKE SCARED PEOPLE." . .   50  A HUNDRED COLLARS . .     175
     "THERE'S SOMETHING I SHOULD LIKE TO ASK YOU, DEAR." .    52  HOME BURIAL . . . .        42
     THOUGH I DON'T LIKE SUCH THINGS 'TWIXT THOSE THAT LOVE.   53  HOME BURIAL . . . .        53
     LEAP UP, LIKE THAT, LIKE THAT, AND LAND SO LIGHTLY . .   53  HOME BURIAL . . . .        76
     THINK OF IT, TALK LIKE THAT AT SUCH A TIME! . . . .     54  HOME BURIAL . . . .        94
     SAYING THEM LIKE THE HEATHEN? WE COULD DROP THEM. . .    58  THE BLACK COTTAGE . .      98
     LIKE BIRDS. THEY STORE A GREAT MANY AWAY. . . . . .      60  BLUEBERRIES . . . .        51
     THEN SANK OUT OF SIGHT LIKE TROLLS UNDERGROUND, . .     62  BLUEBERRIES . . . .        86
     LIKE TWO KINDS OF JEWELS, A VISION FOR THIEVES." . .    62  BLUEBERRIES . . . .       105
     LIKE A DEEP PIECE OF SOME OLD RUNNING RIVER . . . . .    63  A SERVANT TO SERVANTS .    20
     YOU LET THINGS MORE LIKE FEATHERS REGULATE . . . . .    63  A SERVANT TO SERVANTS .    36
     YOUR GOING AND COMING. AND YOU LIKE IT HERE? . . . .    63  A SERVANT TO SERVANTS .    37
     LIKE STANCHIONS IN THE BARN, FROM FLOOR TO CEILING-- .   66  A SERVANT TO SERVANTS .   115
     LIKE A BEAST'S STALL, TO EASE THEIR CONSCIENCES. . .    66  A SERVANT TO SERVANTS .   120
     HE'D PULL HIS BARS APART LIKE BOW AND BOWSTRING, . .    66  A SERVANT TO SERVANTS .   134
     SOMEHOW THE CHANGE WORE OUT LIKE A PRESCRIPTION. . .    67  A SERVANT TO SERVANTS .   154
     I ALMOST THINK IF I COULD DO LIKE YOU, . . . . . .      67  A SERVANT TO SERVANTS .   161
     BUT IT MIGHT BE, COME NIGHT, I SHOULDN'T LIKE IT, . .    67  A SERVANT TO SERVANTS .   163
     I HAVEN'T COURAGE FOR A RISK LIKE THAT. . . . . .       67  A SERVANT TO SERVANTS .   170
     THE WOODCHUCK COULD SAY WHETHER IT'S LIKE HIS . . .     69  AFTER APPLE-PICKING .      40
     SHOUTS LIKE AN ARMY CAPTAIN, 'LET HER COME!' . . . .    71  THE CODE . . . . .         63
     NEVER YOU SAY A THING LIKE THAT TO A MAN, . . . . .     71  THE CODE . . . . .         68
     LIKE MEDITATING, AND THEN I JUST DUG IN . . . . . .     72  THE CODE . . . . .         73
     'THAT GETS YE!' HE SQUEAKED LIKE A SQUEEZED RAT. . .    72  THE CODE . . . . .         78
     LIKE A VIOLA. I DON'T FOLLOW YOU." . . . . . . . .      75  THE GENERATIONS OF MEN     54
     THE SITUATION WAS LIKE THIS: THE ROAD . . . . . .       75  THE GENERATIONS OF MEN     70
     LIKE WILD GEESE ON A LAKE BEFORE A STORM? . . . . .     76  THE GENERATIONS OF MEN     90
     "HE'S NOTHING. LISTEN. WHEN I LEAN LIKE THIS . . . .    77  THE GENERATIONS OF MEN    103
     "TELL ME ABOUT HER. DOES SHE LOOK LIKE ME?" . . . .     77  THE GENERATIONS OF MEN    110
     SHE DOES LOOK LIKE YOU. STAY THE WAY YOU ARE. . . .     77  THE GENERATIONS OF MEN    113
     WHAT DO YOU THINK YOU'RE LIKE TO HEAR TODAY?" . . .     78  THE GENERATIONS OF MEN    141
     BUT WHY TAKE TIME FOR WHAT I'M LIKE TO HEAR? . . .      78  THE GENERATIONS OF MEN    143
     THERE AIN'T NO NAMES QUITE LIKE THE OLD ONES, THOUGH,    80  THE GENERATIONS OF MEN    186
     "I LIKE YOUR 'GOING TO BE.' YOU SAID JUST NOW . . .     80  THE GENERATIONS OF MEN    200
     I'VE BEEN BUILT IN HERE LIKE A BIG CHURCH ORGAN. . .    82  THE HOUSEKEEPER . . .      38
     HE'S JUST DROPPED EVERYTHING. HE'S LIKE A CHILD. . .    83  THE HOUSEKEEPER . . .      55
     LIKE SOME MENFOLK. NO ONE'S AFRAID OF HIM; . . . .      83  THE HOUSEKEEPER . . .      69
     THAN FOLKS LIKE US HAVE ANY BUSINESS WITH. . . . .      85  THE HOUSEKEEPER . . .     112
     BUT ESTELLE DON'T COMPLAIN: SHE'S LIKE HIM THERE. . .    85  THE HOUSEKEEPER . . .     117
     "AND LIKE IT, TOO. IT MAKES IT ALL THE WORSE." . . .    86  THE HOUSEKEEPER . . .     155
     "WHY DO YOU SPEAK LIKE THAT? WHAT DO YOU KNOW? . . .     87  THE HOUSEKEEPER . . .     178
     I CAN'T, AND LEAVE A THING LIKE THAT UNSETTLED. . .     89  THE FEAR . . . . .         15
     DID HE LOOK LIKE----?" / "HE LOOKED LIKE ANYONE. . .    90  THE FEAR . . . . .         31
     ONE OUGHT AS A GOOD VILLAGER TO LIKE IT. . . . . .      94  THE SELF-SEEKER . . .      44
     SOUNDS SOMETHING LIKE. BETTER THAN FARMER'S BEANS . .    97  THE SELF-SEEKER . . .     127
     THE FLOATING HEART, WITH SMALL LEAF LIKE A HEART, . .    98  THE SELF-SEEKER . . .     154
     LIKE A SMALL PISTOL WHEN HE SNAPPED IT SHUT . . . .     98  THE SELF-SEEKER . . .     165
     IT SMELLS TO ME LIKE A DISHONEST TRICK." . . . . .     100  THE SELF-SEEKER . . .     203
     YOU STAND UP TO IT LIKE A PAIR OF COCKS. . . . . .     100  THE SELF-SEEKER . . .     211
     THE WHITE ONE IN HIS TAIL; LIKE ONE WHO TAKES . . .    101  THE WOOD-PILE . . . .      15
     AND NOT ANOTHER LIKE IT COULD I SEE. . . . . . .       101  THE WOOD-PILE . . . .      25
     HAD WOUND STRINGS ROUND AND ROUND IT LIKE A BUNDLE. .   102  THE WOOD-PILE . . . .      31
     LIKE PROFANATION, BY YOUR LEAVE, . . . . . . . . .     102  GOOD HOURS . . . .         15
     MY WOODS--THE YOUNG FIR BALSAMS LIKE A PLACE . . .     106  CHRISTMAS TREES . .        13
     WOULD PAY IN CITIES FOR GOOD TREES LIKE THOSE, . . .   107  CHRISTMAS TREES . .        52
     WHICH HAS ITS SOUNDS, FAMILIAR, LIKE THE ROAR, . . .   108  OLD MAN'S WINTER NIGHT     12
     BUT NOTHING SO LIKE BEATING ON A BOX. . . . . . .      108  OLD MAN'S WINTER NIGHT     14
     OF CHAIRS TURNED UPSIDE DOWN TO SIT LIKE PEOPLE . . .   110  IN THE HOME STRETCH .       6
     MORE THAN SOME WOMEN LIKE THE DISHPAN, JOE; . . . .    111  IN THE HOME STRETCH .      31
     A VIEW." / "AND YET YOU THINK YOU LIKE IT, DEAR?" . .   111  IN THE HOME STRETCH .      35
     I LIKE IT.--BANG GOES SOMETHING BIG AWAY . . . . .     111  IN THE HOME STRETCH .      37
     MORE THAN YOU LIKE TO OWN TO OUT THAT WINDOW." . . .   112  IN THE HOME STRETCH .      45
     WHEN PEOPLE'RE GETTING ON IN LIFE. YOU'LL LIKE IT." .   113  IN THE HOME STRETCH .      94
     AS TO OUR FATE, LIKE FOOLS PAST REASONING WITH. . .    114  IN THE HOME STRETCH .     125
     I LIKE CHAIRS OCCUPYING OTHER CHAIRS . . . . . . .     115  IN THE HOME STRETCH .     156
     "SHOULDN'T YOU LIKE TO KNOW?" / "I'D LIKE TO KNOW . .   116  IN THE HOME STRETCH .     166
```

LIKE (CONTINUED)

	PAGE	TITLE	LINE
LIKE GHOST OF SLEIGH BELLS IN A GHOST OF SNOW)--	119	HYLA BROOK	6
I LIKE TO THINK SOME BOY'S BEEN SWINGING THEM.	121	BIRCHES	3
LIKE GIRLS ON HANDS AND KNEES THAT THROW THEIR HAIR	121	BIRCHES	19
AND LIFE IS TOO MUCH LIKE A PATHLESS WOOD	122	BIRCHES	44
I'D LIKE TO GET AWAY FROM EARTH AWHILE	122	BIRCHES	48
I'D LIKE TO GO BY CLIMBING A BIRCH TREE,	122	BIRCHES	54
OF WHAT YOU CAME FOR AND BECOME LIKE ME,	124	PUTTING IN THE SEED	8
I DIDN'T LIKE THE WAY HE WENT AWAY.	127	THE SMILE	1
HE'S WATCHING FROM THE WOODS AS LIKE AS NOT.	127	THE SMILE	12
WITH SAYING WHAT THEY'D LIKE TO DO TO US	130	THE BONFIRE	14
BUT THE BLACK SPREAD LIKE BLACK DEATH ON THE GROUND,	131	THE BONFIRE	53
LIKE WINTER AND EVENING COMING ON TOGETHER.	131	THE BONFIRE	55
THAT'S WHAT FOR REASONS I SHOULD LIKE TO KNOW--	132	THE BONFIRE	98
LIKE WINGS, REVOLVING IN THE SCENE	138	BROWN'S DESCENT	22
AND CAME DOWN LIKE A COASTING CHILD.	139	BROWN'S DESCENT	44
WE TALKED LIKE BARKING ABOVE THE DIN	140	THE GUM-GATHERER	7
LIKE UNCUT JEWELS, DULL AND ROUGH.	141	THE GUM-GATHERER	31
IF YOU LIKE TO CALL SUCH A SOUND A LAUGH.	142	THE VANISHING RED	3
THE WATER IN DESPERATE STRAITS LIKE FRANTIC FISH,	142	THE VANISHING RED	22
LIKE DARLINGS, BOTH OF THEM. THEY'RE IN THE BARN.--	143	SNOW	25
"WHAT IS HE DOING OUT A NIGHT LIKE THIS?	145	SNOW	68
"YOU LIKE THE RUNT." / "DON'T YOU A LITTLE?" / "WELL,	146	SNOW	94
I DON'T LIKE WHAT HE'S DOING, WHICH IS WHAT	146	SNOW	95
YOU LIKE, AND LIKE HIM FOR." / "OH, YES YOU DO.	146	SNOW	96
YOU LIKE YOUR FUN AS WELL AS ANYONE:	146	SNOW	97
LIKE A WHITE CRUMPLED SPIDER ON HIS KNEE:	147	SNOW	115
JUST THEN, I THOUGHT. IT'S STOOD ERECT LIKE THAT,	147	SNOW	117
MORE LIKE A TUNNEL THAN A HOLE--WAY DOWN	149	SNOW	193
AND QUIVER LIKE THE FRAYED EDGE OF THE DRIFT	149	SNOW	195
BLOWN IN THE WIND. I LIKE THAT--I LIKE THAT.	150	SNOW	196
AND AT THE EAVES. I LIKE IT FROM INSIDE	150	SNOW	208
'WELL THEN,' SHE SAID, AND 'WELL THEN'--LIKE A THREAT.	153	SNOW	289
DO YOU KNOW WHAT SHE'S LIKE? HAVE YOU EVER MET HER?	154	SNOW	313
ITS MOTHER WOULDN'T LET IT CRY LIKE THAT,	154	SNOW	320
ON TURRETS, LIKE CONSTANTINOPLE, DEEP	160	NEW HAMPSHIRE	40
LIKE A LONE ACTOR ON A GLOOMY STAGE--	160	NEW HAMPSHIRE	46
ROSE LIKE A FACTOR'S AT A TRADING STATION.	160	NEW HAMPSHIRE	53
LIKE THOSE WHO FURNISHED ADAM'S SONS WITH WIVES;	161	NEW HAMPSHIRE	79
"I LIKE THIS BETTER." IT WAS REALLY BETTER.	164	NEW HAMPSHIRE	158
HER UNPRUNED GRAPES ARE FLUNG LIKE LARIATS	164	NEW HAMPSHIRE	163
IN MANY MARCHES. AND THEY LIE LIKE WEDGES,	164	NEW HAMPSHIRE	178
AND LIKE THE ACTRESS EXCLAIM "OH, MY GOD" AT?	165	NEW HAMPSHIRE	207
HE DODGED A LOG THAT LIFTED LIKE AN ARM	170	NEW HAMPSHIRE	347
HE DID NOT SEE HOW LIKE A FLYING THING	172	A STAR IN A STONEBOAT	13
IT DREW BACK IN ITS BODY LIKE A SNAIL);	172	A STAR IN A STONEBOAT	18
THAT I AM LIKE TO COMPASS, FOOL OR WISE.	174	A STAR IN A STONEBOAT	57
HAS A MAN, I SHOULD LIKE TO ASK, NO RIGHTS	176	THE STAR-SPLITTER	11
BUT IT SEEMS LIKE SOME WORD SHE LEFT TO BID YOU	180	MAPLE	21
BE A GOOD GIRL--BE LIKE A MAPLE TREE.	180	MAPLE	22
HOW LIKE A MAPLE TREE'S FOR US TO GUESS.	180	MAPLE	23
I HAVE TO LET THEM CALL ME WHAT THEY LIKE."	182	MAPLE	91
COULD IT HAVE BEEN ANOTHER MAPLE LIKE IT?	184	MAPLE	152
LIKE THE TWO STROKES ACROSS A DOLLAR SIGN.	186	THE AX-HELVE	25
OF BENDING LIKE A SWORD ACROSS THE KNEE.	187	THE AX-HELVE	71
LIKE COMING TO A SUDDEN RAILROAD STATION.	189	THE GRINDSTONE	33
IT LOOKED TO HIM LIKE SOME NEW KIND OF HOLLOW	193	PAUL'S WIFE	86
HER WET HAIR HEAVY ON HER LIKE A HELMET,	194	PAUL'S WIFE	109
ACROSS THE LOGS LIKE BACKS OF ALLIGATORS,	195	PAUL'S WIFE	121
PAUL DARKLY, LIKE HER SHADOW. ALL THE LIGHT	195	PAUL'S WIFE	136
SHE WENT OUT LIKE A FIREFLY, AND THAT WAS ALL.	195	PAUL'S WIFE	144
MURPHY'S IDEA WAS THAT A MAN LIKE PAUL	196	PAUL'S WIFE	155
I WAS BORN, I SUPPOSE, LIKE ANYONE,	196	WILD GRAPES	7
AND WAS COME AFTER LIKE EURYDICE	196	WILD GRAPES	12
HOW WOULD SHE LIKE TO SLEEP HER LAST WITH HIM?	200	PLACE FOR A THIRD	36
AND KICK WITH TWO LEGS LIKE AN ARMY MULE.	202	THE WITCH OF COOS	10
AND CARRIED ITSELF LIKE A PILE OF DISHES	203	THE WITCH OF COOS	29
NOT LIKE A MAN, BUT LIKE A CHANDELIER.	204	THE WITCH OF COOS	69
SO THAT IT LOOKED LIKE LIGHTNING OR A SCRIBBLE,	205	THE WITCH OF COOS	88
WITH SOUNDS LIKE THE DRY RATTLING OF A SHUTTER,	206	THE WITCH OF COOS	129
I'M GOING TO TELL THEM SOMETHING THEY WON'T LIKE:	207	PAUPER WITCH OF GRAFTON	2
LIKE, "NO, SHE AIN'T COME BACK FROM KITING YET.	209	PAUPER WITCH OF GRAFTON	80
HE'D LIKE TO TAKE ME THERE AND SHOW IT TO ME.	213	A FOUNTAIN, A BOTTLE	6
ON MARSHALL, LOOK LIKE DONKEY'S EARS.	214	A FOUNTAIN, A BOTTLE	53
YOU DON'T LIKE NATURE. ALL YOU LIKE IS BOOKS.	215	A FOUNTAIN, A BOTTLE	57
THAT, OVERFLOWING LIKE A HORN OF PLENTY,	216	A FOUNTAIN, A BOTTLE	94
OR LIKE THE POETESS'S HEART OF LOVE,	216	A FOUNTAIN, A BOTTLE	95
TRIED TO IMPROVE ON SAILING LIKE A TILE	216	A FOUNTAIN, A BOTTLE	112
BY FLYING LIKE A BIRD (SILENT IN FLIGHT),	216	A FOUNTAIN, A BOTTLE	113
ONLY TO TUMBLE LIKE A STRICKEN BIRD,	216	A FOUNTAIN, A BOTTLE	115
GOOD-LOOKING BOOKS LIKE THAT." HE PICKED ONE FRESH	217	A FOUNTAIN, A BOTTLE	125
THE ATTIC WASPS WENT MISSING BY LIKE BULLETS.	217	A FOUNTAIN, A BOTTLE	130
LIKE A BEADED FUR.	218	I WILL SING YOU ONE-O	37
APPEAR LIKE STANDING	219	I WILL SING YOU ONE-O	66
LIKE DOVE WINGS ON A FIGURE ON A TOMB,	222	TO E.T.	3
LIKE A SHADOW AGAINST THE CURTAIN OF FALLING FLAKES.	223	THE RUNAWAY	8
AND DEAD WEEDS, LIKE A DISAPPEARING SNAKE.	226	THE ONSET	21
LIKE SOME UP-ENDED BOULDER SPLIT IN TWO,	229	TWO LOOK AT TWO	19
LIKE RABBIT AND DEER	235	GATHERING LEAVES	7
OF GLOSSY BIRDS LIKE RIPPLES OVER ROCKS.	240	OUR SINGING STRENGTH	34
LIKE A PISTIL AFTER THE PETALS GO.	241	NEED OF BEING VERSED	4
THEIR MURMUR MORE LIKE THE SIGH WE SIGH	242	NEED OF BEING VERSED	15
AND LIKE THE FLOWERS BESIDE THEM, CHILL AND SHIVER,	245	SPRING POOLS	3
WILL LIKE THE FLOWERS BESIDE THEM SOON BE GONE,	245	SPRING POOLS	4
APPEARED LIKE GOLD IN THE SUNSET SKY,	249	A PECK OF GOLD	6
LIKE LOCKS BLOWN FORWARD IN THE GLEAM OF EYES.	250	ONCE BY THE PACIFIC	6
CHANGE LIKE THIS TO A DEEPER ROAR?	251	BEREFT	2
NOT GAINING BUT NOT LOSING, LIKE A BIRD	258	WEST-RUNNING BROOK	22

LIKE (CONTINUED)

	PAGE	TITLE	LINE
SOME SAY EXISTENCE LIKE A PIROUOT	259	WEST-RUNNING BROOK	45
IT IS BECAUSE LIKE MEN WE LOOK TOO NEAR,	261	A SOLDIER	6
THE MOUNTAIN SEEMED TO LIKE THE STIR,	265	THE BIRTHPLACE	8
I SUFFERED LIKE A METAL BEING CAST.	267	WHAT FIFTY SAID	3
AND THE NORTHERN LIGHTS THAT RUN LIKE TINGLING NERVES.	268	ON LOOKING UP BY CHANCE	3
MAN ACTS MORE LIKE THE POOR BEAR IN A CAGE,	269	THE BEAR	13
AND BENT SOME RAIL WIDE OPEN LIKE A SWITCH,	270	THE EGG AND THE MACHINE	7
HERE IT CAME BREASTING LIKE A HORSE IN SKIRTS.	270	THE EGG AND THE MACHINE	11
TO TOLLING LIKE THE COUNT OF FATE,	273	A LONE STRIKER	2
WHEN INDUSTRY SEEMED LIKE TO DIE	274	A LONE STRIKER	58
THE EXIT HE COMES OUT AT LIKE A BULLET	277	THE WHITE-TAILED HORNET	3
IS LIKE THE PUPIL OF A POINTED GUN.	277	THE WHITE-TAILED HORNET	4
I LIKE TO THINK I AM IN EVERYTHING--	278	THE WHITE-TAILED HORNET	16
HOW LIKE A FLY, HOW VERY LIKE A FLY.	279	THE WHITE-TAILED HORNET	47
LIKE PEOPLE THROWN OUT TO DELAY THE WOLVES.	279	THE WHITE-TAILED HORNET	68
(LIKE WAR AND PESTILENCE	282	A DRUMLIN WOODCHUCK	23
I WONDER HOW I SHOULD LIKE YOU TO COME TO ME	287	A ROADSIDE STAND	50
LIKE WAKING IN A CAGE OF SILVER BARS.	290	OLD BARN AT THE BOTTOM	27
MIGHT SEE THEM ON A RACK LIKE FAMOUS OARS,	290	OLD BARN AT THE BOTTOM	36
LIKE THE LAST PETAL OFF A FLOWER.	291	ON HEART'S BEGINNING TO	12
THE WETTER GROUND LIKE GLASS	301	NEITHER OUT FAR NOR IN	7
WOULD COME IN LIKE YOU HERE:	302	VOICE WAYS	7
LIKE A WHITE PIECE OF RIGID SATIN CLOTH--	302	DESIGN	3
LIKE THE INGREDIENTS OF A WITCHES' BROTH--	302	DESIGN	6
A SNOW-DROP SPIDER, A FLOWER LIKE A FROTH,	302	DESIGN	7
AND DEAD WINGS CARRIED LIKE A PAPER KITE.	302	DESIGN	8
(THIS LIKE FATE BY STARS IS RECKONED),	304	CLEAR AND COLDER	7
IF THIS SEEMS LIKE WITCHCRAFT RATHER,	304	CLEAR AND COLDER	16
YOU LIKE TO HEAR ABOUT GOLD.	310	THE VINDICTIVES	1
LIKE A MANHOLE OPENED TO HELL.	311	THE VINDICTIVES	23
THEN A SMALL RAINBOW LIKE A TRELLIS GATE,	315	IRIS BY NIGHT	17
LIKE A YARDFUL OF SCHOOLBOYS OUT AT RECESS	318	BUILD SOIL	61
I HAVE NO DOUBT LIKE ALL THE LOVES WHEN	318	BUILD SOIL	78
MADE GOOD FOR EVERYONE--THINGS LIKE INVENTIONS--	319	BUILD SOIL	94
(IN THIS IT IS AS MUCH LIKE HATE AS LOVE),	319	BUILD SOIL	105
I FIGURE THAT LIKE ANY BANDYING	321	BUILD SOIL	169
OR WEAVING LIKE A STABLED HORSE:	325	TO A THINKER	7
ALMOST LIKE A CALL TO COME IN	334	COME IN	15
LIKE THE CURL AT THE CORNER OF A SMILE;	335	I COULD GIVE ALL	8
AND LANDED POURING LIKE A WATERFALL,	338	THE MOST OF IT	18
CAUGHT UP LIKE FINGERTIPS	339	THE SUBVERTED FLOWER	12
LIKE A TIGER AT A BONE.	340	THE SUBVERTED FLOWER	29
A HAND HUNG LIKE A PAW,	340	THE SUBVERTED FLOWER	42
AN ARM WORKED LIKE A SAW	340	THE SUBVERTED FLOWER	43
LIKE SOME TENACIOUS BIT	341	THE SUBVERTED FLOWER	67
THAT SUCKS HIS BREATH LIKE A WICKED CAT IN BED.	341	WILLFUL HOMING	4
AND SNATCHES OF VERSE AND SONG OF SCENES LIKE THIS	342	QUEST OF PURPLE-FRINGED	3
THEY COULD ONLY SAY LIKE ANY TWO,	345	DISCOVERY OF MADEIRAS	46
BUT SO IS HISTORY LIKE TO ERR.	347	DISCOVERY OF MADEIRAS	136
LIKE HORACE IN THE TRUE HORATIAN VEIN,	353	THE LESSON FOR TODAY	93
YET LIKE A CHRISTIAN DISCIPLINED TO BEND	353	THE LESSON FOR TODAY	94
ONE AGE IS LIKE ANOTHER FOR THE SOUL.	354	THE LESSON FOR TODAY	113
LIKE ONE POSSESSED.	360	THE RABBIT-HUNTER	9
AND SET UP LIKE A STATUE IN YOUR YARD,	365	OF STONES OF THE PLACE	10
VOICES CONFLICTING LIKE THE CANDIDATES.	368	THE LITERATE FARMER AND	4
LIKE SOMEONE DEAD PERMITTED TO EXIST	368	THE LITERATE FARMER AND	17
THE LOVING'S MADE TO HOLD EACH OTHER LIKE,	371	THE LITERATE FARMER AND	114
LIKE GRAVEYARD MARBLE SCULPTURE IN THE WEATHER,	377	DIRECTIVE	4
NOW SLOWLY CLOSING LIKE A DENT IN DOUGH.	378	DIRECTIVE	47
A BROKEN DRINKING GOBLET LIKE THE GRAIL	379	DIRECTIVE	57
NO PLACE TO GET LOST LIKE TOO FAR IN THE DISTANCE.	379	TOO ANXIOUS FOR RIVERS	11
AND NEEDN'T HAVE FARED INTO SPACE LIKE HIS MASTER	380	TOO ANXIOUS FOR RIVERS	25
THERE, POINTED LIKE THE PIP OF SPADES,	380	AN UNSTAMPED LETTER IN	8
THE PLACE WAS LIKE A CITY PARK,	380	AN UNSTAMPED LETTER IN	11
THAT LIKE A BLANKET TO MY CHIN	380	AN UNSTAMPED LETTER IN	14
LIKE A STAR FRESH FALLEN OUT OF THE SKY.	383	WERE I IN TROUBLE	5
WHERE THE COLD CRACKS LIKE A PISTOL	384	IN THE LONG NIGHT	3
SOME GAS LIKE HELIUM MUST BE INNATE.	387	INNATE HELIUM	6
LIKE A CAUL IN WHICH I WAS BORN AND STILL AM WRAPPED.	390	SKEPTIC	12
LIKE THE IDEAL OF SOME MISTAKEN LOVER.	391	ON BEING IDOLIZED	6
DON'T MIND A LITTLE THING LIKE THE ACTORS FIGHTING.	392	IT BIDS PRETTY FAIR	2
FEELS LIKE MY ARMORY OF HATE:	393	BEYOND WORDS	2
SARCASTIC SCIENCE, SHE WOULD LIKE TO KNOW,	395	WHY WAIT FOR SCIENCE	1
SO, LIKE A HALF-MAD OUTPOST SENTINEL,	396	ANY SIZE WE PLEASE	2
THAT NATIONS LIKE THE CUBAN AND THE SWISS	398	NO HOLY WARS FOR THEM	11
LIKE TROUBLE IN THE BROW ABOVE THE EYES:	399	THE INGENUITIES OF DEBT	3
TAKE SOMETHING LIKE A STAR	403	SOMETHING LIKE A STAR	T
WE MAY TAKE SOMETHING LIKE A STAR	403	SOMETHING LIKE A STAR	24
WAS STILL IN SIGHT LIKE SOMEONE TO DEPEND ON.	404	FROM PLANE TO PLANE	20
"HOEING'S TOO MUCH LIKE WORK FOR DICK," HE ADDED.	404	FROM PLANE TO PLANE	27
"HE LOOKS TO ME LIKE GOING HOME SUCCESSFUL,	405	FROM PLANE TO PLANE	37
I LIKE TO GIVE MY ENEMIES A TRUCE."	406	FROM PLANE TO PLANE	65
I LIKE TO THINK THE SUN'S LIKE YOU IN THAT--	408	FROM PLANE TO PLANE	124
LIKE ADAM AND EVE	413	AWAY!	11
HE DUMPED HIMSELF LIKE A BAG OF BONES,	419	ONE MORE BREVITY	15
LIKE SWEARING OFF ON THE TRAFFIC WORLD.	419	ONE MORE BREVITY	18
COME FRESH FROM AN ELECTION LIKE THE LAST,	423	FOR JOHN F. KENNEDY	54
LIKE A DUM-DUM BULLET--	427	VERSION	13
LIKE A RIPE TOMATO.	427	VERSION	15
LIKE THE CRUMPLED, BETTER-	428	KITTY HAWK	19
LIKE A LITTLE BROTHER	432	KITTY HAWK	118
LIKE A THOUSAND BIRDS.	434	KITTY HAWK	191
LIKE A HURRICANE.	434	KITTY HAWK	211
JUST LIKE PULLMAN CARS,	438	KITTY HAWK	319
ONE WOULD LIKE TO KNOW	438	KITTY HAWK	336
WE DON'T LIKE THAT MUCH.	438	KITTY HAWK	338
LIKE A KITCHEN SPOON	442	KITTY HAWK	442

LIKE, (CONTINUED)
    LIKE A KING AND QUEEN . . . . 442 KITTY HAWK 456
    LIKE DARIUS GREEN . . . . 443 KITTY HAWK 470
    LIKE MALICE PREPENSE. . . . . 450 OBJECTION TO BE STEPPED 11
    LIKE SPLASHING PHOSPHORESCENT PAINT, ... 451 A-WISHING WELL . . . 16
    BUT THAT'S NOT LIKE ME. ON MUCH LESS . . . . 451 A-WISHING WELL . . . 20
    STREAMED OUT LIKE PENNANTS SWALLOW-TAIL. . . . . . . 452 A-WISHING WELL . . . 53
    "SIRE, I'VE BEEN LOOKING ON, AND I DON'T LIKE . . . . 453 HOW HARD TO KEEP FROM 8
    IT WILL COME ROLLING AFTER US LIKE A HOOP." . . . . . 454 HOW HARD TO KEEP FROM 27
    (THE COOK WAS TEMPERAMENTAL LIKE THE KING.) . . . . . 455 HOW HARD TO KEEP FROM 57
    LIKE FLESH, THERE MUST BE SOMETHING LIVING IN IT." . . 456 HOW HARD TO KEEP FROM 91
    (THE KING WAS TEMPERAMENTAL LIKE HIS COOK, ... 456 HOW HARD TO KEEP FROM 95
    HIS MOTHER DIDN'T LIKE THE WAY HE PUT IT, ... 457 HOW HARD TO KEEP FROM 105
    LIKE A PIP SHOT FROM 'TWIXT OUR PINCHING FINGERS." . . 460 HOW HARD TO KEEP FROM 202
    FROM HOLDING FORTH ON FREEDOM LIKE A WHITMAN-- . . . 461 HOW HARD TO KEEP FROM 225
    BUT SUMMONS OUT OF NOWHERE LIKE A JINNI. . . . . . . 461 HOW HARD TO KEEP FROM 240
    LIKE SMALL BOYS WE GOT MAD . . . . 464 MILKY WAY IS A COWPATH 6
    GAVE ME IN TRUTH: I LIKE THE FRANK ADMISSION. . . . . 474 A MASQUE OF REASON . . 37
    I HAVE TO WAIT FOR WORDS LIKE ANYONE. . . . . 475 A MASQUE OF REASON . . 58
    AND I SHOULD LIKE TO KNOW THE REASON WHY. . . . . . . 477 A MASQUE OF REASON . . 104
    AND BID MY WILL AVOUCH IT LIKE MACBETH. . . . . 477 A MASQUE OF REASON . . 112
    THAT COULD, LIKE ANY SPACE, BE TURNED AROUND IN? . . 479 A MASQUE OF REASON . . 161
    SHE'D LIKE TO KNOW HOW YOU WOULD TAKE A PRAYER . . . 479 A MASQUE OF REASON . . 180
    LIKE A BIG EGG AND HATCH A HEAVEN OUT . . . . 484 A MASQUE OF REASON . . 306
    TWO PITCHING ON LIKE THIS TEND TO CONFUSE ME. . . . . 484 A MASQUE OF REASON . . 323
    (THE DEVIL ENTERS LIKE A SAPPHIRE WASP . . . . . . 487 A MASQUE OF REASON . . 389
    LIKE THE ONE MILTON FOUND TO FOOL HIMSELF . . . . 488 A MASQUE OF REASON . . 416
    HE'S ON THAT TENDENCY THAT LIKE THE GULF STREAM, . . 489 A MASQUE OF REASON . . 442
    COME, COME, YOU TALK LIKE AN AGRARIAN. . . . . 496 A MASQUE OF MERCY . . 68
    SHE'LL TAKE TO DRINK AND SEE HOW WE LIKE THAT. . . . 496 A MASQUE OF MERCY . . 85
    MY NAME'S NOT JOE. I DON'T LIKE WHAT SHE SAYS. . . . 500 A MASQUE OF MERCY . . 169
    LIKE WORKING MYSELF UP TO PROPHESY . . . . 501 A MASQUE OF MERCY . . 198
    TO SPRING IT LIKE A DEADFALL AND THE FAULT . . . . 502 A MASQUE OF MERCY . . 231
    LIKE THE ONE JOSHUA GAVE JERICHO. . . . . 504 A MASQUE OF MERCY . . 274
    YOU NEEDN'T SHOUT LIKE THAT, YOU WRETCHED MAN. . . . 508 A MASQUE OF MERCY . . 394
    PAUL MAKES IT COME OUT SO THEY LOOK LIKE CHRISTIANS. . 509 A MASQUE OF MERCY . . 407
    HOW THEY'LL LIKE THAT. PAUL SAID CONSERVATIVES-- . . 509 A MASQUE OF MERCY . . 408
    YES, PAUL, YOU DO SAY THINGS LIKE THAT SOMETIMES. . . 511 A MASQUE OF MERCY . . 486
    (THEY PUT THEIR HANDS TOGETHER LIKE A BOOK . . . . 512 A MASQUE OF MERCY . . 489
    YOU MUST MAKE YOUR DESCENT LIKE EVERYONE. . . . . 514 A MASQUE OF MERCY . . 552
    I'D LIKE TO SEE THE WORLD TRIED ONCE WITHOUT IT. . . 515 A MASQUE OF MERCY . . 575
    TO LOOK AT LONG DIRECTLY (LIKE THE SUN), ... 515 A MASQUE OF MERCY . . 584
    LIKE SHADRACH, MESHACH, AND ABEDNEGO. . . . . . . 516 A MASQUE OF MERCY . . 604
    WE LIKE YOU, DON'T WE, PAUL? (PAUL TAKES HIS WRIST.) . 518 A MASQUE OF MERCY . . 665
    AND LET THAT TELL YOU WHAT YOU THINK, LIKE THAT? . . 519 A MASQUE OF MERCY . . 676
    OUR VERY BEST, OUR LIVES LAID DOWN LIKE JONAH'S, . . 520 A MASQUE OF MERCY . . 720
LIKED
    BECAUSE HE LIKED IT--THAT AN ARGUMENT' . . . . . . 37 DEATH OF THE HIRED MAN 81
    AND SHE LIKED TALK. SHE HAD SEEN GARRISON . . . . 56 THE BLACK COTTAGE . . 52
    DOING THE HAYING. NO ONE LIKED THE BOSS. . . . . 70 THE CODE 32
    BUT WHAT HE LIKED WAS SOMEONE TO ENCOURAGE. . . . 71 THE CODE 43
    THE WAY THE WIRY GANG-BOSS LIKED THE LOGJAM. . . . 170 NEW HAMPSHIRE . . . 345
    HE LIKED TO HAVE IT SLENDER AS A WHIPSTOCK, . . . 187 THE AX-HELVE . . . 69
    IF THE BONES LIKED THE ATTIC, LET THEM HAVE IT. . . 206 THE WITCH OF COOS . . 124
    SHE MIGHT AS WELL HERSELF." BUT HE LIKED BEST . . . 209 PAUPER WITCH OF GRAFTON 83
    AND HE LIKED EVERYTHING I MADE HIM DO. . . . . . 210 PAUPER WITCH OF GRAFTON 100
    NOW WAS SEEN HOW THESE LIKED BELATED SNOW. . . . . 239 OUR SINGING STRENGTH . 25
    UNLESS I LIKED TO SUFFER LOSS OF WORSHIP. . . . . 476 A MASQUE OF REASON . . 75
LIKELIHOOD
    FOR YOU TO DOUBT THE LIKELIHOOD. . . . . 307 PROVIDE, PROVIDE . . 6
LIKELY
    HE THINKS YOUNG WILSON A LIKELY LAD, THOUGH DAFT . . . 36 DEATH OF THE HIRED MAN 65
    NOT LIKELY, WHEN ALL THE YOUNG LORENS DEPLOY. . . . 62 BLUEBERRIES 98
    BUT IT'S MORE LIKELY HE WAS CROSSED IN LOVE, . . . 66 A SERVANT TO SERVANTS 108
    MOST LIKELY I'D HAVE SERVED YOU JUST THE SAME. . . 70 THE CODE 25
    YOU WILL BE LIKELY TO REGARD AS SACRED . . . . . 79 THE GENERATIONS OF MEN 179
    I DON'T KNOW WHERE IT'S LIKELY TO GO BETTER. . . . 122 BIRCHES 53
    IT VERY LIKELY QUICKENS AND REFINES US. . . . . . 321 BUILD SOIL 171
    AND LIKELY TO HAVE BEEN ENOUGH ALONE. . . . . . . 382 TO AN ANCIENT . . . 15
    IT MAY BE WINE, BUT MUCH MORE LIKELY LOVE-- . . . 461 HOW HARD TO KEEP FROM 242
    DOWN A LIKELY HOLE . . . . 468 A REFLEX 3
    OR COURT OF LOVE. / MORE LIKELY ROYAL COURT-- . . . 474 A MASQUE OF REASON . . 25
LIKENESS
    "WAS EVER SUCH A MAN FOR SEEING LIKENESS?" . . . . 151 SNOW 250
    A LIKENESS TO SURPRISE THE THRILLY TOURIST. . . . . 214 A FOUNTAIN, A BOTTLE . 40
LIKES
    AND HE LIKES HAVING THOUGHT OF IT SO WELL . . . . 34 MENDING WALL . . . 44
    STOPS WHEN SHE LIKES: I TELL HER WHEN TO GO. . . . 49 A HUNDRED COLLARS . . 140
    HE'D SAY SHE DOES IT MORE BECAUSE SHE LIKES IT. . . 85 THE HOUSEKEEPER . . 109
    JOHN LIKES TO TELL THE OFFERS HE HAS HAD, ... 86 THE HOUSEKEEPER . . 138
    LIKES TO TELL HOW ONE SPRING . . . . 133 A GIRL'S GARDEN . . 2
    SHE LIKES TO HALT US IN OUR RUNNER TRACKS, ... 238 ON A TREE FALLEN ACROSS 6
    AS WHOSOEVER LIKES THE YOUNG AND SLIGHT . . . . . 375 A YOUNG BIRCH . . . 3
    HE LIKES TO TURN HIS BACK ON GRATITUDE . . . . . 408 FROM PLANE TO PLANE . 130
LIKING
    NOT LIKING TO OWN UP I'D GROWN A SIZE. . . . . . 46 A HUNDRED COLLARS . . 60
    ONE THING YOU CAN'T HELP LIKING ABOUT JOHN, ... 85 THE HOUSEKEEPER . . 115
LILAC
    YET FOR THEM THE LILAC RENEWED ITS LEAF, ... 242 NEED OF BEING VERSED . 17
LILLIPUTIANS
    LILLIPUTIANS WE'RE . . . . 434 KITTY HAWK 197
LIMBED (SEE LOW-LIMBED)
LIME
    OF WOOD OR GRANITE OR LIME . . . . 348 TRIPLE BRONZE . . . 6
    OR AREN'T THE BONES ENOUGH I LIVE TO LIME? . . . . 382 TO AN ANCIENT . . . 18
LIMESTONE
    SOME HALFWAY UP THE LIMESTONE WALL, ... 392 A CLIFF DWELLING . . 5

LIMIT (SEE AEON—LIMIT)
    AND SO ON TO THE LIMIT OF MY NATURE. . . . . 323 BUILD SOIL 242
    THERE IS A LIMIT TO OUR TIME EXTENSION. . . . . 355 THE LESSON FOR TODAY . 144
LIMITED
    ARE LIMITED TO THE ROAD. . . . . 388 MIDDLENESS OF THE ROAD   11
    THEIR NUMBER WOULD SEEM LIMITED TO THREE. . . . . . . 398 NO HOLY WARS FOR THEM .   2
    (HE SEEMS TO HAVE FELT LIMITED TO ONE), ... 456 HOW HARD TO KEEP FROM   71
LIMITLESS
    IT CAN BLAME THIS LIMITLESS TRAIT IN THE HEARTS OF MEN. . . 305 THERE ARE ROUGHLY ZONES 21
    THROUGH A PITCH—DARK LIMITLESS GROVE. . . . . 443 THE DRAFT HORSE . . .   4
LIMITS
    THAT TO NO LIMITS AND BOUNDS HE CAN STAY CONFINED? . . . 305 THERE ARE ROUGHLY ZONES   8
    NO LIMITS TO WHAT ROSE IN RUBBING STICKS . . . . . . 372 THE LITERATE FARMER AND 138
LIMNS
    AND VERY BEAUTIFULLY GOD LIMNS, ... 20 THE TRIAL BY EXISTENCE   37
LIMP
    LIKE A LIMP ROSE—WREATH IN A FAIRY DANCE. . . . . . 28 MY BUTTERFLY   17
    AND NOT ONE BUT HUNG LIMP, NOT ONE WAS LEFT. . . . . 122 BIRCHES   31
    AT THE FIRST DRINK IT RUSTLED AND GREW LIMP. . . . . 194 PAUL'S WIFE 102
LINCOLN
    OF LINCOLN, LAFAYETTE, AND LIBERTY? . . . . 169 NEW HAMPSHIRE 324
    FOR LINCOLN MACVEAGH . . . . 172 A STAR IN A STONEBOAT . D
LINE (SEE SNOW—LINE)
    AND ON A DAY WE MEET TO WALK THE LINE . . . . 33 MENDING WALL   13
    THE LINE WHERE MAN LEAVES OFF AND NATURE STARTS, . . . 171 NEW HAMPSHIRE 379
    HE STOOD ON THE SAFE SIDE OF THE LINE TALKING—— . . . 171 NEW HAMPSHIRE 381
    AS FISH DO WITH THE LINE IN FIRST ALARM. . . . . . . 174 A STAR IN A STONEBOAT . 54
    I LEANED TO LINE THE FIGURES IN . . . . 252 THE PEACEFUL SHEPHERD .   3
    THAT THOUGH THERE IS NO FIXED LINE BETWEEN WRONG AND RIGHT, 305 THERE ARE ROUGHLY ZONES 12
    ESTABLISHED A ROYAL LINE, ... 314 BEARER OF EVIL TIDINGS   30
    IF WHAT YOU'RE PREACHING IS A LINE OF CONDUCT, ... 322 BUILD SOIL 204
    AND THE WAVE LINE A SHAKEN SIGH. . . . . 327 A MISSIVE MISSILE . .   12
    THE LINE MUST BE A JAGGED BLADE. . . . . 327 A MISSIVE MISSILE . .   15
    THE TWO DOTS AND THE RIPPLE LINE. . . . . 328 A MISSIVE MISSILE . .   42
    WHERE MY IMAGINARY LINE . . . . 331 BEECH   1
    IN A SWEEPING LINE. . . . . 342 QUEST OF PURPLE—FRINGED   6
    THE GOLD FOR WHICH THEY LEAVE THE GOLDEN LINE . . . . 358 THE LOST FOLLOWER . .   2
    IN READING, DON'T YOU, BILL?——AT EVERY LINE END . . . 405 FROM PLANE TO PLANE .   50
    I LINK A LINE OF SHADOWY TRACKS . . . . 470 IN WINTER IN THE WOODS   7
LINE—GANG
    HERE COME THE LINE—GANG PIONEERING BY. . . . . 141 THE LINE—GANG . . .   1
    THE LINE—GANG . . . . 141 THE LINE—GANG . . .   T
LINES
    FOR WHOM THESE LINES WHEN THEY SHALL GREET HER EYE. . . 15 WAITING   27
    THE BOUNDARY LINES KEEP IN SO CLOSE TO IT. . . . . . 43 THE MOUNTAIN   95
    IF SUCH UNLIFELIKE LINES KEPT POWER TO STIR . . . . . 56 THE BLACK COTTAGE . .   29
    ONE FOOT WENT THROUGH. THE VIEW WAS ALL IN LINES . . . 101 THE WOOD—PILE   5
    ACROSS THE LINES OF STRAIGHTER DARKER TREES, ... 121 BIRCHES   2
    HE SHOWED ME THAT THE LINES OF A GOOD HELVE . . . . . 187 THE AX—HELVE   72
    TO BE HER ONLY MARRIAGE LINES. . . . . 347 DISCOVERY OF MADEIRAS . 123
    THE LEDGES SHOW LINES RULED SOUTHEAST—NORTHWEST, . . . 377 DIRECTIVE   15
    LINES WRITTEN IN DEJECTION ON THE EVE OF GREAT SUCCESS . 462 LINES IN DEJECTION . .   T
LINE—STORM
    THE LINE—STORM CLOUDS FLY TATTERED AND SWIFT. . . . . 26 A LINE—STORM SONG . .   1
    A LINE—STORM SONG . . . . 26 A LINE—STORM SONG . .   T
LINGER
    YOU WOULDN'T THINK THEY WOULD. HOW SOME THINGS LINGER! . . 37 DEATH OF THE HIRED MAN   72
    YOU LINGER YOUR LITTLE HOUR AND ARE GONE, ... 247 ON GOING UNNOTICED . .   13
    BUT WITHOUT TIME TO LINGER FOR HER STORY. . . . . . 257 THE LOVELY BE CHOOSERS   49
LINGERED
    BUT A LEAF THAT LINGERED BROWN, ...   9 A LATE WALK   10
    HE LINGERED FOR SOME WORD SHE WOULDN'T SAY, ... 143 SNOW   28
    FROM WHERE I LINGERED IN A LULL IN MARCH . . . . . . 234 EVENING A SUGAR ORCHARD   1
LINGERING
    THIS GLIMPSE OF LINGERING PERSON IN ELIZA, ... 200 PLACE FOR A THIRD . .   16
    SOME LINGERING OBJECTION HOLDS YOU BACK. . . . . . . 517 A MASQUE OF MERCY . . 632
LINGERS
    THE FARMHOUSE LINGERS, THOUGH AVERSE TO SQUARE . . . . 231 A BROOK IN THE CITY .   1
    NO LASTING EFFECT OF IT LINGERS. . . . . 266 SITTING BY A BUSH . .   4
    SHE LINGERS FEEDING AT THE TROUGH, ... 280 BLUE RIBBON AT AMESBURY 15
    HE LINGERS TOO, AVERSE TO SLIGHT . . . . 280 BLUE RIBBON AT AMESBURY 19
LINK
    THE MYSTIC LINK TO BIND AND HOLD . . . . 21 THE TRIAL BY EXISTENCE   63
    EACH LINK OF A HUNDREDWEIGHT, ... 312 THE VINDICTIVES . .   64
    YOU LINK AN ARM IN ITS ARM AND YOU LEAN . . . . . . 349 TO A YOUNG WRETCH . .   5
    TO LINK A CHAIN OF MONEY—METAL BANKS. . . . . 358 THE LOST FOLLOWER . .   8
    I LINK A LINE OF SHADOWY TRACKS . . . . 470 IN WINTER IN THE WOODS   7
LINKED (SEE THOUSAND—LINKED)
LINKS
    OF FLASHING LINKS IN THE SUN. . . . . 312 THE VINDICTIVES . . .   75
LIP
    THE SUCCESS OF THE LIP . . . . 447 THE BAD ISLAND——EASTER   8
LIPPED
    NOW QUIVERED TOWARD EACH OTHER, LIPPED . . . . 381 AN UNSTAMPED LETTER IN   34
LIPS
    HE ASKED WITH THE EYES MORE THAN THE LIPS . . . . .   7 LOVE AND A QUESTION .   5
    ON HER LIPS. . . . . 128 THE IMPULSE   12
    HE LAY AND PUFFED HIS LIPS OUT WITH HIS BREATH. . . . 137 "OUT,OUT——"   29
    A LITTLE THROUGH THE LIPS AND THROAT. . . . . 224 THE AIM WAS SONG . .   15
    LOVE AT THE LIPS WAS TOUCH . . . . 226 TO EARTHWARD   1
    AND ITS CHOKECHERRIES LIPS TO KISS GOOD—BY, ... 268 THE BEAR   3
    THEY TAPPED AT MY EYELIDS AND TOUCHED MY LIPS WITH AN
        INVITATION TO GRIEF. . . . . 298 A LEAF—TREADER . .   10
    THE CORNERS OF HIS LIPS . . . . 339 THE SUBVERTED FLOWER   13
    HIS LIPS WERE SUCKED AND BLOWN . . . . 340 THE SUBVERTED FLOWER   27
    SHE PLUCKED HER LIPS FOR IT, ... 341 THE SUBVERTED FLOWER . 69
LIQUOR
    WAIT AND WATCH THE LIQUOR SETTLE. . . . . 304 CLEAR AND COLDER . .   19

LIST
  SHE TALKS AND I AM FAIN TO LIST: . . . . 7 MY NOVEMBER GUEST . . 7
  AND LIST TO THE LOVE OF THESE, ... 10 WIND AND WINDOW FLOWER 2
  ONE SO LONELY WAS FAIN TO LIST, ... 15 IN A VALE 14
  I SHOULD HAVE TO CHECK ON MY LIST . . . . 384 MAKING CERTAIN ANYTHING 14
LISTEN
  NOR VAINLY LISTEN ALL THE NIGHT LONG. . . . . 16 IN A VALE 25
  TO LISTEN ERE WE DARED TO LOOK, ... 18 GOING FOR WATER . . . 18
  LISTEN TO ME. I WON'T COME DOWN THE STAIRS." . . . 52 HOME BURIAL 40
  IN A BOOK ABOUT FERNS? LISTEN TO THAT! . . . . . 63 A SERVANT TO SERVANTS . 35
  "HE'S NOTHING. LISTEN. WHEN I LEAN LIKE THIS . . . 77 THE GENERATIONS OF MEN 103
  LISTEN! HE KICKED A STONE. HEAR THAT, HEAR THAT! . 90 THE FEAR 38
  AND LISTEN--HOW IT OUGHT TO GO! . . . . 224 THE AIM WAS SONG . . 8
  AND WOULD NOT LISTEN TO MY EXPLANATIONS. . . . . . 278 THE WHITE-TAILED HORNET 21
  THEY LISTEN FOR ME IN THE BEDROOM . . . . 294 A RECORD STRIDE . . . 9
  LISTEN AND I WILL TAKE MY DEAREST RISK. . . . . . 320 BUILD SOIL 136
  LISTEN, THEY MURMUR TALKING IN THE DARK . . . . . 415 A CABIN IN THE CLEARING 34
  WHERE I NEED LISTEN TO ITS ROTE NO MORE, ... 447 DOES NO ONE AT ALL EVER 34
  BUT LISTEN TO ME REGISTER . . . . 451 A-WISHING WELL . . . 10
  DON'T LISTEN TO THEIR PLAY OF PARADOXES. . . . . . 460 HOW HARD TO KEEP FROM 193
  (HE STOPS TO LISTEN.) THAT'S A MIGHTY STORM, . . . 502 A MASQUE OF MERCY . 233
  (HE STOPS TO LISTEN AND HIS UNSPOKEN THOUGHT, . . . 502 A MASQUE OF MERCY . 236
  (HE STARTS TO SPEAK, BUT STOPS AGAIN TO LISTEN. . . 502 A MASQUE OF MERCY . 244
  LISTEN, YE! IT'S THE PROLETARIAT! . . . . 508 A MASQUE OF MERCY . 390
LISTENED
  I LISTENED FOR HIS WHETSTONE ON THE BREEZE. . . . . 22 THE TUFT OF FLOWERS . 6
  NOTHING! THEY LISTENED FOR HIM. NOT A RUSTLE. . . . 72 THE CODE 91
  I'VE NEVER LISTENED IN AMONG THE SOUNDS . . . . . . 78 THE GENERATIONS OF MEN 132
  I LISTENED AND I THOUGHT I CAUGHT THE WORD-- . . . 118 THE TELEPHONE . . . 14
  NO ONE BELIEVED. THEY LISTENED AT HIS HEART. . . . 137 "OUT,OUT--" . . . 31
  THREE TIMES HE BARELY STIRRED THE BELL, THEN LISTENED. 143 SNOW 15
  I LISTENED TILL IT ALMOST CLIMBED THE STAIRS . . . 205 THE WITCH OF COOS . 90
  THEY BIT THE GLASS AND LISTENED FOR THE FLAVOR. . . 293 AT WOODWARD'S GARDENS . 27
LISTENING
  THIS HE SAT LISTENING TO TILL SHE GAVE JUDGMENT. . . 76 THE GENERATIONS OF MEN 77
  THE THREE STOOD LISTENING TO A FRESH ACCESS . . . . 143 SNOW 1
  AND ACQUIRE A LISTENING AIR. . . . . 156 THE SOUND OF TREES . 9
LIT (SEE NEON-LIT)
  THE BUTTERFLY AND I HAD LIT UPON, ... 23 THE TUFT OF FLOWERS . 29
  UNTIL THEY HAD LIT THE LAMP INSIDE. . . . . 127 HOUSE FEAR . . . 10
  NO LAMP WAS LIT. NOTHING WAS ON THE TABLE. . . . . 175 THE CENSUS-TAKER . . 35
  SO ONCE YOU ROSE AND LIT THE LIGHT. . . . . 380 AN UNSTAMPED LETTER IN 2
LITERAL
  WE SPEAK THE LITERAL TO INSPIRE . . . . 19 REVELATION 7
LITERALLY
  SOMEONE HAD LITERALLY RUN TO EARTH . . . . 73 THE GENERATIONS OF MEN 7
  LITERALLY FLY. . . . . 434 KITTY HAWK . . . 195
LITERARY
  (AND HENCE SO MANY LITERARY TEARS . . . . 355 THE LESSON FOR TODAY . 149
  WE KNOW THE LITERARY CHATTER. . . . . 418 AMERICA IS HARD TO SEE 66
LITERATE
  THE LITERATE FARMER AND THE PLANET VENUS . . . . . 368 THE LITERATE FARMER AND T
LITERATURE
  THE PRECIOUS LITERATURE IN QUANTITY . . . . 164 NEW HAMPSHIRE . . 167
  BEING THE CREATURE OF LITERATURE I AM, ... 166 NEW HAMPSHIRE . . 240
  IN LITERATURE TO DATE IS HEARD TO COME. . . . . . 167 NEW HAMPSHIRE . . 271
  A LITERATURE THAT SHALL AT ONCE BE SOUND. . . . . 168 NEW HAMPSHIRE . . 285
  IS THE FIRST PLACE IN LITERATURE, I THINK, ... 508 A MASQUE OF MERCY . 376
LITTERED
  THE WOODBINE LEAVES LITTERED THE YARD, ... 7 LOVE AND A QUESTION . 13
LITTER-MUFFLED
  AND MANY LITTER-MUFFLED FLOORS. . . . . 280 BLUE RIBBON AT AMESBURY 24
LITTLE
  I'M GOING OUT TO FETCH THE LITTLE CALF . . . . . . 1 THE PASTURE 5
  THE BRIDEGROOM THOUGHT IT LITTLE TO GIVE . . . . . 8 LOVE AND A QUESTION . 25
  AND LITTLE OF LOVE COULD KNOW. . . . . 11 WIND AND WINDOW FLOWER 16
  THE MEASURE OF THE LITTLE WHILE . . . . 13 FLOWER-GATHERING . . 15
  AND TENDERLY, LIFE'S LITTLE DREAM, ... 20 THE TRIAL BY EXISTENCE 38
  WHO SEE SO LITTLE THEY TELL NO TALES. . . . . . . 24 PAN WITH US . . . 15
  ONE ON A SIDE. IT COMES TO LITTLE MORE: . . . . . 33 MENDING WALL . . . 22
  AT HIS AGE FOR THE LITTLE HE CAN DO? . . . . . . 35 DEATH OF THE HIRED MAN 16
  HE THINKS HE OUGHT TO EARN A LITTLE PAY, ... 35 DEATH OF THE HIRED MAN 19
  "BUT LITTLE." / "ANYTHING? MARY, CONFESS . . . . . 36 DEATH OF THE HIRED MAN 45
  PICKED UP A LITTLE STICK, AND BROUGHT IT BACK . . . 38 DEATH OF THE HIRED MAN 122
  THAN ON HIS BROTHER? THIRTEEN LITTLE MILES . . . . 38 DEATH OF THE HIRED MAN 125
  THE MOON, THE LITTLE SILVER CLOUD, AND SHE. . . . . 40 DEATH OF THE HIRED MAN 163
  PASTURE RAN UP THE SIDE A LITTLE WAY, ... 41 THE MOUNTAIN . . . 29
  WITH LITTLE FERNS IN CREVICES AT HIS ELBOW. . . . . 42 THE MOUNTAIN . . . 62
  ROLLED OUT A LITTLE FARTHER THAN THE REST." . . . . 44 THE MOUNTAIN . . . 99
  LANCASTER BORE HIM--SUCH A LITTLE TOWN, ... 44 A HUNDRED COLLARS . 1
  TO RUN WILD IN THE SUMMER--A LITTLE WILD. . . . . 44 A HUNDRED COLLARS . 5
  AND NOW I'M LEAVING YOU A LITTLE WHILE. . . . . . 50 A HUNDRED COLLARS . 159
  THE DOCTOR SLID A LITTLE DOWN THE PILLOW. . . . . . 51 A HUNDRED COLLARS . 179
  THE LITTLE GRAVEYARD WHERE MY PEOPLE ARE! . . . . . 51 HOME BURIAL . . . 23
  BROAD-SHOULDERED LITTLE SLABS THERE IN THE SUNLIGHT . 52 HOME BURIAL . . . 27
  SHE MOVED THE LATCH A LITTLE. "DON'T--DON'T GO. . . 53 HOME BURIAL . . . 56
  I DO THINK, THOUGH, YOU OVERDO IT A LITTLE. . . . . 53 HOME BURIAL . . . 62
  WITH YOUR OWN HAND--HOW COULD YOU?--HIS LITTLE GRAVE; 53 HOME BURIAL . . . 73
  THE LITTLE COTTAGE WE WERE SPEAKING OF, ... 55 THE BLACK COTTAGE . 5
  A LITTLE COTTAGE THIS HAS ALWAYS SEEMED; . . . . . 56 THE BLACK COTTAGE . 35
  I WOULD HAVE CHANGED THE CREED A VERY LITTLE? . . . 57 THE BLACK COTTAGE . 88
  IS SET ME BACK A LITTLE MORE BEHIND. . . . . . . 68 A SERVANT TO SERVANTS . 175
  WHAT I SEE. IT'S A LITTLE, LITTLE BOY, ... 77 THE GENERATIONS OF MEN 99
  A LITTLE LONGER. I MUSTN'T FEEL TOO HURRIED, . . . 78 THE GENERATIONS OF MEN 146
  HE HOED A LITTLE YESTERDAY FOR ME: . . . . 83 THE HOUSEKEEPER . . 58
  THE LITTLE TIN BOX ON THE CUPBOARD SHELF-- . . . . 86 THE HOUSEKEEPER . . 143
  MOVED IN A LITTLE. THE MAN GRASPED A WHEEL. . . . . 89 THE FEAR 7
  THAT CAME ON, BUT HER BODY ROCKED A LITTLE. . . . . 92 THE FEAR 77

                                                    PAGE TITLE   LINE
LITTLE (CONTINUED)
    A LITTLE BAREFOOT GIRL, WHO IN THE NOISE . . . . 96 THE SELF-SEEKER . . . 92
    OF LITTLE FINGERS ALL KEPT DOWN BUT ONE, ... 98 THE SELF-SEEKER . . 156
    I FORGOT HIM AND LET HIS LITTLE FEAR . . . . 101 THE WOOD-PILE . . . 19
    A LITTLE STRETCH OF MOWING FIELD FOR YOU; . . . . . . 111 IN THE HOME STRETCH . 32
    OF SUCH A LITTLE HOUSE. ONCE LEFT ALONE, ... 111 IN THE HOME STRETCH . 40
    TO CURL A LITTLE FINGER ROUND, ... 123 PEA BRUSH 18
    MADE THE GREAT TREE SEEM AS A LITTLE BIRD . . . . . . 128 THE OFT-REPEATED DREAM 7
    AND WORK WAS LITTLE IN THE HOUSE, ... 128 THE IMPULSE   5
    BUT IN A MOMENT NOT: A LITTLE SPURT . . . . 130 THE BONFIRE 23
    A LITTLE BIT OF EVERYTHING, ... 134 A GIRL'S GARDEN . . 39
    THAT HER LITTLE BLUEBIRD . . . . 135 LAST WORD OF A BLUEBIRD 7
    LITTLE--LESS--NOTHING!--AND THAT ENDED IT. . . . . . 137 "OUT, OUT--" 32
    HE TOLD ME A LITTLE ABOUT HIMSELF. . . . . 140 THE GUM-GATHERER . . 12
    AND REACHING UP WITH A LITTLE KNIFE, ... 141 THE GUM-GATHERER . . 37
    I HATE HIS WRETCHED LITTLE RACKER SECT, ... 144 SNOW 53
    "YOU LIKE THE RUNT." / "DON'T YOU A LITTLE?" / "WELL, 146 SNOW 94
    YOU MAKE A LITTLE FOURSQUARE BLOCK OF AIR, ... 148 SNOW 142
    LAUGHED THE LOUD LAUGH THE BIG LAUGH AT THE LITTLE. . 165 NEW HAMPSHIRE . . . 200
    TAUNTED THE LOFTY LAND WITH LITTLE MEN." . . . . . . 166 NEW HAMPSHIRE . . . 219
    THE LITTLE MEN (IT'S MASSACHUSETTS SPEAKING). . . . . 166 NEW HAMPSHIRE . . . 225
    THEY TAUNT THE LOFTY LAND WITH LITTLE MEN. . . . . . 167 NEW HAMPSHIRE . . . 264
    WE GET WHAT LITTLE MISERY WE CAN . . . . 167 NEW HAMPSHIRE . . . 272
    FOR ALL HER MOUNTAINS FALL A LITTLE SHORT, ... 170 NEW HAMPSHIRE . . . 355
    OR FOR A LITTLE GIRL TO GUESS SOMETIME. . . . . 180 MAPLE 24
    AND THINK A LITTLE, AND GET SOME CITY SCHOOLING. . . 182 MAPLE 74
    AS IF HE DIDN'T KNOW WHAT LITTLE THING . . . . 183 MAPLE 125
    AND IN A LITTLE--A FRENCH TOUCH IN THAT. . . . . . . 188 THE AX-HELVE 100
    AND GREW TO BE A LITTLE BOYISH GIRL . . . . 196 WILD GRAPES   8
    OR A LITTLE CHILD, COMES UP. IT WASN'T TOFFILE: . . . 204 THE WITCH OF COOS . 53
    A LITTLE MORGAN HAD ONE FOREFOOT ON THE WALL, ... 223 THE RUNAWAY   3
    "I THINK THE LITTLE FELLOW'S AFRAID OF THE SNOW. . . 223 THE RUNAWAY   9
    WITH THE LITTLE FELLOW AT ALL. HE'S RUNNING AWAY. . 223 THE RUNAWAY 11
    HE TOOK A LITTLE IN HIS MOUTH, ... 224 THE AIM WAS SONG . .   9
    A LITTLE THROUGH THE LIPS AND THROAT. . . . . 224 THE AIM WAS SONG . . 15
    MY LITTLE HORSE MUST THINK IT QUEER . . . . 224 STOPPING BY WOODS .   5
    A LITTLE FURTHER UP THE MOUNTAINSIDE . . . . 229 TWO LOOK AT TWO . .   2
    BUILDER, IN BUILDING THE LITTLE HOUSE, ... 232 THE KITCHEN CHIMNEY . 1
    A PIERCING LITTLE STAR WAS THROUGH. . . . . 233 LOOKING FOR SUNSET BIRD 20
    OR AT UTMOST A LITTLE RELUCTANT WHIRL . . . . 236 MISGIVING 11
    I'VE TRIED IT FINE WITH LITTLE BREADTH OF LUSTER, . 245 THE FREEDOM OF THE MOON 4
    YOU LINGER YOUR LITTLE HOUR AND ARE GONE, ... 247 ON GOING UNNOTICED . 13
    RAISING A LITTLE, SENDING UP A LITTLE. . . . . 259 WEST-RUNNING BROOK . 63
    AND MADE OF US A LITTLE WHILE-- . . . . 265 THE BIRTHPLACE . . .   9
    THE POCKET OF A LITTLE TURTLE MINE. . . . . 270 THE EGG AND THE MACHINE 23
    HE STOOPED AND STRUCK A LITTLE HUCKLEBERRY . . . . . 278 THE WHITE-TAILED HORNET 38
    BUT LITTLE LOWER THAN THE GODS AND ANGELS. . . . . . 279 THE WHITE-TAILED HORNET 62
    HAVE A LITTLE WHISTLE WE GIVE, ... 282 A DRUMLIN WOODCHUCK . 14
    THEY HAD JUST GIVEN THEMSELVES A LITTLE TWIST . . . . 283 THE GOLD HESPERIDEE .   7
    HIS LITTLE MATTHEW, ALSO FIVE YEARS OLD, ... 283 THE GOLD HESPERIDEE . 13
    A LITTLE NEARER THE SEA. . . . . 285 IN TIME OF CLOUDBURST . 4
    A LITTLE OF FUTURE HARM. . . . . 285 IN TIME OF CLOUDBURST . 8
    THE LITTLE OLD HOUSE WAS OUT WITH A LITTLE NEW SHED . 286 A ROADSIDE STAND . .   1
    ONCE SHOWED TWO LITTLE MONKEYS IN A CAGE . . . . . . 293 AT WOODWARD'S GARDENS . 2
    HE GOT HIS PURPLE LITTLE KNUCKLES STUNG. . . . . . . 293 AT WOODWARD'S GARDENS . 17
    THERE MAY BE LITTLE OR MUCH BEYOND THE GRAVE, ... 300 STRONG SAYING NOTHING . 15
    SANG HALFWAY THROUGH ITS LITTLE INBORN TUNE. . . . . 302 A BIRD SINGING IN SLEEP 2
    BUT WE CAN'T HELP FEELING MORE THAN A LITTLE BETRAYED 305 THERE ARE ROUGHLY ZONES . 1
    GREED HAS BEEN TAUGHT A LITTLE ABNEGATION . . . . . . 319 BUILD SOIL 117
    BUT SWEATING-FULL, DRIPS WINE AND OIL A LITTLE. . . . 323 BUILD SOIL 236
    ONCE TOOK A LITTLE PEBBLE WHEEL . . . . 326 A MISSIVE MISSILE . . 2
    AND TO THOSE CONCERNED HE MAY SEEM A LITTLE LATE. . . 342 WILLFUL HOMING . . . 12
    THEIR LITTLE STORMY SHIP, THAN ON. . . . . 344 DISCOVERY OF MADEIRAS . 20
    AND IT MUST BE A LITTLE MORE IN FAVOR OF MAN, ... 349 OUR HOLD ON THE PLANET 15
    WHO AM TASKED TO SAVE MY OWN A LITTLE WHILE. . . . . 357 A MOTH SEEN IN WINTER . 24
    AND IN WHICH THERE WAS LITTLE PROPERTY RIGHT. . . . . 364 TRESPASS 12
    THEN CAME HIS LITTLE ACKNOWLEDGMENT: . . . . 364 TRESPASS 17
    WEEP FOR WHAT LITTLE THINGS COULD MAKE THEM GLAD. . . 378 DIRECTIVE 44
    BUT THERE ARE LITTLE STREETLIGHTS SHE SHOULD TRUST, . 386 THE FEAR OF MAN . . . 11
    NOR YET THE LITTLE DOTTED IN ME SEEK. . . . . 387 IOTA SUBSCRIPT . . .   2
    DON'T MIND A LITTLE THING LIKE THE ACTORS FIGHTING. . 392 IT BIDS PRETTY FAIR . 2
    BUT PUNY LITTLE STATES CAN ONLY BE. . . . . 398 NO HOLY WARS FOR THEM . 4
    WHICH MAY A LITTLE WHILE BY WAR AND TRADE . . . . . . 399 THE INGENUITIES OF DEBT 7
    BUT JUDGING BY WHAT LITTLE OF IT STANDS, ... 399 THE INGENUITIES OF DEBT 10
    IT GIVES US STRANGELY LITTLE AID, ... 403 SOMETHING LIKE A STAR . 16
    IT ASKS A LITTLE OF US HERE. . . . . 403 SOMETHING LIKE A STAR . 20
    AND DARED TO TASTE THE WOUND A LITTLE KNOWS. . . . . 411 POD OF THE MILKWEED . 18
    I WAS TO TASTE IN LITTLE THE GRIEF . . . . 420 ONE MORE BREVITY . . 50
    THERE IS A CALL TO LIFE A LITTLE STERNER, ... 424 FOR JOHN F. KENNEDY . 66
    FORGIVE, O LORD, MY LITTLE JOKES ON THEE . . . . . . 428 FORGIVE, O LORD.... .   1
    LIKE A LITTLE BROTHER . . . . 432 KITTY HAWK 118
    LITTLE I IMAGINED . . . . 434 KITTY HAWK 188
    THE REASON ARTISTS SHOW SO LITTLE INTEREST . . . . . 461 HOW HARD TO KEEP FROM 230
    AND MAY AS WELL THROW IN A LITTLE SENSE. . . . . . . 482 A MASQUE OF REASON . 237
    ONE SIMPLE LITTLE STATEMENT FROM THE THRONE . . . . . 484 A MASQUE OF REASON . 308
    WOULD YOU TWO PLEASE DRAW IN A LITTLE CLOSER? . . . . 488 A MASQUE OF REASON . 403
    HOW RELATIVELY LITTLE JUSTICE MATTERS. . . . . 499 A MASQUE OF MERCY . 146
    YOU POOR, POOR SWALLOWABLE LITTLE MAN. . . . . 500 A MASQUE OF MERCY . 190
LITTLETON
    AT LITTLETON (FOUR THOUSAND), LITTLETON . . . . 165 NEW HAMPSHIRE . . . 203
    IN LITTLETON IT MAY AS WELL BE ME. . . . . 177 THE STAR-SPLITTER . . 37
LIVE
    TWO THAT DON'T LOVE CAN'T LIVE TOGETHER WITHOUT THEM. 53 HOME BURIAL 54
    BUT TWO THAT DO CAN'T LIVE TOGETHER WITH THEM." . . . 53 HOME BURIAL 55
    THEY LIVE SO FAR AWAY--SHE IS OUT WEST-- . . . . 55 THE BLACK COTTAGE . 19
    "WHO CARES WHAT THEY SAY? IT'S A NICE WAY TO LIVE, . . 61 BLUEBERRIES 54
    WE USED TO LIVE--TEN MILES FROM ANYWHERE. . . . . . . 64 A SERVANT TO SERVANTS 63
    DROP EVERYTHING AND LIVE OUT ON THE GROUND-- . . . . . 67 A SERVANT TO SERVANTS . 162

LIVE (CONTINUED)
    TO LIVE TOGETHER AND THEN PULL APART. . . . . 82 THE HOUSEKEEPER . . . 40
    NO ONE WILL EVER LIVE ON IT AGAIN. . . . . 83 THE HOUSEKEEPER . . . 49
    SHE THINKS IF IT WAS BAD TO LIVE WITH HIM, ... 83 THE HOUSEKEEPER . . . 74
    "AND WE LIVE UP TO IT; OR I DON'T KNOW . . . . 85 THE HOUSEKEEPER . . . 132
    WITH EVERYTHING. WHAT WE LIVE BY WE DIE BY.-- . . . . 94 THE SELF-SEEKER . . . 48
    TO GET SO WE HAD NO ONE LEFT TO LIVE WITH. . . . . . 178 THE STAR-SPLITTER . . 46
    AND TOOK THE FANCY HOME WITH THEM TO LIVE BY. . . . . 182 MAPLE 96
    UNDER A RUINOUS LIVE APPLE TREE . . . . 189 THE GRINDSTONE . . . 20
    WHEN THE GIRL SEEMED TOO WATERLOGGED TO LIVE, ... 194 PAUL'S WIFE 117
    AND THE LIFE I LIVE NOW'S AN EXTRA LIFE . . . . . . 196 WILD GRAPES 14
    I MAY YET LIVE, AS I KNOW OTHERS LIVE, ... 199 WILD GRAPES 100
    WENTWORTH AND WARREN'S BOTH GOOD TOWNS TO LIVE IN, . . 208 PAUPER WITCH OF GRAFTON 30
    ONLY I HAPPEN TO PREFER TO LIVE . . . . 208 PAUPER WITCH OF GRAFTON 31
    WHO USED TO LIVE HERE. THEY WERE ROBINSONS. . . . . . 215 A FOUNTAIN, A BOTTLE . 76
    IN FETID DARKNESS STILL TO LIVE AND RUN--. . . . . . 231 A BROOK IN THE CITY . 17
    ALL WE WHO PREFER TO LIVE . . . . 282 A DRUMLIN WOODCHUCK . 13
    TO LIVE IN VILLAGES, NEXT TO THE THEATER AND STORE, . . 286 A ROADSIDE STAND . . 25
    BUT NOW LIVE EVEN TOGETHER. . . . . 294 A RECORD STRIDE . . . 8
    THE MUSE TAKES CARE OF YOU. YOU LIVE BY WRITING . . . 316 BUILD SOIL 17
    POOR CASTAWAY OF COMMERCE, AND SO LIVE . . . . . . 323 BUILD SOIL 212
    BUT MUST LIVE LIVES OUT MENTALLY AGAPE . . . . . . 351 THE LESSON FOR TODAY . 40
    ABOUT HOW LONG A MAN MAY THINK TO LIVE, ... 354 THE LESSON FOR TODAY . 135
    AT LEAST TO LIVE UNGOLDEN WITH THE POOR, ... 358 THE LOST FOLLOWER . . 18
    FOR ME TO SEND YOU ONE OUT WHERE YOU LIVE . . . . . 365 OF STONES OF THE PLACE 5
    TO LIVE ITS LIFE OUT AS AN ORNAMENT. . . . . 375 A YOUNG BIRCH . . . 22
    OR AREN'T THE BONES ENOUGH I LIVE TO LIME? . . . . . 382 TO AN ANCIENT . . . 18
    WE DO NOT GO UP THERE TO LIVE BY DAY. . . . . 386 A STEEPLE ON THE HOUSE 5
    NOR NEED WE EVER GO UP THERE TO LIVE. . . . . 386 A STEEPLE ON THE HOUSE 6
    WHO ADVISED MAN TO COME AND LIVE THEREIN? . . . . . 400 THE BROKEN DROUGHT . . 14
    AND SHOWED THEM IT CONTAINED A LIVE TEREDO. . . . . . 456 HOW HARD TO KEEP FROM 85
    WHAT AN EXCITING AGE IT IS WE LIVE IN-- . . . . . . 462 HOW HARD TO KEEP FROM 256
    NO, LET'S NOT LIVE THINGS OVER. I DON'T CARE. . . . . 477 A MASQUE OF REASON . . 119
    THE CITY IS ALL RIGHT. TO LIVE IN ONE . . . . 496 A MASQUE OF MERCY . . 69
    A LOFTY BEAUTY NO ONE CAN LIVE UP TO, ... 512 A MASQUE OF MERCY . . 496
    YET NO ONE TURN FROM TRYING TO LIVE UP TO. . . . . . 512 A MASQUE OF MERCY . . 497
    YES, SPOKEN SO WE CAN'T LIVE UP TO IT, ... 512 A MASQUE OF MERCY . . 498
    HIS LOFTY BEAUTY NO ONE CAN LIVE UP TO, ... 513 A MASQUE OF MERCY . . 521
    LIVE AND LET LIVE, BELIEVE AND LET BELIEVE. . . . . . 516 A MASQUE OF MERCY . . 594
LIVED
    "YOU'VE LIVED HERE ALL YOUR LIFE?" / "EVER SINCE HOR . . 44 THE MOUNTAIN . . . 105
    AND SEE THE WAY YOU LIVED, BUT I DON'T KNOW! . . . . 62 A SERVANT TO SERVANTS . 4
    SOMEONE WHO LIVED IN TURNING TO FRESH TASKS . . . . . 102 THE WOOD-PILE . . . 35
    TO SEE IF THE BIRDS LIVED THE FIRST NIGHT THROUGH, . . 110 THE EXPOSED NEST . . 35
    WHEN THE HOUSE WASN'T LIVED IN? I'VE BEEN LOOKING: . . 117 IN THE HOME STRETCH . 192
    HAVEN'T YOU HEARD WHAT WE HAVE LIVED TO LEARN? . . . . 133 THE BONFIRE 109
    BROWN LIVED AT SUCH A LOFTY FARM . . . . 137 BROWN'S DESCENT . . . 1
    AND WHERE I LIVED IN MOUNTAIN LAND . . . . 140 THE GUM-GATHERER . . 10
    YOU'D HAVE TO HAVE BEEN THERE AND LIVED IT. . . . . . 142 THE VANISHING RED . . 11
    TO SAY YOUR MOTHER, HAD SHE LIVED, WOULD BE . . . . . 184 MAPLE 129
    THE TOTE ROAD TO OUR CLEARING WHERE WE LIVED. . . . . 208 PAUPER WITCH OF GRAFTON 25
    SHE WAS 'SHUT IN' FOR LIFE. SHE LIVED HER WHOLE . . . 215 A FOUNTAIN, A BOTTLE . 84
    I LIVED ON AIR . . . . 226 TO EARTHWARD 4
    HAD FED IN CHORUS, AND LIVED TO FLEDGE, ... 253 THE THATCH 15
    THE MILES AND MILES HE LIVED FROM ANYWHERE . . . . . 292 FIGURE IN THE DOORWAY . 11
    AND I ALONE OF US HAVE LIVED TO TELL. . . . . 315 IRIS BY NIGHT . . . 22
    STILL LIVED FOR ONE SONG MORE . . . . 334 COME IN 11
    ONE MAN HAD LIVED ONE HUNDRED YEARS AND EIGHT. . . . . 355 THE LESSON FOR TODAY . 140
    YOU MIGHT NOT NOTICE IF YOU'VE LIVED IN TOWN, ... 370 THE LITERATE FARMER AND 68
    WHEN MAN FIRST LIVED IN CAVES ALONG THE CREEKS?" . . . 372 THE LITERATE FARMER AND 140
LIVELIER
    AND TAKE A LIVELIER VIEW OF THINGS FROM HERE. . . . . 112 IN THE HOME STRETCH . 61
LIVELONG
    AS LONG AS LIGHTLY ALL THEIR LIVELONG SESSIONS, . . . 317 BUILD SOIL 60
    TO DISTURB THEIR PERFECT POISE THE LIVELONG DAY . . . 343 QUEST OF PURPLE-FRINGED 19
LIVES
    I DON'T MEAN ALTOGETHER BY THE LIVES . . . . 56 THE BLACK COTTAGE . . 37
    AND YOU AREN'T DARKENING OTHER PEOPLE'S LIVES-- . . . 65 A SERVANT TO SERVANTS . 99
    SHE HAS ONE WITCH--OLD STYLE. SHE LIVES IN COLEBROOK. . 163 NEW HAMPSHIRE . . . 125
    SO THERE THEY LET THEIR LIVES BE NARROWED IN . . . . 240 OUR SINGING STRENGTH . 31
    FOR THESE HAVE GOVERNED IN OUR LIVES, ... 252 THE PEACEFUL SHEPHERD . 9
    AND BROUGHT OUR VARIOUS LIVES TO PASS. . . . . . . 265 THE BIRTHPLACE . . . 6
    THE WHITE-TAILED HORNET LIVES IN A BALLOON . . . . . 277 THE WHITE-TAILED HORNET 1
    SWARM OVER THEIR LIVES ENFORCING BENEFITS . . . . . 287 A ROADSIDE STAND . . 28
    FAR INTO THE LIVES OF OTHER FOLK. . . . . 292 ON HEART'S BEGINNING TO 45
    IT LIVES LESS IN THE PRESENT . . . . 336 CARPE DIEM 20
    BUT MUST LIVE LIVES OUT MENTALLY AGAPE . . . . . . 351 THE LESSON FOR TODAY . 40
    THEY EVER WILL RETURN TO ALL THEIR LIVES, ... 411 POD OF THE MILKWEED . 3
    THAT COMES OF DOGS' LIVES BEING SO BRIEF, ... 420 ONE MORE BREVITY . . 51
    OUR VERY BEST, OUR LIVES LAID DOWN LIKE JONAH'S, . . . 520 A MASQUE OF MERCY . . 720
    OUR LIVES LAID DOWN IN WAR AND PEACE--MAY NOT . . . . 520 A MASQUE OF MERCY . . 721
LIVID
    WHEN YOU GIVE IT THE LIVID METAL-SAP. . . . . . . 306 A TRIAL RUN 3
LIVING
    LIVING OR DEAD, WHICHEVER ARE TO MIND. . . . . . . 17 THE VANTAGE POINT . . 8
    AND LIVING PEOPLE, AND THINGS THEY UNDERSTAND. . . . . 54 HOME BURIAL 105
    AND LIVING BY A LAKE. I'M PAST SUCH HELP-- . . . . . 67 A SERVANT TO SERVANTS . 156
    HOW DO YOU SEE HIM LIVING WHEN YOU'RE GONE? . . . . . 82 THE HOUSEKEEPER . . . 41
    "I DON'T JUST SEE HIM LIVING MANY YEARS, ... 82 THE HOUSEKEEPER . . . 43
    THEY PLANT DEAD TREES FOR LIVING, AND THE DEAD . . . . 141 THE LINE-GANG . . . 3
    THEY STRING TOGETHER WITH A LIVING THREAD. . . . . . 141 THE LINE-GANG . . . 4
    AND LIVING HIS FIGHT THROUGH WITH HIM, I SUPPOSE." . . 152 SNOW 269
    WHERE I WAS LIVING THEN, NEW HAMPSHIRE OFFERED . . . . 167 NEW HAMPSHIRE . . . 252
    AT PRESENT I AM LIVING IN VERMONT. . . . . 172 NEW HAMPSHIRE . . . 413
    IT MUST BE I WANT LIFE TO GO ON LIVING. . . . . . . 176 THE CENSUS-TAKER . . 64
    TO EARN A LIVING ON THE CONCORD RAILROAD, ... 178 THE STAR-SPLITTER . . 68
    THE LIVING COME WITH GRASSY TREAD . . . . 221 IN A DISUSED GRAVEYARD 1
    THE GRAVEYARD DRAWS THE LIVING STILL, ... 221 IN A DISUSED GRAVEYARD 3

LIVING (CONTINUED)
  "THE ONES WHO LIVING COME TODAY . . . . 221 IN A DISUSED GRAVEYARD   6
  I DOUBT IF YOU'RE AS LIVING AS YOU LOOK." . . . . . 230 TWO LOOK AT TWO . . . 34
  LIVING. THEY GAVE HIM BACK TO HER ALIVE-- . . . . . 230 NOT TO KEEP 5
  NOT LUPINE LIVING ON SAND AND DROUTH. . . . . 248 A PASSING GLIMPSE . . 8
  SOME STILL WERE LIVING IN HERMITAGE. . . . . 253 THE THATCH 16
  ("YOU COULDN'T CALL IT LIVING, FOR IT AIN'T"), . . . 263 THE INVESTMENT . . . 2
  MY OBJECT IN LIVING IS TO UNITE . . . . 277 TWO TRAMPS IN MUD TIME 66
  THAT SHALL ALL LIVING THINGS DISPLACE. . . . . . . 280 BLUE RIBBON AT AMESBURY 28
  WE CAME TO WHERE THERE WAS A LIVING MAN. . . . . . . 292 FIGURE IN THE DOORWAY . 6
  CLEAR TO THE ARCTIC OF EVERY LIVING KIND. . . . . . 305 THERE ARE ROUGHLY ZONES 10
  AS THE LIVING EVER GO YET STAY. . . . . 346 DISCOVERY OF MADEIRAS . 104
  WE WERE WITHHOLDING FROM OUR LAND OF LIVING, ... 348 THE GIFT OUTRIGHT . . 10
  OR OUR NUMBER LIVING WOULDN'T BE STEADILY MORE, . . . 349 OUR HOLD ON THE PLANET 17
  BUT UNMISTAKABLY A LIVING MITE . . . . 357 A CONSIDERABLE SPECK . 8
  AS MEETING SOMEONE LIVING, FACE TO FACE. . . . . . . 382 TO AN ANCIENT . . . 9
  IN WHAT HE HAS TO DO TO EARN A LIVING. . . . . . . 406 FROM PLANE TO PLANE . 63
  WE WERE WITHHOLDING FROM OUR LAND OF LIVING, ... 424 THE GIFT OUTRIGHT . . 10
  A DESIGN FOR LIVING . . . . 435 KITTY HAWK 226
  LIKE FLESH, THERE MUST BE SOMETHING LIVING IN IT." . . 456 HOW HARD TO KEEP FROM 91
  TO EARN A LIVING. I DON'T INTERFERE. . . . . 459 HOW HARD TO KEEP FROM 180
  WE'RE POOR--THAT'S WHY. MY MAN CAN'T EARN A LIVING. . 496 A MASQUE OF MERCY . . 89
LIZARD
  AND CAUGHT ONE SILVER LIZARD BY THE TAIL, ... 237 A HILLSIDE THAW . . . 10
  SHE HAS HER SPELL ON EVERY SINGLE LIZARD. . . . . . 237 A HILLSIDE THAW . . . 22
  ONE LIZARD AT THE END OF EVERY RAY. . . . . 238 A HILLSIDE THAW . . . 34
LIZARDS
  TEN MILLION SILVER LIZARDS OUT OF SNOW! . . . . . . 237 A HILLSIDE THAW . . . 3
LO
  I HAVE BUT TO TURN ON MY ARM, AND LO, ... 17 THE VANTAGE POINT . . 10
  AND LO, IT IS ENDED. . . . . 30 RELUCTANCE 6
  ONE DROP FELL FROM A FERN, AND LO, A RIPPLE . . . . . 225 FOR ONCE SOMETHING . . 12
LOAD (SEE DEMOCRAT-LOAD)
  SILAS UP ON THE CART TO BUILD THE LOAD, ... 36 DEATH OF THE HIRED MAN 68
  TO TEACH HIM HOW TO BUILD A LOAD OF HAY----" . . . . 37 DEATH OF THE HIRED MAN 87
  THERE'S A HAY LOAD A-COMING--WHEN IT COMES. . . . . . 49 A HUNDRED COLLARS . . 132
  OF LOAD ON LOAD OF APPLES COMING IN. . . . . 69 AFTER APPLE-PICKING . 26
  TO LOAD THE LOAD, THINKS I, LOOK FOR TROUBLE. . . . . 71 THE CODE 50
  I BUILT THE LOAD AND TOPPED IT OFF; OLD SANDERS . . . 71 THE CODE 51
  I'D BUILT THE LOAD AND KNEW RIGHT WHERE TO FIND IT. . . 71 THE CODE 71
  THEY ARE DRAGGED TO THE WITHERED BRACKEN BY THE LOAD, . 121 BIRCHES 14
  HER NOT-NICE LOAD, ... 134 A GIRL'S GARDEN . . . 24
  AS IT RAN LIGHT, OR HAD TO BEAR A LOAD. . . . . . . 136 "OUT,OUT--" 8
  A MAN WITH A SWINGING BAG FOR LOAD . . . . 140 THE GUM-GATHERER . . 5
  HE TURNED ON WILLPOWER TO INCREASE THE LOAD . . . . . 189 THE GRINDSTONE . . . 31
  HEARD HOW HE THRASHED THE HORSES ON A LOAD . . . . . 192 PAUL'S WIFE 43
  THEIR RAWHIDE HARNESS FROM THE LOAD TO CAMP. . . . . 192 PAUL'S WIFE 45
  PAUL TOLD THE BOSS THE LOAD WOULD BE ALL RIGHT, . . . 192 PAUL'S WIFE 46
  "THE SUN WILL BRING YOUR LOAD IN"--AND IT DID-- . . . 192 PAUL'S WIFE 47
  I MAY LOAD AND UNLOAD . . . . 235 GATHERING LEAVES . . 13
  AND SETTING OFF THEIR HEAVY POWDER LOAD. . . . . . . 239 OUR SINGING STRENGTH . 29
  AND BRUSH THE MOW WITH THE SUMMER LOAD. . . . . . . 242 NEED OF BEING VERSED . 12
  AND TRY TO STACK THEM IN A BETTER LOAD. . . . . . . 267 THE ARMFUL 12
  THAT HAD EASED ITSELF OF ITS SUMMER LOAD, ... 304 UNHARVESTED 5
  WOULD LOAD IT ONTO CLOUD, ... 337 THE WIND AND THE RAIN . 30
  OR CREAKING WITH A BUGGY LOAD OF GRAIN. . . . . . . 378 DIRECTIVE 32
LOADED
  LOADED WITH ICE A SUNNY WINTER MORNING . . . . . . 121 BIRCHES 6
  HE LOADED AN OLD STONEBOAT WITH THE STAR . . . . . . 173 A STAR IN A STONEBOAT . 26
  LOADED WITH A GUN . . . . 431 KITTY HAWK 104
LOADS
  WITH CINDER LOADS DUMPED DOWN? THE BROOK WAS THROWN . . 231 A BROOK IN THE CITY . 15
LOAF
  WELL, YOU CAN SET THE TABLE WITH THE LOAF. . . . . . 115 IN THE HOME STRETCH . 154
  LET'S SEE YOU FIND YOUR LOAF. I'LL LIGHT THE FIRE. . . 115 IN THE HOME STRETCH . 155
LOATHING
  WITH LOATHING, FOR AGAIN IT TURNED TO FLY. . . . . . 357 A CONSIDERABLE SPECK . 14
LOAVES
  AND SOME ARE LOAVES AND SOME SO NEARLY BALLS . . . . 33 MENDING WALL 17
LOCAL
  HIS HOUSE AMONG THE LOCAL SHEDS AND SHANTIES . . . . 160 NEW HAMPSHIRE . . . 52
  AND LOCAL GREEN SUGGEST. . . . . 388 MIDDLENESS OF THE ROAD 16
LOCALEST
  THE LONGEST-SAVED-UP, RACIEST, LOCALEST . . . . . . 321 BUILD SOIL 161
LOCK
  THEY LEARNED TO RATTLE THE LOCK AND KEY . . . . . . 127 HOUSE FEAR 5
  AFTER HE'D PICKED THE LOCK AND GOT IT STARTED, ... 170 NEW HAMPSHIRE . . . 346
  WITH NO LOCK TO LOCK. . . . . 240 THE LOCKLESS DOOR . . 4
  LEAVING ON ONE WIRE TOOTH A LOCK OF HAIR. . . . . . 269 THE BEAR 9
  TO THINK THAT THOUGH HE COULD NOT LOCK HIMSELF IN, . . 290 OLD BARN AT THE BOTTOM 43
  COULD MISCHIEVOUSLY LOCK HIM IN TO STAY. . . . . . . 290 OLD BARN AT THE BOTTOM 45
  AND LOCK HIM THROUGH CULEBRA CUT. . . . . 418 AMERICA IS HARD TO SEE 57
LOCKED (SEE DOUBLE-LOCKED)
  LOCKED UP FOR YEARS BACK THERE AT THE OLD FARM. . . . 65 A SERVANT TO SERVANTS . 89
  DOORS LOCKED AND CURTAINS DRAWN WILL MAKE NO DIFFERENCE. 89 THE FEAR 16
  WHEN WE LOCKED UP THE HOUSE AT NIGHT, ... 135 LOCKED OUT 1
  WE ALWAYS LOCKED THE FLOWERS OUTSIDE . . . . 135 LOCKED OUT 2
  LOCKED OUT . . . . 135 LOCKED OUT . . . . T
  HER GIFT FOR READING LETTERS LOCKED IN BOXES. . . . . 163 NEW HAMPSHIRE . . . 131
  THE GATE FOR HALF AN HOUR BE LOCKED, ... 273 A LONE STRIKER . . . 7
  THEY COULD BE LOCKED BUT FROM THE OUTSIDE ONLY. . . . 289 OLD BARN AT THE BOTTOM 16
  AND LOCKS THE DOOR. ONE CUSTOMER, LOCKED IN, ... 493 A MASQUE OF MERCY . . 3
  YOU LOCKED THE DOOR, BEL. LET ME HAVE THE KEY. . . . 500 A MASQUE OF MERCY . . 174
  BEYOND THIS GREAT DOOR YOU HAVE LOCKED AGAINST ME, . . 513 A MASQUE OF MERCY . . 532
LOCKING
  A PERSONAL INTEREST IN THE LOCKING UP . . . . 115 IN THE HOME STRETCH . 134
LOCKLESS
  THE LOCKLESS DOOR . . . . 240 THE LOCKLESS DOOR . . T

```
                                                                PAGE  TITLE                  LINE

LOCKS  (SEE PROP-LOCKS)
    LIKE LOCKS BLOWN FORWARD IN THE GLEAM OF EYES. . . . .  . 250 ONCE BY THE PACIFIC  .    6
    ITS LOCKS WERE PROPS--AND THAT REMINDED HIM. .  . . . .  . 290 OLD BARN AT THE BOTTOM    28
    YES, RIGHT I WAS, THE LOCKS WERE PROPS OUTSIDE; . . . .  . 290 OLD BARN AT THE BOTTOM    41
    IT WASN'T SOMEONE AT YOUR LOCKS. .  . . . . . .  . . . .  . 380 AN UNSTAMPED LETTER IN    3
    AND THIS TIME LOCKS IT UP AND LEAVES IT.) . . . . . .  . . 477 A MASQUE OF REASON .  . 108
    AND LOCKS THE DOOR. ONE CUSTOMER, LOCKED IN, .  . . . .  . 493 A MASQUE OF MERCY  . .    3
LODGE
    --I HAVE A PROTEST I WOULD LODGE WITH YOU. .  . . . . .  . 476 A MASQUE OF REASON .  .   87
LODGED
    SET WELL BACK FROM THE ROAD IN RANK LODGED GRASS, . . .  .  55 THE BLACK COTTAGE  .  .    4
    AND LAY LODGED--THOUGH NOT DEAD. . . . . . . . . . . .  . 250 LODGED . . . . . .  .    5
    LODGED . . . . . . . . . . . . . . . . . . . . . . .  . 250 LODGED . . . . . .  .    T
LOFTINESS
    WE GRANT YOUR LOFTINESS THE RIGHT . . . . . . . . . . .  . 403 SOMETHING LIKE A STAR .    2
LOFTY
    BROWN LIVED AT SUCH A LOFTY FARM . . . . . . . . . . .  . 137 BROWN'S DESCENT  . . .    1
    TAUNTED THE LOFTY LAND WITH LITTLE MEN." . . . . . . .  . 166 NEW HAMPSHIRE  . . . . 219
    THEY TAUNT THE LOFTY LAND WITH LITTLE MEN. . . . . . .  . 167 NEW HAMPSHIRE  . . . . 264
    THE PEOPLE OR THE ALREADY LOFTY MOUNTAINS, . . . . . .  . 168 NEW HAMPSHIRE  . . . . 308
    I'D ELEVATE THE ALREADY LOFTY MOUNTAINS. . . . . . . .  . 168 NEW HAMPSHIRE  . . . . 309
    TOO LOFTY AND ORIGINAL TO RAGE. . . . . . . . . . . .  . 378 DIRECTIVE . . . . .  .   52
    A LOFTY BEAUTY NO ONE CAN LIVE UP TO, . . . . . . . .  . 512 A MASQUE OF MERCY  . . 496
    HIS LOFTY BEAUTY NO ONE CAN LIVE UP TO, . . . . . . .  . 513 A MASQUE OF MERCY  . . 521
LOG
    AND SLEPT. THE LOG THAT SHIFTED WITH A JOLT . . . . .  . 108 OLD MAN'S WINTER NIGHT   23
    SHE RESTED ON A LOG AND TOSSED . . . . . . . . . . .  . 128 THE IMPULSE . . . .  .    9
    HE DODGED A LOG THAT LIFTED LIKE AN ARM . . . . . . .  . 170 NEW HAMPSHIRE  . . . . 347
    OUT OF A WHITE-PINE LOG. MURPHY WAS THERE . . . . . .  . 192 PAUL'S WIFE  . . . .  .   55
    THEY'D SLICED THE FIRST SLAB OFF A BIG BUTT LOG, . . .  . 193 PAUL'S WIFE  . . . .  .   62
    WHEN THEY SAW WHAT HAD HAPPENED TO THE LOG, . . . . .  . 193 PAUL'S WIFE  . . . .  .   66
    ON THE NEW WOOD THE WHOLE LENGTH OF THE LOG . . . . .  . 193 PAUL'S WIFE  . . . .  .   70
    THE LOG WAS HOLLOW. THEY WERE SAWING PINE. . . . . .  . 193 PAUL'S WIFE  . . . .  .   74
    WHERE THE LOG DRIVE LAY PRESSED AGAINST THE BOOM, . .  . 194 PAUL'S WIFE  . . . .  . 107
    WHO, LEANING ON A LOG, LOOKED BACK AT PAUL. . . . . .  . 194 PAUL'S WIFE  . . . .  . 110
    GO CONSULT THE LOG. . . . . . . . . . . . . . . . .  . 438 KITTY HAWK . . . . .  . 342
LOGGED
    THEY LOGGED IT THERE LAST WINTER SOME WAY UP. . . . .  .  41 THE MOUNTAIN . . . .  .   42
LOGGING
    THE SAME PAUL AT THE SAME OLD FEATS OF LOGGING. . . .  . 192 PAUL'S WIFE  . . . .  .   30
LOGIC
    AND ALL THEIR LOGIC WOULD FILL MY HEAD: . . . . . .  . 277 TWO TRAMPS IN MUD TIME   59
    MY LIFE-TRAIN LOGIC. I AGREE WITH YOU . . . . . . .  . 325 BUILD SOIL  . . . . .  . 290
    TO BREAK OUR LOGIC IN TOO LONG A FLIGHT, . . . . .  . 370 THE LITERATE FARMER AND   82
    "YOUR TROUBLE IS BUCOLIC LACK OF LOGIC," . . . . .  . 404 FROM PLANE TO PLANE  .    9
    AND HOW BY ITS OWN LOGIC IT CONCENTRATES . . . . .  . 509 A MASQUE OF MERCY  . . 410
    CHRIST CAME TO INTRODUCE A BREAK WITH LOGIC . . . .  . 511 A MASQUE OF MERCY  . . 475
LOGJAM
    THE WAY THE WIRY GANG-BOSS LIKED THE LOGJAM. `. . .  . 170 NEW HAMPSHIRE  . . . . 345
LOGS
    ACROSS THE LOGS LIKE BACKS OF ALLIGATORS, . . . . .  . 195 PAUL'S WIFE  . . . .  . 121
LOITERING
    AND THE MORE LOITERING ARE TURNED . . . . . . . .  .  20 THE TRIAL BY EXISTENCE   25
    FOR THEM MY LOITERING AROUND . . . . . . . . . .  . 466 SOME SCIENCE FICTION .   17
LOLLING
    THERE AMID LOLLING JUNIPER RECLINED, . . . . . . .  .  17 THE VANTAGE POINT  . .    4
LONDON
    THE CRYSTAL PALACE, LONDON. HE'S IMPORTED. . . . .  .  86 THE HOUSEKEEPER  . . . 151
LONE
    THE LAST LONE ASTER IS GONE; . . . . . . . . . .  .  30 RELUCTANCE . . . . .  .   15
    LIKE A LONE ACTOR ON A GLOOMY STAGE-- . . . . . .  . 160 NEW HAMPSHIRE  . . . .   46
    A LONE STRIKER . . . . . . . . . . . . . . . .  . 273 A LONE STRIKER . . . .  .    T
    WITH A LONE COAST GUARD . . . . . . . . . . . .  . 432 KITTY HAWK . . . . .  . 140
LONELINESS
    LONELINESS . . . . . . . . . . . . . . . . . .  . 126 LONELINESS . . . . .  .    T
    THE LONELINESS INCLUDES ME UNAWARES. . . . . . .  . 296 DESERT PLACES  . . . .    8
    AND LONELY AS IT IS, THAT LONELINESS . . . . . .  . 296 DESERT PLACES  . . . .    9
LONELY
    I DWELL IN A LONELY HOUSE I KNOW . . . . . . . .  .   5 GHOST HOUSE  . . . .  .    1
    ONE SO LONELY WAS FAIN TO LIST, . . . . . . . .  .  15 IN A VALE  . . . . .  .   14
    THIS IS A VERY, VERY LONELY PLACE.-- . . . . . .  .  92 THE FEAR . . . . . .  .   90
    TO THE LONELY HOUSE FROM FAR AWAY, . . . . . . .  . 127 HOUSE FEAR . . . . .  .    3
    IT WAS TOO LONELY FOR HER THERE, . . . . . . . .  . 128 THE IMPULSE  . . . .  .    1
    THE INMATES MAY BE LONELY WOMENFOLK. . . . . . .  . 248 THE COCOON . . . . .  .   11
    AND LONELY AS IT IS, THAT LONELINESS . . . . . .  . 296 DESERT PLACES  . . . .    9
    WILL BE MORE LONELY ERE IT WILL BE LESS-- . . .  . 296 DESERT PLACES  . . . .   10
    NO ONE WAS LOOKING AT HIS LONELY CASE; . . . . .  . 396 ANY SIZE WE PLEASE .  .    1
LONESOME
    "DID THEY MAKE SOMETHING LONESOME GO THROUGH YOU? . .  . 114 IN THE HOME STRETCH  . 122
'LONG
    "GO 'LONG," I SAID TO HIM, HE TO HIS HORSE. . . . .  . 168 NEW HAMPSHIRE  . . .  . 300
LONG  (SEE AGE-LONG, LONG-LONG-AFTER-THOUGHT, SO-LONG-KEPT)
    I SHAN'T BE GONE LONG.--YOU COME TOO. . . . . . . .  .   1 THE PASTURE  . . . .  .    4
    I SHAN'T BE GONE LONG.--YOU COME TOO. . . . . . . .  .   1 THE PASTURE  . . . .  .    8
    AND LONG TO KNOW IF STILL I HELD THEM DEAR. . . . .  .   5 INTO MY OWN  . . . .  .   12
    THAT I'VE BEEN LONG AWAY. . . . . . . . . . . . .  .  13 FLOWER-GATHERING . .  .   16
    NOR VAINLY LISTEN ALL THE NIGHT LONG. . . . . . .  .  16 IN A VALE  . . . . .  .   25
    (THIS WAS MY DREAM) AND LOOKED AND PONDERED LONG, . .  .  16 A DREAM PANG . . . .  .    4
    AND THAT WAS MY LONG SCYTHE WHISPERING TO THE GROUND. .  .  17 MOWING . . . . . .  .    2
    MY LONG SCYTHE WHISPERED AND LEFT THE HAY TO MAKE. . .  .  17 MOWING . . . . . .  .   14
    AND HEAR HIS LONG SCYTHE WHISPERING TO THE GROUND, . .  .  23 THE TUFT OF FLOWERS  .   32
    IT WILL BE LONG ERE THE MARSHES RESUME, . . . . .  .  25 NOW CLOSE THE WINDOWS .    5
    IT WILL BE LONG ERE THE EARLIEST BIRD: . . . . .  .  25 NOW CLOSE THE WINDOWS .    6
    BUT IT IS LONG AGO-- . . . . . . . . . . . . .  .  28 MY BUTTERFLY . . . .  .   10
    IT WOULDN'T HAVE TO BE A LONG WAY DOWN . . . . .  .  42 THE MOUNTAIN . . . .  .   69
    BY ANYONE WHO'D COME A LONG WAY UP. . . . . . .  .  43 THE MOUNTAIN . . . .  .   72
    'I CAN'T AND WON'T. YOU'VE BEEN IN LONG ENOUGH: . .  .  48 A HUNDRED COLLARS  . . 114
    WHAT HAD HOW LONG IT TAKES A BIRCH TO ROT . . . .  .  54 HOME BURIAL  . . . .  .   95
```

LONG (CONTINUED)
ONE WASN'T LONG IN LEARNING THAT SHE THOUGHT, ...   56 THE BLACK COTTAGE . . 54
CLING TO IT LONG ENOUGH, AND NOT A DOUBT . . . .   58 THE BLACK COTTAGE . . 107
TO RIPEN TOO LONG. I AM GREATLY TO BLAME.'" . . . . . .   60 BLUEBERRIES 46
"I'VE TOLD YOU HOW ONCE, NOT LONG AFTER WE CAME, ...   61 BLUEBERRIES 67
IT'S SO LONG SINCE I PICKED I ALMOST FORGET . . . . . .   62 BLUEBERRIES 84
THE ADVANTAGES IT HAS, SO LONG AND NARROW, ...   63 A SERVANT TO SERVANTS . 19
OR A LONG RAIN. I SHOULD SOON GET ENOUGH, ...   67 A SERVANT TO SERVANTS . 164
MY LONG TWO-POINTED LADDER'S STICKING THROUGH A TREE . .   68 AFTER APPLE-PICKING . . 1
LONG SLEEP, AS I DESCRIBE ITS COMING ON, ...   69 AFTER APPLE-PICKING . . 41
HE WON'T BE LONG IN THAT CASE. YOU CAN WAIT. . . . . .   81 THE HOUSEKEEPER . . . 18
WE'VE BEEN HERE FIFTEEN YEARS." / "THAT'S A LONG TIME .   82 THE HOUSEKEEPER . . . 39
TO THE DARK HOUSE AFTER SO LONG AN ABSENCE, ...   89 THE FEAR 18
I DIDN'T TRY TOO LONG TO PULL AWAY, ...   93 THE SELF-SEEKER . . . 24
I'VE BOARDED HERE SO LONG, SHE THINKS SHE OWNS ME. . .   94 THE SELF-SEEKER . . . 54
AND IT MAY TAKE HIM I DON'T KNOW HOW LONG. . . . . . .   98 THE SELF-SEEKER . . . 171
AND BE ONE TRAVELER, LONG I STOOD . . . . 105 THE ROAD NOT TAKEN . . 3
WHOSE COMING HOME HAS BEEN TOO LONG DEFERRED, ... 109 THE EXPOSED NEST . . . 22
TO EVERYTHING. HER LIGHT WON'T LAST US LONG. . . . . . 113 IN THE HOME STRETCH . . 71
A BROOK TO NONE BUT WHO REMEMBER LONG. . . . . 119 HYLA BROOK 12
SO LOW FOR LONG, THEY NEVER RIGHT THEMSELVES: . . . . . 121 BIRCHES 16
AND YES, SHE HAS LONG MISTRUSTED . . . . 134 A GIRL'S GARDEN . . . 33
'BOUT OUT!" AND TOOK THE LONG WAY HOME . . . . 140 BROWN'S DESCENT . . . 75
IT'S TOO LONG A STORY TO GO INTO NOW. . . . . 142 THE VANISHING RED . . 10
LONG ENOUGH FOR RECORDING ALL OUR NAMES ON.— . . . . . 143 SNOW 10
"HAD SHE BEEN RINGING LONG? I'LL GET MY WRAPPER. . . . 152 SNOW 275
OFFERED ME NOT LONG SINCE UP BERLIN WAY . . . . 162 NEW HAMPSHIRE 110
THE PLACE IS SILENT ALL DAY LONG, NOR YET . . . . . . 165 NEW HAMPSHIRE 189
AS LONG AS LIFE GOES SO UNTERRIBLY? . . . . 167 NEW HAMPSHIRE 269
AND A LONG BIRD OF PARADISE'S TAIL . . . . 172 A STAR IN A STONEBOAT . 16
FOR THE LEAST SIN, IT WOULDN'T TAKE US LONG . . . . . 177 THE STAR-SPLITTER . . 45
SHE HAD BEEN HAVING A LONG LOOK AT YOU. . . . . 180 MAPLE 15
WHAT HE SOWED WITH HER SLEPT SO LONG A SLEEP, ... 180 MAPLE 36
ONCE LONG AGO HER FATHER HAD PUT HIMSELF OFF.) . . . . 183 MAPLE 111
SO LONG AS HE WOULD LEAVE ENOUGH UNSAID, ... 186 THE AX-HELVE 38
FOR THE HARD WORK. HE CHAFED ITS LONG WHITE BODY . . . 187 THE AX-HELVE 76
BAPTISTE KNEW HOW TO MAKE A SHORT JOB LONG. . . . . . . 187 THE AX-HELVE 80
ALTHOUGH IT WASN'T USUALLY LONG . . . . 192 PAUL'S WIFE 28
IT WASN'T GREASE AT ALL, BUT A LONG SLOT. . . . . . . 193 PAUL'S WIFE 73
I KNOW I LOOKED LONG AT MY CURLED-UP FINGERS, ... 198 WILD GRAPES 87
IN EIGHTY-FIVE." / "AS LONG AGO AS THAT?" . . . . . . 213 A FOUNTAIN, A BOTTLE . 23
"HADN'T YOU LONG SUSPECTED WHERE YOU WERE?" . . . . . . 214 A FOUNTAIN, A BOTTLE . 47
LIFE LONG IN BED, AND WROTE HER THINGS IN BED. . . . . 215 A FOUNTAIN, A BOTTLE . 85
IT WAS LONG I LAY . . . . 217 I WILL SING YOU ONE-O . 1
AND HELD IT LONG ENOUGH FOR NORTH . . . . 224 THE AIM WAS SONG . . 10
IT SHALL NOT MAKE AGAIN ALL WINTER LONG . . . . 226 THE ONSET 4
IN LONG STORMS AN UNDRIFTED FOUR FEET DEEP . . . . . . 226 THE ONSET 15
I LONG FOR WEIGHT AND STRENGTH . . . . 227 TO EARTHWARD 30
SHE COULD NOT TROUBLE HER MIND WITH TOO LONG, ... 229 TWO LOOK AT TWO . . . 23
LONG, LONG BEFORE WE WERE FROM ANY CREATURE. . . . . . 259 WEST-RUNNING BROOK . . 41
EVER A CAUSE THAT WAS LOST TOO LONG, ... 262 HANNIBAL 2
AND IF MEN HAVE WATCHED A LONG TIME . . . . 266 SITTING BY A BUSH . . 9
YOU'LL WAIT A LONG, LONG TIME FOR ANYTHING MUCH . . . . 268 ON LOOKING UP BY CHANCE 1
BUT NOT LONG SINCE IN THE LUMBER CAMPS). . . . . 276 TWO TRAMPS IN MUD TIME 51
WENT LONG SINCE TO THE DOGS UNDER THE TABLE. . . . . . 279 THE WHITE-TAILED HORNET 57
DOWNWARD COMPARISONS. AS LONG ON EARTH . . . . 279 THE WHITE-TAILED HORNET 59
LONG SINCE THEY SWUNG AS THREE INSTEAD OF TWO— . . . . 283 THE GOLD HESPERIDEE . . 25
THE PEOPLE CAN BURN IT AS LONG AS THEY PLEASE; . . . . 291 ON HEART'S BEGINNING TO 16
THEY CAN KEEP IT BURNING AS LONG AS THEY PLEASE; . . . 291 ON HEART'S BEGINNING TO 24
HAD THE BOY NOT PRESUMED TOO CLOSE AND LONG. . . . . . 293 AT WOODWARD'S GARDENS . 21
ALL SUMMER LONG THEY WERE OVERHEAD, MORE LIFTED UP THAN I. 297 A LEAF-TREADER . . . 5
ALL SUMMER LONG I THOUGHT I HEARD THEM THREATENING UNDER
  THEIR BREATH. . . . . 297 A LEAF-TREADER . . . 7
WAS LONG SINCE SLID. . . . . 298 ON TAKING FROM THE TOP 4
AS LONG AS IT TAKES TO PASS . . . . 301 NEITHER OUT FAR NOR IN 5
ON THE LONG BEAD CHAIN OF REPEATED BIRTH, ... 303 A BIRD SINGING IN SLEEP 11
IS A THREAT TO THE HOUSE. BUT THE HOUSE HAS LONG BEEN TRIED. 305 THERE ARE ROUGHLY ZONES 3
AS LONG AS THE DECLARATION GUARDS . . . . 310 IN DIVES' DIVE . . . 3
AS LONG AS LIGHTLY ALL THEIR LIVELONG SESSIONS, ... 317 BUILD SOIL 60
BUT LONG BEFORE I'M INTERPERSONAL, ... 320 BUILD SOIL 143
NOT FOR A LONG, LONG TIME. PLANT, BREED, PRODUCE, . . . 323 BUILD SOIL 214
SO LONG FOR NOTHING. NO REPLY— . . . . 327 A MISSIVE MISSILE . . 26
HAD NOW PERSISTED IN THE WOODS SO LONG . . . . 339 NEVER WOULD BIRDS' SONG 11
FOR LONG THE LADY WOULD DISAPPEAR, ... 344 DISCOVERY OF MADEIRAS . 32
WHERE ALL DAY LONG SHE LAY AND DOZED. . . . . 344 DISCOVERY OF MADEIRAS . 37
HE STAYED LONG ENOUGH TO CARVE ON STONE . . . . 347 DISCOVERY OF MADEIRAS . 121
BUT LEAVING NOT THE CHAIR I LONG HAVE SAT IN . . . . . 350 THE LESSON FOR TODAY . 5
ABOUT HOW LONG A MAN MAY THINK TO LIVE, ... 354 THE LESSON FOR TODAY . 135
LONG SINCE IN SOME ABYSMAL CITY STREET, ... 359 THE LOST FOLLOWER . . 22
TO BREAK OUR LOGIC IN TOO LONG A FLIGHT, ... 370 THE LITERATE FARMER AND 82
LONG SINCE GAVE UP PRETENSE OF KEEPING COVERED. . . . . 377 DIRECTIVE 12
LOCK DOWN THE LONG VALLEY AND THERE STANDS A MOUNTAIN . 379 TOO ANXIOUS FOR RIVERS 1
TWO MEMORIES THAT LONG HAD LAIN . . . . 381 AN UNSTAMPED LETTER IN 33
IN THE LONG NIGHT . . . . 384 IN THE LONG NIGHT . . T
AS LONG THE TREES HAVE STOOD. . . . . 388 MIDDLENESS OF THE ROAD 7
AND LONG ENOUGH GETS RATED AS A CREED: . . . . 394 ETHEREALIZING 2
HAVE STAYED IN SIGHT SO LONG AS AN EXAMPLE. . . . . . . 404 FROM PLANE TO PLANE . 23
FROM HAVING BEATEN ALL DAY LONG IN VAIN . . . . 412 POD OF THE MILKWEED . 38
KNOW WHERE THEY ARE. / THEY'VE BEEN HERE LONG ENOUGH . 413 A CABIN IN THE CLEARING 2
MY HAVING DEPENDED ON HIM SO LONG, ... 421 ONE MORE BREVITY . . 64
AS LONG AS THE GREAT ISSUE WAS TO SEE . . . . 422 FOR JOHN F. KENNEDY . 12
LONG BEFORE HE FLEW IT. . . . . 430 KITTY HAWK 56
HAS BEEN LONG REDRESSED. . . . . 430 KITTY HAWK 79
FROM ITS LONG STAGNATION . . . . 435 KITTY HAWK 240
WHAT HAD LONG BEEN FACED . . . . 439 KITTY HAWK 370
IN ONE LONG INVIDIOUS DRAFT. . . . . 444 THE DRAFT HORSE . . 12
TO SEE HOW LONG THEY SHOULD WAIT . . . . 466 SOME SCIENCE FICTION . 31
THAT GOOD AND BAD SO LONG HAD LASTED. . . . . 467 QUANDARY 6

LONG (CONTINUED)
   TOO LONG I'VE OWED YOU THIS APOLOGY . . . . 475 A MASQUE OF REASON . . 59
   OR METAPHYSICS, LONG THE WORLD'S REPROACH . . . . . 480 A MASQUE OF REASON . . 191
   FOR VERY LONG. WE'RE PLAINLY MADE TO GO. . . . . . . 481 A MASQUE OF REASON . . 233
   THE CRYPT WAS LONG SINCE RIFLED BY THE GREEKS. . . . 483 A MASQUE OF REASON . . 284
   THE TENDENCY, A LONG, LONG NARROW STRIP . . . . . . 489 A MASQUE OF REASON . . 453
   TOO LONG PENT UP IN RIGOROUS CONVENTION-- . . . . . 509 A MASQUE OF MERCY . . 418
   TO LOOK AT LONG DIRECTLY (LIKE THE SUN), ... 515 A MASQUE OF MERCY . . 584
LONG-AFTER-BEDTIME
   OF AT LEAST ONE LONG-AFTER-BEDTIME WALK. . . . . . . 92 THE FEAR 83
LONG-DRAWN
   ACROSS THE HANDLE'S LONG-DRAWN SERPENTINE, ... 186 THE AX-HELVE 24
LONGED
   PIKE SAID WITH TEMPER. AND DICK LONGED TO SAY, . . . 404 FROM PLANE TO PLANE . 8
   DICK LONGED TO SAY, BUT WASN'T SURE ENOUGH . . . . . 407 FROM PLANE TO PLANE . 110
LONGER
   NO LONGER BLOWN HITHER AND THITHER; . . . . 30 RELUCTANCE 14
   NO LONGER THAN THAT?--AND THE FOLLOWING FALL . . . . 59 BLUEBERRIES 11
   A LITTLE LONGER. I MUSTN'T FEEL TOO HURRIED, ... 78 THE GENERATIONS OF MEN 146
   UPON HIS LONGER AXIS, AND . . . . 138 BROWN'S DESCENT . . 23
   FIVE THOUSAND IS NO LONGER HIGH ENOUGH. . . . . . . 169 NEW HAMPSHIRE . . . 334
   ONLY BEWITCHED SO I WOULD LAST HIM LONGER. . . . . . 210 PAUPER WITCH OF GRAFTON 95
   NO LONGER NEEDED? STAUNCH IT AT ITS SOURCE . . . . . 231 A BROOK IN THE CITY . 14
   AND HOW MUCH LONGER A STORY HAS SCIENCE . . . . . . 379 TOO ANXIOUS FOR RIVERS 17
   OF ITS GOING MUCH LONGER UNNOTICED . . . . 465 SOME SCIENCE FICTION . 2
LONGEST
   IT IS TRUE THE LONGEST DROUTH WILL END IN RAIN, . . . 268 ON LOOKING UP BY CHANCE 11
   THE LONGEST PEACE IN CHINA WILL END IN STRIFE. . . . 268 ON LOOKING UP BY CHANCE 12
   THE SUN THEN HAD HIS LONGEST DAY IN HEAVEN, ... 407 FROM PLANE TO PLANE . 90
LONGEST-SAVED-UP
   THE LONGEST-SAVED-UP, RACIEST, LOCALEST . . . . . . 321 BUILD SOIL 161
LONGING
   THE THOUGHT OF SO MUCH CHILDISH LONGING IN VAIN, . . 287 A ROADSIDE STAND . . 33
   WITH MORTAL LONGING MAY BESEECH; . . . . 328 A MISSIVE MISSILE . . 54
   IN LONGING IS NOT AT A PROGRESS-END . . . . 359 THE LOST FOLLOWER . . 28
   ALL IS AN INTERMINABLE CHAIN OF LONGING. . . . . . . 421 ESCAPIST--NEVER . . . 12
LONG-LONG-AFTER-THOUGHT
   AN AFTERTHOUGHT, A LONG-LONG-AFTER-THOUGHT. . . . . 482 A MASQUE OF REASON . . 246
LONG-SLEEVED
   AND WITH LONG-SLEEVED BRANCHES HOLD THEIR SWAY. . . . 376 SOMETHING FOR HOPE . 12
LOOK
   WITH, "LET US LOOK AT THE SKY, ... 7 LOVE AND A QUESTION . 10
   WITH MISCHIEVOUS, VAGRANT, SERAPHIC LOOK, ... 16 IN NEGLECT 4
   I LOOK INTO THE CRATER OF THE ANT. . . . . 17 THE VANTAGE POINT . . 14
   TO LISTEN ERE WE DARED TO LOOK, ... 18 GOING FOR WATER . . 18
   BUT HE TURNED FIRST, AND LED MY EYE TO LOOK . . . . 22 THE TUFT OF FLOWERS . 21
   HE JUMBLED EVERYTHING. I STOPPED TO LOOK . . . . . . 36 DEATH OF THE HIRED MAN 55
   AND NOTHING TO LOOK BACKWARD TO WITH PRIDE, ... 38 DEATH OF THE HIRED MAN 100
   AND NOTHING TO LOOK FORWARD TO WITH HOPE, ... 38 DEATH OF THE HIRED MAN 101
   "I HAVEN'T BEEN. GO, LOOK, SEE FOR YOURSELF. . . . . 40 DEATH OF THE HIRED MAN 155
   OR TURN AND SIT ON AND LOOK OUT AND DOWN, ... 42 THE MOUNTAIN 61
   TO LOOK AND TELL ME LATER HOW IT WAS." . . . . . . 43 THE MOUNTAIN 74
   AND LOOK MYSELF, BUT YOU KNOW HOW IT IS: . . . . . . 43 THE MOUNTAIN 81
   TO RAISE HERSELF AND LOOK AGAIN. HE SPOKE . . . . . 51 HOME BURIAL 5
   SHE LET HIM LOOK, SURE THAT HE WOULDN'T SEE, ... 51 HOME BURIAL 15
   AND TURNED ON HIM WITH SUCH A DAUNTING LOOK, ... 52 HOME BURIAL 33
   TO LOOK AGAIN, AND STILL YOUR SPADE KEPT LIFTING. . . 53 HOME BURIAL 80
   WE PAUSED, THE MINISTER AND I, TO LOOK. . . . . . . 55 THE BLACK COTTAGE . . 8
   HOW WE USED TO PICK BERRIES: WE TOOK ONE LOOK ROUND, . 62 BLUEBERRIES 85
   TO PEOPLE THEY LOOK ON AS HAVING NO RIGHT . . . . . 62 BLUEBERRIES 101
   YOU TAKE THE LAKE. I LOOK AND LOOK AT IT. . . . . . 63 A SERVANT TO SERVANTS . 16
   AROUND HIM TO LOOK AFTER THAT MAKE WASTE. . . . . . 65 A SERVANT TO SERVANTS . 73
   TO LOAD THE LOAD, THINKS I, LOOK OUT FOR TROUBLE. . . 71 THE CODE 50
   "YOU LOOK SO, SITTING OUT HERE IN THE RAIN . . . . . 76 THE GENERATIONS OF MEN 84
   FIRST LET ME LOOK. I SEE RASPBERRY VINES----" . . . 76 THE GENERATIONS OF MEN 97
   "TELL ME ABOUT HER. DOES SHE LOOK LIKE ME?" . . . . 77 THE GENERATIONS OF MEN 110
   SHE DOES LOOK LIKE YOU. STAY THE WAY YOU ARE. . . . 77 THE GENERATIONS OF MEN 113
   OF BOTH OF US. BUT LOOK HOW IT TURNS OUT: . . . . . 85 THE HOUSEKEEPER . . . 106
   "JCEL, I'LL HAVE TO LOOK. I CAN'T GO IN, ... 89 THE FEAR 14
   DID HE LOOK LIKE----?" / "HE LOOKED LIKE ANYONE. . . 90 THE FEAR 31
   "THEY MUST BE TERRIBLE--I MEAN, TO LOOK AT." . . . . 93 THE SELF-SEEKER . . . 17
   "I HAVEN'T DARED TO LOOK AT THEM UNCOVERED. . . . . 93 THE SELF-SEEKER . . . 18
   YOU NEEDN'T LOOK AT ME." / "I DON'T BELIEVE YOU." . . 95 THE SELF-SEEKER . . . 60
   "YOU'LL FIND IT IS. LET YOUR FRIEND LOOK AT IT." . . 99 THE SELF-SEEKER . . . 190
   TO LOOK FOR SOMETHING IT HAD LEFT BEHIND . . . . . . 106 CHRISTMAS TREES . . . 10
   YOU LET ME LOOK THEM OVER." / "YOU COULD LOOK. . . . 106 CHRISTMAS TREES . . . 31
   IN OTHER CHAIRS, AND SOMETHING, COME TO LOOK, ... 110 IN THE HOME STRETCH . 7
   TO LOOK US OVER AND GIVE US HIS IDEA . . . . 115 IN THE HOME STRETCH . 149
   I DON'T STAND STILL AND LOOK AROUND . . . . 124 A TIME TO TALK . . . 3
   AND SINCE THERE WAS NO OTHER WAY TC LOOK, ... 125 AN ENCOUNTER 10
   AND LOOK FOR SKUNK TRACKS . . . . 136 LAST WORD OF A BLUEBIRD 18
   BUT THAT'S NOT SAYING--LOOK, FRED COLE, IT'S TWELVE, . 144 SNOW 55
   HE DOESN'T LOOK ON IT AS ANYTHING." . . . . 145 SNOW 79
   OF BEING MEN WE CAN'T LOOK AT A GOOD FIGHT . . . . . 146 SNOW 100
   A HEIGHT FROM WHICH TO LOOK DOWN CRITICAL . . . . . 169 NEW HAMPSHIRE . . . 314
   OFTEN HE BID ME COME AND HAVE A LOOK . . . . 178 THE STAR-SPLITTER . . 76
   SHE HAD BEEN HAVING A LONG LOOK AT YOU. . . . . . . 180 MAPLE 15
   "JUST ONE LOOK MORE WITH WHAT YOU SAY IN MIND, . . . 184 MAPLE 131
   AND I GIVE UP"; WHICH LAST LOOK CAME TO NOTHING. . . 184 MAPLE 132
   HE HAD TO RUN RIGHT OFF TO LOOK HER UP, ... 191 PAUL'S WIFE 13
   EVERYONE HAD TO HAVE A LOOK AT IT, ... 193 PAUL'S WIFE 78
   AND THAT MADE PAUL IN TURN LOOK BACK . . . . 194 PAUL'S WIFE 111
   ONE OF THEM FIVE YEARS YOUNGER THAN I LOOK-- . . . . 196 WILD GRAPES 18
   WHERE A FOX WOULDN'T THINK TO LOOK FOR IT-- . . . . 198 WILD GRAPES 66
   THEY SAT. SHE CAST ONE DULL, OLD LOOK AT HIM, . . . 201 PLACE FOR A THIRD . . 52
   THEN THAT SAME SMARTY SOMEONE SAID TO LOOK-- . . . . 209 PAUPER WITCH OF GRAFTON 59
   LOOK HERE, YOU TREAT YOUR GUIDE WITH DUE RESPECT . . 214 A FOUNTAIN, A BOTTLE . 49
   ON MARSHALL, LOOK LIKE DONKEY'S EARS. . . . . 214 A FOUNTAIN, A BOTTLE . 53

LOOK (CONTINUED)

TWO LOOK AT TWO . . . . 229 TWO LOOK AT TWO . . . T
IN ONE LAST LOOK THE WAY THEY MUST NOT GO, ... 229 TWO LOOK AT TWO . . . 10
I DOUBT IF YOU'RE AS LIVING AS YOU LOOK." . . . . . 230 TWO LOOK AT TWO . . . 34
HIS HANDS? SHE HAD TO LOOK, TO LOOK AND ASK, ... 230 NOT TO KEEP 8
AND LOOK UP SMALL FROM THE FOREST'S FEET. . . . . . 247 ON GOING UNNOTICED . 10
MAKES THE NEW MOON LOOK ANYTHING BUT NEW . . . . . 247 THE COCOON 3
NOT IN POSITION TO LOOK TOO CLOSE. . . . . 248 A PASSING GLIMPSE . 12
LOOK, LOOK, IT'S WAVING TO US WITH A WAVE . . . . . 258 WEST-RUNNING BROOK . 16
IT IS BECAUSE LIKE MEN WE LOOK TOO NEAR, ... 261 A SOLDIER 6
AND LOOK ELSEWHERE THAN TO STARS AND MOON AND SUN . . 268 ON LOOKING UP BY CHANCE 9
SO THAT HE COULDN'T LOOK INSIDE . . . . 273 A LONE STRIKER . . . 13
THE WATER FOR WHICH WE MAY HAVE TO LOOK . . . . . . 276 TWO TRAMPS IN MUD TIME 33
BUT WHEN HE CAME TO LOOK, NO APPLES THERE . . . . . 284 THE GOLD HESPERIDEE . 38
TO LOOK UPON THE TREE WHEN IT WAS GREEN . . . . . . 284 THE GOLD HESPERIDEE . 53
HE COULD LOOK AT US IN OUR DINER EATING, ... 292 FIGURE IN THE DOORWAY . 21
A LOOK OF PUZZLED DIMNESS TO THEIR EYES . . . . . . 293 AT WOODWARD'S GARDENS . 10
ALL TURN AND LOOK ONE WAY. . . . . 301 NEITHER OUT FAR NOR IN 2
THEY LOOK AT THE SEA ALL DAY. . . . . 301 NEITHER OUT FAR NOR IN 4
AND THE PEOPLE LOOK AT THE SEA. . . . . 301 NEITHER OUT FAR NOR IN 12
THEY CANNOT LOOK OUT FAR. . . . . 301 NEITHER OUT FAR NOR IN 13
THEY CANNOT LOOK IN DEEP. . . . . 301 NEITHER OUT FAR NOR IN 14
WHERE WE STILL LOOK TO ASK THE WHY . . . . 303 AFTERFLAKES 4
AND LOOK FOR WHAT HAD MADE ME STALL, ... 304 UNHARVESTED 3
LET'S HAVE A LOOK AT ANOTHER FIVE. . . . . 310 IN DIVES' DIVE . . . 6
"LOOK AT WHAT HAPPENED. SURELY SOME GOD PINXIT. . . 321 BUILD SOIL 153
COME LOOK AT MY SIGNIFICANT MUD PIE." . . . . . . 321 BUILD SOIL 154
IF IT MAKES YOU LOOK HELPLESS, PLEASE, ... 326 TO A THINKER . . . 23
MADE HER STEAL A LOOK OF FEAR . . . . 340 THE SUBVERTED FLOWER . 37
AND BEGAN TO FLUTTER THE LEAVES TO LOOK . . . . . . 342 A CLOUD SHADOW . . . 2
SHE WOULD NOT LOOK AT THE FATEFUL SHIP. . . . . . . 343 DISCOVERY OF MADEIRAS . 8
A VOICE SAID, LOOK ME IN THE STARS . . . . 362 A QUESTION 1
THAT MADE ME LOOK AGAIN AT THE CLOCK. . . . . 364 TRESPASS 16
LOOK DOWN THE LONG VALLEY AND THERE STANDS A MOUNTAIN . 379 TOO ANXIOUS FOR RIVERS 1
WE NEVER KNEW EXACTLY WHERE TO LOOK, ... 382 TO AN ANCIENT . . . 4
HAVE I NOT WALKED WITHOUT AN UPWARD LOOK . . . . . . 383 BRAVADO 1
IN A SUBORDINATING LOOK OR TONE, ... 385 THE FEAR OF GOD . . 10
BUT THERE'S A TIGHT-SHUT LOOK TO EITHER DOOR . . . . 400 TO THE RIGHT PERSON . 8
I OWN HE DOES LOOK BUSY WHEN THE SUN . . . . 407 FROM PLANE TO PLANE . 104
WHO COME TO LOOK IN ON THEM FROM THE PULPIT. . . . . 414 A CABIN IN THE CLEARING 24
I OPENED THE DOOR SO MY LAST LOOK . . . . 419 ONE MORE BREVITY . . 1
AND TRIED TO LOOK TEN THOUSAND DOLLARS' WORTH. . . . 454 HOW HARD TO KEEP FROM 38
ARE SINGING. YES, AND LOOK, THE TREE IS TROUBLED. . . 473 A MASQUE OF REASON . 15
AND LOOK FOR JUSTICE IN THE CASE OF SEGUB. . . . . . 477 A MASQUE OF REASON . 114
LOOK AT HOW FAR WE'VE LEFT THE CURRENT SCIENCE . . . 480 A MASQUE OF REASON . 194
YOU LOOK AS IF YOU EITHER HOPED OR FEARED . . . . . 488 A MASQUE OF REASON . 411
IF YOU GO NOW.--LOOK HOW HE TAKES NO STEPS! . . . . 489 A MASQUE OF REASON . 439
LOOK, I DON'T NEED THE BIBLE TO CONSULT. . . . . . 495 A MASQUE OF MERCY . 44
LOOK OUT FOR HIM. / "LOOK OUT FOR ME" IS RIGHT. . . 498 A MASQUE OF MERCY . 130
YOU LOOK SO SLEEPLESS.--IF HE'D PROMISE US . . . . 501 A MASQUE OF MERCY . 207
LOOK, WILL YOU LOOK! GOD CAN'T PUT WORDS IN MY MOUTH. 505 A MASQUE OF MERCY . 295
PAUL MAKES IT COME OUT SO THEY LOOK LIKE CHRISTIANS. . 509 A MASQUE OF MERCY . 407
TO LOOK AT LONG DIRECTLY (LIKE THE SUN), ... 515 A MASQUE OF MERCY . 584

LOOKED

AND HE TURNED AND LOOKED AT THE ROAD AFAR . . . . . 7 LOVE AND A QUESTION . 7
THE BRIDEGROOM LOOKED AT THE WEARY ROAD, ... 8 LOVE AND A QUESTION . 21
(THIS WAS MY DREAM) AND LOOKED AND PONDERED LONG, . . 16 A DREAM PANG . . . 4
I LOOKED FOR HIM BEHIND AN ISLE OF TREES; . . . . . 22 THE TUFT OF FLOWERS . 5
AND STOOD IN THE SUN AND LOOKED HIS FILL . . . . . 23 PAN WITH US 4
AND RAVELED A FLOWER AND LOOKED AWAY. . . . . 24 PAN WITH US 29
AND LOOKED AT THE WORLD, AND DESCENDED; . . . . . . 30 RELUCTANCE 4
OR ANYTHING HE LOOKED FOR FROM HIS BROTHER, ... 39 DEATH OF THE HIRED MAN 137
THE DOCTOR LOOKED AT LAFE AND LOOKED AWAY. . . . . . 46 A HUNDRED COLLARS . 49
FIERCE HEADS LOOKED OUT; SMALL BODIES PIVOTED. . . . 59 THE BLACK COTTAGE . 126
AND THEY LOOKED SO SOLEMN-ABSURDLY CONCERNED." . . . 61 BLUEBERRIES 59
YOU OUGHT TO HAVE SEEN HOW IT LOOKED IN THE RAIN, . . 62 BLUEBERRIES 103
AND I LOOKED TO BE HAPPY, AND I WAS, ... 67 A SERVANT TO SERVANTS 152
I LOOKED OVER THE SIDE ONCE IN THE DUST . . . . . . 72 THE CODE 75
OUT OF THE BARN.' SOMEONE LOOKED IN A WINDOW, . . . 72 THE CODE 95
HE LOOKED SO CLEAN DISGUSTED FROM BEHIND . . . . . 72 THE CODE 99
OR LET HIM KNOW THAT HE WAS BEING LOOKED AT. . . . . 72 THE CODE 101
DID HE LOOK LIKE----?" / "HE LOOKED LIKE ANYONE. . . 90 THE FEAR 31
"YOU SEE," THE VOICE SAID. / "OH." SHE LOOKED AND LOOKED. 92 THE FEAR 78
ANNE LOOKED AT THE LARGE LAWYER AT HER SIDE, ... 97 THE SELF-SEEKER . . 117
AND LOOKED DOWN AS FAR AS I COULD . . . . 105 THE ROAD NOT TAKEN . 4
A STRANGER TO OUR YARD, WHO LOOKED THE CITY, ... 106 CHRISTMAS TREES . . 5
ALL OUT-OF-DOORS LOOKED DARKLY IN AT HIM . . . . . 108 OLD MAN'S WINTER NIGHT 1
SHE STOOD AGAINST THE KITCHEN SINK, AND LOOKED . . . 110 IN THE HOME STRETCH . 1
LOOKED IN A DOOR BEHIND HER AND ADDRESSED . . . . . 110 IN THE HOME STRETCH . 11
ANOTHER BLACKENED FACE THRUST IN AND LOOKED . . . . 111 IN THE HOME STRETCH . 18
LOOKED UP TOWARD HEAVEN, AND THERE AGAINST THE BLUE, . 125 AN ENCOUNTER . . . 11
HE NEVER FOUND HER, THOUGH HE LOOKED . . . . 129 THE IMPULSE 21
THEY LOOKED ABOUT FOR SOMEONE TO HAVE DONE IT. . . . 132 THE BONFIRE 89
HE LOOKED BACK UP THE SLIPPERY SLOPE . . . . 139 BROWN'S DESCENT . . 47
IT MUST HAVE LOOKED AS IF THE COURSE . . . . 139 BROWN'S DESCENT . . 65
THEN YOU WOULDN'T HAVE LOOKED ON IT AS JUST A MATTER . 142 THE VANISHING RED . 12
AREN'T LOOKED ON AS MAN-KILLERS, AND ALTHOUGH . . . 150 SNOW 222
WE'VE LOOKED AND LOOKED, BUT AFTER ALL WHERE ARE WE? . 179 THE STAR-SPLITTER . 95
TO MAKE IT GO WELL WITH THE WAY SHE LOOKED. . . . . 181 MAPLE 43
SO SHE LOOKED FOR HERSELF, AS EVERYONE . . . . . . 182 MAPLE 70
IT LOOKED AS IF IT MIGHT BE BADLY THROWN . . . . . 190 THE GRINDSTONE . . 58
THE HOLLOW LOOKED TOO SOUND AND CLEAN AND EMPTY . . . 193 PAUL'S WIFE 83
IT LOOKED TO HIM LIKE SOME NEW KIND OF HOLLOW . . . 193 PAUL'S WIFE 86
WHO, LEANING ON A LOG, LOOKED BACK AT PAUL. . . . . 194 PAUL'S WIFE 110
AND IF HE LOOKED AND FOUND IT, COULDN'T REACH IT-- . . 198 WILD GRAPES . . . 67
I KNOW I LOOKED AT MY CURLED-UP FINGERS, ... 198 WILD GRAPES . . . 87
SHE'D LOOKED ELIZA UP HER SECOND TIME, ... 201 PLACE FOR A THIRD . 58
SO THAT IT LOOKED LIKE LIGHTNING OR A SCRIBBLE, . . . 205 THE WITCH OF COOS . 88

PAGE TITLE   LINE

LOOKED (CONTINUED)
    I FANCIED WHEN I LOOKED AT SIX O'CLOCK . . . . 237 A HILLSIDE THAW . . . 23
    I LOOKED AT NINE: THE SWARM WAS TURNED TO ROCK . . . . 237 A HILLSIDE THAW . . . 26
    GREAT WAVES LOOKED OVER OTHERS COMING IN, ... 250 ONCE BY THE PACIFIC . 2
    YOU COULD NOT TELL, AND YET IT LOOKED AS IF . . . . . 250 ONCE BY THE PACIFIC . 7
    IT LOOKED AS IF A NIGHT OF DARK INTENT . . . . 250 ONCE BY THE PACIFIC . 10
    I HAVE LOOKED DOWN THE SADDEST CITY LANE. . . . . . . 255 ACQUAINTED WITH NIGHT . 4
    AND LOOKED AROUND TO SEE IF HE WAS SEEN. . . . . . . 284 THE GOLD HESPERIDEE . 50
    IN A FIELD I LOOKED INTO GOING PAST, ... 296 DESERT PLACES . . . 2
    I TURNED AND LOOKED BACK UP AT THE SKY, ... 303 AFTERFLAKES 3
    I TURNED AND LOOKED BACK UPWARD. . . . . 303 AFTERFLAKES 11
    SHE LOOKED AND SAW THE SHAME: . . . . 340 THE SUBVERTED FLOWER . 41
    SHE LOOKED AND SAW THE WORST. . . . . 341 THE SUBVERTED FLOWER . 57
    LOOKED, OR AT MOST . . . . 343 QUEST OF PURPLE-FRINGED 22
    LOOKED FORTH ON HER SMALL SON . . . . 366 NOT OF SCHOOL AGE . 14
    EVERY TIME DICK OR PIKE LOOKED UP, THE DOCTOR . . . . 404 FROM PLANE TO PLANE . 18
    I LOOKED ON IT AS A CARNEGIE GRANT . . . . 459 HOW HARD TO KEEP FROM 174
LOOKING (SEE GOOD-LOOKING)
    I WASN'T LOOKING FOR HIM--AND HE'S CHANGED. . . . . . 35 DEATH OF THE HIRED MAN 38
    "JUST AS YOU SAY. HERE'S LOOKING AT YOU, THEN.-- . . . 50 A HUNDRED COLLARS . . 158
    LOOKING BACK OVER HER SHOULDER AT SOME FEAR. . . . . . 51 HOME BURIAL 3
    I GOT FROM LOOKING THROUGH A PANE OF GLASS . . . . . 68 AFTER APPLE-PICKING . 10
    AND LOOKING UP BEWHISKERED OUT OF THE PIT, ... 71 THE CODE 62
    AROUND US, LOOKING OUT OF TREES AND BUSHES . . . . . 90 THE FEAR 46
    "LOOKING ROUND, I SUPPOSE," SAID WILLIS. / "YES, . . . 96 THE SELF-SEEKER . . 101
    BY LOOKING IN THE EARS. BUT I FORGET IT. . . . . . . 96 THE SELF-SEEKER . . 109
    WHEN THE HOUSE WASN'T LIVED IN? I'VE BEEN LOOKING: . . 117 IN THE HOME STRETCH . 192
    HALF LOOKING FOR THE ORCHID CALYPSO." . . . . 125 AN ENCOUNTER . . . 24
    I WAS LOOKING FOR YOU. . . . . 135 LAST WORD OF A BLUEBIRD 3
    WE ARE NOT LOOKING FOR IT ANY MORE." . . . . 185 MAPLE 162
    AND LOOKING FROM IT TO THE POND NEARBY, ... 194 PAUL'S WIFE 96
    THAT SHE WAS LOOKING AT INSTEAD OF HIM. . . . . . . 194 PAUL'S WIFE 113
    IT'S LOOKING FOR ANOTHER DOOR TO TRY. . . . . 205 THE WITCH OF COOS . . 108
    AND A TRAPPER LOOKING IN AT THE DOOR . . . . 211 AN EMPTY THREAT . . 10
    BOTH EITHER LOOKING FOR OR FINDING SOMETHING. . . . . 217 A FOUNTAIN, A BOTTLE . 129
    LOOKING OUT OF A WREATH OF FERN AND CLOUD PUFFS. . . . 225 FOR ONCE SOMETHING . 6
    I ALMOST STUMBLE LOOKING UP AND ROUND, ... 226 THE ONSET 6
    A DOE FROM ROUND A SPRUCE STOOD LOCKING AT THEM . . . 229 TWO LOOK AT TWO . . 15
    A BUCK FROM ROUND THE SPRUCE STOOD LOOKING AT THEM . . 229 TWO LOOK AT TWO . . . 27
    LOOKING FOR A SUNSET BIRD IN WINTER . . . . 232 LOOKING FOR SUNSET BIRD T
    TO RIDGELY TORRENCE ON LAST LOOKING INTO HIS "HESPERIDES" . 248 A PASSING GLIMPSE . D
    LOOKING DOWNHILL TO A FROTHY SHORE? . . . . 251 BEREFT 5
    ON LOOKING UP BY CHANCE AT THE CONSTELLATIONS . . . . 268 ON LOOKING UP BY CHANCE T
    AND TURNED FROM LOOKING UP AND BEING KISSED . . . . . 283 THE GOLD HESPERIDEE . 8
    TO LOOKING DOWN AND YET NOT BEING SAD, ... 283 THE GOLD HESPERIDEE . 9
    LOOKING OUT OF MY LOWER BERTH . . . . 290 ON HEART'S BEGINNING TO 3
    LOOKING THROUGH WREATHS OF ENGINE SMOKE . . . . . . 292 ON HEART'S BEGINNING TO 44
    LOOKING FOR MY OLD SKY-MARKS IN THE BLUE. . . . . . 295 LOST IN HEAVEN . . . 4
    PATIENCE AND LOOKING AWAY AHEAD, ... 376 SOMETHING FOR HOPE . 21
    FROM LOOKING UP TOO MUCH, ... 389 ASTROMETAPHYSICAL . 6
    NO ONE WAS LOOKING AT HIS LONELY CASE; . . . . . . 396 ANY SIZE WE PLEASE . 1
    AND WHEN HE CAUGHT DICK LOOKING ONCE TOO OFTEN, . . . 404 FROM PLANE TO PLANE . 26
    NO ONE HAS SEEN HIM STUMBLE LOOKING BACK. . . . . . 421 ESCAPIST--NEVER . . 2
    "SIRE, I'VE BEEN LOOKING ON, AND I DON'T LIKE . . . . 453 HOW HARD TO KEEP FROM 8
    FOR LOOKING ON AND NOT PARTICIPATING. . . . . 462 HOW HARD TO KEEP FROM 271
    HIS WIFE LIES BY HIM LOOKING AT THE SKY. . . . . . . 473 A MASQUE OF REASON . 3
    BECAUSE YOUR WIFE'S PAST WON'T BEAR LOOKING INTO?-- . . 477 A MASQUE OF REASON . 116
LOOKING-GLASS
    FROM THE FIRELIT LOOKING-GLASS . . . . 11 WIND AND WINDOW FLOWER 23
LOOK-OFF
    WE CAME OUT ON A LOOK-OFF WHERE WE FACED . . . . . . 214 A FOUNTAIN, A BOTTLE . 37
LOOKOUT
    THAT WAS HIS LOOKOUT. I COULD COUNT ON YOU. . . . . . 485 A MASQUE OF REASON . 358
LOOKS
    INTO THE PASTURE. / "THAT LOOKS LIKE A PATH. . . . . 41 THE MOUNTAIN . . . 34
    HE LOOKS ON THE BRIGHT SIDE OF EVERYTHING, ... 64 A SERVANT TO SERVANTS 45
    "NO FETE TODAY," HE SAID. / "IT LOOKS THAT WAY." . . . 74 THE GENERATIONS OF MEN 35
    STRUNG ON YOUR HAIR, WON'T HURT YOUR SUMMER LOOKS. . . 77 THE GENERATIONS OF MEN 123
    MY, BUT HE LOOKS AS IF HE MUST HAVE HEARD!" . . . . 88 THE HOUSEKEEPER . . 204
    AND HOPELESS GRIST ENOUGH IT LOOKS . . . . 140 THE GUM-GATHERER . . 16
    SINCE LAST WE READ THE GAUGE." / "IT LOOKS AS IF . . . 148 SNOW 159
    AND RISING ON HIS HANDS, HE LOOKS IN ON ME . . . . . 176 THE STAR-SPLITTER . . 3
    LOOKS FOR HIMSELF, MORE OR LESS OUTWARDLY. . . . . . 182 MAPLE 71
    SON LOOKS SURPRISED TO SEE ME END A LIE . . . . . . 207 THE WITCH OF COOS . . 145
    IT LOOKS AS IF SOME MAGIC OF THE SUN . . . . 237 A HILLSIDE THAW . . 6
    (HE ALMOST LOOKS RELIGIOUS BUT HE'S NOT), ... 269 THE BEAR 28
    ONE LOOKS OUT LAST FROM THE DARKENED ROOM . . . . . 291 ON HEART'S BEGINNING TO 26
    THAT LOOKS IN ONTO A MOOD APART. . . . . 385 A MOOD APART . . . 8
    "HE LOOKS TO ME LIKE GOING HOME SUCCESSFUL, ... 405 FROM PLANE TO PLANE . 37
    IF IT LOOKS NONE TOO ORDERLY TODAY, ... 423 FOR JOHN F. KENNEDY . 40
    THE LOOKS OF EMPIRE HERE. I'M LEAVING WITH YOU." . . . 453 HOW HARD TO KEEP FROM 9
    (HE DOESN'T RISE, BUT LOOKS AT HER A MOMENT.) . . . . 519 A MASQUE OF MERCY . 683
LOON
    I DON'T KNOW WHAT MADE HER SO LUNAR A LOON; . . . . . 463 LINES IN DEJECTION . 3
LOOP
    BUT A LOOP THE LOOP, ... 441 KITTY HAWK 405
LOOPED
    NO RUNNER TRACKS IN THIS YEAR'S SNOW LOOPED NEAR IT. . . 101 THE WOOD-PILE . . . 26
    AND LOOPED TEN TIMES BACK AND FORTH, ... 312 THE VINDICTIVES . . 67
LOOSE
    AND SCARE OURSELVES. LET WILD FIRE LOOSE WE WILL----" . 130 THE BONFIRE 18
    TO LOOSE THE RESIN AND TAKE IT DOWN . . . . 141 THE GUM-GATHERER . . 38
    AFTER SUCH LOOSE TALK IT WAS NO SURPRISE . . . . . . 177 THE STAR-SPLITTER . . 38
    WE CHOOSE TO SAY IT IS LET LOOSE BY THE DEVIL; . . . . 254 THE FLOOD 5
    THAT DAY, GIVING A LOOSE TO MY SOUL, ... 275 TWO TRAMPS IN MUD TIME 15
    THAT WHEN LET LOOSE UPON THE GRAZING WORLD . . . . . 319 BUILD SOIL 109
    A LOOSE MOUNTAIN . . . . 360 A LOOSE MOUNTAIN . . T
    THAT THE LOOSE MOUNTAIN LATELY SEEN TO GLINT . . . . 361 A LOOSE MOUNTAIN . . 14

		PAGE	TITLE	LINE

LOOSE (CONTINUED)
```
   A WORLD TORN LOOSE WENT BY ME.  . . . . . . . . .   377  ONE STEP BACKWARD TAKEN    12
   WERE LOOSE ALL ROUND THEIR LEGS--YOU COULDN'T SAY . . . .   404  FROM PLANE TO PLANE   .    16
   FOR ME TO BREAK LOOSE . . . . . . . . .   432  KITTY HAWK    . . . .   130
   UPON A METER, STRICT OR LOOSE IAMBIC. . . . . . .   460  HOW HARD TO KEEP FROM     214
   HE CAN'T GET OUT. / HE'S LOOSE! HE'S OUT! / IT'S GOD.  . .   473  A MASQUE OF REASON .  .    17
```
LOOSELY
```
   SAND DUNES HELD LOOSELY IN TAMARISK   . . . . . .    58  THE BLACK COTTAGE   .  .   120
   YOU HAVE ME THERE, BUT LOOSELY, AS I WOULD BE HELD. . . .   306  NOT QUITE SOCIAL    .  .    10
   BUT STRICTLY HELD BY NONE, IS LOOSELY BOUND . . . . .   332  THE SILKEN TENT . . .     9
```
LOOSEN
```
   ITS PETALS LOOSEN AND ARE STROWN;  . . . . . . .   450  OUR DOOM TO BLOOM   .  .    14
```
LOOSING
```
   AND LOOSING THE PENT-UP MUSIC OF OVERNIGHT. . . . . .   236  VALLEY'S SINGING DAY  .    10
```
LOOTED
```
   IS ABOUT TIRED OF BEING LOOTED  . . . . . . . .   419  AMERICA IS HARD TO SEE    81
```
LOP
```
   THAT LOP EACH OTHER OF BOUGHS, BUT NOT A FEW   . . . .   107  CHRISTMAS TREES . . .    34
```
LORD
```
   LORD, IF I WERE TO DREAM OF EVERYONE  . . . . . .    81  THE HOUSEKEEPER . . .    12
   I CAN'T TALK TO HER, AND, LORD, IF I COULD!"  . . . . .    82  THE HOUSEKEEPER . . .    27
   OUR LORD TO SEE. . . . . . . . . . .   331  SYCAMORE  . . . . .     3
   BUT WHETHER STOLEN FROM HER WEDDED LORD   . . . . .   343  DISCOVERY OF MADEIRAS     2
   MEMENTO MORI AND OBEY THE LORD. . . . . . . .   353  THE LESSON FOR TODAY     96
   BUT HELPED THE LORD HER SOUL TO KEEP. . . . . . .   382  THE NIGHT LIGHT . .  .     4
   LORD, I HAVE LOVED YOUR SKY, . . . . . . . .   388  ASTROMETAPHYSICAL   .  .     1
   O'ER WHICH YOU, LORD, HAVE LORDED, . . . . . . .   389  ASTROMETAPHYSICAL   .  .    10
   FORGIVE, O LORD, MY LITTLE JOKES ON THEE . . . . .   428  FORGIVE, O LORD... . .     1
   FORGIVE, O LORD... . . . . . . . . .   428  FORGIVE, O LORD... . .     T
   SOMEONE SAYS THE LORD  . . . . . . . .   438  KITTY HAWK    . . . .   333
   OH, LORD, LET'S NOT GO BACK TO ANYTHING. . . . . .   477  A MASQUE OF REASON .  .   115
   KIPLING INVOKES YOU AS LORD GOD OF HOSTS. . . . . .   479  A MASQUE OF REASON .  .   179
   THAT STARTED OFF LORD GOD OF HOSTESSES.  . . . . .   480  A MASQUE OF REASON .  .   181
   BUT, LORD, WE SHOWED THEM WHAT. THE AUDIENCE  . . . .   482  A MASQUE OF REASON .  .   252
   YOU SEE THE LORD GOD IS A JEALOUS GOD!   . . . . .   504  A MASQUE OF MERCY  .  .   289
```
LORDED
```
   O'ER WHICH YOU, LORD, HAVE LORDED, . . . . . .   389  ASTROMETAPHYSICAL   .  .    10
```
LOREN
```
   "I WONDER YOU DIDN'T SEE LOREN ABOUT."  . . . . .    60  BLUEBERRIES   . . . .    33
   BUT LOREN, THE FATHERLY, OUT FOR A DRIVE."  . . . .    60  BLUEBERRIES   . . . .    39
   I ALMOST PROVOKED POOR LOREN TO MIRTH.  . . . . .    61  BLUEBERRIES   . . . .    68
```
LORENS
```
   OF ALL THE YOUNG CHATTERING LORENS ALIVE,  . . . .    60  BLUEBERRIES   . . . .    38
   WITH THE MOUTHS OF ALL THOSE YOUNG LORENS TO FEED?  . .    60  BLUEBERRIES   . . . .    49
   NOT LIKELY, WHEN ALL THE YOUNG LORENS DEPLOY.  . . .    62  BLUEBERRIES   . . . .    98
```
LOSE
```
   AND LOSE MYSELF AMID SO MANY ALIKE.  . . . . . .    14  WAITING   . . . . .     8
   ONLY TO LOSE IT WHEN HE PIROUETTES,  . . . . . .    14  WAITING   . . . . .    16
   I'M THINKING I HAVE MORE TO LOSE THAN YOU  . . . .    47  A HUNDRED COLLARS   .  .    82
   THAT'S HOW I THINK I DIDN'T LOSE MY HEAD.  . . . .    93  THE SELF-SEEKER . . .    28
   A DOOR. "THERE'S THAT WE DIDN'T LOSE! AND THESE!"--  . .   115  IN THE HOME STRETCH   .   137
   AND GO ALONG WITH YOU ERE YOU LOSE SIGHT . . . .   124  PUTTING IN THE SEED   .     7
   TILL WE LOSE ALL MEASURE OF PACE,  . . . . . .   156  THE SOUND OF TREES  .  .     7
   I LOSE SOME OTHER OFF MY ARMS AND KNEES, . . . .   266  THE ARMFUL    . . . .     2
   IT DIDN'T LOSE ITS TEMPER AT OUR DEMAND  . . . .   349  OUR HOLD ON THE PLANET    2
   'TWAS NOT THE VALUE I STOOD TO LOSE  . . . . .   364  TRESPASS  . . . . .    13
   FROM ALL THE FIGHTS YOU HAD A MIND TO LOSE.  . . .   457  HOW HARD TO KEEP FROM   126
   YOU COULD LOSE BATTLES, YOU COULD LOSE WHOLE WARS,  . .   457  HOW HARD TO KEEP FROM   127
   YOU COULD LOSE ASIA, AFRICA, AND EUROPE, . . . .   457  HOW HARD TO KEEP FROM   128
   ALL YOU CAN SEEM TO DO IS LOSE YOUR TEMPER . . .   478  A MASQUE OF REASON .  .   135
   BE CAREFUL NOT TO LOSE THE PLACE. BE CAREFUL.  . . .   505  A MASQUE OF MERCY  .  .   293
   WHAT'S THIS? / DON'T LOSE THE PLACE. / OLD DANA LYLE,  .   506  A MASQUE OF MERCY  .  .   324
```
LOSERS
```
   YOU TAKE US TWO, WE'RE LOSERS IN THIS STORE,  . . .   496  A MASQUE OF MERCY  .  .    75
   SO LOSERS IN THE CITY, BUT WE'RE GAME:   . . . . .   496  A MASQUE OF MERCY  .  .    76
```
LOSING
```
   NOT GAINING BUT NOT LOSING, LIKE A BIRD  . . . .   258  WEST-RUNNING BROOK  .  .    22
   IT IS LATE AT NIGHT AND STILL I AM LOSING, . . . .   310  IN DIVES' DIVE  . . .     1
   THE SAME WITH GOD AS LOSING, HOW EXPLAIN . . . .   517  A MASQUE OF MERCY  .  .   634
```
LOSS (SEE MOTHER-LOSS)
```
   BE IT MY LOSS. . . . . . . . . .    25  NOW CLOSE THE WINDOWS     4
   BUT LEN WENT AT IT TO MAKE UP THE LOSS.  . . . .    64  A SERVANT TO SERVANTS     65
   MONEY CAN'T PAY ME FOR THE LOSS OF THEM. . . . .    95  THE SELF-SEEKER . . .    72
   HE STOOD WITH BARRELS ROUND HIM--AT A LOSS.  . . .   108  OLD MAN'S WINTER NIGHT     8
   BECAUSE OF THE FEARS OF FIRE AND LOSS  . . . . .   140  THE GUM-GATHERER  . .    21
   AND THE LOSS OF COMMON SENSE!  . . . . . .   282  A DRUMLIN WOODCHUCK   .    24
   THE LOSS TO SONG, THE DANGER OF DEFECTION  . . .   358  THE LOST FOLLOWER   .  .     9
   BACK IN A TIME MADE SIMPLE BY THE LOSS   . . . .   377  DIRECTIVE   . . . .     2
   SO, NEVER AT A LOSS IN SIMILE, . . . . . .   461  HOW HARD TO KEEP FROM   235
   UNLESS I LIKED TO SUFFER LOSS OF WORSHIP.  . . . .   476  A MASQUE OF REASON .  .    75
   SHE'S HAD SOME LOSS SHE CAN'T ACCEPT FROM GOD--  . .   501  A MASQUE OF MERCY  .  .   204
   FROM THE DISCOVERY THAT LOSS FROM FAILURE, . . . .   506  A MASQUE OF MERCY  .  .   321
```
LOSSES
```
   THE ART OF LIFE IS PASSING LOSSES ON.  . . . . .   399  THE INGENUITIES OF DEBT     5
   COULD SAVE IT FROM ITS LOSSES BEING MET. . . . .   399  THE INGENUITIES OF DEBT    12
```
LOST
```
   WHOSE CLUSTERED FRUIT MUST ELSE BE LOST--  . . .    28  OCTOBER   . . . . .    20
   "CAN'T A MAN SPEAK OF HIS OWN CHILD HE'S LOST?"  . .    52  HOME BURIAL   . . . .    35
   AND I THOUGHT I HAD LOST YOU. I LIFTED A SHOUT   . .    62  BLUEBERRIES   . . . .    93
   OF WHAT SHE'S LOST: SHE GOES DOWN ON ONE KNEE  . .    98  THE SELF-SEEKER . . .   160
   HE SEEMS TO HAVE LOST OFF HIS CHRISTIAN NAME."   . .   144  SNOW  . . . . . .    47
   UNDER IT ALL, HIS DOOR SEALED UP AND LOST, . . . .   150  SNOW  . . . . . .   224
   OR GONE OUTDOORS." / "IN WHICH CASE BOTH ARE LOST.  .   154  SNOW  . . . . . .   312
   SMALL TOWNS--LOST NATION, BUNGEY, MUDDY BOO,  . .   165  NEW HAMPSHIRE   . . .   187
   AND LOST THE PLACE NEVER TO READ AGAIN.  . . . .   181  MAPLE   . . . . .    68
   ONE BY ONE I LOST OFF MY HAT AND SHOES,  . . . .   198  WILD GRAPES   . . . .    72
   AND ALL BUT LOST HIMSELF. (A TONGUE OF FIRE  . . .   204  THE WITCH OF COOS   .  .    72
   "YOU'VE LOST IT, THEN?" / "NOT SO BUT I CAN FIND IT.  . .   213  A FOUNTAIN, A BOTTLE   .    20
```

                                                          PAGE TITLE   LINE
LOST (CONTINUED)
    THE VICTORY FOR WHAT IT LOST AND GAINED. . . . . 222 TO E.T.   12
    SOMETHING MORE OF THE DEPTHS--AND THEN I LOST IT. . . . 225 FOR ONCE SOMETHING . . 10
    AND ALL BUT LOST. . . . . 252 TREE AT MY WINDOW . . 12
    WAS THERE EVER A CAUSE TOO LOST, ... 262 HANNIBAL   1
    EVER A CAUSE THAT WAS LOST TOO LONG, ... 262 HANNIBAL   2
    HIS TIME BE LOST, HIS PITTANCE DOCKED. . . . . 273 A LONE STRIKER . . .   8
    WE WERE LOST PIECEMEAL TO THE ANIMALS, ... 279 THE WHITE-TAILED HORNET 67
    HE THOUGHT NO SPECIAL GOODNESS COULD BE LOST . . . . . 284 THE GOLD HESPERIDEE . 34
    SO LOST ON ME IN MY SURFACE FLIGHT. . . . . 292 ON HEART'S BEGINNING TO 41
    SEEING MYSELF WELL LOST ONCE MORE, I SIGHED, ... 295 LOST IN HEAVEN . . .   9
    LOST IN HEAVEN . . . . 295 LOST IN HEAVEN . . .   T
    THAT PAST ITS PRIME LOST PETALS IN THE FLOOD . . . . . 337 THE WIND AND THE RAIN . 33
    THAT PROBABLY IT NEVER WOULD BE LOST. . . . . 339 NEVER WOULD BIRDS' SONG 12
    HAS LOST ITS FOOTING ON MY MOUNTAIN SLOPE . . . . . . 350 TO A YOUNG WRETCH . . 21
    AND LOST THE STARS OF HEAVEN, MAY, OH, MAY . . . . . . 350 TO A YOUNG WRETCH . . 22
    THE LOST FOLLOWER . . . . 358 THE LOST FOLLOWER . .   T
    WHO ONLY HAS AT HEART YOUR GETTING LOST, ... 377 DIRECTIVE   9
    INTO EACH OTHER. BOTH OF THEM ARE LOST. . . . . . . 378 DIRECTIVE 35
    AND IF YOU'RE LOST ENOUGH TO FIND YOURSELF . . . . . 378 DIRECTIVE 36
    NO PLACE TO GET LOST LIKE TOO FAR IN THE DISTANCE. . . . 379 TOO ANXIOUS FOR RIVERS 11
    HE DON'T MIND HAVING LOST A CASE," PIKE SAID; . . . . 404 FROM PLANE TO PLANE . 25
    NO ONE--NOT I--WOULD GIVE THEM UP FOR LOST . . . . . 414 A CABIN IN THE CLEARING 13
    ANOTHER STILL, LOST FAR INTO THE DISTANCE. . . . . . 421 ESCAPIST--NEVER . .   8
    AND NOW, O SEA, YOU'RE LOST BY AEROPLANE. . . . . . . 446 DOES NO ONE AT ALL EVER 13
    TILL YOU HAVE LOST THE SAVOR OF YOUR SALT. . . . . . 446 DOES NO ONE AT ALL EVER 24
    YOU LOST YOUR ARMY AT MOSUL. WHAT HAPPENED? . . . . . 458 HOW HARD TO KEEP FROM 130
    I'VE LOST MY FAITH IN GOD TO CARRY OUT . . . . 497 A MASQUE OF MERCY . 114
    YOU'VE LOST YOUR FAITH IN GOD? HOW WICKED OF YOU. . . . 497 A MASQUE OF MERCY . 117
    YOU'RE SO LOST IN THE VIRTUOSITY . . . . 503 A MASQUE OF MERCY . 259
    I SAY I'D RATHER BE LOST IN THE WOODS . . . . 513 A MASQUE OF MERCY . 514
    LET THE LOST MILLIONS PRAY IT IN THE DARK! . . . . . 521 A MASQUE OF MERCY . 726
LOSTNESS
    LET'S LET MY HEAVENLY LOSTNESS OVERWHELM ME." . . . . 296 LOST IN HEAVEN . . . 12
LOT
    A LOT OF IT, OUT INTO THE BARN FLOOR. . . . . 72 THE CODE 90
    YOU DON'T KNOW WHAT A GENTLE LOT WE ARE: . . . . . . 85 THE HOUSEKEEPER . . 124
    THEY SET A LOT (NOW DON'T THEY?) BY A RECORD . . . . . 207 PAUPER WITCH OF GRAFTON 12
    HE AND A LOT OF CHILDREN CAME OUTSIDE, ... 368 THE LITERATE FARMER AND 6
    THERE'S A LOT YET THAT ISN'T UNDERSTOOD. . . . . . . 372 THE LITERATE FARMER AND 136
    POETS KNOW A LOT. . . . . 429 KITTY HAWK 32
    A LOT WOULD BE A LOT OF FUN. . . . . 451 A-WISHING WELL . . . 25
    THE EUNUCH LAUGHED: "WELL, THAT'S A LOT TO KNOW. . . . 455 HOW HARD TO KEEP FROM 45
    AND HERE'S A LOT OF MONEY. WHO'S THE TAKER? . . . . . 455 HOW HARD TO KEEP FROM 46
    THAT'S WHY WE NEED A LOT OF BRAINS . . . . 467 QUANDARY   8
LOTH
    NOT LOTH TO HAVE EXCUSE TO GO, ... 18 GOING FOR WATER . . .   5
LOTS
    AND DUMPED THE RACKFUL ON HIM IN TEN LOTS. . . . . . 72 THE CODE 74
    IN BUSHEL LOTS--DOESN'T COME ON THE MARKET. . . . . . 97 THE SELF-SEEKER . . 130
    HE WANTS TO GIVE ME LOTS AND LOTS OF MONEY . . . . . 98 THE SELF-SEEKER . . 169
    'CROSS LOTS, 'CROSS WALLS, 'CROSS EVERYTHING, ... 137 BROWN'S DESCENT . .   7
    WHICH GIVES HIM FOR HIMSELF A CHOICE OF LOTS . . . . . 202 PLACE FOR A THIRD . . 81
    MEN WORK ALONE, THEIR LOTS PLOWED FAR APART, ... 299 STRONG SAYING NOTHING . 6
    STILL THERE MUST BE LOTS OF UNSYSTEMATIC . . . . . . 478 A MASQUE OF REASON . 141
LOUD
    COME WITH RAIN, O LOUD SOUTHWESTER! . . . . 11 TO THE THAWING WIND .   1
    "SH! NOT SO LOUD: HE'LL HEAR YOU," MARY SAID. . . . . 35 DEATH OF THE HIRED MAN 31
    TOO LOUD FOR THE DISTANCE YOU WERE, IT TURNED OUT, . . . 62 BLUEBERRIES 94
    I STAND AND MAKE MYSELF REPEAT OUT LOUD . . . . 63 A SERVANT TO SERVANTS . 18
    I ASKED OUT LOUD, SO'S THERE'D BE NO MISTAKE, ... 71 THE CODE 65
    LOUD, A MID-SUMMER AND A MID-WOOD BIRD, ... 119 THE OVEN BIRD . . .   2
    AND SAID OUT LOUD, I COULDN'T BIDE THE SMOTHER . . . . 131 THE BONFIRE 70
    LAUGHED THE LOUD LAUGH THE BIG LAUGH AT THE LITTLE. . . 165 NEW HAMPSHIRE . . . 200
    AND LET OUT A LOUD YELL, AND THREW A BOTTLE, ... 195 PAUL'S WIFE 140
    TO LOUD CRIES FROM MY BROTHER OF "LET GO! . . . . . . 197 WILD GRAPES 46
    NOR STRIKE OUT FIRE FROM EACH OTHER, NOR CRASH OUT LOUD. . 268 ON LOOKING UP BY CHANCE 5
    YOU'D SAY SUFFICIENTLY LOUD, ... 365 A NATURE NOTE . . .   6
    NOT ONLY WARNED HIM WITH A LOUD COMMAND . . . . . . 394 HAEC FABULA DOCET . .   9
    LOUD TALK IN THE OVERLIGHTED HOUSE . . . . 444 ENDS   1
LOUDER
    LOUDER THAN ACTIONS, AND SOMETIMES ACHIEVES IT. . . . . 171 NEW HAMPSHIRE . . . 402
    WE'VE ALL GROWN FOND OF YOU. (PAUL SAYS IT LOUDER, . . . 518 A MASQUE OF MERCY . 667
LOUDEST
    AND DID ITS LOUDEST DAY AND NIGHT . . . . 223 THE AIM WAS SONG . .   3
LOUDLY
    AND THE KEY RATTLED LOUDLY INTO PLACE . . . . 89 THE FEAR 19
    THE PEOPLE THAT HAD LOUDLY PASSED THE DOOR . . . . . . 175 THE CENSUS-TAKER . . 38
    AND IN IT A PIANO LOUDLY PLAYING. . . . . 263 THE INVESTMENT . .   4
    HIS HARD TAIL LOUDLY SMACKED THE FLOOR . . . . 420 ONE MORE BREVITY . . 23
LOUNGE
    HE WOULDN'T LET ME PUT HIM ON THE LOUNGE. . . . . . . 39 DEATH OF THE HIRED MAN 149
    A BUTTONED HAIRCLOTH LOUNGE SPREAD SCROLLING ARMS . . . 55 THE BLACK COTTAGE . . 22
    AGAINST THE LOUNGE BESIDE IT, THOUGH I DOUBT . . . . . 56 THE BLACK COTTAGE . . 28
LOVE (SEE COUNTER-LOVE)
    THE LOVE OF BARE NOVEMBER DAYS . . . . 7 MY NOVEMBER GUEST . . 17
    LOVE AND A QUESTION . . . . 7 LOVE AND A QUESTION . . T
    TO MAR THE LOVE OF TWO . . . . 8 LOVE AND A QUESTION . 30
    AND YET WITH NEITHER LOVE NOR HATE, ... 9 STARS   9
    LOVERS, FORGET YOUR LOVE, ... 10 WIND AND WINDOW FLOWER   1
    AND LIST TO THE LOVE OF THESE, ... 10 WIND AND WINDOW FLOWER   2
    AND LITTLE OF LOVE COULD KNOW. . . . . 11 WIND AND WINDOW FLOWER 16
    FOR THIS IS LOVE AND NOTHING ELSE IS LOVE, ... 12 A PRAYER IN SPRING . . 13
    TO THE EARNEST LOVE THAT LAID THE SWALE IN ROWS, ... 17 MOWING 10
    AND BE MY LOVE IN THE RAIN. . . . . 26 A LINE-STORM SONG . .   8
    COME, BE MY LOVE IN THE WET WOODS, COME, ... 26 A LINE-STORM SONG . . 15
    OUR LOVE CAME BACK AMAIN. . . . . 27 A LINE-STORM SONG . . 30
    AND BE MY LOVE IN THE RAIN. . . . . 27 A LINE-STORM SONG . . 32

LOVE (CONTINUED)
PRECIPITATE IN LOVE, ... 28 MY BUTTERFLY 15
OF A LOVE OR A SEASON? . . . . 30 RELUCTANCE 24
SOMETHING THERE IS THAT DOESN'T LOVE A WALL, ... 33 MENDING WALL 1
SOMETHING THERE IS THAT DOESN'T LOVE A WALL, ... 34 MENDING WALL 35
THOUGH I DON'T LIKE SUCH THINGS 'TWIXT THOSE THAT LOVE. . . 53 HOME BURIAL 53
TWO THAT DON'T LOVE CAN'T LIVE TOGETHER WITHOUT THEM. . . 53 HOME BURIAL 54
SO INCONSOLABLY--IN THE FACE OF LOVE. . . . . . . 53 HOME BURIAL 65
BUT IT'S MORE LIKELY HE WAS CROSSED IN LOVE, ... 66 A SERVANT TO SERVANTS . 108
ANYWAY ALL HE TALKED ABOUT WAS LOVE. . . . . . . 66 A SERVANT TO SERVANTS . 110
SHE HAD TO LIE AND HEAR LOVE THINGS MADE DREADFUL . . . 66 A SERVANT TO SERVANTS . 130
OLD STREAK OF LEATHER--DOESN'T LOVE ME MUCH . . . . 94 THE SELF-SEEKER . . . 33
"RANK WEEDS THAT LOVE THE WATER FROM THE DISHPAN . . . 111 IN THE HOME STRETCH . 30
"GOOD BOYS THEY SEEMED, AND LET THEM LOVE THE CITY. . . 114 IN THE HOME STRETCH . 119
WE LOVE THE THINGS WE LOVE FOR WHAT THEY ARE. . . . . 119 HYLA BROOK 15
LOVE HAS EARTH TO WHICH SHE CLINGS . . . . 120 BOND AND FREE . . . 1
WHERE LOVE HAS LEFT A PRINTED TRACE . . . . 120 BOND AND FREE . . . 7
AND SUCH IS LOVE AND GLAD TO BE. . . . . 120 BOND AND FREE . . . 9
YET SOME SAY LOVE BY BEING THRALL . . . . 120 BOND AND FREE . . . 17
NOT TO RETURN. EARTH'S THE RIGHT PLACE FOR LOVE: . . . 122 BIRCHES 52
HOW LOVE BURNS THROUGH THE PUTTING IN THE SEED . . . 124 PUTTING IN THE SEED . 10
I DIDN'T USE IT OUT OF LOVE OF HIM, ... 144 SNOW 50
FOR LOVE OF IT, AND YET NOT WASTE TIME EITHER. . . . 188 THE AX-HELVE . . . 81
FALLING IN LOVE ACROSS THE TWILIGHT MILLPOND. . . . 195 PAUL'S WIFE . . . 131
AND WHO HAD THOUGHT TO LAY HER WITH HER FIRST LOVE, . . 201 PLACE FOR A THIRD . 46
OR LIKE THE POETESS'S HEART OF LOVE, ... 216 A FOUNTAIN, A BOTTLE . 95
LOVE AT THE LIPS WAS TOUCH . . . . 226 TO EARTHWARD . . . 1
OF ALMOST TOO MUCH LOVE, ... 227 TO EARTHWARD . . . 22
LOVE AND FORGETTING MIGHT HAVE CARRIED THEM . . . . 229 TWO LOOK AT TWO . . 1
HAD MADE THEM CERTAIN EARTH RETURNED THEIR LOVE. . . . 230 TWO LOOK AT TWO . . 42
SHE WOULD REFUSE LOVE SAFE WITH WEALTH AND HONOR! . . 256 THE LOVELY BE CHOOSERS . 6
"FRED, WHERE IS NORTH?" / "NORTH? NORTH IS THERE, MY LOVE. . 257 WEST-RUNNING BROOK . . 1
AND IT IS TIME, STRENGTH, TONE, LIGHT, LIFE, AND LOVE-- . 259 WEST-RUNNING BROOK . . 54
OR SOME EXTRAVAGANCE YOUNG LOVE HAD BEEN TO? . . . . 264 THE INVESTMENT . . . 11
OR OLD LOVE ON AN IMPULSE NOT TO CARE-- . . . . . 264 THE INVESTMENT . . . 12
A LOVE THAT WANTED RE-RENEWING. . . . . 274 A LONE STRIKER . . 46
THESE TWO MUST MAKE ME LOVE IT MORE . . . . . . 276 TWO TRAMPS IN MUD TIME 42
MY RIGHT MIGHT BE LOVE BUT THEIRS WAS NEED. . . . . 277 TWO TRAMPS IN MUD TIME 62
ONLY WHERE LOVE AND NEED ARE ONE, ... 277 TWO TRAMPS IN MUD TIME 69
SO LOVE WILL TAKE BETWEEN THE HANDS A FACE.... . . . 301 MOON COMPASSES . . . 8
HUMAN BEINGS LOVE IT--LOVE IT. . . . . 304 CLEAR AND COLDER . . 22
OF UNSATISFIED LOVE OF DISPLAY, ... 313 THE VINDICTIVES . . . 86
OF UNSATISFIED LOVE OF THE HIGH, ... 313 THE VINDICTIVES . . . 87
WHERE WOMEN PRAY WITH PRIESTS. THERE IS NO LOVE. . . . 318 BUILD SOIL 84
THERE'S ONLY LOVE OF MEN AND WOMEN, LOVE . . . . . 318 BUILD SOIL 85
OF CHILDREN, LOVE OF FRIENDS, OF MEN, OF GOD: . . . 318 BUILD SOIL 86
DIVINE LOVE, HUMAN LOVE, PARENTAL LOVE, ... 318 BUILD SOIL 87
POETRY, ITSELF ONCE MORE, IS BACK IN LOVE. . . . . 318 BUILD SOIL 89
(IN THIS IT IS AS MUCH LIKE HATE AS LOVE), ... 319 BUILD SOIL 105
THE MAN FREE LOVE, THE BUSINESSMAN FREE TRADE, . . . 319 BUILD SOIL 112
WHO LOVE IT WITH A LOVE SO STRONG AND STUPID . . . 322 BUILD SOIL 188
AS MUCH AS LOVE, AND TOO CLOSE IN TO STRIKE . . . . 325 BUILD SOIL 277
BY COUNTLESS SILKEN TIES OF LOVE AND THOUGHT . . . 332 THE SILKEN TENT . . . 10
IS NOT ITS OWN LOVE BACK IN COPY SPEECH, ... 338 THE MOST OF IT . . . 7
WHOSE LOVE WAS SUCH THEY DIDN'T CARE . . . . . . 345 DISCOVERY OF MADEIRAS . 55
BUT PRESENCE OF LOVE THESE HAD IN DEATH . . . . . 346 DISCOVERY OF MADEIRAS . 80
AND LOVE ITSELF WERE GROWING DIM. . . . . . . 347 DISCOVERY OF MADEIRAS . 117
ART AND RELIGION LOVE THE SOMBER CHORD. . . . . . 353 THE LESSON FOR TODAY . 97
OR BEEN THEIR RICHES, FAME, OR LOVE DENIED; . . . . 355 THE LESSON FOR TODAY . 153
AND SEEK THE LOVE OF KIND IN WINTERTIME? . . . . . 356 A MOTH SEEN IN WINTER . 9
NOR WILL YOU FIND LOVE EITHER, NOR LOVE YOU. . . . 356 A MOTH SEEN IN WINTER . 13
COLLECTIVISTIC REGIMENTING LOVE . . . . 357 A CONSIDERABLE SPECK . 25
HE TRUSTS MY LOVE TOO WELL TO DEIGN REPLY. . . . . 359 THE LOST FOLLOWER . . 33
I LOVE TO TOY WITH THE PLATONIC NOTION . . . . . 362 BOEOTIAN 1
THE TROUBLE IS, WITH THAT RECEIPT FOR LOVE, ... 372 THE LITERATE FARMER AND 124
TO FIND 'TWAS THE EFFORT, THE ESSAY OF LOVE. . . . 380 TOO ANXIOUS FOR RIVERS 26
MY LOVE FOR EVERY HEAVEN . . . . 389 ASTROMETAPHYSICAL . . 9
WITH HIM THE LOVE OF COUNTRY MEANS . . . . . . 393 A CASE FOR JEFFERSON . 9
A RULER WHO PRETENDED NOT TO LOVE . . . . 423 FOR JOHN F. KENNEDY . 44
PASSIONATE PREFERENCE SUCH AS LOVE AT SIGHT. . . . 425 ACCIDENTALLY ON PURPOSE 24
LOVE IS ALL ABOUT. . . . . 429 KITTY HAWK 31
IN A LOVE AND HATE . . . . 436 KITTY HAWK 268
AND HE WISHED LOVE WERE THUS AND SO. . . . . . 451 A-WISHING WELL . . . 2
FREE WILL, TRADE, VERSE, THOUGHT, LOVE, SPEECH, COINAGE. . 459 HOW HARD TO KEEP FROM 186
IT MAY BE MINE, BUT MUCH MORE LIKELY LOVE-- . . . 461 HOW HARD TO KEEP FROM 242
'TWIXT WHAT TO LOVE AND WHAT TO HATE. . . . . . 467 QUANDARY 10
LOVE THOU THY NEIGHBOR AS THYSELF, AYE, ... 467 QUANDARY 12
OR COURT OF LOVE. / MORE LIKELY ROYAL COURT-- . . . 474 A MASQUE OF REASON . 25
SUFFER YOURSELF TO BE ADMIRED, MY LOVE, ... 474 A MASQUE OF REASON . 30
I'M NOT IN LOVE. I DIDN'T LOVE THE DOCTOR . . . . 499 A MASQUE OF MERCY . 157
OF THE WORD LOVE CORRECTED. SHE GOT OFF . . . . . 499 A MASQUE OF MERCY . 161
OF THERAPY. / I DON'T LOVE PAUL--AS YET. . . . . 499 A MASQUE OF MERCY . 163
AND I DON'T LOVE YOU EITHER, DO I, KEEPER? . . . . 499 A MASQUE OF MERCY . 165
IS THIS THE LOVE OF GOD YOU PREACHED TO ME? . . . 505 A MASQUE OF MERCY . 306
THERE'S NOT THE LEAST LACK OF THE LOVE OF GOD . . . 505 A MASQUE OF MERCY . 307
I LOVE AND FEAR HIM. YES, BUT I FEAR FOR HIM. . . . 505 A MASQUE OF MERCY . 310
THEY TOOK MY LOVE AND THREW HER DOWN A WELL. . . . 510 A MASQUE OF MERCY . 446
'TWAS LOVELY AND ITS ORIGIN WAS LOVE. . . . . . 511 A MASQUE OF MERCY . 479
LOVED
THE MOWER IN THE DEW HAD LOVED THEM THUS, ... 23 THE TUFT OF FLOWERS . 25
FAILING OF BEING LOVED FOR WHAT SHE IS, ... 257 THE LOVELY BE CHOOSERS 42
THE TIME WHEN MOST I LOVED MY TASK . . . . . . 276 TWO TRAMPS IN MUD TIME 41
LORD, I HAVE LOVED YOUR SKY, ... 388 ASTROMETAPHYSICAL . . 1
HAVE LOVED IT CLEAR AND HIGH, ... 388 ASTROMETAPHYSICAL . . 3
"NATURE I LOVED; AND NEXT TO NATURE, ART." . . . . 393 LUCRETIUS VERSUS POETS 5
LOVELESS
HERE LOVELESS BIRDS NOW FLOCK AS WINTER FRIENDS, . . . 254 A WINTER EDEN . . . 14

LOVELIER
   OR PAUSED TO SAY BENEATH SOME LOVELIER ONE, ... 107 CHRISTMAS TREES . . . 37
LOVELY
   I KNEW A LOVELY WAY TO TELL FOR CERTAIN . . . . 96 THE SELF-SEEKER . . . 108
   WHAT SHE HAD THOUGHT WAS LOVELY, AND WHAT GOOD. . . . . 181 MAPLE 55
   THE WOODS ARE LOVELY, DARK, AND DEEP, ... 224 STOPPING BY WOODS . . 13
   THE LOVELY SHALL BE CHOOSERS . . . . 255 THE LOVELY BE CHOOSERS 1
   THE LOVELY SHALL BE CHOOSERS, SHALL THEY? . . . . . 256 THE LOVELY BE CHOOSERS 7
   YET LEAVE SUCH LOVELY SHAFTS OUTDOORS TO PERISH. . . . 290 OLD BARN AT THE BOTTOM 34
   FROM LOVELY BLOOMING BUT WASTEFUL WEED . . . . . . 376 SOMETHING FOR HOPE . 15
   'TWAS LOVELY AND ITS ORIGIN WAS LOVE. . . . . 511 A MASQUE OF MERCY . . 479
LOVER
   AND DRAWS IT DOWN AS IF IT WERE A LOVER . . . . . . 268 THE BEAR 2
   HER LOVER TO MAKE THE ORDEAL SWIFT . . . . 343 DISCOVERY OF MADEIRAS . 9
   OR SHE AND HER LOVER WOULD SIT OPPOSED . . . . . . 344 DISCOVERY OF MADEIRAS . 38
   HER LOVER SAW THEM SAIL AWAY, ... 347 DISCOVERY OF MADEIRAS . 114
   AND WHEN HER LOVER WAS LEFT ALONE . . . . 347 DISCOVERY OF MADEIRAS . 120
   LIKE THE IDEAL OF SOME MISTAKEN LOVER. . . . . . . 391 ON BEING IDOLIZED . . 6
   I CHOOSE THE STAR-CROSSED AS A STAR-CROSSED LOVER. . . . 510 A MASQUE OF MERCY . . 441
   WHY DO YOU CALL YOURSELF A STAR-CROSSED LOVER? . . . . 510 A MASQUE OF MERCY . . 450
LCVERS
   LOVERS, FORGET YOUR LOVE, ... 10 WIND AND WINDOW FLOWER 1
   THAT OVERTAKEN LOVERS . . . . 335 CARPE DIEM 15
   MANY LOVERS HAVE BEEN DIVORCED . . . . 346 DISCOVERY OF MADEIRAS . 78
LOVER'S
   I HAD A LOVER'S QUARREL WITH THE WORLD. . . . . . . 355 THE LESSON FOR TODAY . 161
LOVES
   SHE LOVES THE BARE, THE WITHERED TREE; . . . . . . 6 MY NOVEMBER GUEST . . 4
   I HAVE NO DOUBT LIKE ALL THE LOVES WHEN . . . . . 318 BUILD SOIL 78
   THANK GOD OUR PRACTICE HOLDS THE LOVES APART, ... 318 BUILD SOIL 81
   HARRISON LOVES MY COUNTRY TOO, ... 393 A CASE FOR JEFFERSON . 1
LOVE'S
   LEAVING LOVE'S ALTERNATIONS, JOY AND GRIEF, ... 317 BUILD SOIL 35
LOVING
   NOT FIREWEED LOVING WHERE WOODS HAVE BURNT-- . . . . 248 A PASSING GLIMPSE . . 6
   GO LOVING BY AT TWILIGHT, ... 335 CARPE DIEM 2
   WE HAVE ONE LOVING AND ONE HATING HAND. . . . . . 371 THE LITERATE FARMER AND 113
   HOW ABOUT LOVING GOD? / YOU MAKE ME SHRUG.-- . . . . 499 A MASQUE OF MERCY . . 164
LOVING'S
   THE LOVING'S MADE TO HOLD EACH OTHER LIKE, ... 371 THE LITERATE FARMER AND 114
LOW
   BEHIND LOW BOUGHS THE TREES LET DOWN OUTSIDE; . . . . 16 A DREAM PANG 10
   FOR WHEN YOU MADE ANSWER, YOUR VOICE WAS AS LOW . . . 62 BLUEBERRIES 95
   SO LOW FOR LONG, THEY NEVER RIGHT THEMSELVES: . . . . 121 BIRCHES 16
   WHEREVER THE GROUND WAS LOW AND WET, ... 123 PEA BRUSH 10
   IN A LOW VOICE SAID, "OH, ... 135 LAST WORD OF A BLUEBIRD 2
   THAT IS CONTENT WITH THE DAYLIGHT LOW, ... 247 ON GOING UNNOTICED . . 6
   HURRYING LOW ABOVE THE GROVE, SOME WAIF . . . . . 249 ACCEPTANCE 9
   THE CLOUDS WERE LOW AND HAIRY IN THE SKIES, ... 250 ONCE BY THE PACIFIC . 5
   SO LOW I BRUSHED THE STRAW WITH MY SLEEVES, ... 253 THE THATCH 18
   YOUR TOP HAS SUNK TOO LOW, ... 298 ON TAKING FROM THE TOP 5
   TO THE LOW ROOF OVER HIS BED, ... 299 WELCOME TO THEIR BELIEF 6
   NOR IS HE OVERJOYED WHEN THEY LIE LOW, ... 334 I COULD GIVE ALL . . 4
   THAT AT ONCE KEPT YOU BURNING LOW AND HID YOU. . . . 351 THE LESSON FOR TODAY . 25
   WITH TWO WHEELS LOW IN THE DITCH . . . . 367 A SERIOUS STEP LIGHTLY 9
   OR LOW AND STORMY; . . . . 388 ASTROMETAPHYSICAL . . 4
   I'LL BET SHE'D HAVE MADE A MELODIOUS LOW . . . . . 463 LINES IN DEJECTION . . 11
   AND LAY THE MAPLE LOW. . . . . 470 IN WINTER IN THE WOODS 4
LOWE
   LOWE IS THE ONLY DOCTOR'S DARED TO SAY SO-- . . . . . 64 A SERVANT TO SERVANTS . 48
LOWER
   GRIM SILENCE ON MY PART AS I SANK LOWER, ... 198 WILD GRAPES 79
   ITS HEART SINKS LOWER UNDER THE SOD. . . . . . . 228 GOOD-BY AND KEEP COLD . 28
   BUT LITTLE LOWER THAN THE GODS AND ANGELS. . . . . 279 THE WHITE-TAILED HORNET 62
   LOOKING OUT OF MY LOWER BERTH . . . . 290 ON HEART'S BEGINNING TO 3
   AS TO WHOSE AGE DESERVES THE LOWER MARK, ... 352 THE LESSON FOR TODAY . 52
LOWER-CHAMBER
   THE LOWER-CHAMBER WINDOW ON THE EAST, ... 9 STORM FEAR 3
LOWERED
   WITH LOWERED EYES A MOMENT TILL HE SAID, ... 144 SNOW 32
   STRIKING IT GENTLY ACROSS HER LOWERED EYES . . . . . 181 MAPLE 42
   MY SASH IS LOWERED WHEN NIGHT COMES ON; . . . . . 251 TREE AT MY WINDOW . . 2
LOWES
   THE TOWN IS FULL OF CHASES, LOWES, AND BAILEYS, . . . 75 THE GENERATIONS OF MEN 48
LOW-LIMBED
   THOSE STONES OUT UNDER THE LOW-LIMBED TREE . . . . . 6 GHOST HOUSE 24
LOWLY
   THE LOWLY PEN IS YET A HOLD . . . . 281 BLUE RIBBON AT AMESBURY 53
LOW-SLUNG
   BENEATH A LOW-SLUNG JUNIPER . . . . 380 AN UNSTAMPED LETTER IN 13
LOW-TRAILING
   WITH CLOUDS LOW-TRAILING AND MOMENTS OF RAIN THAT MISTED. . 74 THE GENERATIONS OF MEN 20
LUCK
   "IT'S GOOD LUCK WHEN YOU MOVE IN TO BEGIN . . . . . 113 IN THE HOME STRETCH . 91
   WITH GOOD LUCK WITH YOUR STOVEPIPE. NEVER MIND, . . . 113 IN THE HOME STRETCH . 92
   INCREDULOUS OF HIS OWN BAD LUCK. . . . . 138 BROWN'S DESCENT . . . 41
   ON NOTHING WORSE THAN TOO MUCH LUCK AND COMFORT. . . . 167 NEW HAMPSHIRE . . . 276
   WHITTIER'S LUCK WITH SKIPPER IRESON AWES ME-- . . . . 317 BUILD SOIL 44
   MANY MEN'S LUCK WITH GREATEST WASHINGTON . . . . . 317 BUILD SOIL 45
   THAT SPOILS THE NIGGER-TRADER'S LUCK . . . . . . 345 DISCOVERY OF MADEIRAS . 58
   A SUPERSTITIOUS CRY FOR FARMERS' LUCK-- . . . . . 407 FROM PLANE TO PLANE . 118
   BUT THEIR LACK OF LUCK . . . . 431 KITTY HAWK 114
   THE SAILORS THROW ME OVERBOARD FOR LUCK, ... 500 A MASQUE OF MERCY . . 182
LUCKILY
   LUCKILY TERMS ARE ALL AGREED UPON. . . . . . . 99 THE SELF-SEEKER . . . 182
   LUCKILY ALL SHE WANTED OF HER NAME THEN . . . . . 180 MAPLE 30
LUCKY
   "LUCKY FCR YOU YOU DID. LUCKY FOR YOU . . . . . . 150 SNOW 213

LUCKY (CONTINUED)
    AND STILL SHE HAD ALL--THEY HAD--THEY THE LUCKY! . . . . 230 NOT TO KEEP 10
    THE SHORE WAS LUCKY IN BEING BACKED BY CLIFF, ... 250 ONCE BY THE PACIFIC . 8
    WILL HE ASCRIBE THIS LUCKY BREAK. . . . . 418 AMERICA IS HARD TO SEE 72
    ALL YOUR EFFECTS WERE MERELY LUCKY BLUNDERS. . . . . 482 A MASQUE OF REASON . . 259
LUCKY'S
    THE WAY THEY GREW ROUND LEIF THE LUCKY'S GERMAN; . . . 197 WILD GRAPES 27
LUCRETIUS
    LUCRETIUS THE EPICUREAN MIGHT TELL US . . . . . . 380 TOO ANXIOUS FOR RIVERS 23
    FOR I THOUGHT EPICURUS AND LUCRETIUS . . . . 393 LUCRETIUS VERSUS POETS 5
    LUCRETIUS VERSUS THE LAKE POETS . . . . 393 LUCRETIUS VERSUS POETS T
LULL
    FROM WHERE I LINGERED IN A LULL IN MARCH . . . . . . 234 EVENING A SUGAR ORCHARD 1
LUMBER
    THAT TROUBLE THE SLEEP OF LUMBER FOLK: . . . . . . 140 THE GUM-GATHERER . . 22
    TO DRIVE PAUL OUT OF ANY LUMBER CAMP . . . . 191 PAUL'S WIFE 1
    THE LUMBER ON PAUL TILL PAUL BEGGED FOR MERCY. . . . . 193 PAUL'S WIFE 61
    BUT NOT LONG SINCE IN THE LUMBER CAMPS). . . . . . 276 TWO TRAMPS IN MUD TIME 51
    THEN CUT DOWN THE TREES WHEN LUMBER GROWN, ... 376 SOMETHING FOR HOPE . . 13
LUMBERING
    PAUL WORKED AT ANYTHING IN LUMBERING. . . . . . . 193 PAUL'S WIFE 57
LUMBERJACKS
    MEN OF THE WOODS AND LUMBERJACKS, ... 276 TWO TRAMPS IN MUD TIME 53
LUMINARY
    ONE LUMINARY CLOCK AGAINST THE SKY . . . . 255 ACQUAINTED WITH NIGHT . 12
LUMPS
    HE SHOWED ME LUMPS OF THE SCENTED STUFF . . . . . 141 THE GUM-GATHERER . . 30
LUNAR
    A BIRD HALF WAKENED IN THE LUNAR NOON . . . . . . 302 A BIRD SINGING IN SLEEP 1
    SOME LUNATIC OR LUNAR WHIM . . . . 390 TWO LEADING LIGHTS . . 18
    I DON'T KNOW WHAT MADE HER SO LUNAR A LOON; . . . . . 463 LINES IN DEJECTION . . 3
LUNATIC
    SOME LUNATIC OR LUNAR WHIM-- . . . . 390 TWO LEADING LIGHTS . . 18
    WILL BE SOME SOULLESS LUNATIC ASYLUM-- . . . . . . 500 A MASQUE OF MERCY . . 187
LUNENBURG
    "WHAT TOWN IS THIS?" I ASKED. / "THIS? LUNENBURG." . . 41 THE MOUNTAIN 19
    "YOU CAN DRIVE ROUND AND KEEP IN LUNENBURG, ... 43 THE MOUNTAIN 93
LUPINE
    NOT LUPINE LIVING ON SAND AND DROUTH. . . . . . . 248 A PASSING GLIMPSE . . 8
LURCH
    BECAUSE HE LEFT IT IN THE LURCH, ... 274 A LONE STRIKER . . . 59
LURCHED
    HE REELED, HE LURCHED, HE BOBBED, HE CHECKED; . . . . 138 BROWN'S DESCENT . . . 37
LURCHING
    AND THREW THEIR LURCHING SHADOWS ON A HOUSE . . . . . 89 THE FEAR 3
LURE (SEE ANTI-LURE)
    IS NOT TO LURE THE CITY TO THE COUNTRY. . . . . . 322 BUILD SOIL 186
LURED
    AND NOW PRAY TELL WHAT LURED YOU WITH FALSE HOPE . . . 356 A MOTH SEEN IN WINTER . 7
LURKING
    THE LURKING FROST IN THE EARTH BENEATH . . . . . 276 TWO TRAMPS IN MUD TIME 38
LURKS
    "THE PLACE IS DESERT, AND LET WHOSO LURKS . . . . 176 THE CENSUS-TAKER . . 57
    THE SADNESS THAT LURKS NEAR THE OPEN WINDOW THERE, . . 287 A ROADSIDE STAND . . 34
    THE HUNTER LURKS . . . . 360 THE RABBIT-HUNTER . . 2
LUST
    WITH THIRST ON HUNGER TO THE POINT OF LUST. . . . . 411 POD OF THE MILKWEED . 26
LUSTER
    I'VE TRIED IT FINE WITH LITTLE BREADTH OF LUSTER, . . . 245 THE FREEDOM OF THE MOON 4
LUSTY
    THIS WAS AN ANTLERED BUCK OF LUSTY NOSTRIL, ... 229 TWO LOOK AT TWO . . . 29
LUXURIANCE
    SUCH WHITE LUXURIANCE OF MAY FOR OURS. . . . . . 233 A BOUNDLESS MOMENT . . 8
LUXURIATING
    IT LIFTS A GAUNT LUXURIATING BEAST . . . . 254 A WINTER EDEN . . . 9
LYING
    YOU'RE HIDING SOMETHING. THAT'S AS BAD AS LYING. . . . 97 THE SELF-SEEKER . . . 132
    HE MIGHT HAVE LEFT IT LYING WHERE IT FELL. . . . . . 173 A STAR IN A STONEBOAT . 39
    SO LYING FORWARD WEAKLY ON THE HANDRAIL . . . . . . 205 THE WITCH OF COOS . . 96
    AND LEFT IT LYING WHERE IT FELL REJECTED. . . . . . 217 A FOUNTAIN, A BOTTLE . 120
LYLE
    WHAT'S THIS? / DON'T LOSE THE PLACE. / OLD DANA LYLE, . 506 A MASQUE OF MERCY . . 324
LYNCH
    HARRIS OF DERRY, AND LYNCH OF BETHLEHEM. . . . . . 167 NEW HAMPSHIRE . . . 261
LYRE
    "BEHOLD MY SON IN RAGS HERE WITH HIS LYRE," . . . . . 459 HOW HARD TO KEEP FROM 169
LYRIC
    OF LYRIC IS A GOLDEN LIGHT DIVINE, ... 358 THE LOST FOLLOWER . . 3

M

MA
    "MA FRIEND, YOU AIN'T KNOW WHAT IT IS YOU'RE ASK." . . . 114 IN THE HOME STRETCH . 105
MABEL
    HER TEACHER'S CERTAINTY IT MUST BE MABEL . . . . . . 179 MAPLE 1
    "ISN'T IT MABEL? I THOUGHT IT WAS MABEL." . . . . . 182 MAPLE 89
    "NO DOUBT YOU'VE HEARD THE OFFICE CALL ME MABEL. . . . 182 MAPLE 90
MACBETH
    AND BID MY WILL AVOUCH IT LIKE MACBETH. . . . . . . 477 A MASQUE OF REASON . . 112
MACHINE
    "MADE ON MACHINE," HE SAID, PLOWING THE GRAIN . . . . 186 THE AX-HELVE . . . 22
    I WONDERED WHAT MACHINE OF AGES GONE . . . . . . 189 THE GRINDSTONE . . . 35
    THE EGG AND THE MACHINE . . . . 269 THE EGG AND THE MACHINE T
    HE RAISED AGAINST THE GODS IN THE MACHINE. . . . . . 270 THE EGG AND THE MACHINE 15
    THE NEXT MACHINE THAT HAS THE POWER TO PASS . . . . . 270 THE EGG AND THE MACHINE 29
    TO SEE IF SOME FORLORN MACHINE . . . . 273 A LONE STRIKER . . . 14

MACHINE (CONTINUED)
     WAS A PRAYER MACHINE FROM TIBET . . . . 397 AN IMPORTER 18
     GOD OF THE MACHINE, ... 442 KITTY HAWK 462
     PEREGRINE MACHINE, ... 442 KITTY HAWK 463
MACHINERY
     BY NATURE MEANT THE WHOLE GODDAM MACHINERY. . . . . . . 393 LUCRETIUS VERSUS POETS   6
     AND AS PICTURESQUE MACHINERY . . . . 397 AN IMPORTER 21
MACHINERY'S
     ALL OTHER FARM MACHINERY'S GONE IN, ... 189 THE GRINDSTONE 11
MACVEAGH
     FOR LINCOLN MACVEAGH . . . . 172 A STAR IN A STONEBOAT .   D
MAD (SEE HALF-MAD)
     MY FATHER'S BROTHER, HE WENT MAD QUITE YOUNG. . . . . . 65 A SERVANT TO SERVANTS . 104
     IS SUPPOSED TO BE MAD." / "I MAY BE MAD." . . . . 76 THE GENERATIONS OF MEN 83
     I THINK WE'RE ALL MAD. TELL ME WHY WE'RE HERE, ... 76 THE GENERATIONS OF MEN 88
     LIKE SMALL BOYS WE GOT MAD . . . . 464 MILKY WAY IS A COWPATH   6
MADAM
     IN OUR GREAT MOMENT WHAT DID YOU DO, MADAM? . . . . . . 477 A MASQUE OF REASON . . 117
MADDENING
     ALL JOINED IN THE MADDENING GAME. . . . . 311 THE VINDICTIVES . . . 32
MADE (SEE MOON-MADE)
     DIMLY TO HAVE MADE OUT MY SECRET PLACE, ... 14 WAITING 15
     A SLENDER TINKLING FALL THAT MADE . . . . 18 GOING FOR WATER . . . 22
     THE DEW WAS GONE THAT MADE HIS BLADE SO KEEN . . . . . 22 THE TUFT OF FLOWERS . 3
     THAT MADE ME HEAR THE WAKENING BIRDS AROUND, ... 23 THE TUFT OF FLOWERS . 31
     THAT FATE HAD MADE THEE FOR THE PLEASURE OF THE WIND, . 29 MY BUTTERFLY 23
     I HAVE COME AFTER THEM AND MADE REPAIR . . . . 33 MENDING WALL 6
     NO ONE HAS SEEN THEM MADE OR HEARD THEM MADE, ... 33 MENDING WALL 10
     TWO OR THREE TIMES--HE MADE ME FEEL SO QUEER-- . . . . 36 DEATH OF THE HIRED MAN 56
     HE WON'T BE MADE ASHAMED TO PLEASE HIS BROTHER." . . . 39 DEATH OF THE HIRED MAN 145
     I MADE THE BED UP FOR HIM THERE TONIGHT. . . . . 39 DEATH OF THE HIRED MAN 151
     AND MADE A WIDESPREAD BRAWL ON COBBLESTONES; . . . . . 40 THE MOUNTAIN 11
     THE DOCTOR MADE A SUBDUED DASH FOR IT, ... 47 A HUNDRED COLLARS . . 73
     HE MADE AS IF TO HOLD IT AT ARM'S LENGTH . . . . 55 THE BLACK COTTAGE . . 9
     BUT HOW COULD THEY BE MADE SO VERY UNLIKE . . . . 57 THE BLACK COTTAGE . . 77
     I'M JUST AS GLAD SHE MADE ME KEEP HANDS OFF, ... 58 THE BLACK COTTAGE . . 104
     FOR WHEN YOU MADE ANSWER, YOUR VOICE WAS AS LOW . . . . 62 BLUEBERRIES 95
     SO THEY MADE THE PLACE COMFORTABLE WITH STRAW, ... 66 A SERVANT TO SERVANTS . 119
     SHE HAD TO LIE AND HEAR LOVE THINGS MADE DREADFUL . . . 66 A SERVANT TO SERVANTS . 130
     MADE SHIFT TO SHELTER THEM WITHOUT THE HELP . . . . . . 73 THE GENERATIONS OF MEN 12
     TO RECONNOITER, AND THEN MADE UP HER MIND . . . . 74 THE GENERATIONS OF MEN 31
     SHE MADE A SUDDEN MOVEMENT TOWARD HER BODICE, ... 74 THE GENERATIONS OF MEN 43
     OF AN ACQUAINTANCE MADE ADVENTUROUSLY." . . . . 78 THE GENERATIONS OF MEN 153
     ALL IS, HE'S MADE UP HIS MIND NOT TO STAND . . . . . . 83 THE HOUSEKEEPER . . . 70
     THE SMELL OF SCORCHING WOOLEN MADE HER FAINT. . . . . . 91 THE FEAR 69
     AND THAT HAS MADE ALL THE DIFFERENCE. . . . . 105 THE ROAD NOT TAKEN . . 20
     MADE ME ASK WOULD THE MOTHER-BIRD RETURN . . . . 109 THE EXPOSED NEST . . 23
     AT WEEDS THE WATER FROM THE SINK MADE TALL. . . . . . . 110 IN THE HOME STRETCH . 3
     BUT JIMMY ONLY MADE HIS JAW RECEDE . . . . 114 IN THE HOME STRETCH . 101
     WHO SAID WITH SERIOUSNESS BEHIND THEIR LAUGH, ... 114 IN THE HOME STRETCH . 104
     MADE THE GREAT TREE SEEM AS A LITTLE BIRD . . . . 128 THE OFT-REPEATED DREAM   7
     MADE THE DIM TREES STAND BACK IN WIDER CIRCLE-- . . . . 130 THE BONFIRE 29
     AND MY FLAME MADE A PINNACLE TO HEAVEN . . . . 130 THE BONFIRE 38
     MADE WIND BY FANNING, SINCE YOU NEVER KNEW . . . . . . 130 THE BONFIRE 42
     SOMETHING OR SOMEONE WATCHING MADE THAT GUST. . . . . . 130 THE BONFIRE 44
     THAT MADE THE STARS BRIGHT . . . . 135 LAST WORD OF A BLUEBIRD 10
     AND MADE ICE ON THE TROUGH . . . . 135 LAST WORD OF A BLUEBIRD 11
     ALMOST MADE HIM COUGH . . . . 135 LAST WORD OF A BLUEBIRD 12
     AND MADE DUST AND DROPPED STOVE-LENGTH STICKS OF WOOD, . 136 "OUT,OUT--" 2
     OR BEEN MADE MASTER OF THE GRANGE." . . . . 138 BROWN'S DESCENT . . . 36
     HE FELL AND MADE THE LANTERN RATTLE . . . . 138 BROWN'S DESCENT . . . 38
     "HE HAD THE SHOVEL. HE'LL HAVE MADE A FIGHT." . . . . . 153 SNOW 279
     "I SEE THE PORTER'S MADE YOUR BED," I TOLD HIM. . . . . 159 NEW HAMPSHIRE . . . 15
     IT MADE THE WORLD SEEM SO MYSTERIOUS. . . . . 163 NEW HAMPSHIRE . . . 134
     THE FARM I MADE MY HOME ON IN THE MOUNTAINS . . . . . . 163 NEW HAMPSHIRE . . . 150
     EMERSON SAID, "THE GOD WHO MADE NEW HAMPSHIRE . . . . . 166 NEW HAMPSHIRE . . . 218
     BEFORE I MADE THE TENTH ACROSS THE THRESHOLD. . . . . . 175 THE CENSUS-TAKER . . 33
     MADE MAPLE FIRST TAKE NOTICE OF HER NAME. . . . . 179 MAPLE 2
     IT MUST HAVE MADE YOUR DIMPLE THERE, AND SAID, ... 180 MAPLE 17
     MADE PEOPLE NOTICE IT--AND NOTICE HER. . . . . 181 MAPLE 50
     (THE ARRANGEMENT MADE A PLEASANT SUNNY CELLAR.) . . . . 181 MAPLE 59
     IT MADE IT SEEM AS IF THERE MUST BE SOMETHING . . . . . 182 MAPLE 94
     WHEN THEY MADE HER RELATED TO THE MAPLES, ... 184 MAPLE 139
     MADE A GIRL'S MARRIAGE, AND RULED IN HER LIFE. . . . . 185 MAPLE 164
     "MADE ON MACHINE," HE SAID, PLOWING THE GRAIN . . . . . 186 THE AX-HELVE 22
     THICK HAND MADE LIGHT OF, STEEL-BLUE CHIN DRAWN DOWN . . 188 THE AX-HELVE 99
     THE THING THAT MADE ME MORE AND MORE AFRAID . . . . . . 190 THE GRINDSTONE . . . 65
     TO SEE IF IT WAS EMPTY. HE MADE OUT IN THERE . . . . . 194 PAUL'S WIFE 90
     HE MADE IN WALKING SLOWLY TO THE BEACH . . . . 194 PAUL'S WIFE 99
     AND THAT MADE PAUL IN TURN LOOK BACK . . . . 194 PAUL'S WIFE 111
     SHE HAD MADE THREE HERSELF TO THREE OF HIS. . . . . . . 199 PLACE FOR A THIRD . . 2
     SOMEHOW MADE HER IMPATIENT WITH THE MAN. . . . . 199 PLACE FOR A THIRD . . 8
     WHILE SHE MADE UP HER MIND HOW MUCH SHE CARED-- . . . . 201 PLACE FOR A THIRD . . 55
     (SHE MADE SHREWD EYES TO SEE WHERE HE CAME IN.) . . . . 201 PLACE FOR A THIRD . . 57
     THAT MADE HIM THROW HIS BARE LEGS OUT OF BED . . . . . 205 THE WITCH OF COOS . . 102
     THE UNCOMMONLY DEEP SNOW HAS MADE HIM THINK . . . . . . 205 THE WITCH OF COOS . . 109
     "TOFFILE, GET NAILS." I MADE HIM NAIL THE DOOR SHUT . . 206 THE WITCH OF COOS . . 119
     THEY MADE HIM KEEP ON GNAWING TILL HE WHINED. . . . . . 209 PAUPER WITCH OF GRAFTON 58
     I MADE HIM GATHER ME WET SNOWBERRIES . . . . 210 PAUPER WITCH OF GRAFTON 97
     I MADE HIM DO IT FOR ME IN THE DARK. . . . . 210 PAUPER WITCH OF GRAFTON 99
     AND HE LIKED EVERYTHING I MADE HIM DO. . . . . 210 PAUPER WITCH OF GRAFTON 100
     THE EARLY MORMONS MADE A SETTLEMENT. . . . . 213 A FOUNTAIN, A BOTTLE . 9
     WE MADE A DAY OF IT OUT OF THE WORLD, ... 214 A FOUNTAIN, A BOTTLE . 33
     (WE MADE IT SECURE AGAINST BEING, I HOPE, ... 228 GOOD-BY AND KEEP COLD . 13
     HAD MADE THEM CERTAIN EARTH RETURNED THEIR LOVE. . . . . 230 TWO LOOK AT TWO . . . 42
     AND MADE IT LEAP MY KNUCKLE, HAVING TOSSED . . . . . . 231 A BROOK IN THE CITY . 7
     THE SPARKS MADE NO ATTEMPT TO BE THE MOON. . . . . . . 234 EVENING A SUGAR ORCHARD 14
     YOU MADE NO SOUND IN THE GRASS WITH YOUR FOOTFALL, . . . 235 VALLEY'S SINGING DAY . 2

```
                                                              PAGE TITLE                      LINE
MADE (CONTINUED)
  AND THE LIGHT BREAKING ON THEM MADE THEM RUN.   . . . . . 237 A HILLSIDE THAW . . .            8
  THEY MADE NO WHITE IMPRESSION ON THE BLACK. .   . . . . . 239 OUR SINGING STRENGTH .          5
  BY THOUSANDS THE BAD WEATHER MADE AKIN. . .     . . . . . 240 OUR SINGING STRENGTH .         32
  MADE QUICK ASIDES, BUT HAVING DONE IN AIR   .   . . . . . 240 OUR SINGING STRENGTH .         40
  THE SHATTERED WATER MADE A MISTY DIN. . . .     . . . . . 250 ONCE BY THE PACIFIC  . . .      1
  TILL DAYLIGHT MADE IT SAFE FOR A FLYER. . .     . . . . . 253 THE THATCH . . . .             27
  WERE MADE IN HEAVEN. IT WASN'T WAVED TO US."    . . . . . 258 WEST-RUNNING BROOK . . .       29
  THEY ARE THE SEA MADE LAND  . . . . . . . .     . . . . . 260 SAND DUNES . . . .              5
  AND MADE OF US A LITTLE WHILE-- . . . . . .     . . . . . 265 THE BIRTHPLACE . . .            9
  AND FOLLOWED IT TO WHERE HE MADE OUT VAGUE  .   . . . . . 270 THE EGG AND THE MACHINE        19
  NOT SO MUCH TIED AS MADE THEM BLEND. . . . .    . . . . . 274 A LONE STRIKER . . .           32
  BUT FOR THE FLY HE MIGHT HAVE MADE ME THINK .   . . . . . 278 THE WHITE-TAILED HORNET        44
  THE MISSED FLY MADE ME DANGEROUSLY SKEPTIC.     . . . . . 279 THE WHITE-TAILED HORNET        49
  AND THIS DAY'S WORK MADE EVEN THAT SEEM DOUBTFUL.  . . .  279 THE WHITE-TAILED HORNET        70
  THREE MADE IT CERTAIN NOTHING FATE COULD DO .   . . . . . 283 THE GOLD HESPERIDEE            27
  HAVE NEVER MADE THE FIRST MOVE TO ASSEMBLE,     . . . . . 291 ON HEART'S BEGINNING TO        30
  MATTER OF FACT HAS MADE THEM BRAVE. . . . .     . . . . . 291 ON HEART'S BEGINNING TO        35
  AND NEVER COULD BE MADE TO UNDERSTAND.  . .     . . . . . 293 AT WOODWARD'S GARDENS .         4
  HE MADE THE SUN A PINPOINT ON THE NOSE  . .     . . . . . 293 AT WOODWARD'S GARDENS .         8
  THE AUTHENTIC SHOES IT WAS MADE IN  . . . .     . . . . . 295 A RECORD STRIDE . . .          27
  HAD MADE IT MUCH MORE EASILY A PREY. . . . .    . . . . . 303 A BIRD SINGING IN SLEEP        14
  AND LOOK FOR WHAT HAD MADE ME STALL, . . . .    . . . . . 304 UNHARVESTED . . . .             3
  THEY MADE HIM SEND OUT A CALL  . . . . . . .    . . . . . 310 THE VINDICTIVES . . .          10
  MADE GOOD FOR EVERYONE--THINGS LIKE INVENTIONS--  . . .  319 BUILD SOIL . . . .             94
  MADE SO WE ALL SHOULD GET THE GOOD OF THEM--    . . . . . 319 BUILD SOIL . . . .             95
  AND MADE FUN OF BY BUSINESS, LAW, AND ART;      . . . . . 322 BUILD SOIL . . . .            190
  THAT SOVIET RUSSIA HAS MADE FASHIONABLE. . .    . . . . . 323 BUILD SOIL . . . .            223
  MADE PUBLICLY IN SCHOOL, ABOVE SUSPICION   .    . . . . . 324 BUILD SOIL . . . .            274
  AND MADE COMMIT TO MEMORY  . . . . . . . . .    . . . . . 331 BEECH . . . .                  8
  IS OF THE SLIGHTEST BONDAGE MADE AWARE. . .     . . . . . 332 THE SILKEN TENT . . .          14
  AS IF SHE MADE IT ACHE . . . . . . . . . . .    . . . . . 339 THE SUBVERTED FLOWER          19
  AND THE EFFORT MADE HIM CHOKE  . . . . . . .    . . . . . 340 THE SUBVERTED FLOWER          28
  MADE HER STEAL A LOOK OF FEAR  . . . . . . .    . . . . . 340 THE SUBVERTED FLOWER          37
  TILL THE PIRATE SAILORS MADE A VOW . . . . .    . . . . . 344 DISCOVERY OF MADEIRAS         24
  BUT THE GIRL FOUGHT THEM AND MADE A SCENE.      . . . . . 345 DISCOVERY OF MADEIRAS         63
  SAFELY MADE THE AFRICAN SHORE;  . . . . . .     . . . . . 347 DISCOVERY OF MADEIRAS        127
  SOMETHING WE WERE WITHHOLDING MADE US WEAK      . . . . . 348 THE GIFT OUTRIGHT . . .         8
  YOU MUST BE MADE MORE SIMPLY WISE THAN I .      . . . . . 356 A MOTH SEEN IN WINTER         19
  WHEN SOMETHING STRANGE ABOUT IT MADE ME THINK.  . . . . . 357 A CONSIDERABLE SPECK .         6
  THAT MADE ME LOOK AGAIN AT THE CLOCK. . . .     . . . . . 364 TRESPASS . . . . .            16
  BUT IT MADE MY PROPERTY MINE ONCE MORE. . .     . . . . . 364 TRESPASS . . . . .            20
  I MADE BUT THE ONE FRIEND. . . . . . . . . .    . . . . . 366 NOT OF SCHOOL AGE . .          4
  THE LOVING'S MADE TO HOLD EACH OTHER LIKE,      . . . . . 371 THE LITERATE FARMER AND      114
  BACK IN A TIME MADE SIMPLE BY THE LOSS  . .     . . . . . 377 DIRECTIVE . . . . .            2
  THE YOUNG SPRUCE MADE A SUITE OF GLADES  . .    . . . . . 380 AN UNSTAMPED LETTER IN         9
  THE ONE YOU MADE, THE OTHER ONE YOU GREW. .     . . . . . 382 TO AN ANCIENT . . . .          2
  YOU MADE THE EOLITH, YOU GREW THE BONE,  . .    . . . . . 382 TO AN ANCIENT . . . .         13
  AND MADE FEEL LESS ALONE THAN I RIGHTLY SHOULD, . . . . . 383 WERE I IN TROUBLE . . .        8
  THAT MADE OUR HOUSE OF LIFE A HOUSE OF WORSHIP? . . . . . 386 A STEEPLE ON THE HOUSE         3
  THAT MADE THEM MILITATE. . . . . . . . . . .    . . . . . 387 THE COURAGE TO BE NEW .       12
  BY THE ROGERS GROUP THEY MADE. . . . . . . .    . . . . . 391 A ROGERS GROUP . . .          12
  I MADE A GOOD TRY. . . . . . . . . . . . . .    . . . . . 391 A WISH TO COMPLY . . .         4
  BUT WANTS IT ALL MADE OVER NEW. . . . . . .     . . . . . 393 A CASE FOR JEFFERSON .         2
  AND HAVING IT ALL MADE OVER NEW. . . . . . .    . . . . . 393 A CASE FOR JEFFERSON .        11
  WHEN SHE HAS MADE THINGS SO WE HAVE TO GO       . . . . . 395 WHY WAIT FOR SCIENCE .         4
  WAS MADE BY GETTING SCIENCE ON THE BRAIN;       . . . . . 398 BURSTING RAPTURE . . .         5
  AND MADE OF BY A BOY; THEN HAVING REACHED       . . . . . 405 FROM PLANE TO PLANE           57
  A RIVALRY THAT MADE THEM BOTH FEEL KINDER.      . . . . . 408 FROM PLANE TO PLANE          119
  REMEMBER HE HAD MADE THE TEST  . . . . . . .    . . . . . 416 AMERICA IS HARD TO SEE         7
  HE MIGHT HAVE BOLDLY MADE THE BLUFF  . . . .    . . . . . 417 AMERICA IS HARD TO SEE        26
  AS CORTEZ ON THE AZTECS MADE. . . . . . . .     . . . . . 419 AMERICA IS HARD TO SEE        84
  NOT A HEAVENLY DOG MADE MANIFEST, . . . . .     . . . . . 419 ONE MORE BREVITY . . .        10
  WHO HAD MADE AN OVERNIGHT DESCENT  . . . . .    . . . . . 421 ONE MORE BREVITY . . .        62
  SOMETHING WE WERE WITHHOLDING MADE US WEAK      . . . . . 424 THE GIFT OUTRIGHT . . .         8
  MADE THEM NO LESS GAY, . . . . . . . . . . .    . . . . . 431 KITTY HAWK . . . .           115
  SOMETHING MADE IT SAD  . . . . . . . . . . .    . . . . . 432 KITTY HAWK . . . .           129
  MANNERS MADE IT HARD, . . . . . . . . . . .     . . . . . 432 KITTY HAWK . . . .           134
  MADE ALL BEING FULL. . . . . . . . . . . . .    . . . . . 433 KITTY HAWK . . . .           174
  WE HAVE MADE A PASS . . . . . . . . . . . .     . . . . . 439 KITTY HAWK . . . .           362
  MADE IT, AS IT WERE, . . . . . . . . . . . .    . . . . . 439 KITTY HAWK . . . .           364
  THAT MADE US STUMBLE PAST. . . . . . . . . .    . . . . . 444 ENDS . . . . . .               2
  THAT SHOULD HAVE MADE THE NEW WORLD NEWLY GREAT . . . . . 446 DOES NO ONE AT ALL EVER        3
  SOME MISTAKE HAD BEEN MADE . . . . . . . . .    . . . . . 449 THE BAD ISLAND--EASTER        49
  THEY WERE MADE TO PARADE, . . . . . . . . .     . . . . . 449 THE BAD ISLAND--EASTER        56
  AND THE MEAL MADE THE BANQUETERS EXCLAIM  .     . . . . . 455 HOW HARD TO KEEP FROM         58
  PROSE MADE OF, GIVEN AN AIR BY CHURCH INTONING. . . . . . 461 HOW HARD TO KEEP FROM        222
  AND NOTHING MADE OF YOUTH. CONSIDER ME,   .     . . . . . 462 HOW HARD TO KEEP FROM        258
  I DON'T KNOW WHAT MADE HER SO LUNAR A LOON;     . . . . . 463 LINES IN DEJECTION . .         3
  I'LL BET SHE'D HAVE MADE A MELODIOUS LOW . .    . . . . . 463 LINES IN DEJECTION . .        11
  AND MADE THE PAPERS' FRONT PAGE. . . . . . .    . . . . . 463 LINES IN DEJECTION . .        24
  I MADE THIS YOU TO BEGUILE  . . . . . . . .     . . . . . 466 SOME SCIENCE FICTION          33
  MADE FOR THE EMPEROR ALEXIUS, . . . . . . .     . . . . . 473 A MASQUE OF REASON .          11
  I TOLD HIM NOT TO SCRATCH: IT MADE IT WORSE.    . . . . . 478 A MASQUE OF REASON .         128
  FOR VERY LONG. WE'RE PLAINLY MADE TO GO. .      . . . . . 481 A MASQUE OF REASON .         233
  I TRUST I MADE IT CLEAR I TOOK YOUR SIDE .      . . . . . 486 A MASQUE OF REASON .         362
  CAN BE MADE NEGLIGIBLE. / WHAT'S YOUR BOOK?     . . . . . 506 A MASQUE OF MERCY .          323
  I NOTICED HOW HE JUST NOW MADE YOU OUT  . .     . . . . . 510 A MASQUE OF MERCY .          454
  DON'T YOU BE MADE FEEL SMALL BY ALL THIS POSING.  . . .  511 A MASQUE OF MERCY .          461
  THAT MADE ALL OTHER OUTRAGE SEEM AS CHILD'S PLAY: . . . . 511 A MASQUE OF MERCY .          476
  BUT SUCH WE ALL ARE MADE IN THE SIGHT OF GOD.   . . . . . 512 A MASQUE OF MERCY .          501
  NERVOUS IS ALL THE GREAT THINGS EVER MADE YOU.  . . . . . 516 A MASQUE OF MERCY .          599
MADEIRAS
  THE DISCOVERY OF THE MADEIRAS  . . . . . . . . . . . . . 343 DISCOVERY OF MADEIRAS .        T
MADISON
  JOHN ADAMS, JEFFERSON, AND MADISON--  . . . . . . . . . . 422 FOR JOHN F. KENNEDY .         26
  WHERE MADISON ATTEMPTED TO ARREST IT. . . . . . . . . . . 458 HOW HARD TO KEEP FROM        156
```

MADNESS
  OF BUSINESS, MIGHT INCREASE INTO A MADNESS. . . . . . . 503 A MASQUE OF MERCY . . 249
MAGI
  DID YOU STAY UP LAST NIGHT (THE MAGI DID) . . . . . 360 A LOOSE MOUNTAIN . . 1
MAGIC
  IT LOOKS AS IF SOME MAGIC OF THE SUN . . . . 237 A HILLSIDE THAW . . . 6
MAGICAL
  AS MAGICAL AS SUNLIGHT ON THE SKIN. . . . . 337 THE WIND AND THE RAIN . 42
MAGNIFIED
  MAGNIFIED APPLES APPEAR AND DISAPPEAR, ... 68 AFTER APPLE-PICKING . 18
MAGNITUDE
  UNDER MAGNITUDE THE SECOND.) . . . . 304 CLEAR AND COLDER . . 9
MAGOON
  YOU GOT IT THE FIRST TIME. AND YOURS?" / "MAGOON. . . . 46 A HUNDRED COLLARS . . 42
  DOCTOR MAGOON." / "A DOCTOR?" / "WELL, A TEACHER." . . . 46 A HUNDRED COLLARS . . 43
MAIANTHEMUM
  DWARF CORNEL, GOLDTHREAD, AND MAIANTHEMUM, ... 355 TIME OUT 5
MAIDENS
  AND THUS IT WAS THE MAIDENS PALE . . . . 15 IN A VALE 3
MAIDS
  HAVE MARRIED BEGGAR MAIDS FROM OFF THE STREETS. . . . 457 HOW HARD TO KEEP FROM 110
MAIL
  PREOCCUPIED WITH FORMIDABLE MAIL, ... 44 A HUNDRED COLLARS . . 9
MAINTAIN
  ALL THEY MAINTAIN THE PATH FOR IS THE COMFORT . . . . 414 A CABIN IN THE CLEARING 7
MAINTAINED
  THE ROAD ALONE MAINTAINED ITSELF IN MUD, ... 239 OUR SINGING STRENGTH . 16
  THAT WAS MAINTAINED AGAINST THE NIGHT, ... 291 ON HEART'S BEGINNING TO 8
MAINTAINING
  I'M WITH YOU IN MAINTAINING TO THE PUBLIC. . . . . . 482 A MASQUE OF REASON . . 251
MAIZE
  THIS THOUGH WE TOOK THE INDIAN NAME FOR MAIZE . . . . 446 DOES NO ONE AT ALL EVER 7
MAJOR
  CANIS MAJOR . . . . 261 CANIS MAJOR . . . . T
  A HALF A DOZEN MAJOR WARS, ... 368 A SERIOUS STEP LIGHTLY 23
MAKE
  MAKE THE SETTLED SNOWBANK STEAM; . . . . 11 TO THE THAWING WIND . 4
  BATHE MY WINDOW, MAKE IT FLOW, ... 11 TO THE THAWING WIND . 7
  AND MAKE US HAPPY IN THE HAPPY BEES, ... 12 A PRAYER IN SPRING . . 7
  AND MAKE US HAPPY IN THE DARTING BIRD . . . . 12 A PRAYER IN SPRING . . 9
  TO MAKE ME SAD TO GO. . . . . 12 FLOWER-GATHERING . . 4
  MY LONG SCYTHE WHISPERED AND LEFT THE HAY TO MAKE. . . . 17 MOWING 14
  AND IN THE HUSH WE JOINED TO MAKE . . . . 18 GOING FOR WATER . . . 19
  WE MAKE OURSELVES A PLACE APART . . . . 19 REVELATION 1
  AND CHECKED MY STEPS TO MAKE PRETENSE . . . . 25 THE DEMIURGE'S LAUGH . 15
  TO MAKE ONE TEXTURE OF FADED BROWN . . . . 25 IN HARDWOOD GROVES . . 3
  MAKE THE DAY SEEM TO US LESS BRIEF. . . . . 27 OCTOBER 9
  WE HAVE TO USE A SPELL TO MAKE THEM BALANCE: . . . . 33 MENDING WALL 18
  HE ONLY SAYS, "GOOD FENCES MAKE GOOD NEIGHBORS." . . . 33 MENDING WALL 27
  "WHY DO THEY MAKE GOOD NEIGHBORS? ISN'T IT . . . . . 34 MENDING WALL 30
  HE SAYS AGAIN, "GOOD FENCES MAKE GOOD NEIGHBORS." . . . 34 MENDING WALL 45
  AND GAVE HIM TEA AND TRIED TO MAKE HIM SMOKE. . . . . 36 DEATH OF THE HIRED MAN 41
  I TRIED TO MAKE HIM TALK ABOUT HIS TRAVELS. . . . . . 36 DEATH OF THE HIRED MAN 42
  HE SAYS THEY TWO WILL MAKE A TEAM FOR WORK: . . . . . 36 DEATH OF THE HIRED MAN 62
  HE SAID HE COULDN'T MAKE THE BOY BELIEVE . . . . . . 37 DEATH OF THE HIRED MAN 82
  SIT DOWN OR LIE DOWN, FRIEND; YOU MAKE ME NERVOUS." . . 47 A HUNDRED COLLARS . . 72
  APART WOULD MAKE ME OUT. GIVE ME MY CHANCE. . . . . 53 HOME BURIAL 61
  YOU MAKE ME ANGRY. I'LL COME DOWN TO YOU. . . . . . 53 HOME BURIAL 68
  FRIENDS MAKE PRETENSE OF FOLLOWING TO THE GRAVE, . . . 54 HOME BURIAL 102
  SOMEWHERE OUT OF THIS HOUSE. HOW CAN I MAKE YOU----" . . 55 HOME BURIAL 113
  HE WON'T MAKE THE FACT THAT THEY'RE RIGHTFULLY HIS . . 60 BLUEBERRIES 31
  I DIDN'T MAKE YOU KNOW HOW GLAD I WAS . . . . 62 A SERVANT TO SERVANTS . 1
  I STAND AND MAKE MYSELF REPEAT OUT LOUD . . . . . . 63 A SERVANT TO SERVANTS . 18
  BUT LEN WENT AT IT TO MAKE UP THE LOSS. . . . . . . 64 A SERVANT TO SERVANTS . 65
  (WOMEN AND MEN WILL MAKE THEM ALL THE SAME.) . . . . 64 A SERVANT TO SERVANTS . 69
  AROUND HIM TO LOOK AFTER THAT MAKE WASTE. . . . . . 65 A SERVANT TO SERVANTS . 73
  AND LET THEM GO AND MAKE THEM TWANG, UNTIL . . . . . 66 A SERVANT TO SERVANTS . 135
  I CAN MAKE OUT OLD GRANDSIR STARK DISTINCTLY-- . . . . 77 THE GENERATIONS OF MEN 104
  AND COME AND MAKE YOUR SUMMER DWELLING HERE, ... 79 THE GENERATIONS OF MEN 166
  BUT DON'T YOU THINK WE SOMETIMES MAKE TOO MUCH . . . . 80 THE GENERATIONS OF MEN 196
  MAKE SO MUCH DIFFERENCE IN HIS MAN'S AFFAIRS. . . . . 83 THE HOUSEKEEPER . . . 54
  TAKE IT YEAR IN, YEAR OUT, HE DOESN'T MAKE MUCH. . . . 85 THE HOUSEKEEPER . . . 103
  DOORS LOCKED AND CURTAINS DRAWN WILL MAKE NO DIFFERENCE. . 89 THE FEAR 16
  "IN THE FIRST PLACE YOU CAN'T MAKE ME BELIEVE IT'S----". . 90 THE FEAR 41
  BECAUSE I MAKE HIM SPIT FIRE AT MY KNUCKLES, ... 94 THE SELF-SEEKER . . . 34
  THE WAY BEN FRANKLIN USED TO MAKE THE KITE STRING. . . 94 THE SELF-SEEKER . . . 35
  "YOU MAKE THAT SOUND AS IF IT WASN'T SO . . . . . . 94 THE SELF-SEEKER . . . 47
  SOMEHOW I'LL MAKE IT RIGHT WITH HER--SHE'LL SEE. . . . 98 THE SELF-SEEKER . . . 150
  WAS CUNNINGLY DEVISED TO MAKE A NOISE . . . . 98 THE SELF-SEEKER . . . 164
  WHERE YOU CAN'T MAKE THEM. WHAT IS IT YOU WANT? . . . 99 THE SELF-SEEKER . . . 185
  "MAKE YOURSELF USEFUL, THEN, AND MAKE IT FOR ME.-- . . 99 THE SELF-SEEKER . . . 188
  HE WENT BEHIND IT TO MAKE HIS LAST STAND. . . . . . 101 THE WOOD-PILE . . . 22
  I WENT TO SHOW YOU HOW TO MAKE IT STAY, ... 109 THE EXPOSED NEST . . 5
  TO MAKE IT ROOT AGAIN AND GROW AFRESH. . . . . . . 109 THE EXPOSED NEST . . 8
  AND MIGHT OUR MEDDLING MAKE HER MORE AFRAID. . . . . 109 THE EXPOSED NEST . . 25
  MORE THAN SO MANY TIMES MAKE ME A LADY . . . . . . 111 IN THE HOME STRETCH . 23
  AND MAKE GOOD FARMERS, AND LEAVE OTHER FELLOWS . . . . 114 IN THE HOME STRETCH . 96
  ACROSS HIS CHEST TO MAKE AS 'TWERE A BOW: . . . . . 114 IN THE HOME STRETCH . 107
  "DID THEY MAKE SOMETHING LONESOME GO THROUGH YOU? . . . 114 IN THE HOME STRETCH . 122
  I HAVE TO MAKE YOU BUILD IT. COME, THE LIGHT." . . . 117 IN THE HOME STRETCH . 200
  IS WHAT TO MAKE OF A DIMINISHED THING. . . . . . . 120 THE OVEN BIRD . . . 14
  TO MAKE NO MORE OF A WALL THAN AN OPEN GATE, ... 124 THE COW IN APPLE TIME . 2
  OH, LET'S NOT WAIT FOR RAIN TO MAKE IT SAFE. . . . . 129 THE BONFIRE 5
  AND HE SAID, "THAT OUGHT TO MAKE YOU . . . . 133 A GIRL'S GARDEN . . . 13
  AND MANY MUST HAVE SEEN HIM MAKE . . . . 137 BROWN'S DESCENT . . . 5
  TO HOLD IT HARD UNTIL THEY MAKE IT FAST, ... 141 THE LINE-GANG . . . 10
  STICK TO HIM, HELEN. MAKE HIM ANSWER YOU. . . . . . 145 SNOW 63
  I SHOULD HAVE THOUGHT, THOUGH, YOU COULD MAKE HIM HEAR YOU." 145 SNOW 67

MAKE (CONTINUED)

	PAGE	TITLE	LINE
HE'LL MAKE A CASE OF IT IF HE SUCCEEDS,	146	SNOW	86
I'VE HAD MY EYE ON IT TO MAKE OUT WHICH:	147	SNOW	120
ONE OF THE LIES WOULD MAKE IT OUT THAT NOTHING	147	SNOW	129
YOU MAKE A LITTLE FOURSQUARE BLOCK OF AIR,	148	SNOW	142
"FRED, AFTER ALL I SAID! YOU SHAN'T MAKE OUT	153	SNOW	285
NOT IF SHE'S THERE." / "WHAT DO YOU MAKE OF IT?"	154	SNOW	321
"THERE'S ONLY ONE THING POSSIBLE TO MAKE,	155	SNOW	322
IF HE THINKS HE IS GOING TO MAKE OUR HOUSE	155	SNOW	341
I SHALL MAKE THE RECKLESS CHOICE	156	THE SOUND OF TREES	20
ANGRILY TRIED TO MAKE ME WRITE A PROTEST	160	NEW HAMPSHIRE	29
AND MAKE THE MOST OF IT FOR BETTER OR WORSE.	161	NEW HAMPSHIRE	65
JUST ENOUGH GOLD TO MAKE THE ENGAGEMENT RINGS	162	NEW HAMPSHIRE	113
I MAKE A VIRTUE OF MY SUFFERING	166	NEW HAMPSHIRE	237
TO WANT TO MAKE NEW HAMPSHIRE PEOPLE OVER.	167	NEW HAMPSHIRE	263
I HAD TO MAKE AN ALMOST FUNNY CHOICE.	170	NEW HAMPSHIRE	361
ON WORDS, AND TRIES HIS WORST TO MAKE WORDS SPEAK	171	NEW HAMPSHIRE	401
SO WHAT IS THIS I MAKE A SORROW OF?)	174	THE CENSUS-TAKER	8
TO MAKE FUN OF MY WAY OF DOING THINGS,	176	THE STAR-SPLITTER	9
TO MAKE IT GO WELL WITH THE WAY SHE LOOKED.	181	MAPLE	43
'TWOULD BE TOO BAD TO MAKE HIM SORRY FOR	183	MAPLE	121
BAPTISTE KNEW HOW TO MAKE A SHORT JOB LONG	187	THE AX-HELVE	80
MIGHTN'T WE MAKE IT WORSE INSTEAD OF BETTER?	191	THE GRINDSTONE	74
TO MAKE A WILLOW WHISTLE ON A SUNDAY	191	PAUL'S WIFE	21
SO THEN, TO MAKE ME WHOLLY SELF-SUPPORTING,	197	WILD GRAPES	36
MY BROTHER TRIED TO MAKE ME LAUGH TO HELP ME.	197	WILD GRAPES	55
DON'T MAKE ME LIE WITH THOSE TWO OTHER WOMEN."	199	PLACE FOR A THIRD	11
LABAN SAID, NO, HE WOULD NOT MAKE HER LIE	199	PLACE FOR A THIRD	12
AND ANXIOUS TO MAKE ALL HE COULD OF IT	200	PLACE FOR A THIRD	17
MOTHER CAN MAKE A COMMON TABLE REAR	202	THE WITCH OF COOS	9
HE BROKE MY TRANCE. DON'T THAT MAKE YOU SUSPICIOUS	202	THE WITCH OF COOS	16
"DON'T MAKE ME GET UP; I'M TOO WARM IN BED."	205	THE WITCH OF COOS	95
TO MAKE A PRESENT OF ME TO EACH OTHER.	207	PAUPER WITCH OF GRAFTON	5
IT'D MAKE MY POSITION STRONGER, THINK,	208	PAUPER WITCH OF GRAFTON	42
TO MAKE IT SURER THAT I WAS A WITCH?	208	PAUPER WITCH OF GRAFTON	44
TO UNDO WHAT HE'D DONE AND MAKE IT RIGHT,	209	PAUPER WITCH OF GRAFTON	79
TO MAKE SO FREE AND KICK UP IN FOLKS' FACES.	210	PAUPER WITCH OF GRAFTON	107
TO MAKE THEM OUT."	212	AN EMPTY THREAT	57
IN DALTON THAT WOULD SOME DAY MAKE HIS FORTUNE.	212	A FOUNTAIN, A BOTTLE	2
WHY MAKE SO MUCH OF FRAGMENTARY BLUE	220	FRAGMENTARY BLUE	1
THOUGH SOME SAVANTS MAKE EARTH INCLUDE THE SKY;	220	FRAGMENTARY BLUE	6
IT SHALL NOT MAKE AGAIN ALL WINTER LONG.	226	THE ONSET	4
AS IF TO ASK, "WHY DON'T YOU MAKE SOME MOTION?	230	TWO LOOK AT TWO	32
I MAKE A GREAT NOISE	234	GATHERING LEAVES	5
TO MAKE A LEAF, IF THERE HAD BEEN ONE, STIR.	238	A HILLSIDE THAW	32
AND MAKE US GET DOWN IN A FOOT OF SNOW	238	ON A TREE FALLEN ACROSS	7
HORDES SPENT THEMSELVES TO MAKE IT WET AND COLD,	239	OUR SINGING STRENGTH	3
TO MAKE IT WORTH LIFE'S WHILE TO WAKE AND SPORT.	254	A WINTER EDEN	20
THOSE FRIENDS KNOW NOTHING OF HER GRIEF TO MAKE IT SHAMEFUL.	256	THE LOVELY BE CHOOSERS	27
AND MAKE THEM SEE IT IN THE WINTER FIRELIGHT.	257	THE LOVELY BE CHOOSERS	34
MAKE HER AMONG THE HUMBLEST EVEN	257	THE LOVELY BE CHOOSERS	39
OUR MISSILES ALWAYS MAKE TOO SHORT AN ARC.	261	A SOLDIER	8
THEY MAKE US CRINGE FOR METAL-POINT ON STONE.	261	A SOLDIER	11
TO WHICH THE FARMER WOULD MAKE REPLY,	263	THE TIMES TABLE	8
THE WORLD HAS ROOM TO MAKE A BEAR FEEL FREE;	269	THE BEAR	11
ONE FAILED TO MAKE THE CLOSING GATE.	273	A LONE STRIKER	4
THESE TWO MUST MAKE ME LOVE IT MORE	276	TWO TRAMPS IN MUD TIME	42
AS MY TWO EYES MAKE ONE IN SIGHT.	277	TWO TRAMPS IN MUD TIME	68
IN HER WE MAKE OURSELVES ACQUAINTED	280	BLUE RIBBON AT AMESBURY	11
AND MAKE UP FOR ITS LACK OF SIZE.	281	A DRUMLIN WOODCHUCK	4
NOT MAKE ME TIRED AND MOROSE.	286	IN TIME OF CLOUDBURST	27
HERE FAR FROM THE CITY WE MAKE OUR ROADSIDE STAND	286	A ROADSIDE STAND	18
TO TRY IF IT WILL NOT MAKE OUR BEING EXPAND,	286	A ROADSIDE STAND	20
AND SO ARE NOTHING TO MAKE HER TREMBLE.	291	ON HEART'S BEGINNING TO	31
SAYS, TO MAKE THIS FALL ELIXIR	303	CLEAR AND COLDER	3
IT WILL MAKE A HOMICIDAL ROAR.	306	A TRIAL RUN	4
MAKE UP YOUR MIND TO DIE IN STATE.	307	PROVIDE, PROVIDE	9
MAKE THE WHOLE STOCK EXCHANGE YOUR OWN!	307	PROVIDE, PROVIDE	10
FOR FEAR IT WOULD MAKE ME CONSERVATIVE WHEN OLD.	308	PRECAUTION	2
BUT TO MAKE BAD MATTERS WORSE	309	NOT ALL THERE	3
MAKE BOLD TO SING IT SO, BUT DO I DARE	317	BUILD SOIL	42
YOU'D MAKE A SORT OF SAFETY-FIRST DICTATOR.	320	BUILD SOIL	130
THE MORAL IS, MAKE A LATE START TO MARKET.	322	BUILD SOIL	181
UNOCCUPIED NEED NOT MAKE US UNEASY.	322	BUILD SOIL	192
I'LL MAKE A COMPACT WITH YOU, MELIBOEUS,	323	BUILD SOIL	220
ENOUGH TO MAKE A SPIRIT MOAN	328	A MISSIVE MISSILE	39
FAR AS WE OFTEN MAKE THEM REACH,	328	A MISSIVE MISSILE	48
DOWNWARD TO MAKE HIM SIT ASTRIDE A DRIFT,	341	WILLFUL HOMING	6
THE BREEZE DISDAINED TO MAKE REPLY:	342	A CLOUD SHADOW	6
FOR FEAR I WOULD MAKE HER MISS THE PLACE.	342	A CLOUD SHADOW	8
HER LOVER TO MAKE THE ORDEAL SWIFT	343	DISCOVERY OF MADEIRAS	9
HE LAUGHED BUT HE DID NOT MAKE YOU LAUGH.	346	DISCOVERY OF MADEIRAS	91
I MAKE MYSELF THIS TIME	348	TRIPLE BRONZE	5
BUT NO ONE EVER HEARD YOU MAKE THE CLAIM.	351	THE LESSON FOR TODAY	28
TO MAKE THEIR VERSE AND THEIR EXCUSES LAME.	351	THE LESSON FOR TODAY	33
I CAN JUST HEAR THE WAY YOU MAKE IT GO:	352	THE LESSON FOR TODAY	54
(MAKE NO MISTAKE ABOUT ITS BEING BONES);	354	THE LESSON FOR TODAY	132
IT TOOK THAT PAUSE TO MAKE HIM REALIZE	355	TIME OUT	1
TO MAKE THE VENTURE OF ETERNITY.	356	A MOTH SEEN IN WINTER	8
YOU MAKE A LABOR OF FLIGHT FOR ONE SO AIRY,	356	A MOTH SEEN IN WINTER	11
OH, WE MAKE A BOAST OF STORING,	359	NOVEMBER	9
WE'LL MAKE IT THREE HUNDRED MORE	367	A SERIOUS STEP LIGHTLY	16
THE IDEA IS NO DOUBT TO MAKE ONE JOB	370	THE LITERATE FARMER AND	71
MAKE YOURSELF UP A CHEERING SONG OF HOW	378	DIRECTIVE	29
THEN MAKE YOURSELF AT HOME. THE ONLY FIELD	378	DIRECTIVE	39
WEEP FOR WHAT LITTLE THINGS COULD MAKE THEM GLAD.	378	DIRECTIVE	44
YOU MAKE ME ASK IF I WOULD GO TO TIME	382	TO AN ANCIENT	16
TO MAKE SURE WHAT STAR I MISSED	384	MAKING CERTAIN ANYTHING	13

- 324 -

MAKE (CONTINUED)
YOU SHOULD BE TEMPTED TO MAKE UP FOR IT . . . . 385 THE FEAR OF GOD . . .   9
SHE TRIES TO MAKE IT IN ONE CATCH OF BREATH, ... 386 THE FEAR OF MAN . . .   3
GOD BLESS THE DEAN AND MAKE HIS DEANSHIP PLENARY. . . . 394 LUCRETIUS VERSUS POETS   12
COULD MAKE MUCH DIFFERENCE TO THE DEAD AND GONE. . . . 397 THE PLANNERS   6
HOW THEY MAKE HASTE TO CRY WITH FINGERS CROSSED, . . . 399 U.S. 1946 KING'S X . .   3
TO MAKE UP FOR A LACK OF MEDITATION. . . . . 400 TO THE RIGHT PERSON . . 14
MAKE SUCH A NOISELESS TUMULT OVER IT . . . . 411 POD OF THE MILKWEED . . 11
ON EITHER HAND TO MAKE HIS COURSE PERHAPS . . . . . . 421 ESCAPIST--NEVER . . .   4
MAKE EVERYBODY WANT TO BE A NATION. . . . . 423 FOR JOHN F. KENNEDY . . 31
I CAN'T MAKE IT SEEM . . . . 430 KITTY HAWK   85
TO MAKE THEMSELVES GLAD . . . . 432 KITTY HAWK   132
WE MAKE NO PRETENSION . . . . 440 KITTY HAWK   378
AS ONE WHO WOULD NOT MAKE A GANYMEDE. . . . . 443 AUSPEX   8
TO MAKE US DIFFERENT IN A SINGLE TRAIT. . . . . 446 DOES NO ONE AT ALL EVER 6
THAT OUGHT TO MAKE THE SUNDAY PRESS. . . . . 451 A--WISHING WELL . . .   19
"MAKE THEM AS HAPPY AS IS GOOD FOR THEM. . . . . 458 HOW HARD TO KEEP FROM 150
FOR HIM TO MAKE A POET OF HIMSELF ON . . . . 459 HOW HARD TO KEEP FROM 175
BEFORE THEY MAKE IT A STATE. . . . . 466 SOME SCIENCE FICTION . 32
WHAT DID YOU TRY TO MAKE YOUR HUSBAND SAY? . . . . . . 477 A MASQUE OF REASON .   118
BETWEEN US, YOU AND I. / I MAKE YOU SEE? . . . . 480 A MASQUE OF REASON .   185
NO, MAKE ME PROPHESY. / AND--YOU--JUST--WON'T? . . . . 494 A MASQUE OF MERCY .   41
ONCE AND FOR ALL. I'M GOING TO MAKE YOU SEE . . . . . 498 A MASQUE OF MERCY .   145
HOW ABOUT LOVING GOD? / YOU MAKE ME SHRUG.-- . . . . . 499 A MASQUE OF MERCY .   164
WHAT GOOD IS THAT? / I'LL MAKE YOU SEE WHAT GOOD. . . . 501 A MASQUE OF MERCY .   196
THE ONE INDECENCY'S TO MAKE A FUSS . . . . 507 A MASQUE OF MERCY .   353
PAUL ONLY MEANS YOU MAKE TOO MUCH OF JUSTICE. . . . . 508 A MASQUE OF MERCY .   384
WHAT DO YOU MAKE OF IT? / THE SAME OLD NOTHING. . . . 512 A MASQUE OF MERCY .   492
DON'T LET HIM MAKE YOU SEE TOO BRIGHT A GATE . . . . . 513 A MASQUE OF MERCY .   536
TOWARD WHAT YOU MAKE ME SEE BEYOND THE WORLD. . . . . 514 A MASQUE OF MERCY .   545
YOU MUST MAKE YOUR DESCENT LIKE EVERYONE. . . . . . . 514 A MASQUE OF MERCY .   552
OUR MAKING ALL THIS EFFORT MORTALS MAKE? . . . . 517 A MASQUE OF MERCY .   635
NOTHING CAN MAKE INJUSTICE JUST BUT MERCY. . . . . . . 521 A MASQUE OF MERCY .   738
MAKE-BELIEVE
I WONDER IF IT'S NOT YOUR MAKE-BELIEVE. . . . . 78 THE GENERATIONS OF MEN 140
BUT 'TWAS NO MAKE-BELIEVE WITH YOU TODAY, ... 109 THE EXPOSED NEST . .   9
FIRST THERE'S THE CHILDREN'S HOUSE OF MAKE-BELIEVE, . . 378 DIRECTIVE   41
MAKERS'
ITS MAKERS' NAME--TIME CANNOT GET THAT WRONG, ... 308 THE WRIGHTS' BIPLANE .   3
MAKES
WHICH GOD MAKES HIS ESPECIAL CARE. . . . . 20 THE TRIAL BY EXISTENCE 32
AND MAKES GAPS EVEN TWO CAN PASS ABREAST. . . . . . . 33 MENDING WALL   4
WHAT MAKES YOU STAND THERE ON ONE LEG LIKE THAT? . . . 47 A HUNDRED COLLARS . .   69
I OUGHT TO KNOW--IT MAKES A DIFFERENCE WHICH: . . . . 56 THE BLACK COTTAGE . .   32
BUT I OWN WHAT YOU SAY MAKES MY HEAD SPIN. . . . . . . 75 THE GENERATIONS OF MEN 60
THAT A BROOK MAKES IN SUCH A WILD DESCENT. . . . . . . 78 THE GENERATIONS OF MEN 133
"AND LIKE IT, TOO. IT MAKES IT ALL THE WORSE." . . . . 86 THE HOUSEKEEPER . .   155
"IT MAKES IT ALL THE WORSE. YOU MUST BE BLIND." . . . 87 THE HOUSEKEEPER . .   163
"SEE HOW IT MAKES HIS NOSE-SIDE BRIGHT, A PROOF . . . 112 IN THE HOME STRETCH . 66
ITS SEEMING BAD FOR A MOMENT MAKES IT SEEM . . . . . 115 IN THE HOME STRETCH . 128
WHO MAKES THE SOLID TREE TRUNKS SOUND AGAIN. . . . . . 119 THE OVEN BIRD . . .   3
TILL DAY MAKES HIM RETRACE HIS FLIGHT, ... 120 BOND AND FREE . . .   13
SOON THE SUN'S WARMTH MAKES THEM SHED CRYSTAL SHELLS . 121 BIRCHES   10
"BROWN MAKES AT SUCH AN HOUR OF NIGHT! . . . . 138 BROWN'S DESCENT . .   33
AT THE SAME TIME YOU CAN'T DENY IT MAKES . . . . . . 149 SNOW   188
THERE QUALITY MAKES UP FOR QUANTITY. . . . . 163 NEW HAMPSHIRE . . .   148
IT MAKES THE GUILD OF NOVEL WRITERS SICK . . . . . . 167 NEW HAMPSHIRE . . .   274
SHE THINKS WHEN THE WIND MAKES A NIGHT OF IT . . . . 209 PAUPER WITCH OF GRAFTON 82
FROM THE HIGH WEST SHE MAKES A GENTLE CAST . . . . . 237 A HILLSIDE THAW . .   20
MAKES THE NEW MOON LOOK ANYTHING BUT NEW . . . . . . 247 THE COCOON   3
SHE MAKES THE WHOLE FLOCK MOVE ALONG. . . . . 281 BLUE RIBBON AT AMESBURY 48
IF IT MAKES YOU LOOK HELPLESS, PLEASE, ... 326 TO A THINKER . . .   23
HAPPINESS MAKES UP IN HEIGHT FOR WHAT IT LACKS IN LENGTH 333 HAPPINESS MAKES UP . . 1
AND THAT DEFENSE MAKES THREE . . . . 349 TRIPLE BRONZE . . .   11
WHICH MAKES THE WAR GOD SEEM NO SPECIAL DUNCE . . . . 350 TO A YOUNG WRETCH . .   17
ITS CONTEMPLATION MAKES US OUT AS SMALL . . . . 352 THE LESSON FOR TODAY . 69
WHICH OFTEN MAKES THE MANUMITTER BITTER." . . . . . . 371 THE LITERATE FARMER AND 91
I DON'T BELIEVE WHAT MAKES YOU RED IN THE FACE . . . 389 SKEPTIC   7
WHICH MAKES OPPOSING IT TO ART ABSURD . . . . 394 LUCRETIUS VERSUS POETS 10
IT MAKES THE BUTTERFLIES INTEMPERATE. . . . . 411 POD OF THE MILKWEED . 22
HIGH PURPOSE MAKES THE HERO RUDE: . . . . 418 AMERICA IS HARD TO SEE 73
IT MAKES THE PROPHET IN US ALL PRESAGE . . . . 424 FOR JOHN F. KENNEDY . 70
IT MAKES US TO HAVE HAD A SEA IN VAIN. . . . . 446 DOES NO ONE AT ALL EVER 16
BUT THOUGH ALMOST ALL--WISE, HE MAKES MISTAKES. . . . 460 HOW HARD TO KEEP FROM 208
FREE VERSE LEAVES OUT THE METER AND MAKES UP . . . . 460 HOW HARD TO KEEP FROM 219
IT MAKES HER MOVE AS IF TO REINFORCE IT. . . . . . . 493 A MASQUE OF MERCY .   7
THE THREATS HE MAKES AGAINST THE CITY EVIL. . . . . . 497 A MASQUE OF MERCY .   115
PAUL MAKES IT COME OUT SO THEY LOOK LIKE CHRISTIANS. . 509 A MASQUE OF MERCY .   407
MAKING
THEN THERE WERE THREE THERE, MAKING A DIM ROW, . . . 40 DEATH OF THE HIRED MAN 162
MAKING THE GRAVEL LEAP AND LEAP IN AIR, ... 53 HOME BURIAL   75
AND MAKING THE BEST OF THEIR WAY BACK TO LIFE . . . . 54 HOME BURIAL   104
MAKING ALLOWANCE, MAKING DUE ALLOWANCE." . . . . . . 77 THE GENERATIONS OF MEN 115
"YOU, WILL, STOP MAKING FACES. COME ROUND HERE . . . 99 THE SELF-SEEKER . .   184
THEIR COMING OUT AND MAKING USEFUL FARMERS." . . . . 114 IN THE HOME STRETCH . 121
MAKING A GREAT SCROLL UPWARD TOWARD THE SKY, ... 143 SNOW   9
(SHE'S MAKING HER CROSS-COUNTRY IN THE FALL). . . . . 268 THE BEAR   6
ON MAKING CERTAIN ANYTHING HAS HAPPENED . . . . 383 MAKING CERTAIN ANYTHING 1
SO THE TWO MAKING GOOD THEIR ABDICATION . . . . 454 HOW HARD TO KEEP FROM   10
OR MAKING VERSE IF THAT IS WHAT YOU'RE BENT ON. . . . 454 HOW HARD TO KEEP FROM   35
BY MAKING ME YOUR MINISTER-VIZIER, ... 457 HOW HARD TO KEEP FROM 120
BUT 'TWAS BY MAKING SWEETBREADS DO . . . . 467 QUANDARY   25
BY MAKING FAILURE OUT OF EQUAL VALUE. . . . . 513 A MASQUE OF MERCY .   526
IN MAKING FOOLS OF PEOPLE EQUALLY. . . . . 513 A MASQUE OF MERCY .   528
OUR MAKING ALL THIS EFFORT MORTALS MAKE? . . . . . . 517 A MASQUE OF MERCY .   635
MALICE
LIKE MALICE PREPENSE. . . . . 450 OBJECTION TO BE STEPPED 11

MALICIOUSLY
   MALICIOUSLY SATISFIED. . . . . 312 THE VINDICTIVES . . . 55
MALLICE
   IT WA'N'T NO SIGN, I S'POSE, WHEN MALLICE HUSE . . . . 208 PAUPER WITCH OF GRAFTON 45
MALMSEY
   BUT IN A BUTT OF MALMSEY I WAS DROWNED. . . . . 510 A MASQUE OF MERCY . . 449
MALVERN
   WE TWO WERE GROPING DOWN A MALVERN SIDE . . . . . . 315 IRIS BY NIGHT . . . 2
MAME
   MAME, WE DON'T KNOW ANY GOOD BERRYING PLACE?' . . . . 61 BLUEBERRIES 77
MAMMON
   (FOR WHICH ASSURANCE MAMMON IS TO THANK). . . . . . 386 THE FEAR OF MAN . . . 10
MAN   (SEE ONE-MAN)
   BUT WHETHER OR NOT A MAN WAS ASKED . . . . 8 LOVE AND A QUESTION . 29
   AH, WHEN TO THE HEART OF MAN . . . . 30 RELUCTANCE 19
   THE DEATH OF THE HIRED MAN . . . . 34 DEATH OF THE HIRED MAN T
   SURELY YOU WOULDN'T GRUDGE THE POOR OLD MAN . . . . 36 DEATH OF THE HIRED MAN 49
   AND THERE I MET A MAN WHO MOVED SO SLOW . . . . . 41 THE MOUNTAIN . . . 16
   SUCH A GREAT MAN. IT DOESN'T SEE HIM OFTEN . . . . 44 A HUNDRED COLLARS . 2
   "A MAN." / "SO I SHOULD HOPE. WHAT KIND OF MAN?" . . . 45 A HUNDRED COLLARS . 25
   "I KNOW HIM: HE'S ALL RIGHT. A MAN'S A MAN. . . . . 45 A HUNDRED COLLARS . 26
   "WHO'S THAT MAN SLEEPING IN THE OFFICE CHAIR? . . . 45 A HUNDRED COLLARS . 29
   MAN THAT KNEW ANYTHING I HAPPENED IN WITH. . . . . 46 A HUNDRED COLLARS . 47
   A MAN? A BRUTE. NAKED ABOVE THE WAIST, ... 46 A HUNDRED COLLARS . 50
   I'LL NOT BE PUT TO BED BY YOU, MY MAN." . . . . . 47 A HUNDRED COLLARS . 78
   'MY MAN' IS IT? YOU TALK LIKE A PROFESSOR." . . . . 47 A HUNDRED COLLARS . 80
   "YOU'D SAY SO, MISTER MAN.--I'M A COLLECTOR." . . . . 48 A HUNDRED COLLARS . 95
   "CAN'T A MAN SPEAK OF HIS OWN CHILD HE'S LOST?" . . . 52 HOME BURIAL . . . 35
   I DON'T KNOW RIGHTLY WHETHER ANY MAN CAN." . . . . 52 HOME BURIAL . . . 38
   A MAN MUST PARTLY GIVE UP BEING A MAN . . . . . . 52 HOME BURIAL . . . 49
   A MAN CAN'T SPEAK OF HIS OWN CHILD THAT'S DEAD." . . . 53 HOME BURIAL . . . 70
   I THOUGHT, WHO IS THAT MAN? I DIDN'T KNOW YOU. . . . 53 HOME BURIAL . . . 78
   WILL ROT THE BEST BIRCH FENCE A MAN CAN BUILD.' . . . 54 HOME BURIAL . . . 93
   BUT WORK! THAT MAN COULD WORK, ESPECIALLY . . . . . 70 THE CODE 36
   FOR THE MAN UP ON TOP, OF THROWING DOWN . . . . . 71 THE CODE 56
   NEVER YOU SAY A THING LIKE THAT TO A MAN, ... 71 THE CODE 68
   ONE OF THE BOYS SINGS OUT, 'WHERE'S THE OLD MAN?' . . 72 THE CODE 83
   I NEVER SAW A MAN LET FAMILY TROUBLES . . . . . . 83 THE HOUSEKEEPER . . 53
   THAT'S NO WAY FOR A MAN TO DO AT HIS AGE: . . . . . 83 THE HOUSEKEEPER . . 63
   IT'S DIFFERENT WITH A MAN, AT LEAST WITH JOHN: . . . 84 THE HOUSEKEEPER . . 79
   THE MAN WAS FOUND. I'D BETTER NAME NO NAMES. . . . 88 THE HOUSEKEEPER . . 188
   "HOW ARE YOU, NEIGHBOR? JUST THE MAN I'M AFTER. . . 88 THE HOUSEKEEPER . . 206
   SHONE ON A MAN AND WOMAN IN THE DOOR . . . . . . 89 THE FEAR 2
   MOVED IN A LITTLE. THE MAN GRASPED A WHEEL. . . . . 89 THE FEAR 7
   "BUT YOUR FLOWERS, MAN, YOU'RE SELLING OUT YOUR FLOWERS." . 95 THE SELF-SEEKER . . 66
   YOU ASK THIS LAWYER MAN. AND IT'S NOT SAFE . . . . 97 THE SELF-SEEKER . . 133
   THE LAWYER MAN IS THINKING OF HIS TRAIN. . . . . . 98 THE SELF-SEEKER . . 168
   ONE AGED MAN--ONE MAN--CAN'T KEEP A HOUSE, ... 108 OLD MAN'S WINTER NIGHT 26
   NO MORE SO THAN BECAME A MAN-- . . . . 139 BROWN'S DESCENT . . 69
   A MAN WITH A SWINGING BAG FOR LOAD . . . . 140 THE GUM-GATHERER . . 5
   WHAT THIS MAN BROUGHT IN A COTTON SACK . . . . . . 141 THE GUM-GATHERER . . 28
   HE IS SAID TO HAVE BEEN THE LAST RED MAN . . . . . 142 THE VANISHING RED . 1
   THE RED MAN GAVE IN POKING ABOUT THE MILL, ... 142 THE VANISHING RED . 15
   AND SAID SOMETHING TO A MAN WITH A MEAL SACK . . . 142 THE VANISHING RED . 27
   THAT THE MAN WITH THE MEAL SACK DIDN'T CATCH--THEN. . . 142 THE VANISHING RED . 28
   AS IF A MAN COULD MOVE THAT SLOW AND MOVE. . . . . 145 SNOW 60
   THAT SORT OF MAN TALKS STRAIGHT-ON ALL HIS LIFE . . . 145 SNOW 64
   LET THE MAN FREEZE AN EAR OR TWO, I SAY.-- . . . . 146 SNOW 102
   TO STOP AT. IF YOU WERE THE KIND OF MAN . . . . . 150 SNOW 215
   THAN THE MAN FIGHTING IT TO KEEP ABOVE IT, ... 151 SNOW 225
   ASK ANY MAN." / HE THREW HER THAT AS SOMETHING . . . 151 SNOW 242
   NOT READING IT. / "WELL, WHAT KIND OF A MAN . . . . 151 SNOW 247
   "WAS EVER SUCH A MAN FOR SEEING LIKENESS?" . . . . 151 SNOW 250
   WE'RE GLAD. OH, SAY NO MORE ABOUT IT, MAN. . . . . 155 SNOW 332
   IS THE DISGRACE IN MAN OR STATE OR NATION. . . . . 159 NEW HAMPSHIRE . . 8
   FAR UP THE BIRCHES OUT OF REACH OF MAN. . . . . . 164 NEW HAMPSHIRE . . 164
   SEEMS TO HAVE BEEN A MAN NAMED JOHN L. DARWIN." . . . 168 NEW HAMPSHIRE . . 299
   I KNEW A MAN WHO FAILING AS A FARMER . . . . . . 168 NEW HAMPSHIRE . . 301
   I KNOW A MAN WHO TOOK A DOUBLE AX . . . . 170 NEW HAMPSHIRE . . 367
   "'NATURE IS CRUEL, MAN IS SICK OF BLOOD': . . . . . 170 NEW HAMPSHIRE . . 371
   THE LINE WHERE MAN LEAVES OFF AND NATURE STARTS, . . . 171 NEW HAMPSHIRE . . 379
   HAS A MAN, I SHOULD LIKE TO ASK, NO RIGHTS . . . . 176 THE STAR-SPLITTER . 11
   AND A MAN WITH A SMOKY LANTERN CHIMNEY? . . . . . 179 THE STAR-SPLITTER . 98
   THIS WAS A MAN, BAPTISTE, WHO STOLE ONE DAY . . . . 185 THE AX-HELVE . . . 6
   A FATHER-TIME-LIKE MAN GOT ON AND RODE, ... 189 THE GRINDSTONE . . 29
   I WONDERED WHO IT WAS THE MAN THOUGHT GROUND-- . . . 190 THE GRINDSTONE . . 45
   NOR WAS I FOR THE MAN SO MUCH CONCERNED. . . . . . 190 THE GRINDSTONE . . 56
   A MAN YOU COULD SAY ALMOST ANYTHING TO . . . . . 192 PAUL'S WIFE . . . 33
   MURPHY'S IDEA WAS THAT A MAN LIKE PAUL . . . . . . 196 PAUL'S WIFE . . . 155
   SOMEHOW MADE HER IMPATIENT WITH THE MAN. . . . . . 199 PLACE FOR A THIRD . 8
   HOUSEKEEPING FOR THE NEXT MAN OUT OF WEDLOCK. . . . 201 PLACE FOR A THIRD . 62
   THE WAY A MAN WITH ONE LEG AND A CRUTCH, ... 204 THE WITCH OF COOS . 52
   NOT LIKE A MAN, BUT LIKE A CHANDELIER. . . . . . 204 THE WITCH OF COOS . 69
   I MEAN A MAN HE KILLED INSTEAD OF ME. . . . . . . 206 THE WITCH OF COOS . 140
   THE POOR OLD MAN. IT WOULD HAVE BEEN ALL RIGHT . . . 209 PAUPER WITCH OF GRAFTON 53
   ON MOOSILAUKE, BUT WOMAN SIGNS TO MAN, ... 210 PAUPER WITCH OF GRAFTON 94
   FOR GOD, MAN, OR BEAST'S SAKE, ... 212 AN EMPTY THREAT . . 36
   THE OLD MAN SERIOUSLY TOOK HIS BEARINGS, ... 214 A FOUNTAIN, A BOTTLE . 35
   TO WHICH MAN SENDS HIS . . . . 219 I WILL SING YOU ONE-O . 50
   TO THE EYE OF MAN . . . . 220 I WILL SING YOU ONE-O . 73
   SINCE MAN BEGAN . . . . 220 I WILL SING YOU ONE-O . 77
   TO DRAG DOWN MAN . . . . 220 I WILL SING YOU ONE-O . 78
   BEFORE MAN CAME TO BLOW IT RIGHT . . . . 223 THE AIM WAS SONG . . 1
   MAN CAME TO TELL IT WHAT WAS WRONG: . . . . 224 THE AIM WAS SONG . . 5
   NOT TO SINK UNDER BEING MAN AND WIFE, ... 264 THE INVESTMENT . . 13
   MAN ACTS MORE LIKE THE POOR BEAR IN A CAGE, ... 269 THE BEAR 13
   THERE WAS A LAW OF GOD OR MAN . . . . 273 A LONE STRIKER . . 5
   AND WARRANT PRUDENCE IN A MAN. . . . . 281 BLUE RIBBON AT AMESBURY 56

```
                                                    PAGE TITLE                    LINE
MAN (CONTINUED)
   TO WALK A GRAVER MAN RESTRAINED IN WRATH. . . . . . .  285 THE GOLD HESPERIDEE    . 60
   WE CAME TO WHERE THERE WAS A LIVING MAN. . . . . . .   292 FIGURE IN THE DOORWAY .  6
   THERE IS SELDOM MORE THAN A MAN TO A HARROWED PIECE. .  299 STRONG SAYING NOTHING .  5
   AS COMPLETE AS THE APPLE HAD GIVEN MAN. . . . . . .    305 UNHARVESTED . . . . .   9
   WHAT COMES OVER A MAN, IS IT SOUL OR MIND-- . . . . .  305 THERE ARE ROUGHLY ZONES  7
   THAT THE CITY'S HOLD ON A MAN IS NO MORE TIGHT . . . . 306 NOT QUITE SOCIAL    . .  7
   I'M MELIBOEUS THE POTATO MAN, . . . . . . . . . . .    316 BUILD SOIL  . . . .     2
   THE MAN FREE LOVE, THE BUSINESSMAN FREE TRADE, . . . . 319 BUILD SOIL  . . . .   112
   THE LAND MAY SEEM TO HAVE ON MAN TO USE IT. . . . . .  322 BUILD SOIL  . . . .   208
   A MAN THE WAY THINGS COME IN PAIRS. . . . . . . . .    326 TO A THINKER  . . . .  14
   THAT A FLOWER HAD MARRED A MAN, . . . . . . . . . .    340 THE SUBVERTED FLOWER  . 49
   THE MAN WAS AMONG THE FIRST IT TOOK. . . . . . . . .   345 DISCOVERY OF MADEIRAS . 59
   A MAN COMES BACK TO A WOMAN AGAIN . . . . . . . . .    346 DISCOVERY OF MADEIRAS . 87
   AND IT MUST BE A LITTLE MORE IN FAVOR OF MAN. . . . .  349 OUR HOLD ON THE PLANET  15
   ABOUT HOW LONG A MAN MAY THINK TO LIVE, . . . . . .    354 THE LESSON FOR TODAY  . 135
   ONE MAN HAD LIVED ONE HUNDRED YEARS AND EIGHT. . . . . 355 THE LESSON FOR TODAY  . 140
   KNOWS THE OLD MAN, AND NOBODY'S SO DEEP . . . . . .    371 THE LITERATE FARMER AND 96
   THE OLD MAN ARGUES SCIENCE CHEAPENED SPEED. . . . . .  371 THE LITERATE FARMER AND 98
   WHEN MAN FIRST LIVED IN CAVES ALONG THE CREEKS?" . . . 372 THE LITERATE FARMER AND 140
   THE FEAR OF MAN . . . . . . . . . . . . . . .          386 THE FEAR OF MAN . . .   T
   WHO ADVISED MAN TO COME AND LIVE THEREIN? . . . . . .  400 THE BROKEN DROUGHT  .  14
   "A MAN HAS GOT TO KEEP HIS EXTRICATION. . . . . . .    406 FROM PLANE TO PLANE .  61
   AND ALL THE GOOD THEY DID FOR MAN OR GOD. . . . . . .  412 POD OF THE MILKWEED .  41
   WHY DON'T THEY ASK THE RED MAN WHERE THEY ARE? . . . . 414 A CABIN IN THE CLEARING 21
   TO ALL THE MODERN WORKS OF MAN . . . . . . . . . .     418 AMERICA IS HARD TO SEE  59
   LET'S KEEP STARRING MAN . . . . . . . . . . . .        441 KITTY HAWK  . . . .   414
   AND A MAN CAME OUT OF THE TREES . . . . . . . . .      444 THE DRAFT HORSE . . .   5
   WE ASSUMED THAT THE MAN HIMSELF . . . . . . . . .      444 THE DRAFT HORSE . . .  17
   OF MAN AND WOMANKIND . . . . . . . . . . . . .         464 MILKY WAY IS A COWPATH  26
   A MAN SITS LEANING BACK AGAINST A PALM. . . . . . .    473 A MASQUE OF REASON  .   2
   THERE'S NO CONNECTION MAN CAN REASON OUT . . . . . .   475 A MASQUE OF REASON  .  50
   AND NO ONE BUT A MAN WOULD THINK THERE WAS. . . . . .  478 A MASQUE OF REASON  . 139
   FOUND OUT THE DISCIPLINE MAN NEEDED MOST . . . . . .   481 A MASQUE OF REASON  . 209
   I'M CURIOUS. AND I'M A GROWN-UP MAN: . . . . . . .     482 A MASQUE OF REASON  . 255
   WHETHER THERE'S ANY PART OF MAN IMMORTAL. . . . . .    483 A MASQUE OF REASON  . 297
   AN EASIER PLACE FOR MAN TO SAVE HIS SOUL IN. . . . .   484 A MASQUE OF REASON  . 317
   WE DON'T BELIEVE THE COMMON MAN SHOULD READ IT. . . .  494 A MASQUE OF MERCY   .  31
   WE'RE POOR--THAT'S WHY. MY MAN CAN'T EARN A LIVING. .  496 A MASQUE OF MERCY   .  89
   LEGITIMIZE THE BROTHERHOOD OF MAN, . . . . . . . .     498 A MASQUE OF MERCY   . 124
   YOU POOR, POOR SWALLOWABLE LITTLE MAN. . . . . . .     500 A MASQUE OF MERCY   . 190
   THE MOB MIGHT HOLD A MAN UP IN THE STREETS . . . . .   503 A MASQUE OF MERCY   . 250
   YOU'RE WORKING IT, OLD MAN. DON'T BE DISCOURAGED. . .  507 A MASQUE OF MERCY   . 347
   YOU NEEDN'T SHOUT LIKE THAT, YOU WRETCHED MAN. . . . . 508 A MASQUE OF MERCY   . 394
MANAGE
   YOU'RE BAD ENOUGH TO MANAGE, WITHOUT HER." . . . . .    94 THE SELF-SEEKER . . .  55
MANAGED
   BEFORE I BURIED HIM, OR I COULDN'T HAVE MANAGED. . . .  72 THE CODE  . . . . .    93
   "IT'S HARD TO TELL YOU HOW I MANAGED IT. . . . . . .    93 THE SELF-SEEKER . . .  22
   THE SOBER WEED HAS MANAGED TO CONTRIVE . . . . . .     412 POD OF THE MILKWEED .  31
MANAGES
   HE MANAGES TO KEEP THE UPPER HAND . . . . . . . .       86 THE HOUSEKEEPER . . . 134
MANCHESTER
   NEW YORK (FIVE MILLION) LAUGHS AT MANCHESTER, . . . .  165 NEW HAMPSHIRE   . . . 201
   MANCHESTER (SIXTY OR SEVENTY THOUSAND) LAUGHS . . . .  165 NEW HAMPSHIRE   . . . 202
MANDATES
   AND HIS MANDATES WERE GIVEN HEED TO . . . . . . .      314 BEARER OF EVIL TIDINGS  31
MANEUVER
   MONEY AND MANEUVER . . . . . . . . . . . . .           430 KITTY HAWK  . . . .    68
MANGER
   ABOVE SOME MORE RELIGION IN A MANGER. . . . . . . .    369 THE LITERATE FARMER AND 35
MANHOLE
   AND SHOWED HIM, THROUGH A MANHOLE IN THE FLOOR, . . .  142 THE VANISHING RED   .  21
   LIKE A MANHOLE OPENED TO HELL. . . . . . . . . .       311 THE VINDICTIVES . . .  23
MANIFEST
   NOT A HEAVENLY DOG MADE MANIFEST, . . . . . . . .      419 ONE MORE BREVITY    .  10
MANIPULATED  (SEE STATE-MANIPULATED)
MAN-KILLERS
   AREN'T LOOKED ON AS MAN-KILLERS, AND ALTHOUGH . . . .  150 SNOW  . . . . . .     222
MANKIND
   IF TIRED OF TREES I SEEK AGAIN MANKIND, . . . . . .     17 THE VANTAGE POINT . .   1
   MANKIND HAD NOT YET GONE ON THE SABBATICAL. . . . . .  161 NEW HAMPSHIRE   . . .  90
   BUT SHE DOES NOT KNOW MANKIND . . . . . . . . .        260 SAND DUNES  . . . .    10
   WITH HOPES OF GETTING MANKIND UNBENIGHTED. . . . . .   371 THE LITERATE FARMER AND 87
   YOU KNOW HOW CUNNINGLY MANKIND IS PLANNED: . . . . .   371 THE LITERATE FARMER AND 112
   FEDERATION OF MANKIND. . . . . . . . . . . . .         387 THE COURAGE TO BE NEW . 8
   BUT OURSELVES--MANKIND, . . . . . . . . . . . .        436 KITTY HAWK  . . . .   267
   OF COATS, OATS, VOTES, TO ALL MANKIND. . . . . . .     450 OUR DOOM TO BLOOM   .   9
   TO SET OUT TO HOMOGENIZE MANKIND . . . . . . . .       509 A MASQUE OF MERCY   . 420
MANKIND'S
   HIS VERY WEAKNESS FOR MANKIND'S ENDEARING. . . . . .   505 A MASQUE OF MERCY   . 309
MANNED  (SEE PILGRIM-MANNED)
MANNER
   AFTER THE MANNER OF OUR STOCK; . . . . . . . . .       139 BROWN'S DESCENT . . .  62
   IN DRESS OR MANNER OF THE GIRL WHO BORE IT. . . . . .  181 MAPLE . . . . . .      53
   HE MAY BE SOME GOOD, IN A MANNER OF SPEAKING. . . . .  407 FROM PLANE TO PLANE   103
MANNERS
   OF GETTING ONE MORE CHANCE TO CHANGE OUR MANNERS? . .  397 THE PLANNERS  . . . .  12
   (OR MERELY MANNERS IT MAY HAVE BEEN), . . . . . . .    420 ONE MORE BREVITY    .  21
   MANNERS MADE IT HARD, . . . . . . . . . . . .          432 KITTY HAWK  . . . .   134
   JUST AS IF NOTHING MATTERED BUT OUR MANNERS. . . . .   488 A MASQUE OF REASON  . 410
MAN'S
   "I KNOW HIM: HE'S ALL RIGHT. A MAN'S A MAN. . . . .     45 A HUNDRED COLLARS   .  26
   HIS WORK'S A MAN'S, OF COURSE, FROM SUN TO SUN, . . .   64 A SERVANT TO SERVANTS  66
   I WAS UP HERE IN SALEM, AT A MAN'S . . . . . . . .      70 THE CODE  . . . . .    30
   MAKE SO MUCH DIFFERENCE IN HIS MAN'S AFFAIRS. . . . .   83 THE HOUSEKEEPER . . .  54
   ALONG THE BUSHES AT THE ROADSIDE--A MAN'S FACE. . . .   89 THE FEAR  . . . . .    11
   AN OLD MAN'S WINTER NIGHT . . . . . . . . . . .        108 OLD MAN'S WINTER NIGHT  T

                                  - 327 -
```

MAN'S (CONTINUED)
DOING A MAN'S WORK, THOUGH A CHILD AT HEART-- . . . . . 137 "OUT,OUT--" 24
ONE MAN'S THREE WOMEN IN A BURIAL ROW . . . . 199 PLACE FOR A THIRD . . 7
BEFORE SHE WENT THE POOR MAN'S WIDOW'S WAY, ... 201 PLACE FOR A THIRD . . 61
THEY WERE A MAN'S HIS FATHER KILLED FOR ME. . . . . . . 206 THE WITCH OF COOS . . 139
MAN'S INGENUITY WAS GOOD. . . . . 274 A LONE STRIKER . . . 33
WITH WHAT WAS ANOTHER MAN'S WORK FOR GAIN. . . . . . . 277 TWO TRAMPS IN MUD TIME 61
AND RESENTFUL OF MAN'S CONDITION. . . . . 286 IN TIME OF CLOUDBURST . 28
MAN'S PRACTICALLY INEXTERMINATE. . . . . 453 A-WISHING WELL . . . 77
"A MAN'S OUT THERE WHO CLAIMS HE KNOWS THE SECRET, . . . 455 HOW HARD TO KEEP FROM 60
WHEN NO MAN'S NAME AND NO NOUN'S ADJECTIVE . . . . . . 461 HOW HARD TO KEEP FROM 239
THE ONLY FREE WILL THERE AT FIRST WAS MAN'S, ... 475 A MASQUE OF REASON . 71
AND THAT FOR MAN'S OWN SAKE AS WELL AS MINE, ... 481 A MASQUE OF REASON . 211
IF EVEN THE FACE OF MAN'S TOO BRIGHT A LIGHT . . . . . 515 A MASQUE OF MERCY . 583
MANSARD
HE'D BUILT A NOBLE MANSARD ROOF WITH BALLS . . . . . 160 NEW HAMPSHIRE . . . 39
MANTLE
BUT IF THIS PROPHET'S MANTLE FELL ON ME . . . . 519 A MASQUE OF MERCY . 686
MANUMITTER
THE SLAVE WILL NEVER THANK HIS MANUMITTER; . . . . . . 371 THE LITERATE FARMER AND 90
WHICH OFTEN MAKES THE MANUMITTER BITTER." . . . . . . 371 THE LITERATE FARMER AND 91
MANUSCRIPT
TO WHERE MY MANUSCRIPT WAS NOT YET DRY; . . . . . . 357 A CONSIDERABLE SPECK . 12
MANY (SEE MANY-MANY-EYED)
THAT VANISHED MANY A SUMMER AGO, ... 5 GHOST HOUSE 2
FULL MANY A TIME TO SAY HIS SAY . . . . 6 GHOST HOUSE 19
AND YET, IN VIEW OF HOW MANY THINGS, ... 6 GHOST HOUSE 29
WITH THE BREATH OF MANY FLOWERS-- . . . . 13 ROSE POGONIAS . . . 7
AND LOSE MYSELF AMID SO MANY ALIKE. . . . . 14 WAITING 8
IT HAS LASTED ME MANY AND MANY A YEAR. . . . . 25 THE DEMIURGE'S LAUGH . 6
AFTER SO MANY YEARS HE STILL KEEPS FINDING . . . . . 37 DEATH OF THE HIRED MAN 74
WE CAN'T IN NATURE GROW TO MANY MORE: . . . . 41 THE MOUNTAIN . . . 26
"BUT REALLY I--I HAVE SO MANY COLLARS." . . . . . . 50 A HUNDRED COLLARS . 167
LIKE BIRDS. THEY STORE A GREAT MANY AWAY. . . . . . 60 BLUEBERRIES 51
IT'S HIGHWAYS, AND HE'S GOT TOO MANY MEN . . . . . . 64 A SERVANT TO SERVANTS 72
"SHE SHOULD, SHOULDN'T SHE?--YOU'RE SO MANY TIMES . . . 77 THE GENERATIONS OF MEN 111
BUT THERE'S A DITE TOO MANY OF THEM FOR COMFORT. . . . 80 THE GENERATIONS OF MEN 189
"I DON'T JUST SEE HIM LIVING MANY YEARS, ... 82 THE HOUSEKEEPER . . 43
NO MATTER HOW FAR AND HOW MANY TIMES . . . . 85 THE HOUSEKEEPER . . 130
SO MANY MILES YOU MIGHT HAVE WALKED YOU WON'T WALK. . . 93 THE SELF-SEEKER . . 12
"I COULD SOON TELL HOW MANY THEY WOULD CUT, ... 106 CHRISTMAS TREES . . 30
MORE THAN SO MANY TIMES MAKE ME A LADY . . . . . . 111 IN THE HOME STRETCH . 23
OF MANY PLATES WITH TOWELS MANY TIMES." . . . . . . 111 IN THE HOME STRETCH . 28
I DOUBT IF THEY HAVE LEFT US MANY GRAPES. . . . . . 117 IN THE HOME STRETCH . 193
THEY WERE CROOKING MANY A TRILLIUM . . . . 123 PEA BRUSH 22
AND MANY MUST HAVE SEEN HIM MAKE . . . . 137 BROWN'S DESCENT . . 5
A MANY TIMES--I DON'T SAY JUST HOW MANY-- . . . . . 147 SNOW 127
IN MANY MARCHES. AND THEY LIE LIKE WEDGES, ... 164 NEW HAMPSHIRE . . . 178
THAT HAD AS MANY MOTIONS AS THE WORLD: . . . . . . 186 THE AX-HELVE . . . 47
AND THEN HE HAD A THOUGHT WORTH MANY OF THESE. . . . . 200 PLACE FOR A THIRD . 32
ELIZA'S HAD TOO MANY OTHER MEN." . . . . 202 PLACE FOR A THIRD . 78
WHICH WASN'T MANY, IN THE TOWN OF WENTWORTH. . . . . 208 PAUPER WITCH OF GRAFTON 22
IT WENT MANY YEARS, ... 240 THE LOCKLESS DOOR . 1
"A SIGH FOR EVERY SO MANY BREATH, ... 263 THE TIMES TABLE . . 9
AND FOR EVERY SO MANY SIGH A DEATH. . . . . 263 THE TIMES TABLE . . 10
SO MANY PRICKLY GRAPPLING FEET AT ONCE. . . . . . . 278 THE WHITE-TAILED HORNET 29
A DEPTH PAST MANY SWINGING DOORS . . . . 280 BLUE RIBBON AT AMESBURY 23
AND MANY LITTER-MUFFLED FLOORS. . . . . 280 BLUE RIBBON AT AMESBURY 24
OF MANY TIMES HIS SIZE. . . . . 287 DEPARTMENTAL . . . 3
JUST WHEN THE COLD WENT DOWN SO MANY BELOW. . . . . . 305 THERE ARE ROUGHLY ZONES 17
TOO MANY FALL FROM GREAT AND GOOD . . . . 307 PROVIDE, PROVIDE . . 5
OF MANY A TREASURE BY NAME . . . . 311 THE VINDICTIVES . . 34
MANY MEN'S LUCK WITH GREATEST WASHINGTON . . . . . . 317 BUILD SOIL 45
DON'T JOIN TOO MANY GANGS. JOIN FEW IF ANY. . . . . 325 BUILD SOIL 280
THE MANY DEATHS ONE MUST HAVE DIED . . . . 336 THE WIND AND THE RAIN . 10
MANY LOVERS HAVE BEEN DIVORCED . . . . 346 DISCOVERY OF MADEIRAS . 78
(THE DEED OF GIFT WAS MANY DEEDS OF WAR) . . . . . . 348 THE GIFT OUTRIGHT . 13
TO MONTHS AND YEARS AND MANY, MANY YEARS. . . . . . 355 THE LESSON FOR TODAY . 139
(AND HENCE SO MANY LITERARY TEARS . . . . 355 THE LESSON FOR TODAY . 149
BUT THERE ARE MANY NIGHTS, THOUGH CLEAR, ... 390 TWO LEADING LIGHTS . 16
HOW MANY THOUSAND OF THEM IN AN ACRE. . . . . 404 FROM PLANE TO PLANE . 17
MANY SHALL COME AWAY AS STRUGGLE-WORN . . . . 412 POD OF THE MILKWEED . 34
(THE DEED OF GIFT WAS MANY DEEDS OF WAR) . . . . . . 424 THE GIFT OUTRIGHT . 13
AND SO WITH HOMESICKNESS IN MANY WAYS. . . . . . . 446 DOES NO ONE AT ALL EVER 10
I KNOW THE QUINTESSENCE OF MANY THINGS. . . . . . . 455 HOW HARD TO KEEP FROM 41
WHICH IS UNUSUAL. SO MANY KINGS . . . . 457 HOW HARD TO KEEP FROM 109
FROM MANY GODS TO THREE, AND THREE TO ONE, ... 498 A MASQUE OF MERCY . 121
THAT WAY'S BEEN TRIED TOO MANY TIMES FOR ME. . . . . 515 A MASQUE OF MERCY . 574
WHO CAN BE MANY GODS TO MANY MEN, ... 516 A MASQUE OF MERCY . 591
MANY-COLORED
AS THE BREEZE RISES, AND TURN MANY-COLORED . . . . . 121 BIRCHES 8
ITS TWO MOTE-SWIMMING MANY-COLORED ENDS . . . . . . 315 IRIS BY NIGHT . . . 27
MANY-MANY-EYED
THE MILL, THOUGH MANY-MANY-EYED, ... 273 A LONE STRIKER . . . 11
MAP
OUR ACTUAL MOUNTAINS GIVEN IN A MAP . . . . 169 NEW HAMPSHIRE . . . 330
BETWEEN TWO BURRS ON THE MAP . . . . 367 A SERIOUS STEP LIGHTLY 1
IN HAVING LEFT THE MAP . . . . 464 MILKY WAY IS A COWPATH 3
MAPLE
STRIPPED TO BARE GROUND, THE MAPLE TREES . . . . . 49 A HUNDRED COLLARS . 135
IT WAS A CORD OF MAPLE, CUT AND SPLIT . . . . . . 101 THE WOOD-PILE . . . 23
MADE MAPLE FIRST TAKE NOTICE OF HER NAME. . . . . . 179 MAPLE 2
SHE ASKED HER FATHER AND HE TOLD HER, "MAPLE-- . . . 179 MAPLE 3
MAPLE IS RIGHT." / "BUT TEACHER TOLD THE SCHOOL . . . 179 MAPLE 4
MAPLE . . . . 179 MAPLE . . . . . T
YOU ASK HER IF SHE KNOWS A MAPLE TREE. . . . . . . 180 MAPLE 8
WELL, YOU WERE NAMED AFTER A MAPLE TREE. . . . . . 180 MAPLE 9
'MAPLE.' I SAID IT TOO: 'YES, FOR HER NAME.' . . . . 180 MAPLE 18

	PAGE	TITLE	LINE

MAPLE (CONTINUED)

BE A GOOD GIRL--BE LIKE A MAPLE TREE.	180	MAPLE	22
HOW LIKE A MAPLE TREE'S FOR US TO GUESS.	180	MAPLE	23
A MAPLE LEAF SHE THOUGHT MUST HAVE BEEN LAID	181	MAPLE	63
FOR THE NAME MAPLE TO HAVE BROUGHT HER TO,	182	MAPLE	78
A MAPLE TREE?" / "BECAUSE MY NAME IS MAPLE?"	182	MAPLE	88
SHE TOLD HIM OF THE BOOKMARK MAPLE LEAF	183	MAPLE	104
ONCE THEY CAME ON A MAPLE IN A GLADE,	184	MAPLE	144
COULD IT HAVE BEEN ANOTHER MAPLE LIKE IT?	184	MAPLE	152
AND ANYWAY IT CAME TOO LATE FOR MAPLE.	184	MAPLE	159
AS MEASURED AGAINST MAPLE, BIRCH, AND OAK,	226	THE ONSET	16
AMONG BARE MAPLE BOUGHS, AND IN THE RARE	234	EVENING A SUGAR ORCHARD	8
FOR MAPLE, BIRCH, AND SPRUCE TO PUSH	376	SOMETHING FOR HOPE	6
I MARK A MAPLE FOR MY OWN	470	IN WINTER IN THE WOODS	3
AND LAY THE MAPLE LOW.	470	IN WINTER IN THE WOODS	4

M-A-P-L-E

| YOU TELL HER THAT IT'S M-A-P-L-E. | 180 | MAPLE | 7 |

MAPLES

THEY KEPT THEIR THOUGHTS AWAY FROM WHEN THE MAPLES	184	MAPLE	136
WHEN THEY MADE HER RELATED TO THE MAPLES,	184	MAPLE	139
MAPLES AND BIRCHES AND TAMARACKS.	228	GOOD-BY AND KEEP COLD	24
FAR IN THE MAPLES, PALE, BUT NOT A GHOST?	233	A BOUNDLESS MOMENT	2
AS SHE FLINGS OVER AND OFF DOWN THROUGH THE MAPLES,	269	THE BEAR	8

MAPLE'S

| TWENTY-FIVE YEARS AGO AT MAPLE'S NAMING | 184 | MAPLE | 149 |

MAPS

| NO ONE WOULD KNOW EXCEPT FOR ANCIENT MAPS | 231 | A BROOK IN THE CITY | 20 |

MAR

| DOUBTLESS BEAR NAMES THAT THE MOSSES MAR. | 6 | GHOST HOUSE | 25 |
| TO MAR THE LOVE OF TWO | 8 | LOVE AND A QUESTION | 30 |

MARBLE

MINERVA'S SNOW-WHITE MARBLE EYES	9	STARS	11
THERE ARE THREE STONES OF SLATE AND ONE OF MARBLE,	52	HOME BURIAL	26
AS IN SOME TOO MUCH CARVEN MARBLE HALL	240	OUR SINGING STRENGTH	42
LIKE GRAVEYARD MARBLE SCULPTURE IN THE WEATHER,	377	DIRECTIVE	4

MARBLES

| SO SURE OF DEATH THE MARBLES RHYME, | 221 | IN A DISUSED GRAVEYARD | 9 |

MARCH

FOR HOG REEVE IN MARCH MEETING HERE IN WARREN.	207	PAUPER WITCH OF GRAFTON	14
IN WARREN AT MARCH MEETING, FOR THE REASON	208	PAUPER WITCH OF GRAFTON	18
HE STOOD THERE BRINGING MARCH AGAINST HIS THOUGHT,	233	A BOUNDLESS MOMENT	3
HAD WE BUT IN US TO ASSUME IN MARCH	233	A BOUNDLESS MOMENT	7
FROM WHERE I LINGERED IN A LULL IN MARCH	234	EVENING A SUGAR ORCHARD	1
MARCH INTO A SHADOWY CLAIM.	264	THE LAST MOWING	10
AND YOU'RE TWO MONTHS BACK IN THE MIDDLE OF MARCH.	275	TWO TRAMPS IN MUD TIME	24
AND STARTED HIS MARCH BACK AGAIN DISCOURSING:	406	FROM PLANE TO PLANE	60

MARCHED

| MARCHED HIMSELF OFF THE FIELD AND HOME. ONE STAYED. | 69 | THE CODE | 8 |

MARCHES

| IN MANY MARCHES. AND THEY LIE LIKE WEDGES, | 164 | NEW HAMPSHIRE | 178 |

MARCHING

| GAVE THEM THEIR MARCHING ORDERS AND WAS MOVING. | 44 | THE MOUNTAIN | 109 |

MARE

| ONLY WHEN SOMEONE'S COMING, AND THE MARE | 49 | A HUNDRED COLLARS | 139 |
| HIS MARE WAS SURE TO OBSERVE THE SPOT | 263 | THE TIMES TABLE | 4 |

MARGIN

| I SKIRTED THE MARGIN ALDERS FOR MILES AND MILES | 342 | QUEST OF PURPLE-FRINGED | 5 |

MARINER

| THE TROUBLE WAS WITH HIM THE MARINER. | 417 | AMERICA IS HARD TO SEE | 16 |
| ANOTHER MARINER, DA GAMA, | 417 | AMERICA IS HARD TO SEE | 20 |

MARJORIE

| AS LESLEY, CAROL, IRMA, MARJORIE, | 181 | MAPLE | 46 |

MARK

THOSE OF US NOT ASLEEP SUBDUED TO MARK	10	STORM FEAR	11
HE COULD NOT HELP BUT MARK,	10	WIND AND WINDOW FLOWER	10
IT ALWAYS SEEMS TO ME A SORT OF MARK	56	THE BLACK COTTAGE	45
TOO MUCH ALIKE TO MARK OR NAME A PLACE BY	101	THE WOOD-PILE	7
WHAT WELL MAY PROVE THE YEAR'S HIGH GIRDLE MARK.	254	A WINTER EDEN	12
SEE NOTHING WORTHY TO HAVE BEEN ITS MARK,	261	A SOLDIER	5
AS TO WHOSE AGE DESERVES THE LOWER MARK,	352	THE LESSON FOR TODAY	52
SO CAN'T GET SAVED, AS SAINT MARK SAYS THEY MUSTN'T.	379	DIRECTIVE	59
I MARK A MAPLE FOR MY OWN	470	IN WINTER IN THE WOODS	3

MARKED

HE MARKED HER THROUGH THE PANE,	10	WIND AND WINDOW FLOWER	9
AND ONCE I MARKED HIS FLIGHT GO ROUND AND ROUND,	22	THE TUFT OF FLOWERS	15
OF THE PLACE MARKED WITH IT--"WAVE OFFERING,	183	MAPLE	106

MARKET

SHE TOOK THE MARKET THINGS FROM WARREN'S ARMS	34	DEATH OF THE HIRED MAN	8
IN BUSHEL LOTS--DOESN'T COME ON THE MARKET.	97	THE SELF-SEEKER	130
THE TRIAL BY MARKET EVERYTHING MUST COME TO.	106	CHRISTMAS TREES	24
IT COMES TO MARKET GOLDEN BROWN;	141	THE GUM-GATHERER	32
AND BRING IT TO MARKET WHEN YOU PLEASE.	141	THE GUM-GATHERER	39
OF BEING IN THE MARKET WITH A CLIMATE."	159	NEW HAMPSHIRE	24
CONSIDERING THE MARKET, THERE ARE MORE	164	NEW HAMPSHIRE	170
TO MARKET 'TIS OUR DESTINY TO GO.	321	BUILD SOIL	172
AND EVEN SUBSOIL AND HARDPAN TO MARKET.	321	BUILD SOIL	178
THE MORAL IS, MAKE A LATE START TO MARKET.	322	BUILD SOIL	181
THAT NONE SHALL EVER SEE YOU COME TO MARKET--	323	BUILD SOIL	213
TO TAKE TO MARKET--I WILL TURN IT UNDER.	323	BUILD SOIL	240
I SAW A BOXFUL IN THE CHRISTMAS MARKET.	488	A MASQUE OF REASON	422

MARKETPLACE

| TO THE SLAVE AUCTION IN SOME MARKETPLACE | 454 | HOW HARD TO KEEP FROM | 32 |
| THE EX-KING STOOD UP IN THE MARKETPLACE | 454 | HOW HARD TO KEEP FROM | 37 |

MARKING

| YET CAN'T HELP MARKING ALL THE TIME | 221 | IN A DISUSED GRAVEYARD | 10 |

MARKS (SEE SKY-MARKS)

| (WHO WOULD YOU BE, I WONDER, BY THOSE MARKS | 356 | A MOTH SEEN IN WINTER | 5 |

MARLOWE
   KIT MARLOWE TAUGHT ME HOW TO SAY MY PRAYERS: .   .   .   . 166 NEW HAMPSHIRE   .   . . 242
MARRED
   AT HAVING THE LANDSCAPE MARRED WITH THE ARTLESS PAINT   . 286 A ROADSIDE STAND   .   . .   9
   THAT A FLOWER HAD MARRED A MAN, ... 340 THE SUBVERTED FLOWER   . 49
MARRIAGE
   AND MARRIAGE RINGS OF THOSE WHO OWNED THE FARM.   .   .   . 162 NEW HAMPSHIRE   .   . . 114
   MADE A GIRL'S MARRIAGE, AND RULED IN HER LIFE. . . . . 185 MAPLE 164
   WHO WAS SHE TO JUDGE MARRIAGE IN A WORLD . . . . . 201 PLACE FOR A THIRD . . 64
   WHOSE BIBLE'S SO CONFUSED IN MARRIAGE COUNSEL?   .   .   . 201 PLACE FOR A THIRD . . 65
   OF THE OCEAN BED FOR A MARRIAGE BED. . . . . . . 345 DISCOVERY OF MADEIRAS . 67
   TO BE THEIR OWN MARRIAGE FEAST FOR THE SHARK. . . . 346 DISCOVERY OF MADEIRAS . 85
   TO BE HER ONLY MARRIAGE LINES. . . . . 347 DISCOVERY OF MADEIRAS . 123
MARRIAGES
   NOTHING TO SAY TO ALL THOSE MARRIAGES!   .   .   .   .   . 199 PLACE FOR A THIRD . .   1
MARRIED (SEE NEVER-MARRIED)
   FATHER AND MOTHER MARRIED, AND MOTHER CAME, ... 66 A SERVANT TO SERVANTS . 126
   MY MOTHER WAS A LANE, YET MIGHT HAVE MARRIED   .   .   . 75 THE GENERATIONS OF MEN   50
   "YES, BUT HE SHOULD HAVE MARRIED HER." / "I KNOW."   .   . 84 THE HOUSEKEEPER . . . 76
   BETTER THAN MARRIED OUGHT TO BE AS GOOD   .   .   .   . 84 THE HOUSEKEEPER . . . 81
   AS MARRIED--THAT'S WHAT HE HAS ALWAYS SAID. . . . . 84 THE HOUSEKEEPER . . . 82
   BUT WHEN I'VE SAID, WHY SHOULDN'T THEY BE MARRIED?   .   . 84 THE HOUSEKEEPER . . . 90
   "I MEAN SHE'S MARRIED--MARRIED SOMEONE ELSE."   .   .   . 87 THE HOUSEKEEPER . . . 180
   "BAD TO GET MARRIED WHEN SHE HAD THE CHANCE?"   .   .   . 88 THE HOUSEKEEPER . . . 184
   SHE MUST HAVE MISSED HERSELF. SO THEY WERE MARRIED, . . 182 MAPLE 95
   THAT PAUL HAD MARRIED A WIFE NOT HIS EQUAL. . . . . 192 PAUL'S WIFE 36
   SO THERE WERE WITNESSES THAT PAUL WAS MARRIED, . . . 195 PAUL'S WIFE 145
   WHO MARRIED HER FOR PLAYMATE MORE THAN HELPMATE, . . . 200 PLACE FOR A THIRD . . 34
   THE ARTHUR AMY I WAS MARRIED TO . . . . 207 PAUPER WITCH OF GRAFTON 16
   THE ARTHUR AMY I WAS MARRIED TO . . . . 208 PAUPER WITCH OF GRAFTON 20
   HE NEVER SAID MUCH AFTER WE WERE MARRIED, ... 209 PAUPER WITCH OF GRAFTON 73
   AS YOU AND I ARE MARRIED TO EACH OTHER, ... 258 WEST-RUNNING BROOK . . 12
   WE'LL BOTH BE MARRIED TO THE BROOK. WE'LL BUILD   .   .   . 258 WEST-RUNNING BROOK . . 13
   HAVE MARRIED BEGGAR MAIDS FROM OFF THE STREETS. . . . 457 HOW HARD TO KEEP FROM   110
MARROW
   CLEAR INTO HER MARROW SPINE. . . . . 463 LINES IN DEJECTION . . 20
MARRY
   "I WONDER WHY HE DOESN'T MARRY HER . . . . 84 THE HOUSEKEEPER . . . 84
   "WHO'D MARRY HER STRAIGHT OUT OF SUCH A MESS?   .   .   . 88 THE HOUSEKEEPER . . . 186
   TO MARRY A PERSIAN PRINCE . . . . 314 BEARER OF EVIL TIDINGS 20
   "APPARENTLY THESE TWO OUGHT TO MARRY. . . . . . . 345 DISCOVERY OF MADEIRAS . 69
MARRYING
   THAT WAS WHAT MARRYING FATHER MEANT TO HER. . . . . 66 A SERVANT TO SERVANTS . 129
   SEVERAL TIMES OVER, AND BY MARRYING FATHER   .   .   .   . 75 THE GENERATIONS OF MEN   56
MARS
   TO SUCH RESORTS OF LIFE AS MARS AND EARTH-- . . . . 174 A STAR IN A STONEBOAT . 48
   SATURN AND MARS . . . . 219 I WILL SING YOU ONE-O . 41
   JUPITER AND MARS, ... 438 KITTY HAWK 318
MARSHALL
   ON MARSHALL, LOOK LIKE DONKEY'S EARS. . . . . . . 214 A FOUNTAIN, A BOTTLE . 53
MARSHES
   IT WILL BE LONG ERE THE MARSHES RESUME, ... 25 NOW CLOSE THE WINDOWS .   5
MARTIN
   THERE'S NOT MUCH WE CAN DO TILL MARTIN GETS HERE.-- . . . 514 A MASQUE OF MERCY . . 557
MARVELOUS
   "MARVELOUS WORLD IN NINETEEN-TWENTY-SIX."   .   .   .   . 372 THE LITERATE FARMER AND 141
MARX
   AND OF THE MESSIANIC RACE, KARL MARX. . . . . . . 515 A MASQUE OF MERCY . . 578
MARX'
   CHRIST'S OR KARL MARX', AND IT WILL SET YOU FREE. . . . 460 HOW HARD TO KEEP FROM   192
MARXIAN
   BY DAY HE'S MARXIAN MUSCOVITE. . . . . 393 A CASE FOR JEFFERSON .   4
MARY
   MARY SAT MUSING ON THE LAMP-FLAME AT THE TABLE, . . . 34 DEATH OF THE HIRED MAN   1
   "SH! NOT SO LOUD: HE'LL HEAR YOU," MARY SAID. . . . . 35 DEATH OF THE HIRED MAN 31
   "BUT LITTLE." / "ANYTHING? MARY, CONFESS . . . . . . 36 DEATH OF THE HIRED MAN 45
MAS
   SOMEONE IN ANCIENT MAS D'AZIL . . . . 326 A MISSIVE MISSILE . . .   1
MASK
   WERE NOT, AS 'TWERE, THE MEREST MASK OF GLOOM, ...   5 INTO MY OWN   3
MASKED
   AND A MASKED MOON HAD SPREAD DOWN COMPASS RAYS   .   .   . 300 MOON COMPASSES . . .   3
MASONRY
   CAN DO A GOOD DEAL TO BAD MASONRY. . . . . 213 A FOUNTAIN, A BOTTLE . 26
MASQUE
   A MASQUE OF REASON . . . . 471 A MASQUE OF REASON . . T
   A MASQUE OF REASON . . . . 473 A MASQUE OF REASON . . T
   A MASQUE OF MERCY . . . . 491 A MASQUE OF MERCY . . T
   A MASQUE OF MERCY . . . . 493 A MASQUE OF MERCY . . T
MASS
   IS BLOCKS SPLIT OFF THE MOUNTAIN MASS-- . . . . . 140 THE GUM-GATHERER . . . 15
   MOST OF ALL THE MASS PRODUCTION . . . . 396 AN IMPORTER 11
   TEACH THOSE ASIANS MASS PRODUCTION? . . . . 397 AN IMPORTER 25
   IS NOTHING BUT AN OUTBREAK OF MASS MERCY, ... 509 A MASQUE OF MERCY . . 417
MASSACHUSETTS
   ANOTHER MASSACHUSETTS POET SAID, ... 166 NEW HAMPSHIRE   . . 220
   THE LITTLE MEN (IT'S MASSACHUSETTS SPEAKING). . . . . 166 NEW HAMPSHIRE   . . 225
   WHEN I LEFT MASSACHUSETTS YEARS AGO . . . . . . 167 NEW HAMPSHIRE   . . 248
   I'D SURE HAD NO SUCH FRIENDS IN MASSACHUSETTS   .   .   .   . 167 NEW HAMPSHIRE   . . 258
   THE GLORIOUS BARDS OF MASSACHUSETTS SEEM . . . . . 167 NEW HAMPSHIRE   . . 262
   IN MASSACHUSETTS, IN VIRGINIA, ... 348 THE GIFT OUTRIGHT . .   4
   IN MASSACHUSETTS, IN VIRGINIA, ... 424 THE GIFT OUTRIGHT . .   4
MASSE
   THAT STRUCK EN MASSE . . . . 218 I WILL SING YOU ONE-O . 35
MASSED
   SOMBER CLOUDS IN THE WEST WERE MASSED. . . . . . . 251 BEREFT   7
MASS-PRODUCING
   MASS-PRODUCING WITH A VENGEANCE. . . . . 397 AN IMPORTER 24

MAST
    SHE WAS CARRIED OUT BESIDE THE MAST, ... 344 DISCOVERY OF MADEIRAS . 36
    WITH AN ARM OF SCRAWNY MAST . . . . 469 FOUR-ROOM SHACK.... . 2
MASTER
    OR BEEN MADE MASTER OF THE GRANGE." . . . . 138 BROWN'S DESCENT . . . 36
    AND DORY AND MASTER WILL SAIL BY FATE . . . . 262 THE FLOWER BOAT . . . 11
    THE MASTER SPEED . . . . 300 THE MASTER SPEED . . T
    TWO SUCH AS YOU WITH SUCH A MASTER SPEED . . . . 300 THE MASTER SPEED . . 10
    I'D SAY, O MASTER OF THE PALACE SCHOOL, ... 351 THE LESSON FOR TODAY . 19
    AND NEEDN'T HAVE FARED INTO SPACE LIKE HIS MASTER . . . 380 TOO ANXIOUS FOR RIVERS 25
    ONCE I TOLD THE MASTER, ... 429 KITTY HAWK 50
    WAS TO MASTER NATURE . . . . 438 KITTY HAWK 323
    DO YOU ACCEPT IT, MASTER JONAS DOVE? . . . . 512 A MASQUE OF MERCY . 512
MATCH
    AS PALE AND DIM AS A MATCH FLAME IN THE SUN; . . . . . 77 THE GENERATIONS OF MEN 100
    I'M NO MATCH--NO, AND DON'T PRETEND TO BE----" . . . . 100 THE SELF-SEEKER . . 217
    AT ONE STROKE (OF A MATCH), BRAD HAD TO TURN . . . . . 178 THE STAR-SPLITTER . . 67
    PAUL WAS ASHAMED OF HER. TO MATCH A HERO . . . . 192 PAUL'S WIFE 37
    TO MATCH YOU DEED FOR DEED AND PLAN FOR PLAN. . . . . . 323 BUILD SOIL 221
    IN A VAULTING MATCH, ... 436 KITTY HAWK 264
MATCHES
    SOME MATCHES HE UNPOCKETED. "FOR FOOD-- . . . . 115 IN THE HOME STRETCH . 138
MATERIAL
    THE MATERIAL . . . . 435 KITTY HAWK 216
    INTO THE MATERIAL. . . . . 436 KITTY HAWK 257
    THE FREEDOM OF THEIR OWN MATERIAL: . . . . 461 HOW HARD TO KEEP FROM 234
MATERIALIZE
    TO MATERIALIZE . . . . 435 KITTY HAWK 231
MATHER
    (ALL MY EYE AND COTTON MATHER!), ... 304 CLEAR AND COLDER . . 18
MATTER
    SPIRIT TO MATTER TILL DEATH COME. . . . . 21 THE TRIAL BY EXISTENCE 64
    WHAT MATTER IF WE GO CLEAR TO THE WEST, ... 27 A LINE-STORM SONG . . 21
    I JUST FOUND WHAT THE MATTER WAS TONIGHT: . . . . . . 46 A HUNDRED COLLARS . . 55
    NO MATTER IF I HAVE NO ERRAND THERE. . . . . 49 A HUNDRED COLLARS . . 144
    NO MATTER IF NOT BRUISED OR SPIKED WITH STUBBLE, . . . 69 AFTER APPLE-PICKING . 34
    "STARK?" HE INQUIRED. "NO MATTER FOR THE PROOF." . . . 74 THE GENERATIONS OF MEN 45
    THOUGH WHAT A NAME SHOULD MATTER BETWEEN US----" . . . 79 THE GENERATIONS OF MEN 158
    NO MATTER HOW FAR AND HOW MANY TIMES . . . . 85 THE HOUSEKEEPER . . 130
    SAY IT RIGHT OUT--NO MATTER FOR HER MOTHER. . . . . . . 88 THE HOUSEKEEPER . . 187
    WITH ALL HER MATTER OF FACT ABOUT THE ICE STORM, . . . 121 BIRCHES 22
    BY ROAD, A MATTER OF SEVERAL MILES. . . . . 140 BROWN'S DESCENT . . 76
    THEN YOU WOULDN'T HAVE LOOKED ON IT AS JUST A MATTER . . 142 THE VANISHING RED . 12
    MUCH SAY IN THE MATTER, AND I'M JUST AS GLAD . . . . . 152 SNOW 257
    THE MATTER WITH THE MID-VICTORIANS . . . . 168 NEW HAMPSHIRE . . . 298
    NO MATTER THAT THE MEANING WAS NOT CLEAR. . . . . . . 185 MAPLE 165
    WON'T THIS WHOLE INSTINCT MATTER BEAR REVISION? . . . . 279 THE WHITE-TAILED HORNET 50
    MATTER OF FACT HAS MADE THEM BRAVE. . . . . 291 ON HEART'S BEGINNING TO 35
    NO MATTER WHAT SOME MAY SAY. . . . . 312 THE VINDICTIVES . . 76
    FROM FORCE TO MATTER AND BACK TO FORCE, ... 325 TO A THINKER . . . 8
    NO MATTER WHERE THEY STOUTLY MEAN TO GET, ... 354 THE LESSON FOR TODAY . 108
    NO MATTER WHAT THE COLOR OF ITS SKIN. . . . . 369 THE LITERATE FARMER AND 51
    AS A MATTER OF FACT THERE ARE TIMES WHEN I AM APT . . . 389 SKEPTIC 10
    WHAT FOR THAT MATTER HAD IT EVER BEEN? . . . . 400 THE BROKEN DROUGHT . 13
    OR INSIDE EITHER FOR THAT MATTER. . . . . 418 AMERICA IS HARD TO SEE 65
    MATTER WAS BEGUN-- . . . . 426 A NEVER NAUGHT SONG . 8
    THAT'S HOW MATTER MATTERED. . . . . 427 VERSION 16
    DEEPER INTO MATTER-- . . . . 435 KITTY HAWK 227
    IS BUT FURTHER MATTER) . . . . 435 KITTY HAWK 235
    MATTER MUSTN'T CURD, ... 442 KITTY HAWK 448
    SENT FOR THE EX-KING IN A PRIVATE MATTER. . . . . . . 456 HOW HARD TO KEEP FROM 97
    YES, BY AND BY. BUT FIRST A LARGER MATTER. . . . . . . 475 A MASQUE OF REASON . 46
    SOMETHING'S THE MATTER, EVERYONE ADMITS. . . . . 514 A MASQUE OF MERCY . 562
    AND YOU SAY JUSTICE DOESN'T REALLY MATTER. . . . . . . 517 A MASQUE OF MERCY . 623
    SAVE THEM TO SAY YOUR PRAYERS ON.--WHAT'S THE MATTER? . . 519 A MASQUE OF MERCY . 682
MATTERED
    TO ANSWER FOR THEMSELVES: WHO SAID IT MATTERED . . . . 294 AT WOODWARD'S GARDENS . 33
    THAT'S HOW MATTER MATTERED. . . . . 427 VERSION 16
    JUST AS IF NOTHING MATTERED BUT OUR MANNERS. . . . . . 488 A MASQUE OF REASON . 410
MATTER-OF-FACT
    MY FLOOR SO HARD AND MATTER-OF-FACT. . . . . 421 ONE MORE BREVITY . . 55
MATTERS
    IT'S YOU IT MATTERS TO, BECAUSE IT'S YOU . . . . 149 SNOW 169
    MUCH MATTERS. YOU MAY WORK FOR ALL OF ME. . . . . . . 159 NEW HAMPSHIRE . . . 5
    BUT TO MAKE BAD MATTERS WORSE . . . . 309 NOT ALL THERE . . . 3
    HOW RELATIVELY LITTLE JUSTICE MATTERS. . . . . 499 A MASQUE OF MERCY . 146
    RELIGION FOR THESE PHILOSOPHIC MATTERS. . . . . 501 A MASQUE OF MERCY . 217
MATTHEW
    AND RAN FOR SHELTER QUOTING MATTHEW ARNOLD: . . . . . 170 NEW HAMPSHIRE . . . 370
    WHICH IS SHEER MATTHEW ARNOLDISM, ... 171 NEW HAMPSHIRE . . . 382
    SQUARE MATTHEW HALE'S YOUNG GRAFTED APPLE TREE . . . . 283 THE GOLD HESPERIDEE . 1
    HIS LITTLE MATTHEW, ALSO FIVE YEARS OLD, ... 283 THE GOLD HESPERIDEE . 13
    SQUARE MATTHEW HALE TOOK OFF HIS SUNDAY HAT . . . . . 284 THE GOLD HESPERIDEE . 45
    IN GRATITUDE FOR WHICH SQUARE MATTHEW VOWED . . . . . 285 THE GOLD HESPERIDEE . 59
MATUREST
    BUT MUST BRING TO THE MEETING THE MATUREST, ... 321 BUILD SOIL 160
MAXIMS
    YOU'RE GOOD AT MAXIMS. SAY ME ONE ON FREEDOM. . . . . 459 HOW HARD TO KEEP FROM 164
MAY---NOT INDEXED--EXCEPT FOR:
    WAS HOT ENOUGH FOR THE FIRST OF MAY, ... 123 PEA BRUSH 6
    SUCH WHITE LUXURIANCE OF MAY FOR OURS. . . . . 233 A BOUNDLESS MOMENT . 8
    YOU'RE ONE MONTH ON IN THE MIDDLE OF MAY. . . . . . . 275 TWO TRAMPS IN MUD TIME 20
    MAY AS EXPECTED WAS A DISAPPOINTMENT, ... 406 FROM PLANE TO PLANE . 88
MAYBE
    SHE THINKS I'M SOCIABLE. I MAYBE AM. . . . . 49 A HUNDRED COLLARS . . 145
    I'VE GOT SOME NEWS THAT MAYBE ISN'T NEWS. . . . . . . 88 THE HOUSEKEEPER . . 210
    "A CLOCK MAYBE." / "DON'T YOU HEAR SOMETHING ELSE?" . . 154 SNOW 316
    MAYBE SHE ONLY WANTS HIM FOR THE CHILDREN." . . . . . 155 SNOW 336

MAYBE (CONTINUED)
    THEN PICK YOUR HOE UP, MAYBE SHOULDER IT, ... 405 FROM PLANE TO PLANE   . 41
    I HEARD A DEEP GROAN--MAYBE OUT OF HIM. . . . . . . 516 A MASQUE OF MERCY . . 611
MAYFLOWER
    BUT, PILGRIM-MANNED, THE MAYFLOWER IN A DREAM . . . 262 IMMIGRANTS   3
    TO TAKE THE MAYFLOWER BACK WHERE HE BELONGED, . . . 370 THE LITERATE FARMER AND 59
MAYN'T---NOT INDEXED
MCCORMIC
    "DEATH'S COME TO JERRY MCCORMIC, ... 288 DEPARTMENTAL   23
MCLAUGHLIN
    SO BRAD MCLAUGHLIN MINGLED RECKLESS TALK . . . . . 176 THE STAR-SPLITTER . . 13
ME---NOT INDEXED--EXCEPT FOR GREEK:
    (THE ME ON OF PLATO), ... 427 VERSION   10
MEADOW
    A SATURATED MEADOW, ...   13 ROSE POGONIAS . . .   1
    HE SAID HE'D COME TO DITCH THE MEADOW FOR ME." . . .   36 DEATH OF THE HIRED MAN 46
    HE'S COME TO HELP YOU DITCH THE MEADOW. . . . . . .   40 DEATH OF THE HIRED MAN 157
    THE FAMILY'S ALL AWAY IN SOME BACK MEADOW. . . . . .   49 A HUNDRED COLLARS . 131
    THERE WERE THREE IN THE MEADOW BY THE BROOK . . . .   69 THE CODE   1
    IN THE MEADOW, BUSY WITH THE NEW-CUT HAY, ... 109 THE EXPOSED NEST   .   3
    IN APRIL BY SUBSIDING MEADOW BROOKS. . . . . 191 PAUL'S WIFE . . .   22
    THE MEADOW GRASS COULD BE CEMENTED DOWN . . . . . . 231 A BROOK IN THE CITY   9
    AND POURS THE ELM-TREE MEADOW FULL OF BLUE, ... 248 THE COCOON   . . .   4
    THERE'S A PLACE CALLED FARAWAY MEADOW . . . . 264 THE LAST MOWING . .   1
    THE MEADOW IS FINISHED WITH MEN. . . . . 264 THE LAST MOWING . .   4
    THE MEADOW IS DONE WITH THE TAME. . . . . 264 THE LAST MOWING . .   14
    WHO SLEPT THERE IN A MOW OF MEADOW HAY . . . . . . 289 OLD BARN AT THE BOTTOM 19
    I FELT THE CHILL OF THE MEADOW UNDERFOOT, ... 342 QUEST OF PURPLE-FRINGED 1
MEADOWSWEET
    AND THAT RIGHT SOON, THAT THE MEADOWSWEET . . . . . 375 SOMETHING FOR HOPE . . 2
    THROUGH MEADOWSWEET AND STEEPLE BUSH . . . . 376 SOMETHING FOR HOPE . . 7
MEAGER
    HER OWN TOO MEAGER HEART . . . . 340 THE SUBVERTED FLOWER . 55
MEAL
    AND SAID SOMETHING TO A MAN WITH A MEAL SACK . . . . 142 THE VANISHING RED .   27
    THAT THE MAN WITH THE MEAL SACK DIDN'T CATCH--THEN. . 142 THE VANISHING RED .   28
    HE GOT HIS FIRST CHANCE TO PREPARE A MEAL . . . . . 455 HOW HARD TO KEEP FROM 55
    AND THE MEAL MADE THE BANQUETERS EXCLAIM . . . . . 455 HOW HARD TO KEEP FROM 58
MEALS
    IT'S SELDOM I GET DOWN EXCEPT FOR MEALS, THOUGH. . .   49 A HUNDRED COLLARS . 146
    FROM COOKING MEALS FOR HUNGRY HIRED MEN . . . . .   64 A SERVANT TO SERVANTS . 50
    HE GETS SOME SORT OF BAKESHOP MEALS TOGETHER, . . .   82 THE HOUSEKEEPER . .   31
    THE MEALS WE'VE HAD NO ONE CAN TAKE FROM US. . . . . 115 IN THE HOME STRETCH . 139
    AS CERTAIN AS THE MEALS WE'VE HAD. I WISH . . . . . 115 IN THE HOME STRETCH . 141
    THE MEALS WE HAVEN'T HAD WERE, ANYWAY. . . . . . . 115 IN THE HOME STRETCH . 142
MEAN
    TO PLEASE THE YELPING DOGS. THE GAPS I MEAN, ...   33 MENDING WALL . . .   9
    IT ALL DEPENDS ON WHAT YOU MEAN BY HOME. . . . . .   38 DEATH OF THE HIRED MAN 114
    I'VE FELT MEAN LATELY; MEAN'S NO NAME FOR IT. . . .   46 A HUNDRED COLLARS .   54
    "WHERE DO YOU MEAN TO GO? FIRST TELL ME THAT. . . .   55 HOME BURIAL 115
    THEY SAY THEY MEAN TO COME AND SUMMER HERE . . . .   55 THE BLACK COTTAGE .   17
    I DON'T MEAN ALTOGETHER BY THE LIVES . . . . . .   56 THE BLACK COTTAGE .   37
    I MEAN BY THE WORLD'S HAVING PASSED IT BY-- . . . .   56 THE BLACK COTTAGE .   43
    WHAT DID HE MEAN? OF COURSE THE EASY WAY . . . . .   57 THE BLACK COTTAGE .   65
    "I DON'T KNOW WHAT PART OF THE PASTURE YOU MEAN." . .   59 BLUEBERRIES   8
    THINKS I, D'YE MEAN IT? 'WHAT WAS THAT YOU SAID?' . .   71 THE CODE   64
    "I ONLY MEAN MY MOTHER WAS A STARK . . . .   75 THE GENERATIONS OF MEN 55
    PERHAPS YOU HAVE THE ART OF WHAT I MEAN. . . . . .   78 THE GENERATIONS OF MEN 131
    WHO ARE THEY FOR?" / "YOU MEAN?--OH, FOR SOME MISS. .   81 THE HOUSEKEEPER . .   10
    "I MEAN ESTELLE HAS ALWAYS HELD THE PURSE." . . . .   84 THE HOUSEKEEPER . .   98
    WE HAVE TO GO." / "YOU MEAN THAT'S JOHN'S IDEA." . .   85 THE HOUSEKEEPER . . 131
    WHAT DO YOU MEAN?--SHE'S DONE HARM TO HERSELF?" . . .   87 THE HOUSEKEEPER . . 179
    "I MEAN SHE'S MARRIED--MARRIED SOMEONE ELSE." . . .   87 THE HOUSEKEEPER . . 180
    "YOU MEAN YOU COULDN'T UNDERSTAND HIS CARING. . . .   91 THE FEAR   50
    "THEY MUST BE TERRIBLE--I MEAN, TO LOOK AT." . . . .   93 THE SELF-SEEKER . .   17
    TO YOU--TO YOU I MEAN--THEY'RE BOTH TOO COMMON." . .   98 THE SELF-SEEKER . . 144
    "YOU DON'T MEAN YOU WILL SIGN THAT THING UNREAD?" . .   99 THE SELF-SEEKER . . 187
    YOU DON'T KNOW WHAT I MEAN ABOUT THE FLOWERS. . . . 100 THE SELF-SEEKER . . 226
    FOR THINGS THAT DON'T EXIST; I MEAN BEGINNINGS. . . 116 IN THE HOME STRETCH . 173
    I MEAN IT SHALL NOT DO IF I CAN BIND IT. . . . . . 130 THE BONFIRE . . .   31
    "IF YOU MEAN HE WAS INCONSIDERATE . . . . 155 SNOW   345
    MEAN LAUGHTER WENT ABOUT THE TOWN THAT DAY . . . . 177 THE STAR-SPLITTER .   40
    I DON'T KNOW WHAT SHE WANTED IT TO MEAN, ... 180 MAPLE   20
    BUT LACKING FAITH IN ANYTHING TO MEAN . . . . . . 184 MAPLE 155
    I MEAN, THEY WON'T PICK YOU IF YOU DON'T THEM." . . . 198 WILD GRAPES . . .   58
    I MEAN A MAN HE KILLED INSTEAD OF ME. . . . . . . 206 THE WITCH OF COOS . 140
    AND I DON'T MEAN JUST SKULLS OF ROGERS' RANGERS . . 210 PAUPER WITCH OF GRAFTON 93
    "YOU MEAN MILES FROM THE MORMON SETTLEMENT? . . . . 214 A FOUNTAIN, A BOTTLE . 48
    (BY WHICH THEY MEAN THE RAIN IS PEARLS SO EARLY, . . 236 VALLEY'S SINGING DAY   12
    THEY CANNOT MEAN TO PLANT IT, NO-- . . . . 238 PLOWMEN   2
    AND WORSHIP APPLES. WHAT ELSE COULD IT MEAN? . . . 284 THE GOLD HESPERIDEE . 54
    YOU HAVE THE MONEY, BUT IF YOU WANT TO BE MEAN, . . 286 A ROADSIDE STAND   .   14
    I MEAN THEY COULD BE TRUSTED TO GIVE THE ALARM . . . 317 BUILD SOIL   . . .   57
    THAN IS? / WHAT SHOULD YOU MEAN BY SOCIALIZED? . . . 319 BUILD SOIL   . . .   93
    TOO MEAN A THOUGHT TO GET MUCH COMFORT OUT OF. . . . 321 BUILD SOIL   . . . 168
    NO MATTER WHERE THEY STOUTLY MEAN TO GET, ... 354 THE LESSON FOR TODAY 108
    WON'T KNOW EXACTLY WHAT I MEAN BY THAT. . . . . . 354 THE LESSON FOR TODAY 121
    I MEAN SO ALTRUISTICALLY MORAL . . . . 354 THE LESSON FOR TODAY 122
    HAS FAILED TO BRING--I MEAN THE GOLDEN AGE. . . . . 358 THE LOST FOLLOWER .   16
    NOT BE MISUNDERSTOOD IN WHAT I MEAN. . . . . . . 386 THE FEAR OF MAN . .   16
    I MEAN THE GREAT FOUR, WASHINGTON, ... 422 FOR JOHN F. KENNEDY   25
    THEY MEAN TO TELL US ALL WAS ROLLING BLIND . . . . 425 ACCIDENTALLY ON PURPOSE   5
    THEY MEAN TO TELL US, THOUGH, THE OMNIBUS . . . . 425 ACCIDENTALLY ON PURPOSE 11
    WHAT DID MEN MEAN BY . . . . 430 KITTY HAWK   . . .   59
    SHE'S SUPPOSED TO MEAN. . . . . 442 KITTY HAWK   . . . 461
    BUT SOME MEAN WHAT THEY SAY. . . . . 445 ENDS   12
    IT'S WHAT MY FATHER MUST MEAN BY DEPARTURE, ... 461 HOW HARD TO KEEP FROM 245
    YOU MEAN THE BURNING BUSH? / THE CHRISTMAS TREE. . . 473 A MASQUE OF REASON . . 6

                                              PAGE TITLE   LINE
MEAN (CONTINUED)
    I MEAN WE SEEM TO KNOW ENOUGH TO ACT ON. . . . . 483 A MASQUE OF REASON . . 290
    PRAY TELL ME WHAT DOES THAT MEAN? ANYTHING? . . . . 484 A MASQUE OF REASON . . 304
    FOR MORE EXCUSES. / WHAT I MEAN TO SAY: . . . . 486 A MASQUE OF REASON . . 367
    GOD'S AFTER ME! / YOU MEAN THE DEVIL IS. . . . . 493 A MASQUE OF MERCY . . 19
    ABOUT A WHALE. / OH, YOU MEAN MOBY DICK . . . . 495 A MASQUE OF MERCY . . 48
    YOU HEARD FROM GOD--I MEAN HAD ORDERS FROM HIM? . . . . 504 A MASQUE OF MERCY . . 277
    YOU SAY IT, PAUL. / YOU MEAN ABOUT SUCCESS, ... 509 A MASQUE OF MERCY . . 409
    YOU MEAN I'M BEING SENT DOWN IN THE CELLAR? . . . . . . 514 A MASQUE OF MERCY . . 551
    ALL YOU MEAN, PAUL, I THINK---- / WILL YOU STAND THERE . . 519 A MASQUE OF MERCY . . 675
    I CAN SEE THAT, IF THAT IS WHAT YOU MEAN. . . . . 520 A MASQUE OF MERCY . . 714
MEANING
    MEANING BY US THEIR TICKET. 'NO,' I SAYS, ... 48 A HUNDRED COLLARS . . 113
    THE MEANING OF IT ALL IS OUT OF YOU; . . . . 78 THE GENERATIONS OF MEN 136
    AND SLOWS HIS HORSE TO A MEANING WALK, ... 124 A TIME TO TALK . . . 2
    OR EVEN NATION'S TO RESTRICT MY MEANING. . . . . 166 NEW HAMPSHIRE . . . 231
    IN HAVING TOO MUCH MEANING. OTHER NAMES, ... 181 MAPLE 45
    SIGNIFIED NOTHING. ROSE COULD HAVE A MEANING, ... 181 MAPLE 47
    THUS HAD A NAME WITH MEANING, GIVEN IN DEATH, ... 185 MAPLE 163
    NO MATTER THAT THE MEANING WAS NOT CLEAR. . . . . 185 MAPLE 165
    A NAME WITH MEANING COULD BRING UP A CHILD, ... 185 MAPLE 166
    (THE MEANING OF THE PASSAGE HAD BEEN HID): . . . . 284 THE GOLD HESPERIDEE . 52
    THE MEANING OF IT IS UNKNOWN, ... 328 A MISSIVE MISSILE . . 43
    HER TONE OF MEANING BUT WITHOUT THE WORDS. . . . . 338 NEVER WOULD BIRDS' SONG 5
    THE ONLY MEANING POSSIBLE FOR NATURE . . . . 393 LUCRETIUS VERSUS POETS 8
    A MEANING I WAS SUPPOSED TO SEEK, ... 421 ONE MORE BREVITY . . 68
    IT HAD TO SEEM UNMEANING TO HAVE MEANING. . . . . 475 A MASQUE OF REASON . . 64
MEANINGLESS
    BETTER A MEANINGLESS NAME, I SHOULD SAY, ... 185 MAPLE 168
    IT WOULD BE MEANINGLESS. IT MIGHT AS WELL . . . . 484 A MASQUE OF REASON . . 321
MEANINGLESSLY
    OF MEANINGLESSLY BEING BROKEN OFF. . . . . 355 THE LESSON FOR TODAY . 148
MEANLY
    WHOSE SPOTTED FLOWERS HANG MEANLY DOWN. . . . . 247 ON GOING UNNOTICED . . 8
MEANS
    THERE THEY HAVE EVERY MEANS PROPER TO DO WITH, ... 65 A SERVANT TO SERVANTS . 98
    WHICH MEANS THE-SEVEN-CAVES-THAT-WE-CAME-OUT-OF. . . . . 76 THE GENERATIONS OF MEN 93
    PRESSED INTO SERVICE MEANS PRESSED OUT OF SHAPE. . . . . 98 THE SELF-SEEKER . . . 149
    AND TOO MUCH WORLD AT ONCE--COULD MEANS BE FOUND. . . . . 109 THE EXPOSED NEST . . 19
    THAT NOW IT MEANS TO STAY. . . . . 156 THE SOUND OF TREES . . 14
    FROM COMPANY MEANS COMING TO OUR SENSES. . . . . 325 BUILD SOIL 292
    SINCE HE MEANS TO COME TO A DOOR HE WILL COME TO A DOOR, . 341 WILLFUL HOMING . . . 9
    (AS YET UNBROUGHT TO EARTH) HE MEANS TO TRY. . . . . . . 359 THE LOST FOLLOWER . . 36
    MEANS THAT A SOUL IS COMING ON THE FLESH. . . . . 386 A STEEPLE ON THE HOUSE 8
    WITH HIM THE LOVE OF COUNTRY MEANS . . . . 393 A CASE FOR JEFFERSON . 9
    AND BEING GOOD FOR THESE MEANS STANDING BY . . . . 398 NO HOLY WARS FOR THEM . 5
    FOR HASTE AND OTHER MEANS. . . . . 415 CLOSED FOR GOOD . . . 12
    MEANS THAT WE APPROVE . . . . 442 KITTY HAWK 439
    WE'RE SAVED, WE'RE SAVED, WHATEVER ELSE IT MEANS. . . . . 476 A MASQUE OF REASON . . 82
    PAUL ONLY MEANS YOU MAKE TOO MUCH OF JUSTICE. . . . . . . 508 A MASQUE OF MERCY . . 384
    AN END YOU CAN'T BY ANY MEANS ACHIEVE, ... 512 A MASQUE OF MERCY . . 509
    BY SOMETHING TO BELIEVE IN, JESSE MEANS . . . . 515 A MASQUE OF MERCY . . 569
    ALL PAUL MEANS, AND I WISH THE DEAD COULD HEAR ME-- . . . 519 A MASQUE OF MERCY . . 674
MEAN'S
    I'VE FELT MEAN LATELY; MEAN'S NO NAME FOR IT. . . . . . . 46 A HUNDRED COLLARS . . 54
MEANT
    AND WELL I KNEW WHAT THE DEMON MEANT. . . . . 25 THE DEMIURGE'S LAUGH . 12
    HE MEANT TO CLEAR THE UPPER PASTURE, TOO. . . . . 36 DEATH OF THE HIRED MAN 52
    HE TRIED THIS SIDE. I'VE ALWAYS MEANT TO GO . . . . 43 THE MOUNTAIN 80
    SUCH A PHRASE COULDN'T HAVE MEANT MUCH TO HER. . . . . . 58 THE BLACK COTTAGE . . 100
    THAT WAS WHAT MARRYING FATHER MEANT TO HER. . . . . 66 A SERVANT TO SERVANTS . 129
    HE THOUGHT YOU MEANT TO FIND FAULT WITH HIS WORK. . . . . 70 THE CODE 16
    THAT'S WHAT THE AVERAGE FARMER WOULD HAVE MEANT. . . . . 70 THE CODE 17
    YOU UNDERSTAND THAT MEANT THE EASY JOB . . . . 71 THE CODE 55
    THEN I WAS CERTAIN I HAD NEVER MEANT . . . . 107 CHRISTMAS TREES . . . 45
    AND EVERY CRASH MEANT ONE LESS TO RETURN . . . . 112 IN THE HOME STRETCH . 57
    AS IF TO PROVE SAWS KNEW WHAT SUPPER MEANT, ... 136 "OUT,OUT--" 15
    AS IF NOT KNOWING WHAT YOU MEANT BY THE WORD STORM." . . 151 SNOW 232
    NOT MEANT FOR US AT ALL." / "NOT MEANT FOR ME? . . . . . 183 MAPLE 114
    OF REALLY NEVER HAVING MEANT TO KEEP IT. . . . . 187 THE AX-HELVE . . . 62
    OWNING A WIFE WITH HIM MEANT OWNING HER. . . . . 196 PAUL'S WIFE 151
    I MEANT, YOU MEANT, THAT NOTHING SHOULD REMAIN . . . . . 222 TO E.T. 9
    THE WIND THE WIND HAD MEANT TO BE-- . . . . 224 THE AIM WAS SONG . . 14
    ONE NIGHT (HE TOLD ME). AND THE BARN HE MEANT . . . . . 289 OLD BARN AT THE BOTTOM 20
    WAS THE ONE I MEANT. OUR DETAILS AGREED. . . . . 289 OLD BARN AT THE BOTTOM 21
    THAT I ASSUME WAS WHAT OUR PASSING TRAIN MEANT. . . . . . 292 FIGURE IN THE DOORWAY . 20
    NOBODY WAS EVER MEANT . . . . 309 HARDSHIP OF ACCOUNTING 3
    TO COMMAND ONLY WHAT YOU MEANT TO DO . . . . 323 BUILD SOIL 232
    I MEANT NOT EVEN IF ASKED, ... 334 COME IN 19
    AND WHAT A SAVING 'TWOULD HAVE MEANT TO ME. . . . . 350 TO A YOUNG WRETCH . . 9
    AND USING FOR APPAREL WHAT WAS MEANT . . . . 385 THE FEAR OF GOD . . . 12
    BY NATURE MEANT THE WHOLE GODDAM MACHINERY. . . . . 393 LUCRETIUS VERSUS POETS 6
    THESE I ASSUME WERE WORDS SO DEEPLY MEANT . . . . 399 THE INGENUITIES OF DEBT 1
    "I THOUGHT YOU MEANT TO BE AN INDIAN CHIEF-- . . . . . . 406 FROM PLANE TO PLANE . 69
    TO TEACH THEM HOW DEMOCRACY IS MEANT. . . . . 423 FOR JOHN F. KENNEDY . 38
    INTO FLESH WAS MEANT . . . . 435 KITTY HAWK 220
    TELL THEM IAMB, JEHOVAH SAID, AND MEANT IT. . . . . 460 HOW HARD TO KEEP FROM . 218
    YES, CALL ME PAGAN, PAUL, AS IF YOU MEANT IT. . . . . . . 513 A MASQUE OF MERCY . . 524
MEANWHILE
    MEANWHILE FEEL OBLIGATION-FREE. . . . . 420 ONE MORE BREVITY . . 34
MEASURE
    THEY ARE YOURS, AND BE THE MEASURE . . . . 13 FLOWER-GATHERING . . 13
    THE MEASURE OF THE LITTLE WHILE . . . . 13 FLOWER-GATHERING . . 15
    TO MEASURE HOW FAR FIFTY YEARS HAVE BROUGHT US. . . . . . 56 THE BLACK COTTAGE . . 46
    TILL WE LOSE ALL MEASURE OF PACE, ... 156 THE SOUND OF TREES . . 7
    FOR NOTHING IN THE MEASURE OF A NEIGHBOR. . . . . 186 THE AX-HELVE . . . 43
    AND GIVE GOOD MEASURE TO THE DEAD, THOUGH THANKLESS. . . 200 PLACE FOR A THIRD . . 20
    AND THEN BY MEASURE BLEW IT FORTH. . . . . 224 THE AIM WAS SONG . . 12

                                    - 333 -

MEASURE (CONTINUED)
   BY MEASURE. IT WAS WORD AND NOTE, ... 224 THE AIM WAS SONG . . 13
MEASURED
   AND PILED--AND MEASURED, FOUR BY FOUR BY EIGHT. . . . . 101 THE WOOD-PILE . . . 24
   AS MEASURED AGAINST MAPLE, BIRCH, AND OAK, ... 226 THE ONSET 16
   AS MEASURED AGAINST THE ALL, ... 282 A DRUMLIN WOODCHUCK . 30
   HE MUST HAVE MEASURED TO THE FURTHER WALL. . . . . . 292 FIGURE IN THE DOORWAY . 9
   AS IF I HAD MEASURED THE COUNTRY . . . . 295 A RECORD STRIDE . . 35
   AND AS IT MEASURED IN HER CALIPERS, ... 301 MOON COMPASSES . . . 6
   AND MEASURED, BUT NOT TAKEN AFTER ALL, ... 443 AUSPEX 3
MEASURING
   I MUST GO MEASURING STONE WALLS, PERCH ON PERCH; . . . 173 A STAR IN A STONEBOAT . 45
MEBBE
   MEBBE I'M WRONG TO TAKE IT AS I DO. . . . . 80 THE GENERATIONS OF MEN 185
MECHANIC
   THE MIXTURE MECHANIC . . . . 442 KITTY HAWK 4P
   IN A BLEND MECHANIC, ... 442 KITTY HAWK 445
MEDDLING
   AND MIGHT OUR MEDDLING MAKE HER MORE AFRAID. . . . . 109 THE EXPOSED NEST . . 25
MEDICINE
   WITH DOCTORING. BUT IT'S NOT MEDICINE-- . . . . . 64 A SERVANT TO SERVANTS . 47
   AND MEDICINE AND REST, AND YOU A WEEK, ... 230 NOT TO KEEP 16
   "IN SHORT, YOU THINK THAT STAR A PATENT MEDICINE . . . 371 THE LITERATE FARMER AND 92
MEDIEVAL
   AND GETTING UP MY MEDIEVAL LATIN, ... 350 THE LESSON FOR TODAY . 8
MEDITATE
   WELL THEN! / AND THAT'S WHAT I'M TO MEDITATE? . . . . 517 A MASQUE OF MERCY . . 627
   MEDITATE NOTHING. LEARN TO CONTEMPLATE. . . . . . 517 A MASQUE OF MERCY . . 628
MEDITATES
   HE MEDITATES THE BREEDER'S ART. . . . . 280 BLUE RIBBON AT AMESBURY 25
MEDITATING
   LIKE MEDITATING, AND THEN I JUST DUG IN . . . . . 72 THE CODE 73
   BUT WHILE MEDITATING . . . . 441 KITTY HAWK 412
MEDITATION
   TO MAKE UP FOR A LACK OF MEDITATION. . . . . 400 TO THE RIGHT PERSON . 14
   IN MERE MEDITATION. . . . . 435 KITTY HAWK 241
MEDLEY
   A DATED POPULAR-SCIENCE MEDLEY ON A MYSTERIOUS LIGHT... . 368 THE LITERATE FARMER AND S
   IN TIME WITH A MEDLEY OF SOTTO CHANTS; . . . . . . 385 A MOOD APART 3
MEEK
   BUT THE CONQUERED GREW MEEK AND STILL. . . . . . . 312 THE VINDICTIVES . . . 52
MEEKLY
   "SO MUCH FOR PROGRESS," SAID DARIUS MEEKLY. . . . . 459 HOW HARD TO KEEP FROM 162
MEET
   WE RAN AS IF TO MEET THE MOON . . . . 18 GOING FOR WATER . . . 9
   AND ON A DAY WE MEET TO WALK THE LINE . . . . . . 33 MENDING WALL . . . 13
   TO MEET HIM IN THE DOORWAY WITH THE NEWS . . . . . 34 DEATH OF THE HIRED MAN 4
   THEY MEET HIM IN THE GENERAL STORE AT NIGHT, ... 44 A HUNDRED COLLARS . . 8
   HE HAD GONE TO THE HOUSE SO'S NOT TO MEET ME. . . . 73 THE CODE 105
   "WHERE SHALL WE MEET AGAIN?" / "NOWHERE BUT HERE . . . 80 THE GENERATIONS OF MEN 208
   ONCE MORE BEFORE WE MEET ELSEWHERE." / "IN RAIN?" . . 81 THE GENERATIONS OF MEN 209
   TO MEET HIM WITH HIS ANSWER AT THE DOOR. . . . . . 201 PLACE FOR A THIRD . . 72
   TWO WINDS WOULD MEET, ... 218 I WILL SING YOU ONE-O . 11
   YOU WENT TO MEET THE SHELL'S EMBRACE OF FIRE . . . . 222 TO E.T. 13
   IS WHERE TWO ROCKS ALMOST MEET, ... 282 A DRUMLIN WOODCHUCK . 25
   IT WELL MAY BE. WE MEET--I DON'T SAY WHEN-- . . . . 321 BUILD SOIL . . . 159
   BEFORE HE CAME TO MEET HIS OWN! . . . . 336 THE WIND AND THE RAIN . 11
   SO SCIENCE AND RELIGION REALLY MEET. . . . . 353 THE LESSON FOR TODAY . 83
   MIND WHEN I MEET WITH IT IN ANY GUISE. . . . . . . 358 A CONSIDERABLE SPECK . 31
   YOU'LL HEAR ALL SORTS OF THINGS. YOU'LL MEET WITH THEM . 369 THE LITERATE FARMER AND 33
MEETING
   PROVISION THERE HAD BEEN FOR JUST SUCH MEETING . . . . 74 THE GENERATIONS OF MEN 38
   MEETING AND PASSING . . . . 118 MEETING AND PASSING . T
   NEITHER REFUSED THE MEETING. BUT THE HAND! . . . . 136 "OUT, OUT--" . . . 18
   FOR HOG REEVE IN MARCH MEETING HERE IN WARREN. . . . 207 PAUPER WITCH OF GRAFTON 14
   IN WARREN AT MARCH MEETING, FOR THE REASON . . . . 208 PAUPER WITCH OF GRAFTON 18
   'TWAS SUNDAY AND SQUARE HALE WAS DRESSED FOR MEETING. . 284 THE GOLD HESPERIDEE . 41
   BUT MUST BRING TO THE MEETING THE MATUREST; . . . . 321 BUILD SOIL . . . 160
   AS MEETING SOMEONE LIVING, FACE TO FACE. . . . . . 382 TO AN ANCIENT . . . 9
MEETS
   NO HABITATION MEETS THE EYE . . . . 392 A CLIFF DWELLING . . 3
MELANCHOLY
   THE MELANCHOLY OF HAVING TO COUNT SOULS . . . . . . 176 THE CENSUS-TAKER . . 61
   ANY MELANCHOLY . . . . 431 KITTY HAWK . . . 97
   INDULGENCE IN YOUR FORM OF MELANCHOLY . . . . . . 498 A MASQUE OF MERCY . . 144
MELIBOEUS
   I'M MELIBOEUS THE POTATO MAN, ... 316 BUILD SOIL . . . 2
   OH, MELIBOEUS, I HAVE HALF A MIND . . . . 316 BUILD SOIL . . . 26
   I KEEP MY EYE ON CONGRESS, MELIBOEUS. . . . . . . 317 BUILD SOIL . . . 54
   PARDON THE ANALOGY, MY MELIBOEUS, ... 318 BUILD SOIL . . . 90
   AND BE JUDGED BY THE OUTCOME, MELIBOEUS. . . . . . 320 BUILD SOIL . . . 135
   LET ME PREACH TO YOU, WILL YOU, MELIBOEUS? . . . . 322 BUILD SOIL . . . 182
   I'LL MAKE A COMPACT WITH YOU, MELIBOEUS, ... 323 BUILD SOIL . . . 220
   IS IT A BARGAIN, SHEPHERD MELIBOEUS? . . . . . . 325 BUILD SOIL . . . 283
MELL (SEE PELL-MELL)
MELLOW
   I THRUST MY HOE IN THE MELLOW GROUND, ... 124 A TIME TO TALK . . . 7
MELODIOUS
   I'LL BET SHE'D HAVE MADE A MELODIOUS LOW . . . . . 463 LINES IN DEJECTION . . 11
MELT
   MELT IT AS THE ICE WILL GO; . . . . 11 TO THE THAWING WIND . 8
   MELT THE GLASS AND LEAVE THE STICKS . . . . 11 TO THE THAWING WIND . 9
   THAT WAS HOW THAT GRIEF STARTED TO MELT. . . . . . 253 THE THATCH 30
   AND NOT MELT SNOW OR START A DORMANT TREE. . . . . 254 A WINTER EDEN . . . 4
   IN CASE THE ROCKS SHOULD MELT AND RUN AGAIN. . . . . 407 FROM PLANE TO PLANE . 95
MELTED
   WAS MELTED DOWN AT NOON, ... 10 WIND AND WINDOW FLOWER 6
   IT MELTED, AND I LET IT FALL AND BREAK. . . . . . 68 AFTER APPLE-PICKING . 13

```
                                                           PAGE TITLE              LINE
MELTED (CONTINUED)
   AND UNDERFOOT SNOW MELTED DOWN TO ICE,         .  .  .  .  . 179 THE STAR-SPLITTER  .  . 80
   AND THOUGHT IT MUST HAVE MELTED. IT WAS GONE.  .  .  .  .  . 194 PAUL'S WIFE  .  .  .  . 105
   FROM SNOW THAT MELTED ONLY YESTERDAY.  .  .  .  .  .  .  . 245 SPRING POOLS  .  .  .  . 12
   ON MELTED MOUNTAIN WATER LED BY FLUME  .  .  .  .  .  .  . 337 THE WIND AND THE RAIN  . 23
MELTING
   AND MELTING FURTHER IN THE WIND TO MUD.  .  .  .  .  .  . 179 THE STAR-SPLITTER  .  . 81
MEMBER
   OF THE STARK FAMILY I'M A MEMBER OF)."  .  .  .  .  .  . 76 THE GENERATIONS OF MEN  81
MEMBERS  (SEE NON-MEMBERS)
   WHEN, TO PLEASE YOUNGER MEMBERS OF THE CHURCH,  .  .  .  . 57 THE BLACK COTTAGE  .  . 85
MEMENTO
   MEMENTO MORI AND OBEY THE LORD.  .  .  .  .  .  .  .  . 353 THE LESSON FOR TODAY  . 96
   I HOLD YOUR DOCTRINE OF MEMENTO MORI.  .  .  .  .  .  . 355 THE LESSON FOR TODAY  . 157
MEMORIES
   SEEKING WITH MEMORIES GROWN DIM O'ER NIGHT  .  .  .  .  . 22 THE TUFT OF FLOWERS  . 13
   ANCESTRAL MEMORIES MIGHT COME TOGETHER.  .  .  .  .  .  . 73 THE GENERATIONS OF MEN  3
   TWO MEMORIES THAT LONG HAD LAIN .  .  .  .  .  .  .  . 381 AN UNSTAMPED LETTER IN  33
MEMORY
   BUT ON THE MEMORY OF ONE ABSENT, MOST,  .  .  .  .  .  . 15 WAITING  .  .  .  .  . 26
   THE MEMORY THAT HE CHOSE THE LIFE;  .  .  .  .  .  .  . 21 THE TRIAL BY EXISTENCE  52
   ADMITS NO MEMORY OF CHOICE,  .  .  .  .  .  .  .  .  . 21 THE TRIAL BY EXISTENCE  54
   THE LASTING MEMORY AT ALL CLEAR,  .  .  .  .  .  .  . 21 THE TRIAL BY EXISTENCE  67
   YOU'D THINK HIS MEMORY MIGHT BE SATISFIED----" .  .  .  . 53 HOME BURIAL  .  .  .  . 66
   "OUT WALKING. EVERY CHILD SHOULD HAVE THE MEMORY  .  .  . 92 THE FEAR  .  .  .  .  . 82
   I HAVEN'T ANY MEMORY--HAVE YOU?--  .  .  .  .  .  .  . 110 THE EXPOSED NEST  .  . 33
   (THIS WAS HER FADED MEMORY OF THE WAY .  .  .  .  .  . 183 MAPLE  .  .  .  .  .  . 110
   NO MEMORY OF HAVING STARRED  .  .  .  .  .  .  .  . 307 PROVIDE, PROVIDE  .  . 16
   AND MADE COMMIT TO MEMORY  .  .  .  .  .  .  .  .  . 331 BEECH  .  .  .  .  .  . 8
MEMPHIS
   WERE SEEN OF OLD AT MEMPHIS ON THE HEIGHTS  .  .  .  . 315 IRIS BY NIGHT  .  .  . 6
MEN
   FAR OFF THE HOMES OF MEN, AND FARTHER STILL,  .  .  .  . 17 THE VANTAGE POINT  .  . 6
   THE GRAVES OF MEN ON AN OPPOSING HILL,  .  .  .  .  . 17 THE VANTAGE POINT  .  . 7
   "MEN WORK TOGETHER," I TOLD HIM FROM THE HEART,  .  .  . 23 THE TUFT OF FLOWERS  . 39
   THAT ALL MEN ARE CREATED FREE AND EQUAL.  .  .  .  . 57 THE BLACK COTTAGE  .  . 61
   SCATTERED OASES WHERE MEN DWELT, BUT MOSTLY  .  .  .  . 58 THE BLACK COTTAGE  .  . 119
   WITH A HOUSEFUL OF HUNGRY MEN TO FEED .  .  .  .  .  . 62 A SERVANT TO SERVANTS . 5
   FROM COOKING MEALS FOR HUNGRY HIRED MEN  .  .  .  .  . 64 A SERVANT TO SERVANTS . 50
   (WOMEN AND MEN WILL MAKE THEM ALL THE SAME.)  .  .  . 64 A SERVANT TO SERVANTS . 69
   IT'S HIGHWAYS, AND HE'S GOT TOO MANY MEN .  .  .  .  . 64 A SERVANT TO SERVANTS . 72
   THE GENERATIONS OF MEN  .  .  .  .  .  .  .  .  . 73 THE GENERATIONS OF MEN  T
   HE KNOWS HE'S KINDER THAN THE RUN OF MEN.  .  .  .  . 84 THE HOUSEKEEPER  .  .  . 80
   YOU KNOW HOW MEN WILL BE RIDICULOUS.  .  .  .  .  . 87 THE HOUSEKEEPER  .  .  . 160
   OFF THERE UPSTAIRS. THE VERY TREAD OF MEN  .  .  .  . 111 IN THE HOME STRETCH  . 38
   IT SOUNDS AS IF IT WERE THE MEN WENT DOWN,  .  .  . 112 IN THE HOME STRETCH  . 56
   DOOR-FILLING MEN BURST IN AND SEIZED THE STOVE.  .  . 113 IN THE HOME STRETCH  . 83
   OF WIRE WITH SOMETHING IN IT FROM MEN TO MEN.  .  . 125 AN ENCOUNTER  .  .  .  . 18
   "OH, BUT WAR'S NOT FOR CHILDREN--IT'S FOR MEN."  .  . 132 THE BONFIRE  .  .  .  . 100
   TO IMPRESS MEN. YOU'VE GOT US SO ASHAMED  .  .  .  . 146 SNOW  .  .  .  .  .  . 99
   OF BEING MEN WE CAN'T LOOK AT A GOOD FIGHT  .  .  . 146 SNOW  .  .  .  .  .  . 100
   TAUNTED THE LOFTY LAND WITH LITTLE MEN."  .  .  .  . 166 NEW HAMPSHIRE  .  .  . 219
   THE LITTLE MEN (IT'S MASSACHUSETTS SPEAKING).  .  . 166 NEW HAMPSHIRE  .  .  . 225
   THEY TAUNT THE LOFTY LAND WITH LITTLE MEN.  .  .  . 167 NEW HAMPSHIRE  .  .  . 264
   AND THAT NOT DWELT IN NOW BY MEN OR WOMEN.  .  .  . 174 THE CENSUS-TAKER  .  . 6
   FOREVER OFF THE LATCH, AS IF RUDE MEN .  .  .  .  . 175 THE CENSUS-TAKER  .  . 28
   I SAW NO MEN THERE AND NO BONES OF MEN THERE.  .  . 175 THE CENSUS-TAKER  .  . 42
   ELIZA'S HAD TOO MANY OTHER MEN."  .  .  .  .  .  . 202 PLACE FOR A THIRD  .  . 78
   IT'S NOT MEN BY SOME MISTAKE?  .  .  .  .  .  .  . 211 AN EMPTY THREAT  .  .  . 21
   WHAT IS IT MEN ARE SHRINKING FROM?  .  .  .  .  . 221 IN A DISUSED GRAVEYARD . 12
   AND TELL THE STONES: MEN HATE TO DIE  .  .  .  . 221 IN A DISUSED GRAVEYARD . 14
   AND SEE HOW MEN HAVE WARRED.  .  .  .  .  .  . 252 THE PEACEFUL SHEPHERD . 10
   (WEST-RUNNING BROOK MEN CALL IT TO THIS DAY.)  .  . 257 WEST-RUNNING BROOK  .  . 3
   WE MEN MUST SEE YOU TO THE CONFINES OF  .  .  . 259 WEST-RUNNING BROOK  .  . 34
   THE MEN SHE COULD NOT DROWN.  .  .  .  .  .  . 260 SAND DUNES  .  .  .  . 8
   MEN LEFT HER A SHIP TO SINK:  .  .  .  .  .  . 260 SAND DUNES  .  .  .  . 13
   IT IS BECAUSE LIKE MEN WE LOOK TOO NEAR,  .  . 261 A SOLDIER  .  .  .  .  . 6
   THE MEADOW IS FINISHED WITH MEN.  .  .  .  . 264 THE LAST MOWING  .  .  . 4
   IT'S NO MORE MEN I'M AFRAID OF;  .  .  .  .  . 264 THE LAST MOWING  .  .  . 13
   AND IF MEN HAVE WATCHED A LONG TIME  .  .  . 266 SITTING BY A BUSH  .  . 9
   MEN OF THE WOODS AND LUMBERJACKS,  .  .  . 276 TWO TRAMPS IN MUD TIME  53
   WITH GODS AND ANGELS, WE WERE MEN AT LEAST,  .  . 279 THE WHITE-TAILED HORNET  61
   I BADE MEN TELL ME WHICH IN BRIEF,  .  .  . 297 LEAVES COMPARED WITH  . 13
   MEN WORK ALONE, THEIR LOTS PLOWED FAR APART,  .  . 299 STRONG SAYING NOTHING . 6
   TO BE A BIRD WHILE WE ARE MEN ON EARTH,  .  .  . 303 A BIRD SINGING IN SLEEP  12
   IT CAN BLAME THIS LIMITLESS TRAIT IN THE HEARTS OF MEN. . 305 THERE ARE ROUGHLY ZONES  21
   THERE'S ONLY LOVE OF MEN AND WOMEN, LOVE  .  . 318 BUILD SOIL  .  .  .  . 85
   OF CHILDREN, LOVE OF FRIENDS, OF MEN, OF GOD:  .  . 318 BUILD SOIL  .  .  .  . 86
   WHEN AFTER TALK WITH OTHER MEN  .  .  .  . 346 DISCOVERY OF MADEIRAS . 86
   SOME STANDING JEST BETWEEN YOU MEN?  .  .  . 346 DISCOVERY OF MADEIRAS . 94
   AND TELL ME TRULY, MEN OF EARTH,  .  .  .  . 362 A QUESTION  .  .  .  . 2
   IT BEST BE LEFT TO GREAT MEN OF HIS KIND .  .  . 372 THE LITERATE FARMER AND 134
   THAT MEN HAVE THOUGHT ABOUT IN VAIN.  .  .  . 381 AN UNSTAMPED LETTER IN  37
   THE MISTAKES OF ANCIENT MEN,  .  .  .  .  . 387 THE COURAGE TO BE NEW . 2
   ALL THE WAY TO MEN.  .  .  .  .  .  .  .  . 426 A NEVER NAUGHT SONG  . 16
   WHAT DID MEN MEAN BY .  .  .  .  .  .  . 430 KITTY HAWK  .  .  .  . 59
   I AT ODDS WITH MEN  .  .  .  .  .  .  . 433 KITTY HAWK  .  .  .  . 178
   MEN WOULD TREAT THIS SKY  .  .  .  .  . 434 KITTY HAWK  .  .  .  . 189
   FLED FROM THE PALACE IN THE GUISE OF MEN.  .  . 454 HOW HARD TO KEEP FROM . 11
   THE QUINTESSENCE OF HORSES, MEN, AND WOMEN."  .  . 455 HOW HARD TO KEEP FROM . 44
   "YOU SAY YOU KNOW THE INWARDNESS OF MEN,  .  . 456 HOW HARD TO KEEP FROM . 98
   TO TROUBLE MEN WITH HAVING TO TAKE SIDES.  .  . 468 FROM IRON  .  .  .  . 2
   WHEREAS MEN PROPHETS ARE RECEIVED WITH HONOR.  .  . 476 A MASQUE OF REASON  . 90
   GET BURNED FOR PROPHECY, MEN ALMOST NEVER.  .  . 478 A MASQUE OF REASON  . 150
   MEN FUMBLE AT THE POSSIBILITIES  .  .  .  . 483 A MASQUE OF REASON  . 275
   SOMETHING ABOUT--(THE THREE MEN LAUGH.)  .  . 487 A MASQUE OF REASON  . 400
   WHAT THE SINS ARE MEN OUGHT TO PERISH FOR.  .  . 503 A MASQUE OF MERCY  .  . 261
   WHO CAN BE MANY GODS TO MANY MEN,  .  .  . 516 A MASQUE OF MERCY  .  . 591
```

MENACINGLY
    HIS STINGING QUARTERS MENACINGLY WORK. . . . . 309 WASPISH 4
MEND
    WATING TO SEE IF SHE WOULD MEND; . . . . 347 DISCOVERY OF MADEIRAS . 112
    AND MEND THE OTHERS UP TO GO AGAIN. . . . . 508 A MASQUE OF MERCY . 371
MENDING
    MENDING WALL . . . . 33 MENDING WALL . . . . T
    OR MENDING FENCE IT ALL COMES BACK TO ME . . . . . 325 BUILD SOIL . . 288
MENDING-TIME
    BUT AT SPRING MENDING-TIME WE FIND THEM THERE. . . . . 33 MENDING WALL 11
MENFOLK
    LIKE SOME MENFOLK. NO ONE'S AFRAID OF HIM; . . . . . 83 THE HOUSEKEEPER . . 69
MENS
    THE MENS ANIMI. . . . . 440 KITTY HAWK . . . 390
MEN'S
    MANY MEN'S LUCK WITH GREATEST WASHINGTON . . . . . 317 BUILD SOIL 45
    (I DO TOO MUCH IN SOME MEN'S EYES.) . . . . . . 327 A MISSIVE MISSILE . . 37
    MEN'S LEGS AND BODIES IN THE GALE . . . . 452 A-WISHING WELL . . 52
MENTAL
    IN ANSWER TO THE MENTAL THRUST. . . . . 332 ALL REVELATION . . . 15
MENTALLY
    BUT MUST LIVE LIVES OUT MENTALLY AGAPE . . . . . 351 THE LESSON FOR TODAY . 40
MENTION
    OR GRASS-BLADE IS LEFT, NOT TO MENTION A STICK, . . 59 BLUEBERRIES 19
    IT WAS WELL WORTH PRELIMINARY MENTION. . . . . 352 THE LESSON FOR TODAY . 59
    IT WAS WELL WORTH PRELIMINARY MENTION. . . . . 352 THE LESSON FOR TODAY . 63
    ARGUMENTS TOO STALE TO MENTION . . . . . . 396 AN IMPORTER . . . 9
    NOT TO MENTION CLUTCH. . . . . 438 KITTY HAWK . . . 332
    AS TOO NEW TO MENTION. . . . . 440 KITTY HAWK . . . 383
MENTIONED
    JOB MENTIONED HIM, AND SO I BROUGHT HIM IN, ... 489 A MASQUE OF REASON . 432
MENTIONLESS
    GOES MENTIONLESS EXCEPT IN BABY-SCHOOL . . . . . 447 DOES NO ONE AT ALL EVER 38
MERCHANT
    THERE CAME TO COURT A MERCHANT SELLING PEARLS, ... 455 HOW HARD TO KEEP FROM 66
MERCIFUL
    WHAT WOULD YOU HAVE GOD IF NOT MERCIFUL? . . . . . 507 A MASQUE OF MERCY . 362
MERCIFULLY
    BUT MERCIFULLY KEPT THE PASSING CROWD . . . . . . 284 THE GOLD HESPERIDEE . 56
    ARE TO BE BOUGHT OUT AND MERCIFULLY GATHERED IN . . 286 A ROADSIDE STAND . 24
MERCY
    THE LUMBER ON PAUL TILL PAUL BEGGED FOR MERCY. . . . 193 PAUL'S WIFE . . 61
    IT MAY BE A MERCY THE DARK CLOSES ROUND US . . . 379 TOO ANXIOUS FOR RIVERS 12
    WHOSE MERCY TO YOU RATHER THAN TO OTHERS . . . 385 THE FEAR OF GOD . . 5
    A MASQUE OF MERCY . . . . 491 A MASQUE OF MERCY . T
    A MASQUE OF MERCY . . . . 493 A MASQUE OF MERCY . T
    MERCY AND JUSTICE ARE A CONTRADICTION. . . . . . 498 A MASQUE OF MERCY . 141
    MERCY, FOR MERCY'S SAKE! / BEL WANTS SOME MERCY.-- . 507 A MASQUE OF MERCY . 345
    KNEEL TO YOUR DOCTOR. HE DISPENSES MERCY.-- . . 507 A MASQUE OF MERCY . 346
    YOU SHOULD BE AN AUTHORITY ON MERCY. . . . . . 508 A MASQUE OF MERCY . 374
    WHERE MERCY IS EXPLICITLY THE SUBJECT. . . . . 508 A MASQUE OF MERCY . 377
    BUT MERCY FIRST AND LAST SHALL BRIGHTEST SHINE-- . 508 A MASQUE OF MERCY . 381
    IS NOTHING BUT AN OUTBREAK OF MASS MERCY, . . . 509 A MASQUE OF MERCY . 417
    THE MERCY ON THE SIN AGAINST THE SERMON. . . . 511 A MASQUE OF MERCY . 477
    THROWN PROSTRATE AT THE MERCY SEAT FOR MERCY. . . 511 A MASQUE OF MERCY . 485
    MERCY IS ONLY TO THE UNDESERVING. . . . . . 512 A MASQUE OF MERCY . 500
    A PENITENT PERHAPS, SELF-THROWN ON MERCY. . . 516 A MASQUE OF MERCY . 610
    MERCY ON ME FOR HAVING THOUGHT I KNEW. . . . 518 A MASQUE OF MERCY . 660
    MERCY ON HIM FOR HAVING ASKED FOR JUSTICE. . . 518 A MASQUE OF MERCY . 662
    THAT NOTHING BUT GOD'S MERCY CAN ASSUAGE. . . 520 A MASQUE OF MERCY . 713
    NOTHING CAN MAKE INJUSTICE JUST BUT MERCY. . . 521 A MASQUE OF MERCY . 738
MERCY-CROSSED
    IT WAS THEIR JUSTICE BEING MERCY-CROSSED. . . 509 A MASQUE OF MERCY . 415
    TO SEE IT, EVIL-CROSSED OR MERCY-CROSSED? . . 510 A MASQUE OF MERCY . 438
    OF STAR-CROSSED, MERCY-CROSSED, OR EVIL-CROSSED . 510 A MASQUE OF MERCY . 440
    WHERE MERCY-CROSSED TO ME SEEMED EVIL-CROSSED. . . 510 A MASQUE OF MERCY . 443
MERCY-JUSTICE
    BUT FROM HIS MERCY-JUSTICE CONTRADICTION. . . . . 498 A MASQUE OF MERCY . 140
MERCY'S
    UPON ITS DOORSTEPS AS AT MERCY'S FEET . . . . . 400 TO THE RIGHT PERSON . 13
    MERCY, FOR MERCY'S SAKE! / BEL WANTS SOME MERCY.-- . 507 A MASQUE OF MERCY . 345
MERE
    AS IF TO SAY MERE LEARNING WAS THE DEVIL . . . . . 400 TO THE RIGHT PERSON . 10
    HE WASN'T OFF A MERE DEGREE; . . . . 417 AMERICA IS HARD TO SEE 17
    THAT'S BECAUSE THOUGH MERE . . . . 434 KITTY HAWK . . . 196
    IN MERE MEDITATION. . . . . 435 KITTY HAWK . . . 241
    THAT IF IT'S NOT A MERE ILLUSION . . . . . . 450 OUR DOOM TO BLOOM . 7
MERELY
    MERELY BECAUSE IT CEASES TO BE TRUE. . . . . . . 58 THE BLACK COTTAGE . 106
    OR EVEN MERELY SEEMED TO PINE . . . . 275 A LONE STRIKER . . 60
    FOR MERELY GIVING YOU ONCE MORE GENTLE PROOF . . 306 NOT QUITE SOCIAL . 6
    HAS BROUGHT HER MERELY VISITING, ... 390 TWO LEADING LIGHTS . 26
    (OR MERELY MANNERS IT MAY HAVE BEEN), ... 420 ONE MORE BREVITY . 21
    IT MERELY WOULD ENTAIL THE PURGE . . . . . . 453 A-WISHING WELL . . 72
    ALL YOUR EFFECTS WERE MERELY LUCKY BLUNDERS. . . 482 A MASQUE OF REASON . 259
    MERELY THE WINDOWS RATTLING IN THE STORM. . . . 504 A MASQUE OF MERCY . 280
    TO COUNT ON JUSTICE TO BE MERELY JUST. . . . . 509 A MASQUE OF MERCY . 425
MEREST
    WERE NOT, AS 'TWERE, THE MEREST MASK OF GLOOM, . . . 5 INTO MY OWN . . . 3
    THAN THE MEREST AIMLESS BREATH OF AIR. . . . . 24 PAN WITH US . . 25
    THAT AND THE MEREST CURL OF CIGARETTE SMOKE-- . . . 131 THE BONFIRE . . . 50
    THE TRACE WOULD HAVE TO BE THE MEREST TRACE . . . 162 NEW HAMPSHIRE . . 120
MERIT
    THAT THE SUPREME MERIT . . . . 435 KITTY HAWK . . . 222
MERITED
    THE CONDEMNED WORLD THE LEGACY WAS MERITED. . . . . 370 THE LITERATE FARMER AND 56

PAGE TITLE   LINE

MERRY
   IN WISHING YOU HEREWITH A MERRY CHRISTMAS. . . . . . . 107 CHRISTMAS TREES . . . 60
MESERVE
   MESERVE, BELITTLED IN THE GREAT SKIN COAT HE WORE. . . . 143 SNOW 5
   MESERVE WAS FIRST TO SPEAK. HE POINTED BACKWARD . . . . 143 SNOW 6
   BROTHER MESERVE. YOU KNOW TO FIND YOUR WAY . . . . . 144 SNOW 37
   AND SAVE HIS LIFE.--ALL RIGHT, COME IN, MESERVE. . . . . 147 SNOW 104
   MR. MESERVE, I'LL LEAVE IT TO YOUR WIFE. . . . . . . 147 SNOW 109
   MESERVE SEEMED TO HEED NOTHING BUT THE LAMP . . . . . 147 SNOW 111
   "I SHOULDN'T WANT TO HURRY YOU, MESERVE. . . . . . . 148 SNOW 153
   "BROTHER MESERVE, TAKE CARE, YOU'LL SCARE YOURSELF . . . 149 SNOW 167
   WELL, NOW I LEAVE YOU, PEOPLE." / "COME, MESERVE, . . . 150 SNOW 197
   "HELLO, MESERVE. YOU'RE THERE, THEN!--AND YOUR WIFE? . . 155 SNOW 329
MESHACH
   LIKE SHADRACH, MESHACH, AND ABEDNEGO. . . . . 516 A MASQUE OF MERCY . 604
MESS
   "WHO'D MARRY HER STRAIGHT OUT OF SUCH A MESS? . . . . . 88 THE HOUSEKEEPER . . . 186
MESSAGE
   NEVERTHELESS, A MESSAGE FROM THE DAWN, ... 23 THE TUFT OF FLOWERS . 30
MESSENGER
   YOU ARE NO COMMON MESSENGER . . . . 327 A MISSIVE MISSILE . 23
MESSIAH
   THE WORLD SEEMS CRYING OUT FOR A MESSIAH. . . . . . 515 A MASQUE OF MERCY . 576
MESSIANIC
   AND OF THE MESSIANIC RACE, KARL MARX. . . . . 515 A MASQUE OF MERCY . 578
MET
   AND THERE I MET A MAN WHO MOVED SO SLOW . . . . . . 41 THE MOUNTAIN 16
   I MET THEM ONE DAY AND EACH HAD A FLOWER . . . . . . 61 BLUEBERRIES 64
   AS YOU CAME UP THE HILL. WE MET. BUT ALL . . . . . . 118 MEETING AND PASSING . 4
   BEFORE WE MET, AND YOU WHAT I HAD PASSED. . . . . . . 119 MEETING AND PASSING . 14
   DO YOU KNOW WHAT SHE'S LIKE? HAVE YOU EVER MET HER? . . 154 SNOW 313
   I MET A LADY FROM THE SOUTH WHO SAID . . . . 159 NEW HAMPSHIRE . . 1
   I MET A TRAVELER FROM ARKANSAS . . . . 159 NEW HAMPSHIRE . . 9
   I MET A CALIFORNIAN WHO WOULD . . . . 159 NEW HAMPSHIRE . . 16
   I MET A POET FROM ANOTHER STATE, ... 159 NEW HAMPSHIRE . . 25
   (THE ONLY OTHER WITCH I EVER MET . . . . 163 NEW HAMPSHIRE . . 126
   OR DOWN A MINE OR AT THE MILL (I MET HIM) . . . . . 289 OLD BARN AT THE BOTTOM 18
   A GIRL OF HIS AGE HE MET . . . . 313 BEARER OF EVIL TIDINGS 14
   WHERE NATURAL FRIENDS ARE MET, WHERE DOGS ARE KEPT, . . 318 BUILD SOIL . . . 83
   TWO SOULS MAY BE TOO WIDELY MET. . . . . 328 A MISSIVE MISSILE . 52
   AS EVER WHEN PHILOSOPHERS ARE MET, ... 354 THE LESSON FOR TODAY . 107
   COULD SAVE IT FROM ITS LOSSES BEING MET. . . . . . . 399 THE INGENUITIES OF DEBT 12
   LATER WHEN WE MET, ... 429 KITTY HAWK . . . 51
METAL (SEE MONEY-METAL)
   WERE METAL THAN IT WAS WHEN THEY WERE WOODEN? . . . . 163 NEW HAMPSHIRE . . 133
   I SUFFERED LIKE A METAL BEING CAST. . . . . 267 WHAT FIFTY SAID . . 3
METALLIC
   THAN AN IMPOVERISHED SOIL, PALE AND METALLIC? . . . . 323 BUILD SOIL . . . 218
METAL-POINT
   THEY MAKE US CRINGE FOR METAL-POINT ON STONE. . . . . 261 A SOLDIER 11
METALS
   A STATE PRODUCING PRECIOUS METALS, STONES, ... 164 NEW HAMPSHIRE . . 165
METAL-SAP
   WHEN YOU GIVE IT THE LIVID METAL-SAP. . . . . . . 306 A TRIAL RUN . . . 3
METAPHOR
   THE METAPHOR, THE SYMBOL LIES! . . . . 327 A MISSIVE MISSILE . 35
METAPHYSICAL
   BETWEEN TWO METAPHYSICAL EXTREMES. . . . . 269 THE BEAR 25
   OF METAPHYSICAL PROFUNDITY . . . . 483 A MASQUE OF REASON . 278
METAPHYSICS
   OR METAPHYSICS, LONG THE WORLD'S REPROACH . . . . . 480 A MASQUE OF REASON . 191
METEOR
   THE METEOR THAT THRUSTS IN WITH NEEDLE BILL, ... 12 A PRAYER IN SPRING . 11
METEORITE
   NOT A METEORITE, BUT AN AVATAR-- . . . . 421 ONE MORE BREVITY . 61
METEORS
   WHERE SHOWERS OF CHARTED METEORS LET FLY. . . . . . 173 A STAR IN A STONEBOAT . 42
METER
   UPON A METER, STRICT OR LOOSE IAMBIC. . . . . . . 460 HOW HARD TO KEEP FROM 214
   THE TUNE IS NOT THAT METER, NOT THAT RHYTHM, ... 460 HOW HARD TO KEEP FROM 216
   FREE VERSE LEAVES OUT THE METER AND MAKES UP . . . . 460 HOW HARD TO KEEP FROM 219
   IT SEEMS TO BE A CHAPTER HEAD IN METER. . . . . . 506 A MASQUE OF MERCY . 327
METHOD
   OR AT LEAST IN A LIFETIME, BY THAT METHOD." . . . . 405 FROM PLANE TO PLANE . 47
MEWLING
   MEWLING AND PUKING IN THE PUBLIC ARMS." . . . . . 170 NEW HAMPSHIRE . . 363
MICA
   OLD DAVIS OWNED A SOLID MICA MOUNTAIN . . . . . . 212 A FOUNTAIN, A BOTTLE . 1
   THE MICA SHEETS WERE BIG AS PLATE-GLASS WINDOWS. . . . 213 A FOUNTAIN, A BOTTLE . 5
   THAT FLICKERS MICA WINGS. HE LIFTS A HAND . . . . . 487 A MASQUE OF REASON . 390
MICROBES
   AS A BRIEF EPIDEMIC OF MICROBES . . . . 352 THE LESSON FOR TODAY . 70
MICROSCOPE
   AND AT THE OTHER END THE MICROSCOPE, ... 269 THE BEAR 19
MICROSCOPIC
   (MICROSCOPIC) . . . . 357 A CONSIDERABLE SPECK . 5
   BUT THIS POOR MICROSCOPIC ITEM NOW! . . . . 358 A CONSIDERABLE SPECK . 27
MID-AIR
   AND OFF A BLOSSOM IN MID-AIR STANDS STILL. . . . . . 12 A PRAYER IN SPRING . 12
MIDDAY
   AT MIDDAY WHEN A SUNNY SUMMER BREEZE . . . . . . 331 THE SILKEN TENT . . . 2
MIDDEN
   THE MIDDEN OF FEAST UPON FEAST, ... 312 THE VINDICTIVES . . . 60
   IN THE KITCHEN MIDDEN . . . . 441 KITTY HAWK . . . 432
MIDDLE
   MURDERED HIM AS LEFT OUT HIS MIDDLE NAME. . . . . . 71 THE CODE 70
   WITH ONE STROKE OF YOUR FINGER IN THE MIDDLE. . . . . 179 THE STAR-SPLITTER . . 91
   THEN SIT DOWN IN THE MIDDLE OF THEM ALL. . . . . . 267 THE ARMFUL . . . 10

MIDDLE (CONTINUED)
    YOU'RE ONE MONTH ON IN THE MIDDLE OF MAY. . . . . . . 275 TWO TRAMPS IN MUD TIME   20
    AND YOU'RE TWO MONTHS BACK IN THE MIDDLE OF MARCH. . . 275 TWO TRAMPS IN MUD TIME   24
    SEIZES THE DEAD BY THE MIDDLE, ... 289 DEPARTMENTAL   37
    THEN IN THE MIDDLE OF THE OPEN SHEET . . . . 357 A CONSIDERABLE SPECK   21
    BUT THE SECRET SITS IN THE MIDDLE AND KNOWS. . . . . . 362 THE SECRET SITS . . .   2
    "YOU WISHED YOUR MIDDLE NAME HAD BEEN TECUMSEH." . . . 406 FROM PLANE TO PLANE   74
    AND PART THEM IN THE MIDDLE WITH A PATH. . . . . 414 A CABIN IN THE CLEARING   4
MIDDLE-AISLE
    OF MIDDLE-AISLE CHURCH CARPET, SISAL HEMP, ... 489 A MASQUE OF REASON . . 454
MIDDLENESS
    THE MIDDLENESS OF THE ROAD . . . . 388 MIDDLENESS OF THE ROAD   T
MIDDLES
    THERE ARE ONLY MIDDLES." / "WHAT IS THIS?" / "THIS LIFE? . 116 IN THE HOME STRETCH . 175
MIDGES
    AND THEN BEYOND THE OPEN WATER, DIM WITH MIDGES, ... 194 PAUL'S WIFE 106
MIDNIGHT
    TO ROUT US OUT TO THINK FOR HIM AT MIDNIGHT . . . . . 155 SNOW 346
    TO THE MIDNIGHT SKY A SUNSET GLOW. . . . . 241 NEED OF BEING VERSED .   2
    IN THE DESERT AT MIDNIGHT IN UTAH, ... 290 ON HEART'S BEGINNING TO   2
    TO A CONE MOUNTAIN IN THE MIDNIGHT HAZE, ... 300 MOON COMPASSES   4
    SETS FORTH FOR HOME AT MIDNIGHT FROM A FRIEND'S-- . . . 386 THE FEAR OF MAN . . .   2
    ON MIDNIGHT PATROL, ... 432 KITTY HAWK 141
MID-SUMMER
    LOUD, A MID-SUMMER AND A MID-WOOD BIRD, ... 119 THE OVEN BIRD   2
    MID-SUMMER IS TO SPRING AS ONE TO TEN. . . . . 120 THE OVEN BIRD   5
MID-VICTORIANS
    WE'VE HEARD AGAINST THE MID-VICTORIANS . . . . 168 NEW HAMPSHIRE 295
    THE MATTER WITH THE MID-VICTORIANS . . . . 168 NEW HAMPSHIRE 298
MID-WASTE
    RETARD MID-WASTE MY COWERING CARAVANS-- . . . . 59 THE BLACK COTTAGE . . 124
MID-WOOD
    LOUD, A MID-SUMMER AND A MID-WOOD BIRD, ... 119 THE OVEN BIRD   2
MIEN
    WITH NO SMALL DIGNITY OF MIEN. . . . . 138 BROWN'S DESCENT . . .   24
MIGHT---NOT INDEXED--EXCEPT FOR:
    HOLD ON WITH ALL YOUR MIGHT WHEN I LET GO." . . . . . 197 WILD GRAPES   40
MIGHTIER
    AND ALL THE MORE THE MIGHTIER THE SHOWER . . . . 337 THE WIND AND THE RAIN. 35
MIGHTN'T---NOT INDEXED
MIGHTY
    A MIGHTY FARMER FLUNG THE HOUSE DOOR WIDE, ... 368 THE LITERATE FARMER AND 5
    SOME OF THEM MIGHTY HUGE, SOME MIGHTY TINY, ... 425 ACCIDENTALLY ON PURPOSE 3
    ALL OF THEM RADIANT AND MIGHTY SHINY. . . . . 425 ACCIDENTALLY ON PURPOSE   4
    WAS ONE MIGHTY CHARGE . . . . 436 KITTY HAWK 254
    (HE STOPS TO LISTEN.) THAT'S A MIGHTY STORM, ... 502 A MASQUE OF MERCY . . 233
MIGRATORY
    THEN ALMOST MIGRATORY . . . . 359 NOVEMBER   2
MILD
    O HUSHED OCTOBER MORNING MILD, ... 27 OCTOBER   1
    O HUSHED OCTOBER MORNING MILD, ... 27 OCTOBER   7
MILE (SEE TWO-THOUSAND-MILE)
    WE PICKED, TILL I FEARED YOU HAD WANDERED A MILE, . . . 62 BLUEBERRIES   92
    THREE HOURS TO DO FOUR MILES--A MILE AN HOUR . . . . . 145 SNOW   58
    SCARCELY A MILE BUT THAT I COME ON ONE, ... 171 NEW HAMPSHIRE 390
    MORE THAN A MILE ACROSS THE WILDERNESS . . . . 195 PAUL'S WIFE 132
    OF COURSE THE BOTTLE FELL SHORT BY A MILE, ... 195 PAUL'S WIFE 142
    IN DUST ONCE MORE. WE FOLLOWED THIS A MILE, ... 215 A FOUNTAIN, A BOTTLE . 67
    AT HOW SLOW I DO A MILE, ... 465 SOME SCIENCE FICTION . 10
MILES
    A HUNDRED MILES AWAY. . . . . 11 WIND AND WINDOW FLOWER 28
    THAN ON HIS BROTHER? THIRTEEN LITTLE MILES . . . . . . 38 DEATH OF THE HIRED MAN 125
    THAT'S FIVE MILES BACK. YOU CAN'T MISTAKE THE PLACE: . . 41 THE MOUNTAIN 41
    CUT SHORT OFF AT BOTH ENDS. IT LIES FIVE MILES . . . . 63 A SERVANT TO SERVANTS   21
    WE USED TO LIVE--TEN MILES FROM ANYWHERE. . . . . . . 64 A SERVANT TO SERVANTS   63
    SO MANY MILES YOU MIGHT HAVE WALKED YOU WON'T WALK. . . 93 THE SELF-SEEKER . . .   12
    AND FILL ANOTHER WITH 'EM FIFTEEN MILES AWAY, ... 116 IN THE HOME STRETCH . 161
    THAT EVERYONE FOR MILES COULD SEE . . . . 137 BROWN'S DESCENT . . .   2
    (TWO MILES IT WAS) TO HIS ABODE. . . . . 139 BROWN'S DESCENT . . .   48
    BY ROAD, A MATTER OF SEVERAL MILES. . . . . 140 BROWN'S DESCENT . . .   76
    AND SET ME FIVE MILES ON MY ROAD . . . . 140 THE GUM-GATHERER . .   3
    THREE HOURS TO DO FOUR MILES--A MILE AN HOUR . . . . . 145 SNOW   58
    AND THREE MILES MORE TO GO!" / "DON'T LET HIM GO. . . . 145 SNOW   62
    IN WOODS SOME TEN MILES FROM A RAILROAD STATION, . . . 160 NEW HAMPSHIRE   41
    A HUNDRED SQUARE MILES ROUND IT IN THE MOUNTAINS: . . . 174 THE CENSUS-TAKER . .   5
    NONE IN THE HUNDRED MILES, NONE IN THE HOUSE, ... 174 THE CENSUS-TAKER . .   11
    NOT ALL THE MILES IT MAY HAVE THOUGHT IT WENT, ... 188 THE GRINDSTONE . . .   6
    "YOU MEAN MILES FROM THE MORMON SETTLEMENT? . . . . . 214 A FOUNTAIN, A BOTTLE . 48
    AND MILES TO GO BEFORE I SLEEP, ... 225 STOPPING BY WOODS . . 15
    AND MILES TO GO BEFORE I SLEEP. . . . . 225 STOPPING BY WOODS . . 16
    THE MILES AND MILES HE LIVED FROM ANYWHERE . . . . . . 292 FIGURE IN THE DOORWAY. 11
    I SKIRTED THE MARGIN ALDERS FOR MILES AND MILES . . . 342 QUEST OF PURPLE-FRINGED 5
    AND SHARING HIS MILES OF EXERCISE. . . . . 420 ONE MORE BREVITY . .   43
    AND FOR MILES AND MILES . . . . 437 KITTY HAWK 288
MILITATE
    THAT MADE THEM MILITATE. . . . . 387 THE COURAGE TO BE NEW   12
MILK
    HER UDDER SHRIVELS AND THE MILK GOES DRY. . . . . . . 125 THE COW IN APPLE TIME. 11
    THAT AS A WITCH I'D OFTEN MILK A BAT . . . . 208 PAUPER WITCH OF GRAFTON 40
    OR MILK THE COW, HE VISITED THE FRUIT, ... 283 THE GOLD HESPERIDEE .   20
    IF NOT, A GLASS OF MILK WILL BE ALL RIGHT." . . . . . 368 THE LITERATE FARMER AND 22
    WITH MILK AND HONEY, IT IS BITTER MILK, ... 411 POD OF THE MILKWEED .   16
MILKING
    HAVEN'T COME DOWN TO THE BARS AT MILKING TIME? . . . . 43 THE MOUNTAIN   86
    WHO ROSE FROM THE MILKING STOOL WITH A CURSE . . . . . 463 LINES IN DEJECTION . . 15
MILKWEED
    THE MILKWEED BRINGS UP TO MY VERY DOOR . . . . 411 POD OF THE MILKWEED .   5
    POD OF THE MILKWEED . . . . 411 POD OF THE MILKWEED .   T

PAGE TITLE   LINE

MILKY
  THE MILKY WAY IS A COWPATH . . . . 464 MILKY WAY IS A COWPATH . . T
  THE MILKY WAY PERHAPS . . . . 464 MILKY WAY IS A COWPATH . . 15
  ALONG THE MILKY WAY . . . . 465 MILKY WAY IS A COWPATH . . 31
MILL
  I DROPPED IN AT THE MILL AND WAS DETAINED." . . . . . 96 THE SELF-SEEKER . . . 100
  THE RED MAN GAVE IN POKING ABOUT THE MILL, ... 142 THE VANISHING RED . . 15
  THE ONLY DECENT TREE HAD BEEN TO MILL . . . . 171 NEW HAMPSHIRE . . . 376
  THE SWINGING MILL BELL CHANGED ITS RATE . . . . . . 273 A LONE STRIKER . . 1
  THE STRAINING MILL BEGAN TO SHAKE. . . . . 273 A LONE STRIKER . . 10
  THE MILL, THOUGH MANY-MANY-EYED, ... 273 A LONE STRIKER . . 11
  OR DOWN A MINE OR AT THE MILL (I MET HIM) . . . . . 289 OLD BARN AT THE BOTTOM 18
MILLENNIUM
  (PERHAPS IT WILL BE NEXT MILLENNIUM.) . . . . 353 THE LESSON FOR TODAY . 103
  THAT THE MILLENNIUM TO WHICH YOU BEND . . . . 359 THE LOST FOLLOWER . . 27
  THE TRUE MILLENNIUM, ... 361 ALMOST TWO THOUSAND . 6
MILLENNIUM'S
  ONE MORE MILLENNIUM'S ABOUT TO END. . . . . 352 THE LESSON FOR TODAY . 46
MILLER
  IN ACTON. AND THE MILLER IS SAID TO HAVE LAUGHED-- . 142 THE VANISHING RED . . 2
  DISGUSTED THE MILLER PHYSICALLY AS COMING . . . . . 142 THE VANISHING RED . . 17
MILLIKAN
  THAT MILLIKAN MOTE? . . . . 391 A WISH TO COMPLY . . 2
MILLION
  NEW YORK (FIVE MILLION) LAUGHS AT MANCHESTER, . . . 165 NEW HAMPSHIRE . . . 201
  TEN MILLION SILVER LIZARDS OUT OF SNOW! . . . . . . 237 A HILLSIDE THAW . . . 3
  WITHIN A MILLION YEARS OF AN IDEA. . . . . 293 AT WOODWARD'S GARDENS . 16
  A MILLION YEARS TO BE PRECISE-- . . . . 326 A MISSIVE MISSILE . . 5
  AS FIFTY MILLION YEARS AGO WE CAME-- . . . . 395 WHY WAIT FOR SCIENCE . 12
MILLIONS
  WAS COGNIZANT. HER HUSBAND WAS WORTH MILLIONS. . . . 163 NEW HAMPSHIRE . . . 136
  LET THE LOST MILLIONS PRAY IT IN THE DARK! . . . . . 521 A MASQUE OF MERCY . 726
MILLPOND
  FALLING IN LOVE ACROSS THE TWILIGHT MILLPOND. . . . 195 PAUL'S WIFE 131
MILLS
  TEN MILLS . . . . 308 TEN MILLS . . . . . T
MILLSTONE
  OVER THE GREAT BIG THUMPING, SHUFFLING MILLSTONE, . . 142 THE VANISHING RED . . 16
MILTON
  "I GUESS SO," PIKE SAID, INNOCENT OF MILTON. . . . . 408 FROM PLANE TO PLANE . 136
  AS KEATS (OR WAS IT MILTON?) SANG . . . . 452 A-WISHING WELL . . 41
  LIKE THE ONE MILTON FOUND TO FOOL HIMSELF . . . . . 488 A MASQUE OF REASON . 416
MILTON'S
  MILTON'S PENTAMETERS GO ON TO SAY, ... 508 A MASQUE OF MERCY . . 380
MIND (SEE A-MIND)
  LIVING OR DEAD, WHICHEVER ARE TO MIND. . . . . . . 17 THE VANTAGE POINT . . 8
  AND THE MIND WHIRLS AND THE HEART SINGS, ... 21 THE TRIAL BY EXISTENCE 47
  I SHOULDN'T MIND HIS BETTERING HIMSELF . . . . . . 35 DEATH OF THE HIRED MAN 25
  HAROLD'S ASSOCIATED IN HIS MIND WITH LATIN. . . . . 37 DEATH OF THE HIRED MAN 78
  SILAS IS WHAT HE IS--WE WOULDN'T MIND HIM-- . . . . 39 DEATH OF THE HIRED MAN 140
  "YOU SAY 'UNLESS.'" / "UNLESS YOU WOULDN'T MIND . . 45 A HUNDRED COLLARS . . 23
  THAT I HAD ON MY MIND TO ASK THE FIRST . . . . . . 46 A HUNDRED COLLARS . . 46
  ON THE SIDEHILL. WE HAVEN'T TO MIND THOSE. . . . . 52 HOME BURIAL . . . 28
  BUT NEVER MIND, THE WELSHMAN GOT IT PLANTED . . . . 57 THE BLACK COTTAGE . . 68
  IT TOOK MY MIND OFF DOUGHNUTS AND SODA BISCUIT . . . 63 A SERVANT TO SERVANTS 26
  MIND YOU, I WAITED TILL LEN SAID THE WORD. . . . . 67 A SERVANT TO SERVANTS 149
  YOU WERE JUST TALKING WHAT WAS IN YOUR MIND, . . . 70 THE CODE 27
  TO RECONNOITER, AND THEN MADE UP HER MIND . . . . . 74 THE GENERATIONS OF MEN 31
  HE MUST HAVE CHANGED HIS MIND AND GONE TO GARLAND'S. 81 THE HOUSEKEEPER . . 17
  ALL IS, HE'S MADE UP HIS MIND NOT TO STAND . . . . 83 THE HOUSEKEEPER . . 70
  WAMPUM, I CALL IT. MIND, WE DON'T COMPLAIN. . . . . 86 THE HOUSEKEEPER . . 153
  YES. THANKS FOR CARING.--DON'T MIND WILL: HE'S SAVAGE. 100 THE SELF-SEEKER . . 224
  WITH GOOD LUCK WITH YOUR STOVEPIPE. NEVER MIND, . . 113 IN THE HOME STRETCH . 92
  DON'T MIND NOW. . . . . 116 IN THE HOME STRETCH . 159
  BUT SHE DON'T MIND NOW. . . . . 133 A GIRL'S GARDEN . . 20
  AND FAILED TO SEE THE GOOD OF. NEVER MIND, ... 147 SNOW 125
  AS IF TO PUT FOREVER OUT OF MIND . . . . 160 NEW HAMPSHIRE . . 42
  OF MIND AND STRONG OF ARM SHOULD FIT TOGETHER, . . . 164 NEW HAMPSHIRE . . 181
  "JUST ONE LOOK MORE WITH WHAT YOU SAY IN MIND, . . . 184 MAPLE 131
  HE HAD IN MIND TO SAY TO A BAD NEIGHBOR . . . . . . 185 THE AX-HELVE . . 16
  I SHOULDN'T MIND HIS BEING OVERJOYED . . . . 186 THE AX-HELVE . . 39
  THAT I CAN SEE. THE MIND--IS NOT THE HEART. . . . . 199 WILD GRAPES . . 99
  TO WISH IN VAIN TO LET GO WITH THE MIND-- . . . . . 199 WILD GRAPES . . 101
  WITH ANYONE BUT THAT SHE HAD A MIND TO, ... 200 PLACE FOR A THIRD . 13
  WHILE SHE MADE UP HER MIND HOW MUCH SHE CARED-- . . 201 PLACE FOR A THIRD . 55
  SHE COULD NOT TROUBLE HER MIND WITH TOO LONG, . . . 229 TWO LOOK AT TWO . 23
  WAS SOMETHING BRUSHED ACROSS MY MIND . . . . 248 A PASSING GLIMPSE . 9
  SHE HOPES TO CUT OFF MIND. . . . . 260 SAND DUNES . . 12
  WITH ALL I HAVE TO HOLD WITH, HAND AND MIND . . . . 267 THE ARMFUL . . 6
  HIS MOOD REJECTING ALL HIS MIND SUGGESTS. . . . . . 269 THE BEAR . . . 15
  I KNEW PRETTY WELL WHAT HE HAD IN MIND: . . . . . . 275 TWO TRAMPS IN MUD TIME 7
  LET HIM LIGHT ON YOUR SKIN UNLESS YOU MIND . . . . 278 THE WHITE-TAILED HORNET 28
  HE HAS A HALF A MIND TO START, ... 280 BLUE RIBBON AT AMESBURY 26
  WITH THOSE IN MIND AT MY BACK . . . . 282 A DRUMLIN WOODCHUCK . 9
  THE POLISHED TRAFFIC PASSED WITH A MIND AHEAD, . . . 286 A ROADSIDE STAND . 7
  ON THE HEART'S BEGINNING TO CLOUD THE MIND . . . . 290 ON HEART'S BEGINNING TO T
  BUT MY HEART WAS BEGINNING TO CLOUD MY MIND. . . . 291 ON HEART'S BEGINNING TO 13
  WHAT COMES OVER A MAN, IS IT SOUL OR MIND-- . . . . 305 THERE ARE ROUGHLY ZONES 7
  MAKE UP YOUR MIND TO DIE IN STATE. . . . . 307 PROVIDE, PROVIDE . 9
  NEVER MIND OF WHAT ACTUAL WORTH, ... 312 THE VINDICTIVES . . 83
  OH, MELIBOEUS, I HAVE HALF A MIND . . . . 316 BUILD SOIL . . . 26
  EXCEPT AS AN ABSTRACTION OF THE MIND. . . . . 318 BUILD SOIL . . . 71
  WE ARE BOTH ROUND BECAUSE THE MIND IS ROUND, . . . 322 BUILD SOIL . . 201
  I WILL GO TO MY RUN-OUT SOCIAL MIND . . . . 323 BUILD SOIL . . 237
  FOR MY MIND TO KEEP WORKING IN YOUR PRESENCE. . . . 325 BUILD SOIL . . 285
  AT LEAST DON'T USE YOUR MIND TOO HARD, ... 326 TO A THINKER . . 35
  THESE THINGS THE MIND HAS PONDERED ON . . . . . . 332 ALL REVELATION . . 8
  STRANGE APPARITION OF THE MIND! . . . . 332 ALL REVELATION . . 10

- 339 -

MIND (CONTINUED)
  HIS MIND TO THINKING ALWAYS OF THE END. . . . . 353 THE LESSON FOR TODAY . . 95
  I HAVE A MIND MYSELF AND RECOGNIZE . . . . 358 A CONSIDERABLE SPECK . . 30
  MIND WHEN I MEET WITH IT IN ANY GUISE. . . . . 358 A CONSIDERABLE SPECK . . 31
  ON ANY SHEET THE LEAST DISPLAY OF MIND. . . . . 358 A CONSIDERABLE SPECK . . 33
  YOUR MIND MISTRUSTED THERE WAS SOMETHING WRONG, ... 369 THE LITERATE FARMER AND 24
  ABOUT IT, THOUGH. WE HAVEN'T GOT THE MIND. . . . . . 372 THE LITERATE FARMER AND 133
  YOU MUST NOT MIND A CERTAIN COOLNESS FROM HIM . . . . . 377 DIRECTIVE 18
  NOR NEED YOU MIND THE SERIAL ORDEAL . . . . 377 DIRECTIVE 20
  IN BODY AND IN MIND, ... 387 THE COURAGE TO BE NEW . 6
  DON'T MIND A LITTLE THING LIKE THE ACTORS FIGHTING. . . 392 IT BIDS PRETTY FAIR . . 2
  BUT HIS MIND IS HARDLY OUT OF HIS TEENS: . . . . . . 393 A CASE FOR JEFFERSON . 8
  SO THAT THE MIND CAN BE ENTIRELY FREED. . . . . . . 395 ETHEREALIZING 4
  HE DON'T MIND HAVING LOST A CASE," PIKE SAID; . . . . 404 FROM PLANE TO PLANE . 25
  "I THINK I'LL CHANGE MY MIND." / "YOU'RE SAYING THAT . . 406 FROM PLANE TO PLANE . 75
  WHEN WE WOULD HAVE TO PUT OUR MIND . . . . 417 AMERICA IS HARD TO SEE 41
  DON'T TRY TO TELL ME WHAT'S ON YOUR MIND, ... 420 ONE MORE BREVITY . . 30
  TILL ACCIDENTALLY IT HIT ON MIND . . . . 425 ACCIDENTALLY ON PURPOSE 6
  MIND YOU, WE ARE MIND. . . . . 434 KITTY HAWK 200
  NEVER MIND WITH WHOM . . . . 436 KITTY HAWK 265
  FROM ALL THE FIGHTS YOU HAD A MIND TO LOSE. . . . . . 457 HOW HARD TO KEEP FROM 126
  TELL TISSAPHERNES NOT TO MIND THE GREEKS. . . . . . 461 HOW HARD TO KEEP FROM 227
  NO FATHOMING THE ASIATIC MIND. . . . . 462 HOW HARD TO KEEP FROM 265
  AND SOME OF THEM MAY MIND . . . . 465 SOME SCIENCE FICTION . 5
  I'VE HAD YOU ON MY MIND A THOUSAND YEARS . . . . . . 475 A MASQUE OF REASON . 47
  (JOB TAKES A FEW STEPS PACING.) DO YOU MIND? . . . . 485 A MASQUE OF REASON . 329
  BUT I DON'T MIND. LET'S LEAVE IT AS IT STOOD. . . . . 485 A MASQUE OF REASON . 334
  SHE DOESN'T MIND NOT OFFERING A DRINK . . . . 496 A MASQUE OF MERCY . 87
  HAD YOU IN MIND TO VISIT ON THE CITY, ... 502 A MASQUE OF MERCY . 224
  WE CAN ALL SEE WHAT'S PASSING IN YOUR MIND. . . . . . 503 A MASQUE OF MERCY . 255
MINDED (SEE FOOD-MINDED, OPEN-MINDED)
MINDS
  BUT BEFORE ONE IS IN IT, THEIR MINDS ARE TURNED . . . 54 HOME BURIAL 103
  WHAT WAS IN ALL OUR MINDS, AND YOU WEREN'T HINTING. . . 70 THE CODE 28
  THEIR MINDS RAN ON CRANNY AND CRACK. . . . . 311 THE VINDICTIVES . . . 31
  SOME MINDS ARE SO CONFOUNDED INTERMENTAL . . . . . . 321 BUILD SOIL 151
  TO STAY OUR MINDS ON AND BE STAID. . . . . 403 SOMETHING LIKE A STAR . 25
  YOU'RE DOING SOMETHING TO OUR MINDS. / I'M NOT.-- . . 504 A MASQUE OF MERCY . 285
  THE BEST MINDS ARE THE BEST AT PREMISES. . . . . . . 510 A MASQUE OF MERCY . 434
MINE---NOT INDEXED--EXCEPT FOR:
  WITH A MINE ON IT THAT WAS WORKED FOR GOLD; . . . . . 162 NEW HAMPSHIRE . . . 111
  THE POCKET OF A LITTLE TURTLE MINE. . . . . 270 THE EGG AND THE MACHINE 23
  OR DOWN A MINE OR AT THE MILL (I MET HIM) . . . . . 289 OLD BARN AT THE BOTTOM 18
  NEVER THE GOLD OF DARKNESS FROM A MINE. . . . . . . 358 THE LOST FOLLOWER . 4
MINERAL
  THE MINERAL DROPS THAT EXPLODE . . . . 388 MIDDLENESS OF THE ROAD 9
  AND ALL TANKED UP WITH MINERAL JUICE, ... 463 LINES IN DEJECTION . . 7
MINERVA'S
  MINERVA'S SNOW-WHITE MARBLE EYES . . . . 9 STARS 11
MINES
  NOT LABORED OUT OF MINES, ... 361 ALMOST TWO THOUSAND . 3
MINGLE
  WE DID THAT DAY WAS MINGLE GREAT AND SMALL . . . . . 118 MEETING AND PASSING . 5
MINGLED (SEE CLOVER-MINGLED)
  MINGLED WITH THESE, SMOOTH BEAN AND WRINKLED PEA), . . 124 PUTTING IN THE SEED . 6
  SO BRAD MCLAUGHLIN MINGLED RECKLESS TALK . . . . . . 176 THE STAR-SPLITTER . . 13
  THEIR BREATHING MINGLED WITH HIS BREATHING. . . . . . 274 A LONE STRIKER . . 41
  OF MINGLED BUTTERFLY AND FLOWER DUST . . . . 412 POD OF THE MILKWEED . 28
  WHERE GOOD AND BAD ARE MINGLED EVERY WHICH WAY, . . . 488 A MASQUE OF REASON . 408
MINIATURE
  WE HEARD THE MINIATURE THUNDER WHERE HE FLED, ... 223 THE RUNAWAY 6
MINISTER
  WE PAUSED, THE MINISTER AND I, TO LOOK. . . . . . . 55 THE BLACK COTTAGE . . 8
MINISTERS
  OF WORDS OR TOYS, IT MINISTERS TO HEALTH. . . . . . 321 BUILD SOIL 170
MINISTER-VIZIER
  BY MAKING ME YOUR MINISTER-VIZIER, ... 457 HOW HARD TO KEEP FROM 120
MINISTRY
  IN HER COMPLACENT MINISTRY OF FEAR, ... 395 WHY WAIT FOR SCIENCE . 2
MINOR
  A MINOR BIRD . . . . 250 A MINOR BIRD . . . T
  YOU HAD NO CHANCE BUT TO BE MINOR, DID YOU? . . . . . 351 THE LESSON FOR TODAY . 23
MINUTE
  THE MINUTE THEY HEARD MY STEP WENT STILL . . . . . . 123 PEA BRUSH 11
  HE'S GETTING UP A MIRACLE THIS MINUTE. . . . . . . 146 SNOW 84
  ARTISTS THE MINUTE THEY SET UP AS ARTISTS, ... 162 NEW HAMPSHIRE . . . 96
  AND BOYS THE MINUTE THEY GET OUT OF COLLEGE. . . . . 162 NEW HAMPSHIRE . . . 98
  HE WAS ALL DUTY TO HER IN A MINUTE: . . . . 191 PAUL'S WIFE 12
  THE MINUTE IT WAS LEFT WITH ME ALONE, ... 197 WILD GRAPES 43
  NEXT MORNING THE MINUTE I WAS ABOUT . . . . 420 ONE MORE BREVITY . . 44
  CUNNINGLY MINUTE. . . . . 426 A NEVER NAUGHT SONG . 20
  AND THERE WAS A MINUTE . . . . 427 VERSION 2
  A TENDENCY. THE MINUTE YOU GET ON ONE . . . . 489 A MASQUE OF REASON . 449
  WELL, YOU'RE AS GOOD AS IN NEW YORK THIS MINUTE-- . . 497 A MASQUE OF MERCY . 92
  ONE MINUTE, MAY I, PAUL?--BEFORE WE LEAVE . . . . . 501 A MASQUE OF MERCY . 216
MIRACLE
  HE'S GETTING UP A MIRACLE THIS MINUTE. . . . . . . 146 SNOW 84
  AND THEN WE WERE VOUCHSAFED THE MIRACLE . . . . . . 315 IRIS BY NIGHT . . . 20
  IT IS NO MIRACLE OUR MOOD IS HIGH. . . . . 423 FOR JOHN F. KENNEDY . 57
MIRACULOUSLY
  (MIRACULOUSLY WITHOUT TASTING FLESH) . . . . 109 THE EXPOSED NEST . . 15
MIRE
  WHERE WHEELS HAVE FRESHLY SLICED THE APRIL MIRE. . . . 225 BLUE-BUTTERFLY DAY . . 8
  THEY MUST BROOD WHERE THEY FELL IN MULCH AND MIRE, . . 253 THE THATCH 25
MIRED
  GOD KNOWS ALL THE COLOR AND FORM OF LEAVES I HAVE TRODDEN
    ON AND MIRED. . . . . 297 A LEAF-TREADER . . 2

MIRTH
    THEY WERE PIPES OF PAGAN MIRTH, ... 24 PAN WITH US   26
    I ALMOST PROVOKED POOR LOREN TO MIRTH . . . . 61 BLUEBERRIES   68
    THE WAY OF UNDERSTANDING IS PARTLY MIRTH. . . . . . 306 NOT QUITE SOCIAL . .   11
MISCELLANY
    HER CROP WAS A MISCELLANY . . . . 134 A GIRL'S GARDEN . . . 37
MISCHIEF
    SPRING IS THE MISCHIEF IN ME, AND I WONDER . . . . . 34 MENDING WALL 28
    THEY SOON SAW HE WOULD DO SOMEONE A MISCHIEF . . . . 66 A SERVANT TO SERVANTS 111
    I HOPE SHE ISN'T GETTING INTO MISCHIEF." . . . . . . 191 PAUL'S WIFE   15
    YOU WERE MORE GUILTY OF MISCHIEF THAN YOU ARE. . . . 488 A MASQUE OF REASON . 412
    THE THING THAT DID WHAT YOU CONSIDER MISCHIEF, . . . 505 A MASQUE OF MERCY . 317
MISCHIEVOUS
    WITH MISCHIEVOUS, VAGRANT, SERAPHIC LOOK, ...   16 IN NEGLECT   4
MISCHIEVOUSLY
    COULD MISCHIEVOUSLY LOCK HIM IN TO STAY. . . . . . . 290 OLD BARN AT THE BOTTOM 45
MISCONSTRUED
    AND HAVING HER EXPOSURE MISCONSTRUED. . . . . 386 THE FEAR OF MAN . . . 14
MISER
    OF CAPITAL, AND CALLING THRIFT A MISER). . . . . . . 363 AN EQUALIZER   4
MISERABLE
    A MISERABLE SIGHT, AND FRIGHTENING, TOO-- . . . . .   35 DEATH OF THE HIRED MAN 36
MISERY
    WE GET WHAT LITTLE MISERY WE CAN . . . . 167 NEW HAMPSHIRE . . . 272
    OUT OF NOT HAVING CAUSE FOR MISERY. . . . . 167 NEW HAMPSHIRE . . . 273
MISGIVING
    MISGIVING . . . . 236 MISGIVING . . . . .   T
    PIKE GRUNTED RATHER GRIMLY WITH MISGIVING . . . . . 405 FROM PLANE TO PLANE . 55
    OF A GREAT MISGIVING. . . . . 435 KITTY HAWK 229
MISGIVINGS
    WHO SAYS WE DON'T? WHO GOT UP THESE MISGIVINGS? . . . 483 A MASQUE OF REASON . 288
MISS
    TO OVERTAKE ME, WHO SHOULD MISS ME HERE . . . . . .   5 INTO MY OWN   11
    TO PICK WHERE NONE COULD MISS THEM . . . . 13 ROSE POGONIAS . . .   11
    WILL HIT OR MISS THE MOON." / IT HIT THE MOON. . . 40 DEATH OF THE HIRED MAN 161
    WHO ARE THEY FOR?" / "YOU MEAN?--OH, FOR SOME MISS. 81 THE HOUSEKEEPER . .   10
    DON'T STOP TO TRY TO NOW. YOU'LL MISS YOUR TRAIN. . 101 THE SELF-SEEKER . . 227
    BUT WHAT WE MISS WE GO TO HIM AND ASK FOR. . . . . 178 THE STAR-SPLITTER . . 50
    THREW ME DOWN GRAPES TO MISS AND SCATTER . . . . . 197 WILD GRAPES   32
    BEYOND WHICH THEY ARE DOOMED TO MISS. . . . . 328 A MISSIVE MISSILE . . 51
    FOR FEAR I WOULD MAKE HER MISS THE PLACE. . . . . . 342 A CLOUD SHADOW . . .   8
    I'M THINKING THE UNBORN WOULD NEVER MISS . . . . . 397 THE PLANNERS   2
    COLUMBUS, AS I SAY, WILL MISS . . . . 418 AMERICA IS HARD TO SEE 67
MISSED
    I NOTICED THAT I MISSED STARS IN THE WEST, ... 40 THE MOUNTAIN   3
    HIS TRAIN BEING LATE, HE MISSED ANOTHER TRAIN . . . 44 A HUNDRED COLLARS . . 15
    BUT SUPPOSE SHE HAD MISSED IT FROM THE CREED, . . . 58 THE BLACK COTTAGE . . 101
    SHE MUST HAVE MISSED HERSELF. SO THEY WERE MARRIED, . 182 MAPLE   95
    I MIGHT NOT HAVE THE CHANCE I MISSED IN LIFE . . . 222 TO E.T.   5
    BLINDLY STRUCK AT MY KNEE AND MISSED. . . . . 251 BEREFT   10
    AND, WITH A TOUCH THAT NEVER MISSED, ... 274 A LONE STRIKER . . . 31
    AT LAST IT WAS A FLY. HE SHOT AND MISSED; . . . . . 278 THE WHITE-TAILED HORNET 42
    BUT THE REAL FLY HE MISSED WOULD NEVER DO; . . . . 279 THE WHITE-TAILED HORNET 48
    THE MISSED FLY MADE ME DANGEROUSLY SKEPTIC. . . . . 279 THE WHITE-TAILED HORNET 49
    AND TWO WAS ALL HE COUNTED (ONE HE MISSED); . . . . 283 THE GOLD HESPERIDEE . 11
    OR MISSED THEIR CHANCE, OR NOT HAVE BEEN THEIR BEST, . 355 THE LESSON FOR TODAY . 152
    ENOUGH TO SEE IF HE WAS GREATLY MISSED. . . . . . . 368 THE LITERATE FARMER AND 18
    MIGHT NOT HAVE MISSED ME WHEN THEY SHOT AND FELL? . 383 BRAVADO   3
    TO MAKE SURE WHAT STAR I MISSED . . . . 384 MAKING CERTAIN ANYTHING 13
    THE BLINDMAN MISSED HIM WITH A BLOW SO VICIOUS . . . 394 HAEC FABULA DOCET . . 12
MISSES
    AS A CHILD MISSES THE UNSAID GOOD-NIGHT . . . . . . 58 THE BLACK COTTAGE . . 102
MISSILE
    A MISSIVE MISSILE . . . . 326 A MISSIVE MISSILE . .   T
MISSILES
    OUR MISSILES ALWAYS MAKE TOO SHORT AN ARC. . . . . 261 A SOLDIER   8
MISSING
    THE ATTIC WASPS WENT MISSING BY LIKE BULLETS. . . . 217 A FOUNTAIN, A BOTTLE . 130
    NOT EVEN MISSING THE CORALROOT FLOWER . . . . 247 ON GOING UNNOTICED . 15
MISSION
    CAN NEVER HOPE TO WAGE A GLOBAL MISSION. . . . . . . 398 NO HOLY WARS FOR THEM 12
    OF MY INCENTIVE--CANCELING MY MISSION. . . . . . . 499 A MASQUE OF MERCY . 148
    A MISSION AS TO HAVE TO TELL NEW YORK . . . . . . 503 A MASQUE OF MERCY . 272
MISSIVE
    A MISSIVE MISSILE . . . . 326 A MISSIVE MISSILE . .   T
MIST
    IS SILVER NOW WITH CLINGING MIST. . . . .   7 MY NOVEMBER GUEST . . 10
    BUT ALL CAME EVERY NIGHT WITH THE MIST; . . . . . . 15 IN A VALE   11
    RETARD THE SUN WITH GENTLE MIST; . . . . 27 OCTOBER   15
    WHEN THAT WAS, THE SOFT MIST . . . . 28 MY BUTTERFLY 18
    THE BLUE'S BUT A MIST FROM THE BREATH OF THE WIND, 60 BLUEBERRIES   25
    THAT SHOUTED IN THE MIST A MONTH AGO, ... 119 HYLA BROOK   5
    IN SNOW AND MIST . . . . 211 AN EMPTY THREAT . .   33
    AROUND WITH MIST AND CLOUD, ... 333 HAPPINESS MAKES UP .   3
    A MIST AND SMOKE EAVESDROPPING ON A HAZE-- . . . . 415 A CABIN IN THE CLEARING 39
    THAN SMOKE AND MIST WHO BETTER COULD APPRAISE . . . 415 A CABIN IN THE CLEARING 41
MISTAKE
    THAT'S FIVE MILES BACK. YOU CAN'T MISTAKE THE PLACE: . 41 THE MOUNTAIN 41
    I ASKED OUT LOUD, SO'S THERE'D BE NO MISTAKE. . . . 71 THE CODE   65
    THAT'S HIS MISTAKE. THE DEAR KNOWS MY INTEREST . . . 84 THE HOUSEKEEPER . .   87
    SO YOUR MISTAKE WAS OURS. HAVEN'T YOU HEARD, THOUGH, 132 THE BONFIRE 103
    SHE NODDED. SO WE'RE SURE THERE'S NO MISTAKE. . . . 180 MAPLE   19
    IT'S NOT MEN BY SOME MISTAKE? . . . . 211 AN EMPTY THREAT . .   21
    TO ASK IF THERE IS SOME MISTAKE. . . . . 224 STOPPING BY WOODS . . 10
    (MAKE NO MISTAKE ABOUT ITS BEING BONES); . . . . . 354 THE LESSON FOR TODAY . 132
    TO AVOID MISTAKE, ... 438 KITTY HAWK 317
    SOME MISTAKE HAD BEEN MADE . . . . 449 THE BAD ISLAND--EASTER 49

PAGE TITLE   LINE

MISTAKEN
    AS TWO IN WHOM THEY WERE PROVED MISTAKEN, ... 16 IN NEGLECT   2
    HE'LL FIND HE'S MISTAKEN. SEE HERE, FOR A WHIM, ... 61 BLUEBERRIES   80
    THEN WHETHER FROM MISTAKEN COURTESY   . . . . 106 CHRISTMAS TREES . . . 26
    AND DARWIN'S PROVED MISTAKEN, NOT THE BIBLE. . . . . . 369 THE LITERATE FARMER AND 46
    LIKE THE IDEAL OF SOME MISTAKEN LOVER. . . . . 391 ON BEING IDOLIZED . .   6
    UNLESS I'M MUCH MISTAKEN IN MYSELF . . . . 495 A MASQUE OF MERCY . . 62
MISTAKES
    THE MISTAKES OF ANCIENT MEN, ... 387 THE COURAGE TO BE NEW .   2
    BUT THOUGH ALMOST ALL-WISE, HE MAKES MISTAKES. . . . . 460 HOW HARD TO KEEP FROM 208
MISTED
    WITH CLOUDS LOW-TRAILING AND MOMENTS OF RAIN THAT MISTED. . 74 THE GENERATIONS OF MEN 20
MISTER
    "YOU'D SAY SO, MISTER MAN.--I'M A COLLECTOR. . . . . . 48 A HUNDRED COLLARS . . 95
    SHYLY BEHIND HER. / "WELL, AND HOW IS MISTER...?" . . . . 96 THE SELF-SEEKER . . . 96
MISTING
    "IT'S RAINING." / "NO, IT'S MISTING; LET'S BE FAIR. . . . . 75 THE GENERATIONS OF MEN 68
MISTRUST
    IF MY MISTRUST IS RIGHT   . . . . 333 HAPPINESS MAKES UP .   12
MISTRUSTED
    AND YES, SHE HAS LONG MISTRUSTED . . . . 134 A GIRL'S GARDEN . .   33
    BUT I MISTRUSTED HE WAS NONE TOO PROUD . . . . . . 209 PAUPER WITCH OF GRAFTON 74
    YOUR MIND MISTRUSTED THERE WAS SOMETHING WRONG, ... 369 THE LITERATE FARMER AND 24
MISTY
    BY A MISTY FEN THAT RANG ALL NIGHT, ... 15 IN A VALE   2
    THE SHATTERED WATER MADE A MISTY DIN. . . . . 250 ONCE BY THE PACIFIC .   1
    ONE MISTY EVENING, ONE ANOTHER'S GUIDE, ... 315 IRIS BY NIGHT . . .   1
MISUNDERSTAND
    MAY NO FATE WILLFULLY MISUNDERSTAND ME   . . . . . . 122 BIRCHES 50
    HE WON'T MISUNDERSTAND YOUR FREEST MOVEMENTS. . . . . 278 THE WHITE-TAILED HORNET 27
    AND BLOW A GALE. IT DIDN'T MISUNDERSTAND . . . . . . 349 OUR HOLD ON THE PLANET   3
MISUNDERSTOOD
    NOT BE MISUNDERSTOOD IN WHAT I MEAN. . . . . 386 THE FEAR OF MAN . . . 16
MITE
    IT NOT A MITE WORSE, SITTING HERE, WE THREE, ... 149 SNOW 189
    I REFUSE TO ADAPT MYSELF A MITE . . . . 166 NEW HAMPSHIRE . . . 234
    BUT UNMISTAKABLY A LIVING MITE . . . . 357 A CONSIDERABLE SPECK .   8
    IT SEEMED I WAS A MITE OF SEDIMENT. . . . . 468 IN A GLASS OF CIDER .   1
MIX
    THEY YELLING MIX TAG, HIDE-AND-SEEK, HOPSCOTCH, ... 318 BUILD SOIL 63
MIXED
    THE WAY HE MIXED THAT IN WITH OTHER THINGS. . . . . . 36 DEATH OF THE HIRED MAN 64
    THE FRUIT MIXED WITH WATER IN LAYERS OF LEAVES, ... 62 BLUEBERRIES 104
    IT WILL HAVE ROARED FIRST AND MIXED SPARKS WITH STARS, . . 130 THE BONFIRE 27
    MIXED READY TO BEGIN THE MORNING RIGHT, ... 302 DESIGN   5
    SO THE EFFECT WHEN THEY ARE MIXED ON CANVAS . . . . . 321 BUILD SOIL 149
MIXER
    WIND, THE SEASON-CLIMATE MIXER, ... 303 CLEAR AND COLDER . .   1
MIXTURE
    THE MIXTURE MECHANIC   . . . . 442 KITTY HAWK 4P
MIX-UP
    HOW IS THAT FOR A MIX-UP, THYATIRA?-- . . . . 485 A MASQUE OF REASON . . 337
MOAB
    IN OR NEAR MOAB . . . . 436 KITTY HAWK 262
MOAN
    ENOUGH TO MAKE A SPIRIT MOAN . . . . 328 A MISSIVE MISSILE . . 39
MOAT
    OUR MOAT AROUND US IS NO MORE A MOAT, ... 446 DOES NO ONE AT ALL EVER 17
MOATED
    OUR CONTINENT NO MORE A MOATED CASTLE. . . . . . . 446 DOES NO ONE AT ALL EVER 18
MOB
    SO AT TIMES THE MOB IS SWAYED . . . . 403 SOMETHING LIKE A STAR . 22
    FROM KING TO MOB TO KING TO MOB TO KING . . . . . . 459 HOW HARD TO KEEP FROM 160
    THE MOB MIGHT HOLD A MAN UP IN THE STREETS . . . . . 503 A MASQUE OF MERCY . . 250
MOBBED
    OR ELSE YOU WERE AFRAID OF BEING MOBBED . . . . . . 497 A MASQUE OF MERCY . . 104
MOBY
    ABOUT A WHALE. / OH, YOU MEAN MOBY DICK . . . . . . 495 A MASQUE OF MERCY . . 48
MOCK
    UNLESS IN BITTERNESS TO MOCK . . . . 238 PLOWMEN   3
    TO BID US A MOCK FAREWELL. . . . . 365 A NATURE NOTE 12
    COULD MOCK AT RICHES IN THE RIGHT IT CLAIMS . . . . . 509 A MASQUE OF MERCY . . 424
MOCKED
    "HOME," HE MOCKED GENTLY. / "YES, WHAT ELSE BUT HOME? . . 38 DEATH OF THE HIRED MAN 113
    PERHAPS HE MOCKED AT US FOR BEING WED, ... 127 THE SMILE   8
    MOCKED ME FOR AN ANSWER. . . . . 429 KITTY HAWK 39
MOCKING
    A SLEEPY SOUND, BUT MOCKING HALF, ... 25 THE DEMIURGE'S LAUGH .   8
    WAS BUT THE MOCKING ECHO OF HIS OWN . . . . 338 THE MOST OF IT . . .   3
MODERATE
    I'D WELCOME ANY MODERATE DISASTER . . . . 190 THE GRINDSTONE . . . 62
MODERATION
    WITH A BUYER'S MODERATION, "THAT WOULD DO." . . . . . 107 CHRISTMAS TREES . . . 38
MODERN
    HE WISHED IT ALL THE MODERN SPEED. . . . . 274 A LONE STRIKER . . . 51
    ALL MODERN, NOTHING ANCIENT IN'T, ... 328 A MISSIVE MISSILE . . 45
    AND SO BEGAN THE MODERN WORLD FOR US. . . . . 351 THE LESSON FOR TODAY . 18
    WITH WHICH THE MODERN WORLD IS BEING SWEPT. . . . . . 357 A CONSIDERABLE SPECK . 26
    TO ALL THE MODERN WORKS OF MAN . . . . 418 AMERICA IS HARD TO SEE 59
    WHO, HAVING FAILED OF THE MODERN SPEED, ... 419 ONE MORE BREVITY . . 12
    A TURNING POINT IN MODERN HISTORY. . . . . 422 FOR JOHN F. KENNEDY . 10
    ON THE GOSPEL OF MODERN SCIENCE. . . . . 466 SOME SCIENCE FICTION . 16
    YOU'RE MODERN; SO THE WHALE YOU THROW ME TO . . . . . 500 A MASQUE OF MERCY . . 186
    THIS MODERN TENDENCY I FIND IN HIM . . . . 505 A MASQUE OF MERCY . . 312
    THAT USHERED IN THIS MODERN LENIENCE, ... 505 A MASQUE OF MERCY . . 318
MODERNS
    SPACE AILS US MODERNS: WE ARE SICK WITH SPACE. . . . . . 352 THE LESSON FOR TODAY . 68

MOIST
    AND SMOOTH AND MOIST IN VERNAL HEAT. . . . . 276 TWO TRAMPS IN MUD TIME   48
MOISTURE
    MOISTURE AND COLOR AND ODOR THICKEN HERE. . . . . . 246 ATMOSPHERE   5
MOLD
    THE WIND WAS ANOTHER LAYER OF MOLD. . . . . 253 THE THATCH   12
    TO THE FRESH AND BLACK OF THE SQUARES OF EARLY MOLD . . 299 STRONG SAYING NOTHING .   9
MOLDED
    WHAT CAN'T BE MOLDED MUST BE CRACKED AND SPRUNG. . . . 267 WHAT FIFTY SAID . . .   6
MOLDING
    THE SOLID MOLDING OF VAST PEAKS OF CLOUD . . . . . . 169 NEW HAMPSHIRE . . . 322
MOLESTED
    YET NOBODY MOLESTED THEM! . . . . 135 LOCKED OUT   7
MOLTEN
    TIME WAS WE WERE MOLTEN, TIME WAS WE WERE VAPOR. . . . 380 TOO ANXIOUS FOR RIVERS   21
    WENT STREAKING MOLTEN DOWN THE WEST. . . . . 381 AN UNSTAMPED LETTER IN   27
MOMENT
    OF THINGS OF MOMENT TO WHICH, THEY WIST, ... 15 IN A VALE   13
    I DOUBT IF I WAS TEMPTED FOR A MOMENT . . . . 106 CHRISTMAS TREES . .   16
    ITS SEEMING BAD FOR A MOMENT MAKES IT SEEM . . . . . 115 IN THE HOME STRETCH . 128
    ON SUNNY DAYS A MOMENT OVERCAST; . . . . 120 THE OVEN BIRD . . .   8
    A MOMENT SOUGHT IN AIR HIS FLOWER OF REST, ... 126 RANGE-FINDING . .   7
    BUT IN A MOMENT NOT: A LITTLE SPURT . . . . 130 THE BONFIRE   23
    OF WIND THAT CAUGHT AGAINST THE HOUSE A MOMENT, . . . 143 SNOW   2
    WITH LOWERED EYES A MOMENT TILL HE SAID, ... 144 SNOW   32
    OR HAVING SEEN AND CREDITED A MOMENT . . . . 169 NEW HAMPSHIRE . . 321
    THEY HOVERED FOR A MOMENT NEAR DISCOVERY, ... 184 MAPLE 153
    HELD IT A MOMENT WHERE IT WAS, TO CALM ME, ... 185 THE AX-HELVE . . .   12
    THERE WAS A MOMENT OF SUSPENSE IN BIRTH . . . . . . 194 PAUL'S WIFE . . . 116
    A MOMENT HE STOOD BALANCING WITH EMOTION, ... 204 THE WITCH OF COOS .   71
    ALMOST THE MOMENT HE WAS GIVEN AN OPENING, ... 206 THE WITCH OF COOS . 115
    WE STOOD A MOMENT SO, IN A STRANGE WORLD, ... 233 A BOUNDLESS MOMENT .   9
    A BOUNDLESS MOMENT . . . . 233 A BOUNDLESS MOMENT .   I
    HE COULD HAVE SLEPT BUT A MOMENT MORE AT BEST. . . . . 235 VALLEY'S SINGING DAY   6
    TO SEPARATE US FOR A PANIC MOMENT. . . . . 259 WEST-RUNNING BROOK .   52
    THE PLACE FOR THE MOMENT IS OURS . . . . 264 THE LAST MOWING . .   15
    THEN FOR A MOMENT ALL THERE WAS WAS SIZE, ... 270 THE EGG AND THE MACHINE 13
    OR IF EVER ASIDE A MOMENT, THEN OUT OF SORTS . . . . 286 A ROADSIDE STAND .   8
    THERE CAME A MOMENT OF CONFUSING LIGHTS, ... 315 IRIS BY NIGHT . . .   4
    A MOMENT AND STILL ASKING GONE. . . . . 332 ALL REVELATION . .   9
    WHEREAT IN A MOMENT OF CROSS UNRUTH . . . . 346 DISCOVERY OF MADEIRAS . 96
    BUT IT WILL HAVE ITS MOMENT TO REFLECT. . . . . . . 356 TIME OUT   14
    EVEN IN A PLAYFUL MOMENT TO CONTEND . . . . 359 THE LOST FOLLOWER .   26
    AND FOR A MOMENT ALL WAS PLAIN . . . . 381 AN UNSTAMPED LETTER IN   36
    WE FEEL IT IN THE MOMENT WE DEPART . . . . 460 HOW HARD TO KEEP FROM 196
    THIS PERFECT MOMENT OF UNBAFFLEMENT, ... 461 HOW HARD TO KEEP FROM 238
    WE KNOW NOT WHAT WE OWE THIS MOMENT TO. . . . . . . 461 HOW HARD TO KEEP FROM 241
    IN OUR GREAT MOMENT WHAT DID YOU DO, MADAM? . . . . . 477 A MASQUE OF REASON . 117
    (HE DOESN'T RISE, BUT LOOKS AT HER A MOMENT.) . . . . 519 A MASQUE OF MERCY . 683
MOMENTOUS
    IN SUNLIGHT NEAR US IN MOMENTOUS SWING . . . . . . 361 A LOOSE MOUNTAIN . .   15
MOMENTS
    WITH CLOUDS LOW-TRAILING AND MOMENTS OF RAIN THAT MISTED. . 74 THE GENERATIONS OF MEN 20
    THE WASTE OF MOMENTS SLEEPING. . . . . 359 NOVEMBER   12
MOMENT'S
    ISN'T GIVEN A MOMENT'S ARREST-- . . . . 288 DEPARTMENTAL . . .   16
MONARCH
    I COULD BE MONARCH OF A DESERT LAND . . . . 58 THE BLACK COTTAGE . . 112
MONARCHIC
    MONARCHIC SOCIALISM, OLIGARCHIC-- . . . . 318 BUILD SOIL . . .   73
MONARCHY
    YOU OFTEN GET IT MOST IN MONARCHY, ... 318 BUILD SOIL . . .   75
MONEY
    TRYING TO COAX HIM OFF WITH POCKET MONEY-- . . . . . 35 DEATH OF THE HIRED MAN   28
    YOU'D BETTER TUCK YOUR MONEY UNDER YOU . . . . . . 47 A HUNDRED COLLARS . .   90
    'TWAS WE LET HIM HAVE MONEY, NOT HE US. . . . . . . 84 THE HOUSEKEEPER . . 101
    HE NEVER TAKES THE MONEY. IF THEY'RE WORTH . . . . . 86 THE HOUSEKEEPER . . 140
    TO SEE WHERE ALL THE MONEY GOES SO FAST. . . . . . 86 THE HOUSEKEEPER . . 159
    MONEY CAN'T PAY ME FOR THE LOSS OF THEM. . . . . . 95 THE SELF-SEEKER . .   72
    THAT WAS WORTH MONEY TO ME? STILL I OWN . . . . . . 95 THE SELF-SEEKER . .   82
    HE WANTS TO GIVE ME LOTS AND LOTS OF MONEY . . . . . 98 THE SELF-SEEKER . . 169
    WAS IT SOME MONEY SUDDENLY COME INTO? . . . . 264 THE INVESTMENT . .   10
    BUT FOR SOME OF THE MONEY, THE CASH, WHOSE FLOW SUPPORTS . 286 A ROADSIDE STAND .   5
    YOU HAVE THE MONEY, BUT IF YOU WANT TO BE MEAN, . . . 286 A ROADSIDE STAND .   14
    WHY, KEEP YOUR MONEY (THIS CROSSLY) AND GO ALONG, . . 286 A ROADSIDE STAND .   15
    AND ASK FOR SOME CITY MONEY TO FEEL IN HAND . . . . . 286 A ROADSIDE STAND .   19
    NO, IN COUNTRY MONEY, THE COUNTRY SCALE OF GAIN, . . . 287 A ROADSIDE STAND .   44
    NEVER ASK OF MONEY SPENT . . . . 309 HARDSHIP OF ACCOUNTING   1
    MONEY AND MANEUVER . . . . 430 KITTY HAWK   68
    "YOU'RE RIGHT," THE EX-KING SAID, "WE'LL NEED SOME MONEY. . 454 HOW HARD TO KEEP FROM   30
    AND HERE'S A LOT OF MONEY. WHO'S THE TAKER? . . . . . 455 HOW HARD TO KEEP FROM   46
    HE IS THE ONE WHO TOOK THE MONEY FOR ME . . . . . . 459 HOW HARD TO KEEP FROM 171
    IF SUCH A THING IS POSSIBLE WITH MONEY. . . . . . . 459 HOW HARD TO KEEP FROM 176
    UNLUCKILY IT WASN'T MONEY ENOUGH . . . . 459 HOW HARD TO KEEP FROM 177
MONEY-METAL
    TO LINK A CHAIN OF MONEY-METAL BANKS. . . . . 358 THE LOST FOLLOWER . .   8
MONKEY
    ARE GOING TO BE, UNLESS THESE MONKEY JOKES . . . . . 369 THE LITERATE FARMER AND 44
    IN AN ALBINO MONKEY IN A JUNGLE, ... 425 ACCIDENTALLY ON PURPOSE   7
MONKEYS
    ONCE SHOWED TWO LITTLE MONKEYS IN A CAGE . . . . . . 293 AT WOODWARD'S GARDENS .   2
    WHAT MONKEYS DID OR DIDN'T UNDERSTAND? . . . . . . 294 AT WOODWARD'S GARDENS . 34
MONKEYS'
    AND THE GLASS WAS THE MONKEYS', NOT THE BOY'S. . . . . 293 AT WOODWARD'S GARDENS . 23
MONOLITHIC
    GREAT MONOLITHIC KNEES THE FORMER TOWN . . . . . . 377 DIRECTIVE   11
MONOTONY
    BUT AS THROUGH THE MONOTONY WE RAN, ... 292 FIGURE IN THE DOORWAY .   5

MONSTER
   AND STRAINING HER RIBS FOR A MONSTER SIGH; . . . . 263 THE TIMES TABLE . . . 7
MONTAUK
   I WET ONE LAST YEAR AT MONTAUK . . . . 294 A RECORD STRIDE . . . 13
MONTH
   THAT SHOUTED IN THE MIST A MONTH AGO, ... 119 HYLA BROOK 5
   YOU'RE ONE MONTH ON IN THE MIDDLE OF MAY. . . . . . 275 TWO TRAMPS IN MUD TIME 20
   BETTER A MONTH FROM NOW WHEN CUTTING POSTS . . . . . 325 BUILD SOIL 287
MONTHS
   FOR MONTHS IT HASN'T KNOWN THE TASTE OF STEEL . . . . . 189 THE GRINDSTONE . . . 15
   AND YOU'RE TWO MONTHS BACK IN THE MIDDLE OF MARCH. . . . 275 TWO TRAMPS IN MUD TIME 24
   WE MUST WAIT TILL SOME MONTHS HENCE IN THE SPRING TO KNOW. . 305 THERE ARE ROUGHLY ZONES 19
   TO MONTHS AND YEARS AND MANY, MANY YEARS. . . . . . 355 THE LESSON FOR TODAY . 139
MONTREAL
   AND TELL ME WHERE YOU'RE OFF FOR--MONTREAL? . . . . . 125 AN ENCOUNTER 21
MOOD
   A CHANGE OF MOOD . . . . 221 DUST OF SNOW 6
   HIS MOOD REJECTING ALL HIS MIND SUGGESTS. . . . . . 269 THE BEAR 15
   LEAVES ARE ALL MY DARKER MOOD. . . . . 297 LEAVES COMPARED WITH . 20
   THAT LOOKS IN ONTO A MOOD APART. . . . . 385 A MOOD APART 8
   A MOOD APART . . . . 385 A MOOD APART . . . . T
   IT IS NO MIRACLE OUR MOOD IS HIGH. . . . . 423 FOR JOHN F. KENNEDY . 57
   GOD, PLEASE, ENOUGH FOR NOW. I'M IN NO MOOD . . . . . 486 A MASQUE OF REASON . . 366
MOODIE
   --THE MOODIE FORESTER . . . . 331 BEECH 13
MOODY
   THAT THOUGH REPRESSED AND MOODY WITH THE WEATHER . . . . 240 OUR SINGING STRENGTH . 51
MOON
   AND RISING FULL MOON, SIT ME DOWN . . . . 14 WAITING 6
   PREVENTING SHADOW UNTIL THE MOON PREVAIL; . . . . . . 14 WAITING 10
   WE RAN AS IF TO MEET THE MOON . . . . 18 GOING FOR WATER . . . 9
   LIKE GNOMES THAT HID US FROM THE MOON, ... 18 GOING FOR WATER . . . 14
   PART OF A MOON WAS FALLING DOWN THE WEST, ... 38 DEATH OF THE HIRED MAN 103
   WILL HIT OR MISS THE MOON." / IT HIT THE MOON. . . . . 40 DEATH OF THE HIRED MAN 161
   THE MOON, THE LITTLE SILVER CLOUD, AND SHE. . . . . . 40 DEATH OF THE HIRED MAN 163
   WHERE THE SUN SHINES NOW NO WARMER THAN THE MOON. . . . 106 CHRISTMAS TREES . . . 19
   HE CONSIGNED TO THE MOON--SUCH AS SHE WAS, ... 108 OLD MAN'S WINTER NIGHT 18
   SO LATE-ARISING--TO THE BROKEN MOON, ... 108 OLD MAN'S WINTER NIGHT 19
   IT IS BY THAT? OR BY THE MOON? THE NEW MOON! . . . . . 113 IN THE HOME STRETCH . 68
   AT DUSK TO WATCH THE MOON DOWN EARLY. . . . . . . 135 LOCKED OUT 13
   AS THE MOON USED TO SEEM WHEN I WAS YOUNGER, ... 197 WILD GRAPES 29
   AND MOON AND STARS, ... 219 I WILL SING YOU ONE-O . 40
   AND SO BE ADDED TO THE MOON UP THERE. . . . . . . 234 EVENING A SUGAR ORCHARD 10
   THE MOON, THOUGH SLIGHT, WAS MOON ENOUGH TO SHOW . . . . 234 EVENING A SUGAR ORCHARD 11
   THE SPARKS MADE NO ATTEMPT TO BE THE MOON. . . . . . 234 EVENING A SUGAR ORCHARD 14
   IT TAKES THE MOON FOR THIS. THE SUN'S A WIZARD . . . . 237 A HILLSIDE THAW . . . 18
   BY ALL I TELL; BUT SO'S THE MOON A WITCH. . . . . . 237 A HILLSIDE THAW . . . 19
   THE MOON WAS WAITING FOR HER CHILL EFFECT. . . . . . 237 A HILLSIDE THAW . . . 25
   I'VE TRIED THE NEW MOON TILTED IN THE AIR . . . . . 245 THE FREEDOM OF THE MOON 1
   THE FREEDOM OF THE MOON . . . . 245 THE FREEDOM OF THE MOON T
   MAKES THE NEW MOON LOOK ANYTHING BUT NEW . . . . . . 247 THE COCOON 3
   AND ANCHORING IT TO AN EARTH AND MOON . . . . . . 248 THE COCOON 14
   THE SUN AND MOON GET CROSSED, BUT THEY NEVER TOUCH, . . . 268 ON LOOKING UP BY CHANCE 4
   AND LOOK ELSEWHERE THAN TO STARS AND MOON AND SUN . . . 268 ON LOOKING UP BY CHANCE 9
   THE HARVEST MOON AND THEN THE HUNTER'S MOON. . . . . 289 OLD BARN AT THE BOTTOM 5
   WELL, THE MOON AFTER THAT, CAME ONE AT LAST . . . . . 289 OLD BARN AT THE BOTTOM 6
   AND A MASKED MOON HAD SPREAD DOWN COMPASS RAYS . . . . 300 MOON COMPASSES . . . 3
   MOON COMPASSES . . . . 300 MOON COMPASSES . . . T
   AND THEN THERE WAS A MOON AND THEN A SCENE . . . . . 315 IRIS BY NIGHT . . . 10
   THE MOON FOR ALL HER LIGHT AND GRACE . . . . . . 390 TWO LEADING LIGHTS . . 12
   BE UNINHABITABLE AS THE MOON. . . . . 400 THE BROKEN DROUGHT . . 12
   "AND THE MOON WAS FULL," . . . . 433 KITTY HAWK 167
   AT THE STARS OR MOON . . . . 442 KITTY HAWK 438
   I ONCE HAD A COW THAT JUMPED OVER THE MOON, ... 462 LINES IN DEJECTION . . 1
   NOT ONTO THE MOON BUT OVER. . . . . 462 LINES IN DEJECTION . . 2
   BUT IF OVER THE MOON I HAD WANTED TO GO . . . . . 463 LINES IN DEJECTION . . 9
   THAT OVERSHOT THE MOON. . . . . 464 MILKY WAY IS A COWPATH 20
   ESTABLISHING ON THE MOON. . . . . 466 SOME SCIENCE FICTION . 24
MOONLIT
   AT MOONLIT SKY AND MOONLIT EARTH. . . . . 290 ON HEART'S BEGINNING TO 4
MOON-MADE
   A VERY SMALL MOON-MADE PRISMATIC BOW, ... 315 IRIS BY NIGHT . . . 18
MOONS
   AND FILL THE SKY AS FULL OF MOONS . . . . 451 A-WISHING WELL . . . 17
   ARE SEEN TO JUGGLE MOONS GALORE. . . . . 451 A-WISHING WELL . . . 24
   DON'T YOU KNOW WHERE NEW MOONS ARE FROM? . . . . . 451 A-WISHING WELL . . . 31
MOON'S
   UPON THE FULL MOON'S SIDE OF THE FIRST HAYCOCK . . . . 14 WAITING 7
   IT WAS THE MOON'S: SHE HELD THEM UNTIL DAY, ... 238 A HILLSIDE THAW . . . 33
MOOR
   WHERE HE FELL A PRISONER TO THE MOOR. . . . . . . 347 DISCOVERY OF MADEIRAS . 128
   BUT THE MOOR STRANGELY ENOUGH BELIEVED . . . . . . 347 DISCOVERY OF MADEIRAS . 129
MOOSILAUKE
   "YOU HEAR THOSE HOUND DOGS SING ON MOOSILAUKE? . . . . 168 NEW HAMPSHIRE . . . 293
   ON MOOSILAUKE, BUT WOMAN SIGNS TO MAN, ... 210 PAUPER WITCH OF GRAFTON 94
MOPPING
   AS I SAT MOPPING HAYSEED FROM MY NECK, ... 72 THE CODE 81
MORAL
   THE MORAL IS, MAKE A LATE START TO MARKET. . . . . . 322 BUILD SOIL 181
   I MEAN SO ALTRUISTICALLY MORAL . . . . 354 THE LESSON FOR TODAY . 122
   THE MORAL IS, IT HARDLY NEED BE SHOWN, ... 394 HAEC FABULA DOCET . . 17
   MORAL . . . . 394 HAEC FABULA DOCET . . 1P
   THE MORAL KIND'S AS BRAVE AS FACING BULLETS." . . . . 405 FROM PLANE TO PLANE . 35
   FROM MORAL BONDAGE TO THE HUMAN RACE. . . . . . . 475 A MASQUE OF REASON . . 70
MORE
   ONLY MORE SURE OF ALL I THOUGHT WAS TRUE. . . . . . 5 INTO MY OWN 14
   HE ASKED WITH THE EYES MORE THAN THE LIPS . . . . . 7 LOVE AND A QUESTION . 5
   THAT, SILENCED BY MY ADVENT, FINDS ONCE MORE, ... 14 WAITING 20

		PAGE	TITLE	LINE
MORE (CONTINUED)				
ANYTHING MORE THAN THE TRUTH WOULD HAVE SEEMED TOO WEAK		17	MOWING	9
AND THE MORE LOITERING ARE TURNED		20	THE TRIAL BY EXISTENCE	25
TO VIEW ONCE MORE THE SACRIFICE		20	THE TRIAL BY EXISTENCE	26
SO THAT HENCEFORTH I WORKED NO MORE ALONE;		23	THE TUFT OF FLOWERS	34
ONE ON A SIDE. IT COMES TO LITTLE MORE:		33	MENDING WALL	22
OF COURSE HE'S NOTHING TO US, ANY MORE		38	DEATH OF THE HIRED MAN	115
WERE FIELDS, A RIVER, AND BEYOND, MORE FIELDS.		40	THE MOUNTAIN	9
WE CAN'T IN NATURE GROW TO MANY MORE:		41	THE MOUNTAIN	26
MORE THAN. A HUNDRED COLLARS, SIZE FOURTEEN.		47	A HUNDRED COLLARS	66
I'M THINKING I HAVE MORE TO LOSE THAN YOU		47	A HUNDRED COLLARS	82
YOU'LL HAVE TO PAY ME MORE THAN TEN A WEEK		48	A HUNDRED COLLARS	116
I'VE SPOILED JEMIMA IN MORE WAYS THAN ONE.		49	A HUNDRED COLLARS	141
ONE IS ALONE, AND HE DIES MORE ALONE.		54	HOME BURIAL	101
SINCE SHE WENT, MORE THAN EVER, BUT BEFORE--		56	THE BLACK COTTAGE	36
AND SAW NOTHING MORE OF EACH OTHER, OR HEARD,		62	BLUEBERRIES	87
I CAN'T EXPRESS MY FEELINGS, ANY MORE		63	A SERVANT TO SERVANTS	7
YOU LET THINGS MORE LIKE FEATHERS REGULATE		63	A SERVANT TO SERVANTS	36
IT WOULD BE DIFFERENT IF MORE PEOPLE CAME,		63	A SERVANT TO SERVANTS	39
LEN SAYS ONE STEADY PULL MORE OUGHT TO DO IT.		64	A SERVANT TO SERVANTS	55
NO MORE PUT OUT IN WHAT THEY DO OR SAY		65	A SERVANT TO SERVANTS	79
KEPT THEM AT HOME; AND IT DOES SEEM MORE HUMAN.		65	A SERVANT TO SERVANTS	96
BUT IT'S MORE LIKELY HE WAS CROSSED IN LOVE,		66	A SERVANT TO SERVANTS	108
AND THERE'S MORE TO IT THAN JUST WINDOW VIEWS		67	A SERVANT TO SERVANTS	155
MORE THAN YOU HAVE YOURSELF, SOME OF THESE NIGHTS.		67	A SERVANT TO SERVANTS	167
IS SET ME BACK A LITTLE MORE BEHIND.		68	A SERVANT TO SERVANTS	175
I SAID THAT MORE THAN HALF AN HOUR AGO.		70	THE CODE	13
IF BY SO DOING HE COULD GET MORE WORK		70	THE CODE	37
MORE THAN WAS NEEDED, SOMETHING MUST BE UP.		72	THE CODE	87
THEY EXCAVATED MORE. 'GO KEEP HIS WIFE		72	THE CODE	94
NO MORE THAN BROUGHT US BACK INTO THE NAME."		75	THE GENERATIONS OF MEN	57
A BEAD OF SILVER WATER MORE OR LESS,		77	THE GENERATIONS OF MEN	122
MORE OF THE SALT WHEREWITH THEY'RE TO BE SALTED.		80	THE GENERATIONS OF MEN	191
ONCE MORE BEFORE WE MEET ELSEWHERE." / "IN RAIN?"		81	THE GENERATIONS OF MEN	209
NOT ANSWERING YOUR KNOCK. I CAN NO MORE		81	THE HOUSEKEEPER	3
HE'D SAY, WHY SHOULD THEY?--NO MORE WORDS THAN THAT."		84	THE HOUSEKEEPER	91
HE'D SAY SHE DOES IT MORE BECAUSE SHE LIKES IT.		85	THE HOUSEKEEPER	109
THERE'S MORE IN IT THAN YOU'RE INCLINED TO SAY.		90	THE FEAR	30
"NOTHING." A PAUSE: THERE SEEMED NO MORE TO SAY.		91	THE FEAR	71
YET MORE I'D HATE TO HOLD MY TREES, EXCEPT		106	CHRISTMAS TREES	21
WORTH THREE CENTS MORE TO GIVE AWAY THAN SELL,		107	CHRISTMAS TREES	56
AND MIGHT OUR MEDDLING MAKE HER MORE AFRAID.		109	THE EXPOSED NEST	25
NO MORE TO TELL? WE TURNED TO OTHER THINGS.		110	THE EXPOSED NEST	32
MORE THAN SO MANY TIMES MAKE ME A LADY		111	IN THE HOME STRETCH	23
"WHAT I'LL BE SEEING MORE OF IN THE YEARS		111	IN THE HOME STRETCH	26
MORE THAN SOME WOMEN LIKE THE DISHPAN, JOE;		111	IN THE HOME STRETCH	31
MORE THAN YOU LIKE TO OWN TO OUT THAT WINDOW."		112	IN THE HOME STRETCH	45
IT WOULD TAKE MORE THAN THEM TO SICKEN YOU--		114	IN THE HOME STRETCH	123
ALTHOUGH YOU DO NO MORE THAN DUMP THEM DOWN."		116	IN THE HOME STRETCH	162
WHEN THERE WAS NO MORE LANTERN IN THE KITCHEN,		117	IN THE HOME STRETCH	201
BUT MORE THAN ONE AS YET. YOUR PARASOL		119	MEETING AND PASSING	8
TOWARD HEAVEN, TILL THE TREE COULD BEAR NO MORE,		122	BIRCHES	56
TO MAKE NO MORE OF A WALL THAN AN OPEN GATE,		124	THE COW IN APPLE TIME	2
AND THINK NO MORE OF WALL-BUILDERS THAN FOOLS.		124	THE COW IN APPLE TIME	3
DONE SO MUCH AND I KNOW NOT HOW MUCH MORE		130	THE BONFIRE	30
OF SOMETHING MORE THAN TINDER-GRASS AND WEED--		131	THE BONFIRE	77
NO MORE TO BUILD ON THERE. AND THEY, SINCE THEY		137	"OUT, OUT--"	33
NO MORE SO THAN BECAME A MAN--		139	BROWN'S DESCENT	69
AND THREE MILES MORE TO GO!" / "DON'T LET HIM GO.		145	SNOW	62
"FINE, FINE." / "AND READY FOR SOME MORE? MY WIFE HERE		147	SNOW	106
MORE THAN YOU WILL US WITH SUCH NIGHTMARE TALK.		149	SNOW	168
MORE LIKE A TUNNEL THAN A HOLE--WAY DOWN		149	SNOW	193
MORE THAN I SHALL OUT IN IT. BUT THE HORSES		150	SNOW	209
YOU'VE DONE MORE THAN YOU HAD A RIGHT TO THINK		150	SNOW	219
WHAT? WE'VE FOUND OUT IN ONE HOUR MORE ABOUT HIM		152	SNOW	252
WE'RE GLAD. OH, SAY NO MORE ABOUT IT, MAN.		155	SNOW	332
AND THEN TAKE OUR ADVICE NO MORE THAN NOTHING,		155	SNOW	347
MORE THAN ANOTHER NOISE		156	THE SOUND OF TREES	4
THEY'D BEEN THERE THEN A HUNDRED YEARS OR MORE.		161	NEW HAMPSHIRE	82
AS FOR WHAT THEY WERE UP TO MORE THAN FISHING--		161	NEW HAMPSHIRE	87
WHAT GOLD MORE INNOCENT COULD ONE HAVE ASKED FOR?		162	NEW HAMPSHIRE	115
MORE THAN ENOUGH LAND FOR A SPECIMEN		163	NEW HAMPSHIRE	145
CONSIDERING THE MARKET, THERE ARE MORE		164	NEW HAMPSHIRE	170
SO MUCH MORE BUSINESSLIKE THAN BUSINESSMEN.		164	NEW HAMPSHIRE	173
"I GO NO MORE TO SUMMER IN NEW HAMPSHIRE.		166	NEW HAMPSHIRE	221
OF ANYTHING MORE SOCIABLE TO SAY:		168	NEW HAMPSHIRE	292
THE MORE THE SENSIBILITIST I AM		170	NEW HAMPSHIRE	343
THE MORE I SEEM TO WANT MY MOUNTAINS WILD;		170	NEW HAMPSHIRE	344
MORE PRACTICAL THAN PEGASUS THE HORSE		173	A STAR IN A STONEBOAT	29
PERHAPS THE WIND THE MORE WITHOUT THE HELP		175	THE CENSUS-TAKER	25
MORE BLAMELESS IN THE SENSE OF BEING LESS		177	THE STAR-SPLITTER	23
LOOKS FOR HIMSELF, MORE OR LESS OUTWARDLY.		182	MAPLE	71
"JUST ONE LOOK MORE WITH WHAT YOU SAY IN MIND,		184	MAPLE	131
WE ARE NOT LOOKING FOR IT ANY MORE."		185	MAPLE	162
AS LEAVING MORE TO NATURE AND HAPPY CHANCE.		185	MAPLE	169
THAT GOT HER NOWHERE; ONE MORE GRADUAL,		187	THE AX-HELVE	49
BAPTISTE WAS ANXIOUS FOR HER; BUT NO MORE		187	THE AX-HELVE	58
AND SOME OF IT ON NO MORE LEGS AND WHEEL		189	THE GRINDSTONE	12
HAS NOTHING ANY MORE TO DO WITH ME,		189	THE GRINDSTONE	21
THE THING THAT MADE ME MORE AND MORE AFRAID		190	THE GRINDSTONE	65
IT NEEDED A TURN MORE, I COULD HAVE CRIED		191	THE GRINDSTONE	72
AND THERE WAS ONE MORE NOT SO FAIR TO PAUL:		192	PAUL'S WIFE	35
MORE CUTTING AND HE HAD THIS IN BOTH HANDS,		194	PAUL'S WIFE	95
MORE THAN A MILE ACROSS THE WILDERNESS		195	PAUL'S WIFE	132
IN ONE WAY: YOU HAVE ONE MORE STEM TO CLING BY,		198	WILD GRAPES	70
AND PROMISE MORE RESISTANCE TO THE PICKER."		198	WILD GRAPES	71
WHO MARRIED HER FOR PLAYMATE MORE THAN HELPMATE,		200	PLACE FOR A THIRD	34
I GUESS HE FOUND HE GOT MORE OUT OF ME		209	PAUPER WITCH OF GRAFTON	76

MORE (CONTINUED)

    IN DUST ONCE MORE. WE FOLLOWED THIS A MILE, ... 215 A FOUNTAIN, A BOTTLE . 67
    AT HAVING EASED HER HEART OF ONE MORE COPY-- . . . . . 217 A FOUNTAIN, A BOTTLE . 135
    STILL MORE UNFETTERED, ... 219 I WILL SING YOU ONE-O . 43
    AND ONE THING MORE THAT WAS NOT THEN TO SAY: . . . . . 222 TO E.T. 11
    THE WAR SEEMED OVER MORE FOR YOU THAN ME, ... 222 TO E.T. 15
    AND SEE YOU PLEASED ONCE MORE WITH WORDS OF MINE? . . . . 222 TO E.T. 20
    SOMETHING MORE OF THE DEPTHS--AND THEN I LOST IT. . . . 225 FOR ONCE SOMETHING . . 10
    THERE IS MORE UNMIXED COLOR ON THE WING . . . . 225 BLUE-BUTTERFLY DAY . . 3
    MORE THAN IF LIFE HAD NEVER BEEN BEGUN. . . . . . . 226 THE ONSET 11
    DREAD FIFTY ABOVE MORE THAN FIFTY BELOW." . . . . . . 228 GOOD-BY AND KEEP COLD . 19
    "GOOD-NIGHT TO WOODS." BUT NOT SO; THERE WAS MORE. . . . 229 TWO LOOK AT TWO . . 14
    "THIS, THEN, IS ALL. WHAT MORE IS THERE TO ASK?" . . . . 229 TWO LOOK AT TWO . . 25
    SHE DARED NO MORE THAN ASK HIM WITH HER EYES . . . . . 231 NOT TO KEEP . . . 19
    AND SEND MORE SPARKS UP CHIMNEY WITH THE SMOKE." . . . . 234 EVENING A SUGAR ORCHARD 6
    HE COULD HAVE SLEPT BUT A MOMENT MORE AT BEST. . . . . 235 VALLEY'S SINGING DAY . 6
    IN SPRING MORE MORTAL SINGERS THAN BELONG . . . . . . 239 OUR SINGING STRENGTH . 19
    NO MORE IT OPENED WITH ALL ONE END . . . . 241 NEED OF BEING VERSED . 9
    THEIR MURMUR MORE LIKE THE SIGH WE SIGH . . . . 242 NEED OF BEING VERSED . 15
    THERE WOULD BE MORE THAN OCEAN-WATER BROKEN . . . . . 250 ONCE BY THE PACIFIC . 13
    WHEN IT SEEMED AS IF I COULD BEAR NO MORE. . . . . . 250 A MINOR BIRD 4
    AND NOW IT IS ONCE MORE THE TIDAL WAVE . . . . 255 THE FLOOD 12
    IT IS YOUR BROOK! I HAVE NO MORE TO SAY." . . . . . . 259 WEST-RUNNING BROOK . 36
    AND BE BUT MORE FREE TO THINK . . . . 261 SAND DUNES 15
    FOR THE ONE MORE CAST-OFF SHELL. . . . . 261 SAND DUNES 16
    HAVE GATHERED PEOPLE TO US MORE AND MORE . . . . . . 262 IMMIGRANTS 2
    MORE THAN HALFWAY UP THE PASS . . . . 263 THE TIMES TABLE . . . 1
    IT'S NO MORE MEN I'M AFRAID OF; . . . . 264 THE LAST MOWING . . 13
    I CATCH NO MORE THAN A RAY . . . . 266 SITTING BY A BUSH . . 2
    MAN ACTS MORE LIKE THE POOR BEAR IN A CAGE, ... 269 THE BEAR 13
    THESE TWO MUST MAKE ME LOVE IT MORE . . . . 276 TWO TRAMPS IN MUD TIME 42
    HE COMES OUT MORE UNERRING THAN A BULLET. . . . . . 277 THE WHITE-TAILED HORNET 6
    AND STILL MORE SECURE AND SNUG, ... 282 A DRUMLIN WOODCHUCK . 7
    ONE MORE, HE THOUGHT, TO TAKE HIM SAFELY THROUGH. . . . 283 THE GOLD HESPERIDEE . 26
    NEXT MORNING TO THE LIGHT OF DAY WAS MORE . . . . . 290 OLD BARN AT THE BOTTOM 26
    I SHOULD FIND IT NO MORE NO LESS INTENSE. . . . . . 291 ON HEART'S BEGINNING TO 20
    AND MORE THAN ONE, TO THEIRS AKIN, ... 292 ON HEART'S BEGINNING TO 39
    THE ALREADY KNOWN HAD ONCE MORE BEEN CONFIRMED . . . . 293 AT WOODWARD'S GARDENS . 18
    SEEING MYSELF WELL LOST ONCE MORE, I SIGHED, ... 295 LOST IN HEAVEN . . . 9
    WILL BE MORE LONELY ERE IT WILL BE LESS-- . . . . . 296 DESERT PLACES . . . 10
    ALL SUMMER LONG THEY WERE OVERHEAD, MORE LIFTED UP THAN I. . 297 A LEAF-TREADER . . . 5
    A SHADE MORE THE COLOR OF SNOW. . . . . 299 WELCOME TO THEIR BELIEF 12
    THERE IS SELDOM MORE THAN A MAN TO A HARROWED PIECE. . . 299 STRONG SAYING NOTHING . 5
    THOUGH THERE'S MORE THAN A DOUBT IF THE WEATHER IS NOT TOO
        COLD . . . . 300 STRONG SAYING NOTHING . 11
    THE LAND MAY VARY MORE; . . . . 301 NEITHER OUT FAR NOR IN 9
    HAD MADE IT MUCH MORE EASILY A PREY. . . . . 303 A BIRD SINGING IN SLEEP 14
    BUT WE CAN'T HELP FEELING MORE THAN A LITTLE BETRAYED . . 305 THERE ARE ROUGHLY ZONES 15
    FOR MERELY GIVING YOU ONCE MORE GENTLE PROOF . . . . . 306 NOT QUITE SOCIAL . . 6
    THAT THE CITY'S HOLD ON A MAN IS NO MORE TIGHT . . . . 306 NOT QUITE SOCIAL . . 7
    TO HIS SUBJECTS TO GATHER THEM MORE. . . . . 310 THE VINDICTIVES . . 11
    BUT WHEN THERE SEEMED NO MORE TO BRING, ... 310 THE VINDICTIVES . . 14
    THEY GAVE NO MORE THOUGHT TO THE KING. . . . . . . 311 THE VINDICTIVES . . 27
    POETRY, ITSELF ONCE MORE, IS BACK IN LOVE. . . . . . 318 BUILD SOIL 89
    BUT DON'T YOU THINK MORE SHOULD BE SOCIALIZED . . . . 319 BUILD SOIL 92
    AND SHALL BE MORE BEFORE WE'RE DONE WITH IT. . . . . 319 BUILD SOIL 118
    THERE IS STILL MORE WE NEVER BRING OR SHOULD BRING; . . . 321 BUILD SOIL 174
    MORE THAT SHOULD BE KEPT BACK--THE SOIL FOR INSTANCE, . . 321 BUILD SOIL 175
    THE WORLD'S SIZE HAS NO MORE TO DO WITH US . . . . . 322 BUILD SOIL 198
    TO BUILD THE SOIL. FOR WHAT IS MORE ACCURSED . . . . 323 BUILD SOIL 217
    WHAT CRIES MORE TO OUR KIND FOR SYMPATHY? . . . . . 323 BUILD SOIL 219
    UNTIL IT CAN CONTAIN ITSELF NO MORE, ... 323 BUILD SOIL 235
    AS THE MORE ECONOMICAL PRODUCER, ... 324 BUILD SOIL 253
    MORE WONDERFUL, MORE BEAUTIFUL PRODUCER? . . . . . 324 BUILD SOIL 254
    ONE MORE WOULD THROW YOU ON THE RIGHT. . . . . . . 325 TO A THINKER 3
    AND SWAY WITH REASON MORE OR LESS. . . . . 326 TO A THINKER 28
    STILL LIVED FOR ONE SONG MORE . . . . 334 COME IN 11
    AND ALL THE MORE THE MIGHTIER THE SHOWER . . . . . 337 THE WIND AND THE RAIN . 35
    AND THERE IS ALWAYS MORE THAN SHOULD BE SAID. . . . . 337 THE WIND AND THE RAIN . 40
    HE MAY FUMBLE WIDE OF THE KNOB A YARD OR MORE, ... 342 WILLFUL HOMING . . . 11
    THE WAY SHE CLUNG TO HIM THE MORE . . . . 343 DISCOVERY OF MADEIRAS . 12
    IT DID MORE DISTANCE UP AND DOWN, ... 344 DISCOVERY OF MADEIRAS . 19
    WITH FAINT HEADSHAKINGS, NO MORE WISE. . . . . . . 344 DISCOVERY OF MADEIRAS . 40
    HE NO MORE DREW THE SMILE HE SOUGHT. . . . . . . 347 DISCOVERY OF MADEIRAS . 118
    SHE WAS OUR LAND MORE THAN A HUNDRED YEARS . . . . . 348 THE GIFT OUTRIGHT . . 2
    POSSESSED BY WHAT WE NOW NO MORE POSSESSED. . . . . 348 THE GIFT OUTRIGHT . . 7
    AND GIVE US MORE THAN OUR SPOKESMAN BARGAINED FOR; . . . 349 OUR HOLD ON THE PLANET 4
    AND IT MUST BE A LITTLE MORE IN FAVOR OF MAN, ... 349 OUR HOLD ON THE PLANET 15
    OR OUR NUMBER LIVING WOULDN'T BE STEADILY MORE, ... 349 OUR HOLD ON THE PLANET 17
    ONE MORE MILLENNIUM'S ABOUT TO END. . . . . 352 THE LESSON FOR TODAY . 46
    I HAD THOUGHT OURS THE MORE PROFOUND DISGRACE: . . . . 353 THE LESSON FOR TODAY . 79
    BEING ALREADY MORE THAN PROVED IN FIGHT, ... 353 THE LESSON FOR TODAY . 91
    YOU MUST BE MADE MORE SIMPLY WISE THAN I . . . . . 356 A MOTH SEEN IN WINTER . 19
    TO TRY IF ONE MORE POPULAR ELECTION . . . . . . 358 THE LOST FOLLOWER . . 12
    BUT IT MADE MY PROPERTY MINE ONCE MORE. . . . . . . 364 TRESPASS 20
    WE'LL MAKE IT THREE HUNDRED MORE . . . . 367 A SERIOUS STEP LIGHTLY 16
    ABOVE SOME MORE RELIGION IN A MANGER. . . . . . . 369 THE LITERATE FARMER AND 35
    "HERE COME MORE STARS TO CHARACTER THE SKIES, ... 370 THE LITERATE FARMER AND 75
    ARE MORE DIVINE THAN ANY BULB OR ARC, ... 370 THE LITERATE FARMER AND 77
    WERE ONCE MORE ON THEIR TRAVELS, ... 376 ONE STEP BACKWARD TAKEN 2
    THERE IS A HOUSE THAT IS NO MORE A HOUSE . . . . . 377 DIRECTIVE 5
    UPON A FARM THAT IS NO MORE A FARM . . . . 377 DIRECTIVE 6
    AND IN A TOWN THAT IS NO MORE A TOWN. . . . . . . 377 DIRECTIVE 7
    THEN FOR THE HOUSE THAT IS NO MORE A HOUSE, ... 378 DIRECTIVE 45
    THE SECOND MORE PECULIARLY YOUR OWN, ... 382 TO AN ANCIENT . . . 14
    TO GIVE THEM STILL MORE BUOYANCY IN FLIGHT. . . . . 387 INNATE HELIUM . . . 5
    THEY WILL TELL YOU MORE AS SOON AS . . . . 387 THE COURAGE TO BE NEW . 13
    OF GETTING ONE MORE CHANCE TO CHANGE OUR MANNERS? . . . 397 THE PLANNERS 12

PAGE TITLE   LINE

MORE (CONTINUED)
    THERE WAS SO MUCH MORE EVERY DAY TO LEARN, ... 398 BURSTING RAPTURE . . 6
    MORE THAN THEY KNOW WHAT COURAGE IS THAT CLAIM . . . . . 405 FROM PLANE TO PLANE . 34
    TO CURRY FAVOR WITH THE DIRT SOME MORE . . . . 405 FROM PLANE TO PLANE . 43
    YOU'D BET YOU GOT MORE WORK DONE IN A DAY, ... 405 FROM PLANE TO PLANE . 46
    WHAT'S MORE, I HATE TO KEEP AFFLICTING WEEDS. . . . . . . 406 FROM PLANE TO PLANE . 64
    THE SAME AS YOUR IDEA, ONLY MORE SO. . . . . 406 FROM PLANE TO PLANE . 81
    AND I SUSPECT IT MAY BE MORE AND MORE SO . . . . 406 FROM PLANE TO PLANE . 82
    FROM KNOWING MORE THAN I KNOW HOW TO THINK WITH. . . . . 407 FROM PLANE TO PLANE . 99
    I OWE THEM MORE TODAY . . . . 415 CLOSED FOR GOOD . . . 5
    A MORE THAN MOSES' EXODUS. . . . . 417 AMERICA IS HARD TO SEE . 36
    HE GOT NO MORE THAN DUNGEON CHAINS . . . . 417 AMERICA IS HARD TO SEE . 44
    ONE MORE BREVITY . . . . 419 ONE MORE BREVITY . . T
    AS IF BESEECHING ME, "PLEASE, NO MORE; . . . . 420 ONE MORE BREVITY . . 24
    AND MORE PREOCCUPATION WITH THE SPORT. . . . . 424 FOR JOHN F. KENNEDY . 69
    SHE WAS OUR LAND MORE THAN A HUNDRED YEARS . . . . 424 THE GIFT OUTRIGHT . . 2
    POSSESSED BY WHAT WE NOW NO MORE POSSESSED. . . . . 424 THE GIFT OUTRIGHT . . 7
    WHICH IS NO MORE THAN GOOD OLD PANTHEISM. . . . . 427 CONCEPT SELF-CONCEIVED . 4
    EVEN MORE ACCURSED . . . . 430 KITTY HAWK 76
    MORE THAN THAT MY THEME . . . . 431 KITTY HAWK 86
    ONE MORE FOND ALAS . . . . 431 KITTY HAWK 90
    BUT HER FATHER MORE-- . . . . 433 KITTY HAWK 151
    MORE THAN YOU CAN SING. . . . . 437 KITTY HAWK 280
    ANY MORE THAN WE HAD TO TO HATE, ... 444 THE DRAFT HORSE . . . 16
    OUR MOAT AROUND US IS NO MORE A MOAT, ... 446 DOES NO ONE AT ALL EVER 17
    OUR CONTINENT NO MORE A MOATED CASTLE. . . . . 446 DOES NO ONE AT ALL EVER 18
    WHERE I NEED LISTEN TO ITS ROTE NO MORE, ... 447 DOES NO ONE AT ALL EVER 34
    "AND ONE THING MORE THAT MAY NOT BE, ... 451 A-WISHING WELL . . . 4
    THE ONE THING MORE OF HIS CONCERN. . . . . 451 A-WISHING WELL . . . 9
    THE ONE THING MORE I WISH THERE WERE. . . . . 451 A-WISHING WELL . . . 11
    YOUR MOTHER'S FOLKS----" / HE STAYED TO HEAR NO MORE, . . 457 HOW HARD TO KEEP FROM 111
    THERE IS NO ACT MORE KINGLY THAN TO GIVE?" . . . . 458 HOW HARD TO KEEP FROM 140
    IN CASE I SHOULD DECIDE TO REIGN SOME MORE-- . . . . . . 458 HOW HARD TO KEEP FROM 148
    IT MAY BE WINE, BUT MUCH MORE LIKELY LOVE-- . . . . 461 HOW HARD TO KEEP FROM 242
    OF MORE THAN ROYAL ATTRIBUTES BETRAYED HIM. . . . . 462 HOW HARD TO KEEP FROM 274
    (OR MORE THAN HALF I'M HALF INCLINED TO SAY)." . . . . . 462 HOW HARD TO KEEP FROM 278
    AS THEY GET MORE NUCLEAR . . . . 466 SOME SCIENCE FICTION . 14
    AND MORE BIGOTED IN RELIANCE . . . . 466 SOME SCIENCE FICTION . 15
    STAYS MORE POPULAR . . . . 469 BUT OUTER SPACE... . . 5
    OR COURT OF LOVE. / MORE LIKELY ROYAL COURT-- . . . . . . 474 A MASQUE OF REASON . 25
    THAT'S ONE THING MORE TO PUT ON YOUR AGENDA. . . . . . . 478 A MASQUE OF REASON . 126
    I'D GIVE MORE FOR ONE LEAST BEFOREHAND REASON . . . . . . 482 A MASQUE OF REASON . 247
    IT WILL BE FOUND THERE'S NO MORE GIVEN THERE . . . . . . 483 A MASQUE OF REASON . 282
    'TWAS HUMAN OF YOU. I EXPECTED MORE . . . . 485 A MASQUE OF REASON . 331
    FOR MORE EXCUSES. / WHAT I MEAN TO SAY: . . . . 486 A MASQUE OF REASON . 367
    YOU WERE MORE GUILTY OF MISCHIEF THAN YOU ARE. . . . . . 488 A MASQUE OF REASON . 412
    MORE TO GIVE HIS REALITY ITS DUE . . . . 489 A MASQUE OF REASON . 433
    MORE THAN IT TOUCHES ME. / YOU MAY COME IN.. . . . . . . 493 A MASQUE OF MERCY . 17
    WHERE HE WAS HOARDING MORE THAN THEY ENJOYED. . . . . . . 503 A MASQUE OF MERCY . 254
    I'D WANT TO BE MORE CERTAIN I WAS CALLED, ... 503 A MASQUE OF MERCY . 270
    HE WROTE ONE BOOK. LET THERE BE NO MORE WRITTEN. . . . . 504 A MASQUE OF MERCY . 290
    (A WHOLE SHELF CASCADES DOWN.) HERE COME SOME MORE. . . . 506 A MASQUE OF MERCY . 341
    TO EASE THE MORE EXTREMELY WOUNDED OUT . . . . 507 A MASQUE OF MERCY . 370
    YOURS MORE THROUGH ROME, MINE MORE THROUGH PALESTINE.-- . 513 A MASQUE OF MERCY . 518
    THEN HOW MUCH MORE THE FACE OF TRUTH MUST BE. . . . . . . 515 A MASQUE OF MERCY . 585
    I SAY WE KEEP HIM TILL WE WRING SOME MORE . . . . 517 A MASQUE OF MERCY . 639
    BUT ONE THING MORE BEFORE THE CURTAIN FALLS.-- . . . . . 519 A MASQUE OF MERCY . 672
    I'M NO MORE GOVERNED BY THE FEAR OF HELL . . . . 520 A MASQUE OF MERCY . 702
    COURAGE IS WHAT IT TAKES AND TAKES THE MORE OF . . . . . 521 A MASQUE OF MERCY . 731
    AS IF I ASKED FOR ONE MORE CHANCE MYSELF . . . . 521 A MASQUE OF MERCY . 736
MOREOVER
    MOREOVER HER VOICE UPON THEIR VOICES CROSSED . . . . . . 339 NEVER WOULD BIRDS' SONG 10
    NEITHER WILL I SHOW. THAT'S TOO BAD MOREOVER. . . . . . . 490 A MASQUE OF REASON . 463
MORGAN
    A LITTLE MORGAN HAD ONE FOREFOOT ON THE WALL, ... 223 THE RUNAWAY 3
    THEN'S WHEN HIS MORGAN LIGHTS OUT THROWING SNOWBALLS . . 407 FROM PLANE TO PLANE . 107
MORI
    MEMENTO MORI AND OBEY THE LORD. . . . . 353 THE LESSON FOR TODAY . 96
    I HOLD YOUR DOCTRINE OF MEMENTO MORI. . . . . 355 THE LESSON FOR TODAY . 157
MORMON
    YOU WON'T SEE ANY MORMON SWIMMING IN IT. . . . . 213 A FOUNTAIN, A BOTTLE . 27
    "YOU MEAN MILES FROM THE MORMON SETTLEMENT? . . . . 214 A FOUNTAIN, A BOTTLE . 48
MORMONS
    THE EARLY MORMONS MADE A SETTLEMENT . . . . 213 A FOUNTAIN, A BOTTLE . 9
MORN
    THEY CLAIM THEY RECOLLECT THE MORN . . . . 452 A-WISHING WELL . . . 38
MORNING (SEE EARLY-MORNING, GOOD-MORNING)
    AND MORNING FOUND THE BREEZE . . . . 11 WIND AND WINDOW FLOWER 27
    I LEFT YOU IN THE MORNING, ... 12 FLOWER-GATHERING . . 1
    AND IN THE MORNING GLOW . . . . 12 FLOWER-GATHERING . . 2
    THE LIGHT FOREVER IS MORNING LIGHT; . . . . 19 THE TRIAL BY EXISTENCE 11
    BUT FROM SHEER MORNING GLADNESS AT THE BRIM. . . . . . . 23 THE TUFT OF FLOWERS . 28
    O HUSHED OCTOBER MORNING MILD, ... 27 OCTOBER 1
    O HUSHED OCTOBER MORNING MILD, ... 27 OCTOBER 7
    NOT FOR THIS MORNING, BUT SOME OTHER TIME: . . . . 41 THE MOUNTAIN 36
    WE'LL GO IN THE MORNING, THAT IS, IF IT'S CLEAR, ... 61 BLUEBERRIES 82
    A SUNNY MORNING, OR TAKE THE RISING WIND . . . . 63 A SERVANT TO SERVANTS 28
    I SKIMMED THIS MORNING FROM THE DRINKING TROUGH . . . . 68 AFTER APPLE-PICKING . 11
    AND BOTH THAT MORNING EQUALLY LAY . . . . 105 THE ROAD NOT TAKEN . 11
    THE FIRST THING IN THE MORNING, OUT WE GO . . . . 117 IN THE HOME STRETCH . 195
    LOADED WITH ICE A SUNNY WINTER MORNING . . . . 121 BIRCHES 6
    DOWN AT THE AVERYS'? WELL, ONE SUNNY MORNING . . . . . . 149 SNOW 175
    HELPLESS. "THERE'S NOTHING WE CAN DO TILL MORNING." . . 155 SNOW 325
    TO HEAVE THEM HIGHER TO THE MORNING STAR? . . . . 169 NEW HAMPSHIRE . . . 319
    BUT THE FIRST THING NEXT MORNING WE REFLECTED . . . . . 177 THE STAR-SPLITTER . 43
    TO KEEP HIS BARGAIN OF THE MORNING WITH ME . . . . 187 THE AX-HELVE 60
    I VERIFIED THE NAME NEXT MORNING: TOFFILE. . . . . 207 THE WITCH OF COOS . 154
    BUT YOU HAD AWAKENED UNDER THE MORNING STAR . . . . . . 235 VALLEY'S SINGING DAY . 4

	PAGE	TITLE	LINE
MORNING (CONTINUED)			
THE DEW OF NIGHT AND MORNING ON HIS BOOT.	283	THE GOLD HESPERIDEE	21
NEXT MORNING TO THE LIGHT OF DAY WAS MORE	290	OLD BARN AT THE BOTTOM	26
MIXED READY TO BEGIN THE MORNING RIGHT,	302	DESIGN	5
SOME MORNING FROM THE BOULDER-BROKEN BEACH	338	THE MOST OF IT	5
NEXT MORNING THE MINUTE I WAS ABOUT	420	ONE MORE BREVITY	44
MORNING-GLORY			
AMONG THE HARPLIKE MORNING-GLORY STRINGS,	38	DEATH OF THE HIRED MAN	107
MORNINGS			
'THREE FOGGY MORNINGS AND ONE RAINY DAY	54	HOME BURIAL	92
MOROSE			
NOT MAKE ME TIRED AND MOROSE	286	IN TIME OF CLOUDBURST	27
MORTAL			
IN SPRING MORE MORTAL SINGERS THAN BELONG	239	OUR SINGING STRENGTH	19
AND THE WORK IS PLAY FOR MORTAL STAKES,	277	TWO TRAMPS IN MUD TIME	70
WITH MORTAL LONGING MAY BESEECH;	328	A MISSIVE MISSILE	54
OBSCURED FROM MORTAL VIEW--	333	HAPPINESS MAKES UP	7
AND BRAIN IS ALL THAT'S LEFT OF MORTAL STUFF,	395	ETHEREALIZING	6
MORTALS			
WHEN REASON-HUNGRY MORTALS ASK FOR REASONS.	478	A MASQUE OF REASON	136
OUR MAKING ALL THIS EFFORT MORTALS MAKE?	517	A MASQUE OF MERCY	635
MORTGAGE			
SUCH AS IT IS. IT ISN'T WORTH THE MORTGAGE."	84	THE HOUSEKEEPER	97
MORTGAGED			
WHO SLEEP IN HOUSES OF THEIR OWN, THOUGH MORTGAGED.	290	OLD BARN AT THE BOTTOM	31
MORTICIAN			
APPEARS A SOLEMN MORTICIAN;	288	DEPARTMENTAL	34
MOSES'			
A MORE THAN MOSES' EXODUS.	417	AMERICA IS HARD TO SEE	36
MOSS			
THE GRAY OF THE MOSS OF WALLS WERE THEY--	23	PAN WITH US	3
(THE WAY IT IS WILL DO FOR MOSS.)	140	THE GUM-GATHERER	18
MOSSES			
DOUBTLESS BEAR NAMES THAT THE MOSSES MAR.	6	GHOST HOUSE	25
UP WHERE THE TREES GROW SHORT, THE MOSSES TALL,	210	PAUPER WITCH OF GRAFTON	96
MOST			
BUT ON THE MEMORY OF ONE ABSENT, MOST,	15	WAITING	26
OFF HE GOES ALWAYS WHEN I NEED HIM MOST.	35	DEATH OF THE HIRED MAN	18
HE WANTED TO GO OVER THAT. BUT MOST OF ALL	37	DEATH OF THE HIRED MAN	85
MOST OF THE CHANGE WE THINK WE SEE IN LIFE	58	THE BLACK COTTAGE	109
MOST LIKELY I'D HAVE SERVED YOU JUST THE SAME.	70	THE CODE	25
AND MAKE THE MOST OF IT FOR BETTER OR WORSE.	161	NEW HAMPSHIRE	65
SHE'S STILL NEW HAMPSHIRE, A MOST RESTFUL STATE.	170	NEW HAMPSHIRE	357
BUT MOST WOULD HAVE TO THINK OF THE EXPENSE.	208	PAUPER WITCH OF GRAFTON	38
AND YET TOO READY TO BELIEVE THE MOST.	233	A BOUNDLESS MOMENT	4
AT MOST HE THINKS OR TWITTERS SOFTLY, "SAFE!	249	ACCEPTANCE	11
AND THING NEXT MOST DIFFUSE TO CLOUD,	251	TREE AT MY WINDOW	6
SO THAT THE FALL OF MOST OF IT IS ALWAYS	259	WEST-RUNNING BROOK	62
AGAINST THE STREAM, THAT MOST WE SEE OURSELVES IN,	260	WEST-RUNNING BROOK	69
IT IS MOST US." / "TODAY WILL BE THE DAY	260	WEST-RUNNING BROOK	72
THE TIME WHEN MOST I LOVED MY TASK	276	TWO TRAMPS IN MUD TIME	41
THE GREAT TREASURE WANTED THE MOST,	312	THE VINDICTIVES	62
YOU OFTEN GET IT MOST IN MONARCHY,	318	BUILD SOIL	75
THE MOST OF IT	338	THE MOST OF IT	T
LOOKED, OR AT MOST	343	QUEST OF PURPLE-FRINGED	22
THE MOST HE ASKED HER EYES TO GRANT	344	DISCOVERY OF MADEIRAS	41
THE MOST EFFICIENT HELP YOU EVER HIRED	375	A YOUNG BIRCH	17
RELIGIOUS FAITH IS A MOST FILLING VAPOR.	386	INNATE HELIUM	1
MOST OF ALL THE MASS PRODUCTION	396	AN IMPORTER	11
THE MOST PRIMITIVE OF ENGINES	397	AN IMPORTER	23
NO HOLY WARS FOR THEM. THE MOST THE SMALL	398	NO HOLY WARS FOR THEM	13
OR AT MOST SOME ANDEAN QUAKE.	418	AMERICA IS HARD TO SEE	71
ONLY A FRACTION OF OURS AT MOST.	421	ONE MORE BREVITY	52
TO THE MOST REMOTE	439	KITTY HAWK	366
THE MOST UNQUESTIONING PAIR	444	THE DRAFT HORSE	13
MOST OF THEM LET GO AND WERE GONE.	452	A-WISHING WELL	54
FOUND OUT THE DISCIPLINE MAN NEEDED MOST	481	A MASQUE OF REASON	209
BUT ALL THE TIME IT'S WHAT WE'RE MOST CONCERNED WITH.	481	A MASQUE OF REASON	229
OF WHAT I VALUED MOST IN HUMAN NATURE.	485	A MASQUE OF REASON	350
A QUESTION WHO WAS GETTING THE MOST OUT	503	A MASQUE OF MERCY	248
AND THE MOST SACRED THING OF ALL'S ABRUPTION.	510	A MASQUE OF MERCY	435
MOSTLY			
SCATTERED OASES WHERE MEN DWELT, BUT MOSTLY	58	THE BLACK COTTAGE	119
MOSTLY AS MUCH BEYOND MY LIFTED HANDS, THOUGH,	197	WILD GRAPES	28
AEONS OF TIME AND STILL IT'S MOSTLY WOMEN	478	A MASQUE OF REASON	149
MOSUL			
YOU LOST YOUR ARMY AT MOSUL. WHAT HAPPENED?	458	HOW HARD TO KEEP FROM	130
MOTE			
THAT MILLIKAN MOTE?	391	A WISH TO COMPLY	2
MOTES			
THE COSMIC MOTES	219	I WILL SING YOU ONE-O	53
MOTE-SWIMMING			
ITS TWO MOTE-SWIMMING MANY-COLORED ENDS	315	IRIS BY NIGHT	27
MOTH			
WITH CODLIN MOTH OR RUSTY PARASITE	283	THE GOLD HESPERIDEE	28
RAN INTO A DORMANT MOTH	287	DEPARTMENTAL	2
ON A WHITE HEAL-ALL, HOLDING UP A MOTH	302	DESIGN	2
THEN STEERED THE WHITE MOTH THITHER IN THE NIGHT?	302	DESIGN	12
TO A MOTH SEEN IN WINTER	356	A MOTH SEEN IN WINTER	T
MOTHER			
THAT'S STANDING BY THE MOTHER. IT'S SO YOUNG	1	THE PASTURE	6
AND SENDS THE CHILDREN DOWN THERE WITH THEIR MOTHER	44	A HUNDRED COLLARS	4
FATHER AND MOTHER MARRIED, AND MOTHER CAME,	66	A SERVANT TO SERVANTS	126
MY MOTHER WAS A LANE, YET MIGHT HAVE MARRIED	75	THE GENERATIONS OF MEN	50
"I ONLY MEAN MY MOTHER WAS A STARK.	75	THE GENERATIONS OF MEN	55
AND SHE'LL COME BACK. BUT, BLESS YOU, I'M HER MOTHER--	82	THE HOUSEKEEPER	26
I BLAME HIS BEING BROUGHT UP BY HIS MOTHER.	83	THE HOUSEKEEPER	56
AND YOU'RE HER MOTHER." / "BUT I DIDN'T ALWAYS.	87	THE HOUSEKEEPER	172

MOTHER (CONTINUED)
   SAY IT RIGHT OUT--NO MATTER FOR HER MOTHER. . . . . . . 88 THE HOUSEKEEPER . . . 187
   ITS MOTHER WOULDN'T LET IT CRY LIKE THAT, ... 154 SNOW 320
   YOUR MOTHER NAMED YOU. YOU AND SHE JUST SAW . . . . . 180 MAPLE 10
   ABOUT YOUR MOTHER THAT PERHAPS MAY HELP." . . . . . . 180 MAPLE 28
   IF SHE COULD FORM SOME NOTION OF HER MOTHER-- . . . . 181 MAPLE 54
   AS IF IT WAS HER MOTHER SPEAKING TO HER. . . . . . . 181 MAPLE 66
   SOMETHING BETWEEN YOUR FATHER AND YOUR MOTHER . . . . 183 MAPLE 113
   AS WELL AS COULD A MOTHER. AND AGAIN . . . . 183 MAPLE 119
   TO SAY YOUR MOTHER, HAD SHE LIVED, WOULD BE . . . . . 184 MAPLE 129
   BEHIND THE MOUNTAIN, WITH A MOTHER AND SON, ... 202 THE WITCH OF COOS . . 2
   MOTHER CAN MAKE A COMMON TABLE REAR . . . . 202 THE WITCH OF COOS . . 9
   UP ATTIC, MOTHER? / BONES--A SKELETON. . . . . . . 203 THE WITCH OF COOS . . 20
   IT'S HARMLESS. MOTHER HEARS IT IN THE NIGHT, ... 203 THE WITCH OF COOS . . 23
   RIGHT PAST BOTH FATHER AND MOTHER, AND NEITHER STOPPED IT. . 203 THE WITCH OF COOS . . 33
   FATHER HAD GONE UPSTAIRS; MOTHER WAS DOWNSTAIRS. . . . 203 THE WITCH OF COOS . . 34
   I DOUBT IF EVEN HIS MOTHER COULD TELL HIM, 'SAKES, . . 223 THE RUNAWAY 12
   WHERE IS HIS MOTHER? HE CAN'T BE OUT ALONE." . . . . 223 THE RUNAWAY 14
   WITH HER FOR MOTHER EVE, A RACE . . . . 280 BLUE RIBBON AT AMESBURY 27
   BEFORE HER MOTHER CAME. . . . . 340 THE SUBVERTED FLOWER . 40
   HER MOTHER WIPED THE FOAM . . . . 341 THE SUBVERTED FLOWER . 71
   ONE DRANK TO HIS MOTHER . . . . 432 KITTY HAWK 127
   "YOU DIE FOR THAT." / "NO, YOU GO ASK YOUR MOTHER." . . 457 HOW HARD TO KEEP FROM 104
   HIS MOTHER DIDN'T LIKE THE WAY HE PUT IT, ... 457 HOW HARD TO KEEP FROM 105
   THE NAME HIS MOTHER GAVE HIM IS TO BLAME . . . . . . 494 A MASQUE OF MERCY . . 35
MOTHER-BIRD
   STOOD UP TO US AS TO A MOTHER-BIRD . . . . 109 THE EXPOSED NEST . . 21
   MADE ME ASK WOULD THE MOTHER-BIRD RETURN . . . . . . 109 THE EXPOSED NEST . . 23
MOTHER-LOSS
   TO TAKE YOUR MOTHER-LOSS OF A FIRST CHILD . . . . . 53 HOME BURIAL 64
MOTHERLY
   OR CHILD, AND THIS IS MOTHERLY RESENTMENT? . . . . . 501 A MASQUE OF MERCY . . 206
MOTHERS
   WHEN WILDER MOTHERS THAN OUR WILDEST NOW . . . . . . 197 WILD GRAPES 50
MOTHER'S
   AND HE ASKED AT HER MOTHER'S HOUSE . . . . 129 THE IMPULSE 23
   THIS WAS HER MOTHER'S CHILDHOOD HOME; . . . . 181 MAPLE 56
   HER MOTHER'S BEDROOM WAS HER FATHER'S STILL, ... 181 MAPLE 60
   WHERE SHE COULD WATCH HER MOTHER'S PICTURE FADING. . . 181 MAPLE 61
   BUT THE HEADBOARD OF MOTHER'S BED IS PUSHED . . . . . 203 THE WITCH OF COOS . . 21
   IT WAS THEN HER MOTHER'S CALL . . . . 340 THE SUBVERTED FLOWER . 35
   YOU'RE WELL DESCENDED ON YOUR MOTHER'S SIDE, ... 457 HOW HARD TO KEEP FROM 108
   YOUR MOTHER'S FOLKS----" / HE STAYED TO HEAR NO MORE, . 457 HOW HARD TO KEEP FROM 111
MOTHS
   IF I HAD MOTHS TO FRIEND AS I HAVE FLOWERS?) . . . . 356 A MOTH SEEN IN WINTER . 6
MOTION
   IT BLOW BUT THAT YOU SAW THE TREES IN MOTION.) . . . . 130 THE BONFIRE 43
   AN AIRSHIP LABORING WITH UNSHIPLIKE MOTION . . . . . 182 MAPLE 82
   NOT ALL THE MOTION, THOUGH, THEY EVER LENT, ... 188 THE GRINDSTONE . . . 5
   AS IF TO ASK, "WHY DON'T YOU MAKE SOME MOTION? . . . . 230 TWO LOOK AT TWO . . 32
   IT IS THIS BACKWARD MOTION TOWARD THE SOURCE, ... 260 WEST-RUNNING BROOK . . 68
MOTIONS
   THAT HAD AS MANY MOTIONS AS THE WORLD: . . . . . . 186 THE AX-HELVE . . . 47
MOTIVE
   A MOTIVE THEN WAS STILL A MOTIVE. . . . . 327 A MISSIVE MISSILE . . 21
MOTIVES
   IS SUCH AN EXECRABLE JUDGE OF MOTIVES . . . . 278 THE WHITE-TAILED HORNET 14
MOTOR
   ITS NAME MIGHT BETTER BE FIRST MOTOR KITE. . . . . . 308 THE WRIGHTS' BIPLANE . 2
   THERE'S WILL AS MOTOR AND THERE'S WILL AS BRAKES. . . . 481 A MASQUE OF REASON . 230
   THE WILL AS BRAKES CAN'T STOP THE WILL AS MOTOR . . . . 481 A MASQUE OF REASON . 232
MOTORCARS
   ON MOTORCARS, I'M ASKED IF I . . . . 139 BROWN'S DESCENT . . . 50
MOTOR-DRILL
   OF TRACTOR-PLOW AND MOTOR-DRILL. . . . . 418 AMERICA IS HARD TO SEE 69
MOTORS
   AND WHEN MOTORS STOP . . . . 439 KITTY HAWK 354
MOTTO
   ALWAYS THE WITCH'S MOTTO ANYWAY. . . . . 207 PAUPER WITCH OF GRAFTON 8
MOTTOED
   A CHEER WENT UP THAT SHOOK THE MOTTOED WALL. . . . . 400 THE BROKEN DROUGHT . . 6
MOUND
   BUT THE CHILD'S MOUND----" / "DON'T, DON'T, DON'T, DON'T,"
     SHE CRIED. . . . . 52 HOME BURIAL 30
   AND ROLL BACK DOWN THE MOUND BESIDE THE HOLE. . . . . 53 HOME BURIAL 77
MOUNT
   BEFORE THE LEAVES CAN MOUNT AGAIN . . . . 26 IN HARDWOOD GROVES . . 5
   THERE IS OUR WILDEST MOUNT--A HEADLESS HORSE. . . . . 267 RIDERS 9
   AND SO TO ROOST, THE LAST TO MOUNT. . . . . 281 BLUE RIBBON AT AMESBURY 44
   WE ALL KNOW HIS ADDRESS, MOUNT HECLA, ICELAND. . . . . 408 FROM PLANE TO PLANE . 143
   PAUL'S CONSTANT THEME. THE SERMON ON THE MOUNT . . . . 511 A MASQUE OF MERCY . . 482
   YOU ALL HAVE READ THE SERMON ON THE MOUNT. . . . . . 511 A MASQUE OF MERCY . . 487
MOUNTAIN
   THE MOUNTAIN HELD THE TOWN AS IN A SHADOW. . . . . . 40 THE MOUNTAIN 1
   THE MOUNTAIN . . . . 40 THE MOUNTAIN . . . . T
   I CROSSED THE RIVER AND SWUNG ROUND THE MOUNTAIN. . . . 41 THE MOUNTAIN 15
   BEYOND THE BRIDGE, WAS NOT THAT OF THE MOUNTAIN, . . . 41 THE MOUNTAIN 21
   THE MOUNTAIN STOOD THERE TO BE POINTED AT. . . . . . 41 THE MOUNTAIN 28
   FROM SUCH A MOUNTAIN--IF IT ISN'T WOODED . . . . . . 42 THE MOUNTAIN 56
   SOMEWHERE IN IRELAND ON A MOUNTAIN TOP." . . . . . . 43 THE MOUNTAIN 76
   IT DOESN'T SEEM SO MUCH TO CLIMB A MOUNTAIN . . . . . 43 THE MOUNTAIN 82
   BY MOUNTAIN RANGES HALF IN SUMMER SNOW, ... 58 THE BLACK COTTAGE . . 116
   OF THE BOULDER-STREWN MOUNTAIN, AND WHEN THEY WILL CROP. . 61 BLUEBERRIES 63
   STRAIGHTAWAY THROUGH THE MOUNTAIN NOTCH . . . . . . 63 A SERVANT TO SERVANTS . 22
   BOWED OUTWARD ON THE MOUNTAIN HALFWAY UP, ... 75 THE GENERATIONS OF MEN 71
   MOUNTAIN INTERVAL . . . . 103 MOUNTAIN INTERVAL . . T
   IF THAT IS WHAT THE MOUNTAIN EVER WAS-- . . . . . . 130 THE BONFIRE 17
   FIVE MOUNTAIN RANGES ONE BEHIND THE OTHER . . . . . 136 "OUT, OUT--" 5

MOUNTAIN (CONTINUED)
  AND WHERE I LIVED IN MOUNTAIN LAND . . . . 140 THE GUM-GATHERER . . 10
  IS BLOCKS SPLIT OFF THE MOUNTAIN MASS-- . . . . 140 THE GUM-GATHERER . . 15
  WAS GUM, THE GUM OF THE MOUNTAIN SPRUCE. . . . . . . 141 THE GUM-GATHERER . . 29
  HE'D BEEN THE HERO OF THE MOUNTAIN CAMPS . . . . . . 191 PAUL'S WIFE 17
  BEHIND THE MOUNTAIN, WITH A MOTHER AND SON, ... 202 THE WITCH OF COOS . . 2
  OLD DAVIS OWNED A SOLID MICA MOUNTAIN . . . . 212 A FOUNTAIN, A BOTTLE . 1
  AND EXPERTS SAID THAT DEEP DOWN IN THE MOUNTAIN . . . 212 A FOUNTAIN, A BOTTLE . 4
  BUT SMITH, OR SOMEONE, CALLED THEM OFF THE MOUNTAIN . 213 A FOUNTAIN, A BOTTLE . 11
  THE MOUNTAIN MAY HAVE SHIFTED SINCE I SAW IT . . . . 213 A FOUNTAIN, A BOTTLE . 22
  COME STRAIGHT DOWN OFF THIS MOUNTAIN JUST AS FAST . . 215 A FOUNTAIN, A BOTTLE . 61
  WE STOPPED BY A MOUNTAIN PASTURE TO SAY, "WHOSE COLT?" . 223 THE RUNAWAY . . . 2
  TRANSFIXED ON MOUNTAIN SLOPES ALMOST ERECT. . . . . . 237 A HILLSIDE THAW . . . 28
  HERE FURTHER UP THE MOUNTAIN SLOPE . . . . 264 THE BIRTHPLACE . . . 1
  THE MOUNTAIN SEEMED TO LIKE THE STIR, ... 265 THE BIRTHPLACE . . . 8
  THE MOUNTAIN PUSHED US OFF HER KNEES. . . . . 265 THE BIRTHPLACE . . . 13
  WHEN IT COMES TO A MOUNTAIN FARM . . . . 285 IN TIME OF CLOUDBURST . 6
  OR BEAUTY REST IN A BEAUTIFUL MOUNTAIN SCENE. . . . . 286 A ROADSIDE STAND . . 13
  TO A CONE MOUNTAIN IN THE MIDNIGHT HAZE, ... 300 MOON COMPASSES . . . 4
  THE MOUNTAIN STOOD EXALTED IN ITS PLACE. . . . . . . 301 MOON COMPASSES . . . 7
  FOR INTEREST, AND I'VE BOUGHT A MOUNTAIN FARM . . . . 316 BUILD SOIL 7
  YOU SHALL GO TO YOUR RUN-OUT MOUNTAIN FARM . . . . . 323 BUILD SOIL 211
  YOU WILL GO TO YOUR RUN-OUT MOUNTAIN FARM . . . . . 323 BUILD SOIL 230
  ON MELTED MOUNTAIN WATER LED BY FLUME . . . . 337 THE WIND AND THE RAIN . 23
  HAS LOST ITS FOOTING ON MY MOUNTAIN SLOPE . . . . . 350 TO A YOUNG WRETCH . . 21
  THE MOUNTAIN HE WAS CLIMBING HAD THE SLANT . . . . . 355 TIME OUT 2
  A LOOSE MOUNTAIN . . . . 360 A LOOSE MOUNTAIN . . T
  THAT THE LOOSE MOUNTAIN LATELY SEEN TO GLINT . . . . 361 A LOOSE MOUNTAIN . . 14
  STILL SAID TO HAUNT THIS SIDE OF PANTHER MOUNTAIN. . . 377 DIRECTIVE 19
  LOOK DOWN THE LONG VALLEY AND THERE STANDS A MOUNTAIN . 379 TOO ANXIOUS FOR RIVERS . 1
  AWAY ON THE MOUNTAIN UP FAR TOO HIGH, ... 383 WERE I IN TROUBLE . . 2
  SPRING WATER IN OUR MOUNTAIN BOSOM SWELLS . . . . . 446 DOES NO ONE AT ALL EVER 22
MOUNTAINS
  THE FARM I MADE MY HOME ON IN THE MOUNTAINS . . . . . 163 NEW HAMPSHIRE . . . 150
  EXCEPTING THAT THEY DIFFER IN THEIR MOUNTAINS. . . . . 165 NEW HAMPSHIRE . . . 212
  THE VERMONT MOUNTAINS STRETCH EXTENDED STRAIGHT; . . . 165 NEW HAMPSHIRE . . . 213
  NEW HAMPSHIRE MOUNTAINS CURL UP IN A COIL. . . . . . 165 NEW HAMPSHIRE . . . 214
  I HAD BEEN COMING TO NEW HAMPSHIRE MOUNTAINS. . . . . 166 NEW HAMPSHIRE . . . 215
  THE PEOPLE OR THE ALREADY LOFTY MOUNTAINS, ... 168 NEW HAMPSHIRE . . . 308
  I'D ELEVATE THE ALREADY LOFTY MOUNTAINS. . . . . . . 168 NEW HAMPSHIRE . . . 309
  IS THAT HER MOUNTAINS AREN'T QUITE HIGH ENOUGH. . . . 169 NEW HAMPSHIRE . . . 311
  ON MOUNTAINS? WHAT HAS GIVEN ME ASSURANCE . . . . . 169 NEW HAMPSHIRE . . . 315
  TO SAY WHAT HEIGHT BECOMES NEW HAMPSHIRE MOUNTAINS, . 169 NEW HAMPSHIRE . . . 316
  OR ANY MOUNTAINS? CAN IT BE SOME STRENGTH . . . . . 169 NEW HAMPSHIRE . . . 317
  OUR ACTUAL MOUNTAINS GIVEN IN A MAP . . . . 169 NEW HAMPSHIRE . . . 330
  THE MORE I SEEM TO WANT MY MOUNTAINS WILD; . . . . . 170 NEW HAMPSHIRE . . . 344
  FOR ALL HER MOUNTAINS FALL A LITTLE SHORT, ... 170 NEW HAMPSHIRE . . . 355
  A HUNDRED SQUARE MILES ROUND IT IN THE MOUNTAINS: . . 174 THE CENSUS-TAKER . . 5
  THROWING A LEG UP OVER OUR FENCE OF MOUNTAINS, . . . 176 THE STAR-SPLITTER . . 2
  BUT THE MOUNTAINS I RAISE . . . . 235 GATHERING LEAVES . . 9
  THROUGH LEVEL MOUNTAINS NOTHING TO THE EYE . . . . . 292 FIGURE IN THE DOORWAY . 2
  THE MOUNTAINS ARE BROUGHT UP NEAR, ... 301 VOICE WAYS 4
  SOME OVER THE MOUNTAINS EAST, ... 312 THE VINDICTIVES . . . 70
  AND ONE WENT OFF TO THE MOUNTAINS . . . . 313 BEARER OF EVIL TIDINGS . 7
  HE TOOK THE ONE TO THE MOUNTAINS. . . . . 313 BEARER OF EVIL TIDINGS . 9
MOUNTAIN'S
  OF AN OLD MOUNTAIN'S CASE . . . . 298 ON TAKING FROM THE TOP 18
MOUNTAINSIDE
  A LITTLE FURTHER UP THE MOUNTAINSIDE . . . . 229 TWO LOOK AT TWO . . . 2
MOUNTED
  AND SOMEONE MOUNTED ON IT RODE IT HARD, ... 189 THE GRINDSTONE . . . 24
  TO SEE HOW THEY WERE MOUNTED FOR THIS WALK. . . . . 204 THE WITCH OF COOS . . 67
  BUT BEING MOUNTED BAREBACK ON THE EARTH? . . . . . . 267 RIDERS 6
MOUNTING
  MOUNTING UNTIL SHE COWERED UNDER HIM. . . . . 51 HOME BURIAL 11
  THEIR EFFORT IS A MOUNTING ECSTASY . . . . 398 BURSTING RAPTURE . . 11
MOUNTS
  AND MOUNTS THE WALL AGAIN WITH WHITED EYES . . . . . 223 THE RUNAWAY 16
MOURN
  THERE IS NONE LEFT TO MOURN THEE IN THE FIELDS. . . . 28 MY BUTTERFLY 7
MOURNED
  THAT ANY SONG IN WHICH HE MOURNED . . . . 336 THE WIND AND THE RAIN . 13
MOURNS
  THE MUSE MOURNS ONE WHO WENT TO HIS RETREAT . . . . . 359 THE LOST FOLLOWER . . 21
MOUSE
  I DON'T WANT IT GIRDLED BY RABBIT AND MOUSE, ... 228 GOOD-BY AND KEEP COLD . 6
MOUSY
  SO MOUSY OR SO FOXY . . . . 416 CLOSED FOR GOOD . . . 29
MOUTH (SEE CANNON-MOUTH-LIKE)
  WITH HIS PIPE IN HIS MOUTH AND HIS BROWN JUG-- . . . 77 THE GENERATIONS OF MEN 105
  HE'S ON HIS ROUNDS NOW WITH HIS TAIL IN HIS MOUTH, . . 94 THE SELF-SEEKER . . . 38
  IT BURSTS AGAINST US AT THE CHIMNEY MOUTH, ... 150 SNOW 207
  FROM THE WAY SHE HAD SET HER POOR OLD MOUTH, ... 201 PLACE FOR A THIRD . . 74
  HE TOOK A LITTLE IN HIS MOUTH, ... 224 THE AIM WAS SONG . . 9
  NOT BLUEBELLS GRACING A TUNNEL MOUTH-- . . . . 248 A PASSING GLIMPSE . . 7
  'TIS NOT ENOUGH ON ROOTS AND IN THE MOUTH, ... 337 THE WIND AND THE RAIN . 37
  UNLESS I PUT IT IN YOUR MOUTH TO SAY. . . . . 354 THE LESSON FOR TODAY . 115
  HE HAS CURSED EVERY RIVER MOUTH . . . . 418 AMERICA IS HARD TO SEE . 53
  LOOK, WILL YOU LOOK! GOD CAN'T PUT WORDS IN MY MOUTH. . 505 A MASQUE OF MERCY . . 295
MOUTHFUL
  AND A MOUTHFUL OF DYESTUFF INSTEAD OF A STING, . . . 309 ONE GUESS 3
MOUTHS
  WITH THE MOUTHS OF ALL THOSE YOUNG LORENS TO FEED? . . 60 BLUEBERRIES 49
MOVE
  "IT'S GOOD LUCK WHEN YOU MOVE IN TO BEGIN . . . . . 113 IN THE HOME STRETCH . 91
  AS IF A MAN COULD MOVE THAT SLOW AND MOVE. . . . . . 145 SNOW 60
  BUT THE WIND DIDN'T MOVE IT IF IT MOVED. . . . . . . 148 SNOW 136
  NOR KNOW THAT HE MIGHT MOVE IT FROM THE SPOT-- . . . 173 A STAR IN A STONEBOAT . 19

PAGE TITLE   LINE

MOVE (CONTINUED)
    AND PLOWED BETWEEN THE ROCKS HE COULDN'T MOVE, ... 177 THE STAR-SPLITTER . . 27
    THEY MOVE IN PLEASURE TOO FAR OFF . . . . 256 THE LOVELY BE CHOOSERS 29
    SHE MAKES THE WHOLE FLOCK MOVE ALONG. . . . . 281 BLUE RIBBON AT AMESBURY 48
    HAVE NEVER MADE THE FIRST MOVE TO ASSEMBLE, ... 291 ON HEART'S BEGINNING TO 30
    HARD TIMES HAVE STRUCK ME AND I'M ON THE MOVE. . . . . 316 BUILD SOIL 5
    NO. I UNOSTENTATIOUSLY MOVE OFF . . . . 324 BUILD SOIL 255
    OF THEM ON THE MOVE. . . . . 442 KITTY HAWK 440
    IT MAKES HER MOVE AS IF TO REINFORCE IT. . . . . . . 493 A MASQUE OF MERCY . . 7
MOVED
    AND THERE I MET A MAN WHO MOVED SO SLOW . . . . 41 THE MOUNTAIN 16
    THAT THING TAKES ALL THE ROOM!" HE MOVED HIS GOAD. . . 41 THE MOUNTAIN 27
    HER FINGERS MOVED THE LATCH FOR ALL REPLY. . . . . . . 52 HOME BURIAL 44
    SHE MOVED THE LATCH A LITTLE. "DON'T--DON'T GO. . . . . 53 HOME BURIAL 56
    I WAS GLAD THOUGH, NO END, WHEN WE MOVED OUT, ... 67 A SERVANT TO SERVANTS 151
    MOVED IN A LITTLE. THE MAN GRASPED A WHEEL. . . . . . . 89 THE FEAR 7
    "THAT LEAF THERE IN YOUR OPEN BOOK! IT MOVED . . . . . 147 SNOW 116
    BUT THE WIND DIDN'T MOVE IT IF IT MOVED. . . . . 148 SNOW 136
    IT MOVED ITSELF. THE WIND'S AT NAUGHT IN HERE. . . . . 148 SNOW 137
    HE MOVED IT ROUGHLY WITH AN IRON BAR, ... 173 A STAR IN A STONEBOAT . 25
    THERE WHERE HE MOVED THE ROCKS TO PLOW THE GROUND . . . 177 THE STAR-SPLITTER . . 26
    OR EARTHSLIDE MOVED AT NIGHT, IT MOVED ITSELF; . . . . 229 TWO LOOK AT TWO . . 12
    NO FOOTSTEP MOVED IT. "THIS IS ALL," THEY SIGHED, . . . 229 TWO LOOK AT TWO . . 13
    AND THEN I SAID THE TRUTH (AND WE MOVED ON). . . . . . 234 A BOUNDLESS MOMENT . . 11
    AND IF SO MOVED UNCURL A HAND IN GREETING. . . . . . . 292 FIGURE IN THE DOORWAY . 22
    BREATHES THERE A BARD WHO ISN'T MOVED . . . . 469 CHOSEN POET OF VERMONT 1
MOVEMENT
    SHE MADE A SUDDEN MOVEMENT TOWARD HER BODICE, ... 74 THE GENERATIONS OF MEN 43
    LEST MOVEMENT SHOULD PROVOKE . . . . 340 THE SUBVERTED FLOWER . 32
MOVEMENTS
    HE WON'T MISUNDERSTAND YOUR FREEST MOVEMENTS. . . . . 278 THE WHITE-TAILED HORNET 27
MOVES
    HE MOVES IN DARKNESS AS IT SEEMS TO ME, ... 34 MENDING WALL 41
    TO LEARN TO SAY (HE MOVES TO JONAH'S FEET.) . . . . . 521 A MASQUE OF MERCY . . 737
MOVIE
    BETWEEN THE PICTURES ON A MOVIE SCREEN . . . . 165 NEW HAMPSHIRE . . . 194
MOVING
    MOVING AMONG TALL HAYCOCKS LIGHTLY PILED, ... 14 WAITING 2
    GAVE THEM THEIR MARCHING ORDERS AND WAS MOVING. . . . . 44 THE MOUNTAIN . . . 109
    "I'M MOVING INTO A SIZE-LARGER SHIRT. . . . . 46 A HUNDRED COLLARS . . 53
    WHERE ARE YOU MOVING OVER TO? STAY STILL. . . . . . . 47 A HUNDRED COLLARS . . 89
    IT WAS HIS PLAN OUR MOVING OVER IN . . . . 64 A SERVANT TO SERVANTS 61
    MOVING A FLOCK OF HENS FROM PLACE TO PLACE. . . . . . 85 THE HOUSEKEEPER . . 126
    OFF ANY STILL OR MOVING THING YOU SAY. . . . . 300 THE MASTER SPEED . . 9
    INSTEAD OF MOVING WITH US AS WE WENT . . . . 315 IRIS BY NIGHT . . . 24
MOVING-PICTURES'
    AND GIVE US THE LIFE OF THE MOVING-PICTURES' PROMISE . . 286 A ROADSIDE STAND . . 21
MOW
    THAT NONE SHOULD MOW THE GRASS THERE . . . . 14 ROSE POGONIAS . . . 23
    KEEP AT THEIR HEELS AND THREATEN TO MOW THEIR LEGS OFF. . 71 THE CODE 46
    WHERE ON A MOW IT WOULD HAVE BEEN SLOW LIFTING. . . . . 71 THE CODE 58
    IF I COULD SEE IT, OR ELSE MOW THE ROOM, ... 205 THE WITCH OF COOS . 105
    AND BRUSH THE MOW WITH THE SUMMER LOAD. . . . . . . 242 NEED OF BEING VERSED . 12
    WE NEVER SHALL MOW IN AGAIN, ... 264 THE LAST MOWING . . 2
    WHO SLEPT THERE IN A MOW OF MEADOW HAY . . . . 289 OLD BARN AT THE BOTTOM 19
MOWED
    WHO MOWED IT IN THE DEW BEFORE THE SUN. . . . . 22 THE TUFT OF FLOWERS . 2
    OF HAVING HOED AND MOWED FOR FIFTY YEARS, ... 404 FROM PLANE TO PLANE . 3
MOWER
    THE MOWER IN THE DEW HAD LOVED THEM THUS, ... 23 THE TUFT OF FLOWERS . 25
MOWERS
    THAT CAN'T STAND MOWERS AND PLOWERS. . . . . 264 THE LAST MOWING . . . 6
MOWING
    THE WOODS COME BACK TO THE MOWING FIELD; . . . . 5 GHOST HOUSE 7
    WHEN I GO UP THROUGH THE MOWING FIELD, ... 8 A LATE WALK 1
    THAT IN THE GENERAL MOWING . . . . 14 ROSE POGONIAS . . . 19
    MOWING . . . . 17 MOWING . . . . . T
    AND DRIVE, THE WAY YOU CAN, YOU KNOW, IN MOWING-- . . . 71 THE CODE 45
    A LITTLE STRETCH OF MOWING FIELD FOR YOU; . . . . . 111 IN THE HOME STRETCH . 32
    PINE, ALDER, PASTURE, MOWING, WELL, AND BROOK. . . . 117 IN THE HOME STRETCH . 197
    BEFORE THE NOT MOWING BRINGS TREES ON, ... 264 THE LAST MOWING . . 8
    THE LAST MOWING . . . . 264 THE LAST MOWING . . . T
MOWN
    BUT HE HAD GONE HIS WAY, THE GRASS ALL MOWN, ... 22 THE TUFT OF FLOWERS . 7
MR.
    YOU KNOW IT, MR. LAWYER. THE SIN IS . . . . 100 THE SELF-SEEKER . . 200
    MR. MESERVE, I'LL LEAVE IT TO YOUR WIFE. . . . . . . 147 SNOW 109
    PUT UP TO CURE THE WORLD BY MR. EDISON." . . . . . . 371 THE LITERATE FARMER AND 93
    THEM IS MY SENTIMENTS, AND, MR. FLOOD, ... 497 A MASQUE OF MERCY . 108
    IF I WERE IN YOUR PLACE, THOUGH, MR. PROPHET, ... 503 A MASQUE OF MERCY . 269
MRS.
    I'D RATHER MRS. CORBIN DIDN'T KNOW; . . . . 94 THE SELF-SEEKER . . 53
    AND BRING HIM UP, AND DON'T LET MRS. CORBIN.-- . . . . 96 THE SELF-SEEKER . . 89
    BOTH THE COLES SAID TOGETHER. MRS. COLE . . . . . . 144 SNOW 34
    MRS. COLE'S VOICE CAME FROM AN INNER ROOM: . . . . . 152 SNOW 271
    MRS. BAPTISTE CAME IN AND ROCKED A CHAIR . . . . . . 186 THE AX-HELVE . . . 46
    MRS. SOMEONE'S BEEN TO ASIA. . . . . 396 AN IMPORTER 1
MUCH
    AND OFTEN THEY BROUGHT SO MUCH TO SAY . . . . 15 IN A VALE 12
    AND IF BY NOON I HAVE TOO MUCH OF THESE, ... 17 THE VANTAGE POINT . . 9
    WHICH SHOWED HOW MUCH GOOD SCHOOL HAD EVER DONE HIM. . . 37 DEATH OF THE HIRED MAN 84
    YOU'LL BE SURPRISED AT HIM--HOW MUCH HE'S BROKEN. . . . 39 DEATH OF THE HIRED MAN 152
    I SAW SO MUCH BEFORE I SLEPT THERE ONCE: . . . . . . 40 THE MOUNTAIN . . . 2
    IT DOESN'T SEEM SO MUCH TO CLIMB A MOUNTAIN . . . . . 43 THE MOUNTAIN . . . 82
    BUT IT'S AS MUCH AS EVER YOU CAN DO, ... 43 THE MOUNTAIN . . . 94
    YOU'RE NOT MUCH FURTHER THAN WHERE KIKE LEFT YOU. . . . 47 A HUNDRED COLLARS . . 70
    NOT SO MUCH LARGER THAN A BEDROOM, IS IT? . . . . . . 51 HOME BURIAL 25
    LET ME INTO YOUR GRIEF. I'M NOT SO MUCH . . . . . . 53 HOME BURIAL 59

	PAGE	TITLE	LINE

MUCH (CONTINUED)

AND OF HER HALF ASLEEP, WAS TOO MUCH FOR ME. . . . . . . 58 THE BLACK COTTAGE . . 92
SUCH A PHRASE COULDN'T HAVE MEANT MUCH TO HER. . . . . . 58 THE BLACK COTTAGE . . 100
BUT I DON'T COUNT ON IT AS MUCH AS LEN. . . . . 64 A SERVANT TO SERVANTS . 44
BY GOOD RIGHTS I OUGHT NOT TO HAVE SO MUCH . . . . 64 A SERVANT TO SERVANTS . 53
BUT WORK AIN'T ALL. LEN UNDERTAKES TOO MUCH. . . . . . . 64 A SERVANT TO SERVANTS . 70
WHILE I FRY THEIR BACON. MUCH THEY CARE! . . . . 65 A SERVANT TO SERVANTS . 78
I'VE HEARD TOO MUCH OF THE OLD-FASHIONED WAY. . . . . . 65 A SERVANT TO SERVANTS . 103
FOR I HAVE HAD TOO MUCH . . . . 69 AFTER APPLE-PICKING . . 27
I SAID IT TO MYSELF AS MUCH AS YOU." . . . . 70 THE CODE 14
YOU WOULDN'T THINK A FELLOW'D NEED MUCH URGING . . . . . 71 THE CODE 59
BUT DON'T YOU THINK WE SOMETIMES MAKE TOO MUCH . . . . . 80 THE GENERATIONS OF MEN 196
WHAT'S WANTED AND HOW MUCH AND WHERE IT IS. . . . . . . 82 THE HOUSEKEEPER . . . 33
MAKE SO MUCH DIFFERENCE IN HIS MAN'S AFFAIRS. . . . . . 83 THE HOUSEKEEPER . . . 54
"THE STRAIN'S BEEN TOO MUCH FOR HER ALL THESE YEARS: . . 84 THE HOUSEKEEPER . . . 77
TAKE IT YEAR IN, YEAR OUT, HE DOESN'T MAKE MUCH. . . . . 85 THE HOUSEKEEPER . . . 103
THAT MUCH TO SELL, THEY'RE WORTH AS MUCH TO KEEP. . . . 86 THE HOUSEKEEPER . . . 141
OLD STREAK OF LEATHER--DOESN'T LOVE ME MUCH . . . . . . 94 THE SELF-SEEKER . . . 33
THEY NEVER EARNED ME SO MUCH AS ONE CENT: . . . . 95 THE SELF-SEEKER . . . 71
AND THOUGHT SHE WOULDN'T VENTURE ON SO MUCH. . . . . . . 97 THE SELF-SEEKER . . . 118
"YES, BUT ALL THAT TAKES TIME, AND I'M AS MUCH . . . . . 99 THE SELF-SEEKER . . . 191
"A THOUSAND WOULDN'T BE A CENT TOO MUCH; . . . . 100 THE SELF-SEEKER . . . 199
TOO MUCH ALIKE TO MARK OR NAME A PLACE BY . . . . 101 THE WOOD-PILE 7
WITHOUT SO MUCH AS WISHING HIM GOOD-NIGHT. . . . . . . 101 THE WOOD-PILE 21
I DALLIED SO MUCH WITH THE THOUGHT OF SELLING. . . . . . 106 CHRISTMAS TREES . . . 25
AND TOO MUCH WORLD AT ONCE--COULD MEANS BE FOUND. . . . 109 THE EXPOSED NEST . . . 19
NOT MUCH OF THAT UNTIL I COME TO WOODS . . . . 111 IN THE HOME STRETCH . 33
"COME FROM THAT WINDOW WHERE YOU SEE TOO MUCH, ... 112 IN THE HOME STRETCH . 60
SO MUCH TOO LIGHT AND AIRY FOR THEIR STRENGTH . . . . . 113 IN THE HOME STRETCH . 87
THEY ALMOST SHOOK ME." / "IT'S ALL SO MUCH . . . . . . 114 IN THE HOME STRETCH . 126
"IT'S ALL SO MUCH WHAT I HAVE ALWAYS WANTED, ... 116 IN THE HOME STRETCH . 164
IF IT IS WHAT YOU WANTED, THEN HOW MUCH . . . . 116 IN THE HOME STRETCH . 167
MUST GET SOMEWHERE. I'VE HEARD YOU SAY AS MUCH. . . . . 117 IN THE HOME STRETCH . 185
ALL OF A FARM IT IS." / " I KNOW THIS MUCH: . . . . . . 117 IN THE HOME STRETCH . 198
AS MUCH AT HOME AS IF THEY'D ALWAYS DANCED THERE. . . . 117 IN THE HOME STRETCH . 204
"I MAY HAVE THOUGHT AS MUCH, BUT NOT ALOUD." . . . . . 118 THE TELEPHONE 18
SOUGHT FOR MUCH AFTER THAT, IT WILL BE FOUND . . . . . 119 HYLA BROOK 2
AND LIFE IS TOO MUCH LIKE A PATHLESS WOOD . . . . 122 BIRCHES 44
SO MUCH AS YOU AND I . . . . 126 LONELINESS 2
OR CARE SO MUCH WHEN THEY COME BACK . . . . 126 LONELINESS 5
THE TRUTH BEING WE ARE AS MUCH . . . . 126 LONELINESS 7
DONE SO MUCH AND I KNOW NOT HOW MUCH MORE . . . . 130 THE BONFIRE 30
COULDN'T BELIEVE THAT SO MUCH BLACK HAD COME THERE . . 132 THE BONFIRE 85
THAT A BOY COUNTS SO MUCH WHEN SAVED FROM WORK. . . . . 136 "OUT,OUT--" 12
NOT MUCH CONCERNED FOR THOSE TO WHOM, ... 139 BROWN'S DESCENT . . . 63
NOT MUCH CONCERNED FOR THEM, I SAY; . . . . 139 BROWN'S DESCENT . . . 68
ALL'S EVER I HEARD OF IT, WHICH ISN'T MUCH. . . . . . . 144 SNOW 54
OR NOT MUCH BETTER. WHY, IT DOESN'T SEEM . . . . 145 SNOW 59
YOU CAN'T GET TOO MUCH WINTER IN THE WINTER.' . . . . . 149 SNOW 184
MUCH SAY IN THE MATTER, AND I'M JUST AS GLAD . . . . . 152 SNOW 257
"BUT HOW MUCH BETTER OFF ARE WE AS IT IS? . . . . 152 SNOW 261
TO DISOBEY YOU. MUCH HIS WIFE'LL THANK YOU." . . . . . 153 SNOW 284
"I THOUGHT YOU'D FEEL YOU'D BEEN TOO MUCH CONCERNED." . 155 SNOW 343
MUCH MATTERS. YOU MAY WORK FOR ALL OF ME. . . . . . . 159 NEW HAMPSHIRE 5
WHY WAS IT SO MUCH GREATER WHEN THE BOXES . . . . 163 NEW HAMPSHIRE 132
NOT EVEN NEW HAMPSHIRE FARMS ARE MUCH FOR SALE. . . . . 163 NEW HAMPSHIRE 149
SO MUCH MORE BUSINESSLIKE THAN BUSINESSMEN. . . . . . . 164 NEW HAMPSHIRE 173
THEIR WARES ARE SO MUCH HARDER TO GET RID OF. . . . . . 164 NEW HAMPSHIRE 174
ON NOTHING WORSE THAN TOO MUCH LUCK AND COMFORT. . . . 167 NEW HAMPSHIRE 276
WHERE I CAME LAST WITH HOPE, BUT NOT MUCH, ... 174 THE CENSUS-TAKER . . . 12
THERE'S NO SUCH NAME." / "TEACHERS DON'T KNOW AS MUCH . 179 MAPLE 5
SO YOU CAN'T HAVE MUCH RECOLLECTION OF HER. . . . . . . 180 MAPLE 14
IN HAVING TOO MUCH MEANING. OTHER NAMES, ... 181 MAPLE 45
NOT SO MUCH AS A SINGLE TREE FOR SHADE, ... 183 MAPLE 102
"SHE AIN'T SPICK TOO MUCH HENGLISH--DAT'S TOO BAD." . . 187 THE AX-HELVE 54
"HAHN, HAHN," HE MUSED, "DON'T NEED MUCH TAKING DOWN." . 187 THE AX-HELVE 79
AND ARROWHEADS ITSELF. MUCH USE FOR YEARS . . . . . . 189 THE GRINDSTONE . . . 38
NOT FOR MYSELF WAS I SO MUCH CONCERNED. . . . . 190 THE GRINDSTONE . . . 51
NOR WAS I FOR THE MAN SO MUCH CONCERNED. . . . . 190 THE GRINDSTONE . . . 56
WASN'T THERE DANGER OF A TURN TOO MUCH? . . . . 191 THE GRINDSTONE . . . 73
EITHER TO PRAISE HER OR SO MUCH AS NAME HER, ... 196 PAUL'S WIFE 153
MOSTLY AS MUCH BEYOND MY LIFTED HANDS, THOUGH, ... 197 WILD GRAPES 28
BUT NOT SO MUCH, PERHAPS, AS A BOY NEEDED. . . . . . . 197 WILD GRAPES 35
MUCH DANGER OF MY PICKING ANYTHING! . . . . 198 WILD GRAPES 59
I DON'T KNOW MUCH ABOUT THE LETTING DOWN; . . . . 198 WILD GRAPES 84
SO MUCH AS MY NOT KNOWING ANYTHING-- . . . . 199 WILD GRAPES 93
BUT COME TO DIE SHE FOUND SHE CARED SO MUCH: . . . . . 199 PLACE FOR A THIRD . . 4
WHILE SHE MADE UP HER MIND HOW MUCH SHE CARED-- . . . . 201 PLACE FOR A THIRD . . 55
AND HOW MUCH LABAN CARED--AND WHY HE CARED. . . . . . . 201 PLACE FOR A THIRD . . 56
HAS ALWAYS BEEN TOO MUCH FOR ME, IT HAS. . . . . 208 PAUPER WITCH OF GRAFTON 35
HE NEVER SAID MUCH AFTER WE WERE MARRIED, ... 209 PAUPER WITCH OF GRAFTON 73
I CAN'T SAY HE'S MUCH HELP! . . . . 211 AN EMPTY THREAT . . . 17
OVER SO MUCH BAY . . . . 211 AN EMPTY THREAT . . . 31
WHY MAKE SO MUCH OF FRAGMENTARY BLUE . . . . 220 FRAGMENTARY BLUE . . . 1
AND ONCE THAT SEEMED TOO MUCH; . . . . 226 TO EARTHWARD 3
OF ALMOST TOO MUCH LOVE, ... 227 TO EARTHWARD 22
WITH NIGHT SO NEAR, BUT NOT MUCH FURTHER UP. . . . . . 229 TWO LOOK AT TWO . . . 3
AS IN SOME TOO MUCH CARVEN MARBLE HALL . . . . 240 OUR SINGING STRENGTH . 42
FROM TOO MUCH DWELLING ON WHAT HAS BEEN. . . . . 242 NEED OF BEING VERSED . 16
SO MUCH AS TO TAKE CARE OF EVENING CHORES. . . . . . . 248 THE COCOON 10
YOUR HEAD SO MUCH CONCERNED WITH OUTER, ... 252 TREE AT MY WINDOW . . 15
MY GREATER GRIEF WAS BY SO MUCH REDUCED . . . . 253 THE THATCH 28
"HOW MUCH TIME HAVE WE?" . . . . 256 THE LOVELY BE CHOOSERS 4
TO THINK MUCH OR MUCH CARE. . . . . 256 THE LOVELY BE CHOOSERS 30
YOU'LL WAIT A LONG, LONG TIME FOR ANYTHING MUCH . . . . 268 ON LOOKING UP BY CHANCE 1
NOT SO MUCH TIED AS MADE THEM BLEND. . . . . 274 A LONE STRIKER . . . 32
BUT IF YOU SO MUCH AS DARE TO SPEAK, ... 275 TWO TRAMPS IN MUD TIME 21
SO MUCH AS THE TRUSTING SORROW OF WHAT IS UNSAID: . . . 286 A ROADSIDE STAND . . 17

MUCH (CONTINUED)
THE THOUGHT OF SO MUCH CHILDISH LONGING IN VAIN, ... 287 A ROADSIDE STAND . . 33
WITH TOO MUCH STRESS ON THE WHO. . . . . 294 A RECORD STRIDE . . 12
I HAVE IT IN ME SO MUCH NEARER HOME . . . . 296 DESERT PLACES . . . 15
IT NEVER WILL SHOW MUCH FLOWER OR FRUIT. . . . . . . 296 LEAVES COMPARED WITH . 4
PERHAPS I HAVE PUT FORTH TOO MUCH STRENGTH AND BEEN TOO
   FIERCE FROM FEAR. . . . . 297 A LEAF-TREADER . . 3
THERE MAY BE LITTLE OR MUCH BEYOND THE GRAVE, ... 300 STRONG SAYING NOTHING . 15
HAD MADE IT MUCH MORE EASILY A PREY. . . . . 303 A BIRD SINGING IN SLEEP 14
MAY MUCH STAY OUT OF OUR STATED PLAN, ... 305 UNHARVESTED 12
THERE IS NOTHING MUCH WE CAN DO FOR THE TREE TONIGHT, . . 305 THERE ARE ROUGHLY ZONES 14
GET CALLED AS MUCH IN CLASHES OF AMBITION. . . . . . 317 BUILD SOIL 40
(IN THIS IT IS AS MUCH LIKE HATE AS LOVE), ... 319 BUILD SOIL 105
WORKS IN THE DARK AS MUCH AGAINST AS FOR US. . . . . 319 BUILD SOIL 106
WE'RE ALWAYS TOO MUCH OUT OR TOO MUCH IN. . . . . . 320 BUILD SOIL 137
WE'RE SO MUCH OUT THAT THE ODDS ARE AGAINST . . . . . 320 BUILD SOIL 139
TOO MEAN A THOUGHT TO GET MUCH COMFORT OUT OF. . . . . 321 BUILD SOIL 168
BUT MUCH AS IN THE END WE BRING FOR SALE THERE, ... 321 BUILD SOIL 173
THEY STILL HANG ON. THAT 'SO MUCH OF THE EARTH'S . . . 322 BUILD SOIL 191
WE ARE TOO MUCH OUT, AND IF WE WON'T DRAW IN . . . . 324 BUILD SOIL 243
OF SPEECH AND THINKING IS SO MUCH MY BETTER . . . . . 324 BUILD SOIL 250
AS MUCH AS LOVE, AND TOO CLOSE IN TO STRIKE . . . . . 325 BUILD SOIL 277
BUT NOT MUCH IN BETWEEN UNLESS A COLLEGE. . . . . . 325 BUILD SOIL 282
DON'T LET IT BOTHER YOU TOO MUCH . . . . 326 TO A THINKER 22
(I DO TOO MUCH IN SOME MEN'S EYES.) . . . . 327 A MISSIVE MISSILE . . 37
OF SO MUCH WARMTH AND LIGHT. . . . . 333 HAPPINESS MAKES UP . . 11
IS TOO MUCH FOR THE SENSES, ... 336 CARPE DIEM 24
YET DID NOT MUCH TO SHORTEN STRIDE. . . . . 336 THE WIND AND THE RAIN 8
AND THOUGH IT WERE AS MUCH AS CLOUD COULD BEAR . . . . 337 THE WIND AND THE RAIN . 29
HE TELLS HER AS MUCH OF BLOOD AND DIRT . . . . . . 346 DISCOVERY OF MADEIRAS . 88
AS HE THINKS WILL DO HER NOT TOO MUCH HURT. . . . . . 346 DISCOVERY OF MADEIRAS . 89
BETWEEN TOO MUCH AND ME. . . . . 349 TRIPLE BRONZE . . . 12
THERE IS MUCH IN NATURE AGAINST US. BUT WE FORGET: . . . 349 OUR HOLD ON THE PLANET 7
THEY'VE TRIED TO GRASP WITH TOO MUCH SOCIAL FACT . . . 351 THE LESSON FOR TODAY . 34
AND GET OUTSIDE OF TOO MUCH BAD STATISTICS, ... 351 THE LESSON FOR TODAY . 37
ON ME AS MUCH AS ANY IS THE JEST. . . . . 355 THE LESSON FOR TODAY . 154
SPENDING YOURSELF TOO MUCH IN SELF-SUPPORT. . . . . . 356 A MOTH SEEN IN WINTER . 12
I CANNOT TOUCH YOUR LIFE, MUCH LESS CAN SAVE, ... 357 A MOTH SEEN IN WINTER . 23
TO EXPRESS HOW MUCH IT DIDN'T WANT TO DIE. . . . . . 357 A CONSIDERABLE SPECK . 18
WERE NOT TOO MUCH TO PAY FOR BIRTH. . . . . 362 A QUESTION 4
SO MUCH IS BEING NOW EXPECTED OF, ... 369 THE LITERATE FARMER AND 41
MUCH NOTICE OF WHAT'S GOING ON IN STARS. . . . . . . 370 THE LITERATE FARMER AND 70
YOU TAKE THE UGLINESS ALL SO MUCH DREAD, ... 371 THE LITERATE FARMER AND 106
BACK OUT OF ALL THIS NOW TOO MUCH FOR US, ... 377 DIRECTIVE 1
THEY THINK TOO MUCH OF HAVING SHADED OUT . . . . . . 378 DIRECTIVE 27
I NEVER SAW SO MUCH SWIFT WATER RUN CLOUDLESS. . . . . 379 TOO ANXIOUS FOR RIVERS 5
AND HOW MUCH LONGER A STORY HAS SCIENCE . . . . . . 379 TOO ANXIOUS FOR RIVERS 17
OR SO MUCH AS UNCROSS MY FEET, ... 381 AN UNSTAMPED LETTER IN 22
TO SAY AS MUCH I WRITE YOU THIS. . . . . 381 AN UNSTAMPED LETTER IN 52
BEWARE OF COMING TOO MUCH TO THE SURFACE . . . . . . 385 THE FEAR OF GOD . . . 11
FROM LOOKING UP TOO MUCH, ... 389 ASTROMETAPHYSICAL . . 6
HE HAD BEEN TOO ALL OUT, TOO MUCH EXTENDED. . . . . . 396 ANY SIZE WE PLEASE . . 12
COULD MAKE MUCH DIFFERENCE TO THE DEAD AND GONE. . . . . 397 THE PLANNERS . . . 6
IT HAPPENED WOULD HAVE VERY MUCH TO SAY. . . . . . . 397 THE PLANNERS . . . 8
THERE WAS SO MUCH MORE EVERY DAY TO LEARN, ... 398 BURSTING RAPTURE . . 6
AS MUCH AS ANYTHING FOR SITUATION. . . . . 400 TO THE RIGHT PERSON . 3
"HOEING'S TOO MUCH LIKE WORK FOR DICK," HE ADDED. . . . 404 FROM PLANE TO PLANE . 27
ISN'T IT PRETTY MUCH THE SAME IDEA? . . . . 405 FROM PLANE TO PLANE . 44
AND JUNE WAS NOT MUCH BETTER, COLD AND RAINY. . . . . 407 FROM PLANE TO PLANE . 89
OUR WORSHIP WAS A THING HE HAD TOO MUCH OF . . . . . 408 FROM PLANE TO PLANE . 132
HE SEEMS TO SAY THE REASON WHY SO MUCH . . . . . . 412 POD OF THE MILKWEED . 53
BUT WHO THERE IS TOO MUCH TO BELIEVE-- . . . . . . 414 A CABIN IN THE CLEARING 31
MUCH AS I OWN I OWE . . . . 415 CLOSED FOR GOOD . . 1
BUT NEVER SO MUCH AS LIFTED CHIN. . . . . 420 ONE MORE BREVITY . . 22
SO MUCH THOSE HEROES KNEW AND UNDERSTOOD-- . . . . . 422 FOR JOHN F. KENNEDY . 24
SO MUCH THEY KNEW AS CONSECRATED SEERS . . . . . . 422 FOR JOHN F. KENNEDY . 27
WE DON'T LIKE THAT MUCH. . . . . 438 KITTY HAWK . . . 338
BUT THAT'S NOT LIKE ME. ON MUCH LESS . . . . 451 A-WISHING WELL . . . 20
AND MUCH, MUCH EASIER TO GET, ... 451 A-WISHING WELL . . . 21
"YOU KNOW SO MUCH, GO ON, INSTRUCT ME FURTHER.. . . . . 458 HOW HARD TO KEEP FROM 146
"SO MUCH FOR PROGRESS," SAID DARIUS MEEKLY. . . . . . 459 HOW HARD TO KEEP FROM 162
IT MAY BE WINE, BUT MUCH MORE LIKELY LOVE-- . . . . . 461 HOW HARD TO KEEP FROM 242
OF ITS GOING MUCH LONGER UNNOTICED . . . . 465 SOME SCIENCE FICTION . 2
GOD NEEDS TIME JUST AS MUCH AS YOU OR I . . . . . . 478 A MASQUE OF REASON . 151
BUT TO MY QUESTION. I AM MUCH IMPRESSED . . . . . . 480 A MASQUE OF REASON . 183
MUCH AS YOUR HUSBAND, JOB, AND I TOGETHER . . . . . 481 A MASQUE OF REASON . 208
YOU HAVE THE IDEA. THERE'S NOT MUCH I CAN TELL YOU. . . 481 A MASQUE OF REASON . 216
THE CHANCES ARE WHEN THERE'S SO MUCH PRETENSE . . . . 483 A MASQUE OF REASON . 277
I WANTED HIM FORCED TO ACKNOWLEDGE SO MUCH. . . . . . 486 A MASQUE OF REASON . 359
UNLESS I'M MUCH MISTAKEN IN MYSELF . . . . 495 A MASQUE OF MERCY . 62
I THOUGHT AS MUCH. YOU HAVE IT ALL ARRANGED. . . . . 508 A MASQUE OF MERCY . 372
PAUL ONLY MEANS YOU MAKE TOO MUCH OF JUSTICE. . . . . 508 A MASQUE OF MERCY . 384
THAN FOUND IN CHURCH. / THAT DOESN'T HELP ME MUCH. . . . 513 A MASQUE OF MERCY . 515
THERE'S NOT MUCH WE CAN DO TILL MARTIN GETS HERE.-- . . 514 A MASQUE OF MERCY . 557
INCLINED TO HOPE FOR MUCH. STILL WHAT WE NEED . . . . 515 A MASQUE OF MERCY . 567
THEN HOW MUCH MORE THE FACE OF TRUTH MUST BE. . . . . 515 A MASQUE OF MERCY . 585
TOO MUCH ALL-FIRED BELIEF AND WE'D BE BACK . . . . . 516 A MASQUE OF MERCY . 602
BUT I'M TOO MUCH AFRAID OF GOD TO CLAIM . . . . . . 520 A MASQUE OF MERCY . 705
MUD
AND MELTING FURTHER IN THE WIND TO MUD. . . . . . . 179 THE STAR-SPLITTER . . 81
THE ROAD ALONE MAINTAINED ITSELF IN MUD, ... 239 OUR SINGING STRENGTH . 16
OUT OF THE MUD TWO STRANGERS CAME . . . . 275 TWO TRAMPS IN MUD TIME 1
TWO TRAMPS IN MUD TIME . . . . 275 TWO TRAMPS IN MUD TIME T
REFLECTED IN THE MUD AND EVEN DUST, ... 279 THE WHITE-TAILED HORNET 65
THE MUD CAME IN ONE COLD . . . . 298 ON TAKING FROM THE TOP 11
COME LOOK AT MY SIGNIFICANT MUD PIE." . . . . 321 BUILD SOIL 154
MUDDY
SMALL TOWNS--LOST NATION, BUNGEY, MUDDY BOO, ... 165 NEW HAMPSHIRE . . . 187

MUDDY (CONTINUED)
   BUT GULPING MUDDY GALLONS . . . . 376 ONE STEP BACKWARD TAKEN   3
MUFFLED (SEE LITTER-MUFFLED)
   FRANTIC IT SOUNDS, THOUGH MUFFLED AND FAR OFF. . . . . . 154 SNOW 319
   IN WHICH HIS FACE WAS MUFFLED TO THE EYES, ... 160 NEW HAMPSHIRE . . . 48
   THOUGH STRANGE AND MUFFLED. . . . . 218 I WILL SING YOU ONE-O . 26
MUFF-THING
   THE FUR-THING, MUFF-THING, ROCKING IN AND OUT . . . . 289 OLD BARN AT THE BOTTOM   8
MUGGER (SEE HUGGER-MUGGER)
MULCH
   THEY MUST BROOD WHERE THEY FELL IN MULCH AND MIRE, . . . 253 THE THATCH 25
MULE
   AND KICK WITH TWO LEGS LIKE AN ARMY MULE. . . . . . . 202 THE WITCH OF COOS . . 10
MULLEIN
   O'ERNIGHT 'TWIXT MULLEIN STALKS A WHEEL OF THREAD . . . 126 RANGE-FINDING . . . 10
MULTIPLICATION
   IS THE MULTIPLICATION TABLE OF LIFE." . . . . 263 THE TIMES TABLE . . . 12
MURDER
   HE NEVER STOPPED TO MURDER ANYONE . . . . 192 PAUL'S WIFE 25
   OF EITHER MURDER OR WAR IN ANY LAND. . . . . 371 THE LITERATE FARMER AND 111
MURDERED
   "HE WAS AFRAID OF BEING ROBBED OR MURDERED. . . . . . 45 A HUNDRED COLLARS . . 31
   MURDERED HIM AS LEFT OUT HIS MIDDLE NAME. . . . . . . 71 THE CODE 70
MURMUR
   THEIR MURMUR MORE LIKE THE SIGH WE SIGH . . . . 242 NEED OF BEING VERSED . 15
   LISTEN, THEY MURMUR TALKING IN THE DARK . . . . . . 415 A CABIN IN THE CLEARING 34
MURMURED
   BUT AT LAST HE MURMURED, "OH," AND AGAIN, "OH." . . . 51 HOME BURIAL 17
   "JUST THE WAY STEFANSSON RUNS ON," I MURMURED, ... 159 NEW HAMPSHIRE . . . 22
MURMURING
   MURMURING SOMETHING QUIET IN HER BREAST, ... 249 ACCEPTANCE 6
MURPHY
   BUT IF THE STORY MURPHY TOLD WAS TRUE, ... 192 PAUL'S WIFE 40
   OUT OF A WHITE-PINE LOG. MURPHY WAS THERE . . . . . 192 PAUL'S WIFE 55
   (MURPHY HAD BEEN THERE WATCHING ALL THE TIME, ... 194 PAUL'S WIFE 114
   NEXT EVENING MURPHY AND SOME OTHER FELLOWS . . . . . 195 PAUL'S WIFE 123
   AND THERE, WELL AFTER DARK, LET MURPHY TELL IT, . . . 195 PAUL'S WIFE 127
   HAS HAD OF PAUL AND HER SINCE MURPHY SAW THEM . . . . 195 PAUL'S WIFE 130
   MURPHY TOLD ME PAUL PUT ON ALL THOSE AIRS . . . . . 195 PAUL'S WIFE 148
MURPHY'S
   MURPHY'S IDEA WAS THAT A MAN LIKE PAUL . . . . . . 196 PAUL'S WIFE 155
MUSCLES
   THE LIFE OF MUSCLES ROCKING SOFT . . . . 276 TWO TRAMPS IN MUD TIME 47
   OUR MUSCLES NEVER COULD AGAIN CONTRACT: . . . . . . 351 THE LESSON FOR TODAY . 38
MUSCOVITE
   BY DAY HE'S MARXIAN MUSCOVITE. . . . . 393 A CASE FOR JEFFERSON . 4
MUSE
   TO MY MUSEUM AND MUSE; . . . . 295 A RECORD STRIDE . . . 30
   THE MUSE TAKES CARE OF YOU. YOU LIVE BY WRITING . . . 316 BUILD SOIL 17
   THE MUSE MOURNS ONE WHO WENT TO HIS RETREAT . . . . 359 THE LOST FOLLOWER . . 21
   FOR MY MUSE TO FLY . . . . 434 KITTY HAWK 184
MUSED
   "HAHN, HAHN," HE MUSED, "DON'T NEED MUCH TAKING DOWN." . 187 THE AX-HELVE 79
MUSEUM
   TO MY MUSEUM AND MUSE; . . . . 295 A RECORD STRIDE . . . 30
   IN THE MUSEUM OF ANTIOCH. . . . . 452 A-WISHING WELL . . . 63
MUSHROOM
   OR BROKEN ITS WHITE NECK OF MUSHROOM STUFF . . . . . 149 SNOW 165
MUSIC (SEE BAND-MUSIC)
   WERE MUSIC ENOUGH FOR HIM, FOR ONE. . . . . 24 PAN WITH US . . . 20
   AS THEY BOTH BITE THE WOOD. IT'S ALL OUR MUSIC. . . . 94 THE SELF-SEEKER . . 43
   AND LOOSING THE PENT-UP MUSIC OF OVERNIGHT. . . . . 236 VALLEY'S SINGING DAY . 10
   BUT GET SOME COLOR AND MUSIC OUT OF LIFE? . . . . . 264 THE INVESTMENT . . . 14
   THRUSH MUSIC--HARK! . . . . 334 COME IN 2
   THRUSH MUSIC WENT-- . . . . 334 COME IN 5
   FROM THAT STRAIN COMES THE EXPRESSION STRAINS OF MUSIC. . 460 HOW HARD TO KEEP FROM 215
   SPARE ME THE SETTING OF MY FATE TO MUSIC. . . . . . 495 A MASQUE OF MERCY . . 58
MUSING
   MARY SAT MUSING ON THE LAMP-FLAME AT THE TABLE, . . . 34 DEATH OF THE HIRED MAN 1
MUSK
   THE FLOW OF--WAS IT MUSK . . . . 227 TO EARTHWARD 6
MUST---NOT INDEXED
MUSTER
   TILL IT CAN MUSTER BREATH INSIDE A HALL . . . . . . 399 THE INGENUITIES OF DEBT 17
MUSTN'T---NOT INDEXED
MUTE
   I KNOW NOT WHO THESE MUTE FOLK ARE . . . . 6 GHOST HOUSE 22
   AND ON THE BAT'S MUTE ANTICS, WHO WOULD SEEM . . . . 14 WAITING 14
MUTTER
   SACRED RIGMAROLES TO MUTTER, ... 396 AN IMPORTER 6
MUZZLE
   AND CRACKED HIS RAGGED MUZZLE. . . . . 339 THE SUBVERTED FLOWER . 14
MY---NOT INDEXED
MYRIAD
   WHERE A MYRIAD SNOWY QUARTZ-STONES LIFT, ... 26 A LINE-STORM SONG . . 3
MYRRH
   THE MYRRH TREE GIVES IT. SMELL THE ROSIN BURNING? . . 473 A MASQUE OF REASON . . 9
MYSELF
   AND LOSE MYSELF AMID SO MANY ALIKE. . . . . 14 WAITING 8
   MYSELF UNSEEN, I SEE IN WHITE DEFINED . . . . . . 17 THE VANTAGE POINT . . 5
   WHAT WAS IT IT WHISPERED? I KNEW NOT WELL MYSELF; . . 17 MOWING 3
   AND LOOK MYSELF, BUT YOU KNOW HOW IT IS: . . . . . 43 THE MOUNTAIN . . . 81
   I'M NOT SO DRUNK I CAN'T TAKE CARE OF MYSELF." . . . 45 A HUNDRED COLLARS . . 38
   BY WHICH I'D BIND MYSELF TO KEEP HANDS OFF . . . . 52 HOME BURIAL . . . 51
   I PROMISED MYSELF TO GET DOWN SOME DAY . . . . . 62 A SERVANT TO SERVANTS . 3
   I STAND AND MAKE MYSELF REPEAT OUT LOUD . . . . . 63 A SERVANT TO SERVANTS . 18
   OF THE GREAT HARVEST I MYSELF DESIRED. . . . . . 69 AFTER APPLE-PICKING . 29
   I SAID IT TO MYSELF AS MUCH AS YOU." . . . . . . 70 THE CODE 14

MYSELF (CONTINUED)
  OR I CAN'T GIVE MYSELF TO HEAR THE VOICES." . . . . 78 THE GENERATIONS OF MEN   147
  I LET MYSELF IN AT THE KITCHEN DOOR. . . . . 81 THE HOUSEKEEPER . . .   1
  I DON'T KNOW WHERE MYSELF. JOHN THINKS I DO. . . . . . 82 THE HOUSEKEEPER . . . 24
  THROUGH THE BED BLANKETS I REMIND MYSELF . . . . 93 THE SELF-SEEKER . . . 19
  BEFORE HE GOES, BECAUSE I HURT MYSELF, ... 98 THE SELF-SEEKER . . . 170
  AND SAW MYSELF--HE WOULD BE ILL-ADVISED----" . . . . . 100 THE SELF-SEEKER . . . 205
  SO WAS I ONCE MYSELF A SWINGER OF BIRCHES.-- . . . . . 122 BIRCHES 41
  TO SEE FOR MYSELF ABOUT THE BIRCH . . . . 123 PEA BRUSH   3
  BY LEANING BACK MYSELF, AS IF THE REINS . . . . . . 132 THE BONFIRE 79
  "WHOSE BUSINESS--IF I TAKE IT ON MYSELF, ... 142 THE VANISHING RED .   6
  "CHRISTIAN ENOUGH I SHOULD CALL THAT MYSELF. . . . . . 144 SNOW 48
  I'VE SEEN THE TIME I'VE HAD TO WORK MYSELF. . . . . . 159 NEW HAMPSHIRE . .   6
  I MAY AS WELL CONFESS MYSELF THE AUTHOR . . . . . . 166 NEW HAMPSHIRE . . 228
  I REFUSE TO ADAPT MYSELF A MITE . . . . 166 NEW HAMPSHIRE . . 234
  I FOUND MYSELF IN A CLOSE CORNER WHERE . . . . . . 170 NEW HAMPSHIRE . . 360
  I ARMED MYSELF AGAINST SUCH BONES AS MIGHT BE . . . . 175 THE CENSUS-TAKER . 43
  DE SECOND GROWT! I CUT MYSELF--TOUGH, TOUGH!" . . . . 186 THE AX-HELVE . . . 31
  NOT FOR MYSELF WAS I SO MUCH CONCERNED. . . . . . . 190 THE GRINDSTONE . . . 51
  AS A GIRL GATHERED FROM THE BIRCH MYSELF . . . . . . 196 WILD GRAPES . . .   4
  AND GIVE MYSELF OUT AS TWO DIFFERENT AGES, ... 196 WILD GRAPES . . . 17
  I WAS JUST COMING TO MYSELF ENOUGH . . . . 203 THE WITCH OF COOS . 44
  AND FELL BACK FROM HIM ON THE FLOOR MYSELF. . . . . . 204 THE WITCH OF COOS . 78
  I PUSHED MYSELF UPSTAIRS, AND IN THE LIGHT . . . . . 205 THE WITCH OF COOS . 97
  OLD AS I AM, I'M GOING TO LET MYSELF . . . . 214 A FOUNTAIN, A BOTTLE . 29
  ME MYSELF IN THE SUMMER HEAVEN, GODLIKE, ... 225 FOR ONCE SOMETHING .   5
  MYSELF AS ONE HIS OWN PRETENSE DECEIVES; . . . . . . 233 A BOUNDLESS MOMENT . 10
  AND THREW MYSELF WET-ELBOWED AND WET-KNEED . . . . . 237 A HILLSIDE THAW . . 12
  SOMETIMES I FEEL MYSELF I CAN HARDLY BEAR . . . . . 287 A ROADSIDE STAND . 32
  SEEING MYSELF WELL LOST ONCE MORE, I SIGHED, ... 295 LOST IN HEAVEN . .   9
  TO SCARE MYSELF WITH MY OWN DESERT PLACES. . . . . . 296 DESERT PLACES . . 16
  I SAID TO MYSELF ALMOST IN PRAYER, ... 306 A TRIAL RUN . . .   1
  I SHOULD MYSELF, ONLY I DON'T KNOW HOW. . . . . . . 316 BUILD SOIL . . . 20
  DON'T LET THE THINGS I SAY AGAINST MYSELF . . . . . 320 BUILD SOIL . . . 131
  TITYRUS, SOMETIMES I'M PERPLEXED MYSELF . . . . . . 321 BUILD SOIL . . . 163
  WHAT I MYSELF HAVE HELD. BUT WHY DECLARE . . . . . . 335 I COULD GIVE ALL . 12
  I MAKE MYSELF THIS TIME . . . . 348 TRIPLE BRONZE . .   5
  I SHOULD NOT CURSE MYSELF WITH IT TO HELL, ... 350 THE LESSON FOR TODAY .   4
  I HAVE A MIND MYSELF AND RECOGNIZE . . . . 358 A CONSIDERABLE SPECK . 30
  I SAVED MYSELF FROM GOING. . . . . 377 ONE STEP BACKWARD TAKEN 11
  MYSELF, IN FORMA PAUPERIS, ... 381 AN UNSTAMPED LETTER IN 51
  WHEN ANY BUT MYSELF PRESUMED TO SAY . . . . 443 AUSPEX 11
  DARE TO SPEAK OUT AND TELL ME ABOUT MYSELF. . . . . 456 HOW HARD TO KEEP FROM 100
  OR FOR MYSELF IN MY RETREAT . . . . 470 IN WINTER IN THE WOODS 11
  MY VARYING OPINION OF MYSELF . . . . 474 A MASQUE OF REASON . 28
  UNLESS I'M MUCH MISTAKEN IN MYSELF . . . . 495 A MASQUE OF MERCY . 62
  YET COULD NOT BRING MYSELF TO SAY A WORD. . . . . . 497 A MASQUE OF MERCY . 99
  LIKE WORKING MYSELF UP TO PROPHESY . . . . 501 A MASQUE OF MERCY . 198
  I WON'T DECEIVE MYSELF ABOUT SUCCESS . . . . 513 A MASQUE OF MERCY . 525
  AS IF I ASKED FOR ONE MORE CHANCE MYSELF . . . . . 521 A MASQUE OF MERCY . 736
MYSTERIOUS
  IT MADE THE WORLD SEEM SO MYSTERIOUS. . . . . 163 NEW HAMPSHIRE . . 134
  A DATED POPULAR-SCIENCE MEDLEY ON A MYSTERIOUS LIGHT... . 368 THE LITERATE FARMER AND S
MYSTERIOUSLY
  IS SO MYSTERIOUSLY PELTED AT US? . . . . 360 A LOOSE MOUNTAIN . .   4
MYSTERY
  THAT'S A HARD MYSTERY OF JEFFERSON'S. . . . . 57 THE BLACK COTTAGE . . 64
  BEFORE THE MYSTERY OF GLASS! . . . . 128 THE OFT-REPEATED DREAM   8
  WITHOUT THE NAME HER PERSONAL MYSTERY. . . . . . . 182 MAPLE 93
  WHAT IS THIS TALKED-OF MYSTERY OF BIRTH . . . . . . 267 RIDERS   5
  SOME MYSTERY BECOMES THE PROUD. . . . . 403 SOMETHING LIKE A STAR .   6
  THAT IS THE MYSTERY YOU MUST ACCEPT.-- . . . . . . 512 A MASQUE OF MERCY . 511
MYSTIC
  THE MYSTIC LINK TO BIND AND HOLD . . . . 21 THE TRIAL BY EXISTENCE 63
MYSTICS
  THAT'S HOW WE FEEL--AND WE'RE NO SPECIAL MYSTICS. . . . 351 THE LESSON FOR TODAY . 42
MYSTIFIED
  BEARING IT CRUSHED AND MYSTIFIED. . . . . 21 THE TRIAL BY EXISTENCE 72
MYTH
  "THE INDIANS HAD A MYTH OF CHICAMOZTOC, ... 76 THE GENERATIONS OF MEN 92
  FORGET THE MYTH. . . . . 413 AWAY! 13
  PERSISTING FROM OLD CHAOS IN THEIR MYTH, ... 511 A MASQUE OF MERCY . 470

N

N
  OF SIGNS THAT WITH N TURNED WRONG AND S TURNED WRONG . . . 286 A ROADSIDE STAND . . 10
NAG'S
  EVER SINCE NAG'S HEAD . . . . 429 KITTY HAWK 23
NAIL (SEE TOE-NAIL)
  PROMISE ME ALL THE SHOOKS I WANT TO NAIL." . . . . . 95 THE SELF-SEEKER . . . 79
  "TOFFILE, GET NAILS." I MADE HIM NAIL THE DOOR SHUT . . . 206 THE WITCH OF COOS . . 119
NAILED
  AGAINST THE ATTIC DOOR: THE DOOR IS NAILED. . . . . . 203 THE WITCH OF COOS . . 22
NAILHEAD
  BUT WHAT HE FOUND HE HAD WAS JUST A NAILHEAD. . . . . 278 THE WHITE-TAILED HORNET 34
  HE STRUCK A SECOND TIME. ANOTHER NAILHEAD. . . . . . 278 THE WHITE-TAILED HORNET 35
  NAILHEAD WITH FLY AND FLY WITH HUCKLEBERRY. . . . . . 279 THE WHITE-TAILED HORNET 46
NAILHEADS
  "THOSE ARE JUST NAILHEADS. THOSE ARE FASTENED DOWN." . . . 278 THE WHITE-TAILED HORNET 36
NAILS
  THE WARPING BOARDS PULL OUT THEIR OWN OLD NAILS . . . 56 THE BLACK COTTAGE . . 49
  "TOFFILE, GET NAILS." I MADE HIM NAIL THE DOOR SHUT . . . 206 THE WITCH OF COOS . . 119
NAIL-SCISSORS
  SOMEONE TOOK CURVED NAIL-SCISSORS AND SNIPPED OFF . . . . 501 A MASQUE OF MERCY . . 201

NAIVENESS
    NAIVENESS ABOUT JUSTICE OUT OF HIM, ... 517 A MASQUE OF MERCY . . 640
NAKED
    ON A HEIGHT OF NAKED PASTURE LAND; . . . . 23 PAN WITH US 7
    A MAN? A BRUTE. NAKED ABOVE THE WAIST, ... 46 A HUNDRED COLLARS . . 50
    THEY BOUND THEM NAKED SO THEY FACED . . . . . . 345 DISCOVERY OF MADEIRAS . 76
NAKEDNESS
    HEROIC IN ITS NAKEDNESS, ... 21 THE TRIAL BY EXISTENCE 43
NAME
    NOT FOR THE SAKE OF CLIMBING. WHAT'S ITS NAME?" . . . . 43 THE MOUNTAIN 90
    "LAFE WAS THE NAME, I THINK?" / "YES, LAYFAYETTE. . . . 46 A HUNDRED COLLARS . . 41
    I'VE FELT MEAN LATELY; MEAN'S NO NAME FOR IT. . . . . 46 A HUNDRED COLLARS . . 54
    WHEN IT OUTGROWS THE WIRE BAND OF ITS NAME TAG. . . . 46 A HUNDRED COLLARS . . 57
    ANYTHING SPECIAL YOU'RE A-MIND TO NAME. . . . . . . 53 HOME BURIAL 52
    "HE'S A THRIFTIER PERSON THAN SOME I COULD NAME." . . . 60 BLUEBERRIES 47
    SOME STRANGE KIND--THEY TOLD ME IT HADN'T A NAME." . . 61 BLUEBERRIES 66
    MURDERED HIM AS LEFT OUT HIS MIDDLE NAME. . . . . . 71 THE CODE 70
    AND THOSE OF THE NAME STARK GATHERED IN BOW, ... 73 THE GENERATIONS OF MEN 4
    NO MORE THAN BROUGHT US BACK INTO THE NAME." . . . . 75 THE GENERATIONS OF MEN 57
    YOU SEE THEY KNOW I HAVEN'T HAD YOUR NAME, ... 79 THE GENERATIONS OF MEN 157
    THOUGH WHAT A NAME SHOULD MATTER BETWEEN US----" . . 79 THE GENERATIONS OF MEN 158
    THE MAN WAS FOUND. I'D BETTER NAME NO NAMES. . . . 88 THE HOUSEKEEPER . . . 188
    AS IF FOR PAPERS THAT MIGHT BEAR THE NAME . . . . 96 THE SELF-SEEKER . . . 98
    YOU ONLY HAVE TO SIGN YOUR NAME. RIGHT--THERE." . . 99 THE SELF-SEEKER . . . 183
    TOO MUCH ALIKE TO MARK OR NAME A PLACE BY . . . . 101 THE WOOD-PILE 7
    WHAT WAS IT? DID YOU CALL ME BY MY NAME? . . . . 118 THE TELEPHONE . . . 15
    AND COMES THAT OTHER FALL WE NAME THE FALL. . . . 120 THE OVEN BIRD . . . 9
    I GUESS I KNOW WHERE I CAN FIND MY NAME . . . . 144 SNOW 39
    HE SEEMS TO HAVE LOST OFF HIS CHRISTIAN NAME." . . 144 SNOW 47
    WHO IN THE NAME OF FLUID INSPIRATION, ... 159 NEW HAMPSHIRE . . . 27
    AND TAKE THEIR NAME. THEY'VE SINCE TOLD ME THEIR NAME-- . 161 NEW HAMPSHIRE . . . 85
    AND I REMEMBER ONE WHOSE NAME APPEARED . . . . 165 NEW HAMPSHIRE . . . 193
    MADE MAPLE FIRST TAKE NOTICE OF HER NAME. . . . 179 MAPLE 2
    THERE'S NO SUCH NAME." / "TEACHERS DON'T KNOW AS MUCH . 179 MAPLE 5
    'MAPLE.' I SAID IT TOO: 'YES, FOR HER NAME.' . . . 180 MAPLE 18
    LUCKILY ALL SHE WANTED OF HER NAME THEN . . . . 180 MAPLE 30
    AS SHE STOOD SAYING HER NAME OVER ALOUD, . . . 181 MAPLE 41
    WHAT WAS IT ABOUT HER NAME? ITS STRANGENESS LAY . 181 MAPLE 44
    FOR THE NAME MAPLE TO HAVE BROUGHT HER TO, . . 182 MAPLE 78
    A MAPLE TREE?" / "BECAUSE MY NAME IS MAPLE?" . . 182 MAPLE 88
    WITHOUT THE NAME HER PERSONAL MYSTERY. . . . 182 MAPLE 93
    A NAME TO CARRY FOR LIFE AND NEVER KNOW . . . 183 MAPLE 116
    THUS HAD A NAME WITH MEANING, GIVEN IN DEATH, . . 185 MAPLE 163
    A NAME WITH MEANING COULD BRING UP A CHILD, . . 185 MAPLE 166
    BETTER A MEANINGLESS NAME, I SHOULD SAY, . . . 185 MAPLE 168
    NAME CHILDREN SOME NAMES AND SEE WHAT YOU DO. . . 185 MAPLE 170
    EITHER TO PRAISE HER OR SO MUCH AS NAME HER, . . 196 PAUL'S WIFE . . . 153
    WHERE WAS HIS GRAVE? DID LABAN KNOW HIS NAME? . . 200 PLACE FOR A THIRD . . 37
    I VERIFIED THE NAME NEXT MORNING: TOFFILE. . . 207 THE WITCH OF COOS . . 154
    WOULD NAME THE HOUR . . . . 217 I WILL SING YOU ONE-O . 4
    TO BEAR FORSAKEN THE PLACE'S NAME. . . . . 241 NEED OF BEING VERSED . 8
    YOUR NAME NOT WRITTEN ON EITHER SIDE. . . . 247 ON GOING UNNOTICED . . 12
    I NAME ALL THE FLOWERS I AM SURE THEY WEREN'T: . . 248 A PASSING GLIMPSE . . 5
    I NEEDN'T CALL YOU BY NAME. . . . . . . 264 THE LAST MOWING . . . 19
    TODAY SHE WOULDN'T KNOW OUR NAME. . . . . 265 THE BIRTHPLACE . . . 11
    GOD ONCE SPOKE TO PEOPLE BY NAME. . . . . 266 SITTING BY A BUSH . . 17
    THEIR NAME WAS CALLED THE GOLD HESPERIDEE. . . 283 THE GOLD HESPERIDEE . 18
    THAT THE NAME GOLD HESPERIDEE WAS RIGHT. . . 284 THE GOLD HESPERIDEE . 30
    ITS NAME MIGHT BETTER BE FIRST MOTOR KITE. . . 308 THE WRIGHTS' BIPLANE . 2
    ITS MAKERS' NAME--TIME CANNOT GET THAT WRONG, . . 308 THE WRIGHTS' BIPLANE . 3
    OF MANY A TREASURE BY NAME . . . . . . 311 THE VINDICTIVES . . . 34
    NAME NAMES AND TELL YOU WHO BY NAME IS WICKED? . . 317 BUILD SOIL 43
    THE NAME OF THE LADY WITH HIS OWN . . . . 347 DISCOVERY OF MADEIRAS 122
    WE HAVE TODAY AND I COULD CALL THEIR NAME . . 351 THE LESSON FOR TODAY . 31
    IT IS AS TRUE AS CAESAR'S NAME WAS KAISER . . 363 AN EQUALIZER . . . 1
    AND THE DOT IN FRONT OF A NAME . . . . . 367 A SERIOUS STEP LIGHTLY 5
    FOR FAMILY AFTER FAMILY NAME. . . . . . 367 A SERIOUS STEP LIGHTLY 15
    FOR OUR NAME FARMING HERE, ... 367 A SERIOUS STEP LIGHTLY 17
    THERE IS A STAR THAT'S SERIOUS BY NAME . . . 369 THE LITERATE FARMER AND 29
    SORRY TO HAVE NO NAME FOR YOU BUT YOU. . . . 382 TO AN ANCIENT . . . 3
    A BLINDMAN BY THE NAME OF LA FONTAINE. . . . 394 HAEC FABULA DOCET . . 1
    "YOU WISHED YOUR MIDDLE NAME HAD BEEN TECUMSEH." . . 406 FROM PLANE TO PLANE . 74
    IN FANCY I RATIFIED HIS NAME, ... 420 ONE MORE BREVITY . . 39
    AND WAS WASTE IN NAME. . . . . 439 KITTY HAWK 372
    THIS THOUGH WE TOOK THE INDIAN NAME FOR MAIZE . . 446 DOES NO ONE AT ALL EVER 7
    AND CHANGED IT TO THE ENGLISH NAME FOR WHEAT. . . 446 DOES NO ONE AT ALL EVER 8
    SO FAR INLAND THE VERY NAME OF OCEAN . . . 447 DOES NO ONE AT ALL EVER 37
    BUT I CALLED IT A NAME. . . . . . . 450 OBJECTION TO BE STEPPED 8
    HIS NAME IS OMAR. I AS A RHODES SCHOLAR . . 459 HOW HARD TO KEEP FROM 188
    WHEN NO MAN'S NAME AND NO NOUN'S ADJECTIVE . . 461 HOW HARD TO KEEP FROM 239
    I AM A NAME FOR BEING PUT UPON. . . . . 474 A MASQUE OF REASON . . 38
    I'M A GREAT STICKLER FOR THE AUTHOR'S NAME. . . 480 A MASQUE OF REASON . 199
    THE NAME HIS MOTHER GAVE HIM IS TO BLAME . . 494 A MASQUE OF MERCY . . 35
    YOU WRONG ME. / WELL THEN, NAME A SINGLE SIN. . . 503 A MASQUE OF MERCY . 262
NAMED
    THE TRIAL BY EXISTENCE NAMED, ... 20 THE TRIAL BY EXISTENCE 19
    NAMED SANDERS, WITH A GANG OF FOUR OR FIVE . . 70 THE CODE 31
    NO, THE FIVE HUNDRED WAS THE SUM THEY NAMED . . 95 THE SELF-SEEKER . . . 73
    WHOLE TOWNSHIPS NAMED BUT WITHOUT POPULATION. . . 165 NEW HAMPSHIRE . . . 209
    SEEMS TO HAVE BEEN A MAN NAMED JOHN L. DARWIN." . . 168 NEW HAMPSHIRE . . . 299
    WELL, YOU WERE NAMED AFTER A MAPLE TREE. . . 180 MAPLE 9
    YOUR MOTHER NAMED YOU. YOU AND SHE JUST SAW . . 180 MAPLE 10
    THEY LEFT THE NAMED . . . . 219 I WILL SING YOU ONE-O . 44
    WAS NAMED FOR HIM INSTEAD OF HER. . . . . 347 DISCOVERY OF MADEIRAS 135
    (A COUNTRY NAMED FOR HIM, A TOWN, ... 418 AMERICA IS HARD TO SEE 46
NAMELESS
    THEY BROUGHT HER TO A NAMELESS ISLE. . . . . . . 347 DISCOVERY OF MADEIRAS . 110

		PAGE TITLE	LINE

NAMES
DOUBTLESS BEAR NAMES THAT THE MOSSES MAR. . . . . . . 6 GHOST HOUSE 25
I DON'T LEARN WHAT THEIR NAMES ARE, LET ALONE . . . . . 65 A SERVANT TO SERVANTS . 82
THERE AIN'T NO NAMES QUITE LIKE THE OLD ONES, THOUGH, . . 80 THE GENERATIONS OF MEN 186
THE MAN WAS FOUND. I'D BETTER NAME NO NAMES. . . . . . 88 THE HOUSEKEEPER . . . 188
AND SAYS THEIR NAMES, AND LEAVES THEM WHERE THEY ARE." . . 98 THE SELF-SEEKER . . . 162
LONG ENOUGH FOR RECORDING ALL OUR NAMES ON.-- . . . . . 143 SNOW 10
IN HAVING TOO MUCH MEANING. OTHER NAMES, ... 181 MAPLE 45
THIS DIFFERENCE FROM OTHER NAMES IT WAS . . . . 181 MAPLE 49
NAME CHILDREN SOME NAMES AND SEE WHAT YOU DO. . . . . . 185 MAPLE 170
NAME NAMES AND TELL YOU WHO BY NAME IS WICKED? . . . . 317 BUILD SOIL 43
BY PROPER NAMES I FIND I DO MY THINKING. . . . . 480 A MASQUE OF REASON . 200
YOU SEEM SO READY AT TRANSLATING NAMES. . . . . 495 A MASQUE OF MERCY . 61
NAME'S
HIS NAME'S JOE, ... 211 AN EMPTY THREAT . . . 12
MY NAME'S NOT JOE. I DON'T LIKE WHAT SHE SAYS. . . . . 500 A MASQUE OF MERCY . 169
NAMING
TWENTY-FIVE YEARS AGO AT MAPLE'S NAMING . . . . 184 MAPLE 149
NAMING STARS TO BOOT . . . . 438 KITTY HAWK 316
NARROW
BURST INTO MY NARROW STALL; . . . . 11 TO THE THAWING WIND . 11
AND DOWN A NARROW PASSAGE FULL OF DOORS, ... 45 A HUNDRED COLLARS . 34
THE ADVANTAGES IT HAS, SO LONG AND NARROW, ... 63 A SERVANT TO SERVANTS . 19
A NARROW PASSAGE ALL THE WAY AROUND. . . . . 66 A SERVANT TO SERVANTS . 116
THE SUN IN THE NEW-CUT NARROW GAP . . . . 123 PEA BRUSH 5
IT SEEMS A NARROW CHOICE THE AGE INSISTS ON. . . . . . 171 NEW HAMPSHIRE . . . 403
THE TENDENCY, A LONG, LONG NARROW STRIP . . . . 489 A MASQUE OF REASON . 453
NARROWED
SO THERE THEY LET THEIR LIVES BE NARROWED IN . . . . 240 OUR SINGING STRENGTH . 31
NASTURTIUM
WE DID FIND ONE NASTURTIUM . . . . 135 LOCKED OUT 8
NATAL
SAND GRAINS SHOULD SUGAR IN THE NATAL DEW . . . . . 58 THE BLACK COTTAGE . . 122
TILL THE SPONGY SOIL AGAIN WAS NATAL WET. . . . . . 349 OUR HOLD ON THE PLANET 10
NATION
IS THE DISGRACE IN MAN OR STATE OR NATION. . . . . . . 159 NEW HAMPSHIRE . . . 8
SMALL TOWNS--LOST NATION, BUNGEY, MUDDY BOO, ... 165 NEW HAMPSHIRE . . . 187
AND NATION NATION. . . . . 220 I WILL SING YOU ONE-O . 79
AND SO'S THE NATION, SO'S THE TOTAL RACE. . . . . . . 355 THE LESSON FOR TODAY . 146
MAKE EVERYBODY WANT TO BE A NATION. . . . . 423 FOR JOHN F. KENNEDY . 31
A NATION HAS TO TAKE ITS NATURAL COURSE . . . . 459 HOW HARD TO KEEP FROM 158
NATIONAL
WE'RE NATIONAL AND ACT AS NATIONALS. . . . . 320 BUILD SOIL 146
ON A NATIONAL BOUNDARY. . . . . 348 TRIPLE BRONZE . . . 10
NATIONALS
WE'RE NATIONAL AND ACT AS NATIONALS. . . . . 320 BUILD SOIL 146
NATIONS
WHETHER IT'S PERSONS PIED OR NATIONS PIED. . . . . . . 321 BUILD SOIL 156
THE WASTE OF NATIONS WARRING. . . . . 360 NOVEMBER 15
THAT NATIONS LIKE THE CUBAN AND THE SWISS . . . . . . 398 NO HOLY WARS FOR THEM . 11
WHAT YOU COMPLAIN OF, ALL THE NATIONS SHARE. . . . . . 398 BURSTING RAPTURE . . 10
IN ANY GAME THE NATIONS WANT TO PLAY. . . . . 424 FOR JOHN F. KENNEDY . 75
NATION'S
OR EVEN NATION'S TO RESTRICT MY MEANING. . . . . . . 166 NEW HAMPSHIRE . . . 231
EQUALLY FOR THE NATION'S CONSTITUTION). . . . . 317 BUILD SOIL 47
NATIVE
WERE NATIVE TO THE GRAIN BEFORE THE KNIFE . . . . . 187 THE AX-HELVE 73
I HAD MY NATIVE SIMILE JARRED. . . . . 265 THE DOOR IN THE DARK . 7
HE CAME AT LAST TO HIS NATIVE SHIRE. . . . . 347 DISCOVERY OF MADEIRAS . 132
HAVE COME DOWN FROM THEIR NATIVE LEDGE . . . . 364 A NATURE NOTE . . . 2
THE ONLY NATIVE TREE THAT DARES TO LEAN, ... 375 A YOUNG BIRCH . . . 8
THEY MUST BY NOW HAVE LEARNED THE NATIVE TONGUE. . . . 414 A CABIN IN THE CLEARING 20
BY CHARACTER, BY TONGUE, BY NATIVE TRAIT, ... 422 FOR JOHN F. KENNEDY . 14
FROM THE PEARL'S HAVING ITS OWN NATIVE WARMTH, ... 456 HOW HARD TO KEEP FROM 90
NATTY
HIS NATTY WINGS WITH SELF-ASSURANCE PERK. . . . . . 309 WASPISH 3
NATURAL
HE BOWED WITH GRACE TO NATURAL LAW, ... 139 BROWN'S DESCENT . . . 60
A NATURAL DEATH, AND VIGILANCE COMMITTEES . . . . . . 159 NEW HAMPSHIRE . . . 19
SOMEONE WAS SAYING IN SUCH NATURAL TONES . . . . . . 182 MAPLE 85
BY SHRINKING THE RAWHIDE TO NATURAL LENGTH. . . . . . 192 PAUL'S WIFE 48
HOWEVER NATURAL? GIVE YOU YOUR BOOKS! . . . . 215 A FOUNTAIN, A BOTTLE . 59
WHERE NATURAL FRIENDS ARE MET, WHERE DOGS ARE KEPT, . . 318 BUILD SOIL 83
A NATION HAS TO TAKE ITS NATURAL COURSE . . . . 459 HOW HARD TO KEEP FROM 158
NATURALLY
WHICH NATURALLY SHE DOESN'T CARE TO SELL. . . . . . 161 NEW HAMPSHIRE . . . 63
AND NATURALLY YOU COULDN'T GO ALONG . . . . 369 THE LITERATE FARMER AND 25
NATURE
WE CAN'T IN NATURE GROW TO MANY MORE: . . . . 41 THE MOUNTAIN . . . 26
JUST TAKING WHAT NATURE IS WILLING TO GIVE, ... 61 BLUEBERRIES . . . 55
I WOULDN'T BE A PRUDE AFRAID OF NATURE. . . . . 170 NEW HAMPSHIRE . . . 366
"'NATURE IS CRUEL, MAN IS SICK OF BLOOD': . . . . . 170 NEW HAMPSHIRE . . . 371
THE LINE WHERE MAN LEAVES OFF AND NATURE STARTS, . . . 171 NEW HAMPSHIRE . . . 379
I'D HATE TO BE A RUNAWAY FROM NATURE. . . . . 171 NEW HAMPSHIRE . . . 397
THE VERY NATURE OF THE SOIL WAS HOT . . . . 173 A STAR IN A STONEBOAT . 21
TO SHOW ITS WORLDLY NATURE AND BEGIN . . . . 174 A STAR IN A STONEBOAT . 51
AS LEAVING MORE TO NATURE AND HAPPY CHANCE. . . . . . 185 MAPLE 169
"FOR GOD'S SAKE, AREN'T YOU FOND OF VIEWING NATURE? . . 215 A FOUNTAIN, A BOTTLE . 56
YOU DON'T LIKE NATURE. ALL YOU LIKE IS BOOKS. . . . . 215 A FOUNTAIN, A BOTTLE . 57
TO DARKEN NATURE AND BE SUMMER WOODS-- . . . . . . 245 SPRING POOLS . . . 8
NO VOICE IN NATURE IS HEARD TO CRY ALOUD . . . . . . 249 ACCEPTANCE 3
IT IS FROM THIS IN NATURE WE ARE FROM. . . . . . . 260 WEST-RUNNING BROOK . 71
AND BRING BACK NATURE IN PEOPLE'S PLACE. . . . . . . 263 THE TIMES TABLE . . 20
AND THE NATURE OF TIME AND SPACE, ... 288 DEPARTMENTAL . . . 11
WHY IS HIS NATURE FOREVER SO HARD TO TEACH . . . . . 305 THERE ARE ROUGHLY ZONES 11
IF HE LEAVES IT TO NATURE TO CARRY OUT THE SENTENCE. . . 307 NOT QUITE SOCIAL . 14
AND SO ON TO THE LIMIT OF MY NATURE. . . . . 323 BUILD SOIL 242
THERE IS MUCH IN NATURE AGAINST US. BUT WE FORGET: . . 349 OUR HOLD ON THE PLANET 12

NATURE (CONTINUED)
    TAKE NATURE ALTOGETHER SINCE TIME BEGAN, ... 349 OUR HOLD ON THE PLANET   13
    INCLUDING HUMAN NATURE, IN PEACE AND WAR, ... 349 OUR HOLD ON THE PLANET   14
    A NATURE NOTE . . . . 364 A NATURE NOTE . . . T
    AND NATURE TOO, BUT THIS IS NOT THE SAME. . . . . . . 369 THE LITERATE FARMER AND 30
    YOUR PROBABLE BRUTE NATURE IS DISCUSSED. . . . . 382 TO AN ANCIENT . . . 11
    BY NATURE MEANT THE WHOLE GODDAM MACHINERY. . . . . . . 393 LUCRETIUS VERSUS POETS 6
    THE ONLY MEANING POSSIBLE FOR NATURE . . . . 393 LUCRETIUS VERSUS POETS 8
    "NATURE I LOVED; AND NEXT TO NATURE, ART." . . . . . . 393 LUCRETIUS VERSUS POETS S
    WAS TO MASTER NATURE . . . . 438 KITTY HAWK 323
    NATURE WITHIN HER INMOST SELF DIVIDES . . . . 468 FROM IRON 1
    I SEE FOR NATURE NO DEFEAT . . . . 470 IN WINTER IN THE WOODS 9
    OF WHAT I VALUED MOST IN HUMAN NATURE. . . . . 485 A MASQUE OF REASON . . 350
    IN NATURE WOULD WIPE OUT ALL HUMAN FAULT. . . . . . . 502 A MASQUE OF MERCY . . 232
NATURED (SEE LIGHT-NATURED)
NATURE'S
    NATURE'S FIRST GREEN IS GOLD, ... 222 NOTHING GOLD CAN STAY . 1
    NATURE'S NEVER QUITE . . . . 442 KITTY HAWK 451
NAUGHT
    AND THOUGHT OF NAUGHT TO SAY, ... 11 WIND AND WINDOW FLOWER 26
    BUT NAUGHT EXTENUATES OR DIMS, ... 20 THE TRIAL BY EXISTENCE 39
    AN OATH OF TOWNS THAT SET THE WILD AT NAUGHT, ... 141 THE LINE-GANG . . . 12
    IT MOVED ITSELF. THE WIND'S AT NAUGHT IN HERE. . . . . 148 SNOW 137
    SEEMS TO OWE NAUGHT TO ANY SINGLE CORD, ... 332 THE SILKEN TENT . . . 8
    TO WALK IN SAYING NAUGHT . . . . 415 CLOSED FOR GOOD . . . 14
    TO NAUGHT BUT HIS OWN FORCE OF WILL. . . . . 418 AMERICA IS HARD TO SEE 70
    THERE WAS NEVER NAUGHT, ... 426 A NEVER NAUGHT SONG . 1
    A NEVER NAUGHT SONG . . . . 426 A NEVER NAUGHT SONG . T
    ALMOST NEXT TO NAUGHT . . . . 426 A NEVER NAUGHT SONG . 30
NAUGHTY
    YOU NAUGHTY KITTEN, YOU SHALL HAVE NO PIE. . . . . . 498 A MASQUE OF MERCY . . 118
NAUSICAA
    CALL HER NAUSICAA, THE UNAFRAID . . . . 78 THE GENERATIONS OF MEN 152
    CALL HER NAUSICAA, AND TAKE A TIMBER . . . . 79 THE GENERATIONS OF MEN 160
NAVY
    SOME DAY OUR NAVY, I PREDICT, ... 418 AMERICA IS HARD TO SEE 55
NAZARENE
    ONCE CHARGED THE NAZARENE WITH HAVING BROUGHT . . . . . 511 A MASQUE OF MERCY . . 465
NEAR
    NOT FAR, BUT NEAR, I STOOD AND SAW IT ALL, ... 16 A DREAM PANG 9
    NEAR ME IT SEEMED: I FELT IT LIKE A WALL . . . . . . 40 THE MOUNTAIN 5
    AND SEES OLD FRIENDS HE SOMEHOW CAN'T GET NEAR. . . . . 44 A HUNDRED COLLARS . . 7
    RAKING THE DOORYARD, WORKING NEAR THE HOUSE. . . . . . 49 A HUNDRED COLLARS . . 128
    BUT I WENT NEAR TO SEE WITH MY OWN EYES. . . . . 54 HOME BURIAL 83
    NO RUNNER TRACKS IN THIS YEAR'S SNOW LOOPED NEAR IT. . . 101 THE WOOD-PILE . . . 26
    WAS THE LAMP TILTED NEAR THEM IN HIS HAND. . . . . . . 108 OLD MAN'S WINTER NIGHT 5
    AND BOOK-LEAF, THAT KEEP NEAR YOU, THEIR REPOSE; . . . 148 SNOW 146
    BESIDE THE TABLE, NEAR THE OPEN BOOK, ... 151 SNOW 246
    IN A TROUT HATCHERY NEAR CANADA, ... 165 NEW HAMPSHIRE . . . 184
    COMES TOO NEAR TO AHAZ' SIN FOR SAFETY. . . . . 171 NEW HAMPSHIRE . . . 393
    AND CAME SO NEAR DEATH IN THE DARK OF YEARS, ... 180 MAPLE 37
    THEY HOVERED FOR A MOMENT NEAR DISCOVERY. . . . . . . 184 MAPLE 153
    BACK ON THE FLOOR, IS FACT OR PRETTY NEAR FACT. . . . . 192 PAUL'S WIFE 53
    I VOW WE MUST BE NEAR THE PLACE FROM WHERE . . . . . . 214 A FOUNTAIN, A BOTTLE . 51
    HAD SPILLED THEM NEAR THE WINDOW, TOWARD THE LIGHT, . . 216 A FOUNTAIN, A BOTTLE . 96
    TO STOP WITHOUT A FARMHOUSE NEAR . . . . 224 STOPPING BY WOODS . . 6
    WITH NIGHT SO NEAR, BUT NOT MUCH FURTHER UP. . . . . . 229 TWO LOOK AT TWO . . . 3
    ACROSS THE WALL, AS NEAR THE WALL AS THEY. . . . . . . 229 TWO LOOK AT TWO . . . 16
    ACROSS THE WALL, AS NEAR THE WALL AS THEY. . . . . . . 229 TWO LOOK AT TWO . . . 28
    AS NEAR A PARADISE AS IT CAN BE . . . . 254 A WINTER EDEN . . . 3
    SO NEAR TO PARADISE ALL PAIRING ENDS: . . . . 254 A WINTER EDEN . . . 13
    IT IS BECAUSE LIKE MEN WE LOOK TOO NEAR, ... 261 A SOLDIER 6
    THE SADNESS THAT LURKS NEAR THE OPEN WINDOW THERE, . . 287 A ROADSIDE STAND . . 34
    THE MOUNTAINS ARE BROUGHT UP NEAR, ... 301 VOICE WAYS 4
    SUPPOSE SOMEONE COMES NEAR ME WHO IN RATE . . . . . . 324 BUILD SOIL 249
    IN SUNLIGHT NEAR US IN MOMENTOUS SWING . . . . 361 A LOOSE MOUNTAIN . . 15
    COLD AS A SPRING AS YET SO NEAR ITS SOURCE, ... 378 DIRECTIVE 51
    THEY DEAL WITH NEAR AND FAR, ... 388 MIDDLENESS OF THE ROAD 12
    I DON'T BELIEVE YOU'RE ANYWHERE NEAR THE LAST, ... 389 SKEPTIC 6
    THAT'S NEAR ENOUGH FOR ME TO THE DIVINE. . . . . 425 ACCIDENTALLY ON PURPOSE 20
    IN OR NEAR MOAB . . . . 436 KITTY HAWK 262
    WE COME NOWHERE NEAR . . . . 442 KITTY HAWK 435
    IT CAME NEAR SPLITTING HER IN HALF. . . . . 452 A-WISHING WELL . . . 43
NEARBY
    NEARBY, ALL DARK IN EVERY GLOSSY WINDOW. . . . . . . 89 THE FEAR 4
    AND LOOKING FROM IT TO THE POND NEARBY, ... 194 PAUL'S WIFE 96
NEARED
    INSTEAD OF PROVING HUMAN WHEN IT NEARED . . . . 338 THE MOST OF IT . . . 14
NEARER
    ON COMING NEARER: "WASN'T SHE AN I-DEAL . . . . 170 NEW HAMPSHIRE . . . 353
    MY BROTHER HAD BEEN NEARER RIGHT BEFORE. . . . . 199 WILD GRAPES 94
    ONE LEVEL NEARER HEAVEN OVERHEAD, ... 254 A WINTER EDEN . . . 7
    ITS CLICK WAS RISING TO A NEARER CLANK. . . . . 270 THE EGG AND THE MACHINE 10
    A LITTLE NEARER THE SEA. . . . . 285 IN TIME OF CLOUDBURST . 4
    I HAVE IT IN ME SO MUCH NEARER HOME . . . . 296 DESERT PLACES . . . 15
    NEARER IN PLIGHT THEIR NEIGHBORS ARE THAN DISTANCE. . . 414 A CABIN IN THE CLEARING 9
NEAREST
    YOU COULDN'T CARE! THE NEAREST FRIENDS CAN GO . . . . 54 HOME BURIAL 97
    THE NEAREST BOUNDARY TO ESCAPE ACROSS. . . . . 167 NEW HAMPSHIRE . . . 253
    AND BRING US TO THE NEAREST LAND; . . . . 346 DISCOVERY OF MADEIRAS . 107
NEARLY
    AND SOME ARE LOAVES AND SOME SO NEARLY BALLS . . . . . 33 MENDING WALL 17
    "MY WORDS ARE NEARLY ALWAYS AN OFFENSE. . . . . 52 HOME BURIAL 45
    "WITH YOU THE FEET HAVE NEARLY BEEN THE SOUL; . . . . . 93 THE SELF-SEEKER . . . 5
    FROM NEARLY EVERYTHING THAT GOES ON ROUND ME. . . . . 166 NEW HAMPSHIRE . . . 238
    TWO INSTRUMENTS OF NEARLY EQUAL HOPE, ... 269 THE BEAR 20
NEARSIGHTEDLY
    AND HOLD IT UP NEARSIGHTEDLY TO READ.) . . . . 512 A MASQUE OF MERCY . . 490

PAGE TITLE   LINE

'NEATH
    SOUNDS NOBLER THERE THAN 'NEATH THE SUN; . . . . 21 THE TRIAL BY EXISTENCE   46
    'NEATH THE ALDER TREE. . . . . 343 QUEST OF PURPLE-FRINGED 20
NECESSARILY
    IT WAS NOT NECESSARILY FROM WANT. . . . . 292 FIGURE IN THE DOORWAY . 14
NECESSARY
    VERY NECESSARY . . . . 430 KITTY HAWK 62
NECESSITIES
    WHO WILL TAKE CARE OF MY NECESSITIES . . . . 99 THE SELF-SEEKER . . . 179
NECK
    WITH THE LEAST STIFFENING OF HER NECK AND SILENCE. . . . 51 HOME BURIAL 14
    AS I SAT MOPPING HAYSEED FROM MY NECK, ... 72 THE CODE 81
    THEY REALIZED FROM THE WAY I SWABBED MY NECK . . . . 72 THE CODE 86
    WERE ROUND MY NECK AND I WAS AT THE PLOW. . . . . 132 THE BONFIRE 80
    HIS NECK, OR THOUGHT TO SPARE HIS CLOTHES. . . . . 138 BROWN'S DESCENT . . . 28
    OR BROKEN ITS WHITE NECK OF MUSHROOM STUFF . . . . 149 SNOW 165
    AGAINST HER NECK, AN ORNAMENT OF GRAPES. . . . . 197 WILD GRAPES 23
    TO TOUCH HER NECK AND HAIR. . . . . 339 THE SUBVERTED FLOWER . 22
    THE STORM GETS DOWN HIS NECK IN AN ICY SOUSE . . . 341 WILLFUL HOMING . . . 3
    THEY ADDED CLASPS ABOUT THE NECK . . . . 346 DISCOVERY OF MADEIRAS . 83
NECKED (SEE CROOK-NECKED)
NEED
    THERE WHERE IT IS WE DO NOT NEED THE WALL: . . . . . 33 MENDING WALL 23
    OFF HE GOES ALWAYS WHEN I NEED HIM MOST. . . . . . 35 DEATH OF THE HIRED MAN 18
    I'LL SEE TO THAT IF THERE IS NEED. HE OUGHT OF RIGHT . . 39 DEATH OF THE HIRED MAN 132
    "REALLY, FRIEND, I CAN'T LET YOU. YOU--MAY NEED THEM." . 50 A HUNDRED COLLARS . 165
    "NOT YOU!--OH, WHERE'S MY HAT? OH, I DON'T NEED IT! . . 52 HOME BURIAL 36
    "HE SEEMS TO BE THRIFTY; AND HASN'T HE NEED, ... 60 BLUEBERRIES 48
    BUT THE THING OF IT IS, I NEED TO BE KEPT. . . . . 68 A SERVANT TO SERVANTS . 172
    YOU WOULDN'T THINK A FELLOW'D NEED MUCH URGING . . . 71 THE CODE 59
    "NOT IN A GLASS CASE, THEN?" / "HE'D NEED A TALL ONE: . 86 THE HOUSEKEEPER . . 148
    HE FELT SOME NEED OF SOFTENING THAT TO ME: . . . . 107 CHRISTMAS TREES . . 43
    BUT THOUGHT HAS NEED OF NO SUCH THINGS, ... 120 BOND AND FREE . . 4
    AND DEMOCRATS WERE SORE IN NEED OF COMFORT: . . . . 165 NEW HAMPSHIRE . . . 197
    "HAHN, HAHN," HE MUSED, "DON'T NEED MUCH TAKING DOWN." . 187 THE AX-HELVE . . . 79
    AND HAVE NO WISH TO WITH THE HEART--NOR NEED, . . . 199 WILD GRAPES . . . 98
    THAT I NEED LEARN TO LET GO WITH THE HEART. . . . . 199 WILD GRAPES . . . 103
    THAT NEED ENDLESS TALK-TALK . . . . 212 AN EMPTY THREAT . . 56
    THE NEED OF BEING VERSED IN COUNTRY THINGS . . . . 241 NEED OF BEING VERSED . T
    AND HEART, IF NEED BE, I WILL DO MY BEST . . . . . 267 THE ARMFUL . . . 7
    FOR THE SHOCKS AND CHANGES WE NEED TO KEEP US SANE. . . 268 ON LOOKING UP BY CHANCE 10
    BE ANY INSTITUTION'S NEED. . . . . 274 A LONE STRIKER . . 55
    MY RIGHT MIGHT BE LOVE BUT THEIRS WAS NEED. . . . . 277 TWO TRAMPS IN MUD TIME 62
    ONLY WHERE LOVE AND NEED ARE ONE, ... 277 TWO TRAMPS IN MUD TIME 69
    THEN ALL I NEED DO IS RUN . . . . 285 IN TIME OF CLOUDBURST . 17
    IF NEED BE OCCUPY A THRONE, ... 307 PROVIDE, PROVIDE . 11
    'TIS TO FIND WHAT THE HATED NEED, ... 312 THE VINDICTIVES . . 82
    UNOCCUPIED NEED NOT MAKE US UNEASY. . . . . . . 322 BUILD SOIL . . . 192
    SO NONE NEED BE AFRAID OF SIZE. . . . . . . 333 ALL REVELATION . . 19
    THAT WISDOM NEED NOT BE OF ATHENS ATTIC, ... 362 BOEOTIAN 2
    WE NEED THE INTERRUPTION OF THE NIGHT . . . . . . 370 THE LITERATE FARMER AND 80
    A GOOD CHEAP ANTI-DARK IS NOW THE NEED. . . . . . 371 THE LITERATE FARMER AND 99
    NO NEED FOR US TO RACK OUR COMMON HEADS . . . . . 372 THE LITERATE FARMER AND 132
    NOR NEED YOU MIND THE SERIAL ORDEAL . . . . . . 377 DIRECTIVE 20
    NOR NEED WE EVER GO UP THERE TO LIVE. . . . . . 386 A STEEPLE ON THE HOUSE 6
    THE MORAL IS, IT HARDLY NEED BE SHOWN, ... 394 HAEC FABULA DOCET . 17
    WITH A NEED THE GALE . . . . 429 KITTY HAWK 26
    (NEED A BODY ASK . . . . 431 KITTY HAWK . . . 106
    FROM THE NEED THEY HAD . . . . 432 KITTY HAWK . . . 131
    WHERE I NEED LISTEN TO ITS ROTE NO MORE, ... 447 DOES NO ONE AT ALL EVER 34
    "YOU'RE RIGHT," THE EX-KING SAID, "WE'LL NEED SOME MONEY. 454 HOW HARD TO KEEP FROM 30
    THEY'VE COME TO FEEL THE NEED OF IS A KIND . . . . 461 HOW HARD TO KEEP FROM 232
    THAT'S WHY WE NEED A LOT OF BRAINS . . . . . . 467 QUANDARY 8
    I NEED SOME HELP ABOUT THIS REASON PROBLEM . . . . 479 A MASQUE OF REASON . 165
    ARE FREEDOMS FROM THE NEED OF ASKING QUESTIONS. . . . 484 A MASQUE OF REASON . 313
    WE CAN'T LEAVE HIM OUT. / NO. NO, WE DON'T NEED TO. . . 486 A MASQUE OF REASON . 378
    LOOK, I DON'T NEED THE BIBLE TO CONSULT. . . . . . 495 A MASQUE OF MERCY . 44
    INCLINED TO HOPE FOR MUCH. STILL WHAT WE NEED . . . 515 A MASQUE OF MERCY . 567
    I OWN THE NEED OF IT HAD SOMEWHAT FADED . . . . . 517 A MASQUE OF MERCY . 625
NEEDED
    THAT I SUDDENLY HEARD--ALL I NEEDED TO HEAR: . . . . 24 THE DEMIURGE'S LAUGH . 5
    MORE THAN WAS NEEDED, SOMETHING MUST BE UP. . . . . 72 THE CODE 87
    SHE HAD THE DARTMOUTH NEEDED TO PRODUCE HIM. . . . 161 NEW HAMPSHIRE . . . 69
    IT NEEDED A TURN MORE, I COULD HAVE CRIED . . . . 191 THE GRINDSTONE . . . 72
    ALL THAT WAS NEEDED WAS TO SAY TO HIM, ... 191 PAUL'S WIFE . . . 2
    BUT NOT SO MUCH, PERHAPS, AS A BOY NEEDED. . . . . 197 WILD GRAPES . . . 35
    BOOKS, I SHOULD SAY!--IF BOOKS ARE WHAT IS NEEDED. . . 216 A FOUNTAIN, A BOTTLE . 92
    NO LONGER NEEDED? STAUNCH IT AT ITS SOURCE . . . . 231 A BROOK IN THE CITY . 14
    YOU HAD BEGUN IT, AND IF THERE NEEDED PROOF-- . . . 236 VALLEY'S SINGING DAY . 15
    ON THEIR PART, THOUGH WITHOUT THE NEEDED INSIGHT. . . 293 AT WOODWARD'S GARDENS . 26
    IS SOCIALISM NEEDED, DO YOU THINK? . . . . . . 318 BUILD SOIL 67
    A SANTA CLAUS WAS NEEDED. AND THERE IS ONE." . . . 408 FROM PLANE TO PLANE . 146
    FOUND OUT THE DISCIPLINE MAN NEEDED MUST . . . . . 481 A MASQUE OF REASON . 209
    PERSONAE NEEDED TO ENACT THE PROBLEM. . . . . . 487 A MASQUE OF REASON . 394
NEEDING
    SO KNOWING--AND YET NEEDING TO BE TOLD . . . . . 506 A MASQUE OF MERCY . 338
NEEDLE
    THE METEOR THAT THRUSTS IN WITH NEEDLE BILL, ... 12 A PRAYER IN SPRING . 11
    AND THE NEEDLE STANDS ON END. . . . . 384 IN THE LONG NIGHT . . 4
NEEDLESS
    NEEDLESS TO SAY TO YOU, MY ARGUMENT . . . . . . 322 BUILD SOIL 185
NEEDLESSLY
    NEEDLESSLY SOON HE HAD HIS AX-HELVES OUT, ... 187 THE AX-HELVE . . . 63
NEEDN'T
    YOU NEEDN'T SMILE--I DIDN'T RECOGNIZE HIM-- . . . . 35 DEATH OF THE HIRED MAN 37
    YOU NEEDN'T BE AFRAID HE'LL LEAVE YOU THIS TIME." . . . 38 DEATH OF THE HIRED MAN 112
    "ESTELLE'S THE ONE. YOU NEEDN'T TALK TO ME." . . . 87 THE HOUSEKEEPER . . 164
    "YOU NEEDN'T THINK YOU'RE GOING TO GET AWAY. . . . 88 THE HOUSEKEEPER . . 195

NEEDN'T (CONTINUED)
    YOU NEEDN'T LOOK AT ME." / "I DON'T BELIEVE YOU." . . . . 95 THE SELF-SEEKER . . . 60
    AND GONE TO SLEEP, SHE NEEDN'T WAKE TO ANSWER." . . . . 143 SNOW 14
    I NEEDN'T CALL YOU BY NAME. . . . . 264 THE LAST MOWING . . . 19
    SO THE THICK-SKINS NEEDN'T ACT THIN-SKINNED . . . . . 295 A RECORD STRIDE . . . 31
    IT NEEDN'T WAIT ON GENERAL REVOLUTION. . . . . . . 324 BUILD SOIL 265
    AND NEEDN'T HAVE FARED INTO SPACE LIKE HIS MASTER . . . 380 TOO ANXIOUS FOR RIVERS 25
    HIS SCIENCE NEEDN'T GET HIM SO UNNERVED. . . . . . 396 ANY SIZE WE PLEASE . . 11
    IT NEEDN'T BE QUITE SO TERRIFIC . . . . 453 A-WISHING WELL . . . 65
    IT NEEDN'T BE QUITE SO GIGANTIC . . . . 453 A-WISHING WELL . . . 67
    I NEEDN'T THINK I HAVE ESCAPED MY DUTY, ... 454 HOW HARD TO KEEP FROM 19
    YOU THOUGHT IT WAS AGREED YOU NEEDN'T GIVE THEM. . . . 478 A MASQUE OF REASON . 144
    HE DOESN'T GO. / YOU NEEDN'T BE SO STERN. . . . . 493 A MASQUE OF MERCY . 11
    YOU NEEDN'T SHOUT LIKE THAT, YOU WRETCHED MAN. . . . . 508 A MASQUE OF MERCY . 394
NEEDS
    BUT WHICH IT ONLY NEEDS THAT WE FULFILL. . . . . . 12 A PRAYER IN SPRING . . 16
    "SAY THAT TO JIMMY HERE. HE NEEDS A FARM." . . . . . 114 IN THE HOME STRETCH . 100
    IT CAN'T TURN EITHER WAY. IT NEEDS THE WIND'S HELP. . . 148 SNOW 135
    IT YET HAS POLES, AND ONLY NEEDS A SPIN . . . . . 174 A STAR IN A STONEBOAT . 50
    GOD NEEDS TIME JUST AS MUCH AS YOU OR I . . . . . 478 A MASQUE OF REASON . 151
    THAT ONLY NEEDS A FINGER TOUCH FROM GOD . . . . . 502 A MASQUE OF MERCY . 230
NEGLECT
    IN NEGLECT . . . . 16 IN NEGLECT . . . . T
    SHE VALUED THE CONSIDERATE NEGLECT . . . . 56 THE BLACK COTTAGE . . 41
    DON'T YOU TWIT. HE'S UNHAPPY. CHURCH NEGLECT . . . . 488 A MASQUE OF REASON . 424
NEGLECTED
    AND NO ONE SEEM NEGLECTING OR NEGLECTED? . . . . . 200 PLACE FOR A THIRD . 29
    BUT NEGLECTED, HOWEVER LIGHTLY, TO LACE . . . . . 265 THE DOOR IN THE DARK . 3
NEGLECTING
    AND NO ONE SEEM NEGLECTING OR NEGLECTED? . . . . . 200 PLACE FOR A THIRD . 29
NEGLIGIBLE
    AT THE EXPENSE OF NEGLIGIBLE FOLK. . . . . 423 FOR JOHN F. KENNEDY . 33
    CAN BE MADE NEGLIGIBLE. / WHAT'S YOUR BOOK? . . . . 506 A MASQUE OF MERCY . 323
NEIGHBOR
    I LET MY NEIGHBOR KNOW BEYOND THE HILL; . . . . . 33 MENDING WALL 12
    "HOW ARE YOU, NEIGHBOR? JUST THE MAN I'M AFTER. . . . 88 THE HOUSEKEEPER . . 206
    A NEIGHBOR OF MINE IN THE VILLAGE . . . . 133 A GIRL'S GARDEN . . . 1
    HE HAD IN MIND TO SAY TO A BAD NEIGHBOR . . . . . 185 THE AX-HELVE 16
    FOR NOTHING IN THE MEASURE OF A NEIGHBOR. . . . . 186 THE AX-HELVE 43
    LOVE THOU THY NEIGHBOR AS THYSELF, AYE, ... 467 QUANDARY 12
NEIGHBORHOOD
    THAT IN THE NEIGHBORHOOD OF HOME AND CHILDREN . . . . 277 THE WHITE-TAILED HORNET 13
    BY HIS COUNTRY AND HIS NEIGHBORHOOD? . . . . . . 469 CHOSEN POET OF VERMONT 4
NEIGHBORS
    HE ONLY SAYS, "GOOD FENCES MAKE GOOD NEIGHBORS." . . . 33 MENDING WALL 27
    "WHY DO THEY MAKE GOOD NEIGHBORS? ISN'T IT . . . . 34 MENDING WALL 30
    HE SAYS AGAIN, "GOOD FENCES MAKE GOOD NEIGHBORS." . . . 34 MENDING WALL 45
    "BUT WHY, WHEN SHE'S WELL OFF? IS IT THE NEIGHBORS, . . 87 THE HOUSEKEEPER . . 168
    THE NEIGHBORS MAY NOT HAVE TAKEN AS THEIR RIGHT . . . 117 IN THE HOME STRETCH . 191
    IT TOOK ME. NEIGHBORS COMING HOME FROM TOWN . . . . 132 THE BONFIRE 84
    NEARER IN PLIGHT THEIR NEIGHBORS ARE THAN DISTANCE. . . 414 A CABIN IN THE CLEARING 9
NEITHER
    AND YET WITH NEITHER LOVE NOR HATE, ... 9 STARS 9
    WHAT SHOULDER DID I SEE HER OVER? NEITHER. . . . . 113 IN THE HOME STRETCH . 69
    NEITHER REFUSED THE MEETING. BUT THE HAND! . . . . 136 "OUT, OUT--" 18
    AND NEITHER WOULD I CHOOSE TO BE A PUKE . . . . . 171 NEW HAMPSHIRE . . . 398
    BUT FROM A SHED WHERE NEITHER OF THEM COULD SEE HIM.) . 194 PAUL'S WIFE 115
    RIGHT PAST BOTH FATHER AND MOTHER, AND NEITHER STOPPED IT. 203 THE WITCH OF COOS . . 33
    NEITHER WAS SONG THAT DAY TO BE SELF-BEGUN. . . . . 236 VALLEY'S SINGING DAY . 14
    PROCLAIMED THE TIME WAS NEITHER WRONG NOR RIGHT. . . . 255 ACQUAINTED WITH NIGHT . 13
    BUT NEITHER ONE WAS THE THIEF . . . . 299 WELCOME TO THEIR BELIEF 15
    NEITHER OUT FAR NOR IN DEEP . . . . 301 NEITHER OUT FAR NOR IN T
    USING NEITHER SPOON NOR SKIMMER, ... 303 CLEAR AND COLDER . . 5
    AND NEITHER GO ON NOR BACK. . . . . 314 BEARER OF EVIL TIDINGS 26
    HE KNEW NOT, NEITHER OF THEM KNEW. . . . . . . 345 DISCOVERY OF MADEIRAS 45
    AND SOON IT IS NEITHER HERE NOR THERE . . . . . 347 DISCOVERY OF MADEIRAS 137
    IS NEITHER ALPHA, ETA, NOR OMEGA, ... 388 IOTA SUBSCRIPT . . . 7
    NEITHER OF THEM WAS BETTER THAN THE OTHER. . . . . 404 FROM PLANE TO PLANE . 1
    NEITHER YOU NOR I . . . . 434 KITTY HAWK 192
    NEITHER WOULD FAIRNESS. YOU HAVE HEARD THE DOCTRINE. . . 485 A MASQUE OF REASON . 356
    NEITHER WILL I SHOW. THAT'S TOO BAD MOREOVER. . . . 490 A MASQUE OF REASON . 463
NEON-LIT
    SWIRL OF NEON-LIT . . . . 439 KITTY HAWK 367
NERVE (SEE SNEEZE-NERVE)
    IN NERVE AND RESOURCE . . . . 448 THE BAD ISLAND--EASTER 39
NERVES
    AND THE NORTHERN LIGHTS THAT RUN LIKE TINGLING NERVES. . . 268 ON LOOKING UP BY CHANCE 3
    IT WILL GATHER SPEED TILL YOUR NERVES PREPARE . . . . 306 A TRIAL RUN 6
NERVOUS
    SIT DOWN OR LIE DOWN, FRIEND; YOU MAKE ME NERVOUS." . . 47 A HUNDRED COLLARS . . 72
    THAT ALL DAY FIGHTS A NERVOUS INWARD RAGE, ... 269 THE BEAR 14
    LET'S CHANGE THE SUBJECT, BOYS, I'M GETTING NERVOUS. . . 516 A MASQUE OF MERCY . 598
    NERVOUS IS ALL THE GREAT THINGS EVER MADE YOU. . . . 516 A MASQUE OF MERCY . 599
NEST
    AWAY FROM ITS NEST, AND I SAID IT WAS YOU. . . . . 62 BLUEBERRIES 89
    THE EXPOSED NEST . . . . 109 THE EXPOSED NEST . . T
    'TWAS A NEST FULL OF YOUNG BIRDS ON THE GROUND . . . . 109 THE EXPOSED NEST . . 13
    AND CUT A FLOWER BESIDE A GROUNDBIRD'S NEST . . . . 126 RANGE-FINDING . . . 2
    BUT THOUGH THEY REJOICED IN THE NEST THEY KEPT, . . . 242 NEED OF BEING VERSED . 22
    OR OVERTAKEN TOO FAR FROM HIS NEST, ... 249 ACCEPTANCE 8
    OF THEIR NEST AGAIN, NOR FIND A PERCH. . . . . . 253 THE THATCH 24
    AS I THOUGHT OF THEM WITHOUT NEST OR ROOST. . . . . 253 THE THATCH 29
NESTER
    BRING THE SINGER, BRING THE NESTER; . . . . . . 11 TO THE THAWING WIND . 2
NEST-FULL
    THE WAY THE NEST-FULL EVERY TIME WE STIRRED . . . . 109 THE EXPOSED NEST . . 20
NESTS
    HE TAKES IT OUT IN BUNCHES LIKE BIG BIRDS' NESTS. . . . 37 DEATH OF THE HIRED MAN 93

```
                                                  PAGE  TITLE                    LINE
NESTS (CONTINUED)
     AND THEIR BUILT OR DRIVEN NESTS. . . . . . . .  . . 127 LONELINESS   . . . .  . 12
     IN NESTS. SHALL I BE COUNTED LESS THAN THEY ARE? . . . 151 SNOW  . . . . .  . 227
NETTLE
     EMBALM HIM WITH ICHOR OF NETTLE. . . . . . . .  . 288 DEPARTMENTAL  . . . .  . 31
NEVER
     THERE WAS NEVER A SOUND BESIDE THE WOOD BUT ONE, . . . .  17 MOWING  . . . . .  .  1
     OH, NEVER THIS WHELMING EAST WIND SWELLS . . . . .  . 27 A LINE-STORM SONG .  . 25
     MY APPLE TREES WILL NEVER GET ACROSS . . . . . . .  . 33 MENDING WALL . . . .  . 25
     YOU NEVER SEE HIM STANDING ON THE HAY  . . . . .  . 37 DEATH OF THE HIRED MAN .  . 94
     SO NOW AND NEVER ANY DIFFERENT."   . . . . . . .  . 38 DEATH OF THE HIRED MAN . 102
     "HE NEVER TOLD US THAT." / "WE KNOW IT, THOUGH." . . .  . 39 DEATH OF THE HIRED MAN . 130
     HE NEVER DID A THING SO VERY BAD.  . . . . . . .  . 39 DEATH OF THE HIRED MAN . 142
     "YOU'VE NEVER CLIMBED IT?" / "I'VE BEEN ON THE SIDES, . .  . 42 THE MOUNTAIN . . . .  . 44
     YOU NEVER SAW IT?" / "I GUESS THERE'S NO DOUBT . .  . 42 THE MOUNTAIN . . . .  . 66
     ABOUT ITS BEING THERE. I NEVER SAW IT. . . . . .  . 42 THE MOUNTAIN . . . .  . 67
     "HE NEVER GOT UP HIGH ENOUGH TO SEE.  . . . . . .  . 43 THE MOUNTAIN . . . .  . 78
     ANYTHING THEY'VE NOT GOT. I NEVER DUN. . . . . .  . 50 A HUNDRED COLLARS  . . 152
     I NEVER NOTICED IT FROM HERE BEFORE. . . . . . .  . 51 HOME BURIAL  . . . .  . 21
     BUT NEVER MIND, THE WELSHMAN GOT IT PLANTED  . .  . 57 THE BLACK COTTAGE  . . 68
     BLACK SHE HAD SCARCELY SEEN, AND YELLOW NEVER. . .  . 57 THE BLACK COTTAGE  . . 76
     IT NEVER GOT SO FAR AS THAT; BUT THE BARE THOUGHT  . .  . 57 THE BLACK COTTAGE  . . 90
     DID EVER YOU FEEL SO? I HOPE YOU NEVER. . . . . .  . 63 A SERVANT TO SERVANTS . 10
     HE WAS BEFORE MY TIME--I NEVER SAW HIM;  . . . .  . 67 A SERVANT TO SERVANTS . 140
     NEVER YOU SAY A THING LIKE THAT TO A MAN,  . . .  . 71 THE CODE  . . . . .  . 68
     YOU NEVER SAW BEFORE. WHAT WILL WE COME TO  . . .  . 76 THE GENERATIONS OF MEN . 86
     I'VE NEVER LISTENED IN AMONG THE SOUNDS  . . . .  . 78 THE GENERATIONS OF MEN . 132
     NOR NEVER WILL BE TO MY WAY OF THINKING. . . . .  . 80 THE GENERATIONS OF MEN . 187
     I NEVER SAW A MAN LET FAMILY TROUBLES . . . . . .  . 83 THE HOUSEKEEPER  . . . 53
     YOU NEVER SAW THIS ROOM BEFORE A SHOW, . . . . .  . 85 THE HOUSEKEEPER  . . . 119
     HE NEVER TAKES THE MONEY. IF THEY'RE WORTH . . .  . 86 THE HOUSEKEEPER  . . . 140
     I'LL NEVER REST TONIGHT UNLESS I KNOW. . . . . .  . 90 THE FEAR  . . . . .  . 32
     TO PUT IT THE RIGHT WAY. HE'D NEVER DARE--  . . .  . 90 THE FEAR  . . . . .  . 37
     THEY NEVER EARNED ME SO MUCH AS ONE CENT:  . . .  . 95 THE SELF-SEEKER  . . . 71
     THEN I WAS CERTAIN I HAD NEVER MEANT  . . . . . .  . 107 CHRISTMAS TREES  . . . 45
     TO LET HIM HAVE THEM. NEVER SHOW SURPRISE! . . .  . 107 CHRISTMAS TREES  . . . 46
     "NEVER WAS I BELADIED SO BEFORE.  . . . . . . . .  . 111 IN THE HOME STRETCH  . 21
     WITH GOOD LUCK WITH YOUR STOVEPIPE. NEVER MIND,  . .  . 113 IN THE HOME STRETCH  . 92
     I NEVER BORE IT WELL WHEN PEOPLE WENT.  . . . . .  . 115 IN THE HOME STRETCH  . 131
     NOR I TO YOU." / "PERHAPS YOU NEVER WERE?"  . . .  . 117 IN THE HOME STRETCH  . 180
     SO LOW FOR LONG, THEY NEVER RIGHT THEMSELVES:  . .  . 121 BIRCHES  . . . . .  . 16
     THAT SMILE! IT NEVER CAME OF BEING GAY. . . . . .  . 127 THE SMILE . . . . .  .  2
     IT NEVER HAD BEEN INSIDE THE ROOM, . . . . . . .  . 128 THE OFT-REPEATED DREAM .  9
     HE NEVER FOUND HER, THOUGH HE LOOKED  . . . . . .  . 129 THE IMPULSE  . . . .  . 21
     MADE WIND BY FANNING, SINCE YOU NEVER KNEW . . .  . 130 THE BONFIRE  . . . .  . 42
     OH, NEVER BY WAY OF ADVICE!  . . . . . . . . . .  . 134 A GIRL'S GARDEN  . . . 46
     AND SHE NEVER SINS BY TELLING THE TALE  . . . . .  . 134 A GIRL'S GARDEN  . . . 47
     HE NEVER LET THE LANTERN DROP. . . . . . . . . .  . 138 BROWN'S DESCENT  . . . 29
     AND FAILED TO SEE THE GOOD OF. NEVER MIND, . . .  . 147 SNOW  . . . . . .  . 125
     BUT NEVER GETS AWAY;  . . . . . . . . . . . . . .  . 156 THE SOUND OF TREES  . . 11
     IT NEVER COULD HAVE HAPPENED IN NEW HAMPSHIRE. .  . 160 NEW HAMPSHIRE  . . .  . 34
     AND NEVER RIGHTLY UNDERSTOOD TILL BRYAN  . . . .  . 168 NEW HAMPSHIRE  . . .  . 296
     WHEREAS I NEVER HAD A GOOD IDEA . . . . . . . . .  . 169 NEW HAMPSHIRE  . . .  . 335
     AND NEVER OVERSTEPPED IT SAVE IN DREAMS. . . . .  . 171 NEW HAMPSHIRE  . . .  . 380
     NEVER TELL ME THAT NOT ONE STAR OF ALL  . . . . .  . 172 A STAR IN A STONEBOAT .  1
     FROM FOLLOWING WALLS I NEVER LIFT MY EYE,  . . .  . 173 A STAR IN A STONEBOAT . 40
     (IT NEVER HAD BEEN DWELT IN, THOUGH, BY WOMEN, . .  . 174 THE CENSUS-TAKER  . . .  7
     AND LOST THE PLACE NEVER TO READ AGAIN. . . . . .  . 181 MAPLE  . . . . . .  . 68
     "YOU'VE NEVER ASKED YOUR FATHER OUTRIGHT, HAVE YOU?" . . 183 MAPLE  . . . . . .  . 108
     A NAME TO CARRY FOR LIFE AND NEVER KNOW  . . . .  . 183 MAPLE  . . . . . .  . 116
     OF REALLY NEVER HAVING MEANT TO KEEP IT. . . . .  . 187 THE AX-HELVE  . . . .  . 62
     HAS NEVER AVAILED THE CUMBERSOME GRINDSTONE  . .  . 188 THE GRINDSTONE  . . . .  2
     HE NEVER STOPPED TO MURDER ANYONE . . . . . . . .  . 192 PAUL'S WIFE  . . . .  . 25
     WE'LL NEVER LET THEM, WILL WE, SON? WE'LL NEVER! . .  . 203 THE WITCH OF COOS  . . 27
     I NEVER COULD HAVE DONE THE THING I DID  . . . .  . 204 THE WITCH OF COOS  . . 65
     WE NEVER COULD FIND OUT WHOSE BONES THEY WERE. .  . 206 THE WITCH OF COOS  . . 137
     HE NEVER SAID MUCH AFTER WE WERE MARRIED,  . . .  . 209 PAUPER WITCH OF GRAFTON 73
     I NEVER SAW SO GOOD A HOUSE DESERTED. . . . . . .  . 215 A FOUNTAIN, A BOTTLE .  . 71
     SHE NEVER TENDED ANYTHING HERSELF. . . . . . . .  . 215 A FOUNTAIN, A BOTTLE .  . 83
     BUT NEVER ANYMORE THE DEAD. . . . . . . . . . . .  . 221 IN A DISUSED GRAVEYARD .  4
     ALWAYS WRONG TO THE LIGHT, SO NEVER SEEING  . . .  . 225 FOR ONCE SOMETHING . .  .  2
     MORE THAN IF LIFE HAD NEVER BEEN BEGUN. . . . . .  . 226 THE ONSET . . . . .  . 11
     I KNOW THAT WINTER DEATH HAS NEVER TRIED . . . .  . 226 THE ONSET . . . . .  . 13
     BUT I NEVER HEARD OF A HOUSE THAT THROVE . . . .  . 232 THE KITCHEN CHIMNEY  . 10
     THAT, THOUGH THEY NEVER EQUAL STARS IN SIZE  . .  . 246 FIREFLIES IN THE GARDEN .  3
     (AND THEY WERE NEVER REALLY STARS AT HEART),  . .  . 246 FIREFLIES IN THE GARDEN .  4
     THAT WATER NEVER DID TO LAND BEFORE. . . . . . .  . 250 ONCE BY THE PACIFIC  .  4
     BUT LET THERE NEVER BE CURTAIN DRAWN  . . . . . .  . 251 TREE AT MY WINDOW  . .  3
     BUT NEVER WAS I FAR OUT OF SIGHT . . . . . . . .  . 253 THE THATCH  . . . .  .  3
     TO TELL ONCE AND ONCE ONLY, FOR THEM NEVER TO FORGET, . 257 THE LOVELY BE CHOOSERS . 32
     HER NEVER HAVING DEIGNED TO TELL THEM. . . . . .  . 257 THE LOVELY BE CHOOSERS . 38
     AND NEVER ONCE DROPS  . . . . . . . . . . . . . .  . 261 CANIS MAJOR  . . . .  .  7
     WE NEVER SHALL MOW IN AGAIN, . . . . . . . . . .  . 264 THE LAST MOWING  . . .  2
     AND NEVER SEEN SUN-SMITTEN SLIME . . . . . . . .  . 266 SITTING BY A BUSH  . . 10
     THE SUN AND MOON GET CROSSED, BUT THEY NEVER TOUCH, . 268 ON LOOKING UP BY CHANCE  4
     HE PACES BACK AND FORTH AND NEVER RESTS  . . . .  . 269 THE BEAR  . . . . .  . 16
     AND, WITH A TOUCH THAT NEVER MISSED,  . . . . . .  . 274 A LONE STRIKER  . . .  . 31
     HE NEVER WOULD ASSUME THAT HE'D  . . . . . . . .  . 274 A LONE STRIKER  . . .  . 54
     YOU'D THINK I NEVER HAD FELT BEFORE . . . . . . .  . 276 TWO TRAMPS IN MUD TIME . 44
     ONE WHO WOULD NEVER HANG ABOVE A BOOKCASE  . . .  . 278 THE WHITE-TAILED HORNET . 17
     BUT THE REAL FLY HE MISSED WOULD NEVER DO;  . . .  . 279 THE WHITE-TAILED HORNET . 48
     THE REQUISITE LIFT OF SPIRIT HAS NEVER BEEN FOUND, . 287 A ROADSIDE STAND  . . . 45
     WHERE'S THIS BARN'S HOUSE? IT NEVER HAD A HOUSE,  . . 289 OLD BARN AT THE BOTTOM .  1
     HAVE NEVER MADE THE FIRST MOVE TO ASSEMBLE,  . .  . 291 ON HEART'S BEGINNING TO 30
     AND NEVER COULD BE MADE TO UNDERSTAND. . . . . .  . 293 AT WOODWARD'S GARDENS .  4
     IT NEVER WILL SHOW MUCH FLOWER OR FRUIT. . . . .  . 296 LEAVES COMPARED WITH  .  4
     SOME THINGS ARE NEVER CLEAR. . . . . . . . . . .  . 301 VOICE WAYS  . . . .  .  1
     WE THINK OF THE TREE. IF IT NEVER AGAIN HAS LEAVES, . 305 THERE ARE ROUGHLY ZONES  4
```

NEVER (CONTINUED)
    THE TREE HAS NO LEAVES AND MAY NEVER HAVE THEM AGAIN. . . 305 THERE ARE ROUGHLY ZONES 18
    BUT IF IT IS DESTINED NEVER AGAIN TO GROW, ... 305 THERE ARE ROUGHLY ZONES 20
    I NEVER DARED BE RADICAL WHEN YOUNG . . . . 308 PRECAUTION   1
    NEVER ASK OF MONEY SPENT . . . . 309 HARDSHIP OF ACCOUNTING 1
    (THE SAYING IS NEVER DONE.) . . . . 312 THE VINDICTIVES . . . 77
    NEVER MIND OF WHAT ACTUAL WORTH, ... 312 THE VINDICTIVES . . . 83
    THAT NEVER YET TO OTHER TWO BEFELL . . . . 315 IRIS BY NIGHT . . . 21
    THERE IS STILL MORE WE NEVER BRING OR SHOULD BRING; . . 321 BUILD SOIL 174
    I OWN I NEVER REALLY WARMED . . . . 326 TO A THINKER . . . 29
    TO TIME IT NEVER SEEMS THAT HE IS BRAVE . . . · . . . 334 I COULD GIVE ALL . . . 1
    NEVER AGAIN WOULD BIRDS' SONG BE THE SAME . . . . . . 338 NEVER WOULD BIRDS' SONG T
    THAT PROBABLY IT NEVER WOULD BE LOST. . . . . 339 NEVER WOULD BIRDS' SONG 12
    NEVER AGAIN WOULD BIRDS' SONG BE THE SAME. . . . . . 339 NEVER WOULD BIRDS' SONG 13
    IT NEVER HAPPENED! DID IT, YOU?" . . . . 346 DISCOVERY OF MADEIRAS . 99
    OUR MUSCLES NEVER COULD AGAIN CONTRACT: . . . . . . 351 THE LESSON FOR TODAY . 38
    WE NEVER COULD RECOVER HUMAN SHAPE, ... 351 THE LESSON FOR TODAY . 39
    I NEVER TAKE MY OWN SIDE IN A QUARREL. . . . . 354 THE LESSON FOR TODAY . 123
    NEVER THE GOLD OF DARKNESS FROM A MINE. . . . . . . 358 THE LOST FOLLOWER . . 4
    IT NEVER REACHES EARTH EXCEPT AS ASHES . . . . 361 A LOOSE MOUNTAIN . . 10
    I NEVER CAME UPON A BLESSED ONE. . . . . 363 AN ANSWER 2
    THE SLAVE WILL NEVER THANK HIS MANUMITTER; . . . . . 371 THE LITERATE FARMER AND 90
    I NEVER SAW SO MUCH SWIFT WATER RUN CLOUDLESS. . . . 379 TOO ANXIOUS FOR RIVERS 5
    I NEVER SHOULD AGAIN BE WARMED, ... 381 AN UNSTAMPED LETTER IN 24
    WE NEVER KNEW EXACTLY WHERE TO LOOK, ... 382 TO AN ANCIENT . . . 4
    THEY WILL NEVER HAVE AGAIN. . . . . 387 THE COURAGE TO BE NEW . 4
    I NEVER HAPPENED TO CONTRAST . . . . 390 TWO LEADING LIGHTS . . 1
    HE NEVER HAS IN ANY PHASE . . . . 390 TWO LEADING LIGHTS . . 5
    HAS NEVER LEARNED TO KNOW HER PLACE. . . . . 390 TWO LEADING LIGHTS . . 13
    I'M THINKING THE UNBORN WOULD NEVER MISS . . . . . . 397 THE PLANNERS . . . 2
    WHAT THEY HAD NEVER HAD OF VITAL BLISS. . . . . . . 397 THE PLANNERS . . . 3
    CAN NEVER HOPE TO WAGE A GLOBAL MISSION. . . . . . . 398 NO HOLY WARS FOR THEM . 12
    AS IT HAS NEVER BEEN TO ME BEFORE. . . . . 411 POD OF THE MILKWEED . 7
    AND I BEGIN TO FEAR THEY NEVER WILL. . . . . 414 A CABIN IN THE CLEARING 6
    TO WHAT WAS NEVER HIS CONCERN . . . . 419 AMERICA IS HARD TO SEE 76
    BUT NEVER SO MUCH AS LIFTED CHIN. . . . . 420 ONE MORE BREVITY . . 22
    ESCAPIST--NEVER . . . . 421 ESCAPIST--NEVER . . . T
    NEVER BELIEVE IT. AT THE VERY WORST . . . . 425 ACCIDENTALLY ON PURPOSE 13
    THERE WAS NEVER NAUGHT, ... 426 A NEVER NAUGHT SONG . 1
    A NEVER NAUGHT SONG . . . . 426 A NEVER NAUGHT SONG . T
    THE RULE IS, NEVER GIVE A CHILD A CHOICE. . . . . . 427 CONCEPT SELF-CONCEIVED 8
    NEVER DID I FAIL . . . . 429 KITTY HAWK 33
    NEVER MIND WITH WHOM . . . . 436 KITTY HAWK 265
    NATURE'S NEVER QUITE . . . . 442 KITTY HAWK 451
    HE NEVER SAID SHE WASN'T YOUNG, ... 444 ENDS 7
    SO, NEVER AT A LOSS IN SIMILE, ... 461 HOW HARD TO KEEP FROM 235
    MIGHT NEVER BRING HER BACK. . . . . 464 MILKY WAY IS A COWPATH 24
    NEVER HAVE I BEEN SAD OR GLAD . . . . 467 QUANDARY 1
    GET BURNED FOR PROPHECY, MEN ALMOST NEVER. . . . . . 478 A MASQUE OF REASON . . 150
    SOCIETY CAN NEVER THINK THINGS OUT: . . . . 481 A MASQUE OF REASON . . 223
    DISINTERESTEDNESS NEVER DID EXIST, ... 485 A MASQUE OF REASON . . 354
    THE DEVIL'S NEVER VERY FAR AWAY. . . . . 487 A MASQUE OF REASON . . 382
    NO, GOD. / I NEVER HEARD OF SUCH A THING. . . . . . 493 A MASQUE OF MERCY . . 20
    I NEVER SAID YOU WEREN'T. I RECOGNIZED YOU. . . . . 498 A MASQUE OF MERCY . . 136
    SO THAT THE CREAM COULD NEVER RISE AGAIN . . . . . . 509 A MASQUE OF MERCY . . 421
NEVER-MARRIED
    A NEVER-MARRIED SISTER'S OF THAT HUSBAND, ... 200 PLACE FOR A THIRD . . 41
NEVERTHELESS
    NEVERTHELESS, A MESSAGE FROM THE DAWN, ... 23 THE TUFT OF FLOWERS . 30
    NEVERTHELESS IT CONSTITUTES A HINT . . . . 361 A LOOSE MOUNTAIN . . 13
    NEVERTHELESS THE LAND WAS MINE: . . . . 364 TRESPASS 3
NEW
    OF NEW WOOD AND OLD WHERE THE WOODPECKER CHOPS; . . . . 6 GHOST HOUSE 9
    READY TO RUN TO HIDING NEW . . . . 18 GOING FOR WATER . . 15
    AND THE WORLD HAD FOUND NEW TERMS OF WORTH. . . . . . 24 PAN WITH US . . . 27
    WHEN I WALKED FORTH AT DAWN TO SEE NEW THINGS, ... 40 THE MOUNTAIN . . . 8
    WHEN ALL WHO WOULD COME SEEKING IN NEW HAMPSHIRE . . . 73 THE GENERATIONS OF MEN 2
    IN A NEW COTTAGE ON THE ANCIENT SPOT. . . . . 79 THE GENERATIONS OF MEN 164
    YOU WERE FOREVER FINDING SOME NEW PLAY. . . . . 109 THE EXPOSED NEST . . 1
    IT IS BY THAT? OR BY THE MOON? THE NEW MOON! . . . . 113 IN THE HOME STRETCH . 68
    A WIRE SHE IS OF SILVER, AS NEW AS WE . . . . 113 IN THE HOME STRETCH . 70
    YOU WON'T DENY THE LANTERN ISN'T NEW. . . . . 116 IN THE HOME STRETCH . 178
    ALL THAT'S NOT NEW IN WHERE WE FIND OURSELVES. . . . . 117 IN THE HOME STRETCH . 182
    NEW IS A WORD FOR FOOLS IN TOWNS WHO THINK . . . . . 117 IN THE HOME STRETCH . 183
    NOTHING SO NEW--SOMETHING WE HAD FORGOTTEN: . . . . . 133 THE BONFIRE . . . 110
    NEW HAMPSHIRE . . . . 157 NEW HAMPSHIRE . . . T
    NEW HAMPSHIRE . . . . 159 NEW HAMPSHIRE . . . T
    IT NEVER COULD HAVE HAPPENED IN NEW HAMPSHIRE. . . . . 160 NEW HAMPSHIRE . . . 34
    I EVER STUMBLED ON IN OLD NEW HAMPSHIRE . . . . . . 160 NEW HAMPSHIRE . . . 36
    JUST SPECIMENS IS ALL NEW HAMPSHIRE HAS, ... 161 NEW HAMPSHIRE . . . 61
    DID YOU BUT KNOW OF HIM, NEW HAMPSHIRE HAS . . . . . 162 NEW HAMPSHIRE . . . 93
    SHE HAS A TOUCH OF GOLD. NEW HAMPSHIRE GOLD-- . . . . 162 NEW HAMPSHIRE . . . 108
    BUT TRUST NEW HAMPSHIRE NOT TO HAVE ENOUGH . . . . . 163 NEW HAMPSHIRE . . . 122
    THE WITCH WAS YOUNG, AND BEAUTIFUL (NEW STYLE), . . . 163 NEW HAMPSHIRE . . . 129
    NEW HAMPSHIRE USED TO HAVE AT SALEM . . . . . 163 NEW HAMPSHIRE . . . 138
    NOT EVEN NEW HAMPSHIRE FARMS ARE MUCH FOR SALE. . . . 163 NEW HAMPSHIRE . . . 149
    APPLES? NEW HAMPSHIRE HAS THEM, BUT UNSPRAYED, ... 164 NEW HAMPSHIRE . . . 159
    NEW HAMPSHIRE RAISES THE CONNECTICUT . . . . 165 NEW HAMPSHIRE . . . 183
    NEW YORK (FIVE MILLION) LAUGHS AT MANCHESTER, ... 165 NEW HAMPSHIRE . . . 201
    ANYTHING I CAN SAY ABOUT NEW HAMPSHIRE . . . . . . 165 NEW HAMPSHIRE . . . 210
    NEW HAMPSHIRE MOUNTAINS CURL UP IN A COIL. . . . . . 165 NEW HAMPSHIRE . . . 214
    I HAD BEEN COMING TO NEW HAMPSHIRE MOUNTAINS. . . . . 166 NEW HAMPSHIRE . . . 215
    EMERSON SAID, "THE GOD WHO MADE NEW HAMPSHIRE . . . . 166 NEW HAMPSHIRE . . . 218
    "I GO NO MORE TO SUMMER IN NEW HAMPSHIRE. . . . . . 166 NEW HAMPSHIRE . . . 221
    BUT WHEN I ASKED TO KNOW WHAT AILED NEW HAMPSHIRE, . . 166 NEW HAMPSHIRE . . . 223
    BECAUSE I WROTE MY NOVELS IN NEW HAMPSHIRE . . . . . 166 NEW HAMPSHIRE . . . 246
    IS NO PROOF THAT I AIMED THEM AT NEW HAMPSHIRE. . . . 166 NEW HAMPSHIRE . . . 247
    NEW HAMPSHIRE, NOT CONNECTICUT, ... 167 NEW HAMPSHIRE . . . 250

                                                          PAGE TITLE   LINE
NEW (CONTINUED)
      RHODE ISLAND, NEW YORK, OR VERMONT WAS THIS: .   .   .   .   .   . 167 NEW HAMPSHIRE   .   . . 251
      WHERE I WAS LIVING THEN, NEW HAMPSHIRE OFFERED .   .   .   . 167 NEW HAMPSHIRE   .   . . 252
      TO WANT TO MAKE NEW HAMPSHIRE PEOPLE OVER. .   .   .   .   . 167 NEW HAMPSHIRE   .   . . 263
      UNDER THE NEW REGIME, AND SO FORBIDDEN. .   .   .   .   .   . 167 NEW HAMPSHIRE   .   . . 279
      THIS, THEN, IS THE NEW FREEDOM WE HEAR TELL OF;   .   .   . 168 NEW HAMPSHIRE   .   . . 283
      THE ONLY FAULT I FIND WITH OLD NEW HAMPSHIRE .   .   .   . 168 NEW HAMPSHIRE   .   . . 310
      TO SAY WHAT HEIGHT BECOMES NEW HAMPSHIRE MOUNTAINS, .   . 169 NEW HAMPSHIRE   .   . . 316
      SHE'S STILL NEW HAMPSHIRE, A MOST RESTFUL STATE.   .   .   . 170 NEW HAMPSHIRE   .   . . 357
      LATELY IN CONVERSE WITH A NEW YORK ALEC .   .   .   .   .   . 170 NEW HAMPSHIRE   .   . . 358
      ABOUT THE NEW SCHOOL OF THE PSEUDO-PHALLIC. .   .   .   . 170 NEW HAMPSHIRE   .   . . 359
      I CHOOSE TO BE A PLAIN NEW HAMPSHIRE FARMER .   .   .   . 172 NEW HAMPSHIRE   .   . . 408
      (FROM, SAY, A PUBLISHER IN NEW YORK CITY). .   .   .   .   . 172 NEW HAMPSHIRE   .   . . 410
      AND RESTFUL JUST TO THINK ABOUT NEW HAMPSHIRE. .   .   . 172 NEW HAMPSHIRE   .   . . 412
      HIS NEW JOB GAVE HIM LEISURE FOR STARGAZING. .   .   .   . 178 THE STAR-SPLITTER   .   . . 75
      BEFORE THEY HEARD OF HIM IN SOME NEW CAMP, ... 192 PAUL'S WIFE   29
      ON THE NEW WOOD THE WHOLE LENGTH OF THE LOG .   .   .   . 193 PAUL'S WIFE   70
      IT LOOKED TO HIM LIKE SOME NEW KIND OF HOLLOW .   .   . 193 PAUL'S WIFE   86
      WITH THE NEW CITY STREET IT HAS TO WEAR .   .   .   .   .   . 231 A BROOK IN THE CITY   .   .   2
      I'VE TRIED THE NEW MOON TILTED IN THE AIR .   .   .   .   . 245 THE FREEDOM OF THE MOON   .   1
      MAKES THE NEW MOON LOOK ANYTHING BUT NEW .   .   .   . 247 THE COCOON   3
      BEHIND NEW BARRIER WALLS (AND LET IT CHAFE!), .   .   . 254 THE FLOOD   3
      IT BREAKS AWAY IN SOME NEW KIND OF SLAUGHTER. .   .   . 254 THE FLOOD   4
      WHAT ARE WE?" / "YOUNG OR NEW?" / "WE MUST BE SOMETHING. . 258 WEST-RUNNING BROOK   .   . 10
      ALL THAT PIANO AND NEW PAINT BACK THERE, ... 264 THE INVESTMENT   .   .   .   9
      AND ON TRACTS LAID NEW TO THE SUN, ... 285 IN TIME OF CLOUDBURST   . 19
      THE LITTLE OLD HOUSE WAS OUT WITH A LITTLE NEW SHED .   . 286 A ROADSIDE STAND   .   .   .   1
      AND SENDING UP NEW SHOOTS .   .   .   . 308 EVIL TENDENCIES CANCEL   .   4
      --THE NEW ENGLAND PRIMER .   .   .   . 331 SYCAMORE   4
      IT'S A NEW PATENTED ELECTRIC LIGHT, ... 369 THE LITERATE FARMER AND   39
      THE COURAGE TO BE NEW .   .   .   . 387 THE COURAGE TO BE NEW .   .   T
      AND THEIR COURAGE TO BE NEW. .   .   .   . 387 THE COURAGE TO BE NEW .   . 16
      BUT WANTS IT ALL MADE OVER NEW. .   .   .   . 393 A CASE FOR JEFFERSON   .   .   2
      AND HAVING IT ALL MADE OVER NEW. .   .   .   . 393 A CASE FOR JEFFERSON   .   . 11
      HAVING INVENTED A NEW HOLOCAUST, ... 399 U.S. 1946 KING'S X .   .   .   1
      A NEW AND BETTER WAY TO IND .   .   .   . 416 AMERICA IS HARD TO SEE   .   2
      THE NEW WORLD CHRISTOPHER COLUMBUS FOUND. .   .   .   . 422 FOR JOHN F. KENNEDY   .   . 15
      NOW CAME ON A NEW ORDER OF THE AGES .   .   .   .   .   . 422 FOR JOHN F. KENNEDY   .   . 19
      "NEW ORDER OF THE AGES" DID WE SAY? .   .   .   .   .   . 423 FOR JOHN F. KENNEDY   .   . 39
      ON A NEW DEPARTURE. .   .   .   . 427 VERSION   3
      BUT IT'S NOT NEW YORK. .   .   .   . 439 KITTY HAWK   .   .   . 344
      AS TOO NEW TO MENTION. .   .   .   . 440 KITTY HAWK   .   .   . 383
      THAT SHOULD HAVE MADE THE NEW WORLD NEWLY GREAT .   .   . 446 DOES NO ONE AT ALL EVER   3
      DON'T YOU KNOW WHERE NEW MOONS ARE FROM? .   .   .   . 451 A-WISHING WELL   .   . 31
      I'M APT TO TELL THEM IN NEW YORK .   .   .   . 452 A-WISHING WELL   .   . 34
      THAT WAS HEARD AS FAR AWAY AS NEW YORK .   .   .   .   . 463 LINES IN DEJECTION   .   . 23
      (WHO HAS BEEN STANDING DAZED WITH NEW IDEAS) .   .   . 489 A MASQUE OF REASON   .   . 441
      YES, BUT NEW YORK WILL DO AS AN EXAMPLE. .   .   .   .   . 496 A MASQUE OF MERCY   .   . 91
      WELL, YOU'RE AS GOOD AS IN NEW YORK THIS MINUTE-- .   . 497 A MASQUE OF MERCY   .   . 92
      OR BAD AS IN NEW YORK. / I KNOW I AM. .   .   .   .   .   . 497 A MASQUE OF MERCY   .   . 93
      A FRACTURE IN THE ROCKS BENEATH NEW YORK .   .   .   . 502 A MASQUE OF MERCY   .   . 229
      A MISSION AS TO HAVE TO TELL NEW YORK .   .   .   .   .   . 503 A MASQUE OF MERCY   .   . 272
      OR THE NEW YORKER. / WHEN WAS THE LAST TIME .   .   .   . 504 A MASQUE OF MERCY   .   . 276
      'TWERE NOTHING NEW IF THAT WERE ALL CHRIST BROUGHT. .   . 511 A MASQUE OF MERCY   .   . 474
NEW-BEGINNING
      WHERE THE GRIST OF THE NEW-BEGINNING BROOKS .   .   .   . 140 THE GUM-GATHERER   .   . 14
NEW-BOUGHTEN
      IN A NEW-BOUGHTEN GRAVE PLOT BY HERSELF, ... 200 PLACE FOR A THIRD   .   . 23
NEW-BUILT
      THIS NEW-BUILT CITY FROM BOTH WORK AND SLEEP. .   .   . 231 A BROOK IN THE CITY   .   . 24
NEWCOMERS
      ONE MUSTN'T BEAR TOO HARD ON THE NEWCOMERS, ... 80 THE GENERATIONS OF MEN 188
NEW-CUT
      IN THE MEADOW, BUSY WITH THE NEW-CUT HAY, ... 109 THE EXPOSED NEST   .   .   3
      THE SUN IN THE NEW-CUT NARROW GAP .   .   .   .   .   . 123 PEA BRUSH   5
NEW-FASHIONED
      INSTEAD OF A NEW-FASHIONED ONE AT AUCTION? .   .   .   . 178 THE STAR-SPLITTER   .   . 65
NEWLY
      THAT SHOULD HAVE MADE THE NEW WORLD NEWLY GREAT .   .   . 446 DOES NO ONE AT ALL EVER   3
      OUR CHANCE OF BEING PEOPLE NEWLY BORN. .   .   .   .   . 446 DOES NO ONE AT ALL EVER 12
NEWNESS
      WITH THEIR EVER BREAKING NEWNESS .   .   .   . 387 THE COURAGE TO BE NEW .   . 15
NEWS
      TO MEET HIM IN THE DOORWAY WITH THE NEWS .   .   .   .   . 34 DEATH OF THE HIRED MAN   4
      ALL ROUND THE COUNTRY FOR THE WEEKLY NEWS, ... 48 A HUNDRED COLLARS   .   . 98
      PUBLISHED IN BOW. YOU KNOW THE WEEKLY NEWS?" .   .   . 48 A HUNDRED COLLARS   .   . 99
      THE NEWS HAS ALWAYS BEEN REPUBLICAN. .   .   .   .   .   . 48 A HUNDRED COLLARS   .   . 111
      I'VE GOT SOME NEWS THAT MAYBE ISN'T NEWS. .   .   .   . 88 THE HOUSEKEEPER   .   . 210
      "WHO WANTS TO HEAR YOUR NEWS, YOU--DREADFUL FOOL?" .   . 89 THE HOUSEKEEPER   .   . 214
      THE NEWS OF A DAY I'VE FORGOTTEN-- .   .   .   .   .   . 110 A PATCH OF OLD SNOW   .   .   7
      AND WHAT'S THE NEWS YOU CARRY--IF YOU KNOW? .   .   .   . 125 AN ENCOUNTER   .   .   . 20
      IT IS IN THE NEWS THAT ALL THESE PITIFUL KIN .   .   .   . 286 A ROADSIDE STAND   .   . 23
      NOT JUST FOR SCIENTIFIC NEWS .   .   .   . 416 AMERICA IS HARD TO SEE   .   5
      HAVEN'T YOU HEARD THE NEWS? WE ALREADY HAVE ONE, .   . 515 A MASQUE OF MERCY   .   . 577
NEWSPAPERS
      LET NEWSPAPERS PROFESS TO FEAR THE WORST! .   .   .   . 318 BUILD SOIL   65
NEW-WORLD
      A NEW-WORLD SONG, FAR OUT OF REACH, ... 24 PAN WITH US   17
NEXT
      FOR THE NEXT FORTY SUMMERS--CALL IT FORTY. .   .   .   . 95 THE SELF-SEEKER   .   . 69
      "I WANTED THERE SHOULD BE SOME THERE NEXT YEAR." .   .   . 97 THE SELF-SEEKER   .   . 123
      "I'M GOING TO PUT YOU ON THE FARM NEXT TO IT." .   .   . 164 NEW HAMPSHIRE   .   .   . 156
      "WHY WON'T THE FARM NEXT TO IT DO FOR YOU?" .   .   .   . 164 NEW HAMPSHIRE   .   .   . 157
      FOR THE NEXT ONE TO OPEN FOR HIMSELF. .   .   .   .   . 175 THE CENSUS-TAKER   .   . 30
      BUT THE FIRST THING NEXT MORNING WE REFLECTED .   .   . 177 THE STAR-SPLITTER   .   . 43
      WAS TO REBUKE HER TEACHER WITH IT NEXT DAY, ... 180 MAPLE   31
      THE NEXT COW MIGHT HAVE LICKED UP OUT AT PASTURE. .   . 184 MAPLE   151
      AT THE NEXT DRINK IT GREW INVISIBLE. .   .   .   .   .   . 194 PAUL'S WIFE   103

NEXT (CONTINUED)
    NEXT EVENING MURPHY AND SOME OTHER FELLOWS . . . . . . 195 PAUL'S WIFE 123
    AS WAS APPARENT FROM WHAT HAPPENED NEXT. . . . . 195 PAUL'S WIFE 138
    TRY TO WEIGH SOMETHING NEXT TIME, SO YOU WON'T . . . . 199 WILD GRAPES 90
    HOUSEKEEPING FOR THE NEXT MAN OUT OF WEDLOCK. . . . . . 201 PLACE FOR A THIRD . . 62
    I VERIFIED THE NAME NEXT MORNING: TOFFILE. . . . . . . 207 THE WITCH OF COOS . . 154
    NEXT TO NOTHING FOR WEIGHT; . . . . 235 GATHERING LEAVES . . 17
    NEXT TO NOTHING FOR COLOR. . . . . 235 GATHERING LEAVES . . 20
    NEXT TO NOTHING FOR USE. . . . . 235 GATHERING LEAVES . . 21
    NEXT DAY THE SCENE WAS PILED AND PUFFED AND DEAD. . . . 239 OUR SINGING STRENGTH . 11
    WHAT WILL NEXT PROVE A ROSE. . . . . 246 THE ROSE FAMILY . . . 8
    AND THING NEXT MOST DIFFUSE TO CLOUD, ... 251 TREE AT MY WINDOW . . 6
    AND AFTER THAT HER NEXT JOY . . . . 256 THE LOVELY BE CHOOSERS 25
    AND BE HER NEXT JOY THIS: . . . . 257 THE LOVELY BE CHOOSERS 37
    HER NEXT STEP ROCKS A BOULDER ON THE WALL . . . . 268 THE BEAR 5
    THE NEXT MACHINE THAT HAS THE POWER TO PASS . . . . . . 270 THE EGG AND THE MACHINE 29
    TO LIVE IN VILLAGES, NEXT TO THE THEATER AND STORE, . . 286 A ROADSIDE STAND . . 25
    AND THEN NEXT DAY AS I COME BACK INTO THE SANE, ... 287 A ROADSIDE STAND . . 49
    NEXT MORNING TO THE LIGHT OF DAY WAS MORE . . . . 290 OLD BARN AT THE BOTTOM 26
    BUT SHEEP IS WHAT I'M GOING INTO NEXT. . . . . 316 BUILD SOIL 10
    GET IN A POEM TOWARD THE NEXT ELECTION. . . . . 316 BUILD SOIL 25
    TO BE ATTEMPTED. GREED MAY WELL COME NEXT. . . . . . . 319 BUILD SOIL 100
    FOR NEXT DEFENSE OUTSIDE . . . . 348 TRIPLE BRONZE . . . 4
    (PERHAPS IT WILL BE NEXT MILLENNIUM.) . . . . 353 THE LESSON FOR TODAY . 103
    AND TURN US INTO THE NEXT SPECIE FOLKS . . . . 369 THE LITERATE FARMER AND 43
    QUESTION OF WHAT WE'RE TURNING INTO NEXT." . . . . . . 369 THE LITERATE FARMER AND 48
    "NATURE I LOVED; AND NEXT TO NATURE, ART." . . . . . . 393 LUCRETIUS VERSUS POETS S
    A HALF COURSE IN IT NEXT YEAR.) AND BESIDES, ... 407 FROM PLANE TO PLANE . 112
    NEXT MORNING THE MINUTE I WAS ABOUT . . . . 420 ONE MORE BREVITY . . 44
    THE GLORY OF A NEXT AUGUSTAN AGE . . . . 424 FOR JOHN F. KENNEDY . 71
    ALMOST NEXT TO NAUGHT . . . . 426 A NEVER NAUGHT SONG . 30
    THERE I NEXT FELL IN . . . . 432 KITTY HAWK 139
    NEXT TIME YOU FIND YOURSELF PRESSED ONTO ONE . . . . . 486 A MASQUE OF REASON . 370
NIBBLED
    I DON'T WANT IT DREAMILY NIBBLED FCR BROWSE . . . . . . 228 GOOD-BY AND KEEP COLD . 7
NICE (SEE NOT-NICE)
    "WHO CARES WHAT THEY SAY? IT'S A NICE WAY TO LIVE, . . 61 BLUEBERRIES 54
    HE'S FOND OF NICE THINGS--TOO FOND, SOME WOULD SAY. . . 85 THE HOUSEKEEPER . . . 116
NICHE
    IN A SMALL NICHE LET INTO IT, THE GIRL . . . . 195 PAUL'S WIFE 134
NICK
    YOU NICK MY SPRUCE UNTIL ITS FIBER CRACKS, ... 349 TO A YOUNG WRETCH . . 3
NIGGER'S
    WHATEVER IT IS THE NIGGER'S GOT." . . . . 345 DISCOVERY OF MADEIRAS . 75
NIGGER-TRADER'S
    THAT SPOILS THE NIGGER-TRADER'S LUCK . . . . 345 DISCOVERY OF MADEIRAS . 58
NIGH (SEE WELL-NIGH)
    FROM A HUMPED BODY NIGH AS BIG'S A BISCUIT. . . . . . . 70 THE CODE 35
NIGHT (SEE ALL-NIGHT, GOOD-NIGHT)
    NIGHT COMES; THE BLACK BATS TUMBLE AND DART; . . . . . 6 GHOST HOUSE 15
    FOR A SHELTER FOR THE NIGHT, ... 7 LOVE AND A QUESTION . 6
    AND QUESTION WHAT OF THE NIGHT TO BE, ... 7 LOVE AND A QUESTION . 11
    WHO LAY THAT NIGHT AWAKE. . . . . 11 WIND AND WINDOW FLOWER 20
    LIKE NOTHING ELSE BY DAY, LIKE GHOSTS BY NIGHT; . . . . 12 A PRAYER IN SPRING . 6
    BY A MISTY FEN THAT RANG ALL NIGHT, ... 15 IN A VALE 2
    BUT ALL CAME EVERY NIGHT WITH THE MIST; . . . . 15 IN A VALE 11
    NOR VAINLY LISTEN ALL THE NIGHT LONG. . . . . 16 IN A VALE 25
    SEEKING WITH MEMORIES GROWN DIM O'ER NIGHT . . . . . . 22 THE TUFT OF FLOWERS . 13
    THAT WROUGHT ON HIM BESIDE HER IN THE NIGHT. . . . . . 38 DEATH OF THE HIRED MAN 110
    BUT ONLY FELT AT NIGHT ITS SHADOWY PRESENCE. . . . . . 41 THE MOUNTAIN 22
    THEY MEET HIM IN THE GENERAL STORE AT NIGHT, ... 44 A HUNDRED COLLARS . . 8
    AFTER ELEVEN O'CLOCK AT NIGHT. TOO TIRED . . . . 45 A HUNDRED COLLARS . . 17
    "NO ROOM," THE NIGHT CLERK SAID, "UNLESS----" . . . . 45 A HUNDRED COLLARS . . 20
    THE NIGHT CLERK BLINKED HIS EYES AND DARED HIM ON. . . 45 A HUNDRED COLLARS . . 28
    THE NIGHT CLERK LED HIM UP THREE FLIGHTS OF STAIRS . . 45 A HUNDRED COLLARS . . 33
    THE NIGHT CLERK CLAPPED A BEDSTEAD ON THE FOOT. . . . . 46 A HUNDRED COLLARS . . 39
    WHEN I'M WITH PEOPLE I DON'T TRUST AT NIGHT." . . . . . 48 A HUNDRED COLLARS . . 92
    I'VE JUST BEGUN THE NIGHT. YOU GET SOME SLEEP. . . . . 50 A HUNDRED COLLARS . . 172
    BY HIS SHOUTS IN THE NIGHT. HE'D SHOUT AND SHOUT . . . 66 A SERVANT TO SERVANTS 131
    BUT IT MIGHT BE, COME NIGHT, I SHOULDN'T LIKE IT, . . . 67 A SERVANT TO SERVANTS 163
    ESSENCE OF WINTER SLEEP IS ON THE NIGHT, ... 68 AFTER APPLE-PICKING . 7
    I'VE HEARD HIM POUNDING IN THE BARN ALL NIGHT. . . . . 71 THE CODE 42
    AT SUCH AN HOUR OF NIGHT, AND ON FOOT TOO? . . . . . . 90 THE FEAR 27
    "WHAT ARE YOU DOING ROUND THIS HOUSE AT NIGHT?" . . . . 91 THE FEAR 70
    "WHAT'S A CHILD DOING AT THIS TIME OF NIGHT----?" . . . 92 THE FEAR 81
    AN OLD MAN'S WINTER NIGHT . . . . 108 OLD MAN'S WINTER NIGHT T
    IN CLOMPING OFF--AND SCARED THE OUTER NIGHT, ... 108 OLD MAN'S WINTER NIGHT 11
    IT'S THUS HE DOES IT OF A WINTER NIGHT. . . . . 108 OLD MAN'S WINTER NIGHT 28
    TO SEE IF THE BIRDS LIVED THE FIRST NIGHT THROUGH, . . 110 THE EXPOSED NEST . . 35
    NIGHT AFTER NIGHT AND STRONGER EVERY NIGHT . . . . . . 113 IN THE HOME STRETCH . 73
    THE FIRST NIGHT AFTER GUESTS HAVE GONE, THE HOUSE . . . 115 IN THE HOME STRETCH . 132
    AND SITS IN SIRIUS' DISC ALL NIGHT, ... 120 BOND AND FREE . . . 12
    ALWAYS AT NIGHT WHEN THEY RETURNED . . . . 127 HOUSE FEAR 2
    AND PREFERRING THE GUT- TO THE INDOOR NIGHT, ... 127 HOUSE FEAR 8
    THROUGH OPENING CLOUDS AT NIGHT WITH DRONING SPEED . . 132 THE BONFIRE 106
    WHEN WE LOCKED UP THE HOUSE AT NIGHT, ... 135 LOCKED OUT 1
    THAT THE NORTH WIND LAST NIGHT . . . . 135 LAST WORD OF A BLUEBIRD 9
    HIS WILD DESCENT FROM THERE ONE NIGHT, ... 137 BROWN'S DESCENT . . 6
    "BROWN MAKES AT SUCH AN HOUR OF NIGHT! . . . . 138 BROWN'S DESCENT . . 33
    "WHAT IS HE DOING OUT A NIGHT LIKE THIS? . . . . 145 SNOW 68
    "IT'S NO NIGHT TO BE OUT." / "HE MAY BE SMALL, ... 145 SNOW 70
    "HE SHAN'T GO--THERE!" / "IT IS A NIGHT, MY DEAR." . . 145 SNOW 80
    WE'RE NOT IN FOR A NIGHT OF HIM. NO SLEEP . . . . 152 SNOW 258
    WHAT SPOILED OUR NIGHT WAS TO HIM JUST HIS FUN. . . . . 155 SNOW 338
    WE'VE HAD A SHARE IN ONE NIGHT OF HIS LIFE. . . . . . . 156 SNOW 349
    WHOSE DUTY WAS AT ANY HOUR OF NIGHT . . . . 163 NEW HAMPSHIRE . . . 140
    ELECTION NIGHT ONCE IN FRANCONIA, ... 165 NEW HAMPSHIRE . . . 195
    FRANCONIA LAUGHS, I FEAR--DID LAUGH THAT NIGHT-- . . . 165 NEW HAMPSHIRE . . . 205

NIGHT (CONTINUED)
AND CANNOT REST FROM PLANNING DAY OR NIGHT . . . . . . 169 NEW HAMPSHIRE . . . 338
OF FROSTY NIGHT AIR ON THE VALE BELOW . . . . 169 NEW HAMPSHIRE . . . 341
THAT SLIP FROM HEAVEN AT NIGHT AND SOFTLY FALL . . . . 172 A STAR IN A STONEBOAT . 2
EXCEPT AT NIGHT TO PLACES IN THE SKY . . . . 173 A STAR IN A STONEBOAT . 41
I RECOLLECT A NIGHT OF BROKEN CLOUDS . . . . 179 THE STAR-SPLITTER . . 79
AND HOW IT STANDS BETWEEN THE NIGHT TONIGHT . . . . . 179 THE STAR-SPLITTER . . 97
TONIGHT?" / AS WELL TONIGHT AS ANY NIGHT. . . . . . . 186 THE AX-HELVE 34
EXCEPT IN TOWNS AT NIGHT, IS NOT A SIN. . . . . . . 189 THE GRINDSTONE . . . 18
OF CARES, AT NIGHT, TO SLEEP; BUT NOTHING TELLS ME . . 199 WILD GRAPES 102
I STAYED THE NIGHT FOR SHELTER AT A FARM . . . . . . 202 THE WITCH OF COOS . . 1
IT'S HARMLESS. MOTHER HEARS IT IN THE NIGHT, ... 203 THE WITCH OF COOS . . 23
THE NIGHT THE BONES CAME UP THE CELLAR STAIRS . . . . 203 THE WITCH OF COOS . . 40
COME DOWN THE STAIRS AT NIGHT AND STAND PERPLEXED . . . 206 THE WITCH OF COOS . . 126
WE WERE ABOUT IT ONE NIGHT IN THE CELLAR. . . . . . . 206 THE WITCH OF COOS . . 142
LAST NIGHT WAS ONE OF HER USUAL OUT. SHE'S KITING. . . 209 PAUPER WITCH OF GRAFTON 81
SHE THINKS WHEN THE WIND MAKES A NIGHT OF IT . . . . . 209 PAUPER WITCH OF GRAFTON 82
AS OFTEN AS HE HAD IN THE TAIL OF THE NIGHT, ... 210 PAUPER WITCH OF GRAFTON 87
IF YOU DON'T WANT TO SPEND THE NIGHT OUTDOORS. . . . . 214 A FOUNTAIN, A BOTTLE . 50
AWAKE THAT NIGHT . . . . 217 I WILL SING YOU ONE-O . 2
AND DID ITS LOUDEST DAY AND NIGHT . . . . 223 THE AIM WAS SONG . . . 3
ALWAYS THE SAME, WHEN ON A FATED NIGHT . . . . 226 THE ONSET 1
I WISH I COULD PROMISE TO LIE IN THE NIGHT . . . . . 228 GOOD-BY AND KEEP COLD . 25
WITH NIGHT SO NEAR, BUT NOT MUCH FURTHER UP. . . . . . 229 TWO LOOK AT TWO . . . 3
OR EARTHSLIDE MOVED AT NIGHT, IT MOVED ITSELF; . . . . 229 TWO LOOK AT TWO . . . 12
OUTSIDE THE SUGARHOUSE ONE NIGHT FOR CHOICE, ... 234 EVENING A SUGAR ORCHARD 2
OR THICKET, OR HOLLOW PLACE FOR THE NIGHT. . . . . . . 236 MISGIVING 8
NOT TILL FROM SEPARATE FLAKES THEY CHANGED AT NIGHT . . 239 OUR SINGING STRENGTH . 7
NOW LET THE NIGHT BE DARK FOR ALL OF ME. . . . . . . 249 ACCEPTANCE 12
LET THE NIGHT BE TOO DARK FOR ME TO SEE . . . . 249 ACCEPTANCE 13
IT LOOKED AS IF A NIGHT OF DARK INTENT . . . . 250 ONCE BY THE PACIFIC . 10
WAS COMING, AND NOT ONLY A NIGHT, AN AGE. . . . . . . 250 ONCE BY THE PACIFIC . 11
MY SASH IS LOWERED WHEN NIGHT COMES ON; . . . . 251 TREE AT MY WINDOW . . 2
I HAVE BEEN ONE ACQUAINTED WITH THE NIGHT. . . . . . . 255 ACQUAINTED WITH NIGHT . 1
ACQUAINTED WITH THE NIGHT . . . . 255 ACQUAINTED WITH NIGHT . T
I HAVE BEEN ONE ACQUAINTED WITH THE NIGHT. . . . . . . 255 ACQUAINTED WITH NIGHT . 14
(FROM SLEEPING GOD KNOWS WHERE LAST NIGHT, ... 276 TWO TRAMPS IN MUD TIME 50
THE LAST TO LET NIGHT DRIVE HER OFF. . . . . 280 BLUE RIBBON AT AMESBURY 16
HIS CHORES FOR ALL THE WINTRY NIGHT. . . . . 280 BLUE RIBBON AT AMESBURY 20
THE NIGHT IS SETTING IN TO BLOW. . . . . 281 BLUE RIBBON AT AMESBURY 49
THE DEW OF NIGHT AND MORNING ON HIS BOOT. . . . . . . 283 THE GOLD HESPERIDEE . 21
DESTROY THEIR SLEEPING AT NIGHT THE ANCIENT WAY. . . . 287 A ROADSIDE STAND . . 31
ONE NIGHT (HE TOLD ME). AND THE BARN HE MEANT . . . . 289 OLD BARN AT THE BOTTOM 20
THAT WAS MAINTAINED AGAINST THE NIGHT, ... 291 ON HEART'S BEGINNING TO 8
THE CLOUDS, THE SOURCE OF RAIN, ONE STORMY NIGHT . . . 295 LOST IN HEAVEN . . . 1
SNOW FALLING AND NIGHT FALLING FAST, OH, FAST . . . . 296 DESERT PLACES . . . 1
LEAVES BY NIGHT AND FLOWERS BY DAY. . . . . 297 LEAVES COMPARED WITH . 16
WAS A SHADE LESS THE COLOR OF NIGHT, ... 299 WELCOME TO THEIR BELIEF 11
THEN STEERED THE WHITE MOTH THITHER IN THE NIGHT? . . . 302 DESIGN 12
PARTLY BECAUSE IT SANG BUT ONCE ALL NIGHT . . . . . . 302 A BIRD SINGING IN SLEEP 3
WE'LL KNOW, WE SAY, THAT THIS WAS THE NIGHT IT DIED. . 305 THERE ARE ROUGHLY ZONES 5
IT IS LATE AT NIGHT AND STILL I AM LOSING, ... 310 IN DIVES' DIVE . . . 1
IRIS BY NIGHT . . . . 315 IRIS BY NIGHT . . . T
TO BETTER ITS PERCH FOR THE NIGHT, ... 334 COME IN 7
A COWARD SAVE AT NIGHT, ... 341 THE SUBVERTED FLOWER . 60
DID YOU STAY UP LAST NIGHT (THE MAGI DID) . . . . . . 360 A LOOSE MOUNTAIN . . 1
AGAINST THE ANCIENT SOVEREIGNTY OF NIGHT. . . . . . . 361 A LOOSE MOUNTAIN . . 8
AND WILL YOU GIVE ME SHELTER FOR THE NIGHT? . . . . . 368 THE LITERATE FARMER AND 21
ITS ACTIONS ANY CLOUDLESS NIGHT WILL SHOW IT. . . . . 370 THE LITERATE FARMER AND 64
OF LIGHTING THE WHOLE NIGHT WITH ONE BIG BLOB . . . . 370 THE LITERATE FARMER AND 72
WE NEED THE INTERRUPTION OF THE NIGHT . . . . 370 THE LITERATE FARMER AND 80
LAST NIGHT YOUR WATCHDOG BARKED ALL NIGHT, ... 380 AN UNSTAMPED LETTER IN 1
ALL NIGHT WITH UNIVERSAL SPACE. . . . . 380 AN UNSTAMPED LETTER IN 17
BESIDE HER ATTIC BED AT NIGHT. . . . . 382 THE NIGHT LIGHT . . . 2
THE NIGHT LIGHT . . . . 382 THE NIGHT LIGHT . . . T
IT IS ON ME BY NIGHT OR DAY, ... 383 THE NIGHT LIGHT . . . 6
WERE I IN TROUBLE WITH NIGHT TONIGHT. . . . . 383 WERE I IN TROUBLE . . 10
IT MIGHT TAKE ME ALL NIGHT. . . . . 384 MAKING CERTAIN ANYTHING 16
IN THE LONG NIGHT . . . . 384 IN THE LONG NIGHT . . T
WE DO NOT GO UP THERE TO SLEEP AT NIGHT. . . . . . . 386 A STEEPLE ON THE HOUSE 4
THAT I HAVE HEARD OF SHONE AT NIGHT. . . . . 390 TWO LEADING LIGHTS . . 6
HE'S FREUDIAN VIENNESE BY NIGHT. . . . . 393 A CASE FOR JEFFERSON . 3
IT WILL NOT DO TO SAY OF NIGHT, ... 403 SOMETHING LIKE A STAR . 4
THAT GIVES OFF FROM A GARDEN GROUND AT NIGHT . . . . . 414 A CABIN IN THE CLEARING 16
I'D BEEN HERE ONE NIGHT . . . . 429 KITTY HAWK 52
BUT THAT NIGHT I STOLE . . . . 432 KITTY HAWK 135
WE ENJOYED AT NIGHT . . . . 437 KITTY HAWK 310
TILL ON SOME FINE NIGHT . . . . 442 KITTY HAWK 454
AND THE NIGHT DREW THROUGH THE TREES . . . . 444 THE DRAFT HORSE . . . 11
OH, THERE HAD ONCE BEEN NIGHT THE FIRST, ... 444 ENDS 3
BUT THIS WAS NIGHT THE LAST. . . . . 444 ENDS 4
FOR A NIGHT OF FROST. . . . . 445 PERIL OF HOPE . . . 12
BUT THEY HAD NOT WALKED FAR INTO THE NIGHT . . . . . . 454 HOW HARD TO KEEP FROM 12
THE NIGHT WE RAN AWAY FROM CTESIPHON). . . . . 462 HOW HARD TO KEEP FROM 270
ENOUGH TO BUILD HIM EVERY NIGHT A PUP TENT . . . . . . 478 A MASQUE OF REASON . . 132
A BOOKSTORE LATE AT NIGHT. THE KEEPER'S WIFE . . . . . 493 A MASQUE OF MERCY . . 1
WITH THE SUSPICION AT THIS HOUR OF NIGHT . . . . 495 A MASQUE OF MERCY . . 53
OR SING AND DANCE ALL NIGHT AND SEE SUNRISE . . . . . 496 A MASQUE OF MERCY . . 71
THIS VERY NIGHT. I HAD THE HALL ALL HIRED, ... 497 A MASQUE OF MERCY . . 95
CAN YOU INTERPRET DREAMS? I DREAMED LAST NIGHT . . . . 501 A MASQUE OF MERCY . . 200
YOU WOULDN'T WANT THE NIGHT CLUBS LAUGHING AT YOU. . . 504 A MASQUE OF MERCY . . 275
NIGHTHAWKS
I DREAM UPON THE NIGHTHAWKS PEOPLING HEAVEN, ... 14 WAITING 11
NIGHTINGALES
AND HARK, THE GOLD ENAMELED NIGHTINGALES . . . . . . 473 A MASQUE OF REASON . . 14
NIGHTMARE
MORE THAN YOU WILL US WITH SUCH NIGHTMARE TALK. . . . 149 SNOW 168
TO SUFFER THE SAME DRIVEN NIGHTMARE OVER. . . . . . . 240 OUR SINGING STRENGTH . 45

NIGHTS
 MORE THAN YOU HAVE YOURSELF, SOME OF THESE NIGHTS. . . . 67 A SERVANT TO SERVANTS . 167
 LAST NIGHT WAS ONE OF HER NIGHTS OUT. SHE'S KITING. . . . 209 PAUPER WITCH OF GRAFTON 81
 BUT THERE ARE MANY NIGHTS, THOUGH CLEAR, ... 390 TWO LEADING LIGHTS . . 16
 "I FLED HIM, DOWN THE NIGHTS AND DOWN THE DAYS; . . . . 494 A MASQUE OF MERCY . . 22
NIL
 ANC SO RENDER NIL . . . . 426 A NEVER NAUGHT SONG . 25
NILLY (SEE WILLY-NILLY)
NINE
 (NINE TIMES REMOVED. CORRECT ME IF I ERR.) . . . . . 79 THE GENERATIONS OF MEN 178
 HE SAYS HE LEFT THE VILLAGE STORE AT NINE: . . . . . 145 SNOW 57
 I COUNTED NINE I HAD NO RIGHT TO COUNT . . . . . . 175 THE CENSUS-TAKER . . 31
 I LOOKED AT NINE: THE SWARM WAS TURNED TO ROCK . . . . 237 A HILLSIDE THAW . . 26
 IF THERE WAS ONE EGG IN IT THERE WERE NINE, ... 270 THE EGG AND THE MACHINE 24
NINETEENTH
 WATCHING OUT OF A NINETEENTH STORY WINDOW . . . . . 182 MAPLE 81
NINETEEN-FIFTY-THREE
 BACK THERE IN 1953 WITH THE HUNTINGTON CAIRNSES . . . 428 KITTY HAWK . . . . D
NINETEEN-FORTY-SIX
 U.S. 1946 KING'S X . . . . 399 U.S. 1946 KING'S X . . T
NINETEEN-TWENTY-SIX
 "MARVELOUS WORLD IN NINETEEN-TWENTY-SIX." . . . . . 372 THE LITERATE FARMER AND 141
NINETY
 OF GOOD FAITH. THERE IS NINETY DOLLARS. . . . . . . 47 A HUNDRED COLLARS . . 86
 MY NINETY ISN'T MINE--YOU WON'T THINK THAT. . . . . . 48 A HUNDRED COLLARS . . 96
NINETY-ODD
 THROUGH NINETY-ODD DEGREES OF ARC, IT SEEMS, ... 269 THE BEAR 24
NO---NOT INDEXED
NOBLE
 HE'D BUILT A NOBLE MANSARD ROOF WITH BALLS . . . . . 160 NEW HAMPSHIRE . . 39
 AS A NOBLE EXPERIMENT. . . . . 466 SOME SCIENCE FICTION . 28
NOBLEMAN'S
 OR GIVING ME A NOBLEMAN'S ESTATE. . . . . 457 HOW HARD TO KEEP FROM 121
NOBLER
 SOUNDS NOBLER THERE THAN 'NEATH THE SUN; . . . . . . 21 THE TRIAL BY EXISTENCE 46
NOBODY
 TO WHIPS AND POLES. THERE'S NOBODY ABOUT. . . . . . 49 A HUNDRED COLLARS . . 136
 YET NOBODY MOLESTED THEM! . . . . 135 LOCKED OUT 7
 NOBODY KNEW IN WHAT DIRECTION, ... 192 PAUL'S WIFE . . . 27
 WHEN SLOWLY (AND NOBODY COMES WITH A LIGHT) . . . . . 228 GOOD-BY AND KEEP COLD . 27
 NOR I NOR NOBODY ELSE MAY SAY, ... 263 THE TIMES TABLE . . 15
 IT IS NOBODY ELSE'S AFFAIR. . . . . 289 DEPARTMENTAL . . . 41
 WHERE NOBODY CAN CALL YOU CRONE. . . . . 307 PROVIDE, PROVIDE . . 12
 NOBODY WAS EVER MEANT . . . . 309 HARDSHIP OF ACCOUNTING 3
 AND NOBODY ELSE AT FAULT, ... 314 BEARER OF EVIL TIDINGS 24
 NOBODY HAS TO CONFIDE IN ME." . . . . 420 ONE MORE BREVITY . . 35
 THAT NOBODY SAW . . . . 449 THE BAD ISLAND--EASTER 52
 BUT NOBODY HAD NOTICED THE CONNECTION), ... 456 HOW HARD TO KEEP FROM 96
NOBODY'S
 KNOWS THE OLD MAN, AND NOBODY'S SO DEEP . . . . . . 371 THE LITERATE FARMER AND 96
NOCTURNES
 FIVE NOCTURNES . . . . 382 FIVE NOCTURNES . . . T
NODDED
 THIS WAS SOME STARK SHE DIDN'T KNOW. HE NODDED. . . . 74 THE GENERATIONS OF MEN 34
 ALL ROUND AND ROUND. THE LATTER HE NODDED "YES" TO, . . 107 CHRISTMAS TREES . . . 36
 SHE NODDED. SO WE'RE SURE THERE'S NO MISTAKE. . . . . 180 MAPLE 19
 GOD NODDED HIS APPROVAL OF AS GOOD. . . . . 422 FOR JOHN F. KENNEDY . 23
NODDING
 NOTHING WOULD DO: HE JUST KEPT NODDING OFF." . . . . 36 DEATH OF THE HIRED MAN 43
 "HE JUST KEPT NODDING HIS HEAD UP AND DOWN. . . . . . 60 BLUEBERRIES 41
NOISE
 I WANTED TO TRY SOMETHING WITH THE NOISE . . . . . . 77 THE GENERATIONS OF MEN 124
 A LITTLE BAREFOOT GIRL, WHO IN THE NOISE . . . . . . 96 THE SELF-SEEKER . . 92
 WAS CUNNINGLY DEVISED TO MAKE A NOISE . . . . . . 98 THE SELF-SEEKER . . 164
 DIED NOT WITHOUT A NOISE OF CRACKLING WOOD-- . . . . 131 THE BONFIRE 76
 THAT JANGLED EVEN ABOVE THE GENERAL NOISE,-- . . . . 142 THE VANISHING RED . . 25
 FOREVER THE NOISE OF THESE . . . . 156 THE SOUND OF TREES . . 3
 MORE THAN ANOTHER NOISE . . . . 156 THE SOUND OF TREES . . 4
 I MAKE A GREAT NOISE . . . . 234 GATHERING LEAVES . . 5
NOISELESS
 ON NOISELESS WING A BEWILDERED BUTTERFLY, ... 22 THE TUFT OF FLOWERS . 12
 MAKE SUCH A NOISELESS TUMULT OVER IT . . . . 411 POD OF THE MILKWEED . 11
NOISY
 SHE STOOD HER GROUND AGAINST THE NOISY STEPS . . . . 92 THE FEAR 76
NOMENCLATURE
 BUT YOU SAY THAT IN COLLEGE NOMENCLATURE . . . . . 393 LUCRETIUS VERSUS POETS 7
 BY SOME NOMENCLATURE. . . . . 438 KITTY HAWK . . . 324
NOMINAL
 TO WATCH A WAR IN NOMINAL ALLIANCE, ... 398 NO HOLY WARS FOR THEM . 6
NOMINATING
 NO ONE IS NOMINATING ME FOR KING. . . . . 462 HOW HARD TO KEEP FROM 260
NON-CONFORMISM
 THAT'S BROWNING AND SHEER CHAPEL NCN-CONFORMISM. . . . 486 A MASQUE OF REASON . . 365
NONE
 WITH NONE AMONG THEM THAT EVER SINGS, ... 6 GHOST HOUSE 28
 TO PICK WHERE NONE COULD MISS THEM . . . . 13 ROSE POGONIAS . . 11
 THAT NONE SHOULD MOW THE GRASS THERE . . . . . . 14 ROSE POGONIAS . . 23
 AND NONE ARE TAKEN BUT WHO WILL, ... 20 THE TRIAL BY EXISTENCE 33
 HIS HEART KNEW PEACE, FOR NONE CAME HERE . . . . . 24 PAN WITH US . . . 11
 THERE IS NONE LEFT TO MOURN THEE IN THE FIELDS. . . . 28 MY BUTTERFLY 7
 WITH NONE TO TREAD AND PUT THEM IN THEIR PLACE. . . . 56 THE BLACK COTTAGE . . 50
 UP AND DOWN STAIRS AND THROUGH THE ROOMS, AND NONE . . 112 IN THE HOME STRETCH . 42
 A BROOK TO NONE BUT WHO REMEMBER LCNG. . . . . . . 119 HYLA BROOK . . . 12
 A GREAT DEAL OF NONE. . . . . 134 A GIRL'S GARDEN . . 40
 "NONE OF MY FAMILY EVER WORKED, OR HAD . . . . . . 159 NEW HAMPSHIRE . . 3
 HE SAID, IN CLIMATE, NONE HAD EVER DIED THERE . . . . 159 NEW HAMPSHIRE . . 18
 AND--WRITING; NONE OF THESE EXCEPT PERHAPS . . . . . 164 NEW HAMPSHIRE . . 166
 NO, NONE OF THESE HAS RAISED ME TO MY THRONE . . . . 169 NEW HAMPSHIRE . . 327
 TO COUNT THE PEOPLE IN IT AND FOUND NONE, ... 174 THE CENSUS-TAKER . . 10
 NONE IN THE HUNDRED MILES, NONE IN THE HOUSE, ... 174 THE CENSUS-TAKER . . 11

NONE (CONTINUED)
NONE NOT IN HIDING FROM THE OUTWARD EYE. . . . . 174 THE CENSUS-TAKER . . 16
IS EXTREME WHERE THEY SHRINK TO NONE AT ALL. . . . . . 176 THE CENSUS-TAKER . . 63
SHE MIGHT HAVE OVERLOOKED. THEY COULD FIND NONE, . . . 183 MAPLE 101
BUT I MISTRUSTED HE WAS NONE TOO PROUD . . . . 209 PAUPER WITCH OF GRAFTON 74
I HAVE NO DOUBT I'D END BY HOLDING NONE. . . . . . . 237 A HILLSIDE THAW . . 17
NONE FLEW BEHIND ME TO BE LEFT ALONE. . . . . 240 OUR SINGING STRENGTH . 48
AND THOUGH NONE TOO SUCCESSFUL AT IT, GUIDERS, ... 267 RIDERS 2
AND THE HARM IS NONE TOO SURE, ... 285 IN TIME OF CLOUDBURST . 9
THEY COULDN'T (THIS CROSSLY): THEY HAD NONE, DIDN'T IT SEE? 287 A ROADSIDE STAND . . 43
WHEN THESE GO THERE WILL BE NONE TO REPLACE THEM. . . . 290 OLD BARN AT THE BOTTOM 40
THEN NONE THE WISER, FRANKLY GAVE IT UP, ... 293 AT WOODWARD'S GARDENS . 29
THEY MIGHT AS WELL HAVE NONE AT ALL. . . . . 297 LEAVES COMPARED WITH . 10
AND NONE WAS LEFT TO PRATE . . . . 298 ON TAKING FROM THE TOP 17
NONE REMAINING IN EXISTENCE . . . . 304 CLEAR AND COLDER . . 8
THAN NONE AT ALL. PROVIDE, PROVIDE! . . . . 307 PROVIDE, PROVIDE . . 21
NONE SHALL BE AS AMBITIOUS AS HE CAN. . . . . 320 BUILD SOIL . . . 121
NONE SHOULD BE AS INGENIOUS AS HE COULD, ... 320 BUILD SOIL . . . 122
LET NONE ASSUME TO TILL THE LAND BUT FARMERS. . . . . 322 BUILD SOIL . . . 209
THAT NONE SHALL EVER SEE YOU COME TO MARKET-- . . . . 323 BUILD SOIL . . . 213
BUT STRICTLY HELD BY NONE, IS LOOSELY BOUND . . . . . 332 THE SILKEN TENT . . . 9
SO NONE NEED BE AFRAID OF SIZE. . . . . 333 ALL REVELATION . . 19
THAT HAVE NONE LEFT TO STAY. . . . . 337 THE WIND AND THE RAIN . 48
I HAVE NONE OF THE TENDERER-THAN-THOU . . . . 357 A CONSIDERABLE SPECK . 24
THEY OFTEN DO, AND NONE THE WISER FOR IT. . . . . . 414 A CABIN IN THE CLEARING 22
IF IT LOOKS NONE TOO ORDERLY TODAY, ... 423 FOR JOHN F. KENNEDY . 40
NONE I DON'T REJECT . . . . 440 KITTY HAWK . . . 382
NONE BUT A COOK'S SON COULD BE SO FOOD-MINDED. . . . . 458 HOW HARD TO KEEP FROM 135
I THOUGHT YOU HAD NONE. SOMEWHERE BACK . . . . . . 482 A MASQUE OF REASON . 240
BUT WARN THE CHILDREN THEY PERHAPS SHOULD HAVE NONE. . . 483 A MASQUE OF REASON . 294
THE POINT WAS IT WAS NONE OF MY CONCERN. . . . . . 485 A MASQUE OF REASON . 335
THINKS WHY NOT TAPER OFF TO NONE AT ALL, ... 498 A MASQUE OF MERCY . 122
NONETHELESS
WAS NONETHELESS THERE READY TO BE FREED . . . . . . 240 OUR SINGING STRENGTH . 52
NONE-TOO-APPARENT
FOR THESE NONE-TOO-APPARENT GAINS . . . . 417 AMERICA IS HARD TO SEE 43
NON-EXISTENCE
WAS THE NON-EXISTENCE . . . . 427 VERSION 8
NON-MEMBERS
OR RATHER SAY NON-MEMBERS IN THE CHURCH, ... 57 THE BLACK COTTAGE . . 86
NONPLUSSED
AT WHICH POINT WE ARE TOTALLY NONPLUSSED. . . . . . 382 TO AN ANCIENT . . . 12
NON-RESISTANCE
ON HER NON-RESISTANCE, ... 427 VERSION 12
NONSENSE
"NONSENSE! SEE WHAT SHE'S DONE! BUT WHO, BUT WHO----?" . 88 THE HOUSEKEEPER . . 185
"BUT IT'S NONSENSE TO THINK HE'D CARE ENOUGH." . . . . 91 THE FEAR 49
"NONSENSE TO THAT! YOU WANT TO SEE HIM SAFE." . . . . 146 SNOW 93
AGAINST MY BROTHER'S NONSENSE. "DROP," HE SAID, . . . 198 WILD GRAPES . . . 75
WOULD PUT AN END TO SUCH FANTASTIC NONSENSE; . . . . 484 A MASQUE OF REASON . 309
I'M GOING TO TAKE THE NONSENSE OUT OF YOU . . . . . 498 A MASQUE OF MERCY . 132
NONSENSICAL (SEE DRUNK-NONSENSICAL)
NOOK
THAT WE SIT SOMETIMES IN THE WAYSIDE NOOK, ... 16 IN NEGLECT 3
NOON
WAS MELTED DOWN AT NOON, ... 10 WIND AND WINDOW FLOWER 6
AND IF BY NOON I HAVE TOO MUCH OF THESE, ... 17 THE VANTAGE POINT . . 9
AND WEARY, SOUGHT AT NOON WITH HIM THE SHADE; . . . . 23 THE TUFT OF FLOWERS . 36
AT NOON RELEASE ANOTHER LEAF; . . . . 27 OCTOBER 13
TILL WELL TOWARD NOON, WHEN THE STORM SETTLED DOWN . . . 74 THE GENERATIONS OF MEN 22
A BIRD HALF WAKENED IN THE LUNAR NOON . . . . 302 A BIRD SINGING IN SLEEP 1
NOONDAY'S
OF WHICH THIS NOONDAY'S THE BEGINNING HOUR. . . . . . 424 FOR JOHN F. KENNEDY . 77
NOR---NOT INDEXED
NORM
FROM NORM TO CRAZY AND BACK TO NORM, ... 325 TO A THINKER . . . 10
NORTH
NORTH OF BOSTON . . . . 31 NORTH OF BOSTON . . T
HE SAYS IT'S NOT REPORTED SO FAR NORTH.-- . . . . . 95 THE SELF-SEEKER . . 87
AND CAME DOWN ON THE NORTH. / HE SAID, "A THOUSAND." . . 107 CHRISTMAS TREES . . 41
WHERE THE FIELD STRETCHES TOWARD THE NORTH . . . . . 131 THE BONFIRE . . . 57
THAT THE NORTH WIND LAST NIGHT . . . . 135 LAST WORD OF A BLUEBIRD 9
BETWEEN ME AND THE NORTH POLE-- . . . . 211 AN EMPTY THREAT . . 25
AND HELD IT LONG ENOUGH FOR NORTH . . . . 224 THE AIM WAS SONG . . 10
FROM NORTH TO SOUTH ACROSS THE BLUE; . . . . 233 LOOKING FOR SUNSET BIRD 19
SOME TO GO FURTHER NORTH TO HUDSON'S BAY, ... 239 OUR SINGING STRENGTH . 22
SOME THAT HAVE COME TOO FAR NORTH BACK AWAY, ... 239 OUR SINGING STRENGTH . 23
"FRED, WHERE IS NORTH?" / "NORTH? NORTH IS THERE, MY LOVE. 257 WEST-RUNNING BROOK . 1
FAR TO NORTH OF THE ST. LAWRENCE. . . . . 304 CLEAR AND COLDER . 11
IT IS VERY FAR NORTH, WE ADMIT, TO HAVE BROUGHT THE PEACH. 305 THERE ARE ROUGHLY ZONES 6
SOME INTO THE COUNTRY NORTH, ... 312 THE VINDICTIVES . . 71
FROM FIFTY NORTH TO FIFTY SOUTH. . . . . 418 AMERICA IS HARD TO SEE 54
NORTHERLY
BY SETTING IT OUT ON A NORTHERLY SLOPE.) . . . . . 228 GOOD-BY AND KEEP COLD . 14
NORTHERN
AND THE NORTHERN LIGHTS THAT RUN LIKE TINGLING NERVES. . 268 ON LOOKING UP BY CHANCE 3
TO OBSERVE THE NORTHERN LIGHT. . . . . 384 IN THE LONG NIGHT . . 8
NORTHWARD
TO NORTHWARD FROM YOUR WINDOW AT THE SINK, ... 114 IN THE HOME STRETCH . 115
NORTHWEST (SEE SOUTHEAST-NORTHWEST, WEST-NORTHWEST)
THAT THE NORTHWEST WIND SHOULD RISE TO SUCH A HEIGHT . . 305 THERE ARE ROUGHLY ZONES 16
NOSE
OF HIS SLIM GOAD ON NOSE AND OFFSIDE FLANK, ... 44 THE MOUNTAIN . . . 108
THE NOSE IS JUST THE SAME, AND SO'S THE CHIN-- . . . . 77 THE GENERATIONS OF MEN 114
LIGHTING HIS PIPE NOW, SQUINTING DOWN HIS NOSE . . . . 112 IN THE HOME STRETCH . 64
HE MADE THE SUN A PINPOINT ON THE NOSE . . . . . . 293 AT WOODWARD'S GARDENS . 8
ONE PUT A THOUGHTFUL HAND UP TO HIS NOSE . . . . . 293 AT WOODWARD'S GARDENS . 14
NOSE-SIDE
"SEE HOW IT MAKES HIS NOSE-SIDE BRIGHT, A PROOF . . . 112 IN THE HOME STRETCH . 66

NOSTRIL
    THIS WAS AN ANTLERED BUCK OF LUSTY NOSTRIL, ... 229 TWO LOOK AT TWO . . . 29
    TO STAB ME IN THE SNEEZE-NERVE OF A NOSTRIL. . . . . . 277 THE WHITE-TAILED HORNET 10
NOT---NOT INDEXED
NOTCH
    STRAIGHTAWAY THROUGH THE MOUNTAIN NOTCH . . . . 63 A SERVANT TO SERVANTS . 22
NOTE
    A NOTE AS FROM A SINGLE PLACE, ... 18 GOING FOR WATER . . . 21
    A NOTE UNRUFFLED . . . . 218 I WILL SING YOU ONE-O . 24
    BY MEASURE. IT WAS WORD AND NOTE, ... 224 THE AIM WAS SONG . . . 13
    A NATURE NOTE . . . . 364 A NATURE NOTE . . . T
    I TOOK NOTE OF WHEN IT OCCURRED, ... 365 A NATURE NOTE . . . 13
    I LEAVE THIS NOTE WITHOUT A STAMP . . . . 380 AN UNSTAMPED LETTER IN 5
    OF RECORD IN MY NOTE BOOK. / WELL, SHE WAS. . . . . 477 A MASQUE OF REASON . . 103
    (SHE STARTLES AT THE SUDDEN NOTE OF KINDNESS.) . . . . 519 A MASQUE OF MERCY . . 691
NOTED
    AT HAVING IN THEIR TOWN A NOTED WITCH: . . . . . . 208 PAUPER WITCH OF GRAFTON 37
NOTEDEST
    THE NOTEDEST ASTRONOMERS . . . . 390 TWO LEADING LIGHTS . . 14
NOTHING
    LIKE NOTHING ELSE BY DAY, LIKE GHOSTS BY NIGHT; . . . . 12 A PRAYER IN SPRING . . 6
    FOR THIS IS LOVE AND NOTHING ELSE IS LOVE, ... 12 A PRAYER IN SPRING . . 13
    NOTHING BUT WHAT WE SOMEHOW CHOSE: . . . . 21 THE TRIAL BY EXISTENCE 69
    NOTHING WOULD DO: HE JUST KEPT NODDING OFF." . . . . 36 DEATH OF THE HIRED MAN 43
    AND NOTHING TO LOOK BACKWARD TO WITH PRIDE, ... 38 DEATH OF THE HIRED MAN 100
    AND NOTHING TO LOOK FORWARD TO WITH HOPE, ... 38 DEATH OF THE HIRED MAN 101
    OF COURSE HE'S NOTHING TO US, ANY MORE . . . . . . 38 DEATH OF THE HIRED MAN 115
    'TWAS NOTHING BUT MY FOOLISH HANGING BACK, ... 46 A HUNDRED COLLARS . . 59
    THERE'S NOTHING I'M AFRAID OF LIKE SCARED PEOPLE. . . . 50 A HUNDRED COLLARS . . 175
    (NOTHING COULD DRAW HER AFTER THOSE TWO SONS, ... 56 THE BLACK COTTAGE . . 40
    AND SAW NOTHING MORE OF EACH OTHER, OR HEARD, ... 62 BLUEBERRIES 87
    THERE'S NOTHING BUT A VOICE-LIKE LEFT INSIDE . . . . 63 A SERVANT TO SERVANTS . 13
    NOTHING! THEY LISTENED FOR HIM. NOT A RUSTLE. . . . . 72 THE CODE 91
    NOTHING WOULD DO BUT THEY MUST FIX A DAY . . . . . . 73 THE GENERATIONS OF MEN 15
    "HE'S NOTHING. LISTEN. WHEN I LEAN LIKE THIS . . . . 77 THE GENERATIONS OF MEN 103
    LEFT HERE WITH NOTHING BUT THE FURNITURE. . . . . . 82 THE HOUSEKEEPER . . . 44
    "NOTHING." IT CAME FROM WELL ALONG THE ROAD. . . . . 91 THE FEAR 67
    "NOTHING." A PAUSE: THERE SEEMED NO MORE TO SAY. . . . 91 THE FEAR 71
    NOTHING IS HIDDEN FROM SOME PEOPLE, ANNE. . . . . . 97 THE SELF-SEEKER . . . 135
    BUT NOTHING SO LIKE BEATING ON A BOX. . . . . . . 108 OLD MAN'S WINTER NIGHT 14
    IT'S NOTHING; IT'S THEIR LEAVING US AT DUSK. . . . . 115 IN THE HOME STRETCH . 130
    BUT FINDING NOTHING, SULLENLY WITHDREW. . . . . . . 126 RANGE-FINDING . . . 14
    OF BURNING FATNESS, AND THEN NOTHING BUT . . . . . 130 THE BONFIRE 24
    NOTHING SO NEW--SOMETHING WE HAD FORGOTTEN: . . . . 133 THE BONFIRE 110
    AND NOTHING HAPPENED: DAY WAS ALL BUT DONE. . . . . 136 "OUT,OUT--" 9
    LITTLE--LESS--NOTHING!--AND THAT ENDED IT. . . . . 137 "OUT,OUT--" 32
    MESERVE SEEMED TO HEED NOTHING BUT THE LAMP . . . . 147 SNOW 111
    ONE OF THE LIES WOULD MAKE IT OUT THAT NOTHING . . . 147 SNOW 129
    HELPLESS. "THERE'S NOTHING WE CAN DO TILL MORNING." . . 155 SNOW 325
    "THE WHOLE TO-DO SEEMS TO HAVE BEEN FOR NOTHING. . . . 155 SNOW 337
    AND THEN TAKE OUR ADVICE NO MORE THAN NOTHING, . . . 155 SNOW 347
    ON NOTHING WORSE THAN TOO MUCH LUCK AND COMFORT. . . . 167 NEW HAMPSHIRE . . . 276
    FROM NOTHING BUT EMBARRASSMENT AND WANT . . . . . 168 NEW HAMPSHIRE . . . 291
    NOTHING NOT BUILT WITH HANDS OF COURSE IS SACRED. . . . 171 NEW HAMPSHIRE . . . 394
    HE NOTICED NOTHING IN IT TO REMARK. . . . . 172 A STAR IN A STONEBOAT . 7
    AND NOTHING BUT THE STUMP OF IT WAS LEFT . . . . . 175 THE CENSUS-TAKER . 20
    NO LAMP WAS LIT. NOTHING WAS ON THE TABLE. . . . . 175 THE CENSUS-TAKER . 35
    NOTHING WAS LEFT TO DO THAT I COULD SEE . . . . . 176 THE CENSUS-TAKER . 54
    SIGNIFIED NOTHING. ROSE COULD HAVE A MEANING, . . . 181 MAPLE 47
    SHE WAS SURE, THOUGH, THERE HAD BEEN NOTHING IN IT. . . 181 MAPLE 69
    AND I GIVE UP"; WHICH LAST LOOK CAME TO NOTHING. . . . 184 MAPLE 132
    AND CUTTING NOTHING NOT CUT DOWN ALREADY. . . . . 185 THE AX-HELVE . . . 9
    "DEN WHEN YOU SAY YOU COME? IT'S COST YOU NOTHING. . . . 186 THE AX-HELVE . . . 33
    FOR NOTHING IN THE MEASURE OF A NEIGHBOR. . . . . 186 THE AX-HELVE . . . 43
    HAS NOTHING ANY MORE TO DO WITH ME, ... 189 THE GRINDSTONE . . 21
    WHAT EVIDENTLY NOTHING COULD CONCLUDE. . . . . . 190 THE GRINDSTONE . . 64
    OF CARES; AT NIGHT, TO SLEEP; BUT NOTHING TELLS ME . . 199 WILD GRAPES . . . 102
    NOTHING TO SAY TO ALL THOSE MARRIAGES! . . . . . 199 PLACE FOR A THIRD . 1
    SO LABAN SAW THE SISTER; AND, SAYING NOTHING . . . . 200 PLACE FOR A THIRD . 44
    I COULD SEE NOTHING. "TOFFILE, I DON'T SEE IT. . . . 205 THE WITCH OF COOS . 99
    YOU CAN COME DOWN FROM EVERYTHING TO NOTHING. . . . 210 PAUPER WITCH OF GRAFTON 103
    AND NOTHING CAME OF ALL HE SAILED. . . . . . . 212 AN EMPTY THREAT . 47
    I MEANT, YOU MEANT, THAT NOTHING SHOULD REMAIN . . . 222 TO E.T. 9
    NOTHING GOLD CAN STAY . . . . 222 NOTHING GOLD CAN STAY . T
    NOTHING GOLD CAN STAY. . . . . 223 NOTHING GOLD CAN STAY . 8
    UPON HIM WHERE HE IS, WITH NOTHING DONE . . . . . 226 THE ONSET 9
    NOTHING WILL BE LEFT WHITE BUT HERE A BIRCH, . . . 226 THE ONSET 22
    HIGH IN THE BREAST. NOTHING BUT WHAT GOOD CARE . . . 230 NOT TO KEEP . . . 15
    AND ALL FOR NOTHING IT HAD EVER DONE, ... 231 A BROOK IN THE CITY . 18
    NEXT TO NOTHING FOR WEIGHT; . . . . 235 GATHERING LEAVES . 17
    NEXT TO NOTHING FOR COLOR. . . . . 235 GATHERING LEAVES . 20
    NEXT TO NOTHING FOR USE. . . . . 235 GATHERING LEAVES . 21
    THEY COULD FIND NOTHING OPEN BUT THE ROAD. . . . . 239 OUR SINGING STRENGTH . 30
    FOR THEM THERE WAS REALLY NOTHING SAD. . . . . . 242 NEED OF BEING VERSED . 21
    THOSE FRIENDS KNOW NOTHING OF HER GRIEF TO MAKE IT SHAMEFUL. 256 THE LOVELY BE CHOOSERS 27
    SEE NOTHING WORTHY TO HAVE BEEN ITS MARK, ... 261 A SOLDIER 5
    YET NOTHING I SHOULD CARE TO LEAVE BEHIND. . . . . 266 THE ARMFUL . . . 5
    BUT NOTHING EVER HAPPENS, NO HARM IS DONE. . . . . 268 ON LOOKING UP BY CHANCE 7
    NOTHING ON EITHER SIDE WAS SAID. . . . . 277 TWO TRAMPS IN MUD TIME 57
    NOTHING BUT FALLIBILITY WAS LEFT US, ... 279 THE WHITE-TAILED HORNET 69
    THREE MADE IT CERTAIN NOTHING FATE COULD DO . . . . 283 THE GOLD HESPERIDEE . 27
    AND SO ARE NOTHING TO MAKE HER TREMBLE. . . . . 291 ON HEART'S BEGINNING TO 31
    THROUGH LEVEL MOUNTAINS NOTHING TO THE EYE . . . . 292 FIGURE IN THE DOORWAY . 2
    WITH NO EXPRESSION, NOTHING TO EXPRESS. . . . . 296 DESERT PLACES . . 12
    THE STRONG ARE SAYING NOTHING . . . . 299 STRONG SAYING NOTHING . T
    BUT THE STRONG ARE SAYING NOTHING UNTIL THEY SEE. . . . 300 STRONG SAYING NOTHING . 16
    "SO WE WON'T SAY NOTHING IS CLEAR." . . . . . . 302 VOICE WAYS 8
    THERE IS NOTHING MUCH WE CAN DO FOR THE TREE TONIGHT, . 305 THERE ARE ROUGHLY ZONES 14

PAGE TITLE   LINE

NOTHING (CONTINUED)
IT IS NOTHING TO ME WHO RUNS THE DIVE. . . . . 310 IN DIVES' DIVE . . . 5
THEY DIVED AND NOTHING WAS FOUND. . . . . 311 THE VINDICTIVES . . . 45
FOR NOTHING DOWN, ALL-OUT-DOORS OF A PLACE, ... 316 BUILD SOIL 8
FOR NOTHING BUT ITS OWN BLIND SATISFACTION . . . . . 319 BUILD SOIL 104
NOTHING COMPARED TO THE PRODUCING OF THEM. . . . . . 324 BUILD SOIL 258
SO LONG FOR NOTHING. NO REPLY-- . . . . 327 A MISSIVE MISSILE . . 26
ALL MODERN, NOTHING ANCIENT IN'T, ... 328 A MISSIVE MISSILE . . 45
AND NOTHING EVER CAME OF WHAT HE CRIED . . . . 338 THE MOST OF IT . . . 9
THERE'S NOTHING BUT INJUSTICE TO BE HAD, ... 352 THE LESSON FOR TODAY . 60
WE'RE EITHER NOTHING OR A GOD'S REGRET. . . . . . . 353 THE LESSON FOR TODAY . 106
SINCE IT WAS NOTHING I KNEW EVIL OF . . . . 358 A CONSIDERABLE SPECK . 28
AND THOUGH THEY'RE NOTHING ANYBODY BEGS, ... 365 OF STONES OF THE PLACE . 3
CARVE NOTHING ON IT. YOU CAN SIMPLY SAY . . . . . . 365 OF STONES OF THE PLACE . 13
AND NOTHING BUT THE TOP A LEAFY GREEN-- . . . . . . 375 A YOUNG BIRCH . . . 7
BUT HAVE ALMOST NOTHING TO DO . . . . 388 MIDDLENESS OF THE ROAD . 13
WE'LL BE ALL RIGHT IF NOTHING GOES WRONG WITH THE LIGHTING. 392 IT BIDS PRETTY FAIR . 4
SHOULD COME TO NOTHING MUST BE FAIRLY FACED. . . . . 412 POD OF THE MILKWEED . 54
HE COULD IMAGINE NOTHING BARRENER. . . . . 417 AMERICA IS HARD TO SEE . 15
YOU'RE RIGHT, THERE'S NOTHING TO DISCUSS. . . . . . 420 ONE MORE BREVITY . . 29
AND YET DONE NOTHING ABOUT IT IN SONG. . . . . . . 421 ONE MORE BREVITY . . 65
"NOTHING CAN GO UP . . . . 437 KITTY HAWK 306
NOTHING WOULD DO. . . . . 449 THE BAD ISLAND--EASTER 48
AS FLY THE ATOMIC SMITHEREENS TO NOTHING. . . . . . 460 HOW HARD TO KEEP FROM 197
ONCE TO HAVE KNOWN IT, NOTHING ELSE WILL DO. . . . . 461 HOW HARD TO KEEP FROM 247
AND NOTHING MADE OF YOUTH. CONSIDER ME, ... 462 HOW HARD TO KEEP FROM 258
SHE'LL GO TO SLEEP. NOTHING KEEPS HER AWAKE . . . . 478 A MASQUE OF REASON . 153
BUT THERE IS NOTHING YOU ARE NOT BEHIND. . . . . . 482 A MASQUE OF REASON . 265
THE OBSCURITY'S A FRAUD TO COVER NOTHING. . . . . . 483 A MASQUE OF REASON . 279
SO THERE IS NOTHING WE CAN DO ABOUT IT . . . . . . 483 A MASQUE OF REASON . 293
THOUGH I HOLD RAYS DETERIORATE TO NOTHING: . . . . . 485 A MASQUE OF REASON . 345
JUST AS IF NOTHING MATTERED BUT OUR MANNERS. . . . . 488 A MASQUE OF REASON . 410
NOTHING HAS BEEN BROUGHT OUT THAT FOR MY PART . . . . 488 A MASQUE OF REASON . 413
I AM SICK, AS SHE SAYS. NOTHING EXHAUSTS ME . . . . 501 A MASQUE OF MERCY . 197
NOTHING WOULD HAPPEN. THAT'S THE THING OF IT. . . . 505 A MASQUE OF MERCY . 300
IT'S NOTHING BUT THE LENDING LIBRARY. . . . . . . 507 A MASQUE OF MERCY . 351
IT'S NOTHING I BROUGHT ON BY WORDS OF MINE. . . . . 507 A MASQUE OF MERCY . 355
THERE'S NOTHING COMING ON US, IS THERE, PAUL? . . . 508 A MASQUE OF MERCY . 395
THE RICH IN SEEING NOTHING BUT INJUSTICE . . . . . 509 A MASQUE OF MERCY . 412
IS NOTHING BUT AN OUTBREAK OF MASS MERCY, ... 509 A MASQUE OF MERCY . 417
'TWERE NOTHING NEW IF THAT WERE ALL CHRIST BROUGHT. . 511 A MASQUE OF MERCY . 474
WHAT DO YOU MAKE OF IT? / THE SAME OLD NOTHING. . . . 512 A MASQUE OF MERCY . 492
MEDITATE NOTHING. LEARN TO CONTEMPLATE. . . . . . 517 A MASQUE OF MERCY . 628
THAT NOTHING BUT GOD'S MERCY CAN ASSUAGE. . . . . . 520 A MASQUE OF MERCY . 713
NOTHING CAN MAKE INJUSTICE JUST BUT MERCY. . . . . . 521 A MASQUE OF MERCY . 738
NOTHINGNESS
THAT SPENDS TO NOTHINGNESS--AND UNRESISTED, ... 259 WEST-RUNNING BROOK . 57
NOTHING'S
NOTHING'S TOO GOOD FOR THEM. WE SAY IT PAYS. . . . . 86 THE HOUSEKEEPER . . . 137
NOTHING'S PORTENTOUS, I AM REASSURED. . . . . . . 318 BUILD SOIL 66
AND IF THIS MAY NOT BE (AND NOTHING'S SURE), ... 358 THE LOST FOLLOWER . . 17
NOTHINGS (SEE GOOD-FOR-NOTHINGS)
NOTICE
HE TOOK NO NOTICE, DID HE? WELL, AT LEAST . . . . . 144 SNOW 49
MADE MAPLE FIRST TAKE NOTICE OF HER NAME. . . . . . 179 MAPLE 2
MADE PEOPLE NOTICE IT--AND NOTICE HER. . . . . . . 181 MAPLE 50
BEFORE NOW POETRY HAS TAKEN NOTICE . . . . 316 BUILD SOIL 28
YOU MIGHT NOT NOTICE IF YOU'VE LIVED IN TOWN, ... 370 THE LITERATE FARMER AND 68
MUCH NOTICE OF WHAT'S GOING ON IN STARS. . . . . . 370 THE LITERATE FARMER AND 70
AND EVEN HE, YOU'LL NOTICE, DODGES OFF . . . . . . 408 FROM PLANE TO PLANE . 141
TAKE NOTICE, HAMAN, HE'S IN FAVOR WITH US." . . . . 455 HOW HARD TO KEEP FROM 65
I'M HEARING FROM HIM NOW, DID YOU BUT NOTICE, ... 504 A MASQUE OF MERCY . 278
NOTICED
I NOTICED THAT I MISSED STARS IN THE WEST, ... 40 THE MOUNTAIN 3
AND A GOOD DISTANCE DOWN MIGHT NOT BE NOTICED . . . . 43 THE MOUNTAIN 71
I NEVER NOTICED IT FROM HERE BEFORE. . . . . 51 HOME BURIAL 21
HE NOTICED NOTHING IN IT TO REMARK. . . . . 172 A STAR IN A STONEBOAT . 7
(THEY EITHER NOTICED IT, OR GOT IT WRONG.) . . . . . 181 MAPLE 51
MAY WELL HAVE NOTICED. SOON ENTIRELY WHITE . . . . 375 A YOUNG BIRCH . . . 4
BUT WHEN NOTICED FIRST . . . . 426 A NEVER NAUGHT SONG . 3
BUT NOBODY HAD NOTICED THE CONNECTION), ... 456 HOW HARD TO KEEP FROM 96
I NOTICED WHEN SHE CALLED UP SAMUEL . . . . 477 A MASQUE OF REASON . 99
HAVEN'T YOU NOTICED ANYTHING (HEAR THAT!) . . . . . 495 A MASQUE OF REASON . 42
I NOTICED HOW HE JUST NOW MADE YOU OUT . . . . . . 510 A MASQUE OF MERCY . 454
NOTION
IF I COULD PUT A NOTION IN HIS HEAD: . . . . 34 MENDING WALL 29
UNLESS LEN TOOK THE NOTION, WHICH HE WON'T, ... 67 A SERVANT TO SERVANTS . 157
IF SHE COULD FORM SOME NOTION OF HER MOTHER-- . . . . 181 MAPLE 54
I LOVE TO TOY WITH THE PLATONIC NOTION . . . . . . 362 BOEOTIAN 1
WE CAN HAVE NO NOTION . . . . 433 KITTY HAWK 158
AND SHE CAN ONLY GIVE THE CLASS A NOTION . . . . . . 447 DOES NO ONE AT ALL EVER 40
GOOD LIBERALS WILL OBJECT MY NOTION . . . . 453 A-WISHING WELL . . . 69
NOTIONS
WITH GOODS TO SELL AND NOTIONS TO IMPART. . . . . . 324 BUILD SOIL 269
I S'POSE YOU HAVE YOUR NOTIONS ON THE VEXED . . . . . 369 THE LITERATE FARMER AND 47
NOT-NICE
HER NOT-NICE LOAD, ... 134 A GIRL'S GARDEN . . . 24
NOTTINGHAM
TODAY AN HONORED ONE IN NOTTINGHAM. . . . . 161 NEW HAMPSHIRE . . . 86
NOUN'S
WHEN NO MAN'S NAME AND NO NOUN'S ADJECTIVE . . . . . 461 HOW HARD TO KEEP FROM 239
NOURISH
HOPE MAY NOT NOURISH A COW OR HORSE, ... 376 SOMETHING FOR HOPE . 23
NOVA
TO BE A NOVA, ... 220 I WILL SING YOU ONE-O . 71
NOVEL
THE RUSSIAN NOVEL IN AMERICA . . . . 167 NEW HAMPSHIRE . . . 268
IT MAKES THE GUILD OF NOVEL WRITERS SICK . . . . . . 167 NEW HAMPSHIRE . . . 274

PAGE TITLE   LINE

NOVELS
   BECAUSE I WROTE MY NOVELS IN NEW HAMPSHIRE . . . . 166 NEW HAMPSHIRE . . . 246
NOVELTY
   IT TOOK THE HALL DOOR FOR THE NOVELTY, ... 205 THE WITCH OF COOS . . 85
   STILL, NOVELTY HAS DOUBTLESS AN ATTRACTION. . . . . . 480 A MASQUE OF REASON . 197
NOVEMBER
   MY NOVEMBER GUEST . . . . 6 MY NOVEMBER GUEST . . T
   THE LOVE OF BARE NOVEMBER DAYS . . . . 7 MY NOVEMBER GUEST . . 17
   NOVEMBER . . . . 359 NOVEMBER . . . . . T
NOVITIATE
   THE SLAVE SERVED HIS NOVITIATE DISHWASHING. . . . . . 455 HOW HARD TO KEEP FROM 54
NOW---NOT INDEXED
NOWADAYS
   WHOM WE ALL HAVE TO THINK OF NOWADAYS, ... 57 THE BLACK COTTAGE . . 87
   "YOU HERE?" I SAID. "WHERE AREN'T YOU NOWADAYS? . . . . 125 AN ENCOUNTER 19
   ALTARS THE WOODS ARE FULL OF NOWADAYS, ... 171 NEW HAMPSHIRE . . . 387
NOWHERE
   I GO NOWHERE ON PURPOSE: I HAPPEN BY.-- . . . . . . 50 A HUNDRED COLLARS . . 154
   "WHERE SHALL WE MEET AGAIN?" / "NOWHERE BUT HERE . . . 80 THE GENERATIONS OF MEN 208
   A HALFWAY COFFEE HOUSE 'TWIXT TOWN AND NOWHERE----" . . 155 SNOW 342
   THAT GOT HER NOWHERE; ONE MORE GRADUAL, ... 187 THE AX-HELVE . . . 49
   THE FIELDS HAD NOWHERE LEFT FOR THEM TO GO; . . . . . 239 OUR SINGING STRENGTH . 26
   IF YOU SHOULD RISE FROM NOWHERE UP TO SOMEWHERE, . . . 385 THE FEAR OF GOD . . . 1
   NOWHERE BUT ON THE BRADFORD INTERVAL . . . . 404 FROM PLANE TO PLANE . 21
   WE COME NOWHERE NEAR . . . . 442 KITTY HAWK . . . 435
   BUT SUMMONS OUT OF NOWHERE LIKE A JINNI. . . . . . . 461 HOW HARD TO KEEP FROM 240
   BUT SINCE WE GOT NOWHERE, ... 464 MILKY WAY IS A COWPATH 5
NOW'S---NOT INDEXED
NUCLEAR
   NO BURST OF NUCLEAR PHENOMENON . . . . 397 THE PLANNERS 4
   AS THEY GET MORE NUCLEAR . . . . 466 SOME SCIENCE FICTION . 14
NUISANCE
   CAN EVER GIVE US IS A NUISANCE BRAWL. . . . . 398 NO HOLY WARS FOR THEM . 14
NUMBER
   NUMBER EIGHTEEN THIS IS. WHAT SIZE DO YOU WEAR?" . . . 46 A HUNDRED COLLARS . . 61
   WHO WANTS TO CUT YOUR NUMBER FOURTEEN THROAT! . . . . 47 A HUNDRED COLLARS . . 84
   I'M A GREAT BOY TO THINK OF NUMBER ONE. . . . . . . 99 THE SELF-SEEKER . . 177
   IT CAN SCARCE BE THAT THEY WOULD BE IN NUMBER . . . . 112 IN THE HOME STRETCH . 53
   A NUMBER IN. BUT WHAT ABOUT THE BROOK . . . . . . 231 A BROOK IN THE CITY . 3
   MY RIGHT TO BE EQUAL IN NUMBER OF CARDS, ... 310 IN DIVES' DIVE . . . 4
   THEN A NUMBER OF US AGREE . . . . 348 TRIPLE BRONZE . . . 9
   OR OUR NUMBER LIVING WOULDN'T BE STEADILY MORE, . . . 349 OUR HOLD ON THE PLANET 17
   HE SPARED IT FROM THE NUMBER OF THE SLAIN, ... 375 A YOUNG BIRCH . . . 13
   FROM NUMBER ONE TO SEVEN, ... 389 ASTROMETAPHYSICAL . 11
   THEIR NUMBER WOULD SEEM LIMITED TO THREE. . . . . . 398 NO HOLY WARS FOR THEM . 2
NUMBERLESS
   THAN NOW THESE NUMBERLESS YEARS THE ELVES, ... 26 A LINE-STORM SONG . . 11
NUMBERS
   ANC TAGS AND NUMBERS IT FOR FUTURE REFERENCE, ... 37 DEATH OF THE HIRED MAN 90
   I WRITE REAL VERSE IN NUMBERS, AS THEY SAY. . . . . . 460 HOW HARD TO KEEP FROM 211
NUMBER'S
   THEIR NUMBER'S--TWENTY-ONE?--THE THING WON'T WORK. . . 153 SNOW 294
NUMEROUS
   THENCE THEY WERE SPRUNG, SO NUMEROUS A TRIBE . . . . 73 THE GENERATIONS OF MEN 10
NURSE
   THE FAMOUS FOSTER NURSE . . . . 464 MILKY WAY IS A COWPATH 25
NURSERY
   I'VE BEEN A-CHOKING LIKE A NURSERY TREE . . . . . . 46 A HUNDRED COLLARS . . 56
NURTURED
   LESS CAREFULLY NURTURED, LESS FRUITFUL THAN THESE, . . . 228 GOOD-BY AND KEEP COLD . 22

O

O (SEE ONE-O)
   COME WITH RAIN, O LOUD SOUTHWESTER! . . . . 11 TO THE THAWING WIND . 1
   O HUSHED OCTOBER MORNING MILD, ... 27 OCTOBER 1
   O HUSHED OCTOBER MORNING MILD, ... 27 OCTOBER 7
   "O FIREMAN, GIVE THE FIRE ANOTHER STOKE, ... 234 EVENING A SUGAR ORCHARD 5
   ALL CRYING, "WE WILL GO WITH YOU, O WIND!" . . . . . 236 MISGIVING 1
   FOR YOU, O TUMULTUOUS FLOWERS, ... 264 THE LAST MOWING . . 16
   O OPENING CLOUDS, BY OPENING ON ME WIDE. . . . . . . 296 LOST IN HEAVEN . . 11
   O YOU WHO BRING THIS TO MY HAND, ... 327 A MISSIVE MISSILE . . 22
   O STORMY, STORMY WORLD, ... 333 HAPPINESS MAKES UP . 1
   I'D SAY, O MASTER OF THE PALACE SCHOOL, ... 351 THE LESSON FOR TODAY . 19
   O PALADINS, THE LESSON FOR TODAY . . . . 353 THE LESSON FOR TODAY . 87
   O STAR (THE FAIREST ONE IN SIGHT), ... 403 SOMETHING LIKE A STAR . 1
   KITTY HAWK, O KITTY, ... 428 KITTY HAWK . . . 1
   FORGIVE, O LORD, MY LITTLE JOKES ON THEE . . . . . . 428 FORGIVE, O LORD... . 1
   FORGIVE, O LORD... . . . . 428 FORGIVE, O LORD... . T
   KITTY HAWK, O KITTY, ... 433 KITTY HAWK . . . 175
   O OCEAN SEA, FOR ALL YOUR BEING VAST, ... 446 DOES NO ONE AT ALL EVER 1
   AND NOW, O SEA, YOU'RE LOST BY AEROPLANE. . . . . . 446 DOES NO ONE AT ALL EVER 13
   GRIND SHELLS, O FUTILE SEA, GRIND EMPTY SHELLS . . . . 446 DOES NO ONE AT ALL EVER 19
   "THE CHOICE IS NOT BETWEEN TWO PEARLS, O KING, ... 456 HOW HARD TO KEEP FROM 74
   "O CITY ON INSECURE ROCK PEDESTAL, ... 506 A MASQUE OF MERCY . 337
OAK
   SAVE THOSE THAT THE OAK IS KEEPING . . . . 30 RELUCTANCE 8
   AS MEASURED AGAINST MAPLE, BIRCH, AND OAK, ... 226 THE ONSET 16
   GOOD BLOCKS OF OAK IT WAS I SPLIT, ... 275 TWO TRAMPS IN MUD TIME 9
   BUT SCRUB OAK, SCRUB OAK AND THE LACK OF EARTH . . . . 292 FIGURE IN THE DOORWAY . 3
OAKS
   THAT KEPT THE OAKS FROM GETTING ANY GIRTH. . . . . . 292 FIGURE IN THE DOORWAY . 4
   HE HAD THE OAKS FOR HEATING AND FOR LIGHT. . . . . . 292 FIGURE IN THE DOORWAY . 15
OAR
   TOGETHER WING TO WING AND OAR TO OAR. . . . . 300 THE MASTER SPEED . . 14

PAGE TITLE   LINE

OARS
   MIGHT SEE THEM ON A RACK LIKE FAMOUS OARS, ... 290 OLD BARN AT THE BOTTOM   36
OASES
   SCATTERED OASES WHERE MEN DWELT, BUT MOSTLY . . . . . . 58 THE BLACK COTTAGE . . 119
OASIS
   A FAIR OASIS IN THE PUREST DESERT. . . . . 473 A MASQUE OF REASON . .   1
OATH
   AN OATH OF TOWNS THAT SET THE WILD AT NAUGHT, ... 141 THE LINE-GANG . . . 12
OATS
   OF COATS, OATS, VOTES, TO ALL MANKIND. . . . . . . 450 OUR DOOM TO BLOOM . .   9
OBEY
   MEMENTO MORI AND OBEY THE LORD. . . . . 353 THE LESSON FOR TODAY . 96
   I BUT OBEY . . . . 413 AWAY! 18
   OR SOMEONE HE HAD TO OBEY . . . . 444 THE DRAFT HORSE . . . 18
OBEYED
   THERE ARE ROUGHLY ZONES WHOSE LAWS MUST BE OBEYED? . . . 305 THERE ARE ROUGHLY ZONES 13
OBEYING
   OBEYING BESTIAL LAWS, ... 341 THE SUBVERTED FLOWER . 59
OBJECT
   OBJECT TO BEING ASKED A CIVIL QUESTION-- . . . . . 192 PAUL'S WIFE 32
   MY OBJECT IN LIVING IS TO UNITE . . . . 277 TWO TRAMPS IN MUD TIME 66
   WHO HAVE NO OTHER OBJECT THAN OUR GOOD. . . . . . 372 THE LITERATE FARMER AND 135
   GOOD LIBERALS WILL OBJECT MY NOTION . . . . 453 A-WISHING WELL . . . 69
OBJECTED
   AND TAKES THE PLAYFULLY OBJECTED RHYME . . . . . . 362 IN A POEM   2
OBJECTION
   OUT WITH IT IF YOU'VE ANY REAL OBJECTION." . . . . . 99 THE SELF-SEEKER . . .197
   THE OBJECTION TO BEING STEPPED ON . . . . 450 OBJECTION TO BE STEPPED T
   SOME LINGERING OBJECTION HOLDS YOU BACK. . . . . . 517 A MASQUE OF MERCY . .632
OBLATE
   HAD GRADUALLY WORN IT AN OBLATE . . . . 190 THE GRINDSTONE . . . 39
OBLIGATION-FREE
   MEANWHILE FEEL OBLIGATION-FREE. . . . . 420 ONE MORE BREVITY . . 34
OBLIGED
   THESE FORCES ARE OBLIGED TO PAY RESPECT TO?" . . . . 176 THE STAR-SPLITTER . . 12
OBLIVION
   INTO OBLIVION WITHOUT A LAWYER. . . . . 462 HOW HARD TO KEEP FROM 263
OBSCURATION
   THE OBSCURATION UPON EARTH. . . . . 20 THE TRIAL BY EXISTENCE 20
OBSCURE
   SO ALMOST CLEAR AND YET OBSCURE. . . . . 327 A MISSIVE MISSILE . . 19
   FOR MY OBSCURE PETITIONER. . . . . 327 A MISSIVE MISSILE . . 29
OBSCURED
   OBSCURED FROM MORTAL VIEW-- . . . . 333 HAPPINESS MAKES UP . .   7
OBSCURITY
   TO SOME OBSCURITY OF CLOUD-- . . . . 403 SOMETHING LIKE A STAR .   3
OBSCURITY'S
   THE OBSCURITY'S A FRAUD TO COVER NOTHING. . . . . 483 A MASQUE OF REASON . 279
OBSERVATORY
   THE CLOISTER AND THE OBSERVATORY SAINT . . . . . 353 THE LESSON FOR TODAY . 81
OBSERVE
   HIS MARE WAS SURE TO OBSERVE THE SPOT . . . . . 263 THE TIMES TABLE . .   4
   TO OBSERVE THE NORTHERN LIGHT. . . . . 384 IN THE LONG NIGHT . .   8
   AS ANY MIGHT OBSERVE, ... 464 MILKY WAY IS A COWPATH 23
   NOT ONLY LAST, BUT FIRST, YOU WILL OBSERVE; . . . 508 A MASQUE OF MERCY . 382
OBSERVED
   ...RECENTLY OBSERVED IN THE WESTERN SKY AT EVENING . . 368 THE LITERATE FARMER AND S
OBSTACLE
   BUT THIS WE KNOW, THE OBSTACLE THAT CHECKED . . . 261 A SOLDIER 12
OBSTINATELY
   IT WAS THE OBSTINATELY GENTLE AIR . . . . . . 356 TIME OUT 12
OBSTRUCTION
   AND YET SHE KNOWS OBSTRUCTION IS IN VAIN: . . . 238 ON A TREE FALLEN ACROSS 9
OBTAIN
   OBTAIN SUCH GRACE OF HOURS . . . . 14 ROSE POGONIAS . . . 22
OBVIOUS
   BUT NOW AT LAST SO OBVIOUS A BOLE . . . . . . 375 A YOUNG BIRCH . . . 16
OCCASION
   WE TAKE OCCASION TO THINK. . . . . 282 A DRUMLIN WOODCHUCK . 20
   YOU'D AS WELL SMILE AS FROWN ON THE OCCASION. . . 490 A MASQUE OF REASON . 465
OCCASIONS
   IN THE AUGUST OCCASIONS OF THE STATE . . . . 422 FOR JOHN F. KENNEDY .   2
OCCLUDED
   IT SWIRLS OCCLUDED IN US UNDER TIGHT . . . . 386 INNATE HELIUM . . .   2
OCCUPANCY
   WE DON'T PRETEND TO COMPLETE OCCUPANCY. . . . 322 BUILD SOIL 193
OCCUPY
   IF NEED BE OCCUPY A THRONE, ... 307 PROVIDE, PROVIDE . . 11
OCCUPYING
   I LIKE CHAIRS OCCUPYING OTHER CHAIRS . . . . 115 IN THE HOME STRETCH .156
OCCUR
   STILL SOMETIMES OCCUR . . . . 433 KITTY HAWK 155
OCCURRED
   "NOW, THE PLACE WHERE THE ACCIDENT OCCURRED----" . 100 THE SELF-SEEKER . . .207
   I TOOK NOTE OF WHEN IT OCCURRED, ... 365 A NATURE NOTE . . . 13
   AND HAVE OCCURRED TO YOU NO DOUBT, ... 381 AN UNSTAMPED LETTER IN 46
OCEAN
   GREATER THAN BEING SHORE TO THE OCEAN-- . . . 247 DEVOTION   2
   TO REACH THE OCEAN? IT MUST BE THE BROOK . . . 258 WEST-RUNNING BROOK .   6
   THERE IS A FELLOW ON THE OCEAN NOW . . . . . 289 OLD BARN AT THE BOTTOM 17
   ONE FOOT IN EACH GREAT OCEAN . . . . 295 A RECORD STRIDE . . . 25
   WHAT NOW IS INLAND SHALL BE OCEAN ISLE, . . . 335 I COULD GIVE ALL . .   6
   I WOULD PICK UP ALL OCEAN LESS ITS SALT, . . . 337 THE WIND AND THE RAIN . 28
   OF THE OCEAN BED FOR A MARRIAGE BED. . . . . 345 DISCOVERY OF MADEIRAS . 67
   THE TURTLE IN TURN ON A ROCK IN THE OCEAN. . . 379 TOO ANXIOUS FOR RIVERS 16
   TWO THOUSAND FEET ABOVE THE OCEAN LEVEL. . . . 400 TO THE RIGHT PERSON .   6
   ON ONE SIDE THE OCEAN, ... 433 KITTY HAWK 164
   O OCEAN SEA, FOR ALL YOUR BEING VAST, ... 446 DOES NO ONE AT ALL EVER 1

OCEAN (CONTINUED)
    THE OCEAN HAD BEEN SPOKEN TO BEFORE. . . . . 447 DOES NO ONE AT ALL EVER   31
    SO FAR INLAND THE VERY NAME OF OCEAN . . . . 447 DOES NO ONE AT ALL EVER   37
    AS COMING FROM A LESSER OCEAN. . . . . 453 A-WISHING WELL   . . .   68
OCEAN'S
    BUT WHEN THE OCEAN'S WORST HAD PASSED . . . . 344 DISCOVERY OF MADEIRAS . 35
OCEAN-WATER
    THERE WOULD BE MORE THAN OCEAN-WATER BROKEN . . . . . 250 ONCE BY THE PACIFIC   . 13
OCHER-WRITTEN
    I HAVE THE OCHER-WRITTEN FLINT, ... 328 A MISSIVE MISSILE . .   41
O'CLOCK
    AFTER ELEVEN O'CLOCK AT NIGHT. TOO TIRED . . . . . . 45 A HUNDRED COLLARS   . . 17
    AT TEN O'CLOCK OF A WINTER EVE. . . . . 102 GOOD HOURS   16
    AT THAT PARTICULAR TIME O'CLOCK, ... 139 BROWN'S DESCENT . . .   64
    I FANCIED WHEN I LOOKED AT SIX O'CLOCK . . . . . . 237 A HILLSIDE THAW . . .   23
    THIS EDEN DAY IS DONE AT TWO O'CLOCK. . . . . . . 254 A WINTER EDEN   . . .   18
    IT MAY HAVE BEEN AT TWO O'CLOCK . . . . 380 AN UNSTAMPED LETTER IN   18
    AT FOUR O'CLOCK I SHOULDER AX, ... 470 IN WINTER IN THE WOODS   5
OCTOBER
    O HUSHED OCTOBER MORNING MILD, ... 27 OCTOBER   1
    O HUSHED OCTOBER MORNING MILD, ... 27 OCTOBER   7
    OCTOBER . . . . 27 OCTOBER   . . . . .   T
ODD (SEE NINETY-ODD)
    AND POLITICIAN AT ODD SEASONS. . . . . 139 BROWN'S DESCENT . . .   70
    IN AN INQUISITIVE POSITION ODD . . . . 412 POD OF THE MILKWEED .   46
ODDS
    WE'RE SO MUCH OUT THAT THE ODDS ARE AGAINST . . . . 320 BUILD SOIL   139
    I AT ODDS WITH MEN . . . . 433 KITTY HAWK   178
ODOR
    IN THE ABYSS OF ODOR AND RUSTLE AT MY BACK, ... 14 WAITING   19
    WHY THE FLOWER HAS ODOR, THE BIRD HAS SONG. . . . . 16 IN A VALE   22
    AND STIFLING HOT WITH THE ODOR OF SAP . . . . . . 123 PEA BRUSH   7
    MOISTURE AND COLOR AND ODOR THICKEN HERE. . . . . 246 ATMOSPHERE   5
ODORS
    THE BREEZE THREE ODORS BROUGHT, ... 29 MY BUTTERFLY   36
O'ER
    O'ER RUINED FENCES THE GRAPEVINES SHIELD . . . . .   5 GHOST HOUSE   6
    O'ER OUR TUMULTUOUS SNOW, ...   9 STARS   2
    RUN THE RATTLING PAGES O'ER; . . . . 11 TO THE THAWING WIND .   13
    SEEKING WITH MEMORIES GROWN DIM O'ER NIGHT . . . . 22 THE TUFT OF FLOWERS .   13
    O'ER WHICH YOU, LORD, HAVE LORDED, ... 389 ASTROMETAPHYSICAL .   10
O'EREAGER
    SNATCHED THEE, O'EREAGER, WITH UNGENTLE GRASP. . . . 29 MY BUTTERFLY   30
O'ERHEAD
    FURTHER O'ERHEAD THAN ALL BUT STARS AND ANGELS-- . . . 132 THE BONFIRE   107
O'ERNIGHT
    O'ERNIGHT 'TWIXT MULLEIN STALKS A WHEEL OF THREAD . . . 126 RANGE-FINDING   . . . 10
OF---NOT INDEXED
OFF (SEE BROKEN-OFF, CAST-OFF, FAR-OFF, LOOK-OFF, WALLED-OFF)
    AND OFF A BLOSSOM IN MID-AIR STANDS STILL, ... 12 A PRAYER IN SPRING . .   12
    FAR OFF THE HOMES OF MEN, AND FARTHER STILL, ... 17 THE VANTAGE POINT .   6
    OFF HE GOES ALWAYS WHEN I NEED HIM MOST. . . . . . 35 DEATH OF THE HIRED MAN   18
    TRYING TO COAX HIM OFF WITH POCKET MONEY-- . . . . 35 DEATH OF THE HIRED MAN   28
    NOTHING WOULD DO: HE JUST KEPT NODDING OFF." . . . . 36 DEATH OF THE HIRED MAN   43
    LIKE BOULDERS BROKEN OFF THE UPPER CLIFF, ... 44 THE MOUNTAIN   98
    YOU CAN'T REST THAT WAY. LET ME PULL YOUR SHOES OFF." . . 47 A HUNDRED COLLARS   . . 76
    WHAT AM I GOING CARRYING OFF THIS BOTTLE?-- . . . . 50 A HUNDRED COLLARS . . 177
    BY WHICH I'D BIND MYSELF TO KEEP HANDS OFF . . . . . 52 HOME BURIAL   51
    I'M JUST AS GLAD SHE MADE ME KEEP HANDS OFF, ... 58 THE BLACK COTTAGE . . 104
    "YOU KNOW WHERE THEY CUT OFF THE WOODS--LET ME SEE-- . . 59 BLUEBERRIES   9
    CUT SHORT OFF AT BOTH ENDS. IT LIES FIVE MILES . . . 63 A SERVANT TO SERVANTS   21
    IT TOOK MY MIND OFF DOUGHNUTS AND SODA BISCUIT . . . 63 A SERVANT TO SERVANTS   26
    THE SCENT OF APPLES: I AM DROWSING OFF. . . . . . . 68 AFTER APPLE-PICKING .   8
    MARCHED HIMSELF OFF THE FIELD AND HOME. ONE STAYED. . . 69 THE CODE   8
    KEEP AT THEIR HEELS AND THREATEN TO MOW THEIR LEGS OFF. . . 71 THE CODE   46
    SO WHEN HE PAIRED OFF WITH ME IN THE HAYFIELD . . . 71 THE CODE   49
    I BUILT THE LOAD AND TOPPED IT OFF; OLD SANDERS . . . 71 THE CODE   51
    THE HAY AND ROLLING IT OFF WHOLESALE, ... 71 THE CODE   57
    I CLEANED THE RACK AND DROVE OUT TO COOL OFF. . . . . 72 THE CODE   80
    A ROCK-STREWN TOWN WHERE FARMING HAS FALLEN OFF, . . . 73 THE GENERATIONS OF MEN   5
    WAS A GIRL; AND SHE HALTED SOME WAY OFF . . . . . . 74 THE GENERATIONS OF MEN   30
    AND DISAPPEARED AND ENDED NOT FAR OFF . . . . . . 75 THE GENERATIONS OF MEN   72
    "IT RESTS WITH US ALWAYS TO CUT HER OFF." . . . . . 80 THE GENERATIONS OF MEN 183
    "HAVEN'T YOU SEEN HIM? STRANGE WHAT SET YOU OFF . . . 81 THE HOUSEKEEPER   . . . 14
    IT'S GONE SO FAR. YOU'VE HEARD? ESTELLE'S RUN OFF." . . 82 THE HOUSEKEEPER   . . . 20
    FARMERS AROUND TWICE AS WELL OFF AS WE . . . . . . 85 THE HOUSEKEEPER   . . . 113
    HE CAN EAT OFF A BARREL FROM THE GROUND. . . . . . 86 THE HOUSEKEEPER   . . . 149
    "BUT WHY, WHEN SHE'S WELL OFF? IS IT THE NEIGHBORS, . . 87 THE HOUSEKEEPER   . . . 168
    BEING CUT OFF FROM FRIENDS?" / "WE HAVE OUR FRIENDS. . . 87 THE HOUSEKEEPER   . . . 169
    LET HIM GET OFF AND HE'LL BE EVERYWHERE . . . . . . 90 THE FEAR   45
    TILL WEISS SHUT OFF THE WATER IN THE WHEEL PIT. . . . 93 THE SELF-SEEKER   . . . 27
    "AWFUL. WHY DIDN'T THEY THROW OFF THE BELT . . . . . 93 THE SELF-SEEKER   . . . 30
    THAT DAY A WOMAN COULDN'T COAX HIM OFF. . . . . . . 94 THE SELF-SEEKER   . . . 37
    WILLIS FLUNG OFF THE BED. "I WASH MY HANDS-- . . . 100 THE SELF-SEEKER   . . . 216
    CARRY HIM OFF THE WAY I MIGHT HAVE GONE, ... 101 THE WOOD-PILE   20
    THE WOOD WAS GRAY AND THE BARK WARPING OFF IT . . . 102 THE WOOD-PILE   29
    TO SELL THEM OFF THEIR FEET TO GO IN CARS . . . . . 106 CHRISTMAS TREES   . . . 17
    COULD HANG ENOUGH ON TO PICK OFF ENOUGH. . . . . . 107 CHRISTMAS TREES   . . . 54
    IN CLOMPING OFF--AND SCARED THE OUTER NIGHT, ... 108 OLD MAN'S WINTER NIGHT   11
    "AND WHAT IS THAT? YOU ONLY PUT ME OFF." . . . . . 111 IN THE HOME STRETCH .   29
    OFF THERE UPSTAIRS. THE VERY TREAD OF MEN . . . . . 111 IN THE HOME STRETCH .   38
    YOU DIDN'T COUNT THEM?" / "NO, THE FURTHER OFF . . . 112 IN THE HOME STRETCH .   51
    AND BANG GOES SOMETHING ELSE AWAY OFF THERE. . . . . 112 IN THE HOME STRETCH .   55
    AT BEDTIME; BUT THE STRANGENESS SOON WEARS OFF." . . . 115 IN THE HOME STRETCH . 135
    POINTED THE DECIMAL OFF WITH ONE DEEP THRUST. . . . . 119 MEETING AND PASSING .   9
    AND GOT THEM OFF THE WILD FLOWERS' BACKS. . . . . . 123 PEA BRUSH   16
    AND LIFT THEMSELVES UP OFF THE GROUND. . . . . . . 123 PEA BRUSH   20
    IF I CAN LEAVE OFF BURYING THE WHITE . . . . 124 PUTTING IN THE SEED .   3

OFF (CONTINUED)
AND TELL ME WHERE YOU'RE OFF FOR--MONTREAL? . . . . . . 125 AN ENCOUNTER 21
ME? I'M NOT OFF FOR ANYWHERE AT ALL. . . . . 125 AN ENCOUNTER 22
WARNING AND TIME TO BE OFF IN FLIGHT: . . . . 127 HOUSE FEAR 7
AND CUT THEM OFF FROM WINDOW LIGHT. . . . . 135 LOCKED OUT 3
HIS TAIL FEATHERS OFF. . . . . 135 LAST WORD OF A BLUEBIRD 13
HE SAW ALL SPOILED. "DON'T LET HIM CUT MY HAND OFF-- . 137 "OUT,OUT--" 25
SHOULD TAKE THE POLISH OFF THE CRUST. . . . . 139 BROWN'S DESCENT . . . 59
IS BLOCKS SPLIT OFF THE MOUNTAIN MASS-- . . . . 140 THE GUM-GATHERER . . . 15
"YOU CAN JUST SEE IT GLANCING OFF THE ROOF . . . . . . 143 SNOW 8
HE SEEMS TO HAVE LOST OFF HIS CHRISTIAN NAME." . . . . 144 SNOW 47
SHORT OFF, AND DIED AGAINST THE WINDOWPANE." . . . . . 149 SNOW 166
SOUNDS FURTHER OFF, IT'S NOT BECAUSE IT'S DYING; . . . 150 SNOW 204
HE HAD COLE WITH HIM TO THE BARN TO SEE HIM OFF. . . . 151 SNOW 244
"BUT HOW MUCH BETTER OFF ARE WE AS IT IS? . . . . . . 152 SNOW 261
FRANTIC IT SOUNDS, THOUGH MUFFLED AND FAR OFF. . . . . 154 SNOW 319
OFF HIS. THE TIME WAS EVENING IN THE PULLMAN. . . . . 159 NEW HAMPSHIRE . . . 14
DANGLING THEIR LEGS AND FISHING OFF A WHARF . . . . . 161 NEW HAMPSHIRE . . . 75
"I'M GOING TO PUT YOU OFF THIS FARM: I WANT IT." . . . 164 NEW HAMPSHIRE . . . 154
THE LINE WHERE MAN LEAVES OFF AND NATURE STARTS, . . . 171 NEW HAMPSHIRE . . . 379
AND RUN OFF IN STRANGE TANGENTS WITH MY ARM, ... 174 A STAR IN A STONEBOAT 53
FOREVER OFF THE LATCH, AS IF RUDE MEN . . . . 175 THE CENSUS-TAKER . . 28
THE STOVE WAS COLD--THE STOVE WAS OFF THE CHIMNEY-- . 175 THE CENSUS-TAKER . . 36
I PICKED UP THE STRAW-DUST-COVERED FLOOR. . . . . . . 175 THE CENSUS-TAKER . . 45
WE DON'T CUT OFF FROM COMING TO CHURCH SUPPERS, . . . 178 THE STAR-SPLITTER . . 49
"I HAVE, AND BEEN PUT OFF SOMETIME, I THINK." . . . . 183 MAPLE 109
ONCE LONG AGO HER FATHER HAD PUT HIMSELF OFF.) . . . . 183 MAPLE 111
AND HOLDS US OFF UNNECESSARILY, ... 183 MAPLE 124
OF SAP AND SNOW ROLLED OFF THE SUGARHOUSE. . . . . . . 184 MAPLE 138
"YOU GIVE HER ONE GOOD CRACK, SHE'S SNAP RAGHT OFF. . 186 THE AX-HELVE 26
HE HAD TO RUN RIGHT OFF TO LOOK HER UP, ... 191 PAUL'S WIFE 13
THE BARK OF A WHOLE TAMARACK OFF WHOLE, ... 191 PAUL'S WIFE 19
AS CLEAN AS BOYS DO OFF A WILLOW TWIG . . . . 191 PAUL'S WIFE 20
THEY'D SLICED THE FIRST SLAB OFF A BIG BUTT LOG, . . . 193 PAUL'S WIFE 62
BLEW IT ONCE OFF HIS HANDS AND ALMOST BROKE IT. . . . 194 PAUL'S WIFE 100
AND WALKED OFF, TALKING TO HERSELF OR PAUL, ... 195 PAUL'S WIFE 120
ONE BY ONE I LOST OFF MY HAT AND SHOES, ... 198 WILD GRAPES 72
BEFORE I STRAIGHTENED THEM AND BRUSHED THE BARK OFF. . 199 WILD GRAPES 88
BE RUN OFF WITH BY BIRCH TREES INTO SPACE." . . . . . 199 WILD GRAPES 91
BUT LEFT AN OPEN DOOR TO COOL THE ROOM OFF . . . . . . 203 THE WITCH OF COOS . 42
I STRUCK THE HAND OFF BRITTLE ON THE FLOOR, ... 204 THE WITCH OF COOS . 77
ANC SET OFF BRISKLY FOR SO SLOW A THING, ... 205 THE WITCH OF COOS . 86
OFF FROM THE HOUSE AS FAR AS WE COULD KEEP . . . . . . 210 PAUPER WITCH OF GRAFTON 90
HE'S SO FAR OFF HE CAN'T SEE WHAT I'VE COME TO. . . . 210 PAUPER WITCH OF GRAFTON 102
AND HE'S OFF SETTING TRAPS-- . . . . 211 AN EMPTY THREAT . . . 28
OFF HERE . . . . 212 AN EMPTY THREAT . . . 51
BUT SMITH, OR SOMEONE, CALLED THEM OFF THE MOUNTAIN . 213 A FOUNTAIN, A BOTTLE . 11
BUT YOU HAVE SAID IT, AND WE'RE OFF TO FIND IT. . . . 213 A FOUNTAIN, A BOTTLE . 28
COME STRAIGHT DOWN OFF THIS MOUNTAIN JUST AS FAST . . 215 A FOUNTAIN, A BOTTLE . 61
HE SHUDDERS HIS COAT AS IF TO THROW OFF FLIES. . . . . 223 THE RUNAWAY 18
ALL WINTER, CUT OFF BY A HILL FROM THE HOUSE. . . . . 228 GOOD-BY AND KEEP COLD 5
WE WILL NOT BE PUT OFF THE FINAL GOAL . . . . 238 ON A TREE FALLEN ACROSS 10
STEER STRAIGHT OFF AFTER SOMETHING INTO SPACE. . . . . 238 ON A TREE FALLEN ACROSS 14
AND SETTING OFF THEIR HEAVY POWDER LOAD. . . . . 239 OUR SINGING STRENGTH . 29
THEY MOVE IN PLEASURE TOO FAR OFF . . . . 256 THE LOVELY BE CHOOSERS 29
THAT WAVE'S BEEN STANDING OFF THIS JUT OF SHORE--" . . 258 WEST-RUNNING BROOK . 18
"THAT WAVE'S BEEN STANDING OFF THIS JUT OF SHORE . . . 258 WEST-RUNNING BROOK . 27
"OH, IF YOU TAKE IT OFF TO LADY-LAND, ... 258 WEST-RUNNING BROOK . 32
SHE HOPES TO CUT OFF MIND. . . . . 260 SAND DUNES 12
THE MOUNTAIN PUSHED US OFF HER KNEES. . . . . 265 THE BIRTHPLACE . . . 13
I'M NOT THE ONE FOR PUTTING OFF THE PROOF. . . . . . . 265 DUST IN THE EYES . . 3
LET IT BE OVERWHELMING, OFF A ROOF . . . . 265 DUST IN THE EYES . . 4
AGAIN COME TO LIFE AND CRAWL OFF, ... 266 SITTING BY A BUSH . . 11
I LOSE SOME OTHER OFF MY ARMS AND KNEES, ... 266 THE ARMFUL 2
BUT THOUGH IT RUNS UNBRIDLED OFF ITS COURSE, ... 268 RIDERS 10
AS SHE FLINGS OVER AND OFF DOWN THROUGH THE MAPLES, . 269 THE BEAR 8
AND ONE OF THEM PUT ME OFF MY AIM . . . . 275 TWO TRAMPS IN MUD TIME 3
A WIND COMES OFF A FROZEN PEAK, ... 275 TWO TRAMPS IN MUD TIME 23
HE ROLLED ME OFF THE FIELD HEAD OVER HEELS . . . . . . 278 THE WHITE-TAILED HORNET 20
THE LAST TO LET NIGHT DRIVE HER OFF. . . . . 280 BLUE RIBBON AT AMESBURY 16
SQUARE MATTHEW HALE TOOK OFF HIS SUNDAY HAT . . . . . 284 THE GOLD HESPERIDEE . 45
AND WAS OFF ON HIS DUTY RUN. . . . . 288 DEPARTMENTAL 7
LIKE THE LAST PETAL OFF A FLOWER. . . . . 291 ON HEART'S BEGINNING TO 12
THEY BREAK THE HANDLE AND THE BINDING OFF IT. . . . . 293 AT WOODWARD'S GARDENS . 28
OFF ANY STILL OR MOVING THING YOU SAY. . . . . 300 THE MASTER SPEED . . 9
'TWAS TO BUY HIMSELF OFF HIS DOOM. . . . . 310 THE VINDICTIVES . . . 6
AND ONE WENT OFF TO THE MOUNTAINS . . . . 313 BEARER OF EVIL TIDINGS 7
TO SELL THE HAY OFF, LET ALONE THE SOIL, ... 321 BUILD SOIL 179
NO. I UNOSTENTATIOUSLY MOVE OFF . . . . 324 BUILD SOIL 255
KEEP OFF EACH OTHER AND KEEP EACH OTHER OFF. . . . . . 324 BUILD SOIL 263
JUST NOW YOU'RE OFF DEMOCRACY . . . . 326 TO A THINKER . . . 15
AND OFF THIS CORNER IN THE WILD, ... 331 BEECH 4
THE SNOW BLOWS ON HIM AND OFF HIM, EXERTING FORCE . . 341 WILLFUL HOMING . . . 5
AND FORCE HER FAREWELL STEP OFF SHORE. . . . . 343 DISCOVERY OF MADEIRAS . 11
FROM A FALLEN TREE AND PUSHING OFF . . . . 347 DISCOVERY OF MADEIRAS . 126
OF MEANINGLESSLY BEING BROKEN OFF. . . . . 355 THE LESSON FOR TODAY . 148
SET OFF ACROSS WHAT I HAD WRITTEN THERE. . . . . 357 A CONSIDERABLE SPECK . 3
TO EASE ATTENTION OFF WHEN OVERTIGHT, ... 370 THE LITERATE FARMER AND 81
GREAT BOULDERS OFF THEIR BALANCE . . . . 376 ONE STEP BACKWARD TAKEN 4
WHOLE CAPES CAKED OFF IN SLICES. . . . . 377 ONE STEP BACKWARD TAKEN 7
OF DETAIL, BURNED, DISSOLVED, AND BROKEN OFF . . . . . 377 DIRECTIVE 3
AND TAKE OFF INTO THE SKIES. . . . . 388 MIDDLENESS OF THE ROAD 3
TO SOME STAR OFF THERE, SAY, A HALF LIGHT-YEAR . . . . 395 WHY WAIT FOR SCIENCE . 7
AND EVEN HE, YOU'LL NOTICE, DODGES OFF . . . . 408 FROM PLANE TO PLANE . 141
ONE KNOCKS ANOTHER OFF FROM WHERE HE CLINGS. . . . . . 411 POD OF THE MILKWEED . 24
THEY KNOCK THE DYESTUFF OFF EACH OTHER'S WINGS-- . . . 411 POD OF THE MILKWEED . 25
AND SPENT AND DUSTED OFF OF THEIR REGALIA, ... 412 POD OF THE MILKWEED . 35
THAT GIVES OFF FROM A GARDEN GROUND AT NIGHT . . . . . 414 A CABIN IN THE CLEARING 16

OFF (CONTINUED)
  HE WASN'T OFF A MERE DEGREE; . . . . 417 AMERICA IS HARD TO SEE   17
  HIS RECKONING WAS OFF A SEA. . . . . 417 AMERICA IS HARD TO SEE   18
  AND SO PUT OFF THE WEARY DAY . . . . 417 AMERICA IS HARD TO SEE   40
  LIKE SWEARING OFF ON THE TRAFFIC WORLD. . . . . . . 419 ONE MORE BREVITY . . 18
  I BROKE OFF BAFFLED. BUT ALL THE SAME, ... 420 ONE MORE BREVITY . . 38
  OFF THESE SANDS OF TIME . . . . 429 KITTY HAWK 47
  OFF ON THE UNBOUNDED . . . . 432 KITTY HAWK 136
  OFF THIS VERY SHORE? . . . . 432 KITTY HAWK 149
  OFF THERE IN THE FOG? . . . . 438 KITTY HAWK 341
  YOU'RE OFF TO XANADU TO HELP THE COOK. . . . . . . 455 HOW HARD TO KEEP FROM   48
  HAVE MARRIED BEGGAR MAIDS FROM OFF THE STREETS. . . 457 HOW HARD TO KEEP FROM   110
  GUARANTEED TO COME SAFELY OFF WITH YOU . . . . . . 457 HOW HARD TO KEEP FROM   125
  FREEDOM TO FLASH OFF INTO WILD CONNECTIONS. . . . . 461 HOW HARD TO KEEP FROM   246
  TO LEAD HIM OFF THE ASIATIC WAY . . . . 462 HOW HARD TO KEEP FROM   262
  I WAS NO WORSE OFF THAN I WAS AT FIRST. . . . . . . 468 IN A GLASS OF CIDER . 6
  TRY TO READ TO HER AND SHE DROPS RIGHT OFF. . . . . 479 A MASQUE OF REASON . 155
  THAT STARTED OFF LORD GOD OF HOSTESSES. . . . . . . 480 A MASQUE OF REASON . 181
  LET'S DO SO NOW. BECAUSE I LET YOU OFF . . . . . . 482 A MASQUE OF REASON . 238
  I'M NOT A CHILD FOR YOU TO PUT ME OFF . . . . . . 482 A MASQUE OF REASON . 256
  I WAS JUST SHOWING OFF TO THE DEVIL, JOB, ... 484 A MASQUE OF REASON . 327
  WE'RE TOO WELL OFF. / SOMEDAY WE THREE SHOULD HAVE 486 A MASQUE OF REASON . 379
  AND EASY TO SEE THROUGH. BUT WHERE'S HE OFF TO? . . 488 A MASQUE OF REASON . 428
  OH, YES, THAT TENDENCY!--OH, DO COME OFF IT. . . . 489 A MASQUE OF REASON . 447
  IT SEEMS TO START RIGHT OFF ACCELERATING. . . . . . 489 A MASQUE OF REASON . 450
  IN THREE QUICK STEPS AS OFF AN ESCALATOR. . . . . . 489 A MASQUE OF REASON . 452
  THINKS WHY NOT TAPER OFF TO NONE AT ALL, ... 498 A MASQUE OF MERCY . 122
  OF THE WORD LOVE CORRECTED. SHE GOT OFF . . . . . 499 A MASQUE OF MERCY . 161
  SOMEONE TOOK CURVED NAIL-SCISSORS AND SNIPPED OFF . 501 A MASQUE OF MERCY . 201
  AND LET HIM GET OFF WITHOUT PROPHESYING? . . . . . 502 A MASQUE OF MERCY . 221
  AND TEAR HIS CLOTHES OFF TO EXAMINE HIM . . . . . 503 A MASQUE OF MERCY . 251
  THERE HE GOES OFF INTO ANOTHER TRANCE. . . . . . . 503 A MASQUE OF MERCY . 264
  (TAKING A WALK OFF DOWN THE STORE DISTRESSED) . . . 503 A MASQUE OF MERCY . 267
  YOU KNOW WHAT LETS US OFF FROM BEING CAREFUL? . . . 505 A MASQUE OF MERCY . 316
  AND CAKE THEIR CONCRETE DIRT OFF IN THE STREETS." . 506 A MASQUE OF MERCY . 334
  BUT BY OUR BITING OFF OUR ADOLESCENCE . . . . . . 508 A MASQUE OF MERCY . 388
  (HE SNAPS ONE BULB OFF. PAUL SNAPS ON ANOTHER.) . . 508 A MASQUE OF MERCY . 393
  OR CLEAR OFF WHAT WE KNOW HIS INTERESTS ARE. . . . 509 A MASQUE OF MERCY . 427
  STILL, NOT SO FAR OFF, COME TO THINK OF IT. . . . . 509 A MASQUE OF MERCY . 428
  I'M GOING NOW. BUT DON'T YOU PUSH ME OFF. . . . . . 518 A MASQUE OF MERCY . 646
  AS IF TO COME, BUT KEEPER WAVES HER OFF.) . . . . 518 A MASQUE OF MERCY . 653
  (STILL STANDING OFF) WE'VE ALL GROWN FOND OF YOU. . 518 A MASQUE OF MERCY . 666
OFF-CHANCE
  ON THE OFF-CHANCE IT MAY BE LACK OF FAITH, ... 515 A MASQUE OF MERCY . 563
OFFENSE
  AND TO WHOM I WAS LIKE TO GIVE OFFENSE. . . . . . . 34 MENDING WALL 34
  "MY WORDS ARE NEARLY ALWAYS AN OFFENSE. . . . . . . 52 HOME BURIAL 45
  IT ROSE IN OFFENSE . . . . 450 OBJECTION TO BE STEPPED   4
OFFER
  MAYN'T I OFFER YOU----?" / "NO, NO, NO, THANK YOU." 50 A HUNDRED COLLARS . 157
  HE DIDN'T EVEN OFFER ME A DRINK . . . . 160 NEW HAMPSHIRE . . 31
  AND OFFER TO PUT ME GENTLY OUT OF MY PAIN. . . . . 287 A ROADSIDE STAND . 51
  WE POETS OFFER YOU ANOTHER: STAR-CROSSED. . . . . . 510 A MASQUE OF MERCY . 439
  BUT LET'S BE SERIOUS ABOUT PAUL'S OFFER. . . . . . 513 A MASQUE OF MERCY . 519
  OUR SACRIFICE--THE BEST WE HAVE TO OFFER, ... 520 A MASQUE OF MERCY . 718
OFFERED
  OFFERED ME NOT LONG SINCE UP BERLIN WAY . . . . . 162 NEW HAMPSHIRE . . 110
  WHERE I WAS LIVING THEN, NEW HAMPSHIRE OFFERED . . 167 NEW HAMPSHIRE . . 252
  THAT COURSE, THEY TELL ME, ISN'T OFFERED THIS YEAR. 171 NEW HAMPSHIRE . . 405
  AND OFFERED HER A HOME TO REST AWHILE . . . . . . 201 PLACE FOR A THIRD . 60
  OFFERED FOR SALE WILD BERRIES IN WOODEN QUARTS, . . 286 A ROADSIDE STAND . 11
  OFFERED AN OPENING TO THE SOURCE OF DEW; . . . . . 295 LOST IN HEAVEN . . 2
OFFERING
  NOT OFFERING A LADY----" / "THERE AGAIN, JOE! . . . 116 IN THE HOME STRETCH . 157
  OF THE PLACE MARKED WITH IT--"WAVE OFFERING, . . . 183 MAPLE 106
  SOMETHING ABOUT WAVE OFFERING, IT SAID." . . . . . 183 MAPLE 107
  SHE DOESN'T MIND NOT OFFERING A DRINK . . . . . . 496 A MASQUE OF MERCY . 87
OFFERS
  JOHN LIKES TO TELL THE OFFERS HE HAS HAD, ... 86 THE HOUSEKEEPER . . 138
OFFICE
  "WHO'S THAT MAN SLEEPING IN THE OFFICE CHAIR? . . . 45 A HUNDRED COLLARS . 29
  "NO DOUBT YOU'VE HEARD THE OFFICE CALL ME MABEL. . 182 MAPLE 90
  WHOSE OFFICE IT IS TO BURY . . . . 288 DEPARTMENTAL . . . 26
  (YOUR BADGE OF OFFICE IS A SPADE). . . . . 327 A MISSIVE MISSILE . 24
OFFICIAL
  AND COME TO REST IN AN OFFICIAL VERDICT. . . . . . 474 A MASQUE OF REASON . 29
OFFICIOUS
  ENRAGED AT WHAT HE COULD BUT THINK OFFICIOUS, . . . 394 HAEC FABULA DOCET . 11
OFFING
  IN THE OFFING THERE . . . . 360 THE RABBIT-HUNTER . 8
OFFSIDE
  OF HIS SLIM GOAD ON NOSE AND OFFSIDE FLANK, ... 44 THE MOUNTAIN . . . 108
OFFSTAGE
  IS WORKED BY HANDS INVISIBLE, OFFSTAGE.) . . . . . 489 A MASQUE OF REASON . 455
OFT
  THAT FRIGHTED THEE SO OFT, IS FLED OR DEAD: . . . . 28 MY BUTTERFLY 3
OFTEN
  AND OFTEN THEY BROUGHT SO MUCH TO SAY . . . . . . 15 IN A VALE 12
  SUCH A GREAT MAN. IT DOESN'T SEE HIM OFTEN . . . . 44 A HUNDRED COLLARS . 2
  I OFTEN THINK OF THE SMOOTH HICKORY BARS. . . . . . 67 A SERVANT TO SERVANTS . 144
  AS ICE STORMS DO. OFTEN YOU MUST HAVE SEEN THEM . . 121 BIRCHES 5
  OFTEN HE BID ME COME AND HAVE A LOOK . . . . . . 178 THE STAR-SPLITTER . 76
  THAT AS A WITCH I'D OFTEN MILK A BAT . . . . . . 208 PAUPER WITCH OF GRAFTON 40
  AS OFTEN AS HE HAD IN THE TAIL OF THE NIGHT, . . . 210 PAUPER WITCH OF GRAFTON 87
  "HOW OFTEN ALREADY YOU'VE HAD TO BE TOLD, ... 228 GOOD-BY AND KEEP COLD . 17
  AS OFTEN AS I'VE SEEN IT DONE BEFORE . . . . . . 237 A HILLSIDE THAW . . 4
  I OFTEN SEE FLOWERS FROM A PASSING CAR . . . . . . 248 A PASSING GLIMPSE . 1
  YOU OFTEN GET IT MOST IN MONARCHY, ... 318 BUILD SOIL 75

OFTEN (CONTINUED)
    FAR AS WE OFTEN MAKE THEM REACH, ... 328 A MISSIVE MISSILE .   48
    WHICH OFTEN MAKES THE MANUMITTER BITTER."   . . . . . 371 THE LITERATE FARMER AND   91
    OH, I HAVE BEEN OFTEN TOO ANXIOUS FOR RIVERS   . . . . 379 TOO ANXIOUS FOR RIVERS   6
    AND WHEN HE CAUGHT DICK LOOKING ONCE TOO OFTEN, . . . 404 FROM PLANE TO PLANE .   26
    THEY OFTEN DO, AND NONE THE WISER FOR IT. . . . . . 414 A CABIN IN THE CLEARING 22
    AS SO OFTEN, ENDED . . . . 431 KITTY HAWK   96
    ASKS OF HIMSELF ONCE IN SO OFTEN   . . . . 453 A-WISHING WELL . . .   74
    WHICH IS WHAT PEOPLE USE IT FOR TOO OFTEN-- . . . . . 494 A MASQUE OF REASON .   29
OFTENER
    OFTENER THAN AS CONFLICTING GOOD AND ILL; . . . . . 350 TO A YOUNG WRETCH . .   16
OFTENTIMES
    AS I SIT HERE, AND OFTENTIMES, I WISH . . . . 58 THE BLACK COTTAGE . . 111
OFT-REPEATED
    THE OFT-REPEATED DREAM . . . . 128 THE OFT-REPEATED DREAM   T
    WAS AFRAID IN AN OFT-REPEATED DREAM . . . . 128 THE OFT-REPEATED DREAM   11
OGRESS
    CUMAEAN SIBYL, CHARMING OGRESS, ... 449 OUR DOOM TO BLOOM . .   1
OH
    OH, GIVE US PLEASURE IN THE FLOWERS TODAY; . . . . . 12 A PRAYER IN SPRING . .   1
    OH, GIVE US PLEASURE IN THE ORCHARD WHITE, ... 12 A PRAYER IN SPRING . .   5
    BUT OH, THE AGITATED HEART . . . . 19 REVELATION   3
    OH, NEVER THIS WHELMING EAST WIND SWELLS . . . . . . 27 A LINE-STORM SONG . .   25
    OH, COME FORTH INTO THE STORM AND ROUT . . . . . . 27 A LINE-STORM SONG . .   31
    OH, JUST ANOTHER KIND OF OUTDOOR GAME, ... 33 MENDING WALL   21
    "OH--AH--FOURTEEN--FOURTEEN." / "FOURTEEN! YOU SAY SO! . 46 A HUNDRED COLLARS . .   63
    TO SEE YOU AS YOU ARE TO SEE THEM." / "OH, ... 49 A HUNDRED COLLARS . . 150
    BUT AT LAST HE MURMURED, "OH," AND AGAIN, "OH." . . . 51 HOME BURIAL   17
    "NOT YOU!--OH, WHERE'S MY HAT? OH, I DON'T NEED IT! . . 52 HOME BURIAL   36
    IF I CAN CHANGE IT. OH, I WON'T, I WON'T" . . . . . 54 HOME BURIAL 107
    "YOU--OH, YOU THINK THE TALK IS ALL. I MUST GO-- . . . 54 HOME BURIAL 112
    MY HAND (OH, I CAN LIFT IT WHEN I HAVE TO). . . . . . 63 A SERVANT TO SERVANTS .   9
    "OH, IF YOU'RE GOING TO USE YOUR EYES, JUST HEAR . . . 76 THE GENERATIONS OF MEN   98
    WHO ARE THEY FOR?" / "YOU MEAN?--OH, FOR SOME MISS. . . 81 THE HOUSEKEEPER . . .   10
    "OH, IF YOU ASK ME THAT, WHAT WILL HE DO? . . . . . 82 THE HOUSEKEEPER . . .   30
    "OH, THAT'S BEEN THERE FOR HAWKS SINCE CHICKEN-TIME. . . 83 THE HOUSEKEEPER . . .   66
    OH, BUT YOU SEE HE HADN'T HAD ENOUGH-- . . . . . . 91 THE FEAR   51
    "YOU SEE," THE VOICE SAID. / "OH." SHE LOOKED AND LOOKED. 92 THE FEAR   78
    OH, WELL, WE'LL SOON BE THROUGH WITH IT. I'M TIRED." . . 96 THE SELF-SEEKER . . .   90
    "OH, GUESS WHICH HAND? MY, MY! ONCE ON A TIME . . . . 96 THE SELF-SEEKER . . . 107
    OH, I KEPT THE FIRST FOR ANOTHER DAY! . . . . 105 THE ROAD NOT TAKEN . .   13
    OF SOMETHING ELSE," SHE LAUGHED. "OH, PUT IT WHERE . . 111 IN THE HOME STRETCH .   15
    (OH, IT WAS WITHOUT PREJUDICE TO ME!) . . . . 119 MEETING AND PASSING .   12
    "OH, LET'S GO UP THE HILL AND SCARE OURSELVES, ... 129 THE BONFIRE   1
    OH, LET'S NOT WAIT FOR RAIN TO MAKE IT SAFE. . . . . 129 THE BONFIRE   5
    I HAD MY COAT. AND OH, I KNEW, I KNEW, ... 131 THE BONFIRE   69
    "OH, BUT WAR'S NOT FOR CHILDREN--IT'S FOR MEN." . . . 132 THE BONFIRE 100
    OH, NEVER BY WAY OF ADVICE! . . . . 134 A GIRL'S GARDEN . . .   46
    IN A LOW VOICE SAID, "OH, ... 135 LAST WORD OF A BLUEBIRD   2
    OH, YES, HE SHOWED JOHN THE WHEEL PIT ALL RIGHT. . . . 142 THE VANISHING RED . .   29
    YOU LIKE, AND LIKE HIM FOR." / "OH, YES YOU DO. . . . 146 SNOW   96
    OH, I'M NOT BLAMING YOU. HE DIDN'T LEAVE YOU . . . . 152 SNOW 256
    AND THEN HER VOICE CAME SCRAPING SLOW: 'OH, YOU, . . . 153 SNOW 290
    WE'RE GLAD. OH, SAY NO MORE ABOUT IT, MAN. . . . . . 155 SNOW 332
    I ASKED HIM, ON MY GUARD. "OH, YES," HE ANSWERED, . . . 159 NEW HAMPSHIRE . . .   13
    OH, IT WAS TERRIBLE AS WELL COULD BE. . . . . 160 NEW HAMPSHIRE . . .   59
    AND LIKE THE ACTRESS EXCLAIM "OH, MY GOD" AT? . . . . 165 NEW HAMPSHIRE . . . 207
    OH NO!--ALTHOUGH, OF COURSE, I COULD HAVE FOUND . . . 190 THE GRINDSTONE . . .   52
    YET OH! THE TEMPTING FLATNESS OF A BOOK, ... 216 A FOUNTAIN, A BOTTLE . 109
    "OH, THAT'S THE PARADISE-IN-BLOOM," I SAID; . . . . . 233 A BOUNDLESS MOMENT .   5
    OH, BLOOD WILL OUT. IT CANNOT BE CONTAINED. . . . . . 255 THE FLOOD   14
    "OH, IF YOU TAKE IT OFF TO LADY-LAND, ... 258 WEST-RUNNING BROOK .   32
    SNOW FALLING AND NIGHT FALLING FAST, OH, FAST . . . . 296 DESERT PLACES . . .   1
    OH, I DON'T BLAME YOU. I SAY TAKE LIFE EASY. . . . . 316 BUILD SOIL   19
    OH, MELIBOEUS, I HAVE HALF A MIND . . . . 316 BUILD SOIL   26
    OH, SLOW UNCOMPREHENDING ME, ... 327 A MISSIVE MISSILE . .   38
    OH, SHOULD A CHILD BE LEFT UNWARNED . . . . 336 THE WIND AND THE RAIN .   12
    AND OH, FOR ONE SO YOUNG . . . . 341 THE SUBVERTED FLOWER .   65
    AND LOST THE STARS OF HEAVEN, MAY, OH, MAY . . . . . 350 TO A YOUNG WRETCH . .   22
    OH, WE MAKE A BOAST OF STORING, ... 359 NOVEMBER   9
    OH, I HAVE BEEN OFTEN TOO ANXIOUS FOR RIVERS . . . . 379 TOO ANXIOUS FOR RIVERS   6
    OH, YEARS AGO--TEN THOUSAND YEARS. . . . . 392 A CLIFF DWELLING . .   13
    OH, MAY THE TIDE BE SOON ENOUGH AT HIGH . . . . . . 395 ETHEREALIZING . . .   13
    OH, BUT NOT TO BOAST, ... 429 KITTY HAWK   22
    OH, BUT FLY WE DID, ... 434 KITTY HAWK 194
    OH, THERE HAD ONCE BEEN NIGHT THE FIRST, ... 444 ENDS   3
    OH, SOME AS SOON WOULD THROW IT ALL . . . . 445 ENDS   9
    "OH, FROM MY KNOWLEDGE OF ITS QUINTESSENCE. . . . . . 456 HOW HARD TO KEEP FROM   87
    LET'S SEE, WHERE ARE WE? OH, WE'RE IN TRANSITION, . . . 462 HOW HARD TO KEEP FROM   254
    OH, I REMEMBER WELL: YOU'RE JOB, MY PATIENT, ... 474 A MASQUE OF REASON .   34
    OH, LORD, LET'S NOT GO BACK TO ANYTHING. . . . . . . 477 A MASQUE OF REASON .   115
    AND TANTALIZE ME WITH ANOTHER "OH, BECAUSE." . . . . 482 A MASQUE OF REASON .   257
    OH, WE KNOW WELL ENOUGH TO GO AHEAD WITH. . . . . . 483 A MASQUE OF REASON .   289
    YOUR COMFORTERS WERE WRONG. / OH, THAT COMMITTEE! . . . 486 A MASQUE OF REASON .   368
    YOU'RE PENSIVE. / OH, I'M THINKING OF THE DEVIL. . . . 486 A MASQUE OF REASON .   376
    ABOUT HIS BLINDNESS. / OH, HE SPEAKS! HE CAN SPEAK! . . 488 A MASQUE OF REASON .   417
    HE'S TWITTING US.--OH, BY THE WAY, YOU HAVEN'T . . . 488 A MASQUE OF REASON .   420
    OH, YES, THAT TENDENCY!--OH, DO COME OFF IT. . . . . 489 A MASQUE OF REASON .   447
    ABOUT A WHALE. / OH, YOU MEAN MOBY DICK . . . . . . 495 A MASQUE OF MERCY . .   48
    I'M SICK. / OF WHAT? / OH, EVERYTHING, I GUESS. . . . 499 A MASQUE OF MERCY . . 155
    OH, NO, YOU'RE NOT. YOU'RE STAYING HERE TONIGHT.-- . . 500 A MASQUE OF MERCY . . 173
    BUT OH, NO, NOT FOR JONAH. I REFUSE . . . . 505 A MASQUE OF MERCY . . 302
    "OH, WHAT IS A KING HERE, ... 512 A MASQUE OF MERCY . . 502
    OH, THERE'S TO BE A FUNERAL ORATION. . . . . 519 A MASQUE OF MERCY . . 678
OHO
    "OHO, OHO!" / "YOU DON'T BELIEVE ME." / "YES, I DO, . . 87 THE HOUSEKEEPER . . . 181
OIL
    AND OIL ARE BURIED OUT OF REACH?" / AGAIN . . . . . 113 IN THE HOME STRETCH .   81

		PAGE	TITLE	LINE

OIL (CONTINUED)
```
    A SWAMP OF CEDAR. CHOKED WITH OIL OF CEDAR  . . . . . . 125 AN ENCOUNTER . . . .    5
    BUT SWEATING-FULL, DRIPS WINE AND OIL A LITTLE. . . . . 323 BUILD SOIL . . . .  236
    WE WOULD POUR OIL ON THE INGLE  . . . . . . . . . . . . 384 IN THE LONG NIGHT  . .    5
    AND ENOUGH DRINK OIL FOR ALL. . . . . . . . . . . . . . 384 IN THE LONG NIGHT  . .   12
O.K.
    COMBED IT DOWN WITH A RAKE AND SAYS, 'O.K.' . . . . . .  71 THE CODE . . . . . .   52
OLD  (SEE WORLD-OLD)
    SO OLD AND FIRM THEY SCARCELY SHOW THE BREEZE, . . . . .   5 INTO MY OWN . . . .    2
    OF NEW WOOD AND OLD WHERE THE WOODPECKER CHOPS; . . . .    6 GHOST HOUSE . . . .    9
    SURELY YOU WOULDN'T GRUDGE THE POOR OLD MAN . . . . . .   36 DEATH OF THE HIRED MAN   49
    AND ROLLED HIS OLD HEAD ON THAT SHARP-EDGED CHAIR-BACK. . 39 DEATH OF THE HIRED MAN  148
    OF LATE YEARS, THOUGH HE KEEPS THE OLD HOMESTEAD  . . .   44 A HUNDRED COLLARS . .    3
    AND SEES OLD FRIENDS HE SOMEHOW CAN'T GET NEAR. . . . .   44 A HUNDRED COLLARS . .    7
    DONE SADLY FROM AN OLD DAGUERREOTYPE. . . . . . . . . .   55 THE BLACK COTTAGE  . .   24
    THE WARPING BOARDS PULL OUT THEIR OWN OLD NAILS . . . .   56 THE BLACK COTTAGE  . .   49
    SHE HAD HER OWN IDEA OF THINGS, THE OLD LADY. . . . . .   56 THE BLACK COTTAGE  . .   51
    OF HER OLD TREMULOUS BONNET IN THE PEW, . . . . . . . .   57 THE BLACK COTTAGE  . .   91
    LIKE A DEEP PIECE OF SOME OLD RUNNING RIVER . . . . . .   63 A SERVANT TO SERVANTS . .   20
    LOCKED UP FOR YEARS BACK THERE AT THE OLD FARM. . . . .   65 A SERVANT TO SERVANTS . .   89
    YOU KNOW THE OLD IDEA--THE ONLY ASYLUM  . . . . . . . .   65 A SERVANT TO SERVANTS . .   93
    I BUILT THE LOAD AND TOPPED IT OFF; OLD SANDERS . . . .   71 THE CODE . . . . . .   51
    BUT THE OLD FOOL SEIZES HIS FORK IN BOTH HANDS, . . . .   71 THE CODE . . . . . .   61
    ONE OF THE BOYS SINGS OUT, 'WHERE'S THE OLD MAN?' . . .   72 THE CODE . . . . . .   83
    IN AN OLD CELLAR HOLE IN A BYROAD . . . . . . . . . . .   73 THE GENERATIONS OF MEN    8
    I CAN MAKE OUT OLD GRANDSIR STARK DISTINCTLY-- . . . .    77 THE GENERATIONS OF MEN  104
    SHE'S AFTER CIDER, THE OLD GIRL, SHE'S THIRSTY; . . . .   77 THE GENERATIONS OF MEN  108
    DOES IT PURPORT TO SPEAK IN? NOT OLD GRANDSIR'S . . . .   79 THE GENERATIONS OF MEN  174
    THERE AIN'T NO NAMES QUITE LIKE THE OLD ONES, THOUGH, . . 80 THE GENERATIONS OF MEN  186
    OF THE OLD STOCK? WHAT COUNTS IS THE IDEALS, . . . . .    80 THE GENERATIONS OF MEN  197
    I'M GETTING TOO OLD FOR MY SIZE, I TELL THEM. . . . . .   81 THE HOUSEKEEPER . . .    5
    I HATE TO THINK OF THE OLD PLACE WHEN WE'RE GONE, . . .   82 THE HOUSEKEEPER . . .   45
    JOHN SAID I WAS TOO OLD TO HAVE GRANDCHILDREN. . . . . .  87 THE HOUSEKEEPER . . .  175
    I'LL TALK TO YOU, OLD WOMAN, AFTERWARD.-- . . . . . . .   88 THE HOUSEKEEPER . . .  209
    OLD STREAK OF LEATHER--DOESN'T LOVE ME MUCH . . . . . .   94 THE SELF-SEEKER . . .   33
    OF HEAVY FOOTSTEPS IN THE OLD FRAME HOUSE, . . . . . . .  96 THE SELF-SEEKER . . .   93
    AN OLD MAN'S WINTER NIGHT . . . . . . . . . . . . . . . 108 OLD MAN'S WINTER NIGHT    T
    THERE'S A PATCH OF OLD SNOW IN A CORNER, . . . . . . . . 110 A PATCH OF OLD SNOW  .    1
    A PATCH OF OLD SNOW . . . . . . . . . . . . . . . . . . 110 A PATCH OF OLD SNOW  .    T
    ON THE OLD PEACH TREES ON THE KNOLL, TO GROPE . . . . . 117 IN THE HOME STRETCH  .  189
    HE SAYS THAT LEAVES ARE OLD AND THAT FOR FLOWERS . . . . 119 THE OVEN BIRD . . . .    4
    TO HAVE A VISION OF US OLD AND DEAD) . . . . . . . . . . 127 THE SMILE . . . . .   10
    LET'S ALL BUT BRING TO LIFE THIS OLD VOLCANO, . . . . . 130 THE BONFIRE . . . . .   16
    GRASS ITS FULL LENGTH, OLD SILVER GOLDENROD, . . . . . . 131 THE BONFIRE . . . . .   62
    SINCE HE WAS OLD ENOUGH TO KNOW, BIG BOY . . . . . . . . 137 "OUT, OUT--" . . . .   23
    WITH HIS TEN CHILDREN UNDER TEN YEARS OLD. . . . . . . . 144 SNOW . . . . . . . .   52
    I EVER STUMBLED ON IN OLD NEW HAMPSHIRE  . . . . . . . . 160 NEW HAMPSHIRE . . .   36
    AS AN OLD BOYHOOD FRIEND, AND ONCE INDEED . . . . . . . 160 NEW HAMPSHIRE . . .   49
    IN DEALING IN "OLD RAGS" IN SAN FRANCISCO. . . . . . . . 160 NEW HAMPSHIRE . . .   58
    I CALL HER OLD. SHE HAS ONE FAMILY . . . . . . . . . . . 161 NEW HAMPSHIRE . . .   70
    SHE HAS ONE WITCH--OLD STYLE. SHE LIVES IN COLEBROOK. . . 163 NEW HAMPSHIRE . . .  125
    YOKEFELLOWS IN THE SAP YOKE FROM OF OLD . . . . . . . . 164 NEW HAMPSHIRE . . .  177
    THE ONLY FAULT I FIND WITH OLD NEW HAMPSHIRE . . . . . . 168 NEW HAMPSHIRE . . .  310
    HE LOADED AN OLD STONEBOAT WITH THE STAR . . . . . . . . 173 A STAR IN A STONEBOAT .   26
    BY BRINGING IT UP TO HIM WHEN HE WAS TOO OLD. . . . . . 183 MAPLE . . . . . .  122
    IT STANDS BESIDE THE SAME OLD APPLE TREE. . . . . . . . 189 THE GRINDSTONE . . .    8
    EXCEPT THAT I REMEMBER HOW OF OLD . . . . . . . . . . . 189 THE GRINDSTONE . . .   22
    THE SAME PAUL AT THE SAME OLD FEATS OF LOGGING. . . . . 192 PAUL'S WIFE . . . .   30
    LABAN WAS OLD AND POOR, YET SEEMED TO CARE; . . . . . . 201 PLACE FOR A THIRD . .   50
    AND SHE WAS OLD AND POOR--BUT SHE CARED, TOO, . . . . . 201 PLACE FOR A THIRD . .   51
    THEY SAT. SHE CAST ONE DULL, OLD LOOK AT HIM, . . . . . 201 PLACE FOR A THIRD . .   52
    FROM THE WAY SHE HAD SET HER POOR OLD MOUTH, . . . . . . 201 PLACE FOR A THIRD . .   74
    OF HIS OLD SONG, 'THE WILD COLONIAL BOY,' . . . . . . . 205 THE WITCH OF COÖS . .  110
    SAID THAT I TOOK HIM OUT IN HIS OLD AGE . . . . . . . . 208 PAUPER WITCH OF GRAFTON   46
    THE POOR OLD MAN. IT WOULD HAVE BEEN ALL RIGHT . . . . . 209 PAUPER WITCH OF GRAFTON   53
    IT'S THE OLD CAPTAIN'S DARK FATE . . . . . . . . . . . . 212 AN EMPTY THREAT . . .   43
    OLD DAVIS OWNED A SOLID MICA MOUNTAIN . . . . . . . . . 212 A FOUNTAIN, A BOTTLE .    1
    "HUH, THAT OLD BATHTUB, WHAT IS THAT TO SEE? . . . . . . 213 A FOUNTAIN, A BOTTLE .   15
    OLD AS I AM, I'M GOING TO LET MYSELF . . . . . . . . . . 214 A FOUNTAIN, A BOTTLE .   29
    THE OLD MAN SERIOUSLY TOOK HIS BEARINGS, . . . . . . . . 214 A FOUNTAIN, A BOTTLE .   35
    "TAKE ONE," OLD DAVIS BADE ME GRACIOUSLY. . . . . . . . 217 A FOUNTAIN, A BOTTLE .  123
    BUT WHERE THIS OLD WALL BURNS A SUNNY CHEEK, . . . . . . 246 ATMOSPHERE . . . .    2
    BUT THE STRANGEST THING: IN THE THICK OLD THATCH, . . . 253 THE THATCH . . . . .   13
    THERE WAS AN OLD, OLD HOUSE RENEWED WITH PAINT, . . . . 263 THE INVESTMENT . . .    3
    OR OLD LOVE ON AN IMPULSE NOT TO CARE-- . . . . . . . . 264 THE INVESTMENT . . .   12
    THEN DESCENDED OF OLD ON THE BUSH. . . . . . . . . . . . 266 SITTING BY A BUSH . .   16
    WHEN I WAS YOUNG MY TEACHERS WERE THE OLD. . . . . . . . 267 WHAT FIFTY SAID . .    1
    NOW I AM OLD MY TEACHERS ARE THE YOUNG. . . . . . . . . 267 WHAT FIFTY SAID . .    5
    HIS LITTLE MATTHEW, THREE FIVE YEARS OLD, . . . . . . . 283 THE GOLD HESPERIDEE  .   13
    SOME WORN OLD TOOL OF MY OWN . . . . . . . . . . . . . . 285 IN TIME OF CLOUDBURST   21
    THE LITTLE OLD HOUSE WAS OUT WITH A LITTLE NEW SHED . . . 286 A ROADSIDE STAND . .    1
    THE OLD BARN AT THE BOTTOM OF THE FOGS. . . . . . . . . 289 OLD BARN AT THE BOTTOM    T
    THE OLD BARN AT THE BOTTOM OF THE FOGS. . . . . . . . . 290 OLD BARN AT THE BOTTOM   23
    AND FOR BACK WALL A CRUMBLING OLD CHIMNEY . . . . . . . 294 A RECORD STRIDE . .    3
    OLD RIVALS OF SAGGING LEATHER, . . . . . . . . . . . . . 294 A RECORD STRIDE . .    6
    ABOUT WHO IS TOO OLD TO GO WALKING, . . . . . . . . . . 294 A RECORD STRIDE . .   11
    LOCKING FOR MY OLD SKY-MARKS IN THE BLUE. . . . . . . . 295 LOST IN HEAVEN . . .    4
    YOU SQUAT OLD PYRAMID. . . . . . . . . . . . . . . . . . 298 ON TAKING FROM THE TOP    2
    OF AN OLD MOUNTAIN'S CASE . . . . . . . . . . . . . . . 298 ON TAKING FROM THE TOP   18
    YOUR OLD SWEET-CYNICAL STRAIN . . . . . . . . . . . . . 302 VOICE WAYS . . . .    6
    FOR FEAR IT WOULD MAKE ME CONSERVATIVE WHEN OLD. . . . . 308 PRECAUTION . . . .    2
    THE OLD DOG BARKS BACKWARD WITHOUT GETTING UP. . . . . . 308 THE SPAN OF LIFE . .    1
    WERE SEEN OF OLD AT MEMPHIS ON THE HEIGHTS . . . . . . . 315 IRIS BY NIGHT . . .    6
    THEY SLOWLY LED OLD LATIN VERSE TO RHYME . . . . . . . . 351 THE LESSON FOR TODAY   16
    THEY ARE PHILOSOPHERS, AND FROM OLD HABIT . . . . . . . 354 THE LESSON FOR TODAY  110
    THE OLD INCURABLE UNTIMELINESS, . . . . . . . . . . . . 356 A MOTH SEEN IN WINTER   15
    TO START THE WORLD OF OLD . . . . . . . . . . . . . . . 361 ALMOST TWO THOUSAND    1
    THE WEST AND KEEP THE OLD TRADITION SAFE. . . . . . . . 365 OF STONES OF THE PLACE   12
```

OLD (CONTINUED)
    KNOWS THE OLD MAN, AND NOBODY'S SO DEEP . . . . 371 THE LITERATE FARMER AND   96
    THE OLD MAN ARGUES SCIENCE CHEAPENED SPEED. . . . . . . 371 THE LITERATE FARMER AND   98
    A FEW OLD PECKER-FRETTED APPLE TREES. . . . . 378 DIRECTIVE   28
    OF AN OLD CEDAR AT THE WATERSIDE . . . . 379 DIRECTIVE   56
    IN THE OLD DAYS IN PERSIA AND PERU. . . . . 408 FROM PLANE TO PLANE . 133
    DICK SAID, TO OLD PIKE INNOCENT OF SHAKESPEARE. . . . . 408 FROM PLANE TO PLANE . 148
    "GUSTIE, OLD BOY, DALMATIAN GUS, ... 420 ONE MORE BREVITY . .   28
    WHICH IS NO MORE THAN GOOD OLD PANTHEISM. . . . . 427 CONCEPT SELF-CONCEIVED   4
    YOUR SEPARATION OF US FROM THE OLD . . . . 446 DOES NO ONE AT ALL EVER   2
    FROM SOME EXTINCT OLD CHIMNEY POT. . . . . 452 A-WISHING WELL . . .   36
    CHANGING AN OLD KING FOR ANOTHER OLD ONE. . . . . 462 HOW HARD TO KEEP FROM 255
    FOR ME AS AN OLD SLOW COACH. . . . . 466 SOME SCIENCE FICTION . 12
    YOU WERE AFFLICTED WITH IN THOSE OLD DAYS. . . . . 475 A MASQUE OF REASON .   61
    A GOOD OLD GET-TOGETHER CELEBRATION. . . . . 487 A MASQUE OF REASON . 380
    WHAT'S THIS? / DON'T LOSE THE PLACE. / OLD DANA LYLE, . 506 A MASQUE OF MERCY . 324
    YOU'RE WORKING IT, OLD MAN. DON'T BE DISCOURAGED. . . . 507 A MASQUE OF MERCY . 347
    THAT BOOK OF YOURS IN THE OLD TESTAMENT . . . . 508 A MASQUE OF MERCY . 375
    OLD ATTIC GRACE AND SPARTAN DISCIPLINE . . . . 511 A MASQUE OF MERCY . 467
    PERSISTING FROM OLD CHAOS IN THEIR MYTH, ... 511 A MASQUE OF MERCY . 470
    WHAT DO YOU MAKE OF IT? / THE SAME OLD NOTHING. . . . . 512 A MASQUE OF MERCY . 492
    YOU POOR OLD SAPE, IF I MAY COIN THE SLANG. . . . . . . 518 A MASQUE OF MERCY . 664
OLD-BELIEVERS
    TWO OLD-BELIEVERS. THEY DID ALL THE TALKING. . . . . . 202 THE WITCH OF COOS . .   3
OLDER
    AND IT WAS OLDER SURE THAN THIS YEAR'S CUTTING, ... 101 THE WOOD-PILE . . .   27
    AS IT GROWS WISER AND OLDER, ... 156 THE SOUND OF TREES .   13
OLD-FASHIONED
    I'VE HEARD TOO MUCH OF THE OLD-FASHIONED WAY. . . . . . 65 A SERVANT TO SERVANTS . 103
    AND AN OLD-FASHIONED SACRIFICE BY FIRE, ... 178 THE STAR-SPLITTER .   64
    AND HIS BE POETRY'S OLD-FASHIONED PRAISE . . . . . . 422 FOR JOHN F. KENNEDY .   5
    'TWAS IN FOR AN OLD-FASHIONED SHAKING DOWN . . . . . . 503 A MASQUE OF MERCY . 273
    DIE SAYING THAT, OLD-FASHIONED SAPIENT, ... 518 A MASQUE OF MERCY . 663
OLD-GOLDEN
    AND ON THE WORN BOOK OF OLD-GOLDEN SONG . . . . 15 WAITING   23
OLD-STONE
    IN EACH HAND, LIKE AN OLD-STONE SAVAGE ARMED. . . . . . 34 MENDING WALL   40
OLD-TIMER
    A GOOD OLD-TIMER DATING BACK ALONG; . . . . 178 THE STAR-SPLITTER .   60
OLIGARCHIC
    MONARCHIC SOCIALISM, OLIGARCHIC-- . . . . 318 BUILD SOIL   73
OLIVIER
    AND AT THE SUMMONS ROLAND, OLIVIER, ... 353 THE LESSON FOR TODAY .   89
OLYMPIC
    PERHAPS FOR AN OLYMPIC TOURNAMENT, ... 474 A MASQUE OF REASON .   24
OMAR
    HIS NAME IS OMAR. I AS A RHODES SCHOLAR . . . . . . 459 HOW HARD TO KEEP FROM 188
OMEGA
    IS NEITHER ALPHA, ETA, NOR OMEGA, ... 388 IOTA SUBSCRIPT . . .   7
OMINOUS
    AND I DREAD THE OMINOUS STAIN OF TAR . . . . 232 THE KITCHEN CHIMNEY .   13
OMNIBUS
    THEY MEAN TO TELL US, THOUGH, THE OMNIBUS . . . . . 425 ACCIDENTALLY ON PURPOSE 11
ON---NOT INDEXED--EXCEPT FOR GREEK:
    (THE ME ON OF PLATO), ... 427 VERSION   10
ONCE
    THAT, SILENCED BY MY ADVENT, FINDS ONCE MORE, ... 14 WAITING   20
    AND TRIES ONCE--TWICE--AND THRICE IF I BE THERE; . . . 15 WAITING   22
    BUT ONCE WITHIN THE WOOD, WE PAUSED . . . . 18 GOING FOR WATER . . .   13
    TO VIEW ONCE MORE THE SACRIFICE . . . . 20 THE TRIAL BY EXISTENCE 26
    I WENT TO TURN THE GRASS ONCE AFTER ONE . . . . . . 22 THE TUFT OF FLOWERS .   1
    AND ONCE I MARKED HIS FLIGHT GO ROUND AND ROUND, . . . 22 THE TUFT OF FLOWERS .   15
    TO THIS LEAN FEEDING, SAVE ONCE A YEAR . . . . . . 24 PAN WITH US   12
    HOW ONCE CONSPIRACY WAS RIFE . . . . 29 MY BUTTERFLY   32
    AND SET THE WALL BETWEEN US ONCE AGAIN. . . . . . . 33 MENDING WALL   14
    I SAW SO MUCH BEFORE I SLEPT THERE ONCE: . . . . . . 40 THE MOUNTAIN   2
    "THE WONDER IS I DIDN'T SEE AT ONCE. . . . . 51 HOME BURIAL   20
    "I'VE TOLD YOU HOW ONCE, NOT LONG AFTER WE CAME, . . . 61 BLUEBERRIES   67
    I'VE BEEN AWAY ONCE--YES, I'VE BEEN BACK. . . . . . . 65 A SERVANT TO SERVANTS . 90
    TELL YOU A STORY OF WHAT HAPPENED ONCE: . . . . . . 70 THE CODE   29
    I LOOKED OVER THE SIDE ONCE IN THE DUST . . . . . . 72 THE CODE   75
    ONCE MORE BEFORE WE MEET ELSEWHERE." / "IN RAIN?" . . 81 THE GENERATIONS OF MEN 209
    A HORSE'S HOOF PAWED ONCE THE HOLLOW FLOOR, ... 89 THE FEAR   5
    "OH, GUESS WHICH HAND? MY, MY! ONCE ON A TIME . . . . 96 THE SELF-SEEKER . . . 107
    IN CLOMPING HERE, HE SCARED IT ONCE AGAIN . . . . . 108 OLD MAN'S WINTER NIGHT 10
    ONCE IN THE STOVE, DISTURBED HIM AND HE SHIFTED, . . . 108 OLD MAN'S WINTER NIGHT 24
    AND TOO MUCH WORLD AT ONCE--COULD MEANS BE FOUND. . . . 109 THE EXPOSED NEST .   19
    OF SUCH A LITTLE HOUSE. ONCE LEFT ALONE, ... 111 IN THE HOME STRETCH .   40
    AND ALL AT ONCE. HE'LL PLAN FOR US AND PLAN . . . . . 115 IN THE HOME STRETCH . 152
    AND THEY SEEM NOT TO BREAK; THOUGH ONCE THEY ARE BOWED 121 BIRCHES   15
    SO WAS I ONCE MYSELF A SWINGER OF BIRCHES. . . . . . 122 BIRCHES   41
    ONCE ON THE KIND OF DAY CALLED "WEATHER BREEDER," . . . 125 AN ENCOUNTER   1
    AND ONCE SHE WENT TO BREAK A BOUGH . . . . 129 THE IMPULSE   13
    AS ONCE IT DID WITH ME UPON AN APRIL. . . . . 130 THE BONFIRE   34
    AS I WALKED ONCE AROUND IT IN POSSESSION. . . . . . . 130 THE BONFIRE   39
    AS AN OLD BOYHOOD FRIEND, AND ONCE INDEED . . . . . 160 NEW HAMPSHIRE . . .   49
    IT SET OUT ONCE TO BE A CITY AND STILL . . . . . . 165 NEW HAMPSHIRE . . . 191
    ELECTION NIGHT ONCE IN FRANCONIA, ... 165 NEW HAMPSHIRE . . . 195
    A LITERATURE THAT SHALL LAST ONCE BE SOUND . . . . . 168 NEW HAMPSHIRE . . . 285
    ONCE SHE FOUND FOR A BOOKMARK IN THE BIBLE . . . . . 181 MAPLE   62
    THEY WENT ON PILGRIMAGE ONCE TO HER FATHER'S . . . . 182 MAPLE   97
    ONCE LONG AGO HER FATHER HAD PUT HIMSELF OFF.) . . . . 183 MAPLE 111
    ONCE THEY CAME ON A MAPLE IN A GLADE, ... 184 MAPLE 144
    TO SEE FOR ONCE THE INSIDE OF HIS HOUSE. . . . . . . 188 THE AX-HELVE   89
    ONCE WHEN THE GRINDSTONE ALMOST JUMPED ITS BEARING . . 190 THE GRINDSTONE . . .   57
    AND WHEN HE RAISED IT DRIPPING ONCE AND TRIED . . . . 190 THE GRINDSTONE . . .   68
    OTHERS BECAUSE HE'D HAD ONE ONCE, A GOOD ONE, ... 191 PAUL'S WIFE   8

ONCE (CONTINUED)

WITH BOTH HIS FEET AT ONCE AGAINST THE CEILING, ... 192 PAUL'S WIFE 51
BLEW IT ONCE OFF HIS HANDS AND ALMOST BROKE IT. . . . . 194 PAUL'S WIFE 100
BUT ONCE I FELT GROUND WITH MY STOCKING FEET . . . . . 198 WILD GRAPES 85
THAT, ONCE GRIEF SETS TO GROWING, GRIEF MAY REST: . . . 200 PLACE FOR A THIRD . . 27
TELL YOU WHAT RALLE THE SIOUX CONTROL ONCE TOLD ME. . . 202 THE WITCH OF COOS . . 13
THE WAY HE DID IN LIFE ONCE; BUT THIS TIME . . . . . 204 THE WITCH OF COOS . . 76
FOR HELPING THEM BE CRUEL ONCE TO HIM. . . . . 206 THE WITCH OF COOS . . 134
YES, WE COULD TOO, SON. TELL THE TRUTH FOR ONCE. . . . 206 THE WITCH OF COOS . . 138
OF ARTHUR AMY'S HAVING ONCE BEEN UP . . . . 207 PAUPER WITCH OF GRAFTON 13
SO NOW THEY'VE DRAGGED IT THROUGH THE LAW COURTS ONCE, . 208 PAUPER WITCH OF GRAFTON 28
YOU SAID YOU KNEW THE PLACE WHERE ONCE, ON KINSMAN, . . 213 A FOUNTAIN, A BOTTLE . 8
IN DUST ONCE MORE. WE FOLLOWED THIS A MILE, ... 215 A FOUNTAIN, A BOTTLE . 67
OF ONCE EXPANDING . . . . 219 I WILL SING YOU ONE-O . 70
ANC SEE YOU PLEASED ONCE MORE WITH WORDS OF MINE? . . . 222 TO E.T. 20
ONCE WHEN THE SNOW OF THE YEAR WAS BEGINNING TO FALL, . 223 THE RUNAWAY 1
THE WIND ONCE BLEW ITSELF UNTAUGHT, ... 223 THE AIM WAS SONG . . 2
ONCE, WHEN TRYING WITH CHIN AGAINST A WELL-CURB, . . . 225 FOR ONCE SOMETHING . . 7
FOR ONCE, THEN, SOMETHING. . . . . 225 FOR ONCE SOMETHING . . T
TRUTH? A PEBBLE OF QUARTZ? FOR ONCE, THEN, SOMETHING. . 225 FOR ONCE SOMETHING . . 15
AND ONCE THAT SEEMED TOO MUCH; . . . . 226 TO EARTHWARD 3
THAT ONCE YOU HAD OPENED THE VALLEY'S SINGING DAY. . . 236 VALLEY'S SINGING DAY . 20
THE TREES THEY'D HAD ENOUGH OF WITH ONCE TRYING . . . 239 OUR SINGING STRENGTH . 28
ONCE BY THE PACIFIC . . . . 250 ONCE BY THE PACIFIC . T
AND NOW IT IS ONCE MORE THE TIDAL WAVE . . . . . . 255 THE FLOOD 12
TO TELL ONCE AND ONCE ONLY, FOR THEM NEVER TO FORGET, . 257 THE LOVELY BE CHOOSERS 32
HOW ONCE SHE WALKED IN BRIGHTNESS, ... 257 THE LOVELY BE CHOOSERS 33
AND NEVER ONCE DROPS . . . . 261 CANIS MAJOR 7
GOD ONCE DECLARED HE WAS TRUE . . . . 266 SITTING BY A BUSH . . 13
GOD ONCE SPOKE TO PEOPLE BY NAME. . . . . 266 SITTING BY A BUSH . . 17
THE SUN ONCE IMPARTED ITS FLAME. . . . . 266 SITTING BY A BUSH . . 18
EXTREMES TOO HARD TO COMPREHEND AT ONCE, ... 266 THE ARMFUL 4
THEN ONCE AGAIN THE SANDBANK LAY SERENE. . . . . . . 270 THE EGG AND THE MACHINE 16
SO MANY PRICKLY GRAPPLING FEET AT ONCE. . . . . . . 278 THE WHITE-TAILED HORNET 29
BUT ONCE COMPARISONS WERE YIELDED DOWNWARD, ... 279 THE WHITE-TAILED HORNET 63
ONCE WE BEGAN TO SEE OUR IMAGES , ... 279 THE WHITE-TAILED HORNET 66
YET ONCE SHE RISES TO THE HEIGHT, ... 281 BLUE RIBBON AT AMESBURY 46
ONCE SHOWED TWO LITTLE MONKEYS IN A CAGE . . . . . . 293 AT WOODWARD'S GARDENS . 2
THE ALREADY KNOWN HAD ONCE MORE BEEN CONFIRMED . . . . 293 AT WOODWARD'S GARDENS . 18
WHO ONCE KEPT SURPASSING EACH OTHER, ... 294 A RECORD STRIDE . . . 7
SEEING MYSELF WELL LOST ONCE MORE, I SIGHED, ... 295 LOST IN HEAVEN . . . 9
PETALS I MAY HAVE ONCE PURSUED. . . . . 297 LEAVES COMPARED WITH . 19
FROM ONE ANOTHER ONCE YOU ARE AGREED . . . . 300 THE MASTER SPEED . . 12
PARTLY BECAUSE IT SANG BUT ONCE ALL NIGHT . . . . . 302 A BIRD SINGING IN SLEEP 3
FOR MERELY GIVING YOU ONCE MORE GENTLE PROOF . . . . 306 NOT QUITE SOCIAL . . 6
WAS ONCE THE BEAUTY ABISHAG, ... 307 PROVIDE, PROVIDE . . 3
OF ONCE HAVING STARTED A WAR, ... 310 THE VINDICTIVES . . . 16
THAT ONCE BETWEEN POST AND POST . . . . 312 THE VINDICTIVES . . . 65
POETRY, ITSELF ONCE MORE, IS BACK IN LOVE. . . . . . 318 BUILD SOIL 89
I SENT YOU ONCE A SONG WITH THE REFRAIN: . . . . . . 324 BUILD SOIL 259
ONCE TOOK A LITTLE PEBBLE WHEEL . . . . 326 A MISSIVE MISSILE . . 2
AND ONCE THEY HAD SHIPPED A CAPTIVE PAIR . . . . . . 345 DISCOVERY OF MADEIRAS . 54
FOR ALWAYS FIGHTING ON BOTH SIDES AT ONCE. . . . . . 350 TO A YOUNG WRETCH . . 18
OF BEING BORN AT ONCE TOO EARLY AND LATE, ... 351 THE LESSON FOR TODAY . 12
THAT AT ONCE KEPT YOU BURNING LOW AND HID YOU. . . . 351 THE LESSON FOR TODAY . 25
IT MIGHT AS WELL AT ONCE BE KINGDOM-COME. . . . . . 353 THE LESSON FOR TODAY . 102
THAT ONCE A YEAR BY HAND OR APPARATUS . . . . 360 A LOOSE MOUNTAIN . . 3
BUT IT MADE MY PROPERTY MINE ONCE MORE. . . . . . . 364 TRESPASS 20
HOW ONCE IN CUTTING BRUSH ALONG THE WALL . . . . . . 375 A YOUNG BIRCH . . . 12
WERE ONCE MORE ON THEIR TRAVELS, ... 376 ONE STEP BACKWARD TAKEN 2
SOMEONE'S ROAD HOME FROM WORK THIS ONCE WAS, ... 378 DIRECTIVE 30
SO ONCE YOU ROSE AND LIT THE LIGHT. . . . . 380 AN UNSTAMPED LETTER IN 2
ONCE DOWN ON MY KNEES TO GROWING PLANTS . . . . . . 385 A MOOD APART 1
THERE ONCE WE LAY AS BLOBS OF JELLYFISH . . . . . . 395 ETHEREALIZING . . . 9
ANC WHEN HE CAUGHT DICK LOOKING ONCE TOO OFTEN, . . . 404 FROM PLANE TO PLANE . 26
TO THEIR SURPRISE RANG ONCE ON STONE ALL DAY . . . . 407 FROM PLANE TO PLANE . 116
ONCE THERE WAS AN ARCHER, ... 427 VERSION 1
THERE WAS ONCE A SONG, ... 428 KITTY HAWK 2
ONCE I TOLD THE MASTER, ... 429 KITTY HAWK 50
ONCE CONSIDERED CRANKS . . . . 443 KITTY HAWK 469
ONCE IN A CALIFORNIA SIERRA . . . . 443 AUSPEX 1
OH, THERE HAD ONCE BEEN NIGHT THE FIRST, ... 444 ENDS 3
(PERHAPS SO CALLED BECAUSE IT MAY HAVE RISEN ONCE) . . 447 THE BAD ISLAND--EASTER 5
ASKS OF HIMSELF ONCE IN SO OFTEN . . . . 453 A-WISHING WELL . . . 74
ONCE TO HAVE KNOWN IT, NOTHING ELSE WILL DO. . . . . 461 HOW HARD TO KEEP FROM 247
I ONCE HAD A COW THAT JUMPED OVER THE MOON, ... 462 LINES IN DEJECTION . . 1
A COW DID THAT ONCE TO A FELLOW . . . . 463 LINES IN DEJECTION . . 14
ONCE I WAS FOOL ENOUGH TO THINK . . . . 467 QUANDARY 20
ESTABLISH ONCE FOR ALL THE PRINCIPLE . . . . 475 A MASQUE OF REASON . . 49
IF I SAID ONCE I SAID A THOUSAND TIMES, ... 478 A MASQUE OF REASON . . 129
YES, BOTH OF US: WE SAW TO THAT AT ONCE. . . . . . 479 A MASQUE OF REASON . . 162
BE HEAVEN AT ONCE AND HAVE IT OVER WITH. . . . . . 484 A MASQUE OF REASON . . 322
ONCE AND FOR ALL. I'M GOING TO MAKE YOU SEE . . . . 498 A MASQUE OF MERCY . . 145
YOU! WHO ARE YOU? I ASKED YOU ONCE BEFORE. . . . . 499 A MASQUE OF MERCY . . 150
ANYTHING WE ONCE THOUGHT WE HAD TO BE. . . . . . . 505 A MASQUE OF MERCY . . 315
ONCE CHARGED THE NAZARENE WITH HAVING BROUGHT . . . . 511 A MASQUE OF MERCY . . 465
I ASK YOU ALL TO READ IT ONCE AGAIN. . . . . 511 A MASQUE OF MERCY . . 488
I'D LIKE TO SEE THE WORLD TRIED ONCE WITHOUT IT. . . . 515 A MASQUE OF MERCY . . 575
FOR ALL THE LIGHT AT ONCE THE SOURCE OF LIGHT-- . . . 515 A MASQUE OF MERCY . . 587
AS ONCE THE PHARAOH DID IT OUT OF SEKHTI . . . . . . 517 A MASQUE OF MERCY . . 641

ONE (SEE TWENTY-ONE)

ONE OF MY WISHES IS THAT THOSE DARK TREES, ... 5 INTO MY OWN 1
THE ORCHARD TREE HAS GROWN ONE COPSE . . . . 5 GHOST HOUSE 8
BUT ON THE MEMORY OF ONE ABSENT, MOST, ... 15 WAITING 26
ONE SO LONELY WAS FAIN TO LIST, ... 15 IN A VALE 14
WHERE BIRD AND FLOWER WERE ONE AND THE SAME. . . . . 15 IN A VALE 20
AND TO THE FOREST EDGE YOU CAME ONE DAY . . . . . . 16 A DREAM PANG . . . 3
THERE WAS NEVER A SOUND BESIDE THE WOOD BUT ONE, . . . 17 MOWING 1

ONE (CONTINUED)
AND A SHOUT GREETS THE DARING ONE. . . . . 21 THE TRIAL BY EXISTENCE   48
"ONE THOUGHT IN AGONY OF STRIFE . . . . 21 THE TRIAL BY EXISTENCE   50
IN THE PAIN THAT HAS BUT ONE CLOSE, ... 21 THE TRIAL BY EXISTENCE   71
I WENT TO TURN THE GRASS ONCE AFTER ONE . . . . 22 THE TUFT OF FLOWERS   1
NOR YET TO DRAW ONE THOUGHT OF OURS TO HIM, ... 23 THE TUFT OF FLOWERS   27
WITH ONE WHOSE THOUGHT I HAD NOT HOPED TO REACH. . . . 23 THE TUFT OF FLOWERS   38
PAN CAME OUT OF THE WOODS ONE DAY-- . . . . 23 PAN WITH US   1
WERE MUSIC ENOUGH FOR HIM, FOR ONE. . . . . 24 PAN WITH US   20
AS OF ONE WHO UTTERLY COULDN'T CARE. . . . . 25 THE DEMIURGE'S LAUGH   9
TO MAKE ONE TEXTURE OF FADED BROWN. . . . . 25 IN HARDWOOD GROVES   3
RELEASE ONE LEAF AT BREAK OF DAY; . . . . 27 OCTOBER   12
ONE FROM OUR TREES, ONE FAR AWAY. . . . . 27 OCTOBER   14
TO RAVEL THEM ONE BY ONE . . . . 30 RELUCTANCE   9
WHERE THEY HAVE LEFT NOT ONE STONE ON A STONE, ... 33 MENDING WALL   7
NO ONE HAS SEEN THEM MADE OR HEARD THEM MADE, ... 33 MENDING WALL   10
ONE ON A SIDE. IT COMES TO LITTLE MORE: . . . . 33 MENDING WALL   22
"I KNOW, THAT'S SILAS' ONE ACCOMPLISHMENT. . . . . . . 37 DEATH OF THE HIRED MAN   88
ONE OF THE GREAT SIGHTS GOING IS TO SEE . . . . 42 THE MOUNTAIN   50
SHELVES ONE COULD REST A KNEE ON GETTING UP-- . . . . 42 THE MOUNTAIN   59
ONE TIME I ASKED A FELLOW CLIMBING IT . . . . 43 THE MOUNTAIN   73
"CAN ONE WALK AROUND IT? WOULD IT BE TOO FAR?" . . . . 43 THE MOUNTAIN   92
AND CARS THAT SHOCK AND RATTLE--AND ONE HOTEL. . . . . 45 A HUNDRED COLLARS   22
AT THE LAST ONE OF WHICH HE KNOCKED AND ENTERED. . . . 45 A HUNDRED COLLARS   35
WHAT MAKES YOU STAND THERE ON ONE LEG LIKE THAT? . . . 47 A HUNDRED COLLARS   69
I'VE SPOILED JEMIMA IN MORE WAYS THAN ONE. . . . . . . 49 A HUNDRED COLLARS   141
"ONE WOULD SUPPOSE THEY MIGHT NOT BE AS GLAD . . . . . 49 A HUNDRED COLLARS   149
THERE ARE THREE STONES OF SLATE AND ONE OF MARBLE, . . 52 HOME BURIAL   26
'THREE FOGGY MORNINGS AND ONE RAINY DAY . . . . 54 HOME BURIAL   92
NO, FROM THE TIME WHEN ONE IS SICK TO DEATH, ... 54 HOME BURIAL   100
ONE IS ALONE, AND HE DIES MORE ALONE. . . . . 54 HOME BURIAL   101
BUT BEFORE ONE IS IN IT, THEIR MINDS ARE TURNED . . . 54 HOME BURIAL   103
"PRETTY," HE SAID. "COME IN. NO ONE WILL CARE." . . . 55 THE BLACK COTTAGE   11
THEY LIVE SO FAR AWAY--ONE IS OUT WEST-- . . . . 55 THE BLACK COTTAGE   19
ONE WASN'T LONG IN LEARNING THAT SHE THOUGHT, ... 56 THE BLACK COTTAGE   54
NO ONE WOULD COVET IT OR THINK IT WORTH . . . . 58 THE BLACK COTTAGE   117
IN THE CAVERNOUS PAIL OF THE FIRST ONE TO COME! . . . 59 BLUEBERRIES   5
AND THE AIR OF THE YOUNGSTERS! NOT ONE OF THEM TURNED, 61 BLUEBERRIES   58
I MET THEM ONE DAY AND EACH HAD A FLOWER . . . . 61 BLUEBERRIES   64
HOW WE USED TO PICK BERRIES: WE TOOK ONE LOOK ROUND, . 62 BLUEBERRIES   85
'WELL, ONE OF US IS.' FOR COMPLAINING IT FLEW . . . . 62 BLUEBERRIES   90
LEN SAYS ONE STEADY PULL MORE OUGHT TO DO IT. . . . . 64 A SERVANT TO SERVANTS   55
ONE CAN SEE WHAT WILL TROUBLE . . . . 69 AFTER APPLE-PICKING   37
ONE HELPER, THRUSTING PITCHFORK IN THE GROUND, ... 69 THE CODE   7
MARCHED HIMSELF OFF THE FIELD AND HOME. ONE STAYED. . 69 THE CODE   8
"YOU DIDN'T KNOW. BUT JAMES IS ONE BIG FOOL. . . . . . 70 THE CODE   15
DOING THE HAYING. NO ONE LIKED THE BOSS. . . . . 70 THE CODE   32
HE WAS ONE OF THE KIND SPORTS CALL A SPIDER, ... 70 THE CODE   33
DAYLIGHT AND LANTERN-LIGHT WERE ONE TO HIM: . . . . . 71 THE CODE   41
ONE OF THE BOYS SINGS OUT, 'WHERE'S THE OLD MAN?' . . 72 THE CODE   83
THERE WAS NO ONE THAT DARED TO STIR HIM UP, ... 72 THE CODE   100
ONLY ONE FROM A FARM NOT FAR AWAY . . . . 74 THE GENERATIONS OF MEN   25
ONE, AND ONE OTHER, YES, FOR THERE WERE TWO. . . . . . 74 THE GENERATIONS OF MEN   28
OF THE ONE BEARING IT DONE IN DETAIL-- . . . . 74 THE GENERATIONS OF MEN   41
AS ONE WHO CLASPS HER HEART. THEY LAUGHED TOGETHER. . 74 THE GENERATIONS OF MEN   44
"ONE OUGHT NOT TO BE THROWN INTO CONFUSION . . . . . . 75 THE GENERATIONS OF MEN   58
NO ONE WENT HOME THAT WAY, THE ONLY HOUSE . . . . . . 76 THE GENERATIONS OF MEN   73
"FOUR CARDS: ONE YOURS, THREE MINE (ONE FOR EACH BRANCH 76 THE GENERATIONS OF MEN 80
NOR GRANNY'S, SURELY. CALL UP ONE OF THEM. . . . . . . 79 THE GENERATIONS OF MEN   175
ONE MUSTN'T BEAR TOO HARD ON THE NEWCOMERS, ... 80 THE GENERATIONS OF MEN   188
HE AND I ONLY HINDER ONE ANOTHER. . . . . 82 THE HOUSEKEEPER   36
AND NO ONE HERE BUT HENS BLOWING ABOUT. . . . . 83 THE HOUSEKEEPER   47
NO ONE WILL EVER LIVE ON IT AGAIN. . . . . 83 THE HOUSEKEEPER   49
COULDN'T ONE TALK TO HER? WHAT DOES SHE SAY? . . . . . 83 THE HOUSEKEEPER   72
ONE THING YOU CAN'T HELP LIKING ABOUT JOHN, ... 85 THE HOUSEKEEPER   115
TWO AT A TIME'S THE RULE, ONE ON EACH ARM, ... 85 THE HOUSEKEEPER   129
THE UPPER SHELF, THE TIN BOX. THAT'S THE ONE. . . . . 86 THE HOUSEKEEPER   144
FOR FIFTY DOLLARS FOR ONE LANGSHANG COCK-- . . . . . . 86 THE HOUSEKEEPER   146
"NOT IN A GLASS CASE, THEN?" / "HE'D NEED A TALL ONE: . 86 THE HOUSEKEEPER   148
"ESTELLE'S THE ONE. YOU NEEDN'T TALK TO ME." . . . . . 87 THE HOUSEKEEPER   164
AT ONE DOOR AS WE ENTERED AT ANOTHER. . . . . 89 THE FEAR   21
IF THE TIME'S COME TO FACE IT, I'M THE ONE . . . . . . 90 THE FEAR   36
"I'LL BE THE ONE, IF ANYBODY GOES! . . . . 91 THE FEAR   54
"THERE'S NO ONE; SO YOU'RE WRONG," HE SAID. / "THERE IS.-- 91 THE FEAR   64
OF AT LEAST ONE LONG-AFTER-BEDTIME WALK. . . . . 92 THE FEAR   83
ONE OUGHT AS A GOOD VILLAGER TO LIKE IT. . . . . 94 THE SELF-SEEKER   44
FIVE HUNDRED--FIVE--FIVE! ONE, TWO, THREE, FOUR,FIVE. 94 THE SELF-SEEKER   59
"YES, THAT'S ONE WAY TO PUT IT--ALL THE FLOWERS . . . 95 THE SELF-SEEKER   67
THEY NEVER EARNED ME SO MUCH AS ONE CENT: . . . . . . 95 THE SELF-SEEKER   71
THE BROKEN ONE SAW ANNE. "WHY, HERE IS ANNE. . . . . . 96 THE SELF-SEEKER   103
OF LITTLE FINGERS ALL KEPT DOWN BUT ONE, ... 98 THE SELF-SEEKER   156
OF WHAT SHE'S LOST: SHE GOES DOWN ON ONE KNEE . . . . 98 THE SELF-SEEKER   160
I'M A GREAT BOY TO THINK OF NUMBER ONE. . . . . 99 THE SELF-SEEKER   177
THE BROKEN ONE WAS TWISTED IN HIS BED. . . . . 100 THE SELF-SEEKER   208
ONE OF YOU HOLD MY HEAD UP FROM THE PILLOW." . . . . . 100 THE SELF-SEEKER   215
OUT WALKING IN THE FROZEN SWAMP ONE GRAY DAY, ... 101 THE WOOD-PILE   1
ONE FOOT WENT THROUGH. THE VIEW WAS ALL IN LINES . . . 101 THE WOOD-PILE   5
THE WHITE ONE IN HIS TAIL; LIKE ONE WHO TAKES . . . . 101 THE WOOD-PILE   15
ONE FLIGHT OUT SIDEWAYS WOULD HAVE UNDECEIVED HIM. . . 101 THE WOOD-PILE   17
WHAT HELD IT, THOUGH, ON ONE SIDE WAS A TREE . . . . . 102 THE WOOD-PILE   32
STILL GROWING, AND ON ONE A STAKE AND PROP, ... 102 THE WOOD-PILE   33
NO ONE AT ALL WITH WHOM TO TALK, ... 102 GOOD HOURS   2
AND BE ONE TRAVELER, LONG I STOOD . . . . 105 THE ROAD NOT TAKEN   3
AND LOOKED DOWN ONE AS FAR AS I COULD . . . . 105 THE ROAD NOT TAKEN   4
I TOOK THE ONE LESS TRAVELED BY, ... 105 THE ROAD NOT TAKEN   19
OR PAUSED TO SAY BENEATH SOME LOVELIER ONE, ... 107 CHRISTMAS TREES   37
TOO BAD I COULDN'T LAY ONE IN A LETTER. . . . . 107 CHRISTMAS TREES   58
I CAN'T HELP WISHING I COULD SEND YOU ONE . . . . . . 107 CHRISTMAS TREES   59

ONE (CONTINUED)
A LIGHT HE WAS TO NO ONE BUT HIMSELF . . . . 108 OLD MAN'S WINTER NIGHT   15
ONE AGED MAN--ONE MAN--CAN'T KEEP A HOUSE, ... 108 OLD MAN'S WINTER NIGHT   26
AND EVERY CRASH MEANT ONE LESS TO RETURN . . . . . . 112 IN THE HOME STRETCH . 57
"A FIT!" SAID ONE, AND BANGED A STOVEPIPE SHOULDER. . . . 113 IN THE HOME STRETCH . 90
"GOD!" ONE SAID WILDLY, AND, WHEN NO ONE SPOKE: . . . . 114 IN THE HOME STRETCH . 99
THE MEALS WE'VE HAD NO ONE CAN TAKE FROM US. . . . . . 115 IN THE HOME STRETCH . 139
TO EMPTY ONE HOUSE OF ALL HOUSEHOLD GOODS . . . . . . 116 IN THE HOME STRETCH . 160
BUT MORE THAN ONE AS YET. YOUR PARASOL . . . . 119 MEETING AND PASSING . 8
POINTED THE DECIMAL OFF WITH ONE DEEP THRUST. . . . . 119 MEETING AND PASSING . 9
MID-SUMMER IS TO SPRING AS ONE TO TEN. . . . . 120 THE OVEN BIRD   . . . 5
ONE BY ONE HE SUBDUED HIS FATHER'S TREES . . . . . . 122 BIRCHES   28
AND NOT ONE BUT HUNG LIMP, NOT ONE WAS LEFT . . . . . 122 BIRCHES   31
BROKEN ACROSS IT, AND ONE EYE IS WEEPING . . . . . . 122 BIRCHES   46
ONE COULD DO WORSE THAN BE A SWINGER OF BIRCHES. . . . 122 BIRCHES   59
ONE OUGHT NOT TO HAVE TO CARE . . . . 126 LONELINESS   1
TOO GLAD FOR THE ONE THING . . . . 126 LONELINESS   8
AND ONLY ONE OF THE TWO . . . . 128 THE OFT-REPEATED DREAM 10
DIVIDE IT? NO! BUT BURN IT AS ONE PILE . . . . 129 THE BONFIRE   9
I WON! BUT I'M SURE NO ONE EVER SPREAD . . . . 132 THE BONFIRE   81
BUT THERE WAS NO ONE. I WAS SOMEWHERE WONDERING . . . 132 THE BONFIRE   90
LIKES TO TELL HOW ONE SPRING . . . . 133 A GIRL'S GARDEN   . . . 2
ONE DAY SHE ASKED HER FATHER . . . . 133 A GIRL'S GARDEN   . . . 5
SHE SAYS SHE THINKS SHE PLANTED ONE . . . . 134 A GIRL'S GARDEN   . . . 27
WE DID FIND ONE NASTURTIUM . . . . 135 LOCKED OUT   8
FIVE MOUNTAIN RANGES ONE BEHIND THE OTHER . . . . . . 136 "OUT,OUT--"   5
NO ONE BELIEVED. THEY LISTENED AT HIS HEART. . . . . 137 "OUT,OUT--"   31
WERE NOT THE ONE DEAD, TURNED TO THEIR AFFAIRS. . . . 137 "OUT,OUT--"   34
HIS WILD DESCENT FROM THERE ONE NIGHT, ... 137 BROWN'S DESCENT   . . . 6
BUT HE GAVE NO ONE ELSE A LAUGHER'S LICENSE. . . . . 142 THE VANISHING RED . . 4
FROM ONE WHO HAD NO RIGHT TO BE HEARD FROM. . . . . . 142 THE VANISHING RED . . 18
HE MAY BE GOOD, BUT ONE THING'S SURE, HE'S TOUGH." . . 145 SNOW   71
"ONE THING: HE DIDN'T DRAG GOD INTO IT." . . . . . . 146 SNOW   81
OUT OF ONE OF THOSE PIOUS SCALAWAGS." . . . . 146 SNOW   92
ONE OF THE LIES WOULD MAKE IT OUT THAT NOTHING . . . . 147 SNOW   129
I'LL HAVE TO TURN THE LEAF IF NO ONE ELSE WILL. . . . 148 SNOW   151
IN ONE ANOTHER, AND HAD GONE TO SLEEP . . . . 148 SNOW   163
TO BREATHE THE AIR ONE WINTER--HAD A ROOM . . . . . . 149 SNOW   174
DOWN AT THE AVERYS'? WELL, ONE SUNNY MORNING . . . . 149 SNOW   175
"BUT WHY, WHEN NO ONE WANTS YOU TO, GO ON? . . . . . 151 SNOW   233
WHAT? WE'VE FOUND OUT IN ONE HOUR MORE ABOUT HIM . . . 152 SNOW   252
"ONE OF TWO THINGS, EITHER SHE'S GONE TO BED . . . . 154 SNOW   311
"THERE'S ONLY ONE THING POSSIBLE TO MAKE, ... 155 SNOW   322
WE'VE HAD A SHARE IN ONE NIGHT OF HIS LIFE. . . . . . 156 SNOW   349
UNTIL I ASKED FOR ONE TO STEADY HIM. . . . . 160 NEW HAMPSHIRE   . . . 32
ONE EACH OF EVERYTHING AS IN A SHOWCASE, ... 161 NEW HAMPSHIRE   . . . 62
SHE HAD ONE PRESIDENT. (PRONOUNCE HIM PURSE, ... 161 NEW HAMPSHIRE   . . . 64
HE'S YOUR ONE CHANCE TO SCORE AGAINST THE STATE.) . . 161 NEW HAMPSHIRE   . . . 66
SHE HAD ONE DANIEL WEBSTER. HE WAS ALL . . . . 161 NEW HAMPSHIRE   . . . 67
I CALL HER OLD. SHE HAS ONE FAMILY . . . . 161 NEW HAMPSHIRE   . . . 70
TODAY AN HONORED ONE IN NOTTINGHAM. . . . . 161 NEW HAMPSHIRE   . . . 86
ONE REAL REFORMER WHO WOULD CHANGE THE WORLD . . . . 162 NEW HAMPSHIRE   . . . 94
AND SHE HAS ONE I DON'T KNOW WHAT TO CALL HIM, ... 162 NEW HAMPSHIRE   . . . 100
WHAT GOLD MORE INNOCENT COULD ONE HAVE ASKED FOR? . . 162 NEW HAMPSHIRE   . . . 115
ONE OF MY CHILDREN RANGING AFTER ROCKS . . . . 162 NEW HAMPSHIRE   . . . 116
SHE HAS ONE WITCH--OLD STYLE. SHE LIVES IN COLEBROOK. 163 NEW HAMPSHIRE   . . . 125
ONE EACH OF EVERYTHING AS IN A SHOWCASE. . . . . . . 163 NEW HAMPSHIRE   . . . 144
SHE'S ONE OF THE TWO BEST STATES IN THE UNION. . . . 164 NEW HAMPSHIRE   . . . 175
ONE THICK WHERE ONE IS THIN AND VICE VERSA. . . . . . 164 NEW HAMPSHIRE   . . . 182
AND I REMEMBER ONE WHOSE NAME APPEARED . . . . 165 NEW HAMPSHIRE   . . . 193
FOR ART'S SAKE ONE COULD ALMOST WISH THEM WORSE . . . 167 NEW HAMPSHIRE   . . . 266
THE CULT OF ONE WHO OWNED HIMSELF "A FOILED . . . . . 171 NEW HAMPSHIRE   . . . 383
SCARCELY A MILE BUT THAT I COME ON ONE, ... 171 NEW HAMPSHIRE   . . . 390
WELL, IF I HAVE TO CHOOSE ONE OR THE OTHER, ... 172 NEW HAMPSHIRE   . . . 407
NEVER TELL ME THAT NOT ONE STAR OF ALL . . . . 172 A STAR IN A STONEBOAT   . 1
SOME LABORER FOUND ONE FADED AND STONE-COLD, ... 172 A STAR IN A STONEBOAT   . 4
THE ONE THING PALPABLE BESIDES THE SOUL . . . . . . 172 A STAR IN A STONEBOAT   . 11
IT BROODED ANT EGGS, AND HAD ONE LARGE WING, ... 172 A STAR IN A STONEBOAT   . 14
ONE NOT SO LARGE FOR FLYING IN A RING, ... 172 A STAR IN A STONEBOAT   . 15
OF THE ONE WORLD COMPLETE IN ANY SIZE . . . . 174 A STAR IN A STONEBOAT   . 56
I CAME AN ERRAND ONE CLOUD-BLOWING EVENING . . . . . 174 THE CENSUS-TAKER   . . 1
OF ONE ROOM AND ONE WINDOW AND ONE DOOR, ... 174 THE CENSUS-TAKER   . . 3
PASSED IN AND SLAMMED IT SHUT EACH ONE BEHIND HIM . . 175 THE CENSUS-TAKER   . . 29
FOR THE NEXT ONE TO OPEN FOR HIMSELF. . . . . 175 THE CENSUS-TAKER   . . 30
AND DOWN BY ONE SIDE WHERE IT LACKED A LEG. . . . . . 175 THE CENSUS-TAKER   . . 37
THIS HOUSE IN ONE YEAR FALLEN TO DECAY . . . . 176 THE CENSUS-TAKER   . . 50
UNLESS TO FIND THAT THERE WAS NO ONE THERE . . . . . 176 THE CENSUS-TAKER   . . 55
"WHAT DO YOU WANT WITH ONE OF THOSE BLAME THINGS?" . . 177 THE STAR-SPLITTER . . 20
I ASKED HIM WELL BEFOREHAND. "DON'T YOU GET ONE!" . . 177 THE STAR-SPLITTER . . 21
"I'LL HAVE ONE IF I SELL MY FARM TO BUY IT." . . . . 177 THE STAR-SPLITTER . . 25
SEEMS TO ME OWES IT TO THE TOWN TO KEEP ONE. . . . . 177 THE STAR-SPLITTER . . 36
IF ONE BY ONE WE COUNTED PEOPLE OUT . . . . 177 THE STAR-SPLITTER . . 44
TO GET SO WE HAD NO ONE LEFT TO LIVE WITH. . . . . . 178 THE STAR-SPLITTER . . 46
OUR THIEF, THE ONE WHO DOES OUR STEALING FROM US, . . 178 THE STAR-SPLITTER . . 48
OF BEING GIVEN ONE FOR CHRISTMAS GIFT, ... 178 THE STAR-SPLITTER . . 55
TO FIND HIMSELF IN ONE. WELL, ALL WE SAID WAS . . . 178 THE STAR-SPLITTER . . 57
INSTEAD OF A NEW-FASHIONED ONE AT AUCTION? . . . . . 178 THE STAR-SPLITTER . . 65
AT ONE STROKE (OF A MATCH), BRAD HAD TO TURN . . . . 178 THE STAR-SPLITTER . . 67
WITH ONE STROKE OF YOUR FINGER IN THE MIDDLE. . . . . 179 THE STAR-SPLITTER . . 91
IT'S A STAR-SPLITTER IF THERE EVER WAS ONE, ... 179 THE STAR-SPLITTER . . 92
ONE COMING THIS WAY INTO LIFE, AND ONE . . . . 180 MAPLE   12
IT CAME BACK VAGUELY AT THE GLASS ONE DAY, ... 181 MAPLE   40
THE HOUSE ONE STORY HIGH IN FRONT, THREE STORIES . . 181 MAPLE   57
(THE HOUSE ONE STORY HIGH IN FRONT, THREE STORIES . . 182 MAPLE   98
IT MAY HAVE BEEN THEIR ONE LAPSE INTO FANCY . . . . . 183 MAPLE   120
"JUST ONE LOOK MORE WITH WHAT YOU SAY IN MIND, . . . 184 MAPLE   131
THEY CLUNG TO WHAT ONE HAD SEEN IN THE OTHER . . . . 184 MAPLE   134
BUT ITS AGE KEPT THEM FROM CONSIDERING THIS ONE. . . 184 MAPLE   148

ONE (CONTINUED)
THIS WAS A MAN, BAPTISTE, WHO STOLE ONE DAY . . . . . . 185 THE AX-HELVE 6
"YOU GIVE HER ONE GOOD CRACK, SHE'S SNAP RAGHT OFF. . . . 186 THE AX-HELVE 26
"COME ON MY HOUSE AND I PUT YOU ONE IN . . . . 186 THE AX-HELVE 29
ONE BACK AND FORWARD, IN AND OUT OF SHADOW, ... 186 THE AX-HELVE 48
THAT GOT HER NOWHERE; ONE MORE GRADUAL, ... 187 THE AX-HELVE 49
HAVE GOT IT ONE STEP FROM THE STARTING PLACE. . . . . . . 189 THE GRINDSTONE . . . 7
ONE SUMMER DAY, ALL DAY I DROVE IT HARD, ... 189 THE GRINDSTONE . . . 23
THE ONE WHO HELD THE WHEEL BACK OR THE ONE . . . . 190 THE GRINDSTONE . . . 46
OR SO OF HAVING ONE, AND THEN BEEN JILTED; . . . . 191 PAUL'S WIFE 7
OTHERS BECAUSE HE'D HAD ONE ONCE, A GOOD ONE, ... 191 PAUL'S WIFE 8
AND OTHERS STILL BECAUSE HE HAD ONE NOW . . . . 191 PAUL'S WIFE 10
NO ONE WAS ANXIOUS TO GET RID OF PAUL. . . . . 191 PAUL'S WIFE 16
AND THERE WAS ONE MORE NOT SO FAIR TO PAUL: . . . . 192 PAUL'S WIFE 35
THE ONE ABOUT HIS JUMPING SO'S TO LAND . . . . 192 PAUL'S WIFE 50
EQUALLY WITH MY WEIGHT IN GRAPES, ONE AUTUMN, ... 196 WILD GRAPES 5
ONE OF THEM FIVE YEARS YOUNGER THAN I LOOK-- . . . . . . 196 WILD GRAPES 18
ONE DAY MY BROTHER LED ME TO A GLADE . . . . 196 WILD GRAPES 19
ONE BUNCH OF THEM, AND THERE BEGAN TO BE . . . . 197 WILD GRAPES 25
IN ONE WAY: YOU HAVE ONE MORE STEM TO CLING BY, ... 198 WILD GRAPES 70
ONE BY ONE I LOST OFF MY HAT AND SHOES, ... 198 WILD GRAPES 72
ONE MAN'S THREE WOMEN IN A BURIAL ROW . . . . 199 PLACE FOR A THIRD . . 7
AND NO ONE SEEM NEGLECTING OR NEGLECTED? . . . . 200 PLACE FOR A THIRD . . 29
THEY SAT. SHE CAST ONE DULL, OLD LOOK AT HIM, ... 201 PLACE FOR A THIRD . . 52
UP ONE FLIGHT FROM THE CELLAR TO THE KITCHEN, ... 203 THE WITCH OF COOS . . 30
THE WAY A MAN WITH ONE LEG AND A CRUTCH, ... 204 THE WITCH OF COOS . . 52
THEN HE CAME AT ME WITH ONE HAND OUTSTRETCHED, ... 204 THE WITCH OF COOS . . 75
(WHERE DID I SEE ONE OF THOSE PIECES LATELY? . . . . . . 205 THE WITCH OF COOS . . 80
TO NO ONE ANYMORE SINCE TOFFILE DIED. . . . . 206 THE WITCH OF COOS . . 131
WE WERE ABOUT IT ONE NIGHT IN THE CELLAR. . . . . 206 THE WITCH OF COOS . . 142
THEY DON'T DISPOSE ME, EITHER ONE OF THEM, ... 207 PAUPER WITCH OF GRAFTON 6
COULDN'T HAVE BEEN THE ONE THEY SAY WAS UP . . . . 207 PAUPER WITCH OF GRAFTON 17
ONE OF THE TIMES WAS WHEN 'TWAS IN THE WARRANT . . . . . 208 PAUPER WITCH OF GRAFTON 23
IN FRONT OF ONE TOWN HALL, I'D LEFT HIM HITCHED . . . . . 208 PAUPER WITCH OF GRAFTON 50
IN FRONT OF EVERY ONE IN GRAFTON COUNTY. . . . . 209 PAUPER WITCH OF GRAFTON 51
LAST NIGHT WAS ONE OF HER NIGHTS OUT. SHE'S KITING. . . . 209 PAUPER WITCH OF GRAFTON 81
IN ONE HIMSELF PERHAPS. . . . . 211 AN EMPTY THREAT . . . 29
UNFORTUNATELY ALL OF ONE KIND, THOUGH. . . . . 216 A FOUNTAIN, A BOTTLE . 99
HAVING TRIED ONE, HAD DROPPED IT AT HIS FEET . . . . . . 217 A FOUNTAIN, A BOTTLE . 119
"TAKE ONE," OLD DAVIS BADE ME GRACIOUSLY. . . . . 217 A FOUNTAIN, A BOTTLE . 123
GOOD-LOOKING BOOKS LIKE THAT." HE PICKED ONE FRESH . . . 217 A FOUNTAIN, A BOTTLE . 125
HE READ IN ONE AND I READ IN ANOTHER, ... 217 A FOUNTAIN, A BOTTLE . 128
AT HAVING EASED HER HEART OF ONE MORE COPY-- . . . . . . 217 A FOUNTAIN, A BOTTLE . 135
ONE DOWN ONE STREET, ... 218 I WILL SING YOU ONE-O . 12
ONE DOWN ANOTHER, ... 218 I WILL SING YOU ONE-O . 13
THEN CAME ONE KNOCK! . . . . 218 I WILL SING YOU ONE-O . 23
THE TOWER SAID, "ONE!" . . . . 218 I WILL SING YOU ONE-O . 27
IN THAT GRAVE ONE . . . . 219 I WILL SING YOU ONE-O . 38
IN ONE SELF STATION. . . . . 219 I WILL SING YOU ONE-O . 67
HOW NO ONE DEAD WILL SEEM TO COME. . . . . 221 IN A DISUSED GRAVEYARD 11
AND ONE THING MORE THAT WAS NOT THEN TO SAY: . . . . . . 222 TO E.T. 11
A LITTLE MORGAN HAD ONE FOREFOOT ON THE WALL, ... 223 THE RUNAWAY 3
ONE DROP FELL FROM A FERN, AND LO, ⊕ RIPPLE . . . . 225 FOR ONCE SOMETHING . . 12
AS ONE WHO OVERTAKEN BY THE END . . . . 226 THE ONSET 7
BUT ONE THING ABOUT IT, IT MUSTN'T GET WARM. . . . . . . 228 GOOD-BY AND KEEP COLD . 16
IN ONE LAST LOOK THE WAY THEY MUST NOT GO, ... 229 TWO LOOK AT TWO . . . 10
AS IF THE EARTH IN ONE UNLOOKED-FOR FAVOR . . . . 230 TWO LOOK AT TWO . . . 41
I ASK AS ONE WHO KNEW THE BROOK, ITS STRENGTH . . . . . . 231 A BROOK IN THE CITY . 5
NO ONE WOULD KNOW EXCEPT IN ANCIENT MAPS . . . . 231 A BROOK IN THE CITY . 20
(AND I KNOW OF ONE THAT DIDN'T THRIVE) . . . . 232 THE KITCHEN CHIMNEY . 11
MYSELF AS ONE HIS OWN PRETENSE DECEIVES; . . . . 233 A BOUNDLESS MOMENT . . 10
OUTSIDE THE SUGARHOUSE ONE NIGHT FOR CHOICE, ... 234 EVENING A SUGAR ORCHARD 2
AND CAUGHT ONE SILVER LIZARD BY THE TAIL, ... 237 A HILLSIDE THAW . . . 10
AND PUT MY FOOT ON ONE WITHOUT AVAIL, ... 237 A HILLSIDE THAW . . . 11
TO MAKE A LEAF, IF THERE HAD BEEN ONE, STIR. . . . . . . 238 A HILLSIDE THAW . . . 32
ONE LIZARD AT THE END OF EVERY RAY. . . . . 238 A HILLSIDE THAW . . . 34
AND, TIRED OF AIMLESS CIRCLING IN ONE PLACE, ... 238 ON A TREE FALLEN ACROSS 13
THE GRASS LAY FLATTENED UNDER ONE GREAT TREAD. . . . . . 239 OUR SINGING STRENGTH . 12
TO ANY ONE PLACE COVER US WITH SONG. . . . . 239 OUR SINGING STRENGTH . 20
WHERE ONE FALSE WING BEAT WOULD HAVE BROUGHT DOWN ALL, . . 240 OUR SINGING STRENGTH . 43
ONE SUCH STORM IN A LIFETIME COULDN'T TEACH THEM . . . . 240 OUR SINGING STRENGTH . 46
NO MORE IT OPENED WITH ALL ONE END . . . . 241 NEED OF BEING VERSED . 9
ONE HAD TO BE VERSED IN COUNTRY THINGS . . . . 242 NEED OF BEING VERSED . 23
ALONE, OR IN ONE ORNAMENT COMBINING . . . . 245 THE FREEDOM OF THE MOON 5
WITH ONE FIRST-WATER STAR ALMOST AS SHINING. . . . . . . 245 THE FREEDOM OF THE MOON 6
HOLDING THE CURVE OF ONE POSITION, ... 247 DEVOTION 3
IS ALL THE SMOKE FROM ONE POOR HOUSE ALONE, ... 248 THE COCOON 5
WITH BUT ONE CHIMNEY IT CAN CALL ITS OWN; . . . . 248 THE COCOON 6
NO ONE FOR HOURS HAS SET A FOOT OUTDOORS . . . . 248 THE COCOON 9
THAT NO ONE ON EARTH WILL EVER FIND? . . . . 248 A PASSING GLIMPSE . . 10
AND I WAS ONE OF THE CHILDREN TOLD . . . . 249 A PECK OF GOLD . . . 3
BUT I WAS ONE OF THE CHILDREN TOLD . . . . 249 A PECK OF GOLD . . . 7
AND I WAS ONE OF THE CHILDREN TOLD, ... 249 A PECK OF GOLD . . . 11
ONE BIRD BEGINS TO CLOSE A FADED EYE; . . . . 249 ACCEPTANCE 7
WORD I HAD NO ONE LEFT BUT GOD. . . . . 251 BEREFT 16
WELL, WE SHOULD SEE WHICH ONE WOULD WIN, ... 253 THE THATCH 8
WE SHOULD SEE WHICH ONE WOULD BE FIRST TO YIELD. . . . . 253 THE THATCH 9
ONE LEVEL HIGHER THAN THE EARTH BELOW, ... 254 A WINTER EDEN 6
ONE LEVEL NEARER HEAVEN OVERHEAD, ... 254 A WINTER EDEN 7
I HAVE BEEN ONE ACQUAINTED WITH THE NIGHT. . . . . 255 ACQUAINTED WITH NIGHT . 1
ONE LUMINARY CLOCK AGAINST THE SKY. . . . . 255 ACQUAINTED WITH NIGHT . 12
I HAVE BEEN ONE ACQUAINTED WITH THE NIGHT. . . . . 255 ACQUAINTED WITH NIGHT . 14
THEN SEND SOME ONE WITH EYES TO SEE . . . . 257 THE LOVELY BE CHOOSERS 46
BE HER LAST JOY HER HEART'S GOING OUT TO THIS ONE . . . . 257 THE LOVELY BE CHOOSERS 50
FLUNG BACKWARD ON ITSELF IN ONE WHITE WAVE, ... 258 WEST-RUNNING BROOK . . 20
AND PIROUETTE, FOREVER IN ONE PLACE, ... 259 WEST-RUNNING BROOK . . 46
FOR THE ONE MORE CAST-OFF SHELL, ... 261 SAND DUNES 16
WITH A STAR IN ONE EYE, ... 261 CANIS MAJOR 3

PAGE TITLE LINE

ONE (CONTINUED)

	PAGE	TITLE	LINE
WAS COUNTING WINTER DINNERS, ONE A HILL,	263	THE INVESTMENT	7
I'M NOT THE ONE FOR PUTTING OFF THE PROOF.	265	DUST IN THE EYES	3
THERE WAS ONE TIME AND ONLY THE ONE	266	SITTING BY A BUSH	5
AND FROM THAT ONE INTAKE OF FIRE	266	SITTING BY A BUSH	7
ONE IMPULSE PERSISTS AS OUR BREATH;	266	SITTING BY A BUSH	19
LEAVING ON ONE WIRE TOOTH A LOCK OF HAIR.	269	THE BEAR	9
THE TELESCOPE AT ONE END OF HIS BEAT,	269	THE BEAR	18
AT ONE EXTREME AGREEING WITH ONE GREEK,	269	THE BEAR	30
AND PROBING WITH ONE FINGER NOT TOO ROUGH,	270	THE EGG AND THE MACHINE	21
IF THERE WAS ONE EGG IN IT THERE WERE NINE,	270	THE EGG AND THE MACHINE	24
ONE FAILED TO MAKE THE CLOSING GATE.	273	A LONE STRIKER	4
THAT ON THE ONE WHO CAME TOO LATE	273	A LONE STRIKER	6
AND IF ONE BROKE BY ANY CHANCE,	273	A LONE STRIKER	24
AND IF HE STOOD ON ONE OF THESE,	274	A LONE STRIKER	38
AND ONE OF THEM PUT ME OFF MY AIM	275	TWO TRAMPS IN MUD TIME	3
YOU'RE ONE MONTH ON IN THE MIDDLE OF MAY.	275	TWO TRAMPS IN MUD TIME	20
AS MY TWO EYES MAKE ONE IN SIGHT.	277	TWO TRAMPS IN MUD TIME	68
ONLY WHERE LOVE AND NEED ARE ONE,	277	TWO TRAMPS IN MUD TIME	69
ONE WHO WOULD NEVER HANG ABOVE A BOOKCASE	278	THE WHITE-TAILED HORNET	17
IN AT ONE DOOR PERHAPS AND OUT ANOTHER,	278	THE WHITE-TAILED HORNET	25
THE ANSWER IS THIS ONE HAS BEEN--	279	BLUE RIBBON AT AMESBURY	4
WITH ONE A SEWELL MIGHT HAVE PAINTED.	280	BLUE RIBBON AT AMESBURY	12
THE ONE WHO GAVE HER ANKLE-BAND,	280	BLUE RIBBON AT AMESBURY	17
ONE THING HAS A SHELVING BANK,	281	A DRUMLIN WOODCHUCK	1
AS ONE WHO SHREWDLY PRETENDS.	282	A DRUMLIN WOODCHUCK	11
AND TWO WAS ALL HE COUNTED (ONE HE MISSED);	283	THE GOLD HESPERIDEE	11
ONE MORE, HE THOUGHT, TO TAKE HIM SAFELY THROUGH.	283	THE GOLD HESPERIDEE	26
BUT ONE DAY WHEN THE FOLIAGE ALL WENT SWISH.	284	THE GOLD HESPERIDEE	32
FROM WITNESSING THE FAULT OF ONE SO PROUD.	284	THE GOLD HESPERIDEE	57
JUST ONE TO INQUIRE WHAT A FARMER'S PRICES ARE.	287	A ROADSIDE STAND	38
AND ONE DID STOP, BUT ONLY TO PLOW UP GRASS	287	A ROADSIDE STAND	39
TO PUT THESE PEOPLE AT ONE STROKE OUT OF THEIR PAIN.	287	A ROADSIDE STAND	48
YET IF HE ENCOUNTERED ONE	288	DEPARTMENTAL	8
ONE CROSSING WITH HURRIED TREAD	288	DEPARTMENTAL	14
THE BODY OF ONE OF THEIR DEAD	288	DEPARTMENTAL	15
NO ONE STANDS ROUND TO STARE.	289	DEPARTMENTAL	40
WELL, THE MOON AFTER THAT, CAME ONE AT LAST	289	OLD BARN AT THE BOTTOM	6
ONE NIGHT (HE TOLD ME). AND THE BARN HE MEANT	289	OLD BARN AT THE BOTTOM	20
WAS THE ONE I MEANT. OUR DETAILS AGREED.	289	OLD BARN AT THE BOTTOM	21
WHEN ONE WILL SAY, "LET US PUT IT OUT."	291	ON HEART'S BEGINNING TO	22
ONE LOOKS OUT LAST FROM THE DARKENED ROOM	291	ON HEART'S BEGINNING TO	26
AND MORE THAN ONE, TO THEIRS AKIN,	292	ON HEART'S BEGINNING TO	39
OF FIRST ONE, THEN THE OTHER, TILL IT BROUGHT	293	AT WOODWARD'S GARDENS	9
ONE PUT A THOUGHTFUL HAND UP TO HIS NOSE	293	AT WOODWARD'S GARDENS	14
I WET ONE LAST YEAR AT MONTAUK	294	A RECORD STRIDE	13
ON ONE I CAN TASTE ATLANTIC,	295	A RECORD STRIDE	23
ONE FOOT IN EACH GREAT OCEAN.	295	A RECORD STRIDE	25
THE CLOUDS, THE SOURCE OF RAIN, ONE STORMY NIGHT	295	LOST IN HEAVEN	1
NO ONE WAS BRIGHT ENOUGH TO IDENTIFY;	295	LOST IN HEAVEN	7
BUT I MAY BE ONE WHO DOES NOT CARE	296	LEAVES COMPARED WITH	5
FOR YOU TO ROLL ONE STONE	298	ON TAKING FROM THE TOP	7
THE MUD CAME IN ONE COLD	298	ON TAKING FROM THE TOP	15
TO INDUCE THE ONE SNOW ON HIS HEAD.	299	WELCOME TO THEIR BELIEF	8
BUT NEITHER ONE WAS THE THIEF	299	WELCOME TO THEIR BELIEF	15
ONE STRINGING A CHAIN OF SEED IN AN OPEN CREASE,	299	STRONG SAYING NOTHING .	7
FROM ONE ANOTHER ONCE YOU ARE AGREED	300	THE MASTER SPEED	12
ALL TURN AND LOOK ONE WAY.	301	NEITHER OUT FAR NOR IN	2
THE GROUND WAS ONE CIRCLE OF SOLID RED.	305	UNHARVESTED	10
ONE GUESS	309	ONE GUESS	T
THAT GOLD SHOULD BE THE ONE THING	311	THE VINDICTIVES	25
ONE INCA PRINCE ON THE RACK,	311	THE VINDICTIVES	41
ONE KNEW OF A BURIAL HOLE	312	THE VINDICTIVES	56
COMMANDED BY ONE SUN-PRIEST,	312	THE VINDICTIVES	73
WHERE ONE ROAD LED TO THE THRONE	313	BEARER OF EVIL TIDINGS	6
AND ONE WENT OFF TO THE MOUNTAINS	313	BEARER OF EVIL TIDINGS	7
HE TOOK THE ONE TO THE MOUNTAINS.	313	BEARER OF EVIL TIDINGS	9
ON ONE HIMALAYAN SHELF;	314	BEARER OF EVIL TIDINGS	34
ONE MISTY EVENING, ONE ANOTHER'S GUIDE,	315	IRIS BY NIGHT	1
COULD CONCENTRATE ANEW AND RISE AS ONE.	315	IRIS BY NIGHT	8
THE ONE YOU HAD THE TALK WITH, YOU REMEMBER,	316	BUILD SOIL	3
I DON'T KNOW WHAT IT WOULD BE. NO ONE KNOWS.	318	BUILD SOIL	77
PHILOSOPHIZED TOGETHER INTO ONE--	318	BUILD SOIL	79
ONE SICKNESS OF THE BODY AND THE SOUL.	318	BUILD SOIL	80
BUT THE WORST ONE OF ALL TO LEAVE UNCURBED,	319	BUILD SOIL	101
THE WORLD'S ONE GLOBE, HUMAN SOCIETY	322	BUILD SOIL	194
I ONLY SPEAK TO YOU AS ONE OF THEM.	323	BUILD SOIL	210
LET ME BE THE ONE	324	BUILD SOIL	260
ONE MORE WOULD THROW YOU ON THE RIGHT.	325	TO A THINKER	3
TWO TEARDROPS, ONE FOR EITHER EYE,	327	A MISSIVE MISSILE	11
ONE TREE, BY BEING DEEPLY WOUNDED,	331	BEECH	6
FROM ONE DAY'S PERFECT WEATHER,	333	HAPPINESS MAKES UP	14
BE ALL FROM THAT ONE DAY	333	HAPPINESS MAKES UP	20
STILL LIVED FOR ONE SONG MORE	334	COME IN	11
THE MANY DEATHS ONE MUST HAVE DIED	336	THE WIND AND THE RAIN	10
I HAVE BEEN ONE NO DWELLING COULD CONTAIN	337	THE WIND AND THE RAIN	43
AND OH, FOR ONE SO YOUNG	341	THE SUBVERTED FLOWER	65
AND I FOR ONE	343	QUEST OF PURPLE-FRINGED	26
BUT DARED NOT TELL HER ALL ONE DAY.	347	DISCOVERY OF MADEIRAS	115
SAY A FRACTION OF ONE PERCENT AT THE VERY LEAST,	349	OUR HOLD ON THE PLANET	16
BUT NO ONE EVER HEARD YOU MAKE THE CLAIM.	351	THE LESSON FOR TODAY	28
ONE MORE MILLENNIUM'S ABOUT TO END.	352	THE LESSON FOR TODAY	46
OR SHOULD I SAY THE HIGHER ONE, FOR DARK.	352	THE LESSON FOR TODAY	53
ONE AS COMPARED WITH GOD AND ONE WITH SPACE.	353	THE LESSON FOR TODAY	78
TO ANY ONE TIME, PLACE, OR HUMAN KIND.	353	THE LESSON FOR TODAY	105
ONE AGE IS LIKE ANOTHER FOR THE SOUL.	354	THE LESSON FOR TODAY	113
ONE MAN HAD LIVED ONE HUNDRED YEARS AND EIGHT.	355	THE LESSON FOR TODAY	140
GOD BLESS HIMSELF CAN NO ONE ELSE BE BLESSED.	355	THE LESSON FOR TODAY	156

ONE (CONTINUED)

I'D HAVE A SHORT ONE READY FOR MY OWN. . . . . . . 355 THE LESSON FOR TODAY . 159
YOU MAKE A LABOR OF FLIGHT FOR ONE SO AIRY, ... 356 A MOTH SEEN IN WINTER . 11
NO ONE CAN KNOW HOW GLAD I AM TO FIND . . . . 358 A CONSIDERABLE SPECK . 32
NO ONE HAS EVER FAILED THE POET RANKS . . . . 358 THE LOST FOLLOWER . . 7
TO TRY IF ONE MORE POPULAR ELECTION . . . . 358 THE LOST FOLLOWER . . 12
THE MUSE MOURNS ONE WHO WENT TO HIS RETREAT . . . . 359 THE LOST FOLLOWER . . 21
IN ONE WILD DAY OF RAIN. . . . . 359 NOVEMBER 6
LIKE ONE POSSESSED, ... 360 THE RABBIT-HUNTER . . 9
WE HAD ONE AGE OF GOLD . . . . 361 ALMOST TWO THOUSAND . 2
BUT THEY'RE ONE THING THAT SHOULD BE DONE BY HALVES. . . 363 A SEMI-REVOLUTION . . 8
I NEVER CAME UPON A BLESSED ONE. . . . . 363 AN ANSWER 2
FOR ME TO SEND YOU ONE OUT WHERE YOU LIVE . . . . . 365 OF STONES OF THE PLACE 5
I'D SHIP A SMOOTH ONE YOU COULD SLAP AND CHAFE, . . . 365 OF STONES OF THE PLACE 9
I CAME TO BUT ONE HOUSE, ... 366 NOT OF SCHOOL AGE . . 3
I MADE BUT THE ONE FRIEND. . . . . 366 NOT OF SCHOOL AGE . . 4
AT THE ONE HOUSE A CHILD WAS OUT . . . . 366 NOT OF SCHOOL AGE . . 5
AS ONE HAVING WAR-COMMAND. . . . . 366 NOT OF SCHOOL AGE . . 12
A PARENT, HIS GENTLER ONE, ... 366 NOT OF SCHOOL AGE . . 13
TO SEE IT SO, THE BRIGHT AND ONLY ONE . . . . 368 THE LITERATE FARMER AND 11
THE IDEA IS NO DOUBT TO MAKE ONE JOB . . . . 370 THE LITERATE FARMER AND 71
OF LIGHTING THE WHOLE NIGHT WITH ONE BIG BLOB . . . . 370 THE LITERATE FARMER AND 72
WE HAVE ONE LOVING AND ONE HATING HAND. . . . . . . 371 THE LITERATE FARMER AND 113
ONE STEP BACKWARD TAKEN . . . . 376 ONE STEP BACKWARD TAKEN T
BUT WITH ONE STEP BACKWARD TAKEN . . . . 377 ONE STEP BACKWARD TAKEN 10
THE ONE YOU MADE, THE OTHER ONE YOU GREW. . . . . . 382 TO AN ANCIENT . . . 2
BUT FOUND ONE IN THE DELTA OF A BROOK, ... 382 TO AN ANCIENT . . . 5
ONE IN A CAVERN WHERE YOU USED TO COOK. . . . . . . 382 TO AN ANCIENT . . . 6
SHOULD BE THE ONLY ONE; . . . . 384 MAKING CERTAIN ANYTHING 6
SOME CLUSTER ONE STAR SHORT. . . . . 384 MAKING CERTAIN ANYTHING 8
AS ONE RANKLY WARM INSIDER . . . . 384 IN THE LONG NIGHT . . 13
FROM BEING NO ONE UP TO BEING SOMEONE, ... 385 THE FEAR OF GOD . . . 2
AS A GIRL NO ONE GALLANILY ATTENDS . . . . 386 THE FEAR OF MAN . . . 1
SHE TRIES TO MAKE IT IN ONE CATCH OF BREATH, ... 386 THE FEAR OF MAN . . . 3
FROM NUMBER ONE TO SEVEN, ... 389 ASTROMETAPHYSICAL . . 11
AND COULD IN ONE BURST OVERWHELM . . . . 390 TWO LEADING LIGHTS . . 8
AND NO ONE TOLD THEM SO . . . . 391 A ROGERS GROUP . . . 9
NO ONE WAS SO FAR TOUCHED . . . . 391 A ROGERS GROUP . . . 11
BUT I'M NO ONE TO QUOTE. . . . . 391 A WISH TO COMPLY . . 5
WITH ONLY ONE VESTIGIAL CREATURE WISH: . . . . 395 ETHEREALIZING 12
NO ONE WAS LOOKING AT HIS LONELY CASE; . . . . 396 ANY SIZE WE PLEASE . . 1
OF GETTING ONE MORE CHANCE TO CHANGE OUR MANNERS? . . 397 THE PLANNERS 12
WILL FIND RELIEF IN ONE BURST. YOU SHALL SEE. . . . . 398 BURSTING RAPTURE . . . 13
THE DROUGHT WAS ONE NO SPIT OF RAIN COULD CURE. . . . 400 THE BROKEN DROUGHT . . 10
IN THE ONE STATE OF OURS THAT IS A SHIRE, ... 400 TO THE RIGHT PERSON . 1
O STAR (THE FAIREST ONE IN SIGHT), ... 403 SOMETHING LIKE A STAR . 1
WITH ONE FOOT ON THE DASHBOARD OF HIS BUGGY . . . . . 404 FROM PLANE TO PLANE . 19
BUT NO ONE FROM THE FEELING WOULD HAVE GUESSED . . . 407 FROM PLANE TO PLANE . 91
A SANTA CLAUS WAS NEEDED. AND THERE IS ONE." . . . . 408 FROM PLANE TO PLANE . 146
ONE KNOCKS ANOTHER OFF FROM WHERE HE CLINGS. . . . . 411 POD OF THE MILKWEED . 24
ONE DAY TOO SWEET FOR BEINGS TO SURVIVE. . . . . . . 412 POD OF THE MILKWEED . 33
WAS LEAVE AS THEIR POSTERITY ONE POD . . . . 412 POD OF THE MILKWEED . 43
THERE IS NO ONE I . . . . 413 AWAY! 14
NO ONE--NOT I--WOULD GIVE THEM UP FOR LOST . . . . . 414 A CABIN IN THE CLEARING 13
AND SCARE ME TO ONE SIDE. . . . . 415 CLOSED FOR GOOD . . . 10
WITHOUT ONE TRINKET FROM ORMUZ . . . . 416 AMERICA IS HARD TO SEE 10
ONE MORE BREVITY . . . . 419 ONE MORE BREVITY . . T
TO BE THE ONE SO DOG-PREFERRED. . . . . 419 ONE MORE BREVITY . . 14
NO ONE HAS SEEN HIM STUMBLE LOOKING BACK. . . . . . 421 ESCAPIST--NEVER . . . 2
WHAT COUNTRY'D BE THE ONE TO DOMINATE . . . . 422 FOR JOHN F. KENNEDY . 13
NO ONE OF HONEST FEELING WOULD APPROVE . . . . 423 FOR JOHN F. KENNEDY . 43
OF ATOMIC ONE. . . . . 426 A NEVER NAUGHT SONG . 7
ONE AND YET DISCRETE . . . . 426 A NEVER NAUGHT SONG . 10
AND I'LL FORGIVE THY GREAT BIG ONE ON ME. . . . . . 428 FORGIVE, O LORD... . . 2
I'D BEEN HERE ONE NIGHT . . . . 429 KITTY HAWK 52
ONE MORE FOND ALAS . . . . 431 KITTY HAWK 90
EACH AND EVERY ONE . . . . 431 KITTY HAWK 103
UNLESS ONE ANOTHER. . . . . 431 KITTY HAWK 113
ONE DRANK TO HIS MOTHER . . . . 432 KITTY HAWK 127
ON ONE SIDE THE OCEAN, ... 433 KITTY HAWK 164
AND ON ONE A WATER . . . . 433 KITTY HAWK 165
WAS ONE MIGHTY CHARGE . . . . 436 KITTY HAWK 254
(NO ONE, I PRESUME, ... 436 KITTY HAWK 266
ONE WOULD LIKE TO KNOW . . . . 438 KITTY HAWK 336
NOT A SINGLE ONE . . . . 440 KITTY HAWK 400
ONE LEAST GERM OR COAL. . . . . 441 KITTY HAWK 418
AS ONE WHO WOULD NOT MAKE A GANYMEDE. . . . . 443 AUSPEX 8
IN ONE LONG INVIDIOUS DRAFT. . . . . 444 THE DRAFT HORSE . . . 12
DOES NO ONE AT ALL EVER FEEL THIS WAY IN THE LEAST? . . 446 DOES NO ONE AT ALL EVER T
FOR ONE THING ALONE, ... 447 THE BAD ISLAND--EASTER 7
BUT ONE THING IS SURE, ... 449 THE BAD ISLAND--EASTER 54
THE STATE'S ONE FUNCTION IS TO GIVE. . . . . 450 OUR DOOM TO BLOOM . . 12
"AND ONE THING MORE THAT MAY NOT BE, ... 451 A-WISHING WELL . . . 4
THE ONE THING MORE OF HIS CONCERN. . . . . 451 A-WISHING WELL . . . 9
THE ONE THING MORE I WISH THERE WERE. . . . . 451 A-WISHING WELL . . . 11
BUT ALL I ASK'S AN EXTRA ONE. . . . . 451 A-WISHING WELL . . . 26
ALL THE SEA WATER IN ONE TIDE . . . . 452 A-WISHING WELL . . . 45
ONE HAS BEEN LATELY ALL THE TALK . . . . 452 A-WISHING WELL . . . 62
AND EYEING ONE HE ONLY WISHED WERE HIS, ... 454 HOW HARD TO KEEP FROM 15
ONE DAY WHEN THE CHIEF COOK WAS SICK AT HEART. . . . 455 HOW HARD TO KEEP FROM 56
A LARGER ONE HE ASKED FIVE HUNDRED FOR. . . . . . . 455 HOW HARD TO KEEP FROM 68
THE KING SAT FAVORING ONE PEARL FOR ITS BIGNESS, . . . 455 HOW HARD TO KEEP FROM 69
(HE SEEMS TO HAVE FELT LIMITED TO ONE), ... 456 HOW HARD TO KEEP FROM 71
BUT THE BIG ONE IS WORTHLESS. BREAK IT OPEN. . . . . 456 HOW HARD TO KEEP FROM 82
MY HEAD FOR IT--YOU'LL FIND THE BIG ONE HOLLOW. . . . 456 HOW HARD TO KEEP FROM 83
NO ONE COULD GET YOU: YOU WOULD COME THROUGH SMILING. . 458 HOW HARD TO KEEP FROM 129
BUT STILL FOOD, FOOD. YOUR ONE IDEA WAS FOOD. . . . . 458 HOW HARD TO KEEP FROM 134
BUT THAT'S A HARD ONE, FOR I HAVE TO ADD: . . . . . 458 HOW HARD TO KEEP FROM 151

ONE (CONTINUED)
    YOU'RE GOOD AT MAXIMS. SAY ME ONE ON FREEDOM. . . . . . . 459 HOW HARD TO KEEP FROM   164
    HE IS THE ONE WHO TOOK THE MONEY FOR ME . . . . 459 HOW HARD TO KEEP FROM   171
    NO ONE CAN GIVE THEM--THEY CAN SCARCE ATTAIN-- . . . . . . 461 HOW HARD TO KEEP FROM   233
    CHANGING AN OLD KING FOR ANOTHER OLD ONE. . . . . 462 HOW HARD TO KEEP FROM   255
    NO ONE IS NOMINATING ME FOR KING. . . . . 462 HOW HARD TO KEEP FROM   260
    THEY SHOULD TRY ONE WASTREL FIRST . . . . 466 SOME SCIENCE FICTION .   29
    I RODE UP ON ONE TILL THE BUBBLE BURST, ... 468 IN A GLASS OF CIDER .   4
    IN ONE TREE'S OVERTHROW . . . . 470 IN WINTER IN THE WOODS   10
    ONE WHO IN THE BEGINNING WAS THE WORD . . . . 475 A MASQUE OF REASON .   56
    YOU'RE NOT A WITCH? / NO. / HAVE YOU EVER BEEN ONE? . . 476 A MASQUE OF REASON .   92
    THAT'S ONE THING MORE TO PUT ON YOUR AGENDA. . . . . . 478 A MASQUE OF REASON .   126
    AND NO ONE BUT A MAN WOULD THINK THERE WAS. . . . . . . 478 A MASQUE OF REASON .   139
    IN CONFIDENCE. THERE'S NO ONE HERE BUT HER, ... 479 A MASQUE OF REASON .   172
    FOR STANDING STILL IN ONE PLACE TRUE FOREVER; . . . . . 480 A MASQUE OF REASON .   192
    I KNEW YOU HAD ONE. BUT THIS ISN'T IT . . . . 482 A MASQUE OF REASON .   241
    I'D GIVE MORE FOR ONE LEAST BEFOREHAND REASON . . . . . 482 A MASQUE OF REASON .   247
    THE FRONT OF BEING ANSWERABLE TO NO ONE . . . . 482 A MASQUE OF REASON .   250
    WE DON'T KNOW ONE ANOTHER; DON'T KNOW YOU; . . . . . . 483 A MASQUE OF REASON .   286
    ONE SIMPLE LITTLE STATEMENT FROM THE THRONE . . . . . . 484 A MASQUE OF REASON .   308
    ONE AT A TIME, PLEASE. I WILL ANSWER JOB FIRST. . . . . 484 A MASQUE OF REASON .   324
    AS IS SET FORTH IN CHAPTERS ONE AND TWO. . . . . 485 A MASQUE OF REASON .   328
    IT'S ON THE INCREASE. HE COULD COUNT ON NO ONE: . . . . 485 A MASQUE OF REASON .   357
    NEXT TIME YOU FIND YOURSELF PRESSED ONTO ONE . . . . . 486 A MASQUE OF REASON .   370
    LIKE THE ONE MILTON FOUND TO FOOL HIMSELF . . . . . . 488 A MASQUE OF REASON .   416
    HOW I SHOULD PRIZE ONE PERSONALLY FROM YOU. . . . . . . 488 A MASQUE OF REASON .   423
    A TENDENCY. THE MINUTE YOU GET ON ONE . . . . 489 A MASQUE OF REASON .   449
    AND LOCKS THE DOOR. ONE CUSTOMER, LOCKED IN, ... 493 A MASQUE OF MERCY .   3
    AND WHY WE WOULDN'T HAVE ONE IN THE STORE. . . . . . . 494 A MASQUE OF MERCY .   30
    THE CITY IS ALL RIGHT. TO LIVE IN ONE . . . . 496 A MASQUE OF MERCY .   69
    I'M NOT A SPORT AND DON'T PRETEND I AM ONE.-- . . . . . 496 A MASQUE OF MERCY .   79
    FROM MANY GODS TO THREE, AND THREE TO ONE, ... 498 A MASQUE OF MERCY .   121
    AT EVERY STATION BUT THE FINAL ONE. . . . . 501 A MASQUE OF MERCY .   195
    ONE MINUTE, MAY I, PAUL?--BEFORE WE LEAVE . . . . . . 501 A MASQUE OF MERCY .   216
    AND ONE TO CAP THE CLIMAX BY COMBINING . . . . 502 A MASQUE OF MERCY .   242
    LIKE THE ONE JOSHUA GAVE JERICHO. . . . . 504 A MASQUE OF MERCY .   274
    HE WROTE ONE BOOK. LET THERE BE NO MORE WRITTEN. . . . 504 A MASQUE OF MERCY .   290
    HOW ARE THEIR VOLUMES FALLEN! / ONLY ONE! . . . . . . 504 A MASQUE OF MERCY .   291
    THE ONE INDECENCY'S TO MAKE A FUSS . . . . 507 A MASQUE OF MERCY .   353
    THERE'S SOME SUCH THING AND NO ONE WILL DENY IT-- . . . 508 A MASQUE OF MERCY .   385
    (HE SNAPS ONE BULB OFF. PAUL SNAPS ON ANOTHER.) . . . . 508 A MASQUE OF MERCY .   393
    STRANGE NO ONE EVER THOUGHT OF IT BEFORE HIM. . . . . . 511 A MASQUE OF MERCY .   478
    A LOFTY BEAUTY NO ONE CAN LIVE UP TO, ... 512 A MASQUE OF MERCY .   496
    YET NO ONE TURN FROM TRYING TO LIVE UP TO. . . . . . . 512 A MASQUE OF MERCY .   497
    HIS LOFTY BEAUTY NO ONE CAN LIVE UP TO, ... 513 A MASQUE OF MERCY .   521
    YET NO ONE TURN AWAY FROM OR IGNORE-- . . . . 513 A MASQUE OF MERCY .   522
    MY DUNGEONEERS, COME FETCH US.--NO ONE ANSWERS. . . . . 514 A MASQUE OF MERCY .   556
    HAVEN'T YOU HEARD THE NEWS? WE ALREADY HAVE ONE, ... 515 A MASQUE OF MERCY .   577
    OF ONE GOD, WE PROVIDE HE SHALL BE ONE . . . . 515 A MASQUE OF MERCY .   590
    OF THE ONE AWFUL GOD. JUST SO THE SAINTS . . . . . . 516 A MASQUE OF MERCY .   596
    THERE'S NO ONE DOWN THERE GETTING TORTURED, SAVE . . . 516 A MASQUE OF MERCY .   609
    BUT ONE THING MORE BEFORE THE CURTAIN FALLS.-- . . . . 519 A MASQUE OF MERCY .   672
    AS IF I ASKED FOR ONE MORE CHANCE MYSELF . . . . . . 521 A MASQUE OF MERCY .   736
ONE-GIRL
    AN IDEAL ONE-GIRL FARM, ... 133 A GIRL'S GARDEN . . .   14
O'NEILL
    MY FRIENDS AND STOKERS, JEFFERS AND O'NEILL. . . . . 516 A MASQUE OF MERCY .   607
ONE-MAN
    I BID YOU TO A ONE-MAN REVOLUTION-- . . . . 324 BUILD SOIL   266
    ALL LANGUAGE IN A ONE-MAN TONGUE-CONFUSION. . . . . . 502 A MASQUE OF MERCY .   243
ONE-O
    I WILL SING YOU ONE-O . . . . 217 I WILL SING YOU ONE-O .   T
ONE-OF-THEM'S
    AS AFTER ONE-OF-THEM'S PROVERBIAL FAILURE . . . . . 412 POD OF THE MILKWEED .   37
ONES
    WITH ALL THY DAZZLING OTHER ONES, ... 28 MY BUTTERFLY   13
    THERE AIN'T NO NAMES QUITE LIKE THE OLD ONES, THOUGH, . . 80 THE GENERATIONS OF MEN 186
    "THE ONES WHO LIVING COME TODAY . . . . 221 IN A DISUSED GRAVEYARD   6
    UNDER A SPELL SO THE WRONG ONES CAN'T FIND IT, . . . 379 DIRECTIVE   58
ONE'S
    SOME ZEALOUS ONE'S LABORIOUS DEVICE. . . . . . . 74 THE GENERATIONS OF MEN 42
    LIKE SOME MENFOLK. NO ONE'S AFRAID OF HIM; . . . . . 83 THE HOUSEKEEPER . . . 69
    AND ONLY BY ONE'S GOING SLIGHTLY TAUT . . . . . . 332 THE SILKEN TENT . . . 12
    AND THE SLAVE SAID, "THE SMALL ONE'S WORTH THE PRICE, . . 456 HOW HARD TO KEEP FROM   81
ONE-SIDED
    'TWAS TOO ONE-SIDED A DIALOGUE, ... 420 ONE MORE BREVITY . . 36
ONETIME
    THOU ONETIME PRINCE OF CONVERSATIONISTS? . . . . . 488 A MASQUE OF REASON .   406
ONE-TWO-THREE
    RHYMED WITH 1 2 3 . . . . 436 KITTY HAWK   275
ONLOOKER'S
    WHO TOOK IN THEM ONLOOKER'S SHARE. . . . . 345 DISCOVERY OF MADEIRAS . 56
ONLOOKING
    EITHER FOR THEM OR THE ONLOOKING WORLD. . . . . . . 415 A CABIN IN THE CLEARING 32
ONLY
    I'LL ONLY STOP TO RAKE THE LEAVES AWAY . . . . . . 1 THE PASTURE   2
    ONLY MORE SURE OF ALL I THOUGHT WAS TRUE. . . . . . 5 INTO MY OWN   14
    AND ONLY PASSED HER BY . . . . 10 WIND AND WINDOW FLOWER 11
    BUT WHICH IT ONLY NEEDS THAT WE FULFILL. . . . . . 12 A PRAYER IN SPRING . . 16
    ONLY TO LOSE IT WHEN HE PIROUETTES, ... 14 WAITING   16
    YOU HAVE ONLY TO ASK ME, AND I CAN TELL. . . . . . 16 IN A VALE   23
    SAVE ONLY ME . . . . 28 MY BUTTERFLY   4
    SAVE ONLY ME . . . . 28 MY BUTTERFLY   6
    HE ONLY SAYS, "GOOD FENCES MAKE GOOD NEIGHBORS." . . . 33 MENDING WALL 27
    NOT OF WOODS ONLY AND THE SHADE OF TREES. . . . . . 34 MENDING WALL 42
    BUT ONLY FELT AT NIGHT ITS SHADOWY PRESENCE. . . . . 41 THE MOUNTAIN 22
    "THERE IS NO VILLAGE--ONLY SCATTERED FARMS. . . . . 41 THE MOUNTAIN 24
    AFTER THAT ONLY TOPS OF TREES, AND CLIFFS . . . . . 41 THE MOUNTAIN 31
    THE ONLY TROUBLE IS WE DISAGREE . . . . 48 A HUNDRED COLLARS . 108

ONLY (CONTINUED)
ONLY WHEN SOMEONE'S COMING, AND THE MARE . . . . 49 A HUNDRED COLLARS . . 139
THEY'RE ONLY TURNING YELLOW WHERE THEY ARE. . . . . . . 50 A HUNDRED COLLARS . . 169
WHITE WAS THE ONLY RACE SHE EVER KNEW. . . . . 57 THE BLACK COTTAGE . . 75
ONLY--THERE WAS THE BONNET IN THE PEW. . . . . 58 THE BLACK COTTAGE . . 99
LOWE IS THE ONLY DOCTOR'S DARED TO SAY SO-- . . . . . . 64 A SERVANT TO SERVANTS . 48
YOU KNOW THE OLD IDEA--THE ONLY ASYLUM . . . . 65 A SERVANT TO SERVANTS . 93
THE ONLY FUN HE HAD. I'VE HEARD THEM SAY, THOUGH, ... 66 A SERVANT TO SERVANTS . 138
MY INSTEP ARCH NOT ONLY KEEPS THE ACHE, ... 68 AFTER APPLE-PICKING . 21
ONLY ONE FROM A FARM NOT FAR AWAY . . . . 74 THE GENERATIONS OF MEN 25
"I ONLY IDLED DOWN." / "I IDLED DOWN." . . . . 74 THE GENERATIONS OF MEN 37
"I ONLY MEAN MY MOTHER WAS A STARK . . . . 75 THE GENERATIONS OF MEN 55
NO ONE WENT HOME THAT WAY, THE ONLY HOUSE . . . . 76 THE GENERATIONS OF MEN 73
HE THINKS I ONLY HAVE TO SAY THE WORD, ... 82 THE HOUSEKEEPER . . . 25
HE AND I ONLY HINDER ONE ANOTHER. . . . . 82 THE HOUSEKEEPER . . . 36
ONLY TOO WELL. I KNEW THERE MUST BE SOMETHING! . . . . 87 THE HOUSEKEEPER . . . 182
"IT'S NOT SO VERY LATE--IT'S ONLY DARK. . . . . 90 THE FEAR 29
YOU ONLY HAVE TO SIGN YOUR NAME. RIGHT--THERE." . . . . 99 THE SELF-SEEKER . . . 183
THESE LATTER ABOUT TO FALL. I THOUGHT THAT ONLY . . . . 102 THE WOOD-PILE . . . 34
"AND WHAT IS THAT? YOU ONLY PUT ME OFF.". . . . . . . 111 IN THE HOME STRETCH . 29
I ONLY SEE THE YEARS. THEY COME AND GO . . . . 112 IN THE HOME STRETCH . 47
BUT JIMMY ONLY MADE HIS JAW RECEDE . . . . 114 IN THE HOME STRETCH . 101
THERE ARE ONLY MIDDLES." / "WHAT IS THIS?" / "THIS LIFE? . 116 IN THE HOME STRETCH . 175
WHOSE ONLY PLAY WAS WHAT HE FOUND HIMSELF, ... 121 BIRCHES 26
SOMETHING INSPIRES THE ONLY COW OF LATE . . . . 124 THE COW IN APPLE TIME . 1
PERHAPS BECAUSE WE GAVE HIM ONLY BREAD . . . . 127 THE SMILE 4
AND ONLY ONE OF THE TWO . . . . 128 THE OFT-REPEATED DREAM 10
WITH A SONG ONLY TO HERSELF . . . . 128 THE IMPULSE 11
"YOU ONLY SAY SO. NOT ANOTHER HOUSE . . . . 145 SNOW 73
WHAT HAPPENS TO HIM IF IT ONLY TAKES . . . . 146 SNOW 90
ONLY YOU WOMEN HAVE TO PUT THESE AIRS ON . . . . 146 SNOW 98
WAS COMING. "GOD." BUT NO, HE ONLY SAID, ... 151 SNOW 239
"THERE'S ONLY ONE THING POSSIBLE TO MAKE, ... 155 SNOW 322
MAYBE SHE ONLY WANTS HIM FOR THE CHILDREN." . . . . . 155 SNOW 336
THE ONLY PERSON REALLY SOILED WITH TRADE . . . . . . 160 NEW HAMPSHIRE . . . 35
(THE ONLY OTHER WITCH I EVER MET . . . . 163 NEW HAMPSHIRE . . . 126
IS ONLY CORNERS, CROSSROADS IN A WOOD). . . . . 165 NEW HAMPSHIRE . . . 192
THERE IS THE PINCH FROM WHICH OUR ONLY OUTCRY . . . . . 167 NEW HAMPSHIRE . . . 270
THE ONLY FAULT I FIND WITH OLD NEW HAMPSHIRE . . . . . 168 NEW HAMPSHIRE . . . 310
TEN THOUSAND FEET INSTEAD OF ONLY FIVE-- . . . . 169 NEW HAMPSHIRE . . . 332
THE ONLY DECENT TREE HAD BEEN TO MILL . . . . 171 NEW HAMPSHIRE . . . 376
IT YET HAS POLES, AND ONLY NEEDS A SPIN . . . . 174 A STAR IN A STONEBOAT . 50
THE ONLY DWELLING IN A WASTE CUT OVER . . . . 174 THE CENSUS-TAKER . . 4
ME ONLY AS I TOOK MY AX TO HEART. . . . . 186 THE AX-HELVE . . . 20
WHAT PASSED BETWEEN US, SHE WAS ONLY FEIGNING. . . . . 187 THE AX-HELVE . . . 57
I LAUGHED INSIDE, AND ONLY CRANKED THE FASTER . . . . . 190 THE GRINDSTONE . . . 60
AND NOW WERE ONLY WASTING PRECIOUS BLADE. . . . . . . 190 THE GRINDSTONE . . . 67
ONLY DISINTERESTEDLY TO DECIDE . . . . 191 THE GRINDSTONE . . . 71
HE ONLY HAD TO BE REMINDED OF-- . . . . 191 PAUL'S WIFE . . . 11
IT WAS THE ONLY GLIMPSE THAT ANYONE . . . . 195 PAUL'S WIFE . . . 129
AND ONLY FREELY TO BE HAD FOR CLIMBING. . . . . 197 WILD GRAPES 30
ONLY YOU HAVE THE ADVANTAGE OF THE GRAPES . . . . . . 198 WILD GRAPES 69
THE ONLY FAULT MY HUSBAND FOUND WITH ME— . . . . . . 203 THE WITCH OF COOS . 36
FROM THE HALL TO THE ONLY FINISHED BEDROOM, ... 205 THE WITCH OF COOS . 91
VOTED THE ONLY TIMES HE EVER VOTED, ... 208 PAUPER WITCH OF GRAFTON 21
ONLY I HAPPEN TO PREFER TO LIVE . . . . 208 PAUPER WITCH OF GRAFTON 31
ONLY BEWITCHED SO I WOULD LAST HIM LONGER. . . . . . . 210 PAUPER WITCH OF GRAFTON 95
ONLY TO TUMBLE LIKE A STRICKEN BIRD, ... 216 A FOUNTAIN, A BOTTLE . 115
IT ONLY GIVES OUR WISH FOR BLUE A WHET. . . . . 220 FRAGMENTARY BLUE . . 8
BUT ONLY SO AN HOUR. . . . . 222 NOTHING GOLD CAN STAY . 4
IT'S ONLY WEATHER.' HE'D THINK SHE DIDN'T KNOW! . . . . 223 THE RUNAWAY 13
THE ONLY OTHER SOUND'S THE SWEEP . . . . 224 STOPPING BY WOODS . . 11
A CHIMNEY THAT ONLY WOULD SERVE TO REMIND ME . . . . . 232 THE KITCHEN CHIMNEY . 19
WAS ONLY ADDING FROST TO SNOW . . . . 233 LOOKING FOR SUNSET BIRD 15
I ONLY HOPE THAT WHEN I AM FREE, ... 236 MISGIVING 13
FROM SNOW THAT MELTED ONLY YESTERDAY. . . . . 245 SPRING POOLS . . . 12
THE DEAR ONLY KNOWS . . . . 246 THE ROSE FAMILY . . . 7
ONLY, OF COURSE, THEY CAN'T SUSTAIN THE PART. . . . . . 246 FIREFLIES IN THE GARDEN 6
THE ONLY LEAF IT DROPS GOES WIDE, ... 247 ON GOING UNNOTICED . 11
HEAVEN GIVES ITS GLIMPSES ONLY TO THOSE . . . . 248 A PASSING GLIMPSE . . 11
WAS COMING, AND NOT ONLY A NIGHT, AN AGE. . . . . . . 250 ONCE BY THE PACIFIC . 11
TO TELL ONCE AND ONCE ONLY, FOR THEM NEVER TO FORGET, . . 257 THE LOVELY BE CHOOSERS 32
THERE WAS ONE TIME AND ONLY THE ONE . . . . 266 SITTING BY A BUSH . . 5
'TIS ONLY TO SIT BACK AND SWAY HIS HEAD . . . . 269 THE BEAR 23
WHICH MAY BE THOUGHT, BUT ONLY SO TO SPEAK. . . . . . . 269 THE BEAR 32
WINTER WAS ONLY PLAYING POSSUM. . . . . 276 TWO TRAMPS IN MUD TIME 30
ONLY WHERE LOVE AND NEED ARE ONE, ... 277 TWO TRAMPS IN MUD TIME 69
ONLY TOO LIBERAL OF OUR COMPLIMENT . . . . 279 THE WHITE-TAILED HORNET 54
AND ONE DID STOP, BUT ONLY TO PLOW UP GRASS . . . . . . 287 A ROADSIDE STAND . . 39
THEY COULD BE LOCKED BUT FROM THE OUTSIDE ONLY. . . . . 289 OLD BARN AT THE BOTTOM 16
ITS ONLY WINDOWS WERE THE CREVICES . . . . 290 OLD BARN AT THE BOTTOM 24
WOULD SOMEONE ONLY ACT IN TIME WE YET . . . . 290 OLD BARN AT THE BOTTOM 35
THEIR LABEL PROP-LOCKS, ONLY SPECIMENS . . . . 290 OLD BARN AT THE BOTTOM 37
THAT LIFE IS ONLY LIFE FOREVERMORE . . . . 300 THE MASTER SPEED . . 13
ALL WOODS AND PASTURE ONLY FIT FOR SHEEP. . . . . . . 316 BUILD SOIL 9
I SHOULD MYSELF, ONLY I DON'T KNOW HOW. . . . . 316 BUILD SOIL 20
THERE'S ONLY DEMOCRATIC SOCIALISM, ... 318 BUILD SOIL 72
THERE'S ONLY LOVE OF MEN AND WOMEN, LOVE . . . . 318 BUILD SOIL 85
WE SOMETIMES ONLY GET THE BAD OF THEM. . . . . 319 BUILD SOIL 97
LET THOSE POSSESS THE LAND, AND ONLY THOSE, ... 322 BUILD SOIL 187
I ONLY SPEAK TO YOU AS ONE OF THEM. . . . . 323 BUILD SOIL 210
TO COMMAND ONLY WHAT YOU MEANT TO DO . . . . 323 BUILD SOIL 232
THE ONLY REVOLUTION THAT IS COMING. . . . . 324 BUILD SOIL 267
NOT EVEN THAT, IT'S ONLY ROCKING. . . . . 325 TO A THINKER 6
IF ONLY ANYONE WERE SURE . . . . 327 A MISSIVE MISSILE . . 20
AND ONLY BY ONE'S GOING SLIGHTLY TAUT . . . . 332 THE SILKEN TENT . . 12
BUT ONLY GRAVE, CONTEMPLATIVE AND GRAVE. . . . . 334 I COULD GIVE ALL . . 5
COULD ONLY HAVE HAD AN INFLUENCE ON BIRDS . . . . . . 338 NEVER WOULD BIRDS' SONG 7
A GIRL COULD ONLY SEE . . . . 340 THE SUBVERTED FLOWER . 48

ONLY (CONTINUED)
I ONLY KNELT AND PUTTING THE BOUGHS ASIDE . . . . . . 343 QUEST OF PURPLE-FRINGED 21
THEY COULD ONLY SAY LIKE ANY TWO, ... 345 DISCOVERY OF MADEIRAS . 46
TO BE HER ONLY MARRIAGE LINES. . . . . 347 DISCOVERY OF MADEIRAS . 123
BUT DOUBTLESS THIS WAS ONLY MY CONCEIT. . . . . . . 353 THE LESSON FOR TODAY . 80
THE ONLY OTHER THERE WAS FAR AWAY . . . . 354 THE LESSON FOR TODAY . 128
BUT I WAS ONLY THERE TO READ THE STONES . . . . . 354 THE LESSON FOR TODAY . 133
ONLY BEGETTER OF ALL ILLS THAT ARE. . . . . 356 A MOTH SEEN IN WINTER . 16
BUT ONLY BY IGNORING . . . . 359 NOVEMBER 11
YES, REVOLUTIONS ARE THE ONLY SALVES, ... 363 A SEMI-REVOLUTION . .   7
FOR ONLY A DOLLAR DOWN. . . . . 367 A SERIOUS STEP LIGHTLY   8
TO SEE IT SO, THE BRIGHT AND ONLY ONE . . . . . . 368 THE LITERATE FARMER AND 11
THE ONLY NATIVE TREE THAT DARES TO LEAN, ... 375 A YOUNG BIRCH . . .   8
NOT ONLY SANDS AND GRAVELS . . . . 376 ONE STEP BACKWARD TAKEN   1
WHO ONLY HAS AT HEART YOUR GETTING LOST, ... 377 DIRECTIVE   9
THEN MAKE YOURSELF AT HOME. THE ONLY FIELD . . . . . 378 DIRECTIVE 39
BUT ONLY A BELILACED CELLAR HOLE, ... 378 DIRECTIVE 46
ONLY WITHIN. INSIDE THE BRAIN . . . . 381 AN UNSTAMPED LETTER IN 32
SHOULD BE THE ONLY ONE; . . . . 384 MAKING CERTAIN ANYTHING   6
THE ONLY THING I WORRY ABOUT IS THE SUN. . . . . . 392 IT BIDS PRETTY FAIR .   3
THE ONLY MEANING POSSIBLE FOR NATURE . . . . . . 393 LUCRETIUS VERSUS POETS   8
NOT ONLY WARNED HIM WITH A LOUD COMMAND . . . . . 394 HAEC FABULA DOCET . .   9
WITH ONLY ONE VESTIGIAL CREATURE WISH: . . . . . 395 ETHEREALIZING . . . 12
ONLY A FEW OF THOSE EVEN IN WHOSE DAY . . . . . . 397 THE PLANNERS   7
BUT PUNY LITTLE STATES CAN ONLY BE. . . . . . . 398 NO HOLY WARS FOR THEM .   4
AND ONLY RESTS, A SERPENT ON ITS CHIN, ... 399 THE INGENUITIES OF DEBT 15
THE SAME AS YOUR IDEA, ONLY MORE SO. . . . . . . 406 FROM PLANE TO PLANE . 81
HE ONLY STAYED TO SET THE SUMMER ON FIRE, ... 407 FROM PLANE TO PLANE . 93
AND ONLY SOME SLIGHT BEAST . . . . 416 CLOSED FOR GOOD . . 28
ONLY A FRACTION OF OURS AT MOST. . . . . 421 ONE MORE BREVITY . . 52
HAD I ONLY SUNG, ... 430 KITTY HAWK 83
WOULD ONLY DISAPPOINT US AT THE LAST . . . . . . 446 DOES NO ONE AT ALL EVER   4
AND SHE CAN ONLY GIVE THE CLASS A NOTION . . . . . 447 DOES NO ONE AT ALL EVER 40
AND EYEING ONE HE ONLY WISHED WERE HIS, ... 454 HOW HARD TO KEEP FROM 15
ONLY LESS HARD WAS IT FOR WASHINGTON. . . . . . 454 HOW HARD TO KEEP FROM 25
NOT OF FOOD ONLY BUT OF EVERYTHING, ... 455 HOW HARD TO KEEP FROM 61
IF WE COULD ONLY STOP THE PROGRESS SOMEWHERE, ... 458 HOW HARD TO KEEP FROM 154
THE ONLY CERTAIN FREEDOM'S IN DEPARTURE. . . . . . 460 HOW HARD TO KEEP FROM 194
IT HAS ITS BEAUTY, ONLY I DON'T WRITE IT. . . . . . 461 HOW HARD TO KEEP FROM 223
THOUGH AS YET THEY ONLY SMILE . . . . 465 SOME SCIENCE FICTION .   9
IF ONLY TO DISCRIMINATE . . . . 467 QUANDARY   9
THE ONLY FREE WILL THERE AT FIRST WAS MAN'S, ... 475 A MASQUE OF REASON . 71
OR IS IT ONLY FOUR? MY EXTRA TWENTY . . . . . . 484 A MASQUE OF REASON . 312
INCLUDING ME, THE ONLY DRAMATIS . . . . 487 A MASQUE OF REASON . 393
ONLY OF SAND, NOT WATER, RUNS THROUGH HERE. . . . . 489 A MASQUE OF REASON . 443
THE COUNTRY'S ONLY USEFUL AS A PLACE . . . . . . 496 A MASQUE OF MERCY . 73
IT'S ONLY FAIR TO KEEPER TO INFORM YOU . . . . . 496 A MASQUE OF MERCY . 80
THAT ONLY NEEDS A FINGER TOUCH FROM GOD . . . . . 502 A MASQUE OF MERCY . 230
HOW ARE THEIR VOLUMES FALLEN! / ONLY ONE! . . . . . 504 A MASQUE OF MERCY . 291
HE MAY BE GOD, BUT ME, I'M ONLY HUMAN: . . . . . 505 A MASQUE OF MERCY . 304
ONLY TO SEE IT SHATTERED EVERY DAY. . . . . . . 508 A MASQUE OF MERCY . 373
NOT ONLY LAST, BUT FIRST, YOU WILL OBSERVE; . . . . 508 A MASQUE OF MERCY . 382
PAUL ONLY MEANS YOU MAKE TOO MUCH OF JUSTICE. . . . 508 A MASQUE OF MERCY . 384
MERCY IS ONLY TO THE UNDESERVING. . . . . . . 512 A MASQUE OF MERCY . 500
DON'T LET ME SCARE YOU. I WAS ONLY TEASING. . . . . 514 A MASQUE OF MERCY . 558
TO BRING FAITH BACK. I'M ONLY LANGUIDLY . . . . . 515 A MASQUE OF MERCY . 566
'TWAS SAID THE LESSER GODS WERE ONLY TRAITS . . . . 516 A MASQUE OF MERCY . 595
AND THAT THEY MAY BE IS THE ONLY PRAYER . . . . . 520 A MASQUE OF MERCY . 723
ON-PENETRATION
BY ON-PENETRATION . . . . 435 KITTY HAWK 232
ONSET
THE ONSET . . . . 226 THE ONSET . . . . .   T
ONSLAUGHT
YOU KNOW THEY SUFFERED FROM A GENERAL ONSLAUGHT. . . . 58 THE BLACK COTTAGE . . 96
ONTO
IN ONTO THE UPPER CHAMBER FLOORS. . . . . . . 253 THE THATCH 35
HE WOULD PUT HIM ONTO THE CASE. . . . . 288 DEPARTMENTAL . . . 12
WOULD LOAD IT ONTO CLOUD. . . . . 337 THE WIND AND THE RAIN 30
THAT LOOKS IN ONTO A MOOD APART. . . . . . . 385 A MOOD APART . . .   8
NOT ONTO THE MOON BUT OVER. . . . . 462 LINES IN DEJECTION .   2
NEXT TIME YOU FIND YOURSELF PRESSED ONTO ONE . . . . 486 A MASQUE OF REASON . 370
ONWARD
SPENDING WHAT ONWARD IMPULSE THEY STILL HAD . . . . 229 TWO LOOK AT TWO . . .   9
OPAQUE
HAD EYES INSCRUTABLY OPAQUE; . . . . 273 A LONE STRIKER . . . 12
OPEN
FEARLESS OF EVER FINDING OPEN LAND, ...   5 INTO MY OWN   7
BENT OVER THE OPEN FIRE, ...   8 LOVE AND A QUESTION . 18
AND SIT BEFORE YOU IN THE OPEN DOOR . . . . . . 79 THE GENERATIONS OF MEN 168
FROM A TWIG'S HAVING LASHED ACROSS IT OPEN. . . . . 122 BIRCHES 47
TO MAKE NO MORE OF A WALL THAN AN OPEN GATE, ... 124 THE COW IN APPLE TIME .   2
"THAT LEAF THERE IN YOUR OPEN BOOK! IT MOVED . . . . 147 SNOW 116
BESIDE THE TABLE, NEAR THE OPEN BOOK, ... 151 SNOW 246
WIDE OPEN AND THE WIND'S BLOWN OUT THE LAMP . . . . 154 SNOW 309
INSIDE THE THRESHOLD OF HIS OPEN BARN. . . . . . 160 NEW HAMPSHIRE . . . 45
BY WORSHIP UNDER GREEN TREES IN THE OPEN. . . . . 171 NEW HAMPSHIRE . . . 389
FOR THE NEXT ONE TO OPEN FOR HIMSELF. . . . . . 175 THE CENSUS-TAKER . . 30
AND THEN BEYOND THE OPEN WATER, DIM WITH MIDGES, . . . 194 PAUL'S WIFE 106
BUT LEFT AN OPEN DOOR TO COOL THE ROOM OFF . . . . 203 THE WITCH OF COOS . 42
HE'S AFTER AN OPEN DOOR TO GET OUTDOORS. . . . . 205 THE WITCH OF COOS . 112
LET'S TRAP HIM WITH AN OPEN DOOR UP ATTIC." . . . . 206 THE WITCH OF COOS . 113
AND SPOKE HIS DOUBTS IN EVERY OPEN PLACE. . . . . 214 A FOUNTAIN, A BOTTLE . 36
OR FLOWER, OR WEARING-STONE, OR OPEN EYE, ... 220 FRAGMENTARY BLUE . .   3
SPREAD OPEN AS I DROPPED THEM HALF-READ THROUGH . . . 222 TO E.T.   2
THEY COULD FIND NOTHING OPEN BUT THE ROAD. . . . . 239 OUR SINGING STRENGTH . 30
WINDS BLOW THE OPEN GRASSY PLACES BLEAK; . . . . . 246 ATMOSPHERE   1
HOLDING OPEN A RESTIVE DOOR, ... 251 BEREFT   4
AND BENT SOME RAIL WIDE OPEN LIKE A SWITCH, ... 270 THE EGG AND THE MACHINE   7

OPEN (CONTINUED)
    THE SADNESS THAT LURKS NEAR THE OPEN WINDOW THERE, . . . 287 A ROADSIDE STAND . . 34
    THAT WAITS ALL DAY IN ALMOST OPEN PRAYER . . . . . . 287 A ROADSIDE STAND . . 35
    HE TOOK THE PROPS DOWN USED FOR PROPPING OPEN, ... 289 OLD BARN AT THE BOTTOM 10
    ONE STRINGING A CHAIN OF SEED IN AN OPEN CREASE, ... 299 STRONG SAYING NOTHING . 7
    AND HE LASHED HIS OPEN PALM . . . . 339 THE SUBVERTED FLOWER . 3
    A BREEZE DISCOVERED MY OPEN BOOK . . . . 342 A CLOUD SHADOW . . . 1
    THEN IN THE MIDDLE OF THE OPEN SHEET . . . . 357 A CONSIDERABLE SPECK . 21
    TO THE OPEN COUNTRY EDGE . . . . 364 A NATURE NOTE . . . 3
    THOUGH THEY DO SAY HE DOESN'T OPEN LETTERS. . . . . . 408 FROM PLANE TO PLANE . 145
    BUT THE BIG ONE IS WORTHLESS. BREAK IT OPEN. . . . . . 456 HOW HARD TO KEEP FROM 82
    OPEN ENOUGH TO FIND OUT WHO IT IS. . . . . 493 A MASQUE OF MERCY . 12
    HOLD ON THERE. LEAVE THAT OPEN WHERE IT LIES. . . . . . 504 A MASQUE OF MERCY . 292
OPENED
    THAT ONCE YOU HAD OPENED THE VALLEY'S SINGING DAY. . . . 236 VALLEY'S SINGING DAY . 20
    NO MORE IT OPENED WITH ALL ONE END . . . . 241 NEED OF BEING VERSED . 9
    LIKE A MANHOLE OPENED TO HELL. . . . . 311 THE VINDICTIVES . . . 23
    I OPENED THE DOOR SO MY LAST LOOK . . . . 419 ONE MORE BREVITY . . 1
    I OPENED THE DOOR AND HE WAS GONE. . . . . 420 ONE MORE BREVITY . . 49
OPENING
    "IF--YOU--DO!" SHE WAS OPENING THE DOOR WIDER. . . . . 55 HOME BURIAL 114
    THROUGH OPENING CLOUDS AT NIGHT WITH DRONING SPEED . . . 132 THE BONFIRE 106
    AND SPREAD THE OPENING, AND YOU'VE GOT A DUGOUT . . . . 193 PAUL'S WIFE 81
    ALMOST THE MOMENT HE WAS GIVEN AN OPENING, ... 206 THE WITCH OF COOS . . 115
    TILL IT CAUGHT WIND AND, OPENING OUT ITS COVERS, ... 216 A FOUNTAIN, A BOTTLE . 111
    WITH SNOWBALLS CUPPED IN EVERY OPENING BUD. . . . . . 239 OUR SINGING STRENGTH . 15
    BEFORE TREES, SEEING THE OPENING, ... 264 THE LAST MOWING . . . 9
    OFFERED AN OPENING TO THE SOURCE OF DEW; . . . . . . 295 LOST IN HEAVEN . . . 2
    O OPENING CLOUDS, BY OPENING ON ME WIDE. . . . . . . 296 LOST IN HEAVEN . . . 11
    HE MIGHT BE OPENING LEAVES OF STONE, ... 364 TRESPASS 9
OPEN-MINDED
    AND OPEN-MINDED. SHE WAS FREE TO QUESTION . . . . . 163 NEW HAMPSHIRE 130
OPENS
    THAT OPENS EARTHWARD, GOOD AND ILL, ... 20 THE TRIAL BY EXISTENCE 35
    (THE DOOR HERE OPENS DARKLY OF ITSELF.) . . . . . . 514 A MASQUE OF MERCY . 550
OPHIR
    HIS CLAIM IT WAS ANOTHER OPHIR. . . . . 417 AMERICA IS HARD TO SEE 24
OPIATE
    IT TASTES AS IF IT MIGHT BE OPIATE. . . . . 411 POD OF THE MILKWEED . 19
OPINION
    IN MY OPINION--THOUGH WE BOTH KNOW POETS . . . . . . 321 BUILD SOIL 176
    MY VARYING OPINION OF MYSELF . . . . 474 A MASQUE OF REASON . . 28
OPPOSED
    THE BARN OPPOSED ACROSS THE WAY, ... 241 NEED OF BEING VERSED . 5
    OR SHE AND HER LOVER WOULD SIT OPPOSED . . . . . . 344 DISCOVERY OF MADEIRAS . 38
OPPOSING
    I DREAM UPON THE OPPOSING LIGHTS OF THE HOUR, ... 14 WAITING 9
    THE GRAVES OF MEN ON AN OPPOSING HILL, ... 17 THE VANTAGE POINT . . 7
    BUT EVEN WHERE, THUS, OPPOSING INTERESTS KILL, ... 350 TO A YOUNG WRETCH . 14
    THEY ARE TO BE THOUGHT OF AS OPPOSING GOODS . . . . . 350 TO A YOUNG WRETCH . 15
    WHICH MAKES OPPOSING IT TO ART ABSURD . . . . 394 LUCRETIUS VERSUS POETS 10
OPPOSITE
    THE OPPOSITE WAS TRUE. THE TREE HAD ME. . . . . . . 197 WILD GRAPES 42
    IS ALWAYS IN THE OPPOSITE DIRECTION. . . . . 358 THE LOST FOLLOWER . . 10
    AND I AWAY IN MY OPPOSITE WOOD . . . . 383 WERE I IN TROUBLE . . 6
    AT EVOLUTION'S OPPOSITE EXTREME. . . . . 395 ETHEREALIZING . . . 10
OPPRESSES
    BUT A SLEEP OPPRESSES THEM AS THEY GO, ... 236 MISGIVING 3
OPTIMISM
    WITH SOME OPTIMISM FOR CHRISTMAS . . . . 466 SOME SCIENCE FICTION . 34
OR---NOT INDEXED
ORACLE
    IT OUGHT TO GIVE A PURER ORACLE." . . . . 78 THE GENERATIONS OF MEN 134
    "I WONDER WHERE YOUR ORACLE IS TENDING. . . . . . . 79 THE GENERATIONS OF MEN 171
    TO QUOTE THE ORACLE OF DELPHI, ... 467 QUANDARY 11
ORATION
    OH, THERE'S TO BE A FUNERAL ORATION. . . . . 519 A MASQUE OF MERCY . 678
ORATOR
    AND WE'RE AN ORATOR. GET UP. STAND UP . . . . 519 A MASQUE OF MERCY . 679
ORATORS
    GOOD ORATORS WILL DO WHEN THEY ARE OUT. . . . . . . 400 THE BROKEN DROUGHT . . 8
ORBIT
    ABOUT WHEN BEST TO HAVE US IN OUR ORBIT, ... 361 A LOOSE MOUNTAIN . . 20
ORCHARD
    THE ORCHARD TREE HAS GROWN ONE COPSE . . . . 5 GHOST HOUSE 8
    OH, GIVE US PLEASURE IN THE ORCHARD WHITE, ... 12 A PRAYER IN SPRING . . 5
    HE IS ALL PINE AND I AM APPLE ORCHARD. . . . . . . 33 MENDING WALL 24
    OF HERE AND THERE A TENT IN GROVE AND ORCHARD. . . . . 73 THE GENERATIONS OF MEN 13
    LET ALONE GROVE OF TREES FOR SUGAR ORCHARD. . . . . . 183 MAPLE 103
    AND THE COLD TO AN ORCHARD SO YOUNG IN THE BARK . . . . 228 GOOD-BY AND KEEP COLD . 2
    AN ORCHARD AWAY AT THE END OF THE FARM . . . . . . 228 GOOD-BY AND KEEP COLD . 4
    KEEP COLD, YOUNG ORCHARD. GOOD-BY AND KEEP COLD. . . . 228 GOOD-BY AND KEEP COLD . 18
    EVENING IN A SUGAR ORCHARD . . . . 234 EVENING IN A SUGAR ORCHARD T
    GOD SAW HIM DANCING IN THE ORCHARD PATH, ... 284 THE GOLD HESPERIDEE . 55
    THE ORCHARD BARE . . . . 445 PERIL OF HOPE . . . 3
    AND THE ORCHARD GREEN, ... 445 PERIL OF HOPE . . . 4
ORCHARD'S
    NO ORCHARD'S THE WORSE FOR THE WINTRIEST STORM; . . . . 228 GOOD-BY AND KEEP COLD . 15
    AND THINK OF AN ORCHARD'S ARBOREAL PLIGHT . . . . . . 228 GOOD-BY AND KEEP COLD . 26
ORCHID
    COME, HOLD IT OUT. DON'T CHANGE.--A RAM'S HORN ORCHID! . . 96 THE SELF-SEEKER . . 112
    A RAM'S HORN ORCHID SEEDPOD FOR A WOODCHUCK . . . . . 97 THE SELF-SEEKER . . 126
    HALF LOOKING FOR THE ORCHID CALYPSO." . . . . . . 125 AN ENCOUNTER . . . 24
ORCHIDS
    YOU HAVEN'T RUN YOUR FORTY ORCHIDS DOWN. . . . . . . 93 THE SELF-SEEKER . . 13
ORCHISES
    A THOUSAND ORCHISES; . . . . 13 ROSE POGONIAS . . . 12
    (PALE ORCHISES), AND SCARED A BRIGHT GREEN SNAKE. . . . . 17 MOWING 12

ORDAINED
     BEHIND THE SCENES, ORDAINED AND ADVERTISED . . . . . . 497 A MASQUE OF MERCY . . 97
ORDEAL
     TO THINK OF SITTING SUCH AN ORDEAL OUT, ... 45 A HUNDRED COLLARS . . 18
     HER LOVER TO MAKE THE ORDEAL SWIFT . . . . 343 DISCOVERY OF MADEIRAS .   9
     NOR NEED YOU MIND THE SERIAL ORDEAL . . . . 377 DIRECTIVE 20
     I WAIVED THE REASON FOR MY ORDEAL--BUT-- . . . . 479 A MASQUE OF REASON . . 170
ORDER
     NOW CAME ON A NEW ORDER OF THE AGES . . . . 422 FOR JOHN F. KENNEDY . 19
     "NEW ORDER OF THE AGES" DID WE SAY? . . . . 423 FOR JOHN F. KENNEDY . 39
ORDERED
     AND LAY HIM WHERE YOU ORDERED HIM TO LIE . . . . 521 A MASQUE OF MERCY . . 734
ORDERLY
     IF IT LOOKS NONE TOO ORDERLY TODAY, ... 423 FOR JOHN F. KENNEDY . 40
ORDERS
     GAVE THEM THEIR MARCHING ORDERS AND WAS MOVING. . . . . 44 THE MOUNTAIN 109
     SO HE WON'T FIND IT HARD TO TAKE HIS ORDERS . . . . . . 481 A MASQUE OF REASON . . 212
     YOU HEARD FROM GOD--I MEAN HAD ORDERS FROM HIM? . . . . 504 A MASQUE OF MERCY . . 277
ORDINARY
     OR NOT AT LEAST THE ORDINARY KIND. . . . . 510 A MASQUE OF MERCY . . 456
ORGAN
     I'VE BEEN BUILT IN HERE LIKE A BIG CHURCH ORGAN. . . . 82 THE HOUSEKEEPER . . . 38
ORGANIZE
     HAD HAD TO ORGANIZE TO STOCK THE GRAVEYARDS . . . . . . 159 NEW HAMPSHIRE   . . . 20
ORGANIZED
     BEFORE THEIR PLAYS AND GAMES WERE ORGANIZED, ... 318 BUILD SOIL 62
ORIGIN
     THE ORIGIN OF ALL THE FAMILY THERE. . . . . 73 THE GENERATIONS OF MEN   9
     'TWAS LOVELY AND ITS ORIGIN WAS LOVE. . . . . 511 A MASQUE OF MERCY . . 479
ORIGINAL
     BUT COUNTER-LOVE, ORIGINAL RESPONSE. . . . . 338 THE MOST OF IT . . .   8
     TOO LOFTY AND ORIGINAL TO RAGE. . . . . 378 DIRECTIVE 52
     THE ORIGINAL? . . . . 430 KITTY HAWK 60
     FALSE PREMISES THAT ARE THE ORIGINAL . . . . 480 A MASQUE OF REASON . . 204
ORIGINALITY
     ANY ORIGINALITY IT SHOWED . . . . 480 A MASQUE OF REASON . . 189
     ANY ORIGINALITY IT SHOWED . . . . 480 A MASQUE OF REASON . . 202
     OF ALL ORIGINALITY, THE SIN . . . . 481 A MASQUE OF REASON . . 205
ORIGINATE
     AND WELL MAY BE WHERE WARS ORIGINATE. . . . . 371 THE LITERATE FARMER AND 109
ORION
     "YOU KNOW ORION ALWAYS COMES UP SIDEWAYS. . . . . . . 176 THE STAR-SPLITTER . .   1
     AS LEO, ORION, AND THE PLEIADES. . . . . 234 EVENING A SUGAR ORCHARD 16
ORION'S
     OR ELSE FUN OF ORION'S HAVING CAUGHT ME. . . . . 176 THE STAR-SPLITTER . . 10
ORMUZ
     WITHOUT ONE TRINKET FROM ORMUZ . . . . 416 AMERICA IS HARD TO SEE 10
ORNAMENT
     AGAINST HER NECK, AN ORNAMENT OF GRAPES. . . . . 197 WILD GRAPES 23
     ALONE, OR IN ONE ORNAMENT COMBINING . . . . 245 THE FREEDOM OF THE MOON 5
     TO LIVE ITS LIFE OUT AS AN ORNAMENT. . . . . 375 A YOUNG BIRCH . . . 22
ORNAMENTS
     THE ORNAMENTS THE GREEK ARTIFICERS . . . . 473 A MASQUE OF REASON . . 10
ORNATE
     FOR WHAT THE DRAB WEED LACKS OF THE ORNATE. . . . . . 411 POD OF THE MILKWEED . 13
ORTHODOX
     SO AS TO JUSTIFY THE ORTHODOX . . . . 515 A MASQUE OF MERCY . . 571
OTHER---NOT INDEXED
OTHER'S---NOT INDEXED
OTHERS---NOT INDEXED
OTHERS'---NOT INDEXED
OTHERWHERE
     THAN WITH BROOKS TAKEN OTHERWHERE IN SONG. . . . . . . 119 HYLA BROOK 14
OTHERWISE
     OR OTHERWISE AN ENVIRONMENTALIST. . . . . 166 NEW HAMPSHIRE   . . . 233
OTHERWORLDLINESS
     AND HOW WAS THAT FOR OTHERWORLDLINESS? . . . . 168 NEW HAMPSHIRE   . . . 306
OUBLIETTE
     WHAT'S REALLY DOWN THERE? / JUST AN OUBLIETTE, ... 516 A MASQUE OF MERCY . . 612
OUGHT
     HE THINKS HE OUGHT TO EARN A LITTLE PAY. . . . . . . 35 DEATH OF THE HIRED MAN 19
     "I THINK HIS BROTHER OUGHT TO HELP, OF COURSE. . . . . 39 DEATH OF THE HIRED MAN 131
     I'LL SEE TO THAT IF THERE IS NEED. HE OUGHT OF RIGHT . . 39 DEATH OF THE HIRED MAN 132
     "THERE OUGHT TO BE A VIEW AROUND THE WORLD . . . . . 42 THE MOUNTAIN 55
     THAT OUGHT TO BE WORTH SEEING." / "IF IT'S THERE. . . 42 THE MOUNTAIN 65
     TOO BAD TO WASTE THEM ALL. YOU OUGHT TO HAVE THEM. . . 47 A HUNDRED COLLARS . . 67
     THEY PAY FOR IT, AND SO THEY OUGHT TO HAVE IT. . . . . 48 A HUNDRED COLLARS . . 104
     I OUGHT TO KNOW--IT MAKES A DIFFERENCE WHICH: . . . . 56 THE BLACK COTTAGE . . 32
     "YOU OUGHT TO HAVE SEEN WHAT I SAW ON MY WAY . . . . . 59 BLUEBERRIES   1
     AND SOME OF THEM RIPE! YOU OUGHT TO HAVE SEEN!" . . . 59 BLUEBERRIES   7
     YOU OUGHT TO HAVE SEEN HOW IT LOOKED IN THE RAIN, . . . 62 BLUEBERRIES 103
     THAT SEEMS TO TELL ME HOW I OUGHT TO FEEL, ... 63 A SERVANT TO SERVANTS . 14
     THAT OUGHT TO BE WORTH SOMETHING, AND MAY YET. . . . . 64 A SERVANT TO SERVANTS . 43
     BY GOOD RIGHTS I OUGHT NOT TO HAVE SO MUCH . . . . . . 64 A SERVANT TO SERVANTS . 53
     LEN SAYS ONE STEADY PULL MORE OUGHT TO DO IT. . . . . 64 A SERVANT TO SERVANTS . 55
     "ONE OUGHT NOT TO BE THROWN INTO CONFUSION . . . . . . 75 THE GENERATIONS OF MEN 58
     "JUST SO--THAT OUGHT TO BE ENOUGH PROTECTION." . . . . 75 THE GENERATIONS OF MEN 66
     IT OUGHT TO GIVE A PURER ORACLE." . . . . 78 THE GENERATIONS OF MEN 134
     "IT OUGHT TO BE IN RAIN. SOMETIME IN RAIN. . . . . . . 81 THE GENERATIONS OF MEN 210
     BETTER THAN MARRIED OUGHT TO BE AS GOOD . . . . 84 THE HOUSEKEEPER . . . 81
     WE WOULDN'T HURT A HEN! YOU OUGHT TO SEE US . . . . . 85 THE HOUSEKEEPER . . . 125
     YOU OUGHT TO HAVE THE KITCHEN TO YOURSELF . . . . . . 88 THE HOUSEKEEPER . . . 193
     ONE OUGHT AS A GOOD VILLAGER TO LIKE IT. . . . . 94 THE SELF-SEEKER . . . 44
     HE THINKS YOU OUGHT TO PAY ME FOR MY FLOWERS. . . . . 100 THE SELF-SEEKER . . . 225
     JOE SAID: "YOU BIG BOYS OUGHT TO FIND A FARM, ... 113 IN THE HOME STRETCH . 95
     ONE OUGHT NOT TO HAVE TO CARE . . . . 126 LONELINESS   1
     AND HE SAID, "THAT OUGHT TO MAKE YOU . . . . 133 A GIRL'S GARDEN . . . 13
     OF WORDS, OR IS IT TONGUES I OUGHT TO SAY?" . . . . . 151 SNOW 249

OUGHT (CONTINUED)
```
    AND OUGHT TO DO SOME GOOD IF SPLITTING STARS  . . . .  179  THE STAR-SPLITTER   .  93
    AND TELL PAUL WHAT HE OUGHT TO DO ABOUT IT. . . . . .  193  PAUL'S WIFE  . . . .  79
    I OUGHT TO KNOW WHAT TREE THE GRAPE IS FRUIT OF. . . .  196  WILD GRAPES  . . . .   6
    THAT EVEN I WOULD BE. THEY OUGHT TO KNOW . . . . . .  208  PAUPER WITCH OF GRAFTON  39
    OUGHT TO BE TOLD TO COME AND TAKE HIM IN." . . . . .  223  THE RUNAWAY  . . . .  21
    AND LISTEN--HOW IT OUGHT TO GO!  . . . . . . . . .  224  THE AIM WAS SONG  . .   8
    SUCH A FINE PULLET OUGHT TO GO . . . . . . . . . .  279  BLUE RIBBON AT AMESBURY   1
    "APPARENTLY THESE TWO OUGHT TO MARRY. . . . . . . .  345  DISCOVERY OF MADEIRAS .  69
    (AND SCIENCE OUGHT TO KNOW) . . . . . . . . . .  361  ALMOST TWO THOUSAND  .   9
    AT LEAST IT OUGHT TO SEND . . . . . . . . . . .  389  ASTROMETAPHYSICAL  . .  19
    SEEMS SOMETHING ARTISTS OUGHT TO CELEBRATE. . . . . .  422  FOR JOHN F. KENNEDY  .   3
    THAT OUGHT TO MAKE THE SUNDAY PRESS. . . . . . . .  451  A-WISHING WELL  . . .  19
    "AT LEAST YOU OUGHT TO DIE FOR WIZARDRY. . . . . . .  457  HOW HARD TO KEEP FROM  115
    (YOU OUGHT TO SEE THE COINS DONE IN COS.) . . . . .  459  HOW HARD TO KEEP FROM  187
    WHAT THE SINS ARE MEN OUGHT TO PERISH FOR. . . . . .  503  A MASQUE OF MERCY  . . 261
OUR---NOT INDEXED
CURS---NOT INDEXED
OURSELVES
    AND SAVE OURSELVES UNAIDED. . . . . . . . . . . .   10  STORM FEAR  . . . . .  18
    WE MAKE OURSELVES A PLACE APART . . . . . . . . . .   19  REVELATION  . . . . .   1
    "WE SHAN'T HAVE THE PLACE TO OURSELVES TO ENJOY-- . . .   62  BLUEBERRIES  . . . .  97
    ALL THAT'S NOT NEW IN WHERE WE FIND OURSELVES. . . . .  117  IN THE HOME STRETCH  . 182
    BEFORE WE SET OURSELVES TO RIGHT THE HOUSE, . . . . .  117  IN THE HOME STRETCH  . 194
    "OH, LET'S GO UP THE HILL AND SCARE OURSELVES, . . . .  129  THE BONFIRE  . . . .   1
    AND SCARE OURSELVES. LET WILD FIRE LOOSE WE WILL----" . .  130  THE BONFIRE  . . . .  18
    WE'D KEPT UP ALL THESE YEARS BETWEEN OURSELVES . . . .  207  THE WITCH OF COOS  . . 146
    AND LEAVE YOU THERE, OURSELVES FORBID TO ENTER-- . . .  259  WEST-RUNNING BROOK  .  35
    AGAINST THE STREAM, THAT MOST WE SEE OURSELVES IN, . . .  260  WEST-RUNNING BROOK  .  69
    IN HER WE MAKE OURSELVES ACQUAINTED . . . . . . . .  280  BLUE RIBBON AT AMESBURY  11
    UNTIL WE FOUND OUT THAT IT WAS OURSELVES . . . . . .  348  THE GIFT OUTRIGHT  . .   9
    SUCH AS WE WERE WE GAVE OURSELVES OUTRIGHT . . . . .  348  THE GIFT OUTRIGHT  . .  12
    UNTIL WE FOUND OUT THAT IT WAS OURSELVES . . . . . .  424  THE GIFT OUTRIGHT  . .   9
    SUCH AS WE WERE WE GAVE OURSELVES OUTRIGHT . . . . .  424  THE GIFT OUTRIGHT  . .  12
    BUT OURSELVES--MANKIND,  . . . . . . . . . . . .  436  KITTY HAWK  . . . . . 267
    WE BLAME OURSELVES. WE'RE GOOD SPORTS, AREN'T WE, BEL?  .  496  A MASQUE OF MERCY  . .  78
OUT  (SEE ALL-OUT-DOORS, IRONING-OUT, RUN-OUT, WORN-OUT)
    I'M GOING OUT TO CLEAN THE PASTURE SPRING; . . . . .    1  THE PASTURE  . . . .   1
    I'M GOING OUT TO FETCH THE LITTLE CALF . . . . . .    1  THE PASTURE  . . . .   5
    BEFORE HE ARRIVES TO SAY IT OUT. . . . . . . . .    6  GHOST HOUSE  . . . .  20
    THOSE STONES OUT UNDER THE LOW-LIMBED TREE . . . . .    6  GHOST HOUSE  . . . .  24
    "COME OUT! COME OUT!"-- . . . . . . . . . . . .   10  STORM FEAR  . . . . .   6
    TURN THE POET OUT OF DOOR. . . . . . . . . . . .   12  TO THE THAWING WIND  .  15
    DIMLY TO HAVE MADE OUT MY SECRET PLACE, . . . . . .   14  WAITING  . . . . . .  15
    TILL SOMEONE REALLY FIND US OUT. . . . . . . . . .   19  REVELATION  . . . . .   4
    HAVING FIRST HEARD THE LIFE READ OUT . . . . . . .   20  THE TRIAL BY EXISTENCE  34
    PAN CAME OUT OF THE WOODS ONE DAY-- . . . . . . . .   23  PAN WITH US  . . . .   1
    A NEW-WORLD SONG, FAR OUT OF REACH, . . . . . . . .   24  PAN WITH US  . . . .  17
    I SHALL NOT FORGET HOW HIS LAUGH RANG OUT. . . . . .   25  THE DEMIURGE'S LAUGH  .  13
    OUT THROUGH THE FIELDS AND THE WOODS . . . . . . .   29  RELUCTANCE  . . . . .   1
    OUT OVER THE CRUSTED SNOW, . . . . . . . . . . .   30  RELUCTANCE  . . . . .  11
    BUT THEY WOULD HAVE THE RABBIT OUT OF HIDING, . . . .   33  MENDING WALL  . . . .   8
    WHAT I WAS WALLING IN OR WALLING OUT, . . . . . . .   34  MENDING WALL  . . . .  33
    "HE'S WORN OUT. HE'S ASLEEP BESIDE THE STOVE. . . . .   35  DEATH OF THE HIRED MAN  33
    "YES, I TOOK CARE TO KEEP WELL OUT OF EARSHOT." . . . .   37  DEATH OF THE HIRED MAN  70
    HE TAKES IT OUT IN BUNCHES LIKE BIG BIRDS' NESTS. . . .   37  DEATH OF THE HIRED MAN  93
    AND SPREAD HER APRON TO IT. SHE PUT OUT HER HAND . . .   38  DEATH OF THE HIRED MAN 106
    OUT OF THE WOODS, WORN OUT UPON THE TRAIL." . . . . .   38  DEATH OF THE HIRED MAN 117
    WARREN LEANED OUT AND TOOK A STEP OR TWO, . . . . .   38  DEATH OF THE HIRED MAN 121
    GOOD GRASSLAND GULLIED OUT, AND IN THE GRASS . . . .   40  THE MOUNTAIN  . . . .  13
    OR TURN AND SIT ON AND LOOK OUT AND DOWN, . . . . .   42  THE MOUNTAIN  . . . .  61
    ROLLED OUT A LITTLE FARTHER THAN THE REST." . . . . .   44  THE MOUNTAIN  . . . .  99
    TO THINK OF SITTING SUCH AN ORDEAL OUT, . . . . . .   45  A HUNDRED COLLARS  . .  18
    'FEEL OUT THE PUBLIC SENTIMENT'--HE SAYS. . . . . .   48  A HUNDRED COLLARS  . . 106
    COMING OUT ON THEM FROM A STRETCH OF WOODS, . . . . .   49  A HUNDRED COLLARS  . . 125
    I LIKE TO FIND FOLKS GETTING OUT IN SPRING. . . . . .   49  A HUNDRED COLLARS  . . 127
    LATER THEY GET OUT FURTHER IN THE FIELDS. . . . . .   49  A HUNDRED COLLARS  . . 129
    I DRINK OUT OF THE BOTTLE--NOT YOUR STYLE. . . . . .   50  A HUNDRED COLLARS  . . 156
    "NOT TILL I SHRINK, WHEN THEY'LL BE OUT OF STYLE." . . .   50  A HUNDRED COLLARS  . . 166
    I'LL PUT THE LIGHT OUT. DON'T YOU WAIT FOR ME: . . . .   50  A HUNDRED COLLARS  . . 171
    "I WILL FIND OUT NOW--YOU MUST TELL ME, DEAR." . . . .   51  HOME BURIAL  . . . .  12
    I MUST GET OUT OF HERE. I MUST GET AIR.-- . . . . .   52  HOME BURIAL  . . . .  37
    APART WOULD MAKE ME OUT. I HAVE MY CHANCE. . . . . .   53  HOME BURIAL  . . . .  61
    OUT IN THE KITCHEN, AND I DON'T KNOW WHY, . . . . .   54  HOME BURIAL  . . . .  82
    THE HEART'S GONE OUT OF IT: WHY KEEP IT UP? . . . . .   54  HOME BURIAL  . . . . 110
    SOMEWHERE OUT OF THIS HOUSE. HOW CAN I MAKE YOU----" . .   55  HOME BURIAL  . . . . 113
    THEY LIVE SO FAR AWAY--ONE IS OUT WEST-- . . . . . .   55  THE BLACK COTTAGE  . .  19
    THAT HAD GONE OUT OF IT, THE FATHER FIRST, . . . . .   56  THE BLACK COTTAGE  . .  38
    THE WARPING BOARDS PULL OUT THEIR OWN OLD NAILS . . . .   56  THE BLACK COTTAGE  . .  49
    IS DUE TO TRUTHS BEING IN AND OUT OF FAVOR. . . . . .   58  THE BLACK COTTAGE  . . 110
    FIERCE HEADS LOOKED OUT; SMALL BODIES PIVOTED. . . . .   59  THE BLACK COTTAGE  . . 126
    BUT GET THE PINE OUT OF THE WAY, YOU MAY BURN . . . .   59  BLUEBERRIES  . . . .  17
    AN EXCUSE FOR KEEPING US OTHER FOLK OUT." . . . . .   60  BLUEBERRIES  . . . .  32
    BUT LOREN, THE FATHERLY, OUT FOR A DRIVE. . . . . .   60  BLUEBERRIES  . . . .  39
    AND THE SUN SHINES OUT WARM: THE VINES MUST BE WET. . .   62  BLUEBERRIES  . . . .  83
    THEN SANK OUT OF SIGHT LIKE TROLLS UNDERGROUND, . . . .   62  BLUEBERRIES  . . . .  86
    TOO LOUD FOR THE DISTANCE YOU WERE, IT TURNED OUT, . . .   62  BLUEBERRIES  . . . .  94
    I STAND AND MAKE MYSELF REPEAT OUT LOUD . . . . . .   63  A SERVANT TO SERVANTS .  18
    IT'S REST I WANT--THERE, I HAVE SAID IT OUT-- . . . .   64  A SERVANT TO SERVANTS .  49
    HE SAYS THE BEST WAY OUT IS ALWAYS THROUGH. . . . . .   64  A SERVANT TO SERVANTS .  56
    AS THAT I CAN SEE NO WAY OUT BUT THROUGH-- . . . . .   64  A SERVANT TO SERVANTS .  58
    NO MORE PUT OUT IN WHAT THEY DO OR SAY . . . . . .   65  A SERVANT TO SERVANTS .  79
    UNTIL THE STRENGTH WAS SHOUTED OUT OF HIM, . . . . .   66  A SERVANT TO SERVANTS . 132
    I WAS GLAD THOUGH, NO END, WHEN WE MOVED OUT, . . . .   67  A SERVANT TO SERVANTS . 151
    SOMEHOW THE CHANGE WORE OUT LIKE A PRESCRIPTION. . . .   67  A SERVANT TO SERVANTS . 154
    DROP EVERYTHING AND LIVE OUT ON THE GROUND-- . . . .   67  A SERVANT TO SERVANTS . 162
    "DON'T LET IT BOTHER YOU. YOU'VE FOUND OUT SOMETHING. . .   70  THE CODE  . . . . .  21
    ALL WIRY ARMS AND LEGS THAT SPREAD OUT WAVY . . . . .   70  THE CODE  . . . . .  34
```

                                                             PAGE TITLE   LINE
OUT (CONTINUED)
        OUT OF HIS HIRED HELP. I'M NOT DENYING . . . . 70 THE CODE 38
        TO LOAD THE LOAD, THINKS I, LOOK OUT FOR TROUBLE. . . 71 THE CODE 50
        AND LOOKING UP BEWHISKERED OUT OF THE PIT. . . . . . 71 THE CODE 62
        I ASKED OUT LOUD, SO'S THERE'D BE NO MISTAKE, ... 71 THE CODE 65
        MURDERED HIM AS LEFT OUT HIS MIDDLE NAME. . . . . . . 71 THE CODE 70
        I CLEANED THE RACK AND DROVE OUT TO COOL OFF. . . . . 72 THE CODE 80
        ONE OF THE BOYS SINGS OUT, 'WHERE'S THE OLD MAN?' . . 72 THE CODE 83
        IF YE WANT HIM, YE CAN GO AND DIG HIM OUT.' . . . . . 72 THE CODE 85
        A LOT OF IT, OUT INTO THE BARN FLOOR. . . . . 72 THE CODE 90
        OUT OF THE BARN.' SOMEONE LOOKED IN A WINDOW, ... 72 THE CODE 95
        WE TENDED TO HIS HAY. WE SAW HIM OUT . . . . 73 THE CODE 107
        THE PAST AND GET SOME STRANGENESS OUT OF IT. . . . . 73 THE GENERATIONS OF MEN 18
        THE YOUNG FOLK HELD SOME HOPE OUT TO EACH OTHER . . . 74 THE GENERATIONS OF MEN 21
        ANYONE ELSE, BUT OUT OF IDLENESS. . . . . 74 THE GENERATIONS OF MEN 27
        "YOU LOOK SO, SITTING OUT HERE IN THE RAIN . . . . . 76 THE GENERATIONS OF MEN 84
        WHICH MEANS THE-SEVEN-CAVES-THAT-WE-CAME-OUT-OF. . . . 76 THE GENERATIONS OF MEN 93
        I CAN MAKE OUT OLD GRANDSIR STARK DISTINCTLY-- . . . 77 THE GENERATIONS OF MEN 104
        HERE'S HOPING SHE GETS HER DRINK AND GETS OUT SAFELY." 77 THE GENERATIONS OF MEN 109
        TO SET THE VOICES SPEAKING OUT OF IT, ... 78 THE GENERATIONS OF MEN 129
        THE MEANING OF IT ALL IS OUT OF YOU; . . . . 78 THE GENERATIONS OF MEN 136
        THE LIFE IS NOT YET ALL GONE OUT OF IT. . . . . 79 THE GENERATIONS OF MEN 165
        LET PEOPLE IN THAN I CAN KEEP THEM OUT. . . . . 81 THE HOUSEKEEPER . . .   4
        I HELP OUT WITH THIS BEADWORK WHAT I CAN." . . . . . 81 THE HOUSEKEEPER . . .   8
        TWO OF YOU OUT WILL LEAVE AN EMPTY HOUSE." . . . . . 82 THE HOUSEKEEPER . . . 42
        TAKE IT YEAR IN, YEAR OUT, HE DOESN'T MAKE MUCH. . . . 85 THE HOUSEKEEPER . . . 103
        OF BOTH OF US. BUT LOOK HOW IT TURNS OUT: . . . . . . 85 THE HOUSEKEEPER . . . 106
        "WHO'D MARRY HER STRAIGHT OUT OF SUCH A MESS? . . . . 88 THE HOUSEKEEPER . . . 186
        SAY IT RIGHT OUT--NO MATTER FOR HER MOTHER. . . . . . 88 THE HOUSEKEEPER . . . 187
        AND TURN DOLL OUT TO PASTURE, RIG AND ALL. . . . . . 88 THE HOUSEKEEPER . . . 201
        COME OUT HERE IF YOU WANT TO HEAR ME TALK.-- . . . . 88 THE HOUSEKEEPER . . . 208
        THE WOMAN SPOKE OUT SHARPLY, "WHOA, STAND STILL!-- . 89 THE FEAR   8
        SEEMED TO WARN SOMEONE TO BE GETTING OUT . . . . . . 89 THE FEAR 20
        AND NOW'S THE TIME TO HAVE IT OUT WITH HIM . . . . . 90 THE FEAR 43
        AROUND US, LOOKING OUT OF TREES AND BUSHES . . . . . 90 THE FEAR 46
        "OUT WALKING. EVERY CHILD SHOULD HAVE THE MEMORY . . 92 THE FEAR 82
        IT TOUCHED, IT STRUCK, IT CLATTERED AND WENT OUT. . . 92 THE FEAR 93
        OF A STARFISH LAID OUT WITH RIGID POINTS." . . . . . 93 THE SELF-SEEKER . . . 20
        I JUST EMBRACED THE SHAFT AND RODE IT OUT-- . . . . . 93 THE SELF-SEEKER . . . 26
        "BUT YOUR FLOWERS, MAN, YOU'RE SELLING OUT YOUR FLOWERS." 95 THE SELF-SEEKER . . . 66
        COME, HOLD IT OUT. DON'T CHANGE.--A RAM'S HORN ORCHID! 96 THE SELF-SEEKER . . . 112
        IF I HAD CHOSEN LEFT. HOLD OUT THE LEFT. . . . . . . 97 THE SELF-SEEKER . . . 114
        WITH A LAWYER AT HAND TO FIND YOU OUT. . . . . 97 THE SELF-SEEKER . . . 134
        PRESSED INTO SERVICE MEANS PRESSED OUT OF SHAPE. . . . 98 THE SELF-SEEKER . . . 149
        NOW RUN.--GET OUT YOUR DOCUMENTS! YOU SEE . . . . . . 99 THE SELF-SEEKER . . . 175
        I'LL PUT YOU OUT WITH ANNE. BE GOOD OR GO." . . . . . 99 THE SELF-SEEKER . . . 186
        OUT WITH IT IF YOU'VE ANY REAL OBJECTION." . . . . . 99 THE SELF-SEEKER . . . 197
        OUT WALKING IN THE FROZEN SWAMP ONE GRAY DAY, ... 101 THE WOOD-PILE   1
        ONE FLIGHT OUT SIDEWAYS WOULD HAVE UNDECEIVED HIM. . . 101 THE WOOD-PILE 17
        HE SAT AND WAITED TILL HE DREW US OUT, ... 106 CHRISTMAS TREES . . .   7
        (FOR THAT WAS ALL THEY FIGURED OUT APIECE)-- . . . . 107 CHRISTMAS TREES . . . 49
        OVER THE SINK OUT THROUGH A DUSTY WINDOW, ... 110 IN THE HOME STRETCH .   2
        "WHAT ARE YOU SEEING OUT THE WINDOW, LADY?" . . . . . 111 IN THE HOME STRETCH . 20
        WHAT ARE YOU SEEING OUT THE WINDOW, LADY?" . . . . . 111 IN THE HOME STRETCH . 25
        MORE THAN YOU LIKE TO OWN TO OUT THAT WINDOW." . . . 112 IN THE HOME STRETCH . 45
        AND OIL ARE BURIED OUT OF REACH?" / AGAIN . . . . . . 113 IN THE HOME STRETCH . 81
        AND PUT EACH OTHER BODILY OUT OF THE HOUSE. . . . . . 114 IN THE HOME STRETCH . 110
        THEIR COMING OUT AND MAKING USEFUL FARMERS." . . . . 114 IN THE HOME STRETCH . 121
        TILL ED BEGINS TO GET OUT ON A SUNDAY . . . . 115 IN THE HOME STRETCH . 148
        TO HELP US, BUT HE'LL TAKE IT OUT IN PLANNING. . . . 115 IN THE HOME STRETCH . 153
        YOU'RE TIRED." / "I'M DRUNK-NONSENSICAL TIRED OUT; . . 116 IN THE HOME STRETCH . 158
        "I DON'T WANT TO FIND OUT WHAT CAN'T BE KNOWN. . . . 116 IN THE HOME STRETCH . 170
        TO DRAG YOU OUT FOR JUST A GOOD-NIGHT CALL . . . . . 117 IN THE HOME STRETCH . 188
        THE FIRST THING IN THE MORNING, OUT WE GO . . . . . . 117 IN THE HOME STRETCH . 195
        THE FIRE GOT OUT THROUGH CRANNIES IN THE STOVE . . . 117 IN THE HOME STRETCH . 202
        BY JUNE OUR BROOK'S RUN OUT OF SONG AND SPEED. . . . 119 HYLA BROOK   1
        WALL WITHIN WALL TO SHUT FEAR OUT. . . . . 120 BOND AND FREE   3
        AS HE WENT OUT AND IN TO FETCH THE COWS-- . . . . . . 121 BIRCHES 24
        UNTIL HE TOOK THE STIFFNESS OUT OF THEM, ... 122 BIRCHES 30
        TO LEARN ABOUT NOT LAUNCHING OUT TOO SOON . . . . . . 122 BIRCHES 33
        SOMETIMES I WANDER OUT OF BEATEN WAYS . . . . 125 AN ENCOUNTER 23
        AND PREFERRING THE OUT- TO THE INDOOR NIGHT, ... 127 HOUSE FEAR   8
        THE FIRE ITSELF CAN PUT IT OUT, AND THAT . . . . . . 130 THE BONFIRE 25
        BY BURNING OUT, AND BEFORE IT BURNS OUT . . . . 130 THE BONFIRE 26
        AND SAID OUT LOUD, I COULDN'T BIDE THE SMOTHER . . . 131 THE BONFIRE 70
        THE TOWN TURNED OUT TO FIGHT FOR ME--THAT HELD ME. . . 131 THE BONFIRE 73
        ABOUT THE SHIPS WHERE WAR HAS FOUND THEM OUT . . . . 132 THE BONFIRE 104
        THE FLOWERS WERE OUT THERE WITH THE THIEVES. . . . . 135 LOCKED OUT   6
        LOCKED OUT . . . . 135 LOCKED OUT . . . . .   T
        AS I WENT OUT A CROW . . . . 135 LAST WORD OF A BLUEBIRD   1
        LEAPED OUT AT THE BOY'S HAND, OR SEEMED TO LEAP-- . . 136 "OUT,OUT--" 16
        "OUT, OUT--" . . . . 136 "OUT,OUT--" . . . . .   T
        HE LAY AND PUFFED HIS LIPS OUT WITH HIS BREATH. . . . 137 "OUT,OUT--" 29
        AND BLEW HIM OUT ON THE ICY CRUST . . . . 137 BROWN'S DESCENT . . . 11
        (BUT SAVED THE LIGHT FROM GOING OUT). . . . . 138 BROWN'S DESCENT . . . 39
        SHOULD SAY OUR STOCK WAS PETERED OUT, ... 139 BROWN'S DESCENT . . . 51
        'BOUT OUT!' AND TOOK THE LONG WAY HOME . . . . 140 BROWN'S DESCENT . . . 75
        WHEREIN WORDS WHETHER BEATEN OUT OR SPOKEN . . . . . 141 THE LINE-GANG   6
        OUT THROUGH THE SHED." / "I GUESS I KNOW MY WAY. . . 144 SNOW 38
        I DIDN'T USE IT OUT OF LOVE OF HIM, ... 144 SNOW 50
        "WHAT IS HE DOING OUT A NIGHT LIKE THIS? . . . . . . 145 SNOW 68
        "IT'S NO NIGHT TO BE OUT." / "HE MAY BE SMALL, . . . 145 SNOW 70
        OUT OF ONE OF THOSE PIOUS SCALAWAGS." . . . . 146 SNOW 92
        BY STRAIGHTENING OUT AND LIFTING A FOREFINGER, . . . 147 SNOW 113
        I'VE HAD MY EYE ON IT TO MAKE OUT WHICH: . . . . . . 147 SNOW 120
        ONE OF THE LIES WOULD MAKE IT OUT THAT NOTHING . . . 147 SNOW 129
        WHO HAVE TO GO OUT INTO IT ALONE." . . . . 149 SNOW 170
        YOU RECOLLECT THE BOY WHO CAME OUT HERE . . . . 149 SNOW 173

OUT (CONTINUED)

	PAGE	TITLE	LINE
BUT BANKED THE DAYLIGHT OUT OF AVERY'S WINDOWS.	149	SNOW	186
MORE THAN I SHALL OUT IN IT. BUT THE HORSES	150	SNOW	209
IN NO TIME OUT TONIGHT. AND YET TOMORROW	151	SNOW	229
WHAT? WE'VE FOUND OUT IN ONE HOUR MORE ABOUT HIM	152	SNOW	252
"FRED, AFTER ALL I SAID! YOU SHAN'T MAKE OUT	153	SNOW	285
WIDE OPEN AND THE WIND'S BLOWN OUT THE LAMP	154	SNOW	309
THAT IS, ASSUMING--THAT SHE HAS GONE OUT.	155	SNOW	323
"FRED, I SHAN'T LET YOU THINK OF GOING OUT."	155	SNOW	326
TO ROUT US OUT TO THINK FOR HIM AT MIDNIGHT	155	SNOW	346
AS IF TO PUT FOREVER OUT OF MIND	160	NEW HAMPSHIRE	42
AND BOYS THE MINUTE THEY GET OUT OF COLLEGE.	162	NEW HAMPSHIRE	98
FAR UP THE BIRCHES OUT OF REACH OF MAN.	164	NEW HAMPSHIRE	164
IT SET OUT ONCE TO BE A CITY AND STILL	165	NEW HAMPSHIRE	191
SHE SAID, "GO READ YOUR OWN BOOKS AND FIND OUT."	166	NEW HAMPSHIRE	227
"WHY, THIS IS HELL, NOR AM I OUT OF IT."	166	NEW HAMPSHIRE	243
OUT OF NOT HAVING CAUSE FOR MISERY.	167	NEW HAMPSHIRE	273
FLOWERS FANNED AND NOT PUT OUT BY ALL THE RAIN	173	A STAR IN A STONEBOAT	23
NOW BRINGING OUT ITS RINGS IN SUGAR OF PITCH;	175	THE CENSUS-TAKER	21
IF ONE BY ONE WE COUNTED PEOPLE OUT	177	THE STAR-SPLITTER	44
UNEATEN, UNWORN OUT, OR UNDISPOSED OF.	178	THE STAR-SPLITTER	52
OUT OF A HOUSE AND SO OUT OF A FARM	178	THE STAR-SPLITTER	66
WAS SETTING OUT, UP TRACK AND DOWN, NOT PLANTS	178	THE STAR-SPLITTER	71
BRADFORD AND I HAD OUT THE TELESCOPE.	179	THE STAR-SPLITTER	82
GOING THE OTHER OUT OF LIFE--YOU KNOW?	180	MAPLE	13
HER PROBLEM WAS TO FIND OUT WHAT IT ASKED	181	MAPLE	52
WATCHING OUT OF A NINETEENTH STORY WINDOW	182	MAPLE	81
THE NEXT COW MIGHT HAVE LICKED UP OUT AT PASTURE.	184	MAPLE	151
TAKING THE CHILD OUT OF THE PARENTS' HANDS.	185	MAPLE	167
ONE BACK AND FORWARD, IN AND OUT OF SHADOW,	186	THE AX-HELVE	48
NEEDLESSLY SOON HE HAD HIS AX-HELVES OUT,	187	THE AX-HELVE	63
HAD BEAUTIES HE HAD TO POINT ME OUT AT LENGTH	187	THE AX-HELVE	67
THAN GRINDING DISCORD OUT OF A GRINDSTONE,	190	THE GRINDSTONE	54
TO DRIVE PAUL OUT OF ANY LUMBER CAMP	191	PAUL'S WIFE	1
OUT OF A WHITE-PINE LOG. MURPHY WAS THERE	192	PAUL'S WIFE	55
TO WANT TO FIND OUT IF HE COULDN'T PILE	193	PAUL'S WIFE	60
TO SEE IF IT WAS EMPTY. HE MADE OUT IN THERE	194	PAUL'S WIFE	90
AND LET OUT A LOUD YELL, AND THREW A BOTTLE,	195	PAUL'S WIFE	140
BUT THE SHOUT REACHED THE GIRL AND PUT HER LIGHT OUT.	195	PAUL'S WIFE	143
SHE WENT OUT LIKE A FIREFLY, AND THAT WAS ALL.	195	PAUL'S WIFE	144
BUT THAT BEGINNING WAS WIPED OUT IN FEAR.	196	WILD GRAPES	10
AND GIVE MYSELF OUT AS TWO DIFFERENT AGES,	196	WILD GRAPES	17
HUNG BABIES OUT ON BRANCHES BY THE HANDS.	197	WILD GRAPES	51
THEN TURNED HIM OUT TO GO ON OTHER ERRANDS	201	PLACE FOR A THIRD	53
HOUSEKEEPING FOR THE NEXT MAN OUT OF WEDLOCK.	201	PLACE FOR A THIRD	62
SO AS TO SORT OF TURN ME OUT OF IT.	203	THE WITCH OF COOS	43
FLASHED OUT AND LICKED ALONG HIS UPPER TEETH.	204	THE WITCH OF COOS	73
"WHAT BONES?" "THE CELLAR BONES--OUT OF THE GRAVE."	205	THE WITCH OF COOS	101
THAT MADE HIM THROW HIS BARE LEGS OUT OF BED	205	THE WITCH OF COOS	102
I WANTED TO PUT OUT THE LIGHT AND SEE	205	THE WITCH OF COOS	104
WE NEVER COULD FIND OUT WHOSE BONES THEY WERE.	206	THE WITCH OF COOS	137
AMONG THE BUTTONS POURED OUT IN HER LAP.	207	THE WITCH OF COOS	153
SAID THAT I TOOK HIM OUT IN HIS OLD AGE	208	PAUPER WITCH OF GRAFTON	46
I GUESS HE FOUND HE GOT MORE OUT OF ME	209	PAUPER WITCH OF GRAFTON	76
LAST NIGHT WAS ONE OF HER NIGHTS OUT. SHE'S KITING.	209	PAUPER WITCH OF GRAFTON	81
AND FROM BARN SMELLS YOU CAN'T WASH OUT OF PLOWED GROUND	210	PAUPER WITCH OF GRAFTON	91
TO MAKE THEM OUT."	212	AN EMPTY THREAT	57
THERE'D BEEN SOME BOSTON PEOPLE OUT TO SEE IT;	212	A FOUNTAIN, A BOTTLE	3
WE MADE A DAY OF IT OUT OF THE WORLD,	214	A FOUNTAIN, A BOTTLE	33
WE CAME OUT ON A LOOK-OFF WHERE WE FACED	214	A FOUNTAIN, A BOTTLE	37
TO FIND OUT WHAT TO DO TO HURT A POEM.	216	A FOUNTAIN, A BOTTLE	108
TO SEND IT SAILING OUT THE ATTIC WINDOW	216	A FOUNTAIN, A BOTTLE	110
TILL IT CAUGHT WIND AND, OPENING OUT ITS COVERS,	216	A FOUNTAIN, A BOTTLE	111
WHERE IS HIS MOTHER? HE CAN'T BE OUT ALONE."	223	THE RUNAWAY	14
"WHOEVER IT IS THAT LEAVES HIM OUT SO LATE,	223	THE RUNAWAY	19
LOCKING OUT OF A WREATH OF FERN AND CLOUD PUFFS.	225	FOR ONCE SOMETHING	6
BLURRED IT, BLOTTED IT OUT. WHAT WAS THAT WHITENESS?	225	FOR ONCE SOMETHING	14
AND NOW FROM HAVING RIDDEN OUT DESIRE	225	BLUE-BUTTERFLY DAY	6
BY SETTING IT OUT ON A NORTHERLY SLOPE.)	228	GOOD-BY AND KEEP COLD	14
THE WEST WAS GETTING OUT OF GOLD,	232	LOOKING FOR SUNSET BIRD	1
TEN MILLION SILVER LIZARDS OUT OF SNOW!	237	A HILLSIDE THAW	3
I BLEW OUT THE LIGHT,	240	THE LOCKLESS DOOR	5
AT BROKEN WINDOWS FLEW OUT AND IN,	242	NEED OF BEING VERSED	14
AND YET NOT OUT BY ANY BROOK OR RIVER,	245	SPRING POOLS	5
TO BLOT OUT AND DRINK UP AND SWEEP AWAY	245	SPRING POOLS	10
KEEPING ITS LIFE SO CLOSE AND OUT OF SIGHT	248	THE COCOON	8
I WANT TO GET OUT OF THE TRAIN AND GO BACK	248	A PASSING GLIMPSE	3
BEFORE GOD'S LAST PUT OUT THE LIGHT WAS SPOKEN.	250	ONCE BY THE PACIFIC	14
OUT IN THE PORCH'S SAGGING FLOOR	251	BEREFT	8
VAGUE DREAM-HEAD LIFTED OUT OF THE GROUND,	251	TREE AT MY WINDOW	5
OUT ALONE IN THE WINTER RAIN,	252	THE THATCH	1
BUT NEVER WAS I FAR OUT OF SIGHT	253	THE THATCH	3
I WOULD NOT GO IN TILL THE LIGHT WENT OUT;	253	THE THATCH	6
IT WOULD NOT GO OUT TILL I CAME IN.	253	THE THATCH	7
I FLUSHED BIRDS OUT OF HOLE AFTER HOLE,	253	THE THATCH	19
WHERE CONIES NOW COME OUT TO SUN AND ROMP,	254	A WINTER EDEN	2
OH, BLOOD WILL OUT. IT CANNOT BE CONTAINED.	255	THE FLOOD	14
I HAVE WALKED OUT IN RAIN--AND BACK IN RAIN.	255	ACQUAINTED WITH NIGHT	2
BE HER LAST JOY HER HEART'S GOING OUT TO THIS ONE	257	THE LOVELY BE CHOOSERS	50
OUT IN THE PLOWED GROUND IN THE COLD A DIGGER,	263	THE INVESTMENT	5
BUT GET SOME COLOR AND MUSIC OUT OF LIFE?	264	THE INVESTMENT	14
I REACHED OUT BLINDLY TO SAVE MY FACE,	265	THE DOOR IN THE DARK	2
WHEN I SPREAD OUT MY HAND HERE TODAY,	266	SITTING BY A BUSH	1
NOR STRIKE OUT FIRE FROM EACH OTHER, NOR CRASH OUT LOUD.	268	ON LOOKING UP BY CHANCE	5
AND FOLLOWED IT TO WHERE HE MADE OUT VAGUE	270	THE EGG AND THE MACHINE	19
OUT OF THE MUD TWO STRANGERS CAME	275	TWO TRAMPS IN MUD TIME	1
WHEN THE SUN IS OUT AND THE WIND IS STILL,	275	TWO TRAMPS IN MUD TIME	19
OUT OF THE WOODS TWO HULKING TRAMPS	276	TWO TRAMPS IN MUD TIME	49

```
                                                            PAGE TITLE                     LINE
OUT (CONTINUED)
    THE EXIT HE COMES OUT AT LIKE A BULLET    . . . . .  . 277 THE WHITE-TAILED HORNET      3
    HE COMES OUT MORE UNERRING THAN A BULLET. . . . . .  . 277 THE WHITE-TAILED HORNET      6
    IN AT ONE DOOR PERHAPS AND OUT ANOTHER, . . . . . .  . 278 THE WHITE-TAILED HORNET     25
    LIKE PEOPLE THROWN OUT TO DELAY THE WOLVES. . . . .  . 279 THE WHITE-TAILED HORNET     68
    AND DON'T COME OUT FOR A WHILE, . . . . . . . . . .  . 282 A DRUMLIN WOODCHUCK       . 18
    THE LITTLE OLD HOUSE WAS OUT WITH A LITTLE NEW SHED    . 286 A ROADSIDE STAND    . .    1
    OR IF EVER ASIDE A MOMENT, THEN OUT OF SORTS   . . .  . 286 A ROADSIDE STAND    . .    8
    ARE TO BE BOUGHT OUT AND MERCIFULLY GATHERED IN   .  . 286 A ROADSIDE STAND    . .   24
    THAT ARE CALCULATED TO SOOTHE THEM OUT OF THEIR WITS, . 287 A ROADSIDE STAND    . .   29
    TO PUT THESE PEOPLE AT ONE STROKE OUT OF THEIR PAIN. . 287 A ROADSIDE STAND    . .   48
    AND OFFER TO PUT ME GENTLY OUT OF MY PAIN.    . . .  . 287 A ROADSIDE STAND    . .   51
    WHOSE WORK IS TO FIND OUT GOD   . . . . . . . . .    . 288 DEPARTMENTAL    . . . .   10
    CARRIES HIM OUT OF THERE. . . . . . . . . . . . .    . 289 DEPARTMENTAL    . . . .   39
    THE GUN REVERSED THAT HE WENT OUT WITH SHOULDERED.   . 289 OLD BARN AT THE BOTTOM     4
    THE FUR-THING, MUFF-THING, ROCKING IN AND OUT   . .  . 289 OLD BARN AT THE BOTTOM     8
    LOOKING OUT OF MY LOWER BERTH   . . . . . . . . .    . 290 ON HEART'S BEGINNING TO    3
    WHEN ONE WILL SAY, "LET US PUT IT OUT."   . . . . .  . 291 ON HEART'S BEGINNING TO   22
    THEY CAN PUT IT OUT WHENEVER THEY PLEASE.   . . . .  . 291 ON HEART'S BEGINNING TO   25
    ONE LOOKS OUT LAST FROM THE DARKENED ROOM   . . . .  . 291 ON HEART'S BEGINNING TO   26
    BUT EARLIER OUT FOR BED TONIGHT,    . . . . . . .    . 292 ON HEART'S BEGINNING TO   40
    THE STARS ARE BROUGHT OUT BRIGHT.   . . . . . . .    . 301 VOICE WAYS    . . . .      5
    NEITHER OUT FAR NOR IN DEEP   . . . . . . . . . .    . 301 NEITHER OUT FAR NOR IN     T
    THEY CANNOT LOOK OUT FAR.   . . . . . . . . . . .    . 301 NEITHER OUT FAR NOR IN    13
    IF SINGING OUT OF SLEEP AND DREAM THAT WAY    . . :  . 303 A BIRD SINGING IN SLEEP   13
    MAY MUCH STAY OUT OF OUR STATED PLAN,   . . . . .    . 305 UNHARVESTED   . . . . .   12
    HAS BEEN THOUGHT OUT AND ACCOUNTED FOR.   . . . .    . 306 A TRIAL RUN   . . . . .   12
    IF HE LEAVES IT TO NATURE TO CARRY OUT THE SENTENCE. . 307 NOT QUITE SOCIAL    . .   14
    THEY MADE HIM SEND OUT A CALL   . . . . . . . . .    . 310 THE VINDICTIVES   . . .   10
    OUT OF TEMPLE AND PALACE AND STORE.   . . . . . .    . 310 THE VINDICTIVES   . . .   13
    AND PUT OUT ITS LIGHT FOR THE FOE.    . . . . . .    . 311 THE VINDICTIVES   . . .   36
    THEIR TONGUES HANGING OUT UNASSUAGED.   . . . . .    . 311 THE VINDICTIVES   . . .   51
    AND WIPE THAT OUT OF THE EARTH.   . . . . . . . .    . 313 THE VINDICTIVES   . . .   84
    LIKE A YARDFUL OF SCHOOLBOYS OUT AT RECESS    . . .  . 318 BUILD SOIL    . . . .     61
    WILL PUT TEN THOUSAND FARMERS OUT OF SHEEP.   . . .  . 319 BUILD SOIL    . . . .    110
    WE'RE ALWAYS TOO MUCH OUT OR TOO MUCH IN.   . . . .  . 320 BUILD SOIL    . . . .    137
    WE'RE SO MUCH OUT THAT THE ODDS ARE AGAINST   . . .  . 320 BUILD SOIL    . . . .    139
    TOO MEAN A THOUGHT TO GET MUCH COMFORT OUT OF.    .  . 321 BUILD SOIL    . . . .    168
    BUT WHAT YOU RAISE OR GROW, WHY, FEED IT OUT,   . .  . 323 BUILD SOIL    . . . .    215
    IT TAKES TEN YEARS OR SO TO CARRY OUT.    . . . . .  . 323 BUILD SOIL    . . . .    226
    TO THINK IT OUT. COME CLOSE, LET US CONSPIRE--   . .  . 323 BUILD SOIL    . . . .    228
    WE ARE TOO MUCH OUT, AND IF WE WON'T DRAW IN    . .  . 324 BUILD SOIL    . . . .    243
    WE'RE TOO UNSEPARATE OUT AMONG EACH OTHER--   . . .  . 324 BUILD SOIL    . . . .    268
    OF WORKING OUT THE REST, THE OTHER HALF.    . . . .  . 324 BUILD SOIL    . . . .    272
    THUS TRUTH'S ESTABLISHED AND BORNE OUT,   . . . . .  . 331 BEECH   . . . . . .       10
    BRING OUT THE STARS, BRING OUT THE FLOWERS,   . . .  . 332 ALL REVELATION    . . .   17
    BUT NO, I WAS OUT FOR STARS:  . . . . . . . . . .    . 334 COME IN   . . . . . .     17
    TILL THEY WERE OUT OF HEARING   . . . . . . . . .    . 335 CARPE DIEM    . . . . .    7
    HE WOULD CRY OUT ON LIFE, THAT WHAT IT WANTS    . .  . 338 THE MOST OF IT    . . .    6
    HE PEERS OUT SHREWDLY INTO THE THICK AND SWIFT.   .  . 341 WILLFUL HOMING    . . .    8
    SHE WAS CARRIED OUT BESIDE THE MAST,    . . . . . .  . 344 DISCOVERY OF MADEIRAS     36
    UNTIL WE FOUND OUT THAT IT WAS OURSELVES    . . . .  . 348 THE GIFT OUTRIGHT   . .    9
    WHO KNOW EXACTLY WHAT IS OUT OF JOINT   . . . . . .  . 351 THE LESSON FOR TODAY      32
    BUT MUST LIVE LIVES OUT MENTALLY AGAPE    . . . . .  . 351 THE LESSON FOR TODAY      40
    ITS CONTEMPLATION MAKES US OUT AS SMALL   . . . . .  . 352 THE LESSON FOR TODAY      69
    TIME OUT    . . . . . . . . . . . . . . . . . .     . 355 TIME OUT    . . . . .      T
    BUT STAY AND HEAR ME OUT. I SURELY THINK    . . . .  . 356 A MOTH SEEN IN WINTER     10
    NOT LABORED OUT OF MINES,   . . . . . . . . . . .    . 361 ALMOST TWO THOUSAND        3
    ALL OUT OF TIME PELL-MELL!  . . . . . . . . . . .    . 365 A NATURE NOTE   . . . .    9
    FOR ME TO SEND YOU ONE OUT WHERE YOU LIVE   . . . .  . 365 OF STONES OF THE PLACE     5
    AT THE ONE HOUSE A CHILD WAS OUT    . . . . . . .    . 366 NOT OF SCHOOL AGE   . .    5
    HE BET IT WAS OUT TODAY,    . . . . . . . . . . .    . 367 NOT OF SCHOOL AGE   . .   27
    CALLED GETTING OUT OF THE WRONG SIDE OF BED.    . .  . 371 THE LITERATE FARMER AND  107
    OR SOON WE'D BAT EACH OTHER OUT OF TOUCH,   . . . .  . 371 THE LITERATE FARMER AND  117
    A BED'S GOT NO RIGHT SIDE TO GET OUT OF.    . . . .  . 372 THE LITERATE FARMER AND  125
    WHEN YOU WERE READING BOOKS OR OUT OF TOWN.   . . .  . 375 A YOUNG BIRCH   . . . .   20
    TO LIVE ITS LIFE OUT AS AN ORNAMENT.    . . . . . .  . 375 A YOUNG BIRCH   . . . .   22
    WILL HAVE CROWDED OUT THE EDIBLE GRASS.   . . . . .  . 376 SOMETHING FOR HOPE  . .    4
    AND CROWD THEM OUT AT A SIMILAR RATE.   . . . . . .  . 376 SOMETHING FOR HOPE  . .    8
    AND THE SUN CAME OUT TO DRY ME.   . . . . . . . .    . 377 ONE STEP BACKWARD TAKEN   14
    BACK OUT OF ALL THIS NOW TOO MUCH FOR US,   . . . .  . 377 DIRECTIVE   . . . . . .    1
    AS IF BY EYE PAIRS OUT OF FORTY FIRKINS.    . . . .  . 378 DIRECTIVE   . . . . . .   22
    THEY THINK TOO MUCH OF HAVING SHADED OUT    . . . .  . 378 DIRECTIVE   . . . . . .   27
    TO LEAVE IT TO THEM TO GET OUT OF THEIR VALLEYS.  .  . 379 TOO ANXIOUS FOR RIVERS     7
    BEFORE SHE MUST PUT OUT THE LIGHT ON THE CHILDREN .  . 379 TOO ANXIOUS FOR RIVERS    18
    KEPT SOME DEW OUT AND SOME HEAT IN,   . . . . . .    . 380 AN UNSTAMPED LETTER IN    15
    IF NOT INDEED FROM SLEEPING OUT,    . . . . . . .    . 381 AN UNSTAMPED LETTER IN    47
    LIKE A STAR FRESH FALLEN OUT OF THE SKY.    . . . .  . 383 WERE I IN TROUBLE   . .    5
    WE WOULD CRAWL OUT FILING SINGLE    . . . . . . .    . 384 IN THE LONG NIGHT   . .    7
    WHAT IF IT SHOULD TURN OUT ETERNITY   . . . . . .    . 386 A STEEPLE ON THE HOUSE     1
    COMPRESSION TO UPLIFT US OUT OF WEIGHT--    . . . .  . 387 INNATE HELIUM   . . . .    3
    WILL BRING HER OUT, DIMINISHED DIM,   . . . . . .    . 390 TWO LEADING LIGHTS  . .   19
    THE PLAY SEEMS OUT FOR AN ALMOST INFINITE RUN.    .  . 392 IT BIDS PRETTY FAIR   .    1
    BUT HIS MIND IS HARDLY OUT OF HIS TEENS:    . . . .  . 393 A CASE FOR JEFFERSON  .    8
    OR BE WIPED OUT. WILL SHE BE ASKED TO SHOW   . . .  . 395 WHY WAIT FOR SCIENCE  .    5
    HE STRETCHED HIS ARMS OUT TO THE DARK OF SPACE   .  . 396 ANY SIZE WE PLEASE  . .    5
    HE HAD BEEN TOO ALL OUT, TOO MUCH EXTENDED.   . . .  . 396 ANY SIZE WE PLEASE  . .   12
    GET PARCELED OUT AMONG THE WINNING GIANTS.    . . .  . 398 NO HOLY WARS FOR THEM .    8
    GOOD ORATORS WILL DO WHEN THEY ARE OUT.   . . . . .  . 400 THE BROKEN DROUGHT  . .    8
    SINCE DARK IS WHAT BRINGS OUT YOUR LIGHT.   . . . .  . 403 SOMETHING LIKE A STAR .    5
    I GET YOU WHEN YOU HOE OUT TO THE RIVER,    . . . .  . 405 FROM PLANE TO PLANE   .   40
    THEN'S WHEN HIS MORGAN LIGHTS OUT THROWING SNOWBALLS . 407 FROM PLANE TO PLANE   .  107
    AND SO IT SEEMS A FLOWER'S COMING OUT   . . . . .    . 411 POD OF THE MILKWEED   .    8
    NOW I OUT WALKING   . . . . . . . . . . . . . .     . 412 AWAY!   . . . . . . .      1
    PUT OUT OF THE PARK.    . . . . . . . . . . . . .    . 413 AWAY!   . . . . . . .     12
    AM PUT OUT WITH   . . . . . . . . . . . . . . .     . 413 AWAY!   . . . . . . .     15
    OR PUT OUT BY.  . . . . . . . . . . . . . . . .     . 413 AWAY!   . . . . . . .     16
    THAT LEANS OUT THIS AND THAT WAY FROM THEIR CHIMNEY. . 414 A CABIN IN THE CLEARING   11
```

OUT (CONTINUED)
  PUTTING THE LAMP OUT HAS NOT PUT THEIR THOUGHT OUT. . . . . 415 A CABIN IN THE CLEARING 36
  OF OUR ENACTING OUT THE DOOM . . . . 417 AMERICA IS HARD TO SEE   38
  AND FOR NOT TURNING OUT A STRAIT, ... 418 AMERICA IS HARD TO SEE   52
  HE WAS AT THE DOOR TO BE LET OUT . . . . 420 ONE MORE BREVITY . . 45
  AND COUNTED OUT. HEROIC DEEDS WERE DONE. . . . . . . 422 FOR JOHN F. KENNEDY   17
  GLORY IS OUT OF DATE IN LIFE AND ART. . . . . 423 FOR JOHN F. KENNEDY   50
  UNTIL WE FOUND OUT THAT IT WAS OURSELVES . . . . . . 424 THE GIFT OUTRIGHT . . 9
  OUT OF COMING-IN . . . . 426 A NEVER NAUGHT SONG   27
  OUT AND DOWN ALONG . . . . 428 KITTY HAWK 7
  OUT OF SORTS WITH FATE, ... 428 KITTY HAWK 11
  OUT TO KILL A DUCK . . . . 431 KITTY HAWK 108
  OUT FROM WHERE WE WERE. . . . . 439 KITTY HAWK 346
  AND A MAN CAME OUT OF THE TREES . . . . 444 THE DRAFT HORSE . . . 5
  STREAMED OUT LIKE PENNANTS SWALLOW-TAIL. . . . . . . 452 A-WISHING WELL . . . 53
  I'M GETTING OUT TONIGHT. HERE, TAKE THE CROWN." . . . 453 HOW HARD TO KEEP FROM   3
  "A MAN'S OUT THERE WHO CLAIMS HE KNOWS THE SECRET, . . 455 HOW HARD TO KEEP FROM   60
  DARE TO SPEAK OUT AND TELL ME ABOUT MYSELF. . . . . 456 HOW HARD TO KEEP FROM   100
  I PICKED YOU OUT A HORSE CALLED SAFETY THIRD, ... 457 HOW HARD TO KEEP FROM   123
  BY SAFETY SECOND OUT OF SAFETY FIRST, ... 457 HOW HARD TO KEEP FROM   124
  UNTIL THE EDDY OF IT EDDIES OUT." . . . . 459 HOW HARD TO KEEP FROM   161
  TO BE A TEST. IT DIDN'T LAST HIM OUT. . . . . 459 HOW HARD TO KEEP FROM   178
  FREE VERSE LEAVES OUT THE METER AND MAKES UP . . . . 460 HOW HARD TO KEEP FROM   219
  BUT SUMMONS OUT OF NOWHERE LIKE A JINNI. . . . . . . 461 HOW HARD TO KEEP FROM   240
  SHE LET OUT A HOWL OF RAGE . . . . 463 LINES IN DEJECTION . . 22
  CAN EVER QUITE PASS OUT OF UTTER GRIEF . . . . 469 WE VAINLY WRESTLE... . 3
  HE CAN'T GET OUT. / HE'S LOOSE! HE'S OUT! / IT'S GOD. . 473 A MASQUE OF REASON . . 17
  THERE'S NO CONNECTION MAN CAN REASON OUT . . . . . . 475 A MASQUE OF REASON . . 50
  AND IT CAME OUT ALL RIGHT. I HAVE NO DOUBT . . . . . 475 A MASQUE OF REASON . . 65
  YOU CALL IT MINE. / WE GROPED IT OUT TOGETHER . . . . 480 A MASQUE OF REASON . . 188
  AS FOR THE EARTH, WE GROPED THAT OUT TOGETHER, ... 481 A MASQUE OF REASON . . 207
  FOUND OUT THE DISCIPLINE MAN NEEDED MOST . . . . . . 481 A MASQUE OF REASON . . 209
  SOCIETY CAN NEVER THINK THINGS OUT: . . . . 481 A MASQUE OF REASON . . 223
  IT HAS TO SEE THEM ACTED OUT BY ACTORS, ... 481 A MASQUE OF REASON . . 224
  YOU'RE GIVING ME. YOU SAY WE GROPED THIS OUT. . . . . 482 A MASQUE OF REASON . . 242
  IT SOUNDS TO ME AS IF YOU THOUGHT IT OUT, ... 482 A MASQUE OF REASON . . 244
  HAS ALL GONE HOME TO BED. THE PLAY'S PLAYED OUT. . . . 482 A MASQUE OF REASON . . 253
  THE ARTIST IN ME CRIES OUT FOR DESIGN. . . . . . . 482 A MASQUE OF REASON . . 261
  YOU COULD END THIS BY SIMPLY COMING OUT . . . . . . 483 A MASQUE OF REASON . . 295
  YOU WON'T GET ANY ANSWERS OUT OF GOD. . . . . 484 A MASQUE OF REASON . . 301
  LIKE A BIG EGG AND HATCH A HEAVEN OUT . . . . 484 A MASQUE OF REASON . . 306
  AND FIND OUT WHETHER HE IS ANY GOOD, ... 484 A MASQUE OF REASON . . 320
  FIRST WHITE, THEN RED, THEN ULTRARED, THEN OUT. . . . 485 A MASQUE OF REASON . . 346
  WE CAN'T LEAVE HIM OUT. / NO. NO, WE DON'T NEED TO. . . 486 A MASQUE OF REASON . . 378
  NOTHING HAS BEEN BROUGHT OUT THAT FOR MY PART . . . . 488 A MASQUE OF REASON . . 413
  OPEN ENOUGH TO FIND OUT WHO IT IS. . . . . 493 A MASQUE OF MERCY . . 12
  TO FIND OUT HOW TO GET AWAY FROM GOD? . . . . 494 A MASQUE OF MERCY . . 28
  BUT OUT OF POLITICS. SHE TOLD ME SO. . . . . 494 A MASQUE OF MERCY . . 38
  I COULD POINT OUT MY SORT OF PASSPORT IN IT. . . . . 495 A MASQUE OF MERCY . . 46
  YOUR RIGHTEOUS INDIGNATION FIZZLED OUT, ... 497 A MASQUE OF MERCY . . 103
  I'M IN THE BIBLE, ALL DONE OUT IN STORY. . . . . . . 497 A MASQUE OF MERCY . . 113
  I'VE LOST MY FAITH IN GOD TO CARRY OUT . . . . . . 497 A MASQUE OF MERCY . . 114
  CHRIST ALMOST OUT OF CHRISTIANITY. . . . . 498 A MASQUE OF MERCY . . 129
  LOOK OUT FOR HIM. / "LOOK OUT FOR ME" IS RIGHT. . . . 498 A MASQUE OF MERCY . . 130
  I'M GOING TO TAKE THE NONSENSE OUT OF YOU . . . . . 498 A MASQUE OF MERCY . . 132
  BIG-CITY TALK. I'M GETTING OUT OF HERE. . . . . . . 500 A MASQUE OF MERCY . . 171
  ALWAYS THE SAME WHEN I SET OUT IN FLIGHT. . . . . . 500 A MASQUE OF MERCY . . 179
  FOR ME TO DISAGREE WITH HIM AND GET SPIT OUT . . . . 500 A MASQUE OF MERCY . . 184
  THERE MAY BE THERE AND GET SPIT OUT AGAIN. . . . . . 500 A MASQUE OF MERCY . . 189
  IF YOU WOULD TAKE THE HANDS OUT OF YOUR HAIR . . . . 500 A MASQUE OF MERCY . . 191
  IN NATURE WOULD WIPE OUT ALL HUMAN FAULT. . . . . . 502 A MASQUE OF MERCY . . 232
  A QUESTION WHO WAS GETTING THE MOST OUT . . . . . . 503 A MASQUE OF MERCY . . 248
  DON'T YOU FEEL SOMETHING? / LEAVE ME OUT OF THIS. . . 504 A MASQUE OF MERCY . . 286
  TO TAKE THE PUNISHMENT OUT OF ALL FAILURE . . . . . 505 A MASQUE OF MERCY . . 313
  BY BEING SPREAD OUT OVER EVERYBODY, ... 506 A MASQUE OF MERCY . . 322
  TRYING TO FLUSH ME OUT. THAT'S ALL IT IS. . . . . . 507 A MASQUE OF MERCY . . 350
  TO EASE THE MORE EXTREMELY WOUNDED OUT . . . . . . 507 A MASQUE OF MERCY . . 370
  LIGHTS OUT, I SAY, SO'S TO ESCAPE ATTENTION. . . . . 508 A MASQUE OF MERCY . . 392
  PAUL MAKES IT COME OUT SO THEY LOOK LIKE CHRISTIANS. . 509 A MASQUE OF MERCY . . 407
  TO SET OUT TO HOMOGENIZE MANKIND . . . . 509 A MASQUE OF MERCY . . 420
  I NOTICED HOW HE JUST NOW MADE YOU OUT . . . . . . 510 A MASQUE OF MERCY . . 454
  OR "TURN THE RASCALS OUT" WOULD DO FOR ME. . . . . . 510 A MASQUE OF MERCY . . 460
  A DARKNESS OUT OF ASIA THAT HAD CROSSED . . . . . . 511 A MASQUE OF MERCY . . 466
  BY MAKING FAILURE OUT OF EQUAL VALUE. . . . . 513 A MASQUE OF MERCY . . 526
  UNLOCK THE DOOR FOR ME. / NOT THAT WAY OUT. . . . . 514 A MASQUE OF MERCY . . 546
  THE WORLD SEEMS CRYING OUT FOR A MESSIAH. . . . . . 515 A MASQUE OF MERCY . . 576
  I HEARD A DEEP GROAN--MAYBE OUT OF HIM. . . . . . . 516 A MASQUE OF MERCY . . 611
  CONTEMPLATE TRUTH UNTIL IT BURNS YOUR EYES OUT. . . . 517 A MASQUE OF MERCY . . 630
  NAIVENESS ABOUT JUSTICE OUT OF HIM, ... 517 A MASQUE OF MERCY . . 640
  AS ONCE THE PHARAOH DID IT OUT OF SEKHTI . . . . . . 517 A MASQUE OF MERCY . . 641
  DON'T WEAR YOUR PANTS OUT PREACHING ON YOUR KNEES. . . 519 A MASQUE OF MERCY . . 681
OUTBREAK
  MY KINGDOM, WHAT AN OUTBREAK! / JOB IS RIGHT. . . . . 484 A MASQUE OF REASON . . 302
  IS NOTHING BUT AN OUTBREAK OF MASS MERCY, ... 509 A MASQUE OF MERCY . . 417
OUTCOME
  AND THEN I'D CLAIM THE CREDIT FOR THE OUTCOME. . . . . 320 BUILD SOIL 129
  AND BE JUDGED BY THE OUTCOME, MELIBOEUS. . . . . . . 320 BUILD SOIL 135
OUTCRY
  THE BOY'S FIRST OUTCRY WAS A RUEFUL LAUGH, ... 136 "OUT, OUT--" 19
  THERE IS THE PINCH FROM WHICH OUR ONLY OUTCRY . . . . 167 NEW HAMPSHIRE . . . 270
OUTDOOR
  OH, JUST ANOTHER KIND OF OUTDOOR GAME, ... 33 MENDING WALL 21
  HALF OF THE OUTDOOR WORK, THOUGH AS FOR THAT, ... 85 THE HOUSEKEEPER . . . 108
  IT TAKES ALL SORTS OF IN- AND OUTDOOR SCHOOLING . . . 470 IT TAKES ALL SORTS... . 1
OUTDOORS
  TO STEP OUTDOORS AND TAKE THE WATER DAZZLE . . . . . 63 A SERVANT TO SERVANTS . 27
  YOU SEE OUR PRETTY THINGS ARE ALL OUTDOORS. . . . . . 85 THE HOUSEKEEPER . . . 110
  TILL I SHAN'T DARE TO SET A FOOT OUTDOORS. . . . . . 90 THE FEAR 47

OUTDOORS (CONTINUED)
```
    GO OUTDOORS IF YOU WANT TO FIGHT. SPARE ME.  .  .  .  .  . 100 THE SELF-SEEKER .  .  . 212
    I'LL GO OUTDOORS, BY GAD, AND WON'T COME BACK."  .  .  .  . 100 THE SELF-SEEKER .  .  . 222
    YOU DON'T SUPPOSE?--SHE WOULDN'T GO OUTDOORS?"  .  .  .  . 154 SNOW  .  .  .  .  .  . 305
    OR GONE OUTDOORS." / "IN WHICH CASE BOTH ARE LOST.  .  .  . 154 SNOW  .  .  .  .  .  . 312
    I CAUGHT THE OWNER OUTDOORS BY HIMSELF  .  .  .  .  .  . 164 NEW HAMPSHIRE .  .  . 152
    BUSY OUTDOORS BY LANTERN-LIGHT WITH SOMETHING  .  .  .  . 176 THE STAR-SPLITTER .  .  . 4
    BUT STANDING OUTDOORS HUNGRY, IN THE COLD,  .  .  .  .  . 189 THE GRINDSTONE .  .  . 17
    HE'S AFTER AN OPEN DOOR TO GET OUTDOORS.  .  .  .  .  . 205 THE WITCH OF COOS .  . 112
    AND BUILT A STONE BAPTISMAL FONT OUTDOORS--  .  .  .  . 213 A FOUNTAIN, A BOTTLE .  . 10
    IF YOU DON'T WANT TO SPEND THE NIGHT OUTDOORS.  .  .  . 214 A FOUNTAIN, A BOTTLE .  . 50
    NO ONE FOR HOURS HAS SET A FOOT OUTDOORS  .  .  .  .  . 248 THE COCOON  .  .  .  . 9
    BY LETTING THE RAIN I KNEW OUTDOORS  .  .  .  .  .  . 253 THE THATCH  .  .  .  . 34
    YET LEAVE SUCH LOVELY SHAFTS OUTDOORS TO PERISH.  .  .  . 290 OLD BARN AT THE BOTTOM 34
OUTER
    ACROSS THE SILL FROM THE OUTER GLOOM.  .  .  .  .  .  . 15 IN A VALE .  .  .  .  . 9
    IN CLOMPING OFF--AND SCARED THE OUTER NIGHT,  .  .  . 108 OLD MAN'S WINTER NIGHT 11
    AND THE BIRDS ON HER OUTER WINDOWSILL,  .  .  .  .  . 215 A FOUNTAIN, A BOTTLE .  . 81
    YOUR HEAD SO MUCH CONCERNED WITH OUTER,  .  .  .  .  . 252 TREE AT MY WINDOW .  . 15
    THE HEARTLESS AND ENORMOUS OUTER BLACK  .  .  .  . 361 A LOOSE MOUNTAIN .  . 17
    THE BIRCH BEGINS TO CRACK ITS OUTER SHEATH  .  .  . 375 A YOUNG BIRCH  .  .  . 1
    FOR THE OUTER DARK  .  .  .  .  .  .  .  .  .  .  . 413 AWAY!  .  .  .  .  .  . 10
    BUT OUTER SPACE,  .  .  .  .  .  .  .  .  .  .  .  . 469 BUT OUTER SPACE... .  .  . 1
    BUT OUTER SPACE...  .  .  .  .  .  .  .  .  .  .  . 469 BUT OUTER SPACE... .  .  . T
    ON THE BLANK CURTAIN ON THE OUTER DOOR.)  .  .  .  . 502 A MASQUE OF MERCY .  . 239
    SOMETHING HAS ALTERED IN THE OUTER DOOR.)  .  .  .  . 507 A MASQUE OF MERCY .  . 344
OUTGROWS
    WHEN IT OUTGROWS THE WIRE BAND OF ITS NAME TAG.  .  .  . 46 A HUNDRED COLLARS  .  . 57
OUTLAWRY
    OUR VENTURE IN REVOLUTION AND OUTLAWRY  .  .  .  .  . 423 FOR JOHN F. KENNEDY .  . 51
OUTLET
    IT WILL HAVE OUTLET, BRAVE AND NOT SO BRAVE.  .  .  . 255 THE FLOOD  .  .  .  .  . 9
OUT-OF-DOORS
    ALL CUT-OF-DOORS LOOKED DARKLY IN AT HIM  .  .  .  . 108 OLD MAN'S WINTER NIGHT 1
    BUT THE WIND OUT-OF-DOORS--YOU KNOW THE SAYING.  .  .  . 130 THE BONFIRE  .  .  .  . 40
OUTPOST
    TO CLOSE THIS OUTPOST BARN AND CLOSE THE SEASON.  .  .  . 289 OLD BARN AT THE BOTTOM 7
    SO, LIKE A HALF-MAD OUTPOST SENTINEL,  .  .  .  .  . 396 ANY SIZE WE PLEASE .  . 2
OUTRAGE
    HOW HAD THE TENDER VERSE ESCAPED THEIR OUTRAGE?  .  .  . 216 A FOUNTAIN, A BOTTLE .  . 105
    OF OUTRAGE--VIOLENCE--THAT BREAKS ACROSS IT.  .  .  . 509 A MASQUE OF MERCY .  . 431
    THAT ALL OTHER OUTRAGE SEEM AS CHILD'S PLAY:  .  .  . 511 A MASQUE OF MERCY .  . 476
OUTRAGEOUS
    A SORDID PEACE OR AN OUTRAGEOUS WAR.  .  .  .  .  .  . 352 THE LESSON FOR TODAY .  . 56
OUTRIGHT
    TO HAVE GIVEN OUTRIGHT FOR THEM ALL SHE GAVE.  .  .  . 57 THE BLACK COTTAGE .  . 59
    "YOU'VE NEVER ASKED YOUR FATHER OUTRIGHT, HAVE YOU?"  .  . 183 MAPLE  .  .  .  .  .  . 108
    SHE HEARD HIM BARK OUTRIGHT.  .  .  .  .  .  .  .  . 341 THE SUBVERTED FLOWER .  . 64
    THE GIFT OUTRIGHT  .  .  .  .  .  .  .  .  .  .  . 348 THE GIFT OUTRIGHT .  . T
    SUCH AS WE WERE WE GAVE OURSELVES OUTRIGHT  .  .  . 348 THE GIFT OUTRIGHT .  . 12
    GIFT OUTRIGHT OF "THE GIFT OUTRIGHT"  .  .  .  .  . 422 FOR JOHN F. KENNEDY .  . S
    THE GIFT OUTRIGHT  .  .  .  .  .  .  .  .  .  .  . 424 THE GIFT OUTRIGHT .  . T
    SUCH AS WE WERE WE GAVE OURSELVES OUTRIGHT  .  .  . 424 THE GIFT OUTRIGHT .  . 12
    TO ASKING FLATLY FOR THE REASON--OUTRIGHT.  .  .  .  . 483 A MASQUE OF REASON .  . 269
OUTSIDE
    BEHIND LOW BOUGHS THE TREES LET DOWN OUTSIDE;  .  .  . 16 A DREAM PANG .  .  .  . 10
    OUTSIDE THERE IN THE ENTRY, FOR I SAW IT."  .  .  .  . 54 HOME BURIAL  .  .  .  . 88
    WE ALWAYS LOCKED THE FLOWERS OUTSIDE .  .  .  .  .  . 135 LOCKED OUT  .  .  .  . 2
    'SO YOU CAN THINK IT'S SIX FEET DEEP OUTSIDE,  .  .  . 149 SNOW  .  .  .  .  .  . 182
    SO HIGH ACROSS THE PANE OUTSIDE. THERE WHERE  .  .  . 149 SNOW  .  .  .  .  .  . 191
    TO LAST HER TILL HE GOT OUTSIDE THE DOOR,  .  .  .  . 151 SNOW  .  .  .  .  .  . 243
    "THE OUTSIDE DOORS AS YET HAVE HELD AGAINST US.  .  . 215 A FOUNTAIN, A BOTTLE .  . 74
    OUTSIDE THE SUGARHOUSE ONE NIGHT FOR CHOICE,  .  .  . 234 EVENING A SUGAR ORCHARD 2
    THE SOUND OF THE CLOSING OUTSIDE DOOR WAS ALL.  .  .  . 235 VALLEY'S SINGING DAY .  . 1
    AND DESCENDED OUTSIDE.  .  .  .  .  .  .  .  .  .  . 241 THE LOCKLESS DOOR .  . 12
    THEY COULD BE LOCKED BUT FROM THE OUTSIDE ONLY.  .  . 289 OLD BARN AT THE BOTTOM 16
    YES, RIGHT I WAS, THE LOCKS WERE PROPS OUTSIDE;  .  . 290 OLD BARN AT THE BOTTOM 41
    WE SIT INDOORS AND TALK OF THE COLD OUTSIDE.  .  .  . 305 THERE ARE ROUGHLY ZONES 1
    NOW IF IT WAS DUSK OUTSIDE,  .  .  .  .  .  .  .  . 334 COME IN  .  .  .  .  . 3
    FOR NEXT DEFENSE OUTSIDE  .  .  .  .  .  .  .  .  . 348 TRIPLE BRONZE  .  .  . 4
    AND GET OUTSIDE OF TOO MUCH BAD STATISTICS,  .  .  . 351 THE LESSON FOR TODAY .  . 37
    THE DANGER NOT AN INCH OUTSIDE  .  .  .  .  .  .  . 363 ASSURANCE .  .  .  .  . 1
    HE AND A LOT OF CHILDREN CAME OUTSIDE,  .  .  .  .  . 368 THE LITERATE FARMER AND 6
    WHO HAD STOPPED OUTSIDE THE FENCE TO SPY,  .  .  .  . 385 A MOOD APART  .  .  .  . 5
    SOMETHING WAS GOING RIGHT OUTSIDE THE HALL.  .  .  . 399 THE BROKEN DROUGHT .  . 2
    THEY COULD NOT SEE IT FROM OUTSIDE--  .  .  .  .  . 418 AMERICA IS HARD TO SEE 64
    SHOULD BE TAKEN OUTSIDE A HOUSE AND BOOK.  .  .  .  . 419 ONE MORE BREVITY .  . 2
OUTSIDERS
    SO AS TO HAVE IT READY FOR OUTSIDERS.  .  .  .  .  . 207 THE WITCH OF COOS .  . 147
OUTSPREAD
    SOMETIMES HE CAME WITH ARMS OUTSPREAD  .  .  .  .  . 138 BROWN'S DESCENT  .  .  . 21
    THE GRIP ON EARTH OF OUTSPREAD FEET,  .  .  .  .  . 276 TWO TRAMPS IN MUD TIME 46
OUTSTRETCHED
    THEN HE CAME AT ME WITH ONE HAND OUTSTRETCHED,  .  . 204 THE WITCH OF COOS .  . 75
OUTWALKED
    I HAVE OUTWALKED THE FURTHEST CITY LIGHT.  .  .  .  . 255 ACQUAINTED WITH NIGHT .  . 3
OUTWARD
    SHE PUSHED HIM OUTWARD WITH HER THROUGH THE DOOR  .  .  . 34 DEATH OF THE HIRED MAN 6
    BOWED OUTWARD ON THE MOUNTAIN HALFWAY UP,  .  .  .  . 75 THE GENERATIONS OF MEN 71
    I HAD SUCH COMPANY OUTWARD BOUND.  .  .  .  .  .  . 102 GOOD HOURS  .  .  .  . 9
    THEN HE FLUNG OUTWARD, FEET FIRST, WITH A SWISH,  .  . 122 BIRCHES  .  .  .  .  . 39
    NONE NOT IN HIDING FROM THE OUTWARD EYE.  .  .  .  . 174 THE CENSUS-TAKER  .  .  . 16
    OR OUTWARD FROM THE VILLAGE,  .  .  .  .  .  .  .  . 335 CARPE DIEM  .  .  .  . 4
OUTWARDLY
    LOOKS FOR HIMSELF, MORE OR LESS OUTWARDLY.  .  .  .  . 182 MAPLE  .  .  .  .  .  . 71
OUTWITTED (SEE UN-OUTWITTED)
```

OVEN
  THE THE OVEN BIRD . . . . 119 THE OVEN BIRD . . . T
OVER
  BENT OVER THE OPEN FIRE, ... 8 LOVE AND A QUESTION . 18
  HUNG OVER HER IN TUNE, ... 10 WIND AND WINDOW FLOWER . 8
  THE SAME LEAVES OVER AND OVER AGAIN! . . . . 25 IN HARDWOOD GROVES . . 1
  COME OVER THE HILLS AND FAR WITH ME, ... 26 A LINE-STORM SONG . . 7
  AND OVER THE WALLS I HAVE WENDED; . . . . 29 RELUCTANCE 2
  OUT OVER THE CRUSTED SNOW, ... 30 RELUCTANCE 11
  HE WANTED TO GO OVER THAT. BUT MOST OF ALL . . . . . . 37 DEATH OF THE HIRED MAN . 85
  WHERE ARE YOU MOVING OVER TO? STAY STILL. . . . . . . 47 A HUNDRED COLLARS . . 89
  OR OVER A HILL OR ROUND A SUDDEN CORNER. . . . . 49 A HUNDRED COLLARS . . 126
  LOOKING BACK OVER HER SHOULDER AT SOME FEAR. . . . . . 51 HOME BURIAL 3
  HE SAID TWICE OVER BEFORE HE KNEW HIMSELF; . . . . . . 52 HOME BURIAL 34
  BLOWN OVER AND OVER THEMSELVES IN IDLENESS. . . . . . . 58 THE BLACK COTTAGE . . 121
  THE PASTURE ALL OVER UNTIL NOT A FERN . . . . 59 BLUEBERRIES 18
  AND OVER THE WALL AND INTO THE ROAD, ... 60 BLUEBERRIES 36
  THINGS OVER AND OVER THAT JUST WON'T STAY DONE. . . . . 64 A SERVANT TO SERVANTS . 52
  IT WAS HIS PLAN OUR MOVING OVER IN . . . . 64 A SERVANT TO SERVANTS . 61
  FROM OVER YOU AS YOU LAY IN YOUR BEDS. . . . . 67 A SERVANT TO SERVANTS . 169
  JAMES WOULD TAKE TIME, OF COURSE, TO CHEW IT OVER . . . 70 THE CODE 18
  HE SAID IT OVER, BUT HE SAID IT SOFTER. . . . . 71 THE CODE 67
  I LOOKED OVER THE SIDE ONCE IN THE DUST . . . . 72 THE CODE 75
  SEVERAL TIMES OVER, AND BY MARRYING FATHER . . . . . . 75 THE GENERATIONS OF MEN . 56
  OVER DESCENDED FROM HER. I BELIEVE . . . . 77 THE GENERATIONS OF MEN . 112
  AND BEGIN OVER----' THERE, SHE'D BETTER STOP. . . . . 80 THE GENERATIONS OF MEN . 194
  I WANT THIS OVER WITH; I'M HOT AND TIRED." . . . . . . 94 THE SELF-SEEKER . . . 50
  TO PAY THE DOCTOR'S BILL AND TIDE ME OVER. . . . . . . 95 THE SELF-SEEKER . . . 74
  OVER STONE WALLS AND ALL ALONG A WOOD . . . . 98 THE SELF-SEEKER . . . 152
  IN HASTE TO GET IT OVER WITH AS YOU.-- . . . . 99 THE SELF-SEEKER . . . 192
  OVER THE SNOW MY CREAKING FEET . . . . 102 GOOD HOURS 13
  YOU LET ME LOOK THEM OVER." / "YOU COULD LOOK. . . . . 106 CHRISTMAS TREES . . . 31
  WE CLIMBED THE PASTURE ON THE SOUTH, CROSSED OVER, . . . 107 CHRISTMAS TREES . . . 40
  THE CUTTER BAR HAD JUST GONE CHAMPING OVER . . . . . . 109 THE EXPOSED NEST . . 14
  OVER THE SINK OUT THROUGH A DUSTY WINDOW . . . . 110 IN THE HOME STRETCH . 2
  OVER THE WHEEL INTO THE SKY-HIGH SEAT, ... 112 IN THE HOME STRETCH . 63
  WHAT SHOULDER DID I SEE HER OVER? NEITHER. . . . . . . 113 IN THE HOME STRETCH . 69
  TO LOOK US OVER AND GIVE US HIS IDEA . . . . 115 IN THE HOME STRETCH . 149
  HE SAYS THE HIGHWAY DUST IS OVER ALL. . . . . 120 THE OVEN BIRD . . . 10
  BEFORE THEM OVER THEIR HEADS TO DRY IN THE SUN. . . . . 121 BIRCHES 20
  BY RIDING THEM DOWN OVER AND OVER AGAIN . . . . 122 BIRCHES 29
  AND THEN COME BACK TO IT AND BEGIN OVER. . . . . 122 BIRCHES 49
  STOOD OVER ME A RESURRECTED TREE, ... 125 AN ENCOUNTER 12
  ANOTHER COLOR OVER A TENTH THE SPACE . . . . 132 THE BONFIRE 82
  THAT I SPREAD COAL-BLACK OVER IN THE TIME . . . . . . 132 THE BONFIRE 83
  OVER THE GREAT BIG THUMPING, SHUFFLING MILLSTONE, . . . 142 THE VANISHING RED . . 16
  OVER HIS SHOULDER WITH HIS PIPESTEM, SAYING, ... 143 SNOW 7
  BUT KEEP STILL IF HE FAILS." / "KEEP STILL ALL OVER. . . 146 SNOW 87
  BUT WHAT GOOD IS MY SAYING IT OVER AND OVER? . . . . . 150 SNOW 218
  THE WHITE CLOUDS OVER THEM ON. . . . . 156 THE SOUND OF TREES . . 23
  WE BOTH OF US TURNED OVER IN OUR GRAVES. . . . . 161 NEW HAMPSHIRE . . . 60
  TO WANT TO MAKE NEW HAMPSHIRE PEOPLE OVER. . . . . . . 167 NEW HAMPSHIRE . . . 263
  THE ONLY DWELLING IN A WASTE CUT OVER . . . . 174 THE CENSUS-TAKER . . 4
  THROWING A LEG UP OVER OUR FENCE OF MOUNTAINS, ... 176 THE STAR-SPLITTER . . 2
  HE TOOK A STRANGE THING TO BE ROGUISH OVER. . . . . . 178 THE STAR-SPLITTER . . 58
  AS SHE STOOD SAYING HER NAME OVER ALOUD, ... 181 MAPLE 41
  AND VIEWED IT OVER HIS GLASSES FUNNY-EYED, ... 190 THE GRINDSTONE . . . 70
  THEY'LL FIND THEY'VE GOT THE WHOLE THING TO DO OVER, . . 207 PAUPER WITCH OF GRAFTON 10
  TO SEE IF THE TOWN WANTED TO TAKE OVER . . . . 208 PAUPER WITCH OF GRAFTON 24
  AND RODE ALL OVER EVERYTHING ON HIM . . . . 208 PAUPER WITCH OF GRAFTON 47
  OVER THE RIDGEPOLE, 'STRIDE OF A BROOMSTICK, ... 210 PAUPER WITCH OF GRAFTON 86
  OVER SO MUCH BAY . . . . 211 AN EMPTY THREAT . . . 31
  BE DRAGGED BY YOU ALL OVER EVERYWHERE----" . . . . . . 214 A FOUNTAIN, A BOTTLE . 30
  ON PLANETS OVER, ... 220 I WILL SING YOU ONE-O . 74
  THE WAR SEEMED OVER MORE FOR YOU THAN ME, ... 222 TO E.T. 15
  HOW OVER, THOUGH, FOR EVEN ME WHO KNEW . . . . 222 TO E.T. 17
  THEY LIE CLOSED OVER IN THE WIND AND CLING . . . . . . 225 BLUE-BUTTERFLY DAY . . 7
  A GREAT WAVE FROM IT GOING OVER THEM, ... 230 TWO LOOK AT TWO . . . 40
  GRIM GIVING TO DO OVER FOR THEM BOTH. . . . . 231 NOT TO KEEP 18
  FLOWING OVER MY ARMS . . . . 235 GATHERING LEAVES . . 11
  MY WINDOW CURTAIN HUNG OVER THE SILL TO WET; . . . . . 236 VALLEY'S SINGING DAY . 17
  OF GLOSSY BIRDS LIKE RIPPLES OVER ROCKS. . . . . 240 OUR SINGING STRENGTH . 34
  TO SUFFER THE SAME DRIVEN NIGHTMARE OVER. . . . . . . 240 OUR SINGING STRENGTH . 45
  BACK OVER THE SILL . . . . 241 THE LOCKLESS DOOR . . 13
  AND BROUGHT IT OVER GLOSSY WATER, GREATER, ... 245 THE FREEDOM OF THE MOON 10
  THEY LAYER OVER IT TOO TOPPLING WEAK . . . . 246 ATMOSPHERE 3
  GREAT WAVES LOOKED OVER OTHERS COMING IN, ... 250 ONCE BY THE PACIFIC . 2
  CAME OVER HOUSES FROM ANOTHER STREET, ... 255 ACQUAINTED WITH NIGHT . 9
  OUR ARM THROWN OVER IT ASLEEP BESIDE IT. . . . . 258 WEST-RUNNING BROOK . . 15
  BUT IT FLOWS OVER US. IT FLOWS BETWEEN US . . . . . . 259 WEST-RUNNING BROOK . . 51
  IT FLOWS BETWEEN US, OVER US, AND WITH US. . . . . . . 259 WEST-RUNNING BROOK . . 53
  OVER BACK WHERE THEY SPEAK OF LIFE AS STAYING . . . . . 263 THE INVESTMENT . . . 1
  AS SHE FLINGS OVER AND OFF DOWN THROUGH THE MAPLES, . . 269 THE BEAR 8
  A CLOUD COMES OVER THE SUNLIT ARCH, ... 275 TWO TRAMPS IN MUD TIME 22
  HE ROLLED ME OFF THE FIELD HEAD OVER HEELS . . . . . . 278 THE WHITE-TAILED HORNET 20
  BEGIN ALL OVER 10 HOPE. . . . . 285 IN TIME OF CLOUDBURST . 20
  SWARM OVER THEIR LIVES ENFORCING BENEFITS . . . . . . 287 A ROADSIDE STAND . . 28
  AND EXCHANGED TROUBLED GLANCES OVER LIFE. . . . . . . 293 AT WOODWARD'S GARDENS . 13
  TO THE LOW ROOF OVER HIS BED, ... 299 WELCOME TO THEIR BELIEF 6
  A SCENT OF RIPENESS FROM OVER A WALL. . . . . 304 UNHARVESTED 1
  WHAT COMES OVER A MAN, IS IT SOUL OR MIND-- . . . . . 305 THERE ARE ROUGHLY ZONES 7
  AT LEAST NOT OVER HALF. . . . . 309 NOT ALL THERE . . . 8
  SOME OVER THE MOUNTAINS EAST, ... 312 THE VINDICTIVES . . . 70
  STOOD CLOSELY OVER US THROUGH WHICH TO GO. . . . . . . 315 IRIS BY NIGHT . . . 19
  WHO FALL ALL OVER EACH OTHER TO BRING SOIL . . . . . . 321 BUILD SOIL 177
  "THROW HIM OVER ALIVE," THEY SAID, ... 345 DISCOVERY OF MADEIRAS . 60
  WE HEARD "'TIS OVER" ROARING. . . . . 359 NOVEMBER 7
  NOT OVER FOUR OR SO. . . . . 366 NOT OF SCHOOL AGE . . 22

OVER (CONTINUED)
    AS FOR THE WOODS' EXCITEMENT OVER YOU . . . . 378 DIRECTIVE   23
    AND DID I NOT TAKE STEPS WOULD BE TIPPED OVER . . . . . 391 ON BEING IDOLIZED . .   5
    GOING OVER MY EYE . . . . 392 A WISH TO COMPLY . .   11
    BUT WANTS IT ALL MADE OVER NEW . . . . 393 A CASE FOR JEFFERSON .   2
    AND HAVING IT ALL MADE OVER NEW . . . . 393 A CASE FOR JEFFERSON .   11
    AND WHEN IT'S OVER WATCH THE WORLD'S SUPPLY . . . . . . 398 NO HOLY WARS FOR THEM .   7
    A FINAL GOING OVER WITH THE HOE . . . . 404 FROM PLANE TO PLANE .   13
    MAKE SUCH A NOISELESS TUMULT OVER IT . . . . 411 POD OF THE MILKWEED .   11
    TO SAY GOD'S EITHER ALL OR OVER ALL? . . . . 427 CONCEPT SELF-CONCEIVED   7
    OVER CURRITUCK . . . . 431 KITTY HAWK 110
    TO START THE WORLD ALL OVER AT . . . . 453 A-WISHING WELL . . .   81
    I ONCE HAD A COW THAT JUMPED OVER THE MOON, ... 462 LINES IN DEJECTION .   1
    NOT ONTO THE MOON BUT OVER . . . . 462 LINES IN DEJECTION .   2
    BUT IF OVER THE MOON I HAD WANTED TO GO . . . . 463 LINES IN DEJECTION .   9
    AS WALLER SAYS. / OR NOT ADMIRED. GO OVER . . . . 474 A MASQUE OF REASON .   31
    NO, LET'S NOT LIVE THINGS OVER. I DON'T CARE. . . . . . 477 A MASQUE OF REASON .   119
    BE HEAVEN AT ONCE AND HAVE IT OVER WITH. . . . . 484 A MASQUE OF REASON .   322
    I GAVE YOU OVER TO HIM, BUT WITH SAFEGUARDS. . . . . . 486 A MASQUE OF REASON .   360
    I STUMBLED OVER IT AND GOT TRIPPED UP. . . . . 489 A MASQUE OF REASON .   446
    SHE WAS LEFT OVER FROM THE BROOK FARM VENTURE. . . . . . 494 A MASQUE OF MERCY .   39
    BY BEING SPREAD OUT OVER EVERYBODY, ... 506 A MASQUE OF MERCY .   322
    THAT OVER. I SHALL HAVE TO RETAIL IT . . . . 509 A MASQUE OF MERCY .   404
    BUT WE ARE TALKING OVER JONAH'S HEAD, ... 509 A MASQUE OF MERCY .   426
    A LIGHT THAT FALLS DIFFUSED OVER MY SHOULDER . . . . . 515 A MASQUE OF MERCY .   580
OVERALLS
    WHAT WOULD I DO? GO IN MY OVERALLS, ... 43 THE MOUNTAIN   84
OVERANXIOUS
    BUT SOMEONE OVERANXIOUS AT HIS PERIL . . . . 394 HAEC FABULA DOCET . .   8
OVERBOARD
    THE SAILORS THROW ME OVERBOARD FOR LUCK, ... 500 A MASQUE OF MERCY . . 182
OVERCAST
    ON SUNNY DAYS A MOMENT OVERCAST; . . . . 120 THE OVEN BIRD . . .   8
OVERCOME
    TO OVERCOME THE FEAR WITHIN THE SOUL . . . . 521 A MASQUE OF MERCY . . 729
OVERCRUELLY
    TO PUNISH ME OVERCRUELLY WOULDN'T BE RIGHT . . . . . . 306 NOT QUITE SOCIAL . .   5
OVERDO
    I DO THINK, THOUGH, YOU OVERDO IT A LITTLE. . . . . . . 53 HOME BURIAL   62
OVERDOG
    THE GREAT OVERDOG, ... 261 CANIS MAJOR   1
    WITH THE GREAT OVERDOG . . . . 261 CANIS MAJOR   11
OVEREAGERNESS
    AND ITS EYES SHUT WITH OVEREAGERNESS . . . . 148 SNOW   161
OVERELATED
    FOR BEING AS OVERELATED . . . . 295 A RECORD STRIDE . . .   34
OVERFERTILE
    HERE I AM OVERFERTILE IN SUGGESTION, ... 169 NEW HAMPSHIRE . . .   337
OVERFLOODED
    FROM BEING OVERFLOODED . . . . 335 CARPE DIEM   16
OVERFLOWING
    THAT, OVERFLOWING LIKE A HORN OF PLENTY, ... 216 A FOUNTAIN, A BOTTLE .   94
OVERHEAD
    AND BE GLAD OF A GOOD ROOF OVERHEAD. . . . . 67 A SERVANT TO SERVANTS . 165
    ONE LEVEL NEARER HEAVEN OVERHEAD, ... 254 A WINTER EDEN . . .   7
    ALL SUMMER LONG THEY WERE OVERHEAD, MORE LIFTED UP THAN I. . 297 A LEAF-TREADER . . .   5
    BUT THE SUN OVERHEAD; . . . . 342 QUEST OF PURPLE-FRINGED   2
    AND RIGHT OVERHEAD, ... 433 KITTY HAWK   171
OVERHEATED
    AND SCURF OF PLANTS, AND WEARY AND OVERHEATED, ... 125 AN ENCOUNTER   6
OVERIMPORTANT
    THE OVERIMPORTANT PAIR. . . . . 299 WELCOME TO THEIR BELIEF   4
OVERJOYED
    I SHOULDN'T MIND HIS BEING OVERJOYED . . . . 186 THE AX-HELVE   39
    (IF OVERJOYED HE WAS) AT HAVING GOT ME . . . . 186 THE AX-HELVE   40
    NOR IS HE OVERJOYED WHEN THEY LIE LOW, ... 334 I COULD GIVE ALL . .   4
OVERLIGHTED
    LOUD TALK IN THE OVERLIGHTED HOUSE . . . . 444 ENDS   1
OVERLONG
    FOSTERED OVERLONG . . . . 430 KITTY HAWK   69
OVERLOOK
    SHE STRETCHED UP TALL TO OVERLOOK THE LIGHT . . . . . . 91 THE FEAR   62
OVERLOOKED
    SHE MIGHT HAVE OVERLOOKED. THEY COULD FIND NONE, . . . 183 MAPLE   101
OVERLOOKING
    AFTER HOURS' OVERLOOKING FROM THE CLIFFS . . . . 174 THE CENSUS-TAKER . .   13
OVERNIGHT
    AND LOOSING THE PENT-UP MUSIC OF OVERNIGHT. . . . . . . 236 VALLEY'S SINGING DAY .   10
    WHO HAD MADE AN OVERNIGHT DESCENT . . . . 421 ONE MORE BREVITY .   62
OVERRULED
    A WOMAN WANTS TO BE OVERRULED. . . . . 344 DISCOVERY OF MADEIRAS .   43
OVERSHOT
    THAT OVERSHOT THE MOON. . . . . 464 MILKY WAY IS A COWPATH   20
OVERSOUND
    HAD ADDED TO THEIR OWN AN OVERSOUND, ... 338 NEVER WOULD BIRDS' SONG   4
OVERSPREAD
    SMALL PRINT OVERSPREAD IT, ... 110 A PATCH OF OLD SNOW .   6
OVERSTEPPED
    AND NEVER OVERSTEPPED IT SAVE IN DREAMS. . . . . 171 NEW HAMPSHIRE . . .   380
OVERTAKE
    TO OVERTAKE ME, WHO SHOULD MISS ME HERE . . . .   5 INTO MY OWN   11
    MY CROWN SHALL OVERTAKE ME, YOU WILL SEE; . . . . . . 454 HOW HARD TO KEEP FROM   26
OVERTAKEN
    AS ONE WHO OVERTAKEN BY THE END . . . . 226 THE ONSET   7
    OR OVERTAKEN TOO FAR FROM HIS NEST, ... 249 ACCEPTANCE   8
    THAT OVERTAKEN LOVERS . . . . 335 CARPE DIEM   15
OVERTAXED
    IT SELDOM OVERTAXED THEIR STRENGTH; . . . . 273 A LONE STRIKER . . .   22

```
                                                PAGE TITLE                    LINE
OVERTAXED (CONTINUED)
    UNTIL OVERTAXED  . . . . . . . . . .  . . . 448 THE BAD ISLAND--EASTER     38
OVERTHROW  (SEE SELF-OVERTHROW)
    BELSHAZZAR'S OVERTHROW,  . . . . . . . . . . 314 BEARER OF EVIL TIDINGS     42
    IN ONE TREE'S OVERTHROW  . . . . . . . . . . 470 IN WINTER IN THE WOODS     10
OVERTIGHT
    TO EASE ATTENTION OFF WHEN OVERTIGHT, . . . . . . . 370 THE LITERATE FARMER AND  81
OVERTIRED
    OF APPLE-PICKING: I AM OVERTIRED  . . . . . . . .  69 AFTER APPLE-PICKING   .  28
OVERTOOK
    THERE OVERTOOK ME AND DREW ME IN  . . . . . . . . 140 THE GUM-GATHERER   . .   1
OVER-WARMTH
    BEYOND AN OVER-WARMTH OF KITCHEN STOVE  . . . . . 186 THE AX-HELVE  . . . . . 35
OVERWHELM
    LET'S LET MY HEAVENLY LOSTNESS OVERWHELM ME."  . . . . 296 LOST IN HEAVEN  . . . 12
    AND COULD IN ONE BURST OVERWHELM  . . . . . . . 390 TWO LEADING LIGHTS . .    8
OVERWHELMING
    LET IT BE OVERWHELMING, OFF A ROOF  . . . . . . . 265 DUST IN THE EYES  . .     4
OVER-WINTER
    OF OVER-WINTER WITH THE LEAST TIP-TOUCH  . . . . . 131 THE BONFIRE  . . . .    46
OVERWISE
    WILL KEEP MY TALK FROM GETTING OVERWISE,  . . . . . 265 DUST IN THE EYES   . .  2
OWE
    SEEMS TO OWE NAUGHT TO ANY SINGLE CORD,  . . . . . . 332 THE SILKEN TENT  . .    8
    TO WHATSOEVER GOD WE OWE THE THANKS.  . . . . . . 358 THE LOST FOLLOWER  . .    6
    YOU OWE IT TO AN ARBITRARY GOD  . . . . . . . . 385 THE FEAR OF GOD  . . .     4
    OF THE TRUTHS WE OWE AN ASIAN?  . . . . . . . . 397 AN IMPORTER  . . . . .    16
    MUCH AS I OWN I OWE . . . . . . . . . . 415 CLOSED FOR GOOD . . .               1
    I OWE THEM MORE TODAY  . . . . . . . . . . 415 CLOSED FOR GOOD . . .            5
    WE KNOW NOT WHAT WE OWE THIS MOMENT TO.  . . . . . 461 HOW HARD TO KEEP FROM   241
OWED
    TOO LONG I'VE OWED YOU THIS APOLOGY  . . . . . . . 475 A MASQUE OF REASON  . .  59
OWES
    SEEMS TO ME OWES IT TO THE TOWN TO KEEP ONE.  . . . . 177 THE STAR-SPLITTER . .  36
    ALL HE OWES TO THE ARTIFICE  . . . . . . . . 418 AMERICA IS HARD TO SEE       68
OWL
    THE WINTER OWL BANKED JUST IN TIME TO PASS  . . . . 445 QUESTIONING FACES   .    1
OWN
    INTO MY OWN  . . . . . . . . . .  . .   5 INTO MY OWN  . . . . .      T
    AND FEEL A SPIRIT KINDRED TO MY OWN;  . . . . . . .  23 THE TUFT OF FLOWERS   .  33
    NOT LIKING TO OWN UP I'D GROWN A SIZE.  . . . . . . .  46 A HUNDRED COLLARS   .  60
    "JUST AS YOU SAY. HAVE IT YOUR OWN WAY, THEN.  . . . .  47 A HUNDRED COLLARS   .  79
    "CAN'T A MAN SPEAK OF HIS OWN CHILD HE'S LOST?"  . . . .  52 HOME BURIAL . . . .  35
    A MAN CAN'T SPEAK OF HIS OWN CHILD THAT'S DEAD."  . . .  53 HOME BURIAL . . . .  70
    WITH YOUR OWN HAND--HOW COULD YOU?--HIS LITTLE GRAVE;  . .  53 HOME BURIAL . . . .  73
    BUT I WENT NEAR TO SEE WITH MY OWN EYES.  . . . . .  54 HOME BURIAL . . . .     83
    OF THE FRESH EARTH FROM YOUR OWN BABY'S GRAVE  . . . .  54 HOME BURIAL . . . .   85
    THE WARPING BOARDS PULL OUT THEIR OWN OLD NAILS  . . .  56 THE BLACK COTTAGE . .  49
    SHE HAD HER OWN IDEA OF THINGS, THE OLD LADY.  . . . .  56 THE BLACK COTTAGE . .  51
    STRANGE HOW SUCH INNOCENCE GETS ITS OWN WAY.  . . . .  57 THE BLACK COTTAGE . .  81
    BUT I OWN WHAT YOU SAY MAKES MY HEAD SPIN.  . . . . .  75 THE GENERATIONS OF MEN  60
    A FRIEND OR TWO AS GOOD AS OWN THE FARM,  . . . . .  84 THE HOUSEKEEPER . . .   96
    ON HIS OWN FARM. HE'S BOSS. BUT AS TO HENS:  . . . . .  86 THE HOUSEKEEPER . . .  135
    THAT WAS WORTH MONEY TO ME? STILL I OWN  . . . . .  95 THE SELF-SEEKER . . .   82
    MORE THAN YOU LIKE TO OWN TO OUT THAT WINDOW."  . . . . 112 IN THE HOME STRETCH   45
    BY ITS OWN POWER SEEMS TO BE UNDONE.  . . . . . . 125 AN ENCOUNTER . . . .     3
    TO LEAP THE DUSTY DEADLINE. FOR MY OWN  . . . . . . 131 THE BONFIRE . . . .     64
    INCREDULOUS OF HIS OWN BAD LUCK.  . . . . . . . 138 BROWN'S DESCENT . . .     41
    OF ITS OWN STUPID LACK OF UNDERSTANDING,  . . . . . 148 SNOW  . . . . .         164
    "I'LL OWN IT'S COLD FOR SUCH A FALL OF SNOW.  . . . . 150 SNOW  . . . . .        201
    SHE SAID, "GO READ YOUR OWN BOOKS AND FIND OUT."  . . . 166 NEW HAMPSHIRE . . .   227
    BEHIND ME ON THE SNOW IN MY OWN YARD  . . . . . . 185 THE AX-HELVE . . . .      7
    HAVING A WHEEL AND FOUR LEGS OF ITS OWN  . . . . . 188 THE GRINDSTONE . . .      1
    AND PUT IT IN MY HANDS TO PICK MY OWN GRAPES.  . . . . 197 WILD GRAPES . . . .    38
    (THE KITCHEN HAD BEEN DARK) I HAD TO OWN . . . . . 205 THE WITCH OF COOS . .    98
    "DON'T DONKEY'S EARS SUGGEST WE SHAKE OUR OWN?"  . . . 215 A FOUNTAIN, A BOTTLE  .  55
    WERE NOT THEIR OWN:  . . . . . . . . . 219 I WILL SING YOU ONE-O  .  56
    MYSELF AS ONE HIS OWN PRETENSE DECEIVES;  . . . . . 233 A BOUNDLESS MOMENT . .   10
    INSISTING ALWAYS ON OUR OWN WAY SO.  . . . . . . 238 ON A TREE FALLEN ACROSS   5
    AND HAS NO LEAVES AT ALL OF ITS OWN;  . . . . . . 247 ON GOING UNNOTICED . .    7
    WITH BUT ONE CHIMNEY IT CAN CALL ITS OWN;  . . . . . 248 THE COCOON . . . .       6
    SPINNING THEIR OWN COCOON DID THEY BUT KNOW IT.  . . . 248 THE COCOON . . . .     16
    THE CURVE OF EARTH, AND STRIKING, BREAK THEIR OWN;  . . . 261 A SOLDIER . . . .   10
    MY OWN STRATEGIC RETREAT  . . . . . . . . . 282 A DRUMLIN WOODCHUCK . .   5
    SOME WORN OLD TOOL OF MY OWN . . . . . . . . 285 IN TIME OF CLOUDBURST    21
    WHO SLEEP IN HOUSES OF THEIR OWN, THOUGH MORTGAGED.  . . 290 OLD BARN AT THE BOTTOM   31
    TO SCARE MYSELF WITH MY OWN DESERT PLACES.  . . . . 296 DESERT PLACES . . .     16
    MAKE THE WHOLE STOCK EXCHANGE YOUR OWN!  . . . . . 307 PROVIDE, PROVIDE . .     10
    FOR NOTHING BUT ITS OWN BLIND SATISFACTION  . . . . 319 BUILD SOIL  . . . .    104
    WE HAVE OUR OWN ROUND SHAPE TO KEEP UNBROKEN.  . . . 322 BUILD SOIL  . . . .    197
    I OWN I NEVER REALLY WARMED  . . . . . . . . 326 TO A THINKER . . . .      29
    BEFORE HE CAME TO MEET HIS OWN!  . . . . . . . 336 THE WIND AND THE RAIN     11
    WAS BUT THE MOCKING ECHO OF HIS OWN  . . . . . . 338 THE MOST OF IT . . .       3
    IS NOT ITS OWN LOVE BACK IN COPY SPEECH,  . . . . . 338 THE MOST OF IT . . .       7
    HAD ADDED TO THEIR OWN AN OVERSOUND,  . . . . . . 338 NEVER WOULD BIRDS' SONG    4
    HER OWN TOO MEAGER HEART  . . . . . . . . . 340 THE SUBVERTED FLOWER      55
    OR FROM HER OWN SELF AGAINST HER WILL  . . . . . . 343 DISCOVERY OF MADEIRAS      3
    TO BE THEIR OWN MARRIAGE FEAST FOR THE SHARK.  . . . . 346 DISCOVERY OF MADEIRAS     85
    THE NAME OF THE LADY WITH HIS OWN  . . . . . . . 347 DISCOVERY OF MADEIRAS    122
    I NEVER TAKE MY OWN SIDE IN A QUARREL.  . . . . . . 354 THE LESSON FOR TODAY    123
    I'D HAVE A SHORT ONE READY FOR MY OWN.  . . . . . 355 THE LESSON FOR TODAY    159
    WHO AM TASKED TO SAVE MY OWN A LITTLE WHILE.  . . . . 357 A MOTH SEEN IN WINTER    24
    WITH INCLINATIONS IT COULD CALL ITS OWN.  . . . . . 357 A CONSIDERABLE SPECK       9
    AND READY AGAIN FOR THE GRASS TO OWN.  . . . . . . 376 SOMETHING FOR HOPE  .     16
    EACH KNOWS HIS OWN DISCERNMENT BEST.  . . . . . . 381 AN UNSTAMPED LETTER IN    43
    THE SECOND MORE PECULIARLY OUR OWN,  . . . . . . 382 TO AN ANCIENT . . .       14
    HE GAVE HIS OWN POOR ILIAC A WRENCH  . . . . . . 394 HAEC FABULA DOCET  . .    13
    "--TAKING HIS OWN SWEET TIME AS IF TO SHOW  . . . . . 404 FROM PLANE TO PLANE   .  24
```

OWN (CONTINUED)
    I OWN HE DOES LOOK BUSY WHEN THE SUN . . . . 407 FROM PLANE TO PLANE . 104
    MUCH AS I OWN I OWE . . . . 415 CLOSED FOR GOOD . . . 1
    TO NAUGHT BUT HIS OWN FORCE OF WILL. . . . . 418 AMERICA IS HARD TO SEE 70
    SHOULD HAVE BEEN--MY OWN . . . . 429 KITTY HAWK 44
    BUT GOD'S OWN DESCENT . . . . 435 KITTY HAWK 219
    IS ITS OWN REWARD. . . . . 438 KITTY HAWK 335
    WE CAN CALL OUR OWN . . . . 440 KITTY HAWK 380
    IN HIS OWN BACKYARD . . . . 441 KITTY HAWK 407
    WHEN TEACHER'S OWN EXPERIENCES FAIL HER . . . . . . 447 DOES NO ONE AT ALL EVER 39
    FROM THE PEARL'S HAVING ITS OWN NATIVE WARMTH, . . . 456 HOW HARD TO KEEP FROM 90
    THE FREEDOM OF THEIR OWN MATERIAL: . . . . 461 HOW HARD TO KEEP FROM 234
    I MARK A MAPLE FOR MY OWN . . . . 470 IN WINTER IN THE WOODS 3
    EXCEPT IN THEIR OWN COUNTRY, THYATIRA . . . . 476 A MASQUE OF REASON . 91
    AND THAT FOR MAN'S OWN SAKE AS WELL AS MINE, ... 481 A MASQUE OF REASON . 211
    (SHE HAS HER OWN GLASS IN A VACANT CHAIR.) . . . . . 496 A MASQUE OF MERCY . 84
    A LANGUAGE OF HIS OWN TO WRITE HIS BOOK IN, ... 502 A MASQUE OF MERCY . 241
    MY TONGUE'S MY OWN, AS TRUE THOMAS USED TO SAY. . . . 505 A MASQUE OF MERCY . 296
    ABOUT OUR OWN OR ANYBODY'S END. . . . . 507 A MASQUE OF MERCY . 354
    AND HOW BY ITS OWN LOGIC IT CONCENTRATES . . . . . . 509 A MASQUE OF MERCY . 410
    I OWN THE NEED OF IT HAD SOMEWHAT FADED . . . . . . 517 A MASQUE OF MERCY . 625
OWNED
    AND MARRIAGE RINGS OF THOSE WHO OWNED THE FARM. . . . 162 NEW HAMPSHIRE . . 114
    I THINK HE OWNED SOME SHARES IN HARVARD COLLEGE.) . . 163 NEW HAMPSHIRE . . 137
    THE CULT OF ONE WHO OWNED HIMSELF "A FOILED . . . . 171 NEW HAMPSHIRE . . 383
    OLD DAVIS OWNED A SOLID MICA MOUNTAIN . . . . 212 A FOUNTAIN, A BOTTLE . 1
    AND JUST BECAUSE WE OWNED TO A WISH FOR RAIN, ... 349 OUR HOLD ON THE PLANET 5
    WE OWNED UP TO OUR WIFE . . . . 464 MILKY WAY IS A COWPATH 14
OWNER
    I CAUGHT THE OWNER OUTDOORS BY HIMSELF . . . . 164 NEW HAMPSHIRE . . 152
OWNING
    OWNING A WIFE WITH HIM MEANT OWNING HER. . . . . . . 196 PAUL'S WIFE . . . 151
    I CAN'T HELP OWNING THE GREAT RELIEF IT WOULD BE . . . 287 A ROADSIDE STAND . 47
OWNS
    AND MY HEART OWNS A DOUBT . . . . 10 STORM FEAR 16
    I'VE BOARDED HERE SO LONG, SHE THINKS SHE OWNS ME. . . 94 THE SELF-SEEKER . . 54
OXBOW
    HIS HANDS HAD WORN THEM SMOOTH AS ANY OXBOW. . . . . 66 A SERVANT TO SERVANTS . 136
OXEN
    WITH WHITE-FACED OXEN, IN A HEAVY CART, ... 41 THE MOUNTAIN . . . 17
    HE DREW THE OXEN TOWARD HIM WITH LIGHT TOUCHES . . . 44 THE MOUNTAIN . . . 107
OX'S
    IT STEAM IN WINTER LIKE AN OX'S BREATH, ... 42 THE MOUNTAIN . . . 51

P

PACE
    TILL WE LOSE ALL MEASURE OF PACE, ... 156 THE SOUND OF TREES . 7
    HE DRAGGED IT THROUGH THE PLOWED GROUND AT A PACE . . 173 A STAR IN A STONEBOAT . 31
    HAD CHECKED THE PACE . . . . 218 I WILL SING YOU ONE-O . 18
    THAT I'M NOT KEEPING PACE . . . . 465 SOME SCIENCE FICTION . 3
PACES
    HE PACES BACK AND FORTH AND NEVER RESTS . . . . . . 269 THE BEAR 16
PACIFIC
    ONCE BY THE PACIFIC . . . . 250 ONCE BY THE PACIFIC . T
    ON THE OTHER PACIFIC, SALT. . . . . 295 A RECORD STRIDE . . 24
    'TWAS TORN FROM HER PACIFIC SIDE. . . . . 452 A-WISHING WELL . . 44
    THAT'S HOW IT WAS FROM THE PACIFIC. . . . . 452 A-WISHING WELL . . 64
PACING
    (JOB TAKES A FEW STEPS PACING.) DO YOU MIND? . . . . 485 A MASQUE OF REASON . 329
PACK
    THE WHOLE FIERCE CONQUERING PACK . . . . 311 THE VINDICTIVES . . 47
PACKED
    ALL PACKED IN SAND TO WAIT THE TRUMP TOGETHER. . . . 270 THE EGG AND THE MACHINE 26
PACKING
    A WHOLE EDITION IN A PACKING CASE . . . . 216 A FOUNTAIN, A BOTTLE . 93
PAD
    TAKING DICTATION ON A PAPER PAD . . . . 182 MAPLE 79
PADDLE
    AND A PADDLE BLADE. . . . . 211 AN EMPTY THREAT . . 6
PAGAN
    THEY WERE PIPES OF PAGAN MIRTH, ... 24 PAN WITH US . . . 26
    THAT SEEMED TOO PAGAN TO OUR LIBERAL YOUTH. . . . . 58 THE BLACK COTTAGE . . 95
    AS DULCET AS A PAGAN TEMPLE GONG! . . . . 488 A MASQUE OF REASON . 419
    I SIMPLY TURN AWAY FROM IT. / YOU PAGAN! . . . . . . 513 A MASQUE OF MERCY . 523
    YES, CALL ME PAGAN, PAUL, AS IF YOU MEANT IT. . . . 513 A MASQUE OF MERCY . 524
PAGE (SEE FRONT-PAGE)
    FOR BEAUTY ON THE ILLUMINATED PAGE . . . . 358 THE LOST FOLLOWER . 15
    ACROSS THE PAGE TO WHERE WE STARTED FROM. . . . . . 405 FROM PLANE TO PLANE . 52
    AND MADE THE PAPERS' FRONT PAGE. . . . . 463 LINES IN DEJECTION . 24
    AND IS REFLECTED FROM THE PRINTED PAGE . . . . . . 515 A MASQUE OF MERCY . 581
PAGEANT
    SOME DAY TO A PAGEANT . . . . 434 KITTY HAWK 190
PAGES
    RUN THE RATTLING PAGES O'ER; . . . . 11 TO THE THAWING WIND . 13
    OF THE TWO PAGES IT WAS PRESSED BETWEEN, ... 181 MAPLE 65
    I SHOULD BETAKE ME BACK TEN THOUSAND PAGES . . . . . 350 THE LESSON FOR TODAY . 6
PAID
    JOHN BOUGHT HIM, AND WE PAID THE BILL WITH BEADS-- . 86 THE HOUSEKEEPER . . 152
    PAID HEED TO WOMEN, YOU'D TAKE MY ADVICE . . . . . . 150 SNOW 216
    WITH AN AIR THAT SAID, "I HAVE PAID MY CALL. . . . . 420 ONE MORE BREVITY . . 46
PAIL
    AND SO WE WENT WITH PAIL AND CAN . . . . 18 GOING FOR WATER . . 2
    IN THE CAVERNOUS PAIL OF THE FIRST ONE TO COME! . . 59 BLUEBERRIES 5
    HER KEEPER, EMPTY PAIL IN HAND, ... 280 BLUE RIBBON AT AMESBURY 18

PAIL (CONTINUED)
   TO WASH THE STEPS WITH PAIL AND RAG . . . . 307 PROVIDE, PROVIDE . . 2
   AND PUT HER FOOT IN THE PAIL; . . . . 463 LINES IN DEJECTION . . 12
PAILS
   OR HOMESPUN CHILDREN WITH CLICKING PAILS . . . . . . 24 PAN WITH US 14
PAIN
   IN THE PAIN THAT HAS BUT ONE CLOSE, ... 21 THE TRIAL BY EXISTENCE 71
   I SHALL NOT LACK FOR PAIN TO KEEP ME AWAKE. . . . . . 166 NEW HAMPSHIRE . . . 241
   THAT IS NOT DASHED WITH PAIN . . . . 227 TO EARTHWARD 18
   INTENT ON GIVING AND TAKING PAIN. . . . . 252 THE THATCH 2
   TO PUT THESE PEOPLE AT ONE STROKE OUT OF THEIR PAIN. . . 287 A ROADSIDE STAND . . 48
   AND OFFER TO PUT ME GENTLY OUT OF MY PAIN. . . . . . 287 A ROADSIDE STAND . . 51
   YOU MUST BE WICKED TO DESERVE SUCH PAIN. . . . . . . 486 A MASQUE OF REASON . 364
PAINS
   THE PAINS OF CONQUERING TO FORCE CHANGE ON. . . . . . 58 THE BLACK COTTAGE . . 118
   "WHAT DID I SAY?" / "ABOUT OUR TAKING PAINS." . . . . 70 THE CODE 11
   WITH THE SAME PAINS YOU USE TO FILL A CUP . . . . . 122 BIRCHES 37
   TO ASK ME IF I THINK IT WORTH THE PAINS . . . . . . 324 BUILD SOIL 271
   ESCAPE FROM SO GREAT PAINS OF LIFE ON EARTH . . . . . 475 A MASQUE OF REASON . 43
PAINT
   THERE WAS AN OLD, OLD HOUSE RENEWED WITH PAINT, . . . 263 THE INVESTMENT . . . 3
   ALL THAT PIANO AND NEW PAINT BACK THERE, ... 264 THE INVESTMENT . . . 9
   AT HAVING THE LANDSCAPE MARRED WITH THE ARTLESS PAINT . 286 A ROADSIDE STAND . . 9
   LIKE SPLASHING PHOSPHORESCENT PAINT, ... 451 A-WISHING WELL . . . 16
PAINTED
   FRESH PAINTED BY THE SHOWER A VELVET BLACK. . . . . . 55 THE BLACK COTTAGE . . 7
   A CLIFF, AND ON THE CLIFF A BOTTLE PAINTED, ... 214 A FOUNTAIN, A BOTTLE . 38
   WITH ONE A SEWELL MIGHT HAVE PAINTED. . . . . 280 BLUE RIBBON AT AMESBURY 12
   I HAVE HAD PAINTED ON THE CELLAR WALL . . . . 516 A MASQUE OF MERCY . . 615
PAIR
   "THAT'S A SMART PAIR OF PUMPS YOU'RE BEADING THERE. . . 81 THE HOUSEKEEPER . . . 9
   FIVE HUNDRED DOLLARS FOR THE PAIR, YOU KNOW." . . . . 93 THE SELF-SEEKER . . 4
   YOU STAND UP TO IT LIKE A PAIR OF COCKS. . . . . . . 100 THE SELF-SEEKER . . 211
   FOR THOUGHT HAS A PAIR OF DAUNTLESS WINGS. . . . . . 120 BOND AND FREE . . . 5
   TIME SOMEONE CAME WITH CART AND PAIR . . . . 123 PEA BRUSH 15
   GOT DRUNK, AND TRACKED THE PAIR UP CATAMOUNT, ... 195 PAUL'S WIFE 124
   SO PEOPLE AND THINGS DON'T PAIR ANYMORE . . . . . . 265 THE DOOR IN THE DARK . 8
   WITH WHAT THEY USED TO PAIR WITH BEFORE. . . . . . . 265 THE DOOR IN THE DARK . 9
   I HAVE A PAIR OF SHOES STANDING, ... 294 A RECORD STRIDE . . 5
   THE OVERIMPORTANT PAIR. . . . . 299 WELCOME TO THEIR BELIEF 4
   AND ONCE THEY HAD SHIPPED A CAPTIVE PAIR . . . . . . 345 DISCOVERY OF MADEIRAS 54
   TWO IN JUNE WERE A PAIR-- . . . . 365 A NATURE NOTE . . . 5
   TO CONFLICT AND PAIR. . . . . 426 A NEVER NAUGHT SONG . 11
   THE MOST UNQUESTIONING PAIR . . . . 444 THE DRAFT HORSE . . 13
PAIRED
   SO WHEN HE PAIRED OFF WITH ME IN THE HAYFIELD . . . . 71 THE CODE 49
PAIRING
   SO NEAR TO PARADISE ALL PAIRING ENDS: . . . . 254 A WINTER EDEN . . . 13
PAIRS
   A MAN THE WAY THINGS COME IN PAIRS. . . . . 326 TO A THINKER 14
   AS IF BY EYE PAIRS OUT OF FORTY FIRKINS. . . . . . . 378 DIRECTIVE 22
PALACE
   THE CRYSTAL PALACE, LONDON. HE'S IMPORTED. . . . . . 86 THE HOUSEKEEPER . . . 151
   OUT OF TEMPLE AND PALACE AND STORE. . . . . 310 THE VINDICTIVES . . . 13
   HAD SERVED AS A PALACE GATE. . . . . 312 THE VINDICTIVES . . . 68
   I'D SAY, O MASTER OF THE PALACE SCHOOL, ... 351 THE LESSON FOR TODAY . 19
   I CAN JUST HEAR YOU CALL YOUR PALACE CLASS: . . . . . 353 THE LESSON FOR TODAY . 84
   FLED FROM THE PALACE IN THE GUISE OF MEN. . . . . . 454 HOW HARD TO KEEP FROM 11
PALADIN
   AND EVERY SHEEPISH PALADIN AND PEER, ... 353 THE LESSON FOR TODAY . 90
PALADINS
   O PALADINS, THE LESSON FOR TODAY . . . . 353 THE LESSON FOR TODAY . 87
PALE
   AND THUS IT WAS THE MAIDENS PALE . . . . 15 IN A VALE 3
   (PALE ORCHISES), AND SCARED A BRIGHT GREEN SNAKE. . . 17 MOWING 12
   AS PALE AND DIM AS A MATCH FLAME IN THE SUN; . . . . 77 THE GENERATIONS OF MEN 100
   LAID SCARLET AND PALE PINK ABOUT HER FEET. . . . . . 184 MAPLE 147
   FAR IN THE MAPLES, PALE, BUT NOT A GHOST? . . . . . 233 A BOUNDLESS MOMENT . . 2
   THAN AN IMPOVERISHED SOIL, PALE AND METALLIC? . . . . 323 BUILD SOIL 218
   THAT WERE PALE AS A GHOST. . . . . 343 QUEST OF PURPLE-FRINGED 24
PALESTINE
   YOURS MORE THROUGH ROME, MINE MORE THROUGH PALESTINE.-- . 513 A MASQUE OF MERCY . 518
PALETTE
   THE COLORS ARE KEPT UNMIXED ON THE PALETTE, ... 320 BUILD SOIL 147
   THEY REMIND ME OF PICTURES ON A PALETTE: . . . . . . 321 BUILD SOIL 152
PALLADIUM
   AN EOLITH PALLADIUM TO GUARD . . . . 365 OF STONES OF THE PLACE 11
PALLIATIVE
   STRAY SCRAPS OF PALLIATIVE REASON . . . . 478 A MASQUE OF REASON . 142
PALLID
   SOME PALLID THING HAD SQUASHED ITS FEATURES FLAT . . . 148 SNOW 160
PALM
   TO CHAFE AND SHUFFLE IN MY CALLOUSED PALM . . . . . . 174 A STAR IN A STONEBOAT . 52
   AND HE LASHED HIS OPEN PALM . . . . 339 THE SUBVERTED FLOWER . 3
   AND SO TO LET PIKE SEEM TO HAVE THE PALM . . . . . . 408 FROM PLANE TO PLANE . 120
   A MAN SITS LEANING BACK AGAINST A PALM. . . . . . . 473 A MASQUE OF REASON . . 2
PALPABLE
   THE ONE THING PALPABLE BESIDES THE SOUL . . . . . . 172 A STAR IN A STONEBOAT . 11
PAMIR
   TILL HE CAME TO THE LAND OF PAMIR. . . . . 313 BEARER OF EVIL TIDINGS 12
PAN
   PAN CAME OUT OF THE WOODS ONE DAY-- . . . . 23 PAN WITH US 1
   PAN WITH US . . . . 23 PAN WITH US . . . . T
   AND BADE HIM LEAVE THE PAN AND STOKE THE ARCH: . . . 234 EVENING A SUGAR ORCHARD 4
PANE
   HE MARKED HER THROUGH THE PANE, ... 10 WIND AND WINDOW FLOWER 9
   WE PRESSED OUR FACES TO THE PANE. "YOU SEE," HE SAID, . 55 THE BLACK COTTAGE . . 14
   I GOT FROM LOOKING THROUGH A PANE OF GLASS . . . . . 68 AFTER APPLE-PICKING . 10

PANE (CONTINUED)
    THAT GATHERS ON THE PANE IN EMPTY ROOMS. . . . . 108 OLD MAN'S WINTER NIGHT   3
    SO HIGH ACROSS THE PANE OUTSIDE. THERE WHERE . . . . . 149 SNOW 191
    AGAINST THE WRONG SIDE OF A WINDOW PANE. . . . . 412 POD OF THE MILKWEED .   39
PANELING
    TO BRING ME TO FOR BROAD-BOARD PANELING. . . . . 215 A FOUNTAIN, A BOTTLE . 70
PANG
    A DREAM PANG . . . . 16 A DREAM PANG . . . .   T
    AND THE SWEET PANG IT COST ME NOT TO CALL . . . . . 16 A DREAM PANG   11
    IT COST THE EARTH AS FIERCE A PANG . . . . 452 A-WISHING WELL . . .   40
PANIC
    TO SEPARATE US FOR A PANIC MOMENT. . . . . 259 WEST-RUNNING BROOK .   52
    BEFORE THEIR PANIC HANDS . . . . 298 ON TAKING FROM THE TOP 13
PANTHEISM
    WHICH IS NO MORE THAN GOOD OLD PANTHEISM. . . . . . . 427 CONCEPT SELF-CONCEIVED   4
PANTHEON
    HIS CHURCH ON EARTH A ROMAN PANTHEON; . . . . 516 A MASQUE OF MERCY . 592
PANTHER
    STILL SAID TO HAUNT THIS SIDE OF PANTHER MOUNTAIN. . . 377 DIRECTIVE   19
PANTING
    AND GONE PANTING BY. . . . . 342 QUEST OF PURPLE-FRINGED 12
PANTS
    DON'T WEAR YOUR PANTS OUT PREACHING ON YOUR KNEES. . . 519 A MASQUE OF MERCY . 681
PAPER (SEE BLACK-PAPER-COVERED, CREPE-PAPER)
    WAS A BLOW-AWAY PAPER THE RAIN . . . . 110 A PATCH OF OLD SNOW .   3
    ITS BED IS LEFT A FADED PAPER SHEET . . . . 119 HYLA BROOK   10
    TAKING DICTATION ON A PAPER PAD . . . . . . 182 MAPLE   79
    AND DEAD WINGS CARRIED LIKE A PAPER KITE. . . . . . 302 DESIGN   8
    ON ANY BUT A PAPER SHEET SO WHITE . . . . . . 357 A CONSIDERABLE SPECK .   2
    OF FRONT-PAGE PAPER EVENTS, ... 367 A SERIOUS STEP LIGHTLY 22
    AS IN THOSE BUOYANT BIRD BONES THIN AS PAPER, ... 387 INNATE HELIUM . . .   4
    IF SO, IT WILL BE IN TOMORROW'S PAPER. . . . . . . 507 A MASQUE OF MERCY . 357
PAPERED
    THAT THERE ALWAYS IS ON THE PAPERED WALLS, ... 232 THE KITCHEN CHIMNEY . 14
PAPERS
    AS IF FOR PAPERS THAT MIGHT BEAR THE NAME . . . 96 THE SELF-SEEKER . .   98
    THE LAWYER GAVE A LAUGH AMONG HIS PAPERS . . . . 98 THE SELF-SEEKER . . 145
    WHEN YOU COME BACK, I'LL HAVE THE PAPERS SIGNED. . . 100 THE SELF-SEEKER . . 213
    SAFETY RAZORS, SUNDAY PAPERS. . . . . 396 AN IMPORTER   14
PAPERS'
    AND MADE THE PAPERS' FRONT PAGE. . . . . 463 LINES IN DEJECTION .   24
PAPER'S
    "YOU SEEM TO SHAPE THE PAPER'S POLICY." . . . . . 48 A HUNDRED COLLARS . 119
PAPHIAN
    AND SAIL FOR SOME VAGUE PAPHIAN BOURN . . . . . . 344 DISCOVERY OF MADEIRAS . 17
PARABOLIC
    THE PARABOLIC CURVE . . . . 464 MILKY WAY IS A COWPATH 21
PARADE
    THEY WERE MADE TO PARADE, ... 449 THE BAD ISLAND--EASTER 56
PARADED
    THEY TRIED TO KEEP HIM CLOTHED, BUT HE PARADED . . . . 66 A SERVANT TO SERVANTS . 122
PARADISE
    EVEN AS ON EARTH, IN PARADISE; . . . . 19 THE TRIAL BY EXISTENCE   4
    WILL GLADLY GIVE UP PARADISE. . . . . 20 THE TRIAL BY EXISTENCE 28
    "DUMPED DOWN IN PARADISE WE ARE AND HAPPY." . . . . 116 IN THE HOME STRETCH . 163
    AS NEAR A PARADISE AS IT CAN BE . . . . 254 A WINTER EDEN . . .   3
    SO NEAR TO PARADISE ALL PAIRING ENDS: . . . . . 254 A WINTER EDEN . . .   13
    THE BIRDS, SEEM ALL ON FIRE WITH PARADISE. . . . . 473 A MASQUE OF REASON .   13
PARADISE-IN-BLOOM
    "OH, THAT'S THE PARADISE-IN-BLOOM," I SAID; . . . . . 233 A BOUNDLESS MOMENT .   5
PARADISE'S
    AND A LONG BIRD OF PARADISE'S TAIL . . . . 172 A STAR IN A STONEBOAT . 16
PARADOXES
    DON'T LISTEN TO THEIR PLAY OF PARADOXES. . . . . . 460 HOW HARD TO KEEP FROM 193
PARAKEET
    AS ANY GUATEMALAN PARAKEET. . . . . 412 POD OF THE MILKWEED .   47
PARALLEL
    AND FELD THEM ABSOLUTELY PARALLEL . . . . 396 ANY SIZE WE PLEASE .   6
PARASITE
    WITH CODLIN MOTH OR RUSTY PARASITE . . . . 283 THE GOLD HESPERIDEE .   28
    TILL ANOTHER PARASITE . . . . 308 EVIL TENDENCIES CANCEL   5
PARASOL
    BUT MORE THAN ONE AS YET. YOUR PARASOL . . . . . 119 MEETING AND PASSING .   8
PARCEL
    FOR EVERY PARCEL I STOOP DOWN TO SEIZE . . . . . 266 THE ARMFUL   1
PARCELED
    GET PARCELED OUT AMONG THE WINNING GIANTS. . . . . 398 NO HOLY WARS FOR THEM . 8
PARDON
    PARDON THE ANALOGY, MY MELIBOEUS, ... 318 BUILD SOIL   90
    KEPT REPEATING PARDON, PARDON; . . . . 397 AN IMPORTER   20
    PARDON MY INTERRUPTION; I'M UNHAPPY. . . . . . . 460 HOW HARD TO KEEP FROM 204
PARENT
    THE FLOWER WAS DIFFERENT FROM THE PARENT SEED. . . . 181 MAPLE   39
    A PARENT, HIS GENTLER ONE, ... 366 NOT OF SCHOOL AGE . . 13
PARENTAL
    DIVINE LOVE, HUMAN LOVE, PARENTAL LOVE, ... 318 BUILD SOIL   87
PARENTS
    OF PLAGIARISM AND HELP OF CHEATING PARENTS. . . . . 325 BUILD SOIL 275
    MY PARENTS WHEN I RAN TO THEM AVERRED . . . . . . 443 AUSPEX   6
PARENTS'
    TAKING THE CHILD OUT OF THE PARENTS' HANDS. . . . . 185 MAPLE 167
    TO BE OUR PARENTS' PSEUDONYMITY . . . . 408 FROM PLANE TO PLANE . 138
PARK
    THE PLACE WAS LIKE A CITY PARK. . . . . 380 AN UNSTAMPED LETTER IN 11
    PUT OUT OF THE PARK. . . . . 413 AWAY!   12
    UNDER THE BANDSTAND IN SUBURBAN PARK. . . . . . 501 A MASQUE OF MERCY . 210
PARLOR
    TO DO WITH WHAT WAS IN THE DARKENED PARLOR? . . . . 54 HOME BURIAL   96

PARLOR (CONTINUED)
  FOR EVERY ROOM A HOUSE HAS--PARLOR, BEDROOM, ... 110 IN THE HOME STRETCH   .   8
PART
  PART OF A MOON WAS FALLING DOWN THE WEST, ... 38 DEATH OF THE HIRED MAN 103
  "I DON'T KNOW WHAT PART OF THE PASTURE YOU MEAN." . . . 59 BLUEBERRIES   8
  GRIM SILENCE ON MY PART AS I SANK LOWER, ... 198 WILD GRAPES   79
  AND SAVED SOME PART . . . . 221 DUST OF SNOW   7
  ONLY, OF COURSE, THEY CAN'T SUSTAIN THE PART. . . . . 246 FIREFLIES IN THE GARDEN   6
  ON THEIR PART, THOUGH WITHOUT THE NEEDED INSIGHT. . . . 293 AT WOODWARD'S GARDENS . 26
  BUT STARS WERE SCARCE IN THAT PART OF THE SKY, ... 295 LOST IN HEAVEN . . .   5
  WAS NOT IN PART OR ALL . . . . 333 HAPPINESS MAKES UP . .   6
  AND WHAT I WOULD NOT PART WITH I HAVE KEPT. . . . . . 335 I COULD GIVE ALL . .   15
  THAT THE FLOWER HAD DONE BUT PART, ... 340 THE SUBVERTED FLOWER . 53
  BUT LET'S GO ON TO WHERE OUR CASES PART, ... 352 THE LESSON FOR TODAY . 64
  IF PART THEY DO. LET ME PROPOSE A START. . . . . . . 352 THE LESSON FOR TODAY . 65
  GO PART WAY DOWN THE LANE, ... 359 NOVEMBER   3
  A PART APPLE IN HIS HAND, ... 366 NOT OF SCHOOL AGE . .   10
  NO PART OF WHICH WE'D HAVE TO WASTE, I SAY, ... 371 THE LITERATE FARMER AND 101
  WHOSE PART SHOULD BE TO TELL . . . . 383 MAKING CERTAIN ANYTHING 3
  "SO I HAVE HEARD AND SO DO IN PART BELIEVE IT," . . . 408 FROM PLANE TO PLANE . 147
  AND PART THEM IN THE MIDDLE WITH A PATH. . . . . . . 414 A CABIN IN THE CLEARING 4
  LEARNING HAS BEEN A PART OF THEIR RELIGION. . . . . . 414 A CABIN IN THE CLEARING 28
  SO IN IT HAVE TO TAKE COURAGEOUS PART. . . . . 423 FOR JOHN F. KENNEDY . 42
  ON OUR HUMAN PART . . . . 436 KITTY HAWK 255
  AND THE BETTER PART . . . . 440 KITTY HAWK 387
  OF AT LEAST SOME PART . . . . 441 KITTY HAWK 424
  WE CAN GIVE THE PART . . . . 441 KITTY HAWK 427
  AS THROW A PART AWAY. . . . . 445 ENDS   10
  YOU REALIZE BY NOW THE PART YOU PLAYED . . . . 475 A MASQUE OF REASON . .   66
  WHETHER THERE'S ANY PART OF MAN IMMORTAL. . . . . . . 483 A MASQUE OF REASON . . 297
  NOTHING HAS BEEN BROUGHT OUT THAT FOR MY PART . . . . 488 A MASQUE OF REASON . . 413
PARTED
  CANNOT BE PARTED NOR BE SWEPT AWAY . . . . 300 THE MASTER SPEED . .   11
PARTIAL
  "YOU SEEM SO PARTIAL TO OUR GREAT-GRANDMOTHER . . . . 79 THE GENERATIONS OF MEN 177
  LESS PARTIAL WITNESSES THAN HE . . . . 418 AMERICA IS HARD TO SEE 62
PARTICIPATE
  SUMMONING ARTISTS TO PARTICIPATE . . . . 422 FOR JOHN F. KENNEDY .   1
PARTICIPATING
  FOR LOOKING ON AND NOT PARTICIPATING. . . . . 462 HOW HARD TO KEEP FROM 271
PARTICLE
  PARTICLE AFLOAT. 439 KITTY HAWK 368
PARTICULAR
  I'M AS PARTICULAR AS ANYONE: . . . . 70 THE CODE   24
  AT THAT PARTICULAR TIME O'CLOCK, ... 139 BROWN'S DESCENT . . .   64
  ON HIS PARTICULAR TIME AND PERSONAL SIGHT. . . . . . 268 ON LOOKING UP BY CHANCE 15
  WHO IN PARTICULAR, WHEN ALL ALIKE . . . . 317 BUILD SOIL   39
PARTICULARLY
  HIS PRESENCE WAS PARTICULARLY THERE. . . . . 407 FROM PLANE TO PLANE . 92
PARTICULARS
  NOR WHAT PARTICULARS THEY REASON FROM, ... 354 THE LESSON FOR TODAY . 109
PARTING
  THE PATH WAS A VAGUE PARTING IN THE GRASS . . . . . . 55 THE BLACK COTTAGE . .   12
  SO WHEN HE CAME TO THE PARTING . . . . 313 BEARER OF EVIL TIDINGS   5
PARTLY
  A MAN MUST PARTLY GIVE UP BEING A MAN . . . . 52 HOME BURIAL   49
  PERHAPS A FILIAL DIFFIDENCE PARTLY KEPT THEM . . . . 184 MAPLE 157
  WAS I DESIRED IN FRIENDSHIP, PARTLY AS SOMEONE . . . 188 THE AX-HELVE   90
  THE FAULT MUST PARTLY HAVE BEEN IN ME. . . . . 251 A MINOR BIRD   5
  PARTLY BECAUSE IT SANG BUT ONCE ALL NIGHT . . . . . . 302 A BIRD SINGING IN SLEEP 3
  PARTLY BECAUSE IT SANG VENTRILOQUIST . . . . 302 A BIRD SINGING IN SLEEP 5
  THE WAY OF UNDERSTANDING IS PARTLY MIRTH. . . . . . . 306 NOT QUITE SOCIAL . .   11
  AND IT IS PARTLY TO COMPEL . . . . 381 AN UNSTAMPED LETTER IN 50
PARTS
  EVERYTHING ITS PARTS CAN DO . . . . 306 A TRIAL RUN   11
PARTY (SEE COCKTAIL-PARTY)
  THAT THE PARTY IN POWER IS SAID TO BE KEEPING FROM US. . 286 A ROADSIDE STAND . .   22
  AND TWENTY FREEDOMS ON THE PARTY DOCKET. . . . . . . 484 A MASQUE OF REASON . . 311
PASS
  AND MAKES GAPS EVEN TWO CAN PASS ABREAST. . . . . . . 33 MENDING WALL   4
  AT LEAST TO PASS BY AND SEE WHO HE WAS, ... 74 THE GENERATIONS OF MEN 32
  THAT WITH EVERY FUTILE PASS . . . . 128 THE OFT-REPEATED DREAM   6
  HE CAME FROM HIGHER UP IN THE PASS . . . . 140 THE GUM-GATHERER . .   13
  THAN WE HAD SEEING HIM PASS BY IN THE ROAD . . . . . 152 SNOW 253
  A BETTER WAY TO PASS THE AFTERNOON . . . . 190 THE GRINDSTONE . . .   53
  SHE COULD CALL UP TO PASS A WINTER EVENING, ... 202 THE WITCH OF COOS . .   5
  MORE THAN HALFWAY UP THE PASS . . . . 263 THE TIMES TABLE . . .   1
  AND BROUGHT OUR VARIOUS LIVES TO PASS. . . . . 265 THE BIRTHPLACE . . .   6
  THE NEXT MACHINE THAT HAS THE POWER TO PASS . . . . . 270 THE EGG AND THE MACHINE 29
  OF ALL THE THOUSAND SELFISH CARS THAT PASS, ... 287 A ROADSIDE STAND . .   37
  I PASS, BUT SCARCELY PASS NO DOUBT, ... 291 ON HEART'S BEGINNING TO 21
  TO COME TO THEIR FINAL PLACE IN EARTH THEY HAD TO PASS ME
    BY, ... 297 A LEAF-TREADER . . .   6
  AS LONG AS IT TAKES TO PASS . . . . 301 NEITHER OUT FAR NOR IN   5
  AT THE PRESENT RATE IT MUST COME TO PASS, ... 375 SOMETHING FOR HOPE . .   1
  WE HAVE MADE A PASS . . . . 439 KITTY HAWK 362
  THE WINTER OWL BANKED JUST IN TIME TO PASS . . . . . 445 QUESTIONING FACES . .   1
  OUR DAYS ALL PASS AWAITING ITS RETURN. . . . . 461 HOW HARD TO KEEP FROM 248
  CAN EVER QUITE PASS OUT OF UTTER GRIEF . . . . 469 WE VAINLY WRESTLE... .   3
  PREDICTED ANYTHING THAT CAME TO PASS. . . . . 476 A MASQUE OF REASON . .   96
PASSAGE
  SHE RAN ON TIPTOE DOWN THE DARKENED PASSAGE . . . . . 34 DEATH OF THE HIRED MAN   3
  AND DOWN A NARROW PASSAGE FULL OF DOORS, ... 45 A HUNDRED COLLARS . .   34
  A NARROW PASSAGE ALL THE WAY AROUND. . . . . 66 A SERVANT TO SERVANTS 116
  OUR PASSAGE TO OUR JOURNEY'S END FOR GOOD, ... 238 ON A TREE FALLEN ACROSS 3
  (THE MEANING OF THE PASSAGE HAD BEEN HID): . . . . . 284 THE GOLD HESPERIDEE .   52
  HE HAD HIS TICKET BOUGHT, HIS PASSAGE EARNED, ... 370 THE LITERATE FARMER AND 58

PASSED
    AND ONLY PASSED HER BY . . . . 10 WIND AND WINDOW FLOWER   11
    BUT AS I SAID IT, SWIFT THERE PASSED ME BY . . . . . . 22 THE TUFT OF FLOWERS .   11
    I MEAN BY THE WORLD'S HAVING PASSED IT BY-- . . . . . 56 THE BLACK COTTAGE . .   43
    YOU CAN'T HAVE PASSED EACH OTHER. I KNOW WHAT: . . . . 81 THE HOUSEKEEPER . . .   16
    AFTERWARD I WENT PAST WHAT YOU HAD PASSED . . . . . . 119 MEETING AND PASSING .   13
    BEFORE WE MET, AND YOU WHAT I HAD PASSED. . . . . . . 119 MEETING AND PASSING .   14
    WHEN THEY HAD PASSED AN HOUR OR SO BEFORE . . . . . . 132 THE BONFIRE   87
    IT'S FROM REGRET FOR SOMETHING YOU HAVE PASSED . . . . 147 SNOW 124
    AFTER A DOWNY STORM, HE PASSED OUR PLACE . . . . 149 SNOW 176
    PASSED IN AND SLAMMED IT SHUT EACH ONE BEHIND HIM . . 175 THE CENSUS-TAKER . .   29
    THE PEOPLE THAT HAD LOUDLY PASSED THE DOOR . . . . . . 175 THE CENSUS-TAKER . .   38
    WHAT PASSED BETWEEN US, SHE WAS ONLY FEIGNING. . . . . 187 THE AX-HELVE   57
    SHE SIGHED AND PASSED UNSCARED ALONG THE WALL. . . . . 229 TWO LOOK AT TWO . .   24
    THEN HE TOO PASSED UNSCARED ALONG THE WALL. . . . . . 230 TWO LOOK AT TWO . .   37
    IN SUMMER WHEN I PASSED THE PLACE, ... 233 LOOKING FOR SUNSET BIRD   5
    AND AS I PASSED ALONG THE EAVES . . . . 253 THE THATCH   17
    I HAVE PASSED BY THE WATCHMAN ON HIS BEAT . . . . . . 255 ACQUAINTED WITH NIGHT   5
    THE POLISHED TRAFFIC PASSED WITH A MIND AHEAD, ... 286 A ROADSIDE STAND . .   7
    BUT WE WHO PASSED WERE NOT TO SEE HIM FALL. . . . . . 292 FIGURE IN THE DOORWAY . 10
    BUT WHEN THE OCEAN'S WORST HAD PASSED . . . . 344 DISCOVERY OF MADEIRAS . 35
    I PASSED WITH SUCH A HIGH I.Q. . . . . 467 QUANDARY   26
PASSERS
    THE PASSERS OF THE PAST . . . . 415 CLOSED FOR GOOD . . .   2
PASSES
    AND THE AWE PASSES WONDER THEN, ... 21 THE TRIAL BY EXISTENCE   59
PASSING
    WE CHANCED IN PASSING BY THAT AFTERNOON . . . . . .   55 THE BLACK COTTAGE . .   1
    DON'T HOLD MY ARM!" / "I SAY IT'S SOMEONE PASSING." . 90 THE FEAR   23
    THOUGH AS FOR THAT, THE PASSING THERE . . . . 105 THE ROAD NOT TAKEN .   9
    "THE BREAD WE BOUGHT IN PASSING AT THE STORE. . . . . 115 IN THE HOME STRETCH . 144
    MEETING AND PASSING . . . . 118 MEETING AND PASSING .   T
    A SUDDEN PASSING BULLET SHOOK IT DRY. . . . . 126 RANGE-FINDING . . .   12
    AND HID FROM ANYONE PASSING. . . . . 134 A GIRL'S GARDEN . . .   25
    DROP IN AND SEE US WHEN YOU'RE PASSING." / "WELL, . . 155 SNOW 333
    EACH OTHER IN PASSING IN THE ROOM UPSTAIRS, ... 180 MAPLE   11
    FROM INWARD FIRES OR BRUSH OF PASSING FEET. . . . . . 239 OUR SINGING STRENGTH .   18
    I OFTEN SEE FLOWERS FROM A PASSING CAR . . . . 248 A PASSING GLIMPSE . .   1
    A PASSING GLIMPSE . . . . 248 A PASSING GLIMPSE . .   T
    BUT MERCIFULLY KEPT THE PASSING CROWD . . . . 284 THE GOLD HESPERIDEE .   56
    THAT I ASSUME WAS WHAT OUR PASSING TRAIN MEANT. . . . 292 FIGURE IN THE DOORWAY . 20
    THE ART OF LIFE IS PASSING LOSSES ON. . . . . 399 THE INGENUITIES OF DEBT   5
    WE CAN ALL SEE WHAT'S PASSING IN YOUR MIND. . . . . . 503 A MASQUE OF MERCY . 255
PASSION
    SLAVE TO A SPRINGTIME PASSION FOR THE EARTH. . . . . . 124 PUTTING IN THE SEED .   9
    IN ALL THE PASSION OF A BROKEN DROUTH. . . . . 337 THE WIND AND THE RAIN . 39
PASSIONATE
    AS I HAVE KNOWN THEM PASSIONATE AND FINE, ... 358 THE LOST FOLLOWER . .   1
    PASSIONATE PREFERENCE SUCH AS LOVE AT SIGHT. . . . . . 425 ACCIDENTALLY ON PURPOSE 24
PASSIONATELY
    TO ALL THOSE FLOWERS THEY PASSIONATELY TROD . . . . . 412 POD OF THE MILKWEED .   42
PASSPORT
    DRAWN ON A SORT OF PASSPORT WITH THE BRANCH . . . . . 74 THE GENERATIONS OF MEN   40
    "YES, STARK. AND YOU?" / "I'M STARK." HE DREW HIS PASSPORT. 74 THE GENERATIONS OF MEN 46
    I COULD POINT OUT MY SORT OF PASSPORT IN IT. . . . . . 495 A MASQUE OF MERCY .   46
PAST   (SEE HALF-PAST)
    THEY MUST GO DOWN PAST THINGS COMING UP. . . . . 26 IN HARDWOOD GROVES .   7
    AND LIVING BY A LAKE. I'M PAST SUCH HELP-- . . . . . . 67 A SERVANT TO SERVANTS 156
    THE PAST AND GET SOME STRANGENESS OUT OF IT. . . . . . 73 THE GENERATIONS OF MEN   18
    SHE PUSHED PAST HIM AND GOT IT FOR HERSELF. . . . . . 90 THE FEAR   34
    AS TO OUR FATE, LIKE FOOLS PAST REASONING WITH. . . . 114 IN THE HOME STRETCH . 125
    AFTERWARD I WENT PAST WHAT YOU HAD PASSED . . . . . . 119 MEETING AND PASSING .   13
    HE SAYS THE EARLY PETAL-FALL IS PAST, ... 120 THE OVEN BIRD   6
    BACK PAST THE SUN TO AN EARTHLY ROOM. . . . . 120 BOND AND FREE . . .   15
    BUT IN NO HUSH THEY STRING IT: THEY GO PAST. . . . . . 141 THE LINE-GANG . . .   8
    RIGHT PAST BOTH FATHER AND MOTHER, AND NEITHER STOPPED IT. 203 THE WITCH OF COOS .   33
    SUMMER WAS PAST AND DAY WAS PAST. . . . . 251 BEREFT   6
    A SLIM DOOR GOT IN PAST MY GUARD, ... 265 THE DOOR IN THE DARK .   5
    I WENT TO SCHOOL TO AGE TO LEARN THE PAST. . . . . . . 267 WHAT FIFTY SAID . .   4
    A DEPTH PAST MANY SWINGING DOORS . . . . 280 BLUE RIBBON AT AMESBURY 23
    AND IF AFTER THE HUNT GOES PAST . . . . 282 A DRUMLIN WOODCHUCK .   21
    IN A FIELD I LOOKED INTO GOING PAST, ... 296 DESERT PLACES   2
    THAN IN THE PAST. THE PRESENT . . . . 336 CARPE DIEM   23
    THAT PAST ITS PRIME LOST PETALS IN THE FLOOD . . . . 337 THE WIND AND THE RAIN . 33
    THE PASSERS OF THE PAST . . . . 415 CLOSED FOR GOOD . . .   2
    WHEN PAST THE LEG I THRUST FOR BAR . . . . 419 ONE MORE BREVITY . .   8
    PAST ELIZABETH CITY . . . . 428 KITTY HAWK   8
    THAT MADE US STUMBLE PAST. . . . . 444 ENDS   2
    FOR THE WOES OF THE PAST . . . . 447 THE BAD ISLAND--EASTER   5
    THAT GO BLINDLY POURING PAST. . . . . 469 FOUR-ROOM SHACK. . . .   4
    BECAUSE YOUR WIFE'S PAST WON'T BEAR LOOKING INTO?-- . 477 A MASQUE OF REASON . 116
PAST-ACTIVE
    ABOUT BEING PAST-ACTIVE SHOES. . . . . 295 A RECORD STRIDE . . .   32
PASTE
    LIGHT WAS A PASTE OF PIGMENT IN OUR EYES. . . . . . . 315 IRIS BY NIGHT   9
PASTED
    GET BEATEN DOWN AND PASTED . . . . 359 NOVEMBER   5
PASTORAL
    A POLITICAL PASTORAL . . . . 316 BUILD SOIL . . . . .   S
PASTURE
    I'M GOING OUT TO CLEAN THE PASTURE SPRING; . . . . . . 1 THE PASTURE   1
    THE PASTURE . . . . 1 THE PASTURE . . . . .   T
    SHE WALKS THE SODDEN PASTURE LANE. . . . . 6 MY NOVEMBER GUEST . .   5
    ON A HEIGHT OF NAKED PASTURE LAND; . . . . 23 PAN WITH US   7
    HE MEANT TO CLEAR THE UPPER PASTURE, TOO. . . . . . . 36 DEATH OF THE HIRED MAN   52
    PASTURE RAN UP THE SIDE A LITTLE WAY, ... 41 THE MOUNTAIN   29
    INTO THE PASTURE. / "THAT LOOKS LIKE A PATH. . . . . . 41 THE MOUNTAIN   34
    TO THE VILLAGE, THROUGH PATTERSON'S PASTURE TODAY: . . 59 BLUEBERRIES   2

	PAGE	TITLE	LINE

PASTURE (CONTINUED)

"I DON'T KNOW WHAT PART OF THE PASTURE YOU MEAN." . . . . . 59 BLUEBERRIES 8
THE PASTURE ALL OVER UNTIL NOT A FERN . . . . 59 BLUEBERRIES 18
WE'LL PICK IN THE PATTERSONS' PASTURE THIS YEAR. . . . . . 61 BLUEBERRIES 81
AND TURN DOLL OUT TO PASTURE, RIG AND ALL. . . . . . . 88 THE HOUSEKEEPER . . 201
PASTURE THEY SPRING IN, SOME IN CLUMPS TOO CLOSE . . . . 107 CHRISTMAS TREES . . . 33
WE CLIMBED THE PASTURE ON THE SOUTH, CROSSED OVER, . . . 107 CHRISTMAS TREES . . . 40
THE EXTENT OF PASTURE I SHOULD STRIP, THREE CENTS . . . 107 CHRISTMAS TREES . . . 48
THEY LEAVE US TO: THAT PASTURE SLOPE THAT SEEMS . . . . 114 IN THE HOME STRETCH . 113
PINE, ALDER, PASTURE, MOWING, WELL, AND BROOK. . . . . . 117 IN THE HOME STRETCH . 197
SHE SCORNS A PASTURE WITHERING TO THE ROOT. . . . . . . 125 THE COW IN APPLE TIME . 6
ON THE BARE UPLAND PASTURE THERE HAD SPREAD . . . . . . 126 RANGE-FINDING . . . 9
THE NEXT COW MIGHT HAVE LICKED UP OUT AT PASTURE. . . . 184 MAPLE 151
WE STOPPED BY A MOUNTAIN PASTURE TO SAY, "WHOSE COLT?" . . 223 THE RUNAWAY 2
AND ON THE PASTURE BARS . . . . 252 THE PEACEFUL SHEPHERD . 2
ALL WOODS AND PASTURE ONLY FIT FOR SHEEP. . . . . . . 316 BUILD SOIL 9
I FARM A PASTURE WHERE THE BOULDERS LIE . . . . 365 OF STONES OF THE PLACE 1
WHO USED YOUR PASTURE FOR A CAMP. . . . . 380 AN UNSTAMPED LETTER IN 7
THROUGH LET-DOWN PASTURE BARS . . . . 465 MILKY WAY IS A COWPATH 30
PASTUREWISE
THE HILLS ARE VERDURED PASTUREWISE; . . . . 19 THE TRIAL BY EXISTENCE 12
PATCH
THERE'S A PATCH OF OLD SNOW IN A CORNER, ... 110 A PATCH OF OLD SNOW . 1
A PATCH OF OLD SNOW . . . . 110 A PATCH OF OLD SNOW . T
HE HAD A TEN-BY-TWENTY GARDEN PATCH. . . . . 292 FIGURE IN THE DOORWAY . 18
PATCHES
THE FIELDS ARE STRIPPED TO LAWN, THE GARDEN PATCHES . . . 49 A HUNDRED COLLARS . . 134
PATENT
SHE WATERS AT THE PATENT FOUNT. . . . . 281 BLUE RIBBON AT AMESBURY 43
"IN SHORT, YOU THINK THAT STAR A PATENT MEDICINE . . . 371 THE LITERATE FARMER AND 92
PATENTED
IT'S A NEW PATENTED ELECTRIC LIGHT, ... 369 THE LITERATE FARMER AND 39
PATH
HALF CLOSES THE GARDEN PATH. . . . . 8 A LATE WALK 4
INTO THE PASTURE. / "THAT LOOKS LIKE A PATH. . . . . . 41 THE MOUNTAIN 34
THERE IS NO PROPER PATH, BUT THOSE THAT HAVE . . . . . 41 THE MOUNTAIN 39
THE PATH WAS A VAGUE PARTING IN THE GRASS . . . . . . 55 THE BLACK COTTAGE . . 12
WITH THOUGHTS OF THE PATH BACK, HOW ROUGH IT WAS . . . . 229 TWO LOOK AT TWO . . . 5
ON UP THE FAILING PATH, WHERE, IF A STONE . . . . . . 229 TWO LOOK AT TWO . . . 11
HE KNEW A PATH THAT WANTED WALKING; . . . . 274 A LONE STRIKER . . . 43
GOD SAW HIM DANCING IN THE ORCHARD PATH, ... 284 THE GOLD HESPERIDEE . 55
TILL I SAW THE PATH WHERE THE SLENDER FOX HAD COME . . . 342 QUEST OF PURPLE-FRINGED 11
AND PART THEM IN THE MIDDLE WITH A PATH. . . . . . . 414 A CABIN IN THE CLEARING 4
ALL THEY MAINTAIN THE PATH FOR IS THE COMFORT . . . . 414 A CABIN IN THE CLEARING 7
PATHETIC
A BAGGY FIGURE, EQUALLY PATHETIC . . . . 269 THE BEAR 33
A FLICKERING, HUMAN PATHETIC LIGHT, ... 291 ON HEART'S BEGINNING TO 7
PATHETICALLY
A ROADSIDE STAND THAT TOO PATHETICALLY PLED, ... 286 A ROADSIDE STAND . . 3
PATHLESS
AND LIFE IS TOO MUCH LIKE A PATHLESS WOOD . . . . . 122 BIRCHES 44
PATHS
DOWN DARK CONVERGING PATHS BETWEEN THE PINES. . . . . 129 THE BONFIRE 7
PATIENCE
PATIENCE AND LOOKING AWAY AHEAD, ... 376 SOMETHING FOR HOPE . 21
PATIENT
OH, I REMEMBER WELL: YOU'RE JOB, MY PATIENT. . . . . 474 A MASQUE OF REASON . 34
PATIENTLY
WE MAY AS WELL GO PATIENTLY ON WITH OUR LIFE, ... 268 ON LOOKING UP BY CHANCE 8
PATINA
THE PATINA OF THIS THE LEAST OF GLOBES. . . . . . . 352 THE LESSON FOR TODAY . 72
PATROL
ON MIDNIGHT PATROL, ... 432 KITTY HAWK 141
PATTER
NOT WITHOUT DUE PATTER . . . . 435 KITTY HAWK 228
PATTERSON
"DOES PATTERSON KNOW WHAT HE HAS, DO YOU THINK?" . . . 60 BLUEBERRIES 28
PATTERSONS'
WE'LL PICK IN THE PATTERSONS' PASTURE THIS YEAR. . . . 61 BLUEBERRIES 81
PATTERSON'S
TO THE VILLAGE, THROUGH PATTERSON'S PASTURE TODAY: . . 59 BLUEBERRIES 2
PAUL
TO DRIVE PAUL OUT OF ANY LUMBER CAMP . . . . . . 191 PAUL'S WIFE 1
"HOW IS THE WIFE, PAUL?"—AND HE'D DISAPPEAR. . . . . 191 PAUL'S WIFE 3
NO ONE WAS ANXIOUS TO GET RID OF PAUL. . . . . . . 191 PAUL'S WIFE 16
"HOW IS THE WIFE, PAUL?" AND HE ALWAYS WENT. . . . . 192 PAUL'S WIFE 24
THE SAME PAUL AT THE SAME OLD FEATS OF LOGGING. . . . 192 PAUL'S WIFE 30
THE QUESTION EVERYWHERE WAS WHY SHOULD PAUL. . . . . 192 PAUL'S WIFE 31
AND THERE WAS ONE MORE NOT SO FAIR TO PAUL: . . . . . 192 PAUL'S WIFE 35
THAT PAUL HAD MARRIED A WIFE NOT HIS EQUAL. . . . . 192 PAUL'S WIFE 36
PAUL WAS ASHAMED OF HER. TO MATCH A HERO . . . . . 192 PAUL'S WIFE 37
YOU KNOW PAUL COULD DO WONDERS. EVERYONE'S . . . . 192 PAUL'S WIFE 42
PAUL TOLD THE BOSS THE LOAD WOULD BE ALL RIGHT, . . . 192 PAUL'S WIFE 46
WELL, THIS IS SUCH A YARN. PAUL SAWED HIS WIFE, . . . 192 PAUL'S WIFE 54
PAUL WORKED AT ANYTHING IN LUMBERING. . . . . . . 193 PAUL'S WIFE 57
THE LUMBER ON PAUL TILL PAUL BEGGED FOR MERCY. . . . 193 PAUL'S WIFE 61
BUT WHEN PAUL PUT HIS FINGER IN THE GREASE, ... 193 PAUL'S WIFE 72
THAT COMES OF HAVING PAUL AROUND THE PLACE. . . . . 193 PAUL'S WIFE 76
AND TELL PAUL WHAT HE OUGHT TO DO ABOUT IT. . . . . 193 PAUL'S WIFE 79
ALL DUG TO GO A-FISHING IN." TO PAUL . . . . . . 193 PAUL'S WIFE 82
PAUL WONDERED HOW IT WOULD RESPOND TO WATER. . . . . 194 PAUL'S WIFE 97
PAUL DRAGGED THE SHALLOWS FOR IT WITH HIS FINGERS, . . 194 PAUL'S WIFE 104
WHO, LEANING ON A LOG, LOOKED BACK AT PAUL. . . . . 194 PAUL'S WIFE 110
AND THAT MADE PAUL IN TURN LOOK BACK . . . . . . 194 PAUL'S WIFE 111
AND WALKED OFF, TALKING TO HERSELF OR PAUL, ... 195 PAUL'S WIFE 120
PAUL TAKING AFTER HER AROUND THE POND. . . . . . 195 PAUL'S WIFE 122
THEY SAW PAUL AND HIS CREATURE KEEPING HOUSE. . . . 195 PAUL'S WIFE 128
HAS HAD OF PAUL AND HER SINCE MURPHY SAW THEM . . . 195 PAUL'S WIFE 130

PAUL (CONTINUED)
  PAUL DARKLY, LIKE HER SHADOW. ALL THE LIGHT . . . . . . 195 PAUL'S WIFE 136
  SO THERE WERE WITNESSES THAT PAUL WAS MARRIED, ... 195 PAUL'S WIFE 145
  EVERYONE HAD BEEN WRONG IN JUDGING PAUL. . . . . 195 PAUL'S WIFE 147
  MURPHY TOLD ME PAUL PUT ON ALL THOSE AIRS . . . . . 195 PAUL'S WIFE 148
  PAUL WAS WHAT'S CALLED A TERRIBLE POSSESSOR. . . . . . 195 PAUL'S WIFE 150
  MURPHY'S IDEA WAS THAT A MAN LIKE PAUL . . . . . . 196 PAUL'S WIFE 155
  KEEPER, YOU COME AND SEE. OR YOU COME, PAUL. . . . . 493 A MASQUE OF MERCY . 13
  YOU DON'T KNOW PAUL: HE'S IN THE BIBLE TOO. . . . . 498 A MASQUE OF MERCY . 127
  I HAD BEFORE. THAT'S WHY I CHANGED TO PAUL-- . . . . 499 A MASQUE OF MERCY . 158
  OF THERAPY. / I DON'T LOVE PAUL--AS YET. . . . . 499 A MASQUE OF MERCY . 163
  ONE MINUTE, MAY I, PAUL?--BEFORE WE LEAVE . . . . 501 A MASQUE OF MERCY . 216
  PAUL ONLY MEANS YOU MAKE TOO MUCH OF JUSTICE. . . . 508 A MASQUE OF MERCY . 384
  (HE SNAPS ONE BULB OFF. PAUL SNAPS ON ANOTHER.) . . . 508 A MASQUE OF MERCY . 393
  THERE'S NOTHING COMING ON US, IS THERE, PAUL? . . . 508 A MASQUE OF MERCY . 395
  PAUL ALMOST HAD POOR KEEPER IN A CORNER . . . . 508 A MASQUE OF MERCY . 401
  OR BE A CHRISTIAN.--PAUL, I WISH YOU'D SAY . . . . 509 A MASQUE OF MERCY . 403
  PAUL MAKES IT COME OUT SO THEY LOOK LIKE CHRISTIANS. . . 509 A MASQUE OF MERCY . 407
  HOW THEY'LL LIKE THAT. PAUL SAID HIS CONSERVATIVES-- . . 509 A MASQUE OF MERCY . 408
  YOU SAY IT, PAUL. / YOU MEAN ABOUT SUCCESS, ... 509 A MASQUE OF MERCY . 409
  YES, PAUL, YOU DO SAY THINGS LIKE THAT SOMETIMES. . . . 511 A MASQUE OF MERCY . 486
  OUR DISAGREEMENT WHEN WE DISAGREE, PAUL, ... 513 A MASQUE OF MERCY . 516
  YES, CALL ME PAGAN, PAUL, AS IF YOU MEANT IT. . . . 513 A MASQUE OF MERCY . 524
  JESSE HAS GIVEN PAUL THE RENT OF IT . . . . 514 A MASQUE OF MERCY . 560
  TO PAUL TO SEE WHAT HE CAN DO WITH IT . . . . 515 A MASQUE OF MERCY . 565
  IS SOMETHING TO BELIEVE IN, DON'T WE, PAUL? . . . 515 A MASQUE OF MERCY . 568
  CRUMPLE HIM ON THE FLOOR. KEEPER AND PAUL . . . 518 A MASQUE OF MERCY . 651
  NOW WE HAVE DONE IT, PAUL. WHAT DID HE SAY? . . . 518 A MASQUE OF MERCY . 656
  WE LIKE YOU, DON'T WE, PAUL? (PAUL TAKES HIS WRIST.) . 518 A MASQUE OF MERCY . 665
  WE'VE ALL GROWN FOND OF YOU. (PAUL SAYS IT LOUDER, . 518 A MASQUE OF MERCY . 667
  ALL PAUL MEANS, AND I WISH THE DEAD COULD HEAR ME-- . 519 A MASQUE OF MERCY . 674
  ALL YOU MEAN, PAUL, I THINK---- / WILL YOU STAND THERE 519 A MASQUE OF MERCY . 675
PAUL'S
  PAUL'S WIFE . . . . 191 PAUL'S WIFE . . . . T
  PAUL'S CONSTANT THEME. THE SERMON ON THE MOUNT . . . 511 A MASQUE OF MERCY . 482
  BUT LET'S BE SERIOUS ABOUT PAUL'S OFFER. . . . . 513 A MASQUE OF MERCY . 519
PAUPER
  THE PAUPER WITCH OF GRAFTON . . . . 207 PAUPER WITCH OF GRAFTON T
PAUPERIS
  MYSELF, IN FORMA PAUPERIS, ... 381 AN UNSTAMPED LETTER IN 51
PAUSE
  "NOTHING." A PAUSE: THERE SEEMED NO MORE TO SAY. . . 91 THE FEAR 71
  THE PAUSE RIGHT THERE, SHE THOUGHT THE DREADED WORD . 151 SNOW 238
  I STOLE FORTH DIMLY IN THE DRIPPING PAUSE . . . 300 MOON COMPASSES . . 1
  AND THE THICK FLAKES FLOATING AT A PAUSE . . . 303 AFTERFLAKES . . . 13
  IT TOOK THAT PAUSE TO MAKE HIM REALIZE . . . 355 TIME OUT 1
PAUSED
  BUT ONCE WITHIN THE WOOD, WE PAUSED . . . . 18 GOING FOR WATER . . 13
  WE PAUSED, THE MINISTER AND I, TO LOOK. . . . 55 THE BLACK COTTAGE . 8
  I PAUSED AND SAID, "I WILL TURN BACK FROM HERE. . 101 THE WOOD-PILE . . 2
  OR PAUSED TO SAY BENEATH SOME LOVELIER ONE, . . 107 CHRISTMAS TREES . . 37
  I PAUSED AND RESTED ON A SORT OF HOOK . . . 125 AN ENCOUNTER . . . 8
  IT PAUSED AS WITH SUSPICION OF MY PEN, . . . 357 A CONSIDERABLE SPECK . 10
  THEN PAUSED AGAIN AND EITHER DRANK OR SMELT-- . 357 A CONSIDERABLE SPECK . 13
PAUSES
  AND, IN THE PAUSES WHEN SHE RAISED HER EYES, . . 182 MAPLE 80
PAUSING (SEE JUST-PAUSING)
PAVEMENTS
  FROM GROWING UNDER PAVEMENTS OF A TOWN; . . . 231 A BROOK IN THE CITY . 10
PAW
  A HAND HUNG LIKE A PAW, ... 340 THE SUBVERTED FLOWER . 42
PAWED
  A HORSE'S HOOF PAWED ONCE THE HOLLOW FLOOR, . . 89 THE FEAR 5
PAWN
  "WE SHOULD HAVE BROUGHT THE CROWN ALONG TO PAWN." . 454 HOW HARD TO KEEP FROM 29
PAY
  HE THINKS HE OUGHT TO EARN A LITTLE PAY, . . . 35 DEATH OF THE HIRED MAN 19
  'ALL RIGHT,' I SAY, 'I CAN'T AFFORD TO PAY . . 35 DEATH OF THE HIRED MAN 22
  THEY PAY FOR IT, AND SO THEY OUGHT TO HAVE IT. . 48 A HUNDRED COLLARS . 104
  YOU'LL HAVE TO PAY ME MORE THAN TEN A WEEK . . 48 A HUNDRED COLLARS . 116
  I'M THERE, AND THEY CAN PAY ME IF THEY LIKE. . 50 A HUNDRED COLLARS . 153
  MONEY CAN'T PAY ME FOR THE LOSS OF THEM. . . 95 THE SELF-SEEKER . . 72
  TO PAY THE DOCTOR'S BILL AND TIDE ME OVER. . . 95 THE SELF-SEEKER . . 74
  HE THINKS YOU OUGHT TO PAY ME FOR MY FLOWERS. . 100 THE SELF-SEEKER . . 225
  WOULD PAY IN CITIES FOR GOOD TREES LIKE THOSE, . 107 CHRISTMAS TREES . . 52
  THESE FORCES ARE OBLIGED TO PAY RESPECT TO?" . 176 THE STAR-SPLITTER . 12
  HE'D SELL A YOKE OF STEERS TO PAY FOR IT. . . 200 PLACE FOR A THIRD . 25
  HE WANTED TO TAKE MY JOB FROM PAY. . . . 275 TWO TRAMPS IN MUD TIME 8
  OR SO WE PAY THE COMPLIMENT TO INSTINCT, . . 279 THE WHITE-TAILED HORNET 53
  AND PAY A DEATH TAX OF FAIRLY POLITE REPENTANCE. . 307 NOT QUITE SOCIAL . 16
  AND HER THOUGHT WAS SHE HAD HAD HER PAY. . . 346 DISCOVERY OF MADEIRAS . 105
  WERE NOT TOO MUCH TO PAY FOR BIRTH. . . . 362 A QUESTION . . . 4
  NO PLOW AMONG THESE ROCKS WOULD PAY. . . . 376 SOMETHING FOR HOPE . 9
  FROM WHAT IT IS WITH HIS. BOTH SERVE FOR PAY. . 485 A MASQUE OF REASON . 353
  KEEPER, BE STILL.--PAY NO ATTENTION TO HIM. . . 494 A MASQUE OF MERCY . 33
PAYING
  BUT IF IT HAD NO THOUGHT OF PAYING HEED . . . 447 DOES NO ONE AT ALL EVER 32
PAYS
  NOTHING'S TOO GOOD FOR THEM. WE SAY IT PAYS. . 86 THE HOUSEKEEPER . . 137
PEA
  PEA BRUSH . . . . 123 PEA BRUSH . . . . T
  MINGLED WITH THESE, SMOOTH BEAN AND WRINKLED PEA), . 124 PUTTING IN THE SEED . 6
PEACE
  HIS HEART KNEW PEACE, FOR NONE CAME HERE . . . 24 PAN WITH US . . . 11
  WEAPONS OF WAR AND IMPLEMENTS OF PEACE . . . 255 THE FLOOD . . . 10
  THE LONGEST PEACE IN CHINA WILL END IN STRIFE. . . 268 ON LOOKING UP BY CHANCE 12
  INCLUDING HUMAN NATURE, IN PEACE AND WAR, . . . 349 OUR HOLD ON THE PLANET 14
  A SORDID PEACE OR AN OUTRAGEOUS WAR. . . . 352 THE LESSON FOR TODAY . 56

PEACE (CONTINUED)
   THE THEME OF WANTON WASTE IN PEACE AND WAR . . . . . 411 POD OF THE MILKWEED . . 6
   BUT BETWEEN PEACE AND WAR AS WE CONCEIVE IT. . . . . 456 HOW HARD TO KEEP FROM . 75
   IN PEACE AND WAR--ESPECIALLY IN WAR. . . . . 481 A MASQUE OF REASON . . 214
   OUR LIVES LAID DOWN IN WAR AND PEACE--MAY NOT . . . . 520 A MASQUE OF MERCY . . 721
PEACEFUL
   THE PEACEFUL SHEPHERD . . . . 252 THE PEACEFUL SHEPHERD . T
PEACH
   ON THE OLD PEACH TREES ON THE KNOLL, TO GROPE . . . . 117 IN THE HOME STRETCH . 189
   BY STARLIGHT IN THE GRASS FOR A LAST PEACH . . . . . 117 IN THE HOME STRETCH . 190
   TO GO THE ROUND OF APPLE, CHERRY, PEACH, ... 117 IN THE HOME STRETCH . 196
   IT IS VERY FAR NORTH, WE ADMIT, TO HAVE BROUGHT THE PEACH. . 305 THERE ARE ROUGHLY ZONES 6
PEAK
   A WIND COMES OFF A FROZEN PEAK, ... 275 TWO TRAMPS IN MUD TIME 23
PEAKS
   THE SOLID MOLDING OF VAST PEAKS OF CLOUD . . . . . . 169 NEW HAMPSHIRE . . . 322
   HOW HIGH I'D THRUST THE PEAKS IN SUMMER SNOW . . . . 169 NEW HAMPSHIRE . . . 339
   TO SET HIMSELF AGAINST THE PEAKS OF SNOW . . . . . . 334 I COULD GIVE ALL . . 2
PEALS
   THEIR SOLEMN PEALS . . . . 219 I WILL SING YOU ONE-O . 55
PEAR
   WHEN PEAR AND CHERRY BLOOM WENT DOWN IN SHOWERS . . . 120 THE OVEN BIRD . . . 7
   AND THE PEAR IS, AND SO'S . . . . 246 THE ROSE FAMILY . . 5
PEARL (SEE SEED-PEARL)
   A SMALLER PEARL HE ASKED A THOUSAND FOR, ... 455 HOW HARD TO KEEP FROM 67
   THE KING SAT FAVORING ONE PEARL FOR ITS BIGNESS, . . . 455 HOW HARD TO KEEP FROM 69
PEARLS
   LIKE PEARLS, AND NOW A SILVER BLADE. . . . . 18 GOING FOR WATER . . . 24
   (BY WHICH THEY MEAN THE RAIN IS PEARLS SO EARLY, . . . 236 VALLEY'S SINGING DAY . 12
   IN BROAD ROUND EARRINGS, GOLD AND JET WITH PEARLS, . . 256 THE LOVELY BE CHOOSERS 15
   THERE CAME TO COURT A MERCHANT SELLING PEARLS, ... 455 HOW HARD TO KEEP FROM 66
   "THE CHOICE IS NOT BETWEEN TWO PEARLS, O KING, ... 456 HOW HARD TO KEEP FROM 74
PEARL'S
   FROM THE PEARL'S HAVING ITS OWN NATIVE WARMTH, ... 456 HOW HARD TO KEEP FROM 90
PEARLY (SEE PEARLY-PEARLY)
PEARLY-PEARLY
   BUT DAWN WAS NOT TO BEGIN THEIR "PEARLY-PEARLY" . . . 236 VALLEY'S SINGING DAY . 11
PEAS
   AFTER A WHILE PICKING PEAS IN HIS GARDEN: . . . . . 73 THE CODE 108
   HE SAID I COULD HAVE TO BUSH MY PEAS. . . . . . . 123 PEA BRUSH 4
   RADISHES, LETTUCE, PEAS, ... 134 A GIRL'S GARDEN . . . 30
PEBBLE
   TRUTH? A PEBBLE OF QUARTZ? FOR ONCE, THEN, SOMETHING. . 225 FOR ONCE SOMETHING . . 15
   A PEBBLE HIT THE ROOF, ... 298 ON TAKING FROM THE TOP 10
   ONCE TOOK A LITTLE PEBBLE WHEEL . . . . 326 A MISSIVE MISSILE . . 2
PEBBLES
   IT IS BUT FIERY PUFFS OF DUST AND PEBBLES, ... 360 A LOOSE MOUNTAIN . . 5
PECK
   A PECK OF GOLD . . . . 249 A PECK OF GOLD . . . T
   "WE ALL MUST EAT OUR PECK OF GOLD." . . . . 249 A PECK OF GOLD . . . 12
   TO PECK HERSELF A PRECIOUS STONE. . . . . 281 BLUE RIBBON AT AMESBURY 42
PECKER-FRETTED
   A FEW OLD PECKER-FRETTED APPLE TREES. . . . . 378 DIRECTIVE 28
PECULIARLY
   THE SECOND MORE PECULIARLY YOUR OWN, ... 382 TO AN ANCIENT . . . 14
PEDAGOGUE
   TELL ME AS PEDAGOGUE TO PEDAGOGUE, ... 351 THE LESSON FOR TODAY . 21
PEDESTAL
   "O CITY ON INSECURE ROCK PEDESTAL, ... 506 A MASQUE OF MERCY . . 337
PEDIGREE
   YOU HAVE A RIGHT TO KNOW YOUR PEDIGREE. . . . . . . 457 HOW HARD TO KEEP FROM 107
PEDIMENT
   IT LIFTED FROM ITS DEWY PEDIMENT . . . . 315 IRIS BY NIGHT . . . 26
PEEP
   I'LL KNOCK SO-FASHION AND PEEP ROUND THE DOOR . . . . 50 A HUNDRED COLLARS . . 173
PEEPER'S
   IT CANNOT CHECK THE PEEPER'S SILVER CROAK; . . . . . 226 THE ONSET 17
PEEPING
   THE FROGS THAT WERE PEEPING A THOUSAND SHRILL . . . . 123 PEA BRUSH 9
PEER
   AND EVERY SHEEPISH PALADIN AND PEER, ... 353 THE LESSON FOR TODAY . 90
PEERS
   HE PEERS OUT SHREWEDLY INTO THE THICK AND SWIFT. . . . 341 WILLFUL HOMING . . . 8
PEGASUS
   MORE PRACTICAL THAN PEGASUS THE HORSE . . . . 173 A STAR IN A STONEBOAT . 29
PEGGED
   I CAN JUST SEE MY TENT PEGGED, ... 211 AN EMPTY THREAT . . . 7
PELF
   BY GRACE OF STATE-MANIPULATED PELF, ... 359 THE LOST FOLLOWER . . 29
PELL-MELL
   AND DINING ROOM--THROWN PELL-MELL IN THE KITCHEN. . . . 110 IN THE HOME STRETCH . 9
   ALL OUT OF TIME PELL-MELL! . . . . 365 A NATURE NOTE . . . 9
PELT
   "YOU PUSH AND I'LL PELT." . . . . 250 LODGED 2
PELTED
   IS SO MYSTERIOUSLY PELTED AT US? . . . . 360 A LOOSE MOUNTAIN . . 4
PELTING
   OF PELTING HEAVEN WITH CHUNKS . . . . 464 MILKY WAY IS A COWPATH 11
PELTS
   AND PELTS WITH SNOW . . . . 9 STORM FEAR 2
PEN
   BUT THE PEN STAYED EXACTLY AS IT WAS, ... 67 A SERVANT TO SERVANTS . 141
   WILL PENCIL DO? THEN, PLEASE, YOUR FOUNTAIN PEN. . . . 100 THE SELF-SEEKER . . . 214
   THE LAWYER GRAVELY CAPPED HIS FOUNTAIN PEN. . . . . . 100 THE SELF-SEEKER . . . 218
   AT HOME IN HER ABIDING PEN, ... 280 BLUE RIBBON AT AMESBURY 14
   SHE GROPES ACROSS THE PEN ALONE . . . . 281 BLUE RIBBON AT AMESBURY 41
   THE LOWLY PEN IS YET A HOLD . . . . 281 BLUE RIBBON AT AMESBURY 53
   IN LESS THAN NO TIME, TONGUE AND PEN, ... 326 TO A THINKER 19

PEN (CONTINUED)
AND I HAD IDLY POISED MY PEN IN AIR . . . . 357 A CONSIDERABLE SPECK . 4
IT PAUSED AS WITH SUSPICION OF MY PEN, ... 357 A CONSIDERABLE SPECK . 10
PENAL
TO THE PENAL COLONY . . . . 466 SOME SCIENCE FICTION . 22
IN SOME WAY NOT SO PENAL AS THE POORHOUSE. . . . . . 478 A MASQUE OF REASON . . 125
PENCIL
WILL PENCIL DO? THEN, PLEASE, YOUR FOUNTAIN PEN. . . . 100 THE SELF-SEEKER . . . 214
PENETRATE
TO PENETRATE THE AIR IN WHICH WE ROLL. . . . . . . 172 A STAR IN A STONEBOAT . 12
PENETRATES
WITH WHICH HE PENETRATES MY BEST DEFENSE . . . . . . 277 THE WHITE-TAILED HORNET 8
PENETRATION (SEE ON-PENETRATION)
PENITENT
A PENITENT PERHAPS, SELF-THROWN ON MERCY. . . . . . . 516 A MASQUE OF MERCY . . 610
PENITENTS
UNLESS FOR PENITENTS WHO TOOK THEIR SEAT . . . . . . 400 TO THE RIGHT PERSON . 12
PENNANTS
STREAMED OUT LIKE PENNANTS SWALLOW-TAIL. . . . . . . 452 A-WISHING WELL . . . 53
PENNONS
THE WAVY UPFLUNG PENNONS OF THE CORN . . . . 404 FROM PLANE TO PLANE . 15
PENSIVE
YOU SHOOK YOUR PENSIVE HEAD AS WHO SHOULD SAY, ... 16 A DREAM PANG 6
YOU'RE PENSIVE. / OH, I'M THINKING OF THE DEVIL. . . . 486 A MASQUE OF REASON . . 376
PENT
TOO LONG PENT UP IN RIGOROUS CONVENTION-- . . . . . 509 A MASQUE OF MERCY . . 418
PENTAMETERS
MILTON'S PENTAMETERS GO ON TO SAY, ... 508 A MASQUE OF MERCY . . 380
PENTATEUCH
WHO RECONCILED THE PENTATEUCH WITH SCIENCE. . . . . . 506 A MASQUE OF MERCY . . 325
PENTHOUSE
WOULD KNOCK THEIR DRUNKEN PENTHOUSE HEADS TOGETHER . . 506 A MASQUE OF MERCY . . 333
PENT-UP
AND LOOSING THE PENT-UP MUSIC OF OVERNIGHT. . . . . . 236 VALLEY'S SINGING DAY . 10
THE TREES THAT HAVE IT IN THEIR PENT-UP BUDS . . . . 245 SPRING POOLS 7
PENULT
ON JOURNEY THE PENULT. . . . . 464 MILKY WAY IS A COWPATH 4
PEOPLE
WHEN I'M WITH PEOPLE I DON'T TRUST AT NIGHT." . . . . 48 A HUNDRED COLLARS . . 92
MY BUSINESS IS TO FIND WHAT PEOPLE WANT: . . . . . . 48 A HUNDRED COLLARS . . 103
THERE'S NOTHING I'M AFRAID OF LIKE SCARED PEOPLE. . . . 50 A HUNDRED COLLARS . . 175
THE LITTLE GRAVEYARD WHERE MY PEOPLE ARE! . . . . . . 51 HOME BURIAL 23
AND LIVING PEOPLE, AND THINGS THEY UNDERSTAND. . . . . 54 HOME BURIAL 105
BY GOING TO HIM OF ALL PEOPLE ON EARTH . . . . . . 61 BLUEBERRIES 69
TO PEOPLE THEY LOOK ON AS HAVING NO RIGHT . . . . . 62 BLUEBERRIES 101
IT WOULD BE DIFFERENT IF MORE PEOPLE CAME, ... 63 A SERVANT TO SERVANTS . 39
LET PEOPLE IN THAN I CAN KEEP THEM OUT. . . . . . . 81 THE HOUSEKEEPER . . . 4
NOTHING IS HIDDEN FROM SOME PEOPLE, ANNE. . . . . . 97 THE SELF-SEEKER . . . 135
OF CHAIRS TURNED UPSIDE DOWN TO SIT LIKE PEOPLE . . . 110 IN THE HOME STRETCH . 6
I NEVER BORE IT WELL WHEN PEOPLE WENT. . . . . . . 115 IN THE HOME STRETCH . 131
OF PEOPLE BROUGHT TO WINDOWS BY A LIGHT . . . . . . 129 THE BONFIRE 11
TO SEE WHAT PEOPLE FOUND SO INTERESTING . . . . . . 148 SNOW 162
WELL, NOW I LEAVE YOU, PEOPLE." / "COME, MESERVE, . . . 150 SNOW 197
PRE-PRIMITIVES OF THE WHITE RACE, DAWN PEOPLE, ... 161 NEW HAMPSHIRE . . . 78
THERE WERE FOUR CANDLES AND FOUR PEOPLE PRESENT. . . . 163 NEW HAMPSHIRE . . . 128
SHE SAID SHE COULDN'T STAND THE PEOPLE IN IT, ... 166 NEW HAMPSHIRE . . . 224
AND WHEN I ASKED TO KNOW WHAT AILED THE PEOPLE, . . . 166 NEW HAMPSHIRE . . . 226
ABOUT THE PEOPLE BEING BETTER THERE . . . . 167 NEW HAMPSHIRE . . . 255
TO WANT TO MAKE NEW HAMPSHIRE PEOPLE OVER. . . . . . 167 NEW HAMPSHIRE . . . 263
I DON'T KNOW WHAT TO SAY ABOUT THE PEOPLE. . . . . . 167 NEW HAMPSHIRE . . . 265
THE PEOPLE OR THE ALREADY LOFTY MOUNTAINS, ... 168 NEW HAMPSHIRE . . . 308
ABOUT IMPROVING PEOPLE IN THE WORLD, ... 169 NEW HAMPSHIRE . . . 336
HER PEOPLE NOT QUITE SHORT ENOUGH FOR ART, ... 170 NEW HAMPSHIRE . . . 356
TO COUNT THE PEOPLE IN IT AND FOUND NONE, ... 174 THE CENSUS-TAKER . . 10
I FOUND NO PEOPLE THAT DARED SHOW THEMSELVES, ... 174 THE CENSUS-TAKER . . 15
THE PEOPLE THAT HAD LOUDLY PASSED THE DOOR . . . . . 175 THE CENSUS-TAKER . . 38
WERE PEOPLE TO THE EAR BUT NOT THE EYE. . . . . . . 175 THE CENSUS-TAKER . . 39
ABOUT THE HOUSE--ABOUT THE PEOPLE NOT THERE. . . . . 175 THE CENSUS-TAKER . . 49
IF ONE BY ONE WE COUNTED PEOPLE OUT . . . . 177 THE STAR-SPLITTER . . 44
MADE PEOPLE NOTICE IT--AND NOTICE HER. . . . . . . 181 MAPLE 50
THE SAME AT DIFFERENT TIMES TO DIFFERENT PEOPLE. . . . 184 MAPLE 156
AND HE'D THANK PEOPLE NOT TO THINK OF HER. . . . . . 196 PAUL'S WIFE 154
THERE'D BEEN SOME BOSTON PEOPLE OUT TO SEE IT: . . . . 212 A FOUNTAIN, A BOTTLE . 3
I WANT TO INTRODUCE YOU TO THE PEOPLE . . . . 215 A FOUNTAIN, A BOTTLE . 75
AND SUCH FEW PEOPLE . . . . 218 I WILL SING YOU ONE-O . 30
HAVE GATHERED PEOPLE TO US MORE AND MORE . . . . . . 262 IMMIGRANTS 2
SO PEOPLE AND THINGS DON'T PAIR ANYMORE . . . . . . 265 THE DOOR IN THE DARK . 8
GOD ONCE SPOKE TO PEOPLE BY NAME. . . . . 266 SITTING BY A BUSH . . 17
LIKE PEOPLE THROWN OUT TO DELAY THE WOLVES. . . . . . 279 THE WHITE-TAILED HORNET 68
TO PUT THESE PEOPLE AT ONE STROKE OUT OF THEIR PAIN. . 287 A ROADSIDE STAND . . 48
GO BRING HIM HOME TO HIS PEOPLE. . . . . 288 DEPARTMENTAL 28
IT SEEMED TO ME, BY THE PEOPLE THERE, ... 291 ON HEART'S BEGINNING TO 9
THE PEOPLE CAN BURN IT AS LONG AS THEY PLEASE; . . . . 291 ON HEART'S BEGINNING TO 16
THAT MIGHT BE PEOPLE AND ARE BUT CEDAR, ... 291 ON HEART'S BEGINNING TO 28
THE PEOPLE ALONG THE SAND . . . . 301 NEITHER OUT FAR NOR IN 1
AND THE PEOPLE LOOK AT THE SEA. . . . . 301 NEITHER OUT FAR NOR IN 12
AND THAT WAS WHY THERE WERE PEOPLE . . . . 314 BEARER OF EVIL TIDINGS 33
OF TYPES, COMPOSITE AND IMAGINED PEOPLE: . . . . . . 317 BUILD SOIL 49
BEFORE WE WERE HER PEOPLE. SHE WAS OURS . . . . . . 348 THE GIFT OUTRIGHT . . 3
THAT CLASS OF PEOPLE DON'T KNOW WHAT WORK IS-- . . . . 405 FROM PLANE TO PLANE . 33
THE GREATEST VOTE A PEOPLE EVER CAST, ... 423 FOR JOHN F. KENNEDY . 55
BEFORE WE WERE HER PEOPLE. SHE WAS OURS . . . . . . 424 THE GIFT OUTRIGHT . . 3
OUR CHANCE OF BEING PEOPLE NEWLY BORN. . . . . . . 446 DOES NO ONE AT ALL EVER 12
WHEN CLEVER PEOPLE ASK ME WHERE . . . . 452 A-WISHING WELL . . . 32
YOU THINK OF FOR YOUR PEOPLE--FEEDING THEM." . . . . 458 HOW HARD TO KEEP FROM 138
A KING MUST GIVE HIS PEOPLE CHARACTER." . . . . . . 458 HOW HARD TO KEEP FROM 142
TELL ME SOME RULE FOR RULING PEOPLE WISELY, ... 458 HOW HARD TO KEEP FROM 147
HOW SHALL I GIVE A PEOPLE CHARACTER?" . . . . 458 HOW HARD TO KEEP FROM 149

PEOPLE (CONTINUED)
 WE CAN'T BE ALWAYS SELLING PEOPLE THINGS. . . . . . . 493 A MASQUE OF MERCY . . 10
 WHICH IS WHAT PEOPLE USE IT FOR TOO OFTEN-- . . . . . 494 A MASQUE OF MERCY . . 29
 SOME PEOPLE WANT YOU NOT TO UNDERSTAND THEM, ... 510 A MASQUE OF MERCY . . 452
 IN MAKING FOOLS OF PEOPLE EQUALLY. . . . . 513 A MASQUE OF MERCY . . 528
PEOPLE'RE
 WHEN PEOPLE'RE GETTING ON IN LIFE. YOU'LL LIKE IT." . . . 113 IN THE HOME STRETCH . 94
PEOPLE'S
 AND YOU AREN'T DARKENING OTHER PEOPLE'S LIVES-- . . . . 65 A SERVANT TO SERVANTS . 99
 I CAN'T KEEP TRACK OF OTHER PEOPLE'S DAUGHTERS. . . . . 81 THE HOUSEKEEPER . . . 11
 "OR DISREGARDING PEOPLE'S CIVIL QUESTIONS-- . . . . . . 151 SNOW 251
 AND BRING BACK NATURE IN PEOPLE'S PLACE. . . . . 263 THE TIMES TABLE . . 20
PEOPLING
 I DREAM UPON THE NIGHTHAWKS PEOPLING HEAVEN, ... 14 WAITING 11
PERCENT
 SAY A FRACTION OF ONE PERCENT AT THE VERY LEAST, ... 349 OUR HOLD ON THE PLANET 16
PERCEPTIBLY
 THAT HANGS PERCEPTIBLY ABOVE THE SCENE. . . . . 412 POD OF THE MILKWEED . 29
 HIS BROW WAS PERCEPTIBLY TROUBLE-CREASED. . . . . . . 420 ONE MORE BREVITY . . 26
PERCH
 SHORT OF THE PERCH THEIR LANGUID FLIGHT WAS TOWARD; . . . 130 THE BONFIRE . . . 37
 I MUST GO MEASURING STONE WALLS, PERCH ON PERCH; . . . . 173 A STAR IN A STONEBOAT . 45
 OF THEIR NEST AGAIN, NOR FIND A PERCH. . . . . 253 THE THATCH 24
 TO BETTER ITS PERCH FOR THE NIGHT, ... 334 COME IN 7
 A PERCH AND RESTING PLACE 'TWIXT WOOD AND WOOD, ... 356 A MOTH SEEN IN WINTER . 2
PERCHANCE
 PERCHANCE HE HALF PREVAILED . . . . 11 WIND AND WINDOW FLOWER 21
PEREGRINE
 PEREGRINE MACHINE, ... 442 KITTY HAWK 463
PERENNIAL
 PERENNIAL AS FLOWERS, ... 465 MILKY WAY IS A COWPATH 33
PERFECT
 THE SWARM DILATING ROUND THE PERFECT TREES. . . . . . 12 A PRAYER IN SPRING . . 8
 SHE SCORED AN ALMOST PERFECT BIRD. . . . . 280 BLUE RIBBON AT AMESBURY 10
 FROM ONE DAY'S PERFECT WEATHER, ... 333 HAPPINESS MAKES UP . 14
 TO DISTURB THEIR PERFECT POISE THE LIVELONG DAY . . . . 343 QUEST OF PURPLE-FRINGED 19
 THIS PERFECT MOMENT OF UNBAFFLEMENT, ... 461 HOW HARD TO KEEP FROM 238
PERFECTLY
 WHERE PERFECTLY IN FORM AND TINT . . . . 327 A MISSIVE MISSILE . . 34
PERFORCE
 SUCH AS EVEN POETS WOULD ADMIT PERFORCE . . . . . . 173 A STAR IN A STONEBOAT . 28
PERHAPS
 PERHAPS IT WAS SOMETHING ABOUT THE HEAT OF THE SUN, . . . 17 MOWING 4
 SOMETHING, PERHAPS, ABOUT THE LACK OF SOUND-- . . . . 17 MOWING 5
 SOME GOOD PERHAPS TO SOMEONE IN THE WORLD. . . . . . 37 DEATH OF THE HIRED MAN 97
 YOU'LL REST EASIER WHEN I'M GONE, PERHAPS-- . . . . . 50 A HUNDRED COLLARS . . 160
 AND PERHAPS HEAR SOME WORD ABOUT THE WEATHER. . . . . 74 THE GENERATIONS OF MEN 33
 PERHAPS YOU HAVE THE ART OF WHAT I MEAN. . . . . . . 78 THE GENERATIONS OF MEN 131
 AND PERHAPS SHE WILL COME, STILL UNAFRAID, ... 79 THE GENERATIONS OF MEN 167
 AND HAVING PERHAPS THE BETTER CLAIM, ... 105 THE ROAD NOT TAKEN . 7
 NOR I TO YOU." / "PERHAPS YOU NEVER WERE?" . . . . . 117 IN THE HOME STRETCH . 180
 PERHAPS BECAUSE WE GAVE HIM ONLY BREAD . . . . . . 127 THE SMILE 4
 PERHAPS BECAUSE HE LET US GIVE INSTEAD . . . . . . 127 THE SMILE 6
 PERHAPS HE MOCKED AT US FOR BEING WED, ... 127 THE SMILE 8
 AND PERHAPS IN THE SPRING . . . . 136 LAST WORD OF A BLUEBIRD 21
 "LET HIM TALK, HELEN, AND PERHAPS HE'LL STAY." . . . . 149 SNOW 171
 TO KEEP HIM--THOUGH PERHAPS YOU DIDN'T QUITE . . . . 153 SNOW 282
 AND--WRITING; NONE OF THESE EXCEPT PERHAPS . . . . . 164 NEW HAMPSHIRE . . 166
 SO NOT TO BE COMPARED, PERHAPS, IN WORTH . . . . . 174 A STAR IN A STONEBOAT . 47
 PERHAPS THE WIND THE MORE WITHOUT THE HELP . . . . . 175 THE CENSUS-TAKER . . 25
 ABOUT YOUR MOTHER THAT PERHAPS MAY HELP." . . . . . 180 MAPLE 28
 PERHAPS A FILIAL DIFFIDENCE PARTLY KEPT THEM . . . . 184 MAPLE 157
 EXCEPT, PERHAPS, A FOOT AT EITHER END. . . . . . . 193 PAUL'S WIFE . . . 71
 BUT NOT SO MUCH, PERHAPS, AS A BOY NEEDED. . . . . . 197 WILD GRAPES . . . 35
 IN ONE HIMSELF PERHAPS. . . . . 211 AN EMPTY THREAT . . 29
 YET DOES PERHAPS FOR ALL THREE. . . . . 212 AN EMPTY THREAT . . 37
 PERHAPS, TO WHERE IT ENDED AT A HOUSE . . . . . . 215 A FOUNTAIN, A BOTTLE . 68
 SINCE EARTH IS EARTH, PERHAPS, NOT HEAVEN (AS YET)-- . . 220 FRAGMENTARY BLUE . 5
 EXCEPT FORGET TO GO IN FEAR PERHAPS. . . . . 231 A BROOK IN THE CITY . 19
 IN AT ONE DOOR PERHAPS AND OUT ANOTHER, ... 278 THE WHITE-TAILED HORNET 25
 AS IF REMINDED--OR AS IF PERHAPS . . . . 293 AT WOODWARD'S GARDENS . 15
 PERHAPS I HAVE PUT FORTH TOO MUCH STRENGTH AND BEEN TOO
  FIERCE FROM FEAR. . . . . 297 A LEAF-TREADER . . 3
 SEEMED TO ARGUE PERHAPS SHE WENT . . . . 343 DISCOVERY OF MADEIRAS . 13
 YOUR LIGHT WAS SPENT PERHAPS AS IN A FOG . . . . . . 351 THE LESSON FOR TODAY . 24
 (PERHAPS IT WILL BE NEXT MILLENNIUM.) . . . . . . 353 THE LESSON FOR TODAY . 103
 THAT IS THE SOURCE PERHAPS OF HUMAN HATE . . . . . 371 THE LITERATE FARMER AND 108
 (LESS BRAVE PERHAPS THAN TRUSTING ARE THE FAIR.) . . . 375 A YOUNG BIRCH . . 10
 PERHAPS BUT TO A TREE . . . . 415 CLOSED FOR GOOD . . 15
 ON EITHER HAND TO MAKE HIS COURSE PERHAPS . . . . . 421 ESCAPIST--NEVER . . 4
 OR PERHAPS A SWAN . . . . 431 KITTY HAWK 109
 (PERHAPS SO CALLED BECAUSE IT MAY HAVE RISEN ONCE) . . 447 THE BAD ISLAND--EASTER 5
 THE MILKY WAY PERHAPS . . . . 464 MILKY WAY IS A COWPATH 15
 PERHAPS FOR AN OLYMPIC TOURNAMENT, ... 474 A MASQUE OF REASON . 24
 THE LETUP'S HEAVENLY. YOU PERHAPS WILL TELL US . . . 474 A MASQUE OF REASON . 41
 BUT WARN THE CHILDREN THEY PERHAPS SHOULD HAVE NONE. . . 483 A MASQUE OF REASON . 294
 PERHAPS THAT EARTH IS GOING TO CRACK SOMEDAY . . . . 484 A MASQUE OF REASON . 305
 A PENITENT PERHAPS, SELF-THROWN ON MERCY. . . . . . 516 A MASQUE OF MERCY . . 610
PERICLES
 PERICLES SENT ASPASIA IN ABSENTIA: . . . . 461 HOW HARD TO KEEP FROM 250
PERIL
 IT VENTURED LESS IN PERIL THAN APPEARS. . . . . . 302 A BIRD SINGING IN SLEEP 8
 BUT SOMEONE OVERANXIOUS AT HIS PERIL . . . . . . 394 HAEC FABULA DOCET . . 8
 PERIL OF HOPE . . . . 445 PERIL OF HOPE . . . T
PERIOD
 TO STOP IT WITH A PERIOD OF INK, ... 357 A CONSIDERABLE SPECK . 5
PERIPATETIC
 WHEN SEDENTARY AND WHEN PERIPATETIC. . . . . . . 269 THE BEAR 34

PAGE TITLE   LINE

PERISH
     BUT IF IT HAD TO PERISH TWICE, ... 220 FIRE AND ICE 5
     YET LEAVE SUCH LOVELY SHAFTS OUTDOORS TO PERISH. . . . . 290 OLD BARN AT THE BOTTOM 34
     AND WHOLLY PERISH. . . . . 469 WE VAINLY WRESTLE... . 4
     WHAT THE SINS ARE MEN OUGHT TO PERISH FOR. . . . . . . 503 A MASQUE OF MERCY . . 261
PERISHING
     "SHINE, PERISHING REPUBLIC." / ROBINSON JEFFERS . . . . 449 OUR DOOM TO BLOOM . . 5
PERK
     HIS NATTY WINGS WITH SELF-ASSURANCE PERK. . . . . . . 309 WASPISH 3
PERMANENCE
     AT A GOOD POINT FOR PLIANT PERMANENCE, ... 458 HOW HARD TO KEEP FROM 155
PERMANENT
     THEY CUT THEMSELVES IN STONE FOR PERMANENT . . . . . . 399 THE INGENUITIES OF DEBT 2
PERMISSIBLE
     AND ALL THE REST FOR THEM PERMISSIBLE EASE. . . . . . 230 NOT TO KEEP 12
PERMISSIVE
     SOMETIMES, WITH HER PERMISSIVE SMILE, ... 345 DISCOVERY OF MADEIRAS . 48
PERMIT
     PERMIT ME." AND HE CRUSHED IT UNDER HIS HEEL . . . . 456 HOW HARD TO KEEP FROM 84
     A SANDBURG. BUT PERMIT ME IN CONCLUSION: . . . . . . 461 HOW HARD TO KEEP FROM 226
PERMITTED
     LIKE SOMEONE DEAD PERMITTED TO EXIST . . . . 368 THE LITERATE FARMER AND 17
PERPETUAL
     "I WISH YOU HAD SEEN HIS PERPETUAL BOW-- . . . . . . 61 BLUEBERRIES 57
     DARKLY ADVANCED WITH A PERPETUAL DAGGER . . . . . . 69 THE CODE 5
PERPLEXED
     HALTING PERPLEXED BEHIND THE BARRIER . . . . 203 THE WITCH OF COOS . . 24
     COME DOWN THE STAIRS AT NIGHT AND STAND PERPLEXED . . 206 THE WITCH OF COOS . . 126
     TITYRUS, SOMETIMES I'M PERPLEXED MYSELF . . . . . . 321 BUILD SOIL 163
PERSCENTED
     A THING THE LEAST BIT DOUBTFULLY PERSCENTED . . . . . 163 NEW HAMPSHIRE . . . 142
PERSIA
     IN THE OLD DAYS IN PERSIA AND PERU. . . . . 408 FROM PLANE TO PLANE . 133
PERSIAN
     TO MARRY A PERSIAN PRINCE . . . . 314 BEARER OF EVIL TIDINGS 20
PERSISTED
     HAD NOW PERSISTED IN THE WOODS SO LONG . . . . . . 339 NEVER WOULD BIRDS' SONG 11
PERSISTING
     AND PERSISTING IN THEFT . . . . 449 THE BAD ISLAND--EASTER 64
     PERSISTING FROM OLD CHAOS IN THEIR MYTH, ... 511 A MASQUE OF MERCY . 470
PERSISTS
     ONE IMPULSE PERSISTS AS OUR BREATH; . . . . 266 SITTING BY A BUSH . . 19
     THE OTHER PERSISTS AS OUR FAITH. . . . . 266 SITTING BY A BUSH . . 20
PERSON
     WHAT ARE YOU GOING TO DO WITH SUCH A PERSON? . . . . 57 THE BLACK COTTAGE . . 80
     "HE'S A THRIFTIER PERSON THAN SOME I COULD NAME." . . 60 BLUEBERRIES 47
     "O'YOU KNOW A PERSON SO RELATED TO HERSELF . . . . 76 THE GENERATIONS OF MEN 82
     TO THE SAME PERSON TWICE. . . . . 134 A GIRL'S GARDEN . . 48
     THE ONLY PERSON REALLY SOILED WITH TRADE . . . . 160 NEW HAMPSHIRE . . . 35
     IT SLOWLY ROSE A PERSON, ROSE A GIRL, ... 194 PAUL'S WIFE 108
     THIS GLIMPSE OF LINGERING PERSON IN ELIZA, ... 200 PLACE FOR A THIRD . 16
     TO THE RIGHT PERSON . . . . 400 TO THE RIGHT PERSON . T
PERSONAE
     PERSONAE NEEDED TO ENACT THE PROBLEM. . . . . . . 487 A MASQUE OF REASON . 394
PERSONAL
     EVERYTHING SAID AS PERSONAL TO HIMSELF. . . . . . 101 THE WOOD-PILE . . . 16
     A PERSONAL INTEREST IN THE LOCKING UP . . . . . 115 IN THE HOME STRETCH . 134
     WITHOUT THE NAME HER PERSONAL MYSTERY. . . . . . 182 MAPLE 93
     IT WAS AS PERSONAL AS HE COULD BE . . . . 183 MAPLE 127
     ON HIS PARTICULAR TIME AND PERSONAL SIGHT. . . . . 268 ON LOOKING UP BY CHANCE 15
     AWAY 'WAY DOWN INSIDE I'M PERSONAL. . . . . . . 320 BUILD SOIL 144
PERSONALLY
     HOW I SHOULD PRIZE ONE PERSONALLY FROM YOU. . . . . 488 A MASQUE OF REASON . 423
PERSONIFIED
     PERSONIFIED, BUT ASK TO BE EXCUSED . . . . 317 BUILD SOIL 51
PERSONNEL
     AT ANYTHING BUT CHANGE OF PERSONNEL. . . . . . . 510 A MASQUE OF MERCY . 458
PERSONS
     WHETHER IT'S PERSONS PIED OR NATIONS PIED. . . . . 321 BUILD SOIL 156
PERSON'S
     THE REASON MIGHT HAVE BEEN SOME OTHER PERSON'S. . . . 482 A MASQUE OF REASON . 264
PERSUADED
     AND PERSUADED TO SEE . . . . 448 THE BAD ISLAND--EASTER 32
PERSUASIVE
     AS IF TO BE PERSUASIVE, ... 340 THE SUBVERTED FLOWER . 44
PERTINAX
     PERTINAX . . . . 308 PERTINAX . . . . . T
PERU
     IN THE OLD DAYS IN PERSIA AND PERU. . . . . 408 FROM PLANE TO PLANE . 133
PESTILENCE
     (LIKE WAR AND PESTILENCE . . . . 282 A DRUMLIN WOODCHUCK . 23
     REBELLION, PESTILENCE, INVASION? / EARTHQUAKE . . . 502 A MASQUE OF MERCY . 225
PETAL
     THE PETAL OF THE ROSE . . . . 227 TO EARTHWARD 15
     WRAP HIM FOR SHROUD IN A PETAL. . . . . 288 DEPARTMENTAL 30
     LIKE THE LAST PETAL OFF A FLOWER. . . . . . . 291 ON HEART'S BEGINNING TO 12
PETAL-FALL
     HE SAYS THE EARLY PETAL-FALL IS PAST, ... 120 THE OVEN BIRD . . . 6
PETALS
     SOFT PETALS FALLEN FROM THE APPLE TREE . . . . 124 PUTTING IN THE SEED . 4
     (SOFT PETALS, YES, BUT NOT SO BARREN QUITE, ... 124 PUTTING IN THE SEED . 5
     LIKE A PISTIL AFTER THE PETALS GO. . . . . . . 241 NEED OF BEING VERSED . 19
     PETALS I MAY HAVE ONCE PURSUED. . . . . 297 LEAVES COMPARED WITH . 19
     THAT PAST ITS PRIME LOST PETALS IN THE FLOOD . . . 337 THE WIND AND THE RAIN . 33
     WHEN THE COLOR FLUSHED TO THE PETALS IT MUST HAVE BEEN-- 343 QUEST OF PURPLE-FRINGED 15
     ITS PETALS LOOSEN AND ARE STROWN; . . . . . . 450 OUR DOOM TO BLOOM . . 14
PETERED
     SHOULD SAY OUR STOCK WAS PETERED OUT, ... 139 BROWN'S DESCENT . . . 51

PETITIONER
    FOR MY OBSCURE PETITIONER. . . . . 327 A MISSIVE MISSILE . . 29
PEW
    OF HER OLD TREMULOUS BONNET IN THE PEW, ... 57 THE BLACK COTTAGE . . 91
    ONLY--THERE WAS THE BONNET IN THE PEW. . . . . 58 THE BLACK COTTAGE . . 99
PHALLIC (SEE PSEUDO-PHALLIC)
PHARAOH
    AS ONCE THE PHARAOH DID IT OUT OF SEKHTI . . . . . . 517 A MASQUE OF MERCY . . 641
PHASE
    HE NEVER HAS IN ANY PHASE . . . . 390 TWO LEADING LIGHTS . . 5
PHENOMENON
    NO BURST OF NUCLEAR PHENOMENON . . . . 397 THE PLANNERS 4
    BUT THERE WAS THIS PHENOMENON: . . . . 452 A-WISHING WELL . . . 55
PHILADELPHIA
    WHO COMES FROM PHILADELPHIA EVERY YEAR . . . . . . 162 NEW HAMPSHIRE . . . 101
PHILOSOPHERS
    AS EVER WHEN PHILOSOPHERS ARE MET, ... 354 THE LESSON FOR TODAY . 107
    THEY ARE PHILOSOPHERS, AND FROM OLD HABIT . . . . . 354 THE LESSON FOR TODAY . 110
    SO DO THEY ALSO ASK PHILOSOPHERS . . . . 414 A CABIN IN THE CLEARING 23
PHILOSOPHIC
    IN PHILOSOPHIC TALK; . . . . 465 SOME SCIENCE FICTION . 8
    RELIGION FOR THESE PHILOSOPHIC MATTERS. . . . . . . 501 A MASQUE OF MERCY . . 217
PHILOSOPHICAL
    OR DIE OF PHILOSOPHICAL DISTENTION. . . . . 351 THE LESSON FOR TODAY . 41
PHILOSOPHIZED
    PHILOSOPHIZED TOGETHER INTO ONE-- . . . . 318 BUILD SOIL 79
PHILOSOPHY
    TO A PHILOSOPHY OF HANG-AND-LET-HANG. . . . . 198 WILD GRAPES 61
PHOEBES
    NOT TO BELIEVE THE PHOEBES WEPT. . . . . 242 NEED OF BEING VERSED . 24
PHOENIX
    OF THE PHOENIX PULLET . . . . 427 VERSION 9
PHOSPHORESCENT
    LIKE SPLASHING PHOSPHORESCENT PAINT, ... 451 A-WISHING WELL . . . 16
PHRASE
    SUCH A PHRASE COULDN'T HAVE MEANT MUCH TO HER. . . . 58 THE BLACK COTTAGE . . 100
PHRASES
    AND TO HEAR HER QUAINT PHRASES--SO REMOVED . . . . 57 THE BLACK COTTAGE . . 62
    (A SKYLARK FOR THEM IN THREE-BEAT PHRASES) . . . . 428 KITTY HAWK 5
PHYSICAL
    BUT PHYSICAL ACTIVITY, I FIND. . . . . 479 A MASQUE OF REASON . . 154
PHYSICALLY
    DISGUSTED THE MILLER PHYSICALLY AS COMING . . . . . 142 THE VANISHING RED . . 17
PHYSICIAN
    I WENT TO THE PHYSICIAN TO COMPLAIN, ... 398 BURSTING RAPTURE . . 1
PHYSICIAN'S
    BUT THE PHYSICIAN'S ANSWER WAS, "THERE, THERE, . . . 398 BURSTING RAPTURE . . 9
PIANO
    AND IN IT A PIANO LOUDLY PLAYING. . . . . 263 THE INVESTMENT . . . 4
    ALL THAT PIANO AND NEW PAINT BACK THERE, ... 264 THE INVESTMENT . . . 9
PIANO'S
    WITH HALF AN EAR TO THE PIANO'S VIGOR. . . . . . . 263 THE INVESTMENT . . . 8
PICK
    TO PICK WHERE NONE COULD MISS THEM . . . . 13 ROSE POGONIAS . . . 11
    I PICK IT UP A DOLLAR AT A TIME . . . . 48 A HUNDRED COLLARS . . 97
    WE'LL PICK IN THE PATTERSONS' PASTURE THIS YEAR. . . 61 BLUEBERRIES 81
    HOW WE USED TO PICK BERRIES: WE TOOK ONE LOOK ROUND, . 62 BLUEBERRIES 85
    TO PICK WHERE THEY'RE PICKING. BUT WE WON'T COMPLAIN. . 62 BLUEBERRIES 102
    APPLES I DIDN'T PICK UPON SOME BOUGH. . . . . 68 AFTER APPLE-PICKING . 5
    NOW GIVE ME YOUR HAND UP.--PICK ME THAT FLOWER." . . 80 THE GENERATIONS OF MEN 207
    I KNEW YOU WOULDN'T LET ME PICK THEM ALL." . . . . 97 THE SELF-SEEKER . . 120
    COULD HANG ENOUGH ON TO PICK OFF ENOUGH. . . . . . 107 CHRISTMAS TREES . . 54
    AND PUT IT IN MY HANDS TO PICK MY OWN GRAPES. . . . 197 WILD GRAPES 38
    I MEAN, THEY WON'T PICK YOU IF YOU DON'T THEM." . . 198 WILD GRAPES 58
    I WOULD PICK UP ALL OCEAN LESS ITS SALT, ... 337 THE WIND AND THE RAIN . 28
    THEN PICK YOUR HOE UP, MAYBE SHOULDER IT, ... 405 FROM PLANE TO PLANE . 41
    PICK UP OUR EYES AND CARRY THEM BACK IDLE . . . . . 405 FROM PLANE TO PLANE . 51
    I PICK A DEAD SHELL UP FROM WHERE THE KELP . . . . 446 DOES NO ONE AT ALL EVER 25
PICKED
    PICKED UP A LITTLE STICK, AND BROUGHT IT BACK . . . 38 DEATH OF THE HIRED MAN 122
    IT'S SO LONG SINCE I PICKED I ALMOST FORGET . . . . 62 BLUEBERRIES 84
    WE PICKED, TILL I FEARED YOU HAD WANDERED A MILE, . . 62 BLUEBERRIES 92
    TWO OR THREE FORKFULS I PICKED LIGHTLY ROUND FOR . . 72 THE CODE 72
    AFTER HE'D PICKED THE LOCK AND GOT IT STARTED, . . . 170 NEW HAMPSHIRE . . . 346
    HAS BEEN PICKED UP WITH STONES TO BUILD A WALL. . . 172 A STAR IN A STONEBOAT . 3
    I PICKED UP OFF THE STRAW-DUST-COVERED FLOOR. . . . 175 THE CENSUS-TAKER . . 45
    GOOD-LOOKING BOOKS LIKE THAT." HE PICKED ONE FRESH . 217 A FOUNTAIN, A BOTTLE . 125
    THE TRAVELER'S EYE PICKED UP A TURTLE TRAIL, . . . 270 THE EGG AND THE MACHINE 17
    AND SAW THEM PICKED UNBRUISED AND IN A DISH, . . . 284 THE GOLD HESPERIDEE . 36
    FROM HER CHIN, PICKED UP HER COMB, ... 341 THE SUBVERTED FLOWER . 72
    I PICKED YOU OUT A HORSE CALLED SAFETY THIRD, . . . 457 HOW HARD TO KEEP FROM . 123
    HIS TENTS BLEW ALL TO PIECES, I PICKED UP . . . . . 478 A MASQUE OF REASON . . 131
PICKER
    AND PROMISE MORE RESISTANCE TO THE PICKER." . . . . 198 WILD GRAPES 71
PICKERS
    AND LESS THAN THE TAN WITH WHICH PICKERS ARE TANNED." . 60 BLUEBERRIES 27
PICKING (SEE APPLE-PICKING)
    BY PICKING THE FADED BLUE . . . . 9 A LATE WALK 14
    FOR THE PICKING. THE RASCAL, HE SAID HE'D BE GLAD . . 61 BLUEBERRIES 71
    TO PICK WHERE THEY'RE PICKING. BUT WE WON'T COMPLAIN. . 62 BLUEBERRIES 102
    AFTER A WHILE PICKING PEAS IN HIS GARDEN: . . . . . 73 THE CODE 108
    MUCH DANGER OF MY PICKING ANYTHING! . . . . 198 WILD GRAPES 59
    AND THE PRINCE ANSWERED, PICKING UP THE PIECES, . . 453 HOW HARD TO KEEP FROM . 7
PICKS
    (THE THRONE COLLAPSES. BUT HE PICKS IT UP . . . . . 477 A MASQUE OF REASON . . 107
PICTURE
    SWING THE PICTURE ON THE WALL; . . . . 11 TO THE THAWING WIND . 12
    TO CATCH IT IN A SORT OF SPECIAL PICTURE . . . . . 55 THE BLACK COTTAGE . . 2

PICTURE (CONTINUED)
  "IT'S AS YOU THROW A PICTURE ON A SCREEN: . . . . . . 78 THE GENERATIONS OF MEN 135
  WHERE SHE COULD WATCH HER MOTHER'S PICTURE FADING. . . 181 MAPLE 61
  GIVES ME BACK IN A SHINING SURFACE PICTURE . . . . 225 FOR ONCE SOMETHING . . 4
  I DISCERNED, AS I THOUGHT, BEYOND THE PICTURE, . . . 225 FOR ONCE SOMETHING . . 8
  THROUGH THE PICTURE, A SOMETHING WHITE, UNCERTAIN, . . 225 FOR ONCE SOMETHING . . 9
  A SHELF'S FOR A CLOCK OR VASE OR PICTURE, ... 232 THE KITCHEN CHIMNEY . 17
  THE PICTURE PRIDE OF HOLLYWOOD. . . . . 307 PROVIDE, PROVIDE . . 4
  THE PICTURE BOOK OF THE TRILOBITE, ... 364 TRESPASS 10
  I'D KNOW HIM BY BLAKE'S PICTURE ANYWHERE. . . . 474 A MASQUE OF REASON . 18
  (I'D KNOW YOU BY BLAKE'S PICTURE ANYWHERE)-- . . 476 A MASQUE OF REASON . 85
  THEY WON'T SHOW IN THE PICTURE. THAT'S TOO BAD. . . 490 A MASQUE OF REASON . 462
PICTURES
  BETWEEN THE PICTURES ON A MOVIE SCREEN . . . . . 165 NEW HAMPSHIRE . . 194
  THEY REMIND ME OF PICTURES ON A PALETTE: . . . . 321 BUILD SOIL . . . 152
PICTURES' (SEE MOVING-PICTURES')
PICTURE'S
  SO THE PICTURE'S CAUGHT . . . . 426 A NEVER NAUGHT SONG . 29
PICTURESQUE
  AND AS PICTURESQUE MACHINERY . . . . 397 AN IMPORTER . . . 21
PIE
  COME LOOK AT MY SIGNIFICANT MUD PIE." . . . . 321 BUILD SOIL . . . 154
  YOU NAUGHTY KITTEN, YOU SHALL HAVE NO PIE. . . . 498 A MASQUE OF MERCY . 118
PIECE
  LIKE A DEEP PIECE OF SOME OLD RUNNING RIVER . . . 63 A SERVANT TO SERVANTS . 20
  SOMETIMES WE DON'T. WE'VE A GOOD PIECE OF SHORE . . 64 A SERVANT TO SERVANTS . 42
  FOR A DOORSILL OR OTHER CORNER PIECE . . . . . 79 THE GENERATIONS OF MEN 163
  HAVE WE A PIECE OF CANDLE IF THE LAMP . . . . 113 IN THE HOME STRETCH . 80
  AND EVERY PIECE I SQUARELY HIT . . . . . . 275 TWO TRAMPS IN MUD TIME 11
  THERE IS SELDOM MORE THAN A MAN TO A HARROWED PIECE. . 299 STRONG SAYING NOTHING . 5
  LIKE A WHITE PIECE OF RIGID SATIN CLOTH-- . . . 302 DESIGN 3
  TO GIVE US A PIECE OF THEIR BILLS. . . . . . 364 A NATURE NOTE . . . 4
  THERE WILL BE NO SUCH PIECE OF FURNITURE. . . . 372 THE LITERATE FARMER AND 130
PIECEMEAL
  WE WERE LOST PIECEMEAL TO THE ANIMALS, ... 279 THE WHITE-TAILED HORNET 67
PIECES (SEE FINGER-PIECES)
  HE'D TEAR TO PIECES, EVEN A BED TO LIE ON. . . . 66 A SERVANT TO SERVANTS . 118
  (WHERE DID I SEE ONE OF THOSE PIECES LATELY? . . 205 THE WITCH OF COOS . 80
  SHE CAUGHT THE PIECES END TO END . . . . . . 274 A LONE STRIKER . . . 30
  AND THE PRINCE ANSWERED, PICKING UP THE PIECES, . . 453 HOW HARD TO KEEP FROM . 7
  HIS TENTS BLEW ALL TO PIECES, I PICKED UP . . . 478 A MASQUE OF REASON . 131
PIED
  WHETHER IT'S PERSONS PIED OR NATIONS PIED. . . . 321 BUILD SOIL . . . 156
PIERCED
  THEY MUST BE PIERCED BY FLOWERS AND PUT . . . . 26 IN HARDWOOD GROVES . . 9
PIERCING
  A PIERCING LITTLE STAR WAS THROUGH. . . . . . 233 LOOKING FOR SUNSET BIRD 20
PIG
  AS REGULARLY AS HE WENT TO FEED THE PIG . . . . 283 THE GOLD HESPERIDEE . 19
  HE HAD A HEN, HE HAD A PIG IN SIGHT. . . . . . 292 FIGURE IN THE DOORWAY . 16
PIGMENT
  LIGHT WAS A PASTE OF PIGMENT IN OUR EYES. . . . 315 IRIS BY NIGHT . . . 9
PIGS
  OUR HENS AND COWS AND PIGS ARE ALWAYS BETTER . . 85 THE HOUSEKEEPER . . 111
PIKE
  THEY BOTH WERE HIRED. AND THOUGH PIKE HAD THE ADVANTAGE . 404 FROM PLANE TO PLANE . 2
  PIKE SAID WITH TEMPER. AND DICK LONGED TO SAY, . . . 404 FROM PLANE TO PLANE . 8
  EVERY TIME DICK OR PIKE LOOKED UP, THE DOCTOR . . 404 FROM PLANE TO PLANE . 18
  HE DON'T MIND HAVING LOST A CASE," PIKE SAID; . . . 404 FROM PLANE TO PLANE . 25
  PIKE GRUNTED RATHER GRIMLY WITH MISGIVING . . . 405 FROM PLANE TO PLANE . 55
  AND SO TO LET PIKE SEEM TO HAVE THE PALM . . . . 408 FROM PLANE TO PLANE . 120
  "I GUESS SO," PIKE SAID, INNOCENT OF MILTON. . . . 408 FROM PLANE TO PLANE . 136
  DICK SAID, TO OLD PIKE INNOCENT OF SHAKESPEARE. . . 408 FROM PLANE TO PLANE . 148
PILE (SEE CHALK-PILE, WOOD-PILE)
  AND THEN THERE WAS A PILE OF WOOD FOR WHICH . . . 101 THE WOOD-PILE . . . 18
  AND THE PILE SOMEWHAT SUNKEN. CLEMATIS . . . . 102 THE WOOD-PILE . . . 30
  THE PILE IS OURS: WE DRAGGED IT BOUGH ON BOUGH . . 129 THE BONFIRE . . . 6
  DIVIDE IT? NO! BUT BURN IT AS ONE PILE . . . . 129 THE BONFIRE . . . 9
  TO WANT TO FIND OUT IF HE COULDN'T PILE . . . . 193 PAUL'S WIFE . . . 60
  AND CARRIED ITSELF LIKE A PILE OF DISHES . . . 203 THE WITCH OF COOS . 29
  AND THE WHOLE PILE IS SLIPPING, BOTTLES, BUNS-- . . 266 THE ARMFUL . . . 3
  AND PILE OF REAL ROCKS HAVE BEEN FOUNDED. . . . 331 BEECH 3
PILED
  HOW DRIFTS ARE PILED, ... 10 STORM FEAR . . . 13
  MOVING AMONG TALL HAYCOCKS LIGHTLY PILED, . . . 14 WAITING 2
  AND PILED--AND MEASURED, FOUR BY FOUR BY EIGHT. . . 101 THE WOOD-PILE . . 24
  BIRCH BOUGHS ENOUGH PILED EVERYWHERE!-- . . . . 123 PEA BRUSH . . . 13
  THAT HAD BUDDED BEFORE THE BOUGHS WERE PILED . . 123 PEA BRUSH . . . 23
  BY SETTING FIRE TO ALL THE BRUSH WE PILED . . . 129 THE BONFIRE . . . 3
  THE WAY WE PILED IT. AND LET'S BE THE TALK . . . 129 THE BONFIRE . . . 10
  NEXT DAY THE SCENE WAS PILED AND PUFFED AND DEAD. . 239 OUR SINGING STRENGTH . 11
  WHERE THESE ARE DRIVEN IN AND PILED, ... 331 BEECH 5
PILGRIM
  YES, PILGRIM NOW INSTEAD OF RUNAWAY, ... 513 A MASQUE OF MERCY . 534
PILGRIMAGE
  THEY WENT ON PILGRIMAGE ONCE TO HER FATHER'S . . 182 MAPLE 97
  OF WHERE THEY WOULD GO ON PILGRIMAGE . . . . 344 DISCOVERY OF MADEIRAS . 25
PILGRIM-MANNED
  BUT, PILGRIM-MANNED, THE MAYFLOWER IN A DREAM . . 262 IMMIGRANTS . . . 3
PILING
  GATHERING UP WINDROWS, PILING COCKS OF HAY, . . . 69 THE CODE 2
  AND SHOW YOU HOW IT'S PILING UP AGAINST YOU. . . 148 SNOW 156
  PILING IT WELL ABOVE THE WINDOWSILLS. . . . . 149 SNOW 179
PILLARED
  FAR IN THE PILLARED DARK . . . . 334 COME IN 13
PILLOW
  AND PROPPED HIMSELF AT BAY AGAINST A PILLOW. . . . 47 A HUNDRED COLLARS . 74
  THE DOCTOR SLID A LITTLE DOWN THE PILLOW. . . . 51 A HUNDRED COLLARS . 179

PILLOW (CONTINUED)
    OF CARRYING HIS PILLOW IN HIS TEETH; . . . . 66 A SERVANT TO SERVANTS . 107
    ONE OF YOU HOLD MY HEAD UP FROM THE PILLOW." . . . . 100 THE SELF-SEEKER . . . 215
PILOT
    PILOT, THOUGH AT BEST YOUR . . . . 440 KITTY HAWK 402
PIN
    AND PINNED WITH A SILVER PIN. . . . . 8 LOVE AND A QUESTION . 24
PINCH
    THERE IS THE PINCH FROM WHICH OUR ONLY OUTCRY . . . . 167 NEW HAMPSHIRE . . . 270
PINCHING
    LIKE A PIP SHOT FROM 'TWIXT OUR PINCHING FINGERS." . . . 460 HOW HARD TO KEEP FROM 202
PINE (SEE WHITE-PINE)
    HE IS ALL PINE AND I AM APPLE ORCHARD. . . . . . . 33 MENDING WALL 24
    OF THEM ANYWHERE UNDER THE SHADE OF THE PINE, ... 59 BLUEBERRIES 16
    BUT GET THE PINE OUT OF THE WAY, YOU MAY BURN . . . . . 59 BLUEBERRIES 17
    PINE, ALDER, PASTURE, MOWING, WELL, AND BROOK. . . . . 117 IN THE HOME STRETCH . 197
    FOR THE DARK PINE THAT KEPT . . . . 128 THE OFT-REPEATED DREAM 2
    THE LOG WAS HOLLOW. THEY WERE SAWING PINE. . . . . . 193 PAUL'S WIFE 74
    "FIRST TIME I EVER SAW A HOLLOW PINE. . . . . . . 193 PAUL'S WIFE 75
    OR EVEN MERELY SEEMED TO PINE . . . . 275 A LONE STRIKER . . . 60
    SOME SHATTERED DISHES UNDERNEATH A PINE, ... 378 DIRECTIVE 42
PINES
    AND EAT THE CONES UNDER HIS PINES, I TELL HIM. . . . . 33 MENDING WALL 26
    DOWN DARK CONVERGING PATHS BETWEEN THE PINES. . . . . 129 THE BONFIRE 7
PINIONS
    GO TILL YOU WET YOUR PINIONS AND ARE QUENCHED. . . . . 356 A MOTH SEEN IN WINTER . 18
PINK
    BUT TURNS TO PINK BETWEEN THE TEETH. . . . . 141 THE GUM-GATHERER . . 33
    LAID SCARLET AND PALE PINK ABOUT HER FEET. . . . . . 184 MAPLE 147
    OF PINK AND WHITE, ... 445 PERIL OF HOPE . . . 7
PINNACLE
    AND MY FLAME MADE A PINNACLE TO HEAVEN . . . . . . 130 THE BONFIRE 38
    THAT IS ITS PINNACLE TO HEAVENWARD . . . . 332 THE SILKEN TENT . . . 6
PINNED (SEE COTTER-PINNED)
    AND PINNED WITH A SILVER PIN. . . . . 8 LOVE AND A QUESTION . 24
PINPOINT
    HE MADE THE SUN A PINPOINT ON THE NOSE . . . . . . 293 AT WOODWARD'S GARDENS . 8
PINXIT
    "LOOK AT WHAT HAPPENED. SURELY SOME GOD PINXIT. . . . . 321 BUILD SOIL 153
PIONEERING
    HERE COME THE LINE-GANG PIONEERING BY. . . . . . . 141 THE LINE-GANG . . . 1
PIOUS
    OUT OF ONE OF THOSE PIOUS SCALAWAGS." . . . . . . 146 SNOW 92
PIP
    THERE, POINTED LIKE THE PIP OF SPADES, ... 380 AN UNSTAMPED LETTER IN 8
    LIKE A PIP SHOT FROM 'TWIXT OUR PINCHING FINGERS." . . . 460 HOW HARD TO KEEP FROM 202
PIPE
    WITH HIS PIPE IN HIS MOUTH AND HIS BROWN JUG-- . . . . 77 THE GENERATIONS OF MEN 105
    LIGHTING HIS PIPE NOW, SQUINTING DOWN HIS NOSE . . . . 112 IN THE HOME STRETCH . 64
PIPES
    HE STOOD IN THE ZEPHYR, PIPES IN HAND, ... 23 PAN WITH US 6
    HE TOSSED HIS PIPES, TOO HARD TO TEACH . . . . . . 24 PAN WITH US 16
    SUCH PIPES KEPT LESS OF POWER TO STIR . . . . . . 24 PAN WITH US 22
    THEY WERE PIPES OF PAGAN MIRTH, ... 24 PAN WITH US 26
    A TRENCH WERE WATER PIPES WERE LAYING ON. . . . . . 394 HAEC FABULA DOCET . . 6
PIPE'S
    BUT THE PIPE'S THERE AND SMOKING, AND THE JUG. . . . . 77 THE GENERATIONS OF MEN 107
PIPESTEM
    OVER HIS SHOULDER WITH HIS PIPESTEM, SAYING, ... 143 SNOW 7
    A BUBBLE ON A PIPESTEM, GROWING BIG. . . . . 283 THE GOLD HESPERIDEE . 24
PIQUED
    HAROLD'S YOUNG COLLEGE-BOY'S ASSURANCE PIQUED HIM. . . . 37 DEATH OF THE HIRED MAN 73
PIRATE
    TILL THE PIRATE SAILORS MADE A VOW . . . . 344 DISCOVERY OF MADEIRAS . 24
    "WHAT WAS THE PIRATE CAPTAIN'S CHAFF? . . . . 346 DISCOVERY OF MADEIRAS . 90
PIROUETTE
    AND PIROUETTE, FOREVER IN ONE PLACE, ... 259 WEST-RUNNING BROOK . . 46
PIROUETTES
    ONLY TO LOSE IT WHEN HE PIROUETTES, ... 14 WAITING 16
PIROUCT
    SOME SAY EXISTENCE LIKE A PIROUOT . . . . 259 WEST-RUNNING BROOK . . 45
PISTIL
    LIKE A PISTIL AFTER THE PETALS GO. . . . . 241 NEED OF BEING VERSED . 4
PISTOL
    LIKE A SMALL PISTOL WHEN HE SNAPPED IT SHUT . . . . . 98 THE SELF-SEEKER . . . 165
    WHERE THE COLD CRACKS LIKE A PISTOL . . . . 384 IN THE LONG NIGHT . . 3
PIT
    AND LOOKING UP BEWHISKERED OUT OF THE PIT, ... 71 THE CODE 62
    THIS IS THE PIT FROM WHICH WE STARKS WERE DIGGED." . . . 76 THE GENERATIONS OF MEN 94
    TILL WEISS SHUT OFF THE WATER IN THE WHEEL PIT. . . . . 93 THE SELF-SEEKER . . . 27
    INSTEAD OF GOING CLEAR DOWN IN THE WHEEL PIT?" . . . . 93 THE SELF-SEEKER . . . 31
    "COME, JOHN," HE SAID, "YOU WANT TO SEE THE WHEEL PIT?" . . 142 THE VANISHING RED . . 19
    OH, YES, HE SHOWED JOHN THE WHEEL PIT ALL RIGHT. . . . . 142 THE VANISHING RED . . 29
PITCH
    HAROLD ALONG BESIDE TO PITCH IT ON." . . . . 37 DEATH OF THE HIRED MAN 69
    NOW BRINGING OUT ITS RINGS IN SUGAR OF PITCH; . . . . 175 THE CENSUS-TAKER . . 21
PITCH-BLACKENED
    WITH THE PITCH-BLACKENED STUB OF AN AX-HANDLE . . . . 175 THE CENSUS-TAKER . . 44
PITCH-DARK
    THROUGH A PITCH-DARK LIMITLESS GROVE. . . . . . . 443 THE DRAFT HORSE . . . 4
PITCHED
    HIS SONG SO PITCHED AS NOT TO EXCITE . . . . 276 TWO TRAMPS IN MUD TIME 27
PITCHER
    JUST HOOK THEM ON THE INSIDE OF THE PITCHER. . . . . 99 THE SELF-SEEKER . . . 174
PITCHER'S
    THE PITCHER'S TOO FULL FOR HER.--THERE'S NO CUP? . . . 99 THE SELF-SEEKER . . . 173
PITCHFORK
    ONE HELPER, THRUSTING PITCHFORK IN THE GROUND, ... 69 THE CODE 7

```
                                                    PAGE TITLE                    LINE
PITCHFORK (CONTINUED)
    HE COULDN'T LAY HANDS ON A PITCHFORK TO HIT HER    . . . . 463 LINES IN DEJECTION .  . 17
PITCHING
    NOW WHAT'S HE DOING? / PITCHING THRONE, I GUESS,   . . . . 474 A MASQUE OF REASON .  . 19
    TWO PITCHING ON LIKE THIS TEND TO CONFUSE ME.  . . . . .  484 A MASQUE OF REASON .  . 323
PITCHY
    WITH PITCHY HANDS TO WAIT FOR RAIN OR SNOW. . . . . . . . 129 THE BONFIRE  . . . .   4
PITH
    A SLENDER LENGTH OF PITH, OR WAS IT PITH?  . . . . . 194 PAUL'S WIFE  . . . .  91
PITIFUL
    BEHIND THE PITIFUL REALITY . . . . . . . . . . . . . 169 NEW HAMPSHIRE  . . . 323
    IT IS IN THE NEWS THAT ALL THESE PITIFUL KIN . . . . 286 A ROADSIDE STAND .  . 23
PITTANCE
    HIS TIME BE LOST, HIS PITTANCE DOCKED.  . . . . . . 273 A LONE STRIKER . . .   8
PITY
    'TIS PITY IF THE CASE REQUIRE  . . . . . . . . . .   19 REVELATION  . . . .   5
    BUT HAVE SOME PITY ON SILAS. DO YOU THINK . . . . .  39 DEATH OF THE HIRED MAN 135
    YOU'LL BE EXPECTING JOHN. I PITY ESTELLE;  . . . . . 88 THE HOUSEKEEPER  . . 191
    I SUPPOSE SHE DESERVES SOME PITY, TOO. . . . . . . . 88 THE HOUSEKEEPER  . . 192
    PITY HE DIDN'T ASK WHAT THEY WERE UP TO  . . . . . . 161 NEW HAMPSHIRE  . . . 83
    BUT HAVE SOME PITY ON US WHO HAVE TO WORK. . . . . . 316 BUILD SOIL  . . . . 21
    AND WHAT I PITY IN YOU IS SOMETHING HUMAN, . . . . . 356 A MOTH SEEN IN WINTER . 14
    BUT GO. YOU ARE RIGHT. MY PITY CANNOT HELP. . . . . . 356 A MOTH SEEN IN WINTER . 17
    CAME UPON THEIR PITY,  . . . . . . . . . . . . . . 433 KITTY HAWK  . . . . 179
PIVOTED
    FIERCE HEADS LOOKED OUT; SMALL BODIES PIVOTED. . . . . . 59 THE BLACK COTTAGE . 126
PLACE
    WHO SHARE THE UNLIT PLACE WITH ME--  . . . . . . . .  6 GHOST HOUSE  . . . . 23
    TO WHITE REST, AND A PLACE OF REST . . . . . . . . .  9 STARS . . . . . .   7
    THAT PLACE MIGHT BE FORGOT;  . . . . . . . . . . . . 14 ROSE POGONIAS  . . . 20
    DIMLY TO HAVE MADE OUT MY SECRET PLACE,  . . . . . . 14 WAITING  . . . . . 15
    EACH CAME SINGLY UNTO HER PLACE,  . . . . . . . . . 15 IN A VALE  . . . . 10
    BACK TO THE PLACE FROM WHICH SHE CAME--  . . . . . . 15 IN A VALE . . . .  17
    A NOTE AS FROM A SINGLE PLACE,  . . . . . . . . . . 18 GOING FOR WATER . . 21
    WE MAKE OURSELVES A PLACE APART  . . . . . . . . . . 19 REVELATION  . . . .  1
    HE BUNDLES EVERY FORKFUL IN ITS PLACE,  . . . . . . 37 DEATH OF THE HIRED MAN 89
    "HOME IS THE PLACE WHERE, WHEN YOU HAVE TO GO THERE,  . 38 DEATH OF THE HIRED MAN 118
    THAT'S FIVE MILES BACK. YOU CAN'T MISTAKE THE PLACE:  . 41 THE MOUNTAIN . .  . 41
    WOODSVILLE'S A PLACE OF SHRIEKS AND WANDERING LAMPS  . 45 A HUNDRED COLLARS .  . 21
    SHE, IN HER PLACE, REFUSED HIM ANY HELP, . . . . . . 51 HOME BURIAL  . . . 13
    ANYWAY THEY WON'T HAVE THE PLACE DISTURBED."  . . . . 55 THE BLACK COTTAGE . 21
    WITH NONE TO TREAD AND PUT THEM IN THEIR PLACE.  . . . 56 THE BLACK COTTAGE . 50
    MAME, WE DON'T KNOW ANY GOOD BERRYING PLACE?'  . . . . 61 BLUEBERRIES  . . . 77
    "WE SHAN'T HAVE THE PLACE TO OURSELVES TO ENJOY--  . . . 62 BLUEBERRIES  . . . 97
    RATHER THAN SEND THEIR FOLKS TO SUCH A PLACE,  . . . . 65 A SERVANT TO SERVANTS . 95
    BUT IT'S NOT SO: THE PLACE IS THE ASYLUM. . . . . . . 65 A SERVANT TO SERVANTS . 97
    SO THEY MADE THE PLACE COMFORTABLE WITH STRAW, . . . . 66 A SERVANT TO SERVANTS . 119
    THE SOUND OF WHICH WAS SILENCE FOR THE PLACE.  . . . . 76 THE GENERATIONS OF MEN 76
    THEY HAVE BEST RIGHT TO BE HEARD IN THIS PLACE."  . . . 79 THE GENERATIONS OF MEN 176
    HE CAN'T FIND ANYONE TO TAKE HER PLACE." . . . . . . 82 THE HOUSEKEEPER  . . 29
    I HATE TO THINK OF THE OLD PLACE WHEN WE'RE GONE, . . . 82 THE HOUSEKEEPER  . . 45
    IF HE COULD SELL THE PLACE, BUT THEN, HE CAN'T:  . . . 83 THE HOUSEKEEPER  . . 48
    MOVING A FLOCK OF HENS FROM PLACE TO PLACE.  . . . . . 85 THE HOUSEKEEPER  . . 126
    AND THE KEY RATTLED LOUDLY INTO PLACE . . . . . . . . 89 THE FEAR  . . . . 19
    "IN THE FIRST PLACE YOU CAN'T MAKE ME BELIEVE IT'S----" . . 90 THE FEAR  . . . . 41
    THIS IS A VERY, LONELY PLACE.--  . . . . . . . . . . 92 THE FEAR  . . . . 90
    ANNE HAS A WAY WITH FLOWERS TO TAKE THE PLACE  . . . . 98 THE SELF-SEEKER  . . 159
    AND YOU CAN'T BLAME ME IN THE PLACE I'M IN.  . . . . . 99 THE SELF-SEEKER  . . 178
    "NOW, THE PLACE WHERE THE ACCIDENT OCCURRED----"  . . . 100 THE SELF-SEEKER  . . 207
    TOO MUCH ALIKE TO MARK OR NAME A PLACE BY  . . . . . . 101 THE WOOD-PILE  . . .  7
    MY WOODS--THE YOUNG FIR BALSAMS LIKE A PLACE . . . . . 106 CHRISTMAS TREES  . . 13
    OF EVER COMING TO THE PLACE AGAIN  . . . . . . . . . 110 THE EXPOSED NEST .  . 34
    NOT TO RETURN. EARTH'S THE RIGHT PLACE FOR LOVE:  . . . 122 BIRCHES  . . . . 52
    TO THE PLACE WHERE JOHN HAS BEEN CUTTING TREES,  . . . 123 PEA BRUSH  . . . .  2
    THE PLACE IT REACHED TO BLACKENED INSTANTLY. . . . . . 131 THE BONFIRE  . . . 48
    OR SHELTER TO PUT INTO FROM THIS PLACE . . . . . . . 145 SNOW . . . . . .  74
    AFTER A DOWNY STORM, HE PASSED OUR PLACE . . . . . . 149 SNOW . . . . . . 176
    SO CLOSE TO OUR DWELLING PLACE? . . . . . . . . . . 156 THE SOUND OF TREES .  5
    THE PLACE IS SILENT ALL DAY LONG, NOR YET  . . . . . . 165 NEW HAMPSHIRE  . . 189
    I'VE GIVEN UP MY SUMMER PLACE IN DUBLIN."  . . . . . . 166 NEW HAMPSHIRE  . . 222
    ABOUT OUR PLACE AMONG THE INFINITIES.  . . . . . . . 168 NEW HAMPSHIRE  . . 305
    "THE PLACE IS DESERT, AND LET WHOSO LURKS  . . . . . . 176 THE CENSUS-TAKER .  . 57
    ABOUT OUR PLACE AMONG THE INFINITIES.  . . . . . . . 177 THE STAR-SPLITTER .  . 19
    AND LOST THE PLACE NEVER TO READ AGAIN.  . . . . . . 181 MAPLE  . . . . .  68
    SO, TILL SHE FOUND HERSELF IN A STRANGE PLACE  . . . . 182 MAPLE  . . . . .  77
    OF THE PLACE MARKED WITH IT--"WAVE OFFERING,  . . . . . 183 MAPLE  . . . . . 106
    HAVE GOT IT ONE STEP FROM THE STARTING PLACE.  . . . . 189 THE GRINDSTONE  . .  7
    THAT COMES OF HAVING PAUL AROUND THE PLACE.  . . . . . 193 PAUL'S WIFE  . . . 76
    BRIGHTLY, AS IF A STAR PLAYED ON THE PLACE, . . . . . 195 PAUL'S WIFE  . . . 135
    PLACE FOR A THIRD  . . . . . . . . . . . . . . . . 199 PLACE FOR A THIRD .  . T
    YOU SAID YOU KNEW THE PLACE WHERE ONCE, ON KINSMAN,  . . 213 A FOUNTAIN, A BOTTLE .  8
    LET'S TALK ABOUT IT." / "LET'S GO SEE THE PLACE."  . . . 213 A FOUNTAIN, A BOTTLE . 16
    AND SPOKE HIS DOUBTS IN EVERY OPEN PLACE.  . . . . . . 214 A FOUNTAIN, A BOTTLE . 36
    I VOW WE MUST BE NEAR THE PLACE FROM WHERE . . . . . 214 A FOUNTAIN, A BOTTLE . 51
    IN ANY ROUGH PLACE WHERE IT CAUGHT. . . . . . . . . 223 THE AIM WAS SONG .  .  4
    IT HADN'T FOUND THE PLACE TO BLOW;  . . . . . . . . 224 THE AIM WAS SONG .  .  6
    NOT THE SAME DOE COME BACK INTO HER PLACE. . . . . . 229 TWO LOOK AT TWO . . 30
    IN SUMMER WHEN I PASSED THE PLACE, . . . . . . . . 233 LOOKING FOR SUNSET BIRD 5
    IN PLACE ACROSS A CLOUD THE SLENDER RAY  . . . . . . 235 VALLEY'S SINGING DAY .  8
    OR THICKET, OR HOLLOW PLACE FOR THE NIGHT.  . . . . . 236 MISGIVING . . . . .  8
    AND, TIRED OF AIMLESS CIRCLING IN ONE PLACE,  . . . . 238 ON A TREE FALLEN ACROSS 13
    THE FLAKES COULD FIND NO LANDING PLACE TO FORM.  . . . 239 OUR SINGING STRENGTH .  2
    TO ANY ONE PLACE COVER US WITH SONG. . . . . . . . 239 OUR SINGING STRENGTH . 20
    AND PIROUETTE, FOREVER IN ONE PLACE,  . . . . . . . 259 WEST-RUNNING BROOK .  46
    AND BRING BACK NATURE IN PEOPLE'S PLACE. . . . . . . 263 THE TIMES TABLE . . 20
    THERE'S A PLACE CALLED FARAWAY MEADOW  . . . . . . . 264 THE LAST MOWING . . .  1
    THE PLACE FOR THE MOMENT IS OURS . . . . . . . . . 264 THE LAST MOWING . . . 15
    HE KNEW ANOTHER PLACE, A WOOD, . . . . . . . . . . 274 A LONE STRIKER . . . 36
```

PLACE (CONTINUED)
TO COME TO THEIR FINAL PLACE IN EARTH THEY HAD TO PASS ME
  BY. . . . . 297 A LEAF-TREADER . . . 6
THE MOUNTAIN STOOD EXALTED IN ITS PLACE. . . . . 301 MOON COMPASSES . . . 7
FOR NOTHING DOWN, ALL-OUT-DOORS OF A PLACE, ... 316 BUILD SOIL 8
AND YET CONVERSION HAS ITS PLACE . . . . 326 TO A THINKER . . . 31
TURNED FROM THE PLACE AND RAN. . . . . 341 THE SUBVERTED FLOWER . 61
FOR FEAR I WOULD MAKE HER MISS THE PLACE. . . . . . . 342 A CLOUD SHADOW . . 8
AND LET US TRY AN UNTOSSED PLACE . . . . 347 DISCOVERY OF MADEIRAS . 108
EARTH'S A HARD PLACE IN WHICH TO SAVE THE SOUL, ... 353 THE LESSON FOR TODAY . 98
TO ANY ONE TIME, PLACE, OR HUMAN KIND. . . . . 353 THE LESSON FOR TODAY . 105
A PERCH AND RESTING PLACE 'TWIXT WOOD AND WOOD, ... 356 A MOTH SEEN IN WINTER . 2
OF THE STONES OF THE PLACE . . . . 365 OF STONES OF THE PLACE . T
"AS LIBERALS WE'RE WILLING TO GIVE PLACE . . . . 369 THE LITERATE FARMER AND 49
HERE ARE YOUR WATERS AND YOUR WATERING PLACE. . . . . 379 DIRECTIVE 61
NO PLACE TO GET LOST LIKE TOO FAR IN THE DISTANCE. . . . 379 TOO ANXIOUS FOR RIVERS 11
THE PLACE WAS LIKE A CITY PARK. . . . . 380 AN UNSTAMPED LETTER IN 11
THE PLACE OF STANDING STILL . . . . 388 MIDDLENESS OF THE ROAD 6
HAS NEVER LEARNED TO KNOW HER PLACE. . . . . 390 TWO LEADING LIGHTS . 13
FROM SOURCE UNKNOWN BUT FROM NO SPECIAL PLACE . . . . 411 POD OF THE MILKWEED . 2
THE RACE'S FUTURE TRIAL PLACE, ... 417 AMERICA IS HARD TO SEE 29
ROUND THE PLACE ON FOOT . . . . 434 KITTY HAWK 204
TO TAUNT OF MINE I KNEW A PLACE TO GO . . . . 447 DOES NO ONE AT ALL EVER 33
THEY STOOD IT IN PLACE . . . . 448 THE BAD ISLAND--EASTER 18
AND STANDS BESIDE, SUPPORTING IT IN PLACE.) . . . . . 474 A MASQUE OF REASON . 23
FOR STANDING STILL IN ONE PLACE TRUE FOREVER; . . . . 480 A MASQUE OF REASON . 192
AN EASIER PLACE FOR MAN TO SAVE HIS SOUL IN. . . . . 484 A MASQUE OF REASON . 317
EXCEPT AS A HARD PLACE TO SAVE HIS SOUL IN, ... 484 A MASQUE OF REASON . 318
THE COUNTRY'S ONLY USEFUL AS A PLACE . . . . 496 A MASQUE OF MERCY . 73
IF I WERE IN YOUR PLACE, THOUGH, MR. PROPHET, ... 503 A MASQUE OF MERCY . 269
BE CAREFUL NOT TO LOSE THE PLACE. BE CAREFUL. . . . . 505 A MASQUE OF MERCY . 293
WHAT'S THIS? / DON'T LOSE THE PLACE. / OLD DANA LYLE, . 506 A MASQUE OF MERCY . 324
THIS IS GOD AT ME IN MY SKULKING PLACE, ... 507 A MASQUE OF MERCY . 349
IS THE FIRST PLACE IN LITERATURE, I THINK, ... 508 A MASQUE OF MERCY . 376
PLACED
THAN FOR HIMSELF, SO PLACED HE COULDN'T HOPE . . . . 187 THE AX-HELVE 59
PLACES
EXCEPT AT NIGHT TO PLACES IN THE SKY . . . . 173 A STAR IN A STONEBOAT . 41
WINDS BLOW THE OPEN GRASSY PLACES BLEAK; . . . . . . 246 ATMOSPHERE 1
SHE CAN THINK OF PLACES THAT ARE NOT THUS . . . . . 291 ON HEART'S BEGINNING TO 32
DESERT PLACES . . . . 296 DESERT PLACES . . . T
TO SCARE MYSELF WITH MY OWN DESERT PLACES. . . . . . 296 DESERT PLACES . . . 16
PLACE'S
TO BEAR FORSAKEN THE PLACE'S NAME. . . . . 241 NEED OF BEING VERSED . 8
PLAGIARISM
OF PLAGIARISM AND HELP OF CHEATING PARENTS. . . . . . 325 BUILD SOIL 275
PLAGUED
TO LET ON HE WAS PLAGUED TO DEATH WITH ME: . . . . . 210 PAUPER WITCH OF GRAFTON 84
PLAIN
BY A PLAIN STATEMENT OF RELATIONSHIP, ... 75 THE GENERATIONS OF MEN 59
FOLKS IN HER DAY WERE GIVEN TO PLAIN SPEAKING. . . . . 79 THE GENERATIONS OF MEN 181
I SAW IT JUST AS PLAIN AS A WHITE PLATE." . . . . . 89 THE FEAR 9
I CHOOSE TO BE A PLAIN NEW HAMPSHIRE FARMER . . . . . 172 NEW HAMPSHIRE . . . 408
AND FOR A MOMENT ALL WAS PLAIN . . . . 381 AN UNSTAMPED LETTER IN 36
AND GOLDEN SEEMS THE SANDY PLAIN. . . . . 392 A CLIFF DWELLING . . 2
PLAINLY
HE SAW IT PLAINLY WHERE HE STOOD, ... 274 A LONE STRIKER . . . 34
PLAINLY WITH AN INTELLIGENCE I DEALT. . . . . 357 A CONSIDERABLE SPECK . 15
FOR VERY LONG. WE'RE PLAINLY MADE TO GO. . . . . . . 481 A MASQUE OF REASON . 233
AND SAYING PLAINLY AND UNEQUIVOCALLY . . . . 483 A MASQUE OF REASON . 296
PLAN
HE HAS A PLAN. YOU MUSTN'T LAUGH AT HIM. . . . . . . 40 DEATH OF THE HIRED MAN 158
IT WAS HIS PLAN OUR MOVING OVER IN . . . . 64 A SERVANT TO SERVANTS . 61
AND ALL AT ONCE. HE'LL PLAN FOR US AND PLAN . . . . 115 IN THE HOME STRETCH . 152
LABAN WAS FORCED TO FALL BACK ON HIS PLAN . . . . . 202 PLACE FOR A THIRD . 79
TO GIVE A PROSPECT TO A PLAN . . . . 281 BLUE RIBBON AT AMESBURY 55
MAY MUCH STAY OUT OF OUR STATED PLAN, ... 305 UNHARVESTED 12
TO MATCH YOU DEED FOR DEED AND PLAN FOR PLAN. . . . . 323 BUILD SOIL 221
A FIVE-YEAR PLAN I CALL SO NOT BECAUSE . . . . 323 BUILD SOIL 225
WILL THEREFORE PLAN TO GO HALFWAY AND STOP. . . . . . 363 A SEMI-REVOLUTION . . 6
PLANE
IT LIFTS EXISTENCE ON A PLANE OF SNOW . . . . 254 A WINTER EDEN . . . 5
FROM PLANE TO PLANE . . . . 404 FROM PLANE TO PLANE . T
AND WE SCALED A PLANE . . . . 434 KITTY HAWK 208
PLANET
OUR HOLD ON THE PLANET . . . . 349 OUR HOLD ON THE PLANET . T
OUR HOLD ON THE PLANET WOULDN'T HAVE SO INCREASED. . . 349 OUR HOLD ON THE PLANET 18
THE LITERATE FARMER AND THE PLANET VENUS . . . . . . 368 THE LITERATE FARMER AND T
PLANETARY
AT SUCH A PLANETARY CHANGE OF STYLE. . . . . 335 I COULD GIVE ALL . . 10
PLANETS
AS ON A FARM, BUT PLANETS, EVENING STARS . . . . . . 178 THE STAR-SPLITTER . . 72
ON PLANETS OVER, ... 220 I WILL SING YOU ONE-O . 74
THE PLANETS SEEM TO INTERFERE IN THEIR CURVES, ... 268 ON LOOKING UP BY CHANCE 6
SOME PLANETS, THE UNBLINKING FOUR, ... 451 A-WISHING WELL . . . 23
PLANK
ANOTHER A ROTTING PLANK, ... 281 A DRUMLIN WOODCHUCK . 2
PLANNED
YOU KNOW HOW CUNNINGLY MANKIND IS PLANNED: . . . . . 371 THE LITERATE FARMER AND 112
PLANNERS
THE PLANNERS . . . . 397 THE PLANNERS . . . . T
WHO WOULD THEY BE? THE GUILD OF SOCIAL PLANNERS . . . 397 THE PLANNERS 10
PLANNING
TO HELP US, BUT HE'LL TAKE IT OUT IN PLANNING. . . . . 115 IN THE HOME STRETCH . 153
AND CANNOT REST FROM PLANNING DAY OR NIGHT . . . . . 169 NEW HAMPSHIRE . . . 338
PLANS
FRIENDS CROWD AROUND ME WITH THEIR FIVE-YEAR PLANS . . 323 BUILD SOIL 222

PLANT
  I SMELL THE EARTH, I SMELL THE BRUISED PLANT, ... 17 THE VANTAGE POINT . . . 13
  TO PLANT AND TEND AND REAP HERSELF, ... 133 A GIRL'S GARDEN . . . 7
  THEY PLANT DEAD TREES FOR LIVING, AND THE DEAD . . . . 141 THE LINE-GANG . . . 3
  THEY CANNOT MEAN TO PLANT IT, NO-- . . . . 238 PLOWMEN 2
  NOT FOR A LONG, LONG TIME. PLANT, BREED, PRODUCE, ... 323 BUILD SOIL 214
  (AND WAS A TEXT ALBEIT DONE IN PLANT). . . . . . . 355 TIME OUT 4
  TO A PLANT CALLED THE SILPHION, ... 452 A-WISHING WELL . . . 49
PLANTED
  BUT NEVER MIND, THE WELSHMAN GOT IT PLANTED . . . . . 57 THE BLACK COTTAGE . . 68
  SHE SAYS SHE THINKS SHE PLANTED ONE . . . . . . 134 A GIRL'S GARDEN . . . 27
PLANTS
  AND SCURF OF PLANTS, AND WEARY AND OVERHEATED, ... 125 AN ENCOUNTER 6
  WAS SETTING OUT, UP TRACK AND DOWN, NOT PLANTS . . . 178 THE STAR-SPLITTER . . 71
  ONCE DOWN ON MY KNEES TO GROWING PLANTS . . . . . 385 A MOOD APART 1
PLASM
  WILL GET THIS PLASM IN ITS GOGGLE GLASS." . . . . . 270 THE EGG AND THE MACHINE 30
PLATE
  I SAW IT JUST AS PLAIN AS A WHITE PLATE," . . . . . 89 THE FEAR 9
  FAR STAR THAT TICKLES FOR ME MY SENSITIVE PLATE . . . 389 SKEPTIC 1
PLATE-GLASS
  THE MICA SHEETS WERE BIG AS PLATE-GLASS WINDOWS. . . . 213 A FOUNTAIN, A BOTTLE . 5
PLATES
  FROM THE SINK WINDOW WHERE I WASH THE PLATES, ... 63 A SERVANT TO SERVANTS . 23
  OF MANY PLATES WITH TOWELS MANY TIMES." . . . . . 111 IN THE HOME STRETCH . 28
  OR BETTER ON DISH PLATES ALL AROUND THE ROOM, ... 320 BUILD SOIL 148
  KNIVES AND FORKS RINGING ON THE SUPPER PLATES, ... 368 THE LITERATE FARMER AND 3
PLATO
  (THE ME ON OF PLATO), ... 427 VERSION 10
  YOU DON'T CATCH WOMEN TRYING TO BE PLATO. . . . . 478 A MASQUE OF REASON . . 140
PLATONIC
  I LOVE TO TOY WITH THE PLATONIC NOTION . . . . . . 362 BOEOTIAN 1
PLAUDITS
  THE JEST SEEMED HIS AND THE PLAUDITS HIS. . . . . . 346 DISCOVERY OF MADEIRAS . 92
PLAY
  BUT SO WITH ALL, FROM BABES THAT PLAY . . . . . . 19 REVELATION 9
  PLAY? PLAY?--WHAT SHOULD HE PLAY? . . . . 24 PAN WITH US 30
  AFRAID OF ME. THERE'S TWO CAN PLAY AT THAT. . . . . . 65 A SERVANT TO SERVANTS . 86
  AND THEN HE'D CROW AS IF HE THOUGHT THAT CHILD'S PLAY-- . . 66 A SERVANT TO SERVANTS . 137
  YOU WERE FOREVER FINDING SOME NEW PLAY. . . . . . 109 THE EXPOSED NEST . . 1
  AS IN THE GAME 'TEN-STEP' THE CHILDREN PLAY." . . . . 114 IN THE HOME STRETCH . 118
  WHOSE ONLY PLAY WAS WHAT HE FOUND HIMSELF, ... 121 BIRCHES 26
  SUMMER OR WINTER, AND COULD PLAY ALONE. . . . . . 121 BIRCHES 27
  TO PLAY----" / "YOU TEND YOUR HORSES AND COME BACK.-- . . 144 SNOW 42
  HE ISN'T WINTER-BROKEN. IT ISN'T PLAY . . . . . . 223 THE RUNAWAY 10
  AS THAT I HAD NO RIGHT TO PLAY . . . . 277 TWO TRAMPS IN MUD TIME 60
  AND THE WORK IS PLAY FOR MORTAL STAKES, ... 277 TWO TRAMPS IN MUD TIME 70
  AND PLAY THE GOOD WITHOUT THE ILL. . . . . . . 336 THE WIND AND THE RAIN . 17
  THE PLAY SEEMS OUT FOR AN ALMOST INFINITE RUN. . . . . 392 IT BIDS PRETTY FAIR . 1
  IN ANY GAME THE NATIONS WANT TO PLAY. . . . . . . 424 FOR JOHN F. KENNEDY . 75
  DON'T LISTEN TO THEIR PLAY OF PARADOXES. . . . . . 460 HOW HARD TO KEEP FROM . 193
  REQUIRED SOMEONE WHO LAUGHINGLY COULD PLAY . . . . . 509 A MASQUE OF MERCY . . 422
  THAT MADE ALL OTHER OUTRAGE SEEM AS CHILD'S PLAY: . . . 511 A MASQUE OF MERCY . . 476
PLAYED
  AS IF SHE PLAYED UNHEARD SOME TENDERNESS . . . . . 38 DEATH OF THE HIRED MAN 109
  SOME FLOWER I PLAYED WITH AS I SAT . . . . 135 LOCKED OUT 12
  BRIGHTLY, AS IF A STAR PLAYED ON THE PLACE, ... 195 PAUL'S WIFE 135
  YOU REALIZE BY NOW THE PART YOU PLAYED . . . . . 475 A MASQUE OF REASON . . 66
  HAS ALL GONE HOME TO BED. THE PLAY'S PLAYED OUT. . . . 482 A MASQUE OF REASON . . 253
  BUT TO THE EVENSONG, AND HAVING PLAYED . . . . . 489 A MASQUE OF REASON . . 436
PLAYER
  THE WAY A PLAYER CURLS AROUND A FOOTBALL. . . . . . 278 THE WHITE-TAILED HORNET 39
PLAYFUL
  EVEN IN A PLAYFUL MOMENT TO CONTEND . . . . . . 359 THE LOST FOLLOWER . . 26
PLAYFULLY
  AND TAKES THE PLAYFULLY OBJECTED RHYME . . . . . . 362 IN A POEM 2
PLAYHOUSE
  THE PLAYTHINGS IN THE PLAYHOUSE OF THE CHILDREN. . . . 378 DIRECTIVE 43
  THIS WAS NO PLAYHOUSE BUT A HOUSE IN EARNEST. . . . . 378 DIRECTIVE 48
  (I STOLE THE GOBLET FROM THE CHILDREN'S PLAYHOUSE.) . . . 379 DIRECTIVE 60
PLAYING
  SPEAKING OR SINGING, OR THE BAND-MUSIC PLAYING. . . . 78 THE GENERATIONS OF MEN 130
  PLAYING OUR FANCY, TO HAVE THE SNOW-LINE RUN . . . . 149 SNOW 190
  AND IN IT A PIANO LOUDLY PLAYING. . . . . . . 263 THE INVESTMENT . . 4
  WINTER WAS ONLY PLAYING POSSUM. . . . . 276 TWO TRAMPS IN MUD TIME 30
  THEN EDDIES PLAYING ROUND A SUNKEN REEF . . . . . 335 I COULD GIVE ALL . . 7
PLAYMATE
  WHO MARRIED HER FOR PLAYMATE MORE THAN HELPMATE, . . . 200 PLACE FOR A THIRD . . 34
PLAYS
  BEFORE THEIR PLAYS AND GAMES WERE ORGANIZED, ... 318 BUILD SOIL 62
  THE SPIRIT PLAYS US STRANGE RELIGIOUS PRANKS . . . . 358 THE LOST FOLLOWER . . 5
PLAY'S
  HAS ALL GONE HOME TO BED. THE PLAY'S PLAYED OUT. . . . 482 A MASQUE OF REASON . . 253
PLAYTHINGS
  THE PLAYTHINGS IN THE PLAYHOUSE OF THE CHILDREN. . . . 378 DIRECTIVE 43
PLEASANT
  "YOU DRIVE AROUND? IT MUST BE PLEASANT WORK." . . . . 49 A HUNDRED COLLARS . 122
  I TOLD HIM THIS IS A PLEASANT LIFE, ... 141 THE GUM-GATHERER . . 34
  (THE ARRANGEMENT MADE A PLEASANT SUNNY CELLAR.) . . . 181 MAPLE 59
PLEASE
  TO PLEASE THE YELPING DOGS. THE GAPS I MEAN, ... 33 MENDING WALL 9
  HE WON'T BE MADE ASHAMED TO PLEASE HIS BROTHER." . . . 39 DEATH OF THE HIRED MAN 145
  BUT, WARREN, PLEASE REMEMBER HOW IT IS: . . . . . 40 DEATH OF THE HIRED MAN 156
  "DON'T TOUCH ME, PLEASE--I SAY, DON'T TOUCH ME, PLEASE. . . 47 A HUNDRED COLLARS . 77
  SO AS TO PLEASE YOU. BUT I MIGHT BE TAUGHT, ... 52 HOME BURIAL . . . 47
  WHEN, TO PLEASE YOUNGER MEMBERS OF THE CHURCH, ... 57 THE BLACK COTTAGE . . 85
  HE'S COMING TOWARDS US. JOEL, GO IN--PLEASE. . . . . 90 THE FEAR 39
  HARK!--I DON'T HEAR HIM NOW. BUT PLEASE GO IN." . . . . 90 THE FEAR 40

PLEASE (CONTINUED)
    WILL PENCIL DO? THEN, PLEASE, YOUR FOUNTAIN PEN. . . . . 100 THE SELF-SEEKER . . . 214
    TO PLEASE THE BOY BY GIVING HIM THE HALF HOUR . . . . . 136 "OUT, OUT--" 11
    AND BRING IT TO MARKET WHEN YOU PLEASE. . . . . 141 THE GUM-GATHERER . . 39
    "WON'T YOU TO PLEASE ME? PLEASE! IF I SAY PLEASE? . . . 147 SNOW 108
    I CAN WASTE AS I PLEASE ON WHOM I PLEASE. . . . . . . 196 WILD GRAPES 15
    IN EVERY WAY YOU MAY PLEASE YOURSELF; . . . . 232 THE KITCHEN CHIMNEY . 2
    BUT PLEASE PLEASE ME IN THE KITCHEN CHIMNEY: . . . . . 232 THE KITCHEN CHIMNEY . 3
    I PUT IT SHINING ANYWHERE I PLEASE. . . . . 245 THE FREEDOM OF THE MOON 7
    THE PEOPLE CAN BURN IT AS LONG AS THEY PLEASE; . . . . 291 ON HEART'S BEGINNING TO 16
    THEY CAN KEEP IT BURNING AS LONG AS THEY PLEASE; . . . 291 ON HEART'S BEGINNING TO 24
    THEY CAN PUT IT OUT WHENEVER THEY PLEASE. . . . . . . 291 ON HEART'S BEGINNING TO 25
    IF IT MAKES YOU LOOK HELPLESS, PLEASE, ... 326 TO A THINKER 23
    BUT IN YOUR FAVOR--PLEASE TO TELL YOUR KING-- . . . . 354 THE LESSON FOR TODAY . 117
    WELL, WOULD I PLEASE GO TO SCHOOL, ... 366 NOT OF SCHOOL AGE . . 23
    PLEASE, MY INVOLUNTARY HOST, ... 381 AN UNSTAMPED LETTER IN 38
    ANY SIZE WE PLEASE . . . . 396 ANY SIZE WE PLEASE . . T
    AS IF BESEECHING ME, "PLEASE, NO MORE; . . . . . . 420 ONE MORE BREVITY . . 24
    THE KINGDOM'S YOURS TO FINISH AS YOU PLEASE. . . . . 453 HOW HARD TO KEEP FROM . 2
    ONE AT A TIME, PLEASE. I WILL ANSWER JOB FIRST. . . . 484 A MASQUE OF REASON . 324
    GOD, PLEASE, ENOUGH FOR NOW. I'M IN NO MOOD . . . . 486 A MASQUE OF REASON . 366
    WOULD YOU TWO PLEASE DRAW IN A LITTLE CLOSER? . . . 488 A MASQUE OF REASON . 403
    AND ALWAYS WILL BE.--PLEASE DON'T GO. STAY, STAY . . 489 A MASQUE OF REASON . 435
    PLEASE, SOMEONE UNDERSTAND. / I UNDERSTAND. . . . . 497 A MASQUE OF MERCY . 110
    PLEASE LET ME HAVE IT. / READ US WHAT IT SAYS. . . . 505 A MASQUE OF MERCY . 294
    (THE CURTAIN STARTS TO FALL.) PLEASE HOLD THE CURTAIN.-- . 519 A MASQUE OF MERCY . 673
PLEASED
    OR BEING VERY YOUNG (AND HE WAS PLEASED . . . . . 127 THE SMILE 9
    BAPTISTE DREW BACK AND SQUINTED AT IT, PLEASED: . . . 188 THE AX-HELVE . . . 101
    AND SEE YOU PLEASED ONCE MORE WITH WORDS OF MINE? . . 222 TO E.T. 20
    IF GOLD PLEASED THE CONQUEROR, WELL, ... 311 THE VINDICTIVES . . 24
PLEASURE
    HER PLEASURE WILL NOT LET ME STAY. . . . . 7 MY NOVEMBER GUEST . . 6
    OH, GIVE US PLEASURE IN THE FLOWERS TODAY; . . . . 12 A PRAYER IN SPRING . . 1
    OH, GIVE US PLEASURE IN THE ORCHARD WHITE; . . . . 12 A PRAYER IN SPRING . . 5
    THAT FATE HAD MADE THEE FOR THE PLEASURE OF THE WIND, . 29 MY BUTTERFLY . . . 23
    THEY MOVE IN PLEASURE TOO FAR OFF . . . . 256 THE LOVELY BE CHOOSERS 29
    AND SEIZE THE DAY OF PLEASURE." . . . . 335 CARPE DIEM 10
    THE WASTE OF PLEASURE WEEPING, ... 360 NOVEMBER 13
PLEAT
    YOU GRASP THE BARK BY A RUGGED PLEAT, ... 247 ON GOING UNNOTICED . . 9
PLED
    A ROADSIDE STAND THAT TOO PATHETICALLY PLED, ... 286 A ROADSIDE STAND . . 3
PLEIADES
    AS LEO, ORION, AND THE PLEIADES. . . . . 234 EVENING A SUGAR ORCHARD 16
PLENARY
    GOD BLESS THE DEAN AND MAKE HIS DEANSHIP PLENARY. . . . 394 LUCRETIUS VERSUS POETS 12
PLENTY
    THAT, OVERFLOWING LIKE A HORN OF PLENTY, ... 216 A FOUNTAIN, A BOTTLE . 94
    WE GET PLENTY FUNERALS AT SEA. . . . . 345 DISCOVERY OF MADEIRAS . 70
PLIANT
    AT A GOOD POINT FOR PLIANT PERMANENCE, ... 458 HOW HARD TO KEEP FROM 155
PLIGHT
    AND THINK OF AN ORCHARD'S ARBOREAL PLIGHT . . . . 228 GOOD-BY AND KEEP COLD . 26
    ANOTHER STILL--YOU SEE YOUR PLIGHT. . . . . . . 325 TO A THINKER . . . 4
    NEARER IN PLIGHT THEIR NEIGHBORS ARE THAN DISTANCE. . . 414 A CABIN IN THE CLEARING 9
PLOD
    AND PLOD: I GO UP TO THE STONE WALL . . . . . . 124 A TIME TO TALK . . . 9
PLOT
    TO GIVE HER A GARDEN PLOT . . . . 133 A GIRL'S GARDEN . . 6
    IN A NEW-BOUGHTEN GRAVE PLOT BY HERSELF, ... 200 PLACE FOR A THIRD . . 23
    TO BUY ELIZA A PLOT TO LIE ALONE IN: . . . . . . 202 PLACE FOR A THIRD . . 80
    AT HIS DEVOTIONS IN A SPECIAL PLOT. . . . . . . 354 THE LESSON FOR TODAY . 130
PLOW (SEE TRACTOR-PLOW)
    NOT FORCING HER HAND WITH HARROW AND PLOW." . . . . 61 BLUEBERRIES 56
    WERE ROUND MY NECK AND I WAS AT THE PLOW. . . . . 132 THE BONFIRE 80
    HER FATHER SAID, TO PLOW; . . . . 133 A GIRL'S GARDEN . . 18
    THERE WHERE HE MOVED THE ROCKS TO PLOW THE GROUND . . 177 THE STAR-SPLITTER . . 26
    A PLOW, THEY SAY, TO PLOW THE SNOW. . . . . . . 238 PLOWMEN 2
    WILL BE TURNED UP BY THE PLOW, ... 285 IN TIME OF CLOUDBURST . 22
    AND ONE DID STOP, BUT ONLY TO PLOW UP GRASS . . . . 287 A ROADSIDE STAND . . 39
    EAT IT OR PLOW IT UNDER WHERE IT STANDS, ... 323 BUILD SOIL 216
    NO PLOW AMONG THESE ROCKS WOULD PAY. . . . . . . 376 SOMETHING FOR HOPE . . 9
PLOWED
    HE DRAGGED IT THROUGH THE PLOWED GROUND AT A PACE . . . 173 A STAR IN A STONEBOAT . 31
    AND PLOWED BETWEEN THE ROCKS HE COULDN'T MOVE, . . . 177 THE STAR-SPLITTER . . 27
    AND FROM BARN SMELLS YOU CAN'T WASH OUT OF PLOWED GROUND . 210 PAUPER WITCH OF GRAFTON 91
    BUT STILL LIES POINTED AS IT PLOWED THE DUST. . . . . 261 A SOLDIER 3
    OUT IN THE PLOWED GROUND IN THE COLD A DIGGER, ... 263 THE INVESTMENT . . . 5
    MEN WORK ALONE, THEIR LOTS PLOWED FAR APART, ... 299 STRONG SAYING NOTHING . 6
PLOWERS
    THAT CAN'T STAND MOWERS AND PLOWERS. . . . . . . 264 THE LAST MOWING . . . 6
PLOWING
    "MADE ON MACHINE," HE SAID, PLOWING THE GRAIN . . . 186 THE AX-HELVE . . . 22
PLOWMEN
    PLOWMEN . . . . 238 PLOWMEN . . . . . T
PLUCKED
    SHE PLUCKED HER LIPS FOR IT, ... 341 THE SUBVERTED FLOWER . 69
PLUM
    THE PLUM, I SUPPOSE. . . . . 246 THE ROSE FAMILY . . . 6
    THE LEAFLESS BLOOM OF A PLUM IS FRESH AND WHITE; . . . 300 STRONG SAYING NOTHING . 10
PLUMAGE
    IN SEPARATE COOPS, HAVING THEIR PLUMAGE DONE. . . . . 85 THE HOUSEKEEPER . . . 121
    HER FLUFF OF PLUMAGE, WHITE AS CHALK. . . . . . . 280 BLUE RIBBON AT AMESBURY 7
PLUME
    WITH SMELL OF BURNING ON EVERY PLUME, ... 120 BOND AND FREE . . . 14
    AND TURNS TO THE WIND TO UNRUFFLE A PLUME, ... 276 TWO TRAMPS IN MUD TIME 26

PLUNDERERS
    AND BE ALL PLUNDERERS CURST. . . . . 312 THE VINDICTIVES 80
PLUNGED
    AND PLUNGED HIMSELF HEAD FOREMOST IN THE TRENCH: . . . . 394 HAEC FABULA DOCET . . . 14
PLUNGING
    OR PLUNGING HEADLONG WITH FIERCE TWANG AFAR; . . . . . 14 WAITING 13
PLYWOOD
    (THE THRONE'S A PLYWOOD FLAT, PREFABRICATED, ... 474 A MASQUE OF REASON . . 21
POCKET
    TRYING TO COAX HIM OFF WITH POCKET MONEY-- . . . . . . 35 DEATH OF THE HIRED MAN 28
    THE SMALL BOOK IN MY POCKET. IT WAS THERE. . . . . . . 217 A FOUNTAIN, A BOTTLE . 133
    THE POCKET OF A LITTLE TURTLE MINE. . . . . 270 THE EGG AND THE MACHINE 23
    HERE'S FIRST A GLOVELESS HAND WARM FROM MY POCKET, . . . 356 A MOTH SEEN IN WINTER . 1
    WE CARRY IN OUR PURSE AND POCKET STILL?) . . . . . . 422 FOR JOHN F. KENNEDY . 22
POCKETS
    TO FIND IF THERE WERE POCKETS IN HIS SKIN, ... 503 A MASQUE OF MERCY . . 252
POD
    POD OF THE MILKWEED . . . . 411 POD OF THE MILKWEED . T
    WAS LEAVE AS THEIR POSTERITY ONE POD . . . . 412 POD OF THE MILKWEED . 43
POEM
    TO FIND OUT WHAT TO DO TO HURT A PCEM. . . . . 216 A FOUNTAIN, A BOTTLE . 108
    GET IN A POEM TOWARD THE NEXT ELECTION. . . . . 316 BUILD SOIL 25
    FOR A POEM THERE USED TO BE ON SPRING. . . . . 342 A CLOUD SHADOW . . . 3
    FOR WHOM WOULD A POEM ON SPRING BE BY? . . . . 342 A CLOUD SHADOW . . . 5
    IN A POEM . . . . 362 IN A POEM . . . . . T
    I GET A POEM, I DESPAIR. . . . . 452 A-WISHING WELL . . . 33
    TO QUOTE THE GREATEST WESTERN POEM YET. . . . . 485 A MASQUE OF REASON . 344
POEMS
    SCATTER POEMS ON THE FLOOR; . . . . 12 TO THE THAWING WIND . 14
    POEMS PRODUCED THAN ANY OTHER THING? . . . . 164 NEW HAMPSHIRE . . . 171
    EXCEPT, IT SEEMED, THE POETESS'S POEMS. . . . . 216 A FOUNTAIN, A BOTTLE . 91
    I SLUMBERED WITH YOUR POEMS ON MY BREAST, ... 222 TO E.T. 1
    YOUR POEMS ON A FARM AND CALL THAT FARMING. . . . . . 316 BUILD SOIL 18
    I AM BROUGHT GUARANTEED YOUNG PRATTLE POEMS . . . . . 324 BUILD SOIL 273
    'TWAS AGE IMPOSED ON POEMS . . . . 335 CARPE DIEM 12
    "AN AFTERWORD" FROM COMPLETE POEMS . . . . 401 AFTERWORD FROM COMPLETE T
POET (SEE SOLDIER-POET)
    TURN THE POET OUT OF DOOR. . . . . 12 TO THE THAWING WIND . 15
    I MET A POET FROM ANOTHER STATE, ... 159 NEW HAMPSHIRE . . . 25
    ANOTHER MASSACHUSETTS POET SAID, ... 166 NEW HAMPSHIRE . . . 220
    FIRST SOLDIER, AND THEN POET, AND THEN BOTH, ... 222 TO E.T. 7
    NO CHOICE IS LEFT A POET, YOU MIGHT ADD, ... 352 THE LESSON FOR TODAY . 61
    NO ONE HAS EVER FAILED THE POET RANKS . . . . 358 THE LOST FOLLOWER . 7
    AS THE POET SAID . . . . 433 KITTY HAWK 168
    A POET WOULD A-WISHING GO, ... 451 A-WISHING WELL . . . 1
    FOR HIM TO MAKE A POET OF HIMSELF ON . . . . 459 HOW HARD TO KEEP FROM 175
    ON BEING CHOSEN POET OF VERMONT . . . . 469 CHOSEN POET OF VERMONT T
    BOTH OF THEM CAUGHT IT FROM BEL'S FAVORITE POET, . . . 511 A MASQUE OF MERCY . . 462
POETESS
    THE POETESS WHO WROTE THE BOOK OF VERSES . . . . . . 215 A FOUNTAIN, A BOTTLE . 78
    THE POETESS HAD SIGHED, I KNEW, IN HEAVEN . . . . . . 217 A FOUNTAIN, A BOTTLE . 134
POETESS'S
    EXCEPT, IT SEEMED, THE POETESS'S POEMS. . . . . 216 A FOUNTAIN, A BOTTLE . 91
    OR LIKE THE POETESS'S HEART OF LOVE, ... 216 A FOUNTAIN, A BOTTLE . 95
    HERE WERE ALL THOSE THE POETESS'S LIFE . . . . 217 A FOUNTAIN, A BOTTLE . 121
POETRY
    HE HAD BEEN AT HIS POETRY, COMPARING . . . . 278 THE WHITE-TAILED HORNET 45
    BEFORE NOW POETRY HAS TAKEN NOTICE . . . . 316 BUILD SOIL 28
    POETRY, ITSELF ONCE MORE, IS BACK IN LOVE. . . . . . . 318 BUILD SOIL 89
    THAT POETRY WITH ALL ITS GOLDEN RAGE . . . . 358 THE LOST FOLLOWER . 14
    A GOLDEN AGE OF POETRY AND POWER . . . . 424 FOR JOHN F. KENNEDY . 76
POETRY'S
    OF DESPERATION THAT WOULD WARRANT POETRY'S . . . . . . 317 BUILD SOIL 34
    THIS HAS BEEN POETRY'S GREAT ANTI-LURE. . . . . 358 THE LOST FOLLOWER . 20
    AND HIS BE POETRY'S OLD-FASHIONED PRAISE . . . . . . 422 FOR JOHN F. KENNEDY . 5
POETS
    NO WONDER POETS SOMETIMES HAVE TO SEEM . . . . 164 NEW HAMPSHIRE . . . 172
    SUCH AS EVEN POETS WOULD ADMIT PERFORCE . . . . 173 A STAR IN A STONEBOAT . 28
    IN MY OPINION--THOUGH WE BOTH KNOW POETS . . . . . . 321 BUILD SOIL 176
    WITH POETS WHO COULD CALMLY TAKE THE FATE . . . . . . 351 THE LESSON FOR TODAY . 11
    LUCRETIUS VERSUS THE LAKE POETS . . . . 393 LUCRETIUS VERSUS POETS T
    POETS KNOW A LOT. . . . . 429 KITTY HAWK 32
    FREEDOM IS SLAVERY SOME POETS TELL US. . . . . 460 HOW HARD TO KEEP FROM 190
    WE POETS OFFER YOU ANOTHER: STAR-CROSSED. . . . . . . 510 A MASQUE OF MERCY . . 439
POET-THINKER
    WHO IN HIS FAVORITE POSE AS POET-THINKER . . . . . . 511 A MASQUE OF MERCY . . 463
POGONIAS
    ROSE POGONIAS . . . . 13 ROSE POGONIAS . . . T
PCINT (SEE METAL-POINT, PIN-POINT)
    THE VANTAGE POINT . . . . 17 THE VANTAGE POINT . . T
    HAD BEAUTIES HE HAD TO POINT ME OUT AT LENGTH . . . . 187 THE AX-HELVE . . . 67
    BELOW THE POINT, AND WERE AT LAST DRIVEN WRINKLED . . . 258 WEST-RUNNING BROOK . 25
    IT MUST AT SOME POINT GRACEFULLY REFRAIN. . . . . . . 319 BUILD SOIL 116
    AT EVERY POINT AND FACET GLOWED . . . . 332 ALL REVELATION . . 14
    THE AGE WHEN FULL UPON YOU. THAT'S MY POINT. . . . . . 351 THE LESSON FOR TODAY . 30
    THAT UNDER ME A POINT OF ROCK . . . . 380 AN UNSTAMPED LETTER IN 19
    AT WHICH POINT WE ARE TOTALLY NONPLUSSED. . . . . . . 382 TO AN ANCIENT . . 12
    WITH THIRST ON HUNGER TO THE POINT OF LUST. . . . . . 411 POD OF THE MILKWEED . 26
    A TURNING POINT IN MODERN HISTORY. . . . . 422 FOR JOHN F. KENNEDY . 10
    AT A GOOD POINT FOR PLIANT PERMANENCE, ... 458 HOW HARD TO KEEP FROM 155
    THE POINT WAS IT WAS NONE OF MY CONCERN. . . . . . . 485 A MASQUE OF REASON . 335
    I COULD POINT OUT MY SORT OF PASSPORT IN IT. . . . . . 495 A MASQUE OF MERCY . 46
POINTED (SEE FEEBLE-POINTED, TWO-POINTED)
    THE MOUNTAIN STOOD THERE TO BE POINTED AT. . . . . . 41 THE MOUNTAIN . . . 28
    POINTED THE DECIMAL OFF WITH ONE DEEP THRUST. . . . . 119 MEETING AND PASSING . 9
    MESERVE WAS FIRST TO SPEAK. HE POINTED BACKWARD . . . 143 SNOW 6
    HE POINTED WITH HIS HAND FROM WHERE IT LAY . . . . . 147 SNOW 114
    POINTED OUR THOUGHTS THE WAY WE POINTED IT, ... 179 THE STAR-SPLITTER . 84

POINTED (CONTINUED)
  WEARING A THIN HEADDRESS OF POINTED LEAVES, ... 196 WILD GRAPES 21
  BUT STILL LIES POINTED AS IT PLOWED THE DUST. . . . . . 261 A SOLDIER 3
  IS LIKE THE PUPIL OF A POINTED GUN. . . . . 277 THE WHITE-TAILED HORNET 4
  HE POINTED ON UP THE ROAD . . . . 366 NOT OF SCHOOL AGE . 11
  THERE, POINTED LIKE THE PIP OF SPADES, ... 380 AN UNSTAMPED LETTER IN 8
POINTS
  OF A STARFISH LAID OUT WITH RIGID POINTS." . . . . . 93 THE SELF-SEEKER . . 20
  ARE BUT THE POINTS AT WHICH IT FINDS RELEASE. . . . . 255 THE FLOOD 11
  THE WAY IT RESTED TWO POINTS ON THE GROUND . . . . . 501 A MASQUE OF MERCY . 194
POISE
  CLEAR TO THE GROUND. HE ALWAYS KEPT HIS POISE . . . . 122 BIRCHES 35
  TO DISTURB THEIR PERFECT POISE THE LIVELONG DAY . . . 343 QUEST OF PURPLE-FRINGED 19
POISED
  IT COULDN'T STIR SO SENSITIVELY POISED . . . . . . 148 SNOW 138
  THE WEIGHT OF AN AX-HEAD POISED ALOFT, ... 276 TWO TRAMPS IN MUD TIME 45
  AND I HAD IDLY POISED MY PEN IN AIR . . . . 357 A CONSIDERABLE SPECK . 4
POISONED
  NO TRUE SOURCE CAN BE POISONED. / THEN THAT'S ALL. . . 514 A MASQUE OF MERCY . 543
POKING
  THE RED MAN GAVE IN POKING ABOUT THE MILL, ... 142 THE VANISHING RED . 15
POLE
  BETWEEN ME AND THE NORTH POLE-- . . . . . . 211 AN EMPTY THREAT . . 25
  NOT THOUGH WE HAVE TO SEIZE EARTH BY THE POLE . . . 238 ON A TREE FALLEN ACROSS 12
  AND ITS SUPPORTING CENTRAL CEDAR POLE, ... 332 THE SILKEN TENT . . 5
  AND THEN NO BIGGER THAN A FISHING POLE, ... 375 A YOUNG BIRCH . . 15
  THAT BRACED HIS FEET AGAINST THE ARCTIC POLE. . . . . 377 DIRECTIVE 17
  SCIENCE STUCK A POLE . . . . 468 A REFLEX 2
POLES
  TO WHIPS AND POLES. THERE'S NOBODY ABOUT. . . . . . 49 A HUNDRED COLLARS . 136
  OR ROOM WITHIN A ROOM, OF HICKORY POLES, ... 66 A SERVANT TO SERVANTS 114
  IT YET HAS POLES, AND ONLY NEEDS A SPIN . . . . . . 174 A STAR IN A STONEBOAT 50
POLICY
  "YOU SEEM TO SHAPE THE PAPER'S POLICY." . . . . . . 48 A HUNDRED COLLARS . 119
POLISH
  SHOULD TAKE THE POLISH OFF THE CRUST. . . . . . . 139 BROWN'S DESCENT . . 59
POLISHED
  THE POLISHED TRAFFIC PASSED WITH A MIND AHEAD, . . . 286 A ROADSIDE STAND . 7
POLITE
  'I'M SURE--I'M SURE'--AS POLITE AS COULD BE. . . . . 61 BLUEBERRIES . . . 75
  THEY WON'T BE TOO FRIENDLY--THEY MAY BE POLITE-- . . . 62 BLUEBERRIES . . . 100
  AND PAY A DEATH TAX OF FAIRLY POLITE REPENTANCE. . . . 307 NOT QUITE SOCIAL . 16
  (WITH A POLITE REGRET TO BE) . . . . 326 TO A THINKER . . 16
  IS HOW TO BE UNHAPPY YET POLITE. . . . . 353 THE LESSON FOR TODAY 88
  NO, NOR LESS POLITE. . . . . 431 KITTY HAWK . . . 116
  THIS IS POLITE SOCIETY YOU'RE IN, ... 488 A MASQUE OF REASON . 407
POLITELY
  YOU KNOW HOW POLITELY HE ALWAYS GOES BY. . . . . . 60 BLUEBERRIES . . . 42
POLITICAL
  A POLITICAL PASTORAL . . . . 316 BUILD SOIL . . . . S
  POLITICAL AMBITION HAS BEEN TAUGHT, ... 319 BUILD SOIL . . . 114
POLITICIAN
  AND POLITICIAN AT ODD SEASONS. . . . . 139 BROWN'S DESCENT . . 70
POLITICIANS
  FOR THE EMBOLDENED POLITICIANS DARING . . . . . . 424 FOR JOHN F. KENNEDY . 61
POLITICS
  IN POLITICS: I'M VERMONT DEMOCRAT-- . . . . 48 A HUNDRED COLLARS . 109
  RETIRED FROM POLITICS AND JOINED THE CHORUS. . . . . 168 NEW HAMPSHIRE . . 297
  TRUST HIM TO HAVE HIS BITTER POLITICS . . . . . . 290 OLD BARN AT THE BOTTOM 29
  TO TAKE A WRITING HAND IN POLITICS. . . . . 316 BUILD SOIL . . . 27
  OF WARS, AND WHAT ARE WARS BUT POLITICS . . . . . . 316 BUILD SOIL . . . 29
  OR POLITICS OF GHIBELLINE OR GUELPH, ... 359 THE LOST FOLLOWER . 30
  THE FREEDOM THEY SEEK IS BY POLITICS, ... 461 HOW HARD TO KEEP FROM 228
  BUT OUT OF POLITICS. SHE TOLD ME SO. . . . . . . 494 A MASQUE OF MERCY . 38
  WHERE HE WOULD HAVE TO QUIT HIS POLITICS . . . . . 509 A MASQUE OF MERCY . 402
POLLYANNA
  AND SHOT. IT'S POLLYANNA NOW OR DEATH. . . . . . . 168 NEW HAMPSHIRE . . 282
POMACE
  HER FACE IS FLECKED WITH POMACE AND SHE DROOLS . . . 124 THE COW IN APPLE TIME 4
POMEGRANATES
  THE STAR OF BETHLEHEM, THE POMEGRANATES, ... 473 A MASQUE OF REASON . 12
POND
  AND LOOKING FROM IT TO THE POND NEARBY, ... 194 PAUL'S WIFE . . . 96
  PAUL TAKING AFTER HER AROUND THE POND. . . . . . . 195 PAUL'S WIFE . . . 122
  IN EVERY PRINT OF A HOOF A POND. . . . . 276 TWO TRAMPS IN MUD TIME 36
PONDERED
  (THIS WAS MY DREAM) AND LOOKED AND PONDERED LONG, . . 16 A DREAM PANG . . . 4
  THESE THINGS THE MIND HAS PONDERED ON . . . . . . 332 ALL REVELATION . . 8
PONDEROUS
  THE PONDEROUS BEAST WENT DOWN . . . . 444 THE DRAFT HORSE . . 9
POOL
  NOW DROPS THAT FLOATED ON THE POOL . . . . 18 GOING FOR WATER . . 23
  FLECKED THE DARK STREAM AND FLECKED THE DARKER POOL . 258 WEST-RUNNING BROOK . 24
  OF WHAT IT IS BY CALLING IT A POOL . . . . 447 DOES NO ONE AT ALL EVER 41
POOLS
  THESE POOLS THAT, THOUGH IN FORESTS, STILL REFLECT . . 245 SPRING POOLS . . . 1
  SPRING POOLS . . . . 245 SPRING POOLS . . . T
POOR
  A HEARTFELT PRAYER FOR THE POOR OF GOD, ... 8 LOVE AND A QUESTION . 27
  SURELY YOU WOULDN'T GRUDGE THE POOR OLD MAN . . . . 36 DEATH OF THE HIRED MAN 49
  POOR SILAS, SO CONCERNED FOR OTHER FOLK, ... 37 DEATH OF THE HIRED MAN 99
  I ALMOST PROVOKED POOR LOREN TO MIRTH . . . . . . 61 BLUEBERRIES . . . 68
  "YOU POOR, DEAR, GREAT, GREAT, GREAT, GREAT GRANNY!" . . 77 THE GENERATIONS OF MEN 116
  AND THE WRETCH KNEW FROM THAT THAT WE WERE POOR. . . . 127 THE SMILE 5
  "SHE KNEW HE HAD, POOR THING, TWO HOURS AGO." . . . . 153 SNOW 278
  TO DRY, FROM POOR TO RICH, OR BACK AGAIN. . . . . . 166 NEW HAMPSHIRE . . 236
  LABAN WAS OLD AND POOR, YET SEEMED TO CARE; . . . . . 201 PLACE FOR A THIRD . 50
  AND SHE WAS OLD AND POOR--BUT SHE CARED, TOO. . . . . 201 PLACE FOR A THIRD . 51
  BEFORE SHE WENT THE POOR MAN'S WIDOW'S WAY, ... 201 PLACE FOR A THIRD . 61

POOR (CONTINUED)
 FROM THE WAY SHE HAD SET HER POOR OLD MOUTH, ... 201 PLACE FOR A THIRD . . 74
 THE POOR OLD MAN. IT WOULD HAVE BEEN ALL RIGHT . . . . . 209 PAUPER WITCH OF GRAFTON 53
 IS ALL THE SMOKE FROM ONE POOR HOUSE ALONE, ... 248 THE COCOON 5
 I'M A POOR UNDERDOG, ... 261 CANIS MAJOR 9
 MAN ACTS MORE LIKE THE POOR BEAR IN A CAGE, ... 269 THE BEAR 13
 SHALL BE IN THE END SCOURED POOR, ... 285 IN TIME OF CLOUDBURST . 11
 POOR EGOTIST, HE HAS NO WAY OF KNOWING . . . . 309 WASPISH 5
 POOR CASTAWAY OF COMMERCE, AND SO LIVE . . . . 323 BUILD SOIL 212
 BUT THIS POOR MICROSCOPIC ITEM NOW! . . . . 358 A CONSIDERABLE SPECK . 27
 AT LEAST TO LIVE UNGOLDEN WITH THE POOR, ... 358 THE LOST FOLLOWER . . 18
 SO THAT THE POOR WON'T HAVE TO STEAL BY STEALTH, ... 363 AN EQUALIZER 7
 HE GAVE HIS OWN POOR ILIAC A WRENCH . . . . 394 HAEC FABULA DOCET . . 13
 SOME POOR FOOL HAS BEEN SAYING IN HIS HEART . . . . . . 423 FOR JOHN F. KENNEDY . 49
 YOU MIGHT THINK TOO POOR- . . . . 428 KITTY HAWK 14
 HAD DONE OR NOT DONE TO OR FOR THE POOR. . . . . 477 A MASQUE OF REASON . . 122
 THE TEST IS ALWAYS HOW WE TREAT THE POOR. . . . . 477 A MASQUE OF REASON . . 123
 IT'S TIME THE POOR WERE TREATED BY THE STATE . . . . . 477 A MASQUE OF REASON . . 124
 JOB HADN'T DONE A THING, POOR INNOCENT. . . . . 478 A MASQUE OF REASON . . 127
 WE'RE POOR—THAT'S WHY. MY MAN CAN'T EARN A LIVING. . . . 496 A MASQUE OF MERCY . . 89
 AND GIVE YOU REST, POOR WANDERING JEW. / I'M NOT . . . . 498 A MASQUE OF MERCY . . 133
 YOU POOR, POOR SWALLOWABLE LITTLE MAN. . . . . 500 A MASQUE OF MERCY . . 190
 PAUL ALMOST HAD POOR KEEPER IN A CORNER . . . . 508 A MASQUE OF MERCY . . 401
 ALL DWARFED AND POOR." . . . . 512 A MASQUE OF MERCY . . 505
 HERE WE ALL FAIL TOGETHER, DWARFED AND POOR. . . . . . . 512 A MASQUE OF MERCY . . 506
 YOU POOR OLD SAPE, IF I MAY COIN THE SLANG. . . . . . . 518 A MASQUE OF MERCY . . 664
POORHOUSE
 WAS THE POORHOUSE, AND THOSE WHO COULD AFFORD, ... 65 A SERVANT TO SERVANTS . 94
 IN SOME WAY NOT SO REAL AS THE POORHOUSE. . . . . 478 A MASQUE OF REASON . . 125
 THAN BY THE FEAR OF THE ASYLUM, JAIL, OR POORHOUSE, . . . 520 A MASQUE OF MERCY . . 703
POOR-SPIRITED
 YOU MIGHT THINK TOO POOR-/SPIRITED TO CARE . . . . . 428 KITTY HAWK . . . 14/15
POPCORN
 AND THOUGH IN TINSEL CHAIN AND POPCORN ROPE . . . . . 350 TO A YOUNG WRETCH . . 19
POPLIN
 POPLIN, STILL CORNERS (SO CALLED NOT BECAUSE . . . . . 165 NEW HAMPSHIRE . . . 188
POPULACE
 OF THE POPULACE, ... 469 BUT OUTER SPACE... . 4
POPULAR
 TO TRY IF ONE MORE POPULAR ELECTION . . . . 358 THE LOST FOLLOWER . . 12
 STAYS MORE POPULAR . . . . 469 BUT OUTER SPACE... . 5
POPULAR-SCIENCE
 A DATED POPULAR-SCIENCE MEDLEY ON A MYSTERIOUS LIGHT... . 368 THE LITERATE FARMER AND S
POPULATION
 WHOLE TOWNSHIPS NAMED BUT WITHOUT POPULATION. . . . . . 165 NEW HAMPSHIRE . . . 209
POPULOUS
 THAN POPULOUS. . . . . 469 BUT OUTER SPACE... . 6
PORCH
 THE BRIDEGROOM CAME FORTH INTO THE PORCH . . . . 7 LOVE AND A QUESTION . 9
 AND SET THEM ON THE PORCH, THEN DREW HIM DOWN . . . . . 34 DEATH OF THE HIRED MAN 9
PORCH'S
 OUT IN THE PORCH'S SAGGING FLOOR . . . . 251 BEREFT 8
PORK
 HE DOTES ON SATURDAY PORK AND BEANS. . . . . 393 A CASE FOR JEFFERSON . 7
PORT
 CAME JUST THEN SAILING INTO PORT . . . . 417 AMERICA IS HARD TO SEE 21
PORTENTOUS
 NOTHING'S PORTENTOUS, I AM REASSURED. . . . . 318 BUILD SOIL 66
PORTENTS
 PORTENTS, PRESENTIMENTS, AND PREMONITIONS . . . . . . 428 KITTY HAWK 1P
PORTER'S
 "I SEE THE PORTER'S MADE YOUR BED," I TOLD HIM. . . . . 159 NEW HAMPSHIRE . . . 15
PORTHOLE'S
 BEHIND THE PORTHOLE'S SLAB OF GLASS . . . . 363 ASSURANCE 2
PORTRAIT
 UNDER A CRAYON PORTRAIT ON THE WALL, ... 55 THE BLACK COTTAGE . . 23
 (WHO SAT FOR STUART'S PORTRAIT, BUT WHO SAT . . . . . 317 BUILD SOIL 46
 "THE PORTRAIT OF THE SOUL OF MY GRANSIR IRA. . . . . . 366 OF STONES OF THE PLACE 15
POSE
 WHO IN HIS FAVORITE POSE AS POET-THINKER . . . . 511 A MASQUE OF MERCY . . 463
POSES
 (HIS WAS THE DOCTRINE OF THE SEVEN POSES) . . . . . . 511 A MASQUE OF MERCY . . 464
POSIES
 THE POSIES ON HER INNER WINDOWSILL, ... 215 A FOUNTAIN, A BOTTLE . 80
POSING
 DON'T YOU BE MADE FEEL SMALL BY ALL THIS POSING. . . . . 511 A MASQUE OF MERCY . . 461
POSITION
 I SAW THE STRANGE POSITION OF HIS HANDS-- . . . . . . 125 AN ENCOUNTER 16
 IT'D MAKE MY POSITION STRONGER, THINK, ... 208 PAUPER WITCH OF GRAFTON 42
 HOLDING THE CURVE OF ONE POSITION, ... 247 DEVOTION 3
 NOT IN POSITION TO LOOK TOO CLOSE. . . . . 248 A PASSING GLIMPSE . . 12
 AND TAKING FORMAL POSITION, ... 288 DEPARTMENTAL 35
 THEY'RE IN THE BEST POSITION OF US ALL . . . . 317 BUILD SOIL 55
 AND WHAT ON THIS IS YOUR DIVINE POSITION? . . . . 398 NO HOLY WARS FOR THEM . 10
 TO CONVEY MY RESPECT FOR YOUR POSITION?" . . . . 408 FROM PLANE TO PLANE . 135
 IN AN INQUISITIVE POSITION ODD . . . . 412 POD OF THE MILKWEED . 46
 WOULD BE IN A POSITION TO COMMAND IT. . . . . 475 A MASQUE OF REASON . . 57
POSSESS
 LET THOSE POSSESS THE LAND, AND ONLY THOSE, ... 322 BUILD SOIL 187
 TO USE THE GIFT YOU DO POSSESS, ... 326 TO A THINKER 27
POSSESSED
 SOMETIMES HE GETS POSSESSED TO KEEP ACCOUNTS . . . . . 86 THE HOUSEKEEPER . . . 158
 POSSESSED BY WHAT WE NOW NO MORE POSSESSED. . . . . . . 348 THE GIFT OUTRIGHT . . 7
 LIKE ONE POSSESSED, ... 360 THE RABBIT-HUNTER . . 9
 POSSESSED BY WHAT WE NOW NO MORE POSSESSED. . . . . . . 424 THE GIFT OUTRIGHT . . 7
POSSESSES
 AND SIMPLY STAYING POSSESSES ALL . . . . 120 BOND AND FREE . . . 18
POSSESSING
 POSSESSING WHAT WE STILL WERE UNPOSSESSED BY, ... 348 THE GIFT OUTRIGHT . . 6

POSSESSING (CONTINUED)
    POSSESSING WHAT WE STILL WERE UNPOSSESSED BY, ... 424 THE GIFT OUTRIGHT . . 6
POSSESSION
    AS I WALKED ONCE AROUND IT IN POSSESSION. . . . . 130 THE BONFIRE 39
    IN SOMEONE'S POSSESSION . . . . 433 KITTY HAWK 156
POSSESSOR
    PAUL WAS WHAT'S CALLED A TERRIBLE POSSESSOR. . . . . . 195 PAUL'S WIFE 150
POSSIBILITIES
    MEN FUMBLE AT THE POSSIBILITIES. . . . . 483 A MASQUE OF REASON . . 275
POSSIBILITY
    ANOTHER POSSIBILITY I THOUGHT OF-- . . . . 502 A MASQUE OF MERCY . . 235
    ANOTHER POSSIBILITY I THOUGHT OF---- . . . . 503 A MASQUE OF MERCY . . 263
POSSIBLE
    "THERE'S ONLY ONE THING POSSIBLE TO MAKE, ... 155 SNOW 322
    'TIS POSSIBLE YOU MAY HAVE SEEN, ... 381 AN UNSTAMPED LETTER IN 40
    THE ONLY MEANING POSSIBLE FOR NATURE . . . . 393 LUCRETIUS VERSUS POETS 8
    IF SUCH A THING IS POSSIBLE WITH MONEY. . . . . . . 459 HOW HARD TO KEEP FROM 176
POSSIBLY
    I DON'T SEE." / "POSSIBLY NOT FOR HERSELF. . . . . . 155 SNOW 335
    AND POSSIBLY MY NOT WRITING IT SHOULD STOP ME . . . . 461 HOW HARD TO KEEP FROM 224
    POSSIBLY JUST WELL-BEING IN THE BODY, ... 461 HOW HARD TO KEEP FROM 243
POSSUM
    WINTER WAS ONLY PLAYING POSSUM. . . . . 276 TWO TRAMPS IN MUD TIME 30
POST (SEE EX-POST-FACTO)
    SO THEY COULD RECOGNIZE THEM. NOT A POST . . . . . 209 PAUPER WITCH OF GRAFTON 56
    AND THE FENCE POST CARRIED A STRAND OF WIRE. . . . . 242 NEED OF BEING VERSED . 20
    THAT ONCE BETWEEN POST AND POST . . . . 312 THE VINDICTIVES . . . 65
POSTERITY
    WAS LEAVE AS THEIR POSTERITY ONE POD . . . . . . 412 POD OF THE MILKWEED . 43
POSTHUMOUS
    AND SUCH SMALL POSTHUMOUS RENOWN . . . . . . 418 AMERICA IS HARD TO SEE 45
POSTPONE
    THAT MIGHT BE CALCULATED TO POSTPONE . . . . . . 190 THE GRINDSTONE . . . 63
POSTS
    IF SOMEONE HADN'T SAID TO GNAW THE POSTS . . . . 209 PAUPER WITCH OF GRAFTON 54
    THEY FOUND HE'D GNAWED THE FOUR POSTS OF HIS BED, . . 209 PAUPER WITCH OF GRAFTON 62
    NOT THAT HE HADN'T GNAWED THE HITCHING POSTS . . . 209 PAUPER WITCH OF GRAFTON 64
    HE DON'T GNAW TREES AND POSTS AND FENCES TOO. . . . 209 PAUPER WITCH OF GRAFTON 67
    BETTER A MONTH FROM NOW WHEN CUTTING POSTS . . . 325 BUILD SOIL 287
POSTSCRIPT
    POSTSCRIPT . . . . 463 LINES IN DEJECTION . . 1P
POSTURE
    IN EVERY LIFELIKE POSTURE OF THE SWARM, ... 237 A HILLSIDE THAW . . . 27
POT
    ACROSS THE LANDSCAPE WITH A WATERING POT . . . . . . 354 THE LESSON FOR TODAY . 129
    FROM SOME EXTINCT OLD CHIMNEY POT. . . . . 452 A-WISHING WELL . . . 36
POTATO
    I'M MELIBOEUS THE POTATO MAN, ... 316 BUILD SOIL . . . 2
    I'M DONE FOREVER WITH POTATO CROPS . . . . 316 BUILD SOIL . . . 11
POTATOES
    A HILL EACH OF POTATOES, ... 134 A GIRL'S GARDEN . . . 29
    AMONG UNEARTHED POTATOES STANDING STILL, ... 263 THE INVESTMENT . . . 6
    I DIDN'T MY POTATOES. I CONSUMED THEM. . . . . . . 316 BUILD SOIL . . . 15
POTS
    (TO KEEP THE POTS OF GOLD FROM BEING FOUND), ... 315 IRIS BY NIGHT . . . 25
POUNCE
    AND WOULD POUNCE TO END IT ALL . . . . 340 THE SUBVERTED FLOWER . 39
POUNCED
    I WATCHED HIM WHERE HE SWOOPED, HE POUNCED, HE STRUCK; . 278 THE WHITE-TAILED HORNET 33
POUND
    WHATEVER THEY COST APIECE OR A POUND, ... 232 THE KITCHEN CHIMNEY . 6
    I KNOW WOOL'S DOWN TO SEVEN CENTS A POUND. . . . . . 316 BUILD SOIL 13
POUNDED
    OF THE ATLANTIC POUNDED. . . . . 432 KITTY HAWK 138
POUNDING
    I'VE HEARD HIM POUNDING IN THE BARN ALL NIGHT. . . . . 71 THE CODE 42
POUR
    MUST FIND WHERE TO POUR ITSELF INTO AND EMPTY? . . . . 379 TOO ANXIOUS FOR RIVERS 4
    WE WOULD POUR OIL ON THE INGLE . . . . 384 IN THE LONG NIGHT . . 5
    TO POUR FRESH RIVERS ON YOU FROM THE LAND, ... 446 DOES NO ONE AT ALL EVER 23
POURED
    ITS LIGHT POURED SOFTLY IN HER LAP. SHE SAW IT . . . . 38 DEATH OF THE HIRED MAN 105
    POURED ON THEM BY HIS PRAYERS PRAYED IN VAIN. . . . . 173 A STAR IN A STONEBOAT . 24
    AND POURED ON WATER (TEARS IT MIGHT HAVE BEEN); . . . 189 THE GRINDSTONE . . . 27
    AMONG THE BUTTONS POURED OUT IN HER LAP. . . . . . 207 THE WITCH OF COOS . . 153
POURING
    AND LANDED POURING LIKE A WATERFALL. . . . . . . 338 THE MOST OF IT . . . 18
    THAT GO BLINDLY POURING PAST. . . . . 469 FOUR-ROOM SHACK... . 4
POURS
    OR HIGHWAY WHERE THE SLOW WHEEL POURS THE SAND. . . . 5 INTO MY OWN 8
    AND POURS THE ELM-TREE MEADOW FULL OF BLUE, ... 248 THE COCOON 4
POWDER
    AND SETTING OFF THEIR HEAVY POWDER LOAD. . . . . . 239 OUR SINGING STRENGTH . 29
    DASH IT WITH SOME SNOW FOR POWDER. . . . . 304 CLEAR AND COLDER . . 15
POWER
    SUCH PIPES KEPT LESS OF POWER TO STIR . . . . . . 24 PAN WITH US 22
    IF SUCH UNLIFELIKE LINES KEPT POWER TO STIR . . . . . 56 THE BLACK COTTAGE . . 29
    BY ITS OWN POWER SEEMS TO BE UNDONE, ... 125 AN ENCOUNTER 3
    BUT POWER OF BLOOD ITSELF RELEASES BLOOD. . . . . . 254 THE FLOOD 6
    THE NEXT MACHINE THAT HAS THE POWER TO PASS . . . . . 270 THE EGG AND THE MACHINE 29
    AND HAVING POWER TO CHANGE HIS AIM IN FLIGHT, ... 277 THE WHITE-TAILED HORNET 5
    THAT THE PARTY IN POWER IS SAID TO BE KEEPING FROM US. . 286 A ROADSIDE STAND . . 22
    THAT YOU MAY HAVE THE POWER OF STANDING STILL-- . . . 300 THE MASTER SPEED . . 8
    "IT IS THIS THAT HAD THE POWER." . . . . 339 THE SUBVERTED FLOWER . 2
    AND YET HE IS A POWER OF LIGHT . . . . 390 TWO LEADING LIGHTS . . 7
    THAT BY BROOK POWER IN THE GARDEN . . . . 397 AN IMPORTER 19
    OF A POWER LEADING FROM ITS STRENGTH AND PRIDE, . . . 424 FOR JOHN F. KENNEDY . 72
    A GOLDEN AGE OF POETRY AND POWER . . . . 424 FOR JOHN F. KENNEDY . 76

POWER (CONTINUED)
    ALL WEALTH AND POWER IN TOO FEW HANDS? . . . . 509 A MASQUE OF MERCY . . 411
POWERFULLY
    AS A GREAT BUCK IT POWERFULLY APPEARED, ... 338 THE MOST OF IT . . . 16
POWERS
    LET THEM THINK TWICE BEFORE THEY USE THEIR POWERS . . . . 245 SPRING POOLS 9
    IS THE REASON THE POWERS PROVIDE . . . . 348 TRIPLE BRONZE . . . 2
    DON'T DISCOUNT OUR POWERS; . . . . 439 KITTY HAWK 361
PRACTICAL
    MORE PRACTICAL THAN PEGASUS THE HORSE . . . . 173 A STAR IN A STONEBOAT . 29
PRACTICALLY
    MAN'S PRACTICALLY INEXTERMINATE. . . . . 453 A-WISHING WELL . . . 77
PRACTICE
    LEAST IN DEMOCRACY. IN PRACTICE, PURE, ... 318 BUILD SOIL 76
    THANK GOD OUR PRACTICE HOLDS THE LOVES APART, ... 318 BUILD SOIL 81
PRAISE
    AND THEY ARE BETTER FOR HER PRAISE. . . . . 7 MY NOVEMBER GUEST . . 20
    THE WAYS YOU FOUND TO SAY THE PRAISE OF COMFORT . . . 150 SNOW 199
    EITHER TO PRAISE HER OR SO MUCH AS NAME HER, ... 196 PAUL'S WIFE . . . 153
    TO CARRY PRAISE OR BLAME TOO FAR, ... 403 SOMETHING LIKE A STAR . 23
    AND HIS BE POETRY'S OLD-FASHIONED PRAISE . . . . . 422 FOR JOHN F. KENNEDY . 5
PRANKS
    THE SPIRIT PLAYS US STRANGE RELIGIOUS PRANKS . . . . 358 THE LOST FOLLOWER . . 5
PRATE
    AND NONE WAS LEFT TO PRATE . . . . 298 ON TAKING FROM THE TOP 17
PRATTLE
    I AM BROUGHT GUARANTEED YOUNG PRATTLE POEMS . . . . . 324 BUILD SOIL 273
PRAY
    WHERE WOMEN PRAY WITH PRIESTS. THERE IS NO LOVE. . . . 318 BUILD SOIL 84
    AND NOW PRAY TELL WHAT LURED YOU WITH FALSE HOPE . . . 356 A MOTH SEEN IN WINTER . 7
    PRAY TELL ME WHAT DOES THAT MEAN? ANYTHING? . . . . 484 A MASQUE OF REASON . . 304
    LET THE LOST MILLIONS PRAY IT IN THE DARK! . . . . 521 A MASQUE OF MERCY . . 726
PRAYED
    POURED ON THEM BY HIS PRAYERS PRAYED IN VAIN. . . . . 173 A STAR IN A STONEBOAT . 24
PRAYER
    A HEARTFELT PRAYER FOR THE POOR OF GOD, ... 8 LOVE AND A QUESTION . 27
    A PRAYER IN SPRING . . . . 12 A PRAYER IN SPRING . . T
    WE RAISED A SIMPLE PRAYER . . . . 14 ROSE POGONIAS . . . 17
    IN PRAYER TO THE DOOR. . . . . 241 THE LOCKLESS DOOR . . 8
    THAT WAITS ALL DAY IN ALMOST OPEN PRAYER . . . . . 287 A ROADSIDE STAND . . 35
    I SAID TO MYSELF ALMOST IN PRAYER, ... 306 A TRIAL RUN 1
    WAS A PRAYER MACHINE FROM TIBET . . . . 397 AN IMPORTER . . . 18
    SHE'D LIKE TO KNOW HOW YOU WOULD TAKE A PRAYER . . . 479 A MASQUE OF REASON . . 180
    FOR THE REVISION OF THE BOOK OF PRAYER . . . . . . 486 A MASQUE OF REASON . . 371
    AND THAT THEY MAY BE IS THE ONLY PRAYER . . . . . 520 A MASQUE OF MERCY . . 723
PRAYERS
    KIT MARLOWE TAUGHT ME HOW TO SAY MY PRAYERS: . . . . 166 NEW HAMPSHIRE . . . 242
    POURED ON THEM BY HIS PRAYERS PRAYED IN VAIN. . . . . 173 A STAR IN A STONEBOAT . 24
    SAVE THEM TO SAY YOUR PRAYERS ON.--WHAT'S THE MATTER? . 519 A MASQUE OF MERCY . 682
PRAYING
    WORTH PRAYING. MAY MY SACRIFICE . . . . 520 A MASQUE OF MERCY . 724
PREACH
    WHY CAN'T HE STAY AT HOME?" / "HE HAD TO PREACH." . . 145 SNOW 69
    LET ME PREACH TO YOU, WILL YOU, MELIBOEUS? . . . . 322 BUILD SOIL . . . 182
    PREACH ON. I THOUGHT YOU WERE ALREADY PREACHING. . . 322 BUILD SOIL . . . 183
    BUT PREACH AND SEE IF I CAN TELL THE DIFFERENCE. . . 322 BUILD SOIL . . . 184
PREACHED
    SOME HAVE PREACHED AND TAUGHT . . . . 438 KITTY HAWK . . . 321
    IS THIS THE LOVE OF GOD YOU PREACHED TO ME? . . . . 505 A MASQUE OF MERCY . 306
PREACHES
    A THOUSAND TIMES. IF THAT'S THE WAY HE PREACHES! . . 152 SNOW 254
PREACHING
    PREACH ON. I THOUGHT YOU WERE ALREADY PREACHING. . . 322 BUILD SOIL . . . 183
    IF WHAT YOU'RE PREACHING IS A LINE OF CONDUCT, . . . 322 BUILD SOIL . . . 204
    DON'T WEAR YOUR PANTS OUT PREACHING ON YOUR KNEES. . 519 A MASQUE OF MERCY . 681
PRECAUTION
    PRECAUTION . . . . 308 PRECAUTION . . . . T
PRECEDENT
    YET ALL THE PRECEDENT IS ON MY SIDE: . . . . . . 226 THE ONSET 12
PRECIOUS
    A STATE PRODUCING PRECIOUS METALS, STONES, ... 164 NEW HAMPSHIRE . . . 165
    THE PRECIOUS LITERATURE IN QUANTITY . . . . . . 164 NEW HAMPSHIRE . . . 167
    AND NOW WERE ONLY WASTING PRECIOUS BLADE. . . . . 190 THE GRINDSTONE . . . 67
    TO PECK HERSELF A PRECIOUS STONE. . . . . . . 281 BLUE RIBBON AT AMESBURY 42
    IN CHESTNUT NOW BECOME A PRECIOUS WOOD . . . . . 290 OLD BARN AT THE BOTTOM 38
    BUT NOT TO TAKE AWAY THE PRECIOUS DARK. . . . . 370 THE LITERATE FARMER AND 79
    LEST HAVING WASTED PRECIOUS HEAT . . . . . . 381 AN UNSTAMPED LETTER IN 23
PRECIPICE
    AND THERE IN A PRECIPICE VALLEY . . . . 313 BEARER OF EVIL TIDINGS 13
PRECIPITATE
    PRECIPITATE IN LOVE, ... 28 MY BUTTERFLY 15
PRECIPITATED
    PRECIPITATED FROM THE DESERT AIR.-- . . . . . . 487 A MASQUE OF REASON . 385
PRECIPITATELY
    PRECIPITATELY THEY RETIRED BACK-CAGE . . . . . . 293 AT WOODWARD'S GARDENS . 24
PRECISE
    A MILLION YEARS TO BE PRECISE-- . . . . 326 A MISSIVE MISSILE . . 5
PREDESTINED
    OR IF PREDESTINED TO DIE LATE, ... 307 PROVIDE, PROVIDE . . 8
PREDICT
    SOME DAY OUR NAVY, I PREDICT, ... 418 AMERICA IS HARD TO SEE 55
PREDICTED
    PREDICTED ANYTHING THAT CAME TO PASS. . . . . . 476 A MASQUE OF REASON . 96
PREFABRICATED
    (THE THRONE'S A PLYWOOD FLAT, PREFABRICATED, . . . 474 A MASQUE OF REASON . 21
PREFER
    I SHOULD PREFER TO HAVE SOME BOY BEND THEM . . . . 121 BIRCHES 23
    HE MIGHT PREFER TO SAY TO HIM DISARMED. . . . . 185 THE AX-HELVE . . . 17

PREFER (CONTINUED)
    ONLY I HAPPEN TO PREFER TO LIVE . . . . 208 PAUPER WITCH OF GRAFTON   31
    ALL WE WHO PREFER TO LIVE . . . . 282 A DRUMLIN WOODCHUCK . 13
    I PREFER TO SING SAFELY IN THE REALM . . . . 317 BUILD SOIL 48
    (AND YOU'VE GOT TO), WHICH WILL YOU PREFER . . . . . 510 A MASQUE OF MERCY . . 437
PREFERENCE
    PASSIONATE PREFERENCE SUCH AS LOVE AT SIGHT. . . . . 425 ACCIDENTALLY ON PURPOSE   24
PREFERRED (SEE DOG-PREFERRED)
    NO DOUBT SHE WOULD HAVE PREFERRED THE FORK. . . . . 463 LINES IN DEJECTION . . 21
PREFERRING
    AND PREFERRING THE OUT- TO THE INDOOR NIGHT, ... 127 HOUSE FEAR 8
PREJUDICE
    (OH, IT WAS WITHOUT PREJUDICE TO ME!) . . . . 119 MEETING AND PASSING . 12
PREJUDICED
    THE STATE ASYLUM. I WAS PREJUDICED; . . . . 65 A SERVANT TO SERVANTS . 91
PRELIMINARY
    I GAVE IT THE PRELIMINARY SPIN, ... 189 THE GRINDSTONE . . . 26
    IT WAS WELL WORTH PRELIMINARY MENTION. . . . . 352 THE LESSON FOR TODAY . 59
    IT WAS WELL WORTH PRELIMINARY MENTION. . . . . 352 THE LESSON FOR TODAY . 63
    (WITH SOME PRELIMINARY HISTORY IN RHYME) . . . . . . 422 FOR JOHN F. KENNEDY . 5
PREMISES
    AND ASK US IF OUR PREMISES ARE RIGHT." . . . . 370 THE LITERATE FARMER AND 83
    FALSE PREMISES THAT ARE THE ORIGINAL . . . . 480 A MASQUE OF REASON . . 204
    THE BEST MINDS ARE THE BEST AT PREMISES. . . . . . . 510 A MASQUE OF MERCY . . 434
PREMONITIONS
    PORTENTS, PRESENTIMENTS, AND PREMONITIONS . . . . . 428 KITTY HAWK 1P
PREOCCUPATION
    AND MORE PREOCCUPATION WITH THE SPORT. . . . . 424 FOR JOHN F. KENNEDY . 69
PREOCCUPIED
    PREOCCUPIED WITH FORMIDABLE MAIL, ... 44 A HUNDRED COLLARS . . 9
PREPARE
    IT WILL GATHER SPEED TILL YOUR NERVES PREPARE . . . 306 A TRIAL RUN 6
    HE GOT HIS FIRST CHANCE TO PREPARE A MEAL . . . . . 455 HOW HARD TO KEEP FROM 55
PREPARED
    SOMEONE HAD BETTER BE PREPARED FOR RAGE. . . . . . . 250 ONCE BY THE PACIFIC . 12
    THAT'S SOMETHING I'M PREPARED TO FACE. . . . . 453 A-WISHING WELL . . . 71
    I'M NOT PREPARED FOR OR THAT JOB HIMSELF . . . . . . 488 A MASQUE OF REASON . . 414
    I'M ALL TURNED ROUND. / THERE IS YOUR WAY PREPARED. . 514 A MASQUE OF MERCY . . 547
PREPENSE
    LIKE MALICE PREPENSE. . . . . 450 OBJECTION TO BE STEPPED 11
PRE-PRIMITIVES
    PRE-PRIMITIVES OF THE WHITE RACE, DAWN PEOPLE, . . . 161 NEW HAMPSHIRE . . . 78
PRESAGE
    IT MAKES THE PROPHET IN US ALL PRESAGE . . . . 424 FOR JOHN F. KENNEDY . 70
PRESCRIBE
    LET'S HOLLER AND ASK HIM IF HE WON'T PRESCRIBE . . . 405 FROM PLANE TO PLANE . 29
PRESCRIPTION
    SOMEHOW THE CHANGE WORE OUT LIKE A PRESCRIPTION. . . 67 A SERVANT TO SERVANTS . 154
PRESENCE
    BUT ONLY FELT AT NIGHT ITS SHADOWY PRESENCE. . . . . 41 THE MOUNTAIN 22
    WAS LED INTO THE PRESENCE OF THE TREE . . . . 283 THE GOLD HESPERIDEE . 14
    MUST LEAVE THEM UNLOCKED TO BETRAY HIS PRESENCE. . . 289 OLD BARN AT THE BOTTOM 15
    FOR MY MIND TO KEEP WORKING IN YOUR PRESENCE. . . . 325 BUILD SOIL 285
    BUT PRESENCE OF LOVE THESE HAD IN DEATH . . . . . . 346 DISCOVERY OF MADEIRAS . 80
    HIS PRESENCE WAS PARTICULARLY THERE. . . . . 407 FROM PLANE TO PLANE . 92
    LADY, AT SUCH A TIME, AND IN THE PRESENCE!-- . . . . 519 A MASQUE OF MERCY . . 684
PRESENT
    THERE WERE FOUR CANDLES AND FOUR PEOPLE PRESENT. . . 163 NEW HAMPSHIRE . . . 128
    AT PRESENT I AM LIVING IN VERMONT. . . . . 172 NEW HAMPSHIRE . . . 413
    TO MAKE A PRESENT OF ME TO EACH OTHER. . . . . 207 PAUPER WITCH OF GRAFTON   5
    TO EXACT FOR A PRESENT GAIN . . . . 285 IN TIME OF CLOUDBURST .   7
    AT PRESENT FROM A COSMICAL DILATION . . . . 320 BUILD SOIL 138
    BUT BID LIFE SEIZE THE PRESENT? . . . . 335 CARPE DIEM 19
    IT LIVES LESS IN THE PRESENT . . . . 336 CARPE DIEM 20
    THAN IN THE PAST. THE PRESENT . . . . 336 CARPE DIEM 23
    TOO PRESENT TO IMAGINE. . . . . 336 CARPE DIEM 26
    THE PRESENT AGE OR YOUR AGE. YOU AND I . . . . 352 THE LESSON FOR TODAY . 49
    AT THE PRESENT RATE IT MUST COME TO PASS, ... 375 SOMETHING FOR HOPE . .   1
    IT IS THE FUTURE THAT CREATES HIS PRESENT. . . . . . 421 ESCAPIST--NEVER . . . 11
PRESENTED
    ON THE END IT PRESENTED TO THE ROAD. . . . . 181 MAPLE 58
    ON THE SIDE IT PRESENTED TO THE ROAD) . . . . 182 MAPLE 99
    THROUGH EVERYTHING PRESENTED, LAND AND TIDE . . . . 267 RIDERS   3
PRESENTIMENTS
    PORTENTS, PRESENTIMENTS, AND PREMONITIONS . . . . . 428 KITTY HAWK 1P
PRESENTLY
    AND PRESENTLY ON THE SCENE . . . . 288 DEPARTMENTAL 33
PRESENTS
    THE BACK SOME FARM PRESENTS US; AND YOUR WOODS . . . 114 IN THE HOME STRETCH . 114
    EVER PRESENTS ITSELF BEFORE US TWICE. . . . . 147 SNOW 130
    WHEN HEAVEN PRESENTS IN SHEETS THE SOLID HUE? . . . 220 FRAGMENTARY BLUE . . .   4
PRESIDENT
    SHE HAD ONE PRESIDENT. (PRONOUNCE HIM PURSE, ... 161 NEW HAMPSHIRE 64
PRESIDENTS
    AND FORTY-FIVE PRESIDENTS. . . . . 368 A SERIOUS STEP LIGHTLY 24
PRESS
    NOR IS THERE WANTING IN THE PRESS . . . . 20 THE TRIAL BY EXISTENCE 41
    SHE MUST NOT KEEP HIM WAITING. TIME WOULD PRESS . . 201 PLACE FOR A THIRD . . 68
    THE WRITER AND TALKER FREE SPEECH AND FREE PRESS. . 319 BUILD SOIL 113
    THAT OUGHT TO MAKE THE SUNDAY PRESS. . . . . 451 A-WISHING WELL . . . 19
    AND PRESS YOUR FATHER INTO BEING KING." . . . . . . 460 HOW HARD TO KEEP FROM 206
PRESSED
    WE PRESSED OUR FACES TO THE PANE. "YOU SEE," HE SAID, . 55 THE BLACK COTTAGE . . 14
    PRESSED INTO SERVICE MEANS PRESSED OUT OF SHAPE. . . 98 THE SELF-SEEKER . . 149
    OF THE TWO PAGES IT WAS PRESSED BETWEEN, ... 181 MAPLE 65
    WHERE THE LOG DRIVE LAY PRESSED AGAINST THE BOOM, . 194 PAUL'S WIFE 107
    NEXT TIME YOU FIND YOURSELF PRESSED ONTO ONE . . . . 486 A MASQUE OF REASON . . 370

PRESSURE
    IT KEEPS THE PRESSURE OF A LADDER-ROUND. . . . . 68 AFTER APPLE-PICKING . 22
    HIS FIRST THOUGHT UNDER PRESSURE WAS A GRAVE . . . . . 200 PLACE FOR A THIRD . 22
    ITS AIRY PRESSURE TURNED TO WATER WEIGHT. . . . . 315 IRIS BY NIGHT . . . 16
PRESTO
    AND PRESTO, THEY'RE UP ALL AROUND YOU AS THICK . . . . . 59 BLUEBERRIES 20
PRESUME
    CONTENT WITH BUD-INSPECTING. THEY PRESUME . . . . . . 254 A WINTER EDEN . . . 15
    (NO ONE, I PRESUME, ... 436 KITTY HAWK 266
    I WON'T PRESUME TO TELL BEL WHERE TO GO. . . . . 519 A MASQUE OF MERCY . 685
PRESUMED
    HAD THE BOY NOT PRESUMED TOO CLOSE AND LONG. . . . . . 293 AT WOODWARD'S GARDENS . 21
    WHEN ANY BUT MYSELF PRESUMED TO SAY . . . . 443 AUSPEX 11
PRESUMING
    A BOY, PRESUMING ON HIS INTELLECT, ... 293 AT WOODWARD'S GARDENS . 1
    PRESUMING ON HER FEMININITY. . . . . 390 TWO LEADING LIGHTS . . 28
    (THINK OF PRESUMING TO CALL HIM GUS), ... 421 ONE MORE BREVITY . . 59
PRETEND
    I'M NO MATCH--NO, AND DON'T PRETEND TO BE----" . . . 100 THE SELF-SEEKER . . 217
    AND, IF YOU ASKED ME, EVEN HELP PRETEND . . . . . . 109 THE EXPOSED NEST . . 7
    I CAN'T PRETEND TO TELL THE WAY IT'S DONE. . . . . . 237 A HILLSIDE THAW . . 5
    WE DON'T PRETEND TO COMPLETE OCCUPANCY. . . . . . . 322 BUILD SOIL . . . 193
    BUT FOR THE FOLLY OF IT, LET'S PRETEND . . . . . . 352 THE LESSON FOR TODAY . 44
    LET US PRETEND THE DEWDROPS FROM THE EAVES . . . . . 415 A CABIN IN THE CLEARING 37
    I'M NOT A SPORT AND DON'T PRETEND I AM ONE.-- . . . 496 A MASQUE OF MERCY . . 79
PRETENDED
    A RULER WHO PRETENDED NOT TO LOVE . . . . 423 FOR JOHN F. KENNEDY . 44
PRETENDS
    AS ONE WHO SHREWDLY PRETENDS . . . . 282 A DRUMLIN WOODCHUCK . 11
PRETENSE
    AND CHECKED MY STEPS TO MAKE PRETENSE . . . . 25 THE DEMIURGE'S LAUGH . 15
    FRIENDS MAKE PRETENSE OF FOLLOWING TO THE GRAVE, . . . 54 HOME BURIAL . . . 102
    MYSELF AS ONE HIS OWN PRETENSE DECEIVES; . . . . . . 233 A BOUNDLESS MOMENT . 10
    LONG SINCE GAVE UP PRETENSE OF KEEPING COVERED. . . . 377 DIRECTIVE . . . 12
    THE CHANCES ARE WHEN THERE'S SO MUCH PRETENSE . . . 483 A MASQUE OF REASON . 277
PRETENSION
    WE MAKE NO PRETENSION . . . . 440 KITTY HAWK 378
PRETTY
    "PRETTY," HE SAID. "COME IN. NO ONE WILL CARE." . . 55 THE BLACK COTTAGE . . 11
    I SEE IT'S A FAIR, PRETTY SHEET OF WATER. . . . . . 63 A SERVANT TO SERVANTS . 17
    I SEE IT'S A FAIR, PRETTY SHEET OF WATER, ... 63 A SERVANT TO SERVANTS . 32
    YOU SEE OUR PRETTY THINGS ARE ALL OUTDOORS. . . . . 85 THE HOUSEKEEPER . . . 110
    UNLESS I DO?" / " A PRETTY INTERLUDE," . . . . . . 99 THE SELF-SEEKER . . 180
    'HEY, THAT'S A PRETTY THOUGHT'--THOSE WERE HIS WORDS-- . 149 SNOW 181
    BACK ON THE FLOOR, IS FACT OR PRETTY NEAR FACT. . . . 192 PAUL'S WIFE . . . 53
    BY THAT TIME I WAS PRETTY WELL REDUCED . . . . . . 198 WILD GRAPES . . . 60
    I KNEW PRETTY WELL WHY HE DROPPED BEHIND . . . . . 275 TWO TRAMPS IN MUD TIME 5
    I KNEW PRETTY WELL WHAT HE HAD IN MIND: . . . . . 275 TWO TRAMPS IN MUD TIME 7
    IN FARMING WELL--OR PRETTY WELL. . . . . 381 AN UNSTAMPED LETTER IN 49
    IT BIDS PRETTY FAIR . . . . 392 IT BIDS PRETTY FAIR . T
    IN LANDOR'S QUATRAIN WOULD BE PRETTY SCENERY. . . . 393 LUCRETIUS VERSUS POETS 9
    ISN'T IT PRETTY MUCH THE SAME IDEA? . . . . 405 FROM PLANE TO PLANE . 44
    HE WILL BE STARTING PRETTY LATE. . . . . 419 AMERICA IS HARD TO SEE 79
    THAT'S THE PRETTY KETTLE! . . . . 442 KITTY HAWK 447
    THEY ARE THINKING OF PRETTY SOON . . . . 466 SOME SCIENCE FICTION . 23
    HE TOO IS PRETTY CIRCUMAMBIENT. . . . . 487 A MASQUE OF REASON . 383
    GOOD, PRETTY GOOD. / WAIT TILL I GET MY KODAK.-- . . 488 A MASQUE OF REASON . 402
    AND FIGURATIVE USE HAVE PRETTY WELL . . . . 488 A MASQUE OF REASON . 425
    ALL OF US GET EACH OTHER PRETTY WRONG. . . . . . . 518 A MASQUE OF MERCY . 655
PREVAIL
    PREVENTING SHADOW UNTIL THE MOON PREVAIL; . . . . . 14 WAITING 10
    IT WERE THE FORCE THAT WOULD AT LAST PREVAIL. . . . 57 THE BLACK COTTAGE . . 83
PREVAILED
    PERCHANCE HE HALF PREVAILED . . . . 11 WIND AND WINDOW FLOWER 21
PREVENT
    I CROUCH DOWN TO PREVENT THEM AS THEY FALL; . . . . 267 THE ARMFUL 9
PREVENTING
    PREVENTING SHADOW UNTIL THE MOON PREVAIL; . . . . . 14 WAITING 10
PREY
    WHILE GREEDY GOOD-DOERS, BENEFICENT BEASTS OF PREY, . . 287 A ROADSIDE STAND . . 27
    HAD MADE IT MUCH MORE EASILY A PREY. . . . . . . 303 A BIRD SINGING IN SLEEP 14
PRICE
    HAVE YOU AGREED TO ANY PRICE?" / "FIVE HUNDRED. . . 94 THE SELF-SEEKER . . 58
    AND SELL HIM INTO SLAVERY? MY PRICE . . . . . . 454 HOW HARD TO KEEP FROM 33
    AND THE SLAVE SAID, "THE SMALL ONE'S WORTH THE PRICE, . . 456 HOW HARD TO KEEP FROM 81
PRICES
    JUST ONE TO INQUIRE WHAT A FARMER'S PRICES ARE. . . . 287 A ROADSIDE STAND . . 38
    OR ELSE WRITE SOMETHING TO IMPROVE FOOD PRICES. . . . 316 BUILD SOIL 24
PRICK
    ALMOST BEFORE THE PRICK OF HOSTILE EARS, ... 302 A BIRD SINGING IN SLEEP 7
PRICKLY
    SO MANY PRICKLY GRAPPLING FEET AT ONCE. . . . . . 278 THE WHITE-TAILED HORNET 29
PRIDE
    THUS ARE WE WHOLLY STRIPPED OF PRIDE . . . . . . 21 THE TRIAL BY EXISTENCE 70
    AND NOTHING TO LOOK BACKWARD TO WITH PRIDE, ... 38 DEATH OF THE HIRED MAN 100
    IF HE HAD ANY PRIDE IN CLAIMING KIN . . . . . . 39 DEATH OF THE HIRED MAN 136
    WITH ALL THIS PRIDE OF ANCESTRY, WE YANKEES? . . . 76 THE GENERATIONS OF MEN 87
    WHOSE PRIDE HAS FAILED TO GET HIM ANYWHERE). . . . 190 THE GRINDSTONE . . 44
    PROUD AND THE PRIDE OF FRIENDS. . . . . 256 THE LOVELY BE CHOOSERS 18
    THE PICTURE PRIDE OF HOLLYWOOD. . . . . 307 PROVIDE, PROVIDE . . 4
    OF A POWER LEADING FROM ITS STRENGTH AND PRIDE, . . . 424 FOR JOHN F. KENNEDY . 72
PRIEST (SEE SUN-PRIEST)
PRIESTS
    WHERE WOMEN PRAY WITH PRIESTS. THERE IS NO LOVE. . . 318 BUILD SOIL 84
PRIME
    THAT PAST ITS PRIME LOST PETALS IN THE FLOOD . . . . 337 THE WIND AND THE RAIN . 33
PRIMER
    IN MY WITCHES' WEATHER PRIMER . . . . 303 CLEAR AND COLDER . . 2

PRIMER (CONTINUED)
   --THE NEW ENGLAND PRIMER . . . . 331 SYCAMORE   4
PRIMING
   A PRIMING COAT OF LEAVES. . . . . 416 CLOSED FOR GOOD . . .   18
PRIMITIVE
   THE MOST PRIMITIVE OF ENGINES   . . . . 397 AN IMPORTER   23
   THAT PRIMITIVE HEAD . . . . 447 THE BAD ISLAND--EASTER   1
PRIMITIVES (SEE PRE-PRIMITIVES)
PRIMPED
   WHOSE SHOES I PRIMPED TO DANCE IN!" / "AND WHERE'S JOHN?" . 81 THE HOUSEKEEPER . . .   13
PRINCE
   ONE INCA PRINCE ON THE RACK, ... 311 THE VINDICTIVES . . .   41
   TO MARRY A PERSIAN PRINCE . . . . 314 BEARER OF EVIL TIDINGS 20
   BUT THE PRINCE DREW AWAY HIS HAND IN TIME . . . . 453 HOW HARD TO KEEP FROM   4
   AND THE PRINCE ANSWERED, PICKING UP THE PIECES, . . . 453 HOW HARD TO KEEP FROM   7
   "LET'S NOT GET SUPERSTITIOUS, SIRE," THE PRINCE SAID. . 454 HOW HARD TO KEEP FROM   28
   THOU ONETIME PRINCE OF CONVERSATIONISTS? . . . . . . 488 A MASQUE OF REASON . . 406
PRINCESS
   A PRINCESS EN ROUTE FROM CHINA . . . . 313 BEARER OF EVIL TIDINGS 19
   AND THE CHILD THAT CAME OF THE PRINCESS . . . . . 314 BEARER OF EVIL TIDINGS 29
PRINCIPLE
   IF NOT AT HEART, AT LEAST ON PRINCIPLE. . . . . . 44 A HUNDRED COLLARS . .   13
   HER GIVING SOMEHOW TOUCHED THE PRINCIPLE . . . . . 57 THE BLACK COTTAGE . .   60
   ESTABLISH ONCE FOR ALL THE PRINCIPLE . . . . 475 A MASQUE OF REASON . .   49
PRINCIPLES
   IN GENERAL IDEAS AND PRINCIPLES. . . . . 479 A MASQUE OF REASON . . 174
PRINT
   SMALL PRINT OVERSPREAD IT, ... 110 A PATCH OF OLD SNOW .   6
   IN EVERY PRINT OF A HOOF A POND. . . . . 276 TWO TRAMPS IN MUD TIME 36
   STILL PRINT THERE AS MY PROXY. . . . . 416 CLOSED FOR GOOD . . .   30
PRINTED
   RIFLING A PRINTED LETTER AS HE TALKS. . . . . . . 44 A HUNDRED COLLARS . .   10
   WHERE LOVE HAS LEFT A PRINTED TRACE . . . . 120 BOND AND FREE . . .   7
   AND IS REFLECTED FROM THE PRINTED PAGE . . . . . . 515 A MASQUE OF MERCY . . 581
PRINTER
   TO COME AS A FOOT PRINTER, ... 416 CLOSED FOR GOOD . . .   27
PRIORITY
   ALL CLAIMING SOME PRIORITY IN STARKNESS. . . . . . 75 THE GENERATIONS OF MEN 49
PRISMATIC
   A VERY SMALL MOON-MADE PRISMATIC BOW, ... 315 IRIS BY NIGHT   . . .   18
PRISON
   A KING FILLED HIS PRISON ROOM . . . . 310 THE VINDICTIVES . . .   2
PRISONER
   WHERE HE FELL A PRISONER TO THE MOOR. . . . . . . 347 DISCOVERY OF MADEIRAS . 128
   THEN I'M A PRISONER? / YOU ARE TONIGHT. . . . . . 500 A MASQUE OF MERCY . . 176
PRISONERS'
   AGAINST THE DAY OF PRISONERS' ENNUI, ... 293 AT WOODWARD'S GARDENS . 31
PRISTINE
   AND THERE'S YOUR PRISTINE EARTH ALL FREED . . . . 376 SOMETHING FOR HOPE . . 14
PRIVATE
   SENT FOR THE EX-KING IN A PRIVATE MATTER. . . . . 456 HOW HARD TO KEEP FROM   97
PRIVATELY
   PRIVATELY--TO HIMSELF, RIGHT NOW, HE'S THINKING . . . 146 SNOW   85
PRIZE
   SUCH AS IT IS, IT PROMISES THE PRIZE . . . . 174 A STAR IN A STONEBOAT . 55
   HOW I SHOULD PRIZE ONE PERSONALLY FROM YOU. . . . . 488 A MASQUE OF REASON . . 423
PROBABLE
   YOUR PROBABLE BRUTE NATURE IS DISCUSSED. . . . . . 382 TO AN ANCIENT   . . .   11
PROBABLY
   PROBABLY, BUT YOU'RE FAR TOO FAST AND STRONG   . . . 325 BUILD SOIL 284
   THAT PROBABLY IT NEVER WOULD BE LOST. . . . . . . 339 NEVER WOULD BIRDS' SONG 12
   IT'S GONE SO FAR SHE'S PROBABLY CAUGHT . . . . . 345 DISCOVERY OF MADEIRAS . 74
PROBES
   STILL PROBES AND DENTS OUR ROCKY COAST . . . . . 418 AMERICA IS HARD TO SEE 50
PROBING
   AND PROBING WITH ONE FINGER NOT TOO ROUGH, ... 270 THE EGG AND THE MACHINE 21
PROBLEM
   HER PROBLEM WAS TO FIND OUT WHAT IT ASKED . . . . 181 MAPLE   52
   SLIPPED IN TO BE MY PROBLEM GUEST. . . . . 419 ONE MORE BREVITY . .   9
   THE PROBLEM FOR THE KING IS JUST HOW STRICT . . . . 460 HOW HARD TO KEEP FROM 198
   I NEED SOME HELP ABOUT THIS REASON PROBLEM . . . . 479 A MASQUE OF REASON . . 165
   PERSONAE NEEDED TO ENACT THE PROBLEM. . . . . . . 487 A MASQUE OF REASON . . 394
PROCEEDS
   AND SPENT THE PROCEEDS ON A TELESCOPE . . . . . . 168 NEW HAMPSHIRE . . . 303
   AND SPENT THE PROCEEDS ON A TELESCOPE . . . . . . 177 THE STAR-SPLITTER . .   17
PROCLAIMED
   AND FROM A CLIFF TOP IS PROCLAIMED . . . . 20 THE TRIAL BY EXISTENCE 17
   A GOVERNOR IT WAS PROCLAIMED THIS TIME, ... 73 THE GENERATIONS OF MEN   1
   PROCLAIMED THE TIME WAS NEITHER WRONG NOR RIGHT. . . . 255 ACQUAINTED WITH NIGHT . 13
PRODDED
   I PRODDED THE EARTH WITH A LAZY TOOL . . . . 385 A MOOD APART   2
PRODIGAL
   (THOUGH PRODIGAL HIMSELF AND A DESPISER . . . . . . 363 AN EQUALIZER   3
PRODUCE
   SHE HAD THE DARTMOUTH NEEDED TO PRODUCE HIM. . . . . 161 NEW HAMPSHIRE . . .   69
   NOT FOR A LONG, LONG TIME. PLANT, BREED, PRODUCE, . . . 323 BUILD SOIL 214
   TO PRODUCE PURPOSE AS THE FITTER BRED: . . . . . . 425 ACCIDENTALLY ON PURPOSE 15
PRODUCED
   POEMS PRODUCED THAN ANY OTHER THING? . . . . 164 NEW HAMPSHIRE   . . . 171
PRODUCER
   OR QUALITY TO WORRY THE PRODUCER . . . . 164 NEW HAMPSHIRE   . . . 168
   AS THE MORE ECONOMICAL PRODUCER, ... 324 BUILD SOIL   253
   MORE WONDERFUL, MORE BEAUTIFUL PRODUCER? . . . . . 324 BUILD SOIL   254
PRODUCING (SEE MASS-PRODUCING)
   A STATE PRODUCING PRECIOUS METALS, STONES, ... 164 NEW HAMPSHIRE   . . . 165
   NOTHING COMPARED TO THE PRODUCING OF THEM. . . . . 324 BUILD SOIL   258
PRODUCT
   A DECENT PRODUCT OF LIFE'S IRONING-OUT; . . . . . . 201 PLACE FOR A THIRD . .   67

PRODUCT (CONTINUED)
    THOUGHT PRODUCT AND FOOD PRODUCT ARE TO ME . . . . . . 324 BUILD SOIL 257
PRODUCTION
    MOST OF ALL THE MASS PRODUCTION . . . . 396 AN IMPORTER 11
    TEACH THOSE ASIANS MASS PRODUCTION? . . . . 397 AN IMPORTER 25
PROFANATION
    LIKE PROFANATION, BY YOUR LEAVE, ... 102 GOOD HOURS 15
PROFESS
    LET NEWSPAPERS PROFESS TO FEAR THE WORST! . . . . . 318 BUILD SOIL 65
PROFESSIONS
    "IT'S WHETHER THESE PROFESSIONS REALLY WORK. . . . . 404 FROM PLANE TO PLANE . 11
PROFESSOR
    "PROFESSOR SQUARE-THE-CIRCLE-TILL-YOU'RE-TIRED? . . . 46 A HUNDRED COLLARS . . 44
    'MY MAN' IS IT? YOU TALK LIKE A PROFESSOR. . . . . . 47 A HUNDRED COLLARS . . 80
PROFFERING
    TO STRETCH A PROFFERING HAND--AND A SPELL-BREAKING. . . 230 TWO LOOK AT TWO . . . 36
PROFILE
    THERE WAS THE BOOK OF PROFILE TALES DECLARING . . . . 423 FOR JOHN F. KENNEDY . 60
PROFIT
    THOUGH THERE'S SMALL PROFIT IN COMPARISONS. . . . . . 64 A SERVANT TO SERVANTS . 68
PROFITABLE
    BEYOND THE TIME OF PROFITABLE GROWTH-- . . . . . . 106 CHRISTMAS TREES . . . 23
PROFOUND
    COULD BE PROFOUND. . . . . 252 TREE AT MY WINDOW . . 8
    I HAD THOUGHT OURS THE MORE PROFOUND DISGRACE; . . . . 353 THE LESSON FOR TODAY . 79
    EQUALLY PROFOUND . . . . 433 KITTY HAWK 180
PROFUNDITY
    OF METAPHYSICAL PROFUNDITY . . . . 483 A MASQUE OF REASON . . 278
PROGRESS
    SUCH IS THE UNCAGED PROGRESS OF THE BEAR. . . . . . 269 THE BEAR 10
    WHAT ARE THE SIMPLE FACTS OF PROGRESS . . . . . . 449 OUR DOOM TO BLOOM . . 2
    WHICH IS THE CREVICE THAT LETS PROGRESS IN. . . . . 458 HOW HARD TO KEEP FROM 153
    IF WE COULD ONLY STOP THE PROGRESS SOMEWHERE, ... 458 HOW HARD TO KEEP FROM 154
    OF PROGRESS ROUND AND ROUND IN CIRCLES . . . . . 459 HOW HARD TO KEEP FROM 159
    "SO MUCH FOR PROGRESS," SAID DARIUS MEEKLY. . . . . 459 HOW HARD TO KEEP FROM 162
    FOR INSTANCE, IS THERE SUCH A THING AS PROGRESS? . . . 484 A MASQUE OF REASON . . 315
PROGRESS-END
    IN LONGING IS NOT AT A PROGRESS-END . . . . . . 359 THE LOST FOLLOWER . . 28
PROHIBITING
    NO, I HAD SET NO PROHIBITING SIGN, ... 364 TRESPASS 1
PROJECTED
    PROJECTED FROM THE LANTERN OF HIS EYES, ... 502 A MASQUE OF MERCY . . 237
PROJECTING
    OF PROJECTING RAY . . . . 440 KITTY HAWK 379
PROLETARIAT
    LISTEN, YE! IT'S THE PROLETARIAT! . . . . . . 508 A MASQUE OF MERCY . . 390
PROLONGED
    WE PROLONGED THE WALK, ... 433 KITTY HAWK 163
PROMINENCE
    WHOSE PROMINENCE HAS BEEN SO VAST. . . . . . . 390 TWO LEADING LIGHTS . . 3
PROMISE
    JOEL, I WON'T--I WON'T--I PROMISE YOU. . . . . . . 91 THE FEAR 52
    PROMISE ME ALL THE SHOOKS I WANT TO NAIL." . . . . . 95 THE SELF-SEEKER . . . 79
    AND PROMISE MORE RESISTANCE TO THE PICKER." . . . . 198 WILD GRAPES . . . 71
    TRIED TO THINK HOW HE COULD EXCEED HIS PROMISE, . . . 200 PLACE FOR A THIRD . . 19
    I WISH I COULD PROMISE TO LIE IN THE NIGHT . . . . 228 GOOD-BY AND KEEP COLD . 25
    AND GIVE US THE LIFE OF THE MOVING-PICTURES' PROMISE . . 286 A ROADSIDE STAND . . 21
    YOU LOOK SO SLEEPLESS.--IF HE'D PROMISE US . . . . . 501 A MASQUE OF MERCY . . 207
PROMISED
    I PROMISED MYSELF TO GET DOWN SOME DAY . . . . . 62 A SERVANT TO SERVANTS . 3
    I PROMISED TOFFILE TO BE CRUEL TO THEM . . . . . 206 THE WITCH OF COÖS . . 133
    THE LEAVES HAD PROMISED THEMSELVES THIS FLIGHT, . . . 236 MISGIVING 6
PROMISES
    SUCH AS IT IS, IT PROMISES THE PRIZE . . . . . . 174 A STAR IN A STONEBOAT . 55
    BUT I HAVE PROMISES TO KEEP, ... 225 STOPPING BY WOODS . . 14
PROMOTE
    AND AS SUCH I PROMOTE YOU TO A SAINT. . . . . . . 476 A MASQUE OF REASON . . 79
PROMPTLY
    HE PROMPTLY GIVES IT BACK, THAT IS IF STILL . . . . 178 THE STAR-SPLITTER . . 51
PRONG
    HE COULD FIND WATER WITH A HAZEL PRONG-- . . . . . 37 DEATH OF THE HIRED MAN 83
PRONOUNCE
    SHE HAD ONE PRESIDENT. (PRONOUNCE HIM PURSE, ... 161 NEW HAMPSHIRE . . . 64
    PRONOUNCE IT HOMER WITH A COCKNEY ROUGH. . . . . 459 HOW HARD TO KEEP FROM 189
PROOF
    FOR THE WOOD WAKES, AND YOU ARE HERE FOR PROOF. . . . 16 A DREAM PANG 14
    "STARK?" HE INQUIRED. "NO MATTER FOR THE PROOF." . . . 74 THE GENERATIONS OF MEN 45
    "SEE HOW IT MAKES HIS NOSE-SIDE BRIGHT, A PROOF . . . 112 IN THE HOME STRETCH . 66
    IS NO PROOF THAT I AIMED THEM AT NEW HAMPSHIRE. . . . 166 NEW HAMPSHIRE . . . 247
    GNAWS IN THE STABLE AIN'T NO PROOF TO ME . . . . . 209 PAUPER WITCH OF GRAFTON 66
    BUT EVERYBODY TOOK IT FOR A PROOF. . . . . 209 PAUPER WITCH OF GRAFTON 68
    YOU HAD BEGUN IT, AND IF THERE NEEDED PROOF-- . . . . 236 VALLEY'S SINGING DAY . 15
    I'M NOT THE ONE FOR PUTTING OFF THE PROOF. . . . . 265 DUST IN THE EYES . . 3
    DEMANDING PROOF. . . . . 298 ON TAKING FROM THE TOP 12
    FOR MERELY GIVING YOU ONCE MORE GENTLE PROOF . . . . 306 NOT QUITE SOCIAL . . 6
    MY PROOF OF BEING NOT UNBOUNDED. . . . . 331 BEECH 9
PROP
    STILL GROWING, AND ON ONE A STAKE AND PROP, ... 102 THE WOOD-PILE . . . 33
PROPENSITY
    BEEN SOCIALIZED--THE FIRST PROPENSITY . . . . . 319 BUILD SOIL 99
PROPER
    THERE IS NO PROPER PATH, BUT THOSE THAT HAVE . . . . 41 THE MOUNTAIN 39
    THERE THEY HAVE EVERY MEANS PROPER TO DO WITH, ... 65 A SERVANT TO SERVANTS . 98
    BY PROPER NAMES I FIND I DO MY THINKING. . . . . . 480 A MASQUE OF REASON . . 200
    HAVE THEY BEEN DOWN? / NOT IN THE PROPER SPIRIT. . . . 516 A MASQUE OF MERCY . . 618
PROPERLY
    I TRUST FEELS PROPERLY DEFIED. . . . . 363 ASSURANCE 4

PROPERTY
   THERE WAS NO QUARREL ABOUT PROPERTY." . . . . 84 THE HOUSEKEEPER . . . 94
   "REASON ENOUGH, THERE WAS NO PROPERTY. . . . . 84 THE HOUSEKEEPER . . . 95
   AND IN WHICH THERE WAS LITTLE PROPERTY RIGHT. . . . . . 364 TRESPASS 12
   BUT IT MADE MY PROPERTY MINE ONCE MORE. . . . . 364 TRESPASS 20
PROPHECY
   GET BURNED FOR PROPHECY, MEN ALMOST NEVER. . . . . . . 478 A MASQUE OF REASON . 150
   TO PROPHESY, AND FULL OF PROPHECY, ... 497 A MASQUE OF MERCY . 98
   THAT'S THE RIGHT STYLE OF COAT FOR PROPHECY . . . . . 501 A MASQUE OF MERCY . 218
   LET'S HAVE SOME PROPHECY. WHAT FORM OF RUIN . . . . . 502 A MASQUE OF MERCY . 222
   IT'S A HARD CASE. IT'S GOT SO PROPHECY . . . . 503 A MASQUE OF MERCY . 257
   AND IF IT'S PROPHECY, WE'LL SEE WHAT HAPPENS. . . . . 505 A MASQUE OF MERCY . 299
PROPHESIED
   WOULD BE AS IF HE PROPHESIED? . . . . 336 THE WIND AND THE RAIN . 14
   THIS ISN'T IT. I HAVEN'T PROPHESIED. . . . . 507 A MASQUE OF MERCY . 348
PROPHESY
   I'M NOT AFRAID TO PROPHESY THE FUTURE, ... 320 BUILD SOIL 134
   NO, MAKE ME PROPHESY. / AND--YOU--JUST--WON'T? . . . . 494 A MASQUE OF MERCY . 41
   TO PROPHESY AGAINST THE CITY EVIL. . . . . 495 A MASQUE OF MERCY . 64
   TO PROPHESY, AND FULL OF PROPHECY, ... 497 A MASQUE OF MERCY . 98
   LIKE WORKING MYSELF UP TO PROPHESY . . . . 501 A MASQUE OF MERCY . 198
PROPHESYING
   AND THEN NOT PROPHESYING. (HE SITS DOWN.) . . . . . 501 A MASQUE OF MERCY . 199
   AND LET HIM GET OFF WITHOUT PROPHESYING? . . . . . . 502 A MASQUE OF MERCY . 221
PROPHET
   THE PROPHET OF DISASTER CEASED TO SHOUT. . . . . . . 399 THE BROKEN DROUGHT . 1
   IT MAKES THE PROPHET IN US ALL PRESAGE . . . . 424 FOR JOHN F. KENNEDY . 70
   A WITCH WAS STRONGER THAN A PROPHET THERE. . . . . . 477 A MASQUE OF REASON . 101
   A PROPHET WITH THE BIBLE FOR CREDENTIALS. . . . . . 498 A MASQUE OF MERCY . 135
   SHALL IT BE TOLD WE HAD A PROPHET CAPTIVE . . . . . . 502 A MASQUE OF MERCY . 220
   IF I WERE IN YOUR PLACE, THOUGH, MR. PROPHET, ... 503 A MASQUE OF MERCY . 269
PROPHETS
   THAT WOMEN PROPHETS SHOULD BE BURNED AS WITCHES, . . . 476 A MASQUE OF REASON . 89
   WHEREAS MEN PROPHETS ARE RECEIVED WITH HONOR. . . . . 476 A MASQUE OF REASON . 90
PROPHET'S
   BUT IF THIS PROPHET'S MANTLE FELL ON ME . . . . . . 519 A MASQUE OF MERCY . 686
PROP-LOCKS
   THEIR LABEL PROP-LOCKS, ONLY SPECIMENS . . . . 290 OLD BARN AT THE BOTTOM 37
PROPORTION
   THE FOUNTAIN IN PROPORTION TO THE BASIN? . . . . . . 169 NEW HAMPSHIRE . . . 326
   WE MAY DOUBT THE JUST PROPORTION OF GOOD TO ILL. . . . 349 OUR HOLD ON THE PLANET 11
PROPOSAL
   YOU SEE THE BEAUTY OF MY PROPOSAL IS . . . . 324 BUILD SOIL 264
PROPOSE
   IF PART THEY DO. LET ME PROPOSE A START. . . . . . . 352 THE LESSON FOR TODAY . 65
   HOW WE PROPOSE TO GET AWAY FROM HERE . . . . 395 WHY WAIT FOR SCIENCE . 3
PROPOSED
   ALL THEY COULD SAY WAS 'GOD!' WHEN YOU PROPOSED . . . 114 IN THE HOME STRETCH . 120
   SINCE YOU PROPOSED IT, I BELIEVE I WILL. . . . . . . 497 A MASQUE OF MERCY . 109
PROPPED
   AND PROPPED HIMSELF AT BAY AGAINST A PILLOW. . . . . . 47 A HUNDRED COLLARS . 74
PROPPING
   HE TOOK THE PROPS DOWN USED FOR PROPPING OPEN, ... 289 OLD BARN AT THE BOTTOM 10
   AND SET THEM UP AGAIN FOR PROPPING SHUT, ... 289 OLD BARN AT THE BOTTOM 11
PROPS
   HE TOOK THE PROPS DOWN USED FOR PROPPING OPEN, ... 289 OLD BARN AT THE BOTTOM 10
   ITS LOCKS WERE PROPS--AND THAT REMINDED HIM. . . . . 290 OLD BARN AT THE BOTTOM 28
   YES, RIGHT I WAS, THE LOCKS WERE PROPS OUTSIDE; . . . 290 OLD BARN AT THE BOTTOM 41
PROSE
   FREE VERSE, SO CALLED, IS REALLY CHERISHED PROSE, . . . 460 HOW HARD TO KEEP FROM 221
   PROSE MADE OF, GIVEN AN AIR BY CHURCH INTONING. . . . 461 HOW HARD TO KEEP FROM 222
PROSPECT
   TO GIVE A PROSPECT TO A PLAN . . . . 281 BLUE RIBBON AT AMESBURY 55
PROSPECTS
   THE PROSPECTS ARE IN WHITE . . . . 416 CLOSED FOR GOOD . . . 20
PROSPER
   I HAD TO PROSPER GOOD AND PUNISH EVIL. . . . . 476 A MASQUE OF REASON . 76
PROSPEROUS
   NO DOUBT IT HAS A SORT OF PROSPEROUS SOUND, ... 94 THE SELF-SEEKER . . . 45
PROSTRATE
   THROWN PROSTRATE AT THE MERCY SEAT FOR MERCY. . . . . 511 A MASQUE OF MERCY . 485
PROTECT
   SOMETHING ELSE TO PROTECT HER FROM HERSELF. . . . . . 163 NEW HAMPSHIRE . . . 147
PROTECTION
   "JUST SO--THAT OUGHT TO BE ENOUGH PROTECTION." . . . . 75 THE GENERATIONS OF MEN 66
PROTEST
   ANGRILY TRIED TO MAKE ME WRITE A PROTEST . . . . . . 160 NEW HAMPSHIRE . . . 29
   --I HAVE A PROTEST I WOULD LODGE WITH YOU. . . . . . 476 A MASQUE OF REASON . 87
PROUD
   AND PROUD, TOO, OF THEMSELVES FOR DOING SO. . . . . . 65 A SERVANT TO SERVANTS . 75
   BUT I MISTRUSTED HE WAS NONE TOO PROUD . . . . 209 PAUPER WITCH OF GRAFTON 74
   PROUD AND THE PRIDE OF FRIENDS. . . . . 256 THE LOVELY BE CHOOSERS 18
   FROM WITNESSING THE FAULT OF ONE SO PROUD. . . . . . 284 THE GOLD HESPERIDEE . 57
   TOO PROUD TO BE BEHOLDEN FOR RELIEF. . . . . 394 HAEC FABULA DOCET . . 19
   SOME MYSTERY BECOMES THE PROUD. . . . . 403 SOMETHING LIKE A STAR . 6
   ALL VERY SPLENDID. I AM FLATTERED PROUD . . . . . . 481 A MASQUE OF REASON . 217
   I SAY YOU SHOULD BE PROUD OF HAVING BEATEN . . . . . 508 A MASQUE OF MERCY . 378
PROUDLY
   BUT INSTEAD I PROUDLY DEVOTE THEM . . . . 295 A RECORD STRIDE . . . 29
PROVE
   WELL, YES." / "HEAR ANYTHING THAT MIGHT PROVE USEFUL?" . 96 THE SELF-SEEKER . . . 102
   ALL THIS TO PROVE WE CARED. WHY IS THERE THEN . . . . 109 THE EXPOSED NEST . . 31
   AS IF TO PROVE SAWS KNEW WHAT SUPPER MEANT, ... 136 "OUT,OUT--" 15
   THE THOUSANDTH TIME MAY PROVE THE CHARM.--THAT LEAF! . . 148 SNOW 134
   THEY'VE GOT IT SETTLED WRONG, AND I CAN PROVE IT. . . . 207 PAUPER WITCH OF GRAFTON 3
   ALL FOUR OF THEM TO SPLINTERS. WHAT DID THAT PROVE? . . 209 PAUPER WITCH OF GRAFTON 63
   WHAT WILL NEXT PROVE A ROSE. . . . . 246 THE ROSE FAMILY . . . 8
   WHAT WELL MAY PROVE THE YEAR'S HIGH GIRDLE MARK. . . . 254 A WINTER EDEN . . . 12

PROVE (CONTINUED)
    DESTINED TO PROVE OUR DESTRUCTION. . . . . 396 AN IMPORTER 12
    PROVE BUT FLYING CHIPS . . . . 439 KITTY HAWK 352
    PROVE AS VAIN A HOP . . . . 439 KITTY HAWK 358
    (I HAVE TO SIN TO PROVE IT ISN'T THAT). . . . . 520 A MASQUE OF MERCY . . 701
PROVED
    AS TWO IN WHOM THEY WERE PROVED MISTAKEN, ... 16 IN NEGLECT 2
    HE PROVED TO BE THE CITY COME AGAIN . . . . 106 CHRISTMAS TREES . . . 9
    BY INSPIRATION. IT PROVED THERE WAS SOMETHING. . . . . 184 MAPLE 135
    BEING ALREADY MORE THAN PROVED IN FIGHT, ... 353 THE LESSON FOR TODAY . 91
    WITH SUCH IT HAS PROVED DANGEROUS AS FRIEND . . . . . 359 THE LOST FOLLOWER . . 25
    AND DARWIN'S PROVED MISTAKEN, NOT THE BIBLE. . . . . . 369 THE LITERATE FARMER AND 46
    AND ALSO PROVED THE WORLD A BALL, ... 416 AMERICA IS HARD TO SEE 3
PROVERBIAL
    AS AFTER ONE-OF-THEM'S PROVERBIAL FAILURE . . . . . 412 POD OF THE MILKWEED . 37
PROVIDE
    PROVIDE, PROVIDE . . . . 307 PROVIDE, PROVIDE . . 1
    THAN NONE AT ALL. PROVIDE, PROVIDE! . . . . 307 PROVIDE, PROVIDE . . 21
    IS THE REASON THE POWERS PROVIDE . . . . 348 TRIPLE BRONZE . . . 2
    OF ONE GOD, WE PROVIDE HE SHALL BE ONE . . . . 515 A MASQUE OF MERCY . . 590
PROVIDENTIAL
    'TWAS PROVIDENTIAL YOU APPLIED TO US, ... 369 THE LITERATE FARMER AND 27
PROVING
    WOULD KEEP HIM NOW FROM PROVING WITH A BITE . . . . . 283 THE GOLD HESPERIDEE . 29
    INSTEAD OF PROVING HUMAN WHEN IT NEARED . . . . 338 THE MOST OF IT . . . 14
PROVISION
    PROVISION THERE HAD BEEN FOR JUST SUCH MEETING . . . . 74 THE GENERATIONS OF MEN 38
PROVOCATION
    JOB, YOU MUST UNDERSTAND MY PROVOCATION. . . . . . . 485 A MASQUE OF REASON . . 347
PROVOKE
    LEST MOVEMENT SHOULD PROVOKE . . . . 340 THE SUBVERTED FLOWER . 32
PROVOKED
    I ALMOST PROVOKED POOR LOREN TO MIRTH . . . . 61 BLUEBERRIES 68
PROW
    NOW STOOD UPON ITS BULGING PROW . . . . 344 DISCOVERY OF MADEIRAS . 23
PROXY
    STILL PRINT THERE AS MY PROXY. . . . . 416 CLOSED FOR GOOD . . . 30
PRUDE
    "CHOOSE YOU WHICH YOU WILL BE--A PRUDE, OR PUKE, . . . 170 NEW HAMPSHIRE . . . 362
    I WOULDN'T BE A PRUDE AFRAID OF NATURE. . . . . . . 170 NEW HAMPSHIRE . . . 366
    "COME, BUT THIS ISN'T CHOOSING--PUKE OR PRUDE?" . . . 171 NEW HAMPSHIRE . . . 406
PRUDENCE
    AND WARRANT PRUDENCE IN A MAN. . . . . 281 BLUE RIBBON AT AMESBURY 56
PRUDENT
    A PRUDENT GRIEF WILL NOT DESPISE SUCH AIDS. . . . . . 200 PLACE FOR A THIRD . . 30
PRUDENTLY
    THEY PRUDENTLY ARE SPINNING THEIR COCOON . . . . . . 248 THE COCOON 13
PRUNING
    OF WHAT WANTS PRUNING, SHINGLING, BREAKING UP. . . . 115 IN THE HOME STRETCH . 150
PRYING
    FOR PRYING BENEATH AND FORCING THE LIDS OF SIGHT, . . 235 VALLEY'S SINGING DAY . 9
PSEUDONYMITY
    TO BE OUR PARENTS' PSEUDONYMITY . . . . 408 FROM PLANE TO PLANE . 138
PSEUDO-PHALLIC
    ABOUT THE NEW SCHOOL OF THE PSEUDO-PHALLIC, ... 170 NEW HAMPSHIRE . . . 359
PSYCHICAL
    THE S'CIETY FOR PSYCHICAL RESEARCH . . . . 163 NEW HAMPSHIRE . . . 135
PSYCHOLOGICAL
    BY PSYCHOLOGICAL EXPERIMENT, ... 293 AT WOODWARD'S GARDENS . 19
PTERODIX
    ON FIRE TO SCARE AWAY THE PTERODIX . . . . 372 THE LITERATE FARMER AND 139
PUBLIC
    'FEEL OUT THE PUBLIC SENTIMENT'--HE SAYS. . . . . . . 48 A HUNDRED COLLARS . . 106
    MEWLING AND PUKING IN THE PUBLIC ARMS." . . . . . . 170 NEW HAMPSHIRE . . . 363
    'TWAS HIS IDEA THAT FOR THE PUBLIC HEALTH, ... 363 AN EQUALIZER 6
    I HEARD A FELLOW IN A PUBLIC LECTURE . . . . 369 THE LITERATE FARMER AND 53
    IN PUBLIC FREEDOM IS BECAUSE THE FREEDOM . . . . . . 461 HOW HARD TO KEEP FROM 231
    I'M WITH YOU IN MAINTAINING TO THE PUBLIC. . . . . . 482 A MASQUE OF REASON . . 251
PUBLICLY
    MADE PUBLICLY IN SCHOOL, ABOVE SUSPICION . . . . . . 324 BUILD SOIL 274
    IN PUBLICLY DISPUTING WHICH IS WORSE, ... 352 THE LESSON FOR TODAY . 48
    I SHRINK FROM BEING PUBLICLY LET DOWN. . . . . 505 A MASQUE OF MERCY . . 305
PUBLISHED
    PUBLISHED IN BOW. YOU KNOW THE WEEKLY NEWS?" . . . . 48 A HUNDRED COLLARS . . 99
    AND HAD IT PUBLISHED. IT WAS ALL ABOUT . . . . . . 215 A FOUNTAIN, A BOTTLE . 79
PUBLISHER
    (FROM, SAY, A PUBLISHER IN NEW YORK CITY). . . . . . 172 NEW HAMPSHIRE . . . 410
    THEY HAD BEEN BROUGHT HOME FROM SOME PUBLISHER . . . 216 A FOUNTAIN, A BOTTLE . 100
PUEBLO
    ON PUEBLO INDIANS AND THEIR ARCHITECTURE . . . . . . 369 THE LITERATE FARMER AND 54
PUFF
    TO GET A PUFF OF BLACK SMOKE FROM THE FLAME, ... 148 SNOW 140
PUFFED
    HE LAY AND PUFFED HIS LIPS OUT WITH HIS BREATH. . . . 137 "OUT, OUT--" 29
    NEXT DAY THE SCENE WAS PILED AND PUFFED AND DEAD. . . 239 OUR SINGING STRENGTH . 11
PUFFS
    LOCKING OUT OF A WREATH OF FERN AND CLOUD PUFFS. . . . 225 FOR ONCE SOMETHING . . 6
    IT IS BUT FIERY PUFFS OF DUST AND PEBBLES, ... 360 A LOOSE MOUNTAIN . . 5
    IT PUFFS THE FACE AND BRUTALIZES SO. . . . . 371 THE LITERATE FARMER AND 105
PUKE
    "CHOOSE YOU WHICH YOU WILL BE--A PRUDE, OR PUKE, . . . 170 NEW HAMPSHIRE . . . 362
    AND NEITHER WOULD I CHOOSE TO BE A PUKE . . . . . . 171 NEW HAMPSHIRE . . . 398
    "COME, BUT THIS ISN'T CHOOSING--PUKE OR PRUDE?" . . . 171 NEW HAMPSHIRE . . . 406
PUKING
    MEWLING AND PUKING IN THE PUBLIC ARMS." . . . . . . 170 NEW HAMPSHIRE . . . 363
PULL
    YOU CAN'T REST THAT WAY. LET ME PULL YOUR SHOES OFF." . . 47 A HUNDRED COLLARS . . 76
    THE WARPING BOARDS PULL OUT THEIR OWN OLD NAILS . . . 56 THE BLACK COTTAGE . . 49

PULL (CONTINUED)
    LEN SAYS ONE STEADY PULL MORE OUGHT TO DO IT. . . . . . . 64 A SERVANT TO SERVANTS . 55
    HE'D PULL HIS BARS APART LIKE BOW AND BOWSTRING, ... 66 A SERVANT TO SERVANTS . 134
    TO LIVE TOGETHER AND THEN PULL APART. . . . . 82 THE HOUSEKEEPER . . . 40
    I DIDN'T TRY TOO LONG TO PULL AWAY, ... 93 THE SELF-SEEKER . . . 24
    WITH SHOUTS AFAR TO PULL THE CABLE TAUT, ... 141 THE LINE-GANG   9
    "AND STRONG OF STALE TOBACCO." / "HE'LL PULL THROUGH." . 145 SNOW 72
    A THOUSAND YARNS WERE UNDER PULL, ... 273 A LONE STRIKER . . . 19
    BUT PULL SO SLOW, WITH SUCH A TWIST, ... 273 A LONE STRIKER . . . 20
    BY NOW, PULL IN YOUR LADDER ROAD BEHIND YOU . . . . . 378 DIRECTIVE 37
    BY ITS TIDAL PULL . . . . 433 KITTY HAWK 173
PULLED
    WHOSE HORSE HAD PULLED HIM SHORT UP IN THE ROAD . . . 168 NEW HAMPSHIRE . . . 289
    I'VE PULLED IT FROM A CRATE OF CROOKED TREES, ... 245 THE FREEDOM OF THE MOON   9
    AND THEN GET SLOWLY, SLOWLY PULLED BACK DOWN. . . . . 370 THE LITERATE FARMER AND 67
    ALMOST PULLED OUR HAIR . . . . 434 KITTY HAWK 210
    IT CAN'T BE PULLED UP BY THE ROOT. . . . . 452 A-WISHING WELL . . . 51
PULLET
    SUCH A FINE PULLET OUGHT TO GO . . . . 279 BLUE RIBBON AT AMESBURY   1
    OF THE PHOENIX PULLET . . . . 427 VERSION   9
PULLEYS
    SNATCHED RIGHT AND LEFT ACROSS THE SILVER PULLEYS. . . . 94 THE SELF-SEEKER . . . 39
PULLMAN
    OFF HIS. THE TIME WAS EVENING IN THE PULLMAN. . . . . 159 NEW HAMPSHIRE . . . 14
    JUST LIKE PULLMAN CARS, ... 438 KITTY HAWK 319
PULLS
    THAT GOD PULLS LIGHTLY UPRIGHT ON ITS HINGES . . . . 474 A MASQUE OF REASON . . 22
    PULLS DOWN THE WINDOW CURTAIN ON THE DOOR . . . . . 493 A MASQUE OF MERCY . .   2
PULPIT
    WHO COME TO LOOK IN ON THEM FROM THE PULPIT. . . . . 414 A CABIN IN THE CLEARING 24
PULPITEERS
    PULPITEERS WILL CENSURE . . . . 434 KITTY HAWK 213
PULSE
    AND THEN--THE WATCHER AT HIS PULSE TOOK FRIGHT. . . . 137 "OUT,OUT--" 30
PUMP
    AND THE DRY PUMP FLUNG UP AN AWKWARD ARM; . . . . . 242 NEED OF BEING VERSED . 19
PUMPKINS
    TOMATOES, BEETS, BEANS, PUMPKINS, CORN, ... 134 A GIRL'S GARDEN . . . 31
PUMPS
    "THAT'S A SMART PAIR OF PUMPS YOU'RE BEADING THERE. . . . 81 THE HOUSEKEEPER . . .   9
PUNG
    BEHIND HER AT THE DASHBOARD OF HIS PUNG." . . . . . 407 FROM PLANE TO PLANE . 108
PUNISH
    AND THE REST WON'T WANT TO PUNISH ME TOO SEVERELY . . . 306 NOT QUITE SOCIAL . .   2
    TO PUNISH ME OVERCRUELLY WOULDN'T BE RIGHT . . . . . 306 NOT QUITE SOCIAL . .   5
    'TWAS TO PUNISH HER, ... 432 KITTY HAWK 150
    I HAD TO PROSPER GOOD AND PUNISH EVIL. . . . . . . 476 A MASQUE OF REASON . 76
PUNISHED
    BY BEING PUNISHED BACK, IT IS NOT FREE: . . . . . . 319 BUILD SOIL 115
    THEY WERE PUNISHED AND BRIBED; . . . . 449 THE BAD ISLAND--EASTER 46
PUNISHMENT
    TO TAKE THE PUNISHMENT OUT OF ALL FAILURE . . . . . 505 A MASQUE OF MERCY . 313
    BUT NOT THE FEAR OF PUNISHMENT FOR SIN . . . . . . 520 A MASQUE OF MERCY . 700
PUNT
    TILL THE AMBASSADORS FROM PUNT OR SOMEWHERE . . . . . 456 HOW HARD TO KEEP FROM 72
PUNY
    BUT PUNY LITTLE STATES CAN ONLY BE. . . . . 398 NO HOLY WARS FOR THEM .   4
PUP
    I CAN REMEMBER WHEN HE WAS A PUP. . . . . 308 THE SPAN OF LIFE . .   2
    ENOUGH TO BUILD HIM EVERY NIGHT A PUP TENT . . . . . 478 A MASQUE OF REASON . 132
PUPIL
    IS LIKE THE PUPIL OF A POINTED GUN. . . . . 277 THE WHITE-TAILED HORNET   4
PURBLIND
    AND SEEK IT ENDLESSLY WITH PURBLIND HASTE; . . . . . 14 WAITING 17
PURE
    BUT THE PURE FATE TO WHICH YOU GO . . . . 21 THE TRIAL BY EXISTENCE 53
    THERE'S NO SUCH THING AS SOCIALISM PURE-- . . . . . 318 BUILD SOIL 70
    LEAST IN DEMOCRACY. IN PRACTICE, PURE, ... 318 BUILD SOIL 76
    ALLUVIUM SO PURE THAT WHEN A BLADE . . . . 407 FROM PLANE TO PLANE . 115
PURER
    IT OUGHT TO GIVE A PURER ORACLE." . . . . 78 THE GENERATIONS OF MEN 134
PUREST
    A FAIR OASIS IN THE PUREST DESERT. . . . . 473 A MASQUE OF REASON .   1
PURGATORY
    OUR WICKED FRIENDS WE SEND TO PURGATORY. . . . . . 519 A MASQUE OF MERCY . 689
PURGE
    IT MERELY WOULD ENTAIL THE PURGE . . . . 453 A-WISHING WELL . . 72
PURIFY
    FOR INSTANCE, WHEN TO PURIFY THE ITZAS . . . . . . 510 A MASQUE OF MERCY . 445
PURITAN
    HE'S PURITAN YANKEE THROUGH AND THROUGH. . . . . . 393 A CASE FOR JEFFERSON .   6
PURITANLY
    SUPPOSE THEY WEREN'T BEHAVING PURITANLY, ... 161 NEW HAMPSHIRE . . . 88
PURPLE
    THE PURPLE LADY'S SLIPPER'S COMMONER." . . . . . . 98 THE SELF-SEEKER . . 142
    "I DIDN'T BRING A PURPLE LADY'S SLIPPER. . . . . . 98 THE SELF-SEEKER . . 143
    HE GOT HIS PURPLE LITTLE KNUCKLES STUNG. . . . . . 293 AT WOODWARD'S GARDENS . 17
    THERE STOOD THE PURPLE SPIRES WITH NO BREATH OF AIR . . 343 QUEST OF PURPLE-FRINGED 17
PURPLE-FRINGED
    THE QUEST OF THE PURPLE-FRINGED . . . . 342 QUEST OF PURPLE-FRINGED   T
PURPLE-STEMMED
    AND THE PURPLE-STEMMED WILD RASPBERRIES GROW. . . . .   5 GHOST HOUSE   5
PURPORT
    DOES IT PURPORT TO SPEAK IN? NOT OLD GRANDSIR'S . . . 79 THE GENERATIONS OF MEN 174
PURPOSE
    I GO NOWHERE ON PURPOSE: I HAPPEN BY.-- . . . . . 50 A HUNDRED COLLARS . 154
    "I HALF SUSPECT YOU KNEW, AND CAME ON PURPOSE . . . . 93 THE SELF-SEEKER . . .   8
    UNLESS OUR PURPOSE IS DOING HARM, ... 263 THE TIMES TABLE . . . 16

PURPOSE (CONTINUED)
   HAVE NO PURPOSE, HAVE NO LEADER, ... 291 ON HEART'S BEGINNING TO   29
   BECAUSE THEIR PURPOSE IS TO FLASH AND SPARK, ... 370 THE LITERATE FARMER AND 78
   HIGH PURPOSE MAKES THE HERO RUDE; . . . . . . 418 AMERICA IS HARD TO SEE   73
   ACCIDENTALLY ON PURPOSE . . . . 425 ACCIDENTALLY ON PURPOSE   T
   HAD NO REAL PURPOSE TILL IT GOT TO US. . . . . 425 ACCIDENTALLY ON PURPOSE 12
   IT MUST HAVE HAD THE PURPOSE FROM THE FIRST . . . 425 ACCIDENTALLY ON PURPOSE 14
   TO PRODUCE PURPOSE AS THE FITTER BRED: . . . . 425 ACCIDENTALLY ON PURPOSE 15
   WE WERE JUST PURPOSE COMING TO A HEAD. . . . . 425 ACCIDENTALLY ON PURPOSE 16
   WHOSE PURPOSE WAS IT? HIS OR HERS OR ITS? . . . 425 ACCIDENTALLY ON PURPOSE 17
   GRANT ME INTENTION, PURPOSE, AND DESIGN-- . . . 425 ACCIDENTALLY ON PURPOSE 19
   PURPOSE WAS EXPRESSED . . . . 437 KITTY HAWK 294
PURSE
   A DOLE OF BREAD, A PURSE, ...   8 LOVE AND A QUESTION . 26
   "I MEAN ESTELLE HAS ALWAYS HELD THE PURSE." . . .   84 THE HOUSEKEEPER . . . 98
   I GUESS ESTELLE AND I HAVE FILLED THE PURSE. . .   84 THE HOUSEKEEPER . . 100
   SHE HAD ONE PRESIDENT. (PRONOUNCE HIM PURSE, . .   161 NEW HAMPSHIRE . . . 64
   HE SLAPPED HIS BREAST TO VERIFY HIS PURSE . .   396 ANY SIZE WE PLEASE. . 13
   WE CARRY IN OUR PURSE AND POCKET STILL?) . . . 422 FOR JOHN F. KENNEDY . 22
PURSUED
   HE GAINED NO FOOTHOLD, BUT PURSUED . . . . . 138 BROWN'S DESCENT . . 19
   PETALS I MAY HAVE ONCE PURSUED. . . . . . 297 LEAVES COMPARED WITH . 19
PURSUER
   HE RUNS FACE FORWARD. HE IS A PURSUER. . . . . 421 ESCAPIST--NEVER . . .   6
PURSUIT
   THAT BACK BEHIND PURSUIT IT COULDN'T REACH THEM; . . 240 OUR SINGING STRENGTH . 47
   THE DEMON OF PURSUIT . . . . 340 THE SUBVERTED FLOWER . 33
   HIS LIFE IS A PURSUIT OF A PURSUIT FOREVER. . . . 421 ESCAPIST--NEVER . . . 10
   'TWAS NO VAIN PURSUIT. . . . . 438 KITTY HAWK . . .   320
PUSH
   AND PUSH THE HEADBOARD OF THE BED AGAINST IT. . . 206 THE WITCH OF COOS .   120
   "YOU PUSH AND I'LL PELT." . . . . 250 LODGED   2
   FOR MAPLE, BIRCH, AND SPRUCE TO PUSH . . . . 376 SOMETHING FOR HOPE . .   6
   TO PUSH THE WOODS BACK FROM AROUND THE HOUSE . . 414 A CABIN IN THE CLEARING   3
   I'M GOING NOW. BUT DON'T YOU PUSH ME OFF. . . . 518 A MASQUE OF MERCY . . 646
PUSHED
   SHE PUSHED HIM OUTWARD WITH HER THROUGH THE DOOR .   34 DEATH OF THE HIRED MAN   6
   SHE PUSHED PAST HIM AND GOT IT FOR HERSELF. . .   90 THE FEAR 34
   BUT THE HEADBOARD OF MOTHER'S BED IS PUSHED . .   203 THE WITCH OF COOS . 21
   I PUSHED MYSELF UPSTAIRS, AND IN THE LIGHT . .   205 THE WITCH OF COOS . 97
   THE MOUNTAIN PUSHED US OFF HER KNEES. . . .   265 THE BIRTHPLACE . . . 13
PUSHING
   PUSHING THE CRUMPLED WATER UP AHEAD, ... 338 THE MOST OF IT . . 17
   FROM A FALLEN TREE AND PUSHING OFF . . . . 347 DISCOVERY OF MADEIRAS   126
PUT
   THEY MUST BE PIERCED BY FLOWERS AND PUT . . .   26 IN HARDWOOD GROVES . .   9
   IF I COULD PUT A NOTION IN HIS HEAD: . . .   34 MENDING WALL . . . 29
   AND PUT HIM ON HIS GUARD. "SILAS IS BACK." . .   34 DEATH OF THE HIRED MAN   5
   AND SPREAD HER APRON TO IT. SHE PUT OUT HER HAND .   38 DEATH OF THE HIRED MAN 106
   HE WOULDN'T LET ME PUT HIM ON THE LOUNGE. . .   39 DEATH OF THE HIRED MAN 149
   I'LL NOT BE PUT TO BED BY YOU, MY MAN." . . .   47 A HUNDRED COLLARS . 78
   "WILL YOU BELIEVE ME IF I PUT IT THERE . . .   48 A HUNDRED COLLARS . 93
   I'LL PUT THE LIGHT OUT. DON'T YOU WAIT FOR ME: .   50 A HUNDRED COLLARS . 171
   OR PUT THE LEAVES ASIDE THAT FRAMED IT IN. . .   55 THE BLACK COTTAGE . 10
   WITH NONE TO TREAD AND PUT THEM IN THEIR PLACE. .   56 THE BLACK COTTAGE . 50
   PUT ON ME, BUT THERE SEEMS NO OTHER WAY. . .   64 A SERVANT TO SERVANTS 54
   NO MORE PUT OUT IN WHAT THEY DO OR SAY . . .   65 A SERVANT TO SERVANTS 79
   ANYTHING THEY PUT IN FOR FURNITURE. . . .   66 A SERVANT TO SERVANTS 117
   THEY FOUND A WAY TO PUT A STOP TO IT. . . .   67 A SERVANT TO SERVANTS 139
   HERE HE IS NOW. THIS BOX! PUT IT AWAY. . . .   88 THE HOUSEKEEPER . . . 198
   TO PUT IT THE RIGHT WAY. HE'D NEVER DARE-- . .   90 THE FEAR 37
   "YES, THAT'S ONE WAY TO PUT IT--ALL THE FLOWERS .   95 THE SELF-SEEKER . . 67
   BUT PUT OUR FLOWERS IN WATER FIRST.--WILL, HELP HER: 99 THE SELF-SEEKER .   172
   I'LL PUT YOU OUT WITH ANNE. BE GOOD OR GO." . .   99 THE SELF-SEEKER .   186
   TO PUT A TREE BETWEEN US WHEN HE LIGHTED, . .   101 THE WOOD-PILE . . . 11
   "WHERE WILL I PUT THIS WALNUT BUREAU, LADY?" . . 110 IN THE HOME STRETCH . 13
   "PUT IT ON TOP OF SOMETHING THAT'S ON TOP . .   111 IN THE HOME STRETCH . 14
   OF SOMETHING ELSE," SHE LAUGHED. "OH, PUT IT WHERE   111 IN THE HOME STRETCH . 15
   "AND WHAT IS THAT? YOU ONLY PUT ME OFF." . .   111 IN THE HOME STRETCH . 29
   AND PUT EACH OTHER BODILY OUT OF THE HOUSE. . . 114 IN THE HOME STRETCH . 110
   I'M GOING TO PUT YOU IN YOUR BED, IF FIRST . .   117 IN THE HOME STRETCH . 199
   THE FIRE ITSELF CAN PUT IT OUT, AND THAT . .   130 THE BONFIRE . . . 25
   IT PUT THE FLAME TIP-DOWN AND DABBED THE GRASS .   131 THE BONFIRE . . . 45
   AND GIVE YOU A CHANCE TO PUT SOME STRENGTH . .   133 A GIRL'S GARDEN . . 15
   THE DOCTOR PUT HIM IN THE DARK OF ETHER. . .   137 "OUT,OUT--" . . . 28
   OR SHELTER TO PUT INTO FROM THIS PLACE . . .   145 SNOW 74
   ONLY YOU WOMEN HAVE TO PUT THESE AIRS ON . .   146 SNOW 98
   AS IF TO PUT FOREVER OUT OF MIND . . . .   160 NEW HAMPSHIRE . . . 42
   "I'M GOING TO PUT YOU OFF THIS FARM: I WANT IT." . 164 NEW HAMPSHIRE . . 154
   "WHERE ARE YOU GOING TO PUT ME? IN THE ROAD?" .   164 NEW HAMPSHIRE . . 155
   "I'M GOING TO PUT YOU ON THE FARM NEXT TO IT." .   164 NEW HAMPSHIRE . . 156
   FLOWERS FANNED AND NOT PUT OUT BY ALL THE RAIN .   173 A STAR IN A STONEBOAT 23
   IF IT COULD PUT A STAR BACK IN ITS COURSE. . .   173 A STAR IN A STONEBOAT 30
   "THE BEST THING THAT WE'RE PUT HERE FOR'S TO SEE;   177 THE STAR-SPLITTER . 33
   SHE PUT HER FINGER IN YOUR CHEEK SO HARD . .   180 MAPLE 16
   BUT FORGOT TO PUT THE LEAF BACK IN CLOSING . .   181 MAPLE 67
   "I HAVE, AND BEEN PUT OFF SOMETIME, I THINK." .   183 MAPLE   109
   ONCE LONG AGO HER FATHER HAD PUT HIMSELF OFF.) .   183 MAPLE   111
   WHEN ALL MY STRENGTH PUT FORTH WAS IN HIS FAVOR,   185 THE AX-HELVE . . . 11
   "COME ON MY HOUSE AND I PUT YOU ONE IN . . .   186 THE AX-HELVE . . . 29
   PUT ON IT FROM WITHOUT. AND THERE ITS STRENGTH LAY   187 THE AX-HELVE . . . 75
   BUT WHEN PAUL PUT HIS FINGER IN THE GREASE, . . 193 PAUL'S WIFE . . . 72
   ALL THOSE GREAT RUFFIANS PUT THEIR THROATS TOGETHER,   195 PAUL'S WIFE . .   139
   BUT THE SHOUT REACHED THE GIRL AND PUT HER LIGHT OUT.   195 PAUL'S WIFE . .   143
   MURPHY TOLD ME PAUL PUT ON ALL THOSE AIRS . .   195 PAUL'S WIFE . .   148
   AND PUT IT IN MY HANDS TO PICK MY OWN GRAPES. .   197 WILD GRAPES . . . 38
   TO DO, AS SHE HAD PUT IT, WHAT WAS RIGHT. . .   201 PLACE FOR A THIRD . 75
   I HAD A VISION OF THEM PUT TOGETHER . . .   204 THE WITCH OF COOS . 68

PUT (CONTINUED)
    I WANTED TO PUT OUT THE LIGHT AND SEE . . . . 205 THE WITCH OF CODS . . 104
    HE GUESSED THEY'D KNOW WHAT HE HAD TO PUT UP WITH. . . . 210 PAUPER WITCH OF GRAFTON 88
    AND PUT MY FOOT ON ONE WITHOUT AVAIL, ... 237 A HILLSIDE THAW . . . 11
    WE WILL NOT BE PUT OFF THE FINAL GOAL . . . . 238 ON A TREE FALLEN ACROSS 10
    I PUT IT SHINING ANYWHERE I PLEASE. . . . . 245 THE FREEDOM OF THE MOON   7
    BEFORE GOD'S LAST PUT OUT THE LIGHT WAS SPOKEN. . . . . 250 ONCE BY THE PACIFIC . 14
    THAT DAY SHE PUT OUR HEADS TOGETHER, ... 252 TREE AT MY WINDOW . . 13
    AND ONE OF THEM PUT ME OFF MY AIM . . . . 275 TWO TRAMPS IN MUD TIME   3
    TRUST HIM THEN NOT TO PUT YOU IN THE WRONG. . . . . . . 278 THE WHITE-TAILED HORNET 26
    TO PUT THESE PEOPLE AT ONE STROKE OUT OF THEIR PAIN. . . 287 A ROADSIDE STAND . . 48
    AND OFFER TO PUT ME GENTLY OUT OF MY PAIN. . . . . . . 287 A ROADSIDE STAND . . 51
    HE WOULD PUT HIM ONTO THE CASE. . . . . 288 DEPARTMENTAL 12
    WHEN ONE WILL SAY, "LET US PUT IT OUT." . . . . 291 ON HEART'S BEGINNING TO 22
    THEY CAN PUT IT OUT WHENEVER THEY PLEASE. . . . . 291 ON HEART'S BEGINNING TO 25
    ONE PUT A THOUGHTFUL HAND UP TO HIS NOSE . . . . 293 AT WOODWARD'S GARDENS . 14
    BUT UNLESS YOU PUT THE RIGHT THING TO ITS ROOT . . . . . 296 LEAVES COMPARED WITH . 3
    PERHAPS I HAVE PUT FORTH TOO MUCH STRENGTH AND BEEN TOO
        FIERCE FROM FEAR. . . . . 297 A LEAF-TREADER 3
    AND PUT OUT ITS LIGHT FOR THE FOE. . . . . 311 THE VINDICTIVES 36
    WILL PUT TEN THOUSAND FARMERS OUT OF SHEEP. . . . . . . 319 BUILD SOIL 110
    I ELECT YOU TO PUT THE CURB ON IT. . . . . 320 BUILD SOIL 126
    WHICH PUT THE THOUGHT INTO SOMEONE'S HEAD . . . . 345 DISCOVERY OF MADEIRAS . 66
    UNLESS I PUT IT IN YOUR MOUTH TO SAY. . . . . 354 THE LESSON FOR TODAY . 115
    AS FINE AS FLOUR PUT THROUGH A BAKER'S SIEVE. . . . . . 365 OF STONES OF THE PLACE   8
    BUT PUT THAT DOWN TO SUPERSTITION, STRANGER. . . . . . 369 THE LITERATE FARMER AND 36
    PUT UP ON TRIAL BY THAT JERSEYITE . . . . 369 THE LITERATE FARMER AND 40
    PUT UP TO CURE THE WORLD BY MR. EDISON." . . . . 371 THE LITERATE FARMER AND 93
    WHILE THE TREES PUT ON THEIR WOODEN RINGS . . . . 376 SOMETHING FOR HOPE . . 11
    AND PUT A SIGN UP CLOSED TO ALL BUT ME. . . . . 378 DIRECTIVE 38
    BEFORE SHE MUST PUT OUT THE LIGHT ON THE CHILDREN . . . 379 TOO ANXIOUS FOR RIVERS 18
    I PUT NO FAITH IN THE SEEMING FACTS OF LIGHT. . . . . . 389 SKEPTIC 4
    IF ANYTHING SHOULD PUT AN END TO THIS, ... 397 THE PLANNERS 1
    THAT PUT AN END TO WHAT WAS GOING ON . . . . 397 THE PLANNERS 5
    PUT OUT OF THE PARK. . . . . 413 AWAY! 12
    AM PUT OUT WITH . . . . 413 AWAY! 15
    OR PUT OUT BY. . . . . 413 AWAY! 16
    PUTTING THE LAMP OUT HAS NOT PUT THEIR THOUGHT OUT. . . 415 A CABIN IN THE CLEARING 36
    AND SO PUT OFF THE WEARY DAY . . . . 417 AMERICA IS HARD TO SEE 40
    WHEN WE WOULD HAVE TO PUT OUR MIND . . . . 417 AMERICA IS HARD TO SEE 41
    OF JUST STAYING PUT, ... 434 KITTY HAWK 206
    SINCE YOU PUT FOOD FIRST IN YOUR REPERTORY. . . . . . . 455 HOW HARD TO KEEP FROM . 50
    TO PUT AN END TO THE KING'S VACILLATION. . . . . 456 HOW HARD TO KEEP FROM . 80
    HIS MOTHER DIDN'T LIKE THE WAY HE PUT IT, ... 457 HOW HARD TO KEEP FROM . 105
    AND PUT HER FOOT IN THE PAIL; . . . . 463 LINES IN DEJECTION . . 12
    TILL I WAS CAUGHT AND PUT TO SHAME, ... 467 QUANDARY 22
    I AM A NAME FOR BEING PUT UPON. . . . . 474 A MASQUE OF REASON . . 38
    'TWAS A GREAT DEMONSTRATION WE PUT ON. . . . . 475 A MASQUE OF REASON . . 53
    THAT'S ONE THING MORE TO PUT ON YOUR AGENDA. . . . . . 478 A MASQUE OF REASON . . 126
    I'M NOT A CHILD FOR YOU TO PUT ME OFF . . . . 482 A MASQUE OF REASON . . 256
    WOULD PUT AN END TO SUCH FANTASTIC NONSENSE. . . . . . 484 A MASQUE OF REASON . . 309
    PUT THAT IN IF IT ISN'T IN ALREADY: . . . . 486 A MASQUE OF REASON . . 372
    LOOK, WILL YOU LOOK! GOD CAN'T PUT WORDS IN MY MOUTH. . 505 A MASQUE OF MERCY . . 295
    (THEY PUT THEIR HANDS TOGETHER LIKE A BOOK . . . . . . 512 A MASQUE OF MERCY . . 489
PUTATIVE
    EXCEPT AS FATHER PUTATIVE TO SORT OF . . . . 498 A MASQUE OF MERCY . . 123
PUTS
    THE BEAR PUTS BOTH ARMS AROUND THE TREE ABOVE HER . . . 268 THE BEAR 1
    I TAKE THE FIRST BOAT. GOD PUTS UP A STORM . . . . . . 500 A MASQUE OF MERCY . . 180
PUTTING
    PUTTING IN THE SEED . . . . 123 PUTTING IN THE SEED . T
    HOW LOVE BURNS THROUGH THE PUTTING IN THE SEED . . . . 124 PUTTING IN THE SEED . 10
    I'M NOT THE ONE FOR PUTTING OFF THE PROOF. . . . . . . 265 DUST IN THE EYES . . . 3
    I ONLY KNELT AND PUTTING THE BOUGHS ASIDE . . . . 343 QUEST OF PURPLE-FRINGED 21
    PUTTING THE LAMP OUT HAS NOT PUT THEIR THOUGHT OUT. . . 415 A CABIN IN THE CLEARING 36
PUZZLE
    "GOOD-BY TO THEM! WE PUZZLE THEM. THEY THINK-- . . . . 114 IN THE HOME STRETCH . 111
    FOR A WOMAN AND A PUZZLE. . . . . 339 THE SUBVERTED FLOWER . 9
    I'M SICK OF THE WHOLE ARTIFICIAL PUZZLE. . . . . 484 A MASQUE OF REASON . . 300
PUZZLED
    A LOOK OF PUZZLED DIMNESS TO THEIR EYES . . . . 293 AT WOODWARD'S GARDENS . 10
PYRAMID
    YOU SQUAT OLD PYRAMID, ... 298 ON TAKING FROM THE TOP   2

Q

QUAINT
    AND TO HEAR HER QUAINT PHRASES--SO REMOVED . . . . . . 57 THE BLACK COTTAGE . . 62
    SOME QUAINT DISSATISFACTION ATE HIM. . . . . 451 A-WISHING WELL . . . 7
    SHE DIDN'T DO IT TO HIM TO BE QUAINT, ... 494 A MASQUE OF MERCY . . 37
QUAKE
    OR AT MOST SOME ANDEAN QUAKE, ... 418 AMERICA IS HARD TO SEE 71
QUAKING
    AT A STAR QUAKING IN THE OTHER END. . . . . 179 THE STAR-SPLITTER . . 78
QUALIFY
    AS SCHOOLMEN OF REPUTE SHOULD QUALIFY . . . . 352 THE LESSON FOR TODAY . 50
QUALITY
    THERE QUALITY MAKES UP FOR QUANTITY. . . . . 163 NEW HAMPSHIRE . . . 148
    OR QUALITY TO WORRY THE PRODUCER . . . . 164 NEW HAMPSHIRE . . . 168
QUANDARY
    QUANDARY . . . . 467 QUANDARY . . . . . . T
    THERE QUANDARY IS AT ITS GREATEST. . . . . 467 QUANDARY 14
QUANTITIES
    AND APPLES IN COMMERCIAL QUANTITIES?" . . . . 159 NEW HAMPSHIRE . . . 12
    BUT NOT GOLD IN COMMERCIAL QUANTITIES, ... 162 NEW HAMPSHIRE . . . 112

QUANTITY
    THERE QUALITY MAKES UP FOR QUANTITY. . . . . 163 NEW HAMPSHIRE . . . 148
    THE PRECIOUS LITERATURE IN QUANTITY . . . . 164 NEW HAMPSHIRE . . . 167
QUARREL
    THERE WAS NO QUARREL ABOUT PROPERTY." . . . . 84 THE HOUSEKEEPER . . . 94
    I NEVER TAKE MY OWN SIDE IN A QUARREL. . . . . 354 THE LESSON FOR TODAY . 123
    I HAD A LOVER'S QUARREL WITH THE WORLD. . . . . 355 THE LESSON FOR TODAY . 161
QUARRY
    MAY SEEM AS IF IT SHOULD HAVE BEEN A QUARRY-- . . . . 377 DIRECTIVE 10
QUARTER
    A WIND TO BLOW IN EARNEST FROM SOME QUARTER, ... 130 THE BONFIRE 33
QUARTERS
    HIS STINGING QUARTERS MENACINGLY WORK. . . . . 309 WASPISH 4
    YOU'VE GOT TO KEEP THE QUARTERS CLEAN." . . . . . . 345 DISCOVERY OF MADEIRAS . 62
QUARTS
    OFFERED FOR SALE WILD BERRIES IN WOODEN QUARTS, . . . 286 A ROADSIDE STAND . . 11
QUARTZ
    TRUTH? A PEBBLE OF QUARTZ? FOR ONCE, THEN, SOMETHING. . . 225 FOR ONCE SOMETHING . . 15
QUARTZ-STONES
    WHERE A MYRIAD SNOWY QUARTZ-STONES LIFT, ... 26 A LINE-STORM SONG . . 3
QUATRAIN
    A YOUNGSTER COMES TO ME WITH HALF A QUATRAIN . . . . 324 BUILD SOIL 270
    IN LANDOR'S QUATRAIN WOULD BE PRETTY SCENERY. . . . . 393 LUCRETIUS VERSUS POETS 9
QUEEN
    THIS IS THE WORD OF YOUR QUEEN." . . . . 288 DEPARTMENTAL . . . 32
    HAD THE QUEEN BACKED HIM TO A CRUISE. . . . . 416 AMERICA IS HARD TO SEE 6
    TO SAVE THE QUEEN FROM FAMILY CENSURE . . . . 416 AMERICA IS HARD TO SEE 11
    LIKE A KING AND QUEEN . . . . 442 KITTY HAWK 456
QUEER
    TWO OR THREE TIMES--HE MADE ME FEEL SO QUEER-- . . . 36 DEATH OF THE HIRED MAN 56
    MY LITTLE HORSE MUST THINK IT QUEER . . . . 224 STOPPING BY WOODS . . 5
QUENCHED
    GO TILL YOU WET YOUR PINIONS AND ARE QUENCHED. . . . . 356 A MOTH SEEN IN WINTER . 18
QUEST
    AS THEY ARE FREE, TO GO IN QUEST . . . . 236 MISGIVING 14
    THE QUEST OF THE PURPLE-FRINGED . . . . 342 QUEST OF PURPLE-FRINGED T
    COMPARISON IS NOT HER QUEST. . . . . 390 TWO LEADING LIGHTS . 23
    YOUR FUGITIVE ESCAPE BECOME A QUEST. . . . . 513 A MASQUE OF MERCY . 535
QUESTING
    YOUR FATHER FEELS US ROUND HIM WITH OUR QUESTING, . . . 183 MAPLE 123
QUESTION
    LOVE AND A QUESTION . . . . 7 LOVE AND A QUESTION . T
    AND QUESTION WHAT OF THE NIGHT TO BE, ... 7 LOVE AND A QUESTION . 11
    ALL FOR ME? AND NOT A QUESTION . . . . 13 FLOWER-GATHERING . . 9
    BUT THE FEET QUESTION "WHITHER?" . . . . 30 RELUCTANCE 18
    THE QUESTION THAT HE FRAMES IN ALL BUT WORDS . . . . 120 THE OVEN BIRD . . . 13
    AND OPEN-MINDED. SHE WAS FREE TO QUESTION . . . . . 163 NEW HAMPSHIRE . . . 130
    BUT HERE IS NOT A QUESTION OF WHAT'S SACRED; . . . . 171 NEW HAMPSHIRE . . . 395
    WHO ASKED THE QUESTION. HE JUST DISAPPEARED-- . . . . 192 PAUL'S WIFE 26
    THE QUESTION EVERYWHERE WAS WHY SHOULD PAUL . . . . . 192 PAUL'S WIFE 31
    OBJECT TO BEING ASKED A CIVIL QUESTION-- . . . . . . 192 PAUL'S WIFE 32
    THE QUESTION IS WHETHER THEY'VE REACHED A DEPTH . . . 317 BUILD SOIL 33
    A QUESTION . . . . 362 A QUESTION . . . . T
    QUESTION OF WHAT WE'RE TURNING INTO NEXT." . . . . . 369 THE LITERATE FARMER AND 48
    OF CEASING-TO-QUESTION-WHAT-DOESN'T-CONCERN-US, ... 379 TOO ANXIOUS FOR RIVERS 9
    BUT, GOD, I HAVE A QUESTION TOO TO RAISE. . . . . . 479 A MASQUE OF REASON . 163
    I HAVE A QUESTION EVEN THERE TO ASK-- . . . . 479 A MASQUE OF REASON . 171
    BUT TO MY QUESTION. I AM MUCH IMPRESSED . . . . . . 480 A MASQUE OF REASON . 183
    TO ASK MY QUESTION. WE DISPARAGE REASON. . . . . . 481 A MASQUE OF REASON . 228
    A QUESTION WHO WAS GETTING THE MOST OUT . . . . . . 503 A MASQUE OF MERCY . 248
QUESTIONED
    "WARREN?" SHE QUESTIONED. / "DEAD," WAS ALL HE ANSWERED. . 40 DEATH OF THE HIRED MAN 166
QUESTIONING
    QUESTIONING FACES . . . . 445 QUESTIONING FACES . . T
QUESTIONS
    I THOUGHT OF QUESTIONS THAT HAVE NO REPLY, ... 22 THE TUFT OF FLOWERS . 19
    "OR DISREGARDING PEOPLE'S CIVIL QUESTIONS-- . . . . . 151 SNOW 251
    ARE FREEDOMS FROM THE NEED OF ASKING QUESTIONS. . . . 484 A MASQUE OF REASON . 313
    (I HOPE YOU KNOW THE GAME CALLED TWENTY QUESTIONS.) . . 484 A MASQUE OF REASON . 314
QUI
    "AH," HE SAID, "QUI VIVE, ... 468 A REFLEX 8
QUICK
    "QUICK!" I SLAMMED TO THE DOOR AND HELD THE KNOB. . . . 206 THE WITCH OF COOS . . 118
    MADE QUICK ASIDES, BUT HAVING DONE IN AIR . . . . . 240 OUR SINGING STRENGTH . 40
    IN THREE QUICK STEPS AS OFF AN ESCALATOR. . . . . . 489 A MASQUE OF REASON . 452
QUICKENS
    IT VERY LIKELY QUICKENS AND REFINES US. . . . . . . 321 BUILD SOIL . . . 171
QUICKSILVER
    A GLOBULE OF QUICKSILVER IN YOUR HAND . . . . 179 THE STAR-SPLITTER . 90
QUIDNUNCS
    INCORRIGIBLE QUIDNUNCS, ... 464 MILKY WAY IS A COWPATH 9
QUIET
    A QUIET LIGHT, AND THEN NOT EVEN THAT. . . . . . . 108 OLD MAN'S WINTER NIGHT 17
    QUIET AND LIGHT AND WARM, IN SPITE OF ALL . . . . . 148 SNOW 143
    IT'S QUIET AS AN EMPTY CHURCH WITHOUT HIM." . . . . . 152 SNOW 260
    MURMURING SOMETHING QUIET IN HER BREAST, ... 249 ACCEPTANCE 6
    AGE SAW TWO QUIET CHILDREN . . . . 335 CARPE DIEM 1
QUILL
    IN A DISPLAY OF UNDERDOWN AND QUILL . . . . 445 QUESTIONING FACES . . 5
QUINTESSENCE
    I KNOW THE QUINTESSENCE OF MANY THINGS. . . . . . . 455 HOW HARD TO KEEP FROM 41
    I KNOW THE QUINTESSENCE OF FOOD, I KNOW . . . . . . 455 HOW HARD TO KEEP FROM 42
    THE QUINTESSENCE OF JEWELS, AND I KNOW . . . . . . 455 HOW HARD TO KEEP FROM 43
    THE QUINTESSENCE OF HORSES, MEN, AND WOMEN." . . . . 455 HOW HARD TO KEEP FROM 44
    IT SEEMS YOU CALL QUINTESSENCE QUINTESSENCE." . . . . 455 HOW HARD TO KEEP FROM 51
    "OH, FROM MY KNOWLEDGE OF ITS QUINTESSENCE. . . . . . 456 HOW HARD TO KEEP FROM 87
    I TOLD YOU I KNEW THE QUINTESSENCE OF JEWELS. . . . . 456 HOW HARD TO KEEP FROM 88

QUIT
  THE RIVER BANK, QUIT WORK DEFIANTLY, ... 405 FROM PLANE TO PLANE . 58
  WHERE HE WOULD HAVE TO QUIT HIS POLITICS . . . . . . 509 A MASQUE OF MERCY . . 402
QUITE
  WHERE WINDS WERE QUITE EXCLUDED, ... 13 ROSE POGONIAS . . . 5
  HE DON'T KNOW WHY HE ISN'T QUITE AS GOOD . . . . . . 39 DEATH OF THE HIRED MAN 143
  MY FATHER'S BROTHER, HE WENT MAD QUITE YOUNG. . . . . 65 A SERVANT TO SERVANTS . 104
  THERE AIN'T NO NAMES QUITE LIKE THE OLD ONES, THOUGH, . . 80 THE GENERATIONS OF MEN 186
  QUITE SOLITARY AND HAVING EQUAL BOUGHS . . . . 107 CHRISTMAS TREES . . . 35
  (SOFT PETALS, YES, BUT NOT SO BARREN QUITE, ... 124 PUTTING IN THE SEED . 5
  TO KEEP HIM--THOUGH PERHAPS YOU DIDN'T QUITE . . . . . 153 SNOW 282
  IS THAT HER MOUNTAINS AREN'T QUITE HIGH ENOUGH. . . . . 169 NEW HAMPSHIRE . . . 311
  HER PEOPLE NOT QUITE SHORT ENOUGH FOR ART, ... 170 NEW HAMPSHIRE . . . 356
  AND IN CONJUNCTION GIVING QUITE A SPREAD. . . . . . . 269 THE BEAR 21
  NOT QUITE SOCIAL . . . . 306 NOT QUITE SOCIAL . . T
  NATURE'S NEVER QUITE . . . . 442 KITTY HAWK 451
  IT NEEDN'T BE QUITE SO TERRIFIC . . . . 453 A-WISHING WELL . . . 65
  IT NEEDN'T BE QUITE SO GIGANTIC . . . . 453 A-WISHING WELL . . . 67
  WON'T SEEM UNHERETICAL QUITE. . . . . 466 SOME SCIENCE FICTION . 20
  CAN EVER QUITE PASS OUT OF UTTER GRIEF . . . . 469 WE VAINLY WRESTLE... . 3
  HOW ARE YOU NOW? I TRUST YOU'RE QUITE RECOVERED, . . . 474 A MASQUE OF REASON . . 35
  YET YOUR FRIEND HERE CAN'T BE QUITE DISREGARDED, . . . 517 A MASQUE OF MERCY . . 638
QUIVER
  AND QUIVER LIKE THE FRAYED EDGE OF THE DRIFT . . . . . 149 SNOW 195
QUIVERED
  NOW QUIVERED TOWARD EACH OTHER, LIPPED . . . . 381 AN UNSTAMPED LETTER IN 34
QUIVERFUL
  A QUIVERFUL TO CHOOSE FROM, SINCE HE WISHED ME . . . . 187 THE AX-HELVE 64
QUIZZICAL
  IN SELF-DEFENSE TO QUIZZICAL INQUIRY: . . . . 365 OF STONES OF THE PLACE 14
QUIZZICALLY
  HE VIEWED THEM QUIZZICALLY WITH JERKS OF HEAD, ... 229 TWO LOOK AT TWO . . . 31
QUOTE
  BUT I'M NO ONE TO QUOTE. . . . . 391 A WISH TO COMPLY . . 5
  I QUOTE HIM WITH RESPECT VERBATIM. . . . . 451 A-WISHING WELL . . . 6
  TO QUOTE THE ORACLE OF DELPHI, ... 467 QUANDARY 11
  TO QUOTE THE GREATEST WESTERN POEM YET. . . . . . . 485 A MASQUE OF REASON . 344
QUOTED
  AND I APTLY QUOTED. . . . . 433 KITTY HAWK 169
QUOTES
  "I'M--BOUND--AWAY!" (HE QUOTES IT TO THE TUNE.) . . . 500 A MASQUE OF MERCY . 172
QUOTING
  AND RAN FOR SHELTER QUOTING MATTHEW ARNOLD: . . . . . 170 NEW HAMPSHIRE . . . 370

R

RABBIT
  BUT THEY WOULD HAVE THE RABBIT OUT OF HIDING, ... 33 MENDING WALL 8
  I DON'T WANT IT GIRDLED BY RABBIT AND MOUSE, ... 228 GOOD-BY AND KEEP COLD . 6
  I'D SUMMON GROUSE, RABBIT, AND DEER TO THE WALL . . . . 228 GOOD-BY AND KEEP COLD . 10
  LIKE RABBIT AND DEER . . . . 235 GATHERING LEAVES . . 7
  AS UNORIGINAL AS ANY RABBIT. . . . . 354 THE LESSON FOR TODAY . 112
RABBIT-HUNTER
  THE RABBIT-HUNTER . . . . 360 THE RABBIT-HUNTER . . T
RACE
  WHITE WAS THE ONLY RACE SHE EVER KNEW. . . . . 57 THE BLACK COTTAGE . . 75
  PRE-PRIMITIVES OF THE WHITE RACE, DAWN PEOPLE, ... 161 NEW HAMPSHIRE . . . 78
  BUT FAINTLY REMINISCENT OF THE RACE . . . . 173 A STAR IN A STONEBOAT . 32
  THESE HANDS HAVE HELPED IT GO, AND EVEN RACE; . . . . . 188 THE GRINDSTONE . . . 4
  WITH THE DEAD RACE OF THE GREAT AUK!" . . . . 212 AN EMPTY THREAT . . 52
  WHO DIED A SOLDIER-POET OF YOUR RACE. . . . . 222 TO E.T. 8
  REDUCE THE BIRTHS OF THE HUMAN RACE, ... 263 THE TIMES TABLE . . 19
  WITH HER FOR MOTHER EVE, A RACE . . . . 280 BLUE RIBBON AT AMESBURY 27
  ANTS ARE A CURIOUS RACE; . . . . 288 DEPARTMENTAL . . . 13
  AS RELIC OF A VANISHED RACE OF TREES-- . . . . 290 OLD BARN AT THE BOTTOM 39
  BETWEEN STARS--ON STARS WHERE NO HUMAN RACE IS. . . . . 296 DESERT PLACES . . . 14
  WITH THE RACE HE CHOSE TO ADOPT: . . . . 314 BEARER OF EVIL TIDINGS 38
  WE BOTH ARE THE BELITTLED HUMAN RACE, ... 353 THE LESSON FOR TODAY . 77
  AND SO'S THE NATION, SO'S THE TOTAL RACE. . . . . . . 355 THE LESSON FOR TODAY . 146
  TO ANY DEMONSTRABLY BETTER RACE, ... 369 THE LITERATE FARMER AND 50
  (BUT WHAT A HUMAN RACE THE WHITE HAS BEEN!) . . . . . 369 THE LITERATE FARMER AND 52
  BEFORE THE INDIAN RACE WAS FURTHER WRONGED. . . . . . 370 THE LITERATE FARMER AND 60
  SEEMS AS EXPRESSIVE OF THE HUMAN RACE . . . . 382 TO AN ANCIENT . . . 8
  AND OF HIS RACE STARVATION SLIM, ... 392 A CLIFF DWELLING . . 12
  CALLING ALL BUTTERFLIES OF EVERY RACE . . . . 411 POD OF THE MILKWEED . 1
  A FRESH START FOR THE HUMAN RACE. . . . . 417 AMERICA IS HARD TO SEE 30
  OF A THINKING RACE . . . . 440 KITTY HAWK 393
  OF THEMSELVES AS A RACE . . . . 448 THE BAD ISLAND--EASTER 22
  IS TOO HARD ON THE HUMAN RACE. . . . . 453 A-WISHING WELL . . . 70
  WITH THE HEADLONG HUMAN RACE. . . . . 465 SOME SCIENCE FICTION . 4
  FROM MORAL BONDAGE TO THE HUMAN RACE. . . . . 475 A MASQUE OF REASON . 70
  AND OF THE MESSIANIC RACE, KARL MARX. . . . . 515 A MASQUE OF MERCY . 578
RACES
  OF WHO BEGAN IT BETWEEN THE TWO RACES. . . . . 142 THE VANISHING RED . . 13
  WE SEE HOW SERIOUSLY THE RACES SWARM . . . . 423 FOR JOHN F. KENNEDY . 34
RACE'S
  THE RACE'S FUTURE TRIAL PLACE, ... 417 AMERICA IS HARD TO SEE 29
RACIEST
  THE LONGEST-SAVED-UP, RACIEST, LOCALEST . . . . . . 321 BUILD SOIL 161
RACING
  AND THEN CAME RACING WILDLY ON AGAIN . . . . 357 A CONSIDERABLE SPECK . 11
RACK
  I CLEANED THE RACK AND DROVE OUT TO COOL OFF. . . . . 72 THE CODE 80
  MIGHT SEE THEM ON A RACK LIKE FAMOUS OARS, ... 290 OLD BARN AT THE BOTTOM 36
  ONE INCA PRINCE ON THE RACK, ... 311 THE VINDICTIVES . . . 41
  NO NEED FOR US TO RACK OUR COMMON HEADS . . . . . . 372 THE LITERATE FARMER AND 132

RACKER
   I HATE HIS WRETCHED LITTLE RACKER SECT, ... 144 SNOW 53
RACKFUL
   AND DUMPED THE RACKFUL ON HIM IN TEN LOTS. . . . . . . 72 THE CODE 74
RADIANCE
   BACK UP A STREAM OF RADIANCE TO THE SKY, ... 300 THE MASTER SPEED . . 3
RADIANT
   ALL OF THEM RADIANT AND MIGHTY SHINY. . . . . 425 ACCIDENTALLY ON PURPOSE 4
RADICAL
   I NEVER DARED BE RADICAL WHEN YOUNG . . . . 308 PRECAUTION 1
RADIO
   'TWAS A RADIO . . . . 436 KITTY HAWK 270
   THEN THE RADIO . . . . 436 KITTY HAWK 277
   AND THE RADIO . . . . 437 KITTY HAWK 296
RADISHES
   RADISHES, LETTUCE, PEAS, ... 134 A GIRL'S GARDEN . . . 30
RADIUM
   OF RADIUM. I KNOW WITH RADIUM . . . . 162 NEW HAMPSHIRE . . . 119
   OF RADIUM OR ANYTHING TO SELL. . . . . 163 NEW HAMPSHIRE . . 123
RAFTER
   HE TOOK HIM DOWN BELOW A CRAMPING RAFTER, ... 142 THE VANISHING RED . . 20
RAG
   TO WASH THE STEPS WITH PAIL AND RAG . . . . 307 PROVIDE, PROVIDE . . 2
RAGE
   SOMEONE HAD BETTER BE PREPARED FOR RAGE. . . . . . . 250 ONCE BY THE PACIFIC . 12
   THAT ALL DAY FIGHTS A NERVOUS INWARD RAGE, ... 269 THE BEAR 14
   THAT POETRY WITH ALL ITS GOLDEN RAGE . . . . . . 358 THE LOST FOLLOWER . 14
   TOO LOFTY AND ORIGINAL TO RAGE. . . . . 378 DIRECTIVE 52
   SHE LET OUT A HOWL OF RAGE . . . . 463 LINES IN DEJECTION . 22
RAGED
   HUNTED AND TORTURED AND RAGED. . . . . 311 THE VINDICTIVES . . 48
RAGGED
   TO ALMOST STRIPS AND TAPES OF RAGGED WHITE . . . . . 239 OUR SINGING STRENGTH . 8
   AND CRACKED HIS RAGGED MUZZLE. . . . . 339 THE SUBVERTED FLOWER . 14
RAGHT
   "YOU GIVE HER ONE GOOD CRACK, SHE'S SNAP RAGHT OFF. . . 186 THE AX-HELVE . . . 26
RAGS
   IN DEALING IN "OLD RAGS" IN SAN FRANCISCO. . . . . . 160 NEW HAMPSHIRE . . . 58
   "BEHOLD MY SON IN RAGS HERE WITH HIS LYRE," . . . . . 459 HOW HARD TO KEEP FROM 169
RAID
   HIS CAN BE NO SUCH EASY RAID . . . . 419 AMERICA IS HARD TO SEE 83
RAIL
   HE GAVE THE SOLID RAIL A HATEFUL KICK. . . . . . . 269 THE EGG AND THE MACHINE 1
   AND BENT SOME RAIL WIDE OPEN LIKE A SWITCH, ... 270 THE EGG AND THE MACHINE 7
   AND WENT TO LEAN AGAINST THE RAIL, ... 345 DISCOVERY OF MADEIRAS . 50
RAILROAD
   IN WOODS SOME TEN MILES FROM A RAILROAD STATION, . . . 160 NEW HAMPSHIRE . . . 41
   TO EARN A LIVING ON THE CONCORD RAILROAD, ... 178 THE STAR-SPLITTER . . 68
   LIKE COMING TO A SUDDEN RAILROAD STATION. . . . . . 189 THE GRINDSTONE . . . 33
   GOING BY AT A RAILROAD RATE, ... 292 ON HEART'S BEGINNING TO 43
RAIN
   THINKS THESE DARK DAYS OF AUTUMN RAIN . . . . . . 6 MY NOVEMBER GUEST . . 2
   COME WITH RAIN, O LOUD SOUTHWESTER! . . . . . . 11 TO THE THAWING WIND . 1
   AND BE MY LOVE IN THE RAIN. . . . . 26 A LINE-STORM SONG . 8
   WHERE THE BOUGHS RAIN WHEN IT BLOWS. . . . . . . 26 A LINE-STORM SONG . 16
   AND BE MY LOVE IN THE RAIN. . . . . 27 A LINE-STORM SONG . 32
   YOU OUGHT TO HAVE SEEN HOW IT LOOKED IN THE RAIN, . . . 62 BLUEBERRIES 103
   UR A LUNG RAIN. I SHOULD SOON GET ENOUGH, ... 67 A SERVANT TO SERVANTS . 164
   BUT RAIN SPOILED ALL. THE DAY BEGAN UNCERTAIN, ... 74 THE GENERATIONS OF MEN 19
   WITH CLOUDS LOW-TRAILING AND MOMENTS OF RAIN THAT MISTED. . 74 THE GENERATIONS OF MEN 20
   ARE THERE," THEY SAID. "IT ISN'T GOING TO RAIN." . . . 74 THE GENERATIONS OF MEN 24
   "NOT FROM THE RAIN. I THINK IT'S GOING TO RAIN." . . . 75 THE GENERATIONS OF MEN 67
   DOES THE RAIN SEEM TO YOU TO COOL THE EYES?" . . . . 75 THE GENERATIONS OF MEN 69
   "YOU LOOK SO, SITTING OUT HERE IN THE RAIN . . . . 76 THE GENERATIONS OF MEN 84
   IT'S GOING TO RAIN." / "I KNOW, AND IT WAS RAINING. . . . 80 THE GENERATIONS OF MEN 201
   ONCE MORE BEFORE WE MEET ELSEWHERE." / "IN RAIN?" . . . 81 THE GENERATIONS OF MEN 209
   "IT OUGHT TO BE IN RAIN. SOMETIME IN RAIN. . . . . . 81 THE GENERATIONS OF MEN 210
   IN RAIN TOMORROW, SHALL WE, IF IT RAINS? . . . . . . 81 THE GENERATIONS OF MEN 211
   WAS A BLOW-AWAY PAPER THE RAIN . . . . 110 A PATCH OF OLD SNOW . 3
   AFTER A RAIN. THEY CLICK UPON THEMSELVES . . . . . . 121 BIRCHES 7
   WITH PITCHY HANDS TO WAIT FOR RAIN OR SNOW. . . . . . 129 THE BONFIRE 4
   OH, LET'S NOT WAIT FOR RAIN TO MAKE IT SAFE. . . . . . 129 THE BONFIRE 5
   FLOWERS FANNED AND NOT PUT OUT BY ALL THE RAIN . . . 173 A STAR IN A STONEBOAT . 23
   WITH ALL THE RAIN AND SNOW OF SEVEN YEARS; . . . . . 210 PAUPER WITCH OF GRAFTON 92
   WHERE DRIVEN RAIN HAD WET AND SWOLLEN THEM. . . . . . 216 A FOUNTAIN, A BOTTLE . 97
   AND THE SMELL OF FIRE DROWNED IN RAIN . . . . . . 232 THE KITCHEN CHIMNEY . 15
   (BY WHICH THEY MEAN THE RAIN IS PEARLS SO EARLY, ... 236 VALLEY'S SINGING DAY . 12
   THE RAIN TO THE WIND SAID, ... 250 LODGED 1
   OUT ALONE IN THE WINTER RAIN, ... 252 THE THATCH 1
   THE RAIN BY RIGHTS WAS SNOW FOR COLD. . . . . . . 253 THE THATCH . . . 11
   BY LETTING THE RAIN I KNEW OUTDOORS . . . . . . 253 THE THATCH 34
   I HAVE WALKED OUT IN RAIN--AND BACK IN RAIN. . . . . . 255 ACQUAINTED WITH NIGHT . 2
   IT IS TRUE THE LONGEST DROUTH WILL END IN RAIN. . . . . 268 ON LOOKING UP BY CHANCE 11
   'TIS THE WORLD-OLD WAY OF THE RAIN . . . . . . 285 IN TIME OF CLOUDBURST . 5
   HE HAD A WELL, HE HAD THE RAIN TO CATCH. . . . . . 292 FIGURE IN THE DOORWAY . 17
   THE CLOUDS, THE SOURCE OF RAIN, ONE STORMY NIGHT . . . 295 LOST IN HEAVEN . . . 1
   THANKS TO A CLEARING RAIN. . . . . 301 VOICE WAYS 3
   BRING ON WIND. BRING RAIN IN TORRENTS-- . . . . . 304 CLEAR AND COLDER . . 13
   THE WIND AND THE RAIN . . . . 336 THE WIND AND THE RAIN . T
   AS STRONG IS RAIN WITHOUT AS WINE WITHIN, ... 337 THE WIND AND THE RAIN . 41
   WHEN THERE WAS RAIN; . . . . 337 THE WIND AND THE RAIN . 44
   RAIN WAS THE TEARS ADOPTED BY MY EYES . . . . . . 337 THE WIND AND THE RAIN . 47
   WE ASKED FOR RAIN. IT DIDN'T FLASH AND ROAR. . . . . . 349 OUR HOLD ON THE PLANET 1
   AND JUST BECAUSE WE OWNED TO A WISH FOR RAIN, ... 349 OUR HOLD ON THE PLANET 5
   IN ONE WILD DAY OF RAIN. . . . . 359 NOVEMBER 6
   THEN THE RAIN STOPPED AND THE BLOWING, ... 377 ONE STEP BACKWARD TAKEN 13
   A RAIN, THOUGH STINGY, HAD BEGUN TO FALL . . . . . 399 THE BROKEN DROUGHT . . 3
   THE DROUGHT WAS ONE NO SPIT OF RAIN COULD CURE. . . . . 400 THE BROKEN DROUGHT . . 10

```
                                                    PAGE TITLE                      LINE
RAINBOW
    THEN A SMALL RAINBOW LIKE A TRELLIS GATE,   . . . . . .  315 IRIS BY NIGHT      . . .  17
    I WONDER! BOW AND RAINBOW AS IT BENT, . . . . . . . .  315 IRIS BY NIGHT      . . .  23
RAINED
    HE'S GOT HAY DOWN THAT'S BEEN RAINED ON THREE TIMES. . . .  83 THE HOUSEKEEPER   . . .  57
RAIN-FRESH
    THE RAIN-FRESH GOLDENROD. . . . . . . . . . . . . . .  27 A LINE-STORM SONG  . .  24
RAINING
    "IT'S RAINING." / "NO, IT'S MISTING; LET'S BE FAIR. . . .  75 THE GENERATIONS OF MEN  68
    IT'S GOING TO RAIN." / "I KNOW, AND IT WAS RAINING. . . .  80 THE GENERATIONS OF MEN  201
RAINS
    IN RAIN TOMORROW, SHALL WE, IF IT RAINS? . . . . . . .  81 THE GENERATIONS OF MEN  211
RAIN-WASHED
    A BLACK-CHEEKED STONE AND STICK OF RAIN-WASHED CHARCOAL.  . 171 NEW HAMPSHIRE   . . .  391
RAINY
    'THREE FOGGY MORNINGS AND ONE RAINY DAY . . . . . . .  54 HOME BURIAL    . . . .  92
    AND JUNE WAS NOT MUCH BETTER, COLD AND RAINY. . . . . . 407 FROM PLANE TO PLANE  .  89
RAISE
    TO RAISE HERSELF AND LOOK AGAIN. HE SPOKE   . . . . . .  51 HOME BURIAL    . . . .  5
    THAN I CAN RAISE MY VOICE OR WANT TO LIFT   . . . . . .  63 A SERVANT TO SERVANTS .  8
    BUT LET ME RAISE THIS CURTAIN ON A SCENE,   . . . . . . 148 SNOW    . . . . . . . 155
    BUT THE MOUNTAINS I RAISE . . . . . . . . . . . . . . 235 GATHERING LEAVES  . .  9
    AS VAIN AS RAISE A VOICE AS A SIGH . . . . . . . . . . 247 ON GOING UNNOTICED  . .  1
    BUT WHAT YOU RAISE OR GROW, WHY, FEED IT OUT,  . . . . . 323 BUILD SOIL   . . . . . 215
    WE WELL MAY RAISE OUR HEADS . . . . . . . . . . . . . 361 ALMOST TWO THOUSAND  .  10
    THEY RAISE IN THEIR INTEMPERANCE A CLOUD  . . . . . . . 411 POD OF THE MILKWEED  .  27
    BUT, GOD, I HAVE A QUESTION TOO TO RAISE.   . . . . . . 479 A MASQUE OF REASON  . . 163
RAISED
    WE RAISED A SIMPLE PRAYER . . . . . . . . . . . . . .  14 ROSE POGONIAS  . . .  17
    SHE RAISED HER VOICE AGAINST THE CLOSING DOOR: . . . . .  89 THE HOUSEKEEPER   . . . 213
    A TREE THAT HAD BEEN DOWN AND RAISED AGAIN-- . . . . . . 125 AN ENCOUNTER  . . . .  13
    NO, NONE OF THESE HAS RAISED ME TO MY THRONE . . . . . . 169 NEW HAMPSHIRE  . . . 327
    AND, IN THE PAUSES WHEN SHE RAISED HER EYES,  . . . . . 182 MAPLE    . . . . . .  80
    AND WHEN HE RAISED IT DRIPPING ONCE AND TRIED . . . . . 190 THE GRINDSTONE   . . .  68
    AND RAISED BOTH HANDS  . . . . . . . . . . . . . . . 241 THE LOCKLESS DOOR   . .  7
    HE RAISED AGAINST THE GODS IN THE MACHINE.  . . . . . . 270 THE EGG AND THE MACHINE  15
    AND RAISED AMONG THE LEAVES AND DULY TOLD,  . . . . . . 283 THE GOLD HESPERIDEE  .  15
    THE BOTTOM OF SEAS RAISED DRY-- . . . . . . . . . . . 285 IN TIME OF CLOUDBURST  .  15
    RAISED THIS TOWER SHAFT  . . . . . . . . . . . . . . 430 KITTY HAWK   . . . .  71
RAISES
    THAT THE BROOK RAISES IN THE EMPTY VALLEY.  . . . . . .  77 THE GENERATIONS OF MEN  125
    NEW HAMPSHIRE RAISES THE CONNECTICUT . . . . . . . . . 165 NEW HAMPSHIRE  . . . 183
RAISING (SEE HAIR-RAISING)
    RAISING A LITTLE, SENDING UP A LITTLE.   . . . . . . . 259 WEST-RUNNING BROOK  .  63
    A SHIP KEEPS RAISING ITS HULL; . . . . . . . . . . . . 301 NEITHER OUT FAR NOR IN  6
    AND RAISING A DUST WITH A TRAIN . . . . . . . . . . . 312 THE VINDICTIVES   . . .  74
RAKE
    I'LL ONLY STOP TO RAKE THE LEAVES AWAY   . . . . . . .  1 THE PASTURE   . . . .  2
    COMBED IT DOWN WITH A RAKE AND SAYS, 'O.K.'  . . . . . .  71 THE CODE   . . . . .  52
RAKING
    RAKING THE DOORYARD, WORKING NEAR THE HOUSE.  . . . . .  49 A HUNDRED COLLARS   . . 128
    RAKING UP AFTER WINTER, AND I SAID,  . . . . . . . . . 164 NEW HAMPSHIRE  . . . 153
RALEIGH
    SOWED IN VAIN BY RALEIGH, . . . . . . . . . . . . . . 431 KITTY HAWK   . . . .  92
    RALEIGH OF THE CLOAK, . . . . . . . . . . . . . . . . 431 KITTY HAWK   . . . .  93
RALLE
    TELL YOU WHAT RALLE THE SIOUX CONTROL ONCE TOLD ME. . . 202 THE WITCH OF COOS   . .  13
RAM'S
    COME, HOLD IT OUT. DON'T CHANGE.--A RAM'S HORN ORCHID!  .  96 THE SELF-SEEKER   . . 112
    A RAM'S HORN! WHAT WOULD I HAVE GOT, I WONDER,  . . . .  96 THE SELF-SEEKER   . . 113
    ANOTHER RAM'S HORN! WHERE DID YOU FIND THOSE,  . . . . .  97 THE SELF-SEEKER   . . 115
    A RAM'S HORN ORCHID SEEDPOD FOR A WOODCHUCK . . . . . .  97 THE SELF-SEEKER   . . 126
    THOUGH THE RAM'S HORN IS SELDOM TO BE HAD . . . . . . .  97 THE SELF-SEEKER   . . 129
    YOU DON'T TELL ME THAT WHERE YOU FOUND A RAM'S HORN . .  97 THE SELF-SEEKER   . . 136
RAN
    TO SEEK THE BROOK IF STILL IT RAN; . . . . . . . . . .  18 GOING FOR WATER   . . .  4
    WE RAN AS IF TO MEET THE MOON  . . . . . . . . . . . .  18 GOING FOR WATER   . . .  9
    SHE RAN ON TIPTOE DOWN THE DARKENED PASSAGE . . . . . .  34 DEATH OF THE HIRED MAN  3
    HE RAN ON HAROLD WILSON--YOU REMEMBER-- . . . . . . . .  36 DEATH OF THE HIRED MAN  58
    PASTURE RAN UP THE SIDE A LITTLE WAY, . . . . . . . . .  41 THE MOUNTAIN   . . .  29
    THE FIRE RAN AND BURNED IT ALL UP BUT THE WALL."  . . .  59 BLUEBERRIES   . . . .  12
    SHE SAID, "AS THE LIGHT ON THE DASHBOARD RAN . . . . .  89 THE FEAR   . . . . .  10
    SO RAN TOGETHER THAT I DIDN'T TRY TO. . . . . . . . . . 112 IN THE HOME STRETCH  .  52
    THE INDWELLING SPIDER RAN TO GREET THE FLY, . . . . . . 126 RANGE-FINDING  . . .  13
    SHE STOOD, AND THEN SHE RAN AND HID  . . . . . . . . . 129 THE IMPULSE   . . . .  19
    BUT SHE ALWAYS RAN AWAY AND LEFT  . . . . . . . . . . 134 A GIRL'S GARDEN   . .  23
    AS IT RAN LIGHT, OR HAD TO BEAR A LOAD.  . . . . . . . 136 "OUT, OUT--"   . . . .  8
    AND RAN FOR SHELTER QUOTING MATTHEW ARNOLD: . . . . . . 170 NEW HAMPSHIRE  . . . 370
    IT WAS THE TREE THE AUTUMN FIRE RAN THROUGH . . . . . . 184 MAPLE    . . . . . . 140
    WITH A THICK THUMBNAIL TO SHOW HOW IT RAN . . . . . . . 186 THE AX-HELVE   . . .  23
    (IT RAN AS IF IT WASN'T GREASED BUT GLUED); . . . . . . 190 THE GRINDSTONE   . . .  61
    THE FAINTEST RESTLESS RUSTLING RAN ALL THROUGH THEM. . . 204 THE WITCH OF COOS   . .  64
    THEN RAN AND SHOUTED, "SHUT THE BEDROOM DOOR, . . . . . 205 THE WITCH OF COOS   . .  93
    THAT SUCH A BROOK RAN WATER. BUT I WONDER . . . . . . . 231 A BROOK IN THE CITY  .  21
    THE SWARM STILL RAN AND SCUTTLED JUST AS FAST. . . . . . 237 A HILLSIDE THAW   . .  24
    AND THOUGH AT THAT THE TARDY RAN, . . . . . . . . . . 273 A LONE STRIKER   . . .  3
    RAN INTO A DORMANT MOTH  . . . . . . . . . . . . . . 287 DEPARTMENTAL   . . . .  2
    BUT AS THROUGH THE MONOTONY WE RAN,  . . . . . . . . . 292 FIGURE IN THE DOORWAY  .  5
    THEIR MINDS RAN ON CRANNY AND CRACK. . . . . . . . . . 311 THE VINDICTIVES   . . .  31
    HE RAN THROUGH THE VALE OF CASHMERE, . . . . . . . . . 313 BEARER OF EVIL TIDINGS  10
    HE RAN THROUGH THE RHODODENDRONS  . . . . . . . . . . 313 BEARER OF EVIL TIDINGS  11
    TURNED FROM THE PLACE AND RAN. . . . . . . . . . . . . 341 THE SUBVERTED FLOWER  .  61
    IT RAN WITH TERROR AND WITH CUNNING CREPT.  . . . . . . 357 A CONSIDERABLE SPECK  .  19
    BUT RAN AGAINST HIM WITH A STAYING HAND. . . . . . . . 394 HAEC FABULA DOCET  . .  10
    MY PARENTS WHEN I RAN TO THEM AVERRED . . . . . . . . . 443 AUSPEX   . . . . . .  6
    AND FATHER'S IN FOR WHAT WE RAN AWAY FROM.  . . . . . . 462 HOW HARD TO KEEP FROM  266
    THE NIGHT WE RAN AWAY FROM CTESIPHON), . . . . . . . . 462 HOW HARD TO KEEP FROM  270
```

PAGE TITLE   LINE

RANG
    BY A MISTY FEN THAT RANG ALL NIGHT, ... 15 IN A VALE   2
    I SHALL NOT FORGET HOW HIS LAUGH RANG OUT.   .   .   .   .   . . 25 THE DEMIURGE'S LAUGH . 13
    TO THEIR SURPRISE RANG ONCE ON STONE ALL DAY   .   .   .   .   .   407 FROM PLANE TO PLANE   . 116
RANGE
    WE FENCE OUR FLOWERS IN AND THE HENS RANGE.   .   .   .   .   . . 86 THE HOUSEKEEPER . . . 136
    A FURTHER RANGE .   .   .   . 271 A FURTHER RANGE .   . . T
RANGED
    IT HAS NOT RANGED, ...   219 I WILL SING YOU ONE-O . 68
RANGE-FINDING
    RANGE-FINDING .   .   .   .   126 RANGE-FINDING   . . .   T
RANGERS
    AND I DON'T MEAN JUST SKULLS OF ROGERS' RANGERS   .   .   .   .   210 PAUPER WITCH OF GRAFTON 93
RANGES
    BY MOUNTAIN RANGES HALF IN SUMMER SNOW, ... 58 THE BLACK COTTAGE . . . 116
    FIVE MOUNTAIN RANGES ONE BEHIND THE OTHER   .   .   .   .   . . 136 "OUT,OUT--"   5
RANGEY
    THE RANGEY BOUGH ANTICIPATED FRUIT .   .   .   .   239 OUR SINGING STRENGTH . 14
RANGING
    ONE OF MY CHILDREN RANGING AFTER ROCKS   .   .   .   .   . . 162 NEW HAMPSHIRE   .   . 116
    THE AGES RANGING ALL THE WAY FROM HOURS   .   .   .   .   . . 355 THE LESSON FOR TODAY . 138
RANK
    SET WELL BACK FROM THE ROAD IN RANK LODGED GRASS, ...   55 THE BLACK COTTAGE .   .   4
    "RANK WEEDS THAT LOVE THE WATER FROM THE DISHPAN   .   .   .   .   111 IN THE HOME STRETCH   . 30
    SOME IGNORANCE TAKES RANK AS INNOCENCE.   .   .   .   .   . . 371 THE LITERATE FARMER AND 88
RANKLY
    AS ONE RANKLY WARM INSIDER   .   .   .   .   384 IN THE LONG NIGHT .   . 13
RANKS
    NO ONE HAS EVER FAILED THE POET RANKS .   .   .   .   358 THE LOST FOLLOWER .   . 7
    IF WHAT YOU SAY IS TRUE, IF WINNING RANKS   .   .   .   .   .   .   517 A MASQUE OF MERCY . 633
RANSOM
    BUT IT WASN'T RANSOM ENOUGH. .   .   .   .   310 THE VINDICTIVES . . .   7
RAPIDEST
    FOR ANY BUT THE RAPIDEST EYE READERS.)   .   .   .   .   .   502 A MASQUE OF MERCY . 246
RAPTURE
    BURSTING RAPTURE .   .   .   .   398 BURSTING RAPTURE   .   . T
RARE
    WITH A GREAT FLOCK OF CHICKENS OF RARE BREEDS   .   .   .   .   .   162 NEW HAMPSHIRE   . . . 102
    AMONG BARE MAPLE BOUGHS, AND IN THE RARE   .   .   .   .   .   234 EVENING A SUGAR ORCHARD 8
RASCAL
    FOR THE PICKING. THE RASCAL, HE SAID HE'D BE GLAD   .   .   .   .   61 BLUEBERRIES 71
    AND HE WAS RICH, AND I WAS STILL A RASCAL.   .   .   .   .   .   160 NEW HAMPSHIRE   .   . . 54
RASCALS
    OR "TURN THE RASCALS OUT" WOULD DO FOR ME.   .   .   .   .   .   510 A MASQUE OF MERCY . 460
RASP
    ON THE LAST SWALLOW'S SWEEP; AND ON THE RASP   .   .   .   .   .   14 WAITING 18
RASPBERRIES
    AND THE PURPLE-STEMMED WILD RASPBERRIES GROW.   .   .   .   .   .   5 GHOST HOUSE   5
    CRANBERRIES IN BOGS AND RASPBERRIES ON TOP.   .   .   .   .   .   61 BLUEBERRIES 62
    AMONG THE RASPBERRIES, AND HEW AND SHAPE IT .   .   .   .   .   .   79 THE GENERATIONS OF MEN 162
RASPBERRY
    AND DANGLE FEET AMONG THE RASPBERRY VINES?"   .   .   .   .   .   75 THE GENERATIONS OF MEN 64
    FIRST LET ME LOOK. I SEE RASPBERRY VINES----"   .   .   .   .   .   76 THE GENERATIONS OF MEN 97
RAT
    'THAT GETS YE!' HE SQUEAKED LIKE A SQUEEZED RAT.   .   .   .   .   72 THE CODE 78
RATE
    THE SWINGING MILL BELL CHANGED ITS RATE   .   .   .   .   .   273 A LONE STRIKER   .   . .   1
    AT WHICH RATE BARRING BROODINESS   .   .   .   .   280 BLUE RIBBON AT AMESBURY 31
    GOING BY AT A RAILROAD RATE, ...   292 ON HEART'S BEGINNING TO 43
    SUPPOSE SOMEONE COMES NEAR ME WHO IN RATE   .   .   .   .   .   324 BUILD SOIL   249
    ALTHOUGH SO COMPROMISED OF AIM AND RATE   .   .   .   .   .   341 WILLFUL HOMING   .   . . 10
    AT THE PRESENT RATE IT MUST COME TO PASS, ...   375 SOMETHING FOR HOPE .   .   1
    AND CROWD THEM OUT AT A SIMILAR RATE.   .   .   .   .   .   376 SOMETHING FOR HOPE .   .   8
    I AM ASSURED AT ANY RATE .   .   .   .   453 A-WISHING WELL   .   . . 76
    IT HAS A RATE DISTINCTLY DIFFERENT .   .   .   .   489 A MASQUE OF REASON . 444
RATED
    AND LONG ENOUGH GETS RATED AS A CREED: .   .   .   .   .   394 ETHEREALIZING   .   . .   2
RATHER
    BUT IT'S NOT ELVES EXACTLY, AND I'D RATHER   .   .   .   .   .   34 MENDING WALL 37
    "I DON'T KNOW WHO I RATHER WOULD HAVE HAVE THEM.   .   .   .   .   50 A HUNDRED COLLARS . 168
    OR RATHER SAY NON-MEMBERS IN THE CHURCH, ...   57 THE BLACK COTTAGE .   . 86
    RATHER THAN SEND THEIR FOLKS TO SUCH A PLACE, ...   65 A SERVANT TO SERVANTS 95
    I'D RATHER YOU'D NOT GO UNLESS YOU MUST.   .   .   .   .   .   68 A SERVANT TO SERVANTS 177
    I'M GOING TO SELL MY SOUL, OR RATHER, FEET.   .   .   .   .   .   92 THE SELF-SEEKER .   . .   3
    I'D RATHER MRS. CORBIN DIDN'T KNOW;   .   .   .   .   94 THE SELF-SEEKER .   . . 53
    I'D RATHER BE THE BEAST THAT SLEEPS THE SLEEP   .   .   .   .   .   150 SNOW   223
    I HAD TO TAKE BY FORCE RATHER THAN BUY.   .   .   .   .   .   163 NEW HAMPSHIRE   .   . 151
    RATHER THAN BETTER. HOW ARE WE TO WRITE   .   .   .   .   .   167 NEW HAMPSHIRE   .   . 267
    RATHER OF WHAT TO FACE OR RUN AWAY FROM.   .   .   .   .   .   171 NEW HAMPSHIRE   .   . 396
    FEW FARMS CHANGED HANDS; SO RATHER THAN SPEND YEARS .   .   .   177 THE STAR-SPLITTER .   . 28
    RATHER THAN TIP A TABLE FOR YOU, LET ME   .   .   .   .   .   .   202 THE WITCH OF COOS .   . 12
    IF THIS SEEMS LIKE WITCHCRAFT RATHER, ...   304 CLEAR AND COLDER   .   . 16
    THE FARMERS RATHER GUESS NOT. .   .   .   .   308 EVIL TENDENCIES CANCEL   2
    RATHER BECAUSE IT TOOK FIVE YEARS AT LEAST   .   .   .   .   .   323 BUILD SOIL   227
    WHOSE MERCY TO YOU RATHER THAN TO OTHERS .   .   .   .   .   .   385 THE FEAR OF GOD .   . .   5
    I RATHER SUSPECT .   .   .   .   392 A WISH TO COMPLY   .   .   9
    THAT RATHER HURT HIS THEORY OF THE DROUGHT   .   .   .   .   .   400 THE BROKEN DROUGHT .   .   4
    PIKE GRUNTED RATHER GRIMLY WITH MISGIVING   .   .   .   .   .   405 FROM PLANE TO PLANE .   . 55
    UNLESS 'TWOULD RATHER WILT THAN FADE."   .   .   .   .   .   450 OUR DOOM TO BLOOM .   . 16
    OR RATHER SUBMIT TO BE SENT   .   .   .   .   466 SOME SCIENCE FICTION . 27
    GOD KNOWS---OR RATHER, YOU KNOW (GOD FORGIVE ME)   .   .   .   .   479 A MASQUE OF REASON . 169
    I SAY I'D RATHER BE LOST IN THE WOODS   .   .   .   .   .   .   513 A MASQUE OF MERCY . 514
RATIFIED
    IN FANCY I RATIFIED HIS NAME, ...   420 ONE MORE BREVITY   .   . 39
RATING
    A FRENCHMAN COULDN'T GET HIS HUMAN RATING!   .   .   .   .   .   186 THE AX-HELVE 45
RATIONALLY
    RATIONALLY OURS, ...   439 KITTY HAWK   365

	PAGE TITLE	LINE

RATIONS
    WHILE YOU SIT WARM AND READ UP BALANCED RATIONS. . . . . 149 SNOW 183
RATTLE
    AND CARS THAT SHOCK AND RATTLE--AND ONE HOTEL. . . . . . 45 A HUNDRED COLLARS . . 22
    THEY LEARNED TO RATTLE THE LOCK AND KEY . . . . 127 HOUSE FEAR 5
    HE FELL AND MADE THE LANTERN RATTLE . . . . 138 BROWN'S DESCENT . . . 38
RATTLED
    AND THE KEY RATTLED LOUDLY INTO PLACE . . . . 89 THE FEAR 19
    THE BUZZ SAW SNARLED AND RATTLED IN THE YARD . . . . . 136 "OUT,OUT--" 1
    AND THE SAW SNARLED AND RATTLED, SNARLED AND RATTLED, . . 136 "OUT,OUT--" 7
    NOT BONES, BUT THE ILL-FITTED WINDOW RATTLED. . . . . 175 THE CENSUS-TAKER . . 46
RATTLING
    COMES SOFTLY RATTLING DOWN. . . . . 9 A LATE WALK 12
    RUN THE RATTLING PAGES O'ER; . . . . 11 TO THE THAWING WIND . 13
    I THINK I HEAR A CLOCK--AND WINDOWS RATTLING. . . . . 153 SNOW 301
    WITH SOUNDS LIKE THE DRY RATTLING OF A SHUTTER, . . . 206 THE WITCH OF COOS . . 129
    MERELY THE WINDOWS RATTLING IN THE STORM. . . . . . 504 A MASQUE OF MERCY . 280
    THAT IS NO WINDOW. THAT'S A SHOWCASE RATTLING. . . . 504 A MASQUE OF MERCY . 282
    THAT IS YOUR ANTIQUES RATTLING ON A SHELF. . . . . . 504 A MASQUE OF MERCY . 283
RAVEL
    TO RAVEL THEM ONE BY ONE . . . . 30 RELUCTANCE 9
RAVELED
    AND RAVELED A FLOWER AND LOOKED AWAY.. . . . . . . 24 PAN WITH US 29
RAVEN
    OF HIS RAVEN COLOR OF HAIR. . . . . 299 WELCOME TO THEIR BELIEF 16
RAVINE
    A DRY RAVINE EMERGED FROM UNDER BOUGHS . . . . . . 41 THE MOUNTAIN 33
RAW
    THERE WOULD BE FISH RAW AND COOKED TOO . . . . . . 384 IN THE LONG NIGHT . . 11
RAWHIDE
    THEIR RAWHIDE HARNESS FROM THE LOAD TO CAMP. . . . . 192 PAUL'S WIFE 45
    BY SHRINKING THE RAWHIDE TO NATURAL LENGTH. . . . . 192 PAUL'S WIFE 48
RAY
    IN PLACE ACROSS A CLOUD THE SLENDER RAY . . . . . . 235 VALLEY'S SINGING DAY . 8
    ONE LIZARD AT THE END OF EVERY RAY. . . . . 238 A HILLSIDE THAW . . . 34
    I CATCH NO MORE THAN A RAY . . . . 266 SITTING BY A BUSH . . 2
    OF CRYSTALS WITH A RAY CATHODE . . . . 332 ALL REVELATION . . . 13
    AN INTIMATION, A SHOT OF RAY, ... 421 ONE MORE BREVITY . . 67
    OF PROJECTING RAY . . . . 440 KITTY HAWK 379
    IS THE RAY WE DART . . . . 440 KITTY HAWK 388
RAYMOND
    BARTLETT OF RAYMOND (NOW OF COLORADO), ... 167 NEW HAMPSHIRE . . . 260
RAYS
    WHEN THE SPENT SUN THROWS UP ITS RAYS ON CLOUD . . . 249 ACCEPTANCE 1
    FOR GATHERING SOLAR RAYS WOULD NOT HAVE HELPED. . . . 293 AT WOODWARD'S GARDENS . 6
    AND A MASKED MOON HAD SPREAD DOWN COMPASS RAYS . . . 300 MOON COMPASSES . . . 3
    OR OF HOW RAYS RETURN UPON THEMSELVES, ... 485 A MASQUE OF REASON . . 343
    THOUGH I HOLD RAYS DETERIORATE TO NOTHING: . . . . . 485 A MASQUE OF REASON . . 345
RAZOR
    HAS GOT A RAZOR EDGE; . . . . 465 MILKY WAY IS A COWPATH 36
RAZORS
    SAFETY RAZORS, SUNDAY PAPERS . . . . 396 AN IMPORTER 14
REACH
    WITH ONE WHOSE THOUGHT I HAD NOT HOPED TO REACH. . . 23 THE TUFT OF FLOWERS . 38
    A NEW-WORLD SONG, FAR OUT OF REACH, ... 24 PAN WITH US 17
    IS THAT THE WAY TO REACH THE TOP FROM HERE?-- . . . 41 THE MOUNTAIN 35
    BLESS YOU, IT'S ALL EXPENSE, THOUGH. REACH ME DOWN . 86 THE HOUSEKEEPER . . . 142
    AND OIL ARE BURIED OUT OF REACH? / AGAIN . . . . . 113 IN THE HOME STRETCH . 81
    A THING AS THAT. IT COULDN'T REACH THE LAMP . . . . 148 SNOW 139
    FAR UP THE BIRCHES OUT OF REACH OF MAN. . . . . . 164 NEW HAMPSHIRE . . . 164
    AND IF HE LOOKED AND FOUND IT, COULDN'T REACH IT-- . 198 WILD GRAPES 67
    THAT BACK BEHIND PURSUIT IT COULDN'T REACH THEM; . . 240 OUR SINGING STRENGTH . 47
    TO REACH THE OCEAN? IT MUST BE THE BROOK . . . . . 258 WEST-RUNNING BROOK . . 6
    YOU WOULD SAY HIS AMBITION WAS TO EXTEND TO REACH . . 305 THERE ARE ROUGHLY ZONES 9
    TO THE TOP OF HIS REACH ON THE WALL . . . . 310 THE VINDICTIVES . . . 4
    FAR AS WE AIM OUR SIGNS TO REACH, ... 328 A MISSIVE MISSILE . . 47
    FAR AS WE OFTEN MAKE THEM REACH, ... 328 A MISSIVE MISSILE . . 48
    MAY REACH TO YOU, BUT CANNOT TOUCH YOUR FATE. . . . 357 A MOTH SEEN IN WINTER . 22
    WE DON'T GO BACK ON GRAPES WE COULDN'T REACH. . . . 496 A MASQUE OF MERCY . . 77
REACHED
    EVERYTHING WENT WELL TILL WE REACHED THE BARN . . . 71 THE CODE 53
    SHE REACHED A HAND TO JOEL FOR SUPPORT: . . . . . 91 THE FEAR 68
    THE PLACE IT REACHED TO BLACKENED INSTANTLY. . . . . 131 THE BONFIRE 48
    BUT THE SHOUT REACHED THE GIRL AND PUT HER LIGHT OUT. . 195 PAUL'S WIFE 143
    I REACHED OUT BLINDLY TO SAVE MY FACE, ... 265 THE DOOR IN THE DARK . 2
    THE QUESTION IS WHETHER THEY'VE REACHED A DEPTH . . . 317 BUILD SOIL 33
    AND MADE OF BY A BOY; THEN HAVING REACHED . . . . 405 FROM PLANE TO PLANE . 57
REACHES
    IT NEVER REACHES EARTH EXCEPT AS ASHES . . . . . . 361 A LOOSE MOUNTAIN . . 10
REACHING
    AND REACHING UP WITH A LITTLE KNIFE, ... 141 THE GUM-GATHERER . . 37
    SAYS OUR REACHING TOWARD . . . . 438 KITTY HAWK 334
    AND REACHING BACK TO HIS RIBS . . . . 444 THE DRAFT HORSE . . . 7
READ (SEE HALF-READ)
    I BROUGHT NOT HERE TO READ, IT SEEMS, BUT HOLD . . . 15 WAITING 24
    HAVING FIRST HEARD THE LIFE READ OUT . . . . 20 THE TRIAL BY EXISTENCE 34
    "MAKE YOURSELF USEFUL, THEN, AND READ IT FOR ME.-- . 99 THE SELF-SEEKER . . . 188
    BUT READ IT, READ IT.--THAT'S RIGHT, DRAW THE CURTAIN: . 99 THE SELF-SEEKER . . . 193
    IF I EVER READ IT. . . . . 110 A PATCH OF OLD SNOW . 8
    SINCE LAST WE READ THE GAUGE." / "IT LOOKS AS IF . . 148 SNOW 159
    WHILE YOU SIT WARM AND READ UP BALANCED RATIONS. . . 149 SNOW 183
    SHE SAID, "GO READ YOUR OWN BOOKS AND FIND OUT." . . 166 NEW HAMPSHIRE . . . 227
    IN WAIT FOR HER THERE. SHE READ EVERY WORD . . . . 181 MAPLE 64
    AND LOST THE PLACE NEVER TO READ AGAIN. . . . . . 181 MAPLE 68
    MAY STILL HAVE BEEN WHAT LED HER ON TO READ, . . . 182 MAPLE 73
    HE READ IN ONE AND I READ IN ANOTHER, ... 217 A FOUNTAIN, A BOTTLE . 128
    TO READ THE GRAVESTONES ON THE HILL; . . . . . . 221 IN A DISUSED GRAVEYARD 2
    TO READ THE STONES AND GO AWAY . . . . 221 IN A DISUSED GRAVEYARD 7

READ (CONTINUED)
    BUT WHEN THEY GROW UP AND CAN READ THIS . . . . 294 A RECORD STRIDE . . .   19
    AND TELL HIM I HAD READ HIS EPITAPH. . . . . 354 THE LESSON FOR TODAY . 126
    BUT I WAS ONLY THERE TO READ THE STONES. . . . . 354 THE LESSON FOR TODAY . 133
    HE FOLLOWINGLY FINGERED AS HE READ, ... 356 TIME OUT   6
    I HAD READ AND THROWN. . . . . 429 KITTY HAWK   21
    SUCH AUSPICES ARE VERY HARD TO READ. . . . . 443 AUSPEX   5
    IS AS EASILY READ . . . . 447 THE BAD ISLAND--EASTER   4
    BUT THE KING SAID, "HAVEN'T I READ SOMEWHERE . . . . . 458 HOW HARD TO KEEP FROM 139
    YOU MUST HAVE READ THE FAMOUS VALENTINE . . . . 461 HOW HARD TO KEEP FROM 249
    TRY TO READ TO HER AND SHE DROPS RIGHT OFF. . . . . . 479 A MASQUE OF REASON . 155
    WE DON'T BELIEVE THE COMMON MAN SHOULD READ IT. . . . 494 A MASQUE OF MERCY . 31
    IS TO BE CIVILIZED, STAY UP AND READ . . . . 496 A MASQUE OF MERCY . 70
    PLEASE LET ME HAVE IT. / READ US WHAT IT SAYS. . . . . 505 A MASQUE OF MERCY . 294
    SOMEONE ELSE READ IT. / NO, YOU READ IT TO US. . . . . 505 A MASQUE OF MERCY . 298
    SOMEONE ELSE READ IT. / NO, YOU ASKED FOR IT. . . . . 506 A MASQUE OF MERCY . 329
    YOU ALL HAVE READ THE SERMON ON THE MOUNT. . . . . . . 511 A MASQUE OF MERCY . 487
    I ASK YOU ALL TO READ IT ONCE AGAIN. . . . . 511 A MASQUE OF MERCY . 488
    AND HOLD IT UP NEARSIGHTEDLY TO READ.) . . . . 512 A MASQUE OF MERCY . 490
    WE'RE READING IT. / WELL, NOW YOU'VE GOT IT READ, . . 512 A MASQUE OF MERCY . 491
READERS
    FOR ANY BUT THE RAPIDEST EYE READERS.) . . . . 502 A MASQUE OF MERCY . 246
READINESS
    IN READINESS TO WEIGH UPON HER. . . . . 256 THE LOVELY BE CHOOSERS 13
READING
    NOT READING IT. / "WELL, WHAT KIND OF A MAN . . . . . 151 SNOW 247
    HER GIFT FOR READING LETTERS LOCKED IN BOXES. . . . . 163 NEW HAMPSHIRE . . . 131
    THE SAME FOR READING AS IT WAS FOR THOUGHT, ... 356 TIME OUT   9
    WHEN YOU WERE READING BOOKS OR OUT OF TOWN. . . . . . 375 A YOUNG BIRCH . . . 20
    IN READING, DON'T YOU, BILL?--AT EVERY LINE END . . 405 FROM PLANE TO PLANE 50
    THE OTHER WAY OF READING BACK AND FORTH, ... 405 FROM PLANE TO PLANE 53
    BY ROCKWELL KENT THAT EVERYBODY'S READING. . . . . . 495 A MASQUE OF MERCY . 49
    HIS FAVORITE READING IS SEED CATALOGUES. . . . . . . 496 A MASQUE OF MERCY . 81
    WE'RE READING IT. / WELL, NOW YOU'VE GOT IT READ, . 512 A MASQUE OF MERCY . 491
READY
    READY TO RUN TO HIDING NEW . . . . 18 GOING FOR WATER . . . 15
    REAL SKY-BLUE, AND HEAVY, AND READY TO DRUM . . . . . 59 BLUEBERRIES   4
    "YOU'RE GETTING READY TO DO SOMETHING FOOLISH." . . . 94 THE SELF-SEEKER . . 51
    "FINE, FINE." / "AND READY FOR SOME MORE? MY WIFE HERE 147 SNOW 106
    SHE HURRIED HER DECISION TO BE READY . . . . 201 PLACE FOR A THIRD . 71
    SO AS TO HAVE IT READY FOR OUTSIDERS. . . . . 207 THE WITCH OF COOS . 147
    BE READY, I THOUGHT, FOR ALMOST ANYTHING. . . . . . . 215 A FOUNTAIN, A BOTTLE 64
    AND YET TOO READY TO BELIEVE THE MOST. . . . . 233 A BOUNDLESS MOMENT .   4
    WAS NONETHELESS THERE READY TO BE FREED . . . . 240 OUR SINGING STRENGTH 52
    WE MUST NOT BE TOO READY TO SCOFF. . . . . 266 SITTING BY A BUSH . . 12
    BUT AS READY TO WIELD AS NOW. . . . . 285 IN TIME OF CLOUDBURST 24
    MIXED READY TO BEGIN THE MORNING RIGHT, ... 302 DESIGN   5
    I'D HAVE A SHORT ONE READY FOR MY OWN. . . . . 355 THE LESSON FOR TODAY . 159
    AND READY AGAIN FOR THE GRASS TO OWN. . . . . 376 SOMETHING FOR HOPE . 16
    YOU SEEM SO READY AT TRANSLATING NAMES. . . . . 495 A MASQUE OF MERCY . 61
REAL
    'TWOULDN'T SEEM REAL TO CLIMB FOR CLIMBING IT." . . . 43 THE MOUNTAIN 88
    REAL SKY-BLUE, AND HEAVY, AND READY TO DRUM . . . . . 59 BLUEBERRIES   4
    WHAT'S THE REAL TROUBLE? WHAT WILL SATISFY HER?" . . . 87 THE HOUSEKEEPER . . 166
    OUT WITH IT IF YOU'VE ANY REAL OBJECTION." . . . . . . 99 THE SELF-SEEKER . . 197
    NOR WAS THE GRASS ITSELF YOUR REAL CONCERN, ... 109 THE EXPOSED NEST . . 10
    ONE REAL REFORMER WHO WOULD CHANGE THE WORLD . . . . 162 NEW HAMPSHIRE . . . 94
    HERE COME REAL STARS TO FILL THE UPPER SKIES, ... 246 FIREFLIES IN THE GARDEN 1
    BUT THE REAL FLY HE MISSED WOULD NEVER DO; . . . . . 279 THE WHITE-TAILED HORNET 48
    OF BEING BROUGHT DOWN TO THE REAL." . . . . 313 THE VINDICTIVES . . 91
    AND PILE OF REAL ROCKS AND HAVE BEEN FOUNDED. . . . . 331 BEECH   3
    HAD NO REAL PURPOSE TILL IT GOT TO US. . . . . 425 ACCIDENTALLY ON PURPOSE 12
    I WRITE REAL VERSE IN NUMBERS, AS THEY SAY. . . . . . 460 HOW HARD TO KEEP FROM 211
    THAN ANYTHING. / HE'S VERY REAL TO ME . . . . 489 A MASQUE OF REASON . 434
REALITY
    BEHIND THE PITIFUL REALITY . . . . 169 NEW HAMPSHIRE . . . 323
    MORE TO GIVE HIS REALITY ITS DUE . . . . 489 A MASQUE OF REASON . 433
REALIZE
    "BUT IF THAT'S ALL--JOEL--YOU REALIZE-- . . . . 92 THE FEAR 87
    IT TOOK THAT PAUSE TO MAKE HIM REALIZE . . . . 355 TIME OUT   1
    YOU REALIZE BY NOW THE PART YOU PLAYED . . . . 475 A MASQUE OF REASON . 66
REALIZED
    THEY REALIZED FROM THE WAY I SWABBED MY NECK . . . . . 72 THE CODE 86
    IN TIME, HAD SHE NOT REALIZED HER DANGER . . . . . . 187 THE AX-HELVE 51
REALIZING
    TO THE LAND VAGUELY REALIZING WESTWARD, ... 348 THE GIFT OUTRIGHT . 14
    BEFORE OUR REALIZING WHAT WE HAVE . . . . 408 FROM PLANE TO PLANE . 128
    TO THE LAND VAGUELY REALIZING WESTWARD, ... 425 THE GIFT OUTRIGHT . 14
REALLY
    TILL SOMEONE FINALLY FIND US OUT. . . . . 19 REVELATION   4
    HE ADDED, IF YOU REALLY CARE TO KNOW, ... 36 DEATH OF THE HIRED MAN 51
    "REALLY, FRIEND, I CAN'T LET YOU. YOU--MAY NEED THEM." 50 A HUNDRED COLLARS . 165
    "BUT REALLY I--I HAVE SO MANY COLLARS." . . . . 50 A HUNDRED COLLARS . 167
    AND AFTER ALL, REALLY THEY'RE EBONY SKINNED: . . . . . 60 BLUEBERRIES 24
    I'LL TELL YOU WHAT THE VOICES REALLY SAY. . . . . . . 78 THE GENERATIONS OF MEN 144
    WAS STARTLED WHEN AN ANSWER REALLY CAME. . . . . 91 THE FEAR 66
    HAD WORN THEM REALLY ABOUT THE SAME, ... 105 THE ROAD NOT TAKEN . 10
    HE STEERED WAS REALLY STRAIGHT AWAY . . . . 139 BROWN'S DESCENT . . 66
    HE HADN'T COME AND HAD HE REALLY STARTED." . . . . . 152 SNOW 277
    THE ONLY PERSON REALLY SOILED WITH TRADE . . . . . . 160 NEW HAMPSHIRE . . . 35
    "I LIKE THIS BETTER." IT WAS REALLY BETTER. . . . . . 164 NEW HAMPSHIRE . . . 158
    OF REALLY NEVER HAVING MEANT TO KEEP IT. . . . . . . 187 THE AX-HELVE 62
    I WONDERED IF HE REALLY THOUGHT IT FAIR . . . . 190 THE GRINDSTONE . . . 48
    REALLY A VERY FEW TO BUILD AND STAY. . . . . 239 OUR SINGING STRENGTH 24
    FOR THEM THERE WAS REALLY NOTHING SAD. . . . . 242 NEED OF BEING VERSED 21
    (AND THEY WERE NEVER REALLY STARS AT HEART), ... 246 FIREFLIES IN THE GARDEN 4
    SOME OF THE DUST WAS REALLY GOLD. . . . . 249 A PECK OF GOLD . . .   8
    WHEN DUST REALLY TOOK IN THE SUN; . . . . 266 SITTING BY A BUSH . .   6

REALLY (CONTINUED)
    IS THE DEED EVER REALLY DONE . . . . 277 TWO TRAMPS IN MUD TIME   71
    THAT REALLY TAKES AWAY INSTEAD OF GIVES. . . . . . 279 THE WHITE-TAILED HORNET 55
    BUT REALLY THAT GOLD WAS NOT HALF . . . . 310 THE VINDICTIVES . . .   18
    I OWN I NEVER REALLY WARMED . . . . 326 TO A THINKER   29
    WERE REALLY AS DARK AS I HEAR SAGES TELL, ... 350 THE LESSON FOR TODAY   . 2
    AND I CONVINCED THAT THEY WERE REALLY SAGES, . . . 350 THE LESSON FOR TODAY   . 3
    SO SCIENCE AND RELIGION REALLY MEET. . . . . 353 THE LESSON FOR TODAY   . 83
    "IT'S WHETHER THESE PROFESSIONS REALLY WORK. . . . 404 FROM PLANE TO PLANE   . 11
    FREE VERSE, SO CALLED, IS REALLY CHERISHED PROSE, . 460 HOW HARD TO KEEP FROM 221
    WORKED UP ABOUT IT. BUT SHE REALLY HASN'T-- . . . . 476 A MASQUE OF REASON .   . 94
    HE ISN'T REALLY GOING, YET HE'S LEAVING. . . . . . 489 A MASQUE OF REASON .   . 440
    TO SEE THAT THE FAIR FIGHT IS REALLY FAIR. . . . . 507 A MASQUE OF MERCY .   . 364
    THE THING THAT REALLY COUNTS, THOUGH, IS THE FORM . 509 A MASQUE OF MERCY .   . 430
    WHAT'S REALLY DOWN THERE? / JUST AN OUBLIETTE, . . 516 A MASQUE OF MERCY .   . 612
    AND YOU SAY JUSTICE DOESN'T REALLY MATTER. . . . . 517 A MASQUE OF MERCY .   . 623
REALM
    I PREFER TO SING SAFELY IN THE REALM . . . . 317 BUILD SOIL   48
    AND DAYIFY THE DARKEST REALM . . . . 390 TWO LEADING LIGHTS . . 9
REAP
    TO PLANT AND TEND AND REAP HERSELF, ... 133 A GIRL'S GARDEN . . .   7
REAR
    MOTHER CAN MAKE A COMMON TABLE REAR . . . . 202 THE WITCH OF COOS . .   9
    TO REAR AGAINST THE INSCRIPTION ON THE WALL. . . . 399 THE INGENUITIES OF DEBT 18
REASCEND
    ASCENDING TO DESCEND TO REASCEND. . . . . 214 A FOUNTAIN, A BOTTLE . 34
REASON
    AND VEXES ME FOR REASON WHY. . . . .   7 MY NOVEMBER GUEST . .   15
    TO YIELD WITH A GRACE TO REASON, ... 30 RELUCTANCE   22
    I MUST BE WONTED TO IT--THAT'S THE REASON. . . . . 51 HOME BURIAL   22
    "REASON ENOUGH, THERE WAS NO PROPERTY. . . . . . . 84 THE HOUSEKEEPER . .   95
    NOT BUT I'VE EVERY REASON NOT TO CARE . . . . . . 146 SNOW   89
    BETWEEN TWO DAYS, THE REASON WHY I SOUGHT . . . . 167 NEW HAMPSHIRE . . .   249
    IT WAS THE BONES. I KNEW THEM--AND GOOD REASON. . . 204 THE WITCH OF COOS . . 59
    IN WARREN AT MARCH MEETING, FOR THE REASON . . . . 208 PAUPER WITCH OF GRAFTON 18
    BUT IT WAS NO REASON I HAD TO GO BECAUSE THEY HAD TO GO. 298 A LEAF-TREADER . . 11
    IF THE REASON WAS IN ME, ... 303 AFTERFLAKES   7
    REASON IN CIRCLES? / NO, REFUSE TO BE . . . . . . 322 BUILD SOIL   206
    AND SWAY WITH REASON MORE OR LESS. . . . . 326 TO A THINKER   28
    IS THE REASON THE POWERS PROVIDE . . . . 348 TRIPLE BRONZE . . .   2
    NOR WHAT PARTICULARS THEY REASON FROM, ... 354 THE LESSON FOR TODAY   109
    HE SEEMS TO SAY THE REASON WHY SO MUCH . . . . . 412 POD OF THE MILKWEED   53
    "I'M A RHODES SCHOLAR--THAT'S THE REASON WHY. . . 455 HOW HARD TO KEEP FROM   52
    THE REASON ARTISTS SHOW SO LITTLE INTEREST . . . 461 HOW HARD TO KEEP FROM 230
    A MASQUE OF REASON . . . . 471 A MASQUE OF REASON . .   T
    A MASQUE OF REASON . . . . 473 A MASQUE OF REASON . .   T
    THERE'S NO CONNECTION MAN CAN REASON OUT . . . . 475 A MASQUE OF REASON .   50
    I WANT TO ASK YOU IF IT STANDS TO REASON . . . . 476 A MASQUE OF REASON .   88
    AND I SHOULD LIKE TO KNOW THE REASON WHY. . . . . 477 A MASQUE OF REASON .   104
    THERE ISN'T ANY UNIVERSAL REASON; . . . . 478 A MASQUE OF REASON .   138
    STRAY SCRAPS OF PALLIATIVE REASON . . . . 478 A MASQUE OF REASON .   142
    I NEED SOME HELP ABOUT THIS REASON PROBLEM . . . 479 A MASQUE OF REASON .   165
    I WAIVED THE REASON FOR MY ORDEAL--BUT-- . . . . 479 A MASQUE OF REASON .   170
    TO ASK MY QUESTION. WE DISPARAGE REASON. . . . . 481 A MASQUE OF REASON .   228
    REASON IS, I SUPPOSED, THE STEERING GEAR. . . . . 481 A MASQUE OF REASON .   231
    FROM TELLING ME YOUR REASON, DON'T ASSUME . . . . 482 A MASQUE OF REASON .   239
    I'D GIVE MORE FOR ONE LEAST BEFOREHAND REASON . . 482 A MASQUE OF REASON .   247
    THE REASON MIGHT HAVE BEEN SOME OTHER PERSON'S. . 482 A MASQUE OF REASON .   264
    TO ASKING FLATLY FOR THE REASON--OUTRIGHT. . . . 483 A MASQUE OF REASON .   269
    I WOULD DO ANYTHING FOR YOU IN REASON. . . . . . 486 A MASQUE OF REASON .   374
REASONER
    A REASONER AND GOOD AS SUCH, ... 326 TO A THINKER   21
REASON-HUNGRY
    WHEN REASON-HUNGRY MORTALS ASK FOR REASONS. . . . 478 A MASQUE OF REASON .   136
REASONING
    AS TO OUR FATE, LIKE FOOLS PAST REASONING WITH. . 114 IN THE HOME STRETCH   125
    BECAUSE ALL REASONING IS IN A CIRCLE. . . . . . . 322 BUILD SOIL   202
REASONS
    THAT'S WHAT FOR REASONS I SHOULD LIKE TO KNOW-- . 132 THE BONFIRE   98
    WHILE I INVESTED HIM WITH REASONS; . . . . 140 BROWN'S DESCENT . .   72
    THEY HAD BOTH OF THEM HAD THEIR REASONS . . . . . 314 BEARER OF EVIL TIDINGS 39
    AND FOR THESE REASONS KEPT FROM BEING GREAT. . . 351 THE LESSON FOR TODAY   13
    YOU'D BE TO BLAME FOR FURNISHING THE REASONS." . . 406 FROM PLANE TO PLANE   68
    WHEN REASON-HUNGRY MORTALS ASK FOR REASONS. . . . 478 A MASQUE OF REASON .   136
    AS TO WHAT REASONS I AGREE TO WAIVE. . . . . . . 479 A MASQUE OF REASON .   167
REASSURANCE
    GREAT IS THE REASSURANCE OF RECALL. . . . . 427 CONCEPT SELF-CONCEIVED 5
REASSURE
    BUT HASTENED BACK TO REASSURE HIS SLAVE . . . . . 457 HOW HARD TO KEEP FROM 112
REASSURED
    NOTHING'S PORTENTOUS, I AM REASSURED. . . . . . . 318 BUILD SOIL   66
REBELLED
    I WOULD NOT BE TAKEN AS EVER HAVING REBELLED. . . 306 NOT QUITE SOCIAL   .   12
REBELLION
    REBELLION, PESTILENCE, INVASION? / EARTHQUAKE . . 502 A MASQUE OF MERCY .   225
REBELS
    NO DOUBT DIRECTED AT OUR HEADS AS REBELS . . . . 361 A LOOSE MOUNTAIN   .   6
REBUKE
    WAS TO REBUKE HER TEACHER WITH IT NEXT DAY, . . . 180 MAPLE   31
    WATER CAME TO REBUKE THE TOO CLEAR WATER. . . . . 225 FOR ONCE SOMETHING . . 11
REBUKED
    HE STOOD REBUKED AND UNEMPLOYED. . . . . 273 A LONE STRIKER . . .   9
RECALL
    THAT STILL, IF I REPENT, I MAY RECALL IT, ... 130 THE BONFIRE   22
    IMMURED ALMOST BEYOND RECALL, ... 280 BLUE RIBBON AT AMESBURY 22
    AND SOMEONE REMINISCENT WILL RECALL . . . . 375 A YOUNG BIRCH . . .   11
    HE DID AS SHAKESPEARE SAYS, YOU MAY RECALL, . . . 400 THE BROKEN DROUGHT . . 7
    GREAT IS THE REASSURANCE OF RECALL. . . . . 427 CONCEPT SELF-CONCEIVED 5

RECEDE
  BUT JIMMY ONLY MADE HIS JAW RECEDE . . . . 114 IN THE HOME STRETCH . 101
RECEIPT
  THE TROUBLE IS, WITH THAT RECEIPT FOR LOVE, ... 372 THE LITERATE FARMER AND 124
RECEIPTED
  RECEIPTED. AND THE COCK IS IN THE YARD." . . . . 86 THE HOUSEKEEPER 147
RECEIVE
  AND FLED TO YOU. BUT YOU RECEIVE ME NOT. . . . . 497 A MASQUE OF MERCY . . 101
RECEIVED
  THE HOPE OF BEING, AS WE SAY, RECEIVED. . . . . 160 NEW HAMPSHIRE 43
  WHEREAS MEN PROPHETS ARE RECEIVED WITH HONOR. . . . . . 476 A MASQUE OF REASON . . 90
RECEIVER'S
  SOMEONE'S RECEIVER'S DOWN. THE HANDLE STUMBLES. . . . . 153 SNOW 295
RECEIVES
  "FROM YOU THE ROAD RECEIVES . . . . 415 CLOSED FOR GOOD . . . 17
RECENT
  ALL FRESH AND SOUND FROM THE RECENT AX. . . . . 123 PEA BRUSH 14
RECENTLY
  ...RECENTLY OBSERVED IN THE WESTERN SKY AT EVENING . . . 368 THE LITERATE FARMER AND S
RECESS
  LIKE A YARDFUL OF SCHOOLBOYS OUT AT RECESS . . . . . . 318 BUILD SOIL 61
RECIPES
  RECIPES FOR TEA WITH BUTTER, ... 396 AN IMPORTER 5
RECITE
  "IT WOULD TAKE ME FOREVER TO RECITE . . . . 117 IN THE HOME STRETCH . 181
  AND FOR WANT OF BOOKS RECITE. . . . . 384 IN THE LONG NIGHT . . 6
RECITING
  I HEAR THE WORLD RECITING . . . . 387 THE COURAGE TO BE NEW . 1
RECKLESS
  WHAT SHOULD THAT RECKLESS ZEPHYR FLING . . . . 29 MY BUTTERFLY 41
  AS RECKLESS AS THE BEST OF THEM TONIGHT, ... 129 THE BONFIRE 2
  I SHALL MAKE THE RECKLESS CHOICE . . . . 156 THE SOUND OF TREES . . 20
  SO BRAD MCLAUGHLIN MINGLED RECKLESS TALK . . . . 176 THE STAR-SPLITTER . . 13
RECKON
  AND SEE IF YOU CAN RECKON OUR COUSINSHIP. . . . . . . 75 THE GENERATIONS OF MEN 62
  "THAT'S WHERE I RECKON SANTA CLAUS COMES IN-- . . . . . 408 FROM PLANE TO PLANE . 137
RECKONED
  (THIS LIKE FATE BY STARS IS RECKONED, ... 304 CLEAR AND COLDER . . 7
RECKONING
  HIS RECKONING WAS OFF A SEA. . . . . 417 AMERICA IS HARD TO SEE 18
RECLAIM
  OURS WAS TO RECLAIM . . . . 439 KITTY HAWK 369
RECLINED
  THERE AMID LOLLING JUNIPER RECLINED, ... 17 THE VANTAGE POINT . . 4
RECOGNITION
  "FEED HIM ANOTHER FEAST OF RECOGNITION." . . . . 456 HOW HARD TO KEEP FROM . 92
RECOGNIZE
  YOU NEEDN'T SMILE--I DIDN'T RECOGNIZE HIM-- . . . . . . 35 DEATH OF THE HIRED MAN 37
  HE DID NOT RECOGNIZE IN THAT SMOOTH COAL . . . . 172 A STAR IN A STONEBOAT . 10
  SO THEY COULD RECOGNIZE THEM. NOT A POST . . . . 209 PAUPER WITCH OF GRAFTON 56
  WE STRUCK A ROAD I DIDN'T RECOGNIZE, ... 215 A FOUNTAIN, A BOTTLE . 65
  AS NOT TO RECOGNIZE IN ME THE EXCEPTION . . . . 278 THE WHITE-TAILED HORNET 15
  I HAVE A MIND MYSELF AND RECOGNIZE . . . . 358 A CONSIDERABLE SPECK . 30
  HE MAY NOT RECOGNIZE FOR HIS. . . . . 418 AMERICA IS HARD TO SEE 48
  I RECOGNIZE THEM. GREEK ARTIFICERS . . . . 490 A MASQUE OF REASON . . 460
RECOGNIZED
  AND RECOGNIZED HIM, THROUGH THE IRON GRAY . . . . . . 160 NEW HAMPSHIRE 47
  AND RECOGNIZED AS SUCH IN RUSSIA ITSELF . . . . 167 NEW HAMPSHIRE 278
  I NEVER SAID YOU WEREN'T. I RECOGNIZED YOU. . . . . . . 498 A MASQUE OF MERCY . . 136
RECOLLECT
  YOU RECOLLECT THE BOY WHO CAME OUT HERE . . . . 149 SNOW 173
  I RECOLLECT A NIGHT OF BROKEN CLOUDS . . . . 179 THE STAR-SPLITTER . . 79
  DID I RECOLLECT . . . . 432 KITTY HAWK 146
  THEY CLAIM THEY RECOLLECT THE MORN . . . . 452 A-WISHING WELL . . . 38
RECOLLECTION
  SO YOU CAN'T HAVE MUCH RECOLLECTION OF HER. . . . . . . 180 MAPLE 14
RECONCILED
  AND THEN BECOMING RECONCILED . . . . 138 BROWN'S DESCENT . . . 42
  WHO RECONCILED THE PENTATEUCH WITH SCIENCE. . . . . . . 506 A MASQUE OF MERCY . . 325
RECONNOITER
  TO RECONNOITER, AND THEN MADE UP HER MIND . . . . . . 74 THE GENERATIONS OF MEN 31
RECONSIDER
  EACH AGE WILL HAVE TO RECONSIDER IT. . . . . 57 THE BLACK COTTAGE . . 70
RECORD
  THEY SET A LOT (NOW DON'T THEY?) BY A RECORD . . . . . 207 PAUPER WITCH OF GRAFTON 12
  A RECORD STRIDE . . . . 294 A RECORD STRIDE . . . T
  IS A RECORD STRIDE OR STRETCH. . . . . 295 A RECORD STRIDE . . . 26
  OF RECORD IN MY NOTE BOOK. / WELL, SHE WAS. . . . . . . 477 A MASQUE OF REASON . . 103
RECORDING
  LONG ENOUGH FOR RECORDING ALL OUR NAMES ON.-- . . . . . 143 SNOW 10
RECOVER
  WE NEVER COULD RECOVER HUMAN SHAPE, ... 351 THE LESSON FOR TODAY . 39
RECOVERED
  HOW ARE YOU NOW? I TRUST YOU'RE QUITE RECOVERED, ... 474 A MASQUE OF REASON . . 35
RECREATION
  AND TAKE YOUR WALK OF RECREATION BACK . . . . 405 FROM PLANE TO PLANE . 42
RECURRING
  RECURRING TILL WE ANSWER FROM WITHIN. . . . . 147 SNOW 133
RED (SEE ROSE-RED)
  AND WEAR HER RED HOOD, ... 136 LAST WORD OF A BLUEBIRD 17
  HE IS SAID TO HAVE BEEN THE LAST RED MAN . . . . 142 THE VANISHING RED . . 1
  THE VANISHING RED . . . . 142 THE VANISHING RED . . T
  THE RED MAN GAVE IN POKING ABOUT THE MILL, ... 142 THE VANISHING RED . . 15
  THEY WEREN'T RED INDIANS BUT VERITABLE . . . . 161 NEW HAMPSHIRE 77
  THAT VARIED IN THEIR HUE FROM RED TO GREEN. . . . . . . 178 THE STAR-SPLITTER . . 73
  AND LAST YEAR'S BERRIES SHINING SCARLET RED. . . . . . 254 A WINTER EDEN 8
  THE GROUND WAS ONE CIRCLE OF SOLID RED. . . . . 305 UNHARVESTED 10
  AND DOTTED IT WITH RED FOR ME, ... 326 A MISSIVE MISSILE . . 3

RED (CONTINUED)
BUT NO, THE COLOR USED IS RED. . . . . 327 A MISSIVE MISSILE . . 13
THE BIG FLAG: THE RED--WHITE-- . . . . 367 NOT OF SCHOOL AGE . . 25
I DON'T BELIEVE WHAT MAKES YOU RED IN THE FACE . . . . 389 SKEPTIC 7
WHY DON'T THEY ASK THE RED MAN WHERE THEY ARE? . . . . 414 A CABIN IN THE CLEARING 21
CAUGHT COLOR FROM THE LAST OF EVENING RED . . . . . 445 QUESTIONING FACES . . 4
FIRST WHITE, THEN RED, THEN ULTRARED, THEN OUT. . . . 485 A MASQUE OF REASON . . 346
AS RED CROSS AMBULANCE COMMANDER-IN-CHIEF . . . . . 507 A MASQUE OF MERCY . . 369
REDISTRIBUTION
A HOLY IMPULSE TOWARDS REDISTRIBUTION. . . . . . . 509 A MASQUE OF MERCY . . 419
REDOUBLING
BY DOUBLING AND REDOUBLING SONG AND TWITTER— . . . . 237 A HILLSIDE THAW . . . 16
REDRESSED
HAS BEEN LONG REDRESSED. . . . . 430 KITTY HAWK 79
REDUCE
REDUCE THE BIRTHS OF THE HUMAN RACE, ... 263 THE TIMES TABLE . . . 19
REDUCED
BY THAT TIME I WAS PRETTY WELL REDUCED . . . . . . 198 WILD GRAPES 60
MY GREATER GRIEF WAS BY SO MUCH REDUCED . . . . . . 253 THE THATCH 28
WHY DID YOU HURT ME SO? I AM REDUCED . . . . 483 A MASQUE OF REASON . . 268
REDUCED HIM TO A SHADOW OF HIMSELF. . . . . 488 A MASQUE OF REASON . . 426
REEDS
ACROSS THE REEDS TO A WINDOW LIGHT. . . . . 15 IN A VALE 5
REEDY
BESIDE A REEDY BROOK THE SCYTHE HAD BARED. . . . . . 22 THE TUFT OF FLOWERS . 24
REEF
IT WILL SHAKE ITS CAST STONE REEF OF FLOOR. . . . . 306 A TRIAL RUN . . . 5
THEN EDDIES PLAYING ROUND A SUNKEN REEF . . . . . 335 I COULD GIVE ALL . . 7
REELED
HE REELED, HE LURCHED, HE BOBBED, HE CHECKED; . . . 138 BROWN'S DESCENT . . . 37
TILL I HAVE REELED AND STUMBLED . . . . 389 ASTROMETAPHYSICAL . . 5
REEVE
FOR HOG REEVE IN MARCH MEETING HERE IN WARREN. . . . . 207 PAUPER WITCH OF GRAFTON 14
REFERENCE
AND TAGS AND NUMBERS IT FOR FUTURE REFERENCE, ... 37 DEATH OF THE HIRED MAN 90
REFINES
IT VERY LIKELY QUICKENS AND REFINES US. . . . . . . 321 BUILD SOIL . . . 171
REFLECT
THESE POOLS THAT, THOUGH IN FORESTS, STILL REFLECT . . 245 SPRING POOLS 1
BUT IT WILL HAVE ITS MOMENT TO REFLECT. . . . . . . 356 TIME OUT . . . 14
ALL WE DO'S REFLECT . . . . 440 KITTY HAWK . . . 384
REFLECTED
BUT THE FIRST THING NEXT MORNING WE REFLECTED . . . . 177 THE STAR-SPLITTER . . 43
REFLECTED IN THE MUD AND EVEN DUST, ... 279 THE WHITE-TAILED HORNET 65
AND IS REFLECTED FROM THE PRINTED PAGE . . . . . . 515 A MASQUE OF MERCY . . 581
REFLECTS
REFLECTS A STANDING GULL. . . . . 301 NEITHER OUT FAR NOR IN 8
REFLEX
A REFLEX . . . . 468 A REFLEX . . . . . T
REFORMED
TO THE REFORMER OR REFORMED. . . . . 326 TO A THINKER 30
REFORMER
ONE REAL REFORMER WHO WOULD CHANGE THE WORLD . . . . 162 NEW HAMPSHIRE . . . 94
TO THE REFORMER OR REFORMED. . . . . 326 TO A THINKER 30
REFORMERS
TO GET THINGS DONE. REFORMERS FAIL TO SEE THAT.-- . . . 478 A MASQUE OF REASON . . 152
REFRACTED
ARE GOD'S WHITE LIGHT REFRACTED INTO COLORS. . . . . 516 A MASQUE OF MERCY . . 597
REFRAIN
IT MUST AT SOME POINT GRACEFULLY REFRAIN. . . . . . 319 BUILD SOIL . . . 116
I SENT YOU ONCE A SONG WITH THE REFRAIN: . . . . . 324 BUILD SOIL . . . 259
HE HAS THE GREATNESS TO REFRAIN. . . . . 390 TWO LEADING LIGHTS . . 11
REFUSAL
HAS HE HAD THE REFUSAL OF MY CHANCE?" . . . . 45 A HUNDRED COLLARS . . 30
REFUSE
AS OTHERS HOLD THEIRS OR REFUSE FOR THEM, ... 106 CHRISTMAS TREES . . 22
I REFUSE TO ADAPT MYSELF A MITE . . . . 166 NEW HAMPSHIRE . . . 234
AND THAT'S WHY I CAN'T DECENTLY REFUSE YOU." . . . . 214 A FOUNTAIN, A BOTTLE . 32
SHE WOULD REFUSE LOVE SAFE WITH WEALTH AND HONOR! . . . 256 THE LOVELY BE CHOOSERS 6
REASON IN CIRCLES? / NO, REFUSE TO BE . . . . . . 322 BUILD SOIL . . . 206
YET YOU REFUSE TO SEE IT IN THE DOCTOR." . . . . . 407 FROM PLANE TO PLANE . 101
BUT OH, NO, NOT FOR JONAH. I REFUSE . . . . 505 A MASQUE OF MERCY . . 302
REFUSED
SHE, IN HER PLACE, REFUSED HIM ANY HELP, ... 51 HOME BURIAL 13
NEITHER REFUSED THE MEETING. BUT THE HAND! . . . . 136 "OUT, OUT--" 18
REGALIA
AND SPENT AND DUSTED OFF OF THEIR REGALIA, ... 412 POD OF THE MILKWEED . 35
REGARD
YOU WILL BE LIKELY TO REGARD AS SACRED . . . . . 79 THE GENERATIONS OF MEN 179
WHY NOT REGARD IT AS A SACRIFICE, ... 178 THE STAR-SPLITTER . . 63
AND SMALL REGARD TO THE FUTURE OF ANY WEED. . . . . 299 STRONG SAYING NOTHING . 2
REGIME
UNDER THE NEW REGIME, AND SO FORBIDDEN. . . . . . . 167 NEW HAMPSHIRE . . . 279
REGIMENTING
COLLECTIVISTIC REGIMENTING LOVE . . . . 357 A CONSIDERABLE SPECK . 25
REGINAE
ABOUT MY CYPRIPEDIUM REGINAE; . . . . 95 THE SELF-SEEKER . . . 86
REGION
OF EVERY KIND EVERYWHERE IN THIS REGION . . . . . 95 THE SELF-SEEKER . . . 68
FOR WHICH THE REGION ROUND WAS KNOWN, ... 364 TRESPASS 11
REGION VOICE SAID, "GO, ... 436 KITTY HAWK . . . 278
REGIONS
AND BROUGHT DOWN SAFELY FROM THE UPPER REGIONS; . . . 196 WILD GRAPES 13
REGISTER
BUT LISTEN TO ME REGISTER . . . . 451 A-WISHING WELL . . . 10
REGRET
OF MY REGRET HUNG NOT ON ALL THE LAND, ... 28 MY BUTTERFLY 19
"YOU'RE DOING THE WISE THING: YOU WON'T REGRET IT. . . 100 THE SELF-SEEKER . . 219

REGRET (CONTINUED)
    IT'S FROM REGRET FOR SOMETHING YOU HAVE PASSED . . . . . 147 SNOW 124
    AS IF REGRET WERE IN IT AND WERE SACRED. . . . . . . 259 WEST-RUNNING BROOK . . 60
    (WITH A POLITE REGRET TO BE) . . . . 326 TO A THINKER . . . 16
    WE'RE EITHER NOTHING OR A GOD'S REGRET. . . . . . . 353 THE LESSON FOR TODAY . 106
REGULAR
    REGULAR VESTRY-TREES WHOLE SUNDAY SCHOOLS . . . . . 107 CHRISTMAS TREES . . . 53
    SO REGULAR THAT IN THE DARK . . . . 380 AN UNSTAMPED LETTER IN 10
    REGULAR VERSE SPRINGS FROM THE STRAIN OF RHYTHM . . . 460 HOW HARD TO KEEP FROM 213
REGULARLY
    AS REGULARLY AS HE WENT TO FEED THE PIG . . . . . . 283 THE GOLD HESPERIDEE . 19
REGULATE
    YOU LET THINGS MORE LIKE FEATHERS REGULATE . . . . . 63 A SERVANT TO SERVANTS . 36
REIGN
    ON WAKING TO FIND VALOR REIGN, ... 19 THE TRIAL BY EXISTENCE 3
    IN CASE I SHOULD DECIDE TO REIGN SOME MORE. . . . 458 HOW HARD TO KEEP FROM 148
    YOU CHANGED ALL THAT. YOU SET ME FREE TO REIGN. . . . 476 A MASQUE OF REASON . . 77
REIGNS
    THAT'S WHY DISCRIMINATION REIGNS. . . . . 467 QUANDARY 7
REINFORCE
    IT MAKES HER MOVE AS IF TO REINFORCE IT. . . . . . 493 A MASQUE OF MERCY . . 7
REINS
    AND I LIE BACK AND RIDE. I TAKE THE REINS . . . . . 49 A HUNDRED COLLARS . . 138
    "NO, HE WON'T, EITHER. HE'LL JUST DROP THE REINS . . . 88 THE HOUSEKEEPER . . . 200
    BY LEANING BACK MYSELF, AS IF THE REINS . . . . . 132 THE BONFIRE 79
REJECT
    NONE I DON'T REJECT . . . . 440 KITTY HAWK 382
REJECTED
    AND LEFT IT LYING WHERE IT FELL REJECTED. . . . . . 217 A FOUNTAIN, A BOTTLE . 120
    I WAS REJECTED BY THE ROYAL BIRD . . . . 443 AUSPEX 7
    HE WAS REJECTED FOR HIS RESERVATIONS! . . . . . . 519 A MASQUE OF MERCY . . 670
REJECTING
    HIS MOOD REJECTING ALL HIS MIND SUGGESTS. . . . . 269 THE BEAR 15
REJOICED
    BUT THOUGH THEY REJOICED IN THE NEST THEY KEPT, . . . 242 NEED OF BEING VERSED . 22
RELAPSE
    WHY GIVE THE CONTROVERSY A RELAPSE? . . . . 407 FROM PLANE TO PLANE . 113
RELATED
    "D'YOU KNOW A PERSON SO RELATED TO HERSELF . . . . 76 THE GENERATIONS OF MEN 82
    WHEN THEY MADE HER RELATED TO THE MAPLES, ... 184 MAPLE 139
RELATION
    IN A RELATION OF ELECTED FRIENDS. . . . . 315 IRIS BY NIGHT . . . 31
RELATIONSHIP
    BY A PLAIN STATEMENT OF RELATIONSHIP, ... 75 THE GENERATIONS OF MEN 59
RELATIVELY
    HOW RELATIVELY LITTLE JUSTICE MATTERS. . . . . . . 499 A MASQUE OF MERCY . 146
RELEASE
    RELEASE ONE LEAF AT BREAK OF DAY; . . . . 27 OCTOBER 12
    AT NOON RELEASE ANOTHER LEAF; . . . . 27 OCTOBER 13
    ARE BUT THE POINTS AT WHICH IT FINDS RELEASE. . . . . 255 THE FLOOD 11
RELEASES
    BUT POWER OF BLOOD ITSELF RELEASES BLOOD. . . . . . 254 THE FLOOD 6
RELEASING
    MY THANKS ARE TO YOU FOR RELEASING ME . . . . . . 475 A MASQUE OF REASON . . 69
RELENT
    HAS DRIED THE DEW AND ALL ITS ROPES RELENT, ... 331 THE SILKEN TENT . . . 3
RELIANCE
    THAT I MAY TRADE ON WITH RELIANCE . . . . 449 OUR DOOM TO BLOOM . . 3
    AND MORE BIGOTED IN RELIANCE . . . . 466 SOME SCIENCE FICTION . 15
RELIC
    AS RELIC OF A VANISHED RACE OF TREES-- . . . . . . 290 OLD BARN AT THE BOTTOM 39
RELIED
    SOME HAVE RELIED ON WHAT THEY KNEW, ... 307 PROVIDE, PROVIDE . . 13
RELIEF
    TO THINK THEIR CASE WAS BEYOND RELIEF-- . . . . . 253 THE THATCH 22
    I CAN'T HELP OWNING THE GREAT RELIEF IT WOULD BE . . . 287 A ROADSIDE STAND . . 47
    TOO PROUD TO BE BEHOLDEN FOR RELIEF, ... 394 HAEC FABULA DOCET . . 19
    WILL FIND RELIEF IN ONE BURST. YOU SHALL SEE. . . . . 398 BURSTING RAPTURE . . 13
RELIEVED
    "WEREN'T YOU RELIEVED TO FIND HE WASN'T DEAD?" . . . . 73 THE CODE 110
RELIGION
    SHE TAUGHT HIM HER TRIBE'S RELIGION: . . . . . . 313 BEARER OF EVIL TIDINGS 17
    SO SCIENCE AND RELIGION REALLY MEET. . . . . . . 353 THE LESSON FOR TODAY . 83
    ART AND RELIGION LOVE THE SOMBER CHORD. . . . . . 353 THE LESSON FOR TODAY . 97
    ABOVE SOME MORE RELIGION IN A MANGER. . . . . . . 369 THE LITERATE FARMER AND 35
    LEARNING HAS BEEN A PART OF THEIR RELIGION. . . . . . 414 A CABIN IN THE CLEARING 28
    LET HIM SEEK HIS RELIGION IN THE CHURCH. . . . . . 494 A MASQUE OF MERCY . . 32
    RELIGION FOR THESE PHILOSOPHIC MATTERS. . . . . . 501 A MASQUE OF MERCY . . 217
    (I WON'T HAVE KEEPER CALLING IT RELIGION.) . . . . . 503 A MASQUE OF MERCY . . 256
RELIGIOUS
    (HE ALMOST LOOKS RELIGIOUS BUT HE'S NOT), ... 269 THE BEAR 28
    THE SPIRIT PLAYS US STRANGE RELIGIOUS PRANKS . . . . 358 THE LOST FOLLOWER . . 5
    RELIGIOUS FAITH IS A MOST FILLING VAPOR. . . . . . 386 INNATE HELIUM . . . 1
    AND CHANGE THE TENOR OF RELIGIOUS THOUGHT. . . . . 475 A MASQUE OF REASON . . 68
    HE'S BEING A RELIGIOUS SNOB FOR FUN. . . . . . . 494 A MASQUE OF MERCY . . 34
    BY A RELIGIOUS AZTEC INDIAN. . . . . 516 A MASQUE OF MERCY . . 616
RELISH
    I DIDN'T RELISH IT ALONG AT FIRST. . . . . 87 THE HOUSEKEEPER . . . 173
RELUCTANCE
    RELUCTANCE . . . . 29 RELUCTANCE . . . . T
RELUCTANT
    OR AT UTMOST A LITTLE RELUCTANT WHIRL . . . . . . 236 MISGIVING 11
RELYING
    RELYING ON ITS BEAUTY, TO THE AIR. . . . . . . 375 A YOUNG BIRCH . . . 9
    RELYING ON HIMSELF AND ON HIS CANE, ... 394 HAEC FABULA DOCET . . 2
REMAIN
    I MEANT, YOU MEANT, THAT NOTHING SHOULD REMAIN . . . . 222 TO E.T. 9
    IT HAD SEEMED DISCREET TO REMAIN THERE . . . . . . 314 BEARER OF EVIL TIDINGS 25

PAGE TITLE   LINE

REMAIN (CONTINUED)
HOW HAPPILY INSTINCTIVE WE REMAIN, ... 425 ACCIDENTALLY ON PURPOSE 22
REMAINED
UNSAID BETWEEN US, BROTHER, AND THIS REMAINED-- . . . 222 TO E.T. 10
HIS WATCHDOG EYE ON WHAT REMAINED . . . . 419 ONE MORE BREVITY . . 5
I HAVE REMAINED RESENTFUL TO THIS DAY . . . . 443 AUSPEX 10
REMAINING
OF THE LAST REMAINING ASTER FLOWER . . . .   9 A LATE WALK . . . 15
NONE REMAINING IN EXISTENCE . . . . 304 CLEAR AND COLDER . . 8
REMARK
HE NOTICED NOTHING IN IT TO REMARK. . . . . 172 A STAR IN A STONEBOAT . 7
REMARKED
JOHN SMITH REMARKED THEM AS HE COASTED BY, ... 161 NEW HAMPSHIRE . . . 74
REMARKING
SHE'S BEAUTIFUL. / YES, SHE WAS JUST REMARKING . . . . 479 A MASQUE OF REASON . . 156
REMEDY
WE'D HAIL THE REMEDY. BUT IT'S BEEN TRIED . . . . . 372 THE LITERATE FARMER AND 122
REMEMBER
AH! I REMEMBER ME . . . . 29 MY BUTTERFLY 31
HE RAN ON HAROLD WILSON--YOU REMEMBER-- . . . . . 36 DEATH OF THE HIRED MAN 58
BUT, WARREN, PLEASE REMEMBER HOW IT IS: . . . . . 40 DEATH OF THE HIRED MAN 156
I CAN REMEMBER WHEN I WORE FOURTEEN. . . . . . . 47 A HUNDRED COLLARS . . 64
DO YOU REMEMBER WHAT IT WAS YOU SAID?" . . . . . 118 THE TELEPHONE . . . 9
A BROOK TO NONE BUT WHO REMEMBER LONG. . . . . . 119 HYLA BROOK 12
AND I REMEMBER ONE WHOSE NAME APPEARED . . . . . 165 NEW HAMPSHIRE . . 193
REMEMBER BIRNAM WOOD! THE WOOD'S IN FLUX!" . . . . 170 NEW HAMPSHIRE . . 373
EXCEPT THAT I REMEMBER HOW OF OLD . . . . 189 THE GRINDSTONE . . 22
I DON'T REMEMBER WHY I EVER CARED. . . . . . . 207 THE WITCH OF COOS . 149
I'LL TELL YOU WHO'D REMEMBER--HEMAN LAPISH. . . . . 208 PAUPER WITCH OF GRAFTON 26
"I'LL TELL YOU WHAT YOU SHOW ME. YOU REMEMBER . . . 213 A FOUNTAIN, A BOTTLE . 7
"IF I REMEMBER RIGHTLY, IT HAD SPRUNG . . . . . 213 A FOUNTAIN, A BOTTLE . 24
AND REMEMBER HOW FINAL A HUSH . . . . 266 SITTING BY A BUSH . 15
I CAN REMEMBER WHEN HE WAS A PUP. . . . . 308 THE SPAN OF LIFE . . 2
TO REMEMBER OR INVENT . . . . 309 HARDSHIP OF ACCOUNTING 4
THE ONE YOU HAD THE TALK WITH, YOU REMEMBER, . . . 316 BUILD SOIL . . . 3
REMEMBER, AND MUST KEEP A SOLEMN FACE.) . . . . . 352 THE LESSON FOR TODAY . 67
THEIR LATEST THAT I REMEMBER, ... 365 A NATURE NOTE . . 15
REMEMBER HOW YOU ENVIED GENERAL SHERMAN. . . . . 406 FROM PLANE TO PLANE . 71
REMEMBER HE HAD MADE THE TEST . . . . 416 AMERICA IS HARD TO SEE 7
(AS I REMEMBER THEY WERE SUMMER STARS . . . . . . 462 HOW HARD TO KEEP FROM 269
TELL HIM HE MAY REMEMBER YOU: YOU'RE JOB. . . . . 474 A MASQUE OF REASON . . 33
OH, I REMEMBER WELL: YOU'RE JOB, MY PATIENT. . . . 474 A MASQUE OF REASON . . 34
YOU MUST REMEMBER HE WAS IN ON THIS. . . . . . . 486 A MASQUE OF REASON . . 377
WELL, BUT REMEMBER THIS IS UNOFFICIAL: . . . . . 506 A MASQUE OF MERCY . 331
REMEMBERED
IN THE BIG BIBLE, AND ALL SHE REMEMBERED . . . . . 183 MAPLE 105
WITH SOMETHING HE REMEMBERED IN HIMSELF, ... 200 PLACE FOR A THIRD . 18
SWOOPS JUST IN TIME TO HIS REMEMBERED TREE. . . . . 249 ACCEPTANCE 10
REMEMBERED THAT EVIL TIDINGS . . . . 313 BEARER OF EVIL TIDINGS 3
REMEMBERING
WHAT KEPT HIM FROM REMEMBERING WHAT IT WAS . . . . 108 OLD MAN'S WINTER NIGHT 6
WHY WOULDN'T I BE SCARED REMEMBERING THAT?" . . . . 132 THE BONFIRE 94
ALL THE WAY HOME I KEPT REMEMBERING . . . . . . 217 A FOUNTAIN, A BOTTLE . 132
REMEMBERS
IF ANYONE REMEMBERS HOW THAT WAS. . . . . 395 WHY WAIT FOR SCIENCE . 13
REMIND
THROUGH THE BED BLANKETS I REMIND MYSELF . . . . . 93 THE SELF-SEEKER . . 19
WELL, THEY REMIND ME OF THE HUE AND CRY . . . . . 168 NEW HAMPSHIRE . . 294
"DO YOU KNOW YOU REMIND ME OF A TREE-- . . . . . 182 MAPLE 87
A CHIMNEY THAT ONLY WOULD SERVE TO REMIND ME . . . 232 THE KITCHEN CHIMNEY . 19
THEY REMIND ME OF PICTURES ON A PALETTE: . . . . . 321 BUILD SOIL . . . 152
DELIVER US FROM COMMITTEES. 'TWILL REMIND ME. . . . 486 A MASQUE OF REASON . . 373
REMINDED
"BEFORE YOU DROP THE CURTAIN--I'M REMINDED: . . . . 149 SNOW 172
HE ONLY HAD TO BE REMINDED OF-- . . . . 191 PAUL'S WIFE . . . 1
ITS LOCKS WERE PROPS--AND THAT REMINDED HIM. . . . 290 OLD BARN AT THE BOTTOM 11
AS IF REMINDED--OR AS IF PERHAPS . . . . 293 AT WOODWARD'S GARDENS . 15
NOR BE REMINDED OF THEM IN A BLOW-- . . . . . . 447 DOES NO ONE AT ALL EVER 36
REMINDS
REMINDS ME OF ALL THAT CAN HAPPEN TO HARM . . . . . 228 GOOD-BY AND KEEP COLD . 3
REMINISCENT
BUT FAINTLY REMINISCENT OF THE RACE . . . . . . 173 A STAR IN A STONEBOAT . 32
AND SOMEONE REMINISCENT WILL RECALL . . . . . . 375 A YOUNG BIRCH . . 11
A REMINISCENT TWINGE OF RHEUMATISM. . . . . . . 474 A MASQUE OF REASON . . 40
REMOTE
TO THE MOST REMOTE . . . . 439 KITTY HAWK . . . 366
REMOTENESS
OR ELSE BY SOME REMOTENESS THAT DEFIED THEM . . . . 216 A FOUNTAIN, A BOTTLE . 107
REMOTEST
THE CHANCE IS THE REMOTEST . . . . 465 SOME SCIENCE FICTION . 1
REMOVED
AND TO HEAR HER QUAINT PHRASES--SO REMOVED . . . . . 57 THE BLACK COTTAGE . 62
(NINE TIMES REMOVED. CORRECT ME IF I ERR.) . . . . 79 THE GENERATIONS OF MEN 178
REND
THERE'S BUTTER SOMEWHERE, TOO." / "LET'S REND THE BREAD. 115 IN THE HOME STRETCH . 145
FOR HIM TO REND . . . . 360 THE RABBIT-HUNTER . . 14
RENDER
AND SO RENDER NIL . . . . 426 A NEVER NAUGHT SONG . 25
RENEW
THEY RENEW TALK OF THE FABLED . . . . 387 THE COURAGE TO BE NEW . 7
RENEWAL
AS HARDLY WORTH RENEWAL. . . . . 252 THE PEACEFUL SHEPHERD . 8
RENEWED
YET FOR THEM THE LILAC RENEWED ITS LEAF, ... 242 NEED OF BEING VERSED . 17
THERE WAS AN OLD, OLD HOUSE RENEWED WITH PAINT, . . . 263 THE INVESTMENT . . . 3
RENEWING (SEE RE-RENEWING)
RENOWN
TO MY UNDUE RENOWN, ... 389 ASTROMETAPHYSICAL . . 18

- 441 -

<table>
<tr><td></td><td>PAGE TITLE</td><td>LINE</td></tr>
</table>

RENOWN (CONTINUED)
    AND SUCH SMALL POSTHUMOUS RENOWN . . . . 418 AMERICA IS HARD TO SEE   45
RENT
    THE COTTAGES LEN BUILT, SOMETIMES WE RENT THEM, ... 64 A SERVANT TO SERVANTS . 41
    THE BATTLE RENT A COBWEB DIAMOND-STRUNG . . . . 126 RANGE-FINDING 1
    JESSE HAS GIVEN PAUL THE RENT OF IT . . . . 514 A MASQUE OF MERCY . . 560
REPAIR
    I HAVE COME AFTER THEM AND MADE REPAIR . . . . . . 33 MENDING WALL 6
REPAIRING
    REPAIRING FENCE AND ROOF; . . . . 367 A SERIOUS STEP LIGHTLY 20
REPEAT
    "I CAN REPEAT THE VERY WORDS YOU WERE SAYING: . . . . 54 HOME BURIAL 91
    I STAND AND MAKE MYSELF REPEAT OUT LOUD . . . . . . 63 A SERVANT TO SERVANTS . 18
    BY HEART AND WHEN ALONE REPEAT. . . . . 403 SOMETHING LIKE A STAR . 10
    LET ME REPEAT: I'M GLAD TO HEAR YOU SAY . . . . . 507 A MASQUE OF MERCY . 360
    BUT TO REPEAT AND GET IT THROUGH YOUR HEAD: . . . . 516 A MASQUE OF MERCY . 600
REPEATED (SEE OFT-REPEATED)
    ON THE LONG BEAD CHAIN OF REPEATED BIRTH, ... 303 A BIRD SINGING IN SLEEP 11
REPEATEDLY
    BUT THOUGH REPEATEDLY HE STROVE . . . . 138 BROWN'S DESCENT . . . 16
REPEATING
    IF THAT WAS HOW SHE FELT, HE KEPT REPEATING. . . . . 200 PLACE FOR A THIRD . 21
    BE SURE TO KEEP REPEATING TO YOURSELF . . . . . . 385 THE FEAR OF GOD . . . 3
    KEPT REPEATING PARDON, PARDON; . . . . 397 AN IMPORTER . . . 20
REPENT
    THAT STILL, IF I REPENT, I MAY RECALL IT, ... 130 THE BONFIRE . . . 22
    SO IF YOU FIND YOU MUST REPENT . . . . 326 TO A THINKER 33
REPENTANCE
    AND PAY A DEATH TAX OF FAIRLY POLITE REPENTANCE. . . . 307 NOT QUITE SOCIAL . 16
REPENTED
    I TURNED AND REPENTED, BUT COMING BACK . . . . . . 102 GOOD HOURS 11
REPERTORY
    SINCE YOU PUT FOOD FIRST IN YOUR REPERTORY. . . . . 455 HOW HARD TO KEEP FROM 50
REPETITION
    COUNTING AN ENDLESS REPETITION. . . . . 247 DEVOTION 4
    TO SO ENDLESS A REPETITION . . . . 286 IN TIME OF CLOUDBURST . 26
REPLACE
    WHEN THESE GO THERE WILL BE NONE TO REPLACE THEM. . . . 290 OLD BARN AT THE BOTTOM 40
REPLIED
    REPLIED SHE HAD AS SOON . . . . 464 MILKY WAY IS A COWPATH 18
REPLY
    I THOUGHT OF QUESTIONS THAT HAVE NO REPLY, ... 22 THE TUFT OF FLOWERS 19
    HER FINGERS MOVED THE LATCH FOR ALL REPLY. . . . . 52 HOME BURIAL . . . 44
    AND THIS IS MY SINCERE REPLY: . . . . 139 BROWN'S DESCENT . . . 52
    TO WHICH THE FARMER WOULD MAKE REPLY, ... 263 THE TIMES TABLE . . 8
    SO LONG FOR NOTHING. NO REPLY-- . . . . 327 A MISSIVE MISSILE . 26
    THE BREEZE DISDAINED TO MAKE REPLY; . . . . . . 342 A CLOUD SHADOW . . 6
    HE TRUSTS MY LOVE TOO WELL TO DEIGN REPLY. . . . . 359 THE LOST FOLLOWER . 33
    AND I REPLY I ALMOST THINK I DO, ... 513 A MASQUE OF MERCY . 531
REPORT
    AND THEY NO DOUBT REPORT . . . . 288 DEPARTMENTAL 20
    YET STILL I MUST REPORT . . . . 384 MAKING CERTAIN ANYTHING 7
REPORTED
    HE SAYS IT'S NOT REPORTED SO FAR NORTH.-- . . . . . 95 THE SELF-SEEKER . . . 87
REPORTS
    BUT HE NO DOUBT REPORTS TO ANY . . . . 288 DEPARTMENTAL 18
REPOSE
    AND BOOK-LEAF, THAT KEEP NEAR YOU, THEIR REPOSE; . . . 148 SNOW 146
    THOUGH FOR ALL ANYONE CAN TELL, REPOSE . . . . 148 SNOW 147
    THE WINGS NOT FOLDED IN REPOSE, BUT SPREAD. . . . . 356 A MOTH SEEN IN WINTER . 4
REPRESENTED
    THIS REPRESENTED AN IMPROVEMENT ON. . . . . . . 189 THE GRINDSTONE . . . 36
REPRESSED
    THAT THOUGH REPRESSED AND MOODY WITH THE WEATHER . . . 240 OUR SINGING STRENGTH . 51
REPROACH (SEE SELF-REPROACH)
    WHEN I WAS SOLD--AND SMALL REPROACH TO HIM. . . . . 459 HOW HARD TO KEEP FROM 172
    WITH TOLERANT REPROACH . . . . 466 SOME SCIENCE FICTION . 11
    OR METAPHYSICS, LONG THE WORLD'S REPROACH . . . . . 480 A MASQUE OF REASON . 191
REPROACHFULLY
    AH, JONAH, JONAH--TWICE--REPROACHFULLY. . . . . . 495 A MASQUE OF MERCY . . 57
REPUBLIC
    "SHINE, PERISHING REPUBLIC." / ROBINSON JEFFERS . . . 449 OUR DOOM TO BLOOM . . 5
REPUBLICAN
    THE NEWS HAS ALWAYS BEEN REPUBLICAN. . . . . . . 48 A HUNDRED COLLARS . 111
    WHEN EVERYTHING HAD GONE REPUBLICAN . . . . . . 165 NEW HAMPSHIRE . . 196
REPULSE
    SLAMS IN HIS FACE. THE BLOW AND THE REPULSE . . . . 518 A MASQUE OF MERCY . 650
REPUTABLE
    (ASK ANY REPUTABLE ROSICRUCIAN) . . . . 363 A SEMI-REVOLUTION . . 3
REPUTE
    AS SCHOOLMEN OF REPUTE SHOULD QUALIFY . . . . . . 352 THE LESSON FOR TODAY . 50
REQUIRE
    'TIS PITY IF THE CASE REQUIRE . . . . 19 REVELATION 5
REQUIRED
    REQUIRED SOMEONE WHO LAUGHINGLY COULD PLAY . . . . . 509 A MASQUE OF MERCY . 422
REQUISITE
    THE REQUISITE LIFT OF SPIRIT HAS NEVER BEEN FOUND, . . 287 A ROADSIDE STAND . . 45
RE-RENEWING
    A LOVE THAT WANTED RE-RENEWING. . . . . 274 A LONE STRIKER . . . 46
RESEARCH
    THE S'CIETY FOR PSYCHICAL RESEARCH . . . . 163 NEW HAMPSHIRE . . . 135
RESENT
    TO SHOW BY DEEDS HE DIDN'T RESENT . . . . 421 ONE MORE BREVITY . . 63
RESENTFUL
    AND RESENTFUL OF MAN'S CONDITION. . . . . 286 IN TIME OF CLOUDBURST . 28
    I HAVE REMAINED RESENTFUL TO THIS DAY . . . . . . 443 AUSPEX 10
    (WHY ARE WE SO RESENTFUL OF DETACHMENT?) . . . . . 462 HOW HARD TO KEEP FROM 272

- 442 -

RESENTMENT
   OR CHILD, AND THIS IS MOTHERLY RESENTMENT? . . . . . . 501 A MASQUE OF MERCY . . 206
RESERVATIONS
   HE WAS REJECTED FOR HIS RESERVATIONS! . . . . 519 A MASQUE OF MERCY . . 670
RESERVE
   WE HAVE STRENGTH OF RESERVE IN US TO BRING. . . . . . 321 BUILD SOIL 162
   IN YOUR RESERVE IS NOT ALLOWED. . . . . 403 SOMETHING LIKE A STAR . . 8
RESERVED
   THE WHICH IT IS RESERVED FOR GOD ABOVE . . . . 12 A PRAYER IN SPRING . . 14
   BESIDE IT ROOM RESERVED; THE SAY A SISTER'S, ... 200 PLACE FOR A THIRD . . 40
   IS RESERVED FOR THE BED OF A FEW SELECTED SEED. . . . 299 STRONG SAYING NOTHING . 4
RESIDUE
   AS A VILE RESIDUE, ... 449 THE BAD ISLAND--EASTER 44
RESIN
   TO LOOSE THE RESIN AND TAKE IT DOWN . . . . 141 THE GUM-GATHERER . . . 38
   TO FRIZZLE RESIN IN A CANDLE FLAME, ... 350 TO A YOUNG WRETCH . . 8
RESIST
   YET FOUND IT EASY TO RESIST. . . . . 274 A LONE STRIKER . . . 35
RESISTANCE (SEE NON-RESISTANCE)
   AND PROMISE MORE RESISTANCE TO THE PICKER." . . . . . 198 WILD GRAPES 71
   SAVE BY SOME STRANGE RESISTANCE IN ITSELF, ... 259 WEST-RUNNING BROOK . . 58
RESORT
   FROM THE SAME GENERAL RESORT, ... 417 AMERICA IS HARD TO SEE 22
RESORTS
   TO SUCH RESORTS OF LIFE AS MARS AND EARTH-- . . . . . 174 A STAR IN A STONEBOAT . 48
RESOURCE
   IN NERVE AND RESOURCE . . . . 448 THE BAD ISLAND--EASTER 39
RESPECT (SEE SELF-RESPECT)
   THESE FORCES ARE OBLIGED TO PAY RESPECT TO?" . . . . 176 THE STAR-SPLITTER . . 12
   AS A BRUTE TRIBUTE OF RESPECT TO BEAUTY. . . . . . . 195 PAUL'S WIFE 141
   LOOK HERE, YOU TREAT YOUR GUIDE WITH DUE RESPECT . . . 214 A FOUNTAIN, A BOTTLE . 49
   TO CONVEY MY RESPECT FOR YOUR POSITION?" . . . . . . 408 FROM PLANE TO PLANE . 135
   I QUOTE HIM WITH RESPECT VERBATIM. . . . . 451 A-WISHING WELL . . . 6
RESPECTFULLY
   SHUFFLED THEIR FEET AS IF TO HINT RESPECTFULLY, . . . 456 HOW HARD TO KEEP FROM 73
RESPITE
   OR RESPITE FROM THE THOUGHT OF RIVALRY. . . . . . . 461 HOW HARD TO KEEP FROM 244
RESPOND
   PAUL WONDERED HOW IT WOULD RESPOND TO WATER. . . . . 194 PAUL'S WIFE 97
RESPONSE
   EYES SEEKING THE RESPONSE OF EYES . . . . 332 ALL REVELATION . . . 16
   BUT COUNTER-LOVE, ORIGINAL RESPONSE. . . . . 338 THE MOST OF IT . . . 8
RESPONSIBILITY
   FELL ALL IN WRINKLES OF RESPONSIBILITY. . . . . . . 201 PLACE FOR A THIRD . . 48
REST
   TO WHITE REST, AND A PLACE OF REST . . . . 9 STARS 7
   SHELVES ONE COULD REST A KNEE ON GETTING UP-- . . . . 42 THE MOUNTAIN 59
   ROLLED OUT A LITTLE FARTHER THAN THE REST." . . . . . 44 THE MOUNTAIN 99
   YOU CAN'T REST THAT WAY. LET ME PULL YOUR SHOES OFF." . 47 A HUNDRED COLLARS . . 76
   YOU'LL REST EASIER WHEN I'M GONE, PERHAPS-- . . . . . 50 A HUNDRED COLLARS . . 160
   IT'S REST I WANT--THERE, I HAVE SAID IT OUT-- . . . . 64 A SERVANT TO SERVANTS . 49
   I'LL NEVER REST TONIGHT UNLESS I KNOW. . . . . . . 90 THE FEAR 32
   "OF COURSE YOU DID. YOU LEFT THE REST FOR SEED, . . . 97 THE SELF-SEEKER . . . 124
   HAD BROUGHT TO REST. . . . . 110 A PATCH OF OLD SNOW . 4
   A MOMENT SOUGHT IN AIR HIS FLOWER OF REST, ... 126 RANGE-FINDING . . . 7
   I COULD, BUT WHAT'S THE SENSE? THE REST WON'T BE . . . 143 SNOW 20
   THE REST IS DOWN.--WHY NO, NO, NOT A WALLOW: . . . . 143 SNOW 23
   GET INTO BED I SAY, AND GET SOME REST. . . . . . . 152 SNOW 265
   AND CANNOT REST FROM PLANNING DAY OR NIGHT . . . . . 169 NEW HAMPSHIRE . . . 338
   THAT, ONCE GRIEF SETS TO GROWING, GRIEF MAY REST: . . . 200 PLACE FOR A THIRD . . 27
   AND OFFERED HER A HOME TO REST AWHILE . . . . 201 PLACE FOR A THIRD . . 60
   AND ALL THE REST FOR THEM PERMISSIBLE EASE. . . . . . 230 NOT TO KEEP 12
   AND MEDICINE AND REST, AND YOU A WEEK, ... 230 NOT TO KEEP 16
   THE FIRST SONGBIRD THAT AWAKENED ALL THE REST. . . . . 235 VALLEY'S SINGING DAY . 5
   IT MAY NOT SEEM BETTER TO ME TO REST. . . . . 236 MISGIVING 16
   ON HIS FOREFEET TO REST. . . . . 261 CANIS MAJOR 8
   THE FULL SIX DAYS. THEN REST A DAY; . . . . 280 BLUE RIBBON AT AMESBURY 30
   OR BEAUTY REST IN A BEAUTIFUL MOUNTAIN SCENE. . . . . 286 A ROADSIDE STAND . . 13
   AND THE REST WON'T WANT TO PUNISH ME TOO SEVERELY . . . 306 NOT QUITE SOCIAL . . 2
   OF WORKING OUT THE REST, THE OTHER HALF. . . . . . . 324 BUILD SOIL 272
   I TAKE MY INCOMPLETENESS WITH THE REST. . . . . . . 355 THE LESSON FOR TODAY . 155
   AND TELL THEM THE REST OF THE STORY IS DREAMING? . . . 379 TOO ANXIOUS FOR RIVERS . 19
   WE CAN REST ASSURED ON EIDER. . . . . 385 IN THE LONG NIGHT . . 15
   WITH THE ABSOLUTE FLIGHT AND REST . . . . 388 MIDDLENESS OF THE ROAD 14
   TO REST FROM HIS BESETTING FEARS. . . . . 392 A CLIFF DWELLING . . 9
   FOR ALL HUMANITY A COMPLETE REST . . . . 405 FROM PLANE TO PLANE . 30
   AND WALK THE REST OF THE WAY. . . . . 444 THE DRAFT HORSE . . 20
   AND COME TO REST IN AN OFFICIAL VERDICT. . . . . . . 474 A MASQUE OF REASON . 29
   TO REST AT TIMES FROM BEING CIVILIZED. . . . . . . 496 A MASQUE OF MERCY . 74
   AND GIVE YOU REST, POOR WANDERING JEW. / I'M NOT . . . 498 A MASQUE OF MERCY . 133
   WHICH IS OUR GREATEST HOPE OF REST FROM WAR. . . . . 516 A MASQUE OF MERCY . 593
RESTED
   THAT RESTED ON THE BANISTER, AND SLID DOWNSTAIRS; . . . 52 HOME BURIAL 32
   I PAUSED AND RESTED ON A SORT OF HOOK . . . . 125 AN ENCOUNTER 8
   SHE RESTED ON A LOG AND TOSSED . . . . 128 THE IMPULSE 9
   ARE RESTED AND IT'S TIME TO SAY GOOD-NIGHT. . . . . . 150 SNOW 210
   THE WAY IT RESTED TWO POINTS ON THE GROUND . . . . . 501 A MASQUE OF MERCY . 194
RESTFUL
   SHE'S STILL NEW HAMPSHIRE, A MOST RESTFUL STATE. . . . 170 NEW HAMPSHIRE . . . 357
   IT'S RESTFUL TO ARRIVE AT A DECISION, ... 172 NEW HAMPSHIRE . . . 411
   AND RESTFUL JUST TO THINK ABOUT NEW HAMPSHIRE. . . . . 172 NEW HAMPSHIRE . . . 412
RESTING
   SOME RESTING FLOWER OF YESTERDAY'S DELIGHT. . . . . . 22 THE TUFT OF FLOWERS . 14
   WAS COILED IN ITS LAST RESTING GRAVE . . . . 312 THE VINDICTIVES . . . 61
   A PERCH AND RESTING PLACE 'TWIXT WOOD AND WOOD, . . . 356 A MOTH SEEN IN WINTER . 2
RESTIVE
   HOLDING OPEN A RESTIVE DOOR, ... 251 BEREFT 4

	PAGE	TITLE	LINE

RESTLESS
THE FAINTEST RESTLESS RUSTLING RAN ALL THROUGH THEM. . . . . 204 THE WITCH OF COOS . . 64
GAVE ME A STRANGELY RESTLESS DAY. . . . . 364 TRESPASS 8
WITH AN INHERITANCE OF RESTLESS DREAM. . . . . 412 POD OF THE MILKWEED . 44
RESTORE
YOU WANTED TO RESTORE THEM TO THEIR RIGHT . . . . . 109 THE EXPOSED NEST . . 17
RESTRAINED
TO WALK A GRAVER MAN RESTRAINED IN WRATH. . . . . . 285 THE GOLD HESPERIDEE . 60
RESTRAINT (SEE SELF-RESTRAINT)
IN SELF-RESTRAINT, IF IN RESTRAINT OF TRADE. . . . . 323 BUILD SOIL 229
I'M TEMPTED TO LET GO RESTRAINT, ... 451 A-WISHING WELL . . . 15
RESTRICT
OR EVEN NATION'S TO RESTRICT MY MEANING. . . . . . . 166 NEW HAMPSHIRE . . . 231
RESTS
"IT RESTS WITH US ALWAYS TO CUT HER OFF." . . . . . 80 THE GENERATIONS OF MEN 183
HE PACES BACK AND FORTH AND NEVER RESTS . . . . . . 269 THE BEAR 16
OR IF HE RESTS FROM SCIENTIFIC TREAD, ... 269 THE BEAR 22
AND WHEN TO STOP IT RESTS WITH YOU. . . . . 306 A TRIAL RUN 14
RESTS ON THE WORLD, AND CLINGING SLOWLY ROLLS. . . . 322 BUILD SOIL 196
AND ONLY RESTS, A SERPENT ON ITS CHIN, ... 399 THE INGENUITIES OF DEBT 15
RESULTANT
BUT A RESULTANT THAT ARISES FROM THEM. . . . . . . 460 HOW HARD TO KEEP FROM 217
RESUME
IT WILL BE LONG ERE THE MARSHES RESUME, ... 25 NOW CLOSE THE WINDOWS . 5
FAR ENOUGH FOR MY THOUGHT-FLOW TO RESUME. . . . . . 324 BUILD SOIL 256
RESURRECTED
STOOD OVER ME A RESURRECTED TREE, ... 125 AN ENCOUNTER 12
RESUSCITATING
AND HE WAS THERE RESUSCITATING FLOWERS . . . . . . 354 THE LESSON FOR TODAY . 131
RETAIL
THAT OVER. I SHALL HAVE TO RETAIL IT . . . . 509 A MASQUE OF MERCY . . 404
RETARD
RETARD THE SUN WITH GENTLE MIST; . . . . 27 OCTOBER 15
RETARD MID-WASTE MY COWERING CARAVANS-- . . . . . 59 THE BLACK COTTAGE . 124
I DON'T SAY RETARD. . . . . 441 KITTY HAWK . . . 410
RETIRED
RETIRED FROM POLITICS AND JOINED THE CHORUS. . . . . 168 NEW HAMPSHIRE . . . 297
PRECIPITATELY THEY RETIRED BACK-CAGE . . . . . . 293 AT WOODWARD'S GARDENS . 24
RETRACE
TILL DAY MAKES HIM RETRACE HIS FLIGHT, ... 120 BOND AND FREE . . . 13
RETREAT (SEE SELF-RETREAT)
MY OWN STRATEGIC RETREAT . . . . 282 A DRUMLIN WOODCHUCK . 5
THE MUSE MOURNS ONE WHO WENT TO HIS RETREAT . . . . 359 THE LOST FOLLOWER . 21
OR FOR MYSELF IN MY RETREAT . . . . 470 IN WINTER IN THE WOODS 11
RETROACTIVE
SALVATION IN OUR CASE IS RETROACTIVE. . . . . . . 476 A MASQUE OF REASON . 81
RETURN
BUT IT SEEMS LIKE THE SEA'S RETURN . . . . 27 A LINE-STORM SONG . 26
MADE ME ASK WOULD THE MOTHER-BIRD RETURN . . . . . 109 THE EXPOSED NEST . 23
AND EVERY CRASH MEANT ONE LESS TO RETURN . . . . . 112 IN THE HOME STRETCH . 57
NOT TO RETURN. EARTH'S THE RIGHT PLACE FOR LOVE: . . . 122 BIRCHES 52
OR RETURN. . . . . 129 THE IMPULSE . . . 18
APPEARING TO RETURN ME HATE FOR HATE . . . . . . 190 THE GRINDSTONE . . 41
THEY EVER WILL RETURN TO ALL THEIR LIVES, ... 411 POD OF THE MILKWEED . 3
AND I MAY RETURN . . . . 413 AWAY! 21
OUR DAYS ALL PASS AWAITING ITS RETURN. . . . . . . 461 HOW HARD TO KEEP FROM 248
OR OF HOW RAYS RETURN UPON THEMSELVES, ... 485 A MASQUE OF REASON . 343
RETURNED
WARREN RETURNED--TOO SOON, IT SEEMED TO HER-- . . . . 40 DEATH OF THE HIRED MAN 164
ALWAYS AT NIGHT WHEN THEY RETURNED . . . . 127 HOUSE FEAR 2
WHEN COLE RETURNED HE FOUND HIS WIFE STILL STANDING . . 151 SNOW 245
HAD MADE THEM CERTAIN EARTH RETURNED THEIR LOVE. . . . 230 TWO LOOK AT TWO . . 42
RETURNS
SUSPICION OF THE INCOME-TAX RETURNS, ... 503 A MASQUE OF MERCY . 247
REVELATION
REVELATION . . . . 19 REVELATION . . . . T
ALL REVELATION . . . . 332 ALL REVELATION . . . T
ALL REVELATION HAS BEEN OURS. . . . . 333 ALL REVELATION . . . 20
REVELRY
IN THEIR REVELRY-- . . . . 432 KITTY HAWK 119
REVERSED
THE SLOPE OF THE EARTH REVERSED. . . . . 285 IN TIME OF CLOUDBURST . 16
THE GUN REVERSED THAT HE WENT OUT WITH SHOULDERED. . . 289 OLD BARN AT THE BOTTOM 4
AND WHEN THAT LEFT ME TO SINK BACK REVERSED . . . . 468 IN A GLASS OF CIDER . 5
I SHOULD HAVE SAID. YOU GOT YOUR AGE REVERSED . . . . 479 A MASQUE OF REASON . 159
REVISION
WON'T THIS WHOLE INSTINCT MATTER BEAR REVISION? . . . 279 THE WHITE-TAILED HORNET 50
WON'T ALMOST ANY THEORY BEAR REVISION? . . . . . 279 THE WHITE-TAILED HORNET 51
FOR THE REVISION OF THE BOOK OF PRAYER . . . . . . 486 A MASQUE OF REASON . 371
REVISITED
AND STILL THE BIRD REVISITED HER YOUNG. . . . . . . 126 RANGE-FINDING . . . 5
REVOLUTION (SEE SEMI-REVOLUTION)
IT NEEDN'T WAIT ON GENERAL REVOLUTION. . . . . . . 324 BUILD SOIL 265
I BID YOU TO A ONE-MAN REVOLUTION-- . . . . . . 324 BUILD SOIL 266
THE ONLY REVOLUTION THAT IS COMING. . . . . 324 BUILD SOIL 267
THE TROUBLE WITH A TOTAL REVOLUTION . . . . . . 363 A SEMI-REVOLUTION . 2
OUR VENTURE IN REVOLUTION AND OUTLAWRY . . . . . 423 FOR JOHN F. KENNEDY . 51
THE SUBJECT OF THE WORKERS' REVOLUTION . . . . . 508 A MASQUE OF MERCY . 398
IN THEIR IMPOVERISHMENT BY REVOLUTION . . . . . 509 A MASQUE OF MERCY . 413
THE REVOLUTION KEEPER'S BRINGING ON . . . . . . 509 A MASQUE OF MERCY . 416
NO REVOLUTION I BROUGHT ON WOULD AIM . . . . . . 510 A MASQUE OF MERCY . 457
REVOLUTIONARIES
A BUNCH OF SMALL-TIME REVOLUTIONARIES.-- . . . . . 509 A MASQUE OF MERCY . 406
REVOLUTIONARY
THE TIMES SEEM REVOLUTIONARY BAD. . . . . 317 BUILD SOIL 32
A REVOLUTIONARY--WHICH OF COURSE YOU CAN'T BE. . . . 510 A MASQUE OF MERCY . 455
REVOLUTIONIST
OR KEEPER IS A REVOLUTIONIST. . . . . 508 A MASQUE OF MERCY . 400

REVOLUTIONISTS
    WHEN YOU CAME IN. WE'RE REVOLUTIONISTS. . . . . . . 508 A MASQUE OF MERCY . . 399
REVOLUTIONS
    YES, REVOLUTIONS ARE THE ONLY SALVES, ... 363 A SEMI-REVOLUTION . .   7
REVOLUTION'S
    A REVOLUTION'S COMING DOWN THE STREET! . . . . . . 508 A MASQUE OF MERCY . . 391
REVOLVING
    LIKE WINGS, REVOLVING IN THE SCENE . . . . 138 BROWN'S DESCENT 22
    AND THE WORLD CAME REVOLVING BACK TO ME, ... 198 WILD GRAPES 86
    WE WATCH A CIRCUS OF REVOLVING DOGS . . . . 362 SYMPATHY WITH UNDER DOG   2
    WHAT SET US ON FIRE AND WHAT SET US REVOLVING, ... 380 TOO ANXIOUS FOR RIVERS 22
REWARD
    TO FIND THAT THE UTMOST REWARD . . . .   19 THE TRIAL BY EXISTENCE   7
    STILL IT WOULDN'T REWARD THE WATCHER TO STAY AWAKE . . 268 ON LOOKING UP BY CHANCE 13
    AS A SMALL SELF-CONFERRED REWARD OF VIRTUE. . . . . . 405 FROM PLANE TO PLANE . 39
    IS ITS OWN REWARD. . . . . 438 KITTY HAWK 335
    IS IT NOT TRUE? AND WHAT WAS MY REWARD? . . . . . . 458 HOW HARD TO KEEP FROM 132
REWARDED
    SHOULD BE REWARDED. . . . . 389 ASTROMETAPHYSICAL . . 12
    YOU'D HAVE REWARDED ME FOR ALL I'VE DONE . . . . . . 457 HOW HARD TO KEEP FROM 119
REWARDS
    WHETHER TIME'S REWARDS ARE FAIR OR UNFAIR. . . . . . 347 DISCOVERY OF MADEIRAS . 138
    WITH FORFEITS AND REWARDS HE UNDERSTOOD-- . . . . . . 476 A MASQUE OF REASON . . 74
RHEUMATISM
    A REMINISCENT TWINGE OF RHEUMATISM. . . . . 474 A MASQUE OF REASON . . 40
RHINE
    THE FOE THRUST BACK UNSAFE BEYOND THE RHINE, ... 222 TO E.T. 18
RHODE
    RHODE ISLAND, NEW YORK, OR VERMONT WAS THIS: . . . . 167 NEW HAMPSHIRE 251
RHODES
    "I'M A RHODES SCHOLAR--THAT'S THE REASON WHY. . . . . 455 HOW HARD TO KEEP FROM   52
    I WAS AT COLLEGE IN THE ISLE OF RHODES." . . . . . . 455 HOW HARD TO KEEP FROM   53
    HIS NAME IS OMAR. I AS A RHODES SCHOLAR . . . . . . 459 HOW HARD TO KEEP FROM 188
RHODODENDRONS
    HE RAN THROUGH THE RHODODENDRONS . . . . 313 BEARER OF EVIL TIDINGS 11
RHYME
    SO SURE OF DEATH THE MARBLES RHYME, ... 221 IN A DISUSED GRAVEYARD   9
    A RHYME OF HAKLUYT . . . . 343 DISCOVERY OF MADEIRAS .   5
    THEY SLOWLY LED OLD LATIN VERSE TO RHYME . . . . . . 351 THE LESSON FOR TODAY . 16
    AND TAKES THE PLAYFULLY OBJECTED RHYME . . . . . . 362 IN A POEM   2
    WOULD I GAIN ANYTHING BY USING RHYME? . . . . 382 TO AN ANCIENT . . . 17
    (WITH SOME PRELIMINARY HISTORY IN RHYME) . . . . . . 422 FOR JOHN F. KENNEDY .   5
RHYMED
    RHYMED WITH 1 2 3 . . . . 436 KITTY HAWK 275
RHYTHM
    REGULAR VERSE SPRINGS FROM THE STRAIN OF RHYTHM . . . 460 HOW HARD TO KEEP FROM 213
    THE TUNE IS NOT THAT METER, NOT THAT RHYTHM, ... 460 HOW HARD TO KEEP FROM 216
RIBBON
    A BLUE RIBBON AT AMESBURY . . . . 279 BLUE RIBBON AT AMESBURY   T
RIBS
    AND STRAINING HER RIBS FOR A MONSTER SIGH; . . . . . 263 THE TIMES TABLE . . .   7
    AND REACHING BACK TO HIS RIBS . . . . 444 THE DRAFT HORSE . . .   7
RICH
    OR FOR THE RICH A CURSE: . . . .   8 LOVE AND A QUESTION . 28
    WHY DOESN'T HE GO THERE? HIS BROTHER'S RICH, ...   39 DEATH OF THE HIRED MAN 128
    AND HE WAS RICH, AND I WAS STILL A RASCAL. . . . . . 160 NEW HAMPSHIRE . . . 54
    HOW DID HE GET SO? (RICH WAS UNDERSTOOD.) . . . . . 160 NEW HAMPSHIRE . . . 57
    TO DRY, FROM POOR TO RICH, OR BACK AGAIN. . . . . . 166 NEW HAMPSHIRE . . . 236
    FOR WHEN ALL THAT WAS ROTTED RICH . . . . 285 IN TIME OF CLOUDBURST . 10
    AGAINST HIS UNACQUAINTANCES THE RICH . . . . 290 OLD BARN AT THE BOTTOM 30
    THE RICH IN SEEING NOTHING BUT INJUSTICE . . . . . . 509 A MASQUE OF MERCY . . 412
RICHES
    OR BEEN THEIR RICHES, FAME, OR LOVE DENIED; . . . . . 355 THE LESSON FOR TODAY . 153
    COULD MOCK AT RICHES IN THE RIGHT IT CLAIMS . . . . . 509 A MASQUE OF MERCY . . 424
RID
    THEIR WARES ARE SO MUCH HARDER TO GET RID OF. . . . . 164 NEW HAMPSHIRE . . . 174
    NO ONE WAS ANXIOUS TO GET RID OF PAUL. . . . . . . 191 PAUL'S WIFE 16
    IN TIME SHE WOULD BE RID OF ALL HER BOOKS. . . . . . 217 A FOUNTAIN, A BOTTLE . 138
    GET RID OF THAT AND THERE'D BE LEFT NO GREAT . . . . 371 THE LITERATE FARMER AND 110
    THEN IT'S NOT LETHAL--TO GET RID OF ME? . . . . . . 516 A MASQUE OF MERCY . . 617
RIDDEN (SEE HABIT-RIDDEN)
    AND NOW FROM HAVING RIDDEN OUT DESIRE . . . . 225 BLUE-BUTTERFLY DAY . .   6
RIDDLE
    "YOU RIDDLE WITH YOUR GENEALOGY, ...   75 THE GENERATIONS OF MEN 53
RIDE
    AND I LIE BACK AND RIDE. I TAKE THE REINS . . . . .   49 A HUNDRED COLLARS . . 138
    BETTER THAN IF HE HAD HAD ME RIDE, ... 140 THE GUM-GATHERER . . .   4
    AND GIVE SOMEONE THE SKIPPER IRESON'S RIDE. . . . . . 163 NEW HAMPSHIRE . . . 143
    AND NOW THE VERY AIR, OF WHAT WE RIDE. . . . . . . 267 RIDERS   4
    TO RIDE THE WHIRLWIND AND THE HURRICANE. . . . . . . 423 FOR JOHN F. KENNEDY . 48
    OUR SAILORS RIDE A BULLET FOR A BOAT. . . . . 446 DOES NO ONE AT ALL EVER 14
RIDERS
    THE SUREST THING THERE IS IS WE ARE RIDERS, ... 267 RIDERS   1
    RIDERS . . . . 267 RIDERS . . . . . .   T
RIDES
    AT ANCHOR SHE RIDES THE SUNNY SOD, ... 262 THE FLOWER BOAT . . .   5
RIDGE
    ON VIMY RIDGE; AND WHEN YOU FELL THAT DAY . . . . . 222 TO E.T. 14
RIDGELY
    TO RIDGELY TORRENCE ON LAST LOOKING INTO HIS "HESPERIDES" . 248 A PASSING GLIMPSE . .   D
RIDGEPOLE
    OVER THE RIDGEPOLE, 'STRIDE OF A BROOMSTICK, ... 210 PAUPER WITCH OF GRAFTON 86
RIDGES
    RIDGES OF SAND, AND DRIFTWOOD STRIPPED OF BARK. . . .   40 THE MOUNTAIN 14
RIDICULOUS
    YOU KNOW HOW MEN WILL BE RIDICULOUS. . . . .   87 THE HOUSEKEEPER . . . 160
RIDING
    SOMETHING I MUST HAVE LEARNED RIDING IN TRAINS . . . .   77 THE GENERATIONS OF MEN 127

RIDING (CONTINUED)
    BY RIDING THEM DOWN OVER AND OVER AGAIN . . . . 122 BIRCHES 29
    THE GRADE SURMOUNTED, WE WERE RIDING HIGH . . . . . 292 FIGURE IN THE DOORWAY . 1
RIFE
    HOW ONCE CONSPIRACY WAS RIFE . . . . 29 MY BUTTERFLY 32
RIFLED
    THE CRYPT WAS LONG SINCE RIFLED BY THE GREEKS. . . . . 483 A MASQUE OF REASON . . 284
RIFLING
    RIFLING A PRINTED LETTER AS HE TALKS. . . . . 44 A HUNDRED COLLARS . . 10
RIG
    AND TURN DOLL OUT TO PASTURE, RIG AND ALL. . . . . . 88 THE HOUSEKEEPER . . . 201
RIGEL
    RIGEL, BELLATRIX, OR ELSE BETELGEUSE, ... 454 HOW HARD TO KEEP FROM 16
RIGHT
    AS THE SUN'S RIGHT WORSHIP IS, ... 13 ROSE POGONIAS 10
    'ALL RIGHT,' I SAY, 'I CAN'T AFFORD TO PAY . . . . . 35 DEATH OF THE HIRED MAN 22
    TO THINK OF THE RIGHT THING TO SAY TOO LATE. . . . . 37 DEATH OF THE HIRED MAN 77
    I'LL SEE TO THAT IF THERE IS NEED. HE OUGHT OF RIGHT . . 39 DEATH OF THE HIRED MAN 132
    RIGHT ON THE TOP, TIP-TOP--A CURIOUS THING. . . . . . 42 THE MOUNTAIN 47
    RIGHT ON THE SUMMIT, ALMOST LIKE A FOUNTAIN. . . . . 42 THE MOUNTAIN 64
    IT MAY NOT BE RIGHT ON THE VERY TOP- . . . . 42 THE MOUNTAIN 68
    "WE CALL IT HOR: I DON'T KNOW IF THAT'S RIGHT." . . . 43 THE MOUNTAIN 91
    "I KNOW HIM: HE'S ALL RIGHT. A MAN'S A MAN. . . . . . 45 A HUNDRED COLLARS . . 26
    RIGHT ON THE COUNTERPANE--THAT I DO TRUST YOU?" . . . 48 A HUNDRED COLLARS . . 94
    AND WELL, IF THEY WEREN'T TRUE WHY KEEP RIGHT ON . . . 58 THE BLACK COTTAGE . . 97
    TO PEOPLE THEY LOOK ON AS HAVING NO RIGHT . . . . . 62 BLUEBERRIES 101
    INCLUDING ME. HE THINKS I'LL BE ALL RIGHT . . . . . 64 A SERVANT TO SERVANTS . 46
    MY FATHER'S BROTHER WASN'T RIGHT. THEY KEPT HIM . . . 65 A SERVANT TO SERVANTS . 88
    I'D BUILT THE LOAD AND KNEW RIGHT WHERE TO FIND IT. . 71 THE CODE 71
    "DISCHARGE ME? NO! HE KNEW I DID JUST RIGHT." . . . . 73 THE CODE 114
    "SEE THAT YOU GET HER GREATNESS RIGHT. DON'T STINT HER." . 77 THE GENERATIONS OF MEN 117
    YOU WILL DO VERY WELL RIGHT WHERE YOU ARE . . . . . 78 THE GENERATIONS OF MEN 145
    THEY HAVE BEST RIGHT TO BE HEARD IN THIS PLACE." . . . 79 THE GENERATIONS OF MEN 176
    IT MUST BE RIGHT TO LEAVE HIM." / "WHICH IS WRONG!" . 83 THE HOUSEKEEPER . . . 75
    SAY IT RIGHT OUT--NO MATTER FOR HER MOTHER. . . . . . 88 THE HOUSEKEEPER . . . 187
    WHAT IF I'M RIGHT, AND SOMEONE ALL THE TIME-- . . . . 90 THE FEAR 22
    TO PUT IT THE RIGHT WAY. HE'D NEVER DARE-- . . . . . 90 THE FEAR 37
    SNATCHED RIGHT AND LEFT ACROSS THE SILVER PULLEYS. . . 94 THE SELF-SEEKER . . . 39
    ER, LET ME SEE. I THINK I'LL TAKE THE RIGHT. . . . . 96 THE SELF-SEEKER . . . 110
    THAT'S SURE TO BE RIGHT, EVEN IF IT'S WRONG. . . . . 96 THE SELF-SEEKER . . . 111
    SOMEHOW I'LL MAKE IT RIGHT WITH HER--SHE'LL SEE. . . 98 THE SELF-SEEKER . . . 150
    YOU ONLY HAVE TO SIGN YOUR NAME. RIGHT--THERE." . . . 99 THE SELF-SEEKER . . . 183
    BUT READ IT, READ IT.--THAT'S RIGHT, DRAW THE CURTAIN: . 99 THE SELF-SEEKER . . . 193
    "FIVE HUNDRED DOLLARS!" / "WHAT WOULD YOU THINK RIGHT?" . 99 THE SELF-SEEKER . . . 198
    YOU WANTED TO RESTORE THEM TO THEIR RIGHT . . . . . 109 THE EXPOSED NEST . . 17
    THE NEIGHBORS MAY NOT HAVE TAKEN AS THEIR RIGHT . . . 117 IN THE HOME STRETCH . 191
    BEFORE WE SET OURSELVES TO RIGHT THE HOUSE, ... 117 IN THE HOME STRETCH . 194
    WHEN I SEE BIRCHES BEND TO LEFT AND RIGHT . . . . . 121 BIRCHES 1
    SO LOW FOR LONG, THEY NEVER RIGHT THEMSELVES: . . . . 121 BIRCHES 16
    NOT TO RETURN. EARTH'S THE RIGHT PLACE FOR LOVE: . . . 122 BIRCHES 52
    JUST WHEN IT SEEMS TO COME IN RIGHT, ... 134 A GIRL'S GARDEN . . . 43
    FROM ONE WHO HAD NO RIGHT TO BE HEARD FROM. . . . . 142 THE VANISHING RED . . 18
    OH, YES, HE SHOWED JOHN THE WHEEL PIT ALL RIGHT. . . 142 THE VANISHING RED . . 29
    WHY DID I CALL HIM THAT?" / "IT'S RIGHT ENOUGH. . . . 144 SNOW 45
    PRIVATELY--TO HIMSELF, RIGHT NOW, HE'S THINKING . . . 146 SNOW 85
    AND SAVE HIS LIFE.--ALL RIGHT, COME IN, MESERVE. . . 147 SNOW 104
    YOU'VE DONE MORE THAN YOU HAD A RIGHT TO THINK . . . 150 SNOW 219
    THE PAUSE RIGHT THERE, SHE THOUGHT THE DREADED WORD . 151 SNOW 238
    TO RIGHT THE WRONG THAT THIS SHOULD HAVE BEEN SO. . . 173 A STAR IN A STONEBOAT . 36
    I COUNTED NINE I HAD NO RIGHT TO COUNT . . . . . . 175 THE CENSUS-TAKER . . 31
    MAPLE IS RIGHT." / "BUT TEACHER TOLD THE SCHOOL . . . 179 MAPLE 4
    TO LEAVE IT TO, WHETHER THE RIGHT TO HOLD . . . . . 188 THE AX-HELVE 91
    HE HAD TO RUN RIGHT OFF TO LOOK HER UP, ... 191 PAUL'S WIFE 13
    PAUL TOLD THE BOSS THE LOAD WOULD BE ALL RIGHT, . . . 192 PAUL'S WIFE 46
    AND THEN LAND SAFELY RIGHT SIDE UP AGAIN, ... 192 PAUL'S WIFE 52
    MY BROTHER HAD BEEN NEARER RIGHT BEFORE. . . . . . . 199 WILD GRAPES 94
    A GOOD DEAL RIGHT; DON'T DO THE LAST THING WRONG. . . 199 PLACE FOR A THIRD . . 10
    SHE WANTED TO DO RIGHT. SHE'D HAVE TO THINK. . . . . 201 PLACE FOR A THIRD . . 49
    TO DO, AS SHE HAD PUT IT, WHAT WAS RIGHT. . . . . . 201 PLACE FOR A THIRD . . 75
    RIGHT PAST BOTH FATHER AND MOTHER, AND NEITHER STOPPED IT. . 203 THE WITCH OF COOS . . 33
    RIGHT'S RIGHT, AND THE TEMPTATION TO DO RIGHT . . . . 208 PAUPER WITCH OF GRAFTON 33
    THE POOR OLD MAN. IT WOULD HAVE BEEN ALL RIGHT . . . 209 PAUPER WITCH OF GRAFTON 53
    TO UNDO WHAT HE'D DONE AND MAKE IT RIGHT, ... 209 PAUPER WITCH OF GRAFTON 79
    WELL THEN, RIGHT HERE IS WHERE I SHOW YOU BOOKS. . . 215 A FOUNTAIN, A BOTTLE . 60
    BEFORE MAN CAME TO BLOW IT RIGHT . . . . 223 THE AIM WAS SONG . . 1
    THAT KEPT THE GROUND, ALMOST DISPUTING RIGHT . . . . 240 OUR SINGING STRENGTH . 36
    PROCLAIMED THE TIME WAS NEITHER WRONG NOR RIGHT. . . 255 ACQUAINTED WITH NIGHT . 13
    THEY THOUGHT ALL CHOPPING WAS THEIRS OF RIGHT. . . . 276 TWO TRAMPS IN MUD TIME 52
    AS THAT I HAD NO RIGHT TO PLAY . . . . 277 TWO TRAMPS IN MUD TIME 60
    MY RIGHT MIGHT BE LOVE BUT THEIRS WAS NEED. . . . . . 277 TWO TRAMPS IN MUD TIME 62
    THEIRS WAS THE BETTER RIGHT--AGREED. . . . . 277 TWO TRAMPS IN MUD TIME 64
    AND SERVED US RIGHT FOR HAVING INSTITUTED . . . . . 279 THE WHITE-TAILED HORNET 58
    THAT THE NAME GOLD HESPERIDEE WAS RIGHT. . . . . . . 284 THE GOLD HESPERIDEE . 30
    YES, RIGHT I WAS, THE LOCKS WERE PROPS OUTSIDE; . . . 290 OLD BARN AT THE BOTTOM 41
    BUT UNLESS YOU PUT THE RIGHT THING TO ITS ROOT . . . 296 LEAVES COMPARED WITH . 3
    MIXED READY TO BEGIN THE MORNING RIGHT, ... 302 DESIGN 5
    TILL ABOUT THE RIGHT CONSISTENCE. . . . . 304 CLEAR AND COLDER . . 6
    THAT THOUGH THERE IS NO FIXED LINE BETWEEN WRONG AND RIGHT, 305 THERE ARE ROUGHLY ZONES 12
    TO PUNISH ME OVERCRUELLY WOULDN'T BE RIGHT . . . . . 306 NOT QUITE SOCIAL . . 5
    MY RIGHT TO BE EQUAL IN NUMBER OF CARDS, ... 310 IN DIVES' DIVE . . . 4
    ONE MORE WOULD THROW YOU ON THE RIGHT. . . . . 325 TO A THINKER 3
    IF MY MISTRUST IS RIGHT . . . . 333 HAPPINESS MAKES UP . 12
    HE THOUGHT, ALL RIGHT, IF YOU WANT THE TRUTH! . . . . 346 DISCOVERY OF MADEIRAS . 97
    BUT GO. YOU ARE RIGHT. MY PITY CANNOT HELP. . . . . 356 A MOTH SEEN IN WINTER . 17
    BUT RIGHT BESIDE YOU BOOKLIKE ON A SHELF, ... 359 THE LOST FOLLOWER . . 31
    AND IN WHICH THERE WAS LITTLE PROPERTY RIGHT. . . . . 364 TRESPASS 12
    AND WOULD I SEE IF HE WAS RIGHT? . . . . 367 NOT OF SCHOOL AGE . . 28
    BUT RIGHT IN HEAVEN WAS SLOWLY BEING SHRUNK . . . . . 368 THE LITERATE FARMER AND 14

                                                                    PAGE TITLE   LINE

RIGHT (CONTINUED)
    IF NOT, A GLASS OF MILK WILL BE ALL RIGHT." . . . . 368 THE LITERATE FARMER AND 22
    AND ASK US IF OUR PREMISES ARE RIGHT." . . . . 370 THE LITERATE FARMER AND 83
    ON THE RIGHT SIDE OF BED WOULD END THE FRAY, ... 372 THE LITERATE FARMER AND 121
    AND FOUND, HE SAYS, A BED HAS NO RIGHT SIDE. . . . . . . 372 THE LITERATE FARMER AND 123
    A BED'S GOT NO RIGHT SIDE TO GET OUT OF. . . . . 372 THE LITERATE FARMER AND 125
    AND THAT RIGHT SOON, THAT THE MEADOWSWEET . . . . 375 SOMETHING FOR HOPE . .   2
    BY RIGHT OF EMINENT DOMAIN. . . . . 390 TWO LEADING LIGHTS . . 10
    WE'LL BE ALL RIGHT IF NOTHING GOES WRONG WITH THE LIGHTING. 392 IT BIDS PRETTY FAIR .   4
    SOMETHING WAS GOING RIGHT OUTSIDE THE HALL. . . . . . . 399 THE BROKEN DROUGHT . .   2
    TO THE RIGHT PERSON . . . . 400 TO THE RIGHT PERSON . .   T
    WE GRANT YOUR LOFTINESS THE RIGHT . . . . 403 SOMETHING LIKE A STAR .   2
    "AND RIGHT YOU ARE. YOU DO THE WAY WE DO . . . . 405 FROM PLANE TO PLANE . . 49
    "ALL RIGHT, LET'S HARMONIZE ABOUT THE DOCTOR. . . . . . 407 FROM PLANE TO PLANE . . 102
    YOU'RE RIGHT, THERE'S NOTHING TO DISCUSS. . . . . 420 ONE MORE BREVITY . .   29
    FINDING HIM IN HIS RIGHT SUPPLIES . . . . 420 ONE MORE BREVITY . .   42
    RIGHT DOWN TO NOW IN GLORY UPON GLORY. . . . . 423 FOR JOHN F. KENNEDY .   53
    A DEMOCRATIC FORM OF RIGHT DIVINE . . . . 424 FOR JOHN F. KENNEDY .   64
    AND RIGHT OVERHEAD, ... 433 KITTY HAWK 171
    AND BY RIGHT DIVINE, ... 442 KITTY HAWK 457
    IT IS RIGHT IN THERE . . . . 445 PERIL OF HOPE   1
    WHEN THE BOUGHS ARE RIGHT . . . . 445 PERIL OF HOPE   5
    LET'S GET MY INCANTATION RIGHT: . . . . 451 A-WISHING WELL . . .   27
    "YOU'RE RIGHT," THE EX-KING SAID, "WE'LL NEED SOME MONEY. 454 HOW HARD TO KEEP FROM 30
    THIS LARRIKIN? ALL RIGHT. YOU COME ALONG. . . . . 455 HOW HARD TO KEEP FROM 47
    YOU HAVE A RIGHT TO KNOW YOUR PEDIGREE. . . . . 457 HOW HARD TO KEEP FROM 107
    ENSLAVE YOURSELF TO THE RIGHT LEADER'S TRUTH, ... 460 HOW HARD TO KEEP FROM 191
    AND GONE RIGHT ON ASTRAY . . . . 465 MILKY WAY IS A COWPATH 29
    AND IT CAME OUT ALL RIGHT. I HAVE NO DOUBT . . . . 475 A MASQUE OF REASON .   65
    TRY TO READ TO HER AND SHE DROPS RIGHT OFF. . . . . . . 479 A MASQUE OF REASON . 155
    THAN THE DAY SHE WAS BORN / THAT'S ABOUT RIGHT, ... 479 A MASQUE OF REASON . 158
    BEFORE I AM TOO LATE TO BE GOT RIGHT . . . . 479 A MASQUE OF REASON . 166
    I'D TELL YOU, JOB---- / ALL RIGHT, DON'T TELL ME, THEN, . 483 A MASQUE OF REASON . 270
    MY KINGDOM, WHAT AN OUTBREAK! / JOB IS RIGHT. . . . . . 484 A MASQUE OF REASON . 302
    WHY NOT RIGHT NOW? / WE CAN'T WITHOUT THE DEVIL. . . . . 487 A MASQUE OF REASON . 381
    IT SEEMS TO START RIGHT OFF ACCELERATING. . . . . 489 A MASQUE OF REASON . 450
    MUST HAVE YOU. THERE, THAT'S JUST THE RIGHT ARRANGEMENT. 489 A MASQUE OF REASON . 457
    THE CITY IS ALL RIGHT. TO LIVE IN ONE . . . . 496 A MASQUE OF MERCY .   69
    LOOK OUT FOR HIM. / "LOOK OUT FOR ME" IS RIGHT. . . . . 498 A MASQUE OF MERCY . 130
    RIGHT BACK IN THE SAME TROUBLE I WAS IN. . . . . 500 A MASQUE OF MERCY . 185
    THAT'S THE RIGHT STYLE OF COAT FOR PROPHECY . . . . . . 501 A MASQUE OF MERCY . 218
    ARE RIGHT. BUT 'TWAS INTENTIONAL INJUSTICE. . . . . . 509 A MASQUE OF MERCY . 414
    COULD MOCK AT RICHES IN THE RIGHT IT CLAIMS . . . . . . 509 A MASQUE OF MERCY . 424
    BUT BEL GETS SOME THINGS RIGHT--AND SHE WAS RIGHT-- . . 519 A MASQUE OF MERCY . 690
    I AM RIGHT, THEN? / --IN GLORIFYING COURAGE. . . . . . 519 A MASQUE OF MERCY . 692
RIGHTEOUS
    YOUR RIGHTEOUS INDIGNATION FIZZLED OUT, ... 497 A MASQUE OF MERCY . 103
RIGHTFULLY
    HE WON'T MAKE THE FACT THAT THEY'RE RIGHTFULLY HIS . . 60 BLUEBERRIES   31
RIGHTLY
    I DON'T KNOW RIGHTLY WHETHER ANY MAN CAN." . . . . . . 52 HOME BURIAL   38
    AND NEVER RIGHTLY UNDERSTOOD TILL BRYAN . . . . 168 NEW HAMPSHIRE . . . 296
    "IF I REMEMBER RIGHTLY, IT HAD SPRUNG . . . . 213 A FOUNTAIN, A BOTTLE . 24
    AND MADE FEEL LESS ALONE THAN I RIGHTLY SHOULD, . . . 383 WERE I IN TROUBLE . .   8
RIGHT'S
    RIGHT'S RIGHT, AND THE TEMPTATION TO DO RIGHT . . . . 208 PAUPER WITCH OF GRAFTON 33
RIGHTS (SEE STATE-RIGHTS)
    BY GOOD RIGHTS I OUGHT NOT TO HAVE SO MUCH . . . . . . 64 A SERVANT TO SERVANTS . 53
    "THE RIGHTS OF THAT ARE HARDER TO GET AT. . . . . . . 84 THE HOUSEKEEPER . . .   99
    HAS A MAN, I SHOULD LIKE TO ASK, NO RIGHTS . . . . . 176 THE STAR-SPLITTER . .   11
    THE RAIN BY RIGHTS WAS SNOW FOR COLD. . . . . 253 THE THATCH   11
    WHAT ARE HER INTERESTS, JOB? / WITCH-WOMEN'S RIGHTS. . 479 A MASQUE OF REASON . 175
RIGID
    OF A STARFISH LAID OUT WITH RIGID POINTS." . . . . . . 93 THE SELF-SEEKER . . .   20
    LIKE A WHITE PIECE OF RIGID SATIN CLOTH-- . . . . . . 302 DESIGN   3
RIGMAROLE
    HEAR MY RIGMAROLE. . . . . 468 A REFLEX   1
RIGMAROLES
    SACRED RIGMAROLES TO MUTTER, ... 396 AN IMPORTER   6
RIGOROUS
    TOO LONG PENT UP IN RIGOROUS CONVENTION-- . . . . . . 509 A MASQUE OF MERCY . . 418
RILL
    IN WATER OF A SLENDER APRIL RILL . . . . 226 THE ONSET   19
RIM
    UNLESS IN THE HORIZON RIM, ... 392 A CLIFF DWELLING . .   4
RING
    THEN HE SHUT DOWN THE TRAP DOOR WITH A RING IN IT . . 142 THE VANISHING RED . .   24
    ONE NOT SO LARGE FOR FLYING IN A RING, ... 172 A STAR IN A STONEBOAT . 15
    AND GATHERED THEM TOGETHER IN A RING. . . . . 315 IRIS BY NIGHT . . .   28
    WE DANCE ROUND IN A RING AND SUPPOSE, ... 362 THE SECRET SITS . . .   1
    AND DOUBLE RING OF FITTED BRASS . . . . 363 ASSURANCE   3
    SOME RUMOR OF HIS WISHING RING . . . . 390 TWO LEADING LIGHTS . . 24
    INTO A LADY'S FINGER RING OR THIMBLE." . . . . 447 DOES NO ONE AT ALL EVER 30
RING-AROUND
    OR JOINED WITH SHEDS IN RING-AROUND A DOORYARD. . . . 289 OLD BARN AT THE BOTTOM   2
RINGING
    "HAD SHE BEEN RINGING LONG? I'LL GET MY WRAPPER. . . 152 SNOW 275
    OR (CHIMES WERE RINGING) CHURCHWARD. . . . . 335 CARPE DIEM   5
    KNIVES AND FORKS RINGING ON THE SUPPER PLATES, . . . 368 THE LITERATE FARMER AND 3
RINGS
    DESCRIBING RINGS OF LANTERN-LIGHT. . . . . 137 BROWN'S DESCENT . . .   8
    JUST ENOUGH GOLD TO MAKE THE ENGAGEMENT RINGS . . . . 162 NEW HAMPSHIRE . . . 113
    AND MARRIAGE RINGS OF THOSE WHO OWNED THE FARM. . . . 162 NEW HAMPSHIRE . . . 114
    NOW BRINGING OUT ITS RINGS IN SUGAR OF PITCH; . . . . 175 THE CENSUS-TAKER . .   21
    HER DEFT HAND SHOWED WITH FINGER RINGS . . . . 273 A LONE STRIKER . . .   28
    WHILE THE TREES PUT ON THEIR WOODEN RINGS . . . . . . 376 SOMETHING FOR HOPE . . 11
    THE THINGS BUT BALLS ALL GOING ROUND IN RINGS. . . . 425 ACCIDENTALLY ON PURPOSE 2

RINK
  ROUND AND ROUND THE RINK . . . . 440 KITTY HAWK 397
RIP
  THEY FALL, THEY RIP THE GRASS, THEY INTERSECT . . . . . 261 A SOLDIER 9
RIPE
  AND ALL RIPE TOGETHER, NOT SOME OF THEM GREEN . . . . 59 BLUEBERRIES 6
  AND SOME OF THEM RIPE! YOU OUGHT TO HAVE SEEN!" . . . . 59 BLUEBERRIES 7
  LIKE A RIPE TOMATO. . . . . 427 VERSION 15
RIPEN
  TO RIPEN TOO LONG. I AM GREATLY TO BLAME.'" . . . . . 60 BLUEBERRIES 46
  WHERE THEY COULD RIPEN SAFELY TO THE EATING. . . . . . 284 THE GOLD HESPERIDEE . 37
RIPENED
  THY LEAVES HAVE RIPENED TO THE FALL; . . . . 27 OCTOBER 2
RIPENESS
  A SCENT OF RIPENESS FROM OVER A WALL. . . . . 304 UNHARVESTED 1
RIPOSTE
  SUMMARY RIPOSTE . . . . 429 KITTY HAWK 28
RIPPLE
  ONE DROP FELL FROM A FERN, AND LO, A RIPPLE . . . . . 225 FOR ONCE SOMETHING . 12
  TWO ROUND DOTS AND A RIPPLE STREAK, ... 327 A MISSIVE MISSILE . . 7
  THE TWO DOTS AND THE RIPPLE LINE. . . . . 328 A MISSIVE MISSILE . . 42
RIPPLES
  OF GLOSSY BIRDS LIKE RIPPLES OVER ROCKS. . . . . . . 240 OUR SINGING STRENGTH . 34
RISE
  HE CAUGHT MY AX EXPERTLY ON THE RISE, ... 185 THE AX-HELVE 10
  RISE OTHERS VASTER YET, ... 260 SAND DUNES 3
  THAT THE NORTHWEST WIND SHOULD RISE TO SUCH A HEIGHT . . 305 THERE ARE ROUGHLY ZONES 16
  COULD CONCENTRATE ANEW AND RISE AS ONE. . . . . . . 315 IRIS BY NIGHT . . . 8
  IF YOU SHOULD RISE FROM NOWHERE UP TO SOMEWHERE, ... 385 THE FEAR OF GOD . . . 1
  THE ROAD AT THE TOP OF THE RISE . . . . 388 MIDDLENESS OF THE ROAD 1
  AND YOUR RISE AND SWOOP, ... 441 KITTY HAWK 404
  SO THAT THE CREAM COULD NEVER RISE AGAIN . . . . . . 509 A MASQUE OF MERCY . 421
  (HE DOESN'T RISE, BUT LOOKS AT HER A MOMENT.) . . . . 519 A MASQUE OF MERCY . 683
RISEN
  THE THOUGHTS MAY NOT HAVE RISEN THAT SO KEEP . . . . 231 A BROOK IN THE CITY . 23
  (PERHAPS SO CALLED BECAUSE IT MAY HAVE RISEN ONCE) . . . 447 THE BAD ISLAND--EASTER 5
RISES
  AS THE BREEZE RISES, AND TURN MANY-COLORED . . . . . 121 BIRCHES 8
  YET ONCE SHE RISES TO THE HEIGHT, ... 281 BLUE RIBBON AT AMESBURY 46
RISING
  AND RISING FULL MOON, SIT ME DOWN . . . . 14 WAITING 6
  A SUNNY MORNING, OR TAKE THE RISING WIND . . . . . . 63 A SERVANT TO SERVANTS . 28
  AND RISING ON HIS HANDS, HE LOOKS IN ON ME . . . . . 176 THE STAR-SPLITTER . . 3
  ITS CLICK WAS RISING TO A NEARER CLANK. . . . . . . 270 THE EGG AND THE MACHINE 10
RISK
  I HAVEN'T COURAGE FOR A RISK LIKE THAT. . . . . . . 67 A SERVANT TO SERVANTS . 170
  WE SAW THE RISK WE TOOK IN DOING GOOD, ... 109 THE EXPOSED NEST . . 27
  ACCORDING AS HE FEARED TO RISK . . . . 138 BROWN'S DESCENT . . . 27
  YOU COULD DO--NOW. YOU KNOW THE RISK YOU TAKE . . . . 150 SNOW 220
  LISTEN AND I WILL TAKE MY DEAREST RISK. . . . . . . 320 BUILD SOIL 136
  IT WAS A RISK I HAD TO TAKE--AND TOOK. . . . . . . 383 BRAVADO 4
RISKING
  LAY IN RISKING SPIRIT . . . . 435 KITTY HAWK 223
RITUAL
  'TIS RITUAL WITH HER TO LAY . . . . 280 BLUE RIBBON AT AMESBURY 29
RIVALRY
  A RIVALRY THAT MADE THEM BOTH FEEL KINDER. . . . . . 408 FROM PLANE TO PLANE . 119
  RIVALRY COMBINED)-- . . . . 436 KITTY HAWK 269
  OR RESPITE FROM THE THOUGHT OF RIVALRY. . . . . . . 461 HOW HARD TO KEEP FROM 244
RIVALS
  OLD RIVALS OF SAGGING LEATHER, ... 294 A RECORD STRIDE . . 6
  (WE'RE RIVALS IN THE BADNESS OF OUR CASE, ... 352 THE LESSON FOR TODAY . 66
RIVER
  ITS TWO BANKS HAVE NOT SHUT UPON THE RIVER; . . . . . 28 MY BUTTERFLY 9
  WERE FIELDS, A RIVER, AND BEYOND, MORE FIELDS. . . . . 40 THE MOUNTAIN 9
  THE RIVER AT THE TIME WAS FALLEN AWAY, ... 40 THE MOUNTAIN 10
  I CROSSED THE RIVER AND SWUNG ROUND THE MOUNTAIN. . . . 41 THE MOUNTAIN 15
  LIKE A DEEP PIECE OF SOME OLD RUNNING RIVER, ... 63 A SERVANT TO SERVANTS . 20
  AND BY A RIVER BANK FOR WATER FLOWERS, ... 98 THE SELF-SEEKER . . 153
  AS STANDING IN THE RIVER ROAD . . . . 139 BROWN'S DESCENT . . 46
  BUT SOON DIVIDES THE RIVER WITH VERMONT. . . . . . 165 NEW HAMPSHIRE . . . 185
  AND A VAGUE ALL-DISTURBING ROAR ABOVE THE RIVER . . . 182 MAPLE 83
  AND YET NOT OUT BY ANY BROOK OR RIVER, ... 245 SPRING POOLS . . . 5
  THAT SAD-WITH-DISTANCE RIVER BEACH . . . . 328 A MISSIVE MISSILE . . 53
  THEN WHAT OF THIS RIVER THAT HAVING ARISEN . . . . . 379 TOO ANXIOUS FOR RIVERS 3
  THE TRUTH IS THE RIVER FLOWS INTO THE CANYON . . . . 379 TOO ANXIOUS FOR RIVERS 8
  I GET YOU WHEN YOU HOE OUT TO THE RIVER, ... 405 FROM PLANE TO PLANE . 40
  THE RIVER BANK, QUIT WORK DEFIANTLY, ... 405 FROM PLANE TO PLANE . 58
  HE HAS CURSED EVERY RIVER MOUTH . . . . 418 AMERICA IS HARD TO SEE 53
RIVERS
  EVER SINCE RIVERS, I WAS GOING TO SAY, ... 258 WEST-RUNNING BROOK . 28
  OH, I HAVE BEEN OFTEN TOO ANXIOUS FOR RIVERS . . . . 379 TOO ANXIOUS FOR RIVERS 6
  TOO ANXIOUS FOR RIVERS -- . . . . 379 TOO ANXIOUS FOR RIVERS T
  TO POUR FRESH RIVERS ON YOU FROM THE LAND, ... 446 DOES NO ONE AT ALL EVER 23
ROAD
  ON THAT DISUSED AND FORGOTTEN ROAD . . . . 6 GHOST HOUSE 13
  AND HE TURNED AND LOOKED AT THE ROAD AFAR . . . . . 7 LOVE AND A QUESTION . 7
  THE BRIDEGROOM LOOKED AT THE WEARY ROAD, ... 8 LOVE AND A QUESTION . 21
  DOORYARD AND ROAD UNGRADED, ... 10 STORM FEAR 14
  THE ROAD IS FORLORN ALL DAY, ... 26 A LINE-STORM SONG . . 2
  AS THE ROAD WINDS WOULD BRING HIM TO HIS DOOR. . . . . 38 DEATH OF THE HIRED MAN 126
  AMY! THERE'S SOMEONE COMING DOWN THE ROAD'" . . . . . 54 HOME BURIAL 111
  SET WELL BACK FROM THE ROAD IN RANK LODGED GRASS, . . . 55 THE BLACK COTTAGE . . 4
  AND OVER THE WALL AND INTO THE ROAD, ... 60 BLUEBERRIES 36
  I S'POSE I'VE GOT TO GO THE ROAD I'M GOING: . . . . . 67 A SERVANT TO SERVANTS . 159
  THE SECOND ROUND THE CURVING HILLSIDE ROAD . . . . . 74 THE GENERATIONS OF MEN 29
  THE SITUATION WAS LIKE THIS: THE ROAD . . . . 75 THE GENERATIONS OF MEN 70
  "YOU SPEAK AS IF THIS WERE A TRAVELED ROAD. . . . . . 90 THE FEAR 24

ROAD (CONTINUED)
   "NOTHING." IT CAME FROM WELL ALONG THE ROAD. . . . . 91 THE FEAR 67
   THE ROAD NOT TAKEN . . . . 105 THE ROAD NOT TAKEN . . T
   WHEN A FRIEND CALLS TO ME FROM THE ROAD . . . . 124 A TIME TO TALK . . . 1
   AND SORRY I EVER LEFT THE ROAD I KNEW, ... 125 AN ENCOUNTER . . . 7
   I WONDER HOW FAR DOWN THE ROAD HE'S GOT. . . . . . . 127 THE SMILE 11
   UPON THE ROAD, TO FLAMES TOO, THOUGH IN FEAR . . . . 131 THE BONFIRE . . . 60
   THE ROAD WOULD FAIL; AND ON THAT SIDE THE FIRE . . . . 131 THE BONFIRE . . . 75
   ALONG A STRETCH OF ROAD; . . . . 134 A GIRL'S GARDEN . . 22
   AS STANDING IN THE RIVER ROAD . . . . 139 BROWN'S DESCENT . . 46
   BY ROAD, A MATTER OF SEVERAL MILES. . . . . 140 BROWN'S DESCENT . . 76
   AND SET ME FIVE MILES ON MY ROAD . . . . 140 THE GUM-GATHERER . . 3
   THAN WE HAD SEEING HIM PASS BY IN THE ROAD . . . . . 152 SNOW 253
   A DROVER WITH ME ON THE ROAD TO BRIGHTON. . . . . . 160 NEW HAMPSHIRE . . 50
   "WHERE ARE YOU GOING TO PUT ME? IN THE ROAD?" . . . . 164 NEW HAMPSHIRE . . 155
   WHOSE HORSE HAD PULLED HIM SHORT UP IN THE ROAD . . . 168 NEW HAMPSHIRE . . 289
   ON THE END IT PRESENTED TO THE ROAD. . . . . 181 MAPLE 58
   ON THE SIDE IT PRESENTED TO THE ROAD) . . . . 182 MAPLE 99
   HE ALWAYS USED TO SING ALONG THE TCTE ROAD. . . . . . 205 THE WITCH OF COOS . 111
   THE TOTE ROAD TO OUR CLEARING WHERE WE LIVED. . . . . 208 PAUPER WITCH OF GRAFTON 25
   WE STRUCK A ROAD I DIDN'T RECOGNIZE, ... 215 A FOUNTAIN, A BOTTLE . 65
   ON A TREE FALLEN ACROSS THE ROAD . . . . 238 ON A TREE FALLEN ACROSS T
   AND ALL GO BACK TO WINTER BUT THE ROAD. . . . . . . 239 OUR SINGING STRENGTH . 10
   THE ROAD ALONE MAINTAINED ITSELF IN MUD, ... 239 OUR SINGING STRENGTH . 16
   THEY COULD FIND NOTHING OPEN BUT THE ROAD. . . . . . 239 OUR SINGING STRENGTH . 30
   THE ROAD BECAME A CHANNEL RUNNING FLOCKS . . . . . . 240 OUR SINGING STRENGTH . 33
   FOR TEAMS THAT CAME BY THE STONY ROAD . . . . . . 241 NEED OF BEING VERSED . 10
   TO CLOSE A ROAD, ABANDON A FARM, ... 263 THE TIMES TABLE . . . 18
   I HAD TO DROP THE ARMFUL IN THE ROAD . . . . 267 THE ARMFUL . . . 11
   HIS HATE HAD ROUSED AN ENGINE UP THE ROAD. . . . . . 270 THE EGG AND THE MACHINE 4
   IN FRONT AT THE EDGE OF THE ROAD WHERE THE TRAFFIC SPED, . 286 A ROADSIDE STAND . . 2
   AND COME TO LEAVE THE ROUTINE ROAD . . . . 304 UNHARVESTED . . . 2
   WHERE ONE ROAD LED TO THE THRONE . . . . 313 BEARER OF EVIL TIDINGS 6
   HE POINTED ON UP THE ROAD. . . . . 366 NOT OF SCHOOL AGE . . 11
   THE ROAD THERE, IF YOU'LL LET A GUIDE DIRECT YOU . . . 377 DIRECTIVE 8
   SOMEONE'S ROAD HOME FROM WORK THIS ONCE WAS, ... 378 DIRECTIVE 30
   BY NOW, PULL IN YOUR LADDER ROAD BEHIND YOU . . . . 378 DIRECTIVE 37
   THE ROAD AT THE TOP OF THE RISE . . . . 388 MIDDLENESS OF THE ROAD 1
   THE MIDDLENESS OF THE ROAD . . . . 388 MIDDLENESS OF THE ROAD T
   ARE LIMITED TO THE ROAD. . . . . 388 MIDDLENESS OF THE ROAD 11
   HAS CUT THIS ROAD TO LAST, ... 415 CLOSED FOR GOOD . . . 4
   THEY LEAVE THE ROAD TO ME . . . . 415 CLOSED FOR GOOD . . . 13
   "FROM YOU THE ROAD RECEIVES . . . . 415 CLOSED FOR GOOD . . . 17
ROADS
   TWO ROADS DIVERGED IN A YELLOW WOOD, ... 105 THE ROAD NOT TAKEN . . 1
   TWO ROADS DIVERGED IN A WOOD, AND I-- . . . . . . 105 THE ROAD NOT TAKEN . . 18
ROADSIDE
   THE ROADSIDE FLOWERS, TOO WET FOR THE BEE, ... 26 A LINE-STORM SONG . . 5
   ALONG THE BUSHES AT THE ROADSIDE--A MAN'S FACE. . . . 89 THE FEAR 11
   A ROADSIDE STAND THAT TOO PATHETICALLY PLED, ... 286 A ROADSIDE STAND . . 3
   A ROADSIDE STAND . . . . 286 A ROADSIDE STAND . . T
   HERE FAR FROM THE CITY WE MAKE OUR ROADSIDE STAND . . 286 A ROADSIDE STAND . . 18
ROAMING
   GAUNT AND DUSTY GRAY WITH ROAMING? . . . . 13 FLOWER-GATHERING . . 6
ROANOKE
   OR SAD ROANOKE, ... 431 KITTY HAWK 89
ROAR
   WHEN I WAS YOUNG. I USED TO USE THE ROAR . . . . . 78 THE GENERATIONS OF MEN 128
   WHICH HAS ITS SOUNDS, FAMILIAR, LIKE THE ROAR . . . . 108 OLD MAN'S WINTER NIGHT 12
   ACROSS THE ROAR AND CHAOS, AND THE WORDS . . . . 170 NEW HAMPSHIRE . . . 350
   AND A VAGUE ALL-DISTURBING ROAR ABOVE THE RIVER . . . 182 MAPLE 83
   CHANGE LIKE THIS TO A DEEPER ROAR? . . . . 251 BEREFT 2
   CONFUSION, AND A ROAR THAT DROWNED THE CRIES . . . . 270 THE EGG AND THE MACHINE 14
   IT WILL MAKE A HOMICIDAL ROAR. . . . . 306 A TRIAL RUN . . . 4
   WE ASKED FOR RAIN. IT DIDN'T FLASH AND ROAR. . . . . 349 OUR HOLD ON THE PLANET 1
ROARED
   AND BELOW ROARED A BROOK HIDDEN IN TREES, ... 76 THE GENERATIONS OF MEN 75
   IT WILL HAVE ROARED FIRST AND MIXED SPARKS WITH STARS, . 130 THE BONFIRE . . . 27
ROARING
   WE HEARD "'TIS OVER" ROARING. . . . . 359 NOVEMBER 7
ROB
   THAN TO ROB THE GRAVE. . . . . 430 KITTY HAWK . . . 77
ROBBED
   "HE WAS AFRAID OF BEING ROBBED OR MURDERED. . . . . . 45 A HUNDRED COLLARS . . 31
ROBBER
   A ROBBER WOULDN'T HAVE HIS FAMILY WITH HIM." . . . . 92 THE FEAR 80
   IT CAN'T BE JUST TO GIVE THE ROBBER A CHANCE . . . . 321 BUILD SOIL 166
ROBBING
   I SEE WHAT YOU ARE UP TO: ROBBING ME . . . . . . 499 A MASQUE OF MERCY . . 147
ROBIN
   THRUSH, BLUEBIRD, BLACKBIRD, SPARROW, AND ROBIN THRONG; . 239 OUR SINGING STRENGTH . 21
ROBINSON
   YOU MUST HAVE HEARD OF CLARA ROBINSON, ... 215 A FOUNTAIN, A BOTTLE . 77
   "SHINE, PERISHING REPUBLIC." / ROBINSON JEFFERS . . . 449 OUR DOOM TO BLOOM . . S
ROBINSONS
   WHO USED TO LIVE HERE. THEY WERE ROBINSONS. . . . . 215 A FOUNTAIN, A BOTTLE . 76
ROCK
   THEIR BULK IN WATER WOULD BE FROZEN ROCK . . . . . 151 SNOW 228
   OF JOSTLING ROCK IN INTERSTELLAR SPACE . . . . . 173 A STAR IN A STONEBOAT . 33
   WITH ROCK AND WASHOUT, AND UNSAFE IN DARKNESS; . . . 229 TWO LOOK AT TWO . . 6
   I LOOKED AT NINE: THE SWARM WAS TURNED TO ROCK . . . 237 A HILLSIDE THAW . . 26
   AT HAVING CULTIVATED ROCK. . . . . 238 PLOWMEN 4
   (THE BLACK STREAM, CATCHING ON A SUNKEN ROCK, ... 258 WEST-RUNNING BROOK . . 19
   FELL SPLINTERLESS AS A CLOVEN ROCK. . . . . . . 275 TWO TRAMPS IN MUD TIME 12
   IN SPECIMEN CRAB IN SPECIMEN ROCK, ... 364 TRESPASS . . . 14
   THE TURTLE IN TURN ON A ROCK IN THE OCEAN. . . . . 379 TOO ANXIOUS FOR RIVERS 16
   THAT UNDER ME A POINT OF ROCK . . . . 380 AN UNSTAMPED LETTER IN 19
   "O CITY ON INSECURE ROCK PEDESTAL, ... 506 A MASQUE OF MERCY . . 337

PAGE TITLE   LINE

ROCKED
    THAT CAME ON, BUT HER BODY ROCKED A LITTLE. . . . . . . 92 THE FEAR 77
    MRS. BAPTISTE CAME IN AND ROCKED A CHAIR . . . . 186 THE AX-HELVE . . . 46
ROCKET
    US HOW BY ROCKET WE MAY HOPE TO STEER . . . . 395 WHY WAIT FOR SCIENCE . 6
ROCKIES
    THIS SIDE THE ROCKIES IN MY ESTIMATION-- . . . . 400 TO THE RIGHT PERSON . 5
ROCKING
    THE LIFE OF MUSCLES ROCKING SOFT . . . . 276 TWO TRAMPS IN MUD TIME   47
    THE FUR-THING, MUFF-THING, ROCKING IN AND OUT . . . . 289 OLD BARN AT THE BOTTOM   8
    NOT EVEN THAT, IT'S ONLY ROCKING, ... 325 TO A THINKER 6
ROCKS
    ONE OF MY CHILDREN RANGING AFTER ROCKS . . . . 162 NEW HAMPSHIRE . . . 116
    THERE WHERE HE MOVED THE ROCKS TO PLOW THE GROUND . . . 177 THE STAR-SPLITTER . . 26
    AND PLOWED BETWEEN THE ROCKS HE COULDN'T MOVE, ... 177 THE STAR-SPLITTER . . 27
    ON SLIPPERY ROCKS BESIDE A WATERFALL. . . . . 210 PAUPER WITCH OF GRAFTON 98
    OF GLOSSY BIRDS LIKE RIPPLES OVER ROCKS. . . . . . . 240 OUR SINGING STRENGTH . 34
    HER NEXT STEP ROCKS A BOULDER ON THE WALL . . . . . . 268 THE BEAR 5
    IS WHERE TWO ROCKS ALMOST MEET, ... 282 A DRUMLIN WOODCHUCK . 6
    AND PILE OF REAL ROCKS HAVE BEEN FOUNDED. . . . . . . 331 BEECH 3
    AND STUMBLED THROUGH THE ROCKS WITH HORNY TREAD, . . . 338 THE MOST OF IT . . . 19
    NO PLOW AMONG THESE ROCKS WOULD PAY. . . . . 376 SOMETHING FOR HOPE . 9
    IN CASE THE ROCKS SHOULD MELT AND RUN AGAIN. . . . . . 407 FROM PLANE TO PLANE . 95
    FROM OUR ROCKS, AND YES, ... 440 KITTY HAWK 385
    A FRACTURE IN THE ROCKS BENEATH NEW YORK . . . . . . 502 A MASQUE OF MERCY . 229
ROCK-STREWN
    A ROCK-STREWN TOWN WHERE FARMING HAS FALLEN OFF, ... 73 THE GENERATIONS OF MEN   5
ROCKWELL
    BY ROCKWELL KENT THAT EVERYBODY'S READING. . . . . . 495 A MASQUE OF MERCY . . 49
ROCKY
    STILL PROBES AND DENTS OUR ROCKY COAST . . . . . . 418 AMERICA IS HARD TO SEE 50
ROD
    AS TAKE HIS GUN--ROD--TO GO HUNTING--FISHING. . . . . 349 TO A YOUNG WRETCH . . 2
RODE
    I JUST EMBRACED THE SHAFT AND RODE IT OUT-- . . . . . 93 THE SELF-SEEKER . . . 26
    AND SOMEONE MOUNTED ON IT RODE IT HARD, ... 189 THE GRINDSTONE . . . 24
    A FATHER-TIME-LIKE MAN GOT ON AND RODE, ... 189 THE GRINDSTONE . . . 29
    AND RODE ALL OVER EVERYTHING ON HIM . . . . 208 PAUPER WITCH OF GRAFTON 47
    AND THE WHITE WATER RODE THE BLACK FOREVER, ... 258 WEST-RUNNING BROOK . . 21
    I RODE UP ON ONE TILL THE BUBBLE BURST, ... 468 IN A GLASS OF CIDER . 4
ROGERS
    A ROGERS GROUP . . . . 391 A ROGERS GROUP . . . T
    BY THE ROGERS GROUP THEY MADE. . . . . 391 A ROGERS GROUP . . . 12
ROGERS'
    AND I DON'T MEAN JUST SKULLS OF ROGERS' RANGERS . . . . 210 PAUPER WITCH OF GRAFTON 93
ROGUISH
    HE TOOK A STRANGE THING TO BE ROGUISH OVER. . . . . . 178 THE STAR-SPLITTER . . 58
ROIL
    LET THE DOWNPOUR ROIL AND TOIL! . . . . 285 IN TIME OF CLOUDBURST . 1
ROLAND
    AND AT THE SUMMONS ROLAND, OLIVIER, ... 353 THE LESSON FOR TODAY . 89
ROLE
    IN THE ROYAL ROLE. . . . . 441 KITTY HAWK 415
ROLL
    AND ROLL BACK DOWN THE MOUND BESIDE THE HOLE. . . . . 53 HOME BURIAL 77
    TO PENETRATE THE AIR IN WHICH WE ROLL. . . . . . . 172 A STAR IN A STONEBOAT . 12
    ROLL STONES DOWN ON OUR HEAD! . . . . 298 ON TAKING FROM THE TOP   1
    FOR YOU TO ROLL ONE STONE . . . . 298 ON TAKING FROM THE TOP   7
ROLLED
    AND ROLLED HIS OLD HEAD ON THAT SHARP-EDGED CHAIR-BACK. . . 39 DEATH OF THE HIRED MAN 148
    ROLLED OUT A LITTLE FARTHER THAN THE REST." . . . . . 44 THE MOUNTAIN . . . 99
    FOOL-LIKE, AND ROLLED HIS EYES AS IF TO SAY . . . . . 114 IN THE HOME STRETCH . 102
    OF SAP AND SNOW ROLLED OFF THE SUGARHOUSE. . . . . . 184 MAPLE 138
    SMOKE ROLLED INSIDE THE SOCKETS OF HIS EYES.) . . . . 204 THE WITCH OF COOS . . 74
    HE ROLLED ME OFF THE FIELD HEAD OVER HEELS . . . . . 278 THE WHITE-TAILED HORNET 20
    THE HUCKLEBERRY ROLLED HIM ON HIS HEAD. . . . . . . 278 THE WHITE-TAILED HORNET 41
    HE ROLLED AN EYE WITH GRATITUDE . . . . 420 ONE MORE BREVITY . . 20
ROLLER
    AND ROLLING IT INLAND ON ROLLER AIR, ... 337 THE WIND AND THE RAIN . 31
ROLLING
    THE HAY AND ROLLING IT OFF WHOLESALE, ... 71 THE CODE 57
    AND ROLLING IT INLAND ON ROLLER AIR, ... 337 THE WIND AND THE RAIN . 31
    AND MIGHT BE ROLLING DEAD BELOW . . . . 344 DISCOVERY OF MADEIRAS . 33
    THEY MEAN TO TELL US ALL WAS ROLLING BLIND . . . . . 425 ACCIDENTALLY ON PURPOSE 5
    IT WILL COME ROLLING AFTER US LIKE A HOOP." . . . . . 454 HOW HARD TO KEEP FROM   27
ROLLS
    AND A WHITE SHIMMERING CONCOURSE ROLLS . . . . 20 THE TRIAL BY EXISTENCE 29
    RESTS ON THE WORLD, AND CLINGING SLOWLY ROLLS. . . . . 322 BUILD SOIL 196
ROMAN
    HIS CHURCH ON EARTH A ROMAN PANTHEON; . . . . 516 A MASQUE OF MERCY . 592
ROME
    SINCE THE FOREST GERMANS SACKED ROME . . . . 311 THE VINDICTIVES . . . 39
    SUCH AS ACCORDING TO BELIEF IN ROME . . . . 315 IRIS BY NIGHT . . . 5
    ATHENS, ROME, FRANCE, BRITAIN, ... 437 KITTY HAWK . . . 290
    THE SIBYL SAID, "GO BACK TO ROME . . . . 449 OUR DOOM TO BLOOM . 5
    YOURS MORE THROUGH ROME, MINE MORE THROUGH PALESTINE.-- . 513 A MASQUE OF MERCY . 518
ROMP
    WHERE CONIES NOW COME OUT TO SUN AND ROMP, ... 254 A WINTER EDEN . . . 2
ROMPS
    THAT ROMPS THROUGH THE DARK. . . . . 261 CANIS MAJOR 12
    AND SINGS AND ROMPS, ... 360 THE RABBIT-HUNTER . . 11
ROOF
    HE SAW NO SMOKE AND HE SAW NO ROOF. . . . . 24 PAN WITH US 9
    AND BE GLAD OF A GOOD ROOF OVERHEAD. . . . . 67 A SERVANT TO SERVANTS . 165
    FOR SUCH A CHARGE, HIS SNOW UPON THE ROOF, ... 108 OLD MAN'S WINTER NIGHT 21
    "YOU CAN JUST SEE IT GLANCING OFF THE ROOF . . . . . 143 SNOW 8
    HE'D BUILT A NOBLE MANSARD ROOF WITH BALLS . . . . . 160 NEW HAMPSHIRE . . . 39
    I WAS ASLEEP STILL UNDER THE DRIPPING ROOF, ... 236 VALLEY'S SINGING DAY . 16

- 450 -

PAGE TITLE   LINE

ROOF (CONTINUED)
    LET IT BE OVERWHELMING, OFF A ROOF . . . . 265 DUST IN THE EYES . . . 4
    A PEBBLE HIT THE ROOF, ... 298 ON TAKING FROM THE TOP . 10
    TO THE LOW ROOF OVER HIS BED, ... 299 WELCOME TO THEIR BELIEF . 6
    BUT WHENEVER THE ROOF CAME WHITE . . . . 299 WELCOME TO THEIR BELIEF . 9
    THAN WHEN ITS WALLS ROSE HIGHER THAN ANY ROOF. . . . 306 NOT QUITE SOCIAL . . . 8
    REPAIRING FENCE AND ROOF; . . . . 367 A SERIOUS STEP LIGHTLY . 20
    A SPIRE AND BELFRY COMING ON THE ROOF . . . . . . 386 A STEEPLE ON THE HOUSE . 7
ROOM (SEE FOUR-ROOM)
    AND A VOICE THAT HAS SOUNDED IN MY ROOM . . . . . 15 IN A VALE 8
    THAT THING TAKES ALL THE ROOM!" HE MOVED HIS GOAD. . . 41 THE MOUNTAIN 27
    "NO ROOM," THE NIGHT CLERK SAID, "UNLESS----" . . . 45 A HUNDRED COLLARS . . 20
    SHARING A ROOM WITH SOMEONE ELSE." / "WHO IS IT?" . . 45 A HUNDRED COLLARS . . 24
    "LAFE, HERE'S A FELLOW WANTS TO SHARE YOUR ROOM." . . 45 A HUNDRED COLLARS . . 36
    THAN IF I WASN'T IN THE ROOM AT ALL. . . . . . . 65 A SERVANT TO SERVANTS . 80
    OR ROOM WITHIN A ROOM, OF HICKORY POLES, ... 66 A SERVANT TO SERVANTS . 114
    YOU NEVER SAW THIS ROOM BEFORE A SHOW, ... 85 THE HOUSEKEEPER . . . 119
    THAT BROUGHT HIM TO THAT CREAKING ROOM WAS AGE. . . . 108 OLD MAN'S WINTER NIGHT . 7
    BEHIND HER WAS CONFUSION IN THE ROOM, ... 110 IN THE HOME STRETCH . 5
    FOR EVERY ROOM A HOUSE HAS--PARLOR, BEDROOM, ... 110 IN THE HOME STRETCH . 8
    AND DINING ROOM--THROWN PELL-MELL IN THE KITCHEN. . . 110 IN THE HOME STRETCH . 9
    BACK PAST THE SUN TO AN EARTHLY ROOM. . . . . . . 120 BOND AND FREE . . . 15
    OF THE ROOM WHERE THEY SLEPT. . . . . 128 THE OFT-REPEATED DREAM . 4
    IT NEVER HAD BEEN INSIDE THE ROOM, ... 128 THE OFT-REPEATED DREAM . 9
    TO BREATHE THE AIR ONE WINTER--HAD A ROOM . . . . . 149 SNOW 174
    THIS ROOM YOU SIT IN. IF YOU THINK THE WIND . . . . 150 SNOW 203
    MRS. COLE'S VOICE CAME FROM AN INNER ROOM: . . . . 152 SNOW 271
    "WHAT DO YOU HEAR?" / "I HEAR AN EMPTY ROOM-- . . . 153 SNOW 299
    OF ONE ROOM AND ONE WINDOW AND ONE DOOR, ... 174 THE CENSUS-TAKER . . 3
    EACH OTHER IN PASSING IN THE ROOM UPSTAIRS, ... 180 MAPLE 11
    BESIDE IT ROOM RESERVED; THE SAY A SISTER'S, ... 200 PLACE FOR A THIRD . . 40
    BUT LEFT AN OPEN DOOR TO COOL THE ROOM OFF . . . . 203 THE WITCH OF COOS . . 42
    IT'S WITH US IN THE ROOM, THOUGH. IT'S THE BONES." . . 205 THE WITCH OF COOS . . 100
    IF I COULD SEE IT, OR ELSE MOW THE ROOM, ... 205 THE WITCH OF COOS . . 105
    IN GOING FROM ROOM TO ROOM IN THE DARK . . . . . 265 THE DOOR IN THE DARK . 1
    THE WORLD HAS ROOM TO MAKE A BEAR FEEL FREE; . . . . 269 THE BEAR 11
    ONE LOOKS OUT LAST FROM THE DARKENED ROOM . . . . . 291 ON HEART'S BEGINNING TO 26
    A KING FILLED HIS PRISON ROOM . . . . 310 THE VINDICTIVES . . . 2
    AS FULL AS THE ROOM COULD HOLD . . . . 310 THE VINDICTIVES . . . 3
    OR BETTER ON DISH PLATES ALL AROUND THE ROOM, . . . 320 BUILD SOIL 148
    IT SEEMED TOO TINY TO HAVE ROOM FOR FEET, ... 357 A CONSIDERABLE SPECK . 16
    BUT ALL HE DID WAS SPREAD THE ROOM . . . . 417 AMERICA IS HARD TO SEE . 37
ROOMS
    THAT GATHERS ON THE PANE IN EMPTY ROOMS. . . . . . 108 OLD MAN'S WINTER NIGHT . 3
    UP AND DOWN STAIRS AND THROUGH THE ROOMS, AND NONE . . 112 IN THE HOME STRETCH . 42
ROOM'S
    AND THE FIRE'S DIED AND THE ROOM'S DARK AND COLD?" . . 154 SNOW 310
ROOST
    YET THINK OF THE SMALL BIRDS AT ROOST AND NOT . . . 151 SNOW 226
    AS I THOUGHT OF THEM WITHOUT NEST OR ROOST.. . . . 253 THE THATCH 29
    AND SO TO ROOST, THE LAST TO MOUNT. . . . . . . 281 BLUE RIBBON AT AMESBURY 44
    THE ROOST IS HER EXTENT OF FLIGHT. . . . . 281 BLUE RIBBON AT AMESBURY 45
ROOT
    "CAN'T YOU AND I GET TO THE ROOT OF IT? . . . . . 87 THE HOUSEKEEPER . . . 165
    TO MAKE IT ROOT AGAIN AND GROW AFRESH. . . . . . 109 THE EXPOSED NEST . . 8
    SHE SCORNS A PASTURE WITHERING TO THE ROOT. . . . . 125 THE COW IN APPLE TIME . 6
    BORNE DOWN UNTIL THE END ALMOST TOOK ROOT, ... 239 OUR SINGING STRENGTH . 13
    AND SING THE WILD FLOWERS UP FROM ROOT AND SEED. . . 240 OUR SINGING STRENGTH . 53
    BUT UNLESS YOU PUT THE RIGHT THING TO ITS ROOT . . . 296 LEAVES COMPARED WITH . 3
    BOLE AND BRANCH AND ROOT . . . . 426 A NEVER NAUGHT SONG . 19
    IT CAN'T BE PULLED UP BY THE ROOT. . . . . 452 A-WISHING WELL . . . 51
    YES, THERE YOU HAVE IT AT THE ROOT OF THINGS. . . . 520 A MASQUE OF MERCY . . 716
ROOTS
    FROM STRIKING AT ANOTHER ALDER'S ROOTS, ... 185 THE AX-HELVE 4
    BUT UP BY ROOTS TO BRING DARK FOLIAGE ON. . . . . 245 SPRING POOLS 6
    IT KEEPS SMOLDERING AT THE ROOTS . . . . 308 EVIL TENDENCIES CANCEL 3
    'TIS NOT ENOUGH ON ROOTS AND IN THE MOUTH, ... 337 THE WIND AND THE RAIN . 37
    AND WHEN WE HAD TAKEN THAT INTO THE ROOTS OF GRAIN, . . 349 OUR HOLD ON THE PLANET 8
ROPE
    AND THOUGH IN TINSEL CHAIN AND POPCORN ROPE . . . . 350 TO A YOUNG WRETCH . . 19
ROPES
    HAS DRIED THE DEW AND ALL ITS ROPES RELENT, ... 331 THE SILKEN TENT . . . 3
ROPY
    BEGIN IN SMUDGE WITH ROPY SMOKE, AND KNOW . . . . 130 THE BONFIRE 21
ROSE
    ROSE POGONIAS . . . . 13 ROSE POGONIAS . . . T
    WILD, EASILY SHATTERED ROSE. . . . . 26 A LINE-STORM SONG . . 14
    WE ROSE TO GO. SUNSET BLAZED ON THE WINDOWS. . . . 59 THE BLACK COTTAGE . . 127
    ROSE LIKE A FACTOR'S AT A TRADING STATION. . . . . 160 NEW HAMPSHIRE . . . 53
    SIGNIFIED NOTHING. ROSE COULD HAVE A MEANING, . . . 181 MAPLE 47
    BUT HADN'T AS IT WENT. (SHE KNEW A ROSE.) . . . . 181 MAPLE 48
    IT SLOWLY ROSE A PERSON, ROSE A GIRL, ... 194 PAUL'S WIFE 108
    THE PETAL OF THE ROSE . . . . 227 TO EARTHWARD . . . 15
    THE ROSE IS A ROSE, ... 246 THE ROSE FAMILY . . . 1
    AND WAS ALWAYS A ROSE. . . . . 246 THE ROSE FAMILY . . . 2
    THAT THE APPLE'S A ROSE, ... 246 THE ROSE FAMILY . . . 4
    WHAT WILL NEXT PROVE A ROSE. . . . . 246 THE ROSE FAMILY . . . 8
    YOU, OF COURSE, ARE A ROSE-- . . . . 246 THE ROSE FAMILY . . . 9
    THE ROSE FAMILY . . . . 246 THE ROSE FAMILY . . . T
    BUT WERE ALWAYS A ROSE. . . . . 246 THE ROSE FAMILY . . . 10
    THAN WHEN ITS WALLS ROSE HIGHER THAN ANY ROOF. . . . 306 NOT QUITE SOCIAL . . . 8
    NO LIMITS TO WHAT ROSE IN RUBBING STICKS . . . . . 372 THE LITERATE FARMER AND 138
    SO ONCE YOU ROSE AND LIT THE LIGHT. . . . . . . 380 AN UNSTAMPED LETTER IN 2
    IT ROSE IN OFFENSE . . . . 450 OBJECTION TO BE STEPPED 4
    WHO ROSE FROM THE MILKING STOOL WITH A CURSE . . . 463 LINES IN DEJECTION . . 15
ROSE-RED
    HER FACE ROSE-RED WITH THE GLOWING COAL . . . . . 8 LOVE AND A QUESTION . 19

ROSES (SEE GATHER-ROSES)
ROSE-WREATH
   LIKE A LIMP ROSE-WREATH IN A FAIRY DANCE. . . . . . . 28 MY BUTTERFLY 17
ROSICRUCIAN
   (ASK ANY REPUTABLE ROSICRUCIAN) . . . . 363 A SEMI-REVOLUTION . . 3
ROSIN
   THE MYRRH TREE GIVES IT. SMELL THE ROSIN BURNING? . . . . 473 A MASQUE OF REASON . . 9
ROT
   WILL ROT THE BEST BIRCH FENCE A MAN CAN BUILD.' . . . . 54 HOME BURIAL 93
   WHAT HAD HOW LONG IT TAKES A BIRCH TO ROT . . . . . 54 HOME BURIAL 95
ROTE
   WHERE I NEED LISTEN TO ITS ROTE NO MORE, ... 447 DOES NO ONE AT ALL EVER 34
ROTTED
   FOR WHEN ALL THAT WAS ROTTED RICH . . . . 285 IN TIME OF CLOUDBURST . 10
ROTTEN
   DON'T SCRATCH! AND WHEN, AS ROTTEN AS HIS SKIN, ... 478 A MASQUE OF REASON . . 130
ROTTING
   AND EVERY TREE UP STOOD A ROTTING TRUNK . . . . . . 175 THE CENSUS-TAKER . . 22
   ANOTHER A ROTTING PLANK, ... 281 A DRUMLIN WOODCHUCK . 2
ROUGH
   WE WEAR OUR FINGERS ROUGH WITH HANDLING THEM. . . . . 33 MENDING WALL 20
   LIKE UNCUT JEWELS, DULL AND ROUGH. . . . . 141 THE GUM-GATHERER . . 31
   FROM END TO END WITH HIS ROUGH HAND SHUT ROUND IT. . . . 187 THE AX-HELVE . . . 77
   IN ANY ROUGH PLACE WHERE IT CAUGHT. . . . . 223 THE AIM WAS SONG . . 4
   TO FEEL THE EARTH AS ROUGH . . . . 227 TO EARTHWARD . . . 31
   WITH THOUGHTS OF THE PATH BACK, HOW ROUGH IT WAS . . . 229 TWO LOOK AT TWO . . 5
   AND PROBING WITH ONE FINGER NOT TOO ROUGH, ... 270 THE EGG AND THE MACHINE 21
   LEAVES FOR SMOOTH AND BARK FOR ROUGH, ... 297 LEAVES COMPARED WITH . 7
   ROUGHLY DISCRIMINATED FOR THE ROUGH. . . . . . . 318 BUILD SOIL 88
   AND TAKE OUR DAILY TIDE BATHS SMOOTH AND ROUGH. . . . 395 ETHEREALIZING . . . 8
   PRONOUNCE IT HOMER WITH A COCKNEY ROUGH. . . . . . 459 HOW HARD TO KEEP FROM 189
ROUGHER
   THAT ALL THEY ASK IS ROUGHER WEATHER, ... 262 THE FLOWER BOAT . . 10
ROUGHLY
   HE MOVED IT ROUGHLY WITH AN IRON BAR, ... 173 A STAR IN A STONEBOAT . 25
   THERE ARE ROUGHLY ZONES . . . . 305 THERE ARE ROUGHLY ZONES T
   THERE ARE ROUGHLY ZONES WHOSE LAWS MUST BE OBEYED? . . . 305 THERE ARE ROUGHLY ZONES 13
   ROUGHLY DISCRIMINATED FOR THE ROUGH. . . . . . . 318 BUILD SOIL 88
ROUND (SEE LADDER-ROUND)
   THE SWARM DILATING ROUND THE PERFECT TREES. . . . . 12 A PRAYER IN SPRING . 8
   AND ONCE I MARKED HIS FLIGHT GO ROUND AND ROUND, . . . 22 THE TUFT OF FLOWERS . 15
   I CROSSED THE RIVER AND SWUNG ROUND THE MOUNTAIN. . . . 41 THE MOUNTAIN . . . 15
   "YOU CAN DRIVE ROUND AND KEEP IN LUNENBURG, ... 43 THE MOUNTAIN . . . 93
   AND A FEW HOUSES SPRINKLED ROUND THE FOOT, ... 43 THE MOUNTAIN . . . 97
   ALL ROUND THE COUNTRY FOR THE WEEKLY NEWS, ... 48 A HUNDRED COLLARS . . 98
   OR OVER A HILL OR ROUND A SUDDEN CORNER. . . . . . 49 A HUNDRED COLLARS . . 126
   I'LL KNOCK SO-FASHION AND PEEP ROUND THE DOOR . . . . 50 A HUNDRED COLLARS . . 173
   THEY EAT THEM THE YEAR ROUND, AND THOSE THEY DON'T EAT . . 60 BLUEBERRIES 52
   HOW WE USED TO PICK BERRIES: WE TOOK ONE LOOK ROUND, . . 62 BLUEBERRIES 85
   BEFORE HE ACTED: HE'S JUST GOT ROUND TO ACT." . . . . 70 THE CODE 19
   TWO OR THREE FORKFULS I PICKED LIGHTLY ROUND FOR . . . 72 THE CODE 72
   THE SECOND ROUND THE CURVING HILLSIDE ROAD . . . . . 74 THE GENERATIONS OF MEN 29
   "WHAT ARE YOU DOING ROUND THIS HOUSE AT NIGHT?" . . . . 91 THE FEAR 70
   "LOOKING ROUND, I SUPPOSE," SAID WILLIS. / "YES, ... 96 THE SELF-SEEKER . . 101
   "YOU, WILL, STOP MAKING FACES. COME ROUND HERE . . . . 99 THE SELF-SEEKER . . 184
   HAD WOUND STRINGS ROUND AND ROUND IT LIKE A BUNDLE. . . . 102 THE WOOD-PILE . . . 31
   ALL ROUND AND ROUND. THE LATTER HE NODDED "YES" TO, . . . 107 CHRISTMAS TREES . . 36
   HE STOOD WITH BARRELS ROUND HIM--AT A LOSS. . . . . . 108 OLD MAN'S WINTER NIGHT 8
   TO COME AS HERE I STAND AND GO THE ROUND . . . . . 111 IN THE HOME STRETCH . 27
   TO GO THE ROUND OF APPLE, CHERRY, PEACH, ... 117 IN THE HOME STRETCH . 196
   TO CURL A LITTLE FINGER ROUND, ... 123 PEA BRUSH 18
   CARE WHEN THE BIRDS COME ROUND THE HOUSE . . . . . 126 LONELINESS 3
   AND SWEEPING ROUND IT WITH A FLAMING SWORD, ... 130 THE BONFIRE . . . 28
   WERE ROUND MY NECK AND I WAS AT THE PLOW. . . . . . 132 THE BONFIRE . . . 80
   AND THEN WENT ROUND IT ON HIS FEET, ... 139 BROWN'S DESCENT . . 61
   AND HALF THE BAG WOUND ROUND HIS HAND. . . . . . . 140 THE GUM-GATHERER . . 6
   WHOSE BUSINESS--BUT WHY TALK ROUND THE BARN?-- . . . . 142 THE VANISHING RED . . 7
   THE THREE STOOD IN THE LAMPLIGHT ROUND THE TABLE . . . . 144 SNOW 31
   THAT'S ALL YOU EVER HEARD HIM CALLED ROUND HERE. . . . . 144 SNOW 46
   FROM NEARLY EVERYTHING THAT GOES ON ROUND ME. . . . . 166 NEW HAMPSHIRE . . . 238
   A HUNDRED SQUARE MILES ROUND IT IN THE MOUNTAINS: . . . 174 THE CENSUS-TAKER . . 5
   YOUR FATHER FEELS US ROUND HIM WITH OUR QUESTING, . . . 183 MAPLE 123
   FROM END TO END WITH HIS ROUGH HAND SHUT ROUND IT. . . . 187 THE AX-HELVE . . . 77
   WHO GAVE HIS LIFE TO KEEP IT GOING ROUND? . . . . . 190 THE GRINDSTONE . . 47
   BUNCHES ALL ROUND ME GROWING IN WHITE BIRCHES, ... 197 WILD GRAPES . . . 26
   THE WAY THEY GREW ROUND LEIF THE LUCKY'S GERMAN; . . . . 197 WILD GRAPES . . . 27
   TO TURN HIM ROUND. HE GOT TO SAYING THINGS . . . . . 209 PAUPER WITCH OF GRAFTON 78
   I ALMOST STUMBLE LOOKING UP AND ROUND, ... 226 THE ONSET . . . 6
   A DOE FROM ROUND A SPRUCE STOOD LOOKING AT THEM . . . . 229 TWO LOOK AT TWO . . 15
   A BUCK FROM ROUND THE SPRUCE STOOD LOOKING AT THEM . . . 229 TWO LOOK AT TWO . . 27
   IN BROAD ROUND EARRINGS, GOLD AND JET WITH PEARLS, . . . 256 THE LOVELY BE CHOOSERS 15
   AND BROAD ROUND SUCHLIKE BROOCH, ... 256 THE LOVELY BE CHOOSERS 16
   IF WE WHO SIGHT ALONG IT ROUND THE WORLD, ... 261 A SOLDIER 4
   STRUNG CHAINS OF WALL ROUND EVERYTHING, ... 265 THE BIRTHPLACE . . 4
   AND ROUND A CORNER, BLIZZARD SNOW FOR DUST, ... 265 DUST IN THE EYES . . 5
   THEIR UPPER BRANCHES ROUND HIM WREATHING, ... 274 A LONE STRIKER . . 40
   AND THE FLY CIRCLED ROUND HIM IN DERISION. . . . . . 278 THE WHITE-TAILED HORNET 43
   NO ONE STANDS ROUND TO STARE. . . . . 289 DEPARTMENTAL . . . 40
   YOUR LEAST TOUCH SETS IT GOING ROUND, ... 306 A TRIAL RUN . . . 13
   AND WE STOOD IN IT SOFTLY CIRCLED ROUND . . . . . . 315 IRIS BY NIGHT . . 29
   WE HAVE OUR OWN ROUND SHAPE TO KEEP UNBROKEN. . . . . 322 BUILD SOIL . . . 197
   WE ARE ROUND FROM THE SAME SOURCE OF ROUNDNESS. . . . . 322 BUILD SOIL . . . 200
   WE ARE BOTH ROUND BECAUSE THE MIND IS ROUND, ... 322 BUILD SOIL . . . 201
   AT LEAST THAT'S WHY THE UNIVERSE IS ROUND. . . . . . 322 BUILD SOIL . . . 203
   TWO ROUND DOTS AND A RIPPLE STREAK, ... 327 A MISSIVE MISSILE . . 7
   TO EVERYTHING ON EARTH THE COMPASS ROUND, ... 332 THE SILKEN TENT . . 11
   THEN EDDIES PLAYING ROUND A SUNKEN REEF . . . . . . 335 I COULD GIVE ALL . . 7
   THAT THE BIRDS THERE IN ALL THE GARDEN ROUND . . . . 338 NEVER WOULD BIRDS' SONG 2

ROUND (CONTINUED)
    AND CARVED THEM ROUND WITH A SCROLL OF VINES. . . . . . 347 DISCOVERY OF MADEIRAS . 124
    WE DANCE ROUND IN A RING AND SUPPOSE, ... 362 THE SECRET SITS . . . 1
    FOR WHICH THE REGION ROUND WAS KNOWN, ... 364 TRESPASS 11
    AND THE FRAY WOULDN'T LAST A SINGLE ROUND. . . . . . . 371 THE LITERATE FARMER AND 118
    IT MAY BE A MERCY THE DARK CLOSES ROUND US . . . . . . 379 TOO ANXIOUS FOR RIVERS . 12
    IT WRAPS A WISP OF SEAWEED ROUND MY LEGS, ... 391 ON BEING IDOLIZED . . 2
    WERE LOOSE ALL ROUND THEIR LEGS--YOU COULDN'T SAY . . . 404 FROM PLANE TO PLANE . 16
    THE THINGS BUT BALLS ALL GOING ROUND IN RINGS. . . . . 425 ACCIDENTALLY ON PURPOSE 2
    SMALL BUT STRONG AND ROUND, ... 433 KITTY HAWK 172
    ROUND THE PLACE ON FOOT . . . . 434 KITTY HAWK 204
    ROUND AND ROUND THE RINK . . . . 440 KITTY HAWK 397
    HALFWAY ROUND THE WORLD. . . . . 448 THE BAD ISLAND--EASTER 12
    OF PROGRESS ROUND AND ROUND IN CIRCLES . . . . 459 HOW HARD TO KEEP FROM 159
    AND ALSO OF THE WAY ALL THINGS COME ROUND, ... 485 A MASQUE OF REASON . 342
    I'M ALL TURNED ROUND. / THERE IS YOUR WAY PREPARED. . . 514 A MASQUE OF MERCY . 547
ROUNDNESS
    WE ARE ROUND FROM THE SAME SOURCE OF ROUNDNESS. . . . . 322 BUILD SOIL 200
ROUNDS
    HE'S ON HIS ROUNDS NOW WITH HIS TAIL IN HIS MOUTH, . . . 94 THE SELF-SEEKER . . . 38
ROUSE
    ROUSE THEM ALL, BOTH THE FREE AND NOT SO FREE . . . . 130 THE BONFIRE 13
    AS WINDS MIGHT ROUSE . . . . 218 I WILL SING YOU ONE-O . 31
ROUSED
    HIS HATE HAD ROUSED AN ENGINE UP THE ROAD. . . . . . 270 THE EGG AND THE MACHINE 4
ROUT
    OH, COME FORTH INTO THE STORM AND ROUT . . . . . . 27 A LINE-STORM SONG . . 31
    TO ROUT US OUT TO THINK FOR HIM AT MIDNIGHT . . . . . 155 SNOW 346
ROUTE
    A PRINCESS EN ROUTE FROM CHINA . . . . 313 BEARER OF EVIL TIDINGS 19
ROUTINE
    AND COME TO LEAVE THE ROUTINE ROAD . . . . 304 UNHARVESTED . . . 2
ROW
    THEN THERE WERE THREE THERE, MAKING A DIM ROW, ... 40 DEATH OF THE HIRED MAN 162
    ALL IN A FAMILY ROW DOWN TO THE YOUNGEST." . . . . 49 A HUNDRED COLLARS . 148
    BUT I HAD THE COTTAGES IN A ROW . . . . 102 GOOD HOURS . . . 3
    SHE THOUGHT OF CHILDREN IN A BURIAL ROW; . . . . . 199 PLACE FOR A THIRD . 5
    THREE CHILDREN IN A BURIAL ROW WERE SAD. . . . . . 199 PLACE FOR A THIRD . 6
    ONE MAN'S THREE WOMEN IN A BURIAL ROW . . . . . . 199 PLACE FOR A THIRD . 7
    THAT ROW OF ICICLES ALONG THE GUTTER . . . . . . 393 BEYOND WORDS . . . 1
    AT THE END OF THE ROW . . . . 450 OBJECTION TO BE STEPPED 1
ROWAN
    THE CLOVER-MINGLED ROWAN ON THE GROUND . . . . . 315 IRIS BY NIGHT . . . 13
ROWE'S
    WHEN I CAME UP FROM ROWE'S I FOUND HIM HERE, ... 35 DEATH OF THE HIRED MAN 34
ROWS
    TO THE EARNEST LOVE THAT LAID THE SWALE IN ROWS, . . . 17 MOWING 10
ROYAL
    ESTABLISHED A ROYAL LINE, ... 314 BEARER OF EVIL TIDINGS 30
    IN THE ROYAL ROLE. . . . . 441 KITTY HAWK 415
    I WAS REJECTED BY THE ROYAL BIRD . . . . 443 AUSPEX 7
    WE ARE IMPATIENT FOR YOUR ROYAL ANSWER." . . . . . 456 HOW HARD TO KEEP FROM 76
    OF ROYAL BLOOD. YOUR FATHER WAS A COOK." . . . . . 457 HOW HARD TO KEEP FROM 103
    "IF YOU HAD BEEN A KING OF ROYAL BLOOD, ... 457 HOW HARD TO KEEP FROM 118
    OF MORE THAN ROYAL ATTRIBUTES BETRAYED HIM. . . . . 462 HOW HARD TO KEEP FROM 274
    OR COURT OF LOVE. / MORE LIKELY ROYAL COURT-- . . . 474 A MASQUE OF REASON . 25
RUB
    I CANNOT RUB THE STRANGENESS FROM MY SIGHT . . . . . 68 AFTER APPLE-PICKING . 9
RUBBING
    FIGHT SUCH A FIRE BY RUBBING NOT BY BEATING. . . . . 131 THE BONFIRE . . . 67
    NO LIMITS TO WHAT ROSE IN RUBBING STICKS . . . . . 372 THE LITERATE FARMER AND 138
RUDE
    FOREVER OFF THE LATCH, AS IF RUDE MEN . . . . . 175 THE CENSUS-TAKER . . 28
    HER FEAR IS BEING SPOKEN BY THE RUDE . . . . . . 386 THE FEAR OF MAN . . . 13
    HIGH PURPOSE MAKES THE HERO RUDE; . . . . 418 AMERICA IS HARD TO SEE 73
    YET SO RUDE IN ITS ART, ... 447 THE BAD ISLAND--EASTER 3
RUDELY
    WITH AUTUMN AND THE FRUIT WAS RUDELY TOSSED, ... 284 THE GOLD HESPERIDEE . 33
RUED
    OF A DAY I HAD RUED. . . . . 221 DUST OF SNOW 8
RUEFUL
    THE BOY'S FIRST OUTCRY WAS A RUEFUL LAUGH, ... 136 "OUT,OUT--" 19
RUFFIANS
    ALL THOSE GREAT RUFFIANS PUT THEIR THROATS TOGETHER, . . 195 PAUL'S WIFE 139
RUG
    AND ON BLACK GROUND A BEAR-SKIN RUG OF SNOW. . . . . 234 EVENING A SUGAR ORCHARD 13
    LIFTED THE RUG THAT BRED THEM ON THE FLOOR . . . . 237 A HILLSIDE THAW . . . 7
RUGGED
    YOU GRASP THE BARK BY A RUGGED PLEAT, ... 247 ON GOING UNNOTICED . . 9
RUIN
    FALLEN TO RUIN IN TEN THOUSAND YEARS . . . . . . 176 THE CENSUS-TAKER . 52
    LET'S HAVE SOME PROPHECY. WHAT FORM OF RUIN . . . . 502 A MASQUE OF MERCY . 222
    (FOR RUIN I ASSUME WAS WHAT IT WAS) . . . . . . 502 A MASQUE OF MERCY . 223
RUINED
    O'ER RUINED FENCES THE GRAPEVINES SHIELD . . . . . 5 GHOST HOUSE 6
RUINOUS
    UNDER A RUINOUS LIVE APPLE TREE . . . . 189 THE GRINDSTONE . . . 20
RUINS
    OF GETTING UP GOOD RUINS, YOU'VE FORGOTTEN . . . . 503 A MASQUE OF MERCY . 260
RULE
    TWO AT A TIME'S THE RULE, ONE ON EACH ARM, ... 85 THE HOUSEKEEPER . . . 129
    IN GOING ON." / "OUR SNOWSTORMS AS A RULE . . . . 150 SNOW 221
    I FEAR, THE CROWN OF RULE, ... 252 THE PEACEFUL SHEPHERD . 6
    YOU DID NOT KNOW THAT SINCE KING CHARLES DID RULE . . 351 THE LESSON FOR TODAY . 22
    TO RULE FIRST ANSWERABLE TO HIGH DESIGN. . . . . . 424 FOR JOHN F. KENNEDY . 65
    THE RULE IS, NEVER GIVE A CHILD A CHOICE. . . . . 427 CONCEPT SELF-CONCEIVED 8
    BUT WAS THERE A RULE . . . . 450 OBJECTION TO BE STEPPED 13
    TELL ME SOME RULE FOR RULING PEOPLE WISELY, ... 458 HOW HARD TO KEEP FROM 147

RULED
    MADE A GIRL'S MARRIAGE, AND RULED IN HER LIFE. . . . . . . 185 MAPLE 164
    THE LEDGES SHOW LINES RULED SOUTHEAST-NORTHWEST, ... 377 DIRECTIVE 15
RULER
    A RULER WHO PRETENDED NOT TO LOVE . . . . 423 FOR JOHN F. KENNEDY . 44
RULING
    TELL ME SOME RULE FOR RULING PEOPLE WISELY, ... 458 HOW HARD TO KEEP FROM 147
RUMBLING
    THEN YOU CAME IN. I HEARD YOUR RUMBLING VOICE . . . . . 53 HOME BURIAL 81
    THE RUMBLING SOUND . . . . 69 AFTER APPLE-PICKING . 25
RUMOR
    SOME RUMOR OF HIS WISHING RING . . . . 390 TWO LEADING LIGHTS . . 24
RUMPLE
    OR BLOW A RUMPLE IN THE COLLIE'S COAT. . . . . . . 148 SNOW 141
RUMPLING
    THE SOIL NOW GETS A RUMPLING SOFT AND DAMP, ... 299 STRONG SAYING NOTHING . 1
RUN
    RUN THE RATTLING PAGES O'ER; . . . . 11 TO THE THAWING WIND . 13
    READY TO RUN TO HIDING NEW . . . . 18 GOING FOR WATER . . . 15
    TO RUN WILD IN THE SUMMER--A LITTLE WILD. . . . . . 44 A HUNDRED COLLARS . . 5
    SOMEONE HAD LITERALLY RUN TO EARTH . . . . 73 THE GENERATIONS OF MEN 7
    IT'S GONE SO FAR. YOU'VE HEARD? ESTELLE'S RUN OFF." . . 82 THE HOUSEKEEPER . . . 20
    IT'S TOO RUN DOWN. THIS IS THE LAST OF IT. . . . . . 83 THE HOUSEKEEPER . . . 50
    HE KNOWS HE'S KINDER THAN THE RUN OF MEN. . . . . . 84 THE HOUSEKEEPER . . . 80
    YOU HAVEN'T RUN YOUR FORTY ORCHIDS DOWN. . . . . . . 93 THE SELF-SEEKER . . . 13
    NOW RUN.--GET OUT YOUR DOCUMENTS! YOU SEE . . . . . 99 THE SELF-SEEKER . . . 175
    BY JUNE OUR BROOK'S RUN OUT OF SONG AND SPEED. . . . 119 HYLA BROOK 1
    WILL RUN AS HUSHED AS WHEN THEY WERE A THOUGHT. . . . 141 THE LINE-GANG . . . 7
    PLAYING OUR FANCY, TO HAVE THE SNOW-LINE RUN . . . . 149 SNOW 190
    RATHER OF WHAT TO FACE OR RUN AWAY FROM. . . . . . 171 NEW HAMPSHIRE . . . 396
    AND RUN OFF IN STRANGE TANGENTS WITH MY ARM, ... 174 A STAR IN A STONEBOAT . 53
    SIDEWAYS, THAT WOULD HAVE RUN HER ON THE STOVE . . . 187 THE AX-HELVE . . . 50
    WHO'D RUN AWAY WITH SOMEONE ELSE AND LEFT HIM; . . . 191 PAUL'S WIFE . . . 9
    HE HAD TO RUN RIGHT OFF TO LOOK HER UP, ... 191 PAUL'S WIFE . . . 13
    BE RUN OFF WITH BY BIRCH TREES INTO SPACE." . . . . 199 WILD GRAPES . . . 91
    IN FETID DARKNESS STILL TO LIVE AND RUN-- . . . . . 231 A BROOK IN THE CITY . 17
    AND THE LIGHT BREAKING ON THEM MADE THEM RUN. . . . 237 A HILLSIDE THAW . . 8
    THE COLOR RUN, ALL SORTS OF WONDER FOLLOW. . . . . 245 THE FREEDOM OF THE MOON 12
    AND THE NORTHERN LIGHTS THAT RUN LIKE TINGLING NERVES. . 268 ON LOOKING UP BY CHANCE 3
    THEN ALL I NEED DO IS RUN . . . . 285 IN TIME OF CLOUDBURST . 17
    ANC WAS OFF ON HIS DUTY RUN. . . . . 288 DEPARTMENTAL . . . 7
    A TRIAL RUN . . . . 306 A TRIAL RUN . . . T
    WOULD RUN IN UNDER IT TO GET MY SHARE. . . . . . . 337 THE WIND AND THE RAIN . 36
    NOW IT TOOK A FITFUL RUN; . . . . 344 DISCOVERY OF MADEIRAS . 21
    I NEVER SAW SO MUCH SWIFT WATER RUN CLOUDLESS. . . . 379 TOO ANXIOUS FOR RIVERS 5
    THE PLAY SEEMS OUT FOR AN ALMOST INFINITE RUN. . . . 392 IT BIDS PRETTY FAIR . 1
    IN CASE THE ROCKS SHOULD MELT AND RUN AGAIN. . . . . 407 FROM PLANE TO PLANE . 95
    OR THE SORROW OF HAVING RUN AWAY. . . . . 420 ONE MORE BREVITY . . 32
    TO HAVE RUN THE EVENT . . . . 437 KITTY HAWK 300
    YOU'VE FINISHED. I'M DISMISSED. I WANT TO RUN . . . 514 A MASQUE OF MERCY . . 544
RUNAWAY
    I'D HATE TO BE A RUNAWAY FROM NATURE. . . . . . . 171 NEW HAMPSHIRE . . . 397
    THE RUNAWAY . . . . 223 THE RUNAWAY . . . T
    YES, PILGRIM NOW INSTEAD OF RUNAWAY, ... 513 A MASQUE OF MERCY . . 534
RUNAWAYS
    WHERE DO THESE SENILE RUNAWAYS ESCAPE FROM? . . . . . 493 A MASQUE OF MERCY . . 15
RUNG
    THERE! THERE'S THE BELL. HE'S RUNG. BUT YOU GO DOWN . . 95 THE SELF-SEEKER . . . 88
RUNNER
    NO RUNNER TRACKS IN THIS YEAR'S SNOW LOOPED NEAR IT. . . 101 THE WOOD-PILE . . . 26
    SHE LIKES TO HALT US IN OUR RUNNER TRACKS, ... 238 ON A TREE FALLEN ACROSS 6
RUNNING (SEE WEST-RUNNING)
    I WAS RUNNING WITH JOY ON THE DEMON'S TRAIL, ... 24 THE DEMIURGE'S LAUGH . 2
    LIKE A DEEP PIECE OF SOME OLD RUNNING RIVER . . . . 63 A SERVANT TO SERVANTS . 20
    WITH THE LITTLE FELLOW AT ALL. HE'S RUNNING AWAY. . . 223 THE RUNAWAY . . . 11
    RUNNING AWAY. . . . . 235 GATHERING LEAVES . . 8
    THE ROAD BECAME A CHANNEL RUNNING FLOCKS . . . . . 240 OUR SINGING STRENGTH . 33
    "WHAT DOES IT THINK IT'S DOING RUNNING WEST . . . . . 257 WEST-RUNNING BROOK . . 4
    OR HE MIGHT BE RUNNING YET. . . . . 313 BEARER OF EVIL TIDINGS 16
    TO LAY THEM LEVEL WITH THE RUNNING WAVE, ... 334 I COULD GIVE ALL . . 3
    IN A RUNNING START, ... 436 KITTY HAWK . . . 258
    RUNNING AWAY FROM HIM YOU THINK YOU ARE, ... 498 A MASQUE OF MERCY . . 139
RUN-OUT
    YOU SHALL GO TO YOUR RUN-OUT MOUNTAIN FARM, ... 323 BUILD SOIL 211
    YOU WILL GO TO YOUR RUN-OUT MOUNTAIN FARM . . . . . 323 BUILD SOIL 230
    I WILL GO TO MY RUN-OUT SOCIAL MIND . . . . . . 323 BUILD SOIL 237
RUNS
    I HAVE MY FANCIES: IT RUNS IN THE FAMILY. . . . . . 65 A SERVANT TO SERVANTS . 87
    SHE RUNS FROM TREE TO TREE WHERE LIE AND SWEETEN . . . 125 THE COW IN APPLE TIME . 7
    "JUST THE WAY STEFANSSON RUNS ON," I MURMURED, ... 159 NEW HAMPSHIRE . . . 22
    THE BROOK RUNS WEST." / "WEST-RUNNING BROOK THEN CALL IT." 257 WEST-RUNNING BROOK . . 2
    IN THAT WHITE WAVE RUNS COUNTER TO ITSELF. . . . . 259 WEST-RUNNING BROOK . . 39
    THE STREAM OF EVERYTHING THAT RUNS AWAY. . . . . . 259 WEST-RUNNING BROOK . . 44
    STANDS STILL AND DANCES, BUT IT RUNS AWAY; . . . . . 259 WEST-RUNNING BROOK . . 47
    IT SERIOUSLY, SADLY, RUNS AWAY . . . . 259 WEST-RUNNING BROOK . . 48
    OUR LIFE RUNS DOWN IN SENDING UP THE CLOCK. . . . . 259 WEST-RUNNING BROOK . . 64
    THE BROOK RUNS DOWN IN SENDING UP OUR LIFE. . . . . 260 WEST-RUNNING BROOK . . 65
    THE SUN RUNS DOWN IN SENDING UP THE BROOK. . . . . 260 WEST-RUNNING BROOK . . 66
    BUT THOUGH IT RUNS UNBRIDLED OFF ITS COURSE, ... 268 RIDERS 10
    IT IS NOTHING TO ME WHO RUNS THE DIVE. . . . . . 310 IN DIVES' DIVE . . . 5
    HE RUNS FACE FORWARD. HE IS A PURSUER. . . . . . 421 ESCAPIST--NEVER . . . 6
    ONLY OF SAND, NOT WATER, RUNS THROUGH HERE. . . . . 489 A MASQUE OF REASON . . 443
RUNT
    "YOU LIKE THE RUNT." / "DON'T YOU A LITTLE?" / "WELL, . 146 SNOW 94
RUNWAY
    FROM THIS RUNWAY BEACH . . . . 434 KITTY HAWK 185

	PAGE	TITLE	LINE
RUNWAY'S			
TO THE RUNWAY'S FAME	430	KITTY HAWK	82
RURAL			
THE RURAL LETTER BOX SAID TOFFILE LAJWAY.	207	THE WITCH OF COOS .	155
NO, IN YOUR RURAL LETTER BOX	380	AN UNSTAMPED LETTER IN	4
AN UNSTAMPED LETTER IN OUR RURAL LETTER BOX	380	AN UNSTAMPED LETTER IN	T
RUSH			
TO RUSH IN SHEETS AND FOOL'S CAPS WHERE THEY SMELLED . .	163	NEW HAMPSHIRE . .	141
BUT IN THE RUSH OF EVERYTHING TO WASTE, ...	300	THE MASTER SPEED .	7
AND WITH THE SWIFT RUSH OF ITS SANDY DREGS	391	ON BEING IDOLIZED .	3
RUSHED			
AND ALL THE AIR RUSHED TO THE SPOT.	452	A-WISHING WELL . . .	46
RUSHES			
THAT SENDS LIGHT RUSTLE RUSHES TO THEIR LEAVES, . . .	378	DIRECTIVE	24
RUSHING			
NO SPEED OF WIND OR WATER RUSHING BY	300	THE MASTER SPEED . .	1
RUSS			
NOT OUR FRIENDS THE RUSS, ...	437	KITTY HAWK	299
RUSSET			
AND EVERY FLECK OF RUSSET SHOWING CLEAR.	68	AFTER APPLE-PICKING .	20
RUSSIA			
SAMOA, RUSSIA, IRELAND I COMPLAIN OF, ...	166	NEW HAMPSHIRE . .	244
AND RECOGNIZED AS SUCH IN RUSSIA ITSELF	167	NEW HAMPSHIRE . .	278
IF WELL IT IS WITH RUSSIA, THEN FEEL FREE	168	NEW HAMPSHIRE . .	280
THE LAST BEING WHAT THEY SEEM TO HAVE IN RUSSIA. . . .	318	BUILD SOIL	74
THAT SOVIET RUSSIA HAS MADE FASHIONABLE.	323	BUILD SOIL	223
RUSSIAN			
THE RUSSIAN NOVEL IN AMERICA	167	NEW HAMPSHIRE . .	268
IT ISN'T BECAUSE HE'S RUSSIAN JEW.	393	A CASE FOR JEFFERSON .	5
RUST			
THAT LIES UNLIFTED NOW, COME DEW, COME RUST, ...	261	A SOLDIER	2
UNTARNISHED BY RUST AND DECAY.	312	THE VINDICTIVES . . .	79
RUSTLE			
IN THE ABYSS OF ODOR AND RUSTLE AT MY BACK, ...	14	WAITING	19
NOTHING! THEY LISTENED FOR HIM. NOT A RUSTLE.	72	THE CODE	91
OR RUSTLE IN A BUSH OR TREE.	328	A MISSIVE MISSILE .	40
THAT SENDS LIGHT RUSTLE RUSHES TO THEIR LEAVES, . . .	378	DIRECTIVE	24
RUSTLED			
AT THE FIRST DRINK IT RUSTLED AND GREW LIMP.	194	PAUL'S WIFE	102
RUSTLING			
THE FAINTEST RESTLESS RUSTLING RAN ALL THROUGH THEM. . .	204	THE WITCH OF COOS .	64
OF RUSTLING ALL DAY	234	GATHERING LEAVES .	6
RUSTY			
WASHED DOWN WITH RUSTY WATER IN A TIN.	189	THE GRINDSTONE . .	16
WITH CODLIN MOTH OR RUSTY PARASITE	283	THE GOLD HESPERIDEE .	28
ALBEIT THROUGH A RUSTY SCREEN, ...	381	AN UNSTAMPED LETTER IN	41
RYAN'S			
COMING DOWN RYAN'S HILL. I THOUGHT 'TWAS HIM.	88	THE HOUSEKEEPER . . .	197

S

	PAGE	TITLE	LINE
S			
OF SIGNS THAT WITH N TURNED WRONG AND S TURNED WRONG .	286	A ROADSIDE STAND . .	10
TO AHMED S. BOKHARI	468	FROM IRON	0
'SA			
'SA THING TO BE COMPARED WITH SPLITTING WOOD.	179	THE STAR-SPLITTER .	94
SABBATICAL			
MANKIND HAD NOT YET GONE ON THE SABBATICAL.	161	NEW HAMPSHIRE . .	90
SACK (SEE SELF-SACK)			
WHAT THIS MAN BROUGHT IN A COTTON SACK	141	THE GUM-GATHERER .	28
AND SAID SOMETHING TO A MAN WITH A MEAL SACK	142	THE VANISHING RED .	27
THAT THE MAN WITH THE MEAL SACK DIDN'T CATCH--THEN. . .	142	THE VANISHING RED .	28
THAT WAS THE SPLENDIDEST SACK	311	THE VINDICTIVES . .	38
SACKED			
SINCE THE FOREST GERMANS SACKED ROME	311	THE VINDICTIVES . . .	39
SACRED			
BUT NOT COME IN ACROSS THE SACRED SILL----"	79	THE GENERATIONS OF MEN	170
YOU WILL BE LIKELY TO REGARD AS SACRED	79	THE GENERATIONS OF MEN	179
NOTHING NOT BUILT WITH HANDS OF COURSE IS SACRED. . . .	171	NEW HAMPSHIRE . .	394
BUT HERE IS NOT A QUESTION OF WHAT'S SACRED;	171	NEW HAMPSHIRE . .	395
AS IF REGRET WERE IN IT AND WERE SACRED.	259	WEST-RUNNING BROOK .	60
SACRED RIGMAROLES TO MUTTER, ...	396	AN IMPORTER	6
AND THE MOST SACRED THING OF ALL'S ABRUPTION.	510	A MASQUE OF MERCY .	435
SACRIFICE			
TO VIEW ONCE MORE THE SACRIFICE	20	THE TRIAL BY EXISTENCE	26
WE DIDN'T CHANGE WITHOUT SOME SACRIFICE, ...	64	A SERVANT TO SERVANTS .	64
WHY NOT REGARD IT AS A SACRIFICE, ...	178	THE STAR-SPLITTER .	63
AND AN OLD-FASHIONED SACRIFICE BY FIRE, ...	178	THE STAR-SPLITTER .	64
DEVOTED ACTORS AT A SACRIFICE--	481	A MASQUE OF REASON .	225
OUR SACRIFICE--THE BEST WE HAVE TO OFFER, ...	520	A MASQUE OF MERCY .	718
WORTH PRAYING. MAY MY SACRIFICE	520	A MASQUE OF MERCY .	724
SACRIFICIAL-VOTIVE			
HIS DEATH WAS SACRIFICIAL-VOTIVE, ...	327	A MISSIVE MISSILE .	18
SACRILEGE			
NOW IF WE'VE HAD ENOUGH OF SACRILEGE, ...	507	A MASQUE OF MERCY .	358
SAD			
THEY ARE TIRELESS FOLK, BUT SLOW AND SAD--	6	GHOST HOUSE . . .	26
TO MAKE ME SAD TO GO.	12	FLOWER-GATHERING .	4
(NOR IS IT SAD TO THEE!)--	28	MY BUTTERFLY	5
AS WE ARE TOO SAD FOR THE OTHER HERE--	126	LONELINESS . . .	9
AND SAD ON A FOUNDATION OF WELL-BEING.	168	NEW HAMPSHIRE . .	286
BUT THE SAD ACCIDENT OF HAVING SEEN	169	NEW HAMPSHIRE . .	329
WHICH SHOWS HOW SAD AN ACCIDENT MAY BE.	169	NEW HAMPSHIRE . .	333
THREE CHILDREN IN A BURIAL ROW WERE SAD.	199	PLACE FOR A THIRD .	6
FOR THEM THERE WAS REALLY NOTHING SAD.	242	NEED OF BEING VERSED	21
TO LOOKING DOWN AND YET NOT BEING SAD, ...	283	THE GOLD HESPERIDEE .	9

SAD (CONTINUED)
    OR SAD ROANOKE, ... 431 KITTY HAWK 89
    SOMETHING MADE IT SAD . . . . 432 KITTY HAWK 129
    NEVER HAVE I BEEN SAD OR GLAD . . . . 467 QUANDARY 1
    JONAH, I'M GLAD, NOT SAD, TO HEAR YOU SAY . . . . 501 A MASQUE OF MERCY . 213
SADDER
    IS SADDER THAN ANY WORDS. . . . . 8 A LATE WALK 8
SADDEST
    HUGHES 2. AND EVERYBODY TO THE SADDEST . . . . . 165 NEW HAMPSHIRE . . . 199
    I HAVE LOOKED DOWN THE SADDEST CITY LANE. . . . . 255 ACQUAINTED WITH NIGHT . 4
    YOUR COURAGE FAILED. THE SADDEST THING IN LIFE . . 497 A MASQUE OF MERCY . . 106
SADDLE
    IMPRINT A SADDLE, AND CALMLY CONSIDER A COURSE. . 341 WILLFUL HOMING . . . 7
SADLY
    DONE SADLY FROM AN OLD DAGUERREOTYPE. . . . . . . 55 THE BLACK COTTAGE . . 24
    IT SERIOUSLY, SADLY, RUNS AWAY . . . . 259 WEST-RUNNING BROOK . . 48
SADNESS
    THE SADNESS THAT LURKS NEAR THE OPEN WINDOW THERE, . 287 A ROADSIDE STAND . . 34
    IN HAPPY SADNESS BY THE YOUNG, ... 336 THE WIND AND THE RAIN . 19
    BUT THERE IS IN THE SADNESS OF HIS EYE . . . . . 359 THE LOST FOLLOWER . . 34
SAD-WITH-DISTANCE
    THAT SAD-WITH-DISTANCE RIVER BEACH . . . . 328 A MISSIVE MISSILE . . 53
SAFE
    THEIR CHARACTERS, OR WHETHER THEY ARE SAFE . . . . 65 A SERVANT TO SERVANTS . 83
    YOU SPOKE OF JOHN'S NOT BEING SAFE TO STAY WITH. . 85 THE HOUSEKEEPER . . . 123
    YOU ASK THIS LAWYER MAN. AND IT'S NOT SAFE . . . . 97 THE SELF-SEEKER . . . 133
    OH, LET'S NOT WAIT FOR RAIN TO MAKE IT SAFE. . . . 129 THE BONFIRE 5
    "NONSENSE TO THAT! YOU WANT TO SEE HIM SAFE." . . 146 SNOW 93
    WE'LL HAVE TO SIT HERE TILL WE KNOW HE'S SAFE." . 152 SNOW 262
    HE STOOD ON THE SAFE SIDE OF THE LINE TALKING-- . 171 NEW HAMPSHIRE . . . 381
    SHE SEEMED TO THINK THAT, TWO THUS, THEY WERE SAFE. . 229 TWO LOOK AT TWO . . 21
    AT MOST HE THINKS OR TWITTERS SOFTLY, "SAFE! . . 249 ACCEPTANCE 11
    TILL DAYLIGHT MADE IT SAFE FOR A FLYER. . . . . . 253 THE THATCH 27
    JUST WHEN WE THINK WE HAVE IT IMPOUNDED SAFE . . . 254 THE FLOOD 2
    SHE WOULD REFUSE LOVE SAFE WITH WEALTH AND HONOR! . 256 THE LOVELY BE CHOOSERS . 6
    THAT CALM SEEMS CERTAINLY SAFE TO LAST TONIGHT. . 268 ON LOOKING UP BY CHANCE 16
    AS SAFE A VEHICLE OF SEED . . . . 281 BLUE RIBBON AT AMESBURY 35
    THE WEST AND KEEP THE OLD TRADITION SAFE. . . . . 365 OF STONES OF THE PLACE 12
    EXCEPT BESIDE A SAFE INSIDE A BANK . . . . 386 THE FEAR OF MAN . . . 9
SAFEGUARDS
    I GAVE YOU OVER TO HIM, BUT WITH SAFEGUARDS. . . . 486 A MASQUE OF REASON . . 360
SAFELY
    HERE'S HOPING SHE GETS HER DRINK AND GETS OUT SAFELY." . 77 THE GENERATIONS OF MEN 109
    AND THEN LAND SAFELY RIGHT SIDE UP AGAIN, ... 192 PAUL'S WIFE 52
    AND BROUGHT DOWN SAFELY FROM THE UPPER REGIONS; . 196 WILD GRAPES 13
    THEY SAFELY GREW IN SLENDER LENGTH. . . . . 273 A LONE STRIKER . . . 23
    ONE MORE, HE THOUGHT, TO TAKE HIM SAFELY THROUGH. . 283 THE GOLD HESPERIDEE . 26
    WHERE THEY COULD RIPEN SAFELY TO THE EATING. . . . 284 THE GOLD HESPERIDEE . 37
    I HAVE SAFELY TRODDEN UNDERFOOT THE LEAVES OF ANOTHER YEAR. . 297 A LEAF-TREADER . . 4
    I PREFER TO SING SAFELY IN THE REALM . . . . . . 317 BUILD SOIL 48
    SAFELY MADE THE AFRICAN SHORE; . . . . 347 DISCOVERY OF MADEIRAS 127
    GUARANTEED TO COME SAFELY OFF WITH YOU . . . . . 457 HOW HARD TO KEEP FROM 125
SAFETY
    COMES TOO NEAR TO AHAZ' SIN FOR SAFETY. . . . . . 171 NEW HAMPSHIRE . . . 393
    I HAVE CROSSED TO SAFETY WITH? FOR I AM THERE, . . 335 I COULD GIVE ALL . . 14
    SAFETY RAZORS, SUNDAY PAPERS . . . . 396 AN IMPORTER 14
    I PICKED YOU OUT A HORSE CALLED SAFETY THIRD, . . 457 HOW HARD TO KEEP FROM 123
    BY SAFETY SECOND OUT OF SAFETY FIRST, ... 457 HOW HARD TO KEEP FROM 124
SAFETY-FIRST
    YOU'D MAKE A SORT OF SAFETY-FIRST DICTATOR. . . . 320 BUILD SOIL 130
SAGES
    WERE REALLY AS DARK AS I HEAR SAGES TELL, ... 350 THE LESSON FOR TODAY . 2
    AND I CONVINCED THAT THEY WERE REALLY SAGES, . . . 350 THE LESSON FOR TODAY . 3
    THAT IN THE LATIN OF OUR FOUNDING SAGES . . . . . 422 FOR JOHN F. KENNEDY . 20
SAGGING
    OUT IN THE PORCH'S SAGGING FLOOR . . . . 251 BEREFT 8
    OLD RIVALS OF SAGGING LEATHER, ... 294 A RECORD STRIDE . . 6
SAID
    "AS ALL MUST BE," I SAID WITHIN MY HEART, ... 22 THE TUFT OF FLOWERS . 9
    BUT AS I SAID IT, SWIFT THERE PASSED ME BY . . . . 22 THE TUFT OF FLOWERS . 11
    FOR THOU ART DEAD, I SAID, ... 29 MY BUTTERFLY 44
    HE SAID IT FOR HIMSELF. I SEE HIM THERE, ... 34 MENDING WALL 38
    AND SHUT IT AFTER HER. "BE KIND," SHE SAID. . . . 34 DEATH OF THE HIRED MAN 7
    BUT I'LL NOT HAVE THE FELLOW BACK," HE SAID. . . . 35 DEATH OF THE HIRED MAN 12
    IF HE LEFT THEN, I SAID, THAT ENDED IT. . . . . . 35 DEATH OF THE HIRED MAN 14
    "SH! NOT SO LOUD: HE'LL HEAR YOU," MARY SAID. . . 35 DEATH OF THE HIRED MAN 31
    HE SAID HE'D COME TO DITCH THE MEADOW FOR ME." . . 36 DEATH OF THE HIRED MAN 46
    HE SAID HE COULDN'T MAKE THE BOY BELIEVE . . . . 37 DEATH OF THE HIRED MAN 82
    "WARREN," SHE SAID, "HE HAS COME HOME TO DIE: . . 38 DEATH OF THE HIRED MAN 111
    "WHAT DID HE SAY?" / "HE SAID THERE WAS A LAKE . . 43 THE MOUNTAIN 75
    "NO ROOM," THE NIGHT CLERK SAID, "UNLESS----" . . 45 A HUNDRED COLLARS . . 20
    "THIS WILL BE YOURS. GOOD-NIGHT," HE SAID, AND WENT. . 46 A HUNDRED COLLARS . . 40
    A GOOD DEAL COMES ON ME WHEN ALL IS SAID. . . . . 48 A HUNDRED COLLARS . . 107
    HE SAID TO GAIN TIME: "WHAT IS IT YOU SEE?" . . . 51 HOME BURIAL 10
    "WHAT IS IT--WHAT?" SHE SAID. / "JUST THAT I SEE." . 51 HOME BURIAL 18
    HE SAID TWICE OVER BEFORE HE KNEW HIMSELF: . . . 52 HOME BURIAL 34
    "THERE, YOU HAVE SAID IT ALL AND YOU FEEL BETTER. . 54 HOME BURIAL 108
    "PRETTY," HE SAID. "COME IN. NO ONE WILL CARE." . 55 THE BLACK COTTAGE . . 11
    WE PRESSED OUR FACES TO THE PANE. "YOU SEE," HE SAID, . 55 THE BLACK COTTAGE . . 14
    FOR THE PICKING. THE RASCAL, HE SAID HE'D BE GLAD . 61 BLUEBERRIES 71
    UNLESS WHEN YOU SAID I WAS KEEPING A BIRD . . . . 62 BLUEBERRIES 88
    AWAY FROM ITS NEST, AND I SAID IT WAS YOU. . . . 62 BLUEBERRIES 89
    IT'S REST I WANT--THERE, I HAVE SAID IT OUT-- . . 64 A SERVANT TO SERVANTS . 49
    MIND YOU, I WAITED TILL LEN SAID THE WORD. . . . 67 A SERVANT TO SERVANTS . 149
    AS I SAID, FOR A WHILE--BUT I DON'T KNOW . . . . 67 A SERVANT TO SERVANTS . 153
    "WHAT IS THERE WRONG?" / "SOMETHING YOU JUST NOW SAID." . 69 THE CODE 10
    I SAID THAT MORE THAN HALF AN HOUR AGO. . . . . . 70 THE CODE 13
    I SAID IT TO MYSELF AS MUCH AS YOU." . . . . . . 70 THE CODE 14

SAID (CONTINUED)
                                                     PAGE TITLE   LINE

THINKS I, D'YE MEAN IT? 'WHAT WAS THAT YOU SAID?' . . . . . 71 THE CODE 64
HE SAID IT OVER, BUT HE SAID IT SOFTER. . . . . . . 71 THE CODE 67
ARE THERE," THEY SAID. "IT ISN'T GOING TO RAIN." . . . . 74 THE GENERATIONS OF MEN . . 24
"NO FETE TODAY," HE SAID. / "IT LOCKS THAT WAY." . . . . 74 THE GENERATIONS OF MEN . . 35
"I LIKE YOUR 'GOING TO BE.' YOU SAID JUST NOW . . . . . 80 THE GENERATIONS OF MEN . . 200
"NO, I DON'T TRUST YOUR EYES. YOU'VE SAID ENOUGH. . . . . 80 THE GENERATIONS OF MEN . . 206
"IT'S YOU," SHE SAID. "I CAN'T GET UP. FORGIVE ME . . . . 81 THE HOUSEKEEPER . . . 2
AS MARRIED—THAT'S WHAT HE HAS ALWAYS SAID. . . . . . 84 THE HOUSEKEEPER . . . 82
BUT WHEN I'VE SAID, WHY SHOULDN'T THEY BE MARRIED? . . . 84 THE HOUSEKEEPER . . . 90
JOHN SAID I WAS TOO OLD TO HAVE GRANDCHILDREN. . . . . 87 THE HOUSEKEEPER . . . 175
ISN'T IT HELL?" HE SAID. "I WANT TC KNOW. . . . . . 88 THE HOUSEKEEPER . . . 207
SHE SAID, "AS THE LIGHT ON THE DASHBOARD RAN . . . . . 89 THE FEAR 10
"YOU'RE NOT TO COME," SHE SAID. "THIS IS MY BUSINESS. . . . 90 THE FEAR 35
"THERE'S NO ONE; SO YOU'RE WRONG," HE SAID. / "THERE IS.— . . 91 THE FEAR 64
"YOU SEE," THE VOICE SAID. / "OH." SHE LOOKED AND LOOKED. . . 92 THE FEAR 78
"LOOKING ROUND, I SUPPOSE," SAID WILLIS. / "YES, ... 96 THE SELF-SEEKER . . . 101
WITH BOTH HANDS HELD BEHIND HER. "GUESS," SHE SAID. . . . 96 THE SELF-SEEKER . . . 106
THE LAWYER SAID. "I'M SORRY, BUT MY TRAIN— . . . . 99 THE SELF-SEEKER . . . 181
"WHAT DID YOU HEAR, FOR INSTANCE?" WILLIS SAID. . . . . 100 THE SELF-SEEKER . . . 206
I PAUSED AND SAID, "I WILL TURN BACK FROM HERE. . . . . 101 THE WOOD-PILE . . . 2
EVERYTHING SAID AS PERSONAL TO HIMSELF. . . . . . . 101 THE WOOD-PILE . . . 16
I SAID, "THERE AREN'T ENOUGH TO BE WORTH WHILE." . . . . 106 CHRISTMAS TREES . . 29
AND CAME DOWN ON THE NORTH. / HE SAID, "A THOUSAND." . . . 107 CHRISTMAS TREES . . 41
"A FIT!" SAID ONE, AND BANGED A STOVEPIPE SHOULDER. . . . 113 IN THE HOME STRETCH . . 90
JOE SAID: "YOU BIG BOYS OUGHT TO FIND A FARM, ... 113 IN THE HOME STRETCH . . 95
"GOD!" ONE SAID WILDLY, AND, WHEN NO ONE SPOKE: . . . . 114 IN THE HOME STRETCH . . 99
WHO SAID WITH SERIOUSNESS THAT MADE THEM LAUGH, ... 114 IN THE HOME STRETCH . . 104
BUT WHO FIRST SAID THE WORD TO COME?" / "MY DEAR, . . . 116 IN THE HOME STRETCH . . 171
DO YOU REMEMBER WHAT IT WAS YOU SAID?" . . . . 118 THE TELEPHONE . . 9
SOMEONE SAID 'COME'—I HEARD IT AS I BOWED." . . . . . 118 THE TELEPHONE . . 17
HE SAID I COULD HAVE TO BUSH MY PEAS. . . . . 123 PEA BRUSH 4
"YOU HERE?" I SAID. "WHERE AREN'T YOU NOWADAYS? . . . . 125 AN ENCOUNTER . . . 19
"AND SCARE YOU TOO?" THE CHILDREN SAID TOGETHER. . . . . 130 THE BONFIRE . . . 19
ANC SAID OUT LOUD, I COULDN'T BIDE THE SMOTHER. . . . . 131 THE BONFIRE . . . 70
AND HE SAID, "WHY NOT?" . . . . 133 A GIRL'S GARDEN . . 8
AND HE SAID, "JUST IT." . . . . 133 A GIRL'S GARDEN . . 12
AND HE SAID, "THAT OUGHT TO MAKE YOU . . . . 133 A GIRL'S GARDEN . . 13
HER FATHER SAID, TO PLOW; . . . . 133 A GIRL'S GARDEN . . 18
WHEN ALL WAS SAID AND DONE, ... 134 A GIRL'S GARDEN . . 38
IN A LOW VOICE SAID, "OH, ... 135 LAST WORD OF A BLUEBIRD 2
AND SAID TO BE GOOD, ... 136 LAST WORD OF A BLUEBIRD 16
CALL IT A DAY, I WISH THEY MIGHT HAVE SAID . . . . . 136 "OUT, OUT—" . . . 10
AND STAMPED AND SAID THINGS TO HIMSELF, ... 138 BROWN'S DESCENT . . 17
"WELL—I—BE—" THAT WAS ALL HE SAID, ... 139 BROWN'S DESCENT . . 45
HE IS SAID TO HAVE BEEN THE LAST RED MAN . . . . . . 142 THE VANISHING RED . . 1
IN ACTON. AND THE MILLER IS SAID TO HAVE LAUGHED— . . . 142 THE VANISHING RED . . 2
"COME, JOHN," HE SAID, "YOU WANT TO SEE THE WHEEL PIT?" . . 142 THE VANISHING RED . . 19
AND SAID SOMETHING TO A MAN WITH A MEAL SACK . . . . . 142 THE VANISHING RED . . 27
SAID IT AT LAST HIMSELF, "GOOD-NIGHT," AND THEN, ... 143 SNOW 29
WITH LOWERED EYES A MOMENT TILL HE SAID, ... 144 SNOW 32
BOTH THE COLES SAID TOGETHER. MRS. COLE . . . . . . 144 SNOW 34
FROM THE LAST THING HE SAID HIMSELF, STONE DEAF . . . . 145 SNOW 65
WAS COMING. "GOD." BUT NO, HE ONLY SAID, ... 151 SNOW 239
DO YOU CALL THAT?" SHE SAID. / "HE HAD THE GIFT . . . 151 SNOW 248
I WANT TO SPEAK TO HER." / "ALL SHE SAID WAS, ... 152 SNOW 276
"FRED, AFTER ALL I SAID! YOU SHAN'T MAKE OUT . . . . 153 SNOW 285
DID SHE LET ON BY ANY WORD SHE SAID . . . . 153 SNOW 287
'WELL THEN,' SHE SAID, AND 'WELL THEN'—LIKE A THREAT. . . 153 SNOW 289
I MET A LADY FROM THE SOUTH WHO SAID . . . . 159 NEW HAMPSHIRE . . . 1
(YOU WON'T BELIEVE SHE SAID IT, BUT SHE SAID IT): . . . . 159 NEW HAMPSHIRE . . . 2
HE SAID, IN CLIMATE, NONE HAD EVER DIED THERE . . . . . 159 NEW HAMPSHIRE . . . 18
A SPECIMEN OF EVERYTHING, I SAID. . . . . 163 NEW HAMPSHIRE . . . 124
RAKING UP AFTER WINTER, AND I SAID, ... 164 NEW HAMPSHIRE . . . 153
EMERSON SAID, "THE GOD WHO MADE NEW HAMPSHIRE . . . . . 166 NEW HAMPSHIRE . . . 218
ANOTHER MASSACHUSETTS POET SAID, ... 166 NEW HAMPSHIRE . . . 220
SHE SAID SHE COULDN'T STAND THE PEOPLE IN IT, ... 166 NEW HAMPSHIRE . . . 224
SHE SAID, "GO READ YOUR OWN BOOKS AND FIND OUT." . . . . 166 NEW HAMPSHIRE . . . 227
BY ME, A STRANGER. THIS IS WHAT HE SAID, ... 168 NEW HAMPSHIRE . . . 290
"GO 'LONG," I SAID TO HIM, HE TO HIS HORSE. . . . . . 168 NEW HAMPSHIRE . . . 300
AND EDUCATED INTO BOARDS, HE SAID. . . . . 171 NEW HAMPSHIRE . . . 377
OF BREATHING TREES SAID SOMETHING OF THE TIME . . . . . 175 THE CENSUS-TAKER . . 26
A WEAPON IN OUR HUMAN FIGHT," HE SAID. . . . . . . 177 THE STAR-SPLITTER . . 24
TO FIND HIMSELF IN ONE. WELL, ALL WE SAID WAS . . . . 178 THE STAR-SPLITTER . . 57
SAID SOME OF THE BEST THINGS WE EVER SAID. . . . . . 179 THE STAR-SPLITTER . . 86
IT MUST HAVE MADE YOUR DIMPLE THERE, AND SAID, ... 180 MAPLE 17
'MAPLE.' I SAID IT TOO: 'YES, FOR HER NAME.' . . . . 180 MAPLE 18
SOMETHING ABOUT WAVE OFFERING, IT SAID." . . . . . . 183 MAPLE 107
"MADE ON MACHINE," HE SAID, PLOWING THE GRAIN . . . . . 186 THE AX-HELVE . . . 22
SOME SAID IT WAS BECAUSE HE HAD NO WIFE, ... 191 PAUL'S WIFE . . . 4
TAKE IT TO HELL FOR ME," THE SAWYER SAID. . . . . . 193 PAUL'S WIFE . . . 77
I SAID I HAD THE TREE. IT WASN'T TRUE. . . . . . . 197 WILD GRAPES . . . 41
"NOW YOU KNOW HOW IT FEELS," MY BROTHER SAID, ... 198 WILD GRAPES . . . 62
AGAINST MY BROTHER'S NONSENSE. "DROP," HE SAID, ... 198 WILD GRAPES . . . 75
MY BROTHER SAID: "DON'T YOU WEIGH ANYTHING? . . . . . 199 WILD GRAPES . . . 89
AND SO SHE SAID TO LABAN, "YOU HAVE DONE . . . . . . 199 PLACE FOR A THIRD . . 9
LABAN SAID, NO, HE WOULD NOT MAKE HER LIE . . . . . . 199 PLACE FOR A THIRD . . 12
IF THAT WAS HOW SHE FELT, OF COURSE, HE SAID. . . . . 200 PLACE FOR A THIRD . . 14
SHE SAID HE MIGHT ATTEND TO IN THE VILLAGE, ... 201 PLACE FOR A THIRD . . 54
HE SAID THE DEAD HAD SOULS, BUT WHEN I ASKED HIM . . . . 202 THE WITCH OF COOS . . 14
TOFFILE, FOR MY SAKE!" "COMPANY?" HE SAID, ... 205 THE WITCH OF COOS . . 94
THE RURAL LETTER BOX SAID TOFFILE LAJWAY. . . . . . 207 THE WITCH OF COOS . . 155
IN WENTWORTH FROM NOW ON; AND WHEN ALL'S SAID, ... 208 PAUPER WITCH OF GRAFTON 32
SAID THAT I TOOK HIM OUT IN HIS OLD AGE . . . . . . 208 PAUPER WITCH OF GRAFTON 46
IF SOMEONE HADN'T SAID TO GNAW THE POSTS . . . . . . 209 PAUPER WITCH OF GRAFTON 54
THEN THAT SAME SMARTY SOMEONE SAID TO LOOK— . . . . 209 PAUPER WITCH OF GRAFTON 59
HE SAID HE HAD, BESIDES. BECAUSE A HORSE . . . . . . 209 PAUPER WITCH OF GRAFTON 65
HE NEVER SAID MUCH AFTER WE WERE MARRIED, ... 209 PAUPER WITCH OF GRAFTON 73

SAID (CONTINUED)
    AND EXPERTS SAID THAT DEEP DOWN IN THE MOUNTAIN . . . . 212 A FOUNTAIN, A BOTTLE .   4
    YOU SAID YOU KNEW THE PLACE WHERE ONCE, ON KINSMAN, .   213 A FOUNTAIN, A BOTTLE .   8
    YOU SAID YOU'D SEEN THE STONE BAPTISMAL FONT. . . . . 213 A FOUNTAIN, A BOTTLE .   13
    BUT YOU HAVE SAID IT, AND WE'RE OFF TO FIND IT. . . . 213 A FOUNTAIN, A BOTTLE .   28
    THAT HAPPENS TO BE BROKEN," DAVIS SAID. . . . . . 215 A FOUNTAIN, A BOTTLE .   73
    THE TOWER SAID, "ONE!" . . . . 218 I WILL SING YOU ONE-O .   27
    "OH, THAT'S THE PARADISE-IN-BLOOM," I SAID; . . . . 233 A BOUNDLESS MOMENT .   5
    AND THEN I SAID THE TRUTH (AND WE MOVED ON). . . . 234 A BOUNDLESS MOMENT .   11
    THE RAIN TO THE WIND SAID, ... 250 LODGED   1
    THE VOICE SAID, "HURL HER DOWN!" . . . . . . 255 THE LOVELY BE CHOOSERS   1
    "TRUST US," THE VOICES SAID. . . . . 257 THE LOVELY BE CHOOSERS   53
    WE'VE TOWER WE TWO. LET'S CHANGE THAT TO WE THREE. . 258 WEST-RUNNING BROOK .   11
    YOU SAID SO." / "NO, TODAY WILL BE THE DAY . . . 260 WEST-RUNNING BROOK .   73
    YOU SAID THE BROOK WAS CALLED WEST-RUNNING BROOK." . 260 WEST-RUNNING BROOK .   74
    "TODAY WILL BE THE DAY OF WHAT WE BOTH SAID." . . . 260 WEST-RUNNING BROOK .   75
    WHAT FIFTY SAID . . . . 267 WHAT FIFTY SAID . .   T
    BUT HE SAID THEN AND STILL WOULD SAY, ... 274 A LONE STRIKER .   56
    NOTHING ON EITHER SIDE WAS SAID. . . . . . . 277 TWO TRAMPS IN MUD TIME   57
    "WRONG SHAPE, WRONG COLOR, AND WRONG SCENT," I SAID. . 278 THE WHITE-TAILED HORNET 40
    THAT THE PARTY IN POWER IS SAID TO BE KEEPING FROM US. . 286 A ROADSIDE STAND . . 22
    WE SAID WELL TWICE TO WHAT WE HAD IN COMMON, . . . 290 OLD BARN AT THE BOTTOM   22
    TO ANSWER FOR THEMSELVES: WHO SAID IT MATTERED . . . 294 AT WOODWARD'S GARDENS . 33
    I SAID TO MYSELF ALMOST IN PRAYER, ... 306 A TRIAL RUN . . .   1
    SOME SAID IT HAD GONE TO THE COAST, ... 312 THE VINDICTIVES . .   69
    AND THERE IS ALWAYS MORE THAN SHOULD BE SAID. . . . 337 THE WIND AND THE RAIN . 40
    I SUNG OR SAID. . . . . 342 QUEST OF PURPLE-FRINGED   4
    SAID THAT THE FALL MIGHT COME AND WHIRL OF LEAVES, . 343 QUEST OF PURPLE-FRINGED 27
    A STOLEN LADY WAS ALL IT SAID. . . . . . . 343 DISCOVERY OF MADEIRAS .   5
    "THROW HIM OVER ALIVE," THEY SAID, ... 345 DISCOVERY OF MADEIRAS . 60
    SOME TOM SAID TO DICK OR HARRY: . . . . . . 345 DISCOVERY OF MADEIRAS . 68
    HE SAID TO THE CAPTAIN, "GIVE COMMAND, ... 346 DISCOVERY OF MADEIRAS . 106
    I'M TELLING YOU. YOU HAVEN'T SAID A THING, . . . 354 THE LESSON FOR TODAY . 114
    A VOICE SAID, LOOK ME IN THE STARS. . . . . . 362 A QUESTION   1
    "YOU SAID IT--THAT'S EXACTLY WHAT IT IS. . . . . 371 THE LITERATE FARMER AND 94
    BUT SPES ALIT AGRICOLAM 'TIS SAID. . . . . . 376 SOMETHING FOR HOPE .   24
    STILL SAID TO HAUNT THIS SIDE OF PANTHER MOUNTAIN. . 377 DIRECTIVE . . .   19
    THAT SOMEONE HAS SAID IS THE END OF THE WORLD. . . . 379 TOO ANXIOUS FOR RIVERS   2
    BE IT SAID AGAINST OR FOR ME, ... 388 ASTROMETAPHYSICAL . .   2
    WELL, I SAID THAT I DID. . . . . 391 A WISH TO COMPLY . .   3
    PIKE SAID WITH TEMPER. AND DICK LONGED TO SAY, . . 404 FROM PLANE TO PLANE .   8
    HE DON'T MIND HAVING LOST A CASE," PIKE SAID; . . . 404 FROM PLANE TO PLANE . 25
    YOU SAID YOURSELF YOU WEREN'T AVOIDING WORK. . . . 405 FROM PLANE TO PLANE . 45
    YOU SAID THE SECOND COMING OF TECUMSEH. . . . . 406 FROM PLANE TO PLANE . 70
    DICK SAID, "YOU'VE BEEN A LESSON IN WORK WISDOM . . 408 FROM PLANE TO PLANE . 122
    SHALL I GO ON OR HAVE I SAID ENOUGH-- . . . . . 408 FROM PLANE TO PLANE . 134
    "I GUESS SO," PIKE SAID, INNOCENT OF MILTON. . . . 408 FROM PLANE TO PLANE . 136
    DICK SAID, TO OLD PIKE INNOCENT OF SHAKESPEARE. . . 408 FROM PLANE TO PLANE . 148
    I SAID I WOULD SEE HOW SIRIUS KEPT . . . . . . 419 ONE MORE BREVITY .   4
    WITH AN AIR THAT SAID, "I HAVE PAID MY CALL." . . . 420 ONE MORE BREVITY .   46
    AS THE POET SAID. . . . . 433 KITTY HAWK 168
    VOICE THAT SAID, "GET SET . . . . 436 KITTY HAWK 271
    REGION VOICE SAID, "GO, ... 436 KITTY HAWK 278
    OF ALL THE THINGS HE MIGHT HAVE SAID, ... 444 ENDS   5
    HE NEVER SAID SHE WASN'T YOUNG, ... 444 ENDS   7
    THE SIBYL SAID, "GO BACK TO ROME . . . . . . 449 OUR DOOM TO BLOOM . .   5
    "IF BUT IT WERE," HE SAID, SAID HE, ... 451 A-WISHING WELL . .   3
    THE KING SAID TO HIS SON: "ENOUGH OF THIS! . . . 453 HOW HARD TO KEEP FROM   1
    THE EX-KING SAID, "YON STAR'S INDIFFERENCE . . . 454 HOW HARD TO KEEP FROM 17
    "LET'S NOT GET SUPERSTITIOUS, SIRE," THE PRINCE SAID. . 454 HOW HARD TO KEEP FROM 28
    "YOU'RE RIGHT," THE EX-KING SAID, "WE'LL NEED SOME MONEY. 454 HOW HARD TO KEEP FROM 30
    WHAT GOOD HE WAS HE BOLDLY SAID, "I'LL TELL YOU: . 454 HOW HARD TO KEEP FROM 40
    THE KING SAID GRANDLY, "EVEN AS WE ARE FED . . . 455 HOW HARD TO KEEP FROM 63
    AND THE SLAVE SAID, "THE SMALL ONE'S WORTH THE PRICE, . 456 HOW HARD TO KEEP FROM 81
    "BUT YES," SHE SAID, "SOME DAY I'LL TELL YOU, DEAR. . 457 HOW HARD TO KEEP FROM 106
    BUT THE KING SAID, "HAVEN'T I READ SOMEWHERE . . 458 HOW HARD TO KEEP FROM 139
    "YOU'RE HOPELESS," SAID THE SLAVE. / "I GUESS I AM; . 458 HOW HARD TO KEEP FROM 144
    I AM ABJECT BEFORE YOU," SAID DARIUS. . . . . . 458 HOW HARD TO KEEP FROM 145
    "SO MUCH FOR PROGRESS," SAID DARIUS MEEKLY. . . . 459 HOW HARD TO KEEP FROM 162
    THE EX-KING SAID. "WE'RE IN THIS THING TOGETHER. . . 459 HOW HARD TO KEEP FROM 170
    TELL THEM IAMB, JEHOVAH SAID, AND MEANT IT. . . . 460 HOW HARD TO KEEP FROM 218
    "AH," HE SAID, "QUI VIVE, ... 468 A REFLEX   8
    I SAID THE INCENSE TREE'S ON FIRE AGAIN. . . . . 473 A MASQUE OF REASON .   5
    IF I SAID ONCE I SAID A THOUSAND TIMES, ... 478 A MASQUE OF REASON . 129
    I SHOULD HAVE SAID. YOU GOT YOUR AGE REVERSED . . 479 A MASQUE OF REASON . 159
    THAT FELLED THE ANGELS, WOLSEY SHOULD HAVE SAID. . . 481 A MASQUE OF REASON . 206
    WHAT DID WE SAY? / YOU SAID THE DEVIL'S IN IT. . . 487 A MASQUE OF REASON . 397
    I THOUGHT YOU JUST NOW SAID IT WAS A GIFT SHOP. . . 494 A MASQUE OF MERCY . 25
    HE SAID THE BIBLE. / I SHOULD HATE TO SCARE YOU . . 495 A MASQUE OF MERCY . 52
    I NEVER SAID YOU WEREN'T. I RECOGNIZED YOU. . . . 498 A MASQUE OF MERCY . 136
    HOW THEY'LL LIKE THAT. PAUL SAID CONSERVATIVES-- . . 509 A MASQUE OF MERCY . 408
    NOT EVERYTHING I SAY IS SAID IN SCORN. . . . . . 510 A MASQUE OF MERCY . 451
    'TWAS SAID THE LESSER GODS WERE ONLY TRAITS . . . 516 A MASQUE OF MERCY . 595
    WHO SAID, "TOO LATE, YOU CANNOT ENTER NOW"? . . . 519 A MASQUE OF MERCY . 669
SAIL
    NO SHIP OF ALL THAT UNDER SAIL OR STEAM . . . . 262 IMMIGRANTS   1
    AND DORY AND MASTER WILL SAIL BY FATE . . . . . 262 THE FLOWER BOAT . .   11
    AND SAIL FOR SOME VAGUE PAPHIAN BOURN . . . . . 344 DISCOVERY OF MADEIRAS . 17
    NOW STANDING CRACKED ITS SAIL AND SPUN; . . . . 344 DISCOVERY OF MADEIRAS . 22
    HER LOVER SAW THEM SAIL AWAY, ... 347 DISCOVERY OF MADEIRAS . 114
SAILED
    AND NOTHING CAME OF ALL HE SAILED. . . . . . . 212 AN EMPTY THREAT . .   47
    BUT SAILED AND LEFT THEM IN THE END. . . . . . 347 DISCOVERY OF MADEIRAS . 113
SAILING
    I'LL SIT AND SEE IF THAT SMALL SAILING CLOUD . . . 40 DEATH OF THE HIRED MAN 160
    TO SEND IT SAILING OUT THE ATTIC WINDOW . . . . 216 A FOUNTAIN, A BOTTLE . 110
    TRIED TO IMPROVE ON SAILING LIKE A TILE . . . . 216 A FOUNTAIN, A BOTTLE . 112
    THEN HE GOUGED A CLUMSY SAILING TROUGH . . . . 347 DISCOVERY OF MADEIRAS . 125

SAILING (CONTINUED)
    FINDING THE EAST BY SAILING WEST. . . . . 416 AMERICA IS HARD TO SEE   8
    CAME JUST THEN SAILING INTO PORT . . . . 417 AMERICA IS HARD TO SEE   21
SAILOR
    AND TELLING THEM HOW SINBAD WAS A SAILOR. . . . . . 447 DOES NO ONE AT ALL EVER 42
SAILORS
    TILL THE PIRATE SAILORS MADE A VOW . . . . 344 DISCOVERY OF MADEIRAS . 24
    OUR SAILORS RIDE A BULLET FOR A BOAT. . . . . 446 DOES NO ONE AT ALL EVER 14
    THE SAILORS THROW ME OVERBOARD FOR LUCK, ... 500 A MASQUE OF MERCY . . 182
SAINT
    THE CLOISTER AND THE OBSERVATORY SAINT . . . . . . 353 THE LESSON FOR TODAY . 81
    SO CAN'T GET SAVED, AS SAINT MARK SAYS THEY MUSTN'T. . . 379 DIRECTIVE 59
    AND AS SUCH I PROMOTE YOU TO A SAINT. . . . . 476 A MASQUE OF REASON . 79
    YOU HEAR HIM, THYATIRA: WE'RE A SAINT. . . . . 476 A MASQUE OF REASON . 80
SAINTS
    OF THE ONE AWFUL GOD. JUST SO THE SAINTS . . . . . . 516 A MASQUE OF MERCY . . 596
SAKE
    FOR THE GRAPES' SAKE, IF THEY WERE ALL, ... 28 OCTOBER   18
    FOR THE GRAPES' SAKE ALONG THE WALL. . . . . 28 OCTOBER   21
    NOT FOR THE SAKE OF CLIMBING. WHAT'S ITS NAME?" . . . 43 THE MOUNTAIN   90
    AND FOR YOUR FAMILY'S SAKE STAY WHERE YOU ARE. . . . 150 SNOW 217
    FOR ART'S SAKE ONE COULD ALMOST WISH THEM WORSE . . . 167 NEW HAMPSHIRE . . . 266
    TOFFILE, FOR MY SAKE!" "COMPANY?" HE SAID, ... 205 THE WITCH OF COOS .   94
    FOR GOD, MAN, OR BEAST'S SAKE, ... 212 AN EMPTY THREAT . . . 36
    "FOR GOD'S SAKE, AREN'T YOU FOND OF VIEWING NATURE? . . 215 A FOUNTAIN, A BOTTLE . 56
    WAS STANDING IDLE FOR HIS SAKE. . . . . 273 A LONE STRIKER . . . 15
    FOR GOOD GRACIOUS' SAKE. . . . . 432 KITTY HAWK 124
    FOR GOOD GRACIOUS' SAKE, ... 438 KITTY HAWK 315
    AND THAT FOR MAN'S OWN SAKE AS WELL AS MINE, ... 481 A MASQUE OF REASON . 211
    BY BEING BAFFLED FOR THE SAKE OF BEING. . . . . 484 A MASQUE OF REASON . 299
    MERCY, FOR MERCY'S SAKE! / BEL WANTS SOME MERCY.-- . . 507 A MASQUE OF MERCY . 345
SAKES
    I DOUBT IF EVEN HIS MOTHER COULD TELL HIM, 'SAKES, . . 223 THE RUNAWAY 12
    FOR HEAVEN AND THE FUTURE'S SAKES. . . . . 277 TWO TRAMPS IN MUD TIME 72
SALE
    NOT EVEN NEW HAMPSHIRE FARMS ARE MUCH FOR SALE. . . . 163 NEW HAMPSHIRE . . . 149
    OFFERED FOR SALE WILD BERRIES IN WOODEN QUARTS, . . . 286 A ROADSIDE STAND . 11
    BUT MUCH AS IN THE END WE BRING FOR SALE THERE, . . . 321 BUILD SOIL 173
SALEM
    I WAS UP HERE IN SALEM, AT A MAN'S . . . . 70 THE CODE   30
    NEW HAMPSHIRE USED TO HAVE AT SALEM . . . . 163 NEW HAMPSHIRE . . . 138
SALESMANSHIP
    BUT IN THE BEST STYLE OF BAD SALESMANSHIP, ... 160 NEW HAMPSHIRE . . . 28
SALMON
    SALMON AND STURGEON, LASHING WITH THEIR TAILS. . . . 142 THE VANISHING RED . 23
SALT
    SOMEONE TO SALT THE HALF-WILD STEER, ... 24 PAN WITH US 13
    MORE OF THE SALT WHEREWITH THEY'RE TO BE SALTED. . . . 80 THE GENERATIONS OF MEN 191
    YOUR TONGUE GIVES SALT OR SUGAR IN YOUR HAND. . . . . 131 THE BONFIRE 47
    NOW NO JOY BUT LACKS SALT, ... 227 TO EARTHWARD 17
    ON THE OTHER PACIFIC, SALT. . . . . 295 A RECORD STRIDE . . 24
    I WOULD PICK UP ALL OCEAN LESS ITS SALT, ... 337 THE WIND AND THE RAIN . 28
    TILL YOU HAVE LOST THE SAVOR OF YOUR SALT. . . . . . 446 DOES NO ONE AT ALL EVER 24
    NOR TASTE ITS SALT, NOR SMELL ITS FISH AND WEED, . . 447 DOES NO ONE AT ALL EVER 35
    NOT EVEN BRACKISH FROM ITS SALT EXPERIENCE, ... 514 A MASQUE OF MERCY . 542
SALTED
    MORE OF THE SALT WHEREWITH THEY'RE TO BE SALTED. . . . 80 THE GENERATIONS OF MEN 191
SALVATION
    AND FORTHWITH FOUND SALVATION IN SURRENDER. . . . . . 348 THE GIFT OUTRIGHT . 11
    AND FORTHWITH FOUND SALVATION IN SURRENDER. . . . . . 424 THE GIFT OUTRIGHT . 11
    SALVATION IN OUR CASE IS RETROACTIVE. . . . . 476 A MASQUE OF REASON . 81
SALVES
    YES, REVOLUTIONS ARE THE ONLY SALVES, ... 363 A SEMI-REVOLUTION .   7
SAME
    WHERE BIRD AND FLOWER WERE ONE AND THE SAME. . . . . 15 IN A VALE 20
    BUT THE LAST CHOICE IS STILL THE SAME; . . . . 21 THE TRIAL BY EXISTENCE 58
    THE SAME LEAVES OVER AND OVER AGAIN! . . . . 25 IN HARDWOOD GROVES . .   1
    WITH A BIG STICK, THE SAME AS WHEN THE COWS . . . . . 43 THE MOUNTAIN 85
    BY THE SAME HAND WORKING IN THE SAME STUFF? . . . . . 57 THE BLACK COTTAGE . 78
    (WOMEN AND MEN WILL MAKE THEM ALL THE SAME.) . . . . 64 A SERVANT TO SERVANTS . 69
    MOST LIKELY I'D HAVE SERVED YOU JUST THE SAME. . . . . 70 THE CODE   25
    THE NOSE IS JUST THE SAME, AND SO'S THE CHIN-- . . . . 77 THE GENERATIONS OF MEN 114
    I KNOW THE WAY HE'S FELT--BUT ALL THE SAME!" . . . . . 84 THE HOUSEKEEPER . . 83
    EVERYTHING GOES THE SAME WITHOUT ME THERE. . . . . . 94 THE SELF-SEEKER . . 40
    HAD WORN THEM REALLY ABOUT THE SAME, ... 105 THE ROAD NOT TAKEN . 10
    WITH THE SAME PAINS YOU USE TO FILL A CUP . . . . . . 122 BIRCHES   37
    THE SAME AS YOU SEIZE CAT'S-CRADLE STRINGS, ... 123 PEA BRUSH 19
    TO THE SAME PERSON TWICE. . . . . 134 A GIRL'S GARDEN . . 48
    MY DEAR, I'M COMING JUST THE SAME. I DIDN'T . . . . . 143 SNOW 26
    AT THE SAME TIME YOU CAN'T DENY IT MAKES . . . . . . 149 SNOW 188
    THE SAME AT DIFFERENT TIMES TO DIFFERENT PEOPLE. . . . 184 MAPLE 156
    IT STANDS BESIDE THE SAME OLD APPLE TREE. . . . . . . 189 THE GRINDSTONE . . .   8
    THE SAME PAUL AT THE SAME OLD FEATS OF LOGGING. . . . 192 PAUL'S WIFE 30
    THEN THAT SAME SMARTY SOMEONE SAID TO LOOK-- . . . . 209 PAUPER WITCH OF GRAFTON 59
    ALWAYS THE SAME, WHEN ON A FATED NIGHT . . . . 226 THE ONSET   1
    NOT THE SAME DOE COME BACK INTO HER PLACE. . . . . . 229 TWO LOOK AT TWO . . 30
    CAN CURE ME OF TO GO AGAIN." THE SAME . . . . 230 NOT TO KEEP 17
    IS WATER WOOD TO SERVE A BROOK THE SAME? . . . . . . 231 A BROOK IN THE CITY . 12
    TO SUFFER THE SAME DRIVEN NIGHTMARE OVER. . . . . . . 240 OUR SINGING STRENGTH . 45
    (NO GIRL'S, OF COURSE, HAS STAYED THE SAME.) . . . . 265 THE BIRTHPLACE . . . 12
    AND NO TWO WERE OF THE SAME CONSTELLATION-- . . . . . 295 LOST IN HEAVEN . .   6
    WE ARE ROUND FROM THE SAME SOURCE OF ROUNDNESS. . . . 322 BUILD SOIL 200
    NEVER AGAIN WOULD BIRDS' SONG BE THE SAME . . . . . . 338 NEVER WOULD BIRDS' SONG T
    NEVER AGAIN WOULD BIRDS' SONG BE THE SAME. . . . . . 339 NEVER WOULD BIRDS' SONG 13
    BUT TREE BY CHARITY IS NOT THE SAME . . . . 350 TO A YOUNG WRETCH . 10
    YES, YES, OF COURSE. WE HAVE THE SAME CONVENTION. . . . 352 THE LESSON FOR TODAY . 57
    WHICH COMES TO THE SAME THING IN DIFFERENT TERMS. . . . 353 THE LESSON FOR TODAY . 76
    TAKE COMFORT IN ABOUT THE SAME COMPLAINT. . . . . . . 353 THE LESSON FOR TODAY . 82

PAGE TITLE   LINE

SAME (CONTINUED)
    THE SAME FOR READING AS IT WAS FOR THOUGHT, ... 356 TIME OUT 9
    IS THAT IT BRINGS THE SAME CLASS UP ON TOP. . . . . . 363 A SEMI-REVOLUTION . . 4
    AND NATURE TOO, BUT THIS IS NOT THE SAME. . . . . . 369 THE LITERATE FARMER AND 30
    THE SAME SIGN HEAVEN SHOWED OUR GUEST. . . . . . . 381 AN UNSTAMPED LETTER IN 42
    THE WAY TO GO AWAY SHOULD BE THE SAME. . . . . . . 395 WHY WAIT FOR SCIENCE . 11
    ISN'T IT PRETTY MUCH THE SAME IDEA? . . . . 405 FROM PLANE TO PLANE . 44
    THE SAME AS YOUR IDEA, ONLY MORE SO. . . . . 406 FROM PLANE TO PLANE . 81
    "IT ISN'T JUST THE SAME, AND SOME DAY, SCHOOLBOY, . . . 406 FROM PLANE TO PLANE . 85
    FROM THE SAME GENERAL RESORT, ... 417 AMERICA IS HARD TO SEE 22
    I BROKE OFF BAFFLED. BUT ALL THE SAME, ... 420 ONE MORE BREVITY . . 38
    THAT BRAINS AND SWEETBREADS WERE THE SAME, ... 467 QUANDARY 21
    WHICH IS THE SAME AS SAYING JONAH, JONAH-- . . . . . 495 A MASQUE OF MERCY . . 56
    ALWAYS THE SAME WHEN I SET OUT IN FLIGHT. . . . . . 500 A MASQUE OF MERCY . 179
    RIGHT BACK IN THE SAME TROUBLE I WAS IN. . . . . . 500 A MASQUE OF MERCY . 185
    WHAT DO YOU MAKE OF IT? / THE SAME OLD NOTHING. . . . 512 A MASQUE OF MERCY . 492
    THE SAME WITH GOD AS LOSING, HOW EXPLAIN . . . . . . 517 A MASQUE OF MERCY . 634
SAMENESS
    IT WAS FAR IN THE SAMENESS OF THE WOOD; . . . . . . 24 THE DEMIURGE'S LAUGH . 1
SAMOA
    SAMOA, RUSSIA, IRELAND I COMPLAIN OF, ... 166 NEW HAMPSHIRE . . 244
SAMUEL
    I NOTICED WHEN SHE CALLED UP SAMUEL . . . . . . 477 A MASQUE OF REASON . 99
SAN
    IN DEALING IN "OLD RAGS" IN SAN FRANCISCO. . . . . . 160 NEW HAMPSHIRE . . . 58
SANCTIFY
    TO SANCTIFY TO WHAT FAR ENDS HE WILL, ... 12 A PRAYER IN SPRING . . 15
SANCTIMONIOUS
    SOME OF THE SANCTIMONIOUS CONCEIT . . . . 146 SNOW 91
SANCTUARY
    WAS THAT TRAMP TAKING SANCTUARY THERE . . . . . . 289 OLD BARN AT THE BOTTOM 14
    THIS IS A BOOKSTORE--NOT A SANCTUARY. . . . . . . 494 A MASQUE OF MERCY . 24
SAND
    OR HIGHWAY WHERE THE SLOW WHEEL POURS THE SAND. . . . 5 INTO MY OWN . . . 8
    RIDGES OF SAND, AND DRIFTWOOD STRIPPED OF BARK. . . . 40 THE MOUNTAIN . . 14
    SAND DUNES HELD LOOSELY IN TAMARISK . . . . . . 58 THE BLACK COTTAGE . 120
    SAND GRAINS SHOULD SUGAR IN THE NATAL DEW . . . . . 58 THE BLACK COTTAGE . 122
    ON SNOW AND SAND AND TURF, I SEE . . . . 120 BOND AND FREE . . 6
    IN GRASS AND SAND, ... 227 TO EARTHWARD . . 28
    NOT LUPINE LIVING ON SAND AND DROUTH. . . . . . 248 A PASSING GLIMPSE . 8
    AND BURY IN SOLID SAND . . . . 260 SAND DUNES . . 7
    SAND DUNES . . . . 260 SAND DUNES . . T
    HE FOUND SUSPICIOUS SAND, AND SURE ENOUGH, ... 270 THE EGG AND THE MACHINE 22
    ALL PACKED IN SAND TO WAIT THE TRUMP TOGETHER. . . . 270 THE EGG AND THE MACHINE 26
    THE PEOPLE ALONG THE SAND . . . . 301 NEITHER OUT FAR NOR IN 1
    HIS CHEEK SMEARED WITH APPLE SAND, ... 366 NOT OF SCHOOL AGE . . 9
    SAND HAS BEEN THRUSTING IN THE SQUARE OF DOOR . . . 399 THE INGENUITIES OF DEBT 13
    ONLY OF SAND, NOT WATER, RUNS THROUGH HERE. . . . 489 A MASQUE OF REASON . 443
SANDBANK
    THEN ONCE AGAIN THE SANDBANK LAY SERENE. . . . . . 270 THE EGG AND THE MACHINE 16
SANDBURG
    A SANDBURG. BUT PERMIT ME IN CONCLUSION: . . . . . 461 HOW HARD TO KEEP FROM 226
SANDERS
    NAMED SANDERS, WITH A GANG OF FOUR OR FIVE . . . . 70 THE CODE 31
    I BUILT THE LOAD AND TOPPED IT OFF; OLD SANDERS . . . 71 THE CODE 51
SANDS
    NOT ONLY SANDS AND GRAVELS . . . . 376 ONE STEP BACKWARD TAKEN 1
    OFF THESE SANDS OF TIME . . . . 429 KITTY HAWK 47
SANDSTORM
    THE BABE BORN TO THE DESERT, THE SANDSTORM . . . . 58 THE BLACK COTTAGE . 123
SANDY
    AND WITH THE SWIFT RUSH OF ITS SANDY DREGS . . . . 391 ON BEING IDOLIZED . . 3
    THERE SANDY SEEMS THE GOLDEN SKY . . . . 392 A CLIFF DWELLING . . 1
    AND GOLDEN SEEMS THE SANDY PLAIN. . . . . . . 392 A CLIFF DWELLING . . 2
SANE
    FOR THE SHOCKS AND CHANGES WE NEED TO KEEP US SANE. . . 268 ON LOOKING UP BY CHANCE 10
    AND THEN NEXT DAY AS I COME BACK INTO THE SANE, . . . 287 A ROADSIDE STAND . . 49
    AND CALM YOURSELF. BE SANE! I HEREBY HOLD . . . . . 501 A MASQUE OF MERCY . 192
SANG
    SANG HALFWAY THROUGH ITS LITTLE INBORN TUNE. . . . . 302 A BIRD SINGING IN SLEEP 2
    PARTLY BECAUSE IT SANG BUT ONCE ALL NIGHT . . . . . 302 A BIRD SINGING IN SLEEP 3
    PARTLY BECAUSE IT SANG VENTRILOQUIST . . . . . . 302 A BIRD SINGING IN SLEEP 5
    I SANG OF DEATH--BUT HAD I KNOWN . . . . 336 THE WIND AND THE RAIN . 9
    AS KEATS (OR WAS IT MILTON?) SANG . . . . 452 A-WISHING WELL . . . 41
SANK
    SHE TURNED AND SANK UPON HER SKIRTS AT THAT, ... 51 HOME BURIAL 8
    THEN SANK OUT OF SIGHT LIKE TROLLS UNDERGROUND, . . . 62 BLUEBERRIES . . . 86
    GRIM SILENCE ON MY PART AS I SANK LOWER, ... 198 WILD GRAPES 79
    SO EDEN SANK TO GRIEF, ... 222 NOTHING GOLD CAN STAY . 6
SANTA
    "THAT'S WHERE I RECKON SANTA CLAUS COMES IN-- . . . . 408 FROM PLANE TO PLANE . 137
    A SANTA CLAUS WAS NEEDED. AND THERE IS ONE." . . . . 408 FROM PLANE TO PLANE . 146
SAP (SEE METAL-SAP)
    AND STIFLING HOT WITH THE ODOR OF SAP . . . . . . 123 PEA BRUSH 7
    YOKEFELLOWS IN THE SAP YOKE FROM OF OLD . . . . . 164 NEW HAMPSHIRE . . 177
    OF SAP AND SNOW ROLLED OFF THE SUGARHOUSE. . . . . 194 MAPLE 138
SAPE
    YOU POOR OLD SAPE, IF I MAY COIN THE SLANG. . . . . 518 A MASQUE OF MERCY . 664
SAPIENT
    DIE SAYING THAT, OLD-FASHIONED SAPIENT, ... 518 A MASQUE OF MERCY . 663
SAPPHIRE
    (THE DEVIL ENTERS LIKE A SAPPHIRE WASP . . . . . 487 A MASQUE OF REASON . 389
SARCASTIC
    SARCASTIC SCIENCE, SHE WOULD LIKE TO KNOW, ... 395 WHY WAIT FOR SCIENCE . 1
SASH
    HE GAVE THE SASH A SHAKE, ... 11 WIND AND WINDOW FLOWER 18
    ASK HELEN HOW FAR UP THE SASH IT'S CLIMBED . . . . 148 SNOW 158
    MY SASH IS LOWERED WHEN NIGHT COMES ON; . . . . . 251 TREE AT MY WINDOW . . 2

SAT
    THEREAFTER I SAT ME AGAINST A TREE. . . . . 25 THE DEMIURGE'S LAUGH . 18
    MARY SAT MUSING ON THE LAMP-FLAME AT THE TABLE, . . 34 DEATH OF THE HIRED MAN   1
    HE SAT THERE CREASED AND SHINING IN THE LIGHT, . . 46 A HUNDRED COLLARS . . 51
    HE SAT AND FIXED HIS CHIN BETWEEN HIS FISTS. . . . 52 HOME BURIAL 41
    AS I SAT MOPPING HAYSEED FROM MY NECK, ... 72 THE CODE 81
    THIS HE SAT LISTENING TO TILL SHE GAVE JUDGMENT. . 76 THE GENERATIONS OF MEN   77
    HE SAT AND WAITED TILL HE DREW US OUT. . . . . . . 106 CHRISTMAS TREES . . 7
    WHERE NOW HE SAT, CONCERNED WITH HE KNEW WHAT, . . 108 OLD MAN'S WINTER NIGHT   16
    SOME FLOWER I PLAYED WITH AS I SAT . . . . 135 LOCKED OUT 12
    OF COURSE SHE HASN'T, THOUGH." THEY BOTH SAT DOWN . 155 SNOW 324
    THEY SAT TOGETHER HALFWAY UP A CLIFF . . . . 195 PAUL'S WIFE 133
    THEY SAT. SHE CAST ONE DULL, OLD LOOK AT HIM, . . . 201 PLACE FOR A THIRD . . 52
    I SAT UP ON THE FLOOR AND SHOUTED, "TOFFILE, . . . 205 THE WITCH OF COOS . 82
    (WHO SAT FOR STUART'S PORTRAIT, BUT WHO SAT . . . . 317 BUILD SOIL 46
    BUT LEAVING NOT THE CHAIR I LONG HAVE SAT IN . . . 350 THE LESSON FOR TODAY . 5
    BEFORE THEY SAT DOWN WEARY ON A BANK . . . . 454 HOW HARD TO KEEP FROM   13
    THE KING SAT FAVORING ONE PEARL FOR ITS BIGNESS, . 455 HOW HARD TO KEEP FROM   69
SATAN
    SOME STILL THINK IS SATAN, ... 443 KITTY HAWK 464
    SATAN, WHAT AILS YOU? WHERE'S THE FAMOUS TONGUE, . 488 A MASQUE OF REASON . .405
SATCHEL
    THE LAWYER WAS ALREADY IN HIS SATCHEL . . . . . . 96 THE SELF-SEEKER . . . 97
SATED
    SHE WHETS A SLEEPY SATED BILL. . . . . 281 BLUE RIBBON AT AMESBURY 40
SATELLITE
    GIVE EARTH ANOTHER SATELLITE. . . . . 451 A-WISHING WELL . . . 29
SATIN
    LIKE A WHITE PIECE OF RIGID SATIN CLOTH-- . . . . 302 DESIGN 3
SATISFACTION
    FOR NOTHING BUT ITS OWN BLIND SATISFACTION . . . . 319 BUILD SOIL 104
    I FAIL TO SEE WHAT FUN, WHAT SATISFACTION . . . . 483 A MASQUE OF REASON . .273
SATISFIED
    YOU'D THINK HIS MEMORY MIGHT BE SATISFIED----" . . 53 HOME BURIAL 66
    AT THE ISLES OF SHOALS, AND SATISFIED HIMSELF . . 161 NEW HAMPSHIRE . . . 76
    BE SATISFIED IF HE'D BE SATISFIED. . . . . 191 THE GRINDSTONE . . . 77
    I WAS SOON SATISFIED FOR THE TIME BEING. . . . . 217 A FOUNTAIN, A BOTTLE .131
    MALICIOUSLY SATISFIED. . . . . 312 THE VINDICTIVES . . . 55
    THE SUN IS SATISFIED WITH DAYS. . . . . 390 TWO LEADING LIGHTS . 4
    HOPE YOU'RE SATISFIED TO LAST. . . . . 469 FOUR-ROOM SHACK... . 7
    YES, YES. / YOU DON'T SEEM SATISFIED. / I AM. . . 486 A MASQUE OF REASON . .375
SATISFY
    WHAT'S THE REAL TROUBLE? WHAT WILL SATISFY HER?" . 87 THE HOUSEKEEPER . . .166
    TO SATISFY A LIFELONG CURIOSITY . . . . 168 NEW HAMPSHIRE . . .304
    TO SATISFY A LIFELONG CURIOSITY . . . . 177 THE STAR-SPLITTER . . 18
    COME, AFTER ALL THESE YEARS--TO SATISFY ME. . . . 482 A MASQUE OF REASON . .254
SATRAP
    MY SATRAP TISSAPHERNES HAS NO END . . . . 459 HOW HARD TO KEEP FROM   166
SATURATED
    A SATURATED MEADOW, ... 13 ROSE POGONIAS . . . 1
    IN WHICH WE TWO STOOD SATURATED, DROWNED. . . . . 315 IRIS BY NIGHT . . . 12
    AND STILL THE AIR WAS SATURATED TOO, ... 315 IRIS BY NIGHT . . . 15
SATURDAY
    HE DOTES ON SATURDAY PORK AND BEANS. . . . . . . 393 A CASE FOR JEFFERSON . 7
SATURN
    SATURN AND MARS . . . . 219 I WILL SING YOU ONE-O . 41
SAVAGE
    IN EACH HAND, LIKE AN OLD-STONE SAVAGE ARMED. . . 34 MENDING WALL 40
    YES. THANKS FOR CARING.--DON'T MIND WILL: HE'S SAVAGE. . 100 THE SELF-SEEKER . .224
    SHE WAS A SAVAGE JUNGLE CAT . . . . 345 DISCOVERY OF MADEIRAS . 64
SAVANTS
    THOUGH SOME SAVANTS MAKE EARTH INCLUDE THE SKY; . 220 FRAGMENTARY BLUE . . 6
SAVE
    AND SAVE OURSELVES UNAIDED. . . . . 10 STORM FEAR 18
    TO THIS LEAN FEEDING, SAVE ONCE A YEAR . . . . . 24 PAN WITH US 12
    SAVE ONLY ME . . . . 28 MY BUTTERFLY 4
    SAVE ONLY ME . . . . 28 MY BUTTERFLY 6
    SAVE THOSE THAT THE OAK IS KEEPING . . . . 30 RELUCTANCE 8
    SOME HUMBLE WAY TO SAVE HIS SELF-RESPECT. . . . . 36 DEATH OF THE HIRED MAN   50
    THE HARD SNOW HELD ME, SAVE WHERE NOW AND THEN . 101 THE WOOD-PILE . . . 4
    AND SAVE HIS LIFE.--ALL RIGHT, COME IN, MESERVE. 147 SNOW 104
    "SAVE US FROM BEING CORNERED BY A WOMAN. . . . . 151 SNOW 236
    AND NEVER OVERSTEPPED IT SAVE IN DREAMS. . . . . 171 NEW HAMPSHIRE . . .380
    WE MAY AS WELL SEE THAT AND SAVE THE DAY." . . . 214 A FOUNTAIN, A BOTTLE . 54
    AND SAVE FOR THE WONDER . . . . 219 I WILL SING YOU ONE-O . 69
    SAVE BY SOME STRANGE RESISTANCE IN ITSELF; . . . 259 WEST-RUNNING BROOK . 58
    I REACHED OUT BLINDLY TO SAVE MY FACE, ... 265 THE DOOR IN THE DARK . 2
    TO SAVE HIM THE EXPENSE OF DOING. . . . . 274 A LONE STRIKER . . . 48
    CONSERVATIVES, THEY DON'T KNOW WHAT TO SAVE. . . 290 OLD BARN AT THE BOTTOM   32
    FOR A HAT I HAD TO SAVE. . . . . 294 A RECORD STRIDE . . 14
    A COWARD SAVE AT NIGHT, ... 341 THE SUBVERTED FLOWER . 60
    EARTH'S A HARD PLACE IN WHICH TO SAVE THE SOUL, . 353 THE LESSON FOR TODAY . 98
    I CANNOT TOUCH YOUR LIFE, MUCH LESS CAN SAVE, . . 357 A MOTH SEEN IN WINTER . 23
    WHO AM TASKED TO SAVE MY OWN A LITTLE WHILE. . . 357 A MOTH SEEN IN WINTER . 24
    COULD SAVE IT FROM ITS LOSSES BEING MET. . . . . 399 THE INGENUITIES OF DEBT 12
    TO SAVE THE QUEEN FROM FAMILY CENSURE. . . . . . 416 AMERICA IS HARD TO SEE 11
    AND SAVE HERSELF FROM BREAKING WINDOW GLASS. . . 445 QUESTIONING FACES . . 2
    AN EASIER PLACE FOR MAN TO SAVE HIS SOUL IN. . . 484 A MASQUE OF REASON . .317
    EXCEPT AS A HARD PLACE TO SAVE HIS SOUL IN, . . . 484 A MASQUE OF REASON . .318
    WHY IS GOD AFTER YOU?--TO SAVE YOUR SOUL? . . . . 494 A MASQUE OF REASON . . 40
    TO BASE HIS CAMPAIGN ON TO SAVE THE WORLD. . . . 514 A MASQUE OF MERCY . .561
    THERE'S NO ONE DOWN THERE GETTING TORTURED, SAVE . 516 A MASQUE OF MERCY . .609
    SAVE THEM TO SAY YOUR PRAYERS ON.--WHAT'S THE MATTER? . 519 A MASQUE OF MERCY . .682
SAVED (SEE LONGEST-SAVED-UP)
    THAT A BOY COUNTS SO MUCH WHEN SAVED FROM WORK. . 136 "OUT,OUT--" 12
    (BUT SAVED THE LIGHT FROM GOING OUT). . . . . . 138 BROWN'S DESCENT . . 39
    AND SAVED SOME PART . . . . 221 DUST OF SNOW 7
    SO AUTOMATICALLY WE ALL WERE SAVED, ... 353 THE LESSON FOR TODAY . 100

SAVED (CONTINUED)
    I SAVED MYSELF FROM GOING. . . . . 377 ONE STEP BACKWARD TAKEN   11
    SO CAN'T GET SAVED, AS SAINT MARK SAYS THEY MUSTN'T. . . 379 DIRECTIVE   59
    THEY SAVED THEMSELVES BY HANGING ON . . . . 452 A-WISHING WELL . . .   48
    WE'RE SAVED, WE'RE SAVED, WHATEVER ELSE IT MEANS. . . 476 A MASQUE OF REASON . .   82
SAVING
    AND SAVING THAT ITS WEIGHT SUGGESTED GOLD . . . . . 172 A STAR IN A STONEBOAT .   5
    AND WHAT A SAVING 'TWOULD HAVE MEANT TO ME. . . . . 350 TO A YOUNG WRETCH . .   9
    OF SAVING AND OF KEEPING, ... 359 NOVEMBER   10
    SUBTERFUGE FOR SAVING FACES, ... 396 AN IMPORTER   7
    IN SAVING HERETICS BY SLAYING THEM, ... 515 A MASQUE OF MERCY . . 572
SAVOR
    TILL YOU HAVE LOST THE SAVOR OF YOUR SALT. . . . . . 446 DOES NO ONE AT ALL EVER 24
SAW
    YET SAW BUT HER WITHIN, ...   8 LOVE AND A QUESTION .   22
    NOT FAR, BUT NEAR, I STOOD AND SAW IT ALL, ... 16 A DREAM PANG   9
    AND TELL YOU THAT I SAW DOES STILL ABIDE. . . . . . 16 A DREAM PANG   12
    HE SAW NO SMOKE AND HE SAW NO ROOF. . . . . 24 PAN WITH US   9
    SINCE FIRST I SAW THEE GLANCE, ... 28 MY BUTTERFLY   12
    ITS LIGHT POURED SOFTLY IN HER LAP. SHE SAW IT . . . 38 DEATH OF THE HIRED MAN 105
    I SAW SO MUCH BEFORE I SLEPT THERE ONCE: . . . . . 40 THE MOUNTAIN   2
    CLEAR TO THE TOP." I SAW THROUGH LEAFY SCREENS . . . 42 THE MOUNTAIN   57
    YOU NEVER SAW IT?" / "I GUESS THERE'S NO DOUBT . . . 42 THE MOUNTAIN   66
    ABOUT ITS BEING THERE. I NEVER SAW IT. . . . . . . 42 THE MOUNTAIN   67
    HE SAW HER FROM THE BOTTOM OF THE STAIRS. . . . . . 51 HOME BURIAL   1
    BEFORE SHE SAW HIM. SHE WAS STARTING DOWN, ... 51 HOME BURIAL   2
    I SAW YOU FROM THAT VERY WINDOW THERE, ... 53 HOME BURIAL   74
    OUTSIDE THERE IN THE ENTRY, FOR I SAW IT." . . . . 54 HOME BURIAL   88
    "YOU OUGHT TO HAVE SEEN WHAT I SAW ON MY WAY . . . . 59 BLUEBERRIES   1
    "HE SAW YOU, THEN? WHAT DID HE DO? DID HE FROWN?" . . 60 BLUEBERRIES   40
    AND SAW NOTHING MORE OF EACH OTHER, OR HEARD, . . . 62 BLUEBERRIES   87
    THEY SOON SAW HE WOULD DO SOMEONE A MISCHIEF . . . 66 A SERVANT TO SERVANTS . 111
    HE WAS BEFORE MY TIME--I NEVER SAW HIM; . . . . . 67 A SERVANT TO SERVANTS . 140
    THAT WAS THE LAST I SAW OR HEARD OF HIM. . . . . . 72 THE CODE   79
    WE TENDED TO HIS HAY. WE SAW HIM OUT . . . . . . 73 THE CODE 107
    YOU NEVER SAW BEFORE. WHAT WILL WE COME TO . . . . 76 THE GENERATIONS OF MEN   86
    I NEVER SAW A MAN LET FAMILY TROUBLES . . . . . . 83 THE HOUSEKEEPER . .   53
    SOMETHING WENT WRONG. I SAW HIM THROW THE HOE . . . 83 THE HOUSEKEEPER . .   60
    YOU NEVER SAW THIS ROOM BEFORE A SHOW, ... 85 THE HOUSEKEEPER . . 119
    I SAW IT JUST AS PLAIN AS A WHITE PLATE," . . . . . 89 THE FEAR   9
    I SAW BY THE WAY YOU WHIPPED UP THE HORSE. . . . . 91 THE FEAR   73
    WHEN I SAW THE SHAFT HAD ME BY THE COAT, ... 93 THE SELF-SEEKER . .   23
    YOU CAN HEAR THE SMALL BUZZ SAWS WHINE, THE BIG SAW . 94 THE SELF-SEEKER . .   41
    THE BROKEN ONE SAW ANNE. "WHY, HERE IS ANNE. . . . 96 THE SELF-SEEKER . . 103
    AND SAW MYSELF--HE WOULD BE ILL-ADVISED----" . . . . 100 THE SELF-SEEKER . . 205
    I SAW NO WINDOW BUT THAT WAS BLACK. . . . . 102 GOOD HOURS   12
    SO WHEN I SAW YOU DOWN ON HANDS AND KNEES . . . . 109 THE EXPOSED NEST . .   2
    WE SAW THE RISK WE TOOK IN DOING GOOD, ... 109 THE EXPOSED NEST . .   27
    HE SAW HIMSELF A FARMER. THEN THERE WAS A FRENCH BOY . . 114 IN THE HOME STRETCH . 103
    AND HAD JUST TURNED FROM WHEN I FIRST SAW YOU . . . 118 MEETING AND PASSING .   3
    I SAW THE STRANGE POSITION OF HIS HANDS-- . . . . 125 AN ENCOUNTER . . .   16
    IT BLOW BUT THAT YOU SAW THE TREES IN MOTION.) . . . 130 THE BONFIRE   43
    THE BUZZ SAW SNARLED AND RATTLED IN THE YARD . . . 136 "OUT,OUT--"   1
    AND THE SAW SNARLED AND RATTLED, SNARLED AND RATTLED, . 136 "OUT,OUT--"   7
    TO TELL THEM "SUPPER." AT THE WORD, THE SAW, . . . 136 "OUT,OUT--"   14
    THE LIFE FROM SPILLING. THEN THE BOY SAW ALL-- . . 137 "OUT,OUT--"   22
    HE SAW ALL SPOILED. "DON'T LET HIM CUT MY HAND OFF-- . 137 "OUT,OUT--"   25
    HE SAW NO STAY UNLESS HE STOVE . . . . 137 BROWN'S DESCENT . .   14
    AND SOME EXCLAIMED WHO SAW AFAR . . . . 138 BROWN'S DESCENT . .   30
    YOU CAN'T GET BACK AND SEE IT AS HE SAW IT. . . . . 142 THE VANISHING RED .   9
    WE SAW HIM SAY ALONG THE ZIGZAG JOURNEY . . . . . 170 NEW HAMPSHIRE . . . 351
    I SAW NO MEN THERE AND NO BONES OF MEN THERE. . . . 175 THE CENSUS-TAKER . .   42
    YOUR MOTHER NAMED YOU. YOU AND SHE JUST SAW. . . . 180 MAPLE   10
    ABOUT THE WAY HE SAW IT WAS WITH YOU . . . . 183 MAPLE 128
    AND, AS YOU MIGHT SAY, SAW THE LADY BORN. . . . . 193 PAUL'S WIFE   56
    TO SLAM END-ON AGAIN AGAINST THE SAW TEETH. . . . . 193 PAUL'S WIFE   64
    WHEN THEY SAW WHAT HAD HAPPENED TO THE LOG, ... 193 PAUL'S WIFE   66
    "FIRST TIME I EVER SAW A HOLLOW PINE. . . . . . . 193 PAUL'S WIFE   75
    THEY SAW PAUL AND HIS CREATURE KEEPING HOUSE. . . . 195 PAUL'S WIFE 128
    HAS HAD OF PAUL AND HER SINCE MURPHY SAW THEM . . . 195 PAUL'S WIFE 130
    SO LABAN SAW THE SISTER, AND, SAYING NOTHING . . . 200 PLACE FOR A THIRD .   44
    SO WHEN SHE SAW HIM COMING IN THE STREET . . . . . 201 PLACE FOR A THIRD .   70
    THE MOUNTAIN MAY HAVE SHIFTED SINCE I SAW IT . . . 213 A FOUNTAIN, A BOTTLE .   22
    I NEVER SAW SO GOOD A HOUSE DESERTED. . . . . . . 215 A FOUNTAIN, A BOTTLE .   71
    AND WE SAW HIM, OR THOUGHT WE SAW HIM, DIM AND GRAY, . 223 THE RUNAWAY . . .   7
    SHE SAW THEM IN THEIR FIELD, THEY HER IN HERS. . . 229 TWO LOOK AT TWO . .   17
    WAS IN HER CLOUDED EYES: THEY SAW NO FEAR THERE. . . 229 TWO LOOK AT TWO . .   20
    I THOUGHT I SAW A BIRD ALIGHT. . . . . 232 LOOKING FOR SUNSET BIRD   4
    AND YET HE THOUGHT HE SAW THE SCENE: . . . . . . 273 A LONE STRIKER . .   17
    THE SPINNER SAW IT AT A GLANCE. . . . . 273 A LONE STRIKER . .   25
    HE SAW IT PLAINLY WHERE HE STOOD, ... 274 A LONE STRIKER . .   34
    AND SAW THEM PICKED UNBRUISED AND IN A DISH, . . . 284 THE GOLD HESPERIDEE .   36
    THEN SUDDENLY HE SAW THE THING HE DID, ... 284 THE GOLD HESPERIDEE .   49
    GOD SAW HIM DANCING IN THE ORCHARD PATH, ... 284 THE GOLD HESPERIDEE .   55
    SOMETHING I SAW OR THOUGHT I SAW . . . . 290 ON HEART'S BEGINNING TO   1
    THIS I SAW WHEN WAKING LATE, ... 292 ON HEART'S BEGINNING TO 42
    I SAW MY SHADOW ON SNOW. . . . . 303 AFTERFLAKES   2
    AGE SAW TWO QUIET CHILDREN . . . . 335 CARPE DIEM   1
    SHE LOOKED AND SAW THE SHAME: . . . . 340 THE SUBVERTED FLOWER .   41
    AN ARM WORKED LIKE A SAW. . . . . 340 THE SUBVERTED FLOWER .   43
    SHE LOOKED AND SAW THE WORST. . . . . 341 THE SUBVERTED FLOWER .   57
    BUT I SAW NO SIGN. . . . . 342 QUEST OF PURPLE-FRINGED   8
    TILL I SAW WHERE THE PATH THE SLENDER FOX HAD COME . 342 QUEST OF PURPLE-FRINGED 11
    HER LOVER SAW THEM SAIL AWAY, ... 347 DISCOVERY OF MADEIRAS . 114
    WE SAW LEAVES GO TO GLORY, ... 359 NOVEMBER   1
    I NEVER SAW SO MUCH SWIFT WATER RUN CLOUDLESS. . . . 379 TOO ANXIOUS FOR RIVERS   5
    ALL I SAW WAS THE LID. . . . . 392 A WISH TO COMPLY . .   10
    ALL I SAW WAS A WINK. . . . . 392 A WISH TO COMPLY . .   13

SAW (CONTINUED)
    THEN I SAW IT ALL. . . . . 434 KITTY HAWK 212
    ANYTHING WE SAW . . . . 438 KITTY HAWK 327
    THAT NOBODY SAW . . . . 449 THE BAD ISLAND--EASTER 52
    YES, BOTH OF US: WE SAW TO THAT AT ONCE. . . . . 479 A MASQUE OF REASON . 162
    I SAW YOU HAD NO FONDNESS FOR COMMITTEES. . . . . 486 A MASQUE OF REASON . 369
    I SAW A BOXFUL IN THE CHRISTMAS MARKET. . . . . . 488 A MASQUE OF REASON . 422
SAWDUST
    THE CELLAR WINDOWS WERE BANKED UP WITH SAWDUST . . . . 204 THE WITCH OF COOS . . 57
SAWED
    WELL, THIS IS SUCH A YARN. PAUL SAWED HIS WIFE . . . 192 PAUL'S WIFE 54
SAWING
    THE LOG WAS HOLLOW. THEY WERE SAWING PINE. . . . . 193 PAUL'S WIFE 74
SAWS
    YOU CAN HEAR THE SMALL BUZZ SAWS WHINE, THE BIG SAW . . 94 THE SELF-SEEKER . . 41
    AS IF TO PROVE SAWS KNEW WHAT SUPPER MEANT, ... 136 "OUT,OUT--" 15
SAWYER
    FOR--I FORGET--THE LAST AMBITIOUS SAWYER . . . . . 193 PAUL'S WIFE 59
    AND THE SAWYER HAD SLAMMED THE CARRIAGE BACK . . . . 193 PAUL'S WIFE 63
    TAKE IT TO HELL FOR ME," THE SAWYER SAID. . . . . . 193 PAUL'S WIFE 77
SAY
    FULL MANY A TIME TO SAY HIS SAY . . . . 6 GHOST HOUSE 19
    BEFORE HE ARRIVES TO SAY IT OUT. . . . . 6 GHOST HOUSE 20
    AND THOUGHT OF NAUGHT TO SAY, ... 11 WIND AND WINDOW FLOWER 26
    AND OFTEN THEY BROUGHT SO MUCH TO SAY . . . . . . 15 IN A VALE 12
    YOU SHOOK YOUR PENSIVE HEAD AS WHO SHOULD SAY, . . . 16 A DREAM PANG 6
    (OR SO WE SAY) THAT IN THE END . . . . 19 REVELATION 6
    THE BIRDS HAVE LESS TO SAY FOR THEMSELVES . . . . . 26 A LINE-STORM SONG . . 9
    AND THE STRANGE BIRDS SAY. . . . . 29 MY BUTTERFLY 45
    THAT WANTS IT DOWN." I COULD SAY "ELVES" TO HIM, . . 34 MENDING WALL 36
    'ALL RIGHT,' I SAY, 'I CAN'T AFFORD TO PAY . . . . 35 DEATH OF THE HIRED MAN 22
    WAIT TILL YOU SEE." / "WHERE DID YOU SAY HE'D BEEN?" . 35 DEATH OF THE HIRED MAN 39
    "HE DIDN'T SAY. I DRAGGED HIM TO THE HOUSE, ... 35 DEATH OF THE HIRED MAN 40
    "WHAT DID HE SAY? DID HE SAY ANYTHING?" . . . . . 36 DEATH OF THE HIRED MAN 44
    "OF COURSE HE DID. WHAT WOULD YOU HAVE HIM SAY? . . 36 DEATH OF THE HIRED MAN 48
    TO THINK OF THE RIGHT THING TO SAY TOO LATE. . . . 37 DEATH OF THE HIRED MAN 77
    "I'D NOT BE IN A HURRY TO SAY THAT." . . . . . . 39 DEATH OF THE HIRED MAN 154
    THAT STARTS UP ON IT SOMEWHERE--I'VE HEARD SAY . . . 42 THE MOUNTAIN 46
    "AS TO THAT I CAN'T SAY. BUT THERE'S THE SPRING, . . 42 THE MOUNTAIN 63
    "WHAT DID HE SAY?" / "HE SAID THERE WAS A LAKE . . . 43 THE MOUNTAIN 75
    "WARM IN DECEMBER, COLD IN JUNE, YOU SAY?" . . . . 44 THE MOUNTAIN 100
    BUT ALL THE FUN'S IN HOW YOU SAY A THING." . . . . 44 THE MOUNTAIN 104
    "YOU SAY 'UNLESS.'" / "UNLESS YOU WOULDN'T MIND . . . 45 A HUNDRED COLLARS . . 23
    WHAT DO YOU SAY?" / "I'LL HAVE TO HAVE A BED." . . . 45 A HUNDRED COLLARS . . 32
    "OH--AH--FOURTEEN--FOURTEEN." / "FOURTEEN! YOU SAY SO! 46 A HUNDRED COLLARS . . 63
    "DON'T TOUCH ME, PLEASE--I SAY, DON'T TOUCH ME, PLEASE. 47 A HUNDRED COLLARS . . 77
    "JUST AS YOU SAY. HAVE IT YOUR OWN WAY, THEN. . . . 47 A HUNDRED COLLARS . . 79
    "YOU'D SAY SO, MISTER MAN.--I'M A COLLECTOR. . . . . 48 A HUNDRED COLLARS . . 95
    "IT'S BUSINESS, BUT I CAN'T SAY IT'S NOT FUN. . . . 49 A HUNDRED COLLARS . . 123
    "JUST AS YOU SAY. HERE'S LOOKING AT YOU, THEN.-- . . 50 A HUNDRED COLLARS . . 158
    I SHOULD SUPPOSE. I CAN'T SAY I SEE HOW.- . . . . 52 HOME BURIAL 48
    THEY SAY THEY MEAN TO COME AND SUMMER HERE . . . . 55 THE BLACK COTTAGE . . 17
    IT MAY NOT BE. I HEARD A FELLOW SAY SO. . . . . . 57 THE BLACK COTTAGE . . 67
    OR RATHER SAY NON-MEMBERS IN THE CHURCH, ... 57 THE BLACK COTTAGE . . 86
    HE HAS BROUGHT THEM ALL UP ON WILD BERRIES, THEY SAY, . 60 BLUEBERRIES 50
    "WHO CARES WHAT THEY SAY? IT'S A NICE WAY TO LIVE, . 61 BLUEBERRIES 54
    HE DIDN'T SAY WHERE THEY HAD BEEN. HE WENT ON: . . . 61 BLUEBERRIES 74
    LOWE IS THE ONLY DOCTOR'S DARED TO SAY SO-- . . . . 64 A SERVANT TO SERVANTS . 48
    NO MORE PUT OUT IN WHAT THEY DO OR SAY . . . . . . 65 A SERVANT TO SERVANTS . 79
    THE ONLY FUN HE HAD. I'VE HEARD THEM SAY, THOUGH, . . 66 A SERVANT TO SERVANTS . 138
    IT GOT SO I WOULD SAY--YOU KNOW, HALF FOOLING-- . . 67 A SERVANT TO SERVANTS . 145
    THE WOODCHUCK COULD SAY WHETHER IT'S LIKE HIS . . . 69 AFTER APPLE-PICKING . 40
    "WHAT DID I SAY?" / "ABOUT OUR TAKING PAINS." . . . 70 THE CODE 11
    'DID YOU SAY, "LET HER COME"?' 'YES, LET HER COME.' . 71 THE CODE 66
    NEVER YOU SAY A THING LIKE THAT TO A MAN, ... 71 THE CODE 66
    "NO! AND YET I DON'T KNOW--IT'S HARD TO SAY. . . . 73 THE CODE 111
    BUT I OWN WHAT YOU SAY MAKES MY HEAD SPIN. . . . . 75 THE GENERATIONS OF MEN 60
    I'LL TELL YOU WHAT THE VOICES REALLY SAY. . . . . 78 THE GENERATIONS OF MEN 144
    "I'LL HARDLY BREATHE." / "THE VOICES SEEM TO SAY----" 78 THE GENERATIONS OF MEN 150
    "I'M WAITING." / "DON'T! THE VOICES SEEM TO SAY: . . 78 THE GENERATIONS OF MEN 151
    "I LET YOU SAY THAT--ON CONSIDERATION." . . . . . 79 THE GENERATIONS OF MEN 154
    "I SHALL SUSPECT----" / "BE GOOD. THE VOICES SAY: . . 79 THE GENERATIONS OF MEN 159
    ANYTHING SHE MAY SAY. BUT LET ME WARN YOU, ... 79 THE GENERATIONS OF MEN 180
    I LET YOU SAY ALL THAT. BUT I MUST GO NOW." . . . . 80 THE GENERATIONS OF MEN 202
    "YOU LET ME SAY IT? ON CONSIDERATION? . . . . . . 80 THE GENERATIONS OF MEN 203
    HOW SHALL WE SAY GOOD-BY IN SUCH A CASE?" . . . . . 80 THE GENERATIONS OF MEN 204
    HE THINKS I ONLY HAVE TO SAY THE WORD, ... 82 THE HOUSEKEEPER . . 25
    I'LL SAY THAT FOR HIM, JOHN'S NO THREATENER . . . . 83 THE HOUSEKEEPER . . 68
    COULDN'T ONE TALK TO HER? WHAT DOES SHE SAY? . . . 83 THE HOUSEKEEPER . . 72
    YOU SAY YOU DON'T KNOW WHERE SHE IS." / "NOR WANT TO! 83 THE HOUSEKEEPER . . 73
    HE'D SAY, WHY SHOULD THEY?--NO MORE WORDS THAN THAT." 84 THE HOUSEKEEPER . . 91
    HE'D SAY SHE DOES IT MORE BECAUSE SHE LIKES IT. . . 85 THE HOUSEKEEPER . . 109
    HE'S FOND OF NICE THINGS--TOO FOND, SOME WOULD SAY. . 85 THE HOUSEKEEPER . . 116
    NOTHING'S TOO GOOD FOR THEM. WE SAY IT PAYS. . . . 86 THE HOUSEKEEPER . . 137
    HE'S BEEN IN A GLASS CASE, AS YOU MAY SAY, ... 86 THE HOUSEKEEPER . . 150
    "IT'S AS I SAY: SHE'S TURNED FROM HIM, THAT'S ALL." . 87 THE HOUSEKEEPER . . 167
    SAY IT RIGHT OUT--NO MATTER FOR HER MOTHER. . . . . 88 THE HOUSEKEEPER . . 187
    DON'T HOLD MY ARM!" / "I SAY IT'S SOMEONE PASSING." . 90 THE FEAR 23
    THERE'S MORE IN IT THAN YOU'RE INCLINED TO SAY. . . 90 THE FEAR 30
    WE MUSTN'T SAY HARD THINGS. YOU MUSTN'T EITHER." . . 91 THE FEAR 53
    "NOTHING." A PAUSE: THERE SEEMED NO MORE TO SAY. . . 91 THE FEAR 71
    "THEY SAY SOME TIME WAS WASTED ON THE BELT-- . . . 94 THE SELF-SEEKER . . 32
    AS IF TO SAY, 'YOU! YOU'RE THE HEART'S DESIRE.' . . 98 THE SELF-SEEKER . . 158
    WHAT DO YOU SAY, WILL? DON'T YOU BE A FOOL, ... 99 THE SELF-SEEKER . . 195
    SO AS TO SAY FOR CERTAIN I WAS HERE . . . . 101 THE WOOD-PILE . . . 8
    AND SAY NO WORD TO TELL ME WHO HE WAS . . . . . . 101 THE WOOD-PILE . . . 12
    OR PAUSED TO SAY BENEATH SOME LOVELIER ONE, ... 107 CHRISTMAS TREES . . 37
    I THOUGHT SO TOO, BUT WASN'T THERE TO SAY SO. . . . 107 CHRISTMAS TREES . . 39

SAY (CONTINUED)
"SAY THAT TO JIMMY HERE. HE NEEDS A FARM." . . . . . 114 IN THE HOME STRETCH . 100
FOOL-LIKE, AND ROLLED HIS EYES AS IF TO SAY . . . . . 114 IN THE HOME STRETCH . 102
ALL THEY COULD SAY WAS 'GOD!' WHEN YOU PROPOSED . . . . 114 IN THE HOME STRETCH . 120
DON'T MIND A WORD I SAY. IT'S A DAY'S WORK . . . . . 116 IN THE HOME STRETCH . 159
MUST GET SOMEWHERE. I'VE HEARD YOU SAY AS MUCH. . . . . 117 IN THE HOME STRETCH . 185
DON'T SAY I DIDN'T, FOR I HEARD YOU SAY-- . . . . . 118 THE TELEPHONE . . . 7
OR DID YOU SAY-- . . . . . 118 THE TELEPHONE . . . 16
YET SOME SAY LOVE BY BEING THRALL . . . . . 120 BOND AND FREE . . . 17
BUT I WAS GOING TO SAY WHEN TRUTH BROKE IN . . . . . 121 BIRCHES 21
TO SEEM TO SAY GOOD-BY; . . . . . 126 LONELINESS 4
WHAT WOULD YOU SAY TO WAR IF IT SHOULD COME? . . . . . 132 THE BONFIRE 97
SHOULD OUR STOCK WAS PETERED OUT, ... 139 BROWN'S DESCENT . . 51
NOT MUCH CONCERNED FOR THEM, I SAY; . . . . . 139 BROWN'S DESCENT . . 68
FOR HE TURNED SUDDENLY GRAVE AS IF TO SAY, ... 142 THE VANISHING RED . . 5
I CALLED YOU UP TO SAY GOOD-NIGHT FROM HERE . . . . . 143 SNOW 17
BEFORE I WENT TO SAY GOOD-MORNING THERE.-- . . . . . 143 SNOW 18
HE LINGERED FOR SOME WORD SHE WOULDN'T SAY, ... 143 SNOW 28
TO ANYTHING ANYONE ELSE MAY SAY. . . . . . 145 SNOW 66
"YOU ONLY SAY SO. NOT ANOTHER HOUSE . . . . . 145 SNOW 73
LET THE MAN FREEZE AN EAR OR TWO, I SAY. . . . . . 146 SNOW 102
"WON'T YOU TO PLEASE ME? PLEASE! IF I SAY PLEASE? . . . 147 SNOW 108
WHAT DID YOUR WIFE SAY ON THE TELEPHONE?" . . . . . 147 SNOW 110
A MANY TIMES--I DON'T SAY JUST HOW MANY-- . . . . . 147 SNOW 127
SO FALSE, THAT WHAT WE ALWAYS SAY IS TRUE. . . . . . 148 SNOW 150
BUT IF YOU'RE GOING--SAY YOU'LL STAY, YOU KNOW. . . . . 148 SNOW 154
THE WAYS YOU FOUND TO SAY THE PRAISE OF COMFORT . . . . 150 SNOW 199
ARE RESTED AND IT'S TIME TO SAY GOOD-NIGHT. . . . . 150 SNOW 210
OF WORDS, OR IS IT TONGUES I OUGHT TO SAY?" . . . . . 151 SNOW 249
MUCH SAY IN THE MATTER, AND I'M JUST AS GLAD . . . . . 152 SNOW 257
GET INTO BED I SAY, AND GET SOME REST. . . . . . 152 SNOW 265
"TRY SPEAKING. SAY 'HELLO!'" / "HELLO. HELLO." . . . . 153 SNOW 298
"WHAT DO YOU SAY IT IS?" / "A BABY'S CRYING! . . . . . 154 SNOW 318
WE'RE GLAD. OH, SAY NO MORE ABOUT IT, MAN. . . . . . 155 SNOW 332
I SHALL HAVE LESS TO SAY, ... 156 THE SOUND OF TREES . 24
THE HOPE OF BEING, AS WE SAY, RECEIVED. . . . . . 160 NEW HAMPSHIRE . . . 43
YOU'LL SAY SHE HAS, BUT THERE THERE ENTERS IN . . . . 163 NEW HAMPSHIRE . . . 146
ANYTHING I CAN SAY ABOUT NEW HAMPSHIRE . . . . . 165 NEW HAMPSHIRE . . . 210
AND HERE I AM AND WHAT AM I TO SAY? . . . . . 166 NEW HAMPSHIRE . . . 216
KIT MARLOWE TAUGHT ME HOW TO SAY MY PRAYERS: . . . . . 166 NEW HAMPSHIRE . . . 242
I DON'T KNOW WHAT TO SAY ABOUT THE PEOPLE. . . . . . 167 NEW HAMPSHIRE . . . 265
TO SAY SO OR BE STOOD AGAINST THE WALL . . . . . 168 NEW HAMPSHIRE . . . 281
OF ANYTHING MORE SOCIABLE TO SAY: . . . . . 168 NEW HAMPSHIRE . . . 292
TO SAY WHAT HEIGHT BECOMES NEW HAMPSHIRE MOUNTAINS, . . . 169 NEW HAMPSHIRE . . . 316
WE SAW HIM SAY ALONG THE ZIGZAG JOURNEY . . . . . 170 NEW HAMPSHIRE . . . 351
WERE DOUBTLESS AS THE WORDS WE HEARD HIM SAY . . . . . 170 NEW HAMPSHIRE . . . 352
EVEN TO SAY THE GROVES WERE GOD'S FIRST TEMPLES . . . . 171 NEW HAMPSHIRE . . . 392
WITH AN INCOME IN CASH OF, SAY, A THOUSAND . . . . . 172 NEW HAMPSHIRE . . . 409
(FROM, SAY, A PUBLISHER IN NEW YORK CITY). . . . . . 172 NEW HAMPSHIRE . . . 410
THOUGH NOT, I SAY, A STAR OF DEATH AND SIN, ... 174 A STAR IN A STONEBOAT . 49
LET HIM SAY WHY IT SHOULD NOT BE DECLARED SO." . . . . 176 THE CENSUS-TAKER . . 60
HE HAD BEEN HEARD TO SAY BY SEVERAL: . . . . . 177 THE STAR-SPLITTER . . 32
TO SAY YOUR MOTHER, HAD SHE LIVED, WOULD BE . . . . . 184 MAPLE 129
"JUST ONE LOOK MORE WITH WHAT YOU SAY IN MIND, ... 184 MAPLE 131
BETTER A MEANINGLESS NAME, I SHOULD SAY, ... 185 MAPLE 168
AND THAT WAS, AS I SAY, AN ALDER BRANCH. . . . . . 185 THE AX-HELVE . . . 5
HE HAD IN MIND TO SAY TO A BAD NEIGHBOR . . . . . 185 THE AX-HELVE . . . 16
HE MIGHT PREFER TO SAY TO HIM DISARMED. . . . . . 185 THE AX-HELVE . . . 17
"DEN WHEN YOU SAY YOU COME? IT'S COST YOU NOTHING. . . . 186 THE AX-HELVE . . . 33
FOR HIM TO HAVE THE SAY WHEN WE WERE DONE. . . . . . 190 THE GRINDSTONE . . . 49
ALL THAT WAS NEEDED WAS TO SAY TO HIM, ... 191 PAUL'S WIFE . . . 2
AS IF TO SAY, "THAT'S SO, HOW IS MY WIFE? . . . . . 191 PAUL'S WIFE . . . 14
A MAN YOU COULD SAY ALMOST ANYTHING TO . . . . . 192 PAUL'S WIFE . . . 33
AND, AS YOU MIGHT SAY, SAW THE LADY BORN. . . . . . 193 PAUL'S WIFE . . . 56
NOTHING TO SAY TO ALL THOSE MARRIAGES! . . . . . 199 PLACE FOR A THIRD . . 1
BESIDE IT ROOM RESERVED; THE SAY A SISTER'S, ... 200 PLACE FOR A THIRD . . 40
THAT'S WHAT I SIT UP IN THE DARK TO SAY-- . . . . . 206 THE WITCH OF COOS . . 130
COULDN'T HAVE BEEN THE ONE THEY SAY WAS UP . . . . . 207 PAUPER WITCH OF GRAFTON 17
HE WA'N'T BUT FIFTEEN AT THE TIME THEY SAY. . . . . . 208 PAUPER WITCH OF GRAFTON 19
I CAN'T SAY HE'S MUCH HELP: . . . . . 211 AN EMPTY THREAT . . 17
I WAS GOING TO SAY; . . . . . 212 AN EMPTY THREAT . . 35
IT'S TO SAY, "YOU AND I--" . . . . . 212 AN EMPTY THREAT . . 48
BOOKS, I SHOULD SAY!--IF BOOKS ARE WHAT IS NEEDED. . . . 216 A FOUNTAIN, A BOTTLE . 92
I COULD NOT SAY, ... 218 I WILL SING YOU ONE-O . 16
SOME SAY THE WORLD WILL END IN FIRE, ... 220 FIRE AND ICE . . . 1
SOME SAY IN ICE. . . . . . 220 FIRE AND ICE . . . 2
TO SAY THAT FOR DESTRUCTION ICE . . . . . 220 FIRE AND ICE . . . 7
THE VERSES IN IT SAY AND SAY: . . . . . 221 IN A DISUSED GRAVEYARD 5
AND ONE THING MORE THAT WAS NOT THEN TO SAY: . . . . . 222 TO E.T. 11
WE STOPPED BY A MOUNTAIN PASTURE TO SAY, "WHOSE COLT?" . . 223 THE RUNAWAY . . . 2
AND WHO'S TO SAY WHERE . . . . . 235 GATHERING LEAVES . . 23
I SHOULD BE WILLING TO SAY AND HELP YOU SAY . . . . . 236 VALLEY'S SINGING DAY . 19
A PLOW, THEY SAY, TO PLOW THE SNOW. . . . . . 238 PLOWMEN 1
TO SAY WHICH BUDS ARE LEAF AND WHICH ARE BLOOM. . . . . 254 A WINTER EDEN . . . 16
WE CHOOSE TO SAY IT IS LET LOOSE BY THE DEVIL; . . . . 254 THE FLOOD 5
BUT NOT TO CALL ME BACK OR SAY GOOD-BY; . . . . . 255 ACQUAINTED WITH NIGHT . 10
EVER SINCE RIVERS, I WAS GOING TO SAY, ... 258 WEST-RUNNING BROOK . 28
IT IS YOUR BROOK! I HAVE NO MORE TO SAY." . . . . . 259 WEST-RUNNING BROOK . 36
SOME SAY EXISTENCE LIKE A PIROUOT . . . . . 259 WEST-RUNNING BROOK . 45
NOR I NOR NOBODY ELSE MAY SAY, ... 263 THE TIMES TABLE . . 15
IF, AS THEY SAY, SOME DUST THROWN IN MY EYES . . . . . 265 DUST IN THE EYES . . 1
THAT IS TO SAY, 'TWAS NOT A CHURCH. . . . . . 274 A LONE STRIKER . . 53
BUT HE SAID THEN AND STILL WOULD SAY, ... 274 A LONE STRIKER . . 56
IF I CAN WITH CONFIDENCE SAY . . . . . 282 A DRUMLIN WOODCHUCK . 25
IT WOULD NOT BE FAIR TO SAY FOR A DOLE OF BREAD, ... 286 A ROADSIDE STAND . . 4
WHEN ONE WILL SAY, "LET US PUT IT OUT." . . . . . 291 ON HEART'S BEGINNING TO 22
WORDS ARE NO GOOD: TO SAY IT WAS A LENS . . . . . 293 AT WOODWARD'S GARDENS . 5
THEY DID NOT HAVE THE WIT TO SAY, ... 297 LEAVES COMPARED WITH . 15

SAY (CONTINUED)

	PAGE	TITLE	LINE
OFF ANY STILL OR MOVING THING YOU SAY.	300	THE MASTER SPEED	9
"SO WE WON'T SAY NOTHING IS CLEAR."	302	VOICE WAYS	8
WE'LL KNOW, WE SAY, THAT THIS WAS THE NIGHT IT DIED.	305	THERE ARE ROUGHLY ZONES	5
YOU WOULD SAY HIS AMBITION WAS TO EXTEND TO REACH	305	THERE ARE ROUGHLY ZONES	9
AS THEY SAY IN WAR.	306	A TRIAL RUN	9
NO MATTER WHAT SOME MAY SAY.	312	THE VINDICTIVES	76
OH, I DON'T BLAME YOU. I SAY TAKE LIFE EASY.	316	BUILD SOIL	19
NOT IF I HAD MY SAY. BOUNDS SHOULD BE SET	320	BUILD SOIL	123
DON'T LET THE THINGS I SAY AGAINST MYSELF	320	BUILD SOIL	131
DON'T LET ME SEEM TO SAY THE EXCHANGE, THE ENCOUNTER,	321	BUILD SOIL	157
IT WELL MAY BE. WE MEET--I DON'T SAY WHEN--	321	BUILD SOIL	159
NEEDLESS TO SAY TO YOU, MY ARGUMENT	322	BUILD SOIL	185
SO SHE THOUGHT SHE HEARD HIM SAY;	340	THE SUBVERTED FLOWER	25
THEY COULD ONLY SAY LIKE ANY TWO,	345	DISCOVERY OF MADEIRAS	46
SAY A FRACTION OF ONE PERCENT AT THE VERY LEAST,	349	OUR HOLD ON THE PLANET	16
I'D SAY, O MASTER OF THE PALACE SCHOOL,	351	THE LESSON FOR TODAY	19
OR SHOULD I SAY THE HIGHER ONE, FOR DARK.	352	THE LESSON FOR TODAY	53
UNLESS I PUT IT IN YOUR MOUTH TO SAY.	354	THE LESSON FOR TODAY	115
TO SEE WHAT ON THE WHOLE THEY HAD TO SAY	354	THE LESSON FOR TODAY	134
AND SOME SAY THERE ARE SIGNS	361	ALMOST TWO THOUSAND	4
IN HAVING ITS UNDEVIABLE SAY.	362	IN A POEM	4
YOU'D SAY SUFFICIENTLY LOUD,	365	A NATURE NOTE	6
CARVE NOTHING ON IT. YOU CAN SIMPLY SAY	365	OF STONES OF THE PLACE	13
SAY ABOUT HALFWAY UP THE WESTERN SKY,	370	THE LITERATE FARMER AND	66
NO PART OF WHICH WE'D HAVE TO WASTE, I SAY,	371	THE LITERATE FARMER AND	101
A CYCLE WE'LL SAY OF A HUNDRED YEARS.	376	SOMETHING FOR HOPE	17
TO SAY AS MUCH I WRITE YOU THIS.	381	AN UNSTAMPED LETTER IN	52
FROM, SAY, THE CROSS OR CROWN.	384	MAKING CERTAIN ANYTHING	12
TO ANOTHER I WOULD SAY,	384	IN THE LONG NIGHT	14
BUT SAY WHAT FANCY WILL,	388	MIDDLENESS OF THE ROAD	8
BUT YOU SAY THAT IN COLLEGE NOMENCLATURE	393	LUCRETIUS VERSUS POETS	7
TO SOME STAR OFF THERE, SAY, A HALF LIGHT-YEAR	395	WHY WAIT FOR SCIENCE	7
IT HAPPENED WOULD HAVE VERY MUCH TO SAY.	397	THE PLANNERS	8
AS IF TO SAY MERE LEARNING WAS THE DEVIL	400	TO THE RIGHT PERSON	10
IT WILL NOT DO TO SAY OF NIGHT,	403	SOMETHING LIKE A STAR	4
SAY SOMETHING TO US WE CAN LEARN	403	SOMETHING LIKE A STAR	9
SAY SOMETHING! AND IT SAYS, "I BURN."	403	SOMETHING LIKE A STAR	11
BUT SAY WITH WHAT DEGREE OF HEAT.	403	SOMETHING LIKE A STAR	12
PIKE SAID WITH TEMPER. AND DICK LONGED TO SAY,	404	FROM PLANE TO PLANE	8
BUT ALL HE DID SAY WAS, "WHAT IS THE SUBJECT?"	404	FROM PLANE TO PLANE	10
WERE LOOSE ALL ROUND THEIR LEGS--YOU COULDN'T SAY	404	FROM PLANE TO PLANE	16
YOU'VE GOT NO SOCIAL CONSCIENCE, AS THEY SAY,	406	FROM PLANE TO PLANE	77
DICK LONGED TO SAY, BUT WASN'T SURE ENOUGH	407	FROM PLANE TO PLANE	110
THOUGH THEY DO SAY HE DOESN'T OPEN LETTERS.	408	FROM PLANE TO PLANE	145
HE SEEMS TO SAY THE REASON WHY SO MUCH	412	POD OF THE MILKWEED	53
THEY SAY HIS FLAGSHIP'S UNLAID GHOST	418	AMERICA IS HARD TO SEE	49
COLUMBUS, AS I SAY, WILL MISS	418	AMERICA IS HARD TO SEE	67
"NEW ORDER OF THE AGES" DID WE SAY?	423	FOR JOHN F. KENNEDY	39
TO SAY GOD'S EITHER ALL OR OVER ALL?	427	CONCEPT SELF-CONCEIVED	7
OF (WE'LL SAY) BASALT	436	KITTY HAWK	261
OR LET'S SAY THE CUP,	437	KITTY HAWK	303
I DON'T SAY RETARD.	441	KITTY HAWK	410
WHEN ANY BUT MYSELF PRESUMED TO SAY	443	AUSPEX	11
AND SOME WILL SAY ALL SORTS OF THINGS,	445	ENDS	11
BUT SOME MEAN WHAT THEY SAY.	445	ENDS	12
AND I MUST SAY IT DEALT	450	OBJECTION TO BE STEPPED	9
"YOU SAY YOU KNOW THE INWARDNESS OF MEN,	456	HOW HARD TO KEEP FROM	98
YOU'RE GOOD AT MAXIMS. SAY ME ONE ON FREEDOM.	459	HOW HARD TO KEEP FROM	164
I WRITE REAL VERSE IN NUMBERS, AS THEY SAY.	460	HOW HARD TO KEEP FROM	211
(OR MORE THAN HALF I'M HALF INCLINED TO SAY)."	462	HOW HARD TO KEEP FROM	278
WE ALWAYS SAY--NOT WHO WON IT,	463	LINES IN DEJECTION	27
YOU WOULDN'T SAY SHE FARED SO VERY BADLY.	477	A MASQUE OF REASON	98
WHAT DID YOU TRY TO MAKE YOUR HUSBAND SAY?	477	A MASQUE OF REASON	118
WITH WHAT YOU SAY WE HAVE ESTABLISHED,	480	A MASQUE OF REASON	184
'TWAS A GREAT DEMONSTRATION IF YOU SAY SO.	481	A MASQUE OF REASON	219
HAVE SOME SAY AS TO WHERE WE'RE HEADED FOR;	482	A MASQUE OF REASON	235
YOU'RE GIVING ME. YOU SAY WE GROPED THIS OUT.	482	A MASQUE OF REASON	242
FOR MORE EXCUSES. / WHAT I MEAN TO SAY:	486	A MASQUE OF REASON	367
WHAT DID WE SAY? / YOU SAID THE DEVIL'S IN IT.	487	A MASQUE OF REASON	397
AND WHAT ELSE DID WE SAY? / WELL, WHAT LED UP--	487	A MASQUE OF REASON	399
YET COULD NOT BRING MYSELF TO SAY A WORD.	497	A MASQUE OF MERCY	99
IF WHAT YOU HAD TO SAY WAS DISAGREEABLE.	497	A MASQUE OF MERCY	105
THE WANDERING JEW--I'M WHO I SAY I AM,	498	A MASQUE OF MERCY	134
ESCAPIST, AS WE SAY--THOUGH YOU ARE NOT	498	A MASQUE OF MERCY	138
THE DOCTORS SAY THE TROUBLE WITH ME IS	499	A MASQUE OF MERCY	156
DON'T LAY YOUR HAND ON ME TO SAY IT, SHAMELESS.	500	A MASQUE OF MERCY	166
OR, AS YOU MIGHT SAY, THROW ME TO THE WHALE--	500	A MASQUE OF MERCY	183
JONAH, I'M GLAD, NOT SAD, TO HEAR YOU SAY	501	A MASQUE OF MERCY	213
MY TONGUE'S MY OWN, AS TRUE THOMAS USED TO SAY.	505	A MASQUE OF MERCY	296
IN WHAT I SAY. DON'T BE SO SILLY, WOMAN.	505	A MASQUE OF MERCY	308
LET ME REPEAT: I'M GLAD TO HEAR YOU SAY	507	A MASQUE OF MERCY	360
I SAY YOU SHOULD BE PROUD OF HAVING BEATEN	508	A MASQUE OF MERCY	378
MILTON'S PENTAMETERS GO ON TO SAY,	508	A MASQUE OF MERCY	380
LIGHTS OUT, I SAY, SO'S TO ESCAPE ATTENTION.	508	A MASQUE OF MERCY	392
OR BE A CHRISTIAN.--PAUL, I WISH YOU'D SAY	509	A MASQUE OF MERCY	403
YOU SAY IT, PAUL. / YOU MEAN ABOUT SUCCESS,	509	A MASQUE OF MERCY	409
NOT EVERYTHING I SAY IS SAID IN SCORN.	510	A MASQUE OF MERCY	451
WE KNOW WHAT'S COMING NOW. / YOU SAY IT, KEEPER,	511	A MASQUE OF MERCY	480
YES, PAUL, YOU DO SAY THINGS LIKE THAT SOMETIMES.	511	A MASQUE OF MERCY	486
WHAT DO YOU SAY TO IT, MY BROTHER'S KEEPER?	512	A MASQUE OF MERCY	513
I SAY I'D RATHER BE LOST IN THE WOODS	513	A MASQUE OF MERCY	514
AND YOU SAY JUSTICE DOESN'T REALLY MATTER.	517	A MASQUE OF MERCY	623
IF WHAT YOU SAY IS TRUE, IF WINNING RANKS	517	A MASQUE OF MERCY	633
YOU'LL TELL ME SOMETIME. ALL YOU SAY HAS GREATNESS.	517	A MASQUE OF MERCY	637
I SAY WE KEEP HIM TILL WE WRING SOME MORE	517	A MASQUE OF MERCY	639
NOW WE HAVE DONE IT, PAUL. WHAT DID HE SAY?	518	A MASQUE OF MERCY	656
WHAT DID HE SAY? I CAN'T HEAR WHAT HE SAYS.	518	A MASQUE OF MERCY	661

SAY (CONTINUED)
    SAVE THEM TO SAY YOUR PRAYERS ON.--WHAT'S THE MATTER? . . . 519 A MASQUE OF MERCY . . 682
    I SHOULD DARE SAY SHE WOULD BE TAKEN CARE OF. . . . . . . 519 A MASQUE OF MERCY . . 687
    THAT IS FOR HIM AND NOT FOR ME TO SAY. . . . . 520 A MASQUE OF MERCY . . 707
    FOR ME TO SAY IT WOULD BE IRRELIGIOUS. . . . . 520 A MASQUE OF MERCY . . 708
    AND IF I SAY WE LIFT HIM FROM THE FLOOR . . . . 521 A MASQUE OF MERCY . . 733
    TO LEARN TO SAY (HE MOVES TO JONAH'S FEET.) . . . . . . 521 A MASQUE OF MERCY . . 737
SAYING
    HE WILL NOT GO BEHIND HIS FATHER'S SAYING, ... 34 MENDING WALL 43
    HE ASKED ME WHAT I THOUGHT OF HAROLD'S SAYING . . . . . 37 DEATH OF THE HIRED MAN 79
    BUT YOU'RE THE DOCTOR, AS THE SAYING IS. . . . . 50 A HUNDRED COLLARS . . 170
    "I CAN REPEAT THE VERY WORDS YOU WERE SAYING: . . . . . 54 HOME BURIAL 91
    YOU COULDN'T TELL HER WHAT THE WEST WAS SAYING, ... 57 THE BLACK COTTAGE . . 71
    SAYING THEM LIKE THE HEATHEN? WE COULD DROP THEM. . . . 58 THE BLACK COTTAGE . . 98
    SHE HAD NO SAYING DARK ENOUGH . . . . 128 THE OFT-REPEATED DREAM 1
    WITH SAYING WHAT THEY'D LIKE TO DO TO US . . . . 130 THE BONFIRE 14
    BUT THE WIND OUT-OF-DOORS--YOU KNOW THE SAYING. . . . . 130 THE BONFIRE 40
    THEN SHOOK HIS LANTERN, SAYING, "ILE'S . . . . 140 BROWN'S DESCENT . . 74
    OVER HIS SHOULDER WITH HIS PIPESTEM, SAYING, ... 143 SNOW 7
    BUT THAT'S NOT SAYING--LOOK, FRED COLE, IT'S TWELVE, . . 144 SNOW 55
    BUT WHAT GOOD IS MY SAYING IT OVER AND OVER? . . . . . 150 SNOW 218
    FLIRTING THEIR WINGS AND SAYING CHICKADEE, ... 151 SNOW 231
    AS SHE STOOD SAYING HER NAME OVER ALOUD, ... 181 MAPLE 41
    SOMEONE WAS SAYING IN SUCH NATURAL TONES . . . . 182 MAPLE 85
    SO LABAN SAW THE SISTER, AND, SAYING NOTHING . . . . . 200 PLACE FOR A THIRD . . 44
    TO TURN HIM ROUND. HE GOT TO SAYING THINGS . . . . . . 209 PAUPER WITCH OF GRAFTON 78
    THIS SAYING GOOD-BY ON THE EDGE OF THE DARK . . . . . . 228 GOOD-BY AND KEEP COLD . 1
    SAYING....AND SHE COULD HAVE HIM. AND BEFORE . . . . . 230 NOT TO KEEP 2
    THE SAYING MAY BE EVER SO TRUE; . . . . 263 THE TIMES TABLE . . 13
    THE STRONG ARE SAYING NOTHING . . . . 299 STRONG SAYING NOTHING . T
    BUT THE STRONG ARE SAYING NOTHING UNTIL THEY SEE. . . . 300 STRONG SAYING NOTHING . 16
    (THE SAYING IS NEVER DONE.) . . . . 312 THE VINDICTIVES . . . 77
    FROM SAYING ON A JURY "HERE'S THE GUILTY." . . . . . . 317 BUILD SOIL 52
    IN INFINITE APPEAL. THEN SAYING "HELL," . . . . 396 ANY SIZE WE PLEASE . . 7
    THE CITY SAYING IT WAS CTESIPHON, ... 399 THE INGENUITIES OF DEBT 6
    "I THINK I'LL CHANGE MY MIND." / "YOU'RE SAYING THAT . . 406 FROM PLANE TO PLANE . 75
    "I'M SAYING IT TO ARGUE HIS IDEA'S . . . . 406 FROM PLANE TO PLANE . 80
    TO WALK IN SAYING NAUGHT . . . . 415 CLOSED FOR GOOD . . . 14
    SOME POOR FOOL HAS BEEN SAYING IN HIS HEART . . . . . . 423 FOR JOHN F. KENNEDY . 49
    SAYING THAT'S THE TUNE, ... 442 KITTY HAWK 446
    AND SAYING PLAINLY AND UNEQUIVOCALLY . . . . 483 A MASQUE OF REASON . . 296
    I'VE HEARD WHAT YOU WERE SAYING--EVERY WORD. . . . . . 487 A MASQUE OF REASON . . 396
    WHICH IS THE SAME AS SAYING JONAH, JONAH-- . . . . . . 495 A MASQUE OF MERCY . . 56
    GOOD FOR YOU, JONAH. THAT'S WHAT I'VE BEEN SAYING. . . . 510 A MASQUE OF MERCY . . 444
    GOOD FOR YOU, JONAH. THAT'S WHAT I'VE BEEN SAYING. . . . 517 A MASQUE OF MERCY . . 636
    DIE SAYING THAT, OLD-FASHIONED SAPIENT, ... 518 A MASQUE OF MERCY . . 663
SAYS
    HE ONLY SAYS, "GOOD FENCES MAKE GOOD NEIGHBORS." . . . . 33 MENDING WALL 27
    HE SAYS AGAIN, "GOOD FENCES MAKE GOOD NEIGHBORS." . . . 34 MENDING WALL 45
    HE SAYS THEY TWO WILL MAKE A TEAM FOR WORK-- . . . . . 36 DEATH OF THE HIRED MAN 62
    FAIRBANKS, HE SAYS TO ME--HE'S EDITOR-- . . . . 48 A HUNDRED COLLARS . . 105
    'FEEL OUT THE PUBLIC SENTIMENT'--HE SAYS. . . . . . . 48 A HUNDRED COLLARS . . 106
    FAIRBANKS, HE SAYS TO ME, 'HELP US THIS YEAR,' . . . . 48 A HUNDRED COLLARS . . 112
    MEANING BY US THEIR TICKET. 'NO,' I SAYS, ... 48 A HUNDRED COLLARS . . 113
    LEN SAYS ONE STEADY PULL.MORE OUGHT TO DO IT. . . . . . 64 A SERVANT TO SERVANTS 55
    HE SAYS THE BEST WAY OUT IS ALWAYS THROUGH. . . . . . 64 A SERVANT TO SERVANTS 56
    COMBED IT DOWN WITH A RAKE AND SAYS, 'O.K.' . . . . . 71 THE CODE 52
    KEEPING HIS HEAD ABOVE. 'DAMN YE,' I SAYS, ... 72 THE CODE 77
    HE SAYS IT'S NOT REPORTED SO FAR NORTH.-- . . . . . . 95 THE SELF-SEEKER . . 87
    AND SAYS THEIR NAMES, AND LEAVES THEM WHERE THEY ARE." . 98 THE SELF-SEEKER . . 162
    HE SAYS THAT LEAVES ARE OLD AND THAT FOR FLOWERS . . . 119 THE OVEN BIRD . . . 4
    HE SAYS THE EARLY PETAL-FALL IS PAST, ... 120 THE OVEN BIRD . . . 6
    HE SAYS THE HIGHWAY DUST IS OVER ALL. . . . . 120 THE OVEN BIRD . . . 10
    SHE SAYS SHE THINKS SHE PLANTED ONE . . . . 134 A GIRL'S GARDEN . . 27
    SHE SAYS, "I KNOW! . . . . 134 A GIRL'S GARDEN . . 44
    HE SAYS HE LEFT THE VILLAGE STORE AT NINE: . . . . . 145 SNOW 57
    SAYS IT WON'T DO. YOU'VE GOT TO GIVE IT UP." . . . . 147 SNOW 107
    "WELL, THERE'S--THE STORM. THAT SAYS I MUST GO ON. . . 151 SNOW 240
    HE SAYS SHE WENT TO LET HIM IN THE BARN.-- . . . . . 155 SNOW 331
    OR SOME SUCH SENSE AS SAYS HOW HIGH SHALL JET . . . . 169 NEW HAMPSHIRE . . . 325
    SAYS, TO MAKE THIS FALL ELIXIR . . . . 303 CLEAR AND COLDER . . 3
    THE SONG SAYS. STEAL AWAY AND STAY AWAY. . . . . . . 325 BUILD SOIL 279
    MY SON IN JERSEY SAYS A FRIEND OF HIS . . . . 371 THE LITERATE FARMER AND 95
    AND FOUND, HE SAYS, A BED HAS NO RIGHT SIDE. . . . . 372 THE LITERATE FARMER AND 123
    SO CAN'T GET SAVED, AS SAINT MARK SAYS THEY MUSTN'T. . . 379 DIRECTIVE 59
    HE DID AS SHAKESPEARE SAYS, YOU MAY RECALL, ... 400 THE BROKEN DROUGHT . . 7
    SAY SOMETHING! AND IT SAYS, "I BURN." . . . . 403 SOMETHING LIKE A STAR . 11
    SOMEONE SAYS THE LORD . . . . 438 KITTY HAWK 333
    SAYS OUR REACHING TOWARD . . . . 438 KITTY HAWK 334
    WHERE GOD SAYS IT, THOUGH. . . . . 438 KITTY HAWK 337
    AS WALLER SAYS. / OR NOT ADMIRED. GO OVER . . . . . 474 A MASQUE OF REASON . . 31
    WHO SAYS WE DON'T? WHO GOT UP THESE MISGIVINGS? . . . 483 A MASQUE OF REASON . . 288
    JOB SAYS THERE'S NO SUCH THING AS EARTH'S BECOMING . . 484 A MASQUE OF REASON . . 316
    MY NAME'S NOT JOE. I DON'T LIKE WHAT SHE SAYS . . . . 500 A MASQUE OF MERCY . . 169
    I AM SICK, AS SHE SAYS. NOTHING EXHAUSTS ME . . . . . 501 A MASQUE OF MERCY . . 197
    PLEASE LET ME HAVE IT. / READ US WHAT IT SAYS. . . . . 505 A MASQUE OF MERCY . . 294
    THERE IS SOME JUSTICE, EVEN AS KEEPER SAYS. . . . . . 509 A MASQUE OF MERCY . . 429
    WHAT DID HE SAY? I CAN'T HEAR WHAT HE SAYS. . . . . . 518 A MASQUE OF MERCY . . 661
    WE'VE ALL GROWN FOND OF YOU. (PAUL SAYS IT LOUDER, . . 518 A MASQUE OF MERCY . . 667
SCALAWAGS
    OUT OF ONE OF THOSE PIOUS SCALAWAGS." . . . . 146 SNOW 92
SCALDING
    (HE STOOD WELL BACK FOR FEAR OF SCALDING SQUIRTS.) . . 270 THE EGG AND THE MACHINE 12
SCALE
    NO, IN COUNTRY MONEY, THE COUNTRY SCALE OF GAIN, . . . 287 A ROADSIDE STAND . . 44
    NOT HALFWAY DOWN THE SCALE OF GRACE. . . . . 326 TO A THINKER . . . 32
    THE FURTHER UP THE SCALE OF WORK YOU GO. . . . . . . 406 FROM PLANE TO PLANE . 83

	PAGE	TITLE	LINE

SCALED
AND WE SCALED A PLANE . . . . 434 KITTY HAWK 208
SCALES
THE SCALES OF TRADE, THE CROSS OF FAITH, ... 252 THE PEACEFUL SHEPHERD . 7
THE CROSS, THE CROWN, THE SCALES MAY ALL . . . . 252 THE PEACEFUL SHEPHERD . 11
SCALP
MY SCALP WILL IN THE COPE . . . . 389 ASTROMETAPHYSICAL . . 15
SCANT
CAN SCANT OR HURRY HER THE LEAST. . . . . 281 BLUE RIBBON AT AMESBURY 38
SCAPEGOAT
THE THANKS AND LET HIM CATCH IT AS A SCAPEGOAT. . . . . 408 FROM PLANE TO PLANE . 140
SCARCE
THE GRAY GRASS IS SCARCE DAPPLED WITH THE SNOW; . . . 28 MY BUTTERFLY 8
IN HAYING TIME, WHEN ANY HELP IS SCARCE. . . . . . . 35 DEATH OF THE HIRED MAN 29
THAT END ALL. AND IT'S SCARCE ENOUGH TO CALL . . . . 111 IN THE HOME STRETCH . 34
IT CAN SCARCE BE THAT THEY WOULD BE IN NUMBER . . . . 112 IN THE HOME STRETCH . 53
BUT STARS WERE SCARCE IN THAT PART OF THE SKY, ... 295 LOST IN HEAVEN . . . 5
THE KING HAD SCARCE CEASED TO WRITHE, ... 311 THE VINDICTIVES . . 21
NO ONE CAN GIVE THEM--THEY CAN SCARCE ATTAIN-- . . . . 461 HOW HARD TO KEEP FROM 233
SCARCELY
SO OLD AND FIRM THEY SCARCELY SHOW THE BREEZE, ... 5 INTO MY OWN 2
A CIRCLE SCARCELY WIDER . . . . 13 ROSE POGONIAS . . . 3
BLACK SHE HAD SCARCELY SEEN, AND YELLOW NEVER. . . . 57 THE BLACK COTTAGE . . 76
SHE STRAYED SO FAR SHE SCARCELY HEARD . . . . . . 129 THE IMPULSE 15
SCARCELY A MILE BUT THAT I COME ON ONE, ... 171 NEW HAMPSHIRE . . . 390
HE GAVE IT SCARCELY A TOUCH, ... 288 DEPARTMENTAL . . . 6
I PASS, BUT SCARCELY PASS NO DOUBT, ... 291 ON HEART'S BEGINNING TO 21
THERE SCARCELY IS A LIGHT IN ALL ITS WALLS, ... 386 THE FEAR OF MAN . . . 8
BUT SCARCELY WAS MY DOOR AJAR, ... 419 ONE MORE BREVITY . . 7
SCARE
"OH, LET'S GO UP THE HILL AND SCARE OURSELVES, ... 129 THE BONFIRE 1
AND SCARE OURSELVES. LET WILD FIRE LOOSE WE WILL----" . 130 THE BONFIRE 18
"AND SCARE YOU TOO?" THE CHILDREN SAID TOGETHER. . . . 130 THE BONFIRE 19
"WHY WOULDN'T IT SCARE ME TO HAVE A FIRE . . . . . 130 THE BONFIRE 20
"SCARE YOU. BUT IF YOU SHRINK FROM BEING SCARED, . . . 132 THE BONFIRE 96
"BROTHER MESERVE, TAKE CARE, YOU'LL SCARE YOURSELF . . 149 SNOW 167
AND TOSSING SO AS TO SCARE . . . . 156 THE SOUND OF TREES . 22
AND GIVE THE TEACHER A SCARE AS FROM HER FATHER. . . . 180 MAPLE 32
THEY CANNOT SCARE ME WITH THEIR EMPTY SPACES . . . . 296 DESERT PLACES . . . 13
TO SCARE MYSELF WITH MY OWN DESERT PLACES. . . . . 296 DESERT PLACES . . . 16
ON FIRE TO SCARE AWAY THE PTERODIX . . . . . . 372 THE LITERATE FARMER AND 139
AND SCARE ME TO ONE SIDE. . . . . 415 CLOSED FOR GOOD . . 10
HE SAID THE BIBLE. / I SHOULD HATE TO SCARE YOU . . . 495 A MASQUE OF MERCY . 52
DON'T LET ME SCARE YOU. I WAS ONLY TEASING. . . . . 514 A MASQUE OF MERCY . 558
SCARED
(PALE ORCHISES), AND SCARED A BRIGHT GREEN SNAKE.. . . 17 MOWING 12
THERE'S NOTHING I'M AFRAID OF LIKE SCARED PEOPLE.. . . 50 A HUNDRED COLLARS . 175
AND HAVING SCARED THE CELLAR UNDER HIM . . . . . 108 OLD MAN'S WINTER NIGHT 9
IN CLOMPING HERE, HE SCARED IT ONCE AGAIN . . . . 108 OLD MAN'S WINTER NIGHT 10
IN CLOMPING OFF--AND SCARED THE OUTER NIGHT, ... 108 OLD MAN'S WINTER NIGHT 11
WHY WOULDN'T I BE SCARED REMEMBERING THAT?" . . . . 132 THE BONFIRE 94
"SCARE YOU. BUT IF YOU SHRINK FROM BEING SCARED, . . . 132 THE BONFIRE 96
SCARES
"IF IT SCARES YOU, WHAT WILL IT DO TO US?" . . . . 132 THE BONFIRE 95
SO BACK AND FORTH. IT ALMOST SCARES . . . . . . 326 TO A THINKER . . . 13
SCARF
IN A WHITE SCARF AGAINST THE FAR-SHORE ALDERS.) . . . 258 WEST-RUNNING BROOK . . 26
SCARIFIED
THAT THEY COULD HEAR TELL OF WAS SCARIFIED. . . . . 209 PAUPER WITCH OF GRAFTON 57
SCARING (SEE DEVIL-SCARING)
SCARLET
LAID SCARLET AND PALE PINK ABOUT HER FEET. . . . . 184 MAPLE 147
AND LAST YEAR'S BERRIES SHINING SCARLET RED. . . . 254 A WINTER EDEN . . . 8
SCARRED
WHEN STIFF AND SORE AND SCARRED . . . . 227 TO EARTHWARD . . . 25
SCARS
IF ALL THE SOUL-AND-BODY SCARS . . . . 362 A QUESTION 3
SCATTER
SCATTER POEMS ON THE FLOOR; . . . . 12 TO THE THAWING WIND . 14
THREW ME DOWN GRAPES TO MISS AND SCATTER . . . . . 197 WILD GRAPES . . . 32
SCATTERED
FOR THOUGH THE GRASS WAS SCATTERED, ... 13 ROSE POGONIAS . . . 13
"THERE IS NO VILLAGE--ONLY SCATTERED FARMS. . . . . 41 THE MOUNTAIN . . . 24
SCATTERED OASES WHERE MEN DWELT, BUT MOSTLY . . . . 58 THE BLACK COTTAGE . 119
SO THE CROWN FELL AND THE CROWN JEWELS SCATTERED. . . . 453 HOW HARD TO KEEP FROM 6
SCENE
BEFORE I CAME TO VIEW THE LEVELED SCENE. . . . . 22 THE TUFT OF FLOWERS . 4
AND CARE FOR THEM IN SUCH A CHANGE OF SCENE, ... 109 THE EXPOSED NEST . . 24
LIKE WINGS, REVOLVING IN THE SCENE. . . . . . . 138 BROWN'S DESCENT . . 22
BUT LET ME RAISE THIS CURTAIN ON A SCENE, ... 148 SNOW 155
NEXT DAY THE SCENE WAS PILED AND PUFFED AND DEAD. . . . 239 OUR SINGING STRENGTH . 11
AND YET HE THOUGHT HE SAW THE SCENE: . . . . . . 273 A LONE STRIKER . . 17
OR BEAUTY REST IN A BEAUTIFUL MOUNTAIN SCENE. . . . 286 A ROADSIDE STAND . . 13
AND PRESENTLY ON THE SCENE . . . . 288 DEPARTMENTAL . . . 33
AND THEN THERE WAS A MOON AND THEN A SCENE . . . . 315 IRIS BY NIGHT . . . 10
BUT THE GIRL FOUGHT THEM AND MADE A SCENE. . . . . 345 DISCOVERY OF MADEIRAS . 63
MAY I IN MY BRIEF BOLT ACROSS THE SCENE . . . . . 386 THE FEAR OF MAN . . 15
THAT HANGS PERCEPTIBLY ABOVE THE SCENE. . . . . . 412 POD OF THE MILKWEED . 29
WHEN THE SCENE WAS SET . . . . 430 KITTY HAWK 54
SCENERY
THE HURT TO THE SCENERY WOULDN'T BE MY COMPLAINT . . . 286 A ROADSIDE STAND . . 16
IN LANDOR'S QUATRAIN WOULD BE PRETTY SCENERY. . . . 393 LUCRETIUS VERSUS POETS 9
BEAT A SUNDIAL IN THE SCENERY-- . . . . 397 AN IMPORTER . . . 22
SCENES
AND SNATCHES OF VERSE AND SONG OF SCENES LIKE THIS . . 342 QUEST OF PURPLE-FRINGED 3
THEY HAVE FOUND OTHER SCENES . . . . 415 CLOSED FOR GOOD . . . 11
BEHIND THE SCENES, ORDAINED AND ADVERTISED . . . . . 497 A MASQUE OF MERCY . . 97

                                                             PAGE TITLE   LINE

SCENT
    THE SCENT OF APPLES: I AM DROWSING OFF. . . . . 68 AFTER APPLE-PICKING .   8
    "WRONG SHAPE, WRONG COLOR, AND WRONG SCENT," I SAID. . . 278 THE WHITE-TAILED HORNET 40
    A SCENT OF RIPENESS FROM OVER A WALL. . . . . 304 UNHARVESTED   1
SCENTED (SEE SWEET-SCENTED)
    HE SHOWED ME LUMPS OF THE SCENTED STUFF . . . . 141 THE GUM-GATHERER . . 30
SCEPTER-BATON
    WAVING SCEPTER-BATON, ... 442 KITTY HAWK 458
SCHEME
    BUT WASTE WAS OF THE ESSENCE OF THE SCHEME. . . . . . 412 POD OF THE MILKWEED . 40
SCHOLAR
    THOUGH A GREAT SCHOLAR, HE'S A DEMOCRAT, ... 44 A HUNDRED COLLARS . . 12
    "I'M A RHODES SCHOLAR--THAT'S THE REASON WHY. . . . . 455 HOW HARD TO KEEP FROM 52
    HIS NAME IS OMAR. I AS A RHODES SCHOLAR . . . . . . 459 HOW HARD TO KEEP FROM 188
SCHOLASTICAL
    TO WAGE A FINE SCHOLASTICAL CONTENTION . . . . . . 352 THE LESSON FOR TODAY . 51
SCHOOL (SEE BABY-SCHOOL)
    HE'S FINISHED SCHOOL, AND TEACHING IN HIS COLLEGE. . . 36 DEATH OF THE HIRED MAN 60
    WHICH SHOWED HOW MUCH GOOD SCHOOL HAD EVER DONE HIM. . . 37 DEATH OF THE HIRED MAN 84
    ABOUT THE NEW SCHOOL OF THE PSEUDO-PHALLIC, ... 170 NEW HAMPSHIRE . . .359
    SOME MAY KNOW WHAT THEY SEEK IN SCHOOL AND CHURCH, . . 173 A STAR IN A STONEBOAT .43
    MAPLE IS RIGHT." / "BUT TEACHER TOLD THE SCHOOL . . . 179 MAPLE 4
    HE KEPT FROM SCHOOL, OR DID HIS BEST TO KEEP-- . . . 188 THE AX-HELVE 84
    WHATEVER SCHOOL AND CHILDREN AND OUR DOUBTS . . . . 188 THE AX-HELVE 85
    I WENT TO SCHOOL TO AGE TO LEARN THE PAST. . . . . . 267 WHAT FIFTY SAID . . . 4
    I GO TO SCHOOL TO YOUTH TO LEARN THE FUTURE. . . . . 267 WHAT FIFTY SAID . . . 8
    LIKE A YARDFUL OF SCHOOL BOYS OUT AT RECESS . . . . 318 BUILD SOIL 61
    MADE PUBLICLY IN SCHOOL, ABOVE SUSPICION . . . . . 324 BUILD SOIL 274
    I'D SAY, O MASTER OF THE PALACE SCHOOL, ... 351 THE LESSON FOR TODAY . 19
    SITS DOWN IN SCHOOL TO TRY IF HE CAN WRITE . . . . . 353 THE LESSON FOR TODAY . 92
    NOT OF SCHOOL AGE . . . . 366 NOT OF SCHOOL AGE . . T
    WELL, WOULD I PLEASE GO TO SCHOOL, ... 366 NOT OF SCHOOL AGE . . 23
    BUT BECOMING AWARE OF SOME BOYS FROM SCHOOL . . . . 385 A MOOD APART 4
    AND THIS SCHOOL WASN'T KEEPING ANYMORE, ... 400 TO THE RIGHT PERSON . 11
    THAT'S WHAT I HAVE TO DO IN SCHOOL, KEEP MINE . . . 407 FROM PLANE TO PLANE . 98
    AND DISCIPLINE SHOULD BE IN SCHOOL AND STATE . . . . 460 HOW HARD TO KEEP FROM 200
    TO A BAD START IT SEEMS IN THE WRONG SCHOOL . . . . 499 A MASQUE OF MERCY . .162
SCHOOLBOY
    "IT ISN'T JUST THE SAME, AND SOME DAY, SCHOOLBOY, . . 406 FROM PLANE TO PLANE . 85
SCHOOLBOYS
    LIKE A YARDFUL OF SCHOOLBOYS OUT AT RECESS . . . . . 318 BUILD SOIL 61
SCHOOLHOUSE
    THERE IS A DISTRICT SCHOOLHOUSE I ADMIRE . . . . . . 400 TO THE RIGHT PERSON . 2
SCHOOLING
    AND THINK A LITTLE, AND GET SOME CITY SCHOOLING. . . . 182 MAPLE 74
    IT TAKES ALL SORTS OF IN- AND OUTDOOR SCHOOLING . . . 470 IT TAKES ALL SORTS... . 1
SCHOOLMEN
    AS SCHOOLMEN OF REPUTE SHOULD QUALIFY . . . . 352 THE LESSON FOR TODAY . 50
SCHOOLS
    REGULAR VESTRY-TREES WHOLE SUNDAY SCHOOLS . . . . . 107 CHRISTMAS TREES . . . 53
SCIENCE (SEE POPULAR-SCIENCE)
    SO SCIENCE AND RELIGION REALLY MEET. . . . . 353 THE LESSON FOR TODAY . 83
    OR SEE WHAT COMES OF SCIENCE AND INVENTION, ... 355 THE LESSON FOR TODAY .143
    (AND SCIENCE OUGHT TO KNOW) . . . . 361 ALMOST TWO THOUSAND . 9
    THE OLD MAN ARGUES SCIENCE CHEAPENED SPEED. . . . . . 371 THE LITERATE FARMER AND 98
    AND HOW MUCH LONGER A STORY HAS SCIENCE . . . . . . 379 TOO ANXIOUS FOR RIVERS 17
    SARCASTIC SCIENCE, SHE WOULD LIKE TO KNOW, ... 395 WHY WAIT FOR SCIENCE . 1
    WHY WAIT FOR SCIENCE TO SUPPLY THE HOW . . . . . . 395 WHY WAIT FOR SCIENCE . 9
    WHY WAIT FOR SCIENCE . . . . 395 WHY WAIT FOR SCIENCE . T
    HIS SCIENCE NEEDN'T GET HIM SO UNNERVED. . . . . . . 396 ANY SIZE WE PLEASE . . 11
    WAS MADE BY GETTING SCIENCE ON THE BRAIN; . . . . . 398 BURSTING RAPTURE . . 5
    THAT SCIENCE MAY HAVE STAKED THE FUTURE ON? . . . . 412 POD OF THE MILKWEED . 52
    ALL THE SCIENCE ZEST . . . . 435 KITTY HAWK 230
    FROM THE SCIENCE SHOP . . . . 439 KITTY HAWK 353
    SCIENCE HAS FAILED TO UNDERSTAND. . . . . 452 A-WISHING WELL . . . 61
    SOME SCIENCE FICTION . . . . 465 SOME SCIENCE FICTION . T
    ON THE GOSPEL OF MODERN SCIENCE, ... 466 SOME SCIENCE FICTION . 16
    SCIENCE STUCK A POLE . . . . 468 A REFLEX 2
    SCIENCE GAVE A STAB . . . . 468 A REFLEX 5
    WHILE SCIENCE GOES SELF-SUPERSEDING ON. . . . . . . 480 A MASQUE OF REASON . .193
    LOOK AT HOW FAR WE'VE LEFT THE CURRENT SCIENCE . . . 480 A MASQUE OF REASON . .194
    FOR ME TO DISAGREE WITH ANY SCIENCE . . . . 500 A MASQUE OF MERCY . .188
    WHO RECONCILED THE PENTATEUCH WITH SCIENCE. . . . . 506 A MASQUE OF MERCY . .325
SCIENTIFIC
    OR IF HE RESTS FROM SCIENTIFIC TREAD, ... 269 THE BEAR 22
    NOT JUST FOR SCIENTIFIC NEWS . . . . 416 AMERICA IS HARD TO SEE 5
    LET'S LEAVE THAT TO THE SCIENTIFIC WITS. . . . . . . 425 ACCIDENTALLY ON PURPOSE 18
    THEN BY A SCIENTIFIC BOOK. . . . . 467 QUANDARY 24
S'CIETY
    THE S'CIETY FOR PSYCHICAL RESEARCH . . . . 163 NEW HAMPSHIRE . . .135
SCISSORS (SEE NAIL-SCISSORS)
SCOFF
    WE MUST NOT BE TOO READY TO SCOFF. . . . . 266 SITTING BY A BUSH . . 12
    AT WHICH MY INCLINATION IS TO SCOFF.) . . . . 355 THE LESSON FOR TODAY .150
SCORCHED
    IN SPITE OF A SCORCHED FOURTH-OF-JULY FEELING. . . . . 132 THE BONFIRE 93
SCORCHING
    THE SMELL OF SCORCHING WOOLEN MADE HER FAINT. . . . . 91 THE FEAR 69
SCORE
    HE'S YOUR ONE CHANCE TO SCORE AGAINST THE STATE.) . . . 161 NEW HAMPSHIRE . . . 66
    THE SCORE WAS EVEN FOR THEM, THREE TO THREE. . . . . 199 PLACE FOR A THIRD . . 3
    SHE WELL MAY SCORE AN EGG-SUCCESS. . . . . 280 BLUE RIBBON AT AMESBURY 32
SCORED
    AS IF WITH SOME IDEA THAT SHE HAD SCORED. . . . . . 98 THE SELF-SEEKER . . .146
    SHE SCORED AN ALMOST PERFECT BIRD. . . . . 280 BLUE RIBBON AT AMESBURY 10
SCORN
    OF WHAT WAS IT? SCORN . . . . 448 THE BAD ISLAND--EASTER 21
    NOT EVERYTHING I SAY IS SAID IN SCORN. . . . . . . 510 A MASQUE OF MERCY . .451

```
                                                    PAGE TITLE              LINE
SCORNFULLY
    SO SCORNFULLY CURLED, . . . . . . . . . . . . . 447 THE BAD ISLAND--EASTER    9
SCORNS
    SHE SCORNS A PASTURE WITHERING TO THE ROOT. . . . . . 125 THE COW IN APPLE TIME .  6
SCOURED
    SHALL BE IN THE END SCOURED POOR, . . . . . . . . 285 IN TIME OF CLOUDBURST   11
SCOURS
    IT SCOURS THE WINDOWPANE WITH SNOW, . . . . . . . 281 BLUE RIBBON AT AMESBURY 50
SCOUTING
    SHE'S GOING TO DO MY SCOUTING IN THE FIELD, . . . . . 98 THE SELF-SEEKER . . . 151
SCRAPING
    AND LET THEM GO SCRAPING AND CREEPING . . . . . . . 30 RELUCTANCE . . . . . 10
    ANE THEN HER VOICE CAME SCRAPING SLOW: 'OH, YOU, . . . 153 SNOW . . . . . 290
SCRAPS
    STRAY SCRAPS OF PALLIATIVE REASON . . . . . . . . 478 A MASQUE OF REASON . . 142
SCRATCH
    AS IT WERE FROM SCRATCH, . . . . . . . . . . . 436 KITTY HAWK . . . . 259
    I TOLD HIM NOT TO SCRATCH: IT MADE IT WORSE. . . . . 478 A MASQUE OF REASON . 128
    DON'T SCRATCH! AND WHEN, AS ROTTEN AS HIS SKIN, . . . 478 A MASQUE OF REASON . 130
SCRATCHED
    JOB SCRATCHED HIS BOILS AND TRIED TO THINK WHAT HE . . 477 A MASQUE OF REASON . 121
SCRAWNY
    WITH AN ARM OF SCRAWNY MAST . . . . . . . . . . 469 FOUR-ROOM SHACK... . . 2
SCREECH
    FOR A SYLVAN SIGN THAT THE BLUE JAY'S SCREECH . . . . 24 PAN WITH US . . . . 18
SCREEN
    "IT'S AS YOU THROW A PICTURE ON A SCREEN: . . . . . 78 THE GENERATIONS OF MEN 135
    THOUGH HARM SHOULD COME OF IT; SO BUILT THE SCREEN . . 109 THE EXPOSED NEST . . 29
    BETWEEN THE PICTURES ON A MOVIE SCREEN . . . . . . 165 NEW HAMPSHIRE . . 194
    SHE GAVE IT THROUGH THE SCREEN DOOR CLOSED BETWEEN THEM: 201 PLACE FOR A THIRD . . 76
    ALBEIT THROUGH A RUSTY SCREEN, . . . . . . . . . 381 AN UNSTAMPED LETTER IN 41
    THE WRITING ON THE SCREEN MUST CHANGE TOO FAST . . . 502 A MASQUE OF MERCY . . 245
SCREENS
    CLEAR TO THE TOP." I SAW THROUGH LEAFY SCREENS . . . . 42 THE MOUNTAIN . . . . 57
SCRIBBLE
    SO THAT IT LOOKED LIKE LIGHTNING OR A SCRIBBLE, . . . 205 THE WITCH OF COOS . . 88
SCRIBES
    UNTIL THE SCRIBES HAD TAKEN DOWN A BOOKFUL . . . . . 518 A MASQUE OF MERCY . . 644
SCRIPT
    IS THROWN IN SCRIPT, AS AT BELSHAZZAR'S FEAST, . . . . 502 A MASQUE OF MERCY . . 238
SCROLL
    MAKING A GREAT SCROLL UPWARD TOWARD THE SKY, . . . . 143 SNOW . . . . . 9
    AND CARVED THEM ROUND WITH A SCROLL OF VINES. . . . . 347 DISCOVERY OF MADEIRAS . 124
SCROLLING
    A BUTTONED HAIRCLOTH LOUNGE SPREAD SCROLLING ARMS . . . 55 THE BLACK COTTAGE . . 22
SCRUB
    BUT SCRUB OAK, SCRUB OAK AND THE LACK OF EARTH . . . . 292 FIGURE IN THE DOORWAY . 3
SCUFFLING
    THE HUNTER SCUFFLING LEAVES GOES BY AT DUSK, . . . . 289 OLD BARN AT THE BOTTOM 3
    THEY WERE BOTH BENT ON SCUFFLING UP . . . . . . . 407 FROM PLANE TO PLANE . 114
SCULPTURE
    LIKE GRAVEYARD MARBLE SCULPTURE IN THE WEATHER, . . . 377 DIRECTIVE . . . . . 4
SCURF
    AND SCURF OF PLANTS, AND WEARY AND OVERHEATED, . . . . 125 AN ENCOUNTER . . . . 6
SCURRYING
    TO DRUM ON THE FLOOR WITH SCURRYING HOOFS . . . . . 241 NEED OF BEING VERSED . 11
SCUTTLED
    THE SWARM STILL RAN AND SCUTTLED JUST AS FAST. . . . 237 A HILLSIDE THAW . . . 24
SCYTHE
    AND THAT WAS MY LONG SCYTHE WHISPERING TO THE GROUND. . 17 MOWING . . . . . . 2
    MY LONG SCYTHE WHISPERED AND LEFT THE HAY TO MAKE. . . 17 MOWING . . . . . . 14
    A LEAPING TONGUE OF BLOOM THE SCYTHE HAD SPARED . . . 22 THE TUFT OF FLOWERS . 23
    BESIDE A REEDY BROOK THE SCYTHE HAD BARED. . . . . . 22 THE TUFT OF FLOWERS . 24
    AND HEAR HIS LONG SCYTHE WHISPERING TO THE GROUND, . . 23 THE TUFT OF FLOWERS . 32
    ARMED WITH A SCYTHE AND SPECTACLES THAT GLOWED, . . . 189 THE GRINDSTONE . . . 30
    YET FURTHER I WENT TO BE BEFORE THE SCYTHE, . . . . . 342 QUEST OF PURPLE-FRINGED 9
SEA (SEE DEEP-SEA)
    AT SEA, ABOUT THE TOWNS WHERE WAR HAS COME . . . . . 132 THE BONFIRE . . . . 105
    EXCEPT WHEN SEA FOG LAID IT DOWN, . . . . . . . . 249 A PECK OF GOLD . . . 2
    SEA WAVES ARE GREEN AND WET, . . . . . . . . . . 260 SAND DUNES . . . . 1
    THEY ARE THE SEA MADE LAND . . . . . . . . . . 260 SAND DUNES . . . . 5
    A LITTLE NEARER THE SEA. . . . . . . . . . . . 285 IN TIME OF CLOUDBURST . 4
    THEY LOOK AT THE SEA ALL DAY. . . . . . . . . . 301 NEITHER OUT FAR NOR IN 4
    AND THE PEOPLE LOOK AT THE SEA. . . . . . . . . . 301 NEITHER OUT FAR NOR IN 12
    WE GET PLENTY FUNERALS AT SEA. . . . . . . . . . 345 DISCOVERY OF MADEIRAS . 70
    HIS RECKONING WAS OFF A SEA. . . . . . . . . . . 417 AMERICA IS HARD TO SEE 18
    O OCEAN SEA, FOR ALL YOUR BEING VAST, . . . . . . . 446 DOES NO ONE AT ALL EVER 1
    AND NOW, O SEA, YOU'RE LOST BY AEROPLANE. . . . . . 446 DOES NO ONE AT ALL EVER 13
    IT MAKES US TO HAVE HAD A SEA IN VAIN. . . . . . . 446 DOES NO ONE AT ALL EVER 16
    GRIND SHELLS, O FUTILE SEA, GRIND EMPTY SHELLS . . . . 446 DOES NO ONE AT ALL EVER 19
    ALL THE SEA WATER IN ONE TIDE . . . . . . . . . 452 A-WISHING WELL . . . 45
SEAL
    THE SEAL YELP . . . . . . . . . . . . . . . 211 AN EMPTY THREAT . . . 19
SEALED
    UNDER IT ALL, HIS DOOR SEALED UP AND LOST, . . . . . 150 SNOW . . . . . . 224
SEARCH
    THERE'S FIVE: THAT'S ALL I CARRY." / "I CAN SEARCH YOU? . 47 A HUNDRED COLLARS . . 88
    AND WHY THEY SEEK IT THERE; FOR WHAT I SEARCH . . . . 173 A STAR IN A STONEBOAT . 44
    BUT THOUGH THEY NOW GAVE UP THE SEARCH FOREVER, . . . 184 MAPLE . . . . . . 133
    THEY COULD NOT GO FLYING ABOUT IN SEARCH . . . . . . 253 THE THATCH . . . . 23
    COME GET HIM—THEY KNEW WHERE TO SEARCH. . . . . . . 275 A LONE STRIKER . . . 62
SEARCHED
    THEY SEARCHED FOR INTO BRAZIL, . . . . . . . . . 311 THE VINDICTIVES . . . 50
SEARCHING
    IT'S WHO FIRST THOUGHT THE THOUGHT. YOU'RE SEARCHING, JOE, 116 IN THE HOME STRETCH . 172
SEAS
    THE BOTTOM OF SEAS RAISED DRY-- . . . . . . . . . 285 IN TIME OF CLOUDBURST . 15
SEA'S
    BUT IT SEEMS LIKE THE SEA'S RETURN . . . . . . . . 27 A LINE-STORM SONG . . 26

                            - 469 -
```

SEASON
    OF A LOVE OR A SEASON? . . . . 30 RELUCTANCE 24
    I HAVE TO BE GONE FOR A SEASON OR SO. . . . . 228 GOOD-BY AND KEEP COLD . 20
    IT MUST BE NOW, THOUGH, IN SEASON . . . . 264 THE LAST MOWING . . 7
    TO CLOSE THIS OUTPOST BARN AND CLOSE THE SEASON. . . . 289 OLD BARN AT THE BOTTOM . 7
    COLDER THAN THE SEASON WARRANTS. . . . . 304 CLEAR AND COLDER . . 14
SEASON-CLIMATE
    WIND, THE SEASON-CLIMATE MIXER, ... 303 CLEAR AND COLDER . . 1
SEASON-ENDING
    A SEASON-ENDING WIND THERE BLEW . . . . 336 THE WIND AND THE RAIN . 3
SEASONS
    AND POLITICIAN AT ODD SEASONS. . . . . 139 BROWN'S DESCENT . . . 70
SEAT
    OVER THE WHEEL INTO THE SKY-HIGH SEAT, ... 112 IN THE HOME STRETCH . 63
    BRING BERRIES UNDER THE WAGON SEAT, ... 141 THE GUM-GATHERER . 26
    HIS SEAT UPON THE INTELLECTUAL THRONE"-- . . . . . 171 NEW HAMPSHIRE . . . 385
    UNLESS FOR PENITENTS WHO TOOK THEIR SEAT . . . . . 400 TO THE RIGHT PERSON . 12
    IN THE SEAT OF MY SENSE. . . . . 450 OBJECTION TO BE STEPPED 6
    THROWN PROSTRATE AT THE MERCY SEAT FOR MERCY. . . . 511 A MASQUE OF MERCY . 485
SEATED
    THAT HAD ME BY THE COAT AS GOOD AS SEATED, ... 125 AN ENCOUNTER 9
SEATS
    WHY NOT TAKE SEATS HERE ON THE CELLAR WALL . . . . 75 THE GENERATIONS OF MEN 63
SEAWEED
    IT WRAPS A WISP OF SEAWEED ROUND MY LEGS, ... 391 ON BEING IDOLIZED . . 2
    WE CAN LIE ON THE BEACH WITH THE SEAWEED . . . . . 395 ETHEREALIZING . . . 7
SECOND
    YET EVERY SECOND SPEAR . . . . 13 ROSE POGONIAS . . . 14
    THE SECOND ROUND THE CURVING HILLSIDE ROAD . . . . . 74 THE GENERATIONS OF MEN 29
    CE SECOND GROWT' I CUT MYSELF--TOUGH, TOUGH!" . . . 186 THE AX-HELVE . . . 31
    SHE'D LOOKED ELIZA UP HER SECOND TIME, ... 201 PLACE FOR A THIRD . 58
    A WIDOW AT HER SECOND HUSBAND'S GRAVE, ... 201 PLACE FOR A THIRD . 59
    HOW WAS IT WITH HIM FOR A SECOND TRIAL. . . . . . . 231 NOT TO KEEP . . . 20
    HE STRUCK A SECOND TIME. ANOTHER NAILHEAD. . . . . 278 THE WHITE-TAILED HORNET 35
    UNDER MAGNITUDE THE SECOND.) . . . . 304 CLEAR AND COLDER . . 9
    THE SECOND SUCH HAS COME, ... 361 ALMOST TWO THOUSAND . 5
    THE SECOND MORE PECULIARLY YOUR OWN, ... 382 TO AN ANCIENT . . 14
    YOU SAID THE SECOND COMING OF TECUMSEH. . . . . . . 406 FROM PLANE TO PLANE . 70
    BY SAFETY SECOND OUT OF SAFETY FIRST, ... 457 HOW HARD TO KEEP FROM 124
    OUR SECOND SECOND-CHILDHOOD CASE TONIGHT. . . . . . 493 A MASQUE OF MERCY . 14
    AND NOT OUR WORST NOR SECOND BEST, OUR BEST, ... 520 A MASQUE OF MERCY . 719
SECOND-CHILDHOOD
    OUR SECOND SECOND-CHILDHOOD CASE TONIGHT. . . . . . 493 A MASQUE OF MERCY . 14
SECONDHAND
    ALL SECONDHAND. DON'T GET EXCITED, FOLKS; . . . . . 507 A MASQUE OF MERCY . 352
SECRECY
    BUT WHAT IS ALL THIS SECRECY ABOUT? . . . . 483 A MASQUE OF REASON . 272
SECRET
    DIMLY TO HAVE MADE OUT MY SECRET PLACE, ... 14 WAITING 15
    THE SECRET OF?" / "AND THEN IT MAY HAVE BEEN . . . . 183 MAPLE 117
    "WE WOULD NOT SEE THE SECRET IF WE COULD NOW: . . . 185 MAPLE 161
    WHATEVER ITS SECRET WAS OF GREATER HEAT . . . . . . 239 OUR SINGING STRENGTH . 17
    TOLD ME MY SECRET MUST BE KNOWN: . . . . 251 BEREFT 12
    THAT THOUGH SHE GRIEVES, HER GRIEF IS SECRET: . . . 256 THE LOVELY BE CHOOSERS 26
    BUT THE SECRET SITS IN THE MIDDLE AND KNOWS. . . . . 362 THE SECRET SITS . . 2
    THE SECRET SITS . . . . 362 THE SECRET SITS . . T
    OR SOME DIM SECRET OF THE GOOD OF WASTE? . . . . . 412 POD OF THE MILKWEED . 49
    "A MAN'S OUT THERE WHO CLAIMS HE KNOWS THE SECRET, . . 455 HOW HARD TO KEEP FROM 60
    HOW DID YOU KNOW THE SECRET OF MY BIRTH?" . . . . . 457 HOW HARD TO KEEP FROM 117
SECRETE
    BUT WHATSOEVER ELSE IT MAY SECRETE, ... 411 POD OF THE MILKWEED . 20
SECRETS
    THEY KEPT THEIR SECRETS AND DIED, ... 312 THE VINDICTIVES . . 54
SECT
    I HATE HIS WRETCHED LITTLE RACKER SECT, ... 144 SNOW 53
    THAT MAY BE CLAMORED AT BY CAUSE AND SECT, ... 356 TIME OUT 13
    WHO AS OF A SECT . . . . 432 KITTY HAWK . . . 142
SECURE
    (WE MADE IT SECURE AGAINST BEING, I HOPE, ... 228 GOOD-BY AND KEEP COLD . 13
    AND STILL MORE SECURE AND SNUG, ... 282 A DRUMLIN WOODCHUCK . 7
SEDENTARY
    WHEN SEDENTARY AND WHEN PERIPATETIC. . . . . 269 THE BEAR 34
SEDIMENT
    IT SEEMED I WAS A MITE OF SEDIMENT . . . . 468 IN A GLASS OF CIDER . 1
SEDUCED
    SEDUCED BACK TO THE LAND BY ANY CLAIM . . . . . . 322 BUILD SOIL 207
SEE
    I DO NOT SEE WHY I SHOULD E'ER TURN BACK, ... 5 INTO MY OWN . . . 9
    MYSELF UNSEEN, I SEE IN WHITE DEFINED . . . . . . 17 THE VANTAGE POINT . 5
    AND THEN HE FLEW AS FAR AS EYE COULD SEE, ... 22 THE TUFT OF FLOWERS . 17
    WHO SEE SO LITTLE THEY TELL NO TALES. . . . . . . 24 PAN WITH US . . . 15
    (THOUGH DOUBTFUL WHETHER HE STAYED TO SEE). . . . . 25 THE DEMIURGE'S LAUGH . 17
    BUT SEE ALL WIND-STIRRED. . . . . 25 NOW CLOSE THE WINDOWS . 8
    HE SAID IT FOR HIMSELF. I SEE HIM THERE, ... 34 MENDING WALL . . . 38
    WAIT TILL YOU SEE." / "WHERE DID YOU SAY HE'D BEEN?" . 35 DEATH OF THE HIRED MAN 39
    TO SEE IF HE WAS TALKING IN HIS SLEEP. . . . . . . 36 DEATH OF THE HIRED MAN 57
    YOU NEVER SEE HIM STANDING ON THE HAY . . . . . . 37 DEATH OF THE HIRED MAN 94
    HE HATES TO SEE A BOY THE FOOL OF BOOKS. . . . . . 37 DEATH OF THE HIRED MAN 98
    I'LL SEE TO THAT IF THERE IS NEED. HE OUGHT OF RIGHT . 39 DEATH OF THE HIRED MAN 132
    YOU MUST GO IN AND SEE WHAT YOU CAN DO. . . . . . 39 DEATH OF THE HIRED MAN 150
    "I HAVEN'T BEEN. GO, LOOK, SEE FOR YOURSELF. . . . 40 DEATH OF THE HIRED MAN 155
    I'LL SIT AND SEE IF THAT SMALL SAILING CLOUD . . . . 40 DEATH OF THE HIRED MAN 160
    WHEN I WALKED FORTH AT DAWN TO SEE NEW THINGS, . . . 40 THE MOUNTAIN . . . 8
    ONE OF THE GREAT SIGHTS GOING IS TO SEE . . . . . 42 THE MOUNTAIN . . . 50
    "HE NEVER GOT UP HIGH ENOUGH TO SEE, ... 43 THE MOUNTAIN . . . 78
    SUCH A GREAT MAN. IT DOESN'T SEE HIM OFTEN . . . . 44 A HUNDRED COLLARS . 2
    "YOU SEE I'M IN WITH EVERYBODY, KNOW 'EM ALL. . . . 49 A HUNDRED COLLARS . 120
    TO SEE YOU AS YOU ARE TO SEE THEM." / "OH, ... 49 A HUNDRED COLLARS . 150

SEE (CONTINUED)
BUT FIRST--LET'S SEE--WHAT WAS I GOING TO ASK YOU? . . . 50 A HUNDRED COLLARS . . 162
ADVANCING TOWARD HER: "WHAT IS IT YOU SEE . . . . . 51 HOME BURIAL 6
HE SAID TO GAIN TIME: "WHAT IS IT YOU SEE?" . . . . 51 HOME BURIAL 10
SHE LET HIM LOOK, SURE THAT HE WOULDN'T SEE, ... 51 HOME BURIAL 15
BLIND CREATURE; AND AWHILE HE DIDN'T SEE. . . . . . 51 HOME BURIAL 16
"WHAT IS IT--WHAT?" SHE SAID. / "JUST THAT I SEE." . . 51 HOME BURIAL 18
"THE WONDER IS I DIDN'T SEE AT ONCE. . . . . 51 HOME BURIAL 20
I SHOULD SUPPOSE. I CAN'T SAY I SEE HOW. . . . . . 52 HOME BURIAL 48
BUT I WENT NEAR TO SEE WITH MY OWN EYES. . . . . . 54 HOME BURIAL 83
WE PRESSED OUR FACES TO THE PANE. "YOU SEE," HE SAID, . 55 THE BLACK COTTAGE . . 14
MOST OF THE CHANGE WE THINK WE SEE IN LIFE . . . . 58 THE BLACK COTTAGE . . 109
"YOU KNOW WHERE THEY CUT OFF THE WOODS--LET ME SEE-- . 59 BLUEBERRIES 9
"I WONDER YOU DIDN'T SEE LOREN ABOUT." . . . . . . 60 BLUEBERRIES 33
HE SPOKE TO HIS WIFE IN THE DOOR, 'LET ME SEE, . . . 61 BLUEBERRIES 76
HE'LL FIND HE'S MISTAKEN. SEE HERE, FOR A WHIM, . . . 61 BLUEBERRIES 80
AND SEE THE WAY YOU LIVED, BUT I DON'T KNOW! . . . . 62 A SERVANT TO SERVANTS . 4
I SEE IT'S A FAIR, PRETTY SHEET OF WATER. . . . . . 63 A SERVANT TO SERVANTS . 17
I SEE IT'S A FAIR, PRETTY SHEET OF WATER, ... 63 A SERVANT TO SERVANTS . 32
I CAN SEE HOW YOU MIGHT. BUT I DON'T KNOW! . . . . 63 A SERVANT TO SERVANTS . 38
AS THAT I CAN SEE NO WAY OUT BUT THROUGH-- . . . . . 64 A SERVANT TO SERVANTS . 58
ONE CAN SEE WHAT WILL TROUBLE . . . . 69 AFTER APPLE-PICKING . 37
AT LEAST TO PASS BY AND SEE WHO HE WAS, ... 74 THE GENERATIONS OF MEN 32
AND SEE IF YOU CAN RECKON OUR COUSINSHIP. . . . . . 75 THE GENERATIONS OF MEN 62
"ON FATHER'S SIDE, IT SEEMS, WE'RE--LET ME SEE----" . . 76 THE GENERATIONS OF MEN 78
WHAT DO WE SEE IN SUCH A HOLE, I WONDER." . . . . 76 THE GENERATIONS OF MEN 91
"YOU MUST BE LEARNED. THAT'S WHAT YOU SEE IN IT?" . . 76 THE GENERATIONS OF MEN 95
"AND WHAT DO YOU SEE?" / "YES, WHAT DO I SEE? . . . 76 THE GENERATIONS OF MEN 96
FIRST LET ME LOOK. I SEE RASPBERRY VINES----" . . . 76 THE GENERATIONS OF MEN 97
WHAT I SEE. IT'S A LITTLE, LITTLE BOY, ... 77 THE GENERATIONS OF MEN 99
"SEE THAT YOU GET HER GREATNESS RIGHT. DON'T STINT HER." 77 THE GENERATIONS OF MEN 117
I WON'T BE TEASED. BUT SEE HOW WET I AM." . . . . 77 THE GENERATIONS OF MEN 119
"I DON'T SEE VERY WELL HOW YOU CAN HELP IT. . . . . 79 THE GENERATIONS OF MEN 155
YOU SEE THEY KNOW I HAVEN'T HAD YOUR NAME, ... 79 THE GENERATIONS OF MEN 157
YOU CAN SEE THAT THERE'S SOMETHING WRONG WITH IT, . . 79 THE GENERATIONS OF MEN 172
I SHOULD FEEL EASIER IF I COULD SEE . . . . . . 80 THE GENERATIONS OF MEN 190
YOU CAN SEE WHAT IS TROUBLING GRANNY, THOUGH. . . . 80 THE GENERATIONS OF MEN 195
"I CAN SEE WE ARE GOING TO BE GOOD FRIENDS." . . . 80 THE GENERATIONS OF MEN 199
HOW DO YOU SEE HIM LIVING WHEN YOU'RE GONE? . . . . 82 THE HOUSEKEEPER . . . 41
"I DON'T JUST SEE HIM LIVING MANY YEARS, ... 82 THE HOUSEKEEPER . . . 43
SKY-HIGH WITH BOTH HANDS. I CAN SEE IT NOW-- . . . 83 THE HOUSEKEEPER . . . 61
YOU SEE OUR PRETTY THINGS ARE ALL OUTDOORS. . . . . 85 THE HOUSEKEEPER . . . 110
WE WOULDN'T HURT A HEN! YOU OUGHT TO SEE A . . . . 85 THE HOUSEKEEPER . . . 125
BUT YOU SEE, DON'T YOU, WE TAKE CARE OF HIM." . . . 86 THE HOUSEKEEPER . . . 154
TO SEE WHERE ALL THE MONEY GOES SO FAST. . . . . . 86 THE HOUSEKEEPER . . . 159
"NONSENSE! SEE WHAT SHE'S DONE! BUT WHO, BUT WHO----?" 88 THE HOUSEKEEPER . . . 185
ON SOMETHING--THERE'S NO HARM. SEE, THERE HE IS! . . 88 THE HOUSEKEEPER . . . 203
YOU MUST HAVE SEEN IT TOO. / "I DIDN'T SEE IT. . . . 89 THE FEAR 12
OH, BUT YOU SEE HE HADN'T HAD ENOUGH-- . . . . . 91 THE FEAR 51
AND IF TO SEE WAS WHAT HE WANTED, WHY, ... 91 THE FEAR 57
HE HAS SEEN ALL THERE WAS TO SEE AND GONE." . . . 91 THE FEAR 58
AND LET YOU SEE." / "YES, DO.--JOEL, GO BACK!" . . 92 THE FEAR 75
"YOU SEE," THE VOICE SAID. / "OH." SHE LOOKED AND LOOKED. 92 THE FEAR 78
"YOU DON'T SEE--I'VE A CHILD HERE BY THE HAND. . . . 92 THE FEAR 79
I WANT TO SEE YOU DO IT. WHEN'S HE COMING?" . . . 93 THE SELF-SEEKER . . . 7
WHAT I CAN GET. YOU SEE THEY HAVE THE FEET, . . . 95 THE SELF-SEEKER . . . 63
ER, LET ME SEE. I THINK I'LL TAKE THE RIGHT. . . . 96 THE SELF-SEEKER . . . 110
YOU SEE ANNE HAS HER LESSON LEARNED BY HEART." . . . 97 THE SELF-SEEKER . . . 122
SOMEHOW I'LL MAKE IT RIGHT WITH HER--SHE'LL SEE. . . 98 THE SELF-SEEKER . . . 150
NOW RUN.--GET OUT YOUR DOCUMENTS! YOU SEE . . . . 99 THE SELF-SEEKER . . . 175
NO, I WILL GO ON FARTHER--AND WE SHALL SEE." . . . 101 THE WOOD-PILE . . . 3
AND NOT ANOTHER LIKE IT COULD I SEE. . . . . . . 101 THE WOOD-PILE . . . 25
TO SEE IF THE BIRDS LIVED THE FIRST NIGHT THROUGH, . . 110 THE EXPOSED NEST . . 35
WILL EVER SLAM THE DOORS." / "I THINK YOU SEE . . . 112 IN THE HOME STRETCH . 44
I ONLY SEE THE YEARS. THEY COME AND GO . . . . . 112 IN THE HOME STRETCH . 47
DIFFERENT FROM EARLY YEARS." / "I SEE THEM, TOO. . . 112 IN THE HOME STRETCH . 50
"COME FROM THAT WINDOW WHERE YOU SEE TOO MUCH, . . . 112 IN THE HOME STRETCH . 60
"SEE HOW IT MAKES HIS NOSE-SIDE BRIGHT, A PROOF . . . 112 IN THE HOME STRETCH . 66
WHAT SHOULDER DID I SEE HER OVER? NEITHER. . . . . 113 IN THE HOME STRETCH . 69
TO SEE US THROUGH OUR FIRST TWO WEEKS. BUT, JOE, . . 113 IN THE HOME STRETCH . 74
I DON'T KNOW WHAT THEY THINK WE SEE IN WHAT . . . . 114 IN THE HOME STRETCH . 112
LET'S SEE YOU FIND YOUR LOAF. I'LL LIGHT THE FIRE. . . 115 IN THE HOME STRETCH . 155
AND ALL THE TIME WE TALKED YOU SEEMED TO SEE . . . 119 MEETING AND PASSING . 10
ON SNOW AND SAND AND TURF, I SEE . . . . 120 BOND AND FREE . . . 6
WHEN I SEE BIRCHES BEND TO LEFT AND RIGHT . . . . 121 BIRCHES 1
YOU MAY SEE THEIR TRUNKS ARCHING IN THE WOODS . . . 121 BIRCHES 17
TO SEE FOR MYSELF ABOUT THE BIRCH . . . . 123 PEA BRUSH 3
TO WATCH ME AND SEE WHAT I CAME TO GET. . . . . . 123 PEA BRUSH 12
WHEN SUPPER'S ON THE TABLE, AND WE'LL SEE . . . . 123 PUTTING IN THE SEED . 2
STILL HE SMILED--DID YOU SEE HIM?--I WAS SURE! . . . 127 THE SMILE 3
THAT EVERYONE FOR MILES COULD SEE . . . . 137 BROWN'S DESCENT . . 2
YOU CAN'T GET BACK AND SEE IT AS HE SAW IT. . . . . 142 THE VANISHING RED . . 9
"COME, JOHN," HE SAID, "YOU WANT TO SEE THE WHEEL PIT?" 142 THE VANISHING RED . . 19
"YOU CAN JUST SEE IT GLANCING OFF THE ROOF . . . . 143 SNOW 8
"I'LL JUST SEE HOW THE HORSES ARE." / "YES, DO," . . 144 SNOW 33
"WAIT AND HE MAY. LET'S SEE WHAT HE WILL DO. . . . 145 SNOW 76
LET'S SEE IF HE WILL THINK OF HER AGAIN. . . . . . 145 SNOW 77
"NONSENSE TO THAT! YOU WANT TO SEE HIM SAFE." . . . 146 SNOW 93
YOU SEE I KNOW--TO GET YOU ON TO THINGS . . . . . 147 SNOW 122
IT WANTS TO SEE HOW YOU WILL TAKE; IF BACKWARD, . . . 147 SNOW 123
AND FAILED TO SEE THE GOOD OF. NEVER MIND, ... 147 SNOW 125
THAT VARIES WITH THE THINGS--BEFORE WE SEE THEM. . . 147 SNOW 128
YOU SEE THE SNOW-WHITE THROUGH THE WHITE OF FROST? . . 148 SNOW 157
TO SEE WHAT PEOPLE FOUND SO INTERESTING . . . . . 148 SNOW 162
AT THE FAR END OF IT YOU SEE A STIR . . . . . . 149 SNOW 194
HE HAD COLE WITH HIM TO THE BARN TO SEE HIM OFF. . . 151 SNOW 244
CONCEAL A WISH TO SEE HIM SHOW THE SPUNK . . . . . 153 SNOW 283
"FRED, SEE IF YOU CAN HEAR WHAT I HEAR. COME." . . 154 SNOW 315

SEE (CONTINUED)

	PAGE	TITLE	LINE
DROP IN AND SEE US WHEN YOU'RE PASSING." / "WELL,	155	SNOW	333
I DON'T SEE." / "POSSIBLY NOT FOR HERSELF.	155	SNOW	335
"I SEE THE PORTER'S MADE YOUR BED," I TOLD HIM.	159	NEW HAMPSHIRE	15
HE DID NOT SEE HOW LIKE A FLYING THING	172	A STAR IN A STONEBOAT	13
NOTHING WAS LEFT TO DO THAT I COULD SEE	176	THE CENSUS-TAKER	54
"THE BEST THING THAT WE'RE PUT HERE FOR'S TO SEE;	177	THE STAR-SPLITTER	33
THE STRONGEST THING THAT'S GIVEN US TO SEE WITH'S	177	THE STAR-SPLITTER	34
AND HE COULD WAIT--WE'D SEE TO HIM TOMORROW.	177	THE STAR-SPLITTER	42
TO SEE IF THERE WAS NOT SOME SPECIAL TREE	183	MAPLE	100
FIGURATIVE ENOUGH TO SEE THE SYMBOL,	184	MAPLE	154
"WE WOULD NOT SEE THE SECRET IF WE COULD NOW:	185	MAPLE	161
NAME CHILDREN SOME NAMES AND SEE WHAT YOU DO.	185	MAPLE	170
TO SEE FOR ONCE THE INSIDE OF HIS HOUSE.	188	THE AX-HELVE	89
"SEE HOW SHE'S COCK HER HEAD!"	188	THE AX-HELVE	102
TO GET IT ANYWHERE THAT I CAN SEE.	188	THE GRINDSTONE	3
THEY SEEMED TO ASK HIM JUST TO SEE HIM GO,	191	PAUL'S WIFE	23
TO SEE IF IT WAS EMPTY. HE MADE OUT IN THERE	194	PAUL'S WIFE	90
TO SEE IF IT WAS ANYONE BEHIND HIM	194	PAUL'S WIFE	112
BUT FROM A SHED WHERE NEITHER OF THEM COULD SEE HIM.)	194	PAUL'S WIFE	115
SO IF YOU SEE ME CELEBRATE TWO BIRTHDAYS,	196	WILD GRAPES	16
THAT I CAN SEE. THE MIND--IS NOT THE HEART.	199	WILD GRAPES	99
(SHE MADE SHREWD EYES TO SEE WHERE HE CAME IN.)	201	PLACE FOR A THIRD	57
TO SEE HOW THEY WERE MOUNTED FOR THIS WALK.	204	THE WITCH OF COOS	67
(WHERE DID I SEE ONE OF THOSE PIECES LATELY?	205	THE WITCH OF COOS	80
I COULD SEE NOTHING. "TOFFILE, I DON'T SEE IT.	205	THE WITCH OF COOS	99
I WANTED TO PUT OUT THE LIGHT AND SEE	205	THE WITCH OF COOS	104
IF I COULD SEE IT, OR ELSE MOW THE ROOM,	205	THE WITCH OF COOS	105
SON LOOKS SURPRISED TO SEE ME END A LIE	207	THE WITCH OF COOS	145
TO SEE IF THE TOWN WANTED TO TAKE OVER	208	PAUPER WITCH OF GRAFTON	24
HE'S SO FAR OFF HE CAN'T SEE WHAT I'VE COME TO.	210	PAUPER WITCH OF GRAFTON	102
I CAN JUST SEE MY TENT PEGGED,	211	AN EMPTY THREAT	7
THERE'D BEEN SOME BOSTON PEOPLE OUT TO SEE IT:	212	A FOUNTAIN, A BOTTLE	3
"HUH, THAT OLD BATHTUB, WHAT IS THAT TO SEE?	213	A FOUNTAIN, A BOTTLE	15
LET'S TALK ABOUT IT." / "LET'S GO SEE THE PLACE."	213	A FOUNTAIN, A BOTTLE	16
YOU WON'T SEE ANY MORMON SWIMMING IN IT.	213	A FOUNTAIN, A BOTTLE	27
WE MAY AS WELL SEE THAT AND SAVE THE DAY."	214	A FOUNTAIN, A BOTTLE	54
TO SEE IF IN A DREAM THEY BROUGHT OF YOU.	222	TO E.T.	4
AND SEE YOU PLEASED ONCE MORE WITH WORDS OF MINE?	222	TO E.T.	20
THE AIM WAS SONG--THE WIND COULD SEE.	224	THE AIM WAS SONG	16
HE WILL NOT SEE ME STOPPING HERE	224	STOPPING BY WOODS	3
AND I SHALL SEE THE SNOW ALL GO DOWNHILL	226	THE ONSET	18
BUT I DON'T SEE WHY IT SHOULD HAVE TO BEAR	232	THE KITCHEN CHIMNEY	18
AND THAT WAS ALL THERE WAS TO SEE	233	LOOKING FOR SUNSET BIRD	11
AS FAR AS I CAN SEE, THIS AUTUMN HAZE	247	THE COCOON	1
I OFTEN SEE FLOWERS FROM A PASSING CAR	248	A PASSING GLIMPSE	1
TO SEE WHAT THEY WERE BESIDE THE TRACK.	248	A PASSING GLIMPSE	4
LET THE NIGHT BE TOO DARK FOR ME TO SEE	249	ACCEPTANCE	13
AND SEE HOW MEN HAVE WARRED.	252	THE PEACEFUL SHEPHERD	10
WELL, WE SHOULD SEE WHICH ONE WOULD WIN,	253	THE THATCH	8
WE SHOULD SEE WHICH ONE WOULD BE FIRST TO YIELD.	253	THE THATCH	9
AND MAKE THEM SEE IT IN THE WINTER FIRELIGHT.	257	THE LOVELY BE CHOOSERS	34
THEN SEND SOME ONE WITH EYES TO SEE	257	THE LOVELY BE CHOOSERS	46
WE MEN MUST SEE YOU TO THE CONFINES OF	259	WEST-RUNNING BROOK	34
"SPEAKING OF CONTRARIES, SEE HOW THE BROOK	259	WEST-RUNNING BROOK	38
AGAINST THE STREAM, THAT MOST WE SEE OURSELVES IN,	260	WEST-RUNNING BROOK	69
SEE NOTHING WORTHY TO HAVE BEEN ITS MARK,	261	A SOLDIER	5
WE CAN JUST SEE THE INFANT UP ASTRIDE,	267	RIDERS	7
TO SEE IF SOME FORLORN MACHINE	273	A LONE STRIKER	14
ONCE WE BEGAN TO SEE OUR IMAGES.	279	THE WHITE-TAILED HORNET	64
WHEN CAME SQUARE HALE WITH LET'S SEE WHAT WE HAD;	283	THE GOLD HESPERIDEE	10
WE MUSTN'T TOUCH THEM YET, BUT SEE AND SEE!	283	THE GOLD HESPERIDEE	16
AND LOOKED AROUND TO SEE IF HE WAS SEEN.	284	THE GOLD HESPERIDEE	50
THEY COULDN'T (THIS CROSSLY): THEY HAD NONE, DIDN'T IT SEE?	287	A ROADSIDE STAND	43
MIGHT SEE THEM ON A RACK LIKE FAMOUS OARS,	290	OLD BARN AT THE BOTTOM	36
BUT WE WHO PASSED WERE NOT TO SEE HIM FALL.	292	FIGURE IN THE DOORWAY	10
BUT THE STRONG ARE SAYING NOTHING UNTIL THEY SEE.	300	STRONG SAYING NOTHING	16
BETWEEN TWO DOWNPOURS TO SEE WHAT THERE WAS.	300	MOON COMPASSES	2
FOR SWEEPING ME AWAY. LET'S SEE, WHERE WAS I?	319	BUILD SOIL	91
BUT PREACH AND SEE IF I CAN TELL THE DIFFERENCE.	322	BUILD SOIL	184
THAT NONE SHALL EVER SEE YOU COME TO MARKET--	323	BUILD SOIL	213
YOU SEE THE BEAUTY OF MY PROPOSAL IS	324	BUILD SOIL	264
ANOTHER STILL--YOU SEE YOUR PLIGHT.	325	TO A THINKER	4
I DON'T SEE BUT YOU MUST CONTINUE	326	TO A THINKER	26
HOW ANYONE CAN FAIL TO SEE	327	A MISSIVE MISSILE	33
OUR LORD TO SEE.	331	SYCAMORE	3
WITH WATER I WOULD SEE THEM WATER-BOWED.	337	THE WIND AND THE RAIN	27
TO SEE TO THE UNBURDENING OF SKIES.	337	THE WIND AND THE RAIN	46
TO SEE IF HE COULD HEAR	340	THE SUBVERTED FLOWER	38
A GIRL COULD ONLY SEE	340	THE SUBVERTED FLOWER	48
BUT WHAT SHE COULD NOT SEE	340	THE SUBVERTED FLOWER	50
AND SEE IF IT WILL HELP HER CASE."	347	DISCOVERY OF MADEIRAS	109
WATING TO SEE IF SHE WOULD MEND;	347	DISCOVERY OF MADEIRAS	112
TO SEE WHAT ON THE WHOLE THEY HAD TO SAY.	354	THE LESSON FOR TODAY	134
OR SEE WHAT COMES OF SCIENCE AND INVENTION,	355	THE LESSON FOR TODAY	143
IT FALTERED: I COULD SEE IT HESITATE:	357	A CONSIDERABLE SPECK	20
TO SEE THE STAR SHOWER KNOWN AS LEONID	360	A LOOSE MOUNTAIN	2
AND WOULD I SEE IF HE WAS RIGHT?	367	NOT OF SCHOOL AGE	28
TO SEE IT SO, THE BRIGHT AND ONLY ONE	368	THE LITERATE FARMER AND	11
ENOUGH TO SEE THEY WERE GREATLY MISSED.	368	THE LITERATE FARMER AND	18
I DIDN'T SEE THE SUN SET. DID IT SET?	368	THE LITERATE FARMER AND	19
YOU'LL SEE IT BE ALLOWED UP JUST SO HIGH,	370	THE LITERATE FARMER AND	65
I SEE WHAT YOU ARE: CAN'T GET YOU EXCITED	370	THE LITERATE FARMER AND	86
DID I SEE IT GO BY,	391	A WISH TO COMPLY	1
AND SEE AS I'M BID.	392	A WISH TO COMPLY	8
I SEE THE CALLUS ON HIS SOLE,	392	A CLIFF DWELLING	10
WILL FIND RELIEF IN ONE BURST. YOU SHALL SEE.	398	BURSTING RAPTURE	13
YOU COULD DO WORSE THAN BOOST ME UP TO SEE."	406	FROM PLANE TO PLANE	84

SEE (CONTINUED)
      YOU SEE IT IN YOURSELF AND IN THE SUN; . . . . 407 FROM PLANE TO PLANE . 100
      YET YOU REFUSE TO SEE IT IN THE DOCTOR." . . . . 407 FROM PLANE TO PLANE . 101
      AND SEE IF WE CAN TELL THE BASS FROM THE SOPRANO. . . . 415 A CABIN IN THE CLEARING 40
      AMERICA IS HARD TO SEE . . . . 416 AMERICA IS HARD TO SEE   T
      AMERICA IS HARD TO SEE. . . . . 418 AMERICA IS HARD TO SEE   61
      THEY COULD NOT SEE IT FROM OUTSIDE-- . . . . 418 AMERICA IS HARD TO SEE   64
      I SAID I WOULD SEE HOW SIRIUS KEPT . . . . 419 ONE MORE BREVITY . .   4
      AS LONG AS THE GREAT ISSUE WAS TO SEE . . . . 422 FOR JOHN F. KENNEDY . 12
      WE SEE HOW SERIOUSLY THE RACES SWARM . . . . 423 FOR JOHN F. KENNEDY . 34
      I CAN SEE NOW MIGHT-- . . . . 429 KITTY HAWK   43
      WE WOULD SEE TO YET-- . . . . 438 KITTY HAWK   330
      LET'S SEE WHERE WE ARE. . . . . 438 KITTY HAWK   339
      AND PERSUADED TO SEE . . . . 448 THE BAD ISLAND--EASTER   32
      AND WHAT DO WE SEE? . . . . 450 OBJECTION TO BE STEPPED 16
      MY CROWN SHALL OVERTAKE ME, YOU WILL SEE; . . . . . . 454 HOW HARD TO KEEP FROM   26
      SEE THAT OUR SLAVE IS ALSO. HE'S IN FAVOR. . . . . . . 455 HOW HARD TO KEEP FROM   64
      (YOU OUGHT TO SEE THE COINS DONE IN COS.) . . . . . . 459 HOW HARD TO KEEP FROM 187
      LET'S SEE, WHERE ARE WE? OH, WE'RE IN TRANSITION, . . . 462 HOW HARD TO KEEP FROM 254
      WE WOULD SEE WHAT WOULD COME . . . . 464 MILKY WAY IS A COWPATH   10
      TO SEE HOW LONG THEY SHOULD WAIT . . . . 466 SOME SCIENCE FICTION . 31
      I SEE FOR NATURE NO DEFEAT . . . . 470 IN WINTER IN THE WOODS   9
      TO GET THINGS DONE. REFORMERS FAIL TO SEE THAT.-- . . . 478 A MASQUE OF REASON . 152
      I'M CHARMED WITH HER. / YES, I COULD SEE YOU WERE. . . . 480 A MASQUE OF REASON . 182
      BETWEEN US, YOU AND I. / I MAKE YOU SEE? . . . . 480 A MASQUE OF REASON . 185
      YOU FAILED TO SEE THE WORTH OF YOUR ACHIEVEMENT. . . . . 480 A MASQUE OF REASON . 187
      IT HAS TO SEE THEM ACTED OUT BY ACTORS, ... 481 A MASQUE OF REASON . 224
      I FAIL TO SEE WHAT FUN, WHAT SATISFACTION . . . . . . 483 A MASQUE OF REASON . 273
      AND EASY TO SEE THROUGH. BUT WHERE'S HE OFF TO? . . . . 488 A MASQUE OF REASON . 428
      KEEPER, YOU COME AND SEE. OR YOU COME, PAUL. . . . . . 493 A MASQUE OF MERCY .   13
      OR SING AND DANCE ALL NIGHT AND SEE SUNRISE . . . . . . 496 A MASQUE OF MERCY .   71
      SHE'LL TAKE TO DRINK AND SEE HOW WE LIKE THAT. . . . . . 496 A MASQUE OF MERCY .   85
      ONCE AND FOR ALL. I'M GOING TO MAKE YOU SEE . . . . . . 498 A MASQUE OF MERCY . 145
      I SEE WHAT YOU ARE UP TO: ROBBING ME . . . . 499 A MASQUE OF MERCY . 147
      WHAT GOOD IS THAT? / I'LL MAKE YOU SEE WHAT GOOD. . . . 501 A MASQUE OF MERCY . 196
      WE CAN ALL SEE WHAT'S PASSING IN YOUR MIND. . . . . . . 503 A MASQUE OF MERCY . 255
      YOU SEE THE LORD GOD IS A JEALOUS GOD! . . . . 504 A MASQUE OF MERCY . 289
      AND IF IT'S PROPHECY, WE'LL SEE WHAT HAPPENS. . . . . . 505 A MASQUE OF MERCY . 299
      I DON'T SEE HOW IT CAN BE TO HIS INTEREST. . . . . . . 505 A MASQUE OF MERCY . 311
      TO SEE THAT THE FAIR FIGHT IS REALLY FAIR. . . . . . . 507 A MASQUE OF MERCY . 364
      ONLY TO SEE IT SHATTERED EVERY DAY. . . . . 508 A MASQUE OF MERCY . 373
      AND IF YOU'VE GOT TO SEE YOUR JUSTICE CROSSED . . . . . 510 A MASQUE OF MERCY . 436
      TO SEE IT, EVIL-CROSSED OR MERCY-CROSSED? . . . . . . 510 A MASQUE OF MERCY . 438
      YOU ASK IF I SEE YONDER SHINING GATE, ... 513 A MASQUE OF MERCY . 530
      DON'T LET HIM MAKE YOU SEE TOO BRIGHT A GATE . . . . . 513 A MASQUE OF MERCY . 536
      TOWARD WHAT YOU MAKE ME SEE BEYOND THE WORLD. . . . . . 514 A MASQUE OF MERCY . 545
      TO PAUL TO SEE WHAT HE CAN DO WITH IT . . . . 515 A MASQUE OF MERCY . 565
      I'D LIKE TO SEE THE WORLD TRIED ONCE WITHOUT IT. . . . . 515 A MASQUE OF MERCY . 575
      THESE TWO ARE STUBBORN CHILDREN, AS YOU SEE. . . . . . 517 A MASQUE OF MERCY . 619
      I DON'T SEE ANY STAIRCASE. / THERE ARE STAIRS. . . . . . 517 A MASQUE OF MERCY . 631
      AND I CAN SEE THAT THE UNCERTAINTY . . . . 520 A MASQUE OF MERCY . 710
      I CAN SEE THAT, IF THAT IS WHAT YOU MEAN. . . . . . . 520 A MASQUE OF MERCY . 714
SEED
      "OF COURSE YOU DID. YOU LEFT THE REST FOR SEED, ... 97 THE SELF-SEEKER . 124
      PUTTING IN THE SEED . . . . 123 PUTTING IN THE SEED .   T
      HOW LOVE BURNS THROUGH THE PUTTING IN THE SEED . . . . 124 PUTTING IN THE SEED .   10
      AND THEN SHE BEGGED THE SEED. . . . . 134 A GIRL'S GARDEN . . .   26
      THE FLOWER WAS DIFFERENT FROM THE PARENT SEED. . . . . 181 MAPLE   39
      AND SING THE WILD FLOWERS UP FROM ROOT AND SEED. . . . . 240 OUR SINGING STRENGTH . 53
      AS SAFE A VEHICLE OF SEED . . . . 281 BLUE RIBBON AT AMESBURY 35
      IS RESERVED FOR THE BED OF A FEW SELECTED SEED. . . . . 299 STRONG SAYING NOTHING .   4
      ONE STRINGING A CHAIN OF SEED IN AN OPEN CREASE, ... 299 STRONG SAYING NOTHING .   7
      THE FLOWERS FADING ON THE SEED TO COME; . . . . 356 TIME OUT   7
      FOR THE SEED OF FOLK . . . . 431 KITTY HAWK   91
      HIS FAVORITE READING IS SEED CATALOGUES. . . . . . . 496 A MASQUE OF MERCY .   81
SEEDLING
      THE STURDY SEEDLING WITH ARCHED BODY COMES . . . . . . 124 PUTTING IN THE SEED .   13
      IT HARDLY COULD HAVE BEEN A TWO-LEAVED SEEDLING . . . . 184 MAPLE   150
SEED-PEARL
      SUPPOSE SOME SEED-PEARL SUN . . . . 384 MAKING CERTAIN ANYTHING   5
SEEDPOD
      BEYOND WHERE THEY WERE WAS A SHATTERED SEEDPOD. . . . . 76 THE GENERATIONS OF MEN   74
      A RAM'S HORN ORCHID SEEDPOD FOR A WOODCHUCK . . . . . 97 THE SELF-SEEKER . 126
SEEING
      THAT OUGHT TO BE WORTH SEEING." / "IF IT'S THERE. . . . 42 THE MOUNTAIN . . .   65
      "WHAT ARE YOU SEEING OUT THE WINDOW, LADY?" . . . . . 111 IN THE HOME STRETCH .   20
      WHAT ARE YOU SEEING OUT THE WINDOW, LADY?" . . . . . 111 IN THE HOME STRETCH .   25
      "WHAT I'LL BE SEEING MORE OF IN THE YEARS . . . . . . 111 IN THE HOME STRETCH .   26
      ADDED: "YOU CAN JUDGE BETTER AFTER SEEING.-- . . . . . 144 SNOW   35
      "WAS EVER SUCH A MAN FOR SEEING LIKENESS?" . . . . . 151 SNOW   250
      THAN WE HAD SEEING HIM PASS BY IN THE ROAD . . . . . . 152 SNOW   253
      ALWAYS WRONG TO THE LIGHT, SO NEVER SEEING . . . . . . 225 FOR ONCE SOMETHING .   2
      THE DIFFICULTY OF SEEING WHAT STOOD STILL, ... 229 TWO LOOK AT TWO . .   18
      BEFORE TREES, SEEING THE OPENING, ... 264 THE LAST MOWING . . .   9
      IN HOPES OF SEEING THE CALM OF HEAVEN BREAK . . . . . 268 ON LOOKING UP BY CHANCE 14
      SEEING MYSELF WELL LOST ONCE MORE, I SIGHED, ... 295 LOST IN HEAVEN . . .   9
      SEEING NO HELP IN WINGS OR FEET . . . . 346 DISCOVERY OF MADEIRAS . 100
      FROM SEEING THIS UNDOUBTED STIR . . . . 381 AN UNSTAMPED LETTER IN   29
      BEFORE I GAVE UP SEEING AND SLEPT . . . . 419 ONE MORE BREVITY . .   3
      THE RICH IN SEEING NOTHING BUT INJUSTICE . . . . . . 509 A MASQUE OF MERCY . 412
SEEK (SEE HIDE-AND-SEEK)
      AND SEEK IT ENDLESSLY WITH PURBLIND HASTE; . . . . . . 14 WAITING   17
      HE MUST SEEK ME WOULD HE UNDO THE WRONG." . . . . . . 16 A DREAM PANG   8
      IF TIRED OF TREES I SEEK AGAIN MANKIND, ... 17 THE VANTAGE POINT . .   1
      TO SEEK THE BROOK IF STILL IT RAN; . . . . 18 GOING FOR WATER . . .   4
      AND SEEK WITH LAUGHTER WHAT TO BRAVE-- . . . . 20 THE TRIAL BY EXISTENCE   14
      THE HEART IS STILL ACHING TO SEEK, ... 30 RELUCTANCE   17
      SOME MAY KNOW WHAT THEY SEEK IN SCHOOL AND CHURCH, . . . 173 A STAR IN A STONEBOAT . 43

SEEK (CONTINUED)
```
    AND WHY THEY SEEK IT THERE; FOR WHAT I SEARCH  . . . . . 173  A STAR IN A STONEBOAT .  44
    WHO NOW WOULD FAIN SEEK SHELTERING WALL, . . . . . . . 236  MISGIVING . . . . .   7
    TO SEEK FOR THE HAPPY ISLES TOGETHER. . . . . . . . . 262  THE FLOWER BOAT . . .  12
    TO SEEK WHAT THEY SEEMED SO TO WANT. . . . . . . . . . 311  THE VINDICTIVES . . .  44
    SEEK CONVERSE COMMON CAUSE AND BROTHERHOOD . . . . . . 350  THE LESSON FOR TODAY .   9
    AND SEEK THE LOVE OF KIND IN WINTERTIME? . . . . . . . 356  A MOTH SEEN IN WINTER .   9
    SEEK NOT IN ME THE BIG I CAPITAL, . . . . . . . . . . 387  IOTA SUBSCRIPT . . .   1
    NOR YET THE LITTLE DOTTED IN ME SEEK. . . . . . . . . 387  IOTA SUBSCRIPT . . .   2
    ANY WHO SEEK HIM SEEK IN HIM THE SEEKER. . . . . . . . 421  ESCAPIST--NEVER . . .   9
    A MEANING I WAS SUPPOSED TO SEEK, . . . . . . . . . . 421  ONE MORE BREVITY . .  68
    THE FREEDOM THEY SEEK IS BY POLITICS, . . . . . . . . 461  HOW HARD TO KEEP FROM 228
    LET HIM SEEK HIS RELIGION IN THE CHURCH. . . . . . . . 494  A MASQUE OF MERCY . .  32
SEEKER (SEE SELF-SEEKER)
    HE SEEKS A SEEKER WHO IN HIS TURN SEEKS . . . . . . . 421  ESCAPIST--NEVER . . .   7
    ANY WHO SEEK HIM SEEK IN HIM THE SEEKER. . . . . . . . 421  ESCAPIST--NEVER . . .   9
SEEKING (SEE SELF-SEEKING)
    SEEKING WITH MEMORIES GROWN DIM O'ER NIGHT . . . . . .  22  THE TUFT OF FLOWERS  .  13
    WHEN ALL WHO WOULD COME SEEKING IN NEW HAMPSHIRE . . .  73  THE GENERATIONS OF MEN   2
    EYES SEEKING THE RESPONSE OF EYES . . . . . . . . . . 332  ALL REVELATION . . .  16
SEEKS
    HE SEEKS A SEEKER WHO IN HIS TURN SEEKS . . . . . . . 421  ESCAPIST--NEVER . . .   7
SEEM
    AND ON THE BAT'S MUTE ANTICS, WHO WOULD SEEM . . . . .  14  WAITING . . . . . .  14
    MAKE THE DAY SEEM TO US LESS BRIEF. . . . . . . . . .  27  OCTOBER . . . . . .   9
    IT DOESN'T SEEM SO MUCH TO CLIMB A MOUNTAIN . . . . .  43  THE MOUNTAIN . . . .  82
    'TWOULDN'T SEEM REAL TO CLIMB FOR CLIMBING IT." . . .  43  THE MOUNTAIN . . . .  88
    THEY SEEM AFRAID. HE WOULDN'T HAVE IT SO: . . . . . .  44  A HUNDRED COLLARS . .  11
    "YOU SEEM TO SHAPE THE PAPER'S POLICY." . . . . . . .  48  A HUNDRED COLLARS . . 119
    KEPT THEM AT HOME; AND IT DOES SEEM MORE HUMAN. . . .  65  A SERVANT TO SERVANTS  96
    YOU TAKE MY CARD--YOU SEEM SO GOOD AT SUCH THINGS-- .  75  THE GENERATIONS OF MEN  61
    DOES THE RAIN SEEM TO YOU TO COOL THE EYES?" . . . .  75  THE GENERATIONS OF MEN  69
    "I'LL HARDLY BREATHE." / "THE VOICES SEEM TO SAY----"  78  THE GENERATIONS OF MEN 150
    "I'M WAITING." / "DON'T! THE VOICES SEEM TO SAY: . .  78  THE GENERATIONS OF MEN 151
    "YOU SEEM SO PARTIAL TO OUR GREAT-GRANDMOTHER . . . .  79  THE GENERATIONS OF MEN 177
    AND THEN THE VOICE AGAIN: "YOU SEEM AFRAID. . . . . .  91  THE FEAR . . . . . .  72
    ITS SEEMING BAD FOR A MOMENT MAKES IT SEEM . . . . . 115  IN THE HOME STRETCH . 128
    AND THEY SEEM NOT TO BREAK; THOUGH ONCE THEY ARE BOWED 121  BIRCHES . . . . . .  15
    TO SEEM TO SAY GOOD-BY; . . . . . . . . . . . . . . 126  LONELINESS . . . . .   4
    MADE THE GREAT TREE SEEM AS A LITTLE BIRD . . . . . . 128  THE OFT-REPEATED DREAM   7
    OR NOT MUCH BETTER. WHY, IT DOESN'T SEEM . . . . . . 145  SNOW . . . . . . .  59
    GOOD! WHY I ASKED--SHE DIDN'T SEEM TO ANSWER.-- . . . 155  SNOW . . . . . . . 330
    IT MADE THE WORLD SEEM SO MYSTERIOUS. . . . . . . . . 163  NEW HAMPSHIRE . . . 134
    NO WONDER POETS SOMETIMES HAVE TO SEEM . . . . . . . 164  NEW HAMPSHIRE . . . 172
    THE GLORIOUS BARDS OF MASSACHUSETTS SEEM . . . . . . 167  NEW HAMPSHIRE . . . 262
    THE MORE I SEEM TO WANT MY MOUNTAINS WILD; . . . . . 170  NEW HAMPSHIRE . . . 344
    IT MADE IT SEEM AS IF THERE MUST BE SOMETHING . . . . 182  MAPLE . . . . . .  94
    AS THE MOON USED TO SEEM WHEN I WAS YOUNGER, . . . . 197  WILD GRAPES . . . .  29
    AND NO ONE SEEM NEGLECTING OR NEGLECTED? . . . . . . 200  PLACE FOR A THIRD . .  29
    I HEARD THEM. TOFFILE DIDN'T SEEM TO HEAR THEM. . . . 206  THE WITCH OF COOS . . 117
    IT DOESN'T SEEM AS IF I'D HAD THE COURAGE . . . . . . 210  PAUPER WITCH OF GRAFTON 106
    I MIGHT HAVE, BUT IT DOESN'T SEEM AS IF. . . . . . . 210  PAUPER WITCH OF GRAFTON 108
    HOW NO ONE DEAD WILL SEEM TO COME. . . . . . . . . . 221  IN A DISUSED GRAVEYARD  11
    IT MAY NOT SEEM BETTER TO ME TO REST. . . . . . . . . 236  MISGIVING . . . . .  16
    AN HOUR OF WINTER DAY MIGHT SEEM TOO SHORT . . . . . 254  A WINTER EDEN . . .  19
    SEEM TO THEM LESS THAN THEY ARE. . . . . . . . . . . 257  THE LOVELY BE CHOOSERS  40
    AND ALL OUR BLANDISHMENTS WOULD SEEM DEFIED, . . . . 268  RIDERS . . . . . .  11
    THE PLANETS SEEM TO INTERFERE IN THEIR CURVES, . . . 268  ON LOOKING UP BY CHANCE  6
    AND THIS DAY'S WORK MADE EVEN THAT SEEM DOUBTFUL. . . 279  THE WHITE-TAILED HORNET 70
    THAT BLINKING COULD NOT SEEM TO BLINK AWAY. . . . . . 293  AT WOODWARD'S GARDENS .  11
    SO WATERY AS TO SEEM SUBMARINE; . . . . . . . . . . 315  IRIS BY NIGHT . . .  11
    THE TIMES SEEM REVOLUTIONARY BAD. . . . . . . . . . . 317  BUILD SOIL . . . .  32
    THE LAST BEING WHAT THEY SEEM TO HAVE IN RUSSIA. . . 318  BUILD SOIL . . . .  74
    MAY SEEM ALMOST EXCLUSIVELY DESIGNED. . . . . . . . . 321  BUILD SOIL . . . . 150
    DON'T LET ME SEEM TO SAY THE EXCHANGE, THE ENCOUNTER, 321  BUILD SOIL . . . . 157
    THE LAND MAY SEEM TO HAVE ON MAN TO USE IT. . . . . . 322  BUILD SOIL . . . . 208
    SO VIVID AS TO SEEM TO SPEAK. . . . . . . . . . . . 327  A MISSIVE MISSILE . .   8
    AND YET 'TWOULD SEEM THAT WHAT IS SUNG . . . . . . . 336  THE WIND AND THE RAIN  18
    AND TO THOSE CONCERNED HE MAY SEEM A LITTLE LATE. . . 342  WILLFUL HOMING . . .  12
    BEGAN ALREADY TO SEEM FORLORN. . . . . . . . . . . . 344  DISCOVERY OF MADEIRAS  18
    WHICH MAKES THE WAR GOD SEEM NO SPECIAL DUNCE . . . . 350  TO A YOUNG WRETCH . .  17
    BUT COME, ENLIGHTENED AS IN TALK YOU SEEM, . . . . . 370  THE LITERATE FARMER AND 61
    MAY SEEM AS IF IT SHOULD HAVE BEEN A QUARRY-- . . . . 377  DIRECTIVE . . . . .  10
    FORGIVE ME IF I SEEM TO BOAST. . . . . . . . . . . . 381  AN UNSTAMPED LETTER IN  39
    DEAN, ADULT EDUCATION MAY SEEM SILLY. . . . . . . . . 393  LUCRETIUS VERSUS POETS   1
    THEIR NUMBER WOULD SEEM LIMITED TO THREE. . . . . . . 398  NO HOLY WARS FOR THEM .   2
    AND SO TO LET PIKE SEEM TO HAVE THE PALM . . . . . . 408  FROM PLANE TO PLANE . 120
    I CAN'T MAKE IT SEEM . . . . . . . . . . . . . . . . 430  KITTY HAWK . . . .  85
    HOW TOTALLY IGNORED I SEEM TO BE. . . . . . . . . . . 462  HOW HARD TO KEEP FROM 259
    WON'T SEEM UNHERETICAL QUITE. . . . . . . . . . . . 466  SOME SCIENCE FICTION .  20
    THE BIRDS, SEEM ALL ON FIRE WITH PARADISE. . . . . . 473  A MASQUE OF REASON . .  13
    IT HAD TO SEEM UNMEANING TO HAVE MEANING. . . . . . . 475  A MASQUE OF REASON . .  64
    ALL YOU CAN SEEM TO DO IS LOSE YOUR TEMPER . . . . . 478  A MASQUE OF REASON . . 135
    DID SEEM UNLIKE YOU, AND I TRIED TO THINK . . . . . . 482  A MASQUE OF REASON . . 263
    I MEAN WE SEEM TO KNOW ENOUGH TO ACT ON. . . . . . . 483  A MASQUE OF REASON . . 290
    YES, YES. / YOU DON'T SEEM SATISFIED. / I AM. . . . . 486  A MASQUE OF REASON . . 375
    YOU SEEM SO READY AT TRANSLATING NAMES. . . . . . . . 495  A MASQUE OF MERCY . .  61
    THAT MADE ALL OTHER OUTRAGE SEEM AS CHILD'S PLAY: . . 511  A MASQUE OF MERCY . . 476
SEEMED
    SEEMED TIPPED WITH WINGS OF COLOR . . . . . . . . . .  13  ROSE POGONIAS . . .  15
    ANYTHING MORE THAN THE TRUTH WOULD HAVE SEEMED TOO WEAK 17  MOWING . . . . . .   9
    IT SEEMED GOD LET THEE FLUTTER FROM HIS GENTLE CLASP,  29  MY BUTTERFLY . . .  27
    WARREN RETURNED--TOO SOON, IT SEEMED TO HER-- . . . .  40  DEATH OF THE HIRED MAN 164
    NEAR ME IT SEEMED: I FELT IT LIKE A WALL . . . . . .  40  THE MOUNTAIN . . . .   5
    IT SEEMED NO HARM TO STOP HIM ALTOGETHER. . . . . . .  41  THE MOUNTAIN . . . .  18
    A LITTLE COTTAGE THIS HAS ALWAYS SEEMED; . . . . . .  56  THE BLACK COTTAGE . .  35
    THAT SEEMED TOO PAGAN TO OUR LIBERAL YOUTH. . . . . .  58  THE BLACK COTTAGE . .  95
    SEEMED TO WARN SOMEONE TO BE GETTING OUT . . . . . .  89  THE FEAR . . . . .  20
```

SEEMED (CONTINUED)
  "NOTHING." A PAUSE: THERE SEEMED NO MORE TO SAY. . . . . 91 THE FEAR 71
  BUT THIRTY DOLLARS SEEMED SO SMALL BESIDE . . . . 107 CHRISTMAS TREES . . 47
  IT ALMOST SEEMED TO COME BALLOONING UP. . . . . 113 IN THE HOME STRETCH . 88
  "GOOD BOYS THEY SEEMED, AND LET THEM LOVE THE CITY. . . 114 IN THE HOME STRETCH . 119
  AND ALL THE TIME WE TALKED YOU SEEMED TO SEE . . . . . 119 MEETING AND PASSING . 10
  THEY SEEMED TO FAIL THE BLUEBIRDS UNDER THEM . . . . . 130 THE BONFIRE 36
  LEAPED OUT AT THE BOY'S HAND, OR SEEMED TO LEAP-- . . . 136 "OUT,OUT--" 16
  AND SOMETIMES SOMETHING SEEMED TO YIELD, ... 138 BROWN'S DESCENT . . 18
  MESERVE SEEMED TO HEED NOTHING BUT THE LAMP . . . . . 147 SNOW 111
  THEY SEEMED TO ASK HIM JUST TO SEE HIM GO, ... 191 PAUL'S WIFE . . . 23
  WHEN THE GIRL SEEMED TOO WATERLOGGED TO LIVE, ... 194 PAUL'S WIFE . . . 117
  LABAN WAS OLD AND POOR, YET SEEMED TO CARE; . . . . . 201 PLACE FOR A THIRD . 50
  EXCEPT, IT SEEMED, THE POETESS'S POEMS. . . . . 216 A FOUNTAIN, A BOTTLE . 91
  THE WAR SEEMED OVER MORE FOR YOU THAN ME, ... 222 TO E.T. 15
  AND ONCE THAT SEEMED TOO MUCH; . . . . 226 TO EARTHWARD . . .   3
  SEEMED STRONG WHEN I WAS YOUNG; . . . . 227 TO EARTHWARD . . . 14
  SHE SEEMED TO THINK THAT, TWO THUS, THEY WERE SAFE. . . 229 TWO LOOK AT TWO . . 21
  WASN'T SHE GLAD NOW? EVERYTHING SEEMED WON, ... 230 NOT TO KEEP . . . 11
  WHEN IT SEEMED AS IF I COULD BEAR NO MORE. . . . . . . 250 A MINOR BIRD . . .   4
  THE MOUNTAIN SEEMED TO LIKE THE STIR, ... 265 THE BIRTHPLACE . .   8
  WHEN INDUSTRY SEEMED LIKE TO DIE . . . . 274 A LONE STRIKER . . 58
  OR EVEN MERELY SEEMED TO PINE . . . . 275 A LONE STRIKER . . 60
  AND THE LIGHT-NATURED TREE SEEMED NOT TO CARE! . . . . 284 THE GOLD HESPERIDEE . 40
  IT SEEMED TO ME, BY THE PEOPLE THERE, ... 291 ON HEART'S BEGINNING TO   9
  AND WHEN THEY CAME IT SEEMED WITH A WILL TO CARRY ME WITH
    THEM TO DEATH. . . . . 297 A LEAF-TREADER . . .   8
  BUT WHEN THERE SEEMED NO MORE TO BRING, ... 310 THE VINDICTIVES . . 14
  TO SEEK WHAT THEY SEEMED SO TO WANT. . . . . 311 THE VINDICTIVES . . 44
  IT HAD SEEMED DISCREET TO REMAIN THERE . . . . 314 BEARER OF EVIL TIDINGS 25
  SEEMED TO ARGUE PERHAPS SHE WENT . . . . 343 DISCOVERY OF MADEIRAS . 13
  THE SHIP IT SEEMED HAD BEEN A SLAVER. . . . . 345 DISCOVERY OF MADEIRAS . 53
  THE JEST SEEMED HIS AND THE PLAUDITS HIS. . . . . . . 346 DISCOVERY OF MADEIRAS . 92
  AND VERY WIDE THE CHOICE THEY SEEMED TO GIVE; . . . . 354 THE LESSON FOR TODAY . 137
  IT SEEMED TOO TINY TO HAVE ROOM FOR FEET, ... 357 A CONSIDERABLE SPECK . 16
  IT SEEMED AS IF I COULDN'T STAND THE STRAIN. . . . . . 398 BURSTING RAPTURE . .   8
  IT SEEMED TO COMFORT US TO CALL IT CORN. . . . . . . 446 DOES NO ONE AT ALL EVER   9
  IT SEEMED I WAS A MITE OF SEDIMENT . . . . 468 IN A GLASS OF CIDER .   1
  WHERE MERCY-CROSSED TO ME SEEMED EVIL-CROSSED. . . . . 510 A MASQUE OF MERCY . 443
SEEING
  AND FEAR OF SEEMING SHORT OF SPEECH, OR WHETHER . . . . 106 CHRISTMAS TREES . . 27
  ITS SEEMING BAD FOR A MOMENT MAKES IT SEEM . . . . . 115 IN THE HOME STRETCH . 128
  I PUT NO FAITH IN THE SEEMING FACTS OF LIGHT. . . . . 389 SKEPTIC   4
SEEMINGLY
  SEEMINGLY HAS CEASED . . . . 435 KITTY HAWK 239
SEEMS
  I BROUGHT NOT HERE TO READ, IT SEEMS, BUT HOLD . . . . 15 WAITING 24
  BUT IT SEEMS LIKE THE SEA'S RETURN . . . . 27 A LINE-STORM SONG . 26
  AND IT SEEMS LIKE THE TIME WHEN, AFTER DOUBT, ... 27 A LINE-STORM SONG . 29
  IT SEEMS FOREVER-- . . . . 28 MY BUTTERFLY . . . 11
  HE MOVES IN DARKNESS AS IT SEEMS TO ME, ... 34 MENDING WALL . . . 41
  IT ALWAYS SEEMS TO ME A SORT OF MARK . . . . 56 THE BLACK COTTAGE . 45
  "HE SEEMS TO BE THRIFTY; AND HASN'T HE NEED, ... 60 BLUEBERRIES . . . 48
  I GUESS YOU'D FIND... IT SEEMS TO ME . . . . 62 A SERVANT TO SERVANTS .   6
  THAT SEEMS TO TELL ME HOW I OUGHT TO FEEL, ... 63 A SERVANT TO SERVANTS . 14
  PUT ON ME, BUT THERE SEEMS NO OTHER WAY. . . . . 64 A SERVANT TO SERVANTS . 54
  "ON FATHER'S SIDE, IT SEEMS, WE'RE--LET ME SEE----" . . 76 THE GENERATIONS OF MEN 78
  SHE SEEMS TO HAVE THE HOUSEWORK, AND BESIDES, ... 85 THE HOUSEKEEPER . . 107
  "IT SEEMS AS IF. AND THAT'S NOT ALL: HE'S HELPLESS . . . 86 THE HOUSEKEEPER . . 156
  THEY LEAVE US TO: THAT PASTURE SLOPE THAT SEEMS . . . . 114 IN THE HOME STRETCH . 113
  SEEMS HAUNTED OR EXPOSED. I ALWAYS TAKE . . . . 115 IN THE HOME STRETCH . 133
  BY ITS OWN POWER SEEMS TO BE UNDONE, ... 125 AN ENCOUNTER . . .   3
  JUST WHEN IT SEEMS TO COME IN RIGHT, ... 134 A GIRL'S GARDEN . . 43
  HE SEEMS TO HAVE LOST OFF HIS CHRISTIAN NAME." . . . . 144 SNOW 47
  "THE WHOLE TO-DO SEEMS TO HAVE BEEN FOR NOTHING. . . . 155 SNOW 337
  SEEMS TO HAVE BEEN A MAN NAMED JOHN L. DARWIN." . . . . 168 NEW HAMPSHIRE . . 299
  IT SEEMS A NARROW CHOICE THE AGE INSISTS ON. . . . . . 171 NEW HAMPSHIRE . . 403
  SEEMS TO ME OWES IT TO THE TOWN TO KEEP ONE. . . . . . 177 THE STAR-SPLITTER . 36
  BUT IT SEEMS LIKE SOME WORD SHE LEFT TO BID YOU . . . . 180 MAPLE 21
  THAT CALM SEEMS CERTAINLY SAFE TO LAST TONIGHT. . . . . 268 ON LOOKING UP BY CHANCE 16
  THE UNIVERSE SEEMS CRAMPED TO YOU AND ME. . . . . . . 269 THE BEAR 12
  THROUGH NINETY-ODD DEGREES OF ARC, IT SEEMS, ... 269 THE BEAR 24
  IT SEEMS AS IF YOU MUST HAVE HEARD. . . . . 280 BLUE RIBBON AT AMESBURY   9
  OR SO THE VOICE OF THE COUNTRY SEEMS TO COMPLAIN. . . . 287 A ROADSIDE STAND . . 46
  SEEMS NOT EVEN IMPRESSED. . . . . 288 DEPARTMENTAL . . . 17
  IF THIS SEEMS LIKE WITCHCRAFT RATHER, ... 304 CLEAR AND COLDER . 16
  IF THIS SEEMS A WITCHES' CHOWDER . . . . 304 CLEAR AND COLDER . 17
  LAWS TO ITSELF, IT SEEMS, AND YET HAVE NO . . . . . . 324 BUILD SOIL . . . 247
  SEEMS TO OWE NAUGHT TO ANY SINGLE CORD; . . . . 332 THE SILKEN TENT . .   8
  TO TIME IT NEVER SEEMS THAT HE IS BRAVE . . . . 334 I COULD GIVE ALL .   1
  SEEMS AS EXPRESSIVE OF THE HUMAN RACE . . . . 382 TO AN ANCIENT . .   8
  THE CITY SEEMS IN-TOPPLING FROM A HEIGHT, ... 386 THE FEAR OF MAN . .   5
  SEEMS TO COME TO AN END . . . . 388 MIDDLENESS OF THE ROAD   2
  IT SEEMS TO GO INTO A WOOD, ... 388 MIDDLENESS OF THE ROAD   5
  BUT IF THAT SEEMS TO TEND . . . . 389 ASTROMETAPHYSICAL . 17
  THERE SANDY SEEMS THE GOLDEN SKY . . . . 392 A CLIFF DWELLING . .   1
  AND GOLDEN SEEMS THE SANDY PLAIN. . . . . 392 A CLIFF DWELLING . .   2
  THE PLAY SEEMS OUT FOR AN ALMOST INFINITE RUN. . . . . 392 IT BIDS PRETTY FAIR .   1
  AND SO IT SEEMS A FLOWER'S COMING OUT . . . . 411 POD OF THE MILKWEED .   8
  HE SEEMS TO SAY THE REASON WHY SO MUCH . . . . 412 POD OF THE MILKWEED . 53
  SEEMS SOMETHING ARTISTS OUGHT TO CELEBRATE. . . . . . 422 FOR JOHN F. KENNEDY .   3
  IT SEEMS YOU CALL QUINTESSENCE QUINTESSENCE." . . . . 455 HOW HARD TO KEEP FROM 51
  (HE SEEMS TO HAVE FELT LIMITED TO ONE), ... 456 HOW HARD TO KEEP FROM 71
  BUT THAT IS AS DARIUS SEEMS TO WANT IT. . . . . 462 HOW HARD TO KEEP FROM 264
  AND TOOK YOUR TIME TO IT. IT SEEMS TO ME . . . . . . 482 A MASQUE OF REASON . 245
  I DID NOT ASK THEN, BUT IT SEEMS AS IF . . . . 482 A MASQUE OF REASON . 266
  YET I SUPPOSE WHAT SEEMS TO US CONFUSION . . . . . . 485 A MASQUE OF REASON . 338
  IT SEEMS TO START RIGHT OFF ACCELERATING. . . . . . . 489 A MASQUE OF REASON . 450

```
                                                      PAGE TITLE                        LINE
SEEMS (CONTINUED)
    TO A BAD START IT SEEMS IN THE WRONG SCHOOL  . . . . .  499 A MASQUE OF MERCY  . . 162
    IT SEEMS TO BE A CHAPTER HEAD IN METER.  . . . . . . .  506 A MASQUE OF MERCY  . . 327
    THEN FURTHER DOWN IT SEEMS TO START FROM WHERE . . . .  506 A MASQUE OF MERCY  . . 335
    THE WORLD SEEMS CRYING OUT FOR A MESSIAH.  . . . . . .  515 A MASQUE OF MERCY  . . 576
SEEN
    NO ONE HAS SEEN THEM MADE OR HEARD THEM MADE,  . . . .   33 MENDING WALL  . . . .  10
    AND SHE LIKED TALK. SHE HAD SEEN GARRISON  . . . . . .   56 THE BLACK COTTAGE . .  52
    BLACK SHE HAD SCARCELY SEEN, AND YELLOW NEVER. . . . .   57 THE BLACK COTTAGE . .  76
    "YOU OUGHT TO HAVE SEEN WHAT I SAW ON MY WAY . . . . .   59 BLUEBERRIES . . . . .   1
    AND SOME OF THEM RIPE! YOU OUGHT TO HAVE SEEN!" . . . .  59 BLUEBERRIES . . . . .   7
    "I WISH YOU HAD SEEN HIS PERPETUAL BOW-- . . . . . . .   61 BLUEBERRIES . . . . .  57
    YOU OUGHT TO HAVE SEEN HOW IT LOOKED IN THE RAIN, . . .  62 BLUEBERRIES . . . . . 103
    I'D SEEN ABOUT ENOUGH OF HIS BULLING TRICKS. . . . . .   71 THE CODE  . . . . . .  47
    WE HAVE SEEN VISIONS--NOW CONSULT THE VOICES. . . . . .  77 THE GENERATIONS OF MEN 126
    "HAVEN'T YOU SEEN HIM? STRANGE WHAT SET YOU OFF . . . .  81 THE HOUSEKEEPER . . .  14
    YOU MUST HAVE SEEN IT TOO." / "I DIDN'T SEE IT. . . . .  89 THE FEAR  . . . . . .  12
    HE HAS SEEN ALL THERE WAS TO SEE AND GONE." . . . . . .  91 THE FEAR  . . . . . .  58
    ISN'T IT SOMETHING I HAVE SEEN BEFORE?" . . . . . . . .  99 THE SELF-SEEKER . . . 189
    THIS AS IT WILL BE SEEN IS OTHER FAR . . . . . . . . . 119 HYLA BROOK  . . . . .  13
    AS ICE STORMS DO. OFTEN YOU MUST HAVE SEEN THEM . . . . 121 BIRCHES . . . . . . .   5
    GOING THE OTHER WAY AND THEY NOT SEEN IT.  . . . . . . 132 THE BONFIRE . . . . .  88
    AND MANY MUST HAVE SEEN HIM MAKE  . . . . . . . . . . 137 BROWN'S DESCENT . . .   5
    I'VE SEEN THE TIME I'VE HAD TO WORK MYSELF. . . . . . . 159 NEW HAMPSHIRE . . . .   6
    OR HAVING SEEN AND CREDITED A MOMENT . . . . . . . . . 169 NEW HAMPSHIRE . . . . 321
    BUT THE SAD ACCIDENT OF HAVING SEEN . . . . . . . . . . 169 NEW HAMPSHIRE . . . . 329
    THEY CLUNG TO WHAT ONE HAD SEEN IN THE OTHER . . . . . 184 MAPLE . . . . . . . . 134
    GRAPES, I KNEW GRAPES FROM HAVING SEEN THEM LAST YEAR. . 197 WILD GRAPES . . . . .  24
    IF ANYONE HAD SEEN ME COMING HOME  . . . . . . . . . . 210 PAUPER WITCH OF GRAFTON 85
    IF SEEN CLEAR,  . . . . . . . . . . . . . . . . . . . 212 AN EMPTY THREAT . . .  54
    YOU SAID YOU'D SEEN THE STONE BAPTISMAL FONT. . . . . . 213 A FOUNTAIN, A BOTTLE .  13
    TWO HAD SEEN TWO, WHICHEVER SIDE YOU SPOKE FROM. . . . 230 TWO LOOK AT TWO . . .  38
    AS OFTEN AS I'VE SEEN IT DONE BEFORE . . . . . . . . . 237 A HILLSIDE THAW . . .   4
    NOW WAS SEEN HOW THESE LIKED BELATED SNOW. . . . . . . 239 OUR SINGING STRENGTH .  25
    AND DROPPED IT IN, AND SEEN THE IMAGE WALLOW, . . . . . 245 THE FREEDOM OF THE MOON 11
    BUT, TREE, I HAVE SEEN YOU TAKEN AND TOSSED, . . . . . 252 TREE AT MY WINDOW . .   9
    AND IF YOU HAVE SEEN ME WHEN I SLEPT, . . . . . . . . . 252 TREE AT MY WINDOW . .  10
    YOU HAVE SEEN ME WHEN I WAS TAKEN AND SWEPT . . . . . . 252 TREE AT MY WINDOW . .  11
    AND NEVER SEEN SUN-SMITTEN SLIME . . . . . . . . . . . 266 SITTING BY A BUSH . .  10
    AND LOOKED AROUND TO SEE IF HE WAS SEEN. . . . . . . . 284 THE GOLD HESPERIDEE .  50
    WERE SEEN OF OLD AT MEMPHIS ON THE HEIGHTS . . . . . . 315 IRIS BY NIGHT . . . .   6
    THAT IN A GOOD GLASS MAY BE SEEN TO CRAWL  . . . . . . 352 THE LESSON FOR TODAY .  71
    A MOTH SEEN IN WINTER  . . . . . . . . . . . . . . . . 356 A MOTH SEEN IN WINTER .   T
    THAT THE LOOSE MOUNTAIN LATELY SEEN TO GLINT . . . . . 361 A LOOSE MOUNTAIN  . .  14
    'TIS POSSIBLE YOU MAY HAVE SEEN, . . . . . . . . . . . 381 AN UNSTAMPED LETTER IN  40
    NOW JUST AHEAD OF HIM WAS SEEN TO YAWN . . . . . . . . 394 HAEC FABULA DOCET . .   5
    NO ONE HAS SEEN HIM STUMBLE LOOKING BACK. . . . . . . . 421 ESCAPIST--NEVER . . .   2
    THEY MUST HAVE SEEN AHEAD WHAT NOW APPEARS: . . . . . . 423 FOR JOHN F. KENNEDY .  28
    TIME HAD SEEN AMASS  . . . . . . . . . . . . . . . . . 429 KITTY HAWK  . . . . .  48
    ARE SEEN TO JUGGLE MOONS GALORE. . . . . . . . . . . . 451 A-WISHING WELL  . . .  24
SEERS
    SO MUCH THEY KNEW AS CONSECRATED SEERS . . . . . . . . 422 FOR JOHN F. KENNEDY .  27
SEES
    THE BEAUTIES SHE SO TRULY SEES, . . . . . . . . . . . .   7 MY NOVEMBER GUEST . .  13
    GOOD ARGUMENTS HE SEES HE MIGHT HAVE USED. . . . . . .  37 DEATH OF THE HIRED MAN  75
    AND SEES OLD FRIENDS HE SOMEHOW CAN'T GET NEAR. . . . .  44 A HUNDRED COLLARS . .   7
    NOW WHEN SHE SEES IN THE VILLAGE . . . . . . . . . . . 134 A GIRL'S GARDEN . . .  41
    I HOPE IF HE IS WHERE HE SEES ME NOW . . . . . . . . . 210 PAUPER WITCH OF GRAFTON 101
SEGUB
    AND LOOK FOR JUSTICE IN THE CASE OF SEGUB. . . . . . . 477 A MASQUE OF REASON  . 114
SEIZE
    THE SAME AS YOU SEIZE CAT'S-CRADLE STRINGS, . . . . . . 123 PEA BRUSH . . . . . .  19
    NOT THOUGH WE HAVE TO SEIZE EARTH BY THE POLE . . . . 238 ON A TREE FALLEN ACROSS 12
    FOR EVERY PARCEL I STOOP DOWN TO SEIZE . . . . . . . . 266 THE ARMFUL  . . . . .   1
    AND SEIZE THE DAY OF PLEASURE." . . . . . . . . . . . . 335 CARPE DIEM  . . . . .  10
    BUT BID LIFE SEIZE THE PRESENT? . . . . . . . . . . . . 335 CARPE DIEM  . . . . .  19
SEIZED
    DOOR-FILLING MEN BURST IN AND SEIZED THE STOVE. . . . . 113 IN THE HOME STRETCH .  83
    OF SEIZING FROM US AS HE MIGHT HAVE SEIZED. . . . . . . 127 THE SMILE . . . . . .   7
SEIZES
    BUT THE OLD FOOL SEIZES HIS FORK IN BOTH HANDS, . . . .  71 THE CODE  . . . . . .  61
    SEIZES THE DEAD BY THE MIDDLE, . . . . . . . . . . . . 289 DEPARTMENTAL  . . . .  37
SEIZING
    OF SEIZING FROM US AS HE MIGHT HAVE SEIZED. . . . . . . 127 THE SMILE . . . . . .   7
SEKHTI
    AS ONCE THE PHARAOH DID IT OUT OF SEKHTI . . . . . . . 517 A MASQUE OF MERCY . . 641
SELDOM
    IT'S SELDOM I GET DOWN EXCEPT FOR MEALS, THOUGH. . . . .  49 A HUNDRED COLLARS . . 146
    THESE DOORSTEPS SELDOM HAVE A VISITOR. . . . . . . . .  56 THE BLACK COTTAGE . .  48
    THOUGH THE RAM'S HORN IS SELDOM TO BE HAD  . . . . . .  97 THE SELF-SEEKER . . . 129
    IT SELDOM OVERTAXED THEIR STRENGTH; . . . . . . . . . . 273 A LONE STRIKER  . . .  22
    THERE IS SELDOM MORE THAN A MAN TO A HARROWED PIECE. . . 299 STRONG SAYING NOTHING .   5
SELECTED
    IS RESERVED FOR THE BED OF A FEW SELECTED SEED. . . . . 299 STRONG SAYING NOTHING .   4
SELF
    IN ONE SELF STATION. . . . . . . . . . . . . . . . . . 219 I WILL SING YOU ONE-O .  67
    OR FROM HER OWN SELF AGAINST HER WILL . . . . . . . . . 343 DISCOVERY OF MADEIRAS .   3
    NATURE WITHIN HER INMOST SELF DIVIDES  . . . . . . . . 468 FROM IRON . . . . . .   1
SELF-AGGRANDIZEMENT
    WHICH FOR NO SORDID SELF-AGGRANDIZEMENT, . . . . . . . 319 BUILD SOIL  . . . . . 103
SELF-AROUSING
    DANGEROUS SELF-AROUSING WORDS TO SOW. . . . . . . . . . 180 MAPLE . . . . . . . .  29
SELF-ASSURANCE
    HIS NATTY WINGS WITH SELF-ASSURANCE PERK. . . . . . . . 309 WASPISH . . . . . . .   3
SELF-BEFRIENDED
    WRAPPED IN AROUND ITSELF AND SELF-BEFRIENDED, . . . . . 396 ANY SIZE WE PLEASE  .  10
SELF-BEGUN
    NEITHER WAS SONG THAT DAY TO BE SELF-BEGUN. . . . . . . 236 VALLEY'S SINGING DAY .  14
```

SELF-CLEAR
    TO BLOW THE EARTH OR ANYTHING SELF-CLEAR; . . . . . . 246 ATMOSPHERE   4
SELF-COLLAPSE
    AT LAST IN SELF-COLLAPSE . . . . 464 MILKY WAY IS A COWPATH   13
SELF-CONCEIVED
    IS THAT THE ALL'S A CONCEPT SELF-CONCEIVED, ... 427 CONCEPT SELF-CONCEIVED   3
    A CONCEPT SELF-CONCEIVED . . . . 427 CONCEPT SELF-CONCEIVED   T
SELF-CONFERRED
    AS A SMALL SELF-CONFERRED REWARD OF VIRTUE. . . . . . . 405 FROM PLANE TO PLANE . 39
SELF-CONSCIOUSNESS
    BEYOND EMBARRASSING SELF-CONSCIOUSNESS . . . . 318 BUILD SOIL 82
SELF-CONTROL
    THE BLOWS THAT A LIFE OF SELF-CONTROL . . . . 275 TWO TRAMPS IN MUD TIME 13
SELF-DEFENSE
    IN SELF-DEFENSE TO QUIZZICAL INQUIRY: . . . . 365 OF STONES OF THE PLACE 14
SELF-EMBRACE
    HE DREW THEM IN FOR WARMTH OF SELF-EMBRACE. . . . . . 396 ANY SIZE WE PLEASE . . 8
SELF-FORGETFULNESS
    WHERE YOU MUST LIE IN SELF-FORGETFULNESS . . . . . 516 A MASQUE OF MERCY . . 613
SELFISH
    OF ALL THE THOUSAND SELFISH CARS THAT PASS, ... 287 A ROADSIDE STAND   . . 37
SELFLESS
    OUR SELFLESS FORAGER JERRY. . . . . 288 DEPARTMENTAL 24
SELF-OVERTHROW
    THAT SELF-SACK AND SELF-OVERTHROW, ... 311 THE VINDICTIVES . . . 37
SELF-REPROACH
    WITHOUT SELF-REPROACH." . . . . 437 KITTY HAWK 286
SELF-RESPECT
    SOME HUMBLE WAY TO SAVE HIS SELF-RESPECT. . . . . . 36 DEATH OF THE HIRED MAN 50
SELF-RESTRAINT
    IN SELF-RESTRAINT, IF IN RESTRAINT OF TRADE. . . . . 323 BUILD SOIL 229
SELF-RETREAT
    SHE WITHDREW BACK IN SELF-RETREAT . . . . 346 DISCOVERY OF MADEIRAS . 101
SELF-SACK
    THAT SELF-SACK AND SELF-OVERTHROW, ... 311 THE VINDICTIVES . . . 37
SELFSAME
    IN THE SELFSAME DAY, ... 433 KITTY HAWK 177
SELF-SEEKER
    THE SELF-SEEKER . . . . 92 THE SELF-SEEKER . . . T
SELF-SEEKING
    AND HER SELF-SEEKING, FITFUL THOUGH IT WAS, ... 182 MAPLE 72
SELF-SUPERSEDING
    WHILE SCIENCE GOES SELF-SUPERSEDING ON. . . . . . 480 A MASQUE OF REASON . 193
SELF-SUPPORT
    SPENDING YOURSELF TOO MUCH IN SELF-SUPPORT. . . . . . 356 A MOTH SEEN IN WINTER . 12
SELF-SUPPORTING
    SO THEN, TO MAKE ME WHOLLY SELF-SUPPORTING, ... 197 WILD GRAPES 36
SELF-TAUGHT
    SELF-TAUGHT. BUT OUR BRUTE SNARLING AND LASHING TAUGHT IT. . 320 BUILD SOIL 120
SELF-THROWN
    A PENITENT PERHAPS, SELF-THROWN ON MERCY. . . . . . 516 A MASQUE OF MERCY . 610
SELL
    HER SONS WON'T SELL THE HOUSE OR THE THINGS IN IT. . . . 55 THE BLACK COTTAGE . 16
    THEY SELL IN THE STORE AND BUY SHOES FOR THEIR FEET." . . 61 BLUEBERRIES 53
    IF HE COULD SELL THE PLACE, BUT THEN, HE CAN'T: . . . . 83 THE HOUSEKEEPER . . . 48
    THAT MUCH TO SELL, THEY'RE WORTH AS MUCH TO KEEP. . . . . 86 THE HOUSEKEEPER . . . 141
    I'M GOING TO SELL MY SOUL, OR RATHER, FEET. . . . . . 92 THE SELF-SEEKER . . . 3
    AND IF YOU'RE GOING TO SELL THEM TO THE DEVIL, ... 93 THE SELF-SEEKER . . . 6
    HE ASKED IF I WOULD SELL MY CHRISTMAS TREES; . . . . . 106 CHRISTMAS TREES . . . 12
    TO SELL THEM OFF THEIR FEET TO GO IN CARS . . . . . 106 CHRISTMAS TREES . . . 17
    WORTH THREE CENTS MORE TO GIVE AWAY THAN SELL, ... 107 CHRISTMAS TREES . . . 56
    A THING TO SELL." I DON'T SUPPOSE THE WORK . . . . . 159 NEW HAMPSHIRE . . . 4
    THE HAVING ANYTHING TO SELL IS WHAT . . . . . 159 NEW HAMPSHIRE . . . 7
    THIS IS CALLED HAVING AN IDEA TO SELL. . . . . . 160 NEW HAMPSHIRE . . . 33
    WHICH NATURALLY SHE DOESN'T CARE TO SELL. . . . . . 161 NEW HAMPSHIRE . . . 63
    OF RADIUM OR ANYTHING TO SELL. . . . . 163 NEW HAMPSHIRE . . . 123
    "I'LL HAVE ONE IF I SELL MY FARM TO BUY IT." . . . . . 177 THE STAR-SPLITTER . 25
    TRYING TO SELL HIS FARM AND THEN NOT SELLING, ... 177 THE STAR-SPLITTER . 29
    SOMETHING TO SELL? THAT WASN'T HOW IT SOUNDED. . . . . 186 THE AX-HELVE 32
    HE'D SELL A YOKE OF STEERS TO PAY FOR IT. . . . . . 200 PLACE FOR A THIRD . 25
    WITH FURS TO SELL. . . . . 211 AN EMPTY THREAT . . 11
    HAD BEEN TOO SHORT TO SELL OR GIVE AWAY. . . . . . 217 A FOUNTAIN, A BOTTLE . 122
    AND ANOTHER TO ASK COULD THEY SELL IT A GALLON OF GAS . . 287 A ROADSIDE STAND . . 42
    I SHOULD SELL FOR WHAT THEY WOULD FETCH. . . . . . 295 A RECORD STRIDE . . 28
    BUT I DON'T CALCULATE TO SELL MY WOOL. . . . . . 316 BUILD SOIL 14
    HAVE TO SELL YOU MY APPLES AND BUY YOURS? . . . . . 321 BUILD SOIL 165
    TO SELL THE HAY OFF, LET ALONE THE SOIL, ... 321 BUILD SOIL 179
    WITH GOODS TO SELL AND NOTIONS TO IMPART. . . . . . 324 BUILD SOIL 269
    TAKE CARE TO SELL YOUR HORSE BEFORE HE DIES . . . . . 399 THE INGENUITIES OF DEBT 4
    AND SELL HIM INTO SLAVERY? MY PRICE . . . . . . 454 HOW HARD TO KEEP FROM 33
SELLING
    "BUT YOUR FLOWERS, MAN, YOU'RE SELLING OUT YOUR FLOWERS." . 95 THE SELF-SEEKER . . . 66
    BUT I'M NOT SELLING THOSE, I'M GIVING THEM; . . . . 95 THE SELF-SEEKER . . . 70
    I DALLIED SO MUCH WITH THE THOUGHT OF SELLING. . . . . 106 CHRISTMAS TREES . . . 25
    FROM SELLING THINGS IN CALIFORNIA. . . . . . 160 NEW HAMPSHIRE . . . 38
    TRYING TO SELL HIS FARM AND THEN NOT SELLING, ... 177 THE STAR-SPLITTER . 29
    WHERE HIS JOB, WHEN HE WASN'T SELLING TICKETS, ... 178 THE STAR-SPLITTER . 70
    THERE CAME TO COURT A MERCHANT SELLING PEARLS, ... 455 HOW HARD TO KEEP FROM 66
    WE CAN'T BE ALWAYS SELLING PEOPLE THINGS. . . . . . 493 A MASQUE OF MERCY . 10
SELLS
    CONTROL OF WHAT IT SELLS OR WHAT IT BUYS. . . . . . 324 BUILD SOIL 248
SEMI-REVOLUTION
    I ADVOCATE A SEMI-REVOLUTION. . . . . 363 A SEMI-REVOLUTION . . 1
    A SEMI-REVOLUTION . . . . 363 A SEMI-REVOLUTION . . T
SENATOR
    NO SENATOR DARES IN TO KICK ASUNDER, ... 362 SYMPATHY WITH UNDER DOG 3
SEND
    THEY'RE YOURS AND WELCOME; LET ME SEND THEM TO YOU.— . . 47 A HUNDRED COLLARS . . 68

SEND (CONTINUED)
    RATHER THAN SEND THEIR FOLKS TO SUCH A PLACE, ... 65 A SERVANT TO SERVANTS . 95
    I CAN'T HELP WISHING I COULD SEND YOU ONE . . . . . . 107 CHRISTMAS TREES . . . 59
    TO SEND IT SAILING OUT THE ATTIC WINDOW . . . . 216 A FOUNTAIN, A BOTTLE . 110
    HOW ELSE? THEY ARE NOT KNOWN TO SEND THE DEAD.— . . . . 230 NOT TO KEEP 6
    AND SEND MORE SPARKS UP CHIMNEY WITH THE SMOKE." . . . . 234 EVENING A SUGAR ORCHARD 6
    THEN SEND SOME ONE WITH EYES TO SEE . . . . 257 THE LOVELY BE CHOOSERS 46
    THEY MADE HIM SEND OUT A CALL . . . . 310 THE VINDICTIVES . . 10
    SEND US A FLOOD AND BID US BE DAMNED AND DROWN. . . . . 349 OUR HOLD ON THE PLANET . 6
    FOR ME TO SEND YOU ONE OUT WHERE YOU LIVE . . . . . . 365 OF STONES OF THE PLACE . 5
    AT LEAST IT OUGHT TO SEND . . . . 389 ASTROMETAPHYSICAL . . 19
    WE SEND OUR WICKED ENEMIES TO HELL, ... 519 A MASQUE OF MERCY . . 688
    OUR WICKED FRIENDS WE SEND TO PURGATORY. . . . . . . 519 A MASQUE OF MERCY . . 689
SENDER
    THE SENDER MUST HAVE HAD TO DIE, ... 327 A MISSIVE MISSILE . 16
SENDING
    RAISING A LITTLE, SENDING UP A LITTLE. . . . . . . 259 WEST-RUNNING BROOK . . 63
    OUR LIFE RUNS DOWN IN SENDING UP THE CLOCK. . . . . . 259 WEST-RUNNING BROOK . . 64
    THE BROOK RUNS DOWN IN SENDING UP OUR LIFE. . . . . . 260 WEST-RUNNING BROOK . . 65
    THE SUN RUNS DOWN IN SENDING UP THE BROOK. . . . . . 260 WEST-RUNNING BROOK . . 66
    AND THERE IS SOMETHING SENDING UP THE SUN. . . . . . 260 WEST-RUNNING BROOK . . 67
    AND SENDING UP NEW SHOOTS . . . . 308 EVIL TENDENCIES CANCEL . 4
    GO IF YOU'RE GOING. / WHO IS SENDING ME? . . . . . . 514 A MASQUE OF MERCY . . 553
SENDS
    THAT SENDS THE FROZEN-GROUND-SWELL UNDER IT . . . . 33 MENDING WALL . . . 2
    AND SENDS THE CHILDREN DOWN THERE WITH THEIR MOTHER . . 44 A HUNDRED COLLARS . . 4
    TO WHICH MAN SENDS HIS . . . . 219 I WILL SING YOU ONE-O . 50
    THAT SENDS LIGHT RUSTLE RUSHES TO THEIR LEAVES, . . . 378 DIRECTIVE 24
SENILE
    WHERE DO THESE SENILE RUNAWAYS ESCAPE FROM? . . . . 493 A MASQUE OF MERCY . . 15
SENSATIONS
    WE'VE HAD ABOUT ENOUGH OF THESE SENSATIONS. . . . . . 508 A MASQUE OF MERCY . . 396
SENSE
    "FROM THE SENSE OF OUR HAVING BEEN TOGETHER— . . . 78 THE GENERATIONS OF MEN 142
    I COULD, BUT WHAT'S THE SENSE? THE REST WON'T BE . . . 143 SNOW 20
    OR SOME SUCH SENSE AS SAYS HOW HIGH SHALL JET . . . . 169 NEW HAMPSHIRE . . . 325
    MORE BLAMELESS IN THE SENSE OF BEING LESS . . . . . 177 THE STAR-SPLITTER . . 23
    "NO, NOT WITH JOHN. THERE WOULDN'T BE NO SENSE. . . . 202 PLACE FOR A THIRD . . 77
    AND THE LOSS OF COMMON SENSE), ... 282 A DRUMLIN WOODCHUCK . 24
    AND UNLESS MY SENSE IS AT FAULT, ... 295 A RECORD STRIDE . . 22
    IN YOUR SENSE OF THE WORD AMBITION HAS . . . . . . 319 BUILD SOIL 98
    FROM SOUND TO SENSE AND BACK TO SOUND. . . . . . . 326 TO A THINKER . . . 12
    I GET THE LASTING SENSE . . . . 333 HAPPINESS MAKES UP . . 10
    FOR SLOWLY EVEN HER SENSE OF HIM . . . . 347 DISCOVERY OF MADEIRAS . 116
    TO FEEL IT CLOSE IN TIGHT AGAINST MY SENSE . . . . . 390 SKEPTIC 11
    WHOLENESS IN A SENSE. . . . . 441 KITTY HAWK 428
    IN THE SEAT OF MY SENSE. . . . . 450 OBJECTION TO BE STEPPED 6
    IT GIVES A SENSE OF LETUP CALCULATED . . . . 475 A MASQUE OF REASON . . 44
    NOT IN THE SENSE OF HAVING TO MY KNOWLEDGE . . . . . 476 A MASQUE OF REASON . . 95
    AND MAY AS WELL THROW IN A LITTLE SENSE. . . . . . 482 A MASQUE OF REASON . . 237
    MY TROUBLE HAS BEEN WITH MY SENSE OF JUSTICE. . . . . 517 A MASQUE OF MERCY . . 622
    I SHOULD HAVE WARNED YOU, THOUGH, MY SENSE OF JUSTICE . 518 A MASQUE OF MERCY . . 657
SENSES
    FROM COMPANY MEANS COMING TO OUR SENSES. . . . . . . 325 BUILD SOIL 292
    IS TOO MUCH FOR THE SENSES, ... 336 CARPE DIEM 24
SENSIBILITIST
    I'M WHAT IS CALLED A SENSIBILITIST, ... 166 NEW HAMPSHIRE . . . 232
    THE MORE THE SENSIBILITIST I AM . . . . 170 NEW HAMPSHIRE . . . 343
SENSIBLE
    AND VERY SENSIBLE. NO STATE CAN BUILD . . . . . . 168 NEW HAMPSHIRE . . . 284
SENSITIVE
    FAR STAR THAT TICKLES FOR ME MY SENSITIVE PLATE . . . 389 SKEPTIC 1
SENSITIVELY
    IT COULDN'T STIR SO SENSITIVELY POISED . . . . . . 148 SNOW 138
SENT
    I WOULDN'T HAVE SERVANT ANYONE OF MINE THERE; . . . . 65 A SERVANT TO SERVANTS . 92
    "IT IS—OR SOMEONE ELSE HE'S SENT TO WATCH. . . . . 90 THE FEAR 42
    BUT HE SENT HER GOOD-BY, ... 136 LAST WORD OF A BLUEBIRD 15
    THEY SENT HIM BACK TO HER. THE LETTER CAME . . . . . 230 NOT TO KEEP 1
    THE APPLE TREES BE SENT TO HEARTHSTONE FLAME. . . . . 231 A BROOK IN THE CITY . 11
    THEY DISAPPEARED AS IF EARTH SENT THEM BACK. . . . . 239 OUR SINGING STRENGTH . 6
    I SENT YOU ONCE A SONG WITH THE REFRAIN: . . . . . 324 BUILD SOIL 259
    AND SENT IT TO ME YEARS AND YEARS— . . . . . . 326 A MISSIVE MISSILE . . 4
    AND SENT HIM TO THE KING TO ADMIRE. . . . . 347 DISCOVERY OF MADEIRAS . 131
    IT SENT ME TO THE GRAVES THE OTHER DAY. . . . . . . 354 THE LESSON FOR TODAY . 127
    IT WAS A THING OF BEAUTY AND WAS SENT . . . . . . 375 A YOUNG BIRCH . . . 21
    THAT'S WHAT A CERTAIN BOMB WAS SENT TO BE." . . . . 398 BURSTING RAPTURE . . 14
    SENT FOR THE EX-KING IN A PRIVATE MATTER. . . . . . 456 HOW HARD TO KEEP FROM 97
    PERICLES SENT ASPASIA IN ABSENTIA: . . . . 461 HOW HARD TO KEEP FROM 250
    OR RATHER SUBMIT TO BE SENT . . . . 466 SOME SCIENCE FICTION . 27
    THIS IS THE SEVENTH TIME I HAVE BEEN SENT . . . . . 495 A MASQUE OF MERCY . . 63
    WE TAKE IT YOU WERE SENT IN HERE FOR HELP. . . . . . 500 A MASQUE OF MERCY . . 177
    YOU MEAN I'M BEING SENT DOWN IN THE CELLAR? . . . . 514 A MASQUE OF MERCY . . 551
SENTENCE
    IF HE LEAVES IT TO NATURE TO CARRY OUT THE SENTENCE. . . 307 NOT QUITE SOCIAL . . 14
SENTENCING
    THE SENTENCING GOES BLITHELY ON ITS WAY . . . . . . 362 IN A POEM 1
SENTIENT
    BUT A HOUSE ISN'T SENTIENT; THE HOUSE . . . . . . 178 THE STAR-SPLITTER . . 61
SENTIMENT
    'FEEL OUT THE PUBLIC SENTIMENT'—HE SAYS. . . . . . 48 A HUNDRED COLLARS . . 106
    IN OUR SUBSCRIPTION TO THE SENTIMENT . . . . 515 A MASQUE OF MERCY . . 589
SENTIMENTAL
    "SICK TALK, SICK TALK, SICK SENTIMENTAL TALK! . . . . 370 THE LITERATE FARMER AND 84
    THEY WERE SENTIMENTAL. . . . . 432 KITTY HAWK 126
SENTIMENTS
    THEM IS MY SENTIMENTS, AND, MR. FLOOD, ... 497 A MASQUE OF MERCY . . 108

SENTINEL
   SO, LIKE A HALF-MAD OUTPOST SENTINEL, ... 396 ANY SIZE WE PLEASE . . . 2
SEPAL
   LAY HIM IN STATE ON A SEPAL. . . . . 288 DEPARTMENTAL 29
SEPARATE
   SEPARATE BEDS, OF COURSE, YOU UNDERSTAND." . . . . 45 A HUNDRED COLLARS . . . 27
   IN SEPARATE COOPS, HAVING THEIR PLUMAGE DONE. . . . . . . 85 THE HOUSEKEEPER . . . 121
   THROUGH THE THIN FROST, ALMOST IN SEPARATE STARS, ... 108 OLD MAN'S WINTER NIGHT . 2
   NOT TILL FROM SEPARATE FLAKES THEY CHANGED AT NIGHT . . . 239 OUR SINGING STRENGTH . 7
   TO SEPARATE US FOR A PANIC MOMENT. . . . . 259 WEST-RUNNING BROOK . . 52
   SEPARATE AND SETTLE. . . . . 442 KITTY HAWK 449
SEPARATENESS
   ITS SEPARATENESS FROM HEAVEN COULD BE WAIVED; . . . . . . 353 THE LESSON FOR TODAY . 101
SEPARATION
   BUT YIELD WHO WILL TO THEIR SEPARATION, ... 277 TWO TRAMPS IN MUD TIME 65
   YOUR SEPARATION OF US FROM THE OLD . . . . 446 DOES NO ONE AT ALL EVER 2
SEPTEMBER
   THE TWENTY-THIRD OF SEPTEMBER, ... 365 A NATURE NOTE 14
   SEPTEMBER THE TWENTY-THIRD. . . . . 365 A NATURE NOTE 16
SERAPHIC
   WITH MISCHIEVOUS, VAGRANT, SERAPHIC LOOK, ... 16 IN NEGLECT 4
SERENE
   AND WHAT THE SOUTH, TO HER SERENE BELIEF. . . . . 57 THE BLACK COTTAGE . . 72
   THEN ONCE AGAIN THE SANDBANK LAY SERENE. . . . . 270 THE EGG AND THE MACHINE 16
SERIAL
   NOR NEED YOU MIND THE SERIAL ORDEAL . . . . 377 DIRECTIVE 20
SERIOUS
   "WHY, IF SHE ISN'T SERIOUS ABOUT IT! . . . . 198 WILD GRAPES 81
   A SERIOUS STEP LIGHTLY TAKEN . . . . 367 A SERIOUS STEP LIGHTLY T
   WITHOUT INQUIRING IF 'TWAS SERIOUS. . . . . 369 THE LITERATE FARMER AND 26
   THERE IS A STAR THAT'S SERIOUS BY NAME . . . . 369 THE LITERATE FARMER AND 29
   AS WELL AS WORDS. / I'M SERIOUS. GOD'S HAD . . . . 478 A MASQUE OF REASON . . 148
   BUT LET'S BE SERIOUS ABOUT PAUL'S OFFER. . . . . 513 A MASQUE OF MERCY . . 519
SERIOUSLY
   THE OLD MAN SERIOUSLY TOOK HIS BEARINGS, ... 214 A FOUNTAIN, A BOTTLE . 35
   IT SERIOUSLY, SADLY, RUNS AWAY . . . . 259 WEST-RUNNING BROOK . . 48
   WE SEE HOW SERIOUSLY THE RACES SWARM . . . . 423 FOR JOHN F. KENNEDY . 34
SERIOUSNESS
   WHO SAID WITH SERIOUSNESS THAT MADE THEM LAUGH, ... 114 IN THE HOME STRETCH . 104
SERMON
   THE MERCY ON THE SIN AGAINST THE SERMON. . . . . 511 A MASQUE OF MERCY . . 477
   PAUL'S CONSTANT THEME. THE SERMON ON THE MOUNT . . . . . 511 A MASQUE OF MERCY . . 482
   YOU ALL HAVE READ THE SERMON ON THE MOUNT. . . . . 511 A MASQUE OF MERCY . . 487
SERPENT
   AND ONLY RESTS, A SERPENT ON ITS CHIN, ... 399 THE INGENUITIES OF DEBT 15
SERPENTINE
   ACROSS THE HANDLE'S LONG-DRAWN SERPENTINE, ... 186 THE AX-HELVE 24
SERPENT'S
   THE SERPENT'S TAIL STUCK DOWN THE SERPENT'S THROAT, . . . 485 A MASQUE OF REASON . . 340
SERVANT
   A SERVANT TO SERVANTS . . . . 62 A SERVANT TO SERVANTS . T
SERVANTS
   A SERVANT TO SERVANTS . . . . 62 A SERVANT TO SERVANTS . T
SERVE
   WILL SERVE ALMOST AS WELL ABOUT VERMONT, ... 165 NEW HAMPSHIRE . . . 211
   IS WATER WOOD TO SERVE A BROOK THE SAME? . . . . 231 A BROOK IN THE CITY . 12
   A CHIMNEY THAT ONLY WOULD SERVE TO REMIND ME . . . . . . 232 THE KITCHEN CHIMNEY . 19
   FOR THE BEES TO COME AND SERVE ITS BEAUTY ARIGHT. . . . 300 STRONG SAYING NOTHING . 12
   FROM WHAT IT IS WITH HIS. BOTH SERVE FOR PAY. . . . . . 485 A MASQUE OF REASON . . 353
SERVED
   MOST LIKELY I'D HAVE SERVED YOU JUST THE SAME. . . . . . 70 THE CODE 25
   AND SERVED US RIGHT FOR HAVING INSTITUTED . . . . 279 THE WHITE-TAILED HORNET 58
   HAD SERVED AS A PALACE GATE. . . . . 312 THE VINDICTIVES . . . 68
   THE SLAVE SERVED HIS NOVITIATE DISHWASHING. . . . . . . 455 HOW HARD TO KEEP FROM 54
SERVICE
   PRESSED INTO SERVICE MEANS PRESSED OUT OF SHAPE. . . . . 98 THE SELF-SEEKER . . . 149
SESSIONS
   AS LONG AS LIGHTLY ALL THEIR LIVELONG SESSIONS, ... 317 BUILD SOIL 60
SET   (SEE FIRM-SET)
   OR THOSE SHOULD NOT SET FORTH UPON MY TRACK . . . . . . 5 INTO MY OWN 10
   AND SET THE WALL BETWEEN US ONCE AGAIN. . . . . 33 MENDING WALL 14
   AND SET THEM ON THE PORCH, THEN DREW HIM DOWN . . . . . . 34 DEATH OF THE HIRED MAN 9
   SET WELL BACK FROM THE ROAD IN RANK LODGED GRASS, . . . 55 THE BLACK COTTAGE . . 4
   IS SET ME BACK A LITTLE MORE BEHIND. . . . . 68 A SERVANT TO SERVANTS . 175
   TO SET THE VOICES SPEAKING OUT OF IT, ... 78 THE GENERATIONS OF MEN 129
   "HAVEN'T YOU SEEN HIM? STRANGE WHAT SET YOU OFF . . . . 81 THE HOUSEKEEPER . . . 14
   TILL I SHAN'T DARE TO SET A FOOT OUTDOORS. . . . . 90 THE FEAR 47
   TRYING, I THOUGHT, TO SET IT UP ON END, ... 109 THE EXPOSED NEST . . . 4
   TO WHICH THEY SET IT TRUE BY EYE; AND THEN . . . . 113 IN THE HOME STRETCH . 85
   WELL, YOU CAN SET THE TABLE WITH THE LOAF. . . . . 115 IN THE HOME STRETCH . 154
   BEFORE WE SET OURSELVES TO RIGHT THE HOUSE, ... 117 IN THE HOME STRETCH . 194
   BUT DIPPED ITS TOP AND SET ME DOWN AGAIN. . . . . 122 BIRCHES 57
   AND SET ME FIVE MILES ON MY ROAD . . . . 140 THE GUM-GATHERER . . 3
   TO SET YOUR BREAST TO THE BARK OF TREES . . . . 141 THE GUM-GATHERER . . 35
   AN OATH OF TOWNS THAT SET THE WILD AT NAUGHT, ... 141 THE LINE-GANG . . . 12
   IF HE HAD STAYED. THE LEAST THING SET HIM GOING. . . . . 152 SNOW 259
   I SHALL SET FORTH FOR SOMEWHERE, ... 156 THE SOUND OF TREES . 19
   ARTISTS THE MINUTE THEY SET UP AS ARTISTS, ... 162 NEW HAMPSHIRE . . . 96
   IT SET OUT ONCE TO BE A CITY AND STILL . . . . 165 NEW HAMPSHIRE . . . 191
   AND SET HERSELF BACK WHERE SHE STARTED FROM. . . . . . . 187 THE AX-HELVE 53
   FROM THE WAY SHE HAD SET HER POOR OLD MOUTH, ... 201 PLACE FOR A THIRD . . 74
   AND SET OFF BRISKLY FOR SO SLOW A THING, ... 205 THE WITCH OF COOS . . 86
   THEY SET A LOT (NOW DON'T THEY?) BY A RECORD . . . . . . 207 PAUPER WITCH OF GRAFTON 12
   I KNOW OF SOME FOLKS THAT'D BE SET UP . . . . 208 PAUPER WITCH OF GRAFTON 36
   THOUGH SET SO FAR . . . . 219 I WILL SING YOU ONE-O . 64
   NO ONE FOR HOURS HAS SET A FOOT OUTDOORS . . . . 248 THE COCOON 9
   THAT WILL STEAL FORTH AFTER THE SUN IS SET . . . . 276 TWO TRAMPS IN MUD TIME 39
   IT SET ITSELF TO KEEP THOSE THREE ALIVE; . . . . 283 THE GOLD HESPERIDEE . 5

SET (CONTINUED)
    AND SET THEM UP AGAIN FOR PROPPING SHUT, ... 289 OLD BARN AT THE BOTTOM   11
    NOT IF I HAD MY SAY. BOUNDS SHOULD BE SET . . . . . . 320 BUILD SOIL 123
    THERE IS AN AEON-LIMIT SET . . . . 328 A MISSIVE MISSILE . . 50
    TO SET HIMSELF AGAINST THE PEAKS OF SNOW . . . . . . 334 I COULD GIVE ALL . . . 2
    WAS NOT SET FORTH IN THE LADING BILL. . . . . 343 DISCOVERY OF MADEIRAS . 4
    SET OFF ACROSS WHAT I HAD WRITTEN THERE. . . . . 357 A CONSIDERABLE SPECK . 3
    YET MUST HAVE HAD A SET OF THEM COMPLETE . . . . . . 357 A CONSIDERABLE SPECK . 17
    NO, I HAD SET NO PROHIBITING SIGN, ... 364 TRESPASS 1
    AND SET UP LIKE A STATUE IN YOUR YARD, ... 365 OF STONES OF THE PLACE   10
    I DIDN'T SEE THE SUN SET. DID IT SET? . . . . 368 THE LITERATE FARMER AND 19
    WHAT SET US ON FIRE AND WHAT SET US REVOLVING, ... 380 TOO ANXIOUS FOR RIVERS   22
    HAVE SET THE DARK ASIDE FOR HERS. . . . . 390 TWO LEADING LIGHTS . . 15
    TO SET HERSELF BESIDE THE SUN, ... 390 TWO LEADING LIGHTS . . 20
    HE ONLY STAYED TO SET THE SUMMER ON FIRE, ... 407 FROM PLANE TO PLANE . . 93
    I SET HIM WATER, I SET HIM FOOD. . . . . 419 ONE MORE BREVITY . . 19
    WHEN THE SCENE WAS SET . . . . 430 KITTY HAWK 54
    VOICE THAT SAID, "GET SET . . . . 436 KITTY HAWK 271
    FROM CHILDHOOD HAS MY HEART BEEN SET. . . . . 451 A-WISHING WELL . . . 22
    SHOULD BE ENOUGH TO SET YOU UP IN BUSINESS-- . . . . . 454 HOW HARD TO KEEP FROM   34
    CHRIST'S OR KARL MARX', AND IT WILL SET YOU FREE. . . . 460 HOW HARD TO KEEP FROM 192
    YOU CHANGED ALL THAT. YOU SET ME FREE TO REIGN. . . . 476 A MASQUE OF REASON . 77
    AS IS SET FORTH IN CHAPTERS ONE AND TWO. . . . . . . 485 A MASQUE OF REASON . 328
    ALWAYS THE SAME WHEN I SET OUT IN FLIGHT. . . . . . . 500 A MASQUE OF MERCY . 179
    TO SET OUT TO HOMOGENIZE MANKIND . . . . 509 A MASQUE OF MERCY . 420
SETS
    THE SUNBURNED HILLSIDE SETS MY FACE AGLOW, ... 17 THE VANTAGE POINT . . 11
    THAT, ONCE GRIEF SETS TO GROWING, GRIEF MAY REST: . . . 200 PLACE FOR A THIRD . . 27
    YOUR LEAST TOUCH SETS IT GOING ROUND, ... 306 A TRIAL RUN 13
    THE SUN SETS THE EXAMPLE IN THE DAY." . . . . 370 THE LITERATE FARMER AND 74
    SETS FORTH FOR HOME AT MIDNIGHT FROM A FRIEND'S-- . . . 386 THE FEAR OF MAN . . . 2
SETTING
    SETTING THE THING THAT IS SUPREME. . . . . 20 THE TRIAL BY EXISTENCE   40
    BY SETTING FIRE TO ALL THE BRUSH WE PILED . . . . . 129 THE BONFIRE 3
    AND SETTING SUN TO HYLA BROOK, I GAVE IT . . . . . . 131 THE BONFIRE 58
    WAS SETTING OUT, UP TRACK AND DOWN, NOT PLANTS . . . . 178 THE STAR-SPLITTER . . 71
    AND HE'S OFF SETTING TRAPS-- . . . . 211 AN EMPTY THREAT . . 28
    BY SETTING IT OUT ON A NORTHERLY SLOPE.) . . . . . . 228 GOOD-BY AND KEEP COLD . 14
    AND SETTING OFF THEIR HEAVY POWDER LOAD. . . . . . . 239 OUR SINGING STRENGTH . 29
    THE NIGHT IS SETTING IN TO BLOW. . . . . 281 BLUE RIBBON AT AMESBURY 49
    SPARE ME THE SETTING OF MY FATE TO MUSIC. . . . . . . 495 A MASQUE OF MERCY . . 58
SETTLE
    WHEN HIS TIME COMES TO DIE AND SETTLE DOWN. . . . . . 202 PLACE FOR A THIRD . . 82
    WAIT AND WATCH THE LIQUOR SETTLE. . . . . 304 CLEAR AND COLDER . . 19
    SEPARATE AND SETTLE. . . . . 442 KITTY HAWK 449
SETTLED
    MAKE THE SETTLED SNOWBANK STEAM; . . . . 11 TO THE THAWING WIND . . 4
    TILL WELL TOWARD NOON, WHEN THE STORM SETTLED DOWN . . . 74 THE GENERATIONS OF MEN   22
    ESTELLE'S TO TAKE ME WHEN SHE'S SETTLED DOWN. . . . . . 82 THE HOUSEKEEPER . . . 35
    I JUST WANT TO GET SETTLED IN MY LIFE, ... 95 THE SELF-SEEKER . . . 76
    IT'S NOT SO BAD IN THE COUNTRY, SETTLED DOWN, ... 113 IN THE HOME STRETCH . 93
    WHOSE CLAIM IS GOOD TO BEING SETTLED HERE . . . . . 161 NEW HAMPSHIRE . . . 71
    NOW THAT THEY'VE GOT IT SETTLED WHOSE I BE, ... 207 PAUPER WITCH OF GRAFTON 1
    THEY'VE GOT IT SETTLED WRONG, AND I CAN PROVE IT. . . . 207 PAUPER WITCH OF GRAFTON 3
    NOW IF YOU THREE HAVE SETTLED ANYTHING . . . . . . 490 A MASQUE OF REASON . 464
SETTLEMENT
    THE EARLY MORMONS MADE A SETTLEMENT . . . . 213 A FOUNTAIN, A BOTTLE . 9
    "YOU MEAN MILES FROM THE MORMON SETTLEMENT? . . . . . 214 A FOUNTAIN, A BOTTLE . 48
SETTLES
    (WHEN THE DUST SETTLES IT SHOULD BE APPARENT . . . . 507 A MASQUE OF MERCY . . 343
SEVEN
    WHICH MEANS THE-SEVEN-CAVES-THAT-WE-CAME-OUT-OF. . . . . 76 THE GENERATIONS OF MEN   93
    LAUGHS AT FRANCONIA (SEVEN HUNDRED), AND . . . . . . 165 NEW HAMPSHIRE . . . 204
    WITH ALL THE RAIN AND SNOW OF SEVEN YEARS; . . . . . 210 PAUPER WITCH OF GRAFTON 92
    "SEVEN LEVELS OF THE WORLD." . . . . 256 THE LOVELY BE CHOOSERS   3
    YOU KNOW THEM--SEVEN IN ALL." . . . . 257 THE LOVELY BE CHOOSERS 52
    I KNOW WOOL'S DOWN TO SEVEN CENTS A POUND. . . . . . 316 BUILD SOIL 13
    FROM NUMBER ONE TO SEVEN, ... 389 ASTROMETAPHYSICAL . . 11
    HE HAS BEEN BEGGING THROUGH THE SEVEN CITIES . . . . 459 HOW HARD TO KEEP FROM 182
    TO BE THE AUTHOR OF THE SEVEN FREEDOMS: . . . . . . 459 HOW HARD TO KEEP FROM 185
    (HIS WAS THE DOCTRINE OF THE SEVEN POSES) . . . . . . 511 A MASQUE OF MERCY . . 464
SEVENTH
    THIS IS THE SEVENTH TIME I HAVE BEEN SENT . . . . . 495 A MASQUE OF MERCY . . 63
SEVENTY
    MANCHESTER (SIXTY OR SEVENTY THOUSAND) LAUGHS . . . . 165 NEW HAMPSHIRE . . . 202
SEVERAL
    SEVERAL TIMES OVER, AND BY MARRYING FATHER . . . . . 75 THE GENERATIONS OF MEN   56
    IN SEVERAL BEAUTY THAT THOUGHT FARES FAR . . . . . . 121 BOND AND FREE . . . 19
    BY ROAD, A MATTER OF SEVERAL MILES. . . . . 140 BROWN'S DESCENT . . 76
    OF SEVERAL BOOKS AGAINST THE WORLD IN GENERAL. . . . . 166 NEW HAMPSHIRE . . . 229
    HE HAD BEEN HEARD TO SAY BY SEVERAL: . . . . 177 THE STAR-SPLITTER . . 32
    THIS LIGHT'S BEEN GOING ON FOR SEVERAL YEARS, ... 369 THE LITERATE FARMER AND 31
SEVERELY
    AND THE REST WON'T WANT TO PUNISH ME TOO SEVERELY . . . 306 NOT QUITE SOCIAL . . 2
SEVERITY
    IN WHICH WE ACT IS A SEVERITY, ... 520 A MASQUE OF MERCY . . 711
SEW
    SO'S TO TAKE ANY COMFORT. I CAN SEW: . . . . 81 THE HOUSEKEEPER . . . 7
SEWELL
    WITH ONE A SEWELL MIGHT HAVE PAINTED. . . . . 280 BLUE RIBBON AT AMESBURY 12
SEWER
    DEEP IN A SEWER DUNGEON UNDER STONE . . . . 231 A BROOK IN THE CITY . 16
SH
    "SH! NOT SO LOUD: HE'LL HEAR YOU," MARY SAID. . . . . 35 DEATH OF THE HIRED MAN   31
SHACK
    THERE HE HAD BUILT HIS STOLEN SHACK. . . . . 140 THE GUM-GATHERER . . 19
    IT HAD TO BE A STOLEN SHACK . . . . 140 THE GUM-GATHERER . . 20
    FOUR-ROOM SHACK ASPIRING HIGH . . . . 469 FOUR-ROOM SHACK... . . 1

SHACK (CONTINUED)
    FOUR-ROOM SHACK... . . . . 469 FOUR-ROOM SHACK... . . I
SHADE
    AND WEARY, SOUGHT AT NOON WITH HIM THE SHADE; . . . . . 23 THE TUFT OF FLOWERS . 36
    THEY FALL FROM GIVING SHADE ABOVE, ... 25 IN HARDWOOD GROVES . . 2
    TO FILL THE TREES WITH ANOTHER SHADE, ... 26 IN HARDWOOD GROVES . . 6
    NOT OF WOODS ONLY AND THE SHADE OF TREES. . . . . . . 34 MENDING WALL 42
    OF THEM ANYWHERE UNDER THE SHADE OF THE PINE, ... 59 BLUEBERRIES 16
    YOU HAD BEGUN, AND GAVE THEM BACK THEIR SHADE. . . . . 109 THE EXPOSED NEST . . 30
    NOT SO MUCH AS A SINGLE TREE FOR SHADE, ... 183 MAPLE 102
    THAT FLOWERS CAN'T BLOOM IN THE SHADE OF; . . . . . . 264 THE LAST MOWING . . 12
    WAS A SHADE LESS THE COLOR OF NIGHT, ... 299 WELCOME TO THEIR BELIEF 11
    A SHADE MORE THE COLOR OF SNOW. . . . . 299 WELCOME TO THEIR BELIEF 12
SHADED
    THEY THINK TOO MUCH OF HAVING SHADED OUT . . . . 378 DIRECTIVE 27
SHADOW
    PREVENTING SHADOW UNTIL THE MOON PREVAIL; . . . . . . 14 WAITING 10
    BEYOND THE SHADOW OF A DOUBT; . . . . 20 THE TRIAL BY EXISTENCE 36
    THE MOUNTAIN HELD THE TOWN AS IN A SHADOW. . . . . . . 40 THE MOUNTAIN 1
    GREAT GRANITE TERRACES IN SUN AND SHADOW, ... 42 THE MOUNTAIN 58
    ONE BACK AND FORWARD, IN AND OUT OF SHADOW, ... 186 THE AX-HELVE 48
    THE SHADOW OF THE APPLE TREE IS THIN . . . . 189 THE GRINDSTONE . . . 9
    PAUL DARKLY, LIKE HER SHADOW. ALL THE LIGHT . . . . . 195 PAUL'S WIFE 136
    LIKE A SHADOW AGAINST THE CURTAIN OF FALLING FLAKES. . . 223 THE RUNAWAY 8
    WHAT ARE YOU, IN THE SHADOW OF TREES . . . . 247 ON GOING UNNOTICED . . 3
    I SAW MY SHADOW ON SNOW. . . . . 303 AFTERFLAKES 2
    THAT SHADOW OF MINE SHOULD SHOW IN FORM . . . . 303 AFTERFLAKES 8
    AGAINST THE SHAPELESS SHADOW OF STORM, ... 303 AFTERFLAKES 9
    NO SHADOW CROSSED BUT OURS . . . . 333 HAPPINESS MAKES UP . . 21
    AND A CLOUD SHADOW CROSSED HER FACE . . . . 342 A CLOUD SHADOW . . . 7
    A CLOUD SHADOW . . . . 342 A CLOUD SHADOW . . . T
    OR SHADOW, BUT A CAVERN HOLE, ... 392 A CLIFF DWELLING . . 7
    REDUCED HIM TO A SHADOW OF HIMSELF. . . . . 488 A MASQUE OF REASON . . 426
SHADOWS
    AND THREW THEIR LURCHING SHADOWS ON A HOUSE . . . . . 89 THE FEAR 3
SHADOWY
    BUT ONLY FELT AT NIGHT ITS SHADOWY PRESENCE. . . . . . 41 THE MOUNTAIN 22
    MARCH INTO A SHADOWY CLAIM. . . . . 264 THE LAST MOWING . . . 10
    THE SHADOWY HARE . . . . 360 THE RABBIT-HUNTER . . 13
    I LINK A LINE OF SHADOWY TRACKS . . . . 470 IN WINTER IN THE WOODS 7
SHADRACH
    LIKE SHADRACH, MESHACH, AND ABEDNEGO. . . . . 516 A MASQUE OF MERCY . . 604
SHAFT
    WHEN I SAW THE SHAFT HAD ME BY THE COAT; . . . . . . 93 THE SELF-SEEKER . . . 23
    I JUST EMBRACED THE SHAFT AND RODE IT OUT-- . . . . . 93 THE SELF-SEEKER . . . 26
    WHEN HE SHOT A SHAFT . . . . 427 VERSION 3
    AND THE SHAFT GOT BLUNTED . . . . 427 VERSION 11
    RAISED THIS TOWER SHAFT . . . . 430 KITTY HAWK 71
    WITH A CRACK OF A BROKEN SHAFT. . . . . 444 THE DRAFT HORSE . . 10
SHAFTS
    YET LEAVE SUCH LOVELY SHAFTS OUTDOORS TO PERISH. . . . 290 OLD BARN AT THE BOTTOM 34
SHAKE
    HE GAVE THE SASH A SHAKE, ... 11 WIND AND WINDOW FLOWER 18
    "DROP OR I'LL SHAKE THE TREE AND SHAKE YOU DOWN." . . . 198 WILD GRAPES 78
    "DON'T DONKEY'S EARS SUGGEST WE SHAKE OUR OWN?" . . . . 215 A FOUNTAIN, A BOTTLE . 55
    HE GIVES HIS HARNESS BELLS A SHAKE . . . . 224 STOPPING BY WOODS . . 9
    THAT WHEN THEY'RE GATHERED SHAKE . . . . 227 TO EARTHWARD . . . 11
    THE STRAINING MILL BEGAN TO SHAKE. . . . . 273 A LONE STRIKER . . . 10
    IT WILL SHAKE ITS CAST STONE REEF OF FLOOR. . . . . . 306 A TRIAL RUN 5
SHAKEN
    BUT THOUGHT HAS SHAKEN HIS ANKLES FREE. . . . . 120 BOND AND FREE . . . 10
    AND THE WAVE LINE A SHAKEN SIGH. . . . . 327 A MISSIVE MISSILE . . 12
    I FELT MY STANDPOINT SHAKEN . . . . 377 ONE STEP BACKWARD TAKEN 8
    AND WE ARE SHAKEN. BUT IT ISN'T EARTHQUAKE. . . . . . 502 A MASQUE OF MERCY . . 234
SHAKES
    MY BREATHING SHAKES THE BLUET LIKE A BREEZE, ... 17 THE VANTAGE POINT . . 12
SHAKESPEARE
    HE DID AS SHAKESPEARE SAYS, YOU MAY RECALL, ... 400 THE BROKEN DROUGHT . . 7
    DICK SAID, TO OLD PIKE INNOCENT OF SHAKESPEARE. . . . . 408 FROM PLANE TO PLANE . 148
SHAKING
    'TWAS IN FOR AN OLD-FASHIONED SHAKING DOWN . . . . . . 503 A MASQUE OF MERCY . . 273
SHALL---NOT INDEXED
SHALLOW
    AND THE SHALLOW WATERS AFLUTTER WITH WIND . . . . . . 27 A LINE-STORM SONG . . 19
SHALLOWS
    PAUL DRAGGED THE SHALLOWS FOR IT WITH HIS FINGERS, . . . 194 PAUL'S WIFE 104
SHAME
    SOME CRIED SHAME ON ME NOT TO BLANKET HIM, ... 209 PAUPER WITCH OF GRAFTON 52
    SHE LOOKED AND SAW THE SHAME: . . . . 340 THE SUBVERTED FLOWER . 41
    ALBEIT NOT WITHOUT SOME SHAME OF FACE, ... 396 ANY SIZE WE PLEASE . . 4
    TILL I WAS CAUGHT AND PUT TO SHAME, ... 467 QUANDARY 22
SHAMEFUL
    THOSE FRIENDS KNOW NOTHING OF HER GRIEF TO MAKE IT SHAMEFUL. 256 THE LOVELY BE CHOOSERS 27
SHAMEFULLY
    THEY TAKE ADVANTAGE OF HIM SHAMEFULLY, ... 65 A SERVANT TO SERVANTS . 74
SHAMELESS
    DON'T LAY YOUR HAND ON ME TO SAY IT, SHAMELESS. . . . . 500 A MASQUE OF MERCY . . 166
SHAN'T---NOT INDEXED
SHANTIES
    HIS HOUSE AMONG THE LOCAL SHEDS AND SHANTIES . . . . . 160 NEW HAMPSHIRE . . . 52
SHAPE
    "YOU SEEM TO SHAPE THE PAPER'S POLICY." . . . . 48 A HUNDRED COLLARS . . 119
    AMONG THE RASPBERRIES, AND HEW AND SHAPE IT . . . . . 79 THE GENERATIONS OF MEN 162
    PRESSED INTO SERVICE MEANS PRESSED OUT OF SHAPE. . . . 98 THE SELF-SEEKER . . . 149
    IF BY ANY CHANGE OF SHAPE . . . . 260 SAND DUNES 11
    "WRONG SHAPE, WRONG COLOR, AND WRONG SCENT," I SAID. . . 278 THE WHITE-TAILED HORNET 40
    THIS BIPLANE IS THE SHAPE OF HUMAN FLIGHT. . . . . . . 308 THE WRIGHTS' BIPLANE . 1
    WITH EVERY KNOWN SHAPE OF THE STUFF. . . . . 310 THE VINDICTIVES . . . 5

SHAPE (CONTINUED)
    WE HAVE OUR OWN ROUND SHAPE TO KEEP UNBROKEN. . . . . . . 322 BUILD SOIL 197
    WE NEVER COULD RECOVER HUMAN SHAPE, ... 351 THE LESSON FOR TODAY . 39
    THE SHAPE OF LEAVES WILL SHOW . . . . 416 CLOSED FOR GOOD . . . 23
SHAPED (SEE SUN-SHAPED)
SHAPELESS
    AGAINST THE SHAPELESS SHADOW OF STORM, ... 303 AFTERFLAKES 9
SHAPES
    WHICH FLOWS IN SHAPES AS TALL AS TREES . . . . 9 STARS 3
    ALL SHAPES AND COLORS OF FLOWERS, ... 264 THE LAST MOWING . . . 18
    LET CLOUD SHAPES SWARM! . . . . 308 PERTINAX 2
SHAPING
    AND STARTED SHAPING MY LIFE TO HIS, ... 420 ONE MORE BREVITY . . 41
SHARE
    WHO SHARE THE UNLIT PLACE WITH ME-- . . . . 6 GHOST HOUSE 23
    "LAFE, HERE'S A FELLOW WANTS TO SHARE YOUR ROOM." . . . 45 A HUNDRED COLLARS . . 36
    WE'VE HAD A SHARE IN ONE NIGHT OF HIS LIFE. . . . . . 156 SNOW 349
    MY SHARE AT LEAST, LEST I BE EMPTY-IDLE. . . . . . . 324 BUILD SOIL . . . 262
    AND I COULD SHARE TIME'S LACK OF JOY OR GRIEF . . . . 335 I COULD GIVE ALL . . 9
    WOULD RUN IN UNDER IT TO GET MY SHARE. . . . . 337 THE WIND AND THE RAIN . 36
    WHO TOOK IN THEM ONLOOKER'S SHARE. . . . . 345 DISCOVERY OF MADEIRAS . 56
    A VIRTUE IN WHICH WE ALL MAY SHARE. . . . . 376 SOMETHING FOR HOPE . 19
    WHAT YOU COMPLAIN OF, ALL THE NATIONS SHARE. . . . . . 398 BURSTING RAPTURE . . 10
    AND DONE YEOMAN SHARE . . . . 434 KITTY HAWK . . . 205
SHARED
    THE BRIDE WHO SHARED THE CRUST HE BROKE TO EAT, ... 359 THE LOST FOLLOWER . . 23
SHARES
    I THINK HE OWNED SOME SHARES IN HARVARD COLLEGE.) . . . 163 NEW HAMPSHIRE . . . 137
SHARING
    SHARING A ROOM WITH SOMEONE ELSE." / "WHO IS IT?" . . . 45 A HUNDRED COLLARS . . 24
    AND SHARING HIS MILES OF EXERCISE. . . . . 420 ONE MORE BREVITY . . 43
    BUT THE GOSPEL OF SHARING, ... 449 THE BAD ISLAND--EASTER 60
SHARK
    TO BE THEIR OWN MARRIAGE FEAST FOR THE SHARK. . . . . 346 DISCOVERY OF MADEIRAS . 85
SHARP
    WAS THAT WE'D GROUND IT SHARP AND HADN'T KNOWN, ... 190 THE GRINDSTONE . . 66
SHARP-EDGED
    AND ROLLED HIS OLD HEAD ON THAT SHARP-EDGED CHAIR-BACK. . 39 DEATH OF THE HIRED MAN 148
SHARPENED
    FOR ALL I KNEW IT MAY HAVE SHARPENED SPEARS . . . . . 189 THE GRINDSTONE . . . 37
SHARPLY
    THE WOMAN SPOKE OUT SHARPLY, "WHOA, STAND STILL!-- . . . 89 THE FEAR 8
SHATTER
    SHATTER IT INWARD ON THE UNSWEPT FLOORS. . . . . . . 216 A FOUNTAIN, A BOTTLE . 104
SHATTERED
    AND IS NOT SHATTERED INTO DYES, ... 19 THE TRIAL BY EXISTENCE 10
    WILD, EASILY SHATTERED ROSE. . . . . 26 A LINE-STORM SONG . . 14
    BEYOND WHERE THEY WERE WAS A SHATTERED SEEDPOD. . . . . 76 THE GENERATIONS OF MEN 74
    THE SHATTERED WATER MADE A MISTY DIN. . . . . 250 ONCE BY THE PACIFIC . 1
    SOME SHATTERED DISHES UNDERNEATH A PINE, ... 378 DIRECTIVE 42
    ONLY TO SEE IT SHATTERED EVERY DAY. . . . . 508 A MASQUE OF MERCY . . 373
SHATTERING
    AS GREAT AS THOSE IS SHATTERING TO THE FRAME . . . . . 111 IN THE HOME STRETCH . 39
    SHATTERING AND AVALANCHING ON THE SNOW CRUST-- . . . . 121 BIRCHES 11
SHAVINGS
    BUT NOW HE BRUSHED THE SHAVINGS FROM HIS KNEE . . . . 188 THE AX-HELVE . . . 94
SHE---NOT INDEXED
SHEATH
    THE BIRCH BEGINS TO CRACK ITS OUTER SHEATH . . . . . 375 A YOUNG BIRCH . . . 1
SHEBA
    AS SHEBA CAME TO SOLOMON. . . . . 390 TWO LEADING LIGHTS . . 21
SHED
    SOON THE SUN'S WARMTH MAKES THEM SHED CRYSTAL SHELLS . . 121 BIRCHES 10
    OUT THROUGH THE SHED." / "I GUESS I KNOW MY WAY. . . . 144 SNOW 38
    CARVED IN THE SHED TO TELL ME WHO I AM . . . . 144 SNOW 40
    THERE'S BEEN ENOUGH SHED WITHOUT SHEDDING MINE. . . . 170 NEW HAMPSHIRE . . 372
    BUT FROM A SHED WHERE NEITHER OF THEM COULD SEE HIM.) . . 194 PAUL'S WIFE . . . 115
    TILL I FILL THE WHOLE SHED, ... 235 GATHERING LEAVES . 15
    THE LITTLE OLD HOUSE WAS OUT WITH A LITTLE NEW SHED . . 286 A ROADSIDE STAND . 1
    IF I SHED SUCH A DARKNESS, ... 303 AFTERFLAKES . . . 6
SHE'D---NOT INDEXED
SHEDDING
    SHOULDERING ITS WAY AND SHEDDING THE EARTH CRUMBS. . . . 124 PUTTING IN THE SEED . 14
    THERE'S BEEN ENOUGH SHED WITHOUT SHEDDING MINE. . . . 170 NEW HAMPSHIRE . . 372
SHEDS
    HIS HOUSE AMONG THE LOCAL SHEDS AND SHANTIES . . . . 160 NEW HAMPSHIRE . . . 52
    OR JOINED WITH SHEDS IN RING-AROUND A DOORYARD. . . . 289 OLD BARN AT THE BOTTOM 2
SHEEP
    ALL WOODS AND PASTURE ONLY FIT FOR SHEEP. . . . . . 316 BUILD SOIL 9
    BUT SHEEP IS WHAT I'M GOING INTO NEXT. . . . . . . 316 BUILD SOIL 10
    AT THIRTY CENTS A BUSHEL. GIVE ME SHEEP. . . . . . 316 BUILD SOIL 12
    I'LL DRESS UP IN SHEEP'S CLOTHING AND EAT SHEEP. . . . 316 BUILD SOIL 16
    WILL PUT TEN THOUSAND FARMERS OUT OF SHEEP. . . . . 319 BUILD SOIL . . . 110
    WHEN INSTEAD OF SHEEP . . . . 437 KITTY HAWK . . . 311
SHEEPISH
    AND EVERY SHEEPISH PALADIN AND PEER, ... 353 THE LESSON FOR TODAY . 90
SHEEP'S
    I'LL DRESS UP IN SHEEP'S CLOTHING AND EAT SHEEP. . . . 316 BUILD SOIL 16
SHEER
    BUT FROM SHEER MORNING GLADNESS AT THE BRIM. . . . . 23 THE TUFT OF FLOWERS . 28
    WITH DEPTHS BEHIND HIM SHEER A HUNDRED FEET-- . . . . 42 THE MOUNTAIN . . . 60
    WHICH IS SHEER MATTHEW ARNOLDISM, ... 171 NEW HAMPSHIRE . . 382
    SOME TURN IN SHEER, IN SHELLEYAN DEJECTION . . . . . 358 THE LOST FOLLOWER . 11
    THAT'S BROWNING AND SHEER CHAPEL NON-CONFORMISM. . . . 486 A MASQUE OF REASON . 365
SHEET
    I SEE IT'S A FAIR, PRETTY SHEET OF WATER. . . . . . 63 A SERVANT TO SERVANTS . 17
    I SEE IT'S A FAIR, PRETTY SHEET OF WATER, ... 63 A SERVANT TO SERVANTS . 32
    ITS BED IS LEFT A FADED PAPER SHEET . . . . 119 HYLA BROOK 10

SHEET (CONTINUED)
   ON ANY BUT A PAPER SHEET SO WHITE . . . . 357 A CONSIDERABLE SPECK . 2
   THEN IN THE MIDDLE OF THE OPEN SHEET . . . . 357 A CONSIDERABLE SPECK . 21
   ON ANY SHEET THE LEAST DISPLAY OF MIND. . . . . . . 358 A CONSIDERABLE SPECK . 33
SHEETS
   TO RUSH IN SHEETS AND FOOL'S CAPS WHERE THEY SMELLED . . 163 NEW HAMPSHIRE . . . 141
   THE MICA SHEETS WERE BIG AS PLATE-GLASS WINDOWS. . . . 213 A FOUNTAIN, A BOTTLE . 5
   WHEN HEAVEN PRESENTS IN SHEETS THE SOLID HUE? . . . . 220 FRAGMENTARY BLUE . . 4
SHELF
   THE LITTLE TIN BOX ON THE CUPBOARD SHELF-- . . . . . 86 THE HOUSEKEEPER . . . 143
   THE UPPER SHELF, THE TIN BOX. THAT'S THE ONE. . . . . 86 THE HOUSEKEEPER . . . 144
   DON'T BUILD ME A CHIMNEY UPON A SHELF. . . . . . . 232 THE KITCHEN CHIMNEY . 4
   ON ONE HIMALAYAN SHELF; . . . . 314 BEARER OF EVIL TIDINGS 34
   BUT RIGHT BESIDE YOU BOOKLIKE ON A SHELF, ... 359 THE LOST FOLLOWER . . 31
   THAT IS YOUR ANTIQUES RATTLING ON A SHELF. . . . . . 504 A MASQUE OF MERCY . . 283
   (A WHOLE SHELF CASCADES DOWN.) HERE COME SOME MORE. . . 506 A MASQUE OF MERCY . . 341
SHELF'S
   A SHELF'S FOR A CLOCK OR VASE OR PICTURE, ... 232 THE KITCHEN CHIMNEY . 17
SHELL
   FOR THE ONE MORE CAST-OFF SHELL. . . . . 261 SAND DUNES 16
   TORPEDO-LIKE, WITH SHELL OF GRITTY LEATHER, ... 270 THE EGG AND THE MACHINE 25
   HER WELL-TURNED EGG'S BROWN STURDY SHELL, ... 281 BLUE RIBBON AT AMESBURY 34
   I PICK A DEAD SHELL UP FROM WHERE THE KELP . . . . . 446 DOES NO ONE AT ALL EVER 25
SHE'LL---NOT INDEXED
SHELLEYAN
   SOME TURN IN SHEER, IN SHELLEYAN DEJECTION . . . . . 358 THE LOST FOLLOWER . . 11
SHELLS
   TO THE ANCIENT LANDS WHERE IT LEFT THE SHELLS . . . . 27 A LINE-STORM SONG . . 27
   SOON THE SUN'S WARMTH MAKES THEM SHED CRYSTAL SHELLS . . 121 BIRCHES 10
   GRIND SHELLS, O FUTILE SEA, GRIND EMPTY SHELLS . . . . 446 DOES NO ONE AT ALL EVER 19
SHELL'S
   YOU WENT TO MEET THE SHELL'S EMBRACE OF FIRE . . . . 222 TO E.T. 13
SHELTER
   FOR A SHELTER FOR THE NIGHT, ... 7 LOVE AND A QUESTION . 6
   MADE SHIFT TO SHELTER THEM WITHOUT THE HELP . . . . . 73 THE GENERATIONS OF MEN 12
   "UNDER THE SHELTER OF THE FAMILY TREE." . . . . . . 75 THE GENERATIONS OF MEN 65
   OR SHELTER TO PUT INTO FROM THIS PLACE . . . . . . 145 SNOW 74
   AND RAN FOR SHELTER QUOTING MATTHEW ARNOLD: . . . . . 170 NEW HAMPSHIRE . . . 370
   I STAYED THE NIGHT FOR SHELTER AT A FARM . . . . . . 202 THE WITCH OF COOS . . 1
   AND WILL YOU GIVE ME SHELTER FOR THE NIGHT? . . . . . 368 THE LITERATE FARMER AND 21
SHELTERED
   BEHIND WHICH I WAS SHELTERED FROM A WIND. . . . . . 40 THE MOUNTAIN 6
SHELTERING
   WHO NOW WOULD FAIN SEEK SHELTERING WALL, ... 236 MISGIVING 7
SHELVES
   SHELVES ONE COULD REST A KNEE ON GETTING UP-- . . . . 42 THE MOUNTAIN 59
   THEY WERE NOT SLEEPING IN THE SHELVES OF BUNKS. . . . 175 THE CENSUS-TAKER . . 41
SHELVING
   ONE THING HAS A SHELVING BANK, ... 281 A DRUMLIN WOODCHUCK . 1
SHEPHERD
   THE PEACEFUL SHEPHERD . . . . 252 THE PEACEFUL SHEPHERD . T
   IS IT A BARGAIN, SHEPHERD MELIBOEUS? . . . . 325 BUILD SOIL . . . 283
SHERMAN
   REMEMBER HOW YOU ENVIED GENERAL SHERMAN. . . . . . . 406 FROM PLANE TO PLANE . 71
   WILLIAM TECUMSEH SHERMAN. WHY TECUMSEH?" . . . . . . 406 FROM PLANE TO PLANE . 72
SHE'S---NOT INDEXED
SHIELD
   O'ER RUINED FENCES THE GRAPEVINES SHIELD . . . . . . 5 GHOST HOUSE 6
SHIFT
   MADE SHIFT TO SHELTER THEM WITHOUT THE HELP . . . . . 73 THE GENERATIONS OF MEN 12
SHIFTED
   AND SLEPT. THE LOG THAT SHIFTED WITH A JOLT . . . . . 108 OLD MAN'S WINTER NIGHT 23
   ONCE IN THE STOVE, DISTURBED HIM AND HE SHIFTED, . . . 108 OLD MAN'S WINTER NIGHT 24
   THE MOUNTAIN MAY HAVE SHIFTED SINCE I SAW IT . . . . 213 A FOUNTAIN, A BOTTLE . 22
   A BLINDING HEADLIGHT SHIFTED GLARE . . . . 383 WERE I IN TROUBLE . . 3
SHIMMERING
   AND A WHITE SHIMMERING CONCOURSE ROLLS . . . . . . 20 THE TRIAL BY EXISTENCE 29
SHINE
   YOU KNOW THE KIND. THEN LET THE SUN SHINE ON IT!" . . . 42 THE MOUNTAIN 54
   IN HAVING GRANTED YOU ALL AGES SHINE . . . . 354 THE LESSON FOR TODAY . 118
   "SHINE, PERISHING REPUBLIC." / ROBINSON JEFFERS . . . 449 OUR DOOM TO BLOOM . . S
   BUT MERCY FIRST AND LAST SHALL BRIGHTEST SHINE-- . . . 508 A MASQUE OF MERCY . . 381
SHINES
   AND THE SUN SHINES OUT WARM: THE VINES MUST BE WET. . . 62 BLUEBERRIES 83
   WHERE THE SUN SHINES NOW NO WARMER THAN THE MOON. . . . 106 CHRISTMAS TREES . . . 19
SHINGLING
   OF WHAT WANTS PRUNING, SHINGLING, BREAKING UP. . . . . 115 IN THE HOME STRETCH . 150
SHINING
   HE SAT THERE CREASED AND SHINING IN THE LIGHT, ... 46 A HUNDRED COLLARS . . 51
   UP TO THEIR SHINING EYES IN SNOW. . . . . 102 GOOD HOURS 4
   GIVES ME BACK IN A SHINING SURFACE PICTURE . . . . . 225 FOR ONCE SOMETHING . . 4
   WITH ONE FIRST-WATER STAR ALMOST AS SHINING. . . . . 245 THE FREEDOM OF THE MOON 4
   I PUT IT SHINING ANYWHERE I PLEASE. . . . . 245 THE FREEDOM OF THE MOON 7
   AND LAST YEAR'S BERRIES SHINING SCARLET RED. . . . . 254 A WINTER EDEN . . . 8
   WITH THE SUN SHINING THROUGH. . . . . 303 AFTERFLAKES 15
   HER SHINING HAIR DISPLACED. . . . . 339 THE SUBVERTED FLOWER . 17
   I LEFT LIGHT SHINING ON AN EMPTY STAGE . . . . . . 497 A MASQUE OF MERCY . . 100
   YOU ASK IF I SEE YONDER SHINING GATE, ... 513 A MASQUE OF MERCY . . 530
SHINY
   AT THE SHINY DESERT WITH SPOTS OF GLOOM . . . . . . 291 ON HEART'S BEGINNING TO 27
   ALL OF THEM RADIANT AND MIGHTY SHINY. . . . . 425 ACCIDENTALLY ON PURPOSE 4
SHIP
   MEN LEFT HER A SHIP TO SINK: . . . . 260 SAND DUNES 13
   NO SHIP OF ALL THAT UNDER SAIL OR STEAM . . . . . . 262 IMMIGRANTS 1
   A SHIP KEEPS RAISING ITS HULL; . . . . 301 NEITHER OUT FAR NOR IN 6
   SHE WOULD NOT LOOK AT THE FATEFUL SHIP. . . . . . . 343 DISCOVERY OF MADEIRAS . 8
   THEIR LITTLE STORMY SHIP, THAN ON. . . . . 344 DISCOVERY OF MADEIRAS . 20
   THE SHIP IT SEEMED HAD BEEN A SLAVER. . . . . 345 DISCOVERY OF MADEIRAS . 53

SHIP (CONTINUED)
AND THE SHIP LAY IN THE BAY FOR A WHILE . . . . 347 DISCOVERY OF MADEIRAS . 111
I'D SHIP A SMOOTH ONE YOU COULD SLAP AND CHAFE, . . . 365 OF STONES OF THE PLACE   9
BEEN BROUGHT IN A SHIP . . . . 447 THE BAD ISLAND--EASTER   11
SHIPPED
AND ONCE THEY HAD SHIPPED A CAPTIVE PAIR . . . . . . 345 DISCOVERY OF MADEIRAS . 54
SHIPS
ABOUT THE SHIPS WHERE WAR HAS FOUND THEM OUT . . . 132 THE BONFIRE 104
AND CHILDREN IN THE SHIPS AND IN THE TOWNS? . . . . . 132 THE BONFIRE 108
THOUGH OUR KITING SHIPS . . . . 439 KITTY HAWK 351
SHIRE
HE CAME AT LAST TO HIS NATIVE SHIRE. . . . . . . 347 DISCOVERY OF MADEIRAS . 132
IN THE ONE STATE OF OURS THAT IS A SHIRE, ... 400 TO THE RIGHT PERSON . 1
SHIRT
FUMBLING THE BUTTONS IN A WELL-STARCHED SHIRT. . . . . 46 A HUNDRED COLLARS . . 52
"I'M MOVING INTO A SIZE-LARGER SHIRT. . . . . 46 A HUNDRED COLLARS . . 53
SHIVER
AND LIKE THE FLOWERS BESIDE THEM, CHILL AND SHIVER, . . 245 SPRING POOLS 3
SHIVERED
AND A COLD CHILL SHIVERED ACROSS THE LAKE. . . . . . 63 A SERVANT TO SERVANTS . 31
SHIVERY
FULL OF LANK, SHIVERY, HALF-DROWNED BIRDS . . . . . 85 THE HOUSEKEEPER . . . 120
SHOALS
AT THE ISLES OF SHOALS, AND SATISFIED HIMSELF . . . . 161 NEW HAMPSHIRE . . . 76
SHOCK
AND CARS THAT SHOCK AND RATTLE--AND ONE HOTEL. . . . . 45 A HUNDRED COLLARS . . 22
SHOCKS
FOR THE SHOCKS AND CHANGES WE NEED TO KEEP US SANE. . . 268 ON LOOKING UP BY CHANCE 10
SHOD (SEE DRY-SHOD)
SHOE
AND MY SHOE AND MY STOCKING . . . . 413 AWAY! 3
SHOEING
WHEN SHOEING HOME ACROSS THE WHITE, ... 232 LOOKING FOR SUNSET BIRD 3
SHOES
"NOT THAT WAY, WITH YOUR SHOES ON KIKE'S WHITE BED. . . 47 A HUNDRED COLLARS . . 75
YOU CAN'T REST THAT WAY. LET ME PULL YOUR SHOES OFF." . 47 A HUNDRED COLLARS . . 76
YOU COULD SIT THERE WITH THE STAINS ON YOUR SHOES . . 54 HOME BURIAL 84
THEY SELL IN THE STORE AND BUY SHOES FOR THEIR FEET." . 61 BLUEBERRIES 53
WHOSE SHOES I PRIMPED TO DANCE IN!" / "AND WHERE'S JOHN?" 81 THE HOUSEKEEPER . . . 13
I WALKED SO LIGHT ON AIR IN HEAVY SHOES . . . . . 132 THE BONFIRE 92
ONE BY ONE I LOST OFF MY HAT AND SHOES, ... 198 WILD GRAPES 72
BUT WELCOMED FOR THE CHANCE TO LAVE MY SHOES . . . . 215 A FOUNTAIN, A BOTTLE . 66
I HAVE A PAIR OF SHOES STANDING, ... 294 A RECORD STRIDE . . 5
I TOUCH MY TONGUE TO THE SHOES NOW, ... 295 A RECORD STRIDE . . 21
THE AUTHENTIC SHOES IT WAS MADE IN . . . . 295 A RECORD STRIDE . . 27
ABOUT BEING PAST-ACTIVE SHOES. . . . . 295 A RECORD STRIDE . . 32
SHONE
SHONE ON A MAN AND WOMAN IN THE DOOR . . . . 89 THE FEAR 2
FURTHER THAN TARGET EVER SHOWED OR SHONE. . . . . . 262 A SOLDIER 14
THAT I HAVE HEARD OF SHONE AT NIGHT. . . . . 390 TWO LEADING LIGHTS . . 6
SHOOK
YOU SHOOK YOUR PENSIVE HEAD AS WHO SHOULD SAY, . . . 16 A DREAM PANG 6
THEY ALMOST SHOOK ME." / "IT'S ALL SO MUCH . . . . 114 IN THE HOME STRETCH . 126
A SUDDEN PASSING BULLET SHOOK IT DRY. . . . . . . 126 RANGE-FINDING . . . 12
THEN SHOOK HIS LANTERN, SAYING, "ILE'S . . . . . 140 BROWN'S DESCENT . . 74
SHOOK DOWN ON ME . . . . 221 DUST OF SNOW 2
SHOOK WHATEVER IT WAS LAY THERE AT BOTTOM, ... 225 FOR ONCE, SOMETHING . 13
A CHEER WENT UP THAT SHOOK THE MOTTOED WALL. . . . . 400 THE BROKEN DROUGHT . . 6
SHOOKS
PROMISE ME ALL THE SHOOKS I WANT TO NAIL." . . . . 95 THE SELF-SEEKER . . . 79
SHOOT
I DON'T WANT YOU SHOULD SHOOT ME IN THE HEAD.-- . . . 50 A HUNDRED COLLARS . . 176
SHOOTS
AND SENDING UP NEW SHOOTS . . . . 308 EVIL TENDENCIES CANCEL   4
SHOP
OF WALLED-OFF GROUND WHERE A SHOP HAD STOOD, ... 133 A GIRL'S GARDEN . . . 11
FROM THE SCIENCE SHOP . . . . 439 KITTY HAWK 353
I THOUGHT YOU JUST NOW SAID IT WAS A GIFT SHOP. . . . 494 A MASQUE OF MERCY . . 25
SHORE (SEE FAR-SHORE)
SOMETIMES WE DON'T. WE'VE A GOOD PIECE OF SHORE . . . 64 A SERVANT TO SERVANTS . 42
GREATER THAN BEING SHORE TO THE OCEAN-- . . . . . . 247 DEVOTION 2
AND THOUGHT OF DOING SOMETHING TO THE SHORE . . . . 250 ONCE BY THE PACIFIC . 3
THE SHORE WAS LUCKY IN BEING BACKED BY CLIFF, ... 250 ONCE BY THE PACIFIC . 8
LOOKING DOWNHILL TO A FROTHY SHORE? . . . . . . 251 BEREFT 5
THAT WAVE'S BEEN STANDING OFF THIS JUT OF SHORE--" . . 258 WEST-RUNNING BROOK . . 18
"THAT WAVE'S BEEN STANDING OFF THIS JUT OF SHORE . . . 258 WEST-RUNNING BROOK . . 27
HAS BEEN HER ANXIOUS CONVOY IN TO SHORE. . . . . . 262 IMMIGRANTS 4
AND FORCE HER FAREWELL STEP OFF SHORE. . . . . . 343 DISCOVERY OF MADEIRAS . 11
SAFELY MADE THE AFRICAN SHORE; . . . . 347 DISCOVERY OF MADEIRAS . 127
ON OUR CISATLANTIC SHORE . . . . 367 A SERIOUS STEP LIGHTLY 14
OFF THIS VERY SHORE? . . . . 432 KITTY HAWK 149
SHORT
WITH ANYONE TO DEATH, COMES SO FAR SHORT . . . . . 54 HOME BURIAL 98
CUT SHORT OFF AT BOTH ENDS. IT LIES FIVE MILES . . . 63 A SERVANT TO SERVANTS . 21
AND FEAR OF SEEMING SHORT OF SPEECH, OR WHETHER . . . 106 CHRISTMAS TREES . . . 27
SHORT OF THE PERCH THEIR LANGUID FLIGHT WAS TOWARD; . . 130 THE BONFIRE 37
SHORT OFF, AND DIED AGAINST THE WINDOWPANE." . . . . 149 SNOW 166
WHOSE HORSE HAD PULLED HIM SHORT UP IN THE ROAD . . . 168 NEW HAMPSHIRE . . . 289
FOR ALL HER MOUNTAINS FALL A LITTLE SHORT, ... 170 NEW HAMPSHIRE . . . 355
HER PEOPLE NOT QUITE SHORT ENOUGH FOR ART, ... 170 NEW HAMPSHIRE . . . 356
BAPTISTE KNEW HOW TO MAKE A SHORT JOB LONG . . . . 187 THE AX-HELVE . . . 80
TOP-HEAVY WITH A HEAVINESS HIS SHORT, ... 188 THE AX-HELVE . . . 98
SHORT OF A FIGHTING WORD. YOU HAVE THE ANSWERS. . . . 192 PAUL'S WIFE . . . 34
OF COURSE THE BOTTLE FELL SHORT BY A MILE, ... 195 PAUL'S WIFE . . . 142
UP WHERE THE TREES GROW SHORT, THE MOSSES TALL, . . . 210 PAUPER WITCH OF GRAFTON 96
HAD BEEN TOO SHORT TO SELL OR GIVE AWAY. . . . . . 217 A FOUNTAIN, A BOTTLE . 122
AN HOUR OF WINTER DAY MIGHT SEEM TOO SHORT . . . . . 254 A WINTER EDEN . . . 19
OUR MISSILES ALWAYS MAKE TOO SHORT AN ARC. . . . . 261 A SOLDIER 8

```
                                                              PAGE TITLE                      LINE
SHORT (CONTINUED)
    I'D HAVE A SHORT ONE READY FOR MY OWN.  .   .   .   .   .   . 355 THE LESSON FOR TODAY  .  159
    "IN SHORT, YOU THINK THAT STAR A PATENT MEDICINE  .   .   .   . 371 THE LITERATE FARMER AND   92
    SOME CLUSTER ONE STAR SHORT.  .   .   .   .   .   .   .   .   . 384 MAKING CERTAIN ANYTHING    8
    SHORT OF ANYWHERE,  .   .   .   .   .   .   .   .   .   .   .   . 439 KITTY HAWK  .   .   .   . 356
SHORTCUT
    WILL GIVE US BY SHORTCUT THE FINAL STAGE  .   .   .   .   .   . 358 THE LOST FOLLOWER  .   .   13
SHORTEN
    YET DID NOT MUCH TO SHORTEN STRIDE.  .   .   .   .   .   .   . 336 THE WIND AND THE RAIN  .    8
SHORTENED
    THAT HUMAN HISTORY SHOULD NOT BE SHORTENED.  .   .   .   .   . 397 THE PLANNERS  .   .   .   .  14
SHORTHAND
    SHE LEARNED SHORTHAND, WHATEVER SHORTHAND MAY  .   .   .   . 182 MAPLE  .   .   .   .   .   .  75
SHOT  (SEE STAR-SHOT)
    AND SHOT. IT'S POLLYANNA NOW OR DEATH.   .   .   .   .   .   . 168 NEW HAMPSHIRE  .   .   . 282
    AND TRIPPED THE BODY, SHOT THE SPIRIT ON .   .   .   .   .   . 262 A SOLDIER  .   .   .   .   .  13
    AT LAST IT WAS A FLY. HE SHOT AND MISSED;  .   .   .   .   . 278 THE WHITE-TAILED HORNET   42
    ANOTHER SHOT THROUGH GLASS,  .   .   .   .   .   .   .   .   . 298 ON TAKING FROM THE TOP    11
    MIGHT NOT HAVE MISSED ME WHEN THEY SHOT AND FELL?  .   .   . 383 BRAVADO  .   .   .   .   .    3
    AN INTIMATION, A SHOT OF RAY,   .   .   .   .   .   .   .   . 421 ONE MORE BREVITY  .   .   .  67
    WHEN HE SHOT A SHAFT  .   .   .   .   .   .   .   .   .   .   . 427 VERSION  .   .   .   .   .    3
    LIKE A PIP SHOT FROM 'TWIXT OUR PINCHING FINGERS."  .   .   . 460 HOW HARD TO KEEP FROM   202
SHOTGUN
    OR WITH A SHOTGUN FOR A STRAY BLACK BEAR?  .   .   .   .   .  43 THE MOUNTAIN  .   .   .   .  87
SHOULD---NOT INDEXED
SHOULDER
    LOOKING BACK OVER HER SHOULDER AT SOME FEAR.   .   .   .   .  51 HOME BURIAL  .   .   .   .    3
    WHAT SHOULDER DID I SEE HER OVER? NEITHER.   .   .   .   . 113 IN THE HOME STRETCH  .  69
    "A FIT!" SAID ONE, AND BANGED A STOVEPIPE SHOULDER.  .   . 113 IN THE HOME STRETCH  .  90
    OVER HIS SHOULDER WITH HIS PIPESTEM, SAYING,  .   .   .   . 143 SNOW  .   .   .   .   .   .    7
    AND MY HEAD SWAYS TO MY SHOULDER  .   .   .   .   .   .   . 156 THE SOUND OF TREES  .   .  16
    INVISIBLE HANDS CROWDED ON HER SHOULDER  .   .   .   .   . 256 THE LOVELY BE CHOOSERS   12
    THEN PICK YOUR HOE UP, MAYBE SHOULDER IT,  .   .   .   .   . 405 FROM PLANE TO PLANE  .  41
    AT FOUR O'CLOCK I SHOULDER AX,  .   .   .   .   .   .   .   . 470 IN WINTER IN THE WOODS    5
    A LIGHT THAT FALLS DIFFUSED OVER MY SHOULDER  .   .   .   . 515 A MASQUE OF MERCY  .   . 580
SHOULDERED  (SEE BROAD-SHOULDERED)
    THE GUN REVERSED THAT HE WENT OUT WITH SHOULDERED.  .   . 289 OLD BARN AT THE BOTTOM     4
SHOULDERING
    SHOULDERING ITS WAY AND SHEDDING THE EARTH CRUMBS.  .   . 124 PUTTING IN THE SEED  .  14
SHOULDERS
    UP AT HIS SHOULDERS, DRAGGING YELLOW STRANDS  .   .   .   . 125 AN ENCOUNTER  .   .   .  17
    SHE SHOULDERS WITH A WING SO STRONG  .   .   .   .   .   . 281 BLUE RIBBON AT AMESBURY  47
SHOULDN'T---NOT INDEXED
SHOUT
    THE WHIPPOORWILL IS COMING TO SHOUT  .   .   .   .   .   .   .   6 GHOST HOUSE  .   .   .   .  16
    AND A SHOUT GREETS THE DARING ONE.  .   .   .   .   .   .   .  21 THE TRIAL BY EXISTENCE    48
    AND I THOUGHT I HAD LOST YOU. I LIFTED A SHOUT .   .   .   .  62 BLUEBERRIES  .   .   .   .  93
    BY HIS SHOUTS IN THE NIGHT. HE'D SHOUT AND SHOUT  .   .   .  66 A SERVANT TO SERVANTS . 131
    AND SHOUT FROM WHERE I AM, 'WHAT IS IT?'  .   .   .   .   . 124 A TIME TO TALK  .   .   .    5
    "SHOUT, SHE MAY HEAR YOU." / "SHOUTING IS NO GOOD."  .   . 154 SNOW  .   .   .   .   .   . 303
    BUT THE SHOUT REACHED THE GIRL AND PUT HER LIGHT OUT.  . 195 PAUL'S WIFE  .   .   .   . 143
    I HEARD HIM SHOUT "WHAT A THING IT IS!"  .   .   .   .   . 346 DISCOVERY OF MADEIRAS  .  93
    THAT BLEW SO HE HAD TO SHOUT.  .   .   .   .   .   .   .   . 366 NOT OF SCHOOL AGE  .   .    8
    THE PROPHET OF DISASTER CEASED TO SHOUT.  .   .   .   .   . 399 THE BROKEN DROUGHT  .    1
    FILLED ME WITH TO SHOUT  .   .   .   .   .   .   .   .   .   . 429 KITTY HAWK  .   .   .   .  27
    YOU NEEDN'T SHOUT LIKE THAT, YOU WRETCHED MAN.  .   .   . 508 A MASQUE OF MERCY  .   . 394
SHOUTED
    UNTIL THE STRENGTH WAS SHOUTED OUT OF HIM,  .   .   .   .  66 A SERVANT TO SERVANTS . 132
    THAT SHOUTED IN THE MIST A MONTH AGO,  .   .   .   .   .   . 119 HYLA BROOK  .   .   .   .    5
    I SAT UP ON THE FLOOR AND SHOUTED, "TOFFILE,  .   .   .   . 205 THE WITCH OF COOS  .   .  82
    THEN RAN AND SHOUTED, "SHUT THE BEDROOM DOOR,  .   .   . 205 THE WITCH OF COOS  .   .  93
SHOUTING
    "DO GO ALONG WITH HIM AND STOP HIS SHOUTING."  .   .   .   .  89 THE HOUSEKEEPER  .   . 212
    "SHOUT, SHE MAY HEAR YOU." / "SHOUTING IS NO GOOD."  .   . 154 SNOW  .   .   .   .   .   . 303
SHOUTS
    BY HIS SHOUTS IN THE NIGHT. HE'D SHOUT AND SHOUT  .   .   .  66 A SERVANT TO SERVANTS . 131
    SHOUTS LIKE AN ARMY CAPTAIN, 'LET HER COME!'  .   .   .   .  71 THE CODE  .   .   .   .   .  63
    WITH SHOUTS AFAR TO PULL THE CABLE TAUT,  .   .   .   .   . 141 THE LINE-GANG  .   .   .    9
SHOVE
    TO GIVE DEVELOPMENTS THE FINAL SHOVE  .   .   .   .   .   . 369 THE LITERATE FARMER AND   42
SHOVEL
    "HE HAD THE SHOVEL. HE'LL HAVE MADE A FIGHT."  .   .   .   . 153 SNOW  .   .   .   .   .   . 279
SHOW
    SO OLD AND FIRM THEY SCARCELY SHOW THE BREEZE,  .   .   .   .   5 INTO MY OWN  .   .   .   .    2
    "SHOW HIM THIS WAY. I'M NOT AFRAID OF HIM.  .   .   .   .   .  45 A HUNDRED COLLARS  .   .  37
    I WAS JUST GETTING THROUGH WHAT THE FIELD HAD TO SHOW  .  60 BLUEBERRIES  .   .   .   .  35
    COME HERE--I'LL SHOW YOU--IN THAT APPLE TREE.  .   .   .   .  83 THE HOUSEKEEPER  .   .  62
    YOU NEVER SAW THIS ROOM BEFORE A SHOW,  .   .   .   .   .   .  85 THE HOUSEKEEPER  .   . 119
    I'LL SHOW YOU. HERE YOU ARE." / "WHAT'S THIS?" / "A BILL--  .  86 THE HOUSEKEEPER  .   . 145
    TO LET HIM HAVE THEM. NEVER SHOW SURPRISE!  .   .   .   . 107 CHRISTMAS TREES  .   .   .  46
    I WENT TO SHOW YOU HOW TO MAKE IT STAY,  .   .   .   .   . 109 THE EXPOSED NEST  .   .    5
    AND SHOW YOU HOW IT'S PILING UP AGAINST YOU.  .   .   .   . 148 SNOW  .   .   .   .   .   . 156
    CONCEAL A WISH TO SEE HIM SHOW THE SPUNK  .   .   .   .   . 153 SNOW  .   .   .   .   .   . 283
    TO SHOW THE LEVEL OF INTELLIGENCE  .   .   .   .   .   .   . 168 NEW HAMPSHIRE  .   .   . 287
    TO SHOW ITS WORLDLY NATURE AND BEGIN  .   .   .   .   .   . 174 A STAR IN A STONEBOAT  .  51
    I FOUND NO PEOPLE THAT DARED SHOW THEMSELVES,  .   .   . 174 THE CENSUS-TAKER  .   .  15
    WITH A THICK THUMBNAIL TO SHOW HOW IT RAN  .   .   .   . 186 THE AX-HELVE  .   .   .   .  23
    EVER SINCE, JUST TO SHOW THEM, HE HAD SLIPPED  .   .   . 191 PAUL'S WIFE  .   .   .   .  18
    HE'D LIKE TO TAKE ME THERE AND SHOW IT TO ME.  .   .   . 213 A FOUNTAIN, A BOTTLE  .    6
    "I'LL TELL YOU WHAT YOU SHOW ME. YOU REMEMBER  .   .   . 213 A FOUNTAIN, A BOTTLE  .    7
    WELL THEN, RIGHT HERE IS WHERE I SHOW YOU BOOKS.  .   . 215 A FOUNTAIN, A BOTTLE  .  60
    I'LL SHOW YOU HOW SHE HAD HER SILLS EXTENDED  .   .   . 216 A FOUNTAIN, A BOTTLE  .  86
    THAN FLOWERS WILL SHOW FOR DAYS UNLESS THEY HURRY.  . 225 BLUE-BUTTERFLY DAY  .    4
    AS GILT TO GOLD THAT WOULDN'T SHOW.  .   .   .   .   .   . 233 LOOKING FOR SUNSET BIRD   16
    THE MOON, THOUGH SLIGHT, WAS MOON ENOUGH TO SHOW  . 234 EVENING A SUGAR ORCHARD   11
    AND SHOW ON THE WATER ITS CRYSTAL TEETH.  .   .   .   . 276 TWO TRAMPS IN MUD TIME    40
    ALL COIFFURED TO A WINTER SHOW,  .   .   .   .   .   .   . 279 BLUE RIBBON AT AMESBURY    2
    BUT LET HIM SHOW THEM HOW THE WEAPON WORKED.  .   .   . 293 AT WOODWARD'S GARDENS  .   7
```

SHOW (CONTINUED)
    IT NEVER WILL SHOW MUCH FLOWER OR FRUIT. . . . . 296 LEAVES COMPARED WITH .   4
    THAT SHADOW OF MINE SHOULD SHOW IN FORM . . . . 303 AFTERFLAKES   8
    ITS ACTIONS ANY CLOUDLESS NIGHT WILL SHOW IT. . . . . . 370 THE LITERATE FARMER AND 64
    OF BABY GREEN AND SHOW THE WHITE BENEATH. . . . . 375 A YOUNG BIRCH   2
    THE LEDGES SHOW LINES RULED SOUTHEAST-NORTHWEST, ... 377 DIRECTIVE   15
    OR BE WIPED OUT. WILL SHE BE ASKED TO SHOW . . . . 395 WHY WAIT FOR SCIENCE .   5
    "--TAKING HIS OWN SWEET TIME AS IF TO SHOW . . . . 404 FROM PLANE TO PLANE .   24
    I'LL SHOW YOU WHY IT ISN'T--NOT TODAY. . . . . 406 FROM PLANE TO PLANE .   86
    THE SHAPE OF LEAVES WILL SHOW . . . . 416 CLOSED FOR GOOD . . .   23
    AND WITH THE GOLD IN HAND TO SHOW FOR . . . . 417 AMERICA IS HARD TO SEE   23
    BUT LET HIM SHOW HIS HAUGHTY STERN . . . . 419 AMERICA IS HARD TO SEE   75
    TO SHOW BY DEEDS HE DIDN'T RESENT . . . . 421 ONE MORE BREVITY . .   63
    TO SHOW THE EVOLUTION HOW TO STEER. . . . . 425 ACCIDENTALLY ON PURPOSE   10
    THE REASON ARTISTS SHOW SO LITTLE INTEREST . . . . 461 HOW HARD TO KEEP FROM   230
    SHOW YOURSELF, SON.--I'LL GET BACK ON MY THRONE . . . . 487 A MASQUE OF REASON .   386
    THEY WON'T SHOW IN THE PICTURE. THAT'S TOO BAD. . . . . 490 A MASQUE OF REASON .   462
    NEITHER WILL I SHOW. THAT'S TOO BAD MOREOVER. . . . . . 490 A MASQUE OF REASON .   463
SHOWCASE
    ONE EACH OF EVERYTHING AS IN A SHOWCASE, ... 161 NEW HAMPSHIRE . . .   62
    ONE EACH OF EVERYTHING AS IN A SHOWCASE. . . . . 163 NEW HAMPSHIRE . . .   144
    STAYS TALKING WITH THE KEEPER AT A SHOWCASE. . . . . . . 493 A MASQUE OF MERCY .   4
    THAT IS NO WINDOW. THAT'S A SHOWCASE RATTLING. . . . . . 504 A MASQUE OF MERCY .   282
SHOWDOWN
    LET'S HAVE A SHOWDOWN AS AN EVIDENCE . . . . 47 A HUNDRED COLLARS .   85
SHOWED
    WHICH SHOWED HOW MUCH GOOD SCHOOL HAD EVER DONE HIM. . . 37 DEATH OF THE HIRED MAN   84
    BUT THE SIGNS SHOWED WHAT IT HAD DONE IN SPRING; . . . . 40 THE MOUNTAIN   12
    BESIDE THE LAKE FROM WHERE THAT DAY I SHOWED YOU . . . . 64 A SERVANT TO SERVANTS   62
    HE SHOWED ME LUMPS OF THE SCENTED STUFF . . . . 141 THE GUM-GATHERER . .   30
    AND SHOWED HIM, THROUGH A MANHOLE IN THE FLOOR, ... 142 THE VANISHING RED .   21
    OH, YES, HE SHOWED JOHN THE WHEEL PIT ALL RIGHT. . . . . 142 THE VANISHING RED .   29
    THAT SHOWED ITSELF IN DENDROPHOBIA. . . . . 171 NEW HAMPSHIRE . . .   375
    HE SHOWED ME THAT THE LINES OF A GOOD HELVE . . . . . . 187 THE AX-HELVE . . .   72
    MY SMALL WRISTS STRETCHING TILL THEY SHOWED THE BANJO
        STRINGS. . . . . 198 WILD GRAPES   80
    WELL, I SHOWED ARTHUR AMY SIGNS ENOUGH . . . . 210 PAUPER WITCH OF GRAFTON 89
    OR THAT SHOWED WITH THE LAPSE OF TIME TOO VAIN . . . . . 262 HANNIBAL   3
    FURTHER THAN TARGET EVER SHOWED OR SHONE. . . . . 262 A SOLDIER   14
    HER DEFT HAND SHOWED WITH FINGER RINGS. . . . . 273 A LONE STRIKER . .   28
    HE SHOWED NOT THE LEAST SURPRISE. . . . . 288 DEPARTMENTAL   4
    ONCE SHOWED TWO LITTLE MONKEYS IN A CAGE . . . . 293 AT WOODWARD'S GARDENS   2
    THE SAME SIGN HEAVEN SHOWED YOUR GUEST. . . . . 381 AN UNSTAMPED LETTER IN   42
    AND SHOWED THEM IT CONTAINED A LIVE TEREDO. . . . . . . 456 HOW HARD TO KEEP FROM   85
    ANY ORIGINALITY IT SHOWED . . . . 480 A MASQUE OF REASON .   189
    ANY ORIGINALITY IT SHOWED . . . . 480 A MASQUE OF REASON .   202
    BUT, LORD, WE SHOWED THEM WHAT. THE AUDIENCE . . . . . . 482 A MASQUE OF REASON .   252
SHOWER
    FRESH PAINTED BY THE SHOWER A VELVET BLACK. . . . . . . 55 THE BLACK COTTAGE . .   7
    STUCK INTO HIS BERRIES AS FRESH AS A SHOWER; . . . . . . 61 BLUEBERRIES   65
    "TO COCK THE HAY?--BECAUSE IT'S GOING TO SHOWER? . . . . 70 THE CODE   12
    AND ALL THE MORE THE MIGHTIER THE SHOWER . . . . 337 THE WIND AND THE RAIN   35
    IT GENTLY THREW US A GLITTERING SHOWER DOWN. . . . . . . 349 OUR HOLD ON THE PLANET   7
    TO SEE THE STAR SHOWER KNOWN AS LECNID . . . . 360 A LOOSE MOUNTAIN . .   2
SHOWERS
    WHEN PEAR AND CHERRY BLOOM WENT DOWN IN SHOWERS . . . . 120 THE OVEN BIRD . . .   7
    WHERE SHOWERS OF CHARTED METEORS LET FLY. . . . . 173 A STAR IN A STONEBOAT   42
SHOWING
    AND EVERY FLECK OF RUSSET SHOWING CLEAR. . . . . 68 AFTER APPLE-PICKING .   20
    BUT A FEW WEEDS AND STUBBLE SHOWING LAST. . . . . 296 DESERT PLACES   4
    I WAS JUST SHOWING OFF TO THE DEVIL, JOB, ... 484 A MASQUE OF REASON .   327
SHOWN
    AS MAY BE SHOWN BY A SIMPLE CALCULATION. . . . . 107 CHRISTMAS TREES . . .   57
    WELL, SOMETHING FOR A SNOWSTORM TO HAVE SHOWN . . . . . 240 OUR SINGING STRENGTH   49
    THE MORAL IS, IT HARDLY NEED BE SHOWN, ... 394 HAEC FABULA DOCET .   17
SHOWS
    WHICH SHOWS HOW SAD AN ACCIDENT MAY BE. . . . . 169 NEW HAMPSHIRE . . .   333
SHREWD
    (SHE MADE SHREWD EYES TO SEE WHERE HE CAME IN.) . . . . 201 PLACE FOR A THIRD . .   57
SHREWDLY
    'I HAVE LEFT THOSE THERE BERRIES, I SHREWDLY SUSPECT, . . 60 BLUEBERRIES   45
    AS ONE WHO SHREWDLY PRETENDS . . . . 282 A DRUMLIN WOODCHUCK   11
    HE PEERS OUT SHREWDLY INTO THE THICK AND SWIFT. . . . . 341 WILLFUL HOMING . . .   8
SHRIEKS
    WOODSVILLE'S A PLACE OF SHRIEKS AND WANDERING LAMPS . . 45 A HUNDRED COLLARS . .   21
SHRILL
    THE FROGS THAT WERE PEEPING A THOUSAND SHRILL . . . . . 123 PEA BRUSH   9
SHRINK
    "NOT TILL I SHRINK, WHEN THEY'LL BE OUT OF STYLE." . . . 50 A HUNDRED COLLARS . .   166
    "SCARE YOU. BUT IF YOU SHRINK FROM BEING SCARED, ... 132 THE BONFIRE   96
    IS EXTREME WHERE THEY SHRINK TO NONE AT ALL. . . . . . . 176 THE CENSUS-TAKER . .   63
    I SHRINK FROM BEING PUBLICLY LET DOWN. . . . . 505 A MASQUE OF MERCY .   305
SHRINKING
    SHE WITHDREW, SHRINKING FROM BENEATH HIS ARM . . . . . . 52 HOME BURIAL   31
    BY SHRINKING THE RAWHIDE TO NATURAL LENGTH. . . . . . . 192 PAUL'S WIFE   48
    WHAT IS IT MEN ARE SHRINKING FROM? . . . . 221 IN A DISUSED GRAVEYARD   12
SHRIVELS
    HER UDDER SHRIVELS AND THE MILK GOES DRY. . . . . 125 THE COW IN APPLE TIME   11
SHROUD
    WRAP HIM FOR SHROUD IN A PETAL. . . . . 288 DEPARTMENTAL   30
    OR WRAPPED AS IN A SHROUD, ... 333 HAPPINESS MAKES UP .   4
SHRUG
    HOW ABOUT LOVING GOD? / YOU MAKE ME SHRUG.-- . . . . . . 499 A MASQUE OF MERCY .   164
SHRUNK
    BUT RIGHT IN HEAVEN WAS SLOWLY BEING SHRUNK . . . . . . 368 THE LITERATE FARMER AND   14
SHRUNKEN
    AND THE SUN SHRUNKEN YELLOW IN SMOKE. . . . . 141 THE GUM-GATHERER . .   24

SHUDDERS
  HE SHUDDERS HIS COAT AS IF TO THROW OFF FLIES. . . . . . . 223 THE RUNAWAY 18
SHUFFLE
  TO CHAFE AND SHUFFLE IN MY CALLOUSED PALM   . . . . 174 A STAR IN A STONEBOAT . 52
  THE TOENAIL CLICK AND SHUFFLE OF HIS FEET, ... 269 THE BEAR 17
SHUFFLED
  SHUFFLED THEIR FEET AS IF TO HINT RESPECTFULLY, ... 456 HOW HARD TO KEEP FROM 73
SHUFFLING
  OVER THE GREAT BIG THUMPING, SHUFFLING MILLSTONE, ... 142 THE VANISHING RED . . 16
SHUT (SEE TIGHT-SHUT)
  ITS TWO BANKS HAVE NOT SHUT UPON THE RIVER; . . . . . . 28 MY BUTTERFLY 9
  AND SHUT IT AFTER HER. "BE KIND," SHE SAID. . . . . . . 34 DEATH OF THE HIRED MAN 7
  EVERYTHING'S SHUT SOMETIMES EXCEPT THE BARN; . . . . . . 49 A HUNDRED COLLARS . . 130
  THERE NOW, YOU GET SOME SLEEP." / HE SHUT THE DOOR. . . 50 A HUNDRED COLLARS . . 178
  TILL WEISS SHUT OFF THE WATER IN THE WHEEL PIT. . . . . 93 THE SELF-SEEKER . . . 27
  LIKE A SMALL PISTOL WHEN HE SNAPPED IT SHUT . . . . . . 98 THE SELF-SEEKER . . . 165
  WALL WITHIN WALL TO SHUT FEAR OUT. . . . . 120 BOND AND FREE 3
  THEN HE SHUT DOWN THE TRAP DOOR WITH A RING IN IT . . . 142 THE VANISHING RED . . 24
  AND ITS EYES SHUT WITH OVEREAGERNESS . . . . 148 SNOW 161
  PASSED IN AND SLAMMED IT SHUT EACH ONE BEHIND HIM . . . 175 THE CENSUS-TAKER . . . 29
  THE DOOR WAS STILL BECAUSE I HELD IT SHUT . . . . . . 175 THE CENSUS-TAKER . . . 47
  FROM END TO END WITH HIS ROUGH HAND SHUT ROUND IT. . . 187 THE AX-HELVE 77
  AND SHUT MY EYES AGAINST THE SUN, MY EARS . . . . . . 198 WILD GRAPES 74
  THEN RAN AND SHOUTED, "SHUT THE BEDROOM DOOR, ... 205 THE WITCH OF COOS . . 93
  "TOFFILE, GET NAILS." I MADE HIM NAIL THE DOOR SHUT . . 206 THE WITCH OF COOS . . 119
  "TO SHUT YOU UP I'LL TELL YOU WHAT I'LL DO: . . . . . 213 A FOUNTAIN, A BOTTLE . 17
  SHE WAS 'SHUT IN' FOR LIFE. SHE LIVED HER WHOLE . . . 215 A FOUNTAIN, A BOTTLE . 84
  WITH LIFTED SNOUT AND EYES (IF ANY) SHUT . . . . . . 269 THE BEAR 27
  AND SET THEM UP AGAIN FOR PROPPING SHUT, ... 289 OLD BARN AT THE BOTTOM 11
  HIS EYES AS GOOD (OR BAD) AS SHUT . . . . 418 AMERICA IS HARD TO SEE 58
  MY EYELIDS SO I COULDN'T SHUT MY EYES . . . . 501 A MASQUE OF MERCY . . 202
SHUTTER
  WITH SOUNDS LIKE THE DRY RATTLING OF A SHUTTER, . . . 206 THE WITCH OF COOS . . 129
SHYLY
  SHYLY BEHIND HER. / "WELL, AND HOW IS MISTER...?" . . . 96 THE SELF-SEEKER . . . 96
SI
  "I CAN'T THINK SI EVER HURT ANYONE." . . . . 39 DEATH OF THE HIRED MAN 146
SIBYL
  CUMAEAN SIBYL, CHARMING OGRESS, ... 449 OUR DOOM TO BLOOM . . 1
  THE SIBYL SAID, "GO BACK TO ROME . . . . 449 OUR DOOM TO BLOOM . . 5
SICK
  NO, FROM THE TIME WHEN ONE IS SICK TO DEATH, ... 54 HOME BURIAL 100
  IT MAKES THE GUILD OF NOVEL WRITERS SICK . . . . . . 167 NEW HAMPSHIRE . . . 274
  "'NATURE IS CRUEL, MAN IS SICK OF BLOOD': . . . . . . 170 NEW HAMPSHIRE . . . 371
  SPACE AILS US MODERNS: WE ARE SICK WITH SPACE. . . . . 352 THE LESSON FOR TODAY . 68
  "SICK TALK, SICK TALK, SICK SENTIMENTAL TALK! . . . . 370 THE LITERATE FARMER AND 84
  AND EVERYBODY'S BEING SICK FOR CHRISTMAS. . . . . . 407 FROM PLANE TO PLANE . 106
  ONE DAY WHEN THE CHIEF COOK WAS SICK AT HEART. . . . . 455 HOW HARD TO KEEP FROM 56
  TILL ON A DAY THE KING, BEING SICK AT HEART . . . . 456 HOW HARD TO KEEP FROM 94
  I'M SICK OF THE WHOLE ARTIFICIAL PUZZLE. . . . . . . 484 A MASQUE OF REASON . 300
  I'M SICK. / OF WHAT? / OH, EVERYTHING, I GUESS. . . . 499 A MASQUE OF MERCY . . 155
  LET ME ALONE. / I'M SICK. JOE'S SICK. THE WORLD'S SICK. . 500 A MASQUE OF MERCY . . 167
  I AM SICK, AS SHE SAYS. NOTHING EXHAUSTS ME . . . . . 501 A MASQUE OF MERCY . . 197
SICKEN
  IT WOULD TAKE MORE THAN THEM TO SICKEN YOU-- . . . . 114 IN THE HOME STRETCH . 123
  AND I'M AFRAID. (THE BULB LIGHTS SICKEN DOWN. . . . . 520 A MASQUE OF MERCY . . 695
SICKNESS
  ONE SICKNESS OF THE BODY AND THE SOUL. . . . . . . 318 BUILD SOIL 80
  IS IN THE SIGN OF SICKNESS IN THE WINTER . . . . . . 407 FROM PLANE TO PLANE . 105
SIDE (SEE NOSE-SIDE)
  UPON THE FULL MOON'S SIDE OF THE FIRST HAYCOCK . . . . 14 WAITING 7
  ONE ON A SIDE. IT COMES TO LITTLE MORE: . . . . . . 33 MENDING WALL . . . 22
  SLIPPED TO HER SIDE, CAUGHT UP HER HAND AND WAITED. . . 40 DEATH OF THE HIRED MAN 165
  PASTURE RAN UP THE SIDE A LITTLE WAY, ... 41 THE MOUNTAIN . . . 29
  "I DON'T ADVISE YOUR TRYING FROM THIS SIDE. . . . . . 41 THE MOUNTAIN . . . 38
  THAT'S WHY I DON'T ADVISE YOUR TRYING THIS SIDE. . . . 43 THE MOUNTAIN . . . 79
  HE TRIED THIS SIDE. I'VE ALWAYS MEANT TO GO . . . . 43 THE MOUNTAIN . . . 80
  HE LOOKS ON THE BRIGHT SIDE OF EVERYTHING, ... 64 A SERVANT TO SERVANTS 45
  I LOOKED OVER THE SIDE ONCE IN THE DUST . . . . . . 72 THE CODE 75
  "ON FATHER'S SIDE, IT SEEMS, WE'RE--LET ME SEE----" . . 76 THE GENERATIONS OF MEN 78
  ANNE LOOKED AT THE LARGE LAWYER AT HER SIDE, ... 97 THE SELF-SEEKER . . . 117
  I HAVE TO KEEP ON THE GOOD SIDE OF ANNE. . . . . . . 99 THE SELF-SEEKER . . . 176
  WHAT HELD IT, THOUGH, ON ONE SIDE WAS A TREE . . . . 102 THE WOOD-PILE . . . 32
  THE ROAD WOULD FAIL; AND ON THAT SIDE THE FIRE . . . 131 THE BONFIRE 75
  HE STOOD ON THE SAFE SIDE OF THE LINE TALKING-- . . . 171 NEW HAMPSHIRE . . . 381
  AND DOWN BY ONE SIDE WHERE IT LACKED A LEG. . . . . 175 THE CENSUS-TAKER . . 37
  ON THE SIDE IT PRESENTED TO THE ROAD) . . . . 182 MAPLE 99
  AND THEN LAND SAFELY RIGHT SIDE UP AGAIN, ... 192 PAUL'S WIFE 52
  YET ALL THE PRECEDENT IS ON MY SIDE: . . . . 226 THE ONSET 12
  TWO HAD SEEN TWO, WHICHEVER SIDE YOU SPOKE FROM. . . . 230 TWO LOOK AT TWO . . 38
  ACROSS EACH OTHER AND SIDE BY SIDE THEY LAY. . . . . 237 A HILLSIDE THAW . . 29
  YOUR NAME NOT WRITTEN ON EITHER SIDE. . . . . 247 ON GOING UNNOTICED . 12
  NOTHING ON EITHER SIDE WAS SAID. . . . . 277 TWO TRAMPS IN MUD TIME 57
  WITH BOUGHTEN FRIENDSHIP AT YOUR SIDE . . . . 307 PROVIDE, PROVIDE . . 20
  WE TWO WERE GROPING DOWN A MALVERN SIDE . . . . . . 315 IRIS BY NIGHT . . . 2
  FROM SIDE TO SIDE IN ARGUMENT, ... 326 TO A THINKER . . . 34
  IN THE CLIFF'S TALUS ON THE OTHER SIDE. . . . . . . 338 THE MOST OF IT . . 11
  I NEVER TAKE MY OWN SIDE IN A QUARREL. . . . . . . 354 THE LESSON FOR TODAY . 123
  CALLED GETTING OUT OF THE WRONG SIDE OF BED. . . . . 371 THE LITERATE FARMER AND 107
  ON THE RIGHT SIDE OF BED WOULD END THE FRAY, ... 372 THE LITERATE FARMER AND 121
  AND FOUND, HE SAYS, A BED HAS NO RIGHT SIDE. . . . . 372 THE LITERATE FARMER AND 123
  A BED'S GOT NO RIGHT SIDE TO GET OUT OF. . . . . . . 372 THE LITERATE FARMER AND 125
  STILL SAID TO HAUNT THIS SIDE OF PANTHER MOUNTAIN. . . 377 DIRECTIVE 19
  THIS SIDE THE ROCKIES IN MY ESTIMATION-- . . . . . . 400 TO THE RIGHT PERSON . 5
  AGAINST THE WRONG SIDE OF A WINDOWPANE. . . . . . . 412 POD OF THE MILKWEED . 39
  AND SCARE ME TO ONE SIDE. . . . . 415 CLOSED FOR GOOD . . 10
  ON ONE SIDE THE OCEAN, ... 433 KITTY HAWK 164
  'TWAS TORN FROM HER PACIFIC SIDE. . . . . 452 A-WISHING WELL . . . 44

SIDE (CONTINUED)
     YOU'RE WELL DESCENDED ON YOUR MOTHER'S SIDE, ... 457 HOW HARD TO KEEP FROM   108
     I TRUST I MADE IT CLEAR I TOOK YOUR SIDE . . . . 486 A MASQUE OF REASON . . 362
     I HAVE BEEN FIGHTING ON THE ANGELS' SIDE. . . . . . . 520 A MASQUE OF MERCY . . 706
SIDED (SEE ONE-SIDED)
SIDEHILL
     ON THE SIDEHILL. WE HAVEN'T TO MIND THOSE. . . . . 52 HOME BURIAL 28
SIDELONG
     SIDELONG, FULL ON MY CHEEK, ... 29 MY BUTTERFLY 40
SIDES
     "YOU'VE NEVER CLIMBED IT?" / "I'VE BEEN ON THE SIDES, . . 42 THE MOUNTAIN 44
     BETRAY YOU INTO TAKING SIDES AGAINST ME, ... 320 BUILD SOIL 132
     FOR ALWAYS FIGHTING ON BOTH SIDES AT ONCE. . . . . . . 350 TO A YOUNG WRETCH . . 18
     TO TROUBLE MEN WITH HAVING TO TAKE SIDES. . . . . . . 468 FROM IRON 2
SIDEWAYS
     ONE FLIGHT OUT SIDEWAYS WOULD HAVE UNDECEIVED HIM. . . 101 THE WOOD-PILE 17
     "YOU KNOW ORION ALWAYS COMES UP SIDEWAYS. . . . . . . 176 THE STAR-SPLITTER . . 1
     SIDEWAYS, THAT WOULD HAVE RUN HER ON THE STOVE . . . . 187 THE AX-HELVE 50
SIDING
     TO BOTHER ME BY SIDING WITH THE DOCTOR. . . . . 406 FROM PLANE TO PLANE . 76
SIERRA
     ONCE IN A CALIFORNIA SIERRA . . . . 443 AUSPEX 1
SIEVE
     AS FINE AS FLOUR PUT THROUGH A BAKER'S SIEVE. . . . . 365 OF STONES OF THE PLACE 8
SIGH
     I SHALL BE TELLING THIS WITH A SIGH . . . . 105 THE ROAD NOT TAKEN . 16
     THEIR MURMUR MORE LIKE THE SIGH WE SIGH . . . . 242 NEED OF BEING VERSED . 15
     AS VAIN TO RAISE A VOICE AS A SIGH . . . . 247 ON GOING UNNOTICED . . 1
     AND STRAINING HER RIBS FOR A MONSTER SIGH; . . . . . . 263 THE TIMES TABLE . . . 7
     "A SIGH FOR EVERY SO MANY BREATH, ... 263 THE TIMES TABLE . . . 9
     AND FOR EVERY SO MANY SIGH A DEATH. . . . . 263 THE TIMES TABLE . . . 10
     AND THE WAVE LINE A SHAKEN SIGH. . . . . 327 A MISSIVE MISSILE . . 12
SIGHED
     BUT HE SIGHED UPON THE SILL, ... 11 WIND AND WINDOW FLOWER 17
     THE POETESS HAD SIGHED, I KNEW, IN HEAVEN . . . . . . 217 A FOUNTAIN, A BOTTLE . 134
     NO FOOTSTEP MOVED IT. "THIS IS ALL," THEY SIGHED, . . 229 TWO LOOK AT TWO . . . 13
     SHE SIGHED AND PASSED UNSCARED ALONG THE WALL. . . . . 229 TWO LOOK AT TWO . . . 24
     SEEING MYSELF WELL LOST ONCE MORE, I SIGHED, ... 295 LOST IN HEAVEN . . . 9
     HE SIGHED HIMSELF A COUPLE OF GROANS, ... 419 ONE MORE BREVITY . . 16
SIGHT
     WITHOUT THE GIFT OF SIGHT. . . . . 9 STARS 12
     A MISERABLE SIGHT, AND FRIGHTENING, TOO-- . . . . 35 DEATH OF THE HIRED MAN 36
     THEN SANK OUT OF SIGHT LIKE TROLLS UNDERGROUND, ... 62 BLUEBERRIES 86
     I CANNOT RUB THE STRANGENESS FROM MY SIGHT . . . . 68 AFTER APPLE-PICKING . 9
     AND CAUGHT SIGHT OF HIM TREADING-WATER-LIKE, ... 72 THE CODE 76
     OF SOMETHING INTERPOSED BETWEEN THEIR SIGHT . . . . . 109 THE EXPOSED NEST . . 18
     AND GO ALONG WITH YOU ERE YOU LOSE SIGHT . . . . 124 PUTTING IN THE SEED . 7
     FOR PRYING BENEATH AND FORCING THE LIDS OF SIGHT, . . . 235 VALLEY'S SINGING DAY . 9
     KEEPING ITS LIFE SO CLOSE AND OUT OF SIGHT . . . . . . 248 THE COCOON 8
     BUT NEVER WAS I FAR OUT OF SIGHT . . . . 253 THE THATCH 3
     IF WE WHO SIGHT ALONG IT ROUND THE WORLD, ... 261 A SOLDIER 4
     ON HIS PARTICULAR TIME AND PERSONAL SIGHT. . . . . . . 268 ON LOOKING UP BY CHANCE 15
     AS MY TWO EYES MAKE ONE IN SIGHT. . . . . 277 TWO TRAMPS IN MUD TIME 68
     HE HAD A HEN, HE HAD A PIG IN SIGHT. . . . . 292 FIGURE IN THE DOORWAY . 16
     WHICH I ACCEPTED WITH IMPATIENT SIGHT, ... 295 LOST IN HEAVEN . . . 3
     A SPECK THAT WOULD HAVE BEEN BENEATH MY SIGHT . . . . 357 A CONSIDERABLE SPECK . 1
     AND BLUE FLAG, THE GREAT SIGHT-- . . . . 367 NOT OF SCHOOL AGE . . 26
     EVERY STAR IN SIGHT. . . . . 384 MAKING CERTAIN ANYTHING 15
     O STAR (THE FAIREST ONE IN SIGHT), ... 403 SOMETHING LIKE A STAR . 1
     WAS STILL IN SIGHT LIKE SOMEONE TO DEPEND ON. . . . . . 404 FROM PLANE TO PLANE . 20
     HAVE STAYED IN SIGHT SO LONG AS AN EXAMPLE. . . . . . . 404 FROM PLANE TO PLANE . 23
     PASSIONATE PREFERENCE SUCH AS LOVE AT SIGHT. . . . . . 425 ACCIDENTALLY ON PURPOSE 24
     THE UPLIFTED SIGHT . . . . 437 KITTY HAWK 309
     WHEN AT SIGHT OF YOU HE THOUGHT OF ME. . . . . 461 HOW HARD TO KEEP FROM . 253
     BUT SUCH WE ALL ARE MADE IN THE SIGHT OF GOD. . . . . . 512 A MASQUE OF MERCY . . 501
     BE FOUND ACCEPTABLE IN HEAVEN'S SIGHT. . . . . 520 A MASQUE OF MERCY . . 722
     BE FOUND ACCEPTABLE IN HEAVEN'S SIGHT. . . . . 520 A MASQUE OF MERCY . . 725
SIGHTS
     ONE OF THE GREAT SIGHTS GOING IS TO SEE . . . . 42 THE MOUNTAIN 50
SIGMAS
     THE SIGMAS AND TAUS . . . . 219 I WILL SING YOU ONE-O . 46
SIGN
     FOR A SYLVAN SIGN THAT THE BLUE JAY'S SCREECH . . . . . 24 PAN WITH US 18
     THERE MAY NOT HAVE BEEN THE GHOST OF A SIGN . . . . . . 59 BLUEBERRIES 15
     YOU ONLY HAVE TO SIGN YOUR NAME. RIGHT--THERE." . . . . 99 THE SELF-SEEKER . . 183
     "YOU DON'T MEAN YOU WILL SIGN THAT THING UNREAD?" . . . . 99 THE SELF-SEEKER . . 187
     LIKE THE TWO STROKES ACROSS A DOLLAR SIGN. . . . . . . 186 THE AX-HELVE 25
     IF I WAS TO CONSENT TO GIVE SOME SIGN . . . . 208 PAUPER WITCH OF GRAFTON 43
     IT WA'N'T NO SIGN, I S'POSE, WHEN MALLICE HUSE . . . . 208 PAUPER WITCH OF GRAFTON 45
     OR GIVE SOME SIGN OF LIFE? BECAUSE YOU CAN'T. . . . . 230 TWO LOOK AT TWO . . . 33
     BUT I SAW NO SIGN. . . . . 342 QUEST OF PURPLE-FRINGED 8
     NO, I HAD SET NO PROHIBITING SIGN, ... 364 TRESPASS 1
     AND PUT A SIGN UP CLOSED TO ALL BUT ME. . . . . 378 DIRECTIVE 38
     THE SAME SIGN HEAVEN SHOWED YOUR GUEST. . . . . 381 AN UNSTAMPED LETTER IN . 42
     IS IN THE SIGN OF SICKNESS IN THE WINTER . . . . 407 FROM PLANE TO PLANE . 105
     BUT JONAH GIVES NO SIGN OF HAVING HEARD.) . . . . . . 518 A MASQUE OF MERCY . . 668
SIGNALS
     "I WONDER WHAT THOSE SIGNALS ARE . . . . 138 BROWN'S DESCENT . . . 32
SIGNED
     WHEN YOU COME BACK, I'LL HAVE THE PAPERS SIGNED. . . . 100 THE SELF-SEEKER . . . 213
SIGNIFICANT
     COME LOOK AT MY SIGNIFICANT MUD PIE." . . . . 321 BUILD SOIL 154
SIGNIFIED
     SIGNIFIED NOTHING. ROSE COULD HAVE A MEANING, ... 181 MAPLE 47
SIGNIFIES
     AND SIGNIFIES THE SURENESS OF THE SOUL, ... 332 THE SILKEN TENT . . . 7
SIGNIFY
     WHAT SIGNIFY A DONKEY'S EARS AND BOTTLE, ... 215 A FOUNTAIN, A BOTTLE . 58

PAGE TITLE   LINE

SIGNIFY (CONTINUED)
  I WONDER IF IT WOULDN'T SIGNIFY . . . . 365 OF STONES OF THE PLACE   4
SIGNS
  BUT THE SIGNS SHOWED WHAT IT HAD DONE IN SPRING: . . . . 40 THE MOUNTAIN   12
  WELL, I SHOWED ARTHUR AMY SIGNS ENOUGH   . . . . . . 210 PAUPER WITCH OF GRAFTON 89
  ON MOOSILAUKE, BUT WOMAN SIGNS TO MAN, ... 210 PAUPER WITCH OF GRAFTON 94
  BUT CERTAIN SIGNS OF BURIED TURTLE'S EGG; . . . . . . 270 THE EGG AND THE MACHINE 20
  OF SIGNS THAT WITH N TURNED WRONG AND S TURNED WRONG . . 286 A ROADSIDE STAND   . . 10
  FAR AS WE AIM OUR SIGNS TO REACH, ... 328 A MISSIVE MISSILE . . 47
  AND SOME SAY THERE ARE SIGNS . . . . 361 ALMOST TWO THOUSAND .   4
SILAS
  AND PUT HIM ON HIS GUARD. "SILAS IS BACK."   . . . . . 34 DEATH OF THE HIRED MAN   5
  SILAS DECLARES YOU'LL HAVE TO GET HIM BACK. . . . . . 36 DEATH OF THE HIRED MAN   61
  SILAS UP ON THE CART TO BUILD THE LOAD, ... 36 DEATH OF THE HIRED MAN   68
  "WELL, THOSE DAYS TROUBLE SILAS LIKE A DREAM. . . . . . 37 DEATH OF THE HIRED MAN   71
  IN THE UNLOADING. SILAS DOES THAT WELL. . . . . 37 DEATH OF THE HIRED MAN   92
  POOR SILAS, SO CONCERNED FOR OTHER FOLK, ... 37 DEATH OF THE HIRED MAN   99
  "SILAS HAS BETTER CLAIM ON US YOU THINK   . . . . . . 38 DEATH OF THE HIRED MAN 124
  SILAS HAS WALKED THAT FAR NO DOUBT TODAY. . . . . . . 38 DEATH OF THE HIRED MAN 127
  BUT HAVE SOME PITY ON SILAS. DO YOU THINK   . . . . . 39 DEATH OF THE HIRED MAN 135
  SILAS IS WHAT HE IS--WE WOULDN'T MIND HIM-- . . . . . 39 DEATH OF THE HIRED MAN 140
SILAS'
  "I KNOW, THAT'S SILAS' ONE ACCOMPLISHMENT. . . . . . 37 DEATH OF THE HIRED MAN   88
SILENCE
  WITH THE LEAST STIFFENING OF HER NECK AND SILENCE. . . . 51 HOME BURIAL   14
  THE SOUND OF WHICH WAS SILENCE FOR THE PLACE. . . . . 76 THE GENERATIONS OF MEN   76
  IN SILENCE, IF IN THIS HE IS AGGRIEVED, ... 176 THE CENSUS-TAKER . .   58
  BREAK SILENCE NOW OR BE FOREVER SILENT, ... 176 THE CENSUS-TAKER . .   59
  GRIM SILENCE ON MY PART AS I SANK LOWER, ... 198 WILD GRAPES   79
  THE DEAD WAS BOUND TO SILENCE: ASK THE SISTER. . . . . 200 PLACE FOR A THIRD . . 43
  IN WANTING TO SILENCE ANY SONG. . . . . 251 A MINOR BIRD   8
SILENCED
  THAT, SILENCED BY MY ADVENT, FINDS ONCE MORE, ... 14 WAITING   20
  I AM IMPOSED ON, SILENCED AND DISCOURAGED. . . . . . . 324 BUILD SOIL   251
SILENT
  THE PLACE IS SILENT ALL DAY LONG, NOR YET   . . . . . 165 NEW HAMPSHIRE . . . 189
  BREAK SILENCE NOW OR BE FOREVER SILENT. . . . . 176 THE CENSUS-TAKER . .   59
  BY FLYING LIKE A BIRD (SILENT IN FLIGHT, ... 216 A FOUNTAIN, A BOTTLE . 113
SILENTLY
  IF THE TREES MUST, LET THEM SILENTLY TOSS; . . . . . . 25 NOW CLOSE THE WINDOWS .   2
  THEY SLOWLY AND SILENTLY AGED. . . . . 312 THE VINDICTIVES . .   53
  THEN I AROSE AND SILENTLY WANDERED HOME, ... 343 QUEST OF PURPLE-FRINGED 25
SILKEN
  SHE IS AS IN A FIELD A SILKEN TENT . . . . 331 THE SILKEN TENT . . .   1
  THE SILKEN TENT . . . . 331 THE SILKEN TENT . . .   T
  BY COUNTLESS SILKEN TIES OF LOVE AND THOUGHT . . . . 332 THE SILKEN TENT . . .   10
SILL
  BUT HE SIGHED UPON THE SILL, ... 11 WIND AND WINDOW FLOWER   17
  ACROSS THE SILL FROM THE OUTER GLOOM. . . . . 15 IN A VALE   9
  BUT NOT COME IN ACROSS THE SACRED SILL----" . . . . . 79 THE GENERATIONS OF MEN 170
  MY WINDOW CURTAIN HUNG OVER THE SILL TO WET; . . . . . 236 VALLEY'S SINGING DAY . 17
  I CLIMBED ON THE SILL . . . . 241 THE LOCKLESS DOOR . .   11
  BACK OVER THE SILL . . . . 241 THE LOCKLESS DOOR . .   13
SILLIEST
  BUT THE SILLIEST EVASION . . . . 397 AN IMPORTER   15
SILLS
  I'LL SHOW YOU HOW SHE HAD HER SILLS EXTENDED . . . . 216 A FOUNTAIN, A BOTTLE . 86
SILLY
  DEAN, ADULT EDUCATION MAY SEEM SILLY. . . . . 393 LUCRETIUS VERSUS POETS   1
  IN WHAT I SAY. DON'T BE SO SILLY, WOMAN. . . . . . . 505 A MASQUE OF MERCY . . 308
SILPHION
  TO A PLANT CALLED THE SILPHION, ... 452 A-WISHING WELL   . . .   49
  IN BRANCHES OF THE SILPHION . . . . 452 A-WISHING WELL   . . .   58
SILT
  WE DATE YOU BY YOUR DEPTH IN SILT AND DUST . . . . . 382 TO AN ANCIENT . . .   10
SILVER
  IS SILVER NOW WITH CLINGING MIST. . . . .   7 MY NOVEMBER GUEST . .   10
  AND PINNED WITH A SILVER PIN. . . . .   8 LOVE AND A QUESTION .   24
  LIKE PEARLS, AND NOW A SILVER BLADE. . . . . 18 GOING FOR WATER . . .   24
  THE MOON, THE LITTLE SILVER CLOUD, AND SHE. . . . . . 40 DEATH OF THE HIRED MAN 163
  A BEAD OF SILVER WATER MORE OR LESS, ... 77 THE GENERATIONS OF MEN 122
  SNATCHED RIGHT AND LEFT ACROSS THE SILVER PULLEYS. . . . 94 THE SELF-SEEKER . .   39
  A WIRE SHE IS OF SILVER, AS NEW AS WE . . . . 113 IN THE HOME STRETCH .   70
  AND STRAINING CABLES WET WITH SILVER DEW. . . . . . . 126 RANGE-FINDING . . .   11
  GRASS ITS FULL LENGTH, OLD SILVER GOLDENROD, ... 131 THE BONFIRE   62
  IT CANNOT CHECK THE PEEPER'S SILVER CROAK; . . . . . . 226 THE ONSET   17
  TEN MILLION SILVER LIZARDS OUT OF SNOW! . . . . 237 A HILLSIDE THAW . . .   3
  AND CAUGHT ONE SILVER LIZARD BY THE TAIL, ... 237 A HILLSIDE THAW . . .   10
  OR CROOK-NECKED GOLDEN SQUASH WITH SILVER WARTS, ... 286 A ROADSIDE STAND   . . 12
  LIKE WAKING IN A CAGE OF SILVER BARS. . . . . 290 OLD BARN AT THE BOTTOM   27
SILVERY
  BRIGHT-BLACK-EYED SILVERY CREATURE, BRUSHED WITH BROWN, . 356 A MOTH SEEN IN WINTER .   3
SIMILAR
  AND CROWD THEM OUT AT A SIMILAR RATE. . . . . 376 SOMETHING FOR HOPE . .   8
SIMILE
  I HAD MY NATIVE SIMILE JARRED. . . . . 265 THE DOOR IN THE DARK .   7
  SO, NEVER AT A LOSS IN SIMILE, ... 461 HOW HARD TO KEEP FROM 235
  MUST HAVE BEEN HIS SUCCESS IN SIMILE . . . . 461 HOW HARD TO KEEP FROM 252
SIMMER
  FIRST YOU LET THE SUMMER SIMMER, ... 303 CLEAR AND COLDER   . .   4
SIMPLE
  SHE'S GLAD HER SIMPLE WORSTED GRAY . . . .   7 MY NOVEMBER GUEST . .   9
  WE RAISED A SIMPLE PRAYER . . . . 14 ROSE POGONIAS . . .   17
  AS MAY BE SHOWN BY A SIMPLE CALCULATION. . . . . 107 CHRISTMAS TREES . . .   57
  BACK IN A TIME MADE SIMPLE BY THE LOSS . . . . 377 DIRECTIVE   2
  TO FARMING FOR A SIMPLE WAY TO EARN; . . . . 398 BURSTING RAPTURE   . .   3
  WHAT ARE THE SIMPLE FACTS OF PROGRESS . . . . 449 OUR DOOM TO BLOOM . .   2
  ONE SIMPLE LITTLE STATEMENT FROM THE THRONE . . . . . 484 A MASQUE OF REASON . . 308

SIMPLE (CONTINUED)
    THEIR CASE IS NOT SO SIMPLE. YOU ARE GOOD. . . . . . . 517 A MASQUE OF MERCY . . 620
SIMPLY
    ALL SIMPLY IN THE SPRINGING OF THE YEAR. . . . . 12 A PRAYER IN SPRING . . . 4
    SOME SPIRIT TO STAND SIMPLY FORTH, ... 20 THE TRIAL BY EXISTENCE . 42
    IS TO DECIDE IT SIMPLY ISN'T TRUE. . . . . 57 THE BLACK COTTAGE . . 66
    AND SIMPLY STAYING POSSESSES ALL . . . . 120 BOND AND FREE 18
    THAT WOULDN'T BUDGE, UNTIL THEY SIMPLY STRETCHED . . . 192 PAUL'S WIFE 44
    BEGGED SIMPLY FOR THE GRAVE. THE SISTER'S FACE . . . . 201 PLACE FOR A THIRD . . 47
    THEY SIMPLY LAY WHERE SOMEONE NOW AND THEN, ... 217 A FOUNTAIN, A BOTTLE . 118
    OTHERS ON BEING SIMPLY TRUE. . . . . 307 PROVIDE, PROVIDE . . . 14
    YOU MUST BE MADE MORE SIMPLY WISE THAN I . . . . 356 A MOTH SEEN IN WINTER . 19
    SO WE WON'T SIMPLY TAKE IT AND ABSORB IT. . . . . 361 A LOOSE MOUNTAIN . . . 21
    CARVE NOTHING ON IT. YOU CAN SIMPLY SAY . . . . 365 OF STONES OF THE PLACE . 13
    AND SIMPLY MUST EVOLVE TO STAY AWAKE. . . . . 372 THE LITERATE FARMER AND 127
    SIMPLY BECAUSE THEY DON'T KNOW WHERE THEY ARE. . . . . . 414 A CABIN IN THE CLEARING . 14
    YOU COULD END THIS BY SIMPLY COMING OUT . . . . 483 A MASQUE OF REASON . 295
    I SIMPLY TURN AWAY FROM IT. / YOU PAGAN! . . . . 513 A MASQUE OF MERCY . . 523
SIN
    YOU KNOW IT, MR. LAWYER. THE SIN IS . . . . 100 THE SELF-SEEKER . . . 200
    COMES TOO NEAR TO AHAZ' SIN FOR SAFETY. . . . . 171 NEW HAMPSHIRE 393
    THOUGH NOT, I SAY, A STAR OF DEATH AND SIN, ... 174 A STAR IN A STONEBOAT . 49
    FOR THE LEAST SIN, IT WOULDN'T TAKE US LONG . . . . . . 177 THE STAR-SPLITTER . . 45
    EXCEPT IN TOWNS AT NIGHT, IS NOT A SIN. . . . . 189 THE GRINDSTONE 18
    THIS WAS THE SIN THAT AHAZ WAS FORBID . . . . 284 THE GOLD HESPERIDEE . 51
    IS AN UNPARDONABLE SIN IN FARMING. . . . . 322 BUILD SOIL 180
    APROPOS OF SIN, ... 432 KITTY HAWK 145
    OF ALL ORIGINALITY, THE SIN . . . . 481 A MASQUE OF REASON . 205
    YOU WRONG ME. / WELL THEN, NAME A SINGLE SIN. . . . . . 503 A MASQUE OF MERCY . . 262
    THE MERCY ON THE SIN AGAINST THE SERMON. . . . . 511 A MASQUE OF MERCY . . 477
    BUT NOT THE FEAR OF PUNISHMENT FOR SIN . . . . 520 A MASQUE OF MERCY . . 700
    (I HAVE TO SIN TO PROVE IT ISN'T THAT). . . . . 520 A MASQUE OF MERCY . . 701
SINBAD
    AND TELLING THEM HOW SINBAD WAS A SAILOR. . . . . 447 DOES NO ONE AT ALL EVER 42
SINCE
    SINCE FIRST I SAW THEE GLANCE, ... 28 MY BUTTERFLY 12
    THE BOY YOU HAD IN HAYING FOUR YEARS SINCE. . . . . . . 36 DEATH OF THE HIRED MAN . 59
    "YOU'VE LIVED HERE ALL YOUR LIFE?" / "EVER SINCE HOR . . 44 THE MOUNTAIN 105
    "KNOWN IT SINCE I WAS YOUNG." / "THEN YOU KNOW ME. . . . 48 A HUNDRED COLLARS . . 100
    SINCE SHE WENT, MORE THAN EVER, BUT BEFORE-- . . . . . 56 THE BLACK COTTAGE . . 36
    IT'S SO LONG SINCE I PICKED I ALMOST FORGET . . . . . . 62 BLUEBERRIES 84
    "TWO WEEKS SINCE." / "SHE'S IN EARNEST, IT APPEARS." . . 82 THE HOUSEKEEPER . . . 22
    "OH, THAT'S BEEN THERE FOR HAWKS SINCE CHICKEN-TIME. . . 83 THE HOUSEKEEPER . . . 66
    AND SINCE IT WAS COMING UP HAD TO COME. . . . . 123 PEA BRUSH 24
    AND SINCE THERE WAS NO OTHER WAY TO LOOK, ... 125 AN ENCOUNTER 10
    AND SINCE THERE WERE BUT TWO OF THEM, ... 128 THE IMPULSE 3
    MADE WIND BY FANNING, SINCE YOU NEVER KNEW . . . . . . 130 THE BONFIRE 42
    SINCE HE WAS OLD ENOUGH TO KNOW, BIG BOY . . . . 137 "OUT,OUT--" 23
    NO MORE TO BUILD ON THERE. AND THEY, SINCE THEY . . . . 137 "OUT,OUT--" 33
    THERE ON THE TABLE, EVER SINCE I CAME, ... 147 SNOW 118
    SINCE LAST WE READ THE GAUGE." / "IT LOOKS AS IF . . . . 148 SNOW 159
    AND TAKE THEIR NAME. THEY'VE SINCE TOLD ME THEIR NAME-- . 161 NEW HAMPSHIRE 85
    OFFERED ME NOT LONG SINCE UP BERLIN WAY . . . . 162 NEW HAMPSHIRE 110
    A QUIVERFUL TO CHOOSE FROM, SINCE HE WISHED ME . . . . . 187 THE AX-HELVE 64
    EVER SINCE, JUST TO SHOW THEM, HE HAD SLIPPED . . . . . 191 PAUL'S WIFE 18
    HAS HAD OF PAUL AND HER SINCE MURPHY SAW THEM . . . . . 195 PAUL'S WIFE 130
    TO NO ONE ANYMORE SINCE TOFFILE DIED. . . . . 206 THE WITCH OF COOS . . 131
    LET THEM STAY IN THE ATTIC SINCE THEY WENT THERE. . . . 206 THE WITCH OF COOS . . 132
    THE MOUNTAIN MAY HAVE SHIFTED SINCE I SAW IT . . . . . . 213 A FOUNTAIN, A BOTTLE . 22
    SINCE MAN BEGAN . . . . 220 I WILL SING YOU ONE-O . 77
    SINCE EARTH IS EARTH, PERHAPS, NOT HEAVEN (AS YET)-- . . 220 FRAGMENTARY BLUE . . 5
    AND SINCE THEY GREW DULLER . . . . 235 GATHERING LEAVES . . 18
    SINCE EVER THEY FLUNG ABROAD IN SPRING . . . . 236 MISGIVING 5
    EVER SINCE RIVERS, I WAS GOING TO SAY, ... 258 WEST-RUNNING BROOK . 28
    BUT NOT LONG SINCE IN THE LUMBER CAMPS). . . . . 276 TWO TRAMPS IN MUD TIME . 51
    WENT LONG SINCE TO THE DOGS UNDER THE TABLE. . . . . . . 279 THE WHITE-TAILED HORNET . 57
    LONG SINCE THEY SWUNG AS THREE INSTEAD OF TWO-- . . . . 283 THE GOLD HESPERIDEE . 25
    WAS LONG SINCE SLID. . . . . 298 ON TAKING FROM THE TOP . 4
    SINCE THE FOREST GERMANS SACKED ROME . . . . 311 THE VINDICTIVES . . . 39
    HOW, AGES AND AGES SINCE, ... 313 BEARER OF EVIL TIDINGS . 18
    SINCE HE MEANS TO COME TO A DOOR HE WILL COME TO A DOOR, . 341 WILLFUL HOMING 9
    TAKE NATURE ALTOGETHER SINCE TIME BEGAN, ... 349 OUR HOLD ON THE PLANET . 13
    YOU DID NOT KNOW THAT SINCE KING CHARLES DID RULE . . . 351 THE LESSON FOR TODAY . 22
    SINCE IT WAS NOTHING I KNEW EVIL OF . . . . 358 A CONSIDERABLE SPECK . 28
    LONG SINCE IN SOME ABYSMAL CITY STREET, ... 359 THE LOST FOLLOWER . . 22
    LONG SINCE GAVE UP PRETENSE OF KEEPING COVERED. . . . . 377 DIRECTIVE 12
    SINCE DARK IS WHAT BRINGS OUT YOUR LIGHT. . . . . 403 SOMETHING LIKE A STAR . 5
    SINCE YOU BRING UP THE SUBJECT OF THE SUN. . . . . . . 408 FROM PLANE TO PLANE . 125
    AND THINGS HAVE BEEN GOING SO STRANGELY SINCE, ... 421 ONE MORE BREVITY . . 56
    EVER SINCE NAG'S HEAD . . . . 429 KITTY HAWK 23
    SINCE YOU PUT FOOD FIRST IN YOUR REPERTORY. . . . . . . 455 HOW HARD TO KEEP FROM . 50
    BUT SINCE WE GOT NOWHERE, ... 464 MILKY WAY IS A COWPATH . 5
    THE CRYPT WAS LONG SINCE RIFLED BY THE GREEKS. . . . . . 483 A MASQUE OF REASON . 284
    SINCE I CAME IN? / HEAR WHAT? THAT ARMY TRUCK? . . . . . 495 A MASQUE OF MERCY . . 43
    SINCE YOU PROPOSED IT, I BELIEVE I WILL. . . . . 497 A MASQUE OF MERCY . . 109
    EVER SINCE ALEXANDER GREECED THE WORLD. . . . . 511 A MASQUE OF MERCY . . 473
SINCERE
    AND THIS IS MY SINCERE REPLY: . . . . 139 BROWN'S DESCENT . . . 52
    SINCERE OR INSINCERE, ... 444 ENDS 6
SING
    BUT THAT HE KNOWS IN SINGING NOT TO SING. . . . . 120 THE OVEN BIRD 12
    WITH WHATEVER IT IS THEY SING; . . . . 126 LONELINESS 6
    HE WOULD COME BACK AND SING." . . . . 136 LAST WORD OF A BLUEBIRD 22
    "YOU HEAR THOSE HOUND DOGS SING ON MOOSILAUKE? . . . . . 168 NEW HAMPSHIRE 293
    HE ALWAYS USED TO SING ALONG THE TOTE ROAD. . . . . . . 205 THE WITCH OF COOS . . 111
    I WILL SING YOU ONE-O . . . . 217 I WILL SING YOU ONE-O . 1
    BUT THESE ARE FLOWERS THAT FLY AND ALL BUT SING: . . . . 225 BLUE-BUTTERFLY DAY . . 5
    A TALKING TWITTER ALL THEY HAD TO SING. . . . . 240 OUR SINGING STRENGTH . 38

SING (CONTINUED)
   AND SING THE WILD FLOWERS UP FROM ROOT AND SEED. . . . . 240 OUR SINGING STRENGTH . 53
   AND NOT SING BY MY HOUSE ALL DAY; . . . . 250 A MINOR BIRD 2
   A LEG AKIMBO WITH WHICH HE CAN SING, ... 309 ONE GUESS 2
   MAKE BOLD TO SING IT SO, BUT DO I DARE . . . . . . 317 BUILD SOIL 42
   I PREFER TO SING SAFELY IN THE REALM . . . . 317 BUILD SOIL 48
   THOUGH IT STILL COULD SING. . . . . 334 COME IN 8
   MORE THAN YOU CAN SING. . . . . 437 KITTY HAWK 280
   OR SING AND DANCE ALL NIGHT AND SEE SUNRISE . . . . . 496 A MASQUE OF MERCY . . 71
SINGER
   BRING THE SINGER, BRING THE NESTER; . . . . 11 TO THE THAWING WIND . 2
   THERE IS A SINGER EVERYONE HAS HEARD, ... 119 THE OVEN BIRD . . . 1
   I'M NOT A FREE-VERSE SINGER. HE WAS WRONG THERE. . . . 460 HOW HARD TO KEEP FROM 209
SINGERS
   IN SPRING MORE MORTAL SINGERS THAN BELONG . . . . . 239 OUR SINGING STRENGTH . 19
SINGING
   NO BIRD IS SINGING NOW, AND IF THERE IS, ... 25 NOW CLOSE THE WINDOWS . 3
   AND BRUIT OUR SINGING DOWN, ... 26 A LINE-STORM SONG . . 18
   SPEAKING OR SINGING, AND THE BAND-MUSIC PLAYING. . . . 78 THE GENERATIONS OF MEN 130
   BUT THAT HE KNOWS IN SINGING NOT TO SING. . . . . . 120 THE OVEN BIRD . . . 12
   WAS SINGING IN IT SWEET AND SWIFT. . . . . 233 LOOKING FOR SUNSET BIRD 8
   NO BIRD WAS SINGING IN IT NOW. . . . . 233 LOOKING FOR SUNSET BIRD 9
   THE VALLEY'S SINGING DAY . . . . 235 VALLEY'S SINGING DAY . T
   THAT ONCE YOU HAD OPENED THE VALLEY'S SINGING DAY. . . 236 VALLEY'S SINGING DAY . 20
   OUR SINGING STRENGTH . . . . 239 OUR SINGING STRENGTH . T
   THE COUNTRY'S SINGING STRENGTH THUS BROUGHT TOGETHER, . 240 OUR SINGING STRENGTH . 50
   ON A BIRD SINGING IN ITS SLEEP . . . . 302 A BIRD SINGING IN SLEEP T
   IF SINGING OUT OF SLEEP AND DREAM THAT WAY . . . . . 303 A BIRD SINGING IN SLEEP 13
   I LEANED ON WITH A SINGING TRUST . . . . 336 THE WIND AND THE RAIN . 5
   YET SINGING BUT DIONE IN THE WOOD . . . . 351 THE LESSON FOR TODAY . 14
   ARE SINGING. YES, AND LOOK, THE TREE IS TROUBLED. . . 473 A MASQUE OF REASON . . 15
SINGLE
   A NOTE AS FROM A SINGLE PLACE, ... 18 GOING FOR WATER . . . 21
   BEFORE IT STAINED A SINGLE HUMAN BREAST. . . . . . 126 RANGE-FINDING . . . 3
   WITHOUT A SINGLE LEAF TO SPEND ON AUTUMN, ... 175 THE CENSUS-TAKER . . 23
   NOT SO MUCH AS A SINGLE TREE FOR SHADE, ... 183 MAPLE 102
   A SINGLE LEAF WAS ON A BOUGH, ... 233 LOOKING FOR SUNSET BIRD 10
   SHE HAS HER SPELL ON EVERY SINGLE LIZARD. . . . . . 237 A HILLSIDE THAW . . . 22
   A SINGLE FLOWER AS YET TO BLOOM. . . . . 276 TWO TRAMPS IN MUD TIME 28
   THE EARTH HAD A SINGLE LIGHT AFAR, ... 291 ON HEART'S BEGINNING TO 6
   SEEMS TO OWE NAUGHT TO ANY SINGLE CORD, ... 332 THE SILKEN TENT . . . 8
   AND THE FRAY WOULDN'T LAST A SINGLE ROUND. . . . . . 371 THE LITERATE FARMER AND 118
   WE WOULD CRAWL OUT FILING SINGLE . . . . 384 IN THE LONG NIGHT . . 7
   EVERY SINGLE THING . . . . 426 A NEVER NAUGHT SONG . 13
   OF A SINGLE SUN . . . . 440 KITTY HAWK 398
   NOT A SINGLE ONE . . . . 440 KITTY HAWK 400
   TO MAKE US DIFFERENT IN A SINGLE TRAIT. . . . . . . 446 DOES NO ONE AT ALL EVER 6
   YOU WRONG ME. / WELL THEN, NAME A SINGLE SIN. . . . 503 A MASQUE OF MERCY . . 262
SINGLE-FILE
   ON THE BACKS OF A SINGLE-FILE HOST, ... 312 THE VINDICTIVES . . . 72
SINGLY
   EACH CAME SINGLY UNTO HER PLACE, ... 15 IN A VALE 10
SINGS
   WITH NONE AMONG THEM THAT EVER SINGS, ... 6 GHOST HOUSE 28
   AND THE MIND WHIRLS AND THE HEART SINGS, ... 21 THE TRIAL BY EXISTENCE 47
   ONE OF THE BOYS SINGS OUT, 'WHERE'S THE OLD MAN?' . . . 72 THE CODE 83
   AND SINGS AND ROMPS, ... 360 THE RABBIT-HUNTER . . 11
SINGULAR
   OF COURSE, IN THE ABSTRACT HIGH SINGULAR . . . . . . 478 A MASQUE OF REASON . . 137
SINISTER
   SOMETHING SINISTER IN THE TONE . . . . 251 BEREFT 11
   SO SINISTER? YOU SPOKE TO SOMEONE DOWN THERE. . . . . 516 A MASQUE OF MERCY . . 606
SINISTER-GRAVE
   LIFE IS NOT SO SINISTER-GRAVE. . . . . 291 ON HEART'S BEGINNING TO 34
SINK
   FROM THE SINK WINDOW WHERE I WASH THE PLATES, ... 63 A SERVANT TO SERVANTS . 23
   SHE STOOD AGAINST THE KITCHEN SINK, AND LOOKED . . . . 110 IN THE HOME STRETCH . 1
   OVER THE SINK OUT THROUGH A DUSTY WINDOW . . . . . . 110 IN THE HOME STRETCH . 2
   AT WEEDS THE WATER FROM THE SINK MADE TALL. . . . . . 110 IN THE HOME STRETCH . 3
   TO NORTHWARD FROM YOUR WINDOW AT THE SINK, ... 114 IN THE HOME STRETCH . 115
   MEN LEFT HER A SHIP TO SINK: . . . . 260 SAND DUNES 13
   NOT TO SINK UNDER BEING MAN AND WIFE, ... 264 THE INVESTMENT . . . 13
   (SO AS NOT TO SINK), ... 440 KITTY HAWK 399
   AND WHEN THAT LEFT ME TO SINK BACK REVERSED . . . . . 468 IN A GLASS OF CIDER . 5
SINKING
   THE FLOWER OF CITIES FROM SINKING AND WITHERING FAINT. . 286 A ROADSIDE STAND . . 6
SINKS
   ITS HEART SINKS LOWER UNDER THE SOD. . . . . 228 GOOD-BY AND KEEP COLD . 28
SINNED
   AGAIN AS IN THE DAYS WHEN AHAZ SINNED . . . . 171 NEW HAMPSHIRE . . . 388
SINS
   AND SHE NEVER SINS BY TELLING THE TALE . . . . . . 134 A GIRL'S GARDEN . . . 47
   WHAT THE SINS ARE MEN OUGHT TO PERISH FOR. . . . . . 503 A MASQUE OF MERCY . . 261
SINUS
   AND AT THE SINUS UNDER WATER A FIST . . . . 98 THE SELF-SEEKER . . . 155
SIOUX
   TELL YOU WHAT RALLE THE SIOUX CONTROL ONCE TOLD ME. . . 202 THE WITCH OF COOS . . 13
SIRE
   "SIRE, I'VE BEEN LOOKING ON, AND I DON'T LIKE . . . . 453 HOW HARD TO KEEP FROM 8
   "LET'S NOT GET SUPERSTITIOUS, SIRE," THE PRINCE SAID. . 454 HOW HARD TO KEEP FROM 28
SIRIUS
   I SAID I WOULD SEE HOW SIRIUS KEPT . . . . 419 ONE MORE BREVITY . . 4
   I MIGHT EVEN CLAIM, HE WAS SIRIUS . . . . 421 ONE MORE BREVITY . . 58
   ALDEBARAN, CAPELLA, SIRIUS . . . . 462 HOW HARD TO KEEP FROM 268
SIRIUS'
   AND SITS IN SIRIUS' DISC ALL NIGHT, ... 120 BOND AND FREE . . . 12
SISAL
   OF MIDDLE-AISLE CHURCH CARPET, SISAL HEMP, ... 489 A MASQUE OF REASON . . 454

SISTER
      HIS SISTER STOOD BESIDE THEM IN HER APRON   . . . . 136 "OUT,OUT--" 13
      THE DOCTOR, WHEN HE COMES. DON'T LET HIM, SISTER!" . . . 137 "OUT,OUT--" 26
      THE DEAD WAS BOUND TO SILENCE: ASK THE SISTER. . . . . . 200 PLACE FOR A THIRD . . 43
      SO LABAN SAW THE SISTER, AND, SAYING NOTHING   . . . . . 200 PLACE FOR A THIRD . . 44
      THE SISTER HAD NOT COME ACROSS THIS LABAN;   . . . . . . 201 PLACE FOR A THIRD . . 66
SISTER'S
      BESIDE IT ROOM RESERVED; THE SAY A SISTER'S, ... 200 PLACE FOR A THIRD . . 40
      A NEVER-MARRIED SISTER'S OF THAT HUSBAND, ... 200 PLACE FOR A THIRD . . 41
      BEGGED SIMPLY FOR THE GRAVE. THE SISTER'S FACE . . . . . 201 PLACE FOR A THIRD . . 47
SIT
      AND RISING FULL MOON, SIT ME DOWN   . . . . 14 WAITING 6
      THAT WE SIT SOMETIMES IN THE WAYSIDE NOOK, ... 16 IN NEGLECT 3
      TO SIT BESIDE HER ON THE WOODEN STEPS. . . . . 34 DEATH OF THE HIRED MAN   10
      I'LL SIT AND SEE IF THAT SMALL SAILING CLOUD   . . . . . 40 DEATH OF THE HIRED MAN 160
      OR TURN AND SIT ON AND LOOK OUT AND DOWN, ... 42 THE MOUNTAIN 61
      SIT DOWN OR LIE DOWN, FRIEND; YOU MAKE ME NERVOUS." . . 47 A HUNDRED COLLARS . . 72
      YOU COULD SIT THERE WITH THE STAINS ON YOUR SHOES . . . 54 HOME BURIAL 84
      WHY NOT SIT DOWN IF YOU ARE IN NO HASTE? . . . . 56 THE BLACK COTTAGE . . 47
      AS I SIT HERE, AND OFTENTIMES, I WISH   . . . . 58 THE BLACK COTTAGE . . 111
      AND SIT BEFORE YOU IN THE OPEN DOOR   . . . . 79 THE GENERATIONS OF MEN 168
      WITH ME TO SIT AND TELL HIM EVERYTHING, ... 82 THE HOUSEKEEPER . . . 32
      OF CHAIRS TURNED UPSIDE DOWN TO SIT LIKE PEOPLE   . . . 110 IN THE HOME STRETCH . 6
      SIT DOWN, SIT DOWN. HOW DID YOU FIND THE HORSES?" . . . 147 SNOW 105
      WHILE YOU SIT WARM AND READ UP BALANCED RATIONS. . . . 149 SNOW 183
      THIS ROOM YOU SIT IN. IF YOU THINK THE WIND . . . . . 150 SNOW 203
      WE'LL HAVE TO SIT HERE TILL WE KNOW HE'S SAFE." . . . 152 SNOW 262
      AND SIT UP BY ME AND TAKE HOLD OF ME. . . . . 205 THE WITCH OF COOS . . 103
      THAT'S WHAT I SIT UP IN THE DARK TO SAY--   . . . . . . 206 THE WITCH OF COOS . . 130
      THEN SIT DOWN IN THE MIDDLE OF THEM ALL. . . . . 267 THE ARMFUL 10
      'TIS ONLY TO SIT BACK AND SWAY HIS HEAD   . . . . 269 THE BEAR 23
      I CAN SIT FORTH EXPOSED TO ATTACK, ... 282 A DRUMLIN WOODCHUCK . 10
      WE SIT INDOORS AND TALK OF THE COLD OUTSIDE. . . . . . 305 THERE ARE ROUGHLY ZONES 1
      DOWNWARD TO MAKE HIM SIT ASTRIDE A DRIFT, ... 341 WILLFUL HOMING . . . 6
      OR SHE AND HER LOVER WOULD SIT OPPOSED   . . . . 344 DISCOVERY OF MADEIRAS . 38
SITS
      AND SITS IN SIRIUS' DISC ALL NIGHT, ... 120 BOND AND FREE . . . 12
      HE SITS BACK ON HIS FUNDAMENTAL BUTT   . . . . 269 THE BEAR 26
      SITS DOWN IN SCHOOL TO TRY IF HE CAN WRITE   . . . . . 353 THE LESSON FOR TODAY . 92
      BUT THE SECRET SITS IN THE MIDDLE AND KNOWS.   . . . . 362 THE SECRET SITS . . . 2
      THE SECRET SITS . . . . 362 THE SECRET SITS . . . T
      A MAN SITS LEANING BACK AGAINST A PALM.   . . . . . . 473 A MASQUE OF REASON . . 2
      JOB'S WIFE SITS UP.) / WELL, IF WE AREN'T ALL HERE, . 487 A MASQUE OF REASON . . 392
      AND THEN NOT PROPHESYING. (HE SITS DOWN.)   . . . . . 501 A MASQUE OF MERCY . . 199
      (STILL ON HIS KNEES, HE SITS BACK ON HIS HEELS.) . . 519 A MASQUE OF MERCY . . 671
SITTING
      TO THINK OF SITTING SUCH AN ORDEAL OUT, ... 45 A HUNDRED COLLARS . . 18
      "YOU LOOK SO, SITTING OUT HERE IN THE RAIN   . . . . . 76 THE GENERATIONS OF MEN 84
      OUR SITTING HERE BY LANTERN-LIGHT TOGETHER   . . . . . 116 IN THE HOME STRETCH . 176
      SITTING OR STANDING AS HE CHOSE, ... 138 BROWN'S DESCENT . . . 26
      IT NOT A MITE WORSE, SITTING HERE, WE THREE;   . . . . 149 SNOW 189
      WE CAN'T BE ANY HELP BY SITTING HERE   . . . . 152 SNOW 268
      NO STEP, THOUGH. IF SHE'S THERE SHE'S SITTING DOWN." . 153 SNOW 302
      SITTING BY A BUSH IN BROAD SUNLIGHT   . . . . 266 SITTING BY A BUSH . . T
SITUATION
      THE SITUATION WAS LIKE THIS: THE ROAD   . . . . 75 THE GENERATIONS OF MEN 70
      TOO LARGE A SITUATION. YOU AND I   . . . . 351 THE LESSON FOR TODAY . 35
      AS MUCH AS ANYTHING FOR SITUATION.   . . . . 400 TO THE RIGHT PERSON . 3
      HOW HARD IT IS TO KEEP FROM BEING KING WHEN IT'S IN YOU AND
          IN THE SITUATION. . . . . 453 HOW HARD TO KEEP FROM . T
      WHEN IT'S IN YOU AND IN THE SITUATION.   . . . . . . 454 HOW HARD TO KEEP FROM 21
      WHEN IT'S IN YOU AND IN THE SITUATION.   . . . . . . 462 HOW HARD TO KEEP FROM 276
SIX   (SEE NINETEEN-TWENTY-SIX, NINETEEN-FORTY-SIX)
      'SO YOU CAN THINK IT'S SIX FEET DEEP OUTSIDE,   . . . 149 SNOW 182
      HE GOT A GOOD GLASS FOR SIX HUNDRED DOLLARS.   . . . 178 THE STAR-SPLITTER . . 74
      I FANCIED WHEN I LOOKED AT SIX O'CLOCK   . . . . . . 237 A HILLSIDE THAW . . . 23
      THE FULL SIX DAYS. THEN REST A DAY;   . . . . 280 BLUE RIBBON AT AMESBURY 30
SIXTH
      GIVE HER THE COMFORT FOR HER SIXTH OF KNOWING   . . . 257 THE LOVELY BE CHOOSERS 43
SIXTY
      WE WERE BUT SIXTY VOTERS LAST ELECTION.   . . . . . . 41 THE MOUNTAIN 25
      MANCHESTER (SIXTY OR SEVENTY THOUSAND) LAUGHS   . . . 165 NEW HAMPSHIRE . . . 202
      SIXTY YEARS AGO. . . . . 428 KITTY HAWK 9
SIXTY-FIVE
      IN OUR THREE HUNDRED DAYS AND SIXTY-FIVE   . . . . . 412 POD OF THE MILKWEED . 32
SIZE
      NOT LIKING TO OWN UP I'D GROWN A SIZE.   . . . . . . 46 A HUNDRED COLLARS . . 60
      NUMBER EIGHTEEN THIS IS. WHAT SIZE DO YOU WEAR?" . . 46 A HUNDRED COLLARS . . 61
      MORE THAN A HUNDRED COLLARS, SIZE FOURTEEN.   . . . . 47 A HUNDRED COLLARS . . 66
      I'M GETTING TOO OLD FOR MY SIZE, I TELL THEM.   . . . 81 THE HOUSEKEEPER . . . 5
      OF THE ONE WORLD COMPLETE IN ANY SIZE . . . . 174 A STAR IN A STONEBOAT 56
      THAT, THOUGH THEY NEVER EQUAL STARS IN SIZE . . . . 246 FIREFLIES IN THE GARDEN 3
      THEN FOR A MOMENT ALL THERE WAS WAS SIZE, ... 270 THE EGG AND THE MACHINE 13
      AND MAKE UP FOR ITS LACK OF SIZE. . . . . 281 A DRUMLIN WOODCHUCK . 4
      OF MANY TIMES HIS SIZE.   . . . . 287 DEPARTMENTAL 3
      THE WORLD'S SIZE HAS NO MORE TO DO WITH US   . . . . 322 BUILD SOIL 198
      SO NONE NEED BE AFRAID OF SIZE. . . . . 333 ALL REVELATION . . . 19
      ANY SIZE WE PLEASE   . . . . 396 ANY SIZE WE PLEASE . . T
      OF A SIZE TITANIC   . . . . 442 KITTY HAWK 443
SIZE-LARGER
      "I'M MOVING INTO A SIZE-LARGER SHIRT.   . . . . 46 A HUNDRED COLLARS . . 53
SKELETON
      UP ATTIC, MOTHER? / BONES--A SKELETON.   . . . . . . 203 THE WITCH OF COOS . . 20
      IS SOMETIMES FOUND A SKELETON   . . . . 452 A-WISHING WELL . . . 59
SKELETONS
      "THE CITY'S GROTESQUE IRON SKELETONS   . . . . 506 A MASQUE OF MERCY . . 332
SKEPTIC
      THE MISSED FLY MADE ME DANGEROUSLY SKEPTIC. . . . . . 279 THE WHITE-TAILED HORNET 49

SKEPTIC (CONTINUED)
    SKEPTIC . . . . 389 SKEPTIC . . . . . T
SKEPTICS
    DOWN BURNING SKEPTICS IN THE CELLAR FURNACE . . . . . 516 A MASQUE OF MERCY . . 603
SKIES
    HERE COME REAL STARS TO FILL THE UPPER SKIES, ... 246 FIREFLIES IN THE GARDEN 1
    THE CLOUDS WERE LOW AND HAIRY IN THE SKIES, ... 250 ONCE BY THE PACIFIC . 5
    TO GIVE IT COZIER SKIES . . . . 281 A DRUMLIN WOODCHUCK . 3
    THUS CONCENTRATING EARTH AND SKIES . . . . 333 ALL REVELATION . . . 18
    TO SEE TO THE UNBURDENING OF SKIES. . . . . 337 THE WIND AND THE RAIN . 46
    "HERE COME MORE STARS TO CHARACTER THE SKIES, ... 370 THE LITERATE FARMER AND 75
    AND TAKE OFF INTO THE SKIES. . . . . 388 MIDDLENESS OF THE ROAD 3
    INTO EARTH AND SKIES . . . . 435 KITTY HAWK 233
SKIFF
    A SMALL SKIFF . . . . 211 AN EMPTY THREAT . . . 5
SKILLFUL
    EXECUTIVES OF SKILLFUL EXECUTION . . . . 363 A SEMI-REVOLUTION . . 5
SKIMMED
    I SKIMMED THIS MORNING FROM THE DRINKING TROUGH . . . 68 AFTER APPLE-PICKING . 11
SKIMMER
    USING NEITHER SPOON NOR SKIMMER, ... 303 CLEAR AND COLDER . . 5
SKIN (SEE BEAR-SKIN)
    HIS SKIN AND HIS HAIR AND HIS EYES WERE GRAY, ... 23 PAN WITH US . . . 2
    MESERVE, BELITTLED IN THE GREAT SKIN COAT HE WORE. . . 143 SNOW 5
    IT MIGHT HAVE BEEN THE SKIN A SNAKE HAD CAST . . . . 194 PAUL'S WIFE . . . 92
    UNTIL I'D HAD HIM WORN TO SKIN AND BONES, ... 208 PAUPER WITCH OF GRAFTON 48
    LET HIM LIGHT ON YOUR SKIN UNLESS YOU MIND . . . . . 278 THE WHITE-TAILED HORNET 28
    AS MAGICAL AS SUNLIGHT ON THE SKIN. . . . . 337 THE WIND AND THE RAIN . 42
    NO MATTER WHAT THE COLOR OF ITS SKIN. . . . . 369 THE LITERATE FARMER AND 51
    DON'T SCRATCH! AND WHEN, AS ROTTEN AS HIS SKIN, . . . 478 A MASQUE OF REASON . . 130
    TO FIND IF THERE WERE POCKETS IN HIS SKIN, ... 503 A MASQUE OF MERCY . . 252
SKINNED (SEE THIN-SKINNED)
    AND AFTER ALL, REALLY THEY'RE EBONY SKINNED: . . . . 60 BLUEBERRIES 24
SKINS (SEE THICK-SKINS)
SKIPPER
    AND GIVE SOMEONE THE SKIPPER IRESON'S RIDE. . . . . 163 NEW HAMPSHIRE . . . 143
    WHITTIER'S LUCK WITH SKIPPER IRESON AWES ME-- . . . . 317 BUILD SOIL 44
SKIPPING
    THEN CAME IN DANCING, SKIPPING WITH HIS LIFE . . . . 170 NEW HAMPSHIRE . . . 349
SKIRT
    THAT HUNG IN BOTH HANDS, HOT AGAINST HER SKIRT. . . . 91 THE FEAR 63
SKIRTED
    I SKIRTED THE MARGIN ALDERS FOR MILES AND MILES . . . 342 QUEST OF PURPLE-FRINGED 5
SKIRTS
    SHE TURNED AND SANK UPON HER SKIRTS AT THAT, ... 51 HOME BURIAL 8
    HERE IT CAME BREASTING LIKE A HORSE IN SKIRTS. . . . 270 THE EGG AND THE MACHINE 11
SKULKING
    THIS IS GOD AT ME IN MY SKULKING PLACE, ... 507 A MASQUE OF MERCY . . 349
SKULL
    BRUSHING THEIR CHALKY SKULL WITH CHALKY FINGERS, . . 206 THE WITCH OF COOS . . 128
SKULLS
    AND I DON'T MEAN JUST SKULLS OF ROGERS' RANGERS . . . 210 PAUPER WITCH OF GRAFTON 93
SKUNK
    AND LOOK FOR SKUNK TRACKS . . . . 136 LAST WORD OF A BLUEBIRD 18
SKY
    THE FADED EARTH, THE HEAVY SKY, ... 7 MY NOVEMBER GUEST . . 12
    WITH, "LET US LOOK AT THE SKY, ... 7 LOVE AND A QUESTION . 10
    DRAGGING THE WHOLE SKY WITH IT TO THE HILLS. . . . . 38 DEATH OF THE HIRED MAN 104
    WHERE ITS BLACK BODY CUT INTO THE SKY. . . . . . . 40 THE MOUNTAIN . . . 4
    SHE BELLOWS ON A KNOLL AGAINST THE SKY. . . . . . . 125 THE COW IN APPLE TIME . 10
    AND I THINK THE SKY DARKENED WITH A CLOUD . . . . . 131 THE BONFIRE 54
    THEY STRING AN INSTRUMENT AGAINST THE SKY . . . . . 141 THE LINE-GANG . . . 5
    MAKING A GREAT SCROLL UPWARD TOWARD THE SKY, ... 143 SNOW 9
    TO TAP THE UPPER SKY AND DRAW A FLOW . . . . 169 NEW HAMPSHIRE . . . 340
    AGAINST THE SKY TO BREAK HIS BACK FOR HIM, ... 170 NEW HAMPSHIRE . . . 348
    EXCEPT AT NIGHT TO PLACES IN THE SKY . . . . 173 A STAR IN A STONEBOAT . 41
    THOUGH SOME SAVANTS MAKE EARTH INCLUDE THE SKY; . . . 220 FRAGMENTARY BLUE . . 6
    TO THE MIDNIGHT SKY A SUNSET GLOW. . . . . 241 NEED OF BEING VERSED . 2
    THE TOTAL SKY ALMOST WITHOUT DEFECT, ... 245 SPRING POOLS . . . 2
    APPEARED LIKE GOLD IN THE SUNSET SKY, ... 249 A PECK OF GOLD . . . 6
    IT IS THE CHANGE TO DARKNESS IN THE SKY. . . . . . 249 ACCEPTANCE 5
    ONE LUMINARY CLOCK AGAINST THE SKY . . . . 255 ACQUAINTED WITH NIGHT . 12
    THEN LETS IT SNAP BACK UPRIGHT IN THE SKY. . . . . 268 THE BEAR 4
    AT MOONLIT SKY AND MOONLIT EARTH; . . . . 290 ON HEART'S BEGINNING TO 4
    THE SKY HAD HERE AND THERE A STAR; . . . . 290 ON HEART'S BEGINNING TO 5
    BUT STARS WERE SCARCE IN THAT PART OF THE SKY, . . . 295 LOST IN HEAVEN . . . 5
    BACK UP A STREAM OF RADIANCE TO THE SKY, ... 300 THE MASTER SPEED . . 3
    I TURNED AND LOOKED BACK UP AT THE SKY, ... 303 AFTERFLAKES 3
    THE WHOLE SKY WAS BLUE; . . . . 303 AFTERFLAKES 12
    SOMETHING ABOUT A KINGDOM IN THE SKY . . . . . . 359 THE LOST FOLLOWER . . 35
    ...RECENTLY OBSERVED IN THE WESTERN SKY AT EVENING . 368 THE LITERATE FARMER AND 5
    SAY ABOUT HALFWAY UP THE WESTERN SKY, ... 370 THE LITERATE FARMER AND 66
    LIKE A STAR FRESH FALLEN OUT OF THE SKY. . . . . . 383 WERE I IN TROUBLE . . 5
    LORD, I HAVE LOVED YOUR SKY, ... 388 ASTROMETAPHYSICAL . . 1
    THERE SANDY SEEMS THE GOLDEN SKY . . . . 392 A CLIFF DWELLING . . 1
    MEN WOULD TREAT THIS SKY . . . . 434 KITTY HAWK 189
    I'M ALWAYS FOR A BETTER SKY, ... 451 A-WISHING WELL . . . 13
    AND FILL THE SKY AS FULL OF MOONS . . . . 451 A-WISHING WELL . . . 17
    FOR THE VISIONS IN THE SKY . . . . 469 FOUR-ROOM SHACK... . 3
    HIS WIFE LIES BY HIM LOOKING AT THE SKY. . . . . . 473 A MASQUE OF REASON . 3
SKY-BLUE
    REAL SKY-BLUE, AND HEAVY, AND READY TO DRUM . . . . 59 BLUEBERRIES 4
SKY-FLAKES
    AND WITH THESE SKY-FLAKES DOWN IN FLURRY ON FLURRY . 225 BLUE-BUTTERFLY DAY . . 2
SKY-HIGH
    SKY-HIGH WITH BOTH HANDS. I CAN SEE IT NOW-- . . . . 83 THE HOUSEKEEPER . . . 61
    OVER THE WHEEL INTO THE SKY-HIGH SEAT, ... 112 IN THE HOME STRETCH . 63

SKYLARK
   (A SKYLARK FOR THEM IN THREE-BEAT PHRASES) . . . . . . 428 KITTY HAWK . . . . S
SKY-MARKS
   LOOKING FOR MY OLD SKY-MARKS IN THE BLUE. . . . . . . 295 LOST IN HEAVEN . . . 4
SKYSCRAPERS
   WHAT ARE TELEPHONES, SKYSCRAPERS, ... 396 AN IMPORTER 13
SLAB
   THEY'D SLICED THE FIRST SLAB OFF A BIG BUTT LOG, . . . 193 PAUL'S WIFE 62
   BEHIND THE PORTHOLE'S SLAB OF GLASS . . . . 363 ASSURANCE 2
   ON A CERTAIN SLAB . . . . 436 KITTY HAWK 260
SLAB-BUILT
   TO A SLAB-BUILT, BLACK-PAPER-COVERED HOUSE . . . . . 174 THE CENSUS-TAKER . . 2
SLABS
   BROAD-SHOULDERED LITTLE SLABS THERE IN THE SUNLIGHT . . . 52 HOME BURIAL 27
SLAIN
   EVEN THE BRAVEST THAT ARE SLAIN . . . . 19 THE TRIAL BY EXISTENCE 1
   HE SPARED IT FROM THE NUMBER OF THE SLAIN, ... 375 A YOUNG BIRCH . . . 13
   THAT IF HE HAD HIM SLAIN IT WOULDN'T BE . . . . . 457 HOW HARD TO KEEP FROM 113
SLAM
   WILL EVER SLAM THE DOORS." / "I THINK YOU SEE . . . . 112 IN THE HOME STRETCH . 44
   TO SLAM END-ON AGAIN AGAINST THE SAW TEETH. . . . . . 193 PAUL'S WIFE 64
SLAMBANGING
   SOMETHING WAS GOING TO GO WITH THEIR SLAMBANGING. . . . 193 PAUL'S WIFE 68
SLAMMED
   PASSED IN AND SLAMMED IT SHUT EACH ONE BEHIND HIM . . . 175 THE CENSUS-TAKER . . 29
   AND THE SAWYER HAD SLAMMED THE CARRIAGE BACK . . . . 193 PAUL'S WIFE 63
   "QUICK!" I SLAMMED TO THE DOOR AND HELD THE KNOB. . . . 206 THE WITCH OF COOS . 118
SLAMS
   SLAMS IN HIS FACE, THE BLOW AND THE REPULSE . . . . . 518 A MASQUE OF MERCY . 650
   THE CELLAR DOOR SWINGS WIDE AND SLAMS AGAIN.) . . . . 520 A MASQUE OF MERCY . 696
SLANG
   YOU POOR OLD SAPE, IF I MAY COIN THE SLANG. . . . . . 518 A MASQUE OF MERCY . 664
SLANT
   AND THE SLANT SPIRITS TROOPING BY . . . . 20 THE TRIAL BY EXISTENCE 21
   THE MOUNTAIN HE WAS CLIMBING HAD THE SLANT . . . . . 355 TIME OUT 2
SLAP
   FROM THE SLAP I HAD JUST NOW GIVEN ITS HAND. . . . . 205 THE WITCH OF COOS . . 89
   I'D SHIP A SMOOTH ONE YOU COULD SLAP AND CHAFE, . . . 365 OF STONES OF THE PLACE 9
SLAPPED
   HE SLAPPED HIS BREAST TO VERIFY HIS PURSE. . . . . . 396 ANY SIZE WE PLEASE . . 13
SLATE
   THERE ARE THREE STONES OF SLATE AND ONE OF MARBLE, . . . 52 HOME BURIAL 26
SLAUGHTER
   IT BREAKS AWAY IN SOME NEW KIND OF SLAUGHTER. . . . . 254 THE FLOOD 4
SLAVE
   SLAVE TO A SPRINGTIME PASSION FOR THE EARTH. . . . . 124 PUTTING IN THE SEED . 9
   THE SLAVE WILL NEVER THANK HIS MANUMITTER; . . . . . 371 THE LITERATE FARMER AND 90
   TO THE SLAVE AUCTION IN SOME MARKETPLACE. . . . . . 454 HOW HARD TO KEEP FROM 32
   THE SLAVE SERVED HIS NOVITIATE DISHWASHING. . . . . 455 HOW HARD TO KEEP FROM 54
   SEE THAT OUR SLAVE IS ALSO. HE'S IN FAVOR. . . . . . 455 HOW HARD TO KEEP FROM 64
   THOUGHT OF THE KITCHEN SLAVE AND HAD HIM IN . . . . 456 HOW HARD TO KEEP FROM 79
   AND THE SLAVE SAID, "THE SMALL ONE'S WORTH THE PRICE, . . 456 HOW HARD TO KEEP FROM 81
   BUT HASTENED BACK TO REASSURE HIS SLAVE . . . . . 457 HOW HARD TO KEEP FROM 112
   "YOU'RE HOPELESS," SAID THE SLAVE. / "I GUESS I AM; . . 458 HOW HARD TO KEEP FROM 144
SLAVER
   THE SHIP IT SEEMED HAD BEEN A SLAVER. . . . . 345 DISCOVERY OF MADEIRAS . 53
SLAVER'S
   BEFORE THEY WERE HURLED FROM THE SLAVER'S DECK. . . . 346 DISCOVERY OF MADEIRAS . 82
SLAVERY
   AND SELL HIM INTO SLAVERY? MY PRICE . . . . 454 HOW HARD TO KEEP FROM 33
   FREEDOM IS SLAVERY SOME POETS TELL US. . . . . . . 460 HOW HARD TO KEEP FROM 190
SLAVES
   NOR JUST TO FREE THE SLAVES, THOUGH IT DID BOTH. . . . 56 THE BLACK COTTAGE . . 57
SLAY
   ANYTHING TO SLAY . . . . 431 KITTY HAWK 112
SLAYING
   IN SAVING HERETICS BY SLAYING THEM, ... 515 A MASQUE OF MERCY . 572
   WHAT'S ALL THIS TALK OF SLAYING DOWN IN CELLARS-- . . . 516 A MASQUE OF MERCY . 605
SLEEP
   TO SEE IF HE WAS TALKING IN HIS SLEEP. . . . . . . 36 DEATH OF THE HIRED MAN 57
   AND SLEEP ON IT, THE WAY I ALWAYS DO . . . . 48 A HUNDRED COLLARS . 91
   LIE DOWN--LET YOURSELF GO AND GET SOME SLEEP. . . . . 50 A HUNDRED COLLARS . 161
   I'VE JUST BEGUN THE NIGHT. YOU GET SOME SLEEP. . . . . 50 A HUNDRED COLLARS . 172
   THERE NOW, YOU GET SOME SLEEP." / HE SHUT THE DOOR. . . 50 A HUNDRED COLLARS . 178
   ESSENCE OF WINTER SLEEP IS ON THE NIGHT, ... 68 AFTER APPLE-PICKING . 7
   UPON MY WAY TO SLEEP BEFORE IT FELL, ... 68 AFTER APPLE-PICKING . 15
   THIS SLEEP OF MINE, WHATEVER SLEEP IT IS. . . . . . 69 AFTER APPLE-PICKING . 38
   LONG SLEEP, AS I DESCRIBE ITS COMING ON, ... 69 AFTER APPLE-PICKING . 41
   OR JUST SOME HUMAN SLEEP. . . . . 69 AFTER APPLE-PICKING . 42
   THAT TROUBLE THE SLEEP OF LUMBER FOLK: . . . . . . 140 THE GUM-GATHERER . . 22
   DRESSED, BUT DISHEVELED FROM SOME HOURS OF SLEEP; . . . 143 SNOW 4
   AND GONE TO SLEEP, SHE NEEDN'T WAKE TO ANSWER." . . . 143 SNOW 14
   IN ONE ANOTHER, AND HAD GONE TO SLEEP . . . . . . 148 SNOW 163
   SORRY I HAD TO BREAK IN ON YOUR SLEEP." . . . . . 150 SNOW 212
   I'D RATHER BE THE BEAST THAT SLEEPS THE SLEEP . . . . 150 SNOW 223
   WE'RE NOT IN FOR A NIGHT OF HIM. NO SLEEP . . . . . 152 SNOW 258
   WHAT HE SOWED WITH HER SLEPT SO LONG A SLEEP, ... 180 MAPLE 36
   OF CARES, AT NIGHT, TO SLEEP; BUT NOTHING TELLS ME . . 199 WILD GRAPES . . . 102
   HOW WOULD SHE LIKE TO SLEEP HER LAST WITH HIM? . . . . 200 PLACE FOR A THIRD . 36
   I WENT TO SLEEP BEFORE I WENT TO BED, ... 203 THE WITCH OF COOS . 37
   AND GIVE UP SLEEP. . . . . 218 I WILL SING YOU ONE-O . 8
   AND MILES TO GO BEFORE I SLEEP, ... 225 STOPPING BY WOODS . 15
   AND MILES TO GO BEFORE I SLEEP. . . . . 225 STOPPING BY WOODS . 16
   THIS NEW-BUILT CITY FROM BOTH WORK AND SLEEP. . . . . 231 A BROOK IN THE CITY . 24
   BUT A SLEEP OPPRESSES THEM AS THEY GO, ... 236 MISGIVING 3
   AND BY TEACHING THEM HOW TO SLEEP THE SLEEP ALL DAY, . . 287 A ROADSIDE STAND . . 30
   WHO SLEEP IN HOUSES OF THEIR OWN, THOUGH MORTGAGED. . . 290 OLD BARN AT THE BOTTOM 31
   ON A BIRD SINGING IN ITS SLEEP . . . . 302 A BIRD SINGING IN SLEEP T

SLEEP (CONTINUED)
  IF SINGING OUT OF SLEEP AND DREAM THAT WAY . . . . . . 303 A BIRD SINGING IN SLEEP   13
  IN INCANDESCENT LAMPS AND ENDING SLEEP. . . . . . . 371 THE LITERATE FARMER AND   97
  IN SLEEP OR SLOWNESS IS THE DEADLY CRIME. . . . . . 371 THE LITERATE FARMER AND   103
  HE GAVE UP SLEEP HIMSELF SOME TIME AGO, ... 371 THE LITERATE FARMER AND   104
  WE CAN'T BE TRUSTED TO THE SLEEP WE TAKE, ... 372 THE LITERATE FARMER AND   126
  IT GAVE BAD DREAMS AND BROKEN SLEEP, ... 382 THE NIGHT LIGHT . . .   3
  WE DO NOT GO UP THERE TO SLEEP AT NIGHT. . . . . . 386 A STEEPLE ON THE HOUSE   4
  NOT TO GO TO SLEEP, ... 438 KITTY HAWK   313
  YOU GO TO SLEEP. GOD MUST AWAIT EVENTS, ... 478 A MASQUE OF REASON . .   147
  SHE'LL GO TO SLEEP. NOTHING KEEPS HER AWAKE . . . . 478 A MASQUE OF REASON . .   153
  THE VERY SLEEP WE SLEEP IS AN EXAMPLE. . . . . . . 509 A MASQUE OF MERCY . .   432
SLEEPERS
  I DON'T BELIEVE THE SLEEPERS IN THIS HOUSE . . . . . 413 A CABIN IN THE CLEARING   1
SLEEPING
  WHEN OTHERS ARE SLEEPING. . . . . 30 RELUCTANCE   12
  "WHO'S THAT MAN SLEEPING IN THE OFFICE CHAIR? . . . 45 A HUNDRED COLLARS . .   29
  THEY WERE NOT SLEEPING IN THE SHELVES OF BUNKS. . . 175 THE CENSUS-TAKER . .   41
  FROM SLEEPING WARM . . . . 218 I WILL SING YOU ONE-O .   32
  (FROM SLEEPING GOD KNOWS WHERE LAST NIGHT, ... 276 TWO TRAMPS IN MUD TIME   50
  DESTROY THEIR SLEEPING AT NIGHT THE ANCIENT WAY. . . 287 A ROADSIDE STAND . .   31
  THE WASTE OF MOMENTS SLEEPING. . . . . 359 NOVEMBER   12
  IF NOT INDEED FROM SLEEPING OUT, ... 381 AN UNSTAMPED LETTER IN   47
SLEEPLESS
  YOU LOOK SO SLEEPLESS.--IF HE'D PROMISE US . . . . . 501 A MASQUE OF MERCY . .   207
SLEEPS
  I'D RATHER BE THE BEAST THAT SLEEPS THE SLEEP . . . . 150 SNOW   223
SLEEPY
  A SLEEPY SOUND, BUT MOCKING HALF, ... 25 THE DEMIURGE'S LAUGH .   8
  SHE WHETS A SLEEPY SATED BILL. . . . . 281 BLUE RIBBON AT AMESBURY   40
SLEEVED (SEE LONG-SLEEVED)
SLEEVES
  AND BRUSHED WITH BUTTONS UPON SLEEVES, ... 135 LOCKED OUT   5
  SO LOW I BRUSHED THE STRAW WITH MY SLEEVES, ... 253 THE THATCH   18
SLEIGH
  LIKE GHOST OF SLEIGH BELLS IN A GHOST OF SNOW)-- . . 119 HYLA BROOK   6
SLEIGHT
  BY SLEIGHT OF WING . . . . 334 COME IN   6
SLENDER
  A SLENDER TINKLING FALL THAT MADE . . . . 18 GOING FOR WATER . . .   22
  AND A FLAME SLENDER AS THE HEPATICAS, ... 131 THE BONFIRE   51
  HE LIKED TO HAVE IT SLENDER AS A WHIPSTOCK, ... 187 THE AX-HELVE   69
  A SLENDER LENGTH OF PITH, OR WAS IT PITH? . . . . . 194 PAUL'S WIFE   91
  IN WATER OF A SLENDER APRIL RILL . . . . 226 THE ONSET   19
  IN PLACE ACROSS A CLOUD THE SLENDER RAY . . . . . 235 VALLEY'S SINGING DAY .   8
  THEY SAFELY GREW IN SLENDER LENGTH. . . . . 273 A LONE STRIKER . . .   23
  EACH SWUNG IN DANGER ON ITS SLENDER TWIG, ... 283 THE GOLD HESPERIDEE .   23
  TILL I SAW THE PATH WHERE THE SLENDER FOX HAD COME . 342 QUEST OF PURPLE-FRINGED   11
SLEPT
  I SAW SO MUCH BEFORE I SLEPT THERE ONCE: . . . . . 40 THE MOUNTAIN . . .   2
  AND SLEPT. THE LOG THAT SHIFTED WITH A JOLT . . . 108 OLD MAN'S WINTER NIGHT   23
  AND EASED HIS HEAVY BREATHING, BUT STILL SLEPT. . . 108 OLD MAN'S WINTER NIGHT   25
  OF THE ROOM WHERE THEY SLEPT. . . . . 128 THE OFT-REPEATED DREAM   4
  WHAT HE SOWED WITH HER SLEPT SO LONG A SLEEP, . . . 180 MAPLE   36
  THE CRIB HE SLEPT IN--AND AS SURE'S YOU'RE BORN . . 209 PAUPER WITCH OF GRAFTON   61
  HE COULD HAVE SLEPT BUT A MOMENT MORE AT BEST. . . 235 VALLEY'S SINGING DAY .   6
  AND IF YOU HAVE SEEN ME WHEN I SLEPT, ... 252 TREE AT MY WINDOW . .   10
  WHO SLEPT THERE IN A MOW OF MEADOW HAY . . . . . 289 OLD BARN AT THE BOTTOM   19
  THE THINGS FORBIDDEN THAT WHILE THE CUSTOMS SLEPT . 335 I COULD GIVE ALL . .   13
  I LET IT LIE THERE TILL I HOPE IT SLEPT. . . . . 358 A CONSIDERABLE SPECK .   29
  BEFORE I GAVE UP SEEING AND SLEPT . . . . 419 ONE MORE BREVITY . .   3
SLICED
  THEY'D SLICED THE FIRST SLAB OFF A BIG BUTT LOG, . . 193 PAUL'S WIFE   62
  WHERE WHEELS HAVE FRESHLY SLICED THE APRIL MIRE. . . 225 BLUE-BUTTERFLY DAY . .   8
SLICES
  WHOLE CAPES CAKED OFF IN SLICES. . . . . 377 ONE STEP BACKWARD TAKEN   7
SLID
  THE DOCTOR SLID A LITTLE DOWN THE PILLOW. . . . . 51 A HUNDRED COLLARS . .   179
  THAT RESTED ON THE BANISTER, AND SLID DOWNSTAIRS; . 52 HOME BURIAL   32
  THE FINGER-PIECES SLID IN ALL DIRECTIONS. . . . . 204 THE WITCH OF COOS . .   79
  WAS LONG SINCE SLID. . . . . 298 ON TAKING FROM THE TOP   4
SLIDES
  THE TWO CONVERGING SLIDES, THE AVALANCHES, ... 214 A FOUNTAIN, A BOTTLE .   52
SLIGHT
  THOUGH SLIGHT, WAS A DEMAND. SHE FELT THE TUG. . . 217 A FOUNTAIN, A BOTTLE .   137
  THE MOON, THOUGH SLIGHT, WAS MOON ENOUGH TO SHOW . 234 EVENING A SUGAR ORCHARD 11
  HE LINGERS TOO, AVERSE TO SLIGHT . . . . 280 BLUE RIBBON AT AMESBURY   19
  AS WHOSOEVER LIKES THE YOUNG AND SLIGHT . . . . . 375 A YOUNG BIRCH . . .   3
  AND ONLY SOME SLIGHT BEAST . . . . 416 CLOSED FOR GOOD . .   28
SLIGHTEST
  IS OF THE SLIGHTEST BONDAGE MADE AWARE. . . . . . 332 THE SILKEN TENT . .   14
  NOR FIND IN DEW THE SLIGHTEST CLOUDY TRACE. . . . . 361 A LOOSE MOUNTAIN . .   12
SLIGHTLY
  ANOTHER SOFTER GLOBE THAT SLIGHTLY FLATTENED . . . 322 BUILD SOIL   195
  AND ONLY BY ONE'S GOING SLIGHTLY TAUT. . . . . . . 332 THE SILKEN TENT . .   12
SLIM
  OF HIS SLIM GOAD ON NOSE AND OFFSIDE FLANK, ... 44 THE MOUNTAIN . . .   108
  STRAIGHT UP AND DOWN OF TALL SLIM TREES . . . . . 101 THE WOOD-PILE . . .   6
  A SLIM DOOR GOT IN PAST MY GUARD, ... 265 THE DOOR IN THE DARK .   5
  AND OF HIS RACE STARVATION SLIM, ... 392 A CLIFF DWELLING . .   12
SLIME
  AND NEVER SEEN SUN-SMITTEN SLIME . . . . 266 SITTING BY A BUSH . .   10
SLIM-JIM
  ON YOUR SLIM-JIM ARM." . . . . 133 A GIRL'S GARDEN . .   16
SLING
  IS SOMETHING IN A BALEARIC SLING . . . . 361 A LOOSE MOUNTAIN . .   16
SLIP
  THAT SLIP FROM HEAVEN AT NIGHT AND SOFTLY FALL . . . 172 A STAR IN A STONEBOAT .   2

SLIP (CONTINUED)
    TO THE DARKENING, WINDY VILLAGE SLIP. . . . . 343 DISCOVERY OF MADEIRAS .   7
SLIPPED
    SLIPPED TO HER SIDE, CAUGHT UP HER HAND AND WAITED. . . . 40 DEATH OF THE HIRED MAN 165
    EVER SINCE, JUST TO SHOW THEM, HE HAD SLIPPED . . . . 191 PAUL'S WIFE   18
    TOGETHER, AND TOGETHER SLIPPED; . . . . 381 AN UNSTAMPED LETTER IN   35
    SLIPPED IN TO BE MY PROBLEM GUEST, ... 419 ONE MORE BREVITY . .   9
SLIPPER
    YOU DIDN'T FIND A YELLOW LADY'S SLIPPER. . . . . . 97 THE SELF-SEEKER . . . 137
    WHERE IS IT NOW, THE YELLOW LADY'S SLIPPER?" . . . . 97 THE SELF-SEEKER . . . 140
    "I DIDN'T BRING A PURPLE LADY'S SLIPPER. . . . . . 98 THE SELF-SEEKER . . . 143
SLIPPER'S
    THE PURPLE LADY'S SLIPPER'S COMMONER." . . . . . . 98 THE SELF-SEEKER . . . 142
SLIPPERY
    HE LOOKED BACK UP THE SLIPPERY SLOPE . . . . 139 BROWN'S DESCENT . . . 47
    HE COULDN'T CLIMB THAT SLIPPERY SLOPE; . . . . . . 139 BROWN'S DESCENT . . . 56
    ON SLIPPERY ROCKS BESIDE A WATERFALL. . . . . . . 210 PAUPER WITCH OF GRAFTON 98
SLIPPING
    SLIPPING FROM CLUMSY CLUTCHES TOWARD THE CEILING. . . . 113 IN THE HOME STRETCH . 89
    AND THE WHOLE PILE IS SLIPPING, BOTTLES, BUNS-- . . . 266 THE ARMFUL   3
SLOGAN
    THE ANDREW JACKSON SLOGAN OF VAE VICTIS . . . . . 510 A MASQUE OF MERCY . . 459
SLOPE
    TO A SLOPE WHERE THE CATTLE KEEP THE LAWN. . . . . 17 THE VANTAGE POINT . .   3
    AND LEAVE THE SLOPE BEHIND THE HOUSE ALL BARE, . . . 106 CHRISTMAS TREES . . . 18
    THEY LEAVE US TO: THAT PASTURE SLOPE THAT SEEMS . . . 114 IN THE HOME STRETCH . 113
    HE LOOKED BACK UP THE SLIPPERY SLOPE . . . . 139 BROWN'S DESCENT . . . 47
    HE COULDN'T CLIMB THAT SLIPPERY SLOPE; . . . . . . 139 BROWN'S DESCENT . . . 56
    BY SETTING IT OUT ON A NORTHERLY SLOPE.) . . . . . 228 GOOD-BY AND KEEP COLD . 14
    HERE FURTHER UP THE MOUNTAIN SLOPE . . . . 264 THE BIRTHPLACE   1
    THE SLOPE OF THE EARTH REVERSED. . . . . 285 IN TIME OF CLOUDBURST . 16
    TO THE OTHER END OF THE SLOPE. . . . . 285 IN TIME OF CLOUDBURST . 18
    HAS LOST ITS FOOTING ON MY MOUNTAIN SLOPE . . . . . 350 TO A YOUNG WRETCH . . 21
    BUT THE THING WAS THE SLOPE IT GAVE HIS HEAD: . . . . 356 TIME OUT   8
SLOPES
    TRANSFIXED ON MOUNTAIN SLOPES ALMOST ERECT. . . . . 237 A HILLSIDE THAW . . . 28
SLOT
    IT WASN'T GREASE AT ALL, BUT A LONG SLOT. . . . . 193 PAUL'S WIFE 73
SLOUGH
    SUCH AS THAT FLESH IS SOMETHING WE CAN SLOUGH . . . 395 ETHEREALIZING   3
SLOW
    OR HIGHWAY WHERE THE SLOW WHEEL POURS THE SAND. . . .   5 INTO MY OWN   8
    THEY ARE TIRELESS FOLK, BUT SLOW AND SAD-- . . . .   6 GHOST HOUSE 26
    BEGIN THE HOURS OF THIS DAY SLOW. . . . . 27 OCTOBER   8
    SLOW, SLOW! . . . . 28 OCTOBER 17
    AND THERE I MET A MAN WHO MOVED SO SLOW . . . . . 41 THE MOUNTAIN 16
    DRAWING THE SLOW WAVES WHITER AND WHITER AND WHITER. . . 63 A SERVANT TO SERVANTS . 25
    WHERE ON A MOW IT WOULD HAVE BEEN SLOW LIFTING. . . . 71 THE CODE 58
    WITH THE SLOW SMOKELESS BURNING OF DECAY. . . . . 102 THE WOOD-PILE 40
    AS IF A MAN COULD MOVE THAT SLOW AND MOVE. . . . . 145 SNOW 60
    AND THEN HER VOICE CAME SCRAPING SLOW: 'OH, YOU, . . . 153 SNOW 290
    AND SLOW ME DOWN--AND I ABRUPTLY SLOWED, ... 189 THE GRINDSTONE . . . 32
    AND SET OFF BRISKLY FOR SO SLOW A THING, ... 205 THE WITCH OF COOS . . 86
    BUT PULL SO SLOW, WITH SUCH A TWIST, ... 273 A LONE STRIKER . . . 20
    OH, SLOW UNCOMPREHENDING ME, ... 327 A MISSIVE MISSILE . . 38
    AT HOW SLOW I DO A MILE, ... 465 SOME SCIENCE FICTION . 10
    FOR ME AS AN OLD SLOW COACH. . . . . 466 SOME SCIENCE FICTION . 12
SLOWED
    AND SLOW ME DOWN--AND I ABRUPTLY SLOWED, ... 189 THE GRINDSTONE . . . 32
SLOWER
    FASTER OR SLOWER AS HE CHANCED, ... 138 BROWN'S DESCENT . . . 25
SLOWLY
    THAT SLOWLY DAWNED BEHIND THE TREES, ... 18 GOING FOR WATER . . . 10
    AND HIS VOICE DIED DOWN SLOWLY FROM EXHAUSTION. . . . 66 A SERVANT TO SERVANTS . 133
    WHEN THE HEAT SLOWLY HAZES AND THE SUN . . . . . 125 AN ENCOUNTER   2
    HE MADE IN WALKING SLOWLY TO THE BEACH . . . . . 194 PAUL'S WIFE 99
    IT SLOWLY ROSE A PERSON, ROSE A GIRL, ... 194 PAUL'S WIFE 108
    AND LAUGHED. THEN SHE CLIMBED SLOWLY TO HER FEET, . . . 194 PAUL'S WIFE 119
    WHEN SLOWLY (AND NOBODY COMES WITH A LIGHT) . . . . 228 GOOD-BY AND KEEP COLD 27
    BY WALKING SLOWLY ON SOME EVENING LATER . . . . . 245 THE FREEDOM OF THE MOON   8
    DANCED SLOWLY ON IT TILL HE TROD IT FLAT. . . . . 284 THE GOLD HESPERIDEE . 48
    THEY SLOWLY AND SILENTLY AGED. . . . . 312 THE VINDICTIVES . . . 53
    RESTS ON THE WORLD, AND CLINGING SLOWLY ROLLS. . . . 322 BUILD SOIL 196
    FOR SLOWLY EVEN HER SENSE OF HIM . . . . 347 DISCOVERY OF MADEIRAS . 116
    THEY SLOWLY LED OLD LATIN VERSE TO RHYME . . . . . 351 THE LESSON FOR TODAY . 16
    BUT I SLOWLY UNDERSTOOD. . . . . 366 NOT OF SCHOOL AGE . . 18
    BUT RIGHT IN HEAVEN WAS SLOWLY BEING SHRUNK . . . . 368 THE LITERATE FARMER AND 14
    AND THEN GET SLOWLY, SLOWLY PULLED BACK DOWN. . . . 370 THE LITERATE FARMER AND 67
    NOW SLOWLY CLOSING LIKE A DENT IN DOUGH. . . . . . 378 DIRECTIVE 47
SLOWNESS
    IN SLEEP OR SLOWNESS IS THE DEADLY CRIME. . . . . 371 THE LITERATE FARMER AND 103
    MY SLOWNESS WITH THEIR SPEED . . . . 415 CLOSED FOR GOOD . . .   9
SLOWS
    AND SLOWS HIS HORSE TO A MEANING WALK, ... 124 A TIME TO TALK . . .   2
SLUMBER
    THERE IS NO SLUMBER IN ITS JUICE FOR THEM. . . . . 411 POD OF THE MILKWEED . 23
SLUMBERED
    I SLUMBERED WITH YOUR POEMS ON MY BREAST, ... 222 TO E.T.   1
SLUMBERING
    DISTURBED THE SLUMBERING VILLAGE STREET . . . . . 102 GOOD HOURS 14
SLUMBERS
    THAT SLUMBERS IN A BRUTE. . . . . 340 THE SUBVERTED FLOWER . 34
SLUMPED
    SLUMPED WAY DOWN IN A CHAIR, WITH BOTH HIS FEET . . . 72 THE CODE 97
SLUNG (SEE LOW-SLUNG)
SMACKED
    HIS HARD TAIL LOUDLY SMACKED THE FLOOR . . . . . 420 ONE MORE BREVITY . . 23
    IN SPITE OF THE WAY HIS TAIL HAD SMACKED . . . . . 421 ONE MORE BREVITY . . 54

SMALL (SEE INFRA-SMALL, JEWEL-SMALL)
    IT IS UNDER THE SMALL, DIM, SUMMER STAR. . . . . . .   6 GHOST HOUSE   21
    I'LL SIT AND SEE IF THAT SMALL SAILING CLOUD . . . . . 40 DEATH OF THE HIRED MAN 160
    SO SMALL THE WINDOW FRAMES THE WHOLE OF IT. . . . . . . 51 HOME BURIAL . . .   24
    FIERCE HEADS LOOKED OUT; SMALL BODIES PIVOTED. . . . .   59 THE BLACK COTTAGE . . 126
    THOUGH THERE'S SMALL PROFIT IN COMPARISONS. . . . . .   64 A SERVANT TO SERVANTS . 68
    YOU CAN HEAR THE SMALL BUZZ SAWS WHINE, THE BIG SAW .   94 THE SELF-SEEKER . . . 41
    THE FLOATING HEART, WITH SMALL LEAF LIKE A HEART, . . . 98 THE SELF-SEEKER . . . 154
    LIKE A SMALL PISTOL WHEN HE SNAPPED IT SHUT . . . . . . 98 THE SELF-SEEKER . . . 165
    A SMALL BIRD FLEW BEFORE ME. HE WAS CAREFUL . . . . . 101 THE WOOD-PILE . . .   10
    BUT THIRTY DOLLARS SEEMED SO SMALL BESIDE . . . . . . 107 CHRISTMAS TREES . . . 47
    THREE CENTS SO SMALL BESIDE THE DOLLAR FRIENDS . . . . 107 CHRISTMAS TREES . . . 50
    SMALL PRINT OVERSPREAD IT, ... 110 A PATCH OF OLD SNOW .   6
    WE DID THAT DAY WAS MINGLE GREAT AND SMALL . . . . . 118 MEETING AND PASSING .   5
    SMALL GOOD TO ANYTHING GROWING WILD, ... 123 PEA BRUSH   21
    WITH NO SMALL DIGNITY OF MIEN. . . . . 138 BROWN'S DESCENT . . . 24
    "IT'S NO NIGHT TO BE OUT." / "HE MAY BE SMALL, ... 145 SNOW   70
    YET THINK OF THE SMALL BIRDS AT ROOST AND NOT . . . . 151 SNOW 226
    SMALL TOWNS--LOST NATION, BUNGEY, MUDDY BOO, ... 165 NEW HAMPSHIRE . . . 187
    IN A SMALL NICHE LET INTO IT, THE GIRL . . . . . . 195 PAUL'S WIFE 134
    MY SMALL WRISTS STRETCHING TILL THEY SHOWED THE BANJO
       STRINGS. . . . . 198 WILD GRAPES   80
    A SMALL SKIFF . . . . 211 AN EMPTY THREAT . . .   5
    THE SMALL BOOK IN MY POCKET. IT WAS THERE. . . . . . 217 A FOUNTAIN, A BOTTLE . 133
    A WHIR AMONG WHITE BRANCHES GREAT AND SMALL, ... 240 OUR SINGING STRENGTH . 41
    AND LOOK UP SMALL FROM THE FOREST'S FEET. . . . . . 247 ON GOING UNNOTICED .   10
    HIS SMALL FIST BURIED IN THE BUSHY HIDE. . . . . . . 267 RIDERS   8
    IT WILL BE BECAUSE, THOUGH SMALL . . . . 282 A DRUMLIN WOODCHUCK . 29
    SOME GIANT TREES HAVE BLOOM SO SMALL . . . . 297 LEAVES COMPARED WITH .   9
    AND SMALL REGARD TO THE FUTURE OF ANY WEED. . . . . 299 STRONG SAYING NOTHING .   2
    IF DESIGN GOVERN IN A THING SO SMALL. . . . . . . 302 DESIGN 14
    THEN A SMALL RAINBOW LIKE A TRELLIS GATE, ... 315 IRIS BY NIGHT . . . 17
    A VERY SMALL MOON-MADE PRISMATIC BOW, ... 315 IRIS BY NIGHT . . . 18
    ITS CONTEMPLATION MAKES US OUT AS SMALL . . . . . . 352 THE LESSON FOR TODAY . 69
    LOOKED FORTH ON HER SMALL SON . . . . 366 NOT OF SCHOOL AGE .   14
    SO SMALL AS TO BE VIRTUALLY GONE, ... 368 THE LITERATE FARMER AND 15
    SO SMALL AM I AS AN ATTENTION BEGGAR. . . . . . . 388 IOTA SUBSCRIPT . .   5
    NO HOLY WARS FOR THEM. THE MOST THE SMALL . . . . . 398 NO HOLY WARS FOR THEM . 13
    AS A SMALL SELF-CONFERRED REWARD OF VIRTUE. . . . . 405 FROM PLANE TO PLANE . 39
    AND SUCH SMALL POSTHUMOUS RENOWN . . . . 418 AMERICA IS HARD TO SEE 45
    SMALL BUT STRONG AND ROUND, ... 433 KITTY HAWK 172
    THOUGH AN EARTH SO SMALL, ... 440 KITTY HAWK 374
    I WAS SWOOPED DOWN UPON WHEN I WAS SMALL, ... 443 AUSPEX   2
    AND THE SLAVE SAID, "THE SMALL ONE'S WORTH THE PRICE, . 456 HOW HARD TO KEEP FROM   81
    WHEN I WAS SOLD--AND SMALL REPROACH TO HIM. . . . . 459 HOW HARD TO KEEP FROM 172
    LIKE SMALL BOYS WE GOT MAD . . . . 464 MILKY WAY IS A COWPATH   6
    YOU KNOW, THERE MAY HAVE BEEN A SMALL TEMBLOR. . . . 507 A MASQUE OF MERCY . 356
    DON'T YOU BE MADE FEEL SMALL BY ALL THIS POSING. . . 511 A MASQUE OF MERCY . 461
    MY SMALL FRESH-WATER SPRING GETS DROWNED OF COURSE. . . 513 A MASQUE OF MERCY . 539
SMALLER
    A SMALLER PEARL HE ASKED A THOUSAND FOR, ... 455 HOW HARD TO KEEP FROM 67
SMALL-TIME
    A BUNCH OF SMALL-TIME REVOLUTIONARIES.-- . . . . . 509 A MASQUE OF MERCY . 406
SMART
    "THAT'S A SMART PAIR OF PUMPS YOU'RE BEADING THERE. . . 81 THE HOUSEKEEPER . . .   9
    HE THINKS HE'S SMART. HE THINKS HE CAN CONVINCE ME . 485 A MASQUE OF REASON . 351
SMARTY
    THEN THAT SAME SMARTY SOMEONE SAID TO LOOK-- . . . . 209 PAUPER WITCH OF GRAFTON 59
    THE SMARTY SOMEONE WHO SPOILED EVERYTHING . . . . . 209 PAUPER WITCH OF GRAFTON 70
SMASH
    WHAT I THINK HE WILL DO, IS LET THINGS SMASH. . . . 83 THE HOUSEKEEPER . . . 51
SMEARED
    HIS CHEEK SMEARED WITH APPLE SAND, ... 366 NOT OF SCHOOL AGE . .   9
SMELL
    I SMELL THE EARTH, I SMELL THE BRUISED PLANT, . . . 17 THE VANTAGE POINT . . 13
    THE SMELL OF THE WET FEATHERS IN THE HEAT! . . . . 85 THE HOUSEKEEPER . . 122
    THE SMELL OF SCORCHING WOOLEN MADE HER FAINT. . . . 91 THE FEAR   69
    WITH SMELL OF BURNING ON EVERY PLUME, ... 120 BOND AND FREE . . . 14
    AND THE SMELL OF FIRE DROWNED IN RAIN. . . . . . . 232 THE KITCHEN CHIMNEY . 15
    NOR TASTE ITS SALT, NOR SMELL ITS FISH AND WEED, . . 447 DOES NO ONE AT ALL EVER 35
    THE MYRRH TREE GIVES IT. SMELL THE ROSIN BURNING? . . 473 A MASQUE OF REASON .   9
SMELLED
    TO RUSH IN SHEETS AND FOOL'S CAPS WHERE THEY SMELLED . . 163 NEW HAMPSHIRE . . . 141
SMELLING
    SO SMELLING THEIR SWEETNESS WOULD BE NO THEFT. . . . 305 UNHARVESTED 14
    ACROSS THE LIGHT SNOW HOMEWARD SMELLING GREEN. . . . 349 TO A YOUNG WRETCH .   6
SMELLS
    IT SMELLS TO ME LIKE A DISHONEST TRICK." . . . . . 100 THE SELF-SEEKER . . 203
    AND FROM BARN SMELLS YOU CAN'T WASH OUT OF PLOWED GROUND . 210 PAUPER WITCH OF GRAFTON 91
SMELT
    THEN PAUSED AGAIN AND EITHER DRANK OR SMELT-- . . . 357 A CONSIDERABLE SPECK . 13
SMILE
    YOU NEEDN'T SMILE--I DIDN'T RECOGNIZE HIM-- . . . . 35 DEATH OF THE HIRED MAN 37
    SOMETHING DOWN THERE TO SMILE AT IN THE DUST. . . . 119 MEETING AND PASSING . 11
    THAT SMILE! IT NEVER CAME OF BEING GAY. . . . . . 127 THE SMILE   2
    THE SMILE . . . . 127 THE SMILE . . . .   T
    WITH ALWAYS SOMETHING IN HER SMILE. . . . . 265 THE BIRTHPLACE . . . 10
    LIKE THE CURL AT THE CORNER OF A SMILE; . . . . . 335 I COULD GIVE ALL . .   8
    HE SMILED FOR HER TO SMILE, ... 339 THE SUBVERTED FLOWER .   5
    AND ANOTHER SORT OF SMILE . . . . 339 THE SUBVERTED FLOWER . 11
    SOMETIMES, WITH HER PERMISSIVE SMILE, ... 345 DISCOVERY OF MADEIRAS . 48
    HE NO MORE DREW THE SMILE HE SOUGHT. . . . . . . 347 DISCOVERY OF MADEIRAS . 118
    THOUGH AS YET THEY ONLY SMILE . . . . 465 SOME SCIENCE FICTION .   9
    TO BRUSH AWAY A DISRESPECTFUL SMILE. . . . . . . 487 A MASQUE OF REASON . 391
    NO--NO, THAT'S NOT A SMILE THERE. THAT'S A GRIN. . . 488 A MASQUE OF REASON . 404
    YOU'D AS WELL SMILE AS FROWN ON THE OCCASION. . . . 490 A MASQUE OF REASON . 465
SMILED
    AND SMILED, AND WHEN SHE DID NOT TURN, SPOKE GENTLY, . . 111 IN THE HOME STRETCH . 19

SMILED (CONTINUED)
    STILL HE SMILED--DID YOU SEE HIM?--I WAS SURE! . . . . . 127 THE SMILE   3
    HE SMILED FOR HER TO SMILE, ... 339 THE SUBVERTED FLOWER .   5
SMILING
    NO ONE COULD GET YOU: YOU WOULD COME THROUGH SMILING. . 458 HOW HARD TO KEEP FROM 129
SMITH
    JOHN SMITH REMARKED THEM AS HE COASTED BY, ... 161 NEW HAMPSHIRE . . .   74
    BUT SMITH, OR SOMEONE, CALLED THEM OFF THE MOUNTAIN . . 213 A FOUNTAIN, A BOTTLE . 11
SMITHEREENS
    BLOWING IT ALL TO SMITHEREENS . . . . 393 A CASE FOR JEFFERSON . 10
    AS FLY THE ATOMIC SMITHEREENS TO NOTHING. . . . . . 460 HOW HARD TO KEEP FROM 197
SMITTEN (SEE SUN-SMITTEN)
SMOKE
    HE SAW NO SMOKE AND HE SAW NO ROOF. . . . . . . 24 PAN WITH US . . .   9
    AND GAVE HIM TEA AND TRIED TO MAKE HIM SMOKE. . . . . 36 DEATH OF THE HIRED MAN 41
    BEGIN IN SMUDGE WITH ROPY SMOKE, AND KNOW . . . . . 130 THE BONFIRE 21
    THAT AND THE MEREST CURL OF CIGARETTE SMOKE-- . . . . 131 THE BONFIRE . . . 50
    AND THE SUN SHRUNKEN YELLOW IN SMOKE. . . . . . . 141 THE GUM-GATHERER . . . 24
    TO GET A PUFF OF BLACK SMOKE FROM THE FLAME, ... 148 SNOW 140
    UNSCORCHED, UNBLACKENED, EVEN, BY ANY SMOKE. . . . . 184 MAPLE 142
    SMOKE ROLLED INSIDE THE SOCKETS OF HIS EYES.) . . . . 204 THE WITCH OF COOS . . 74
    OF WHAT WAS EITHER CLOUD OR SMOKE . . . . 233 LOOKING FOR SUNSET BIRD 18
    AND SEND MORE SPARKS UP CHIMNEY WITH THE SMOKE." . . . 234 EVENING A SUGAR ORCHARD 6
    IS ALL THE SMOKE FROM ONE POOR HOUSE ALONE, ... 248 THE COCOON . . .   5
    I WANT TO TELL THEM THAT WITH ALL THIS SMOKE . . . . 248 THE COCOON . . .   12
    LOOKING THROUGH WREATHS OF ENGINE SMOKE . . . . . 292 ON HEART'S BEGINNING TO 44
    I AM THE GUARDIAN WRAITH OF STARLIT SMOKE . . . . . 414 A CABIN IN THE CLEARING 10
    I AM THE DAMPER COUNTERPART OF SMOKE, ... 414 A CABIN IN THE CLEARING 15
    A MIST AND SMOKE EAVESDROPPING ON A HAZE-- . . . . . 415 A CABIN IN THE CLEARING 39
    THAN SMOKE AND MIST WHO BETTER COULD APPRAISE . . . . 415 A CABIN IN THE CLEARING 41
SMOKELESS
    WITH THE SLOW SMOKELESS BURNING OF DECAY. . . . . . 102 THE WOOD-PILE . . . 40
SMOKING
    THE CHIMNEY, THOUGH, KEEPS UP A GOOD BRISK SMOKING. . . 49 A HUNDRED COLLARS . . 137
    BUT THE PIPE'S THERE AND SMOKING, AND THE JUG. . . . . 77 THE GENERATIONS OF MEN 107
SMOKY
    OF WASTE LEAVES AT MY SMOKY LANTERN CHIMNEY . . . . 176 THE STAR-SPLITTER . .   8
    AND A MAN WITH A SMOKY LANTERN CHIMNEY? . . . . . 179 THE STAR-SPLITTER . . 98
SMOLDERING
    IT KEEPS SMOLDERING AT THE ROOTS . . . . 308 EVIL TENDENCIES CANCEL   3
SMOOTH
    BETWEEN THEM THEY WILL LAY THIS FARM AS SMOOTH! . . . 36 DEATH OF THE HIRED MAN 63
    HIS HANDS HAD WORN THEM SMOOTH AS ANY OXBOW. . . . . 66 A SERVANT TO SERVANTS . 136
    I OFTEN THINK OF THE SMOOTH HICKORY BARS. . . . . . 67 A SERVANT TO SERVANTS . 144
    MINGLED WITH THESE, SMOOTH BEAN AND WRINKLED PEA), . . 124 PUTTING IN THE SEED .   6
    HE DID NOT RECOGNIZE IN THAT SMOOTH COAL . . . . . 172 A STAR IN A STONEBOAT . 10
    STANDING ALONE WITH SMOOTH ARMS LIFTED UP, ... 184 MAPLE 145
    AND SMOOTH AND MOIST IN VERNAL HEAT. . . . . . . 184 MAPLE 145
    AND THE GROUND ALMOST COVERED SMOOTH IN SNOW, ... 276 TWO TRAMPS IN MUD TIME 48
    LEAVES FOR SMOOTH AND BARK FOR ROUGH, ... 296 DESERT PLACES . . .   3
    I'D SHIP A SMOOTH ONE YOU COULD SLAP AND CHAFE, . . . 297 LEAVES COMPARED WITH .   7
    AND TAKE OUR DAILY TIDE BATHS SMOOTH AND ROUGH. . . . 365 OF STONES OF THE PLACE   9
SMOOTH-LAID   395 ETHEREALIZING . . .   8
    SMOOTH-LAID LIKE THATCH WITH THE HEAVY DEW, ...   8 A LATE WALK   3
SMOTE
    THEY SO SMOTE THE GARDEN BED . . . . 250 LODGED   3
SMOTHER
    AND SAID OUT LOUD, I COULDN'T BIDE THE SMOTHER . . . . 131 THE BONFIRE 70
    AND FIGHT IN A SMOTHER . . . . 218 I WILL SING YOU ONE-O . 14
SMOTHERED
    ALL ANIMALS ARE SMOTHERED IN THEIR LAIRS. . . . . . 296 DESERT PLACES . . .   6
SMUDGE
    BEGIN IN SMUDGE WITH ROPY SMOKE, AND KNOW . . . . . 130 THE BONFIRE 21
SMUDGED
    AND NOW AND THEN A SMUDGED, INFERNAL FACE . . . . . 110 IN THE HOME STRETCH . 10
SMUGGLER'S
    AS IN A SMUGGLER'S AT THE DIAMOND FIELDS, ... 503 A MASQUE OF MERCY . . 253
SNAIL
    IT DREW BACK IN ITS BODY LIKE A SNAIL); . . . . . . 172 A STAR IN A STONEBOAT 18
SNAKE
    (PALE ORCHISES), AND SCARED A BRIGHT GREEN SNAKE. . . . 17 MOWING 12
    THE SNAKE STOOD UP FOR EVIL IN THE GARDEN-- . . . . . 188 THE AX-HELVE 97
    IT MIGHT HAVE BEEN THE SKIN A SNAKE HAD CAST . . . . 194 PAUL'S WIFE 92
    AND DEAD WEEDS, LIKE A DISAPPEARING SNAKE. . . . . . 226 THE ONSET 21
    WAS A HOLLOW-HEADED SNAKE. . . . . 367 A SERIOUS STEP LIGHTLY   2
    THE BURRS WERE HILLS, THE SNAKE WAS A STREAM, ... 367 A SERIOUS STEP LIGHTLY   3
SNAP
    "YOU GIVE HER ONE GOOD CRACK, SHE'S SNAP RIGHT OFF. . . 186 THE AX-HELVE 26
    THEN LETS IT SNAP BACK UPRIGHT IN THE SKY. . . . . . 268 THE BEAR   4
    OR THE WIND TO SNAP THEIR WALKING STICK, ... 344 DISCOVERY OF MADEIRAS . 29
SNAPPED
    LIKE A SMALL PISTOL WHEN HE SNAPPED IT SHUT . . . . . 98 THE SELF-SEEKER . . 165
    AT SUCH A TIME AS THIS. HE SNAPPED IT NOW. . . . . . 98 THE SELF-SEEKER . . 166
    BUT NOW HE SNAPPED HIS EYES THREE TIMES; . . . . . . 140 BROWN'S DESCENT . . 73
SNAPS
    (HE SNAPS ONE BULB OFF. PAUL SNAPS ON ANOTHER.) . . . 508 A MASQUE OF MERCY . . 393
SNARLED
    THE BUZZ SAW SNARLED AND RATTLED IN THE YARD . . . . 136 "OUT, OUT--"   1
    AND THE SAW SNARLED AND RATTLED, SNARLED AND RATTLED, . 136 "OUT, OUT--"   7
SNARLING
    SELF-TAUGHT. BUT OUR BRUTE SNARLING AND LASHING TAUGHT IT. 320 BUILD SOIL 120
SNATCH
    BUT SUDDEN WINDS THAT SNATCH THEM FROM OUR HANDS . . . 112 IN THE HOME STRETCH . 43
    AND HALF GRANT WHAT I WISH AND SNATCH ME AWAY . . . . 122 BIRCHES 51
    THERE WAS A SUDDEN FLASH OF ARM, A SNATCH, ... 293 AT WOODWARD'S GARDENS . 22
SNATCHED
    SNATCHED THEE, O'EREAGER, WITH UNGENTLE GRASP. . . . . 29 MY BUTTERFLY 30
    THE WONDER WAS THE TENTS WEREN'T SNATCHED AWAY . . . . 67 A SERVANT TO SERVANTS . 168

SNATCHED (CONTINUED)
    SNATCHED RIGHT AND LEFT ACROSS THE SILVER PULLEYS. . . . 94 THE SELF-SEEKER . . . 39
SNATCHES
    AND SNATCHES OF VERSE AND SONG OF SCENES LIKE THIS . . . 342 QUEST OF PURPLE-FRINGED 3
SNEERED
    WE'RE VERY SORRY FOR YOU." / WILLIS SNEERED: . . . . . 100 THE SELF-SEEKER . . . 220
SNEERING
    "THERE YOU GO SNEERING NOW!" / "I'M NOT, I'M NOT! . . . . 53 HOME BURIAL 67
SNEEZE-NERVE
    TO STAB ME IN THE SNEEZE-NERVE OF A NOSTRIL. . . . . . 277 THE WHITE-TAILED HORNET 10
SNIPPED
    SOMEONE TOOK CURVED NAIL-SCISSORS AND SNIPPED OFF . . . 501 A MASQUE OF MERCY . . 201
SNOB
    HE'S BEING A RELIGIOUS SNOB FOR FUN. . . . . 494 A MASQUE OF MERCY . . 34
SNORT
    BUT NO, NOT YET. A SNORT TO BID THEM WAIT. . . . . . 229 TWO LOOK AT TWO . . . 26
SNORTED
    AND SNORTED AT US. AND THEN HE HAD TO BOLT. . . . . . 223 THE RUNAWAY 5
SNOUT
    WITH LIFTED SNOUT AND EYES (IF ANY) SHUT . . . . . 269 THE BEAR 27
    THAT CUT THE SNOUT IN HALF, ... 340 THE SUBVERTED FLOWER . 46
SNOW
    BEFORE THE COMING OF THE SNOW, ... 7 MY NOVEMBER GUEST . . 18
    O'ER OUR TUMULTUOUS SNOW, ... 9 STARS 2
    AND PELTS WITH SNOW . . . . 9 STORM FEAR 2
    CONCERNED WITH ICE AND SNOW, ... 10 WIND AND WINDOW FLOWER 14
    AND BINDING ALL IS THE HUSHED SNOW. . . . . 20 THE TRIAL BY EXISTENCE 15
    THE GRAY GRASS IS SCARCE DAPPLED WITH THE SNOW; . . . . 28 MY BUTTERFLY 8
    OUT OVER THE CRUSTED SNOW, ... 30 RELUCTANCE 11
    BY MOUNTAIN RANGES HALF IN SUMMER SNOW, ... 58 THE BLACK COTTAGE . . 116
    THE HARD SNOW HELD ME, SAVE WHERE NOW AND THEN . . . . 101 THE WOOD-PILE . . . 4
    NO RUNNER TRACKS IN THIS YEAR'S SNOW LOOPED NEAR IT. . . 101 THE WOOD-PILE . . . 26
    UP TO THEIR SHINING EYES IN SNOW. . . . . 102 GOOD HOURS 4
    OVER THE SNOW MY CREAKING FEET . . . . 102 GOOD HOURS 13
    WHEN BETWEEN WHIRLS OF SNOW NOT COME TO LIE . . . . . 106 CHRISTMAS TREES . . . 3
    FOR SUCH A CHARGE, HIS SNOW UPON THE ROOF, ... 108 OLD MAN'S WINTER NIGHT 21
    THERE'S A PATCH OF OLD SNOW IN A CORNER, ... 110 A PATCH OF OLD SNOW . 1
    A PATCH OF OLD SNOW . . . . 110 A PATCH OF OLD SNOW . T
    LIKE GHOST OF SLEIGH BELLS IN A GHOST OF SNOW)-- . . . 119 HYLA BROOK 6
    ON SNOW AND SAND AND TURF, I SEE . . . . 120 BOND AND FREE . . . 6
    SHATTERING AND AVALANCHING ON THE SNOW CRUST-- . . . . 121 BIRCHES 11
    WITH PITCHY HANDS TO WAIT FOR RAIN OR SNOW. . . . . . 129 THE BONFIRE 4
    IN THE SNOW WITH AN AX-- . . . . 136 LAST WORD OF A BLUEBIRD 19
    GULPED SNOW, AND THEN BLEW FREE AGAIN--THE COLES, . . . 143 SNOW 3
    SNOW. . . . . 143 SNOW . . . . . . T
    AND FOUND ME BANKING UP THE HOUSE WITH SNOW. . . . . 149 SNOW 177
    THE SNOW AGAINST THE WINDOW CAUGHT HIS EYE. . . . . 149 SNOW 180
    "I'LL OWN IT'S COLD FOR SUCH A FALL OF SNOW. . . . . 150 SNOW 201
    YOU'RE FURTHER UNDER IN THE SNOW--THAT'S ALL-- . . . . 150 SNOW 205
    HOW HIGH I'D THRUST THE PEAKS IN SUMMER SNOW . . . . 169 NEW HAMPSHIRE . . . 339
    AND UNDERFOOT SNOW MELTED DOWN TO ICE, ... 179 THE STAR-SPLITTER . . 80
    OF SAP AND SNOW ROLLED OFF THE SUGARHOUSE. . . . . 184 MAPLE 138
    BEHIND ME ON THE SNOW IN MY OWN YARD . . . . . 185 THE AX-HELVE 7
    UPON IT NOW; ITS FEET ARE FAST IN SNOW. . . . . . 189 THE GRINDSTONE . . . 10
    MIGHT JUST AS WELL BE ICE AND THE CLOTHES SNOW. . . . 203 THE WITCH OF COOS . . 39
    AND SWOLLEN TIGHT AND BURIED UNDER SNOW. . . . . . 204 THE WITCH OF COOS . . 56
    AND SWOLLEN TIGHT AND BURIED UNDER SNOW. . . . . . 204 THE WITCH OF COOS . . 58
    THE UNCOMMONLY DEEP SNOW HAS MADE HIM THINK . . . . . 205 THE WITCH OF COOS . . 109
    WITH ALL THE RAIN AND SNOW OF SEVEN YEARS; . . . . 210 PAUPER WITCH OF GRAFTON 92
    IN SNOW AND MIST . . . . 211 AN EMPTY THREAT . . . 33
    THE SNOW FELL DEEP . . . . 218 I WILL SING YOU ONE-O . 9
    THE DUST OF SNOW . . . . 221 DUST OF SNOW 3
    DUST OF SNOW . . . . 221 DUST OF SNOW . . . . T
    ONCE WHEN THE SNOW OF THE YEAR WAS BEGINNING TO FALL, . . 223 THE RUNAWAY 1
    "I THINK THE LITTLE FELLOW'S AFRAID OF THE SNOW. . . . 223 THE RUNAWAY 9
    TO WATCH HIS WOODS FILL UP WITH SNOW. . . . . . . 224 STOPPING BY WOODS . . 4
    AT LAST THE GATHERED SNOW LETS DOWN AS WHITE . . . . 226 THE ONSET 2
    THE EARTH BUT IT HAS FAILED: THE SNOW MAY HEAP . . . . 226 THE ONSET 14
    AND I SHALL SEE THE SNOW ALL GO DOWNHILL . . . . . 226 THE ONSET 18
    WAS ONLY ADDING FROST TO SNOW . . . . 233 LOOKING FOR SUNSET BIRD 15
    AND ON BLACK GROUND A BEAR-SKIN RUG OF SNOW. . . . . 234 EVENING A SUGAR ORCHARD 13
    TEN MILLION SILVER LIZARDS OUT OF SNOW! . . . . . 237 A HILLSIDE THAW . . . 3
    A PLOW, THEY SAY, TO PLOW THE SNOW. . . . . . . 238 PLOWMEN 1
    AND MAKE US GET DOWN IN A FOOT OF SNOW . . . . . 238 ON A TREE FALLEN ACROSS 7
    NOW WAS SEEN HOW THESE LIKED BELATED SNOW. . . . . 239 OUR SINGING STRENGTH . 25
    FROM SNOW THAT MELTED ONLY YESTERDAY. . . . . . . 245 SPRING POOLS 12
    THE RAIN BY RIGHTS WAS SNOW FOR COLD. . . . . . . 253 THE THATCH 11
    AND NOT MELT SNOW OR START A DORMANT TREE. . . . . . 254 A WINTER EDEN . . . 4
    IT LIFTS EXISTENCE ON A PLANE OF SNOW. . . . . . 254 A WINTER EDEN . . . 5
    AND ROUND A CORNER, BLIZZARD SNOW FOR DUST, ... 265 DUST IN THE EYES . . 5
    IT SCOURS THE WINDOWPANE WITH SNOW; . . . . . . 281 BLUE RIBBON AT AMESBURY 50
    SNOW FALLING AND NIGHT FALLING FAST, OH, FAST . . . . 296 DESERT PLACES . . . 1
    AND THE GROUND ALMOST COVERED SMOOTH IN SNOW, ... 296 DESERT PLACES . . . 3
    A BLANKER WHITENESS OF BENIGHTED SNOW . . . . . . 296 DESERT PLACES . . . 11
    NOW UP, MY KNEE, TO KEEP ON TOP OF ANOTHER YEAR OF SNOW. . 298 A LEAF-TREADER . . . 12
    TO INDUCE THE ONE SNOW ON HIS HEAD. . . . . . . 299 WELCOME TO THEIR BELIEF 8
    A SHADE MORE THE COLOR OF SNOW. . . . . 299 WELCOME TO THEIR BELIEF 12
    I SAW MY SHADOW ON SNOW. . . . . 303 AFTERFLAKES 2
    DASH IT WITH SOME SNOW FOR POWDER. . . . . . . 304 CLEAR AND COLDER . . 15
    TO SET HIMSELF AGAINST THE PEAKS OF SNOW . . . . . 334 I COULD GIVE ALL . . 2
    THE SNOW BLOWS ON HIM AND OFF HIM, EXERTING FORCE . . . 341 WILLFUL HOMING . . . 5
    ACROSS THE LIGHT SNOW HOMEWARD SMELLING GREEN. . . . . 349 TO A YOUNG WRETCH . . 6
    BENEATH THE BRUSH OF SNOW." . . . . 416 CLOSED FOR GOOD . . 24
    ACROSS THE TINTED SNOW. . . . . 470 IN WINTER IN THE WOODS 8
    (ENTERING HATLESS IN A WHIRL OF SNOW) . . . . . . 493 A MASQUE OF MERCY . . 18
    THERE'S NOT A FOOTPRINT TO IT IN THE SNOW. . . . . 501 A MASQUE OF MERCY . . 212
SNOWBALLS
    WITH SNOWBALLS CUPPED IN EVERY OPENING BUD. . . . . 239 OUR SINGING STRENGTH . 15

SNOWBALLS (CONTINUED)
    THEN'S WHEN HIS MORGAN LIGHTS OUT THROWING SNOWBALLS . . . 407 FROM PLANE TO PLANE   . 107
SNOWBANK
    MAKE THE SETTLED SNOWBANK STEAM;   . . . . 11 TO THE THAWING WIND   .   4
SNOWBERRIES
    I MADE HIM GATHER ME WET SNOWBERRIES . . . . 210 PAUPER WITCH OF GRAFTON 97
SNOW-DROP
    A SNOW-DROP SPIDER, A FLOWER LIKE A FROTH, ... 302 DESIGN   7
SNOWED
    IT SNOWED IN SPRING ON EARTH SO DRY AND WARM . . . . 239 OUR SINGING STRENGTH .   1
    DID GRASS AND GARDEN GROUND CONFESS IT SNOWED, ... 239 OUR SINGING STRENGTH .   9
SNOWFALL
    IN THE THICK OF A TEEMING SNOWFALL . . . . 303 AFTERFLAKES   1
SNOWING
    THOUGHT HE'D JUST CALL TO TELL US IT WAS SNOWING. . . . 155 SNOW   340
    IT IS SNOWING A FLAKE: AND HE HALF KNEW . . . . . . 276 TWO TRAMPS IN MUD TIME 29
SNOW-LINE
    PLAYING OUR FANCY, TO HAVE THE SNOW-LINE RUN   . . . . 149 SNOW   190
SNOWS
    NO, IT TOOK ALL THE SNOWS THAT CLUNG . . . . 299 WELCOME TO THEIR BELIEF   5
SNOWSTORM
    WELL, SOMETHING FOR A SNOWSTORM TO HAVE SHOWN . . . . 240 OUR SINGING STRENGTH . 49
SNOWSTORMS
    IN GOING ON." / "OUR SNOWSTORMS AS A RULE   . . . . . 150 SNOW   221
SNOW-WHITE
    THOSE STARS LIKE SOME SNOW-WHITE   . . . .   9 STARS 10
    MINERVA'S SNOW-WHITE MARBLE EYES   . . . .   9 STARS 11
    AND CLIMB BLACK BRANCHES UP A SNOW-WHITE TRUNK . . . . 122 BIRCHES 55
    YOU SEE THE SNOW-WHITE THROUGH THE WHITE OF FROST?   . . 148 SNOW   157
    GHASTLY SNOW-WHITE. . . . . 360 THE RABBIT-HUNTER . .   6
SNOWY
    WHERE A MYRIAD SNOWY QUARTZ-STONES LIFT, ... 26 A LINE-STORM SONG   . .   3
    STOPPING BY WOODS ON A SNOWY EVENING . . . . 224 STOPPING BY WOODS . .   T
SNUG
    AND STILL MORE SECURE AND SNUG, ... 282 A DRUMLIN WOODCHUCK   .   7
SO---NOT INDEXED
SOBER
    THE WHIR OF SOBER BIRDS . . . .   8 A LATE WALK   6
    THE SOBER WEED HAS MANAGED TO CONTRIVE   . . . . . . 412 POD OF THE MILKWEED   . 31
SO-CALLED
    I'VE COME TO THINK NO SO-CALLED HIDDEN VALUE'S . . . . 483 A MASQUE OF REASON . . 280
SOCIABLE
    SHE THINKS I'M SOCIABLE. I MAYBE AM. . . . . 49 A HUNDRED COLLARS . . 145
    OF ANYTHING MORE SOCIABLE TO SAY: . . . . 168 NEW HAMPSHIRE . . . 292
SOCIAL
    FOR TO BE SOCIAL IS TO BE FORGIVING. . . . . 178 THE STAR-SPLITTER . . 47
    NOT QUITE SOCIAL . . . . 306 NOT QUITE SOCIAL   . .   T
    I WILL GO TO MY RUN-OUT SOCIAL MIND   . . . . . . 323 BUILD SOIL   237
    THEY'VE TRIED TO GRASP WITH TOO MUCH SOCIAL FACT . . . 351 THE LESSON FOR TODAY . 34
    WHO WOULD THEY BE? THE GUILD OF SOCIAL PLANNERS . . . 397 THE PLANNERS 10
    YOU'VE GOT NO SOCIAL CONSCIENCE, AS THEY SAY, ... 406 FROM PLANE TO PLANE . 77
    YOU CAN'T CLAIM YOU'RE A SOCIAL VISIONARY." . . . . . 406 FROM PLANE TO PLANE . 79
    BEL IS A SOLITARY SOCIAL DRINKER. . . . . 496 A MASQUE OF MERCY . . 86
SOCIALISM
    IS SOCIALISM NEEDED, DO YOU THINK? . . . . 318 BUILD SOIL   67
    WE HAVE IT NOW. FOR SOCIALISM IS . . . . 318 BUILD SOIL   68
    THERE'S NO SUCH THING AS SOCIALISM PURE-- . . . . . 318 BUILD SOIL   70
    THERE'S ONLY DEMOCRATIC SOCIALISM, ... 318 BUILD SOIL   72
    MONARCHIC SOCIALISM, OLIGARCHIC-- . . . . 318 BUILD SOIL   73
SOCIALIZED
    BUT DON'T YOU THINK MORE SHOULD BE SOCIALIZED   . . . . 319 BUILD SOIL   92
    THAN IS? / WHAT SHOULD YOU MEAN BY SOCIALIZED? . . . . 319 BUILD SOIL   93
    BEEN SOCIALIZED--THE FIRST PROPENSITY . . . . . . 319 BUILD SOIL   99
SOCIETY
    THE WORLD'S ONE GLOBE, HUMAN SOCIETY   . . . . . . 322 BUILD SOIL   194
    SOCIETY CAN NEVER THINK THINGS OUT: . . . . 481 A MASQUE OF REASON . . 223
    THIS IS POLITE SOCIETY YOU'RE IN, ... 488 A MASQUE OF REASON . . 407
SOCKETS
    SMOKE ROLLED INSIDE THE SOCKETS OF HIS EYES.) . . . . 204 THE WITCH OF COOS . . 74
SOD
    ITS HEART SINKS LOWER UNDER THE SOD. . . . . 228 GOOD-BY AND KEEP COLD . 28
    AT ANCHOR SHE RIDES THE SUNNY SOD, ... 262 THE FLOWER BOAT . . .   5
SODA
    IT TOOK MY MIND OFF DOUGHNUTS AND SODA BISCUIT . . . . 63 A SERVANT TO SERVANTS . 26
SODDEN
    SHE WALKS THE SODDEN PASTURE LANE. . . . .   6 MY NOVEMBER GUEST . .   5
SO-FASHION
    I'LL KNOCK SO-FASHION AND PEEP ROUND THE DOOR . . . . 50 A HUNDRED COLLARS . . 173
SOFT
    WHEN THAT WAS, THE SOFT MIST . . . . 28 MY BUTTERFLY 18
    SOFT PETALS FALLEN FROM THE APPLE TREE . . . . . . 124 PUTTING IN THE SEED .   4
    (SOFT PETALS, YES, BUT NOT SO BARREN QUITE, ... 124 PUTTING IN THE SEED .   5
    AND FEEL IT LESS. HEAR THE SOFT BOMBS OF DUST . . . . 150 SNOW   206
    THE LIFE OF MUSCLES ROCKING SOFT . . . . 276 TWO TRAMPS IN MUD TIME 47
    THE SOIL NOW GETS A RUMPLING SOFT AND DAMP, ... 299 STRONG SAYING NOTHING .   1
    ADMITTEDLY AN ELOQUENCE SO SOFT . . . . 338 NEVER WOULD BIRDS' SONG   6
SOFTEN
    SO THE FIRM FIRMAMENT WON'T SOFTEN.   . . . . 453 A-WISHING WELL . . . 75
SOFTENING
    HE FELT SOME NEED OF SOFTENING THAT TO ME: . . . . . 107 CHRISTMAS TREES . . . 43
SOFTER
    HE SAID IT OVER, BUT HE SAID IT SOFTER. . . . . . . 71 THE CODE 67
    YOU AND I, DEAR, WILL GO WITH SOFTER STEPS . . . . . 111 IN THE HOME STRETCH . 41
    ANOTHER SOFTER GLOBE THAT SLIGHTLY FLATTENED   . . . . 322 BUILD SOIL   195
SOFTLY
    COMES SOFTLY RATTLING DOWN. . . . .   9 A LATE WALK 12
    ITS LIGHT POURED SOFTLY IN HER LAP. SHE SAW IT . . . . 38 DEATH OF THE HIRED MAN 105

SOFTLY (CONTINUED)
    I'LL CALL HER SOFTLY SO THAT IF SHE'S WISE . . . . . . 143 SNOW   13
    THAT SLIP FROM HEAVEN AT NIGHT AND SOFTLY FALL . . . . . 172 A STAR IN A STONEBOAT .   2
    AT MOST HE THINKS OR TWITTERS SOFTLY, "SAFE!   . . . . . 249 ACCEPTANCE   11
    AND WE STOOD IN IT SOFTLY CIRCLED ROUND . . . . 315 IRIS BY NIGHT   . . .   29
SOIL (SEE WIND-SOIL)
    WHEN, JUST AS THE SOIL TARNISHES WITH WEED, ... 124 PUTTING IN THE SEED   . 12
    EVER TO GRIND TO SOIL FOR GRASS. . . . . 140 THE GUM-GATHERER   . . 17
    THE VERY NATURE OF THE SOIL WAS HOT   . . . . 173 A STAR IN A STONEBOAT .   21
    IS CARRY SOME GARDEN SOIL . . . . 285 IN TIME OF CLOUDBURST .   3
    THE SOIL NOW GETS A RUMPLING SOFT AND DAMP, ... 299 STRONG SAYING NOTHING .   1
    BUILD SOIL . . . . 316 BUILD SOIL   . . . .   T
    MORE THAT SHOULD BE KEPT BACK--THE SOIL FOR INSTANCE, . . 321 BUILD SOIL   175
    WHO FALL ALL OVER EACH OTHER TO BRING SOIL . . . . . . 321 BUILD SOIL   177
    TO SELL THE HAY OFF, LET ALONE THE SOIL, ... 321 BUILD SOIL   179
    TO BUILD THE SOIL. FOR WHAT IS MORE ACCURSED   . . . . . 323 BUILD SOIL   217
    THAN AN IMPOVERISHED SOIL, PALE AND METALLIC? . . . . . 323 BUILD SOIL   218
    BUILD SOIL. TURN THE FARM IN UPON ITSELF . . . . 323 BUILD SOIL   234
    TILL THE SPONGY SOIL AGAIN WAS NATAL WET. . . . . 349 OUR HOLD ON THE PLANET 10
    ENRICHING SOIL AND INCREASING STOCK. . . . . 367 A SERIOUS STEP LIGHTLY 19
SOILED
    THE ONLY PERSON REALLY SOILED WITH TRADE . . . . 160 NEW HAMPSHIRE   . . . 35
SOJOURN
    THEN I WAS WRONG: THE TOWN OF MY SOJOURN, ... 41 THE MOUNTAIN   20
SOLAR
    FOR GATHERING SOLAR RAYS WOULD NOT HAVE HELPED. . . . . 293 AT WOODWARD'S GARDENS .   6
SOLD
    I WONDER IF HE'S SOLD HIS FARM, ... 138 BROWN'S DESCENT . . . 35
    IT WAS THE BAD AX-HELVE SOMEONE HAD SOLD ME-- . . . . . 186 THE AX-HELVE . . . 21
    WHEN I WAS SOLD--AND SMALL REPROACH TO HIM. . . . . . . 459 HOW HARD TO KEEP FROM 172
SOLDIER
    FIRST SOLDIER, AND THEN POET, AND THEN BOTH, ... 222 TO E.T.   7
    A SOLDIER . . . . 261 A SOLDIER . . . . .   T
SOLDIER-POET
    WHO DIED A SOLDIER-POET OF YOUR RACE. . . . . 222 TO E.T.   8
SOLE
    I SEE THE CALLUS ON HIS SOLE, ... 392 A CLIFF DWELLING . . 10
    ALL THOSE WHO TRY TO GO IT SOLE ALONE, ... 394 HAEC FABULA DOCET . . 18
SOLEMN
    THEIR SOLEMN PEALS . . . . 219 I WILL SING YOU ONE-O . 55
    AND LEAPING ON IT WITH A SOLEMN BOUND, ... 284 THE GOLD HESPERIDEE . 47
    APPEARS A SOLEMN MORTICIAN; . . . . 288 DEPARTMENTAL . . . 34
    REMEMBER, AND MUST KEEP A SOLEMN FACE.) . . . . 352 THE LESSON FOR TODAY . 67
SOLEMN-ABSURDLY
    AND THEY LOOKED SO SOLEMN-ABSURDLY CONCERNED." . . . . . 61 BLUEBERRIES 59
SOLID
    WHO MAKES THE SOLID TREE TRUNKS SOUND AGAIN. . . . . . 119 THE OVEN BIRD . . .   3
    THE SOLID MOLDING OF VAST PEAKS OF CLOUD. . . . . . . 169 NEW HAMPSHIRE   . . . 322
    OLD DAVIS OWNED A SOLID MICA MOUNTAIN . . . . 212 A FOUNTAIN, A BOTTLE .   1
    WHEN HEAVEN PRESENTS IN SHEETS THE SOLID HUE? . . . . . 220 FRAGMENTARY BLUE . .   4
    AND BURY IN SOLID SAND . . . . 260 SAND DUNES   7
    HE GAVE THE SOLID RAIL A HATEFUL KICK. . . . . 269 THE EGG AND THE MACHINE 1
    THE GROUND WAS ONE CIRCLE OF SOLID RED. . . . . 305 UNHARVESTED 10
SOLITARY
    QUITE SOLITARY AND HAVING EQUAL BOUGHS   . . . . 107 CHRISTMAS TREES . . . 35
    WITH A SOLITARY FRIEND, ... 384 IN THE LONG NIGHT . .   2
    BEL IS A SOLITARY SOCIAL DRINKER. . . . . 496 A MASQUE OF MERCY . . 86
SOLITUDE
    FOR CHANGE OF SOLITUDE. . . . . 333 HAPPINESS MAKES UP . . 24
SOLOMON
    AS SHEBA CAME TO SOLOMON. . . . . 390 TWO LEADING LIGHTS . . 21
SO-LONG-KEPT
    TILL THE SO-LONG-KEPT . . . . 437 KITTY HAWK 293
SOMBER
    SOMBER CLOUDS IN THE WEST WERE MASSED. . . . . 251 BEREFT   7
    ART AND RELIGION LOVE THE SOMBER CHORD. . . . . 353 THE LESSON FOR TODAY . 97
SOME
    I SHOULD NOT BE WITHHELD BUT THAT SOME DAY . . . . . . 5 INTO MY OWN   5
    THOSE STARS LIKE SOME SNOW-WHITE . . . . 9 STARS 10
    OF THOSE WHO FOR SOME GOOD DISCERNED . . . . 20 THE TRIAL BY EXISTENCE 27
    SOME SPIRIT TO STAND SIMPLY FORTH, ... 20 THE TRIAL BY EXISTENCE 42
    SOME RESTING FLOWER OF YESTERDAY'S DELIGHT. . . . . . . 22 THE TUFT OF FLOWERS . 14
    AS WHERE SOME FLOWER LAY WITHERING ON THE GROUND. . . . . 22 THE TUFT OF FLOWERS . 16
    HOWEVER IT IS IN SOME OTHER WORLD . . . . 26 IN HARDWOOD GROVES . . 11
    ALL SONG OF THE WOODS IS CRUSHED LIKE SOME . . . . . . 26 A LINE-STORM SONG . . 13
    AND SOME ARE LOAVES AND SOME SO NEARLY BALLS . . . . . 33 MENDING WALL . . . 17
    SOME HUMBLE WAY TO SAVE HIS SELF-RESPECT. . . . . . . 36 DEATH OF THE HIRED MAN 50
    YOU WOULDN'T THINK THEY WOULD. HOW SOME THINGS LINGER! . . 37 DEATH OF THE HIRED MAN 72
    SOME GOOD PERHAPS TO SOMEONE IN THE WORLD. . . . . . . 37 DEATH OF THE HIRED MAN 97
    AS IF SHE PLAYED UNHEARD SOME TENDERNESS . . . . . . 38 DEATH OF THE HIRED MAN 109
    BUT HAVE SOME PITY ON SILAS. DO YOU THINK . . . . . . 39 DEATH OF THE HIRED MAN 135
    NOT FOR THIS MORNING, BUT SOME OTHER TIME: . . . . . . 41 THE MOUNTAIN 36
    THEY LOGGED IT THERE LAST WINTER SOME WAY UP. . . . . . 41 THE MOUNTAIN 42
    TO HAVE SOME HEAD OF WATER FROM ABOVE, ... 43 THE MOUNTAIN 70
    THE FAMILY'S ALL AWAY IN SOME BACK MEADOW. . . . . . . 49 A HUNDRED COLLARS . . 131
    AS IF SHE HAD SOME SORT OF CURVATURE. . . . . 49 A HUNDRED COLLARS . . 143
    LIE DOWN--LET YOURSELF GO AND GET SOME SLEEP. . . . . . 50 A HUNDRED COLLARS . . 161
    I'VE JUST BEGUN THE NIGHT. YOU GET SOME SLEEP. . . . . . 50 A HUNDRED COLLARS . . 172
    THERE NOW, YOU GET SOME SLEEP." / HE SHUT THE DOOR. . . . 50 A HUNDRED COLLARS . . 178
    LOOKING BACK OVER HER SHOULDER AT SOME FEAR. . . . . . 51 HOME BURIAL   3
    WITH WOMENFOLK. WE COULD HAVE SOME ARRANGEMENT . . . . . 52 HOME BURIAL 50
    SHE HAD AT SOME COST TAUGHT THEM AFTER YEARS.) . . . . . 56 THE BLACK COTTAGE . . 42
    SHE HAD SOME ART OF HEARING AND YET NOT . . . . 57 THE BLACK COTTAGE . . 73
    AND ALL RIPE TOGETHER, NOT SOME OF THEM GREEN . . . . . 59 BLUEBERRIES   6
    AND SOME OF THEM RIPE! YOU OUGHT TO HAVE SEEN!" . . . . . 59 BLUEBERRIES   7
    "HE'S A THRIFTIER PERSON THAN SOME I COULD NAME." . . . . 60 BLUEBERRIES 47
    SOME STRANGE KIND--THEY TOLD ME IT HADN'T A NAME." . . . . 61 BLUEBERRIES 66
    THERE HAD BEEN SOME BERRIES--BUT THOSE WERE ALL GONE. . . 61 BLUEBERRIES 73

SOME (CONTINUED)

	PAGE TITLE	LINE
I PROMISED MYSELF TO GET DOWN SOME DAY	62 A SERVANT TO SERVANTS	3
LIKE A DEEP PIECE OF SOME OLD RUNNING RIVER	63 A SERVANT TO SERVANTS	20
WE DIDN'T CHANGE WITHOUT SOME SACRIFICE,	64 A SERVANT TO SERVANTS	64
SOME THOUGHT HE HAD BEEN BITTEN BY A DOG,	65 A SERVANT TO SERVANTS	105
OR SO THE STORY GOES. IT WAS SOME GIRL.	66 A SERVANT TO SERVANTS	109
MORE THAN YOU HAVE YOURSELF, SOME OF THESE NIGHTS.	67 A SERVANT TO SERVANTS	167
APPLES I DIDN'T PICK UPON SOME BOUGH.	68 AFTER APPLE-PICKING	5
OR JUST SOME HUMAN SLEEP.	69 AFTER APPLE-PICKING	42
THE PAST AND GET SOME STRANGENESS OUT OF IT.	73 THE GENERATIONS OF MEN	18
THE YOUNG FOLK HELD SOME HOPE OUT TO EACH OTHER	74 THE GENERATIONS OF MEN	21
WAS A GIRL; AND SHE HALTED SOME WAY OFF	74 THE GENERATIONS OF MEN	30
AND PERHAPS HEAR SOME WORD ABOUT THE WEATHER.	74 THE GENERATIONS OF MEN	33
THIS WAS SOME STARK SHE DIDN'T KNOW. HE NODDED.	74 THE GENERATIONS OF MEN	34
SOME ZEALOUS ONE'S LABORIOUS DEVICE.	74 THE GENERATIONS OF MEN	42
ALL CLAIMING SOME PRIORITY IN STARKNESS.	75 THE GENERATIONS OF MEN	49
"IS THIS SOME TRANCE YOU ARE WITHDRAWING INTO?"	78 THE GENERATIONS OF MEN	148
AND THOSE WILL BEAR SOME KEEPING STILL ABOUT."	80 THE GENERATIONS OF MEN	198
WHO ARE THEY FOR?" / "YOU MEAN?--OH, FOR SOME MISS.	81 THE HOUSEKEEPER	10
HE GETS SOME SORT OF BAKESHOP MEALS TOGETHER,	82 THE HOUSEKEEPER	31
LIKE SOME MENFOLK. NO ONE'S AFRAID OF HIM;	83 THE HOUSEKEEPER	69
HE'S FOND OF NICE THINGS--TOO FOND, SOME WOULD SAY.	85 THE HOUSEKEEPER	116
I SUPPOSE SHE DESERVES SOME PITY, TOO.	88 THE HOUSEKEEPER	192
I'VE GOT SOME NEWS THAT MAYBE ISN'T NEWS.	88 THE HOUSEKEEPER	210
"THEY SAY SOME TIME WAS WASTED ON THE BELT--	94 THE SELF-SEEKER	32
THAT MUST BE IT. SOME DAYS HE WON'T STAY ON.	94 THE SELF-SEEKER	36
"I WANTED THERE SHOULD BE SOME THERE NEXT YEAR."	97 THE SELF-SEEKER	123
NOTHING IS HIDDEN FROM SOME PEOPLE, ANNE.	97 THE SELF-SEEKER	135
AS IF WITH SOME IDEA THAT SHE HAD SCORED.	98 THE SELF-SEEKER	146
"WHO'S WE?--SOME STOCKHOLDERS IN BOSTON?	100 THE SELF-SEEKER	221
PASTURE THEY SPRING IN, SOME IN CLUMPS TOO CLOSE	107 CHRISTMAS TREES	33
OR PAUSED TO SAY BENEATH SOME LOVELIER ONE,	107 CHRISTMAS TREES	37
HE FELT SOME NEED OF SOFTENING THAT TO ME:	107 CHRISTMAS TREES	43
YOU WERE FOREVER FINDING SOME NEW PLAY.	109 THE EXPOSED NEST	1
MORE THAN SOME WOMEN LIKE THE DISHPAN, JOE;	111 IN THE HOME STRETCH	31
THE BACK SOME FARM PRESENTS US; AND YOUR WOODS	114 IN THE HOME STRETCH	114
SOME MATCHES HE UNPOCKETED. "FOR FOOD--	115 IN THE HOME STRETCH	138
YET SOME SAY LOVE BY BEING THRALL	120 BOND AND FREE	17
I LIKE TO THINK SOME BOY'S BEEN SWINGING THEM.	121 BIRCHES	3
I SHOULD PREFER TO HAVE SOME BOY BEND THEM	121 BIRCHES	23
SOME BOY TOO FAR FROM TOWN TO LEARN BASEBALL,	121 BIRCHES	25
A WIND TO BLOW IN EARNEST FROM SOME QUARTER,	130 THE BONFIRE	33
AND GIVE YOU A CHANCE TO PUT SOME STRENGTH	133 A GIRL'S GARDEN	15
SOME FLOWER I PLAYED WITH AS I SAT	135 LOCKED OUT	12
AND SOME EXCLAIMED WHO SAW AFAR	138 BROWN'S DESCENT	30
SOME GUTTURAL EXCLAMATION OF SURPRISE	142 THE VANISHING RED	14
DRESSED, BUT DISHEVELED FROM SOME HOURS OF SLEEP;	143 SNOW	4
HE LINGERED FOR SOME WORD SHE WOULDN'T SAY,	143 SNOW	28
SOME OF THE SANCTIMONIOUS CONCEIT	146 SNOW	91
"FINE, FINE." / "AND READY FOR SOME MORE? MY WIFE HERE	147 SNOW	106
SOME PALLID THING HAD SQUASHED ITS FEATURES FLAT	148 SNOW	160
GET INTO BED I SAY, AND GET SOME REST.	152 SNOW	265
SOME DAY WHEN THEY ARE IN VOICE.	156 THE SOUND OF TREES	21
IN WOODS SOME TEN MILES FROM A RAILROAD STATION,	160 NEW HAMPSHIRE	41
I THINK HE OWNED SOME SHARES IN HARVARD COLLEGE.)	163 NEW HAMPSHIRE	137
OR ANY MOUNTAINS? CAN IT BE SOME STRENGTH	169 NEW HAMPSHIRE	317
OR SOME SUCH SENSE AS SAYS HOW HIGH SHALL JET	169 NEW HAMPSHIRE	325
SOME LABORER FOUND ONE FADED AND STONE-COLD,	172 A STAR IN A STONEBOAT	4
SOME MAY KNOW WHAT THEY SEEK IN SCHOOL AND CHURCH,	173 A STAR IN A STONEBOAT	43
WHERE I CAME LAST WITH SOME HOPE, BUT NOT MUCH,	174 THE CENSUS-TAKER	12
SOME SYMPATHY WAS WASTED ON THE HOUSE,	178 THE STAR-SPLITTER	59
SAID SOME OF THE BEST THINGS WE EVER SAID.	179 THE STAR-SPLITTER	86
AND OUGHT TO DO SOME GOOD IF SPLITTING STARS	179 THE STAR-SPLITTER	93
BUT IT SEEMS LIKE SOME WORD SHE LEFT TO BID YOU	180 MAPLE	21
IF SHE COULD FORM SOME NOTION OF HER MOTHER--	181 MAPLE	54
AND THINK A LITTLE, AND GET SOME CITY SCHOOLING.	182 MAPLE	74
TO SEE IF THERE WAS NOT SOME SPECIAL TREE	183 MAPLE	100
NAME CHILDREN SOME NAMES AND SEE WHAT YOU DO.	185 MAPLE	170
AND SOME OF IT ON NO MORE LEGS AND WHEEL	189 THE GRINDSTONE	12
SOME SAID IT WAS BECAUSE HE HAD NO WIFE,	191 PAUL'S WIFE	4
BEFORE THEY HEARD OF HIM IN SOME NEW CAMP,	192 PAUL'S WIFE	29
INSTEAD OF WHICH SHE WAS SOME HALF-BREED SQUAW.	192 PAUL'S WIFE	39
IT LOOKED TO HIM LIKE SOME NEW KIND OF HOLLOW	193 PAUL'S WIFE	86
NEXT EVENING MURPHY AND SOME OTHER FELLOWS	195 PAUL'S WIFE	123
WHICH GAVE HIM SOME TIME TO HIMSELF TO EAT,	197 WILD GRAPES	34
I KNOW OF SOME FOLKS THAT'D BE SET UP	208 PAUPER WITCH OF GRAFTON	36
IF I WAS TO CONSENT TO GIVE SOME SIGN	208 PAUPER WITCH OF GRAFTON	43
SOME CRIED SHAME ON ME NOT TO BLANKET HIM,	209 PAUPER WITCH OF GRAFTON	52
IT'S NOT MEN BY SOME MISTAKE?	211 AN EMPTY THREAT	21
THERE'D BEEN SOME BOSTON PEOPLE OUT TO SEE IT:	212 A FOUNTAIN, A BOTTLE	3
A FOUNTAIN, A BOTTLE, A DONKEY'S EARS, AND SOME BOOKS	212 A FOUNTAIN, A BOTTLE	T
NO DOUBT IT'S GROWN UP SOME TO WOODS AROUND IT.	213 A FOUNTAIN, A BOTTLE	21
THEY HAD BEEN BROUGHT HOME FROM SOME PUBLISHER	216 A FOUNTAIN, A BOTTLE	100
OR ELSE BY SOME REMOTENESS THAT DEFIED THEM	216 A FOUNTAIN, A BOTTLE	107
THOUGH SOME SAVANTS MAKE EARTH INCLUDE THE SKY;	220 FRAGMENTARY BLUE	6
SOME SAY THE WORLD WILL END IN FIRE,	220 FIRE AND ICE	1
SOME SAY IN ICE.	220 FIRE AND ICE	2
AND SAVED SOME PART	221 DUST OF SNOW	7
THROUGH SOME DELAY, AND CALL YOU TO YOUR FACE	222 TO E.T.	6
TO ASK IF THERE IS SOME MISTAKE.	224 STOPPING BY WOODS	10
LIKE SOME UP-ENDED BOULDER SPLIT IN TWO,	229 TWO LOOK AT TWO	19
AS IF TO ASK, "WHY DON'T YOU MAKE SOME MOTION?	230 TWO LOOK AT TWO	32
OR GIVE SOME SIGN OF LIFE? BECAUSE YOU CAN'T.	230 TWO LOOK AT TWO	33
IT LOOKS AS IF SOME MAGIC OF THE SUN	237 A HILLSIDE THAW	6
SOME TO GO FURTHER NORTH TO HUDSON'S BAY,	239 OUR SINGING STRENGTH	22
SOME THAT HAVE COME TOO FAR NORTH BACK AWAY,	239 OUR SINGING STRENGTH	23
AS IN SOME TOO MUCH CARVEN MARBLE HALL	240 OUR SINGING STRENGTH	42
BY WALKING SLOWLY ON SOME EVENING LATER	245 THE FREEDOM OF THE MOON	8

SOME (CONTINUED)

	PAGE	TITLE	LINE
SOME OF THE BLOWING DUST WAS GOLD.	249	A PECK OF GOLD	4
SOME OF THE DUST WAS REALLY GOLD.	249	A PECK OF GOLD	8
HURRYING LOW ABOVE THE GROVE, SOME WAIF	249	ACCEPTANCE	9
SOME STILL WERE LIVING IN HERMITAGE.	253	THE THATCH	16
ON SOME WILD APPLE-TREE'S YOUNG TENDER BARK,	254	A WINTER EDEN	11
IT BREAKS AWAY IN SOME NEW KIND OF SLAUGHTER.	254	THE FLOOD	4
THEN SEND SOME ONE WITH EYES TO SEE	257	THE LOVELY BE CHOOSERS	46
SOME SAY EXISTENCE LIKE A PIROUOT	259	WEST-RUNNING BROOK	45
SAVE BY SOME STRANGE RESISTANCE IN ITSELF,	259	WEST-RUNNING BROOK	58
WAS IT SOME MONEY SUDDENLY COME INTO?	264	THE INVESTMENT	10
OR SOME EXTRAVAGANCE YOUNG LOVE HAD BEEN TO?	264	THE INVESTMENT	11
BUT GET SOME COLOR AND MUSIC OUT OF LIFE?	264	THE INVESTMENT	14
IF, AS THEY SAY, SOME DUST THROWN IN MY EYES	265	DUST IN THE EYES	1
I LOSE SOME OTHER OFF MY ARMS AND KNEES,	266	THE ARMFUL	2
AND BENT SOME RAIL WIDE OPEN LIKE A SWITCH,	270	THE EGG AND THE MACHINE	7
TO SEE IF SOME FORLORN MACHINE	273	A LONE STRIKER	14
WE ALLOW SOME TIME FOR GUILE	282	A DRUMLIN WOODCHUCK	17
IS CARRY SOME GARDEN SOIL	285	IN TIME OF CLOUDBURST	3
SOME FORCE HAS BUT TO APPLY,	285	IN TIME OF CLOUDBURST	13
SOME WORN OLD TOOL OF MY OWN	285	IN TIME OF CLOUDBURST	21
BUT FOR SOME OF THE MONEY, THE CASH, WHOSE FLOW SUPPORTS	286	A ROADSIDE STAND	5
AND ASK FOR SOME CITY MONEY TO FEEL IN HAND	286	A ROADSIDE STAND	19
SOME GIANT TREES HAVE BLOOM SO SMALL	297	LEAVES COMPARED WITH	9
SOME THINGS ARE NEVER CLEAR.	301	VOICE WAYS	1
THEN TAKE SOME LEFTOVER WINTER	304	CLEAR AND COLDER	10
DASH IT WITH SOME SNOW FOR POWDER.	304	CLEAR AND COLDER	15
WE MUST WAIT TILL SOME MONTHS HENCE IN THE SPRING TO KNOW.	305	THERE ARE ROUGHLY ZONES	19
SOME OF YOU WILL BE GLAD I DID WHAT I DID,	306	NOT QUITE SOCIAL	1
SOME HAVE RELIED ON WHAT THEY KNEW,	307	PROVIDE, PROVIDE	13
SOME SAID IT HAD GONE TO THE COAST,	312	THE VINDICTIVES	69
SOME OVER THE MOUNTAINS EAST,	312	THE VINDICTIVES	70
SOME INTO THE COUNTRY NORTH,	312	THE VINDICTIVES	71
NO MATTER WHAT SOME MAY SAY.	312	THE VINDICTIVES	76
BUT HAVE SOME PITY ON US WHO HAVE TO WORK.	316	BUILD SOIL	21
EVEN WHILE WE TALK SOME CHEMIST AT COLUMBIA	319	BUILD SOIL	107
IT MUST AT SOME POINT GRACEFULLY REFRAIN.	319	BUILD SOIL	116
SOME MINDS ARE SO CONFOUNDED INTERMENTAL	321	BUILD SOIL	151
"LOOK AT WHAT HAPPENED. SURELY SOME GOD PINXIT.	321	BUILD SOIL	153
(I DO TOO MUCH IN SOME MEN'S EYES.)	327	A MISSIVE MISSILE	37
FROM SOME TREE-HIDDEN CLIFF ACROSS THE LAKE.	338	THE MOST OF IT	4
SOME MORNING FROM THE BOULDER-BROKEN BEACH	338	THE MOST OF IT	5
LIKE SOME TENACIOUS BIT	341	THE SUBVERTED FLOWER	67
AND SAIL FOR SOME VAGUE PAPHIAN BOURN	344	DISCOVERY OF MADEIRAS	17
SOME TOM SAID TO DICK OR HARRY:	345	DISCOVERY OF MADEIRAS	68
SOME STANDING JEST BETWEEN YOU MEN?	346	DISCOVERY OF MADEIRAS	94
AND FOLLOW SOME DEVELOPMENT OF STATE,	355	THE LESSON FOR TODAY	142
SOME TURN IN SHEER, IN SHELLEYAN DEJECTION	358	THE LOST FOLLOWER	11
LONG SINCE IN SOME ABYSMAL CITY STREET,	359	THE LOST FOLLOWER	22
AND SOME SAY THERE ARE SIGNS	361	ALMOST TWO THOUSAND	4
ABOVE SOME MORE RELIGION IN A MANGER.	369	THE LITERATE FARMER AND	35
SOME IGNORANCE TAKES RANK AS INNOCENCE.	371	THE LITERATE FARMER AND	88
HE GAVE UP SLEEP HIMSELF SOME TIME AGO,	371	THE LITERATE FARMER AND	104
AND LEAVING SOME THINGS TO TAKE THEIR COURSE.	376	SOMETHING FOR HOPE	22
SOME SHATTERED DISHES UNDERNEATH A PINE,	378	DIRECTIVE	42
KEPT SOME DEW OUT AND SOME HEAT IN,	380	AN UNSTAMPED LETTER IN	15
SUPPOSE SOME SEED-PEARL SUN	384	MAKING CERTAIN ANYTHING	5
SOME CLUSTER ONE STAR SHORT.	384	MAKING CERTAIN ANYTHING	8
BUT BECOMING AWARE OF SOME BOYS FROM SCHOOL	385	A MOOD APART	4
SOME GAS LIKE HELIUM MUST BE INNATE.	387	INNATE HELIUM	6
SOME LUNATIC OR LUNAR WHIM	390	TWO LEADING LIGHTS	18
SOME RUMOR OF HIS WISHING RING	390	TWO LEADING LIGHTS	24
LIKE THE IDEAL OF SOME MISTAKEN LOVER.	391	ON BEING IDOLIZED	6
SOME HALFWAY UP THE LIMESTONE WALL,	392	A CLIFF DWELLING	1
WHAT OF IT, THOUGH? I GOT SOME WILLY-NILLY	393	LUCRETIUS VERSUS POETS	2
TO SOME STAR OFF THERE, SAY, A HALF LIGHT-YEAR	395	WHY WAIT FOR SCIENCE	7
ALBEIT NOT WITHOUT SOME SHAME OF FACE,	396	ANY SIZE WE PLEASE	4
TO SOME OBSCURITY OF CLOUD--	403	SOMETHING LIKE A STAR	3
SOME MYSTERY BECOMES THE PROUD.	403	SOMETHING LIKE A STAR	6
TO CURRY FAVOR WITH THE DIRT SOME MORE.	405	FROM PLANE TO PLANE	43
HE MAY BE SOME GOOD, IN A MANNER OF SPEAKING.	407	FROM PLANE TO PLANE	103
OR SUME DIM SECRET OF THE GOOD OF WASTE?	412	POD OF THE MILKWEED	49
AND ONLY SOME SLIGHT BEAST	416	CLOSED FOR GOOD	28
OR AT MOST SOME ANDEAN QUAKE,	418	AMERICA IS HARD TO SEE	71
(WITH SOME PRELIMINARY HISTORY IN RHYME)	422	FOR JOHN F. KENNEDY	5
THEY ARE OUR WARDS WE THINK TO SOME EXTENT	423	FOR JOHN F. KENNEDY	36
SOME POOR FOOL HAS BEEN SAYING IN HIS HEART	423	FOR JOHN F. KENNEDY	49
SOME OF THEM MIGHTY HUGE, SOME MIGHTY TINY,	425	ACCIDENTALLY ON PURPOSE	3
FOR SOME KIND OF FLIGHT	430	KITTY HAWK	55
AND SOME OTHER FOLLY.	431	KITTY HAWK	94
SOME KIND OF COMMITTEE	431	KITTY HAWK	101
SOME HAVE PREACHED AND TAUGHT	438	KITTY HAWK	321
BY SOME NOMENCLATURE.	438	KITTY HAWK	324
IT'S SOME KIND OF TOWN,	439	KITTY HAWK	343
OF AT LEAST SOME PART	441	KITTY HAWK	424
TILL ON SOME FINE NIGHT	442	KITTY HAWK	454
SOME STILL THINK IS SATAN,	443	KITTY HAWK	464
OH, SOME AS SOON WOULD THROW IT ALL	445	ENDS	9
AND SOME WILL SAY ALL SORTS OF THINGS,	445	ENDS	11
BUT SOME MEAN WHAT THEY SAY.	445	ENDS	12
SOME MISTAKE HAD BEEN MADE	449	THE BAD ISLAND--EASTER	49
SOME CHANGE IN THE LAW	449	THE BAD ISLAND--EASTER	51
SOME QUAINT DISSATISFACTION ATE HIM.	451	A-WISHING WELL	7
SOME PLANETS, THE UNBLINKING FOUR,	451	A-WISHING WELL	23
FROM SOME EXTINCT OLD CHIMNEY POT.	452	A-WISHING WELL	36
SOME OF THEM GAVE WAY AT THE WRIST.	452	A-WISHING WELL	56
"YOU'RE RIGHT," THE EX-KING SAID, "WE'LL NEED SOME MONEY.	454	HOW HARD TO KEEP FROM	30
TO THE SLAVE AUCTION IN SOME MARKETPLACE	454	HOW HARD TO KEEP FROM	32

	PAGE	TITLE	LINE

SOME (CONTINUED)

TELL ME SOME RULE FOR RULING PEOPLE WISELY, ... 458 HOW HARD TO KEEP FROM 147
IN CASE I SHOULD DECIDE TO REIGN SOME MORE. . . . . . . 458 HOW HARD TO KEEP FROM 148
FREEDOM IS SLAVERY SOME POETS TELL US. . . . . 460 HOW HARD TO KEEP FROM 190
TO WHERE AS SOME ALLEGE . . . . 465 MILKY WAY IS A COWPATH 34
AND SOME OF THEM MAY MIND . . . . 465 SOME SCIENCE FICTION . 5
SOME SCIENCE FICTION . . . . 465 SOME SCIENCE FICTION . T
WITH SOME OPTIMISM FOR CHRISTMAS . . . . 466 SOME SCIENCE FICTION . 34
IN SOME WAY NOT SO PENAL AS THE POORHOUSE. . . . . . 478 A MASQUE OF REASON . 125
I NEED SOME HELP ABOUT THIS REASON PROBLEM . . . . . 479 A MASQUE OF REASON . 165
HAVE SOME SAY AS TO WHERE WE'RE HEADED FOR; . . . . . 482 A MASQUE OF REASON . 235
THE REASON MIGHT HAVE BEEN SOME OTHER PERSON'S. . . . . 482 A MASQUE OF REASON . 264
OF SOME KIND. WE COULD HAVE CHARADES. . . . . . . 489 A MASQUE OF REASON . 430
WILL BE SOME SOULLESS LUNATIC ASYLUM-- . . . . . 500 A MASQUE OF MERCY . 187
SHE'S HAD SOME LOSS SHE CAN'T ACCEPT FROM GOD-- . . . 501 A MASQUE OF MERCY . 204
IS THAT IT? SOME UTOPIAN BELIEF-- . . . . . 501 A MASQUE OF MERCY . 205
LET'S HAVE SOME PROPHECY. WHAT FORM OF RUIN . . . . 502 A MASQUE OF MERCY . 222
(A WHOLE SHELF CASCADES DOWN.) HERE COME SOME MORE. . . . 506 A MASQUE OF MERCY . 341
MERCY, FOR MERCY'S SAKE! / BEL WANTS SOME MERCY.-- . . . 507 A MASQUE OF MERCY . 345
THERE'S SOME SUCH THING AND NO ONE WILL DENY IT-- . . . 508 A MASQUE OF MERCY . 385
TO SOME OF KEEPER'S FRIENDS THAT COME IN HERE, ... 509 A MASQUE OF MERCY . 405
THERE IS SOME JUSTICE, EVEN AS KEEPER SAYS. . . . . 509 A MASQUE OF MERCY . 429
SOME PEOPLE WANT YOU NOT TO UNDERSTAND THEM, ... 510 A MASQUE OF MERCY . 452
SOME LINGERING OBJECTION HOLDS YOU BACK. . . . . . 517 A MASQUE OF MERCY . 632
I SAY WE KEEP HIM TILL WE WRING SOME MORE . . . . 517 A MASQUE OF MERCY . 639
BUT BEL GETS SOME THINGS RIGHT--AND SHE WAS RIGHT-- . . 519 A MASQUE OF MERCY . 690

SOMEBODY

A SOMEBODY--DIRECTOR IN THE BANK." . . . . 39 DEATH OF THE HIRED MAN 129

SOMEBODY'S

IT HAD TO BE AT SOMEBODY'S EXPENSE. . . . . 481 A MASQUE OF REASON . 222

SOMEDAY

IN DALTON THAT WOULD SOMEDAY MAKE HIS FORTUNE. . . . 212 A FOUNTAIN, A BOTTLE . 2
WELL, TAKE ME THERE." / "SOMEDAY I WILL." / "TODAY." . . 213 A FOUNTAIN, A BOTTLE . 14
"IT ISN'T JUST THE SAME, AND SOMEDAY, SCHOOLBOY,' . . . 406 FROM PLANE TO PLANE . 85
SOMEDAY OUR NAVY, I PREDICT, ... 418 AMERICA IS HARD TO SEE 55
SOMEDAY TO A PAGEANT . . . . 434 KITTY HAWK . . . 190
WHICH SOMEDAY SHOULD BE . . . . 436 KITTY HAWK . . . 274
SOMEDAY I MUST GO INTO THAT. . . . . 453 A-WISHING WELL . . . 78
"BUT YES," SHE SAID, "SOMEDAY I'LL TELL YOU, DEAR. . . 457 HOW HARD TO KEEP FROM 106
TO THANK YOU SOMEDAY FOR THE WAY YOU HELPED ME . . . 475 A MASQUE OF REASON . 48
PERHAPS THAT EARTH IS GOING TO CRACK SOMEDAY . . . 484 A MASQUE OF REASON . 305
WE'RE TOO WELL OFF. / SOMEDAY WE THREE SHOULD HAVE . . 486 A MASQUE OF REASON . 379

SOMEHOW

NOTHING BUT WHAT WE SOMEHOW CHOSE; . . . . . . 21 THE TRIAL BY EXISTENCE 69
SOMETHING YOU SOMEHOW HAVEN'T TO DESERVE." . . . . 38 DEATH OF THE HIRED MAN 120
AND SEES OLD FRIENDS HE SOMEHOW CAN'T GET NEAR. . . . 44 A HUNDRED COLLARS . 7
HER GIVING SOMEHOW TOUCHED THE PRINCIPLE . . . . 57 THE BLACK COTTAGE . 60
SOMEHOW THE CHANGE WORE OUT LIKE A PRESCRIPTION. . . . 67 A SERVANT TO SERVANTS 154
SOMEHOW I'LL MAKE IT RIGHT WITH HER--SHE'LL SEE. . . . 98 THE SELF-SEEKER . . 150
SOMEHOW MADE HER IMPATIENT WITH THE MAN. . . . . 199 PLACE FOR A THIRD . 8
SOMEHOW MUST HAVE GOTTEN ABROAD, ... 251 BEREFT 14

SOMEONE

TILL SOMEONE REALLY FIND US OUT. . . . . . . 19 REVELATION . . . 4
SOMEONE TO SALT THE HALF-WILD STEER, ... 24 PAN WITH US . . . 13
'SOMEONE ELSE CAN.' 'THEN SOMEONE ELSE WILL HAVE TO.' . 35 DEATH OF THE HIRED MAN 24
WHEN HE BEGINS LIKE THAT, THERE'S SOMEONE AT HIM . . . 35 DEATH OF THE HIRED MAN 27
SOME GOOD PERHAPS TO SOMEONE IN THE WORLD. . . . 37 DEATH OF THE HIRED MAN 97
SHARING A ROOM WITH SOMEONE ELSE." / "WHO IS IT?" . . 45 A HUNDRED COLLARS . 24
"AMY! DON'T GO TO SOMEONE ELSE THIS TIME. . . . . 52 HOME BURIAL . . . 39
DON'T CARRY IT TO SOMEONE ELSE THIS TIME. . . . . 53 HOME BURIAL . . . 57
AMY! THERE'S SOMEONE COMING DOWN THE ROAD!" . . . 54 HOME BURIAL . . . 111
THEY SOON SAW HE WOULD DO SOMEONE A MISCHIEF . . . 66 A SERVANT TO SERVANTS 111
BUT WHAT HE LIKED WAS SOMEONE TO ENCOURAGE. . . . 71 THE CODE 43
OUT OF THE BARN.' SOMEONE LOOKED IN A WINDOW, . . . 72 THE CODE 95
SOMEONE HAD LITERALLY RUN TO EARTH . . . . . 73 THE GENERATIONS OF MEN 7
"I MEAN SHE'S MARRIED--MARRIED SOMEONE ELSE." . . . 87 THE HOUSEKEEPER . . 180
JOHN'S ALMOST HERE. I'VE HAD MY EYE ON SOMEONE . . . 88 THE HOUSEKEEPER . . 196
SEEMED TO WARN SOMEONE TO BE GETTING OUT . . . . 89 THE FEAR 20
WHAT IF I'M RIGHT, AND SOMEONE ALL THE TIME-- . . . 90 THE FEAR 22
DON'T HOLD MY ARM!" / "I SAY IT'S SOMEONE PASSING." . . 90 THE FEAR 23
"IT IS--OR SOMEONE ELSE HE'S SENT TO WATCH. . . . 90 THE FEAR 42
SOMEONE WHO LIVED IN TURNING TO FRESH TASKS . . . 102 THE WOOD-PILE . . . 35
SOMEONE SAID 'COME'--I HEARD IT AS I BOWED." . . . 118 THE TELEPHONE . . 17
TIME SOMEONE CAME WITH CART AND PAIR . . . . 123 PEA BRUSH 15
SOMETHING OR SOMEONE WATCHING MADE THAT GUST. . . . 130 THE BONFIRE . . . 44
THEY LOOKED ABOUT FOR SOMEONE TO HAVE DONE IT. . . . 132 THE BONFIRE . . . 89
WAS SOMEONE WHO HAD JUST COME BACK ASHAMED . . . 160 NEW HAMPSHIRE . . . 37
AND GIVE SOMEONE THE SKIPPER IRESON'S RIDE. . . . 163 NEW HAMPSHIRE . . . 143
A TELESCOPE. SOMEONE IN EVERY TOWN . . . . 177 THE STAR-SPLITTER . 35
SOMEONE WAS SAYING IN SUCH NATURAL TONES . . . 182 MAPLE 85
IT WAS THE BAD AX-HELVE SOMEONE HAD SOLD ME-- . . . 186 THE AX-HELVE . . . 21
WAS I DESIRED IN FRIENDSHIP, PARTLY AS SOMEONE . . . 188 THE AX-HELVE . . . 90
AND SOMEONE MOUNTED ON IT RODE IT HARD, ... 189 THE GRINDSTONE . . 24
WHO'D RUN AWAY WITH SOMEONE ELSE AND LEFT HIM; . . . 191 PAUL'S WIFE . . . 9
STRUCK THE HARD CELLAR BOTTOM. AND THEN SOMEONE . . 204 THE WITCH OF COOS . . 50
WHEN I CAN HURT SOMEONE BY DOING IT . . . . 208 PAUPER WITCH OF GRAFTON 34
IF SOMEONE HADN'T SAID TO GNAW THE POSTS . . . 209 PAUPER WITCH OF GRAFTON 54
THEN THAT SAME SMARTY SOMEONE SAID TO LOOK-- . . . 209 PAUPER WITCH OF GRAFTON 59
THE SMARTY SOMEONE WHO SPOILED EVERYTHING . . . 209 PAUPER WITCH OF GRAFTON 70
BUT SMITH, OR SOMEONE, CALLED THEM OFF THE MOUNTAIN . . 213 A FOUNTAIN, A BOTTLE . 11
THEY SIMPLY LAY WHERE SOMEONE NOW AND THEN, . . . 217 A FOUNTAIN, A BOTTLE . 118
SOMEONE HAD BETTER BE PREPARED FOR RAGE. . . . 250 ONCE BY THE PACIFIC . 12
WOULD SOMEONE ONLY ACT IN TIME WE YET . . . . 290 OLD BARN AT THE BOTTOM 35
THEY CAN LEAVE IT TO SOMEONE ELSE TO TEND. . . . 291 ON HEART'S BEGINNING TO 18
SUPPOSE SOMEONE COMES NEAR ME WHO IN RATE . . . 324 BUILD SOIL . . . 249
SOMEONE IN ANCIENT MAS D'AZIL . . . . . 326 A MISSIVE MISSILE . 1
AND WANTED SOMEONE NOW TO KNOW . . . . . 327 A MISSIVE MISSILE . 17

SOMEONE (CONTINUED)
  AND SOMEONE ELSE ADDITIONAL TO HIM, ... 338 THE MOST OF IT 15
  LIKE SOMEONE DEAD PERMITTED TO EXIST . . . . 368 THE LITERATE FARMER AND 17
  AND SOMEONE REMINISCENT WILL RECALL . . . . 375 A YOUNG BIRCH . . . 11
  THAT SOMEONE HAS SAID IS THE END OF THE WORLD. . . . 379 TOO ANXIOUS FOR RIVERS . 2
  IT WASN'T SOMEONE AT YOUR LOCKS. . . . . 380 AN UNSTAMPED LETTER IN . 3
  AS MEETING SOMEONE LIVING, FACE TO FACE. . . . . . 382 TO AN ANCIENT . . . 9
  FROM BEING NO ONE UP TO BEING SOMEONE, ... 385 THE FEAR OF GOD . . . 2
  WHERE SOMEONE USED TO CLIMB AND CRAWL . . . . . 392 A CLIFF DWELLING . . . 8
  BUT SOMEONE OVERANXIOUS AT HIS PERIL . . . . . 394 HAEC FABULA DOCET . . 8
  WAS STILL IN SIGHT LIKE SOMEONE TO DEPEND ON. . . . 404 FROM PLANE TO PLANE . . 20
  SOMEONE SAYS THE LORD . . . . 438 KITTY HAWK 333
  LANDS ON SOMEONE HARD . . . . 441 KITTY HAWK 406
  OR SOMEONE HE HAD TO OBEY . . . . 444 THE DRAFT HORSE . . . 18
  WHERE SOMEONE SOMEONE ELSE BEGAT . . . . . . 453 A-WISHING WELL . . . 80
  MIGHT HAVE DETERIORATED HAD NOT SOMEONE . . . . 456 HOW HARD TO KEEP FROM . 78
  NOW SOMEONE CAN LIGHT UP THE BURNING BUSH . . . 490 A MASQUE OF REASON . . 458
  PLEASE, SOMEONE UNDERSTAND. / I UNDERSTAND. . . . 497 A MASQUE OF MERCY . . 110
  THAT SOMEONE IN THE CREW CONNECTS WITH ME. . . . 500 A MASQUE OF MERCY . . 181
  SOMEONE TOOK CURVED NAIL-SCISSORS AND SNIPPED OFF . 501 A MASQUE OF MERCY . . 201
  SOMEONE ELSE READ IT. / NO, YOU READ IT TO US. . . 505 A MASQUE OF MERCY . . 298
  SOMEONE ELSE READ IT. / NO. YOU ASKED FOR IT. . . 506 A MASQUE OF MERCY . . 329
  REQUIRED SOMEONE WHO LAUGHINGLY COULD PLAY . . . 509 A MASQUE OF MERCY . . 422
  SO SINISTER? YOU SPOKE TO SOMEONE DOWN THERE. . . 516 A MASQUE OF MERCY . . 606
SOMEONE'S
  ONLY WHEN SOMEONE'S COMING, AND THE MARE . . . . 49 A HUNDRED COLLARS . . 139
  SOMEONE'S RECEIVER'S DOWN. THE HANDLE STUMBLES. . . 153 SNOW 295
  WHICH PUT THE THOUGHT INTO SOMEONE'S HEAD . . . . 345 DISCOVERY OF MADEIRAS . 66
  SOMEONE'S ROAD HOME FROM WORK THIS ONCE WAS, . . . 378 DIRECTIVE 30
  MRS. SOMEONE'S BEEN TO ASIA. . . . . 396 AN IMPORTER . . . 1
  IN SOMEONE'S POSSESSION . . . . 433 KITTY HAWK . . . 156
  SOMEONE'S CAUGHT IN THE BRANCHES. / SO THERE IS. . . 473 A MASQUE OF REASON . 16
SOMETHING
  PERHAPS IT WAS SOMETHING ABOUT THE HEAT OF THE SUN, . 17 MOWING 4
  SOMETHING, PERHAPS, ABOUT THE LACK OF SOUND-- . . . 17 MOWING 5
  IT WAS SOMETHING AMONG THE LEAVES I SOUGHT . . . . 25 THE DEMIURGE'S LAUGH . 16
  SOMETHING THERE IS THAT DOESN'T LOVE A WALL, . . . 33 MENDING WALL . . . 1
  SOMETHING THERE IS THAT DOESN'T LOVE A WALL, . . . 34 MENDING WALL . . . 35
  THAT SOUNDS LIKE SOMETHING YOU HAVE HEARD BEFORE? . . 36 DEATH OF THE HIRED MAN 53
  SOMETHING YOU SOMEHOW HAVEN'T TO DESERVE." . . . . 38 DEATH OF THE HIRED MAN 120
  HOLD ON, THERE'S SOMETHING I DON'T THINK OF NOW . . 46 A HUNDRED COLLARS . . 45
  I'M SORT OF SOMETHING FOR IT AT THE FRONT. . . . . 48 A HUNDRED COLLARS . . 102
  "THERE'S SOMETHING I SHOULD LIKE TO ASK YOU, DEAR." . 52 HOME BURIAL . . . 42
  TELL ME ABOUT IT IF IT'S SOMETHING HUMAN. . . . . 53 HOME BURIAL . . . 58
  THAT OUGHT TO BE WORTH SOMETHING, AND MAY YET. . . . 64 A SERVANT TO SERVANTS . 43
  "WHAT IS THERE WRONG?" / "SOMETHING YOU JUST NOW SAID.. 69 THE CODE 10
  "DON'T LET IT BOTHER YOU. YOU'VE FOUND OUT SOMETHING. . 70 THE CODE 21
  MORE THAN WAS NEEDED, SOMETHING MUST BE UP. . . . . 72 THE CODE 87
  HE COULDN'T KEEP AWAY FROM DOING SOMETHING." . . . 73 THE CODE 109
  I WANTED TO TRY SOMETHING WITH THE NOISE . . . . . 77 THE GENERATIONS OF MEN 124
  SOMETHING I MUST HAVE LEARNED RIDING IN TRAINS . . . 77 THE GENERATIONS OF MEN 127
  YOU CAN SEE THAT THERE'S SOMETHING WRONG WITH IT, . . 79 THE GENERATIONS OF MEN 172
  SOMETHING WENT WRONG. I SAW HIM THROW THE HOE . . . 83 THE HOUSEKEEPER . . 60
  HE'S GIVEN HER TIME TO THINK OF SOMETHING ELSE. . . 84 THE HOUSEKEEPER . . 86
  ONLY TOO WELL. I KNEW THERE MUST BE SOMETHING! . . . 87 THE HOUSEKEEPER . . 182
  ON SOMETHING--THERE'S NO HARM. SEE, THERE HE IS! . . 88 THE HOUSEKEEPER . . 203
  "YOU'RE GETTING READY TO DO SOMETHING FOOLISH." . . 94 THE SELF-SEEKER . . 51
  SOUNDS SOMETHING LIKE. BETTER THAN FARMER'S BEANS . . 97 THE SELF-SEEKER . . 127
  YOU'RE HIDING SOMETHING. THAT'S AS BAD AS LYING. . . 97 THE SELF-SEEKER . . 132
  ISN'T IT SOMETHING I HAVE SEEN BEFORE?" . . . . . 99 THE SELF-SEEKER . . 189
  TO LOOK FOR SOMETHING IT HAD LEFT BEHIND . . . . . 106 CHRISTMAS TREES . . 10
  OF SOMETHING INTERPOSED BETWEEN THEIR SIGHT . . . . 109 THE EXPOSED NEST . . 18
  IN OTHER CHAIRS, AND SOMETHING, COME TO LOOK, . . . 110 IN THE HOME STRETCH . 7
  "PUT IT ON TOP OF SOMETHING THAT'S ON TOP . . . . 111 IN THE HOME STRETCH . 14
  OF SOMETHING ELSE," SHE LAUGHED. "OH, PUT IT WHERE . 111 IN THE HOME STRETCH . 15
  I LIKE IT.--BANG GOES SOMETHING BIG AWAY . . . . 111 IN THE HOME STRETCH . 37
  AND BANG GOES SOMETHING ELSE AWAY OFF THERE. . . . 112 IN THE HOME STRETCH . 55
  IT'S SOMETHING, THOUGH, TO KNOW WE'RE GOING TO HAVE HER 113 IN THE HOME STRETCH . 72
  "DID THEY MAKE SOMETHING LONESOME GO THROUGH YOU? . . 114 IN THE HOME STRETCH . 122
  SOMETHING DOWN THERE TO SMILE AT IN THE DUST. . . . 119 MEETING AND PASSING . 11
  SOMETHING INSPIRES THE ONLY COW OF LATE . . . . . 124 THE COW IN APPLE TIME . 1
  OF WIRE WITH SOMETHING IN IT FROM MEN TO MEN. . . . 125 AN ENCOUNTER . . . 18
  SOMETHING OR SOMEONE WATCHING MADE THAT GUST. . . . 130 THE BONFIRE . . . 44
  OF SOMETHING MORE THAN TINDER-GRASS AND WEED-- . . . 131 THE BONFIRE . . . 77
  NOTHING SO NEW--SOMETHING WE HAD FORGOTTEN: . . . . 133 THE BONFIRE . . . 110
  GOT HIM BY SOMETHING HE HAD ON . . . . 137 BROWN'S DESCENT . . 10
  AND SOMETIMES SOMETHING SEEMED TO YIELD, ... 138 BROWN'S DESCENT . . 18
  HE'S CELEBRATING SOMETHING STRANGE. . . . . . . 138 BROWN'S DESCENT . . 34
  AND SAID SOMETHING TO A MAN WITH A MEAL SACK . . . 142 THE VANISHING RED . . 27
  OR SOMETHING NOT FAR FROM IT ON THE TABLE. . . . . 147 SNOW 112
  IT'S FROM REGRET FOR SOMETHING YOU HAVE PASSED . . . 147 SNOW 124
  ASK ANY MAN." / HE THREW HER THAT AS SOMETHING . . . 151 SNOW 242
  "A CLOCK MAYBE." / "DON'T YOU HEAR SOMETHING ELSE?" . 154 SNOW 316
  SOMETHING ELSE TO PROTECT HER FROM HERSELF. . . . 163 NEW HAMPSHIRE . . . 147
  OF BREATHING TREES SAID SOMETHING OF THE TIME . . . 175 THE CENSUS-TAKER . . 26
  BUSY OUTDOORS BY LANTERN-LIGHT WITH SOMETHING . . . 176 THE STAR-SPLITTER . . 4
  ABOUT THE DIFFERENT TREES, AND SOMETHING, TOO, . . . 180 MAPLE 27
  IT MADE IT SEEM AS IF THERE MUST BE SOMETHING . . . 182 MAPLE 94
  SOMETHING ABOUT WAVE OFFERING, IT SAID." . . . . 183 MAPLE 107
  SOMETHING BETWEEN YOUR FATHER AND YOUR MOTHER . . . 183 MAPLE 113
  SOMETHING A FATHER COULDN'T TELL A DAUGHTER . . . . 183 MAPLE 118
  BY INSPIRATION. IT PROVED THERE WAS SOMETHING. . . . 184 MAPLE 135
  WHAT IT WAS ALL ABOUT. THERE MIGHT BE SOMETHING . . 185 THE AX-HELVE . . . 15
  SOMETHING TO SELL? THAT WASN'T HOW IT SOUNDED. . . . 186 THE AX-HELVE . . . 32
  I WAS FOR LEAVING SOMETHING TO THE WHETTER. . . . 191 THE GRINDSTONE . . 75
  SOMETHING WAS GOING TO GO WITH THEIR SLAMBANGING. . . 193 PAUL'S WIFE . . . 68
  SOMETHING HAD LEFT A BROAD BLACK STREAK OF GREASE . . 193 PAUL'S WIFE . . . 69
  BUT I, WITH SOMETHING OF THE BABY GRIP . . . . . 197 WILD GRAPES . . . 48

SOMETHING (CONTINUED)
    TRY TO WEIGH SOMETHING NEXT TIME, SO YOU WON'T . . . . . 199 WILD GRAPES 90
    WITH SOMETHING HE REMEMBERED IN HIMSELF, ... 200 PLACE FOR A THIRD . . 18
    BUT WON'T, SHOULD BE BURNED AT THE STAKE OR SOMETHING. . 202 THE WITCH OF COOS . . 6
    THAT THERE'S SOMETHING THE DEAD ARE KEEPING BACK? . . . 202 THE WITCH OF COOS . . 17
    YES, THERE'S SOMETHING THE DEAD ARE KEEPING BACK. . . . 202 THE WITCH OF COOS . . 18
    I'M GOING TO TELL THEM SOMETHING THEY WON'T LIKE: . . . 207 PAUPER WITCH OF GRAFTON 2
    BY HAVING ME A WITCH. OR SOMETHING HAPPENED . . . . . . 209 PAUPER WITCH OF GRAFTON 77
    BOTH EITHER LOOKING FOR OR FINDING SOMETHING. . . . . . 217 A FOUNTAIN, A BOTTLE . 129
    THROUGH THE PICTURE, A SOMETHING WHITE, UNCERTAIN, . . . 225 FOR ONCE SOMETHING . . 9
    FOR ONCE, THEN, SOMETHING . . . . 225 FOR ONCE SOMETHING . . T
    SOMETHING MORE OF THE DEPTHS--AND THEN I LOST IT. . . . 225 FOR ONCE SOMETHING . . 10
    TRUTH? A PEBBLE OF QUARTZ? FOR ONCE, THEN, SOMETHING. . 225 FOR ONCE SOMETHING . . 15
    BUT SOMETHING HAS TO BE LEFT TO GOD. . . . . 228 GOOD-BY AND KEEP COLD . 29
    THEN, AS IF THEY WERE SOMETHING THAT, THOUGH STRANGE, . 229 TWO LOOK AT TWO . . . 22
    STEER STRAIGHT OFF AFTER SOMETHING INTO SPACE. . . . . 238 ON A TREE FALLEN ACROSS 14
    WELL, SOMETHING FOR A SNOWSTORM TO HAVE SHOWN . . . . . 240 OUR SINGING STRENGTH . 49
    WAS SOMETHING BRUSHED ACROSS MY MIND . . . . 248 A PASSING GLIMPSE . . 9
    MURMURING SOMETHING QUIET IN HER BREAST, ... 249 ACCEPTANCE 6
    AND THOUGHT OF DOING SOMETHING TO THE SHORE . . . . . . 250 ONCE BY THE PACIFIC . . 3
    AND OF COURSE THERE MUST BE SOMETHING WRONG . . . . . . 251 A MINOR BIRD 7
    SOMETHING SINISTER IN THE TONE . . . . 251 BEREFT 11
    IS YET--WELL, SOMETHING THEY KNOW, HE AND SHE. . . . . 256 THE LOVELY BE CHOOSERS 24
    WHAT ARE WE?" / "YOUNG OR NEW?" / "WE MUST BE SOMETHING. 258 WEST-RUNNING BROOK . . 10
    "YES, YOU HAVE, TOO. GO ON. YOU THOUGHT OF SOMETHING." 259 WEST-RUNNING BROOK . . 37
    AND THERE IS SOMETHING SENDING UP THE SUN. . . . . . . 260 WEST-RUNNING BROOK . . 67
    WITH ALWAYS SOMETHING IN HER SMILE. . . . . 265 THE BIRTHPLACE . . . 10
    SOMETHING I SAW OR THOUGHT I SAW . . . . 290 ON HEART'S BEGINNING TO 1
    WERE EVIDENTLY SOMETHING HE COULD BEAR. . . . . 292 FIGURE IN THE DOORWAY . 12
    MAY SOMETHING GO ALWAYS UNHARVESTED! . . . . 305 UNHARVESTED 11
    APPLES OR SOMETHING FORGOTTEN AND LEFT, ... 305 UNHARVESTED 13
    OR ELSE WRITE SOMETHING TO IMPROVE FOOD PRICES. . . . . 316 BUILD SOIL 24
    BUT SOMETHING IN IT STILL IS INCOMPLETE. . . . . 337 THE WIND AND THE RAIN . 25
    SOMETHING WE WERE WITHHOLDING MADE US WEAK . . . . . . 348 THE GIFT OUTRIGHT . . 8
    THERE'S ALWAYS SOMETHING TO BE SORRY FOR, ... 352 THE LESSON FOR TODAY . 55
    AND WHAT I PITY IN YOU IS SOMETHING HUMAN, ... 356 A MOTH SEEN IN WINTER . 14
    WHEN SOMETHING STRANGE ABOUT IT MADE ME THINK. . . . . 357 A CONSIDERABLE SPECK . 6
    SOMETHING ABOUT A KINGDOM IN THE SKY . . . . 359 THE LOST FOLLOWER . . 35
    IS SOMETHING IN A BALEARIC SLING . . . . 361 A LOOSE MOUNTAIN . . 16
    SOMETHING WHERE I COULD GO-- . . . . 366 NOT OF SCHOOL AGE . . 19
    YOUR MIND MISTRUSTED THERE WAS SOMETHING WRONG, ... 369 THE LITERATE FARMER AND 24
    SOMETHING FOR HOPE . . . . 375 SOMETHING FOR HOPE . . T
    'TWAS SOMETHING WE KNEW ALL ABOUT TO BEGIN WITH . . . . 380 TOO ANXIOUS FOR RIVERS 24
    SUCH AS THAT FLESH IS SOMETHING WE CAN SLOUGH . . . . . 395 ETHEREALIZING 3
    SOMETHING WAS GOING RIGHT OUTSIDE THE HALL. . . . . . . 399 THE BROKEN DROUGHT . . 2
    SAY SOMETHING TO US WE CAN LEARN . . . . 403 SOMETHING LIKE A STAR . 9
    TAKE SOMETHING LIKE A STAR . . . . 403 SOMETHING LIKE A STAR . T
    SAY SOMETHING! AND IT SAYS, "I BURN." . . . . 403 SOMETHING LIKE A STAR . 11
    BUT DOES TELL SOMETHING IN THE END. . . . . 403 SOMETHING LIKE A STAR . 17
    WE MAY TAKE SOMETHING LIKE A STAR . . . . 403 SOMETHING LIKE A STAR . 24
    SOMETHING ELUDES HIM. IS IT FOOD TO EAT? . . . . 412 POD OF THE MILKWEED . 48
    THERE HAD BEEN SOMETHING STRANGELY WRONG . . . . 416 AMERICA IS HARD TO SEE 13
    SEEMS SOMETHING ARTISTS OUGHT TO CELEBRATE. . . . . . . 422 FOR JOHN F. KENNEDY . 3
    SOMETHING WE WERE WITHHOLDING MADE US WEAK . . . . . . 424 THE GIFT OUTRIGHT . . 8
    SOMETHING MADE IT SAD . . . . 432 KITTY HAWK 129
    SOMETHING IN IT FOR THEM? . . . . 448 THE BAD ISLAND--EASTER 33
    THAT'S SOMETHING I'M PREPARED TO FACE. . . . . 453 A-WISHING WELL . . . 71
    LIKE FLESH, THERE MUST BE SOMETHING LIVING IN IT." . . 456 HOW HARD TO KEEP FROM 91
    AND HE MAY HAVE TO TURN TO SOMETHING ELSE . . . . 459 HOW HARD TO KEEP FROM 179
    HERE BY OUR ATOLL. / SOMETHING BYZANTINE. . . . . 474 A MASQUE OF REASON . . 20
    SOMETHING ABOUT--(THE THREE MEN LAUGH.) . . . . 487 A MASQUE OF REASON . . 400
    I'M GOING TO TELL YOU SOMETHING, JONAS DOVE. . . . . . 498 A MASQUE OF MERCY . . 131
    I HAVE TO TELL YOU SOMETHING THAT WILL SPOIL . . . . . 498 A MASQUE OF MERCY . . 143
    YOU STICK TO EARTHQUAKE, YOU HAVE SOMETHING THERE-- . . 503 A MASQUE OF MERCY . . 265
    SOMETHING WE'LL KNOW WE'RE GETTING WHEN WE GET IT. . . 503 A MASQUE OF MERCY . . 266
    YOU'RE DOING SOMETHING TO OUR MINDS. / I'M NOT.-- . . . 504 A MASQUE OF MERCY . . 285
    DON'T YOU FEEL SOMETHING? / LEAVE ME OUT OF THIS. . . . 504 A MASQUE OF MERCY . . 286
    SOMETHING HAS ALTERED IN THE OUTER DOOR.) . . . . 507 A MASQUE OF MERCY . . 344
    IS SOMETHING TO BELIEVE IN, DON'T WE, PAUL? . . . . . . 515 A MASQUE OF MERCY . . 568
    BY SOMETHING TO BELIEVE IN, JESSE MEANS . . . . 515 A MASQUE OF MERCY . . 569
    SOMETHING TO BE FANATICAL ABOUT, ... 515 A MASQUE OF MERCY . . 570
SOMETHING'S
    SOMETHING'S THE MATTER, EVERYONE ADMITS. . . . . 514 A MASQUE OF MERCY . . 562
SOMETIME
    "IT OUGHT TO BE IN RAIN. SOMETIME IN RAIN. . . . . . . 81 THE GENERATIONS OF MEN 210
    OR FOR A LITTLE GIRL TO GUESS SOMETIME. . . . . 180 MAPLE 24
    "I HAVE, AND BEEN PUT OFF SOMETIME, I THINK." . . . . . 183 MAPLE 109
    YOU'LL TELL ME SOMETIME. ALL YOU SAY HAS GREATNESS. . . 517 A MASQUE OF MERCY . . 637
SOMETIMES
    THAT WE SIT SOMETIMES IN THE WAYSIDE NOOK, ... 16 IN NEGLECT 3
    SOMETIMES HE JOINS THEM FOR A DAY OR TWO . . . . 44 A HUNDRED COLLARS . . 6
    EVERYTHING'S SHUT SOMETIMES EXCEPT THE BARN; . . . . . 49 A HUNDRED COLLARS . . 130
    I TASTE IN THEM SOMETIMES THE FLAVOR OF SOOT. . . . . . 59 BLUEBERRIES 23
    THE COTTAGES LEN BUILT, SOMETIMES WE RENT THEM, ... 64 A SERVANT TO SERVANTS . 41
    SOMETIMES WE DON'T. WE'VE A GOOD PIECE OF SHORE . . . . 64 A SERVANT TO SERVANTS . 42
    BUT DON'T YOU THINK WE SOMETIMES MAKE TOO MUCH . . . . 80 THE GENERATIONS OF MEN 196
    SOMETIMES HE GETS POSSESSED TO KEEP ACCOUNTS . . . . . 86 THE HOUSEKEEPER . . . 158
    SOMETIMES I WANDER OUT OF BEATEN WAYS . . . . 125 AN ENCOUNTER 23
    AND SOMETIMES SOMETHING SEEMED TO YIELD, ... 138 BROWN'S DESCENT . . . 18
    SOMETIMES HE CAME WITH ARMS OUTSPREAD . . . . 138 BROWN'S DESCENT . . . 21
    SOMETIMES AS AN AUTHORITY . . . . 139 BROWN'S DESCENT . . . 49
    SOMETIMES WHEN I WATCH TREES SWAY, ... 156 THE SOUND OF TREES . . 17
    NO WONDER POETS SOMETIMES HAVE TO SEEM . . . . 164 NEW HAMPSHIRE 172
    LOUDER THAN ACTIONS, AND SOMETIMES ACHIEVES IT. . . . . 171 NEW HAMPSHIRE 402
    HAVE HAD TO DO WITH IT--SHE SOMETIMES WONDERED. . . . . 182 MAPLE 76
    AND SOMETIMES LAUGHED AT WHAT IT WAS BETWEEN THEM. . . 200 PLACE FOR A THIRD . . 35
    LET THEM STAY IN THE ATTIC. WHEN THEY SOMETIMES . . . . 206 THE WITCH OF COOS . . 125
    IT'S SOMETIMES DIM . . . . 212 AN EMPTY THREAT . . . 40

SOMETIMES (CONTINUED)
  SOMETIMES I FEEL MYSELF I CAN HARDLY BEAR . . . . . . 287 A ROADSIDE STAND . . 32
  WE SOMETIMES ONLY GET THE BAD OF THEM. . . . . 319 BUILD SOIL . . . 97
  TITYRUS, SOMETIMES I'M PERPLEXED MYSELF . . . . 321 BUILD SOIL . . . 163
  SOMETIMES, WITH HER PERMISSIVE SMILE, ... 345 DISCOVERY OF MADEIRAS . 48
  STILL SOMETIMES OCCUR . . . . 433 KITTY HAWK . . . 155
  IS SOMETIMES FOUND A SKELETON . . . . 452 A-WISHING WELL . . 59
  SOMETIMES SHE THINKS SHE HAS AND GETS HERSELF . . . . 476 A MASQUE OF REASON . . 93
  THOUGH INCIDENTALLY I SOMETIMES WONDER . . . . 481 A MASQUE OF REASON . 220
  YES, PAUL, YOU DO SAY THINGS LIKE THAT SOMETIMES. . . 511 A MASQUE OF MERCY . 486
  (SOMETIMES I THINK YOU ARE TOO SURE YOU HAVE BEEN.) . 520 A MASQUE OF MERCY . 709
SOMEWHAT
  AND THE PILE SOMEWHAT SUNKEN. CLEMATIS . . . . 102 THE WOOD-PILE . . . 30
  SOMEWHAT (ALIQUID). . . . . 434 KITTY HAWK . . . 199
  I OWN THE NEED OF IT HAD SOMEWHAT FADED . . . . . . 517 A MASQUE OF MERCY . 625
SOMEWHERE
  THAT STARTS UP ON IT SOMEWHERE--I'VE HEARD SAY . . . 42 THE MOUNTAIN 46
  SOMEWHERE IN IRELAND ON A MOUNTAIN TOP." . . . . . . 43 THE MOUNTAIN . . . 76
  SOMEWHERE OUT OF THIS HOUSE. HOW CAN I MAKE YOU----". 55 HOME BURIAL . . . 113
  "I'M SURE SHE WON'T COME BACK. SHE'S HIDING SOMEWHERE. 82 THE HOUSEKEEPER . . 23
  SOMEWHERE TO WALK----" / "THE HIGHWAY, AS IT HAPPENS-- 92 THE FEAR 85
  OR SOMEWHERE ELSE: I WAS JUST FAR FROM HOME. . . . . 101 THE WOOD-PILE . . . 9
  SOMEWHERE AGES AND AGES HENCE: . . . . 105 THE ROAD NOT TAKEN . 17
  THERE'S BUTTER SOMEWHERE, TOO." / "LET'S REND THE BREAD. 115 IN THE HOME STRETCH . 145
  MUST GET SOMEWHERE. I'VE HEARD YOU SAY AS MUCH. . . . 117 IN THE HOME STRETCH . 185
  THROWN FROM SOMEWHERE AGAINST THEIR WALLPAPER . . . . 129 THE BONFIRE . . . 12
  BUT THERE WAS NO ONE. I WAS SOMEWHERE WONDERING . . . 132 THE BONFIRE . . . 90
  A HOLE IN SOMEWHERE WITH HIS HEEL. . . . . 138 BROWN'S DESCENT . . 15
  I SHALL SET FORTH FOR SOMEWHERE, ... 156 THE SOUND OF TREES . 19
  SOMEWHERE MUST BE THE GRAVE OF THE YOUNG BOY . . . . 200 PLACE FOR A THIRD . 33
  AS SOONER OR LATER WE HAVE TO CEASE SOMEWHERE. . . . 379 TOO ANXIOUS FOR RIVERS 10
  IF YOU SHOULD RISE FROM NOWHERE UP TO SOMEWHERE, . . 385 THE FEAR OF GOD . . 1
  FOR GETTING BACK SOMEWHERE OR FURTHER ON." . . . . . 420 ONE MORE BREVITY . 48
  TILL THE AMBASSADORS FROM PUNT OR SOMEWHERE . . . . . 456 HOW HARD TO KEEP FROM 72
  BUT THE KING SAID, "HAVEN'T I READ SOMEWHERE . . . . 458 HOW HARD TO KEEP FROM 139
  IF WE COULD ONLY STOP THE PROGRESS SOMEWHERE, ... 458 HOW HARD TO KEEP FROM 154
  I THOUGHT YOU HAD NONE. SOMEWHERE BACK . . . . 482 A MASQUE OF REASON . 240
SON
  SON, YOU DO AS YOU'RE TOLD! YOU TAKE THE TIMBER-- . . 80 THE GENERATIONS OF MEN 192
  WHAT, SON?" / "THEN I SHOULD THINK YOU'D TRY TO FIND . 92 THE FEAR 84
  BEHIND THE MOUNTAIN, WITH A MOTHER AND SON, ... 202 THE WITCH OF COOS . 2
  WE'LL NEVER LET THEM, WILL WE, SON? WE'LL NEVER! . . 203 THE WITCH OF COOS . 27
  YES, WE COULD TOO, SON. TELL THE TRUTH FOR ONCE. . . 206 THE WITCH OF COOS . 138
  SON KNOWS THE STORY: BUT 'TWAS NOT FOR HIM . . . . . 206 THE WITCH OF COOS . 143
  SON LOOKS SURPRISED TO SEE ME END A LIE . . . . . . 207 THE WITCH OF COOS . 145
  BUT ISLANDS OF THE BLESSED, BLESS YOU, SON, ... 363 AN ANSWER . . . 1
  LOOKED FORTH ON HER SMALL SON . . . . 366 NOT OF SCHOOL AGE . 14
  MY SON IN JERSEY SAYS A FRIEND OF HIS . . . . 371 THE LITERATE FARMER AND 95
  FOR A SON ASTRAY . . . . 433 KITTY HAWK . . . 181
  THE KING SAID TO HIS SON: "ENOUGH OF THIS! . . . . . 453 HOW HARD TO KEEP FROM 1
  NONE BUT A COOK'S SON COULD BE SO FOOD-MINDED. . . . 458 HOW HARD TO KEEP FROM 135
  "BEHOLD MY SON IN RAGS HERE WITH HIS LYRE," . . . . . 459 HOW HARD TO KEEP FROM 169
  MY SON AND I HAVE TASTED IT AND KNOW. . . . . 460 HOW HARD TO KEEP FROM 195
  SHOW YOURSELF, SON.--I'LL GET BACK ON MY THRONE . . . 487 A MASQUE OF REASON . 386
SONG
  AND ON THE WORN BOOK OF OLD-GOLDEN SONG . . . . . . 15 WAITING 23
  WHY THE FLOWER HAS ODOR, THE BIRD HAS SONG. . . . . . 16 IN A VALE . . . 22
  I HAD WITHDRAWN IN FOREST, AND MY SONG . . . . 16 A DREAM PANG . . . 1
  A NEW-WORLD SONG, FAR OUT OF REACH, ... 24 PAN WITH US . . . 17
  A LINE-STORM SONG . . . . 26 A LINE-STORM SONG . T
  ALL SONG OF THE WOODS IS CRUSHED LIKE SOME . . . . . 26 A LINE-STORM SONG . 13
  BY JUNE OUR BROOK'S RUN OUT OF SONG AND SPEED. . . . 119 HYLA BROOK . . . 1
  THAN WITH BROOKS TAKEN OTHERWHERE IN SONG. . . . . . 119 HYLA BROOK . . . 14
  WITH A SONG ONLY TO HERSELF . . . . 128 THE IMPULSE . . . 11
  OF HIS OLD SONG, 'THE WILD COLONIAL BOY,' . . . . . 205 THE WITCH OF COOS . 110
  BUT ALL THE BURDEN OF ITS BODY SONG), ... 216 A FOUNTAIN, A BOTTLE . 114
  THE AIM WAS SONG . . . . 223 THE AIM WAS SONG . T
  IT BLEW TOO HARD--THE AIM WAS SONG. . . . . 224 THE AIM WAS SONG . 7
  THE AIM WAS SONG--THE WIND COULD SEE. . . . . 224 THE AIM WAS SONG . 16
  AS MAY BE IN DARK WOODS, AND WITH A SONG . . . . . . 226 THE ONSET . . . 3
  NEITHER WAS SONG THAT DAY TO BE SELF-BEGUN. . . . . . 236 VALLEY'S SINGING DAY 14
  BY DOUBLING AND REDOUBLING SONG AND TWITTER-- . . . . 237 A HILLSIDE THAW . 16
  TO ANY ONE PLACE COVER US WITH SONG. . . . . 239 OUR SINGING STRENGTH . 20
  IN WANTING TO SILENCE ANY SONG. . . . . 251 A MINOR BIRD . . . 8
  FOR THE GENEROUS TEARS OF YOUTH AND SONG? . . . . . . 262 HANNIBAL . . . 4
  HIS SONG SO PITCHED AS NOT TO EXCITE . . . . 276 TWO TRAMPS IN MUD TIME 27
  I SENT YOU ONCE A SONG WITH THE REFRAIN: . . . . . . 324 BUILD SOIL . . . 259
  THE SONG SAYS. STEAL AWAY AND STAY AWAY. . . . . . . 325 BUILD SOIL . . . 279
  STILL LIVED FOR ONE SONG MORE . . . . 334 COME IN . . . 11
  THAT ANY SONG IN WHICH HE MOURNED . . . . 336 THE WIND AND THE RAIN . 13
  NEVER AGAIN WOULD BIRDS' SONG BE THE SAME . . . . . . 338 NEVER WOULD BIRDS' SONG T
  BE THAT AS MAY BE, SHE WAS IN THEIR SONG. . . . . . . 339 NEVER WOULD BIRDS' SONG 9
  NEVER AGAIN WOULD BIRDS' SONG BE THE SAME. . . . . . 339 NEVER WOULD BIRDS' SONG 13
  AND SNATCHES OF VERSE AND SONG OF SCENES LIKE THIS . 342 QUEST OF PURPLE-FRINGED 3
  THE LOSS TO SONG, THE DANGER OF DEFECTION . . . . . . 358 THE LOST FOLLOWER . 9
  MAKE YOURSELF UP A CHEERING SONG OF HOW . . . . 378 DIRECTIVE . . . 29
  I STOPPED MY SONG AND ALMOST HEART, ... 385 A MOOD APART . . . 6
  THE URGE OF A SONG: . . . . 413 AWAY! 19
  AND YET DONE NOTHING ABOUT IT IN SONG. . . . . 421 ONE MORE BREVITY . 65
  A NEVER NAUGHT SONG . . . . 426 A NEVER NAUGHT SONG . T
  THERE WAS ONCE A SONG, ... 428 KITTY HAWK . . . 2
  JEWELS AND HORSES, WOMEN, WINE, AND SONG." . . . . . 455 HOW HARD TO KEEP FROM 62
SONGBIRD
  THE FIRST SONGBIRD THAT AWAKENED ALL THE REST. . . . 235 VALLEY'S SINGING DAY . 5
SON-OF-A-BITCH
  SON-OF-A-BITCH? YOU BET SHE WAS AN I-DEAL." . . . . . 170 NEW HAMPSHIRE . . . 354
SONS
  HER SONS WON'T SELL THE HOUSE OR THE THINGS IN IT. . 55 THE BLACK COTTAGE . . 16

SONS (CONTINUED)
    THEN THE TWO SONS, TILL SHE WAS LEFT ALONE. . . . . . . 56 THE BLACK COTTAGE . . 39
    (NOTHING COULD DRAW HER AFTER THOSE TWO SONS. . . . . . 56 THE BLACK COTTAGE . . 40
    LIKE THOSE WHO FURNISHED ADAM'S SONS WITH WIVES; . . . 161 NEW HAMPSHIRE . . . 79
SOON
    WITH LAUGHTER WHEN SHE FOUND US SOON. . . . . 18 GOING FOR WATER . . . 16
    "I WANT HIM TO: HE'LL HAVE TO SOON OR LATE." . . . . . 35 DEATH OF THE HIRED MAN 32
    WARREN RETURNED--TOO SOON, IT SEEMED TO HER-- . . . . 40 DEATH OF THE HIRED MAN 164
    THEY SOON SAW HE WOULD DO SOMEONE A MISCHIEF . . . . . 66 A SERVANT TO SERVANTS 111
    OR A LONG RAIN. I SHOULD SOON GET ENOUGH, ... 67 A SERVANT TO SERVANTS 164
    NOT IF HE VALUES WHAT HE IS. GOD, I'D AS SOON . . . . . 71 THE CODE 69
    OH, WELL, WE'LL SOON BE THROUGH WITH IT. I'M TIRED." . 96 THE SELF-SEEKER . . . 90
    "I COULD SOON TELL HOW MANY THEY WOULD CUT, ... 106 CHRISTMAS TREES . . . 30
    AT BEDTIME; BUT THE STRANGENESS SOON WEARS OFF." . . . 115 IN THE HOME STRETCH . 135
    SOON THE SUN'S WARMTH MAKES THEM SHED CRYSTAL SHELLS . 121 BIRCHES 10
    TO LEARN ABOUT NOT LAUNCHING OUT TOO SOON . . . . . . 122 BIRCHES 33
    BLOODROOT, AND VIOLETS SO SOON TO BE NOW. . . . . . . 131 THE BONFIRE 52
    BUT SOON DIVIDES THE RIVER WITH VERMONT. . . . . . . 165 NEW HAMPSHIRE . . . 185
    NEEDLESSLY SOON HE HAD HIS AX-HELVES OUT, ... 187 THE AX-HELVE . . . 63
    I WAS SOON SATISFIED FOR THE TIME BEING. . . . . . . 217 A FOUNTAIN, A BOTTLE . 131
    THEY MUST HAVE HALTED SOON IN ANY CASE . . . . 229 TWO LOOK AT TWO . . 4
    AND THAT WAS WHAT THE BOUGHS WERE FULL OF SOON. . . . 234 EVENING A SUGAR ORCHARD 17
    THEY'D SOON EXHAUSTED ALL THERE WAS IN FLYING; . . . . 239 OUR SINGING STRENGTH . 27
    WILL LIKE THE FLOWERS BESIDE THEM SOON BE GONE, . . . 245 SPRING POOLS . . . 4
    WHAT SOON ENOUGH HE WOULD KNOW? . . . . 314 BEARER OF EVIL TIDINGS 44
    AND SOON IT IS NEITHER HERE NOR THERE . . . . 347 DISCOVERY OF MADEIRAS . 137
    OR SOON WE'D BAT EACH OTHER OUT OF TOUCH, ... 371 THE LITERATE FARMER AND 117
    MAY WELL HAVE NOTICED. SOON ENTIRELY WHITE . . . . . 375 A YOUNG BIRCH . . . 4
    AND THAT RIGHT SOON, THAT THE MEADOWSWEET . . . . . . 375 SOMETHING FOR HOPE . . 2
    SO BROODINGLY SOON IN EVERY DIRECTION. . . . . 379 TOO ANXIOUS FOR RIVERS 13
    THEY WILL TELL YOU MORE AS SOON AS . . . . 387 THE COURAGE TO BE NEW . 13
    OH, MAY THE TIDE BE SOON ENOUGH AT HIGH . . . . . . 395 ETHEREALIZING . . . 13
    IT WAS THE DROUGHT OF DESERTS. EARTH WOULD SOON . . . 400 THE BROKEN DROUGHT . . 11
    "AND SOON FOR LACK OF SUN, ... 416 CLOSED FOR GOOD . . . 19
    OH, SOME AS SOON WOULD THROW IT ALL . . . . 445 ENDS 9
    REPLIED SHE HAD AS SOON . . . . 464 MILKY WAY IS A COWPATH 18
    THEY ARE THINKING OF PRETTY SOON . . . . 466 SOME SCIENCE FICTION . 23
SOONER
    SOONER OR LATER CAME AND LEANED, HALF KNELT, ... 56 THE BLACK COTTAGE . . 27
    AS SOONER OR LATER WE HAVE TO CEASE SOMEWHERE. . . . 379 TOO ANXIOUS FOR RIVERS 10
    I SHOULD HAVE SPOKEN SOONER HAD I FOUND . . . . . . 475 A MASQUE OF REASON . . 54
SOOT
    I TASTE IN THEM SOMETIMES THE FLAVOR OF SOOT. . . . . 59 BLUEBERRIES 23
SOOTHE
    THAT ARE CALCULATED TO SOOTHE THEM OUT OF THEIR WITS, . 287 A ROADSIDE STAND . . 29
SOPHISTRY
    AND EARS ARE LENT TO ANY SOPHISTRY . . . . 488 A MASQUE OF REASON . . 409
SOPRANO
    AND SEE IF WE CAN TELL THE BASS FROM THE SOPRANO. . . . 415 A CABIN IN THE CLEARING 40
SORDID
    WHICH FOR NO SORDID SELF-AGGRANDIZEMENT, ... 319 BUILD SOIL 103
    A SORDID PEACE OR AN OUTRAGEOUS WAR. . . . . 352 THE LESSON FOR TODAY . 56
SORE
    AND DEMOCRATS WERE SORE IN NEED OF COMFORT: . . . . . 165 NEW HAMPSHIRE . . . 197
    WHEN STIFF AND SORE AND SCARRED . . . . 227 TO EARTHWARD . . . 25
SORROW
    MY SORROW, WHEN SHE'S HERE WITH ME, ... 6 MY NOVEMBER GUEST . . 1
    THIS IS NOT SORROW, THOUGH; IT'S JUST THE VAPORS, . . . 167 NEW HAMPSHIRE . . . 277
    HOW, TO MY SORROW, HOW HAVE I ATTAINED . . . . 169 NEW HAMPSHIRE . . . 313
    SO WHAT IS THIS I MAKE A SORROW OF?) . . . . 174 THE CENSUS-TAKER . . 8
    FILLED ME WITH NO LESS SORROW THAN THE HOUSES . . . . 176 THE CENSUS-TAKER . . 51
    SO MUCH AS THE TRUSTING SORROW OF WHAT IS UNSAID: . . . 286 A ROADSIDE STAND . . 17
    THE SORROW OF HAVING BEEN LEFT BEHIND, ... 420 ONE MORE BREVITY . . 31
    OR THE SORROW OF HAVING RUN AWAY. . . . . 420 ONE MORE BREVITY . . 32
    FOR THE APPARENTLY UNMEANING SORROW . . . . 475 A MASQUE OF REASON . . 60
SORRY
    SORRY THERE IS NO CUP TO GIVE YOU A DRINK. . . . . . 50 A HUNDRED COLLARS . . 155
    WHETHER I AM GLAD, SORRY, OR ANYTHING. . . . . 63 A SERVANT TO SERVANTS . 12
    THE LAWYER SAID. "I'M SORRY, BUT MY TRAIN-- . . . . . 99 THE SELF-SEEKER . . . 181
    WE'RE VERY SORRY FOR YOU." / WILLIS SNEERED: . . . . 100 THE SELF-SEEKER . . . 220
    AND SORRY I COULD NOT TRAVEL BOTH . . . . 105 THE ROAD NOT TAKEN . . 2
    AND SORRY I EVER LEFT THE ROAD I KNEW, ... 125 AN ENCOUNTER . . . 7
    SORRY I HAD TO BREAK IN ON YOUR SLEEP." . . . . . . 150 SNOW 212
    'TWOULD BE TOO BAD TO MAKE HIM SORRY FOR . . . . . . 183 MAPLE 121
    THERE'S ALWAYS SOMETHING TO BE SORRY FOR, ... 352 THE LESSON FOR TODAY . 55
    SORRY TO HAVE NO NAME FOR YOU BUT YOU. . . . . 382 TO AN ANCIENT . . . 3
    BUT THE SORRY STORY . . . . 430 KITTY HAWK . . . 78
SORT
    AND WHISPERS WITH A SORT OF STIFLED BARK, ... 9 STORM FEAR 4
    I'M SORT OF SOMETHING FOR IT AT THE FRONT. . . . . . 48 A HUNDRED COLLARS . . 102
    YOU KNOW WHAT THAT IS, SORT OF DOUBLE-DYED; . . . . . 48 A HUNDRED COLLARS . . 110
    AS IF SHE HAD SOME SORT OF CURVATURE, ... 49 A HUNDRED COLLARS . . 143
    TO CATCH IT IN A SORT OF SPECIAL PICTURE . . . . . . 55 THE BLACK COTTAGE . . 2
    IT ALWAYS SEEMS TO ME A SORT OF MARK . . . . 56 THE BLACK COTTAGE . . 45
    IN FATHER'S BUILDING HIM A SORT OF CAGE, ... 66 A SERVANT TO SERVANTS . 113
    A SORT OF CATCHALL FULL OF ATTIC CLUTTER. . . . . . 67 A SERVANT TO SERVANTS . 143
    AND SORT OF WAITING TO BE ASKED ABOUT IT, ... 72 THE CODE 82
    DRAWN ON A SORT OF PASSPORT WITH THE BRANCH . . . . . 74 THE GENERATIONS OF MEN 40
    HE GETS SOME SORT OF BAKESHOP MEALS TOGETHER, ... 82 THE HOUSEKEEPER . . 31
    HE'LL SORT OF SWEAR THE TIME AWAY. HE'S AWFUL! . . . . 83 THE HOUSEKEEPER . . 52
    NO DOUBT IT HAS A SORT OF PROSPEROUS SOUND, ... 94 THE SELF-SEEKER . . . 45
    I PAUSED AND RESTED ON A SORT OF HOOK . . . . 125 AN ENCOUNTER . . . 8
    THAT SORT OF MAN TALKS STRAIGHT-ON ALL HIS LIFE . . . 145 SNOW 64
    THERE IS A SORT OF TUNNEL IN THE FROST-- . . . . . . 149 SNOW 192
    SO AS TO SORT OF TURN ME OUT OF IT. . . . . 203 THE WITCH OF COOS . . 43
    YOU'D MAKE A SORT OF SAFETY-FIRST DICTATOR. . . . . . 320 BUILD SOIL . . . 130
    AND ANOTHER SORT OF SMILE . . . . 339 THE SUBVERTED FLOWER . 11
    I COULD POINT OUT MY SORT OF PASSPORT IN IT. . . . . 495 A MASQUE OF MERCY . . 46

SORT (CONTINUED)
  EXCEPT AS FATHER PUTATIVE TO SORT OF . . . . 498 A MASQUE OF MERCY . . 123
SORTS
  THE COLOR RUN, ALL SORTS OF WONDER FOLLOW. . . . . . 245 THE FREEDOM OF THE MOON 12
  OR IF EVER ASIDE A MOMENT, THEN OUT OF SORTS . . . . 286 A ROADSIDE STAND . . 8
  YOU'LL HEAR ALL SORTS OF THINGS. YOU'LL MEET WITH THEM . 369 THE LITERATE FARMER AND 33
  OUT OF SORTS WITH FATE, ... 428 KITTY HAWK 11
  AND SOME WILL SAY ALL SORTS OF THINGS, ... 445 ENDS 11
  IT TAKES ALL SORTS OF IN- AND OUTDOOR SCHOOLING . . . 470 IT TAKES ALL SORTS... . 1
  IT TAKES ALL SORTS... . . . . 470 IT TAKES ALL SORTS... . T
SO'S---NOT INDEXED
SOTTO
  IN TIME WITH A MEDLEY OF SOTTO CHANTS; . . . . 385 A MOOD APART 3
SOUGHT (SEE FAR-SOUGHT)
  AND WHERE THEY SOUGHT WITHOUT THE SWORD . . . . 19 THE TRIAL BY EXISTENCE 5
  AND WEARY, SOUGHT AT NOON WITH HIM THE SHADE; . . . . 23 THE TUFT OF FLOWERS . 36
  IT WAS SOMETHING AMONG THE LEAVES I SOUGHT . . . . . . 25 THE DEMIURGE'S LAUGH . 16
  SOUGHT FOR MUCH AFTER THAT, IT WILL BE FOUND . . . . 119 HYLA BROOK 2
  A MOMENT SOUGHT IN AIR HIS FLOWER OF REST, ... 126 RANGE-FINDING . . . 7
  BETWEEN TWO DAYS, THE REASON WHY I SOUGHT . . . . . . 167 NEW HAMPSHIRE . . 249
  HE NO MORE DREW THE SMILE HE SOUGHT. . . . . 347 DISCOVERY OF MADEIRAS 118
  WE SOUGHT HOWEVER CRUDELY TO DEFEAT . . . . 446 DOES NO ONE AT ALL EVER 11
SOUL (SEE SOUL-FROM-SOUL)
  I'M GOING TO SELL MY SOUL, OR RATHER, FEET. . . . . . 92 THE SELF-SEEKER . . . 3
  "WITH YOU THE FEET HAVE NEARLY BEEN THE SOUL; . . . . 93 THE SELF-SEEKER . . . 5
  THE ONE THING PALPABLE BESIDES THE SOUL . . . . . . 172 A STAR IN A STONEBOAT . 11
  THERE'S NOT A SOUL . . . . 211 AN EMPTY THREAT . . . 23
  INTO THE DARKNESS. IT GRIEVED MY SOUL, ... 253 THE THATCH 20
  THAT DAY, GIVING A LOOSE TO MY SOUL, ... 275 TWO TRAMPS IN MUD TIME 15
  WHAT COMES OVER A MAN, IS IT SOUL OR MIND-- . . . . . 305 THERE ARE ROUGHLY ZONES 7
  ONE SICKNESS OF THE BODY AND THE SOUL. . . . . 318 BUILD SOIL 80
  AND SIGNIFIES THE SURENESS OF THE SOUL, ... 332 THE SILKEN TENT . . . 7
  EARTH'S A HARD PLACE IN WHICH TO SAVE THE SOUL, . . . 353 THE LESSON FOR TODAY . 98
  ONE AGE IS LIKE ANOTHER FOR THE SOUL. . . . . 354 THE LESSON FOR TODAY . 113
  "THE PORTRAIT OF THE SOUL OF MY GRANSIR IRA. . . . . . 366 OF STONES OF THE PLACE 15
  BUT HELPED THE LORD HER SOUL TO KEEP. . . . . 382 THE NIGHT LIGHT . . . 4
  TO BE THE CURTAIN OF THE INMOST SOUL. . . . . 385 THE FEAR OF GOD . . . 13
  MEANS THAT A SOUL IS COMING ON THE FLESH. . . . . . . 386 A STEEPLE ON THE HOUSE 8
  ASKED ABOUT MY SOUL . . . . 432 KITTY HAWK 143
  AN EASIER PLACE FOR MAN TO SAVE HIS SOUL IN. . . . . . 484 A MASQUE OF REASON . 317
  EXCEPT AS A HARD PLACE TO SAVE HIS SOUL IN, ... 484 A MASQUE OF REASON . 318
  WHY IS GOD AFTER YOU?--TO SAVE YOUR SOUL? . . . . . . 494 A MASQUE OF MERCY . . 40
  AND GREAT IT IS. BUT FEAR IS OF THE SOUL. . . . . . . 519 A MASQUE OF MERCY . . 694
  TO OVERCOME THE FEAR WITHIN THE SOUL . . . . 521 A MASQUE OF MERCY . . 729
SOUL-AND-BODY
  IF ALL THE SOUL-AND-BODY SCARS . . . . 362 A QUESTION 3
SOUL-FROM-SOUL
  ACROSS THE SOUL-FROM-SOUL ABYSS, ... 328 A MISSIVE MISSILE . . 49
SOULLESS
  WILL BE SOME SOULLESS LUNATIC ASYLUM-- . . . . 500 A MASQUE OF MERCY . . 187
SOULS
  THE GATHERING OF THE SOULS FOR BIRTH, ... 20 THE TRIAL BY EXISTENCE 18
  THE SPEEDING OF DEVOTED SOULS . . . . 20 THE TRIAL BY EXISTENCE 31
  THE MELANCHOLY OF HAVING TO COUNT SOULS . . . . . . 176 THE CENSUS-TAKER . . 61
  HE SAID THE DEAD HAD SOULS, BUT WHEN I ASKED HIM . . 202 THE WITCH OF COOS . . 14
  HOW COULD THAT BE--I THOUGHT THE DEAD WERE SOULS-- . . 202 THE WITCH OF COOS . . 15
  TWO SOULS MAY BE TOO WIDELY MET. . . . . 328 A MISSIVE MISSILE . . 52
  WE HAVE TO STAY AFRAID DEEP IN OUR SOULS . . . . . . 520 A MASQUE OF MERCY . . 717
SOUL'S
  OF THE SOUL'S ETHEREAL . . . . 436 KITTY HAWK 256
SOUND
  THERE WAS NEVER A SOUND BESIDE THE WOOD BUT ONE, . . . 17 MOWING 1
  SOMETHING, PERHAPS, ABOUT THE LACK OF SOUND-- . . . . 17 MOWING 5
  THE SOUND WAS BEHIND ME INSTEAD OF BEFORE, ... 25 THE DEMIURGE'S LAUGH . 7
  A SLEEPY SOUND, BUT MOCKING HALF, ... 25 THE DEMIURGE'S LAUGH . 8
  THE RUMBLING SOUND . . . . 69 AFTER APPLE-PICKING . 25
  THE SOUND OF WHICH WAS SILENCE FOR THE PLACE. . . . . 76 THE GENERATIONS OF MEN 76
  IT'S AS SOUND AS THE DAY WHEN IT WAS CUT-- . . . . . 80 THE GENERATIONS OF MEN 193
  NO DOUBT IT HAS A SORT OF PROSPEROUS SOUND. . . . . . 94 THE SELF-SEEKER . . 45
  "YOU MAKE THAT SOUND AS IF IT WASN'T SO . . . . 94 THE SELF-SEEKER . . 47
  I HAD THE SOUND OF A VIOLIN; . . . . 102 GOOD HOURS 6
  WHO MAKES THE SOLID TREE TRUNKS SOUND AGAIN. . . . . 119 THE OVEN BIRD . . . 3
  ALL FRESH AND SOUND FROM THE RECENT AX. . . . . . . 123 PEA BRUSH 14
  IF YOU LIKE TO CALL SUCH A SOUND A LAUGH. . . . . . . 142 THE VANISHING RED . . 3
  THE SOUND OF TREES . . . . 156 THE SOUND OF TREES . . T
  A LITERATURE THAT SHALL AT ONCE BE SOUND . . . . . . 168 NEW HAMPSHIRE . . 285
  THE HOLLOW LOOKED TOO SOUND AND CLEAN AND EMPTY . . . 193 PAUL'S WIFE . . . 83
  THE SOUND OF THE CLOSING OUTSIDE DOOR WAS ALL. . . . . 235 VALLEY'S SINGING DAY . 1
  YOU MADE NO SOUND IN THE GRASS WITH YOUR FOOTFALL, . . 235 VALLEY'S SINGING DAY . 2
  I HAVE STOOD STILL AND STOPPED THE SOUND OF FEET . . . 255 ACQUAINTED WITH NIGHT . 7
  JUST AS HE WAS, WITHOUT AN UTTERED SOUND . . . . . . 284 THE GOLD HESPERIDEE . 43
  FOR THE SQUEAL OF BRAKES, THE SOUND OF A STOPPING CAR, . 287 A ROADSIDE STAND . . 36
  FROM SOUND TO SENSE AND BACK TO SOUND. . . . . 326 TO A THINKER . . . 12
  OF THE INNER SOUND; . . . . 433 KITTY HAWK 166
  AT LESS THAN THE SPEED OF SOUND . . . . 466 SOME SCIENCE FICTION . 18
  DON'T ANY OF YOU HEAR A SOUND? / THE STORM! . . . . . 504 A MASQUE OF MERCY . . 279
SOUNDED
  AND A VOICE THAT HAS SOUNDED IN MY ROOM . . . . 15 IN A VALE 8
  SOMETHING TO SELL? THAT WASN'T HOW IT SOUNDED. . . . . 186 THE AX-HELVE . . . 32
SOUNDS
  SOUNDS NOBLER THERE THAN 'NEATH THE SUN; . . . . . . 21 THE TRIAL BY EXISTENCE 46
  THAT SOUNDS LIKE SOMETHING YOU HAVE HEARD BEFORE? . . . 36 DEATH OF THE HIRED MAN 53
  CRUEL--IT SOUNDS. I S'POSE THEY DID THE BEST . . . . 66 A SERVANT TO SERVANTS . 124
  I'VE NEVER LISTENED IN AMONG THE SOUNDS . . . . . . 78 THE GENERATIONS OF MEN 132
  SOUNDS SOMETHING LIKE. BETTER THAN FARMER'S BEANS . . . 97 THE SELF-SEEKER . . 127
  WHICH HAS ITS SOUNDS, FAMILIAR, LIKE THE ROAR . . . . 108 OLD MAN'S WINTER NIGHT 12
  IT SOUNDS AS IF IT WERE THE MEN WENT DOWN, ... 112 IN THE HOME STRETCH . 56
  SOUNDS FURTHER OFF, IT'S NOT BECAUSE IT'S DYING; . . . 150 SNOW 204

SOUNDS (CONTINUED)
    YOU KNOW--IT SOUNDS THAT WAY, AND YES, I HEAR--   . . . 153 SNOW 300
    FRANTIC IT SOUNDS, THOUGH MUFFLED AND FAR OFF. .   . . . 154 SNOW 319
    WITH SOUNDS LIKE THE DRY RATTLING OF A SHUTTER,   . . . 206 THE WITCH OF COOS . 129
    IT SOUNDS TO ME AS IF YOU THOUGHT IT OUT, ... 482 A MASQUE OF REASON . 244
SOUND'S
    THE ONLY OTHER SOUND'S THE SWEEP . . . . 224 STOPPING BY WOODS .   11
SOURCE
    NO LONGER NEEDED? STAUNCH IT AT ITS SOURCE . . .   . . 231 A BROOK IN THE CITY   14
    IT IS THIS BACKWARD MOTION TOWARD THE SOURCE, ... 260 WEST-RUNNING BROOK . . 68
    THE TRIBUTE OF THE CURRENT TO THE SOURCE.   . . .   . . 260 WEST-RUNNING BROOK . . 70
    THE CLOUDS, THE SOURCE OF RAIN, ONE STORMY NIGHT   . . 295 LOST IN HEAVEN . . . 1
    OFFERED AN OPENING TO THE SOURCE OF DEW; . . .   . . . 295 LOST IN HEAVEN .   . . 2
    WE ARE ROUND FROM THE SAME SOURCE OF ROUNDNESS.   . . 322 BUILD SOIL 200
    THAT IS THE SOURCE PERHAPS OF HUMAN HATE. . . .   . . 371 THE LITERATE FARMER AND 108
    COLD AS A SPRING AS YET SO NEAR ITS SOURCE, ... 378 DIRECTIVE 51
    FROM SOURCE UNKNOWN BUT FROM NO SPECIAL PLACE   . . . . 411 POD OF THE MILKWEED   2
    I CAN COUNT ON MY SOURCE TO SPRING AGAIN, ... 514 A MASQUE OF MERCY . 541
    NO TRUE SOURCE CAN BE POISONED. / THEN THAT'S ALL. . . 514 A MASQUE OF MERCY . 543
    FOR ALL THE LIGHT AT ONCE THE SOURCE OF LIGHT--   . . 515 A MASQUE OF MERCY . 587
SOUSE
    THE STORM GETS DOWN HIS NECK IN AN ICY SOUSE   . . . . 341 WILLFUL HOMING . . . 3
SOUTH
    AND WHAT THE SOUTH, TO HER SERENE BELIEF. . . . .   . 57 THE BLACK COTTAGE .   . 72
    WE CLIMBED THE PASTURE ON THE SOUTH, CROSSED OVER, . . . 107 CHRISTMAS TREES . . . 40
    I MET A LADY FROM THE SOUTH WHO SAID . . . . .   . 159 NEW HAMPSHIRE 1
    TO BE CONVERTED INTO SOUTH, ... 224 THE AIM WAS SONG .   11
    FROM NORTH TO SOUTH ACROSS THE BLUE; . . . . 233 LOOKING FOR SUNSET BIRD 19
    FROM FIFTY NORTH TO FIFTY SOUTH. . . . . 418 AMERICA IS HARD TO SEE 54
SOUTHEAST-NORTHWEST
    THE LEDGES SHOW LINES RULED SOUTHEAST-NORTHWEST,   . . . 377 DIRECTIVE 15
SOUTHWESTER
    COME WITH RAIN, O LOUD SOUTHWESTER! . . . . 11 TO THE THAWING WIND . 1
SOVEREIGNTY
    AGAINST THE ANCIENT SOVEREIGNTY OF NIGHT. . . . .   . 361 A LOOSE MOUNTAIN . . 8
    IN THEIR ATTEMPTS AT SOVEREIGNTY AND FORM. . . .   . 423 FOR JOHN F. KENNEDY . 35
SOVIET
    THAT SOVIET RUSSIA HAS MADE FASHIONABLE. . . . .   . . 323 BUILD SOIL 223
SOW
    DANGEROUS SELF-AROUSING WORDS TO SOW. . . . . .   . 180 MAPLE 29
SOWED
    WHAT HE SOWED WITH HER SLEPT SO LONG A SLEEP, ... 180 MAPLE 36
    SOWED IN VAIN BY RALEIGH, ... 431 KITTY HAWK 92
SPACE
    ANOTHER COLOR OVER A TENTH THE SPACE . . . . .   . 132 THE BONFIRE 82
    OF JOSTLING ROCK IN INTERSTELLAR SPACE. . . . .   . 173 A STAR IN A STONEBOAT . 33
    BE RUN OFF WITH BY BIRCH TREES INTO SPACE." . .   . . 199 WILD GRAPES 91
    STEER STRAIGHT OFF AFTER SOMETHING INTO SPACE. .   . . 238 ON A TREE FALLEN ACROSS 14
    AND THE NATURE OF TIME AND SPACE, ... 288 DEPARTMENTAL 11
    SPACE AILS US MODERNS: WE ARE SICK WITH SPACE. .   . . 352 THE LESSON FOR TODAY . 68
    ONE AS COMPARED WITH GOD AND ONE WITH SPACE. . .   . . 353 THE LESSON FOR TODAY . 78
    AND NEEDN'T HAVE FARED INTO SPACE LIKE HIS MASTER   . . 380 TOO ANXIOUS FOR RIVERS 25
    ALL NIGHT WITH UNIVERSAL SPACE. . . . . 380 AN UNSTAMPED LETTER IN 17
    I DON'T BELIEVE I BELIEVE YOU'RE THE LAST IN SPACE, . . 389 SKEPTIC 5
    HE STRETCHED HIS ARMS OUT TO THE DARK OF SPACE .   . . 396 ANY SIZE WE PLEASE . 5
    HE THOUGHT IF HE COULD HAVE HIS SPACE ALL CURVED,   . . 396 ANY SIZE WE PLEASE . 9
    ANYWHERE IN SPACE. . . . . 440 KITTY HAWK 394
    BUT OUTER SPACE, ... 469 BUT OUTER SPACE. . . 1
    BUT OUTER SPACE... . . . . 469 BUT OUTER SPACE... . . T
    WHEN TIME WAS FOUND TO BE A SPACE DIMENSION . .   . . 479 A MASQUE OF REASON . 160
    THAT COULD, LIKE ANY SPACE, BE TURNED AROUND IN?   . . 479 A MASQUE OF REASON . 161
SPACES
    THEY CANNOT SCARE ME WITH THEIR EMPTY SPACES   . . . . 296 DESERT PLACES .   . . 13
SPADE
    TO LOOK AGAIN, AND STILL YOUR SPADE KEPT LIFTING. . . . 53 HOME BURIAL 80
    YOU HAD STOOD THE SPADE UP AGAINST THE WALL . .   . . . 54 HOME BURIAL 87
    (YOUR BADGE OF OFFICE IS A SPADE). . . . . 327 A MISSIVE MISSILE . . 24
SPADES
    SPADES TAKE UP LEAVES . . . . 234 GATHERING LEAVES . . 1
    THERE, POINTED LIKE THE PIP OF SPADES, ... 380 AN UNSTAMPED LETTER IN 8
SPAN
    THE SPAN OF LIFE . . . . 308 THE SPAN OF LIFE . . T
SPANISH
    THE FRENCH, THE SPANISH, AND THE DUTCH WERE DOWNED . . 422 FOR JOHN F. KENNEDY . 16
SPARE
    GO OUTDOORS IF YOU WANT TO FIGHT. SPARE ME. . .   . . 100 THE SELF-SEEKER . . 212
    BUT DARED NOT SPARE TO DO THE BEST WE COULD. . .   . . 109 THE EXPOSED NEST . . 28
    HIS NECK, OR THOUGHT TO SPARE HIS CLOTHES. . . .   . . 138 BROWN'S DESCENT . . 28
    TO HAVE THE BEST HE HAD, OR HAD TO SPARE-- . . .   . . 187 THE AX-HELVE 65
    TO SPARE THEM ANY TROUBLE. DOUBLE TROUBLE'S . .   . . 207 PAUPER WITCH OF GRAFTON 7
    AS IF HE COULD NOT SPARE . . . . 339 THE SUBVERTED FLOWER . 21
    IF GOD WOULD SPARE THEM TO DIE OF AGE. . . . . 344 DISCOVERY OF MADEIRAS . 26
    BUT LET ME INTO IT AND I WILL SPARE YOU. . . . .   . . 457 HOW HARD TO KEEP FROM 116
    SPARE ME THE SETTING OF MY FATE TO MUSIC. . . .   . . 495 A MASQUE OF MERCY . 58
SPARED
    A LEAPING TONGUE OF BLOOM THE SCYTHE HAD SPARED   . . . 22 THE TUFT OF FLOWERS . 23
    HE SPARED IT FROM THE NUMBER OF THE SLAIN, ... 375 A YOUNG BIRCH . . . 13
SPARES
    SPARES TO STRIKE FOR THE COMMON GOOD, ... 275 TWO TRAMPS IN MUD TIME 14
SPARK
    BECAUSE THEIR PURPOSE IS TO FLASH AND SPARK, ... 370 THE LITERATE FARMER AND 78
SPARKS
    IT WILL HAVE ROARED FIRST AND MIXED SPARKS WITH STARS, . 130 THE BONFIRE 27
    AND SEND MORE SPARKS UP CHIMNEY WITH THE SMOKE." . . . 234 EVENING A SUGAR ORCHARD 6
    THE SPARKS MADE NO ATTEMPT TO BE THE MOON. . . .   . . 234 EVENING A SUGAR ORCHARD 14
SPARROW
    THRUSH, BLUEBIRD, BLACKBIRD, SPARROW, AND ROBIN THRONG; . 239 OUR SINGING STRENGTH . 21

SPARTAN
  OLD ATTIC GRACE AND SPARTAN DISCIPLINE . . . . 511 A MASQUE OF MERCY . . 467
SPEAK
  AND THAT WAS WHY IT WHISPERED AND DID NOT SPEAK. . . . . 17 MOWING 6
  WE SPEAK THE LITERAL TO INSPIRE . . . . 19 REVELATION 7
  MUST SPEAK AND TELL US WHERE THEY ARE. . . . . 19 REVELATION 12
  AND COULD NOT SPEAK, ... 29 MY BUTTERFLY 39
  HE MAY NOT SPEAK OF IT, AND THEN HE MAY. . . . . 40 DEATH OF THE HIRED MAN 159
  "CAN'T A MAN SPEAK OF HIS OWN CHILD HE'S LOST?" . . . . 52 HOME BURIAL . . . 35
  I DON'T KNOW HOW TO SPEAK OF ANYTHING . . . . . . 52 HOME BURIAL . . . 46
  A MAN CAN'T SPEAK OF HIS OWN CHILD THAT'S DEAD." . . . 53 HOME BURIAL . . . 70
  "YOU CAN'T BECAUSE YOU DON'T KNOW HOW TO SPEAK. . . . 53 HOME BURIAL . . . 71
  YOU WANT THE TRUTH. I SPEAK BUT BY THE VOICES.. . . . 79 THE GENERATIONS OF MEN 156
  OR IT WOULD SPEAK IN DIALECT. WHOSE VOICE . . . . . 79 THE GENERATIONS OF MEN 173
  DOES IT PURPORT TO SPEAK IN? NOT OLD GRANDSIR'S . . . 79 THE GENERATIONS OF MEN 174
  "WHY DO YOU SPEAK LIKE THAT? WHAT DO YOU KNOW? . . . . 87 THE HOUSEKEEPER . . . 178
  "YOU SPEAK AS IF THIS WERE A TRAVELED ROAD. . . . . . 90 THE FEAR 24
  AND DIDN'T ANSWER--DIDN'T SPEAK-- . . . . 129 THE IMPULSE . . . 17
  MESERVE WAS FIRST TO SPEAK. HE POINTED BACKWARD . . . . 143 SNOW 6
  I WANT TO SPEAK TO HER." / "ALL SHE SAID WAS, . . . 152 SNOW 276
  SHE DIDN'T DARE TO SPEAK WHEN HE WAS HERE. . . . 153 SNOW 293
  IT'S STRANGE SHE DOESN'T WANT TO SPEAK TO US." . . . . 154 SNOW 314
  ON WORDS, AND TRIES HIS WORST TO MAKE WORDS SPEAK . . . 171 NEW HAMPSHIRE . . . 401
  IN ANY WAY THE WORLD KNEW HOW TO SPEAK. . . . . . 196 PAUL'S WIFE . . . 157
  IF I WAS NOT TO SPEAK OF IT TO YOU . . . . 222 TO E.T. 19
  OVER BACK WHERE THEY SPEAK OF LIFE AS STAYING . . . . 263 THE INVESTMENT . . . 1
  WHICH MAY BE THOUGHT, BUT ONLY SO TO SPEAK. . . . . . 269 THE BEAR 32
  BUT IF YOU SO MUCH AS DARE TO SPEAK, ... 275 TWO TRAMPS IN MUD TIME 21
  I TURNED TO SPEAK TO GOD . . . . 309 NOT ALL THERE . . . 1
  GOD TURNED TO SPEAK TO ME . . . . 309 NOT ALL THERE . . . 5
  I ONLY SPEAK TO YOU AS ONE OF THEM. . . . . 323 BUILD SOIL 210
  SO VIVID AS TO SEEM TO SPEAK. . . . . 327 A MISSIVE MISSILE . . 8
  IT CANNOT SPEAK AS FAR AS THIS. . . . . 328 A MISSIVE MISSILE . . 55
  AND FINDING, WASN'T DISPOSED TO SPEAK. . . . . . . 421 ONE MORE BREVITY . . 69
  DARE TO SPEAK OUT AND TELL ME ABOUT MYSELF. . . . . 456 HOW HARD TO KEEP FROM 100
  AND SPEAK TO HIM BEFORE THE OTHERS COME. . . . . . 474 A MASQUE OF REASON . 32
  YET YOU DON'T SPEAK. LET FOOLS BEMUSE THEMSELVES . . . 484 A MASQUE OF REASON . 298
  ABOUT HIS BLINDNESS. / OH, HE SPEAKS! HE CAN SPEAK! . . 488 A MASQUE OF REASON . 417
  THAT WAS WHERE MY ENGAGEMENT WAS TO SPEAK . . . . 497 A MASQUE OF MERCY . 94
  (HE STARTS TO SPEAK, BUT STOPS AGAIN TO LISTEN. . . . 502 A MASQUE OF MERCY . 244
SPEAKER
  SO FAR AS HE, THE SPEAKER, WAS CONCERNED . . . . . . 370 THE LITERATE FARMER AND 57
SPEAKING
  SPEAKING OF WHO'S AFRAID OF WHO, HOWEVER, ... 47 A HUNDRED COLLARS . . 81
  THE LITTLE COTTAGE WE WERE SPEAKING OF, ... 55 THE BLACK COTTAGE . . 5
  TO SET THE VOICES SPEAKING OUT OF IT, ... 78 THE GENERATIONS OF MEN 129
  SPEAKING OR SINGING, AND THE BAND-MUSIC PLAYING. . . . 78 THE GENERATIONS OF MEN 130
  FOLKS IN HER DAY WERE GIVEN TO PLAIN SPEAKING. . . . 79 THE GENERATIONS OF MEN 181
  "WELL THEN, IT'S GRANNY SPEAKING: 'I DUNNOW! . . . . 80 THE GENERATIONS OF MEN 184
  "TRY SPEAKING. SAY 'HELLO!'" / "HELLO. HELLO." . . . 153 SNOW 298
  "KEEP SPEAKING, THEN." / "HELLO. HELLO. HELLO.-- . . . 154 SNOW 304
  THE LITTLE MEN (IT'S MASSACHUSETTS SPEAKING)-- . . . . 166 NEW HAMPSHIRE . . . 225
  AS IF IT WAS HER MOTHER SPEAKING TO HER. . . . . . 181 MAPLE 66
  "SPEAKING OF CONTRARIES, SEE HOW THE BROOK . . . . . 259 WEST-RUNNING BROOK . . 38
  HE MAY BE SOME GOOD, IN A MANNER OF SPEAKING. . . . . 407 FROM PLANE TO PLANE . 103
SPEAKS
  BUT ALWAYS GOD SPEAKS AT THE END: . . . . 21 THE TRIAL BY EXISTENCE 49
  SO THAT SHE ALMOST SPEAKS. . . . . 257 THE LOVELY BE CHOOSERS 51
  ABOUT HIS BLINDNESS. / OH, HE SPEAKS! HE CAN SPEAK! . . 488 A MASQUE OF REASON . 417
SPEAR
  YET EVERY SECOND SPEAR . . . . 13 ROSE POGONIAS . . . 14
SPEARS
  FOR ALL I KNEW IT MAY HAVE SHARPENED SPEARS . . . . . 189 THE GRINDSTONE . . . 37
SPECIAL
  ANYTHING SPECIAL YOU'RE A-MIND TO NAME. . . . . . 53 HOME BURIAL . . . 52
  TO CATCH IT IN A SORT OF SPECIAL PICTURE . . . . . 55 THE BLACK COTTAGE . . 2
  TO TAKE THEM AS AGAINST A SPECIAL STATE . . . . . 166 NEW HAMPSHIRE . . . 230
  HE HAD A SPECIAL TERROR OF THE FLUX . . . . . . 171 NEW HAMPSHIRE . . . 374
  TO SEE IF THERE WAS NOT SOME SPECIAL TREE . . . . 183 MAPLE 100
  AND WEREN'T THERE SPECIAL CEMETERY FLOWERS, ... 200 PLACE FOR A THIRD . . 26
  HE THOUGHT NO SPECIAL GOODNESS COULD BE LOST . . . . 284 THE GOLD HESPERIDEE . 34
  WILL THE SPECIAL JANIZARY . . . . 288 DEPARTMENTAL . . . 25
  WHICH MAKES THE WAR GOD SEEM NO SPECIAL DUNCE . . . 350 TO A YOUNG WRETCH . . 17
  THAT'S HOW WE FEEL--AND WE'RE NO SPECIAL MYSTICS. . . 351 THE LESSON FOR TODAY . 42
  AT HIS DEVOTIONS IN A SPECIAL PLOT. . . . . . . 354 THE LESSON FOR TODAY . 130
  FROM SOURCE UNKNOWN BUT FROM NO SPECIAL PLACE . . . 411 POD OF THE MILKWEED . 2
SPECIE
  AND TURN US INTO THE NEXT SPECIE FOLKS . . . . . . 369 THE LITERATE FARMER AND 43
SPECIMEN
  A SPECIMEN OF BERYL WITH A TRACE . . . . 162 NEW HAMPSHIRE . . . 118
  A SPECIMEN OF EVERYTHING, I SAID. . . . . 163 NEW HAMPSHIRE . . . 124
  MORE THAN ENOUGH LAND FOR A SPECIMEN . . . . . . 163 NEW HAMPSHIRE . . . 145
  IN SPECIMEN CRAB IN SPECIMEN ROCK, ... 364 TRESPASS 14
SPECIMENS
  JUST SPECIMENS IS ALL NEW HAMPSHIRE HAS, ... 161 NEW HAMPSHIRE . . . 61
  THEIR LABEL PROP-LOCKS, ONLY SPECIMENS . . . . . . 290 OLD BARN AT THE BOTTOM 37
SPECK
  A SPECK THAT WOULD HAVE BEEN BENEATH MY SIGHT . . . . 357 A CONSIDERABLE SPECK . 1
  THIS WAS NO DUST SPECK BY MY BREATHING BLOWN, ... 357 A CONSIDERABLE SPECK . 7
  A CONSIDERABLE SPECK . . . . 357 A CONSIDERABLE SPECK . T
SPECKLED
  IT IS SPECKLED WITH GRIME AS IF . . . . 110 A PATCH OF OLD SNOW . 5
SPECTACLES
  ARMED WITH A SCYTHE AND SPECTACLES THAT GLOWED. . . . 189 THE GRINDSTONE . . . 30
SPECTER
  A BARKLESS SPECTER. HE HAD HALTED TOO, ... 125 AN ENCOUNTER 14
  NO HUMAN SPECTER AT THE FEAST . . . . 281 BLUE RIBBON AT AMESBURY 37

PAGE TITLE LINE

SPECTER-LIKE
 WHAT THINGS FOR DREAM THERE ARE WHEN SPECTER-LIKE,   . . . 14 WAITING 1
SPECULATION
 SPECULATION, ... 219 I WILL SING YOU ONE-O . 51
SPED
 IN FRONT AT THE EDGE OF THE ROAD WHERE THE TRAFFIC SPED,   . 286 A ROADSIDE STAND . . 2
SPEECH
 AND DREAMING, AS IT WERE, HELD BROTHERLY SPEECH   . . . . 23 THE TUFT OF FLOWERS . 37
 AND FEAR OF SEEMING SHORT OF SPEECH, OR WHETHER   . . . 106 CHRISTMAS TREES . . 27
 THE WRITER AND TALKER FREE SPEECH AND FREE PRESS. . . . 319 BUILD SOIL . . . 113
 OF SPEECH AND THINKING IS SO MUCH MY BETTER . . . . . 324 BUILD SOIL . . . 250
 IS NOT ITS OWN LOVE BACK IN COPY SPEECH, ... 338 THE MOST OF IT . . 7
 AS A FIGURE OF SPEECH . . . . 434 KITTY HAWK . . . 186
 FREE WILL, TRADE, VERSE, THOUGHT, LOVE, SPEECH, COINAGE. . 459 HOW HARD TO KEEP FROM 186
SPEED
 BY JUNE OUR BROOK'S RUN OUT OF SONG AND SPEED. . . . . 119 HYLA BROOK . . . 1
 THROUGH OPENING CLOUDS AT NIGHT WITH DRONING SPEED . . . 132 THE BONFIRE . . . 106
 IN FRONT OF TWENTY OTHERS' WRIGGLING SPEED-- . . . . 237 A HILLSIDE THAW . . 13
 HE WISHED IT ALL THE MODERN SPEED. . . . . . . 274 A LONE STRIKER . . 51
 NO SPEED OF WIND OR WATER RUSHING BY . . . . . 300 THE MASTER SPEED . 1
 BUT YOU HAVE SPEED FAR GREATER. YOU CAN CLIMB . . . 300 THE MASTER SPEED . 2
 THE MASTER SPEED . . . . 300 THE MASTER SPEED . T
 TWO SUCH AS YOU WITH SUCH A MASTER SPEED . . . . 300 THE MASTER SPEED . 10
 IT WILL GATHER SPEED TILL YOUR NERVES PREPARE . . . 306 A TRIAL RUN . . . 6
 THE OLD MAN ARGUES SCIENCE CHEAPENED SPEED. . . . . 371 THE LITERATE FARMER AND 98
 MY SLOWNESS WITH THEIR SPEED . . . . 415 CLOSED FOR GOOD . . 9
 WHO, HAVING FAILED OF THE MODERN SPEED, ... 419 ONE MORE BREVITY . 12
 AT LESS THAN THE SPEED OF SOUND . . . . . . 466 SOME SCIENCE FICTION . 18
 OR EVEN THE SPEED OF LIGHT . . . . 466 SOME SCIENCE FICTION . 19
SPEEDING
 THE SPEEDING OF DEVOTED SOULS . . . . . . 20 THE TRIAL BY EXISTENCE 31
SPELL
 WE HAVE TO USE A SPELL TO MAKE THEM BALANCE: . . . 33 MENDING WALL . . 18
 I BLAMED IT ON THE HOT SPELL WE'VE BEEN HAVING. . . . 46 A HUNDRED COLLARS . . 58
 SHE HAS HER SPELL ON EVERY SINGLE LIZARD. . . . 237 A HILLSIDE THAW . . 22
 THE SPELL THAT SO COULD HOLD THEM AS THEY WERE . . . 237 A HILLSIDE THAW . . 30
 UNDER A SPELL SO THE WRONG ONES CAN'T FIND IT, . . . 379 DIRECTIVE 58
 INDULGING AN ABSURD DRAMATIC SPELL. . . . . . 396 ANY SIZE WE PLEASE . 3
SPELL-BREAKING
 TO STRETCH A PROFFERING HAND--AND A SPELL-BREAKING. . 230 TWO LOOK AT TWO . . . 36
SPEND
 WITHOUT A SINGLE LEAF TO SPEND ON AUTUMN, ... 175 THE CENSUS-TAKER . . 23
 FEW FARMS CHANGED HANDS; SO RATHER THAN SPEND YEARS . . 177 THE STAR-SPLITTER . . 28
 IF YOU DON'T WANT TO SPEND THE NIGHT OUTDOORS. . . . 214 A FOUNTAIN, A BOTTLE . 50
SPENDER
 WHERE THE SPENDER THINKS IT WENT. . . . . . . 309 HARDSHIP OF ACCOUNTING 2
SPENDING
 SPENDING WHAT ONWARD IMPULSE THEY STILL HAD . . . . 229 TWO LOOK AT TWO . . . 9
 SPENDING YOURSELF TOO MUCH IN SELF-SUPPORT. . . . . 356 A MOTH SEEN IN WINTER . 12
SPENDS
 THAT SPENDS TO NOTHINGNESS--AND UNRESISTED, ... 259 WEST-RUNNING BROOK . . 57
SPENT
 HE SPENT HIMSELF, THE LABOR OF HIS AX, ... 102 THE WOOD-PILE . . 37
 THE BREEZES WERE SO SPENT WITH WINTER BLOWING . . . 130 THE BONFIRE . . . 35
 AND SPENT THE PROCEEDS ON A TELESCOPE . . . . . 168 NEW HAMPSHIRE . . . 303
 OR BRANCH TO WHISTLE AFTER WHAT WAS SPENT. . . . . 175 THE CENSUS-TAKER . . 24
 AND SPENT THE PROCEEDS ON A TELESCOPE . . . . . 177 THE STAR-SPLITTER . . 17
 HORDES SPENT THEMSELVES TO MAKE IT WET AND COLD, . . 239 OUR SINGING STRENGTH . 3
 WHEN THE SPENT SUN THROWS UP ITS RAYS ON CLOUD . . . 249 ACCEPTANCE . . . 1
 I SPENT ON THE UNIMPORTANT WOOD. . . . . . . 275 TWO TRAMPS IN MUD TIME 16
 NEVER ASK OF MONEY SPENT . . . . 309 HARDSHIP OF ACCOUNTING 1
 YOUR LIGHT WAS SPENT PERHAPS AS IN A FOG . . . . 351 THE LESSON FOR TODAY . 24
 AND SPENT AND DUSTED OFF OF THEIR REGALIA, ... 412 POD OF THE MILKWEED . 35
SPES
 BUT SPES ALIT AGRICOLAM 'TIS SAID. . . . . . . 376 SOMETHING FOR HOPE . 24
SPHERE
 FORGETTING THAT AS FITTED TO THE SPHERE, ... 261 A SOLDIER 7
 NOT EVEN STOOPING FROM ITS SPHERE, ... 403 SOMETHING LIKE A STAR . 19
SPHERES
 ON SUCCESSIVE SPHERES . . . . 437 KITTY HAWK . . . 285
 TO EMBROIL THE VERY GODS ABOUT THEIR SPHERES . . . 511 A MASQUE OF MERCY . 471
SPHEROID
 SPHEROID THAT KICKED AND STRUGGLED IN ITS GAIT, . . . 190 THE GRINDSTONE . . . 40
SPICK
 "SHE AIN'T SPICK TOO MUCH HENGLISH--DAT'S TOO BAD." . . 187 THE AX-HELVE . . . 54
SPIDER
 HE WAS ONE OF THE KIND SPORTS CALL A SPIDER, . . . 70 THE CODE 33
 THE INDWELLING SPIDER RAN TO GREET THE FLY, . . . 126 RANGE-FINDING . . . 13
 LIKE A WHITE CRUMPLED SPIDER ON HIS KNEE: . . . 147 SNOW 115
 I FOUND A DIMPLED SPIDER, FAT AND WHITE, ... 302 DESIGN 1
 A SNOW-DROP SPIDER, A FLOWER LIKE A FROTH, . . . 302 DESIGN 7
 WHAT BROUGHT THE KINDRED SPIDER TO THAT HEIGHT, . . . 302 DESIGN 11
SPIKED
 NO MATTER IF NOT BRUISED OR SPIKED WITH STUBBLE, . . . 69 AFTER APPLE-PICKING . 34
 I GUESS THEY THOUGHT I'D SPIKED HIM IN THE TEMPLE . . . 72 THE CODE . . . 92
 THE WINDFALLS SPIKED WITH STUBBLE AND WORM-EATEN. . . 125 THE COW IN APPLE TIME . 8
SPIKES
 NOT WITHOUT FEEBLE-POINTED SPIKES OF FLOWERS . . . 17 MOWING 11
SPILLED
 HAD SPILLED THEM NEAR THE WINDOW, TOWARD THE LIGHT, . . . 216 A FOUNTAIN, A BOTTLE . 96
SPILLING
 THE LIFE FROM SPILLING. THEN THE BOY SAW ALL-- . . . 137 "OUT,OUT--" . . . 22
SPILLS
 AND SPILLS THE UPPER BOULDERS IN THE SUN, ... 33 MENDING WALL . . 3
SPIN
 BUT I OWN WHAT YOU SAY MAKES MY HEAD SPIN. . . . . 75 THE GENERATIONS OF MEN 60
 IT YET HAS POLES, AND ONLY NEEDS A SPIN . . . . 174 A STAR IN A STONEBOAT . 50
 I GAVE IT THE PRELIMINARY SPIN, ... 189 THE GRINDSTONE . . 26

SPIN (CONTINUED)
  THE SPINNER STILL WAS THERE TO SPIN. . . . . 273 A LONE STRIKER . . . 26
SPINE
  BENDS SQUARE IN WOODS, AN IRON SPINE . . . . 331 BEECH 2
  CLEAR INTO HER MARROW SPINE. . . . . 463 LINES IN DEJECTION . . 20
SPINES
  ARE INCH-DEEP WITH THE FROSTY SPINES AND BRISTLES-- . . . 42 THE MOUNTAIN 53
SPINNER
  THE SPINNER SAW IT AT A GLANCE. . . . . 273 A LONE STRIKER . . . 25
  THE SPINNER STILL WAS THERE TO SPIN. . . . . 273 A LONE STRIKER . . . 26
SPINNING
  THEY PRUDENTLY ARE SPINNING THEIR COCOON . . . . . . 248 THE COCOON 13
  SPINNING THEIR OWN COCOON DID THEY BUT KNOW IT. . . . 248 THE COCOON 16
SPIRE
  A SPIRE AND BELFRY COMING ON THE ROOF . . . . 386 A STEEPLE ON THE HOUSE 7
SPIRES
  WHERE HOUSES ALL ARE CHURCHES AND HAVE SPIRES. . . . 106 CHRISTMAS TREES . . 14
  THERE STOOD THE PURPLE SPIRES WITH NO BREATH OF AIR . . 343 QUEST OF PURPLE-FRINGED 17
SPIRIT
  SOME SPIRIT TO STAND SIMPLY FORTH, ... 20 THE TRIAL BY EXISTENCE 42
  SPIRIT TO MATTER TILL DEATH COME. . . . . 21 THE TRIAL BY EXISTENCE 64
  AND FEEL A SPIRIT KINDRED TO MY OWN; . . . . 23 THE TUFT OF FLOWERS . 33
  AND TRIPPED THE BODY, SHOT THE SPIRIT ON . . . . . . 262 A SOLDIER 13
  THE REQUISITE LIFT OF SPIRIT HAS NEVER BEEN FOUND, . . 287 A ROADSIDE STAND . . 45
  ENOUGH TO MAKE A SPIRIT MOAN . . . . 328 A MISSIVE MISSILE . . 39
  HER SPIRIT FADED AS FAR AWAY . . . . 346 DISCOVERY OF MADEIRAS . 103
  THE SPIRIT PLAYS US STRANGE RELIGIOUS PRANKS . . . . 358 THE LOST FOLLOWER . . 5
  THE KINDRED SPIRIT OF AN INNER HAZE? . . . . 415 A CABIN IN THE CLEARING 42
  LAY IN RISKING SPIRIT . . . . 435 KITTY HAWK 223
  SPIRIT ENTERS FLESH . . . . 435 KITTY HAWK 246
  HIS SPIRIT HAD TO COME. APPARENTLY . . . . 477 A MASQUE OF REASON . 100
  HAVE THEY BEEN DOWN? / NOT IN THE PROPER SPIRIT. . . 516 A MASQUE OF MERCY . . 618
SPIRITED (SEE ABSENT-SPIRITED, POOR-SPIRITED)
SPIRITS
  AND THE SLANT SPIRITS TROOPING BY . . . . 20 THE TRIAL BY EXISTENCE 21
  FOLKS THINK A WITCH WHO HAS FAMILIAR SPIRITS . . . . 202 THE WITCH OF COOS . . 4
SPIRTS
  SUMMONING SPIRTS ISN'T "BUTTON, BUTTON, ... 202 THE WITCH OF COOS . . 7
SPIT
  BECAUSE I MAKE HIM SPIT FIRE AT MY KNUCKLES, ... 94 THE SELF-SEEKER . . 34
  THE BITTER WORDS SHE SPIT . . . . 341 THE SUBVERTED FLOWER . 66
  THE DROUGHT WAS ONE NO SPIT OF RAIN COULD CURE. . . 400 THE BROKEN DROUGHT . 10
  FOR ME TO DISAGREE WITH HIM AND GET SPIT OUT . . . . 500 A MASQUE OF MERCY . . 184
  THERE MAY BE THERE AND GET SPIT OUT AGAIN. . . . . . 500 A MASQUE OF MERCY . . 189
SPITE
  IN SPITE OF A SCORCHED FOURTH-OF-JULY FEELING. . . . 132 THE BONFIRE 93
  QUIET AND LIGHT AND WARM, IN SPITE OF ALL . . . . . 148 SNOW 143
  IN SPITE OF THE WAY HIS TAIL HAD SMACKED . . . . . . 421 ONE MORE BREVITY . . 54
SPLASHED
  AND THEN IN THE FAR-DISTANT WATER SPLASHED, ... 338 THE MOST OF IT . . . 12
SPLASHING
  LIKE SPLASHING PHOSPHORESCENT PAINT, ... 451 A-WISHING WELL . . . 16
SPLATTERED
  DID IN FACT GET SPLATTERED . . . . 427 VERSION 14
SPLENDID
  ALL VERY SPLENDID. I AM FLATTERED PROUD . . . . . 481 A MASQUE OF REASON . 217
SPLENDIDEST
  THAT WAS THE SPLENDIDEST SACK . . . . 311 THE VINDICTIVES . . 38
SPLINTER
  LEAVES TO STRIP AND BRANCHES SPLINTER, ... 304 CLEAR AND COLDER . . 12
SPLINTERLESS
  FELL SPLINTERLESS AS A CLOVEN ROCK. . . . . 275 TWO TRAMPS IN MUD TIME 12
SPLINTERS
  ALL FOUR OF THEM TO SPLINTERS. WHAT DID THAT PROVE? . . 209 PAUPER WITCH OF GRAFTON 63
SPLIT
  IT WAS A CORD OF MAPLE, CUT AND SPLIT . . . . 101 THE WOOD-PILE . . . 23
  IS BLOCKS SPLIT OFF THE MOUNTAIN MASS-- . . . . . . 140 THE GUM-GATHERER . . 15
  BECAUSE IT DIDN'T DO A THING BUT SPLIT . . . . . . 179 THE STAR-SPLITTER . . 88
  A STAR IN TWO OR THREE, THE WAY YOU SPLIT . . . . . 179 THE STAR-SPLITTER . . 89
  LIKE SOME UP-ENDED BOULDER SPLIT IN TWO, ... 229 TWO LOOK AT TWO . . 19
  GOOD BLOCKS OF OAK IT WAS I SPLIT, ... 275 TWO TRAMPS IN MUD TIME 9
SPLITTER (SEE STAR-SPLITTER)
SPLITTING
  AND OUGHT TO DO SOME GOOD IF SPLITTING STARS . . . . 179 THE STAR-SPLITTER . . 93
  'SA THING TO BE COMPARED WITH SPLITTING WOOD. . . . 179 THE STAR-SPLITTER . . 94
  AND CAUGHT ME SPLITTING WOOD IN THE YARD. . . . . . 275 TWO TRAMPS IN MUD TIME 2
  IT CAME NEAR SPLITTING HER IN HALF. . . . . 452 A-WISHING WELL . . . 43
SPOIL
  I MUST NOT SPOIL YOUR CHRISTMAS WITH CONTRITION. . . 350 TO A YOUNG WRETCH . . 12
  I HAVE TO TELL YOU SOMETHING THAT WILL SPOIL . . . . 498 A MASQUE OF MERCY . . 143
SPOILED
  I'VE SPOILED JEMIMA IN MORE WAYS THAN ONE. . . . . . 49 A HUNDRED COLLARS . . 141
  BUT RAIN SPOILED ALL. THE DAY BEGAN UNCERTAIN, . . . 74 THE GENERATIONS OF MEN 19
  HE SAW ALL SPOILED. "DON'T LET HIM CUT MY HAND OFF-- . . 137 "OUT,OUT--" . . . 25
  WHAT SPOILED OUR NIGHT WAS TO HIM JUST HIS FUN. . . 155 SNOW 338
  THE SMARTY SOMEONE WHO SPOILED EVERYTHING . . . . . 209 PAUPER WITCH OF GRAFTON 70
SPOILS
  THAT SPOILS THE NIGGER-TRADER'S LUCK . . . . 345 DISCOVERY OF MADEIRAS . 58
  WHICH SPOILS YOUR FIGURE OF THE AMBULANCE. . . . . . 508 A MASQUE OF MERCY . . 383
SPOKE
  AND HE SPOKE THE BRIDEGROOM FAIR. . . . . 7 LOVE AND A QUESTION . 2
  TO RAISE HERSELF AND LOOK AGAIN. HE SPOKE . . . . . 51 HOME BURIAL . . . 5
  HE SPOKE TO HIS WIFE IN THE DOOR, 'LET ME SEE, . . . 61 BLUEBERRIES 76
  YOU SPOKE OF JOHN'S NOT BEING SAFE TO STAY WITH. . . 85 THE HOUSEKEEPER . . 123
  THE WOMAN SPOKE OUT SHARPLY, "WHOA, STAND STILL"-- . . 89 THE FEAR 8
  JOEL!" SHE SPOKE AS IF SHE COULDN'T TURN. . . . . . 92 THE FEAR 91
  AND SMILED, AND WHEN SHE DID NOT TURN, SPOKE GENTLY, . . 111 IN THE HOME STRETCH . 19

SPOKE (CONTINUED)
    "GOD!" ONE SAID WILDLY, AND, WHEN NO ONE SPOKE: . . . . 114 IN THE HOME STRETCH . 99
    YOU SPOKE FROM THAT FLOWER ON THE WINDOWSILL-- . . . . 118 THE TELEPHONE . . . 8
    AND SPOKE HIS DOUBTS IN EVERY OPEN PLACE. . . . . . 214 A FOUNTAIN, A BOTTLE . 36
    THEY SPOKE TO THEMSELVES . . . . 218 I WILL SING YOU ONE-O . 29
    THEY SPOKE OF THE SUN . . . . 219 I WILL SING YOU ONE-O . 39
    AND SPOKE OF THE LETTERED, ... 219 I WILL SING YOU ONE-O . 45
    THEY SPOKE FOR THE CLOCK . . . . 219 I WILL SING YOU ONE-O . 57
    TWO HAD SEEN TWO, WHICHEVER SIDE YOU SPOKE FROM. . . . 230 TWO LOOK AT TWO . . 38
    GOD ONCE SPOKE TO PEOPLE BY NAME. . . . . 266 SITTING BY A BUSH . 17
    THEY SPOKE TO THE FUGITIVE IN MY HEART AS IF IT WERE LEAF
       TO LEAF. . . . . 298 A LEAF-TREADER . . . 9
    THOUGH WITH EVERY WORD HE SPOKE . . . . 340 THE SUBVERTED FLOWER . 26
    BUT SPOKE TO ME IN A GALE . . . . 366 NOT OF SCHOOL AGE . 7
    SO I SPOKE IN TERMS OF ADOPTION THUS; . . . . . . 420 ONE MORE BREVITY . 27
    SO SINISTER? YOU SPOKE TO SOMEONE DOWN THERE. . . . . 516 A MASQUE OF MERCY . 606
SPOKEN
    WHEREIN WORDS WHETHER BEATEN OUT OR SPOKEN . . . . 141 THE LINE-GANG . . . 6
    DORKINGS BECAUSE THEY'RE SPOKEN OF BY CHAUCER, ... 162 NEW HAMPSHIRE . . 106
    SUSSEX BECAUSE THEY'RE SPOKEN OF BY HERRICK. . . . . 162 NEW HAMPSHIRE . . 107
    WOULDN'T BE SPOKEN TO ABOUT A WIFE . . . . 196 PAUL'S WIFE . . . 156
    BEFORE GOD'S LAST PUT OUT THE LIGHT WAS SPOKEN. . . . 250 ONCE BY THE PACIFIC . 14
    HER FEAR IS BEING SPOKEN BY THE RUDE . . . . . . 386 THE FEAR OF MAN . . 13
    THE OCEAN HAD BEEN SPOKEN TO BEFORE. . . . . . . 447 DOES NO ONE AT ALL EVER 31
    I SHOULD HAVE SPOKEN SOONER HAD I FOUND . . . . . 475 A MASQUE OF REASON . 54
    YES, SPOKEN SO WE CAN'T LIVE UP TO IT, ... 512 A MASQUE OF MERCY . 498
SPOKESMAN
    AND GIVE US MORE THAN OUR SPOKESMAN BARGAINED FOR; . . 349 OUR HOLD ON THE PLANET 4
SPONGY
    TILL THE SPONGY SOIL AGAIN WAS NATAL WET. . . . . . 349 OUR HOLD ON THE PLANET 10
SPOOL
    ALL DAY FROM SPOOL TO LESSER SPOOL, ... 273 A LONE STRIKER . . 21
SPOON
    USING NEITHER SPOON NOR SKIMMER, ... 303 CLEAR AND COLDER . 5
    LIKE A KITCHEN SPOON . . . . 442 KITTY HAWK . . . 442
SPOONS
    NO BETTER THAN SPOONS, ... 234 GATHERING LEAVES . . 2
SPORT
    TO MAKE IT WORTH LIFE'S WHILE TO WAKE AND SPORT. . . . 254 A WINTER EDEN . . 20
    AND MORE PREOCCUPATION WITH THE SPORT. . . . . . 424 FOR JOHN F. KENNEDY . 69
    I'M NOT A SPORT AND DON'T PRETEND I AM ONE.-- . . . 496 A MASQUE OF MERCY . 79
SPORTING
    YOU'RE SPORTING THERE. I'LL BET YOU'RE GOOD AT IT. . . 502 A MASQUE OF MERCY . 219
SPORTS
    HE WAS ONE OF THE KIND SPORTS CALL A SPIDER, ... 70 THE CODE 33
    WE BLAME OURSELVES. WE'RE GOOD SPORTS, AREN'T WE, BEL? . 496 A MASQUE OF MERCY . 78
S'POSE
    CRUEL--IT SOUNDS. I S'POSE THEY DID THE BEST . . . . 66 A SERVANT TO SERVANTS . 124
    I S'POSE I'VE GOT TO GO THE ROAD I'M GOING: . . . . 67 A SERVANT TO SERVANTS . 159
    IT WA'N'T NO SIGN, I S'POSE, WHEN MALLICE HUSE . . . 208 PAUPER WITCH OF GRAFTON 45
    I S'POSE YOU HAVE YOUR NOTIONS ON THE VEXED . . . . 369 THE LITERATE FARMER AND 47
SPOT
    BEFORE WE LEFT THE SPOT, ... 14 ROSE POGONIAS . . 18
    IN A NEW COTTAGE ON THE ANCIENT SPOT. . . . . . . 79 THE GENERATIONS OF MEN 164
    NOR KNOW THAT HE MIGHT MOVE IT FROM THE SPOT-- . . . 173 A STAR IN A STONEBOAT . 19
    HIS MARE WAS SURE TO OBSERVE THE SPOT . . . . . . 263 THE TIMES TABLE . 4
    THAT SPOT OF BLACK IS NOT A STAIN . . . . 392 A CLIFF DWELLING . 6
    AND ALL THE AIR RUSHED TO THE SPOT. . . . . . . 452 A-WISHING WELL . . 46
SPOTS
    AT THE SHINY DESERT WITH SPOTS OF GLOOM . . . . . 291 ON HEART'S BEGINNING TO 27
SPOTTED
    WHOSE SPOTTED FLOWERS HANG MEANLY DOWN. . . . . . 247 ON GOING UNNOTICED . . 8
SPOUSE
    OUR UN-OUTWITTED SPOUSE . . . . 464 MILKY WAY IS A COWPATH 17
SPRAWLING
    SPRAWLING ABOUT THE KITCHEN WITH THEIR TALK . . . . 65 A SERVANT TO SERVANTS . 77
SPRAY
    WITH THE HISS OF SPRAY; . . . . 218 I WILL SING YOU ONE-O . 10
SPRAYS
    FROM SPRAYS OF HONEYSUCKLE . . . . 227 TO EARTHWARD . . . 10
SPREAD
    AND SPREAD HER APRON TO IT. SHE PUT OUT HER HAND . . . 38 DEATH OF THE HIRED MAN 106
    A BUTTONED HAIRCLOTH LOUNGE SPREAD SCROLLING ARMS . . . 55 THE BLACK COTTAGE . 22
    ALL WIRY ARMS AND LEGS THAT SPREAD OUT WAVY . . . . 70 THE CODE 34
    ON THE BARE UPLAND PASTURE THERE HAD SPREAD . . . . 126 RANGE-FINDING . . 9
    BUT THE BLACK SPREAD LIKE BLACK DEATH ON THE GROUND, . 131 THE BONFIRE . . . 53
    I WON! BUT I'M SURE NO ONE EVER SPREAD . . . . . 132 THE BONFIRE . . . 81
    THAT I SPREAD COAL-BLACK OVER IN THE TIME . . . . 132 THE BONFIRE . . . 83
    WE SPREAD OUR TWO LEGS AS WE SPREAD ITS THREE, . . . 179 THE STAR-SPLITTER . 83
    AND SPREAD THE OPENING, AND YOU'VE GOT A DUGOUT . . . 193 PAUL'S WIFE . . . 81
    SPREAD OPEN AS I DROPPED THEM HALF-READ THROUGH . . . 222 TO E.T. 2
    WHEN I SPREAD OUT MY HAND HERE TODAY, ... 266 SITTING BY A BUSH . 1
    AND IN CONJUNCTION GIVING QUITE A SPREAD. . . . . . 269 THE BEAR . . . 21
    AMONG THE HARPLIKE SPREAD OF STRINGS. . . . . . . 274 A LONE STRIKER . . 29
    YOUR BASE HAS SPREAD TOO WIDE, ... 298 ON TAKING FROM THE TOP 6
    AND A MASKED MOON HAD SPREAD DOWN COMPASS RAYS . . . 300 MOON COMPASSES . 3
    "BEFORE THE THING HAS TIME TO SPREAD. . . . . . . 345 DISCOVERY OF MADEIRAS 61
    THE WINGS NOT FOLDED IN REPOSE, BUT SPREAD. . . . . 356 A MOTH SEEN IN WINTER . 4
    BUT ALL HE DID WAS SPREAD THE ROOM . . . . 417 AMERICA IS HARD TO SEE 37
    BY BEING SPREAD OUT OVER EVERYBODY, ... 506 A MASQUE OF MERCY . 322
SPREADING
    THAT SPREADING IN THE EVENING AIR BOTH WAYS . . . . 247 THE COCOON . . . 2
SPRING
    I'M GOING OUT TO CLEAN THE PASTURE SPRING; . . . . 1 THE PASTURE . . . 1
    A PRAYER IN SPRING . . . . 12 A PRAYER IN SPRING . T
    BUT AT SPRING MENDING-TIME WE FIND THEM THERE. . . . 33 MENDING WALL . . . 11
    SPRING IS THE MISCHIEF IN ME, AND I WONDER . . . . 34 MENDING WALL . . . 28

SPRING (CONTINUED)
    BUT THE SIGNS SHOWED WHAT IT HAD DONE IN SPRING: .   .   .   .   40 THE MOUNTAIN   12
    "AS TO THAT I CAN'T SAY. BUT THERE'S THE SPRING,   .   .   .   42 THE MOUNTAIN   63
    "BUT A LAKE'S DIFFERENT. WHAT ABOUT THE SPRING?"   .   .   .   43 THE MOUNTAIN   77
    I LIKE TO FIND FOLKS GETTING OUT IN SPRING.   .   .   .   .   49 A HUNDRED COLLARS   .   .   .   127
    PASTURE THEY SPRING IN, SOME IN CLUMPS TOO CLOSE   .   .   .   .   107 CHRISTMAS TREES   .   .   .   33
    MID-SUMMER IS TO SPRING AS ONE TO TEN.   .   .   .   .   .   .   120 THE OVEN BIRD   5
    LIKES TO TELL HOW ONE SPRING   .   .   .   .   133 A GIRL'S GARDEN   .   .   .   2
    AND PERHAPS IN THE SPRING   .   .   .   .   136 LAST WORD OF A BLUEBIRD   21
    WHEN THERE WAS WATER IN THE CELLAR IN SPRING   .   .   .   .   204 THE WITCH OF COOS   .   .   49
    IT IS BLUE-BUTTERFLY DAY HERE IN SPRING, ...   225 BLUE-BUTTERFLY DAY   .   .   1
    SINCE EVER THEY FLUNG ABROAD IN SPRING   .   .   .   .   .   236 MISGIVING   5
    IT SNOWED IN SPRING ON EARTH SO DRY AND WARM   .   .   .   .   239 OUR SINGING STRENGTH   .   1
    IN SPRING MORE MORTAL SINGERS THAN BELONG   .   .   .   .   239 OUR SINGING STRENGTH   .   19
    SPRING POOLS   .   .   .   .   245 SPRING POOLS   .   .   .   .   T
    WAS A SPRING WITH A BROKEN DRINKING GLASS, ...   263 THE TIMES TABLE   .   .   .   2
    MY FATHER BUILT, ENCLOSED A SPRING, ...   265 THE BIRTHPLACE   .   .   .   3
    HE KNEW A SPRING THAT WANTED DRINKING;   .   .   .   .   .   .   274 A LONE STRIKER   .   .   .   44
    WE MUST WAIT TILL SOME MONTHS HENCE IN THE SPRING TO KNOW.   .   305 THERE ARE ROUGHLY ZONES   19
    FOR A POEM THERE USED TO BE ON SPRING.   .   .   .   .   .   .   342 A CLOUD SHADOW   .   .   .   3
    FOR WHOM WOULD A POEM ON SPRING BE BY?   .   .   .   .   .   342 A CLOUD SHADOW   .   .   .   5
    COLD AS A SPRING AS YET SO NEAR ITS SOURCE, ...   378 DIRECTIVE   51
    THAT CHANGES WINTER INTO SPRING   .   .   .   .   390 TWO LEADING LIGHTS   .   .   25
    SPRING WATER IN OUR MOUNTAIN BOSOM SWELLS   .   .   .   .   446 DOES NO ONE AT ALL EVER   22
    TO SPRING IT LIKE A DEADFALL AND THE FAULT   .   .   .   .   502 A MASQUE OF MERCY   .   231
    MY SMALL FRESH-WATER SPRING GETS DROWNED OF COURSE.   .   .   513 A MASQUE OF MERCY   .   539
    I CAN COUNT ON MY SOURCE TO SPRING AGAIN, ...   514 A MASQUE OF MERCY   .   541
SPRINGING
    ALL SIMPLY IN THE SPRINGING OF THE YEAR.   .   .   .   .   .   .   12 A PRAYER IN SPRING   .   .   4
    THE FUTURE STATE IS SPRINGING EVEN NOW   .   .   .   .   .   .   506 A MASQUE OF MERCY   .   320
SPRINGS
    FROM HIDDEN GRAPEVINE SPRINGS   .   .   .   .   227 TO EARTHWARD   7
    REGULAR VERSE SPRINGS FROM THE STRAIN OF RHYTHM   .   .   .   460 HOW HARD TO KEEP FROM   213
SPRINGTIME
    SLAVE TO A SPRINGTIME PASSION FOR THE EARTH.   .   .   .   .   124 PUTTING IN THE SEED   .   .   9
SPRINKLED
    AND A FEW HOUSES SPRINKLED ROUND THE FOOT, ...   43 THE MOUNTAIN   97
SPROUT-LANDS
    AND SPROUT-LANDS FLOURISH WHERE THE AX HAS GONE.   .   .   .   73 THE GENERATIONS OF MEN   6
SPRUCE
    WAS GUM, THE GUM OF THE MOUNTAIN SPRUCE.   .   .   .   .   .   141 THE GUM-GATHERER   .   .   29
    A DOE FROM ROUND A SPRUCE STOOD LOOKING AT THEM   .   .   .   229 TWO LOOK AT TWO   .   .   15
    A BUCK FROM ROUND THE SPRUCE STOOD LOOKING AT THEM   .   .   229 TWO LOOK AT TWO   .   .   27
    YOU NICK MY SPRUCE UNTIL ITS FIBER CRACKS, ...   349 TO A YOUNG WRETCH   .   .   3
    FOR MAPLE, BIRCH, AND SPRUCE TO PUSH   .   .   .   .   .   .   376 SOMETHING FOR HOPE   .   .   6
    THE YOUNG SPRUCE MADE A SUITE OF GLADES   .   .   .   .   .   380 AN UNSTAMPED LETTER IN   9
SPRUNG
    THENCE THEY WERE SPRUNG, SO NUMEROUS A TRIBE   .   .   .   .   73 THE GENERATIONS OF MEN   10
    "IF I REMEMBER RIGHTLY, IT HAD SPRUNG   .   .   .   .   .   .   213 A FOUNTAIN, A BOTTLE   .   24
    WHAT CAN'T BE MOLDED MUST BE CRACKED AND SPRUNG.   .   .   .   267 WHAT FIFTY SAID   .   .   .   6
SPUN
    NOW STANDING CRACKED ITS SAIL AND SPUN;   .   .   .   .   .   .   344 DISCOVERY OF MADEIRAS   .   22
SPUNK
    CONCEAL A WISH TO SEE HIM SHOW THE SPUNK   .   .   .   .   .   153 SNOW   283
SPURT
    BUT IN A MOMENT NOT: A LITTLE SPURT   .   .   .   .   .   .   130 THE BONFIRE   23
SPY
    WHO HAD STOPPED OUTSIDE THE FENCE TO SPY, ...   385 A MOOD APART   5
SQUAD
    OF THE HIVE'S ENQUIRY SQUAD   .   .   .   .   288 DEPARTMENTAL   9
SQUARE
    "PROFESSOR SQUARE-THE-CIRCLE-TILL-YOU'RE-TIRED?   .   .   .   .   46 A HUNDRED COLLARS   .   .   44
    A HUNDRED SQUARE MILES ROUND IT IN THE MOUNTAINS: .   .   .   174 THE CENSUS-TAKER   .   .   5
    THE FARMHOUSE LINGERS, THOUGH AVERSE TO SQUARE   .   .   .   231 A BROOK IN THE CITY   .   .   1
    SQUARE MATTHEW HALE'S YOUNG GRAFTED APPLE TREE   .   .   .   .   283 THE GOLD HESPERIDEE   .   1
    WHEN CAME SQUARE HALE WITH LET'S SEE WHAT WE HAD: .   .   .   283 THE GOLD HESPERIDEE   .   10
    'TWAS SUNDAY AND SQUARE HALE WAS DRESSED FOR MEETING.   .   .   284 THE GOLD HESPERIDEE   .   41
    SQUARE MATTHEW HALE TOOK OFF HIS SUNDAY HAT   .   .   .   .   284 THE GOLD HESPERIDEE   .   45
    IN GRATITUDE FOR WHICH SQUARE MATTHEW VOWED   .   .   .   .   285 THE GOLD HESPERIDEE   .   59
    BENDS SQUARE IN WOODS, AN IRON SPINE   .   .   .   .   .   .   331 BEECH   2
    SAND HAS BEEN THRUSTING IN THE SQUARE OF DOOR   .   .   .   .   399 THE INGENUITIES OF DEBT   13
SQUARELY
    AND EVERY PIECE I SQUARELY HIT   .   .   .   .   275 TWO TRAMPS IN MUD TIME   11
SQUARES
    TO THE FRESH AND BLACK OF THE SQUARES OF EARLY MOLD   .   .   299 STRONG SAYING NOTHING   .   9
SQUASH
    OR CROOK-NECKED GOLDEN SQUASH WITH SILVER WARTS,   .   .   .   286 A ROADSIDE STAND   .   .   12
SQUASHED
    SOME PALLID THING HAD SQUASHED ITS FEATURES FLAT   .   .   .   148 SNOW   160
SQUAT
    YOU SQUAT OLD PYRAMID, ...   298 ON TAKING FROM THE TOP   2
SQUAW
    INSTEAD OF WHICH SHE WAS SOME HALF-BREED SQUAW.   .   .   .   192 PAUL'S WIFE   39
SQUEAKED
    'THAT GETS YE!' HE SQUEAKED LIKE A SQUEEZED RAT.   .   .   .   72 THE CODE   78
SQUEAL
    FOR THE SQUEAL OF BRAKES, THE SOUND OF A STOPPING CAR,   .   287 A ROADSIDE STAND   .   .   36
SQUEEZE
    THE LACK OF LIBERTY, THE SQUEEZE OF LAW   .   .   .   .   .   460 HOW HARD TO KEEP FROM   199
SQUEEZED
    'THAT GETS YE!' HE SQUEAKED LIKE A SQUEEZED RAT.   .   .   .   72 THE CODE   78
SQUINTED
    BAPTISTE DREW BACK AND SQUINTED AT IT, PLEASED: .   .   .   188 THE AX-HELVE   .   .   .   101
SQUINTING
    LIGHTING HIS PIPE NOW, SQUINTING DOWN HIS NOSE   .   .   .   .   112 IN THE HOME STRETCH   .   64
SQUIRTS
    (HE STOOD WELL BACK FOR FEAR OF SCALDING SQUIRTS.)   .   .   270 THE EGG AND THE MACHINE   12

PAGE TITLE   LINE

ST.
      FAR TO NORTH OF THE ST. LAWRENCE. . . . . 304 CLEAR AND COLDER   . . 11
STAB
      TO STAB ME IN THE SNEEZE-NERVE OF A NOSTRIL. . . . . 277 THE WHITE-TAILED HORNET 10
      OR GIVE HER A STAB OF THE TINE, ... 463 LINES IN DEJECTION . . 18
      SCIENCE GAVE A STAB . . . . 468 A REFLEX   5
STABBED
      WITH BREAKING STEP I STABBED THE DUST, ... 336 THE WIND AND THE RAIN   7
      DELIBERATELY STABBED HIM DEAD. . . . . 444 THE DRAFT HORSE . . .   8
STABLE
      GNAWS IN THE STABLE AIN'T NO PROOF TO ME . . . . . 209 PAUPER WITCH OF GRAFTON 66
STABLED
      OR WEAVING LIKE A STABLED HORSE: . . . . 325 TO A THINKER   7
STACK
      AND TRY TO STACK THEM IN A BETTER LOAD. . . . . . 267 THE ARMFUL 12
STAFF
      I'D LAY MY HAND ON HIS HAND ON HIS STAFF, ... 354 THE LESSON FOR TODAY . 124
STAGE
      LIKE A LONE ACTOR ON A GLOOMY STAGE-- . . . . . . 160 NEW HAMPSHIRE 46
      WILL GIVE US BY SHORTCUT THE FINAL STAGE . . . . . 358 THE LOST FOLLOWER . . 13
      I LEFT LIGHT SHINING ON AN EMPTY STAGE . . . . . 497 A MASQUE OF MERCY . . 100
STAGNATION
      FROM ITS LONG STAGNATION . . . . 435 KITTY HAWK 240
STAID
      TO STAY OUR MINDS ON AND BE STAID. . . . . 403 SOMETHING LIKE A STAR . 25
STAIN
      I CRAVE THE STAIN . . . . 227 TO EARTHWARD 20
      AND I DREAD THE OMINOUS STAIN OF TAR . . . . . . 232 THE KITCHEN CHIMNEY . 13
      THAT SPOT OF BLACK IS NOT A STAIN . . . . 392 A CLIFF DWELLING . . .   6
STAINED
      BEFORE IT STAINED A SINGLE HUMAN BREAST. . . . . . 126 RANGE-FINDING . . .   3
      OR STAINED BY VEGETATION FROM ABOVE, ... 214 A FOUNTAIN, A BOTTLE . 39
      THAT WHEN IT HAS SWEPT BY, LEAVES SUMMITS STAINED. . . 255 THE FLOOD 13
STAINS
      YOU COULD SIT THERE WITH THE STAINS ON YOUR SHOES . . . 54 HOME BURIAL 84
STAIR
      AND BEGAN TO BOUNCE DOWN A GRANITE STAIR, ... 383 WERE I IN TROUBLE . .   4
STAIRCASE
      I DON'T SEE ANY STAIRCASE. / THERE ARE STAIRS. . . . 517 A MASQUE OF MERCY . . 631
STAIRS
      THE NIGHT CLERK LED HIM UP THREE FLIGHTS OF STAIRS . . . 45 A HUNDRED COLLARS . . 33
      HE SAW HER FROM THE BOTTOM OF THE STAIRS . . . . 51 HOME BURIAL   1
      LISTEN TO ME. I WON'T COME DOWN THE STAIRS." . . . . 52 HOME BURIAL 40
      AND I CREPT DOWN THE STAIRS AND UP THE STAIRS . . . . 53 HOME BURIAL 79
      UP AND DOWN STAIRS AND THROUGH THE ROOMS, AND NONE . . . 112 IN THE HOME STRETCH . 42
      THE NIGHT THE BONES CAME UP THE CELLAR STAIRS . . . . 203 THE WITCH OF COOS . . 40
      BEGAN THE STAIRS, TWO FOOTSTEPS FOR EACH STEP, . . . 204 THE WITCH OF COOS . . 51
      I LISTENED TILL IT ALMOST CLIMBED THE STAIRS . . . . 205 THE WITCH OF COOS . . 90
      THE STEPS BEGAN TO CLIMB THE ATTIC STAIRS. . . . . 206 THE WITCH OF COOS . 116
      COME DOWN THE STAIRS AT NIGHT AND STAND PERPLEXED . . 206 THE WITCH OF COOS . 126
      I DON'T SEE ANY STAIRCASE. / THERE ARE STAIRS. . . . 517 A MASQUE OF MERCY . . 631
STAKE
      STILL GROWING, AND ON ONE A STAKE AND PROP, ... 102 THE WOOD-PILE . . . 33
      BUT WON'T, SHOULD BE BURNED AT THE STAKE OR SOMETHING. . . 202 THE WITCH OF COOS . .   6
STAKED
      THAT SCIENCE MAY HAVE STAKED THE FUTURE ON? . . . . 412 POD OF THE MILKWEED . 52
STAKES
      AND THE WORK IS PLAY FOR MORTAL STAKES, ... 277 TWO TRAMPS IN MUD TIME 70
STALE
      "AND STRONG OF STALE TOBACCO." / "HE'LL PULL THROUGH." . 145 SNOW 72
      ARGUMENTS TOO STALE TO MENTION . . . . 396 AN IMPORTER   9
STALEMATE
      BETTER THAN ALL THE STALEMATE AN'S AND IFS. . . . . 423 FOR JOHN F. KENNEDY . 59
STALK
      AND HOLDING BY THE STALK, ... 118 THE TELEPHONE . . . 13
STALKS
      O'ERNIGHT 'TWIXT MULLEIN STALKS A WHEEL OF THREAD . . . 126 RANGE-FINDING . . . 10
STALL
      BURST INTO MY NARROW STALL; . . . . 11 TO THE THAWING WIND . 11
      LIKE A BEAST'S STALL, TO EASE THEIR CONSCIENCES. . . . 66 A SERVANT TO SERVANTS . 120
      WHEN OTHER CREATURES HAVE GONE TO STALL AND BIN, . . . 223 THE RUNAWAY 20
      AND LOOK FOR WHAT HAD MADE ME STALL, ... 304 UNHARVESTED   3
STAMP
      THE FINAL FLAT OF THE HOE'S APPROVAL STAMP . . . . . 299 STRONG SAYING NOTHING .   3
      I LEAVE THIS NOTE WITHOUT A STAMP . . . . 380 AN UNSTAMPED LETTER IN   5
STAMPED
      THAT WAS WELL! AND HE STAMPED A HOOF. . . . . . . 24 PAN WITH US 10
      AND STAMPED AND SAID THINGS TO HIMSELF, ... 138 BROWN'S DESCENT . . . 17
STAMPEDE
      BUT IF I THOUGHT TO STOP THE WET STAMPEDE, ... 237 A HILLSIDE THAW . . .   9
STANCHIONS
      LIKE STANCHIONS IN THE BARN, FROM FLOOR TO CEILING-- . . . 66 A SERVANT TO SERVANTS . 115
STAND
      SOME SPIRIT TO STAND SIMPLY FORTH, ... 20 THE TRIAL BY EXISTENCE 42
      WHAT MAKES YOU STAND THERE ON ONE LEG LIKE THAT? . . . 47 A HUNDRED COLLARS . . 69
      I STAND AND MAKE MYSELF REPEAT OUT LOUD . . . . . 63 A SERVANT TO SERVANTS . 18
      TO STAND TOGETHER ON THE CRATER'S VERGE . . . . . 73 THE GENERATIONS OF MEN 16
      ALL IS, HE'S MADE UP HIS MIND NOT TO STAND . . . . 83 THE HOUSEKEEPER . . 70
      WHAT HE HAS GOT TO STAND." / "WHERE IS ESTELLE? . . . 83 THE HOUSEKEEPER . . 71
      THE WOMAN SPOKE OUT SHARPLY, "WHOA, STAND STILL!-- . . . 89 THE FEAR   8
      AND I CAN'T STAND IT. JOEL, LET ME GO!" . . . . . 91 THE FEAR 48
      WHAT DO YOU WANT, DEAR? COME, STAND BY THE BED; . . . 96 THE SELF-SEEKER . . 104
      YOU STAND UP TO IT LIKE A PAIR OF COCKS. . . . . . 100 THE SELF-SEEKER . . 211
      HE WENT BEHIND IT TO MAKE HIS LAST STAND. . . . . 101 THE WOOD-PILE . . . 22
      TO COME AS HERE I STAND AND GO THE ROUND . . . . . 111 IN THE HOME STRETCH . 27
      WE STAND HERE DREAMING. HURRY! CALL THEM BACK!" . . . 113 IN THE HOME STRETCH . 77
      I DON'T STAND STILL AND LOOK AROUND . . . . . . 124 A TIME TO TALK . . .   3
      MADE THE DIM TREES STAND BACK IN WIDER CIRCLE-- . . . . 130 THE BONFIRE 29

STAND (CONTINUED)
  IT WON'T LIE DOWN. THEN LET IT STAND. WHO CARES?" . . . . 148 SNOW 152
  SHE SAID SHE COULDN'T STAND THE PEOPLE IN IT, ... 166 NEW HAMPSHIRE . . . 224
  THAN THE GRINDSTONE CAN BOAST TO STAND OR GO. . . . . . 189 THE GRINDSTONE . . . 13
  COME DOWN THE STAIRS AT NIGHT AND STAND PERPLEXED . . . 206 THE WITCH OF COOS . . 126
  THAT CAN'T STAND MOWERS AND PLOWERS. . . . . 264 THE LAST MOWING . . . 6
  A ROADSIDE STAND THAT TOO PATHETICALLY PLED, ... 286 A ROADSIDE STAND . . 3
  A ROADSIDE STAND . . . . 286 A ROADSIDE STAND . . T
  HERE FAR FROM THE CITY WE MAKE OUR ROADSIDE STAND . . . 286 A ROADSIDE STAND . . 18
  I COULD STAND WHOLE DAYFULS OF IT. . . . . 304 CLEAR AND COLDER . . 20
  BUT STAND YOUR GROUND, ... 306 A TRIAL RUN . . . 8
  IT GRIEVES ME TO HAVE HAD YOU STAND . . . . 327 A MISSIVE MISSILE . . 25
  IT WILL STAND FORTH, ENTIRELY WHITE IN BARK, ... 375 A YOUNG BIRCH . . . 6
  SO UNDERMINES MY BAREFOOT STAND I TOTTER, ... 391 ON BEING IDOLIZED . . 4
  IT SEEMED AS IF I COULDN'T STAND THE STRAIN. . . . . . 398 BURSTING RAPTURE . . 8
  ALL YOU MEAN, PAUL, I THINK---- / WILL YOU STAND THERE . 519 A MASQUE OF MERCY . 675
  AND WE'RE AN ORATOR. GET UP. STAND UP . . . . . . 519 A MASQUE OF MERCY . 679
STANDING
  THAT'S STANDING BY THE MOTHER. IT'S SO YOUNG . . . . 1 THE PASTURE . . . 6
  YOU NEVER SEE HIM STANDING ON THE HAY . . . . . 37 DEATH OF THE HIRED MAN 94
  UNLIKE OTHER FOLKS AS YOUR STANDING THERE . . . . . 53 HOME BURIAL 60
  WHAT WAS HE STANDING STILL FOR IN THE BUSHES?" . . . 90 THE FEAR 28
  WHAT COULDN'T HE DO TO US STANDING HERE! . . . . . 91 THE FEAR 56
  SITTING OR STANDING AS HE CHOSE, ... 138 BROWN'S DESCENT . . . 26
  AS STANDING IN THE RIVER ROAD . . . . 139 BROWN'S DESCENT . . . 46
  OR EVEN THOUGHT OF STANDING THERE . . . . . . 139 BROWN'S DESCENT . . . 57
  I'VE KEPT BROWN STANDING IN THE COLD . . . . . . 140 BROWN'S DESCENT . . . 71
  WHEN COLE RETURNED HE FOUND HIS WIFE STILL STANDING . 151 SNOW 245
  I FOUND HIM STANDING AT THE CLOSE OF DAY . . . . . 160 NEW HAMPSHIRE . . . 44
  AND STANDING AT OUR LEISURE TILL THE DAY BROKE, . . . 179 THE STAR-SPLITTER . . 85
  STANDING ALONE WITH SMOOTH ARMS LIFTED UP, ... 184 MAPLE 145
  BUT STANDING OUTDOORS HUNGRY, IN THE COLD, ... 189 THE GRINDSTONE . . . 17
  AND, ANYWAY, ITS STANDING IN THE YARD . . . . . . 189 THE GRINDSTONE . . . 19
  APPEAR LIKE STANDING . . . . 219 I WILL SING YOU ONE-O 66
  WHAT WOULD IT TAKE MY STANDING THERE FOR, ... 251 BEREFT 3
  THAT WAVE'S BEEN STANDING OFF THIS JUT OF SHORE--" . . 258 WEST-RUNNING BROOK . . 18
  "THAT WAVE'S BEEN STANDING OFF THIS JUT OF SHORE . . . 258 WEST-RUNNING BROOK . . 27
  AMONG UNEARTHED POTATOES STANDING STILL, ... 263 THE INVESTMENT . . . 6
  WAS STANDING IDLE FOR HIS SAKE. . . . . 273 A LONE STRIKER . . . 15
  I HAVE A PAIR OF SHOES STANDING, ... 294 A RECORD STRIDE . . . 5
  THAT YOU MAY HAVE THE POWER OF STANDING STILL-- . . . 300 THE MASTER SPEED . . 8
  REFLECTS A STANDING GULL. . . . . 301 NEITHER OUT FAR NOR IN 8
  SUPPOSE HIS GHOST IS STANDING BY . . . . 327 A MISSIVE MISSILE . . 30
  SHE WAS STANDING TO THE WAIST . . . . 339 THE SUBVERTED FLOWER . 15
  NOW STANDING CRACKED ITS SAIL AND SPUN; . . . . . 344 DISCOVERY OF MADEIRAS 22
  SOME STANDING JEST BETWEEN YOU MEN? . . . . . . 346 DISCOVERY OF MADEIRAS 94
  IT GIVES UP STANDING STRAIGHT AND GOES DOWN SWISHING. . 349 TO A YOUNG WRETCH . . 4
  THE PLACE OF STANDING STILL . . . . 388 MIDDLENESS OF THE ROAD 6
  AND BEING GOOD FOR THESE MEANS STANDING BY . . . . 398 NO HOLY WARS FOR THEM . 5
  THERE ARE FEW INSTITUTIONS STANDING HIGHER . . . . 400 TO THE RIGHT PERSON . 4
  FOR STANDING STILL IN ONE PLACE TRUE FOREVER; . . . 480 A MASQUE OF REASON . 192
  (WHO HAS BEEN STANDING DAZED WITH NEW IDEAS) . . . 489 A MASQUE OF REASON . 441
  (STILL STANDING OFF) WE'VE ALL GROWN FOND OF YOU. . . 518 A MASQUE OF MERCY . 666
STANDPOINT
  I FELT MY STANDPOINT SHAKEN . . . . 377 ONE STEP BACKWARD TAKEN 8
STANDS
  A TREE BESIDE THE WALL STANDS BARE, ... 9 A LATE WALK . . . 9
  AND OFF A BLOSSOM IN MID-AIR STANDS STILL. . . . . 12 A PRAYER IN SPRING . 12
  AND HOW IT STANDS BETWEEN THE NIGHT TONIGHT . . . 179 THE STAR-SPLITTER . . 97
  IT STANDS BESIDE THE SAME OLD APPLE TREE. . . . . 189 THE GRINDSTONE . . . 8
  STANDS STILL AND DANCES, BUT IT RUNS AWAY; . . . . 259 WEST-RUNNING BROOK . . 47
  NO ONE STANDS ROUND TO STARE. . . . . 289 DEPARTMENTAL . . . 40
  EAT IT OR PLOW IT UNDER WHERE IT STANDS, ... 323 BUILD SOIL . . . 216
  LOOK DOWN THE LONG VALLEY AND THERE STANDS A MOUNTAIN . 379 TOO ANXIOUS FOR RIVERS 1
  THE ELEPHANT STANDS ON THE BACK OF A TURTLE; . . . 379 TOO ANXIOUS FOR RIVERS 15
  AND THE NEEDLE STANDS ON END. . . . . 384 IN THE LONG NIGHT . . 4
  BUT JUDGING BY WHAT LITTLE OF IT STANDS, ... 399 THE INGENUITIES OF DEBT 10
  AND STANDS BESIDE, SUPPORTING IT IN PLACE.) . . . 474 A MASQUE OF REASON . 23
  I WANT TO ASK YOU IF IT STANDS TO REASON . . . . 476 A MASQUE OF REASON . 88
  KNEEL BY HIM. BEL STANDS UP BESIDE HER CHAIR . . . 518 A MASQUE OF MERCY . 652
STANDSTILL
  AND BLIND ME TO A STANDSTILL IF IT MUST. . . . . . 265 DUST IN THE EYES . . 6
STAPLES
  HER GREAT WEIGHT CREAKS THE BARBED WIRE IN ITS STAPLES . 269 THE BEAR 7
STAR
  IT IS UNDER THE SMALL, DIM, SUMMER STAR. . . . . . 6 GHOST HOUSE 21
  TO FIND FUSED IN ANOTHER STAR. . . . . 121 BOND AND FREE . . . 20
  TO HEAVE THEM HIGHER TO THE MORNING STAR? . . . . 169 NEW HAMPSHIRE . . . 319
  NEVER TELL ME THAT NOT ONE STAR OF ALL . . . . . 172 A STAR IN A STONEBOAT . 1
  A STAR IN A STONEBOAT . . . . 172 A STAR IN A STONEBOAT . T
  HE LOADED AN OLD STONEBOAT WITH THE STAR . . . . 173 A STAR IN A STONEBOAT . 26
  IF IT COULD PUT A STAR BACK IN ITS COURSE. . . . . 173 A STAR IN A STONEBOAT . 30
  SURE THAT THOUGH NOT A STAR OF DEATH AND BIRTH, . . . 174 A STAR IN A STONEBOAT . 46
  THOUGH NOT, I SAY, A STAR OF DEATH AND SIN, ... 174 A STAR IN A STONEBOAT . 49
  AT A STAR QUAKING IN THE OTHER END. . . . . . 179 THE STAR-SPLITTER . . 78
  A STAR IN TWO OR THREE, THE WAY YOU SPLIT . . . . 179 THE STAR-SPLITTER . . 89
  BRIGHTLY, AS IF A STAR PLAYED ON THE PLACE, ... 195 PAUL'S WIFE . . . 135
  WAS FROM THE GIRL HERSELF, THOUGH, NOT FROM A STAR, . . 195 PAUL'S WIFE . . . 137
  THE UTMOST STAR . . . . 219 I WILL SING YOU ONE-O 62
  A PIERCING LITTLE STAR WAS THROUGH. . . . . . 233 LOOKING FOR SUNSET BIRD 20
  BUT YOU HAD AWAKENED UNDER THE MORNING STAR . . . 235 VALLEY'S SINGING DAY . 4
  WITH ONE FIRST-WATER STAR ALMOST AS SHINING. . . . 245 THE FREEDOM OF THE MOON 6
  WITH A STAR IN ONE EYE, ... 261 CANIS MAJOR . . . 3
  TURNING HER FOREHEAD WITH A STAR, ... 263 THE TIMES TABLE . . . 6
  THE SKY HAD HERE AND THERE A STAR; . . . . . . 290 ON HEART'S BEGINNING TO 5
  OR A STAR COMING TO DILATE THE SUN. . . . . . 317 BUILD SOIL . . . 59
  THE SYMBOL STAR IT LIFTS AGAINST YOUR CEILING . . . 350 TO A YOUNG WRETCH . . 23
  TO SEE THE STAR SHOWER KNOWN AS LEONID . . . . 360 A LOOSE MOUNTAIN . . 2

STAR (CONTINUED)
        "I STOPPED TO COMPLIMENT YOU ON THIS STAR   . . . . . . 368 THE LITERATE FARMER AND   9
        THERE IS A STAR THAT'S SERIOUS BY NAME   . . . . 369 THE LITERATE FARMER AND   29
        WILL TELL YOU IT'S THE STAR OF BETHLEHEM . . . . 369 THE LITERATE FARMER AND   34
        WHAT'S A STAR DOING BIG AS A BASEBALL?   . . . . 369 THE LITERATE FARMER AND   37
        BETWEEN US TWO IT'S NOT A STAR AT ALL.   . . . . 369 THE LITERATE FARMER AND   38
        IS NOT A STAR?" / "BELIEVE IT? WHY, I KNOW IT.   . . . 370 THE LITERATE FARMER AND   63
        "IN SHORT, YOU THINK THAT STAR A PATENT MEDICINE   . . . 371 THE LITERATE FARMER AND   92
        LIKE A STAR FRESH FALLEN OUT OF THE SKY.   . . . . . . 383 WERE I IN TROUBLE   . .   5
        WHAT STAR IF ANY FELL.   . . . . 383 MAKING CERTAIN ANYTHING   4
        SOME CLUSTER ONE STAR SHORT.   . . . . 384 MAKING CERTAIN ANYTHING   8
        BY ANNOUNCING A STAR DOWN .   . . . 384 MAKING CERTAIN ANYTHING   11
        TO MAKE SURE WHAT STAR I MISSED   . . . . 384 MAKING CERTAIN ANYTHING   13
        EVERY STAR IN SIGHT.   . . . . 384 MAKING CERTAIN ANYTHING   15
        FAR STAR THAT TICKLES FOR ME MY SENSITIVE PLATE   . . . 389 SKEPTIC   1
        TO SOME STAR OFF THERE, SAY, A HALF LIGHT-YEAR . . . . . 395 WHY WAIT FOR SCIENCE .   7
        O STAR (THE FAIREST ONE IN SIGHT), ... 403 SOMETHING LIKE A STAR .   1
        TAKE SOMETHING LIKE A STAR   . . . . 403 SOMETHING LIKE A STAR .   T
        WE MAY TAKE SOMETHING LIKE A STAR   . . . . 403 SOMETHING LIKE A STAR .   24
        THE STAR ITSELF--HEAVEN'S GREATEST STAR, ... 421 ONE MORE BREVITY   . .   60
        THE STAR OF BETHLEHEM, THE POMEGRANATES, ... 473 A MASQUE OF REASON .   12
STARCHED (SEE WELL-STARCHED)
STAR-CROSSED
        WE POETS OFFER YOU ANOTHER: STAR-CROSSED.   . . . . . . 510 A MASQUE OF MERCY .   439
        OF STAR-CROSSED, MERCY-CROSSED, OR EVIL-CROSSED   . . . 510 A MASQUE OF MERCY .   440
        I CHOOSE THE STAR-CROSSED AS A STAR-CROSSED LOVER.   . . 510 A MASQUE OF MERCY .   441
        WHY DO YOU CALL YOURSELF A STAR-CROSSED LOVER? . . . . . 510 A MASQUE OF MERCY .   450
STARE
        NO ONE STANDS ROUND TO STARE.   . . . . 289 DEPARTMENTAL   40
        SO DIFFERENT FROM THE HARD AND LEVEL STARE   . . . . . 356 TIME OUT   10
STARFISH
        OF A STARFISH LAID OUT WITH RIGID POINTS."   . . . . . . 93 THE SELF-SEEKER . . .   20
STARGAZING
        HIS NEW JOB GAVE HIM LEISURE FOR STARGAZING.   . . . . . 178 THE STAR-SPLITTER . .   75
STARK
        AND THOSE OF THE NAME STARK GATHERED IN BOW, ... 73 THE GENERATIONS OF MEN   4
        THIS WAS SOME STARK SHE DIDN'T KNOW. HE NODDED.   . . . . 74 THE GENERATIONS OF MEN   34
        "STARK?" HE INQUIRED. "NO MATTER FOR THE PROOF."   . . . 74 THE GENERATIONS OF MEN   45
        "YES, STARK. AND YOU?" / "I'M STARK." HE DREW HIS PASSPORT. 74 THE GENERATIONS OF MEN   46
        "I ONLY MEAN MY MOTHER WAS A STARK .   . . . 75 THE GENERATIONS OF MEN   55
        OF THE STARK FAMILY I'M A MEMBER OF)."   . . . . 76 THE GENERATIONS OF MEN   81
        I CAN MAKE OUT OLD GRANDSIR STARK DISTINCTLY--   . . . . 77 THE GENERATIONS OF MEN 104
        BLESS YOU, IT ISN'T GRANDSIR STARK, IT'S GRANNY;   . . . 77 THE GENERATIONS OF MEN 106
STARKNESS
        ALL CLAIMING SOME PRIORITY IN STARKNESS.   . . . . 75 THE GENERATIONS OF MEN   49
STARKS
        WOULD HAVE BEEN STARKS, AND DOUBTLESS HERE TODAY."   . . 75 THE GENERATIONS OF MEN   52
        THIS IS THE PIT FROM WHICH WE STARKS WERE DIGGED."   . . 76 THE GENERATIONS OF MEN   94
STARLIGHT
        BY STARLIGHT IN THE GRASS FOR A LAST PEACH   . . . . . . 117 IN THE HOME STRETCH . 190
STARLIKE
        ACHIEVE AT TIMES A VERY STARLIKE START.   . . . . 246 FIREFLIES IN THE GARDEN   5
STARLIT
        I AM THE GUARDIAN WRAITH OF STARLIT SMOKE   . . . . . . 414 A CABIN IN THE CLEARING 10
STARRED
        NO MEMORY OF HAVING STARRED   . . . . 307 PROVIDE, PROVIDE   .   16
STARRING
        LET'S KEEP STARRING MAN   . . . . 441 KITTY HAWK   414
STARRY
        DOWN FROM THE STARS TO FREEZE THE DEW AS STARRY.   . . . 169 NEW HAMPSHIRE   . . .   342
STARS
        STARS   . . . .   9 STARS   . . . . . .   T
        THOSE STARS LIKE SOME SNOW-WHITE   . . . .   9 STARS   10
        THAT THE STARS WERE ALMOST FADED AWAY . . . . 15 IN A VALE   15
        I NOTICED THAT I MISSED STARS IN THE WEST, ... 40 THE MOUNTAIN   3
        THROUGH THE THIN FROST, ALMOST IN SEPARATE STARS,   . . 108 OLD MAN'S WINTER NIGHT   2
        IT WILL HAVE ROARED FIRST AND MIXED SPARKS WITH STARS,   130 THE BONFIRE   27
        FURTHER O'ERHEAD THAN ALL BUT STARS AND ANGELS--   . . . 132 THE BONFIRE   107
        THAT MADE THE STARS BRIGHT   . . . . 135 LAST WORD OF A BLUEBIRD 10
        DOWN FROM THE STARS TO FREEZE THE DEW AS STARRY.   . . . 169 NEW HAMPSHIRE   . . .   342
        HE WAS NOT USED TO HANDLING STARS THROWN DARK   . . . . 172 A STAR IN A STONEBOAT .   8
        OF HEAVENLY STARS WITH HUGGER-MUGGER FARMING.   . . . . 176 THE STAR-SPLITTER . .   14
        AS ON A FARM, BUT PLANETS, EVENING STARS .   . . . 178 THE STAR-SPLITTER . .   72
        AND OUGHT TO DO SOME GOOD IF SPLITTING STARS   . . . . . 179 THE STAR-SPLITTER . .   93
        AND MOON AND STARS, ... 219 I WILL SING YOU ONE-O . 40
        HERE COME REAL STARS TO FILL THE UPPER SKIES, ... 246 FIREFLIES IN THE GARDEN   1
        THAT, THOUGH THEY NEVER EQUAL STARS IN SIZE .   . . . . 246 FIREFLIES IN THE GARDEN   3
        (AND THEY WERE NEVER REALLY STARS AT HEART), ... 246 FIREFLIES IN THE GARDEN   4
        BETWEEN THE DOTTED STARS, ... 252 THE PEACEFUL SHEPHERD   4
        AND LOOK ELSEWHERE THAN TO STARS AND MOON AND SUN   . . . 268 ON LOOKING UP BY CHANCE   9
        BUT STARS WERE SCARCE IN THAT PART OF THE SKY, ... 295 LOST IN HEAVEN   . . .   5
        BETWEEN STARS--ON STARS WHERE NO HUMAN RACE IS.   . . . 296 DESERT PLACES   . . .   14
        THE STARS ARE BROUGHT OUT BRIGHT.   . . . . 301 VOICE WAYS   5
        (THIS LIKE FATE BY STARS IS RECKONED), ... 304 CLEAR AND COLDER   .   7
        BRING OUT THE STARS, BRING OUT THE FLOWERS, ... 332 ALL REVELATION   . . .   17
        BUT NO, I WAS OUT FOR STARS: .   . . . 334 COME IN   17
        AND LOST THE STARS OF HEAVEN, MAY, OH, MAY   . . . . . . 350 TO A YOUNG WRETCH   . . 22
        A VOICE SAID, LOOK ME IN THE STARS .   . . . 362 A QUESTION   1
        MUCH NOTICE OF WHAT'S GOING ON IN STARS.   . . . . 370 THE LITERATE FARMER AND 70
        "HERE COME MORE STARS TO CHARACTER THE SKIES, ... 370 THE LITERATE FARMER AND 75
        OF CAUTION UNDER STARS THAT VERY WELL   . . . . 383 BRAVADO   2
        WE WERE COUNTING STARS, ... 437 KITTY HAWK   312
        NAMING STARS TO BOOT   . . . . 438 KITTY HAWK   316
        AT THE STARS OR MOON   . . . . 442 KITTY HAWK   438
        OF DUSTY WEEDS TO TAKE A DRINK OF STARS.   . . . . 454 HOW HARD TO KEEP FROM   14
        AND SUPERSTITION WINS. HE BLAMES THE STARS, ... 462 HOW HARD TO KEEP FROM   267
        (AS I REMEMBER THEY WERE SUMMER STARS, ... 462 HOW HARD TO KEEP FROM   269
        A-FORAGING ON STARS, ... 465 MILKY WAY IS A COWPATH   32

PAGE TITLE   LINE

STARS'
  FROM TWO STARS' HAVING COALESCED . . . . 381 AN UNSTAMPED LETTER IN   26
STAR'S
  THE EX-KING SAID, "YON STAR'S INDIFFERENCE . . . . . 454 HOW HARD TO KEEP FROM   17
STAR-SHOT
  THE HARM WAS DONE: FROM HAVING BEEN STAR-SHOT . . . . 173 A STAR IN A STONEBOAT . 20
STAR-SPLITTER
  THE STAR-SPLITTER . . . . 176 THE STAR-SPLITTER . . T
  THAT TELESCOPE WAS CHRISTENED THE STAR-SPLITTER, . . . 179 THE STAR-SPLITTER . . 87
  IT'S A STAR-SPLITTER IF THERE EVER WAS ONE, ... 179 THE STAR-SPLITTER . . 92
START
  ACHIEVE AT TIMES A VERY STARLIKE START. . . . . . . 246 FIREFLIES IN THE GARDEN 5
  AND NOT MELT SNOW OR START A DORMANT TREE. . . . . . 254 A WINTER EDEN 4
  I STRAIN AT LESSONS FIT TO START A SUTURE. . . . . . 267 WHAT FIFTY SAID . . . 7
  HE HAS A HALF A MIND TO START, ... 280 BLUE RIBBON AT AMESBURY 26
  IT WILL START HAIR-RAISING CURRENTS OF AIR . . . . . 306 A TRIAL RUN 2
  THE MORAL IS, MAKE A LATE START TO MARKET. . . . . . 322 BUILD SOIL 181
  IF PART THEY DO. LET ME PROPOSE A START. . . . . . . 352 THE LESSON FOR TODAY . 65
  TO START THE WORLD OF OLD . . . . 361 ALMOST TWO THOUSAND . 1
  AND IF OUR GETTING UP TO START THE DAY . . . . . . 372 THE LITERATE FARMER AND 120
  A FRESH START FOR THE HUMAN RACE. . . . . 417 AMERICA IS HARD TO SEE 30
  'TIS A CONFUSION IT WAS OURS TO START . . . . . . 423 FOR JOHN F. KENNEDY . 41
  IN A RUNNING START, ... 436 KITTY HAWK 258
  TO START THE WORLD ALL OVER AT. . . . . 453 A-WISHING WELL . . . 81
  IT SEEMS TO START RIGHT OFF ACCELERATING. . . . . . 489 A MASQUE OF REASON . . 450
  TO A BAD START IT SEEMS IN THE WRONG SCHOOL . . . . . 499 A MASQUE OF MERCY . . 162
  WHERE SHALL I START IN? WHERE MY EYES FELL FIRST? . . 506 A MASQUE OF MERCY . . 326
  THEN FURTHER DOWN IT SEEMS TO START FROM WHERE . . . . 506 A MASQUE OF MERCY . . 335
STARTED
  YOU MUST BE GETTING STARTED BACK TO TOWN." . . . . . 111 IN THE HOME STRETCH . 17
  HE HADN'T COME AND HAD HE REALLY STARTED." . . . . . 152 SNOW 277
  THEY STARTED UP. FRED TOOK THE TELEPHONE. . . . . . 155 SNOW 328
  AFTER HE'D PICKED THE LOCK AND GOT IT STARTED, ... 170 NEW HAMPSHIRE . . . 346
  AND SET HERSELF BACK WHERE SHE STARTED FROM. . . . . 187 THE AX-HELVE . . . 53
  THAT WAS THE WAY HE STARTED COURTING ME. . . . . . 209 PAUPER WITCH OF GRAFTON 72
  WHERE THE CHIMNEY STARTED ABOVE THE STOVE. . . . . . 232 THE KITCHEN CHIMNEY . 12
  IT STARTED A GRIEF WITHIN A GRIEF, ... 253 THE THATCH . . . 21
  THAT WAS HOW THAT GRIEF STARTED TO MELT. . . . . . 253 THE THATCH . . . 30
  OF ONCE HAVING STARTED A WAR, ... 310 THE VINDICTIVES . . . 16
  STARTED CHAIRS THUNDERING ON THE KITCHEN FLOOR, . . . 368 THE LITERATE FARMER AND 2
  AND STARTED DOWN THE GULLY. . . . . 377 ONE STEP BACKWARD TAKEN 6
  ACROSS THE PAGE TO WHERE WE STARTED FROM. . . . . . 405 FROM PLANE TO PLANE . 52
  AND STARTED HIS MARCH BACK AGAIN DISCOURSING: . . . . 406 FROM PLANE TO PLANE . 60
  AND STARTED SHAPING MY LIFE TO HIS, ... 420 ONE MORE BREVITY . 41
  THEY STARTED TO WANE. . . . . 448 THE BAD ISLAND--EASTER 40
  WE STARTED TO EXULT . . . . 464 MILKY WAY IS A COWPATH 2
  THAT STARTED OFF LORD GOD OF HOSTESSES. . . . . . 480 A MASQUE OF REASON . 181
  WE CAN GO BACK TO WHERE WE STARTED FROM. . . . . . 507 A MASQUE OF MERCY . . 359
STARTING
  BEFORE SHE SAW HIM. SHE WAS STARTING DOWN, ... 51 HOME BURIAL . . . 2
  I'M HERE--SO FAR--AND STARTING ON AGAIN. . . . . . 143 SNOW 12
  HAVE GOT IT ONE STEP FROM THE STARTING PLACE. . . . . 189 THE GRINDSTONE . . . 7
  WHEN STARTING CLEAR AT DAWN . . . . 333 HAPPINESS MAKES UP . . 15
  HE WILL BE STARTING PRETTY LATE. . . . . 419 AMERICA IS HARD TO SEE 79
  SO THAT BECAUSE WE'RE ALWAYS STARTING FRESH . . . . . 510 A MASQUE OF MERCY . . 433
STARTLE
  WHY, I MIGHT WAKE HER UP AND STARTLE HER. . . . . . 58 THE BLACK COTTAGE . . 93
STARTLED
  WAS STARTLED WHEN AN ANSWER REALLY CAME. . . . . . 91 THE FEAR 66
STARTLES
  (SHE STARTLES AT THE SUDDEN NOTE OF KINDNESS.) . . . . 519 A MASQUE OF MERCY . . 691
STARTS
  THAT STARTS UP ON IT SOMEWHERE--I'VE HEARD SAY . . . . 42 THE MOUNTAIN . . . 46
  THE LINE WHERE MAN LEAVES OFF AND NATURE STARTS, . . . 171 NEW HAMPSHIRE . . . 379
  (HE STARTS TO SPEAK, BUT STOPS AGAIN TO LISTEN. . . . 502 A MASQUE OF MERCY . . 244
  (THE CURTAIN STARTS TO FALL.) PLEASE HOLD THE CURTAIN.-- 519 A MASQUE OF MERCY . . 673
STARVATION
  LET THEM SUFFER STARVATION AND DIE . . . . . . 313 THE VINDICTIVES . . . 90
  AND OF HIS RACE STARVATION SLIM, ... 392 A CLIFF DWELLING . . 12
STARVE
  HERE ALL STARVE TOGETHER, ... 512 A MASQUE OF MERCY . . 504
STATE
  THE STATE ASYLUM. I WAS PREJUDICED; . . . . . . 65 A SERVANT TO SERVANTS . 91
  AFFECTION OR THE WANT OF IT IN THAT STATE. . . . . . 65 A SERVANT TO SERVANTS . 102
  IS THE DISGRACE IN MAN OR STATE OR NATION. . . . . . 159 NEW HAMPSHIRE . . . 8
  WHO BOASTED OF HIS STATE AS BEAUTIFUL . . . . . . 159 NEW HAMPSHIRE . . . 10
  TALK CALIFORNIA--A STATE SO BLESSED, ... 159 NEW HAMPSHIRE . . . 17
  I MET A POET FROM ANOTHER STATE, ... 159 NEW HAMPSHIRE . . . 25
  HE'S YOUR ONE CHANCE TO SCORE AGAINST THE STATE.) . . . 161 NEW HAMPSHIRE . . . 66
  A STATE PRODUCING PRECIOUS METALS, STONES, ... 164 NEW HAMPSHIRE . . . 165
  TO TAKE THEM AS AGAINST A SPECIAL STATE . . . . . . 166 NEW HAMPSHIRE . . . 230
  AND VERY SENSIBLE. NO STATE CAN BUILD . . . . . . 168 NEW HAMPSHIRE . . . 284
  SHE'S STILL NEW HAMPSHIRE, A MOST RESTFUL STATE. . . . 170 NEW HAMPSHIRE . . . 357
  LAY HIM IN STATE ON A SEPAL. . . . . 288 DEPARTMENTAL . . . 29
  MAKE UP YOUR MIND TO DIE IN STATE. . . . . . . 307 PROVIDE, PROVIDE . . 9
  AN INCONSISTENCY. THE STATE SHALL BE . . . . . . 324 BUILD SOIL . . . 246
  AND COULD IT BE BROUGHT UNDER STATE CONTROL, ... 353 THE LESSON FOR TODAY . 99
  AND FOLLOW SOME DEVELOPMENT OF STATE, ... 355 THE LESSON FOR TODAY . 142
  TO FRIGHTEN CHURCH OR STATE . . . . 384 MAKING CERTAIN ANYTHING 10
  I DON'T BELIEVE I BELIEVE A THING YOU STATE. . . . . 389 SKEPTIC 3
  IN THE ONE STATE OF OURS THAT IS A SHIRE, ... 400 TO THE RIGHT PERSON . 1
  HE'LL FIND THAT ASIATIC STATE . . . . 419 AMERICA IS HARD TO SEE 80
  IN THE AUGUST OCCASIONS OF THE STATE . . . . . . 422 FOR JOHN F. KENNEDY . 2
  IT WAS IN A STATE . . . . 426 A NEVER NAUGHT SONG . 6
  AND DISCIPLINE SHOULD BE IN SCHOOL AND STATE . . . . 460 HOW HARD TO KEEP FROM 200
  BEFORE THEY MAKE IT A STATE. . . . . 466 SOME SCIENCE FICTION . 32
  IT'S TIME THE POOR WERE TREATED BY THE STATE . . . . 477 A MASQUE OF REASON . . 124
  THE FUTURE STATE IS SPRINGING EVEN NOW . . . . . . 506 A MASQUE OF MERCY . . 320

                                                            PAGE TITLE   LINE

STATE (CONTINUED)
     THE BASIC THREE THE STATE IS FOUNDED ON. . . . . 520 A MASQUE OF MERCY . . 704
STATED
     (STATED IN LENGTHS OF HIM IT MIGHT NOT BE.) . . . . . . 198 WILD GRAPES 77
     AND GOT THE UNITED STATES STATED. . . . . 295 A RECORD STRIDE . . . 36
     MAY MUCH STAY OUT OF OUR STATED PLAN, ... 305 UNHARVESTED 12
STATE-MANIPULATED
     BY GRACE OF STATE-MANIPULATED PELF, ... 359 THE LOST FOLLOWER . . . 29
STATEMENT
     BY A PLAIN STATEMENT OF RELATIONSHIP, ... 75 THE GENERATIONS OF MEN 59
     ONE SIMPLE LITTLE STATEMENT FROM THE THRONE . . . . . 484 A MASQUE OF REASON . . 308
STATE-RIGHTS
     A STATE-RIGHTS FREE-TRADE DEMOCRAT. WHAT'S THAT? . . . 324 BUILD SOIL 245
STATES
     IT WASN'T JUST TO KEEP THE STATES TOGETHER. . . . . . 56 THE BLACK COTTAGE . . 56
     SHE'S ONE OF THE TWO BEST STATES IN THE UNION. . . . . 164 NEW HAMPSHIRE . . . 175
     BOTH ARE DELIGHTFUL STATES FOR THEIR ABSURDLY . . . . 165 NEW HAMPSHIRE . . . 186
     AND GOT THE UNITED STATES STATED. . . . . 295 A RECORD STRIDE . . . 36
     JOIN THE UNITED STATES AND JOIN THE FAMILY-- . . . . . 325 BUILD SOIL 281
     STATES STRONG ENOUGH TO DO GOOD ARE BUT FEW. . . . . . 398 NO HOLY WARS FOR THEM . 1
     BUT PUNY LITTLE STATES CAN ONLY BE. . . . . 398 NO HOLY WARS FOR THEM . 4
STATE'S
     AND VINDICATE THE STATE'S HUMANITY. . . . . 159 NEW HAMPSHIRE 21
     THE STATE'S ONE FUNCTION IS TO GIVE. . . . . 450 OUR DOOM TO BLOOM . . 12
STATION
     YOU HAD US FOR A HALFWAY STATION . . . . 150 SNOW 214
     IN WOODS SOME TEN MILES FROM A RAILROAD STATION, . . . 160 NEW HAMPSHIRE 41
     ROSE LIKE A FACTOR'S AT A TRADING STATION. . . . . . . 160 NEW HAMPSHIRE 53
     AS UNDER-TICKET-AGENT AT A STATION . . . . 178 THE STAR-SPLITTER . . 69
     LIKE COMING TO A SUDDEN RAILROAD STATION. . . . . . . 189 THE GRINDSTONE . . . 33
     IN ONE SELF STATION. . . . . 219 I WILL SING YOU ONE-O . 67
     AT EVERY STATION BUT THE FINAL ONE. . . . . 501 A MASQUE OF MERCY . . 195
STATISTICS
     AND GET OUTSIDE OF TOO MUCH BAD STATISTICS, ... 351 THE LESSON FOR TODAY . 37
STATUE
     AND SET UP LIKE A STATUE IN YOUR YARD, ... 365 OF STONES OF THE PLACE   10
STAUNCH
     NO LONGER NEEDED? STAUNCH IT AT ITS SOURCE . . . . . . 231 A BROOK IN THE CITY . 14
STAVES
     FAILED TO CRUSH THEIR BARREL STAVES . . . . 344 DISCOVERY OF MADEIRAS . 28
STAY
     HER PLEASURE WILL NOT LET ME STAY. . . . .   7 MY NOVEMBER GUEST . . 6
     "STAY WHERE YOU ARE UNTIL OUR BACKS ARE TURNED!" . . . 33 MENDING WALL 19
     WHERE ARE YOU MOVING OVER TO? STAY STILL. . . . . . . 47 A HUNDRED COLLARS . . 89
     THINGS OVER AND OVER THAT JUST WON'T STAY DONE. . . . . 64 A SERVANT TO SERVANTS . 52
     SHE DOES LOOK LIKE YOU. STAY THE WAY YOU ARE. . . . . 77 THE GENERATIONS OF MEN 113
     "YES, YOU MUST GO; WE CAN'T STAY HERE FOREVER. . . . . 77 THE GENERATIONS OF MEN 120
     BUT WHEN I'M GONE--OF COURSE I CAN'T STAY HERE: . . . 82 THE HOUSEKEEPER . . . 34
     YOU SPOKE OF JOHN'S NOT BEING SAFE TO STAY WITH. . . . 85 THE HOUSEKEEPER . . . 123
     THAT MUST BE IT. SOME DAYS HE WON'T STAY ON. . . . . . 94 THE SELF-SEEKER . . . 36
     I WENT TO SHOW YOU HOW TO MAKE IT STAY, ... 109 THE EXPOSED NEST . . 5
     BUT SWINGING DOESN'T BEND THEM DOWN TO STAY . . . . . 121 BIRCHES 4
     HE SAW NO STAY UNLESS HE STOVE . . . . 137 BROWN'S DESCENT . . . 14
     WHY CAN'T HE STAY AT HOME?" / "HE HAD TO PREACH." . . 145 SNOW 69
     BUT IF YOU'RE GOING--SAY YOU'LL STAY, YOU KNOW. . . . 148 SNOW 154
     "LET HIM TALK, HELEN, AND PERHAPS HE'LL STAY." . . . . 149 SNOW 171
     AND BEING WHERE YOU ARE, YOU WANT TO STAY. . . . . . . 150 SNOW 200
     AND FOR YOUR FAMILY'S SAKE STAY WHERE YOU ARE. . . . . 150 SNOW 217
     THAT NOW IT MEANS TO STAY. . . . . 156 THE SOUND OF TREES . . 14
     LET THEM STAY IN THE ATTIC. WHEN THEY SOMETIMES . . . 206 THE WITCH OF COÖS . . 125
     LET THEM STAY IN THE ATTIC SINCE THEY WENT THERE. . . 206 THE WITCH OF COÖS . . 132
     I STAY; . . . . 210 AN EMPTY THREAT . . . 1
     TOMORROW DEAD WILL COME TO STAY." . . . . 221 IN A DISUSED GRAVEYARD   8
     NOTHING GOLD CAN STAY . . . . 222 NOTHING GOLD CAN STAY . T
     NOTHING GOLD CAN STAY. . . . . 223 NOTHING GOLD CAN STAY . 8
     AND THEY END BY BIDDING HIM STAY WITH THEM. . . . . . 236 MISGIVING 4
     THE THOUGHT OF MY ATTEMPTING SUCH A STAY! . . . . . . 238 A HILLSIDE THAW . . . 35
     REALLY A VERY FEW TO BUILD AND STAY. . . . . 239 OUR SINGING STRENGTH . 24
     STILL IT WOULDN'T REWARD THE WATCHER TO STAY AWAKE . . 268 ON LOOKING UP BY CHANCE 13
     THEY KNEW THEY HAD BUT TO STAY THEIR STAY . . . . . . 277 TWO TRAMPS IN MUD TIME   58
     COULD MISCHIEVOUSLY LOCK HIM IN TO STAY. . . . . 290 OLD BARN AT THE BOTTOM   45
     MAY MUCH STAY OUT OF OUR STATED PLAN, ... 305 UNHARVESTED 12
     THAT TO NO LIMITS AND BOUNDS HE CAN STAY CONFINED? . . 305 THERE ARE ROUGHLY ZONES 36
     DECIDED TO STAY THERE HIMSELF. . . . . 314 BEARER OF EVIL TIDINGS   36
     THE SONG SAYS. STEAL AWAY AND STAY AWAY. . . . . 325 BUILD SOIL 279
     THAT HAVE NONE LEFT TO STAY. . . . . 337 THE WIND AND THE RAIN   48
     AS THE LIVING EVER GO YET STAY. . . . . 346 DISCOVERY OF MADEIRAS . 104
     BUT STAY AND HEAR ME OUT. I SURELY THINK . . . . 356 A MOTH SEEN IN WINTER . 10
     DID YOU STAY UP LAST NIGHT (THE MAGI DID) . . . . . . 360 A LOOSE MOUNTAIN . . 1
     OF SUCH AN UNACCOUNTABLE STAY . . . . 364 TRESPASS 6
     AND SIMPLY MUST EVOLVE TO STAY AWAKE. . . . . 372 THE LITERATE FARMER AND 127
     STAY UNASSUMING. IF FOR LACK OF LICENSE . . . . 385 THE FEAR OF GOD . . . 7
     TO STAY OUR MINDS ON AND BE STAID. . . . . 403 SOMETHING LIKE A STAR . 25
     TO STAY TOO CONFINED. . . . . 434 KITTY HAWK 202
     BUT TO STAY AWAKE . . . . 438 KITTY HAWK 314
     AND ALWAYS WILL BE.--PLEASE DON'T GO. STAY, STAY . . . 489 A MASQUE OF REASON . . 435
     IS TO BE CIVILIZED, STAY UP AND READ . . . . 496 A MASQUE OF MERCY . . 70
     WE HAVE TO STAY AFRAID DEEP IN OUR SOULS . . . . 520 A MASQUE OF MERCY . . 717
STAYED
     (THOUGH DOUBTFUL WHETHER HE STAYED TO SEE). . . . . . 25 THE DEMIURGE'S LAUGH . 17
     BUT THE PEN STAYED EXACTLY AS IT WAS, ... 67 A SERVANT TO SERVANTS . 141
     MARCHED HIMSELF OFF THE FIELD AND HOME. ONE STAYED. . 69 THE CODE 8
     THEY HEADED FOR THE BARN: I STAYED WHERE I WAS. . . . 72 THE CODE 88
     IF HE HAD STAYED. THE LEAST THING SET HIM GOING. . . . 152 SNOW 259
     I STAYED THE NIGHT FOR SHELTER AT A FARM . . . . 202 THE WITCH OF COÖS . . 1
     (NO GIRL'S, OF COURSE, HAS STAYED THE SAME.) . . . . . 265 THE BIRTHPLACE . . . 12
     SO THEY STAYED AND DECLARED A VILLAGE . . . . 314 BEARER OF EVIL TIDINGS   27
     HE STAYED LONG ENOUGH TO CARVE ON STONE . . . . 347 DISCOVERY OF MADEIRAS . 121

STAYED (CONTINUED)
HAVE STAYED IN SIGHT SO LONG AS AN EXAMPLE. . . . . . . 404 FROM PLANE TO PLANE   .   23
HE ONLY STAYED TO SET THE SUMMER ON FIRE, ... 407 FROM PLANE TO PLANE   .   93
YOUR MOTHER'S FOLKS----" / HE STAYED TO HEAR NO MORE, . 457 HOW HARD TO KEEP FROM 111
STAYING
EACH LAID ON OTHER A STAYING HAND . . . .   18 GOING FOR WATER . . .   17
AND SIMPLY STAYING POSSESSES ALL . . . . 120 BOND AND FREE . . .   18
OVER BACK WHERE THEY SPEAK OF LIFE AS STAYING . . . . 263 THE INVESTMENT . . .   1
BUT RAN AGAINST HIM WITH A STAYING HAND. . . . . . . 394 HAEC FABULA DOCET . .   10
OF JUST STAYING PUT, ... 434 KITTY HAWK 206
MY STAYING BACK BEHIND . . . . 465 SOME SCIENCE FICTION .   6
OH, NO, YOU'RE NOT. YOU'RE STAYING HERE TONIGHT.-- . . 500 A MASQUE OF MERCY . 173
WHERE ARE YOU STAYING--ANYWHERE IN TOWN? . . . . . . 501 A MASQUE OF MERCY . 209
STAYS
STAYS MORE POPULAR . . . . 469 BUT OUTER SPACE.... .   5
STAYS TALKING WITH THE KEEPER AT A SHOWCASE. . . . . 493 A MASQUE OF MERCY .   4
STEADFAST
AND STEADFAST AS KEATS' EREMITE, ... 403 SOMETHING LIKE A STAR .   18
STEADILY
OR OUR NUMBER LIVING WOULDN'T BE STEADILY MORE, . . . 349 OUR HOLD ON THE PLANET   17
STEADY (SEE JEWEL-STEADY)
LEN SAYS ONE STEADY PULL MORE OUGHT TO DO IT. . . .   64 A SERVANT TO SERVANTS .   55
UNTIL I ASKED FOR ONE TO STEADY HIM. . . . . . . 160 NEW HAMPSHIRE . . .   32
BUT STILL I AM STEADY AND UNACCUSING. . . . . . . 310 IN DIVES' DIVE . . .   2
STEAL
INTO THEIR VASTNESS I SHOULD STEAL AWAY, ...   5 INTO MY OWN   6
WAITING TO STEAL A STEP ON US WHENEVER . . . . . . 114 IN THE HOME STRETCH . 116
THAT WILL STEAL FORTH AFTER THE SUN IS SET . . . . . 276 TWO TRAMPS IN MUD TIME   39
AND BE SO VERY STRIKING. STEAL AWAY, ... 325 BUILD SOIL 278
THE SONG SAYS. STEAL AWAY AND STAY AWAY. . . . . . 325 BUILD SOIL 279
MADE HER STEAL A LOOK OF FEAR . . . . 340 THE SUBVERTED FLOWER .   37
SO THAT THE POOR WON'T HAVE TO STEAL BY STEALTH, . . . 363 AN EQUALIZER   7
IS TO STEAL THE GLORY . . . . 430 KITTY HAWK   74
STEALING
OUR THIEF, THE ONE WHO DOES OUR STEALING FROM US, . . 178 THE STAR-SPLITTER . .   48
STEALTH
SO THAT THE POOR WON'T HAVE TO STEAL BY STEALTH, . . . 363 AN EQUALIZER   7
STEALTHILY
IS STEALTHILY CONTRIVING WOOL FROM JUTE . . . . . . 319 BUILD SOIL 108
STEAM
MAKE THE SETTLED SNOWBANK STEAM; . . . .   11 TO THE THAWING WIND .   4
IT STEAM IN WINTER LIKE AN OX'S BREATH, ...   42 THE MOUNTAIN   51
STOOD UNIFORM IN BUCKETS, AND THE STEAM . . . . . . 184 MAPLE 137
NO SHIP OF ALL THAT UNDER SAIL OR STEAM . . . . . . 262 IMMIGRANTS   1
STEED
AND COME NOT BACK WITH STEED . . . . 415 CLOSED FOR GOOD . . .   7
STEEL
FOR MONTHS IT HASN'T KNOWN THE TASTE OF STEEL . . . . 189 THE GRINDSTONE . . .   15
STEEL-BLUE
THICK HAND MADE LIGHT OF, STEEL-BLUE CHIN DRAWN DOWN . . 188 THE AX-HELVE   99
STEEL-BRIGHT
STEEL-BRIGHT JUNE-GRASS, AND BLACKENING HEADS OF CLOVER. . 109 THE EXPOSED NEST . .   12
STEEPLE
AND THEN A STEEPLE. . . . . 218 I WILL SING YOU ONE-O .   28
STEEPLE BUSH . . . . 373 STEEPLE BUSH . . . .   T
AND STEEPLE BUSH, NOT GOOD TO EAT, ... 376 SOMETHING FOR HOPE . .   3
THROUGH MEADOWSWEET AND STEEPLE BUSH . . . . . . 376 SOMETHING FOR HOPE . .   7
WAS BUT THE STEEPLE ON OUR HOUSE OF LIFE . . . . . 386 A STEEPLE ON THE HOUSE   2
A STEEPLE ON THE HOUSE . . . . 386 A STEEPLE ON THE HOUSE   T
STEER
SOMEONE TO SALT THE HALF-WILD STEER, ...   24 PAN WITH US   13
STEER STRAIGHT OFF AFTER SOMETHING INTO SPACE. . . . . 238 ON A TREE FALLEN ACROSS   14
US HOW BY ROCKET WE MAY HOPE TO STEER . . . . . . 395 WHY WAIT FOR SCIENCE .   6
TO SHOW THE EVOLUTION HOW TO STEER. . . . . 425 ACCIDENTALLY ON PURPOSE   10
STEERED
HE STEERED WAS REALLY STRAIGHT AWAY . . . . 139 BROWN'S DESCENT . . .   66
THEN STEERED THE WHITE MOTH THITHER IN THE NIGHT? . . . 302 DESIGN   12
STEERING
REASON IS, I SUPPOSED, THE STEERING GEAR. . . . . . 481 A MASQUE OF REASON . . 231
STEERS
HE'D SELL A YOKE OF STEERS TO PAY FOR IT. . . . . . 200 PLACE FOR A THIRD . .   25
STEFANSSON
"JUST THE WAY STEFANSSON RUNS ON," I MURMURED, ... 159 NEW HAMPSHIRE . . .   22
STELLAR
WHAT IN BEING STELLAR . . . . 442 KITTY HAWK 460
STEM
STEM END AND BLOSSOM END, ...   68 AFTER APPLE-PICKING .   19
UPON THE STEPS WITH BITTEN STEM. . . . . 135 LOCKED OUT   9
WITH NO SUSPICION IN STEM END OR BLOSSOM END . . . . 164 NEW HAMPSHIRE . . . 160
IN ONE WAY: YOU HAVE ONE MORE STEM TO CLING BY, . . . 198 WILD GRAPES   70
THE FOLIAGE FOLLOW HIM, LEAF AND STEM; . . . . . . 236 MISGIVING   2
AS ANYONE WHO EVER BROKE ITS STEM . . . . 411 POD OF THE MILKWEED .   17
STEMMED (SEE PURPLE-STEMMED)
STEMS
AND CAST ITS FLOWERS AND ALL THE STEMS BUT THREE, . . . 283 THE GOLD HESPERIDEE .   4
STEP (SEE TEN-STEP)
WAITING FOR WARREN. WHEN SHE HEARD HIS STEP, ...   34 DEATH OF THE HIRED MAN   2
WARREN LEANED OUT AND TOOK A STEP OR TWO, ...   38 DEATH OF THE HIRED MAN 121
SHE TOOK A DOUBTFUL STEP AND THEN UNDID IT . . . .   51 HOME BURIAL   4
TO STEP OUTDOORS AND TAKE THE WATER DAZZLE . . . . .   63 A SERVANT TO SERVANTS .   27
IN LEAVES NO STEP HAD TRODDEN BLACK. . . . . . . 105 THE ROAD NOT TAKEN .   12
WAITING TO STEAL A STEP ON US WHENEVER . . . . . . 114 IN THE HOME STRETCH . 116
THE MINUTE THEY HEARD MY STEP WENT STILL . . . . . 123 PEA BRUSH   11
NO STEP, THOUGH. IF SHE'S THERE SHE'S SITTING DOWN." . . 153 SNOW 302
HAVE GOT IT ONE STEP FROM THE STARTING PLACE. . . . . 189 THE GRINDSTONE . . .   7
I HAD NOT TAKEN THE FIRST STEP IN KNOWLEDGE; . . . . 199 WILD GRAPES   95
BEGAN THE STAIRS, TWO FOOTSTEPS FOR EACH STEP, ... 204 THE WITCH OF COOS . .   51
HER NEXT STEP ROCKS A BOULDER ON THE WALL . . . . . 268 THE BEAR   5

PAGE TITLE LINE

STEP (CONTINUED)
THE LAST STEP TAKEN FOUND YOUR HEFT . . . . . 325 TO A THINKER 1
WITH BREAKING STEP I STABBED THE DUST, ... 336 THE WIND AND THE RAIN . 7
AND FORCE HER FAREWELL STEP OFF SHORE. . . . . . . 343 DISCOVERY OF MADEIRAS . 11
A SERIOUS STEP LIGHTLY TAKEN . . . . 367 A SERIOUS STEP LIGHTLY T
ONE STEP BACKWARD TAKEN . . . . 376 ONE STEP BACKWARD TAKEN T
BUT WITH ONE STEP BACKWARD TAKEN . . . . 377 ONE STEP BACKWARD TAKEN 10
THE FIRST TOOL I STEP ON . . . . 450 OBJECTION TO BE STEPPED 17
STEPPED
I STEPPED ON THE TOE . . . . 450 OBJECTION TO BE STEPPED 2
THE OBJECTION TO BEING STEPPED ON . . . . 450 OBJECTION TO BE STEPPED T
STEPS
OUR FALTERING FEW STEPS ON . . . . 9 STARS 6
AND CHECKED MY STEPS TO MAKE PRETENSE . . . . . 25 THE DEMIURGE'S LAUGH . 15
TO SIT BESIDE HER ON THE WOODEN STEPS. . . . . . 34 DEATH OF THE HIRED MAN 10
SHE STOOD HER GROUND AGAINST THE NOISY STEPS . . . 92 THE FEAR 76
YOU AND I, DEAR, WILL GO WITH SOFTER STEPS . . . . 111 IN THE HOME STRETCH . 41
UPON THE STEPS WITH BITTEN STEM. . . . . 135 LOCKED OUT 9
THE STEPS BEGAN TO CLIMB THE ATTIC STAIRS. . . . . 206 THE WITCH OF COOS . 116
HERE WE, IN OUR IMPATIENCE OF THE STEPS, ... 259 WEST-RUNNING BROOK . 42
TO WASH THE STEPS WITH PAIL AND RAG . . . . . . 307 PROVIDE, PROVIDE . 2
AND DID I NOT TAKE STEPS WOULD BE TIPPED OVER . . . 391 ON BEING IDOLIZED . 5
(JOB TAKES A FEW STEPS PACING,) DO YOU MIND? . . . 485 A MASQUE OF REASON . 329
IF YOU GO NOW.--LOOK HOW HE TAKES NO STEPS! . . . . 489 A MASQUE OF REASON . 439
IN THREE QUICK STEPS AS OFF AN ESCALATOR. . . . . 489 A MASQUE OF REASON . 452
(JONAH STEPS ON THE THRESHOLD AS THE DOOR . . . . . 518 A MASQUE OF MERCY . 649
STERN
THE DISCIPLINE OF FARMING WAS SO STERN, ... 398 BURSTING RAPTURE . . 7
BUT LET HIM SHOW HIS HAUGHTY STERN . . . . 419 AMERICA IS HARD TO SEE 75
HE DOESN'T GO. / YOU NEEDN'T BE SO STERN. . . . . 493 A MASQUE OF MERCY . 11
STERNER
THERE IS A CALL TO LIFE A LITTLE STERNER, ... 424 FOR JOHN F. KENNEDY . 66
STICK
HE BORE A GREEN-WHITE STICK IN HIS HAND, ... 7 LOVE AND A QUESTION . 3
PICKED UP A LITTLE STICK, AND BROUGHT IT BACK . . . 38 DEATH OF THE HIRED MAN 122
WITH A BIG STICK, THE SAME AS WHEN THE COWS . . . . 43 THE MOUNTAIN . . . 85
OR GRASS-BLADE IS LEFT, NOT TO MENTION A STICK, . . 59 BLUEBERRIES 19
STICK TO HIM, HELEN. MAKE HIM ANSWER YOU. . . . . 145 SNOW 63
A BLACK-CHEEKED STONE AND STICK OF RAIN-WASHED CHARCOAL. . 171 NEW HAMPSHIRE . . 391
AND WARN THEM AWAY WITH A STICK FOR A GUN.) . . . . 228 GOOD-BY AND KEEP COLD . 11
OR THE WIND TO SNAP THEIR WALKING STICK, ... 344 DISCOVERY OF MADEIRAS . 29
I STICK TO THAT. BUT TALK ABOUT CONFUSION!-- . . . . 485 A MASQUE OF REASON . 336
YOU STICK TO EARTHQUAKE, YOU HAVE SOMETHING THERE-- . 503 A MASQUE OF MERCY . 265
STICKING
MY LONG TWO-POINTED LADDER'S STICKING THROUGH A TREE . 68 AFTER APPLE-PICKING . 1
"YOUR TROUBLE IS NOT STICKING TO THE SUBJECT," . . . 404 FROM PLANE TO PLANE . 7
STICKLER
I'M A GREAT STICKLER FOR THE AUTHOR'S NAME. . . . . 480 A MASQUE OF REASON . 199
STICKS
MELT THE GLASS AND LEAVE THE STICKS . . . . . . 11 TO THE THAWING WIND . 9
AND MADE DUST AND DROPPED STOVE-LENGTH STICKS OF WOOD, . 136 "OUT, OUT--" 2
NO LIMITS TO WHAT ROSE IN RUBBING STICKS . . . . . 372 THE LITERATE FARMER AND 138
STIFF
WHEN STIFF AND SORE AND SCARRED . . . . 227 TO EARTHWARD 25
ON WINGS TOO STIFF TO FLAP . . . . 464 MILKY WAY IS A COWPATH 1
STIFFENING
WITH THE LEAST STIFFENING OF HER NECK AND SILENCE. . . 51 HOME BURIAL 14
STIFFNESS
UNTIL HE TOOK THE STIFFNESS OUT OF THEM, ... 122 BIRCHES 30
STIFLED
AND WHISPERS WITH A SORT OF STIFLED BARK, ... 9 STORM FEAR 4
STIFLING
AND THE AIR WAS STIFLING SWEET . . . . 13 ROSE POGONIAS . . . 6
AND STIFLING HOT WITH THE ODOR OF SAP . . . . . . 123 PEA BRUSH 7
STILL
AND LONG TO KNOW IF STILL I HELD THEM DEAR. . . . . 5 INTO MY OWN . . . 12
AND OFF A BLOSSOM IN MID-AIR STANDS STILL. . . . . 12 A PRAYER IN SPRING . 12
AND TELL YOU THAT I SAW DOES STILL ABIDE. . . . . . 16 A DREAM PANG . . . 12
FAR OFF THE HOMES OF MEN, AND FARTHER STILL, ... 17 THE VANTAGE POINT . 6
TO SEEK THE BROOK IF STILL IT RAN; . . . . 18 GOING FOR WATER . . 4
OF DARING SHOULD BE STILL TO DARE. . . . . 19 THE TRIAL BY EXISTENCE 8
BUT THE LAST CHOICE IS STILL THE SAME; . . . . . . 21 THE TRIAL BY EXISTENCE 58
THOUGH WE CHOOSE GREATLY, STILL TO LACK . . . . . 21 THE TRIAL BY EXISTENCE 66
AND THE DEAD LEAVES LIE HUDDLED AND STILL, ... 30 RELUCTANCE 13
THE HEART IS STILL ACHING TO SEEK, ... 30 RELUCTANCE 17
AFTER SO MANY YEARS HE STILL KEEPS FINDING . . . . 37 DEATH OF THE HIRED MAN 74
HE'D KEEP SO STILL ABOUT HIM ALL THIS TIME?" . . . . 39 DEATH OF THE HIRED MAN 138
WHERE ARE YOU MOVING OVER TO? STAY STILL. . . . . 47 A HUNDRED COLLARS . 89
AND LATER STILL THEY ALL GET DRIVEN IN: . . . . . 49 A HUNDRED COLLARS . 133
TO LOOK AGAIN, AND STILL YOUR SPADE KEPT LIFTING. . . 53 HOME BURIAL . . . 80
TOWARD HEAVEN STILL, ... 68 AFTER APPLE-PICKING . 2
"YOU KNOW WE MIGHT NOT BE AND STILL BE COUSINS: . . . 75 THE GENERATIONS OF MEN 47
ANYONE UPON EARTH AND STILL HER CHILDREN . . . . . 75 THE GENERATIONS OF MEN 51
"YOU MUST BE VERY STILL; YOU MUSTN'T TALK." . . . . 78 THE GENERATIONS OF MEN 149
AND PERHAPS SHE WILL COME, STILL UNAFRAID, ... 79 THE GENERATIONS OF MEN 167
AND THOSE WILL BEAR SOME KEEPING STILL ABOUT." . . . 80 THE GENERATIONS OF MEN 198
THE WOMAN SPOKE OUT SHARPLY, "WHOA, STAND STILL!-- . . 89 THE FEAR 8
WHAT WAS HE STANDING STILL FOR IN THE BUSHES?" . . . 90 THE FEAR 28
THAT WAS WORTH MONEY TO ME? STILL I OWN . . . . . 95 THE SELF-SEEKER . . 82
STILL GROWING, AND ON ONE A STAKE AND PROP, ... 102 THE WOOD-PILE . . . 33
AND EASED HIS HEAVY BREATHING, BUT STILL SLEPT. . . . 108 OLD MAN'S WINTER NIGHT 25
EVEN WORSE STILL, AND SO ON DOWN, DOWN, DOWN. . . . 115 IN THE HOME STRETCH . 129
ALL STILL . . . . 118 THE TELEPHONE . . . 4
FROM STUMPS STILL BLEEDING THEIR LIFE AWAY. . . . . 123 PEA BRUSH 8
THE MINUTE THEY HEARD MY STEP WENT STILL. . . . . 123 PEA BRUSH 11
I DON'T STAND STILL AND LOOK AROUND . . . . . . 124 A TIME TO TALK . . . 3
AND STILL THE BIRD REVISITED HER YOUNG. . . . . . 126 RANGE-FINDING . . . 5
STILL HE SMILED--DID YOU SEE HIM?--I WAS SURE! . . . 127 THE SMILE 3

- 522 -

STILL (CONTINUED)
THAT STILL, IF I REPENT, I MAY RECALL IT, ... 130 THE BONFIRE 22
"WHY, LETT, STILL UP? LETT, I'M AT COLE'S. I'M LATE. . . . 143 SNOW 16
BUT KEEP STILL IF HE FAILS." / "KEEP STILL ALL OVER. . . . 146 SNOW 87
WHEN COLE RETURNED HE FOUND HIS WIFE STILL STANDING . . . 151 SNOW 245
AND HE WAS RICH, AND I WAS STILL A RASCAL. . . . . . . 160 NEW HAMPSHIRE . . 54
POPLIN, STILL CORNERS (SO CALLED NOT BECAUSE . . . . . 165 NEW HAMPSHIRE . . 188
BECAUSE IT BOASTS A WHISKY STILL--BECAUSE . . . . . . 165 NEW HAMPSHIRE . . 190
IT SET OUT ONCE TO BE A CITY AND STILL . . . . 165 NEW HAMPSHIRE . . 191
SHE'S STILL NEW HAMPSHIRE, A MOST RESTFUL STATE. . . . 170 NEW HAMPSHIRE . . 357
THE DOOR WAS STILL BECAUSE I HELD IT SHUT . . . . . . 175 THE CENSUS-TAKER . 47
HE PROMPTLY GIVES IT BACK, THAT IS IF STILL . . . . . 178 THE STAR-SPLITTER . 51
HER MOTHER'S BEDROOM WAS HER FATHER'S STILL, ... 181 MAPLE 60
MAY STILL HAVE BEEN WHAT LED HER ON TO READ, ... 182 MAPLE 73
AND OTHERS STILL BECAUSE HE HAD ONE NOW . . . . . . 191 PAUL'S WIFE . . . 10
HE CLIMBED STILL HIGHER AND BENT THE TREE TO EARTH . . 197 WILD GRAPES . . . 37
AND STILL I CLUNG. I LET MY HEAD FALL BACK, ... 198 WILD GRAPES . . . 73
AS STILL I HAVE NOT LEARNED TO WITH THE HEART, ... 199 WILD GRAPES . . . 97
STILL GOING EVERY WHICH WAY IN THE JOINTS, THOUGH, . . 205 THE WITCH OF COOS . 87
STILL MORE UNFETTERED, ... 219 I WILL SING YOU ONE-O . 43
THE GRAVEYARD DRAWS THE LIVING STILL, ... 221 IN A DISUSED GRAVEYARD . 3
SPENDING WHAT ONWARD IMPULSE THEY STILL HAD . . . . . 229 TWO LOOK AT TWO . . 9
THE DIFFICULTY OF SEEING WHAT STOOD STILL, ... 229 TWO LOOK AT TWO . . 18
"THIS MUST BE ALL." IT WAS ALL. STILL THEY STOOD, . . . 230 TWO LOOK AT TWO . . 39
AND STILL SHE HAD ALL--THEY HAD--THEY THE LUCKY! . . . 230 NOT TO KEEP . . . 10
IN FETID DARKNESS STILL TO LIVE AND RUN-- . . . . . . 231 A BROOK IN THE CITY . 17
I WAS ASLEEP STILL UNDER THE DRIPPING ROOF. . . . . . 236 VALLEY'S SINGING DAY . 16
THE SWARM STILL RAN AND SCUTTLED JUST AS FAST. . . . . 237 A HILLSIDE THAW . . 24
AND STILL THEY FAILED OF ANY LASTING HOLD. . . . . . 239 OUR SINGING STRENGTH . 4
THESE POOLS THAT, THOUGH IN FORESTS, STILL REFLECT . . 245 SPRING POOLS . . . 1
AND STILL THE WOODS SWEEP LEAFILY ON, ... 247 ON GOING UNNOTICED . 14
SOME STILL WERE LIVING IN HERMITAGE. . . . . 253 THE THATCH . . . 16
I HAVE STOOD STILL AND STOPPED THE SOUND OF FEET . . . 255 ACQUAINTED WITH NIGHT . 7
AND FURTHER STILL AT AN UNEARTHLY HEIGHT . . . . . . 255 ACQUAINTED WITH NIGHT . 11
BUT SHE STOOD STRAIGHT STILL, ... 256 THE LOVELY BE CHOOSERS . 14
"YES, WE CAN LET HER AND STILL TRIUMPH." . . . . . . 256 THE LOVELY BE CHOOSERS . 20
STANDS STILL AND DANCES, BUT IT RUNS AWAY; . . . . . 259 WEST-RUNNING BROOK . 47
BUT STILL LIES POINTED AS IT PLOWED THE DUST. . . . . 261 A SOLDIER 3
AMONG UNEARTHED POTATOES STANDING STILL, ... 263 THE INVESTMENT . . 6
ALL CREATURES STILL WARMLY SUSPIRE. . . . . 266 SITTING BY A BUSH . 8
STILL IT WOULDN'T REWARD THE WATCHER TO STAY AWAKE . . 268 ON LOOKING UP BY CHANCE . 13
THE SPINNER STILL WAS THERE TO SPIN. . . . . 273 A LONE STRIKER . . 26
THAT'S WHERE THE HUMAN STILL CAME IN. . . . . 273 A LONE STRIKER . . 27
BUT HE SAID THEN AND STILL WOULD SAY, ... 274 A LONE STRIKER . . 56
WHEN THE SUN IS OUT AND THE WIND IS STILL, ... 275 TWO TRAMPS IN MUD TIME . 19
AND STILL MORE SECURE AND SNUG, ... 282 A DRUMLIN WOODCHUCK . 7
THAT STILL FOR ANOTHER DAY, ... 282 A DRUMLIN WOODCHUCK . 26
THAT STILL TOOK FROM ITS TOP . . . . 298 ON TAKING FROM THE TOP . 19
THAT YOU MAY HAVE THE POWER OF STANDING STILL-- . . . 300 THE MASTER SPEED . . 8
OFF ANY STILL OR MOVING THING YOU SAY. . . . . . . 300 THE MASTER SPEED . . 9
WHERE WE STILL LOOK TO ASK THE WHY . . . . 303 AFTERFLAKES . . . 4
IT IS LATE AT NIGHT AND STILL I AM LOSING, ... 310 IN DIVES' DIVE . . 1
BUT STILL I AM STEADY AND UNACCUSING. . . . . 310 IN DIVES' DIVE . . 2
THE TALE IS STILL BOASTINGLY TOLD . . . . 311 THE VINDICTIVES . . 33
BUT THE CONQUERED GREW MEEK AND STILL. . . . . . . 312 THE VINDICTIVES . . 52
AND STILL THE AIR WAS SATURATED TOO, ... 315 IRIS BY NIGHT . . 15
THERE IS STILL MORE WE NEVER BRING OR SHOULD BRING; . . 321 BUILD SOIL 174
THEY STILL HANG ON. THAT SO MUCH OF THE EARTH'S . . . 322 BUILD SOIL 191
ANOTHER STILL--YOU SEE YOUR PLIGHT. . . . . 325 TO A THINKER . . . 4
A MOTIVE THEN WAS STILL A MOTIVE. . . . . 327 A MISSIVE MISSILE . 21
A MOMENT AND STILL ASKING GONE. . . . . 332 ALL REVELATION . . 9
THOUGH IT STILL COULD SING. . . . . 334 COME IN 8
STILL LIVED FOR ONE SONG MORE . . . . 334 COME IN 11
BUT SOMETHING IN IT STILL IS INCOMPLETE. . . . . . . 337 THE WIND AND THE RAIN . 25
AND STILL THE HORROR CLUNG. . . . . 341 THE SUBVERTED FLOWER . 70
BUT WE WERE ENGLAND'S, STILL COLONIALS, ... 348 THE GIFT OUTRIGHT . 5
POSSESSING WHAT WE STILL WERE UNPOSSESSED BY, ... 348 THE GIFT OUTRIGHT . 6
BUT STILL UNSTORIED, ARTLESS, UNENHANCED, ... 348 THE GIFT OUTRIGHT . 15
IT THREW US ANOTHER AND THEN ANOTHER STILL, ... 349 OUR HOLD ON THE PLANET . 9
CARELESS AND STILL . . . . 360 THE RABBIT-HUNTER . 1
IS STILL WITHHOLDING IN THE ZODIAC . . . . 361 A LOOSE MOUNTAIN . 18
AND STILL IT'S BAD ENOUGH TO BADLY WOUND, ... 372 THE LITERATE FARMER AND 119
STILL SAID TO HAUNT THIS SIDE OF PANTHER MOUNTAIN. . . 377 DIRECTIVE 19
THE DARKEST OF IT STILL TO DREAD. . . . . 383 THE NIGHT LIGHT . . 8
YET STILL I MUST REPORT . . . . 384 MAKING CERTAIN ANYTHING 7
TO GIVE THEM STILL MORE BUOYANCY IN FLIGHT. . . . . . 387 INNATE HELIUM . . 5
THE PLACE OF STANDING STILL . . . . 388 MIDDLENESS OF THE ROAD . 6
LIKE A CAUL IN WHICH I WAS BORN AND STILL AM WRAPPED. . 390 SKEPTIC 12
WAS STILL IN SIGHT LIKE SOMEONE TO DEPEND ON. . . . . 404 FROM PLANE TO PLANE . 20
AND STILL I DOUBT IF THEY KNOW WHERE THEY ARE. . . . . 414 A CABIN IN THE CLEARING . 5
STILL PRINT THERE AS MY PROXY. . . . . 416 CLOSED FOR GOOD . . 30
ON HOW TO CROWD BUT STILL BE KIND. . . . . 417 AMERICA IS HARD TO SEE . 42
STILL PROBES AND DENTS OUR ROCKY COAST . . . . . . 418 AMERICA IS HARD TO SEE . 50
ANOTHER STILL, LOST FAR INTO THE DISTANCE. . . . . . 421 ESCAPIST--NEVER . . 8
WE CARRY IN OUR PURSE AND POCKET STILL?) . . . . . . 422 FOR JOHN F. KENNEDY . 22
BUT WE WERE ENGLAND'S, STILL COLONIALS, ... 424 THE GIFT OUTRIGHT . 5
POSSESSING WHAT WE STILL WERE UNPOSSESSED BY, ... 424 THE GIFT OUTRIGHT . 6
BUT STILL UNSTORIED, ARTLESS, UNENHANCED, ... 425 THE GIFT OUTRIGHT . 15
STILL SOMETIMES OCCUR . . . . 433 KITTY HAWK . . . 155
EARTH IS STILL OUR FATE. . . . . 437 KITTY HAWK . . . 308
IT'S STILL KITTY HAWK. . . . . 439 KITTY HAWK . . . 347
SOME STILL THINK IS SATAN. . . . . 443 KITTY HAWK . . . 464
BUT STILL FOOD, FOOD. YOUR ONE IDEA WAS FOOD. . . . . 458 HOW HARD TO KEEP FROM . 134
SHE WANTS TO KNOW WHY THERE IS STILL INJUSTICE. . . . 477 A MASQUE OF REASON . 110
STILL THERE MUST BE LOTS OF UNSYSTEMATIC . . . . . . 478 A MASQUE OF REASON . 141
AEONS OF TIME AND STILL IT'S MOSTLY WOMEN . . . . . 478 A MASQUE OF REASON . 149
FOR STANDING STILL IN ONE PLACE TRUE FOREVER; . . . . 480 A MASQUE OF REASON . 192
STILL, NOVELTY HAS DOUBTLESS AN ATTRACTION. . . . . . 480 A MASQUE OF REASON . 197

STILL (CONTINUED)
   GOD, WHO INVENTED EARTH? / WHAT, STILL AWAKE? . . . . . 480 A MASQUE OF REASON . . 201
   KEEPER, BE STILL.--PAY NO ATTENTION TO HIM. . . . . . 494 A MASQUE OF MERCY . . 33
   KEEPER, BE STILL. HE KNOWS WHAT BOOK HE WANTS. . . . . 495 A MASQUE OF MERCY . . 51
   STILL, NOT SO FAR OFF, COME TO THINK OF IT. . . . . . 509 A MASQUE OF MERCY . . 428
   INCLINED TO HOPE FOR MUCH. STILL WHAT WE NEED . . . . . 515 A MASQUE OF MERCY . . 567
   (STILL STANDING OFF) WE'VE ALL GROWN FOND OF YOU. . . . 518 A MASQUE OF MERCY . . 666
   (STILL ON HIS KNEES, HE SITS BACK ON HIS HEELS.) . . . 519 A MASQUE OF MERCY . . 671
STILLY
   SO THE STILLY AIR . . . . 434 KITTY HAWK 209
STING
   AND A MOUTHFUL OF DYESTUFF INSTEAD OF A STING. . . . . 309 ONE GUESS 3
STINGING
   HIS STINGING QUARTERS MENACINGLY WORK. . . . . 309 WASPISH 4
STINGY
   A RAIN, THOUGH STINGY, HAD BEGUN TO FALL . . . . . . 399 THE BROKEN DROUGHT . . 3
STINT
   "SEE THAT YOU GET HER GREATNESS RIGHT. DON'T STINT HER." . 77 THE GENERATIONS OF MEN 117
STIR
   SUCH PIPES KEPT LESS OF POWER TO STIR . . . . 24 PAN WITH US 22
   IF SUCH UNLIFELIKE LINES KEPT POWER TO STIR . . . . . 56 THE BLACK COTTAGE . . 29
   THERE WAS NO ONE THAT DARED TO STIR HIM UP, ... 72 THE CODE 100
   AS THE STIR CRACKS AND CRAZES THEIR ENAMEL. . . . . . 121 BIRCHES 9
   IT COULDN'T STIR SO SENSITIVELY POISED . . . . 148 SNOW 138
   AT THE FAR END OF IT YOU SEE A STIR . . . . 149 SNOW 194
   WITH AN EVER VAGUER AND VAGUER STIR, ... 236 MISGIVING 10
   TO MAKE A LEAF, IF THERE HAD BEEN ONE, STIR. . . . . . 238 A HILLSIDE THAW . . 32
   THE MOUNTAIN SEEMED TO LIKE THE STIR, ... 265 THE BIRTHPLACE . . 8
   SHE DARED NOT STIR A FOOT, ... 340 THE SUBVERTED FLOWER . 31
   FROM SEEING THIS UNDOUBTED STIR . . . . 381 AN UNSTAMPED LETTER IN 29
STIRRED (SEE WIND-STIRRED)
   THE WAY THE NEST-FULL EVERY TIME WE STIRRED . . . . . 109 THE EXPOSED NEST . . 20
   THREE TIMES HE BARELY STIRRED THE BELL, THEN LISTENED. . . 143 SNOW 15
   THEY WERE BOTH STIRRED THAT HE SHOULD HAVE DIVINED . . . 182 MAPLE 92
   NOT A BREEZE STIRRED, BUT JUST THE BREATH OF AIR . . . 194 PAUL'S WIFE . . . 98
   TREMBLED AND STIRRED, ... 219 I WILL SING YOU ONE-O . 63
   I DON'T WANT IT STIRRED BY THE HEAT OF THE SUN. . . . . 228 GOOD-BY AND KEEP COLD . 12
   NOW ASKED ASYLUM--AND I WAS STIRRED . . . . 419 ONE MORE BREVITY . . 13
   TO KEEP ALL THINGS STIRRED . . . . 442 KITTY HAWK . . . 444
STOCK
   OF THE OLD STOCK? WHAT COUNTS IS THE IDEALS, ... 80 THE GENERATIONS OF MEN 197
   SHOULD SAY OUR STOCK WAS PETERED OUT, ... 139 BROWN'S DESCENT . . 51
   AFTER THE MANNER OF OUR STOCK; . . . . 139 BROWN'S DESCENT . . 62
   HAD HAD TO ORGANIZE TO STOCK THE GRAVEYARDS . . . . . 159 NEW HAMPSHIRE . . . 20
   ENOUGH TO STOCK A VILLAGE LIBRARY-- . . . . 216 A FOUNTAIN, A BOTTLE . 98
   I SHALL WILL TO THE COMMON STOCK OF AIR MY BREATH . . . 307 NOT QUITE SOCIAL . . 15
   MAKE THE WHOLE STOCK EXCHANGE YOUR OWN! . . . . 307 PROVIDE, PROVIDE . . 10
   ENRICHING SOIL AND INCREASING STOCK, ... 367 A SERIOUS STEP LIGHTLY 19
STOCKHOLDERS
   "WHO'S WE?--SOME STOCKHOLDERS IN BOSTON? . . . . . . 100 THE SELF-SEEKER . . 221
STOCKING
   BUT ONCE I FELT GROUND WITH MY STOCKING FEET . . . . . 198 WILD GRAPES . . . 85
   AND MY SHOE AND MY STOCKING . . . . 413 AWAY! 3
STOKE
   AND BADE HIM LEAVE THE PAN AND STOKE THE ARCH: . . . . 234 EVENING A SUGAR ORCHARD 4
   "O FIREMAN, GIVE THE FIRE ANOTHER STOKE, ... 234 EVENING A SUGAR ORCHARD 5
STOKERS
   MY FRIENDS AND STOKERS, JEFFERS AND O'NEILL. . . . . 516 A MASQUE OF MERCY . 607
STOLE
   THIS WAS A MAN, BAPTISTE, WHO STOLE ONE DAY . . . . . 185 THE AX-HELVE . . . 6
   I STOLE FORTH DIMLY IN THE DRIPPING PAUSE . . . . . . 300 MOON COMPASSES . . 1
   (I STOLE THE GOBLET FROM THE CHILDREN'S PLAYHOUSE.) . . 379 DIRECTIVE . . . 60
   BUT THAT NIGHT I STOLE . . . . 432 KITTY HAWK . . . 135
STOLEN
   THERE HE HAD BUILT HIS STOLEN SHACK. . . . . 140 THE GUM-GATHERER . . 19
   IT HAD TO BE A STOLEN SHACK . . . . 140 THE GUM-GATHERER . . 20
   A STOLEN LADY WAS COMING ON BOARD, ... 343 DISCOVERY OF MADEIRAS . 1
   BUT WHETHER STOLEN FROM HER WEDDED LORD . . . . . . 343 DISCOVERY OF MADEIRAS . 2
   A STOLEN LADY WAS ALL IT SAID. . . . . 343 DISCOVERY OF MADEIRAS . 5
   AND THE BAY WHERE HIS STOLEN LADY DIED . . . . . . 347 DISCOVERY OF MADEIRAS . 134
STONE (SEE HEARTH-STONE, OLD-STONE, WEARING-STONE)
   WHERE THEY HAVE LEFT NOT ONE STONE ON A STONE, ... 33 MENDING WALL . . . 7
   BRINGING A STONE GRASPED FIRMLY BY THE TOP . . . . . 34 MENDING WALL . . . 39
   LISTEN! HE KICKED A STONE. HEAR THAT, HEAR THAT! . . . 90 THE FEAR 38
   OVER STONE WALLS AND ALL ALONG A WOOD . . . . 98 THE SELF-SEEKER . . 152
   AND PLOD: I GO UP TO THE STONE WALL . . . . 124 A TIME TO TALK . . 9
   FROM THE LAST THING HE SAID HIMSELF, STONE DEAF . . . . 145 SNOW 65
   A BLACK-CHEEKED STONE AND STICK OF RAIN-WASHED CHARCOAL. . 171 NEW HAMPSHIRE . . . 391
   IT WENT FOR BUILDING STONE, AND I, AS THOUGH . . . . . 173 A STAR IN A STONEBOAT . 34
   I MUST GO MEASURING STONE WALLS, PERCH ON PERCH; . . . 173 A STAR IN A STONEBOAT . 45
   AN EMPTINESS FLAYED TO THE VERY STONE. . . . . 174 THE CENSUS-TAKER . . 14
   UNDER HE DIDN'T CARE HOW GREAT A STONE . . . . 200 PLACE FOR A THIRD . 24
   AND BUILT A STONE BAPTISMAL FONT OUTDOORS-- . . . . . 213 A FOUNTAIN, A BOTTLE . 10
   YOU SAID YOU'D SEEN THE STONE BAPTISMAL FONT. . . . . 213 A FOUNTAIN, A BOTTLE . 13
   WITH STONE AND LEAD TO UNPROTECTED GLASS: . . . . . 216 A FOUNTAIN, A BOTTLE . 103
   AND NOW HE COMES AGAIN WITH CLATTER OF STONE, ... 223 THE RUNAWAY . . . 15
   ON UP THE FAILING PATH, WHERE, IF A STONE . . . . . 229 TWO LOOK AT TWO . . 11
   DEEP IN A SEWER DUNGEON UNDER STONE . . . . 231 A BROOK IN THE CITY . 16
   THEY MAKE US CRINGE FOR METAL-POINT ON STONE. . . . . 261 A SOLDIER . . . 11
   HE HAD ATTACKED IT WITH A CLUB OR STONE . . . . . . 270 THE EGG AND THE MACHINE 6
   TO PECK HERSELF A PRECIOUS STONE. . . . . 281 BLUE RIBBON AT AMESBURY 42
   THE WOOD OF IT CHANGED TO STONE, ... 285 IN TIME OF CLOUDBURST . 23
   FOR YOU TO ROLL ONE STONE . . . . 298 ON TAKING FROM THE TOP 7
   IT WILL SHAKE ITS CAST STONE REEF OF FLOOR. . . . . . 306 A TRIAL RUN . . . 5
   HE STAYED LONG ENOUGH TO CARVE ON STONE . . . . . . 347 DISCOVERY OF MADEIRAS . 121
   I WOULD HAVE WRITTEN OF ME ON MY STONE: . . . . . . 355 THE LESSON FOR TODAY . 160
   HE MIGHT BE OPENING LEAVES OF STONE, ... 364 TRESPASS . . . 9
   THEY CUT THEMSELVES IN STONE FOR PERMANENT . . . . . 399 THE INGENUITIES OF DEBT 2

| | | PAGE TITLE | LINE |

STONE (CONTINUED)
```
    TO THEIR SURPRISE RANG ONCE ON STONE ALL DAY     . . . . . 407 FROM PLANE TO PLANE   . 116
    FROM THIS BALL OF STONE,  . . . . . . . . . . . . . . . . 440 KITTY HAWK  . . . . . . 381
    HAS THAT TONNAGE OF STONE . . . . . . . . . . . . . . . . 447 THE BAD ISLAND--EASTER   10
    THEY WERE DAYS ON THAT STONE.  . . . . . . . . . . . . . . 448 THE BAD ISLAND--EASTER   13
STONEBOAT
    A STAR IN A STONEBOAT  . . . . . . . . . . . . . . . . . . 172 A STAR IN A STONEBOAT .   T
    HE LOADED AN OLD STONEBOAT WITH THE STAR . . . . . . . . . 173 A STAR IN A STONEBOAT .  26
STONE-COLD
    SOME LABORER FOUND ONE FADED AND STONE-COLD,  . . . . . . 172 A STAR IN A STONEBOAT .   4
STONES  (SEE QUARTZ-STONES)
    THOSE STONES OUT UNDER THE LOW-LIMBED TREE . . . . . . . .   6 GHOST HOUSE   . . . . .  24
    THERE ARE THREE STONES OF SLATE AND ONE OF MARBLE,  . . .  52 HOME BURIAL   . . . . .  26
    BUT I UNDERSTAND: IT IS NOT THE STONES,  . . . . . . . . .  52 HOME BURIAL   . . . . .  29
    A STATE PRODUCING PRECIOUS METALS, STONES,  . . . . . . . 164 NEW HAMPSHIRE   . . . . 165
    HAS BEEN PICKED UP WITH STONES TO BUILD A WALL.  . . . . . 172 A STAR IN A STONEBOAT .   3
    AND LIE IN STONES AND BUSHES UNRETRIEVED.  . . . . . . . . 216 A FOUNTAIN, A BOTTLE  . 116
    TO READ THE STONES AND GO AWAY . . . . . . . . . . . . . . 221 IN A DISUSED GRAVEYARD    7
    AND TELL THE STONES: MEN HATE TO DIE . . . . . . . . . . . 221 IN A DISUSED GRAVEYARD   14
    ROLL STONES DOWN ON OUR HEAD!  . . . . . . . . . . . . . . 298 ON TAKING FROM THE TOP    1
    BUT I WAS ONLY THERE TO READ THE STONES  . . . . . . . . . 354 THE LESSON FOR TODAY  . 133
    OF THE STONES OF THE PLACE . . . . . . . . . . . . . . . . 365 OF STONES OF THE PLACE    T
STONY
    FOR TEAMS THAT CAME BY THE STONY ROAD  . . . . . . . . . . 241 NEED OF BEING VERSED  .  10
STOOD
    NOT FAR, BUT NEAR, I STOOD AND SAW IT ALL,  . . . . . . .  16 A DREAM PANG  . . . . .   9
    AND STOOD IN THE SUN AND LOOKED HIS FILL . . . . . . . . .  23 PAN WITH US   . . . . .   4
    HE STOOD IN THE ZEPHYR, PIPES IN HAND,  . . . . . . . . .  23 PAN WITH US   . . . . .   6
    THE MOUNTAIN STOOD THERE TO BE POINTED AT.  . . . . . . .  41 THE MOUNTAIN  . . . . .  28
    YOU HAD STOOD THE SPADE UP AGAINST THE WALL . . . . . . .  54 HOME BURIAL   . . . . .  87
    AS TALKING--YOU STOOD UP BESIDE ME, YOU KNOW."  . . . . .  62 BLUEBERRIES   . . . . .  96
    "SHE'S LET IT WORRY HER. YOU STOOD THE STRAIN,  . . . . .  87 THE HOUSEKEEPER   . . . 171
    AND THE BACK OF THE GIG THEY STOOD BESIDE  . . . . . . . .  89 THE FEAR  . . . . . . .   6
    SHE STOOD HER GROUND AGAINST THE NOISY STEPS . . . . . . .  92 THE FEAR  . . . . . . .  76
    STOOD FOR A WHILE UNNOTICED, WITH HER HANDS  . . . . . . .  96 THE SELF-SEEKER   . . .  95
    AND BE ONE TRAVELER, LONG I STOOD  . . . . . . . . . . . . 105 THE ROAD NOT TAKEN  . .   3
    HE STOOD WITH BARRELS ROUND HIM--AT A LOSS. . . . . . . . 108 OLD MAN'S WINTER NIGHT    8
    STOOD UP TO US AS TO A MOTHER-BIRD.  . . . . . . . . . . . 109 THE EXPOSED NEST  . . .  21
    SHE STOOD AGAINST THE KITCHEN SINK, AND LOOKED . . . . . . 110 IN THE HOME STRETCH   .   1
    STOOD OVER ME A RESURRECTED TREE,  . . . . . . . . . . . . 125 AN ENCOUNTER  . . . . .  12
    SHE STOOD, AND THEN SHE RAN AND HID  . . . . . . . . . . . 129 THE IMPULSE   . . . . .  19
    OF WALLED-OFF GROUND WHERE A SHOP HAD STOOD,  . . . . . . 133 A GIRL'S GARDEN   . . .  11
    HIS SISTER STOOD BESIDE THEM IN HER APRON  . . . . . . . . 136 "OUT,OUT--"   . . . . .  13
    THE THREE STOOD LISTENING TO A FRESH ACCESS. . . . . . . . 143 SNOW  . . . . . . . . .   1
    THE THREE STOOD IN THE LAMPLIGHT ROUND THE TABLE . . . . . 144 SNOW  . . . . . . . . .  31
    JUST THEN, I THOUGHT. IT'S STOOD ERECT LIKE THAT,  . . . . 147 SNOW  . . . . . . . . . 117
    TO SAY SO OR BE STOOD AGAINST THE WALL . . . . . . . . . . 168 NEW HAMPSHIRE   . . . . 281
    HE STOOD ON THE SAFE SIDE OF THE LINE TALKING-- . . . . . 171 NEW HAMPSHIRE   . . . . 381
    AND EVERY TREE UP STOOD A ROTTING TRUNK  . . . . . . . . . 175 THE CENSUS-TAKER  . . .  22
    HOW DIFFERENT FROM THE WAY IT EVER STOOD?  . . . . . . . . 179 THE STAR-SPLITTER   . .  99
    AS SHE STOOD SAYING HER NAME OVER ALOUD,  . . . . . . . . 181 MAPLE   . . . . . . . .  41
    STOOD UNIFORM IN BUCKETS, AND THE STEAM  . . . . . . . . . 184 MAPLE   . . . . . . . . 137
    AND STOOD THE AX THERE ON ITS HORSE'S HOOF,  . . . . . . . 188 THE AX-HELVE  . . . . .  95
    THE SNAKE STOOD UP FOR EVIL IN THE GARDEN-- . . . . . . . 188 THE AX-HELVE  . . . . .  97
    AND LEFT STOOD UP ON END INSIDE THE TREE . . . . . . . . . 194 PAUL'S WIFE   . . . . .  93
    WHERE A WHITE BIRCH HE KNEW OF STOOD ALONE,  . . . . . . . 196 WILD GRAPES   . . . . .  20
    A MOMENT HE STOOD BALANCING WITH EMOTION,  . . . . . . . . 204 THE WITCH OF COOS   . .  71
    HE STOOD BESIDE AND LEAVE HIS TRADEMARK ON THEM,  . . . . 209 PAUPER WITCH OF GRAFTON  55
    WITH BARBED-WIRE BINDING. THEY STOOD FACING THIS,  . . . . 229 TWO LOOK AT TWO   . . .   8
    A DOE FROM ROUND A SPRUCE STOOD LOOKING AT THEM  . . . . . 229 TWO LOOK AT TWO   . . .  15
    THE DIFFICULTY OF SEEING WHAT STOOD STILL,  . . . . . . . 229 TWO LOOK AT TWO   . . .  18
    A BUCK FROM ROUND THE SPRUCE STOOD LOOKING AT THEM . . . . 229 TWO LOOK AT TWO   . . .  27
    "THIS MUST BE ALL." IT WAS ALL. STILL THEY STOOD,  . . . . 230 TWO LOOK AT TWO   . . .  39
    HE STOOD THERE BRINGING MARCH AGAINST HIS THOUGHT,  . . . 233 A BOUNDLESS MOMENT  . .   3
    WE STOOD A MOMENT SO, IN A STRANGE WORLD,  . . . . . . . . 233 A BOUNDLESS MOMENT  . .   9
    NOW THE CHIMNEY WAS ALL OF THE HOUSE THAT STOOD,  . . . . 241 NEED OF BEING VERSED  .   3
    I HAVE STOOD STILL AND STOPPED THE SOUND OF FEET . . . . . 255 ACQUAINTED WITH NIGHT .   7
    BUT SHE STOOD STRAIGHT STILL,  . . . . . . . . . . . . . . 256 THE LOVELY BE CHOOSERS   14
    (HE STOOD WELL BACK FOR FEAR OF SCALDING SQUIRTS.) . . . . 270 THE EGG AND THE MACHINE  12
    HE STOOD REBUKED AND UNEMPLOYED.  . . . . . . . . . . . . 273 A LONE STRIKER  . . . .   9
    HE SAW IT PLAINLY WHERE HE STOOD,  . . . . . . . . . . . . 274 A LONE STRIKER  . . . .  34
    AND IF HE STOOD ON ONE OF THESE,  . . . . . . . . . . . . 274 A LONE STRIKER  . . . .  38
    IF--IF HE STOOD! ENOUGH OF IFS!  . . . . . . . . . . . . . 274 A LONE STRIKER  . . . .  42
    HE STOOD UNSHAKEN, AND IF GRIM AND GAUNT,  . . . . . . . . 292 FIGURE IN THE DOORWAY .  13
    THEY STOOD ARMS LACED TOGETHER AT THE BARS,  . . . . . . . 293 AT WOODWARD'S GARDENS .  12
    THE MOUNTAIN STOOD EXALTED IN ITS PLACE.  . . . . . . . . 301 MOON COMPASSES  . . . .   7
    IN WHICH WE TWO STOOD SATURATED, DROWNED.  . . . . . . . . 315 IRIS BY NIGHT   . . . .  12
    STOOD CLOSELY OVER US THROUGH WHICH TO GO.  . . . . . . . 315 IRIS BY NIGHT   . . . .  19
    AND WE STOOD IN IT SOFTLY CIRCLED ROUND  . . . . . . . . . 315 IRIS BY NIGHT   . . . .  29
    THERE STOOD THE PURPLE SPIRES WITH NO BREATH OF AIR  . . . 343 QUEST OF PURPLE-FRINGED  17
    NOW STOOD UPON ITS BULGING PROW  . . . . . . . . . . . . . 344 DISCOVERY OF MADEIRAS .  23
    'TWAS NOT THE VALUE I STOOD TO LOSE  . . . . . . . . . . . 364 TRESPASS  . . . . . . .  13
    AND THERE ON AN EQUALITY WE STOOD.  . . . . . . . . . . . 368 THE LITERATE FARMER AND   7
    AS LONG THE TREES HAVE STOOD.  . . . . . . . . . . . . . . 388 MIDDLENESS OF THE ROAD    7
    THEY STOOD IT IN PLACE.  . . . . . . . . . . . . . . . . . 448 THE BAD ISLAND--EASTER   18
    THE EX-KING STOOD UP IN THE MARKETPLACE  . . . . . . . . . 454 HOW HARD TO KEEP FROM    37
    I STOOD BY JOB. I MAY HAVE TURNED ON YOU.  . . . . . . . . 477 A MASQUE OF REASON  . . 120
    BUT I DON'T MIND. LET'S LEAVE IT AS IT STOOD.  . . . . . . 485 A MASQUE OF REASON  . . 334
STOOL
    WHO ROSE FROM THE MILKING STOOL WITH A CURSE . . . . . . . 463 LINES IN DEJECTION  . .  15
STOOP
    FOR EVERY PARCEL I STOOP DOWN TO SEIZE . . . . . . . . . . 266 THE ARMFUL  . . . . . .   1
STOOPED
    THEN LIGHTLY STOOPED TO IT AND FLUTTERING CLUNG.  . . . . 126 RANGE-FINDING   . . . .   8
    HE STOOPED AND STRUCK A LITTLE HUCKLEBERRY . . . . . . . . 278 THE WHITE-TAILED HORNET  38
STOOPING
    NOT EVEN STOOPING FROM ITS SPHERE,  . . . . . . . . . . . 403 SOMETHING LIKE A STAR .  19
```

STOP
```
I'LL ONLY STOP TO RAKE THE LEAVES AWAY . . . . . . . .   1 THE PASTURE . . . .   2
IT SEEMED NO HARM TO STOP HIM ALTOGETHER. . . . . . .  41 THE MOUNTAIN . . . .  18
THEY FOUND A WAY TO PUT A STOP TO IT. . . . . . . . .  67 A SERVANT TO SERVANTS . 139
AND BEGIN OVER----' THERE, SHE'D BETTER STOP. . . . .  80 THE GENERATIONS OF MEN 194
"DO GO ALONG WITH HIM AND STOP HIS SHOUTING." . . . .  89 THE HOUSEKEEPER . . . 212
"YOU, WILL, STOP MAKING FACES. COME ROUND HERE . . . .  99 THE SELF-SEEKER . . . 184
DON'T STOP TO TRY TO NOW. YOU'LL MISS YOUR TRAIN. . . 101 THE SELF-SEEKER . . . 227
BETWEEN TWO BOYS AND NOT FEEL BOUND TO STOP IT. . . . 146 SNOW . . . . . . 101
TO STOP AT. IF YOU WERE THE KIND OF MAN . . . . . . . 150 SNOW . . . . . . 215
I DO NOT KNOW--I CANNOT STOP TO TELL: . . . . . . . . 173 A STAR IN A STONEBOAT .  38
TO STOP WITHOUT A FARMHOUSE NEAR . . . . . . . . . . 224 STOPPING BY WOODS . .   6
I HAD TO STOP AND LIFT MY FACE; . . . . . . . . . . 233 LOOKING FOR SUNSET BIRD   6
THE HARVEST SHALL STOP? . . . . . . . . . . . . . . 235 GATHERING LEAVES . .  24
BUT IF I THOUGHT TO STOP THE WET STAMPEDE, . . . . . 237 A HILLSIDE THAW . . .   9
AND ONE DID STOP, BUT ONLY TO PLOW UP GRASS . . . . . 287 A ROADSIDE STAND . .  39
AND WHEN TO STOP IT RESTS WITH YOU. . . . . . . . . 306 A TRIAL RUN . . . .  14
TO STOP IT WITH A PERIOD OF INK, . . . . . . . . . 357 A CONSIDERABLE SPECK .   5
WILL THEREFORE PLAN TO GO HALFWAY AND STOP. . . . . . 363 A SEMI-REVOLUTION . .   6
HE WILL NOT STOP FOR GRATITUDE. . . . . . . . . . 418 AMERICA IS HARD TO SEE  74
AND WHEN MOTORS STOP . . . . . . . . . . . . . . . 439 KITTY HAWK . . . . 354
IF WE COULD ONLY STOP THE PROGRESS SOMEWHERE, . . . . 458 HOW HARD TO KEEP FROM 154
AND POSSIBLY MY NOT WRITING IT SHOULD STOP ME . . . . 461 HOW HARD TO KEEP FROM 224
THE WILL AS BRAKES CAN'T STOP THE WILL AS MOTOR . . . 481 A MASQUE OF REASON . 232
WHO KEEPS OUR BOOKSTORE ANNALS. / STOP IT, KEEPER.-- . 499 A MASQUE OF MERCY . . 152
STOPPED
HE JUMBLED EVERYTHING. I STOPPED TO LOOK . . . . . . .  36 DEATH OF THE HIRED MAN  55
HE NEVER STOPPED TO MURDER ANYONE . . . . . . . . . 192 PAUL'S WIFE . . . .  25
RIGHT PAST BOTH FATHER AND MOTHER, AND NEITHER STOPPED IT. . 203 THE WITCH OF COOS . .  33
AND HAVE STOPPED DYING NOW FOREVER. . . . . . . . . 221 IN A DISUSED GRAVEYARD  15
WE STOPPED BY A MOUNTAIN PASTURE TO SAY, "WHOSE COLT?" . . 223 THE RUNAWAY . . . .   2
I HAVE STOOD STILL AND STOPPED THE SOUND OF FEET . . . 255 ACQUAINTED WITH NIGHT .   7
FOR STOPPING WHERE THEY HAD STOPPED. . . . . . . . . 314 BEARER OF EVIL TIDINGS  40
"I STOPPED TO COMPLIMENT YOU ON THIS STAR . . . . . . 368 THE LITERATE FARMER AND  9
THEN THE RAIN STOPPED AND THE BLOWING, . . . . . . . 377 ONE STEP BACKWARD TAKEN  13
WHO HAD STOPPED OUTSIDE THE FENCE TO SPY, . . . . . . 385 A MOOD APART . . . .   5
I STOPPED MY SONG AND ALMOST HEART, . . . . . . . . 385 A MOOD APART . . . .   6
HE HAD TO BE STOPPED BY THE SWORD OF BRUTUS. . . . . 454 HOW HARD TO KEEP FROM  24
STOPPING
WE'RE STOPPING FOR THE FORTNIGHT DOWN AT DEAN'S." . . .  92 THE FEAR . . . . .  86
HE WILL NOT SEE ME STOPPING HERE . . . . . . . . . 224 STOPPING BY WOODS . .   3
STOPPING BY WOODS ON A SNOWY EVENING . . . . . . . 224 STOPPING BY WOODS . .   T
FOR THE SQUEAL OF BRAKES, THE SOUND OF A STOPPING CAR, . 287 A ROADSIDE STAND . .  36
FOR STOPPING WHERE THEY HAD STOPPED. . . . . . . . . 314 BEARER OF EVIL TIDINGS  40
STOPS
STOPS WHEN SHE LIKES: I TELL HER WHEN TO GO. . . . .  49 A HUNDRED COLLARS . . 140
(HE STOPS TO LISTEN.) THAT'S A MIGHTY STORM, . . . . 502 A MASQUE OF MERCY . . 233
(HE STOPS TO LISTEN AND HIS UNSPOKEN THOUGHT, . . . . 502 A MASQUE OF MERCY . . 236
(HE STARTS TO SPEAK, BUT STOPS AGAIN TO LISTEN. . . . 502 A MASQUE OF MERCY . . 244
STORE
THEY MEET HIM IN THE GENERAL STORE AT NIGHT, . . . . .  44 A HUNDRED COLLARS . .   8
LIKE BIRDS. THEY STORE A GREAT MANY AWAY. . . . . . .  60 BLUEBERRIES . . . .  51
THEY SELL IN THE STORE AND BUY SHOES FOR THEIR FEET." .  61 BLUEBERRIES . . . .  53
"THE BREAD WE BOUGHT IN PASSING AT THE STORE. . . . . 115 IN THE HOME STRETCH . 144
HE SAYS HE LEFT THE VILLAGE STORE AT NINE: . . . . . 145 SNOW . . . . . . .  57
TO LIVE IN VILLAGES, NEXT TO THE THEATER AND STORE, . . 286 A ROADSIDE STAND . .  25
OUT OF TEMPLE AND PALACE AND STORE. . . . . . . . . 310 THE VINDICTIVES . . .  13
YOU CAN'T COME IN! (KNOCK, KNOCK) THE STORE IS CLOSED! . 493 A MASQUE OF MERCY . .   8
AND WHY WE WOULDN'T HAVE ONE IN THE STORE. . . . . . 494 A MASQUE OF MERCY . .  30
YOU TAKE US TWO, WE'RE LOSERS IN THIS STORE, . . . . 496 A MASQUE OF MERCY . .  75
(TAKING A WALK OFF DOWN THE STORE DISTRESSED) . . . . 503 A MASQUE OF MERCY . . 267
IT IS THE CELLAR TO MY STORE.--WHAT HO, DOWN THERE! . . 514 A MASQUE OF MERCY . . 555
IT IS THE CELLAR TO MY STORE, BUT NOT MY CELLAR. . . . 514 A MASQUE OF MERCY . . 559
STORIES
THE HOUSE ONE STORY HIGH IN FRONT, THREE STORIES . . . 181 MAPLE . . . . . .  57
(THE HOUSE ONE STORY HIGH IN FRONT, THREE STORIES . . 182 MAPLE . . . . . .  98
THE WIDESPREAD DOUBLE DOORS TWO STORIES HIGH. . . . . 289 OLD BARN AT THE BOTTOM  12
STORING
OH, WE MAKE A BOAST OF STORING, . . . . . . . . . . 359 NOVEMBER . . . . .   9
STORK
I THINK I GET IT VIA STORK . . . . . . . . . . . . 452 A-WISHING WELL . . .  35
STORM (SEE LINE-STORM)
STORM FEAR . . . . . . . . . . . . . . . . . . .   9 STORM FEAR . . . .   T
OH, COME FORTH INTO THE STORM AND ROUT . . . . . . .  27 A LINE-STORM SONG . .  31
WHEN A STORM THREATENED FROM THE DRAGON'S DEN, . . . .  63 A SERVANT TO SERVANTS  30
TILL WELL TOWARD NOON, WHEN THE STORM SETTLED DOWN . .  74 THE GENERATIONS OF MEN  22
LIKE WILD GEESE ON A LAKE BEFORE A STORM? . . . . . .  76 THE GENERATIONS OF MEN  90
WITH ALL HER MATTER OF FACT ABOUT THE ICE STORM, . . . 121 BIRCHES . . . . . .  22
THE ILLIMITABLE DARK AND COLD AND STORM, . . . . . . 148 SNOW . . . . . . . 144
AFTER A DOWNY STORM, HE PASSED OUR PLACE . . . . . . 149 SNOW . . . . . . . 176
AS IF NOT KNOWING WHAT YOU MEANT BY THE WORD STORM." . 151 SNOW . . . . . . . 232
"WELL, THERE'S--THE STORM. THAT SAYS I MUST GO ON. . . 151 SNOW . . . . . . . 240
THEY LEFT THE STORM . . . . . . . . . . . . . . . 218 I WILL SING YOU ONE-O .  34
NO ORCHARD'S THE WORSE FOR THE WINTRIEST STORM; . . . 228 GOOD-BY AND KEEP COLD  15
WAS WROUGHT THROUGH TREES WITHOUT A BREATH OF STORM . . 238 A HILLSIDE THAW . . .  31
ONE SUCH STORM IN A LIFETIME COULDN'T TEACH THEM . . . 240 OUR SINGING STRENGTH .  46
AGAINST THE SHAPELESS SHADOW OF STORM, . . . . . . . 303 AFTERFLAKES . . . .   9
LET CHAOS STORM! . . . . . . . . . . . . . . . . 308 PERTINAX . . . . .   1
THE STORM GETS DOWN HIS NECK IN AN ICY SOUSE . . . . 341 WILLFUL HOMING . . .   3
I TAKE THE FIRST BOAT. GOD PUTS UP A STORM . . . . . 500 A MASQUE OF MERCY . . 180
(HE STOPS TO LISTEN.) THAT'S A MIGHTY STORM, . . . . 502 A MASQUE OF MERCY . . 233
DON'T ANY OF YOU HEAR A SOUND? / THE STORM! . . . . . 504 A MASQUE OF MERCY . . 279
MERELY THE WINDOWS RATTLING IN THE STORM. . . . . . 504 A MASQUE OF MERCY . . 280
BEYOND THE STORM, BEYOND THE UNIVERSE. . . . . . . . 513 A MASQUE OF MERCY . . 533
STORMS
AND ALL OUR STORMS COME UP TOWARD THE HOUSE, . . . . .  63 A SERVANT TO SERVANTS  24
AS ICE STORMS DO. OFTEN YOU MUST HAVE SEEN THEM . . . 121 BIRCHES . . . . . .   5
IN LONG STORMS AN UNDRIFTED FOUR FEET DEEP . . . . . 226 THE ONSET . . . . .  15
```

STORMY
    THE CLOUDS, THE SOURCE OF RAIN, ONE STORMY NIGHT . . . . . 295 LOST IN HEAVEN 1
    O STORMY, STORMY WORLD, ... 333 HAPPINESS MAKES UP . . 1
    THEIR LITTLE STORMY SHIP, THAN ON. . . . . 344 DISCOVERY OF MADEIRAS . 20
    OR LOW AND STORMY; . . . . 388 ASTROMETAPHYSICAL . . 4

STORY
    AND WHITTIER, AND HAD HER STORY OF THEM. . . . . . . 56 THE BLACK COTTAGE . . . 53
    OR SO THE STORY GOES. IT WAS SOME GIRL. . . . . . . 66 A SERVANT TO SERVANTS . 109
    TELL YOU A STORY OF WHAT HAPPENED ONCE: . . . . 70 THE CODE 29
    IT'S TOO LONG A STORY TO GO INTO NOW. . . . . 142 THE VANISHING RED . . 10
    THE HOUSE ONE STORY HIGH IN FRONT, THREE STORIES . . . 181 MAPLE 57
    WATCHING OUT OF A NINETEENTH STORY WINDOW . . . . 182 MAPLE 81
    (THE HOUSE ONE STORY HIGH IN FRONT, THREE STORIES . . . 182 MAPLE 98
    BUT IF THE STORY MURPHY TOLD WAS TRUE, ... 192 PAUL'S WIFE 40
    SON KNOWS THE STORY: BUT 'TWAS NOT FOR HIM . . . . . 206 THE WITCH OF COOS . . 143
    BUT I SHOULD AWAKE TO CONFIRM YOUR STORY YET; . . . . 236 VALLEY'S SINGING DAY . 18
    BUT WITHOUT TIME TO LINGER FOR HER STORY. . . . . . 257 THE LOVELY BE CHOOSERS 49
    AND SO THE STORY WASN'T TOLD IN GATH; . . . . . . 284 THE GOLD HESPERIDEE . 58
    THERE WERE SUNS OF STORY AND VAUNT . . . . 311 THE VINDICTIVES . . . 49
    THE STORY IS SHE DIED OF THOUGHT. . . . . 347 DISCOVERY OF MADEIRAS . 119
    AND WERE AN EPITAPH TO BE MY STORY . . . . 355 THE LESSON FOR TODAY . 158
    AND THEN TO END THE STORY . . . . 359 NOVEMBER 4
    AND THERE'S A STORY IN A BOOK ABOUT IT: . . . . . . 377 DIRECTIVE 13
    AND HOW MUCH LONGER A STORY HAS SCIENCE . . . . . . 379 TOO ANXIOUS FOR RIVERS 17
    AND TELL THEM THE REST OF THE STORY IS DREAMING? . . . 379 TOO ANXIOUS FOR RIVERS 19
    HAS JUSTIFIED ITSELF IN FREEDOM'S STORY . . . . . . 423 FOR JOHN F. KENNEDY . 52
    BUT THE SORRY STORY . . . . 430 KITTY HAWK 78
    THERE IS A STORY YOU MAY HAVE FORGOTTEN . . . . . . 495 A MASQUE OF MERCY . . 47
    I'M IN THE BIBLE, ALL DONE OUT IN STORY. . . . . . 497 A MASQUE OF MERCY . . 113
    WHY, WHAT A STORY, AT THIS TIME OF YEAR . . . . . 501 A MASQUE OF MERCY . . 211

STOUTLY
    AS OUR COMPARISONS WERE STOUTLY UPWARD . . . . . 279 THE WHITE-TAILED HORNET 60
    NO MATTER WHERE THEY STOUTLY MEAN TO GET, ... 354 THE LESSON FOR TODAY . 108

STOVE
    "HE'S WORN OUT. HE'S ASLEEP BESIDE THE STOVE. . . . . 35 DEATH OF THE HIRED MAN 33
    AGAINST THE STOVE, THE HOTTEST DAY THAT SUMMER. . . . 72 THE CODE 98
    ONCE IN THE STOVE, DISTURBED HIM AND HE SHIFTED, . . . 108 OLD MAN'S WINTER NIGHT 24
    THE STOVE! BEFORE THEY GO! KNOCK ON THE WINDOW; . . . 113 IN THE HOME STRETCH . 75
    "THEY'RE NOT GONE YET." / "WE'VE GOT TO HAVE THE STOVE, . . 113 IN THE HOME STRETCH . 78
    DOOR-FILLING MEN BURST IN AND SEIZED THE STOVE. . . . 113 IN THE HOME STRETCH . 83
    THE STOVE IS NOT, AND YOU ARE NOT TO ME, ... 117 IN THE HOME STRETCH . 179
    THE FIRE GOT OUT THROUGH CRANNIES IN THE STOVE . . . . 117 IN THE HOME STRETCH . 202
    HE SAW NO STAY UNLESS HE STOVE . . . . 137 BROWN'S DESCENT . . 14
    THE STOVE WAS COLD--THE STOVE WAS OFF THE CHIMNEY-- . . 175 THE CENSUS-TAKER . . 36
    BEYOND AN OVER-WARMTH OF KITCHEN STOVE . . . . . . 186 THE AX-HELVE . . . 35
    SIDEWAYS, THAT WOULD HAVE RUN HER ON THE STOVE . . . . 187 THE AX-HELVE . . . 50
    WHERE THE CHIMNEY STARTED ABOVE THE STOVE. . . . . 232 THE KITCHEN CHIMNEY . 12

STOVE-LENGTH
    AND MADE DUST AND DROPPED STOVE-LENGTH STICKS OF WOOD, . . 136 "OUT, OUT--" 2

STOVEPIPE
    CAME UP THE JOINTED STOVEPIPE IN THEIR HANDS, ... 113 IN THE HOME STRETCH . 86
    "A FIT!" SAID ONE, AND BANGED A STOVEPIPE SHOULDER. . . 113 IN THE HOME STRETCH . 90
    WITH GOOD LUCK WITH YOUR STOVEPIPE. NEVER MIND, . . . 113 IN THE HOME STRETCH . 92

STOVE-WINDOW
    AND WARM STOVE-WINDOW LIGHT. . . . . 11 WIND AND WINDOW FLOWER 24

STRAIGHT
    IT WAS ALL HE COULD DO TO KEEP A STRAIGHT FACE." . . . 61 BLUEBERRIES 78
    "WHO'D MARRY HER STRAIGHT OUT OF SUCH A MESS? . . . . 88 THE HOUSEKEEPER . . 186
    STRAIGHT UP AND DOWN OF TALL SLIM TREES . . . . . 101 THE WOOD-PILE . . . 6
    HE STEERED WAS REALLY STRAIGHT AWAY . . . . . . 139 BROWN'S DESCENT . . 66
    THE VERMONT MOUNTAINS STRETCH EXTENDED STRAIGHT; . . . 165 NEW HAMPSHIRE . . . 213
    COME STRAIGHT DOWN OFF THIS MOUNTAIN JUST AS FAST . . . 215 A FOUNTAIN, A BOTTLE . 61
    AND ALL HIS TAIL THAT ISN'T HAIR UP STRAIGHT. . . . 223 THE RUNAWAY 17
    STEER STRAIGHT OFF AFTER SOMETHING INTO SPACE. . . . . 238 ON A TREE FALLEN ACROSS 14
    BUT SHE STOOD STRAIGHT STILL, ... 256 THE LOVELY BE CHOOSERS 14
    IT GIVES UP STANDING STRAIGHT AND GOES DOWN SWISHING. . . 349 TO A YOUNG WRETCH . . 4
    TO GO STRAIGHT HOME, WE WOULDN'T KEEP HIM, WOULD WE?-- . . 501 A MASQUE OF MERCY . . 208

STRAIGHTAWAY
    STRAIGHTAWAY THROUGH THE MOUNTAIN NOTCH . . . . . 63 A SERVANT TO SERVANTS . 22

STRAIGHTENED
    BEFORE I STRAIGHTENED THEM AND BRUSHED THE BARK OFF. . . 199 WILD GRAPES 88

STRAIGHTENING
    BY STRAIGHTENING OUT AND LIFTING A FOREFINGER, ... 147 SNOW 113

STRAIGHTER
    ACROSS THE LINES OF STRAIGHTER DARKER TREES, ... 121 BIRCHES 2

STRAIGHTNESS
    A CROOKED STRAIGHTNESS YET NO LESS A STRAIGHTNESS. . . 421 ESCAPIST--NEVER . . . 5

STRAIGHT-ON
    THAT SORT OF MAN TALKS STRAIGHT-ON ALL HIS LIFE . . . 145 SNOW 64

STRAIN
    "SHE'S LET IT WORRY HER. YOU STOOD THE STRAIN, ... 87 THE HOUSEKEEPER . . 171
    FREE FROM THE LEAST KNOT, EQUAL TO THE STRAIN . . . . 187 THE AX-HELVE . . . 70
    I STRAIN AT LESSONS FIT TO START A SUTURE. . . . . 267 WHAT FIFTY SAID . . 7
    YOUR OLD SWEET-CYNICAL STRAIN . . . . 302 VOICE WAYS 6
    (IN-LEANING UNDER THE STRAIN), ... 312 THE VINDICTIVES . . 66
    IT SEEMED AS IF I COULDN'T STAND THE STRAIN. . . . . 398 BURSTING RAPTURE . . 8
    REGULAR VERSE SPRINGS FROM THE STRAIN OF RHYTHM . . . 460 HOW HARD TO KEEP FROM 213
    FROM THAT STRAIN COMES THE EXPRESSION STRAINS OF MUSIC. . 460 HOW HARD TO KEEP FROM 215
    THAT STRAIN AGAIN! GIVE ME EXCESS OF IT! . . . . . 488 A MASQUE OF REASON . 418

STRAINING
    HE'S TRYING TO LIFT, STRAINING TO LIFT HIMSELF." . . . 37 DEATH OF THE HIRED MAN 95
    WITH STRAINING IN THE WORLD'S EMBRACE. . . . . . 120 BOND AND FREE . . . 8
    AND STRAINING CABLES WET WITH SILVER DEW. . . . . . 126 RANGE-FINDING . . . 11
    AND STRAINING HER RIBS FOR A MONSTER SIGH; . . . . 263 THE TIMES TABLE . . 7
    THE STRAINING MILL BEGAN TO SHAKE. . . . . 273 A LONE STRIKER . . . 10
    AND HER WINGS STRAINING SUDDENLY ASPREAD . . . . . 445 QUESTIONING FACES . . 3

STRAINS
    FROM THAT STRAIN COMES THE EXPRESSION STRAINS OF MUSIC. . 460 HOW HARD TO KEEP FROM 215

STRAIN'S
    "THE STRAIN'S BEEN TOO MUCH FOR HER ALL THESE YEARS: . . . 84 THE HOUSEKEEPER . . . 77
STRAIT
    WHO FAILED TO FIND OR FORCE A STRAIT . . . . 212 AN EMPTY THREAT . . . 44
    AND FOR NOT TURNING OUT A STRAIT, ... 418 AMERICA IS HARD TO SEE 52
STRAITS
    THE WATER IN DESPERATE STRAITS LIKE FRANTIC FISH, . . . 142 THE VANISHING RED . . 22
STRAND
    AND THE FENCE POST CARRIED A STRAND OF WIRE. . . . . . 242 NEED OF BEING VERSED . 20
    FOR ALL THE USE YOU ARE ALONG THE STRAND. . . . . . 446 DOES NO ONE AT ALL EVER 20
STRANDS
    UP AT HIS SHOULDERS, DRAGGING YELLOW STRANDS . . . . . 125 AN ENCOUNTER 17
STRANGE
    AND THE STRANGE BIRDS SAY. . . . . 29 MY BUTTERFLY 45
    STRANGE HOW SUCH INNOCENCE GETS ITS OWN WAY. . . . . . 57 THE BLACK COTTAGE . . 81
    SOME STRANGE KIND--THEY TOLD ME IT HADN'T A NAME." . . . 61 BLUEBERRIES 66
    "THEN I DON'T KNOW. IT MUST BE STRANGE ENOUGH. . . . . 78 THE GENERATIONS OF MEN 139
    "HAVEN'T YOU SEEN HIM? STRANGE WHAT SET YOU OFF . . . . 81 THE HOUSEKEEPER . . . 14
    I ALWAYS HAVE FELT STRANGE WHEN WE CAME HOME . . . . . 89 THE FEAR 17
    I SAW THE STRANGE POSITION OF HIS HANDS-- . . . . . 125 AN ENCOUNTER 16
    HE'S CELEBRATING SOMETHING STRANGE. . . . . 138 BROWN'S DESCENT . . . 34
    IT'S STRANGE SHE DOESN'T WANT TO SPEAK TO US." . . . . 154 SNOW 314
    AND RUN OFF IN STRANGE TANGENTS WITH MY ARM, ... 174 A STAR IN A STONEBOAT . 53
    HE TOOK A STRANGE THING TO BE ROGUISH OVER. . . . . 178 THE STAR-SPLITTER . . 58
    SO, TILL SHE FOUND HERSELF IN A STRANGE PLACE . . . . 182 MAPLE 77
    THOUGH STRANGE AND MUFFLED. . . . . 218 I WILL SING YOU ONE-O . 26
    THEN, AS IF THEY WERE SOMETHING THAT, THOUGH STRANGE, . 229 TWO LOOK AT TWO . . 22
    WE STOOD A MOMENT SO, IN A STRANGE WORLD, ... 233 A BOUNDLESS MOMENT . 9
    SAVE BY SOME STRANGE RESISTANCE IN ITSELF, ... 259 WEST-RUNNING BROOK . 58
    STRANGE APPARITION OF THE MIND! . . . . 332 ALL REVELATION . . . 10
    WHEN SOMETHING STRANGE ABOUT IT MADE ME THINK. . . . 357 A CONSIDERABLE SPECK . 6
    THE SPIRIT PLAYS US STRANGE RELIGIOUS PRANKS . . . . 358 THE LOST FOLLOWER . 5
    OF THE STRANGE DEVOTION . . . . 433 KITTY HAWK 159
    THERE'S A STRANGE LIGHT ON EVERYTHING TODAY. . . . . 473 A MASQUE OF REASON . 8
    STRANGE NO ONE EVER THOUGHT OF IT BEFORE HIM. . . . . 511 A MASQUE OF MERCY . 478
STRANGELY
    I DWELL WITH A STRANGELY ACHING HEART . . . . 6 GHOST HOUSE 11
    "STRANGELY, IT'S ANYTHING THEY WISH TO GIVE." . . . . 78 THE GENERATIONS OF MEN 138
    BUT THE MOOR STRANGELY ENOUGH BELIEVED . . . . . . 347 DISCOVERY OF MADEIRAS . 129
    GAVE ME A STRANGELY RESTLESS DAY. . . . . 364 TRESPASS 8
    IT GIVES US STRANGELY LITTLE AID, ... 403 SOMETHING LIKE A STAR . 16
    THERE HAD BEEN SOMETHING STRANGELY WRONG . . . . . . 416 AMERICA IS HARD TO SEE 13
    AND THINGS HAVE BEEN GOING SO STRANGELY SINCE, ... 421 ONE MORE BREVITY . . 56
STRANGENESS
    I CANNOT RUB THE STRANGENESS FROM MY SIGHT . . . . . 68 AFTER APPLE-PICKING . 9
    THE PAST AND GET SOME STRANGENESS OUT OF IT. . . . . 73 THE GENERATIONS OF MEN 18
    AT BEDTIME; BUT THE STRANGENESS SOON WEARS OFF." . . . 115 IN THE HOME STRETCH . 135
    WHAT WAS IT ABOUT HER NAME? ITS STRANGENESS LAY . . . 181 MAPLE 44
    SHE FAILS FROM STRANGENESS TO A WAY OF LIFE . . . . . 257 THE LOVELY BE CHOOSERS 44
STRANGER
    A STRANGER CAME TO THE DOOR AT EVE, ... 7 LOVE AND A QUESTION . 1
    STRANGER, YOU AND I." . . . . 7 LOVE AND A QUESTION . 12
    "STRANGER, I WISH I KNEW." . . . . 8 LOVE AND A QUESTION . 16
    THAN WAS THE HOUND THAT CAME A STRANGER TO US . . . . 38 DEATH OF THE HIRED MAN 116
    A STRANGER TO OUR YARD, WHO LOOKED THE CITY, ... 106 CHRISTMAS TREES . . 5
    BY ME, A STRANGER. THIS IS WHAT HE SAID, ... 168 NEW HAMPSHIRE . . . 290
    BUT PUT THAT DOWN TO SUPERSTITION, STRANGER. . . . . 369 THE LITERATE FARMER AND 36
    WRETCHEDNESS IN A STRANGER FRIGHTENS ME . . . . . . 493 A MASQUE OF MERCY . 16
STRANGER-COUSINS
    OF STRANGER-COUSINS, IN A FAMILY TREE . . . . 74 THE GENERATIONS OF MEN 39
STRANGERS
    OUT OF THE MUD TWO STRANGERS CAME . . . . 275 TWO TRAMPS IN MUD TIME 1
    HE WAITED (THEY WERE STRANGERS) . . . . 335 CARPE DIEM 6
    WITH VIOLENCE. THE GREEKS WERE HARDLY STRANGERS . . . 511 A MASQUE OF MERCY . . 468
STRANGEST
    BUT THE STRANGEST THING: IN THE THICK OLD THATCH, . . . 253 THE THATCH 13
    I SHOULDN'T BE SURPRISED. / THE STRANGEST LIGHT! . . . 473 A MASQUE OF REASON . 7
STRANGLED
    AND STRANGLED THE WRETCH WITH A STRING. . . . . . . 310 THE VINDICTIVES . . 17
STRAPPING
    I WAS A STRAPPING GIRL OF TWENTY THEN. . . . . . . 209 PAUPER WITCH OF GRAFTON 69
STRATAGEM
    BY WHAT STRATAGEM . . . . 448 THE BAD ISLAND--EASTER 27
STRATEGIC
    MY OWN STRATEGIC RETREAT . . . . 282 A DRUMLIN WOODCHUCK . 5
STRAW
    SO THEY MADE THE PLACE COMFORTABLE WITH STRAW, ... 66 A SERVANT TO SERVANTS . 119
    SO LOW I BRUSHED THE STRAW WITH MY SLEEVES, ... 253 THE THATCH 18
    AND HAVING HID IT IN THEIR BEDDING STRAW . . . . . . 293 AT WOODWARD'S GARDENS . 30
STRAW-DUST-COVERED
    I PICKED UP OFF THE STRAW-DUST-COVERED FLOOR. . . . . 175 THE CENSUS-TAKER . . 45
STRAY
    "I DARE NOT--TOO FAR IN HIS FOOTSTEPS STRAY-- . . . . 16 A DREAM PANG 7
    OR WITH A SHOTGUN FOR A STRAY BLACK BEAR? . . . . . 43 THE MOUNTAIN . . . 87
    STRAY SCRAPS OF PALLIATIVE REASON . . . . 478 A MASQUE OF REASON . 142
STRAYED
    SHE STRAYED SO FAR SHE SCARCELY HEARD . . . . . . 129 THE IMPULSE 15
STREAK
    OLD STREAK OF LEATHER--DOESN'T LOVE ME MUCH . . . . . 94 THE SELF-SEEKER . . 33
    SOMETHING HAD LEFT A BROAD BLACK STREAK OF GREASE . . . 193 PAUL'S WIFE 69
    BETWEEN THE DOTTED FEET A STREAK OF TAIL, ... 270 THE EGG AND THE MACHINE 18
    TWO ROUND DOTS AND A RIPPLE STREAK, ... 327 A MISSIVE MISSILE . . 7
STREAKING
    WENT STREAKING MOLTEN DOWN THE WEST. . . . . 381 AN UNSTAMPED LETTER IN 27
STREAM
    (THE BLACK STREAM, CATCHING ON A SUNKEN ROCK, ... 258 WEST-RUNNING BROOK . 19
    FLECKED THE DARK STREAM AND FLECKED THE DARKER POOL . . 258 WEST-RUNNING BROOK . 24
    THE STREAM OF EVERYTHING THAT RUNS AWAY. . . . . . 259 WEST-RUNNING BROOK . 44

STREAM (CONTINUED)
 AGAINST THE STREAM, THAT MOST WE SEE OURSELVES IN, . . . 260 WEST-RUNNING BROOK . . 69
 BACK UP A STREAM OF RADIANCE TO THE SKY, ... 300 THE MASTER SPEED . . . 3
 AND BACK THROUGH HISTORY UP THE STREAM OF TIME. . . . . 300 THE MASTER SPEED . . . 4
 THE BURRS WERE HILLS, THE SNAKE WAS A STREAM, ... 367 A SERIOUS STEP LIGHTLY . 3
 HE'S ON THAT TENDENCY THAT LIKE THE GULF STREAM, ... 489 A MASQUE OF REASON . . 442
STREAMED
 STREAMED OUT LIKE PENNANTS SWALLOW-TAIL. . . . . . . 452 A-WISHING WELL 53
STREAMS (SEE COUNTER-STREAMS)
 IN STREAMS AND CROSS- AND COUNTER-STREAMS . . . . . . 20 THE TRIAL BY EXISTENCE 22
 (WE KNOW THE VALLEY STREAMS THAT WHEN AROUSED . . . . . 378 DIRECTIVE 53
STREET
 DISTURBED THE SLUMBERING VILLAGE STREET . . . . 102 GOOD HOURS 14
 SO WHEN SHE SAW HIM COMING IN THE STREET . . . . 201 PLACE FOR A THIRD . . 70
 ONE DOWN ONE STREET, ... 218 I WILL SING YOU ONE-O . 12
 WITH THE NEW CITY STREET IT HAS TO WEAR . . . . 231 A BROOK IN THE CITY . 2
 CAME OVER HOUSES FROM ANOTHER STREET, ... 255 ACQUAINTED WITH NIGHT . 9
 LONG SINCE IN SOME ABYSMAL CITY STREET, ... 359 THE LOST FOLLOWER . . 22
 THEY WAITED IN THE STREET, ... 391 A ROGERS GROUP . . . 2
 CAME TAP-TAP-TAPPING DOWN THE VILLAGE STREET, ... 394 HAEC FABULA DOCET . . 3
 A REVOLUTION'S COMING DOWN THE STREET! . . . . 508 A MASQUE OF MERCY . . 391
STREETLIGHTS
 BUT THERE ARE LITTLE STREETLIGHTS SHE SHOULD TRUST, . . . 386 THE FEAR OF MAN . . . 11
STREETS
 TO LIGHTED CITY STREETS WE, TOO, HAVE KNOWN, ... 112 IN THE HOME STRETCH . 58
 HAVE MARRIED BEGGAR MAIDS FROM OFF THE STREETS. . . . . 457 HOW HARD TO KEEP FROM 110
 THE MOB MIGHT HOLD A MAN UP IN THE STREETS . . . . . . 503 A MASQUE OF MERCY . . 250
 AND CAKE THEIR CONCRETE DIRT OFF IN THE STREETS." . . . 506 A MASQUE OF MERCY . . 334
STRENGTH
 I COUNT OUR STRENGTH, ... 10 STORM FEAR 9
 UNTIL THE STRENGTH WAS SHOUTED OUT OF HIM, ... 66 A SERVANT TO SERVANTS . 132
 SO MUCH TOO LIGHT AND AIRY FOR THEIR STRENGTH . . . . . 113 IN THE HOME STRETCH . 87
 AND GIVE YOU A CHANCE TO PUT SOME STRENGTH . . . . . . 133 A GIRL'S GARDEN . . . 15
 OR ANY MOUNTAINS? CAN IT BE SOME STRENGTH . . . . . . 169 NEW HAMPSHIRE 317
 WHEN ALL MY STRENGTH PUT FORTH WAS IN HIS FAVOR, ... 185 THE AX-HELVE 11
 PUT ON IT FROM WITHOUT. AND THERE ITS STRENGTH LAY . . . 187 THE AX-HELVE 75
 I LONG FOR WEIGHT AND STRENGTH . . . . 227 TO EARTHWARD 30
 I ASK AS ONE WHO KNEW THE BROOK, ITS STRENGTH . . . . . 231 A BROOK IN THE CITY . 5
 OUR SINGING STRENGTH . . . . 239 OUR SINGING STRENGTH . T
 THE COUNTRY'S SINGING STRENGTH THUS BROUGHT TOGETHER, . . 240 OUR SINGING STRENGTH . 50
 AND IT IS TIME, STRENGTH, TONE, LIGHT, LIFE, AND LOVE-- . 259 WEST-RUNNING BROOK . . 54
 IT SELDOM OVERTAXED THEIR STRENGTH; . . . . 273 A LONE STRIKER . . . 22
 PERHAPS I HAVE PUT FORTH TOO MUCH STRENGTH AND BEEN TOO
  FIERCE FROM FEAR. . . . . 297 A LEAF-TREADER . . . 3
 AND EVERY GUST THAT GATHERS STRENGTH AND HEAVES . . . . 305 THERE ARE ROUGHLY ZONES 2
 WE HAVE STRENGTH OF RESERVE IN US TO BRING. . . . . . 321 BUILD SOIL 162
 OF A POWER LEADING FROM ITS STRENGTH AND PRIDE, ... 424 FOR JOHN F. KENNEDY . 72
STRENGTHS
 AND BOTH OF OUR UNITED STRENGTHS, TO DO IT." . . . . . 213 A FOUNTAIN, A BOTTLE . 19
STRESS
 WITH TOO MUCH STRESS ON THE WHO. . . . . 294 A RECORD STRIDE . . . 12
STRETCH
 COMING OUT ON THEM FROM A STRETCH OF WOODS, ... 49 A HUNDRED COLLARS . . 125
 IN THE HOME STRETCH . . . . 110 IN THE HOME STRETCH . T
 A LITTLE STRETCH OF MOWING FIELD FOR YOU; . . . . . . 111 IN THE HOME STRETCH . 32
 ALONG A STRETCH OF ROAD; . . . . 134 A GIRL'S GARDEN . . . 22
 THE VERMONT MOUNTAINS STRETCH EXTENDED STRAIGHT; . . . . 165 NEW HAMPSHIRE 213
 TO STRETCH A PROFFERING HAND--AND A SPELL-BREAKING. . . 230 TWO LOOK AT TWO . . . 36
 WHERE HE CAN STRETCH AND HOLD HIS HIGHEST FEAST . . . . 254 A WINTER EDEN 10
 IS A RECORD STRIDE OR STRETCH. . . . . 295 A RECORD STRIDE . . . 26
 TO KNOW THE HAND I STRETCH IMPULSIVELY . . . . 356 A MOTH SEEN IN WINTER . 20
STRETCHED
 BUT STRETCHED AWAY UNTO THE EDGE OF DOOM. . . . . . . 5 INTO MY OWN 4
 SHE STRETCHED UP TALL TO OVERLOOK THE LIGHT . . . . . 91 THE FEAR 62
 THAT WOULDN'T BUDGE, UNTIL THEY SIMPLY STRETCHED . . . . 192 PAUL'S WIFE 44
 HE STRETCHED HER EITHER ARM . . . . 339 THE SUBVERTED FLOWER . 18
 HE STRETCHED HIS ARMS OUT TO THE DARK OF SPACE . . . . 396 ANY SIZE WE PLEASE . . 5
STRETCHER
 THAT'S WHAT IS CALLED A STRETCHER. BUT I GUESS . . . . 192 PAUL'S WIFE 49
STRETCHES
 WHERE THE FIELD STRETCHES TOWARD THE NORTH . . . . . . 131 THE BONFIRE 57
STRETCHING
 MY SMALL WRISTS STRETCHING TILL THEY SHOWED THE BANJO
  STRINGS. . . . . 198 WILD GRAPES 80
STREW
 THAT, AS IT DID THE FOREST STREW, ... 336 THE WIND AND THE RAIN . 4
STREWN (SEE BOULDER-STREWN, ROCK-STREWN)
STRICKEN
 THE STRICKEN FLOWER BENT DOUBLE AND SO HUNG. . . . . . 126 RANGE-FINDING . . . 4
 ONLY TO TUMBLE LIKE A STRICKEN BIRD, ... 216 A FOUNTAIN, A BOTTLE . 115
 THEN HE COULD ENTER ON THE STRICKEN FIELD . . . . . . 507 A MASQUE OF MERCY . . 365
 THEN HE COULD ENTER ON THE STRICKEN FIELD . . . . . . 507 A MASQUE OF MERCY . . 368
STRICT
 IF HE WA'N'T KEPT STRICT WATCH OF, AND IT ENDED . . . . 66 A SERVANT TO SERVANTS . 112
 THE PROBLEM FOR THE KING IS JUST HOW STRICT . . . . . 460 HOW HARD TO KEEP FROM 198
 UPON A METER, STRICT OR LOOSE IAMBIC. . . . . 460 HOW HARD TO KEEP FROM 214
STRICTLY
 BUT STRICTLY HELD BY NONE, IS LOOSELY BOUND . . . . . 332 THE SILKEN TENT . . . 9
STRIDE
 TO HIS DOWNHILL, EARLY-MORNING STRIDE, ... 140 THE GUM-GATHERER . . 2
 A RECORD STRIDE . . . . 294 A RECORD STRIDE . . . T
 IS A RECORD STRIDE OR STRETCH. . . . . 295 A RECORD STRIDE . . . 26
 YET DID NOT MUCH TO SHORTEN STRIDE. . . . . 336 THE WIND AND THE RAIN . 8
'STRIDE
 OVER THE RIDGEPOLE, 'STRIDE OF A BROOMSTICK, ... 210 PAUPER WITCH OF GRAFTON 86
STRIFE
 "ONE THOUGHT IN AGONY OF STRIFE . . . . 21 THE TRIAL BY EXISTENCE 50
 THE LONGEST PEACE IN CHINA WILL END IN STRIFE. . . . . 268 ON LOOKING UP BY CHANCE 12

```
                                                       PAGE TITLE                    LINE
STRIKE
    NOR STRIKE OUT FIRE FROM EACH OTHER, NOR CRASH OUT LOUD.  .  . 268 ON LOOKING UP BY CHANCE     5
    SPARES TO STRIKE FOR THE COMMON GOOD, .  .  .  .  .  .  .  . 275 TWO TRAMPS IN MUD TIME       14
    AS MUCH AS LOVE, AND TOO CLOSE IN TO STRIKE .  .  .  .  .  . 325 BUILD SOIL .  .  .  .  . 277
    WHILE WITH THE HATING OTHER HAND WE STRIKE. .  .  .  .  .  . 371 THE LITERATE FARMER AND 115
    SO WE CAN HANG TOGETHER IN A STRIKE. .  .  .  .  .  .  .  . 498 A MASQUE OF MERCY  .  . 125
STRIKER
    A LONE STRIKER  .  .  .  .  .  .  .  .  .  .  .  .  .  .  . 273 A LONE STRIKER  .  .  .     T
STRIKING
    STRIKING IT GENTLY ACROSS HER LOWERED EYES  .  .  .  .  .  . 181 MAPLE  .  .  .  .  .  .      42
    FROM STRIKING AT ANOTHER ALDER'S ROOTS,  .  .  .  .  .  .  . 185 THE AX-HELVE  .  .  .  .      4
    THE CURVE OF EARTH, AND STRIKING, BREAK THEIR OWN;  .  .  . 261 A SOLDIER .  .  .  .  .      10
    AND BE SO VERY STRIKING. STEAL AWAY,  .  .  .  .  .  .  .  . 325 BUILD SOIL  .  .  .  .  . 278
STRING
    THE WAY BEN FRANKLIN USED TO MAKE THE KITE STRING.  .  .  .  94 THE SELF-SEEKER  .  .  .      35
    THEY STRING TOGETHER WITH A LIVING THREAD.  .  .  .  .  .  . 141 THE LINE-GANG  .  .  .       4
    THEY STRING AN INSTRUMENT AGAINST THE SKY  .  .  .  .  .  . 141 THE LINE-GANG  .  .  .       5
    BUT IN NO HUSH THEY STRING IT: THEY GO PAST .  .  .  .  .  . 141 THE LINE-GANG  .  .  .       8
    AND STRANGLED THE WRETCH WITH A STRING.  .  .  .  .  .  .  . 310 THE VINDICTIVES .  .  .      17
    I'M APT TO STRING ALONG WITH THYATIRA.  .  .  .  .  .  .  . 479 A MASQUE OF REASON .  . 168
STRINGING
    ONE STRINGING A CHAIN OF SEED IN AN OPEN CREASE,  .  .  .  . 299 STRONG SAYING NOTHING .      7
STRINGS
    AMONG THE HARPLIKE MORNING-GLORY STRINGS,  .  .  .  .  .  .  38 DEATH OF THE HIRED MAN 107
    HAD WOUND STRINGS ROUND AND ROUND IT LIKE A BUNDLE.  .  .  . 102 THE WOOD-PILE  .  .  .      31
    THE SAME AS YOU SEIZE CAT'S-CRADLE STRINGS,  .  .  .  .  .  . 123 PEA BRUSH .  .  .  .  .      19
    MY SMALL WRISTS STRETCHING TILL THEY SHOWED THE BANJO
      STRINGS.  .  .  .  .  .  .  .  .  .  .  .  .  .  .  .  . 198 WILD GRAPES  .  .  .  .      80
    AMONG THE HARPLIKE SPREAD OF STRINGS.  .  .  .  .  .  .  .  . 274 A LONE STRIKER  .  .  .      29
STRIP
    THE EXTENT OF PASTURE I SHOULD STRIP, THREE CENTS .  .  .  . 107 CHRISTMAS TREES  .  .  .      48
    LEAVES TO STRIP AND BRANCHES SPLINTER,  .  .  .  .  .  .  . 304 CLEAR AND COLDER  .  .      12
    THE TENDENCY, A LONG, LONG NARROW STRIP  .  .  .  .  .  .  . 489 A MASQUE OF REASON .  . 453
STRIPPED
    THUS ARE WE WHOLLY STRIPPED OF PRIDE  .  .  .  .  .  .  .  .  21 THE TRIAL BY EXISTENCE      70
    RIDGES OF SAND, AND DRIFTWOOD STRIPPED OF BARK.  .  .  .  .  40 THE MOUNTAIN  .  .  .  .      14
    THE FIELDS ARE STRIPPED TO LAWN, THE GARDEN PATCHES  .  .  .  49 A HUNDRED COLLARS  .  . 134
    STRIPPED TO BARE GROUND, THE MAPLE TREES .  .  .  .  .  .  .  49 A HUNDRED COLLARS  .  . 135
    THROUGH A HOUSE STRIPPED OF EVERYTHING  .  .  .  .  .  .  . 216 A FOUNTAIN, A BOTTLE  .  90
STRIPS
    TO ALMOST STRIPS AND TAPES OF RAGGED WHITE  .  .  .  .  .  . 239 OUR SINGING STRENGTH  .       8
STROKE
    AT ONE STROKE (OF A MATCH), BRAD HAD TO TURN .  .  .  .  .  . 178 THE STAR-SPLITTER  .  .      67
    WITH ONE STROKE OF YOUR FINGER IN THE MIDDLE.  .  .  .  .  . 179 THE STAR-SPLITTER  .  .      91
    A BRUSH HAD LEFT A CROOKED STROKE  .  .  .  .  .  .  .  .  . 233 LOOKING FOR SUNSET BIRD  17
    TO PUT THESE PEOPLE AT ONE STROKE OUT OF THEIR PAIN.  .  .  . 287 A ROADSIDE STAND  .  .      48
    AS SURELY AS IT KEEPS THE STROKE AND TIME  .  .  .  .  .  . 362 IN A POEM  .  .  .  .  .       3
STROKED
    AND STROKED IT WITH A HORNY-HANDED KINDNESS.  .  .  .  .  . 217 A FOUNTAIN, A BOTTLE  . 127
STROKES
    LIKE THE TWO STROKES ACROSS A DOLLAR SIGN.  .  .  .  .  .  . 186 THE AX-HELVE  .  .  .  .      25
STROLLED
    STROLLED THITHER, NOT EXPECTING HE WOULD FIND  .  .  .  .  .  74 THE GENERATIONS OF MEN      26
STRONG
    BUT DID NOT ENTER, THOUGH THE WISH WAS STRONG:  .  .  .  .   16 A DREAM PANG .  .  .  .       5
    "AND STRONG OF STALE TOBACCO." / "HE'LL PULL THROUGH."  . 145 SNOW  .  .  .  .  .  .  .      72
    AND ARE A FIGURE OF THE WAY THE STRONG  .  .  .  .  .  .  . 164 NEW HAMPSHIRE  .  .  . 180
    OF MIND AND STRONG OF ARM SHOULD FIT TOGETHER,  .  .  .  . 164 NEW HAMPSHIRE  .  .  . 181
    IF THE WISH HADN'T BEEN TOO STRONG IN ME .  .  .  .  .  .  . 204 THE WITCH OF COOS  .  .      66
    I CRAVED STRONG SWEETS, BUT THOSE  .  .  .  .  .  .  .  .  . 227 TO EARTHWARD .  .  .  .      13
    SEEMED STRONG WHEN I WAS YOUNG;  .  .  .  .  .  .  .  .  .  . 227 TO EARTHWARD .  .  .  .      14
    SHE SHOULDERS WITH A WING SO STRONG  .  .  .  .  .  .  .  . 281 BLUE RIBBON AT AMESBURY     47
    THE STRONG ARE SAYING NOTHING  .  .  .  .  .  .  .  .  .  . 299 STRONG SAYING NOTHING .       T
    BUT THE STRONG ARE SAYING NOTHING UNTIL THEY SEE.  .  .  . 300 STRONG SAYING NOTHING .      16
    WHO LOVE IT WITH A LOVE SO STRONG AND STUPID  .  .  .  .  . 322 BUILD SOIL  .  .  .  . 188
    PROBABLY, BUT YOU'RE FAR TOO FAST AND STRONG  .  .  .  .  . 325 BUILD SOIL  .  .  .  . 284
    AS STRONG IS RAIN WITHOUT AS WINE WITHIN,  .  .  .  .  .  . 337 THE WIND AND THE RAIN  .      41
    STATES STRONG ENOUGH TO DO GOOD ARE BUT FEW.  .  .  .  .  . 398 NO HOLY WARS FOR THEM  .       1
    SMALL BUT STRONG AND ROUND,  .  .  .  .  .  .  .  .  .  .  . 433 KITTY HAWK  .  .  .  . 172
    TO BE STRONG, CAREFUL, THRIFTY, DILIGENT,  .  .  .  .  .  . 505 A MASQUE OF MERCY  .  . 314
STRONGER
    NIGHT AFTER NIGHT AND STRONGER EVERY NIGHT  .  .  .  .  .  . 113 IN THE HOME STRETCH  .      73
    IT'D MAKE MY POSITION STRONGER, THINK,  .  .  .  .  .  .  . 208 PAUPER WITCH OF GRAFTON     42
    THE BLOW CAN BE NO STRONGER THAN THE CLUTCH.  .  .  .  .  . 371 THE LITERATE FARMER AND 116
    A WITCH WAS STRONGER THAN A PROPHET THERE.  .  .  .  .  .  . 477 A MASQUE OF REASON .  . 101
STRONGEST
    THE STRONGEST THING THAT'S GIVEN US TO SEE WITH'S  .  .  . 177 THE STAR-SPLITTER  .  .      34
STROVE
    BUT THOUGH REPEATEDLY HE STROVE .  .  .  .  .  .  .  .  .  . 138 BROWN'S DESCENT  .  .  .      16
STROWN
    ITS PETALS LOOSEN AND ARE STROWN;  .  .  .  .  .  .  .  .  . 450 OUR DOOM TO BLOOM  .  .      14
STRUCK
    "THERE ARE BEES IN THIS WALL." HE STRUCK THE CLAPBOARDS,  .  59 THE BLACK COTTAGE  .  . 125
    THAT STRUCK THE EARTH,  .  .  .  .  .  .  .  .  .  .  .  .  .  69 AFTER APPLE-PICKING  .      33
    IT TOUCHED, IT STRUCK, IT CLATTERED AND WENT OUT.  .  .  .  92 THE FEAR .  .  .  .  .  .      93
    THE HOUR HAD NOT YET STRUCK FOR BEING GOOD, .  .  .  .  . 161 NEW HAMPSHIRE  .  .  .      89
    STRUCK THE HARD CELLAR BOTTOM. AND THEN SOMEONE  .  .  . 204 THE WITCH OF COOS  .  .      50
    I STRUCK THE HAND OFF BRITTLE ON THE FLOOR, .  .  .  .  . 204 THE WITCH OF COOS  .  .      77
    WE STRUCK A ROAD I DIDN'T RECOGNIZE,  .  .  .  .  .  .  .  . 215 A FOUNTAIN, A BOTTLE  .      65
    THAT STRUCK EN MASSE  .  .  .  .  .  .  .  .  .  .  .  .  . 218 I WILL SING YOU ONE-O  .      35
    BLINDLY STRUCK AT MY KNEE AND MISSED.  .  .  .  .  .  .  . 251 BEREFT .  .  .  .  .  .  .      10
    I WATCHED HIM WHERE HE SWOOPED, HE POUNCED, HE STRUCK;  . 278 THE WHITE-TAILED HORNET     33
    HE STRUCK A SECOND TIME. ANOTHER NAILHEAD.  .  .  .  .  . 278 THE WHITE-TAILED HORNET     35
    HE STOOPED AND STRUCK A LITTLE HUCKLEBERRY  .  .  .  .  . 278 THE WHITE-TAILED HORNET     38
    HARD TIMES HAVE STRUCK ME AND I'M ON THE MOVE.  .  .  .  . 316 BUILD SOIL  .  .  .  .  .       5
    WELL, WHEN AT LENGTH THE FEVER STRUCK .  .  .  .  .  .  . 345 DISCOVERY OF MADEIRAS  .      57
    AND STRUCK ME A BLOW  .  .  .  .  .  .  .  .  .  .  .  .  . 450 OBJECTION TO BE STEPPED       5
```

STRUGGLE
    IT COSTS NO INWARD STRUGGLE NOT TO GO, ... 10 STORM FEAR   7
    WHITE FEATHERS FROM THE STRUGGLE OF WHOSE BREAST . . . . 258 WEST-RUNNING BROOK . . 23
STRUGGLED
    SPHEROID THAT KICKED AND STRUGGLED IN ITS GAIT, ... 190 THE GRINDSTONE   . . . 40
STRUGGLE-WORN
    MANY SHALL COME AWAY AS STRUGGLE-WORN . . . . 412 POD OF THE MILKWEED . 34
STRUNG (SEE DIAMOND-STRUNG)
    STRUNG ON YOUR HAIR, WON'T HURT YOUR SUMMER LOOKS. . . . . 77 THE GENERATIONS OF MEN 123
    STRUNG CHAINS OF WALL ROUND EVERYTHING, ... 265 THE BIRTHPLACE 4
STUART'S
    (WHO SAT FOR STUART'S PORTRAIT, BUT WHO SAT . . . . . 317 BUILD SOIL 46
STUB
    WITH THE PITCH-BLACKENED STUB OF AN AX-HANDLE . . . . 175 THE CENSUS-TAKER . . 44
STUBBLE
    I ENTER ALONE UPON THE STUBBLE FIELD, ... 14 WAITING 3
    NO MATTER IF NOT BRUISED OR SPIKED WITH STUBBLE, ... 69 AFTER APPLE-PICKING . 34
    THE WINDFALLS SPIKED WITH STUBBLE AND WORM-EATEN. . . . 125 THE COW IN APPLE TIME 8
    BUT A FEW WEEDS AND STUBBLE SHOWING LAST. . . . . . . 296 DESERT PLACES 4
STUBBORN
    THE STUBBORN THING, THE WAY IT JARS YOUR ARM!-- . . . . 153 SNOW 296
    THESE TWO ARE STUBBORN CHILDREN, AS YOU SEE. . . . . . 517 A MASQUE OF MERCY . 619
STUCK
    STUCK INTO HIS BERRIES AS FRESH AS A SHOWER; . . . . . 61 BLUEBERRIES 65
    OF DEAD LEAVES STUCK TOGETHER BY THE HEAT-- . . . . . 119 HYLA BROOK 11
    THEN FLED FOR FEAR OF GETTING STUCK IN LAVA . . . . . 407 FROM PLANE TO PLANE . 94
    SCIENCE STUCK A POLE . . . . 468 A REFLEX 2
    THE SERPENT'S TAIL STUCK DOWN THE SERPENT'S THROAT, . . . 485 A MASQUE OF REASON . 340
STUDIED
    HE STUDIED LATIN, LIKE THE VIOLIN, ... 37 DEATH OF THE HIRED MAN 80
STUDYING
    STUDYING GENEALOGY WITH ME . . . . 76 THE GENERATIONS OF MEN 85
STUFF
    BY THE SAME HAND WORKING IN THE SAME STUFF? . . . . . 57 THE BLACK COTTAGE . . 78
    SWEET-SCENTED STUFF WHEN THE BREEZE DREW ACROSS IT. . . . 136 "OUT,OUT--" 3
    HE SHOWED ME LUMPS OF THE SCENTED STUFF . . . . . . 141 THE GUM-GATHERER . . 30
    OR BROKEN ITS WHITE NECK OF MUSHROOM STUFF . . . . . 149 SNOW 165
    WITH EVERY KNOWN SHAPE OF THE STUFF. . . . . 310 THE VINDICTIVES . . . 5
    AND BRAIN IS ALL THAT'S LEFT OF MORTAL STUFF, ... 395 ETHEREALIZING 6
STULTIFY
    TO STULTIFY THE DEUTERONOMIST . . . . 475 A MASQUE OF REASON . 67
STUMBLE
    I ALMOST STUMBLE LOOKING UP AND ROUND, ... 226 THE ONSET 6
    SHE HEARD HIM STUMBLE FIRST . . . . 341 THE SUBVERTED FLOWER . 62
    NO ONE HAS SEEN HIM STUMBLE LOOKING BACK. . . . . . 421 ESCAPIST--NEVER . . . 2
    THAT MADE US STUMBLE PAST. . . . . 444 ENDS 2
STUMBLED
    I EVER STUMBLED ON IN OLD NEW HAMPSHIRE . . . . . . 160 NEW HAMPSHIRE . . . 36
    AND STUMBLED THROUGH THE ROCKS WITH HORNY TREAD, ... 338 THE MOST OF IT . . . 19
    TILL I HAVE REELED AND STUMBLED . . . . 389 ASTROMETAPHYSICAL . . 5
    I STUMBLED OVER IT AND GOT TRIPPED UP. . . . . . . 489 A MASQUE OF REASON . 446
STUMBLES
    SOMEONE'S RECEIVER'S DOWN. THE HANDLE STUMBLES. . . . . 153 SNOW 295
STUMBLING
    AND ANOTHER STUMBLING AFTER A HALTING CART. . . . . . 299 STRONG SAYING NOTHING . 8
STUMP
    AND NOTHING BUT THE STUMP OF IT WAS LEFT . . . . . . 175 THE CENSUS-TAKER . . 20
STUMPS
    FROM STUMPS STILL BLEEDING THEIR LIFE AWAY. . . . . . 123 PEA BRUSH 8
STUNG
    IT WAS THAT STUNG. . . . . 227 TO EARTHWARD 16
    HE STUNG ME FIRST AND STUNG ME AFTERWARD. . . . . . 278 THE WHITE-TAILED HORNET 19
    HE GOT HIS PURPLE LITTLE KNUCKLES STUNG. . . . . . 293 AT WOODWARD'S GARDENS 17
STUPID
    OF ITS OWN STUPID LACK OF UNDERSTANDING, ... 148 SNOW 164
    WHO LOVE IT WITH A LOVE SO STRONG AND STUPID . . . . . 322 BUILD SOIL 188
STURDY
    THE STURDY SEEDLING WITH ARCHED BODY COMES . . . . . 124 PUTTING IN THE SEED . 13
    HER WELL-TURNED EGG'S BROWN STURDY SHELL, ... 281 BLUE RIBBON AT AMESBURY 34
STURGEON
    SALMON AND STURGEON, LASHING WITH THEIR TAILS. . . . . 142 THE VANISHING RED . . 23
STYLE
    I DRINK OUT OF THE BOTTLE--NOT YOUR STYLE. . . . . . 50 A HUNDRED COLLARS . 156
    "NOT TILL I SHRINK, WHEN THEY'LL BE OUT OF STYLE." . . . . 50 A HUNDRED COLLARS . 166
    STYLE UPON STYLE IN DRESS AND THOUGHT AT LAST . . . . 117 IN THE HOME STRETCH . 184
    BUT IN THE BEST STYLE OF BAD SALESMANSHIP, ... 160 NEW HAMPSHIRE   . · . 28
    SHE HAS ONE WITCH--OLD STYLE. SHE LIVES IN COLEBROOK. . . 163 NEW HAMPSHIRE . . . 125
    THE WITCH WAS YOUNG, AND BEAUTIFUL (NEW STYLE), . . . 163 NEW HAMPSHIRE . . . 129
    HER STYLE, WERE ALL THE FANCY'S TALK. . . . . . . 280 BLUE RIBBON AT AMESBURY 8
    ANYWAY. THAT IS MY STYLE OF DICTATOR. . . . . . . 323 BUILD SOIL 233
    AT SUCH A PLANETARY CHANGE OF STYLE. . . . . . . 335 I COULD GIVE ALL . . 10
    THAT'S THE RIGHT STYLE OF COAT FOR PROPHECY . . . . . 501 A MASQUE OF MERCY . 218
SUBDUED
    THOSE OF US NOT ASLEEP SUBDUED TO MARK . . . . . . 10 STORM FEAR 11
    THE DOCTOR MADE A SUBDUED DASH FOR IT, ... 47 A HUNDRED COLLARS . 73
    ONE BY ONE HE SUBDUED HIS FATHER'S TREES . . . . . . 122 BIRCHES 28
    SUBDUED THE GROWTH OF EARTH TO GRASS, ... 265 THE BIRTHPLACE . . . 5
SUBJECT
    AND HATED TO BE TWITTED ON THE SUBJECT; . . . . . . 191 PAUL'S WIFE 5
    WHO WERE JUST ON THE SUBJECT WHEN YOU CAME. . . . . 369 THE LITERATE FARMER AND 28
    "YOUR TROUBLE IS NOT STICKING TO THE SUBJECT," . . . . 404 FROM PLANE TO PLANE . 7
    BUT ALL HE DID SAY WAS, "WHAT IS THE SUBJECT?" . . . . 404 FROM PLANE TO PLANE . 10
    SINCE YOU BRING UP THE SUBJECT OF THE SUN. . . . . . 408 FROM PLANE TO PLANE . 125
    WHERE MERCY IS EXPLICITLY THE SUBJECT. . . . . . . 508 A MASQUE OF MERCY . 377
    THE SUBJECT OF THE WORKERS' REVOLUTION . . . . . . 508 A MASQUE OF MERCY . 398
    LET'S CHANGE THE SUBJECT, BOYS, I'M GETTING NERVOUS. . . . 516 A MASQUE OF MERCY . 598
SUBJECTS
    TO HIS SUBJECTS TO GATHER THEM MORE. . . . . 310 THE VINDICTIVES . . . 11

                                                              PAGE TITLE   LINE
SUBJECTS (CONTINUED)
    AND HIS SUBJECTS WRUNG ALL THEY COULD WRING . . . . . . 310 THE VINDICTIVES . . . 12
SUBLIME
    INTO THE SUBLIME. . . . . 429 KITTY HAWK 46
SUBMARINE
    SO WATERY AS TO SEEM SUBMARINE; . . . . 315 IRIS BY NIGHT . . . 11
SUBMISSION
    WAS TO LEARN HIS SUBMISSION TO UNREASON; . . . . . . 481 A MASQUE OF REASON . 210
SUBMIT
    DO I SUBMIT TO BEING SUPPLIED BY HIM . . . . 324 BUILD SOIL 252
    OR RATHER SUBMIT TO BE SENT . . . . 466 SOME SCIENCE FICTION . 27
SUBORDINATING
    IN A SUBORDINATING LOOK OR TONE, ... 385 THE FEAR OF GOD . . 10
SUBSCRIPT
    'TIS THE IOTA SUBSCRIPT OF THE GREEK. . . . . 387 IOTA SUBSCRIPT . . . 4
    IOTA SUBSCRIPT . . . . 387 IOTA SUBSCRIPT . . . T
    THE LETTER YOU WILL FIND ME SUBSCRIPT TO . . . . . . 388 IOTA SUBSCRIPT . . . 6
SUBSCRIPTION
    IN OUR SUBSCRIPTION TO THE SENTIMENT . . . . 515 A MASQUE OF MERCY . . 589
SUBSIDES
    THEN LEAF SUBSIDES TO LEAF. . . . . 222 NOTHING GOLD CAN STAY . 5
SUBSIDING
    IN APRIL BY SUBSIDING MEADOW BROOKS. . . . . 191 PAUL'S WIFE 22
SUBSOIL
    AND EVEN SUBSOIL AND HARDPAN TO MARKET. . . . . . . 321 BUILD SOIL 178
SUBSTANCE
    AND EVEN SUBSTANCE LAPSING UNSUBSTANTIAL; . . . . . 259 WEST-RUNNING BROOK . . 55
SUBSTANTIATION
    IN SUBSTANTIATION. . . . . 435 KITTY HAWK 224
SUBSTITUTE
    "I WON'T ACCEPT THE SUBSTITUTE. IT'S EMPTY." . . . 214 A FOUNTAIN, A BOTTLE . 43
    FOR BRAINS THERE IS NO SUBSTITUTE. . . . . 467 QUANDARY 16
SUBTERFUGE
    SUBTERFUGE FOR SAVING FACES, ... 396 AN IMPORTER 7
SUBURBAN
    UNDER THE BANDSTAND IN SUBURBAN PARK. . . . . 501 A MASQUE OF MERCY . . 210
SUBVERTED
    THE SUBVERTED FLOWER . . . . 339 THE SUBVERTED FLOWER . T
SUCCEED
    VIRTUE MAY FAIL AND WICKEDNESS SUCCEED. . . . . . . 475 A MASQUE OF REASON . . 52
SUCCEEDS
    HE'LL MAKE A CASE OF IT IF HE SUCCEEDS, ... 146 SNOW 86
SUCCESS (SEE EGG-SUCCESS)
    FULL OF SUCCESS, WITH THAT FOOT ON THE DASHBOARD, . . . 405 FROM PLANE TO PLANE . 38
    THE SUCCESS OF THE LIP . . . . 447 THE BAD ISLAND--EASTER 8
    MUST HAVE BEEN HIS SUCCESS IN SIMILE . . . . 461 HOW HARD TO KEEP FROM 252
    LINES WRITTEN IN DEJECTION ON THE EVE OF GREAT SUCCESS . 462 LINES IN DEJECTION . . T
    YOU SAY IT, PAUL. / YOU MEAN ABOUT SUCCESS, ... 509 A MASQUE OF MERCY . . 409
    FAILURE IS FAILURE, BUT SUCCESS IS FAILURE. . . . . 512 A MASQUE OF MERCY . . 507
    I WON'T DECEIVE MYSELF ABOUT SUCCESS . . . . 513 A MASQUE OF MERCY . . 525
SUCCESSFUL
    AND THOUGH NONE TOO SUCCESSFUL AT IT, GUIDERS, ... 267 RIDERS 2
    "HE LOOKS TO ME LIKE GOING HOME SUCCESSFUL, ... 405 FROM PLANE TO PLANE . 37
SUCCESSFULLY
    AND BE SUCCESSFULLY CONVEYED. . . . . 327 A MISSIVE MISSILE . . 32
SUCCESSIVE
    ON SUCCESSIVE SPHERES . . . . 437 KITTY HAWK 285
SUCH
    OBTAIN SUCH GRACE OF HOURS . . . . 14 ROSE POGONIAS . . . 22
    SUCH PIPES KEPT LESS OF POWER TO STIR . . . . 24 PAN WITH US 22
    FROM SUCH A MOUNTAIN--IF IT ISN'T WOODED . . . . . . 42 THE MOUNTAIN 56
    LANCASTER BORE HIM--SUCH A LITTLE TOWN, ... 44 A HUNDRED COLLARS . . 1
    SUCH A GREAT MAN. IT DOESN'T SEE HIM OFTEN . . . . . 44 A HUNDRED COLLARS . . 2
    TO THINK OF SITTING SUCH AN ORDEAL OUT, ... 45 A HUNDRED COLLARS . . 18
    AND TURNED ON HIM WITH SUCH A DAUNTING LOOK, ... 52 HOME BURIAL 33
    THOUGH I DON'T LIKE SUCH THINGS 'TWIXT THOSE THAT LOVE. . 53 HOME BURIAL 53
    THINK OF IT, TALK LIKE THAT AT SUCH A TIME! . . . . . 54 HOME BURIAL 94
    IF SUCH UNLIFELIKE LINES KEPT POWER TO STIR . . . . . 56 THE BLACK COTTAGE . . 29
    WHAT ARE YOU GOING TO DO WITH SUCH A PERSON? . . . . 57 THE BLACK COTTAGE . . 80
    STRANGE HOW SUCH INNOCENCE GETS ITS OWN WAY. . . . . 57 THE BLACK COTTAGE . . 81
    SUCH A PHRASE COULDN'T HAVE MEANT MUCH TO HER. . . . . 58 THE BLACK COTTAGE . . 100
    RATHER THAN SEND THEIR FOLKS TO SUCH A PLACE, ... 65 A SERVANT TO SERVANTS . 95
    A BRIDE, TO HELP TAKE CARE OF SUCH A CREATURE, ... 66 A SERVANT TO SERVANTS . 127
    AND LIVING BY A LAKE. I'M PAST SUCH HELP-- . . . . . 67 A SERVANT TO SERVANTS . 156
    PROVISION THERE HAD BEEN FOR JUST SUCH MEETING . . . . 74 THE GENERATIONS OF MEN 38
    YOU TAKE MY CARD--YOU SEEM SO GOOD AT SUCH THINGS-- . . 75 THE GENERATIONS OF MEN 61
    WHAT DO WE SEE IN SUCH A HOLE, I WONDER." . . . . . 76 THE GENERATIONS OF MEN 91
    THAT A BROOK MAKES IN SUCH A WILD DESCENT. . . . . . 78 THE GENERATIONS OF MEN 133
    YOU THINK YOU'D BEST TEMPT HER AT SUCH A TIME?" . . . 79 THE GENERATIONS OF MEN 182
    HOW SHALL WE SAY GOOD-BY IN SUCH A CASE?" . . . . . 80 THE GENERATIONS OF MEN 204
    SUCH AS IT IS. IT ISN'T WORTH THE MORTGAGE." . . . . 84 THE HOUSEKEEPER . . . 97
    "WHO'D MARRY HER STRAIGHT OUT OF SUCH A MESS? . . . . 88 THE HOUSEKEEPER . . . 186
    AT SUCH AN HOUR OF NIGHT, AND ON FOOT TOO? . . . . . 90 THE FEAR 27
    SUCH AS IT'S GOING TO BE, AND KNOW THE WORST, ... 95 THE SELF-SEEKER . . . 77
    AT SUCH A TIME AS THIS. HE SNAPPED IT NOW. . . . . . 98 THE SELF-SEEKER . . . 166
    I HAD SUCH COMPANY OUTWARD BOUND. . . . . 102 GOOD HOURS 9
    HE CONSIGNED TO THE MOON--SUCH AS SHE WAS, ... 108 OLD MAN'S WINTER NIGHT 18
    FOR SUCH A CHARGE, HIS SNOW UPON THE ROOF, ... 108 OLD MAN'S WINTER NIGHT 21
    AND CARE FOR THEM IN SUCH A CHANGE OF SCENE, ... 109 THE EXPOSED NEST . . 24
    OF SUCH A LITTLE HOUSE. ONCE LEFT ALONE, ... 111 IN THE HOME STRETCH . 40
    ENDS AND BEGINNINGS--THERE ARE NO SUCH THINGS. . . . . 116 IN THE HOME STRETCH . 174
    BUT THOUGHT HAS NEED OF NO SUCH THINGS. . . . . . . 120 BOND AND FREE . . . 4
    AND SUCH IS LOVE AND GLAD TO BE. . . . . 120 BOND AND FREE . . . 9
    SUCH HEAPS OF BROKEN GLASS TO SWEEP AWAY . . . . . . 121 BIRCHES 12
    FIGHT SUCH A FIRE BY RUBBING NOT BY BEATING. . . . . 131 THE BONFIRE 67
    BROWN LIVED AT SUCH A LOFTY FARM . . . . 137 BROWN'S DESCENT . . 1
    "BROWN MAKES AT SUCH AN HOUR OF NIGHT! . . . . 138 BROWN'S DESCENT . . . 33
    IF YOU LIKE TO CALL SUCH A SOUND A LAUGH. . . . . . 142 THE VANISHING RED . . 3

SUCH (CONTINUED)
HE'LL BE DEAD--DEAD AND BURIED." / "SUCH A TROUBLE! . . . . 146 SNOW 88
MORE THAN YOU WILL US WITH SUCH NIGHTMARE TALK. . . . . 149 SNOW 168
NOW YOU AND I WOULD GO TO NO SUCH LENGTH. . . . . . 149 SNOW 187
"I'LL OWN IT'S COLD FOR SUCH A FALL OF SNOW. . . . . . 150 SNOW 201
"WAS EVER SUCH A MAN FOR SEEING LIKENESS?" . . . . . 151 SNOW 250
I'D SURE HAD NO SUCH FRIENDS IN MASSACHUSETTS . . . . 167 NEW HAMPSHIRE . . 258
AND RECOGNIZED AS SUCH IN RUSSIA ITSELF . . . . . . 167 NEW HAMPSHIRE . . 278
OR SOME SUCH SENSE AS SAYS HOW HIGH SHALL JET . . . . . 169 NEW HAMPSHIRE . . 325
SUCH AS EVEN POETS WOULD ADMIT PERFORCE . . . . . . 173 A STAR IN A STONEBOAT . 28
TO SUCH RESORTS OF LIFE AS MARS AND EARTH-- . . . . . 174 A STAR IN A STONEBOAT . 48
SUCH AS IT IS, IT PROMISES THE PRIZE . . . . 174 A STAR IN A STONEBOAT . 55
I ARMED MYSELF AGAINST SUCH BONES AS MIGHT BE . . . . . 175 THE CENSUS-TAKER . . 43
AFTER SUCH LOOSE TALK IT WAS NO SURPRISE . . . . . . 177 THE STAR-SPLITTER . . 38
THERE'S NO SUCH NAME." / "TEACHERS DON'T KNOW AS MUCH . . . 179 MAPLE 5
SOMEONE WAS SAYING IN SUCH NATURAL TONES . . . . . . 182 MAPLE 85
SUCH DOUBTS OF EDUCATION SHOULD DEPEND . . . . 188 THE AX-HELVE . . . 92
SUCH WERE THE BITTER THOUGHTS TO WHICH I TURNED. . . . . 190 THE GRINDSTONE . . 50
WELL, THIS IS SUCH A YARN. PAUL SAWED HIS WIFE . . . . 192 PAUL'S WIFE . . . 54
ACQUIRED ANCESTRALLY IN JUST SUCH TREES . . . . . . 197 WILD GRAPES . . . 49
A PRUDENT GRIEF WILL NOT DESPISE SUCH AIDS. . . . . . 200 PLACE FOR A THIRD . 30
TO SUCH A GHOST-- . . . . 212 AN EMPTY THREAT . . 49
AND SUCH FEW PEOPLE . . . . 218 I WILL SING YOU ONE-O . 30
AND SUCH AS IS DONE TO THEIR WOOD WITH AN AX-- . . . . 228 GOOD-BY AND KEEP COLD . 23
THAT SUCH A BROOK RAN WATER. BUT I WONDER . . . . . 231 A BROOK IN THE CITY . 21
I JUDGED THAT SUCH A CRYSTAL CHILL . . . . 233 LOOKING FOR SUNSET BIRD 14
SUCH WHITE LUXURIANCE OF MAY FOR OURS. . . . . . . 233 A BOUNDLESS MOMENT . 8
THE THOUGHT OF MY ATTEMPTING SUCH A STAY! . . . . . 238 A HILLSIDE THAW . . 35
ONE SUCH STORM IN A LIFETIME COULDN'T TEACH THEM . . . . 240 OUR SINGING STRENGTH . 46
SUCH WAS LIFE IN THE GOLDEN GATE: . . . . 249 A PECK OF GOLD . . 9
IT GOES BY MIGHT OF BEING SUCH A FLOOD . . . . . . 255 THE FLOOD 7
OR SUCH IS THE TALK AT THE FARMHOUSE: . . . . . . 264 THE LAST MOWING . . 3
SUCH IS THE UNCAGED PROGRESS OF THE BEAR. . . . . . 269 THE BEAR 10
BUT PULL SO SLOW, WITH SUCH A TWIST, ... 273 A LONE STRIKER . . 20
SUCH IS THE INSTINCT OF IT I ALLOW. . . . . . . 277 THE WHITE-TAILED HORNET 11
IS SUCH AN EXECRABLE JUDGE OF MOTIVES . . . . . . 278 THE WHITE-TAILED HORNET 14
SUCH A FINE PULLET OUGHT TO GO . . . . 279 BLUE RIBBON AT AMESBURY 1
AT THOSE WHO'D DONE HIM SUCH A WRONG AS THAT, ... 284 THE GOLD HESPERIDEE . 44
HIS BUSINESS WASN'T WITH SUCH. . . . . 288 DEPARTMENTAL . . . 5
YET LEAVE SUCH LOVELY SHAFTS OUTDOORS TO PERISH. . . . . 290 OLD BARN AT THE BOTTOM 34
TWO SUCH AS YOU WITH SUCH A MASTER SPEED . . . . . . 300 THE MASTER SPEED . . 10
IF I SHED SUCH A DARKNESS, ... 303 AFTERFLAKES . . . 6
THAT THE NORTHWEST WIND SHOULD RISE TO SUCH A HEIGHT . . . 305 THERE ARE ROUGHLY ZONES 16
SUCH AS ACCORDING TO BELIEF IN ROME . . . . 315 IRIS BY NIGHT . . 5
TO AFFIRM THERE IS SUCH A THING AS EVIL . . . . . . 317 BUILD SOIL . . . 50
THERE'S NO SUCH THING AS SOCIALISM PURE-- . . . . . 318 BUILD SOIL . . . 70
A REASONER AND GOOD AS SUCH, ... 326 TO A THINKER . . 21
AT SUCH A PLANETARY CHANGE OF STYLE. . . . . . . 335 I COULD GIVE ALL . 10
I TRIED TO TELL HER "THERE'S NO SUCH THING!" . . . . . 342 A CLOUD SHADOW . . 4
WHOSE LOVE WAS SUCH THEY DIDN'T CARE . . . . . . 345 DISCOVERY OF MADEIRAS . 55
SUCH AS WE WERE WE GAVE OURSELVES OUTRIGHT . . . . . 348 THE GIFT OUTRIGHT . 12
SUCH AS SHE WAS, SUCH AS SHE WOULD BECOME. . . . . . 348 THE GIFT OUTRIGHT . 16
WITH SUCH IT HAS PROVED DANGEROUS AS FRIEND . . . . . 359 THE LOST FOLLOWER . 25
THE SECOND SUCH HAS COME, ... 361 ALMOST TWO THOUSAND 5
OF SUCH AN UNACCOUNTABLE STAY . . . . 364 TRESPASS 6
DECLARE THAT IF SUCH INDIANS INHERITED . . . . . . 369 THE LITERATE FARMER AND 55
THERE WILL BE NO SUCH PIECE OF FURNITURE. . . . . . 372 THE LITERATE FARMER AND 130
COMING ON SUCH AN ANCIENT HUMAN TRACE . . . . . . 382 TO AN ANCIENT . . 7
SUCH AS THAT FLESH IS SOMETHING WE CAN SLOUGH . . . . 395 ETHEREALIZING . . 3
MAKE SUCH A NOISELESS TUMULT OVER IT . . . . . . 411 POD OF THE MILKWEED . 11
AND SUCH SMALL POSTHUMOUS RENOWN . . . . 418 AMERICA IS HARD TO SEE 45
HIS CAN BE NO SUCH EASY RAID . . . . 419 AMERICA IS HARD TO SEE 83
WHO WAS THE FIRST TO THINK OF SUCH A THING. . . . . 422 FOR JOHN F. KENNEDY . 6
SUCH AS WE WERE WE GAVE OURSELVES OUTRIGHT . . . . . 424 THE GIFT OUTRIGHT . 12
SUCH AS SHE WAS, SUCH AS SHE WOULD BECOME. . . . . . 425 THE GIFT OUTRIGHT . 16
PASSIONATE PREFERENCE SUCH AS LOVE AT SIGHT. . . . . 425 ACCIDENTLY ON PURPOSE 24
THERE WAS SUCH A LIE . . . . 430 KITTY HAWK . . . 67
SUCH AUSPICES ARE VERY HARD TO READ. . . . . . . 443 AUSPEX 5
IF SUCH A THING IS POSSIBLE WITH MONEY. . . . . . 459 HOW HARD TO KEEP FROM 176
THAT THERE WAS SUCH A THING AS BAD. . . . . . . 467 QUANDARY 2
I PASSED WITH SUCH A HIGH I.Q. . . . . 467 QUANDARY 26
AND AS SUCH I PROMOTE YOU TO A SAINT. . . . . . . 476 A MASQUE OF REASON . 79
SUCH DEVILISH INGENUITY OF TORTURE. . . . . . . 482 A MASQUE OF REASON . 262
WOULD PUT AN END TO SUCH FANTASTIC NONSENSE; . . . . 484 A MASQUE OF REASON . 309
FOR INSTANCE, IS THERE SUCH A THING AS PROGRESS? . . . 484 A MASQUE OF REASON . 315
JOB SAYS THERE'S NO SUCH THING AS EARTH'S BECOMING . . . 484 A MASQUE OF REASON . 316
YOU MUST BE WICKED TO DESERVE SUCH PAIN. . . . . . 486 A MASQUE OF REASON . 364
NO, GOD. / I NEVER HEARD OF SUCH A THING. . . . . 493 A MASQUE OF MERCY . 20
THERE'S SOME SUCH THING AND NO ONE WILL DENY IT-- . . . 508 A MASQUE OF MERCY . 385
BUT SUCH WE ALL ARE MADE IN THE SIGHT OF GOD. . . . . 512 A MASQUE OF MERCY . 501
LADY, AT SUCH A TIME, AND IN THE PRESENCE!-- . . . . 519 A MASQUE OF MERCY . 684
SUCHLIKE
AND BROAD ROUND SUCHLIKE BROOCH, ... 256 THE LOVELY BE CHOOSERS 16
SUCKED
HIS LIPS WERE SUCKED AND BLOWN . . . . 340 THE SUBVERTED FLOWER . 27
SUCKS
AT THE FLAME BURNING DOWNWARD AS HE SUCKS IT." . . . . 112 IN THE HOME STRETCH . 65
THAT SUCKS HIS BREATH LIKE A WICKED CAT IN BED. . . . 341 WILLFUL HOMING . . 4
THE WAVE SUCKS BACK AND WITH THE LAST OF WATER . . . . 391 ON BEING IDOLIZED . 1
SUCTION
TEACH YOUR GRANDMOTHER EGG SUCTION. . . . . . . 397 AN IMPORTER . . . 26
SUDDEN
OR OVER A HILL OR ROUND A SUDDEN CORNER. . . . . . 49 A HUNDRED COLLARS . 126
SHE MADE A SUDDEN MOVEMENT TOWARD HER BODICE, ... 74 THE GENERATIONS OF MEN 43
BUT SUDDEN WINDS THAT SNATCH THEM FROM OUR HANDS . . . 112 IN THE HOME STRETCH . 43
A SUDDEN PASSING BULLET SHOOK IT DRY. . . . . . . 126 RANGE-FINDING . . 12
SUDDEN AND SWIFT AND LIGHT AS THAT . . . . 129 THE IMPULSE . . 25
LIKE COMING TO A SUDDEN RAILROAD STATION. . . . . . 189 THE GRINDSTONE . . 33

SUDDEN (CONTINUED)
   THERE WAS A SUDDEN FLASH OF ARM, A SNATCH, ... 293 AT WOODWARD'S GARDENS . 22
   THEY ARE TOO SUDDEN TO BE CREDIBLE. . . . . 415 A CABIN IN THE CLEARING 33
   (SHE STARTLES AT THE SUDDEN NOTE OF KINDNESS.) . . . . 519 A MASQUE OF MERCY . . 691
SUDDENLY
   THAT SUDDENLY ABOVE THE BEES IS HEARD, ...   12 A PRAYER IN SPRING . .   10
   THAT I SUDDENLY HEARD--ALL I NEEDED TO HEAR: . . . . . 24 THE DEMIURGE'S LAUGH .   5
   FLICKERING ACROSS ITS BOSOM. SUDDENLY . . . .   69 THE CODE   6
   FOR HE TURNED SUDDENLY GRAVE AS IF TO SAY, ... 142 THE VANISHING RED . .   5
   SO SUDDENLY I FLUNG THE DOOR WIDE ON HIM. . . . . . . 204 THE WITCH OF COOS . .   70
   AND SUDDENLY, WITHOUT A JERK OR TWITCH, ... 237 A HILLSIDE THAW . . .   21
   WAS IT SOME MONEY SUDDENLY COME INTO? . . . . 264 THE INVESTMENT . . .   10
   THEN SUDDENLY HE SAW THE THING HE DID, ...   284 THE GOLD HESPERIDEE .   49
   AND HER WINGS STRAINING SUDDENLY ASPREAD . . . . . .   445 QUESTIONING FACES . .   3
SUFFER
   WE SUFFER THEM BY THE DAY . . . . 156 THE SOUND OF TREES . .   6
   TO SUFFER THE SAME DRIVEN NIGHTMARE OVER. . . . . . . 240 OUR SINGING STRENGTH .   45
   LET THEM SUFFER STARVATION AND DIE . . . .   313 THE VINDICTIVES . . .   90
   SUFFER YOURSELF TO BE ADMIRED, MY LOVE, ... 474 A MASQUE OF REASON . .   30
   UNLESS I LIKED TO SUFFER LOSS OF WORSHIP. . . . . . . 476 A MASQUE OF REASON . .   75
   SUFFER A FRIEND TO TRY TO WORD YOU BETTER. . . . . . . 519 A MASQUE OF MERCY . .   677
SUFFERED
   YOU KNOW THEY SUFFERED FROM A GENERAL ONSLAUGHT. . . . 58 THE BLACK COTTAGE . .   96
   I SUFFERED LIKE A METAL BEING CAST. . . . . 267 WHAT FIFTY SAID . . .   3
SUFFERING
   I MAKE A VIRTUE OF MY SUFFERING . . . .   166 NEW HAMPSHIRE   . . .   237
SUFFICE
   AND WOULD SUFFICE. . . . .   220 FIRE AND ICE   9
SUFFICIENTLY
   YOU'D SAY SUFFICIENTLY LOUD, ...   365 A NATURE NOTE . . .   6
SUGAR
   SAND GRAINS SHOULD SUGAR IN THE NATAL DEW . . . . . .   58 THE BLACK COTTAGE . .   122
   YOUR TONGUE GIVES SALT OR SUGAR IN YOUR HAND. . . . . 131 THE BONFIRE   47
   NOW BRINGING OUT ITS RINGS IN SUGAR OF PITCH; . . . . 175 THE CENSUS-TAKER   . .   21
   LET ALONE GROVE OF TREES FOR SUGAR ORCHARD. . . . . . 183 MAPLE   103
   EVENING IN A SUGAR ORCHARD   . . . . 234 EVENING A SUGAR ORCHARD   T
SUGARHOUSE
   OF SAP AND SNOW ROLLED OFF THE SUGARHOUSE. . . . . . . 184 MAPLE   138
   OUTSIDE THE SUGARHOUSE ONE NIGHT FOR CHOICE, ... 234 EVENING A SUGAR ORCHARD   2
SUGGEST
   "DON'T DONKEY'S EARS SUGGEST WE SHAKE OUR OWN?" . . . 215 A FOUNTAIN, A BOTTLE .   55
   AND LOCAL GREEN SUGGEST. . . . .   388 MIDDLENESS OF THE ROAD   16
   "UNLESS IT'S SWEETBREADS," YOU SUGGEST . . . .   467 QUANDARY   17
SUGGESTED
   AND SAVING THAT ITS WEIGHT SUGGESTED GOLD . . . . . . 172 A STAR IN A STONEBOAT .   5
SUGGESTION
   FOR ITS SUGGESTION OF WHAT DREAMS! . . . .   20 THE TRIAL BY EXISTENCE   24
   HERE I AM OVERFERTILE IN SUGGESTION, ...   169 NEW HAMPSHIRE . . .   337
SUGGESTS
   HIS MOOD REJECTING ALL HIS MIND SUGGESTS. . . . . . . 269 THE BEAR   15
SUIT
   YOU THOUGHT TO SUIT YOURSELF. I'VE NOT AGREED . . . . 478 A MASQUE OF REASON . . 145
SUITE
   THE YOUNG SPRUCE MADE A SUITE OF GLADES . . . . 380 AN UNSTAMPED LETTER IN   9
SULLENLY
   BUT FINDING NOTHING, SULLENLY WITHDREW. . . . . 126 RANGE-FINDING   . . .   14
SULPHUR
   WHAT'S THAT SULPHUR BLUR . . . .   438 KITTY HAWK   340
SUM
   NO, THE FIVE HUNDRED WAS THE SUM THEY NAMED . . . . .   95 THE SELF-SEEKER . . .   73
SUMMARY
   SUMMARY RIPOSTE . . . .   429 KITTY HAWK   28
SUMMER (SEE MID-SUMMER)
   THAT VANISHED MANY A SUMMER AGO, ...   5 GHOST HOUSE   2
   IT IS UNDER THE SMALL, DIM, SUMMER STAR. . . . . . .   6 GHOST HOUSE   21
   IT'S ALWAYS COLD IN SUMMER, WARM IN WINTER. . . . . .   42 THE MOUNTAIN   49
   TO RUN WILD IN THE SUMMER--A LITTLE WILD. . . . . . .   44 A HUNDRED COLLARS . .   5
   THEY SAY THEY MEAN TO COME AND SUMMER HERE . . . . .   55 THE BLACK COTTAGE . .   17
   BY MOUNTAIN RANGES HALF IN SUMMER SNOW, ...   58 THE BLACK COTTAGE . .   116
   AGAINST THE STOVE, THE HOTTEST DAY THAT SUMMER. . . .   72 THE CODE   98
   STRUNG ON YOUR HAIR, WON'T HURT YOUR SUMMER LOOKS. . . 77 THE GENERATIONS OF MEN 123
   AND COME AND MAKE YOUR SUMMER DWELLING HERE, ...   79 THE GENERATIONS OF MEN 166
   FOOTPRINTS IN SUMMER DUST AS IF WE DREW . . . . . .   118 MEETING AND PASSING .   6
   SUMMER OR WINTER, AND COULD PLAY ALONE. . . . . 121 BIRCHES   27
   "I GO NO MORE TO SUMMER IN NEW HAMPSHIRE. . . . . . . 166 NEW HAMPSHIRE . . .   221
   I'VE GIVEN UP MY SUMMER PLACE IN DUBLIN." . . . . . . 166 NEW HAMPSHIRE . . .   222
   HOW HIGH I'D THRUST THE PEAKS IN SUMMER SNOW . . . .   169 NEW HAMPSHIRE . . .   339
   ONE SUMMER DAY, ALL DAY I DROVE IT HARD, ...   189 THE GRINDSTONE . . .   23
   I'LL FIND THAT FOUNTAIN IF IT TAKES ALL SUMMER, . . . 213 A FOUNTAIN, A BOTTLE .   18
   ME MYSELF IN THE SUMMER HEAVEN, GODLIKE, ...   225 FOR ONCE SOMETHING . .   5
   IN SUMMER WHEN I PASSED THE PLACE, ...   233 LOOKING FOR SUNSET BIRD   5
   AND BRUSH THE MOW WITH THE SUMMER LOAD. . . . . 242 NEED OF BEING VERSED .   12
   TO DARKEN NATURE AND BE SUMMER WOODS-- . . . .   245 SPRING POOLS   8
   SUMMER WAS PAST AND DAY WAS PAST. . . . . 251 BEREFT   6
   WHERE SUMMER BIRDS HAD BEEN GIVEN HATCH, ...   253 THE THATCH   14
   IF HE FULFILLED AT LAST HIS SUMMER WISH, ...   284 THE GOLD HESPERIDEE .   35
   COME BACK THAT WAY A SUMMER HENCE, ...   291 ON HEART'S BEGINNING TO 19
   ALL SUMMER LONG THEY WERE OVERHEAD, MORE LIFTED UP THAN I. 297 A LEAF-TREADER . . . 5
   ALL SUMMER LONG I THOUGHT I HEARD THEM THREATENING UNDER
      THEIR BREATH. . . . .   297 A LEAF-TREADER . . .   7
   FIRST YOU LET THE SUMMER SIMMER, ...   303 CLEAR AND COLDER . .   4
   THAT HAD EASED ITSELF OF ITS SUMMER LOAD, ... 304 UNHARVESTED   5
   THE WEATHER'S ALTERNATIONS, SUMMER AND WINTER, . . .   317 BUILD SOIL   36
   AT MIDDAY WHEN A SUNNY SUMMER BREEZE . . . .   331 THE SILKEN TENT . . .   2
   IN THE CAPRICIOUSNESS OF SUMMER AIR . . . .   332 THE SILKEN TENT . . .   13
   FOR SUMMER WAS DONE. . . . .   343 QUEST OF PURPLE-FRINGED 28
   HE ONLY STAYED TO SET THE SUMMER ON FIRE, ... 407 FROM PLANE TO PLANE .   93
   HE BESTOWS SUMMER ON US AND ESCAPES . . . .   408 FROM PLANE TO PLANE .   127

SUMMER (CONTINUED)
    (AS I REMEMBER THEY WERE SUMMER STARS . . . . 462 HOW HARD TO KEEP FROM   269
SUMMERS
    FOR THE NEXT FORTY SUMMERS--CALL IT FORTY. . . . . . . 95 THE SELF-SEEKER . . .   69
SUMMERTIME
    IN SUMMERTIME WITH A WITCHING WAND, ... 276 TWO TRAMPS IN MUD TIME   34
SUMMIT
    RIGHT ON THE SUMMIT, ALMOST LIKE A FOUNTAIN. . . . . . 42 THE MOUNTAIN   64
SUMMITS
    THAT WHEN IT HAS SWEPT BY, LEAVES SUMMITS STAINED. . . 255 THE FLOOD   13
    AND SUMMITS SHALL BE IMMERSED, ... 285 IN TIME OF CLOUDBURST   14
SUMMON
    I'D SUMMON GROUSE, RABBIT, AND DEER TO THE WALL . . . . 228 GOOD-BY AND KEEP COLD   10
SUMMONING
    SUMMONING SPIRTS ISN'T "BUTTON, BUTTON, ... 202 THE WITCH OF COOS . .   7
    AND NOW THEY ANSWER HIS SUMMONING BLAST . . . . 236 MISGIVING   9
    SUMMONING ARTISTS TO PARTICIPATE . . . . 422 FOR JOHN F. KENNEDY   1
SUMMONS
    THE FINAL SUMMONS INTO CHURCH WAS BEATING. . . . . . . 284 THE GOLD HESPERIDEE .   42
    AND AT THE SUMMONS ROLAND, OLIVIER, ... 353 THE LESSON FOR TODAY .   89
    BUT SUMMONS OUT OF NOWHERE LIKE A JINNI. . . . . 461 HOW HARD TO KEEP FROM   240
SUN
    PERHAPS IT WAS SOMETHING ABOUT THE HEAT OF THE SUN, . 17 MOWING   4
    SOUNDS NOBLER THERE THAN 'NEATH THE SUN; . . . . 21 THE TRIAL BY EXISTENCE   46
    WHO MOWED IT IN THE DEW BEFORE THE SUN. . . . .   22 THE TUFT OF FLOWERS .   2
    AND STOOD IN THE SUN AND LOOKED HIS FILL . . . . 23 PAN WITH US   4
    AND THE WHIMPER OF HAWKS BESIDE THE SUN . . . . 24 PAN WITH US   19
    RETARD THE SUN WITH GENTLE MIST; . . . . 27 OCTOBER   15
    AND SPILLS THE UPPER BOULDERS IN THE SUN, ...   33 MENDING WALL   3
    ALL THROUGH JULY UNDER THE BLAZING SUN, ...   36 DEATH OF THE HIRED MAN   67
    YOU KNOW THE KIND. THEN LET THE SUN SHINE ON IT!" . .   42 THE MOUNTAIN   54
    GREAT GRANITE TERRACES IN SUN AND SHADOW, ...   42 THE MOUNTAIN   58
    AND THE SUN SHINES OUT WARM: THE VINES MUST BE WET. .   62 BLUEBERRIES   83
    HIS WORK'S A MAN'S, OF COURSE, FROM SUN TO SUN. . . .   64 A SERVANT TO SERVANTS   66
    AS PALE AND DIM AS A MATCH FLAME IN THE SUN; . . . . . 77 THE GENERATIONS OF MEN 100
    AND THAT THRUST UP TO BLOSSOM IN THE SUN . . . . 98 THE SELF-SEEKER . . .   157
    WHERE THE SUN SHINES NOW NO WARMER THAN THE MOON. . . 106 CHRISTMAS TREES . . .   19
    AS BETTER THAN THE SUN IN ANY CASE . . . . 108 OLD MAN'S WINTER NIGHT   20
    BACK PAST THE SUN TO AN EARTHLY ROOM. . . . . 120 BOND AND FREE   15
    BEFORE THEM OVER THEIR HEADS TO DRY IN THE SUN. . . . 121 BIRCHES   20
    THE SUN IN THE NEW-CUT NARROW GAP . . . . 123 PEA BRUSH   5
    WHEN THE HEAT SLOWLY HAZES AND THE SUN . . . .   125 AN ENCOUNTER   2
    AND SETTING SUN TO HYLA BROOK, I GAVE IT . . . . . .   131 THE BONFIRE   58
    AND THE SUN SHRUNKEN YELLOW IN SMOKE. . . . . 141 THE GUM-GATHERER . . .   24
    "THE SUN WILL BRING YOUR LOAD IN"--AND IT DID-- . . . 192 PAUL'S WIFE   47
    AND SHUT MY EYES AGAINST THE SUN, MY EARS . . . . . . 198 WILD GRAPES   74
    THEY SPOKE OF THE SUN . . . . 219 I WILL SING YOU ONE-O .   39
    I DON'T WANT IT STIRRED BY THE HEAT OF THE SUN. . . . 228 GOOD-BY AND KEEP COLD   12
    BEFORE IT CHANGES TO DIAMONDS IN THE SUN), ... 236 VALLEY'S SINGING DAY .   13
    THE HILLSIDE ON THE DAY THE SUN LETS GO . . . . 237 A HILLSIDE THAW . . .   2
    IT LOOKS AS IF SOME MAGIC OF THE SUN . . . . 237 A HILLSIDE THAW . . .   6
    WHEN THE SPENT SUN THROWS UP ITS RAYS ON CLOUD . . . . 249 ACCEPTANCE   1
    WHERE CONIES NOW COME OUT TO SUN AND ROMP . . . . . . 254 A WINTER EDEN   2
    THE SUN RUNS DOWN IN SENDING UP THE BROOK. . . . . . . 260 WEST-RUNNING BROOK .   66
    AND THERE IS SOMETHING SENDING UP THE SUN. . . . . . . 260 WEST-RUNNING BROOK .   67
    WHEN DUST REALLY TOOK IN THE SUN; . . . . 266 SITTING BY A BUSH . .   6
    THE SUN ONCE IMPARTED ITS FLAME. . . . . 266 SITTING BY A BUSH . .   18
    THE SUN AND MOON GET CROSSED, BUT THEY NEVER TOUCH, . 268 ON LOOKING UP BY CHANCE   4
    AND LOOK ELSEWHERE THAN TO STARS AND MOON AND SUN, . . 268 ON LOOKING UP BY CHANCE   9
    THE SUN WAS WARM BUT THE WIND WAS CHILL. . . . . . .   275 TWO TRAMPS IN MUD TIME   17
    WHEN THE SUN IS OUT AND THE WIND IS STILL, ...   275 TWO TRAMPS IN MUD TIME   19
    THAT WILL STEAL FORTH AFTER THE SUN IS SET . . . . .   276 TWO TRAMPS IN MUD TIME   39
    AND ON TRACTS LAID NEW TO THE SUN, ...   285 IN TIME OF CLOUDBURST   19
    HE MADE THE SUN A PINPOINT ON THE NOSE . . . .   293 AT WOODWARD'S GARDENS .   8
    THEY MIGHT NOT UNDERSTAND THE SUN ITSELF. . . . . . . 294 AT WOODWARD'S GARDENS   36
    WITH THE SUN SHINING THROUGH. . . . . 303 AFTERFLAKES   15
    OF FLASHING LINKS IN THE SUN. . . . . 312 THE VINDICTIVES . . .   75
    BEFORE THE FRAGMENTS OF A FORMER SUN . . . .   315 IRIS BY NIGHT   7
    OR A STAR COMING TO DILATE THE SUN. . . . . 317 BUILD SOIL   59
    THE LAST OF THE LIGHT OF THE SUN . . . .   334 COME IN   9
    BUT THE SUN OVERHEAD; . . . . 342 QUEST OF PURPLE-FRINGED   2
    IN SUNSET LIGHT, YOU'D THINK IT WAS THE SUN . . . . . 368 THE LITERATE FARMER AND 12
    I DIDN'T SEE THE SUN SET. DID IT SET? . . . . 368 THE LITERATE FARMER AND 19
    THE SUN SETS THE EXAMPLE IN THE DAY." . . . . 370 THE LITERATE FARMER AND 74
    AND THE SUN CAME OUT TO DRY ME. . . . . 377 ONE STEP BACKWARD TAKEN 14
    SUPPOSE SOME SEED-PEARL SUN . . . . 384 MAKING CERTAIN ANYTHING   5
    THE SUN IS SATISFIED WITH DAYS. . . . . 390 TWO LEADING LIGHTS .   4
    TO SET HERSELF BESIDE THE SUN. . . . . 390 TWO LEADING LIGHTS .   20
    THE ONLY THING I WORRY ABOUT IS THE SUN. . . . . 392 IT BIDS PRETTY FAIR   3
    TODAY I WANT TO TALK ABOUT THE SUN. . . . . 406 FROM PLANE TO PLANE   87
    THE SUN THEN HAD HIS LONGEST DAY IN HEAVEN, ... 407 FROM PLANE TO PLANE   90
    YOU SEE IT IN YOURSELF AND IN THE SUN; . . . .   407 FROM PLANE TO PLANE   100
    I OWN HE DOES LOOK BUSY WHEN THE SUN . . . .   407 FROM PLANE TO PLANE   104
    SINCE YOU BRING UP THE SUBJECT OF THE SUN. . . . . . . 408 FROM PLANE TO PLANE   125
    "AND SOON FOR LACK OF SUN, ...   416 CLOSED FOR GOOD . . .   19
    OF A SINGLE SUN . . . . 440 KITTY HAWK   398
    TO LOOK AT LONG DIRECTLY (LIKE THE SUN), ... 515 A MASQUE OF MERCY .   584
SUN-ASSAULTER
    AND THE DAFT SUN-ASSAULTER, HE . . . . 28 MY BUTTERFLY   2
SUN-BORDERED
    WHERE AN IRREGULAR SUN-BORDERED CLOUD . . . .   69 THE CODE   4
SUNBURNED
    THE SUNBURNED HILLSIDE SETS MY FACE AGLOW, ... 17 THE VANTAGE POINT . .   11
    HE LAID HIM DOWN ON THE SUNBURNED EARTH . . . .   24 PAN WITH US   28
SUNDAY
    REGULAR VESTRY-TREES WHOLE SUNDAY SCHOOLS . . . . . . 107 CHRISTMAS TREES . . .   53
    TILL ED BEGINS TO GET OUT ON A SUNDAY . . . . 115 IN THE HOME STRETCH .   148
    I WALKED DOWN ALONE SUNDAY AFTER CHURCH . . . . 123 PEA BRUSH   1

		PAGE	TITLE	LINE
SUNDAY (CONTINUED)				
TO MAKE A WILLOW WHISTLE ON A SUNDAY	. . . . . .	191	PAUL'S WIFE	21
'TWAS SUNDAY AND SQUARE HALE WAS DRESSED FOR MEETING.		284	THE GOLD HESPERIDEE	41
SQUARE MATTHEW HALE TOOK OFF HIS SUNDAY HAT	. . . .	284	THE GOLD HESPERIDEE	45
SAFETY RAZORS, SUNDAY PAPERS,	. . . .	396	AN IMPORTER	14
THAT OUGHT TO MAKE THE SUNDAY PRESS.	. . . .	451	A-WISHING WELL	19
SUNDIAL				
BEAT A SUNDIAL IN THE SCENERY--	. . . .	397	AN IMPORTER	22
SUNG				
AND YET 'TWOULD SEEM THAT WHAT IS SUNG	. . . . .	336	THE WIND AND THE RAIN	18
I SUNG OR SAID.	. . . .	342	QUEST OF PURPLE-FRINGED	4
THAT SHOULD IF NOT BE TALKED THEN SUNG ABOUT.	. . . .	411	POD OF THE MILKWEED	9
I SHOULD HAVE HAD COLUMBUS SUNG	. . . .	417	AMERICA IS HARD TO SEE	34
I MIGHT WELL HAVE SUNG	. . . .	428	KITTY HAWK	5
TO HAVE UP AND SUNG	. . . .	429	KITTY HAWK	41
HAD I ONLY SUNG,	. . . .	430	KITTY HAWK	83
THAT I MIGHT HAVE SUNG.	. . . .	431	KITTY HAWK	99
SUNK				
YOUR TOP HAS SUNK TOO LOW,	. . . .	298	ON TAKING FROM THE TOP	5
THAT HADN'T SUNK THE WAY IT SHOULD HAVE SUNK,	. . . .	368	THE LITERATE FARMER AND	13
SUNKEN				
AND THE PILE SOMEWHAT SUNKEN. CLEMATIS	. . . . .	102	THE WOOD-PILE	30
(THE BLACK STREAM, CATCHING ON A SUNKEN ROCK,	. . . .	258	WEST-RUNNING BROOK	19
THEN EDDIES PLAYING ROUND A SUNKEN REEF	. . . . . .	335	I COULD GIVE ALL	7
SUNLIGHT				
BROAD-SHOULDERED LITTLE SLABS THERE IN THE SUNLIGHT	. .	52	HOME BURIAL	27
SITTING BY A BUSH IN BROAD SUNLIGHT	. . . .	266	SITTING BY A BUSH	T
AS MAGICAL AS SUNLIGHT ON THE SKIN.	. . . . . .	337	THE WIND AND THE RAIN	42
IN SUNLIGHT NEAR US IN MOMENTOUS SWING	. . . . .	361	A LOOSE MOUNTAIN	15
SUNLIT				
A CLOUD COMES OVER THE SUNLIT ARCH,	. . . .	275	TWO TRAMPS IN MUD TIME	22
SUNNY				
A SUNNY MORNING, OR TAKE THE RISING WIND	. . . .	63	A SERVANT TO SERVANTS	28
ON SUNNY DAYS A MOMENT OVERCAST;	. . . .	120	THE OVEN BIRD	8
LOADED WITH ICE A SUNNY WINTER MORNING	. . . . .	121	BIRCHES	6
DOWN AT THE AVERYS'? WELL, ONE SUNNY MORNING	. . .	149	SNOW	175
(THE ARRANGEMENT MADE A PLEASANT SUNNY CELLAR.)	. .	181	MAPLE	59
BUT WHERE THIS OLD WALL BURNS A SUNNY CHEEK,	. . .	246	ATMOSPHERE	2
AT ANCHOR SHE RIDES THE SUNNY SOD,	. . . . . .	262	THE FLOWER BOAT	5
AT MIDDAY WHEN A SUNNY SUMMER BREEZE	. . . . . .	331	THE SILKEN TENT	2
SUN-PRIEST				
COMMANDED BY ONE SUN-PRIEST,	. . . .	312	THE VINDICTIVES	73
SUNRISE				
OR SING AND DANCE ALL NIGHT AND SEE SUNRISE	. . . .	496	A MASQUE OF MERCY	71
SUNS				
THERE WERE SUNS OF STORY AND VAUNT	. . . . . .	311	THE VINDICTIVES	49
SUN'S				
AS THE SUN'S RIGHT WORSHIP IS,	. . . .	13	ROSE POGONIAS	10
SOON THE SUN'S WARMTH MAKES THEM SHED CRYSTAL SHELLS	.	121	BIRCHES	10
IT TAKES THE MOON FOR THIS. THE SUN'S A WIZARD	. . .	237	A HILLSIDE THAW	18
AND THE SUN'S BRILLIANT BALL	. . . .	333	HAPPINESS MAKES UP	5
I LIKE TO THINK THE SUN'S LIKE YOU IN THAT--	. . .	408	FROM PLANE TO PLANE	124
SUNSET				
WE ROSE TO GO. SUNSET BLAZED ON THE WINDOWS.	. . .	59	THE BLACK COTTAGE	127
UNDER THE SUNSET FAR INTO VERMONT.	. . . . . .	136	"OUT, OUT--"	6
LOOKING FOR A SUNSET BIRD IN WINTER	. . . . . .	232	LOOKING FOR SUNSET BIRD	T
TO THE MIDNIGHT SKY A SUNSET GLOW.	. . . . . .	241	NEED OF BEING VERSED	2
APPEARED LIKE GOLD IN THE SUNSET SKY,	. . . . .	249	A PECK OF GOLD	6
IN SUNSET LIGHT, YOU'D THINK IT WAS THE SUN	. . . .	368	THE LITERATE FARMER AND	12
SUN-SHAPED				
SUN-SHAPED AND JEWEL-SMALL,	. . . .	13	ROSE POGONIAS	2
SUNSHINE				
BUT IF WE MUST, IN SUNSHINE." SO SHE WENT.	. . . .	81	THE GENERATIONS OF MEN	212
SUN-SMITTEN				
AND NEVER SEEN SUN-SMITTEN SLIME	. . . .	266	SITTING BY A BUSH	10
SUPERSEDING (SEE SELF-SUPERSEDING)				
SUPERSTITION				
BUT PUT THAT DOWN TO SUPERSTITION, STRANGER.	. . .	369	THE LITERATE FARMER AND	36
AND SUPERSTITION WINS. HE BLAMES THE STARS,	. . . .	462	HOW HARD TO KEEP FROM	267
SUPERSTITIOUS				
A SUPERSTITIOUS CRY FOR FARMERS' LUCK--	. . . . .	407	FROM PLANE TO PLANE	118
"LET'S NOT GET SUPERSTITIOUS, SIRE," THE PRINCE SAID.	.	454	HOW HARD TO KEEP FROM	28
SUPPER				
TO TELL THEM "SUPPER." AT THE WORD, THE SAW,	. . .	136	"OUT, OUT--"	14
AS IF TO PROVE SAWS KNEW WHAT SUPPER MEANT,	. . .	136	"OUT, OUT--"	15
WHERE WAS MY SUPPER? WHERE WAS ANYONE'S?	. . . .	175	THE CENSUS-TAKER	34
KNIVES AND FORKS RINGING ON THE SUPPER PLATES,	. . .	368	THE LITERATE FARMER AND	3
SUPPERS				
WE DON'T CUT OFF FROM COMING TO CHURCH SUPPERS,	. .	178	THE STAR-SPLITTER	49
SUPPER'S				
WHEN SUPPER'S ON THE TABLE, AND WE'LL SEE	. . . .	123	PUTTING IN THE SEED	2
SUPPLIED				
DO I SUBMIT TO BEING SUPPLIED BY HIM	. . . . . .	324	BUILD SOIL	252
SUPPLIES				
FINDING HIM IN HIS RIGHT SUPPLIES	. . . . . .	420	ONE MORE BREVITY	42
SUPPLY				
WHY WAIT FOR SCIENCE TO SUPPLY THE HOW	. . . .	395	WHY WAIT FOR SCIENCE	9
AND WHEN IT'S OVER WATCH THE WORLD'S SUPPLY	. . . .	398	NO HOLY WARS FOR THEM	7
SUPPORT (SEE SELF-SUPPORT)				
SHE REACHED A HAND TO JOEL FOR SUPPORT:	. . . . .	91	THE FEAR	68
SUPPORTING (SEE SELF-SUPPORTING)				
AND ITS SUPPORTING CENTRAL CEDAR POLE,	. . . . .	332	THE SILKEN TENT	5
AND STANDS BESIDE, SUPPORTING IT IN PLACE.)	. . .	474	A MASQUE OF REASON	23
I WAS SUPPORTING YOU FOR FEAR YOU'D FAINT	. . . .	518	A MASQUE OF MERCY	647
SUPPORTS				
BUT FOR SOME OF THE MONEY, THE CASH, WHOSE FLOW SUPPORTS		286	A ROADSIDE STAND	5
SUPPOSE				
"I DON'T SUPPOSE THE WATER'S CHANGED AT ALL.	. . . .	44	THE MOUNTAIN	101

SUPPOSE (CONTINUED)
"ONE WOULD SUPPOSE THEY MIGHT NOT BE AS GLAD . . . .   49 A HUNDRED COLLARS . . 149
SUPPOSE YOU AREN'T AWAKE WHEN I COME BACK?" . . . . .   50 A HUNDRED COLLARS . . 164
I SHOULD SUPPOSE. I CAN'T SAY I SEE HOW. . . . .   52 HOME BURIAL 48
BUT SUPPOSE SHE HAD MISSED IT FROM THE CREED, ...   58 THE BLACK COTTAGE . . 101
I SUPPOSE SHE DESERVES SOME PITY, TOO. . . . .   88 THE HOUSEKEEPER . . . 192
"LOOKING ROUND, I SUPPOSE," SAID WILLIS. / "YES, . . .   96 THE SELF-SEEKER . . . 101
"YES, I SUPPOSE YOU'LL WANT TO, BUT I SHOULDN'T. . . . 152 SNOW 263
AND LIVING HIS FIGHT THROUGH WITH HIM, I SUPPOSE." . . 152 SNOW 269
YOU DON'T SUPPOSE?--SHE WOULDN'T GO OUTDOORS?" . . . . 154 SNOW 305
A THING TO SELL." I DON'T SUPPOSE THE WORK . . . . . . 159 NEW HAMPSHIRE . . .   4
SUPPOSE THEY WEREN'T BEHAVING PURITANLY, ... 161 NEW HAMPSHIRE . . . 88
I WAS BORN, I SUPPOSE, LIKE ANYONE, ... 196 WILD GRAPES   7
TO TELL THE TRUTH, SUPPOSE THE TIME HAD COME. . . . . . 207 THE WITCH OF COOS . 144
THE PLUM, I SUPPOSE. . . . . 246 THE ROSE FAMILY . . .   6
SUPPOSE SOMEONE COMES NEAR ME WHO IN RATE . . . . 324 BUILD SOIL 249
SUPPOSE YOU'VE NO DIRECTION IN YOU, ... 326 TO A THINKER 25
SUPPOSE HIS GHOST IS STANDING BY . . . . 327 A MISSIVE MISSILE . . 30
WE DANCE ROUND IN A RING AND SUPPOSE, ... 362 THE NIGHT LIGHT . . .   1
WHO HAVE, AS I SUPPOSE, AHEAD . . . . 383 THE SECRET SITS . . .   7
SUPPOSE SOME SEED-PEARL SUN . . . . 384 MAKING CERTAIN ANYTHING   5
YET I SUPPOSE WHAT SEEMS TO US CONFUSION . . . . 485 A MASQUE OF REASON . 338
SUPPOSED
SHE HAD SUPPOSED THE WAR DECIDED THAT. . . . .   57 THE BLACK COTTAGE . . 79
IS SUPPOSED TO BE MAD." / "I MAY BE MAD." . . . .   76 THE GENERATIONS OF MEN 83
JUST WHAT AM I SUPPOSED TO DO ABOUT IT? . . . . 322 BUILD SOIL 205
A MEANING I WAS SUPPOSED TO SEEK, ... 421 ONE MORE BREVITY   . . 68
SHE'S SUPPOSED TO MEAN. . . . . 442 KITTY HAWK 461
THE WORD I WANTED. YOU WOULD HAVE SUPPOSED . . . . . . 475 A MASQUE OF REASON . . 55
REASON IS, I SUPPOSED, THE STEERING GEAR. . . . . 481 A MASQUE OF REASON . 231
SUPPOSING
JUST SUPPOSING I-- . . . . 430 KITTY HAWK 57
SUPREME
SETTING THE THING THAT IS SUPREME. . . . .   20 THE TRIAL BY EXISTENCE 40
THAT THE SUPREME MERIT . . . . 435 KITTY HAWK 222
SURE
ONLY MORE SURE OF ALL I THOUGHT WAS TRUE. . . . .   5 INTO MY OWN 14
HIS WORKING DAYS ARE DONE; I'M SURE OF IT." . . . . . .   39 DEATH OF THE HIRED MAN 153
SHE LET HIM LOOK, SURE THAT HE WOULDN'T SEE, ...   51 HOME BURIAL 15
'I'M SURE--I'M SURE'--AS POLITE AS COULD BE. . . . . .   61 BLUEBERRIES 75
IT'S GOT SO I DON'T EVEN KNOW FOR SURE . . . .   63 A SERVANT TO SERVANTS 11
AND I WON'T ASK HIM--IT'S NOT SURE ENOUGH. . . . . . .   67 A SERVANT TO SERVANTS 158
"I'M SURE SHE WON'T COME BACK. SHE'S HIDING SOMEWHERE.   82 THE HOUSEKEEPER . . . 23
ARE YOU SURE---" / "YES, I'M SURE!" / "--IT WAS A FACE?" 89 THE FEAR 13
THE DOCTOR'S SURE YOU'RE GOING TO WALK AGAIN?" . . . .   93 THE SELF-SEEKER . . . 15
THAT'S SURE TO BE RIGHT, EVEN IF IT'S WRONG. . . . . .   96 THE SELF-SEEKER . . 111
AND IT WAS OLDER SURE THAN THIS YEAR'S CUTTING, ... 101 THE WOOD-PILE . . . 27
STILL HE SMILED--DID YOU SEE HIM?--I WAS SURE! . . . . 127 THE SMILE   3
I WON! BUT I'M SURE NO ONE EVER SPREAD . . . . 132 THE BONFIRE 81
HE MAY BE GOOD, BUT ONE THING'S SURE, HE'S TOUGH." . . 145 SNOW 71
I'D SURE HAD NO SUCH FRIENDS IN MASSACHUSETTS . . . . . 167 NEW HAMPSHIRE . . . 258
SURE THAT THOUGH NOT A STAR OF DEATH AND BIRTH, ... 174 A STAR IN A STONEBOAT 46
SHE NODDED. SO WE'RE SURE THERE'S NO MISTAKE. . . . . . 180 MAPLE 19
SHE WAS SURE, THOUGH, THERE HAD BEEN NOTHING IN IT. . . 181 MAPLE 69
TOFFILE AGREED TO THAT, AND SURE ENOUGH, ... 206 THE WITCH OF COOS . 114
SO SURE OF DEATH THE MARBLES RHYME, ... 221 IN A DISUSED GRAVEYARD   9
SHE COULD BE SURE THERE WAS NO HIDDEN ILL . . . . 230 NOT TO KEEP   3
I NAME ALL THE FLOWERS I AM SURE THEY WEREN'T: . . . . 248 A PASSING GLIMPSE . .   5
HIS MARE WAS SURE TO OBSERVE THE SPOT . . . . 263 THE TIMES TABLE . . .   4
HE FOUND SUSPICIOUS SAND, AND SURE ENOUGH, ... 270 THE EGG AND THE MACHINE 22
AND THE HARM IS NONE TOO SURE, ... 285 IN TIME OF CLOUDBURST . 9
THERE SURE ENOUGH WAS AN APPLE TREE . . . . 304 UNHARVESTED   4
IF ONLY ANYONE WERE SURE . . . . 327 A MISSIVE MISSILE . . 20
AND IF THIS MAY NOT BE (AND NOTHING'S SURE), ... 358 THE LOST FOLLOWER . . 17
BUT BEDS--IN LESS THAN FIFTY YEARS HE'S SURE . . . . . 372 THE LITERATE FARMER AND 129
TO MAKE SURE WHAT STAR I MISSED . . . . 384 MAKING CERTAIN ANYTHING 13
BE SURE TO KEEP REPEATING TO YOURSELF . . . . 385 THE FEAR OF GOD . . .   3
I GRANT YOU--IF YOU'RE SURE ABOUT THE WORD. . . . . . . 394 LUCRETIUS VERSUS POETS 11
ARE ABSOLUTELY SURE TO COME TO GRIEF. . . . . 394 HAEC FABULA DOCET . . 20
YET IN HIS HEART HE WAS UNSHAKEN SURE . . . . 400 FROM THE BROKEN DROUGHT 9
DICK LONGED TO SAY, BUT WASN'T SURE ENOUGH . . . . . . 407 FROM PLANE TO PLANE . 110
AND I WASN'T SURE I WAS TALKING DOG. . . . . 420 ONE MORE BREVITY   . . 37
SO CLOSE YET SURE TO BE ABIDED BY, ... 423 FOR JOHN F. KENNEDY . 56
I WAS, TO BE SURE, ... 428 KITTY HAWK 10
SURE SHE HASN'T ERRED . . . . 442 KITTY HAWK 452
BUT ONE THING IS SURE, ... 449 THE BAD ISLAND--EASTER 54
TO AVOID WHAT HE WASN'T SURE HE WANTED. . . . . 453 HOW HARD TO KEEP FROM   5
THIS TIME AN ALL-NIGHT BANQUET, TO BE SURE, ... 458 HOW HARD TO KEEP FROM 133
(SOMETIMES I THINK YOU ARE TOO SURE YOU HAVE BEEN.) . . 520 A MASQUE OF MERCY . 709
SURELY
SURELY YOU WOULDN'T GRUDGE THE POOR OLD MAN . . . . . .   36 DEATH OF THE HIRED MAN 49
WENT SURELY TO THE CIDER-APPLE HEAP . . . .   69 AFTER APPLE-PICKING . 35
NOR GRANNY'S, SURELY. CALL UP ONE OF THEM. . . . . . .   79 THE GENERATIONS OF MEN 175
"LOOK AT WHAT HAPPENED. SURELY SOME GOD PINXIT. . . . . 321 BUILD SOIL 153
BUT STAY AND HEAR ME OUT. I SURELY THINK . . . . 356 A MOTH SEEN IN WINTER   10
AS SURELY AS IT KEEPS THE STROKE AND TIME . . . . 362 IN A POEM   3
HE'S SURELY GOT IT IN FOR COTS AND BEDS. . . . . 372 THE LITERATE FARMER AND 131
SURENESS
AND SIGNIFIES THE SURENESS OF THE SOUL. . . . . 332 THE SILKEN TENT . . .   7
SURER
TO MAKE IT SURER THAT I WAS A WITCH? . . . . 208 PAUPER WITCH OF GRAFTON 44
SURE'S
THE CRIB HE SLEPT IN--AND AS SURE'S YOU'RE BORN . . . . 209 PAUPER WITCH OF GRAFTON 61
SUREST
THE SUREST THING THERE IS IS WE ARE RIDERS, ... 267 RIDERS   1
SURFACE
GIVES ME BACK IN A SHINING SURFACE PICTURE . . . . . . 225 FOR ONCE SOMETHING . .   4
SO LOST ON ME IN MY SURFACE FLIGHT. . . . . 292 ON HEART'S BEGINNING TO 41

SURFACE (CONTINUED)
   BEWARE OF COMING TOO MUCH TO THE SURFACE . . . . 385 THE FEAR OF GOD . . . 11
   THAN ON THE SURFACE. IF THERE EVER WAS, ... 483 A MASQUE OF REASON . . 283
SURGING
   SURGING, THE GRASSES DIZZIED ME OF THOUGHT, ... 29 MY BUTTERFLY 35
SURLY
   WHOEVER THE SURLY FREEDOM TOOK . . . . 364 TRESPASS 5
SURMOUNTED
   THE GRADE SURMOUNTED, WE WERE RIDING HIGH . . . . . 292 FIGURE IN THE DOORWAY . 1
SURPASSING
   WHO ONCE KEPT SURPASSING EACH OTHER, ... 294 A RECORD STRIDE . . 7
SURPRISE
   SHALL NOT DISSEMBLE THEIR SURPRISE . . . . 19 THE TRIAL BY EXISTENCE 2
   TO LET HIM HAVE THEM. NEVER SHOW SURPRISE! . . . . . 107 CHRISTMAS TREES . . . 46
   SOME GUTTURAL EXCLAMATION OF SURPRISE . . . . . . 142 THE VANISHING RED . . 14
   AFTER SUCH LOOSE TALK IT WAS NO SURPRISE . . . . . 177 THE STAR-SPLITTER . . 38
   A LIKENESS TO SURPRISE THE THRILLY TOURIST. . . . . 214 A FOUNTAIN, A BOTTLE . 40
   HE SHOWED NOT THE LEAST SURPRISE. . . . . 288 DEPARTMENTAL . . . 4
   TO THEIR SURPRISE RANG ONCE ON STONE ALL DAY . . . 407 FROM PLANE TO PLANE . 116
SURPRISED
   YOU'LL BE SURPRISED AT HIM--HOW MUCH HE'S BROKEN. . . . 39 DEATH OF THE HIRED MAN 152
   I SHOULDN'T BE SURPRISED IF IN THIS WORLD . . . . . 57 THE BLACK COTTAGE . . 82
   SON LOOKS SURPRISED TO SEE ME END A LIE . . . . . 207 THE WITCH OF COOS . . 145
   I SHOULDN'T BE SURPRISED. / THE STRANGEST LIGHT! . . . 473 A MASQUE OF REASON . . 7
SURRENDER
   AND FORTHWITH FOUND SALVATION IN SURRENDER. . . . . . 348 THE GIFT OUTRIGHT . . 11
   WITH GRACE AND NOT TOO FORMAL A SURRENDER . . . . . 408 FROM PLANE TO PLANE . 121
   AND FORTHWITH FOUND SALVATION IN SURRENDER. . . . . 424 THE GIFT OUTRIGHT . . 11
SURROUNDED
   THOUGH BY A WORLD OF DOUBT SURROUNDED. . . . . . 331 BEECH 12
SURROUNDING
   FROM THE SURROUNDING DESERT; JUST TODAY . . . . . 489 A MASQUE OF REASON . . 445
SURVIVE
   ONE DAY TOO SWEET FOR BEINGS TO SURVIVE. . . . . . 412 POD OF THE MILKWEED . 33
SURVIVING
   IN THE SURVIVING BOOK WE FIND . . . . 450 OUR DOOM TO BLOOM . . 10
SUSPECT
   'I HAVE LEFT THOSE THERE BERRIES, I SHREWDLY SUSPECT, . . 60 BLUEBERRIES 45
   "I SHALL SUSPECT----" / "BE GOOD. THE VOICES SAY: . . 79 THE GENERATIONS OF MEN 159
   "I HALF SUSPECT YOU KNEW, AND CAME ON PURPOSE . . . . 93 THE SELF-SEEKER . . 8
   AS I SUSPECT YOU HAVE. A TOWN DEBARS . . . . . . 370 THE LITERATE FARMER AND 69
   TO SUSPECT THE HUMAN TRAIT . . . . 387 THE COURAGE TO BE NEW . 10
   I RATHER SUSPECT . . . . 392 A WISH TO COMPLY . . 9
   AND I SUSPECT IT MAY BE MORE AND MORE SO . . . . . 406 FROM PLANE TO PLANE . 82
SUSPECTED
   "HADN'T YOU LONG SUSPECTED WHERE YOU WERE?" . . . . 214 A FOUNTAIN, A BOTTLE . 47
SUSPECTING
   IN TIME TO KEEP ME FROM SUSPECTING HIM . . . . . 187 THE AX-HELVE 61
SUSPENDED
   THE DAY I SWUNG SUSPENDED WITH THE GRAPES, ... 196 WILD GRAPES 11
SUSPENSE
   THERE WAS A MOMENT OF SUSPENSE IN BIRTH . . . . . 194 PAUL'S WIFE 116
SUSPICION
   WITH NO SUSPICION IN STEM END OR BLOSSOM END . . . 164 NEW HAMPSHIRE . . . 160
   MADE PUBLICLY IN SCHOOL, ABOVE SUSPICION . . . . . 324 BUILD SOIL 274
   IT PAUSED AS WITH SUSPICION OF MY PEN, ... 357 A CONSIDERABLE SPECK . 10
   IN HER SUSPICION YOU'RE NO FEMINIST. . . . . . 479 A MASQUE OF REASON . 177
   WITH THE SUSPICION AT THIS HOUR OF NIGHT . . . . . 495 A MASQUE OF MERCY . . 53
   SUSPICION OF THE INCOME-TAX RETURNS, ... 503 A MASQUE OF MERCY . 247
SUSPICIOUS
   HE BROKE MY TRANCE. DON'T THAT MAKE YOU SUSPICIOUS . . 202 THE WITCH OF COOS . . 16
   HE FOUND SUSPICIOUS SAND, AND SURE ENOUGH, ... 270 THE EGG AND THE MACHINE 22
SUSPIRE
   ALL CREATURES STILL WARMLY SUSPIRE. . . . . . . 266 SITTING BY A BUSH . . 8
SUSSEX
   SUSSEX BECAUSE THEY'RE SPOKEN OF BY HERRICK. . . . 162 NEW HAMPSHIRE . . . 107
SUSTAIN
   ONLY, OF COURSE, THEY CAN'T SUSTAIN THE PART. . . . 246 FIREFLIES IN THE GARDEN 6
SUTURE
   I STRAIN AT LESSONS FIT TO START A SUTURE. . . . . 267 WHAT FIFTY SAID . . . 7
SWABBED
   THEY REALIZED FROM THE WAY I SWABBED MY NECK . . . 72 THE CODE 86
SWALE
   TO THE EARNEST LOVE THAT LAID THE SWALE IN ROWS, . . . 17 MOWING 10
SWALLOWABLE
   YOU POOR, POOR SWALLOWABLE LITTLE MAN. . . . . . 500 A MASQUE OF MERCY . 190
SWALLOWED
   WAS SWALLOWED UP IN LEAVES THAT BLEW ALWAY; . . . . 16 A DREAM PANG 2
SWALLOW'S
   ON THE LAST SWALLOW'S SWEEP; AND ON THE RASP . . . 14 WAITING 18
SWALLOW-TAIL
   STREAMED OUT LIKE PENNANTS SWALLOW-TAIL. . . . . 452 A-WISHING WELL . . . 53
SWAMP
   OUT WALKING IN THE FROZEN SWAMP ONE GRAY DAY, . . . 101 THE WOOD-PILE . . . 1
   TO WARM THE FROZEN SWAMP AS BEST IT COULD . . . . 102 THE WOOD-PILE . . . 39
   A SWAMP OF CEDAR. CHOKED WITH OIL OF CEDAR . . . . 125 AN ENCOUNTER 5
   A WINTER GARDEN IN AN ALDER SWAMP, ... 254 A WINTER EDEN . . . 1
SWAMPS
   THE ALDER SWAMPS . . . . 360 THE RABBIT-HUNTER . . 5
SWAN
   OR PERHAPS A SWAN . . . . 431 KITTY HAWK 109
SWAP
   "DICK WISHES HE COULD SWAP JOBS WITH THE DOCTOR. . . . 404 FROM PLANE TO PLANE . 28
SWAPPING
   THE FISHERMAN'S SWAPPING A YARN FOR A YARN . . . . 262 THE FLOWER BOAT . . . 1
SWARM
   THE SWARM DILATING ROUND THE PERFECT TREES. . . . . 12 A PRAYER IN SPRING . . 8
   THE SWARM STILL RAN AND SCUTTLED JUST AS FAST. . . . 237 A HILLSIDE THAW . . . 24

SWARM (CONTINUED)
    I LOOKED AT NINE: THE SWARM WAS TURNED TO ROCK . . . . . 237 A HILLSIDE THAW . . . 26
    IN EVERY LIFELIKE POSTURE OF THE SWARM, ... 237 A HILLSIDE THAW . . . 27
    SWARM OVER THEIR LIVES ENFORCING BENEFITS . . . . 287 A ROADSIDE STAND . . . 28
    LET CLOUD SHAPES SWARM! . . . . 308 PERTINAX 2
    WE SEE HOW SERIOUSLY THE RACES SWARM . . . . 423 FOR JOHN F. KENNEDY . 34
SWARMING
    THEY'RE GOING. WATCH THIS HUSKY SWARMING UP . . . . . 112 IN THE HOME STRETCH . 62
SWARTHY
    HOW SWARTHY I MUST BE. . . . . 303 AFTERFLAKES 10
SWAY
    I FEEL THE LADDER SWAY AS THE BOUGHS BEND. . . . . . . 68 AFTER APPLE-PICKING . 23
    SOMETIMES WHEN I WATCH TREES SWAY, ... 156 THE SOUND OF TREES . 17
    'TIS ONLY TO SIT BACK AND SWAY HIS HEAD . . . . 269 THE BEAR 23
    AND SWAY WITH REASON MORE OR LESS. . . . . 326 TO A THINKER 28
    AND WITH LONG-SLEEVED BRANCHES HOLD THEIR SWAY. . . . 376 SOMETHING FOR HOPE . 12
SWAYED
    SO WHEN AT TIMES THE MOB IS SWAYED . . . . 403 SOMETHING LIKE A STAR . 22
SWAYS
    AND MY HEAD SWAYS TO MY SHOULDER . . . . 156 THE SOUND OF TREES . 16
    AND BACK AND FORTH HE SWAYS FROM CHEEK TO CHEEK, . . . 269 THE BEAR 29
    SO THAT IN GUYS IT GENTLY SWAYS AT EASE, ... 331 THE SILKEN TENT . . . 4
SWEAR
    HE'LL SORT OF SWEAR THE TIME AWAY. HE'S AWFUL! . . . . 83 THE HOUSEKEEPER . . . 52
    WILL ANYBODY SWEAR THAT ISN'T IT? . . . . 368 THE LITERATE FARMER AND 20
SWEARING
    LIKE SWEARING OFF ON THE TRAFFIC WORLD. . . . . . . 419 ONE MORE BREVITY . . 18
SWEATING-FULL
    BUT SWEATING-FULL, DRIPS WINE AND OIL A LITTLE. . . . 323 BUILD SOIL 236
SWEEP
    ON THE LAST SWALLOW'S SWEEP; AND ON THE RASP . . . . 14 WAITING 18
    SUCH HEAPS OF BROKEN GLASS TO SWEEP AWAY . . . . . 121 BIRCHES 12
    THE ONLY OTHER SOUND'S THE SWEEP . . . . 224 STOPPING BY WOODS . 11
    TO BLOT OUT AND DRINK UP AND SWEEP AWAY . . . . . 245 SPRING POOLS . . . 10
    AND STILL THE WOODS SWEEP LEAFILY ON, ... 247 ON GOING UNNOTICED . 14
SWEEPING
    AND SWEEPING ROUND IT WITH A FLAMING SWORD, ... 130 THE BONFIRE . . . 28
    FOR SWEEPING ME AWAY. LET'S SEE, WHERE WAS I? . . . 319 BUILD SOIL 91
    IN A SWEEPING LINE. . . . . 342 QUEST OF PURPLE-FRINGED 6
SWEEPS
    WHEN A GREAT TIDE OF ARGUMENT SWEEPS IN . . . . . 513 A MASQUE OF MERCY . 538
SWEET
    AS SWEET COMPANIONS AS MIGHT BE HAD. . . . . . . 6 GHOST HOUSE . . . 30
    AND THE AIR WAS STIFLING SWEET. . . . . 13 ROSE POGONIAS . . . 6
    AND THE SWEET PANG IT COST ME NOT TO CALL . . . . 16 A DREAM PANG . . . 11
    CAN BUT GIVE EAR TO THAT SWEET CRY . . . . . . 20 THE TRIAL BY EXISTENCE 23
    AND HAVE TO HUNT FOR IN SWEET FERN AND HARDHACK; . . 197 WILD GRAPES . . . 33
    AS SWEET AS I COULD BEAR; . . . . 226 TO EARTHWARD . . . 2
    THAT CROSSED ME FROM SWEET THINGS, ... 227 TO EARTHWARD . . . 5
    THE SWEFT OF BITTER BARK . . . . 227 TO EARTHWARD . . . 23
    WAS SINGING IN IT SWEET AND SWIFT. . . . . . . 233 LOOKING FOR SUNSET BIRD 8
    "--TAKING HIS OWN SWEET TIME AS IF TO SHOW . . . 404 FROM PLANE TO PLANE . 24
    ITS FLOWERS' DISTILLED HONEY IS SO SWEET . . . . 411 POD OF THE MILKWEED . 21
    IN BEING SWEET TO THESE EPHEMERALS . . . . . . 412 POD OF THE MILKWEED . 30
    ONE DAY TOO SWEET FOR BEINGS TO SURVIVE. . . . . 412 POD OF THE MILKWEED . 33
SWEETBREADS
    "UNLESS IT'S SWEETBREADS," YOU SUGGEST . . . . . 467 QUANDARY 17
    THAT BRAINS AND SWEETBREADS WERE THE SAME, . . . 467 QUANDARY 21
    BUT 'TWAS BY MAKING SWEETBREADS DO . . . . . . 467 QUANDARY 25
SWEET-CYNICAL
    YOUR OLD SWEET-CYNICAL STRAIN . . . . 302 VOICE WAYS 6
SWEETEN
    SHE RUNS FROM TREE TO TREE WHERE LIE AND SWEETEN . . . 125 THE COW IN APPLE TIME . 7
SWEETEST
    THE FACT IS THE SWEETEST DREAM THAT LABOR KNOWS. . . . 17 MOWING 13
SWEETNESS
    AND FRESHEN IN THIS AIR OF WITHERING SWEETNESS; . . . 15 WAITING 25
    SO SMELLING THEIR SWEETNESS WOULD BE NO THEFT. . . . 305 UNHARVESTED 14
SWEETS
    I CRAVED STRONG SWEETS, BUT THOSE . . . . 227 TO EARTHWARD . . . 13
SWEET-SCENTED
    SWEET-SCENTED STUFF WHEN THE BREEZE DREW ACROSS IT. . . 136 "OUT,OUT--" 3
SWELL (SEE FROZEN-GROUND-SWELL)
SWELLS
    OH, NEVER THIS WHELMING EAST WIND SWELLS . . . . . 27 A LINE-STORM SONG . . 25
    SPRING WATER IN OUR MOUNTAIN BOSOM SWELLS . . . . 446 DOES NO ONE AT ALL EVER 22
SWEPT
    SHE SWEPT THE HEAVENS, TURNING ON HER HEEL, . . . 74 THE GENERATIONS OF MEN 36
    AND SWEPT OF LEATHERN LEAVES, BUT LEFT THE BARK . . 184 MAPLE 141
    YOU HAVE SEEN ME WHEN I WAS TAKEN AND SWEPT . . . 252 TREE AT MY WINDOW . 11
    THAT WHEN IT HAS SWEPT BY, LEAVES SUMMITS STAINED. . . 255 THE FLOOD 13
    CANNOT BE PARTED NOR BE SWEPT AWAY . . . . . . 300 THE MASTER SPEED . 11
    THE DAY SWEPT CLEARLY ON . . . . 333 HAPPINESS MAKES UP . 16
    WITH WHICH THE MODERN WORLD IS BEING SWEPT. . . . 357 A CONSIDERABLE SPECK . 26
SWERVING
    NOT JUST A SWERVING, BUT A THROWING BACK, ... 259 WEST-RUNNING BROOK . 59
SWIFT
    BUT AS I SAID IT, SWIFT THERE PASSED ME BY . . . . 22 THE TUFT OF FLOWERS . 11
    THE LINE-STORM CLOUDS FLY TATTERED AND SWIFT. . . . 26 A LINE-STORM SONG . 1
    SUDDEN AND SWIFT AND LIGHT AS THAT . . . . . . 129 THE IMPULSE . . . 25
    WAS SINGING IN IT SWEET AND SWIFT. . . . . . . 233 LOOKING FOR SUNSET BIRD 8
    HE PEERS OUT SHREWDLY INTO THE THICK AND SWIFT. . . 341 WILLFUL HOMING . . 8
    HER LOVER TO MAKE THE ORDEAL SWIFT . . . . . . 343 DISCOVERY OF MADEIRAS . 9
    I NEVER SAW SO MUCH SWIFT WATER RUN CLOUDLESS. . . 379 TOO ANXIOUS FOR RIVERS 5
    AND WITH THE SWIFT RUSH OF ITS SANDY DREGS . . . 391 ON BEING IDOLIZED . . 3
SWIFTNESS
    AND YOU WERE GIVEN THIS SWIFTNESS, NOT FOR HASTE . . . 300 THE MASTER SPEED . . 5

		PAGE	TITLE	LINE

SWIM
BUT AFTER A TIME ALLOWED FOR IT TO SWIM, ... 338 THE MOST OF IT . . . 13
SWIMMING (SEE MOTE-SWIMMING)
YOU WON'T SEE ANY MORMON SWIMMING IN IT. . . . . 213 A FOUNTAIN, A BOTTLE . 27
SWING
SWING THE PICTURE ON THE WALL; . . . . 11 TO THE THAWING WIND . 12
IN SUNLIGHT NEAR US IN MOMENTOUS SWING . . . . . . 361 A LOOSE MOUNTAIN . . 15
SWINGER
SO WAS I ONCE MYSELF A SWINGER OF BIRCHES. . . . . . 122 BIRCHES 41
ONE COULD DO WORSE THAN BE A SWINGER OF BIRCHES. . . . 122 BIRCHES 59
SWINGING
THE SWINGING LANTERN LENGTHENED TO THE GROUND, ... 92 THE FEAR 92
I LIKE TO THINK SOME BOY'S BEEN SWINGING THEM. . . . . 121 BIRCHES 3
BUT SWINGING DOESN'T BEND THEM DOWN TO STAY. . . . . 121 BIRCHES 4
A MAN WITH A SWINGING BAG FOR LOAD . . . . 140 THE GUM-GATHERER . . 5
THE SWINGING MILL BELL CHANGED ITS RATE . . . . . . 273 A LONE STRIKER . . . 1
A DEPTH PAST MANY SWINGING DOORS . . . . 280 BLUE RIBBON AT AMESBURY 23
SWINGS
THE CELLAR DOOR SWINGS WIDE AND SLAMS AGAIN.) . . . . 520 A MASQUE OF MERCY . 696
SWIRL
I HAD THE SWIRL AND ACHE . . . . 227 TO EARTHWARD 9
SWIRL OF NEON-LIT . . . . 439 KITTY HAWK . . 367
SWIRLED
THE DAYS YOU WERE NOT SWIRLED . . . . 333 HAPPINESS MAKES UP . . 2
SWIRLS
IT SWIRLS OCCLUDED IN US UNDER TIGHT . . . . 386 INNATE HELIUM . . . 2
SWISH
WITH A SWISH IN THE GRASS. "WHAT IF THE OTHERS . . . . 74 THE GENERATIONS OF MEN 23
THEN HE FLUNG OUTWARD, FEET FIRST, WITH A SWISH, . . . 122 BIRCHES 39
BUT ONE DAY WHEN THE FOLIAGE ALL WENT SWISH . . . . 284 THE GOLD HESPERIDEE . 32
SWISHING
IT GIVES UP STANDING STRAIGHT AND GOES DOWN SWISHING. . . 349 TO A YOUNG WRETCH . . 4
SWISS
THAT NATIONS LIKE THE CUBAN AND THE SWISS . . . . . 398 NO HOLY WARS FOR THEM . 11
SWITCH
AND BENT SOME RAIL WIDE OPEN LIKE A SWITCH, ... 270 THE EGG AND THE MACHINE 7
SWOLLEN
AND SWOLLEN TIGHT AND BURIED UNDER SNOW. . . . . . . 204 THE WITCH OF COOS . . 56
AND SWOLLEN TIGHT AND BURIED UNDER SNOW. . . . . . . 204 THE WITCH OF COOS . . 58
WHERE DRIVEN RAIN HAD WET AND SWOLLEN THEM. . . . . . 216 A FOUNTAIN, A BOTTLE . 97
SWOOP
AND YOUR RISE AND SWOOP, ... 441 KITTY HAWK 404
SWOOPED
I WATCHED HIM WHERE HE SWOOPED, HE POUNCED, HE STRUCK; . . 278 THE WHITE-TAILED HORNET 33
I WAS SWOOPED DOWN UPON WHEN I WAS SMALL, ... 443 AUSPEX 2
SWOOPS
SWOOPS JUST IN TIME TO HIS REMEMBERED TREE. . . . . . 249 ACCEPTANCE . . . 10
SWORD
AND WHERE THEY SOUGHT WITHOUT THE SWORD . . . . . . 19 THE TRIAL BY EXISTENCE 5
AND SWEEPING ROUND IT WITH A FLAMING SWORD, ... 130 THE BONFIRE 28
OF BENDING LIKE A SWORD ACROSS THE KNEE. . . . . . 187 THE AX-HELVE . . . 71
AS WELL HAVE BEEN THE SWORD. . . . . 252 THE PEACEFUL SHEPHERD . 12
HE HAD TO BE STOPPED BY THE SWORD OF BRUTUS. . . . . 454 HOW HARD TO KEEP FROM . 24
SWORE
THEY SWORE ALL THE GOLD SHOULD GO BACK . . . . . . 311 THE VINDICTIVES . . . 29
SWUNG
I CROSSED THE RIVER AND SWUNG ROUND THE MOUNTAIN. . . . 41 THE MOUNTAIN 15
AS HE SWUNG TOWARD THEM HOLDING UP THE HAND, ... 136 "OUT,OUT--" . . . 20
OF YEAR OR DAY THE WAY IT SWUNG A DOOR . . . . . . 175 THE CENSUS-TAKER . . 27
THE DAY I SWUNG SUSPENDED WITH THE GRAPES, ... 196 WILD GRAPES . . . 11
EACH SWUNG IN DANGER ON ITS SLENDER TWIG, ... 283 THE GOLD HESPERIDEE . 23
LONG SINCE THEY SWUNG AS THREE INSTEAD OF TWO-- . . . 283 THE GOLD HESPERIDEE . 25
SYCAMORE
SYCAMORE . . . . 331 SYCAMORE . . . . T
SYLVAN
FOR A SYLVAN SIGN THAT THE BLUE JAY'S SCREECH . . . . 24 PAN WITH US . . . 18
SYMBOL
FIGURATIVE ENOUGH TO SEE THE SYMBOL, ... 184 MAPLE 154
THE METAPHOR, THE SYMBOL LIES! . . . . 327 A MISSIVE MISSILE . . 35
THE SYMBOL STAR IT LIFTS AGAINST YOUR CEILING . . . . 350 TO A YOUNG WRETCH . . 23
A SYMBOL WAS ALL HE COULD HOPE TO CONVEY, ... 421 ONE MORE BREVITY . . 66
AND HOLDING IT FAR FORWARD FOR A SYMBOL . . . . . . 446 DOES NO ONE AT ALL EVER 27
WHICH IS THE SYMBOL OF ETERNITY . . . . 485 A MASQUE OF REASON . 341
SYMPATHIZE
I SYMPATHIZE. I KNOW JUST HOW IT FEELS . . . . . . 37 DEATH OF THE HIRED MAN 76
SYMPATHY
SOME SYMPATHY WAS WASTED ON THE HOUSE, ... 178 THE STAR-SPLITTER . . 59
WHAT CRIES MORE TO OUR KIND FOR SYMPATHY? . . . . . 323 BUILD SOIL 219
ON OUR SYMPATHY WITH THE UNDER DOG . . . . 362 SYMPATHY WITH UNDER DOG T
OF ASKING ANY SYMPATHY OF HIM? . . . . 405 FROM PLANE TO PLANE . 32
YES, WE DO TOO, WITH SYMPATHY, MY FRIEND. . . . . . 497 A MASQUE OF MERCY . 102
SYRUP
A CIDER SYRUP. HAVING TASTED FRUIT, ... 124 THE COW IN APPLE TIME . 5
SYSTEMATIC
AT LEAST I WILL NOT HAVE IT SYSTEMATIC. . . . . . . 362 BOEOTIAN 4

T

TABLE
MARY SAT MUSING ON THE LAMP-FLAME AT THE TABLE, ... 34 DEATH OF THE HIRED MAN 1
WELL, YOU CAN SET THE TABLE WITH THE LOAF. . . . . . 115 IN THE HOME STRETCH . 154
WHEN SUPPER'S ON THE TABLE, AND WE'LL SEE . . . . . 123 PUTTING IN THE SEED . 2
THE THREE STOOD IN THE LAMPLIGHT ROUND THE TABLE . . . 144 SNOW 31
OR SOMETHING NOT FAR FROM IT ON THE TABLE. . . . . . 147 SNOW 112
THERE ON THE TABLE, EVER SINCE I CAME, ... 147 SNOW 118
BESIDE THE TABLE, NEAR THE OPEN BOOK, ... 151 SNOW 246

TABLE (CONTINUED)
  NO LAMP WAS LIT. NOTHING WAS ON THE TABLE. . . . . . . 175 THE CENSUS-TAKER . . 35
  THEY WERE NOT ON THE TABLE WITH THEIR ELBOWS. . . . . 175 THE CENSUS-TAKER . . 40
  MOTHER CAN MAKE A COMMON TABLE REAR . . . . 202 THE WITCH OF COOS . . 9
  RATHER THAN TIP A TABLE FOR YOU, LET ME . . . . . 202 THE WITCH OF COOS . . 12
  THE TIMES TABLE . . . . 263 THE TIMES TABLE . . . T
  IS THE MULTIPLICATION TABLE OF LIFE." . . . . . 263 THE TIMES TABLE . . . 12
  WENT LONG SINCE TO THE DOGS UNDER THE TABLE. . . . . 279 THE WHITE-TAILED HORNET 57
TABLECLOTH
  AN ANT ON THE TABLECLOTH . . . . 287 DEPARTMENTAL 1
TABLES
  HE THINKS THAT CHAIRS AND TABLES WILL ENDURE, ... 372 THE LITERATE FARMER AND 128
TACITURN
  BUT TO BE WHOLLY TACITURN . . . . 403 SOMETHING LIKE A STAR . 7
TACKLE
  THEN WITH TACKLE UNKNOWN . . . . 448 THE BAD ISLAND--EASTER 17
TAFT
  IF I'M EXPECTED TO ELECT BILL TAFT. . . . . . . 48 A HUNDRED COLLARS . . 117
TAG
  WHEN IT OUTGROWS THE WIRE BAND OF ITS NAME TAG. . . . 46 A HUNDRED COLLARS . . 57
  THEY YELLING MIX TAG, HIDE-AND-SEEK, HOPSCOTCH, . . . 318 BUILD SOIL 63
TAGS
  AND TAGS AND NUMBERS IT FOR FUTURE REFERENCE, . . . 37 DEATH OF THE HIRED MAN 90
TAIL (SEE SWALLOW-TAIL)
  HE'S ON HIS ROUNDS NOW WITH HIS TAIL IN HIS MOUTH, . . 94 THE SELF-SEEKER . . . 38
  THE WHITE ONE IN HIS TAIL; LIKE ONE WHO TAKES . . . 101 THE WOOD-PILE . . . 15
  HIS TAIL FEATHERS OFF. . . . . 135 LAST WORD OF A BLUEBIRD 13
  AND A LONG BIRD OF PARADISE'S TAIL . . . . . 172 A STAR IN A STONEBOAT . 16
  AS OFTEN AS HE HAD IN THE TAIL OF THE NIGHT, . . . 210 PAUPER WITCH OF GRAFTON 87
  AND ALL HIS TAIL THAT ISN'T HAIR UP STRAIGHT. . . . 223 THE RUNAWAY 17
  THAT FLASHES TAIL THROUGH LAST YEAR'S WITHERED BRAKE . 226 THE ONSET 20
  AND CAUGHT ONE SILVER LIZARD BY THE TAIL, ... 237 A HILLSIDE THAW . . . 10
  BETWEEN THE DOTTED FEET A STREAK OF TAIL, ... 270 THE EGG AND THE MACHINE 18
  AND HEAD TO TAIL THEN FIRMLY CURLED . . . . . 419 ONE MORE BREVITY . . 17
  HIS HARD TAIL LOUDLY SMACKED THE FLOOR . . . . 420 ONE MORE BREVITY . . 23
  IN SPITE OF THE WAY HIS TAIL HAD SMACKED . . . . 421 ONE MORE BREVITY . . 54
  AND HAD CAUGHT MY COW BY THE TAIL, ... 463 LINES IN DEJECTION . . 10
  THE SERPENT'S TAIL STUCK DOWN THE SERPENT'S THROAT, . 485 A MASQUE OF REASON . . 340
TAILED (SEE WHITE-TAILED)
TAILS
  SALMON AND STURGEON, LASHING WITH THEIR TAILS. . . . . 142 THE VANISHING RED . . 23
TAKE
  THAT COULD TAKE ME FROM BESIDE YOU . . . . . . 13 FLOWER-GATHERING . . 11
  THEY HAVE TO TAKE YOU IN." / "I SHOULD HAVE CALLED IT . 38 DEATH OF THE HIRED MAN 119
  TO TAKE HIM IN, AND MIGHT BE WILLING TO-- . . . . 39 DEATH OF THE HIRED MAN 133
  I'D TAKE YOU, BUT I'M BOUND THE OTHER WAY." . . . . 42 THE MOUNTAIN . . . 43
  I'M NOT SO DRUNK I CAN'T TAKE CARE OF MYSELF." . . . 45 A HUNDRED COLLARS . . 38
  AND I LIE BACK AND RIDE. I TAKE THE REINS . . . . 49 A HUNDRED COLLARS . . 138
  TO TAKE YOUR MOTHER-LOSS OF A FIRST CHILD . . . . 53 HOME BURIAL 64
  YOU TAKE THE LAKE. I LOOK AND LOOK AT IT. . . . . 63 A SERVANT TO SERVANTS . 16
  TO STEP OUTDOORS AND TAKE THE WATER DAZZLE . . . . 63 A SERVANT TO SERVANTS . 27
  A SUNNY MORNING, OR TAKE THE RISING WIND . . . . 63 A SERVANT TO SERVANTS . 28
  THEY TAKE ADVANTAGE OF HIM SHAMEFULLY, ... 65 A SERVANT TO SERVANTS . 74
  A BRIDE, TO HELP TAKE CARE OF SUCH A CREATURE, . . . 66 A SERVANT TO SERVANTS . 127
  WHAT FORM MY DREAMING WAS ABOUT TO TAKE. . . . . 68 AFTER APPLE-PICKING . 17
  JAMES WOULD TAKE TIME, OF COURSE, TO CHEW IT OVER . . 70 THE CODE 18
  YOU TAKE MY CARD--YOU SEEM SO GOOD AT SUCH THINGS-- . 75 THE GENERATIONS OF MEN 61
  WHY NOT TAKE SEATS HERE ON THE CELLAR WALL . . . . 75 THE GENERATIONS OF MEN 63
  BUT WHY TAKE TIME FOR WHAT I'M LIKE TO HEAR? . . . 78 THE GENERATIONS OF MEN 143
  CALL HER NAUSICAA, AND TAKE A TIMBER . . . . . 79 THE GENERATIONS OF MEN 160
  MEBBE I'M WRONG TO TAKE IT AS I DO. . . . . . 80 THE GENERATIONS OF MEN 185
  SON, YOU DO AS YOU'RE TOLD! YOU TAKE THE TIMBER-- . . 80 THE GENERATIONS OF MEN 192
  SO'S TO TAKE ANY COMFORT. I CAN SEW: . . . . 81 THE HOUSEKEEPER . . . 7
  HE CAN'T FIND ANYONE TO TAKE HER PLACE." . . . . 82 THE HOUSEKEEPER . . . 29
  ESTELLE'S TO TAKE ME WHEN SHE'S SETTLED DOWN. . . . 82 THE HOUSEKEEPER . . . 35
  I TAKE IT. WHAT WAS HIS WAS ALWAYS HERS. . . . . 84 THE HOUSEKEEPER . . . 93
  TAKE IT YEAR IN, YEAR OUT, HE DOESN'T MAKE MUCH. . . 85 THE HOUSEKEEPER . . . 103
  WE'RE NOT ALLOWED TO TAKE THEM UPSIDE DOWN, . . . 85 THE HOUSEKEEPER . . . 127
  BUT YOU SEE, DON'T YOU, WE TAKE CARE OF HIM." . . . 86 THE HOUSEKEEPER . . . 154
  DON'T YOU BE HARD ON ME. I HAVE TO TAKE . . . . 95 THE SELF-SEEKER . . . 62
  ER, LET ME SEE. I THINK I'LL TAKE THE RIGHT. . . . 96 THE SELF-SEEKER . . . 110
  ANNE HAS A WAY WITH FLOWERS TO TAKE THE PLACE . . . 98 THE SELF-SEEKER . . . 159
  AND IT MAY TAKE HIM I DON'T KNOW HOW LONG. . . . 98 THE SELF-SEEKER . . . 171
  WHO WILL TAKE CARE OF MY NECESSITIES . . . . . 99 THE SELF-SEEKER . . . 179
  AND TAKE A LIVELIER VIEW OF THINGS FROM HERE. . . . 112 IN THE HOME STRETCH . 61
  IT WOULD TAKE MORE THAN THEM TO SICKEN YOU-- . . . 114 IN THE HOME STRETCH . 123
  SEEMS HAUNTED OR EXPOSED. I ALWAYS TAKE . . . . 115 IN THE HOME STRETCH . 133
  THE MEALS WE'VE HAD NO ONE CAN TAKE FROM US. . . . 115 IN THE HOME STRETCH . 139
  TO HELP US, BUT HE'LL TAKE IT OUT IN PLANNING. . . . 115 IN THE HOME STRETCH . 153
  "IT WOULD TAKE ME FOREVER TO RECITE . . . . . 117 IN THE HOME STRETCH . 181
  SHOULD TAKE THE POLISH OFF THE CRUST. . . . . 139 BROWN'S DESCENT . . . 59
  TO LOOSE THE RESIN AND TAKE IT DOWN . . . . . 141 THE GUM-GATHERER . . 38
  "WHOSE BUSINESS--IF I TAKE IT ON MYSELF, ... 142 THE VANISHING RED . . 6
  IT WANTS TO SEE HOW YOU WILL TAKE; IF BACKWARD, . . 147 SNOW 123
  "BROTHER MESERVE, TAKE CARE, YOU'LL SCARE YOURSELF . 149 SNOW 167
  PAID HEED TO WOMEN, YOU'D TAKE MY ADVICE . . . . 150 SNOW 216
  YOU COULD DO--NOW. YOU KNOW THE RISK YOU TAKE . . . 150 SNOW 220
  AND THEN TAKE OUR ADVICE NO MORE THAN NOTHING, . . . 155 SNOW 347
  AND TAKE THEIR NAME. THEY'VE SINCE TOLD ME THEIR NAME-- 161 NEW HAMPSHIRE . . . 85
  I HAD TO TAKE BY FORCE RATHER THAN BUY. . . . . 163 NEW HAMPSHIRE . . . 151
  TO TAKE THEM AS AGAINST A SPECIAL STATE . . . . 166 NEW HAMPSHIRE . . . 230
  FOR THE LEAST SIN, IT WOULDN'T TAKE US LONG . . . 177 THE STAR-SPLITTER . . 45
  HE HAD TO TAKE THE BEST WAY HE KNEW HOW . . . . 178 THE STAR-SPLITTER . . 56
  MADE MAPLE FIRST TAKE NOTICE OF HER NAME. . . . 179 MAPLE 2
  THEN TOOK IT FROM ME--AND I LET HIM TAKE IT. . . . 185 THE AX-HELVE . . . 13
  TAKE IT TO HELL FOR ME," THE SAWYER SAID. . . . 193 PAUL'S WIFE 77
  (THEY TREATED IT AS HIS.) "YOU TAKE A JACKKNIFE, . . 193 PAUL'S WIFE 80
  HE THOUGH HE'D BETTER TAKE HIS JACKKNIFE TO. . . . 193 PAUL'S WIFE 87

TAKE (CONTINUED)

	PAGE TITLE	LINE
"HERE, TAKE A TREETOP, I'LL GET DOWN ANOTHER.	197 WILD GRAPES	39
AND SIT UP BY ME AND TAKE HOLD OF ME.	205 THE WITCH OF COOS	103
TO SEE IF THE TOWN WANTED TO TAKE OVER	208 PAUPER WITCH OF GRAFTON	24
HE'D LIKE TO TAKE ME THERE AND SHOW IT TO ME.	213 A FOUNTAIN, A BOTTLE	6
WELL, TAKE ME THERE." / "SOME DAY I WILL." / "TODAY."	213 A FOUNTAIN, A BOTTLE	14
"TAKE ONE," OLD DAVIS BADE ME GRACIOUSLY.	217 A FOUNTAIN, A BOTTLE	123
"WHY NOT TAKE TWO OR THREE?" / "TAKE ALL YOU WANT.	217 A FOUNTAIN, A BOTTLE	124
OUGHT TO BE TOLD TO COME AND TAKE HIM IN."	223 THE RUNAWAY	21
I TAKE AWAY MY HAND	227 TO EARTHWARD	26
SPADES TAKE UP LEAVES	234 GATHERING LEAVES	1
SO MUCH AS TO TAKE CARE OF EVENING CHORES.	248 THE COCOON	10
WHAT WOULD IT TAKE MY STANDING THERE FOR,	251 BEREFT	3
"TAKE TWENTY YEARS.	256 THE LOVELY BE CHOOSERS	5
TAKE UP THE TASK BEYOND HER CHOOSING."	256 THE LOVELY BE CHOOSERS	11
"OH, IF YOU TAKE IT OFF TO LADY-LAND,	258 WEST-RUNNING BROOK	32
HE WANTED TO TAKE MY JOB FOR PAY.	275 TWO TRAMPS IN MUD TIME	8
SHE TAKES HER TIME TO TAKE HER FILL.	281 BLUE RIBBON AT AMESBURY	39
WE TAKE OCCASION TO THINK.	282 A DRUMLIN WOODCHUCK	20
ONE MORE, HE THOUGHT, TO TAKE HIM SAFELY THROUGH.	283 THE GOLD HESPERIDEE	26
I HOPE THEY WON'T TAKE IT FOR CENSURE.	294 A RECORD STRIDE	20
SO LOVE WILL TAKE BETWEEN THE HANDS A FACE....	301 MOON COMPASSES	8
THEN TAKE SOME LEFTOVER WINTER	304 CLEAR AND COLDER	10
OH, I DON'T BLAME YOU. I SAY TAKE LIFE EASY.	316 BUILD SOIL	19
TO TAKE A WRITING HAND IN POLITICS.	316 BUILD SOIL	27
WHAT SHOULD YOU DO? / I'D LET THINGS TAKE THEIR COURSE	320 BUILD SOIL	128
LISTEN AND I WILL TAKE MY DEAREST RISK.	320 BUILD SOIL	136
TO CATCH THEM AND TAKE TOLL OF THEM IN TRANSIT.	321 BUILD SOIL	167
AND DO WHAT I COMMAND YOU. I TAKE CARE	323 BUILD SOIL	231
TO TAKE TO MARKET--I WILL TURN IT UNDER.	323 BUILD SOIL	240
AND WHAT TAKE HENCE OR LEAVE BEHIND,	332 ALL REVELATION	7
TAKE NATURE ALTOGETHER SINCE TIME BEGAN,	349 OUR HOLD ON THE PLANET	13
AS GAY FOR YOU TO TAKE YOUR FATHER'S AX	349 TO A YOUNG WRETCH	1
AS TAKE HIS GUN--ROD--TO GO HUNTING--FISHING.	349 TO A YOUNG WRETCH	2
WITH POETS WHO COULD CALMLY TAKE THE FATE	351 THE LESSON FOR TODAY	11
BUT HOW TO TAKE THE CURSE, TRAGIC OR COMIC.	352 THE LESSON FOR TODAY	62
TAKE COMFORT IN ABOUT THE SAME COMPLAINT.	353 THE LESSON FOR TODAY	82
I NEVER TAKE MY OWN SIDE IN A QUARREL.	354 THE LESSON FOR TODAY	123
I TAKE MY INCOMPLETENESS WITH THE REST.	355 THE LESSON FOR TODAY	155
SO WE WON'T SIMPLY TAKE IT AND ABSORB IT.	361 A LOOSE MOUNTAIN	21
WE NOW AND THEN SHOULD TAKE AN EQUALIZER.	363 AN EQUALIZER	8
TO TAKE THE MAYFLOWER BACK WHERE HE BELONGED,	370 THE LITERATE FARMER AND	59
BUT NOT TO TAKE AWAY THE PRECIOUS DARK.	370 THE LITERATE FARMER AND	79
YOU TAKE THE UGLINESS ALL SO MUCH DREAD,	371 THE LITERATE FARMER AND	106
WE CAN'T BE TRUSTED TO THE SLEEP WE TAKE,	372 THE LITERATE FARMER AND	126
AND LEAVING SOME THINGS TO TAKE THEIR COURSE.	376 SOMETHING FOR HOPE	22
IT WAS A RISK I HAD TO TAKE--AND TOOK.	383 BRAVADO	4
IT MIGHT TAKE ME ALL NIGHT.	384 MAKING CERTAIN ANYTHING	16
AND TAKE OFF INTO THE SKIES.	388 MIDDLENESS OF THE ROAD	3
AND DID I NOT TAKE STEPS WOULD BE TIPPED OVER	391 ON BEING IDOLIZED	5
AND TAKE OUR DAILY TIDE BATHS SMOOTH AND ROUGH.	395 ETHEREALIZING	8
TAKE CARE TO SELL YOUR HORSE BEFORE HE DIES	399 THE INGENUITIES OF DEBT	4
TAKE SOMETHING LIKE A STAR	403 SOMETHING LIKE A STAR	T
WE MAY TAKE SOMETHING LIKE A STAR	403 SOMETHING LIKE A STAR	24
NOW TAKE THE DOCTOR--" / THEY WERE GIVING CORN	404 FROM PLANE TO PLANE	12
AND TAKE YOUR WALK OF RECREATION BACK	405 FROM PLANE TO PLANE	42
OF HIS ASTRONOMY. (HE'D HAVE TO TAKE	407 FROM PLANE TO PLANE	111
WILL OF ITSELF TAKE FIRE AND LIGHT THE WORLD UP.	414 A CABIN IN THE CLEARING	27
WILL IN TOW THIS DERELICT	418 AMERICA IS HARD TO SEE	56
SO IN IT HAVE TO TAKE COURAGEOUS PART.	423 FOR JOHN F. KENNEDY	42
ALL CONCERN TO TAKE	432 KITTY HAWK	120
WE MAY TAKE THE VIEW	436 KITTY HAWK	251
WILL TAKE THAT TIME	445 PERIL OF HOPE	11
I'M GETTING OUT TONIGHT. HERE, TAKE THE CROWN."	453 HOW HARD TO KEEP FROM	3
OF DUSTY WEEDS TO TAKE A DRINK OF STARS."	454 HOW HARD TO KEEP FROM	14
HOW WOULD IT BE FOR YOU TO TAKE YOUR FATHER	454 HOW HARD TO KEEP FROM	31
TAKE NOTICE, HAMAN, HE'S IN FAVOR WITH US."	455 HOW HARD TO KEEP FROM	65
A NATION HAS TO TAKE ITS NATURAL COURSE	459 HOW HARD TO KEEP FROM	158
AND IF SHE DON'T TAKE CARE	465 MILKY WAY IS A COWPATH	37
TO TAKE LIFE AT A WALK	465 SOME SCIENCE FICTION	7
TO TROUBLE MEN WITH HAVING TO TAKE SIDES.	468 FROM IRON	2
SHE'D LIKE TO KNOW HOW YOU WOULD TAKE A PRAYER	479 A MASQUE OF REASON	180
SO HE WON'T FIND IT HARD TO TAKE HIS ORDERS	481 A MASQUE OF REASON	212
SO HE WON'T FIND IT HARD TO TAKE HIS WAR.	481 A MASQUE OF REASON	215
AND, TOO, TAKE CARE OF TWENTY OF THE FOUR	484 A MASQUE OF REASON	310
HERE, TAKE MY HAND. / (HE TAKES IT AND ALIGHTS	489 A MASQUE OF REASON	451
YOU TAKE US TWO, WE'RE LOSERS IN THIS STORE,	496 A MASQUE OF MERCY	75
I TAKE TO DRINK--AT LEAST I TAKE A DRINK.	496 A MASQUE OF MERCY	83
SHE'LL TAKE TO DRINK AND SEE HOW WE LIKE THAT.	496 A MASQUE OF MERCY	85
I'M GOING TO TAKE THE NONSENSE OUT OF YOU	498 A MASQUE OF MERCY	132
I'LL TAKE TO DRINK--AT LEAST I'LL TAKE A DRINK.	500 A MASQUE OF MERCY	168
WE TAKE IT YOU WERE SENT IN HERE FOR HELP.	500 A MASQUE OF MERCY	177
I TAKE THE FIRST BOAT. GOD PUTS UP A STORM	500 A MASQUE OF MERCY	180
IF YOU WOULD TAKE THE HANDS OUT OF YOUR HAIR	500 A MASQUE OF MERCY	191
TO TAKE THE PUNISHMENT OUT OF ALL FAILURE	505 A MASQUE OF MERCY	313
FROM DISILLUSIONMENT. YOU'VE HAD TO TAKE IT.	518 A MASQUE OF MERCY	648

TAKEN

	PAGE TITLE	LINE
AND NONE ARE TAKEN BUT WHO WILL,	20 THE TRIAL BY EXISTENCE	33
AND GOD HAS TAKEN A FLOWER OF GOLD	21 THE TRIAL BY EXISTENCE	61
THE ROAD NOT TAKEN	105 THE ROAD NOT TAKEN	T
THE NEIGHBORS MAY NOT HAVE TAKEN AS THEIR RIGHT	117 IN THE HOME STRETCH	191
(AND TAKEN WITH IT ALL THE HYLA BREED	119 HYLA BROOK	4
THAN WITH BROOKS TAKEN OTHERWHERE IN SONG.	119 HYLA BROOK	14
I HAD NOT TAKEN THE FIRST STEP IN KNOWLEDGE;	199 WILD GRAPES	95
AND TAKEN THUS INTO THE FAMILY.	216 A FOUNTAIN, A BOTTLE	101
BUT, TREE, I HAVE SEEN YOU TAKEN AND TOSSED,	252 TREE AT MY WINDOW	9
YOU HAVE SEEN ME WHEN I WAS TAKEN AND SWEPT	252 TREE AT MY WINDOW	11
I WOULD NOT BE TAKEN AS EVER HAVING REBELLED.	306 NOT QUITE SOCIAL	12

TAKEN (CONTINUED)
    LET THEIR TRAPPINGS BE TAKEN AWAY. . . . . 313 THE VINDICTIVES 89
    HAD TAKEN ALL THE WATER IT COULD AS DEW, ... 315 IRIS BY NIGHT 14
    BEFORE NOW POETRY HAS TAKEN NOTICE . . . . 316 BUILD SOIL 28
    THAT THEY MAY BE ABUSED AND TAKEN ADVANTAGE OF . . . 322 BUILD SOIL 189
    THE LAST STEP TAKEN FOUND YOUR HEFT . . . . 325 TO A THINKER 1
    AND WHEN WE HAD TAKEN THAT INTO THE ROOTS OF GRAIN, . . 349 OUR HOLD ON THE PLANET . 8
    IN HAVING TAKEN ARTIFICIAL LIGHT . . . . 361 A LOOSE MOUNTAIN . . 7
    A SERIOUS STEP LIGHTLY TAKEN . . . . 367 A SERIOUS STEP LIGHTLY . T
    ONE STEP BACKWARD TAKEN . . . . 376 ONE STEP BACKWARD TAKEN . T
    BUT WITH ONE STEP BACKWARD TAKEN . . . . 377 ONE STEP BACKWARD TAKEN . 10
    (IT WILL BE TAKEN DOWN BEFORE IT FALLS.) . . . . . . 386 THE FEAR OF MAN 7
    GOD, HAVE YOU TAKEN COGNIZANCE OF THIS? . . . . . . 398 NO HOLY WARS FOR THEM . 9
    SHOULD BE TAKEN OUTSIDE A HOUSE AND BOOK. . . . . . 419 ONE MORE BREVITY . . . 2
    AND MEASURED, BUT NOT TAKEN AFTER ALL, ... 443 AUSPEX 3
    THE BEST, I'M TOLD, I EVER HAVE HAD TAKEN. . . . . . 476 A MASQUE OF REASON . . 86
    WOULD BETTER HAVE BEEN TAKEN TO YOUR DEPTH." . . . . 506 A MASQUE OF MERCY . . 340
    UNTIL THE SCRIBES HAD TAKEN DOWN A BOOKFUL . . . . . 518 A MASQUE OF MERCY . . 644
    I SHOULD DARE SAY SHE WOULD BE TAKEN CARE OF. . . . 519 A MASQUE OF MERCY . . 687
TAKER (SEE CENSUS-TAKER)
    AND HERE'S A LOT OF MONEY. WHO'S THE TAKER? . . . . 455 HOW HARD TO KEEP FROM . 46
TAKES
    HE TAKES IT OUT IN BUNCHES LIKE BIG BIRDS' NESTS. . . 37 DEATH OF THE HIRED MAN . 93
    THAT THING TAKES ALL THE ROOM!" HE MOVED HIS GOAD. . 41 THE MOUNTAIN 27
    WHAT HAD HOW LONG IT TAKES A BIRCH TO ROT . . . . . 54 HOME BURIAL 95
    "HE IS A FOOL IF THAT'S THE WAY HE TAKES ME." . . . 70 THE CODE 20
    HE NEVER TAKES THE MONEY. IF THEY'RE WORTH . . . . 86 THE HOUSEKEEPER . . 140
    "YES, BUT ALL THAT TAKES TIME, AND I'M AS MUCH . . . 99 THE SELF-SEEKER . . . 191
    THE WHITE ONE IN HIS TAIL; LIKE ONE WHO TAKES . . . 101 THE WOOD-PILE . . . 15
    WHAT HAPPENS TO HIM IF IT ONLY TAKES . . . . . . 146 SNOW 90
    I'LL FIND THAT FOUNTAIN IF IT TAKES ALL SUMMER, . . 213 A FOUNTAIN, A BOTTLE . 18
    IT TAKES THE MOON FOR THIS. THE SUN'S A WIZARD . . . 237 A HILLSIDE THAW . . . 18
    THAT REALLY TAKES AWAY INSTEAD OF GIVES. . . . . . 279 THE WHITE-TAILED HORNET . 55
    SHE TAKES HER TIME TO TAKE HER FILL. . . . . 281 BLUE RIBBON AT AMESBURY . 39
    AS LONG AS IT TAKES TO PASS . . . . 301 NEITHER OUT FAR NOR IN . 5
    THE MUSE TAKES CARE OF YOU. YOU LIVE BY WRITING . . 316 BUILD SOIL 17
    IT TAKES TEN YEARS OR SO TO CARRY OUT, ... 323 BUILD SOIL 226
    AND TAKES THE PLAYFULLY OBJECTED RHYME . . . . . 362 IN A POEM 2
    SOME IGNORANCE TAKES RANK AS INNOCENCE. . . . . . 371 THE LITERATE FARMER AND . 88
    IT TAKES ALL SORTS OF IN- AND OUTDOOR SCHOOLING . . 470 IT TAKES ALL SORTS... . 1
    IT TAKES ALL SORTS... . . . . 470 IT TAKES ALL SORTS... . 1
    (JOB TAKES A FEW STEPS PACING.) DO YOU MIND? . . . 485 A MASQUE OF REASON . . 329
    IF YOU GO NOW.--LOOK HOW HE TAKES NO STEPS! . . . 489 A MASQUE OF REASON . . 439
    HERE, TAKE MY HAND. / (HE TAKES IT AND ALIGHTS . . 489 A MASQUE OF REASON . . 451
    (HE GOES AND TAKES IT FROM THE DOOR HIMSELF.) . . 500 A MASQUE OF MERCY . . 175
    WE LIKE YOU, DON'T WE, PAUL? (PAUL TAKES HIS WRIST.) . 518 A MASQUE OF MERCY . . 665
    COURAGE IS WHAT IT TAKES AND TAKES THE MORE OF . . 521 A MASQUE OF MERCY . . 731
TAKING
    JUST TAKING WHAT NATURE IS WILLING TO GIVE, ... 61 BLUEBERRIES 55
    "WHAT DID I SAY?" / "ABOUT OUR TAKING PAINS." . . . 70 THE CODE 11
    TAKING DICTATION ON A PAPER PAD . . . . 182 MAPLE 79
    TAKING THE CHILD OUT OF THE PARENTS' HANDS. . . . . 185 MAPLE 167
    "HAHN, HAHN," HE MUSED, "DON'T NEED MUCH TAKING DOWN." . 187 THE AX-HELVE 79
    HE'D BEEN HARD AT IT TAKING BOARDS AWAY . . . . . 193 PAUL'S WIFE 58
    PAUL TAKING AFTER HER AROUND THE POND. . . . . . 195 PAUL'S WIFE 122
    INTENT ON GIVING AND TAKING PAIN. . . . . 252 THE THATCH 2
    AND TAKING FORMAL POSITION, ... 288 DEPARTMENTAL 35
    WAS THAT TRAMP TAKING SANCTUARY THERE . . . . . 289 OLD BARN AT THE BOTTOM . 14
    ON TAKING FROM THE TOP TO BROADEN THE BASE . . . 298 ON TAKING FROM THE TOP . T
    BETRAY YOU INTO TAKING SIDES AGAINST ME, ... 320 BUILD SOIL 132
    CONTENT WITH CONTEMPLATING, TAKING IN, ... 399 THE INGENUITIES OF DEBT . 16
    "--TAKING HIS OWN SWEET TIME AS IF TO SHOW . . . . 404 FROM PLANE TO PLANE . 24
    WON'T FIND A FORMULA FOR TAKING CARE OF. . . . . 488 A MASQUE OF REASON . . 415
    (TAKING A WALK OFF DOWN THE STORE DISTRESSED) . . . 503 A MASQUE OF MERCY . . 267
TALE
    THE TALE OF EARTH'S UNHONORED THINGS . . . . . . 21 THE TRIAL BY EXISTENCE . 45
    AND SHE NEVER SINS BY TELLING THE TALE . . . . . 134 A GIRL'S GARDEN . . . 47
    I KNEW A TALE OF A BETTER KIND. . . . . 291 ON HEART'S BEGINNING TO . 14
    THE TALE IS STILL BOASTINGLY TOLD . . . . 311 THE VINDICTIVES . . . 33
    AND LET THE CAPTAIN TELL HIM A TALE. . . . . . . 345 DISCOVERY OF MADEIRAS . 51
    THE TALE OF THE VOYAGE HE HAD ACHIEVED, ... 347 DISCOVERY OF MADEIRAS . 130
TALENTS
    WHY DON'T YOU USE YOUR TALENTS AS A WRITER . . . . 316 BUILD SOIL 22
TALES
    WHO SEE SO LITTLE THEY TELL NO TALES. . . . . . . 24 PAN WITH US 15
    THERE WAS THE BOOK OF PROFILE TALES DECLARING . . . 423 FOR JOHN F. KENNEDY . 60
TALK (SEE TALK-TALK)
    I TRIED TO MAKE HIM TALK ABOUT HIS TRAVELS. . . . . 36 DEATH OF THE HIRED MAN . 42
    'MY MAN' IS IT? YOU TALK LIKE A PROFESSOR. . . . . 47 A HUNDRED COLLARS . . 80
    AND TALK ABOUT YOUR EVERYDAY CONCERNS. . . . . . 54 HOME BURIAL 86
    THINK OF IT, TALK LIKE THAT AT SUCH A TIME! . . . . 54 HOME BURIAL 94
    "YOU--OH, YOU THINK THE TALK IS ALL. I MUST GO-- . . 54 HOME BURIAL 112
    AND SHE LIKED TALK. SHE HAD SEEN GARRISON . . . . 56 THE BLACK COTTAGE . . 52
    SPRAWLING ABOUT THE KITCHEN WITH THEIR TALK . . . . 65 A SERVANT TO SERVANTS . 77
    "YOU MUST BE VERY STILL; YOU MUSTN'T TALK." . . . . 78 THE GENERATIONS OF MEN . 149
    I CAN'T TALK TO HER, AND, LORD, IF I COULD!" . . . 82 THE HOUSEKEEPER . . 27
    COULDN'T ONE TALK TO HER? WHAT DOES SHE SAY? . . . 83 THE HOUSEKEEPER . . 72
    "ESTELLE'S THE ONE. YOU NEEDN'T TALK TO ME." . . . 87 THE HOUSEKEEPER . . 164
    COME OUT HERE IF YOU WANT TO HEAR ME TALK.-- . . . 88 THE HOUSEKEEPER . . 208
    I'LL TALK TO YOU, OLD WOMAN, AFTERWARD.-- . . . . 88 THE HOUSEKEEPER . . 209
    NO ONE AT ALL WITH WHOM TO TALK, ... 102 GOOD HOURS 2
    I HEARD YOU TALK. . . . . 118 THE TELEPHONE . . . 6
    NO, NOT AS THERE IS A TIME TO TALK. . . . . . . 124 A TIME TO TALK . . . 6
    A TIME TO TALK . . . . 124 A TIME TO TALK . . . T
    THE WAY WE PILED IT. AND LET'S BE THE TALK . . . . 129 THE BONFIRE 10
    WHOSE BUSINESS--BUT WHY TALK ROUND THE BARN?-- . . 142 THE VANISHING RED . . 7
    MORE THAN YOU WILL US WITH SUCH NIGHTMARE TALK. . . 149 SNOW 168
    "LET HIM TALK, HELEN, AND PERHAPS HE'LL STAY." . . . 149 SNOW 171

TALK (CONTINUED)

WHAT DID HE COME IN FOR?--TO TALK AND VISIT? . . . . . . 155 SNOW 339
TALK CALIFORNIA--A STATE SO BLESSED, ... 159 NEW HAMPSHIRE . . . 17
SO BRAD MCLAUGHLIN MINGLED RECKLESS TALK . . . . 176 THE STAR-SPLITTER . . 13
AFTER SUCH LOOSE TALK IT WAS NO SURPRISE . . . . 177 THE STAR-SPLITTER . . 38
LET'S TALK ABOUT IT." / "LET'S GO SEE THE PLACE." . . . 213 A FOUNTAIN, A BOTTLE . 16
(TO HEAR US TALK) . . . . 238 ON A TREE FALLEN ACROSS S
OR SUCH IS THE TALK AT THE FARMHOUSE: . . . . 264 THE LAST MOWING . . 3
WILL KEEP MY TALK FROM GETTING OVERWISE, ... 265 DUST IN THE EYES . . 2
HER STYLE, WERE ALL THE FANCY'S TALK. . . . . 280 BLUE RIBBON AT AMESBURY 8
WE SIT INDOORS AND TALK OF THE COLD OUTSIDE. . . . . . 305 THERE ARE ROUGHLY ZONES 1
THE ONE YOU HAD THE TALK WITH, YOU REMEMBER, ... 316 BUILD SOIL 3
EVEN WHILE WE TALK SOME CHEMIST AT COLUMBIA . . . . . . 319 BUILD SOIL 107
WHEN AFTER TALK WITH OTHER MEN . . . . 346 DISCOVERY OF MADEIRAS . 86
BUT COME, ENLIGHTENED AS IN TALK YCU SEEM, ... 370 THE LITERATE FARMER AND 61
"SICK TALK, SICK TALK, SICK SENTIMENTAL TALK! . . . . . 370 THE LITERATE FARMER AND 84
IT DOESN'T DO YOU ANY GOOD TO TALK. . . . . 370 THE LITERATE FARMER AND 85
THEY RENEW TALK OF THE FABLED . . . . 387 THE COURAGE TO BE NEW . 7
TALK FAHRENHEIT, TALK CENTIGRADE. . . . . 403 SOMETHING LIKE A STAR . 13
TODAY I WANT TO TALK ABOUT THE SUN. . . . . 406 FROM PLANE TO PLANE . 87
SO IT WAS IN TALK . . . . 433 KITTY HAWK 162
TALK ALOFT . . . . 438 KITTY HAWK 2P
LOUD TALK IN THE OVERLIGHTED HOUSE . . . . 444 ENDS 1
ONE HAS BEEN LATELY ALL THE TALK . . . . 452 A-WISHING WELL . . . 62
ALONG THE AEGEAN COAST. THAT'S ALL THEY TALK OF." . . . 459 HOW HARD TO KEEP FROM 168
WITH ALL THIS TALK ABOUT THE HOPE OF YOUTH . . . . . . 462 HOW HARD TO KEEP FROM 257
IN PHILOSOPHIC TALK; . . . . 465 SOME SCIENCE FICTION . 8
I STICK TO THAT. BUT TALK ABOUT CONFUSION!-- . . . . . 485 A MASQUE OF REASON . 336
COME, COME, YOU TALK LIKE AN AGRARIAN. . . . . 496 A MASQUE OF MERCY . 68
IT'S GREENWICH VILLAGE COCKTAIL-PARTY TALK-- . . . . . 500 A MASQUE OF MERCY . 170
BIG-CITY TALK. I'M GETTING OUT OF HERE. . . . . 500 A MASQUE OF MERCY . 171
WHAT'S ALL THIS TALK OF SLAYING DOWN IN CELLARS-- . . . 516 A MASQUE OF MERCY . 605
TALKED

SHE ALWAYS, WHEN SHE TALKED ABOUT THE WAR, ... 56 THE BLACK COTTAGE . 26
ANYWAY ALL HE TALKED ABOUT WAS LOVE. . . . . 66 A SERVANT TO SERVANTS . 110
AND ALL THE TIME WE TALKED YOU SEEMED TO SEE . . . . . 119 MEETING AND PASSING . 10
WE TALKED LIKE BARKING ABOVE THE DIN . . . . 140 THE GUM-GATHERER . . 7
DO YOU KNOW, WHAT WE TALKED ABOUT WAS KNOWLEDGE? . . . 188 THE AX-HELVE 82
THAT SHOULD IF NOT BE TALKED THEN SUNG ABOUT. . . . . 411 POD OF THE MILKWEED . 9
TALKED-OF

WHAT IS THIS TALKED-OF MYSTERY OF BIRTH . . . . 267 RIDERS 5
TALKER

THE WRITER AND TALKER FREE SPEECH AND FREE PRESS. . . . 319 BUILD SCIL 113
TALKING

TO SEE IF HE WAS TALKING IN HIS SLEEP. . . . . 36 DEATH OF THE HIRED MAN 57
NOW WE ARE GETTING ON TOGETHER--TALKING. . . . . . . 48 A HUNDRED COLLARS . 101
AS TALKING--YOU STOOD UP BESIDE ME, YOU KNOW." . . . . 62 BLUEBERRIES 96
YOU WERE JUST TALKING WHAT WAS IN YOUR MIND, ... 70 THE CODE 27
BUT WHAT'S THE USE OF TALKING WHEN IT'S DONE? . . . . 87 THE HOUSEKEEPER . . 176
"NOT TALKING." / "NO." / "WHY, YES, I HEAR--WHAT IS IT?" 154 SNOW 317
HE STOOD ON THE SAFE SIDE OF THE LINE TALKING-- . . . . 171 NEW HAMPSHIRE . . . 381
AND WALKED OFF, TALKING TO HERSELF OR PAUL, ... 195 PAUL'S WIFE 120
TWO OLD-BELIEVERS. THEY DID ALL THE TALKING. . . . . 202 THE WITCH OF COOS . 3
A TALKING TWITTER ALL THEY HAD TO SING. . . . . 240 OUR SINGING STRENGTH . 38
NOT ALL YOUR LIGHT TONGUES TALKING ALOUD . . . . . . 252 TREE AT MY WINDOW . 7
NOR WAS THIS JUST A WAY OF TALKING . . . . 274 A LONE STRIKER . . 47
LISTEN, THEY MURMUR TALKING IN THE DARK . . . . 415 A CABIN IN THE CLEARING 34
AND I WASN'T SURE I WAS TALKING DOG. . . . . 420 ONE MORE BREVITY . . 37
I'M TALKING NOT FREE VERSE BUT BLANK VERSE NOW. . . . . 460 HOW HARD TO KEEP FROM 212
JUST AS WE WILL BE TALKING ANYWAY . . . . 482 A MASQUE OF REASON . 236
STAYS TALKING WITH THE KEEPER AT A SHOWCASE. . . . . . 493 A MASQUE OF MERCY . 4
BUT WE ARE TALKING OVER JONAH'S HEAD, ... 509 A MASQUE OF MERCY . 426
TALKS

SHE TALKS AND I AM FAIN TO LIST: . . . . 7 MY NOVEMBER GUEST . 7
RIFLING A PRINTED LETTER AS HE TALKS. . . . . 44 A HUNDRED COLLARS . 10
THAT SORT OF MAN TALKS STRAIGHT-ON ALL HIS LIFE . . . 145 SNOW 64
THEY ARE THAT THAT TALKS OF GOING . . . . 156 THE SOUND OF TREES . 10
AND THAT TALKS NO LESS FOR KNOWING, ... 156 THE SOUND OF TREES . 12
TALK-TALK

THAT NEED ENDLESS TALK-TALK . . . . 212 AN EMPTY THREAT . . 56
TALL

WHICH FLOWS IN SHAPES AS TALL AS TREES . . . . 9 STARS 3
THAN THE TREES AROUND WERE TALL; . . . . 13 ROSE POGONIAS . . . 4
MOVING AMONG TALL HAYCOCKS LIGHTLY PILED, ... 14 WAITING 2
AT A TALL TUFT OF FLOWERS BESIDE A BROOK, ... 22 THE TUFT OF FLOWERS . 22
"NOT IN A GLASS CASE, THEN?" / "HE'D NEED A TALL ONE: . 86 THE HOUSEKEEPER . . 148
SHE STRETCHED UP TALL TO OVERLOOK THE LIGHT . . . . . 91 THE FEAR 62
STRAIGHT UP AND DOWN OF TALL SLIM TREES . . . . . . 101 THE WOOD-PILE . . . 6
AT WEEDS THE WATER FROM THE SINK MADE TALL. . . . . . 110 IN THE HOME STRETCH . 3
BLADE-END UP AND FIVE FEET TALL, ... 124 A TIME TO TALK . . 8
UP WHERE THE TREES GROW SHORT, THE MOSSES TALL, . . . 210 PAUPER WITCH OF GRAFTON 96
AND IN IT, TALL AS TREES, WERE CLIFFS; . . . . 274 A LONE STRIKER . . 37
TALON

HE HANGS ON UPSIDE DOWN WITH TALON FEET . . . . 412 POD OF THE MILKWEED . 45
HE ALMOST HAS IT IN HIS TALON CLUTCH. . . . . 412 POD OF THE MILKWEED . 50
TALUS

IN THE CLIFF'S TALUS ON THE OTHER SIDE, ... 338 THE MOST OF IT . . 11
TAMARACK

THE BARK OF A WHOLE TAMARACK OFF WHOLE, ... 191 PAUL'S WIFE 19
TAMARACKS

MAPLES AND BIRCHES AND TAMARACKS. . . . . 228 GOOD-BY AND KEEP COLD . 24
TAMARISK

SAND DUNES HELD LOOSELY IN TAMARISK . . . . 58 THE BLACK COTTAGE . 120
TAME

THE MEADOW IS DONE WITH THE TAME. . . . . 264 THE LAST MOWING . . 14
TAMELY

CAME TAMELY BACK IN FRONT OF ME, THE DROVER, ... 240 OUR SINGING STRENGTH . 44

TAN
    AND LESS THAN THE TAN WITH WHICH PICKERS ARE TANNED." . . 60 BLUEBERRIES 27
    TO DRY OR WASH OR TAN, I DON'T KNOW WHICH . . . . . . 197 WILD GRAPES 52
TANGENTS
    AND RUN OFF IN STRANGE TANGENTS WITH MY ARM, ... 174 A STAR IN A STONEBOAT . 53
TANGLE
    UP FROM THE TANGLE OF WITHERED WEEDS . . . . 8 A LATE WALK 7
    I THOUGHT A FEW MIGHT TANGLE, AS THEY DID, ... 234 EVENING A SUGAR ORCHARD 7
TANGLED
    TOSSED, TANGLED, WHIRLED AND WHIRLED ABOVE, ... 28 MY BUTTERFLY 16
TANKED
    AND ALL TANKED UP WITH MINERAL JUICE, ... 463 LINES IN DEJECTION . . 7
TANNED
    AND LESS THAN THE TAN WITH WHICH PICKERS ARE TANNED." . . 60 BLUEBERRIES 27
TANTALIZE
    AND TANTALIZE ME WITH ANOTHER "OH, BECAUSE." . . . . 482 A MASQUE OF REASON . 257
TAP (SEE TAP-TAP-TAPPING)
    TO TAP THE UPPER SKY AND DRAW A FLOW . . . . 169 NEW HAMPSHIRE . . . 340
TAPER
    THINKS WHY NOT TAPER OFF TO NONE AT ALL, ... 498 A MASQUE OF MERCY . 122
TAPES
    TO ALMOST STRIPS AND TAPES OF RAGGED WHITE . . . . 239 OUR SINGING STRENGTH . 8
TAPPED
    THEY TAPPED AT MY EYELIDS AND TOUCHED MY LIPS WITH AN
        INVITATION TO GRIEF. . . . . 298 A LEAF-TREADER . . . 10
TAPPING (SEE TAP-TAP-TAPPING)
TAP-TAP-TAPPING
    CAME TAP-TAP-TAPPING DOWN THE VILLAGE STREET, ... 394 HAEC FABULA DOCET . . 3
TAR
    AND I DREAD THE OMINOUS STAIN OF TAR . . . . 232 THE KITCHEN CHIMNEY . 13
TAR-BANDED
    AMONG TAR-BANDED ANCIENT CHERRY TREES, ... 55 THE BLACK COTTAGE . . 3
TARDY
    AND THOUGH AT THAT THE TARDY RAN, ... 273 A LONE STRIKER . . . 3
TARGET
    FURTHER THAN TARGET EVER SHOWED OR SHONE. . . . . . 262 A SOLDIER 14
TARNISH
    A TARNISH THAT GOES AT A TOUCH OF THE HAND, ... 60 BLUEBERRIES 26
TARNISHES
    WHEN, JUST AS THE SOIL TARNISHES WITH WEED, ... 124 PUTTING IN THE SEED . 12
TASK
    TAKE UP THE TASK BEYOND HER CHOOSING." . . . . . . 256 THE LOVELY BE CHOOSERS 11
    THE TIME WHEN MOST I LOVED MY TASK . . . . 276 TWO TRAMPS IN MUD TIME 41
TASKED
    WHO AM TASKED TO SAVE MY OWN A LITTLE WHILE. . . . . 357 A MOTH SEEN IN WINTER . 24
TASKS
    SOMEONE WHO LIVED IN TURNING TO FRESH TASKS . . . . 102 THE WOOD-PILE . . . 35
TASTE
    I TASTE IN THEM SOMETIMES THE FLAVOR OF SOOT. . . . 59 BLUEBERRIES 23
    FOR MONTHS IT HASN'T KNOWN THE TASTE OF STEEL . . . 189 THE GRINDSTONE . . . 15
    ON ONE I CAN TASTE ATLANTIC, ... 295 A RECORD STRIDE . . 23
    A DEVELOPED TASTE IN VASES, ... 396 AN IMPORTER 8
    AND DARED TO TASTE THE WOUND A LITTLE KNOWS. . . . 411 POD OF THE MILKWEED . 18
    I WAS TO TASTE IN LITTLE THE GRIEF . . . . 420 ONE MORE BREVITY . . 50
    NOR TASTE ITS SALT, NOR SMELL ITS FISH AND WEED, . . . 447 DOES NO ONE AT ALL EVER 35
TASTED
    A CIDER SYRUP. HAVING TASTED FRUIT, ... 124 THE COW IN APPLE TIME . 5
    FROM WHAT I'VE TASTED OF DESIRE . . . . 220 FIRE AND ICE 3
    MY SON AND I HAVE TASTED IT AND KNOW. . . . . 460 HOW HARD TO KEEP FROM 195
TASTES
    IT TASTES AS IF IT MIGHT BE OPIATE. . . . . 411 POD OF THE MILKWEED . 19
TASTING
    (MIRACULOUSLY WITHOUT TASTING FLESH) . . . . 109 THE EXPOSED NEST . . 15
TATTERED
    THE LINE-STORM CLOUDS FLY TATTERED AND SWIFT. . . . . 26 A LINE-STORM SONG . . 1
TATTERS
    WILL LEAVE THEIR TATTERS HUNG ON BARB AND THORN.) . . . 379 DIRECTIVE 54
TAUGHT (SEE SELF-TAUGHT)
    SO AS TO PLEASE YOU. BUT I MIGHT BE TAUGHT, ... 52 HOME BURIAL 47
    SHE HAD AT SOME COST TAUGHT THEM AFTER YEARS.) . . . . 56 THE BLACK COTTAGE . . 42
    KIT MARLOWE TAUGHT ME HOW TO SAY MY PRAYERS: . . . . 166 NEW HAMPSHIRE . . . 242
    SHE TAUGHT HIM HER TRIBE'S RELIGION: . . . . 313 BEARER OF EVIL TIDINGS 17
    POLITICAL AMBITION HAS BEEN TAUGHT, ... 319 BUILD SOIL 114
    GREED HAS BEEN TAUGHT A LITTLE ABNEGATION . . . . . 319 BUILD SOIL 117
    SELF-TAUGHT. BUT OUR BRUTE SNARLING AND LASHING TAUGHT IT. 320 BUILD SOIL 120
    SOME HAVE PREACHED AND TAUGHT . . . . 438 KITTY HAWK 321
TAUNT
    THEY TAUNT THE LOFTY LAND WITH LITTLE MEN. . . . . . 167 NEW HAMPSHIRE . . . 264
    OTHERS TAUNT ME WITH HAVING KNELT AT WELL-CURBS . . . 225 FOR ONCE SOMETHING . . 1
    YOU MAY TAUNT ME WITH NOT BEING ABLE TO FLEE THE EARTH. . 306 NOT QUITE SOCIAL . . 9
    TO TAUNT OF MINE I KNEW A PLACE TO GO . . . . 447 DOES NO ONE AT ALL EVER 33
TAUNTED
    TAUNTED THE LOFTY LAND WITH LITTLE MEN." . . . . . . 166 NEW HAMPSHIRE . . . 219
TAURUS
    ARIES AND TAURUS, ... 429 KITTY HAWK 37
TAUS
    THE SIGMAS AND TAUS . . . . 219 I WILL SING YOU ONE-O . 46
TAUT
    TAUT WITH THE DEW FROM GARDEN BED TO EAVES, ... 38 DEATH OF THE HIRED MAN 108
    WITH SHOUTS AFAR TO PULL THE CABLE TAUT, ... 141 THE LINE-GANG . . . 9
    AND ONLY BY ONE'S GOING SLIGHTLY TAUT . . . . 332 THE SILKEN TENT . . 12
TAX (SEE INCOME-TAX)
    AND PAY A DEATH TAX OF FAIRLY POLITE REPENTANCE. . . . 307 NOT QUITE SOCIAL . . 16
TEA
    AND GAVE HIM TEA AND TRIED TO MAKE HIM SMOKE. . . . . 36 DEATH OF THE HIRED MAN 41
    RECIPES FOR TEA WITH BUTTER, ... 396 AN IMPORTER 5
TEACH
    HE TOSSED HIS PIPES, TOO HARD TO TEACH . . . . . . 24 PAN WITH US 16

TEACH (CONTINUED)
    TO TEACH HIM HOW TO BUILD A LOAD OF HAY----" . . . . . 37 DEATH OF THE HIRED MAN . 87
    "HE THINKS IF HE COULD TEACH HIM THAT, HE'D BE . . . . . 37 DEATH OF THE HIRED MAN . 96
    ONE SUCH STORM IN A LIFETIME COULDN'T TEACH THEM . . . 240 OUR SINGING STRENGTH . 46
    WHY IS HIS NATURE FOREVER SO HARD TO TEACH . . . . ' . 305 THERE ARE ROUGHLY ZONES 11
    TEACH THOSE ASIANS MASS PRODUCTION? . . . . 397 AN IMPORTER 25
    TEACH YOUR GRANDMOTHER EGG SUCTION. . . . . . . 397 AN IMPORTER 26
    TO TEACH THEM HOW DEMOCRACY IS MEANT. . . . . . 423 FOR JOHN F. KENNEDY . 38
TEACHER
    DOCTOR MAGOON." / "A DOCTOR?" / "WELL, A TEACHER." . . 46 A HUNDRED COLLARS . . 43
    MAPLE IS RIGHT." / "BUT TEACHER TOLD THE SCHOOL . . 179 MAPLE 4
    AS FATHERS ABOUT CHILDREN, YOU TELL TEACHER. . . . 180 MAPLE 6
    WAS TO REBUKE HER TEACHER WITH IT NEXT DAY, . . . 180 MAPLE 31
    AND GIVE THE TEACHER A SCARE AS FROM HER FATHER. . . 180 MAPLE 32
TEACHERS
    THERE'S NO SUCH NAME." / "TEACHERS DON'T KNOW AS MUCH . 179 MAPLE 5
    WHEN I WAS YOUNG MY TEACHERS WERE THE OLD. . . . . 267 WHAT FIFTY SAID . . 1
    NOW I AM OLD MY TEACHERS ARE THE YOUNG. . . . . . 267 WHAT FIFTY SAID . . 5
TEACHER'S
    HER TEACHER'S CERTAINTY IT MUST BE MABEL . . . . . 179 MAPLE 1
    WHEN TEACHER'S OWN EXPERIENCES FAIL HER . . . . . 447 DOES NO ONE AT ALL EVER 39
TEACHING
    HE'S FINISHED SCHOOL, AND TEACHING IN HIS COLLEGE. . . 36 DEATH OF THE HIRED MAN 60
    AND BY TEACHING THEM HOW TO SLEEP THE SLEEP ALL DAY, . 287 A ROADSIDE STAND . . 30
TEAM
    HE SAYS THEY TWO WILL MAKE A TEAM FOR WORK: . . . . 36 DEATH OF THE HIRED MAN 62
TEAMS
    FOR TEAMS THAT CAME BY THE STONY ROAD . . . . . . 241 NEED OF BEING VERSED . 10
TEAR
    HE'D TEAR TO PIECES, EVEN A BED TO LIE ON. . . . . 66 A SERVANT TO SERVANTS . 118
    AND TEAR HIS CLOTHES OFF TO EXAMINE HIM . . . . . 503 A MASQUE OF MERCY . . 251
TEARDROPS
    TWO TEARDROPS, ONE FOR EITHER EYE, ... 327 A MISSIVE MISSILE . . 11
TEARS
    AND POURED ON WATER (TEARS IT MIGHT HAVE BEEN); . . 189 THE GRINDSTONE . . . 27
    OF TEARS, THE AFTERMARK . . . . 227 TO EARTHWARD . . . 21
    FOR THE GENEROUS TEARS OF YOUTH AND SONG? . . . . 262 HANNIBAL 4
    IS WHETHER THE TWO DOTS WERE TEARS, ... 327 A MISSIVE MISSILE . . 10
    NOT TEARS BUT DROPS OF BLOOD INSTEAD. . . . . . 327 A MISSIVE MISSILE . . 14
    RAIN WAS THE TEARS ADOPTED BY MY EYES . . . . . 337 THE WIND AND THE RAIN . 47
    (AND HENCE SO MANY LITERARY TEARS . . . . . . 355 THE LESSON FOR TODAY . 149
TEASE
    BEHIND LIGHT WORDS THAT TEASE AND FLOUT, ... 19 REVELATION 2
    AND A TEMPTATION TO THE TEASE. . . . . . . 326 TO A THINKER . . . 24
TEASED
    I WON'T BE TEASED. BUT SEE HOW WET I AM." . . . . 77 THE GENERATIONS OF MEN 119
TEASING
    DON'T LET ME SCARE YOU. I WAS ONLY TEASING. . . . 514 A MASQUE OF MERCY . . 558
    THEY FAIL ME. NOW I'M TEASING YOU AGAIN. . . . . 516 A MASQUE OF MERCY . . 608
TECHNICAL
    "DON'T BE TOO TECHNICAL.--YOU HAVE THREE CARDS." . . 76 THE GENERATIONS OF MEN 79
TECUMSEH
    YOU SAID THE SECOND COMING OF TECUMSEH. . . . . 406 FROM PLANE TO PLANE . 70
    WILLIAM TECUMSEH SHERMAN. WHY TECUMSEH?" . . . . 406 FROM PLANE TO PLANE . 72
    "YOU WISHED YOUR MIDDLE NAME HAD BEEN TECUMSEH." . . 406 FROM PLANE TO PLANE . 74
TEEMING
    IN THE THICK OF A TEEMING SNOWFALL . . . . . . 303 AFTERFLAKES 1
TEENS
    BUT HIS MIND IS HARDLY OUT OF HIS TEENS: . . . . 393 A CASE FOR JEFFERSON . 8
TEETH
    OF CARRYING HIS PILLOW IN HIS TEETH; . . . . . 66 A SERVANT TO SERVANTS . 107
    BUT TURNS TO PINK BETWEEN THE TEETH. . . . . . 141 THE GUM-GATHERER . . 33
    TO SLAM END-ON AGAIN AGAINST THE SAW TEETH. . . . 193 PAUL'S WIFE . . . 64
    FLASHED OUT AND LICKED ALONG HIS UPPER TEETH. . . . 204 THE WITCH OF COOS . . 73
    AND SHOW ON THE WATER ITS CRYSTAL TEETH. . . . . 276 TWO TRAMPS IN MUD TIME 40
TELEGRAPH
    THEY BRING THE TELEPHONE AND TELEGRAPH. . . . . 141 THE LINE-GANG . . . 13
TELEPHONE
    THE TELEPHONE . . . . 118 THE TELEPHONE . . . T
    THEY BRING THE TELEPHONE AND TELEGRAPH. . . . . 141 THE LINE-GANG . . . 13
    GETTING NO ANSWER, CLOSED THE TELEPHONE. . . . . 143 SNOW 30
    WHAT DID YOUR WIFE SAY ON THE TELEPHONE?" . . . . 147 SNOW 110
    THEY STARTED UP. FRED TOOK THE TELEPHONE. . . . . 155 SNOW 328
TELEPHONES
    HE WON'T COME BACK, AND IF HE TELEPHONES, ... 152 SNOW 266
    WHAT ARE TELEPHONES, SKYSCRAPERS, ... 396 AN IMPORTER . . . 13
TELEPHONING
    COLE HAD BEEN TELEPHONING IN THE DARK. . . . . . 152 SNOW 270
TELESCOPE
    AND SPENT THE PROCEEDS ON A TELESCOPE . . . . . 168 NEW HAMPSHIRE . . 303
    AND SPENT THE PROCEEDS ON A TELESCOPE . . . . . 177 THE STAR-SPLITTER . . 17
    AND BOUGHT THE TELESCOPE WITH WHAT IT CAME TO. . . 177 THE STAR-SPLITTER . . 31
    A TELESCOPE. SOMEONE IN EVERY TOWN . . . . . 177 THE STAR-SPLITTER . . 35
    ABOUT HIS TELESCOPE. BEYOND THE AGE . . . . . 178 THE STAR-SPLITTER . . 54
    BRADFORD AND I HAD OUT THE TELESCOPE. . . . . 179 THE STAR-SPLITTER . . 82
    THAT TELESCOPE WAS CHRISTENED THE STAR-SPLITTER, . . 179 THE STAR-SPLITTER . . 87
    THE TELESCOPE AT ONE END OF HIS BEAT, ... 269 THE BEAR 18
TELESCOPIC
    (TELESCOPIC) . . . . 360 A LOOSE MOUNTAIN . . S
TELL
    BUT IT WERE VAIN TO TELL HER SO, ... 7 MY NOVEMBER GUEST . . 19
    YOU HAVE ONLY TO ASK ME, AND I CAN TELL. . . . . 16 IN A VALE 23
    AND TELL YOU THAT I SAW DOES STILL ABIDE. . . . . 16 A DREAM PANG . . . 12
    MUST SPEAK AND TELL US WHERE THEY ARE. . . . . 19 REVELATION . . . 12
    WHO SEE SO LITTLE THEY TELL NO TALES. . . . . 24 PAN WITH US . . . 15
    AND EAT THE CONES UNDER HIS PINES, I TELL HIM. . . . 33 MENDING WALL . . . 26
    "I WONDER WHAT'S BETWEEN THEM." / "I CAN TELL YOU. . . 39 DEATH OF THE HIRED MAN 139
    TO LOOK AND TELL ME LATER HOW IT WAS." . . . . 43 THE MOUNTAIN . . . 74

TELL (CONTINUED)
     STOPS WHEN SHE LIKES: I TELL HER WHEN TO GO. . . . . .   49 A HUNDRED COLLARS . . 140
     "I WILL FIND OUT NOW--YOU MUST TELL ME, DEAR." . . . .   51 HOME BURIAL 12
     "YOU DON'T," SHE CHALLENGED. "TELL ME WHAT IT IS." . .   51 HOME BURIAL 19
     TELL ME ABOUT IT IF IT'S SOMETHING HUMAN. . . . . . .   53 HOME BURIAL 58
     "WHERE DO YOU MEAN TO GO? FIRST TELL ME THAT. . . . .   55 HOME BURIAL 115
     YOU COULDN'T TELL HER WHAT THE WEST WAS SAYING, . . .   57 THE BLACK COTTAGE . 71
     BUT HE THOUGHT A BIG THOUGHT--I COULD TELL BY HIS EYE-- 60 BLUEBERRIES 43
     TO TELL IF HE KNEW. BUT THE YEAR HAD BEEN BAD. . . . .   61 BLUEBERRIES 72
     THAT SEEMS TO TELL ME HOW I OUGHT TO FEEL, ...   63 A SERVANT TO SERVANTS 14
     AND I COULD TELL . . . .   68 AFTER APPLE-PICKING 16
     TELL YOU A STORY OF WHAT HAPPENED ONCE: . . . .   70 THE CODE 29
     I THINK WE'RE ALL MAD. TELL ME WHY WE'RE HERE, ...   76 THE GENERATIONS OF MEN 88
     "TELL ME ABOUT HER. DOES SHE LOOK LIKE ME?" . . . . .   77 THE GENERATIONS OF MEN 110
     I'LL TELL YOU WHAT THE VOICES REALLY SAY. . . . . . .   78 THE GENERATIONS OF MEN 144
     I'M GETTING TOO OLD FOR MY SIZE, I TELL THEM. . . . .   81 THE HOUSEKEEPER . .   5
     WITH ME TO SIT AND TELL HIM EVERYTHING, ...   82 THE HOUSEKEEPER . . 32
     I TELL THEM THEY CAN'T GET ME THROUGH THE DOOR, THOUGH: 82 THE HOUSEKEEPER . . 37
     JOHN LIKES TO TELL THE OFFERS HE HAS HAD, ...   86 THE HOUSEKEEPER . . 138
     IN WAYS THAT I CAN HARDLY TELL YOU OF. . . . .   86 THE HOUSEKEEPER . . 157
     "IT'S HARD TO TELL YOU HOW I MANAGED IT. . . . .   93 THE SELF-SEEKER . . 22
     YOU'VE GOT TO TELL ME HOW FAR THIS IS GONE: . . . . .   94 THE SELF-SEEKER . . 57
     I HAD A LETTER FROM BURROUGHS--DID I TELL YOU?-- . . .   95 THE SELF-SEEKER . . 85
     TELL ME WHAT IS IT?" / ANNE JUST WAGGED HER DRESS, . .   96 THE SELF-SEEKER . . 105
     I KNEW A LOVELY WAY TO TELL FOR CERTAIN . . . .   96 THE SELF-SEEKER . . 108
     YOU DON'T TELL ME THAT WHERE YOU FOUND A RAM'S HORN . .   97 THE SELF-SEEKER . . 136
     WHAT DID I TELL YOU? WHAT? I'D BLUSH, I WOULD. . . . .   97 THE SELF-SEEKER . . 138
     AND SAY NO WORD TO TELL ME WHO HE WAS . . . . 101 THE WOOD-PILE . . . 12
     "I COULD SOON TELL HOW MANY THEY WOULD CUT, ... 106 CHRISTMAS TREES . . 30
     NO MORE TO TELL? WE TURNED TO OTHER THINGS. . . . . . 110 THE EXPOSED NEST .   32
     "NO: FOR BESIDES THE THINGS I TELL YOU OF, ... 112 IN THE HOME STRETCH 46
     HOW DARK IT'S GETTING. CAN YOU TELL WHAT TIME . . . . 113 IN THE HOME STRETCH 67
     YOU DON'T WANT ME TO TELL IF I DON'T KNOW." . . . . . 116 IN THE HOME STRETCH 169
     "FIRST TELL ME WHAT IT WAS YOU THOUGHT YOU HEARD." . . 118 THE TELEPHONE . . . 10
     AND TELL ME WHERE YOU'RE OFF FOR--MONTREAL? . . . . . 125 AN ENCOUNTER 21
     ALWAYS--I TELL YOU THIS THEY LEARNED-- . . . . 127 HOUSE FEAR   1
     I WASN'T GOING TO TELL YOU AND I MUSTN'T. . . . . . . 133 THE BONFIRE 112
     LIKES TO TELL HOW ONE SPRING . . . . 133 A GIRL'S GARDEN . .   2
     I JUST CAME TO TELL YOU . . . . 135 LAST WORD OF A BLUEBIRD 5
     TO TELL LESLEY (WILL YOU?) . . . . 135 LAST WORD OF A BLUEBIRD 6
     TO TELL THEM "SUPPER." AT THE WORD, THE SAW, ... 136 "OUT, OUT--" 14
     I THINK I'LL JUST CALL UP MY WIFE AND TELL HER . . . . 143 SNOW 11
     CARVED IN THE SHED TO TELL ME WHO I AM . . . . 144 SNOW 40
     IF IT DON'T TELL ME WHERE I AM, I USED . . . . 144 SNOW 41
     THOUGH FOR ALL ANYONE CAN TELL, REPOSE . . . . 148 SNOW 147
     THOUGHT HE'D JUST CALL TO TELL US IT WAS SNOWING. . . 155 SNOW 340
     THIS, THEN, IS THE NEW FREEDOM WE HEAR TELL OF; . . . 168 NEW HAMPSHIRE . . . 283
     THAT COURSE, THEY TELL ME, ISN'T OFFERED THIS YEAR. . 171 NEW HAMPSHIRE . . . 405
     NEVER TELL ME THAT NOT ONE STAR OF ALL . . . . 172 A STAR IN A STONEBOAT   1
     I DO NOT KNOW--I CANNOT STOP TO TELL: . . . . 173 A STAR IN A STONEBOAT 38
     COULD TELL THE TIME OF YEAR WHEN EVERY TREE . . . . . 175 THE CENSUS-TAKER . . 18
     AS FATHERS ABOUT CHILDREN, YOU TELL TEACHER. . . . . 180 MAPLE   6
     YOU TELL HER THAT IT'S M-A-P-L-E. . . . . 180 MAPLE   7
     BY AND BY I WILL TELL YOU ALL I KNOW . . . . 180 MAPLE 26
     SOMETHING A FATHER COULDN'T TELL A DAUGHTER . . . . . 183 MAPLE 118
     BUT ALL HE HAD TO TELL ME IN FRENCH-ENGLISH . . . . . 185 THE AX-HELVE 18
     AND TELL PAUL WHAT HE OUGHT TO DO ABOUT IT. . . . . . 193 PAUL'S WIFE 79
     AND THERE, WELL AFTER DARK, LET MURPHY TELL IT, . . . 195 PAUL'S WIFE 127
     TELL YOU WHAT RALLE THE SIOUX CONTROL ONCE TOLD ME. . 202 THE WITCH OF COOS . 13
     YOU WOULDN'T WANT TO TELL HIM WHAT WE HAVE . . . . . 203 THE WITCH OF COOS . 19
     AND BRING THE CHALK-PILE DOWN. "I'LL TELL YOU WHAT-- 205 THE WITCH OF COOS . 107
     YES, WE COULD TOO, SON. TELL THE TRUTH FOR ONCE. . . 206 THE WITCH OF COOS . 138
     TO TELL THE TRUTH, SUPPOSE THE TIME HAD COME. . . . . 207 THE WITCH OF COOS . 144
     COULD TELL YOU WHY HE EVER CARED HIMSELF.... . . . . 207 THE WITCH OF COOS . 151
     I'M GOING TO TELL THEM SOMETHING THEY WON'T LIKE: . . 207 PAUPER WITCH OF GRAFTON 2
     I'LL TELL YOU WHO'D REMEMBER--HEMAN LAPISH. . . . . . 208 PAUPER WITCH OF GRAFTON 26
     THAT THEY COULD HEAR TELL OF WAS SCARIFIED. . . . . . 209 PAUPER WITCH OF GRAFTON 57
     AND WON'T TELL . . . . 211 AN EMPTY THREAT . . 15
     "I'LL TELL YOU WHAT YOU SHOW ME. YOU REMEMBER . . . . 213 A FOUNTAIN, A BOTTLE   7
     "TO SHUT YOU UP I'LL TELL YOU WHAT I'LL DO: . . . . . 213 A FOUNTAIN, A BOTTLE 17
     AND TELL ME WHETHER . . . . 217 I WILL SING YOU ONE-O   5
     AND TELL THE STONES: MEN HATE TO DIE . . . . 221 IN A DISUSED GRAVEYARD 14
     I DOUBT IF EVEN HIS MOTHER COULD TELL HIM, 'SAKES, . . 223 THE RUNAWAY 12
     MAN CAME TO TELL IT WHAT WAS WRONG: . . . . 224 THE AIM WAS SONG . .   5
     I CAN'T PRETEND TO TELL THE WAY IT'S DONE. . . . . . 237 A HILLSIDE THAW . .   5
     BY ALL I TELL; BUT SO'S THE MOON A WITCH. . . . . . . 237 A HILLSIDE THAW . . 19
     I WANT TO TELL THEM THAT WITH ALL THIS SMOKE . . . . 248 THE COCOON 12
     THAT ARE GONE BEFORE I CAN TELL WHAT THEY ARE. . . . 248 A PASSING GLIMPSE .   2
     YOU COULD NOT TELL, AND YET IT LOOKED AS IF . . . . . 250 ONCE BY THE PACIFIC   7
     THEY TELL ME THE COTTAGE WHERE WE DWELT, ... 253 THE THATCH 31
     TO TELL ONCE AND ONCE ONLY, FOR THEM NEVER TO FORGET, 257 THE LOVELY BE CHOOSERS 32
     BUT GIVE HER FRIENDS, FOR THEN SHE DARE NOT TELL . . 257 THE LOVELY BE CHOOSERS 35
     HER NEVER HAVING DEIGNED TO TELL THEM. . . . . 257 THE LOVELY BE CHOOSERS 38
     THAT'S WHAT I ALWAYS TELL MY WIFE . . . . 263 THE TIMES TABLE . . 11
     THE GATHERER CAN ALWAYS TELL . . . . 280 BLUE RIBBON AT AMESBURY 33
     "WHERE, WHERE IN HEAVEN AM I? BUT DON'T TELL ME! . . 295 LOST IN HEAVEN . . . 10
     I BADE MEN TELL ME WHICH IN BRIEF, ... 297 LEAVES COMPARED WITH   13
     WHY HURRY TO TELL BELSHAZZAR . . . . 314 BEARER OF EVIL TIDINGS 43
     AND I ALONE OF US HAVE LIVED TO TELL. . . . . 315 IRIS BY NIGHT . . . 22
     NAME NAMES AND TELL YOU WHO BY NAME IS WICKED? . . . 317 BUILD SOIL 43
     WERE I DICTATOR, I'LL TELL YOU WHAT I'D DO. . . . . . 320 BUILD SOIL 127
     IT'S HARD TO TELL WHICH IS THE WORSE ABHORRENCE, . . 321 BUILD SOIL 155
     BUT PREACH AND SEE IF I CAN TELL THE DIFFERENCE. . . 322 BUILD SOIL 184
     I CAN TELL BETTER AFTER I GET HOME, ... 325 BUILD SOIL 286
     I TRIED TO TELL HER "THERE'S NO SUCH THING!" . . . . 342 A CLOUD SHADOW . . .   4
     "YOU TELL ME AND I'LL TELL YOU. . . . . 345 DISCOVERY OF MADEIRAS 47
     AND LET THE CAPTAIN TELL HIM A TALE. . . . . 345 DISCOVERY OF MADEIRAS 51
     DON'T TELL ME IF YOU DON'T WANT TO, THEN." . . . . . 346 DISCOVERY OF MADEIRAS 95

TELL (CONTINUED)
```
BUT CARED NOT TELL HER ALL ONE DAY.               347 DISCOVERY OF MADEIRAS . 115
WERE REALLY AS DARK AS I HEAR SAGES TELL,         350 THE LESSON FOR TODAY  .   2
TELL ME AS PEDAGOGUE TO PEDAGOGUE,                351 THE LESSON FOR TODAY  .  21
BUT IN YOUR FAVOR--PLEASE TO TELL YOUR KING--     354 THE LESSON FOR TODAY  . 117
AND TELL HIM I HAD READ HIS EPITAPH.              354 THE LESSON FOR TODAY  . 126
AND NOW PRAY TELL WHAT LURED YOU WITH FALSE HOPE  356 A MOTH SEEN IN WINTER .   7
AND TELL ME TRULY, MEN OF EARTH,                  362 A QUESTION  . . . .      2
WILL TELL YOU IT'S THE STAR OF BETHLEHEM .        369 THE LITERATE FARMER AND 34
AND TELL THEM THE REST OF THE STORY IS DREAMING?  379 TOO ANXIOUS FOR RIVERS  19
"YOU CHILDREN MAY DREAM IT AND TELL IT TOMORROW." 379 TOO ANXIOUS FOR RIVERS  20
LUCRETIUS THE EPICUREAN MIGHT TELL US             380 TOO ANXIOUS FOR RIVERS  23
TO TELL YOU IT WAS JUST A TRAMP                   380 AN UNSTAMPED LETTER IN   6
WHOSE PART SHOULD BE TO TELL                       383 MAKING CERTAIN ANYTHING  3
THEY WILL TELL YOU MORE AS SOON AS                387 THE COURAGE TO BE NEW .  13
YOU TELL THEM WHAT TO DO                          387 THE COURAGE TO BE NEW .  14
WHEN ANY AMATEUR CAN TELL IT NOW?                 395 WHY WAIT FOR SCIENCE  .  10
TELL US WHAT ELEMENTS YOU BLEND.                  403 SOMETHING LIKE A STAR .  15
BUT DOES TELL SOMETHING IN THE END.               403 SOMETHING LIKE A STAR .  17
AND SEE IF WE CAN TELL THE BASS FROM THE SOPRANO. 415 A CABIN IN THE CLEARING  40
DON'T TRY TO TELL ME WHAT'S ON YOUR MIND,         420 ONE MORE BREVITY  . .    30
THEY MEAN TO TELL US ALL WAS ROLLING BLIND,       425 ACCIDENTALLY ON PURPOSE  5
THEY MEAN TO TELL US, THOUGH, THE OMNIBUS         425 ACCIDENTALLY ON PURPOSE 11
TELL ME WHY THE EAST                              435 KITTY HAWK  . . . .    238
UNDERTAKE TO TELL HER                             442 KITTY HAWK  . . . .    459
AND TELL YOUR CLIENTELE AT HOME                   450 OUR DOOM TO BLOOM  . .   6
I'M APT TO TELL THEM IN NEW YORK                  452 A-WISHING WELL  . . .   34
DON'T LET YOUR FATHER TELL YOU WHAT TO BE."       454 HOW HARD TO KEEP FROM   36
WHAT GOOD HE WAS HE BOLDLY SAID, "I'LL TELL YOU:  454 HOW HARD TO KEEP FROM   40
"BUT TELL US HOW YOU KNEW," DARIUS CRIED.         456 HOW HARD TO KEEP FROM   86
DARE TO SPEAK OUT AND TELL ME ABOUT MYSELF.       456 HOW HARD TO KEEP FROM  100
WHAT AILS ME? TELL ME. WHY AM I UNHAPPY?"         457 HOW HARD TO KEEP FROM  101
"BUT YES," SHE SAID, "SOME DAY I'LL TELL YOU, DEAR. 457 HOW HARD TO KEEP FROM 106
TELL ME SOME RULE FOR RULING PEOPLE WISELY,       458 HOW HARD TO KEEP FROM  147
WHERE HOMER BEGGED. HE'LL TELL YOU ABOUT FREEDOM. 459 HOW HARD TO KEEP FROM  183
FREEDOM IS SLAVERY SOME POETS TELL US.            460 HOW HARD TO KEEP FROM  190
TELL THEM IAMB, JEHOVAH SAID, AND MEANT IT.       460 HOW HARD TO KEEP FROM  218
TELL TISSAPHERNES NOT TO MIND THE GREEKS.         461 HOW HARD TO KEEP FROM  227
BUT DON'T TELL ME IT WASN'T HIS DISPLAY           462 HOW HARD TO KEEP FROM  273
TELL HIM HE MAY REMEMBER YOU: YOU'RE JOB.         474 A MASQUE OF REASON  .   33
THE LETUP'S HEAVENLY. YOU PERHAPS WILL TELL US    474 A MASQUE OF REASON  .   41
YOU HAVE THE IDEA. THERE'S NOT MUCH I CAN TELL YOU. 481 A MASQUE OF REASON  . 216
I'D TELL YOU, JOB---- / ALL RIGHT, DON'T TELL ME, THEN, 483 A MASQUE OF REASON . 270
PRAY TELL ME WHAT DOES THAT MEAN? ANYTHING?       484 A MASQUE OF REASON  .  304
I'M GOING TO TELL JOB WHY I TORTURED HIM,         484 A MASQUE OF REASON  .  325
I'M GOING TO TELL YOU SOMETHING, JONAS DOVE.      498 A MASQUE OF MERCY  .   131
I HAVE TO TELL YOU SOMETHING THAT WILL SPOIL      498 A MASQUE OF MERCY  .   143
A MISSION AS TO HAVE TO TELL NEW YORK .           503 A MASQUE OF MERCY  .   272
I AM YOUR CONVERT. TELL ME WHAT I THINK.          517 A MASQUE OF MERCY  .   621
YOU'LL TELL ME SOMETIME. ALL YOU SAY HAS GREATNESS. 517 A MASQUE OF MERCY  . 637
AND LET THAT TELL YOU WHAT YOU THINK, LIKE THAT?  519 A MASQUE OF MERCY  .   676
I WON'T PRESUME TO TELL BEL WHERE TO GO.          519 A MASQUE OF MERCY  .   685
```
TELLING
```
I SHALL BE TELLING THIS WITH A SIGH              105 THE ROAD NOT TAKEN  .   16
AND SHE NEVER SINS BY TELLING THE TALE            134 A GIRL'S GARDEN  . .    47
AND FOR MY TELLING HIM WHERE I'D BEEN             140 THE GUM-GATHERER  . .    9
"BECAUSE NO TELLING BUT IT MAY HAVE BEEN          183 MAPLE  . . . . .       112
I'M TELLING YOU. YOU HAVEN'T SAID A THING,        354 THE LESSON FOR TODAY  114
AND TELLING THEM HOW SINBAD WAS A SAILOR.         447 DOES NO ONE AT ALL EVER 42
FROM TELLING ME YOUR REASON, DON'T ASSUME         482 A MASQUE OF REASON  .  239
```
TELLS
```
OF CARES, AT NIGHT, TO SLEEP; BUT NOTHING TELLS ME 199 WILD GRAPES  . . .   102
AND ANYWAY THIS TELLS ME WHERE I AM."             214 A FOUNTAIN, A BOTTLE  .  46
HE TELLS HER AS MUCH OF BLOOD AND DIRT            346 DISCOVERY OF MADEIRAS .  88
```
TEMBLOR
```
YOU KNOW, THERE MAY HAVE BEEN A SMALL TEMBLOR.    507 A MASQUE OF MERCY  .   356
```
TEMPER
```
IT DIDN'T LOSE ITS TEMPER AT OUR DEMAND           349 OUR HOLD ON THE PLANET   2
PIKE SAID WITH TEMPER. AND DICK LONGED TO SAY,    404 FROM PLANE TO PLANE  .   8
ALL YOU CAN SEEM TO DO IS LOSE YOUR TEMPER        478 A MASQUE OF REASON  .  135
```
TEMPERAMENTAL
```
(THE COOK WAS TEMPERAMENTAL LIKE THE KING.)       455 HOW HARD TO KEEP FROM   57
(THE KING WAS TEMPERAMENTAL LIKE HIS COOK,        456 HOW HARD TO KEEP FROM   95
```
TEMPERATURE
```
THROUGH TEMPERATURE OF ABSOLUTE ZERO?             395 WHY WAIT FOR SCIENCE  .   8
```
TEMPEST
```
THE TREE THE TEMPEST WITH A CRASH OF WOOD         238 ON A TREE FALLEN ACROSS  1
```
TEMPLE
```
A TEMPLE OF THE HEAT.                              13 ROSE POGONIAS  . . .     8
I GUESS THEY THOUGHT I'D SPIKED HIM IN THE TEMPLE. 72 THE CODE  . . . .       92
OUT OF TEMPLE AND PALACE AND STORE.               310 THE VINDICTIVES  . .    13
AS DULCET AS A PAGAN TEMPLE GONG!                 488 A MASQUE OF REASON  .  419
```
TEMPLES
```
EVEN TO SAY THE GROVES WERE GOD'S FIRST TEMPLES   171 NEW HAMPSHIRE  . . .   392
```
TEMPT
```
YOU THINK YOU'D BEST TEMPT HER AT SUCH A TIME?"    79 THE GENERATIONS OF MEN 182
```
TEMPTATION
```
RIGHT'S RIGHT, AND THE TEMPTATION TO DO RIGHT     208 PAUPER WITCH OF GRAFTON 33
AND A TEMPTATION TO THE TEASE.                    326 TO A THINKER  . . .     24
```
TEMPTED
```
I DOUBT IF I WAS TEMPTED FOR A MOMENT             106 CHRISTMAS TREES  . .    16
I SHOULD BE TEMPTED TO FORGET,                    252 THE PEACEFUL SHEPHERD .   5
YOU SHOULD BE TEMPTED TO MAKE UP FOR IT           385 THE FEAR OF GOD  . .     9
I'M TEMPTED TO LET GO RESTRAINT,                  451 A-WISHING WELL  . . .   15
THE TEMPTER COMES TO ME AND I AM TEMPTED.         485 A MASQUE OF REASON  .  348
```
TEMPTER
```
THE TEMPTER COMES TO ME AND I AM TEMPTED.         485 A MASQUE OF REASON  .  348
```

TEMPTING
   YET OH! THE TEMPTING FLATNESS OF A BOOK, ... 216 A FOUNTAIN, A BOTTLE . 109
TEN
   YOU'LL HAVE TO PAY ME MORE THAN TEN A WEEK . . . . . . 48 A HUNDRED COLLARS . . 116
   WE USED TO LIVE--TEN MILES FROM ANYWHERE. . . . . . . 64 A SERVANT TO SERVANTS . 63
   THERE WERE TEN THOUSAND THOUSAND FRUIT TO TOUCH, ... 69 AFTER APPLE-PICKING . 30
   AND DUMPED THE RACKFUL ON HIM IN TEN LOTS. . . . . . 72 THE CODE 74
   AT TEN O'CLOCK OF A WINTER EVE. . . . . 102 GOOD HOURS 16
   MID-SUMMER IS TO SPRING AS ONE TO TEN. . . . . . . 120 THE OVEN BIRD . . . 5
   WITH HIS TEN CHILDREN UNDER TEN YEARS OLD. . . . . . 144 SNOW 52
   IN WOODS SOME TEN MILES FROM A RAILROAD STATION, ... 160 NEW HAMPSHIRE . . . 41
   TEN THOUSAND FEET INSTEAD OF ONLY FIVE-- . . . . . . 169 NEW HAMPSHIRE . . . 332
   FALLEN TO RUIN IN TEN THOUSAND YEARS . . . . 176 THE CENSUS-TAKER . . 52
   TEN MILLION SILVER LIZARDS OUT OF SNOW! . . . . . . 237 A HILLSIDE THAW . . . 3
   TEN MILLS . . . . 308 TEN MILLS . . . . . T
   AND LOOPED TEN TIMES BACK AND FORTH, ... 312 THE VINDICTIVES . . . 67
   WILL PUT TEN THOUSAND FARMERS OUT OF SHEEP. . . . . . 319 BUILD SOIL 110
   IT TAKES TEN YEARS OR SO TO CARRY OUT, ... 323 BUILD SOIL 226
   I SHOULD BETAKE ME BACK TEN THOUSAND PAGES . . . . . 350 THE LESSON FOR TODAY . 6
   OH, YEARS AGO--TEN THOUSAND YEARS. . . . . 392 A CLIFF DWELLING . 13
   AND TRIED TO LOOK TEN THOUSAND DOLLARS' WORTH. . . . . 454 HOW HARD TO KEEP FROM 38
TENACIOUS
   LIKE SOME TENACIOUS BIT . . . . 341 THE SUBVERTED FLOWER . 67
TEN-BY-TWENTY
   HE HAD A TEN-BY-TWENTY GARDEN PATCH. . . . . 292 FIGURE IN THE DOORWAY . 18
TEND
   TO PLANT AND TEND AND REAP HERSELF, ... 133 A GIRL'S GARDEN . . . 7
   TO PLAY----" / "YOU TEND YOUR HORSES AND COME BACK.-- . . 144 SNOW 42
   THEY CAN LEAVE IT TO SOMEONE ELSE TO TEND. . . . . . 291 ON HEART'S BEGINNING TO 18
   BUT IF THAT SEEMS TO TEND . . . . 389 ASTROMETAPHYSICAL . 17
   TWO PITCHING ON LIKE THIS TEND TO CONFUSE ME. . . . . 484 A MASQUE OF REASON . 323
TENDED
   WE TENDED TO HIS HAY. WE SAW HIM OUT . . . . . . 73 THE CODE 107
   AND HOW SHE TENDED BOTH, OR HAD THEM TENDED: . . . . 215 A FOUNTAIN, A BOTTLE . 82
   SHE NEVER TENDED ANYTHING HERSELF. . . . . 215 A FOUNTAIN, A BOTTLE . 83
TENDENCIES
   EVIL TENDENCIES CANCEL . . . . 308 EVIL TENDENCIES CANCEL T
TENDENCY
   HE'S ON THAT TENDENCY THAT LIKE THE GULF STREAM, . . . 489 A MASQUE OF REASON . 442
   OH, YES, THAT TENDENCY!--OH, DO COME OFF IT. . . . . 489 A MASQUE OF REASON . 447
   A TENDENCY. THE MINUTE YOU GET ON ONE . . . . . . 489 A MASQUE OF REASON . 449
   THE TENDENCY, A LONG, LONG NARROW STRIP . . . . . 489 A MASQUE OF REASON . 453
   THIS MODERN TENDENCY I FIND IN HIM . . . . 505 A MASQUE OF MERCY . 312
TENDER
   HOW HAD THE TENDER VERSE ESCAPED THEIR OUTRAGE? . . . 216 A FOUNTAIN, A BOTTLE . 105
   ON SOME WILD APPLE-TREE'S YOUNG TENDER BARK, ... 254 A WINTER EDEN . . . 11
TENDERER-THAN-THOU
   I HAVE NONE OF THE TENDERER-THAN-THOU . . . . . . 357 A CONSIDERABLE SPECK . 24
TENDER-HEADED
   WITH THE TENDER-HEADED FLOWER. . . . . 339 THE SUBVERTED FLOWER . 4
TENDERLY
   AND TENDERLY, LIFE'S LITTLE DREAM, ... 20 THE TRIAL BY EXISTENCE 38
   A BLUEBIRD COMES TENDERLY UP TO ALIGHT . . . . . . 275 TWO TRAMPS IN MUD TIME 25
   TENDERLY BE KEPT . . . . 432 KITTY HAWK 123
TENDERNESS
   AS IF SHE PLAYED UNHEARD SOME TENDERNESS . . . . . 38 DEATH OF THE HIRED MAN 109
TENDING
   "I WONDER WHERE YOUR ORACLE IS TENDING. . . . . . 79 THE GENERATIONS OF MEN 171
TENOR
   AND CHANGE THE TENOR OF RELIGIOUS THOUGHT. . . . . 475 A MASQUE OF REASON . 68
TEN-STEP
   AS IN THE GAME 'TEN-STEP' THE CHILDREN PLAY." . . . 114 IN THE HOME STRETCH . 118
TENT
   OF HERE AND THERE A TENT IN GROVE AND ORCHARD. . . . 73 THE GENERATIONS OF MEN 13
   I CAN JUST SEE MY TENT PEGGED, ... 211 AN EMPTY THREAT . . 7
   SHE IS AS IN A FIELD A SILKEN TENT . . . . 331 THE SILKEN TENT . . . 1
   THE SILKEN TENT . . . . 331 THE SILKEN TENT . . . T
   ENOUGH TO BUILD HIM EVERY NIGHT A PUP TENT . . . . 478 A MASQUE OF REASON . 132
TENTH
   ANOTHER COLOR OVER A TENTH THE SPACE . . . . . . 132 THE BONFIRE 82
   BEFORE I MADE THE TENTH ACROSS THE THRESHOLD. . . . 175 THE CENSUS-TAKER . . 33
TENTS
   THE WONDER WAS THE TENTS WEREN'T SNATCHED AWAY . . . 67 A SERVANT TO SERVANTS . 168
   HIS TENTS BLEW ALL TO PIECES, I PICKED UP . . . . 478 A MASQUE OF REASON . 131
TEREDO
   AND SHOWED THEM IT CONTAINED A LIVE TEREDO. . . . . 456 HOW HARD TO KEEP FROM 85
TERMS
   AND THE WORLD HAD FOUND NEW TERMS OF WORTH. . . . . 24 PAN WITH US 27
   LUCKILY TERMS ARE ALL AGREED UPON. . . . . 99 THE SELF-SEEKER . . 182
   WHICH COMES TO THE SAME THING IN DIFFERENT TERMS. . . 353 THE LESSON FOR TODAY . 76
   SO I SPOKE IN TERMS OF ADOPTION THUS: . . . . . . 420 ONE MORE BREVITY . 27
TERRACES
   GREAT GRANITE TERRACES IN SUN AND SHADOW, ... 42 THE MOUNTAIN 58
TERRAM
   AND VER ASPERGIT TERRAM FLORIBUS . . . . 351 THE LESSON FOR TODAY . 15
TERRIBLE
   "THEY MUST BE TERRIBLE--I MEAN, TO LOOK AT." . . . 93 THE SELF-SEEKER . . 17
   OH, IT WAS TERRIBLE AS WELL COULD BE. . . . . . 160 NEW HAMPSHIRE . . 59
   PAUL WAS WHAT'S CALLED A TERRIBLE POSSESSOR. . . . 195 PAUL'S WIFE 150
   WHEN HATE GAVE A TERRIBLE LAUGH, ... 311 THE VINDICTIVES . . . 22
TERRIBLY
   HAD TERRIBLY COMPLETED. . . . . 341 THE SUBVERTED FLOWER . 56
TERRIFIC
   IT NEEDN'T BE QUITE SO TERRIFIC . . . . 453 A-WISHING WELL . . . 65
TERRIFIED
   AND HER FACE CHANGED FROM TERRIFIED TO DULL. . . . 51 HOME BURIAL 9
TERROR
   HE HAD A SPECIAL TERROR OF THE FLUX . . . . . . 171 NEW HAMPSHIRE . . 374

TERROR (CONTINUED)
    IT RAN WITH TERROR AND WITH CUNNING CREPT. . . . . 357 A CONSIDERABLE SPECK . 19
    BY A GREAT EAGLE BIRD IN ALL ITS TERROR. . . . . 443 AUSPEX 4
TESSELLATION
    ACROSS THE TESSELLATION OF THE FLOOR, ... 399 THE INGENUITIES OF DEBT 14
TEST
    REMEMBER HE HAD MADE THE TEST . . . . 416 AMERICA IS HARD TO SEE   7
    TO BE A TEST. IT DIDN'T LAST HIM OUT. . . . . 459 HOW HARD TO KEEP FROM 178
    THE TEST IS ALWAYS HOW WE TREAT THE POOR. . . . . . 477 A MASQUE OF REASON . . 123
TESTAMENT
    THAT BOOK OF YOURS IN THE OLD TESTAMENT . . . . . . 508 A MASQUE OF MERCY . . 375
TESTIFIED
    IN BOOK ON BOOK HAVE TESTIFIED . . . . 418 AMERICA IS HARD TO SEE 63
TESTS
    I CAN'T HELP THINKING THOSE ARE TESTS TO GO BY. . . . 162 NEW HAMPSHIRE . . . 99
TEXT
    (AND WAS A TEXT ALBEIT DONE IN PLANT). . . . . . . 355 TIME OUT 4
TEXTURE
    TO MAKE ONE TEXTURE OF FADED BROWN . . . . 25 IN HARDWOOD GROVES . . 3
THAN (SEE TENDERER-THAN-THOU)
    HE ASKED WITH THE EYES MORE THAN THE LIPS . . . . . 7 LOVE AND A QUESTION . 5
    IS SADDER THAN ANY WORDS. . . . . 8 A LATE WALK 8
    THAN THE TREES AROUND WERE TALL; . . . . . . 13 ROSE POGONIAS . . . 4
    ANYTHING MORE THAN THE TRUTH WOULD HAVE SEEMED TOO WEAK . 17 MOWING 9
    SOUNDS NOBLER THERE THAN 'NEATH THE SUN; . . . . . 21 THE TRIAL BY EXISTENCE 46
    THAN THE MEREST AIMLESS BREATH OF AIR. . . . . . 24 PAN WITH US 25
    THAN NOW THESE NUMBERLESS YEARS THE ELVES, ... 26 A LINE-STORM SONG . . 11
    WAS IT EVER LESS THAN A TREASON . . . . . . 30 RELUCTANCE 20
    THAN WAS THE HOUND THAT CAME A STRANGER TO US . . . 38 DEATH OF THE HIRED MAN 116
    THAN ON HIS BROTHER? THIRTEEN LITTLE MILES . . . 38 DEATH OF THE HIRED MAN 125
    HE MAY BE BETTER THAN APPEARANCES. . . . . . 39 DEATH OF THE HIRED MAN 134
    ROLLED OUT A LITTLE FARTHER THAN THE REST." . . . . 44 THE MOUNTAIN 99
    WAS NO BIGGER THAN A----" WHAT, I DID NOT HEAR. . . 44 THE MOUNTAIN 106
    MORE THAN A HUNDRED COLLARS, SIZE FOURTEEN. . . 47 A HUNDRED COLLARS . . 66
    YOU'RE NOT MUCH FURTHERER THAN WHERE KIKE LEFT YOU. . 47 A HUNDRED COLLARS . . 70
    I'M THINKING I HAVE MORE TO LOSE THAN YOU . . . . 47 A HUNDRED COLLARS . . 82
    YOU'LL HAVE TO PAY ME MORE THAN TEN A WEEK . . . 48 A HUNDRED COLLARS . . 116
    I'VE SPOILED JEMIMA IN MORE WAYS THAN ONE. . . . 49 A HUNDRED COLLARS . . 141
    NOT SO MUCH LARGER THAN A BEDROOM, IS IT? . . . 51 HOME BURIAL 25
    SINCE SHE WENT, MORE THAN EVER, BUT BEFORE-- . . 56 THE BLACK COTTAGE . . 36
    NO LONGER THAN THAT?--AND THE FOLLOWING FALL . . 59 BLUEBERRIES 11
    AND LESS THAN THE TAN WITH WHICH PICKERS ARE TANNED." . 60 BLUEBERRIES 27
    "HE'S A THRIFTIER PERSON THAN SOME I COULD NAME." . . 60 BLUEBERRIES 47
    THAN I CAN RAISE MY VOICE OR WANT TO LIFT . . . . 63 A SERVANT TO SERVANTS . 8
    THAN IF I WASN'T IN THE ROOM AT ALL. . . . . . 65 A SERVANT TO SERVANTS . 80
    RATHER THAN SEND THEIR FOLKS TO SUCH A PLACE, . . . 65 A SERVANT TO SERVANTS . 95
    WORSE THAN NO GOOD TO THEM, AND THEY NO GOOD . . . 65 A SERVANT TO SERVANTS . 100
    AND THERE'S MORE TO IT THAN JUST WINDOW VIEWS . . . 67 A SERVANT TO SERVANTS . 155
    MORE THAN YOU HAVE YOURSELF, SOME OF THESE NIGHTS. . 67 A SERVANT TO SERVANTS . 167
    I SAID THAT MORE THAN HALF AN HOUR AGO. . . . . 70 THE CODE 13
    MORE THAN WAS NEEDED, SOMETHING MUST BE UP. . . . 72 THE CODE 87
    NO MORE THAN BROUGHT US BACK INTO THE NAME." . . . 75 THE GENERATIONS OF MEN 57
    LET PEOPLE IN THAN I CAN KEEP THEM OUT. . . . . 81 THE HOUSEKEEPER . . . 4
    HE KNOWS HE'S KINDER THAN THE RUN OF MEN. . . . 84 THE HOUSEKEEPER . . . 80
    BETTER THAN MARRIED OUGHT TO BE AS GOOD . . . . 84 THE HOUSEKEEPER . . . 81
    HE'D SAY, WHY SHOULD THEY?--NO MORE WORDS THAN THAT." . 84 THE HOUSEKEEPER . . . 91
    THAN FOLKS LIKE US HAVE ANY BUSINESS WITH. . . . 85 THE HOUSEKEEPER . . . 112
    SHE WON'T COME BACK--IT'S WORSE THAN THAT--SHE CAN'T." . 87 THE HOUSEKEEPER . . . 177
    THERE'S MORE IN IT THAN YOU'RE INCLINED TO SAY. . . 90 THE FEAR 30
    SOUNDS SOMETHING LIKE. BETTER THAN FARMER'S BEANS . . 97 THE SELF-SEEKER . . . 127
    AND IT WAS OLDER SURE THAN THIS YEAR'S CUTTING, . . 101 THE WOOD-PILE . . . 27
    WHERE THE SUN SHINES NOW NO WARMER THAN THE MOON. . . 106 CHRISTMAS TREES . . 19
    WORTH THREE CENTS MORE TO GIVE AWAY THAN SELL, . . . 107 CHRISTMAS TREES . . 56
    AS BETTER THAN THE SUN IN ANY CASE . . . . . 108 OLD MAN'S WINTER NIGHT 20
    MORE THAN SO MANY TIMES MAKE ME A LADY . . . . 111 IN THE HOME STRETCH . 23
    MORE THAN SOME WOMEN LIKE THE DISHPAN, JOE; . . . 111 IN THE HOME STRETCH . 31
    MORE THAN YOU LIKE TO OWN TO OUT THAT WINDOW." . . . 112 IN THE HOME STRETCH . 45
    IT WOULD TAKE MORE THAN THEM TO SICKEN YOU-- . . . 114 IN THE HOME STRETCH . 123
    ALTHOUGH YOU DO NO MORE THAN DUMP THEM DOWN." . . . 116 IN THE HOME STRETCH . 162
    THE FIGURE OF OUR BEING LESS THAN TWO . . . . . 118 MEETING AND PASSING . 7
    BUT MORE THAN ONE AS YET. YOUR PARASOL . . . . 119 MEETING AND PASSING . 8
    THAN WITH BROOKS TAKEN OTHERWHERE IN SONG. . . . 119 HYLA BROOK 14
    ONE COULD DO WORSE THAN BE A SWINGER OF BIRCHES. . . 122 BIRCHES 59
    TO MAKE NO MORE OF A WALL THAN AN OPEN GATE, . . . 124 THE COW IN APPLE TIME . 2
    AND THINK NO MORE OF WALL-BUILDERS THAN FOOLS. . . 124 THE COW IN APPLE TIME . 3
    OF SOMETHING MORE THAN TINDER-GRASS AND WEED-- . . 131 THE BONFIRE 77
    FURTHER O'ERHEAD THAN ALL BUT STARS AND ANGELS-- . . 132 THE BONFIRE 107
    NO MORE SO THAN BECAME A MAN-- . . . . . . 139 BROWN'S DESCENT . . 69
    BETTER THAN IF HE HAD HAD ME RIDE, ... 140 THE GUM-GATHERER . . 4
    THEY THROW A FOREST DOWN LESS CUT THAN BROKEN. . . 141 THE LINE-GANG . . . 2
    MORE THAN YOU WILL US WITH SUCH NIGHTMARE TALK. . . 149 SNOW 168
    MORE LIKE A TUNNEL THAN A HOLE--WAY DOWN . . . . 149 SNOW 193
    MORE THAN I SHALL OUT IN IT. BUT THE HORSES . . . 150 SNOW 209
    YOU'VE DONE MORE THAN YOU HAD A RIGHT TO THINK . . 150 SNOW 219
    THAN THE MAN FIGHTING IT TO KEEP ABOVE IT, . . . 151 SNOW 225
    IN NESTS. SHALL I BE COUNTED LESS THAN THEY ARE? . . 151 SNOW 227
    THAN WE HAD SEEING HIM PASS BY IN THE ROAD . . . 152 SNOW 253
    AND THEN TAKE OUR ADVICE NO MORE THAN NOTHING, . . 155 SNOW 347
    MORE THAN ANOTHER NOISE . . . . 156 THE SOUND OF TREES . 4
    AS FOR WHAT THEY WERE UP TO MORE THAN FISHING-- . . 161 NEW HAMPSHIRE . . . 87
    WERE METAL THAN IT WAS WHEN THEY WERE WOODEN? . . 163 NEW HAMPSHIRE . . . 133
    MORE THAN ENOUGH LAND FOR A SPECIMEN . . . . . 163 NEW HAMPSHIRE . . . 145
    I HAD TO TAKE BY FORCE RATHER THAN BUY. . . . . 163 NEW HAMPSHIRE . . . 151
    POEMS PRODUCED THAN ANY OTHER THING? . . . . . 164 NEW HAMPSHIRE . . . 171
    SO MUCH MORE BUSINESSLIKE THAN BUSINESSMEN. . . . 164 NEW HAMPSHIRE . . . 173
    NO LESS THAN ENGLAND, FRANCE, AND ITALY. . . . 166 NEW HAMPSHIRE . . . 245
    THAN THOSE I LEFT BEHIND. I THOUGHT THEY WEREN'T. . 167 NEW HAMPSHIRE . . . 256
    RATHER THAN BETTER. HOW ARE WE TO WRITE . . . . 167 NEW HAMPSHIRE . . . 267

	PAGE	TITLE	LINE
THAN (CONTINUED)			
ON NOTHING WORSE THAN TOO MUCH LUCK AND COMFORT.	167	NEW HAMPSHIRE	276
LOUDER THAN ACTIONS, AND SOMETIMES ACHIEVES IT.	171	NEW HAMPSHIRE	402
MORE PRACTICAL THAN PEGASUS THE HORSE.	173	A STAR IN A STONEBOAT	29
FILLED ME WITH NO LESS SORROW THAN THE HOUSES	176	THE CENSUS-TAKER	51
FEW FARMS CHANGED HANDS; SO RATHER THAN SPEND YEARS	177	THE STAR-SPLITTER	28
THAN FOR HIMSELF, SO PLACED HE COULDN'T HOPE	187	THE AX-HELVE	59
THAN THE GRINDSTONE CAN BOAST TO STAND OR GO.	189	THE GRINDSTONE	13
THAN GRINDING DISCORD OUT OF A GRINDSTONE.	190	THE GRINDSTONE	54
MORE THAN A MILE ACROSS THE WILDERNESS	195	PAUL'S WIFE	132
ONE OF THEM FIVE YEARS YOUNGER THAN I LOOK--	196	WILD GRAPES	18
WHEN WILDER MOTHERS THAN OUR WILDEST NOW	197	WILD GRAPES	50
WHO MARRIED HER FOR PLAYMATE MORE THAN HELPMATE,	200	PLACE FOR A THIRD	34
RATHER THAN TIP A TABLE FOR YOU, LET ME	202	THE WITCH OF COOS	12
THE ATTIC WAS LESS TO US THAN THE CELLAR.	206	THE WITCH OF COOS	123
THAN LIFE'S VICTORIES OF DOUBT	212	AN EMPTY THREAT	55
THE WAR SEEMED OVER MORE FOR YOU THAN ME,	222	TO E.T.	15
BUT NOW FOR ME THAN YOU--THE OTHER WAY.	222	TO E.T.	16
DEEPER DOWN IN THE WELL THAN WHERE THE WATER	225	FOR ONCE SOMETHING	3
THAN FLOWERS WILL SHOW FOR DAYS UNLESS THEY HURRY.	225	BLUE-BUTTERFLY DAY	4
MORE THAN IF LIFE HAD NEVER BEEN BEGUN.	226	THE ONSET	11
DREAD FIFTY ABOVE MORE THAN FIFTY BELOW."	228	GOOD-BY AND KEEP COLD	19
LESS CAREFULLY NURTURED, LESS FRUITFUL THAN THESE,	228	GOOD-BY AND KEEP COLD	22
SHE DARED NO MORE THAN ASK HIM WITH HER EYES	231	NOT TO KEEP	19
NO BETTER THAN SPOONS,	234	GATHERING LEAVES	2
THAT DROPS THEM NO FURTHER THAN WHERE THEY WERE.	236	MISGIVING	12
IN SPRING MORE MORTAL SINGERS THAN BELONG	239	OUR SINGING STRENGTH	19
LESS THAN THE CORALROOT, YOU KNOW,	247	ON GOING UNNOTICED	5
GREATER THAN BEING SHORE TO THE OCEAN--	247	DEVOTION	2
THERE WOULD BE MORE THAN OCEAN-WATER BROKEN	250	ONCE BY THE PACIFIC	13
ONE LEVEL HIGHER THAN THE EARTH BELOW,	254	A WINTER EDEN	6
BLOOD HAS BEEN HARDER TO DAM BACK THAN WATER.	254	THE FLOOD	1
SEEM TO THEM LESS THAN THEY ARE.	257	THE LOVELY BE CHOOSERS	40
FURTHER THAN TARGET EVER SHOWED OR SHONE.	262	A SOLDIER	14
MORE THAN HALFWAY UP THE PASS	263	THE TIMES TABLE	1
THAN THERE WAS EVER ANY HOPE,	264	THE BIRTHPLACE	2
I CATCH NO MORE THAN A RAY	266	SITTING BY A BUSH	2
AND LOOK ELSEWHERE THAN TO STARS AND MOON AND SUN	268	ON LOOKING UP BY CHANCE	9
HE COMES OUT MORE UNERRING THAN A BULLET.	277	THE WHITE-TAILED HORNET	6
BUT LITTLE LOWER THAN THE GODS AND ANGELS.	279	THE WHITE-TAILED HORNET	62
DEARER TO HIM THAN ANY BARNYARD BRUTE,	283	THE GOLD HESPERIDEE	2
AND MORE THAN ONE, TO THEIRS AKIN,	292	ON HEART'S BEGINNING TO	39
ALL SUMMER LONG THEY WERE OVERHEAD, MORE LIFTED UP THAN I.	297	A LEAF-TREADER	5
THERE IS SELDOM MORE THAN A MAN TO A HARROWED PIECE.	299	STRONG SAYING NOTHING	5
THOUGH THERE'S MORE THAN A DOUBT IF THE WEATHER IS NOT TOO			
COLD	300	STRONG SAYING NOTHING	11
IT VENTURED LESS IN PERIL THAN IT APPEARS.	302	A BIRD SINGING IN SLEEP	8
COLDER THAN THE SEASON WARRANTS.	304	CLEAR AND COLDER	14
BUT WE CAN'T HELP FEELING MORE THAN A LITTLE BETRAYED	305	THERE ARE ROUGHLY ZONES	15
THAN WHEN ITS WALLS ROSE HIGHER THAN ANY ROOF.	306	NOT QUITE SOCIAL	8
THAN NONE AT ALL. PROVIDE, PROVIDE!	307	PROVIDE, PROVIDE	21
THAN IS? / WHAT SHOULD YOU MEAN BY SOCIALIZED?	319	BUILD SOIL	93
THAN HAS THE UNIVERSE'S. WE ARE BALLS,	322	BUILD SOIL	199
THAN AN IMPOVERISHED SOIL, PALE AND METALLIC?	323	BUILD SOIL	218
IN LESS THAN NO TIME, TONGUE AND PEN,	326	TO A THINKER	19
THAN IN THE FUTURE ALWAYS,	336	CARPE DIEM	21
THAN IN THE PAST. THE PRESENT	336	CARPE DIEM	23
AND THERE IS ALWAYS MORE THAN SHOULD BE SAID.	337	THE WIND AND THE RAIN	40
OTHER THAN BASE AND FETID:	340	THE SUBVERTED FLOWER	52
THEIR LITTLE STORMY SHIP, THAN ON.	344	DISCOVERY OF MADEIRAS	20
SHE WAS OUR LAND MORE THAN A HUNDRED YEARS	348	THE GIFT OUTRIGHT	2
AND GIVE US MORE THAN OUR SPOKESMAN BARGAINED FOR;	349	OUR HOLD ON THE PLANET	4
OFTENER THAN AS CONFLICTING GOOD AND ILL;	350	TO A YOUNG WRETCH	16
BEING ALREADY MORE THAN PROVED IN FIGHT,	353	THE LESSON FOR TODAY	91
YOU MUST BE MADE MORE SIMPLY WISE THAN I	356	A MOTH SEEN IN WINTER	19
ARE MORE DIVINE THAN ANY BULB OR ARC,	370	THE LITERATE FARMER AND	77
THE BLOW CAN BE NO STRONGER THAN THE CLUTCH,	371	THE LITERATE FARMER AND	116
BUT BEDS--IN LESS THAN FIFTY YEARS HE'S SURE	372	THE LITERATE FARMER AND	129
WHO HAVE NO OTHER OBJECT THAN OUR GOOD.	372	THE LITERATE FARMER AND	135
(LESS BRAVE PERHAPS THAN TRUSTING ARE THE FAIR.)	375	A YOUNG BIRCH	10
AT FIRST TO BE NO BIGGER THAN A CANE,	375	A YOUNG BIRCH	14
AND THEN NO BIGGER THAN A FISHING POLE,	375	A YOUNG BIRCH	15
NOW LEFT'S NO BIGGER THAN A HARNESS GALL.	378	DIRECTIVE	40
AND MADE FEEL LESS ALONE THAN I RIGHTLY SHOULD,	383	A YOUNG BIRCH	8
THAN AS WATCHER OF THE VOID,	383	MAKING CERTAIN ANYTHING	2
WHOSE MERCY TO YOU RATHER THAN TO OTHERS,	385	THE FEAR OF GOD	5
NEITHER OF THEM WAS BETTER THAN THE OTHER.	404	FROM PLANE TO PLANE	1
MORE THAN THEY KNOW WHAT COURAGE IS THAT CLAIM	405	FROM PLANE TO PLANE	34
YOU COULD DO WORSE THAN BOOST ME UP TO SEE."	406	FROM PLANE TO PLANE	84
FROM KNOWING MORE THAN I KNOW HOW TO THINK WITH.	407	FROM PLANE TO PLANE	99
NEARER IN PLIGHT THEIR NEIGHBORS ARE THAN DISTANCE.	414	A CABIN IN THE CLEARING	9
BUT LIFTS NO HIGHER THAN A GARDEN GROWS.	414	A CABIN IN THE CLEARING	17
I AM NO FURTHER FROM THEIR FATE THAN YOU ARE.	414	A CABIN IN THE CLEARING	19
THAN SMOKE AND MIST WHO BETTER COULD APPRAISE	415	A CABIN IN THE CLEARING	41
THAT BETTER THAN DA GAMA'S GOLD	417	AMERICA IS HARD TO SEE	27
A MORE THAN MOSES' EXODUS.	417	AMERICA IS HARD TO SEE	36
HE GOT NO MORE THAN DUNGEON CHAINS	417	AMERICA IS HARD TO SEE	44
LESS PARTIAL WITNESSES THAN HE	418	AMERICA IS HARD TO SEE	62
BETTER THAN ALL THE STALEMATE AN'S AND IFS.	423	FOR JOHN F. KENNEDY	59
SHE WAS OUR LAND MORE THAN A HUNDRED YEARS	424	THE GIFT OUTRIGHT	2
WHICH IS NO MORE THAN GOOD OLD PANTHEISM.	427	CONCEPT SELF-CONCEIVED	4
FASTER THAN MY TREAD--	428	KITTY HAWK	18
THAN TO ROB THE GRAVE.	430	KITTY HAWK	77
MORE THAN THAT MY THEME	431	KITTY HAWK	86
MORE THAN YOU CAN SING.	437	KITTY HAWK	280
THAN A BOLT OF LEVIN,	441	KITTY HAWK	409
ANY MORE THAN WE HAD TO TO HATE,	444	THE DRAFT HORSE	16
UNLESS 'TWOULD RATHER WILT THAN FADE."	450	OUR DOOM TO BLOOM	16

THAN (CONTINUED)
 THERE IS NO ACT MORE KINGLY THAN TO GIVE?" . . . . . 458 HOW HARD TO KEEP FROM 140
 I CLAIM TO BE NO BETTER THAN I AM. . . . . 460 HOW HARD TO KEEP FROM 210
 OF MORE THAN ROYAL ATTRIBUTES BETRAYED HIM. . . . . 462 HOW HARD TO KEEP FROM 274
 (OR MORE THAN HALF I'M HALF INCLINED TO SAY)." . . . 462 HOW HARD TO KEEP FROM 278
 THAN WHICH THERE IS NO INDIGNITY WORSE. . . . . . 463 LINES IN DEJECTION . 13
 AT LESS THAN THE SPEED OF SOUND . . . . 466 SOME SCIENCE FICTION . 18
 I WAS NO WORSE OFF THAN I WAS AT FIRST. . . . . . 468 IN A GLASS OF CIDER . 6
 THAN POPULOUS. . . . . 469 BUT OUTER SPACE... . 6
 A WITCH WAS STRONGER THAN A PROPHET THERE. . . . . 477 A MASQUE OF REASON . 101
 THAN THE DAY SHE WAS BORN / THAT'S ABOUT RIGHT, . . 479 A MASQUE OF REASON . 158
 THAN ALL THE JUSTIFYING EX-POST-FACTO . . . . . . 482 A MASQUE OF REASON . 248
 THAN ON THE SURFACE. IF THERE EVER WAS, ... 483 A MASQUE OF REASON . 283
 THAN I COULD UNDERSTAND AND WHAT I GET . . . . . . 485 A MASQUE OF REASON . 332
 IS ALMOST LESS THAN I CAN UNDERSTAND. . . . . . . 485 A MASQUE OF REASON . 333
 YOU WERE MORE GUILTY OF MISCHIEF THAN YOU ARE. . . . 488 A MASQUE OF REASON . 412
 THAN ANYTHING. / HE'S VERY REAL TO ME . . . . . . 489 A MASQUE OF REASON . 434
 MORE THAN IT TOUCHES ME. / YOU MAY COME IN. . . . . 493 A MASQUE OF MERCY . 17
 WHERE HE WAS HOARDING MORE THAN THEY ENJOYED. . . . 503 A MASQUE OF MERCY . 254
 THAN FOUND IN CHURCH. / THAT DOESN'T HELP ME MUCH. . 513 A MASQUE OF MERCY . 515
 THAN BY THE FEAR OF THE ASYLUM, JAIL, OR POORHOUSE, . 520 A MASQUE OF MERCY . 703
THANK
 MAYN'T I OFFER YOU----?" / "NO, NO, NO, THANK YOU." . 50 A HUNDRED COLLARS . 157
 TO DISOBEY YOU. MUCH HIS WIFE'LL THANK YOU." . . . 153 SNOW 284
 SHE DIDN'T THANK ME?" / "WHEN I TOLD HER 'GONE,' . . 153 SNOW 288
 AND HE'D THANK PEOPLE NOT TO THINK OF HER. . . . . 196 PAUL'S WIFE 154
 TOO LATE THOUGH, NOW, HE HAD HIMSELF TO THANK. . . . 270 THE EGG AND THE MACHINE 9
 THANK GOD OUR PRACTICE HOLDS THE LOVES APART, . . . 318 BUILD SOIL 81
 THE SLAVE WILL NEVER THANK HIS MANUMITTER; . . . . 371 THE LITERATE FARMER AND 90
 (FOR WHICH ASSURANCE MAMMON IS TO THANK). . . . . 386 THE FEAR OF MAN . . 10
 TO THANK HIM FOR. HE DOESN'T WANT OUR THANKS. . . . 408 FROM PLANE TO PLANE . 129
 TO THANK YOU SOMEDAY FOR THE WAY YOU HELPED ME . . . 475 A MASQUE OF REASON . 48
THANKED
 AND ZEAL WOULD NOT BE THANKED THAT CUT IT DOWN . . . 375 A YOUNG BIRCH . . . 19
THANKLESS
 AND GIVE GOOD MEASURE TO THE DEAD, THOUGH THANKLESS. . 200 PLACE FOR A THIRD . . 20
THANKS
 YES. THANKS FOR CARING.--DON'T MIND WILL: HE'S SAVAGE. 100 THE SELF-SEEKER . . . 224
 THANKS TO A CLEARING RAIN. . . . . 301 VOICE WAYS . . . 3
 TO WHATSOEVER GOD WE OWE THE THANKS. . . . . . . 358 THE LOST FOLLOWER . 6
 TO WORK WITH, BILL. BUT YOU WON'T HAVE MY THANKS. . . 408 FROM PLANE TO PLANE . 123
 TO THANK HIM FOR. HE DOESN'T WANT OUR THANKS. . . . 408 FROM PLANE TO PLANE . 129
 THE THANKS AND LET HIM CATCH IT AS A SCAPEGOAT. . . . 408 FROM PLANE TO PLANE . 140
 UNTO YOU THE THANKS . . . . 443 KITTY HAWK . . . 465
 THANKS TO YOU AND THANKS . . . . 443 KITTY HAWK . . . 467
 MY THANKS ARE TO YOU FOR RELEASING ME . . . . . . 475 A MASQUE OF REASON . 69
THAT---NOT INDEXED
THATCH
 SMOOTH-LAID LIKE THATCH WITH THE HEAVY DEW, ... 8 A LATE WALK . . . 3
 THE THATCH . . . . 252 THE THATCH . . . . T
 BUT THE STRANGEST THING: IN THE THICK OLD THATCH, . . 253 THE THATCH 13
 ITS WIND-TORN THATCH GOES NOW UNMENDED; . . . . . 253 THE THATCH 32
THAT'D---NOT INDEXED
THAT'S---NOT INDEXED
THAW
 UNTIL THE JANUARY THAW . . . . 139 BROWN'S DESCENT . . 58
 A HILLSIDE THAW . . . . 237 A HILLSIDE THAW . . . T
THAWING
 TO THE THAWING WIND . . . . 11 TO THE THAWING WIND . T
THE---NOT INDEXED
THEATER
 TO LIVE IN VILLAGES, NEXT TO THE THEATER AND STORE, . . 286 A ROADSIDE STAND . . 25
THEE
 THAT FRIGHTED THEE SO OFT, IS FLED OR DEAD: . . . . 28 MY BUTTERFLY 3
 (NOR IS IT SAD TO THEE!)-- . . . . 28 MY BUTTERFLY 5
 THERE IS NONE LEFT TO MOURN THEE IN THE FIELDS. . . . 28 MY BUTTERFLY 7
 SINCE FIRST I SAW THEE GLANCE, ... 28 MY BUTTERFLY 12
 AND I WAS GLAD FOR THEE, ... 28 MY BUTTERFLY 20
 THAT FATE HAD MADE THEE FOR THE PLEASURE OF THE WIND, . 29 MY BUTTERFLY 23
 IT SEEMED GOD LET THEE FLUTTER FROM HIS GENTLE CLASP, . 29 MY BUTTERFLY 27
 THEN FEARFUL HE HAD LET THEE WIN . . . . 29 MY BUTTERFLY 28
 SNATCHED THEE, O'EREAGER, WITH UNGENTLE GRASP. . . . 29 MY BUTTERFLY 30
 FORGIVE, O LORD, MY LITTLE JOKES ON THEE . . . . . 428 FORGIVE, O LORD... . 1
THEFT
 SO SMELLING THEIR SWEETNESS WOULD BE NO THEFT. . . . 305 UNHARVESTED 14
 AND PERSISTING IN THEFT . . . . 449 THE BAD ISLAND--EASTER 64
THEIR---NOT INDEXED
THEIRS---NOT INDEXED
THEM---NOT INDEXED
THEME
 HERE FIRST MY THEME BECOMES EMBARRASSING. . . . . 166 NEW HAMPSHIRE . . 217
 OUR AGE-LONG THEME, FOR THE UNCERTAINTY . . . . . 317 BUILD SOIL 37
 THE AGE-LONG THEME IS AGE'S. . . . . 335 CARPE DIEM . . . 11
 THE THEME OF WANTON WASTE IN PEACE AND WAR . . . . 411 POD OF THE MILKWEED . 6
 ON WHAT SHOULD BE THEIR DAYLONG THEME CONTINUED. . . 415 A CABIN IN THE CLEARING 35
 MORE THAN THAT MY THEME . . . . 431 KITTY HAWK . . . 86
 PAUL'S CONSTANT THEME. THE SERMON ON THE MOUNT . . . 511 A MASQUE OF MERCY . 482
THEM'S (SEE ONE-OF-THEM'S)
THEMSELVES
 THE BIRDS HAVE LESS TO SAY FOR THEMSELVES . . . . 26 A LINE-STORM SONG . . 9
 BLOWN OVER AND OVER THEMSELVES IN IDLENESS . . . . 58 THE BLACK COTTAGE . 121
 AND PROUD, TOO, OF THEMSELVES FOR DOING SO. . . . . 65 A SERVANT TO SERVANTS 75
 AFTER A RAIN. THEY CLICK UPON THEMSELVES . . . . . 121 BIRCHES 7
 SO LOW FOR LONG, THEY NEVER RIGHT THEMSELVES: . . . 121 BIRCHES 16
 AND LIFT THEMSELVES UP OFF THE GROUND. . . . . . 123 PEA BRUSH 20
 BUT WITH EACH OTHER AND THEMSELVES . . . . 127 LONELINESS 11
 BEFORE, THAT IS, THEY ARE THEMSELVES ACCEPTED, . . . 162 NEW HAMPSHIRE . . . 97

THEMSELVES (CONTINUED)
    I FOUND NO PEOPLE THAT DARED SHOW THEMSELVES, ... 174 THE CENSUS-TAKER . . 15
    TO JUDGE THEM BY THE WAY THEY CAUGHT THEMSELVES . . . . 193 PAUL'S WIFE 65
    THEY SPOKE TO THEMSELVES . . . . 218 I WILL SING YOU ONE-O . 29
    THE LEAVES HAD PROMISED THEMSELVES THIS FLIGHT, ... 236 MISGIVING 6
    HORDES SPENT THEMSELVES TO MAKE IT WET AND COLD, ... 239 OUR SINGING STRENGTH . 3
    THEY HAD JUST GIVEN THEMSELVES A LITTLE TWIST . . . . . 283 THE GOLD HESPERIDEE . 7
    WHERE THEY WON'T HAVE TO THINK FOR THEMSELVES ANYMORE; . . 287 A ROADSIDE STAND . . 26
    TO ANSWER FOR THEMSELVES: WHO SAID IT MATTERED . . . . 294 AT WOODWARD'S GARDENS . 33
    THEY CUT THEMSELVES IN STONE FOR PERMANENT . . . . . . 399 THE INGENUITIES OF DEBT 2
    TO MAKE THEMSELVES GLAD . . . . 432 KITTY HAWK 132
    OF THEMSELVES AS A RACE . . . . 448 THE BAD ISLAND--EASTER 22
    THEY SAVED THEMSELVES BY HANGING ON . . . . 452 A-WISHING WELL . . . 48
    WHEN LEFT TO GUESS FOREVER FOR THEMSELVES. . . . . . . 483 A MASQUE OF REASON . . 276
    YET YOU DON'T SPEAK. LET FOOLS BEMUSE THEMSELVES . . . . 484 A MASQUE OF REASON . . 298
    OR OF HOW RAYS RETURN UPON THEMSELVES, ... 485 A MASQUE OF REASON . . 343
THEN---NOT INDEXED
THENCE
    THENCE THEY WERE SPRUNG, SO NUMEROLS A TRIBE . . . . . . 73 THE GENERATIONS OF MEN 10
THEN'S---NOT INDEXED
THEODOSIA
    THEODOSIA BURR . . . . 432 KITTY HAWK 148
THEOLOGISTS
    EXCUSES TRUMPED UP BY YOU FOR THEOLOGISTS. . . . . . . 482 A MASQUE OF REASON . . 249
THEOLOGIZED
    HE IS THE FELLOW WHO THEOLOGIZED . . . . 498 A MASQUE OF MERCY . 128
THEORY
    BUT THE THEORY NOW GOES . . . . 246 THE ROSE FAMILY . . . 3
    WON'T ALMOST ANY THEORY BEAR REVISION? . . . . 279 THE WHITE-TAILED HORNET 51
    A THEORY IF YOU HOLD IT HARD ENOUGH . . . . 394 ETHEREALIZING . . . 1
    I HAVE A THEORY, BUT IT HARDLY DOES. . . . . 395 WHY WAIT FOR SCIENCE . 14
    THAT RATHER HURT HIS THEORY OF THE DROUGHT . . . . . . 400 THE BROKEN DROUGHT . 4
THERAPY
    OF THERAPY. / I DON'T LOVE PAUL--AS YET. . . . . 499 A MASQUE OF MERCY . 163
THERE---NOT INDEXED
THEREAFTER
    THEREAFTER I SAT ME AGAINST A TREE. . . . . 25 THE DEMIURGE'S LAUGH . 18
THERE'D---NOT INDEXED
THEREFORE
    WILL THEREFORE PLAN TO GO HALFWAY AND STOP. . . . . . . 363 A SEMI-REVOLUTION . . 6
THEREFROM
    AND BROKEN IT, AND USED THEREFROM . . . . 21 THE TRIAL BY EXISTENCE 62
THEREIN
    WHO ADVISED MAN TO COME AND LIVE THEREIN? . . . . . . 400 THE BROKEN DROUGHT . 14
THERE'S---NOT INDEXED
THESE---NOT INDEXED
THEY---NOT INDEXED
THEY'D---NOT INDEXED
THEY'LL---NOT INDEXED
THEY'RE---NOT INDEXED
THEY'VE---NOT INDEXED
THICK
    AND PRESTO, THEY'RE UP ALL AROUND YOU AS THICK . . . . . 59 BLUEBERRIES 20
    THICK END TO THIN END AND THIN END TO THICK END, ... 164 NEW HAMPSHIRE . . . 179
    ONE THICK WHERE ONE IS THIN AND VICE VERSA. . . . . . . 164 NEW HAMPSHIRE . . . 182
    WITH A THICK THUMBNAIL TO SHOW HOW IT RAN . . . . . . 186 THE AX-HELVE . . . 23
    THICK HAND MADE LIGHT OF, STEEL-BLUE CHIN DRAWN DOWN . . 188 THE AX-HELVE . . . 99
    BUT THE STRANGEST THING: IN THE THICK OLD THATCH, ... 253 THE THATCH 13
    IN THE THICK OF A TEEMING SNOWFALL . . . . 303 AFTERFLAKES 1
    AND THE THICK FLAKES FLOATING AT A PAUSE . . . . 303 AFTERFLAKES 13
    HE PEERS OUT SHREWEDLY INTO THE THICK AND SWIFT. . . . . 341 WILLFUL HOMING . . . 8
THICKEN
    MOISTURE AND COLOR AND ODOR THICKEN HERE. . . . . . . 246 ATMOSPHERE 5
THICKET
    OR THICKET, OR HOLLOW PLACE FOR THE NIGHT. . . . . . . 236 MISGIVING 8
THICK-SKINS
    SO THE THICK-SKINS NEEDN'T ACT THIN-SKINNED . . . . . . 295 A RECORD STRIDE . . . 31
THIEF
    OUR THIEF, THE ONE WHO DOES OUR STEALING FROM US, ... 178 THE STAR-SPLITTER . . 48
    BUT NEITHER ONE WAS THE THIEF . . . . 299 WELCOME TO THEIR BELIEF 15
    IN BEING A THIEF . . . . 449 THE BAD ISLAND--EASTER 63
THIEVES
    LIKE TWO KINDS OF JEWELS, A VISION FOR THIEVES." . . . . 62 BLUEBERRIES 105
    THE FLOWERS WERE OUT THERE WITH THE THIEVES. . . . . . 135 LOCKED OUT 6
THIMBLE
    INTO A LADY'S FINGER RING OR THIMBLE." . . . . 447 DOES NO ONE AT ALL EVER 30
THIN
    THROUGH THE THIN FROST, ALMOST IN SEPARATE STARS, ... 108 OLD MAN'S WINTER NIGHT 2
    THICK END TO THIN END AND THIN END TO THICK END, ... 164 NEW HAMPSHIRE . . . 179
    ONE THICK WHERE ONE IS THIN AND VICE VERSA. . . . . . . 164 NEW HAMPSHIRE . . . 182
    THE SHADOW OF THE APPLE TREE IS THIN . . . . 189 THE GRINDSTONE . . . 9
    WEARING A THIN HEADDRESS OF POINTED LEAVES, ... 196 WILD GRAPES 21
    AS IN THOSE BUOYANT BIRD BONES THIN AS PAPER, ... 387 INNATE HELIUM . . . 4
THINE
    THINE EMULOUS FOND FLOWERS ARE DEAD, TOO, ... 28 MY BUTTERFLY 1
THING (SEE FUR-THING, MUFF-THING)
    SETTING THE THING THAT IS SUPREME. . . . . 20 THE TRIAL BY EXISTENCE 40
    THE WORK OF HUNTERS IS ANOTHER THING: . . . . 33 MENDING WALL 5
    TO THINK OF THE RIGHT THING TO SAY TOO LATE. . . . . . 37 DEATH OF THE HIRED MAN 77
    HE NEVER DID A THING SO VERY BAD. . . . . 39 DEATH OF THE HIRED MAN 142
    THAT THING TAKES ALL THE ROOM!" HE MOVED HIS GOAD. . . . 41 THE MOUNTAIN 27
    RIGHT ON THE TOP, TIP-TOP--A CURIOUS THING. . . . . . . 42 THE MOUNTAIN 47
    BUT ALL THE FUN'S IN HOW YOU SAY A THING." . . . . . . 44 THE MOUNTAIN 104
    WHAT WAS IT BROUGHT YOU UP TO THINK IT THE THING . . . . 53 HOME BURIAL 63
    BUT THE THING OF IT IS, I NEED TO BE KEPT. . . . . . . 68 A SERVANT TO SERVANTS 172
    NEVER YOU SAY A THING LIKE THAT TO A MAN, ... 71 THE CODE 68
    HAS BEEN TO KEEP THE THING FROM BREAKING UP. . . . . . 84 THE HOUSEKEEPER . . . 88

THING (CONTINUED)

	PAGE TITLE	LINE
ONE THING YOU CAN'T HELP LIKING ABOUT JOHN,	85 THE HOUSEKEEPER	115
I CAN'T, AND LEAVE A THING LIKE THAT UNSETTLED.	89 THE FEAR	15
"YOU DON'T MEAN YOU WILL SIGN THAT THING UNREAD?"	99 THE SELF-SEEKER	187
"YOU'RE DOING THE WISE THING: YOU WON'T REGRET IT.	100 THE SELF-SEEKER	219
THAT WAS A THING WE COULD NOT WAIT TO LEARN.	109 THE EXPOSED NEST	26
THE FIRST THING IN THE MORNING, OUT WE GO	117 IN THE HOME STRETCH	195
IS WHAT TO MAKE OF A DIMINISHED THING.	120 THE OVEN BIRD	14
TOO GLAD FOR THE ONE THING	126 LONELINESS	8
A CHILDLIKE THING.	133 A GIRL'S GARDEN	4
WHEN IT'S JUST THAT I HOLD WITH GETTING A THING DONE WITH."	142 THE VANISHING RED	8
FROM THE LAST THING HE SAID HIMSELF, STONE DEAF	145 SNOW	65
"ONE THING: HE DIDN'T DRAG GOD INTO IT."	146 SNOW	81
A THING AS THAT. IT COULDN'T REACH THE LAMP	148 SNOW	139
MAY BE THE THING YOU HAVEN'T, YET YOU GIVE IT.	148 SNOW	148
SOME PALLID THING HAD SQUASHED ITS FEATURES FLAT	148 SNOW	160
IF HE HAD STAYED. THE LEAST THING SET HIM GOING.	152 SNOW	259
"SHE KNEW HE HAD, POOR THING, TWO HOURS AGO."	153 SNOW	278
THEIR NUMBER'S--TWENTY-ONE?--THE THING WON'T WORK.	153 SNOW	294
THE STUBBORN THING, THE WAY IT JARS YOUR ARM!--	153 SNOW	296
"THERE'S ONLY ONE THING POSSIBLE TO MAKE,	155 SNOW	322
A THING TO SELL." I DON'T SUPPOSE THE WORK	159 NEW HAMPSHIRE	4
A THING THE LEAST BIT DOUBTFULLY PERSCENTED	163 NEW HAMPSHIRE	142
POEMS PRODUCED THAN ANY OTHER THING?	164 NEW HAMPSHIRE	171
THE ONE THING PALPABLE BESIDES THE SOUL	172 A STAR IN A STONEBOAT	11
HE DID NOT SEE HOW LIKE A FLYING THING	172 A STAR IN A STONEBOAT	13
"THE BEST THING THAT WE'RE PUT HERE FOR'S TO SEE;	177 THE STAR-SPLITTER	33
THE STRONGEST THING THAT'S GIVEN US TO SEE WITH'S	177 THE STAR-SPLITTER	34
BUT THE FIRST THING NEXT MORNING WE REFLECTED	177 THE STAR-SPLITTER	43
HE TOOK A STRANGE THING TO BE ROGUISH OVER.	178 THE STAR-SPLITTER	58
BECAUSE IT DIDN'T DO A THING BUT SPLIT	179 THE STAR-SPLITTER	88
'SA THING TO BE COMPARED WITH SPLITTING WOOD.	179 THE STAR-SPLITTER	94
AS IF HE DIDN'T KNOW WHAT LITTLE THING	183 MAPLE	125
FROM THINKING IT COULD BE A THING SO BRIDAL.	184 MAPLE	158
THE THING THAT MADE ME MORE AND MORE AFRAID	190 THE GRINDSTONE	65
A GOOD DEAL RIGHT; DON'T DO THE LAST THING WRONG.	199 PLACE FOR A THIRD	10
I NEVER COULD HAVE DONE THE THING I DID	204 THE WITCH OF COOS	65
AND SET OFF BRISKLY FOR SO SLOW A THING.	205 THE WITCH OF COOS	86
THEY'LL FIND THEY'VE GOT THE WHOLE THING TO DO OVER,	207 PAUPER WITCH OF GRAFTON	10
AND ONE THING MORE THAT WAS NOT THEN TO SAY:	222 TO E.T.	11
BUT ONE THING ABOUT IT, IT MUSTN'T GET WARM.	228 GOOD-BY AND KEEP COLD	16
AND THING NEXT MOST DIFFUSE TO CLOUD,	251 TREE AT MY WINDOW	6
BUT THE STRANGEST THING: IN THE THICK OLD THATCH,	253 THE THATCH	13
BUT IT'S JUST THE KIND OF A THING THAT YOU	263 THE TIMES TABLE	14
THE SUREST THING THERE IS IS WE ARE RIDERS,	267 RIDERS	1
BUT HE WOULDN'T ADVISE A THING TO BLOSSOM.	276 TWO TRAMPS IN MUD TIME	32
ONE THING HAS A SHELVING BANK,	281 A DRUMLIN WOODCHUCK	1
THEN SUDDENLY HE SAW THE THING HE DID,	284 THE GOLD HESPERIDEE	49
TO ASK ME A THING OR TWO	294 A RECORD STRIDE	10
BUT UNLESS YOU PUT THE RIGHT THING TO ITS ROOT	296 LEAVES COMPARED WITH	3
OFF ANY STILL OR MOVING THING YOU SAY.	300 THE MASTER SPEED	9
IF DESIGN GOVERN IN A THING SO SMALL.	302 DESIGN	14
FOR FINDING A THING TO DO THAT THOUGH NOT FORBID	306 NOT QUITE SOCIAL	3
THAT GOLD SHOULD BE THE ONE THING	311 THE VINDICTIVES	25
WERE A DANGEROUS THING TO BEAR.	313 BEARER OF EVIL TIDINGS	4
TO AFFIRM THERE IS SUCH A THING AS EVIL	317 BUILD SOIL	50
THERE'S NO SUCH THING AS SOCIALISM PURE--	318 BUILD SOIL	70
MAY NOT BE THE IMPORTANT THING AT LAST.	321 BUILD SOIL	158
I TRIED TO TELL HER "THERE'S NO SUCH THING!"	342 A CLOUD SHADOW	61
"BEFORE THE THING HAS TIME TO SPREAD.	345 DISCOVERY OF MADEIRAS	61
I HEARD HIM SHOUT 'WHAT A THING IT IS!'	346 DISCOVERY OF MADEIRAS	93
WHICH COMES TO THE SAME THING IN DIFFERENT TERMS.	353 THE LESSON FOR TODAY	76
I'M TELLING YOU. YOU HAVEN'T SAID A THING,	354 THE LESSON FOR TODAY	114
BUT THE THING WAS THE SLOPE IT GAVE HIS HEAD:	356 TIME OUT	8
BUT THEY'RE ONE THING THAT SHOULD BE DONE BY HALVES.	363 A SEMI-REVOLUTION	8
IT WAS A THING OF BEAUTY AND WAS SENT	375 A YOUNG BIRCH	21
I DON'T BELIEVE I BELIEVE A THING YOU STATE.	389 SKEPTIC	3
DON'T MIND A LITTLE THING LIKE THE ACTORS FIGHTING.	392 IT BIDS PRETTY FAIR	2
THE ONLY THING I WORRY ABOUT IS THE SUN.	392 IT BIDS PRETTY FAIR	3
GOOD IS A THING THAT THEY, THE GREAT, CAN DO,	398 NO HOLY WARS FOR THEM	3
THE IMPORTANT THING IS NOT TO GET BOGGED DOWN	406 FROM PLANE TO PLANE	62
OUR WORSHIP WAS A THING HE HAD TOO MUCH OF	408 FROM PLANE TO PLANE	132
WHO WAS THE FIRST TO THINK OF SUCH A THING.	422 FOR JOHN F. KENNEDY	6
COLONIAL HAD BEEN THE THING TO BE	422 FOR JOHN F. KENNEDY	11
THE UNIVERSE IS BUT THE THING OF THINGS,	425 ACCIDENTALLY ON PURPOSE	1
EVERY SINGLE THING	426 A NEVER NAUGHT SONG	13
FOR ONE THING ALONE,	447 THE BAD ISLAND--EASTER	7
BUT ONE THING IS SURE,	449 THE BAD ISLAND--EASTER	54
"AND ONE THING MORE THAT MAY NOT BE,	451 A-WISHING WELL	4
THE ONE THING MORE OF HIS CONCERN.	451 A-WISHING WELL	9
THE ONE THING MORE I WISH THERE WERE.	451 A-WISHING WELL	11
THE EX-KING SAID. "WE'RE IN THIS THING TOGETHER.	459 HOW HARD TO KEEP FROM	170
IF SUCH A THING IS POSSIBLE WITH MONEY.	459 HOW HARD TO KEEP FROM	176
THAT THERE WAS SUCH A THING AS BAD.	467 QUANDARY	2
THE THING WAS TO GET NOW AND THEN ELATED.	468 IN A GLASS OF CIDER	8
THERE YOU GO ASKING FOR THE VERY THING	477 A MASQUE OF REASON	105
THAT'S ONE THING MORE TO PUT ON YOUR AGENDA.	478 A MASQUE OF REASON	126
JOB HADN'T DONE A THING, POOR INNOCENT.	478 A MASQUE OF REASON	127
FOR INSTANCE, IS THERE SUCH A THING AS PROGRESS?	484 A MASQUE OF REASON	315
JOB SAYS THERE'S NO SUCH THING AS EARTH'S BECOMING	484 A MASQUE OF REASON	316
NO, GOD. / I NEVER HEARD OF SUCH A THING.	493 A MASQUE OF MERCY	20
YOUR COURAGE FAILED. THE SADDEST THING IN LIFE	497 A MASQUE OF MERCY	106
IS THAT THE BEST THING IN IT SHOULD BE COURAGE.	497 A MASQUE OF MERCY	107
AN ANALYST'S THE LATEST THING IN DOCTORS.	499 A MASQUE OF MERCY	153
NOTHING WOULD HAPPEN. THAT'S THE THING OF IT.	505 A MASQUE OF MERCY	300
THE THING THAT DID WHAT YOU CONSIDER MISCHIEF,	505 A MASQUE OF MERCY	317
THERE'S SOME SUCH THING AND NO ONE WILL DENY IT--	508 A MASQUE OF MERCY	385
THE THING THAT REALLY COUNTS, THOUGH, IS THE FORM	509 A MASQUE OF MERCY	430

                                                    PAGE TITLE   LINE
THING (CONTINUED)
    AND THE MOST SACRED THING OF ALL'S ABRUPTION. . . . . . 510 A MASQUE OF MERCY . . 435
    BUT ONE THING MORE BEFORE THE CURTAIN FALLS.-- . . . . . 519 A MASQUE OF MERCY . . 672
THINGS
    AND YET, IN VIEW OF HOW MANY THINGS, ...   6 GHOST HOUSE 29
    WHAT THINGS FOR DREAM THERE ARE WHEN SPECTER-LIKE, . . .   14 WAITING   1
    OF THINGS OF MOMENT TO WHICH, THEY WIST, ...   15 IN A VALE 13
    THE TALE OF EARTH'S UNHONORED THINGS . . . .   21 THE TRIAL BY EXISTENCE   45
    THEY MUST GO DOWN PAST THINGS COMING UP. . . . . . .   26 IN HARDWOOD GROVES . .   7
    AND THERE WERE OTHER THINGS: . . . .   29 MY BUTTERFLY 26
    TO GO WITH THE DRIFT OF THINGS, ...   30 RELUCTANCE 21
    SHE TOOK THE MARKET THINGS FROM WARREN'S ARMS . . . .   34 DEATH OF THE HIRED MAN   8
    THE WAY HE MIXED THAT IN WITH OTHER THINGS. . . . . .   36 DEATH OF THE HIRED MAN   64
    YOU WOULDN'T THINK THEY WOULD. HOW SOME THINGS LINGER! .   37 DEATH OF THE HIRED MAN   72
    WHEN I WALKED FORTH AT DAWN TO SEE NEW THINGS. . . . .   40 THE MOUNTAIN   8
    THOUGH I DON'T LIKE SUCH THINGS 'TWIXT THOSE THAT LOVE. .   53 HOME BURIAL 53
    AND LIVING PEOPLE, AND THINGS THEY UNDERSTAND. . . . .   54 HOME BURIAL 105
    HER SONS WON'T SELL THE HOUSE OR THE THINGS IN IT. . .   55 THE BLACK COTTAGE . . 16
    SHE HAD HER OWN IDEA OF THINGS, THE OLD LADY. . . . .   56 THE BLACK COTTAGE . . 51
    FROM THE WORLD'S VIEW TODAY OF ALL THOSE THINGS. . . .   57 THE BLACK COTTAGE . . 63
    OF WHERE ALL THE BERRIES AND OTHER THINGS GROW, . . .   61 BLUEBERRIES 61
    YOU LET THINGS MORE LIKE FEATHERS REGULATE . . . . .   63 A SERVANT TO SERVANTS . 36
    THINGS OVER AND OVER THAT JUST WON'T STAY DONE. . . .   64 A SERVANT TO SERVANTS . 52
    SHE HAD TO LIE AND HEAR LOVE THINGS MADE DREADFUL . . .   66 A SERVANT TO SERVANTS . 130
    I DIDN'T WANT THE BLAME IF THINGS WENT WRONG. . . . .   67 A SERVANT TO SERVANTS . 150
    TO DO WORK BETTER OR FASTER--THOSE TWO THINGS. . . . .   70 THE CODE 23
    YOU TAKE MY CARD--YOU SEEM SO GOOD AT SUCH THINGS-- . .   75 THE GENERATIONS OF MEN   61
    WHAT I THINK HE WILL DO, IS LET THINGS SMASH. . . . .   83 THE HOUSEKEEPER . . . 51
    I THOUGHT THE GROWING THINGS WOULD DO HIM GOOD. . . .   83 THE HOUSEKEEPER . . . 59
    YOU SEE OUR PRETTY THINGS ARE ALL OUTDOORS. . . . . .   85 THE HOUSEKEEPER . . . 110
    HE'S FOND OF NICE THINGS--TOO FOND, SOME WOULD SAY. . .   85 THE HOUSEKEEPER . . . 116
    WE MUSTN'T SAY HARD THINGS. YOU MUSTN'T EITHER." . . .   91 THE FEAR 53
    OF TREES AND CRACK OF BRANCHES, COMMON THINGS, ...   108 OLD MAN'S WINTER NIGHT   13
    NO MORE TO TELL? WE TURNED TO OTHER THINGS. . . . . .   110 THE EXPOSED NEST . . . 32
    "NO; FOR BESIDES THE THINGS I TELL YOU OF, ...   112 IN THE HOME STRETCH . 46
    AND TAKE A LIVELIER VIEW OF THINGS FROM HERE. . . . .   112 IN THE HOME STRETCH . 61
    WE DROP OUR EYES OR TURN TO OTHER THINGS, ...   114 IN THE HOME STRETCH . 117
    FOR THINGS THAT DON'T EXIST; I MEAN BEGINNINGS. . . .   116 IN THE HOME STRETCH . 173
    ENDS AND BEGINNINGS--THERE ARE NO SUCH THINGS. . . . .   116 IN THE HOME STRETCH . 174
    WE LOVE THE THINGS WE LOVE FOR WHAT THEY ARE. . . . .   119 HYLA BROOK 15
    BUT I THOUGHT HAS NEED OF NO SUCH THINGS, ...   120 BOND AND FREE . . .   4
    THEY MIGHT BE GOOD FOR GARDEN THINGS . . . .   123 PEA BRUSH 17
    THERE WERE ENOUGH THINGS TO BE THOUGHT OF THEN. . . .   131 THE BONFIRE 56
    OF ALL THINGS BUT WEED. . . . .   134 A GIRL'S GARDEN . . . 28
    HOW VILLAGE THINGS GO, ...   134 A GIRL'S GARDEN . . . 42
    AND STAMPED AND SAID THINGS TO HIMSELF, ...   138 BROWN'S DESCENT . . . 17
    YOU SEE I KNOW--TO GET YOU ON TO THINGS . . . . . .   147 SNOW 122
    THINGS MUST EXPECT TO COME IN FRONT OF US . . . . .   147 SNOW 126
    THAT VARIES WITH THE THINGS--BEFORE WE SEE THEM. . . .   147 SNOW 128
    "ONE OF TWO THINGS, EITHER SHE'S GONE TO BED . . . .   154 SNOW 311
    FROM SELLING THINGS IN CALIFORNIA. . . . .   160 NEW HAMPSHIRE . . .   38
    TO MAKE FUN OF MY WAY OF DOING THINGS, ...   176 THE STAR-SPLITTER . .   9
    "WHAT DO YOU WANT WITH ONE OF THOSE BLAME THINGS?" . .   177 THE STAR-SPLITTER . . 20
    SAID SOME OF THE BEST THINGS WE EVER SAID. . . . . .   179 THE STAR-SPLITTER . . 86
    WAITING FOR THINGS TO HAPPEN IN THEIR FAVOR. . . . .   204 THE WITCH OF COOS . . 63
    TO TURN HIM ROUND. HE GOT TO SAYING THINGS . . . . .   209 PAUPER WITCH OF GRAFTON 78
    LIFE LONG IN BED, AND WROTE HER THINGS IN BED. . . . .   215 A FOUNTAIN, A BOTTLE . 85
    THAT CROSSED ME FROM SWEET THINGS, ...   227 TO EARTHWARD   5
    THE NEED OF BEING VERSED IN COUNTRY THINGS . . . . .   241 NEED OF BEING VERSED .   T
    ONE HAD TO BE VERSED IN COUNTRY THINGS . . . . . .   242 NEED OF BEING VERSED . 23
    SO PEOPLE AND THINGS DON'T PAIR ANYMORE . . . . . .   265 THE DOOR IN THE DARK .   8
    THAT SHALL ALL LIVING THINGS DISPLACE. . . . . . .   280 BLUE RIBBON AT AMESBURY 28
    IT'S KNOWING WHAT TO DO WITH THINGS THAT COUNTS. . . .   294 AT WOODWARD'S GARDENS . 37
    SOME THINGS ARE NEVER CLEAR. . . . .   301 VOICE WAYS   1
    THROUGH THE INTERSTICES OF THINGS AJAR . . . . . .   303 A BIRD SINGING IN SLEEP 10
    MADE GOOD FOR EVERYONE--THINGS LIKE INVENTIONS-- . . .   319 BUILD SOIL 94
    WHAT SHOULD YOU DO? / I'D LET THINGS TAKE THEIR COURSE .   320 BUILD SOIL 128
    DON'T LET THE THINGS I SAY AGAINST MYSELF . . . . .   320 BUILD SOIL 131
    A MAN THE WAY THINGS COME IN PAIRS. . . . .   326 TO A THINKER 14
    THESE THINGS THE MIND HAS PONDERED ON . . . .   332 ALL REVELATION . . .   8
    THE THINGS FORBIDDEN THAT WHILE THE CUSTOMS SLEPT . . .   335 I COULD GIVE ALL . . 13
    YOU'LL HEAR ALL SORTS OF THINGS. YOU'LL MEET WITH THEM .   369 THE LITERATE FARMER AND 33
    SO BUSY YOURSELF WITH OTHER THINGS . . . .   376 SOMETHING FOR HOPE . . 10
    AND LEAVING SOME THINGS TO TAKE THEIR COURSE. . . . .   376 SOMETHING FOR HOPE . . 22
    WEEP FOR WHAT LITTLE THINGS COULD MAKE THEM GLAD. . . .   378 DIRECTIVE 44
    THINGS MUST HAVE HAPPENED TO YOU, YES, ...   381 AN UNSTAMPED LETTER IN   45
    WHEN SHE HAS MADE THINGS SO WE HAVE TO GO . . . . .   395 WHY WAIT FOR SCIENCE .   4
    AND THINGS HAVE BEEN GOING SO STRANGELY SINCE, ...   421 ONE MORE BREVITY . . 56
    THE UNIVERSE IS BUT THE THING OF THINGS, ...   425 ACCIDENTALLY ON PURPOSE   1
    THE THINGS BUT BALLS ALL GOING ROUND IN RINGS. . . . .   425 ACCIDENTALLY ON PURPOSE   2
    THINGS THEY THINK SHE WORE . . . .   433 KITTY HAWK 154
    THOSE TWO THINGS WE CAN'T. . . . .   441 KITTY HAWK 419
    TO KEEP ALL THINGS STIRRED . . . .   442 KITTY HAWK 444
    OF ALL THE THINGS HE MIGHT HAVE SAID, ...   444 ENDS   5
    AND SOME WILL SAY ALL SORTS OF THINGS, ...   445 ENDS 11
    I KNOW THE QUINTESSENCE OF MANY THINGS. . . . . . .   455 HOW HARD TO KEEP FROM   41
    AS WELL AS OF YOUR HUNDRED OTHER THINGS. . . . . . .   456 HOW HARD TO KEEP FROM   99
    NO, LET'S NOT LIVE THINGS OVER. I DON'T CARE. . . . .   477 A MASQUE OF REASON . . 119
    TO GET THINGS DONE. REFORMERS FAIL TO SEE THAT.-- . . .   478 A MASQUE OF REASON . . 152
    SO IT'S IMPORTANT WHO FIRST THINKS OF THINGS? . . . .   480 A MASQUE OF REASON . . 198
    SOCIETY CAN NEVER THINK THINGS OUT: . . . .   481 A MASQUE OF REASON . . 223
    WORTH GOING AFTER. GET DOWN INTO THINGS, ...   483 A MASQUE OF REASON . . 281
    AND ALSO OF THE WAY ALL THINGS COME ROUND, ...   485 A MASQUE OF REASON . . 342
    WE CAN'T BE ALWAYS SELLING PEOPLE THINGS. . . . . .   493 A MASQUE OF MERCY . . 10
    YES, PAUL, YOU DO SAY THINGS LIKE THAT SOMETIMES. . . .   511 A MASQUE OF MERCY . . 486
    NERVOUS IS ALL THE GREAT THINGS EVER MADE YOU. . . . .   516 A MASQUE OF MERCY . . 599
    BUT BEL GETS SOME THINGS RIGHT--AND SHE WAS RIGHT-- . .   519 A MASQUE OF MERCY . . 690
    YES, THERE YOU HAVE IT AT THE ROOT OF THINGS. . . . .   520 A MASQUE OF MERCY . . 716

                                 - 555 -

PAGE TITLE   LINE

THING'S
HE MAY BE GOOD, BUT ONE THING'S SURE, HE'S TOUGH." . . . 145 SNOW 71

THINK
AND GIVE US NOT TO THINK SO FAR AWAY . . . . . . 12 A PRAYER IN SPRING . . 2
YOU WOULDN'T THINK THEY WOULD. HOW SOME THINGS LINGER! . . 37 DEATH OF THE HIRED MAN 72
TO THINK OF THE RIGHT THING TO SAY TOO LATE. . . . . 37 DEATH OF THE HIRED MAN 77
"SILAS HAS BETTER CLAIM ON US YOU THINK . . . . . 38 DEATH OF THE HIRED MAN 124
"I THINK HIS BROTHER OUGHT TO HELP, OF COURSE. . . . . 39 DEATH OF THE HIRED MAN 131
BUT HAVE SOME PITY ON SILAS. DO YOU THINK . . . . . 39 DEATH OF THE HIRED MAN 135
"I CAN'T THINK SI EVER HURT ANYONE." . . . . . 39 DEATH OF THE HIRED MAN 146
TO THINK OF SITTING SUCH AN ORDEAL CUT, ... 45 A HUNDRED COLLARS . . 18
"LAFE WAS THE NAME, I THINK? / "YES, LAYFAYETTE. . . . 46 A HUNDRED COLLARS . . 41
HOLD ON, THERE'S SOMETHING I DON'T THINK OF NOW . . . 46 A HUNDRED COLLARS . . 45
AND COME TO THINK I MUST HAVE BACK AT HOME . . . . 47 A HUNDRED COLLARS . . 65
MY NINETY ISN'T MINE--YOU WON'T THINK THAT. . . . . 48 A HUNDRED COLLARS . . 96
I DO THINK, THOUGH, YOU OVERDO IT A LITTLE. . . . . 53 HOME BURIAL 62
WHAT WAS IT BROUGHT YOU UP TO THINK IT THE THING . . . 53 HOME BURIAL 63
YOU'D THINK HIS MEMORY MIGHT BE SATISFIED----" . . . 53 HOME BURIAL 66
THINK OF IT, TALK LIKE THAT AT SUCH A TIME! . . . . 54 HOME BURIAL 94
"YOU--OH, YOU THINK THE TALK IS ALL. I MUST GO-- . . . 54 HOME BURIAL 112
WHOM WE ALL HAVE TO THINK OF NOWADAYS, ... 57 THE BLACK COTTAGE . . 87
MOST OF THE CHANGE WE THINK WE SEE IN LIFE . . . . 58 THE BLACK COTTAGE . . 109
NO ONE WOULD COVET IT OR THINK IT WORTH . . . . . 58 THE BLACK COTTAGE . . 117
"DOES PATTERSON KNOW WHAT HE HAS, DO YOU THINK?" . . . 60 BLUEBERRIES 28
I OFTEN THINK OF THE SMOOTH HICKORY BARS. . . . . 67 A SERVANT TO SERVANTS 144
I ALMOST THINK IF I COULD DO LIKE YOU, ... 67 A SERVANT TO SERVANTS 161
YOU WOULDN'T THINK A FELLOW'D NEED MUCH URGING . . . 71 THE CODE 59
"NOT FROM THE RAIN. I THINK IT'S GOING TO RAIN." . . . 75 THE GENERATIONS OF MEN 67
I THINK WE'RE ALL MAD. TELL ME WHY WE'RE HERE, . . . 76 THE GENERATIONS OF MEN 88
"YES, IT'S IMPORTANT, THOUGH YOU THINK IT ISN'T. . . . 77 THE GENERATIONS OF MEN 118
WHAT DO YOU THINK YOU'RE LIKE TO HEAR TODAY?" . . . 78 THE GENERATIONS OF MEN 141
YOU THINK YOU'D BEST TEMPT HER AT SUCH A TIME?" . . . 79 THE GENERATIONS OF MEN 182
BUT DON'T YOU THINK WE SOMETIMES MAKE TOO MUCH . . . 80 THE GENERATIONS OF MEN 196
I HATE TO THINK OF THE OLD PLACE WHEN WE'RE GONE, . . . 82 THE HOUSEKEEPER . . . 45
WHAT I THINK HE WILL DO, IS LET THINGS SMASH. . . . 83 THE HOUSEKEEPER . . . 51
HE'S GIVEN HER TIME TO THINK OF SOMETHING ELSE. . . . 84 THE HOUSEKEEPER . . . 86
"THEN IT'S ALL UP. I THINK I'LL GET AWAY. . . . . 88 THE HOUSEKEEPER . . . 190
"YOU NEEDN'T THINK YOU'RE GOING TO GET AWAY. . . . . 88 THE HOUSEKEEPER . . . 195
"BUT IT'S NONSENSE TO THINK HE'D CARE ENOUGH." . . . 91 THE FEAR 49
WHAT, SON?" / "THEN I SHOULD THINK YOU'D TRY TO FIND . . 92 THE FEAR 84
YOU WON'T THINK ANYTHING. YOU UNDERSTAND? . . . . 92 THE FEAR 88
WHAT DOES HE THINK?--HOW ARE THE BLESSED FEET? . . . 93 THE SELF-SEEKER . . . 14
THAT'S HOW I THINK I DIDN'T LOSE MY HEAD. . . . . 93 THE SELF-SEEKER . . . 28
"YOU HAVE ME THERE. BUT THAT--YOU DIDN'T THINK . . . 95 THE SELF-SEEKER . . . 81
ER, LET ME SEE. I THINK I'LL TAKE THE RIGHT. . . . 96 THE SELF-SEEKER . . . 110
I'M A GREAT BOY TO THINK OF NUMBER ONE. . . . . 99 THE SELF-SEEKER . . . 177
"FIVE HUNDRED DOLLARS!" / "WHAT WOULD YOU THINK RIGHT?" . 99 THE SELF-SEEKER . . . 198
"I THINK--I THINK--FROM WHAT I HEARD TODAY-- . . . 100 THE SELF-SEEKER . . . 204
WHO WAS SO FOOLISH AS TO THINK WHAT HE THOUGHT, . . . 101 THE WOOD-PILE . . . 13
A VIEW." / "AND YET YOU THINK YOU LIKE IT, DEAR?" . . . 111 IN THE HOME STRETCH . 35
WILL EVER SLAM THE DOORS." / "I THINK YOU SEE . . . 112 IN THE HOME STRETCH . 44
"GOOD-BY TO THEM! WE PUZZLE THEM. THEY THINK-- . . . 114 IN THE HOME STRETCH . 111
I DON'T KNOW WHAT THEY THINK WE SEE IN WHAT . . . . 114 IN THE HOME STRETCH . 112
NEW IS A WORD FOR FOOLS IN TOWNS WHO THINK . . . . 117 IN THE HOME STRETCH . 183
I LIKE TO THINK SOME BOY'S BEEN SWINGING THEM.. . . . 121 BIRCHES 3
YOU'D THINK THE INNER DOME OF HEAVEN HAD FALLEN. . . . 121 BIRCHES 13
AND THINK NO MORE OF WALL-BUILDERS THAN FOOLS.. . . . 124 THE COW IN APPLE TIME 3
THERE CAME A GUST. (YOU USED TO THINK THE TREES . . . 130 THE BONFIRE 41
AND I THINK THE SKY DARKENED WITH A CLOUD . . . . 131 THE BONFIRE 54
DON'T THINK BROWN EVER GAVE UP HOPE . . . . . 139 BROWN'S DESCENT . . 54
I THINK I'LL JUST CALL UP MY WIFE AND TELL HER . . . 143 SNOW 11
TRY TO THINK WHAT HE DID WITH ALL THAT TIME. . . . 145 SNOW 61
LET'S SEE IF HE WILL THINK OF HER AGAIN. . . . . 145 SNOW 77
"YOU THINK SO, DO YOU? YOU DON'T KNOW THE KIND. . . . 146 SNOW 83
'SO YOU CAN THINK IT'S SIX FEET DEEP OUTSIDE, . . . 149 SNOW 182
THIS ROOM YOU SIT IN. IF YOU THINK THE WIND . . . . 150 SNOW 203
YOU'VE DONE MORE THAN YOU HAD A RIGHT TO THINK . . . 150 SNOW 219
YET THINK OF THE SMALL BIRDS AT ROOST AND NOT . . . 151 SNOW 226
YOU DIDN'T THINK YOU'D KEEP HIM AFTER ALL. . . . . 152 SNOW 255
I THINK I HEAR A CLOCK--AND WINDOWS RATTLING. . . . 153 SNOW 301
"FRED, I SHAN'T LET YOU THINK OF GOING OUT." . . . 155 SNOW 326
"YOU THINK YOU HAVEN'T BEEN CONCERNED YOURSELF." . . . 155 SNOW 344
TO ROUT US OUT TO THINK FOR HIM AT MIDNIGHT . . . . 155 SNOW 346
(IN VERSE I THINK) AGAINST THE VOLSTEAD ACT. . . . 160 NEW HAMPSHIRE . . . 30
I THINK HE OWNED SOME SHARES IN HARVARD COLLEGE.) . . . 163 NEW HAMPSHIRE . . . 137
AND RESTFUL JUST TO THINK ABOUT NEW HAMPSHIRE.. . . . 172 NEW HAMPSHIRE . . . 412
AND NOT, AS YOU MIGHT THINK, A FLYING CAR, ... 173 A STAR IN A STONEBOAT 27
OR SO HE TRIED TO THINK TO AVOID BLAME. . . . . 180 MAPLE 34
AND THINK A LITTLE, AND GET SOME CITY SCHOOLING. . . . 182 MAPLE 74
"I HAVE, AND BEEN PUT OFF SOMETIME, I THINK." . . . 183 MAPLE 109
AND HE'D THANK PEOPLE NOT TO THINK OF HER. . . . . 196 PAUL'S WIFE 154
WHERE A FOX WOULDN'T THINK TO LOOK FOR IT-- . . . 198 WILD GRAPES . . . 66
HOLD TIGHT AWHILE TILL I THINK WHAT TO DO. . . . . 198 WILD GRAPES . . . 82
TRIED TO THINK HOW HE COULD EXCEED HIS PROMISE. . . . 200 PLACE FOR A THIRD . . 19
SHE WANTED TO DO RIGHT. SHE'D HAVE TO THINK. . . . 201 PLACE FOR A THIRD . . 49
FOLKS THINK A WITCH WHO HAS FAMILIAR SPIRITS . . . 202 THE WITCH OF COOS . . 4
THE UNCOMMONLY DEEP SNOW HAS MADE HIM THINK . . . 205 THE WITCH OF COOS . . 109
WE THINK THEY HAD A GRAVE DOWN IN THE CELLAR. . . . 206 THE WITCH OF COOS . . 135
BUT MOST WOULD HAVE TO THINK OF THE EXPENSE. . . . 208 PAUPER WITCH OF GRAFTON 38
IT'D MAKE MY POSITION STRONGER, THINK, ... 208 PAUPER WITCH OF GRAFTON 42
I THINK I KNOW ENOUGH OF HATE . . . . . . 220 FIRE AND ICE . . . 6
I THINK THEY WOULD BELIEVE THE LIE. . . . . . 221 IN A DISUSED GRAVEYARD 16
"I THINK THE LITTLE FELLOW'S AFRAID OF THE SNOW. . . . 223 THE RUNAWAY . . . 9
IT'S ONLY WEATHER.' HE'D THINK SHE DIDN'T KNOW! . . . 223 THE RUNAWAY . . . 13
WHOSE WOODS THESE ARE I THINK I KNOW. . . . . . 224 STOPPING BY WOODS . . 1
MY LITTLE HORSE MUST THINK IT QUEER . . . . . 224 STOPPING BY WOODS . . 5
AND THINK OF AN ORCHARD'S ARBOREAL PLIGHT . . . . 228 GOOD-BY AND KEEP COLD 26
SHE SEEMED TO THINK THAT, TWO THUS, THEY WERE SAFE. . . 229 TWO LOOK AT TWO . . 21

THINK (CONTINUED)

TO THINK TO KNOW THE COUNTRY AND NOT KNOW	. . . . .	237	A HILLSIDE THAW . . .	1
BUT JUST TO ASK US WHO WE THINK WE ARE	. . . .	238	ON A TREE FALLEN ACROSS	4
LET THEM THINK TWICE BEFORE THEY USE THEIR POWERS	. . .	245	SPRING POOLS	9
THE HEART CAN THINK OF NO DEVOTION	. . . .	247	DEVOTION	1
TO THINK THEIR CASE WAS BEYOND RELIEF--	. . . .	253	THE THATCH	22
JUST WHEN WE THINK WE HAVE IT IMPOUNDED SAFE	. . .	254	THE FLOOD	2
TO THINK MUCH OR MUCH CARE.	. . . . . .	256	THE LOVELY BE CHOOSERS	30
"WHAT DOES IT THINK IT'S DOING RUNNING WEST	. . . .	257	WEST-RUNNING BROOK . .	4
AND BE BUT MORE FREE TO THINK	. . . .	261	SAND DUNES	15
YOU'D THINK I NEVER HAD FELT BEFORE	. . . . .	276	TWO TRAMPS IN MUD TIME	44
I LIKE TO THINK I AM IN EVERYTHING--	. . . .	278	THE WHITE-TAILED HORNET	16
BUT FOR THE FLY HE MIGHT HAVE MADE ME THINK .	. .	278	THE WHITE-TAILED HORNET	44
WE TAKE OCCASION TO THINK.	. . . . . .	282	A DRUMLIN WOODCHUCK .	20
WHERE THEY WON'T HAVE TO THINK FOR THEMSELVES ANYMORE;	. .	287	A ROADSIDE STAND . .	26
TO THINK THAT THOUGH HE COULD NOT LOCK HIMSELF IN,	. .	290	OLD BARN AT THE BOTTOM	43
SHE CAN THINK OF PLACES THAT ARE NOT THUS	. . .	291	ON HEART'S BEGINNING TO	32
WE THINK OF THE TREE. IF IT NEVER AGAIN HAS LEAVES,	. .	305	THERE ARE ROUGHLY ZONES	4
IS SOCIALISM NEEDED, DO YOU THINK?	. . . .	318	BUILD SOIL	67
BUT DON'T YOU THINK MORE SHOULD BE SOCIALIZED	. .	319	BUILD SOIL	92
IT IS JUST FOOL ENOUGH TO THINK ITSELF	. . . .	319	BUILD SOIL	119
TO THINK IT OUT. COME CLOSE, LET US CONSPIRE--	. .	323	BUILD SOIL	228
TO ASK ME IF I THINK IT WORTH THE PAINS	. . . .	324	BUILD SOIL	271
YOU WOULD NOT THINK YOU KNEW ENOUGH TO JUDGE	. .	351	THE LESSON FOR TODAY	29
ABOUT HOW LONG A MAN MAY THINK TO LIVE,	. . . .	354	THE LESSON FOR TODAY	135
BUT STAY AND HEAR ME OUT. I SURELY THINK	. . .	356	A MOTH SEEN IN WINTER	10
WHEN SOMETHING STRANGE ABOUT IT MADE ME THINK.	. .	357	A CONSIDERABLE SPECK	6
IN SUNSET LIGHT, YOU'D THINK IT WAS THE SUN	. . .	368	THE LITERATE FARMER AND	12
ALTHOUGH AT TIMES WE THINK IT DISAPPEARS.	. . .	369	THE LITERATE FARMER AND	32
"IN SHORT, YOU THINK THAT STAR A PATENT MEDICINE	. .	371	THE LITERATE FARMER AND	92
THEY THINK TOO MUCH OF HAVING SHADED OUT	. . .	378	DIRECTIVE	27
WHERE I COULD THINK OF NO THOROUGHFARE,	. . .	383	WERE I IN TROUBLE .	1
I HONESTLY THINK . . .	. . . .	392	A WISH TO COMPLY .	12
ENRAGED AT WHAT HE COULD BUT THINK OFFICIOUS;	. .	394	HAEC FABULA DOCET .	11
THESE ANYWAY MIGHT THINK IT WAS IMPORTANT	. . .	397	THE PLANNERS . . .	13
"I THINK I'LL CHANGE MY MIND." / "YOU'RE SAYING THAT	. .	406	FROM PLANE TO PLANE	75
FROM KNOWING MORE THAN I KNOW HOW TO THINK WITH.	. .	407	FROM PLANE TO PLANE	99
I LIKE TO THINK THE SUN'S LIKE YOU IN THAT--	. . .	408	FROM PLANE TO PLANE	124
DON'T THINK I LEAVE . . .	. . . . . .	413	AWAY!	9
(THINK OF PRESUMING TO CALL HIM GUS),	. . .	421	ONE MORE BREVITY .	59
WHO WAS THE FIRST TO THINK OF SUCH A THING.	. .	422	FOR JOHN F. KENNEDY	6
THEY ARE OUR WARDS WE THINK TO SOME EXTENT	. .	423	FOR JOHN F. KENNEDY	36
YOU MIGHT THINK TOO POOR-	. . . . . .	428	KITTY HAWK . . .	14
THINGS THEY THINK SHE WORE	. . . . . .	433	KITTY HAWK . . .	154
THAT HAS THOUGHT TO THINK.	. . . . . .	440	KITTY HAWK . . .	401
SOME STILL THINK IS SATAN,	. . . . . .	443	KITTY HAWK . . .	464
I THINK I GET IT VIA STORK	. . . . . .	452	A-WISHING WELL . .	35
I NEEDN'T THINK I HAVE ESCAPED MY DUTY,	. . .	454	HOW HARD TO KEEP FROM	19
YOU THINK OF FOR YOUR PEOPLE--FEEDING THEM."	. .	458	HOW HARD TO KEEP FROM	138
ONCE I WAS FOOL ENOUGH TO THINK .	. . . . .	467	QUANDARY	20
JOB SCRATCHED HIS BOILS AND TRIED TO THINK WHAT HE	. .	477	A MASQUE OF REASON .	121
AND NO ONE BUT A MAN WOULD THINK THERE WAS.	. . .	478	A MASQUE OF REASON .	139
SOCIETY CAN NEVER THINK THINGS OUT:	. . . .	481	A MASQUE OF REASON .	223
DID SEEM UNLIKE YOU, AND I TRIED TO THINK	. . .	482	A MASQUE OF REASON .	263
I'VE COME TO THINK NO SO-CALLED HIDDEN VALUE'S	. .	483	A MASQUE OF REASON .	280
FOR THIS I THINK. I FIND IT HARD,	. . . .	487	A MASQUE OF REASON .	387
WHO ARE YOU? / WHO ARE YOU? / I THINK YOU KNOW,	. .	495	A MASQUE OF MERCY .	60
RUNNING AWAY FROM HIM YOU THINK YOU ARE,	. . .	498	A MASQUE OF MERCY .	139
IS THE FIRST PLACE IN LITERATURE, I THINK,	. . .	508	A MASQUE OF MERCY .	376
STILL, NOT SO FAR OFF, COME TO THINK OF IT.	. . .	509	A MASQUE OF MERCY .	428
I THINK MY TROUBLE'S WITH THE CRISISES	. . .	510	A MASQUE OF MERCY .	442
KEEPER, I'M GLAD YOU THINK IT BEAUTIFUL.	. . .	512	A MASQUE OF MERCY .	494
AND I REPLY I ALMOST THINK I DO,	. . . .	513	A MASQUE OF MERCY .	531
I AM YOUR CONVERT. TELL ME WHAT I THINK.	. . .	517	A MASQUE OF MERCY .	621
I THINK I MAY HAVE GOT GOD WRONG ENTIRELY.	. . .	518	A MASQUE OF MERCY .	654
ALL YOU MEAN, PAUL, I THINK---- / WILL YOU STAND THERE	. .	519	A MASQUE OF MERCY .	675
AND LET THAT TELL YOU WHAT YOU THINK, LIKE THAT?	. .	519	A MASQUE OF MERCY .	676
FOR WHAT YOU THINK YOUR DOCTOR THINKS, WHY DON'T YOU?	. .	519	A MASQUE OF MERCY .	680
(SOMETIMES I THINK YOU ARE TOO SURE YOU HAVE BEEN.)	. .	520	A MASQUE OF MERCY .	709

THINKER (SEE POET-THINKER)

TO A THINKER	. . . . . .	325	TO A THINKER	T

THINKING

I'M THINKING I HAVE MORE TO LOSE THAN YOU	. . . .	47	A HUNDRED COLLARS . .	82
I'VE LAIN AWAKE THINKING OF YOU, I'LL WARRANT,	. . .	67	A SERVANT TO SERVANTS	166
NOR NEVER WILL BE TO MY WAY OF THINKING.	. . .	80	THE GENERATIONS OF MEN	187
THE LAWYER MAN IS THINKING OF HIS TRAIN.	. . .	98	THE SELF-SEEKER . .	168
TO FLAMES WITHOUT TWICE THINKING, WHERE IT VERGES	. .	131	THE BONFIRE . . .	59
BUT THEN, I DOUBT HE'S THINKING OF HIMSELF.	. . .	145	SNOW	78
PRIVATELY--TO HIMSELF, RIGHT NOW, HE'S THINKING	. .	146	SNOW	85
I CAN'T HELP THINKING THOSE ARE TESTS TO GO BY.	. .	162	NEW HAMPSHIRE . . .	99
FROM THINKING IT COULD BE A THING SO BRIDAL.	. .	184	MAPLE	158
(I'M THINKING CHIEFLY OF THE WHEELBARROW.)	. . .	189	THE GRINDSTONE . .	14
A THOUGHT THAT WANTED FURTHER THINKING;	. . .	274	A LONE STRIKER . .	45
OF SPEECH AND THINKING IS SO MUCH MY BETTER	. .	324	BUILD SOIL	250
WHAT I WAS THINKING WHEN YOU INTERRUPTED	. . .	325	BUILD SOIL	289
YOU CALL THIS THINKING, BUT IT'S WALKING.	. . .	325	TO A THINKER . . .	5
HIS MIND TO THINKING ALWAYS OF THE END.	. . .	353	THE LESSON FOR TODAY	95
I'M THINKING THE UNBORN WOULD NEVER MISS	. . .	397	THE PLANNERS . . .	2
OF A THINKING RACE . . .	. . . . .	440	KITTY HAWK . . .	393
THEY ARE THINKING OF PRETTY SOON	. . . .	466	SOME SCIENCE FICTION	23
BY PROPER NAMES I FIND I DO MY THINKING.	. . .	480	A MASQUE OF REASON .	200
YOU'RE PENSIVE. / OH, I'M THINKING OF THE DEVIL.	. .	486	A MASQUE OF REASON .	376
HE'S THINKING OF, IT WASN'T DOWN A WELL,	. . .	510	A MASQUE OF MERCY .	448

THINKS

THINKS THESE DARK DAYS OF AUTUMN RAIN	. . . .	6	MY NOVEMBER GUEST .	2
SHE THINKS I HAVE NO EYE FOR THESE,	. . . .	7	MY NOVEMBER GUEST .	14
HE THINKS HE OUGHT TO EARN A LITTLE PAY,	. . .	35	DEATH OF THE HIRED MAN	19
HE THINKS YOUNG WILSON A LIKELY LAD, THOUGH DAFT	. .	36	DEATH OF THE HIRED MAN	65

	PAGE TITLE	LINE

THINKS (CONTINUED)

HE THINKS IF HE COULD HAVE ANOTHER CHANCE . . . . 37 DEATH OF THE HIRED MAN 86
"HE THINKS IF HE COULD TEACH HIM THAT, HE'D BE . . . . . 37 DEATH OF THE HIRED MAN 96
SHE THINKS I'M SOCIABLE. I MAYBE AM. . . . . 49 A HUNDRED COLLARS . 145
"IF HE THINKS ALL THE FRUIT THAT GROWS WILD IS FOR HIM, . 61 BLUEBERRIES 79
INCLUDING ME. HE THINKS I'LL BE ALL RIGHT . . . . . 64 A SERVANT TO SERVANTS . 46
TO LOAD THE LOAD, THINKS I, LOOK OUT FOR TROUBLE. . . . 71 THE CODE 50
THINKS I, D'YE MEAN IT? 'WHAT WAS THAT YOU SAID?' . . . 71 THE CODE 64
HE THINKS IT'S DARK, AND IT'S FLOODED WITH DAYLIGHT." . 77 THE GENERATIONS OF MEN 102
I DON'T KNOW WHERE MYSELF. JOHN THINKS I DO. . . . . 82 THE HOUSEKEEPER . . 24
HE THINKS I ONLY HAVE TO SAY THE WORD, ... 82 THE HOUSEKEEPER . . 25
SHE THINKS IF IT WAS BAD TO LIVE WITH HIM, ... 83 THE HOUSEKEEPER . . 74
"HE THINKS I'LL HOBBLE. IT'S BOTH LEGS AND FEET." . . 93 THE SELF-SEEKER . . 16
I'VE BOARDED HERE SO LONG, SHE THINKS SHE OWNS ME. . . 94 THE SELF-SEEKER . . 54
HE THINKS YOU OUGHT TO PAY ME FOR MY FLOWERS. . . . . 100 THE SELF-SEEKER . . 225
SHE SAYS SHE THINKS SHE PLANTED ONE . . . . . . 134 A GIRL'S GARDEN . . 27
IF HE THINKS HE IS GOING TO MAKE OUR HOUSE . . . . 155 SNOW 341
THAT WHEN IT THINKS IT HAS ESCAPED THE FOX . . . . 198 WILD GRAPES . . . 64
SHE THINKS WHEN THE WIND MAKES A NIGHT OF IT . . . 209 PAUPER WITCH OF GRAFTON 82
AT MOST HE THINKS OR TWITTERS SOFTLY, "SAFE! . . . 249 ACCEPTANCE . . . 11
WHERE THE SPENDER THINKS IT WENT. . . . . 309 HARDSHIP OF ACCOUNTING 2
AS HE THINKS WILL DO HER NOT TOO MUCH HURT. . . . . 346 DISCOVERY OF MADEIRAS 89
HE THINKS THAT CHAIRS AND TABLES WILL ENDURE, . . . 372 THE LITERATE FARMER AND 128
AND THIS IS NOT BECAUSE SHE THINKS OF DEATH. . . . 386 THE FEAR OF MAN . . 4
SOMETIMES SHE THINKS SHE HAS AND GETS HERSELF . . . 476 A MASQUE OF REASON . 93
SO IT'S IMPORTANT WHO FIRST THINKS OF THINGS? . . . 480 A MASQUE OF REASON . 198
HE THINKS HE'S SMART. HE THINKS HE CAN CONVINCE ME . 485 A MASQUE OF REASON . 351
THINKS WHY NOT TAPER OFF TO NONE AT ALL, ... 498 A MASQUE OF MERCY . 122
FOR WHAT YOU THINK YOUR DOCTOR THINKS, WHY DON'T YOU? . 519 A MASQUE OF MERCY . 680

THIN-SKINNED

SO THE THICK-SKINS NEEDN'T ACT THIN-SKINNED . . . . . 295 A RECORD STRIDE . . 31

THIRD (SEE TWENTY-THIRD)

PLACE FOR A THIRD . . . . 199 PLACE FOR A THIRD . T
HER THIRD JOY THAT THOUGH NOW THEY CANNOT HELP BUT KNOW, . 256 THE LOVELY BE CHOOSERS 28
NOT A HALF, NOT A THIRD, NOT A TITHE. . . . . . . 310 THE VINDICTIVES . . 20
I PICKED YOU OUT A HORSE CALLED SAFETY THIRD, ... 457 HOW HARD TO KEEP FROM 123

THIRST

WITH THIRST ON HUNGER TO THE POINT OF LUST. . . . . 411 POD OF THE MILKWEED . 26

THIRSTY

SHE'S AFTER CIDER, THE OLD GIRL, SHE'S THIRSTY; . . . . 77 THE GENERATIONS OF MEN 108

THIRTEEN

THAN ON HIS BROTHER? THIRTEEN LITTLE MILES . . . . . 38 DEATH OF THE HIRED MAN 125

THIRTY

"A THOUSAND TREES WOULD COME TO THIRTY DOLLARS." . . . 107 CHRISTMAS TREES . . 44
BUT THIRTY DOLLARS SEEMED SO SMALL BESIDE . . . . 107 CHRISTMAS TREES . . 47
AT THIRTY CENTS A BUSHEL. GIVE ME SHEEP. . . . . . 316 BUILD SOIL . . . 12
IN WIND-SOIL TO A DEPTH OF THIRTY FEET, ... 365 OF STONES OF THE PLACE 6

THIS---NOT INDEXED

THITHER

NO LONGER BLOWN HITHER AND THITHER; . . . . . . 30 RELUCTANCE . . . 14
STROLLED THITHER, NOT EXPECTING HE WOULD FIND . . . . 74 THE GENERATIONS OF MEN 26
THEN STEERED THE WHITE MOTH THITHER IN THE NIGHT? . . 302 DESIGN 12

THOMAS

MY TONGUE'S MY OWN, AS TRUE THOMAS USED TO SAY. . . . 505 A MASQUE OF MERCY . 296

THOMISM

SO YOU'VE BEEN BOHNING UP ON THOMISM TOO. . . . . . 505 A MASQUE OF MERCY . 297

THOMPSON'S

HAVEN'T YOU HEARD OF THOMPSON'S "HOUND OF HEAVEN"? . . 494 A MASQUE OF MERCY . 21

THORN

WILL LEAVE THEIR TATTERS HUNG ON BARB AND THORN.) . . 379 DIRECTIVE 54

THOROUGH

I HAVE BEEN SO INSTINCTIVELY THOROUGH . . . . . . 282 A DRUMLIN WOODCHUCK . 31

THOROUGHFARE

WHERE I COULD THINK OF NO THOROUGHFARE, ... 383 WERE I IN TROUBLE . 1

THOROUGHLY

BUT HOW THOROUGHLY DEPARTMENTAL. . . . . 289 DEPARTMENTAL . . . 43

THOSE---NOT INDEXED

THOU (SEE TENDERER-THAN-THOU)

THOU DIDST NOT KNOW, WHO TOTTERED, WANDERING ON HIGH, . 28 MY BUTTERFLY . . . 22
FOR THOU ART DEAD, I SAID, ... 29 MY BUTTERFLY . . . 44
LOVE THOU THY NEIGHBOR AS THYSELF, AYE, ... 467 QUANDARY 12
AND HATE HIM AS THYSELF THOU HATEST. . . . . . . 467 QUANDARY 13
THOU ONETIME PRINCE OF CONVERSATIONISTS? . . . . . 488 A MASQUE OF REASON . 406

THOUGH---NOT INDEXED

THOUGHT (SEE LONG-LONG-AFTER-THOUGHT)

ONLY MORE SURE OF ALL I THOUGHT WAS TRUE. . . . . . 5 INTO MY OWN . . . 14
AND THE THOUGHT OF THE HEART'S DESIRE. . . . . . 8 LOVE AND A QUESTION . 20
THE BRIDEGROOM THOUGHT IT LITTLE TO GIVE . . . . . 8 LOVE AND A QUESTION . 25
DISTURBED, I DOUBT NOT, BY MY THOUGHT, ... 9 A LATE WALK . . . 11
AND THOUGHT OF NAUGHT TO SAY, ... 11 WIND AND WINDOW FLOWER 26
"ONE THOUGHT IN AGONY OF STRIFE . . . . . . 21 THE TRIAL BY EXISTENCE 50
I THOUGHT OF QUESTIONS THAT HAVE NO REPLY, ... 22 THE TUFT OF FLOWERS . 19
NOR YET TO DRAW ONE THOUGHT OF OURS TO HIM, ... 23 THE TUFT OF FLOWERS . 27
WITH ONE WHOSE THOUGHT I HAD NOT HOPED TO REACH. . . 23 THE TUFT OF FLOWERS . 38
SURGING, THE GRASSES DIZZIED ME OF THOUGHT, ... 29 MY BUTTERFLY . . . 35
AND HE LIKES HAVING THOUGHT OF IT SO WELL . . . . 34 MENDING WALL . . . 44
HE ASKED ME WHAT I THOUGHT OF HAROLD'S SAYING . . . 37 DEATH OF THE HIRED MAN 79
I THOUGHT, WHO IS THAT MAN? I DIDN'T KNOW YOU. . . 53 HOME BURIAL . . . 78
ONE WASN'T LONG IN LEARNING THAT SHE THOUGHT, . . . 56 THE BLACK COTTAGE . 54
IT NEVER GOT SO FAR AS THAT; BUT THE BARE THOUGHT . . 57 THE BLACK COTTAGE . 90
BUT HE THOUGHT A BIG THOUGHT--I COULD TELL BY HIS EYE-- . 60 BLUEBERRIES . . . 43
AND I THOUGHT I HAD LOST YOU. I LIFTED A SHOUT . . 62 BLUEBERRIES . . . 93
SOME THOUGHT HE HAD BEEN BITTEN BY A DOG, ... 65 A SERVANT TO SERVANTS 105
AND THEN HE'D CROW AS IF HE THOUGHT THAT CHILD'S PLAY-- . 66 A SERVANT TO SERVANTS 137
HE THOUGHT YOU MEANT TO FIND FAULT WITH HIS WORK. . . 70 THE CODE 16
I GUESS THEY THOUGHT I'D SPIKED HIM IN THE TEMPLE . . 72 THE CODE 92
I THOUGHT THE GROWING THINGS WOULD DO HIM GOOD. . . 83 THE HOUSEKEEPER . . 59
COMING DOWN RYAN'S HILL. I THOUGHT 'TWAS HIM. . . . 88 THE HOUSEKEEPER . . 197

THOUGHT (CONTINUED)
AND THOUGHT SHE WOULDN'T VENTURE ON SO MUCH. . . . . . 97 THE SELF-SEEKER . . . 118
WHO WAS SO FOOLISH AS TO THINK WHAT HE THOUGHT. . . . . 101 THE WOOD-PILE . . . 13
HE THOUGHT THAT I WAS AFTER HIM FOR A FEATHER-- . . . . 101 THE WOOD-PILE . . . 14
THESE LATTER ABOUT TO FALL. I THOUGHT THAT ONLY . . . . 102 THE WOOD-PILE . . . 34
AND I THOUGHT I HAD THE FOLK WITHIN: . . . . 102 GOOD HOURS 5
I HADN'T THOUGHT OF THEM AS CHRISTMAS TREES. . . . . . 106 CHRISTMAS TREES . . . 15
I DALLIED SO MUCH WITH THE THOUGHT OF SELLING. . . . . 106 CHRISTMAS TREES . . . 25
I THOUGHT SO TOO, BUT WASN'T THERE TO SAY SO. . . . . 107 CHRISTMAS TREES . . . 39
TRYING, I THOUGHT, TO SET IT UP ON END, ... 109 THE EXPOSED NEST . . . 4
IT'S WHO FIRST THOUGHT THE THOUGHT. YOU'RE SEARCHING, JOE, . 116 IN THE HOME STRETCH . . 172
STYLE UPON STYLE IN DRESS AND THOUGHT AT LAST . . . . . 117 IN THE HOME STRETCH . . 184
"FIRST TELL ME WHAT IT WAS YOU THOUGHT YOU HEARD." . . . 118 THE TELEPHONE . . . 10
I LISTENED AND I THOUGHT I CAUGHT THE WORD-- . . . . . 118 THE TELEPHONE . . . 14
"I MAY HAVE THOUGHT AS MUCH, BUT NOT ALOUD." . . . . . 118 THE TELEPHONE . . . 18
BUT THOUGHT HAS NEED OF NO SUCH THINGS, ... 120 BOND AND FREE . . . 4
FOR THOUGHT HAS A PAIR OF DAUNTLESS WINGS. . . . . . . 120 BOND AND FREE . . . 5
BUT THOUGHT HAS SHAKEN HIS ANKLES FREE. . . . . 120 BOND AND FREE . . . 10
THOUGHT CLEAVES THE INTERSTELLAR GLOOM . . . . 120 BOND AND FREE . . . 11
IN SEVERAL BEAUTY THAT THOUGHT FARES FAR . . . . 121 BOND AND FREE . . . 19
THERE WERE ENOUGH THINGS TO BE THOUGHT OF THEN. . . . . 131 THE BONFIRE . . . 56
AND HEAT SO CLOSE IN; BUT THE THOUGHT OF ALL . . . . . 131 THE BONFIRE . . . 71
MY DEARS, MY DEARS, YOU THOUGHT THAT--WE ALL THOUGHT IT. . 132 THE BONFIRE . . . 102
I ALWAYS THOUGHT IT MUST HAVE BEEN . . . . 135 LOCKED OUT . . . 11
HIS NECK, OR THOUGHT TO SPARE HIS CLOTHES. . . . . . . 138 BROWN'S DESCENT . . 28
OR EVEN THOUGHT OF STANDING THERE . . . . 139 BROWN'S DESCENT . . 57
WILL RUN AS HUSHED AS WHEN THEY WERE A THOUGHT. . . . . 141 THE LINE-GANG . . . 7
I THOUGHT I WOULD.--I KNOW, BUT, LETT--I KNOW-- . . . . 143 SNOW 19
THE DEAR KNOWS. I DETEST THE THOUGHT OF HIM-- . . . . 144 SNOW 51
I SHOULD HAVE THOUGHT, THOUGH, YOU COULD MAKE HIM HEAR YOU." 145 SNOW 67
JUST THEN, I THOUGHT. IT'S STOOD ERECT LIKE THAT, . . . 147 SNOW 117
'HEY, THAT'S A PRETTY THOUGHT'--THOSE WERE HIS WORDS-- . . 149 SNOW 181
WE THOUGHT YOU WERE DECIDING NOT TO GO-- . . . . 150 SNOW 198
THE PAUSE RIGHT THERE, SHE THOUGHT THE DREADED WORD . . . 151 SNOW 238
THOUGHT HE'D JUST CALL TO TELL US IT WAS SNOWING. . . . 155 SNOW 340
"I THOUGHT YOU'D FEEL YOU'D BEEN TOO MUCH CONCERNED." . . 155 SNOW 343
THAN THOSE I LEFT BEHIND. I THOUGHT THEY WEREN'T. . . . 167 NEW HAMPSHIRE . . . 256
I THOUGHT THEY COULDN'T BE. AND YET THEY WERE. . . . . 167 NEW HAMPSHIRE . . . 257
WHILE I THOUGHT WHAT TO DO THAT COULD BE DONE-- . . . . 175 THE CENSUS-TAKER . . 48
WHAT SHE HAD THOUGHT WAS LOVELY, AND WHAT GOOD. . . . . 181 MAPLE 55
A MAPLE LEAF SHE THOUGHT MUST HAVE BEEN LAID . . . . . 181 MAPLE 63
"ISN'T IT MABEL? I THOUGHT IT WAS MABEL." . . . . . . 182 MAPLE 89
WAS WHAT HE THOUGHT OF--NOT ME, BUT MY AX, ... 185 THE AX-HELVE . . . 19
NOT ALL THE MILES IT MAY HAVE THOUGHT IT WENT, ... 188 THE GRINDSTONE . . . 6
I WONDERED WHO IT WAS THE MAN THOUGHT GROUND-- . . . . 190 THE GRINDSTONE . . . 45
I WONDERED IF HE REALLY THOUGHT IT FAIR . . . . 190 THE GRINDSTONE . . . 48
AND THOUGHT IT MUST HAVE MELTED. IT WAS GONE. . . . . 194 PAUL'S WIFE . . . 105
SHE THOUGHT OF CHILDREN IN A BURIAL ROW; . . . . 199 PLACE FOR A THIRD . . 5
HIS FIRST THOUGHT UNDER PRESSURE WAS A GRAVE . . . . . 200 PLACE FOR A THIRD . . 22
HE THOUGHT OF EVERGREEN AND EVERLASTING. . . . . 200 PLACE FOR A THIRD . . 31
AND THEN HE HAD A THOUGHT WORTH MANY OF THESE. . . . . 200 PLACE FOR A THIRD . . 32
AND WHO HAD THOUGHT TO LAY HER WITH HER FIRST LOVE, . . . 201 PLACE FOR A THIRD . . 46
HOW COULD THAT BE--I THOUGHT THE DEAD WERE SOULS-- . . . 202 THE WITCH OF COOS . . 15
AND THOUGHT I HEARD HIM DOWNSTAIRS IN THE CELLAR. . . . 203 THE WITCH OF COOS . . 47
"I THOUGHT YOU WERE A GUIDE." / "I AM A GUIDE, ... 214 A FOUNTAIN, A BOTTLE . 31
BE READY, I THOUGHT, FOR ALMOST ANYTHING. . . . . . . 215 A FOUNTAIN, A BOTTLE . 64
AND WE SAW HIM, OR THOUGHT WE SAW HIM, DIM AND GRAY, . . 223 THE RUNAWAY . . . 7
I DISCERNED, AS I THOUGHT, BEYOND THE PICTURE, ... 225 FOR ONCE SOMETHING . . 8
I THOUGHT I SAW A BIRD ALIGHT. . . . . 232 LOOKING FOR SUNSET BIRD 4
HE STOOD THERE BRINGING MARCH AGAINST HIS THOUGHT, . . . 233 A BOUNDLESS MOMENT . . 3
I THOUGHT A FEW MIGHT TANGLE, AS THEY DID, ... 234 EVENING A SUGAR ORCHARD 7
BUT IF I THOUGHT TO STOP THE WET STAMPEDE, ... 237 A HILLSIDE THAW . . . 9
THE THOUGHT OF MY ATTEMPTING SUCH A STAY! . . . . . . 238 A HILLSIDE THAW . . . 35
AND I THOUGHT OF THE DOOR . . . . 240 THE LOCKLESS DOOR . . 3
AND THOUGHT OF DOING SOMETHING TO THE SHORE . . . . . . 250 ONCE BY THE PACIFIC . 3
AS I THOUGHT OF THEM WITHOUT NEST OR ROOST. . . . . . 253 THE THATCH . . . 29
"YES, YOU HAVE, TOO. GO ON. YOU THOUGHT OF SOMETHING." . 259 WEST-RUNNING BROOK . . 37
WHICH MAY BE THOUGHT, BUT ONLY SO TO SPEAK. . . . . . 269 THE BEAR . . . 32
AND YET HE THOUGHT HE SAW THE SCENE: . . . . 273 A LONE STRIKER . . 17
A THOUGHT THAT WANTED FURTHER THINKING. . . . . 274 A LONE STRIKER . . 45
THEY THOUGHT ALL CHOPPING WAS THEIRS OF RIGHT. . . . . 276 TWO TRAMPS IN MUD TIME 52
ONE MORE, HE THOUGHT, TO TAKE HIM SAFELY THROUGH. . . . 283 THE GOLD HESPERIDEE . 26
HE THOUGHT NO SPECIAL GOODNESS COULD BE LOST . . . . . 284 THE GOLD HESPERIDEE . 34
THE THOUGHT OF SO MUCH CHILDISH LONGING IN VAIN, ... 287 A ROADSIDE STAND . . 33
SOMETHING I SAW OR THOUGHT I SAW . . . . 290 ON HEART'S BEGINNING TO 1
ALL SUMMER LONG I THOUGHT I HEARD THEM THREATENING UNDER
    THEIR BREATH. . . . . 297 A LEAF-TREADER . . . 7
GRIEF MAY HAVE THOUGHT IT WAS GRIEF. . . . . 299 WELCOME TO THEIR BELIEF 1
CARE MAY HAVE THOUGHT IT WAS CARE. . . . . 299 WELCOME TO THEIR BELIEF 2
GRIEF MAY HAVE THOUGHT IT WAS GRIEF. . . . . 299 WELCOME TO THEIR BELIEF 13
CARE MAY HAVE THOUGHT IT WAS CARE. . . . . 299 WELCOME TO THEIR BELIEF 14
HAS BEEN THOUGHT OUT AND ACCOUNTED FOR. . . . . 306 A TRIAL RUN . . . 12
THEY GAVE NO MORE THOUGHT TO THE KING. . . . . 311 THE VINDICTIVES . . 27
IF EARTH WERE THOUGHT ABOUT TO CHANGE ITS AXIS, ... 317 BUILD SOIL . . . 58
TOO MEAN A THOUGHT TO GET MUCH COMFORT OUT OF. . . . . 321 BUILD SOIL . . . 168
PREACH ON. I THOUGHT YOU WERE ALREADY PREACHING. . . . 322 BUILD SOIL . . . 183
THE THOUGHT I HAVE, AND MY FIRST IMPULSE IS . . . . . 323 BUILD SOIL . . . 239
THE THOUGHT FROM THAT THOUGHT--I WILL TURN IT UNDER. . . 323 BUILD SOIL . . . 241
THOUGHT PRODUCT AND FOOD PRODUCT ARE TO ME . . . . . . 324 BUILD SOIL . . . 257
BY COUNTLESS SILKEN TIES OF LOVE AND THOUGHT . . . . . 332 THE SILKEN TENT . . 10
BEFORE I THOUGHT THE WILTED TO EXALT . . . . 337 THE WIND AND THE RAIN . 26
HE THOUGHT HE KEPT THE UNIVERSE ALONE; . . . . 338 THE MOST OF IT . . 1
SO SHE THOUGHT SHE HEARD HIM SAY; . . . . 340 THE SUBVERTED FLOWER . 25
WHICH PUT THE THOUGHT INTO SOMEONE'S HEAD . . . . . . 345 DISCOVERY OF MADEIRAS . 66
HE THOUGHT, ALL RIGHT, IF YOU WANT THE TRUTH! . . . . . 346 DISCOVERY OF MADEIRAS . 97
AND HER THOUGHT WAS SHE HAD HAD HER PAY. . . . . 346 DISCOVERY OF MADEIRAS . 105
THE STORY IS SHE DIED OF THOUGHT. . . . . 347 DISCOVERY OF MADEIRAS . 119
THEY ARE TO BE THOUGHT OF AS OPPOSING GOODS . . . . . . 350 TO A YOUNG WRETCH . . 15

THOUGHT (CONTINUED)
```
    I HAD THOUGHT OURS THE MORE PROFOUND DISGRACE;  .  .  .  .  .  353 THE LESSON FOR TODAY  .   79
    THE SAME FOR READING AS IT WAS FOR THOUGHT,  .  .  .  .  .  .  356 TIME OUT  .  .  .  .  .    9
    THAT MEN HAVE THOUGHT ABOUT IN VAIN.  .  .  .  .  .  .  .  .  381 AN UNSTAMPED LETTER IN    37
    FOR I THOUGHT EPICURUS AND LUCRETIUS  .  .  .  .  .  .  .  .  393 LUCRETIUS VERSUS POETS    5
    HE THOUGHT IF HE COULD HAVE HIS SPACE ALL CURVED,  .  .  .  396 ANY SIZE WE PLEASE  .  .    9
    "I THOUGHT YOU MEANT TO BE AN INDIAN CHIEF--  .  .  .  .  .  406 FROM PLANE TO PLANE  .    69
    PUTTING THE LAMP OUT HAS NOT PUT THEIR THOUGHT OUT.  .  .  415 A CABIN IN THE CLEARING   36
    INAUDIBLY IN THOUGHT.  .  .  .  .  .  .  .  .  .  .  .  .  .  415 CLOSED FOR GOOD  .  .  .   16
    THERE WAS ALWAYS THOUGHT.  .  .  .  .  .  .  .  .  .  .  .  .  426 A NEVER NAUGHT SONG  .     2
    BUT THE FORCE OF THOUGHT.  .  .  .  .  .  .  .  .  .  .  .  .  426 A NEVER NAUGHT SONG  .    31
    EVER THOUGHT TO FLY.  .  .  .  .  .  .  .  .  .  .  .  .  .  .  434 KITTY HAWK  .  .  .  .   193
    THOUGHT OF IN THE LARGE  .  .  .  .  .  .  .  .  .  .  .  .  .  436 KITTY HAWK  .  .  .  .   253
    ALL THERE WAS TO THOUGHT  .  .  .  .  .  .  .  .  .  .  .  .  438 KITTY HAWK  .  .  .  .   322
    THAT HAS THOUGHT TO THINK.  .  .  .  .  .  .  .  .  .  .  .  .  440 KITTY HAWK  .  .  .  .   401
    GETTING THOUGHT EXPRESSED.  .  .  .  .  .  .  .  .  .  .  .  .  442 KITTY HAWK  .  .  .  .   436
    BUT IF IT HAD NO THOUGHT OF PAYING HEED  .  .  .  .  .  .  .  447 DOES NO ONE AT ALL EVER   32
    IAN THOUGHT TO ATTAIN,  .  .  .  .  .  .  .  .  .  .  .  .  .  449 THE BAD ISLAND--EASTER    58
    THOUGHT OF THE KITCHEN SLAVE AND HAD HIM IN .  .  .  .  .  .  456 HOW HARD TO KEEP FROM     79
    BUT ALL YOU THOUGHT OF GIVING ME WAS FOOD.  .  .  .  .  .  .  457 HOW HARD TO KEEP FROM    122
    HE WRITES FREE VERSE, I'M TOLD, AND HE IS THOUGHT .  .  .  459 HOW HARD TO KEEP FROM    184
    FREE WILL, TRADE, VERSE, THOUGHT, LOVE, SPEECH, COINAGE.  .  459 HOW HARD TO KEEP FROM    186
    OR RESPITE FROM THE THOUGHT OF RIVALRY.  .  .  .  .  .  .  .  461 HOW HARD TO KEEP FROM    244
    WHEN AT SIGHT OF YOU HE THOUGHT OF ME.  .  .  .  .  .  .  .  461 HOW HARD TO KEEP FROM    253
    AND CHANGE THE TENOR OF RELIGIOUS THOUGHT.  .  .  .  .  .  .  475 A MASQUE OF REASON  .     68
    YOU THOUGHT IT WAS AGREED YOU NEEDN'T GIVE THEM.  .  .  .  478 A MASQUE OF REASON  .    144
    YOU THOUGHT TO SUIT YOURSELF. I'VE NOT AGREED  .  .  .  .  478 A MASQUE OF REASON  .    145
    I THOUGHT YOU HAD NONE. SOMEWHERE BACK  .  .  .  .  .  .  .  482 A MASQUE OF REASON  .    240
    IT SOUNDS TO ME AS IF YOU THOUGHT IT OUT,  .  .  .  .  .  .  482 A MASQUE OF REASON  .    244
    I THOUGHT THERE WERE TO BE FESTIVITIES  .  .  .  .  .  .  .  488 A MASQUE OF REASON  .    429
    I THOUGHT YOU JUST NOW SAID IT WAS A GIFT SHOP.  .  .  .  .  494 A MASQUE OF MERCY  .  .   25
    I JUST THOUGHT IF YOU HAD A COPY HANDY,  .  .  .  .  .  .  .  495 A MASQUE OF MERCY  .  .   45
    WAS WHAT I THOUGHT OF. / HAVE YOU ANY GROUNDS,  .  .  .  .  502 A MASQUE OF MERCY  .  .  226
    ANOTHER POSSIBILITY I THOUGHT OF--  .  .  .  .  .  .  .  .  .  502 A MASQUE OF MERCY  .  .  235
    (HE STOPS TO LISTEN AND HIS UNSPOKEN THOUGHT,  .  .  .  .  502 A MASQUE OF MERCY  .  .  236
    ANOTHER POSSIBILITY I THOUGHT OF----  .  .  .  .  .  .  .  .  503 A MASQUE OF MERCY  .  .  263
    ANYTHING WE ONCE THOUGHT WE HAD TO BE.  .  .  .  .  .  .  .  505 A MASQUE OF MERCY  .  .  315
    THE THOUGHT THAT ADDED CUBITS TO YOUR HEIGHT  .  .  .  .  .  506 A MASQUE OF MERCY  .  .  339
    I THOUGHT AS MUCH. YOU HAVE IT ALL ARRANGED.  .  .  .  .  .  508 A MASQUE OF MERCY  .  .  372
    STRANGE NO ONE EVER THOUGHT OF IT BEFORE HIM.  .  .  .  .  511 A MASQUE OF MERCY  .  .  478
    MERCY ON ME FOR HAVING THOUGHT I KNEW.  .  .  .  .  .  .  .  518 A MASQUE OF MERCY  .  .  660
THOUGHT-FLOW
    FAR ENOUGH FOR MY THOUGHT-FLOW TO RESUME.  .  .  .  .  .  .  324 BUILD SOIL  .  .  .  .  256
THOUGHTFUL
    ONE PUT A THOUGHTFUL HAND UP TO HIS NOSE  .  .  .  .  .  .  293 AT WOODWARD'S GARDENS  .   14
THOUGHTS
    POINTED OUR THOUGHTS THE WAY WE POINTED IT,  .  .  .  .  .  179 THE STAR-SPLITTER  .  .   84
    THEY KEPT THEIR THOUGHTS AWAY FROM WHEN THE MAPLES  .  .  184 MAPLE  .  .  .  .  .  .  136
    SUCH WERE THE BITTER THOUGHTS TO WHICH I TURNED.  .  .  .  190 THE GRINDSTONE  .  .  .   50
    WITH THOUGHTS OF THE PATH BACK, HOW ROUGH IT WAS  .  .  .  229 TWO LOOK AT TWO  .  .  .    5
    THE THOUGHTS MAY NOT HAVE RISEN THAT SO KEEP  .  .  .  .  231 A BROOK IN THE CITY  .    23
    HE LEFT HER TO HER THOUGHTS AWHILE  .  .  .  .  .  .  .  .  345 DISCOVERY OF MADEIRAS  .   49
THOUSAND  (SEE TWO-THOUSAND-MILE)
    A THOUSAND ORCHISES;  .  .  .  .  .  .  .  .  .  .  .  .  .  .   13 ROSE POGONIAS  .  .  .   12
    WHERE IT WILL TROUBLE US A THOUSAND YEARS.  .  .  .  .  .  .   57 THE BLACK COTTAGE  .  .   69
    THERE WERE TEN THOUSAND THOUSAND FRUIT TO TOUCH,  .  .  .   69 AFTER APPLE-PICKING  .    30
    "A THOUSAND WOULDN'T BE A CENT TOO MUCH;  .  .  .  .  .  .  100 THE SELF-SEEKER  .  .  .  199
    AND CAME DOWN ON THE NORTH. / HE SAID, "A THOUSAND."  .  .  107 CHRISTMAS TREES  .  .  .   41
    "A THOUSAND CHRISTMAS TREES!--AT WHAT APIECE?".  .  .  .  .  107 CHRISTMAS TREES  .  .  .   42
    "A THOUSAND TREES WOULD COME TO THIRTY DOLLARS."  .  .  .  107 CHRISTMAS TREES  .  .  .   44
    A THOUSAND CHRISTMAS TREES I DIDN'T KNOW I HAD!  .  .  .  .  107 CHRISTMAS TREES  .  .  .   55
    THE FROGS THAT WERE PEEPING A THOUSAND SHRILL  .  .  .  .  123 PEA BRUSH  .  .  .  .  .    9
    A THOUSAND TIMES.  IF THAT'S THE WAY HE PREACHES!  .  .  .  152 SNOW  .  .  .  .  .  .  254
    MANCHESTER (SIXTY OR SEVENTY THOUSAND) LAUGHS  .  .  .  .  165 NEW HAMPSHIRE  .  .  .  202
    AT LITTLETON (FOUR THOUSAND), LITTLETON  .  .  .  .  .  .  .  165 NEW HAMPSHIRE  .  .  .  203
    TEN THOUSAND FEET INSTEAD OF ONLY FIVE--  .  .  .  .  .  .  169 NEW HAMPSHIRE  .  .  .  332
    FIVE THOUSAND IS NO LONGER HIGH ENOUGH.  .  .  .  .  .  .  .  169 NEW HAMPSHIRE  .  .  .  334
    WITH AN INCOME IN CASH OF, SAY, A THOUSAND  .  .  .  .  .  172 NEW HAMPSHIRE  .  .  .  409
    FALLEN TO RUIN IN TEN THOUSAND YEARS  .  .  .  .  .  .  .  .  176 THE CENSUS-TAKER  .  .   52
    A THOUSAND YARNS WERE WOUND UP PULL,  .  .  .  .  .  .  .  273 A LONE STRIKER  .  .  .   19
    OF ALL THE THOUSAND SELFISH CARS THAT PASS,  .  .  .  .  .  287 A ROADSIDE STAND  .  .   37
    WILL PUT TEN THOUSAND FARMERS OUT OF SHEEP.  .  .  .  .  .  319 BUILD SOIL  .  .  .  .  110
    I SHOULD BETAKE ME BACK TEN THOUSAND PAGES  .  .  .  .  .  350 THE LESSON FOR TODAY  .    6
    IT IS ALMOST THE YEAR TWO THOUSAND  .  .  .  .  .  .  .  .  361 ALMOST TWO THOUSAND  .     1
    A HUNDRED THOUSAND DAYS  .  .  .  .  .  .  .  .  .  .  .  .  367 A SERIOUS STEP LIGHTLY    21
    OH, YEARS AGO--TEN THOUSAND YEARS.  .  .  .  .  .  .  .  .  392 A CLIFF DWELLING  .  .   13
    TWO THOUSAND FEET ABOVE THE OCEAN LEVEL.  .  .  .  .  .  .  400 TO THE RIGHT PERSON  .     6
    HOW MANY THOUSAND OF THEM IN AN ACRE.  .  .  .  .  .  .  .  404 FROM PLANE TO PLANE  .    17
    LIKE A THOUSAND BIRDS.  .  .  .  .  .  .  .  .  .  .  .  .  .  434 KITTY HAWK  .  .  .  .   191
    AND TRIED TO LOOK TEN THOUSAND DOLLARS' WORTH.  .  .  .  .  454 HOW HARD TO KEEP FROM     38
    A SMALLER PEARL HE ASKED A THOUSAND FOR,  .  .  .  .  .  .  455 HOW HARD TO KEEP FROM     67
    I'VE HAD YOU ON MY MIND A THOUSAND YEARS  .  .  .  .  .  .  475 A MASQUE OF REASON  .  .   47
    IF I SAID ONCE I SAID A THOUSAND TIMES,  .  .  .  .  .  .  .  478 A MASQUE OF REASON  .  .  129
    SHE NOW FELT YOUNGER BY A THOUSAND YEARS  .  .  .  .  .  .  479 A MASQUE OF REASON  .  .  157
THOUSAND-LINKED
    THE GREAT THOUSAND-LINKED GOLD CHAIN,  .  .  .  .  .  .  .  312 THE VINDICTIVES  .  .  .   63
THOUSANDS
    BY THOUSANDS THE BAD WEATHER MADE AKIN.  .  .  .  .  .  .  .  240 OUR SINGING STRENGTH  .   32
THOUSANDTH
    THE THOUSANDTH TIME MAY PROVE THE CHARM.--THAT LEAF!  .  .  148 SNOW  .  .  .  .  .  .  134
THRALL
    YET SOME SAY LOVE BY BEING THRALL  .  .  .  .  .  .  .  .  .  120 BOND AND FREE  .  .  .   17
THRASHED
    HEARD HOW HE THRASHED THE HORSES ON A LOAD  .  .  .  .  .  192 PAUL'S WIFE  .  .  .  .   43
THREAD
    O'ERNIGHT 'TWIXT MULLEIN STALKS A WHEEL OF THREAD  .  .  .  126 RANGE-FINDING  .  .  .   10
    THEY STRING TOGETHER WITH A LIVING THREAD.  .  .  .  .  .  141 THE LINE-GANG  .  .  .    4
```

THREAT
  'WELL THEN,' SHE SAID, AND 'WELL THEN'--LIKE A THREAT. . . 153 SNOW 289
  AN EMPTY THREAT . . . . 210 AN EMPTY THREAT . . .   T
  IS A THREAT TO THE HOUSE. BUT THE HOUSE HAS LONG BEEN TRIED. 305 THERE ARE ROUGHLY ZONES   3
  TO BE THE BEARER OF AN EMPTY THREAT. . . . . 505 A MASQUE OF MERCY . . 303
THREATEN
  KEEP AT THEIR HEELS AND THREATEN TO MOW THEIR LEGS OFF. . . 71 THE CODE 46
THREATENED
  WHEN A STORM THREATENED FROM THE DRAGON'S DEN, ... 63 A SERVANT TO SERVANTS . 30
THREATENER
  I'LL SAY THAT FOR HIM, JOHN'S NO THREATENER . . . . . . 83 THE HOUSEKEEPER . . . 68
THREATENING
  ALL SUMMER LONG I THOUGHT I HEARD THEM THREATENING UNDER
    THEIR BREATH. . . . . 297 A LEAF-TREADER . . .   7
THREATS
  THE THREATS HE MAKES AGAINST THE CITY EVIL. . . . . 497 A MASQUE OF MERCY . . 115
THREE (SEE FORTY-THREE, NINETEEN-FIFTY-THREE, ONE-TWO-THREE)
  THE BREEZE THREE ODORS BROUGHT, ... 29 MY BUTTERFLY 36
  TWO OR THREE TIMES--HE MADE ME FEEL SO QUEER-- . . . . 36 DEATH OF THE HIRED MAN 56
  THEN THERE WERE THREE THERE, MAKING A DIM ROW, ... 40 DEATH OF THE HIRED MAN 162
  THE NIGHT CLERK LED HIM UP THREE FLIGHTS OF STAIRS . . . 45 A HUNDRED COLLARS . . 33
  THERE ARE THREE STONES OF SLATE AND ONE OF MARBLE, . . . 52 HOME BURIAL 26
  'THREE FOGGY MORNINGS AND ONE RAINY DAY . . . . 54 HOME BURIAL 92
  BESIDE IT, AND THERE MAY BE TWO OR THREE . . . . . . 68 AFTER APPLE-PICKING .   4
  THERE WERE THREE IN THE MEADOW BY THE BROOK . . . . . 69 THE CODE   1
  TWO OR THREE FORKFULS I PICKED LIGHTLY ROUND FOR . . . 72 THE CODE 72
  "DON'T BE TOO TECHNICAL.--YOU HAVE THREE CARDS." . . . 76 THE GENERATIONS OF MEN 79
  "FOUR CARDS: ONE YOURS, THREE MINE (ONE FOR EACH BRANCH . 76 THE GENERATIONS OF MEN 80
  HE'S GOT HAY DOWN THAT'S BEEN RAINED ON THREE TIMES. . . 83 THE HOUSEKEEPER . . . 57
  FIVE HUNDRED--FIVE--FIVE! ONE, TWO, THREE, FOUR,FIVE. . 94 THE SELF-SEEKER . . . 59
  THE EXTENT OF PASTURE I SHOULD STRIP, THREE CENTS . . . 107 CHRISTMAS TREES . . . 48
  THREE CENTS SO SMALL BESIDE THE DOLLAR FRIENDS . . . . 107 CHRISTMAS TREES . . . 50
  WORTH THREE CENTS MORE TO GIVE AWAY THAN SELL, ... 107 CHRISTMAS TREES . . . 56
  IN WINTER AFTER HALF-PAST THREE. . . . . 137 BROWN'S DESCENT . . .   4
  BUT NOW HE SNAPPED HIS EYES THREE TIMES; . . . . . . 140 BROWN'S DESCENT . . . 73
  THE THREE STOOD LISTENING TO A FRESH ACCESS . . . . . 143 SNOW   1
  THREE TIMES HE BARELY STIRRED THE BELL, THEN LISTENED. . 143 SNOW 15
  THREE HOURS TO HERE! BUT THAT WAS ALL UPHILL; . . . . 143 SNOW 22
  THE THREE STOOD IN THE LAMPLIGHT ROUND THE TABLE . . . 144 SNOW 31
  THREE HOURS TO DO FOUR MILES--A MILE AN HOUR . . . . . 145 SNOW 58
  AND THREE MILES MORE TO GO!" / "DON'T LET HIM GO. . . . 145 SNOW 62
  AND BY SO DOING GIVE THESE THREE, LAMP, DOG, ... 148 SNOW 145
  IT NOT A MITE WORSE, SITTING HERE, WE THREE, ... 149 SNOW 189
  WE MUST HAVE BEEN ASLEEP: IT'S THREE AND AFTER." . . . 152 SNOW 274
  WE SPREAD OUR TWO LEGS AS WE SPREAD ITS THREE, ... 179 THE STAR-SPLITTER . . 83
  A STAR IN TWO OR THREE, THE WAY YOU SPLIT . . . . . . 179 THE STAR-SPLITTER . . 89
  THE HOUSE ONE STORY HIGH IN FRONT, THREE STORIES . . . 181 MAPLE 57
  (THE HOUSE ONE STORY HIGH IN FRONT, THREE STORIES . . . 182 MAPLE 98
  SHE HAD MADE THREE HERSELF TO THREE OF HIS. . . . . . 199 PLACE FOR A THIRD . .   2
  THE SCORE WAS EVEN FOR THEM, THREE TO THREE. . . . . . 199 PLACE FOR A THIRD . .   3
  THREE CHILDREN IN A BURIAL ROW WERE SAD. . . . . . . 199 PLACE FOR A THIRD . .   6
  ONE MAN'S THREE WOMEN IN A BURIAL ROW . . . . 199 PLACE FOR A THIRD . .   7
  YET DOES PERHAPS FOR ALL THREE. . . . . 212 AN EMPTY THREAT . . . 37
  "WHY NOT TAKE TWO OR THREE?" / "TAKE ALL YOU WANT. . . 217 A FOUNTAIN, A BOTTLE . 124
  WE'VE SAID WE TWO. LET'S CHANGE THAT TO WE THREE. . . . 258 WEST-RUNNING BROOK . . 11
  AND CAST ITS FLOWERS AND ALL THE STEMS BUT THREE; . . . 283 THE GOLD HESPERIDEE .   4
  IT SET ITSELF TO KEEP THOSE THREE ALIVE; . . . . . . 283 THE GOLD HESPERIDEE .   5
  AND DOWNY WAX THE THREE BEGAN TO THRIVE. . . . . . . 283 THE GOLD HESPERIDEE .   6
  LONG SINCE THEY SWUNG AS THREE INSTEAD OF TWO-- . . . . 283 THE GOLD HESPERIDEE . 25
  THREE MADE IT CERTAIN NOTHING FATE COULD DO . . . . . 283 THE GOLD HESPERIDEE . 27
  AND THAT DEFENSE MAKES THREE . . . . 349 TRIPLE BRONZE . . . 11
  IT IS TURNING THREE HUNDRED YEARS . . . . 367 A SERIOUS STEP LIGHTLY 13
  WE'LL MAKE IT THREE HUNDRED MORE . . . . 367 A SERIOUS STEP LIGHTLY 16
  THEIR NUMBER WOULD SEEM LIMITED TO THREE. . . . . . . 398 NO HOLY WARS FOR THEM .   2
  IN OUR THREE HUNDRED DAYS AND SIXTY-FIVE . . . . . . 412 POD OF THE MILKWEED . 32
  WE'RE TOO WELL OFF. / SOMEDAY WE THREE SHOULD HAVE . . . 486 A MASQUE OF REASON . 379
  SOMETHING ABOUT--(THE THREE MEN LAUGH.) . . . . . . 487 A MASQUE OF REASON . 400
  IN THREE QUICK STEPS AS OFF AN ESCALATOR. . . . . . . 489 A MASQUE OF REASON . 452
  NOW IF YOU THREE HAVE SETTLED ANYTHING . . . . 490 A MASQUE OF REASON . 464
  FROM MANY GODS TO THREE, AND THREE TO ONE, ... 498 A MASQUE OF MERCY . . 121
  THE BASIC THREE THE STATE IS FOUNDED ON. . . . . . . 520 A MASQUE OF MERCY . . 704
THREE-BEAT
  (A SKYLARK FOR THEM IN THREE-BEAT PHRASES) . . . . . 428 KITTY HAWK . . . .   S
THRESHOLD
  INSIDE THE THRESHOLD OF HIS OPEN BARN, ... 160 NEW HAMPSHIRE . . . 45
  TO BE BELOW THE THRESHOLD OF COMMERCIAL; . . . . . . 162 NEW HAMPSHIRE . . . 121
  BEFORE I MADE THE TENTH ACROSS THE THRESHOLD. . . . . . 175 THE CENSUS-TAKER . . 33
  ACROSS THE THRESHOLD IN THE TWILIGHT FLED HIM. . . . . 289 OLD BARN AT THE BOTTOM   9
  (JONAH STEPS ON THE THRESHOLD AS THE DOOR . . . . . . 518 A MASQUE OF MERCY . . 649
THREW
  JOHN THREW THE DOOR WIDE BUT HE DIDN'T ENTER. . . . . . 88 THE HOUSEKEEPER . . 205
  AND THREW THEIR LURCHING SHADOWS ON A HOUSE . . . . . . 89 THE FEAR   3
  ASK ANY MAN." / HE THREW HAT THAT AS SOMETHING . . . . 151 SNOW 242
  AND LET OUT A LOUD YELL, AND THREW A BOTTLE, ... 195 PAUL'S WIFE 140
  THREW ME DOWN GRAPES TO MISS AND SCATTER . . . . . . 197 WILD GRAPES 32
  AND THREW MYSELF WET-ELBOWED AND WET-KNEED . . . . . 237 A HILLSIDE THAW . . 12
  IT GENTLY THREW US A GLITTERING SHOWER DOWN. . . . . . 349 OUR HOLD ON THE PLANET   7
  IT THREW US ANOTHER AND THEN ANOTHER STILL, ... 349 OUR HOLD ON THE PLANET   9
  THEY TOOK MY LOVE AND THREW HER DOWN A WELL. . . . . . 510 A MASQUE OF MERCY . . 446
THRICE
  AND TRIES ONCE--TWICE--AND THRICE IF I BE THERE; . . . 15 WAITING 22
THRIFT
  OF CAPITAL, AND CALLING THRIFT A MISER). . . . . . . 363 AN EQUALIZER   4
THRIFTIER
  "HE'S A THRIFTIER PERSON THAN SOME I COULD NAME." . . . 60 BLUEBERRIES 47
THRIFTY
  "HE SEEMS TO BE THRIFTY; AND HASN'T HE NEED, ... 60 BLUEBERRIES 48
  TO BE STRONG, CAREFUL, THRIFTY, DILIGENT, ... 505 A MASQUE OF MERCY . . 314

                                                    PAGE TITLE   LINE

THRILLY
    A LIKENESS TO SURPRISE THE THRILLY TOURIST. . . . . . . 214 A FOUNTAIN, A BOTTLE . 40
THRIVE
    (AND I KNOW OF ONE THAT DIDN'T THRIVE) . . . . . . 232 THE KITCHEN CHIMNEY . 11
    AND DOWNY WAX THE THREE BEGAN TO THRIVE. . . . . . . 283 THE GOLD HESPERIDEE . 6
THROAT
    THE DOCTOR CAUGHT HIS THROAT CONVULSIVELY. . . . . . 46 A HUNDRED COLLARS . . 62
    WHO WANTS TO CUT YOUR NUMBER FOURTEEN THROAT! . . . . 47 A HUNDRED COLLARS . . 84
    A LITTLE THROUGH THE LIPS AND THROAT. . . . . 224 THE AIM WAS SONG . . 15
    THE SERPENT'S TAIL STUCK DOWN THE SERPENT'S THROAT, . . 485 A MASQUE OF REASON . 340
THROATS
    ALL THOSE GREAT RUFFIANS PUT THEIR THROATS TOGETHER, . . 195 PAUL'S WIFE 139
    THEY FILLED THEIR THROATS . . . . 219 I WILL SING YOU ONE-O . 48
THRONE
    TOWARD THE THRONE TO WITNESS THERE . . . . . . 20 THE TRIAL BY EXISTENCE 30
    NO, NONE OF THESE HAS RAISED ME TO MY THRONE . . . . 169 NEW HAMPSHIRE . . . 327
    HIS SEAT UPON THE INTELLECTUAL THRONE"-- . . . . . 171 NEW HAMPSHIRE . . . 385
    IF NEED BE OCCUPY A THRONE, ...'. . . . . 307 PROVIDE, PROVIDE . . 11
    WHERE ONE ROAD LED TO THE THRONE . . . . 313 BEARER OF EVIL TIDINGS 6
    ON A CLIFF FOR A THRONE. . . . . 448 THE BAD ISLAND--EASTER 19
    NOW WHAT'S HE DOING? / PITCHING THRONE, I GUESS, . . . 474 A MASQUE OF REASON . . 19
    (THE THRONE COLLAPSES. BUT HE PICKS IT UP . . . . . 477 A MASQUE OF REASON . . 107
    ONE SIMPLE LITTLE STATEMENT FROM THE THRONE . . . . . 484 A MASQUE OF REASON . . 308
    SHOW YOURSELF, SON.--I'LL GET BACK ON MY THRONE . . . 487 A MASQUE OF REASON . . 386
    I WANT YOU IN MY GROUP BESIDE THE THRONE-- . . . . . 489 A MASQUE OF REASON . . 456
THRONE'S
    (THE THRONE'S A PLYWOOD FLAT, PREFABRICATED, ... 474 A MASQUE OF REASON . . 21
THRONG
    THRUSH, BLUEBIRD, BLACKBIRD, SPARROW, AND ROBIN THRONG; . 239 OUR SINGING STRENGTH . 21
    A HEALTHY INDEPENDENCE OF THE THRONG, ... 424 FOR JOHN F. KENNEDY . 63
    WAS THEIR CYNICAL THRONG . . . . 448 THE BAD ISLAND--EASTER 28
THROUGH---NOT INDEXED
THROVE
    BUT I NEVER HEARD OF A HOUSE THAT THROVE . . . . . . 232 THE KITCHEN CHIMNEY . 10
THROW
    "IT'S AS YOU THROW A PICTURE ON A SCREEN: . . . . . 78 THE GENERATIONS OF MEN 135
    SOMETHING WENT WRONG. I SAW HIM THROW THE HOE . . . . 83 THE HOUSEKEEPER . . . 60
    "AWFUL. WHY DIDN'T THEY THROW OFF THE BELT . . . . . 93 THE SELF-SEEKER . . . 30
    LIKE GIRLS ON HANDS AND KNEES THAT THROW THEIR HAIR . . 121 BIRCHES 19
    THEY THROW A FOREST DOWN LESS CUT THAN BROKEN. . . . 141 THE LINE-GANG 2
    THAT MADE HIM THROW HIS BARE LEGS OUT OF BED . . . . 205 THE WITCH OF COOS . . 102
    HE SHUDDERS HIS COAT AS IF TO THROW OFF FLIES. . . . 223 THE RUNAWAY 18
    ONE MORE WOULD THROW YOU ON THE RIGHT. . . . . . . 325 TO A THINKER 3
    "THROW HIM OVER ALIVE," THEY SAID, ... 345 DISCOVERY OF MADEIRAS . 60
    OH, SOME AS SOON WOULD THROW IT ALL . . . . 445 ENDS 9
    AS THROW A PART AWAY. . . . . 445 ENDS 10
    I ASK OF YOU. GRIND THIS I THROW YOU BACK . . . . . 447 DOES NO ONE AT ALL EVER 29
    AND MAY AS WELL THROW IN A LITTLE SENSE. . . . . . 482 A MASQUE OF REASON . . 237
    THE SAILORS THROW ME OVERBOARD FOR LUCK, ... 500 A MASQUE OF MERCY . . 182
    OR, AS YOU MIGHT SAY, THROW ME TO THE WHALE-- . . . 500 A MASQUE OF MERCY . . 183
    YOU'RE MODERN; SO THE WHALE YOU THROW ME TO . . . . 500 A MASQUE OF MERCY . . 186
THROWING
    FOR THE MAN UP ON TOP, OF THROWING DOWN . . . . . 71 THE CODE 56
    THROWING A LEG UP OVER OUR FENCE OF MOUNTAINS, . . . 176 THE STAR-SPLITTER . . 2
    NOT JUST A SWERVING, BUT A THROWING BACK, ... 259 WEST-RUNNING BROOK . . 59
    IT HAS THIS THROWING BACKWARD ON ITSELF . . . . . 259 WEST-RUNNING BROOK . . 61
    THEN'S WHEN HIS MORGAN LIGHTS OUT THROWING SNOWBALLS . . 407 FROM PLANE TO PLANE . 107
THROWN (SEE SELF-THROWN)
    "ONE OUGHT NOT TO BE THROWN INTO CONFUSION . . . . . 75 THE GENERATIONS OF MEN 58
    AND DINING ROOM--THROWN PELL-MELL IN THE KITCHEN. . . . 110 IN THE HOME STRETCH . 9
    THROWN FROM SOMEWHERE AGAINST THEIR WALLPAPER. . . . 129 THE BONFIRE 12
    HE WAS NOT USED TO HANDLING STARS THROWN DARK . . . . 172 A STAR IN A STONEBOAT . 8
    IT LOOKED AS IF HE MIGHT BE BADLY THROWN. . . . . . 190 THE GRINDSTONE . . . 58
    THROWN AWAY . . . . 211 AN EMPTY THREAT . . . 32
    BOOKS WERE NOT THROWN IRREVERENTLY ABOUT. . . . . . 216 A FOUNTAIN, A BOTTLE . 117
    WITH CINDER LOADS DUMPED DOWN? THE BROOK WAS THROWN . . 231 A BROOK IN THE CITY . 15
    OUR ARM THROWN OVER IT ASLEEP BESIDE IT. . . . . . 258 WEST-RUNNING BROOK . . 15
    IF, AS THEY SAY, SOME DUST THROWN IN MY EYES . . . . 265 DUST IN THE EYES . . 1
    LIKE PEOPLE THROWN OUT TO DELAY THE WOLVES. . . . . 279 THE WHITE-TAILED HORNET 68
    GOOD GLOOM ON HER WAS THROWN AWAY. . . . . 383 THE NIGHT LIGHT . . . 5
    I HAD READ AND THROWN. . . . . 429 KITTY HAWK 21
    IS THROWN IN SCRIPT, AS AT BELSHAZZAR'S FEAST, ... 502 A MASQUE OF MERCY . . 238
    THROWN PROSTRATE AT THE MERCY SEAT FOR MERCY. . . . . 511 A MASQUE OF MERCY . . 485
THROWS
    THROWS DOWN IN FRONT OF US IS NOT TO BAR . . . . . 238 ON A TREE FALLEN ACROSS 2
    WHEN THE SPENT SUN THROWS UP ITS RAYS ON CLOUD . . . 249 ACCEPTANCE 1
THRUSH
    THRUSH, BLUEBIRD, BLACKBIRD, SPARROW, AND ROBIN THRONG; . 239 OUR SINGING STRENGTH . 21
    THRUSH MUSIC--HARK! . . . . 334 COME IN 2
    THRUSH MUSIC WENT-- . . . . 334 COME IN 14
THRUSH'S
    IN A THRUSH'S BREAST. . . . . 334 COME IN 12
THRUST
    AND THAT THRUST UP TO BLOSSOM IN THE SUN . . . . . 98 THE SELF-SEEKER . . . 157
    ANOTHER BLACKENED FACE THRUST IN AND LOOKED . . . . 111 IN THE HOME STRETCH . 18
    POINTED THE DECIMAL OFF WITH ONE DEEP THRUST. . . . . 119 MEETING AND PASSING . 9
    I THRUST MY HOE IN THE MELLOW GROUND, ... 124 A TIME TO TALK . . . 7
    AND THRUST HANDS IN AND HELD MY FACE AWAY. . . . . 131 THE BONFIRE 66
    HOW HIGH I'D THRUST THE PEAKS IN SUMMER SNOW . . . . 169 NEW HAMPSHIRE . . . 339
    THE FOE THRUST BACK UNSAFE BEYOND THE RHINE . . . . 222 TO E.T. 18
    IN ANSWER TO THE MENTAL THRUST. . . . . 332 ALL REVELATION . . . 15
    WHEN PAST THE LEG I THRUST FOR BAR . . . . 419 ONE MORE BREVITY . . 8
THRUSTING
    ONE HELPER, THRUSTING PITCHFORK IN THE GROUND, ... 69 THE CODE 7
    SAND HAS BEEN THRUSTING IN THE SQUARE OF DOOR . . . . 399 THE INGENUITIES OF DEBT 13
THRUSTS
    THE METEOR THAT THRUSTS IN WITH NEEDLE BILL, ... 12 A PRAYER IN SPRING . . 11
    A HEAD THRUSTS IN AS FOR THE VIEW, ... 332 ALL REVELATION . . . 1

THRUSTS (CONTINUED)
    BUT WHERE IT IS IT THRUSTS IN FROM . . . . 332 ALL REVELATION 2
    OR WHAT IT IS IT THRUSTS INTO . . . . 332 ALL REVELATION 3
THUMB
    BLUEBERRIES AS BIG AS THE END OF YOUR THUMB, ... 59 BLUEBERRIES 3
    TO FEEL OF BETWEEN THUMB AND FINGERS; . . . . 266 SITTING BY A BUSH . . 3
THUMBNAIL
    WITH A THICK THUMBNAIL TO SHOW HOW IT RAN . . . . . 186 THE AX-HELVE 23
THUMPING
    OVER THE GREAT BIG THUMPING, SHUFFLING MILLSTONE, . . . 142 THE VANISHING RED . . 16
    TO FEED HIS THUMPING GRUBS AS BIG AS HE IS. . . . . 278 THE WHITE-TAILED HORNET 31
THUNDER
    WE HEARD THE MINIATURE THUNDER WHERE HE FLED, ... 223 THE RUNAWAY 6
THUNDERCLAP
    TO HEAR IT WRECK IN A THUNDERCLAP. . . . . 306 A TRIAL RUN 7
THUNDERING
    STARTED CHAIRS THUNDERING ON THE KITCHEN FLOOR, . . . 368 THE LITERATE FARMER AND 2
THUS
    AND THUS IT WAS THE MAIDENS PALE . . . . 15 IN A VALE 3
    AND THUS IT IS I KNOW SO WELL . . . . 16 IN A VALE 21
    BUT 'TIS NOT TRUE THAT THUS I DWELT ALOOF, ... 16 A DREAM PANG 13
    THUS ARE WE WHOLLY STRIPPED OF PRIDE . . . . 21 THE TRIAL BY EXISTENCE 70
    THE MOWER IN THE DEW HAD LOVED THEM THUS, ... 23 THE TUFT OF FLOWERS . 25
    IT'S THUS HE DOES IT OF A WINTER NIGHT. . . . . . . 108 OLD MAN'S WINTER NIGHT 28
    THUS HAD A NAME WITH MEANING, GIVEN IN DEATH, ... 185 MAPLE 163
    AND TAKEN THUS INTO THE FAMILY. . . . . 216 A FOUNTAIN, A BOTTLE . 101
    SHE SEEMED TO THINK THAT, TWO THUS, THEY WERE SAFE. . . 229 TWO LOOK AT TWO . . . 21
    THUS TILL HE HAD THEM ALMOST FEELING DARED . . . . . 230 TWO LOOK AT TWO . . . 35
    THE COUNTRY'S SINGING STRENGTH THUS BROUGHT TOGETHER, . 240 OUR SINGING STRENGTH . 50
    SHE CAN THINK OF PLACES THAT ARE NOT THUS . . . . . 291 ON HEART'S BEGINNING TO 32
    THUS TRUTH'S ESTABLISHED AND BORNE OUT, ... 331 BEECH 10
    THUS CONCENTRATING EARTH AND SKIES . . . . 333 ALL REVELATION . . . 18
    BUT EVEN WHERE, THUS, OPPOSING INTERESTS KILL, ... 350 TO A YOUNG WRETCH . . 14
    THUS FORESIGHT DOES IT AND LAISSEZ-FAIRE, ... 376 SOMETHING FOR HOPE . 18
    AT BEING THUS EXPOUNDED TO HIMSELF . . . . 405 FROM PLANE TO PLANE . 56
    SO I SPOKE IN TERMS OF ADOPTION THUS: . . . . 420 ONE MORE BREVITY . . 27
    AND THUS FASTENED ON . . . . 438 KITTY HAWK 328
    AND HE WISHED LOVE WERE THUS AND SO. . . . . 451 A-WISHING WELL . . . 2
THY
    THY LEAVES HAVE RIPENED TO THE FALL; . . . . 27 OCTOBER 2
    WITH ALL THY DAZZLING OTHER ONES, ... 28 MY BUTTERFLY 13
    BUT THE WILD TOUCH OF THY DYE-DUSTY WING' . . . . . 29 MY BUTTERFLY 42
    AND I'LL FORGIVE THY GREAT BIG ONE ON ME. . . . . . 428 FORGIVE, O LORD... . 2
    LOVE THOU THY NEIGHBOR AS THYSELF, AYE, ... 467 QUANDARY 12
THYATIRA
    YOU HEAR HIM, THYATIRA: WE'RE A SAINT. . . . . . . 476 A MASQUE OF REASON . 80
    EXCEPT IN THEIR OWN COUNTRY, THYATIRA. . . . . . . 476 A MASQUE OF REASON . 91
    I'M APT TO STRING ALONG WITH THYATIRA. . . . . . . 479 A MASQUE OF REASON . 168
    HOW IS THAT FOR A MIX-UP, THYATIRA?— . . . . 485 A MASQUE OF REASON . 337
THYSELF
    LOVE THOU THY NEIGHBOR AS THYSELF, AYE, ... 467 QUANDARY 12
    AND HATE HIM AS THYSELF THOU HATEST. . . . . 467 QUANDARY 13
TIBET
    WAS A PRAYER MACHINE FROM TIBET . . . . 397 AN IMPORTER 18
TICK
    FROM FAR AWAY THERE CAME AN ANSWERING TICK, ... 269 THE EGG AND THE MACHINE 2
    AND THEN ANOTHER TICK. HE KNEW THE CODE: . . . . . 270 THE EGG AND THE MACHINE 3
TICKET (SEE UNDER-TICKET-AGENT)
    MEANING BY US THEIR TICKET. 'NO,' I SAYS, ... 48 A HUNDRED COLLARS . 113
    HE HAD HIS TICKET BOUGHT, HIS PASSAGE EARNED, ... 370 THE LITERATE FARMER AND 58
TICKETS
    WHERE HIS JOB, WHEN HE WASN'T SELLING TICKETS, ... 178 THE STAR-SPLITTER . 70
TICKLES
    WHERE YOUR FACE BURNS AND TICKLES WITH THE COBWEBS . . 122 BIRCHES 45
    FAR STAR THAT TICKLES FOR ME MY SENSITIVE PLATE . . . 389 SKEPTIC 1
TIDAL
    AND NOW IT IS ONCE MORE THE TIDAL WAVE . . . . . . 255 THE FLOOD 12
    BY ITS TIDAL PULL . . . . 433 KITTY HAWK 173
TIDE
    TO PAY THE DOCTOR'S BILL AND TIDE ME OVER. . . . . . 95 THE SELF-SEEKER . . 74
    THROUGH EVERYTHING PRESENTED, LAND AND TIDE . . . . . 267 RIDERS 3
    AND TAKE OUR DAILY TIDE BATHS SMOOTH AND ROUGH. . . . 395 ETHEREALIZING . . . 8
    OH, MAY THE TIDE BE SOON ENOUGH AT HIGH . . . . . . 395 ETHEREALIZING . . . 13
    ALL THE SEA WATER IN ONE TIDE . . . . 452 A-WISHING WELL . . . 45
    WHEN A GREAT TIDE OF ARGUMENT SWEEPS IN . . . . . . 513 A MASQUE OF MERCY . 538
TIDINGS
    THE BEARER OF EVIL TIDINGS, ... 313 BEARER OF EVIL TIDINGS 1
    REMEMBERED THAT EVIL TIDINGS . . . . 313 BEARER OF EVIL TIDINGS 3
    THE BEARER OF EVIL TIDINGS . . . . 313 BEARER OF EVIL TIDINGS T
    AND THE BEARER OF EVIL TIDINGS . . . . 314 BEARER OF EVIL TIDINGS 35
    AS FOR HIS EVIL TIDINGS, ... 314 BEARER OF EVIL TIDINGS 41
TIED
    NOT SO MUCH TIED AS MADE THEM BLEND. . . . . 274 A LONE STRIKER . . . 32
TIES
    THE TIES GAVE, ... 129 THE IMPULSE 26
    BY COUNTLESS SILKEN TIES OF LOVE AND THOUGHT . . . . 332 THE SILKEN TENT . . . 10
TIGER
    LIKE A TIGER AT A BONE. . . . . 340 THE SUBVERTED FLOWER . 29
TIGHT
    HOLD TIGHT AWHILE TILL I THINK WHAT TO DO. . . . . . 198 WILD GRAPES 82
    AND SWOLLEN TIGHT AND BURIED UNDER SNOW. . . . . . 204 THE WITCH OF COOS . 56
    AND SWOLLEN TIGHT AND BURIED UNDER SNOW. . . . . . 204 THE WITCH OF COOS . 58
    THAT THE CITY'S HOLD ON A MAN IS NO MORE TIGHT . . . 306 NOT QUITE SOCIAL . . 7
    IT SWIRLS OCCLUDED IN US UNDER TIGHT . . . . 386 INNATE HELIUM . . . 2
    TO FEEL IT CLOSE IN TIGHT AGAINST MY SENSE . . . . . 390 SKEPTIC 11
TIGHT-SHUT
    BUT THERE'S A TIGHT-SHUT LOOK TO EITHER DOOR . . . . 400 TO THE RIGHT PERSON . 8

TILE
   TRIED TO IMPROVE ON SAILING LIKE A TILE . . . . 216 A FOUNTAIN, A BOTTLE . 112
TILL
   TILL EVEN THE COMFORTING BARN GROWS FAR AWAY, ... 10 STORM FEAR 15
   TILL SOMEONE REALLY FIND US OUT. . . . . 19 REVELATION 4
   SPIRIT TO MATTER TILL DEATH COME. . . . . 21 THE TRIAL BY EXISTENCE . 64
   WAIT TILL YOU SEE." / "WHERE DID YOU SAY HE'D BEEN?" . . . 35 DEATH OF THE HIRED MAN . 39
   "PROFESSOR SQUARE-THE-CIRCLE-TILL-YOU'RE-TIRED? . . . . . 46 A HUNDRED COLLARS . . 44
   "NCT TILL I SHRINK, WHEN THEY'LL BE OUT OF STYLE." . . . . 50 A HUNDRED COLLARS . . 166
   THEN THE TWO SONS, TILL SHE WAS LEFT ALONE. . . . . . . 56 THE BLACK COTTAGE . . 39
   WE PICKED, TILL I FEARED YOU HAD WANDERED A MILE, ... 62 BLUEBERRIES 92
   JUST AS YOU WILL TILL IT BECOMES A HABIT. . . . . 67 A SERVANT TO SERVANTS . 147
   MIND YOU, I WAITED TILL LEN SAID THE WORD. . . . . . . 67 A SERVANT TO SERVANTS . 149
   EVERYTHING WENT WELL TILL WE REACHED THE BARN . . . . . 71 THE CODE 53
   TILL WELL TOWARD NOON, WHEN THE STORM SETTLED DOWN . . . . 74 THE GENERATIONS OF MEN 22
   THIS HE SAT LISTENING TO TILL SHE GAVE JUDGMENT. . . . . 76 THE GENERATIONS OF MEN 77
   TILL I SHAN'T DARE TO SET A FOOT OUTDOORS. . . . . . . 90 THE FEAR 47
   TILL WEISS SHUT OFF THE WATER IN THE WHEEL PIT. . . . . . 93 THE SELF-SEEKER . . . 27
   I WENT TILL THERE WERE NO COTTAGES FOUND. . . . . 102 GOOD HOURS 10
   HE SAT AND WAITED TILL HE DREW US OUT, ... 106 CHRISTMAS TREES . . . 7
   TILL ED BEGINS TO GET OUT ON A SUNDAY . . . . 115 IN THE HOME STRETCH . 148
   TILL DAY MAKES HIM RETRACE HIS FLIGHT, ... 120 BOND AND FREE . . . 13
   TOWARD HEAVEN, TILL THE TREE COULD BEAR NO MORE, ... 122 BIRCHES 56
   FOR WHAT THEY'D BETTER WAIT TILL WE HAVE DONE. . . . . . 130 THE BONFIRE 15
   WITH LOWERED EYES A MOMENT TILL HE SAID, ... 144 SNOW 32
   RECURRING TILL WE ANSWER FROM WITHIN. . . . . 147 SNOW 133
   TO LAST HER TILL HE GOT OUTSIDE THE DOOR, ... 151 SNOW 243
   WE'LL HAVE TO SIT HERE TILL WE KNOW HE'S SAFE." . . . . . 152 SNOW 262
   HELPLESS. "THERE'S NOTHING WE CAN DO TILL MORNING." . . . 155 SNOW 325
   TILL WE LOSE ALL MEASURE OF PACE, ... 156 THE SOUND OF TREES . . 7
   AND NEVER RIGHTLY UNDERSTOOD TILL BRYAN . . . . 168 NEW HAMPSHIRE . . . 296
   TILL HAVING FAILED AT HUGGER-MUGGER FARMING . . . . . . 177 THE STAR-SPLITTER . . 15
   AND STANDING AT OUR LEISURE TILL THE DAY BROKE, ... 179 THE STAR-SPLITTER . . 85
   SO, TILL SHE FOUND HERSELF IN A STRANGE PLACE . . . . . 182 MAPLE 77
   THE LUMBER ON PAUL TILL PAUL BEGGED FOR MERCY. . . . . . 193 PAUL'S WIFE 61
   MY SMALL WRISTS STRETCHING TILL THEY SHOWED THE BANJO
     STRINGS. . . . . 198 WILD GRAPES 80
   HOLD TIGHT AWHILE TILL I THINK WHAT TO DO. . . . . . . 198 WILD GRAPES 82
   I LISTENED TILL IT ALMOST CLIMBED THE STAIRS . . . . . 205 THE WITCH OF COOS . . 90
   THEY MADE HIM KEEP ON GNAWING TILL HE WHINED. . . . . . 209 PAUPER WITCH OF GRAFTON 58
   TILL IT CAUGHT WIND AND, OPENING OUT ITS COVERS, ... 216 A FOUNTAIN, A BOTTLE . 111
   THUS TILL HE HAD THEM ALMOST FEELING DARED . . . . . . 230 TWO LOOK AT TWO . . 35
   TILL I FILL THE WHOLE SHED, ... 235 GATHERING LEAVES . . 15
   NOT TILL FROM SEPARATE FLAKES THEY CHANGED AT NIGHT . . . 239 OUR SINGING STRENGTH . 7
   I WOULD NOT GO IN TILL THE LIGHT WENT OUT; . . . . . . 253 THE THATCH 6
   IT WOULD NOT GO OUT TILL I CAME IN. . . . . 253 THE THATCH 7
   TILL DAYLIGHT MADE IT SAFE FOR A FLYER. . . . . 253 THE THATCH 27
   I GAVE UP FIRE FOR FORM TILL I WAS COLD. . . . . 267 WHAT FIFTY SAID . . . 2
   DANCED SLOWLY ON IT TILL HE TROD IT FLAT. . . . . . . 284 THE GOLD HESPERIDEE . 48
   OF FIRST ONE, THEN THE OTHER, TILL IT BROUGHT . . . . . 293 AT WOODWARD'S GARDENS . 9
   TILL ABOUT THE RIGHT CONSISTENCE. . . . . 304 CLEAR AND COLDER . . 6
   WE MUST WAIT TILL SOME MONTHS HENCE IN THE SPRING TO KNOW. . 305 THERE ARE ROUGHLY ZONES 19
   IT WILL GATHER SPEED TILL YOUR NERVES PREPARE . . . . . 306 A TRIAL RUN 6
   TILL ANOTHER PARASITE . . . . 308 EVIL TENDENCIES CANCEL 5
   HE TOLD THEM TO DIVE TILL THEY DROWNED. . . . . 311 THE VINDICTIVES . . . 46
   TILL HE CAME TO THE LAND OF PAMIR. . . . . 313 BEARER OF EVIL TIDINGS 12
   LET NONE ASSUME TO TILL THE LAND BUT FARMERS. . . . . . 322 BUILD SOIL 209
   TILL THEY WERE OUT OF HEARING . . . . 335 CARPE DIEM 7
   TILL I SAW THE PATH WHERE THE SLENDER FOX HAD COME . . . 342 QUEST OF PURPLE-FRINGED 11
   TILL THE PIRATE SAILORS MADE A VOW . . . . 344 DISCOVERY OF MADEIRAS . 24
   TILL HER HEART ALMOST CEASED TO BEAT. . . . . 346 DISCOVERY OF MADEIRAS . 102
   TILL THE SPONGY SOIL AGAIN WAS NATAL WET. . . . . . . 349 OUR HOLD ON THE PLANET 10
   GO TILL YOU WET YOUR PINIONS AND ARE QUENCHED. . . . . . 356 A MOTH SEEN IN WINTER . 18
   I LET IT LIE THERE TILL I HOPE IT SLEPT. . . . . . . 358 A CONSIDERABLE SPECK . 29
   TILL I HAVE REELED AND STUMBLED . . . . 389 ASTROMETAPHYSICAL . . 5
   TILL IT CAN MUSTER BREATH INSIDE A HALL . . . . 399 THE INGENUITIES OF DEBT 17
   TILL EVEN I HAVE CEASED . . . . 416 CLOSED FOR GOOD . . 26
   TILL ACCIDENTALLY IT HIT ON MIND . . . . 425 ACCIDENTALLY ON PURPOSE 6
   TILL DARWIN CAME TO EARTH UPON A YEAR . . . . 425 ACCIDENTALLY ON PURPOSE 9
   HAD NO REAL PURPOSE TILL IT GOT TO US. . . . . 425 ACCIDENTALLY ON PURPOSE 12
   TILL THE SO-LONG-KEPT . . . . 437 KITTY HAWK 293
   TILL WE CAME TO BE . . . . 440 KITTY HAWK 391
   TILL ON SOME FINE NIGHT . . . . 442 KITTY HAWK 454
   TILL YOU HAVE LOST THE SAVOR OF YOUR SALT. . . . . . . 446 DOES NO ONE AT ALL EVER 24
   TILL IT FLAKED FROM THE LEDGE. . . . . 448 THE BAD ISLAND--EASTER 15
   THE BUD MUST BLOOM TILL BLOWSY BLOWN . . . . 450 OUR DOOM TO BLOOM . . 13
   TILL THE AMBASSADORS FROM PUNT OR SOMEWHERE . . . . . . 456 HOW HARD TO KEEP FROM 72
   TILL ON A DAY THE KING, BEING SICK AT HEART . . . . . . 456 HOW HARD TO KEEP FROM 94
   TILL I WAS CAUGHT AND PUT TO SHAME, ... 467 QUANDARY 22
   I RODE UP ON ONE TILL THE BUBBLE BURST, ... 468 IN A GLASS OF CIDER . 4
   GOOD, PRETTY GOOD. / WAIT TILL I GET MY KODAK.-- . . . . 488 A MASQUE OF REASON . 402
   THERE'S NOT MUCH WE CAN DO TILL MARTIN GETS HERE.-- . . . 514 A MASQUE OF MERCY . . 557
   I SAY WE KEEP HIM TILL WE WRING SOME MORE . . . . . . 517 A MASQUE OF MERCY . . 639
TILTED
   WAS THE LAMP TILTED NEAR THEM IN HIS HAND. . . . . . . 108 OLD MAN'S WINTER NIGHT 5
   I'VE TRIED THE NEW MOON TILTED IN THE AIR . . . . . . 245 THE FREEDOM OF THE MOON 1
TIMBER
   CALL HER NAUSICAA, AND TAKE A TIMBER . . . . 79 THE GENERATIONS OF MEN 160
   SON, YOU DO AS YOU'RE TOLD! YOU TAKE THE TIMBER-- . . . . 80 THE GENERATIONS OF MEN 192
TIME (SEE CHICKEN-TIME, FATHER-TIME-LIKE, MENDING-TIME, SMALL-TIME)
   FULL MANY A TIME TO SAY HIS SAY . . . . 6 GHOST HOUSE . . . 19
   AND IT SEEMS LIKE THE TIME WHEN, AFTER DOUBT, ... 27 A LINE-STORM SONG . . 29
   IN HAYING TIME, WHEN ANY HELP IS SCARCE. . . . . . . 35 DEATH OF THE HIRED MAN 29
   YOU NEEDN'T BE AFRAID HE'LL LEAVE YOU THIS TIME." . . . . 38 DEATH OF THE HIRED MAN 112
   HE'D KEEP SO STILL ABOUT HIM ALL THIS TIME?" . . . . . 39 DEATH OF THE HIRED MAN 138
   THE RIVER AT THE TIME WAS FALLEN AWAY, ... 40 THE MOUNTAIN 10
   NOT FOR THIS MORNING, BUT SOME OTHER TIME . . . . . . 41 THE MOUNTAIN 36
   ONE TIME I ASKED A FELLOW CLIMBING IT . . . . 43 THE MOUNTAIN 73

TIME (CONTINUED)

HAVEN'T COME DOWN TO THE BARS AT MILKING TIME? . . . . . 43 THE MOUNTAIN 86
YOU GOT IT THE FIRST TIME. AND YOURS?" / "MAGOON. . . . . 46 A HUNDRED COLLARS . . 42
I PICK IT UP A DOLLAR AT A TIME . . . . 48 A HUNDRED COLLARS . . 97
IT'S TIME YOU TURNED AROUND AND BOOSTED US. . . . . . 48 A HUNDRED COLLARS . . 115
HE SAID TO GAIN TIME: "WHAT IS IT YOU SEE?" . . . . . 51 HOME BURIAL 10
"AMY! DON'T GO TO SOMEONE ELSE THIS TIME. . . . . . 52 HOME BURIAL 39
DON'T CARRY IT TO SOMEONE ELSE THIS TIME. . . . . . 53 HOME BURIAL 57
THINK OF IT, TALK LIKE THAT AT SUCH A TIME! . . . . . 54 HOME BURIAL 94
NO, FROM THE TIME WHEN ONE IS SICK TO DEATH, ... 54 HOME BURIAL 100
DO YOU KNOW BUT FOR HER THERE WAS A TIME . . . . . . 57 THE BLACK COTTAGE . . 84
"WHY, THERE HASN'T BEEN TIME FOR THE BUSHES TO GROW. . . 59 BLUEBERRIES 13
COMING AND GOING ALL THE TIME, THEY ARE: . . . . . 65 A SERVANT TO SERVANTS 81
HE WAS BEFORE MY TIME--I NEVER SAW HIM; . . . . . . 67 A SERVANT TO SERVANTS 140
"IT'S TIME I TOOK MY TURN UPSTAIRS IN JAIL"-- . . . . 67 A SERVANT TO SERVANTS 146
JAMES WOULD TAKE TIME, OF COURSE, TO CHEW IT OVER . . . 70 THE CODE 18
A GOVERNOR IT WAS PROCLAIMED THIS TIME, ... 73 THE GENERATIONS OF MEN 1
BUT WHY TAKE TIME FOR WHAT I'M LIKE TO HEAR? . . . . 78 THE GENERATIONS OF MEN 143
YOU THINK YOU'D BEST TEMPT HER AT SUCH A TIME?" . . . 79 THE GENERATIONS OF MEN 182
WE'VE BEEN HERE FIFTEEN YEARS." / "THAT'S A LONG TIME . 82 THE HOUSEKEEPER . . . 39
HE'LL SORT OF SWEAR THE TIME AWAY. HE'S AWFUL! . . . 83 THE HOUSEKEEPER . . . 52
HE'S GIVEN HER TIME TO THINK OF SOMETHING ELSE. . . . 84 THE HOUSEKEEPER . . . 86
WHAT IF I'M RIGHT, AND SOMEONE ALL THE TIME-- . . . . 90 THE FEAR 22
AND NOW'S THE TIME TO HAVE IT OUT WITH HIM . . . . . 90 THE FEAR 43
"WHAT'S A CHILD DOING AT THIS TIME OF NIGHT----?" . . . 92 THE FEAR 81
"THEY SAY SOME TIME WAS WASTED ON THE BELT-- . . . . 94 THE SELF-SEEKER . . . 32
"OH, GUESS WHICH HAND? MY, MY! ONCE ON A TIME . . . 96 THE SELF-SEEKER . . . 107
AT SUCH A TIME AS THIS. HE SNAPPED IT NOW. . . . . 98 THE SELF-SEEKER . . . 166
"YES, BUT ALL THAT TAKES TIME, AND I'M AS MUCH . . . 99 THE SELF-SEEKER . . . 191
HALF THE TIME I DON'T KNOW WHAT'S TROUBLING ME.-- . . 99 THE SELF-SEEKER . . . 194
BEYOND THE TIME OF PROFITABLE GROWTH-- . . . . . . 106 CHRISTMAS TREES . . 23
THE WAY THE NEST-FULL EVERY TIME WE STIRRED . . . . 109 THE EXPOSED NEST . . 20
HOW DARK IT'S GETTING. CAN YOU TELL WHAT TIME . . . 113 IN THE HOME STRETCH 67
AND ALL THE TIME WE TALKED YOU SEEMED TO SEE . . . . 119 MEETING AND PASSING 10
TIME SOMEONE CAME WITH CART AND PAIR . . . . . . 123 PEA BRUSH 15
NO, NOT AS THERE IS A TIME TO TALK. . . . . 124 A TIME TO TALK . . 6
A TIME TO TALK . . . . 124 A TIME TO TALK . . T
THE COW IN APPLE TIME . . . . 124 THE COW IN APPLE TIME T
WARNING AND TIME TO BE OFF IN FLIGHT: . . . . . 127 HOUSE FEAR 7
THAT I SPREAD COAL-BLACK OVER IN THE TIME . . . . 132 THE BONFIRE 83
THE TIME I DREAMED THE DOOR WAS TRIED . . . . . 135 LOCKED OUT 4
AT THAT PARTICULAR TIME O'CLOCK, ... 139 BROWN'S DESCENT . . 64
THEY KEPT THEIR HEADS AND TOOK THEIR TIME TO IT . . 143 SNOW 24
TRY TO THINK WHAT HE DID WITH ALL THAT TIME. . . . 145 SNOW 61
THE THOUSANDTH TIME MAY PROVE THE CHARM.--THAT LEAF! . 148 SNOW 134
AT THE SAME TIME YOU CAN'T DENY IT MAKES . . . . . 149 SNOW 188
ARE RESTED AND IT'S TIME TO SAY GOOD-NIGHT. . . . . 150 SNOW 210
IN NO TIME OUT TONIGHT. AND YET TOMORROW . . . . . 151 SNOW 229
I'VE SEEN THE TIME I'VE HAD TO WORK MYSELF. . . . . 159 NEW HAMPSHIRE . . 6
OFF HIS. THE TIME WAS EVENING IN THE PULLMAN. . . . 159 NEW HAMPSHIRE . . 14
THE TIME WAS AUTUMN, BUT HOW ANYONE . . . . . . 175 THE CENSUS-TAKER . 17
COULD TELL THE TIME OF YEAR WHEN EVERY TREE . . . . 175 THE CENSUS-TAKER . 18
OF BREATHING TREES SAID SOMETHING OF THE TIME . . . 175 THE CENSUS-TAKER . 26
IN TIME, HAD SHE NOT REALIZED HER DANGER. . . . . 187 THE AX-HELVE . . . 51
IN TIME TO KEEP ME FROM SUSPECTING HIM . . . . . 187 THE AX-HELVE . . . 61
FOR LOVE OF IT, AND YET NOT WASTE TIME EITHER. . . . 188 THE AX-HELVE . . . 81
"FIRST TIME I EVER SAW A HOLLOW PINE. . . . . . 193 PAUL'S WIFE . . . 75
(MURPHY HAD BEEN THERE WATCHING ALL THE TIME, . . . 194 PAUL'S WIFE . . . 114
WHICH GAVE HIM SOME TIME TO HIMSELF TO EAT, . . . 197 WILD GRAPES . . . 34
BY THAT TIME I WAS PRETTY WELL REDUCED . . . . . 198 WILD GRAPES . . . 60
TRY TO WEIGH SOMETHING NEXT TIME, SO YOU WON'T . . 199 WILD GRAPES . . . 90
SHE'D LOOKED ELIZA UP HER SECOND TIME, ... 201 PLACE FOR A THIRD . 58
SHE MUST NOT KEEP HIM WAITING. TIME WOULD PRESS . . 201 PLACE FOR A THIRD . 68
WHEN HIS TIME COMES TO DIE AND SETTLE DOWN. . . . 202 PLACE FOR A THIRD . 82
THE WAY HE DID IN LIFE ONCE; BUT THIS TIME . . . 204 THE WITCH OF COOS . 144
TO TELL THE TRUTH, SUPPOSE THE TIME HAD COME. . . . 207 THE WITCH OF COOS . 166
I COULD HAVE TOLD THEM ANY TIME THIS TWELVEMONTH . . 207 PAUPER WITCH OF GRAFTON 15
HE WASN'T BUT FIFTEEN AT THE TIME THEY SAY. . . . 208 PAUPER WITCH OF GRAFTON 19
I WAS SOON SATISFIED FOR THE TIME BEING. . . . . 217 A FOUNTAIN, A BOTTLE 131
IN TIME SHE WOULD BE RID OF ALL HER BOOKS. . . . . 217 A FOUNTAIN, A BOTTLE 138
YET CAN'T HELP MARKING ALL THE TIME . . . . . . 221 IN A DISUSED GRAVEYARD 10
SWOOPS JUST IN TIME TO HIS REMEMBERED TREE. . . . 249 ACCEPTANCE . . . 10
PROCLAIMED THE TIME WAS NEITHER WRONG NOR RIGHT. . . 255 ACQUAINTED WITH NIGHT 13
"HOW MUCH TIME HAVE WE?" . . . . 256 THE LOVELY BE CHOOSERS 4
BUT WITHOUT TIME TO LINGER FOR HER STORY. . . . . 257 THE LOVELY BE CHOOSERS 49
AND IT IS TIME, STRENGTH, TONE, LIGHT, LIFE, AND LOVE-- 259 WEST-RUNNING BROOK . 54
OR THAT SHOWED WITH THE LAPSE OF TIME TOO VAIN . . . 262 HANNIBAL 3
THERE WAS ONE TIME AND ONLY THE ONE . . . . . 266 SITTING BY A BUSH . 5
AND IF MEN HAVE WATCHED A LONG TIME . . . . . . 266 SITTING BY A BUSH . 9
YOU'LL WAIT A LONG, LONG TIME FOR ANYTHING MUCH . . 268 ON LOOKING UP BY CHANCE 1
ON HIS PARTICULAR TIME AND PERSONAL SIGHT. . . . . 268 ON LOOKING UP BY CHANCE 15
HIS TIME BE LOST, HIS PITTANCE DOCKED. . . . . . 273 A LONE STRIKER . . 8
TWO TRAMPS IN MUD TIME . . . . 275 TWO TRAMPS IN MUD TIME T
THE TIME WHEN MOST I LOVED MY TASK . . . . . . 276 TWO TRAMPS IN MUD TIME 41
HE STRUCK A SECOND TIME. ANOTHER NAILHEAD. . . . 278 THE WHITE-TAILED HORNET 35
SHE TAKES HER TIME TO TAKE HER FILL. . . . . . 281 BLUE RIBBON AT AMESBURY 39
WE ALLOW SOME TIME FOR GUILE . . . . 282 A DRUMLIN WOODCHUCK 17
IN TIME OF CLOUDBURST . . . . 285 IN TIME OF CLOUDBURST T
AND THE NATURE OF TIME AND SPACE; . . . . . . 288 DEPARTMENTAL . . . 11
WOULD SOMEONE ONLY ACT IN TIME WE YET . . . . . 290 OLD BARN AT THE BOTTOM 35
AND BACK THROUGH HISTORY UP THE STREAM OF TIME. . . 300 THE MASTER SPEED . 4
ITS MAKERS' NAME--TIME CANNOT GET THAT WRONG, . . . 308 THE WRIGHTS' BIPLANE 3
FROM ALL DIVISION TIME OR FOE CAN BRING . . . . . 315 IRIS BY NIGHT . . 30
NOT FOR A LONG, LONG TIME. PLANT, BREED, PRODUCE, . . 323 BUILD SOIL . . . 214
IN LESS THAN NO TIME, TONGUE AND PEN, ... 326 TO A THINKER . . . 19
TO TIME IT NEVER SEEMS THAT HE IS BRAVE . . . . 334 I COULD GIVE ALL . 1
I COULD GIVE ALL TO TIME . . . . 334 I COULD GIVE ALL . T
I COULD GIVE ALL TO TIME EXCEPT--EXCEPT . . . . . 335 I COULD GIVE ALL . 11

TIME (CONTINUED)

PAGE TITLE   LINE

BUT I MUST FORTH AT DUSK, MY TIME OF DAY, ... 337 THE WIND AND THE RAIN . 45
BUT AFTER A TIME ALLOWED FOR IT TO SWIM, ... 338 THE MOST OF IT 13
IT IS GETTING DARK AND TIME HE DREW TO A HOUSE, . . . 341 WILLFUL HOMING 1
THIS WAS NO LADY'S TIME OF YEAR. . . . . 344 DISCOVERY OF MADEIRAS . 31
"BEFORE THE THING HAS TIME TO SPREAD. . . . . 345 DISCOVERY OF MADEIRAS . 61
I MAKE MYSELF THIS TIME . . . . 348 TRIPLE BRONZE 5
TAKE NATURE ALTOGETHER SINCE TIME BEGAN, ... 349 OUR HOLD ON THE PLANET 13
AND TO FORGET THE ANCIENT LENGTHS OF TIME, ... 351 THE LESSON FOR TODAY . 17
WE CAN'T APPRAISE THE TIME IN WHICH WE ACT. . . . . . 352 THE LESSON FOR TODAY . 43
TO ANY ONE TIME, PLACE, OR HUMAN KIND. . . . . 353 THE LESSON FOR TODAY . 105
THERE IS A LIMIT TO OUR TIME EXTENSION. . . . . 355 THE LESSON FOR TODAY . 144
TIME OUT . . . . 355 TIME OUT . . . . . . T
AS SURELY AS IT KEEPS THE STROKE AND TIME . . . . . . 362 IN A POEM 3
ALL OUT OF TIME PELL-MELL! . . . . 365 A NATURE NOTE 9
THAT'S THE TIME KNOCKING AT A DOOR DID GOOD. . . . . 368 THE LITERATE FARMER AND 8
AND WHO KNOWS WHERE WE CAN'T GET! WASTING TIME . . . 371 THE LITERATE FARMER AND 102
HE GAVE UP SLEEP HIMSELF SOME TIME AGO, ... 371 THE LITERATE FARMER AND 104
BACK IN A TIME MADE SIMPLE BY THE HAND . . . . 377 DIRECTIVE 2
TIME WAS WE WERE MOLTEN, TIME WAS WE WERE VAPOR. . . 380 TOO ANXIOUS FOR RIVERS 21
YOU MAKE ME ASK IF I WOULD GO TO TIME . . . . 382 TO AN ANCIENT 16
IN TIME WITH A MEDLEY OF SOTTO CHANTS; . . . . 385 A MOOD APART 3
THE TIME HAD BEEN WHEN ANYONE COULD TURN . . . . . . 398 BURSTING RAPTURE . . . 2
EVERY TIME DICK OR PIKE LOOKED UP, THE DOCTOR . . . . 404 FROM PLANE TO PLANE . 18
"—TAKING HIS OWN SWEET TIME AS IF TO SHOW . . . . . 404 FROM PLANE TO PLANE . 24
FOR THE TIME BEING AND WITH THEIR CONSENT, ... 423 FOR JOHN F. KENNEDY . 37
OFF THESE SANDS OF TIME . . . . 429 KITTY HAWK 47
TIME HAD SEEN AMASS . . . . 429 KITTY HAWK 48
WILL TAKE THAT TIME . . . . 445 PERIL OF HOPE 11
THE WINTER OWL BANKED JUST IN TIME TO PASS . . . . . 445 QUESTIONING FACES . . 1
BUT THE PRINCE DREW AWAY HIS HAND IN TIME . . . . . . 453 HOW HARD TO KEEP FROM 4
THIS TIME AN ALL-NIGHT BANQUET, TO BE SURE, ... 458 HOW HARD TO KEEP FROM 133
YOU SHOULDN'T UNDERSTAND IT AT THE TIME. . . . . . . 475 A MASQUE OF REASON . . 63
AND THIS TIME LOCKS IT UP AND LEAVES IT.) . . . . . . 477 A MASQUE OF REASON . . 108
IT'S TIME THE POOR WERE TREATED BY THE STATE . . . . 477 A MASQUE OF REASON . . 124
AEONS OF TIME AND STILL IT'S MOSTLY WOMEN . . . . . . 478 A MASQUE OF REASON . . 149
GOD NEEDS TIME JUST AS MUCH AS YOU OR I . . . . 478 A MASQUE OF REASON . . 151
WHEN TIME WAS FOUND TO BE A SPACE DIMENSION . . . . . 479 A MASQUE OF REASON . . 160
BUT ALL THE TIME IT'S WHAT WE'RE MOST CONCERNED WITH. 481 A MASQUE OF REASON . . 229
AND TOOK YOUR TIME TO IT. IT SEEMS TO ME . . . . . . 482 A MASQUE OF REASON . . 245
DON'T KNOW WHAT TIME IT IS. WE DON'T KNOW, DON'T WE? . 483 A MASQUE OF REASON . . 287
ONE AT A TIME, PLEASE. I WILL ANSWER JOB FIRST. . . . 484 A MASQUE OF REASON . . 324
NEXT TIME YOU FIND YOURSELF PRESSED ONTO ONE . . . . 486 A MASQUE OF REASON . . 370
THIS IS THE SEVENTH TIME I HAVE BEEN SENT . . . . . . 495 A MASQUE OF MERCY . . 63
WHY, WHAT A STORY. AT THIS TIME OF YEAR . . . . 501 A MASQUE OF MERCY . . 211
OR THE NEW YORKER. / WHEN WAS THE LAST TIME . . . . . 504 A MASQUE OF MERCY . . 276
WHEN THAT FADES I FADE—EVERY TIME I FADE. . . . . . 518 A MASQUE OF MERCY . . 659
LADY, AT SUCH A TIME, AND IN THE PRESENCE!— . . . . 519 A MASQUE OF MERCY . . 684

TIMER (SEE OLD-TIMER)
TIMES
TIMES WERE CHANGED FROM WHAT THEY WERE: . . . . 24 PAN WITH US 21
TWO OR THREE TIMES—HE MADE ME FEEL SO QUEER— . . . 36 DEATH OF THE HIRED MAN 56
SEVERAL TIMES OVER, AND BY MARRYING RATHER . . . . . 75 THE GENERATIONS OF MEN 56
"SHE SHOULD, SHOULDN'T SHE?—YOU'RE SO MANY TIMES . . 77 THE GENERATIONS OF MEN 111
(NINE TIMES REMOVED. CORRECT ME IF I ERR.) . . . . . 79 THE GENERATIONS OF MEN 178
HE'S GOT HAY DOWN THAT'S BEEN RAINED ON THREE TIMES. . 83 THE HOUSEKEEPER . . . 57
NO MATTER HOW FAR AND HOW MANY TIMES . . . . 85 THE HOUSEKEEPER . . . 130
MORE THAN SO MANY TIMES MAKE ME A LADY . . . . 111 IN THE HOME STRETCH . 23
OF MANY PLATES WITH TOWELS MANY TIMES." . . . . 111 IN THE HOME STRETCH . 28
BUT NOW HE SNAPPED HIS EYES THREE TIMES; . . . . . . 140 BROWN'S DESCENT . . . 73
THREE TIMES HE BARELY STIRRED THE BELL, THEN LISTENED. 143 SNOW 15
A MANY TIMES—I DON'T SAY JUST HOW MANY— . . . . . 147 SNOW 127
A THOUSAND TIMES. IF THAT'S THE WAY HE PREACHES! . . 152 SNOW 254
OF EARLY TIMES AS TWICE THE HEIGHT THEY ARE— . . . . 169 NEW HAMPSHIRE 331
THE SAME AT DIFFERENT TIMES TO DIFFERENT PEOPLE. . . 184 MAPLE 156
VOTED THE ONLY TIMES HE EVER VOTED, ... 208 PAUPER WITCH OF GRAFTON 21
ONE OF THE TIMES WAS WHEN 'TWAS IN THE WARRANT . . . 208 PAUPER WITCH OF GRAFTON 23
ACHIEVE AT TIMES A VERY STARLIKE START. . . . . 246 FIREFLIES IN THE GARDEN 5
THE TIMES TABLE . . . . 263 THE TIMES TABLE . . . T
OF MANY TIMES HIS SIZE. . . . . 287 DEPARTMENTAL 1
AND LOOPED TEN TIMES BACK AND FORTH, ... 312 THE VINDICTIVES . . . 67
HARD TIMES HAVE STRUCK ME AND I'M ON THE MOVE. . . . 316 BUILD SOIL 5
THE TIMES SEEM REVOLUTIONARY BAD. . . . . 317 BUILD SOIL 32
I DOUBT IF YOU'RE CONVINCED THE TIMES ARE BAD. . . . 317 BUILD SOIL 53
ALTHOUGH AT TIMES WE THINK IT DISAPPEARS. . . . . . . 369 THE LITERATE FARMER AND 32
AS A MATTER OF FACT THERE ARE TIMES WHEN I AM APT . . 389 SKEPTIC 10
SO WHEN AT TIMES THE MOB IS SWAYED . . . . 403 SOMETHING LIKE A STAR . 22
IF I SAID ONCE I SAID A THOUSAND TIMES, ... 478 A MASQUE OF REASON . . 129
TO REST AT TIMES FROM BEING CIVILIZED. . . . . 496 A MASQUE OF MERCY . . 74
THAT WAY'S BEEN TRIED TOO MANY TIMES FOR ME. . . . . 515 A MASQUE OF MERCY . . 574

TIME'S
TWO AT A TIME'S THE RULE, ONE ON EACH ARM, ... 85 THE HOUSEKEEPER . . . 129
IF THE TIME'S COME TO FACE IT, I'M THE ONE . . . . . 90 THE FEAR 36
AND I COULD SHARE TIME'S LACK OF JOY OR GRIEF . . . . 335 I COULD GIVE ALL . . . 9
WHETHER TIME'S REWARDS ARE FAIR OR UNFAIR. . . . . . 347 DISCOVERY OF MADEIRAS . 138

TIN
THE LITTLE TIN BOX ON THE CUPBOARD SHELF— . . . . . 86 THE HOUSEKEEPER . . . 143
THE UPPER SHELF, THE TIN BOX. THAT'S THE ONE. . . . . 86 THE HOUSEKEEPER . . . 144
WASHED DOWN WITH RUSTY WATER IN A TIN. . . . . 189 THE GRINDSTONE . . . 16

TINDER-GRASS
OF SOMETHING MORE THAN TINDER-GRASS AND WEED— . . . 131 THE BONFIRE 77

TINE
OR GIVE HER A STAB OF THE TINE, ... 463 LINES IN DEJECTION . . 18

TINGED
THAT TINGED THE ATMOSPHERE. . . . . 13 ROSE POGONIAS . . . 16

TINGLING
AND THE NORTHERN LIGHTS THAT RUN LIKE TINGLING NERVES. 268 ON LOOKING UP BY CHANCE 3

TINKLING
  A SLENDER TINKLING FALL THAT MADE . . . . 18 GOING FOR WATER . . . 22
TINSEL
  AND THOUGH IN TINSEL CHAIN AND POPCORN ROPE . . . . . 350 TO A YOUNG WRETCH . . 19
TINT
  WHERE PERFECTLY IN FORM AND TINT . . . . 327 A MISSIVE MISSILE . . 34
TINTED
  ACROSS THE TINTED SNOW. . . . . 470 IN WINTER IN THE WOODS   8
TINY
  IT SEEMED TOO TINY TO HAVE ROOM FOR FEET, ... 357 A CONSIDERABLE SPECK . 16
  SOME OF THEM MIGHTY HUGE, SOME MIGHTY TINY, ... 425 ACCIDENTALLY ON PURPOSE 3
TIP
  RATHER THAN TIP A TABLE FOR YOU, LET ME . . . . . 202 THE WITCH OF COOS . . 12
  BUT IF YOU WILL ACCEPT THE TIP, ... 326 TO A THINKER 18
TIP-DOWN
  IT PUT THE FLAME TIP-DOWN AND DABBED THE GRASS . . . . 131 THE BONFIRE 45
TIPPED
  SEEMED TIPPED WITH WINGS OF COLOR . . . . 13 ROSE POGONIAS . . . 15
  AND DID I NOT TAKE STEPS WOULD BE TIPPED OVER . . . . 391 ON BEING IDOLIZED . . 5
TIPTOE
  SHE RAN ON TIPTOE DOWN THE DARKENED PASSAGE . . . . . 34 DEATH OF THE HIRED MAN   3
TIPTOED
  I TIPTOED THE FLOOR, ... 240 THE LOCKLESS DOOR . . 6
TIP-TOP
  RIGHT ON THE TOP, TIP-TOP--A CURIOUS THING. . . . . . 42 THE MOUNTAIN 47
TIP-TOUCH
  OF OVER-WINTER WITH THE LEAST TIP-TOUCH . . . . . . 131 THE BONFIRE 46
TIRED (SEE AUTUMN-TIRED)
  IF TIRED OF TREES I SEEK AGAIN MANKIND, ... 17 THE VANTAGE POINT . . 1
  AFTER ELEVEN O'CLOCK AT NIGHT. TOO TIRED . . . . . . 45 A HUNDRED COLLARS . . 17
  "PROFESSOR SQUARE-THE-CIRCLE-TILL-YOU'RE-TIRED? . . . 46 A HUNDRED COLLARS . . 44
  I WANT THIS OVER WITH; I'M HOT AND TIRED." . . . . . 94 THE SELF-SEEKER . . . 50
  OH, WELL, WE'LL SOON BE THROUGH WITH IT. I'M TIRED." . . 96 THE SELF-SEEKER . . . 90
  YOU'RE TIRED." / "I'M DRUNK-NONSENSICAL TIRED OUT; . . 116 IN THE HOME STRETCH . 158
  AND, TIRED OF AIMLESS CIRCLING IN ONE PLACE, ... 238 ON A TREE FALLEN ACROSS 13
  NOT MAKE ME TIRED AND MOROSE . . . . 286 IN TIME OF CLOUDBURST . 27
  IS ABOUT TIRED OF BEING LOOTED . . . . 419 AMERICA IS HARD TO SEE 81
TIRELESS
  THEY ARE TIRELESS FOLK, BUT SLOW AND SAD-- . . . . . 6 GHOST HOUSE 26
  THE TIRELESS BUT INEFFECTUAL HANDS . . . . 128 THE OFT-REPEATED DREAM 5
'TIS
  WHETHER 'TIS IN US TO ARISE WITH DAY . . . . 10 STORM FEAR 17
  BUT 'TIS NOT TRUE THAT THUS I DWELT ALOOF, ... 16 A DREAM PANG . . . 13
  'TIS PITY IF THE CASE REQUIRE . . . . 19 REVELATION 5
  'TIS OF THE ESSENCE OF LIFE HERE, ... 21 THE TRIAL BY EXISTENCE 65
  'TIS ONLY TO SIT BACK AND SWAY HIS HEAD . . . . . . 269 THE BEAR 23
  'TIS RITUAL WITH HER TO LAY . . . . 280 BLUE RIBBON AT AMESBURY 29
  'TIS THE WORLD-OLD WAY OF THE RAIN . . . . 285 IN TIME OF CLOUDBURST . 5
  'TIS TO FIND WHAT THE HATED NEED, ... 312 THE VINDICTIVES . . 82
  TO MARKET 'TIS OUR DESTINY TO GO. . . . . 321 BUILD SOIL 172
  'TIS NOT ENOUGH ON ROOTS AND IN THE MOUTH, ... 337 THE WIND AND THE RAIN . 37
  WE HEARD "'TIS OVER" ROARING. . . . . 359 NOVEMBER 7
  BUT SPES ALIT AGRICOLAM 'TIS SAID. . . . . 376 SOMETHING FOR HOPE . . 24
  'TIS POSSIBLE YOU MAY HAVE SEEN, ... 381 AN UNSTAMPED LETTER IN 40
  'TIS THE IOTA SUBSCRIPT OF THE GREEK. . . . . . . 387 IOTA SUBSCRIPT . . . 4
  'TIS A CONFUSION IT WAS OURS TO START . . . . . . 423 FOR JOHN F. KENNEDY . 41
  THAT IS THE FEAR OF GOD WHEREOF 'TIS WRITTEN. . . . . 520 A MASQUE OF MERCY . . 699
TISSAPHERNES
  MY SATRAP TISSAPHERNES HAS NO END . . . . 459 HOW HARD TO KEEP FROM 166
  TELL TISSAPHERNES NOT TO MIND THE GREEKS. . . . . . 461 HOW HARD TO KEEP FROM 227
TITANIC
  OF A SIZE TITANIC . . . . 442 KITTY HAWK 443
TITHE
  NOT A HALF, NOT A THIRD, NOT A TITHE. . . . . . . 310 THE VINDICTIVES . . 20
TITYRUS
  WHY, TITYRUS! BUT YOU'VE FORGOTTEN ME. . . . . . 316 BUILD SOIL 1
  I MAY BE WRONG, BUT, TITYRUS, TO ME . . . . . . 317 BUILD SOIL 31
  TITYRUS, SOMETIMES I'M PERPLEXED MYSELF . . . . . 321 BUILD SOIL 163
TO---NOT INDEXED
TOAD
  THAT HAS NO DUST-BATH NOW FOR THE TOAD. . . . . . . 6 GHOST HOUSE 14
TOBACCO
  ENOUGH AT LEAST TO BUY TOBACCO WITH, ... 35 DEATH OF THE HIRED MAN 20
  "AND STRONG OF STALE TOBACCO." / "HE'LL PULL THROUGH." . 145 SNOW 72
TODAY
  OH, GIVE US PLEASURE IN THE FLOWERS TODAY; . . . . . 12 A PRAYER IN SPRING . 1
  I FOUND THAT WING BROKEN TODAY! . . . . 29 MY BUTTERFLY . . . 43
  SILAS HAS WALKED THAT FAR NO DOUBT TODAY. . . . . . 38 DEATH OF THE HIRED MAN 127
  FROM THE WORLD'S VIEW TODAY OF ALL THOSE THINGS. . . . 57 THE BLACK COTTAGE . 63
  TO THE VILLAGE, THROUGH PATTERSON'S PASTURE TODAY: . . 59 BLUEBERRIES 2
  "NO FETE TODAY," HE SAID. / "IT LOOKS THAT WAY." . . . 74 THE GENERATIONS OF MEN 35
  WOULD HAVE BEEN STARKS, AND DOUBTLESS HERE TODAY." . . 75 THE GENERATIONS OF MEN 52
  WHAT DO YOU THINK YOU'RE LIKE TO HEAR TODAY?" . . . . 78 THE GENERATIONS OF MEN 141
  "WILLIS, I DIDN'T WANT YOU HERE TODAY: . . . . . 92 THE SELF-SEEKER . . 1
  "I THINK--I THINK--FROM WHAT I HEARD TODAY-- . . . 100 THE SELF-SEEKER . . 204
  BUT 'TWAS NO MAKE-BELIEVE WITH YOU TODAY, ... 109 THE EXPOSED NEST . . 9
  FROM HERE TODAY, ... 118 THE TELEPHONE . . . 2
  IN BEARING THERE TODAY IS HERS, ... 134 A GIRL'S GARDEN . . 35
  TODAY AN HONORED ONE IN NOTTINGHAM. . . . . . . 161 NEW HAMPSHIRE . . . 86
  WELL, TAKE ME THERE." / "SOME DAY I WILL." / "TODAY." . 213 A FOUNTAIN, A BOTTLE . 14
  "THE ONES WHO LIVING COME TODAY . . . . 221 IN A DISUSED GRAVEYARD 6
  IT IS MOST US." / "TODAY WILL BE THE DAY . . . . . 260 WEST-RUNNING BROOK . 72
  YOU SAID SO." / "NO, TODAY WILL BE THE DAY . . . . 260 WEST-RUNNING BROOK . 73
  "TODAY WILL BE THE DAY OF WHAT WE BOTH SAID." . . . 260 WEST-RUNNING BROOK . 75
  TODAY SHE WOULDN'T KNOW OUR NAME. . . . . 265 THE BIRTHPLACE . . 11
  WHEN I SPREAD OUT MY HAND HERE TODAY, ... 266 SITTING BY A BUSH . 1
  THE LESSON FOR TODAY . . . . 350 THE LESSON FOR TODAY . T
  WE HAVE TODAY AND I COULD CALL THEIR NAME . . . . . 351 THE LESSON FOR TODAY . 31

TODAY (CONTINUED)

	PAGE	TITLE	LINE
O PALADINS, THE LESSON FOR TODAY	353	THE LESSON FOR TODAY	87
HE BET IT WAS OUT TODAY,	367	NOT OF SCHOOL AGE	27
AND THERE TODAY WE ARE.	367	A SERIOUS STEP LIGHTLY	12
I'LL SHOW YOU WHY IT ISN'T--NOT TODAY.	406	FROM PLANE TO PLANE	86
TODAY I WANT TO TALK ABOUT THE SUN.	406	FROM PLANE TO PLANE	87
I OWE THEM MORE TODAY	415	CLOSED FOR GOOD	5
TODAY IS FOR MY CAUSE A DAY OF DAYS.	422	FOR JOHN F. KENNEDY	4
IF IT LOOKS NONE TOO ORDERLY TODAY,	423	FOR JOHN F. KENNEDY	40
THERE'S A STRANGE LIGHT ON EVERYTHING TODAY.	473	A MASQUE OF REASON	8
FROM THE SURROUNDING DESERT; JUST TODAY	489	A MASQUE OF REASON	445

TO-DO

	PAGE	TITLE	LINE
"THE WHOLE TO-DO SEEMS TO HAVE BEEN FOR NOTHING.	155	SNOW	337

TOE

	PAGE	TITLE	LINE
I STEPPED ON THE TOE	450	OBJECTION TO BE STEPPED	2

TOENAIL

	PAGE	TITLE	LINE
THE TOENAIL CLICK AND SHUFFLE OF HIS FEET,	269	THE BEAR	17

TOES

	PAGE	TITLE	LINE
(AND THAT'S WHAT THEIR TOES ARE TOWARDS),	294	A RECORD STRIDE	4

TOFFILE

	PAGE	TITLE	LINE
TOFFILE HAD GONE TO BED ALONE AND LEFT ME,	203	THE WITCH OF COOS	41
WHEN I HEARD TOFFILE UPSTAIRS IN THE BEDROOM	203	THE WITCH OF COOS	46
OR A LITTLE CHILD, COMES UP. IT WASN'T TOFFILE:	204	THE WITCH OF COOS	53
I SAT UP ON THE FLOOR AND SHOUTED, "TOFFILE,	205	THE WITCH OF COOS	82
TOFFILE, FOR MY SAKE!" "COMPANY?" HE SAID,	205	THE WITCH OF COOS	94
I COULD SEE NOTHING. "TOFFILE, I DON'T SEE IT.	205	THE WITCH OF COOS	99
TOFFILE AGREED TO THAT, AND SURE ENOUGH,	206	THE WITCH OF COOS	114
I HEARD THEM. TOFFILE DIDN'T SEEM TO HEAR THEM.	206	THE WITCH OF COOS	117
"TOFFILE, GET NAILS." I MADE HIM NAIL THE DOOR SHUT	206	THE WITCH OF COOS	119
TO NO ONE ANYMORE SINCE TOFFILE DIED.	206	THE WITCH OF COOS	131
I PROMISED TOFFILE TO BE CRUEL TO THEM	206	THE WITCH OF COOS	133
TOFFILE, IF HE WERE HERE, I DON'T BELIEVE	207	THE WITCH OF COOS	150
I VERIFIED THE NAME NEXT MORNING: TOFFILE.	207	THE WITCH OF COOS	154
THE RURAL LETTER BOX SAID TOFFILE LAJWAY.	207	THE WITCH OF COOS	155

TOGA-TOGS

	PAGE	TITLE	LINE
LEST BOTH SHOULD BITE HIM IN THE TOGA-TOGS.	362	SYMPATHY WITH UNDER DOG	4

TOGETHER (SEE GET-TOGETHER)

	PAGE	TITLE	LINE
"WHETHER THEY WORK TOGETHER OR APART."	22	THE TUFT OF FLOWERS	10
"MEN WORK TOGETHER," I TOLD HIM FROM THE HEART,	23	THE TUFT OF FLOWERS	39
"WHETHER THEY WORK TOGETHER OR APART."	23	THE TUFT OF FLOWERS	40
NOW WE ARE GETTING ON TOGETHER--TALKING.	48	A HUNDRED COLLARS	101
TWO THAT DON'T LOVE CAN'T LIVE TOGETHER WITHOUT THEM.	53	HOME BURIAL	54
BUT TWO THAT DO CAN'T LIVE TOGETHER WITH THEM."	53	HOME BURIAL	55
IT WASN'T JUST TO KEEP THE STATES TOGETHER,	56	THE BLACK COTTAGE	56
AND ALL RIPE TOGETHER, NOT SOME OF THEM GREEN	59	BLUEBERRIES	6
ANCESTRAL MEMORIES MIGHT COME TOGETHER.	73	THE GENERATIONS OF MEN	3
TO STAND TOGETHER ON THE CRATER'S VERGE	73	THE GENERATIONS OF MEN	16
AS ONE WHO CLASPS HER HEART. THEY LAUGHED TOGETHER.	74	THE GENERATIONS OF MEN	44
"FROM THE SENSE OF OUR HAVING BEEN TOGETHER--	78	THE GENERATIONS OF MEN	142
HE GETS SOME SORT OF BAKESHOP MEALS TOGETHER,	82	THE HOUSEKEEPER	31
TO LIVE TOGETHER AND THEN PULL APART.	82	THE HOUSEKEEPER	40
ALL WE CAN HOLD TOGETHER BY THE LEGS.	85	THE HOUSEKEEPER	128
SO RAN TOGETHER THAT I DIDN'T TRY TO.	112	IN THE HOME STRETCH	52
OUR SITTING HERE BY LANTERN-LIGHT TOGETHER	116	IN THE HOME STRETCH	176
OF DEAD LEAVES STUCK TOGETHER BY THE HEAT--	119	HYLA BROOK	11
"AND SCARE YOU TOO?" THE CHILDREN SAID TOGETHER.	130	THE BONFIRE	19
LIKE WINTER AND EVENING COMING ON TOGETHER.	131	THE BONFIRE	55
THEY STRING TOGETHER WITH A LIVING THREAD.	141	THE LINE-GANG	4
BOTH THE COLES SAID TOGETHER. MRS. COLE	144	SNOW	34
OF MIND AND STRONG OF ARM SHOULD FIT TOGETHER,	164	NEW HAMPSHIRE	181
THEY SAT TOGETHER HALFWAY UP A CLIFF	195	PAUL'S WIFE	133
ALL THOSE GREAT RUFFIANS PUT THEIR THROATS TOGETHER,	195	PAUL'S WIFE	139
I HAD A VISION OF THEM PUT TOGETHER	204	THE WITCH OF COOS	68
BY TYING TOGETHER	218	I WILL SING YOU ONE-O	20
THE COUNTRY'S SINGING STRENGTH THUS BROUGHT TOGETHER,	240	OUR SINGING STRENGTH	50
THAT DAY SHE PUT OUR HEADS TOGETHER,	252	TREE AT MY WINDOW	13
TO SEEK FOR THE HAPPY ISLES TOGETHER.	262	THE FLOWER BOAT	12
ALL PACKED IN SAND TO WAIT THE TRUMP TOGETHER.	270	THE EGG AND THE MACHINE	26
THEY STOOD ARMS LACED TOGETHER AT THE BARS,	293	AT WOODWARD'S GARDENS	12
BUT NOW LIVE EVEN TOGETHER.	294	A RECORD STRIDE	8
TOGETHER WING TO WING AND OAR TO OAR.	300	THE MASTER SPEED	14
AND GATHERED THEM TOGETHER IN A RING.	315	IRIS BY NIGHT	28
PHILOSOPHIZED TOGETHER INTO ONE--	318	BUILD SOIL	79
AND LESS IN BOTH TOGETHER	336	CARPE DIEM	22
BUMPED HEADS TOGETHER DULLY	376	ONE STEP BACKWARD TAKEN	5
TOGETHER, AND TOGETHER SLIPPED;	381	AN UNSTAMPED LETTER IN	35
THE EX-KING SAID. "WE'RE IN THIS THING TOGETHER.	459	HOW HARD TO KEEP FROM	170
YOU CALL IT MINE. / WE GROPED IT OUT TOGETHER.	480	A MASQUE OF REASON	188
AS FOR THE EARTH, WE GROPED THAT OUT TOGETHER,	481	A MASQUE OF REASON	207
MUCH AS YOUR HUSBAND, JOB, AND I TOGETHER	481	A MASQUE OF REASON	208
TOGETHER WE WILL GO WITH YOU ALONG.	489	A MASQUE OF REASON	437
SO WE CAN HANG TOGETHER IN A STRIKE.	498	A MASQUE OF MERCY	125
WOULD KNOCK THEIR DRUNKEN PENTHOUSE HEADS TOGETHER	506	A MASQUE OF MERCY	333
(THEY PUT THEIR HANDS TOGETHER LIKE A BOOK	506	A MASQUE OF MERCY	489
HERE ALL STARVE TOGETHER,	512	A MASQUE OF MERCY	504
HERE WE ALL FAIL TOGETHER, DWARFED AND POOR.	512	A MASQUE OF MERCY	506

TOGS (SEE TOGA-TOGS)

TOIL

	PAGE	TITLE	LINE
LET THE DOWNPOUR ROIL AND TOIL!	285	IN TIME OF CLOUDBURST	1

TOKEN

	PAGE	TITLE	LINE
FOR THIS TOKEN FLIGHT,	443	KITTY HAWK	466

TOLD

	PAGE	TITLE	LINE
"MEN WORK TOGETHER," I TOLD HIM FROM THE HEART,	23	THE TUFT OF FLOWERS	39
"I TOLD HIM SO LAST HAYING, DIDN'T I?	35	DEATH OF THE HIRED MAN	13
"HE NEVER TOLD US THAT." / "WE KNOW IT, THOUGH."	39	DEATH OF THE HIRED MAN	130
SOME STRANGE KIND--THEY TOLD ME IT HADN'T A NAME."	61	BLUEBERRIES	66
"I'VE TOLD YOU HOW ONCE, NOT LONG AFTER WE CAME,	61	BLUEBERRIES	67
THE HAND THAT KNOWS HIS BUSINESS WON'T BE TOLD	70	THE CODE	22

TOLD (CONTINUED)
THEY TOLD ME AFTERWARD. FIRST THEY FORKED HAY, ... 72 THE CODE 89
SON, YOU DO AS YOU'RE TOLD! YOU TAKE THE TIMBER-- . . . 80 THE GENERATIONS OF MEN 192
"I TOLD YOU, WILLIS, WHEN YOU FIRST CAME IN. . . . . . 95 THE SELF-SEEKER . . . 61
BUT, ANNE, I'M TROUBLED; HAVE YOU TOLD ME ALL? . . . . 97 THE SELF-SEEKER . . . 131
AS TOLD TO A CHILD . . . . 135 LOCKED OUT 5
AS TOLD TO A CHILD . . . . 135 LAST WORD OF A BLUEBIRD 5
HE TOLD ME A LITTLE ABOUT HIMSELF. . . . . 140 THE GUM-GATHERER . . 12
I TOLD HIM THIS IS A PLEASANT LIFE, ... 141 THE GUM-GATHERER . . 34
WELL, THERE'S--" SHE TOLD FRED AFTERWARD THAT IN . . . 151 SNOW 237
SHE DIDN'T THANK ME?" / "WHEN I TOLD HER 'GONE,' . . . 153 SNOW 288
"I SEE THE PORTER'S MADE YOUR BED," I TOLD HIM. . . . 159 NEW HAMPSHIRE . . . 15
AND TAKE THEIR NAME. THEY'VE SINCE TOLD ME THEIR NAME-- . 161 NEW HAMPSHIRE . . . 85
SHE ASKED HER FATHER AND HE TOLD HER, "MAPLE-- . . . . 179 MAPLE 3
MAPLE IS RIGHT." / "BUT TEACHER TOLD THE SCHOOL . . . . 179 MAPLE 4
SHE TOLD HIM OF THE BOOKMARK MAPLE LEAF . . . . . . 183 MAPLE 104
BUT IF THE STORY MURPHY TOLD WAS TRUE, ... 192 PAUL'S WIFE 40
PAUL TOLD THE BOSS THE LOAD WOULD BE ALL RIGHT, ... 192 PAUL'S WIFE 46
MURPHY TOLD ME PAUL PUT ON ALL THOSE AIRS . . . . . 195 PAUL'S WIFE 148
TELL YOU WHAT RALLE THE SIOUX CONTROL ONCE TOLD ME. . . 202 THE WITCH OF COOS . . 13
I COULD HAVE TOLD THEM ANY TIME THIS TWELVEMONTH . . . 207 PAUPER WITCH OF GRAFTON 15
OUGHT TO BE TOLD TO COME AND TAKE HIM IN." . . . . . 223 THE RUNAWAY 21
"HOW OFTEN ALREADY YOU'VE HAD TO BE TOLD, ... 228 GOOD-BY AND KEEP COLD 17
AND I WAS ONE OF THE CHILDREN TOLD . . . . 249 A PECK OF GOLD . . . 3
BUT I WAS ONE OF THE CHILDREN TOLD . . . . 249 A PECK OF GOLD . . . 7
AND I WAS ONE OF THE CHILDREN TOLD, ... 249 A PECK OF GOLD . . . 11
TOLD ME MY SECRET MUST BE KNOWN: . . . . 251 BEREFT 12
HE TOLD THE DISTANCE, "I AM ARMED FOR WAR. . . . . . 270 THE EGG AND THE MACHINE 28
AND RAISED AMONG THE LEAVES AND DULY TOLD, ... 283 THE GOLD HESPERIDEE . 15
AND SO THE STORY WASN'T TOLD IN GATH; . . . . . . 284 THE GOLD HESPERIDEE . 58
ONE NIGHT (HE TOLD ME). AND THE BARN HE MEANT . . . . 289 OLD BARN AT THE BOTTOM 20
THE TALE IS STILL BOASTINGLY TOLD . . . . 311 THE VINDICTIVES . . . 33
TOLD THEM IN WHAT LAKE TO DIVE . . . . 311 THE VINDICTIVES . . . 43
HE TOLD THEM TO DIVE TILL THEY DROWNED. . . . . . . 311 THE VINDICTIVES . . . 46
AND NO ONE TOLD THEM SO . . . . 391 A ROGERS GROUP . . . 9
DICK TOLD HIM TO BE FAIRER TO THE DOCTOR: . . . . . 405 FROM PLANE TO PLANE . 36
ONCE I TOLD THE MASTER, ... 429 KITTY HAWK 50
WERE THEY TOLD THEY WERE FREE . . . . 448 THE BAD ISLAND--EASTER 31
I TOLD YOU I KNEW THE QUINTESSENCE OF JEWELS. . . . . 456 HOW HARD TO KEEP FROM 88
FOR HAVING LIED BUT HAVING TOLD THE TRUTH. . . . . . 457 HOW HARD TO KEEP FROM 114
HE WRITES FREE VERSE, I'M TOLD, AND HE IS THOUGHT . . . 459 HOW HARD TO KEEP FROM 184
THE BEST, I'M TOLD, I EVER HAVE HAD TAKEN. . . . . . 476 A MASQUE OF REASON . 86
I TOLD HIM NOT TO SCRATCH: IT MADE IT WORSE. . . . . 478 A MASQUE OF REASON . 128
BUT OUT OF POLITICS. SHE TOLD ME SO. . . . . . . 494 A MASQUE OF MERCY . . 38
SHALL IT BE TOLD WE HAD A PROPHET CAPTIVE . . . . . 502 A MASQUE OF MERCY . . 220
SO KNOWING--AND YET NEEDING TO BE TOLD . . . . . . 506 A MASQUE OF MERCY . . 338
TOLERANT
WITH TOLERANT REPROACH . . . . 466 SOME SCIENCE FICTION . 11
(HE LEANS AWAY IN TOLERANT DISTASTE.) . . . . . . 504 A MASQUE OF MERCY . . 287
TOLERATED
GOD HARDLY TOLERATED WITH HIS FEET; . . . . 352 THE LESSON FOR TODAY . 75
TOLL
TO CATCH THEM AND TAKE TOLL OF THEM IN TRANSIT. . . . 321 BUILD SOIL 167
TOLLING
TO TOLLING LIKE THE COUNT OF FATE, ... 273 A LONE STRIKER . . . 2
TOM
SOME TOM SAID TO DICK OR HARRY: . . . . 345 DISCOVERY OF MADEIRAS . 68
TOMATO
LIKE A RIPE TOMATO. . . . . 427 VERSION 15
TOMATOES
TOMATOES, BEETS, BEANS, PUMPKINS, CORN, ... 134 A GIRL'S GARDEN . . . 31
TOMB
LIKE DOVE WINGS ON A FIGURE ON A TOMB, ... 222 TO E.T. 3
TOMORROW
TOMORROW THEY MAY FORM AND GO. . . . . 27 OCTOBER 6
THEY'LL BE THERE TOMORROW, OR EVEN TONIGHT. . . . . 62 BLUEBERRIES 99
IN RAIN TOMORROW, SHALL WE, IF IT RAINS? . . . . . 81 THE GENERATIONS OF MEN 211
IN NO TIME OUT TONIGHT. AND YET TOMORROW . . . . . 151 SNOW 229
AND HE COULD WAIT--WE'D SEE TO HIM TOMORROW. . . . . 177 THE STAR-SPLITTER . 42
TOMORROW DEAD WILL COME TO STAY." . . . . 221 IN A DISUSED GRAVEYARD 8
"YOU CHILDREN MAY DREAM IT AND TELL IT TOMORROW." . . . 379 TOO ANXIOUS FOR RIVERS 20
TOMORROW'S
TOMORROW'S WIND, IF IT BE WILD, ... 27 OCTOBER 3
IF SO, IT WILL BE IN TOMORROW'S PAPER. . . . . . 507 A MASQUE OF MERCY . 357
TON
TO DRIVE MY TON OF CAR . . . . 388 MIDDLENESS OF THE ROAD 10
TONAGHT
TONAGHT?" / AS WELL TONIGHT AS ANY NIGHT. . . . . . 186 THE AX-HELVE 34
TONE
SOMETHING SINISTER IN THE TONE . . . . 251 BEREFT 11
AND IT IS TIME, STRENGTH, TONE, LIGHT, LIFE, AND LOVE-- . 259 WEST-RUNNING BROOK . 54
HER TONE OF MEANING BUT WITHOUT THE WORDS. . . . . . 338 NEVER WOULD BIRDS' SONG 5
IN A SUBORDINATING LOOK OR TONE, ... 385 THE FEAR OF GOD . . 10
(HE TRIED TO IMITATE DICK'S TONE OF VOICE.) . . . . . 406 FROM PLANE TO PLANE . 73
TONES
SOMEONE WAS SAYING IN SUCH NATURAL TONES . . . . . 182 MAPLE 85
TONGUE
IT TOTTERS WHEN SHE LICKS IT WITH HER TONGUE. . . . . 1 THE PASTURE 7
A LEAPING TONGUE OF BLOOM THE SCYTHE HAD SPARED . . . 22 THE TUFT OF FLOWERS . 23
YOUR TONGUE GIVES SALT OR SUGAR IN YOUR HAND. . . . . 131 THE BONFIRE 47
AND ALL BUT LOST HIMSELF. (A TONGUE OF FIRE . . . . 204 THE WITCH OF COOS . . 72
I TOUCH MY TONGUE TO THE SHOES NOW, ... 295 A RECORD STRIDE . . 21
IN LESS THAN NO TIME, TONGUE AND PEN, ... 326 TO A THINKER 19
IT WERE UNWORTHY OF THE TONGUE . . . . 336 THE WIND AND THE RAIN . 15
THAT WILL NOT LEAVE THE TONGUE. . . . . 341 THE SUBVERTED FLOWER . 68
THEY MUST BY NOW HAVE LEARNED THE NATIVE TONGUE. . . . 414 A CABIN IN THE CLEARING 20
BY CHARACTER, BY TONGUE, BY NATIVE TRAIT, ... 422 FOR JOHN F. KENNEDY . 14
IT WAS ON MY TONGUE . . . . 429 KITTY HAWK 40

		PAGE	TITLE	LINE

TONGUE (CONTINUED)

	PAGE TITLE	LINE
THAT IS ALL MY TONGUE.	430 KITTY HAWK	84
SATAN, WHAT AILS YOU? WHERE'S THE FAMOUS TONGUE,	488 A MASQUE OF REASON	405

TONGUE-CONFUSION

ALL LANGUAGE IN A ONE-MAN TONGUE-CONFUSION.	502 A MASQUE OF MERCY	243

TONGUES

OF WORDS, OR IS IT TONGUES I OUGHT TO SAY?"	151 SNOW	249
NOT ALL YOUR LIGHT TONGUES TALKING ALOUD	252 TREE AT MY WINDOW	7
THEIR TONGUES HANGING OUT UNASSUAGED.	311 THE VINDICTIVES	51

TONGUE'S

MY TONGUE'S MY OWN, AS TRUE THOMAS USED TO SAY.	505 A MASQUE OF MERCY	296

TONIGHT

BUT WHATE'ER YOU DO TONIGHT,	11 TO THE THAWING WIND	6
I MADE THE BED UP FOR HIM THERE TONIGHT.	39 DEATH OF THE HIRED MAN	151
I JUST FOUND WHAT THE MATTER WAS TONIGHT:	46 A HUNDRED COLLARS	55
THEY'LL BE THERE TOMORROW, OR EVEN TONIGHT.	62 BLUEBERRIES	99
I'LL NEVER REST TONIGHT UNLESS I KNOW.	90 THE FEAR	32
YOU CAN TONIGHT, AND GO. IT'S ALMOST DARK;	111 IN THE HOME STRETCH	16
YOU COME TO FETCH ME FROM MY WORK TONIGHT	123 PUTTING IN THE SEED	1
AS RECKLESS AS THE BEST OF THEM TONIGHT,	129 THE BONFIRE	2
LET'S NOT CARE WHAT WE DO WITH IT TONIGHT.	129 THE BONFIRE	8
IN NO TIME OUT TONIGHT. AND YET TOMORROW	151 SNOW	229
AND HOW IT STANDS BETWEEN THE NIGHT TONIGHT	179 THE STAR-SPLITTER	97
TONAGHT?" / AS WELL TONIGHT AS ANY NIGHT.	186 THE AX-HELVE	34
BUT TONIGHT I DON'T CARE ENOUGH TO LIE--	207 THE WITCH OF COOS	148
BUT TONIGHT I WILL BARK	261 CANIS MAJOR	10
THAT CALM SEEMS CERTAINLY SAFE TO LAST TONIGHT.	268 ON LOOKING UP BY CHANCE	16
BUT EARLIER OUT FOR BED TONIGHT,	292 ON HEART'S BEGINNING TO	40
BUT THE WEATHER IS CLEAR TONIGHT,	301 VOICE WAYS	2
THERE IS NOTHING MUCH WE CAN DO FOR THE TREE TONIGHT,	305 THERE ARE ROUGHLY ZONES	14
WERE I IN TROUBLE WITH NIGHT TONIGHT.	383 WERE I IN TROUBLE	10
BUT SHE CAN TRUST IT NOT TO FALL TONIGHT.	386 THE FEAR OF MAN	6
I CAN'T EXPLAIN--TONIGHT AT LEAST.	420 ONE MORE BREVITY	25
I'M GETTING OUT TONIGHT. HERE, TAKE THE CROWN."	453 HOW HARD TO KEEP FROM	3
OUR SECOND SECOND-CHILDHOOD CASE TONIGHT.	493 A MASQUE OF MERCY	14
OH, NO, YOU'RE NOT. YOU'RE STAYING HERE TONIGHT.--	500 A MASQUE OF MERCY	173
THEN I'M A PRISONER? / YOU ARE TONIGHT.	500 A MASQUE OF MERCY	176
EVEN BEFORE I CAME IN HERE TONIGHT.	517 A MASQUE OF MERCY	626

TONNAGE

HAS THAT TONNAGE OF STONE	447 THE BAD ISLAND--EASTER	10

TOO---NOT INDEXED

TOOK

THEY LEAVE US SO TO THE WAY WE TOOK,	16 IN NEGLECT	1
SHE TOOK THE MARKET THINGS FROM WARREN'S ARMS	34 DEATH OF THE HIRED MAN	8
"YES, I TOOK CARE TO KEEP WELL OUT OF EARSHOT."	37 DEATH OF THE HIRED MAN	70
WARREN LEANED OUT AND TOOK A STEP OR TWO,	38 DEATH OF THE HIRED MAN	121
SHE TOOK A DOUBTFUL STEP AND THEN UNDID IT	51 HOME BURIAL	4
HOW WE USED TO PICK BERRIES: WE TOOK ONE LOOK ROUND,	62 BLUEBERRIES	85
IT TOOK MY MIND OFF DOUGHNUTS AND SODA BISCUIT	63 A SERVANT TO SERVANTS	26
BECAUSE HIS VIOLENCE TOOK ON THE FORM	66 A SERVANT TO SERVANTS	106
"IT'S TIME I TOOK MY TURN UPSTAIRS IN JAIL"--	67 A SERVANT TO SERVANTS	146
UNLESS LEN TOOK THE NOTION, WHICH HE WON'T,	67 A SERVANT TO SERVANTS	157
"YOU TOOK AN AWKWARD WAY. DID HE DISCHARGE YOU?"	73 THE CODE	113
THEN TOOK THE OTHER, AS JUST AS FAIR,	105 THE ROAD NOT TAKEN	6
I TOOK THE ONE LESS TRAVELED BY,	105 THE ROAD NOT TAKEN	19
WE SAW THE RISK WE TOOK IN DOING GOOD,	109 THE EXPOSED NEST	27
UNTIL HE TOOK THE STIFFNESS OUT OF THEM,	122 BIRCHES	30
I TOOK WHAT FRONT THERE WAS BESIDE. I KNELT	131 THE BONFIRE	65
IT TOOK ME. NEIGHBORS COMING HOME FROM TOWN .	132 THE BONFIRE	84
AND THEN--THE WATCHER AT HIS PULSE TOOK FRIGHT.	137 "OUT, OUT--"	30
'BOUT OUT!" AND TOOK THE LONG WAY HOME	140 BROWN'S DESCENT	75
HE TOOK HIM DOWN BELOW A CRAMPING RAFTER,	142 THE VANISHING RED	20
THEY KEPT THEIR HEADS AND TOOK THEIR TIME TO IT	143 SNOW	24
HE TOOK NO NOTICE, DID HE? WELL, AT LEAST	144 SNOW	49
THEY STARTED UP. FRED TOOK THE TELEPHONE.	155 SNOW	328
I KNOW A MAN WHO TOOK A DOUBLE AX	170 NEW HAMPSHIRE	367
CIRCUITOUS WANDERER," AND "TOOK DEJECTEDLY	171 NEW HAMPSHIRE	384
HE TOOK A STRANGE THING TO BE ROGUISH OVER.	178 THE STAR-SPLITTER	58
AND TOOK THE FANCY HOME WITH THEM TO LIVE BY.	182 MAPLE	96
THEY ALWAYS TOOK THEIR HOLIDAYS IN AUTUMN.	184 MAPLE	143
THEN TOOK IT FROM ME--AND I LET HIM TAKE IT.	185 THE AX-HELVE	13
ME ONLY AS I TOOK MY AX TO HEART.	186 THE AX-HELVE	20
NOT FOR ME TO ASK WHICH, WHEN WHAT HE TOOK	187 THE AX-HELVE	66
IT TOOK THE HALL DOOR FOR THE NOVELTY,	205 THE WITCH OF COOS	85
SAID THAT I TOOK HIM OUT IN HIS OLD AGE	208 PAUPER WITCH OF GRAFTON	46
BUT EVERYBODY TOOK IT FOR A PROOF.	209 PAUPER WITCH OF GRAFTON	68
THE OLD MAN SERIOUSLY TOOK HIS BEARINGS,	214 A FOUNTAIN, A BOTTLE	35
HE TOOK A LITTLE IN HIS MOUTH.	224 THE AIM WAS SONG	9
BORNE DOWN UNTIL THE END ALMOST TOOK ROOT,	239 OUR SINGING STRENGTH	13
YOU TOOK AS A TROPHY OF THE HOUR.	247 ON GOING UNNOTICED	16
WHEN DUST REALLY TOOK IN THE SUN;	266 SITTING BY A BUSH	6
AND THEN TOOK THE VEIL AND WITHDREW,	266 SITTING BY A BUSH	14
SQUARE MATTHEW HALE TOOK OFF HIS SUNDAY HAT	284 THE GOLD HESPERIDEE	45
HE TOOK THE PROPS DOWN USED FOR PROPPING OPEN,	289 OLD BARN AT THE BOTTOM	10
THAT STILL TOOK FROM ITS TOP	298 ON TAKING FROM THE TOP	19
NO, IT TOOK ALL THE SNOWS THAT CLUNG	299 WELCOME TO THEIR BELIEF	5
AND TOOK THE GOLD CANDLESTICKS HOME.	311 THE VINDICTIVES	40
HE TOOK THE ONE TO THE MOUNTAINS.	313 BEARER OF EVIL TIDINGS	9
TOOK HIM HOME TO HER BOWER.	313 BEARER OF EVIL TIDINGS	15
RATHER BECAUSE IT TOOK FIVE YEARS AT LEAST	323 BUILD SOIL	227
ONCE TOOK A LITTLE PEBBLE WHEEL	326 A MISSIVE MISSILE	2
NOW IT TOOK A FITFUL RUN;	344 DISCOVERY OF MADEIRAS	21
WHO TOOK IN THEM ONLOOKER'S SHARE.	345 DISCOVERY OF MADEIRAS	56
THE MAN WAS AMONG THE FIRST IT TOOK.	345 DISCOVERY OF MADEIRAS	59
IT TOOK THAT PAUSE TO MAKE HIM REALIZE	355 TIME OUT	1
WHOEVER THE SURLY FREEDOM TOOK	364 TRESPASS	5
I TOOK NOTE OF WHEN IT OCCURRED,	365 A NATURE NOTE	13
IT WAS A RISK I HAD TO TAKE--AND TOOK.	383 BRAVADO	4

TOOK (CONTINUED)
  UNLESS FOR PENITENTS WHO TOOK THEIR SEAT . . . . . . 400 TO THE RIGHT PERSON . . 12
  WHEN WE TOOK THAT FALL . . . . 435 KITTY HAWK 217
  AND TOOK OUR HORSE BY THE HEAD . . . . 444 THE DRAFT HORSE . . . 6
  THIS THOUGH WE TOOK THE INDIAN NAME FOR MAIZE . . . . 446 DOES NO ONE AT ALL EVER . 7
  HE IS THE ONE WHO TOOK THE MONEY FOR ME . . . . . . 459 HOW HARD TO KEEP FROM . 171
  AND TOOK YOUR TIME TO IT. IT SEEMS TO ME . . . . . 482 A MASQUE OF REASON . 245
  I TOOK CARE OF YOU. AND BEFORE YOU DIED . . . . . . 486 A MASQUE OF REASON . 361
  I TRUST I MADE IT CLEAR I TOOK YOUR SIDE . . . . . 486 A MASQUE OF REASON . 362
  SOMEONE TOOK CURVED NAIL-SCISSORS AND SNIPPED OFF . . 501 A MASQUE OF MERCY . 201
  THEY TOOK MY LOVE AND THREW HER DOWN A WELL. . . . . 510 A MASQUE OF MERCY . 446
TOOL
  THEY JUDGED ME BY THEIR APPROPRIATE TOOL. . . . . . 276 TWO TRAMPS IN MUD TIME . 54
  SOME WORN OLD TOOL OF MY OWN . . . . 285 IN TIME OF CLOUDBURST . 21
  I PRODDED THE EARTH WITH A LAZY TOOL . . . . 385 A MOOD APART . . . 2
  TURNED INTO A TOOL? . . . . 450 OBJECTION TO BE STEPPED . 15
  THE FIRST TOOL I STEP ON . . . . 450 OBJECTION TO BE STEPPED . 17
TOOLS
  TOOLS AND WEAPONS . . . . 468 FROM IRON 5
TOOTH
  LEAVING ON ONE WIRE TOOTH A LOCK OF HAIR. . . . . . 269 THE BEAR 9
TOP (SEE TIP-TOP)
  AND FROM A CLIFF TOP IS PROCLAIMED . . . . 20 THE TRIAL BY EXISTENCE . 17
  BRINGING A STONE GRASPED FIRMLY BY THE TOP . . . . . 34 MENDING WALL 39
  IS THAT THE WAY TO REACH THE TOP FROM HERE?-- . . . . 41-THE MOUNTAIN 35
  RIGHT ON THE TOP, TIP-TOP--A CURIOUS THING. . . . . 42 THE MOUNTAIN 47
  CLEAR TO THE TOP." I SAW THROUGH LEAFY SCREENS . . . 42 THE MOUNTAIN 57
  IT MAY NOT BE RIGHT ON THE VERY TOP: . . . . 42 THE MOUNTAIN 68
  SOMEWHERE IN IRELAND ON A MOUNTAIN TOP." . . . . . 43 THE MOUNTAIN 76
  CRANBERRIES IN BOGS AND RASPBERRIES ON TOP . . . . . 61 BLUEBERRIES 62
  FOR THE MAN UP ON TOP, OF THROWING DOWN . . . . . . 71 THE CODE 56
  "PUT IT ON TOP OF SOMETHING THAT'S ON TOP . . . . . 111 IN THE HOME STRETCH . 14
  TO THE TOP BRANCHES, CLIMBING CAREFULLY . . . . . . 122 BIRCHES 36
  BUT DIPPED ITS TOP AND SET ME DOWN AGAIN. . . . . . 122 BIRCHES 57
  FROM THE BARE TOP OF WHICH THERE IS A VIEW . . . . . 195 PAUL'S WIFE 125
  NOW UP, MY KNEE, TO KEEP ON TOP OF ANOTHER YEAR OF SNOW. . 298 A LEAF-TREADER . . . 12
  YOUR TOP HAS SUNK TOO LOW, ... 298 ON TAKING FROM THE TOP . 5
  ON TAKING FROM THE TOP TO BROADEN THE BASE . . . . . 298 ON TAKING FROM THE TOP . T
  THAT STILL TOOK FROM ITS TOP . . . . 298 ON TAKING FROM THE TOP . 19
  TO THE TOP OF HIS REACH ON THE WALL . . . . 310 THE VINDICTIVES . . . 4
  IS THAT IT BRINGS THE SAME CLASS UP ON TOP. . . . . 363 A SEMI-REVOLUTION . . 4
  AND NOTHING BUT THE TOP A LEAFY GREEN-- . . . . . . 375 A YOUNG BIRCH . . . 7
  THE ROAD AT THE TOP OF THE RISE . . . . 388 MIDDLENESS OF THE ROAD . 1
TOP-HEAVY
  TOP-HEAVY WITH A HEAVINESS HIS SHORT, ... 188 THE AX-HELVE 98
TOPPED
  I BUILT THE LOAD AND TOPPED IT OFF; OLD SANDERS . . . 71 THE CODE 51
TOPPLING (SEE IN-TOPPLING)
  THEY EDDY OVER IT TOO TOPPLING WEAK . . . . 246 ATMOSPHERE 3
TOPS
  AFTER THAT ONLY TOPS OF TREES, AND CLIFFS . . . . . 41 THE MOUNTAIN 31
  'TWOULD BE AMONG THE TOPS OF TREES, ... 274 A LONE STRIKER . . . 39
TORN (SEE WIND-TORN)
  IN THE WOOD-WORLD'S TORN DESPAIR . . . . 26 A LINE-STORM SONG . . 10
  A WORLD TORN LOOSE WENT BY ME. . . . . 377 ONE STEP BACKWARD TAKEN 12
  'TWAS TORN FROM HER PACIFIC SIDE. . . . . 452 A-WISHING WELL . . . 44
TORPEDO-LIKE
  TORPEDO-LIKE, WITH SHELL OF GRITTY LEATHER, ... 270 THE EGG AND THE MACHINE 25
TORRENCE
  TO RIDGELY TORRENCE ON LAST LOOKING INTO HIS "HESPERIDES" . 248 A PASSING GLIMPSE . . D
TORRENTS
  BRING ON WIND. BRING RAIN IN TORRENTS-- . . . . . . 304 CLEAR AND COLDER . . 13
TORTURE
  SUCH DEVILISH INGENUITY OF TORTURE . . . . 482 A MASQUE OF REASON . 262
  AND TRUST IT WON'T BE ADDING TO THE TORTURE. . . . . 484 A MASQUE OF REASON . 326
TORTURED
  HUNTED AND TORTURED AND RAGED. . . . . 311 THE VINDICTIVES . . . 48
  I'M GOING TO TELL JOB WHY I TORTURED HIM, ... 484 A MASQUE OF REASON . 325
  THERE'S NO ONE DOWN THERE GETTING TORTURED, SAVE . . . 516 A MASQUE OF MERCY . 609
TOSS
  AND WOULD HAVE TURNED TO TOSS THE GRASS TO DRY; . . . 22 THE TUFT OF FLOWERS . 20
  IF THE TREES MUST, LET THEM SILENTLY TOSS; . . . . . 25 NOW CLOSE THE WINDOWS . 2
TOSSED
  HE TOSSED HIS PIPES, TOO HARD TO TEACH . . . . . . 24 PAN WITH US 16
  TOSSED, TANGLED, WHIRLED AND WHIRLED ABOVE, ... 28 MY BUTTERFLY 16
  AND BROKE IT IN HIS HAND AND TOSSED IT BY. . . . . . 38 DEATH OF THE HIRED MAN . 123
  SHE RESTED ON A LOG AND TOSSED . . . . 128 THE IMPULSE 9
  AND MADE IT LEAP MY KNUCKLE, HAVING TOSSED . . . . . 231 A BROOK IN THE CITY . 7
  BUT, TREE, I HAVE SEEN YOU TAKEN AND TOSSED, ... 252 TREE AT MY WINDOW . 9
  WITH AUTUMN AND THE FRUIT WAS RUDELY TOSSED, ... 284 THE GOLD HESPERIDEE . 33
TOSSING
  AND TOSSING SO AS TO SCARE . . . . 156 THE SOUND OF TREES . 22
TOTAL
  THE TOTAL SKY ALMOST WITHOUT DEFECT, ... 245 SPRING POOLS . . . 2
  AND SO'S THE NATION, SO'S THE TOTAL RACE. . . . . . 355 THE LESSON FOR TODAY . 146
  THE TROUBLE WITH A TOTAL REVOLUTION . . . . 363 A SEMI-REVOLUTION . . 2
TOTALLY
  AT WHICH POINT WE ARE TOTALLY NONPLUSSED. . . . . . 382 TO AN ANCIENT . . . 12
  HOW TOTALLY IGNORED I SEEM TO BE. . . . . 462 HOW HARD TO KEEP FROM . 259
TOTE
  HE ALWAYS USED TO SING ALONG THE TOTE ROAD. . . . . 205 THE WITCH OF COOS . . 111
  THE TOTE ROAD TO OUR CLEARING WHERE WE LIVED. . . . . 208 PAUPER WITCH OF GRAFTON 25
TOTTER
  SO UNDERMINES MY BAREFOOT STAND I TOTTER, ... 391 ON BEING IDOLIZED . . 4
TOTTERED
  THOU DIDST NOT KNOW, WHO TOTTERED, WANDERING ON HIGH, . . 28 MY BUTTERFLY 22
TOTTERS
  IT TOTTERS WHEN SHE LICKS IT WITH HER TONGUE. . . . . 1 THE PASTURE 7

TOUCH (SEE TIP-TOUCH)
  BUT THE WILD TOUCH OF THY DYE-DUSTY WING! . . . . 29 MY BUTTERFLY 42
  "DON'T TOUCH ME, PLEASE--I SAY, DON'T TOUCH ME, PLEASE. . . . 47 A HUNDRED COLLARS . . 77
  A TARNISH THAT GOES AT A TOUCH OF THE HAND, ... 60 BLUEBERRIES 26
  THERE WERE TEN THOUSAND THOUSAND FRUIT TO TOUCH, . . . 69 AFTER APPLE-PICKING . 30
  JOHN HALL TOUCH ME! NOT IF HE KNOWS HIS FRIENDS. . . . . 83 THE HOUSEKEEPER . . . 67
  SHE HAS A TOUCH OF GOLD. NEW HAMPSHIRE GOLD-- . . 162 NEW HAMPSHIRE . . 108
  AND IN A LITTLE--A FRENCH TOUCH IN THAT. . . . . 188 THE AX-HELVE . . 100
  THE CREEPY EDGE OF IT WITH WARY TOUCH, ... 190 THE GRINDSTONE . . 69
  LOVE AT THE LIPS WAS TOUCH . . . . . . 226 TO EARTHWARD 1
  THE SUN AND MOON GET CROSSED, BUT THEY NEVER TOUCH, . . 268 ON LOOKING UP BY CHANCE 4
  AND, WITH A TOUCH THAT NEVER MISSED, ... 274 A LONE STRIKER . . 31
  WE MUSTN'T TOUCH THEM YET, BUT SEE AND SEE! . . . . 283 THE GOLD HESPERIDEE . 16
  HE GAVE IT SCARCELY A TOUCH, ... 288 DEPARTMENTAL . . . 6
  I TOUCH MY TONGUE TO THE SHOES NOW, ... 295 A RECORD STRIDE . . 21
  YOUR LEAST TOUCH SETS IT GOING ROUND, ... 306 A TRIAL RUN . . . 13
  TO TOUCH HER NECK AND HAIR. . . . . . 339 THE SUBVERTED FLOWER . 22
  MAY REACH TO YOU, BUT CANNOT TOUCH YOUR FATE. . . 357 A MOTH SEEN IN WINTER . 22
  I CANNOT TOUCH YOUR LIFE, MUCH LESS CAN SAVE, . . 357 A MOTH SEEN IN WINTER . 23
  OF WHICH YOU FEEL NO LEAST TOUCH ON YOUR FACE . . 361 A LOOSE MOUNTAIN . 11
  OR SOON WE'D BAT EACH OTHER OUT OF TOUCH, . . . 371 THE LITERATE FARMER AND 117
  WE WOULD WANT TO TOUCH, ... 438 KITTY HAWK . . . 331
  AROUND HIM SO IT WOULDN'T TOUCH AND HURT HIM. . . 478 A MASQUE OF REASON . 133
  THAT ONLY NEEDS A FINGER TOUCH FROM GOD . . . . 502 A MASQUE OF MERCY . 230
TOUCHED
  HER GIVING SOMEHOW TOUCHED THE PRINCIPLE . . . . 57 THE BLACK COTTAGE . 60
  IT TOUCHED, IT STRUCK, IT CLATTERED AND WENT OUT. . 92 THE FEAR . . . 93
  AND THE AGED ELM, THOUGH TOUCHED WITH FIRE; . . . 242 NEED OF BEING VERSED . 18
  THEY TAPPED AT MY EYELIDS AND TOUCHED MY LIPS WITH AN
    INVITATION TO GRIEF. . . . . . . 298 A LEAF-TREADER . . . 10
  AM TOUCHED BY THAT UNINTIMATE LIGHT . . . . 383 WERE I IN TROUBLE . 7
  NO ONE WAS SO FAR TOUCHED . . . . . . 391 A ROGERS GROUP . . 11
TOUCHES
  HE DREW THE OXEN TOWARD HIM WITH LIGHT TOUCHES . . . . 44 THE MOUNTAIN . . . 107
  MORE THAN IT TOUCHES ME. / YOU MAY COME IN. . . . 493 A MASQUE OF MERCY . 17
TOUCHING
  AS TOUCHING AS A BASKETFUL OF EGGS, ... 365 OF STONES OF THE PLACE 2
TOUGH
  HE MAY BE GOOD, BUT ONE THING'S SURE, HE'S TOUGH." . . 145 SNOW 71
  DE SECOND GROWT' I CUT MYSELF--TOUGH, TOUGH!" . . . . 186 THE AX-HELVE . . 31
TOURIST
  A LIKENESS TO SURPRISE THE THRILLY TOURIST. . . . 214 A FOUNTAIN, A BOTTLE . 40
TOURNAMENT
  PERHAPS FOR AN OLYMPIC TOURNAMENT, ... 474 A MASQUE OF REASON . 24
TOW
  WILL TAKE IN TOW THIS DERELICT . . . . . 418 AMERICA IS HARD TO SEE 56
TOWARD
  TOWARD THE THRONE TO WITNESS THERE . . . . 20 THE TRIAL BY EXISTENCE 30
  HE DREW THE OXEN TOWARD HIM WITH LIGHT TOUCHES . . . 44 THE MOUNTAIN . . . 107
  ADVANCING TOWARD HER: "WHAT IS IT YOU SEE . . . 51 HOME BURIAL . . . 6
  AND ALL OUR STORMS COME UP TOWARD THE HOUSE, . . 63 A SERVANT TO SERVANTS . 24
  TOWARD HEAVEN STILL, ... 68 AFTER APPLE-PICKING . 2
  WITH AN EYE ALWAYS LIFTED TOWARD THE WEST . . . 69 THE CODE . . . 3
  TILL WELL TOWARD NOON, WHEN THE STORM SETTLED DOWN . 74 THE GENERATIONS OF MEN 22
  SHE MADE A SUDDEN MOVEMENT TOWARD HER BODICE, . . 74 THE GENERATIONS OF MEN 43
  SLIPPING FROM CLUMSY CLUTCHES TOWARD THE CEILING, . 113 IN THE HOME STRETCH . 89
  TOWARD HEAVEN, TILL THE TREE COULD BEAR NO MORE, . . 122 BIRCHES 56
  LOOKED UP TOWARD HEAVEN, AND THERE AGAINST THE BLUE, . 125 AN ENCOUNTER . . . 11
  SHORT OF THE PERCH THEIR LANGUID FLIGHT WAS TOWARD; . 130 THE BONFIRE . . . 37
  WHERE THE FIELD STRETCHES TOWARD THE NORTH . . . 131 THE BONFIRE . . . 57
  AS HE SWUNG TOWARD THEM HOLDING UP THE HAND, . . . 136 "OUT,OUT--" . . . 20
  MAKING A GREAT SCROLL UPWARD TOWARD THE SKY, . . . 143 SNOW 9
  HAD SPILLED THEM NEAR THE WINDOW, TOWARD THE LIGHT, . 216 A FOUNTAIN, A BOTTLE . 96
  IT IS THIS BACKWARD MOTION TOWARD THE SOURCE, . . 260 WEST-RUNNING BROOK . 68
  GET IN A POEM TOWARD THE NEXT ELECTION. . . . 316 BUILD SOIL . . . 25
  NOW QUIVERED TOWARD EACH OTHER, LIPPED . . . 381 AN UNSTAMPED LETTER IN 34
  SAYS OUR REACHING TOWARD . . . . . . 438 KITTY HAWK . . . 334
  TOWARD WHAT YOU MAKE ME SEE BEYOND THE WORLD. . . 514 A MASQUE OF MERCY . 545
TOWARDS
  HE'S COMING TOWARDS US. JOEL, GO IN--PLEASE. . . 90 THE FEAR . . . 39
  (AND THAT'S WHAT THEIR TOES ARE TOWARDS), . . . 294 A RECORD STRIDE . 4
  A HOLY IMPULSE TOWARDS REDISTRIBUTION. . . . . 509 A MASQUE OF MERCY . 419
TOWELS
  OF MANY PLATES WITH TOWELS MANY TIMES." . . . 111 IN THE HOME STRETCH . 28
TOWER
  WISHING THE TOWER . . . . 217 I WILL SING YOU ONE-O . 3
  OF THE TOWER CLOCK . . . . 218 I WILL SING YOU ONE-O . 19
  THE TOWER SAID, "ONE!" . . . . . . 218 I WILL SING YOU ONE-O . 27
  RAISED THIS TOWER SHAFT . . . . . . 430 KITTY HAWK . . . 71
TOWN
  THE MOUNTAIN HELD THE TOWN AS IN A SHADOW. . . . 40 THE MOUNTAIN . . . 1
  AND YET BETWEEN THE TOWN AND IT I FOUND, . . . 40 THE MOUNTAIN . . . 7
  "WHAT TOWN IS THIS?" I ASKED. / "THIS? LUNENBURG." . 41 THE MOUNTAIN . . . 19
  THEN I WAS WRONG: THE TOWN OF MY SOJOURN, . . . 41 THE MOUNTAIN . . . 20
  LANCASTER BORE HIM--SUCH A LITTLE TOWN, . . . 44 A HUNDRED COLLARS . 1
  HE'S INTO EVERYTHING IN TOWN. THIS YEAR . . . 64 A SERVANT TO SERVANTS . 71
  A ROCK-STREWN TOWN WHERE FARMING HAS FALLEN OFF, . . 73 THE GENERATIONS OF MEN 5
  THAT NOW NOT ALL THE HOUSES LEFT IN TOWN . . . 73 THE GENERATIONS OF MEN 11
  THE TOWN IS FULL OF CHASES, LOWES, AND BAILEYS, . . 75 THE GENERATIONS OF MEN 48
  DRAWN INTO TOWN ABOUT THIS CELLAR HOLE . . . 76 THE GENERATIONS OF MEN 89
  YOU MUST BE GETTING STARTED BACK TO TOWN. . . . 111 IN THE HOME STRETCH . 17
  SOME BOY TOO FAR FROM TOWN TO LEARN BASEBALL, . . 121 BIRCHES 25
  THE WOODS AND TOWN ON FIRE BY ME, AND ALL . . . 131 THE BONFIRE . . . 72
  THE TOWN TURNED OUT TO FIGHT FOR ME--THAT HELD ME. . 131 THE BONFIRE . . . 73
  IT TOOK ME. NEIGHBORS COMING HOME FROM TOWN . . . 132 THE BONFIRE . . . 84
  WE KNOW WHO WHEN THEY COME TO TOWN . . . . 141 THE GUM-GATHERER . . 25
  A HALFWAY COFFEE HOUSE 'TWIXT TOWN AND NOWHERE----" . 155 SNOW 342
  A TELESCOPE. SOMEONE IN EVERY TOWN . . . . 177 THE STAR-SPLITTER . 35

PAGE TITLE   LINE

TOWN (CONTINUED)
  SEEMS TO ME OWES IT TO THE TOWN TO KEEP ONE. . . . . . 177 THE STAR-SPLITTER . . . 36
  MEAN LAUGHTER WENT ABOUT THE TOWN THAT DAY . . . . . 177 THE STAR-SPLITTER . . . 40
  HE FOUND THE GRAVE A TOWN OR TWO AWAY, ... 200 PLACE FOR A THIRD . . . 38
  WHICH WASN'T MANY, IN THE TOWN OF WENTWORTH. . . . . 208 PAUPER WITCH OF GRAFTON 22
  TO SEE IF THE TOWN WANTED TO TAKE OVER . . . . . 208 PAUPER WITCH OF GRAFTON 24
  AT HAVING IN THEIR TOWN A NOTED WITCH: . . . . . 208 PAUPER WITCH OF GRAFTON 37
  IN FRONT OF ONE TOWN HALL, I'D LEFT HIM HITCHED . . . . 208 PAUPER WITCH OF GRAFTON 50
  FROM GROWING UNDER PAVEMENTS OF A TOWN; . . . . . 231 A BROOK IN THE CITY . . 10
  DUST ALWAYS BLOWING ABOUT THE TOWN, ... 249 A PECK OF GOLD . . . 1
  TO COME AT THE FISHER TOWN . . . . . 260 SAND DUNES 6
  WAS WHAT SHOULD BE A TOWN. . . . . . 367 A SERIOUS STEP LIGHTLY . 6
  YOU MIGHT NOT NOTICE IF YOU'VE LIVED IN TOWN, ... 370 THE LITERATE FARMER AND . 68
  AS I SUSPECT YOU HAVE. A TOWN DEBARS . . . . . 370 THE LITERATE FARMER AND . 69
  WHEN YOU WERE READING BOOKS OR OUT OF TOWN. . . . . 375 A YOUNG BIRCH . . . 20
  AND IN A TOWN THAT IS NO MORE A TOWN. . . . . 377 DIRECTIVE 7
  GREAT MONOLITHIC KNEES THE FORMER TOWN . . . . . 377 DIRECTIVE 11
  GOOD FRIENDS IN TOWN. . . . . . 413 AWAY! 6
  (A COUNTRY NAMED FOR HIM, A TOWN, ... 418 AMERICA IS HARD TO SEE . 46
  IT'S SOME KIND OF TOWN, ... 439 KITTY HAWK 343
  WHERE ARE YOU STAYING--ANYWHERE IN TOWN? . . . . . 501 A MASQUE OF MERCY . . 209
TOWN-BRED
  THE TOWN-BRED FARMER FAILED TO UNDERSTAND. . . . . 69 THE CODE 9
TOWNS
  NEW IS A WORD FOR FOOLS IN TOWNS WHO THINK . . . . . 117 IN THE HOME STRETCH . 183
  AT SEA, ABOUT THE TOWNS WHERE WAR HAS COME . . . . . 132 THE BONFIRE 105
  AND CHILDREN IN THE SHIPS AND IN THE TOWNS? . . . . . 132 THE BONFIRE 108
  AN OATH OF TOWNS THAT SET THE WILD AT NAUGHT, ... 141 THE LINE-GANG . . . 12
  SMALL TOWNS--LOST NATION, BUNGEY, MUDDY BOO, ... 165 NEW HAMPSHIRE . . . 187
  THERE'S BUNGEY; AND FOR BUNGEY THERE ARE TOWNS, ... 165 NEW HAMPSHIRE . . . 208
  EXCEPT IN TOWNS AT NIGHT, IS NOT A SIN. . . . . . 189 THE GRINDSTONE . . . 18
  FLATTERED I MUST BE TO HAVE TWO TOWNS FIGHTING . . . . 207 PAUPER WITCH OF GRAFTON 4
  WENTWORTH AND WARREN'S BOTH GOOD TOWNS TO LIVE IN, . . . 208 PAUPER WITCH OF GRAFTON 30
TOWNSHIP
  HOR IS THE TOWNSHIP, AND THE TOWNSHIP'S HOR-- . . . . . 43 THE MOUNTAIN 96
TOWNSHIPS
  WHOLE TOWNSHIPS NAMED BUT WITHOUT POPULATION. . . . . 165 NEW HAMPSHIRE . . . 209
TOWNSHIP'S
  HOR IS THE TOWNSHIP, AND THE TOWNSHIP'S HOR-- . . . . . 43 THE MOUNTAIN 96
TOY
  I LOVE TO TOY WITH THE PLATONIC NOTION . . . . . 362 BOEOTIAN 1
  AS CIRCUS DAY OF TOY BALLOONS. . . . . . 451 A-WISHING WELL . . . 18
TOYS
  OF WORDS OR TOYS, IT MINISTERS TO HEALTH. . . . . 321 BUILD SOIL 170
TRACE
  AND LEFT NO TRACE BUT THE CELLAR WALLS, ... 5 GHOST HOUSE 3
  WHERE LOVE HAS LEFT A PRINTED TRACE . . . . . 120 BOND AND FREE . . . 7
  A SPECIMEN OF BERYL WITH A TRACE . . . . . 162 NEW HAMPSHIRE . . . 118
  THE TRACE WOULD HAVE TO BE THE MEREST TRACE . . . . . 162 NEW HAMPSHIRE . . . 120
  NOR FIND IN DEW THE SLIGHTEST CLOUDY TRACE. . . . . 361 A LOOSE MOUNTAIN . . 12
  COMING ON SUCH AN ANCIENT HUMAN TRACE . . . . . 382 TO AN ANCIENT . . . 7
  THERE WAS NOT A TRACE . . . . . 440 KITTY HAWK 392
  NOT A TRACE OF IT'S LEFT . . . . . 449 THE BAD ISLAND--EASTER 59
TRACK
  OR THOSE SHOULD NOT SET FORTH UPON MY TRACK . . . . . 5 INTO MY OWN 10
  I CAN'T KEEP TRACK OF OTHER PEOPLE'S DAUGHTERS. . . . . 81 THE HOUSEKEEPER . . . 11
  WAS SETTING OUT, UP TRACK AND DOWN, NOT PLANTS. . . . 178 THE STAR-SPLITTER . . 71
  TO SEE WHAT THEY WERE BESIDE THE TRACK. . . . . 248 A PASSING GLIMPSE . . 4
  HE WISHED WHEN HE HAD HAD THE TRACK ALONE . . . . . 270 THE EGG AND THE MACHINE 5
  OF HER CELESTIAL TRACK, ... 464 MILKY WAY IS A COWPATH 22
TRACKED
  GOT DRUNK, AND TRACKED THE PAIR UP CATAMOUNT, ... 195 PAUL'S WIFE 124
TRACKS
  NO RUNNER TRACKS IN THIS YEAR'S SNOW LOOPED NEAR IT. . . . 101 THE WOOD-PILE . . . 26
  AND LOOK FOR SKUNK TRACKS . . . . . 136 LAST WORD OF A BLUEBIRD 18
  SHE LIKES TO HALT US IN OUR RUNNER TRACKS, ... 238 ON A TREE FALLEN ACROSS 6
  I LINK A LINE OF SHADOWY TRACKS. . . . . . 470 IN WINTER IN THE WOODS 7
TRACTOR-PLOW
  OF TRACTOR-PLOW AND MOTOR-DRILL. . . . . . 418 AMERICA IS HARD TO SEE 69
TRACTS
  AND ON TRACTS LAID NEW TO THE SUN, ... 285 IN TIME OF CLOUDBURST . 19
TRADE (SEE FREE-TRADE)
  WHICH GIVES THEM THE ADVANTAGE IN THE TRADE. . . . . 95 THE SELF-SEEKER . . . 64
  THE ONLY PERSON REALLY SOILED WITH TRADE . . . . . 160 NEW HAMPSHIRE . . . 35
  AND THE FUR TRADE, ... 210 AN EMPTY THREAT . . . 4
  THE SCALES OF TRADE, THE CROSS OF FAITH, ... 252 THE PEACEFUL SHEPHERD . 7
  THE MAN FREE LOVE, THE BUSINESSMAN FREE TRADE, ... 319 BUILD SOIL 112
  IN SELF-RESTRAINT, IF IN RESTRAINT OF TRADE. . . . . 323 BUILD SOIL 229
  WHICH MAY A LITTLE WHILE BY WAR AND TRADE . . . . . 399 THE INGENUITIES OF DEBT 7
  THAT I MAY TRADE ON WITH RELIANCE . . . . . 449 OUR DOOM TO BLOOM . . 3
  FREE WILL, TRADE, VERSE, THOUGHT, LOVE, SPEECH, COINAGE. . 459 HOW HARD TO KEEP FROM 186
TRADEMARK
  HE STOOD BESIDE AND LEAVE HIS TRADEMARK ON THEM, . . . 209 PAUPER WITCH OF GRAFTON 55
TRADER'S (SEE NIGGER-TRADER'S)
TRADING
  ROSE LIKE A FACTOR'S AT A TRADING STATION. . . . . 160 NEW HAMPSHIRE . . . 53
TRADITION
  THE WEST AND KEEP THE OLD TRADITION SAFE. . . . . 365 OF STONES OF THE PLACE 12
TRAFFIC
  IN FRONT AT THE EDGE OF THE ROAD WHERE THE TRAFFIC SPED, . 286 A ROADSIDE STAND . . 2
  THE POLISHED TRAFFIC PASSED WITH A MIND AHEAD, ... 286 A ROADSIDE STAND . . 7
  LIKE SWEARING OFF ON THE TRAFFIC WORLD. . . . . 419 ONE MORE BREVITY . . 18
TRAGIC
  BUT HOW TO TAKE THE CURSE, TRAGIC OR COMIC. . . . . 352 THE LESSON FOR TODAY . 62
TRAGICALLY
  LIFE MAY BE TRAGICALLY BAD, AND I . . . . . 317 BUILD SOIL 41
TRAIL
  I KNEW SO WELL, WHOSE GARMENTS TRAIL . . . . . 15 IN A VALE 4

TRAIL (CONTINUED)
   I WAS RUNNING WITH JOY ON THE DEMON'S TRAIL, ...   24 THE DEMIURGE'S LAUGH . 2
   OUT OF THE WOODS, WORN OUT UPON THE TRAIL." .   .   .   .   38 DEATH OF THE HIRED MAN 117
   (THOUGH THESE WHEN NOT IN USE TO FLY AND TRAIL .   .   .   172 A STAR IN A STONEBOAT   17
   THE TRAVELER'S EYE PICKED UP A TURTLE TRAIL,   .   .   .   270 THE EGG AND THE MACHINE 17
TRAILING (SEE LOW-TRAILING)
   YEARS AFTERWARDS, TRAILING THEIR LEAVES ON THE GROUND   .   121 BIRCHES   .   . 18
TRAIN (SEE LIFE-TRAIN)
   HIS TRAIN BEING LATE, HE MISSED ANOTHER TRAIN   .   .   .   44 A HUNDRED COLLARS . 15
   THE LAWYER MAN IS THINKING OF HIS TRAIN.   .   .   .   98 THE SELF-SEEKER . . 168
   THE LAWYER SAID. "I'M SORRY, BUT MY TRAIN-- .   .   .   99 THE SELF-SEEKER . . 181
   DON'T STOP TO TRY TO NOW. YOU'LL MISS YOUR TRAIN. .   101 THE SELF-SEEKER . . 227
   I WANT TO GET OUT OF THE TRAIN AND GO BACK .   .   .   248 A PASSING GLIMPSE .   3
   THAT I ASSUME WAS WHAT OUR PASSING TRAIN MEANT.   .   292 FIGURE IN THE DOORWAY   20
   AND RAISING A DUST WITH A TRAIN .   .   .   .   .   .   312 THE VINDICTIVES .   74
TRAINS
   SOMETHING I MUST HAVE LEARNED RIDING IN TRAINS   .   .   77 THE GENERATIONS OF MEN 127
TRAIN'S
   I WONDER WHERE MY LAWYER IS. HIS TRAIN'S IN.   .   .   94 THE SELF-SEEKER . . 49
TRAIT
   IT CAN BLAME THIS LIMITLESS TRAIT IN THE HEARTS OF MEN. .   305 THERE ARE ROUGHLY ZONES 21
   TO SUSPECT THE HUMAN TRAIT .   .   .   .   .   .   387 THE COURAGE TO BE NEW . 10
   BY CHARACTER, BY TONGUE, BY NATIVE TRAIT,   .   .   .   422 FOR JOHN F. KENNEDY . 14
   TO MAKE US DIFFERENT IN A SINGLE TRAIT.   .   .   .   446 DOES NO ONE AT ALL EVER   6
TRAITS
   'TWAS SAID THE LESSER GODS WERE ONLY TRAITS   .   .   516 A MASQUE OF MERCY . 595
TRAMP
   WAS THAT TRAMP TAKING SANCTUARY THERE .   .   .   .   289 OLD BARN AT THE BOTTOM 14
   THE CHEAPEST TRAMP THAT CAME ALONG THAT WAY .   .   290 OLD BARN AT THE BOTTOM 44
   TO TELL YOU IT WAS JUST A TRAMP .   .   .   .   .   380 AN UNSTAMPED LETTER IN   6
   AND THEN YOUR TRAMP ASTROLOGER .   .   .   .   .   381 AN UNSTAMPED LETTER IN 28
TRAMPING
   THE HOUSE WAS FULL OF TRAMPING, AND THE DARK,   .   .   113 IN THE HOME STRETCH . 82
TRAMPS
   TWO TRAMPS IN MUD TIME .   .   .   .   275 TWO TRAMPS IN MUD TIME   T
   OUT OF THE WOODS TWO HULKING TRAMPS .   .   .   .   276 TWO TRAMPS IN MUD TIME 49
TRANCE
   "IS THIS SOME TRANCE YOU ARE WITHDRAWING INTO?" .   .   78 THE GENERATIONS OF MEN 148
   HE BROKE MY TRANCE. DON'T THAT MAKE YOU SUSPICIOUS .   202 THE WITCH OF COOS . 16
   THERE HE GOES OFF INTO ANOTHER TRANCE.   .   .   .   503 A MASQUE OF MERCY . 264
TRANSFIXED
   TRANSFIXED ON MOUNTAIN SLOPES ALMOST ERECT.   .   .   237 A HILLSIDE THAW .   . 28
TRANSFORMED
   TRANSFORMED FROM CHRONIC TO ACUTE AND BLOODY?   .   .   317 BUILD SOIL   .   .   . 30
TRANSIT
   TO CATCH THEM AND TAKE TOLL OF THEM IN TRANSIT.   .   321 BUILD SOIL   .   . 167
TRANSITION
   LET'S SEE, WHERE ARE WE? OH, WE'RE IN TRANSITION, .   462 HOW HARD TO KEEP FROM 254
TRANSLATED
   AND IT THE FISHPOLE. SO I WAS TRANSLATED,   .   .   .   197 WILD GRAPES .   . 45
   THAT WHEN I AM TRANSLATED .   .   .   .   .   .   389 ASTROMETAPHYSICAL . 14
TRANSLATING
   YOU SEEM SO READY AT TRANSLATING NAMES.   .   .   .   495 A MASQUE OF MERCY . 61
TRAP
   THEN HE SHUT DOWN THE TRAP DOOR WITH A RING IN IT .   .   142 THE VANISHING RED . 24
   LET'S TRAP HIM WITH AN OPEN DOOR UP ATTIC." .   .   .   206 THE WITCH OF COOS . 113
   ENOUGH TO BAIT THE TRAP OF THE IDEAL .   .   .   .   508 A MASQUE OF MERCY . 386
   AND LEAVING IT BEHIND US IN THE TRAP. .   .   .   .   508 A MASQUE OF MERCY . 389
TRAPPER
   AND A TRAPPER LOOKING IN AT THE DOOR .   .   .   .   211 AN EMPTY THREAT .   . 10
TRAPPINGS
   LET THEIR TRAPPINGS BE TAKEN AWAY. .   .   .   .   313 THE VINDICTIVES .   . 89
TRAPS
   AND HE'S OFF SETTING TRAPS-- .   .   .   .   .   .   211 AN EMPTY THREAT .   . 28
TRAVEL
   AND SORRY I COULD NOT TRAVEL BOTH .   .   .   .   105 THE ROAD NOT TAKEN .   2
   CAN IT BE FOREIGN TRAVEL IN THE ALPS? .   .   .   .   169 NEW HAMPSHIRE .   . 320
TRAVELED
   "YOU SPEAK AS IF THIS WERE A TRAVELED ROAD. .   .   90 THE FEAR .   .   .   24
   I TOOK THE ONE LESS TRAVELED BY, ...   105 THE ROAD NOT TAKEN . 19
TRAVELER
   AND BE ONE TRAVELER, LONG I STOOD .   .   .   .   105 THE ROAD NOT TAKEN .   3
   I MET A TRAVELER FROM ARKANSAS .   .   .   .   .   159 NEW HAMPSHIRE .   .   9
   "TRAVELER, I'M GLAD YOU ASKED ABOUT THAT LIGHT. .   368 THE LITERATE FARMER AND 23
   FOR TRAVELER THERE COULD DO ME NO GOOD .   .   .   383 WERE I IN TROUBLE .   9
TRAVELER'S
   THE TRAVELER'S EYE PICKED UP A TURTLE TRAIL,   .   .   270 THE EGG AND THE MACHINE 17
   BY WAY OF TRAVELER'S AID, ...   391 A ROGERS GROUP .   .   10
TRAVELS
   I TRIED TO MAKE HIM TALK ABOUT HIS TRAVELS.   .   .   36 DEATH OF THE HIRED MAN 42
   WERE ONCE MORE ON THEIR TRAVELS, ...   376 ONE STEP BACKWARD TAKEN   2
TREAD
   WITH NONE TO TREAD AND PUT THEM IN THEIR PLACE.   .   56 THE BLACK COTTAGE . 50
   OFF THERE UPSTAIRS. THE VERY TREAD OF MEN .   .   111 IN THE HOME STRETCH . 38
   THE LIVING COME WITH GRASSY TREAD .   .   .   .   221 IN A DISUSED GRAVEYARD   1
   THE GRASS LAY FLATTENED UNDER ONE GREAT TREAD. .   239 OUR SINGING STRENGTH . 12
   OR IF HE RESTS FROM SCIENTIFIC TREAD, ...   269 THE BEAR .   .   .   22
   ONE CROSSING WITH HURRIED TREAD. .   .   .   .   288 DEPARTMENTAL .   . 14
   AND STUMBLED THROUGH THE ROCKS WITH HORNY TREAD, .   338 THE MOST OF IT .   . 19
   FASTER THAN MY TREAD-- .   .   .   .   .   .   428 KITTY HAWK .   . 18
TREADER (SEE LEAF-TREADER)
TREADING
   AS IF FOR FEAR OF TREADING UPON ME. .   .   .   125 AN ENCOUNTER .   .   . 15
   I HAVE BEEN TREADING ON LEAVES ALL DAY UNTIL I AM
     AUTUMN-TIRED. .   .   .   .   297 A LEAF-TREADER .   .   1
TREADING-WATER-LIKE
   AND CAUGHT SIGHT OF HIM TREADING-WATER-LIKE, .   .   72 THE CODE .   .   .   76

TREASON
    WAS IT EVER LESS THAN A TREASON . . . .   30 RELUCTANCE 20
TREASURE
    OF THEIR WORTH FOR YOU TO TREASURE, ...   13 FLOWER-GATHERING . . . 14
    CONSIDER WHAT THEY TREASURE UNDER GLASS, ...   290 OLD BARN AT THE BOTTOM 33
    OF MANY A TREASURE BY NAME . . . .   311 THE VINDICTIVES . . . 34
    THE GREAT TREASURE WANTED THE MOST, ...   312 THE VINDICTIVES . . . 62
TREAT
    LOOK HERE, YOU TREAT YOUR GUIDE WITH DUE RESPECT . .   214 A FOUNTAIN, A BOTTLE . 49
    MEN WOULD TREAT THIS SKY . . . .   434 KITTY HAWK 189
    THE TEST IS ALWAYS HOW WE TREAT THE POOR. . . . . .   477 A MASQUE OF REASON . . 123
TREATED
    (THEY TREATED IT AS HIS.) "YOU TAKE A JACKKNIFE, . .   193 PAUL'S WIFE 80
    IT'S TIME THE POOR WERE TREATED BY THE STATE . . . .   477 A MASQUE OF REASON . . 124
TREE   (SEE ELM-TREE)
    THE ORCHARD TREE HAS GROWN ONE COPSE . . . .   5 GHOST HOUSE 8
    THOSE STONES OUT UNDER THE LOW-LIMBED TREE . . . . .   6 GHOST HOUSE 24
    SHE LOVES THE BARE, THE WITHERED TREE; . . . .   6 MY NOVEMBER GUEST . . 4
    A TREE BESIDE THE WALL STANDS BARE, ...   9 A LATE WALK 9
    THEREAFTER I SAT ME AGAINST A TREE. . . . .   25 THE DEMIURGE'S LAUGH . 18
    I'VE BEEN A-CHOKING LIKE A NURSERY TREE . . . . . .   46 A HUNDRED COLLARS . . 56
    MY LONG TWO-POINTED LADDER'S STICKING THROUGH A TREE   68 AFTER APPLE-PICKING . 1
    OF STRANGER-COUSINS, IN A FAMILY TREE . . . .   74 THE GENERATIONS OF MEN 39
    "UNDER THE SHELTER OF THE FAMILY TREE." . . . . . .   75 THE GENERATIONS OF MEN 65
    COME HERE--I'LL SHOW YOU--IN THAT APPLE TREE. . . .   83 THE HOUSEKEEPER . . . 62
    UNDER WHAT BEECH TREE, ON WHAT WOODCHUCK'S KNOLL?" .   97 THE SELF-SEEKER . . . 116
    TO PUT A TREE BETWEEN US WHEN HE LIGHTED, ...   101 THE WOOD-PILE 11
    WHAT HELD IT, THOUGH, ON ONE SIDE WAS A TREE . . . .   102 THE WOOD-PILE 32
    WHO MAKES THE SOLID TREE TRUNKS SOUND AGAIN. . . . .   119 THE OVEN BIRD 3
    AND SO NOT CARRYING THE TREE AWAY . . . .   122 BIRCHES 34
    I'D LIKE TO GO BY CLIMBING A BIRCH TREE, ...   122 BIRCHES 54
    TOWARD HEAVEN, TILL THE TREE COULD BEAR NO MORE, . .   122 BIRCHES 56
    SOFT PETALS FALLEN FROM THE APPLE TREE . . . .   124 PUTTING IN THE SEED . 4
    SHE RUNS FROM TREE TO TREE WHERE LIE AND SWEETEN . .   125 THE COW IN APPLE TIME. 7
    STOOD OVER ME A RESURRECTED TREE, ...   125 AN ENCOUNTER 12
    A TREE THAT HAD BEEN DOWN AND RAISED AGAIN-- . . . .   125 AN ENCOUNTER 13
    MADE THE GREAT TREE SEEM AS A LITTLE BIRD . . . . .   128 THE OFT-REPEATED DREAM 7
    OF WHAT THE TREE MIGHT DO. . . . .   128 THE OFT-REPEATED DREAM 12
    OR FELLED TREE. . . . .   128 THE IMPULSE 8
    THAT A CIDER-APPLE TREE . . . .   134 A GIRL'S GARDEN . . . 34
    THEY WILL COME BUDDING BOUGHS FROM TREE TO TREE, . .   151 SNOW 230
    THE ONLY DECENT TREE HAD BEEN TO MILL . . . .   171 NEW HAMPSHIRE 376
    COULD TELL THE TIME OF YEAR WHEN EVERY TREE . . . .   175 THE CENSUS-TAKER . . 18
    AND EVERY TREE UP STOOD A ROTTING TRUNK . . . . . .   175 THE CENSUS-TAKER . . 22
    YOU ASK HER IF SHE KNOWS A MAPLE TREE. . . . .   180 MAPLE 8
    WELL, YOU WERE NAMED AFTER A MAPLE TREE. . . . . . .   180 MAPLE 9
    BE A GOOD GIRL--BE LIKE A MAPLE TREE. . . . .   180 MAPLE 22
    "DO YOU KNOW YOU REMIND ME OF A TREE-- . . . .   182 MAPLE 87
    A MAPLE TREE?" / "BECAUSE MY NAME IS MAPLE?" . . . .   182 MAPLE 88
    TO SEE IF THERE WAS NOT SOME SPECIAL TREE . . . . .   183 MAPLE 100
    NOT SO MUCH AS A SINGLE TREE FOR SHADE, ...   183 MAPLE 102
    IT WAS THE TREE THE AUTUMN FIRE RAN THROUGH . . . .   184 MAPLE 140
    IT STANDS BESIDE THE SAME OLD APPLE TREE. . . . . .   189 THE GRINDSTONE . . . 8
    THE SHADOW OF THE APPLE TREE IS THIN . . . .   189 THE GRINDSTONE . . . 9
    UNDER A RUINOUS LIVE APPLE TREE . . . .   189 THE GRINDSTONE . . . 20
    AND LEFT STOOD UP ON END INSIDE THE TREE . . . . . .   194 PAUL'S WIFE 93
    THE HUNDRED YEARS THE TREE MUST HAVE BEEN GROWING. .   194 PAUL'S WIFE 94
    WHAT TREE MAY NOT THE FIG BE GATHERED FROM? . . . .   196 WILD GRAPES 1
    I OUGHT TO KNOW WHAT TREE THE GRAPE IS FRUIT OF. . .   196 WILD GRAPES 6
    HE CLIMBED STILL HIGHER AND BENT THE TREE TO EARTH .   197 WILD GRAPES 37
    I SAID I HAD THE TREE. IT WASN'T TRUE. . . . .   197 WILD GRAPES 41
    THE OPPOSITE WAS TRUE. THE TREE HAD ME. . . . . . .   197 WILD GRAPES 42
    "DROP OR I'LL SHAKE THE TREE AND SHAKE YOU DOWN." .   198 WILD GRAPES 78
    I'LL BEND THE TREE DOWN AND LET YOU DOWN BY IT." . .   198 WILD GRAPES 83
    FROM A HEMLOCK TREE . . . .   221 DUST OF SNOW 4
    IN GOING TWICE AROUND THE TREE . . . .   233 LOOKING FOR SUNSET BIRD 12
    ON EVERY TREE A BUCKET WITH A LID, ...   234 EVENING A SUGAR ORCHARD 12
    THE TREE THE TEMPEST WITH A CRASH OF WOOD . . . . .   238 ON A TREE FALLEN ACROSS 1
    ON A TREE FALLEN ACROSS THE ROAD . . . .   238 ON A TREE FALLEN ACROSS T
    SWOOPS JUST IN TIME TO HIS REMEMBERED TREE. . . . .   249 ACCEPTANCE 10
    TREE AT MY WINDOW, WINDOW TREE, ...   251 TREE AT MY WINDOW . . 1
    TREE AT MY WINDOW . . . .   251 TREE AT MY WINDOW . . T
    BUT, TREE, I HAVE SEEN YOU TAKEN AND TOSSED, ...   252 TREE AT MY WINDOW . . 9
    AND NOT MELT SNOW OR START A DORMANT TREE. . . . . .   254 A WINTER EDEN 4
    THE BEAR PUTS BOTH ARMS AROUND THE TREE ABOVE HER .   268 THE BEAR 1
    SQUARE MATTHEW HALE'S YOUNG GRAFTED APPLE TREE . . .   283 THE GOLD HESPERIDEE . 1
    WAS LED INTO THE PRESENCE OF THE TREE . . . .   283 THE GOLD HESPERIDEE . 14
    UNDER OR ON THE TREE, OR ANYWHERE, ...   284 THE GOLD HESPERIDEE . 39
    AND THE LIGHT-NATURED TREE SEEMED NOT TO CARE! . . .   284 THE GOLD HESPERIDEE . 40
    TO LOOK UPON THE TREE WHEN IT WAS GREEN . . . . . .   284 THE GOLD HESPERIDEE . 53
    EVER TO HAVE TREE BLOOM OR BEAR. . . . .   296 LEAVES COMPARED WITH 6
    LEAVES AND BARK MAY BE TREE ENOUGH. . . . .   297 LEAVES COMPARED WITH 8
    THERE SURE ENOUGH WAS AN APPLE TREE . . . .   304 UNHARVESTED 4
    WE THINK OF THE TREE. IF IT NEVER AGAIN HAS LEAVES, . 305 THERE ARE ROUGHLY ZONES 4
    THERE IS NOTHING MUCH WE CAN DO FOR THE TREE TONIGHT. 305 THERE ARE ROUGHLY ZONES 14
    THE TREE HAS NO LEAVES AND MAY NEVER HAVE THEM AGAIN. 305 THERE ARE ROUGHLY ZONES 18
    OR RUSTLE IN A BUSH OR TREE. . . . .   328 A MISSIVE MISSILE . . 40
    A WITNESS TREE . . . .   329 A WITNESS TREE . . . T
    ONE TREE, BY BEING DEEPLY WOUNDED, ...   331 BEECH 6
    HAS BEEN IMPRESSED AS WITNESS TREE . . . .   331 BEECH 7
    DID CLIMB THE TREE . . . .   331 SYCAMORE 2
    'NEATH THE ALDER TREE. . . . .   343 QUEST OF PURPLE-FRINGED 20
    FROM A FALLEN TREE AND PUSHING OFF . . . .   347 DISCOVERY OF MADEIRAS . 126
    I COULD HAVE BOUGHT YOU JUST AS GOOD A TREE . . . .   350 TO A YOUNG WRETCH . . 7
    BUT TREE BY CHARITY IS NOT THE SAME . . . .   350 TO A YOUNG WRETCH . . 10
    AS TREE BY ENTERPRISE AND EXPEDITION. . . . .   350 TO A YOUNG WRETCH . . 11
    MY TREE, A CAPTIVE IN YOUR WINDOW BAY, ...   350 TO A YOUNG WRETCH . . 20
    THE ONLY NATIVE TREE THAT DARES TO LEAN, ...   375 A YOUNG BIRCH 8

			PAGE	TITLE	LINE

TREE (CONTINUED)
PERHAPS BUT TO A TREE . . . . 415 CLOSED FOR GOOD . . . 15
IT IS ALL THE TREE . . . . 426 A NEVER NAUGHT SONG . 17
FROM THE APPLE TREE. . . . . 435 KITTY HAWK 218
YOU MEAN THE BURNING BUSH? / THE CHRISTMAS TREE. . . 473 A MASQUE OF REASON . . 6
THE MYRRH TREE GIVES IT. SMELL THE ROSIN BURNING? . . 473 A MASQUE OF REASON . . 9
ARE SINGING. YES, AND LOOK, THE TREE IS TROUBLED. . . 473 A MASQUE OF REASON . . 15
TREE-AND-FARMHOUSE
ABOVE A HAZY TREE-AND-FARMHOUSE CLUSTER . . . . . 245 THE FREEDOM OF THE MOON 2
TREE-HIDDEN
FROM SOME TREE-HIDDEN CLIFF ACROSS THE LAKE. . . . 338 THE MOST OF IT . . . 4
TREE'S (SEE APPLE-TREE'S)
HOW LIKE A MAPLE TREE'S FOR US TO GUESS. . . . . 180 MAPLE 23
A TREE'S LEAVES MAY BE EVER SO GOOD, ... 296 LEAVES COMPARED WITH . 1
IN ONE TREE'S OVERTHROW . . . . 470 IN WINTER IN THE WOODS 10
I SAID THE INCENSE TREE'S ON FIRE AGAIN. . . . . 473 A MASQUE OF REASON . . 5
TREES (SEE VESTRY-TREES)
ONE OF MY WISHES IS THAT THOSE DARK TREES, ... 5 INTO MY OWN 1
THE DESOLATE, DESERTED TREES, ... 7 MY NOVEMBER GUEST . . 11
WHICH FLOWS IN SHAPES AS TALL AS TREES . . . . . 9 STARS 3
THE SWARM DILATING ROUND THE PERFECT TREES. . . . 12 A PRAYER IN SPRING . . 8
THAN THE TREES AROUND WERE TALL; . . . . . . 13 ROSE POGONIAS . . . 4
BEHIND LOW BOUGHS THE TREES LET DOWN OUTSIDE; . . . 16 A DREAM PANG . . . 10
IF TIRED OF TREES I SEEK AGAIN MANKIND, ... 17 THE VANTAGE POINT . . 1
THAT SLOWLY DAWNED BEHIND THE TREES, ... 18 GOING FOR WATER . . . 10
I LOOKED FOR HIM BEHIND AN ISLE OF TREES; . . . . 22 THE TUFT OF FLOWERS . 5
IF THE TREES MUST, LET THEM SILENTLY TOSS; . . . . 25 NOW CLOSE THE WINDOWS . 2
TO FILL THE TREES WITH ANOTHER SHADE, ... 26 IN HARDWOOD GROVES . . 6
ONE FROM OUR TREES, ONE FAR AWAY. . . . . . . 27 OCTOBER 14
MY APPLE TREES WILL NEVER GET ACROSS . . . . . 33 MENDING WALL 25
NOT OF WOODS ONLY AND THE SHADE OF TREES. . . . . 34 MENDING WALL 42
AND THEN THERE WAS A WALL OF TREES WITH TRUNKS; . . . 41 THE MOUNTAIN 30
AFTER THAT ONLY TOPS OF TREES, AND CLIFFS . . . . 41 THE MOUNTAIN 31
STRIPPED TO BARE GROUND, THE MAPLE TREES . . . . 49 A HUNDRED COLLARS . . 135
AMONG TAR-BANDED ANCIENT CHERRY TREES, ... 55 THE BLACK COTTAGE . . 3
AND BELOW ROARED A BROOK HIDDEN IN TREES, ... 76 THE GENERATIONS OF MEN 75
AROUND US, LOOKING OUT OF TREES AND BUSHES . . . . 90 THE FEAR 46
STRAIGHT UP AND DOWN OF TALL SLIM TREES . . . . 101 THE WOOD-PILE . . . 6
CHRISTMAS TREES . . . . 105 CHRISTMAS TREES . . . T
HE ASKED IF I WOULD SELL MY CHRISTMAS TREES; . . . 106 CHRISTMAS TREES . . . 12
I HADN'T THOUGHT OF THEM AS CHRISTMAS TREES. . . . 106 CHRISTMAS TREES . . . 15
YET MORE I'D HATE TO HOLD MY TREES, EXCEPT . . . . 106 CHRISTMAS TREES . . . 21
"A THOUSAND CHRISTMAS TREES!--AT WHAT APIECE?" . . . 107 CHRISTMAS TREES . . . 42
"A THOUSAND TREES WOULD COME TO THIRTY DOLLARS." . . 107 CHRISTMAS TREES . . . 44
WOULD PAY IN CITIES FOR GOOD TREES LIKE THOSE, . . . 107 CHRISTMAS TREES . . . 52
A THOUSAND CHRISTMAS TREES I DIDN'T KNOW I HAD! . . . 107 CHRISTMAS TREES . . . 55
OF TREES AND CRACK OF BRANCHES, COMMON THINGS, . . . 108 OLD MAN'S WINTER NIGHT 13
ON THE OLD PEACH TREES ON THE KNOLL, TO GROPE . . . 117 IN THE HOME STRETCH . 189
ACROSS THE LINES OF STRAIGHTER DARKER TREES, . . . 121 BIRCHES 2
ONE BY ONE HE SUBDUED HIS FATHER'S TREES . . . . 122 BIRCHES 28
TO THE PLACE WHERE JOHN HAS BEEN CUTTING TREES, . . . 123 PEA BRUSH 2
MADE THE DIM TREES STAND BACK IN WIDER CIRCLE-- . . . 130 THE BONFIRE 29
THERE CAME A GUST. (YOU USED TO THINK THE TREES . . . 130 THE BONFIRE 41
IT BLOW BUT THAT YOU SAW THE TREES IN MOTION.) . . . 130 THE BONFIRE 43
AND EVEN FRUIT TREES. . . . . 134 A GIRL'S GARDEN . . . 32
WALLS WERE ALL BURIED, TREES WERE FEW: . . . . . 137 BROWN'S DESCENT . . . 13
TO SET YOUR BREAST TO THE BARK OF TREES . . . . . 141 THE GUM-GATHERER . . 35
THEY PLANT DEAD TREES FOR LIVING, AND THE DEAD . . . 141 THE LINE-GANG . . . 3
I WONDER ABOUT THE TREES. . . . . 156 THE SOUND OF TREES . . 1
THE SOUND OF TREES . . . . 156 THE SOUND OF TREES . . T
SOMETIMES WHEN I WATCH TREES SWAY, ... 156 THE SOUND OF TREES . . 17
AND WENT ALONE AGAINST A GROVE OF TREES; . . . . 170 NEW HAMPSHIRE . . . 368
BY WORSHIP UNDER GREEN TREES IN THE OPEN. . . . . 171 NEW HAMPSHIRE . . . 389
OF BREATHING TREES SAID SOMETHING OF THE TIME . . . 175 THE CENSUS-TAKER . . 26
ABOUT THE DIFFERENT TREES, AND SOMETHING, TOO, . . . 180 MAPLE 27
LET ALONE GROVE OF TREES FOR SUGAR ORCHARD. . . . 183 MAPLE 103
ACQUIRED ANCESTRALLY IN JUST SUCH TREES . . . . . 197 WILD GRAPES 49
BE RUN OFF WITH BY BIRCH TREES INTO SPACE." . . . . 199 WILD GRAPES 91
HE DON'T GNAW TREES AND POSTS AND FENCES TOO. . . . 209 PAUPER WITCH OF GRAFTON 67
UP WHERE THE TREES GROW SHORT, THE MOSSES TALL, . . . 210 PAUPER WITCH OF GRAFTON 96
MY BUSINESS AWHILE IS WITH DIFFERENT TREES, ... 228 GOOD-BY AND KEEP COLD . 21
THE APPLE TREES BE SENT TO HEARTHSTONE FLAME. . . . 231 A BROOK IN THE CITY . 11
THEY WERE CONTENT TO FIGURE IN THE TREES . . . . 234 EVENING A SUGAR ORCHARD 15
WAS WROUGHT THROUGH TREES WITHOUT A BREATH OF STORM . 238 A HILLSIDE THAW . . . 31
THE TREES THEY'D HAD ENOUGH OF WITH ONCE TRYING . . . 239 OUR SINGING STRENGTH . 28
THE TREES THAT HAVE IN THEIR PENT-UP BUDS . . . . 245 SPRING POOLS . . . 7
I'VE PULLED IT FROM A CRATE OF CROOKED TREES, . . . 245 THE FREEDOM OF THE MOON 9
WHAT ARE YOU, IN THE SHADOW OF TREES . . . . . 247 ON GOING UNNOTICED . 3
BEFORE THE NOT MOWING BRINGS TREES ON, ... 264 THE LAST MOWING . . . 8
BEFORE TREES, SEEING THE OPENING, ... 264 THE LAST MOWING . . . 9
THE TREES ARE ALL I'M AFRAID OF, ... 264 THE LAST MOWING . . . 11
AND NOW HER LAP IS FULL OF TREES. . . . . . . 265 THE BIRTHPLACE . . . 14
AND IN IT, TALL AS TREES, WERE CLIFFS; . . . . . 274 A LONE STRIKER . . . 37
'TWOULD BE AMONG THE TOPS OF TREES, ... 274 A LONE STRIKER . . . 39
AS RELIC OF A VANISHED RACE OF TREES-- . . . . . 290 OLD BARN AT THE BOTTOM 39
THAT FAR LIGHT FLICKERS BECAUSE OF TREES. . . . . 291 ON HEART'S BEGINNING TO 15
SOME GIANT TREES HAVE BLOOM SO SMALL . . . . . 297 LEAVES COMPARED WITH . 9
WHILE THE TREES PUT ON THEIR WOODEN RINGS . . . . 376 SOMETHING FOR HOPE . . 11
THEN CUT DOWN THE TREES WHEN LUMBER GROWN, ... 376 SOMETHING FOR HOPE . . 13
A FEW OLD PECKER-FRETTED APPLE TREES. . . . . . 378 DIRECTIVE 28
AS LONG THE TREES HAVE STOOD. . . . . 388 MIDDLENESS OF THE ROAD 7
AND A MAN CAME OUT OF THE TREES . . . . 444 THE DRAFT HORSE . . . 5
AND THE NIGHT DREW THROUGH THE TREES . . . . . 444 THE DRAFT HORSE . . . 11
AGAINST THE TREES I GO. . . . . 470 IN WINTER IN THE WOODS 2
TREETOP
"HERE, TAKE A TREETOP, I'LL GET DOWN ANOTHER. . . . 197 WILD GRAPES 39
TRELLIS
THEN A SMALL RAINBOW LIKE A TRELLIS GATE, ... 315 IRIS BY NIGHT . . . 17

TREMBLE
    AND SO ARE NOTHING TO MAKE HER TREMBLE. . . . . 291 ON HEART'S BEGINNING TO 31
    I DID MY WIFELY DUTY. I SHOULD TREMBLE! . . . . 478 A MASQUE OF REASON . . 134
TREMBLED
    TREMBLED AND STIRRED, ... 219 I WILL SING YOU ONE-O . 63
TREMULOUS
    AND THEN ON TREMULOUS WING CAME BACK TO ME. . . . . . . 22 THE TUFT OF FLOWERS . 18
    OF HER OLD TREMULOUS BONNET IN THE PEW, ... 57 THE BLACK COTTAGE . . 91
TRENCH
    A TRENCH WERE WATER PIPES WERE LAYING ON. . . . . . . 394 HAEC FABULA DOCET . . 6
    AND PLUNGED HIMSELF HEAD FOREMOST IN THE TRENCH: . . . . 394 HAEC FABULA DOCET . . 14
TREND
    OF WHAT HAD BEEN FOR CENTURIES THE TREND; . . . . . . 422 FOR JOHN F. KENNEDY . 9
TRESPASS
    TRESPASS . . . . 364 TRESPASS . . . . . T
    TRESPASS AND ENCROACH . . . . 437 KITTY HAWK 284
TRESPASSED
    I WAS BEING TRESPASSED ON AND AGAINST. . . . . 364 TRESPASS 4
TRIAL
    THE TRIAL BY EXISTENCE . . . . 19 THE TRIAL BY EXISTENCE T
    THE TRIAL BY EXISTENCE NAMED, ... 20 THE TRIAL BY EXISTENCE 19
    THE TRIAL BY MARKET EVERYTHING MUST COME TO. . . . . . 106 CHRISTMAS TREES . . . 24
    HOW WAS IT WITH HIM FOR A SECOND TRIAL. . . . . . . 231 NOT TO KEEP 20
    A TRIAL RUN . . . . 306 A TRIAL RUN . . . . T
    PUT UP ON TRIAL BY THAT JERSEYITE . . . . 369 THE LITERATE FARMER AND 40
    THE RACE'S FUTURE TRIAL PLACE, ... 417 AMERICA IS HARD TO SEE 29
    BUT IT WAS OF THE ESSENCE OF THE TRIAL . . . . 475 A MASQUE OF REASON . . 62
    A TRIAL GROUND WHERE HE CAN TRY HIMSELF . . . . . . 484 A MASQUE OF REASON . . 319
TRIBAL
    IN THE FLOOR OF A TRIBAL CAVE, ... 312 THE VINDICTIVES . . . 57
TRIBE
    THENCE THEY WERE SPRUNG, SO NUMEROUS A TRIBE . . . . . 73 THE GENERATIONS OF MEN 10
TRIBE'S
    SHE TAUGHT HIM HER TRIBE'S RELIGION: . . . . 313 BEARER OF EVIL TIDINGS 17
TRIBUTE
    AS A BRUTE TRIBUTE OF RESPECT TO BEAUTY. . . . . . . 195 PAUL'S WIFE 141
    THE TRIBUTE OF THE CURRENT TO THE SOURCE. . . . . . . 260 WEST-RUNNING BROOK . . 70
TRICK
    AND HARD TO EXPLAIN AS A CONJUROR'S TRICK." . . . . . 59 BLUEBERRIES 21
    IT SMELLS TO ME LIKE A DISHONEST TRICK." . . . . . . 100 THE SELF-SEEKER . . . 203
    THEY LAUGHED AS IF THEY HAD TURNED A TRICK. . . . . . 344 DISCOVERY OF MADEIRAS . 30
TRICKS
    I'D SEEN ABOUT ENOUGH OF HIS BULLING TRICKS . . . . . . 71 THE CODE 47
TRIED
    AND GAVE HIM TEA AND TRIED TO MAKE HIM SMOKE. . . . . . 36 DEATH OF THE HIRED MAN 41
    I TRIED TO MAKE HIM TALK ABOUT HIS TRAVELS. . . . . . 36 DEATH OF THE HIRED MAN 42
    HE TRIED THIS SIDE. I'VE ALWAYS MEANT TO GO . . . . . 43 THE MOUNTAIN 80
    THEY TRIED TO KEEP HIM CLOTHED, BUT HE PARADED . . . . . 66 A SERVANT TO SERVANTS . 122
    THE TIME I DREAMED THE DOOR WAS TRIED . . . . 135 LOCKED OUT 4
    ANGRILY TRIED TO MAKE ME WRITE A PROTEST . . . . . . 160 NEW HAMPSHIRE . . . 29
    OR SO HE TRIED TO THINK TO AVOID BLAME. . . . . . . 180 MAPLE 34
    HE TRIED IT AT THE EYEHOLE IN THE AX-HEAD. . . . . . 187 THE AX-HELVE 78
    AND WHEN HE RAISED IT DRIPPING ONCE AND TRIED . . . . . 190 THE GRINDSTONE . . . 68
    MY BROTHER TRIED TO MAKE ME LAUGH TO HELP ME. . . . . 197 WILD GRAPES 55
    TRIED TO THINK HOW HE COULD EXCEED HIS PROMISE, ... 200 PLACE FOR A THIRD . . 19
    TRIED TO IMPROVE ON SAILING LIKE A TILE . . . . . . 216 A FOUNTAIN, A BOTTLE . 112
    HAVING TRIED ONE, HAD DROPPED IT AT HIS FEET . . . . . 217 A FOUNTAIN, A BOTTLE . 119
    I KNOW THAT WINTER DEATH HAS NEVER TRIED . . . . . . 226 THE ONSET 13
    I'VE TRIED THE NEW MOON TILTED IN THE AIR . . . . . . 245 THE FREEDOM OF THE MOON 1
    I'VE TRIED IT FINE WITH LITTLE BREADTH OF LUSTER, ... 245 THE FREEDOM OF THE MOON 4
    WE HAVE IDEAS YET THAT WE HAVEN'T TRIED. . . . . . . 268 RIDERS 12
    DOWN IF YOU TRIED. . . . . 298 ON TAKING FROM THE TOP 8
    IS A THREAT TO THE HOUSE. BUT THE HOUSE HAS LONG BEEN TRIED. 305 THERE ARE ROUGHLY ZONES 3
    I TRIED TO TELL HER "THERE'S NO SUCH THING!" . . . . . 342 A CLOUD SHADOW . . . 4
    THEY'VE TRIED TO GRASP WITH TOO MUCH SOCIAL FACT . . . . 351 THE LESSON FOR TODAY . 34
    WE'D HAIL THE REMEDY. BUT IT'S BEEN TRIED . . . . . . 372 THE LITERATE FARMER AND 122
    (HE TRIED TO IMITATE DICK'S TONE OF VOICE.) . . . . . 406 FROM PLANE TO PLANE . 73
    EACH TRIED TO BE THE FIRST AT GETTING IN . . . . . . 407 FROM PLANE TO PLANE . 117
    WITH EVERY COAST HE TRIED ALONG. . . . . 416 AMERICA IS HARD TO SEE 14
    OF YOUNG AMBITION EAGER TO BE TRIED, ... 424 FOR JOHN F. KENNEDY . 73
    AND TRIED TO LOOK TEN THOUSAND DOLLARS' WORTH. . . . . 454 HOW HARD TO KEEP FROM 38
    JOB SCRATCHED HIS BOILS AND TRIED TO THINK WHAT HE . . . 477 A MASQUE OF REASON . . 121
    DID SEEM UNLIKE YOU, AND I TRIED TO THINK . . . . . . 482 A MASQUE OF REASON . . 263
    BEFORE THE DOOR'S SO VIOLENTLY TRIED . . . . 493 A MASQUE OF MERCY . . 6
    THAT WAY'S BEEN TRIED TOO MANY TIMES FOR ME. . . . . . 515 A MASQUE OF MERCY . . 574
    I'D LIKE TO SEE THE WORLD ONCE WITHOUT IT. . . . . . 515 A MASQUE OF MERCY . . 575
TRIES
    AND TRIES ONCE--TWICE--AND THRICE IF I BE THERE; . . . . 15 WAITING 22
    ON WORDS, AND TRIES HIS WORST TO MAKE WORDS SPEAK . . . 171 NEW HAMPSHIRE . . . 401
    SHE TRIES TO MAKE IT IN ONE CATCH OF BREATH, ... 386 THE FEAR OF MAN . . . 3
TRILLIUM
    THEY WERE CROOKING MANY A TRILLIUM . . . . 123 PEA BRUSH 22
TRILOBITE
    THE PICTURE BOOK OF THE TRILOBITE, ... 364 TRESPASS 10
TRINKET
    WITHOUT ONE TRINKET FROM ORMUZ . . . . 416 AMERICA IS HARD TO SEE 10
TRIPLE
    TRIPLE BRONZE . . . . 348 TRIPLE BRONZE . . . T
TRIPPED
    AND TRIPPED THE BODY, SHOT THE SPIRIT ON . . . . . . 262 A SOLDIER 13
    I STUMBLED OVER IT AND GOT TRIPPED UP. . . . . . . 489 A MASQUE OF REASON . . 446
TRIUMPH
    TO EVIL, NO IMPORTANT TRIUMPH WON, ... 226 THE ONSET 10
    "YES, WE CAN LET HER AND STILL TRIUMPH." . . . . . . 256 THE LOVELY BE CHOOSERS 20
    AND SO IT WENT WITH TRIUMPH AFTER TRIUMPH . . . . . . 456 HOW HARD TO KEEP FROM 93
TRIVIA
    LEFT TRIVIA BEHIND; . . . . 464 MILKY WAY IS A COWPATH 28

```
                                              PAGE TITLE                      LINE
TRIVIAL
   AND OF ALL BUT ITS TRIVIAL FOLIAGE FREE, . . . . . . . 304 UNHARVESTED . . . . . 6
TROD
   WE TROD UNCOMFORTABLY ON CRUNCHING GLASS . . . . . . 216 A FOUNTAIN, A BOTTLE . 89
   DANCED SLOWLY ON IT TILL HE TROD IT FLAT. . . . . . . 284 THE GOLD HESPERIDEE . 48
   TO ALL THOSE FLOWERS THEY PASSIONATELY TROD . . . . . 412 POD OF THE MILKWEED . 42
TRODDEN
   IN LEAVES NO STEP HAD TRODDEN BLACK. . . . . . . . . 105 THE ROAD NOT TAKEN . 12
   GOD KNOWS ALL THE COLOR AND FORM OF LEAVES I HAVE TRODDEN
      ON AND MIRED. . . . . . . . . . . . . . . . . . 297 A LEAF-TREADER . . . 2
   I HAVE SAFELY TRODDEN UNDERFOOT THE LEAVES OF ANOTHER YEAR. 297 A LEAF-TREADER . . . 4
TROLLEY
   A TROLLEY CAR THEY HAILED . . . . . . . . . . . . . 391 A ROGERS GROUP . . . 5
TROLLS
   THEN SANK OUT OF SIGHT LIKE TROLLS UNDERGROUND, . . . 62 BLUEBERRIES . . . . 86
TROOPING
   AND THE SLANT SPIRITS TROOPING BY . . . . . . . . . 20 THE TRIAL BY EXISTENCE 21
TROPHY
   YOU TOOK AS A TROPHY OF THE HOUR. . . . . . . . . . 247 ON GOING UNNOTICED . 16
   HIS JAPANESE CREPE-PAPER GLOBE FOR TROPHY? . . . . . 278 THE WHITE-TAILED HORNET 18
TROUBLE
   "WELL, THOSE DAYS TROUBLE SILAS LIKE A DREAM. . . . . 37 DEATH OF THE HIRED MAN 71
   THE ONLY TROUBLE IS WE DISAGREE . . . . . . . . . . 48 A HUNDRED COLLARS . 108
   WHERE IT WILL TROUBLE US A THOUSAND YEARS. . . . . . 57 THE BLACK COTTAGE . 69
   ONE CAN SEE WHAT WILL TROUBLE . . . . . . . . . . . 69 AFTER APPLE-PICKING . 37
   TO LOAD THE LOAD, THINKS I, LOOK OUT FOR TROUBLE. . . 71 THE CODE . . . . . 50
   WHAT'S THE REAL TROUBLE? WHAT WILL SATISFY HER?" . . 87 THE HOUSEKEEPER . . 166
   THAT TROUBLE THE SLEEP OF LUMBER FOLK: . . . . . . . 140 THE GUM-GATHERER . 22
   HE'LL BE DEAD--DEAD AND BURIED." / "SUCH A TROUBLE! . 146 SNOW . . . . . . 88
   TO SPARE THEM ANY TROUBLE. DOUBLE TROUBLE'S . . . . . 207 PAUPER WITCH OF GRAFTON 7
   SHE COULD NOT TROUBLE HER MIND WITH TOO LONG, . . . . 229 TWO LOOK AT TWO . . 23
   OR IT MIGHT GET YOU INTO TROUBLE WITH ME. . . . . . 320 BUILD SOIL . . . 133
   THE TROUBLE WITH A TOTAL REVOLUTION . . . . . . . . 363 A SEMI-REVOLUTION . 2
   THE TROUBLE IS, WITH THAT RECEIPT FOR LOVE, . . . . . 372 THE LITERATE FARMER AND 124
   WERE I IN TROUBLE . . . . . . . . . . . . . . . . 383 WERE I IN TROUBLE . 1
   WERE I IN TROUBLE WITH NIGHT TONIGHT. . . . . . . . 383 WERE I IN TROUBLE . 10
   LIKE TROUBLE IN THE BROW ABOVE THE EYES: . . . . . . 399 THE INGENUITIES OF DEBT 3
   "YOUR TROUBLE IS NOT STICKING TO THE SUBJECT," . . . 404 FROM PLANE TO PLANE . 7
   "YOUR TROUBLE IS BUCOLIC LACK OF LOGIC," . . . . . . 404 FROM PLANE TO PLANE . 9
   THE TROUBLE WAS WITH HIM THE MARINER. . . . . . . . 417 AMERICA IS HARD TO SEE 16
   OF TROUBLE WITH IT IN HIS GRECIAN CITIES . . . . . . 459 HOW HARD TO KEEP FROM 167
   AND THAT IS HALF THE TROUBLE WITH THE WORLD. . . . . 462 HOW HARD TO KEEP FROM 277
   TO TROUBLE MEN WITH HAVING TO TAKE SIDES. . . . . . 468 FROM IRON . . . . 2
   THE DOCTORS SAY THE TROUBLE WITH ME IS . . . . . . . 499 A MASQUE OF MERCY . 156
   RIGHT BACK IN THE SAME TROUBLE I WAS IN. . . . . . . 500 A MASQUE OF MERCY . 185
   MY TROUBLE HAS BEEN WITH MY SENSE OF JUSTICE. . . . . 517 A MASQUE OF MERCY . 622
TROUBLE-CREASED
   HIS BROW WAS PERCEPTIBLY TROUBLE-CREASED. . . . . . 420 ONE MORE BREVITY . 26
TROUBLED
   BUT, ANNE, I'M TROUBLED; HAVE YOU TOLD ME ALL? . . . 97 THE SELF-SEEKER . . 131
   YOU WANTED IT FOR ME." / "A TROUBLED CONSCIENCE! . . 116 IN THE HOME STRETCH . 168
   AND IT HAD ALMOST GIVEN HIM TROUBLED DREAMS . . . . . 290 OLD BARN AT THE BOTTOM 42
   AND EXCHANGED TROUBLED GLANCES OVER LIFE. . . . . . 293 AT WOODWARD'S GARDENS . 13
   HAD COME TO A TROUBLED HALT. . . . . . . . . . . . 314 BEARER OF EVIL TIDINGS 22
   ARE SINGING. YES, AND LOOK, THE TREE IS TROUBLED. . 473 A MASQUE OF REASON . 15
TROUBLES
   I NEVER SAW A MAN LET FAMILY TROUBLES . . . . . . . 83 THE HOUSEKEEPER . . 53
TROUBLE'S
   TO SPARE THEM ANY TROUBLE. DOUBLE TROUBLE'S . . . . . 207 PAUPER WITCH OF GRAFTON 7
   I THINK MY TROUBLE'S WITH THE CRISISES . . . . . . . 510 A MASQUE OF MERCY . 442
TROUBLING
   YOU CAN SEE WHAT IS TROUBLING GRANNY, THOUGH. . . . . 80 THE GENERATIONS OF MEN 195
   HALF THE TIME I DON'T KNOW WHAT'S TROUBLING ME.-- . . 99 THE SELF-SEEKER . . 194
TROUGH
   I SKIMMED THIS MORNING FROM THE DRINKING TROUGH . . . 68 AFTER APPLE-PICKING . 11
   AND MADE ICE ON THE TROUGH . . . . . . . . . . . 135 LAST WORD OF A BLUEBIRD 11
   SHE LINGERS FEEDING AT THE TROUGH, . . . . . . . . 280 BLUE RIBBON AT AMESBURY 15
   THEN HE GOUGED A CLUMSY SAILING TROUGH . . . . . . . 347 DISCOVERY OF MADEIRAS . 125
T'ROUGH
   DEN WHERE'S YOUR HAX-EAD FLYING T'ROUGH DE HAIR?" . . 186 THE AX-HELVE . . . 27
TROUT
   IN A TROUT HATCHERY NEAR CANADA, . . . . . . . . . 165 NEW HAMPSHIRE . . . 184
TROUT-FISHING
   DEER-HUNTING AND TROUT-FISHING. THERE'S A BROOK . . 42 THE MOUNTAIN . . . . 45
TRUCE
   I LIKE TO GIVE MY ENEMIES A TRUCE." . . . . . . . . 406 FROM PLANE TO PLANE . 65
TRUCK
   SINCE I CAME IN? / HEAR WHAT? THAT ARMY TRUCK? . . . 495 A MASQUE OF MERCY . 43
TRUCKS
   TRUCKS GOING BY TO WAR. A WAR IS ON. . . . . . . . 504 A MASQUE OF MERCY . 281
TRUE
   ONLY MORE SURE OF ALL I THOUGHT WAS TRUE. . . . . . 5 INTO MY OWN . . . 14
   BUT 'TIS NOT TRUE THAT THUS I DWELT ALOOF, . . . . . 16 A DREAM PANG . . . 13
   THOUGH I KNEW THAT I HUNTED WAS NO TRUE GOD. . . . . 24 THE DEMIURGE'S LAUGH . 3
   IS TO DECIDE IT SIMPLY ISN'T TRUE. . . . . . . . . 57 THE BLACK COTTAGE . 66
   AND WELL, IF THEY WEREN'T TRUE WHY KEEP RIGHT ON . . 58 THE BLACK COTTAGE . 97
   MERELY BECAUSE IT CEASES TO BE TRUE. . . . . . . . 58 THE BLACK COTTAGE . 106
   IT WILL TURN TRUE AGAIN, FOR SO IT GOES. . . . . . . 58 THE BLACK COTTAGE . 108
   "WELL, IF IT'S TRUE! YOURS ARE NO COMMON FEET. . . . 93 THE SELF-SEEKER . . 10
   TO WHICH THEY SET IT BY EYE; AND THEN . . . . . . . 113 IN THE HOME STRETCH . 85
   SO FALSE, THAT WHAT WE ALWAYS SAY IS TRUE. . . . . . 148 SNOW . . . . . . 150
   BUT IF THE STORY MURPHY TOLD WAS TRUE, . . . . . . . 192 PAUL'S WIFE . . . 40
   I SAID I HAD THE TREE. IT WASN'T TRUE. . . . . . . 197 WILD GRAPES . . . 41
   THE OPPOSITE WAS TRUE. THE TREE HAD ME. . . . . . . 197 WILD GRAPES . . . 42
   THE SAYING MAY BE EVER SO TRUE; . . . . . . . . . 263 THE TIMES TABLE . . 13
   GOD ONCE DECLARED HE WAS TRUE . . . . . . . . . . 266 SITTING BY A BUSH . 13
   IT IS TRUE THE LONGEST DROUTH WILL END IN RAIN, . . 268 ON LOOKING UP BY CHANCE 11
   IT IS COTTER-PINNED, IT IS BEDDED TRUE. . . . . . . 306 A TRIAL RUN . . . 10
```

TRUE (CONTINUED)

OTHERS ON BEING SIMPLY TRUE. . . . . 307 PROVIDE, PROVIDE . . 14
"I DON'T BELIEVE IT! IT ISN'T TRUE! . . . . 346 DISCOVERY OF MADEIRAS . 98
LIKE HORACE IN THE TRUE HORATIAN VEIN, ... 353 THE LESSON FOR TODAY . 93
THE TRUE MILLENNIUM, ... 361 ALMOST TWO THOUSAND . 6
IT IS AS TRUE AS CAESAR'S NAME WAS KAISER . . . . . 363 AN EQUALIZER 1
IS IT NOT TRUE? AND WHAT WAS MY REWARD? . . . . . . 458 HOW HARD TO KEEP FROM 132
FOR STANDING STILL IN ONE PLACE TRUE FOREVER; . . . 480 A MASQUE OF REASON . 192
MY TONGUE'S MY OWN, AS TRUE THOMAS USED TO SAY. . . 505 A MASQUE OF MERCY . 296
NO TRUE SOURCE CAN BE POISONED. / THEN THAT'S ALL. . 514 A MASQUE OF MERCY . 543
IF WHAT YOU SAY IS TRUE, IF WINNING RANKS . . . . . 517 A MASQUE OF MERCY . 633

TRULY

THE BEAUTIES SHE SO TRULY SEES, ... 7 MY NOVEMBER GUEST . 13
AND TRULY IT WAS FAIR ENOUGH FOR FLOWERS . . . . . 233 A BOUNDLESS MOMENT . . 6
AND TELL ME TRULY, MEN OF EARTH. . . . . 362 A QUESTION 2

TRUMP

ALL PACKED IN SAND TO WAIT THE TRUMP TOGETHER. . . . 270 THE EGG AND THE MACHINE 26

TRUMPED

EXCUSES TRUMPED UP BY YOU FOR THEOLOGISTS. . . . . 482 A MASQUE OF REASON . 249

TRUNK

AND CLIMB BLACK BRANCHES UP A SNOW-WHITE TRUNK . . . 122 BIRCHES 55
AND EVERY TREE UP STOOD A ROTTING TRUNK . . . . . 175 THE CENSUS-TAKER . . 22

TRUNKS

AND THEN THERE WAS A WALL OF TREES WITH TRUNKS; . . 41 THE MOUNTAIN . . . 30
WHO MAKES THE SOLID TREE TRUNKS SOUND AGAIN. . . . 119 THE OVEN BIRD . . . 3
YOU MAY SEE THEIR TRUNKS ARCHING IN THE WOODS . . . 121 BIRCHES 17

TRUST

WHEN I'M WITH PEOPLE I DON'T TRUST AT NIGHT." . . . 48 A HUNDRED COLLARS . . 92
RIGHT ON THE COUNTERPANE--THAT I DO TRUST YOU?" . . 48 A HUNDRED COLLARS . . 94
"NO, I DON'T TRUST YOUR EYES. YOU'VE SAID ENOUGH. . 80 THE GENERATIONS OF MEN 206
BUT TRUST NEW HAMPSHIRE NOT TO HAVE ENOUGH . . . . 163 NEW HAMPSHIRE . . 122
"TRUST US," THE VOICES SAID. . . . . 257 THE LOVELY BE CHOOSERS 53
CAN TRUST ITSELF TO GO BY CONTRARIES . . . . . . 258 WEST-RUNNING BROOK . 7
TRUST HIM THEN NOT TO PUT YOU IN THE WRONG. . . . 278 THE WHITE-TAILED HORNET 26
TRUST HIM TO HAVE HIS BITTER POLITICS . . . . . . 290 OLD BARN AT THE BOTTOM 29
BUT TRUST MY INSTINCT--I'M A BARD. . . . . 326 TO A THINKER . . . 36
I LEANED ON WITH A SINGING TRUST . . . . 336 THE WIND AND THE RAIN . 5
I TRUST FEELS PROPERLY DEFIED. . . . . 363 ASSURANCE 4
BUT SHE CAN TRUST IT NOT TO FALL TONIGHT. . . . . 386 THE FEAR OF MAN . . 6
BUT THERE ARE LITTLE STREETLIGHTS SHE SHOULD TRUST, 386 THE FEAR OF MAN . . 11
I TRUST IT IS. HERE'S WHERE I LAY ASIDE . . . . . 474 A MASQUE OF REASON . 27
HOW ARE YOU NOW? I TRUST YOU'RE QUITE RECOVERED, . 474 A MASQUE OF REASON . 35
AND TRUST IT WON'T BE ADDING TO THE TORTURE. . . . 484 A MASQUE OF REASON . 326
I TRUST I MADE IT CLEAR I TOOK YOUR SIDE. . . . . 486 A MASQUE OF REASON . 362
TRUST ME TO HELP YOU FIND THE BOOK YOU WANT. . . . 495 A MASQUE OF MERCY . 50
I CAN'T TRUST GOD TO BE UNMERCIFUL. . . . . . . 497 A MASQUE OF MERCY . 116
YOU CAN'T TRUST GOD TO BE UNMERCIFUL. . . . . . . 501 A MASQUE OF MERCY . 214
YOU CAN'T TRUST GOD TO BE UNMERCIFUL. . . . . . . 507 A MASQUE OF MERCY . 361

TRUSTED

I TRUSTED THE BROOK BARRIER, BUT FEARED . . . . . 131 THE BONFIRE . . . 74
I MEAN THEY COULD BE TRUSTED TO GIVE THE ALARM . . 317 BUILD SOIL 57
WE CAN'T BE TRUSTED TO THE SLEEP WE TAKE, ... 372 THE LITERATE FARMER AND 126

TRUSTING

TRUSTING FEATHERS AND INWARD FIRE . . . . 253 THE THATCH 26
SO MUCH AS THE TRUSTING SORROW OF WHAT IS UNSAID: . 286 A ROADSIDE STAND . . 17
(LESS BRAVE PERHAPS THAN TRUSTING ARE THE FAIR.) . 375 A YOUNG BIRCH . . . 10

TRUSTS

HE TRUSTS MY LOVE TOO WELL TO DEIGN REPLY. . . . . 359 THE LOST FOLLOWER . . 33

TRUTH

ANYTHING MORE THAN THE TRUTH WOULD HAVE SEEMED TOO WEAK. 17 MOWING 9
YOU WANT THE TRUTH. I SPEAK BUT BY THE VOICES. . . 79 THE GENERATIONS OF MEN 156
BUT I WAS GOING TO SAY WHEN TRUTH BROKE IN . . . . 121 BIRCHES 21
THE TRUTH BEING WE ARE AS MUCH . . . . 126 LONELINESS 7
YES, WE COULD TOO, SON. TELL THE TRUTH FOR ONCE. . 206 THE WITCH OF COOS . 138
TO TELL THE TRUTH, SUPPOSE THE TIME HAD COME. . . . 207 THE WITCH OF COOS . 144
TRUTH? A PEBBLE OF QUARTZ? FOR ONCE, THEN, SOMETHING. 225 FOR ONCE SOMETHING . 15
AND THEN I SAID THE TRUTH (AND WE MOVED ON). . . . 234 A BOUNDLESS MOMENT . 11
BUT WHEREVER THE TRUTH MAY BE-- . . . . 301 NEITHER OUT FAR NOR IN 10
HE THOUGHT, ALL RIGHT, IF YOU WANT THE TRUTH! . . . 346 DISCOVERY OF MADEIRAS . 97
THE TRUTH IS THE RIVER FLOWS INTO THE CANYON . . . 379 TOO ANXIOUS FOR RIVERS 8
FOR HAVING LIED BUT HAVING TOLD THE TRUTH. . . . . 457 HOW HARD TO KEEP FROM 114
ENSLAVE YOURSELF TO THE RIGHT LEADER'S TRUTH, . . . 460 HOW HARD TO KEEP FROM 191
GAVE ME IN TRUTH: I LIKE THE FRANK ADMISSION. . . . 474 A MASQUE OF REASON . 37
I GIVE YOU CREDIT FOR. MY FORTE IS TRUTH, ... 480 A MASQUE OF REASON . 190
THEN HOW MUCH MORE THE FACE OF TRUTH MUST BE. . . . 515 A MASQUE OF MERCY . 585
CONTEMPLATE TRUTH UNTIL IT BURNS YOUR EYES OUT. . . 517 A MASQUE OF MERCY . 630

TRUTHS

IS DUE TO TRUTHS BEING IN AND OUT OF FAVOR. . . . 58 THE BLACK COTTAGE . 110
TO THE TRUTHS WE KEEP COMING BACK AND BACK TO. . . 58 THE BLACK COTTAGE . 114
OF THE TRUTHS WE OWE AN ASIAN? . . . . 397 AN IMPORTER . . . 16

TRUTH'S

THUS TRUTH'S ESTABLISHED AND BORNE OUT, ... 331 BEECH 10

TRY

AND TRY IF WE CANNOT FEEL FORSAKEN. . . . . . . 16 IN NEGLECT 5
THEY MIGHT AS WELL NOT TRY TO GO AT ALL. . . . . 54 HOME BURIAL . . . 99
THAT TURNED THEM ON THE WORLD, AND TRY TO FATHOM . 73 THE GENERATIONS OF MEN 17
I WANTED TO TRY SOMETHING WITH THE NOISE . . . . . 77 THE GENERATIONS OF MEN 124
WHAT, SON?" / "THEN I SHOULD THINK YOU'D TRY TO FIND 92 THE FEAR 84
TO TRY TO HELP ME DRIVE A BETTER BARGAIN." . . . . 93 THE SELF-SEEKER . . 9
I DIDN'T TRY TOO LONG TO PULL AWAY, ... 93 THE SELF-SEEKER . . 24
DON'T STOP TO TRY TO NOW. YOU'LL MISS YOUR TRAIN. . 101 THE SELF-SEEKER . . 227
SO RAN TOGETHER THAT I DIDN'T TRY TO. . . . . . . 112 IN THE HOME STRETCH . 52
TRY TO THINK WHAT HE DID WITH ALL THAT TIME. . . . 145 SNOW 61
HE KNOWS WHAT HE CAN DO, OR HE WOULDN'T TRY. . . . 152 SNOW 264
"TRY SPEAKING. SAY 'HELLO!'" / "HELLO. HELLO." . . 153 SNOW 298
NOT NOW--AT LEAST I SHOULDN'T TRY TOO HARD NOW. . . 180 MAPLE 25
TRY TO WEIGH SOMETHING NEXT TIME, SO YOU WON'T . . 199 WILD GRAPES . . . 90
AND HOLD THE DOOR. BUT THE BONES DIDN'T TRY . . . 204 THE WITCH OF COOS . 61

```
                                                              PAGE TITLE                          LINE
TRY (CONTINUED)
    IT'S LOOKING FOR ANOTHER DOOR TO TRY. . . . . . . .  . . . 205 THE WITCH OF COOS  . .  108
    A FLOWER TO TRY ITS CURRENTS WHERE THEY CROSSED. . . . . . 231 A BROOK IN THE CITY  .    8
    AS YOU MIGHT TRY A JEWEL IN YOUR HAIR. . . . . . . . . . . 245 THE FREEDOM OF THE MOON   3
    AND TRY TO STACK THEM IN A BETTER LOAD. . . . . . . . . . . 267 THE ARMFUL . . . . .   12
    TO TRY IF IT WILL NOT MAKE OUR BEING EXPAND, . . . . . . . 286 A ROADSIDE STAND  . .   20
    AND I ASK ALL TO TRY TO FORGIVE ME . . . . . . . . . . . . 295 A RECORD STRIDE . . .   33
    AND LET US TRY AN UNTOSSED PLACE . . . . . . . . . . . . . 347 DISCOVERY OF MADEIRAS . 108
    SITS DOWN IN SCHOOL TO TRY IF HE CAN WRITE . . . . . . . . 353 THE LESSON FOR TODAY .   92
    TO TRY IF ONE MORE POPULAR ELECTION . . . . . . . . . . . 358 THE LOST FOLLOWER . .   12
    (AS YET UNBROUGHT TO EARTH) HE MEANS TO TRY. . . . . . . . 359 THE LOST FOLLOWER . .   36
    I MADE A GOOD TRY. . . . . . . . . . . . . . . . . . . . . 391 A WISH TO COMPLY  . .    4
    ALL THOSE WHO TRY TO GO IT SOLE ALONE, . . . . . . . . . . 394 HAEC FABULA DOCET . .   18
    DON'T TRY TO TELL ME WHAT'S ON YOUR MIND, . . . . . . . . 420 ONE MORE BREVITY  . .   30
    I'LL TRY YOU IN THE KITCHEN FIRST CN FOOD . . . . . . . . 455 HOW HARD TO KEEP FROM   49
    THEY SHOULD TRY ONE WASTREL FIRST . . . . . . . . . . . . 466 SOME SCIENCE FICTION .  29
    WHAT DID YOU TRY TO MAKE YOUR HUSBAND SAY? . . . . . . . . 477 A MASQUE OF REASON .  118
    TRY TO READ TO HER AND SHE DROPS RIGHT OFF. . . . . . . . . 479 A MASQUE OF REASON .  155
    A TRIAL GROUND WHERE HE CAN TRY HIMSELF . . . . . . . . . 484 A MASQUE OF REASON .  319
    TO TRY ANOTHER. / JESSE BEL'S A GIRL . . . . . . . . . . . 499 A MASQUE OF MERCY .  159
    SUFFER A FRIEND TO TRY TO WORD YOU BETTER. . . . . . . . . 519 A MASQUE OF MERCY . .  677
TRYING
    TRYING TO COAX HIM OFF WITH POCKET MONEY-- . . . . . . . . .  35 DEATH OF THE HIRED MAN   28
    HE'S TRYING TO LIFT, STRAINING TO LIFT HIMSELF." . . . . . .  37 DEATH OF THE HIRED MAN   95
    "I DON'T ADVISE YOUR TRYING FROM THIS SIDE. . . . . . . . .  41 THE MOUNTAIN . . . . .  38
    THAT'S WHY I DON'T ADVISE YOUR TRYING THIS SIDE. . . . . . .  43 THE MOUNTAIN . . . . .  79
    (I MAY HAVE KNOCKED HIM DOWN); BUT MY JUST TRYING . . . . .  72 THE CODE . . . . . .  103
    WHAT ARE THEY TRYING TO DO TO ME, THESE TWO?" . . . . . . .  89 THE HOUSEKEEPER . .  211
    TRYING, I THOUGHT, TO SET IT UP ON END, . . . . . . . . . . 109 THE EXPOSED NEST . .    4
    FOREVER TRYING THE WINDOW LATCH . . . . . . . . . . . . . . 128 THE OFT-REPEATED DREAM   3
    TRYING TO TURN ITSELF BACKWARD OR FORWARD, . . . . . . . . 147 SNOW . . . . . . . .  119
    TRYING TO SELL HIS FARM AND THEN NOT SELLING, . . . . . . . 177 THE STAR-SPLITTER  .   29
    ONCE, WHEN TRYING WITH CHIN AGAINST A WELL-CURB, . . . . . 225 FOR ONCE SOMETHING .    7
    THE TREES THEY'D HAD ENOUGH OF WITH ONCE TRYING . . . . . . 239 OUR SINGING STRENGTH   28
    YOU DON'T CATCH WOMEN TRYING TO BE PLATO. . . . . . . . . . 478 A MASQUE OF REASON .  140
    TRYING TO FLUSH ME OUT. THAT'S ALL IT IS. . . . . . . . . 507 A MASQUE OF MERCY . .  350
    YET NO ONE TURN FROM TRYING TO LIVE UP TO. . . . . . . . . 512 A MASQUE OF MERCY . .  497
TUCK
    YOU'D BETTER TUCK YOUR MONEY UNDER YOU . . . . . . . . . . .  47 A HUNDRED COLLARS . .  90
TUFT
    THE TUFT OF FLOWERS . . . . . . . . . . . . . . . . . . . .  22 THE TUFT OF FLOWERS  .   T
    AT A TALL TUFT OF FLOWERS BESIDE A BROOK, . . . . . . . . .  22 THE TUFT OF FLOWERS  .  22
TUG
    MY FEET TUG AT THE FLOOR . . . . . . . . . . . . . . . . . 156 THE SOUND OF TREES . .  15
    THOUGH SLIGHT, WAS A DEMAND. SHE FELT THE TUG. . . . . . . 217 A FOUNTAIN, A BOTTLE .  137
TUGGED
    AND TUGGED IT FROM HIS FIRST TOO CERTAIN HOLD, . . . . . . 172 A STAR IN A STONEBOAT .   6
TUMBLE
    NIGHT COMES; THE BLACK BATS TUMBLE AND DART; . . . . . . . .   6 GHOST HOUSE . . . . .  15
    ONLY TO TUMBLE LIKE A STRICKEN BIRD, . . . . . . . . . . . 216 A FOUNTAIN, A BOTTLE .  115
TUMBLED
    WHEN THEY WERE HALTED BY A TUMBLED WALL . . . . . . . . . 229 TWO LOOK AT TWO . . .    7
TUMBLING
    AND HERE COME ALL YOUR GREAT BOOKS TUMBLING DOWN! . . . . . 504 A MASQUE OF MERCY . .  288
TUMULT
    IN THE TUMULT OF FREE LEAVES ON HIGH. . . . . . . . . . . . 247 ON GOING UNNOTICED . .    2
    MAKE SUCH A NOISELESS TUMULT OVER IT . . . . . . . . . . . 411 POD OF THE MILKWEED .   11
TUMULTUOUS
    O'ER OUR TUMULTUOUS SNOW, . . . . . . . . . . . . . . . . .   9 STARS . . . . . . . .    2
    FOR YOU, O TUMULTUOUS FLOWERS, . . . . . . . . . . . . . . 264 THE LAST MOWING . . .   16
TUNE
    HUNG OVER HER IN TUNE, . . . . . . . . . . . . . . . . . .  10 WIND AND WINDOW FLOWER   8
    AND BEATING INSECTS AT THEIR GRITTY TUNE. . . . . . . . . . 190 THE GRINDSTONE . . . .  55
    SANG HALFWAY THROUGH ITS LITTLE INBORN TUNE. . . . . . . . 302 A BIRD SINGING IN SLEEP  2
    SAYING THAT'S THE TUNE, . . . . . . . . . . . . . . . . . 442 KITTY HAWK . . . . . .  446
    THE TUNE IS NOT THAT METER, NOT THAT RHYTHM, . . . . . . . 460 HOW HARD TO KEEP FROM  216
    "I'M--BOUND--AWAY!" (HE QUOTES IT TO THE TUNE.) . . . . . . 500 A MASQUE OF MERCY . .  172
TUNNEL
    THERE IS A SORT OF TUNNEL IN THE FROST-- . . . . . . . . . 149 SNOW . . . . . . . .  192
    MORE LIKE A TUNNEL THAN A HOLE--WAY DOWN . . . . . . . . . 149 SNOW . . . . . . . .  193
    NOT BLUEBELLS GRACING A TUNNEL MOUTH-- . . . . . . . . . . 248 A PASSING GLIMPSE . .    7
TURBULENCE
    A TURBULENCE HE HAD THE BETTER OF. . . . . . . . . . . . . 423 FOR JOHN F. KENNEDY  .  45
TURF
    CN SNOW AND SAND AND TURF, I SEE . . . . . . . . . . . . . 120 BOND AND FREE . . . .    6
TURN
    I DO NOT SEE WHY I SHOULD E'ER TURN BACK, . . . . . . . . .   5 INTO MY OWN . . . .     9
    TURN THE POET OUT OF DOOR. . . . . . . . . . . . . . . . .  12 TO THE THAWING WIND  .  15
    I HAVE BUT TO TURN ON MY ARM, AND LO, . . . . . . . . . . .  17 THE VANTAGE POINT . .  10
    I WENT TO TURN THE GRASS ONCE AFTER ONE . . . . . . . . . .  22 THE TUFT OF FLOWERS  .   1
    OR TURN AND SIT ON AND LOOK OUT AND DOWN, . . . . . . . . .  42 THE MOUNTAIN . . . . .  61
    IT WILL TURN TRUE AGAIN, FOR SO IT GOES. . . . . . . . . .  58 THE BLACK COTTAGE . .  108
    "IT'S TIME I TOOK MY TURN UPSTAIRS IN JAIL"-- . . . . . . .  67 A SERVANT TO SERVANTS  146
    AND TURN DOLL OUT TO PASTURE, RIG AND ALL. . . . . . . . .  88 THE HOUSEKEEPER . .  201
    JOEL!" SHE SPOKE AS IF SHE COULDN'T TURN. . . . . . . . . .  92 THE FEAR . . . . . .   91
    I PAUSED AND SAID, "I WILL TURN BACK FROM HERE. . . . . . 101 THE WOOD-PILE . . .     2
    AND SMILED, AND WHEN SHE DID NOT TURN, SPOKE GENTLY, . . . 111 IN THE HOME STRETCH  .  19
    WE DROP OUR EYES OR TURN TO OTHER THINGS, . . . . . . . . 114 IN THE HOME STRETCH  117
    AS THE BREEZE RISES, AND TURN MANY-COLORED . . . . . . . . 121 BIRCHES . . . . . . .    8
    TRYING TO TURN ITSELF BACKWARD OR FORWARD, . . . . . . . . 147 SNOW . . . . . . . .  119
    IT CAN'T TURN EITHER WAY. IT NEEDS THE WIND'S HELP. . . . 148 SNOW . . . . . . . .  135
    I'LL HAVE TO TURN THE LEAF IF NO ONE ELSE WILL. . . . . . 148 SNOW . . . . . . . .  151
    AT ONE STROKE (OF A MATCH), BRAD HAD TO TURN . . . . . . . 178 THE STAR-SPLITTER . .  67
    IT NEEDED A TURN MORE, I COULD HAVE CRIED . . . . . . . . 191 THE GRINDSTONE . . . .  72
    WASN'T THERE DANGER OF A TURN TOO MUCH? . . . . . . . . . 191 THE GRINDSTONE . . . .  73
    AND THAT MADE PAUL IN TURN LOOK BACK . . . . . . . . . . . 194 PAUL'S WIFE . . . . .  111
    SO AS TO SORT OF TURN ME OUT OF IT. . . . . . . . . . . . 203 THE WITCH OF COOS  . .  43
    TO TURN HIM ROUND. HE GOT TO SAYING THINGS . . . . . . . 209 PAUPER WITCH OF GRAFTON  78
```

TURN (CONTINUED)
IN USING THE YARD TO BACK AND TURN AROUND; . . . . . 287 A ROADSIDE STAND . . 40
NOW LICHENS ARE DUE TO HAVE THEIR TURN. . . . . . . 297 LEAVES COMPARED WITH . 12
ALL TURN AND LOOK ONE WAY. . . . . 301 NEITHER OUT FAR NOR IN . 2
THEY TURN THEIR BACK ON THE LAND. . . . . 301 NEITHER OUT FAR NOR IN . 3
BUILD SOIL. TURN THE FARM IN UPON ITSELF . . . . . . 323 BUILD SOIL 234
TO TAKE TO MARKET--I WILL TURN IT UNDER. . . . . . . 323 BUILD SOIL 240
THE THOUGHT FROM THAT THOUGHT--I WILL TURN IT UNDER. . . 323 BUILD SOIL 241
SOME TURN IN SHEER, IN SHELLEYAN DEJECTION . . . . . 358 THE LOST FOLLOWER . . 11
AND TURN US INTO THE NEXT SPECIE FOLKS . . . . 369 THE LITERATE FARMER AND 43
THE TURTLE IN TURN ON A ROCK IN THE OCEAN. . . . . . 379 TOO ANXIOUS FOR RIVERS 16
AND AS I WOKE AFRAID TO TURN . . . . 380 AN UNSTAMPED LETTER IN 21
WHAT IF IT SHOULD TURN OUT ETERNITY . . . . 386 A STEEPLE ON THE HOUSE 1
THE TIME HAD BEEN WHEN ANYONE COULD TURN . . . . . . 398 BURSTING RAPTURE . . 2
HE LIKES TO TURN HIS BACK ON GRATITUDE . . . . 408 FROM PLANE TO PLANE . 130
HE SEEKS A SEEKER WHO IN HIS TURN SEEKS . . . . . . 421 ESCAPIST--NEVER . . 7
AND HE MAY HAVE TO TURN TO SOMETHING ELSE . . . . . . 459 HOW HARD TO KEEP FROM 179
AND TURN THE GOLD ENAMELED ARTIFICIAL BIRDS ON. . . . . 490 A MASQUE OF REASON . 459
KEEPER, I'LL TURN ON YOU IF YOU KEEP ON. . . . . . . 503 A MASQUE OF MERCY . 268
OR "TURN THE RASCALS OUT" WOULD DO FOR ME. . . . . . 510 A MASQUE OF MERCY . 460
YET NO ONE TURN FROM TRYING TO LIVE UP TO. . . . . . 512 A MASQUE OF MERCY . 497
AND YET CAN'T TURN YOUR BACK ON OR IGNORE, ... 512 A MASQUE OF MERCY . 510
YET NO ONE TURN AWAY FROM OR IGNORE-- . . . . 513 A MASQUE OF MERCY . 522
I SIMPLY TURN AWAY FROM IT. / YOU PAGAN! . . . . . . 513 A MASQUE OF MERCY . 523
TURNED (SEE WELL-TURNED)
AND HE TURNED AND LOOKED AT THE ROAD AFAR . . . . . . 7 LOVE AND A QUESTION . 7
AND THE MORE LOITERING ARE TURNED . . . . 20 THE TRIAL BY EXISTENCE 25
AND WOULD HAVE TURNED TO TOSS THE GRASS TO DRY; . . . 22 THE TUFT OF FLOWERS . 20
BUT HE TURNED FIRST, AND LED MY EYE TO LOOK . . . . . 22 THE TUFT OF FLOWERS . 21
"STAY WHERE YOU ARE UNTIL OUR BACKS ARE TURNED!" . . . 33 MENDING WALL . . . 19
HE TURNED TO THE HOTEL TO FIND A BED. . . . . 45 A HUNDRED COLLARS . 19
IT'S TIME YOU TURNED AROUND AND BOOSTED US. . . . . . 48 A HUNDRED COLLARS . 115
SHE TURNED AND SANK UPON HER SKIRTS AT THAT, ... 51 HOME BURIAL . . . 8
AND TURNED ON HIM WITH SUCH A DAUNTING LOOK, ... 52 HOME BURIAL . . . 33
BUT BEFORE ONE IS IN IT, THEIR MINDS ARE TURNED . . . 54 HOME BURIAL . . . 103
AND THE AIR OF THE YOUNGSTERS! NOT ONE OF THEM TURNED, . 61 BLUEBERRIES . . . 58
TOO LOUD FOR THE DISTANCE YOU WERE, IT TURNED OUT, . . . 62 BLUEBERRIES . . . 94
THAT TURNED THEM ON THE WORLD, AND TRY TO FATHOM . . . 73 THE GENERATIONS OF MEN 17
"IT'S AS I SAY: SHE'S TURNED FROM HIM, THAT'S ALL." . . 87 THE HOUSEKEEPER . . 167
I TURNED AND REPENTED, BUT COMING BACK . . . . . . 102 GOOD HOURS . . . 11
NO MORE TO TELL? WE TURNED TO OTHER THINGS. . . . . . 110 THE EXPOSED NEST . . 32
OF CHAIRS TURNED UPSIDE DOWN TO SIT LIKE PEOPLE . . . 110 IN THE HOME STRETCH . 6
AND THEN THEY ALL TURNED TO WITH DEAFENING BOOTS . . . 114 IN THE HOME STRETCH . 109
AND HAD JUST TURNED FROM WHEN I FIRST SAW YOU . . . . 118 MEETING AND PASSING . 3
THE TOWN TURNED OUT TO FIGHT FOR ME--THAT HELD ME. . . 131 THE BONFIRE . . . 73
WHILE THEY HAD BACKS TURNED, THAT IT HADN'T BEEN THERE . 132 THE BONFIRE . . . 86
WERE NOT THE ONE DEAD, TURNED TO THEIR AFFAIRS. . . . 137 "OUT,OUT--" . . . 34
FOR HE TURNED SUDDENLY GRAVE AS IF TO SAY, ... 142 THE VANISHING RED . . 5
WE BOTH OF US TURNED OVER IN OUR GRAVES. . . . . . . 161 NEW HAMPSHIRE . . 60
HE TURNED ON WILLPOWER TO INCREASE THE LOAD . . . . . 189 THE GRINDSTONE . . 31
THEN TURNED HIM OUT TO GO ON OTHER ERRANDS . . . . . 190 THE GRINDSTONE . . 50
I LOOKED AT NINE: THE SWARM WAS TURNED TO ROCK . . . . 201 PLACE FOR A THIRD . 53
AS EVER SHE TURNED HER HOME WITH COD . . . . 237 A HILLSIDE THAW . . 26
AND TURNED FROM LOOKING UP AND BEING KISSED . . . . . 262 THE FLOWER BOAT . . 7
WILL BE TURNED UP BY THE PLOW, ... 283 IN TIME OF CLOUDBURST . 8
OF SIGNS THAT WITH N TURNED WRONG AND S TURNED WRONG . . 285 IN TIME OF CLOUDBURST . 22
I TURNED AND LOOKED BACK UP AT THE SKY, ... 286 A ROADSIDE STAND . 10
I TURNED AND LOOKED BACK UPWARD. . . . . 303 AFTERFLAKES . . . 3
I TURNED TO SPEAK TO GOD . . . . 303 AFTERFLAKES . . . 11
GOD TURNED TO SPEAK TO ME . . . . 309 NOT ALL THERE . . 1
ITS AIRY PRESSURE TURNED TO WATER WEIGHT. . . . . . 309 NOT ALL THERE . . 5
TURNED FROM THE PLACE AND RAN. . . . . 315 IRIS BY NIGHT . . 16
THEY LAUGHED AS IF THEY HAD TURNED A TRICK. . . . . . 341 THE SUBVERTED FLOWER . 61
WITH LOATHING, FOR AGAIN IT TURNED TO FLY. . . . . . 344 DISCOVERY OF MADEIRAS . 30
THE WORKMEN ALL TURNED TO AND BURIED HIM. . . . . . 357 A CONSIDERABLE SPECK . 14
BEFORE THEY TURNED FROM EVERYTHING TO HAY. . . . . . 394 HAEC FABULA DOCET . 16
TURNED INTO A TOOL? . . . . 404 FROM PLANE TO PLANE . 14
TURNED INTO A WEAPON. . . . . 450 OBJECTION TO BE STEPPED 15
I STOOD BY JOB. I MAY HAVE TURNED ON YOU. . . . . . 450 OBJECTION TO BE STEPPED 18
THAT COULD, LIKE ANY SPACE, BE TURNED AROUND IN? . . . 477 A MASQUE OF REASON . 120
THE KEEPER'S WIFE HAS HARDLY TURNED AWAY. . . . . . 479 A MASQUE OF REASON . 161
I'M ALL TURNED ROUND. / THERE IS YOUR WAY PREPARED. . . 493 A MASQUE OF MERCY . 5
                                                    514 A MASQUE OF MERCY . 547
TURNING
THEY'RE ONLY TURNING YELLOW WHERE THEY ARE. . . . . . 50 A HUNDRED COLLARS . 169
SHE SWEPT THE HEAVENS, TURNING ON HER HEEL. . . . . . 74 THE GENERATIONS OF MEN 36
SOMEONE WHO LIVED IN TURNING TO FRESH TASKS . . . . . 102 THE WOOD-PILE . . 35
HER BACK. SHE ALWAYS ANSWERED WITHOUT TURNING. . . . 110 IN THE HOME STRETCH . 12
TURNING HER FOREHEAD WITH A STAR, ... 263 THE TIMES TABLE . . 6
IT IS TURNING THREE HUNDRED YEARS . . . . 367 A SERIOUS STEP LIGHTLY 13
QUESTION OF WHAT WE'RE TURNING INTO NEXT." . . . . . 369 THE LITERATE FARMER AND 48
AND FOR NOT TURNING OUT A STRAIT, ... 418 AMERICA IS HARD TO SEE 52
A TURNING POINT IN MODERN HISTORY. . . . . 422 FOR JOHN F. KENNEDY . 10
TURNS
SHE'S GOT SO SHE TURNS IN AT EVERY HOUSE . . . . . . 49 A HUNDRED COLLARS . 142
OF BOTH OF US. BUT LOOK HOW IT TURNS OUT: . . . . . 85 THE HOUSEKEEPER . . 106
BUT TURNS TO PINK BETWEEN THE TEETH. . . . . 141 THE GUM-GATHERER . 33
AND TURNS TO THE WIND TO UNRUFFLE A PLUME, ... 276 TWO TRAMPS IN MUD TIME 26
TURRETS
ON TURRETS, LIKE CONSTANTINOPLE, DEEP . . . . 160 NEW HAMPSHIRE . . 40
TURTLE
THE TRAVELER'S EYE PICKED UP A TURTLE TRAIL, ... 270 THE EGG AND THE MACHINE 17
THE POCKET OF A LITTLE TURTLE MINE. . . . . 270 THE EGG AND THE MACHINE 23
THE ELEPHANT STANDS ON THE BACK OF A TURTLE; . . . . 379 TOO ANXIOUS FOR RIVERS 15
THE TURTLE IN TURN ON A ROCK IN THE OCEAN. . . . . . 379 TOO ANXIOUS FOR RIVERS 16
TURTLE'S
BUT CERTAIN SIGNS OF BURIED TURTLE'S EGG; . . . . . 270 THE EGG AND THE MACHINE 20

TWAIN
    AND WHERE THE TWO EXIST IN TWAIN . . . . 277 TWO TRAMPS IN MUD TIME   63
    EVERYONE KNOWS THE GLORY OF THE TWAIN . . . . 423 FOR JOHN F. KENNEDY   .   46
TWANG
    OR PLUNGING HEADLONG WITH FIERCE TWANG AFAR; . . . . . 14 WAITING   13
    AND LET THEM GO AND MAKE THEM TWANG, UNTIL . . . . .   66 A SERVANT TO SERVANTS . 135
'TWAS
    'TWAS NOTHING BUT MY FOOLISH HANGING BACK, ...   46 A HUNDRED COLLARS   . . 59
    'TWAS WE LET HIM HAVE MONEY, NOT HE US. . . . .   84 THE HOUSEKEEPER   . . 101
    COMING DOWN RYAN'S HILL. I THOUGHT 'TWAS HIM. . . . .   88 THE HOUSEKEEPER   . . 197
    BUT 'TWAS NO MAKE-BELIEVE WITH YOU TODAY, ...   109 THE EXPOSED NEST   . .   9
    'TWAS A NEST FULL OF YOUNG BIRDS ON THE GROUND . . . . 109 THE EXPOSED NEST   . .   13
    SON KNOWS THE STORY: BUT 'TWAS NOT FOR HIM . . . . . 206 THE WITCH OF COOS   . . 143
    ONE OF THE TIMES WAS WHEN 'TWAS IN THE WARRANT . . . . 208 PAUPER WITCH OF GRAFTON 23
    YET, AFTER ALL, 'TWAS NOT DIVINE, ...   274 A LONE STRIKER   . . .   52
    THAT IS TO SAY, 'TWAS NOT A CHURCH. . . . .   274 A LONE STRIKER   . . .   53
    'TWAS DISILLUSION UPON DISILLUSION. . . . .   279 THE WHITE-TAILED HORNET 66
    'TWAS SUNDAY AND SQUARE HALE WAS DRESSED FOR MEETING. . 284 THE GOLD HESPERIDEE .   41
    SO 'TWAS WITH NOT UNGRATEFUL CONSTERNATION, ... 295 LOST IN HEAVEN   . . .   8
    'TWAS TO BUY HIMSELF OFF HIS DOOM. . . . . 310 THE VINDICTIVES   . . .   6
    'TWAS AGE IMPOSED ON POEMS . . . .   335 CARPE DIEM   12
    'TWAS HIS IDEA THAT FOR THE PUBLIC HEALTH, ... 363 AN EQUALIZER   6
    'TWAS NOT THE VALUE I STOOD TO LOSE . . . . 364 TRESPASS   13
    WITHOUT INQUIRING IF 'TWAS SERIOUS. . . . . 364 TRESPASS   13
    'TWAS PROVIDENTIAL YOU APPLIED TO US, ... 369 THE LITERATE FARMER AND 26
    'TWAS SOMETHING WE KNEW ALL ABOUT TO BEGIN WITH . . . 369 THE LITERATE FARMER AND 27
    TO FIND 'TWAS THE EFFORT, THE ESSAY OF LOVE. . . . . 380 TOO ANXIOUS FOR RIVERS   24
    BUT NOW 'TWAS THERE AS ELSEWHERE, ANY GAIN . . . . . 380 TOO ANXIOUS FOR RIVERS   26
    'TWAS TOO ONE-SIDED A DIALOGUE, ... 398 BURSTING RAPTURE   . .   4
    'TWAS TO PUNISH HER, ... 420 ONE MORE BREVITY   . .   36
    'TWAS A RADIO . . . . 432 KITTY HAWK   150
    'TWAS NO VAIN PURSUIT. . . . . 436 KITTY HAWK   270
    'TWAS AN END FOREGONE . . . . 438 KITTY HAWK   320
    'TWAS TORN FROM HER PACIFIC SIDE. . . . . 438 KITTY HAWK   326
    HE'S A GOOD BOY. 'TWAS AT MY INSTIGATION. . . . . . 452 A-WISHING WELL   . . .   44
    BUT 'TWAS BY MAKING SWEETBREADS DO . . . . 459 HOW HARD TO KEEP FROM   173
    'TWAS A GREAT DEMONSTRATION WE PUT ON. . . . . . . 467 QUANDARY   25
    'TWAS A GREAT DEMONSTRATION IF YOU SAY SO. . . . . 475 A MASQUE OF REASON   .   53
    'TWAS HUMAN OF YOU. I EXPECTED MORE . . . . 481 A MASQUE OF REASON   . 219
    'TWAS IN FOR AN OLD-FASHIONED SHAKING DOWN . . . . 485 A MASQUE OF REASON   . 331
    ARE RIGHT. BUT 'TWAS INTENTIONAL INJUSTICE. . . . 503 A MASQUE OF MERCY   . 273
    'TWAS LOVELY AND ITS ORIGIN WAS LOVE. . . . . . . 509 A MASQUE OF MERCY   . 414
    'TWAS SAID THE LESSER GODS WERE ONLY TRAITS . . . 511 A MASQUE OF MERCY   . 479
                                                       516 A MASQUE OF MERCY   . 595
TWELVE
    BUT THAT'S NOT SAYING--LOOK, FRED COLE, IT'S TWELVE, . . 144 SNOW   55
TWELVEMONTH
    I COULD HAVE TOLD THEM ANY TIME THIS TWELVEMONTH . . . 207 PAUPER WITCH OF GRAFTON 15
TWENTY   (SEE NINETEEN-TWENTY-SIX, TEN-BY-TWENTY)
    TWENTY FOR THIS COCK, TWENTY-FIVE FOR THAT. . . . . . 86 THE HOUSEKEEPER   . . 139
    I WAS A STRAPPING GIRL OF TWENTY THEN. . . . . 209 PAUPER WITCH OF GRAFTON 69
    IN FRONT OF TWENTY OTHERS' WRIGGLING SPEED-- . . . . 237 A HILLSIDE THAW   . .   13
    "TAKE TWENTY YEARS. . . . . 256 THE LOVELY BE CHOOSERS   5
    WHERE WERE THEY ALL NOT TWENTY YEARS AGO? . . . . . 378 DIRECTIVE   26
    AND, TOO, TAKE CARE OF TWENTY OF THE FOUR. . . . . 484 A MASQUE OF REASON   . 310
    AND TWENTY FREEDOMS ON THE PARTY DOCKET. . . . . . 484 A MASQUE OF REASON   . 311
    OR IS IT ONLY FOUR? MY EXTRA TWENTY . . . . 484 A MASQUE OF REASON   . 312
    (I HOPE YOU KNOW THE GAME CALLED TWENTY QUESTIONS.) . 484 A MASQUE OF REASON   . 314
TWENTY-FIVE
    TWENTY FOR THIS COCK, TWENTY-FIVE FOR THAT. . . . . 86 THE HOUSEKEEPER   . . 139
    TWENTY-FIVE YEARS AGO AT MAPLE'S NAMING . . . . . . 104 MAPLE   149
TWENTY-FOUR-HOUR
    GIVE US A GOOD CHEAP TWENTY-FOUR-HOUR DAY, ... 371 THE LITERATE FARMER AND 100
TWENTY-ONE
    THEIR NUMBER'S--TWENTY-ONE?--THE THING WON'T WORK. . . 153 SNOW   294
TWENTY-THIRD
    THE TWENTY-THIRD OF SEPTEMBER, ... 365 A NATURE NOTE   . .   14
    SEPTEMBER THE TWENTY-THIRD. . . . . 365 A NATURE NOTE   . .   16
'TWERE
    WERE NOT, AS 'TWERE, THE MEREST MASK OF GLOOM, . . .   5 INTO MY OWN   3
    ACROSS HIS CHEST TO MAKE AS 'TWERE A BOW: . . . . . 114 IN THE HOME STRETCH . 107
    'TWERE NOTHING NEW IF THAT WERE ALL CHRIST BROUGHT. . 511 A MASQUE OF MERCY   . 474
TWICE
    AND TRIES ONCE--TWICE--AND THRICE IF I BE THERE; . . . 15 WAITING   22
    HE SAID TWICE OVER BEFORE HE KNEW HIMSELF: . . . . . 52 HOME BURIAL   . . .   34
    FARMERS AROUND TWICE AS WELL OFF AS WE . . . . . .   85 THE HOUSEKEEPER   . . 113
    TO FLAMES WITHOUT TWICE THINKING, WHERE IT VERGES . . 131 THE BONFIRE   . . .   59
    TO THE SAME PERSON TWICE. . . . . 134 A GIRL'S GARDEN   . .   48
    EVER PRESENTS ITSELF BEFORE US TWICE. . . . . 147 SNOW   130
    OF EARLY TIMES AS TWICE THE HEIGHT THEY ARE-- . . . 169 NEW HAMPSHIRE   . . 331
    BUT IF IT HAD TO PERISH TWICE, ... 220 FIRE AND ICE   . .   5
    IN GOING TWICE AROUND THE TREE. . . . . 233 LOOKING FOR SUNSET BIRD 12
    LET THEM THINK TWICE BEFORE THEY USE THEIR POWERS. . 245 SPRING POOLS   . .   9
    WE SAID WELL TWICE TO WHAT WE HAD IN COMMON, . . . 290 OLD BARN AT THE BOTTOM 22
    AH, JONAH, JONAH--TWICE--REPROACHFULLY. . . . . . 495 A MASQUE OF MERCY   .   57
TWIG
    AS CLEAN AS BOYS DO OFF A WILLOW TWIG . . . . 191 PAUL'S WIFE   . . .   20
    EACH SWUNG IN DANGER ON ITS SLENDER TWIG, ... 283 THE GOLD HESPERIDEE .   23
TWIG'S
    FROM A TWIG'S HAVING LASHED ACROSS IT OPEN. . . . . 122 BIRCHES   47
TWILIGHT
    FALLING IN LOVE ACROSS THE TWILIGHT MILLPOND. . . . 195 PAUL'S WIFE   . . . 131
    ACROSS THE THRESHOLD IN THE TWILIGHT FLED HIM. . . . 289 OLD BARN AT THE BOTTOM   9
    GO LOVING BY AT TWILIGHT. . . . . 335 CARPE DIEM   . . .   2
'TWILL
    DELIVER US FROM COMMITTEES. 'TWILL REMIND ME. . . . 486 A MASQUE OF REASON   . 373
TWINGE
    A REMINISCENT TWINGE OF RHEUMATISM. . . . . 474 A MASQUE OF REASON   . . 40

TWIST
        BUT PULL SO SLOW, WITH SUCH A TWIST, ... 273 A LONE STRIKER . . . 20
        THEY HAD JUST GIVEN THEMSELVES A LITTLE TWIST . . . . 283 THE GOLD HESPERIDEE . 7
TWISTED
        THE BROKEN ONE WAS TWISTED IN HIS BED. . . . . . . 100 THE SELF-SEEKER . . . 208
TWIT
        DON'T YOU TWIT. HE'S UNHAPPY. CHURCH NEGLECT . . . . 488 A MASQUE OF REASON . . 424
TWITCH
        AND SUDDENLY, WITHOUT A JERK OR TWITCH, ... 237 A HILLSIDE THAW . . . 21
TWITTED
        AND HATED TO BE TWITTED ON THE SUBJECT; . . . . . . 191 PAUL'S WIFE 5
TWITTER
        BY DOUBLING AND REDOUBLING SONG AND TWITTER-- . . . . 237 A HILLSIDE THAW . . . 16
        A TALKING TWITTER ALL THEY HAD TO SING. . . . . . . 240 OUR SINGING STRENGTH . 38
TWITTERS
        AT MOST HE THINKS OR TWITTERS SOFTLY, "SAFE! . . . . 249 ACCEPTANCE 11
TWITTING
        HE'S TWITTING US.--OH, BY THE WAY, YOU HAVEN'T . . . . 488 A MASQUE OF REASON . . 420
'TWIXT
        THOUGH I DON'T LIKE SUCH THINGS 'TWIXT THOSE THAT LOVE. . 53 HOME BURIAL 53
        O'ERNIGHT 'TWIXT MULLEIN STALKS A WHEEL OF THREAD . . . 126 RANGE-FINDING . . . 10
        A HALFWAY COFFEE HOUSE 'TWIXT TOWN AND NOWHERE----" . . 155 SNOW 342
        A PERCH AND RESTING PLACE 'TWIXT WOOD AND WOOD, ... 356 A MOTH SEEN IN WINTER . 2
        LIKE A PIP SHOT FROM 'TWIXT OUR PINCHING FINGERS." . . . 460 HOW HARD TO KEEP FROM 202
        'TWIXT WHAT TO LOVE AND WHAT TO HATE. . . . . 467 QUANDARY 10
TWO   (SEE ONE-TWO-THREE)
        THOUGH TWO, CLOSE-KEEPING, ARE LASS AND LAD-- . . . . 6 GHOST HOUSE 27
        TO MAR THE LOVE OF TWO . . . . 8 LOVE AND A QUESTION . 30
        TWO AND A CHILD, ... 10 STORM FEAR 10
        AS TWO IN WHOM THEY WERE PROVED MISTAKEN, ... 16 IN NEGLECT 2
        ITS TWO BANKS HAVE NOT SHUT UPON THE RIVER; . . . . . 28 MY BUTTERFLY . . . 9
        AND MAKES GAPS EVEN TWO CAN PASS ABREAST. . . . . . 33 MENDING WALL . . . 4
        TWO OR THREE TIMES--HE MADE ME FEEL SO QUEER-- . . . . 36 DEATH OF THE HIRED MAN 56
        HE SAYS THEY TWO WILL MAKE A TEAM FOR WORK: . . . . . 36 DEATH OF THE HIRED MAN 62
        WARREN LEANED OUT AND TOOK A STEP OR TWO, ... 38 DEATH OF THE HIRED MAN 121
        SOMETIMES HE JOINS THEM FOR A DAY OR TWO . . . . . . 44 A HUNDRED COLLARS . 6
        TWO THAT DON'T LOVE CAN'T LIVE TOGETHER WITHOUT THEM. . . 53 HOME BURIAL 54
        BUT TWO THAT DO CAN'T LIVE TOGETHER WITH THEM." . . . . 53 HOME BURIAL 55
        A FRONT WITH JUST A DOOR BETWEEN TWO WINDOWS, ... 55 THE BLACK COTTAGE . 6
        THEN THE TWO SONS, TILL SHE WAS LEFT ALONE. . . . . . 56 THE BLACK COTTAGE . 39
        (NOTHING COULD DRAW HER AFTER THOSE TWO SONS. . . . . 56 THE BLACK COTTAGE . 40
        IT WAS TWO YEARS AGO--OR NO!--CAN IT BE . . . . . . 59 BLUEBERRIES 10
        LIKE TWO KINDS OF JEWELS, A VISION FOR THIEVES." . . . . 62 BLUEBERRIES 105
        AFRAID OF ME. THERE'S TWO CAN PLAY AT THAT. . . . . . 65 A SERVANT TO SERVANTS . 86
        BESIDE IT, AND THERE MAY BE TWO OR THREE . . . . . . 68 AFTER APPLE-PICKING . 4
        TO DO WORK BETTER OR FASTER--THOSE TWO THINGS. . . . . 70 THE CODE 23
        TWO OR THREE FORKFULS I PICKED LIGHTLY ROUND FOR . . . 72 THE CODE 72
        ONE, AND ONE OTHER, YES, FOR THERE WERE TWO. . . . . 74 THE GENERATIONS OF MEN 28
        "TWO WEEKS SINCE." / "SHE'S IN EARNEST, IT APPEARS." . . 82 THE HOUSEKEEPER . . 22
        TWO OF YOU OUT WILL LEAVE AN EMPTY HOUSE." . . . . . 82 THE HOUSEKEEPER . . 42
        A FRIEND OR TWO AS GOOD AS OWN THE FARM. . . . . . 84 THE HOUSEKEEPER . . 96
        TWO AT A TIME'S THE RULE, ONE ON EACH ARM, ... 85 THE HOUSEKEEPER . . 129
        WHAT ARE THEY TRYING TO DO TO ME, THESE TWO?" . . . . 89 THE HOUSEKEEPER . . 211
        FIVE HUNDRED--FIVE--FIVE! ONE, TWO, THREE, FOUR, FIVE. . 94 THE SELF-SEEKER . . 59
        "THIS IS BETWEEN YOU TWO APPARENTLY. . . . . 100 THE SELF-SEEKER . . 209
        TWO ROADS DIVERGED IN A YELLOW WOOD, ... 105 THE ROAD NOT TAKEN . 1
        TWO ROADS DIVERGED IN A WOOD, AND I--. . . . . . . 105 THE ROAD NOT TAKEN . 18
        TO SEE US THROUGH OUR FIRST TWO WEEKS. BUT, JOE, . . . 113 IN THE HOME STRETCH . 74
        THE FIGURE OF OUR BEING LESS THAN TWO . . . . 118 MEETING AND PASSING . 7
        AND ONLY ONE OF THE TWO . . . . 128 THE OFT-REPEATED DREAM 10
        AND SINCE THERE WERE BUT TWO OF THEM, ... 128 THE IMPULSE 3
        (TWO MILES IT WAS) TO HIS ABODE. . . . . 139 BROWN'S DESCENT . . 48
        OF WHO BEGAN IT BETWEEN THE TWO RACES. . . . . . . 142 THE VANISHING RED . 13
        BETWEEN TWO BOYS AND NOT FEEL BOUND TO STOP IT. . . . 146 SNOW 101
        LET THE MAN FREEZE AN EAR OR TWO, I SAY.-- . . . . . 146 SNOW 102
        IT WON'T BE FOR AN HOUR OR TWO." / "WELL THEN-- . . . 152 SNOW 267
        "SHE KNEW HE HAD, POOR THING, TWO HOURS AGO." . . . . 153 SNOW 278
        "ONE OF TWO THINGS, EITHER SHE'S GONE TO BED . . . . . 154 SNOW 311
        SO IT WOULD BE ACCEPTED BY TWO CLASSES, ... 162 NEW HAMPSHIRE . . 95
        SHE'S ONE OF THE TWO BEST STATES IN THE UNION. . . . . 164 NEW HAMPSHIRE . . 175
        VERMONT'S THE OTHER. AND THE TWO HAVE BEEN . . . . . 164 NEW HAMPSHIRE . . 176
        HUGHES 2, AND EVERYBODY TO THE SADDEST . . . . . . 165 NEW HAMPSHIRE . . 199
        BETWEEN TWO DAYS, THE REASON WHY I SOUGHT . . . . . 167 NEW HAMPSHIRE . . 249
        WE SPREAD OUR TWO LEGS AS WE SPREAD ITS THREE, ... 179 THE STAR-SPLITTER . 83
        A STAR IN TWO OR THREE, THE WAY YOU SPLIT . . . . . 179 THE STAR-SPLITTER . 89
        OF THE TWO PAGES IT WAS PRESSED BETWEEN, ... 181 MAPLE 65
        LIKE THE TWO STROKES ACROSS A DOLLAR SIGN. . . . . . 186 THE AX-HELVE . . . 25
        SO IF YOU SEE ME CELEBRATE TWO BIRTHDAYS, ... 196 WILD GRAPES . . . 16
        AND GIVE MYSELF OUT AS TWO DIFFERENT AGES, ... 196 WILD GRAPES . . . 17
        DON'T MAKE ME LIE WITH THOSE TWO OTHER WOMEN." . . . . 199 PLACE FOR A THIRD . 11
        HE FOUND THE GRAVE A TOWN OR TWO AWAY. . . . . . . 200 PLACE FOR A THIRD . 38
        TWO WITCHES . . . . 202 TWO WITCHES . . . T
        TWO OLD-BELIEVERS. THEY DID ALL THE TALKING. . . . . 202 THE WITCH OF COOS . 3
        AND KICK WITH TWO LEGS LIKE AN ARMY MULE. . . . . . 202 THE WITCH OF COOS . 10
        BEGAN THE STAIRS, TWO FOOTSTEPS FOR EACH STEP, ... 204 THE WITCH OF COOS . 51
        FLATTERED I MUST BE TO HEAR TWO TOWNS FIGHTING . . . . 207 PAUPER WITCH OF GRAFTON 4
        THE TWO CONVERGING SLIDES, THE AVALANCHES, ... 214 A FOUNTAIN, A BOTTLE . 52
        "WHY NOT TAKE TWO OR THREE?" / "TAKE ALL YOU WANT. . . 217 A FOUNTAIN, A BOTTLE . 124
        TWO WINDS WOULD MEET, ... 218 I WILL SING YOU ONE-O . 11
        TWO LOOK AT TWO . . . . 229 TWO LOOK AT TWO . . T
        LIKE SOME UP-ENDED BOULDER SPLIT IN TWO, ... 229 TWO LOOK AT TWO . . 19
        SHE SEEMED TO THINK THAT, TWO THUS, THEY WERE SAFE. . . 229 TWO LOOK AT TWO . . 21
        TWO HAD SEEN TWO, WHICHEVER SIDE YOU SPOKE FROM. . . . 230 TWO LOOK AT TWO . . 38
        THIS EDEN DAY IS DONE AT TWO O'CLOCK. . . . . 254 A WINTER EDEN . . . 18
        WE'VE SAID WE TWO. LET'S CHANGE THAT TO WE THREE. . . . 258 WEST-RUNNING BROOK . 11
        TWO INSTRUMENTS OF NEARLY EQUAL HOPE, ... 269 THE BEAR 20
        BETWEEN TWO METAPHYSICAL EXTREMES. . . . . 269 THE BEAR 25
        TWO TRAMPS IN MUD TIME . . . . 275 TWO TRAMPS IN MUD TIME T

TWO (CONTINUED)

OUT OF THE MUD TWO STRANGERS CAME . . . . 275 TWO TRAMPS IN MUD TIME 1
AND YOU'RE TWO MONTHS BACK IN THE MIDDLE OF MARCH. . . . 275 TWO TRAMPS IN MUD TIME 24
THESE TWO MUST MAKE ME LOVE IT MORE . . . . 276 TWO TRAMPS IN MUD TIME 42
OUT OF THE WOODS TWO HULKING TRAMPS . . . . 276 TWO TRAMPS IN MUD TIME 49
AND WHERE THE TWO EXIST IN TWAIN . . . . 277 TWO TRAMPS IN MUD TIME 63
AS MY TWO EYES MAKE ONE IN SIGHT. . . . . 277 TWO TRAMPS IN MUD TIME 68
IS WHERE TWO ROCKS ALMOST MEET, ... 282 A DRUMLIN WOODCHUCK 6
AND TWO WAS ALL HE COUNTED (ONE HE MISSED); . . . . 283 THE GOLD HESPERIDEE 11
BUT TWO FOR A BEGINNING WASN'T BAD. . . . . 283 THE GOLD HESPERIDEE 12
LONG SINCE THEY SWUNG AS THREE INSTEAD OF TWO-- . . . 283 THE GOLD HESPERIDEE 25
THE WIDESPREAD DOUBLE DOORS TWO STORIES HIGH. . . . . 289 OLD BARN AT THE BOTTOM 12
ONCE SHOWED TWO LITTLE MONKEYS IN A CAGE . . . . . 293 AT WOODWARD'S GARDENS 2
WITH A DOOR OF TWO BROAD BOARDS . . . . 294 A RECORD STRIDE 2
TO ASK ME A THING OR TWO . . . . 294 A RECORD STRIDE 10
TWO ENTIRELY DIFFERENT GRANDCHILDREN . . . . 294 A RECORD STRIDE 17
AND NO TWO WERE OF THE SAME CONSTELLATION-- . . . . 295 LOST IN HEAVEN 6
TWO SUCH AS YOU WITH SUCH A MASTER SPEED . . . . . 300 THE MASTER SPEED 10
BETWEEN TWO DOWNPOURS TO SEE WHAT THERE WAS. . . . . 300 MOON COMPASSES 2
WE TWO WERE GROPING DOWN A MALVERN SIDE . . . . . 315 IRIS BY NIGHT 2
IN WHICH WE TWO STOOD SATURATED, DROWNED. . . . . . 315 IRIS BY NIGHT 12
THAT NEVER YET TO OTHER TWO BEFELL . . . . 315 IRIS BY NIGHT 21
ITS TWO MOTE-SWIMMING MANY-COLORED ENDS . . . . . . 315 IRIS BY NIGHT 27
TWO ROUND DOTS AND A RIPPLE STREAK, ... 327 A MISSIVE MISSILE 7
IS WHETHER THE TWO DOTS WERE TEARS, ... 327 A MISSIVE MISSILE 10
TWO TEARDROPS, ONE FOR EITHER EYE, ... 327 A MISSIVE MISSILE 11
THE TWO DOTS AND THE RIPPLE LINE. . . . . 328 A MISSIVE MISSILE 42
TWO SOULS MAY BE TOO WIDELY MET. . . . . 328 A MISSIVE MISSILE 52
AGE SAW TWO QUIET CHILDREN . . . . 335 CARPE DIEM 1
WHEN THE CLAP OF TWO CONVERGING WAVES . . . . . . 344 DISCOVERY OF MADEIRAS 27
THEY COULD ONLY SAY LIKE ANY TWO, ... 345 DISCOVERY OF MADEIRAS 46
"APPARENTLY THESE TWO OUGHT TO MARRY. . . . . . . 345 DISCOVERY OF MADEIRAS 69
OR A COMBINATION OF THE TWO, ... 345 DISCOVERY OF MADEIRAS 72
IT IS ALMOST THE YEAR TWO THOUSAND . . . . 361 ALMOST TWO THOUSAND T
TWO IN JUNE WERE A PAIR-- . . . . 365 A NATURE NOTE 5
BETWEEN TWO BURRS ON THE MAP . . . . 367 A SERIOUS STEP LIGHTLY 1
WITH TWO WHEELS LOW IN THE DITCH . . . . 367 A SERIOUS STEP LIGHTLY 9
BETWEEN US TWO IT'S NOT A STAR AT ALL. . . . . . . 369 THE LITERATE FARMER AND 38
OF COUNTRY WHERE TWO VILLAGE CULTURES FADED . . . . . 378 DIRECTIVE 34
IT MAY HAVE BEEN AT TWO O'CLOCK . . . . 380 AN UNSTAMPED LETTER IN 18
FROM TWO STARS' HAVING COALESCED . . . . 381 AN UNSTAMPED LETTER IN 26
TWO MEMORIES THAT LONG HAD LAIN . . . . 381 AN UNSTAMPED LETTER IN 33
YOUR CLAIMS TO IMMORTALITY WERE TWO. . . . . 382 TO AN ANCIENT 1
THE TWO IN THE CELESTIAL CAST . . . . 390 TWO LEADING LIGHTS 2
TWO LEADING LIGHTS . . . . 390 TWO LEADING LIGHTS T
TWO THOUSAND FEET ABOVE THE OCEAN LEVEL. . . . . . 400 TO THE RIGHT PERSON 6
IT HAS TWO ENTRIES FOR COEDUCATION. . . . . 400 TO THE RIGHT PERSON 7
THOSE TWO THINGS WE CAN'T. . . . . 441 KITTY HAWK 419
WE TWO COME IN FLIGHT . . . . 442 KITTY HAWK 455
SO THE TWO MAKING GOOD THEIR ABDICATION . . . . . 454 HOW HARD TO KEEP FROM 10
"THE CHOICE IS NOT BETWEEN TWO PEARLS, O KING, ... 456 HOW HARD TO KEEP FROM 74
TWO PITCHING ON LIKE THIS TEND TO CONFUSE ME. . . . . 484 A MASQUE OF REASON 323
AS IS SET FORTH IN CHAPTERS ONE AND TWO. . . . . . 485 A MASQUE OF REASON 328
WOULD YOU TWO PLEASE DRAW IN A LITTLE CLOSER? . . . . 488 A MASQUE OF REASON 403
YOU TAKE US TWO, WE'RE LOSERS IN THIS STORE, ... 496 A MASQUE OF MERCY 75
THE WAY IT RESTED TWO POINTS ON THE GROUND . . . . 501 A MASQUE OF MERCY 194
THESE TWO ARE STUBBORN CHILDREN, AS YOU SEE. . . . . 517 A MASQUE OF MERCY 619

TWO-DOOR
A TWO-DOOR BURROW I DUG. . . . . 282 A DRUMLIN WOODCHUCK 8

TWO-LEAVED
IT HARDLY COULD HAVE BEEN A TWO-LEAVED SEEDLING . . . 184 MAPLE 150

TWO-POINTED
MY LONG TWO-POINTED LADDER'S STICKING THROUGH A TREE . . 68 AFTER APPLE-PICKING 1

TWO-THOUSAND-MILE
IN ITS TWO-THOUSAND-MILE COAST; . . . . 212 AN EMPTY THREAT 45

'TWOULD
'TWOULD BE TOO BAD TO MAKE HIM SORRY FOR . . . . . 183 MAPLE 121
'TWOULD BE AMONG THE TOPS OF TREES, ... 274 A LONE STRIKER 39
AND YET 'TWOULD SEEM THAT WHAT IS SUNG . . . . . . 336 THE WIND AND THE RAIN 18
AND WHAT A SAVING 'TWOULD HAVE MEANT TO ME. . . . . 350 TO A YOUNG WRETCH 9
UNLESS 'TWOULD RATHER WILT THAN FADE." . . . . . . 450 OUR DOOM TO BLOOM 16

'TWOULDN'T
'TWOULDN'T SEEM REAL TO CLIMB FOR CLIMBING IT." . . . 43 THE MOUNTAIN 88

TYING
BY TYING TOGETHER . . . . 218 I WILL SING YOU ONE-O 20

TYPES
OF TYPES, COMPOSITE AND IMAGINED PEOPLE: . . . . . 317 BUILD SOIL 49

U

UDDER
HER UDDER SHRIVELS AND THE MILK GOES DRY. . . . . . 125 THE COW IN APPLE TIME 11

UGLINESS
YOU TAKE THE UGLINESS ALL SO MUCH CREAD, ... 371 THE LITERATE FARMER AND 106

ULTRARED
FIRST WHITE, THEN RED, THEN ULTRARED, THEN OUT. . . . 485 A MASQUE OF REASON 346

UNACCOUNTABLE
OF SUCH AN UNACCOUNTABLE STAY . . . . 364 TRESPASS 6

UNACCUSING
BUT STILL I AM STEADY AND UNACCUSING. . . . . . . 310 IN DIVES' DIVE 2

UNACQUAINTANCES
AGAINST HIS UNACQUAINTANCES THE RICH . . . . 290 OLD BARN AT THE BOTTOM 30

UNAFRAID
CALL HER NAUSICAA, THE UNAFRAID, ... 78 THE GENERATIONS OF MEN 152
AND PERHAPS SHE WILL COME, STILL UNAFRAID, ... 79 THE GENERATIONS OF MEN 167

UNAIDED
AND SAVE OURSELVES UNAIDED. . . . . 10 STORM FEAR 18

UNANNOYED
    THEN DISCONCERTED AND NOT UNANNOYED, ... 278 THE WHITE-TAILED HORNET 37
UNASSUAGED
    THEIR TONGUES HANGING OUT UNASSUAGED. . . . . 311 THE VINDICTIVES . . . 51
UNASSUMING
    STAY UNASSUMING. IF FOR LACK OF LICENSE . . . . . . 385 THE FEAR OF GOD . . . 7
    HOW YOUNG AND UNASSUMING . . . . 391 A ROGERS GROUP . . . 1
UNAWARES
    THE LONELINESS INCLUDES ME UNAWARES. . . . . 296 DESERT PLACES . . . 8
UNBAFFLEMENT
    THIS PERFECT MOMENT OF UNBAFFLEMENT, ... 461 HOW HARD TO KEEP FROM 238
UNBELIEF
    THAT WOULD BE UNBELIEF AND ATHEISM. . . . . 482 A MASQUE OF REASON . . 260
UNBENIGHTED
    WITH HOPES OF GETTING MANKIND UNBENIGHTED. . . . . 371 THE LITERATE FARMER AND 87
UNBLACKENED
    UNSCORCHED, UNBLACKENED, EVEN, BY ANY SMOKE. . . . . 184 MAPLE 142
UNBLANKETED
    AND IF I'D LEFT HIM HITCHED UNBLANKETED . . . . . . 208 PAUPER WITCH OF GRAFTON 49
UNBLINKING
    SOME PLANETS, THE UNBLINKING FOUR, ... 451 A-WISHING WELL . . . 23
UNBORN
    I'M THINKING THE UNBORN WOULD NEVER MISS . . . . . . 397 THE PLANNERS 2
UNBOUNDED
    MY PROOF OF BEING NOT UNBOUNDED. . . . . 331 BEECH 9
    OFF ON THE UNBOUNDED . . . . 432 KITTY HAWK 136
UNBRIDLED
    BUT THOUGH IT RUNS UNBRIDLED OFF ITS COURSE, ... 268 RIDERS 10
UNBROKEN
    WE HAVE OUR OWN ROUND SHAPE TO KEEP UNBROKEN. . . . . 322 BUILD SOIL 197
UNBROUGHT
    (AS YET UNBROUGHT TO EARTH) HE MEANS TO TRY. . . . . 359 THE LOST FOLLOWER . . 36
UNBRUISED
    AND SAW THEM PICKED UNBRUISED AND IN A DISH, ... 284 THE GOLD HESPERIDEE . 36
UNBURDENING
    TO SEE TO THE UNBURDENING OF SKIES. . . . . 337 THE WIND AND THE RAIN . 46
UNCAGED
    SUCH IS THE UNCAGED PROGRESS OF THE BEAR. . . . . . 269 THE BEAR 10
UNCERTAIN
    AS THE UNCERTAIN HARVEST; KEEP US HERE . . . . . . 12 A PRAYER IN SPRING . . 3
    BUT RAIN SPOILED ALL. THE DAY BEGAN UNCERTAIN, . . . 74 THE GENERATIONS OF MEN 19
    THROUGH THE PICTURE, A SOMETHING WHITE, UNCERTAIN, . . 225 FOR ONCE SOMETHING . . 9
    IF THIS UNCERTAIN AGE IN WHICH WE DWELL . . . . . . 350 THE LESSON FOR TODAY . 1
UNCERTAINTY
    OUR AGE-LONG THEME, FOR THE UNCERTAINTY . . . . . . 317 BUILD SOIL 37
    AND I CAN SEE THAT THE UNCERTAINTY . . . . 520 A MASQUE OF MERCY . . 710
UNCOMFORTABLY
    WE TROD UNCOMFORTABLY ON CRUNCHING GLASS . . . . . . 216 A FOUNTAIN, A BOTTLE . 89
UNCOMMONLY
    THE UNCOMMONLY DEEP SNOW HAS MADE HIM THINK . . . . . 205 THE WITCH OF COOS . . 109
UNCOMPLAININGLY
    I HELD ON UNCOMPLAININGLY FOR LIFE. . . . . 197 WILD GRAPES 54
UNCOMPREHENDING
    OH, SLOW UNCOMPREHENDING ME, ... 327 A MISSIVE MISSILE . . 38
UNCONCERN
    WHOSE LIFELONG UNCONCERN . . . . 465 MILKY WAY IS A COWPATH 42
UNCOVERED
    "I HAVEN'T DARED TO LOOK AT THEM UNCOVERED. . . . . . 93 THE SELF-SEEKER . . . 18
    OF HISSING ON THE YET UNCOVERED GROUND, ... 226 THE ONSET 5
UNCROSS
    OR SO MUCH AS UNCROSS MY FEET, ... 381 AN UNSTAMPED LETTER IN 22
UNCURBED
    BUT THE WORST ONE OF ALL TO LEAVE UNCURBED, ... 319 BUILD SOIL 101
UNCURL
    AND IF SO MOVED UNCURL A HAND IN GREETING. . . . . . 292 FIGURE IN THE DOORWAY . 22
UNCUT
    LIKE UNCUT JEWELS, DULL AND ROUGH. . . . . 141 THE GUM-GATHERER . . 31
UNDEBATABLY
    TO THE WORLD'S UNDEBATABLY DARK AGES, ... 350 THE LESSON FOR TODAY . 7
UNDECEIVED
    ONE FLIGHT OUT SIDEWAYS WOULD HAVE UNDECEIVED HIM. . . 101 THE WOOD-PILE . . . 17
UNDER
    IT IS UNDER THE SMALL, DIM, SUMMER STAR. . . . . . .   6 GHOST HOUSE 21
    THOSE STONES OUT UNDER THE LOW-LIMBED TREE . . . . .   6 GHOST HOUSE 24
    UNDER THE EAVES. . . . . 29 MY BUTTERFLY 47
    THAT SENDS THE FROZEN-GROUND-SWELL UNDER IT . . . . . 33 MENDING WALL 2
    AND EAT THE CONES UNDER HIS PINES, I TELL HIM. . . . . 33 MENDING WALL 26
    ALL THROUGH JULY UNDER THE BLAZING SUN, ... 36 DEATH OF THE HIRED MAN 67
    A DRY RAVINE EMERGED FROM UNDER BOUGHS . . . . . . 41 THE MOUNTAIN 33
    YOU'D BETTER TUCK YOUR MONEY UNDER YOU . . . . . . 47 A HUNDRED COLLARS . . 90
    MOUNTING UNTIL SHE COWERED UNDER HIM. . . . . 51 HOME BURIAL 11
    UNDER A CRAYON PORTRAIT ON THE WALL, ... 55 THE BLACK COTTAGE . . 23
    OF THEM ANYWHERE UNDER THE SHADE OF THE PINE, ... 59 BLUEBERRIES 16
    UNDER THOSE CIRCUMSTANCES, WOULD YOU NOW? . . . . . 71 THE CODE 60
    'I LEFT HIM IN THE BARN UNDER THE HAY. . . . . . . 72 THE CODE 84
    "UNDER THE SHELTER OF THE FAMILY TREE." . . . . . . 75 THE GENERATIONS OF MEN 65
    UNDER WHAT BEECH TREE, ON WHAT WOODCHUCK'S KNOLL?" . . 97 THE SELF-SEEKER . . . 116
    AND AT THE SINUS UNDER WATER A FIST . . . . 98 THE SELF-SEEKER . . . 155
    AND HAVING SCARED THE CELLAR UNDER HIM . . . . 108 OLD MAN'S WINTER NIGHT   9
    THEY SEEMED TO FAIL THE BLUEBIRDS UNDER THEM . . . . 130 THE BONFIRE 36
    UNDER THE SUNSET FAR INTO VERMONT. . . . . 136 "OUT,OUT--" 6
    BRING BERRIES UNDER THE WAGON SEAT, ... 141 THE GUM-GATHERER . . 26
    WITH HIS TEN CHILDREN UNDER TEN YEARS OLD. . . . . . 144 SNOW 52
    YOU'RE FURTHER UNDER IN THE SNOW--THAT'S ALL-- . . . . 150 SNOW 205
    UNDER IT ALL, HIS DOOR SEALED UP AND LOST, ... 150 SNOW 224
    UNDER THE WATCHFUL EYE OF HAWK AND EAGLE-- . . . . . 162 NEW HAMPSHIRE . . . 105
    UNDER THE NEW REGIME, AND SO FORBIDDEN. . . . . . . 167 NEW HAMPSHIRE . . . 279
    BY WORSHIP UNDER GREEN TREES IN THE OPEN. . . . . . 171 NEW HAMPSHIRE . . . 389

UNDER (CONTINUED)
UNDER A RUINOUS LIVE APPLE TREE . . . . 189 THE GRINDSTONE . . . 20
HIS FIRST THOUGHT UNDER PRESSURE WAS A GRAVE . . . . 200 PLACE FOR A THIRD . . 22
UNDER HE DIDN'T CARE HOW GREAT A STONE; . . . . . . 200 PLACE FOR A THIRD . . 24
AND SWOLLEN TIGHT AND BURIED UNDER SNOW. . . . . . . 204 THE WITCH OF COOS . . 56
AND SWOLLEN TIGHT AND BURIED UNDER SNOW. . . . . . . 204 THE WITCH OF COOS . . 58
AROUND, AND UNDER . . . . 220 I WILL SING YOU ONE-O . 75
ITS HEART SINKS LOWER UNDER THE SOD. . . . . 228 GOOD-BY AND KEEP COLD . 28
UNDER THE FORMAL WRITING, HE WAS THERE, ... 230 NOT TO KEEP 4
FROM GROWING UNDER PAVEMENTS OF A TOWN; . . . . . . 231 A BROOK IN THE CITY . 10
DEEP IN A SEWER DUNGEON UNDER STONE . . . . 231 A BROOK IN THE CITY . 16
IF FROM ITS BEING KEPT FOREVER UNDER, ... 231 A BROOK IN THE CITY . 22
BUT YOU HAD AWAKENED UNDER THE MORNING STAR . . . . 235 VALLEY'S SINGING DAY . 4
I WAS ASLEEP STILL UNDER THE DRIPPING ROOF, ... 236 VALLEY'S SINGING DAY . 16
THE GRASS LAY FLATTENED UNDER ONE GREAT TREAD. . . . 239 OUR SINGING STRENGTH . 12
NO SHIP OF ALL THAT UNDER SAIL OR STEAM . . . . . . 262 IMMIGRANTS 1
UNDER THE HAND OF THE VILLAGE BARBER, ... 262 THE FLOWER BOAT . . . 2
NOT TO SINK UNDER BEING MAN AND WIFE, ... 264 THE INVESTMENT . . . 13
A THOUSAND YARNS WERE UNDER PULL, ... 273 A LONE STRIKER . . . 19
WENT LONG SINCE TO THE DOGS UNDER THE TABLE. . . . . 279 THE WHITE-TAILED HORNET 57
WE DIVE DOWN UNDER THE FARM. . . . . 282 A DRUMLIN WOODCHUCK . 16
UNDER OR ON THE TREE, OR ANYWHERE, ... 284 THE GOLD HESPERIDEE . 39
CONSIDER WHAT THEY TREASURE UNDER GLASS, ... 290 OLD BARN AT THE BOTTOM 33
ALL SUMMER LONG I THOUGHT I HEARD THEM THREATENING UNDER
    THEIR BREATH. . . . . 297 A LEAF-TREADER . . . 7
UNDER MAGNITUDE THE SECOND.) . . . . 304 CLEAR AND COLDER . . 9
WHERE UNDER DEEP ASH AND CHARCOAL . . . . 312 THE VINDICTIVES . . 58
(IN-LEANING UNDER THE STRAIN) . . . . 312 THE VINDICTIVES . . 66
EAT IT OR PLOW IT UNDER WHERE IT STANDS, ... 323 BUILD SOIL 216
TO TAKE TO MARKET--I WILL TURN IT UNDER. . . . . . . 323 BUILD SOIL 240
THE THOUGHT FROM THAT THOUGHT--I WILL TURN IT UNDER. . 323 BUILD SOIL 241
WOULD RUN IN UNDER IT TO GET MY SHARE. . . . . 337 THE WIND AND THE RAIN . 36
AND COULD IT BE BROUGHT UNDER STATE CONTROL, ... 353 THE LESSON FOR TODAY . 99
FIRST UNDER UP AND THEN AGAIN DOWN UNDER, ... 362 SYMPATHY WITH UNDER DOG 1
ON OUR SYMPATHY WITH THE UNDER DOG. . . . . 362 SYMPATHY WITH UNDER DOG T
UNDER A SPELL SO THE WRONG ONES CAN'T FIND IT, . . . 379 DIRECTIVE 58
THAT UNDER ME A POINT OF ROCK . . . . 380 AN UNSTAMPED LETTER IN 19
OF CAUTION UNDER STARS THAT VERY WELL . . . . 383 BRAVADO 2
IT SWIRLS OCCLUDED IN US UNDER TIGHT . . . . 386 INNATE HELIUM . . . 2
PERMIT ME." AND HE CRUSHED IT UNDER HIS HEEL . . . . 456 HOW HARD TO KEEP FROM 84
UNDER THE BANDSTAND IN SUBURBAN PARK. . . . . 501 A MASQUE OF MERCY . . 210
UNDERBRUSH
AND FORCED THE UNDERBRUSH--AND THAT WAS ALL. . . . . 338 THE MOST OF IT . . . 20
UNDERDOG
I'M A POOR UNDERDOG, ... 261 CANIS MAJOR 9
UNDERDOWN
IN A DISPLAY OF UNDERDOWN AND QUILL . . . . 445 QUESTIONING FACES . . 5
UNDERFOOT
AND UNDERFOOT SNOW MELTED DOWN TO ICE, ... 179 THE STAR-SPLITTER . . 80
I DROVE THEM UNDERFOOT IN BITS OF FLIGHT . . . . . . 240 OUR SINGING STRENGTH . 35
I HAVE SAFELY TRODDEN UNDERFOOT THE LEAVES OF ANOTHER YEAR. 297 A LEAF-TREADER . . . 4
I FELT THE CHILL OF THE MEADOW UNDERFOOT, ... 342 QUEST OF PURPLE-FRINGED 1
UNDERGROUND
THEN SANK OUT OF SIGHT LIKE TROLLS UNDERGROUND, . . . 62 BLUEBERRIES 86
EITHER TO HAVE GONE GROPING UNDERGROUND . . . . . . 119 HYLA BROOK 3
UNDERGROUNDS
OR UNDERGROUNDS, FOR CONFIDENCE IN EARTHQUAKE? . . . 502 A MASQUE OF MERCY . . 227
UNDERGROWTH
TO WHERE IT BENT IN THE UNDERGROWTH; . . . . 105 THE ROAD NOT TAKEN . . 5
UNDERMINES
SO UNDERMINES MY BAREFOOT STAND I TOTTER, ... 391 ON BEING IDOLIZED . . 4
UNDERNEATH
SOME SHATTERED DISHES UNDERNEATH A PINE, ... 378 DIRECTIVE 42
UNDERSTAND
BEEN UP, I UNDERSTAND, HAVE CLIMBED FROM LADD'S. . . 41 THE MOUNTAIN 40
SEPARATE BEDS, OF COURSE, YOU UNDERSTAND." . . . . . 45 A HUNDRED COLLARS . . 27
BUT I UNDERSTAND: IT IS NOT THE STONES, ... 52 HOME BURIAL 29
AND LIVING PEOPLE, AND THINGS THEY UNDERSTAND. . . . 54 HOME BURIAL 105
THE TOWN-BRED FARMER FAILED TO UNDERSTAND. . . . . . 69 THE CODE 9
BUT I KNOW YOU DON'T UNDERSTAND OUR WAYS. . . . . . 70 THE CODE 26
YOU UNDERSTAND THAT MEANT THE EASY JOB . . . . 71 THE CODE 55
"YOU MEAN YOU COULDN'T UNDERSTAND HIS CARING. . . . 91 THE FEAR 50
YOU WON'T THINK ANYTHING. YOU UNDERSTAND? . . . . . 92 THE FEAR 88
YOU UNDERSTAND THAT WE HAVE TO BE CAREFUL. . . . . . 92 THE FEAR 89
A BURNING-GLASS THEY COULD NOT UNDERSTAND . . . . . 293 AT WOODWARD'S GARDENS . 3
AND NEVER COULD BE MADE TO UNDERSTAND. . . . . 293 AT WOODWARD'S GARDENS . 4
WHAT MONKEYS DID OR DIDN'T UNDERSTAND? . . . . 294 AT WOODWARD'S GARDENS . 34
THEY MIGHT NOT UNDERSTAND A BURNING-GLASS. . . . . . 294 AT WOODWARD'S GARDENS . 35
THEY MIGHT NOT UNDERSTAND THE SUN ITSELF. . . . . . 294 AT WOODWARD'S GARDENS . 36
SCIENCE HAS FAILED TO UNDERSTAND. . . . . 452 A-WISHING WELL . . . 61
YOU SHOULDN'T UNDERSTAND IT AT THE TIME. . . . . . . 475 A MASQUE OF REASON . . 63
THAN I COULD UNDERSTAND AND WHAT I GET . . . . 485 A MASQUE OF REASON . 332
IS ALMOST LESS THAN I CAN UNDERSTAND. . . . . 485 A MASQUE OF REASON . 333
JOB, YOU MUST UNDERSTAND MY PROVOCATION. . . . . . . 485 A MASQUE OF REASON . 347
PLEASE, SOMEONE UNDERSTAND. / I UNDERSTAND. . . . . 497 A MASQUE OF MERCY . . 110
WHAT DON'T I UNDERSTAND? IT'S EASY ENOUGH. . . . . . 497 A MASQUE OF MERCY . . 112
SOME PEOPLE WANT YOU NOT TO UNDERSTAND THEM, ... 510 A MASQUE OF MERCY . . 452
BUT I WANT YOU TO UNDERSTAND ME WRONG. . . . . 510 A MASQUE OF MERCY . . 453
UNDERSTANDING
THE UNDERSTANDING OF A FRIEND. . . . . 19 REVELATION 8
OF ITS OWN STUPID LACK OF UNDERSTANDING, ... 148 SNOW 164
THE WAY OF UNDERSTANDING IS PARTLY MIRTH. . . . . . 306 NOT QUITE SOCIAL . . 11
UNDERSTOOD
HOW DID HE GET SO? (RICH WAS UNDERSTOOD.) . . . . . 160 NEW HAMPSHIRE . . . 57
AND NEVER RIGHTLY UNDERSTOOD TILL BRYAN . . . . . . 168 NEW HAMPSHIRE . . . 296
THEN ON BAPTISTE, AS IF SHE UNDERSTOOD . . . . 187 THE AX-HELVE . . . 56
BUT I SLOWLY UNDERSTOOD. . . . . 366 NOT OF SCHOOL AGE . . 18
THERE'S A LOT YET THAT ISN'T UNDERSTOOD. . . . . . . 372 THE LITERATE FARMER AND 136

UNDERSTOOD (CONTINUED)
    AS IF HE DIDN'T CARE WHO UNDERSTOOD HIM, ... 405 FROM PLANE TO PLANE . 59
    SO MUCH THOSE HEROES KNEW AND UNDERSTOOD-- . . . . 422 FOR JOHN F. KENNEDY . 24
    THERE HAD TO BE, I UNDERSTOOD, ... 467 QUANDARY 3
    WHEN HE FINDS HIS VERSE IS UNDERSTOOD . . . . 469 CHOSEN POET OF VERMONT . 2
    WITH FORFEITS AND REWARDS HE UNDERSTOOD-- . . . . . . 476 A MASQUE OF REASON . . 74
UNDERTAKE
    UNDERTAKE TO TELL HER . . . . 442 KITTY HAWK 459
UNCERTAKES
    BUT WORK AIN'T ALL. LEN UNDERTAKES TOO MUCH. . . . . . 64 A SERVANT TO SERVANTS . 70
UNDER-TICKET-AGENT
    AS UNDER-TICKET-AGENT AT A STATION . . . . 178 THE STAR-SPLITTER . . 69
UNDERTOOK
    BEFORE I UNDERTOOK SO DELICATE . . . . 503 A MASQUE OF MERCY . . 271
UNDESERVING
    MERCY IS ONLY TO THE UNDESERVING. . . . . 512 A MASQUE OF MERCY . . 500
UNDEVIABLE
    IN HAVING ITS UNDEVIABLE SAY. . . . . 362 IN A POEM 4
UNDID
    SHE TOOK A DOUBTFUL STEP AND THEN UNDID IT . . . . . . 51 HOME BURIAL 4
UNDISPOSED
    UNEATEN, UNWORN OUT, OR UNDISPOSED OF. . . . . . . 178 THE STAR-SPLITTER . . 52
UNDO
    HE MUST SEEK ME WOULD HE UNDO THE WRONG." . . . . . . 16 A DREAM PANG 8
    TO UNDO WHAT HE'D DONE AND MAKE IT RIGHT, ... 209 PAUPER WITCH OF GRAFTON 79
    TO UNDO THE WRONG. . . . . 430 KITTY HAWK 72
UNDONE
    BY ITS OWN POWER SEEMS TO BE UNDONE, ... 125 AN ENCOUNTER 3
UNDOUBTED
    FROM SEEING THIS UNDOUBTED STIR . . . . 381 AN UNSTAMPED LETTER IN 29
UNDRIFTED
    IN LONG STORMS AN UNDRIFTED FOUR FEET DEEP . . . . . 226 THE ONSET 15
UNDUE
    TO MY UNDUE RENOWN, ... 389 ASTROMETAPHYSICAL . . 18
UNEARTHED
    AMONG UNEARTHED POTATOES STANDING STILL, ... 263 THE INVESTMENT . . . 6
UNEARTHLY
    EACH CIRCLING EACH WITH VAGUE UNEARTHLY CRY, ... 14 WAITING 12
    AND FURTHER STILL AT AN UNEARTHLY HEIGHT . . . . . 255 ACQUAINTED WITH NIGHT . 11
UNEASY
    UNOCCUPIED NEED NOT MAKE US UNEASY. . . . . 322 BUILD SOIL 192
UNEATEN
    UNEATEN, UNWORN OUT, OR UNDISPOSED OF. . . . . . . 178 THE STAR-SPLITTER . . 52
UNEMPLOYED
    HE STOOD REBUKED AND UNEMPLOYED. . . . . . . 273 A LONE STRIKER . . . 9
    OF AN UNEMPLOYED HOE. . . . . 450 OBJECTION TO BE STEPPED 3
UNENHANCED
    BUT STILL UNSTORIED, ARTLESS, UNENHANCED, ... 348 THE GIFT OUTRIGHT . . 15
    BUT STILL UNSTORIED, ARTLESS, UNENHANCED, ... 425 THE GIFT OUTRIGHT . . 15
UNEQUIVOCALLY
    AND SAYING PLAINLY AND UNEQUIVOCALLY . . . . . . 483 A MASQUE OF REASON . . 296
UNERRING
    HE COMES OUT MORE UNERRING THAN A BULLET. . . . . . 277 THE WHITE-TAILED HORNET 6
UNEXPECTED
    MY UNEXPECTED KNOCKING AT THE DOOR . . . . . . 368 THE LITERATE FARMER AND 1
UNFAIR
    WHETHER TIME'S REWARDS ARE FAIR OR UNFAIR. . . . . . 347 DISCOVERY OF MADEIRAS . 138
UNFETTERED
    STILL MORE UNFETTERED, ... 219 I WILL SING YOU ONE-O . 43
UNFOLD
    YOU COME TO ME AND I'LL UNFOLD TO YOU . . . . . . 323 BUILD SOIL 224
UNFORTUNATELY
    UNFORTUNATELY ALL OF ONE KIND, THOUGH. . . . . . 216 A FOUNTAIN, A BOTTLE . 99
UNGENTLE
    SNATCHED THEE, O'EREAGER, WITH UNGENTLE GRASP. . . . . 29 MY BUTTERFLY 30
    IT COULDN'T BE CALLED UNGENTLE. . . . . . . 289 DEPARTMENTAL 42
UNGOLDEN
    AT LEAST TO LIVE UNGOLDEN WITH THE POOR, ... 358 THE LOST FOLLOWER . . 18
    ENDURING WHAT THE UNGOLDEN MUST ENDURE. . . . . . 358 THE LOST FOLLOWER . . 19
UNGRADED
    DOORYARD AND ROAD UNGRADED, ... 10 STORM FEAR 14
UNGRATEFUL
    SO 'TWAS WITH NOT UNGRATEFUL CONSTERNATION, ... 295 LOST IN HEAVEN . . . 8
UNHAPPY
    IS HOW TO BE UNHAPPY YET POLITE. . . . . . . 353 THE LESSON FOR TODAY . 88
    WHAT AILS ME? TELL ME. WHY AM I UNHAPPY?" . . . . . 457 HOW HARD TO KEEP FROM 101
    PARDON MY INTERRUPTION; I'M UNHAPPY. . . . . . . 460 HOW HARD TO KEEP FROM 204
    DON'T YOU TWIT. HE'S UNHAPPY. CHURCH NEGLECT . . . . . 488 A MASQUE OF REASON . . 424
UNHARVESTED
    UNHARVESTED . . . . 304 UNHARVESTED . . . . T
    MAY SOMETHING GO ALWAYS UNHARVESTED! . . . . . . 305 UNHARVESTED 11
UNHEARD
    AS IF SHE PLAYED UNHEARD SOME TENDERNESS . . . . . 38 DEATH OF THE HIRED MAN 109
UNHERALDED
    IN BRINGING CHANGE UNHERALDED ON THE UNREADY. . . . . 320 BUILD SOIL 125
UNHERETICAL
    WON'T SEEM UNHERETICAL QUITE. . . . . . . 466 SOME SCIENCE FICTION . 20
UNHITCH
    AND THIS BILL." / "WHAT'S THE HURRY? HE'LL UNHITCH." . . . 88 THE HOUSEKEEPER . . . 199
UNHONORED
    THE TALE OF EARTH'S UNHONORED THINGS . . . . . . 21 THE TRIAL BY EXISTENCE 45
UNHOUSE
    (BUT NOT UNHOUSE). . . . . 218 I WILL SING YOU ONE-O . 33
UNIFORM
    STOOD UNIFORM IN BUCKETS, AND THE STEAM . . . . . 184 MAPLE 137
    TO WEAR THE UNIFORM OF WHO YOU ARE, ... 385 THE FEAR OF GOD . . . 8
UNIMPORTANT
    I SPENT ON THE UNIMPORTANT WOOD. . . . . 275 TWO TRAMPS IN MUD TIME 16

PAGE TITLE   LINE

UNINHABITABLE
  BE UNINHABITABLE AS THE MOON. . . . . 400 THE BROKEN DROUGHT . . 12
UNINNOCENT
  HOWEVER UNINNOCENT THEY MAY HAVE BEEN . . . . . . 161 NEW HAMPSHIRE . . . 80
UNINTIMATE
  AM TOUCHED BY THAT UNINTIMATE LIGHT . . . . . . 383 WERE I IN TROUBLE . . 7
UNION
  SHE'S ONE OF THE TWO BEST STATES IN THE UNION. . . . 164 NEW HAMPSHIRE . . . 175
UNITARIAN
  KEEPER'S THE KIND OF UNITARIAN . . . . 498 A MASQUE OF MERCY . . 119
UNITE
  MY OBJECT IN LIVING IS TO UNITE . . . . 277 TWO TRAMPS IN MUD TIME 66
UNITED
  AND BOTH OF OUR UNITED STRENGTHS, TO DO IT." . . . 213 A FOUNTAIN, A BOTTLE . 19
  AND GOT THE UNITED STATES STATED. . . . . . . 295 A RECORD STRIDE . . . 36
  JOIN THE UNITED STATES AND JOIN THE FAMILY-- . . . 325 BUILD SOIL 281
UNIVERSAL
  THE UNIVERSAL CATARACT OF DEATH . . . . 259 WEST-RUNNING BROOK . . 56
  THEY END UP IN THE UNIVERSAL WHOLE . . . . . . 354 THE LESSON FOR TODAY . 111
  IN THE UNIVERSAL CRISIS. . . . . 377 ONE STEP BACKWARD TAKEN 9
  ALL NIGHT WITH UNIVERSAL SPACE. . . . . 380 AN UNSTAMPED LETTER IN 17
  THE UNIVERSAL BLUE . . . . 388 MIDDLENESS OF THE ROAD 15
  THERE ISN'T ANY UNIVERSAL REASON; . . . . . . 478 A MASQUE OF REASON . . 138
  YOU ARE THE UNIVERSAL FUGITIVE-- . . . . 498 A MASQUE OF MERCY . . 137
UNIVERSALS
  BUT THESE ARE UNIVERSALS, NOT CONFINED . . . . . 353 THE LESSON FOR TODAY . 104
UNIVERSE
  THE UNIVERSE SEEMS CRAMPED TO YOU AND ME. . . . . 269 THE BEAR 12
  AT LEAST THAT'S WHY THE UNIVERSE IS ROUND. . . . . 322 BUILD SOIL 203
  HE THOUGHT HE KEPT THE UNIVERSE ALONE; . . . . . 338 THE MOST OF IT . . . 1
  THE UNIVERSE MAY OR MAY NOT BE VERY IMMENSE. . . . 389 SKEPTIC 9
  AND HUGGED HIMSELF FOR ALL HIS UNIVERSE. . . . . 396 ANY SIZE WE PLEASE . . 14
  THE UNIVERSE IS BUT THE THING OF THINGS, ... 425 ACCIDENTALLY ON PURPOSE 1
  OF THE UNIVERSE. . . . . 440 KITTY HAWK 377
  HAD FOR THE UNIVERSE . . . . 464 MILKY WAY IS A COWPATH 27
  THIS UNIVERSE OF OURS . . . . 465 MILKY WAY IS A COWPATH 35
  BEYOND THE STORM, BEYOND THE UNIVERSE. . . . . . 513 A MASQUE OF MERCY . . 533
UNIVERSE'S
  THAN HAS THE UNIVERSE'S. WE ARE BALLS, ... 322 BUILD SOIL 199
UNKIND
  OR WILLFULLY UNKIND. . . . . 339 THE SUBVERTED FLOWER . 7
UNKNOWN
  AND INTO THE WILD UNKNOWN, ... 313 BEARER OF EVIL TIDINGS 8
  THE MEANING OF IT IS UNKNOWN, ... 328 A MISSIVE MISSILE . . 43
  FROM SOURCE UNKNOWN BUT FROM NO SPECIAL PLACE . . . 411 POD OF THE MILKWEED . 2
  INTO THE UNKNOWN, ... 429 KITTY HAWK 45
  THEN WITH TACKLE UNKNOWN . . . . 448 THE BAD ISLAND--EASTER 17
UNLAID
  THEY SAY HIS FLAGSHIP'S UNLAID GHOST . . . . . . 418 AMERICA IS HARD TO SEE 49
UNLEAVENED
  UNLEAVENED BATCH. . . . . 298 ON TAKING FROM THE TOP 16
UNLESS
  "NO ROOM," THE NIGHT CLERK SAID, "UNLESS----" . . . 45 A HUNDRED COLLARS . . 20
  "YOU SAY 'UNLESS.'" / "UNLESS YOU WOULDN'T MIND . . 45 A HUNDRED COLLARS . . 23
  UNLESS WHEN YOU SAID I WAS KEEPING A BIRD . . . . 62 BLUEBERRIES 88
  UNLESS LEN TOOK THE NOTION, WHICH HE WON'T, . . . 67 A SERVANT TO SERVANTS 157
  I'D RATHER YOU'D NOT GO UNLESS YOU MUST. . . . . 68 A SERVANT TO SERVANTS 177
  I'LL NEVER REST TONIGHT UNLESS I KNOW. . . . . . 90 THE FEAR 32
  UNLESS I DO?" / " A PRETTY INTERIOR," . . . . . 99 THE SELF-SEEKER . . . 180
  HE SAW NO STAY UNLESS HE STOVE . . . . 137 BROWN'S DESCENT . . . 14
  UNLESS TO FIND THAT THERE WAS NO ONE THERE . . . . 176 THE CENSUS-TAKER . . 55
  UNLESS IT BE . . . . 212 AN EMPTY THREAT . . 42
  IT'S HELL FOR KNEES UNLESS DONE HELL-FOR-LEATHER." . 215 A FOUNTAIN, A BOTTLE . 63
  THAN FLOWERS WILL SHOW FOR DAYS UNLESS THEY HURRY. . 225 BLUE-BUTTERFLY DAY . 4
  UNLESS IN BITTERNESS TO MOCK . . . . 238 PLOWMEN 3
  UNLESS OUR PURPOSE IS DOING HARM, ... 263 THE TIMES TABLE . . 16
  LET HIM LIGHT ON YOUR SKIN UNLESS YOU MIND . . . . 278 THE WHITE-TAILED HORNET 28
  AND UNLESS MY SENSE IS AT FAULT, ... 295 A RECORD STRIDE . . 22
  BUT UNLESS YOU PUT THE RIGHT THING TO ITS ROOT . . . 296 LEAVES COMPARED WITH . 3
  BUT NOT MUCH IN BETWEEN UNLESS A COLLEGE. . . . . 325 BUILD SOIL 282
  UNLESS IT WAS THE EMBODIMENT THAT CRASHED . . . . 338 THE MOST OF IT . . . 10
  UNLESS I PUT IT IN YOUR MOUTH TO SAY. . . . . . 354 THE LESSON FOR TODAY . 115
  UNLESS IT WAS COMING TO FOLK . . . . 365 A NATURE NOTE . . . 11
  ARE GOING TO BE, UNLESS THESE MONKEY JOKES . . . . 369 THE LITERATE FARMER AND 44
  UNLESS A GOVERNMENT INTERFERES. . . . . 376 SOMETHING FOR HOPE . . 20
  UNLESS IN THE HORIZON RIM, ... 392 A CLIFF DWELLING . . 4
  UNLESS FOR PENITENTS WHO TOOK THEIR SEAT . . . . 400 TO THE RIGHT PERSON . 12
  UNLESS I'M WRONG . . . . 413 AWAY! 17
  UNLESS ONE ANOTHER. . . . . 431 KITTY HAWK 113
  UNLESS 'TWOULD RATHER WILT THAN FADE." . . . . . 450 OUR DOOM TO BLOOM . . 16
  "THEY CAN'T HAVE CHARACTER UNLESS THEY'RE FED." . . 458 HOW HARD TO KEEP FROM 143
  "UNLESS IT'S SWEETBREADS," YOU SUGGEST . . . . . 467 QUANDARY 17
  UNLESS I LIKED TO SUFFER LOSS OF WORSHIP. . . . . 476 A MASQUE OF REASON . . 75
  UNLESS I'M MUCH MISTAKEN IN MYSELF . . . . . . 495 A MASQUE OF MERCY . . 62
UNLIFELIKE
  IF SUCH UNLIFELIKE LINES KEPT POWER TO STIR . . . . 56 THE BLACK COTTAGE . . 29
UNLIFTED
  THAT LIES UNLIFTED NOW, COME DEW, COME RUST, . . . 261 A SOLDIER 2
UNLIGHTED
  TO LAMPS UNLIGHTED AND FIRE GONE GRAY, ... 127 HOUSE FEAR 4
UNLIKE
  UNLIKE OTHER FOLKS AS YOUR STANDING THERE . . . . 53 HOME BURIAL 60
  BUT HOW COULD THEY BE MADE SO VERY UNLIKE . . . . 57 THE BLACK COTTAGE . . 77
  BECAUSE UNLIKE THE BEES THEY HAVE NO HIVES, . . . 411 POD OF THE MILKWEED . 4
  DID SEEM UNLIKE YOU, AND I TRIED TO THINK . . . . 482 A MASQUE OF REASON . 263
UNLIT
  WHO SHARE THE UNLIT PLACE WITH ME-- . . . . . . 6 GHOST HOUSE 23

- 588 -

UNLOAD
    I MAY LOAD AND UNLOAD . . . . 235 GATHERING LEAVES . . 13
UNLOADING
    IN THE UNLOADING. SILAS DOES THAT WELL. . . . . . . 37 DEATH OF THE HIRED MAN   92
UNLOCK
    UNLOCK THE DOOR FOR ME. / NOT THAT WAY OUT. . . . . . 514 A MASQUE OF MERCY . . 546
UNLOCKED
    TO HAVE INSIDE THE HOUSE WITH DOORS UNLOCKED. . . . . 65 A SERVANT TO SERVANTS . 84
    MUST LEAVE THEM UNLOCKED TO BETRAY HIS PRESENCE. . . 289 OLD BARN AT THE BOTTOM   15
UNLOOKED-FOR
    AS IF THE EARTH IN ONE UNLOOKED-FOR FAVOR . . . . . 230 TWO LOOK AT TWO . . . 41
UNLUCKILY
    UNLUCKILY IT WASN'T MONEY ENOUGH . . . . 459 HOW HARD TO KEEP FROM   177
UNMATED
    DEAD WEEDS AND UNMATED BIRDS, ... 11 WIND AND WINDOW FLOWER   15
UNMEANING
    FOR THE APPARENTLY UNMEANING SORROW . . . . . . 475 A MASQUE OF REASON . . 60
    IT HAD TO SEEM UNMEANING TO HAVE MEANING. . . . . 475 A MASQUE OF REASON . . 64
UNMENDED
    ITS WIND-TORN THATCH GOES NOW UNMENDED; . . . . . 253 THE THATCH 32
UNMERCIFUL
    I CAN'T TRUST GOD TO BE UNMERCIFUL. . . . . . . 497 A MASQUE OF MERCY . . 116
    YOU CAN'T TRUST GOD TO BE UNMERCIFUL. . . . . . . 501 A MASQUE OF MERCY . . 214
    YOU CAN'T TRUST GOD TO BE UNMERCIFUL. . . . . . . 507 A MASQUE OF MERCY . . 361
UNMISTAKABLY
    BUT UNMISTAKABLY A LIVING MITE . . . . 357 A CONSIDERABLE SPECK . 8
UNMIXED
    THERE IS MORE UNMIXED COLOR ON THE WING . . . . . 225 BLUE-BUTTERFLY DAY . . 3
    THE COLORS ARE KEPT UNMIXED ON THE PALETTE, ... 320 BUILD SOIL . . . 147
UNNATURAL
    HELD HIGH AT SO UNNATURAL A LEVEL. . . . . 255 THE FLOOD 8
UNNECESSARILY
    AND HOLDS US OFF UNNECESSARILY, ... 183 MAPLE 124
UNNERVED
    HIS SCIENCE NEEDN'T GET HIM SO UNNERVED. . . . . . 396 ANY SIZE WE PLEASE . . 11
UNNOTICED
    STOOD FOR A WHILE UNNOTICED, WITH HER HANDS . . . . 96 THE SELF-SEEKER . . 95
    ON GOING UNNOTICED . . . . 247 ON GOING UNNOTICED . . T
    OF ITS GOING MUCH LONGER UNNOTICED . . . . 465 SOME SCIENCE FICTION . 2
UNOCCUPIED
    UNOCCUPIED NEED NOT MAKE US UNEASY. . . . . . . 322 BUILD SOIL . . . 192
UNOFFICIAL
    (BUT THIS WAS DREAMY UNOFFICIAL COUNTING) . . . . 175 THE CENSUS-TAKER . . 32
    WELL, BUT REMEMBER THIS IS UNOFFICIAL: . . . . . 506 A MASQUE OF MERCY . . 331
UNORIGINAL
    AS UNORIGINAL AS ANY RABBIT. . . . . 354 THE LESSON FOR TODAY . 112
UNOSTENTATIOUSLY
    NO. I UNOSTENTATIOUSLY MOVE OFF . . . . 324 BUILD SOIL . . . 255
UN-OUTWITTED
    OUR UN-OUTWITTED SPOUSE . . . . 464 MILKY WAY IS A COWPATH   17
UNPARDONABLE
    IS AN UNPARDONABLE SIN IN FARMING. . . . . 322 BUILD SOIL . . . 180
UNPOCKETED
    SOME MATCHES HE UNPOCKETED. "FOR FOOD-- . . . . . 115 IN THE HOME STRETCH . 138
UNPOSSESSED
    POSSESSING WHAT WE STILL WERE UNPOSSESSED BY, . . . 348 THE GIFT OUTRIGHT . . 6
    POSSESSING WHAT WE STILL WERE UNPOSSESSED BY, . . . 424 THE GIFT OUTRIGHT . . 6
UNPROTECTED
    WITH STONE AND LEAD TO UNPROTECTED GLASS: . . . . 216 A FOUNTAIN, A BOTTLE . 103
UNPRUNED
    HER UNPRUNED GRAPES ARE FLUNG LIKE LARIATS . . . . 164 NEW HAMPSHIRE . . . 163
UNQUESTIONING
    THE MOST UNQUESTIONING PAIR . . . . 444 THE DRAFT HORSE . . . 13
UNREAD
    "YOU DON'T MEAN YOU WILL SIGN THAT THING UNREAD?" . . . 99 THE SELF-SEEKER . . 187
UNREADY
    IN BRINGING CHANGE UNHERALDED ON THE UNREADY. . . . 320 BUILD SOIL . . . 125
UNREASON
    WAS TO LEARN HIS SUBMISSION TO UNREASON; . . . . . 481 A MASQUE OF REASON . . 210
UNRESISTED
    THAT SPENDS TO NOTHINGNESS--AND UNRESISTED, ... 259 WEST-RUNNING BROOK . . 57
UNREST
    ARE YOU AND I EAVESDROPPING ON THEIR UNREST-- . . . 415 A CABIN IN THE CLEARING   38
UNRETRIEVED
    AND LIE IN STONES AND BUSHES UNRETRIEVED. . . . . 216 A FOUNTAIN, A BOTTLE . 116
UNRUFFLE
    AND TURNS TO THE WIND TO UNRUFFLE A PLUME, ... 276 TWO TRAMPS IN MUD TIME   26
UNRUFFLED
    A NOTE UNRUFFLED . . . . 218 I WILL SING YOU ONE-O . 24
UNRUTH
    WHEREAT IN A MOMENT OF CROSS UNRUTH . . . . . . 346 DISCOVERY OF MADEIRAS . 96
UNSAFE
    THE FOE THRUST BACK UNSAFE BEYOND THE RHINE, . . . 222 TO E.T. 18
    WITH ROCK AND WASHOUT, AND UNSAFE IN DARKNESS; . . . 229 TWO LOOK AT TWO . . 6
UNSAID
    AS A CHILD MISSES THE UNSAID GOOD-NIGHT . . . . . 58 THE BLACK COTTAGE . . 102
    SO LONG AS HE WOULD LEAVE ENOUGH UNSAID, ... 186 THE AX-HELVE . . . 38
    UNSAID BETWEEN US, BROTHER, AND THIS REMAINED-- . . 222 TO E.T. 10
    SO MUCH AS THE TRUSTING SORROW OF WHAT IS UNSAID: . . 286 A ROADSIDE STAND . . 17
UNSATISFIED
    LET THEM DIE OF UNSATISFIED GREED, ... 313 THE VINDICTIVES . . 85
    OF UNSATISFIED LOVE OF DISPLAY, ... 313 THE VINDICTIVES . . 86
    OF UNSATISFIED LOVE OF THE HIGH, ... 313 THE VINDICTIVES . . 87
UNSATISFYING
    UNSATISFYING TO US EACH. . . . . 328 A MISSIVE MISSILE . . 46
UNSCARED
    SHE SIGHED AND PASSED UNSCARED ALONG THE WALL. . . . 229 TWO LOOK AT TWO . . . 24
    THEN HE TOO PASSED UNSCARED ALONG THE WALL. . . . . 230 TWO LOOK AT TWO . . . 37

UNSCORCHED
   UNSCORCHED, UNBLACKENED, EVEN, BY ANY SMOKE. . . . . . 184 MAPLE 142
UNSCRUPULOUSLY
   USED THESE UNSCRUPULOUSLY TO BRING ME . . . . 188 THE AX-HELVE 88
UNSEEN
   MYSELF UNSEEN, I SEE IN WHITE DEFINED . . . . . 17 THE VANTAGE POINT . . 5
UNSEPARATE
   WE'RE TOO UNSEPARATE OUT AMONG EACH OTHER-- . . . . 324 BUILD SOIL . . . 268
   WE'RE TOO UNSEPARATE. AND GOING HOME . . . . . 325 BUILD SOIL . . . 291
UNSETTLED
   I CAN'T, AND LEAVE A THING LIKE THAT UNSETTLED. . . 89 THE FEAR 15
UNSHAKEN
   HE STOOD UNSHAKEN, AND IF GRIM AND GAUNT, ... 292 FIGURE IN THE DOORWAY . 13
   YET IN HIS HEART HE WAS UNSHAKEN SURE . . . . . . 400 THE BROKEN DROUGHT . . 9
UNSHIPLIKE
   AN AIRSHIP LABORING WITH UNSHIPLIKE MOTION . . . . 182 MAPLE 82
UNSOCIAL
   AND BE AS UNSOCIAL WITH IT AS I CAN. . . . . . . 323 BUILD SOIL . . . 238
UNSOCIALIZED
   UNSOCIALIZED, IS INGENUITY: . . . . 319 BUILD SOIL . . . 102
UNSOILED
   UNVULGAR, UNSOILED, AND IDEAL. . . . . . . 313 THE VINDICTIVES . . . 88
UNSPARING
   WOULD EMPTY IT UNSPARING ON THE FLOWER . . . . 337 THE WIND AND THE RAIN . 32
UNSPOKEN
   (HE STOPS TO LISTEN AND HIS UNSPOKEN THOUGHT, . . . 502 A MASQUE OF MERCY . . 236
UNSPRAYED
   APPLES? NEW HAMPSHIRE HAS THEM, BUT UNSPRAYED, . . 164 NEW HAMPSHIRE . . . 159
UNSTAMPED
   AN UNSTAMPED LETTER IN OUR RURAL LETTER BOX . . . 380 AN UNSTAMPED LETTER IN   T
UNSTORIED
   BUT STILL UNSTORIED, ARTLESS, UNENHANCED, ... 348 THE GIFT OUTRIGHT . . 15
   BUT STILL UNSTORIED, ARTLESS, UNENHANCED, ... 425 THE GIFT OUTRIGHT . . 15
UNSUBSTANTIAL
   AND EVEN SUBSTANCE LAPSING UNSUBSTANTIAL; . . . . 259 WEST-RUNNING BROOK . . 55
UNSWEPT
   SHATTER IT INWARD ON THE UNSWEPT FLOORS. . . . . 216 A FOUNTAIN, A BOTTLE . 104
UNSYSTEMATIC
   STILL THERE MUST BE LOTS OF UNSYSTEMATIC . . . . 478 A MASQUE OF REASON . 141
UNTARNISHED
   UNTARNISHED BY RUST AND DECAY. . . . . 312 THE VINDICTIVES . . . 79
UNTAUGHT
   THE WIND ONCE BLEW ITSELF UNTAUGHT, ... 223 THE AIM WAS SONG . . 2
UNTERRIBLY
   AS LONG AS LIFE GOES SO UNTERRIBLY? . . . . . 167 NEW HAMPSHIRE . . . 269
UNTIDY
   IF HE'S UNTIDY NOW, WHAT WILL HE BE----?" . . . . 87 THE HOUSEKEEPER . . 162
UNTIL
   PREVENTING SHADOW UNTIL THE MOON PREVAIL; . . . 14 WAITING 10
   "STAY WHERE YOU ARE UNTIL OUR BACKS ARE TURNED!" . . 33 MENDING WALL . . . 19
   UNTIL THE BUSHES ALL ALONG ITS BANKS . . . . . 42 THE MOUNTAIN . . . 52
   MOUNTING UNTIL SHE COWERED UNDER HIM. . . . . 51 HOME BURIAL . . . 11
   THE PASTURE ALL OVER UNTIL NOT A FERN . . . . 59 BLUEBERRIES . . . 18
   UNTIL THE STRENGTH WAS SHOUTED OUT OF HIM, . . . 66 A SERVANT TO SERVANTS . 132
   AND LET THEM GO AND MAKE THEM TWANG, UNTIL . . . 66 A SERVANT TO SERVANTS . 135
   BUT WAIT UNTIL I GIVE YOU A HAND UP. . . . . 77 THE GENERATIONS OF MEN 121
   WITH FLOWERS IN HER LAP UNTIL THEY FADE, . . . 79 THE GENERATIONS OF MEN 169
   NOT MUCH OF THAT UNTIL I COME TO WOODS . . . 111 IN THE HOME STRETCH . 33
   UNTIL HE TOOK THE STIFFNESS OUT OF THEM, . . . 122 BIRCHES 30
   UNTIL THEY HAD LIT THE LAMP INSIDE. . . . . 127 HOUSE FEAR . . . 10
   UNTIL THE JANUARY THAW . . . . 139 BROWN'S DESCENT . . 58
   TO HOLD IT HARD UNTIL THEY MAKE IT FAST, . . . 141 THE LINE-GANG . . . 10
   UNTIL I ASKED FOR ONE TO STEADY HIM. . . . . 160 NEW HAMPSHIRE . . . 32
   THAT WOULDN'T BUDGE, UNTIL THEY SIMPLY STRETCHED . 192 PAUL'S WIFE . . . 44
   UNTIL I'D HAD HIM WORN TO SKIN AND BONES, . . . 208 PAUPER WITCH OF GRAFTON 48
   IT WAS THE MOON'S: SHE HELD THEM UNTIL DAY, . . . 238 A HILLSIDE THAW . . . 33
   BORNE DOWN UNTIL THE END ALMOST TOOK ROOT, . . . 239 OUR SINGING STRENGTH . 13
   I HAVE BEEN TREADING ON LEAVES ALL DAY UNTIL I AM
      AUTUMN-TIRED. . . . . 297 A LEAF-TREADER . . . 1
   BUT THE STRONG ARE SAYING NOTHING UNTIL THEY SEE. . . 300 STRONG SAYING NOTHING . 16
   UNTIL IT CAN CONTAIN ITSELF NO MORE, ... 323 BUILD SOIL . . . 235
   UNTIL WE FOUND OUT THAT IT WAS OURSELVES . . . 348 THE GIFT OUTRIGHT . . 9
   YOU NICK MY SPRUCE UNTIL ITS FIBER CRACKS, . . . 349 TO A YOUNG WRETCH . . 3
   UNTIL WE FOUND OUT THAT IT WAS OURSELVES . . . 424 THE GIFT OUTRIGHT . . 9
   UNTIL HERBERT HOOVER . . . . 430 KITTY HAWK 70
   UNTIL OVERTAXED . . . . 448 THE BAD ISLAND--EASTER   38
   UNTIL THE EDDY OF IT EDDIES OUT." . . . . . 459 HOW HARD TO KEEP FROM   161
   CONTEMPLATE TRUTH UNTIL IT BURNS YOUR EYES OUT. . . 517 A MASQUE OF MERCY . 630
   UNTIL THE SCRIBES HAD TAKEN DOWN A BOOKFUL . . . 518 A MASQUE OF MERCY . 644
UNTIMELINESS
   THE OLD INCURABLE UNTIMELINESS, ... 356 A MOTH SEEN IN WINTER . 15
UNTO
   BUT STRETCHED AWAY UNTO THE EDGE OF DOOM. . . . 5 INTO MY OWN 4
   EACH CAME SINGLY UNTO HER PLACE, ... 15 IN A VALE 10
   UNTO YOU THE THANKS . . . . 443 KITTY HAWK . . . 465
   NOT FIND A BARKEEP UNTO JOVE IN ME? . . . . 443 AUSPEX 9
   WHEN UNTO EARTH HER FIRST WAS BORN. . . . . 452 A-WISHING WELL . . . 39
UNTOSSED
   AND LET US TRY AN UNTOSSED PLACE . . . . 347 DISCOVERY OF MADEIRAS . 108
UNUSUAL
   WHICH IS UNUSUAL. SO MANY KINGS . . . . . 457 HOW HARD TO KEEP FROM   109
UNVULGAR
   UNVULGAR, UNSOILED, AND IDEAL. . . . . . 313 THE VINDICTIVES . . . 88
UNWARNED
   OH, SHOULD A CHILD BE LEFT UNWARNED . . . . 336 THE WIND AND THE RAIN . 12
UNWILLING
   AND DROPPED MY EYES, UNWILLING TO EXPLAIN. . . . 255 ACQUAINTED WITH NIGHT . 6

UNWORN
   UNEATEN, UNWORN OUT, OR UNDISPOSED OF. . . . . 178 THE STAR-SPLITTER . . 52
UNWORTHY
   IT WERE UNWORTHY OF THE TONGUE . . . . 336 THE WIND AND THE RAIN . 15
UNWRITTEN (SEE BETTER-LEFT-UNWRITTEN)
UP (SEE CURLED-UP, FRAME-UP, GROWN-UP, HIGHER-UP, LONGEST-SAVED-UP, MIX-UP, PENT-UP)
   WHEN I GO UP THROUGH THE MOWING FIELD, ... 8 A LATE WALK 1
   UP FROM THE TANGLE OF WITHERED WEEDS . . . . 8 A LATE WALK 7
   WAS SWALLOWED UP IN LEAVES THAT BLEW ALWAY; . . . . . 16 A DREAM PANG 2
   WILL GLADLY GIVE UP PARADISE. . . . . 20 THE TRIAL BY EXISTENCE 28
   THEY MUST GO DOWN PAST THINGS COMING UP. . . . . . . 26 IN HARDWOOD GROVES . . 7
   WHEN I CAME UP FROM ROWE'S I FOUND HIM HERE, ... 35 DEATH OF THE HIRED MAN 34
   SILAS UP ON THE CART TO BUILD THE LOAD, ... 36 DEATH OF THE HIRED MAN 68
   PICKED UP A LITTLE STICK, AND BROUGHT IT BACK . . . . . 38 DEATH OF THE HIRED MAN 122
   I MADE THE BED UP FOR HIM THERE TONIGHT. . . . . . . 39 DEATH OF THE HIRED MAN 151
   SLIPPED TO HER SIDE, CAUGHT UP HER HAND AND WAITED. . . . 40 DEATH OF THE HIRED MAN 165
   PASTURE RAN UP THE SIDE A LITTLE WAY. . . . . 41 THE MOUNTAIN 29
   BEEN UP, I UNDERSTAND, HAVE CLIMBED FROM LADD'S. . . . . 41 THE MOUNTAIN 40
   THEY LOGGED IT THERE LAST WINTER SOME WAY UP. . . . . 41 THE MOUNTAIN 42
   THAT STARTS UP ON IT SOMEWHERE--I'VE HEARD SAY . . . . 42 THE MOUNTAIN 46
   SHELVES ONE COULD REST A KNEE ON GETTING UP-- . . . . 42 THE MOUNTAIN 59
   BY ANYONE WHO'D COME A LONG WAY UP. . . . . 43 THE MOUNTAIN 72
   "HE NEVER GOT UP HIGH ENOUGH TO SEE. . . . . 43 THE MOUNTAIN 78
   LATELY WHEN COMING UP TO LANCASTER, ... 44 A HUNDRED COLLARS . . 14
   THE NIGHT CLERK LED HIM UP THREE FLIGHTS OF STAIRS . . . 45 A HUNDRED COLLARS . . 33
   NOT LIKING TO OWN UP I'D GROWN A SIZE. . . . . . . 46 A HUNDRED COLLARS . . 60
   I PICK IT UP A DOLLAR AT A TIME . . . . 48 A HUNDRED COLLARS . . 97
   THE CHIMNEY, THOUGH, KEEPS UP A GOOD BRISK SMOKING. . . . 49 A HUNDRED COLLARS . . 137
   FROM UP THERE ALWAYS?--FOR I WANT TO KNOW." . . . . . 51 HOME BURIAL 7
   A MAN MUST PARTLY GIVE UP BEING A MAN . . . . 52 HOME BURIAL 49
   WHAT WAS IT BROUGHT YOU UP TO THINK IT THE THING . . . . 53 HOME BURIAL 63
   LEAP UP, LIKE THAT, LIKE THAT, AND LAND SO LIGHTLY . . . 53 HOME BURIAL 76
   AND I CREPT DOWN THE STAIRS AND UP THE STAIRS . . . . . 53 HOME BURIAL 79
   YOU HAD STOOD THE SPADE UP AGAINST THE WALL . . . . . 54 HOME BURIAL 87
   THE HEART'S GONE OUT OF IT: WHY KEEP IT UP? . . . . . 54 HOME BURIAL 110
   WHY, I MIGHT WAKE HER UP AND STARTLE HER. . . . . . 58 THE BLACK COTTAGE . . 93
   THE FIRE RAN AND BURNED IT ALL UP BUT THE WALL." . . . . 59 BLUEBERRIES 12
   AND PRESTO, THEY'RE UP ALL AROUND YOU AS THICK . . . . 59 BLUEBERRIES 20
   "HE JUST KEPT NODDING HIS HEAD UP AND DOWN. . . . . . 60 BLUEBERRIES 41
   HE HAS BROUGHT THEM ALL UP ON WILD BERRIES, THEY SAY, . . 60 BLUEBERRIES 50
   AS TALKING--YOU STOOD UP BESIDE ME, YOU KNOW." . . . . 62 BLUEBERRIES 96
   AND ALL OUR STORMS COME UP TOWARD THE HOUSE, ... 63 A SERVANT TO SERVANTS . 24
   BUT LEN WENT AT IT TO MAKE UP THE LOSS. . . . . . . 64 A SERVANT TO SERVANTS . 65
   LOCKED UP FOR YEARS BACK THERE AT THE OLD FARM. . . . . 65 A SERVANT TO SERVANTS . 89
   I SHAN'T CATCH UP IN THIS WORLD, ANYWAY. . . . . . . 68 A SERVANT TO SERVANTS . 176
   GATHERING UP WINDROWS, PILING COCKS OF HAY, ... 69 THE CODE 2
   I WAS UP HERE IN SALEM, AT A MAN'S . . . . 70 THE CODE 30
   FOR THE MAN UP ON TOP, OF THROWING DOWN . . . . . . 71 THE CODE 56
   AND LOOKING UP BEWHISKERED OUT OF THE PIT, ... 71 THE CODE 62
   MORE THAN WAS NEEDED, SOMETHING MUST BE UP. . . . . . 72 THE CODE 87
   THERE WAS NO ONE THAT DARED TO STIR HIM UP, ... 72 THE CODE 100
   TO RECONNOITER, AND THEN MADE UP HER MIND . . . . . . 74 THE GENERATIONS OF MEN 31
   BOWED OUTWARD ON THE MOUNTAIN HALFWAY UP, ... 75 THE GENERATIONS OF MEN 71
   BUT WAIT UNTIL I GIVE YOU A HAND UP. . . . . 77 THE GENERATIONS OF MEN 121
   NOR GRANNY'S, SURELY. CALL UP ONE OF THEM. . . . . . 79 THE GENERATIONS OF MEN 175
   NOW GIVE ME YOUR HAND UP.--PICK ME THAT FLOWER." . . . . 80 THE GENERATIONS OF MEN 207
   "IT'S YOU," SHE SAID. "I CAN'T GET UP. FORGIVE ME . . . 81 THE HOUSEKEEPER . . . 2
   I BLAME HIS BEING BROUGHT UP BY HIS MOTHER. . . . . . 83 THE HOUSEKEEPER . . . 56
   ALL IS, HE'S MADE UP HIS MIND NOT TO STAND . . . . . 83 THE HOUSEKEEPER . . . 70
   HAS BEEN TO KEEP THE THING FROM BREAKING UP. . . . . . 84 THE HOUSEKEEPER . . . 88
   "AND WE LIVE UP TO IT; OR I DON'T KNOW . . . . . . 85 THE HOUSEKEEPER . . . 132
   "THEN IT'S ALL UP. I THINK I'LL GET AWAY. . . . . . 88 THE HOUSEKEEPER . . . 190
   SHE WON'T GET FAR BEFORE THE WHEELS HANG UP . . . . . 88 THE HOUSEKEEPER . . . 202
   SHE STRETCHED UP TALL TO OVERLOOK THE LIGHT . . . . . 91 THE FEAR 62
   I SAW BY THE WAY YOU WHIPPED UP THE HORSE. . . . . . 91 THE FEAR 73
   AND BRING HIM UP, AND DON'T LET MRS. CORBIN.-- . . . . 96 THE SELF-SEEKER . . . 89
   WILLIS BROUGHT UP BESIDES THE BOSTON LAWYER . . . . . 96 THE SELF-SEEKER . . . 91
   AND THAT THRUST UP TO BLOSSOM IN THE SUN . . . . . . 98 THE SELF-SEEKER . . . 157
   YOU STAND UP TO IT LIKE A PAIR OF COCKS. . . . . . . 100 THE SELF-SEEKER . . . 211
   ONE OF YOU HOLD MY HEAD UP FROM THE PILLOW." . . . . . 100 THE SELF-SEEKER . . . 215
   STRAIGHT UP AND DOWN OF TALL SLIM TREES . . . . . . 101 THE WOOD-PILE . . . 6
   UP TO THEIR SHINING EYES IN SNOW. . . . . 102 GOOD HOURS 4
   TRYING, I THOUGHT, TO SET IT UP ON END, ... 109 THE EXPOSED NEST . . 4
   STOOD UP TO US AS TO A MOTHER-BIRD . . . . 109 THE EXPOSED NEST . . 21
   UP AND DOWN STAIRS AND THROUGH THE ROOMS, AND NONE . . . 112 IN THE HOME STRETCH . 42
   BUT NOW ARE GIVING UP FOR COUNTRY DARKNESS." . . . . 112 IN THE HOME STRETCH . 59
   THEY'RE GOING. WATCH THIS HUSKY SWARMING UP . . . . . 112 IN THE HOME STRETCH . 62
   CAME UP THE JOINTED STOVEPIPE IN THEIR HANDS, ... 113 IN THE HOME STRETCH . 86
   IT ALMOST SEEMED TO COME BALLOONING UP, ... 113 IN THE HOME STRETCH . 88
   A PERSONAL INTEREST IN THE LOCKING UP . . . . 115 IN THE HOME STRETCH . 134
   OF WHAT WANTS PRUNING, SHINGLING, BREAKING UP. . . . . 115 IN THE HOME STRETCH . 150
   AS YOU CAME UP THE HILL. WE MET. BUT ALL . . . . . 118 MEETING AND PASSING . 4
   OR FLOURISHED AND COME UP IN JEWELWEED, ... 119 HYLA BROOK 7
   UP TO THE BRIM, AND EVEN ABOVE THE BRIM. . . . . . 122 BIRCHES 38
   AND CLIMB BLACK BRANCHES UP A SNOW-WHITE TRUNK . . . . 122 BIRCHES 55
   AND LIFT THEMSELVES UP OFF THE GROUND. . . . . . . 123 PEA BRUSH 20
   AND SINCE IT WAS COMING UP HAD TO COME. . . . . . . 123 PEA BRUSH 24
   BLADE-END UP AND FIVE FEET TALL, ... 124 A TIME TO TALK . . . 8
   AND PLOD: I GO UP TO THE STONE WALL . . . . 124 A TIME TO TALK . . . 9
   LOCKED UP TOWARD HEAVEN, AND THERE AGAINST THE BLUE, . . 125 AN ENCOUNTER . . . 11
   UP AT HIS SHOULDERS, DRAGGING YELLOW STRANDS . . . . . 125 AN ENCOUNTER . . . 17
   "OH, LET'S GO UP THE HILL AND SCARE OURSELVES, ... 129 THE BONFIRE 1
   WHEN WE LOCKED UP THE HOUSE AT NIGHT, ... 135 LOCKED OUT 1
   AS HE SWUNG TOWARD THEM HOLDING UP THE HAND, ... 136 "OUT,OUT--" 20
   TO EVERYTHING, HE GAVE IT UP . . . . 139 BROWN'S DESCENT . . 43
   HE LOOKED BACK UP THE SLIPPERY SLOPE . . . . 139 BROWN'S DESCENT . . 47
   DON'T THINK BROWN EVER GAVE UP HOPE . . . . 139 BROWN'S DESCENT . . 54
   HE CAME FROM HIGHER UP IN THE PASS . . . . 140 THE GUM-GATHERER . . 13

UP (CONTINUED)

	PAGE	TITLE	LINE
AND REACHING UP WITH A LITTLE KNIFE,	141	THE GUM-GATHERER	37
I THINK I'LL JUST CALL UP MY WIFE AND TELL HER	143	SNOW	11
"WHY, LETT, STILL UP? LETT, I'M AT COLE'S. I'M LATE.	143	SNOW	16
I CALLED YOU UP TO SAY GOOD-NIGHT FROM HERE	143	SNOW	17
HE'S GETTING UP A MIRACLE THIS MINUTE.	146	SNOW	84
SAYS IT WON'T DO. YOU'VE GOT TO GIVE IT UP."	147	SNOW	107
AND SHOW YOU HOW IT'S PILING UP AGAINST YOU.	148	SNOW	156
ASK HELEN HOW FAR UP THE SASH IT'S CLIMBED	148	SNOW	158
AND FOUND ME BANKING UP THE HOUSE WITH SNOW.	149	SNOW	177
WHILE YOU SIT WARM AND READ UP BALANCED RATIONS.	149	SNOW	183
UNDER IT ALL, HIS DOOR SEALED UP AND LOST,	150	SNOW	224
THEY STARTED UP. FRED TOOK THE TELEPHONE.	155	SNOW	328
PITY HE DIDN'T ASK WHAT THEY WERE UP TO --	161	NEW HAMPSHIRE	83
AS FOR WHAT THEY WERE UP TO MORE THAN FISHING--	161	NEW HAMPSHIRE	87
ARTISTS THE MINUTE THEY SET UP AS ARTISTS,	162	NEW HAMPSHIRE	96
OFFERED ME NOT LONG SINCE UP BERLIN WAY	162	NEW HAMPSHIRE	110
THERE QUALITY MAKES UP FOR QUANTITY.	163	NEW HAMPSHIRE	148
RAKING UP AFTER WINTER, AND I SAID,	164	NEW HAMPSHIRE	153
FAR UP THE BIRCHES OUT OF REACH OF MAN.	164	NEW HAMPSHIRE	164
NEW HAMPSHIRE MOUNTAINS CURL UP IN A COIL.	165	NEW HAMPSHIRE	214
I'VE GIVEN UP MY SUMMER PLACE IN DUBLIN."	166	NEW HAMPSHIRE	222
WHOSE HORSE HAD PULLED HIM SHORT UP IN THE ROAD	168	NEW HAMPSHIRE	289
HAS BEEN PICKED UP WITH STONES TO BUILD A WALL.	172	A STAR IN A STONEBOAT	3
AND EVERY TREE UP STOOD A ROTTING TRUNK	175	THE CENSUS-TAKER	22
I PICKED UP OFF THE STRAW-DUST-COVERED FLOOR.	175	THE CENSUS-TAKER	45
"YOU KNOW ORION ALWAYS COMES UP SIDEWAYS.	176	THE STAR-SPLITTER	1
THROWING A LEG UP OVER OUR FENCE OF MOUNTAINS,	176	THE STAR-SPLITTER	2
WAS SETTING OUT, UP TRACK AND DOWN, NOT PLANTS	178	THE STAR-SPLITTER	71
UP THE BRASS BARREL, VELVET BLACK INSIDE,	179	THE STAR-SPLITTER	77
BY BRINGING IT UP TO HIM WHEN HE WAS TOO OLD.	183	MAPLE	122
AND I GIVE UP"; WHICH LAST LOOK CAME TO NOTHING.	184	MAPLE	132
BUT THOUGH THEY NOW GAVE UP THE SEARCH FOREVER,	184	MAPLE	133
STANDING ALONE WITH SMOOTH ARMS LIFTED UP,	184	MAPLE	145
THE NEXT COW MIGHT HAVE LICKED UP OUT AT PASTURE.	184	MAPLE	151
SHE USED HER HANDS TO COVER UP HER EYES.	184	MAPLE	160
A NAME WITH MEANING COULD BRING UP A CHILD,	185	MAPLE	166
AND CAUGHT HERSELF UP BODILY, CHAIR AND ALL,	187	THE AX-HELVE	52
THE SNAKE STOOD UP FOR EVIL IN THE GARDEN--	188	THE AX-HELVE	97
HE HAD TO RUN RIGHT OFF TO LOOK HER UP,	191	PAUL'S WIFE	13
AND THEN LAND SAFELY RIGHT SIDE UP AGAIN,	192	PAUL'S WIFE	52
AND LEFT STOOD UP ON END INSIDE THE TREE	194	PAUL'S WIFE	93
GOT DRUNK, AND TRACKED THE PAIR UP CATAMOUNT,	195	PAUL'S WIFE	124
THEY SAT TOGETHER HALFWAY UP A CLIFF	195	PAUL'S WIFE	133
IT CAUGHT ME UP AS IF I WERE THE FISH	197	WILD GRAPES	44
"WHAT ARE YOU DOING UP THERE IN THOSE GRAPES?	198	WILD GRAPES	56
WHILE SHE MADE UP HER MIND HOW MUCH SHE CARED--	201	PLACE FOR A THIRD	55
SHE'D LOOKED ELIZA UP HER SECOND TIME,	201	PLACE FOR A THIRD	58
SHE COULD CALL UP TO PASS A WINTER EVENING,	202	THE WITCH OF COOS	5
UP ATTIC, MOTHER? / BONES--A SKELETON.	203	THE WITCH OF COOS	20
UP ONE FLIGHT FROM THE CELLAR TO THE KITCHEN,	203	THE WITCH OF COOS	30
THE NIGHT THE BONES CAME UP THE CELLAR STAIRS	203	THE WITCH OF COOS	40
OR A LITTLE CHILD, COMES UP. IT WASN'T TOFFILE:	204	THE WITCH OF COOS	53
THE CELLAR WINDOWS WERE BANKED UP WITH SAWDUST	204	THE WITCH OF COOS	57
I SAT UP ON THE FLOOR AND SHOUTED, "TOFFILE,	205	THE WITCH OF COOS	82
IT'S COMING UP TO YOU." IT HAD ITS CHOICE	205	THE WITCH OF COOS	83
BEFORE I GOT UP TO DO ANYTHING;	205	THE WITCH OF COOS	92
"DON'T MAKE ME GET UP; I'M TOO WARM IN BED."	205	THE WITCH OF COOS	95
AND SIT UP BY ME AND TAKE HOLD OF ME.	205	THE WITCH OF COOS	103
LET'S TRAP HIM WITH AN OPEN DOOR UP ATTIC."	206	THE WITCH OF COOS	113
UP ATTIC THAT WE'D EVER WANT AGAIN.	206	THE WITCH OF COOS	122
THAT'S WHAT I SIT UP IN THE DARK TO SAY--	206	THE WITCH OF COOS	130
WE'D KEPT UP ALL THESE YEARS BETWEEN OURSELVES	207	THE WITCH OF COOS	146
OF ARTHUR AMY'S HAVING ONCE BEEN UP	207	PAUPER WITCH OF GRAFTON	13
COULDN'T HAVE BEEN THE ONE THEY SAY WAS UP	207	PAUPER WITCH OF GRAFTON	17
I KNOW OF SOME FOLKS THAT'D BE SET UP	208	PAUPER WITCH OF GRAFTON	36
HE GUESSED THEY'D KNOW WHAT HE HAD TO PUT UP WITH.	210	PAUPER WITCH OF GRAFTON	88
UP WHERE THE TREES GROW SHORT, THE MOSSES TALL,	210	PAUPER WITCH OF GRAFTON	96
TO MAKE SO FREE AND KICK UP IN FOLKS' FACES.	210	PAUPER WITCH OF GRAFTON	107
"TO SHUT YOU UP I'LL TELL YOU WHAT I'LL DO:	213	A FOUNTAIN, A BOTTLE	17
NO DOUBT IT'S GROWN UP SOME TO WOODS AROUND IT.	213	A FOUNTAIN, A BOTTLE	21
OUR BUSINESS FIRST'S UP ATTIC WITH HER BOOKS."	216	A FOUNTAIN, A BOTTLE	88
AND GIVE UP SLEEP.	218	I WILL SING YOU ONE-O	8
AND ALL HIS TAIL THAT ISN'T HAIR UP STRAIGHT.	223	THE RUNAWAY	17
TO WATCH HIS WOODS FILL UP WITH SNOW.	224	STOPPING BY WOODS	4
I ALMOST STUMBLE LOOKING UP AND ROUND,	226	THE ONSET	6
GIVES UP HIS ERRAND, AND LETS DEATH DESCEND	226	THE ONSET	8
A LITTLE FURTHER UP THE MOUNTAINSIDE	229	TWO LOOK AT TWO	2
WITH NIGHT SO NEAR, BUT NOT MUCH FURTHER UP.	229	TWO LOOK AT TWO	3
ON UP THE FAILING PATH, WHERE, IF A STONE	229	TWO LOOK AT TWO	11
AND SEND MORE SPARKS UP CHIMNEY WITH THE SMOKE."	234	EVENING A SUGAR ORCHARD	6
AND SO BE ADDED TO THE MOON UP THERE.	234	EVENING A SUGAR ORCHARD	10
SPADES TAKE UP LEAVES	234	GATHERING LEAVES	1
AND SING THE WILD FLOWERS UP FROM ROOT AND SEED.	240	OUR SINGING STRENGTH	53
AND THE DRY PUMP FLUNG UP AN AWKWARD ARM;	242	NEED OF BEING VERSED	19
BUT UP BY ROOTS TO BRING DARK FOLIAGE ON.	245	SPRING POOLS	6
TO BLOT OUT AND DRINK UP AND SWEEP AWAY	245	SPRING POOLS	10
ENGAGED UP THERE WITH THE LIGHT AND BREEZE?	247	ON GOING UNNOTICED	4
AND LOOK UP SMALL FROM THE FOREST'S FEET.	247	ON GOING UNNOTICED	10
WHEN THE SPENT SUN THROWS UP ITS RAYS ON CLOUD	249	ACCEPTANCE	1
LEAVES GOT UP IN A COIL AND HISSED,	251	BEREFT	9
TAKE UP THE TASK BEYOND HER CHOOSING."	256	THE LOVELY BE CHOOSERS	11
RAISING A LITTLE, SENDING UP A LITTLE.	259	WEST-RUNNING BROOK	63
OUR LIFE RUNS DOWN IN SENDING UP THE CLOCK.	259	WEST-RUNNING BROOK	64
THE BROOK RUNS DOWN IN SENDING UP OUR LIFE.	260	WEST-RUNNING BROOK	65
THE SUN RUNS DOWN IN SENDING UP THE BROOK.	260	WEST-RUNNING BROOK	66
AND THERE IS SOMETHING SENDING UP THE SUN.	260	WEST-RUNNING BROOK	67
BUT UP FROM WHERE THEY DIE	260	SAND DUNES	2

UP (CONTINUED)
MORE THAN HALFWAY UP THE PASS . . . . 263 THE TIMES TABLE . . . 1
HERE FURTHER UP THE MOUNTAIN SLOPE . . . . 264 THE BIRTHPLACE . . . 1
I GAVE UP FIRE FOR FORM TILL I WAS COLD. . . . . . . 267 WHAT FIFTY SAID . . . 2
WE CAN JUST SEE THE INFANT UP ASTRIDE, ... 267 RIDERS 7
ON LOOKING UP BY CHANCE AT THE CONSTELLATIONS . . . . 268 ON LOOKING UP BY CHANCE T
HIS HATE HAD ROUSED AN ENGINE UP THE ROAD. . . . . . 270 THE EGG AND THE MACHINE 4
THE TRAVELER'S EYE PICKED UP A TURTLE TRAIL, ... 270 THE EGG AND THE MACHINE 17
A BLUEBIRD COMES TENDERLY UP TO ALIGHT . . . . 275 TWO TRAMPS IN MUD TIME 25
AND MAKE UP FOR ITS LACK OF SIZE. . . . . 281 A DRUMLIN WOODCHUCK . 4
AND TURNED FROM LOOKING UP AND BEING KISSED . . . . . 283 THE GOLD HESPERIDEE . 8
WILL BE TURNED UP BY THE PLOW, ... 285 IN TIME OF CLOUDBURST . 22
AND ONE DID STOP, BUT ONLY TO PLOW UP GRASS . . . . . 287 A ROADSIDE STAND . . 39
AND SET THEM UP AGAIN FOR PROPPING SHUT, ... 289 OLD BARN AT THE BOTTOM 11
ALL UP AND DOWN IT. SO THAT WAKING THERE . . . . . . 290 OLD BARN AT THE BOTTOM 25
ONE PUT A THOUGHTFUL HAND UP TO HIS NOSE . . . . . . 293 AT WOODWARD'S GARDENS . 14
THEN NONE THE WISER, FRANKLY GAVE IT UP, ... 293 AT WOODWARD'S GARDENS . 29
BUT WHEN THEY GROW UP AND CAN READ THIS . . . . . . 294 A RECORD STRIDE . . 19
ALL SUMMER LONG THEY WERE OVERHEAD, MORE LIFTED UP THAN I. 297 A LEAF-TREADER . . . 5
NOW UP, MY KNEE, TO KEEP ON TOP OF ANOTHER YEAR OF SNOW. 298 A LEAF-TREADER . . . 12
BACK UP A STREAM OF RADIANCE TO THE SKY, ... 300 THE MASTER SPEED . . 3
AND BACK THROUGH HISTORY UP THE STREAM OF TIME. . . . 300 THE MASTER SPEED . . 4
THE MOUNTAINS ARE BROUGHT UP NEAR, ... 301 VOICE WAYS 4
ON A WHITE HEAL-ALL, HOLDING UP A MOTH . . . . 302 DESIGN 2
I TURNED AND LOOKED BACK UP AT THE SKY, ... 303 AFTERFLAKES 3
MAKE UP YOUR MIND TO DIE IN STATE. . . . . 307 PROVIDE, PROVIDE . . 9
THE OLD DOG BARKS BACKWARD WITHOUT GETTING UP. . . . 308 THE SPAN OF LIFE . . 1
AND SENDING UP NEW SHOOTS . . . . 308 EVIL TENDENCIES CANCEL 4
HE DRAWS HIMSELF UP TO HIS FULL EXTENT. . . . . . . 309 WASPISH 2
I'VE HAD TO GIVE MY INTERVAL FARM UP . . . . 316 BUILD SOIL 6
I'LL DRESS UP IN SHEEP'S CLOTHING AND EAT SHEEP. . . . 316 BUILD SOIL 16
WE SHALL BE DRIVEN IN. I WAS BROUGHT UP . . . . . . 324 BUILD SOIL 244
HAPPINESS MAKES UP IN HEIGHT FOR WHAT IT LACKS IN LENGTH 333 HAPPINESS MAKES UP . . T
I WOULD PICK UP ALL OCEAN LESS ITS SALT, ... 337 THE WIND AND THE RAIN . 28
PUSHING THE CRUMPLED WATER UP AHEAD, ... 338 THE MOST OF IT . . . 17
CAUGHT UP LIKE FINGERTIPS . . . . 339 THE SUBVERTED FLOWER . 12
FROM HER CHIN, PICKED UP HER COMB, ... 341 THE SUBVERTED FLOWER . 72
IT DID MORE DISTANCE UP AND DOWN, ... 344 DISCOVERY OF MADEIRAS . 19
IT GIVES UP STANDING STRAIGHT AND GOES DOWN SWISHING. . 349 TO A YOUNG WRETCH . . 4
AND GETTING UP MY MEDIEVAL LATIN, ... 350 THE LESSON FOR TODAY . 8
THEY END UP IN THE UNIVERSAL WHOLE. . . . . 354 THE LESSON FOR TODAY . 111
AS OF A BOOK HELD UP BEFORE HIS EYES . . . . 355 TIME OUT 3
DID YOU STAY UP LAST NIGHT (THE MAGI DID) . . . . . 360 A LOOSE MOUNTAIN . . 1
FIRST UNDER UP AND THEN AGAIN DOWN UNDER, ... 362 SYMPATHY WITH UNDER DOG 1
IS THAT IT BRINGS THE SAME CLASS UP ON TOP. . . . . . 363 A SEMI-REVOLUTION . . 4
AND SET UP LIKE A STATUE IN YOUR YARD, ... 365 OF STONES OF THE PLACE 10
HE POINTED ON UP THE ROAD . . . . 366 NOT OF SCHOOL AGE . . 11
PUT ON TRIAL BY THAT JERSEYITE . . . . 369 THE LITERATE FARMER AND 40
YOU'LL SEE IT BE ALLOWED UP JUST SO HIGH, ... 370 THE LITERATE FARMER AND 65
SAY ABOUT HALFWAY UP THE WESTERN SKY, ... 370 THE LITERATE FARMER AND 66
PUT UP TO CURE THE WORLD BY MR. EDISON." . . . . . . 371 THE LITERATE FARMER AND 93
HE GAVE UP SLEEP HIMSELF SOME TIME AGO, ... 371 THE LITERATE FARMER AND 104
AND IF OUR GETTING UP TO START THE DAY . . . . 372 THE LITERATE FARMER AND 120
LONG SINCE GAVE UP PRETENSE OF KEEPING COVERED. . . . 377 DIRECTIVE 12
MAKE YOURSELF UP A CHEERING SONG OF HOW . . . . . . 378 DIRECTIVE 29
AND PUT A SIGN UP CLOSED TO ALL BUT ME. . . . . . . 378 DIRECTIVE 38
AWAY ON THE MOUNTAIN UP FAR TOO HIGH, ... 383 WERE I IN TROUBLE . . 2
IF YOU SHOULD RISE FROM NOWHERE UP TO SOMEWHERE, . . . 385 THE FEAR OF GOD . . . 1
FROM BEING NO ONE UP TO BEING SOMEONE, ... 385 THE FEAR OF GOD . . . 2
YOU SHOULD BE TEMPTED TO MAKE UP FOR IT . . . . . . 385 THE FEAR OF GOD . . . 9
WE DO NOT GO UP THERE TO SLEEP AT NIGHT. . . . . . . 386 A STEEPLE ON THE HOUSE 4
WE DO NOT GO UP THERE TO LIVE BY DAY. . . . . 386 A STEEPLE ON THE HOUSE 5
NOR NEED WE EVER GO UP THERE TO LIVE. . . . . 386 A STEEPLE ON THE HOUSE 6
FROM LOOKING UP TOO MUCH, ... 389 ASTROMETAPHYSICAL . . 6
ME UP, NOT DOWN. . . . . 389 ASTROMETAPHYSICAL . . 20
SOME HALFWAY UP THE LIMESTONE WALL, ... 392 A CLIFF DWELLING . . 5
A CHEER WENT UP THAT SHOOK THE MOTTOED WALL. . . . . 400 THE BROKEN DROUGHT . . 6
TO MAKE UP FOR A LACK OF MEDITATION. . . . . 400 TO THE RIGHT PERSON . 14
EVERY TIME DICK OR PIKE LOOKED UP, THE DOCTOR . . . . 404 FROM PLANE TO PLANE . 18
THEN PICK YOUR HOE UP, MAYBE SHOULDER IT, ... 405 FROM PLANE TO PLANE . 41
PICK UP OUR EYES AND CARRY THEM BACK IDLE . . . . . 405 FROM PLANE TO PLANE . 51
THE FURTHER UP THE SCALE OF WORK YOU GO. . . . . . . 406 FROM PLANE TO PLANE . 83
YOU COULD DO WORSE THAN BOOST ME UP TO SEE." . . . . 406 FROM PLANE TO PLANE . 84
THEY WERE BOTH BENT ON SCUFFLING UP . . . . 407 FROM PLANE TO PLANE . 114
SINCE YOU BRING UP THE SUBJECT OF THE SUN. . . . . . 408 FROM PLANE TO PLANE . 125
UP CHIMNEY TO AVOID THE WORST OF IT. . . . . 408 FROM PLANE TO PLANE . 142
THE MILKWEED BRINGS UP TO MY VERY DOOR . . . . 411 POD OF THE MILKWEED . 5
NO ONE--NOT I--WOULD GIVE THEM UP FOR LOST . . . . . 414 A CABIN IN THE CLEARING 13
WILL OF ITSELF TAKE FIRE AND LIGHT THE WORLD UP. . . . 414 A CABIN IN THE CLEARING 27
BEFORE I GAVE UP SEEING AND SLEPT . . . . 419 ONE MORE BREVITY . . 3
TO HAVE UP AND SUNG . . . . 429 KITTY HAWK 41
TO CATCH UP WITH US? . . . . 435 KITTY HAWK 243
"NOTHING CAN GO UP . . . . 437 KITTY HAWK 306
I PICK A DEAD SHELL UP FROM WHERE THE KELP . . . . . 446 DOES NO ONE AT ALL EVER 25
IT CAN'T BE PULLED UP BY THE ROOT. . . . . 452 A-WISHING WELL . . . 51
AND THE PRINCE ANSWERED, PICKING UP THE PIECES, . . . 453 HOW HARD TO KEEP FROM 7
SHOULD BE ENOUGH TO SET YOU UP IN BUSINESS-- . . . . 454 HOW HARD TO KEEP FROM 34
THE EX-KING STOOD UP IN THE MARKETPLACE . . . . . . 454 HOW HARD TO KEEP FROM 37
FREE VERSE LEAVES OUT THE METER AND MAKES UP . . . . 460 HOW HARD TO KEEP FROM 219
AND ALL TANKED UP WITH MINERAL JUICE, ... 463 LINES IN DEJECTION . 7
WE HAVEN'T CAUGHT UP WITH MY COW. . . . . 463 LINES IN DEJECTION . 8
WE OWNED UP TO OUR WIFE . . . . 464 MILKY WAY IS A COWPATH 14
I RODE UP ON ONE TILL THE BUBBLE BURST, ... 468 IN A GLASS OF CIDER . 4
WORKED UP ABOUT IT. BUT SHE REALLY HASN'T-- . . . . 476 A MASQUE OF REASON . 94
I NOTICED WHEN SHE CALLED UP SAMUEL . . . . 477 A MASQUE OF REASON . 99
(THE THRONE COLLAPSES. BUT HE PICKS IT UP . . . . . 477 A MASQUE OF REASON . 107
AND THIS TIME LOCKS IT UP AND LEAVES IT.) . . . . . 477 A MASQUE OF REASON . 108
HIS TENTS BLEW ALL TO PIECES, I PICKED UP . . . . . 478 A MASQUE OF REASON . 131

PAGE TITLE   LINE

UP (CONTINUED)
    EXCUSES TRUMPED UP BY YOU FOR THEOLOGISTS. . . . . . 482 A MASQUE OF REASON . . 249
    WHO SAYS WE DON'T? WHO GOT UP THESE MISGIVINGS? . . . 483 A MASQUE OF REASON . . 288
    JOB'S WIFE SITS UP.) / WELL, IF WE AREN'T ALL HERE, . . 487 A MASQUE OF REASON . . 392
    WE'VE WAKED HER UP. / I HAVEN'T BEEN ASLEEP. . . . . 487 A MASQUE OF REASON . . 395
    AND WHAT ELSE DID WE SAY? / WELL, WHAT LED UP-- . . . 487 A MASQUE OF REASON . . 399
    I STUMBLED OVER IT AND GOT TRIPPED UP. . . . . . . 489 A MASQUE OF REASON . . 446
    NOW SOMEONE CAN LIGHT UP THE BURNING BUSH . . . . . 490 A MASQUE OF REASON . . 458
    IS TO BE CIVILIZED, STAY UP AND READ . . . . 496 A MASQUE OF MERCY . . 70
    BY WAITING UP INSTEAD OF GETTING UP. . . . . 496 A MASQUE OF MERCY . . 72
    I SEE WHAT YOU ARE UP TO: ROBBING ME . . . . 499 A MASQUE OF MERCY . . 147
    I TAKE THE FIRST BOAT. GOD PUTS UP A STORM . . . . . 500 A MASQUE OF MERCY . . 180
    LIKE WORKING MYSELF UP TO PROPHESY . . . . 501 A MASQUE OF MERCY . . 198
    THE MOB MIGHT HOLD A MAN UP IN THE STREETS . . . . . 503 A MASQUE OF MERCY . . 250
    OF GETTING UP GOOD RUINS, YOU'VE FORGOTTEN . . . . . 503 A MASQUE OF MERCY . . 260
    SO YOU'VE BEEN BOHNING UP ON THOMISM TOO. . . . . . 505 A MASQUE OF MERCY . . 297
    IT'S TOO BIG FOR HIM. HELP HIM HOLD IT UP. . . . . . 506 A MASQUE OF MERCY . . 328
    THE FOLLY CRASHES AND THE DUST GOES UP. . . . . . . 506 A MASQUE OF MERCY . . 342
    AND MEND THE OTHERS UP TO GO AGAIN. . . . . 508 A MASQUE OF MERCY . . 371
    TOO LONG PENT UP IN RIGOROUS CONVENTION-- . . . . . 509 A MASQUE OF MERCY . . 418
    AND HOLD IT UP NEARSIGHTEDLY TO READ.) . . . . . . 512 A MASQUE OF MERCY . . 490
    A LOFTY BEAUTY NO ONE CAN LIVE UP TO, ... 512 A MASQUE OF MERCY . . 496
    YET NO ONE TURN FROM TRYING TO LIVE UP TO. . . . . . 512 A MASQUE OF MERCY . . 497
    YES, SPOKEN SO WE CAN'T LIVE UP TO IT, ... 512 A MASQUE OF MERCY . . 498
    HIS LOFTY BEAUTY NO ONE CAN LIVE UP TO, ... 513 A MASQUE OF MERCY . . 521
    KNEEL BY HIM. BEL STANDS UP BESIDE HER CHAIR . . . . 518 A MASQUE OF MERCY . . 652
    AND WE'RE AN ORATOR. GET UP. STAND UP . . . . . . 519 A MASQUE OF MERCY . . 679
    GIVE ME A HAND UP, IF WE ARE AGREED. . . . . 520 A MASQUE OF MERCY . . 715
UP-ENDED
    LIKE SOME UP-ENDED BOULDER SPLIT IN TWO, ... 229 TWO LOOK AT TWO . . . 19
UPFLUNG
    THE WAVY UPFLUNG PENNONS OF THE CORN . . . . 404 FROM PLANE TO PLANE . 15
UPHILL
    THE BEST WAY IS TO COME UPHILL WITH ME . . . . . . 133 THE BONFIRE 113
    THREE HOURS TO HERE! BUT THAT WAS ALL UPHILL; . . . . 143 SNOW 22
UPLAND
    ON THE BARE UPLAND PASTURE THERE HAD SPREAD . . . . . 126 RANGE-FINDING . . . 9
UPLIFT
    COMPRESSION TO UPLIFT US OUT OF WEIGHT-- . . . . . . 387 INNATE HELIUM . . . 3
UPLIFTED
    THE UPLIFTED SIGHT . . . . 437 KITTY HAWK 309
UPON---NOT INDEXED
UPPER
    AND SPILLS THE UPPER BOULDERS IN THE SUN, ... 33 MENDING WALL 3
    HE MEANT TO CLEAR THE UPPER PASTURE, TOO. . . . . . 36 DEATH OF THE HIRED MAN 52
    LIKE BOULDERS BROKEN OFF THE UPPER CLIFF, ... 44 THE MOUNTAIN 98
    THERE IN THE UPPER CHAMBER IN THE ELL, ... 67 A SERVANT TO SERVANTS . 142
    HE MANAGES TO KEEP THE UPPER HAND . . . . 86 THE HOUSEKEEPER . . . 134
    THE UPPER SHELF, THE TIN BOX. THAT'S THE ONE. . . . . 86 THE HOUSEKEEPER . . . 144
    TO TAP THE UPPER SKY AND DRAW A FLOW . . . . 169 NEW HAMPSHIRE 340
    AND BROUGHT DOWN SAFELY FROM THE UPPER REGIONS; . . . 196 WILD GRAPES 13
    FLASHED OUT AND LICKED ALONG HIS UPPER TEETH. . . . . 204 THE WITCH OF COOS . . 73
    HERE COME REAL STARS TO FILL THE UPPER SKIES, ... 246 FIREFLIES IN THE GARDEN 1
    IN ONTO THE UPPER CHAMBER FLOORS. . . . . 253 THE THATCH 35
    THEIR UPPER BRANCHES ROUND HIM WREATHING, ... 274 A LONE STRIKER . . . 40
UPPER-WINDOW
    OF A CERTAIN UPPER-WINDOW LIGHT. . . . . 253 THE THATCH 4
UPRIGHT
    HE DANCES UPRIGHT . . . . 261 CANIS MAJOR 5
    THEN LETS IT SNAP BACK UPRIGHT IN THE SKY. . . . . . 268 THE BEAR 4
    THAT GOD PULLS LIGHTLY UPRIGHT ON ITS HINGES . . . . 474 A MASQUE OF REASON . 22
UPSIDE
    WE'RE NOT ALLOWED TO TAKE THEM UPSIDE DOWN, ... 85 THE HOUSEKEEPER . . . 127
    OF CHAIRS TURNED UPSIDE DOWN TO SIT LIKE PEOPLE . . . 110 IN THE HOME STRETCH . 6
    HE HANGS ON UPSIDE DOWN WITH TALON FEET . . . . . . 412 POD OF THE MILKWEED . 45
UPSILON
    BUT UPSILON WHICH IS THE GREEK FOR YOU. . . . . . . 388 IOTA SUBSCRIPT . . . 8
UPSTAIRS
    "IT'S TIME I TOOK MY TURN UPSTAIRS IN JAIL"-- . . . . 67 A SERVANT TO SERVANTS . 146
    OFF THERE UPSTAIRS. THE VERY TREAD OF MEN . . . . . 111 IN THE HOME STRETCH . 38
    AND CAME UPSTAIRS ALONE--AND GAVE THAT LAUGH, ... 142 THE VANISHING RED . . 26
    EACH OTHER IN PASSING IN THE ROOM UPSTAIRS, ... 180 MAPLE 11
    FATHER HAD GONE UPSTAIRS; MOTHER WAS DOWNSTAIRS. . . . 203 THE WITCH OF COOS . . 34
    WHEN I HEARD TOFFILE UPSTAIRS IN THE BEDROOM . . . . 203 THE WITCH OF COOS . . 46
    I PUSHED MYSELF UPSTAIRS, AND IN THE LIGHT . . . . . 205 THE WITCH OF COOS . . 97
UPSTART
    CHARGE THAT TO UPSTART INEXPERIENCE. . . . . 378 DIRECTIVE 25
UPWARD
    MAKING A GREAT SCROLL UPWARD TOWARD THE SKY, ... 143 SNOW 9
    AS OUR COMPARISONS WERE STOUTLY UPWARD . . . . . . 279 THE WHITE-TAILED HORNET 60
    I TURNED AND LOOKED BACK UPWARD. . . . . 303 AFTERFLAKES 11
    HAVE I NOT WALKED WITHOUT AN UPWARD LOOK . . . . . . 383 BRAVADO 1
    OUR BEST GUIDE UPWARD FURTHER TO THE LIGHT, ... 425 ACCIDENTALLY ON PURPOSE 23
URANIUM
    OF CRUDE URANIUM. . . . . 464 MILKY WAY IS A COWPATH 12
URGE
    THERE IS THE GALE TO URGE BEHIND . . . . 26 A LINE-STORM SONG . . 17
    THE URGE OF A SONG: . . . . 413 AWAY! 19
URGING
    YOU WOULDN'T THINK A FELLOW'D NEED MUCH URGING . . . . 71 THE CODE 59
US---NOT INDEXED
U.S.
    U.S. 1946 KING'S X . . . . 399 U.S. 1946 KING'S X . . T
USE
    WE HAVE TO USE A SPELL TO MAKE THEM BALANCE: . . . . 33 MENDING WALL 18
    "OH, IF YOU'RE GOING TO USE YOUR EYES, JUST HEAR . . . 76 THE GENERATIONS OF MEN 98
    WHEN I WAS YOUNG. I USED TO USE THE ROAR . . . . . . 78 THE GENERATIONS OF MEN 128
    MY FINGERS ARE ABOUT ALL I'VE THE USE OF . . . . . . 81 THE HOUSEKEEPER . . . 6
    BUT WHAT'S THE USE OF TALKING WHEN IT'S DONE? . . . . 87 THE HOUSEKEEPER . . . 176

USE (CONTINUED)
   AND SO AT LAST TO LEARN TO USE THEIR WINGS. . . . . . . 110 THE EXPOSED NEST . . . 36
   WITH THE SAME PAINS YOU USE TO FILL A CUP . . . . . . 122 BIRCHES 37
   I DIDN'T USE IT OUT OF LOVE OF HIM, ... 144 SNOW 50
   HE KNEW TOO WELL FOR ANY EARTHLY USE . . . . . . 171 NEW HAMPSHIRE . . . 378
   (THOUGH THESE WHEN NOT IN USE TO FLY AND TRAIL . . . . 172 A STAR IN A STONEBOAT . 17
   AND ARROWHEADS ITSELF. MUCH USE FOR YEARS . . . . . 189 THE GRINDSTONE . . . 38
   NEXT TO NOTHING FOR USE. . . . . 235 GATHERING LEAVES . . 21
   LET THEM THINK TWICE BEFORE THEY USE THEIR POWERS . . . 245 SPRING POOLS 9
   WHY DON'T YOU USE YOUR TALENTS AS A WRITER . . . . . 316 BUILD SOIL 22
   THE LAND MAY SEEM TO HAVE ON MAN TO USE IT. . . . . . 322 BUILD SOIL . . . 208
   TO USE THE GIFT YOU DO POSSESS, ... 326 TO A THINKER . . . 27
   AT LEAST DON'T USE YOUR MIND TOO HARD, ... 326 TO A THINKER . . . 35
   AND USE HIS HANDS IN FLIGHT. . . . . 341 THE SUBVERTED FLOWER . 63
   YOU MAY NOT WANT TO USE IT AND YOU MAY. . . . . . . 353 THE LESSON FOR TODAY . 86
   KING'S X--NO FAIRS TO USE IT ANYMORE! . . . . . . 399 U.S. 1946 KING'S X . . 4
   USE LANGUAGE WE CAN COMPREHEND. . . . . 403 SOMETHING LIKE A STAR . 14
   FROM ALL THIS WAGERY. BUT WHAT'S THE USE . . . . . 405 FROM PLANE TO PLANE . 31
   "BE CAREFUL HOW YOU USE YOUR INFLUENCE. . . . . . . 406 FROM PLANE TO PLANE . 66
   THEY WERE OF NO USE. . . . . 432 KITTY HAWK . . . 133
   FOR ALL THE USE YOU ARE ALONG THE STRAND. . . . . . 446 DOES NO ONE AT ALL EVER 20
   AND FIGURATIVE USE HAVE PRETTY WELL . . . . 488 A MASQUE OF REASON . 425
   WELL, I COULD USE A BOOK. / WHAT BOOK? / A BIBLE. . . . 494 A MASQUE OF MERCY . 27
   WHICH IS WHAT PEOPLE USE IT FOR TOO OFTEN-- . . . . 494 A MASQUE OF MERCY . 29
USED
   AND BROKEN IT, AND USED THEREFROM . . . . 21 THE TRIAL BY EXISTENCE 62
   GOOD ARGUMENTS HE SEES HE MIGHT HAVE USED. . . . . . 37 DEATH OF THE HIRED MAN 75
   HOW WE USED TO PICK BERRIES: WE TOOK ONE LOOK ROUND, . . 62 BLUEBERRIES 85
   WE USED TO LIVE--TEN MILES FROM ANYWHERE. . . . . . 64 A SERVANT TO SERVANTS . 63
   WHEN I WAS YOUNG. I USED TO USE THE ROAR . . . . . 78 THE GENERATIONS OF MEN 128
   THE WAY BEN FRANKLIN USED TO MAKE THE KITE STRING. . . . 94 THE SELF-SEEKER . . . 35
   THERE CAME A GUST. (YOU USED TO THINK THE TREES . . . 130 THE BONFIRE . . . 41
   IF IT DON'T TELL ME WHERE I AM. I USED . . . . . 144 SNOW 41
   NEW HAMPSHIRE USED TO HAVE AT SALEM . . . . . . 163 NEW HAMPSHIRE . . . 138
   HE WAS NOT USED TO HANDLING STARS THROWN DARK . . . . 172 A STAR IN A STONEBOAT . 8
   SHE USED HER HANDS TO COVER UP HER EYES. . . . . . 184 MAPLE 160
   USED THESE UNSCRUPULOUSLY TO BRING ME . . . . . . 188 THE AX-HELVE . . . 88
   AS THE MOON USED TO SEEM WHEN I WAS YOUNGER, ... 197 WILD GRAPES . . . 29
   HE ALWAYS USED TO SING ALONG THE TOTE ROAD. . . . . 205 THE WITCH OF COOS . 111
   WHO USED TO LIVE HERE. THEY WERE ROBINSONS. . . . . 215 A FOUNTAIN, A BOTTLE . 76
   OF CASTLES I USED TO BUILD IN AIR. . . . . 232 THE KITCHEN CHIMNEY . 20
   WITH WHAT THEY USED TO PAIR WITH BEFORE. . . . . . 265 THE DOOR IN THE DARK . 9
   HE TOOK THE PROPS DOWN USED FOR PROPPING OPEN, ... 289 OLD BARN AT THE BOTTOM 10
   BUT NO, THE COLOR USED IS RED. . . . . 327 A MISSIVE MISSILE . 13
   FOR A POEM THERE USED TO BE ON SPRING. . . . . . . 342 A CLOUD SHADOW . . 3
   WHO USED YOUR PASTURE FOR A CAMP. . . . . 380 AN UNSTAMPED LETTER IN 7
   ONE IN A CAVERN WHERE YOU USED TO COOK. . . . . . 382 TO AN ANCIENT . . . 6
   WHERE SOMEONE USED TO CLIMB AND CRAWL . . . . . . 392 A CLIFF DWELLING . . 8
   MY TONGUE'S MY OWN, AS TRUE THOMAS USED TO SAY. . . . . 505 A MASQUE OF MERCY . 296
USEFUL
   WELL, YES." / "HEAR ANYTHING THAT MIGHT PROVE USEFUL?" . 96 THE SELF-SEEKER . . 102
   "MAKE YOURSELF USEFUL, THEN, AND READ IT FOR ME.-- . . 99 THE SELF-SEEKER . . 188
   AND LEAVE IT THERE FAR FROM A USEFUL FIREPLACE . . . 102 THE WOOD-PILE . . . 38
   THEIR COMING OUT AND MAKING USEFUL FARMERS." . . . . 114 IN THE HOME STRETCH . 121
   THE COUNTRY'S ONLY USEFUL AS A PLACE . . . . . . 496 A MASQUE OF MERCY . 73
USHERED
   THAT USHERED IN THIS MODERN LENIENCE, ... 505 A MASQUE OF MERCY . 318
USING
   IN USING THE YARD TO BACK AND TURN AROUND; . . . . . 287 A ROADSIDE STAND . . 40
   USING NEITHER SPOON NOR SKIMMER, ... 303 CLEAR AND COLDER . . 5
   WOULD I GAIN ANYTHING BY USING RHYME? . . . . . . 382 TO AN ANCIENT . . . 17
   AND USING FOR APPAREL WHAT WAS MEANT . . . . . . 385 THE FEAR OF GOD . . 12
USUALLY
   ALTHOUGH IT WASN'T USUALLY LONG . . . . 192 PAUL'S WIFE . . . 28
UTAH
   IN THE DESERT AT MIDNIGHT IN UTAH, ... 290 ON HEART'S BEGINNING TO 2
UTMOST
   TO FIND THAT THE UTMOST REWARD . . . . 19 THE TRIAL BY EXISTENCE 7
   THE UTMOST STAR . . . . 219 I WILL SING YOU ONE-O . 62
   OR AT UTMOST A LITTLE RELUCTANT WHIRL . . . . . . 236 MISGIVING 11
UTOPIAN
   IS THAT IT? SOME UTOPIAN BELIEF-- . . . . 501 A MASQUE OF MERCY . 205
UTTER
   AND YOU, YOU... YOU, YOU UTTER.... . . . . . . 393 BEYOND WORDS . . . 3
   CAN EVER QUITE PASS OUT OF UTTER GRIEF . . . . . . 469 WE VAINLY WRESTLE... . 3
UTTERED
   UTTERED ALONE . . . . 219 I WILL SING YOU ONE-O . 61
   JUST AS HE WAS, WITHOUT AN UTTERED SOUND . . . . . 284 THE GOLD HESPERIDEE . 43
   IS JUST AS GOOD AS WHEN I UTTERED IT. . . . . . . 480 A MASQUE OF REASON . 196
UTTERLY
   AS OF ONE WHO UTTERLY COULDN'T CARE. . . . . . . 25 THE DEMIURGE'S LAUGH . 9
UTTERMOST
   AGAINST THE UTTERMOST OF EARTH. . . . . 21 THE TRIAL BY EXISTENCE 44

V

VACANT
   (SHE HAS HER OWN GLASS IN A VACANT CHAIR.) . . . . . 496 A MASQUE OF MERCY . . 84
VACILLATION
   TO PUT AN END TO THE KING'S VACILLATION. . . . . . 456 HOW HARD TO KEEP FROM 80
VAE
   THE ANDREW JACKSON SLOGAN OF VAE VICTIS . . . . . 510 A MASQUE OF MERCY . 459
VAGANT (SEE EXTRA-VAGANT)
VAGRANT
   WITH MISCHIEVOUS, VAGRANT, SERAPHIC LOOK, ... 16 IN NEGLECT 4
VAGUE
   EACH CIRCLING EACH WITH VAGUE UNEARTHLY CRY, ... 14 WAITING 12

VAGUE (CONTINUED)
    THE PATH WAS A VAGUE PARTING IN THE GRASS . . . . . . 55 THE BLACK COTTAGE . . 12
    AND A VAGUE ALL-DISTURBING ROAR ABOVE THE RIVER . . . . 182 MAPLE 83
    VAGUE DREAM-HEAD LIFTED OUT OF THE GROUND, ... 251 TREE AT MY WINDOW . .   5
    AND FOLLOWED IT TO WHERE HE MADE OUT VAGUE . . . . . . 270 THE EGG AND THE MACHINE 19
    AND SAIL FOR SOME VAGUE PAPHIAN BOURN . . . . 344 DISCOVERY OF MADEIRAS . 17
    IN HER VAGUE DESIGN . . . . 442 KITTY HAWK 453
VAGUELY
    IT CAME BACK VAGUELY AT THE GLASS ONE DAY, ... 181 MAPLE 40
    TO THE LAND VAGUELY REALIZING WESTWARD, ... 348 THE GIFT OUTRIGHT . . 14
    TO THE LAND VAGUELY REALIZING WESTWARD, ... 425 THE GIFT OUTRIGHT . . 14
VAGUER
    WITH AN EVER VAGUER AND VAGUER STIR, ... 236 MISGIVING 10
VAIN
    BUT IT WERE VAIN TO TELL HER SO, ...   7 MY NOVEMBER GUEST . . 19
    EXPEND THEIR BLOOM IN VAIN. . . . . 26 A LINE-STORM SONG . .   6
    POURED ON THEM BY HIS PRAYERS PRAYED IN VAIN. . . . . 173 A STAR IN A STONEBOAT . 24
    TO WISH IN VAIN TO LET GO WITH THE MIND-- . . . . . . 199 WILD GRAPES 101
    AND YET HE KNOWS OBSTRUCTION IS IN VAIN: . . . . 238 ON A TREE FALLEN ACROSS 9
    AS VAIN TO RAISE A VOICE AS A SIGH . . . . 247 ON GOING UNNOTICED . .   1
    OR THAT SHOWED WITH THE LAPSE OF TIME TOO VAIN . . . . 262 HANNIBAL   3
    THE THOUGHT OF SO MUCH CHILDISH LONGING IN VAIN, . . . 287 A ROADSIDE STAND . . 33
    THAT MEN HAVE THOUGHT ABOUT IN VAIN. . . . . 381 AN UNSTAMPED LETTER IN 37
    FROM HAVING BEATEN ALL DAY LONG IN VAIN . . . . 412 POD OF THE MILKWEED . 38
    SOWED IN VAIN BY RALEIGH, ... 431 KITTY HAWK 92
    'TWAS NO VAIN PURSUIT. . . . . 438 KITTY HAWK 320
    PROVE AS VAIN A HOP . . . . 439 KITTY HAWK 358
    IT MAKES US TO HAVE HAD A SEA IN VAIN. . . . . 446 DOES NO ONE AT ALL EVER 16
    ALL WAS IN VAIN, ... 449 THE BAD ISLAND--EASTER 47
VAINLY
    NO, NOT VAINLY THERE DID I DWELL, ... 16 IN A VALE 24
    NOR VAINLY LISTEN ALL THE NIGHT LONG. . . . . 16 IN A VALE 25
    WE VAINLY WRESTLE WITH THE BLIND BELIEF . . . . 469 WE VAINLY WRESTLE... .   1
    WE VAINLY WRESTLE... . . . . 469 WE VAINLY WRESTLE... .   T
VALE
    WHEN I WAS YOUNG, WE DWELT IN A VALE . . . . 15 IN A VALE   1
    IN A VALE . . . . 15 IN A VALE . . . . .   T
    OF FROSTY NIGHT AIR ON THE VALE BELOW . . . . 169 NEW HAMPSHIRE . . . 341
    HE RAN THROUGH THE VALE OF CASHMERE, ... 313 BEARER OF EVIL TIDINGS 10
VALENTINE
    YOU MUST HAVE READ THE FAMOUS VALENTINE . . . . 461 HOW HARD TO KEEP FROM 249
VALLACOLID
    HE MIGHT HAVE FOOLED VALLADOLID. . . . . 417 AMERICA IS HARD TO SEE 31
VALLEY
    AT WOODED VALLEY AND WOODED HILL. . . . . 23 PAN WITH US   5
    THAT THE BROOK RAISES IN THE EMPTY VALLEY. . . . . . . 77 THE GENERATIONS OF MEN 125
    "BUT WHAT ABOUT YOUR FLORA OF THE VALLEY?" . . . . . . 95 THE SELF-SEEKER . . . 80
    TO OTHER HILLS ACROSS A KETTLE VALLEY. . . . . 195 PAUL'S WIFE 126
    AND THERE IN A PRECIPICE VALLEY . . . . 313 BEARER OF EVIL TIDINGS 13
    (WE KNOW THE VALLEY STREAMS THAT WHEN AROUSED . . . . 378 DIRECTIVE 53
    LOOK DOWN THE LONG VALLEY AND THERE STANDS A MOUNTAIN . 379 TOO ANXIOUS FOR RIVERS 1
VALLEYS
    TO LEAVE IT TO THEM TO GET OUT OF THEIR VALLEYS. . . . 379 TOO ANXIOUS FOR RIVERS 7
VALLEY'S
    THE VALLEY'S SINGING DAY . . . . 235 VALLEY'S SINGING DAY . T
    THAT ONCE YOU HAD OPENED THE VALLEY'S SINGING DAY. . . 236 VALLEY'S SINGING DAY . 20
VALOR
    ON WAKING TO FIND VALOR REIGN, ... 19 THE TRIAL BY EXISTENCE   3
VALUE
    'TWAS NOT THE VALUE I STOOD TO LOSE . . . . 364 TRESPASS 13
    BY MAKING FAILURE OUT OF EQUAL VALUE. . . . . 513 A MASQUE OF MERCY . . 526
VALUED
    SHE VALUED THE CONSIDERATE NEGLECT . . . . 56 THE BLACK COTTAGE . . 41
    OF WHAT I VALUED MOST IN HUMAN NATURE. . . . . 485 A MASQUE OF REASON . . 350
VALUES
    NOT IF HE VALUES WHAT HE IS. GOD, I'D AS SOON . . . . . 71 THE CODE 69
VALUE'S
    I'VE COME TO THINK NO SO-CALLED HIDDEN VALUE'S . . . . 483 A MASQUE OF REASON . . 280
VANISH
    AND THE HOOFPRINTS VANISH AWAY. . . . . 26 A LINE-STORM SONG . .   4
VANISHED
    THAT VANISHED MANY A SUMMER AGO, ...   5 GHOST HOUSE   2
    IN THAT VANISHED ABODE THERE FAR APART . . . .   6 GHOST HOUSE 12
    AS RELIC OF A VANISHED RACE OF TREES-- . . . . 290 OLD BARN AT THE BOTTOM 39
    THAT VANISHED INTO THE BLACK . . . . 311 THE VINDICTIVES . . 35
VANISHING
    THE VANISHING RED . . . . 142 THE VANISHING RED . .   T
VANTAGE
    THE VANTAGE POINT . . . . 17 THE VANTAGE POINT . .   T
VAPOR
    TIME WAS WE WERE MOLTEN; TIME WAS WE WERE VAPOR. . . . 380 TOO ANXIOUS FOR RIVERS 21
    RELIGIOUS FAITH IS A MOST FILLING VAPOR. . . . . 386 INNATE HELIUM   1
VAPORS
    THIS IS NOT SORROW, THOUGH; IT'S JUST THE VAPORS, . . . 167 NEW HAMPSHIRE . . . 277
VARIED
    THAT VARIED IN THEIR HUE FROM RED TO GREEN. . . . . . . 178 THE STAR-SPLITTER . . 73
VARIES
    THAT VARIES WITH THE THINGS--BEFORE WE SEE THEM. . . . . 147 SNOW 128
VARIOUS
    AND BROUGHT OUR VARIOUS LIVES TO PASS. . . . . 265 THE BIRTHPLACE . . .   6
VARY
    THE LAND MAY VARY MORE; . . . . 301 NEITHER OUT FAR NOR IN   9
VARYING
    MY VARYING OPINION OF MYSELF . . . . 474 A MASQUE OF REASON . . 28
VASE
    A SHELF'S FOR A CLOCK OR VASE OR PICTURE, ... 232 THE KITCHEN CHIMNEY . 17
VASES
    A DEVELOPED TASTE IN VASES, ... 396 AN IMPORTER   8

VAST
  THE SOLID MOLDING OF VAST PEAKS OF CLOUD . . . . 169 NEW HAMPSHIRE   . . . 322
  WITH WHOSE VAST WHEELS . . . . 219 I WILL SING YOU ONE-O . 58
  WHOSE PROMINENCE HAS BEEN SO VAST. . . . . 390 TWO LEADING LIGHTS . .   3
  O OCEAN SEA, FOR ALL YOUR BEING VAST, ... 446 DOES NO ONE AT ALL EVER 1
  SO AMBITIOUSLY VAST, ... 447 THE BAD ISLAND--EASTER   2
VASTER
  RISE OTHERS VASTER YET, ... 260 SAND DUNES   3
VASTNESS
  INTO THEIR VASTNESS I SHOULD STEAL AWAY, ...   5 INTO MY OWN   . . .   6
VAULT
  WITH INTENT TO VAULT . . . . 436 KITTY HAWK   263
VAULTING
  IN A VAULTING MATCH, ... 436 KITTY HAWK   264
VAUNT
  THERE WERE SUNS OF STORY AND VAUNT . . . . 311 THE VINDICTIVES . . . 49
VEGETATION
  OR STAINED BY VEGETATION FROM ABOVE, ... 214 A FOUNTAIN, A BOTTLE . 39
VEHICLE
  AS SAFE A VEHICLE OF SEED . . . . 281 BLUE RIBBON AT AMESBURY 35
VEIL
  WHEN THE FROSTY WINDOW VEIL . . . . 10 WIND AND WINDOW FLOWER 5
  AND THEN TOOK THE VEIL AND WITHDREW, ... 266 SITTING BY A BUSH   . 14
VEIN
  LIKE HORACE IN THE TRUE HORATIAN VEIN, ... 353 THE LESSON FOR TODAY . 93
VELVET
  FRESH PAINTED BY THE SHOWER A VELVET BLACK. . . . . 55 THE BLACK COTTAGE . . 7
  UP THE BRASS BARREL, VELVET BLACK INSIDE, ... 179 THE STAR-SPLITTER . . 77
VENGEANCE
  MASS-PRODUCING WITH A VENGEANCE. . . . . 397 AN IMPORTER   24
VENTRILOQUIST
  PARTLY BECAUSE IT SANG VENTRILOQUIST . . . . 302 A BIRD SINGING IN SLEEP 5
VENTURE
  AND THOUGHT SHE WOULDN'T VENTURE ON SO MUCH. . . . . 97 THE SELF-SEEKER . . . 118
  TO MAKE THE VENTURE OF ETERNITY . . . . 356 A MOTH SEEN IN WINTER . 8
  FOR HER INVESTMENT IN HIS VENTURE. . . . . 416 AMERICA IS HARD TO SEE 12
  OUR VENTURE IN REVOLUTION AND OUTLAWRY . . . . . . 423 FOR JOHN F. KENNEDY . 51
  OUR INSTINCTIVE VENTURE . . . . 435 KITTY HAWK   214
  SHE WAS LEFT OVER FROM THE BROOK FARM VENTURE. . . . 494 A MASQUE OF MERCY . . 39
VENTURED
  IT VENTURED LESS IN PERIL THAN APPEARS. . . . . . . 302 A BIRD SINGING IN SLEEP 8
VENUS
  THE LITERATE FARMER AND THE PLANET VENUS . . . . . . 368 THE LITERATE FARMER AND T
VER
  AND VER ASPERGIT TERRAM FLORIBUS . . . . 351 THE LESSON FOR TODAY . 15
VERBATIM
  I QUOTE HIM WITH RESPECT VERBATIM. . . . . 451 A-WISHING WELL   . . . 6
VERDICT
  AND COME TO REST IN AN OFFICIAL VERDICT. . . . . . . 474 A MASQUE OF REASON . . 29
VERDURED
  THE HILLS ARE VERDURED PASTUREWISE; . . . . 19 THE TRIAL BY EXISTENCE 12
VERGE
  TO STAND TOGETHER ON THE CRATER'S VERGE . . . . . . 73 THE GENERATIONS OF MEN 16
  AND SO HE BROUGHT THEM TO THE VERGE OF FROST. . . . . 284 THE GOLD HESPERIDEE . 31
VERGES
  TO FLAMES WITHOUT TWICE THINKING, WHERE IT VERGES . . . 131 THE BONFIRE 59
VERIFIED
  I VERIFIED THE NAME NEXT MORNING: TOFFILE. . . . . . 207 THE WITCH OF COOS . . 154
  THE ISLAND HE FOUND WAS VERIFIED. . . . . 347 DISCOVERY OF MADEIRAS . 133
VERIFY
  HE SLAPPED HIS BREAST TO VERIFY HIS PURSE . . . . . 396 ANY SIZE WE PLEASE . . 13
VERILY
  I VERILY BELIEVE . . . . 333 HAPPINESS MAKES UP . . 18
VERITABLE
  THEY WEREN'T RED INDIANS BUT VERITABLE . . . . . . 161 NEW HAMPSHIRE   . . . 77
VERMONT
  IN POLITICS: I'M VERMONT DEMOCRAT-- . . . . 48 A HUNDRED COLLARS . . 109
  UNDER THE SUNSET FAR INTO VERMONT. . . . . 136 "OUT,OUT--"   6
  BUT SOON DIVIDES THE RIVER WITH VERMONT. . . . . . . 165 NEW HAMPSHIRE   . . . 185
  WILL SERVE ALMOST AS WELL ABOUT VERMONT, ... 165 NEW HAMPSHIRE   . . . 211
  THE VERMONT MOUNTAINS STRETCH EXTENDED STRAIGHT; . . . 165 NEW HAMPSHIRE   . . . 213
  RHODE ISLAND, NEW YORK, OR VERMONT WAS THIS: . . . . 167 NEW HAMPSHIRE   . . . 251
  AT PRESENT I AM LIVING IN VERMONT. . . . . 172 NEW HAMPSHIRE   . . . 413
  IN A VERMONT BEDROOM CLOSET . . . . 294 A RECORD STRIDE . . . 1
  ON BEING CHOSEN POET OF VERMONT . . . . 469 CHOSEN POET OF VERMONT   T
VERMONT'S
  VERMONT'S THE OTHER. AND THE TWO HAVE BEEN . . . . . 164 NEW HAMPSHIRE   . . . 176
VERNAL
  AND SMOOTH AND MOIST IN VERNAL HEAT. . . . . 276 TWO TRAMPS IN MUD TIME 48
VERSA
  ONE THICK WHERE ONE IS THIN AND VICE VERSA. . . . . . 164 NEW HAMPSHIRE   . . . 182
VERSE (SEE FREE-VERSE)
  (IN VERSE I THINK) AGAINST THE VOLSTEAD ACT. . . . . 160 NEW HAMPSHIRE   . . . 30
  HOW HAD THE TENDER VERSE ESCAPED THEIR OUTRAGE? . . . 216 A FOUNTAIN, A BOTTLE . 105
  VERSE COULD BE WRITTEN ON THE CERTAINTY . . . . . . 277 THE WHITE-TAILED HORNET 7
  AND SNATCHES OF VERSE AND SONG OF SCENES LIKE THIS . . 342 QUEST OF PURPLE-FRINGED 3
  THEY SLOWLY LED OLD LATIN VERSE TO RHYME . . . . . . 351 THE LESSON FOR TODAY . 16
  TO MAKE THEIR VERSE AND THEIR EXCUSES LAME. . . . . . 351 THE LESSON FOR TODAY . 33
  TO KEEP OUR ABSTRACT VERSE FROM BEING DRY. . . . . . 395 ETHEREALIZING . . . 14
  THIS VERSE THAT IN ACKNOWLEDGMENT I BRING . . . . . 422 FOR JOHN F. KENNEDY . 7
  OR MAKING VERSE IF THAT IS WHAT YOU'RE BENT ON. . . . 454 HOW HARD TO KEEP FROM 35
  HE WRITES FREE VERSE, I'M TOLD, AND HE IS THOUGHT . . 459 HOW HARD TO KEEP FROM 184
  FREE WILL, TRADE, VERSE, THOUGHT, LOVE, SPEECH, COINAGE. 459 HOW HARD TO KEEP FROM 186
  I WRITE REAL VERSE IN NUMBERS, AS THEY SAY. . . . . . 460 HOW HARD TO KEEP FROM 211
  I'M TALKING NOT FREE VERSE BUT BLANK VERSE NOW. . . . 460 HOW HARD TO KEEP FROM 212
  REGULAR VERSE SPRINGS FROM THE STRAIN OF RHYTHM . . . 460 HOW HARD TO KEEP FROM 213
  FREE VERSE LEAVES OUT THE METER AND MAKES UP . . . . 460 HOW HARD TO KEEP FROM 219
  FREE VERSE, SO CALLED, IS REALLY CHERISHED PROSE, . . . 460 HOW HARD TO KEEP FROM 221

VERSE (CONTINUED)
    WHEN HE FINDS HIS VERSE IS UNDERSTOOD . . . . 469 CHOSEN POET OF VERMONT .   2
VERSED
    THE NEED OF BEING VERSED IN COUNTRY THINGS . . . . . 241 NEED OF BEING VERSED .   T
    ONE HAD TO BE VERSED IN COUNTRY THINGS   . . . . . . 242 NEED OF BEING VERSED . 23
VERSES
    THE POETESS WHO WROTE THE BOOK OF VERSES . . . . . . 215 A FOUNTAIN, A BOTTLE . 78
    THE VERSES IN IT SAY AND SAY: . . . . 221 IN A DISUSED GRAVEYARD   5
VERSION
    VERSION . . . . 427 VERSION . . . . .   T
VERSUS
    LUCRETIUS VERSUS THE LAKE POETS . . . . 393 LUCRETIUS VERSUS POETS   T
VERY
    AND VERY BEAUTIFULLY GOD LIMNS, ... 20 THE TRIAL BY EXISTENCE   37
    HE NEVER DID A THING SO VERY BAD. . . . . 39 DEATH OF THE HIRED MAN 142
    "WHERE IS YOUR VILLAGE? VERY FAR FROM HERE?" . . . . 41 THE MOUNTAIN 23
    IT MAY NOT BE RIGHT ON THE VERY TOP: . . . . 42 THE MOUNTAIN 68
    I SAW YOU FROM THAT VERY WINDOW THERE, ... 53 HOME BURIAL 74
    "I CAN REPEAT THE VERY WORDS YOU WERE SAYING: . . . . 54 HOME BURIAL 91
    BUT HOW COULD THEY BE MADE SO VERY UNLIKE . . . . . . 57 THE BLACK COTTAGE . . 77
    I WOULD HAVE CHANGED THE CREED A VERY LITTLE? . . . . 57 THE BLACK COTTAGE . . 88
    YOU WILL DO VERY WELL RIGHT WHERE YOU ARE . . . . . . 78 THE GENERATIONS OF MEN 145
    "YOU MUST BE VERY STILL; YOU MUSTN'T TALK." . . . . . 78 THE GENERATIONS OF MEN 149
    "I DON'T SEE VERY WELL HOW YOU CAN HELP IT. . . . . . 79 THE GENERATIONS OF MEN 155
    "IT'S NOT SO VERY LATE--IT'S ONLY DARK. . . . . 90 THE FEAR   29
    THIS IS A VERY, VERY LONELY PLACE.-- . . . . 92 THE FEAR   90
    WE'RE VERY SORRY FOR YOU." / WILLIS SNEERED: . . . . 100 THE SELF-SEEKER . . 220
    OFF THERE UPSTAIRS. THE VERY TREAD OF MEN . . . . . 111 IN THE HOME STRETCH . 38
    OR BEING VERY YOUNG (AND HE WAS PLEASED . . . . . . 127 THE SMILE   9
    OUR VERY LIFE DEPENDS ON EVERYTHING'S . . . . 147 SNOW 132
    AND VERY SENSIBLE. NO STATE CAN BUILD . . . . 168 NEW HAMPSHIRE . . . 284
    THE VERY NATURE OF THE SOIL WAS HOT   . . . . 173 A STAR IN A STONEBOAT   21
    AN EMPTINESS FLAYED TO THE VERY STONE. . . . . 174 THE CENSUS-TAKER . 14
    REALLY A VERY FEW TO BUILD AND STAY. . . . . 239 OUR SINGING STRENGTH   24
    ACHIEVE AT TIMES A VERY STARLIKE START. . . . . . . 246 FIREFLIES IN THE GARDEN   5
    AND NOW THE VERY AIR, OF WHAT WE RIDE. . . . . 267 RIDERS   4
    THE FACTORY WAS VERY FINE; . . . . 274 A LONE STRIKER . . 50
    HOW LIKE A FLY, HOW VERY LIKE A FLY. . . . . 279 THE WHITE-TAILED HORNET 47
    IT IS VERY FAR NORTH, WE ADMIT, TO HAVE BROUGHT THE PEACH. . . 305 THERE ARE ROUGHLY ZONES   6
    A VERY SMALL MOON-MADE PRISMATIC BOW, ... 315 IRIS BY NIGHT . . 18
    HERE ON THIS VERY CAMPUS YEARS AGO. . . . . 316 BUILD SOIL   4
    TO KNOW IF ANYTHING IS VERY WRONG. . . . . 317 BUILD SOIL 56
    IT VERY LIKELY QUICKENS AND REFINES US. . . . . . . 321 BUILD SOIL 171
    AND BE SO VERY STRIKING. STEAL AWAY, ... 325 BUILD SOIL 278
    WERE DAYS SO VERY FEW . . . . 333 HAPPINESS MAKES UP .   8
    IN THE VERY HOUR . . . . 342 QUEST OF PURPLE-FRINGED 14
    SAY A FRACTION OF ONE PERCENT AT THE VERY LEAST, . . 349 OUR HOLD ON THE PLANET 16
    THE AGE MAY VERY WELL HAVE BEEN TO BLAME . . . . . . 351 THE LESSON FOR TODAY   26
    AND VERY WIDE THE CHOICE THEY SEEMED TO GIVE; . . . . 354 THE LESSON FOR TODAY . 137
    OF CAUTION UNDER STARS THAT VERY WELL . . . . 383 BRAVADO   2
    THE UNIVERSE MAY OR MAY NOT BE VERY IMMENSE. . . . . 389 SKEPTIC   9
    IT HAPPENED WOULD HAVE VERY MUCH TO SAY. . . . . . . 397 THE PLANNERS . . .   8
    THE MILKWEED BRINGS UP TO MY VERY DOOR . . . . 411 POD OF THE MILKWEED   5
    NEVER BELIEVE IT. AT THE VERY WORST . . . . 425 ACCIDENTALLY ON PURPOSE 13
    WHY WAS IT SO VERY, ... 430 KITTY HAWK . . . 61
    VERY NECESSARY . . . . 430 KITTY HAWK . . . 62
    OFF THIS VERY SHORE? . . . . 432 KITTY HAWK . . . 149
    WE'RE NOT VERY FAR . . . . 439 KITTY HAWK . . . 345
    SUCH AUSPICES ARE VERY HARD TO READ. . . . . 443 AUSPEX   5
    SO FAR INLAND THE VERY NAME OF OCEAN . . . . 447 DOES NO ONE AT ALL EVER 37
    YOU WOULDN'T SAY SHE FARED SO VERY BADLY. . . . . . . 477 A MASQUE OF REASON . 98
    THERE YOU GO ASKING FOR THE VERY THING . . . . 477 A MASQUE OF REASON . 105
    ALL VERY SPLENDID. I AM FLATTERED PROUD . . . . . . 481 A MASQUE OF REASON . 217
    FOR VERY LONG. WE'RE PLAINLY MADE TO GO. . . . . . . 481 A MASQUE OF REASON . 233
    THE DEVIL'S NEVER VERY FAR AWAY. . . . . 487 A MASQUE OF REASON . 382
    THAN ANYTHING. / HE'S VERY REAL TO ME . . . . 489 A MASQUE OF REASON . 434
    THIS VERY NIGHT. I HAD THE HALL ALL HIRED, ... 497 A MASQUE OF MERCY . 95
    HIS VERY WEAKNESS FOR MANKIND'S ENDEARING. . . . . . 505 A MASQUE OF MERCY . 309
    THE VERY SLEEP WE SLEEP IS AN EXAMPLE. . . . . 509 A MASQUE OF MERCY . 432
    TO EMBROIL THE VERY GODS ABOUT THEIR SPHERES . . . . 511 A MASQUE OF MERCY . 471
    OUR VERY BEST, OUR LIVES LAID DOWN LIKE JONAH'S, . . 520 A MASQUE OF MERCY . 720
VESTIGIAL
    WITH ONLY ONE VESTIGIAL CREATURE WISH: . . . . 395 ETHEREALIZING . . . 12
VESTRY-TREES
    REGULAR VESTRY-TREES WHOLE SUNDAY SCHOOLS . . . . . 107 CHRISTMAS TREES . . 53
VEXED
    I S'POSE YOU HAVE YOUR NOTIONS ON THE VEXED . . . . . 369 THE LITERATE FARMER AND 47
VEXES
    AND VEXES ME FOR REASON WHY. . . . .   7 MY NOVEMBER GUEST . . 15
VIA
    I THINK I GET IT VIA STORK . . . . 452 A-WISHING WELL . . 35
VICE
    ONE THICK WHERE ONE IS THIN AND VICE VERSA. . . . . . 164 NEW HAMPSHIRE . . . 182
VICIOUS
    THE BLINDMAN MISSED HIM WITH A BLOW SO VICIOUS . . . 394 HAEC FABULA DOCET . 12
VICTIS
    THE ANDREW JACKSON SLOGAN OF VAE VICTIS . . . . . . 510 A MASQUE OF MERCY . 459
VICTORIANS (SEE MID-VICTORIANS)
VICTORIES
    THAN LIFE'S VICTORIES OF DOUBT . . . . 212 AN EMPTY THREAT . . 55
VICTORY
    THE VICTORY FOR WHAT IT LOST AND GAINED. . . . . . . 222 TO E.T.   12
VIENNESE
    HE'S FREUDIAN VIENNESE BY NIGHT. . . . . 393 A CASE FOR JEFFERSON .   3
VIEW
    AND YET, IN VIEW OF HOW MANY THINGS, ...   6 GHOST HOUSE   29
    TO VIEW ONCE MORE THE SACRIFICE . . . . 20 THE TRIAL BY EXISTENCE 26
    BEFORE I CAME TO VIEW THE LEVELED SCENE. . . . . . . 22 THE TUFT OF FLOWERS .   4

VIEW (CONTINUED)
  I HAVE CLIMBED THE HILLS OF VIEW . . . . 30 RELUCTANCE 3
  "THERE OUGHT TO BE A VIEW AROUND THE WORLD . . . . . 42 THE MOUNTAIN . . . 55
  FROM THE WORLD'S VIEW TODAY OF ALL THOSE THINGS. . . . 57 THE BLACK COTTAGE . . 63
  ONE FOOT WENT THROUGH. THE VIEW WAS ALL IN LINES . . . 101 THE WOOD-PILE . . 5
  A VIEW." / "AND YET YOU THINK YOU LIKE IT, DEAR?" . . . 111 IN THE HOME STRETCH . 35
  AND TAKE A LIVELIER VIEW OF THINGS FROM HERE. . . . . 112 IN THE HOME STRETCH . 61
  THERE WAS A GATE I HAD LEANED AT FOR THE VIEW . . . . 118 MEETING AND PASSING . 2
  FROM THE BARE TOP OF WHICH THERE IS A VIEW . . . . . 195 PAUL'S WIFE . . . 125
  A HEAD THRUSTS IN AS FOR THE VIEW, ... 332 ALL REVELATION . . . 1
  OBSCURED FROM MORTAL VIEW-- . . . . 333 HAPPINESS MAKES UP . . 7
  WE MAY TAKE THE VIEW . . . . 436 KITTY HAWK . . . 251
VIEWED
  AND VIEWED IT OVER HIS GLASSES FUNNY-EYED, ... 190 THE GRINDSTONE . . . 70
  HE VIEWED THEM QUIZZICALLY WITH JERKS OF HEAD, ... 229 TWO LOOK AT TWO . . 31
VIEWING
  "FOR GOD'S SAKE, AREN'T YOU FOND OF VIEWING NATURE? . . 215 A FOUNTAIN, A BOTTLE . 56
VIEWS
  AND THERE'S MORE TO IT THAN JUST WINDOW VIEWS . . . . 67 A SERVANT TO SERVANTS . 155
VIGILANCE
  A NATURAL DEATH, AND VIGILANCE COMMITTEES . . . . . 159 NEW HAMPSHIRE . . . 19
VIGOR
  WITH HALF AN EAR TO THE PIANO'S VIGOR. . . . . . . 263 THE INVESTMENT . . 8
VILE
  AS A VILE RESIDUE, ... 449 THE BAD ISLAND--EASTER 44
VILEST
  YOU WERE BELITTLED INTO VILEST WORMS . . . . 352 THE LESSON FOR TODAY . 74
VILLAGE
  "WHERE IS YOUR VILLAGE? VERY FAR FROM HERE?" . . . . 41 THE MOUNTAIN 23
  "THERE IS NO VILLAGE--ONLY SCATTERED FARMS. . . . . 41 THE MOUNTAIN . . . 24
  TO THE VILLAGE, THROUGH PATTERSON'S PASTURE TODAY: . . 59 BLUEBERRIES . . . 2
  CATERWAUL TO THE HILLS AROUND THE VILLAGE . . . . . 94 THE SELF-SEEKER . . . 42
  DISTURBED THE SLUMBERING VILLAGE STREET . . . . . . 102 GOOD HOURS . . . 14
  A NEIGHBOR OF MINE IN THE VILLAGE . . . . 133 A GIRL'S GARDEN . . 1
  NOW WHEN SHE SEES IN THE VILLAGE . . . . 134 A GIRL'S GARDEN . . 41
  HOW VILLAGE THINGS GO, ... 134 A GIRL'S GARDEN . . 42
  HE SAYS HE LEFT THE VILLAGE STORE AT NINE: . . . . . 145 SNOW 57
  SHE SAID HE MIGHT ATTEND TO IN THE VILLAGE, ... 201 PLACE FOR A THIRD . . 54
  ENOUGH TO STOCK A VILLAGE LIBRARY-- . . . . 216 A FOUNTAIN, A BOTTLE . 98
  HIS HOUSE IS IN THE VILLAGE, THOUGH; . . . . 224 STOPPING BY WOODS . . 2
  UNDER THE HAND OF THE VILLAGE BARBER, ... 262 THE FLOWER BOAT . . 2
  SO THEY STAYED AND DECLARED A VILLAGE . . . . 314 BEARER OF EVIL TIDINGS 27
  OR OUTWARD FROM THE VILLAGE, ... 335 CARPE DIEM 4
  TO THE DARKENING, WINDY VILLAGE SLIP. . . . . . . 343 DISCOVERY OF MADEIRAS . 7
  OF COUNTRY WHERE TWO VILLAGE CULTURES FADED . . . . 378 DIRECTIVE 34
  CAME TAP-TAP-TAPPING DOWN THE VILLAGE STREET, ... 394 HAEC FABULA DOCET . . 3
  IT'S GREENWICH VILLAGE COCKTAIL-PARTY TALK-- . . . . 500 A MASQUE OF MERCY . . 170
VILLAGER
  ONE OUGHT AS A GOOD VILLAGER TO LIKE IT. . . . . . 94 THE SELF-SEEKER . . . 44
VILLAGES
  TO LIVE IN VILLAGES, NEXT TO THE THEATER AND STORE, . . 286 A ROADSIDE STAND . . 25
VIMY
  ON VIMY RIDGE; AND WHEN YOU FELL THAT DAY . . . . . 222 TO E.T. 14
VINDICATE
  AND VINDICATE THE STATE'S HUMANITY. . . . . 159 NEW HAMPSHIRE . . . 21
VINDICTIVES
  THE VINDICTIVES . . . . 310 THE VINDICTIVES . . . T
VINE
  AND ALDER AND GRAPE VINE ENTANGLEMENT, ... 131 THE BONFIRE 63
VINES
  AND THE SUN SHINES OUT WARM: THE VINES MUST BE WET. . . 62 BLUEBERRIES 83
  AND DANGLE FEET AMONG THE RASPBERRY VINES?" . . . . 75 THE GENERATIONS OF MEN 64
  FIRST LET ME LOOK. I SEE RASPBERRY VINES----" . . . 76 THE GENERATIONS OF MEN 97
  AND CARVED THEM ROUND WITH A SCROLL OF VINES. . . . . 347 DISCOVERY OF MADEIRAS . 124
VIOLA
  LIKE A VIOLA. I DON'T FOLLOW YOU." . . . . 75 THE GENERATIONS OF MEN 54
VIOLENCE
  BECAUSE HIS VIOLENCE TOOK ON THE FORM . . . . . . 66 A SERVANT TO SERVANTS . 106
  OF OUTRAGE--VIOLENCE--THAT BREAKS ACROSS IT. . . . . 509 A MASQUE OF MERCY . 431
  WITH VIOLENCE. THE GREEKS WERE HARDLY STRANGERS . . . 511 A MASQUE OF MERCY . 468
  TO THE IDEA OF VIOLENCE. IT FLOURISHED, ... 511 A MASQUE OF MERCY . 469
VIOLENTLY
  BEFORE THE DOOR'S SO VIOLENTLY TRIED . . . . 493 A MASQUE OF MERCY . . 6
VIOLETS
  BLOODROOT, AND VIOLETS SO SOON TO BE NOW. . . . . . 131 THE BONFIRE 52
VIOLIN
  HE STUDIED LATIN, LIKE THE VIOLIN, ... 37 DEATH OF THE HIRED MAN 80
  I HAD THE SOUND OF A VIOLIN; . . . . 102 GOOD HOURS 6
VIRGIL'S
  FOR YOUR NOT HAVING WON TO VIRGIL'S FAME. . . . . . 351 THE LESSON FOR TODAY . 27
VIRGIN
  IN VIRGIN WRAPPER FROM DEEP IN THE BOX, ... 217 A FOUNTAIN, A BOTTLE . 126
VIRGINIA
  IN MASSACHUSETTS, IN VIRGINIA, ... 348 THE GIFT OUTRIGHT . . 4
  IN MASSACHUSETTS, IN VIRGINIA, ... 424 THE GIFT OUTRIGHT . . 4
VIRTUALLY
  SO SMALL AS TO BE VIRTUALLY GONE, ... 368 THE LITERATE FARMER AND 15
VIRTUE
  I MAKE A VIRTUE OF MY SUFFERING . . . . 166 NEW HAMPSHIRE . . . 237
  A VIRTUE IN WHICH WE ALL MAY SHARE . . . . 376 SOMETHING FOR HOPE . . 19
  AS A SMALL SELF-CONFERRED REWARD OF VIRTUE. . . . . 405 FROM PLANE TO PLANE . 39
  VIRTUE MAY FAIL AND WICKEDNESS SUCCEED. . . . . . . 475 A MASQUE OF REASON . 52
  AND IF IT DID, IT WOULDN'T BE A VIRTUE. . . . . . . 485 A MASQUE OF REASON . 355
VIRTUOSITY
  YOU'RE SO LOST IN THE VIRTUOSITY . . . . 503 A MASQUE OF MERCY . 259
VISIBLY
  AND NOT DISFIGURED VISIBLY. HIS FACE? . . . . . . 230 NOT TO KEEP 7

PAGE TITLE   LINE

VISION
    LIKE TWO KINDS OF JEWELS, A VISION FOR THIEVES." . . . . . 62 BLUEBERRIES 105
    TO HAVE A VISION OF US OLD AND DEAD). . . . . 127 THE SMILE 10
    I HAD A VISION OF THEM PUT TOGETHER . . . . 204 THE WITCH OF COOS . . 68
VISIONARY
    YOU CAN'T CLAIM YOU'RE A SOCIAL VISIONARY." . . . . . . 406 FROM PLANE TO PLANE . 79
VISIONS
    WE HAVE SEEN VISIONS--NOW CONSULT THE VOICES. . . . . . 77 THE GENERATIONS OF MEN 126
    VISIONS OF HALF THE WORLD BURNED BLACK . . . . . . 140 THE GUM-GATHERER . . 23
    FOR THE VISIONS IN THE SKY . . . . 469 FOUR-ROOM SHACK.... . 3
VISIT
    FOR A FRIENDLY VISIT. . . . . 124 A TIME TO TALK . . . 10
    WHAT DID HE COME IN FOR?--TO TALK AND VISIT? . . . . . 155 SNOW 339
    HAD YOU IN MIND TO VISIT ON THE CITY, ... 502 A MASQUE OF MERCY . 224
VISITED
    OR MILK THE COW, HE VISITED THE FRUIT, ... 283 THE GOLD HESPERIDEE . 20
VISITING
    HAS BROUGHT HER MERELY VISITING, ... 390 TWO LEADING LIGHTS . 26
    OF VISITING WITH THE EQUALLY BEWILDERED. . . . . . . 414 A CABIN IN THE CLEARING 8
VISITOR
    THESE DOORSTEPS SELDOM HAVE A VISITOR. . . . . . . 56 THE BLACK COTTAGE . 48
    THAT'S WHEN I WENT AS VISITOR TO HIS HOUSE. . . . . . 278 THE WHITE-TAILED HORNET 22
    AS VISITOR AT MY HOUSE HE IS BETTER. . . . . . . 278 THE WHITE-TAILED HORNET 23
VITAL
    WHAT THEY HAD NEVER HAD OF VITAL BLISS. . . . . . 397 THE PLANNERS 3
VITRIOL
    OF VITRIOL OR ARSENATE OF LEAD, ... 164 NEW HAMPSHIRE . . 161
VIVE
    "AH," HE SAID, "QUI VIVE, ... 468 A REFLEX 8
VIVID
    SO VIVID AS TO SEEM TO SPEAK. . . . . 327 A MISSIVE MISSILE . . 8
VIZIER (SEE MINISTER-VIZIER)
VOCATION
    MY AVOCATION AND MY VOCATION . . . . 277 TWO TRAMPS IN MUD TIME 67
VOICE
    AND A VOICE THAT HAS SOUNDED IN MY ROOM . . . . . . 15 IN A VALE 8
    TO WHICH YOU GIVE THE ASSENTING VOICE." . . . . . 21 THE TRIAL BY EXISTENCE 56
    THEN YOU CAME IN. I HEARD YOUR RUMBLING VOICE . . . . 53 HOME BURIAL . . . 81
    FOR WHEN YOU MADE ANSWER, YOUR VOICE WAS AS LOW . . . 62 BLUEBERRIES 95
    THAN I CAN RAISE MY VOICE OR WANT TO LIFT . . . . 63 A SERVANT TO SERVANTS . 8
    AND HIS VOICE DIED DOWN SLOWLY FROM EXHAUSTION. . . . . 66 A SERVANT TO SERVANTS . 133
    OR IT WOULD SPEAK IN DIALECT. WHOSE VOICE . . . . . 79 THE GENERATIONS OF MEN 173
    SHE RAISED HER VOICE AGAINST THE CLOSING DOOR: . . . . 89 THE HOUSEKEEPER . . . 213
    AND THEN THE VOICE AGAIN: "YOU SEEM AFRAID. . . . . 91 THE FEAR 72
    "YOU SEE," THE VOICE SAID. / "OH." SHE LOCKED AND LOOKED. . 92 THE FEAR 78
    IN A LOW VOICE SAID, "OH, ... 135 LAST WORD OF A BLUEBIRD 2
    MRS. COLE'S VOICE CAME FROM AN INNER ROOM: . . . . . 152 SNOW 271
    AND THEN HER VOICE CAME SCRAPING SLOW: 'OH, YOU, ... 153 SNOW 290
    SOME DAY WHEN THEY ARE IN VOICE . . . . 156 THE SOUND OF TREES . 21
    I CALLED THE FIREMAN WITH A CAREFUL VOICE . . . . . 234 EVENING A SUGAR ORCHARD 3
    AS VAIN TO RAISE A VOICE AS A SIGH . . . . . . 247 ON GOING UNNOTICED . . 1
    NO VOICE IN NATURE IS HEARD TO CRY ALOUD . . . . . 249 ACCEPTANCE 3
    THE VOICE SAID, "HURL HER DOWN!" . . . . . . 255 THE LOVELY BE CHOOSERS 1
    THE VOICE ASKED, "YOU CAN LET HER CHOOSE?" . . . . 256 THE LOVELY BE CHOOSERS 19
    OR SO THE VOICE OF THE COUNTRY SEEMS TO COMPLAIN. . . . 287 A ROADSIDE STAND . 46
    VOICE WAYS . . . . 301 VOICE WAYS . . . . T
    FOR ALL THE VOICE IN ANSWER HE COULD WAKE . . . . . 338 THE MOST OF IT . . 2
    FROM HAVING HEARD THE DAYLONG VOICE OF EVE . . . . . 338 NEVER WOULD BIRDS' SONG 3
    MOREOVER HER VOICE UPON THEIR VOICES CROSSED . . . . . 339 NEVER WOULD BIRDS' SONG 10
    A VOICE SAID, LOOK ME IN THE STARS . . . . . . 362 A QUESTION 1
    (HE TRIED TO IMITATE DICK'S TONE OF VOICE.) . . . . 406 FROM PLANE TO PLANE . 73
    WHY GO ON FURTHER WITH CONFUSING VOICE . . . . . 427 CONCEPT SELF-CONCEIVED 6
    VOICE THAT SAID, "GET SET . . . . 436 KITTY HAWK . . . 271
    REGION VOICE SAID, "GO, ... 436 KITTY HAWK . . . 278
VOICE-LIKE
    THERE'S NOTHING BUT A VOICE-LIKE LEFT INSIDE . . . . 63 A SERVANT TO SERVANTS . 13
VOICES
    FROM WHICH THE LABORERS' VOICES LATE HAVE DIED, ... 14 WAITING 4
    WE HAVE SEEN VISIONS--NOW CONSULT THE VOICES. . . . . 77 THE GENERATIONS OF MEN 126
    TO SET THE VOICES SPEAKING OUT OF IT, ... 78 THE GENERATIONS OF MEN 129
    THE VOICES GIVE YOU WHAT YOU WISH TO HEAR." . . . . 78 THE GENERATIONS OF MEN 137
    I'LL TELL YOU WHAT THE VOICES REALLY SAY. . . . . 78 THE GENERATIONS OF MEN 144
    OR I CAN'T GIVE MYSELF TO HEAR THE VOICES." . . . . 78 THE GENERATIONS OF MEN 147
    "I'LL HARDLY BREATHE." / "THE VOICES SEEM TO SAY----" . . 78 THE GENERATIONS OF MEN 150
    "I'M WAITING." / "DON'T! THE VOICES SEEM TO SAY: . . . 78 THE GENERATIONS OF MEN 151
    YOU WANT THE TRUTH. I SPEAK BUT BY THE VOICES. . . . 79 THE GENERATIONS OF MEN 156
    "I SHALL SUSPECT----" / "BE GOOD. THE VOICES SAY: . . . 79 THE GENERATIONS OF MEN 159
    THE VOICES, "HOW FAR DOWN?" . . . . 255 THE LOVELY BE CHOOSERS 2
    "TRUST US," THE VOICES SAID. . . . . 257 THE LOVELY BE CHOOSERS 53
    MOREOVER HER VOICE UPON THEIR VOICES CROSSED . . . . 339 NEVER WOULD BIRDS' SONG 10
    VOICES CONFLICTING LIKE THE CANDIDATES. . . . . . 368 THE LITERATE FARMER AND 4
VOID
    TO FILL THE ABYSS'S VOID WITH EMPTINESS. . . . . . 259 WEST-RUNNING BROOK . . 49
    THAN AS WATCHER OF THE VOID, ... 383 MAKING CERTAIN ANYTHING 2
VOLCANO
    LET'S ALL BUT BRING TO LIFE THIS OLD VOLCANO, ... 130 THE BONFIRE 16
VOLSTEAD
    (IN VERSE I THINK) AGAINST THE VOLSTEAD ACT. . . . . 160 NEW HAMPSHIRE . . . 30
VOLUMES
    HOW ARE THEIR VOLUMES FALLEN! / ONLY ONE! . . . . 504 A MASQUE OF MERCY . 291
VOTE
    THE GREATEST VOTE A PEOPLE EVER CAST, ... 423 FOR JOHN F. KENNEDY . 55
VOTED
    VOTED THE ONLY TIMES HE EVER VOTED, ... 208 PAUPER WITCH OF GRAFTON 21
VOTERS
    WE WERE BUT SIXTY VOTERS LAST ELECTION. . . . . . 41 THE MOUNTAIN . . . 25
VOTES
    OF COATS, OATS, VOTES, TO ALL MANKIND. . . . . . 450 OUR DOOM TO BLOOM . . 9

VOTING
   FOREVER VOTING AND HARANGUING FOR IT. . . . . 461 HOW HARD TO KEEP FROM   229
VOTIVE   (SEE SACRIFICIAL—VOTIVE)
VOUCHSAFE
   IT WOULDN'T HURT YOU TO VOUCHSAFE THE FAITHFUL. . . . . 478 A MASQUE OF REASON . . 143
VOUCHSAFED
   AS IS VOUCHSAFED TO FEATHERED BREED. . . . . 281 BLUE RIBBON AT AMESBURY 36
   AND THEN WE WERE VOUCHSAFED THE MIRACLE . . . . . . 315 IRIS BY NIGHT . . . 20
VOW
   I VOW WE MUST BE NEAR THE PLACE FROM WHERE . . . . . 214 A FOUNTAIN, A BOTTLE . 51
   TILL THE PIRATE SAILORS MADE A VOW . . . . 344 DISCOVERY OF MADEIRAS . 24
VOWED
   IN GRATITUDE FOR WHICH SQUARE MATTHEW VOWED . . . . . 285 THE GOLD HESPERIDEE . 59
VOYAGE
   THE TALE OF THE VOYAGE HE HAD ACHIEVED, ... 347 DISCOVERY OF MADEIRAS . 130

W

WAGE
   TO WAGE A FINE SCHOLASTICAL CONTENTION . . . . . 352 THE LESSON FOR TODAY . 51
   CAN NEVER HOPE TO WAGE A GLOBAL MISSION. . . . . . . 398 NO HOLY WARS FOR THEM . 12
WAGERY
   FROM ALL THIS WAGERY. BUT WHAT'S THE USE . . . . . . 405 FROM PLANE TO PLANE . 31
WAGES
   ANY FIXED WAGES, THOUGH I WISH I COULD.' . . . . . . 35 DEATH OF THE HIRED MAN   23
WAGGED
   TELL ME WHAT IS IT?" / ANNE JUST WAGGED HER DRESS, . . 96 THE SELF-SEEKER . . . 105
WAGON
   BRING BERRIES UNDER THE WAGON SEAT, ... 141 THE GUM-GATHERER . . 26
   BESIDES THE WEAR OF IRON WAGON WHEELS . . . . 377 DIRECTIVE 14
WAIF
   HURRYING LOW ABOVE THE GROVE, SOME WAIF . . . . . . 249 ACCEPTANCE 9
WAIL
   TO THE DREARY WAIL . . . . 429 KITTY HAWK 29
WAIST
   A MAN? A BRUTE. NAKED ABOVE THE WAIST, ... 46 A HUNDRED COLLARS . . 50
   SHE WAS STANDING TO THE WAIST . . . . 339 THE SUBVERTED FLOWER . 15
   WITH A LENGTH OF CORDAGE ABOUT THE WAIST. . . . . . 346 DISCOVERY OF MADEIRAS . 77
WAIT
   (AND WAIT TO WATCH THE WATER CLEAR, I MAY): . . . . . 1 THE PASTURE 3
   WAIT TILL YOU SEE." / "WHERE DID YOU SAY HE'D BEEN?" . . 35 DEATH OF THE HIRED MAN   39
   AND HAD FOUR HOURS TO WAIT AT WOODSVILLE JUNCTION . . 45 A HUNDRED COLLARS . . 16
   I'LL PUT THE LIGHT OUT. DON'T YOU WAIT FOR ME: . . . . 50 A HUNDRED COLLARS . . 171
   BUT WAIT UNTIL I GIVE YOU A HAND UP. . . . . 77 THE GENERATIONS OF MEN 121
   HE WON'T BE LONG IN THAT CASE. YOU CAN WAIT. . . . . 81 THE HOUSEKEEPER . . . 18
   "WELL, WAIT--IT'S COMMON--IT'S TOO COMMON." / "COMMON? . 97 THE SELF-SEEKER . . . 141
   "WELL, ANNE, GO, DEARIE. OUR AFFAIR WILL WAIT. . . . . 98 THE SELF-SEEKER . . . 167
   THAT WAS A THING WE COULD NOT WAIT TO LEARN. . . . . 109 THE EXPOSED NEST . . 26
   WITH PITCHY HANDS TO WAIT FOR RAIN OR SNOW. . . . . 129 THE BONFIRE 4
   OH, LET'S NOT WAIT FOR RAIN TO MAKE IT SAFE. . . . . 129 THE BONFIRE 5
   FOR WHAT THEY'D BETTER WAIT TILL WE HAVE DONE. . . . 130 THE BONFIRE 15
   "WAIT AND HE MAY. LET'S SEE WHAT HE WILL DO. . . . . 145 SNOW 76
   "AND LEAVE THE CHILDREN?" / "WAIT AND CALL AGAIN. . . 154 SNOW 307
   AND HE COULD WAIT--WE'D SEE TO HIM TOMORROW. . . . . 177 THE STAR-SPLITTER . . 42
   IN WAIT FOR HER THERE. SHE READ EVERY WORD . . . . . 181 MAPLE 64
   BUT NO, NOT YET. A SNORT TO BID THEM WAIT. . . . . . 229 TWO LOOK AT TWO . . . 26
   YOU'LL WAIT A LONG, LONG TIME FOR ANYTHING MUCH . . . 268 ON LOOKING UP BY CHANCE 1
   ALL PACKED IN SAND TO WAIT THE TRUMP TOGETHER. . . . 270 THE EGG AND THE MACHINE 26
   WAIT AND WATCH THE LIQUOR SETTLE. . . . . 304 CLEAR AND COLDER . . 19
   WE MUST WAIT TILL SOME MONTHS HENCE IN THE SPRING TO KNOW. . 305 THERE ARE ROUGHLY ZONES 19
   I WAIT FOR FORM. . . . . 308 PERTINAX 3
   IT NEEDN'T WAIT ON GENERAL REVOLUTION. . . . . . . 324 BUILD SOIL 265
   BUT THOUGH WE ALL MAY BE INCLINED TO WAIT . . . . . 355 THE LESSON FOR TODAY . 141
   THEN ALL THERE IS TO DO IS WAIT . . . . 376 SOMETHING FOR HOPE . . 5
   YOU WAIT! . . . . 393 BEYOND WORDS . . . 4
   WHY WAIT FOR SCIENCE TO SUPPLY THE HOW . . . . . . 395 WHY WAIT FOR SCIENCE . 9
   WHY WAIT FOR SCIENCE . . . . 395 WHY WAIT FOR SCIENCE . T
   ALL THAT CAN WAIT FOR THE LIGHT OF DAY. . . . . . . 420 ONE MORE BREVITY . . 33
   TO SEE HOW LONG THEY SHOULD WAIT . . . . 466 SOME SCIENCE FICTION . 31
   I HAVE TO WAIT FOR WORDS LIKE ANYONE. . . . . . . 475 A MASQUE OF REASON . . 58
   GOOD, PRETTY GOOD. / WAIT TILL I GET MY KODAK.-- . . . 488 A MASQUE OF REASON . . 402
WAITED
   SLIPPED TO HER SIDE, CAUGHT UP HER HAND AND WAITED. . . 40 DEATH OF THE HIRED MAN 165
   MIND YOU, I WAITED TILL LEN SAID THE WORD. . . . . . 67 A SERVANT TO SERVANTS . 149
   HE SAT AND WAITED TILL HE DREW US OUT, ... 106 CHRISTMAS TREES . . 7
   HE WAITED (THEY WERE STRANGERS) . . . . 335 CARPE DIEM 6
   THEY WAITED IN THE STREET, ... 391 A ROGERS GROUP . . . 2
   THEY WAITED ON WAS WRONG. . . . . 391 A ROGERS GROUP . . . 8
   THAT WAITED FOR THE BOTTOM TO FERMENT . . . . 468 IN A GLASS OF CIDER . 2
   I'D CATCH ANOTHER BUBBLE IF I WAITED. . . . . . . 468 IN A GLASS OF CIDER . 7
WAITING
   WAITING . . . . 14 WAITING . . . . . T
   WAITING FOR WARREN. WHEN SHE HEARD HIS STEP, ... 34 DEATH OF THE HIRED MAN   2
   AND SORT OF WAITING TO BE ASKED ABOUT IT, ... 72 THE CODE 82
   "I'M WAITING." / "DON'T! THE VOICES SEEM TO SAY: . . . 78 THE GENERATIONS OF MEN 151
   WAITING TO STEAL A STEP ON US WHENEVER . . . . . . 114 IN THE HOME STRETCH . 116
   SHE MUST NOT KEEP HIM WAITING. TIME WOULD PRESS . . . 201 PLACE FOR A THIRD . . 68
   WAITING FOR THINGS TO HAPPEN IN THEIR FAVOR. . . . . 204 THE WITCH OF COOS . . 63
   THE MOON WAS WAITING FOR HER CHILL EFFECT. . . . . 237 A HILLSIDE THAW . . 25
   WAITING WAS TO BRING, ... 426 A NEVER NAUGHT SONG . 14
   BY WAITING UP INSTEAD OF GETTING UP. . . . . . . 496 A MASQUE OF MERCY . . 72
WAITS
   THAT WAITS ALL DAY IN ALMOST OPEN PRAYER . . . . . 287 A ROADSIDE STAND . . 35
WAIVE
   AS TO WHAT REASONS I AGREE TO WAIVE. . . . . . . 479 A MASQUE OF REASON . . 167

WAIVED
    ITS SEPARATENESS FROM HEAVEN COULD BE WAIVED; . . . . . . 353 THE LESSON FOR TODAY . 101
    I WAIVED THE REASON FOR MY ORDEAL--BUT-- . . . . . . 479 A MASQUE OF REASON . 170
WAKE
    WHY, I MIGHT WAKE HER UP AND STARTLE HER. . . . . . 58 THE BLACK COTTAGE . 93
    AND GONE TO SLEEP, SHE NEEDN'T WAKE TO ANSWER." . . . 143 SNOW . . 14
    TO MAKE IT WORTH LIFE'S WHILE TO WAKE AND SPORT. . . . 254 A WINTER EDEN . . 20
    FOR ALL THE VOICE IN ANSWER HE COULD WAKE . . . . 338 THE MOST OF IT . . . 2
WAKED
    WE'VE WAKED HER UP. / I HAVEN'T BEEN ASLEEP. . . . . 487 A MASQUE OF REASON . 395
WAKENED
    A BIRD HALF WAKENED IN THE LUNAR NOON . . . . . . 302 A BIRD SINGING IN SLEEP   1
WAKENING
    THAT MADE ME HEAR THE WAKENING BIRDS AROUND, ... 23 THE TUFT OF FLOWERS . 31
WAKES
    FOR THE WOOD WAKES, AND YOU ARE HERE FOR PROOF. . . . 16 A DREAM PANG . . . 14
WAKING
    ON WAKING TO FIND VALOR REIGN, ... 19 THE TRIAL BY EXISTENCE   3
    ALL UP AND DOWN IT. SO THAT WAKING THERE . . . . 290 OLD BARN AT THE BOTTOM 25
    LIKE WAKING IN A CAGE OF SILVER BARS. . . . . . 290 OLD BARN AT THE BOTTOM 27
    THIS I SAW WHEN WAKING LATE, ... 292 ON HEART'S BEGINNING TO 42
WALK
    A LATE WALK . . . . 8 A LATE WALK . . . . T
    AND ON A DAY WE MEET TO WALK THE LINE . . . . . 33 MENDING WALL . . . 13
    "CAN ONE WALK AROUND IT? WOULD IT BE TOO FAR?" . . . 43 THE MOUNTAIN . . 92
    OF AT LEAST ONE LONG-AFTER-BEDTIME WALK. . . . . 92 THE FEAR . . . 83
    SOMEWHERE TO WALK----" / "THE HIGHWAY, AS IT HAPPENS-- 92 THE FEAR . . . 85
    SO MANY MILES YOU MIGHT HAVE WALKED YOU WON'T WALK. . 93 THE SELF-SEEKER . . 12
    THE DOCTOR'S SURE YOU'RE GOING TO WALK AGAIN?" . . . 93 THE SELF-SEEKER . . 15
    WHETHER HE'S EVER GOING TO WALK AGAIN. . . . . 100 THE SELF-SEEKER . . 202
    I HAD FOR MY WINTER EVENING WALK-- . . . . . 102 GOOD HOURS . . . 1
    "WHEN I WAS JUST AS FAR AS I COULD WALK . . . . 118 THE TELEPHONE . . 1
    AND SLOWS HIS HORSE TO A MEANING WALK, ... 124 A TIME TO TALK . . 2
    THE BOARD WE HAD LAID DOWN TO WALK DRY-SHOD ON . . 204 THE WITCH OF COOS . 48
    TO SEE HOW THEY WERE MOUNTED FOR THIS WALK. . . 204 THE WITCH OF COOS . 67
    TO WALK A GRAVER MAN RESTRAINED IN WRATH. . . . 285 THE GOLD HESPERIDEE . 60
    AND TAKE YOUR WALK OF RECREATION BACK . . . . 405 FROM PLANE TO PLANE . 42
    TO WALK IN SAYING NAUGHT . . . . 415 CLOSED FOR GOOD . . 14
    WE PROLONGED THE WALK, ... 433 KITTY HAWK . . . 163
    EVEN AT A WALK. . . . . 439 KITTY HAWK . . . 349
    AND WALK THE REST OF THE WAY. . . . . . . 444 THE DRAFT HORSE . . 20
    TO TAKE LIFE AT A WALK . . . . 465 SOME SCIENCE FICTION . 7
    (TAKING A WALK OFF DOWN THE STORE DISTRESSED) . . . 503 A MASQUE OF MERCY . 267
WALKED
    YOU WALKED A WAY BESIDE ME . . . . 12 FLOWER-GATHERING . 3
    SILAS HAS WALKED THAT FAR NO DOUBT TODAY. . . . 38 DEATH OF THE HIRED MAN 127
    WHEN I WALKED FORTH AT DAWN TO SEE NEW THINGS, . . . 40 THE MOUNTAIN . . 8
    SO MANY MILES YOU MIGHT HAVE WALKED YOU WON'T WALK. . 93 THE SELF-SEEKER . . 12
    I WALKED DOWN ALONE SUNDAY AFTER CHURCH . . . . 123 PEA BRUSH . . . 1
    AS I WALKED ONCE AROUND IT IN POSSESSION. . . . 130 THE BONFIRE . . 39
    I WALKED SO LIGHT ON AIR IN HEAVY SHOES . . . . 132 THE BONFIRE . . 92
    OF WATER WE WALKED ALONG BESIDE. . . . . . 140 THE GUM-GATHERER . 8
    AND WALKED OFF, TALKING TO HERSELF OR PAUL, . . 195 PAUL'S WIFE . . 120
    I HAVE WALKED OUT IN RAIN--AND BACK IN RAIN. . . 255 ACQUAINTED WITH NIGHT . 2
    HOW ONCE SHE WALKED IN BRIGHTNESS, ... 257 THE LOVELY BE CHOOSERS 33
    HAVE I NOT WALKED WITHOUT AN UPWARD LOOK . . . 383 BRAVADO . . . 1
    BUT THEY HAD NOT WALKED FAR INTO THE NIGHT . . . 454 HOW HARD TO KEEP FROM 12
WALKING
    "OUT WALKING. EVERY CHILD SHOULD HAVE THE MEMORY . 92 THE FEAR . . . 82
    OUT WALKING IN THE FROZEN SWAMP ONE GRAY DAY, . . 101 THE WOOD-PILE . . 1
    HE MADE IN WALKING SLOWLY TO THE BEACH . . . 194 PAUL'S WIFE . . 99
    BY WALKING SLOWLY ON SOME EVENING LATER . . . 245 THE FREEDOM OF THE MOON 8
    HE KNEW A PATH THAT WANTED WALKING; . . . . 274 A LONE STRIKER . . 43
    ABOUT WHO IS TOO OLD TO GO WALKING, ... 294 A RECORD STRIDE . 11
    YOU CALL THIS THINKING, BUT IT'S WALKING. . . . 325 TO A THINKER . . 5
    OR THE WIND TO SNAP THEIR WALKING STICK, . . . 344 DISCOVERY OF MADEIRAS 29
    NOW I OUT WALKING . . . . 412 AWAY! 1
WALKS
    SHE WALKS THE SODDEN PASTURE LANE. . . . . . . 6 MY NOVEMBER GUEST . . 5
WALL
    A TREE BESIDE THE WALL STANDS BARE, ... 9 A LATE WALK . . . 9
    SWING THE PICTURE ON THE WALL; . . . . . . 11 TO THE THAWING WIND . 12
    FOR THE GRAPES' SAKE ALONG THE WALL, ... 28 OCTOBER . . . 21
    SOMETHING THERE IS THAT DOESN'T LOVE A WALL, . . 33 MENDING WALL . . . 1
    MENDING WALL . . . . 33 MENDING WALL . . . T
    AND SET THE WALL BETWEEN US ONCE AGAIN. . . . . 33 MENDING WALL . . 14
    WE KEEP THE WALL BETWEEN US AS WE GO. . . . . 33 MENDING WALL . . 15
    THERE WHERE IT IS WE DO NOT NEED THE WALL: . . . 33 MENDING WALL . . 23
    BEFORE I BUILT A WALL I'D ASK TO KNOW . . . . 34 MENDING WALL . . 32
    SOMETHING THERE IS THAT DOESN'T LOVE A WALL, . . 34 MENDING WALL . . 35
    NEAR ME IT SEEMED: I FELT IT LIKE A WALL. . . . 40 THE MOUNTAIN . . 5
    AND THEN THERE WAS A WALL OF TREES WITH TRUNKS; . 41 THE MOUNTAIN . . 30
    YOU HAD STOOD THE SPADE UP AGAINST THE WALL . . . 54 HOME BURIAL . . 87
    UNDER A CRAYON PORTRAIT ON THE WALL. . . . . 55 THE BLACK COTTAGE . 23
    "THERE ARE BEES IN THIS WALL." HE STRUCK THE CLAPBOARDS, 59 THE BLACK COTTAGE . 125
    THE FIRE RAN AND BURNED IT ALL UP BUT THE WALL." . . 59 BLUEBERRIES . . . 12
    AND OVER THE WALL AND INTO THE ROAD, ... 60 BLUEBERRIES . . . 36
    WHY NOT TAKE SEATS HERE ON THE CELLAR WALL . . . 75 THE GENERATIONS OF MEN 63
    HIS ICICLES ALONG THE WALL TO KEEP; . . . . 108 OLD MAN'S WINTER NIGHT 22
    A CANNON-MOUTH-LIKE HOLE WAS IN THE WALL, . . . 113 IN THE HOME STRETCH . 84
    AS I WENT DOWN THE HILL ALONG THE WALL . . . 118 MEETING AND PASSING . 1
    WALL WITHIN WALL TO SHUT FEAR OUT. . . . . . 120 BOND AND FREE . . . 3
    AND PLOD: I GO UP TO THE STONE WALL . . . . 124 A TIME TO TALK . . 9
    TO MAKE NO MORE OF A WALL THAN AN OPEN GATE, . . 124 THE COW IN APPLE TIME . 2
    TO SAY SO OR BE STOOD AGAINST THE WALL . . . 168 NEW HAMPSHIRE . . 281
    HAS BEEN PICKED UP WITH STONES TO BUILD A WALL. . . 172 A STAR IN A STONEBOAT . 3
    A LITTLE MORGAN HAD ONE FOREFOOT ON THE WALL, . . 223 THE RUNAWAY . . . 3
    AND MOUNTS THE WALL AGAIN WITH WHITED EYES . . . 223 THE RUNAWAY . . . 16

WALL (CONTINUED)
I'D SUMMON GROUSE, RABBIT, AND DEER TO THE WALL . . . . 228 GOOD-BY AND KEEP COLD . 10
WHEN THEY WERE HALTED BY A TUMBLED WALL . . . . . . 229 TWO LOOK AT TWO . . . 7
ACROSS THE WALL, AS NEAR THE WALL AS THEY. . . . . . 229 TWO LOOK AT TWO . . . 16
SHE SIGHED AND PASSED UNSCARED ALONG THE WALL. . . . . 229 TWO LOOK AT TWO . . . 24
ACROSS THE WALL, AS NEAR THE WALL AS THEY. . . . . . 229 TWO LOOK AT TWO . . . 28
THEN HE TOO PASSED UNSCARED ALONG THE WALL. . . . . 230 TWO LOOK AT TWO . . . 37
WHO NOW WOULD FAIN SEEK SHELTERING WALL . . . . . . 236 MISGIVING 7
BUT WHERE THIS OLD WALL BURNS A SUNNY CHEEK, ... 246 ATMOSPHERE 2
INSCRIPTION FOR A GARDEN WALL . . . . 246 ATMOSPHERE 5
STRUNG CHAINS OF WALL ROUND EVERYTHING, ... 265 THE BIRTHPLACE . . . 4
HER NEXT STEP ROCKS A BOULDER ON THE WALL . . . . . 268 THE BEAR 5
HE LEANS AGAINST THE DUSTY WALL . . . . 280 BLUE RIBBON AT AMESBURY 21
HE MUST HAVE MEASURED TO THE FURTHER WALL. . . . . . 292 FIGURE IN THE DOORWAY . 9
AND FOR BACK WALL A CRUMBLING OLD CHIMNEY . . . . . 294 A RECORD STRIDE . . 3
A SCENT OF RIPENESS FROM OVER A WALL. . . . . . . 304 UNHARVESTED 1
TO THE TOP OF HIS REACH ON THE WALL . . . . 310 THE VINDICTIVES . . 4
FROM INSIDE THE GARDEN WALL . . . . 340 THE SUBVERTED FLOWER . 36
A WALL TOO HARD FOR CRIME . . . . 348 TRIPLE BRONZE . . . 7
HOW ONCE IN CUTTING BRUSH ALONG THE WALL . . . . . 375 A YOUNG BIRCH . . . 12
SOME HALFWAY UP THE LIMESTONE WALL, ... 392 A CLIFF DWELLING . . 5
TO REAR AGAINST THE INSCRIPTION ON THE WALL. . . . . 399 THE INGENUITIES OF DEBT 18
A CHEER WENT UP THAT SHOOK THE MOTTOED WALL. . . . . 400 THE BROKEN DROUGHT . 6
I HAVE HAD PAINTED ON THE CELLAR WALL . . . . . . 516 A MASQUE OF MERCY . . 615
WALL-BUILDERS
AND THINK NO MORE OF WALL-BUILDERS THAN FOOLS. . . . 124 THE COW IN APPLE TIME . 3
WALLED
SO DESERT IT WOULD HAVE TO BE, SO WALLED . . . . . 58 THE BLACK COTTAGE . . 115
WALLED-OFF
OF WALLED-OFF GROUND WHERE A SHOP HAD STOOD, . . . 133 A GIRL'S GARDEN . . . 11
WALLER
AS WALLER SAYS. / OR NOT ADMIRED. GO OVER . . . . 474 A MASQUE OF REASON . . 31
WALLING
WHAT I WAS WALLING IN OR WALLING OUT, ... 34 MENDING WALL 33
WALLOW
THE DEMON AROSE FROM HIS WALLOW TO LAUGH, ... 25 THE DEMIURGE'S LAUGH . 10
THE REST IS DOWN.--WHY NO, NO, NOT A WALLOW: . . . 143 SNOW 23
AND DROPPED IT IN, AND SEEN THE IMAGE WALLOW, . . . 245 THE FREEDOM OF THE MOON 11
WALLPAPER
THROWN FROM SOMEWHERE AGAINST THEIR WALLPAPER. . . . 129 THE BONFIRE 12
WALLS
AND LEFT NO TRACE BUT THE CELLAR WALLS, ... 5 GHOST HOUSE 3
THE GRAY OF THE MOSS OF WALLS WERE THEY-- . . . . . 23 PAN WITH US 3
AND OVER THE WALLS I HAVE WENDED; . . . . 29 RELUCTANCE 2
OVER STONE WALLS AND ALL ALONG A WOOD . . . . . . 98 THE SELF-SEEKER . . . 152
'CROSS LOTS, 'CROSS WALLS, 'CROSS EVERYTHING, . . . 137 BROWN'S DESCENT . . 7
WALLS WERE ALL BURIED, TREES WERE FEW: . . . . . 137 BROWN'S DESCENT . . 13
FROM FOLLOWING WALLS I NEVER LIFT MY EYE, ... 173 A STAR IN A STONEBOAT . 40
I MUST GO MEASURING STONE WALLS, PERCH ON PERCH; . . 173 A STAR IN A STONEBOAT . 45
THAT THERE ALWAYS IS ON THE PAPERED WALLS, ... 232 THE KITCHEN CHIMNEY . 14
BEHIND NEW BARRIER WALLS (AND LET IT CHAFE!), . . . 254 THE FLOOD 3
THAN WHEN ITS WALLS ROSE HIGHER THAN ANY ROOF. . . . 306 NOT QUITE SOCIAL . . 8
THERE SCARCELY IS A LIGHT IN ALL ITS WALLS, ... 336 THE FEAR OF MAN . . 8
WALNUT
"WHERE WILL I PUT THIS WALNUT BUREAU, LADY?" . . . . 110 IN THE HOME STRETCH . 13
WAMPUM
WAMPUM, I CALL IT. MIND, WE DON'T COMPLAIN. . . . . 86 THE HOUSEKEEPER . . . 153
WAND
AND A GEM-FLOWER WAVED IN A WAND! . . . . 29 MY BUTTERFLY 37
IN SUMMERTIME WITH A WITCHING WAND, ... 276 TWO TRAMPS IN MUD TIME 34
WANDER
SOMETIMES I WANDER OUT OF BEATEN WAYS . . . . . . 125 AN ENCOUNTER 23
WANDERED
WE PICKED, TILL I FEARED YOU HAD WANDERED A MILE, . . 62 BLUEBERRIES 92
THEN I AROSE AND SILENTLY WANDERED HOME, ... 343 QUEST OF PURPLE-FRINGED 25
WANDERER
CIRCUITOUS WANDERER," AND "TOOK DEJECTEDLY . . . . 171 NEW HAMPSHIRE . . . 384
WANDERING
THOU DIDST NOT KNOW, WHO TOTTERED, WANDERING ON HIGH, . 28 MY BUTTERFLY 22
WOODSVILLE'S A PLACE OF SHRIEKS AND WANDERING LAMPS . 45 A HUNDRED COLLARS . . 21
WANDERING TO AND FRO . . . . 428 KITTY HAWK 12
AND GIVE YOU REST, POOR WANDERING JEW. / I'M NOT . . 498 A MASQUE OF MERCY . . 133
THE WANDERING JEW--I'M WHO I SAY I AM, ... 498 A MASQUE OF MERCY . . 134
WANE
THEY STARTED TO WANE. . . . . 448 THE BAD ISLAND--EASTER 40
WANT
"I WANT HIM TO: HE'LL HAVE TO SOON OR LATE." . . . 35 DEATH OF THE HIRED MAN 32
"WARREN!" / "BUT DID HE? I JUST WANT TO KNOW." . . . 36 DEATH OF THE HIRED MAN 47
"I SHOULDN'T CLIMB IT IF I DIDN'T WANT TO-- . . . . 43 THE MOUNTAIN . . . 89
MY BUSINESS IS TO FIND WHAT PEOPLE WANT: . . . . . 48 A HUNDRED COLLARS . . 103
BECAUSE I WANT THEIR DOLLAR? I DON'T WANT . . . . 50 A HUNDRED COLLARS . . 151
I DON'T WANT YOU SHOULD SHOOT ME IN THE HEAD.-- . . . 50 A HUNDRED COLLARS . . 176
FROM UP THERE ALWAYS?--FOR I WANT TO KNOW." . . . . 51 HOME BURIAL 7
THAN I CAN RAISE MY VOICE OR WANT TO LIFT . . . . 63 A SERVANT TO SERVANTS 8
IT'S REST I WANT--THERE, I HAVE SAID IT OUT-- . . . 64 A SERVANT TO SERVANTS 49
IT'S NOT THAT LEN DON'T WANT THE BEST FOR ME. . . . 64 A SERVANT TO SERVANTS 60
AFFECTION OR THE WANT OF IT IN THAT STATE. . . . . 65 A SERVANT TO SERVANTS 102
I DIDN'T WANT THE BLAME IF THINGS WENT WRONG. . . . 67 A SERVANT TO SERVANTS 150
IF YE WANT HIM, YE CAN GO AND DIG HIM OUT.' . . . . 72 THE CODE 85
YOU WANT THE TRUTH. I SPEAK BUT BY THE VOICES. . . . 79 THE GENERATIONS OF MEN 156
YOU SAY YOU DON'T KNOW WHERE SHE IS." / "NOR WANT TO! . 83 THE HOUSEKEEPER . . 73
ISN'T IT HELL?" HE SAID. "I WANT TO KNOW. . . . . 88 THE HOUSEKEEPER . . 207
COME OUT HERE IF YOU WANT TO HEAR ME TALK.-- . . . 88 THE HOUSEKEEPER . . 208
GIVE ME THE LANTERN." / "YOU DON'T WANT THE LANTERN." . 90 THE FEAR 33
"WHAT DO YOU WANT?" SHE CRIED TO ALL THE DARK. . . . 91 THE FEAR 61
WHAT DO YOU WANT?" SHE CRIED, AND THEN HERSELF . . . 91 THE FEAR 65
"WILLIS, I DIDN'T WANT YOU HERE TODAY: . . . . . 92 THE SELF-SEEKER . . 1
I WANT TO SEE YOU DO IT. WHEN'S HE COMING?" . . . . 93 THE SELF-SEEKER . . 7

WANT (CONTINUED)

	PAGE TITLE	LINE
I WANT THIS OVER WITH; I'M HOT AND TIRED."	94 THE SELF-SEEKER	50
IT'S THAT OR FIGHT, AND I DON'T WANT TO FIGHT--	95 THE SELF-SEEKER	75
I JUST WANT TO GET SETTLED IN MY LIFE,	95 THE SELF-SEEKER	76
PROMISE ME ALL THE SHOOKS I WANT TO NAIL."	95 THE SELF-SEEKER	79
WHAT DO YOU WANT, DEAR? COME, STAND BY THE BED;	96 THE SELF-SEEKER	104
WHERE YOU CAN'T MAKE THEM. WHAT IS IT YOU WANT?	99 THE SELF-SEEKER	185
WHERE I COME IN IS WHAT I WANT TO KNOW.	100 THE SELF-SEEKER	210
GO OUTDOORS IF YOU WANT TO FIGHT. SPARE ME.	100 THE SELF-SEEKER	212
WHATEVER ELSE WE WANT FOR. AND A LIGHT.	113 IN THE HOME STRETCH	79
YOU DON'T WANT ME TO TELL IF I DON'T KNOW."	116 IN THE HOME STRETCH	169
"I DON'T WANT TO FIND OUT WHAT CAN'T BE KNOWN.	116 IN THE HOME STRETCH	170
"COME, JOHN," HE SAID, "YOU WANT TO SEE THE WHEEL PIT?"	142 THE VANISHING RED	19
I WANT YOU HERE WITH ME, FRED.--LEAVE HIM HERE,	144 SNOW	36
"NONSENSE TO THAT! YOU WANT TO SEE HIM SAFE."	146 SNOW	93
"I SHOULDN'T WANT TO HURRY YOU, MESERVE,	148 SNOW	153
AND BEING WHERE YOU ARE. YOU WANT TO STAY."	150 SNOW	200
YOUR WIFE--SHE DOESN'T WANT YOU TO. WE DON'T.	151 SNOW	234
AND YOU YOURSELF DON'T WANT TO. WHO ELSE IS THERE?"	151 SNOW	235
"YES, I SUPPOSE YOU'LL WANT TO, BUT I SHOULDN'T.	152 SNOW	263
I WANT TO SPEAK TO HER." / "ALL SHE SAID WAS,	152 SNOW	276
IT'S STRANGE SHE DOESN'T WANT TO SPEAK TO US.	154 SNOW	314
"I'M GOING TO PUT YOU OFF THIS FARM: I WANT IT."	164 NEW HAMPSHIRE	154
TO WANT TO MAKE NEW HAMPSHIRE PEOPLE OVER.	167 NEW HAMPSHIRE	263
FROM NOTHING BUT EMBARRASSMENT AND WANT.	168 NEW HAMPSHIRE	291
THE MORE I SEEM TO WANT MY MOUNTAINS WILD;	170 NEW HAMPSHIRE	344
IT MUST BE I WANT LIFE TO GO ON LIVING.	176 THE CENSUS-TAKER	64
"WHAT DO YOU WANT WITH ONE OF THOSE BLAME THINGS?"	177 THE STAR-SPLITTER	20
TO WANT TO FIND OUT IF HE COULDN'T PILE	193 PAUL'S WIFE	60
YOU WOULDN'T WANT TO TELL HIM WHAT WE HAVE	203 THE WITCH OF COOS	19
UP ATTIC THAT WE'D EVER WANT AGAIN.	206 THE WITCH OF COOS	122
THAT IS, IF FACTS IS WHAT THEY WANT TO GO BY.	207 PAUPER WITCH OF GRAFTON	11
"SO'S EVERYTHING." / "I WANT MY FOUNTAIN."	214 A FOUNTAIN, A BOTTLE	44
IF YOU DON'T WANT TO SPEND THE NIGHT OUTDOORS.	214 A FOUNTAIN, A BOTTLE	50
I WANT TO INTRODUCE YOU TO THE PEOPLE	215 A FOUNTAIN, A BOTTLE	75
"WHY NOT TAKE TWO OR THREE?" / "TAKE ALL YOU WANT.	217 A FOUNTAIN, A BOTTLE	124
I DON'T WANT IT GIRDLED BY RABBIT AND MOUSE,	228 GOOD-BY AND KEEP COLD	6
I DON'T WANT IT DREAMILY NIBBLED FOR BROWSE	228 GOOD-BY AND KEEP COLD	7
BY DEER, AND I DON'T WANT IT BUDDED BY GROUSE.	228 GOOD-BY AND KEEP COLD	8
I DON'T WANT IT STIRRED BY THE HEAT OF THE SUN.	228 GOOD-BY AND KEEP COLD	12
I WANT TO TELL THEM THAT WITH ALL THIS SMOKE	248 THE COCOON	12
I WANT TO GET OUT OF THE TRAIN AND GO BACK	248 A PASSING GLIMPSE	3
FOR WANT OF HIS APPROVAL, WHY,	275 A LONE STRIKER	61
YOU HAVE THE MONEY, BUT IF YOU WANT TO BE MEAN,	286 A ROADSIDE STAND	14
IT WAS NOT NECESSARILY FROM WANT.	292 FIGURE IN THE DOORWAY	14
AND THE REST WON'T WANT TO PUNISH ME TOO SEVERELY	306 NOT QUITE SOCIAL	2
TO SEEK WHAT THEY SEEMED SO TO WANT.	311 THE VINDICTIVES	44
WAS THAT IN WHAT SHE DOES NOT WANT	344 DISCOVERY OF MADEIRAS	42
DON'T TELL ME IF YOU DON'T WANT TO, THEN."	346 DISCOVERY OF MADEIRAS	95
HE THOUGHT, ALL RIGHT, IF YOU WANT THE TRUTH!	346 DISCOVERY OF MADEIRAS	97
YOU MAY NOT WANT TO USE IT AND YOU MAY.	353 THE LESSON FOR TODAY	86
TO EXPRESS HOW MUCH IT DIDN'T WANT TO DIE.	357 A CONSIDERABLE SPECK	18
AND FOR WANT OF BOOKS RECITE.	384 IN THE LONG NIGHT	6
TODAY I WANT TO TALK ABOUT THE SUN.	406 FROM PLANE TO PLANE	87
TO THANK HIM FOR. HE DOESN'T WANT OUR THANKS.	408 FROM PLANE TO PLANE	129
MAKE EVERYBODY WANT TO BE A NATION.	423 FOR JOHN F. KENNEDY	31
IN ANY GAME THE NATIONS WANT TO PLAY.	424 FOR JOHN F. KENNEDY	75
WE WOULD WANT TO TOUCH,	438 KITTY HAWK	331
I WANT HIM TO BE ANYTHING HE HAS TO.	459 HOW HARD TO KEEP FROM	181
BUT THAT IS AS DARIUS SEEMS TO WANT IT.	462 HOW HARD TO KEEP FROM	264
I WANT TO ASK YOU IF IT STANDS TO REASON	476 A MASQUE OF REASON	88
YOU'D BE THE LAST TO WANT ME TO BELIEVE	482 A MASQUE OF REASON	258
IF YOU DON'T WANT TO. I DON'T WANT TO KNOW.	483 A MASQUE OF REASON	271
I WANT YOU IN MY GROUP BESIDE THE THRONE--	489 A MASQUE OF REASON	456
TRUST ME TO HELP YOU FIND THE BOOK YOU WANT.	495 A MASQUE OF MERCY	50
I'D WANT TO BE MORE CERTAIN I WAS CALLED,	503 A MASQUE OF MERCY	270
YOU WOULDN'T WANT THE NIGHT CLUBS LAUGHING AT YOU.	504 A MASQUE OF MERCY	275
SOME PEOPLE WANT YOU NOT TO UNDERSTAND THEM,	510 A MASQUE OF MERCY	452
BUT I WANT YOU TO UNDERSTAND ME WRONG.	510 A MASQUE OF MERCY	453
YOU'VE FINISHED. I'M DISMISSED. I WANT TO RUN	514 A MASQUE OF MERCY	544

WA'N'T

IF HE WA'N'T KEPT STRICT WATCH OF, AND IT ENDED	66 A SERVANT TO SERVANTS	112
HE WA'N'T BUT FIFTEEN AT THE TIME THEY SAY.	208 PAUPER WITCH OF GRAFTON	19
IT WA'N'T NO SIGN, I S'POSE, WHEN MALLICE HUSE	208 PAUPER WITCH OF GRAFTON	45

WANTED

HE WANTED TO GO OVER THAT. BUT MOST OF ALL	37 DEATH OF THE HIRED MAN	85
I WANTED TO TRY SOMETHING WITH THE NOISE	77 THE GENERATIONS OF MEN	124
WHAT'S WANTED AND HOW MUCH AND WHERE IT IS.	82 THE HOUSEKEEPER	33
AND IF TO SEE WAS WHAT HE WANTED, WHY,	91 THE FEAR	57
"I WANTED THERE SHOULD BE SOME THERE NEXT YEAR."	97 THE SELF-SEEKER	123
BECAUSE IT WAS GRASSY AND WANTED WEAR;	105 THE ROAD NOT TAKEN	8
YOU WANTED TO RESTORE THEM TO THEIR RIGHT	109 THE EXPOSED NEST	17
WHAT WE HAVE ALWAYS WANTED, I CONFESS	115 IN THE HOME STRETCH	127
"IT'S ALL SO MUCH WHAT I HAVE ALWAYS WANTED,	116 IN THE HOME STRETCH	164
I CAN'T BELIEVE IT'S WHAT YOU WANTED, TOO."	116 IN THE HOME STRETCH	165
IF IT IS WHAT YOU WANTED, THEN HOW MUCH	116 IN THE HOME STRETCH	167
YOU WANTED IT FOR ME." / "A TROUBLED CONSCIENCE!	116 IN THE HOME STRETCH	168
WANTED ME TO BRING WORD	135 LAST WORD OF A BLUEBIRD	8
I DON'T KNOW WHAT SHE WANTED IT TO MEAN,	180 MAPLE	20
LUCKILY ALL SHE WANTED ALL HER NAME THEN	180 MAPLE	30
OF WHERE ELIZA WANTED NOT TO LIE,	201 PLACE FOR A THIRD	45
SHE WANTED TO DO RIGHT. SHE'D HAVE TO THINK.	201 PLACE FOR A THIRD	49
I WANTED TO PUT OUT THE LIGHT AND SEE	205 THE WITCH OF COOS	104
SHE HADN'T FOUND THE FINGER-BONE SHE WANTED	207 THE WITCH OF COOS	152
TO SEE IF THE TOWN WANTED TO TAKE OVER	208 PAUPER WITCH OF GRAFTON	24
HE KNEW A PATH THAT WANTED WALKING;	274 A LONE STRIKER	43
HE KNEW A SPRING THAT WANTED DRINKING;	274 A LONE STRIKER	44
A THOUGHT THAT WANTED FURTHER THINKING;	274 A LONE STRIKER	45

WANTED (CONTINUED)
  A LOVE THAT WANTED RE-RENEWING. . . . . 274 A LONE STRIKER . . . 46
  HE WANTED TO TAKE MY JOB FOR PAY. . . . . 275 TWO TRAMPS IN MUD TIME   8
  THE GREAT TREASURE WANTED THE MOST, ... 312 THE VINDICTIVES . . . 62
  AND WANTED SOMEONE NOW TO KNOW . . . . 327 A MISSIVE MISSILE . . 17
  WANTED US TO GET DOWN . . . . 444 THE DRAFT HORSE . . . 19
  TO AVOID WHAT HE WASN'T SURE HE WANTED. . . . . 453 HOW HARD TO KEEP FROM   5
  BUT IF OVER THE MOON I HAD WANTED TO GO . . . . 463 LINES IN DEJECTION . . 9
  THE WORD I WANTED. YOU WOULD HAVE SUPPOSED . . . 475 A MASQUE OF REASON . . 55
  I WANTED HIM FORCED TO ACKNOWLEDGE SO MUCH. . . 486 A MASQUE OF REASON . . 359
WANTING
  NOR IS THERE WANTING IN THE PRESS . . . . 20 THE TRIAL BY EXISTENCE 41
  IN WANTING TO SILENCE ANY SONG. . . . . 251 A MINOR BIRD   8
WANTON
  THE THEME OF WANTON WASTE IN PEACE AND WAR . . . 411 POD OF THE MILKWEED .   6
WANTS
  THAT WANTS IT DOWN." I COULD SAY "ELVES" TO HIM, 34 MENDING WALL 36
  "LAFE, HERE'S A FELLOW WANTS TO SHARE YOUR ROOM." 45 A HUNDRED COLLARS . . 36
  WHO WANTS TO CUT YOUR NUMBER FOURTEEN THROAT! . . 47 A HUNDRED COLLARS . . 84
  SHE WANTS OUR HENS TO BE THE BEST THERE ARE. . . 85 THE HOUSEKEEPER . . . 118
  "WHO WANTS TO HEAR YOUR NEWS, YOU--DREADFUL FOOL?" 89 THE HOUSEKEEPER . . . 214
  HE WANTS TO GIVE ME LOTS AND LOTS OF MONEY . . . 98 THE SELF-SEEKER . . . 169
  OF WHAT WANTS PRUNING, SHINGLING, BREAKING UP. . 115 IN THE HOME STRETCH . 150
  IT WANTS TO SEE HOW YOU WILL TAKE; IF BACKWARD, . 147 SNOW 123
  "BUT WHY, WHEN NO ONE WANTS YOU TO, GO ON? . . . 151 SNOW 233
  THAT WANTS ME AS A WAR MIGHT IF IT CAME. . . . . 151 SNOW 241
  SHE HAS HIM, THEN, THOUGH WHAT SHE WANTS HIM FOR 155 SNOW 334
  MAYBE SHE ONLY WANTS HIM FOR THE CHILDREN." . . 155 SNOW 336
  HE WANTS TO GIVE THE EDUCATIONAL . . . . 162 NEW HAMPSHIRE . . . 103
  OF DOOR AND HEADBOARD. WHERE IT WANTS TO GET . . 203 THE WITCH OF COOS . . 25
  HE WOULD CRY OUT ON LIFE, THAT WHAT IT WANTS . . 338 THE MOST OF IT . . .   6
  A WOMAN WANTS TO BE OVERRULED. . . . . 344 DISCOVERY OF MADEIRAS 43
  BUT WANTS IT ALL MADE OVER NEW. . . . . 393 A CASE FOR JEFFERSON   2
  SHE WANTS TO KNOW WHY THERE IS STILL INJUSTICE. . 477 A MASQUE OF REASON . . 110
  KEEPER, BE STILL. HE KNOWS WHAT BOOK HE WANTS. . 495 A MASQUE OF MERCY . . 51
  MERCY, FOR MERCY'S SAKE! / BEL WANTS SOME MERCY.-- 507 A MASQUE OF MERCY . . 345
WAR
  "THAT WAS THE FATHER AS HE WENT TO WAR. . . . . 55 THE BLACK COTTAGE . . 25
  SHE ALWAYS, WHEN SHE TALKED ABOUT THE WAR, . . . 56 THE BLACK COTTAGE . . 26
  WHATEVER ELSE THE CIVIL WAR WAS FOR, ... 56 THE BLACK COTTAGE . . 55
  SHE HAD SUPPOSED THE WAR DECIDED THAT. . . . . . 57 THE BLACK COTTAGE . . 79
  WHAT WOULD YOU SAY TO WAR IF IT SHOULD COME? . . 132 THE BONFIRE 97
  ABOUT THE SHIPS WHERE WAR HAS FOUND THEM OUT . . 132 THE BONFIRE 104
  AT SEA, ABOUT THE TOWNS WHERE WAR HAS COME . . . 132 THE BONFIRE 105
  WAR IS FOR EVERYONE, FOR CHILDREN TOO. . . . . . 133 THE BONFIRE 111
  THAT WANTS ME AS A WAR MIGHT IF IT CAME. . . . . 151 SNOW 241
  THE WAR SEEMED OVER MORE FOR YOU THAN ME, . . . 222 TO E.T. 15
  WEAPONS OF WAR AND IMPLEMENTS OF PEACE . . . . . 255 THE FLOOD 10
  HE TOLD THE DISTANCE, "I AM ARMED FOR WAR. . . . 270 THE EGG AND THE MACHINE 28
  (LIKE WAR AND PESTILENCE . . . . 282 A DRUMLIN WOODCHUCK . 23
  AS THEY SAY IN WAR. . . . . 306 A TRIAL RUN   9
  OF ONCE HAVING STARTED A WAR, ... 310 THE VINDICTIVES . . . 16
  (THE DEED OF GIFT WAS MANY DEEDS OF WAR) . . . . 348 THE GIFT OUTRIGHT . . 13
  INCLUDING HUMAN NATURE, IN PEACE AND WAR, . . . 349 OUR HOLD ON THE PLANET 14
  WHICH MAKES THE WAR GOD SEEM NO SPECIAL DUNCE . . 350 TO A YOUNG WRETCH . . 17
  A SORDID PEACE OR AN OUTRAGEOUS WAR. . . . . . . 352 THE LESSON FOR TODAY . 56
  OF EITHER MURDER OR WAR IN ANY LAND. . . . . . . 371 THE LITERATE FARMER AND 111
  TO WATCH A WAR IN NOMINAL ALLIANCE, ... 398 NO HOLY WARS FOR THEM   6
  AND BEEN THE FIRST WITH IT TO WIN A WAR, ... 399 U.S. 1946 KING'S X .   2
  WHICH MAY A LITTLE WHILE BY WAR AND TRADE . . . 399 THE INGENUITIES OF DEBT 7
  THE THEME OF WANTON WASTE IN PEACE AND WAR . . . 411 POD OF THE MILKWEED .   6
  (THE DEED OF GIFT WAS MANY DEEDS OF WAR) . . . . 424 THE GIFT OUTRIGHT . . 13
  BUT BETWEEN PEACE AND WAR AS WE CONCEIVE IT. . . 456 HOW HARD TO KEEP FROM 75
  THAT'S WHAT AT THE END OF A WAR . . . . 463 LINES IN DEJECTION . . 26
  IN PEACE AND WAR--ESPECIALLY IN WAR. . . . . . . 481 A MASQUE OF REASON . . 214
  SO HE WON'T FIND IT HARD TO TAKE HIS WAR. . . . 481 A MASQUE OF REASON . . 215
  TRUCKS GOING BY TO WAR. A WAR IS ON. . . . . . . 504 A MASQUE OF MERCY . . 281
  WHICH IS OUR GREATEST HOPE OF REST FROM WAR. . . 516 A MASQUE OF MERCY . . 593
  OUR LIVES LAID DOWN IN WAR AND PEACE--MAY NOT . . 520 A MASQUE OF MERCY . . 721
WAR-COMMAND
  AS ONE HAVING WAR-COMMAND. . . . . 366 NOT OF SCHOOL AGE . . 12
WARDS
  THEY ARE OUR WARDS WE THINK TO SOME EXTENT . . . 423 FOR JOHN F. KENNEDY . 36
WARES
  THEIR WARES ARE SO MUCH HARDER TO GET RID OF. . 164 NEW HAMPSHIRE . . . 174
WARM
  AND WARM STOVE-WINDOW LIGHT. . . . . 11 WIND AND WINDOW FLOWER 24
  IT'S ALWAYS COLD IN SUMMER, WARM IN WINTER. . . 42 THE MOUNTAIN 49
  "WARM IN DECEMBER, COLD IN JUNE, YOU SAY?" . . . 44 THE MOUNTAIN 100
  YOU AND I KNOW ENOUGH TO KNOW IT'S WARM . . . . 44 THE MOUNTAIN 102
  COMPARED WITH COLD, AND COLD COMPARED WITH WARM. 44 THE MOUNTAIN 103
  AND THE SUN SHINES OUT WARM: THE VINES MUST BE WET. 62 BLUEBERRIES 83
  TO WARM THE FROZEN SWAMP AS BEST IT COULD . . . 102 THE WOOD-PILE 39
  QUIET AND LIGHT AND WARM, IN SPITE OF ALL . . . 148 SNOW 143
  WHILE YOU SIT WARM AND READ UP BALANCED RATIONS. 149 SNOW 183
  "DON'T MAKE ME GET UP; I'M TOO WARM IN BED." . . 205 THE WITCH OF COOS . . 95
  FROM SLEEPING WARM . . . . 218 I WILL SING YOU ONE-O 32
  BUT ONE THING ABOUT IT, IT MUSTN'T GET WARM. . . 228 GOOD-BY AND KEEP COLD 16
  IT SNOWED IN SPRING ON EARTH SO DRY AND WARM . . 239 OUR SINGING STRENGTH   1
  THE SUN WAS WARM BUT THE WIND WAS CHILL. . . . . 275 TWO TRAMPS IN MUD TIME 17
  HERE'S FIRST A GLOVELESS HAND WARM FROM MY POCKET, 356 A MOTH SEEN IN WINTER   1
  AS ONE RANKLY WARM INSIDER . . . . 384 IN THE LONG NIGHT . . 13
WARMED
  I OWN I NEVER REALLY WARMED . . . . 326 TO A THINKER 29
  I NEVER SHOULD AGAIN BE WARMED, ... 381 AN UNSTAMPED LETTER IN 24
WARMER
  WHERE THE SUN SHINES NOW NO WARMER THAN THE MOON. . . . 106 CHRISTMAS TREES . . . 19

PAGE TITLE   LINE

WARMLY
    ALL CREATURES STILL WARMLY SUSPIRE. . . . . 266 SITTING BY A BUSH . . 8
WARMTH (SEE OVER-WARMTH)
    SOON THE SUN'S WARMTH MAKES THEM SHED CRYSTAL SHELLS . . 121 BIRCHES 10
    AND I WAS BURROWING IN DEEP FOR WARMTH, ... 149 SNOW 178
    OF SO MUCH WARMTH AND LIGHT. . . . . 333 HAPPINESS MAKES UP . 11
    HE DREW THEM IN FOR WARMTH OF SELF-EMBRACE. . . . . . 396 ANY SIZE WE PLEASE . 8
    FROM THE PEARL'S HAVING ITS OWN NATIVE WARMTH, ... 456 HOW HARD TO KEEP FROM 90
WARN
    ANYTHING SHE MAY SAY. BUT LET ME WARN YOU, ... 79 THE GENERATIONS OF MEN 180
    SEEMED TO WARN SOMEONE TO BE GETTING OUT . . . . . . 89 THE FEAR 20
    AND WARN THEM AWAY WITH A STICK FOR A GUN.) . . . . . 228 GOOD-BY AND KEEP COLD . 11
    TO WARN AGAINST THE DANGER . . . . 335 CARPE DIEM 14
    BUT WARN THE CHILDREN THEY PERHAPS SHOULD HAVE NONE. . . 483 A MASQUE OF REASON . 294
WARNED
    NOT ONLY WARNED HIM WITH A LOUD COMMAND . . . . . . 394 HAEC FABULA DOCET . . 9
    I SHOULD HAVE WARNED YOU, THOUGH, MY SENSE OF JUSTICE . 518 A MASQUE OF MERCY . 657
WARNING
    WARNING AND TIME TO BE OFF IN FLIGHT: . . . . 127 HOUSE FEAR 7
WARPING
    THE WARPING BOARDS PULL OUT THEIR OWN OLD NAILS . . . 56 THE BLACK COTTAGE . 49
    THE WOOD WAS GRAY AND THE BARK WARPING OFF IT . . . . 102 THE WOOD-PILE . . . 29
WARRANT
    I'VE LAIN AWAKE THINKING OF YOU, I'LL WARRANT, ... 67 A SERVANT TO SERVANTS . 166
    ONE OF THE TIMES WAS WHEN 'TWAS IN THE WARRANT . . . . 208 PAUPER WITCH OF GRAFTON 23
    AND WARRANT PRUDENCE IN A MAN. . . . . 281 BLUE RIBBON AT AMESBURY 56
    OF DESPERATION THAT WOULD WARRANT POETRY'S . . . . . 317 BUILD SOIL 34
WARRANTS
    COLDER THAN THE SEASON WARRANTS. . . . . 304 CLEAR AND COLDER . 14
WARRED
    AND SEE HOW MEN HAVE WARRED. . . . . 252 THE PEACEFUL SHEPHERD . 10
WARREN
    WAITING FOR WARREN. WHEN SHE HEARD HIS STEP, ... 34 DEATH OF THE HIRED MAN 2
    "WARREN!" / "BUT DID HE? I JUST WANT TO KNOW." . . . 36 DEATH OF THE HIRED MAN 47
    WARREN, I WISH YOU COULD HAVE HEARD THE WAY . . . . 36 DEATH OF THE HIRED MAN 54
    "WARREN," SHE SAID, "HE HAS COME HOME TO DIE: . . . . 38 DEATH OF THE HIRED MAN 111
    WARREN LEANED OUT AND TOOK A STEP OR TWO, ... 38 DEATH OF THE HIRED MAN 121
    BUT, WARREN, PLEASE REMEMBER HOW IT IS: . . . . . . 40 DEATH OF THE HIRED MAN 156
    WARREN RETURNED--TOO SOON, IT SEEMED TO HER-- . . . . 40 DEATH OF THE HIRED MAN 164
    "WARREN?" SHE QUESTIONED. / "DEAD," WAS ALL HE ANSWERED. . 40 DEATH OF THE HIRED MAN 166
    AMONG US: IT WAS JUST A WARREN FARMER . . . . 168 NEW HAMPSHIRE . . . 288
    FOR HOG REEVE IN MARCH MEETING HERE IN WARREN. . . . . 207 PAUPER WITCH OF GRAFTON 14
    IN WARREN AT MARCH MEETING, FOR THE REASON . . . . . 208 PAUPER WITCH OF GRAFTON 18
WARREN'S
    SHE TOOK THE MARKET THINGS FROM WARREN'S ARMS . . . . 34 DEATH OF THE HIRED MAN 8
    WENTWORTH AND WARREN'S BOTH GOOD TOWNS TO LIVE IN, . . 208 PAUPER WITCH OF GRAFTON 30
WARRING
    THE WASTE OF NATIONS WARRING. . . . . 360 NOVEMBER 15
WARS
    OF WARS, AND WHAT ARE WARS BUT POLITICS . . . . . . 316 BUILD SOIL 29
    A HALF A DOZEN MAJOR WARS, ... 368 A SERIOUS STEP LIGHTLY 23
    AND WELL MAY BE WHERE WARS ORIGINATE. . . . . 371 THE LITERATE FARMER AND 109
    NO HOLY WARS FOR THEM . . . . 398 NO HOLY WARS FOR THEM . T
    NO HOLY WARS FOR THEM. THE MOST THE SMALL . . . . . 398 NO HOLY WARS FOR THEM . 13
    YOU COULD LOSE BATTLES, YOU COULD LOSE WHOLE WARS, . . 457 HOW HARD TO KEEP FROM 127
WAR'S
    "OH, BUT WAR'S NOT FOR CHILDREN--IT'S FOR MEN." . . . 132 THE BONFIRE 100
WARTS
    OR CROOK-NECKED GOLDEN SQUASH WITH SILVER WARTS, . . . 286 A ROADSIDE STAND . . 12
WARY
    THE CREEPY EDGE OF IT WITH WARY TOUCH, ... 190 THE GRINDSTONE . . . 69
WAS---NOT INDEXED
WASH
    FROM THE SINK WINDOW WHERE I WASH THE PLATES, ... 63 A SERVANT TO SERVANTS . 23
    WILLIS FLUNG OFF THE BED. "I WASH MY HANDS-- . . . . 100 THE SELF-SEEKER . . . 216
    TO DRY OR WASH OR TAN, I DON'T KNOW WHICH . . . . . 197 WILD GRAPES 52
    AND FROM BARN SMELLS YOU CAN'T WASH OUT OF PLOWED GROUND . 210 PAUPER WITCH OF GRAFTON 91
    TO WASH THE STEPS WITH PAIL AND RAG . . . . 307 PROVIDE, PROVIDE . . 2
WASHED (SEE RAIN-WASHED)
    WASHED DOWN WITH RUSTY WATER IN A TIN. . . . . . . 189 THE GRINDSTONE . . . 16
WASHING
    AND WASHING DISHES AFTER THEM--FROM DOING . . . . . 64 A SERVANT TO SERVANTS . 51
WASHINGTON
    MANY MEN'S LUCK WITH GREATEST WASHINGTON . . . . . . 317 BUILD SOIL 45
    I MEAN THE GREAT FOUR, WASHINGTON. . . . . 422 FOR JOHN F. KENNEDY . 25
    ONLY LESS HARD WAS IT FOR WASHINGTON. . . . . 454 HOW HARD TO KEEP FROM 25
WASHOUT
    WITH ROCK AND WASHOUT, AND UNSAFE IN DARKNESS; . . . 229 TWO LOOK AT TWO . . . 6
WASN'T---NOT INDEXED
WASP
    (THE DEVIL ENTERS LIKE A SAPPHIRE WASP . . . . . . 487 A MASQUE OF REASON . . 389
WASPISH
    WASPISH . . . . 309 WASPISH . . . . . T
WASPS
    THE ATTIC WASPS WENT MISSING BY LIKE BULLETS. . . . . 217 A FOUNTAIN, A BOTTLE . 130
WASTE (SEE MID-WASTE)
    SHOULD WASTE THEM ALL. . . . . 27 OCTOBER 4
    TOO BAD TO WASTE THEM ALL. YOU OUGHT TO HAVE THEM. . . 47 A HUNDRED COLLARS . . 67
    AROUND HIM TO LOOK AFTER THAT MAKE WASTE. . . . . . 65 A SERVANT TO SERVANTS . 73
    THE ONLY DWELLING IN A WASTE CUT OVER . . . . . . 174 THE CENSUS-TAKER . . 4
    I CAME AS CENSUS-TAKER TO THE WASTE . . . . 174 THE CENSUS-TAKER . . 9
    OF WASTE LEAVES AT MY SMOKY LANTERN CHIMNEY . . . . . 176 THE STAR-SPLITTER . . 8
    FOR LOVE OF IT, AND YET NOT WASTE TIME EITHER. . . . 188 THE AX-HELVE 81
    I CAN WASTE AS I PLEASE ON WHOM I PLEASE. . . . . . 196 WILD GRAPES 15
    TO GO TO WASTE AND GO WILD IN, ... 264 THE LAST MOWING . . . 17
    BUT IN THE RUSH OF EVERYTHING TO WASTE, ... 300 THE MASTER SPEED . . 7
    THE WASTE OF MOMENTS SLEEPING. . . . . 359 NOVEMBER 12
    THE WASTE OF PLEASURE WEEPING, ... 360 NOVEMBER 13

- 606 -

WASTE (CONTINUED)
    THE WASTE OF NATIONS WARRING. . . . . 360 NOVEMBER 15
    NO PART OF WHICH WE'D HAVE TO WASTE, I SAY. . . . . . 371 THE LITERATE FARMER AND 101
    THE THEME OF WANTON WASTE IN PEACE AND WAR. . . . . . 411 POD OF THE MILKWEED . . 6
    BUT WASTE WAS OF THE ESSENCE OF THE SCHEME. . . . . . 412 POD OF THE MILKWEED . 40
    OR SOME DIM SECRET OF THE GOOD OF WASTE? . . . . . . 412 POD OF THE MILKWEED . 49
    AS A FACT OF WASTE . . . . 439 KITTY HAWK 371
    AND WAS WASTE IN NAME. . . . . 439 KITTY HAWK 372
WASTED
    "THEY SAY SOME TIME WAS WASTED ON THE BELT-- . . . . 94 THE SELF-SEEKER . . . 32
    SOME SYMPATHY WAS WASTED ON THE HOUSE, ... 178 THE STAR-SPLITTER . . 59
    ANYTHING FURTHER HAD BEEN WASTED ON HER, ... 180 MAPLE 33
    TO INSURE THEIR NOT BEING WASTED ON ME. . . . . . . 187 THE AX-HELVE 68
    A YEAR OF LEAVES WAS WASTED. . . . . 359 NOVEMBER 8
    LEST HAVING WASTED PRECIOUS HEAT . . . . 381 AN UNSTAMPED LETTER IN 23
WASTEFUL
    FROM LOVELY BLOOMING BUT WASTEFUL WEED . . . . 376 SOMETHING FOR HOPE . . 15
WASTING
    AND NOW WERE ONLY WASTING PRECIOUS BLADE. . . . . . 190 THE GRINDSTONE . . . 67
    AND WHO KNOWS WHERE WE CAN'T GET! WASTING TIME . . . . 371 THE LITERATE FARMER AND 102
WASTREL
    THEY SHOULD TRY ONE WASTREL FIRST . . . . 466 SOME SCIENCE FICTION . 29
WATCH
    (AND WAIT TO WATCH THE WATER CLEAR, I MAY): . . . . . 1 THE PASTURE 3
    IF HE WA'N'T KEPT STRICT WATCH OF, AND IT ENDED . . . 66 A SERVANT TO SERVANTS . 112
    "IT IS--OR SOMEONE ELSE HE'S SENT TO WATCH. . . . . . 90 THE FEAR 42
    "WATCH FOR HIM, WILL YOU, WILL? YOU LET HIM IN. . . . 94 THE SELF-SEEKER . . . 52
    THE LAWYER WORE A WATCH THE CASE OF WHICH . . . . . 98 THE SELF-SEEKER . . . 163
    THEY'RE GOING. WATCH THIS HUSKY SWARMING UP . . . . 112 IN THE HOME STRETCH . 62
    TO WATCH ME AND SEE WHAT I CAME TO GET. . . . . . . 123 PEA BRUSH 12
    AT DUSK TO WATCH THE MOON DOWN EARLY. . . . . 135 LOCKED OUT 13
    SOMETIMES WHEN I WATCH TREES SWAY, ... 156 THE SOUND OF TREES . 17
    WHERE SHE COULD WATCH HER MOTHER'S PICTURE FADING. . . 181 MAPLE 61
    I'LL DOUBLE THEIRS FOR BOTH OF THEM--YOU WATCH ME. . . 207 PAUPER WITCH OF GRAFTON 9
    TO WATCH HIS WOODS FILL UP WITH SNOW. . . . . 224 STOPPING BY WOODS . . 4
    TO ANY WATCH THEY KEEP? . . . . 301 NEITHER OUT FAR NOR IN 16
    WAIT AND WATCH THE LIQUOR SETTLE. . . . . 304 CLEAR AND COLDER . . 19
    TO WATCH THIS END DELUXE. . . . . 361 ALMOST TWO THOUSAND . 13
    WE WATCH A CIRCUS OF REVOLVING DOGS . . . . 362 SYMPATHY WITH UNDER DOG 2
    YET THERE TO WATCH THE DARKNESS COMING ON-- . . . . . 368 THE LITERATE FARMER AND 16
    TO WATCH A WAR IN NOMINAL ALLIANCE, ... 398 NO HOLY WARS FOR THEM . 6
    AND WHEN IT'S OVER WATCH THE WORLD'S SUPPLY . . . . . 398 NO HOLY WARS FOR THEM . 7
WATCHDOG
    LAST NIGHT YOUR WATCHDOG BARKED ALL NIGHT, ... 380 AN UNSTAMPED LETTER IN 1
    HIS WATCHDOG EYE ON WHAT REMAINED . . . . 419 ONE MORE BREVITY . . 5
WATCHED
    AND IF MEN HAVE WATCHED A LONG TIME . . . . 266 SITTING BY A BUSH . . 9
    I WATCHED HIM WHERE HE SWOOPED, HE POUNCED, HE STRUCK; . 278 THE WHITE-TAILED HORNET 33
    OF BEING WATCHED FROM FORTY CELLAR HOLES . . . . . . 378 DIRECTIVE 21
WATCHER
    AND THEN--THE WATCHER AT HIS PULSE TOOK FRIGHT. . . . 137 "OUT,CUT--" 30
    STILL IT WOULDN'T REWARD THE WATCHER TO STAY AWAKE . . 268 ON LOOKING UP BY CHANCE 13
    THAN AS WATCHER OF THE VOID, ... 383 MAKING CERTAIN ANYTHING 2
WATCHFUL
    UNDER THE WATCHFUL EYE OF HAWK AND EAGLE-- . . . . . 162 NEW HAMPSHIRE . . . 105
WATCHING
    (WE CALL THAT BULLING). I'D BEEN WATCHING HIM. . . . 71 THE CODE 48
    ON THROUGH THE WATCHING FOR THAT EARLY BIRTH . . . . 124 PUTTING IN THE SEED . 11
    HE'S WATCHING FROM THE WOODS AS LIKE AS NOT. . . . . 127 THE SMILE 12
    SOMETHING OR SOMEONE WATCHING MADE THAT GUST. . . . . 130 THE BONFIRE 44
    WATCHING OUT OF A NINETEENTH STORY WINDOW . . . . . 182 MAPLE 81
    (MURPHY HAD BEEN THERE WATCHING ALL THE TIME, ... 194 PAUL'S WIFE 114
WATCHMAN
    I HAVE PASSED BY THE WATCHMAN ON HIS BEAT . . . . . 255 ACQUAINTED WITH NIGHT . 5
WATER (SEE FIRST-WATER, FRESH-WATER, OCEAN-WATER, TREADING-WATER-LIKE)
    (AND WAIT TO WATCH THE WATER CLEAR, I MAY): . . . . . 1 THE PASTURE 3
    GOING FOR WATER . . . . 18 GOING FOR WATER . . . T
    HE COULD FIND WATER WITH A HAZEL PRONG-- . . . . . . 37 DEATH OF THE HIRED MAN 83
    TO HAVE SOME HEAD OF WATER FROM ABOVE, ... 43 THE MOUNTAIN 70
    THE FRUIT MIXED WITH WATER IN LAYERS OF LEAVES, . . . 62 BLUEBERRIES 104
    I SEE IT'S A FAIR, PRETTY SHEET OF WATER. . . . . . 63 A SERVANT TO SERVANTS . 17
    TO STEP OUTDOORS AND TAKE THE WATER DAZZLE . . . . . 63 A SERVANT TO SERVANTS . 27
    I SEE IT'S A FAIR, PRETTY SHEET OF WATER, ... 63 A SERVANT TO SERVANTS . 32
    A BEAD OF SILVER WATER MORE OR LESS, ... 77 THE GENERATIONS OF MEN 122
    TILL WEISS SHUT OFF THE WATER IN THE WHEEL PIT. . . . 93 THE SELF-SEEKER . . . 27
    AND BY A RIVER BANK FOR WATER FLOWERS. . . . . 98 THE SELF-SEEKER . . . 153
    AND AT THE SINUS UNDER WATER A FIST . . . . 98 THE SELF-SEEKER . . . 155
    BUT PUT OUR FLOWERS IN WATER FIRST.--WILL, HELP HER: . 99 THE SELF-SEEKER . . . 172
    AT WEEDS THE WATER FROM THE SINK MADE TALL. . . . . 110 IN THE HOME STRETCH . 3
    "RANK WEEDS THAT LOVE THE WATER FROM THE DISHPAN . . . 111 IN THE HOME STRETCH . 30
    OF WATER WE WALKED ALONG BESIDE. . . . . 140 THE GUM-GATHERER . . 8
    THE WATER IN DESPERATE STRAITS LIKE FRANTIC FISH, . . 142 THE VANISHING RED . . 22
    THEIR BULK IN WATER WOULD BE FROZEN ROCK . . . . . . 151 SNOW 228
    WASHED DOWN WITH RUSTY WATER IN A TIN. . . . . 189 THE GRINDSTONE . . . 16
    AND POURED ON WATER (TEARS IT MIGHT HAVE BEEN); . . . 189 THE GRINDSTONE . . . 27
    PAUL WONDERED HOW IT WOULD RESPOND TO WATER. . . . . 194 PAUL'S WIFE 97
    AND THEN BEYOND THE OPEN WATER, DIM WITH MIDGES, . . . 194 PAUL'S WIFE 106
    WHEN THERE WAS WATER IN THE CELLAR IN SPRING . . . . 204 THE WITCH OF COOS . . 49
    DEEPER DOWN IN THE WELL THAN WHERE THE WATER . . . . 225 FOR ONCE SOMETHING . . 3
    WATER CAME TO REBUKE THE TOO CLEAR WATER. . . . . . 225 FOR ONCE SOMETHING . . 11
    IN WATER OF A SLENDER APRIL RILL . . . . 226 THE ONSET 19
    IS WATER WOOD TO SERVE A BROOK THE SAME? . . . . . . 231 A BROOK IN THE CITY . 12
    THAT SUCH A BROOK RAN WATER. BUT I WONDER . . . . . 231 A BROOK IN THE CITY . 21
    AND BROUGHT IT OVER GLOSSY WATER, GREATER, ... 245 THE FREEDOM OF THE MOON 10
    THE SHATTERED WATER MADE A MISTY DIN. . . . . 250 ONCE BY THE PACIFIC . 1
    THAT WATER NEVER DID TO LAND BEFORE. . . . . 250 ONCE BY THE PACIFIC . 4
    BLOOD HAS BEEN HARDER TO DAM BACK THAN WATER. . . . . 254 THE FLOOD 1
    AND THE WHITE WATER RODE THE BLACK FOREVER, ... 258 WEST-RUNNING BROOK . . 21

WATER (CONTINUED)

		PAGE	TITLE	LINE
IT IS FROM THAT IN WATER WE WERE FROM		259	WEST-RUNNING BROOK	40
IT FLOWS BESIDE US IN THIS WATER BROOK,		259	WEST-RUNNING BROOK	50
BY CRAMPING THE WHEEL ON A WATER BAR,		263	THE TIMES TABLE	5
THE WATER FOR WHICH WE MAY HAVE TO LOOK		276	TWO TRAMPS IN MUD TIME	33
BE GLAD OF WATER, BUT DON'T FORGET		276	TWO TRAMPS IN MUD TIME	37
AND SHOW ON THE WATER ITS CRYSTAL TEETH.		276	TWO TRAMPS IN MUD TIME	40
NO SPEED OF WIND OR WATER RUSHING BY		300	THE MASTER SPEED	1
THE WATER COMES ASHORE,		301	NEITHER OUT FAR NOR IN	11
HAD TAKEN ALL THE WATER IT COULD AS DEW,		315	IRIS BY NIGHT	14
ITS AIRY PRESSURE TURNED TO WATER WEIGHT.		315	IRIS BY NIGHT	16
ON MELTED MOUNTAIN WATER LED BY FLUME		337	THE WIND AND THE RAIN	23
WITH WATER I WOULD SEE THEM WATER-BOWED.		337	THE WIND AND THE RAIN	27
BUT GIVE ME WATER HEAVY ON THE HEAD		337	THE WIND AND THE RAIN	38
AND THEN IN THE FAR-DISTANT WATER SPLASHED,		338	THE MOST OF IT	12
PUSHING THE CRUMPLED WATER UP AHEAD,		338	THE MOST OF IT	17
A BROOK THAT WAS THE WATER OF THE HOUSE,		378	DIRECTIVE	50
I NEVER SAW SO MUCH SWIFT WATER RUN CLOUDLESS.		379	TOO ANXIOUS FOR RIVERS	5
THE WAVE SUCKS BACK AND WITH THE LAST OF WATER.		391	ON BEING IDOLIZED	1
A TRENCH WERE WATER PIPES WERE LAYING ON.		394	HAEC FABULA DOCET	6
I SET HIM WATER, I SET HIM FOOD.		419	ONE MORE BREVITY	19
AND ON ONE A WATER		433	KITTY HAWK	165
SPRING WATER IN OUR MOUNTAIN BOSOM SWELLS		446	DOES NO ONE AT ALL EVER	22
ALL THE SEA WATER IN ONE TIDE		452	A-WISHING WELL	45
ONLY OF SAND, NOT WATER, RUNS THROUGH HERE.		489	A MASQUE OF REASON	443

WATER-BOWED

		PAGE	TITLE	LINE
WITH WATER I WOULD SEE THEM WATER-BOWED.		337	THE WIND AND THE RAIN	27

WATERFALL

		PAGE	TITLE	LINE
ON SLIPPERY ROCKS BESIDE A WATERFALL.		210	PAUPER WITCH OF GRAFTON	98
AND LANDED POURING LIKE A WATERFALL,		338	THE MOST OF IT	18

WATERING

		PAGE	TITLE	LINE
ACROSS THE LANDSCAPE WITH A WATERING POT		354	THE LESSON FOR TODAY	129
HERE ARE YOUR WATERS AND YOUR WATERING PLACE.		379	DIRECTIVE	61

WATERLOGGED

		PAGE	TITLE	LINE
WHEN THE GIRL SEEMED TOO WATERLOGGED TO LIVE,		194	PAUL'S WIFE	117

WATERS

		PAGE	TITLE	LINE
AND THE SHALLOW WATERS AFLUTTER WITH WIND		27	A LINE-STORM SONG	19
EVEN AGAINST THE WAY ITS WATERS WENT.		119	HYLA BROOK	9
THESE FLOWERY WATERS AND THESE WATERY FLOWERS		245	SPRING POOLS	11
SHE WATERS AT THE PATENT FOUNT.		281	BLUE RIBBON AT AMESBURY	43
HERE ARE YOUR WATERS AND YOUR WATERING PLACE.		379	DIRECTIVE	61

WATER'S

		PAGE	TITLE	LINE
"I DON'T SUPPOSE THE WATER'S CHANGED AT ALL.		44	THE MOUNTAIN	101

WATERSIDE

		PAGE	TITLE	LINE
OF AN OLD CEDAR AT THE WATERSIDE		379	DIRECTIVE	56

WATERY

		PAGE	TITLE	LINE
THESE FLOWERY WATERS AND THESE WATERY FLOWERS		245	SPRING POOLS	11
SO WATERY AS TO SEEM SUBMARINE;		315	IRIS BY NIGHT	11

WATING

		PAGE	TITLE	LINE
WATING TO SEE IF SHE WOULD MEND;		347	DISCOVERY OF MADEIRAS	112

WAVE

		PAGE	TITLE	LINE
OF THE FAR-DISTANT BREAKING WAVE.		20	THE TRIAL BY EXISTENCE	16
OF THE PLACE MARKED WITH IT--"WAVE OFFERING,		183	MAPLE	106
SOMETHING ABOUT WAVE OFFERING, IT SAID."		183	MAPLE	107
A GREAT WAVE FROM IT GOING OVER THEM,		230	TWO LOOK AT TWO	40
AND NOW IT IS ONCE MORE THE TIDAL WAVE		255	THE FLOOD	12
LOCK, LOOK, IT'S WAVING TO US WITH A WAVE		258	WEST-RUNNING BROOK	16
FLUNG BACKWARD ON ITSELF IN ONE WHITE WAVE,		258	WEST-RUNNING BROOK	20
IN THAT WHITE WAVE RUNS COUNTER TO ITSELF.		259	WEST-RUNNING BROOK	39
IN AN EXTRA-VAGANT WAVE.		294	A RECORD STRIDE	16
WIND GOES FROM FARM TO FARM IN WAVE ON WAVE,		300	STRONG SAYING NOTHING	13
AND THE WAVE LINE A SHAKEN SIGH.		327	A MISSIVE MISSILE	12
TO LAY THEM LEVEL WITH THE RUNNING WAVE,		334	I COULD GIVE ALL	3
THE WAVE SUCKS BACK AND WITH THE LAST OF WATER		391	ON BEING IDOLIZED	1
THIS WIDE FLIGHT WE WAVE		442	KITTY HAWK	437

WAVED

		PAGE	TITLE	LINE
AND A GEM-FLOWER WAVED IN A WAND!		29	MY BUTTERFLY	37
WERE MADE IN HEAVEN. IT WASN'T WAVED TO US."		258	WEST-RUNNING BROOK	29

WAVES

		PAGE	TITLE	LINE
DRAWING THE SLOW WAVES WHITER AND WHITER AND WHITER.		63	A SERVANT TO SERVANTS	25
ERECT, BUT NOT WITHOUT ITS WAVES, AS WHEN		188	THE AX-HELVE	96
GREAT WAVES LOOKED OVER OTHERS COMING IN,		250	ONCE BY THE PACIFIC	2
SEA WAVES ARE GREEN AND WET,		260	SAND DUNES	1
WHEN THE CLAP OF TWO CONVERGING WAVES		344	DISCOVERY OF MADEIRAS	27
AS IF TO COME, BUT KEEPER WAVES HER OFF.)		518	A MASQUE OF MERCY	653

WAVE'S

		PAGE	TITLE	LINE
THAT WAVE'S BEEN STANDING OFF THIS JUT OF SHORE--"		258	WEST-RUNNING BROOK	18
"THAT WAVE'S BEEN STANDING OFF THIS JUT OF SHORE		258	WEST-RUNNING BROOK	27

WAVING

		PAGE	TITLE	LINE
LOCK, LOOK, IT'S WAVING TO US WITH A WAVE		258	WEST-RUNNING BROOK	16
WAVING SCEPTER-BATON,		442	KITTY HAWK	458

WAVY

		PAGE	TITLE	LINE
ALL WIRY ARMS AND LEGS THAT SPREAD OUT WAVY		70	THE CODE	34
THE WAVY UPFLUNG PENNONS OF THE CORN		404	FROM PLANE TO PLANE	15

WAX

		PAGE	TITLE	LINE
AND DOWNY WAX THE THREE BEGAN TO THRIVE.		283	THE GOLD HESPERIDEE	6

WAXED

		PAGE	TITLE	LINE
WELL THEY FLOURISHED AND WAXED		448	THE BAD ISLAND--EASTER	34

WAY

		PAGE	TITLE	LINE
YOU WALKED A WAY BESIDE ME		12	FLOWER-GATHERING	3
THEY LEAVE US SO TO THE WAY WE TOOK,		16	IN NEGLECT	1
BUT HE HAD GONE HIS WAY, THE GRASS ALL MOWN,		22	THE TUFT OF FLOWERS	7
I KNOW THAT THIS IS THE WAY IN OURS.		26	IN HARDWOOD GROVES	12
BEGUILE US IN THE WAY YOU KNOW.		27	OCTOBER	11
SOME HUMBLE WAY TO SAVE HIS SELF-RESPECT.		36	DEATH OF THE HIRED MAN	50
WARREN, I WISH YOU COULD HAVE HEARD THE WAY		36	DEATH OF THE HIRED MAN	54
THE WAY HE MIXED THAT IN WITH OTHER THINGS.		36	DEATH OF THE HIRED MAN	64
"NO, BUT HE HURT MY HEART THE WAY HE LAY		39	DEATH OF THE HIRED MAN	147

WAY (CONTINUED)

PASTURE RAN UP THE SIDE A LITTLE WAY,	41	THE MOUNTAIN	29
IS THAT THE WAY TO REACH THE TOP FROM HERE?--	41	THE MOUNTAIN	35
THEY LOGGED IT THERE LAST WINTER SOME WAY UP.	41	THE MOUNTAIN	42
I'D TAKE YOU, BUT I'M BOUND THE OTHER WAY."	42	THE MOUNTAIN	43
IT WOULDN'T HAVE TO BE A LONG WAY DOWN	42	THE MOUNTAIN	69
BY ANYONE WHO'D COME A LONG WAY UP.	43	THE MOUNTAIN	72
"SHOW HIM THIS WAY. I'M NOT AFRAID OF HIM.	45	A HUNDRED COLLARS	37
"NOT THAT WAY, WITH YOUR SHOES ON KIKE'S WHITE BED.	47	A HUNDRED COLLARS	75
YOU CAN'T REST THAT WAY. LET ME PULL YOUR SHOES OFF."	47	A HUNDRED COLLARS	76
"JUST AS YOU SAY. HAVE IT YOUR OWN WAY, THEN.	47	A HUNDRED COLLARS	79
AND SLEEP ON IT, THE WAY I ALWAYS DO	48	A HUNDRED COLLARS	91
AND MAKING THE BEST OF THEIR WAY BACK TO LIFE	54	HOME BURIAL	104
WHAT DID HE MEAN? OF COURSE THE EASY WAY .	57	THE BLACK COTTAGE	65
STRANGE HOW SUCH INNOCENCE GETS ITS OWN WAY.	57	THE BLACK COTTAGE	81
"YOU OUGHT TO HAVE SEEN WHAT I SAW ON MY WAY	59	BLUEBERRIES	1
THAT'S ALWAYS THE WAY WITH THE BLUEBERRIES, THOUGH:	59	BLUEBERRIES	14
BUT GET THE PINE OUT OF THE WAY, YOU MAY BURN	59	BLUEBERRIES	17
"WHO CARES WHAT THEY SAY? IT'S A NICE WAY TO LIVE,	61	BLUEBERRIES	54
AND SEE THE WAY YOU LIVED, BUT I DON'T KNOW!	62	A SERVANT TO SERVANTS	4
PUT ON ME, BUT THERE SEEMS NO OTHER WAY.	64	A SERVANT TO SERVANTS	54
HE SAYS THE BEST WAY OUT IS ALWAYS THROUGH.	64	A SERVANT TO SERVANTS	56
AS THAT I CAN SEE NO WAY OUT BUT THROUGH--	64	A SERVANT TO SERVANTS	58
I'VE HEARD TOO MUCH OF THE OLD-FASHIONED WAY.	65	A SERVANT TO SERVANTS	103
A NARROW PASSAGE ALL THE WAY AROUND.	66	A SERVANT TO SERVANTS	116
THEY FOUND A WAY TO PUT A STOP TO IT.	67	A SERVANT TO SERVANTS	139
UPON MY WAY TO SLEEP BEFORE IT FELL,	68	AFTER APPLE-PICKING	15
"HE IS A FOOL IF THAT'S THE WAY HE TAKES ME."	70	THE CODE	20
AND DRIVE, THE WAY YOU CAN, YOU KNOW, IN MOWING--	71	THE CODE	45
THEY REALIZED FROM THE WAY I SWABBED MY NECK	72	THE CODE	86
SLUMPED WAY DOWN IN A CHAIR, WITH BOTH HIS FEET	72	THE CODE	97
"YOU TOOK AN AWKWARD WAY. DID HE DISCHARGE YOU?"	73	THE CODE	113
WAS A GIRL; AND SHE HALTED SOME WAY OFF	74	THE GENERATIONS OF MEN	30
"NO FETE TODAY," HE SAID. / "IT LOOKS THAT WAY."	74	THE GENERATIONS OF MEN	35
NO ONE WENT HOME THAT WAY, THE ONLY HOUSE	76	THE GENERATIONS OF MEN	73
SHE DOES LOOK LIKE YOU. STAY THE WAY YOU ARE.	77	THE GENERATIONS OF MEN	113
NOR NEVER WILL BE TO MY WAY OF THINKING.	80	THE GENERATIONS OF MEN	187
"HOW SHALL WE?" / "WILL YOU LEAVE THE WAY TO ME?"	80	THE GENERATIONS OF MEN	205
THAT'S NO WAY FOR A MAN TO DO AT HIS AGE:	83	THE HOUSEKEEPER	63
I CAN'T EXPLAIN IT ANY OTHER WAY.	84	THE HOUSEKEEPER	78
I KNOW THE WAY HE'S FELT--BUT ALL THE SAME!"	84	THE HOUSEKEEPER	83
WHAT CHILDISHNESS HE WOULDN'T GIVE WAY TO.	86	THE HOUSEKEEPER	133
BUT IT'S JUST FUN THE WAY HE GETS BEDEVILED--	87	THE HOUSEKEEPER	161
TO PUT IT THE RIGHT WAY. HE'D NEVER DARE--	90	THE FEAR	37
I SAW BY THE WAY YOU WHIPPED UP THE HORSE.	91	THE FEAR	73
THE WAY BEN FRANKLIN USED TO MAKE THE KITE STRING.	94	THE SELF-SEEKER	35
"YES, THAT'S ONE WAY TO PUT IT--ALL THE FLOWERS	95	THE SELF-SEEKER	67
FOR THE FRIENDS IT MIGHT BRING ME. BY THE WAY,	95	THE SELF-SEEKER	84
I KNEW A LOVELY WAY TO TELL FOR CERTAIN	96	THE SELF-SEEKER	108
ANNE HAS A WAY WITH FLOWERS TO TAKE THE PLACE	98	THE SELF-SEEKER	159
CARRY HIM OFF THE WAY I MIGHT HAVE GONE,	101	THE WOOD-PILE	20
YET KNOWING HOW WAY LEADS ON TO WAY,	105	THE ROAD NOT TAKEN	14
THE WAY THE NEST-FULL EVERY TIME WE STIRRED	109	THE EXPOSED NEST	20
EVEN AGAINST THE WAY ITS WATERS WENT.	119	HYLA BROOK	9
KICKING HIS WAY DOWN THROUGH THE AIR TO THE GROUND.	122	BIRCHES	40
SHOULDERING ITS WAY AND SHEDDING THE EARTH CRUMBS.	124	PUTTING IN THE SEED	14
AND SINCE THERE WAS NO OTHER WAY TO LOOK,	125	AN ENCOUNTER	10
I DIDN'T LIKE THE WAY HE WENT AWAY.	127	THE SMILE	1
THE WAY WE PILED IT. AND LET'S BE THE TALK	129	THE BONFIRE	10
GOING THE OTHER WAY AND THEY NOT SEEN IT.	132	THE BONFIRE	88
THE BEST WAY IS TO COME UPHILL WITH ME	133	THE BONFIRE	113
OH, NEVER BY WAY OF ADVICE!	134	A GIRL'S GARDEN	46
'BOUT OUT!" AND TOOK THE LONG WAY HOME	140	BROWN'S DESCENT	75
TO BE COMING HOME THE WAY I WAS,	140	THE GUM-GATHERER	11
(THE WAY IT IS WILL DO FOR MOSS.)	140	THE GUM-GATHERER	18
BROTHER MESERVE. YOU KNOW TO FIND YOUR WAY .	144	SNOW	37
OUT THROUGH THE SHED." / "I GUESS I KNOW MY WAY.	144	SNOW	38
IT CAN'T TURN EITHER WAY. IT NEEDS THE WIND'S HELP.	148	SNOW	135
MORE LIKE A TUNNEL THAN A HOLE--WAY DOWN	149	SNOW	193
A THOUSAND TIMES. IF THAT'S THE WAY HE PREACHES!	152	SNOW	254
THAT IT WAS ANY WAY BUT WHAT IT WAS.	153	SNOW	286
THE STUBBORN THING, THE WAY IT JARS YOUR ARM!--	153	SNOW	296
YOU KNOW--IT SOUNDS THAT WAY, AND YES, I HEAR--	153	SNOW	300
"JUST THE WAY STEFANSSON RUNS ON," I MURMURED,	159	NEW HAMPSHIRE	22
OFFERED ME NOT LONG SINCE UP BERLIN WAY	162	NEW HAMPSHIRE	110
AND ARE A FIGURE OF THE STRONG	164	NEW HAMPSHIRE	180
THE WAY THE WIRY GANG-BOSS LIKED THE LOGJAM.	170	NEW HAMPSHIRE	345
OF YEAR OR DAY THE WAY IT SWUNG A DOOR	175	THE CENSUS-TAKER	27
TO MAKE FUN OF MY WAY OF DOING THINGS,	176	THE STAR-SPLITTER	9
HE HAD TO TAKE THE BEST WAY HE KNEW HOW	178	THE STAR-SPLITTER	56
POINTED OUR THOUGHTS THE WAY WE POINTED IT,	179	THE STAR-SPLITTER	84
A STAR IN TWO OR THREE, THE WAY YOU SPLIT	179	THE STAR-SPLITTER	89
HOW DIFFERENT FROM THE WAY IT EVER STOOD?	179	THE STAR-SPLITTER	99
ONE COMING THIS WAY INTO LIFE, AND ONE	180	MAPLE	12
TO MAKE IT GO WELL WITH THE WAY SHE LOOKED.	181	MAPLE	43
(THIS WAS HER FADED MEMORY OF THE WAY .	183	MAPLE	110
ABOUT THE WAY HE SAW IT WAS WITH YOU	183	MAPLE	128
A BETTER WAY TO PASS THE AFTERNOON	190	THE GRINDSTONE	53
TO JUDGE THEM BY THE WAY THEY CAUGHT THEMSELVES	193	PAUL'S WIFE	65
IN ANY WAY THE WORLD KNEW HOW TO SPEAK.	196	PAUL'S WIFE	157
THE WAY THEY GREW ROUND LEIF THE LUCKY'S GERMAN;	197	WILD GRAPES	27
IN ONE WAY: YOU HAVE ONE MORE STEM TO CLING BY,	198	WILD GRAPES	70
SHE WENT HER WAY. BUT LABAN HAVING CAUGHT	200	PLACE FOR A THIRD	15
BEFORE SHE WENT THE POOR MAN'S WIDOW'S WAY,	201	PLACE FOR A THIRD	61
FROM THE WAY SHE HAD SET HER POOR OLD MOUTH,	201	PLACE FOR A THIRD	74
THE WAY A MAN WITH ONE LEG AND A CRUTCH,	204	THE WITCH OF COOS	52
THE WAY HE DID IN LIFE ONCE; BUT THIS TIME	204	THE WITCH OF COOS	76
STILL GOING EVERY WHICH WAY IN THE JOINTS, THOUGH,	205	THE WITCH OF COOS	87

WAY (CONTINUED)

	PAGE	TITLE	LINE
THAT WAS THE WAY HE STARTED COURTING ME.	209	PAUPER WITCH OF GRAFTON	72
ALL THE WAY HOME I KEPT REMEMBERING	217	A FOUNTAIN, A BOTTLE	132
THE WAY A CROW	221	DUST OF SNOW	1
BUT NOW FOR ME THAN YOU--THE OTHER WAY.	222	TO E.T.	16
IN ONE LAST LOOK THE WAY THEY MUST NOT GO,	229	TWO LOOK AT TWO	10
IN EVERY WAY YOU MAY PLEASE YOURSELF;	232	THE KITCHEN CHIMNEY	2
I CAN'T PRETEND TO TELL THE WAY IT'S DONE.	237	A HILLSIDE THAW	5
INSISTING ALWAYS ON OUR OWN WAY SO.	238	ON A TREE FALLEN ACROSS	5
OF WAY WITH ME FROM APATHY OF WING,	240	OUR SINGING STRENGTH	37
THE BARN OPPOSED ACROSS THE WAY,	241	NEED OF BEING VERSED	5
SHE FAILS FROM STRANGENESS TO A WAY OF LIFE	257	THE LOVELY BE CHOOSERS	44
THE WAY I CAN WITH YOU--AND YOU WITH ME--	258	WEST-RUNNING BROOK	8
ALL THE WAY TO THE WEST	261	CANIS MAJOR	6
AND THEN I KNOW OF NO BETTER WAY	263	THE TIMES TABLE	17
NOR WAS THIS JUST A WAY OF TALKING	274	A LONE STRIKER	47
AND LET THE OTHER GO ON A WAY.	275	TWO TRAMPS IN MUD TIME	6
THEY HAD NO WAY OF KNOWING A FOOL.	276	TWO TRAMPS IN MUD TIME	56
THE WAY A PLAYER CURLS AROUND A FOOTBALL.	278	THE WHITE-TAILED HORNET	39
'TIS THE WORLD-OLD WAY OF THE RAIN.	285	IN TIME OF CLOUDBURST	5
DESTROY THEIR SLEEPING AT NIGHT THE ANCIENT WAY.	287	A ROADSIDE STAND	31
AND ANOTHER TO ASK THE WAY TO WHERE IT WAS BOUND;	287	A ROADSIDE STAND	41
THE CHEAPEST TRAMP THAT CAME ALONG THAT WAY	290	OLD BARN AT THE BOTTOM	44
COME BACK THAT WAY A SUMMER HENCE,	291	ON HEART'S BEGINNING TO	19
ALL TURN AND LOOK ONE WAY.	301	NEITHER OUT FAR NOR IN	2
IF SINGING OUT OF SLEEP AND DREAM THAT WAY	303	A BIRD SINGING IN SLEEP	13
THE WAY OF UNDERSTANDING IS PARTLY MIRTH.	306	NOT QUITE SOCIAL	11
POOR EGOTIST, HE HAS NO WAY OF KNOWING	309	WASPISH	5
"THE BEST WAY TO HATE IS THE WORST.	312	THE VINDICTIVES	81
AND LEAPFROG IN EACH OTHER'S WAY--ALL'S WELL.	318	BUILD SOIL	64
A MAN THE WAY THINGS COME IN PAIRS.	326	TO A THINKER	14
THE WAY SHE CLUNG TO HIM THE MORE	343	DISCOVERY OF MADEIRAS	12
I CAN JUST HEAR THE WAY YOU MAKE IT GO:	352	THE LESSON FOR TODAY	54
I'M HAVING THE WHOLE ARGUMENT MY WAY--	354	THE LESSON FOR TODAY	116
THE AGES RANGING ALL THE WAY FROM HOURS	355	THE LESSON FOR TODAY	138
GO PART WAY DOWN THE LANE,	359	NOVEMBER	3
THE SENTENCING GOES BLITHELY ON ITS WAY	362	IN A POEM	1
THAT HADN'T SUNK THE WAY IT SHOULD HAVE SUNK,	368	THE LITERATE FARMER AND	13
OF ELECTRICITY IN BULK THE WAY	370	THE LITERATE FARMER AND	73
BY WAY OF TRAVELER'S AID,	391	A ROGERS GROUP	10
THE WAY TO GO AWAY SHOULD BE THE SAME.	395	WHY WAIT FOR SCIENCE	11
TO FARMING FOR A SIMPLE WAY TO EARN;	398	BURSTING RAPTURE	3
"AND RIGHT YOU ARE. YOU DO THE WAY WE DO	405	FROM PLANE TO PLANE	49
THE OTHER WAY OF READING BACK AND FORTH,	405	FROM PLANE TO PLANE	53
THAT LEANS OUT THIS AND THAT WAY FROM THEIR CHIMNEY.	414	A CABIN IN THE CLEARING	11
A NEW AND BETTER WAY TO IND	416	AMERICA IS HARD TO SEE	2
OF BEING IN EACH OTHER'S WAY,	417	AMERICA IS HARD TO SEE	39
EXCEPT AS IT DENIED HIM WAY	419	AMERICA IS HARD TO SEE	77
IN SPITE OF THE WAY HIS TAIL HAD SMACKED	421	ONE MORE BREVITY	54
ALL THE WAY TO MEN.	426	A NEVER NAUGHT SONG	16
AND WALK THE REST OF THE WAY.	444	THE DRAFT HORSE	20
DOES NO ONE AT ALL EVER FEEL THIS WAY IN THE LEAST?	446	DOES NO ONE AT ALL EVER	T
SOME OF THEM GAVE WAY AT THE WRIST	452	A-WISHING WELL	56
BEFORE THEY GAVE WAY AT THE FIST.	452	A-WISHING WELL	57
HIS MOTHER DIDN'T LIKE THE WAY HE PUT IT,	457	HOW HARD TO KEEP FROM	105
TO LEAD HIM OFF THE ASIATIC WAY	462	HOW HARD TO KEEP FROM	262
THE MILKY WAY IS A COWPATH	464	MILKY WAY IS A COWPATH	T
THE MILKY WAY PERHAPS	464	MILKY WAY IS A COWPATH	15
WAS WOMAN'S WAY OF LIFE.	464	MILKY WAY IS A COWPATH	16
ALONG THE MILKY WAY	465	MILKY WAY IS A COWPATH	31
TO THANK YOU SOMEDAY FOR THE WAY YOU HELPED ME	475	A MASQUE OF REASON	48
I ANSWER FLATLY: THAT'S THE WAY IT IS,	477	A MASQUE OF REASON	111
IN SOME WAY NOT SO PENAL AS THE POORHOUSE.	478	A MASQUE OF REASON	125
AND ALSO OF THE WAY ALL THINGS COME ROUND,	485	A MASQUE OF REASON	342
WHERE GOOD AND BAD ARE MINGLED EVERY WHICH WAY,	488	A MASQUE OF REASON	408
HE'S TWITTING US.--OH, BY THE WAY, YOU HAVEN'T	488	A MASQUE OF REASON	420
HOW DID YOU KNOW THAT WAY TO BREAK MY HEART?	495	A MASQUE OF MERCY	59
THE WAY IT RESTED TWO POINTS ON THE GROUND	501	A MASQUE OF MERCY	194
THERE IS NO BETTER WAY OF HAVING IT.	512	A MASQUE OF MERCY	508
UNLOCK THE DOOR FOR ME. / NOT THAT WAY OUT.	514	A MASQUE OF MERCY	546
I'M ALL TURNED ROUND. / THERE IS YOUR WAY PREPARED.	514	A MASQUE OF MERCY	547

'WAY

| AWAY 'WAY DOWN INSIDE I'M PERSONAL. | 320 | BUILD SOIL | 144 |

WAYS

I'VE SPOILED JEMIMA IN MORE WAYS THAN ONE.	49	A HUNDRED COLLARS	141
BUT I KNOW YOU DON'T UNDERSTAND OUR WAYS.	70	THE CODE	26
IN WAYS THAT I CAN HARDLY TELL YOU OF.	86	THE HOUSEKEEPER	157
SOMETIMES I WANDER OUT OF BEATEN WAYS	125	AN ENCOUNTER	23
THE WAYS YOU FOUND TO SAY THE PRAISE OF COMFORT	150	SNOW	199
THAT SPREADING IN THE EVENING AIR BOTH WAYS	247	THE COCOON	2
VOICE WAYS	301	VOICE WAYS	T
"I WOULDN'T HOE BOTH WAYS FOR ANYBODY!"	405	FROM PLANE TO PLANE	48
AND SO WITH HOMESICKNESS IN MANY WAYS	446	DOES NO ONE AT ALL EVER	10

WAY'S

| THAT WAY'S BEEN TRIED TOO MANY TIMES FOR ME. | 515 | A MASQUE OF MERCY | 574 |

WAYSIDE

| THAT WE SIT SOMETIMES IN THE WAYSIDE NOOK, | 16 | IN NEGLECT | 3 |
| THE WAYSIDE BLUE AND INNOCENT HEAL-ALL? | 302 | DESIGN | 10 |

WE---NOT INDEXED

WEAK

ANYTHING MORE THAN THE TRUTH WOULD HAVE SEEMED TOO WEAK	17	MOWING	9
WEAK FOLIAGE THAT IS BLOWN UPON AND BENT,	119	HYLA BROOK	8
THEY EDDY OVER IT TOO TOPPLING WEAK	246	ATMOSPHERE	3
SOMETHING WE WERE WITHHOLDING MADE US WEAK	348	THE GIFT OUTRIGHT	8
SOMETHING WE WERE WITHHOLDING MADE US WEAK	424	THE GIFT OUTRIGHT	8

WEAKLY

| SO LYING FORWARD WEAKLY ON THE HANDRAIL | 205 | THE WITCH OF COOS | 96 |
| SHE CAME DOWN WEAKLY AND BLINDLY LED | 343 | DISCOVERY OF MADEIRAS | 6 |

PAGE TITLE   LINE

WEAKNESS
    HIS VERY WEAKNESS FOR MANKIND'S ENDEARING. . . . . . . 505 A MASQUE OF MERCY . . 309
WEALTH
    SHE WOULD REFUSE LOVE SAFE WITH WEALTH AND HONOR! . . . . 256 THE LOVELY BE CHOOSERS   6
    AND WHEN WE GET TOO FAR APART IN WEALTH, ... 363 AN EQUALIZER   5
    ALL WEALTH AND POWER IN TOO FEW HANDS? . . . . 509 A MASQUE OF MERCY . . 411
WEAPON
    A BOARD IS THE BEST WEAPON IF YOU HAVE IT. . . . . . . 131 THE BONFIRE   68
    A WEAPON IN OUR HUMAN FIGHT," HE SAID. . . . . 177 THE STAR-SPLITTER . .   24
    BUT LET HIM SHOW THEM HOW THE WEAPON WORKED. . . . . . 293 AT WOODWARD'S GARDENS .   7
    THE WEAPON SHOULD BE . . . . 450 OBJECTION TO BE STEPPED   14
    TURNED INTO A WEAPON. . . . . 450 OBJECTION TO BE STEPPED   18
WEAPONS
    WEAPONS OF WAR AND IMPLEMENTS OF PEACE . . . . 255 THE FLOOD   10
    TOOLS AND WEAPONS . . . . 468 FROM IRON   5
WEAR
    WE WEAR OUR FINGERS ROUGH WITH HANDLING THEM. . . . . 33 MENDING WALL   20
    NUMBER EIGHTEEN THIS IS. WHAT SIZE DO YOU WEAR?" . . . 46 A HUNDRED COLLARS . .   61
    BECAUSE IT WAS GRASSY AND WANTED WEAR; . . . . 105 THE ROAD NOT TAKEN . .   8
    AND WEAR HER RED HOOD, ... 136 LAST WORD OF A BLUEBIRD   17
    WITH THE NEW CITY STREET IT HAS TO WEAR . . . . 231 A BROOK IN THE CITY .   2
    BESIDES THE WEAR OF IRON WAGON WHEELS . . . . 377 DIRECTIVE   14
    TO WEAR THE UNIFORM OF WHO YOU ARE, ... 385 THE FEAR OF GOD . . .   8
    TO WEAR A CRUTCH. . . . . 389 ASTROMETAPHYSICAL . .   8
    DON'T WEAR YOUR PANTS OUT PREACHING ON YOUR KNEES. . . 519 A MASQUE OF MERCY . . 681
WEARINESS
    WHERE ALL MY WEARINESS HAD GONE AND WHY . . . . . . 132 THE BONFIRE   91
    AND WEARINESS AND FAULT; . . . . 227 TO EARTHWARD   19
WEARING
    WEARING A THIN HEADDRESS OF POINTED LEAVES, ... 196 WILD GRAPES   21
WEARING-STONE
    CR FLOWER, OR WEARING-STONE, OR OPEN EYE, ... 220 FRAGMENTARY BLUE . .   3
WEARS
    AT BEDTIME; BUT THE STRANGENESS SOON WEARS OFF." . . . 115 IN THE HOME STRETCH . 135
WEARY
    THE BRIDEGROOM LOOKED AT THE WEARY ROAD, ...   8 LOVE AND A QUESTION .   21
    AND WEARY, SOUGHT AT NOON WITH HIM THE SHADE; . . . . 23 THE TUFT OF FLOWERS .   36
    IT'S WHEN I'M WEARY OF CONSIDERATIONS, ... 122 BIRCHES   43
    AND SCURF OF PLANTS, AND WEARY AND OVERHEATED, ... 125 AN ENCOUNTER   6
    AND SO PUT OFF THE WEARY DAY . . . . 417 AMERICA IS HARD TO SEE   40
    BEFORE THEY SAT DOWN WEARY ON A BANK . . . . 454 HOW HARD TO KEEP FROM   13
WEATHER
    AND PERHAPS HEAR SOME WORD ABOUT THE WEATHER. . . . . 74 THE GENERATIONS OF MEN   33
    ONCE ON THE KIND OF DAY CALLED "WEATHER BREEDER," . . . 125 AN ENCOUNTER   1
    OF EARTHLY WEATHER, ... 218 I WILL SING YOU ONE-O .   25
    IT'S ONLY WEATHER.' HE'D THINK SHE DIDN'T KNOW! . . . 223 THE RUNAWAY   13
    BY THOUSANDS THE BAD WEATHER MADE AKIN. . . . . . . 240 OUR SINGING STRENGTH .   32
    THAT THOUGH REPRESSED AND MOODY WITH THE WEATHER . . . 240 OUR SINGING STRENGTH .   51
    MINE WITH INNER, WEATHER. . . . . 252 TREE AT MY WINDOW . .   16
    THAT ALL THEY ASK IS ROUGHER WEATHER, ... 262 THE FLOWER BOAT . . .   10
    THOUGH THERE'S MORE THAN A DOUBT IF THE WEATHER IS NOT TOO
        COLD . . . . 300 STRONG SAYING NOTHING .   11
    BUT THE WEATHER IS CLEAR TONIGHT, ... 301 VOICE WAYS   2
    IN MY WITCHES' WEATHER PRIMER . . . . 303 CLEAR AND COLDER . .   2
    FROM ONE DAY'S PERFECT WEATHER, ... 333 HAPPINESS MAKES UP .   14
    LIKE GRAVEYARD MARBLE SCULPTURE IN THE WEATHER, . . . 377 DIRECTIVE   4
WEATHERED
    THAT LED US TO A WEATHERED WINDOWSILL. . . . . . . 55 THE BLACK COTTAGE . .   13
WEATHER'S
    THE WEATHER'S ALTERNATIONS, SUMMER AND WINTER, ... 317 BUILD SOIL   36
WEAVING
    OR WEAVING LIKE A STABLED HORSE: . . . . 325 TO A THINKER   7
WEBSTER
    SHE HAD ONE DANIEL WEBSTER. HE WAS ALL . . . . . . 161 NEW HAMPSHIRE . . .   67
    THE DANIEL WEBSTER EVER WAS OR SHALL BE. . . . . . . 161 NEW HAMPSHIRE . . .   68
WED
    PERHAPS HE MOCKED AT US FOR BEING WED, ... 127 THE SMILE   8
WE'D---NOT INDEXED
WEDDED
    BUT WHETHER STOLEN FROM HER WEDDED LORD . . . . . . 343 DISCOVERY OF MADEIRAS   2
WEDDING (SEE FUNERAL-WEDDING)
    BE HER FIRST JOY HER WEDDING, ... 256 THE LOVELY BE CHOOSERS   22
    THAT THOUGH A WEDDING, ... 256 THE LOVELY BE CHOOSERS   23
    HOW FOR A CHANGE WOULD A WEDDING BE?-- . . . . . . 345 DISCOVERY OF MADEIRAS   71
WEDGE
    THEY GAVE IT THE WEDGE . . . . 448 THE BAD ISLAND--EASTER   14
WEDGES
    IN MANY MARCHES. AND THEY LIE LIKE WEDGES, ... 164 NEW HAMPSHIRE . . . 178
    WHERE ASIA WEDGES AFRICA FROM EUROPE. . . . . . . 176 THE CENSUS-TAKER . .   53
WEDLOCK
    HOUSEKEEPING FOR THE NEXT MAN OUT OF WEDLOCK. . . . . 201 PLACE FOR A THIRD .   62
WEED
    WHEN, JUST AS THE SOIL TARNISHES WITH WEED, ... 124 PUTTING IN THE SEED .   12
    OF SOMETHING MORE THAN TINDER-GRASS AND WEED-- . . . . 131 THE BONFIRE   77
    OF ALL THINGS BUT WEED. . . . . 134 A GIRL'S GARDEN . . .   28
    AND SMALL REGARD TO THE FUTURE OF ANY WEED. . . . . 299 STRONG SAYING NOTHING .   2
    FROM LOVELY BLOOMING BUT WASTEFUL WEED . . . . . . 376 SOMETHING FOR HOPE .   15
    FOR WHAT THE DRAB WEED LACKS OF THE ORNATE. . . . . 411 POD OF THE MILKWEED .   13
    THE SOBER WEED HAS MANAGED TO CONTRIVE . . . . . . 412 POD OF THE MILKWEED .   31
    NOR TASTE ITS SALT, NOR SMELL ITS FISH AND WEED, . . . 447 DOES NO ONE AT ALL EVER 35
WEEDING
    FROM WEEDING GARDEN BEDS . . . . 361 ALMOST TWO THOUSAND .   11
WEEDS
    UP FROM THE TANGLE OF WITHERED WEEDS . . . .   8 A LATE WALK   7
    DEAD WEEDS AND UNMATED BIRDS, ... 11 WIND AND WINDOW FLOWER   15
    AT WEEDS THE WATER FROM THE SINK MADE TALL. . . . . 110 IN THE HOME STRETCH .   3
    "RANK WEEDS THAT LOVE THE WATER FROM THE DISHPAN . . . 111 IN THE HOME STRETCH .   30
    IN ALTERNATION WITH THE WEEDS, THE FIELD, ... 112 IN THE HOME STRETCH .   48

WEEDS (CONTINUED)
  AND DEAD WEEDS, LIKE A DISAPPEARING SNAKE. . . . . . . 226 THE ONSET 21
  BUT A FEW WEEDS AND STUBBLE SHOWING LAST. . . . . . 296 DESERT PLACES . . . 4
  WHAT'S MORE, I HATE TO KEEP AFFLICTING WEEDS. . . . . 406 FROM PLANE TO PLANE . 64
  OF DUSTY WEEDS TO TAKE A DRINK OF STARS. . . . . . . 454 HOW HARD TO KEEP FROM . 14
WEEK
  YOU'LL HAVE TO PAY ME MORE THAN TEN A WEEK . . . . . 48 A HUNDRED COLLARS . 116
  AND MEDICINE AND REST, AND YOU A WEEK, ... 230 NOT TO KEEP 16
WEEKLY
  ALL ROUND THE COUNTRY FOR THE WEEKLY NEWS, ... 48 A HUNDRED COLLARS . 98
  PUBLISHED IN BOW. YOU KNOW THE WEEKLY NEWS?" . . . . 48 A HUNDRED COLLARS . 99
WEEKS
  "TWO WEEKS SINCE." / "SHE'S IN EARNEST, IT APPEARS." . . 82 THE HOUSEKEEPER . . . 22
  TO SEE US THROUGH OUR FIRST TWO WEEKS. BUT, JOE, . . . 113 IN THE HOME STRETCH . 74
WEEP
  WEEP FOR WHAT LITTLE THINGS COULD MAKE THEM GLAD. . . . 378 DIRECTIVE 44
  YET SO WE'LL HAVE TO WEEP BECAUSE WE CAN'T. . . . . 512 A MASQUE OF MERCY . 499
WEEPING
  BROKEN ACROSS IT, AND ONE EYE IS WEEPING . . . . . . 122 BIRCHES 46
  THE WASTE OF PLEASURE WEEPING, ... 360 NOVEMBER 13
WEIGH
  MY BROTHER SAID: "DON'T YOU WEIGH ANYTHING? . . . . . 199 WILD GRAPES 89
  TRY TO WEIGH SOMETHING NEXT TIME, SO YOU WON'T . . . . 199 WILD GRAPES 90
  IN READINESS TO WEIGH UPON HER. . . . . 256 THE LOVELY BE CHOOSERS 13
WEIGHING
  IT WASN'T MY NOT WEIGHING ANYTHING . . . . 199 WILD GRAPES 92
WEIGHT
  AND SAVING THAT ITS WEIGHT SUGGESTED GOLD . . . . . 172 A STAR IN A STONEBOAT . 5
  EQUALLY WITH MY WEIGHT IN GRAPES, ONE AUTUMN, ... 196 WILD GRAPES 5
  I LONG FOR WEIGHT AND STRENGTH . . . . 227 TO EARTHWARD 30
  NEXT TO NOTHING FOR WEIGHT; . . . . 235 GATHERING LEAVES . . 17
  HER GREAT WEIGHT CREAKS THE BARBED WIRE IN ITS STAPLES . 269 THE BEAR 7
  THE WEIGHT OF AN AX-HEAD POISED ALOFT, ... 276 TWO TRAMPS IN MUD TIME 45
  ITS AIRY PRESSURE TURNED TO WATER WEIGHT. . . . . . 315 IRIS BY NIGHT . . . 16
  COMPRESSION TO UPLIFT US OUT OF WEIGHT-- . . . . . . 387 INNATE HELIUM . . . 3
  INTO HAVING WEIGHT. . . . . 426 A NEVER NAUGHT SONG . 5
WEISS
  TILL WEISS SHUT OFF THE WATER IN THE WHEEL PIT. . . . 93 THE SELF-SEEKER . . . 27
WELCOME
  THEY'RE YOURS AND WELCOME; LET ME SEND THEM TO YOU.-- . 47 A HUNDRED COLLARS . . 68
  MY WELCOME DIFFERED FROM NO OTHER WELCOME. . . . . . 186 THE AX-HELVE . . . 36
  I'D WELCOME ANY MODERATE DISASTER . . . . 190 THE GRINDSTONE . . . 62
  WHETHER ELIZA WOULD BE WELCOME THERE. . . . . . . 200 PLACE FOR A THIRD . 42
  THEY WERE WELCOME TO THEIR BELIEF, ... 299 WELCOME TO THEIR BELIEF 3
  THEY WERE WELCOME TO THEIR BELIEF . . . . 299 WELCOME TO THEIR BELIEF T
WELCOMED
  BUT WELCOMED FOR THE CHANCE TO LAVE MY SHOES . . . . 215 A FOUNTAIN, A BOTTLE . 66
WELL
  THE FOOTPATH DOWN TO THE WELL IS HEALED. . . . . . 6 GHOST HOUSE 10
  I KNEW SO WELL, WHOSE GARMENTS TRAIL . . . . 15 IN A VALE 4
  AND THUS IT IS I KNOW SO WELL . . . . 16 IN A VALE 21
  WELL I KNOW WHERE TO HIE ME--IN THE DAWN, ... 17 THE VANTAGE POINT . . 2
  WHAT WAS IT IT WHISPERED? I KNEW NOT WELL MYSELF; . . . 17 MOWING 3
  THE WELL WAS DRY BESIDE THE DOOR, ... 18 GOING FOR WATER . . 1
  SO ALL WHO HIDE TO WELL AWAY . . . . 19 REVELATION 11
  THAT WAS WELL! AND HE STAMPED A HOOF. . . . . . . 24 PAN WITH US 10
  AND WELL I KNEW WHAT THE DEMON MEANT. . . . . . . 25 THE DEMIURGE'S LAUGH . 12
  AND HE LIKES HAVING THOUGHT OF IT SO WELL . . . . . 34 MENDING WALL . . . 44
  "YES, I TOOK CARE TO KEEP WELL OUT OF EARSHOT." . . . 37 DEATH OF THE HIRED MAN 70
  "WELL, THOSE DAYS TROUBLE SILAS LIKE A DREAM. . . . . 37 DEATH OF THE HIRED MAN 71
  IN THE UNLOADING. SILAS DOES THAT WELL. . . . . . . 37 DEATH OF THE HIRED MAN 92
  DOCTOR MAGOON." / "A DOCTOR?" / "WELL, A TEACHER." . . 46 A HUNDRED COLLARS . 43
  I ALMOST KNOW THEIR FARMS AS WELL AS THEY DO." . . . 49 A HUNDRED COLLARS . 121
  THEY MIGHT AS WELL NOT TRY TO GO AT ALL. . . . . . 54 HOME BURIAL 99
  SET WELL BACK FROM THE ROAD IN RANK LODGED GRASS, . . . 55 THE BLACK COTTAGE . . 4
  AND WELL, IF THEY WEREN'T TRUE WHY KEEP RIGHT ON . . . 58 THE BLACK COTTAGE . 97
  "WELL, ONE OF US IS." FOR COMPLAINING IT FLEW . . . . 62 BLUEBERRIES 90
  BUT I WAS WELL . . . . 68 AFTER APPLE-PICKING . 14
  EVERYTHING WENT WELL TILL WE REACHED THE BARN . . . . 71 THE CODE 53
  TILL WELL TOWARD NOON, WHEN THE STORM SETTLED DOWN . . 74 THE GENERATIONS OF MEN 22
  YOU WILL DO VERY WELL RIGHT WHERE YOU ARE . . . . . 78 THE GENERATIONS OF MEN 145
  "I DON'T SEE VERY WELL HOW YOU CAN HELP IT. . . . . 79 THE GENERATIONS OF MEN 155
  "WELL THEN, IT'S GRANNY SPEAKING: 'I DUNNOW! . . . . 80 THE GENERATIONS OF MEN 184
  FARMERS AROUND TWICE AS WELL OFF AS WE . . . . . . 85 THE HOUSEKEEPER . . . 113
  "BUT WHY, WHEN SHE'S WELL OFF? IS IT THE NEIGHBORS, . . 87 THE HOUSEKEEPER . . . 168
  ONLY TOO WELL. I KNEW THERE MUST BE SOMETHING! . . . 87 THE HOUSEKEEPER . . . 182
  "NOTHING." IT CAME FROM WELL ALONG THE ROAD. . . . . 91 THE FEAR 67
  "WELL, IF IT'S TRUE! YOURS ARE NO COMMON FEET. . . . 93 THE SELF-SEEKER . . . 10
  OH, WELL, WE'LL SOON BE THROUGH WITH IT. I'M TIRED." . 96 THE SELF-SEEKER . . . 90
  SHYLY BEHIND HER. / "WELL, AND HOW IS MISTER...?" . . 96 THE SELF-SEEKER . . . 96
  WELL, YES." / "HEAR ANYTHING THAT MIGHT PROVE USEFUL?" . 96 THE SELF-SEEKER . . . 102
  "WELL, WAIT--IT'S COMMON--IT'S TOO COMMON." / "COMMON? . 97 THE SELF-SEEKER . . . 141
  "WELL, ANNE, GO, DEARIE. OUR AFFAIR WILL WAIT. . . . 98 THE SELF-SEEKER . . . 167
  I NEVER BORE IT WELL WHEN PEOPLE WENT. . . . . . . 115 IN THE HOME STRETCH . 131
  WELL, YOU CAN SET THE TABLE WITH THE LOAF. . . . . 115 IN THE HOME STRETCH . 154
  PINE, ALDER, PASTURE, MOWING, WELL, AND BROOK. . . . 117 IN THE HOME STRETCH . 197
  "WELL, SO I CAME." . . . . 118 THE TELEPHONE . . . 19
  WELL IF IT DOESN'T WITH ITS DRAFT BRING ON . . . . . 130 THE BONFIRE 32
  "WELL--I--BE--" THAT WAS ALL HE SAID, ... 139 BROWN'S DESCENT . . . 45
  FRED COLE, YOU'RE GOING TO LET HIM!" / "WELL, AREN'T YOU? 144 SNOW 43
  HE TOOK NO NOTICE, DID HE? WELL, AT LEAST . . . . . 144 SNOW 49
  "YOU LIKE THE RUNT." / "DON'T YOU A LITTLE?" / "WELL, . 146 SNOW 94
  YOU LIKE YOUR FUN AS WELL AS ANYONE; . . . . . . 146 SNOW 97
  DOWN AT THE AVERYS'? WELL, ONE SUNNY MORNING . . . . 149 SNOW 175
  PILING IT WELL ABOVE THE WINDOWSILLS. . . . . . . 149 SNOW 179
  WELL, NOW I LEAVE YOU, PEOPLE." / "COME, MESERVE, . . 150 SNOW 197
  WELL, THERE'S-- SHE TOLD FRED AFTERWARD THAT IN . . . 151 SNOW 237
  "WELL, THERE'S--THE STORM. THAT SAYS I MUST GO ON. . . 151 SNOW 240

WELL (CONTINUED)
    NOT READING IT. / "WELL, WHAT KIND OF A MAN . . . . . 151 SNOW 247
    IT WON'T BE FOR AN HOUR OR TWO." / "WELL THEN-- . . . 152 SNOW 267
    "WELL THEN," SHE SAID, AND "WELL THEN"--LIKE A THREAT. 153 SNOW 289
    DROP IN AND SEE US WHEN YOU'RE PASSING." / "WELL, . . 155 SNOW 333
    OH, IT WAS TERRIBLE AS WELL COULD BE. . . . . 160 NEW HAMPSHIRE . . 59
    WILL SERVE ALMOST AS WELL ABOUT VERMONT, ... 165 NEW HAMPSHIRE . . 211
    I MAY AS WELL CONFESS MYSELF THE AUTHOR . . . . . . 166 NEW HAMPSHIRE . . 228
    IF WELL IT IS WITH RUSSIA, THEN FEEL FREE . . . . . 168 NEW HAMPSHIRE . . 280
    WELL, THEY REMIND ME OF THE HUE AND CRY . . . . . . 168 NEW HAMPSHIRE . . 294
    HE KNEW TOO WELL FOR ANY EARTHLY USE . . . . 171 NEW HAMPSHIRE . . 378
    WELL, IF I HAVE TO CHOOSE ONE OR THE OTHER, ... 172 NEW HAMPSHIRE . . 407
    YET ASK WHERE ELSE IT COULD HAVE GONE AS WELL, . . . 173 A STAR IN A STONEBOAT . 37
    I ASKED HIM WELL BEFOREHAND. "DON'T YOU GET ONE!" . . 177 THE STAR-SPLITTER . . 21
    IN LITTLETON IT MAY AS WELL BE ME." . . . . 177 THE STAR-SPLITTER . . 37
    TO FIND HIMSELF IN ONE. WELL, ALL WE SAID WAS . . . 178 THE STAR-SPLITTER . . 57
    WELL, YOU WERE NAMED AFTER A MAPLE TREE. . . . . . . 180 MAPLE 9
    TO MAKE IT GO WELL WITH THE WAY SHE LOOKED. . . . . 181 MAPLE 43
    AS WELL AS COULD A MOTHER. AND AGAIN . . . . 183 MAPLE 119
    I DIDN'T KNOW HIM WELL ENOUGH TO KNOW . . . . 185 THE AX-HELVE . . . 14
    TONIGHT?" / AS WELL TONIGHT AS ANY NIGHT. . . . . . 186 THE AX-HELVE . . . 34
    WELL, THIS IS SUCH A YARN. PAUL SAWED HIS WIFE . . . 192 PAUL'S WIFE 54
    AND THERE, WELL AFTER DARK, LET MURPHY TELL IT, . . 195 PAUL'S WIFE 127
    BY THAT TIME I WAS PRETTY WELL REDUCED . . . . . . 198 WILD GRAPES 60
    MIGHT JUST AS WELL BE ICE AND THE CLOTHES SNOW. . . 203 THE WITCH OF COOS . . 39
    SHE MIGHT AS WELL HERSELF." BUT HE LIKED BEST . . . 209 PAUPER WITCH OF GRAFTON 83
    WELL, I SHOWED ARTHUR AMY SIGNS ENOUGH . . . . . . 210 PAUPER WITCH OF GRAFTON 89
    WELL, TAKE ME THERE." / "SOME DAY I WILL." / "TODAY." 213 A FOUNTAIN, A BOTTLE . 14
    "WELL, IF I HAVEN'T BROUGHT YOU TO THE FOUNTAIN, . . 214 A FOUNTAIN, A BOTTLE . 41
    WE MAY AS WELL SEE THAT AND SAVE THE DAY." . . . . 214 A FOUNTAIN, A BOTTLE . 54
    WELL THEN, RIGHT HERE IS WHERE I SHOW YOU BOOKS. . . 215 A FOUNTAIN, A BOTTLE . 60
    DEEPER DOWN IN THE WELL THAN WHERE THE WATER . . . 225 FOR ONCE SOMETHING . . 3
    WELL, SOMETHING FOR A SNOWSTORM TO HAVE SHOWN . . . 240 OUR SINGING STRENGTH . 49
    AS WELL HAVE BEEN THE SWORD. . . . . 252 THE PEACEFUL SHEPHERD . 12
    WELL, WE SHOULD SEE WHICH ONE WOULD WIN, ... 253 THE THATCH 8
    WHAT WELL MAY PROVE THE YEAR'S HIGH GIRDLE MARK. . . 254 A WINTER EDEN . . . 12
    IS YET--WELL, SOMETHING THEY KNOW, HE AND SHE. . . 256 THE LOVELY BE CHOOSERS 24
    THEY CAN LEAVE HER A HUT AS WELL; . . . . 260 SAND DUNES 14
    WE MAY AS WELL GO PATIENTLY ON WITH OUR LIFE, . . . 268 ON LOOKING UP BY CHANCE 8
    (HE STOOD WELL BACK FOR FEAR OF SCALDING SQUIRTS.) . 270 THE EGG AND THE MACHINE 12
    I KNEW PRETTY WELL WHY HE DROPPED BEHIND . . . . . 275 TWO TRAMPS IN MUD TIME 5
    I KNEW PRETTY WELL WHAT HE HAD IN MIND: . . . . . 275 TWO TRAMPS IN MUD TIME 7
    SHE WELL MAY SCORE AN EGG-SUCCESS. . . . . 280 BLUE RIBBON AT AMESBURY 32
    WELL, THE MOON AFTER THAT, CAME ONE AT LAST . . . . 289 OLD BARN AT THE BOTTOM 6
    WE SAID WELL TWICE TO WHAT WE HAD IN COMMON, . . . 290 OLD BARN AT THE BOTTOM 22
    HE HAD A WELL, HE HAD THE RAIN TO CATCH. . . . . . 292 FIGURE IN THE DOORWAY . 17
    SEEING MYSELF WELL LOST ONCE MORE, I SIGHED, . . . 295 LOST IN HEAVEN . . . 9
    THEY MIGHT AS WELL HAVE NONE AT ALL. . . . . . . 297 LEAVES COMPARED WITH . 10
    IF GOLD PLEASED THE CONQUEROR, WELL, ... 311 THE VINDICTIVES . . . 24
    AND LEAPFROG IN EACH OTHER'S WAY--ALL'S WELL. . . . 318 BUILD SOIL 64
    TO BE ATTEMPTED. GREED MAY WELL COME NEXT. . . . . 319 BUILD SOIL 100
    IT WELL MAY BE. WE MEET--I DON'T SAY WHEN-- . . . 321 BUILD SOIL 159
    WELL, WHEN AT LENGTH THE FEVER STRUCK . . . . . . 345 DISCOVERY OF MADEIRAS . 57
    THE AGE MAY VERY WELL HAVE BEEN TO BLAME . . . . . 351 THE LESSON FOR TODAY . 26
    IT WAS WELL WORTH PRELIMINARY MENTION. . . . . . . 352 THE LESSON FOR TODAY . 59
    IT WAS WELL WORTH PRELIMINARY MENTION. . . . . . . 352 THE LESSON FOR TODAY . 63
    IT MIGHT AS WELL AT ONCE BE KINGDOM-COME. . . . . 353 THE LESSON FOR TODAY . 102
    HE TRUSTS MY LOVE TOO WELL TO DEIGN REPLY. . . . . 359 THE LOST FOLLOWER . . 33
    WE WELL MAY RAISE OUR HEADS . . . . 361 ALMOST TWO THOUSAND . 10
    BUT WELL MAY BE LACONIC, EVEN BOEOTIAN. . . . . . 362 BOEOTIAN 3
    WELL, WOULD I PLEASE GO TO SCHOOL, ... 366 NOT OF SCHOOL AGE . . 23
    AND WELL MAY BE WHERE WARS ORIGINATE. . . . . . . 371 THE LITERATE FARMER AND 109
    MAY WELL HAVE NOTICED. SOON ENTIRELY WHITE . . . . 375 A YOUNG BIRCH . . . 4
    IN FARMING WELL--OR PRETTY WELL. . . . . 381 AN UNSTAMPED LETTER IN 49
    OF CAUTION UNDER STARS THAT VERY WELL . . . . . . 383 BRAVADO 2
    WELL, I SAID THAT I DID. . . . . 391 A WISH TO COMPLY . . 3
    I MIGHT WELL HAVE SUNG . . . . 428 KITTY HAWK 5
    WELL THEY FLOURISHED AND WAXED . . . . 448 THE BAD ISLAND--EASTER 34
    A-WISHING WELL . . . . 451 A-WISHING WELL . . T
    THE EUNUCH LAUGHED: "WELL, THAT'S A LOT TO KNOW. . . 455 HOW HARD TO KEEP FROM 45
    AS WELL AS OF YOUR HUNDRED OTHER THINGS. . . . . . 456 HOW HARD TO KEEP FROM 99
    YOU'RE WELL DESCENDED ON YOUR MOTHER'S SIDE, . . . 457 HOW HARD TO KEEP FROM 108
    HE ANSWERED HER BACK, "WELL, WHO BEGUN IT?" . . . . 463 LINES IN DEJECTION . . 25
    OH, I REMEMBER WELL: YOU'RE JOB, MY PATIENT. . . . 474 A MASQUE OF REASON . . 34
    WELL, AFTER ALL THESE YEARS! / THIS IS MY WIFE. . . 476 A MASQUE OF REASON . . 83
    OF RECORD IN MY NOTE BOOK. / WELL, SHE WAS. . . . . 477 A MASQUE OF REASON . . 103
    WE MAY AS WELL GO BACK TO THE BEGINNING . . . . . 477 A MASQUE OF REASON . . 113
    AS WELL AS WORDS. / I'M SERIOUS. GOD'S HAD . . . . 478 A MASQUE OF REASON . . 148
    AND THAT FOR MAN'S OWN SAKE AS WELL AS MINE, . . . 481 A MASQUE OF REASON . . 211
    WE'RE GOING ANYWAY AND MAY AS WELL . . . . 482 A MASQUE OF REASON . . 234
    AND MAY AS WELL THROW IN A LITTLE SENSE. . . . . . 482 A MASQUE OF REASON . . 237
    OH, WE KNOW WELL ENOUGH TO GO AHEAD WITH. . . . . 483 A MASQUE OF REASON . . 289
    IT WOULD BE MEANINGLESS. IT MIGHT AS WELL . . . . 484 A MASQUE OF REASON . . 321
    WE'RE TOO WELL OFF. / SOMEDAY WE THREE SHOULD HAVE . 486 A MASQUE OF REASON . . 379
    JOB'S WIFE SITS UP.) / WELL, IF WE AREN'T ALL HERE, . 487 A MASQUE OF REASON . . 392
    AND WHAT ELSE DID WE SAY? / WELL, WHAT LED UP-- . . 487 A MASQUE OF REASON . . 399
    AND FIGURATIVE USE HAVE PRETTY WELL . . . . 488 A MASQUE OF REASON . . 425
    YOU'D AS WELL SMILE AS FROWN ON THE OCCASION. . . . 490 A MASQUE OF REASON . . 465
    WELL, I COULD USE A BOOK. / WHAT BOOK? / A BIBLE. . 494 A MASQUE OF MERCY . . 27
    WELL, YOU'RE AS GOOD AS IN NEW YORK THIS MINUTE-- . 497 A MASQUE OF MERCY . . 92
    YOU WRONG ME. / WELL THEN, NAME A SINGLE SIN. . . . 503 A MASQUE OF MERCY . . 262
    WELL, BUT REMEMBER THIS IS UNOFFICIAL. . . . . . . 506 A MASQUE OF MERCY . . 331
    THEY TOOK MY LOVE AND THREW HER DOWN A WELL. . . . 510 A MASQUE OF MERCY . . 446
    HE'S THINKING OF, IT WASN'T DOWN A WELL, ... 510 A MASQUE OF MERCY . . 448
    WE'RE READING IT. / WELL, NOW YOU'VE GOT IT READ, . 512 A MASQUE OF MERCY . . 491
    WELL THEN! / AND THAT'S WHAT I'M TO MEDITATE? . . . 517 A MASQUE OF MERCY . . 627
WE'LL---NOT INDEXED

PAGE TITLE   LINE

WELL—BEING
    AND SAD ON A FOUNDATION OF WELL—BEING. . . . . 168 NEW HAMPSHIRE . . . 286
    POSSIBLY JUST WELL—BEING IN THE BODY, ... 461 HOW HARD TO KEEP FROM 243
WELL—CURB
    ONCE, WHEN TRYING WITH CHIN AGAINST A WELL—CURB, . . . 225 FOR ONCE SOMETHING . . 7
WELL—CURBS
    OTHERS TAUNT ME WITH HAVING KNELT AT WELL—CURBS . . . 225 FOR ONCE SOMETHING . . 1
WELL—NIGH
    ACROSS THE GULF OF WELL—NIGH EVERYTHING . . . . . 356 A MOTH SEEN IN WINTER . 21
WELL—STARCHED
    FUMBLING THE BUTTONS IN A WELL—STARCHED SHIRT. . . . 46 A HUNDRED COLLARS . . 52
WELL—TURNED
    HER WELL—TURNED EGG'S BROWN STURDY SHELL, ... 281 BLUE RIBBON AT AMESBURY 34
WELL—WINED
    LET THEM GET WELL—WINED . . . . 413 AWAY! 7
WELSHMAN
    BUT NEVER MIND, THE WELSHMAN GOT IT PLANTED . . . . . 57 THE BLACK COTTAGE . . 68
WENDED
    AND OVER THE WALLS I HAVE WENDED; . . . . 29 RELUCTANCE 2
WENT
    BEFORE THE LAST WENT, HEAVY WITH DEW, ... 15 IN A VALE . . . 16
    AND SO WE WENT WITH PAIL AND CAN . . . . 18 GOING FOR WATER . . . 2
    I WENT TO TURN THE GRASS ONCE AFTER ONE . . . . . 22 THE TUFT OF FLOWERS . 1
    BRUSHING THE DIRT FROM HIS EYE AS HE WENT; . . . . 25 THE DEMIURGE'S LAUGH . 11
    "THIS WILL BE YOURS. GOOD—NIGHT," HE SAID, AND WENT. . . 46 A HUNDRED COLLARS . . 40
    BUT I WENT NEAR TO SEE WITH MY OWN EYES. . . . . 54 HOME BURIAL . . . 83
    "THAT WAS THE FATHER AS HE WENT TO WAR.— . . . . . 55 THE BLACK COTTAGE . . 25
    SINCE SHE WENT, MORE THAN EVER, BUT BEFORE—— . . . 56 THE BLACK COTTAGE . . 36
    HE DIDN'T SAY WHERE THEY HAD BEEN. HE WENT ON: . . 61 BLUEBERRIES . . . 74
    BUT LEN WENT AT IT TO MAKE UP THE LOSS. . . . . . 64 A SERVANT TO SERVANTS . 65
    MY FATHER'S BROTHER, HE WENT MAD QUITE YOUNG. . . . 65 A SERVANT TO SERVANTS . 104
    I DIDN'T WANT THE BLAME IF THINGS WENT WRONG. . . . 67 A SERVANT TO SERVANTS . 150
    WENT SURELY TO THE CIDER—APPLE HEAP . . . . . . 69 AFTER APPLE—PICKING . 35
    EVERYTHING WENT WELL TILL WE REACHED THE BARN . . . 71 THE CODE . . . 53
    I WENT ABOUT TO KILL HIM FAIR ENOUGH." . . . . . 73 THE CODE . . . 112
    NO ONE WENT HOME THAT WAY, THE ONLY HOUSE . . . . 76 THE GENERATIONS OF MEN 73
    BUT IF WE MUST, IN SUNSHINE." SO SHE WENT. . . . . 81 THE GENERATIONS OF MEN 212
    SOMETHING WENT WRONG. I SAW HIM THROW THE HOE . . . 83 THE HOUSEKEEPER . . 60
    IT TOUCHED, IT STRUCK, IT CLATTERED AND WENT OUT. . . 92 THE FEAR . . . 93
    ONE FOOT WENT THROUGH. THE VIEW WAS ALL IN LINES . . 101 THE WOOD—PILE . . 5
    HE WENT BEHIND IT TO MAKE HIS LAST STAND. . . . . 101 THE WOOD—PILE . . 22
    I WENT TILL THERE WERE NO COTTAGES FOUND. . . . . 102 GOOD HOURS . . . 10
    I WENT TO SHOW YOU HOW TO MAKE IT STAY, ... 109 THE EXPOSED NEST . . 5
    IT SOUNDS AS IF IT WERE THE MEN WENT DOWN, ... 112 IN THE HOME STRETCH . 56
    I NEVER BORE IT WELL WHEN PEOPLE WENT. . . . . . 115 IN THE HOME STRETCH . 131
    AS I WENT DOWN THE HILL ALONG THE WALL . . . . . 118 MEETING AND PASSING . 1
    AFTERWARD I WENT PAST WHAT YOU HAD PASSED . . . . 119 MEETING AND PASSING . 13
    EVEN AGAINST THE WAY ITS WATERS WENT. . . . . . 119 HYLA BROOK . . . 9
    WHEN PEAR AND CHERRY BLOOM WENT DOWN IN SHOWERS . . 120 THE OVEN BIRD . . 7
    AS HE WENT OUT AND IN TO FETCH THE COWS—— . . . . 121 BIRCHES . . . 24
    THE MINUTE THEY HEARD MY STEP WENT STILL . . . . 123 PEA BRUSH . . . 11
    I DIDN'T LIKE THE WAY HE WENT AWAY. . . . . . . 127 THE SMILE . . . 1
    AND ONCE SHE WENT TO BREAK A BOUGH. . . . . . . 129 THE IMPULSE . . . 13
    AS I WENT OUT A CROW . . . . 135 LAST WORD OF A BLUEBIRD 1
    AND THEN WENT ROUND IT ON HIS FEET, ... 139 BROWN'S DESCENT . . 61
    BEFORE I WENT TO SAY GOOD—MORNING THERE.—— . . . . 143 SNOW 18
    THOSE WERE HIS WORDS, AND HE WENT HOME AND ALL . . 149 SNOW 185
    HE SAYS SHE WENT TO LET HIM IN THE BARN.—— . . . 155 SNOW 331
    AND WENT ALONE AGAINST A GROVE OF TREES; . . . . 170 NEW HAMPSHIRE . . 368
    IT WENT FOR BUILDING STONE, AND I, AS THOUGH . . . 173 A STAR IN A STONEBOAT . 34
    MEAN LAUGHTER WENT ABOUT THE TOWN THAT DAY . . . 177 THE STAR—SPLITTER . 40
    BUT HADN'T AS IT WENT. (SHE KNEW A ROSE.) . . . . 181 MAPLE . . . 48
    THEY WENT ON PILGRIMAGE ONCE TO HER FATHER'S . . . 182 MAPLE . . . 97
    NOT ALL THE MILES IT MAY HAVE THOUGHT IT WENT, . . 188 THE GRINDSTONE . . 6
    "HOW IS THE WIFE, PAUL?" AND HE ALWAYS WENT. . . . 192 PAUL'S WIFE . . . 24
    SHE WENT OUT LIKE A FIREFLY, AND THAT WAS ALL. . . 195 PAUL'S WIFE . . . 144
    SHE WENT HER WAY. BUT LABAN HAVING CAUGHT . . . . 200 PLACE FOR A THIRD . 15
    BEFORE SHE WENT THE POOR MAN'S WIDOW'S WAY, ... 201 PLACE FOR A THIRD . 61
    I WENT TO SLEEP BEFORE I WENT TO BED, ... 203 THE WITCH OF COOS . 37
    LET HIM STAY IN THE ATTIC SINCE THEY WENT THERE. . . 206 THE WITCH OF COOS . 132
    THE ATTIC WASPS WENT MISSING BY LIKE BULLETS. . . . 217 A FOUNTAIN, A BOTTLE . 130
    YOU WENT TO MEET THE SHELL'S EMBRACE OF FIRE . . . 222 TO E.T. . . . 13
    AS FAR AS YOU WENT FROM THE DOOR, WHICH WAS NOT FAR; . 235 VALLEY'S SINGING DAY . 3
    IT WENT MANY YEARS, ... 240 THE LOCKLESS DOOR . 1
    I WOULD NOT GO IN TILL THE LIGHT WENT OUT; . . . . 253 THE THATCH . . . 6
    I WENT TO SCHOOL TO AGE TO LEARN THE PAST. . . . . 267 WHAT FIFTY SAID . . 4
    THAT'S WHEN I WENT AS VISITOR TO HIS HOUSE. . . . . 278 THE WHITE—TAILED HORNET 22
    WENT LONG SINCE TO THE DOGS UNDER THE TABLE. . . . 279 THE WHITE—TAILED HORNET 57
    AS REGULARLY AS HE WENT TO FEED THE PIG . . . . . 283 THE GOLD HESPERIDEE . 19
    BUT ONE DAY WHEN THE FOLIAGE ALL WENT SWISH . . . 284 THE GOLD HESPERIDEE . 32
    THE GUN REVERSED THAT HE WENT OUT WITH SHOULDERED. . 289 OLD BARN AT THE BOTTOM 4
    JUST WHEN THE COLD WENT DOWN SO MANY BELOW. . . . 305 THERE ARE ROUGHLY ZONES 17
    WHERE THE SPENDER THINKS IT WENT. . . . . . . 309 HARDSHIP OF ACCOUNTING 2
    AND ONE WENT OFF TO THE MOUNTAINS . . . . . . 313 BEARER OF EVIL TIDINGS 7
    INSTEAD OF MOVING WITH US AS WE WENT . . . . . . 315 IRIS BY NIGHT . . 24
    WE WENT FROM HOUSE TO WOOD . . . . 333 HAPPINESS MAKES UP . 23
    THRUSH MUSIC WENT—— . . . . 334 COME IN . . . 14
    YET FURTHER I WENT TO BE BEFORE THE SCYTHE, . . . 342 QUEST OF PURPLE—FRINGED 9
    SEEMED TO ARGUE PERHAPS SHE WENT . . . . . . 343 DISCOVERY OF MADEIRAS . 13
    AND WENT TO LEAN AGAINST THE RAIL, ... 345 DISCOVERY OF MADEIRAS . 50
    AND WENT EMBRACED TO THE COLD AND DARK . . . . . 346 DISCOVERY OF MADEIRAS . 84
    THE MUSE MOURNS ONE WHO WENT TO HIS RETREAT . . . 359 THE LOST FOLLOWER . 21
    A WORLD TORN LOOSE WENT BY ME. . . . . 377 ONE STEP BACKWARD TAKEN 12
    WENT STREAKING MOLTEN DOWN THE WEST. . . . . . 381 AN UNSTAMPED LETTER IN 27
    THEN FROM THE WORK YOU WENT ABOUT . . . . . . 381 AN UNSTAMPED LETTER IN 48
    WENT BY WITH CLANGING GONG . . . . 391 A ROGERS GROUP . . 6
    I WENT TO THE PHYSICIAN TO COMPLAIN, ... 398 BURSTING RAPTURE . . 1
    A CHEER WENT UP THAT SHOOK THE MOTTOED WALL. . . . 400 THE BROKEN DROUGHT . . 6

WENT (CONTINUED)
    WHEN THE CHANCE WENT BY . . . . 434 KITTY HAWK 183
    THE PONDEROUS BEAST WENT DOWN . . . . 444 THE DRAFT HORSE . . . 9
    AND SO IT WENT WITH TRIUMPH AFTER TRIUMPH . . . . . 456 HOW HARD TO KEEP FROM 93
WENTWORTH
    WHICH WASN'T MANY, IN THE TOWN OF WENTWORTH. . . . . 208 PAUPER WITCH OF GRAFTON 22
    WENTWORTH AND WARREN'S BOTH GOOD TOWNS TO LIVE IN, . . 208 PAUPER WITCH OF GRAFTON 30
    IN WENTWORTH FROM NOW ON; AND WHEN ALL'S SAID, ... 208 PAUPER WITCH OF GRAFTON 32
WEPT
    NOT TO BELIEVE THE PHOEBES WEPT. . . . . 242 NEED OF BEING VERSED . 24
    I MAY HAVE WEPT THAT ANY SHOULD HAVE DIED . . . . . 355 THE LESSON FOR TODAY . 151
    WHILE ANOTHER WEPT. . . . . 432 KITTY HAWK 128
WE'RE---NOT INDEXED
WERE---NOT INDEXED
WEREN'T---NOT INDEXED
WEST
    WHAT MATTER IF WE GO CLEAR TO THE WEST, ... 27 A LINE-STORM SONG . . 21
    PART OF A MOON WAS FALLING DOWN THE WEST, ... 38 DEATH OF THE HIRED MAN 103
    I NOTICED THAT I MISSED STARS IN THE WEST, ... 40 THE MOUNTAIN . . . 3
    THEY LIVE SO FAR AWAY--ONE IS OUT WEST-- . . . . . 55 THE BLACK COTTAGE . . 19
    YOU COULDN'T TELL HER WHAT THE WEST WAS SAYING, . . . 57 THE BLACK COTTAGE . . 71
    WITH AN EYE ALWAYS LIFTED TOWARD THE WEST . . . . . 69 THE CODE 3
    TO GO WEST TO A WORSE FIGHT WITH THE DESERT. . . . . 213 A FOUNTAIN, A BOTTLE . 12
    THE WEST WAS GETTING OUT OF GOLD, ... 232 LOOKING FOR SUNSET BIRD 1
    FROM THE HIGH WEST SHE MAKES A GENTLE CAST . . . . . 251 BEREFT 7
    SOMBER CLOUDS IN THE WEST WERE MASSED. . . . . . . 237 A HILLSIDE THAW . . 20
    THE BROOK RUNS WEST." / "WEST-RUNNING BROOK THEN CALL IT." 257 WEST-RUNNING BROOK . . 2
    "WHAT DOES IT THINK IT'S DOING RUNNING WEST . . . . 257 WEST-RUNNING BROOK . . 4
    ALL THE WAY TO THE WEST . . . . 261 CANIS MAJOR . . . 6
    THAT HAD DIED IN THE WEST . . . . 334 COME IN 10
    THE WEST AND KEEP THE OLD TRADITION SAFE. . . . . . 365 OF STONES OF THE PLACE 12
    WENT STREAKING MOLTEN DOWN THE WEST. . . . . . . 381 AN UNSTAMPED LETTER IN 27
    FINDING THE EAST BY SAILING WEST. . . . . 416 AMERICA IS HARD TO SEE 8
WESTERN
    ...RECENTLY OBSERVED IN THE WESTERN SKY AT EVENING . . . 368 THE LITERATE FARMER AND 5
    SAY ABOUT HALFWAY UP THE WESTERN SKY, ... 370 THE LITERATE FARMER AND 66
    TO QUOTE THE GREATEST WESTERN POEM YET. . . . . . 485 A MASQUE OF REASON . . 344
WESTERNERS
    WESTERNERS INHERIT . . . . 435 KITTY HAWK 225
WEST-NORTHWEST
    HAS BEEN WEST-NORTHWEST. . . . . 435 KITTY HAWK 236
    ALWAYS WEST-NORTHWEST, ... 437 KITTY HAWK 291
WEST-RUNNING
    WEST-RUNNING BROOK . . . . 243 WEST-RUNNING BROOK . . T
    THE BROOK RUNS WEST." / "WEST-RUNNING BROOK THEN CALL IT." 257 WEST-RUNNING BROOK . . 2
    (WEST-RUNNING BROOK MEN CALL IT TO THIS DAY.) . . . . 257 WEST-RUNNING BROOK . . 3
    WEST-RUNNING BROOK . . . . 257 WEST-RUNNING BROOK . . T
    YOU SAID THE BROOK WAS CALLED WEST-RUNNING BROOK." . . 260 WEST-RUNNING BROOK . . 74
WESTWARD
    TO THE LAND VAGUELY REALIZING WESTWARD, ... 348 THE GIFT OUTRIGHT . . 14
    TO THE LAND VAGUELY REALIZING WESTWARD, ... 425 THE GIFT OUTRIGHT . . 14
WET
    THE ROADSIDE FLOWERS, TOO WET FOR THE BEE, ... 26 A LINE-STORM SONG . . 5
    COME, BE MY LOVE IN THE WET WOODS, COME, ... 26 A LINE-STORM SONG . . 15
    FOR WILDING BROOCH, SHALL WET YOUR BREAST . . . . . 27 A LINE-STORM SONG . . 23
    AND THE SUN SHINES OUT WARM: THE VINES MUST BE WET. . . 62 BLUEBERRIES 83
    I WON'T BE TEASED. BUT SEE HOW WET I AM." . . . . . 77 THE GENERATIONS OF MEN 119
    THE SMELL OF THE WET FEATHERS IN THE HEAT! . . . . . 85 THE HOUSEKEEPER . . 122
    WHEREVER THE GROUND WAS LOW AND WET, ... 123 PEA BRUSH 10
    AND STRAINING CABLES WET WITH SILVER DEW. . . . . . 126 RANGE-FINDING . . 11
    TO ANY CHANGE FROM HOT TO COLD, FROM WET . . . . . 166 NEW HAMPSHIRE . . 235
    HER WET HAIR HEAVY ON HER LIKE A HELMET, ... 194 PAUL'S WIFE . . . 109
    I MADE HIM GATHER ME WET SNOWBERRIES . . . . . . 210 PAUPER WITCH OF GRAFTON 97
    WHERE DRIVEN RAIN HAD WET AND SWOLLEN THEM. . . . . 216 A FOUNTAIN, A BOTTLE . 97
    MY WINDOW CURTAIN HUNG OVER THE SILL TO WET; . . . . 236 VALLEY'S SINGING DAY . 17
    BUT IF I THOUGHT TO STOP THE WET STAMPEDE, ... 237 A HILLSIDE THAW . . 9
    HORDES SPENT THEMSELVES TO MAKE IT WET AND COLD, . . . 239 OUR SINGING STRENGTH . 3
    SEA WAVES ARE GREEN AND WET, ... 260 SAND DUNES 1
    I WET ONE LAST YEAR AT MONTAUK . . . . 294 A RECORD STRIDE . . 13
    THE OTHER I WET AT THE CLIFF HOUSE . . . . 294 A RECORD STRIDE . . 15
    THE LAST WET FIELDS AND DRIPPING HEDGES HOME. . . . . 315 IRIS BY NIGHT . . . 3
    TO WET THEIR FEET. . . . . 337 THE WIND AND THE RAIN . 24
    TILL THE SPONGY SOIL AGAIN WAS NATAL WET. . . . . . 349 OUR HOLD ON THE PLANET 10
    GO TILL YOU WET YOUR PINIONS AND ARE QUENCHED. . . . 356 A MOTH SEEN IN WINTER . 18
    ON THE WET FLAGS BEFORE A CRUCIFIX . . . . 516 A MASQUE OF MERCY . . 614
WET-ELBOWED
    AND THREW MYSELF WET-ELBOWED AND WET-KNEED . . . . . 237 A HILLSIDE THAW . . . 12
WET-KNEED
    AND THREW MYSELF WET-ELBOWED AND WET-KNEED . . . . . 237 A HILLSIDE THAW . . . 12
WETTER
    THE WETTER GROUND LIKE GLASS . . . . 301 NEITHER OUT FAR NOR IN 7
WE'VE---NOT INDEXED
WHALE
    ABOUT A WHALE. / OH, YOU MEAN MOBY DICK . . . . . 495 A MASQUE OF MERCY . . 48
    OR, AS YOU MIGHT SAY, THROW ME TO THE WHALE-- . . . . 500 A MASQUE OF MERCY . . 183
    YOU'RE MODERN; SO THE WHALE YOU THROW ME TO . . . . 500 A MASQUE OF MERCY . . 186
WHARF
    DANGLING THEIR LEGS AND FISHING OFF A WHARF . . . . . 161 NEW HAMPSHIRE . . . 75
    AT THAT DATE WITH A WHARF ALREADY BUILT, ... 161 NEW HAMPSHIRE . . . 84
WHAT---NOT INDEXED
WHATE'ER
    BUT WHATE'ER YOU DO TONIGHT, ... 11 TO THE THAWING WIND . 6
WHATEVER
    WHATEVER ELSE THE CIVIL WAR WAS FOR, ... 56 THE BLACK COTTAGE . . 55
    THIS SLEEP OF MINE, WHATEVER SLEEP IT IS. . . . . . 69 AFTER APPLE-PICKING . 38
    WHATEVER ELSE WE WANT FOR. AND A LIGHT. . . . . . 113 IN THE HOME STRETCH . 79
    WITH WHATEVER IT IS THEY SING; . . . . 126 LONELINESS 6
    TO GIVE WHATEVER MIGHT CHANCE TO BE, ... 127 HOUSE FEAR 6

```
                                                         PAGE TITLE                          LINE
WHATEVER (CONTINUED)
      SHE LEARNED SHORTHAND, WHATEVER SHORTHAND MAY  . . . .  182 MAPLE  . . . . .    75
      WHATEVER SCHOOL AND CHILDREN AND OUR DOUBTS  . . . . .  188 THE AX-HELVE  . . . .   85
      SHOOK WHATEVER IT WAS LAY THERE AT BOTTOM,  . . . . .   225 FOR ONCE SOMETHING .   13
      WHATEVER THEY COST APIECE OR A POUND,  . . . . . . .    232 THE KITCHEN CHIMNEY   6
      WHATEVER ITS SECRET WAS OF GREATER HEAT  . . . . . .    239 OUR SINGING STRENGTH  17
      TO WHATEVER THE KNOCK  . . . . . . . . . . . . .       241 THE LOCKLESS DOOR .   15
      WHATEVER IT IS THE NIGGER'S GOT."  . . . . . . . .     345 DISCOVERY OF MADEIRAS  75
      WHATEVER I ACCORDED IT OF FATE.  . . . . . . . .       357 A CONSIDERABLE SPECK .  23
      WHATEVER KULTUR  . . . . . . . . . . . . . .          449 THE BAD ISLAND--EASTER  55
      WE'RE SAVED, WE'RE SAVED, WHATEVER ELSE IT MEANS. . .   476 A MASQUE OF REASON .   82
WHAT'LL---NOT INDEXED
WHAT'S---NOT INDEXED
WHATSOEVER
      TO WHATSOEVER GOD WE OWE THE THANKS.  . . . . . . .     358 THE LOST FOLLOWER  .    6
      BUT WHATSOEVER ELSE IT MAY SECRETE,  . . . . . . .     411 POD OF THE MILKWEED .  20
WHEAT
      AND CHANGED IT TO THE ENGLISH NAME FOR WHEAT.  . . .    446 DOES NO ONE AT ALL EVER  8
WHEEL
      OR HIGHWAY WHERE THE SLOW WHEEL POURS THE SAND.  . . .    5 INTO MY OWN  . . . .    8
      MOVED IN A LITTLE. THE MAN GRASPED A WHEEL. . . . .      89 THE FEAR  . . . . .    7
      TILL WEISS SHUT OFF THE WATER IN THE WHEEL PIT. . . .    93 THE SELF-SEEKER  .    27
      INSTEAD OF GOING CLEAR DOWN IN THE WHEEL PIT?"  . . .    93 THE SELF-SEEKER  .    31
      OVER THE WHEEL INTO THE SKY-HIGH SEAT,  . . . . .       112 IN THE HOME STRETCH .  63
      O'ERNIGHT 'TWIXT MULLEIN STALKS A WHEEL OF THREAD . .   126 RANGE-FINDING  . .    10
      "COME, JOHN," HE SAID, "YOU WANT TO SEE THE WHEEL PIT?" .  142 THE VANISHING RED .  19
      OH, YES, HE SHOWED JOHN THE WHEEL PIT ALL RIGHT. . .   142 THE VANISHING RED  .   29
      HAVING A WHEEL AND FOUR LEGS OF ITS OWN  . . . . .     188 THE GRINDSTONE  . .     1
      AND SOME OF IT ON NO MORE LEGS AND WHEEL. . . . .      189 THE GRINDSTONE  . .    12
      THE ONE WHO HELD THE WHEEL BACK OR THE ONE  . . . .    190 THE GRINDSTONE  . .    46
      BY CRAMPING THE WHEEL ON A WATER BAR,  . . . . . .     263 THE TIMES TABLE .  .    5
      ONCE TOOK A LITTLE PEBBLE WHEEL  . . . . . . . .       326 A MISSIVE MISSILE  .    2
WHEELBARROW
      SHE WHEELED THE DUNG IN THE WHEELBARROW  . . . . .     134 A GIRL'S GARDEN .  .   21
      (I'M THINKING CHIEFLY OF THE WHEELBARROW.)  . . . .    189 THE GRINDSTONE  . .    14
WHEELED
      SHE WHEELED THE DUNG IN THE WHEELBARROW  . . . . .     134 A GIRL'S GARDEN .  .   21
WHEELRUT'S
      IN EVERY WHEELRUT'S NOW A BROOK,  . . . . . . .        276 TWO TRAMPS IN MUD TIME  35
WHEELS
      SHE WON'T GET FAR BEFORE THE WHEELS HANG UP  . . . .    88 THE HOUSEKEEPER .  . 202
      WITH WHOSE VAST WHEELS . . . . . . . . . . . .         219 I WILL SING YOU ONE-O .  58
      WHERE WHEELS HAVE FRESHLY SLICED THE APRIL MIRE. . .   225 BLUE-BUTTERFLY DAY .    8
      WITH TWO WHEELS LOW IN THE DITCH  . . . . . . .        367 A SERIOUS STEP LIGHTLY  9
      BESIDES THE WEAR OF IRON WAGON WHEELS  . . . . . .     377 DIRECTIVE  . . . .    14
WHELMING
      OH, NEVER THIS WHELMING EAST WIND SWELLS . . . . .      27 A LINE-STORM SONG .   25
WHEN---NOT INDEXED
WHENCE
      DEEP INTO THE EARTH WHENCE IT CAME.  . . . . . .       311 THE VINDICTIVES  . .   30
      I CAN BUT WONDER WHENCE  . . . . . . . . . .           333 HAPPINESS MAKES UP .    9
WHENEVER
      WAITING TO STEAL A STEP ON US WHENEVER  . . . . .      114 IN THE HOME STRETCH . 116
      THEY CAN PUT IT OUT WHENEVER THEY PLEASE. . . . .      291 ON HEART'S BEGINNING TO  25
      BUT WHENEVER THE ROOF CAME WHITE  . . . . . . .        299 WELCOME TO THEIR BELIEF  9
WHEN'S---NOT INDEXED
WHERE---NOT INDEXED
WHERE-ALL
      AND WHERE-ALL I'D BEEN.  . . . . . . . . . .           432 KITTY HAWK  . . .    144
WHEREAS
      WHEREAS I NEVER HAD A GOOD IDEA . . . . . . .          169 NEW HAMPSHIRE  . .   335
      WHEREAS MEN PROPHETS ARE RECEIVED WITH HONOR. . . .    476 A MASQUE OF REASON .   90
WHEREAT
      WHEREAT IN A MOMENT OF CROSS UNRUTH  . . . . . .       346 DISCOVERY OF MADEIRAS  96
WHEREIN
      WHEREIN WORDS WHETHER BEATEN OUT OR SPOKEN  . . . .    141 THE LINE-GANG  . .     6
WHEREOF
      THAT IS THE FEAR OF GOD WHEREOF 'TIS WRITTEN. . . .    520 A MASQUE OF MERCY  .  699
WHERE'S---NOT INDEXED
WHEREVER
      WHEREVER THE GROUND WAS LOW AND WET,  . . . . .        123 PEA BRUSH . . . .     10
      IN OTHER WORDS, I KNOW WHEREVER I AM,  . . . . . .     166 NEW HAMPSHIRE  . .    239
      BUT WHEREVER THE TRUTH MAY BE--  . . . . . . .         301 NEITHER OUT FAR NOR IN  10
WHEREWITH
      MORE OF THE SALT WHEREWITH THEY'RE TO BE SALTED. . .    80 THE GENERATIONS OF MEN  191
WHEREWITHAL
      BUT HOW ABOUT THE WHEREWITHAL?  . . . . . . .          416 AMERICA IS HARD TO SEE  4
WHET
      IT ONLY GIVES OUR WISH FOR BLUE A WHET.  . . . . .     220 FRAGMENTARY BLUE  .     8
WHETHER
      BUT WHETHER OR NOT A MAN WAS ASKED  . . . . . .          8 LOVE AND A QUESTION    29
      WHETHER 'TIS IN US TO ARISE WITH DAY  . . . . .         10 STORM FEAR  . . .     17
      "WHETHER THEY WORK TOGETHER OR APART."  . . . . .       22 THE TUFT OF FLOWERS    10
      "WHETHER THEY WORK TOGETHER OR APART."  . . . . .       23 THE TUFT OF FLOWERS    40
      (THOUGH DOUBTFUL WHETHER HE STAYED TO SEE). . . .       25 THE DEMIURGE'S LAUGH   17
      I DON'T KNOW RIGHTLY WHETHER ANY MAN CAN."  . . . .     52 HOME BURIAL  . . .    38
      WHETHER I AM GLAD, SORRY, OR ANYTHING,  . . . . .       63 A SERVANT TO SERVANTS  12
      THEIR CHARACTERS, OR WHETHER THEY ARE SAFE  . . . .     65 A SERVANT TO SERVANTS  83
      THE WOODCHUCK COULD SAY WHETHER IT'S LIKE HIS . . .     69 AFTER APPLE-PICKING    40
      WHETHER HE'S EVER GOING TO WALK AGAIN. . . . . .       100 THE SELF-SEEKER  . . 202
      THEN WHETHER FROM MISTAKEN COURTESY  . . . . . .       106 CHRISTMAS TREES  .    26
      AND FEAR OF SEEMING SHORT OF SPEECH, OR WHETHER . .    106 CHRISTMAS TREES  .    27
      WHEREIN WORDS WHETHER BEATEN OUT OR SPOKEN  . . . .    141 THE LINE-GANG  . .     6
      YOU CAN'T FEAR WHETHER SHE HAS LEFT THE DOOR . . .    154 SNOW  . . . . . .    308
      TO LEAVE IT TO, WHETHER THE RIGHT TO HOLD  . . . .    188 THE AX-HELVE  . . .    91
      WHETHER ELIZA WOULD BE WELCOME THERE.  . . . . .      200 PLACE FOR A THIRD .    42
      AND TELL ME WHETHER  . . . . . . . . . . .            217 I WILL SING YOU ONE-O   5
      AND WHETHER THE FARMER DRANK OR NOT  . . . . . .      263 THE TIMES TABLE .  .     3
```

WHETHER (CONTINUED)
    THE QUESTION IS WHETHER THEY'VE REACHED A DEPTH . . . . 317 BUILD SOIL 33
    WHETHER IT'S PERSONS PIED OR NATIONS PIED. . . . . . . 321 BUILD SOIL 156
    IS WHETHER THE TWO DOTS WERE TEARS, ... 327 A MISSIVE MISSILE . . 10
    HE KNEW NOT WHETHER HOMEWARD, ... 335 CARPE DIEM 3
    BUT WHETHER STOLEN FROM HER WEDDED LORD . . . . . . 343 DISCOVERY OF MADEIRAS . 2
    WHETHER TIME'S REWARDS ARE FAIR OR UNFAIR. . . . . . 347 DISCOVERY OF MADEIRAS . 138
    "IT'S WHETHER THESE PROFESSIONS REALLY WORK. . . . . 404 FROM PLANE TO PLANE . 11
    WHETHER THERE'S ANY PART OF MAN IMMORTAL. . . . . . 483 A MASQUE OF REASON . 297
    AND FIND OUT WHETHER HE IS ANY GOOD, ... 484 A MASQUE OF REASON . 320
WHETS
    SHE WHETS A SLEEPY SATED BILL. . . . . 281 BLUE RIBBON AT AMESBURY 40
WHETSTONE
    I LISTENED FOR HIS WHETSTONE ON THE BREEZE. . . . . 22 THE TUFT OF FLOWERS . 6
WHETTER
    I WAS FOR LEAVING SOMETHING TO THE WHETTER. . . . . 191 THE GRINDSTONE . . . 75
WHICH---NOT INDEXED
WHICHEVER
    LIVING OR DEAD, WHICHEVER ARE TO MIND. . . . . . 17 THE VANTAGE POINT . . 8
    TWO HAD SEEN TWO, WHICHEVER SIDE YOU SPOKE FROM. . . 230 TWO LOOK AT TWO . . . 38
WHIFFS
    COURAGE IS IN THE AIR IN BRACING WHIFFS . . . . . 423 FOR JOHN F. KENNEDY . 58
WHILE
    THE MEASURE OF THE LITTLE WHILE . . . . . . 13 FLOWER-GATHERING . . 15
    WHILE SO CONFUSED WITH FLOWERS. . . . . . 14 ROSE POGONIAS . . . 24
    AND NOW I'M LEAVING YOU A LITTLE WHILE. . . . 50 A HUNDRED COLLARS . . 159
    AROUND AND AROUND US. AND THEN FOR A WHILE . . 62 BLUEBERRIES . . . 91
    WHILE I FRY THEIR BACON. MUCH THEY CARE! . . . 65 A SERVANT TO SERVANTS . 78
    AS I SAID, FOR A WHILE--BUT I DON'T KNOW! . . . 67 A SERVANT TO SERVANTS . 153
    AFTER A WHILE PICKING PEAS IN HIS GARDEN: . . . 73 THE CODE . . . 108
    WHILE WE KNOW DEFINITELY WHERE HE IS. . . . 90 THE FEAR . . . 44
    STOOD FOR A WHILE UNNOTICED, WITH HER HANDS . . 96 THE SELF-SEEKER . . 95
    I SAID, "THERE AREN'T ENOUGH TO BE WORTH WHILE." . 106 CHRISTMAS TREES . . 29
    WHILE THEY HAD BACKS TURNED, THAT IT HADN'T BEEN THERE . 132 THE BONFIRE . . 86
    WHILE I INVESTED HIM WITH REASONS; . . . . . 140 BROWN'S DESCENT . . 72
    WHILE YOU SIT WARM AND READ UP BALANCED RATIONS. . . 149 SNOW . . . 183
    WHILE I THOUGHT WHAT TO DO THAT COULD BE DONE-- . . 175 THE CENSUS-TAKER . 48
    WHILE SHE MADE UP HER MIND HOW MUCH SHE CARED-- . 201 PLACE FOR A THIRD . 55
    TO MAKE IT WORTH LIFE'S WHILE TO WAKE AND SPORT. . 254 A WINTER EDEN . . 20
    AND MADE OF US A LITTLE WHILE-- . . . . . . 265 THE BIRTHPLACE . . 9
    AND DON'T COME OUT FOR A WHILE, ... 282 A DRUMLIN WOODCHUCK . 18
    WHILE GREEDY GOOD-DOERS, BENEFICENT BEASTS OF PREY, . 287 A ROADSIDE STAND . . 27
    TO BE A BIRD WHILE WE ARE MEN ON EARTH, ... 303 A BIRD SINGING IN SLEEP 12
    EVEN WHILE WE TALK SOME CHEMIST AT COLUMBIA . . . 319 BUILD SOIL . . . 107
    THE THINGS FORBIDDEN THAT WHILE THE CUSTOMS SLEPT . 335 I COULD GIVE ALL . . 13
    HE EYED HER FOR A WHILE . . . . 339 THE SUBVERTED FLOWER . 8
    AND THE SHIP LAY IN THE BAY FOR A WHILE . . . . 347 DISCOVERY OF MADEIRAS . 111
    WHO AM TASKED TO SAVE MY OWN A LITTLE WHILE. . . . 357 A MOTH SEEN IN WINTER . 24
    WHILE WITH THE HATING OTHER HAND WE STRIKE. . . . 371 THE LITERATE FARMER AND 115
    WHILE THE TREES PUT ON THEIR WOODEN RINGS . . . 376 SOMETHING FOR HOPE . 11
    WHICH MAY A LITTLE WHILE BY WAR AND TRADE . . . 399 THE INGENUITIES OF DEBT 7
    WHILE HAVING ITS BELIEFS DISPUTED. . . . . . 419 AMERICA IS HARD TO SEE 82
    WHILE ANOTHER WEPT. . . . . 432 KITTY HAWK . . . 128
    BUT WHILE MEDITATING . . . . 441 KITTY HAWK . . . 412
    OR SO FOR A WHILE; . . . . 448 THE BAD ISLAND--EASTER 37
    WHILE SCIENCE GOES SELF-SUPERSEDING ON. . . . . 480 A MASQUE OF REASON . 193
WHIM
    HE'LL FIND HE'S MISTAKEN. SEE HERE, FOR A WHIM, . . 61 BLUEBERRIES . . . 80
    SOME LUNATIC OR LUNAR WHIM . . . . 390 TWO LEADING LIGHTS . 18
WHIMPER
    AND THE WHIMPER OF HAWKS BESIDE THE SUN . . . . 24 PAN WITH US . . . 19
WHINE
    YOU CAN HEAR THE SMALL BUZZ SAWS WHINE, THE BIG SAW . . 94 THE SELF-SEEKER . . 41
WHINED
    THEY MADE HIM KEEP ON GNAWING TILL HE WHINED. . . 209 PAUPER WITCH OF GRAFTON 58
WHIPPED
    I SAW BY THE WAY YOU WHIPPED UP THE HORSE. . . . 91 THE FEAR . . . 73
    BY HAVING HIM WHIPPED EVERY DAY AFRESH . . . . 517 A MASQUE OF MERCY . 642
WHIPPOORWILL
    THE WHIPPOORWILL IS COMING TO SHOUT . . . . . 6 GHOST HOUSE . . . 16
WHIPPOORWILLS
    FOUR OR FIVE WHIPPOORWILLS . . . . 364 A NATURE NOTE . . 1
WHIPS
    TO WHIPS AND POLES. THERE'S NOBODY ABOUT. . . . 49 A HUNDRED COLLARS . 136
WHIPSTOCK
    HE LIKED TO HAVE IT SLENDER AS A WHIPSTOCK, . . . 187 THE AX-HELVE . . 69
WHIR
    THE WHIR OF SOBER BIRDS . . . . 8 A LATE WALK . . . 6
    A WHIR AMONG WHITE BRANCHES GREAT AND SMALL, . . . 240 OUR SINGING STRENGTH . 41
WHIRL
    OR AT UTMOST A LITTLE RELUCTANT WHIRL . . . . 236 MISGIVING . . . 11
    SAID THAT THE FALL MIGHT COME AND WHIRL OF LEAVES, . . 343 QUEST OF PURPLE-FRINGED 27
    (ENTERING HATLESS IN A WHIRL OF SNOW) . . . . 493 A MASQUE OF MERCY . 18
WHIRLED
    TOSSED, TANGLED, WHIRLED AND WHIRLED ABOVE, . . . 28 MY BUTTERFLY . . 16
    BEING WHIRLED AND WHIRLED . . . . 440 KITTY HAWK . . . 396
WHIRLING
    ITS WHIRLING FRENZIES . . . . 219 I WILL SING YOU ONE-O . 65
    OF WHIRLING HANDS AND ARMS ABOUT THE HEAD . . . 277 THE WHITE-TAILED HORNET 9
WHIRLS
    AND THE MIND WHIRLS AND THE HEART SINGS, . . . 21 THE TRIAL BY EXISTENCE 47
    WHEN BETWEEN WHIRLS OF SNOW NOT COME TO LIE . . . 106 CHRISTMAS TREES . . 3
    AND WHIRLS OF FOLIAGE NOT YET LAID, THERE DROVE . . 106 CHRISTMAS TREES . . 4
WHIRLWIND
    TO RIDE THE WHIRLWIND AND THE HURRICANE. . . . . 423 FOR JOHN F. KENNEDY . 48
WHISKY
    BECAUSE IT BOASTS A WHISKY STILL--BECAUSE . . . . 165 NEW HAMPSHIRE . . 190

WHISPERED
    WHAT WAS IT IT WHISPERED? I KNEW NOT WELL MYSELF; . . . . . . 17 MOWING 3
    AND THAT WAS WHY IT WHISPERED AND DID NOT SPEAK. . . . . . . 17 MOWING 6
    MY LONG SCYTHE WHISPERED AND LEFT THE HAY TO MAKE. . . . . . 17 MOWING 14
WHISPERING
    AND THAT WAS MY LONG SCYTHE WHISPERING TO THE GROUND. . . . 17 MOWING 2
    AND HEAR HIS LONG SCYTHE WHISPERING TO THE GROUND, ... 23 THE TUFT OF FLOWERS . 32
WHISPERS
    AND WHISPERS WITH A SORT OF STIFLED BARK, ... 9 STORM FEAR 4
WHISTLE
    OR BRANCH TO WHISTLE AFTER WHAT WAS SPENT. . . . . 175 THE CENSUS-TAKER . . 24
    TO MAKE A WILLOW WHISTLE ON A SUNDAY . . . . 191 PAUL'S WIFE 21
    HAVE A LITTLE WHISTLE WE GIVE, ... 282 A DRUMLIN WOODCHUCK . 14
WHITE (SEE GREEN-WHITE, SNOW-WHITE)
    TO WHITE REST, AND A PLACE OF REST . . . . 9 STARS 7
    FIND THE BROWN BENEATH THE WHITE; . . . . 11 TO THE THAWING WIND . 5
    OH, GIVE US PLEASURE IN THE ORCHARD WHITE, ... 12 A PRAYER IN SPRING . 5
    MYSELF UNSEEN, I SEE IN WHITE DEFINED . . . . 17 THE VANTAGE POINT . 5
    THE LIGHT OF HEAVEN FALLS WHOLE AND WHITE . . . . 19 THE TRIAL BY EXISTENCE 9
    AND A WHITE SHIMMERING CONCOURSE ROLLS . . . . 20 THE TRIAL BY EXISTENCE 29
    "NOT THAT WAY, WITH YOUR SHOES ON KIKE'S WHITE BED. . . . . 47 A HUNDRED COLLARS . 75
    WHITE WAS THE ONLY RACE SHE EVER KNEW. . . . . 57 THE BLACK COTTAGE . 75
    I SAW IT JUST AS PLAIN AS A WHITE PLATE," . . . . 89 THE FEAR 9
    THE WHITE ONE IN HIS TAIL; LIKE ONE WHO TAKES . . . . . . 101 THE WOOD-PILE . . . 15
    IF I CAN LEAVE OFF BURYING THE WHITE . . . . 124 PUTTING IN THE SEED . 3
    LIKE A WHITE CRUMPLED SPIDER ON HIS KNEE: . . . . 147 SNOW 115
    YOU SEE THE SNOW-WHITE THROUGH THE WHITE OF FROST? . . . . 148 SNOW 157
    OR BROKEN ITS WHITE NECK OF MUSHROOM STUFF . . . . 149 SNOW 165
    THE WHITE CLOUDS OVER THEM ON. . . . . 156 THE SOUND OF TREES . 23
    PRE-PRIMITIVES OF THE WHITE RACE, DAWN PEOPLE, ... 161 NEW HAMPSHIRE . . . 78
    A COMPANY WE CALLED THE WHITE CORPUSCLES, ... 163 NEW HAMPSHIRE . . . 139
    FOR THE HARD WORK. HE CHAFED ITS LONG WHITE BODY . . . . 187 THE AX-HELVE . . . 76
    WHERE A WHITE BIRCH HE KNEW OF STOOD ALONE, ... 196 WILD GRAPES . . . 20
    BUNCHES ALL ROUND ME GROWING IN WHITE BIRCHES, ... 197 WILD GRAPES . . . 26
    THROUGH THE PICTURE, A SOMETHING WHITE, UNCERTAIN, ... 225 FOR ONCE SOMETHING . 9
    AT LAST THE GATHERED SNOW LETS DOWN AS WHITE . . . . . . 226 THE ONSET 2
    NOTHING WILL BE LEFT WHITE BUT HERE A BIRCH, ... 226 THE ONSET 22
    WHEN SHOEING HOME ACROSS THE WHITE, ... 232 LOOKING FOR SUNSET BIRD 3
    SUCH WHITE LUXURIANCE OF MAY FOR OURS. . . . . 233 A BOUNDLESS MOMENT . 8
    THEY MADE NO WHITE IMPRESSION ON THE BLACK. . . . . . . 239 OUR SINGING STRENGTH 5
    TO ALMOST STRIPS AND TAPES OF RAGGED WHITE . . . . 239 OUR SINGING STRENGTH 8
    A WHIR AMONG WHITE BRANCHES GREAT AND SMALL, ... 240 OUR SINGING STRENGTH 41
    FLUNG BACKWARD ON ITSELF IN ONE WHITE WAVE, ... 258 WEST-RUNNING BROOK . 20
    AND THE WHITE WATER RODE THE BLACK FOREVER, ... 258 WEST-RUNNING BROOK . 21
    WHITE FEATHERS FROM THE STRUGGLE OF WHOSE BREAST . . . . . 258 WEST-RUNNING BROOK . 23
    IN A WHITE SCARF AGAINST THE FAR-SHORE ALDERS.) . . . . . 258 WEST-RUNNING BROOK . 26
    IN THAT WHITE WAVE RUNS COUNTER TO ITSELF. . . . . . . 259 WEST-RUNNING BROOK . 39
    HER FLUFF OF PLUMAGE, WHITE AS CHALK, ... 280 BLUE RIBBON AT AMESBURY 7
    BUT WHENEVER THE ROOF CAME WHITE . . . . 299 WELCOME TO THEIR BELIEF 9
    THE LEAFLESS BLOOM OF A PLUM IS FRESH AND WHITE; . . . . . 300 STRONG SAYING NOTHING 10
    I FOUND A DIMPLED SPIDER, FAT AND WHITE, ... 302 DESIGN 1
    ON A WHITE HEAL-ALL, HOLDING UP A MOTH . . . . 302 DESIGN 2
    LIKE A WHITE PIECE OF RIGID SATIN CLOTH-- . . . . 302 DESIGN 3
    WHAT HAD THAT FLOWER TO DO WITH BEING WHITE, ... 302 DESIGN 9
    THEN STEERED THE WHITE MOTH THITHER IN THE NIGHT? . . . . 302 DESIGN 12
    ON ANY BUT A PAPER SHEET SO WHITE . . . . 357 A CONSIDERABLE SPECK 2
    THE BIG FLAG: THE RED--WHITE-- . . . . 367 NOT OF SCHOOL AGE . 25
    (BUT WHAT A HUMAN RACE THE WHITE HAS BEEN!) . . . . . . 369 THE LITERATE FARMER AND 52
    OF BABY GREEN AND SHOW THE WHITE BENEATH, ... 375 A YOUNG BIRCH . . . 2
    MAY WELL HAVE NOTICED. SOON ENTIRELY WHITE . . . . 375 A YOUNG BIRCH . . . 4
    IT WILL STAND FORTH, ENTIRELY WHITE IN BARK, ... 375 A YOUNG BIRCH . . . 6
    AND FRIES A COUPLE OF EBON ATOMS WHITE, ... 389 SKEPTIC 2
    THE PROSPECTS ARE IN WHITE . . . . 416 CLOSED FOR GOOD . . 20
    OF PINK AND WHITE, ... 445 PERIL OF HOPE . . . 7
    FIRST WHITE, THEN RED, THEN ULTRARED, THEN OUT. . . . . . 485 A MASQUE OF REASON . 346
    ARE GOD'S WHITE LIGHT REFRACTED INTO COLORS. . . . . . . 516 A MASQUE OF MERCY . 597
WHITED
    AND MOUNTS THE WALL AGAIN WITH WHITED EYES . . . . . . 223 THE RUNAWAY 16
WHITE-FACED
    WITH WHITE-FACED OXEN, IN A HEAVY CART, ... 41 THE MOUNTAIN . . . 17
WHITENESS
    BLURRED IT, BLOTTED IT OUT. WHAT WAS THAT WHITENESS? . . . 225 FOR ONCE SOMETHING . 14
    A BLANKER WHITENESS OF BENIGHTED SNOW . . . . 296 DESERT PLACES . . . 11
WHITE-PINE
    CUT OF A WHITE-PINE LOG. MURPHY WAS THERE . . . . 192 PAUL'S WIFE 55
WHITER
    DRAWING THE SLOW WAVES WHITER AND WHITER AND WHITER. . . . 63 A SERVANT TO SERVANTS . 25
WHITE-TAILED
    THE WHITE-TAILED HORNET LIVES IN A BALLOON . . . . 277 THE WHITE-TAILED HORNET 1
    THE WHITE-TAILED HORNET . . . . 277 THE WHITE-TAILED HORNET T
WHITHER
    BUT THE FEET QUESTION "WHITHER?" . . . . 30 RELUCTANCE 18
    AND WHITHER IT WILL BE WITHDRAWN, ... 332 ALL REVELATION . . . 6
WHITMAN
    FROM HOLDING FORTH ON FREEDOM LIKE A WHITMAN-- . . . . . 461 HOW HARD TO KEEP FROM 225
WHITTIER
    AND WHITTIER, AND HAD HER STORY OF THEM. . . . . 56 THE BLACK COTTAGE . . 53
WHITTIER'S
    WHITTIER'S LUCK WITH SKIPPER IRESON AWES ME-- . . . . . 317 BUILD SOIL 44
WHO---NOT INDEXED
WHOA
    THE WOMAN SPOKE OUT SHARPLY, "WHOA, STAND STILL!-- . . . . 89 THE FEAR 8
WHO'D---NOT INDEXED
WHOEVER
    "WHOEVER IT IS THAT LEAVES HIM OUT SO LATE, ... 223 THE RUNAWAY 19
    WHOEVER THE SURLY FREEDOM TOOK . . . . 364 TRESPASS 5
WHOLE
    THE LIGHT OF HEAVEN FALLS WHOLE AND WHITE . . . . 19 THE TRIAL BY EXISTENCE 9
    DRAGGING THE WHOLE SKY WITH IT TO THE HILLS. . . . . . . 38 DEATH OF THE HIRED MAN 104

WHOLE (CONTINUED)
    SO SMALL THE WINDOW FRAMES THE WHOLE OF IT. . . . . . . 51 HOME BURIAL 24
    REGULAR VESTRY-TREES WHOLE SUNDAY SCHOOLS . . . . 107 CHRISTMAS TREES . . . 53
    "THE WHOLE TO-DO SEEMS TO HAVE BEEN FOR NOTHING. . . . . 155 SNOW 337
    WHOLE TOWNSHIPS NAMED BUT WITHOUT POPULATION. . . . . . 165 NEW HAMPSHIRE . . . 209
    THE BARK OF A WHOLE TAMARACK OFF WHOLE, ... 191 PAUL'S WIFE 19
    ON THE NEW WOOD THE WHOLE LENGTH OF THE LOG . . . . . . 193 PAUL'S WIFE 70
    THEY'LL FIND THEY'VE GOT THE WHOLE THING TO DO OVER, . . 207 PAUPER WITCH OF GRAFTON 10
    SHE WAS 'SHUT IN' FOR LIFE. SHE LIVED HER WHOLE . . . . 215 A FOUNTAIN, A BOTTLE . 84
    A WHOLE EDITION IN A PACKING CASE . . . . 216 A FOUNTAIN, A BOTTLE . 93
    TILL I FILL THE WHOLE SHED, ... 235 GATHERING LEAVES . . 15
    AND THE WHOLE PILE IS SLIPPING, BOTTLES, BUNS-- . . . . 266 THE ARMFUL 3
    WON'T THIS WHOLE INSTINCT MATTER BEAR REVISION? . . . . 279 THE WHITE-TAILED HORNET 50
    SHE MAKES THE WHOLE FLOCK MOVE ALONG. . . . . 281 BLUE RIBBON AT AMESBURY 48
    THE WHOLE SKY WAS BLUE; . . . . 303 AFTERFLAKES 12
    I COULD STAND WHOLE DAYFULS OF IT. . . . . 304 CLEAR AND COLDER . . 20
    MAKE THE WHOLE STOCK EXCHANGE YOUR OWN! . . . . 307 PROVIDE, PROVIDE . . 10
    THE WHOLE FIERCE CONQUERING PACK . . . . 311 THE VINDICTIVES . . . 47
    THEY END UP IN THE UNIVERSAL WHOLE . . . . 354 THE LESSON FOR TODAY . 111
    I'M HAVING THE WHOLE ARGUMENT MY WAY-- . . . . 354 THE LESSON FOR TODAY . 116
    TO SEE WHAT ON THE WHOLE THEY HAD TO SAY . . . . 354 THE LESSON FOR TODAY . 134
    OF LIGHTING THE WHOLE NIGHT WITH ONE BIG BLOB . . . . . 370 THE LITERATE FARMER AND 72
    WHOLE CAPES CAKED OFF IN SLICES. . . . . 377 ONE STEP BACKWARD TAKEN 7
    DRINK AND BE WHOLE AGAIN BEYOND CONFUSION. . . . . 379 DIRECTIVE 62
    BY NATURE MEANT THE WHOLE GODDAM MACHINERY. . . . . . . 393 LUCRETIUS VERSUS POETS 6
    THE WHOLE YGGDRASILL. . . . . 426 A NEVER NAUGHT SONG . 26
    BEACHES WHERE THE WHOLE . . . . 432 KITTY HAWK 137
    IF NOT OF THE WHOLE, ... 441 KITTY HAWK 423
    YOU COULD LOSE BATTLES, YOU COULD LOSE WHOLE WARS, . . . 457 HOW HARD TO KEEP FROM 127
    I'M SICK OF THE WHOLE ARTIFICIAL PUZZLE. . . . . 484 A MASQUE OF REASON . 300
    (A WHOLE SHELF CASCADES DOWN.) HERE COME SOME MORE. . . 506 A MASQUE OF MERCY . 341
WHOLENESS
    THE HOLINESS OF WHOLENESS . . . . 440 KITTY HAWK 3P
    WHOLENESS IN A SENSE. . . . . 441 KITTY HAWK 428
WHOLESALE
    THE HAY AND ROLLING IT OFF WHOLESALE, ... 71 THE CODE 57
WHOLLY
    THUS ARE WE WHOLLY STRIPPED OF PRIDE . . . . 21 THE TRIAL BY EXISTENCE 70
    SO THEN, TO MAKE ME WHOLLY SELF-SUPPORTING, ... 197 WILD GRAPES 36
    BUT TO BE WHOLLY TACITURN . . . . 403 SOMETHING LIKE A STAR . 7
    AND WHOLLY PERISH. 469 WE VAINLY WRESTLE... . 4
WHOM---NOT INDEXED
WHO'S---NOT INDEXED
WHOSE---NOT INDEXED
WHOSO
    "THE PLACE IS DESERT, AND LET WHOSO LURKS . . . . 176 THE CENSUS-TAKER . . 57
WHOSOEVER
    AS WHOSOEVER LIKES THE YOUNG AND SLIGHT . . . . 375 A YOUNG BIRCH . . . 3
WHY---NOT INDEXED
WICKED
    NAME NAMES AND TELL YOU WHO BY NAME IS WICKED? . . . . . 317 BUILD SOIL 43
    THAT SUCKS HIS BREATH LIKE A WICKED CAT IN BED. . . . . 341 WILLFUL HOMING . . . 4
    YOU MUST BE WICKED TO DESERVE SUCH PAIN. . . . . 486 A MASQUE OF REASON . 364
    YOU'VE LOST YOUR FAITH IN GOD? HOW WICKED OF YOU. . . . 497 A MASQUE OF MERCY . 117
    WE SEND OUR WICKED ENEMIES TO HELL, ... 519 A MASQUE OF MERCY . 688
    OUR WICKED FRIENDS WE SEND TO PURGATORY. . . . . 519 A MASQUE OF MERCY . 689
WICKEDNESS
    VIRTUE MAY FAIL AND WICKEDNESS SUCCEED. . . . . 475 A MASQUE OF REASON . 52
WIDE
    WIDE FIELDS OF ASPHODEL FORE'ER, ... 19 THE TRIAL BY EXISTENCE 6
    JOHN THREW THE DOOR WIDE BUT HE DIDN'T ENTER. . . . . . 88 THE HOUSEKEEPER . . . 205
    THEY LEARNED TO LEAVE THE HOUSE DOOR WIDE . . . . 127 HOUSE FEAR 9
    WIDE OPEN AND THE WIND'S BLOWN OUT THE LAMP . . . . . . 154 SNOW 309
    SO SUDDENLY I FLUNG THE DOOR WIDE ON HIM. . . . . 204 THE WITCH OF COOS . 70
    MY WINDOW WAS WIDE; . . . . 241 THE LOCKLESS DOOR . . 10
    THE ONLY LEAF IT DROPS GOES WIDE, ... 247 ON GOING UNNOTICED . 11
    AND BENT SOME RAIL WIDE OPEN LIKE A SWITCH, ... 270 THE EGG AND THE MACHINE 7
    O OPENING CLOUDS, BY OPENING ON ME WIDE. . . . . 296 LOST IN HEAVEN . . . 11
    YOUR BASE HAS SPREAD TOO WIDE, ... 298 ON TAKING FROM THE TOP 6
    HE MAY FUMBLE WIDE OF THE KNOB A YARD OR MORE, ... 342 WILLFUL HOMING . . . 11
    THE INFINITE'S BEING SO WIDE . . . . 348 TRIPLE BRONZE . . . 1
    AND VERY WIDE THE CHOICE THEY SEEMED TO GIVE; . . . . . 354 THE LESSON FOR TODAY . 137
    A MIGHTY FARMER FLUNG THE HOUSE DOOR WIDE, ... 368 THE LITERATE FARMER AND 5
    THIS WIDE FLIGHT WE WAVE . . . . 442 KITTY HAWK 437
    THE CELLAR DOOR SWINGS WIDE AND SLAMS AGAIN.) . . . . . 520 A MASQUE OF MERCY . 696
WIDELY
    TWO SOULS MAY BE TOO WIDELY MET. . . . . 328 A MISSIVE MISSILE . 52
WIDER
    A CIRCLE SCARCELY WIDER . . . . 13 ROSE POGONIAS . . . 3
    "IF--YOU--DO'" SHE WAS OPENING THE DOOR WIDER. . . . . . 55 HOME BURIAL 114
    MADE THE DIM TREES STAND BACK IN WIDER CIRCLE-- . . . . 130 THE BONFIRE 29
WIDESPREAD
    AND MADE A WIDESPREAD BRAWL ON COBBLESTONES. . . . . . . 40 THE MOUNTAIN . . . 11
    THE WIDESPREAD DOUBLE DOORS TWO STORIES HIGH. . . . . . 289 OLD BARN AT THE BOTTOM 12
WIDOW
    A WIDOW AT HER SECOND HUSBAND'S GRAVE, ... 201 PLACE FOR A THIRD . 59
WIDOW'S
    BEFORE SHE WENT THE POOR MAN'S WIDOW'S WAY, ... 201 PLACE FOR A THIRD . 61
WIELD
    BUT AS READY TO WIELD AS NOW. . . . . 285 IN TIME OF CLOUDBURST 24
WIFE
    HE SPOKE TO HIS WIFE IN THE DOOR, 'LET ME SEE, ... 61 BLUEBERRIES 76
    THEY EXCAVATED MORE. 'GO KEEP HIS WIFE . . . . 72 THE CODE 94
    THE HILL WIFE . . . . 126 THE HILL WIFE . . . T
    I THINK I'LL JUST CALL UP MY WIFE AND TELL HER . . . . . 143 SNOW 11
    TO THEIRS. I'M GOING TO CALL HIS WIFE AGAIN." . . . . . 145 SNOW 75
    "FINE, FINE." / "AND READY FOR SOME MORE? MY WIFE HERE . 147 SNOW 106
    MR. MESERVE, I'LL LEAVE IT TO YOUR WIFE. . . . . 147 SNOW 109
    WHAT DID YOUR WIFE SAY ON THE TELEPHONE?" . . . . 147 SNOW 110

WIFE (CONTINUED)
    YOUR WIFE--SHE DOESN'T WANT YOU TO. WE DON'T. .   .   .   . 151 SNOW   234
    WHEN COLE RETURNED HE FOUND HIS WIFE STILL STANDING .   .   . 151 SNOW   245
    "HELLO, MESERVE. YOU'RE THERE, THEN!--AND YOUR WIFE? .   .   . 155 SNOW   329
    "HOW IS THE WIFE, PAUL?"--AND HE'D DISAPPEAR. .   .   .   .   . 191 PAUL'S WIFE .   .   .   3
    SOME SAID IT WAS BECAUSE HE HAD NO WIFE, ... 191 PAUL'S WIFE .   .   .   4
    PAUL'S WIFE .   .   .   . 191 PAUL'S WIFE .   .   .   T
    AS IF TO SAY, "THAT'S SO, HOW IS MY WIFE? .   .   .   .   .   . 191 PAUL'S WIFE .   .   . 14
    "HOW IS THE WIFE, PAUL?" AND HE ALWAYS WENT. .   .   .   .   . 191 PAUL'S WIFE .   .   . 14
    THAT PAUL HAD MARRIED A WIFE NOT HIS EQUAL. .   .   .   .   . 192 PAUL'S WIFE .   .   . 24
    WELL, THIS IS SUCH A YARN. PAUL SAWED HIS WIFE .   .   .   . 192 PAUL'S WIFE .   .   . 36
    ABOUT HIS WIFE TO KEEP HER TO HIMSELF. .   .   .   .   .   . 192 PAUL'S WIFE .   .   . 54
    OWNING A WIFE WITH HIM MEANT OWNING HER. .   .   .   .   .   . 195 PAUL'S WIFE .   .   . 149
    WOULDN'T BE SPOKEN TO ABOUT A WIFE .   .   .   . 196 PAUL'S WIFE .   .   . 151
    THAT'S WHAT I ALWAYS TELL MY WIFE .   .   .   . 196 PAUL'S WIFE .   .   . 156
    NOT TO SINK UNDER BEING MAN AND WIFE, ... 263 THE TIMES TABLE .   . 11
    HE IS HUSBAND, SHE IS WIFE. .   .   .   . 264 THE INVESTMENT   .   . 13
    WE OWNED UP TO OUR WIFE .   .   .   . 291 ON HEART'S BEGINNING TO 36
    HIS WIFE LIES BY HIM LOOKING AT THE SKY. .   .   .   .   .   . 464 MILKY WAY IS A COWPATH   14
    WELL, AFTER ALL THESE YEARS! / THIS IS MY WIFE. .   .   .   . 473 A MASQUE OF REASON   .   3
    (MY WIFE GETS IN AHEAD OF ME WITH HERS.) .   .   .   .   .   . 476 A MASQUE OF REASON   . 83
    JOB'S WIFE SITS UP.) / WELL, IF WE AREN'T ALL HERE, .   .   . 479 A MASQUE OF REASON   . 164
    A BOOKSTORE LATE AT NIGHT. THE KEEPER'S WIFE .   .   .   .   . 487 A MASQUE OF REASON   . 392
    THE KEEPER'S WIFE HAS HARDLY TURNED AWAY .   .   .   .   .   . 493 A MASQUE OF MERCY   .   1
    .   .   .   . 493 A MASQUE OF MERCY   .   5
WIFE'LL
    TO DISOBEY YOU. MUCH HIS WIFE'LL THANK YOU." .   .   .   .   . 153 SNOW   284
WIFELY
    I DID MY WIFELY DUTY. I SHOULD TREMBLE! .   .   .   .   .   . 478 A MASQUE OF REASON   . 134
WIFE'S
    BECAUSE YOUR WIFE'S PAST WON'T BEAR LOOKING INTO?-- .   .   . 477 A MASQUE OF REASON   . 116
WILD (SEE HALF-WILD)
    AND THE PURPLE-STEMMED WILD RASPBERRIES GROW. .   .   .   .   .   5 GHOST HOUSE .   .   .   5
    WILD, EASILY SHATTERED ROSE. .   .   .   . 26 A LINE-STORM SONG . 14
    TOMORROW'S WIND, IF IT BE WILD, ... 27 OCTOBER   3
    BUT THE WILD TOUCH OF THY DYE-DUSTY WING! .   .   .   .   . 29 MY BUTTERFLY .   .   . 42
    TO RUN WILD IN THE SUMMER--A LITTLE WILD. .   .   .   .   . 44 A HUNDRED COLLARS .   5
    HE HAS BROUGHT THEM ALL UP ON WILD BERRIES, THEY SAY, .   . 60 BLUEBERRIES .   .   . 50
    "IF HE THINKS ALL THE FRUIT THAT GROWS WILD IS FOR HIM, .   . 61 BLUEBERRIES .   .   . 79
    LIKE WILD GEESE ON A LAKE BEFORE A STORM? .   .   .   .   . 76 THE GENERATIONS OF MEN   90
    THAT A BROOK MAKES IN SUCH A WILD DESCENT. .   .   .   .   . 78 THE GENERATIONS OF MEN 133
    AND GOT THEM OFF THE WILD FLOWERS' BACKS. .   .   .   .   . 123 PEA BRUSH 16
    SMALL GOOD TO ANYTHING GROWING WILD, ... 123 PEA BRUSH 21
    AND TOO WILD, ... 128 THE IMPULSE .   .   .   2
    AND SCARE OURSELVES. LET WILD FIRE LOOSE WE WILL----" .   . 130 THE BONFIRE .   .   . 18
    HIS WILD DESCENT FROM THERE ONE NIGHT, ... 137 BROWN'S DESCENT .   .   6
    AN OATH OF TOWNS THAT SET THE WILD AT NAUGHT, ... 141 THE LINE-GANG .   .   . 12
    ADVANTAGES OF GROWING ALMOST WILD. .   .   .   . 162 NEW HAMPSHIRE .   .   . 104
    THE MORE I SEEM TO WANT MY MOUNTAINS WILD; .   .   .   .   . 170 NEW HAMPSHIRE .   .   . 344
    WILD GRAPES .   .   .   . 196 WILD GRAPES .   .   .   T
    OF HIS OLD SONG, 'THE WILD COLONIAL BOY,' .   .   .   .   . 205 THE WITCH OF COOS . 110
    AND SING THE WILD FLOWERS UP FROM ROOT AND SEED. .   .   . 240 OUR SINGING STRENGTH . 53
    ON SOME WILD APPLE-TREE'S YOUNG TENDER BARK, ... 254 A WINTER EDEN .   .   . 11
    TO GO TO WASTE AND GO WILD IN, ... 264 THE LAST MOWING .   . 17
    OFFERED FOR SALE WILD BERRIES IN WOODEN QUARTS, .   .   . 286 A ROADSIDE STAND .   . 11
    AND INTO THE WILD UNKNOWN, ... 313 BEARER OF EVIL TIDINGS   8
    AND OFF THIS CORNER IN THE WILD, ... 331 BEECH   4
    IN ONE WILD DAY OF RAIN. .   .   .   . 359 NOVEMBER   6
    FREEDOM TO FLASH OFF INTO WILD CONNECTIONS. .   .   .   . 461 HOW HARD TO KEEP FROM   246
WILDER
    WHEN WILDER MOTHERS THAN OUR WILDEST NOW .   .   .   .   . 197 WILD GRAPES 50
WILDERNESS
    MORE THAN A MILE ACROSS THE WILDERNESS .   .   .   .   .   . 195 PAUL'S WIFE 132
WILDEST
    WHEN WILDER MOTHERS THAN OUR WILDEST NOW .   .   .   .   . 197 WILD GRAPES 50
    THERE IS OUR WILDEST MOUNT--A HEADLESS HORSE. .   .   .   . 267 RIDERS   9
WILDING
    FOR WILDING BROOCH, SHALL WET YOUR BREAST .   .   .   .   . 27 A LINE-STORM SONG . 23
WILDLY
    "GOD!" ONE SAID WILDLY, AND, WHEN NO ONE SPOKE: .   .   . 114 IN THE HOME STRETCH . 99
    AND THEN CAME RACING WILDLY ON AGAIN .   .   .   .   .   . 357 A CONSIDERABLE SPECK . 11
WILL---NOT INDEXED--EXCEPT FOR:
    A BOY'S WILL .   .   .   .   3 A BOY'S WILL .   .   .   T
    AND NONE ARE TAKEN BUT WHO WILL, ... 20 THE TRIAL BY EXISTENCE   33
    "WATCH FOR HIM, WILL YOU, WILL? YOU LET HIM IN. .   .   . 94 THE SELF-SEEKER .   . 52
    BUT PUT OUR FLOWERS IN WATER FIRST.--WILL, HELP HER: .   . 99 THE SELF-SEEKER .   . 172
    "YOU, WILL, STOP MAKING FACES. COME ROUND HERE .   .   .   . 99 THE SELF-SEEKER .   . 184
    WHAT DO YOU SAY, WILL? DON'T YOU BE A FOOL, ... 99 THE SELF-SEEKER .   . 195
    YES. THANKS FOR CARING.--DON'T MIND WILL: HE'S SAVAGE. . 100 THE SELF-SEEKER .   . 224
    HAD IT BEEN THE WILL OF THE WIND, WAS LEFT .   .   .   . 241 NEED OF BEING VERSED .   7
    AND WHEN THEY CAME IT SEEMED WITH A WILL TO CARRY ME WITH
        THEM TO DEATH, ... 297 A LEAF-TREADER .   .   8
    NOR CHIEFLY THAT YOU MAY GO WHERE YOU WILL, ... 300 THE MASTER SPEED .   .   6
    I SHALL WILL TO THE COMMON STOCK OF AIR MY BREATH .   . 307 NOT QUITE SOCIAL .   . 15
    OR FROM HER OWN SELF AGAINST HER WILL .   .   .   .   .   . 343 DISCOVERY OF MADEIRAS .   3
    TO NAUGHT BUT HIS OWN FORCE OF WILL. .   .   .   .   .   . 418 AMERICA IS HARD TO SEE   70
    FREE WILL, TRADE, VERSE, THOUGHT, LOVE, SPEECH, COINAGE. . 459 HOW HARD TO KEEP FROM   186
    THE ONLY FREE WILL THERE AT FIRST WAS MAN'S, ... 475 A MASQUE OF REASON   . 71
    AND BID MY WILL AVOUCH IT LIKE MACBETH. .   .   .   .   . 477 A MASQUE OF REASON   . 112
    THERE'S WILL AS MOTOR AND THERE'S WILL AS BRAKES. .   . 481 A MASQUE OF REASON   . 230
    THE WILL AS BRAKES CAN'T STOP THE WILL AS MOTOR .   .   . 481 A MASQUE OF REASON   . 232
WILLFUL
    WILLFUL HOMING .   .   .   . 341 WILLFUL HOMING .   .   .   T
WILLFULLY
    MAY NO FATE WILLFULLY MISUNDERSTAND ME .   .   .   .   . 122 BIRCHES 50
    OR WILLFULLY UNKIND. .   .   .   . 339 THE SUBVERTED FLOWER .   7
WILLIAM
    WILLIAM TECUMSEH SHERMAN. WHY TECUMSEH?" .   .   .   .   . 406 FROM PLANE TO PLANE . 72
WILLING
    TO TAKE HIM IN, AND MIGHT BE WILLING TO-- .   .   .   .   . 39 DEATH OF THE HIRED MAN 133

WILLING (CONTINUED)
  JUST TAKING WHAT NATURE IS WILLING TO GIVE, ... 61 BLUEBERRIES 55
  I SHOULD BE WILLING TO SAY AND HELP YOU SAY . . . . . . 236 VALLEY'S SINGING DAY . 19
  "AS LIBERALS WE'RE WILLING TO GIVE PLACE . . . . 369 THE LITERATE FARMER AND 49
WILLIS
  "WILLIS, I DIDN'T WANT YOU HERE TODAY: . . . . 92 THE SELF-SEEKER . . . 1
  "I TOLD YOU, WILLIS, WHEN YOU FIRST CAME IN. . . . . . 95 THE SELF-SEEKER . . . 61
  WILLIS BROUGHT UP BESIDES THE BOSTON LAWYER . . . . . 96 THE SELF-SEEKER . . . 91
  "LOOKING ROUND, I SUPPOSE," SAID WILLIS. / "YES, . . . 96 THE SELF-SEEKER . . . 101
  "WHAT DID YOU HEAR, FOR INSTANCE?" WILLIS SAID. . . . 100 THE SELF-SEEKER . . . 206
  WILLIS FLUNG OFF THE BED. "I WASH MY HANDS-- . . . . 100 THE SELF-SEEKER . . . 216
  WE'RE VERY SORRY FOR YOU." / WILLIS SNEERED: . . . . 100 THE SELF-SEEKER . . . 220
  "WILLIS, BRING ANNE BACK WITH YOU WHEN YOU COME. . . . 100 THE SELF-SEEKER . . . 223
WILLOUGHBY
  OUR WILLOUGHBY! HOW DID YOU HEAR OF IT? . . . . 63 A SERVANT TO SERVANTS . 33
WILLOW
  AS CLEAN AS BOYS DO OFF A WILLOW TWIG . . . . 191 PAUL'S WIFE 20
  TO MAKE A WILLOW WHISTLE ON A SUNDAY . . . . 191 PAUL'S WIFE 21
WILLPOWER
  HE TURNED ON WILLPOWER TO INCREASE THE LOAD . . . . 189 THE GRINDSTONE . . . 31
WILLY-NILLY
  WHAT OF IT, THOUGH? I GOT SOME WILLY-NILLY . . . . . 393 LUCRETIUS VERSUS POETS 2
WILSON
  HE RAN ON HAROLD WILSON--YOU REMEMBER-- . . . . . . 36 DEATH OF THE HIRED MAN 58
  HE THINKS YOUNG WILSON A LIKELY LAD, THOUGH DAFT . . . 36 DEATH OF THE HIRED MAN 65
  EASTON GOES DEMOCRATIC, WILSON 4 . . . . 165 NEW HAMPSHIRE . . . 198
WILT
  UNLESS 'TWOULD RATHER WILT THAN FADE." . . . . 450 OUR DOOM TO BLOOM . . 16
WILTED
  THOUGH I FOUND YOUR HAND FULL OF WILTED FERN, ... 109 THE EXPOSED NEST . . 11
  BEFORE I THOUGHT THE WILTED TO EXALT . . . . 337 THE WIND AND THE RAIN 26
WIN
  TO WIN HER FOR THE FLIGHT . . . . 11 WIND AND WINDOW FLOWER 22
  THEN FEARFUL HE HAD LET THEE WIN . . . . 29 MY BUTTERFLY 28
  WELL, WE SHOULD SEE WHICH ONE WOULD WIN, ... 253 THE THATCH 8
  AND BE EXHIBITED, AND WIN. . . . . 279 BLUE RIBBON AT AMESBURY 3
  AND BEEN THE FIRST WITH IT TO WIN A WAR, ... 399 U.S. 1946 KING'S X . 2
WIND
  AUTUMN, YES, WINTER WAS IN THE WIND; . . . . 8 LOVE AND A QUESTION . 15
  WHEN THE WIND WORKS AGAINST US IN THE DARK, ... 9 STORM FEAR 1
  WIND AND WINDOW FLOWER . . . . 10 WIND AND WINDOW FLOWER T
  HE WAS A WINTER WIND, ... 10 WIND AND WINDOW FLOWER 13
  TO THE THAWING WIND . . . . 11 TO THE THAWING WIND . T
  SO CLOSE THE WINDOWS AND NOT HEAR THE WIND, ... 25 NOW CLOSE THE WINDOWS . 7
  AND THE SHALLOW WATERS AFLUTTER WITH WIND . . . . . 27 A LINE-STORM SONG . . 19
  OH, NEVER THIS WHELMING EAST WIND SWELLS . . . . . 27 A LINE-STORM SONG . . 25
  TOMORROW'S WIND, IF IT BE WILD, ... 27 OCTOBER 3
  THAT FATE HAD MADE THEE FOR THE PLEASURE OF THE WIND, . 29 MY BUTTERFLY 23
  BEHIND WHICH I WAS SHELTERED FROM A WIND. . . . . . 40 THE MOUNTAIN 6
  THE BLUE'S BUT A MIST FROM THE BREATH OF THE WIND, . . 60 BLUEBERRIES 25
  A SUNNY MORNING, OR TAKE THE RISING WIND . . . . . 63 A SERVANT TO SERVANTS . 28
  A WIND TO BLOW IN EARNEST FROM SOME QUARTER, ... 130 THE BONFIRE 33
  BUT THE WIND OUT-OF-DOORS--YOU KNOW THE SAYING. . . . 130 THE BONFIRE 40
  MADE WIND BY FANNING, SINCE YOU NEVER KNEW . . . . 130 THE BONFIRE 42
  THAT THE NORTH WIND LAST NIGHT . . . . 135 LAST WORD OF A BLUEBIRD 9
  OF WIND THAT CAUGHT AGAINST THE HOUSE A MOMENT, . . . 143 SNOW 2
  BUT THE WIND DIDN'T MOVE IT IF IT MOVED. . . . . . 148 SNOW 136
  BLOWN IN THE WIND. I LIKE THAT--I LIKE THAT. . . . . 150 SNOW 196
  THIS ROOM YOU SIT IN. IF YOU THINK THE WIND . . . . 150 SNOW 203
  PERHAPS THE WIND THE MORE WITHOUT THE HELP . . . . 175 THE CENSUS-TAKER . . 25
  AND MELTING FURTHER IN THE WIND TO MUD. . . . . . 179 THE STAR-SPLITTER . . 81
  SHE THINKS WHEN THE WIND MAKES A NIGHT OF IT . . . . 209 PAUPER WITCH OF GRAFTON 82
  TILL IT CAUGHT WIND AND, OPENING OUT ITS COVERS, . . 216 A FOUNTAIN, A BOTTLE . 111
  THE WIND ONCE BLEW ITSELF UNTAUGHT, ... 223 THE AIM WAS SONG . . 2
  THE WIND THE WIND HAD MEANT TO BE-- . . . . 224 THE AIM WAS SONG . . 14
  THE AIM WAS SONG--THE WIND COULD SEE. . . . . . . 224 THE AIM WAS SONG . . 16
  OF EASY WIND AND DOWNY FLAKE. . . . . 224 STOPPING BY WOODS . . 12
  THEY LIE CLOSED OVER IN THE WIND AND CLING . . . . 225 BLUE-BUTTERFLY DAY . . 7
  HE HALTED IN THE WIND, AND--WHAT WAS THAT . . . . . 233 A BOUNDLESS MOMENT . . 1
  ALL CRYING, "WE WILL GO WITH YOU, O WIND!" . . . . 236 MISGIVING 1
  HAD IT BEEN THE WILL OF THE WIND, WAS LEFT . . . . 241 NEED OF BEING VERSED . 7
  ALL THE DUST THE WIND BLEW HIGH . . . . 249 A PECK OF GOLD . . . 5
  THE RAIN TO THE WIND SAID, ... 250 LODGED 1
  WHERE HAD I HEARD THIS WIND BEFORE . . . . 251 BEREFT 1
  THE WIND WAS ANOTHER LAYER OF MOLD. . . . . 253 THE THATCH 12
  THE SUN WAS WARM BUT THE WIND WAS CHILL, ... 275 TWO TRAMPS IN MUD TIME 17
  WHEN THE SUN IS OUT AND THE WIND IS STILL, ... 275 TWO TRAMPS IN MUD TIME 19
  A WIND COMES OFF A FROZEN PEAK, ... 275 TWO TRAMPS IN MUD TIME 23
  AND TURNS TO THE WIND TO UNRUFFLE A PLUME, ... 276 TWO TRAMPS IN MUD TIME 26
  AGAINST THE DARK AND WIND AND COLD . . . . 281 BLUE RIBBON AT AMESBURY 54
  WIND GOES FROM FARM TO FARM IN WAVE ON WAVE, . . . 300 STRONG SAYING NOTHING . 13
  NO SPEED OF WIND OR WATER RUSHING BY . . . . . . 300 THE MASTER SPEED . . 1
  WIND, THE SEASON-CLIMATE MIXER, ... 303 CLEAR AND COLDER . . 1
  BRING ON WIND. BRING RAIN IN TORRENTS-- . . . . . 304 CLEAR AND COLDER . . 13
  WIND SHE BREWS A HEADY KETTLE. . . . . 304 CLEAR AND COLDER . . 21
  THAT THE NORTHWEST WIND SHOULD RISE TO SUCH A HEIGHT . 305 THERE ARE ROUGHLY ZONES 16
  A SEASON-ENDING WIND THERE BLEW . . . . 336 THE WIND AND THE RAIN . 3
  THE WIND AND THE RAIN . . . . 336 THE WIND AND THE RAIN T
  OR THE WIND TO SNAP THEIR WALKING STICK, ... 344 DISCOVERY OF MADEIRAS . 29
  SO JEWEL-STEADY IN THE WIND AND DUST. . . . . . . 386 THE FEAR OF MAN . . . 12
  COLUMBUS MAY HAVE WORKED THE WIND . . . . 416 AMERICA IS HARD TO SEE 1
WINDBREAK
  FOR A WINDBREAK . . . . 211 AN EMPTY THREAT . . . 24
WINDFALLS
  THE WINDFALLS SPIKED WITH STUBBLE AND WORM-EATEN. . . 125 THE COW IN APPLE TIME . 8
WINDHAM
  AS HALL OF WINDHAM, GAY OF ATKINSON, ... 167 NEW HAMPSHIRE . . . 259
WINDOW (SEE STOVE-WINDOW, UPPER-WINDOW)
  WITHOUT A WINDOW LIGHT. . . . . 7 LOVE AND A QUESTION . 8

WINDOW (CONTINUED)

	PAGE	TITLE	LINE
THE LOWER-CHAMBER WINDOW ON THE EAST,	9	STORM FEAR	3
SHE A WINDOW FLOWER,	10	WIND AND WINDOW FLOWER	3
WHEN THE FROSTY WINDOW VEIL	10	WIND AND WINDOW FLOWER	5
WIND AND WINDOW FLOWER	10	WIND AND WINDOW FLOWER	T
BATHE MY WINDOW, MAKE IT FLOW,	11	TO THE THAWING WIND	7
ACROSS THE REEDS TO A WINDOW LIGHT.	15	IN A VALE	5
SO SMALL THE WINDOW FRAMES THE WHOLE OF IT.	51	HOME BURIAL	24
I SAW YOU FROM THAT VERY WINDOW THERE,	53	HOME BURIAL	74
FROM THE SINK WINDOW WHERE I WASH THE PLATES,	63	A SERVANT TO SERVANTS	23
AND THERE'S MORE TO IT THAN JUST WINDOW VIEWS	67	A SERVANT TO SERVANTS	155
OUT OF THE BARN.' SOMEONE LOOKED IN A WINDOW,	72	THE CODE	95
NEARBY, ALL DARK IN EVERY GLOSSY WINDOW.	89	THE FEAR	4
I SAW NO WINDOW BUT THAT WAS BLACK.	102	GOOD HOURS	12
OVER THE SINK OUT THROUGH A DUSTY WINDOW	110	IN THE HOME STRETCH	2
"WHAT ARE YOU SEEING OUT THE WINDOW, LADY?"	111	IN THE HOME STRETCH	20
WHAT ARE YOU SEEING OUT THE WINDOW, LADY?"	111	IN THE HOME STRETCH	25
MORE THAN YOU LIKE TO OWN TO OUT THAT WINDOW."	112	IN THE HOME STRETCH	45
"COME FROM THAT WINDOW WHERE YOU SEE TOO MUCH,	112	IN THE HOME STRETCH	60
THE STOVE! BEFORE THEY GO! KNOCK ON THE WINDOW;	113	IN THE HOME STRETCH	75
TO NORTHWARD FROM YOUR WINDOW AT THE SINK,	114	IN THE HOME STRETCH	115
FOREVER TRYING THE WINDOW LATCH	128	THE OFT-REPEATED DREAM	3
AND CUT THEM OFF FROM WINDOW LIGHT.	135	LOCKED OUT	3
THE SNOW AGAINST THE WINDOW CAUGHT HIS EYE.	149	SNOW	180
FROM THE WINDOW OR THE DOOR.	156	THE SOUND OF TREES	18
OF ONE ROOM AND ONE WINDOW AND ONE DOOR,	174	THE CENSUS-TAKER	3
NOT BONES, BUT THE ILL-FITTED WINDOW RATTLED.	175	THE CENSUS-TAKER	46
WATCHING OUT OF A NINETEENTH STORY WINDOW	182	MAPLE	81
"EXCUSE ME IF I ASK YOU IN A WINDOW	215	A FOUNTAIN, A BOTTLE	72
HAD SPILLED THEM NEAR THE WINDOW, TOWARD THE LIGHT,	216	A FOUNTAIN, A BOTTLE	96
TO SEND IT SAILING OUT THE ATTIC WINDOW	216	A FOUNTAIN, A BOTTLE	110
MY WINDOW GLASS	218	I WILL SING YOU ONE-O	36
MY WINDOW CURTAIN HUNG OVER THE SILL TO WET;	236	VALLEY'S SINGING DAY	17
MY WINDOW WAS WIDE;	241	THE LOCKLESS DOOR	10
TREE AT MY WINDOW, WINDOW TREE,	251	TREE AT MY WINDOW	1
TREE AT MY WINDOW	251	TREE AT MY WINDOW	T
THE SADNESS THAT LURKS NEAR THE OPEN WINDOW THERE,	287	A ROADSIDE STAND	34
MY TREE, A CAPTIVE IN YOUR WINDOW BAY,	350	TO A YOUNG WRETCH	20
AND SAVE HERSELF FROM BREAKING WINDOW GLASS.	445	QUESTIONING FACES	2
PULLS DOWN THE WINDOW CURTAIN ON THE DOOR	493	A MASQUE OF MERCY	2
THAT IS NO WINDOW. THAT'S A SHOWCASE RATTLING.	504	A MASQUE OF MERCY	282

WINDOWPANE

SHORT OFF, AND DIED AGAINST THE WINDOWPANE."	149	SNOW	166
IT SCOURS THE WINDOWPANE WITH SNOW,	281	BLUE RIBBON AT AMESBURY	50
AGAINST THE WRONG SIDE OF A WINDOWPANE.	412	POD OF THE MILKWEED	39

WINDOWS

NOW CLOSE THE WINDOWS AND HUSH ALL THE FIELDS:	25	NOW CLOSE THE WINDOWS	1
SO CLOSE THE WINDOWS AND NOT HEAR THE WIND,	25	NOW CLOSE THE WINDOWS	7
NOW CLOSE THE WINDOWS	25	NOW CLOSE THE WINDOWS	T
A FRONT WITH JUST A DOOR BETWEEN TWO WINDOWS,	55	THE BLACK COTTAGE	6
WE ROSE TO GO. SUNSET BLAZED ON THE WINDOWS.	59	THE BLACK COTTAGE	127
OF PEOPLE BROUGHT TO WINDOWS BY A LIGHT	129	THE BONFIRE	11
BUT BANKED THE DAYLIGHT OUT OF AVERY'S WINDOWS.	149	SNOW	186
I THINK I HEAR A CLOCK--AND WINDOWS RATTLING.	153	SNOW	301
THE CELLAR WINDOWS WERE BANKED UP WITH SAWDUST	204	THE WITCH OF COOS	57
THE MICA SHEETS WERE BIG AS PLATE-GLASS WINDOWS.	213	A FOUNTAIN, A BOTTLE	5
AT BROKEN WINDOWS FLEW OUT AND IN,	242	NEED OF BEING VERSED	14
ITS ONLY WINDOWS WERE THE CREVICES	290	OLD BARN AT THE BOTTOM	24
AND TO THE WINDOWS OF ITS FENESTRATION,	400	TO THE RIGHT PERSON	9
MERELY THE WINDOWS RATTLING IN THE STORM.	504	A MASQUE OF MERCY	280

WINDOWSILL

THAT LED US TO A WEATHERED WINDOWSILL.	55	THE BLACK COTTAGE	13
YOU SPOKE FROM THAT FLOWER ON THE WINDOWSILL--	118	THE TELEPHONE	8
THE POSIES ON HER INNER WINDOWSILL,	215	A FOUNTAIN, A BOTTLE	80
AND THE BIRDS ON HER OUTER WINDOWSILL,	215	A FOUNTAIN, A BOTTLE	81
TO GLASSED-IN CHILDREN AT THE WINDOWSILL.	445	QUESTIONING FACES	6

WINDOWSILLS

PILING IT WELL ABOVE THE WINDOWSILLS.	149	SNOW	179

WINDROW

LIES IN A WINDROW, BRITTLE-DRY AND BLACK,	446	DOES NO ONE AT ALL EVER	26

WINDROWS

GATHERING UP WINDROWS, PILING COCKS OF HAY,	69	THE CODE	2

WINDS

WHEN WINTRY WINDS DO BLOW!--	9	STARS	4
WHERE WINDS WERE QUITE EXCLUDED,	13	ROSE POGONIAS	5
AS THE ROAD WINDS WOULD BRING HIM TO HIS DOOR.	38	DEATH OF THE HIRED MAN	126
BUT SUDDEN WINDS THAT SNATCH THEM FROM OUR HANDS	112	IN THE HOME STRETCH	43
TWO WINDS WOULD MEET,	218	I WILL SING YOU ONE-O	11
AS WINDS MIGHT ROUSE	218	I WILL SING YOU ONE-O	31
WINDS BLOW THE OPEN GRASSY PLACES BLEAK;	246	ATMOSPHERE	1
FROM GEORGES BANK WHEN WINDS WERE BLOWING.	262	THE FLOWER BOAT	8

WIND'S

IT CAN'T TURN EITHER WAY. IT NEEDS THE WIND'S HELP.	148	SNOW	135
IT MOVED ITSELF. THE WIND'S AT NAUGHT IN HERE.	148	SNOW	137
WIDE OPEN AND THE WIND'S BLOWN OUT THE LAMP	154	SNOW	309

WIND-SOIL

IN WIND-SOIL TO A DEPTH OF THIRTY FEET,	365	OF STONES OF THE PLACE	6

WIND-STIRRED

BUT SEE ALL WIND-STIRRED.	25	NOW CLOSE THE WINDOWS	8

WIND-TORN

ITS WIND-TORN THATCH GOES NOW UNMENDED;	253	THE THATCH	32

WINDY

TO THE DARKENING, WINDY VILLAGE SLIP.	343	DISCOVERY OF MADEIRAS	7

WINE

BUT SWEATING-FULL, DRIPS WINE AND OIL A LITTLE.	323	BUILD SOIL	236
AS STRONG IS RAIN WITHOUT AS WINE WITHIN,"	337	THE WIND AND THE RAIN	41
JEWELS AND HORSES, WOMEN, WINE, AND SONG."	455	HOW HARD TO KEEP FROM	62
IT MAY BE WINE, BUT MUCH MORE LIKELY LOVE--	461	HOW HARD TO KEEP FROM	242

WINED   (SEE WELL-WINED)
WING
    ON NOISELESS WING A BEWILDERED BUTTERFLY, ... 22 THE TUFT OF FLOWERS . 12
    AND THEN ON TREMULOUS WING CAME BACK TO ME. . . . . . . 22 THE TUFT OF FLOWERS . 18
    BUT THE WILD TOUCH OF THY DYE-DUSTY WING! . . . . . . 29 MY BUTTERFLY 42
    I FOUND THAT WING BROKEN TODAY! . . . . 29 MY BUTTERFLY 43
    IT BROODED ANT EGGS, AND HAD ONE LARGE WING, ... 172 A STAR IN A STONEBOAT . 14
    THERE IS MORE UNMIXED COLOR ON THE WING . . . . 225 BLUE-BUTTERFLY DAY . 3
    OF WAY WITH ME FROM APATHY OF WING, ... 240 OUR SINGING STRENGTH . 37
    WHERE ONE FALSE WING BEAT WOULD HAVE BROUGHT DOWN ALL, . 240 OUR SINGING STRENGTH . 43
    SHE SHOULDERS WITH A WING SO STRONG . . . . 281 BLUE RIBBON AT AMESBURY 47
    TOGETHER WING TO WING AND OAR TO OAR. . . . . 300 THE MASTER SPEED . . 14
    HE HAS DUST IN HIS EYES AND A FAN FOR A WING, ... 309 ONE GUESS. 1
    BY SLEIGHT OF WING . . . . 334 COME IN 6
WINGS
    SEEMED TIPPED WITH WINGS OF COLOR . . . . 13 ROSE POGONIAS . . . 15
    WITH THOSE GREAT CARELESS WINGS, ... 29 MY BUTTERFLY 24
    AND SO AT LAST TO LEARN TO USE THEIR WINGS. . . . . . 110 THE EXPOSED NEST . . 36
    FOR THOUGHT HAS A PAIR OF DAUNTLESS WINGS. . . . . . 120 BOND AND FREE . . . 5
    LIKE WINGS, REVOLVING IN THE SCENE . . . . 138 BROWN'S DESCENT . . 22
    FLIRTING THEIR WINGS AND SAYING CHICKADEE, ... 151 SNOW 231
    LIKE DOVE WINGS ON A FIGURE ON A TOMB, ... 222 TO E.T. 3
    AND DEAD WINGS CARRIED LIKE A PAPER KITE. . . . . . . 302 DESIGN 8
    HIS NATTY WINGS WITH SELF-ASSURANCE PERK. . . . . . . 309 WASPISH 3
    SEEING NO HELP IN WINGS OR FEET . . . . 346 DISCOVERY OF MADEIRAS . 100
    THE WINGS NOT FOLDED IN REPOSE, BUT SPREAD. . . . . . 356 A MOTH SEEN IN WINTER . 4
    THE COUNTLESS WINGS THAT FROM THE INFINITE . . . . . 411 POD OF THE MILKWEED . 10
    THEY KNOCK THE DYESTUFF OFF EACH OTHER'S WINGS-- . . . 411 POD OF THE MILKWEED . 25
    AND HER WINGS STRAINING SUDDENLY ASPREAD . . . . . . 445 QUESTIONING FACES . 3
    ON WINGS TOO STIFF TO FLAP . . . . 464 MILKY WAY IS A COWPATH 1
    THAT FLICKERS MICA WINGS. HE LIFTS A HAND . . . . . 487 A MASQUE OF REASON . . 390
WINK
    ALL I SAW WAS A WINK. . . . . 392 A WISH TO COMPLY . 13
WINNING
    GET PARCELED OUT AMONG THE WINNING GIANTS. . . . . . 398 NO HOLY WARS FOR THEM . 8
    IF WHAT YOU SAY IS TRUE, IF WINNING RANKS . . . . . 517 A MASQUE OF MERCY . 633
WINS
    AND SUPERSTITION WINS. HE BLAMES THE STARS, ... 462 HOW HARD TO KEEP FROM 267
WINTER   (SEE OVER-WINTER)
    AUTUMN, YES, WINTER WAS IN THE WIND; . . . .   8 LOVE AND A QUESTION . 15
    AND HE A WINTER BREEZE. . . . . 10 WIND AND WINDOW FLOWER 4
    HE WAS A WINTER WIND, ... 10 WIND AND WINDOW FLOWER 13
    IN WINTER HE COMES BACK TO US. I'M DONE." . . . . . 35 DEATH OF THE HIRED MAN 30
    THEY LOGGED IT THERE LAST WINTER SOME WAY UP. . . . . 41 THE MOUNTAIN 42
    IT'S ALWAYS COLD IN SUMMER, WARM IN WINTER. . . . . . 42 THE MOUNTAIN 49
    IT STEAM IN WINTER LIKE AN OX'S BREATH, ... 42 THE MOUNTAIN 51
    ESSENCE OF WINTER SLEEP IS ON THE NIGHT, ... 68 AFTER APPLE-PICKING . 7
    I HAD FOR MY WINTER EVENING WALK-- . . . . 102 GOOD HOURS 1
    AT TEN O'CLOCK OF A WINTER EVE. . . . . 102 GOOD HOURS 16
    AN OLD MAN'S WINTER NIGHT . . . . 108 OLD MAN'S WINTER NIGHT T
    IT'S THUS HE DOES IT OF A WINTER NIGHT. . . . . . . 108 OLD MAN'S WINTER NIGHT 28
    LOADED WITH ICE A SUNNY WINTER MORNING . . . . . . 121 BIRCHES 6
    SUMMER OR WINTER, AND COULD PLAY ALONE. . . . . . . 121 BIRCHES 27
    THE BREEZES WERE SO SPENT WITH WINTER BLOWING . . . . 130 THE BONFIRE 35
    LIKE WINTER AND EVENING COMING ON TOGETHER. . . . . . 131 THE BONFIRE 55
    IN WINTER AFTER HALF-PAST THREE. . . . . 137 BROWN'S DESCENT . . 4
    TO BREATHE THE AIR ONE WINTER--HAD A ROOM . . . . . 149 SNOW 174
    YOU CAN'T GET TOO MUCH WINTER IN THE WINTER.' . . . . 149 SNOW 184
    RAKING UP AFTER WINTER, AND I SAID, ... 164 NEW HAMPSHIRE . . . 153
    SHE COULD CALL UP TO PASS A WINTER EVENING, ... 202 THE WITCH OF COOS . 5
    ESPECIALLY IN WINTER WHEN THE BED . . . . 203 THE WITCH OF COOS . 38
    IT SHALL NOT MAKE AGAIN ALL WINTER LONG . . . . . . 226 THE ONSET 4
    I KNOW THAT WINTER DEATH HAS NEVER TRIED . . . . . . 226 THE ONSET 13
    ALL WINTER, CUT OFF BY A HILL FROM THE HOUSE. . . . . 228 GOOD-BY AND KEEP COLD 5
    LOOKING FOR A SUNSET BIRD IN WINTER . . . . . . 232 LOOKING FOR SUNSET BIRD T
    AND ALL GO BACK TO WINTER BUT THE ROAD. . . . . 239 OUR SINGING STRENGTH 10
    FROM WHICH NO WINTER GALE CAN HOPE TO BLOW IT-- . . . 248 THE COCOON 15
    OUT ALONE IN THE WINTER RAIN, ... 252 THE THATCH 1
    A WINTER GARDEN IN AN ALDER SWAMP, ... 254 A WINTER EDEN . . . 1
    A WINTER EDEN . . . . 254 A WINTER EDEN . . . T
    HERE LOVELESS BIRDS NOW FLOCK AS WINTER FRIENDS, . . . 254 A WINTER EDEN . . . 14
    AN HOUR OF WINTER DAY MIGHT SEEM TOO SHORT . . . . . 254 A WINTER EDEN . . . 19
    AND MAKE THEM SEE IT IN THE WINTER FIRELIGHT. . . . . 257 THE LOVELY BE CHOOSERS 34
    WAS COUNTING WINTER DINNERS, ONE A HILL, ... 263 THE INVESTMENT . . 7
    WINTER WAS ONLY PLAYING POSSUM. . . . . 276 TWO TRAMPS IN MUD TIME 30
    ALL COIFFURED TO A WINTER SHOW, ... 279 BLUE RIBBON AT AMESBURY 2
    THEN TAKE SOME LEFTOVER WINTER . . . . 304 CLEAR AND COLDER . 10
    THE WEATHER'S ALTERNATIONS, SUMMER AND WINTER, ... 317 BUILD SOIL 36
    TO A MOTH SEEN IN WINTER . . . . 356 A MOTH SEEN IN WINTER . T
    THAT CHANGES WINTER INTO SPRING . . . . 390 TWO LEADING LIGHTS . 25
    IS IN THE SIGN OF SICKNESS IN THE WINTER . . . . . 407 FROM PLANE TO PLANE . 105
    AND SO ON INTO WINTER . . . . 416 CLOSED FOR GOOD . . 25
    THE WINTER OWL BANKED JUST IN TIME TO PASS . . . . . 445 QUESTIONING FACES . 1
    IN WINTER IN THE WOODS ALONE . . . . 470 IN WINTER IN THE WOODS 1
    IN WINTER IN THE WOODS... . . . . 470 IN WINTER IN THE WOODS T
WINTER-BROKEN
    HE ISN'T WINTER-BROKEN. IT ISN'T PLAY . . . . 223 THE RUNAWAY 10
WINTERTIME
    AND SEEK THE LOVE OF KIND IN WINTERTIME? . . . . . 356 A MOTH SEEN IN WINTER . 9
WINTRIEST
    NO ORCHARD'S THE WORSE FOR THE WINTRIEST STORM; . . . 228 GOOD-BY AND KEEP COLD . 15
WINTRY
    WHEN WINTRY WINDS DO BLOW!-- . . . .   9 STARS 4
    HIS CHORES FOR ALL THE WINTRY NIGHT. . . . . . . 280 BLUE RIBBON AT AMESBURY 20
WIPE
    AND WIPE THAT OUT OF THE EARTH. . . . . 313 THE VINDICTIVES . . 84
    IN NATURE WOULD WIPE OUT ALL HUMAN FAULT. . . . . . 502 A MASQUE OF MERCY . 232

WIPED
BUT THAT BEGINNING WAS WIPED OUT IN FEAR . . . . 196 WILD GRAPES 10
HER MOTHER WIPED THE FOAM . . . . 341 THE SUBVERTED FLOWER . 71
OR BE WIPED OUT. WILL SHE BE ASKED TO SHOW . . . . . . 395 WHY WAIT FOR SCIENCE . 5
WIRE (SEE BARBED-WIRE)
WHEN IT OUTGROWS THE WIRE BAND OF ITS NAME TAG. . . . . 46 A HUNDRED COLLARS . 57
A WIRE SHE IS OF SILVER, AS NEW AS WE . . . . 113 IN THE HOME STRETCH . 70
OF WIRE WITH SOMETHING IN IT FROM MEN TO MEN. . . . . 125 AN ENCOUNTER 18
AND THE FENCE POST CARRIED A STRAND OF WIRE. . . . . . 242 NEED OF BEING VERSED . 20
HER GREAT WEIGHT CREAKS THE BARBED WIRE IN ITS STAPLES . 269 THE BEAR 7
LEAVING ON ONE WIRE TOOTH A LOCK OF HAIR. . . . . . 269 THE BEAR 9
WIRES
ON GLOSSY WIRES ARTISTICALLY BENT . . . . 309 WASPISH 1
WIRY
ALL WIRY ARMS AND LEGS THAT SPREAD OUT WAVY . . . . . 70 THE CODE 34
THE WAY THE WIRY GANG-BOSS LIKED THE LOGJAM. . . . . . 170 NEW HAMPSHIRE . . 345
WISDOM
HEARING THE LATTER WISDOM OF THE WORLD. . . . . . . 57 THE BLACK COTTAGE . 74
THAT WISDOM NEED NOT BE OF ATHENS ATTIC, ... 362 BOEOTIAN 3
DICK SAID, "YOU'VE BEEN A LESSON IN WORK WISDOM . . . 408 FROM PLANE TO PLANE . 122
OF GENESIS BEHIND. THE WISDOM THERE, THOUGH, ... 480 A MASQUE OF REASON . 195
IT COMES DOWN TO A DOUBT ABOUT THE WISDOM . . . . . . 483 A MASQUE OF REASON . 291
THERE YOU HAVE THE BEGINNING OF ALL WISDOM. . . . . . 501 A MASQUE OF MERCY . 215
FOR WISDOM THAT CAN HAVE NO COUNTERWISDOM. . . . . . 515 A MASQUE OF MERCY . 588
WISE (SEE ALL-WISE)
"YOU'RE DOING THE WISE THING: YOU WON'T REGRET IT. . . 100 THE SELF-SEEKER . . 219
I'LL CALL HER SOFTLY SO THAT IF SHE'S WISE . . . . . 143 SNOW 13
THAT I AM LIKE TO COMPASS, FOOL OR WISE. . . . . . . 174 A STAR IN A STONEBOAT . 57
WITH FAINT HEADSHAKINGS, NO MORE WISE. . . . . 344 DISCOVERY OF MADEIRAS . 40
YOU MUST BE MADE MORE SIMPLY WISE THAN I . . . . . . 356 A MOTH SEEN IN WINTER . 19
AND THEY IN THE ESTIMATION OF THE WISE . . . . 370 THE LITERATE FARMER AND 76
IF IT WAS NOT WISE, ... 435 KITTY HAWK 237
WISELY
TELL ME SOME RULE FOR RULING PEOPLE WISELY, ... 458 HOW HARD TO KEEP FROM 147
WISER
AS IT GROWS WISER AND OLDER, ... 156 THE SOUND OF TREES . 13
THEN NONE THE WISER, FRANKLY GAVE IT UP, ... 293 AT WOODWARD'S GARDENS . 29
THAT NO ECONOMIST WAS EVER WISER . . . . 363 AN EQUALIZER . . . 2
THEY OFTEN DO, AND NONE THE WISER FOR IT. . . . . . 414 A CABIN IN THE CLEARING 22
WISH
"STRANGER, I WISH I KNEW." . . . . 8 LOVE AND A QUESTION . 16
BUT DID NOT ENTER, THOUGH THE WISH WAS STRONG: . . . 16 A DREAM PANG . . . 5
ANY FIXED WAGES, THOUGH I WISH I COULD. . . . . . . 35 DEATH OF THE HIRED MAN 23
WARREN, I WISH YOU COULD HAVE HEARD THE WAY . . . . 36 DEATH OF THE HIRED MAN 54
AS I SIT HERE, AND OFTENTIMES, I WISH . . . . 58 THE BLACK COTTAGE . 111
"I WISH YOU HAD SEEN HIS PERPETUAL BOW-- . . . . . 61 BLUEBERRIES . . . 57
"I WISH I KNEW HALF WHAT THE FLOCK OF THEM KNOW . . . 61 BLUEBERRIES . . . 60
THE VOICES GIVE YOU WHAT YOU WISH TO HEAR." . . . . 78 THE GENERATIONS OF MEN 137
"STRANGELY, IT'S ANYTHING THEY WISH TO GIVE." . . . . 78 THE GENERATIONS OF MEN 138
I WISH THAT EVERYTHING ON EARTH WERE JUST . . . . . 115 IN THE HOME STRETCH . 140
AS CERTAIN AS THE MEALS WE'VE HAD. I WISH . . . . . 115 IN THE HOME STRETCH . 141
AND HALF GRANT WHAT I WISH AND SNATCH ME AWAY . . . 122 BIRCHES 51
CALL IT A DAY, I WISH THEY MIGHT HAVE SAID . . . . . 136 "OUT,OUT--" 10
CONCEAL A WISH TO SEE HIM SHOW THE SPUNK . . . . . 153 SNOW 283
WHY DO WE WISH TO BEAR . . . . 156 THE SOUND OF TREES . 2
FOR ART'S SAKE ONE COULD ALMOST WISH THEM WORSE . . 167 NEW HAMPSHIRE . . 266
AND HAVE NO WISH TO WITH THE HEART--NOR NEED, . . . 199 WILD GRAPES . . . 98
TO WISH IN VAIN TO LET GO WITH THE MIND-- . . . . . 199 WILD GRAPES . . . 101
IF THE WISH HADN'T BEEN TOO STRONG IN ME . . . . . 204 THE WITCH OF COOS . 66
IT ONLY GIVES OUR WISH FOR BLUE A WHET. . . . . . 220 FRAGMENTARY BLUE . 8
I WISH I COULD PROMISE TO LIE IN THE NIGHT . . . . . 228 GOOD-BY AND KEEP COLD . 25
IF HE FULFILLED AT LAST HIS SUMMER WISH. . . . . . 284 THE GOLD HESPERIDEE . 35
AND JUST BECAUSE WE OWNED TO A WISH FOR RAIN, . . . 349 OUR HOLD ON THE PLANET 5
A WISH TO COMPLY . . . . 391 A WISH TO COMPLY . . 1
IT'S A WISH TO COMPLY . . . . 392 A WISH TO COMPLY . . 7
WITH ONLY ONE VESTIGIAL CREATURE WISH: . . . . . . 395 ETHEREALIZING . . . 12
THE ONE THING MORE I WISH THERE WERE. . . . . . . 451 A-WISHING WELL . . 11
"I WISH I MAY, I WISH I MIGHT" . . . . 451 A-WISHING WELL . . 28
OR BE A CHRISTIAN.--PAUL, I WISH YOU'D SAY . . . . 509 A MASQUE OF MERCY . 403
ALL PAUL MEANS, AND I WISH THE DEAD COULD HEAR ME-- . 519 A MASQUE OF MERCY . 674
WISHED
AND WISHED HER HEART IN A CASE OF GOLD . . . . . . 8 LOVE AND A QUESTION . 23
THE BRIDEGROOM WISHED HE KNEW. . . . . 8 LOVE AND A QUESTION . 32
YOU ACT AS IF YOU WISHED YOU HADN'T COME. . . . . . 47 A HUNDRED COLLARS . 71
A QUIVERFUL TO CHOOSE FROM, SINCE HE WISHED ME . . . 187 THE AX-HELVE . . . 64
I HAVE WISHED A BIRD WOULD FLY AWAY, ... 250 A MINOR BIRD . . . 1
HE WISHED WHEN HE HAD HAD THE TRACK ALONE . . . . 270 THE EGG AND THE MACHINE 5
HE WISHED IT ALL THE MODERN SPEED. . . . . 274 A LONE STRIKER . . 51
"YOU WISHED YOUR MIDDLE NAME HAD BEEN TECUMSEH." . . 406 FROM PLANE TO PLANE . 74
AND HE WISHED LOVE WERE THUS AND SO. . . . . . . 451 A-WISHING WELL . . 2
AND EYEING ONE HE ONLY WISHED WERE HIS, ... 454 HOW HARD TO KEEP FROM 15
WISHES
ONE OF MY WISHES IS THAT THOSE DARK TREES, ... 5 INTO MY OWN . . . 1
"DICK WISHES HE COULD SWAP JOBS WITH THE DOCTOR. . . 404 FROM PLANE TO PLANE . 28
NOT WITHOUT CONSULTATION WITH THEIR WISHES: . . . . 458 HOW HARD TO KEEP FROM 152
WISHING (SEE A-WISHING)
WITHOUT SO MUCH AS WISHING HIM GOOD-NIGHT. . . . . 101 THE WOOD-PILE . . . 21
I CAN'T HELP WISHING I COULD SEND YOU ONE . . . . 107 CHRISTMAS TREES . . 59
IN WISHING YOU HEREWITH A MERRY CHRISTMAS. . . . . 107 CHRISTMAS TREES . . 60
WISHING THE TOWER . . . . 217 I WILL SING YOU ONE-O . 3
SOME RUMOR OF HIS WISHING RING . . . . 390 TWO LEADING LIGHTS . 24
WISP
IT WRAPS A WISP OF SEAWEED ROUND MY LEGS, ... 391 ON BEING IDOLIZED . 2
WIST
OF THINGS OF MOMENT TO WHICH, THEY WIST, ... 15 IN A VALE 13
AND GLAD FOR ME, I WIST. . . . . 28 MY BUTTERFLY . . . 21
WIT
THEY DID NOT HAVE THE WIT TO SAY, ... 297 LEAVES COMPARED WITH . 15

WIT (CONTINUED)
    (NOR I) HAVE WIT . . . . 360 THE RABBIT-HUNTER . . 17
WITCH
    THE FLOWERS OF THE WITCH HAZEL WITHER; . . . . . . 30 RELUCTANCE 16
    SHE HAS ONE WITCH--OLD STYLE. SHE LIVES IN COLEBROOK. . 163 NEW HAMPSHIRE . . . 125
    (THE ONLY OTHER WITCH I EVER MET . . . . 163 NEW HAMPSHIRE . . . 126
    THE WITCH WAS YOUNG, AND BEAUTIFUL (NEW STYLE), . . . 163 NEW HAMPSHIRE . . . 129
    FOLKS THINK A WITCH WHO HAS FAMILIAR SPIRITS . . . . 202 THE WITCH OF COOS . . 4
    THE WITCH OF COOS . . . . 202 THE WITCH OF COOS . . T
    THE PAUPER WITCH OF GRAFTON . . . . 207 PAUPER WITCH OF GRAFTON T
    AT HAVING IN THEIR TOWN A NOTED WITCH: . . . . . . 208 PAUPER WITCH OF GRAFTON 37
    THAT AS A WITCH I'D OFTEN MILK A BAT . . . . 208 PAUPER WITCH OF GRAFTON 40
    TO MAKE IT SURER THAT I WAS A WITCH? . . . . 208 PAUPER WITCH OF GRAFTON 44
    BY HAVING ME A WITCH. OR SOMETHING HAPPENED . . . . 209 PAUPER WITCH OF GRAFTON 77
    BY ALL I TELL; BUT SO'S THE MOON A WITCH. . . . . . 237 A HILLSIDE THAW . . . 19
    THE WITCH THAT CAME (THE WITHERED HAG) . . . . . . 307 PROVIDE, PROVIDE . . 1
    YOU'RE NOT A WITCH? / NO. / HAVE YOU EVER BEEN ONE? . 476 A MASQUE OF REASON . 92
    THE WITCH OF ENDOR WAS A FRIEND OF MINE. . . . . . 476 A MASQUE OF REASON . 97
    A WITCH WAS STRONGER THAN A PROPHET THERE. . . . . 477 A MASQUE OF REASON . 101
WITCHCRAFT
    IF THIS SEEMS LIKE WITCHCRAFT RATHER, ... 304 CLEAR AND COLDER . . 16
    BUT SHE WAS BURNED FOR WITCHCRAFT. / THAT IS NOT . . 477 A MASQUE OF REASON . 102
WITCHES
    TWO WITCHES . . . . 202 TWO WITCHES . . . . T
    THAT WOMEN PROPHETS SHOULD BE BURNED AS WITCHES, . . 476 A MASQUE OF REASON . 89
WITCHES'
    LIKE THE INGREDIENTS OF A WITCHES' BROTH-- . . . . 302 DESIGN 6
    IN MY WITCHES' WEATHER PRIMER . . . . 303 CLEAR AND COLDER . . 2
    IF THIS SEEMS A WITCHES' CHOWDER . . . . 304 CLEAR AND COLDER . . 17
WITCHING
    IN SUMMERTIME WITH A WITCHING WAND, ... 276 TWO TRAMPS IN MUD TIME 34
WITCH'S
    ALWAYS THE WITCH'S MOTTO ANYWAY. . . . . 207 PAUPER WITCH OF GRAFTON 8
WITCH-WOMEN'S
    WHAT ARE HER INTERESTS, JOB? / WITCH-WOMEN'S RIGHTS. . 479 A MASQUE OF REASON . 175
WITH---NOT INDEXED
WITHDRAWING
    "IS THIS SOME TRANCE YOU ARE WITHDRAWING INTO?" . . 78 THE GENERATIONS OF MEN 148
WITHDRAWN
    I HAD WITHDRAWN IN FOREST, AND MY SONG . . . . . 16 A DREAM PANG 1
    THE CITY HAD WITHDRAWN INTO ITSELF . . . . 105 CHRISTMAS TREES . . . 1
    AND WHITHER IT WILL BE WITHDRAWN, ... 332 ALL REVELATION . . . 6
WITHDREW
    SHE WITHDREW, SHRINKING FROM BENEATH HIS ARM . . . 52 HOME BURIAL 31
    BUT FINDING NOTHING, SULLENLY WITHDREW. . . . . . 126 RANGE-FINDING . . . 14
    AND THEN TOOK THE VEIL AND WITHDREW, ... 266 SITTING BY A BUSH . . 14
    SHE WITHDREW BACK IN SELF-RETREAT . . . . 346 DISCOVERY OF MADEIRAS . 101
WITHER
    THE FLOWERS OF THE WITCH HAZEL WITHER; . . . . . 30 RELUCTANCE 16
WITHERED
    SHE LOVES THE BARE, THE WITHERED TREE; . . . . . 6 MY NOVEMBER GUEST . . 4
    UP FROM THE TANGLE OF WITHERED WEEDS . . . . . . 8 A LATE WALK 7
    I FOUND IT WITH THE WITHERED LEAVES . . . . . . 29 MY BUTTERFLY 46
    THEY ARE DRAGGED TO THE WITHERED BRACKEN BY THE LOAD, 121 BIRCHES 14
    THEY MIGHT FIND FUEL THERE, IN WITHERED BRAKE, . . 131 THE BONFIRE 61
    THAT FLASHES TAIL THROUGH LAST YEAR'S WITHERED BRAKE . 226 THE ONSET 20
    THE WITCH THAT CAME (THE WITHERED HAG) . . . . . 307 PROVIDE, PROVIDE . . 1
WITHERING
    AND FRESHEN IN THIS AIR OF WITHERING SWEETNESS; . . 15 WAITING 25
    AS WHERE SOME FLOWER LAY WITHERING ON THE GROUND. . . 22 THE TUFT OF FLOWERS . 16
    SHE SCORNS A PASTURE WITHERING TO THE ROOT. . . . 125 THE COW IN APPLE TIME . 6
    THE FLOWER OF CITIES FROM SINKING AND WITHERING FAINT. 286 A ROADSIDE STAND . . 6
WITHHELD
    I SHOULD NOT BE WITHHELD BUT THAT SOME DAY . . . . 5 INTO MY OWN 5
WITHHOLDING
    SOMETHING WE WERE WITHHOLDING MADE US WEAK . . . . 348 THE GIFT OUTRIGHT . . 8
    WE WERE WITHHOLDING FROM OUR LAND OF LIVING, . . . 348 THE GIFT OUTRIGHT . . 10
    IS STILL WITHHOLDING IN THE ZODIAC . . . . 361 A LOOSE MOUNTAIN . . 18
    SOMETHING WE WERE WITHHOLDING MADE US WEAK . . . . 424 THE GIFT OUTRIGHT . . 8
    WE WERE WITHHOLDING FROM OUR LAND OF LIVING, . . . 424 THE GIFT OUTRIGHT . . 10
WITHIN
    WITHIN, THE BRIDE IN THE DUSK ALONE . . . . . . 8 LOVE AND A QUESTION . 17
    YET SAW BUT HER WITHIN, ... 8 LOVE AND A QUESTION . 22
    AS WITNESS ALL WITHIN . . . . 11 WIND AND WINDOW FLOWER 19
    BUT ONCE WITHIN THE WOOD, WE PAUSED . . . . . . 18 GOING FOR WATER . . 13
    "AS ALL MUST BE," I SAID WITHIN MY HEART, ... 22 THE TUFT OF FLOWERS . 9
    OR ROOM WITHIN A ROOM, OF HICKORY POLES, ... 66 A SERVANT TO SERVANTS 114
    AND I THOUGHT I HAD THE FOLK WITHIN: . . . . . . 102 GOOD HOURS 5
    I SHOULD BE WRITING TO WITHIN THE HOUR . . . . . 107 CHRISTMAS TREES . . . 51
    WALL WITHIN WALL TO SHUT FEAR OUT. . . . . . . 120 BOND AND FREE . . . 3
    RECURRING TILL WE ANSWER FROM WITHIN. . . . . . 147 SNOW 133
    OTHERS BECAUSE HE'D COME WITHIN A DAY . . . . . 191 PAUL'S WIFE 6
    IT STARTED A GRIEF WITHIN A GRIEF, ... 253 THE THATCH 21
    WITHIN A MILLION YEARS OF AN IDEA. . . . . . . 293 AT WOODWARD'S GARDENS . 16
    AS STRONG IS RAIN WITHOUT AS WINE WITHIN, ... 337 THE WIND AND THE RAIN . 41
    ONLY WITHIN. INSIDE THE BRAIN . . . . 381 AN UNSTAMPED LETTER IN 32
    NATURE WITHIN HER INMOST SELF DIVIDES . . . . . 468 FROM IRON 1
    TO OVERCOME THE FEAR WITHIN THE SOUL . . . . . 521 A MASQUE OF MERCY . . 729
WITHOUT
    WITHOUT A WINDOW LIGHT. . . . . 7 LOVE AND A QUESTION . 8
    WITHOUT THE GIFT OF SIGHT. . . . . 9 STARS 12
    NOT WITHOUT FEEBLE-POINTED SPIKES OF FLOWERS . . . 17 MOWING 11
    THE BARREN BOUGHS WITHOUT THE LEAVES, ... 18 GOING FOR WATER . . 11
    WITHOUT THE BIRDS, WITHOUT THE BREEZE. . . . . . 18 GOING FOR WATER . . 12
    AND WHERE THEY SOUGHT WITHOUT THE SWORD . . . . 19 THE TRIAL BY EXISTENCE 5
    TWO THAT DON'T LOVE CAN'T LIVE TOGETHER WITHOUT THEM. 53 HOME BURIAL 54
    WE DIDN'T CHANGE WITHOUT SOME SACRIFICE, ... 64 A SERVANT TO SERVANTS 64
    OF COURSE THEY HAD TO FEED HIM WITHOUT DISHES. . . 66 A SERVANT TO SERVANTS 121

                                                        PAGE TITLE   LINE
WITHOUT (CONTINUED)
    MADE SHIFT TO SHELTER THEM WITHOUT THE HELP . . . . . . 73 THE GENERATIONS OF MEN   12
    EVERYTHING GOES THE SAME WITHOUT ME THERE. . . . . 94 THE SELF-SEEKER . . .   40
    YOU'RE BAD ENOUGH TO MANAGE, WITHOUT HER." . . . . . .   94 THE SELF-SEEKER . . .   55
    WITHOUT SO MUCH AS WISHING HIM GOOD-NIGHT. . . . . 101 THE WOOD-PILE   21
    AND COULD NOT DO WITHOUT AND KEEP ITS CHRISTMAS. . . . . 106 CHRISTMAS TREES . . .   11
    (MIRACULOUSLY WITHOUT TASTING FLESH) . . . . 109 THE EXPOSED NEST . . .   15
    HER BACK. SHE ALWAYS ANSWERED WITHOUT TURNING. . . . . . 110 IN THE HOME STRETCH .   12
    (OH, IT WAS WITHOUT PREJUDICE TO ME!) . . . . 119 MEETING AND PASSING .   12
    TO FLAMES WITHOUT TWICE THINKING, WHERE IT VERGES . . . 131 THE BONFIRE   59
    DIED NOT WITHOUT A NOISE OF CRACKLING WOOD-- . . . . . 131 THE BONFIRE   76
    IT'S QUIET AS AN EMPTY CHURCH WITHOUT HIM." . . . . . . 152 SNOW   260
    WHOLE TOWNSHIPS NAMED BUT WITHOUT POPULATION. . . . . . 165 NEW HAMPSHIRE . . .   209
    THERE'S BEEN ENOUGH SHED WITHOUT SHEDDING MINE. . . . . 170 NEW HAMPSHIRE . . .   372
    WITHOUT A SINGLE LEAF TO SPEND ON AUTUMN, ... 175 THE CENSUS-TAKER . .   23
    PERHAPS THE WIND THE MORE WITHOUT THE HELP . . . . 175 THE CENSUS-TAKER . .   25
    WITHOUT THE NAME HER PERSONAL MYSTERY. . . . . 182 MAPLE   93
    PUT ON IT FROM WITHOUT. AND THERE ITS STRENGTH LAY . . 187 THE AX-HELVE   75
    ERECT, BUT NOT WITHOUT ITS WAVES, AS WHEN . . . . 188 THE AX-HELVE   96
    TO STOP WITHOUT A FARMHOUSE NEAR . . . . 224 STOPPING BY WOODS .   6
    AND PUT MY FOOT ON ONE WITHOUT AVAIL. . . . . 237 A HILLSIDE THAW . .   11
    AND SUDDENLY, WITHOUT A JERK OR TWITCH, ... 237 A HILLSIDE THAW . .   21
    WAS WROUGHT THROUGH TREES WITHOUT A BREATH OF STORM . . 238 A HILLSIDE THAW . .   31
    DEBATING WHAT TO DO WITHOUT AN AX. . . . . 238 ON A TREE FALLEN ACROSS   8
    THE TOTAL SKY ALMOST WITHOUT DEFECT. . . . . 245 SPRING POOLS . . .   2
    AS I THOUGHT OF THEM WITHOUT NEST OR ROOST. . . . . . . 253 THE THATCH   29
    BUT WITHOUT TIME TO LINGER FOR HER STORY. . . . . 257 THE LOVELY BE CHOOSERS   49
    JUST AS HE WAS, WITHOUT AN UTTERED SOUND . . . . 284 THE GOLD HESPERIDEE .   43
    THE OTHER WITHOUT DEMUR AGREES. . . . . 291 ON HEART'S BEGINNING TO   23
    WITHOUT INDULGING A "NOT FOR US!" . . . . 291 ON HEART'S BEGINNING TO   33
    ON THEIR PART, THOUGH WITHOUT THE NEEDED INSIGHT. . . . 293 AT WOODWARD'S GARDENS .   26
    THE OLD DOG BARKS BACKWARD WITHOUT GETTING UP. . . . . . 308 THE SPAN OF LIFE . .   1
    AND PLAY THE GOOD WITHOUT THE ILL. . . . . 336 THE WIND AND THE RAIN .   17
    AS STRONG IS RAIN WITHOUT AS WINE WITHIN, ... 337 THE WIND AND THE RAIN .   41
    HER TONE OF MEANING BUT WITHOUT THE WORDS. . . . . 338 NEVER WOULD BIRDS' SONG   5
    NOT ENTIRELY WITHOUT CONSENT. . . . . 344 DISCOVERY OF MADEIRAS .   14
    WITHOUT INQUIRING IF 'TWAS SERIOUS. . . . . 369 THE LITERATE FARMER AND   26
    I LEAVE THIS NOTE WITHOUT A STAMP . . . . 380 AN UNSTAMPED LETTER IN   5
    HAVE I NOT WALKED WITHOUT AN UPWARD LOOK . . . . 383 BRAVADO   1
    ALBEIT NOT WITHOUT SOME SHAME OF FACE, ... 396 ANY SIZE WE PLEASE .   4
    WITHOUT ONE TRINKET FROM ORMUZ . . . . 416 AMERICA IS HARD TO SEE   10
    FIRM IN OUR FREE BELIEFS WITHOUT DISMAY, ... 424 FOR JOHN F. KENNEDY .   74
    NOT WITHOUT DUE PATTER . . . . 435 KITTY HAWK   228
    WITHOUT SELF-REPROACH." . . . . 437 KITTY HAWK   286
    NOT WITHOUT CONSULTATION WITH THEIR WISHES; . . . . . . 458 HOW HARD TO KEEP FROM   152
    INTO OBLIVION WITHOUT A LAWYER. . . . . 462 HOW HARD TO KEEP FROM   263
    WHY NOT RIGHT NOW? / WE CAN'T WITHOUT THE DEVIL. . . . . 487 A MASQUE OF REASON .   381
    AND LET HIM GET OFF WITHOUT PROPHESYING? . . . . 502 A MASQUE OF MERCY .   221
    I'D LIKE TO SEE THE WORLD TRIED ONCE WITHOUT IT. . . . . 515 A MASQUE OF MERCY .   575
WITH'S
    THE STRONGEST THING THAT'S GIVEN US TO SEE WITH'S . . . 177 THE STAR-SPLITTER .   34
WITNESS
    AS WITNESS ALL WITHIN . . . . 11 WIND AND WINDOW FLOWER   19
    TOWARD THE THRONE TO WITNESS THERE . . . . 20 THE TRIAL BY EXISTENCE   30
    A WITNESS TREE . . . . 329 A WITNESS TREE . . .   T
    HAS BEEN IMPRESSED AS WITNESS TREE . . . . 331 BEECH   7
    WITNESS HOW HARD IT WAS FOR JULIUS CAESAR. . . . . 454 HOW HARD TO KEEP FROM   22
WITNESSES
    SO THERE WERE WITNESSES THAT PAUL WAS MARRIED, ... 195 PAUL'S WIFE   145
    LESS PARTIAL WITNESSES THAN HE . . . . 418 AMERICA IS HARD TO SEE   62
WITNESSING
    FROM WITNESSING THE FAULT OF ONE SO PROUD. . . . . 284 THE GOLD HESPERIDEE .   57
WITS
    THAT ARE CALCULATED TO SOOTHE THEM OUT OF THEIR WITS, . 287 A ROADSIDE STAND . .   29
    LET'S LEAVE THAT TO THE SCIENTIFIC WITS. . . . . 425 ACCIDENTALLY ON PURPOSE   18
WIVES
    LIKE THOSE WHO FURNISHED ADAM'S SONS WITH WIVES; . . . . 161 NEW HAMPSHIRE . . .   79
WIZARD
    IT TAKES THE MOON FOR THIS. THE SUN'S A WIZARD . . . . . 237 A HILLSIDE THAW . . .   18
WIZARDRY
    "AT LEAST YOU OUGHT TO DIE FOR WIZARDRY. . . . . 457 HOW HARD TO KEEP FROM   115
WOE
    BY HARBORING WOE IN THE BRIDAL HOUSE, ...   8 LOVE AND A QUESTION .   31
    OR THE WOE WERE NOT EARTHLY WOE . . . . 21 THE TRIAL BY EXISTENCE   55
    THE GROUNDWORK OF ALL FAITH IS HUMAN WOE. . . . . 352 THE LESSON FOR TODAY .   58
WOES
    FOR THE WOES OF THE PAST . . . . 447 THE BAD ISLAND--EASTER   5
WOKE
    THAT WHEN IT WOKE AND CAME TO LIFE AGAIN . . . . 181 MAPLE   38
    AND AS I WOKE AFRAID TO TURN . . . . 380 AN UNSTAMPED LETTER IN   21
WOLSEY
    THAT FELLED THE ANGELS, WOLSEY SHOULD HAVE SAID. . . . . 481 A MASQUE OF REASON .   206
WOLVES
    LIKE PEOPLE THROWN OUT TO DELAY THE WOLVES. . . . . . . 279 THE WHITE-TAILED HORNET   68
WOMAN
    GOD, WHAT A WOMAN! AND IT'S COME TO THIS, ...   53 HOME BURIAL . . .   69
    I'LL TALK TO YOU, OLD WOMAN, AFTERWARD.-- . . . . 88 THE HOUSEKEEPER . . .   209
    SHONE ON A MAN AND WOMAN IN THE DOOR . . . . 89 THE FEAR   2
    THE WOMAN SPOKE OUT SHARPLY, "WHOA, STAND STILL!-- . . . 89 THE FEAR   8
    THAT DAY A WOMAN COULDN'T COAX HIM OFF. . . . .   94 THE SELF-SEEKER . . .   37
    "SAVE US FROM BEING CORNERED BY A WOMAN. . . . . 151 SNOW   236
    ON MOOSILAUKE, BUT WOMAN SIGNS TO MAN, ... 210 PAUPER WITCH OF GRAFTON   94
    FOR A WOMAN AND A PUZZLE. . . . . 339 THE SUBVERTED FLOWER .   9
    A WOMAN WANTS TO BE OVERRULED. . . . . 344 DISCOVERY OF MADEIRAS .   43
    A MAN COMES BACK TO A WOMAN AGAIN . . . . 346 DISCOVERY OF MADEIRAS .   87
    BUT NO, A WOMAN HAS TO BE HER AGE, ... 458 HOW HARD TO KEEP FROM   157
    AND SHE'S A WOMAN: SHE'S NOT INTERESTED . . . . 479 A MASQUE OF REASON .   173
    IN WHAT I SAY. DON'T BE SO SILLY, WOMAN. . . . . 505 A MASQUE OF MERCY .   308

WOMANKIND
    BUT WITH NO COMPANION OF WOMANKIND . . . . 344 DISCOVERY OF MADEIRAS . 15
    OF MAN AND WOMANKIND . . . . 464 MILKY WAY IS A COWPATH 26
WOMAN'S
    WAS WOMAN'S WAY OF LIFE. . . . . 464 MILKY WAY IS A COWPATH 16
WOMEN
    (WOMEN AND MEN WILL MAKE THEM ALL THE SAME.) . . . . . 64 A SERVANT TO SERVANTS 69
    MORE THAN SOME WOMEN LIKE THE DISHPAN, JOE; . . . . . 111 IN THE HOME STRETCH . 31
    ONLY YOU WOMEN HAVE TO PUT THESE AIRS ON . . . . . . 146 SNOW 98
    PAID HEED TO WOMEN, YOU'D TAKE MY ADVICE . . . . . . 150 SNOW 216
    AND THAT NOT DWELT IN NOW BY MEN OR WOMEN. . . . . . 174 THE CENSUS-TAKER . . 6
    (IT NEVER HAD BEEN DWELT IN, THOUGH, BY WOMEN, ... 174 THE CENSUS-TAKER . . 7
    ONE MAN'S THREE WOMEN IN A BURIAL ROW . . . . 199 PLACE FOR A THIRD . . 7
    DON'T MAKE ME LIE WITH THOSE TWO OTHER WOMEN." . . . . 199 PLACE FOR A THIRD . . 11
    WHERE WOMEN PRAY WITH PRIESTS. THERE IS NO LOVE. . . . 318 BUILD SOIL 84
    THERE'S ONLY LOVE OF MEN AND WOMEN, LOVE . . . . . . 318 BUILD SOIL 85
    I CRY, "DO WORK FOR WOMEN--ALL THE HELP . . . . . . 447 DOES NO ONE AT ALL EVER 28
    THE QUINTESSENCE OF HORSES, MEN, AND WOMEN." . . . . . 455 HOW HARD TO KEEP FROM 44
    JEWELS AND HORSES, WOMEN, WINE, AND SONG." . . . . . 455 HOW HARD TO KEEP FROM 62
    THAT WOMEN PROPHETS SHOULD BE BURNED AS WITCHES, . . . 476 A MASQUE OF REASON . 89
    YOU DON'T CATCH WOMEN TRYING TO BE PLATO. . . . . . . 478 A MASQUE OF REASON . 140
    AEONS OF TIME AND STILL IT'S MOSTLY WOMEN . . . . . . 478 A MASQUE OF REASON . 149
    YOU HAVE IT IN FOR WOMEN, SHE BELIEVES. . . . . . . 479 A MASQUE OF REASON . 178
WOMENFOLK
    WITH WOMENFOLK. WE COULD HAVE SOME ARRANGEMENT . . . . 52 HOME BURIAL 50
    THE INMATES MAY BE LONELY WOMENFOLK. . . . . 248 THE COCOON 11
WOMEN'S (SEE WITCH-WOMEN'S)
WON
    I WON! BUT I'M SURE NO ONE EVER SPREAD . . . . . . 132 THE BONFIRE 81
    TO EVIL, NO IMPORTANT TRIUMPH WON, ... 226 THE ONSET 10
    WASN'T SHE GLAD NOW? EVERYTHING SEEMED WON, ... 230 NOT TO KEEP 11
    FOR YOUR NOT HAVING WON TO VIRGIL'S FAME. . . . . . 351 THE LESSON FOR TODAY . 27
    ELIZABETH THE FIRST AND ENGLAND WON. . . . . 422 FOR JOHN F. KENNEDY . 18
    AND HAVE WON THE CROWN, ... 437 KITTY HAWK 302
    WE ALWAYS SAY--NOT WHO WON IT, ... 463 LINES IN DEJECTION . 27
    THERE CAN BE NO DISPUTING WHO HAS WON-- . . . . . 507 A MASQUE OF MERCY . 367
WONDER
    AND THE AWE PASSES WONDER THEN, ... 21 THE TRIAL BY EXISTENCE 59
    SPRING IS THE MISCHIEF IN ME, AND I WONDER . . . . 34 MENDING WALL . . . 28
    "I WONDER WHAT'S BETWEEN THEM." / "I CAN TELL YOU. . . . 39 DEATH OF THE HIRED MAN 139
    "THE WONDER IS I DIDN'T SEE AT ONCE. . . . . 51 HOME BURIAL 20
    "I WONDER YOU DIDN'T SEE LOREN ABOUT." . . . . . . 60 BLUEBERRIES 33
    NO WONDER I WAS GLAD TO GET AWAY. . . . . 67 A SERVANT TO SERVANTS 148
    THE WONDER WAS THE TENTS WEREN'T SNATCHED AWAY . . . . 67 A SERVANT TO SERVANTS 168
    WHAT DO WE SEE IN SUCH A HOLE, I WONDER." . . . . . 76 THE GENERATIONS OF MEN 91
    I WONDER IF IT'S NOT YOUR MAKE-BELIEVE. . . . . . . 78 THE GENERATIONS OF MEN 140
    "I WONDER WHERE YOUR ORACLE IS TENDING. . . . . . . 79 THE GENERATIONS OF MEN 171
    "I WONDER WHY HE DOESN'T MARRY HER . . . . 84 THE HOUSEKEEPER . . 84
    "THE WONDER IS IT HADN'T BEEN YOUR HEAD." . . . . . 93 THE SELF-SEEKER . . 21
    I WONDER WHERE MY LAWYER IS. HIS TRAIN'S IN. . . . . 94 THE SELF-SEEKER . . 49
    A RAM'S HORN! WHAT WOULD I HAVE GOT, I WONDER, ... 96 THE SELF-SEEKER . .113
    IN COMMON LAW, I WONDER." / "BUT I ASK, ... 111 IN THE HOME STRETCH . 24
    I WONDER HOW FAR DOWN THE ROAD HE'S GOT. . . . . . 127 THE SMILE 11
    "I WONDER WHAT THOSE SIGNALS ARE . . . . 138 BROWN'S DESCENT . . 32
    I WONDER IF HE'S SOLD HIS FARM, ... 138 BROWN'S DESCENT . . 35
    I WONDER ABOUT THE TREES. . . . . 156 THE SOUND OF TREES . 1
    NO WONDER POETS SOMETIMES HAVE TO SEEM . . . . . . 164 NEW HAMPSHIRE . . .172
    TO WONDER WHERE THE COLD WAS COMING FROM, ... 203 THE WITCH OF COOS . 45
    AND SAVE FOR THE WONDER . . . . 219 I WILL SING YOU ONE-O . 69
    THAT A BROOK RAN WATER. BUT I WONDER . . . . . . 231 A BROOK IN THE CITY . 21
    THE COLOR RUN, ALL SORTS OF WONDER FOLLOW. . . . . . 245 THE FREEDOM OF THE MOON 12
    AND WONDER AT HER WHERE SHE IS, ... 257 THE LOVELY BE CHOOSERS 47
    AND WORDS TO WONDER IN HER HEARING HOW SHE CAME THERE, . 257 THE LOVELY BE CHOOSERS 48
    I WONDER HOW I SHOULD LIKE YOU TO COME TO ME . . . . 287 A ROADSIDE STAND . . 50
    I WONDER! BOW AND RAINBOW AS IT BENT, ... 315 IRIS BY NIGHT . . . 23
    I CAN BUT WONDER WHENCE . . . . 333 HAPPINESS MAKES UP . 9
    (WHO WOULD YOU BE, I WONDER, BY THOSE MARKS . . . . . 356 A MOTH SEEN IN WINTER . 5
    I WONDER IF IT WOULDN'T SIGNIFY . . . . 365 OF STONES OF THE PLACE 4
    THOUGH INCIDENTALLY I SOMETIMES WONDER . . . . . . 481 A MASQUE OF REASON . 220
WONDERED
    HAVE HAD TO DO WITH IT--SHE SOMETIMES WONDERED. . . . 182 MAPLE 76
    I WONDERED WHAT MACHINE OF AGES GONE . . . . 189 THE GRINDSTONE . . 35
    I WONDERED WHO IT WAS THE MAN THOUGHT GROUND-- . . . . 190 THE GRINDSTONE . . 45
    I WONDERED IF HE REALLY THOUGHT IT FAIR . . . . . . 190 THE GRINDSTONE . . 48
    PAUL WONDERED HOW IT WOULD RESPOND TO WATER. . . . . 194 PAUL'S WIFE . . . 97
    AND WONDERED WITH ME THERE . . . . 366 NOT OF SCHOOL AGE . 15
WONDERFUL
    MORE WONDERFUL, MORE BEAUTIFUL PRODUCER? . . . . . 324 BUILD SOIL 254
WONDERING
    BUT THERE WAS NO ONE. I WAS SOMEWHERE WONDERING . . . 132 THE BONFIRE 90
WONDERS
    YOU KNOW PAUL COULD DO WONDERS. EVERYONE'S . . . . . 192 PAUL'S WIFE . . . 42
WON'T--NOT INDEXED
WONTED
    I MUST BE WONTED TO IT--THAT'S THE REASON. . . . . . 51 HOME BURIAL 22
    BUT I GOT WONTED TO IT. AND BESIDES-- . . . . . . 87 THE HOUSEKEEPER . . 174
WOOD (SEE MID-WOOD)
    OF NEW WOOD AND OLD WHERE THE WOODPECKER CHOPS; . . . 6 GHOST HOUSE . . . 9
    FOR THE WOOD WAKES, AND YOU ARE HERE FOR PROOF. . . . 16 A DREAM PANG . . . 14
    THERE WAS NEVER A SOUND BESIDE THE WOOD BUT ONE, . . . 17 MOWING 1
    BUT ONCE WITHIN THE WOOD, WE PAUSED . . . . 18 GOING FOR WATER . . 13
    IT WAS FAR IN THE SAMENESS OF THE WOOD; . . . . . . 24 THE DEMIURGE'S LAUGH . 1
    AS THEY BOTH BITE THE WOOD. IT'S ALL OUR MUSIC. . . . 94 THE SELF-SEEKER . . 43
    OVER STONE WALLS AND ALL ALONG A WOOD . . . . . . 98 THE SELF-SEEKER . .152
    AND THEN THERE WAS A PILE OF WOOD FOR WHICH . . . . 101 THE WOOD-PILE . . 18
    THE WOOD WAS GRAY AND THE BARK WARPING OFF IT . . . . 102 THE WOOD-PILE . . 29
    TWO ROADS DIVERGED IN A YELLOW WOOD, ... 105 THE ROAD NOT TAKEN . 1
    TWO ROADS DIVERGED IN A WOOD, AND I-- . . . . . . 105 THE ROAD NOT TAKEN . 18

PAGE TITLE   LINE

WOOD (CONTINUED)

THE WOOD." / "WHAT KIND OF YEARS?" / "WHY, LATTER YEARS--	. 112 IN THE HOME STRETCH	. 49
AND LIFE IS TOO MUCH LIKE A PATHLESS WOOD	. 122 BIRCHES	. 44
DIED NOT WITHOUT A NOISE OF CRACKLING WOOD--	. 131 THE BONFIRE	. 76
AND MADE DUST AND DROPPED STOVE-LENGTH STICKS OF WOOD,	. 136 "OUT, OUT--"	. 2
IS ONLY CORNERS, CROSSROADS IN A WOOD).	. 165 NEW HAMPSHIRE	. 192
REMEMBER BIRNAM WOOD! THE WOOD'S IN FLUX!"	. 170 NEW HAMPSHIRE	. 373
'SA THING TO BE COMPARED WITH SPLITTING WOOD.	. 179 THE STAR-SPLITTER	. 94
ON THE NEW WOOD THE WHOLE LENGTH OF THE LOG	. 193 PAUL'S WIFE	. 70
AND SUCH AS IS DONE TO THEIR WOOD WITH AN AX--	. 228 GOOD-BY AND KEEP COLD	. 23
IS WATER WOOD TO SERVE A BROOK THE SAME?	. 231 A BROOK IN THE CITY	. 12
THE TREE THE TEMPEST WITH A CRASH OF WOOD	. 238 ON A TREE FALLEN ACROSS	. 1
HE KNEW ANOTHER PLACE, A WOOD,	. 274 A LONE STRIKER	. 36
AND CAUGHT ME SPLITTING WOOD IN THE YARD.	. 275 TWO TRAMPS IN MUD TIME	. 2
I SPENT ON THE UNIMPORTANT WOOD.	. 275 TWO TRAMPS IN MUD TIME	. 16
THE WOOD OF IT CHANGED TO STONE,	. 285 IN TIME OF CLOUDBURST	. 23
IN CHESTNUT NOW BECOME A PRECIOUS WOOD	. 290 OLD BARN AT THE BOTTOM	. 38
SO MAY ITS BARK, SO MAY ITS WOOD;	. 296 LEAVES COMPARED WITH	. 2
WE WENT FROM HOUSE TO WOOD	. 333 HAPPINESS MAKES UP	. 23
OF WOOD OR GRANITE OR LIME	. 348 TRIPLE BRONZE	. 6
YET SINGING BUT DIONE IN THE WOOD	. 351 THE LESSON FOR TODAY	. 14
A PERCH AND RESTING PLACE 'TWIXT WOOD AND WOOD,	. 356 A MOTH SEEN IN WINTER	. 2
AND I AWAY IN MY OPPOSITE WOOD	. 383 WERE I IN TROUBLE	. 6
IT SEEMS TO GO INTO A WOOD,	. 388 MIDDLENESS OF THE ROAD	5

WOODBINE

THE WOODBINE LEAVES LITTERED THE YARD,	. 7 LOVE AND A QUESTION	. 13
THE WOODBINE BERRIES WERE BLUE,	. 8 LOVE AND A QUESTION	. 14

WOODCHUCK

THE WOODCHUCK COULD SAY WHETHER IT'S LIKE HIS	. 69 AFTER APPLE-PICKING	. 40
AND FOR THE BACKWOODS WOODCHUCK. YOU'RE THE GIRL!	. 97 THE SELF-SEEKER	. 125
A RAM'S HORN ORCHID SEEDPOD FOR A WOODCHUCK	. 97 THE SELF-SEEKER	. 126
A DRUMLIN WOODCHUCK	. 281 A DRUMLIN WOODCHUCK	. T

WOODCHUCK'S

UNDER WHAT BEECH TREE, ON WHAT WOODCHUCK'S KNOLL?"	. 97 THE SELF-SEEKER	. 116

WOODED

AT WOODED VALLEY AND WOODED HILL.	. 23 PAN WITH US	. 5
FROM SUCH A MOUNTAIN--IF IT ISN'T WOODED	. 42 THE MOUNTAIN	. 56

WOODEN

TO SIT BESIDE HER ON THE WOODEN STEPS.	. 34 DEATH OF THE HIRED MAN	10
WERE METAL THAN IT WAS WHEN THEY WERE WOODEN?	. 163 NEW HAMPSHIRE	. 133
OFFERED FOR SALE WILD BERRIES IN WOODEN QUARTS;	. 286 A ROADSIDE STAND	. 11
WHILE THE TREES PUT ON THEIR WOODEN RINGS	. 376 SOMETHING FOR HOPE	. 11

WOODPECKER

OF NEW WOOD AND OLD WHERE THE WOODPECKER CHOPS;	. 6 GHOST HOUSE	. 9

WOOD-PILE

THE WOOD-PILE	. 101 THE WOOD-PILE	. T

WOODS

THE WOODS COME BACK TO THE MOWING FIELD;	. 5 GHOST HOUSE	. 7
AND BY THE BROOK OUR WOODS WERE THERE.	. 18 GOING FOR WATER	. 8
PAN CAME OUT OF THE WOODS ONE DAY--	. 23 PAN WITH US	. 1
ALL SONG OF THE WOODS IS CRUSHED LIKE SOME	. 26 A LINE-STORM SONG	. 13
COME, BE MY LOVE IN THE WET WOODS, COME,	. 26 A LINE-STORM SONG	. 15
OUT THROUGH THE FIELDS AND THE WOODS	. 29 RELUCTANCE	. 1
NOT OF WOODS ONLY AND THE SHADE OF TREES.	. 34 MENDING WALL	. 42
OUT OF THE WOODS, WORN OUT UPON THE TRAIL."	. 38 DEATH OF THE HIRED MAN	117
COMING OUT ON THEM FROM A STRETCH OF WOODS,	. 49 A HUNDRED COLLARS	. 125
"YOU KNOW WHERE THEY CUT OFF THE WOODS--LET ME SEE--	. 59 BLUEBERRIES	. 9
MY WOODS--THE YOUNG FIR BALSAMS LIKE A PLACE	. 106 CHRISTMAS TREES	. 13
NOT MUCH OF THAT UNTIL I COME TO WOODS	. 111 IN THE HOME STRETCH	. 33
THE BACK SOME FARM PRESENTS US; AND YOUR WOODS	. 114 IN THE HOME STRETCH	. 114
YOU MAY SEE THEIR TRUNKS ARCHING IN THE WOODS.	. 121 BIRCHES	. 17
HE'S WATCHING FROM THE WOODS AS LIKE AS NOT.	. 127 THE SMILE	. 12
THE WOODS AND TOWN ON FIRE BY ME, AND ALL	. 131 THE BONFIRE	. 72
IN WOODS SOME TEN MILES FROM A RAILROAD STATION,	. 160 NEW HAMPSHIRE	. 41
ALTARS THE WOODS ARE FULL OF NOWADAYS,	. 171 NEW HAMPSHIRE	. 387
BUT THAT WAS IN THE WOODS, TO HOLD MY HAND	. 185 THE AX-HELVE	. 3
NO DOUBT IT'S GROWN UP SOME TO WOODS AROUND IT.	. 213 A FOUNTAIN, A BOTTLE	. 21
WHOSE WOODS THESE ARE I THINK I KNOW.	. 224 STOPPING BY WOODS	. 1
TO WATCH HIS WOODS FILL UP WITH SNOW.	. 224 STOPPING BY WOODS	. 4
BETWEEN THE WOODS AND FROZEN LAKE	. 224 STOPPING BY WOODS	. 7
STOPPING BY WOODS ON A SNOWY EVENING	. 224 STOPPING BY WOODS	. T
THE WOODS ARE LOVELY, DARK, AND DEEP,	. 224 STOPPING BY WOODS	. 13
AS MAY BE IN DARK WOODS, AND WITH A SONG	. 226 THE ONSET	. 3
"GOOD-NIGHT TO WOODS." BUT NOT SO; THERE WAS MORE.	. 229 TWO LOOK AT TWO	. 14
TO DARKEN NATURE AND BE SUMMER WOODS--	. 245 SPRING POOLS	. 8
AND STILL THE WOODS SWEEP LEAFILY ON,	. 247 ON GOING UNNOTICED	. 14
NOT FIREWEED LOVING WHERE WOODS HAVE BURNT--	. 248 A PASSING GLIMPSE	. 6
OUT OF THE WOODS TWO HULKING TRAMPS	. 276 TWO TRAMPS IN MUD TIME	. 49
MEN OF THE WOODS AND LUMBERJACKS,	. 276 TWO TRAMPS IN MUD TIME	. 53
THE WOODS AROUND IT HAVE IT--IT IS THEIRS.	. 296 DESERT PLACES	. 5
ALL WOODS AND PASTURE ONLY FIT FOR SHEEP.	. 316 BUILD SOIL	. 9
BENDS SQUARE IN WOODS, AN IRON SPINE	. 331 BEECH	. 2
AS I CAME TO THE EDGE OF THE WOODS,	. 334 COME IN	. 1
TOO DARK IN THE WOODS FOR A BIRD	. 334 COME IN	. 5
HAD NOW PERSISTED IN THE WOODS SO LONG	. 339 NEVER WOULD BIRDS' SONG	11
IT IS YOUR CHRISTMASES AGAINST MY WOODS.	. 350 TO A YOUNG WRETCH	. 13
BUSYING BY MY WOODS AND BROOK	. 364 TRESPASS	. 7
IT WAS BLOWN WOODS AND NO END.	. 366 NOT OF SCHOOL AGE	. 2
TO PUSH THE WOODS BACK FROM AROUND THE HOUSE	. 414 A CABIN IN THE CLEARING	3
IN WINTER IN THE WOODS ALONE	. 470 IN WINTER IN THE WOODS	1
IN WINTER IN THE WOODS...	. 470 IN WINTER IN THE WOODS	T
I SAY I'D RATHER BE LOST IN THE WOODS	. 513 A MASQUE OF MERCY	. 514

WOODS'

AS FOR THE WOODS' EXCITEMENT OVER YOU	. 378 DIRECTIVE	. 23

WOOD'S

REMEMBER BIRNAM WOOD! THE WOOD'S IN FLUX!"	. 170 NEW HAMPSHIRE	. 373

WOODSHED

THAT FLOATS AGAINST THE CEILING OF THE WOODSHED.	. 277 THE WHITE-TAILED HORNET	2

WOODSVILLE
    AND HAD FOUR HOURS TO WAIT AT WOODSVILLE JUNCTION . . .   45 A HUNDRED COLLARS . .   16
WOODSVILLE'S
    WOODSVILLE'S A PLACE OF SHRIEKS AND WANDERING LAMPS . . .   45 A HUNDRED COLLARS . .   21
WOODWARD'S
    AT WOODWARD'S GARDENS . . . . 293 AT WOODWARD'S GARDENS .   T
WOOD-WORLD'S
    IN THE WOOD-WORLD'S TORN DESPAIR . . . .   26 A LINE-STORM SONG . .   10
WOOL
    THE AIR WAS FULL OF DUST OF WOOL. . . . . 273 A LONE STRIKER   18
    BUT I DON'T CALCULATE TO SELL MY WOOL. . . . . . . 316 BUILD SOIL   14
    IS STEALTHILY CONTRIVING WOOL FROM JUTE . . . . . . 319 BUILD SOIL 108
WOOLEN
    THE SMELL OF SCORCHING WOOLEN MADE HER FAINT. . . . .   91 THE FEAR   69
WOOL'S
    I KNOW WOOL'S DOWN TO SEVEN CENTS A POUND. . . . . . 316 BUILD SOIL   13
WORD
    IT WILL BE HARD FOR THEM TO KEEP THEIR WORD. . . . .   55 THE BLACK COTTAGE . .   20
    MIND YOU, I WAITED TILL LEN SAID THE WORD. . . . . .   67 A SERVANT TO SERVANTS . 149
    AND PERHAPS HEAR SOME WORD ABOUT THE WEATHER. . . . .   74 THE GENERATIONS OF MEN   33
    HE THINKS I ONLY HAVE TO SAY THE WORD, ...   82 THE HOUSEKEEPER . . .   25
    AND SAY NO WORD TO TELL ME WHO HE WAS . . . . . . 101 THE WOOD-PILE   12
    DON'T MIND A WORD I SAY. IT'S A DAY'S WORK . . . . . 116 IN THE HOME STRETCH . 159
    BUT WHO FIRST SAID THE WORD TO COME?" / "MY DEAR, . . 116 IN THE HOME STRETCH . 171
    NEW IS A WORD FOR FOOLS IN TOWNS WHO THINK . . . . 117 IN THE HOME STRETCH . 183
    "END IS A GLOOMY WORD." / "IS IT TOO LATE . . . . 117 IN THE HOME STRETCH . 187
    I LISTENED AND I THOUGHT I CAUGHT THE WORD-- . . . 118 THE TELEPHONE   14
    HER WORD . . . . 126 LONELINESS . . . . .   S
    HER WORD . . . . 127 THE SMILE . . . . . .   S
    WANTED ME TO BRING WORD . . . . 135 LAST WORD OF A BLUEBIRD   8
    THE LAST WORD OF A BLUEBIRD . . . . 135 LAST WORD OF A BLUEBIRD   T
    TO TELL THEM "SUPPER." AT THE WORD, THE SAW, ... 136 "OUT, OUT--"   14
    HE LINGERED FOR SOME WORD SHE WOULDN'T SAY, ... 143 SNOW   28
    AS IF NOT KNOWING WHAT YOU MEANT BY THE WORD STORM." . 151 SNOW 232
    THE PAUSE RIGHT THERE, SHE THOUGHT THE DREADED WORD . 151 SNOW 238
    DID SHE LET ON BY ANY WORD SHE SAID . . . . 153 SNOW 287
    BUT IT SEEMS LIKE SOME WORD SHE LEFT TO BID YOU . . . 180 MAPLE   21
    IN WAIT FOR HER THERE. SHE READ EVERY WORD . . . . 181 MAPLE   64
    SHORT OF A FIGHTING WORD. YOU HAVE THE ANSWERS. . . . 192 PAUL'S WIFE   34
    IN THAT GRAVE WORD . . . . 219 I WILL SING YOU ONE-O .   60
    BY MEASURE. IT WAS WORD AND NOTE, ... 224 THE AIM WAS SONG . .   13
    WORD I WAS IN THE HOUSE ALONE . . . . 251 BEREFT   13
    WORD I WAS IN MY LIFE ALONE, ... 251 BEREFT   15
    WORD I HAD NO ONE LEFT BUT GOD. . . . . 251 BEREFT   16
    THEN WORD GOES FORTH IN FORMIC: . . . . 288 DEPARTMENTAL   22
    THIS IS THE WORD OF YOUR QUEEN." . . . . 288 DEPARTMENTAL   32
    BUT EVEN AT THE WORD . . . . 298 ON TAKING FROM THE TOP   9
    IN YOUR SENSE OF THE WORD AMBITION HAS . . . . . . 319 BUILD SOIL   98
    THOUGH WITH EVERY WORD HE SPOKE . . . . 340 THE SUBVERTED FLOWER .   26
    I GRANT YOU--IF YOU'RE SURE ABOUT THE WORD. . . . . 394 LUCRETIUS VERSUS POETS   11
    ACTION IS THE WORD. . . . . 442 KITTY HAWK 450
    "ANOTHER WORD THAT BOTHERS ME IS FREEDOM. . . . . . 459 HOW HARD TO KEEP FROM 163
    THE WORD I WANTED. YOU WOULD HAVE SUPPOSED . . . . 475 A MASQUE OF REASON .   55
    ONE WHO IN THE BEGINNING WAS THE WORD . . . . . . 475 A MASQUE OF REASON .   56
    I'VE HEARD WHAT YOU WERE SAYING--EVERY WORD. . . . . 487 A MASQUE OF REASON . 396
    YET COULD NOT BRING MYSELF TO SAY A WORD. . . . . . 497 A MASQUE OF MERCY .   99
    OF THE WORD LOVE CORRECTED. SHE GOT OFF . °. . . . 499 A MASQUE OF MERCY . 161
    SUFFER A FRIEND TO TRY TO WORD YOU BETTER. . . . . . 519 A MASQUE OF MERCY . 677
WORDS
    IS SADDER THAN ANY WORDS. . . . .   8 A LATE WALK   8
    BEHIND LIGHT WORDS THAT TEASE AND FLOUT, ...   19 REVELATION   2
    "MY WORDS ARE NEARLY ALWAYS AN OFFENSE. . . . . . .   52 HOME BURIAL   45
    "I CAN REPEAT THE VERY WORDS YOU WERE SAYING: . . . .   54 HOME BURIAL   91
    IT WAS THE WORDS 'DESCENDED INTO HADES' . . . . . .   58 THE BLACK COTTAGE . .   94
    HE'D SAY, WHY SHOULD THEY?--NO MORE WORDS THAN THAT." .   84 THE HOUSEKEEPER . . .   91
    THE QUESTION THAT HE FRAMES IN ALL BUT WORDS . . . . 120 THE OVEN BIRD . . .   13
    WHEREIN WORDS WHETHER BEATEN OUT OR SPOKEN . . . . 141 THE LINE-GANG . . .   6
    'HEY, THAT'S A PRETTY THOUGHT'--THOSE WERE HIS WORDS-- 149 SNOW 181
    THOSE WERE HIS WORDS, AND HE WENT HOME AND ALL . . . 149 SNOW 185
    OF WORDS, OR IS IT TONGUES I OUGHT TO SAY?" . . . . 151 SNOW 249
    IN OTHER WORDS, I KNOW WHEREVER I AM, ... 166 NEW HAMPSHIRE . . . 239
    ACROSS THE ROAR AND CHAOS, AND THE WORDS . . . . . 170 NEW HAMPSHIRE . . . 350
    WERE DOUBTLESS AS THE WORDS WE HEARD HIM SAY . . . . 170 NEW HAMPSHIRE . . . 352
    ON WORDS, AND TRIES HIS WORST TO MAKE WORDS SPEAK . . 171 NEW HAMPSHIRE . . . 401
    DANGEROUS SELF-AROUSING WORDS TO SOW. . . . . . . 180 MAPLE   29
    SHE ALMOST WROTE THE WORDS DOWN ON HER KNEE, ... 182 MAPLE   86
    AND SEE YOU PLEASED ONCE MORE WITH WORDS OF MINE? . . 222 TO E.T.   20
    AND WORDS TO WONDER IN HER HEARING HOW SHE CAME THERE, 257 THE LOVELY BE CHOOSERS 48
    WORDS ARE NO GOOD: TO SAY IT WAS A LENS . . . . . . 293 AT WOODWARD'S GARDENS .   5
    OF WORDS OR TOYS, IT MINISTERS TO HEALTH. . . . . . 321 BUILD SOIL 170
    HER TONE OF MEANING BUT WITHOUT THE WORDS. . . . . . 338 NEVER WOULD BIRDS' SONG   5
    THE BITTER WORDS SHE SPIT . . . . 341 THE SUBVERTED FLOWER .   66
    BEYOND WORDS . . . . 393 BEYOND WORDS . . . .   T
    THESE I ASSUME WERE WORDS SO DEEPLY MEANT . . . . . 399 THE INGENUITIES OF DEBT   1
    IN A FLIGHT OF WORDS, ... 434 KITTY HAWK 187
    THE AUTHOR OF THESE WORDS, ... 465 MILKY WAY IS A COWPATH   41
    I HAVE TO WAIT FOR WORDS LIKE ANYONE. . . . . . . 475 A MASQUE OF REASON .   58
    AS WELL AS WORDS. / I'M SERIOUS. GOD'S HAD . . . . 478 A MASQUE OF REASON . 148
    LOOK, WILL YOU LOOK! GOD CAN'T PUT WORDS IN MY MOUTH. 505 A MASQUE OF MERCY . 295
    IT'S NOTHING I BROUGHT ON BY WORDS OF MINE. . . . . 507 A MASQUE OF MERCY . 355
WORE
    I CAN REMEMBER WHEN I WORE FOURTEEN. . . . .   47 A HUNDRED COLLARS . .   64
    SOMEHOW THE CHANGE WORE OUT LIKE A PRESCRIPTION. . . .   67 A SERVANT TO SERVANTS . 154
    THE LAWYER WORE A WATCH THE CASE OF WHICH . . . . .   98 THE SELF-SEEKER . . 163
    SHE WORE HER CAPE; HER HAT WAS IN HER HAND. . . . . 110 IN THE HOME STRETCH .   4
    MESERVE, BELITTLED IN THE GREAT SKIN COAT HE WORE. . . 143 SNOW   5
    THINGS THEY THINK SHE WORE . . . . 433 KITTY HAWK 154

		PAGE	TITLE	LINE

WORK

"WHETHER THEY WORK TOGETHER OR APART."	. . . . . .	22	THE TUFT OF FLOWERS	10
"MEN WORK TOGETHER," I TOLD HIM FROM THE HEART,	. . . .	23	THE TUFT OF FLOWERS	39
"WHETHER THEY WORK TOGETHER OR APART."	. . . .	23	THE TUFT OF FLOWERS	40
THE WORK OF HUNTERS IS ANOTHER THING:	. . . .	33	MENDING WALL	5
HE SAYS THEY TWO WILL MAKE A TEAM FOR WORK:	. . . .	36	DEATH OF THE HIRED MAN	62
"YOU DRIVE AROUND? IT MUST BE PLEASANT WORK."	. . .	49	A HUNDRED COLLARS	122
BUT WORK AIN'T ALL. LEN UNDERTAKES TOO MUCH.	. . .	64	A SERVANT TO SERVANTS	70
BLESS YOU, OF COURSE YOU'RE KEEPING ME FROM WORK,	. . .	67	A SERVANT TO SERVANTS	171
THERE'S WORK ENOUGH TO DO--THERE'S ALWAYS THAT;	. . .	68	A SERVANT TO SERVANTS	173
HE THOUGHT YOU MEANT TO FIND FAULT WITH HIS WORK.	. . .	70	THE CODE	16
TO DO WORK BETTER OR FASTER--THOSE TWO THINGS.	. . .	70	THE CODE	23
BUT WORK! THAT MAN COULD WORK, ESPECIALLY	. . . .	70	THE CODE	36
IF BY SO DOING HE COULD GET MORE WORK	. . . . .	70	THE CODE	37
HALF OF THE OUTDOOR WORK, THOUGH AS FOR THAT,	. . .	85	THE HOUSEKEEPER	108
THE CITY WORK TO DO. THERE'S NOT ENOUGH	. . . .	114	IN THE HOME STRETCH	97
DON'T MIND A WORD I SAY. IT'S A DAY'S WORK	. . . .	116	IN THE HOME STRETCH	159
YOU COME TO FETCH ME FROM MY WORK TONIGHT	. . . .	123	PUTTING IN THE SEED	1
AND WORK WAS LITTLE IN THE HOUSE,	. . . . . .	128	THE IMPULSE	5
SO SHE HAD TO WORK IT ALL BY HAND,	. . . . .	133	A GIRL'S GARDEN	19
THAT A BOY COUNTS SO MUCH WHEN SAVED FROM WORK.	. . .	136	"OUT, OUT--"	12
DOING A MAN'S WORK, THOUGH A CHILD AT HEART--	. . .	137	"OUT, OUT--"	24
THEIR NUMBER'S--TWENTY-ONE?--THE THING WON'T WORK.	. . .	153	SNOW	294
A THING TO SELL." I DON'T SUPPOSE THE WORK	. . . .	159	NEW HAMPSHIRE	4
MUCH MATTERS. YOU MAY WORK FOR ALL OF ME.	. . .	159	NEW HAMPSHIRE	5
I'VE SEEN THE TIME I'VE HAD TO WORK MYSELF.	. . .	159	NEW HAMPSHIRE	6
FOR THE HARD WORK. HE CHAFED ITS LONG WHITE BODY	. .	187	THE AX-HELVE	76
SO AFTER WORK THAT EVENING HE CAME BACK	. . . .	194	PAUL'S WIFE	88
THIS NEW-BUILT CITY FROM BOTH WORK AND SLEEP.	. . .	231	A BROOK IN THE CITY	24
WITH WHAT WAS ANOTHER MAN'S WORK FOR GAIN.	. . .	277	TWO TRAMPS IN MUD TIME	61
AND THE WORK IS PLAY FOR MORTAL STAKES,	. . . .	277	TWO TRAMPS IN MUD TIME	70
AND THIS DAY'S WORK MADE EVEN THAT SEEM DOUBTFUL.	. .	279	THE WHITE-TAILED HORNET	70
WHOSE WORK IS TO FIND OUT GOD	. . . . .	288	DEPARTMENTAL	10
MEN WORK ALONE, THEIR LOTS PLOWED FAR APART,	. . .	299	STRONG SAYING NOTHING .	6
WHAT WORKED FOR THEM MIGHT WORK FOR YOU.	. . . .	307	PROVIDE, PROVIDE	15
HIS STINGING QUARTERS MENACINGLY WORK.	. . . .	309	WASPISH	4
BUT HAVE SOME PITY ON US WHO HAVE TO WORK.	. . .	316	BUILD SOIL	21
THE CHISEL WORK OF AN ENORMOUS GLACIER	. . . .	377	DIRECTIVE	16
SOMEONE'S ROAD HOME FROM WORK THIS ONCE WAS,	. . .	378	DIRECTIVE	30
THEN FROM THE WORK YOU WENT ABOUT	. . . . .	381	AN UNSTAMPED LETTER IN	48
"IT'S WHETHER THESE PROFESSIONS REALLY WORK.	. . .	404	FROM PLANE TO PLANE	11
"HOEING'S TOO MUCH LIKE WORK FOR DICK," HE ADDED.	. .	404	FROM PLANE TO PLANE	27
THAT CLASS OF PEOPLE DON'T KNOW WHAT WORK IS--	. .	405	FROM PLANE TO PLANE	33
YOU SAID YOURSELF YOU WEREN'T AVOIDING WORK.	. . .	405	FROM PLANE TO PLANE	45
YOU'D BET YOU GOT MORE WORK DONE IN A DAY,	. . .	405	FROM PLANE TO PLANE	46
THE RIVER BANK, QUIT WORK DEFIANTLY,	. . . .	405	FROM PLANE TO PLANE	58
THE FURTHER UP THE SCALE OF WORK YOU GO.	. . . .	406	FROM PLANE TO PLANE	83
DICK SAID, "YOU'VE BEEN A LESSON IN WORK WISDOM	. .	408	FROM PLANE TO PLANE	122
TO WORK WITH, BILL. BUT YOU WON'T HAVE MY THANKS.	. .	408	FROM PLANE TO PLANE	123
I CRY, "DO WORK FOR WOMEN--ALL THE HELP	. . . .	447	DOES NO ONE AT ALL EVER	28
AND THE GREAT KING INQUIRE WHOSE WORK IT WAS.	. . .	455	HOW HARD TO KEEP FROM	59

WORKED

SO THAT HENCEFORTH I WORKED NO MORE ALONE;	. . . .	23	THE TUFT OF FLOWERS	34
BUT GLAD WITH HIM, I WORKED AS WITH HIS AID,	. . .	23	THE TUFT OF FLOWERS	35
YOU'VE WORKED AROUND THE FOOT OF ALL YOUR LIFE.	. . .	43	THE MOUNTAIN	83
"NONE OF MY FAMILY EVER WORKED, OR HAD	. . . .	159	NEW HAMPSHIRE	3
WITH A MINE ON IT THAT WAS WORKED FOR GOLD;	. . .	162	NEW HAMPSHIRE	111
PAUL WORKED AT ANYTHING IN LUMBERING.	. . . .	193	PAUL'S WIFE	57
BUT LET HIM SHOW THEM HOW THE WEAPON WORKED.	. . .	293	AT WOODWARD'S GARDENS	7
WHAT WORKED FOR THEM MIGHT WORK FOR YOU.	. . . .	307	PROVIDE, PROVIDE	15
AN ARM WORKED LIKE A SAW	. . . . .	340	THE SUBVERTED FLOWER	43
COLUMBUS MAY HAVE WORKED THE WIND	. . . . .	416	AMERICA IS HARD TO SEE	1
WORKED UP ABOUT IT. BUT SHE REALLY HASN'T--	. . .	476	A MASQUE OF REASON	94
IS WORKED BY HANDS INVISIBLE, OFFSTAGE.)	. . . .	489	A MASQUE OF REASON	455

WORKERS'

THE SUBJECT OF THE WORKERS' REVOLUTION	. . . . .	508	A MASQUE OF MERCY	398

WORKING

HIS WORKING DAYS ARE DONE; I'M SURE OF IT."	. . .	39	DEATH OF THE HIRED MAN	153
RAKING THE DOORYARD, WORKING NEAR THE HOUSE.	. . .	49	A HUNDRED COLLARS	128
BY THE SAME HAND WORKING IN THE SAME STUFF?	. . .	57	THE BLACK COTTAGE	78
WHERE I WAS WORKING AT THE CHOPPING BLOCK,	. . .	185	THE AX-HELVE	8
OF WORKING OUT THE REST, THE OTHER HALF.	. . . .	324	BUILD SOIL	272
FOR MY MIND TO KEEP WORKING IN YOUR PRESENCE.	. . .	325	BUILD SOIL	285
LIKE WORKING MYSELF UP TO PROPHESY	. . . . .	501	A MASQUE OF MERCY	198
YOU'RE WORKING IT, OLD MAN. DON'T BE DISCOURAGED.	. .	507	A MASQUE OF MERCY	347

WORKMEN

THE WORKMEN ALL TURNED TO AND BURIED HIM.	. . . .	394	HAEC FABULA DOCET	16

WORKS

WHEN THE WIND WORKS AGAINST US IN THE DARK,	. . .	9	STORM FEAR	1
BUT HE WORKS WHEN HE WORKS AS HARD AS I DO--	. . .	64	A SERVANT TO SERVANTS	67
WORKS IN THE DARK AS MUCH AGAINST AS FOR US.	. . .	319	BUILD SOIL	106
AND HIS HOUND WORKS	. . . . .	360	THE RABBIT-HUNTER	7
TO ALL THE MODERN WORKS OF MAN	. . . . .	418	AMERICA IS HARD TO SEE	59

WORK'S

HIS WORK'S A MAN'S, OF COURSE, FROM SUN TO SUN,	. . .	64	A SERVANT TO SERVANTS	66

WORLD (SEE NEW-WORLD)

AND THE WORLD HAD FOUND NEW TERMS OF WORTH.	. . .	24	PAN WITH US	27
HOWEVER IT IS IN SOME OTHER WORLD	. . . .	26	IN HARDWOOD GROVES	11
AND LOOKED AT THE WORLD, AND DESCENDED:	. . . .	30	RELUCTANCE	4
SOME GOOD PERHAPS TO SOMEONE IN THE WORLD.	. . .	37	DEATH OF THE HIRED MAN	97
"THERE OUGHT TO BE A VIEW AROUND THE WORLD	. . .	42	THE MOUNTAIN	55
HEARING THE LATTER WISDOM OF THE WORLD.	. . . .	57	THE BLACK COTTAGE	74
I SHOULDN'T BE SURPRISED IF IN THIS WORLD	. . .	57	THE BLACK COTTAGE	82
I SHAN'T CATCH UP IN THIS WORLD, ANYWAY.	. . . .	68	A SERVANT TO SERVANTS	176
AND HELD AGAINST THE WORLD OF HOARY GRASS.	. . .	68	AFTER APPLE-PICKING	12
THAT TURNED THEM ON THE WORLD, AND TRY TO FATHOM	. .	73	THE GENERATIONS OF MEN	17
AND TOO MUCH WORLD AT ONCE--COULD MEANS BE FOUND.	. .	109	THE EXPOSED NEST	19
THAT CASED THE WORLD, AND HE WAS GONE!	. . . .	137	BROWN'S DESCENT	12

WORLD (CONTINUED)
    VISIONS OF HALF THE WORLD BURNED BLACK . . . . . . 140 THE GUM-GATHERER . . 23
    ONE REAL REFORMER WHO WOULD CHANGE THE WORLD . . . . 162 NEW HAMPSHIRE . . . 94
    IT MADE THE WORLD SEEM SO MYSTERIOUS. . . . . . . 163 NEW HAMPSHIRE . . . 134
    OF SEVERAL BOOKS AGAINST THE WORLD IN GENERAL. . . . 166 NEW HAMPSHIRE . . . 229
    ABOUT IMPROVING PEOPLE IN THE WORLD, ... 169 NEW HAMPSHIRE . . . 336
    OF THE ONE WORLD COMPLETE IN ANY SIZE. . . . . . 174 A STAR IN A STONEBOAT . 56
    THAT HAD AS MANY MOTIONS AS THE WORLD: . . . . . 186 THE AX-HELVE . . . 47
    IN ANY WAY THE WORLD KNEW HOW TO SPEAK. . . . . . 196 PAUL'S WIFE . . . 157
    AND THE WORLD CAME REVOLVING BACK TO ME, ... 198 WILD GRAPES . . . 86
    WHO WAS SHE TO JUDGE MARRIAGE IN A WORLD . . . . . 201 PLACE FOR A THIRD . 64
    WE MADE A DAY OF IT OUT OF THE WORLD, ... 214 A FOUNTAIN, A BOTTLE . 33
    SOME SAY THE WORLD WILL END IN FIRE, ... 220 FIRE AND ICE . . 1
    WE STOOD A MOMENT SO, IN A STRANGE WORLD, ... 233 A BOUNDLESS MOMENT . 9
    TO HIDE IN THE WORLD . . . . 241 THE LOCKLESS DOOR . 19
    THE WORLD WAS A BLACK INVISIBLE FIELD. . . . . . 253 THE THATCH . . 10
    "SEVEN LEVELS OF THE WORLD." . . . . 256 THE LOVELY BE CHOOSERS . 3
    IF WE WHO SIGHT ALONG IT ROUND THE WORLD, ... 261 A SOLDIER . . . 4
    THE WORLD HAS ROOM TO MAKE A BEAR FEEL FREE; . . . 269 THE BEAR . . . 11
    THAT HE AND THE WORLD ARE FRIENDS. . . . . . . 282 A DRUMLIN WOODCHUCK . 12
    THAT WHEN LET LOOSE UPON THE GRAZING WORLD . . . . 319 BUILD SOIL . . . 109
    RESTS ON THE WORLD, AND CLINGING SLOWLY ROLLS. . . . 322 BUILD SOIL . . . 196
    THOUGH BY A WORLD OF DOUBT SURROUNDED. . . . . . 331 BEECH 12
    O STORMY, STORMY WORLD, ... 333 HAPPINESS MAKES UP . 1
    AND SO BEGAN THE MODERN WORLD FOR US. . . . . . 351 THE LESSON FOR TODAY . 18
    I HAD A LOVER'S QUARREL WITH THE WORLD. . . . . . 355 THE LESSON FOR TODAY . 161
    WITH WHICH THE MODERN WORLD IS BEING SWEPT. . . . . 357 A CONSIDERABLE SPECK . 26
    TO START THE WORLD OF OLD . . . . 361 ALMOST TWO THOUSAND . 1
    THE CONDEMNED WORLD THE LEGACY WAS MERITED. . . . . 370 THE LITERATE FARMER AND 56
    PUT UP TO CURE THE WORLD BY MR. EDISON." . . . . 371 THE LITERATE FARMER AND 93
    "MARVELOUS WORLD IN NINETEEN—TWENTY—SIX." . . . . 372 THE LITERATE FARMER AND 141
    A WORLD TORN LOOSE WENT BY ME. . . . . 377 ONE STEP BACKWARD TAKEN 12
    THAT SOMEONE HAS SAID IS THE END OF THE WORLD. . . . 379 TOO ANXIOUS FOR RIVERS . 2
    THE WORLD AS WE KNOW IS AN ELEPHANT'S HOWDAH; . . . 379 TOO ANXIOUS FOR RIVERS . 14
    I HEAR THE WORLD RECITING . . . . 387 THE COURAGE TO BE NEW . 1
    THE WORLD DESERT, ... 412 AWAY! 2
    WILL OF ITSELF TAKE FIRE AND LIGHT THE WORLD UP. . . 414 A CABIN IN THE CLEARING 27
    EITHER FOR THEM OR THE ONLOOKING WORLD. . . . . . 415 A CABIN IN THE CLEARING 32
    AND ALSO PROVED THE WORLD A BALL, ... 416 AMERICA IS HARD TO SEE . 3
    LIKE SWEARING OFF ON THE TRAFFIC WORLD. . . . . . 419 ONE MORE BREVITY . . 18
    THE NEW WORLD CHRISTOPHER COLUMBUS FOUND. . . . . 422 FOR JOHN F. KENNEDY . 15
    WE KNOW OF NO WORLD . . . . 440 KITTY HAWK . . . 395
    THAT SHOULD HAVE MADE THE NEW WORLD NEWLY GREAT . . 446 DOES NO ONE AT ALL EVER 3
    HALFWAY ROUND THE WORLD. . . . . 448 THE BAD ISLAND—EASTER 12
    THIS WORLD WERE GOOD ENOUGH FOR ME." . . . . . . 451 A-WISHING WELL . . 5
    (I DON'T CARE HOW THE WORLD GETS BY.) . . . . . 451 A-WISHING WELL . . 14
    TO START THE WORLD ALL OVER AT. . . . . 453 A-WISHING WELL . . 81
    AND THAT IS HALF THE TROUBLE WITH THE WORLD. . . . 462 HOW HARD TO KEEP FROM 277
    EVER SINCE ALEXANDER GREECED THE WORLD. . . . . . 511 A MASQUE OF MERCY . 473
    TOWARD WHAT YOU MAKE ME SEE BEYOND THE WORLD. . . . 514 A MASQUE OF MERCY . 545
    TO BASE HIS CAMPAIGN ON TO SAVE THE WORLD. . . . . 514 A MASQUE OF MERCY . 561
    I'D LIKE TO SEE THE WORLD TRIED ONCE WITHOUT IT. . . 515 A MASQUE OF MERCY . 575
    THE WORLD SEEMS CRYING OUT FOR A MESSIAH. . . . . 515 A MASQUE OF MERCY . 576
WORLD-FLOWERS
    AND BED OF WORLD-FLOWERS SO AS NOT TO BLIND ME. . . . 515 A MASQUE OF MERCY . 582
WORLDLY
    TO SHOW ITS WORLDLY NATURE AND BEGIN . . . . . . 174 A STAR IN A STONEBOAT . 51
WORLD-OLD
    'TIS THE WORLD-OLD WAY OF THE RAIN . . . . . . 285 IN TIME OF CLOUDBURST . 5
WORLD'S (SEE WOOD-WORLD'S)
    BUT THE WORLD'S EVIL. I WON'T HAVE GRIEF SO . . . . 54 HOME BURIAL . . . 106
    I MEAN BY THE WORLD'S HAVING PASSED IT BY-- . . . 56 THE BLACK COTTAGE . 43
    FROM THE WORLD'S VIEW TODAY OF ALL THOSE THINGS. . . 57 THE BLACK COTTAGE . 63
    WITH STRAINING IN THE WORLD'S EMBRACE. . . . . . 120 BOND AND FREE . . 8
    ABOUT THE WORLD'S DESPAIR; . . . . 309 NOT ALL THERE . . 2
    THE WORLD'S ONE GLOBE, HUMAN SOCIETY . . . . . . 322 BUILD SOIL . . . 194
    THE WORLD'S SIZE HAS NO MORE TO DO WITH US . . . . 322 BUILD SOIL . . . 198
    TO THE WORLD'S UNDEBATABLY DARK AGES, ... 350 THE LESSON FOR TODAY . 7
    AS GRAVE AS HE ABOUT THE WORLD'S DEFEAT. . . . . 359 THE LOST FOLLOWER . 24
    AND WHEN IT'S OVER WATCH THE WORLD'S SUPPLY . . . . 398 NO HOLY WARS FOR THEM . 7
    OR METAPHYSICS, LONG THE WORLD'S REPROACH . . . . 480 A MASQUE OF REASON . 191
    LET ME ALONE. / I'M SICK. JOE'S SICK. THE WORLD'S SICK. . 500 A MASQUE OF MERCY . 167
WORM-EATEN
    THE WINDFALLS SPIKED WITH STUBBLE AND WORM-EATEN. . . 125 THE COW IN APPLE TIME . 8
WORMS
    YOU WERE BELITTLED INTO VILEST WORMS . . . . . . 352 THE LESSON FOR TODAY . 74
WORN (SEE STRUGGLE-WORN)
    AND ON THE WORN BOOK OF OLD-GOLDEN SONG . . . . . 15 WAITING . . . 23
    "HE'S WORN OUT. HE'S ASLEEP BESIDE THE STOVE. . . . 35 DEATH OF THE HIRED MAN 33
    OUT OF THE WOODS, WORN OUT UPON THE TRAIL." . . . 38 DEATH OF THE HIRED MAN 117
    HIS HANDS HAD WORN THEM SMOOTH AS ANY OXBOW. . . . 66 A SERVANT TO SERVANTS . 136
    HAD WORN THEM REALLY ABOUT THE SAME, ... 105 THE ROAD NOT TAKEN . 10
    AND EVERY LEAF OF FOLIAGE SHE'D WORN . . . . . . 184 MAPLE 146
    HAD GRADUALLY WORN IT AN OBLATE . . . . 190 THE GRINDSTONE . . 39
    UNTIL I'D HAD HIM WORN TO SKIN AND BONES, ... 208 PAUPER WITCH OF GRAFTON 48
    SOME WORN OLD TOOL OF MY OWN . . . . 285 IN TIME OF CLOUDBURST . 21
WORN-OUT
    INFIRM, WORN-OUT, AND BROKEN ON ITS HANDS; . . . . 399 THE INGENUITIES OF DEBT 9
WORRY
    "SHE'S LET IT WORRY HER. YOU STOOD THE STRAIN, . . . 87 THE HOUSEKEEPER . . 171
    OR QUALITY TO WORRY THE PRODUCER . . . . 164 NEW HAMPSHIRE . . 168
    THE ONLY THING I WORRY ABOUT IS THE SUN. . . . . 392 IT BIDS PRETTY FAIR . 3
WORSE
    WORSE THAN NO GOOD TO THEM, AND THEY NO GOOD . . . 65 A SERVANT TO SERVANTS . 100
    "AND LIKE IT, TOO. IT MAKES IT ALL THE WORSE." . . . 86 THE HOUSEKEEPER . . 155
    "IT MAKES IT ALL THE WORSE. YOU MUST BE BLIND." . . 87 THE HOUSEKEEPER . . 163
    SHE WON'T COME BACK--IT'S WORSE THAN THAT--SHE CAN'T." . 87 THE HOUSEKEEPER . . 177
    "I'M GOING TO BE WORSE INSTEAD OF BETTER. . . . . 94 THE SELF-SEEKER . . 56

PAGE TITLE   LINE

WORSE (CONTINUED)
    EVEN WORSE STILL, AND SO ON DOWN, DOWN, DOWN. . . . . . . 115 IN THE HOME STRETCH . 129
    ONE COULD DO WORSE THAN BE A SWINGER OF BIRCHES. . . . . . 122 BIRCHES 59
    IT NOT A MITE WORSE, SITTING HERE, WE THREE, ... 149 SNOW 189
    AND MAKE THE MOST OF IT FOR BETTER OR WORSE. . . . . . . 161 NEW HAMPSHIRE . . . 65
    FOR ART'S SAKE ONE COULD ALMOST WISH THEM WORSE . . . . . 167 NEW HAMPSHIRE . . . 266
    ON NOTHING WORSE THAN TOO MUCH LUCK AND COMFORT. . . . . 167 NEW HAMPSHIRE . . . 276
    MIGHTN'T WE MAKE IT WORSE INSTEAD OF BETTER? . . . . . . 191 THE GRINDSTONE . . . 74
    TO GO WEST TO A WORSE FIGHT WITH THE DESERT. . . . . . . 213 A FOUNTAIN, A BOTTLE . 12
    NO ORCHARD'S THE WORSE FOR THE WINTRIEST STORM; . . . . . 228 GOOD-BY AND KEEP COLD . 15
    BUT TO MAKE BAD MATTERS WORSE . . . . 309 NOT ALL THERE . . . 3
    IT'S HARD TO TELL WHICH IS THE WORSE ABHORRENCE, ... 321 BUILD SOIL 155
    IN PUBLICLY DISPUTING WHICH IS WORSE, ... 352 THE LESSON FOR TODAY . 48
    I COULD BE WORSE EMPLOYED . . . . 383 MAKING CERTAIN ANYTHING 1
    YOU COULD DO WORSE THAN BOOST ME UP TO SEE." . . . . . 406 FROM PLANE TO PLANE . 84
    THAN WHICH THERE IS NO INDIGNITY WORSE. . . . . . . 463 LINES IN DEJECTION . 13
    I WAS NO WORSE OFF THAN I WAS AT FIRST. . . . . . . 468 IN A GLASS OF CIDER . 6
    I TOLD HIM NOT TO SCRATCH: IT MADE IT WORSE. . . . . . 478 A MASQUE OF REASON . 128
WORSHIP
    AS THE SUN'S RIGHT WORSHIP IS, ... 13 ROSE POGONIAS . . . 10
    BY WORSHIP UNDER GREEN TREES IN THE OPEN. . . . . . . 171 NEW HAMPSHIRE . . . 389
    OUR WORSHIP, HUMOR, CONSCIENTIOUSNESS . . . . 279 THE WHITE-TAILED HORNET 56
    AND WORSHIP APPLES. WHAT ELSE COULD IT MEAN? . . . . . 284 THE GOLD HESPERIDEE . 54
    THAT MADE OUR HOUSE OF LIFE A HOUSE OF WORSHIP? . . . . 386 A STEEPLE ON THE HOUSE 3
    OUR WORSHIP WAS A THING HE HAD TOO MUCH OF . . . . . 408 FROM PLANE TO PLANE . 132
    UNLESS I LIKED TO SUFFER LOSS OF WORSHIP. . . . . . . 476 A MASQUE OF REASON . 75
WORSHIPED
    AND AVOID BEING WORSHIPED AS A GOD. . . . . 408 FROM PLANE TO PLANE . 131
WORST
    "I SHALL LAUGH THE WORST LAUGH I EVER LAUGHED. . . . . . 54 HOME BURIAL 89
    BUT BEHIND'S BEHIND. THE WORST THAT YOU CAN DO . . . . . 68 A SERVANT TO SERVANTS . 174
    SUCH AS IT'S GOING TO BE, AND KNOW THE WORST, ... 95 THE SELF-SEEKER . . 77
    ON WORDS, AND TRIES HIS WORST TO MAKE WORDS SPEAK . . . . 171 NEW HAMPSHIRE . . . 401
    THE WORST IT CAN DO TO ME . . . . 285 IN TIME OF CLOUDBURST . 2
    "THE BEST WAY TO HATE IS THE WORST. . . . . 312 THE VINDICTIVES . . 81
    LET NEWSPAPERS PROFESS TO FEAR THE WORST! . . . . . . 318 BUILD SOIL 65
    BUT THE WORST ONE OF ALL TO LEAVE UNCURBED, ... 319 BUILD SOIL 101
    SHE LOOKED AND SAW THE WORST. . . . . 341 THE SUBVERTED FLOWER . 57
    BUT WHEN THE OCEAN'S WORST HAD PASSED . . . . . . 344 DISCOVERY OF MADEIRAS . 35
    UP CHIMNEY TO AVOID THE WORST OF IT. . . . . . . 408 FROM PLANE TO PLANE . 142
    NEVER BELIEVE IT. AT THE VERY WORST . . . . 425 ACCIDENTALLY ON PURPOSE 13
    OF ALL CRIMES THE WORST . . . . 430 KITTY HAWK 73
    THAT WE FEAR THE WORST. . . . . 445 PERIL OF HOPE . . . 8
    AND NOT OUR WORST NOR SECOND BEST, OUR BEST, ... 520 A MASQUE OF MERCY . 719
WORSTED
    SHE'S GLAD HER SIMPLE WORSTED GRAY . . . . 7 MY NOVEMBER GUEST . . 9
WORTH
    OF THEIR WORTH FOR YOU TO TREASURE, ... 13 FLOWER-GATHERING . . 14
    AND THE WORLD HAD FOUND NEW TERMS OF WORTH. . . . . . 24 PAN WITH US 27
    THAT OUGHT TO BE WORTH SEEING." / "IF IT'S THERE. . . . . 42 THE MOUNTAIN . . . 65
    NO ONE WOULD COVET IT OR THINK IT WORTH . . . . . . 58 THE BLACK COTTAGE . 117
    THAT OUGHT TO BE WORTH SOMETHING, AND MAY YET. . . . . 64 A SERVANT TO SERVANTS . 43
    AS OF NO WORTH. . . . . 69 AFTER APPLE-PICKING . 36
    SUCH AS IT IS. IT ISN'T WORTH THE MORTGAGE." . . . . 84 THE HOUSEKEEPER . . 97
    HE NEVER TAKES THE MONEY. IF THEY'RE WORTH . . . . . 86 THE HOUSEKEEPER . . 140
    THAT MUCH TO SELL, THEY'RE WORTH AS MUCH TO KEEP. . . . 86 THE HOUSEKEEPER . . 141
    THAT WAS WORTH MONEY TO ME? STILL I OWN . . . . . 95 THE SELF-SEEKER . . 82
    I SAID, "THERE AREN'T ENOUGH TO BE WORTH WHILE." . . . 106 CHRISTMAS TREES . . 29
    WORTH THREE CENTS MORE TO GIVE AWAY THAN SELL, ... 107 CHRISTMAS TREES . . 56
    WAS COGNIZANT. HER HUSBAND WAS WORTH MILLIONS. . . . . 163 NEW HAMPSHIRE . . . 136
    SO NOT TO BE COMPARED, PERHAPS, IN WORTH . . . . . 174 A STAR IN A STONEBOAT . 47
    AND THEN HE HAD A THOUGHT WORTH MANY OF THESE. . . . . 200 PLACE FOR A THIRD . 32
    AS HARDLY WORTH RENEWAL. . . . . 252 THE PEACEFUL SHEPHERD . 8
    TO MAKE IT WORTH LIFE'S WHILE TO WAKE AND SPORT. . . . 254 A WINTER EDEN . . . 20
    NEVER MIND OF WHAT ACTUAL WORTH, ... 312 THE VINDICTIVES . . 83
    TO ASK ME IF I THINK IT WORTH THE PAINS . . . . . 324 BUILD SOIL . . . 271
    IT WAS WELL WORTH PRELIMINARY MENTION. . . . . . 352 THE LESSON FOR TODAY . 59
    IT WAS WELL WORTH PRELIMINARY MENTION. . . . . . 352 THE LESSON FOR TODAY . 63
    AND FOR ALL IT'S WORTH . . . . 436 KITTY HAWK . . . 247
    AND TRIED TO LOOK TEN THOUSAND DOLLARS' WORTH. . . . . 454 HOW HARD TO KEEP FROM 38
    AND THE SLAVE SAID, "THE SMALL ONE'S WORTH THE PRICE, . . 456 HOW HARD TO KEEP FROM 81
    YOU FAILED TO SEE THE WORTH OF YOUR ACHIEVEMENT. . . . 480 A MASQUE OF REASON . 187
    WORTH GOING AFTER. GET DOWN INTO THINGS, ... 483 A MASQUE OF REASON . 281
    WORTH PRAYING. MAY MY SACRIFICE . . . . 520 A MASQUE OF MERCY . 724
WORTHLESS
    AS ANYBODY. WORTHLESS THOUGH HE IS, ... 39 DEATH OF THE HIRED MAN 144
    BUT THE BIG ONE IS WORTHLESS. BREAK IT OPEN. . . . . 456 HOW HARD TO KEEP FROM 82
WORTHY
    SEE NOTHING WORTHY TO HAVE BEEN ITS MARK, ... 261 A SOLDIER 5
WOULD---NOT INDEXED
WOULDN'T---NOT INDEXED
WOUND
    HAD WOUND STRINGS ROUND AND ROUND IT LIKE A BUNDLE. . . . 102 THE WOOD-PILE . . . 31
    AND HALF THE BAG WOUND ROUND HIS HAND. . . . . . . 140 THE GUM-GATHERER . . 6
    AND STILL IT'S BAD ENOUGH TO BADLY WOUND, ... 372 THE LITERATE FARMER AND 119
    AND DARED TO TASTE THE WOUND A LITTLE KNOWS. . . . . 411 POD OF THE MILKWEED . 18
WOUNDED
    AND WOUNDED ON HIS BLADE. SO FAR FROM CARING, ... 190 THE GRINDSTONE . . . 59
    ONE TREE, BY BEING DEEPLY WOUNDED, ... 331 BEECH 6
    TO EASE THE MORE EXTREMELY WOUNDED OUT . . . . . . 507 A MASQUE OF MERCY . 370
WRACK
    THAT LIFE HAS FOR US ON THE WRACK . . . . 21 THE TRIAL BY EXISTENCE 68
WRAITH
    I AM THE GUARDIAN WRAITH OF STARLIT SMOKE . . . . . . 414 A CABIN IN THE CLEARING 10
WRAP
    WRAP HIM FOR SHROUD IN A PETAL. . . . . 288 DEPARTMENTAL 30
WRAPPED
    OR WRAPPED AS IN A SHROUD, ... 333 HAPPINESS MAKES UP . . 4

WRAPPED (CONTINUED)
    LIKE A CAUL IN WHICH I WAS BORN AND STILL AM WRAPPED.   . . . 390 SKEPTIC   12
    WRAPPED IN AROUND ITSELF AND SELF-BEFRIENDED, ... 396 ANY SIZE WE PLEASE . . 10
WRAPPER
    ABOUT MY FACE AND BODY AND THROUGH MY WRAPPER, ... 63 A SERVANT TO SERVANTS . 29
    "HAD SHE BEEN RINGING LONG? I'LL GET MY WRAPPER. . . .   . 152 SNOW 275
    IN VIRGIN WRAPPER FROM DEEP IN THE BOX, ... 217 A FOUNTAIN, A BOTTLE . 126
WRAPS
    IT WRAPS A WISP OF SEAWEED ROUND MY LEGS, ... 391 ON BEING IDOLIZED . . 2
WRATH
    TO WALK A GRAVER MAN RESTRAINED IN WRATH. . . .   . 285 THE GOLD HESPERIDEE . 60
WREATH (SEE ROSE-WREATH)
    LOOKING OUT OF A WREATH OF FERN AND CLOUD PUFFS.   . . 225 FOR ONCE SOMETHING . . 6
WREATHING
    THEIR UPPER BRANCHES ROUND HIM WREATHING, ... 274 A LONE STRIKER . . . 40
WREATHS
    LOOKING THROUGH WREATHS OF ENGINE SMOKE . . . . .   . 292 ON HEART'S BEGINNING TO 44
WRECK
    SO AS TO WRECK THE ENGINE IN THE DITCH. . . . .   . 270 THE EGG AND THE MACHINE 8
    TO HEAR IT WRECK IN A THUNDERCLAP. . . . . .   . 306 A TRIAL RUN 7
WRECKAGE
    AMID THE WRECKAGE OF A FORMER HOME? . . . . 116 IN THE HOME STRETCH . 177
WRECKED
    HOW THE WRECKERS WRECKED . . . . 432 KITTY HAWK 147
WRECKERS
    HOW THE WRECKERS WRECKED . . . . 432 KITTY HAWK 147
WRENCH
    HE GAVE HIS OWN POOR ILIAC A WRENCH . . . . 394 HAEC FABULA DOCET . . 13
WRESTLE
    WE VAINLY WRESTLE WITH THE BLIND BELIEF . . . . .   . 469 WE VAINLY WRESTLE... . 1
    WE VAINLY WRESTLE... . . . . 469 WE VAINLY WRESTLE... . T
WRETCH
    AND THE WRETCH KNEW FROM THAT THAT WE WERE POOR. . . .   . 127 THE SMILE 5
    AND STRANGLED THE WRETCH WITH A STRING. . . . . .   . 310 THE VINDICTIVES . . 17
    TO A YOUNG WRETCH . . . . 349 TO A YOUNG WRETCH . . T
WRETCHED
    I HATE HIS WRETCHED LITTLE RACKER SECT, ... 144 SNOW 53
    YOU NEEDN'T SHOUT LIKE THAT, YOU WRETCHED MAN. . . .   . 508 A MASQUE OF MERCY . 394
WRETCHEDNESS
    WRETCHEDNESS IN A STRANGER FRIGHTENS ME . . . . .   . 493 A MASQUE OF MERCY . . 16
WRIGGLERS
    AND DANCED IN YELLOW WRIGGLERS ON THE CEILING, ... 117 IN THE HOME STRETCH . 203
WRIGGLING
    IN FRONT OF TWENTY OTHERS' WRIGGLING SPEED-- . . . .   . 237 A HILLSIDE THAW . . . 13
WRIGHT
    FOR IT WAS WRIT IN HEAVEN DOUBLY WRIGHT. . . . .   . 308 THE WRIGHTS' BIPLANE . 4
    TO THE BROTHERS WRIGHT, ... 443 KITTY HAWK 468
WRIGHTS'
    THE WRIGHTS' BIPLANE . . . . 308 THE WRIGHTS' BIPLANE . T
WRING
    AND HIS SUBJECTS WRUNG ALL THEY COULD WRING . . . .   . 310 THE VINDICTIVES . . 12
    I SAY WE KEEP HIM TILL WE WRING SOME MORE . . . .   . 517 A MASQUE OF MERCY . 639
WRINKLED
    MINGLED WITH THESE, SMOOTH BEAN AND WRINKLED PEA), ... 124 PUTTING IN THE SEED . 6
    BELOW THE POINT, AND WERE AT LAST DRIVEN WRINKLED . . .   . 258 WEST-RUNNING BROOK . 25
WRINKLES
    FELL ALL IN WRINKLES OF RESPONSIBILITY. . . . . .   . 201 PLACE FOR A THIRD . 48
WRIST
    SOME OF THEM GAVE WAY AT THE WRIST . . . . 452 A-WISHING WELL . . 56
    WE LIKE YOU, DON'T WE, PAUL? (PAUL TAKES HIS WRIST.) . .   . 518 A MASQUE OF MERCY . 665
WRISTS
    MY SMALL WRISTS STRETCHING TILL THEY SHOWED THE BANJO
        STRINGS. . . . . 198 WILD GRAPES 80
WRIT
    FOR IT WAS WRIT IN HEAVEN DOUBLY WRIGHT. . . . . .   . 308 THE WRIGHTS' BIPLANE . 4
WRITE
    ANGRILY TRIED TO MAKE ME WRITE A PROTEST . . . . .   . 160 NEW HAMPSHIRE . . 29
    RATHER THAN BETTER. HOW ARE WE TO WRITE . . . .   . 167 NEW HAMPSHIRE . . 267
    OR ELSE WRITE SOMETHING TO IMPROVE FOOD PRICES. . . .   . 316 BUILD SOIL . . . 24
    SITS DOWN IN SCHOOL TO TRY IF HE CAN WRITE . . . .   . 353 THE LESSON FOR TODAY . 92
    TO SAY AS MUCH I WRITE YOU THIS. . . . . 381 AN UNSTAMPED LETTER IN 52
    SO ANYONE CAN WRITE TO HIM WHO HAS TO; . . . . .   . 408 FROM PLANE TO PLANE . 144
    I WRITE REAL VERSE IN NUMBERS, AS THEY SAY. . . . .   . 460 HOW HARD TO KEEP FROM 211
    IT HAS ITS BEAUTY, ONLY I DON'T WRITE IT. . . . .   . 461 HOW HARD TO KEEP FROM 223
    A LANGUAGE OF HIS OWN TO WRITE HIS BOOK IN, ... 502 A MASQUE OF MERCY . 241
WRITER
    WHY DON'T YOU USE YOUR TALENTS AS A WRITER . . . .   . 316 BUILD SOIL 22
    THE WRITER AND TALKER FREE SPEECH AND FREE PRESS. . . .   . 319 BUILD SOIL . . . 113
WRITERS
    IT MAKES THE GUILD OF NOVEL WRITERS SICK . . . . .   . 167 NEW HAMPSHIRE . . 274
WRITES
    HE WRITES FREE VERSE, I'M TOLD, AND HE IS THOUGHT . . .   . 459 HOW HARD TO KEEP FROM 184
WRITHE
    THE KING HAD SCARCE CEASED TO WRITHE, ... 311 THE VINDICTIVES . . 21
WRITING
    I SHOULD BE WRITING TO WITHIN THE HOUR . . . .   . 107 CHRISTMAS TREES . . 51
    AND--WRITING; NONE OF THESE EXCEPT PERHAPS . . . .   . 164 NEW HAMPSHIRE . . 166
    UNDER THE FORMAL WRITING, HE WAS THERE, ... 230 NOT TO KEEP 4
    THE MUSE TAKES CARE OF YOU. YOU LIVE BY WRITING . . . .   . 316 BUILD SOIL . . . 17
    TO TAKE A WRITING HAND IN POLITICS. . . . . .   . 316 BUILD SOIL 27
    AND POSSIBLY MY NOT WRITING IT SHOULD STOP ME . . . .   . 461 HOW HARD TO KEEP FROM 224
    THE WRITING ON THE SCREEN MUST CHANGE TOO FAST . . .   . 502 A MASQUE OF MERCY . 245
WRITTEN (SEE OCHER-WRITTEN)
    YOUR NAME NOT WRITTEN ON EITHER SIDE. . . . . .   . 247 ON GOING UNNOTICED . 12
    VERSE COULD BE WRITTEN ON THE CERTAINTY . . . . .   . 277 THE WHITE-TAILED HORNET 7
    I WOULD HAVE WRITTEN OF ME ON MY STONE: . . . . .   . 355 THE LESSON FOR TODAY . 160
    SET OFF ACROSS WHAT I HAD WRITTEN THERE. . . . . .   . 357 A CONSIDERABLE SPECK . 3
    (IS IT NOT WRITTEN ON THE DOLLAR BILL . . . . .   . 422 FOR JOHN F. KENNEDY . 21

WRITTEN (CONTINUED)
    AS HAVE I NOT WRITTEN, ... 437 KITTY HAWK 292
    LINES WRITTEN IN DEJECTION ON THE EVE OF GREAT SUCCESS . . 462 LINES IN DEJECTION . . T
    HE WROTE ONE BOOK. LET THERE BE NO MORE WRITTEN. . . . . 504 A MASQUE OF MERCY . . 290
    THAT IS THE FEAR OF GOD WHEREOF 'TIS WRITTEN. . . . . . 520 A MASQUE OF MERCY . . 699
WRONG
    HE MUST SEEK ME WOULD HE UNDO THE WRONG." . . . . . 16 A DREAM PANG . . . 8
    THEN I WAS WRONG: THE TOWN OF MY SOJOURN, ... 41 THE MOUNTAIN . . . 20
    IF ANYTHING SHOULD HAPPEN TO BE WRONG. . . . . . . 47 A HUNDRED COLLARS . . 83
    AND WOULD FEEL IF I WASN'T ALL GONE WRONG. . . . . . 63 A SERVANT TO SERVANTS . 15
    I DIDN'T WANT THE BLAME IF THINGS WENT WRONG. . . . . 67 A SERVANT TO SERVANTS . 150
    "WHAT IS THERE WRONG?" / "SOMETHING YOU JUST NOW SAID." . 69 THE CODE 10
    YOU CAN SEE THAT THERE'S SOMETHING WRONG WITH IT, . . . 79 THE GENERATIONS OF MEN 172
    MEBBE I'M WRONG TO TAKE IT AS I DO. . . . . 80 THE GENERATIONS OF MEN 185
    SOMETHING WENT WRONG. I SAW HIM THROW THE HOE . . . . 83 THE HOUSEKEEPER . . . 60
    IT MUST BE RIGHT TO LEAVE HIM." / "WHICH IS WRONG'" . . 83 THE HOUSEKEEPER . . . 75
    "THERE'S NO ONE; SO YOU'RE WRONG," HE SAID. / "THERE IS.-- 91 THE FEAR 64
    THAT'S SURE TO BE RIGHT, EVEN IF IT'S WRONG. . . . . 96 THE SELF-SEEKER . . . 111
    TO RIGHT THE WRONG THAT THIS SHOULD HAVE BEEN SO. . . . 173 A STAR IN A STONEBOAT . 36
    (THEY EITHER NOTICED IT, OR GOT IT WRONG.) . . . . . 181 MAPLE 51
    EVERYONE HAD BEEN WRONG IN JUDGING PAUL. . . . . . 195 PAUL'S WIFE . . . 147
    A GOOD DEAL RIGHT; DON'T DO THE LAST THING WRONG. . . . 199 PLACE FOR A THIRD . . 10
    THEY'VE GOT IT SETTLED WRONG, AND I CAN PROVE IT. . . . 207 PAUPER WITCH OF GRAFTON 3
    MAN CAME TO TELL IT WHAT WAS WRONG: . . . . . 224 THE AIM WAS SONG . . 5
    ALWAYS WRONG TO THE LIGHT, SO NEVER SEEING . . . . 225 FOR ONCE SOMETHING . . 2
    AND OF COURSE THERE MUST BE SOMETHING WRONG. . . . . 251 A MINOR BIRD . . . 7
    PROCLAIMED THE TIME WAS NEITHER WRONG NOR RIGHT. . . . 255 ACQUAINTED WITH NIGHT . 13
    TRUST HIM THEN NOT TO PUT YOU IN THE WRONG. . . . . 278 THE WHITE-TAILED HORNET 26
    "WRONG SHAPE, WRONG COLOR, AND WRONG SCENT," I SAID. . . 278 THE WHITE-TAILED HORNET 40
    AT THOSE WHO'D DONE HIM SUCH A WRONG AS THAT, ... 284 THE GOLD HESPERIDEE . . 44
    OF SIGNS THAT WITH N TURNED WRONG AND S TURNED WRONG . . 286 A ROADSIDE STAND . . 10
    THAT THOUGH THERE IS NO FIXED LINE BETWEEN WRONG AND RIGHT, 305 THERE ARE ROUGHLY ZONES 12
    ITS MAKERS' NAME--TIME CANNOT GET THAT WRONG, ... 308 THE WRIGHTS' BIPLANE . 3
    I MAY BE WRONG, BUT, TITYRUS, TO ME . . . . 317 BUILD SOIL . . . 31
    TO KNOW IF ANYTHING IS VERY WRONG. . . . . 317 BUILD SOIL . . . 56
    YOUR MIND MISTRUSTED THERE WAS SOMETHING WRONG, . . . 369 THE LITERATE FARMER AND 24
    CALLED GETTING OUT OF THE WRONG SIDE OF BED. . . . . 371 THE LITERATE FARMER AND 107
    UNDER A SPELL SO THE WRONG ONES CAN'T FIND IT, ... 379 DIRECTIVE 58
    THEY WAITED ON WAS WRONG. . . . . 391 A ROGERS GROUP . . . 8
    WE'LL BE ALL RIGHT IF NOTHING GOES WRONG WITH THE LIGHTING. 392 IT BIDS PRETTY FAIR . 4
    AGAINST THE WRONG SIDE OF A WINDOWPANE. . . . . . . 412 POD OF THE MILKWEED . 39
    UNLESS I'M WRONG. . . . . 413 AWAY! 17
    THERE HAD BEEN SOMETHING STRANGELY WRONG . . . . . 416 AMERICA IS HARD TO SEE 13
    TO BREAK WITH FOLLOWERS WHEN IN THE WRONG, ... 424 FOR JOHN F. KENNEDY . 62
    TO UNDO THE WRONG. . . . . 430 KITTY HAWK 72
    I'M NOT A FREE-VERSE SINGER. HE WAS WRONG THERE. . . . 460 HOW HARD TO KEEP FROM 209
    YOUR COMFORTERS WERE WRONG. / OH, THAT COMMITTEE! . . . 486 A MASQUE OF REASON . 368
    TO A BAD START IT SEEMS IN THE WRONG SCHOOL . . . . 499 A MASQUE OF MERCY . 162
    YOU WRONG ME. / WELL THEN, NAME A SINGLE SIN. . . . . 503 A MASQUE OF MERCY . 262
    BUT I WANT YOU TO UNDERSTAND ME WRONG. . . . . . . 510 A MASQUE OF MERCY . 453
    I THINK I MAY HAVE GOT GOD WRONG ENTIRELY. . . . . . 518 A MASQUE OF MERCY . 654
    ALL OF US GET EACH OTHER PRETTY WRONG. . . . . . . 518 A MASQUE OF MERCY . 655
WRONGED
    BEFORE THE INDIAN RACE WAS FURTHER WRONGED. . . . . 370 THE LITERATE FARMER AND 60
WROTE
    BECAUSE I WROTE MY NOVELS IN NEW HAMPSHIRE . . . . 166 NEW HAMPSHIRE . . 246
    SHE ALMOST WROTE THE WORDS DOWN ON HER KNEE, ... 182 MAPLE 86
    THE POETESS WHO WROTE THE BOOK OF VERSES . . . . . 215 A FOUNTAIN, A BOTTLE . 78
    LIFE LONG IN BED, AND WROTE HER THINGS IN BED. . . . . 215 A FOUNTAIN, A BOTTLE . 85
    HE WROTE ONE BOOK. LET THERE BE NO MORE WRITTEN. . . . 504 A MASQUE OF MERCY . 290
WROUGHT
    THAT WROUGHT ON HIM BESIDE HER IN THE NIGHT. . . . 38 DEATH OF THE HIRED MAN 110
    WAS WROUGHT THROUGH TREES WITHOUT A BREATH OF STORM . . 238 A HILLSIDE THAW . . . 31
WRUNG
    AND HIS SUBJECTS WRUNG ALL THEY COULD WRING . . . . . 310 THE VINDICTIVES . . . 12

X

X
    KING'S X--NO FAIRS TO USE IT ANYMORE! . . . . 399 U.S. 1946 KING'S X . . 4
    U.S. 1946 KING'S X . . . . 399 U.S. 1946 KING'S X . . T
XANADU
    YOU'RE OFF TO XANADU TO HELP THE COOK. . . . . . . 455 HOW HARD TO KEEP FROM 48

Y

YAK
    THERE IN THE LAND OF THE YAK. . . . . 314 BEARER OF EVIL TIDINGS 28
YANKEE
    HE'S PURITAN YANKEE THROUGH AND THROUGH. . . . . . 393 A CASE FOR JEFFERSON . 6
YANKEES
    WITH ALL THIS PRIDE OF ANCESTRY, WE YANKEES? . . . 76 THE GENERATIONS OF MEN 87
    YANKEES ARE WHAT THEY ALWAYS WERE. . . . . . . 139 BROWN'S DESCENT . . 53
    HARD IF, THOUGH CAST AWAY FOR LIFE WITH YANKEES, . . . 186 THE AX-HELVE 44
YARD
    THE WOODBINE LEAVES LITTERED THE YARD, ... 7 LOVE AND A QUESTION . 13
    WITH THE BROOK GOING BY BELOW THE YARD, ... 82 THE HOUSEKEEPER . . 46
    RECEIPTED. AND THE COCK IS IN THE YARD." . . . . 86 THE HOUSEKEEPER . . 147
    A STRANGER TO OUR YARD, WHO LOOKED THE CITY, ... 106 CHRISTMAS TREES . . 5
    THE BUZZ SAW SNARLED AND RATTLED IN THE YARD . . . . 136 "OUT,OUT--" . . . 1
    BEHIND ME ON THE SNOW IN MY OWN YARD . . . . . 185 THE AX-HELVE . . . 7
    AND, ANYWAY, ITS STANDING IN THE YARD. . . . . . 189 THE GRINDSTONE . . . 19
    AND CAUGHT ME SPLITTING WOOD IN THE YARD. . . . . 275 TWO TRAMPS IN MUD TIME 2
    IN USING THE YARD TO BACK AND TURN AROUND; . . . . . 287 A ROADSIDE STAND . . 40

PAGE TITLE   LINE

YARD (CONTINUED)
  HE MAY FUMBLE WIDE OF THE KNOB A YARD OR MORE, ... 342 WILLFUL HOMING . . . 11
  AND SET UP LIKE A STATUE IN YOUR YARD, ... 365 OF STONES OF THE PLACE 10
YARDFUL
  LIKE A YARDFUL OF SCHOOLBOYS OUT AT RECESS . . . . . 318 BUILD SOIL 61
YARN
  WELL, THIS IS SUCH A YARN. PAUL SAWED HIS WIFE . . . . 192 PAUL'S WIFE 54
  THE FISHERMAN'S SWAPPING A YARN FOR A YARN . . . . 262 THE FLOWER BOAT . . 1
YARNS
  A THOUSAND YARNS WERE UNDER PULL, ... 273 A LONE STRIKER . . 19
YAWN
  NOW JUST AHEAD OF HIM WAS SEEN TO YAWN . . . . . 394 HAEC FABULA DOCET . 5
YAWNING
  OF YAWNING LENSES. . . . . 219 I WILL SING YOU ONE-O . 54
YE
  KEEPING HIS HEAD ABOVE. 'DAMN YE,' I SAYS, ... 72 THE CODE 77
  'THAT GETS YE!' HE SQUEAKED LIKE A SQUEEZED RAT. . . . 72 THE CODE 78
  IF YE WANT HIM, YE CAN GO AND DIG HIM OUT.' . . . . 72 THE CODE 85
  WHAT SHE BROUGHT BACK WOULD AMAZE YE. . . . . . 396 AN IMPORTER . . . 2
  LISTEN, YE! IT'S THE PROLETARIAT! . . . . 508 A MASQUE OF MERCY . . 390
YEAR (SEE FIVE-YEAR, LIGHT-YEAR)
  ALL SIMPLY IN THE SPRINGING OF THE YEAR. . . . . . 12 A PRAYER IN SPRING . . 4
  TO THIS LEAN FEEDING, SAVE ONCE A YEAR . . . . . 24 PAN WITH US . . . 12
  IT HAS LASTED ME MANY AND MANY A YEAR. . . . . . 25 THE DEMIURGE'S LAUGH . 6
  FAIRBANKS, HE SAYS TO ME, 'HELP US THIS YEAR,' . . . 48 A HUNDRED COLLARS . . 112
  WHERE THEY WERE BOYS. THEY HAVEN'T COME THIS YEAR. . . 55 THE BLACK COTTAGE . . 18
  THEY EAT THEM THE YEAR ROUND, AND THOSE THEY DON'T EAT . . 60 BLUEBERRIES . . . 52
  TO TELL IF HE KNEW. BUT THE YEAR HAD BEEN BAD. . . . 61 BLUEBERRIES . . . 72
  WE'LL PICK IN THE PATTERSONS' PASTURE THIS YEAR. . . . 61 BLUEBERRIES . . . 81
  HE'S INTO EVERYTHING IN TOWN. THIS YEAR . . . . . 64 A SERVANT TO SERVANTS . 71
  TAKE IT YEAR IN, YEAR OUT, HE DOESN'T MAKE MUCH. . . . 85 THE HOUSEKEEPER . . 103
  "I WANTED THERE SHOULD BE SOME THERE NEXT YEAR." . . . 97 THE SELF-SEEKER . . 123
  WHO COMES FROM PHILADELPHIA EVERY YEAR . . . . . 162 NEW HAMPSHIRE . . . 101
  THAT COURSE, THEY TELL ME, ISN'T OFFERED THIS YEAR. . . 171 NEW HAMPSHIRE . . . 405
  COULD TELL THE TIME OF YEAR WHEN EVERY TREE . . . . 175 THE CENSUS-TAKER . . 18
  OF YEAR OR DAY THE WAY IT SWUNG A DOOR . . . . . 175 THE CENSUS-TAKER . . 27
  THIS HOUSE IN ONE YEAR FALLEN TO DECAY . . . . . 176 THE CENSUS-TAKER . . 50
  WHERE THEY GROW FEWER AND FEWER EVERY YEAR . . . . 176 THE CENSUS-TAKER . . 62
  GRAPES, I KNEW GRAPES FROM HAVING SEEN THEM LAST YEAR. . . 197 WILD GRAPES . . . 24
  ONCE WHEN THE SNOW OF THE YEAR WAS BEGINNING TO FALL, . . 223 THE RUNAWAY . . . 1
  THE DARKEST EVENING OF THE YEAR. . . . . . . 224 STOPPING BY WOODS . . 8
  OR EVEN ANOTHER YEAR, ... 282 A DRUMLIN WOODCHUCK . 27
  I WET ONE LAST YEAR AT MONTAUK . . . . 294 A RECORD STRIDE . . 13
  I HAVE SAFELY TRODDEN UNDERFOOT THE LEAVES OF ANOTHER YEAR. . 297 A LEAF-TREADER . . 4
  NOW UP, MY KNEE, TO KEEP ON TOP OF ANOTHER YEAR OF SNOW. . 298 A LEAF-TREADER . . 12
  THIS WAS NO LADY'S TIME OF YEAR. . . . . . . 344 DISCOVERY OF MADEIRAS . 31
  A YEAR OF LEAVES WAS WASTED. . . . . 359 NOVEMBER . . . 8
  THAT ONCE A YEAR BY HAND OR APPARATUS . . . . . 360 A LOOSE MOUNTAIN . . 3
  IT IS ALMOST THE YEAR TWO THOUSAND . . . . . . 361 ALMOST TWO THOUSAND . T
  A HALF COURSE IN IT NEXT YEAR.) AND BESIDES, . . . 407 FROM PLANE TO PLANE . 112
  TILL DARWIN CAME TO EARTH UPON A YEAR . . . . . 425 ACCIDENTALLY ON PURPOSE 9
  WHY, WHAT A STORY. AT THIS TIME OF YEAR . . . . . 501 A MASQUE OF MERCY . . 211
YEARNER
  AND BRAVER FOR THE EARNER, LEARNER, YEARNER. . . . . 424 FOR JOHN F. KENNEDY . 67
YEARS
  THAN NOW THESE NUMBERLESS YEARS THE ELVES, ... 26 A LINE-STORM SONG . . 11
  THE BOY YOU HAD IN HAYING FOUR YEARS SINCE. . . . . 36 DEATH OF THE HIRED MAN 59
  AFTER SO MANY YEARS HE STILL KEEPS FINDING . . . . 37 DEATH OF THE HIRED MAN 74
  OF LATE YEARS, THOUGH HE KEEPS THE OLD HOMESTEAD . . . 44 A HUNDRED COLLARS . . 3
  ANYTHING IN HER AFTER ALL THE YEARS. . . . . . 56 THE BLACK COTTAGE . . 30
  SHE HAD AT SOME COST TAUGHT THEM AFTER YEARS.) . . . 56 THE BLACK COTTAGE . . 42
  TO MEASURE HOW FAR FIFTY YEARS HAVE BROUGHT US. . . . 56 THE BLACK COTTAGE . . 46
  WHERE IT WILL TROUBLE US A THOUSAND YEARS. . . . . 57 THE BLACK COTTAGE . . 69
  IT WAS TWO YEARS AGO--OR NO!--CAN IT BE . . . . . 59 BLUEBERRIES . . . 10
  LOCKED UP FOR YEARS BACK THERE AT THE OLD FARM. . . . 65 A SERVANT TO SERVANTS . 89
  WE'VE BEEN HERE FIFTEEN YEARS." / "THAT'S A LONG TIME . . 82 THE HOUSEKEEPER . . 39
  "I DON'T JUST SEE HIM LIVING MANY YEARS, ... 82 THE HOUSEKEEPER . . 43
  "THE STRAIN'S BEEN TOO MUCH FOR HER ALL THESE YEARS: . . 84 THE HOUSEKEEPER . . 77
  "WHAT I'LL BE SEEING MORE OF IN THE YEARS . . . . 111 IN THE HOME STRETCH . 26
  I ONLY SEE THE YEARS. THEY COME AND GO . . . . . 112 IN THE HOME STRETCH . 47
  THE WOOD." / "WHAT KIND OF YEARS?" / "WHY, LATTER YEARS-- . 112 IN THE HOME STRETCH . 49
  DIFFERENT FROM EARLY YEARS." / "I SEE THEM, TOO. . . . 112 IN THE HOME STRETCH . 50
  YEARS AFTERWARDS, TRAILING THEIR LEAVES ON THE GROUND . . 121 BIRCHES 18
  WITH HIS TEN CHILDREN UNDER TEN YEARS OLD. . . . . 144 SNOW 52
  THEY'D BEEN THERE THEN A HUNDRED YEARS OR MORE. . . . 161 NEW HAMPSHIRE . . . 82
  WHEN I LEFT MASSACHUSETTS YEARS AGO . . . . . . 167 NEW HAMPSHIRE . . . 248
  FALLEN TO RUIN IN TEN THOUSAND YEARS . . . . . 176 THE CENSUS-TAKER . . 52
  FEW FARMS CHANGED HANDS; SO RATHER THAN SPEND YEARS . . 177 THE STAR-SPLITTER . . 28
  AND CAME SO NEAR DEATH IN THE DARK OF YEARS, . . . 180 MAPLE 37
  TWENTY-FIVE YEARS AGO AT MAPLE'S NAMING . . . . . 184 MAPLE 149
  AND ARROWHEADS ITSELF. MUCH USE FOR YEARS . . . . 189 THE GRINDSTONE . . 38
  THE HUNDRED YEARS THE TREE MUST HAVE BEEN GROWING. . . 194 PAUL'S WIFE . . . 94
  ONE OF THEM FIVE YEARS YOUNGER THAN I LOOK-- . . . 196 WILD GRAPES . . . 18
  IT LEFT THE CELLAR FORTY YEARS AGO . . . . . . 203 THE WITCH OF COOS . . 28
  WE'D KEPT UP ALL THESE YEARS BETWEEN OURSELVES . . . 207 THE WITCH OF COOS . . 146
  WITH ALL THE RAIN AND SNOW OF SEVEN YEARS; . . . . 210 PAUPER WITCH OF GRAFTON 92
  A LEAK AND EMPTIED THEN. AND FORTY YEARS . . . . 213 A FOUNTAIN, A BOTTLE . 25
  IT WENT MANY YEARS, ... 240 THE LOCKLESS DOOR . . 1
  ITS LIFE OF HUNDREDS OF YEARS HAS ENDED . . . . . 253 THE THATCH . . . 33
  "TAKE TWENTY YEARS. . . . . 256 THE LOVELY BE CHOOSERS 5
  HIS LITTLE MATTHEW, ALSO FIVE YEARS OLD, ... 283 THE GOLD HESPERIDEE . 13
  WITHIN A MILLION YEARS OF AN IDEA. . . . . . . 293 AT WOODWARD'S GARDENS . 16
  HERE ON THIS VERY CAMPUS YEARS AGO. . . . . . 316 BUILD SOIL . . . 4
  IT TAKES TEN YEARS OR SO TO CARRY OUT, ... 323 BUILD SOIL . . . 226
  RATHER BECAUSE IT TOOK FIVE YEARS AT LEAST . . . . 323 BUILD SOIL . . . 227
  AND SENT IT TO ME YEARS AND YEARS-- . . . . . . 326 A MISSIVE MISSILE . . 4
  A MILLION YEARS TO BE PRECISE-- . . . . . . 326 A MISSIVE MISSILE . . 5
  SHE WAS OUR LAND MORE THAN A HUNDRED YEARS . . . . 348 THE GIFT OUTRIGHT . . 2

YEARS (CONTINUED)   PAGE TITLE   LINE

TO MONTHS AND YEARS AND MANY, MANY YEARS.   . . . . . 355 THE LESSON FOR TODAY . 139
ONE MAN HAD LIVED ONE HUNDRED YEARS AND EIGHT.   . . . . 355 THE LESSON FOR TODAY . 140
IT IS TURNING THREE HUNDRED YEARS   . . . . . 367 A SERIOUS STEP LIGHTLY 13
THIS LIGHT'S BEEN GOING ON FOR SEVERAL YEARS, ... 369 THE LITERATE FARMER AND 31
OF THE LAST FIFTY YEARS ARE ALL A LIBEL, ... 369 THE LITERATE FARMER AND 45
BUT BEDS--IN LESS THAN FIFTY YEARS HE'S SURE   . . . . 372 THE LITERATE FARMER AND 129
A CYCLE WE'LL SAY OF A HUNDRED YEARS.   . . . . 376 SOMETHING FOR HOPE .   17
WHERE WERE THEY ALL NOT TWENTY YEARS AGO?   . . . . 378 DIRECTIVE   26
OH, YEARS AGO--TEN THOUSAND YEARS.   . . . . 392 A CLIFF DWELLING .   13
AS FIFTY MILLION YEARS AGO WE CAME--   . . . . 395 WHY WAIT FOR SCIENCE . 12
OF HAVING HOED AND MOWED FOR FIFTY YEARS, ... 404 FROM PLANE TO PLANE .   3
SHE WAS OUR LAND MORE THAN A HUNDRED YEARS   . . . . 424 THE GIFT OUTRIGHT . .   2
SIXTY YEARS AGO.   . . . . 428 KITTY HAWK   9
THEN FOR YEARS AND YEARS   . . . . 437 KITTY HAWK 287
I'VE HAD YOU ON MY MIND A THOUSAND YEARS .   . . . . 475 A MASQUE OF REASON . 47
WELL, AFTER ALL THESE YEARS! / THIS IS MY WIFE. . . . . 476 A MASQUE OF REASON . 83
SHE NOW FELT YOUNGER BY A THOUSAND YEARS .   . . . . 479 A MASQUE OF REASON . 157
COME, AFTER ALL THESE YEARS--TO SATISFY ME.   . . . . 482 A MASQUE OF REASON . 254
NOW AFTER ALL THESE YEARS YOU MIGHT INDULGE ME. . . . . 483 A MASQUE OF REASON . 267
I FLED HIM, DOWN THE ARCHES OF THE YEARS."   . . . . 494 A MASQUE OF MERCY . 23
YEAR'S
NO RUNNER TRACKS IN THIS YEAR'S SNOW LOOPED NEAR IT. . . . 101 THE WOOD-PILE . . . 26
AND IT WAS OLDER SURE THAN THIS YEAR'S CUTTING, . . . 101 THE WOOD-PILE . . . 27
OR EVEN LAST YEAR'S OR THE YEAR'S BEFORE.   . . . . 101 THE WOOD-PILE . . . 28
THAT FLASHES TAIL THROUGH LAST YEAR'S WITHERED BRAKE . . 226 THE ONSET 20
A YOUNG BEECH CLINGING TO ITS LAST YEAR'S LEAVES. . . . 234 A BOUNDLESS MOMENT . 12
AND LAST YEAR'S BERRIES SHINING SCARLET RED.   . . . . 254 A WINTER EDEN . . .   8
WHAT WELL MAY PROVE THE YEAR'S HIGH GIRDLE MARK. . . . 254 A WINTER EDEN . . . 12
YELL
AND LET OUT A LOUD YELL, AND THREW A BOTTLE, ... 195 PAUL'S WIFE 140
YELLING
THEY YELLING MIX TAG, HIDE-AND-SEEK, HOPSCOTCH, . . . 318 BUILD SOIL 63
YELLOW
AND THE CAGED YELLOW BIRD . . . . 10 WIND AND WINDOW FLOWER   7
THEY'RE ONLY TURNING YELLOW WHERE THEY ARE.   . . . . 50 A HUNDRED COLLARS . 169
BLACK SHE HAD SCARCELY SEEN, AND YELLOW NEVER.   . . . . 57 THE BLACK COTTAGE . 76
YOU DIDN'T FIND A YELLOW LADY'S SLIPPER.   . . . . 97 THE SELF-SEEKER . . 137
WHERE IS IT NOW, THE YELLOW LADY'S SLIPPER?"   . . . . 97 THE SELF-SEEKER . . 140
TWO ROADS DIVERGED IN A YELLOW WOOD, ... 105 THE ROAD NOT TAKEN .   1
AND DANCED IN YELLOW WRIGGLERS ON THE CEILING, ... 117 IN THE HOME STRETCH . 203
UP AT HIS SHOULDERS, DRAGGING YELLOW STRANDS   . . . . 125 AN ENCOUNTER . . . 17
AND THE SUN SHRUNKEN YELLOW IN SMOKE.   . . . . 141 THE GUM-GATHERER . 24
YELP
THE SEAL YELP . . . . 211 AN EMPTY THREAT . . . 19
YELPING
TO PLEASE THE YELPING DOGS. THE GAPS I MEAN, ... 33 MENDING WALL   9
YELPS
AND YELPS DELIGHT . . . . 360 THE RABBIT-HUNTER . 10
YEOMAN
AND DONE YEOMAN SHARE . . . . 434 KITTY HAWK 205
YES
AUTUMN, YES, WINTER WAS IN THE WIND;   . . . .   8 LOVE AND A QUESTION . 15
"YES, I TOOK CARE TO KEEP WELL OUT OF EARSHOT." . . . . 37 DEATH OF THE HIRED MAN 70
"HOME," HE MOCKED GENTLY. / "YES, WHAT ELSE BUT HOME? . . 38 DEATH OF THE HIRED MAN 113
"LAFE WAS THE NAME, I THINK?" / "YES, LAYFAYETTE. . . . 46 A HUNDRED COLLARS . 41
I'VE BEEN AWAY ONCE--YES, I'VE BEEN AWAY.   . . . . 65 A SERVANT TO SERVANTS 90
'DID YOU SAY, "LET HER COME"?' 'YES, LET HER COME.' . . . 71 THE CODE 66
ONE, AND ONE OTHER, YES, FOR THERE WERE TWO.   . . . . 74 THE GENERATIONS OF MEN 28
"YES, STARK, AND YOU?" / "I'M STARK." HE DREW HIS PASSPORT. 74 THE GENERATIONS OF MEN 46
"AND WHAT DO YOU SEE?" / "YES, WHAT DO I SEE?   . . . . 76 THE GENERATIONS OF MEN 96
"YES, IT'S IMPORTANT, THOUGH YOU THINK IT ISN'T. . . . . 77 THE GENERATIONS OF MEN 118
"YES, YOU MUST GO; WE CAN'T STAY HERE FOREVER.   . . . . 77 THE GENERATIONS OF MEN 120
"YES, WHAT'S IT ALL ABOUT? WHEN DID SHE GO?"   . . . . 82 THE HOUSEKEEPER . . 21
"YES, BUT HE SHOULD HAVE MARRIED HER." / "I KNOW." . . . 84 THE HOUSEKEEPER . . 76
"OHO, OHO!" / "YOU DON'T BELIEVE ME." / "YES, I DO, . . . 87 THE HOUSEKEEPER . . 181
ARE YOU SURE----" / "YES, I'M SURE!" / "--IT WAS A FACE?" . 89 THE FEAR 13
AND LET YOU SEE." / "YES, DO.--JOEL, GO BACK!"   . . . . 92 THE FEAR 75
AND IT'S OUR LIFE." / "YES, WHEN IT'S NOT OUR DEATH." . . 94 THE SELF-SEEKER . . 46
"YES, THAT'S ONE WAY TO PUT IT--ALL THE FLOWERS . . . . 95 THE SELF-SEEKER . . 67
"LOOKING ROUND, I SUPPOSE," SAID WILLIS. / "YES, ... 96 THE SELF-SEEKER . . 101
WELL, YES." / "HEAR ANYTHING THAT MIGHT PROVE USEFUL?" . . 96 THE SELF-SEEKER . . 102
"YES, BUT ALL THAT YEARS DIGGING, AND I'M AS MUCH . . . . 99 THE SELF-SEEKER . . 191
YES. THANKS FOR CARING.--DON'T MIND WILL: HE'S SAVAGE. . . 100 THE SELF-SEEKER . . 224
ALL ROUND AND ROUND. THE LATTER HE NODDED "YES" TO, . . . 107 CHRISTMAS TREES . . 36
(SOFT PETALS, YES, BUT NOT SO BARREN QUITE, ... 124 PUTTING IN THE SEED .   5
AND YES, SHE HAS LONG MISTRUSTED . . . . 134 A GIRL'S GARDEN . . 33
OH, YES, HE SHOWED JOHN THE WHEEL PIT ALL RIGHT. . . . . 142 THE VANISHING RED . 29
"I'LL JUST SEE HOW THE HORSES ARE." / "YES, DO," . . . . 144 SNOW 33
YOU LIKE, AND LIKE HIM FOR." / "OH, YES YOU DO. . . . . 146 SNOW 96
"YES, I SUPPOSE YOU'LL WANT TO, BUT I SHOULDN'T. . . . . 152 SNOW 263
YOU KNOW--IT SOUNDS THAT WAY, AND YES, I HEAR-- . . . . 153 SNOW 300
"NOT TALKING." / "NO." / "WHY, YES, I HEAR--WHAT IS IT?" . 154 SNOW 317
I ASKED HIM, ON MY GUARD. "OH, YES," HE ANSWERED, ... 159 NEW HAMPSHIRE . . 13
'MAPLE.' I SAID IT TOO: 'YES, FOR HER NAME.'   . . . . 180 MAPLE 18
YES, THERE'S SOMETHING THE DEAD ARE KEEPING BACK. . . . . 202 THE WITCH OF COOS . 18
YES, WE COULD TOO, SON. TELL THE TRUTH FOR ONCE. . . . . 206 THE WITCH OF COOS . 138
"YES, LET HER CHOOSE. . . . . 256 THE LOVELY BE CHOOSERS 10
"YES, WE CAN LET HER AND STILL TRIUMPH." .   . . . . 256 THE LOVELY BE CHOOSERS 20
"YES, YOU HAVE, TOO. GO ON. YOU THOUGHT OF SOMETHING." . . 259 WEST-RUNNING BROOK . 37
YES, RIGHT I WAS, THE LOCKS WERE PROPS OCCURING; . . . . 290 OLD BARN AT THE BOTTOM 41
YES; YES, OF COURSE. WE HAVE THE SAME CONVENTION. . . . . 352 THE LESSON FOR TODAY . 57
YES, REVOLUTIONS ARE THE ONLY SALVES, ... 363 A SEMI-REVOLUTION .   7
AND YES, MY LAND WAS HARDLY FENCED.   . . . . 364 TRESPASS   2
THINGS MUST HAVE HAPPENED TO YOU, YES, ... 381 AN UNSTAMPED LETTER IN 45
AND YES, ALTHOUGH IT IS A FLOWER THAT FLOWS   . . . . 411 POD OF THE MILKWEED . 15
FROM OUR ROCKS, AND YES, ... 440 KITTY HAWK 385
"BUT YES," SHE SAID, "SOME DAY I'LL TELL YOU, DEAR. . . . 457 HOW HARD TO KEEP FROM 106

YES (CONTINUED)
    "YES, BUT GIVE CHARACTER AND NOT JUST FOOD. . . . . 458 HOW HARD TO KEEP FROM   141
    ARE SINGING. YES, AND LOOK, THE TREE IS TROUBLED. . . . . 473 A MASQUE OF REASON . .   15
    BUT, YES, I'M FINE, EXCEPT FOR NOW AND THEN . . . . 474 A MASQUE OF REASON . .   39
    YES, BY AND BY. BUT FIRST A LARGER MATTER. . . . . 475 A MASQUE OF REASON . .   46
    SHE'S BEAUTIFUL. / YES, SHE WAS JUST REMARKING . . . . . . 479 A MASQUE OF REASON . . 156
    YES, BOTH OF US: WE SAW TO THAT AT ONCE. . . . . 479 A MASQUE OF REASON . . 162
    I'M CHARMED WITH HER. / YES, I COULD SEE YOU WERE. . . . . 480 A MASQUE OF REASON . . 182
    YOUR KINGDOM, YES, YOUR KINGDOM COME ON EARTH. . . . . . . 484 A MASQUE OF REASON . . 303
    YES, YES. / YOU DON'T SEEM SATISFIED. / I AM. . . . . . . 486 A MASQUE OF REASON . . 375
    OH, YES, THAT TENDENCY!--OH, DO COME OFF IT. . . . . 489 A MASQUE OF REASON . . 447
    YES, BUT NEW YORK WILL DO AS AN EXAMPLE. . . . . 496 A MASQUE OF MERCY . .   91
    YES, WE DO TOO, WITH SYMPATHY, MY FRIEND. . . . . 497 A MASQUE OF MERCY . . 102
    I LOVE AND FEAR HIM. YES, BUT I FEAR FOR HIM. . . . . . . 505 A MASQUE OF MERCY . . 310
    YES, PAUL, YOU DO SAY THINGS LIKE THAT SOMETIMES. . . . . . 511 A MASQUE OF MERCY . . 486
    YES, SPOKEN SO WE CAN'T LIVE UP TO IT, ... 512 A MASQUE OF MERCY . . 498
    YES, CALL ME PAGAN, PAUL, AS IF YOU MEANT IT. . . . . . . 513 A MASQUE OF MERCY . . 524
    YES, PILGRIM NOW INSTEAD OF RUNAWAY, ... 513 A MASQUE OF MERCY . . 534
    YES, THERE YOU HAVE IT AT THE ROOT OF THINGS. . . . . . . 520 A MASQUE OF MERCY . . 716
YESTERDAY
    NOT YESTERDAY I LEARNED TO KNOW . . . .   7 MY NOVEMBER GUEST . .   16
    HE HOED A LITTLE YESTERDAY FOR ME: . . . . 83 THE HOUSEKEEPER . . .   58
    FROM SNOW THAT MELTED ONLY YESTERDAY. . . . . 245 SPRING POOLS   12
YESTERDAY'S
    SOME RESTING FLOWER OF YESTERDAY'S DELIGHT. . . . . 22 THE TUFT OF FLOWERS .   14
YET
    AND YET, IN VIEW OF HOW MANY THINGS, ...   6 GHOST HOUSE   29
    YET SAW BUT HER WITHIN, ...   8 LOVE AND A QUESTION .   22
    AND YET WITH NEITHER LOVE NOR HATE, ...   9 STARS   9
    YET EVERY SECOND SPEAR . . . . 13 ROSE POGONIAS . . .   14
    NOR YET TO DRAW ONE THOUGHT OF OURS TO HIM, ... 23 THE TUFT OF FLOWERS .   27
    NOR YET DID I. . . . . 29 MY BUTTERFLY   25
    AND YET BETWEEN THE TOWN AND IT I FOUND, ... 40 THE MOUNTAIN   7
    SHE HAD SOME ART OF HEARING AND YET NOT . . . . 57 THE BLACK COTTAGE . .   73
    THAT OUGHT TO BE WORTH SOMETHING, AND MAY YET. . . . . . . 64 A SERVANT TO SERVANTS . 43
    "NO! AND YET I DON'T KNOW--IT'S HARD TO SAY. . . . . 73 THE CODE   111
    MY MOTHER WAS A LANE, YET MIGHT HAVE MARRIED . . . . 75 THE GENERATIONS OF MEN 50
    THE LIFE IS NOT YET ALL GONE OUT OF IT. . . . . 79 THE GENERATIONS OF MEN 165
    YET KNOWING HOW WAY LEADS ON TO WAY, ... 105 THE ROAD NOT TAKEN .   14
    AND WHIRLS OF FOLIAGE NOT YET LAID, THERE DROVE . . . . . 106 CHRISTMAS TREES . .   4
    YET DID IN COUNTRY FASHION IN THAT THERE . . . . 106 CHRISTMAS TREES . .   6
    YET MORE I'D HATE TO HOLD MY TREES, EXCEPT . . . . 106 CHRISTMAS TREES . .   21
    A VIEW." / "AND YET YOU THINK YOU LIKE IT, DEAR?" . . . . 111 IN THE HOME STRETCH .   35
    "THEY'RE NOT GONE YET." / "WE'VE GOT TO HAVE THE STOVE, . 113 IN THE HOME STRETCH .   78
    BUT MORE THAN ONE AS YET. YOUR PARASOL . . . . 119 MEETING AND PASSING .   8
    YET SOME SAY LOVE BY BEING THRALL . . . . 120 BOND AND FREE . . .   17
    YET NOBODY MOLESTED THEM! . . . . 135 LOCKED OUT   7
    MAY BE THE THING YOU HAVEN'T, YET YOU GIVE IT. . . . . . . 148 SNOW   148
    YET THINK OF THE SMALL BIRDS AT ROOST AND NOT . . . . . . 151 SNOW   226
    IN NO TIME OUT TONIGHT. AND YET TOMORROW . . . . 151 SNOW   229
    THE HOUR HAD NOT YET STRUCK FOR BEING GOOD, ... 161 NEW HAMPSHIRE . . .   89
    MANKIND HAD NOT YET GONE ON THE SABBATICAL. . . . . 161 NEW HAMPSHIRE . . .   90
    THE PLACE IS SILENT ALL DAY LONG, NOR YET . . . . 165 NEW HAMPSHIRE . . .   189
    I THOUGHT THEY COULDN'T BE. AND YET THEY WERE. . . . . . . 167 NEW HAMPSHIRE . . .   257
    YET ASK WHERE ELSE IT COULD HAVE GONE AS WELL, ... 173 A STAR IN A STONEBOAT . 37
    IT YET HAS POLES, AND ONLY NEEDS A SPIN . . . . 174 A STAR IN A STONEBOAT . 50
    ADMITTED; AND YET, WHAT WAS THAT TO HIM? . . . . 186 THE AX-HELVE   28
    FOR LOVE OF IT, AND YET NOT WASTE TIME EITHER. . . . . . . 188 THE AX-HELVE   81
    I MAY YET LIVE, AS I KNOW OTHERS LIVE, ... 199 WILD GRAPES   100
    LABAN WAS OLD AND POOR, YET SEEMED TO CARE; . . . . 201 PLACE FOR A THIRD .   50
    LIKE, "NO, SHE AIN'T COME BACK FROM KITING YET. . . . . . 209 PAUPER WITCH OF GRAFTON 80
    YET DOES PERHAPS FOR ALL THREE. . . . . 212 AN EMPTY THREAT . .   37
    "THE OUTSIDE DOORS AS YET HAVE HELD AGAINST US. . . . . . 215 A FOUNTAIN, A BOTTLE . 74
    YET OH! THE TEMPTING FLATNESS OF A BOOK, ... 216 A FOUNTAIN, A BOTTLE . 109
    (THOUGH NOT YET LIGHT) . . . . 218 I WILL SING YOU ONE-O . 7
    SINCE EARTH IS EARTH, PERHAPS, NOT HEAVEN (AS YET)-- . . . 220 FRAGMENTARY BLUE . .   5
    YET CAN'T HELP MARKING ALL THE TIME . . . . 221 IN A DISUSED GRAVEYARD 10
    OF HISSING ON THE YET UNCOVERED GROUND, ... 226 THE ONSET   5
    YET ALL THE PRECEDENT IS ON MY SIDE: . . . . 226 THE ONSET   12
    BUT NO, NOT YET. A SNORT TO BID THEM WAIT. . . . . 229 TWO LOOK AT TWO . .   26
    YET NOT ENOUGH. A BULLET THROUGH AND THROUGH, ... 230 NOT TO KEEP   14
    AND YET TOO READY TO BELIEVE THE MOST. . . . . 233 A BOUNDLESS MOMENT .   4
    BUT I SHOULD AWAKE TO CONFIRM YOUR STORY YET; . . . . . . 236 VALLEY'S SINGING DAY . 18
    AND YET SHE KNOWS OBSTRUCTION IS IN VAIN: . . . . 238 ON A TREE FALLEN ACROSS 9
    YET FOR THEM THE LILAC RENEWED ITS LEAF, ... 242 NEED OF BEING VERSED . 17
    AND YET NOT OUT BY ANY BROOK OR RIVER, ... 245 SPRING POOLS   5
    YOU COULD NOT TELL, AND YET IT LOOKED AS IF . . . . 250 ONCE BY THE PACIFIC .   7
    IS YET--WELL, SOMETHING THEY KNOW, HE AND SHE. . . . . . . 256 THE LOVELY BE CHOOSERS 24
    "IT WASN'T, YET IT WAS. IF NOT TO YOU, ... 258 WEST-RUNNING BROOK .   30
    RISE OTHERS VASTER YET, ... 260 SAND DUNES   3
    YET NOTHING I SHOULD CARE TO LEAVE BEHIND. . . . . 266 THE ARMFUL   5
    WE HAVE IDEAS YET THAT WE HAVEN'T TRIED. . . . . 268 RIDERS   12
    AND YET HE THOUGHT HE SAW THE SCENE: . . . . 273 A LONE STRIKER . . .   17
    YET FOUND IT EASY TO RESIST. . . . . 274 A LONE STRIKER . . .   35
    YET, AFTER ALL, 'TWAS NOT DIVINE, ... 274 A LONE STRIKER . . .   52
    A SINGLE FLOWER AS YET TO BLOOM. . . . . 276 TWO TRAMPS IN MUD TIME 28
    YET HOW ABOUT THE INSECT CERTAINTY . . . . 277 THE WHITE-TAILED HORNET 12
    YET ONCE SHE RISES TO THE HEIGHT, ... 281 BLUE RIBBON AT AMESBURY 46
    THE LOWLY PEN IS YET A HOLD . . . . 281 BLUE RIBBON AT AMESBURY 53
    TO LOOKING DOWN AND YET NOT BEING SAD, ... 283 THE GOLD HESPERIDEE .   9
    WE MUSTN'T TOUCH THEM YET, BUT SEE AND SEE! . . . . 283 THE GOLD HESPERIDEE .   16
    YET IF HE ENCOUNTERED ONE . . . . 288 DEPARTMENTAL   8
    YET LEAVE SUCH LOVELY SHAFTS OUTDOORS TO PERISH. . . . . . 290 OLD BARN AT THE BOTTOM 34
    WOULD SOMEONE ONLY ACT IN TIME WE YET . . . . 290 OLD BARN AT THE BOTTOM 35
    YET WASN'T ENJOINED AND WASN'T EXPECTED, CLEARLY. . . . . 306 NOT QUITE SOCIAL . .   4
    OR HE MIGHT BE RUNNING YET. . . . . 313 BEARER OF EVIL TIDINGS 16
    THAT NEVER YET TO OTHER TWO BEFELL . . . . 315 IRIS BY NIGHT . . .   21
    LAWS TO ITSELF, IT SEEMS, AND YET HAVE NO . . . . 324 BUILD SOIL   247

YET (CONTINUED)
    AND YET CONVERSION HAS ITS PLACE . . . . 326 TO A THINKER   31
    SO ALMOST CLEAR AND YET OBSCURE. . . . . 327 A MISSIVE MISSILE . .   19
    AND YET NOT KNOW THEY HAVE IT. . . . . 335 CARPE DIEM   18
    YET DID NOT MUCH TO SHORTEN STRIDE. . . . . 336 THE WIND AND THE RAIN .   8
    AND YET 'TWOULD SEEM THAT WHAT IS SUNG . . . . 336 THE WIND AND THE RAIN . 18
    YET FURTHER I WENT TO BE BEFORE THE SCYTHE, ... 342 QUEST OF PURPLE-FRINGED   9
    AS THE LIVING EVER GO YET STAY. . . . . 346 DISCOVERY OF MADEIRAS . 104
    YET SINGING BUT DIONE IN THE WOOD . . . . 351 THE LESSON FOR TODAY . 14
    IS HOW TO BE UNHAPPY YET POLITE. . . . . 353 THE LESSON FOR TODAY . 88
    YET LIKE A CHRISTIAN DISCIPLINED TO BEND . . . . . . 353 THE LESSON FOR TODAY . 94
    TO WHERE MY MANUSCRIPT WAS NOT YET DRY; . . . . 357 A CONSIDERABLE SPECK . 12
    YET MUST HAVE HAD A SET OF THEM COMPLETE . . . . . . 357 A CONSIDERABLE SPECK . 17
    (AS YET UNBROUGHT TO EARTH) HE MEANS TO TRY. . . . . 359 THE LOST FOLLOWER . . 36
    ALOOF YET NOT ALOOF, ... 367 A SERIOUS STEP LIGHTLY   18
    YET THERE TO WATCH THE DARKNESS COMING ON-- . . . . . 368 THE LITERATE FARMER AND 16
    THERE'S A LOT YET THAT ISN'T UNDERSTOOD. . . . . . . 372 THE LITERATE FARMER AND 136
    COLD AS A SPRING AS YET SO NEAR ITS SOURCE, ... 378 DIRECTIVE   51
    YET LEFT ME FREELY FACE TO FACE . . . . 380 AN UNSTAMPED LETTER IN 16
    YET STILL I MUST REPORT . . . . 384 MAKING CERTAIN ANYTHING   7
    NOR YET THE LITTLE DOTTED IN ME SEEK. . . . . 387 IOTA SUBSCRIPT . . .   2
    AND YET HE IS A POWER OF LIGHT . . . . 390 TWO LEADING LIGHTS . .   7
    YET IN HIS HEART HE WAS UNSHAKEN SURE . . . . 400 THE BROKEN DROUGHT . .   9
    YET YOU REFUSE TO SEE IT IN THE DOCTOR." . . . . . . 407 FROM PLANE TO PLANE . 101
    A CROOKED STRAIGHTNESS YET NO LESS A STRAIGHTNESS. . . 421 ESCAPIST--NEVER . . .   5
    AND YET DONE NOTHING ABOUT IT IN SONG. . . . . 421 ONE MORE BREVITY . .   65
    SO CLOSE YET SURE TO BE ABIDED BY, ... 423 FOR JOHN F. KENNEDY . 56
    AND YET FOR ALL THIS HELP OF HEAD AND BRAIN . . . . . 425 ACCIDENTALLY ON PURPOSE 21
    ONE AND YET DISCRETE . . . . 426 A NEVER NAUGHT SONG . 10
    WE WOULD SEE TO YET-- . . . . 438 KITTY HAWK 330
    YET SO RUDE IN ITS ART, ... 447 THE BAD ISLAND--EASTER   3
    THOUGH AS YET THEY ONLY SMILE . . . . 465 SOME SCIENCE FICTION .   9
    FOR YET ANOTHER BLOW. . . . . 470 IN WINTER IN THE WOODS 12
    IS THAT YOUR ANSWER? / NO, FOR I HAVE YET . . . . . . 481 A MASQUE OF REASON . 227
    YET YOU DON'T SPEAK. LET FOOLS BEMUSE THEMSELVES . . . 484 A MASQUE OF REASON . 298
    YET I SUPPOSE WHAT SEEMS TO US CONFUSION . . . . . . 485 A MASQUE OF REASON . 338
    TO QUOTE THE GREATEST WESTERN POEM YET. . . . . . . 485 A MASQUE OF REASON . 344
    HE ISN'T REALLY GOING, YET HE'S LEAVING. . . . . . . 489 A MASQUE OF REASON . 440
    YET COULD NOT BRING MYSELF TO SAY A WORD. . . . . . . 497 A MASQUE OF MERCY .   99
    OF THERAPY. / I DON'T LOVE PAUL--AS YET. . . . . . . 499 A MASQUE OF MERCY . 163
    SO KNOWING--AND YET NEEDING TO BE TOLD . . . . 506 A MASQUE OF MERCY . 338
    YET NO ONE TURN FROM TRYING TO LIVE UP TO. . . . . . 512 A MASQUE OF MERCY . 497
    YET SO WE'LL HAVE TO WEEP BECAUSE WE CAN'T. . . . . . 512 A MASQUE OF MERCY . 499
    AND YET CAN'T TURN YOUR BACK ON OR IGNORE, ... 512 A MASQUE OF MERCY . 510
    YET NO ONE TURN AWAY FROM OR IGNORE-- . . . . 513 A MASQUE OF MERCY . 522
    YET YOUR FRIEND HERE CAN'T BE QUITE DISREGARDED. . . . 517 A MASQUE OF MERCY . 638
YGGDRASILL
    THE WHOLE YGGDRASILL. . . . . 426 A NEVER NAUGHT SONG . 26
YIELD
    TO YIELD WITH A GRACE TO REASON, ... 30 RELUCTANCE 22
    AND SOMETIMES SOMETHING SEEMED TO YIELD, ... 138 BROWN'S DESCENT . .   18
    AND BURNING TO YIELD FLOWERS INSTEAD OF GRAIN, ... 173 A STAR IN A STONEBOAT . 22
    WE SHOULD SEE WHICH ONE WOULD BE FIRST TO YIELD. . . . 253 THE THATCH   9
    BUT YIELD WHO WILL TO THEIR SEPARATION, ... 277 TWO TRAMPS IN MUD TIME 65
YIELDED
    BUT ONCE COMPARISONS WERE YIELDED DOWNWARD, ... 279 THE WHITE-TAILED HORNET 63
YOKE
    YOKEFELLOWS IN THE SAP YOKE FROM OF OLD . . . . . . 164 NEW HAMPSHIRE . . . 177
    HE'D SELL A YOKE OF STEERS TO PAY FOR IT. . . . . . . 200 PLACE FOR A THIRD . . 25
YOKEFELLOWS
    YOKEFELLOWS IN THE SAP YOKE FROM OF OLD . . . . . . 164 NEW HAMPSHIRE . . . 177
YON
    THE EX-KING SAID, "YON STAR'S INDIFFERENCE . . . . . 454 HOW HARD TO KEEP FROM   17
YONDER
    YOU ASK IF I SEE YONDER SHINING GATE, ... 513 A MASQUE OF MERCY . 530
YORK
    NEW YORK (FIVE MILLION) LAUGHS AT MANCHESTER, ... 165 NEW HAMPSHIRE . . . 201
    RHODE ISLAND, NEW YORK, OR VERMONT WAS THIS: . . . . 167 NEW HAMPSHIRE . . . 251
    LATELY IN CONVERSE WITH A NEW YORK ALEC . . . . . . 170 NEW HAMPSHIRE . . . 358
    (FROM, SAY, A PUBLISHER IN NEW YORK CITY). . . . . . 172 NEW HAMPSHIRE . . . 410
    BUT IT'S NOT NEW YORK. . . . . 439 KITTY HAWK 344
    I'M APT TO TELL THEM IN NEW YORK . . . . 452 A-WISHING WELL . . . 34
    THAT WAS HEARD AS FAR AWAY AS NEW YORK . . . . 463 LINES IN DEJECTION . 23
    YES, BUT NEW YORK WILL DO AS AN EXAMPLE. . . . . . . 496 A MASQUE OF MERCY .   91
    WELL, YOU'RE AS GOOD AS IN NEW YORK THIS MINUTE-- . . . 497 A MASQUE OF MERCY .   92
    OR BAD AS IN NEW YORK. / I KNOW I AM. . . . . 497 A MASQUE OF MERCY .   93
    A FRACTURE IN THE ROCKS BENEATH NEW YORK . . . . . . 502 A MASQUE OF MERCY . 229
    A MISSION AS TO HAVE TO TELL NEW YORK . . . . 503 A MASQUE OF MERCY . 272
YORKER
    OR THE NEW YORKER. / WHEN WAS THE LAST TIME . . . . . 504 A MASQUE OF MERCY . 276
YOU---NOT INDEXED
YOU'D---NOT INDEXED
YOU'LL---NOT INDEXED
'OUNG
    THAT'S STANDING BY THE MOTHER. IT'S SO YOUNG . . . . . 1 THE PASTURE   6
    WHEN I WAS YOUNG, WE DWELT IN A VALE . . . . 15 IN A VALE   1
    HE THINKS YOUNG WILSON A LIKELY LAD, THOUGH DAFT . . . 36 DEATH OF THE HIRED MAN 65
    HAROLD'S YOUNG COLLEGE-BOY'S ASSURANCE PIQUED HIM. . . 37 DEATH OF THE HIRED MAN 73
    "KNOWN IT SINCE I WAS YOUNG." / "THEN YOU KNOW ME. . . 48 A HUNDRED COLLARS . 100
    OF ALL THE YOUNG CHATTERING LORENS ALIVE, ... 60 BLUEBERRIES   38
    WITH THE MOUTHS OF ALL THOSE YOUNG LORENS TO FEED? . . 60 BLUEBERRIES   49
    NOT LIKELY, WHEN ALL THE YOUNG LORENS DEPLOY. . . . . 62 BLUEBERRIES   98
    MY FATHER'S BROTHER, HE WENT MAD QUITE YOUNG. . . . . 65 A SERVANT TO SERVANTS 104
    AND ACCOMMODATE HER YOUNG LIFE TO HIS. . . . . 66 A SERVANT TO SERVANTS 131
    THE YOUNG FOLK HELD SOME HOPE OUT TO EACH OTHER . . . 74 THE GENERATIONS OF MEN 21
    WHEN I WAS YOUNG. I USED TO USE THE ROAR . . . . . . 78 THE GENERATIONS OF MEN 128
    MY WOODS--THE YOUNG FIR BALSAMS LIKE A PLACE . . . . . 106 CHRISTMAS TREES . . 13
    'TWAS A NEST FULL OF YOUNG BIRDS ON THE GROUND . . . . 109 THE EXPOSED NEST . . 13

YOUNG (CONTINUED)
    WE'D CARE TO KNOW, FOR WE ARE NOT YOUNG NOW.-- . . . . 112 IN THE HOME STRETCH . 54
    AND STILL THE BIRD REVISITED HER YOUNG. . . . . . . 126 RANGE-FINDING . . . 5
    OR BEING VERY YOUNG (AND HE WAS PLEASED . . . . . . 127 THE SMILE 9
    THE WITCH WAS YOUNG, AND BEAUTIFUL (NEW STYLE), . . . 163 NEW HAMPSHIRE . . . 129
    SOMEWHERE MUST BE THE GRAVE OF THE YOUNG BOY . . . . 200 PLACE FOR A THIRD . 33
    ALL IS, IF I'D A-KNOWN WHEN I WAS YOUNG . . . . . . 210 PAUPER WITCH OF GRAFTON 104
    SEEMED STRONG WHEN I WAS YOUNG; . . . . 227 TO EARTHWARD . . . 14
    AND THE COLD TO AN ORCHARD SO YOUNG IN THE BARK . . . 228 GOOD-BY AND KEEP COLD . 2
    KEEP COLD, YOUNG ORCHARD. GOOD-BY AND KEEP COLD. . . . 228 GOOD-BY AND KEEP COLD . 18
    A YOUNG BEECH CLINGING TO ITS LAST YEAR'S LEAVES. . . . 234 A BOUNDLESS MOMENT . 12
    ON SOME WILD APPLE-TREE'S YOUNG TENDER BARK, ... 254 A WINTER EDEN . . . 11
    WHAT ARE WE?" / "YOUNG OR NEW?" / "WE MUST BE SOMETHING. . 258 WEST-RUNNING BROOK . 10
    OR SOME EXTRAVAGANCE YOUNG LOVE HAD BEEN TO? . . . . 264 THE INVESTMENT . . 11
    WHEN I WAS YOUNG MY TEACHERS WERE THE OLD. . . . . 267 WHAT FIFTY SAID . . 1
    NOW I AM OLD MY TEACHERS ARE THE YOUNG. . . . . . . 267 WHAT FIFTY SAID . . 5
    SQUARE MATTHEW HALE'S YOUNG GRAFTED APPLE TREE . . . 283 THE GOLD HESPERIDEE . 1
    BEGINNING WHEN HE WAS YOUNG, ... 299 WELCOME TO THEIR BELIEF 7
    I NEVER DARED BE RADICAL WHEN YOUNG . . . . 308 PRECAUTION 1
    I AM BROUGHT GUARANTEED YOUNG PRATTLE POEMS . . . . 324 BUILD SOIL . . . 273
    IN HAPPY SADNESS BY THE YOUNG, ... 336 THE WIND AND THE RAIN . 19
    AND OH, FOR ONE SO YOUNG . . . . 341 THE SUBVERTED FLOWER . 65
    TO A YOUNG WRETCH . . . . 349 TO A YOUNG WRETCH . . T
    HE WAS TOO YOUNG TO GO, ... 366 NOT OF SCHOOL AGE . 21
    AS WHOSOEVER LIKES THE YOUNG AND SLIGHT . . . . . 375 A YOUNG BIRCH . . . 3
    A YOUNG BIRCH . . . . 375 A YOUNG BIRCH . . . T
    THE YOUNG SPRUCE MADE A SUITE OF GLADES . . . . . 380 AN UNSTAMPED LETTER IN 9
    HOW YOUNG AND UNASSUMING . . . . 391 A ROGERS GROUP . . 1
    IF I HAD HAD MY CHANCE WHEN YOUNG . . . . 417 AMERICA IS HARD TO SEE 33
    OF YOUNG AMBITION EAGER TO BE TRIED, ... 424 FOR JOHN F. KENNEDY . 73
    WHEN I CAME HERE YOUNG . . . . 428 KITTY HAWK . . . 6
    AS A YOUNG ALASTOR . . . . 430 KITTY HAWK . . . 53
    HE NEVER SAID SHE WASN'T YOUNG, ... 444 ENDS 7
YOUNGER
    WHEN, .TO PLEASE YOUNGER MEMBERS OF THE CHURCH, ... 57 THE BLACK COTTAGE . 85
    ONE OF THEM FIVE YEARS YOUNGER THAN I LOOK-- . . . . 196 WILD GRAPES . . . 18
    AS THE MOON USED TO SEEM WHEN I WAS YOUNGER, ... 197 WILD GRAPES . . . 29
    SHE NOW FELT YOUNGER BY A THOUSAND YEARS . . . . . 479 A MASQUE OF REASON . 157
YOUNGEST
    ALL IN A FAMILY ROW DOWN TO THE YOUNGEST." . . . . . 49 A HUNDRED COLLARS . 148
YOUNGSTER
    A YOUNGSTER COMES TO ME WITH HALF A QUATRAIN . . . . 324 BUILD SOIL . . . 270
YOUNGSTERS
    AND THE AIR OF THE YOUNGSTERS! NOT ONE OF THEM TURNED, . . 61 BLUEBERRIES . . . 58
YOUR---NOT INDEXED
YOU'RE---NOT INDEXED
YOURS---NOT INDEXED
YOURSELF
    "I HAVEN'T BEEN. GO, LOOK, SEE FOR YOURSELF. . . . . 40 DEATH OF THE HIRED MAN 155
    LIE DOWN--LET YOURSELF GO AND GET SOME SLEEP. . . . 50 A HUNDRED COLLARS . 161
    MORE THAN YOU HAVE YOURSELF, SOME OF THESE NIGHTS. . . . 67 A SERVANT TO SERVANTS . 167
    YOU OUGHT TO HAVE THE KITCHEN TO YOURSELF . . . . 88 THE HOUSEKEEPER . . 193
    DON'T YOU DEFEND YOURSELF. IF IT WAS THERE, ... 97 THE SELF-SEEKER . . 139
    "MAKE YOURSELF USEFUL, THEN, AND READ IT FOR ME.-- . . . 99 THE SELF-SEEKER . . 188
    HOW CAN YOU HELP YOURSELF? / "I CALLED HIM BROTHER. . . 144 SNOW 44
    "BROTHER MESERVE, TAKE CARE, YOU'LL SCARE YOURSELF . . 149 SNOW 167
    AND YOU YOURSELF DON'T WANT TO. WHO ELSE IS THERE?" . . 151 SNOW 235
    "YOU THINK YOU HAVEN'T BEEN CONCERNED YOURSELF." . . . 155 SNOW 344
    IN EVERY WAY YOU MAY PLEASE YOURSELF; . . . . . . 232 THE KITCHEN CHIMNEY . 2
    SPENDING YOURSELF TOO MUCH IN SELF-SUPPORT. . . . . 356 A MOTH SEEN IN WINTER . 12
    OR EVEN BETTER GODLIKE IN YOURSELF. . . . . . . 359 THE LOST FOLLOWER . 32
    SO BUSY YOURSELF WITH OTHER THINGS . . . . 376 SOMETHING FOR HOPE . 10
    MAKE YOURSELF UP A CHEERING SONG OF HOW . . . . . 378 DIRECTIVE 29
    AND IF YOU'RE LOST ENOUGH TO FIND YOURSELF . . . . 378 DIRECTIVE 36
    THEN MAKE YOURSELF AT HOME. THE ONLY FIELD . . . . 378 DIRECTIVE 39
    BE SURE TO KEEP REPEATING TO YOURSELF . . . . . . 385 THE FEAR OF GOD . . 3
    YOU SAID YOURSELF YOU WEREN'T AVOIDING WORK. . . . . 405 FROM PLANE TO PLANE . 45
    YOU SEE IT IN YOURSELF AND IN THE SUN; . . . . . 407 FROM PLANE TO PLANE . 100
    ENSLAVE YOURSELF TO THE RIGHT LEADER'S TRUTH, . . . 460 HOW HARD TO KEEP FROM 191
    SUFFER YOURSELF TO BE ADMIRED, MY LOVE, ... 474 A MASQUE OF REASON . 30
    YOU THOUGHT TO SUIT YOURSELF. I'VE NOT AGREED . . . 478 A MASQUE OF REASON . 145
    NEXT TIME YOU FIND YOURSELF PRESSED ONTO ONE . . . 486 A MASQUE OF REASON . 370
    SHOW YOURSELF, SON.--I'LL GET BACK ON MY THRONE . . 487 A MASQUE OF REASON . 386
    THESE OTHERS DON'T. / YOU DON'T YOURSELF ENTIRELY. . . 497 A MASQUE OF MERCY . 111
    AND CALM YOURSELF. BE SANE! I HEREBY HOLD . . . . 501 A MASQUE OF MERCY . 192
    WHY DO YOU CALL YOURSELF A STAR-CROSSED LOVER? . . . 510 A MASQUE OF MERCY . 450
YOUTH
    THAT SEEMED TOO PAGAN TO OUR LIBERAL YOUTH. . . . . 58 THE BLACK COTTAGE . 95
    FOR THE GENEROUS TEARS OF YOUTH AND SONG? . . . . 262 HANNIBAL 4
    I GO TO SCHOOL TO YOUTH TO LEARN THE FUTURE. . . . 267 WHAT FIFTY SAID . . 8
    WITH ALL THIS TALK ABOUT THE HOPE OF YOUTH . . . 462 HOW HARD TO KEEP FROM 257
    AND NOTHING MADE OF YOUTH. CONSIDER ME, ... 462 HOW HARD TO KEEP FROM 258
YOUTHFUL
    OF YOUTHFUL FORMS AND YOUTHFUL FACES. . . . . . 102 GOOD HOURS 8
YOU'VE---NOT INDEXED

Z

ZACCHEUS
    ZACCHEUS HE . . . . 331 SYCAMORE 1
ZEAL
    AND ZEAL WOULD NOT BE THANKED THAT CUT IT DOWN . . . . 375 A YOUNG BIRCH . . . 19
ZEALOT
    A ZEALOT FULL OF FLUID INSPIRATION, ... 159 NEW HAMPSHIRE . . . 26
ZEALOUS
    SOME ZEALOUS ONE'S LABORIOUS DEVICE. . . . . . . 74 THE GENERATIONS OF MEN 42

ZEPHYR   PAGE TITLE   LINE
    HE STOOD IN THE ZEPHYR, PIPES IN HAND, ... 23 PAN WITH US 6
    WHAT SHOULD THAT RECKLESS ZEPHYR FLING   . . . . 29 MY BUTTERFLY 41
ZERO
    THROUGH TEMPERATURE OF ABSOLUTE ZERO? . . . . 395 WHY WAIT FOR SCIENCE . 8
ZEST
    ALL THE SCIENCE ZEST . . . . 435 KITTY HAWK 230
ZIGZAG
    WE SAW HIM SAY ALONG THE ZIGZAG JOURNEY . . . . 170 NEW HAMPSHIRE . . . 351
ZODIAC
    IS STILL WITHHOLDING IN THE ZODIAC . . . . 361 A LOOSE MOUNTAIN . . 18
    "BUT CYGNUS ISN'T IN THE ZODIAC," . . . . 407 FROM PLANE TO PLANE . 109
    TO THE ZODIAC . . . . 429 KITTY HAWK 35
ZONES
    THERE ARE ROUGHLY ZONES . . . . 305 THERE ARE ROUGHLY ZONES T
    THERE ARE ROUGHLY ZONES WHOSE LAWS MUST BE OBEYED? . . 305 THERE ARE ROUGHLY ZONES 13